44th

EDITION

CAMRA's GOOD BEER GUIDE 2017

Edited by Roger Protz

Head of Publishing Simon Hall
Project Managers Emma Haines, Susannah Lord
Assistant Editors Ione Brown, Simon Tuite
Project Assistance Katie Button, Julie Hudson
Sales & Marketing David Birkett

CAMRA

BOOKS

Barge & Barrel, Elland, West Yorkshire, p558

BARGE & BARREL
Real Ales & Brew House

Special thanks to 180,000 CAMRA members who carried out research for the pub entries; the Campaign's Regional Directors and Area Organisers, who co-ordinated the pub entries; the Campaign's Brewery Liaison Co-ordinators and Brewery Liaison Officers, who carried out research for the brewery entries; Rick Pickup and Andy Shaw for assistance co-ordinating the brewery entries; Michael Slaughter for advising on heritage pubs; Alex Presland for technical support; all CAMRA's staff and CAMRA's National Executive for their help and support.

Thanks also to the publicans, breweries and others who have kindly contributed their photographs.

Photo credits: [Key: t = top; b = bottom; c=centre; l = left; r = right] Cover: (l) Hemis/Alamy Stock Photo, (r) Brian North; p2: Tim Green/flickr; p4: (br) Cath Harries; p10: (bl) Peter Cripps; p15: (bl) Keith Whitmore; p16: Cath Harries; p18: (bl, bc) Frank Gaymonds, (br) Tim Williams; p19: (bl) Tim Williams, (br) Frank Gaymonds.

Design: Colour pages design: Keith Holmes, Thames Street Studio; cover design: Dale Tomlinson. Typeset in Knockout and Dax.

Maps & illustrations: Pubs section maps: David and Morag Perrot, PerroCarto; illustrations Hannah Moore.

Production: Database, typesetting of listings and indexes: AMA Dataset Ltd, Preston.

Printing: Printed and bound in the UK by CPI William Clowes, Beccles, Suffolk.

Published by the Campaign for Real Ale Ltd, 230 Hatfield Road, St Albans, Herts, AL1 4LW. www.camra.org.uk

Contents

About The Good Beer Guide

It's a unique guide to pubs and beer

The Good Beer Guide, first and foremost, will take you to great pubs serving great beer. But that's only one part of its role. It also directs you to breweries and their ales as well as to the essential outlets in towns and rural areas where you can enjoy them.

Constant companion for pubs and breweries

Pubs are the central core of the guide, the essential outlets for real ale. But the *Good Beer Guide* has always played a dual role, with its Breweries section complementing the pub listings by detailing all the producers of cask beer and their regular ales. As well as listing some 4,500 of the finest outlets for real ale and the ever-growing number of breweries, we also look at the the campaigns to save pubs, curtail the powers of giant pub companies and the threats posed by takeovers by global brewers: see the Introduction on pages 6–9 and also pages 684–685.

Comprehensive breweries section

The *Good Beer Guide* includes a comprehensive listing of all British breweries and their core beers. Breweries are monitored on a regular basis and each brewery is visited by CAMRA members, who speak to the brewer and check on the beers being produced before reporting to the Guide. As soon as a new brewery comes on stream, a liaison officer will be appointed to ensure the Breweries section of the Guide is accurate and up to date and readers are aware of the increased choice available.

Democratically selected entries

The way in which pubs are chosen is equally meticulous. Much of CAMRA's 180,000 membership is involved and those members who cannot be active or attend regular meetings are invited to recommend pubs via email or branch websites. Branch areas are broken down into local sections so pubs can be monitored regularly. The quality of beer in each pub is checked using a national beer scoring system. Special branch meetings are convened once a year where short-lists are presented and then members vote on the final selection for the Guide.

Regular inspections

The entries in most pub guides are chosen either by small editorial teams or by members of the public, whose recommendations are not necessarily checked. However, every pub that appears in this Guide has been visited regularly, often weekly, by CAMRA members. We offer full entries, with no unchecked 'lucky dip' sections of pubs sent in at random. Readers' recommendations are passed to local CAMRA branches, who take this feedback into account during their survey work.

It's not only about quality beer

The key driving force of the Guide – beer quality – has not changed over 44 years. However, the Guide also takes account of the history and architecture of pubs and such important aspects as food, family and disabled facilities, gardens, special events such as mini-beer festivals, and even the standard of the toilets. CAMRA volunteers are called on to be minor essayists, describing in detail all aspects of the pubs they choose. We know, from the feedback we receive, that users of the Guide need full information about pubs before embarking on journeys to visit them.

Town & country pubs

In addition to full descriptions, users want a good spread of pubs. Unlike some guides that concentrate on rural pubs, we recognise that most people live in towns and cities and expect a good selection of pubs in those areas. But we don't neglect suburban and country pubs: on the contrary, CAMRA campaigns for the survival of rural pubs that are often vital hubs of their isolated communities.

We strive hard to ensure that all areas of the country are covered. Each county or region has an allocation of pubs based on a scientific calculation of population, number of licensed premises and the level of 'tourist penetration'. As a result, the Guide's reach is unparalleled.

'all areas of the country are covered... the Guide's reach is unparalleled '

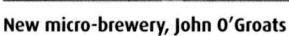

New micro-brewery, John O'Groats

Famous Thames-side inn the Dove, Hammersmith

 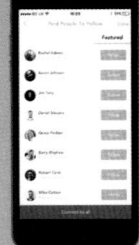 
Proudly independent

Unlike many of our competitors, all entries are free. CAMRA is a proudly independent organisation and there are no hidden costs of appearing in the *Good Beer Guide*. Guides that charge for entries restrict consumer choice as not all publicans can afford the fees demanded. CAMRA is a broad church and the Guide reflects that by choosing pubs across a wide spectrum that will appeal to people from all walks of life, regardless of income and background.

Keeping up to date

The Campaign has more than 200 branches. Each branch surveys the pubs in its area and monitors not only the quality of the cask beer in each one but also watches for change of ownership or management that could affect the range of ale on offer and the overall standard of the pub. In addition, branch officers liaise frequently with breweries in their areas and keep a close eye on the local brewing scene.

There is a cynical saying in the publishing world that 'all guide books are out of date as soon as they appear'. That's not the case with the *Good Beer Guide*. Thanks to modern technology, the Guide is checked and re-checked many times before publication. Checking doesn't stop there: both CAMRA's national website and its monthly newspaper *What's Brewing* publish regular information about and updates to the Guide, including pubs that have closed or where beer quality has declined. These changes are also reflected in the Good Beer Guide mobile app that, alongside an e-book and sat-nav POI file, give readers access to the Guide in many different formats (see p1031). This regular checking, along with the pubs and breweries databases underpinning the Guide, means that CAMRA and the *Good Beer Guide* share an unrivalled electronic storehouse of information about pubs and breweries.

Additional resources

There are limits to the size of the *Good Beer Guide*. We believe – thanks to our members' efforts and the recommendations sent in by readers – that we offer a choice of the very best pubs throughout the country. But the Guide is complemented by other resources, including local pub guides produced by CAMRA branches which are available at beer festivals and local outlets and the online **www.whatpub.com** – CAMRA's official guide to all known real ale outlets in the country.

CAMRA also produces a great and constantly expanding range of other books on the subjects of beer, brewing and pubs. Some of these are highlighted at the back of this book on pages 1027–1028. The full list of CAMRA books can be found at **www.camra.org.uk/books**

Introduction

Real ale: the beer of the moment

The real ale revolution goes roaring on. In the Breweries section, one word is repeated time and time again: NEW. There are now some 1,540 breweries operating in Britain. More than 200 opened between the 2016 Guide and this edition, and almost without exception they brew cask-conditioned beer for a growing audience of drinkers.

As well as new breweries, many others report they are moving to bigger premises or enlarging existing plant to cope with the demand for their beers. The choice is now astonishing. Alongside such staple brews as Mild, Bitter and Golden Ale, brewers have revived such famous old styles as Porter and IPA. They widen the boundaries of beer appreciation with ales aged in whisky and wine oak barrels. They add fruit, herbs, spices and coffee beans to their beers, and embrace such European styles as Belgian Saisons and Sours.

In an overall declining beer market, real ale's share is impressive. It is not only in growth but, according to the latest Cask Report – produced independently by CAMRA – it accounts for:

The latest Cask Report shows growing demand for real ale

 55 per cent of the total ale market and

That share is projected to grow to 70 per cent by 2020 and will account for 20 per cent of the total draught beer sector

As the ale market includes such national and expensively promoted keg brands as Guinness, John Smith's and Tetley, this is a remarkable achievement by the cask beer sector. With the exception of a handful of brands from large regional brewers, such as Fuller's London Pride, Greene King's IPA and Charles Wells's Bombardier, cask beers enjoy no TV or poster promotions. Word of mouth plays a powerful role in presenting real ale to the widest possible number of drinkers. The availability of a large range of beers is aided by CAMRA beer festivals – local, regional and national – held throughout the year (see pages 18–19).

Pubs: closing and opening

It is a curious anomaly of the beer and pub world that while real ale is witnessing encouraging growth, the places where cask beer is consumed – and can only be consumed – continue to suffer. Pubs close at the rate of 21 a week, closures that often rip the heart out of local communities. In The great British pub section (pages 10–12) we focus on both closures and the heartening development of new types of drinking establishments, such as micro or 'pop-up' pubs and larger bars in train stations and old industrial buildings. Cafés and restaurants that have resisted serving real ale in the past are now offering it to customers, aided by new forms of packaging such as Key Casks.

Closures are the result in part of sales of deeply discounted beer in supermarkets. But there are other factors at play. CAMRA has been concerned for many years at the way in which the giant national pub companies or 'pubcos' charge inflated rents from their publicans and 'top dollar' prices for the beers they supply through a restrictive system known as 'the tie'. The tie means publicans can only buy beers from the pubcos' lists. These are often national beers that the pubcos buy cheaply from brewers who can afford to pay discounted prices that are beyond the reach of smaller producers.

The two main pubcos, Enterprise Inns and Punch Taverns, have crippling levels of debt as a result of a pub buying spree in the early years of this century that led to serious financial difficulties during the economic crash in 2007 and 2008. The two companies are reducing their debts by selling pubs, many of them perfectly viable but which are attractive to property developers keen to turn them into private housing.

Particular concern was created in 2015 when Punch sold for £53.5 million 158 pubs – described as 'non-core businesses' – to New River Retail, a property company whose approach to property development is 'unlocking and creating capital growth through the introduction of

CAMRA provides comprehensive guidance for CAMRA branches, community groups and parish councils wishing to nomiate local pubs as Assets of Community Value

new and complementary uses' such as building convenience stores on adjoining car parks, often working with the Co-op. New River previously bought 202 pubs from Marston's in 2012 for £900 million: to date three of those pubs now have Co-op stores alongside but the pubs remain in business.

CAMRA has been at the forefront of a campaign to save pubs and rein in the powers of the pubcos. It worked closely with the Government to ensure the adoption of a robust Pubs Code, including the all-important option for tied tenants to become untied, enabling them to buy beer at much lower prices free of the tie. It negotiated successfully with Punch, New River and the Co-op and won a pledge that pubs would not be closed without consultation.

CAMRA's national chairman, Colin Valentine, spoke at a rally at the Roscoe Head in Liverpool, which has been in every edition of the *Good Beer Guide* since 1974, and was one of the Punch outlets sold to New River. Tenant Carol Ross has run the pub with her family for many years and was worried it could be turned into a Co-op store. A spokesman for New River told the Guide it had no plans to close any pubs bought from Punch. In July 2016, Punch Taverns announced it planned to sell a further 400 pubs that were not 'core businesses' over the next four years.

Battle for MRO

CAMRA has been at the heart of the campaign to tackle the power of the large pubcos, those with 500 tenanted pubs or more. The practices of the pubcos have had a severe impact on the 13,000 tenants in England and Wales who are 'tied' to their pub companies for the supply of beer and other products. Issues raised by CAMRA and pubs campaigners include:

- Opaque methods of calculating rents that resulted in inflated and unfair rents

- Pubco monopoly over the supply of tied beer and other products. This leads to licensees paying well above market prices for beer and having a restricted choice of brands they can stock

- Widespread allegations of unfair treatment of tenants

- Pubcos attempting to circumvent the principle that tied licensees should be no worse off than free-of-tie publicans

As a result of intense lobbying, the Government agreed to introduce a Pubs Code and to appoint a Pubs Adjudicator who would act as an ombudsman and would settle disputes between licensees and the pubcos. At the heart of the code was the Market Rent Only (MRO) option. MRO will allow tenants to negotiate a contract with their pubcos which will allow them to become 'free of tie' and able to buy beer and other products on the open market, paying their pubcos only market rents.

The Pubs Code was due to come into law in May 2016 but was delayed as a result of drafting errors. It was finally introduced in July 2016 and contains the key right for tenants to trigger the MRO process at the time of rent assessment, which must be provided every five years. Tied tenants of pubcos with more than 500 pubs will have access to the MRO process and will be able to obtain a free-of-tie rent comparison by requesting an MRO offer.

The delay in implementing the code meant that a number of pubco tenants who faced rent assessments in May 2016 missed out on the chance to apply for MRO. The pubcos were obdurate and refused to make MRO retrospective. At the same time, a number of campaigners representing tenants expressed their doubts over the appointment of Paul Newby as the Pubs Adjudicator. He worked for many years for Fleurets, the specialist property company heavily involved in the pubs market where he represented pubcos as well as tenants.

His appointment was vigorously criticised in parliament by Greg Mulholland MP and in July, the Business, Innovation and Skills parliamentary committee called for Mr Newby to be replaced by someone who would be even-handed between pubs and tenants. There are also fears that the pubcos will water down or get round MRO with the use of lawyers and attempts to bamboozle tenants with dubious claims about the benefits of keeping the tie. Again, continuing vigilance is vital.

A rally at the Roscoe Head, Liverpool in 2016. New owners have no plans to close the pub that has appeared in every edition of the *Good Beer Guide*

CAMRA's community pubs campaign stresses the vital role of local pubs

Rocky road to prohibition

A worrying move to introduce severe restrictions on the consumption of alcohol came in a report in 2016 by the UK's Chief Medical Officers for England, Wales, Scotland and Northern Ireland. They reduced the previous recommended weekly units of alcohol of 21 for men and 14 for women to just 14 units a week for both sexes. While CAMRA fully supports moderate and sensible drinking, it joined other organisations in criticising the new recommendation and its lack of scientific support and pointed to higher recommended safe units in several other countries (see graphic to right).

The new guideline was heavily influenced by the Institute of Alcohol Studies, which is funded by the Alliance House Foundation, whose former name was the UK Temperance Alliance. The alliance in turn developed from the Temperance Movement in the United States that campaigned for Prohibition in the 20th century. The Chief Medical Officers also took evidence from the Alcohol Health Alliance that claims alcohol consumption has increased in the UK in recent decades. This claim contradicts official figures compiled by HM Revenue & Customs, which collects all the taxes and duties on alcohol, and reveals that sales in the UK have fallen by close to 20 per cent over the past decade.

The Chief Medical Officers also said there is no safe minimum level of alcohol consumption and England's CMO, Professor Dame Sally Davies, declared that when she is offered a glass of white wine she thinks 'cancer'. On the other hand, evidence from the School of Public Health at Harvard University, the American Stroke Association, Tufts University in Massachusetts, and the National Public Health Institute in Helsinki, Finland, indicates that the moderate consumption of beer can protect against strokes, diabetes, heart attacks, dementia, gall stones and bone disease. The American Chemical Society is conducting research into the natural chemicals present in the hop plant that could be key ingredients in the fight against cancer.

CAMRA chairman Colin Valentine says the revised guidelines 'lack credibility, are the result of inappropriately selective scientific evidence and are out of line with international standards. We believe guidance should be specific to individuals and the product of a wider range of factors, rather than the result of a one-size-fits-all approach that is both inappropriate and illustrative of an over-protective and interfering mind-set.'

He pointed to the evidence compiled by researchers at Oxford University and published by CAMRA in a study called Friends on Tap (see box page 12) showing that pub-goers are likely to drink less if those around them are behaving in a measured way and are, as a result, likely to be less tolerant of socially inappropriate behaviour. The lead researcher, Professor Robin Dunbar, concluded that drinking socially and in moderation was good for individuals, the communities to which they belong and to society as a whole.

Further evidence of falling levels of alcohol abuse came in June 2016 with research by the Local Alcohol Profile for England that revealed that hospital admissions for under 18s had fallen by half and women by 42 per cent since 2008/9. Admissions for under 40s dropped by 12.5 per cent over the past five years.

The concern is that, in spite of a body of scientific evidence that disputes the Chief Medical Officers' recommendations, the new weekly units have been accepted almost without criticism by both media and Government. If the recommended units are 14 today they could be slashed still further in future years and, unless countered, could take the country on the road to Prohibition.

CAMRA examines its role

In a fast-changing beer world, CAMRA took the decision to consult its growing membership, now more than 180,000 strong, about the future role of the Campaign. When CAMRA was founded in the early 1970s, beer production was dominated by the 'Big Six' national brewers who also owned or controlled a majority of the country's pubs. Regional and family brewers were in decline and real ale was under threat from such national keg brands as Double Diamond and Watney's Red.

The landscape has changed. The Big Six have gone and have been replaced by global brewers such as AB InBev, Carlsberg, Heineken and Molson Coors. While regional and smaller brewers own pubs, most are now controlled by the pubcos discussed above.

ALCOHOL UNITS GUIDELINES:
Weekly consumption
(UK Units – Men)

34 Units
Spain

25 Units
USA & Canada

21 Units
Ireland & Denmark

14 Units
United Kingdom

In 2016, CAMRA launched its Revitalisation Project, a fundamental review of its future positioning, purpose and strategy

Sales of cask beer are riding high but they have been joined by a new range of 'craft keg' beers brewed by an increasing number of artisan brewers. Apart from the extravagant price of some craft keg products, many CAMRA members have no problem with beers that encourage people to drink products free from mass advertising and global brewers' influence.

CAMRA stands for the Campaign *for* Real Ale. It was founded to save cask beer from oblivion in the 1970s but recognises there are other traditional styles of beer. For example, it has for some 20 years supported the independence of Budweiser Budvar in the Czech Republic from possible takeover by its American namesake and accepts that genuine lager beers have a long and noble history.

Faced by such a dramatically different beer scene, CAMRA decided in 2016 to launch the Revitalisation Project that seeks to involve as many members as possible in deciding the Campaign's future positioning, purpose and strategy.

A Steering Committee was set up to run the programme, chaired by Michael Hardman MBE, one of CAMRA's founding members in 1971. He oversaw and in a number of cases spoke about the review at more than 50 consultation meetings throughout the UK. While the meetings in the main were aimed at CAMRA members, there have also been meetings to seek the opinions of groups such as MPs, cider makers, publicans and members of the British Guild of Beer Writers.

In April 2016, CAMRA members were sent a consultation document Shaping the Future and asked, in the first of a series of surveys, who they thought CAMRA should represent in future. More than 23,000 members responded and their views, together with those collected from the consultation meetings, will be used by the Steering Group when they make recommendations to the Campaign's National Executive at the end of 2016. The executive will then make a proposal at the 2017 Members' Weekend in Bournemouth when it's hoped that CAMRA's future position, purpose and strategy will be agreed.

Whatever the outcome and whether or not CAMRA embraces other styles of beer, real ale will remain its heart beat. The *Good Beer Guide* believes, with quiet passion and undiminished enthusiasm, that beer brewed from natural ingredients, sent from the brewery in an unfinished state, allowed to mature slowly and organically in its container in a pub cellar, and served fresh and bursting with the rich smack of malt and hops, offers both the finest drinking experience and manifestation of the brewer's art.

Here's to the future!

BEER BREXIT

The decision in June 2016 to leave the European Union should have no impact on beer production. The British Government will continue to levy taxes and duties, and CAMRA will carry on arguing the case for lower levels of beer duty. While cuts or freezes on duty in recent budgets have been welcome, the UK still pays far higher levels of duty than most of its former partners in the EU. These high rates are one reason for pub closures as drinkers opt for cheaper supermarkets beers.

In July 2016, the British Beer and Pub Association reported that beer sales had increased by 1.5 per cent in the second quarter of the year. 31 million extra pints were consumed between April and June. Both Marston's and JD Wetherspoon said there had been no loss of sales in their pubs following the EU referendum.

The great British pub
The big fightback

While traditional pubs continue to close, new and often radically different outlets are opening. There are now more than 250 micropubs while other drinking outlets are springing up under railway arches and other unlikely places. But a campaign is still needed urgently to save much-loved community locals.

The current state of the Great British Pub is – like the famous curate's egg – good and bad in parts. Traditional pubs that have been at the heart of towns, cities and villages for centuries continue to close at the alarming rate of 21 a week – though the closure rate is falling. These closures often rip the heart out of communities, robbing local people of the chance to enjoy a convivial drink in company.

As we show in this section, there is now strong evidence that, in an increasingly fragmented society, visits to the pub help social cohesion and play an important role in people's health and welfare. When we lose a pub, we lose more than just the ability to order a pint.

There are many linked and overlapping reasons for the spate of pub closures. In 1951 there were 73,421 pubs in England and Wales and within 20 years that figure had fallen to 64,087. By 2016, the total stood at 52,750.

Some decline was inevitable. Post Second World War, the pub was the main outlet for community activity. Now it has to compete on the high street with a range of restaurants, takeaways and coffee shops all fighting for the 'leisure pound'. Added to this, the appeal of multi-channel television and the ability to download films or watch major sporting events encourages people to stay – and drink – at home.

Drinking at home is aided and abetted by supermarkets and shops that sell alcohol at massive discounts. Beer in particular is used to draw people into stores to do their weekly or daily shop. If beer is offered as a 'loss leader', the stores make up the shortfall through the wide range of other goods bought by customers. The policy encourages the sale and consumption of cheap alcohol, a fact conveniently overlooked by those sections of the media and the 'health lobby' that paint the pub as the main cause of alcohol abuse.

Pubs enjoy none of the advantages of the 'off-trade'. They have to pay the full rate of VAT on food and drink and, as a result of often crippling levels of rent as well as heating, staff and other running costs, many have to charge high prices for beer. While cuts in excise duty in recent budgets have been welcome, Britain remains one of the most expensive countries in Europe for beer.

Victims of the property scramble

Another major cause of the decline in the number of pubs is their attraction to property speculators. Writing in the Morning Advertiser, newspaper of the pub trade, in June 2016, Tony Leonard, who runs the Snowdrop Inn in Lewes and the Roebuck Inn in Laughton, East Sussex, said: 'This week, the only pub in a nearby village will be sold at auction to the highest bidder, widely expected to be a property developer. With the knock of a hammer, hundreds of years of history, a heart of a community, will be wiped out. The villagers had looked into buying it but the asking price was too high to make it viable. So it will probably be replaced by holiday homes for rich Londoners.

'Another nearby pub has recently been sold to a developer and will be turned into luxury housing. Another met the same fate last year. As property prices in the South East soar, the sad truth is that our pubs, no matter how successful, are worth more as development sites than as ongoing businesses.'

One of the pubs mentioned by Tony Leonard was the Lamb at Ripe. It was sold for £367,000 – £67,000 more than its guide price. Villagers attempted to raise funds to buy and save the Lamb but were defeated by the amount demanded.

The sale of pubs to property developers is often favoured by the bigger pub companies. The likes of Enterprise Inns and Punch Taverns are saddled with such vast mountains of debt that they sell off perfectly viable community pubs to help their 'bottom line' accounts. Punch reduced its debts by £3.7 million when it sold the Star in St John's Wood and the Old White Bear in Hampstead, both in North-west London. The Star was popular with cricket fans visiting Lord's and had served such luminaries as Dustin Hoffman and Sir Paul McCartney. It was sold to a property developer and is now – an ironic

Lamb, Ripe: Locals tried to save it but price was too high

Tally Ho, Finchley: For sale

Butcher's Arms, Herne: First micropub

Fuller's Parcel Yard is inside London King's Cross station

fate – an estate agent's. The Old White Bear, which dated back to the early 18th century, enjoyed a good reputation for food as well as beer but was sold to a property developer registered in the Isle of Man and is now a six-bedroom family home.

It's not just the pubcos that close much-loved community locals. Craig and Karen Douglas run the Bree Louise a few yards from Euston Station in London and are faced by a Compulsory Purchase Order. If HS2, the high speed line to Birmingham, goes ahead, the new tracks will be driven straight through the houses and the pub close to the terminus.

The Bree Louise is the current North London CAMRA Pub of the Year for 2016/17, the second time it has held the award. Craig and Karen have spent 13 years turning round a rundown, failing pub originally called the Jolly Gardeners: Bree Louise is named after their daughter, who died shortly after her birth. The pub today is a shrine to real ale. It has no fewer than 23 handpumps and concentrates on ales from small, independent breweries. A petition to save the pub will be launched as soon as the legislation for HS2 to proceed gets Royal Assent.

New pubs opening

All is not doom and gloom. New pubs are opening. In June 2016, JD Wetherspoon said it planned to open eight pubs and a hotel in the following two months. The first new outlet is the Booking Office at Edinburgh's main Waverley Station. Other new pubs were planned for Merseyside, North Ayrshire, West London, Cambridgeshire, Kent and Devon.

JDW chief executive John Hutson said the group would open 15 new pubs between 2016 and 2017. Welcome though these openings are, they have to be set against the sale of some 80 JDW pubs in 2016. Particular concern has been raised about the future of one of North London's most famous pubs, the Tally Ho at Tally Ho Corner, Finchley, once a stopping point for coaches in the 18th and 19th centuries. The Enfield & Barnet branch of CAMRA has applied to the local council for an Asset of Community Value listing for the Tally Ho in a bid to keep it as pub when it is sold by Wetherspoon.

Major railway stations now offer good beer to thirsty travellers. In London, Euston, Paddington, King's Cross and St Pancras have specialist pubs and Fuller's Parcel Yard at King's Cross has become one of the Chiswick brewery's most successful and popular outlets in the capital. Sheffield, Newcastle and York are among a number of regional stations with excellent bars in elegant and ornate station buildings and, as noted above, have now been joined by Edinburgh Waverley.

Micropub boom

Pop-up or micropubs are now a fixture. In just a few short years, the number of micropubs has grown to 251 and 29 of them now have in-house breweries. Many of them are based in empty buildings. The first of the breed, the Butcher's Arms in Herne, Kent, was opened in 2015 by Martyn Hillier and, as the name implies, was previously a butcher's shop. Others are based in a variety of premises, including old funeral parlours, pet shops and disused areas of railway stations.

By their very nature, micropubs are tiny. The Butchers Arms, for example, has room for 10 people sitting and 20 standing. One of the latest new micropubs is the Bumble Inn in Westgate, Peterborough, which offers visitors an excellent comparison between new and older style drinking places. The Bumble Inn, run by Tom Beran, is in a former pharmacy and can accommodate 35 people. It's just a few yards from Oakham Brewery Tap, a cavernous building that was once a Labour Exchange and claims to be the biggest brewpub in Europe. A second micropub was under construction in Peterborough in 2016, based in a former bookmaker's in Church Street.

At Monkseaton in Tyne & Wear a new micropub called the Left Luggage Room is based in a building used for storing bags and parcels in the train station, now part of the Metro line. Council approval for the site was given in June 2016 and the pub will be run by engineer Steven Buckley and former solicitor Andrew Findley, who share a passion for cask and craft beer.

Inspired by this small – in every sense – revolution, larger licensed premises have appeared that often bear little resemblance to the popular concept of the British public house. Manchester in particular has a number of new outlets that make use of redundant space in old warehouses and underneath railway arches and tracks.

The Knott, opposite Deansgate Station, is a two-storey, bright and airy building with a wide range of cask and modern keg beers, as well as highly regarded food, with vegetarian and vegan options. It stands beneath the bridge that carries both trains and the Metro, with a constant rumble of traffic above, and dispenses beer from many independent breweries in the North West, including Brewsmiths from Ramsbottom. The notion that CAMRA is concerned only with traditional pubs is dispelled by the fact that the Knott has been the local Pub of the Year in 2010, 2012 and 2015.

The Piccadilly Tap stands in the arcade that leads to Piccadilly Station. It has seats on the pavement and the large room inside has a bar devoid of either handpumps or keg fonts, with beer dispensed from taps in the wall, with a cool room behind. Again, the emphasis is on local breweries' beers that can also be supplied in takeaway containers for customers embarking on trains.

Close to Piccadilly, Beer Nouveau is also based in old railway buildings in, believe it or not, Temperance Street. It's a new small brewery but owner Steve Dunkley plans to add both a tasting room and a facility where customers can brew their own beer.

Saving pubs

Pubs don't have to close. There are scores of pubs throughout the country that have been saved as a result of people pooling their time and resources to keep their locals open. And there are several organisations on hand that will help with advice on how to raise money and create provident or co-operative groups to run pubs.

Such well publicised victories as the Ivy House in Nunhead, South London, and the Fox & Goose in Hebden Bridge, West Yorkshire, were made possible by the advice of local CAMRA branches, Co-operative & Mutual Solutions, the Plunkett Society and Pub is the Hub – the last-named created by Prince Charles, the Prince of Wales, to save threatened local amenities such as village shops and pubs.

The first and most important step when a pub is threatened with closure is to apply to the local authority for an ACV – Asset of Community Value, a form of protection brought in by the Localism Act of 2011. This not only gives the pub an important listing but also brings in a cooling-off period that enables people to raise the necessary funds to buy the pub and stops the pub's owner from selling it. If local people form a co-op or provident society, they can encourage others in the community to become shareholders and help raise funds. For example, the Ivy House raised £100,000 when it formed a co-operative.

There are currently 1,500 pubs in the UK that have ACV support and a further 1,000 were expected to receive listings during 2016. In Aylesbury in Buckinghamshire, all the town's pubs have been listed as ACVs thanks to a local CAMRA initiative. In Otley, West Yorkshire, the Otley Pub Club, chaired by Andy FitzGerald with the support of Greg Mulholland, MP for Leeds North-west and chair of the Parliamentary Pub Group, has applied to get ACV status for all 20 pubs in the town.

Steps to take

If your favourite pub is under threat, first contact your local CAMRA branch: **www.camra.org.uk/ branches**. Set up an action or steering group and speak to your local council and get them to list the pub as a community asset.

For full details of how to use the Localism Act, go to **www.gov.uk** and follow the links to 'a Plain English Guide to the Localism Act'.

Seek help, advice and possible funding from the Plunkett Foundation: www.plunkett.co.uk; Co-operative & Mutual Solutions: **www.cms.coop**; and Pub is the Hub: **www.pubisthehub.org.uk**.

Why going to the pub is good for you

'Pubs, and small community pubs in particular, provide a safe environment in which to meet old and new friends face to face over a drink. The pub offers an enriching environment where we have the opportunity to meet a greater diversity of people from all walks of life than we might otherwise be able to do' – this is one of the key findings from a special report, commissioned by CAMRA in 2016, 'Friends on Tap – the role of pubs at the heart of the community'.

The report and analysis, carried out by Professor Robin Dunbar and a team from the Department of Experimental Psychology at the University of Oxford, said nothing is more significant, both to people's lives and to the national economy, than health and happiness: 'The more friends you have, the happier and healthier you are.'

And health and happiness are enhanced by having a local pub and visiting it on a regular occasion, Professor Dunbar found. 'People who said they have a "local" or those who patronise small community pubs have more close friends on whom they can depend for support, are more satisfied with their lives and feel more embedded in their local communities than those who said they do not have a local pub,' he added.

A key part of the research for the report was a special poll conducted by YouGov on behalf of CAMRA in which 2,254 adults, distributed by age, sex and region, were asked about their use of pubs

and their overall sense of health and wellbeing. The poll showed that people were most likely to drink alcohol at home with friends (57%), with the second most common location being in a pub with food – 41% of drinkers say the pub is the place where they regularly drink alcohol.

Significantly, the people polled regarded the pub as a relatively safe place to drink and to avoid binge drinking, as well as the best place to socialise with friends after their own or friend's homes. Professor Dunbar and his team said one of the advantages of social drinking in venues like a community pub is that people tend to drink less than when they are on their own.

The report added that 'a limited alcohol intake improves wellbeing and some (though not all) social skills... These findings suggest that pubs in general, and local community pubs in particular, may have unseen social benefits.

'Being more engaged with your local community and being involved more frequently in conversations with other individuals can have substantial benefits by reducing loneliness, which in turn is likely to have significant health and wellbeing benefits...Pubs serve an important hub function, by providing a venue at which people can meet.'

The full report can be read at **www.camra.org/pubs-wellbeing**.

Pub of the Year
Once it was a nightclub, now it's the best pub in Britain

Licensee Grant Cook of the Sandford Park Alehouse – CAMRA's Pub of the Year (See page 175)

A former Cheltenham nightclub that now boasts 10 handpumps for cask beer and cider was, in February 2016, crowned CAMRA National Pub of the Year 2015, just three years after being converted to a pub.

Owner Grant Cook was on holiday in Thailand when he put in a bid for the Grade-II listed Georgian building. Now named the Sandford Park Alehouse, Grant has installed additional walls, a Georgian-style stairwell and a new roof. He has converted a dance floor into his beer cellar.

The beer range includes Gloucester Cascade, Elland Lucky Dip, Oakham Citra, Harvey's Sussex Best, Shepherd Neame Spitfire, Purity Mad Goose, OffBeat Off the Rails and Wye Valley Butty Bach.

Grant Cook spent 10 years running pubs in Leicester then spent 15 years working in IT before deciding to move back into the pub trade. 'I wanted a bit of fun,' he said. 'This is hard work but there's definitely fun, too. It's astonishing to think we've been open less than three years but we've won this award.

'At every stage of the competition, we've been delighted to get to the next round and then to emerge from the list of the final four pubs.'

Pub of the Year organiser Paul Ainsworth says the judges were impressed on every level by the Sandford Park – especially the quality and choice of real ales. 'The judges appreciated the stylish modern interior, knowledgeable, welcoming staff and lively atmosphere,' he added.

As well as good beer and food, the pub also stages an annual cheese and cider festival.

The three other finalists in the Pub of the Year competition were:

Drovers Rest, Monkhill, Carlisle, Cumbria
(see page 98)
A 400 year-old pub close to Hadrian's Wall, it was part of the World War One government-controlled State Management Scheme: there are artefacts from the period on the walls. Four changing beers often come from far afield and the Drover's has a good reputation for its food.

Kelham Island Tavern, Sheffield
(see page 549)
A former winner of the national award, the tavern was saved from closure in 2002 and now draws customers from all parts of the country to savour beers served from 12 handpumps: the range always includes mild, porter and stout. There's an attractive beer garden and regular folk and quiz nights.

Yard of Ale, St Peter's, Kent
(see page 231)
This is a member of the fast-growing micro or pop-up pub sector based in shops and other buildings that have gone out of business. The Yard of Ale stands in the former stable block that housed horses for a local funeral parlour. Drinkers can enjoy three changing beers plus cider surrounded by old riding equipment.

CAMRA's National Pub of the Year competition considers all the criteria that make for a good pub. The competition is judged by the Campaign's 180,000-plus members. Each branch selects its top pub. The branch winners are entered into 16 regional competitions, with the regional winners battling it out to reach the final stages of the competition. Look out for the ♈ symbol against pub entries in the Guide and see 'Award-winning pubs' on pages 1021 – 1022 for the winning branch pubs.

Club of the Year
Seaside club fights off stiff competition to take top prize

Members of the Albatross in Bexhill proudly display their Club of the Year award (See page 451)

The Albatross RAFA Club in Bexhill-on-Sea, East Sussex, walked away with CAMRA's National Club of the Year award for 2016, seeing off intense competition from 28,000 clubs throughout the country.

CAMRA joined forces with *Club Mirror* magazine three years ago in the quest each year to find the club most committed to top quality real ale in welcoming surroundings.

The Albatross, run by the Royal Air Force Association, was singled out for praise by the judges for the quality of its cask beers, often sourced from such local brewers as Dark Star, Rother Valley and Weltons. The club stages beer festivals in April and September and has a full diary of social events, including jazz, folk and quiz nights.

Club of the Year final judge Keith Spencer, said: 'The Albatross offers a wide range of beer and cider, which are kept in excellent condition, but that is only part of the story. The bar staff and steward are part of a bigger team that makes the Albatross the epitome of what a community asset should be. Everyone connected to the club ensures the welcome is warm for everyone that enters.

'On a visit before Christmas, the club was holding a mince pie and raffle evening for local OAPs and it was bursting at the seams with happy customers.'

John Holland, chairman of CAMRA's Clubs Advisory Group and organiser of the competition, added: 'The Campaign's Club of the Year award goes from strength to strength as more and more clubs show great commitment to quality real ale.'

The other finalists in the Club of the Year competition were:

Cheltenham Motor Club, Cheltenham, Gloucestershire (see page 175)
The club was previously a pub called the Crown and in its current form was National Club of the Year in 2013 and has won many local and regional prizes. As well as local real ales from Moor of Bristol and other small breweries, the club stages beer festivals and meet-the-brewer evenings.

Kinver Constitutional Club, Kinver, Staffordshire (see page 423)
This is another former pub and the building dates from 1902. The club serves no fewer than 18 real ales, concentrating on small breweries throughout the Midlands. It has won many local awards from CAMRA and is home to many sporting activities.

Orpington Liberal Club, Orpington, South-east London (see page 304)
Real ale features strongly at the club, which serves more than 200 different cask beers a year. It concentrates on beers from small, independent producers and also serves cider and perry. Beer festivals are staged twice a year and there are regular live folk and blues evenings.

The Club of the Year competition is run by CAMRA in conjunction with the journal *Club Mirror* to find the best real ale clubs in the country. One of the criteria for entry into the competition is that clubs must admit CAMRA members, both men and women. A number of the best real ale clubs feature in the *Good Beer Guide* alongside recommended pubs. As well as admitting CAMRA members, many will also admit non-members carrying a copy of this book. See individual entries for more information.

A tale of three beer cities
Norwich, Sheffield and Derby lay claims to be top ale destination

Norwich is called the City of Ale. Not to be outdone, Sheffield says it's the World's Best Beer City while Derby chips in with the immodest claim that it's the Beer Capital of the World. Which city is the best? The rivalry could be described as bitter but also friendly.

The race to be top of the casks started in Norwich in 2011 with the first City of Ale festival. It was the brainchild of Dawn Leeder and Phil Cutter, a duo from sharply different backgrounds but with a shared passion for good beer and pubs. Dawn is a college lecturer and in her spare time runs a database called PintPicker that lists the beers she has sampled and annotated: more than 16,500 beers are currently listed. Phil is the landlord of the famous Murderers pub close to Norwich castle: its name stems from a grisly murder that took place there in the 19th century.

While they work closely and in perfect harmony with the local CAMRA branch, Dawn and Phil wanted something different to a static beer festival and favoured an event that would celebrate the community role of the pub.

They were also keen to turn the spotlight on the revival of brewing in Norwich and Norfolk. In the 1960s and 70s, a giant London brewer, Watneys, bought and closed all three breweries in the city and flooded their pubs throughout the county with keg beers and lager. Today, there are some 40 Norfolk breweries, with five in the city of Norwich, and pubs now offer a rich choice of beers from East Anglia and further afield.

City of Ale, a 10-day event in May and June, embraces the whole community. Pubs have large banners promoting the event, which is also publicised by the daily and evening newspapers, radio and TV stations, and on the sides of local buses.

The opening ceremony also reaches out to the community, with a horse-drawn brewer's dray transporting local dignitaries – including both the Lord Mayor and the Sheriff – from City Hall to the Roman Catholic cathedral for welcoming speeches and a selection of local brewers' beers. But City of Ale

is about more than beer drinking. There are meet-the-brewer discussions, beer tastings conducted by leading beer writers, and talks from farmers and grain merchants who stress Norfolk's key role as a major producer of the finest malting barley.

Sheffield is one of the biggest cities in the UK with a population of 551,000 while Derby has 248,000 and Norwich just 132,000. But size is not everything. Sheffield, in common with Norwich, has had to recover a lost brewing tradition. It was once home to two Bass breweries along with plants owned by Wards and Whitbread. One by one, they closed and it seemed 'Steel City' had lost its proud brewing tradition.

The revival began with the late Dave Wickett who opened the Fat Cat pub dedicated to cask beer, to which he added the Kelham Island Brewery in 1990. Beer was firmly back on the Sheffield map when Kelham Island's Pale Rider won the prestigious Champion Beer of Britain award in 2004. When the government introduced Progressive Beer Duty in 2002, which means small breweries pay reduced rates of tax, brewing took off like a Victorian steam train.

Today, there are 23 breweries in Sheffield and the city is on course to overtake the number that existed in the peak years of the 19th century. In the wider Sheffield City Region, which covers Barnsley, Bassetlaw, Chesterfield, the Derbyshire Dales, Doncaster, North-east Derbyshire and Rotherham, the overall total of breweries stands at 57. The number includes such substantial producers as Kelham Island, Acorn in Barnsley and the multi award-winning Thornbridge at Bakewell.

Sheffield has become a beer destination as a result of the availability of a fine range of ales in pubs throughout the city, including the Kelham Island Tavern, which has twice been named CAMRA's national pub of the year. As soon as you step off the train you can sample beers on Platform 1b in the Sheffield Tap, a magnificent restoration of the former Edwardian First Class refreshment room at Midland Station. Usually, three of the beers come from the on-site Tapped Brewery that stands alongside in the former dining room.

Phil Cutter and Dawn Leeder, creators of City of Ale

Sheffield Tap, at the city's Midland station

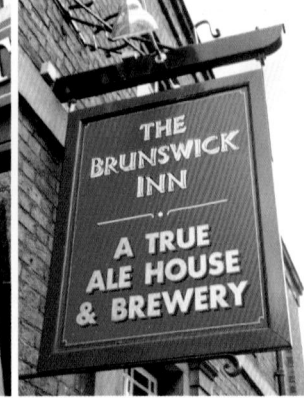

Good beer is flourishing in Derby's many fine pubs (Flower Pot far left)

Sheffield celebrates the return of beer and brewing with an annual Beer Week in March, in its third year in 2017. It was the inspiration of Jules Gray, a local beer writer who also runs the Hop Hideout beer shop. Beer Week is supported by the University of Sheffield, which has produced reports to highlight the city's creative talent. In 2016, it commissioned beer writer Pete Brown to produce a booklet, The World's Best Beer City, that covers the history and revival of brewing in the region.

Beer Week includes Meet the Brewer evenings, beer dinners and brewery tours, with a total of 66 events over 10 days. SIBA, the Society of Independent Brewers, has held its annual BeerX in the city for the past four years, an event that includes a trade show, beer awards and beer festival. Local brewers combine together as the Sheffield Breweries Co-operative to participate in the city's Food Festival in May and in October CAMRA makes a major contribution with its Steel City Beer & Cider Festival. The festival, now in its 42nd year, kept the real ale flag flying during the dog days of the 1970s and 80s and now offers more than 200 beers and ciders at the Kelham Island Industrial Museum.

The friendly rivalry between Derby and Sheffield has led to CAMRA branches in both cities organising an annual Beer Census to calculate the number of different and unique ales available on the bar in a given day. As a result of its sheer size, Sheffield came top with 385 different ales with Derby accounting for an impressive 200.

Derby is no slouch where good beer is concerned. The city lost its last major brewery, Offiler's, in the 1960s, bought and closed by the large London brewer Charrington, which in turn was bought and closed by Bass in neighbouring Burton-on-Trent. But beer has bounced back. There are now 14 breweries in Derby, with more than 60 in the county of Derbyshire. A survey in 1976 found there were only 17 real ales on sale in the city and none came from a local brewer.

Today, pubs feature a growing range of beers from breweries in the city and the county.

The local CAMRA branch stages one of the most respected beer festivals in the country, the Chapter Festival, which will celebrate 40 years in 2017. The festival is attended by around 10,000 drinkers. The 2016 festival was used to launch a book by local CAMRA members on the Demise and Rise of Brewing in Derby while in June that year, Good Beer Guide editor Roger Protz spoke at the prestigious Derby Book Festival that featured such luminaries as Dame Joan Bakewell and James Naughtie. Protz was joined by Rachel Matthews of the local Dancing Duck Brewery, who spoke about her role as a 'brewster' and took a large audience through a tasting of her beers in the Old Bell coaching inn.

The local CAMRA branch organises an Ale Trail in May that takes drinkers on a tour of pubs offering the overlooked Mild Ale style and the branch now plans to run a winter ale festival from 2017 as well as the main festival in July. Visitors to Derby are confronted by a superb choice of pubs in which to enjoy the city's breweries' beers. Just yards from the train station, the Brunswick Inn offers its own home-brewed ales in a superb pub built by a Victorian railway company alongside workers' cottages. Next door, the Alexandra Hotel serves beers from Castle Rock Brewery in Nottingham. Closer to the city centre, pubs include Dancing Duck Brewery's Exeter Arms; the Falstaff, the tap for Falstaff brewery; the Flowerpot, which is home to another brewery, Frontier; and Derby Brewing Company's Greyhound.

Neatly squaring the circle, Derby for three years was home to CAMRA's National Winter Ales Festival. In 2017, the torch will pass to Norwich. This means the 'Fair City' will offer the winter festival in February, City of Ale in May and June, and the CAMRA festival in October.

Three cities: friendly rivalry but combining to showcase good beer and great pubs and underscoring Britain's dynamic beer revolution.

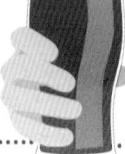

NUMBER OF REAL ALES AVAILABLE, BY CITY:		NUMBER OF BREWERIES IN EACH CITY & THEIR REGION:			
Derby	200	Derby	14	Derbyshire	60
Norwich:	254	Norwich	5	Norfolk	40
Sheffield:	385	Sheffield	23	Sheffield City Region	37

CAMRA beer festivals

Showcasing our rich ale heritage

The great British beer revival is reflected in the growing number of festivals dedicated to our national drink. There are around 200 festivals organised by CAMRA throughout the year – local, regional and national – and they are accompanied by beer events run by other organisations. The Campaign welcomes all beer festivals but believes its own events offer something special.

With a growing emphasis on pale and golden beers, CAMRA is keen to stress through its festivals that the UK offers a much broader choice. Festivals stress the rich heritage of British brewing by offering dark as well as pale beers. There are many festivals run in the colder times of the year that feature dark milds, porters and stouts, culminating in the National Winter Ales Festival that will move in 2017 to Norwich following three successful years in Derby.

Dark beers are also available at festivals held in warmer months, stressing that such styles can be just as refreshing as paler ones. New, innovative styles also feature, including beers stored in oak and those made with the addition of herbs, spices and fruit. A number of festivals now follow the lead of Leicester by stressing in their programmes beers that are suitable for vegans and vegetarians.

Real ale is a perishable drink and needs a little loving care and attention to be served in tip-top condition. All festivals are staffed by CAMRA volunteers who bring pride and passion to the events but who also have wide experience in serving cask beer. CAMRA is running training courses to attract more volunteers to festivals who will be well versed in such vital matters as beer temperature, checking to see when a cask has 'dropped bright' and is ready to serve, and pouring the perfect pint.

Just about every CAMRA festival will also feature cider and perry, drinks growing fast in popularity.

There's no hard sell at CAMRA festivals. The atmosphere is relaxed and many events will offer small tasters of beer so visitors can sample before buying. Prices for both entry and beer are kept as low as possible – in sharp contrast to rival events – as the main aim of CAMRA festivals is to act as showcases for cask beer, not to make money.

A number of festivals are run in conjunction with pubs and clubs as well as charities that range from local hospices to, at a national level, Help for Heroes and other important causes.

Venues range in size, but wherever possible there will be ample seating – to avoid 'vertical drinking' – with family rooms where visitors can leave children in the care of trained staff. Beer's diversity is spotlighted by talks and tastings while live entertainment ranges from jazz, folk and blues to light classical.

Food is an important feature. Depending on the size of a festival, it will range from snacks to bigger offerings. In Manchester, a CAMRA festival has incorporated 'street food' and many events concentrate on food made by local artisans who share the ideals of craft brewers.

When you visit a CAMRA festival you will be helping the local economy. £3.5 million is spent every year buying beer and cider from producers and festival undoubtedly boost trade and tourism wherever they are held. It's estimated that the Great British Beer Festival held in London contributes £10 million to the capital as the crowds that flock to Olympia also use public transport, stay in hotels and use restaurants throughout the capital.

Food – and beer – for thought. Now turn the page to see all the festivals arranged for your pleasure and delight in 2017.

London Olympia: Home to the Great British Beer Festival, one of the world's top beer events

CAMRA beer festivals through the year

January
Cambridge – Winter
Colchester – Winter
Ely – Winter
Exeter – Winter
Manchester
Salisbury – Winter

February
Norwich – National Winter
 Ales
Atherton – Bent & Bongs Beer
 Bash
Bradford
Chappel – Winter
Chelmsford – Winter
Chesterfield
Darlington – Spring
Dorchester
Dover – White Cliffs Winter
Fleetwood
Gosport – Winter
Hucknall
Jersey – Winter
Liverpool
Luton
Pendle
Redditch
Rugby
Stevenage
Stockton – Ale & Arty
Tewkesbury – Winter

March
Brighton – Sussex
Bristol
Bromley
Burton upon Trent

Chippenham
Horsham – Equinox
Leeds
Leicester
London Drinker
Loughborough
Oldham
Seascale
St Neots – Booze on the Ouse
Walsall
Wantage
Wigan
Winchester

April
Bath
Bolton
Bury St Edmunds –
 East Anglian
Coventry
Doncaster
Farnham
Glenrothes – Kingdom of Fife
Gloucester
Hull
Isle of Man
Larbert – Falkirk
Maldon
Mansfield
New Mills
Newcastle upon Tyne
Paisley
Thanet

May
Aberdeen
Banbury
Barnsley

Bexley
Cambridge
Clitheroe
Colchester
Halifax
Kidderminster
Kingston
Lincoln
Macclesfield
Newark
Newport – Tredegar House
 Folk Festival
Newport (Gwent)
Reading
Stourbridge
Wrexham –
 North Wales
Yapton
Yaxley

June
Braintree
Bromsgrove
Glasgow
Greater Manchester –
 Cider & Perry Festival
Hitchin
Lewes – South Downs
Old Harlow – Gibberd Garden
Salisbury
Skipton
Southampton
Stockport
Stratford-Upon-Avon
Tenterden – Kent & East
 Sussex Railway
Thurrock
Wolverhampton

July

Bishop's Stortford
Canterbury – Kent
Chelmsford – Summer
Chorlton
Derby
Devizes
Ealing
Edinburgh – Scottish
Hereford – Beer on the Wye
Maidenhead
Market Bosworth – Rail Ale
Stafford
Stowmarket – Summer
Winchcombe – Cotswold
Woodcote – Steam Fair
Wyke Regis – Wykefest

August

London – Great British
Clacton-on-Sea
Darlington
Durham
Grantham
Manchester – National
    Cycling Centre
Peterborough
Swansea
Worcester

September

Barnsley
Belper – Amber Valley
Bridgnorth – Severn Valley
Bromley
Burnley
Cannock
Cardiff – Great Welsh
Chappel
Cockermouth – Taste Cumbria
    (Jennings)
Crewe – Rail Ale

East Malling (Kent)
Faversham – Hop
Harbury
Hinckley
Jersey
Melton Mowbray
Minehead – West Somerset
    Railway
Morecambe
Moreton-in Marsh –
    North Cotswolds
Plymouth
Scunthorpe
Shrewsbury
St Albans
St Helens
Tamworth
Ulverston
Westmorland
York

October

Alloa
Ascot
Basingstoke – Hampshire
    Octoberfest
Bedford
Birmingham
Carmarthen
Chesterfield – Market
Eastbourne
Egremont (Cumbria)
Falmouth
Gainsborough
Huddersfield – Oktoberfest
Kendal – Westmorland
Louth
Lytham
Matlock
Milton Keynes – Concrete Pint
Norwich
Nottingham

Oxford
Poole
Richmond (North Yorkshire)
Sheffield – Steel City
Solihull
South Woodham Ferrers
Southport
Spa Valley Railway
    (West Kent)
St Ives (Cambs) – Booze on
    the Ouse
Stoke-on-Trent – Potteries
Sunderland
Swindon
Troon – Ayrshire
Twickenham
Wakefield
Weymouth
Woolston – Southampton
Worthing

November

Belfast
Carlisle
Chester – Cheshire
Dudley
Grimsby
Harwich & Parkeston
Heathrow
Redhill
Rochdale
Rochford
Saltburn
Shifnal
Uttoxeter
Watford
Woking

December

London – Pig's Ear

Cask Marque

Champions of beer quality

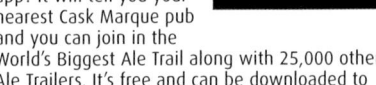

CAMRA are the consumer champions of cask ale and Cask Marque play a similar role within the industry in promoting cask. Together we do our very best to make sure every pint is in perfect condition.

For anyone who has ever been served a pint of beer which is warm, flat, stale or sour, you will know what a dispiriting and depressing experience this is. This is why it is so important to have an industry 'watchdog' like Cask Marque with a watching brief on how this unique product is kept, conditioned, served and promoted.

From humble beginnings, back in 1998, when only 250 pubs passed the Cask Marque inspection, Cask Marque has grown in stature, respect and size. Who would have predicted that today almost 10,000 pubs would pass the rigorous Cask Marque inspection procedure?

Every Cask Marque accredited pub receives unannounced inspections; the pub does not know when the assessor will call. This means that pubs are kept on their toes where quality is concerned.

Every call involves inspecting the cask ale on sale that day, whatever time it is.

Cask Marque want you to experience the beer as the brewer intended it to be served. A pint at cellar temperature, brilliant clarity, clean aroma, and a crisp refreshing tingle from well conditioned beer. If these standards aren't met, the pub doesn't achieve Cask Marque status.

All the Cask Marque assessors are brewers and trade quality technicians and they know their stuff. They are beer experts and won't settle for second best. And if those standards aren't met, they help the outlet by offering advice and training to make sure they meet the quality you demand.

While you can view information on the Cask Marque pubs listed by going to the website www.cask-marque.co.uk , why don't you download for FREE the CaskFinder app? It will tell you your nearest Cask Marque pub and you can join in the World's Biggest Ale Trail along with 25,000 other Ale Trailers. It's free and can be downloaded to iPhones and Android phones.

So while it's good to have a range of beers available on the bar (as most pubs do in this edition of the Good Beer Guide), it's great to have the reassurance that the beers are also independently, and impartially, checked for quality, which is why all pubs which have Cask Marque accreditation have the symbol alongside their listing. This means you're guaranteed a great quality pint.

From Grain to Glass

As well as checking beer in the glass and inspecting cellars Cask Marque also now check breweries to ensure they are compliant with best practice and distributors regarding the handling of beer in the supply chain. This all helps ensure that pubs receive beer in the best possible condition. This is all part of our Grain to Glass programme of which more can be found on the Cask Marque website **www.cask-marque.co.uk/ grain-to-glass**.

A Cask Marque assessor checking a beer for clarity.

The World's Biggest Ale Trail

Ale trails have long been a successful promotion by brewers encouraging drinkers to visit their pubs. Now we have developed the World's Biggest Ale Trail covering nearly 10,000 pubs. Using the CaskFinder app you can discover great pubs to visit and at the same time register your visit and win prizes.

The App records:
- Which pubs you have visited
- Your position in a league table of visits
- How many more visits you need to hit the next level of prizes
- Pubs located nearby that you have not yet visited
- Create your own ale trail for friends to join in

To join the ale trail download CaskFinder App FREE on Android or iPhone and register. Then to record your visits simply scan the QR code on the Cask Marque certificate prominently displayed in pubs.

What prizes can you win?
Registration entitles you to receive the Ale Trailer Newsletter updating you on Cask Marque, Cask Marque pubs' activities and special offers.

The prizes linked to the Ale Trail are:
- Scan 50 barcodes and receive a Cask Marque fridge magnet bottle opener.
- Scan 100 barcodes and receive a Cask Marque t-shirt and 100 scans badge and join the Cask Marque forum and be part of consumer research into cask.

- Scan 250 barcodes and receive a Cask Marque branded pint glass.
- Scan 500 barcodes and become a Cask Marque Ambassador. As well as appearing on our website and being invited to any regional events we may run, get a free place on our Beer Appreciation Course.
- Scan 750 barcodes and win a Cask Marque fleece and climb up the leader board.
- Scan 1000 barcodes and win 4 x 17oz breughel glasses, a 1000 scan badge, a personalised certificate and receive a Cask Marque thermometer to measure temperature of beer in the glass. You are getting nearer to the top of the leader board!
- Scan 2000 barcodes and win a CaskFinder hat, pen and a pack of 6 coasters.

Beer Festivals

If you love Beer Festivals you are in the right place. The CaskFinder app shows all official CAMRA Beer Festivals as well as those being run in Cask Marque pubs across the country. Tapping on the Festivals icon gives a map of your local area and highlights events taking place with further details available – only festivals which can guarantee great beer are shown so make a night of it and visit your nearest beer festival now!

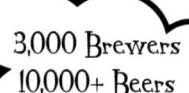

All about beer

The meaning of beer
Craft beer and real ale are one and the same

The sign outside the Gregorian pub in Bermondsey, South-east London, serves to pinpoint a problem facing the modern brewing industry. By offering 'Craft Beer and Real Ale', the casual observer might draw the conclusion that real ale is not a craft product, to the annoyance of the craftsmen and women who work hard to make it. The *Good Beer Guide* has no doubt that real ale is a craft product but the word 'craft' has become a source of dispute.

Large and even global brewers claim today to make craft beer and, for a small number of brewers, the term means 'anything but real ale' in the mistaken belief that younger drinkers don't want to touch beer that comes out of a handpump and a cask – ignoring the proven fact that the biggest swing to real ale is among young drinkers.

The problem with 'craft beer' is that it has no industry definition. CAMRA's annual conference has agreed that 'while real ale is craft beer, not all craft beer is real ale' – an attitude that reaches out to all artisan brewers. The Campaign appreciates that not all outlets for beer are suitable for storing and serving cask-conditioned beer – though the problems can be exaggerated – and there is room in the market for new types of beer called 'craft keg'.

Modern keg beers have little in common with the beers of the 1960s and 70s, such as Red Barrel and Double Diamond, which gave rise to CAMRA's consumer backlash. Today's keg beers are filtered but not always pasteurised and, while served colder than real ale, are not heavily carbonated. In effect, they are identical to the draught beers produced by thousands of independent breweries in the United States. Several new beer festivals in Britain offer a range of craft keg beers but not exclusively so: some offer cask ale as well. Any events that encourage people to sample the pleasures of good beer are to be welcomed.

But in spite of the sound and fury generated by one or two craft keg brewers, it's important to keep its support in proportion. It's a small niche and the big success story of recent years is cask-conditioned real ale.

The *Good Beer Guide* remains committed to real ale not because we're hidebound but because we believe it's a beer style that's not only rooted in Britain's heritage and traditions but one that also offers the finest drinking experience for pub-goers. It's not a beer of the past but the beer of the moment.

Real ale reaches out to drinkers who seek beers made naturally from the finest ingredients. It's possible to make something called 'beer' with rice, maize and corn syrup, and flavoured with green juice squeezed from pulverised hops. The world's biggest beer brand, American Budweiser, even lists rice before barley malt on its label. But cask beer brewers prefer to use the finest malting barley along with hops left in their natural state. They may blend in darker malts and other grains, such as wheat or oats, but they avoid the cheap adjuncts used by the producers of global brands.

Consumers are increasingly concerned by the way food and drink are made. They don't want products trunked half-way round the world and stuffed with preservatives to keep them in edible or drinkable condition. Neither are they impressed by dubious advertising that masks the fact that a 'Belgian' lager is brewed in Wales and 'Australian' and 'French' ones are manufactured in Manchester. Drinkers seek confirmation that their beers are made locally from ingredients grown by farmers who use the finest forms of husbandry.

Thanks to the work of such companies as Warminster Maltings in Wiltshire and Branthill Farm in Norfolk, it's now possible to trace where barley is grown, down to the precise fields where it's harvested. Hop growers are developing new varieties that require fewer agri-chemicals and allow natural predators such as ladybirds to kill the mites that attack the plants.

As we show in the following section, brewers are reaching out to a growing number of vegetarians and vegans by producing beers that have not been 'fined' or cleared with the aid of isinglass made from fish bladders.

As pub entry after pub entry in this Guide proves, more and more publicans are opting for a good range of local cask beers. Their efforts are underscored by CAMRA's LocAle scheme that encourages publicans to source some of their beers from breweries within a 30-mile radius and reduce carbon footprints as a result. For more information on the scheme see **www.camra.org.uk/locale**.

The finished 'real' product is a beer that's neither filtered nor pasteurised and is pulled to the pub bar without the use of applied gas pressure. In all its forms – from the palest pale ale to the blackest stout – it's the perfection of beer and the best of British.

Hop growers are developing new varieties that require fewer agri-chemicals

The unstoppable beer revolution
Revival and innovation bring fresh pleasure to drinkers

There's never been a better time to enjoy beer. The days when brewers made just mild and bitter are long gone and pubs and beer festivals now offer a vast range of styles, both old and new. Today you will find beers made with the addition of fruits, herbs, chocolate, coffee, ginger, lemon grass, pumpkin, coriander and even chilli peppers. But the style that continues to make waves is a revival from the 19th century – India Pale Ale or IPA for short.

In its hey-day, it was a truly revolutionary beer: long before golden lager, it was the first pale beer, made possible by the new technologies of the industrial revolution. Paler malts, better quality hops and an improved scientific understanding of water, yeast and fermentation combined to produce a beer ideally suited for export to 'the Raj' in the blistering climate of the Indian sub-continent.

IPA's impact was both dramatic and brief. By the end of the 19th century it had been marginalised in colonial countries by new golden lager beers served cold with the aid of ice while in Britain strong IPAs were replaced by lower-strength pale ales. In recent years, however, brewers on both sides of the Atlantic have discovered a passion for this almost-lost style. With greater strength than pale ale or bitter and more heavily hopped, IPA offers the complex flavours many discerning drinkers demand today.

Scores of British brewers have added their interpretations of IPA to their portfolios while in the US it has become the most popular style produced by craft brewers. Always keen to 'push the envelope', a number of American brewers have developed stronger Double IPAs and Imperials IPAs. The trend is for 'hop-forward' beers with a citrus aroma from New World varieties, though some American brewers are curbing their enthusiasm for massively hopped beers with more manageable 'session IPAs' while

British brewers are rediscovering the subtle but aromatic delights of English hops.

More recent innovations are based on two Belgian beer styles. Saison was originally, as the name implies, a seasonal beer brewed to refresh farm workers bringing in the harvest. It's now made on a regular commercial basis and, in sharp contrast to hoppy IPAs, drinkers are relishing its more rounded and malty character. Sour beer, on the other hand, is a challenging drink that attempts to replicate the lambic beers of the Senne Valley region that are fermented with wild yeasts in the atmosphere. A true lambic should be aged in wood and several British brewers, including Elgood's and Wild Beer, are keeping to the true path. Expect tart, acidic, woody, yeasty and cider-like notes.

For several years, a number of brewers have experimented with storing beer in casks sourced from wine and whisky producers. There's no doubt that beers served from oak vessels that previously held Bourbon, Cognac, single malt whisky and wine have new depths of aroma and flavour. A more recent development has seen beer stored in freshly-made casks that allow the oak, smoke and vanilla flavours of the wood to permeate the beer. Two pubs in West Yorkshire, the Junction in Castleford and the Duck & Drake in Leeds, specialise in serving beers from the wood and will offer the same beer in both metal and oak casks in order that drinkers can test and taste the difference.

Saison is a traditional style reinvented by a new generation of brewers

How beer is brewed
Craft beer and real ale are one and the same

Barley is beer's building block. Other grain can be used and many brewers blend in small amounts of wheat or oats and even rye, but barley is the preferred grain because it works in perfect harmony with hops and yeast.

But barley has to be turned into malt before brewing can begin. Once it's harvested, the grain is taken to a maltings where it's steeped in water to absorb moisture, then spread on heated floors or inside rotating drums where it starts to germinate. Once germination is under way, the grain is transferred to an oven known as a kiln. Heat dries the grain and, depending on the temperature, produces pale or darker malts.

All beer, regardless of colour, is made mainly from pale malt as it has the highest level of enzymes – natural chemical catalysts – that are crucial to the brewing process. Higher malting temperatures produce brown, black and chocolate malts, which are used for colour and flavour in darker beers. Roasted barley, which is not malted, is often featured in stouts while a method similar to toffee-making produces specialist crystal malts used for colour and flavour. Depending on the mix of malts the brewer chooses, the grain will contribute aromas and flavours similar to Horlicks, Ovaltine, oatmeal biscuits, Ryvita, almonds and other nuts, as well as notes of honey, butterscotch, caramel, tobacco and vanilla.

Hops: the vital seasoning

The annual harvest also produces beer's other key ingredient: hops. In common with grain, hops need good soil, in this case loamy or sandy soil that retains a good supply of water. Kent, Herefordshire and Worcestershire are the main hop-growing counties of England. Hops grow at great speed in the spring and summer and once harvested they are dried by warm air in special sheds or oast houses. Hops contain acids, oils and resins that deliver bitterness to beer along with fragrant aromas of spice, pepper, grass, cedar wood and citrus fruit. The oils and tannins in the plant help stabilise beer and prevent infection. English hops are prized for their spice and pepper notes. Fuggles and Goldings are the best known traditional varieties but new hops have been introduced in recent years, including First Gold, Boadicea, Endeavour and Jester: the last two have been bred to give the aromas and flavours of grapefruit, mango and tropical fruits demanded by many modern brewers.

The brewing process

When malt reaches the brewery it's ground in a mill into a powder called grist. Grist and pure hot water flow into the mash tun, where the porridge-like mixture of grain and water starts the brewing process. Pure water can come from springs, bore holes or from the public supply. It will be thoroughly filtered, and brewers often add such sulphates as gypsum and magnesium to enhance the flavours of malt and hops. The mixture is left to stand in the mash tun for some two hours and during that time enzymes in the malt convert the remaining starch into fermentable sugar.

When starch conversion is complete, the brewer and his team will run the sweet extract, called wort, to a second vessel, the copper, where it's vigorously boiled with hops. The hops are usually added in stages: at the start of the boil, half way through and just before the end in order to extract the maximum aroma and bitterness from the plants.

The copper boil lasts between 1½ and 2 hours. The hopped wort is passed through a cooler to lower the temperature and is then pumped to fermenting vessels. These can be open or closed, upright or horizontal, but it's here that the liquid starts the conversion to alcohol with the aid of yeast. Yeast is a fungus that feeds on sugary liquids. Every brewery will have its own yeast culture that's carefully guarded and stored, as it gives its own important 'house character' to the beer.

Ale fermentation is rapid and lasts for a week – it's a method known as 'warm fermentation' to distinguish it from the cold fermentation method used to make genuine lager. Yeast converts malt sugar into alcohol and carbon dioxide and creates a dense, rocky blanket on top of the liquid. It also produces natural chemical compounds called esters that give off aromas reminiscent of apples, oranges, pear drops, banana, liquorice, molasses and, in especially strong beers, fresh leather. These add to the complexity of the finished beer.

Eventually the yeast will be overcome by the alcohol it has created and the yeast blanket is skimmed from the vessel. The beer will rest for several days in conditioning tanks to mature and to purge unwanted rough alcohols and esters.

Then comes the major divide in the world of brewing. One route leads to filtered, pasteurised and carbonated beer. The other creates Britain's great contribution to the world of beer: cask-conditioned ale. Cask ale is unique as it's not finished in the brewery but in the pub cellar. From conditioning tanks, it's racked into casks. Finings may be added to clear the beer (see Fishy Business below). Additional hops may be placed in the casks for extra aroma and flavour and brewing sugar can be added to encourage a strong secondary fermentation.

The beer that reaches the pub cellar is said to be 'still working' as remaining yeast turns the final sugars into alcohol and CO_2. Casks have to be vented to allow the natural gas to escape. A cask has two openings: a bung at the flat end where a tap is inserted to serve the beer; and a shive hole on top. A soft porous peg of wood, a spile, is knocked into the shive, enabling some of the CO_2 to escape. As fermentation dies down, the soft spile is replaced after 24 hours by a hard one that leaves some gas in the cask: this gives the beer its natural sparkle, known as 'condition'.

Inside the cask, finings sink to the floor, attracting yeast in suspension. When the publican is satisfied that the beer has 'dropped bright', plastic tubes or 'lines' are attached to the tap and the beer is drawn by a suction pump activated by a handpump on the bar. The recommended serving temperature for real ale is 11 or 12°C. Some golden summer beers are served between 8 and 10°C and they may go through a special cooler below the bar.

Fishy business

A growing number of breweries listed in the Guide say their beers are suitable for vegetarians and vegans. Cask beers that are traditionally 'fined' to remove yeast use a clearing agent known as isinglass that's made from fish bladders and many drinkers – not just those who avoid meat, fish and dairy products – dislike the practice. Alternatives are being sought. For example, the Marble Brewery in Manchester, which brews organic beers, clears them with either silica or Irish moss but other brewers don't consider Irish moss to be effective. Experts at the Centre for Bio-energy and Brewing Science at the University of Nottingham are analysing a new role for the hop plant as a clearing agent for beer, cask ale in particular. Scientists are looking at recycling 'spent' hops used in the brewing process to attract yeast and enable beer to 'drop bright'.

Justin Hawke and brewing team at Moor Beer

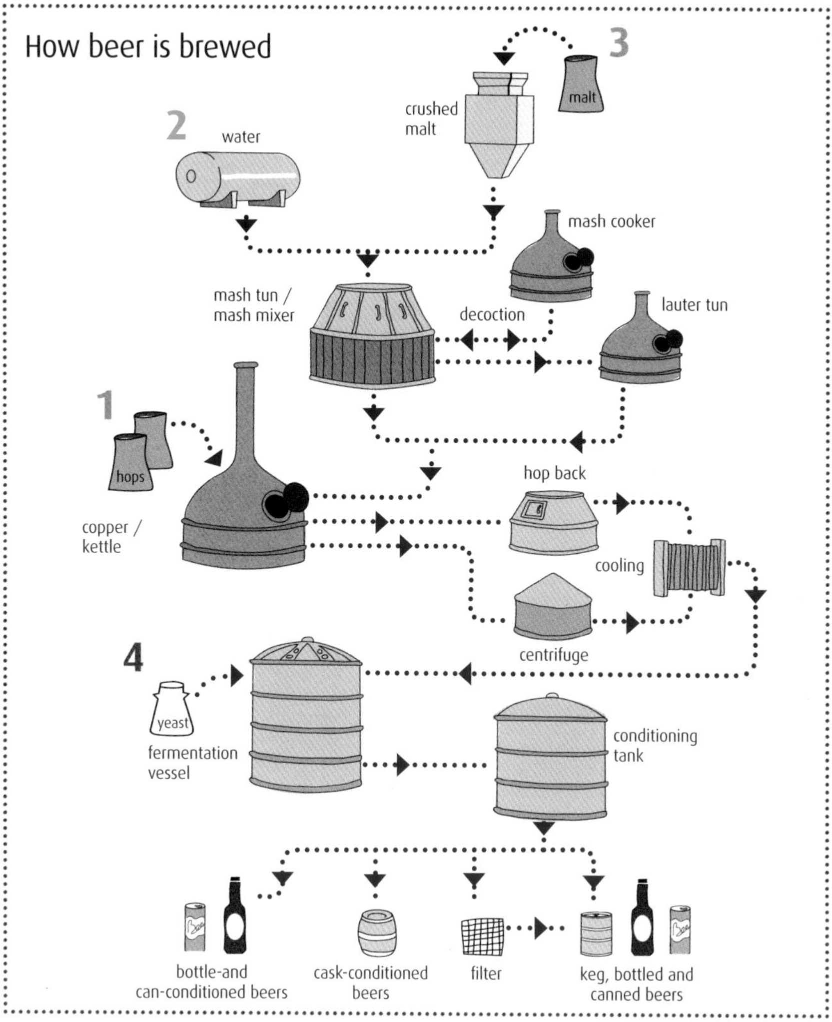

How beer is brewed

3 malt

2 water

crushed malt

mash cooker

mash tun / mash mixer

decoction

lauter tun

1 hops

copper / kettle

hop back

cooling

centrifuge

4 yeast

fermentation vessel

conditioning tank

bottle-and can-conditioned beers

cask-conditioned beers

filter

keg, bottled and canned beers

Beer is made from just four ingredients:

1 HOPS: There are around two dozen hop varieties in England, ranging from the Golding and the Fuggle, first grown in the 18th and 19th centuries, to more modern ones, such as Boadicea and Endeavour. Hops can be used in the brewery either as whole flowers or ground and compressed into pellets.

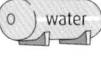
2 WATER: Pure water, called 'liquor' by brewers, can come from springs, bore holes or from the public supply. It will be thoroughly filtered, and brewers often add such sulphates as gypsum and magnesium to enhance the flavours of malt and hops.

3 MALT: Maltsters steep barley in water to absorb moisture, then spread it on heated floors or inside rotating drums where it starts to germinate. Once germination is under way, the grain is transferred to an oven known as a kiln. Heat dries the grain and, depending on the temperature, produces pale or darker malts.

4 YEAST: Yeast is a type of fungus that feeds on sugary liquids. Every brewery will have its own yeast culture that's carefully guarded and stored, as it gives its own important 'house character' to the beer. Brewers keep samples of their yeast cultures in a special bank in Norwich in case they need a fresh supply.

The easiest solution is not to fine beer and several brewers are now following this course. Justin Hawke runs Moor Beer brewery in Bristol and avoids isinglass as he believes it strips flavour from beer. He produces a wide range of cask beer that are served slightly cloudy in pubs and he says he has not had any negative feedback from publicans or drinkers.

New methods of packaging

The growing interest in good beer has seen it move from traditional pubs to new venues, such as bars, restaurants and micropubs. Many of these outlets lack cellars where beer can be stored and served in the conventional manner. As a result, a number of breweries are now using one-trip 'key kegs' that take up little space, can be kept close to the bar if the temperature is controlled, and remove the need for the breweries to pick up the empties.

As the name suggests, a key keg is designed for modern keg beers. It's made up of a plastic container that looks like a large brown urn. Inside a sterile bag holds the beer. Keg beers are filtered and the kegs are connected to gas cylinders at the point of delivery, with the gas replacing the beer as it's served.

As a result of small venues asking for real ale, key kegs now have a variant called a key cask. The principle is the same, with the beer inside a bag in the container, but the gas – either carbon dioxide or oxygen – sits in a second bag on top of the beer. When the serving tap is turned, beer is replaced as the bag of gas pushes down. As the gas does not come into contact with the beer, which is neither filtered nor pasteurised and contains live yeast, key casks are acceptable to CAMRA. The system is similar, though on a smaller scale, to the one used by the Zerodegrees brewpubs (see Breweries section) where the beer is stored in large tanks under bags of air that drive the beer to the bar.

Beer appreciation

We can increase our appreciation of beer by sampling and tasting. Gently swirl the liquid in the glass to release the aroma or the 'nose' and discover the malt, hop and fruit notes that emerge. Allow the beer to trickle over the tongue, which picks up bitterness, sweetness and salt, and enjoy the palate or 'mouthfeel' as the beer coats the cheeks. Finally, the beer passes down the back of the throat in what is known as the 'finish'.

On the nose you may find a rich biscuit or Ovaltine-like malt character. Hops will add their own distinctive note. English hops deliver a restrained spicy, peppery, earthy, wood and resinous note. American hops are renowned for their profound citrus notes, with grapefruit to the fore. German hops are called 'noble' varieties and offer cedar wood, mint, pine kernels and lemon zest. New Zealand hops have a vinous fruit character. One leading variety, Nelson Sauvin, is so called as a result of flavours similar to Sauvignon wine.

Fruit may be detected and this comes from both hops and yeast. A sulphur or salty note is derived from the water, which will have had sulphates added to replicate the famous salty waters of Burton-on-Trent, home of classic pale ale brewing.

In the mouth, the malt may have a delicious juicy note while hop bitterness will build, balancing any fruitiness. Finally the finish should combine all the elements of malt, hops and fruit into a satisfying, dry finale. The flavour characteristics of a particular beer will depend on its style: see the British beer styles section that follows. Suffice it to say that a Mild Ale will offer a pronounced malt and caramel note, with restrained bitterness, while Bitters and IPAs will have a robust hop character, Porters and Stouts a roasted and toasted grain note, while Barley Wines are fruity and vinous, and Old Ales will often have a slight hint of sourness allied to ripe malt, gentle hops and notes of leather and tobacco.

Tasting beer can be carried out in the home but greater appreciation will emerge if a group of people take part – and there's no better place to do it than in a pub. Many pubs now stage regular beer festivals, with a wide choice of beers available. If festivals are not held in your local but it has a good range on the bar, ask whether a room or part of the bar could be set aside for a tasting event.

Glasses should be either half-pint beer glasses or the large ones used for red wine. You will need fresh water and a supply of crackers to allow tasters to clean their palates between beers. Scoring sheets add to the enjoyment of the event, especially if you want to name a 'best beer'. The sheets should be divided into marks out of 10 for appearance, aroma, palate and finish. Usually, not more than six beers are judged in a single event.

Depending on the availability of beer, you could base a tasting round just one style, such as Mild, Bitter or Porter & Stout. However, it's unlikely that many pubs would have six versions of a single style, so it's best to have a mixed event. It's advisable to work up from the lowest strength: it would be difficult to judge a Mild after a Barley Wine.

Marks for appearance will be based on the clarity of the beer when the glass is held up to the light. Does it have a good head of foam, which indicates the beer has what brewers call 'condition'. The absence of foam means the beer is flat. Some beers, such as wheat beers, are designed to have a cloudy appearance, and this should be borne in mind when marking.

Marks for aroma will be based on the appeal of the beer as it's sniffed. Is there a good balance of malt, hops and fruit or is the beer overly malty or, conversely, too bitter? If you are judging bitter beers, including IPA, then expect to find the balance tilted towards hops and bitterness. Palate is based on the appeal of the beer in the mouth:

you would mark down for cloying sweetness or harsh bitterness, and give higher marks when both characteristics are in balance. Finally, the finish: is the beer harmonious as it passes over the back of the tongue and down the throat, well-balanced between malt, hops and fruit, ending neither too malty nor too bitter. Again, marks in this section will be guided by the style of beer: you would expect a roasted grain character from a Stout or Porter.

If it's not possible to organise a tasting event of your own, bear in mind that many CAMRA festivals stage beer tastings, often hosted by experts in the field. Monitor the festivals listed in this Guide (see pages 18–19).

Alan Hinkes: Top mountaineer is a flag waver for British ale

Alan Hinkes raises the flag for British beer. When he's not climbing he's enjoying a pint or two and telling his legion of followers on Twitter about his latest discoveries.

People listen to him because he's one of Britain's leading mountaineers. He's climbed Everest five times, scaled K2 and Kanchenjunga and he was the first Briton to reach the summit of Manashu. He's the only Brit to climb all 14 peaks of more than 8,000 metres in the Himalaya and Karakoram ranges in Nepal, Tibet and Pakistan.

It's thirsty work and when he's not shinning up sheer rock faces, surrounded by snow and ice, he relaxes with a good beer. Climbing in Scotland in the summer of 2016, he regaled his supporters with notes and images of new beers he found there, such as those from Burnside Brewery in Aberdeenshire and he regularly sends reports on beer sightings and tastings when he's climbing in Cumbria.

Alan was born in 1954 and took up rock climbing in Yorkshire while he was a student at Northallerton Grammar School. From there he went on to face the more demanding heights of the Alps, where he climbed the North Face of Eiger, and then tackled the Himalayas.

'Northallerton pubs were dominated by Cameron's and John Smith's,' he recalls. 'I drank Cameron's Strongarm and when I discovered Theakston's I had their Bitter and Old Peculier.'

On the other side of the Pennines, while climbing in Cumbria, he found and has kept a life-long love for Jennings Bitter – 'a gorgeous beer' – which he drank in two pubs in Keswick, the Twa Dogs and the George.

He goes all misty-eyed when he thinks back to the first tastes he had of some of his favourite beers: Bateman's from Lincolnshire, Batham's and Ma Pardoe's from the Black Country and the beers from the long-closed Castle Eden Brewery in Co Durham. But of all the British beers he has sampled, his favourite remains Timothy Taylor Landlord from Keighley, West Yorkshire.

He says his doctor has told him he should have a couple of pints when he comes down from a peak. 'Beer is full of iron, carbohydrates, protein, vitamin B – and a bit of alcohol,' he says. He makes sure there's always beer on hand for relaxing after a climb. In 1994, he and his companions took a home-brewing kit 5,000 metres up K2. They boiled water on a paraffin stove and, then in Alan's words, had to 'nurture the beer' to stop it freezing at night and getting too hot during the day.

Alan is great friends with another beer-loving mountaineer, Sir Chris Bonington, who is one of the founders of the co-operative that saved the Old Crown pub and brewery in Hesket Newmarket in Cumbria.

'Chris and I were searching for the Yeti in Nepal when he had to formally open the Old Crown,' Alan says. 'There was no email or internet then, so he had to do it by Telex.' Fittingly, most of the beers from the brewery behind the pub are named after such Cumbrian peaks as Scafell and Helvellyn, well known to both climbers.

Alan wasn't too impressed with the beers when he first tasted them. 'They were just like home-brew, no better than the beer I made on K2. But since then, they've put proper brewing kit in and the beers are wonderful now.'

He's not enamoured of some of the new breed of powerfully hopped beers. He likes beers with balance such as Black Sheep, London Pride – 'and I still love Jenning's Bitter'. When he's in Cumbria he's partial to the ales from the Keswick Brewery, founded by Sue Harrison in 2006, which specialises in golden ales with 'thirst' in the names.

Alan Hinkes is heavily involved in the Duke of Edinburgh's award scheme and works with Best of British to promote the Three Peaks Challenge. He was awarded an OBE in 2006 and is an Honorary Citizen of Northallerton and a former Yorkshireman of the Year.

On the beer front, he writes for OG magazine and will continue to recommend fine ales from near and far, especially those – important to a mountaineer – that offer good balance.

British beer styles

British beer is constantly evolving. The days when brewers produced just Mild and Bitter are long gone. The new wave of artisan brewers have thrown caution to the wind and now embrace both new styles and recreations of such traditional beers as IPA, Porter and Stout.

They don't confine their beer styles to this country but look abroad for inspiration. Two sharply-contrasting Belgian styles, lambic and saison, add to the delights of current drinking: lambic, made by 'wild fermentation', has been renamed Sour in both the UK and the US and can also be made with the addition of fruit.

One or two brewers are experimenting with a rare German style called Gose, made in the Leipzig area, a beer made with the addition of salt. India Pale Ale has been restored from near oblivion and has become a world-wide phenomenon with brewers here, the US, Australia, New Zealand, Scandinavia, Belgium, Germany, Italy and even Russia making their interpretations. Modern British versions of IPA often lean heavily on the American model and are described as 'hop forward' as a result of their profound citrus hop character. Golden Ale, which transformed British brewing in the 1980s, continues to be made in abundance along with new versions of Pale Ale that are a hymn to the hop plant. But it must not be forgotten that Bitter remains, overwhelmingly, the most popular type of beer, a style that is intrinsically British with its copper and bronze colour and fine balance between malt and hops. Mild, though much diminished these days, is still around and remains popular in parts of the Midlands, Wales and North-west England. It's a style with history and tradition on its side and needs more support.

PORTER & STOUT

Porter was a London beer that created the first commercial brewing industry in the world in the early 18th century. Its name came from its popularity with London porters who needed calories to help sustain them in their hard manual labour. The origins of the beer are disputed but the most recent research suggests Porter, first called 'Entire', was blended in the brewery from pale, mild and aged or 'stale' beer. The strongest version of Porter was called Stout Porter, later shortened to just Stout.

Porter and Stout were exported from London to the rest of the British Isles and, as a result, Arthur Guinness built his own Porter brewery in Dublin. During World War One, when the British government restricted the use of malt, heavily roasted versions in particular, in order to divert grain and energy to bread making and the arms industry, Guinness and other Irish brewers came to dominate the market. In recent years, Porter and Stout have returned to popularity in Britain, the United States and Australasia, with brewers digging into old recipes books to create genuine versions of the style.

Look for a jet-black colour and expect a dark and roasted grain character with burnt fruit, espresso or cappuccino coffee, liquorice and molasses. The beer should have a deep bitterness to balance the richness of malt and fruit. Milk Stout, made by a few brewers, uses lactose or 'milk sugar' to give a creamy character to the beer.

MILD

Mild developed in the 18th and 19th centuries as drinkers started to demand a slightly sweeter and less aggressively hopped beer than Porter. Mild Ale was drunk primarily by industrial and agricultural workers who needed to refresh themselves after long hours of arduous labour. Early Milds were much stronger than modern versions, which tend to fall into the 3% to 3.5% category though a number of brewers are bringing strength back to the style. Mild is usually dark brown in colour, due to the use of well-roasted malts or roasted barley, though there are paler versions such as Banks's Mild and Timothy Taylor's Golden Best. Look for a rich malty aroma and flavour, with hints of dark fruit, chocolate, coffee and caramel, with a gentle underpinning of hop bitterness.

OLD ALE

Old Ale is another style from the 18th century, stored for many months or even years in wooden vessels where the beer picked up some lactic sourness from wild yeasts and tannins in the wood. As a result of the sour taste, it was dubbed 'stale' by drinkers and the beer was one of the components of the early Porters. In recent years, Old Ale has made a return to popularity, due primarily to the success of such beers as Theakston's Old Peculier and Gales' Prize Old Ale. Contrary to expectations, Old Ales do not have to be especially strong and can be no more than 4% alcohol. Neither do they have to be dark: Old Ale can be pale and bursting with lush malt, tart fruit and spicy hops. Darker versions will have a more profound malt character, with powerful hints of roasted grain, dark fruit, polished leather and fresh tobacco. The hallmark of the style is a lengthy period of maturation, often in bottle rather than cask.

BARLEY WINE

Barley Wine dates from the 18th and 19th centuries when England was often at war with France and it was the duty of patriots, usually from the upper classes, to drink ale rather than French claret. Barley Wine had to be strong – often between 10% and 12% – and was stored for as long as 18 months or two years. Fuller's Vintage Ale (8.5%) is a bottle-conditioned version of its Golden Pride and is brewed with four different varieties of malts and hops every year. Expect massive sweet malt and ripe fruit of the pear drop, mandarin orange and lemon type, with chocolate and coffee if darker malts are used. Hop rates are generous and produce bitterness and peppery, grassy and floral notes.

BITTER

At the turn of the 19th and 20th centuries, brewers built large estate of 'tied' pubs and they moved away from beers stored for months or years and developed 'running beers' that could be served after a few days of conditioning in pub cellars. Bitter was a new type of running beer: it developed from Pale Ale but was usually copper coloured or deep bronze due to the use of slightly darker malts, such as crystal, that gave the beer fullness of palate. Best is a stronger version of Bitter but there is considerable crossover. Bitter falls into the 3.4% to 3.9% band while Best Bitter is 4% upwards, though a number of brewers call their ordinary Bitter 'best'. A further development of the style comes in the shape of Strong Bitter of 5% or more: Fuller's ESB and Greene King Abbot are well-known examples. With ordinary Bitter, look for spicy, peppery and grassy hop character, a powerful bitterness, tangy fruit and juicy/nutty malt. With best and strong Bitters, malt and fruit character will tend to dominate but hop aroma and bitterness are still crucial to the style, often achieved by 'late hopping' during the copper boil or by adding additional hops to casks as they leave the brewery.

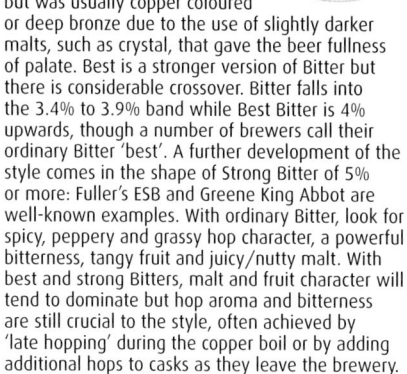

BURTON ALE

As the name suggests, the origins of Burton Ale lie in Burton-on-Trent, but the style became so popular in the 18th and 19th centuries that most brewers had 'a Burton' in their portfolio and the expression 'gone for a Burton' entered the English language. Bass in Burton at one time had six different versions of the beer, ranging from 6% to 11.5%: the strongest versions were exported to Russia and the Baltic States. In the 20th century, Burton was overtaken in popularity by Pale Ale and Bitter but it was revived with great success in the late 1970s with the launch of Ind Coope Draught Burton Ale. When Allied Breweries broke up, the beer was owned by Carlsberg, who stopped production in 2015. But the style has been recreated by Burton Bridge Brewery in its home town. Other versions of the style exist under different names: Young's Winter Warmer was originally called Burton. Bass No 1, brewed occasionally, is called a barley wine but is in fact the last remaining version of a Bass Burton Ale. Look for a bright amber colour, a rich malt and fruit character underscored by a solid resinous and cedar wood hop note.

PALE ALE

According to a legend in the 19th century, when a sailing ship bound for India with a cargo of IPA foundered off the coast at Liverpool, the casks were brought ashore and news of both the colour and taste of Pale Ale spread throughout the country. IPAs were brewed for the domestic market as a result but the Burton brewers were keen to produce versions with lower alcohol and hop rates that didn't require months to mature. The spread of the railway system allowed brewers in Burton to move beer around the country at speed and Pale Ale was dubbed 'the beer of the railway age' as a result. The clamour for Pale Ale was so great that brewers from London, Liverpool and Manchester opened second breweries in Burton to make use of the mineral-rich water to make their own versions of the style. From the early 20th century, Bitter began to overtake Pale Ale in popularity and a result Pale Ale became mainly a bottled product. A true pale ale should be different to Bitter, similar in colour and style to IPA and brewed without the addition of coloured malts. It should have spicy/resinous aroma and palate with biscuit malt and tart fruit from the hops. Many beers called Bitter today should properly be labelled Pale Ale.

IPA

India Pale Ale changed the face of brewing in the 19th century. The new technologies of the Industrial Revolution enabled brewers to use pale malts to design beers that were pale bronze in colour. The first 'India Ales' were brewed in London and were probably based on October Beers that were matured for many months and were ideally suited to a long sea journey to India. But London was soon eclipsed by Burton-on-Trent with its spring waters rich in minerals that brought out the fullest flavours of malt and hops. 19th century IPAs were high in both alcohol and hops to keep them in good condition during the journey to the colonies. Its life span was brief, driven out of Africa and India by German lager beer. But the style has made a big comeback in recent years and is now made in abundance throughout the world. Look for a big peppery hop aroma and palate balanced by juicy malt and tart citrus fruit.

GOLDEN ALE

Golden Ales have become so popular with both drinkers and brewers that the style now has its own category in the annual Champion Beer of Britain competition. Exmoor Gold, Hop Back Summer Lightning and Rooster's Yankee started the trend in the early 1980s and other brewers quickly followed in a rush to wean younger drinkers from mass-produced lager to the pleasures of cask ale. The style is different to Pale Ale in two critical ways: Golden Ale is paler, often brewed with lager malt or specially produced low colour ale malt and, as a result, hops are allowed to give full expression, balancing sappy malt with luscious fruit, floral, herbal, spicy and resinous notes. While brewers of Pale Ale tend to use such traditional English hop varieties as Fuggles and Goldings, imported hops from North America, the Czech Republic, Germany, Slovenia and New Zealand give radically different notes to Golden Ale. As a result these beers offer a new and exciting drinking experience. They are often served colder than draught Bitter and some brewers, such as Fuller's, have installed special cooling devices to ensure the beer reaches the glass at an acceptably refreshing temperature.

SCOTTISH BEERS

Historically, Scottish beers tend to be darker and maltier than beers south of the border, the reflection of a colder climate where beer needs to be nourishing. It's an urban myth, though, that Scottish beers are less heavily hopped than

English ones. The classic traditional styles are Light, Heavy and Export, which are not dissimilar to Mild, Bitter and IPA. They are also known as 60, 70 and 80 Shilling ales from a 19th century system of invoicing beers according to strength. A 'Wee Heavy' or 90 Shilling Ale, now rare, is the Scottish equivalent of barley wine. Many of the newer brewers in Scotland are producing beers lighter in colour and with pronounced hop character.

WHEAT BEER

Wheat beer is a style closely associated with Bavaria and Belgium and its popularity in Britain has encouraged many brewers to add wheat beers to their portfolios. The title is something of a misnomer as all 'wheat beers' are a blend of malted barley as well as wheat, as the latter grain is difficult to brew with and needs the addition of barley, which acts as a natural filter during the mashing stage. But wheat, if used with special yeast cultures developed for brewing the style, gives distinctive aromas and flavours, such as clove, banana and bubblegum, that make it a complex and refreshing beer. The Belgian version of wheat beer often has the addition of herbs and spices, such as milled coriander seeds and orange peel – a habit that dates back to medieval times.

FRUIT/SPECIALITY BEERS

Brewers endlessly search for new flavours to reach out to a wider audience for their beers. The popularity in Britain of Belgian fruit beers has not gone unnoticed and now many domestic brewers are using fruit in their beer. Others have gone the extra mile and add honey, herbs, heather, spice and even spirits – brandy and rum feature in a number of speciality beers, while beers matured in Bourbon, whisky and Cognac casks have become a major development in both this country and the U.S. It's important to dispel the belief that fruit and honey beers are sweet: the ingredients add new dimensions to the brewing process and are highly fermentable, with the result that beers that use the likes of cherries or raspberries are dry and quenching rather than cloying.

SOUR BEER

Also known simply as 'Sours', this is a style brewed in both the UK and US by brewers fascinated by Belgian lambic beer, made by 'wild' or spontaneous fermentation. Instead of carefully cultivated brewer's yeast, lambic is left open to the atmosphere to allow wild yeasts to attack the sugars in the extract known as wort and begin the fermentation process. Elgood's brewery in Wisbech, Cambridgeshire, makes a fine example of lambic as it has the 'cool ships' or open cooling trays that enable the wort to be attacked by passing yeasts. Following the first fermentation, true lambics are stored in wooden casks for a year or more. The main wild yeast, Brettanomyces, is used by modern brewers to inoculate their worts and gain the required sour or acidic character. Other good examples of British sours come from Wild Beer, Kernel and Burning Sky.

SAISON

Saison is another Belgian beer style now finding favour in Britain and other countries. It originates in Wallonia, the French-speaking region of Belgium, and was a seasonal beer brewed by farmers to refresh their labourers during the busy harvest period. Such leading Saison brewers as Dupont, based on a farm, now brew their beers on a full-time basis. In sharp contrast to lambic, Saison should have a rich malty/fruity palate balanced by earthy, spicy and peppery hops. Some Saisons are made with the addition of 'botanicals' such as ginger, black pepper and aniseed. British interpretations come from Adnams, Brew By Numbers, Partizan and Poppyland.

Insist on quality beer

Real ale, when it's conditioned with care, should be bright, sparkling, with a lively head and served cool and refreshing (though some beers, such as wheat beers, may be intentionally cloudy). As a consumer, forking out a high price for beer, don't be afraid to take your pint back to the bar if it is not in good condition. Bar staff should replace it and might not be aware of an issue unless you tell them.

Also, please go back to the bar if you are served a short measure – less than a pint (or half-pint) of liquid in the glass. It's an outrageous rip-off. CAMRA beer festivals serve beer in oversize glasses that ensure drinkers always get the amount of beer they have paid for. Most pub owners refuse to use oversize glasses, preferring brim-measure glasses that allow them consistently to serve short measures. It's a scandal. Don't put up with it.

Take your pint back to the bar if:

- Your beer is served either too warm or too cold. Real ale should be served cool – around 11–12°C. It's a myth that it should be served at room temperature. Warm beer tastes bad, as the temperature creates unpleasant off flavours. But bear in mind that some Golden Ales are meant to be served cooler than other styles.

- Your beer smells of acetone, vinegar or stale bread.

- The pint has no head, is totally flat and out of condition.

- It's not only flat but hazy and has yeast particles or protein floating in the liquid.

Ten of the best

Roger Protz offers his choice of some of the best interpretations of classic beers

BITTER: Otter Bitter

Superb balance of biscuit malt and pungent, spicy and peppery hops, with a dry and bitter finish with orange fruit notes.

BEST BITTER: Blue Monkey Sanctuary

Copper-coloured, with strong notes of biscuit malt and butterscotch, balanced by herbal and fruity hops from American and German varieties.

PORTER & STOUT: Dancing Duck Dark Drake

An oatmeal stout with rich creamy malt and strong notes of caramel and liquorice. There's an espresso coffee character in the velvety finish.

STRONG BITTER: Grain India Pale Ale

Maris Otter malt gives a fine toasted grain note, balanced by fruity and spicy hops, leading to a long, bittersweet and finally dry finish.

GOLDEN ALE: Hawkshead Cumbrian Five Hop

Three English and two American hops deliver pungent tropical fruit and herbal aromas and flavours with a solid juicy malt backbone.

MILD: Rudgate Ruby Mild

Strong mild with roasted grain, rich chocolate, burnt fruit and bitter hops resins: hoppy for the style with a bittersweet, creamy finish.

BARLEY WINE: Darwin Extinction

Recreation of a 1920s barley wine with massive fruit and warming alcohol, the sweetness cut by piny and peppery hops.

SPECIALITY: Titanic Plum Porter

Roasted grain, coffee and liquorice are joined by a big hit of tart fruit and spicy hops: the plum notes linger on into the rich finish.

SOUR: Wild Beer Somerset Wild

Oak-aged beer fermented with wild yeasts from Somerset orchards. Tart, tongue-curling, acidic but dangerously drinkable and refreshing with a delicious tart lemon note.

SCOTTISH: Stewart Edinburgh No.3

A traditional Scottish 'heavy', dark copper coloured, with a big toasted/roasted grain aroma and palate but with a persistent, gentle underpinning of peppery hops. A meal in a glass.

CAMRA's Beers of the Year

The beers listed below are CAMRA's Beers of the Year. They were short-listed for the 2016 Champion Beer of Britain competition, held at the Great British Beer Festival in August, or the Champion Winter Beer of Britain competition, held in February that year. Each beer was found by a panel of trained CAMRA judges to be consistently outstanding in its category and they all receive a 🍺 against their entry in the Breweries section. In the Champion Beer of Britain finals, the best beers from each category in both competitions are judged together to decide the overall national winner. For the full results visit **www.camra.org.uk/cbob**.

BEST BITTERS
B&T, Dragon Slayer
Bank Top, Flat Cap
Bath, Gem
Bathams, Best Bitter
Castle Rock, Elsie Mo
Colchester, No. 1
Leeds, Best
Moorhouse's,
    Pride of Pendle
Nene Valley, Bitter
Ossett, Big Red Bitter
Salopian, Darwins Origin
Sambrook's, Junction Ale
Surrey Hills, Shere Drop
Swannay, Scapa Special
Tiny Rebel, Cwtch
Tryst, Carronade Pale Ale
Twisted Oak, Spun Gold
Waen, Pamplemousse

BITTERS
Acorn, Barnsley Bitter
Ashover, Light Rale
Born in the Borders,
    Game Bird
Buntingford, Twitchell
Hawkshead, Bitter
Jennings, Cumberland Ale
Lincoln Green, Marion
Orkney, Raven
Otley, O1
Otter, Amber
Penpont, Creation Pale Ale
Purity, Pure Gold
Salopian, Shropshire Gold
Sambrook's, Wandle Ale
Timothy Taylor, Boltmaker
Tiny Rebel, Hank
Windsor & Eton,
    Windsor Knot
Woodforde's, Wherry

BARLEY WINES
& STRONG ALES
Adnams, Tally Ho
Blue Anchor, Spingo Special
Broughton, Old Jock
Buffy's, 9X
Darwin, Extinction Ale
Hoggleys, Yuletide Ale
Hopshackle,
    Double Momentum
Kent, Twelfth Night
Kinver, Over the Edge
Moor, Old Freddy Walker
Orkney, Skull Splitter
Outstanding, Imperial IPA
Robinsons, Old Tom
Tiny Rebel, Hadouken
Tring, Death or Glory

GOLDEN ALES
Blue Monkey, Infinity
Brass Castle, Sunshine
Fyne, Jarl
Golden Triangle, Mosaic City
Grey Trees, Diggers Gold
Marble, Lagonda IPA
RCH, Pitchfork
Salopian, Oracle
Surrey Hills, Greensand IPA

MILDS
Acorn, Darkness
Church End, Gravediggers Ale
Facer's, Mountain Mild
Mighty Oak, Oscar Wilde
Nottingham, Rock Ale Mild Beer
Prospect, Nutty Slack
RCH, Hewish Mild
Triple fff, Pressed Rat & Warthog
Williams, Black

OLD ALES
& STRONG MILDS
Adnams, Old Ale
Beowulf, Dark Raven
Brampton, Mild
Castle Rock, Midnight Owl
Driftwood, Alfie's Revenge
Exe Valley, Winter Glow
Isle of Skye, Skye Black
Jacobi, Dr Harries Dark Magic
Leeds, Midnight Bell
Marble, Chocolate Marble
Old Dairy, Snow Top
Palmers, Tally Ho!
Peakstones Rock, Black Hole
Purple Moose, Ochr Tywyll y
    Mws/Dark Side of the Moose
Timothy Taylor, Ram Tam
Watermill, Shih Tzu Faced
Windswept, Wolf

PORTERS
8 Sail, Victorian Porter
Acorn, Old Moor Porter
Ayr, Rabbie's Porter
By The Horns, Lambeth Walk
Dunham Massey, Dunham Porter
Eden St Andrews, Seggie Porter
Elland, 1872 Porter
Facer's, North Star Porter
Fownes, King Korvak's Saga
Longdog, Lamplight Porter
North Cotswold, Hung,
    Drawn 'n' Portered
Pied Bull, Black Bull Porter
Raw, Anubis Porter
RCH, Old Slug Porter
Red Fox, Black Fox Porter
VOG, Dark Matter

SPECIALITY BEERS
Binghams, Vanilla Stout
Harviestoun, Schiehallion
Marble, Earl Grey IPA
Moonshine, Chocolate Orange
    Stout
Peak, Chatsworth Gold
Saltaire, Triple Chocoholic
Skinner's, Hops n Honey
Tiny Rebel, Loki
Titanic, Plum Porter

STOUTS
Ascot, Anastasia's Imperial Stout
Beartown, Polar Eclipse
Cairngorm, Black Gold
Dark Star, Imperial
Mauldons, Black Adder
Ossett, Treacle Stout
Penzance, Scilly Stout
Plain, Inncognito
Thornbridge, Saint Petersburg
    Imperial Russian Stout
Titanic, Stout
Tudor, Black Mountain Stout
Wibblers, Crafty Stoat
Wilson Potter, In the Black

STRONG BITTERS
Adnams, Ghost Ship
Black Sheep, Riggwelter
Castle Rock, Screech Owl
Dark Star, Revelation
Hawkshead, NZPA
Heavy Industry, 77
Kinver, Half Centurion
Otter, Head
Tryst, RAJ IPA

**CHAMPION
WINTER BEER
OF BRITAIN**
Marble,
Chocolate Marble

Vanilla STOUT

**CHAMPION BEER
OF BRITAIN 2016**
Binghams,
Vanilla Stout

Courage Directors; Wells Eagle IPA; Young's Bitter, London Gold, Special; 3 changing beers (sourced nationally) ℍ
A recently refurbished two-bar pub with a pleasant walled patio garden. Lunches are served daily and evening meals on weekdays only. Current guest beers with tasting notes are listed on the website. Peacock Auction Rooms and Bedford Rugby Club are close by. A guest house behind the pub provides five en-suite letting bedrooms. Charles Wells Pub of the Year and Cask Ale Pub of the Year 2014 and local CAMRA Pub of the Year 2016. ⛢✿🚪◑♿🅿🖫(4,5,7)🕸🛜

King's Arms
24 St Mary's Street, MK42 0AS
🕓 11-11; 12-midnight Fri & Sat; 2-9 Sun ☎ (01234) 354494
🌐 thekingsarmsbedford.com
Greene King IPA; 3 changing beers ℍ
Busy former coaching inn that has been a public house since 1230. It has several interconnecting rooms and a conservatory providing a quiet area. There is a quiz on Monday evening, free pool on Tuesday, TV poker on Thursday and top local bands live every Saturday evening. A selection of bottled beers is available. No food at weekends. ⛢✿◑≠(St Johns)♣●🅿🖫🛜

Three Cups ℒ ✅
45 Newnham Street, MK40 3JR (200yds S of A4280 near rugby ground)
🕓 12-11; 11-11.30 Fri & Sat; 12-10.30 Sun
☎ (01234) 352153
Greene King IPA; Morland Old Speckled Hen; 5 changing beers ℍ
Comfortable inn dating from the 1770s, now a Greene King Local Hero pub offering local microbrewery beers. Seven real ales are always available, including at least two from White Park Brewery, which holds the lease. Tasting thirds are available for all beers. Locally sourced home-cooked lunches are served. Old wood panelling helps retain some of the pub's original character. Five minutes from the town centre and close to Bedford Blues rugby ground. Local CAMRA Town Pub of the Year 2015. ⛢✿◑♿♣●🅿🖫(4,5,7)🕸🛜

Wellington Arms ℒ
40-42 Wellington Street, MK40 2JX (N of town centre)
🕓 12-11; 12-10.30 Sun ☎ (01234) 308033
🌐 thewelly.wix.com/bedford
Adnams Southwold Bitter; B&T Shefford Bitter, Black Dragon Mild; 9 changing beers ℍ
This street-corner local operated by B&T Brewery retains a traditional style and offers a wide selection of ever-changing regional and microbrewery beers from 12 handpumps. A rotating range of ciders is served from two further handpumps. Draught Belgian and Dutch beers plus a wide range of bottled Belgian beers are also available. There is a courtyard for drinkers and smokers. A friendly pub with a mixed clientele, it can get busy on Friday and Saturday evenings. ✿●

Biggleswade

Golden Pheasant ℒ ✅
71 High Street, SG18 0JH
🕓 12-11.30; 12-midnight Fri; 11-midnight Sat
☎ (01767) 313653 🌐 goldenpheasantpub.co.uk
Wells Eagle IPA; 5 changing beers ℍ
Lively pub in the middle of town where you will often find an animated conversation at the bar. A

four-minute walk from the railway station brings you to this single-room hostelry furnished with simple, cushioned dark-wood chairs and benches, and with large windows looking out on the High Street. Six handpumps offer a range of beer strengths and styles, showcasing both local and far-flung brewers, as well as still cider from nearby Franklin's and one more cider or perry. Q✿≠♣●🚪🛜🛜

New Inn Ale House & Kitchen 🍽 ℒ ✅
Market Square, SG18 8AS
🕓 10-11.30 (12.30am Thu); 9am-1am Fri & Sat
☎ (01767) 222938 🌐 thenewinnalehouseandkitchen.co.uk
Greene King IPA; 7 changing beers ℍ
This 2016 local CAMRA Pub of the Year is deceptively spacious and comfortably furnished. It usually has three ciders and eight ales on handpump – four from Greene King and four, often local ales, free from tie. Although food is served this does not detract from the needs of those who prefer to simply enjoy a pint or two, neither do the large-screen TVs which usually show muted news channels or rugby. Mini beer festivals are held on an ad hoc basis. Q⛢✿◑≠●🚪🖫🛜

Wheatsheaf ✅
5 Lawrence Road, SG18 0LS
🕓 11-4, 7-11.30; 11-midnight Fri & Sat; 12-11 Sun
☎ (01767) 222220
Greene King IPA; 2 changing beers ℍ
Unspoilt, comfortably furnished, single-room pub with three reasonably priced ales all in excellent condition due to the prize-winning cellarmanship of the landlord. Regulars playing traditional pub games help create a friendly atmosphere and although sport features on the pub's screens it is unobtrusive. Fifty years ago the pub as social hub would have been the norm and this one, fortunately, continues the tradition. The well-tended garden is a pleasant spot to while away the hours in the summer months. ⛢✿≠♣🛜🛜

Bolnhurst

Plough ℒ
Kimbolton Road, MK44 2EX (on W side of B660 S of turning to Thurleigh) TL088587
🕓 12-3, 6.30-11; 12-3 Sun; closed Mon ☎ (01234) 376274
🌐 bolnhurst.com
3 changing beers (sourced regionally; often Adnams) ℍ
Award-winning pub restaurant dating back to Tudor times, serving excellent food and beer. The main bar has a wood-burning stove, and a second room is used for diners and functions. Up to three real ales are available, usually including one from Adnams. Outside is a large garden with decking beside a small pond. The pub has no signage, just a small notice at the entrance to the car park. Closed from Christmas until the second week of January each year. Q⛢✿◑♿🅿🛜🛜

REAL ALE BREWERIES
Ampthill Ampthill (NEW)
B&T Shefford
Brewhouse & Kitchen 🍺 Bedford (NEW)
Charles Wells Bedford
Leighton Buzzard Leighton Buzzard
White Park Cranfield

Broom

Cock ★ [L] ✔

23 High Street, SG18 9NA
🕐 12-11; 12-10 Sun ☎ (01767) 314411
🌐 thecockatbroom.co.uk
Greene King Abbot; Sharp's Doom Bar; Woodforde's Wherry; 2 changing beers (sourced regionally) [G]
Grade II-listed free house, with its nationally important historic pub interior, four cosy rooms with flagstone floors and several fireplaces. A restaurant section serves locally sourced food every day and hosts monthly themed food evenings. Up to five ales are available direct from the cellar, usually including a beer from Tring Brewery, plus three local Franklin's ciders. Pub games are played including darts and Northants skittles. The pub has a strong community focus with live music, mini beer festivals and a campsite.
Q🐴❀◐◑⛺♣🍎P🐾📶

Carlton

Fox 🏆 [L]

High Street, MK43 7LA
🕐 12-11; 12-10.30 Sun ☎ (01234) 720235
🌐 thefoxatcarlton.pub
Fuller's London Pride; Wells Eagle IPA; 2 changing beers [H]
A charming, thatched community pub with a warm welcome and an attractive garden popular with families. Guest beers are often from local microbreweries. Good-value, home-cooked lunches are served daily and evening meals Wednesday to Saturday. There is a regular quiz on Thursday evenings, occasional themed food evenings and an annual spring beer and cider festival, with an outhouse in the garden used as an additional bar. Local CAMRA Country Pub of the Year 2016. Q🐴❀◐◑♿♣P🚌(25)🐾📶

Clapham

Horse & Groom

15 High Street, MK41 6EQ
🕐 12-11; 12-10.30 Sun ☎ (01234) 217502
🌐 horseandgroomatclapham.co.uk
Greene King IPA, Abbot; 1 changing beer [H]
Attractive old coaching inn with comfortable, divided seating areas, including the former coach yard now roofed in to provide extra accommodation. Guest ales are not always from Greene King. There is a strong emphasis on food, with meals ranging from a lunchtime sandwich menu and afternoon tea to evening main meals, with a roast on Sunday. The patio includes an improved children's play area and the large garden beyond runs down to the River Great Ouse.
Q🐴❀◐◑♿P🚌(50,51)🐾📶

Clophill

Stone Jug

10 Back Street, MK45 4BY (550yds off A6 at N end of village) TL083381
🕐 12-3.30, 6-11; 12-midnight Fri & Sat; 12-10.30 Sun
☎ (01525) 860526 🌐 stonejug.co.uk
B&T Shefford Bitter; Otter Amber; St Austell Trelawny; 2 changing beers [H]
Originally three 16th-century cottages, this popular village local has an L-shaped bar that serves two drinking areas and a family/function room. Excellent home-made lunches are available Tuesday to Saturday. The three guest beers are often from local breweries, the cider is Westons. Picnic benches at the front and a rear patio garden offer space for outdoor drinking in fine weather. Parking can be difficult at busy times. Local CAMRA Pub of the Year 2014. Q🐴❀◐♣🍎P🚌(44,81)🐾

Dunstable

Gary Cooper ✔

Grove Park, Court Drive, LU5 4GP
🕐 8am-midnight (1am Fri & Sat) ☎ (01582) 471452
Adnams Broadside; Greene King Abbot; Ruddles Best Bitter; 7 changing beers [H]
This modern Wetherspoon bar is named after the famous Hollywood star who attended the local grammar school between 1910-13. Situated in Grove Park leisure area, its patio overlooks the Grove House gardens with buses stopping opposite. It tends to be very busy on Friday and Saturday nights and be prepared for a long hike to the upstairs loos. A selection of up to seven guest ales is available, often local. Good value meals are served in the large and airy bar. 🐴◐◑♿🍎🚌📶

Globe [L]

43 Winfield Street, LU6 1LS
🕐 12-11 (midnight Fri & Sat); 12-10.30 Sun
☎ (01582) 512300
B&T Shefford Bitter, Black Dragon Mild, Edwin Taylor's Extra Stout, SOD; Everards Tiger Best Bitter; 5 changing beers [H]
Popular beer destination and community local where 13 handpumps feature a good range of regular B&T beers, five ever-changing microbrewery beers, a real cider and a perry. Over 20 Belgian beers also also available. Bare boards, bar stools, breweriana and a famous plank at the end of the bar create a traditional town pub atmosphere buzzing with conversation. Acoustic music night is Tuesday. Regular beer festivals are hosted. Former Bedfordshire and South Bedfordshire CAMRA Pub of the Year.
Q🐴♿♣🍎🚌(70)🐾

Pheasant Inn [L]

208 West Street, LU6 1NX
🕐 11-11 (11.30 Fri & Sat); 12-11.30 Sun ☎ (01582) 662706
🌐 the-pheasant-inn-dunstable.co.uk
Courage Directors; Sharp's Doom Bar; 4 changing beers [H]
Pub plus hotel/B&B, located just out of the town centre, with a large main bar and a large function room selling six real ales. Traditional pub games are played and all major sports are screened via Sky and BT Sport. Outside are a covered and heated front smoking area, rear garden, large umbrellas and a car park. Free curry is served on Friday and free pizza on Saturday evenings (drinks must be purchased). An annual beer festival is hosted and live music on occasion. 🐴🛏◐◑♿♣P🚌🐾📶

Victoria [L]

69 West Street, LU6 1ST
🕐 11-11.30 (midnight Fri & Sat); 12-midnight Sun
☎ (01582) 662682 🌐 victoriapub.co.uk
House beer (by Tring); 3 changing beers [H]
Popular town-centre pub that usually offers three varying ales from microbreweries plus a house beer from Tring Brewery. Good-value food and daily specials are available at lunchtimes including the renowned Sunday roasts, Thai curry on the first

Tuesday of the month and steak on the third Tuesday. Darts, dominoes and crib are popular as well as televised sports in the bar. There is a separate function room available. 🕮🌗♣🖵

Dunton

March Hare 🄻
34 High Street, SG18 8RN
🕭 6-11 (midnight Thu); 3-midnight Fri & Sat; 12-10.30 Sun
☎ (01767) 448093 ⊕ duntonvillage.org.uk/pub/home.htm
4 changing beers 🄷
At heart this is a beer pub, offering an adventurous range of local and national beers across four handpumps. Three varieties of Franklin's cider come from the nearby farm and beer and cider festivals are held regularly. The pub will provide warmed plates if you bring in or order your own food in the evening. A folk music session features on the first Tuesday of the month. Friendly conversation at the bar is the only distraction from enjoying a peaceful pint. Opens at noon Friday and Saturday in summer. Q🕮🌗♣🌙🖵(188)🐾🛜

Flitton

Jolly Coopers 🄻 ✅
Wardhedges, MK45 5ED
🕭 12-3 (not Mon), 5.30-11.30; 12-midnight Fri; 12-12.30am Sat; 12-10 Sun ☎ (01525) 303648 ⊕ jollycoopersflitton.co.uk
Wells Eagle IPA; 2 changing beers 🄷
In a quiet hamlet at the east end of Flitton, the landlord and lady here take obvious pride in this wonderful country community pub. Two ever-changing and varied guest ales are available alongside the regular Eagle. Traditional British food is served in the bar and separate restaurant, with a choice of menus. There is a large garden to the rear and a patio with spectacular floral displays in the summer months. Dogs are welcome in the flagstoned bar. 🕭🕮🌗🚻♣🅿🐾🛜

Harlington

Carpenters Arms
Sundon Road, LU5 6LS
🕭 12-3, 6-11.30; 12-midnight Fri & Sat; 12-11 Sun
☎ (01525) 872384 ⊕ thecarpentersarmsharlington.com
Greene King IPA; Thwaites Wainwright; Woodforde's Wherry; 1 changing beer (sourced nationally) 🄷
Situated in the heart of Harlington, this low beamed watch-your-head traditional village pub was first licensed in 1790 and has listings of landlords from then until the present. Three regular and one changing guest ales are available. Bottled gluten-free beers are stocked from Hambleton Ales. Food is reasonably priced with good helpings; Monday is burger night. The railway station and bus service along with a range of country walks make this a popular stop-off.
Q🕭🕮🌗🚻♣🅿🖵(42)🐾🛜

Heath & Reach

Axe & Compass 🄻
Leighton Road, LU7 0AA
🕭 12-midnight ☎ (01525) 237394
⊕ theaxeandcompass.co.uk
3 changing beers 🄷
This village community pub has been a free house since 2014. The older front bar, with its low beams, is a lounge and dining area while the rear public

bar has gaming machines, pool table and a TV screen. The large garden includes a children's play area. Regular beers are from Tring and Leighton Buzzard Brewing Co and guests often come from local breweries such as White Park, XT and Concrete Cow. Accommodation is available in a separate lodge. 🕭🕮🛏🌗♣🅿🖵(150)🐾🛜

Henlow

Engineers Arms 🄻
68 High Street, SG16 6AA
🕭 12-midnight (1am Fri & Sat); 12-10.30 Sun
☎ (01462) 812284 ⊕ engineersarms.co.uk
10 changing beers 🄷
Multi award-winning pub recognised for the quality of its beers and ciders, with the ales sometimes supplemented with two from specially commissioned wooden barrels, along with eight ciders and perries. The entrance leads directly into a bar with sports-related memorabilia and wide-screen TVs while the door to the left takes the visitor to a quieter bar with a library, local photographs and a collection of bottles and advertising jugs. The February cider festival and October beer festival are legendary.
🕭🕮🅰♣🐝🖵(188,190)🐾🛜

Old Transporter Ale House 🄻
300 Hitchin Road, SG16 6DP
🕭 3-10.30; 12-11 Fri & Sat; 12-9 Sun; closed Mon
☎ (01462) 817410 ⊕ theoldtransporter.co.uk
6 changing beers 🄶
Bedfordshire's first micropub, near RAF Henlow, is a single-room establishment run mainly as an ale house, its walls adorned with transport-themed memorabilia. It serves six ales (sometimes more) direct from the cask from local and regional brewers, plus a large range of still ciders and a selection of wines and spirits. There are regular charity events, quizzes, darts and a fortnightly Friday meat raffle, plus occasional live bands. Seasonal mini beer festivals are held, often featuring dark ales. Summer opening hours may vary. 🕭♣🐝🖵(71,188,190)🐾🛜

Houghton Conquest

Knife & Cleaver 🄻
The Grove, MK45 3LA (opp parish church)
🕭 7am-midnight; 7am-7 Sun ☎ (01234) 930789
⊕ theknifeandcleaver.com
Wells Eagle IPA, Bombardier; 2 changing beers 🄷
A smart pub and restaurant with accommodation, reopened in 2012 after extensive refurbishment and run by partners who previously kept a restaurant in France. The food is of high quality and prepared using fresh, locally sourced ingredients wherever possible. Nine en-suite bedrooms are housed in a separate block behind the secluded, family friendly rear garden. A good base for walks on the nearby Greensand Ridge. Awarded an AA Gold for food 2013-2015. 🕭🕮🛏🌗🚻🅿🖵(42)🐾🛜

Leighton Buzzard

Bald Buzzard Alehouse 🄻
6 Hockliffe Street, LU7 1HJ
🕭 12-9 (10 Fri & Sat); closed Sun & Mon ☎ 07581 146491
⊕ baldbuzzard.co.uk

Leighton Buzzard Restoration Ale; Oakham JHB; 6 changing beers (sourced locally; often Dark Star, Red Squirrel, Thornbridge) Ⓖ
CAMRA award winner for Best New Pub that opened its doors in July 2015 and has been so successful it has featured on BBC Look East and BBC Three Counties radio. The small but perfectly formed premises has a bespoke chiller room with sliding glass doors behind the bar containing 12 casks on stillage and three or four ciders. Simple home-cooked Scotch eggs, ploughman's lunches, pork pies and more are available.
Q❀❶🌂♣👐🍴🚐(70,150)❀

Black Lion 🍷

20 High Street, LU7 1EA
🕓 12-11 (midnight Fri & Sat); 12-10.30 Sun
☎ (01525) 853725
Draught Bass; Nethergate Suffolk County Best Bitter; Oakham Bishops Farewell; 5 changing beers Ⓗ
A traditional alehouse with 17th-century origins, the atmosphere is enhanced by exposed beams, wooden floors and an open fire. Eight handpumps often feature beers from Hook Norton, North Cotswold and local microbreweries such as Leighton Buzzard and XT. Eighty bottled continental beers and eight guest real ciders are also available. There is a large paved garden. Bar snacks are served and bring-your-own cold lunches are welcome. Local CAMRA Pub of the Year 2015 and 2016. Q❀❶♣👐(70,150)❀

Red Lion

1 North Street, LU7 1EF
🕓 10-11 (midnight Fri & Sat); 11-11 Sun ☎ (01525) 374350
Black Sheep Ale; Greene King Abbot; 1 changing beer Ⓗ
A 17th-century building that is a town-centre institution. An old-fashioned pub with old-fashioned values, the manager of 20 years offers a warm welcome. The public bar has all of the traditional pub games and the main bar resembles a living room with comfy chairs, a large fish tank, TV and the pub's dog wandering around. As well as the well-kept ales there is Westons Old Rosie real cider plus a selection of Irish and Scottish single malt whiskies. ♣👐🚐(70,150)❀🌐

Swan Hotel ✅

50 High Street, LU7 1EA
🕓 6 (7 Mon & Sat)-midnight; 7-11.30 Sun ☎ (01525) 380170
Greene King Abbot; Ruddles Best Bitter; Sharp's Doom Bar; 7 changing beers (sourced nationally) Ⓗ
Dating from the 17th century, this former coaching inn has been renovated by Wetherspoon. With good-value food and 39 guest rooms, the Swan is busy and bustling for much of the week. Friendly staff operate one long bar serving two rooms, a conservatory and a courtyard. Guest beers may come from local microbreweries such as Tring, Vale, Concrete Cow and Oxfordshire Ales, and real cider is available in the summer months. Families are welcome until 10pm. Events include beer festivals twice a year. Q❀❶🌂♣👐🚐(70,150)🌐

Luton

Black Horse

23 Hastings Street, LU1 5BE
🕓 3-11 (1am Fri); 1-1am Sat; 1-11 Sun ☎ (01582) 965290
3 changing beers Ⓗ

Two or three varying ales are available here and there is often a fourth at weekends. The jukebox is popular as well as the pool table. Food is served every morning and lunchtime but the bar does not open until 3pm weekdays and 1pm weekends. Outside is a covered courtyard and a seating area for smokers. ❀❶➼♣P❀

Bricklayers Arms

High Town Road, LU2 0DD
🕓 12-11 (midnight Fri & Sat); 12-10.30 Sun
☎ (01582) 611017 ⊕ bricklayersarmsluton.co.uk
Batemans XB; 5 changing beers Ⓗ
The six busy handpumps dispense a choice of light, amber or dark beer from an ever-changing range of guest ales from local and national breweries, often including a mild and an Oakham brew, with draught Belgian beers also available. This quirky town-centre pub has been run by the same landlady for over 30 years. It is popular with Hatters fans on match days, with TVs in both bars. Quiz night is Monday. Two changing real ciders are always available. ❀♣♣👐❀🌐

English Rose

46 Old Bedford Road, LU2 7PA
🕓 1 (4 Mon)-11; 12-11 Fri-Sun ☎ (01582) 723889
4 changing beers (sourced nationally) Ⓗ
Traditional one-room, CAMRA-friendly, street-corner pub which serves up to 600 different ales per year. A pub since 1845, it was originally called the Rabbit – this area was then called Coney Heath, coney being the old word for rabbit. In 1919 this was one of four pubs in which the dissidents met before marching into town and eventually ransacking and burning down the town hall. Back in the '50s celebrity Diana Dors courted and then wed the landlord's son. ❀🌂➼♣👐🚐(24,25,26)

Great Northern

63 Bute Street, LU1 2EY
🕓 11-11; 11-10.30 Sun ☎ (01582) 729311
St Austell Tribute Ⓗ
This may be the smallest pub in Luton but it is one of the friendliest, and has been run by the same landlady since 1985. Its name was changed in the 1860s when the Great Northern Railway was built right on its doorstep. It still retains Victorian green wall tiles together with a table featuring quirky brass pint glass holders at each corner. St Austell beers are served, with Tribute on handpump and Proper Job available in bottles. There is a smoking area at the rear. ➼♣

Moggerhanger

Guinea ✅

Bedford Road, MK44 3RG
🕓 12-11 (midnight Fri & Sat); 12-10.30 Sun
☎ (01767) 640388 ⊕ guineamoggerhanger.co.uk
Courage Directors; Wells Eagle IPA; Young's Bitter; 1 changing beer Ⓗ
Large 18th-century village pub with beamed ceilings in a prominent position on the main road in the heart of the village. There is a garden at the front and car parks at the side and rear. The main bar has a drinking area and two areas beyond for diners. A separate games bar has hood skittles. Freshly prepared food is available every day (not Sun eve). Q❀🌂❀❶🌂♣P🚐(73,188)❀🌐

Odell

Bell

81 High Street, MK43 7AS

🌀 11.30-11; 12-10.30 Sun ☎ (01234) 910850

🌐 thebellinodell.com

Greene King IPA, Abbot; 3 changing beers Ⓗ

Handsome, thatched village pub with a large garden near the River Great Ouse. With the Harrold-Odell Country Park just down the lane, this is a popular stop for walkers. Sympathetic refurbishment and a series of linked but distinct seating areas help retain a traditional pub atmosphere. Good-value, high quality food includes a Sunday roast, steak and chips night Monday and pie and chips night Tuesday. Local CAMRA Most Improved Pub 2016.

Q🌳🏵️🌰🕽🅿️🚻(25,26)🐾

Potton

Rising Sun Ⓛ ✅

11 Everton Road, SG19 2PA

☎ (01767) 260231 🌐 risingsunpotton.co.uk

Wells Eagle IPA, Bombardier; 5 changing beers Ⓗ

Licensed as a beer house in 1836, this large, popular community pub is open plan, divided by low walls and wooden beams. It features a covered well and a snug with comfy seating. There is an upstairs function room with rooftop terrace and an outside patio area. At the bar there are seven ales, usually four from the Wells group, an Oakham ale, two guest ales plus one rotating real cider. Beer festivals are hosted twice a year and home-cooked food is served daily until 9.30pm.

🌳🏵️🕽🍻🅿️🚻(188/190)🐾🛜

Renhold

Polhill Arms ✅

25 Wilden Road, MK41 0JP (at Salph End)

🌀 12 (4.30 Mon)-11; 12-10.30 Sun ☎ (01234) 771398

🌐 polhillarms.co.uk

Hardys & Hansons Bitter; 5 changing beers Ⓗ

One-bar family-friendly village local with a welcoming atmosphere and large garden, play area and restaurant. An interesting collection of pub and brewery artefacts is displayed, as well as R101 Airship memorabilia. Traditional pub food is served, including fish and chips (not Sun or Mon eves). Live entertainment and quiz nights feature regularly, with darts and skittles also played. Five guest beers are usually on the bar, plus two real ciders in the winter months increasing to four in the summer. Local CAMRA Cider Pub of the Year 2016. 🌳🏵️🕽🍀🍻🅿️🚻(27)🐾🛜

Salford

Red Lion Hotel Ⓛ

Wavendon Road, MK17 8AZ (2 miles N of M1 jct 13) SP934389

🌀 11-2.30, 6-11; 12-2.30, 6-10.30 Sun ☎ (01908) 583117

🌐 redlionhotel.eu

Wells Eagle IPA, Bombardier Ⓗ

Friendly, traditional country hotel serving a fine choice of home-cooked food in the bar and restaurant. The cosy bar is heated by an open fire in the winter and offers a selection of interesting board games. The large garden includes a covered area and a secure children's playground. Six rooms

are available for overnight accommodation. A quiet pub and village but convenient for access to the motorway. Q🌳🏵️🌰🕽🍻🅿️🛜

Sandy

Sir William Peel Ⓛ ✅

39 High Street, SG19 1AG

🌀 12-midnight; 12-10.30 Sun ☎ (01767) 680607

🌐 sirwilliampeel.webs.com

Batemans XB; 3 changing beers Ⓗ

Community- and charity-focused pub with plenty of bright outdoor areas at the front and rear. The open-plan interior features a U-shaped bar, with a library and digital jukebox to the right. The old stables at the back serve as the stillage for the April beer and July cider festivals and as a makeshift stage for music events. An Oakham ale, two guests, Belgian beers and real cider complete the line-up. Monthly quizzes are held.

🌳🏵️🚲🍀🍻🅿️🚻(73,188,190)🐾🛜

Sharnbrook

Swan with Two Nicks

High Street, MK44 1PF

🌀 12-3, 6 (5 Fri & Sat)-11; 12-6 Sun ☎ (01234) 781585

🌐 swanwith2nicks.co.uk

Wells Eagle IPA; Young's London Gold; 2 changing beers Ⓗ

Friendly village pub with a rear courtyard and patio garden. Home-cooked quality lunches and evening meals are served, using locally sourced ingredients where possible and including daily specials, pies and fresh fish. A selection of award-winning wines is also available by the glass or bottle. There is a live music session every other week. This is a good base for many local walks and nature reserves near the River Great Ouse. 🌳🏵️🕽🅿️🚻(25,26,50)🐾🛜

Shefford

Brewery Tap

14 North Bridge Street, SG17 5DH

🌀 11.30-11; 12-10.30 Sun ☎ (01462) 628448

B&T Shefford Bitter, Shefford Dark Mild, Dragon Slayer; Everards Tiger Best Bitter; 2 changing beers Ⓗ

Renamed by the nearby B&T Brewery in 1996, the Tap is primarily a drinkers' pub, offering four regular ales plus two guests which are usually stronger beers. Breweriana decorate an open-plan interior divided into two distinct areas with a family room at the rear. Lunchtime pies and rolls are available. Darts, dominoes and cribbage teams are supported, as is a golf society. The rear patio garden is heated on cool evenings. Car park access is through the archway beside the pub.

🌳🏵️🍀🅿️🚻(71,72)🐾

Souldrop

Bedford Arms Ⓛ

High Street, MK44 1EY (½ mile W of A6)

🌀 12-3, 4.30-11; 12-midnight Fri & Sat; 12-11 Sun; closed Mon ☎ (01234) 781384 🌐 bedfordarmssouldrop.co.uk

Black Sheep Best Bitter; Greene King IPA; 3 changing beers Ⓗ

Large village pub created partly from a 17th-century hop and ale house. Guest beers are often from local microbreweries, the cider in summer is usually from Saxby's and nearby Evershed. The restaurant has a central open fireplace and offers traditional, hearty pub favourites with daily specials and a roast on Sunday. A games room with skittles runs off the main bar. The spacious garden with pétanque is popular with families in summer. ► ❀ ◑ ◐ ᵬ ♣ ♠ P ⊟ (26) ❀ ♥

Stanbridge

Five Bells
Station Road, LU7 9JF
❂ 11-11 (11.30 Sat); 12-10.30 Sun ☎ (01525) 210224
⊕ fivebellsstanbridge.co.uk
Fuller's London Pride; Gale's Seafarers Ale; 2 changing beers Ⓗ
A Fuller's-owned country pub set in extensive and attractive grounds with wooden floors, two real fires, a cosy snug and very low beams. A separate 80-seater restaurant in the 18th-century wing offers good-quality food and can be used for weddings and other functions. The pub is named after the nearby church which originally had five bells but subsequently acquired a sixth. Guest ales are usually from Fuller's/Gale's and may occasionally include one from a local microbrewery. ► ❀ ◑ ◐ ᵬ ♣ P ⊟ (70) ❀ ♥

Toddington

Oddfellows Arms
2 Congar Lane, LU5 6BP
❂ 5-11; 1-11 Sat & Sun ☎ (01525) 872021
Adnams Broadside; Fuller's London Pride; 2 changing beers Ⓗ
Attractive 700-year-old two-bar pub facing the village green with a heavily beamed bar featuring a vast collection of pumpclips, and a games room with a pool table. With two regular real ales and a wide selection on the two guest handpumps, there is always plenty of choice. The regular real cider is Westons Old Rosie and there is often an alternative. The patio garden is popular in summer and has shelter for smokers. ♣ ♠ ⊟ (42,E) ❀ ♥

Totternhoe

Old Farm Inn
16 Church Road, LU6 1RE
❂ 5-midnight Mon; 12-3, 5-11; 12-midnight Fri & Sat; 12-11 Sun ☎ (01582) 674053 ⊕ oldfarminndunstable.co.uk
Fuller's London Pride, ESB; 2 changing beers Ⓗ
Located in the conservation area of Church End Totternhoe, this charming village pub boasts two inglenooks. The public bar with its low boarded ceiling is where you will find good conversation and where traditional pub games are played. Dogs are welcome in the front bar and there is a child-friendly garden. Monday is folk music night, Thursday is quiz night. Tasty, home-cooked food is

served including popular Sunday roasts (no food Mon or Sun eves). Beer festivals are held in May and August. Q ► ❀ ◑ ◐ ᵬ ♣ ♠ P ⊟ (61) ❀ ♥

Wingfield

Plough ✓
Tebworth Road, LU7 9QH
❂ 12-3, 5.30-midnight; 12-10.30 Sun ☎ (01525) 873077
⊕ theploughinn.com
Fuller's London Pride, ESB; Gales HSB; 1 changing beer Ⓗ
Charming thatched village inn dating from the 17th century, decorated with paintings of rural scenes and ploughs. Beware the low beams! Good home-cooked food is served daily (no food Sunday evening). There are tables outside at the front and to the rear is a conservatory which can be booked as a function room. Beyond the conservatory is a lovely garden. A quiz is held fortnightly on a Sunday. ► ❀ ◑ ◐ ♣ P ❀ ♥

Wootton

Chequers Ⓛ
Hall End, MK43 9HP (NW edge of village) SP001457
❂ 12-11 ☎ (01234) 930464 ⊕ chequerswootton.co.uk
Wells Eagle IPA; 2 changing beers Ⓗ
Originally a farmhouse, this handsome old free house retains a wealth of heavy wooden beams and period features. A wide range of guest beers is offered, often from local microbreweries. An interesting, quality menu is served in the restaurant and good-value bar food is available throughout the pub (no food Sun eve). The large, pleasant garden is popular in fine weather. Q ► ❀ ◑ ◐ ᵬ ♣ P ⊟ (68) ❀ ♥

Wrestlingworth

Chequers Ⓛ
43 High Street, SG19 2EP
❂ 12-3 (not Mon), 5-11; 12-midnight Fri & Sat; 12-10.30 Sun
☎ (01767) 631818 ⊕ chequersfreehouse.co.uk
Adnams Southwold Bitter; Woodforde's Wherry; 4 changing beers (often Black Sheep, Mauldons) Ⓗ
You will find a cheerful welcome at this attractive listed building at the heart of a small village. Now a free house, it has six handpumps, with a couple of higher strength bitters alongside the regulars. There is a long bar, a small room set aside for diners and a lunchtime suntrap patio. Locally sourced food is offered and the pub will happily cater for walking groups (no food Sun eve and Mon). Darts, pétanque and (muted) Sky Sports are available. Q ► ❀ ◑ ◐ ♣ P ⊟ (188) ❀ ♥

Choosing pubs

CAMRA members and branches choose the pubs listed in the Good Beer Guide. There is no payment for entry, and pubs are inspected on a regular basis by personal visits; publicans are not sent a questionnaire once a year, as is the case with some pub guides. CAMRA branches monitor all the pubs in their areas, and the choice of pubs for the guide is often the result of democratic vote at branch meetings. However, recommendations from readers are welcomed and will be passed on to the relevant branch: write to Good Beer Guide, CAMRA, 230 Hatfield Road, St Albans, Hertfordshire, AL1 4LW; or send an email to: **gbgeditor@camra.org.uk**

Public transport information

Leave the car behind and travel to the pub by bus, train or tram

Using public transport is an excellent way to get to the pub, but many people use it irregularly, and systems can be slightly different from place to place. So, below are some useful websites and phone numbers where you can find all the information you might need.

Combined travel information

The national **Traveline** system gives information on all rail and local bus services throughout England, Scotland and Wales. Calls are put through to a local call centre and if necessary your call will be switched through to a more relevant one. There are also services for mobiles, including a next-bus text service and smart-phone app. The website offers other services including timetables and a journey planner with mapping:

- 0871 200 22 33
  www.traveline.org.uk

The **Transport Direct** website uniquely offers information for door-to-door travel by public transport, bicycle and car around England, Scotland and Wales. The site provides street-level mapping of transport stops and stations, places and addresses and can generate route maps for various types of journeys:

- **www.transportdirect.info**

LONDON

In London use Traveline or **Transport for London (TfL)** travel services. TfL provides information and route planning for all of London's transport networks, including London Underground and Overground, Docklands Light Railway, National Rail, buses, River Buses, Tramlink, Barclays Cycles and cycle routes. Detailed ticketing information helps you find the most cost effective ways to travel in London. There are also live departure boards, service and traffic updates; mobile services and more:

- 020 7222 1234
  www.tfl.gov.uk

Train travel

National Rail Enquiries covers the whole of Great Britain's rail network and provides service information, ticketing, online journey planning and other information.

- 08457 48 49 50
  www.nationalrail.co.uk

Coach travel

The two main UK coach companies are **National Express** and **Scottish Citylink**. Between them, they serve everywhere from Cornwall to the Highlands. Their websites offer timetables, journey planning, ticketing and route mapping, along with other useful information.

- National Express: 08717 81 81 81
  www.nationalexpress.com

- Scottish Citylink: 08705 50 50 50
  www.citylink.co.uk

Northern Ireland & islands

For travel outside mainland Britain but within the area of this Guide, information is available from the following companies:

NORTHERN IRELAND
- Translink: 028 9066 6630
  www.translink.co.uk

ISLE OF MAN
- Isle of Man Transport: 01624 662 525
  www.iombusandrail.info

JERSEY
- Liberty Bus: 01534 828 555
  www.libertybus.je

GUERNSEY
- Island Coachways: 01481 720 210
  www.buses.gg

Public transport symbols in the Guide

Pub entries in the Guide include helpful symbols to show if there are stations and/or bus routes close to a pub. There are symbols for railway stations (≠); tram or light rail stations (Ⓡ); London Underground, Overground or DLR stations (⊖); and bus routes (🚌). See the 'Key to symbols' on the inside front cover for more details.

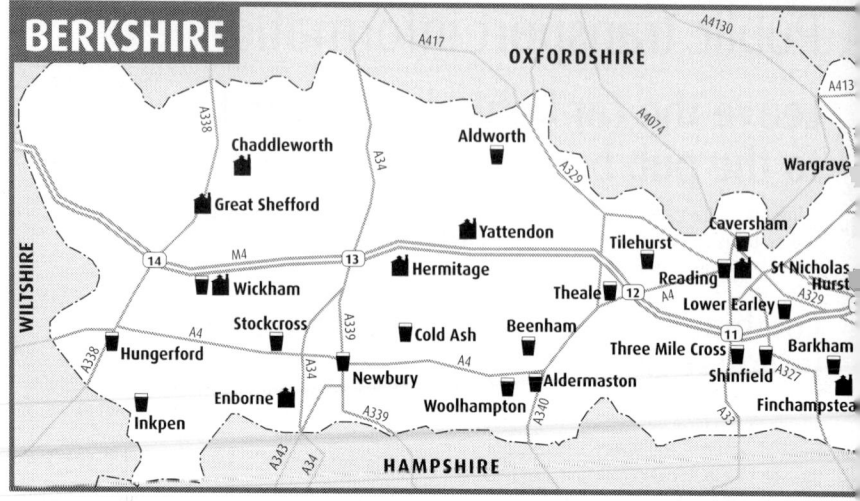

BERKSHIRE

Aldermaston

Butt Inn

Station Road, RG7 4LA

☼ 11.30-11; 12-10.30 Sun ☎ (0118) 971 3309
🌐 thebuttinn.biz

Sharp's Doom Bar; 2 changing beers (sourced nationally; often Otter, Theakston) 🅷

Named after the archery butts in the field opposite, the Butt reopened after a major refurbishment in 2012. Originally built in the 1920s, the pub is well situated for enjoying the surrounding countryside and Kennet & Avon Canal. Three pumps supply Doom Bar and two rotating guests, with local brewers often featuring, including West Berkshire and Indigenous. Good food is served throughout. 🏵🛏🌮⮯P🛜

Aldworth

Bell Inn ★ 🅛

Bell Lane, RG8 9SE (250yds off B4009)

☼ 11-3, 6-11; 12-3, 7-10.30 Sun; closed Mon
☎ (01635) 578272

Arkell's 3B, Moonlight; West Berkshire Maggs' Magnificent Mild; house beer (by West Berkshire); 2 changing beers (sourced locally; often Loose Cannon, West Berkshire) 🅷

This village-centre inn on the Berkshire Downs is an unspoilt gem with a historic interior. It has welcomed beer drinkers for over 250 years and been in the hands of the same family for over half of that period. It is famed for a vast range of hot filled rolls and scrumptious desserts. Outside is a spacious sunny garden. Local ciders from Tutts Clump and Red Dog are popular, alongside Lilley's from Somerset. A former national, regional and branch CAMRA Pub of the Year. Q🕭🏵🌮♣🍴P🛜

Ascot

Duke of Edinburgh ✅

Woodside Road, Woodside, SL4 2DP (near Ascot end of Woodside Rd) SU928709

☼ 11-11; 12-6.30 Sun ☎ (01344) 882736
🌐 thedukeofedinburgh.com

Arkell's Wiltshire Gold, 3B, Kingsdown; 1 changing beer (often Arkell's) 🅷

Licensees Nick and Annie have run this friendly Arkell's tied house since 1998. A good selection of Arkell's ales is always available including seasonal beers. The pub successfully combines both a destination restaurant and a more traditional bar. Less than a mile from Ascot Racecourse, it is a lively place on race days. The large well-kept garden includes an aviary. Mottos and proverbs adorn the walls except in a corner of the bar set aside for football memorabilia. 🏵🌮🛆♣🐾🛜

Barkham

Bull 🅛

Barkham Road, RG41 4TL (on B3349 jct with Barkham St)

☼ 12-11; 12-7 Sun ☎ (0118) 976 2816
🌐 thebullbarkham.com

Gales HSB; Rebellion Smuggler; St Austell Tribute; Sharp's Doom Bar; Timothy Taylor Landlord; 1 changing beer (sourced regionally; often Ringwood) 🅷

Traditional village pub with separate drinking and dining areas, although meals are served throughout at the weekend. The bar is pleasantly relaxing with an inglenook fireplace and the restaurant is sited in a Grade II-listed former smithy. The menu features British and Thai dishes cooked to order, and separate tapas and children's menus are available. A pub quiz is hosted on Monday nights. LocAle has recently been reintroduced and is proving popular. Dogs are allowed in the bar area only. Q🏵🌮🛆P🚆(3)🐾

Beenham

Six Bells 🅛

The Green, RG7 5NX (at Bucklebury end of main road through village)

☼ 12-2.30 (not Mon), 6-11; 12-2.30, 6.30-11 Sat; 12-3 Sun
☎ (0118) 971 3368 🌐 thesixbells.co.uk

West Berkshire Good Old Boy; 2 changing beers (sourced locally; often Loddon) 🅷

A welcoming and comfortable two-bar village local, delightfully decorated with items recalling the diverse backgrounds and world travels of the owners. The name commemorates the recasting of the parish church bells following a 1794 fire. After

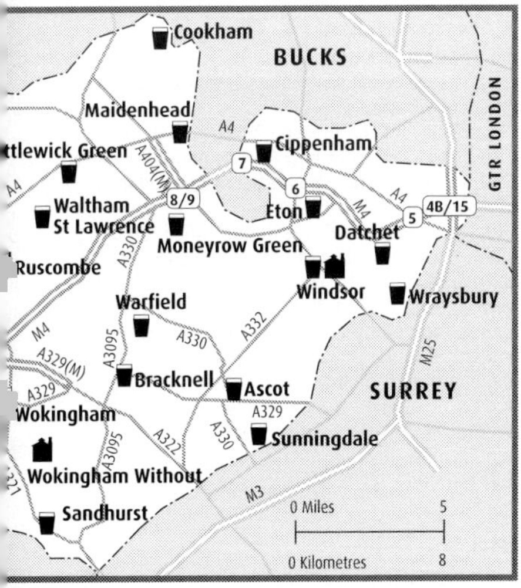

your home-cooked meal, you can play a range of board games in front of open fires or in the conservatory. Two guest beers from local breweries are on offer alongside Good Old Boy. Accommodation is in four bedrooms, and there are conference facilities. Q❀🛏◐◑⛺🍎P🚌(104)📶

Bracknell

Cannie Man 🄻 ✔

Bywood, Hanworth, RG12 7RF

🕐 12-11 (11.30 Fri & Sat); 12-10.30 Sun ☎ (01344) 307620

Fuller's London Pride; 3 changing beers (sourced nationally; often Brains, Rebellion, West Berkshire) 🄷

A well-run community pub in an estate location where visitors are assured of a warm welcome. Four handpumps adorn the bar of this free house, serving an ever-changing selection including a LocAle. A linchpin of the community, the pub hosts darts, pool and football teams as well as sponsoring local charitable and community events. Two TV screens show sports events and there is live entertainment most Saturday evenings. Limited outdoor seating is available at the front. ♣P🚌(171,172)📶

Old Manor 🄻 ✔

Grenville Place, RG12 1BP (at Met Office/College roundabout jct with Church Rd)

🕐 8am-midnight (1am Fri & Sat) ☎ (01344) 304490

Greene King Abbot; Ruddles Best Bitter; 6 changing beers (sourced nationally; often Loddon, Rebellion, Titanic) 🄷

Visitors to this ex-manor house should explore the fascinating rooms and alcoves in the original Tudor building that make this well-frequented Wetherspoon pub unique and very attractive. Highly rated locally and a previous CAMRA branch Pub of the Year, up to eight real ales are served including at least one LocAle, plus a real cider. Guide or working dogs only are allowed in the pub. Just 10 minutes' walk from Bracknell train and bus stations. Q🐴❀◐◑♿⇌🍎P🚌🐾📶

Caversham

Fox & Hounds 🏆 🄻

51 Gosbrook Road, RG4 8BN

🕐 12-midnight; 12-11 Sun ☎ 07540 816293

🌐 foxandhoundscaversham.co.uk

8 changing beers 🄷

Local CAMRA Pub of the Year 2015 and 2016, just off Caversham centre and catering for a varied clientele. A changing range of eight beers is served alongside four real ciders and perries, often from local producers. Quiz night every Thursday is a popular draw. TVs often show sport, and darts and pool are played. The food range has expanded and now rolls are on offer Monday-Friday daytime, with burgers on Saturday until 6pm and roasts on Sunday 1-6pm. 🐴❀◐♣🍎P🚌(25,28,800)🐾📶

Cippenham

Barleycorn 🄻

151 Lower Cippenham Lane, SL1 5DS

🕐 12-midnight (12.30am Fri & Sat); 12-11.30 Sun

☎ (01628) 603115

Shepherd Neame Spitfire; 6 changing beers (sourced nationally) 🄷

A traditional single-bar pub, recently refurbished, with seating on one side and a pool table on the other, catering for a strong local following. Around the walls is a large collection of bottles and jugs. Of the six guest ales there is always one from Rebellion and a strong ale. The remaining four guests come from around the country. There are a couple of TVs for sport, and occasional live music. A free public car park is nearby. Q❀♣P🚌(5)🐾📶

Cold Ash

Castle Inn 🄻 ✔

Cold Ash Hill, RG18 9PS

🕐 11.30-11.30 (midnight Fri & Sat); 11.30-11 Sun

☎ (01635) 863232 🌐 thecastleatcoldash.co.uk

Courage Best Bitter; Fuller's London Pride; Sharp's Doom Bar; West Berkshire Good Old Boy; 2 changing beers (sourced nationally) 🄷

19th-century inn, tastefully refurbished and with a traditional pub feel, in the same family for over 20 years. It is known for its good food including popular pensioners' weekday lunches. As well as the regular beers, including a local brew from West Berkshire Brewery, it serves two guest ales and a real cider. Monday is quiz night and a meat raffle is held on Friday. 🐴❀◐◑♣🍎P🚌(101)🐾📶

Cookham

Bounty 🄻

Cock Marsh, SL8 5RG (over railway bridge from Bourne End or walk along Cookham towpath) SU890872

REAL ALE BREWERIES

Binghams Ruscombe
Bond Wokingham Without (NEW)
Butts Great Shefford
Dickens ▮ Reading
Elusive Finchampstead (NEW)
Hermitage Hermitage
Hop King Reading (brewing suspended)
Indigenous Chaddleworth
INNformal ▮ Wickham
Siren Craft Finchampstead
Two Cocks Enborne
West Berkshire Yattendon
Windsor & Eton Windsor
Zerodegrees ▮ Reading

⚙ 12-11 ☎ (01628) 520056 ⊕ thebountypub.com
Rebellion IPA, Mutiny; 1 changing beer (sourced locally; often Rebellion) Ⓗ
Located on National Trust's Cock Marsh between Cookham village and Bourne End, this quirky, characterful pub is only accessible on foot or by boat. Dogs, walkers and children are made very welcome. The boat-shaped bar is packed with nautical knick-knacks and daft jokes. Bar billiards can be played while listening to '60s music. Food is available until 8pm. Live events feature throughout the summer, including Mikron Theatre. Summer weekends can be busy. Note the reduced winter opening hours – noon to dusk weekends only.
Ⓓ⊕◑≈♣⊟🐾

Old Swan Uppers
The Pound, SL6 9QE
⚙ 11.30-midnight (10.30 Mon; 11 Tue & Wed); 11.30-10.30 Sun ☎ (01628) 523573 ⊕ theoldswanuppers.co.uk
Brains Rev James; Brakspear Bitter; Butcombe Bitter; Courage Best Bitter; Fuller's London Pride Ⓗ
Friendly, cosy pub with flagstone floors and a wood-burning stove. Its name stems from the ancient activity of swan upping or marking of the swans on the River Thames. The front bar accommodates drinkers, with a separate restaurant and lounge to the rear. Choose from a traditional pub menu (burgers, fish and chips, pies, steaks) and a tapas-style menu with a selection of around 20 plates. ⊕◑≈P⊟(37)🐾🐕

Datchet
Royal Stag Ⓛ ✅
The Green, SL3 9JH
⚙ 10-midnight ☎ (01753) 584231
Fuller's London Pride; Windsor & Eton Guardsman; 2 changing beers (sourced locally)
Next to the church, the pub is reputed to be the oldest village house – ring-counting of roof timbers dates it to 1494. It may have been an ale house in the 1500s called the Five Bells, later changed to the High Flyer and then to the Royal Stag in 1796. Two regular beers are supplemented by Windsor & Eton seasonals/specials. The front part of the pub is for drinking and the restaurant is to the rear, serving home-made food. Outside is a large patio-style seating area. Quiz night is Tuesday.
Q⊘⊕◑≈P⊟(60)🐾🐕

Eton
George Inn Ⓛ
77 High Street, SL4 6AF
⚙ 8am-11; 8am-10 Sun ☎ (01753) 861797
⊕ georgeinn-eton.co.uk
Windsor & Eton Windsor Knot, Guardsman; 4 changing beers (sourced locally) Ⓗ
Windsor & Eton Brewery's first pub is on a prominent street corner facing Eton Bridge. The recent refurbishment is now complete, including a new bar which hosts six ales all from the brewery. Wooden floors and lighting by carriage lamps and candles create a warm atmosphere. The range of Windsor & Eton beers can change depending on the number of specials/seasonals on tap. The garden restaurant is available for private parties. Real cider is on offer in the summer months.
Q⊕☞◑≈♣⊟(60)🐾🐕

Watermans Arms Ⓛ ✅
Brocas Street, SL4 6BW
⚙ 12-11.30 (midnight Sat); 12-11 Sun ☎ (01753) 861001
⊕ watermans-eton.com
Adnams Ghost Ship; Brakspear Bitter; Skinner's Cornish Knocker; Windsor & Eton Knight of the Garter; Wychwood Hobgoblin; house beer (by Caledonian); 2 changing beers Ⓗ
Situated close to the River Thames and Eton Bridge, this welcoming pub dates back to 1682. It serves up to eight ales – the two guests can include a beer from a local micro and Harveys Best. The house beer is brewed by Caledonian, reflecting the landlady's roots. The decor is a mixture of tartan wallpaper and rowing memorabilia including a large skiff rescued from the nearby former Eton Boathouse. In summer the courtyard garden is popular. The Sunday roast is recommended.
⊕◑≈♣⊟(60)🐾🐕

Hungerford
John o' Gaunt Ⓛ ✅
14 Bridge Street, RG17 0EG (30yds N of canal bridge)
⚙ 11-11; 12-10.30 Sun ☎ (01488) 683535
⊕ john-o-gaunt-hungerford.co.uk
Loddon Hullabaloo; Two Cocks 1643 Cavalier; 4 changing beers (sourced regionally; often INNformal, Windsor & Eton) Ⓗ
A listed 16th-century building set in the heart of a historic town. A plaque above the fireplace gives information about John o' Gaunt. In addition to a changing selection of six real ales and four real ciders there are numerous bottled beers, many from Belgium. Locally sourced food is available lunchtimes and evenings, all day Friday-Sunday.
Q⊘⊕◑≈♣⊟P⊟🐾🐕

Inkpen
Swan Inn Ⓛ
Craven Road, Lower Green, RG17 9DX
⚙ 12-2.30, 7-11; 12-11 Sat; 12-4 Sun; closed Mon & Tue ☎ (01488) 668326 ⊕ theswaninn-organics.co.uk
Butts Jester, Traditional; 1 changing beer (sourced locally; often Butts) Ⓗ
A splendid traditional rural inn situated close to the famous Combe Gibbet in an area popular with walkers and cyclists. It is divided into several drinking and dining areas on different levels and is ramped for wheelchair access. Organic food features prominently on the menu and Butts organic beers are always available on handpump. There is a separate restaurant. Quiz and darts nights alternate every Thursday – darts is played in a flagstoned games room. Ten en-suite bedrooms provide accommodation.
Q⊘☞⊞◑≈♣⊟P⊟(3)🐾🐕

Littlewick Green
Cricketers
Coronation Road, SL6 3RA
⚙ 12-11 ☎ (01628) 822888 ⊕ cricketers-berkshire.co.uk
Badger First Call, K&B Sussex Bitter, Tanglefoot Ⓗ
This pub is in a quintessential British pub location overlooking the village green and cricket pitch which featured in the TV programme Midsomer Murders. For the summer there is a newly refurbished terrace area to the front, overlooking the green. In winter wood-burning stoves keep the pub cosy. Hall & Woodhouse seasonal beers are

sometimes available. A traditional menu offers a range of quality pub food as well as daily specials. Q ⌂ ❀ ◑ ▯ ▭ ❀ ☍

Lower Earley

Seven Red Roses ✅
19 Maiden Place, RG6 3HA
❂ 11-11 (midnight Thu-Sat); 12-midnight Sun
☎ (0118) 935 4103 ⊕ thesevenredrosesrlowerearley.co.uk
St Austell Tribute; Sharp's Doom Bar; 1 changing beer Ⓗ
Community pub in the Maiden Lane housing estate precinct in Maiden Place, Lower Earley. All types of sport are shown in HD on three big screens, from athletics to diving. A good variety of food is served noon-9pm every day, from king-size mixed grills to burgers in baskets. There is entertainment most weekends, including live bands, discos and the (in)famous karaoke evenings.
⌂ ❀ ☎ ◑ ⅄ ♣ ▭ (21) ☍

Maidenhead

Bear Ⓛ ✅
8-10 High Street, SL6 1QJ
❂ 8am-midnight; 8am-11 Sun ☎ (01628) 763030
Greene King Abbot; Sharp's Doom Bar; 6 changing beers Ⓗ
A short walk from the town hall, this former coaching inn became a Wetherspoon in 2009 and has an open-plan bar with several different seating areas, including a drinking area outside at the front. A spiral staircase leads to an upper floor with an additional bar and comfy sofas. The 10 handpumps dispense up to six guest ales, many from local breweries. Two or three ciders are often available including Mr Whitehead's.
⌂ ❀ ◑ ⇄ ● ▭ ☍

Grenfell Arms Ⓛ ✅
22 Oldfield Road, SL6 1TW
❂ 10-midnight; 11-11 Sun ☎ (01628) 620705
⊕ grenfellarmsmaidenhead.co.uk
Greene King IPA, IPA Gold; 6 changing beers Ⓗ
A welcoming wood-panelled two-room pub situated a short walk from the town centre and the Thames, with eight recently refurbished bedrooms. There are eight handpumps on the bar – four Greene King, including a seasonal, and four rotating guests from local micros. Two real ciders are offered, normally Orchard Pig and Hogan's. Breakfast is available from 10am and traditional pub food lunchtimes and evenings. The garden has had a recent makeover.
Q ⌂ ❀ ☎ ◑ ♣ ● ▭ (53,75) ❀ ☍

Moneyrow Green

White Hart Ⓛ ✅
SL6 2ND
❂ 12-11 (10 Mon); 12-11.30 Fri; 12-9 Sun ☎ (01628) 621460
⊕ thewhitehartholyport.co.uk
Greene King IPA; 3 changing beers Ⓗ
A welcoming, traditional pub half a mile south of the village. Alongside the IPA, one LocAle and two non-Greene King guest beers are available. The wood-panelled lounge features leather sofas and log fires in winter. The larger public bar has wooden flooring, a TV and traditional pub games including bar billiards. There is a quiz night Monday, open mic Tuesday and Joker Jackpot

Sunday. Outside is a large, fenced beer garden with a pétanque pitch and children's play area.
⌂ ❀ ◑ ♣ P ▭ (53) ❀ ☍

Newbury

Cow & Cask Ⓛ
1 Inches Yard, Market Street, RG14 5DP
❂ 12-2 (not Tue & Wed), 4.30-9; 12-2, 4.30-10 Fri; 12-10 Sat; closed Sun & Mon ☎ 07517 658071 ⊕ cowandcask.co.uk
3 changing beers (sourced regionally; often Indigenous, Longdog, Ramsbury) Ⓖ
Berkshire's first micropub is housed in a shop near Newbury's former cattle market site. A large blackboard lists details of up to four beers and two ciders, often including Tutts Clump. Pumpclips from beers served since the November 2014 opening decorate the walls. Landlord Ian cheerfully serves visitors and regulars from the small bar in the far corner of the room. Conversation flourishes, with most drinkers seated around the two tables. Snacks are available and include pork pies and pickled eggs. Q ⇄ ♣ ● ▭ ❀

Hatchet Inn Ⓛ
12 Market Place, RG14 5BD
❂ 7am-midnight; 7am-1am Fri & Sat ☎ (01635) 277560
Greene King Abbot; Ruddles Best Bitter; Sharp's Doom Bar; changing beers (often Ramsbury, Two Cocks, Wild Weather) Ⓗ
Grade II-listed building in Newbury's Market Place that underwent extensive and sensitive refurbishment before being reopened by JD Wetherspoon, under its original name, in 2011. At least three of the four or five guest ales are from local breweries such as Two Cocks, Wild Weather and Ramsbury. Two real ciders are usually available. The pub is handily positioned for transport links and the shopping area.
Q ⌂ ❀ ☎ ◑ ⅄ ⇄ ● P ▭ ☍

King Charles Tavern ▼ Ⓛ ✅
54 Cheap Street, RG14 5BX
❂ 11.30-midnight (1am Thu-Sat); 12-midnight Sun
☎ (01635) 36695 ⊕ kctavern.com
West Berkshire Good Old Boy; house beer (by Greene King); 6 changing beers (sourced nationally; often Adnams, Butts, St Austell) Ⓗ
Close to the train and bus stations, this welcoming family-friendly town-centre pub is local CAMRA's 2016 Pub of the Year. Referred to by its clientele as the KC or KCT, it features eclectic British food, fresh flowers, nice decorative touches and an old map of Newbury on the ceiling. Walk through the narrow passages at the rear to discover an intimate and charming patio. ⌂ ❀ ◑ ⇄ ▭ ❀ ☍

Reading

Alehouse Ⓛ
2 Broad Street, RG1 2BH
❂ 11-11; 12-10.30 Sun ☎ (0118) 950 8119
⊕ the-alehouse-reading.co.uk
9 changing beers Ⓗ
The Alehouse has a unique and quirky atmosphere and is the perfect antidote to town-centre bars. The pub champions many microbreweries (local and from further afield), with varied pumpclips festooning the walls and ceiling as evidence. It is the only pub in Reading that regularly serves mead, as well as an excellent range of cider and perry. Like a fine whisky, not all will appreciate the

unique character of this traditional pub – but those who do come back for more. Local CAMRA Cider Pub of the Year 2014. ≠●☷⌨❀

Castle Tap
120 Castle Street, RG1 7RJ
✪ 11-11.30 (midnight Fri & Sat); 11-10.30 Sun
☎ (0118) 958 0473 ⊕ thecastletap.co.uk
4 changing beers Ⓗ
Winner of the local CAMRA branch's Phoenix Award for most revitalised pub, the Castle Tap was a welcome addition to the real ale scene. Alongside the ever-changing selection of ales and ciders there is an excellent range of British and foreign bottled beers. Fantastic cheeseboards are on the menu most of the time. There is a room at the back that can be used for meetings and events.
☷❀♣●P❀

Eldon Arms ❂
19 Eldon Terrace, RG1 4DX
✪ 12-3, 5-11; 12-11.30 Fri & Sat; 12-11 Sun
☎ (0118) 327 7247 ⊕ eldonarmsreading.co.uk
Wadworth IPA, 6X, Bishops Tipple, Swordfish; 2 changing beers (sourced regionally) Ⓗ
Reopened by Wadworth in 2015 after a major makeover (the two-bar set-up is now a single room), this pub is in the quiet back streets between London Road and Kings Road but only 10 minutes' walk from town. Alongside the Wadworth ales there are a couple of unusual guest beers. Traditional South African food is available alongside pub classics. ☷❀◖●☷❀🛜

Foresters Arms ❂
79-81 Brunswick Street, RG1 6NY
✪ 4-11; 12-midnight Sat; 12-11 Sun ☎ (0118) 376 9128
2 changing beers Ⓗ
Back-street local with two bars linked by a long side corridor, making a welcome return to the Guide. The front bar is a home-from-home, carpeted, with a fire and TV sport. The rear room hosts a pool table. To the rear is a recently renovated garden, ideal for a summer evening pint. The new licensees are enthusiastic about cask and encourage the locals to help choose the beers.
☷❀≠(West)♣☷❀🛜

Greyfriar
53 Greyfriars Road, RG1 1PA
✪ 12-11 (midnight Fri & Sat); 12-8 Sun ☎ (0118) 958 0560
⊕ thegreyfriarreading.co.uk
6 changing beers Ⓗ
A pub that came back from a long period of closure, now enjoying a new lease of life under independent ownership. An ever-changing range of six real ales from microbreweries, unusual keg beers and a variety of craft gins are on offer. Regular events include quiz nights, film nights and tap takeovers. Easily accessible from the station main entrance. ☷◖≠♣☷❀🛜

Hop Leaf
163-165 Southampton Street, RG1 2QZ
✪ 12-11.30 (12.30am Fri & Sat) ☎ (0118) 931 4700
Downton New Forest Ale; Hop Back Citra, Crop Circle, Summer Lightning; 2 changing beers Ⓗ
A traditional local with pub games such as bar billiards, crib and backgammon (featuring regular competitions in each), as well as a pinball machine. Owned by the brewery, the pub stocks six Hop Back beers plus a selection of ciders and perries. A variety of pub snacks is available. Fans of

classic rock will enjoy the landlord's choice in music. A good range of daily newspapers is provided. ☷♣●☷(5,6,11)❀

Nag's Head ⓛ
5 Russell Street, RG1 7XD
✪ 12-11 (midnight Fri); 11-midnight Sat ☎ 07765 880137
⊕ nagsheadreading.com
12 changing beers Ⓗ
In under a decade the Nag's has established itself as a premier ale and cider venue, winning the local CAMRA branch Pub of the Year award multiple times. Pies and baguettes are available during the week, with a roast on Sundays. An eclectic mix of bottled beers is stocked. Numerous board games are available above the (tuned and working) upright piano which is next to the popular dartboard. Gets busy on Reading FC match days.
☷❀◖≠(West)♣●P☷❀🛜

Purple Turtle ❂
9 Gun Street, RG1 2JR
✪ 11-3am ☎ (0118) 959 7196 ⊕ purpleturtlebar.com/reading
4 changing beers Ⓗ
Celebrating its 25th year in 2015, the Purple Turtle is Reading's longest-running independent pub. While many people will associate the pub with the trappings of noisy misspent youth, it underwent a major overhaul in 2013/14. The revitalised bar offers real ale and cider as well as its infamous late opening. Beer choice is eclectic – you never know what you'll see from one week to the next.
❀♿≠●☷🛜

St Nicholas Hurst

Wheelwright's Arms ❂
Davis Way, RG10 0TR (off B3030 opp entrance to Dinton Pastures) SU787716
✪ 11.30-3, 5.30 (5 Thu)-11; 12-11.30 Fri & Sat; 12-10.30 Sun
☎ (0118) 934 4100 ⊕ thewheelwrightsarms.co.uk
Wadworth IPA, Horizon, 6X, Farmer's Glory, Bishops Tipple, Swordfish; 2 changing beers (sourced nationally; often Batemans, St Austell) Ⓗ
Formerly a wheelwright's workshop, this is now a classic country pub popular with locals, walkers and cyclists. It has two bars with low beams plus a dining area (available to book for functions). Five or six Wadworth beers are available plus one or two guest ales and two real ciders. Good pub food is served lunchtimes and evenings (no food Sun). Families are welcome with children until 8.30pm. Newspapers are provided. The garden has a heated, covered patio and a separate smoking area. Q☷❀◖♿●P☷(128)❀

Sandhurst

Rose & Crown ⓛ ❂
108 High Street, GU47 8HA (on A321, 7 mins' walk W of railway station)
✪ 12-11 (midnight Fri & Sat); 12-10.30 Sun
☎ (01252) 878938 ⊕ roseandcrownsandhurst.info
Otter Bitter; 6 changing beers (sourced nationally; often Caledonian, Hammerpot, Redemption) Ⓗ
Renowned for a varied selection of six ales, always including a local ale sold at a reduced price. Previously local CAMRA branch Pub of the Year, two beer festivals are held at Easter and Halloween with around 20 real ales and ciders. The pub has a good reputation for food including hand-made

Pieminister pies (no food Mon). Children and dogs are welcome. Live music sessions feature most Friday and Saturday nights. Craft fairs are held monthly May-September. Sport is shown on TV with the volume turned down.
ॐ❀◖▶≈♣P🖵(194)❀ 🤝

Shinfield

Bell & Bottle
37 School Green, RG2 9EE
✪ 12-11 ☎ (0118) 988 3563
Plain Sheep Dip; 3 changing beers Ⓗ
Spacious yet cosy free house facing the village green with a real community feel. Although primarily a drinkers' pub, a good range of pub grub is served lunchtimes and evenings (until 5pm Sun). A local ale is often available. A games area hosts pool and darts, and Monday is poker night. There is a garden for fine weather and a real fire if it is cold. The interior is fully accessible, with a disabled toilet. Children and dogs are welcome.
ॐ❀◖▶♣P🖵(3)❀🤝

Stockcross

Rising Sun Ⓛ
Ermin Street, RG20 8LG
✪ 12-2.30, 6-11; 12-11 Sat; 12-10.30 Sun; closed Mon
☎ (01488) 608335 ⊕ therisingsunstockcross.com
West Berkshire Mr Chubb's Lunchtime Bitter, Good Old Boy; 2 changing beers (sourced locally) Ⓗ
A welcoming traditional village local which reopened in April 2015 following a period of closure. There are usually four ales available on handpump. West Berkshire Good Old Boy and Mr Chubb's are the regulars alongside two changing beers, almost always from local breweries. Good-value pub grub, mainly locally sourced, is served lunchtimes and evenings. There is live folk music every other Sunday evening and a quiz night on the second Tuesday of the month.
Q ॐ❀◖▶P🖵(4)❀🤝

Sunningdale

Royal Oak Ⓛ ✔
19 Station Road, SL5 0QL
✪ 12-11 (midnight Fri & Sat); 12-10.30 Sun
☎ (01344) 623625 ⊕ oaksunningdale.co.uk
Greene King IPA; Morland Hen's Tooth; Rebellion Smuggler; house beer (by Hardys & Hansons); 2 changing beers (sourced locally; often Ascot, Windsor & Eton) Ⓗ
Warm, friendly Greene King Local Heroes pub in a village setting with a good cross-section of customers. The landlord is very knowledgeable regarding the beers on offer and displays excellent cellarmanship skills. A simple lunchtime food menu is home cooked, complementing a changing beer selection which always includes at least one LocAle. A large garden hosts barbecues in the summer and a beer festival is held during the late May bank holiday. Q ॐ❀◖▶♣P🖵(9)❀🤝

Theale

Bull
41 High Street, RG7 5AH
✪ 12-11.30; 12-10 Sun ☎ (0118) 930 3478
⊕ thebullattheale.co.uk

Wadworth IPA, 6X; 1 changing beer (often Wadworth) Ⓗ
Originally the brewery tap of Blatch of Theale, many of the brewery buildings have been preserved and can be viewed through the car park or the ivy-clad entrance further up the road. The pub was refurbished a couple of years ago and is now a comfortable family-friendly outlet. A number of screens show sporting events. There is a function room that can be booked for parties.
ॐ❀◖▶&≈P🖵(1)❀🤝

Three Mile Cross

Swan Ⓛ
Basingstoke Road, RG7 1AT
✪ 11-1, 2-11; 11-3, 7-11 Sat; 11-4 Sun ☎ (0118) 988 3674
Fuller's London Pride; Loddon Hoppit; Timothy Taylor Boltmaker, Landlord; 1 changing beer Ⓗ
Grade II-listed 17th-century pub, occupied by the current licensees for over 30 years. Being near to the Madejski Stadium, the Swan has a large rugby/football crowd on match days. Locally produced hearty home-cooked food is served. Look out for the inglenook fireplace and the brass plaques in the loos, where famous visitors have had their visits to the pub's facilities recorded for posterity.
ॐ❀◖▶&P🖵(72,82)🤝

Tilehurst

Royal Oak
69 Westwood Glen, RG31 5NW
✪ 2-11; 12-midnight Fri & Sat; 12-11 Sun ☎ (0118) 941 6056
⊕ theroyaloak-tilehurst.co.uk
4 changing beers Ⓗ
Perched at the summit of a steep driveway and pre-dating most of the surrounding suburban housing, this charmingly quirky building has been frequently extended and lies close to an old drovers' route. The lovely grassed beer garden is ideal for a lazy summer's pint. The pub is now owned by Greene King but has retained the original agreement, allowing the sourcing of interesting guest beers to continue.
ॐ❀♣P🖵(33)❀

Waltham St Lawrence

Bell Ⓛ
The Street, RG10 0JJ
✪ 12-3, 5-11; 12-11 Sat; 12-10.30 Sun ☎ (0118) 934 1788
⊕ thebellwalthamstlawrence.co.uk
Loddon Hoppit; 4 changing beers Ⓗ
Picturesque, 14th-century, village-owned pub, popular with locals, discerning drinkers and food lovers. Visitors will find log fires in winter and a good-sized beer garden for sunny summer days. Ales are mainly locally sourced and supplemented by up to eight ciders and perries. High-quality food is served, also locally sourced where possible. Runner-up local CAMRA branch Cider Pub of the Year. A gem of a country inn. Q ॐ❀◖▶●🖵(4)❀

Warfield

Plough & Harrow ✔
Newell Green, RG42 6AE (jct with Warfield St)
✪ 12-11; 12-10.30 Sun ☎ (01344) 300701
⊕ theploughandharrowwarfield.com

Greene King London Glory, Abbot, IPA Reserve; house beer (by Greene King); 2 changing beers (sourced nationally; often St Austell, Skinner's) ⊞
Friendly community local dating from the late-18th century, providing a welcome for families, children, dogs and even horses, who have their own space in the parking area. Four handpumps serve beers from the Greene King stable and changing guest ales. Patrons can take advantage of a real log fire during the winter months and the large beer garden outside in summer. Home-made traditional pub food is served from award-winning suppliers. Mini beer and cider festivals have featured in recent years. Q❄☺◑&▲♣P🖵(53)❀🐾

Wargrave

Wargrave & District Snooker Club
Woodclyffe Hostel, Church Street, RG10 8EP
◑ 7-11; closed Sat & Sun ☎ (0118) 940 3508
1 changing beer ⊞
The club opens weekday evenings and shares the building with the local library. The regularly changing beers reflect members' recommendations, with two on in the winter months and one in the summer. Bar billiards, darts, chess, cards and books are available. The TV's default is off. Visitors may show this Guide or CAMRA membership card for entry (£3 fee to use the snooker tables). The phone number given is the chairman's. Winner of CAMRA branch Club of the Year for several years. ≠♣🖵(850)❀

Wickham

Five Bells 🅛 ✅
Baydon Road, RG20 8HH
◑ 12-3, 5-11; 12-11 Sat; 12-10.30 Sun ☎ (01488) 657300
⊕ fivebellswickham.co.uk
INNformal INNDeep; 8 changing beers (sourced regionally; often Loose Cannon, Two Cocks, Wild Weather Ales) ⊞
The INNformal Brewery tap and winner of two previous CAMRA awards is local CAMRA Cider Pub of the Year 2016. This rural inn attracts beer and cider aficionados with its helpful staff, quality food and long bar featuring nine regional cask ales and eight ciders. The thatched roof, exposed beams and open log fire give the pub a traditional feel. A large garden is popular in summer. Live acoustic music plays outside on occasional summer Saturday afternoons. Q❄☺🕮◑♣P❀🐾🛜

Windsor

Acre 🅛 ✅
Donnelly House, Victoria Street, SL4 1EN
◑ 11-11 (midnight Fri & Sat); 12-10.30 Sun
☎ (01753) 841083 ⊕ theacrewindsor.com
Windsor & Eton Guardsman; 2 changing beers ⊞
Formerly the Liberal Club but now a free house open to all. The name refers to the adjacent Bachelors Acre. Three ales are on offer, with Windsor & Eton's Guardsman a permanent feature and two regularly changing guests, usually from local breweries. Live music is hosted every Saturday night plus an open mic night on the first Monday of the month. Two screens show live sporting events and there are excellent facilities for darts. Two function rooms are available for hire. ❄◑≠♣🖵(77)🛜

Carpenters Arms ✅
4 Market Street, SL1 1PB
◑ 11-11 (midnight Fri & Sat) ☎ (01753) 863739
Fuller's London Pride; St Austell Nicholson's Pale Ale; Sharp's Doom Bar; 5 changing beers (sourced nationally) ⊞
Situated on a narrow cobbled street close to the castle, this excellent, recently refurbished, Nicholson's pub has been voted local CAMRA Pub of the Year several times. The elegantly decorated interior is on three levels, the lowest of which is reputed to house a passageway to the castle. Ashby's Brewery tiles are retained on the floor by the entrance, harking back to the pub's former owners. The three regular beers are supplemented by five interesting guests, usually including something dark. ◑≠🖵(71,702)🛜

Vansittart Arms 🅛 ✅
105 Vansittart Road, SL4 5DD
◑ 12-11 (11.30 Thu; midnight Fri); 10.30-midnight Sat; 10.30-11 Sun ☎ (01753) 865988
⊕ vansittartarmswindsor.co.uk
Fuller's Oliver's Island, London Pride, ESB; Gale's Seafarers Ale; 1 changing beer ⊞
Known to all as the Vanni, this popular and well-run Fuller's pub is worth the 10-minute walk from the town centre. The ale range includes the current Fuller's seasonal beer. There is a separate pool room which has a small book swap library, and a good selection of daily newspapers is also available. The large garden is ideal for summer barbecues and is can be hired for functions. Breakfast is served weekends, 10.30am-1pm. Parking may be difficult.
Q❄☺◑≠♣🖵(71,702)🐾🛜

Wokingham

Crispin 🅛
45 Denmark Street, RG40 2AY (opp library)
◑ 2-11; 12-midnight Fri & Sat; 12-10.30 Sun
☎ (0118) 978 0309 ⊕ crispinpub.co.uk
4 changing beers (often Binghams, Hogs Back, Loddon) ⊞
One of the oldest inns in Wokingham, named after Saint Crispin who is the patron saint of cobblers (hence the pub sign). There are four constantly changing real ales on offer from the single bar. No food is served but you can bring your own takeaway to enjoy with a drink and there are free bar snacks on Sunday lunchtimes. Beer and cider festivals are held throughout the year. There is a modern jukebox. Please note the mid-week opening times. ☺≠♣P🖵(4)🐾🛜

Queen's Head 🍷 🅛 ✅
23 The Terrace, RG40 1BP
◑ 12-11 (12.30am Fri & Sat); 12-10.30 Sun
☎ (0118) 978 1221 ⊕ queensheadwokingham.co.uk
Greene King London Glory, Abbot; house beer (by Greene King); 3 changing beers (sourced locally; often Bond Brews, Loddon, West Berkshire) ⊞
This 15th-century timber cruck-framed inn with low ceilings and beams is on the Wokingham Society's Heritage Trail. Now a Greene King Local Heroes pub, it serves three Greene King beers plus three ales from local breweries. Beer paddles with three third-pints make it easier to sample several different ales. The real fire creates a cosy feel in winter and the large rear garden has a covered area. Food is only available on specials nights.

Children are welcome up to 8pm. County Pub of the Year 2015 and local CAMRA branch Pub of the Year 2016. ⌂❀⇄♣🖵(4)❀🎜

White Horse

Easthampstead Road, RG40 3AF (50yds NW of Heathlands Rd)

🕮 12-11; 12-6 Sun ☎ (0118) 979 7402

🌐 whitehorsewokingham.co.uk

Greene King IPA, Abbot; 1 changing beer (sourced nationally) Ⓗ

A country pub with a relaxed atmosphere and views across the fields. Staff and locals offer a friendly welcome. There are three handpulls, two serving beers from the Greene King stable and the third an ever-changing guest. The freshly prepared food menu is available both lunchtimes and evenings and the dining area can be reserved for functions (no food Sun eve). There is a bar and garden menu for lighter meals. Ingredients are sourced from selected independent producers. A choice of newspapers is available.
Q⌂❀◑♣♦P❀🎜

Woolhampton

Rowbarge

Station Road, RG7 5SH

🕮 11-11; 11-10.30 Sun ☎ (0118) 971 2213

Brunning & Price Original; changing beers (often Indigenous, Tring, Wild Weather) Ⓗ

The pub has a single bar leading to a large restaurant area with cosy alcoves, offering both à la carte and pub food menus featuring freshly cooked produce. The large garden, frequented by walkers, cyclists and dog owners, sits alongside the Kennet & Avon Canal. There is a barbecue and outside bar in the warmer months. Beer festivals feature in the summer with a selection of local brews. ⌂❀◑♦⇄♣P🖵❀🎜

Wraysbury

Perseverance ✅

2 High Street, TW19 5DB

🕮 12-11; 12-8 Sun ☎ (01784) 482375 🌐 thepercy.co.uk

Otter Ale; 3 changing beers (sourced nationally) Ⓗ

Comfortable pub with several seating areas. The larger front room has soft sofas, a piano and a large inglenook fireplace with a real log fire. Another seating area, again with an open fire, leads through to the rear dining area, which has well-stocked bookshelves. To the rear of the building is a delightful garden. Three guest ales are always varied and sourced from some of the more interesting breweries around the country. Regular beer festivals are held. Quiz night is Thursday.
Q⌂❀◑♣♦P🖵(60,305)❀🎜

Old Swan Uppers, Cookham (Photo: Bob Steel)

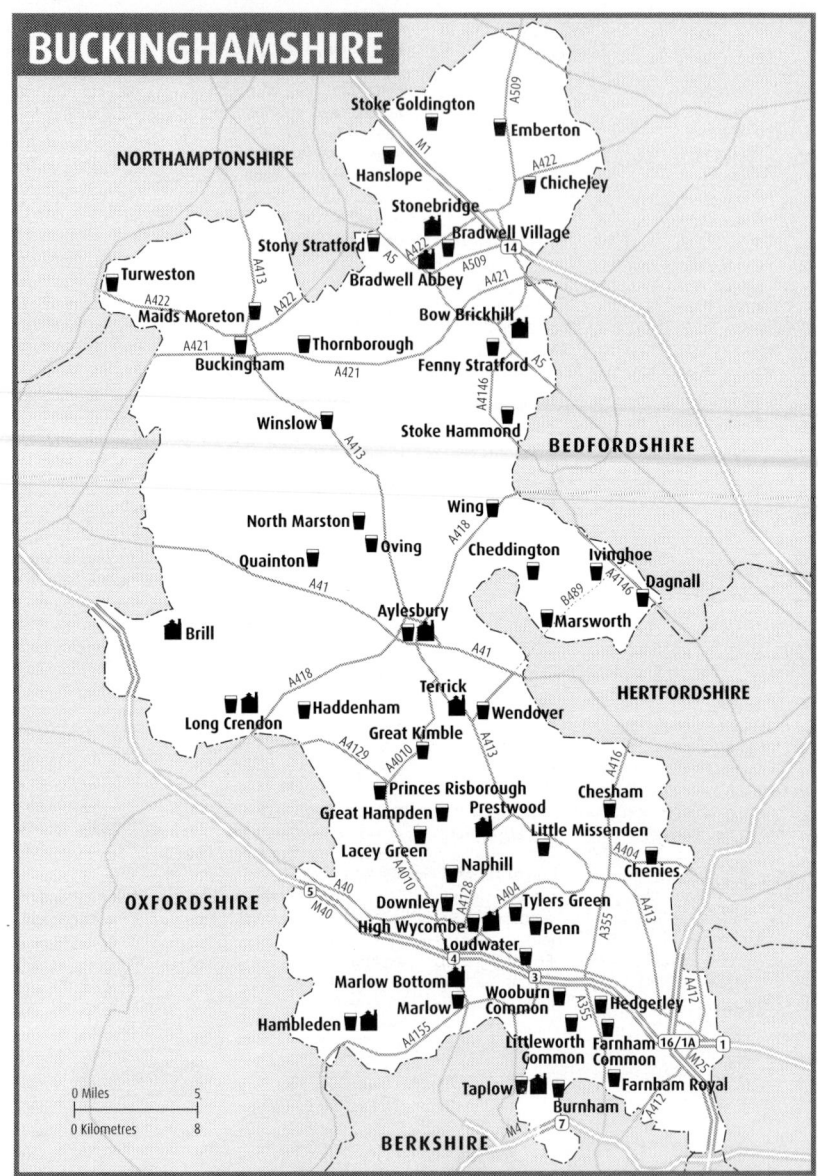

BUCKINGHAMSHIRE

NORTHAMPTONSHIRE

Stoke Goldington
Emberton
Hanslope
Chicheley
Stonebridge
Stony Stratford
Bradwell Village
Turweston
Bradwell Abbey
Maids Moreton
Bow Brickhill
Thornborough
Buckingham
Fenny Stratford
Winslow
Stoke Hammond
BEDFORDSHIRE

North Marston
Wing
Oving
Cheddington
Ivinghoe
Quainton
Dagnall
Aylesbury
Marsworth
Brill
Terrick
HERTFORDSHIRE
Haddenham
Wendover
Long Crendon
Great Kimble
Princes Risborough
Chesham
Great Hampden
Prestwood
Lacey Green
Little Missenden
Naphill
Chenies
OXFORDSHIRE
Downley
Tylers Green
High Wycombe
Penn
Loudwater
Marlow Bottom
Wooburn
Common
Hedgerley
Marlow
Hambleden
Littleworth
Farnham
Common
Common
Taplow
Farnham Royal
Burnham

0 Miles 5
0 Kilometres 8

BERKSHIRE

Aylesbury

Bricklayers Arms

Walton Terrace, HP21 7QY
🕑 11-3, 5-midnight (1am Fri); 11-1am Sat; 12-11 Sun
☎ (01296) 482930 ⊕ bricklayersarmsaylesbury.co.uk
Fuller's London Pride; 2 changing beers (sourced
regionally) Ⓗ
Originally part of the hamlet of Walton, this 17th-
century pub is situated on a crossroads, just round
the corner from Walton pond, once a centre for
breeding the famous Aylesbury Duck. The pub has
a timber-beamed interior on several levels, with a
function room at the rear. A fire provides a warm
welcome in the winter, while a sizeable enclosed
garden at the back is a suntrap in the summer.
❀◐♪≠P🖵 (50,55,300)

Farmers' Bar at King's Head Ⓛ

Market Square, HP20 2RW
🕑 11-11; 12-10.30 Sun ☎ (01296) 718812
⊕ farmersbar.co.uk
Chiltern Pale Ale, Beechwood Bitter; 2 changing
beers Ⓗ
When Chiltern Brewery took over the running of the
Farmers' Bar for the National Trust it became
the first bar in the country to be no-smoking and
free from piped music. Dating from circa 1455, this
is the oldest courtyard inn in England and was
donated by the Rothschild family in 1924. Ales are
often used in cooking – lunches here are made
from ingredients freshly sourced from local
suppliers. A former local CAMRA Pub of the Year.
Q❀♿◐♿≠♠🖵🛜

Hop Pole Inn L

83 Bicester Road, HP19 9AZ (near Gatehouse Industrial Area)

🕓 11-11 (midnight Fri & Sat); 11-10.30 Sun

☎ (01296) 482129 🌐 hoppolepub.com

Vale Best IPA, Gravitas; 8 changing beers (often Aylesbury) ⊞

'Aylesbury's Permanent Beer Festival' is home to the Aylesbury Brewhouse and shop which opened in December 2011. The individual brews feature regularly in the pub, but may not last very long. This is Vale's sister brewery – the pub is the brewery's main outlet, featuring Vale beers plus a selection from other small brewers. A friendly welcome as well as good food adds to the attraction (no food Mon). Children are welcome until 9pm if dining. 😸◗🍴🚐😺

Old Millwrights Arms ✪

83 Walton Road, HP21 7SN

🕓 12-11 (midnight Fri); 9am-midnight Sat

☎ (01296) 488161 🌐 oldmillwrightsarms.com

Greene King IPA; 8 changing beers ⊞

Nine handpumps greet you as you enter this pub, dispensing four ales from the Greene King stable and, as part of the Local Heroes scheme, five mainly locally brewed ales. Pump takeovers from one of many local breweries also feature regularly. The open-plan pub has three distinct areas and excellent food can be enjoyed throughout, as well as in the outdoor space to the rear. 😸◗🚆P🚐😺

Bradwell Village

Victoria Inn ✪

Vicarage Road, MK13 9AQ

🕓 3-11; 12-11 Sat & Sun ☎ (01908) 312769

4 changing beers (sourced regionally; often Everards, Hart Family Brewers, Tring) ⊞/Ⓐ

A stone-built pub with a tiled roof. As you enter, the bar, with its four handpumps, is directly in front of you. To the right is a room with a pool table and dartboard, to the left is another room with tables and chairs and an open fireplace. Exposed beams and low ceilings create a comfortable and relaxed atmosphere. Behind the pub is a large beer garden with swings. 😸😺🍂P🚐😺🛜

Buckingham

Mitre

2 Mitre Street, MK18 1DW

🕓 5-11 (midnight Fri); 12-midnight Sat; 12-10.30 Sun

☎ (01280) 813080 🌐 themitre.org.uk

5 changing beers (sourced regionally; often Banks's, Oakham, Tring) ⊞

A short walk from the centre of Buckingham takes you to the town's oldest pub. As you would expect from a free house, the Mitre has changing and interesting beers, often featuring guests from Animal Brewing and Oakham specials. A cosy atmosphere is enhanced by a real open fire in winter. There are board games to play and books can be borrowed from the lending shelf. Major sporting events are shown on five large-screen TVs including one in the garden. 😸😺🍂P😺🛜

Burnham

Bee

1 Britwell Road, SL1 8AG

🕓 11-11 (1am Fri & Sat); 12-10.30 Sun ☎ (01628) 665789

Brakspear Bitter; Wychwood Hobgoblin; 1 changing beer (sourced nationally) ⊞

Grade II-listed inn on the corner at the top of Burnham High Street with a large L-shaped bar. The friendly pub boasts a charming interior and a popular decked area with tables at the front where you can watch the world go by. The guest ale is from the Marston's stable. Entertainment includes open mic on Tuesdays and live music on Saturdays. A cider festival is hosted in July. Q😸😺🍴P🚐(53,68)😺🛜

Cheddington

Old Swan

58 High Street, LU7 0RQ

🕓 12-11 ☎ (01296) 662171

🌐 theoldswancheddington.co.uk

Young's Bitter; 3 changing beers (sourced locally) ⊞

You are assured of a warm welcome at this pretty thatched Grade II-listed free house which dates back some 400 years. In the hands of a new landlord since January 2015, the pub has been sympathetically refurbished, keeping its low beams and fireplaces. A 10-minute walk from the Grand Union Canal and close to the Ridgeway Path and Ashridge Estate, it is popular with walkers and visitors. Four real ales are available, some from local breweries. 😸😺◗🚆P🚐(164)😺🛜

Chenies

Red Lion L

Latimer Road, WD3 6ED (off A404 between Chorleywood and Little Chalfont)

🕓 11-2.30, 5.30-11; 12-10.30 Sun ☎ (01923) 282722

🌐 redlionchenies.co.uk

Vale Best IPA; Wadworth 6X; house beer (by Rebellion); 1 changing beer (sourced nationally) ⊞

A frequent Guide entry with three regular local beers and one guest, described by its long-standing landlord as an autarchic free house – a genuinely run private free house. It is a pub first and foremost serving high-quality good-value food, not a restaurant serving beer. Walkers and dogs are welcome – Chenies Manor is nearby with some good walks in surrounding countryside. An excellent pub for a get-together and chat with no music or TV. Q😸😺◗P🚐(336)😺

Chesham

Black Cat ✪

Lycrome Road, Lye Green, HP5 3LF (off A416)

SP977034

Aylesbury 🍺 Aylesbury
Bootlegger 🍺 High Wycombe (NEW)
Bucks Star Milton Keynes: Stonebridge
Chiltern Terrick
Concrete Cow Bradwell Abbey
Fisher's High Wycombe
Hillfire Aylesbury (NEW)
Hornes Bow Brickhill (NEW)
Malt Prestwood
moogBREW Taplow (NEW)
Old Luxters Hambleden
Rebellion Marlow Bottom
Vale Brill
XT Long Crendon

✪ 9am-2.30, 5-11 (7 Mon); 9am-11 Sat; 12-10 Sun
☎ (01494) 773966 ⊕ blackcatchesham.co.uk
Timothy Taylor Landlord; Young's Bitter; 1 changing beer (sourced nationally; often Brains, Fuller's, Young's) Ⓗ
On the outskirts of Chesham, this is a cosy, single-bar pub with a warm welcome for all. Those wishing to eat can do so in the bar decorated with a plethora of black cat memorabilia, or in the back room that doubles as a dining area. Games players are well catered for with darts, quiz, dominoes and crib played on various evenings. The spacious garden with play area is ideal for families. Open for breakfast 9am-noon. Q ⌂ ✿ ◑ ◆ P ⏚ (730) ♣ ☞

Chicheley

Chester Arms
Bedford Road, MK16 9JE
✪ 12-midnight ☎ (01234) 391214 ⊕ the-chester-arms.co.uk
Sharp's Doom Bar; Tring Side Pocket for a Toad; 2 changing beers (sourced locally; often Concrete Cow, White Park) Ⓗ
Family-run pub offering a variety of freshly prepared food and a range of real ales, many from local breweries. The menu changes seasonally and food is served all day. Rooms are on different levels, which greatly adds to the pub's character. The room to the left of the entrance is informal, with bench seats, tables, chairs and a large-screen TV, while the areas to the right are set for dining. Outside there are gardens to the front and rear. Q ⌂ ✿ ◑ ◆ P ⏚ (40) ♣ ☞

Dagnall

Red Lion
21 Main Road North, HP4 1QZ
✪ 12-11; 12-10.30 Sun ☎ (01442) 843020
⊕ theredliondagnall.co.uk
Sharp's Doom Bar; 2 changing beers (sourced regionally) Ⓗ
Dating from 1740, this is a well-run free house offering a warm welcome and well-kept beers. Warmed by an open fire and a wood-burning stove, it is popular with locals and walkers alike. Home-made, good-value food using fresh ingredients is available all week. Local watercolour views by a village artist hang on the dining room walls. Quiz and darts team and local interest groups meet here regularly. Dogs (in the bar) and children are welcome. ⌂ ✿ ◑ ◆ P ♣ ☞

Downley

De Spencer Arms ✔
The Common, HP13 5YQ (across common from village on flint track beyond end of Plomer Green Lane)
✪ 12-11 (midnight Fri & Sat); 12-10.30 Sun
☎ (01494) 535511 ⊕ ledespencersarms.co.uk
Fuller's London Pride, ESB; 2 changing beers Ⓗ
Named after Francis Dashwood, the notorious 15th Baron le Despencer, whose family still own the surrounding estate, this traditional village pub offers four real ales, as well as good wines and home-cooked food. It is popular with walkers and cyclists and just a quarter mile by road or across the common from the village hall bus stop. Quiz nights, music nights, beer and food events add to the attraction of this cosy flint pub on Downley Common. ✿ ◑ ◆ P ♣ ☞

Emberton

Bell & Bear Ⓛ
12 High Street, MK46 5DH
✪ 5-10 Mon; 12-2.30, 5-11 Tue-Thu; 12-11 Fri & Sat; 12-8 Sun
☎ (01234) 711565 ⊕ bellandbear.net
4 changing beers (sourced regionally; often Banks's, Leighton Buzzard, Marston's) Ⓗ
A stone-built Grade II-listed pub with a slate roof. It serves a variety of interesting beers and real ciders, always including at least one local beer and local cider from Virtual Orchard and Woughton Orchard. The old building houses a long narrow bar with a Northamptonshire skittles table in the far corner. There is a separate restaurant for fine dining – booking in advance is recommended. Parking is on the street outside.
Q ⌂ ✿ ◑ Å ◆ ◑ P ⏚ (21) ♣ ☞

Farnham Common

Stag & Hounds Ⓛ ✔
18 The Broadway, SL2 3QQ
✪ 12-midnight (1am Fri & Sat) ☎ (01753) 647716
⊕ stagnhounds.co.uk
Greene King IPA, IPA Gold; Hardys & Hansons Olde Trip; Morland Old Speckled Hen; Ruddles County; 5 changing beers Ⓗ
Cosy one-room pub with comfy sofas and beer casks as stools. The cellar can be viewed through a window near the side entrance. Ten beers are generally available, five from local and national microbreweries and five from the Greene King stable. A good selection of ciders is also on offer, and bottled beers from around the world. A beer bat serves three third-pint glasses, allowing a good number of the ales to be tasted. The TV is only turned on for major sporting events.
Q ⌂ ✿ ◑ ◆ ◑ P ⏚ (X74) ♣ ☞

Farnham Royal

Emperor Ⓛ
Blackpond Lane, SL2 3EG SU959842
✪ 12-11 (midnight Fri & Sat); 12-10.30 Sun
☎ (01753) 643006 ⊕ theemperorfarnhamcommon.co.uk
Fuller's London Pride; 2 changing beers (sourced locally; often Andwells, Rebellion, Windsor & Eton) Ⓗ
An old pub, but with a contemporary air about it. The front area, furnished with comfy seating and many cushions, is perfect for relaxing with a pint, and there is a cosy lower area with a large table. To the rear is a room dedicated to dining. Outside is a pleasant garden and covered seating area. Live music is usually hosted monthly on a Saturday. Supplementing the London Pride are two or three constantly changing ales. No food is served Sunday evening. Q ⌂ ✿ ◑ P ⏚ (X74) ♣ ☞

Fenny Stratford

Red Lion
11 Lock View Lane, Simpson Road, MK1 1BY
✪ 12-11 (midnight Fri & Sat); 12-10.30 Sun
☎ (01908) 372317
3 changing beers (sourced nationally; often Camerons, Gale's, Woodforde's) Ⓗ
A popular lockside pub on the Grand Union Canal. The landlord is a real ale enthusiast and keeps a rolling choice of up to three ales, selected to contrast in style and strength. Up to five real ciders are also available including Old Rosie, Rosie's Pig,

Thatchers Cheddar Valley and Heritage. There is a quiet room as you enter and beyond is the main bar with TV and pool table. Through the bar a corridor leads to the canalside garden.
🐴❀🚆♣🍎P🚌(18)🐾📶

Great Hampden

Hampden Arms [L]
Great Missenden, HP16 9RQ
⏲ 12-3, 6-midnight; 12-3.30, 6-11.30 Sun
☎ (01494) 488255 🌐 thehampdenarms.co.uk
Fuller's London Pride; Rebellion IPA; 1 changing beer (sourced locally) [H]
This picturesque pub in the heart of the Chilterns offers excellent real ales and high-quality food. Three ales are on handpump, with an emphasis on local breweries such as Rebellion, Chiltern, Malt, Vale and Tring. An à la carte menu is complemented by specials including Greek signature dishes, and a lunchtime snack menu. The pub's large garden is available for parties and events of all kinds as well as for simply enjoying in fine weather. Q❀◑♿🍎P📶

Great Kimble

Swan [L]
Lower Icknield Way, HP17 9TR
⏲ 12-3.30, 5-10 Mon-Wed; 12-3.30, 5-11; 12-7 Sun
☎ (01844) 275288 🌐 kimbleswan.co.uk
3 changing beers (sourced locally) [H]
Facing the village green, this 18th-century pub has been a committed supporter of LocAle, with a rotating selection of beers from nearby breweries on its three handpumps. Set in the lee of the Chiltern Hills Area of Outstanding Natural Beauty, it offers a warm welcome to walkers and cyclists. A family-run and owned local, the pub has a policy of sourcing food from local suppliers. Opening hours may vary, particularly in the winter.
❀🛏◑♿🚆♣P🚌(300)🐾📶

Haddenham

Rising Sun [L] ✔
9 Thame Road, HP17 8EN
⏲ 12-2.30, 5-11; 12-midnight Fri & Sat; 12-10.30 Sun
☎ (01844) 291744
XT Four; 5 changing beers (sourced locally) [H]
New tenants introduced a different beer philosophy and six handpumps in 2015. As XT's brewery tap, it looks like the Riser is destined to remain the best ale house in the immediate neighbourhood. The removal of the pool table, jukebox, dartboards and live music, and the introduction of comfy chairs and quiet spaces, has resulted in a sea change for locals.
Q❀🚆(Haddenham & Thame Parkway)🍎🚌(280)🐾📶

Hambleden

Stag & Huntsman [L]
Henley-on-Thames, RG9 6RP
⏲ 12-11 (1am Fri & Sat) ☎ (01491) 571227
🌐 thestagandhuntsman.co.uk
Rebellion IPA, Smuggler; Sharp's Doom Bar; 2 changing beers [H]
Historic pub in this beautiful unspoilt village that has recently been refurbished while keeping its old-fashioned charm. It serves four hand-drawn real ales including Sharp's Doom Bar and Rebellion IPA plus a wide variety of local beers. Nestled in the Chilterns, midway between Marlow and Henley, just up from the River Thames, the village has outstanding scenery often featured in Midsomer Murders. Q🐴❀🛏◑♿P🐾📶

Hanslope

Cock
35 High Street, MK19 7LQ
⏲ 4-11; 12-11 Sat & Sun ☎ (01908) 510553
Greene King IPA; 2 changing beers (sourced regionally; often Great Oakley, Magpie, Red Squirrel) [H]
A pub with one large L-shaped room that has a pool table, dartboard and large-screen TV at one end; at the other end is a real fire. The bar is directly in front of you as you enter and serves Greene King IPA and two guest ales. There is BT Sport on the TV and live music is staged once a month. 🐴❀♿♣P🚌(33,33A)🐾📶

Hedgerley

White Horse 🏆 [L]
Village Lane, SL2 3UY (in old village, near church)
⏲ 11-2.30, 5-11; 11-11 Sat; 12-10.30 Sun ☎ (01753) 643225
Rebellion IPA; 7 changing beers (often Mallinsons, Mighty Oak, Oakham) [G]
CAMRA branch Pub of the Year on numerous occasions, this village local has an impressive range of real ales. New breweries are a feature, as well as favourites from Oakham, Mallinsons and Mighty Oak. A draft Belgian beer and three real ciders are also available. This classic pub has a well-tended garden and a heated, covered patio area. Regular beer festivals are held – the largest is over the Whitsun weekend and is a must for real ale enthusiasts. Q🐴❀◑♣🍎P🐾📶

High Wycombe

Belle Vue ✔
45 Gordon Road, HP13 6EQ
⏲ 4.30-11; 3.30-midnight Fri; 12-1am Sat; 12-10.30 Sun
☎ (01494) 524728 🌐 thebv.pub
Adnams Broadside; Sharp's Doom Bar; 4 changing beers [H]
Near the railway station, the pub is a friendly traditional community pub and a regular in the Guide for the past 10 years. It has six ales, four ciders and a real fire, and holds occasional beer festivals. There is live music, regular quiz nights, a literary society, knitting circle, ukulele club, vinyl night, folk sessions, occasional charity events, film nights and even Christmas carol 'shouting'! There is also a permanent art exhibition. The ciders are from Westons. ❀🛏🚆♣🍎🚌🐾📶

Bootlegger [L]
Amersham Hill, HP13 6NQ
⏲ 4-11 Mon-Wed; 12-midnight Thu-Sat; 12-11 Sun
☎ (01494) 525457 🌐 thebootleggerpub.co.uk
10 changing beers (sourced locally) [H]
Recently refurbished ale house directly opposite the railway station. The front bar was extended by removing a wall to provide improved customer access to the handpumps. Bearing left from the entrance is another small room with armchairs. Outside is a large secluded garden with decking. There is a comprehensive beer menu containing

tasting notes for the 300 speciality beers and ciders sourced worldwide. The bottled beers are in glass-fronted chiller cabinets. ⛪&⇄♠🚍🐾🛜

Ivinghoe

Rose & Crown 𝕃
Vicarage Lane, LU7 9EQ
🍺 5 (4 Thu)-11; 12-11 Sat & Sun ☎ (01296) 668472
🌐 roseandcrownivinghoe.com
St Austell Trelawny; Tring Moongazing; 2 changing beers (sourced nationally) 🅷
Hidden away down a one-way street, this village pub dating from 1690 offers a warm welcome, with an open fire and slate floor. It is popular with locals, cyclists and walkers as well as campers from the nearby campsite in summer. A free house, it serves a good choice of regular beers and guests. A quiz is hosted monthly. Dogs (in the bar area only) and children are welcome. Recommended parking is in Ladysmith Road, Wellcroft Road and beside the village green. Q❁🐾⛪◖Å➕🚍(61)🐾🛜

Lacey Green

Black Horse ✪
Main Road, HP27 0QU
🍺 12-3 (not Mon), 5-11; 12-11 Thu; 12-midnight Fri & Sat; 12-11 Sun ☎ (01844) 345195 🌐 blackhorse-pub.co.uk
3 changing beers 🅷
This friendly village pub, located in the heart of the Chilterns, offers four draught ales, three changing regularly, plus a good selection of bottled beers and one regularly changing real cider. Excellent home-cooked and freshly prepared food is available including a traditional Sunday lunch (children under six eat free). Walkers, cyclists and children are welcome and there is a play area in the garden. Full English breakfast is served Tuesday-Saturday. Q⛪◖&♣♠P🚍🛜

Pink & Lily 𝕃 ✪
Pink Road, Parslows Hillock, HP27 0RJ
🍺 12-midnight; 12-10 Sun ☎ (01494) 489857
🌐 pink-lily.com
Sharp's Doom Bar; 3 changing beers (sourced locally) 🅷
This 300-year-old historic pub, where World War I poet Rupert Brooke was a regular, has flourished since reopening in 2013. It is a free house offering fine food and four real ales, including three guests from local breweries. The garden includes heated outdoor dining, a barbecue and a children's play area. A games room is available for adults and children. Muddy boots and (well-behaved) dogs are welcome. Q🐾⛪◖&♣P🐾🛜

Whip Inn 𝕃
Pink Road, HP27 0PG
🍺 11-11 (midnight Fri & Sat); 12-10.30 Sun
☎ (01844) 344060 🌐 thewhipinn.co.uk
6 changing beers (sourced nationally) 🅷
High in the Chilterns, easily accessible by bus, and popular with real ale fans, ramblers and cyclists, this pub is renowned for its variety of ales. It has six handpumps serving more than 900 different beers per annum, from local breweries, micros and nationals. It also offers three real ciders and holds regular beer festivals. An excellent range of reasonably priced food is on offer. There is an attractive enclosed garden overlooking the Lacey Green Windmill. Q⛪◖♣♠P🚍(300)🐾🛜

Little Missenden

Crown Inn ♛
HP7 0RD (off A413, between Amersham and Gt Missenden)
🍺 11-2.30, 6-11; 12-3, 7-10.30 Sun ☎ (01494) 862571
🌐 thecrownlittlemissenden.co.uk
St Austell Tribute; 3 changing beers (sourced regionally; often Otter) 🅷
Lovely 300-year-old pub set in the Chilterns, an Area of Outstanding Natural Beauty, and popular with walkers, cyclists and locals. A regular in the Guide, it has been in the same family for almost 100 years. A real fire welcomes you in winter and four ever-changing beers are available. Old photos of the pub and village adorn the walls. There are three en-suite letting rooms converted from original barns. Local CAMRA branch Pub of the Year 2016. Q⛪🛏◖♣♠P🐾🛜

Littleworth Common

Blackwood Arms
Common Lane, SL1 8PP SU937863
🍺 12-11; 12-9 Sun; closed Mon ☎ (01753) 645672
🌐 theblackwoodarms.net
Brakspear Bitter, Oxford Gold; Wychwood Hobgoblin; 3 changing beers 🅷
A delightful Victorian country pub brought back to life by an enthusiastic couple after a long period of closure. Close to Burnham Beeches and popular with walkers and diners, it has a roaring fire in winter and an attractive garden with plenty of seating for the summer. Three guest ales are on offer – one from the Marston's group plus two free of tie. Dog- and horse-friendly, hay is provided. Cider is available in summer only.
Q🐾⛪◖♣♠P🐾🛜

Long Crendon

Eight Bells 𝕃 ✪
51 High Street, HP18 9AL
🍺 12-11; 10-11 Sat & Sun ☎ (01844) 208244
🌐 8bellspub.com
Ringwood Best Bitter; XT Four; 2 changing beers 🅷
The Eight Bells was refurbished internally in 2014, but retains the charm and character of a village pub. It is renowned for slaking the thirst of ale aficionados – XT Four from less than a mile away and Ringwood Bitter are permanent fixtures on two of the four handpumps, joined by guest ales from across the country. Long Crendon cider is also an attraction, and diners can enjoy a good menu featuring local produce. Beer festivals are held over the Easter weekend and August bank holiday. Q⛪◖♣♠P🚍(110)🐾🛜

Loudwater

General Havelock
114 Kingsmead Road, HP11 1HZ
🍺 12-2.30, 5.30-11; 12-11 Fri & Sat; 12-10.30 Sun
☎ (01494) 520391 🌐 generalhavelock.co.uk
Fuller's London Pride, ESB, 1845; 3 changing beers 🅷
In its 27th consecutive year in the Guide and run by the same family since Fuller's acquired it in 1986, the General Havelock remains popular with all ages. The interior has an eclectic selection of bric-a-brac and antiques. Six ales are available at all times including a range of seasonals and guests. Meals are served lunchtimes (not Sat) and Friday

evenings. The pub has a cosy feel in winter while the garden makes for a peaceful haven in summer. ✿◖♣P🚻(35)🐾❦🛜

Maids Moreton

Wheatsheaf 🍺
Main Street, MK18 1QR
✿ 12-11; 12-10.30 Sun; closed Mon ☎ (01280) 822903
⊕ thewheatsheafmaidsmoreton.com
Shepherd Neame Spitfire; Tring Side Pocket for a Toad; 2 changing beers (sourced nationally; often Binghams, Rooster's, Twickenham) Ⓗ
A family-run, traditional village inn, full of character with a thatched roof, low ceilings and exposed beams. In the bar there is an inglenook fireplace with a wood-burning stove. Food is available in the bar and restaurant – à la carte is offered Tuesday to Saturday, roast lunches only on Sunday. There is a large garden at the rear of the pub. The restaurant can be hired for private parties. Q🕭✿◖♣P🚻(60)🐾🛜

Marlow

Royal British Legion Ⓛ ⊘
Station Approach, SL7 1NT (50yds from train station)
✿ 7-11 (midnight Fri); 11-3, 7-midnight Sat; 11-4 Sun ☎ (01628) 486659 ⊕ rblmarlow.co.uk
Jennings Bitter; 5 changing beers Ⓗ
Effectively a free house, this friendly RBL members' club offers four handpumped ales from four independent breweries, with a Derbyshire beer usually among the selection. Home of the Marlow Jazz Club, music features regularly on a Saturday night. Pool, darts and crib are encouraged. The hall is available for hire. Show a CAMRA membership card or copy of the Guide for entry. CAMRA Regional Club of the Year 2014. ✿♿🚆♣♥P🚻🛜

Marsworth

Anglers Retreat Ⓛ
Startops End, HP23 4LJ (opp Startops Reservoir car park)
✿ 11-midnight; 12-10.30 Sun ☎ (01442) 822250
St Austell Tribute; Tring Side Pocket for a Toad; 2 changing beers (sourced locally; often Aylesbury, Chiltern, Leighton Buzzard) Ⓗ
Close to the Grand Union Canal and Tring Reservoirs, this is a lovely inn with a real fire, an aviary in the garden and a duck pond. Four beers, mostly local, are available and beer festivals feature regularly. Great-value food is served all day, plus roasts on Sundays. Pizzas are cooked in a traditional wood-fired oven (choose your own topping) on Monday evenings 5-9pm. The pub hosts open mic nights on Thursdays and poker nights on Sundays. Q🕭✿🛏◖♣P🚻(164)🐾🛜

Red Lion Ⓛ ⊘
90 Vicarage Road, HP23 4LU (opp church)
✿ 11-3, 5-11; 11-11 Sat; 12-10.30 Sun ☎ (01296) 668366
⊕ redlionmarsworth.co.uk
Fuller's London Pride; 5 changing beers (sourced locally) Ⓗ
A traditional village pub dating from the 17th century, close to the Grand Union Canal. The London Pride is complemented by four to five guests, mostly from local breweries, and regular mini-fests feature up to 10 beers. Home-cooked food is available in the public bar, where there is a real fire, and in the upstairs restaurant area. Bar

billiards, darts and shove-ha'penny are played. Outside, there is seating in front of the pub and behind is a lovely garden. Q🕭✿◖♣♥P🚻(164)🐾🛜

Naphill

Wheel ⊘
100 Main Road, HP14 4QA
✿ 12 (4.30 Mon)-11; 12-10.30 Sun ☎ (01494) 562210
⊕ thewheelnaphill.com
Greene King IPA, IPA Reserve; 2 changing beers Ⓗ
A traditional 18th-century village pub in the heart of the Chilterns. It offers four excellent cask ales including two regularly changing guests and good-quality, home-cooked pub meals. Two bars and a large dining area are available for all – walkers, cyclists, families – and dogs and muddy boots are welcome too. There is a large garden to the front and a secluded, smoker-friendly courtyard at the rear. Two large beer festivals are held each year and are not to be missed. Q✿🛏◖♣P🚻🐾🛜

North Marston

Pilgrim Ⓛ
25 High Street, MK18 3PD
✿ 12-3, 5-11 (midnight Fri); 12-midnight Sat; 12-6 Sun; closed Mon ☎ (01296) 670969 ⊕ thepilgrimpub.co.uk
Sharp's Doom Bar; XT Four Ⓗ
Following a campaign by regulars to save their local pub, this pub is now family-owned. There is a true community spirit here and the locals regularly help out. It has a spacious bar area with a large fireplace at each end. Freshly prepared seasonal food is served featuring home-grown produce from the pub's vegetable patch. The garden enjoys superb views of the Vale of Aylesbury. Listed as an Asset of Community Value. ✿◖♿♥P🚻🛜

Oving

Black Boy Ⓛ
Church Lane, HP22 4HN
✿ 12-11; 12-5.30 Sun; closed Mon ☎ (01296) 641258
⊕ theblackboyoving.co.uk
3 changing beers (sourced locally) Ⓗ
A pleasure to visit, this charming 17th-century pub has a cosy interior with a roaring fire in winter. The carpeted restaurant opposite the bar is divided from the drinking area by a wooden mesh around an archway. The music is '60s and '70s and not intrusive. Good fresh seasonal food is served. ✿◖♥P🐾🛜

Penn

Red Lion Ⓛ ⊘
Elm Road, HP10 8LF
✿ 11-11; 12-10.30 Sun ☎ (01494) 813107
⊕ redlionpenn.co.uk
Chiltern Beechwood Bitter; 1 changing beer Ⓗ
Since the takeover of this 16th-century pub by the people running the Royal Standard of England at Forty Green, there has been a major refurbishment. The layout of the tables is geared towards dining and the bar billiards table has gone. A stunning example of an old English inn, it features exposed wooden beams, bricks and wood panelling, with settles and church pew-style seating. The pub overlooks the village green and pond. Q✿◖P🚻🐾🛜

Princes Risborough

Bird in Hand ⓛ
47 Station Road, HP27 9DE
✪ 12-11 (midnight Fri & Sat) ☎ (01844) 345602
Chiltern Beechwood Bitter; Greene King IPA, Abbot; 3 changing beers Ⓗ
Situated in a residential area near Princes Risborough station, this Greene King house has been recently rejuvenated and now offers six real ales on handpump, three of which are LocAles. It is a thriving community venue and offers a warm welcome. It has a compact L-shaped drinking area and a beer garden and drinking area outside. The pub proudly displays its certificate listing it as an Asset of Community Value. Parking can be tricky nearby. ❀❶⇒♣🖵👹📶

Quainton

George & Dragon ⓛ
32 The Green, HP22 4AR
✪ 12-2.30, 5-11; 12-11 Sat; 12-3, 6-10.30 Sun; closed Mon
☎ (01296) 655436 ⊕ georgeanddragonquainton.co.uk
6 changing beers Ⓗ
Free house always offering LocAles from Hook Norton, Vale and XT plus two guests. Parts of this well-maintained and delightful pub date back to the 1700s, with traditional English features such as inglenook fireplaces, beams and a quarry-tiled floor. The friendly public bar offers darts, a jukebox and TV while the saloon bar is dedicated to dining, with home-cooked food served in both areas. Regular beer festivals are held overlooking the green in summer. ⛵❀❶&♣🖵🖵(16)

Stoke Goldington

Lamb ⓛ
Main Street, MK16 8NR
✪ 12 (5 Mon)-11; 12-7 Sun ☎ (01908) 551233
⊕ thelambatstokegoldington.co.uk
Tring Brock Bitter, Death or Glory; 2 changing beers (sourced regionally) Ⓗ
Situated in the village a few miles from Milton Keynes and Northampton on the B526. The bar area has a dartboard and a Northamptonshire skittles table. Home-cooked food is available featuring local seasonal produce (no food Mon). The cider is typically Old Rosie. The Lamb has ample parking and encourages walking groups to park early, order food before their walk, returning later to enjoy a drink and their meal. The garden has a stage for music events. Q⛵❀🍴❶♣P👹

Stoke Hammond

Three Locks ⓛ ✔
Leighton Road, MK17 9DD
✪ 11.30-11 (midnight Fri & Sat) ☎ (01525) 270214
⊕ thethreelocks.co.uk
Sharp's Doom Bar; 4 changing beers (sourced regionally; often Concrete Cow, Leighton Buzzard, Tring) Ⓗ
This popular canalside hostelry likes to support breweries in the area, with three out of the four changing beers usually local. The cider can come from nearby producers Virtual Orchard or

Woughton Orchard, or may be sourced from traditional producers around the country. A beer festival is held over the late May bank holiday. The pub is particularly popular in summer, with customers arriving by road and narrowboat. The long narrow building has the bar at one end and the restaurant at the other. There is plenty of outdoor seating alongside the locks.
⛵❀❶&♣🖵🖵(70)👹📶

Stony Stratford

White Horse ⓛ
49 High Street, MK11 1AA
✪ 2-11 ☎ (01908) 567082
1 changing beer (often Frog Island, XT) Ⓗ
A small pub with only one bar. The building, with its coach arch to the side, probably dates back to the 18th century. Although there are three handpumps, they are not all in use at quiet times, but one ale will always be from a local brewery. A large-screen TV shows sport and other programmes when there are no big matches. Q♣🖵(6,90)👹📶

Taplow

Oak & Saw ⓛ
Rectory Road, SL6 0ET
✪ 4-9.30 Mon; 12-11 (midnight Fri); 12-10.30 Sun
☎ (01628) 604074 ⊕ oakandsaw.co.uk
Brakspear Bitter; Sharp's Doom Bar; 1 changing beer (sourced locally) Ⓗ
Situated opposite the village green and church in an idyllic setting, this pub offers good pub food and three real ales including the Rebellion monthly. A large decked patio to the rear is popular in the summer. The pub holds a steak evening every Saturday night with a free bottle of wine. There are quizzes on the second and fourth Sundays of month. A covered area is available for smokers. Dogs are permitted in the non-dining area.
Q⛵❀❶P👹📶

Thornborough

Two Brewers
Bridge Street, MK18 2DN
✪ 12-2 (not Mon, Tue & Thu), 6-11; 11.30-3, 7-10 Sun
☎ (01280) 812020
Hook Norton Hooky Gold; St Austell Tribute; 1 changing beer (sourced regionally; often Cottage, Morland) Ⓗ
A quintessential old country pub, run by the same friendly landlord for almost 30 years. Set in a tranquil village, it has a cosy snug with an inglenook fireplace and a larger main bar with a wood-burning stove, pool tables and darts. On Wednesday lunchtimes drinks are half price for OAPs. Q⛵❀♣P👹

Turweston

Stratton Arms
Main Street, NN13 5JX
✪ 12-2.30, 4-10; 12-midnight Fri & Sat; 12-10 Sun
☎ (01280) 704956
Sharp's Doom Bar; Timothy Taylor Golden Best, Landlord; 2 changing beers (sourced nationally; often Adnams, Otter, Shepherd Neame) Ⓗ
A stone-built pub with a slate roof set in a quiet village with five real ales on handpump. Major matches are shown on TV but the volume is low

enough for conversation. Food is available Friday to Sunday (booking advisable). Outside there are extensive lawns often used for barbecues and functions in summer. Q⏚☕🍴♣P🐾📶

Tylers Green

Horse & Jockey ✪
Church Road, HP10 8EG (nr top of Hammersley Lane)
☼ 12-midnight; 12-6 Sun ☎ (01494) 815963
⊕ horseandjockeytylersgreen.com
Adnams Southwold Bitter; Black Sheep Best Bitter; Fuller's London Pride; Greene King Abbot; Sharp's Doom Bar; 1 changing beer Ⓗ
Opened as an inn in 1821, this is a traditional pub near the distinctive Tylers Green church. The single bar is U-shaped – the larger area on the left has dining tables and on the right is a dartboard. There are five regular ales and one guest plus two real ciders from Westons. Food is available 12-2pm and 6-10pm all week, with pensioners' specials Monday to Wednesday. Q☕🍴♿♣🐾P🚲(31)

Wendover

Pack Horse
29 Tring Road, HP22 6NR
☼ 12-11 (midnight Fri & Sat) ☎ (01296) 622075
Fuller's Chiswick Bitter, London Pride; 1 changing beer Ⓗ
Small, friendly village pub dating from 1769 and situated at the end of a terrace of thatched houses known as Anne Boleyn Cottages. On the Ridgeway Path, it has been owned by the same family for over 50 years. They also run the White Swan, another Fuller's pub in the village that deserves a visit. The wall above the bar is decorated with RAF squadron badges, denoting connections with nearby RAF Halton. The pub runs men's and women's darts, dominoes and cribbage teams. ⏚♣🚲

Wing

Queen's Head Ⓛ
9 High Street, LU7 0NS
☼ 11.30-3, 5.30-11; 11.30-11 Fri & Sat; 12-10.30 Sun; closed Mon ☎ (01296) 688268 ⊕ thequeensheadwing.co.uk
Wells Bombardier; 3 changing beers (often Wells) Ⓗ
A 16th-century village-centre free house with a comfortable public bar and restaurant. LocAle-

accredited, guests are from nearby Tring, Vale or other micros. The restaurant at the rear has a well-deserved reputation. Log fires in winter months enhance the welcoming atmosphere and the pub is TV-free. A large garden has a patio and a covered, heated smoking area. There is ample car parking. ☕🍴♿P🚲(100,150)

Winslow

George Inn Ⓛ
16 Market Square, MK18 3AB
☼ 2 (12 Thu)-11; 12-midnight Fri & Sat; 12-10.30 Sun
☎ (01296) 709290
Vale Best IPA, Red Kite, Gravitas; 4 changing beers (sourced nationally; often Milton, Scarborough, Vale) Ⓗ
A 200-year-old listed building standing at one corner of the old Market Square, purchased by Vale and completely refurbished in early 2015. The main bar has tables and chairs and a red leather curved bench seat in the bay window. There is another room leading from the bar, also with red leather bench seating. Both rooms have a real fire. As well as real ales, the pub specialises in world beers and fine whiskies. The cider is typically Old Rosie or Rosie's Pig. Q♣🐾P🚲(50,X60)🐾

Wooburn Common

Royal Standard Ⓛ
Wooburn Common Lane, HP10 0JS (follow signs to Odds Farm)
☼ 12-11; 12-10.30 Sun ☎ (01628) 521121
⊕ theroyalstandard.biz
Caledonian Deuchars IPA Ⓗ; Hop Back Summer Lightning Ⓖ; St Austell Tribute; 7 changing beers Ⓗ
Ever-popular semi-rural pub with a congenial ambience in the bar, catering for diners and discerning drinkers alike. Ten real ales, five direct from the cask, alongside many real ciders, make this venue an important flagship pub in the area. There is always at least one dark beer on offer – either a stout, porter or dark mild. Two beer festivals are held, one over the May Day weekend, the other on the last weekend in October. Quiz night is the second Monday of the month. Q☕🍴♿🐾P🐾📶

Kitchen of an inn

In the evening we reached a village where I had determined to pass the night. As we drove into the great gateway of the inn, I saw on one side the light of a rousing kitchen fire beaming through a window. I entered, and admired for the hundredth time that picture of convenience, neatness, and broad honest enjoyment, the kitchen of an English inn. It was of spacious dimension, hung around by copper and tin vessels, highly polished, and decorated here and there with a Christmas green. Hams, tongues, and flitches of bacon were suspended from the ceiling; a smoke-jack made its ceaseless clanking behind the fireplace, and a clock ticked in one corner. A well-scoured deal table extended along one side of the kitchen, with a cold round of beef, and other hearty viands upon it, over which two foaming tankards of ale seemed mounting guard. Travellers of inferior order were preparing to attack this stout repast, while others sat smoking or gossiping over their ale, on two high-backed oaken settles beside the fire.
Washington Irving, Travelling at Christmas, 1884

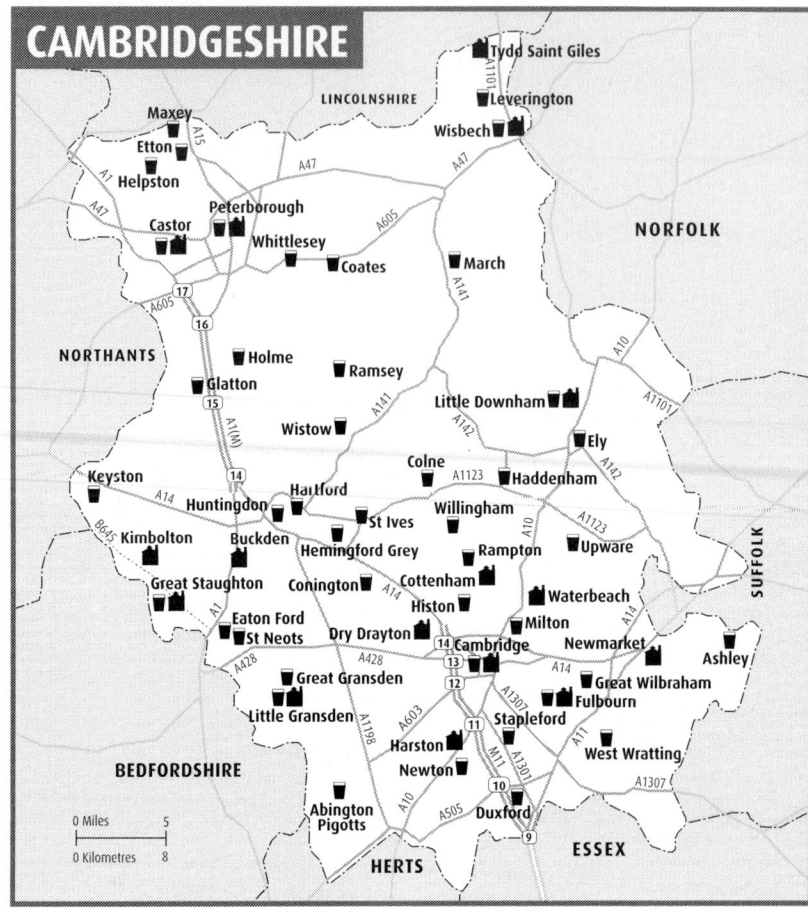

CAMBRIDGESHIRE

Tydd Saint Giles

LINCOLNSHIRE

Leverington

Maxey

Wisbech

Etton

Helpston

Castor

Peterborough

Whittlesey

Coates

March

NORFOLK

NORTHANTS

Holme

Ramsey

Glatton

Little Downham

Wistow

Ely

Keyston

Colne

Haddenham

Huntingdon

Hartford

Willingham

Kimbolton

Buckden

St Ives

Rampton

Upware

Hemingford Grey

Great Staughton

Conington

Cottenham

Waterbeach

SUFFOLK

Histon

Eaton Ford

Milton

St Neots

Dry Drayton

Cambridge

Newmarket

Ashley

Great Gransden

Great Wilbraham

Fulbourn

Little Gransden

Stapleford

Harston

West Wratting

BEDFORDSHIRE

Newton

Abington Pigotts

Duxford

ESSEX

0 Miles 5

0 Kilometres 8

HERTS

Abington Pigotts

Pig & Abbot

High Street, SG8 0SD (off A505 through Litlington)
☼ 12-3, 6-11; 12-11 Sat; 12-10.30 Sun ☎ (01763) 853515
⊕ pigandabbot.co.uk
Adnams Southwold Bitter; Fuller's London Pride; 2 changing beers (often Humpty Dumpty, Mighty Oak, Woodforde's) Ⓗ
Located in a surprisingly remote part of the south Cambridgeshire countryside, this Queen Anne period pub offers a warm welcome. The interior has exposed oak beams and two fireplaces, including a large inglenook with a wood-burning stove. A comfortable restaurant offers home-made traditional pub food and specialises in fresh fish and chips, steak and kidney puddings and pies. Two guest beers are stocked, often including a beer from Burton Bridge, Humpty Dumpty, Mighty Oak, Timothy Taylor or Woodforde's. Q☽❀❶❷♣P❀

Ashley

Crown Inn ♛

24 Newmarket Road, CB8 9DR
☼ 3-11 (9 Mon); 12-11 Sat; 12-10 Sun ☎ (01638) 730117
⊕ thecrowninnashley.co.uk
Mighty Oak IPA; 2 changing beers Ⓗ
A real village community local. The front bar houses the dartboard, pool table and TV while the rear bar is given over to comfortable seating. There are tables out front and at the rear there is additional parking, a covered smoking area and an enclosed garden. The pub is home to darts, pool and pétanque teams. The beer choice is always of interest and frequently includes a dark ale. Real ciders, direct from the box, are also available.
☽❀❶♣♣P❀❀

Cambridge

Cambridge Blue

85 Gwydir Street, CB1 2LG
☼ 12 (11 Sat)-11; 12-10.30 Sun ☎ (01223) 471680
⊕ the-cambridgeblue.co.uk
14 changing beers Ⓗ/Ⓖ
Busy single-bar pub with a large extension leading to the garden and heated marquee. Breweriana and pumpclips provide the decoration. Up to 14 beers sourced from microbreweries nationally are served by handpump or gravity from the tap room. A number of ciders and perries and a large selection of bottled beers are also sold. The main beer festival is held in June. Wholesome home-cooked food using locally sourced ingredients is available all day. A former CAMRA County Pub of the Year. Q☽❀❶❷♣♣➓❀❀

Castle Inn

38 Castle Street, CB3 0AJ

✪ 11.30-11 ☎ (01223) 353194

⊕ thecastleinncambridge.com

Adnams Lighthouse, Southwold Bitter, Explorer, Ghost Ship, Broadside; 4 changing beers ℍ

Acquired by Adnams in 1994 and respectfully renovated by the brewery, this family-run pub offers a great selection of the brewery's own beers plus its seasonal offerings and two or more changing guests. Originally two buildings, they have been combined to create a number of separate drinking areas on two floors, including a downstairs snug. To the rear is a suntrap garden next to the mound of the long-gone castle. Excellent food is served every session including a wide selection of specials. Q ⌂ ♿ ✿ ⊕ 🖐 🚍 (B) ♣ 🎵 🛜

Devonshire Arms 🄻

1 Devonshire Road, CB1 2BH

✪ 12 (midnight Fri & Sat); 12-10.30 Sun

☎ (01223) 316610 ⊕ individualpubs.co.uk/devonshire

Milton Pegasus; 6 changing beers (sourced locally) ℍ

Rescued from decline and opened in 2010 as Milton Brewery's first pub in Cambridge, the building has been impressively renovated, with front and rear drinking areas offering a mixture of wooden booths and larger tables. Five Milton beers are usually available including at least one dark beer, plus changing guests from other micros. Bottled beers and Moravka unpasteurised lager are also kept. Good-quality food is on offer every session except Sunday evening, including pizzas cooked in the pub's stone bake oven. A former CAMRA branch Pub of the Year.

Q ⌂ ♿ ✿ ⊕ ⇄ 🖐 🚍 ♣ 🛜

Elm Tree

16a Orchard Street, CB1 1JT

✪ 11-11; 12-10.30 Sun ☎ (01223) 502632

⊕ theelmtreecambridge.co.uk

10 changing beers (sourced nationally) ℍ

Relaxed back-street pub decorated with breweriana, quirky bric-a-brac, photos and Belgian flags. The single bar has a long seating area extending to the back. Ten handpumps dispense three beers from B&T and Wells, while the remainder offer changing guest ales. A cider or perry is also served. Complementing these is a choice of around 200 bottled Belgian beers if you need advice. Regular live music features. Credit cards are not accepted. ⌂ ♿ ♣ 🖐 🚍 (PR3,X5) ♣

Flying Pig 🄻

106 Hills Road, CB2 1LQ

✪ 12-11 (midnight Fri); 7-11 Sat & Sun ☎ (01223) 354623

Crouch Vale Brewers Gold; 10 changing beers ℍ

Cosy and friendly pub with a local feel despite being on a main road. The walls and ceiling are adorned with an eclectic collection of old posters. Basic pub grub is served weekday lunchtimes only. In the evenings the intimate lighting is enhanced by candles on the tables. Beers from local breweries are regularly available, as well as craft keg beers. Live music features most Tuesday/Thursday evenings and some Saturdays.

⌂ ✿ ⊕ ⇄ 🚍 (Various) 🛜

Free Press

7 Prospect Row, CB1 1DU

✪ 12-11 (midnight Fri & Sat) ☎ (01223) 368337

⊕ freepresspub.com

Greene King XX Mild, IPA, Abbot; 4 changing beers (often Greene King) ℍ

Intimate, friendly pub serving high-quality food and great beer, including the rare XX Mild and Greene King's seasonals and guests. A pub for over 120 years, it just survived the 1970s Kite area redevelopment, with only the tiny snug remaining from the original pub. The building is identified by CAMRA as having a regionally important historic pub interior. It was named after a temperance movement newspaper that lasted for just one edition. A walled garden is at the rear.

Q ⌂ ♿ ✿ ⊕ ♣ 🖐 ⊕ 🚍 ♣

Geldart ✅

1 Ainsworth Street, CB1 2PF (off Mill Rd via Kingston & Sturton streets)

✪ 5-11.30 (1am Fri); 1-1am Sat; 12-midnight Sun; closed Mon

☎ (01223) 314264 ⊕ the-geldart.co.uk

Caledonian Deuchars IPA; St Austell Tribute; Young's Special; 5 changing beers (sourced nationally) ℍ

Large back-street corner pub with two bars decorated with film and music memorabilia. The left side has real ale and a wide selection of malt whiskies and rums, and is used by the regulars. The larger right side mainly serves diners. Five changing guest ales from Punch Finest Cask and SIBA Direct always include a dark beer. Good home-made food including 'hot rocks' is available in both bars. Regular live music and functions are hosted. ⌂ ✿ ⊕ ♣ 🛜

Haymakers 🄻

54 High Street, CB4 1NG

✪ 12-11 (midnight Fri & Sat); 12-10.30 Sun

☎ (01223) 311077 ⊕ individualpubs.co.uk/haymakers

Milton Pegasus; 7 changing beers (often Milton) ℍ

Reopened in 2013, this is Milton Brewery's second pub in Cambridge and is popular with locals and employees from the nearby science park. There are a number of drinking areas - one either side of the door, a snug with bar access, and another room off to one side. Eight real ales, four real ciders or perries plus Moravka unpasteurised lager are on offer. Food includes pizzas to take away. The car park has been converted into the largest pub cycle park in Cambridge, leaving a few spaces for cars. Local CAMRA branch Most Improved (City) Pub in 2014. ⌂ ✿ ⊕ 🖐 P 🚍 ♣ 🛜

REAL ALE BREWERIES

Bexar County Peterborough
BlackBar Harston
Calverley's Cambridge
Cambridge 🍺 Cambridge
Castor Castor
Crafty Beers Newmarket
Draycott Buckden
Elgood & Sons Ltd Wisbech
Fellows Cottenham
Lord Conrad's Dry Drayton
Mile Tree Wisbech
Milton Waterbeach
Moonshine Fulbourn
Oakham 🍺 Peterborough
Red Great Staughton
Son of Sid 🍺 Little Gransden
Three Blind Mice Little Downham
Tinshed Kimbolton
Turpin's 🍺 Cambridge (NEW)
Tydd Steam Tydd Saint Giles
Xtreme Peterborough: Woodston

Kingston Arms ✪

33 Kingston Street, CB1 2NU
✪ 12-2.30, 5-11; 11-midnight Fri & Sat; 11-11 Sun
☎ (01223) 319414 ⊕ kingston-arms.co.uk
Crouch Vale Brewers Gold; Hop Back Summer Lightning; Oakham JHB; Thornbridge Jaipur IPA; Timothy Taylor Landlord; Woodforde's Wherry; 4 changing beers Ⓗ

Classic side-street pub just off Mill Road, equally popular with diners and drinkers. Twelve handpumps serve regular and changing guest beers including at least one dark beer, as well as a changing cider and perry. A selection of Belgian and other bottled beers is stocked and monthly beer festivals are held in the warmer months. Food is available all sessions, with breakfast from 11am on Saturdays and Sundays. The walled garden has canopies and heaters and is popular all year round. Q🏰🛏🕸🕯🍴≈♣🐶🖵🐾❄🖤

Live & Let Live

40 Mawson Road, CB1 2EA
✪ 11.30-2.30 (not Wed & Thu), 5.30-11; 11.30-2.30, 6-11 Sun; 12-2.30, 7-11 Sun ☎ (01223) 460261
Nethergate Umbel Ale; Oakham Citra; 3 changing beers Ⓗ

Wood panelling and railway and beer memorabilia add to the atmosphere at this discreet corner local just off Mill Road. The single bar has a small snug to the rear. The beer range usually includes an additional Oakham brew (frequently Green Devil) and often a mild or stout. Three changing ciders or perries are also offered. There is an outstanding collection of rums from around the world, and occasional rum festivals. Food is restricted to snacks. A former winner of CAMRA branch Dark Ale Award and 2015 Cider Pub of the Year. Q≈♣🐶🖵🐾🖤

Maypole ⓛ

20a Portugal Place, CB5 8AF
✪ 11.30-midnight (1am Fri & Sat); 12-11.30 Sun
☎ (01223) 352999 ⊕ maypolefreehouse.co.uk
12 changing beers Ⓗ

The Maypole has been in the capable hands of the same family since 1982, initially as tenants and now as owners. It has become a showcase for quality beers and offers up to 16 beers, including LocAles, with micros predominating. There are two rooms downstairs, a large function room upstairs and a large partly covered patio at the front. Food focuses on home-cooked Italian dishes and English pub classics. 🕸🕯🍴🐶🖵🐾❄🖤

Mill ⓛ ✪

14 Mill Lane, CB2 1RX
✪ 11-11 (midnight Thu-Sat) ☎ (01223) 311829
⊕ themillpubcambridge.co.uk
7 changing beers (sourced locally) Ⓗ

Set in a honeypot location next to the Mill Pond on the River Cam, the building has been refurbished – improvements include an especially attractive wood-panelled side room. The bar has eight handpumps, including one for cider. Free of tie, there is a strong commitment to local beers, including those brewed at sister pub the Cambridge Brew House. Tasty food is cooked on the premises using locally sourced ingredients wherever possible. A vintage radiogram is used for playing vinyl records. Local CAMRA branch Pub of the Year 2015. 🛏🍴🐶🐾🖤

Pint Shop

10 Peas Hill, CB2 3PN
✪ 12-11 (midnight Fri); 11-midnight Sat; 11-11 Sun
☎ (01223) 352293 ⊕ pintshop.co.uk
6 changing beers Ⓗ

Impressive Georgian townhouse, once the university pensions office. The building has been refurbished, with multiple rooms across two floors providing a variety of drinking and dining areas. Six changing real ales are joined by 10 craft keg beers from the UK and the rest of the world. The terraced patio garden is no-smoking and a separate smokers' alley is behind the main bar. Food is upmarket, ranging from full meals to home-made cold bar snacks available at all times. 🛏🕸🍴🐶🖤

Queen Edith ⓛ

Wulfstan Way, CB1 8QN
✪ 12-11 (midnight Fri & Sat); 12-10.30 Sun
☎ (01223) 244536 ⊕ individualpubs.co.uk/queenedith
Milton Pegasus; 7 changing beers (often Milton) Ⓗ

The first new-build pub in Cambridge for around 30 years, this is Milton Brewery's third pub in Cambridge. A pub of the same name was sited to the rear of the current building and was demolished to make way for housing. Featuring mock Georgian design inside and out, the larger bar to the left of the entrance has big windows on two sides and a wood-burning stove. The second bar has wooden booths down one side. Q🏰🛏🕸🕯🍴🐶♣🐶🅿🖵🐾❄🖤

Castor

Prince of Wales Feathers ⓛ

38 Peterborough Road, PE5 7AL
✪ 12-11.30 (1am Fri & Sat); 12-midnight Sun
☎ (01733) 380222 ⊕ princeofwalesfeathers.co.uk
7 changing beers Ⓗ/Ⓖ

This 17th-century stone-built inn has an open-plan layout with the bar in the centre and different areas for dining, pool, darts and TV. There are seven real ales including one served from the cellar, and a changing real cider and perry are stocked at all times. Lunches are served daily, evening meals weekdays only – steak night is Thursday. Live music is hosted most Saturdays and a quiz on Sunday evening. Outside there are two areas for drinkers with benches and parasols. 🛏🕸🕯🍴♣🐶🖵🐾🐾🖤

Coates

Vine ⓛ

4 South Green, PE7 2BJ
✪ 4-11; 12-midnight Fri; 9am-11 Sat; 12-11 Sun
☎ (01733) 840343 ⊕ vinefreehouse.wordpress.com
3 changing beers Ⓗ

Lively bar/lounge and separate restaurant with its own bar. In the summer of 2013 a private investor secured ownership of the pub from Charles Wells to make it officially a free house, now fully refurbished, including a new kitchen. Meals are served lunchtimes and evenings, and breakfast on Saturdays. The varying beer list includes a LocAle. The large outdoor area includes nine pétanque terrains and a children's play area. Local buses pass in front of the building. Winter opening hours vary. Q🏰🛏🕸🕯🍴🐶♣🐶🅿🖵(33)🐾🖤

Colne

Green Man ⓛ
1 East Street, PE28 3LZ
✪ 12-2.30 (not Mon), 5-11; 12-11 Fri-Sun ☎ (01487) 840368
⊕ greenmancolne.co.uk
Oakham Inferno; Sharp's Doom Bar; 3 changing beers (sourced locally; often Elgood's, Star) Ⓗ
Picturesque 17th-century village local in an old Fenland fruit-growing area. The corrugated roof covers an original thatch. This busy, friendly pub provides a public bar with pool, darts and TV, and a warm, sociable lounge with a modern dining area extension serving good food. Quiz nights feature fortnightly. Outside, the garden has a children's play area and hosts barbecues in summer. There is camping nearby at Earith Lakes.
☎❀◑♠♣P🖳(21,22)❀ 🤝

Conington

White Swan
Elsworth Road, CB23 4LN
✪ 12-11; 12-10.30 Sun ☎ (01954) 267251
⊕ theswan.edgedevelop.co.uk
Adnams Southwold Bitter, Ghost Ship; 1 changing beer Ⓖ
Sturdy 18th-century brick building fronted by an impressive sward for alfresco drinking and children's amusement. The main bar has a tiled floor and a brick fireplace occupied by a fine cast-iron stove. It has been extended into the old cellar, the real ales being served by gravity from behind the new low bar. Food is high quality and good value (no meals Sun eve). The pub has recently been saved by a consortium of locals and is now free of tie. Q☎❀◑♣♠P❀ 🤝

Duxford

Plough
57 St Peter's Street, CB22 4RP
✪ 11-11 ☎ (01223) 833170 ⊕ theduxfordplough.co.uk
Adnams Southwold Bitter; Everards Tiger Best Bitter; 2 changing beers Ⓗ
This thatched building was first recorded as a pub in 1851. The single bar is divided into two distinct areas, one laid out for diners, the other for drinkers. The nearest pub to Duxford Airfield and the Imperial War Museum, it is full of aviation memorabilia. Local beers are often available. Food is prepared on site and served daily except Monday. The pub is home to Duxford United football club, the local badminton players and two darts teams. ☎❀◑♠♣P🖳(7)❀ 🤝

Eaton Ford

Barley Mow ✪
27 Crosshall Road, PE19 7AB
✪ 11.30-11 (midnight Thu-Sat); 12-10.30 Sun
☎ (01480) 474435 ⊕ barleystneots.co.uk
Greene King IPA, Abbot; 1 changing beer Ⓗ
Simple one-bar community pub with a wide variety of activities focused on the regulars including live music events and seasonal celebrations. The decor is a mix of plaster, brick and wood panel, and a long service counter dominates the centre of the bar. Images of past pub social events adorn the walls, some dating back to the early part of the last century. There is a large beer garden with an extensive children's play area. ☎❀◑♣♠P🖳(X5) 🤝

Ely

Drayman's Son 🏆 ⓛ
29a Forehill, CB7 4AA
✪ 5-10.30 Mon-Wed; 11-11 Thu-Sat; 12-10.30 Sun
☎ (01353) 662920
Jo C's Norfolk Kiwi; 10 changing beers Ⓖ
Small welcoming micropub in former shop premises with a nostalgia theme of old railway signs, posters and musical scores. Six real ales are usually available and up to 10 at times, mostly sourced from local microbreweries and others further afield. The cellar is in a temperature-controlled back room and drinks are usually delivered to your table. More than 20 ciders are available, many sourced locally. The pub supports local produce including Ely Gin. ☎♿≍♣♠🖳❀ 🤝

Prince Albert ⓛ ✪
62 Silver Street, CB7 4JF (opp cathedral car park)
✪ 11-11.30; 12-10.30 Sun ☎ (01353) 663494
Greene King XX Mild, IPA, Abbot; 5 changing beers (sourced nationally) Ⓗ
Friendly back-street local, a short walk from historic Ely Cathedral. It was once the officer's mess for the local militia. The front area of the pub is mainly for drinking but towards the rear there are separate dining areas, a conservatory and patio for fine dining. It has 10 handpumps offering up to five guest beers and a guest cider, and is a rare outlet for XX Mild. Free from music, TV and fruit machines, this is a relaxing pub with pleasant bar room banter. Q❀◑♿≍♣🖳❀ 🤝

Etton

Golden Pheasant ⓛ
1 Main Road, PE6 7DA
✪ 12-2.30 (not Mon), 5-11; 12-11 Fri-Sun ☎ (01733) 252387
⊕ thegoldenpheasant.net
Adnams Broadside; Greene King Abbot; 3 changing beers (often Grainstore, Tydd Steam, Woodforde's) Ⓗ
An impressive stone-built Grade II-listed former manor house, now boasting five handpumps dispensing two permanent and three changing (mostly local) beers in the larger bar. There is ample parking, a spacious garden and children's play area. A separate restaurant accommodates up to 30 diners and a permanent marquee with bar caters for functions of up to 150. The pub is a meeting place for several local groups and on the Green Wheel cycle route from Peterborough. It hosts an annual beer festival in spring. A former CAMRA Gold Award winner. Q❀◑♿♣♠P🖳(22)

Fulbourn

Six Bells ✪
9 High Street, CB21 5DH
✪ 11.30-2.30, 5-midnight; 11.30-2am Fri; 12-2am Sat; 12-11
Sun ☎ (01223) 880244 ⊕ thesixbellsfulbourn.co.uk
Adnams Southwold Bitter, Broadside; Greene King IPA; Woodforde's Wherry; 2 changing beers Ⓗ
Traditional thatched village pub, previously a coaching inn. The main bar has low ceilings, a real fire and many cosy corners. The food is locally sourced and home cooked, served in the bar or the separate dining room (no food Sun or Mon eves). The function room hosts a trad jazz club on the first and third Wednesdays of the month. For the warmer months, there is one of the largest beer gardens in the area. A regular in this Guide.
☎❀◑♿♣♠P🖳❀ 🤝

Glatton

Addison Arms L
Sawtry Road, PE28 5RZ
⚙ 11-3, 5-11; 11-11 Fri-Sun ☎ (01487) 830410
⊕ addisonarms.co.uk
Adnams Broadside; house beer (by Digfield) H**; 2
changing beers (sourced locally; often Grainstore,
Nene Valley)** H/G
Grade II-listed pub built at the start of the 18th
century and named after the playwright and
politician Joseph Addison (co-founder of The
Spectator), who was a relative of the first landlord.
The pub offers at least three real ales and a real
cider, with a focus on local producers. Food
prepared from fresh locally sourced supplies is
another popular attraction, and there is a thriving
Sunday night quiz. The house beer Addison Ale is
Digfield Shacklebush. Q ❧ ⊛ ◑ ⅄ ⚘ ⚘ P ⊟ (46) ❀ ☎

Great Gransden

Crown & Cushion
2 West Street, SG19 3AT
⚙ 5.30-11; 4-11 Fri; 12-11 Sat; 12-10 Sun; closed Mon
☎ (01767) 677214 ⊕ crownandcushion.com
**3 changing beers (sourced regionally; often
Adnams)** H
Picture-postcard village pub with a thatched roof
and oak beams, believed to date partly from the
16th century. The lounge and dining area features
a large fireplace with wood-burning stove. This
busy village pub has much to offer including live
music on Thursdays. An interesting menu focusing
on Indonesian cuisine is served Friday evenings, all
day Saturdays and Sundays, and at other times by
prior arrangement. Three guest beers are available.
Q ❧ ⊛ ◑ ⅄ ⚘ P ⊟ ☎

Great Staughton

White Hart
56 The Highway, PE19 5DA (on B645)
⚙ 12-2.30, 4-11 (midnight Fri); 12-11 Sat & Sun
☎ (01480) 861131 ⊕ whitehartgreatstaughton.co.uk
Batemans XB, XXXB; 1 changing beer H
Passing through the narrow entrance to this fine
small former coaching inn takes you back to the
days of horse-drawn coaches. The building dates
back to 1630 and although extended and altered,
still warrants a Grade II listing. As well as the main
bar there is a small room at the front and a
restaurant to the rear. Traditional pub food is
served 12-2.30pm, 6-9pm Thursday-Saturday and
12-3pm Sunday. Q ❧ ⊛ ◑ ◐ P ⊟ ❀ ☎

Great Wilbraham

Carpenters Arms L
10 High Sreet, CB21 5JD
⚙ 11.30-3, 6.30-11; 11.30-3 Sun; closed Mon & Tue
☎ (01223) 882093 ⊕ carpentersarmsgastropub.co.uk
**Crafty Beers Carpenter's Cask; 2 changing beers
(often Crafty Beers)** H
The public bar stocks up to three real ales, mostly
from Crafty Beers, and occasional guest ales. Crafty
Beers started out in the stables at the rear of the
pub, but moved in early 2016 to larger premises in
Stetchworth. The bar billiards table is in regular
use. The pub serves both traditional pub food and a
menu reflecting the owners' previous experience

running an award-winning restaurant in France.
Parts of the building date back to the 17th century.
Local CAMRA LocAle pub (rural) 2014. ⊛ ◑ ⅃ ⚘ P ☎

Haddenham

Three Kings ◎
1 Station Road, CB6 3XD
⚙ 11-11; 11.30-10 Sun ☎ (01353) 749080
⊕ threekingsely.co.uk
**Greene King IPA; 3 changing beers (sourced
nationally)** H
This 17th-century building has been updated over
time but retains its rustic framework and charm
with plenty of exposed old beams, cosy areas and
an inglenook fireplace. While this village pub
focuses on fine food, it is also keen to promote
high-quality ales and is well supported by local
drinkers. A real cider has been introduced. At the
rear is a relaxing courtyard drinking area and a
large car park. Q ❧ ⊛ ◑ ⅃ ⚘ P ⊟

Hartford

King of the Belgians L
27 Main Street, PE29 1XU (Main St is the old village high
street which runs parallel to the B1514 from Huntingdon
to St Ives)
⚙ 11-11 (midnight Fri & Sat); 12-10.30 Sun
☎ (01480) 52030 ⊕ kingofthebelgians.com
**4 changing beers (sourced locally; often Elgood's,
Great Oakley, Nene Valley)**
A 16th-century inn in a picturesque setting. This
genuine community pub actively and generously
supports local charities. It hosts an annual beer
festival in May and a mini festival in late August.
An ever-changing selection of four real ales and
ciders is available daily, and good-value food
including Sunday roasts and takeaway pizza. Oak
beams and a copper-topped bar characterise the
public bar. There is a separate quiet dining area.
Entertainment includes regular quizzes, games
nights and an open mic night on the first Monday
of the month. ❧ ⊛ ◑ ⚘ ⚘ P ⊟ ❀ ☎

Helpston

Bluebell L
10 Woodgate, PE6 7ED
⚙ 11-3, 5-11; 11-11 Sat; 12-10.30 Sun ☎ (01733) 252394
⊕ bluebellhelpston.pub
**Fuller's London Pride; house beer (by Star); 2
changing beers (often Adnams, Nene Valley)** H
Quiet 17th-century stone village pub with its main
entrance at the side. It has two wood-panelled
bars, a number of dining areas, and a snug named
after local poet John Clare who worked in the pub
as a pot boy and lived next door. The beer range
includes Fuller's London Pride and 10 Woodgate
Bitter, a house beer brewed by Star Brewery, plus
two rotating guest beers from breweries around
the country. Good-value food is served lunchtime
and evenings. Q ❧ ⊛ ◑ ⅃ ⚘ P ⊟ ❀ ☎

Hemingford Grey

Cock L
47 High Street, PE28 9BJ (off A14 SE of Huntingdon)
⚙ 11.30-3, 6 (5 Fri)-11; 11.30-11 Sat; 12-10.30 Sun
☎ (01480) 463609 ⊕ cambscuisine.com
**Brewsters Hophead; Elgood's Cambridge Bitter; Great
Oakley Wagtail; 1 changing beer** H

This village inn and restaurant has won local, regional and national awards. The cosy pub interior has been refurbished to provide more comfortable facilities and is popular with locals who enjoy the locally sourced beers and real Cromwell cider produced in the village. The separate restaurant features an extensive fish board, meat, game, and excellent home-made sausages (booking essential at all times). During the summer, occasional beer festivals are held in the beer garden. Q✿❀◑&ΛPⱤ(5)✿🕾

Histon

Red Lion
27 High Street, CB24 9JD
✪ 10.30-11 (midnight Fri); 12-11 Sun ☎ (01223) 564437
🌐 theredlionhiston.co.uk
Adnams Ghost Ship; Lacons Falcon Ale; Oakham Bishops Farewell; Tring Side Pocket for a Toad; 5 changing beers (often Batemans) Ⓗ
The two bars of this free house are adorned with a wonderful collection of breweriana and historic photos. The left-hand bar features the TV, and the right-hand bar, which is quieter and child-free, is home to the nine handpumps. Guest beers always include a mild. There are also Belgian and German beers on draught, a range of continental bottled beers and two ciders and a perry. Two beer festivals are hosted each year – an Easter aperitif and the main event in September. Local CAMRA branch Dark Beer Pub 2014. ❀◑&♣♥PⱤ🕾

Holme

Admiral Wells Ⓛ
41 Station Road, PE7 3PH (jct of B660 and Yaxley Rd)
✪ 11-2.30, 5-11; 11.30-11 Sat; 11.30-10.30 Sun
☎ (01487) 831214 🌐 admiralwells.co.uk
Adnams Southwold Bitter, Broadside; Digfield Shacklebush; Oakham JHB; 2 changing beers Ⓗ
Victorian inn named after one of Nelson's pall bearers and officially built on the lowest land in the UK. It has two bar/lounge areas in a modern contemporary style. Excellent food is served in the lounge area and in the conservatory dining room. There is also a function room at the rear plus a children's play area. Next to the old Holme railway station and the East Coast mainline, the walls are adorned with photographs from steam railway days. Six real ales are usually available and a cider in summer. Quiz night is Tuesday. Q✿❀◑&♣♥P✿🕾

Huntingdon

Falcon ♥ Ⓛ
Market Hill, PE29 3NR
✪ 11-midnight (1am Fri & Sat); 12-midnight Sun
☎ (01480) 457416 🌐 falconhuntingdon.co.uk
Elgood's Black Dog; Marston's EPA; Potbelly Best; 15 changing beers (often Great Oakley, Marston's, Nobby's) Ⓗ
The Falcon is now an established venue after reopening in December 2014 following a six-year closure and a lengthy campaign by local community groups. This former coaching inn used to be Oliver Cromwell's recruiting station and the gates from the Market Square were once the entrance to Huntingdon Prison. A varied selection of beers is served from up to 15 handpumps, along with a range of real ciders. Good-value food is

available every day. For something a little different try the afternoon tea served by staff in period costumes. Q✿❀◑◐⇌♣♥🖫✿

Old Bridge Hotel Ⓛ ✅
1 High Street, PE29 3TQ (at S end of High St on ring road, by river)
✪ 11-11; 11-10.30 Sun ☎ (01480) 424300
🌐 huntsbridge.com
3 changing beers (sourced locally; often Hart Family Brewers, Nene Valley) Ⓗ
A handsome ivy-clad hotel in an 18th-century former private bank at the southern end of the High Street. It has a prominent position on the banks of the River Great Ouse close to riverside footpaths. Imaginative and high-quality food is served in the terrace restaurant, the covered patio and the garden area. Drinkers can also relax in the bar or lounge. The award-winning Old Bridge Wine Shop offers wine tasting as a diversion and there is an emphasis on local and regional beers. The bus station is a short walk away. Q✿❀◑◐&Λ♣PⱤ✿🕾

Keyston

Pheasant Ⓛ
Loop Road, PE28 0RE (on B663, 1 mile S of A14, E of Thrapston)
✪ 12-3, 6-11; 12-11 Fri & Sat; 12-5 Sun; closed Mon
☎ (01832) 710241 🌐 thepheasant-keyston.co.uk
Adnams Southwold Bitter; 2 changing beers Ⓗ
The village is named after Ketil's Stone, probably an Anglo-Saxon boundary marker. Created from a row of thatched cottages in an idyllic setting, the pub offers high-quality food, fine wines and well-kept cask ales. There is a splendid lounge bar and three dining areas. Regularly changing guest beers are offered, usually from Nene Valley or Digfield. Food is served 12-2pm, 6.30-9.30pm Tuesday to Saturday, 12-3.30pm Sunday. One of the few pubs included in the first version of the Good Beer Guide, in 1972. Q✿❀◑◐P✿🕾

Leverington

Rising Sun Inn Ⓛ
Dowgate Road, PE13 5DH
✪ 12-2.30, 6-11; 12-11 Fri; 12-4 Sun ☎ (01945) 583754
Elgood's Cambridge Bitter; 1 changing beer Ⓗ
Comfortably furnished village local with an enclosed garden. Dating back to at least 1872, the pub was refurbished three years ago. The bar still retains the feel of a true village local and serves two changing beers from the Elgood's range. Well known for good-value quality food, Wednesday is steak night and Thursday is curry night. The restaurant hosts regular themed nights. Dogs and children are welcome. Closing time may be earlier if there is no trade. ❀◑♣P✿

Little Downham

Plough
106 Main Street, CB6 2SX (W end of village)
✪ 12-3 (not Mon), 6-11; 12-midnight Fri & Sat; 12-3, 6-10.30 Sun ☎ (01353) 698297
3 changing beers (sourced regionally) Ⓗ
An early-Victorian Grade II-listed inn, well preserved in character and charm. Three changing regional cask ales are normally on offer and there is an annual beer festival held in early September.

Excellent Thai cuisine is available to eat in or take away. The pub has a good community spirit and supports traditional pub games and local customs. Children are welcome until 9pm. ❀◑♣P🖳 (125)

Little Gransden

Chequers 🅛
71 Main Road, SG19 3DW
✪ 12-2, 7-11; 12-11 Fri & Sat; 12-6, 7-10.30 Sun
☎ (01767) 677348 ⊕ chequersgransden.co.uk
4 changing beers (sourced locally) 🅗
Village inn owned and run by the same family for over 60 years and in this Guide for 20. The unspoilt middle bar, with its wooden benches and roaring fire, is a favourite spot to pick up on the local gossip. The pub's Son of Sid brewhouse supplies the bar and local beer festivals. Fish and chips are a highlight on Friday night (booking essential). Pickled Pig cider is nearly always available. Winner of numerous CAMRA awards. Q❀◑⅄♣P🖳🐾 🛜

March

Ship Inn 🅛
1 Nene Parade, PE15 8TD
✪ 11-11 Mon & Tue; 9am-12.30am Wed-Fri; 9am-1am Sat; 9am-10.30 Sun ☎ (01354) 607878
Timothy Taylor Landlord; Woodforde's Wherry; 4 changing beers 🅗
Thatched Grade II-listed riverside pub built in 1680 with extensive riverside moorings. The unusual carved wood beams are said to have 'fallen off a barge' during the building of Ely Cathedral. A quaint wobbly floor and wall lead to the toilets and to a small games room. Reopened in 2010 as a free house, after a major refit, it has a friendly and welcoming atmosphere and a large collection of pumpclips. It has been a Guide regular since 2012. Now serving breakfast Wednesday to Sunday.
Q🏠❀&♣●🖳(33,46.)🐾🛜

Maxey

Blue Bell 🅛
39 High Street, PE6 9EE
✪ 5.30 (1 Sat)-11.30; 12-7, 8.30-11.30 Sun
☎ (01778) 348182
Abbeydale Absolution; Fuller's London Pride, ESB; Oakham Bishops Farewell; 5 changing beers (often Woodforde's) 🅗
Originally a limestone barn, it was converted many years ago and reflects the rural setting in which it is found. A popular meeting place for groups including birdwatchers and golfers, paraphernalia of country life adorns the stone walls and shelves of the two-roomed interior. Nine handpumps dispense a range of quality ales from large and small breweries far and wide. A former local CAMRA Pub of the Year and CAMRA branch Gold Award winner in July 2014.
Q❀♣P🖳(22,413)🐾🛜

Milton

White Horse
22 High Street, CB24 6AJ
✪ 11-11 (midnight Fri & Sat); 12-10.30 Sun
☎ (01223) 860327 ⊕ whitehorsemilton.co.uk
Greene King Abbot; Sharp's Doom Bar; 4 changing beers (sourced regionally) 🅗

A community-focused pub offering an extensive food menu. The lounge is partly divided at the front by a large old fireplace and has a cosy seating area and a rear area with tables. The smaller public bar has pool and darts. Set back from the road, there is outside seating at the front of the building and at the back is the garden with children's play area and a large car park. Disabled access is from the car park. 🏠❀◑&♣●P🖳🐾🛜

Newton

Queen's Head
CB22 7PG
✪ 11.30-2.30, 6-11; 12-2.30, 7-10.30 Sun ☎ (01223) 870436
Adnams Southwold Bitter, Broadside; 2 changing beers 🅖
This village local is one of a handful to have appeared in every edition of the Guide. The list of landlords since 1729, displayed on the wall in the simply furnished public bar, has just 18 entries. The cosy lounge has a welcoming fire in the colder months. Simple but excellent food centres on soup and sandwiches. Guest beers are often Adnams seasonals. The King and Kaiser are reputed to have stopped here for a pint in the early 1900s.
Q◑⅄♣●P🖳(31)

Peterborough

Brewery Tap 🅛 ✅
80 Westgate, PE1 2AA
✪ 12-11 (2am Fri & Sat); 12-10.30 Sun ☎ (01733) 358500
⊕ thebrewery-tap.com
Oakham JHB, Inferno, Citra, Scarlet Macaw, Bishops Farewell; 4 changing beers (sourced regionally) 🅗
Housed in a former 1930s labour exchange, this claims to be one of Europe's largest brewpubs. The small brewery can be seen through large windows, where limited editions of beers are brewed. The 12 ales usually on offer are mainly from the Oakham range. A mezzanine floor area with some brewing artefacts is incorporated in the pub's modern design. Authentic Thai food is served. Entertainment includes live music and an open mic night on Sundays. Close to bus and rail stations.
◑⇌●P🖳🛜

Coalheavers Arms
5 Park Street, Woodston, PE2 9BH
✪ 12-2 (not Mon-Wed), 5-11; 12-11 Fri & Sat; 12-10.30 Sun
☎ (01733) 565664 ⊕ individualpubs.co.uk/coalheavers
Milton Justinian, Sparta; 4 changing beers 🅗
Friendly one-roomed back-street community pub dating back to the 1850s. Bombers Drop, the house beer, is one of the Milton beers on offer, alongside up to four guest ales. Cider, Belgian bottled beers and an English unpasteurised lager are also stocked. Home-made pies are available all week, and fresh rolls on Friday. Beer festivals are held in spring and autumn and the large garden is popular with families in the summer. A free quiz is hosted on Sunday nights. Busy on football match days.
Q🏠❀♣●🖳🖵(5,6,46)🐾🛜

Draper's Arms 🅛 ✅
29-31 Cowgate, PE1 1LZ
✪ 8am-midnight (1am Fri & Sat) ☎ (01733) 847570
Courage Directors; Greene King Abbot; Ruddles Best Bitter; Sharp's Doom Bar; Woodforde's Wherry; 5 changing beers 🅗

A converted former draper's shop dating from circa 1899, this is one of two Wetherspoon pubs in the city. The spacious interior includes a row of popular intimate wood-panelled booths. The beers, often from local microbreweries, are dispensed through 10 handpumps. Food is served all day and regular beer and wine festivals are held throughout the year. Quiz night is Wednesday. A regular top 10-listed real ale pub within the Wetherspoon chain. Close to bus and rail stations. Q✿🌑🕭🛇🌭🏠🖵🛜

Hand & Heart ★ ⓛ
12 Highbury Street, PE1 3BE
🕓 3-11.30 (midnight Fri); 11-midnight Sat; 12-11.30 Sun
☎ (01733) 564653 ⊕ thehandandheart.com
5 changing beers (sourced regionally) Ⓗ

A 1930s back-street pub that features in CAMRA's National Inventory of Historic Pub Interiors for its unspoilt interior. There is a main bar to the front and a quiet room to the rear connected by a drinking corridor. Five handpumps often feature some hard-to-find real ales. The large garden has a bar and stage used for beer festivals and music events. Live music plays on the second Thursday of the month and a cheese club is held on the last Thursday. Local CAMRA Pub of the Year 2015. Q✿♣🖵(1)🐾🛜

Heron ⓛ
Heron Court, Southfields Drive, Stanground, PE2 8QB (¼ mile from A605 in Southfields Estate)
🕓 3 (12 Sat)-1am; 12-11 Sun ☎ (01733) 704693
⊕ heronpub.co.uk
4 changing beers (sourced locally) Ⓗ

Estate pub opened in 1959 with one large bar/lounge and a patio outside. Following speculation that the pub was to be demolished and turned into flats, it reopened in 2014 after refurbishment by a real ale-loving team, and is now a member of the Oakademy of Excellence. A range of local ales has been introduced from brewers including Tydd Steam, Castor Ales and Star. Children are welcome 12-7pm. Quiz night is Tuesday. Note that last entry is 11pm on Friday and Saturday. Presented with a Gold Award by the local CAMRA branch in 2015. 🌭✿♣🛑🖵(3,20)🐾🛜

Palmerston Arms ⓛ
82 Oundle Road, PE2 9PA (on main A605 road S of city centre)
🕓 3 (12 Fri & Sat)-midnight; 12-11.30 Sun
☎ (01733) 565865 ⊕ palmerston-arms.co.uk
Batemans Gold, XXXB Ⓖ**; Castle Rock Harvest Pale; Oakham Citra** Ⓗ**/**Ⓖ**; 10 changing beers (sourced regionally)** Ⓖ

Popular 400-year-old listed stone-built locals' pub. Owned by Batemans, three of its beers are rotated alongside nine or more changing ales, including some from Oakham. Traditional cider, perries and an extensive range of malt whiskies are also available. Most beers are served straight from the cellar which can be seen through a large glass window. Rolls and a variety of snacks tempt customers. Live music features most weekends and occasional philosophy nights. Busy on football match days. ✿♣🛑🖵(1,24)🐾🛜

Ploughman ⓛ
1 Staniland Way, Werrington, PE4 6NA
🕓 4-11; 12-midnight Fri & Sat; 12-11 Sun ☎ (01733) 327696
⊕ theploughman-werrington.co.uk
10 changing beers (sourced regionally) Ⓗ

This rejuvenated two-roomed community pub has been brought to the forefront of the city's real ale outlets by the enthusiastic licensee. Ten handpumps serve beers from breweries both local and from afar. An annual beer festival is held early in July. Many activities are hosted including charity events and live music at weekends. Local CAMRA branch Pub of the Year in 2014. ♣♣🛑🖵(1,22)

Woolpack ♈
29 North Street, Stanground, PE2 8HR (in old part of Stanground village by River Nene)
🕓 12 (2 Mon & Tue)-11; 12-11.30 Sat ☎ (01733) 753544
Adnams Southwold Bitter; Timothy Taylor Landlord; 2 changing beers (sourced locally; often Exit 33, Star) Ⓗ

Originally constructed in 1711, it still has a medieval wall in the garden. The old barn used to be the village mortuary – last used in the 1850s and said to be haunted. The beer garden leads to the old River Nene with boat moorings available. The L-shaped bar has a TV and dartboard and is decorated with a collection of old photos and militaria. Two guest beers are available. Entertainment includes a quiz on Sunday night and occasional live music. Local CAMRA branch Pub of the Year 2016. Q🌭✿🌑♣♠🐾🛜

Rampton

Black Horse
6 High Street, CB24 8QE
🕓 6-11; 12-4 Sun; closed Mon ☎ (01954) 251867
10 changing beers Ⓗ

Former Greene King pub that has been a free house for some time. At least one of the beers is likely to be a local ale, and all are guaranteed to be interesting. Beers can be served in third-pint glasses if you are not sure what to try. The interior comprises two bars separated by an archway. Both are smart and comfortable, with the left side mainly for diners. There is a large garden to the rear and car parking either side. 🌭✿🕭🛑♣🅿🐾

Ramsey

Jolly Sailor ⓛ ✅
43 Great Whyte, PE26 1HH
🕓 11-11 ☎ (01487) 813388 ⊕ jollysailorramsey.co.uk
Greene King Abbot; St Austell Tribute; Woodforde's Wherry; 2 changing beers Ⓗ

Grade II-listed building that has been a pub for over 400 years. The three linked rooms are on slightly different levels and feature wooden beams which date from various periods as the pub has been extended over the years. On the walls are pictures and artefacts depicting Ramsey history. A friendly and welcoming venue which attracts a varied clientele of all ages, it hosts occasional charity nights plus acoustic music sessions. Guest beers are available at the weekend. Good-value home-cooked food is served every day. Q✿🕭🛑♣🖵(31)🛜

St Ives

Oliver Cromwell ⓛ
13 Wellington Street, PE27 5AZ
🕓 11-11 (11.30 Thu; 12.30am Fri & Sat); 12-11 Sun
☎ (01480) 465601 ⊕ theolivercromwell.co.uk
Adnams Southwold Bitter; Oakham JHB; Woodforde's Wherry; 3 changing beers (often Nene Valley, Nethergate) Ⓗ

A popular pub near the town quay, old town bridge and chapel. A true free house, it offers three regular and three rotating beers, often from local breweries. Local Cromwell cider is always available and a selection of Belgian bottled beers is stocked. Lunchtime meals are freshly prepared using local ingredients. Live music is hosted every Thursday evening and a quiz on the first Tuesday of the month. The rear patio is a suntrap in the summer. ⬤◗⬤🚌😺

Royal Oak 🅛 ✅

13 Crown Street, PE27 5EB
🕐 11-11; 11-2am Fri & Sat; 12-midnight Sun
☎ (01480) 462586
Oakham Inferno; Sharp's Doom Bar; Wychwood Hobgoblin; 3 changing beers (often Nobby's, Oakham, Tydd Steam) Ⓗ

Busy town-centre pub, one of a number of historic listed inns in the town, whose most famous inhabitant was Oliver Cromwell. Despite the date 1502 over the door, most of the building is 18th century. The room layout and character were happily preserved in a sensitive renovation in the 1990s. A changing choice of three guest beers, often from local breweries, is complemented by several ciders and, unusually, perry. Live music features on Saturday evenings. 🛏️⬤♣♠🚌😺🛜

St Neots

Olde Sun 🅛

11 Huntingdon Street, PE19 1BL
🕐 12-11 ☎ (01480) 216863 ⊕ yeoldesun.moonfruit.com
Woodforde's Wherry; 5 changing beers (often Adnams, Elgood's, Woodforde's) Ⓗ

Low-beamed and cosy traditional town-centre pub with two large inglenook fireplaces, three bar areas, a dining area and a secluded patio. The jukebox is zoned allowing quiet areas for conversation. Shove-ha'penny and bar billiards are played. Five constantly changing guest beers come from various regional breweries including Adnams, Elgood's, Marston's, Thwaites and Woodforde's. A mild and other dark beers are usually among the range. Good home-cooked food includes a menu of traditional pub fare and blackboard specials. ⬤◗♠🚌(X5)😺

Pig 'n' Falcon 🅛

9 New Street, PE19 1AE (behind Barretts department store)
🕐 11-midnight (2.30am Fri & Sat) ☎ 07951 785678
⊕ pignfalcon.co.uk
Batemans Gold; Greene King IPA Ⓗ, Abbot Ⓖ; Potbelly Best Ⓗ; 5 changing beers (often Potbelly) Ⓖ

Busy town-centre free house with up to eight real ales and four real ciders, focusing on microbreweries and unusual beers including milds, porters and stouts. It also has a good range of bottled ciders and UK and foreign bottled beers including Trappist ales. Four beer festivals are held each year. Live blues and rock nights are hosted Wednesday-Sunday. Outside is a large and imaginative covered and heated beer garden. 🛏️♣♠🚌🚌(X5)😺🛜

Stapleford

Three Horseshoes

2 Church Street, CB22 5DS

🕐 12-2.30, 5-11; 12-midnight Fri & Sat; 12-10.30 Sun
☎ (01223) 503402
Adnams Ghost Ship, Broadside; Dark Star Hophead; Nene Valley Bitter; Woodforde's Wherry; 2 changing beers (sourced regionally) Ⓗ

Friendly village local on the southern fringe of Cambridge. Popular with the local community, the pub also attracts regular visitors from surrounding villages. The interior is divided into three areas – the entrance leads to the main bar with pool table, a small games room to the left and a large room to the right. One guest ale is always a dark beer. There is also a selection of bottled beers including Belgian ales. Local CAMRA Most Improved Rural Pub 2014 and Dark Ale Pub 2015. 🛏️⬤◗♣♠🚌P😺🛜

Upware

Five Miles Inn

Old School Lane, CB7 5ZR
🕐 11-11 (midnight Fri & Sat) ☎ (01353) 721654
⊕ fivemilesinn.co.uk
Morland Old Speckled Hen; 3 changing beers (sourced nationally) Ⓗ

Located off the beaten track, next to the River Cam and overlooking part of the Fens, the pub's full name is The Five Miles From Anywhere No Hurry Inn. Four ales are on handpump with an occasional fifth beer from a cask during the summer. Local Pickled Pig cider is available. A good selection of food is served in the bar and separate restaurant. Live music features most Friday evenings. Visitor moorings and services are provided for narrowboats/motor cruisers and there is a large car park for those arriving by land. 🛏️⬤◗👶🅰♣♠P😺🛜

West Wratting

Chestnut Tree

1 Mill Road, CB21 5LT
🕐 12-3 (not Mon), 5.30-11.30; 12-midnight Fri & Sat; 12-10.30 Sun ☎ (01223) 290384 ⊕ chestnuttreepub.co.uk
Greene King IPA; 3 changing beers Ⓗ

Welcoming two-bar locals' pub with ample car parking and an attractive rear garden. The public bar, with dark wood furniture and red upholstery, has an extension with a pool table. The saloon bar is used more for dining. The pub hosts darts and pool teams and also has a small lending library. Acquired by the present owners from Greene King in 2012, it is now free of tie – the guest beers are mainly from microbreweries, including local suppliers. A changing real cider is also available. CAMRA branch Pub of the Year 2014. Q🛏️⬤◗♣♠P🚌(19)😺

Whittlesey

Boat Inn 🅛

2 Ramsey Road, PE7 1DR
🕐 4 (11 Fri-Sun)-midnight ☎ (01733) 202488
⊕ quinnboatinn.wordpress.com
Elgood's Cambridge Bitter, Golden Newt Ⓗ; 3 changing beers Ⓗ/Ⓖ

This 11th-century inn is mentioned in the Domesday Book. It attracts locals, anglers and visitors, who all receive a warm welcome. The lounge has an unusual boat-shaped bar and hosts a whisky club on the second Friday of the month. Up to seven traditional ciders and perries supplement the real ales, with some served direct from the cask. Open mic music nights are occasional Tuesdays and Fridays. Outside is a pétanque terrain. Good-value accommodation is offered. Closing times can vary as the pub has a 24-hour licence. ☺☜⌺☖♣♠P☏(31)☺♥ 🛜

Hubs Place
No. 1, 12 Market Place, PE7 1AB
✪ 12-2, 5-midnight; 12-1am Fri & Sat; 12-11 Sun; closed Mon
☏ (01733) 204199 ⊕ hubs-place.co.uk
Fuller's London Pride; 1 changing beer Ⓗ
Pleasant and comfortable bar opened by a lottery winner in 2010. Formerly solicitors' offices, its three rooms have been refurbished in a cream and red colour scheme but retain some of the original wood panelling. A large patio is to the rear. The guest ale is usually from Woodforde's and other real ales may be available on special occasions such as the Whittlesea Straw Bear Festival. Closed Tuesday and Wednesday lunchtimes in winter.
☺☖♠P☏(31,33)🛜

Letter B ⓛ
53-57 Church Street, PE7 1DE
✪ 5-11; 3.30-midnight Fri; 12-midnight Sat; 12-11 Sun
☏ (01733) 206975 ⊕ theletterb.co.uk
Sharp's Doom Bar; 4 changing beers Ⓗ
A friendly and welcoming community pub dating back more than 200 years. It was called the Bee for a while but is now the Letter B – said to be so named because there were so many pubs in Whittlesey they ran out of names. A beer festival takes place in January (Straw Bear weekend). Up to 10 ciders and perries are available. Quiz nights are held on alternate Tuesdays and Sundays, and popular charity events are hosted. A former winner of CAMRA Gold Awards, Cider Pub of the Year 2015 and branch Cider Pub of the Year 2016.
Q☺☜⌺♣♠☐(31,33)☺♥🛜

New Crown ✪
58 High Causeway, PE7 1QA
✪ 12-3.30am ☏ (01733) 205134
Sharp's Doom Bar; 1 changing beer (sourced nationally) Ⓗ
Grade II-listed mid-17th century two-roomed thatched pub with wooden decor and beamed ceilings. It has a friendly local atmosphere and is home to a mischievous ghost. Two real ales are on offer, more during the Straw Bear Festival, one of which changes regularly. Good home-cooked food is available Tuesday to Sunday. Darts is played here and there is a separate pool room. Whittlesey Town Bowling Club is next door. Well-behaved dogs are welcome in the front bar only.
☺⌺◑☖♠P☐(31,33)☺♥🛜

Willingham

Bank Micropub
High Street, CB24 5ES
✪ 6-10 Tue; 5.30-11 (10 Wed); closed Sun & Mon
☏ (01954) 200045 ⊕ thebankmicropub.co.uk
6 changing beers Ⓖ
The Bank was converted from a former village bank branch and opened in 2012. Although not a full-sized pub, 'micro' is perhaps a misnomer here. It has a short bar that, along with some of the furniture, was rescued from a closed pub and renovated. Photographs of local interest adorn the walls. Up to six real ales are available direct from the cask, with regional and local beers featuring strongly. One real ale is on KeyKeg. Canned beers from small English breweries are also available.
Q♠☐☺

Wisbech

Red Lion ⓛ
32 North Brink, PE13 1JR
✪ 11.30-3, 6 (5 Fri)-11; 11.30-3, 7-midnight Sat; 12-11 Sun
☏ (01945) 582022
Elgood's Black Dog, Cambridge Bitter; 1 changing beer Ⓗ
This is the nearest Elgood's pub to the brewery and is very comfortable, with a pleasant, relaxed atmosphere. Drinkers and diners are well catered for with quality ales and excellent food served seven days a week in the revamped split-level restaurant. There is a bar to the front and dining room to the rear. The main access is via a side passage which links the North Brink road to the rear car park and patio area. Wheelchair access is from both the front and rear. The outdoor drinking area is popular on sunny days. Q☺◑☖P☐(X1)🛜

Wistow

Three Horseshoes
Mill Road, PE28 2QQ
✪ 6-10 Mon; 12-3, 6-11; 12-10 Sat; 12-4 Sun
☏ (01487) 822270
Adnams Southwold Bitter, Ghost Ship Ⓗ
Multi-roomed brick and thatch 18th-century inn opposite the village church. Though always a pub, the building has evolved over time – part was once a blacksmith's and it provided accommodation for workers employed in church rebuilding work in the 18th century. Traditional pub food is available daily. A quiz is held once a month. Families are welcome in both bars and there is a covered smoking area outside. ☺☜◑☖♠P☐☐(30)🛜

Cask beer

Real ale is often described as 'beer from a barrel' and pubs are said to have 'barrels behind the bar'. In fact, barrels are large containers, too big for most bars. The correct generic term for the containers for real ale is cask and casks come in the following sizes:
Pin – 4.5 gallons
Firkin (from old Dutch word meaning fourth) – 9 gallons
Kilderkin (from old Dutch word meaning small cask) – 18 gallons
Barrel – 36 gallons
Hogshead – 54 gallons

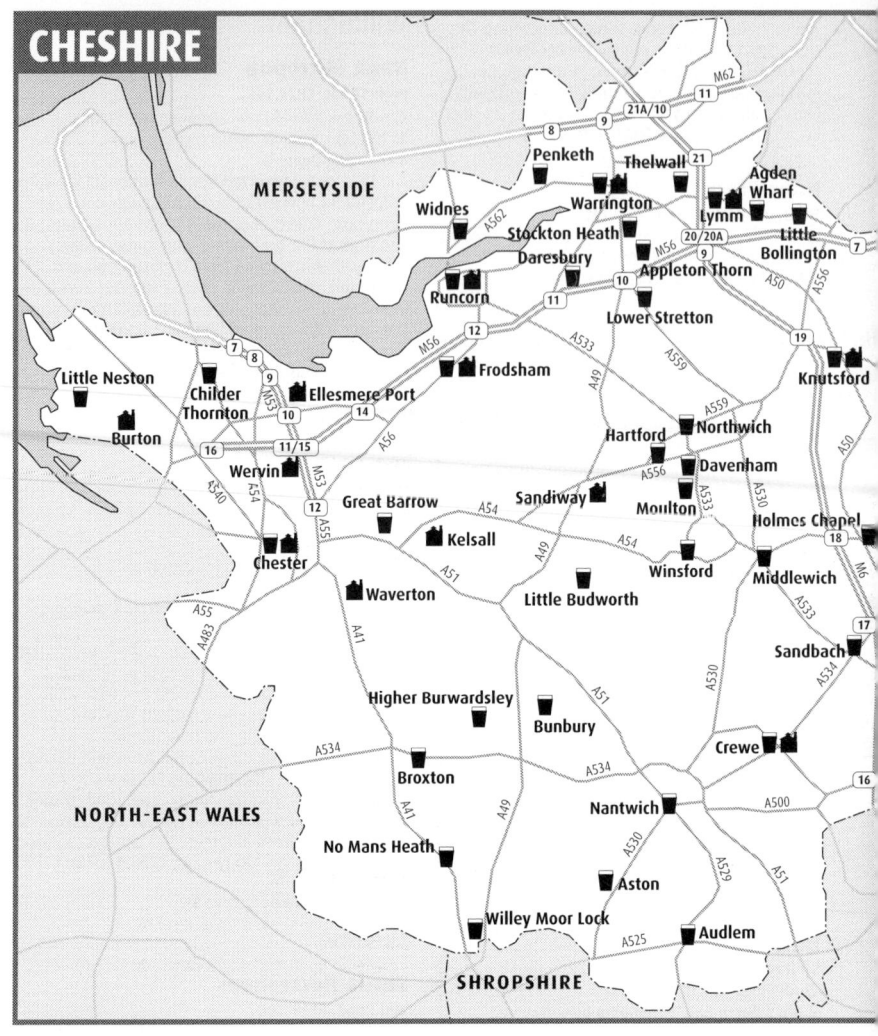

CHESHIRE

MERSEYSIDE

NORTH-EAST WALES

SHROPSHIRE

Agden Wharf

Barn Owl ⅃
Warrington Lane, WA13 0SW (on Bridgewater Canal, off A56)
✪ 12-11 ☎ (01925) 752020 ⊕ thebarnowlinn.co.uk
Thwaites Original, Wainwright, Lancaster Bomber; 3 changing beers (sourced regionally) ⓗ
Situated alongside the Bridgewater Canal, there are fine views across the Cheshire countryside from the pub, the heated, covered terrace and the canalside patio area. Three regular beers are complemented by up to three guest ales, mainly from independent breweries, including at least one LocAle. Renowned for food, it can be busy at mealtimes. ⏴⏵⏴⏵⏴P⏵

Alsager

Lodge ♥ ⅃
88 Crewe Road, ST7 2JA (jct Crewe Rd/Station Rd)
✪ 4-11 (midnight Fri); 2-midnight Sat; 2-11 Sun
☎ (01270) 873669
8 changing beers (sourced nationally) ⓗ

Unspoilt, traditional and friendly community pub. Up to eight regularly changing real ales in a variety of styles are available and up to three real ciders. A range of continental beers is also kept on draught and in bottle. The walled rear garden offers seating and tables. A variety of events ranging from live music to film nights is hosted, otherwise this is a quiet pub for conversation. There is access from the rear into the garden for cycles. Q⏴⏵⏴⏵⏴P⏵(3)⏴

Appleton Thorn

Appleton Thorn Village Hall
Stretton Road, WA4 4RT
✪ 7.30-11.30 Thu-Sat; 1-4, 7.30-10.30 Sun; closed Mon-Wed
☎ (01925) 261187 ⊕ appletonthornvillagehall.co.uk
7 changing beers (sourced nationally) ⓗ
Local CAMRA Club of the Year 2016, regional and national CAMRA award certificates line the walls at this thriving village hall venue. A beamed ceiling, stained-glass sandstone-framed windows and period agricultural tools add to the traditional atmosphere. A cosy lounge opens through to the main function room with a pool room off. Friendly

Audlem

Lord Combermere L ✓
The Square, CW3 0AQ
🌣 12-midnight ☎ (01270) 812277
⊕ thelordcombermere.co.uk
Greene King IPA; Salopian Darwins Origin; Timothy Taylor Landlord; 3 changing beers (sourced locally) ⊞
A regular entry in the Guide in recent years, this is a friendly, modern, open-plan pub. The bar area attracts walkers and their dogs as well as locals, while dining areas, a lounge with TV sport, a patio and garden cater for families. Lunchtime and evening menus include gluten-free meals. The well-kept beers are a mixture of national and local ales. Quiz night is Tuesday, live music plays on Thursday and/or Sunday. ᔓ❀◑ᕼ💷(73)🐾 ♿

Bollington

Poachers Inn L
95 Ingersley Road, SK10 5RE
🌣 12-2 (not Mon), 5.30-11; 12-midnight Sat; 12-11 Sun
☎ (01625) 572086 ⊕ thepoachers.org
Storm Beauforts Ale; Weetwood Old Dog Bitter; 3 changing beers (sourced locally; often Happy Valley) ⊞
Friendly and welcoming family-run community free house near the Gritstone Trail. An enthusiastic supporter of LocAle, it offers two regular beers and three rotating guests including one from nearby Happy Valley. Real cider is also on handpump, with world beers in bottles. It has a real coal fire in winter and a suntrap garden for the summer months. Well-regarded, good-value, home-prepared food is sourced locally. Events include Wednesday pie night and a monthly quiz for local charities. ᔓ❀◑ᕼ💷(10,392)🐾 ♿

Vale Inn L ✓
29-31 Adlington Road, SK10 5JT
🌣 12-2.30, 5-11; 12-11 Fri & Sat; 12-10.30 Sun
☎ (01625) 575147 ⊕ valeinn.co.uk
6 changing beers (sourced locally; often Bollington) ⊞
Terraced free house dating from the 1890s. The brewery tap for the nearby Bollington Brewing Company, it features up to six of its beers, an occasional guest and two real ciders/perries. The part-wooded beer garden overlooks the recreation and cricket ground, making it the ideal spot for a lazy Saturday watching the sport. The popular Middlewood Way and Macclesfield Canal are nearby. ᔓ❀◑ᕼ💷(10,392)🐾 ♿

staff will oblige with a taster of seven regularly changing beers, several ciders and perries. Reasonably priced lunches are served on Sunday afternoons. Q ᔓ❀◑♿♣●💷🚆(8E)🐾

Aston

Bhurtpore L
Wrenbury Road, CW5 8DQ (just off A530)
🌣 12-11.30 (midnight Fri & Sat); 12-11 Sun
☎ (01270) 780917 ⊕ bhurtpore.co.uk
11 changing beers (sourced nationally) ⊞
A friendly, family-run local featuring in the Guide for the past 24 years. The pub has four distinct drinking areas and a separate restaurant. Wall displays and artefacts reflect the history of the venue and its surrounding area. A wide selection of real ales to suit all tastes is kept alongside an equally interesting collection of Belgian bottled beers. The pub offers a great range of home-prepared, locally sourced food and has a deserved reputation for excellent curries. The Vintage Japanese Motorcycle Club meets here.
Q ᔓ❀◑♿▲🚆(Wrenbury)●💷(72)🐾 ♿

Broxton

Sandstone L
Nantwich Road, CH3 9JH (on A534, E of A41)
🌣 12-3, 6-11; 12-11 Sat & Sun ☎ (01829) 782333
⊕ thesandstone.co.uk
Stonehouse Station Bitter; 3 changing beers (sourced locally; often Liverpool Organic, Wincle, Sandstone) ⊞
This 17th-century inn is set in superb countryside and provides an ideal refreshment stop for walkers on the Sandstone Trail. The pub is part-owned by Sandstone Brewery whose beers feature regularly on the bar along with ales from other local micros. High-quality food is served in both the main bar with its impressive logburner and conservatory restaurant. Well-behaved children and dogs are welcome. ᔓ❀◑ᕼ💷🐾 ♿

Bunbury

Nag's Head
Vicarage Lane, CW6 9PB (beside church hall)
🌑 6-11; 12-midnight Sat; 12-10.30 Sun ☎ (01829) 260027
Coach House Postlethwaite; 3 changing beers (sourced regionally) Ⓗ
A prominent three-storey Georgian free house, frequented by actors filming the ITV series Home Fires. The pub has two rooms plus a pool/TV sports room adjoining the lounge. The interior is largely unchanged over the years with some lovely old features still to be found including original oak beams and wattle and daub walls. Up to six cask ales are on offer. There is a large car park and garden area to the rear. ⏰🏵️◗&P

Chelford

Egerton Arms Ⓛ
Knutsford Road, SK11 9BB
🌑 12-11 (1am Fri & Sat) ☎ (01625) 861366
⊕ chelfordegertonarms.co.uk
Wells Bombardier; 5 changing beers (sourced locally; often Tatton, Copper Dragon) Ⓗ
Originally a 15th-century stables, this is now a large single room with rural decor, real fires and an intimate atmosphere. The pub offers excellent food and a good range of beer. Regular beer and food events are hosted, including food matching with local brewers' beers. Live music, often jazz, plays on the last Friday of the month. Quiz night is the last Thursday of the month. Real cider is available in summer. Opens later mid-week at 3pm through January and February, closed Mondays all year except bank holidays.
⏰🏵️◗&≒♣P☷(27,27A,27B)😺🛜

Chester

Brewery Tap Ⓛ
52-54 Lower Bridge Street, CH1 1RU
🌑 12-11; 12-10.30 Sun ☎ (01244) 340999 ⊕ the-tap.co.uk
7 changing beers (sourced nationally) Ⓗ
Occupying a Jacobean great hall, the building features an ornate sandstone fireplace, tapestries and stone floors that create a superb ambience. It is a fitting winner of CAMRA's Heritage Conservation and Conversion to Pub Use award. Food is inventive, freshly prepared and locally sourced. Seven ales are available, with the brewery's own Spitting Feathers beers complemented by a range of guests including many from other local microbreweries. Reached by steps from street level. Q◗♣●☷🛜

Cellar
19-21 City Road, CH1 3AE
🌑 12 (4 Mon)-1am; 12-2am Fri & Sat; 12-midnight Sun
☎ (01244) 318950 ⊕ thecellarchester.co.uk
6 changing beers (sourced nationally; often Burning Sky, Deva Craft, Hawkshead) Ⓗ
Friendly, modern bar which is actually at street level despite the name. Six changing ales and three ciders are served by enthusiastic, knowledgeable staff. Live music and TV sport feature regularly, particularly at weekends. Locally sourced pies, paninis and Scotch eggs are available, with free bacon sandwiches on Sundays. A winner of several recent CAMRA branch awards including Pub of the Year. Dogs are welcome except Friday and Saturday nights when the bar can be busy. An extensive bottled beer range is kept. ≒●😺🛜

Cross Keys
2 Duke Street, CH1 1RP
🌑 12-11; 12-10.30 Sun; closed Mon ☎ (01244) 344460
⊕ crosskeyschester.co.uk
Joule's Blonde, Pale Ale, Slumbering Monk; 2 changing beers (often Deva Craft, Joule's) Ⓗ
Attractive Victorian red-brick building, featuring a stylish interior with etched mirrors, oak floors, wood panelling and a log fire. Specially commissioned stained-glass windows depict other hostelries in the Joule's estate. A large upstairs room (the Slaughtered Lamb) is available for functions. A small beer terrace in front of the building catches the afternoon sun. Three permanent beers, one seasonal beer, one guest and one cider are available. Food is served Wednesday to Sunday. Live Irish music nights are held on the second and fourth Wednesdays of the month. ⏰🏵️◗●☷🛜

Lodge Bar
8-10 Hoole Road, Hoole, CH2 3NH (on A56 ½ mile from railway station and ring road)
🌑 11-11 (midnight Fri & Sat) ☎ (01244) 324971
⊕ lodgebar.co.uk
3 changing beers (sourced nationally; often Abbeydale, Rudgate, Salopian) Ⓗ
Lounge-style bar, part of the Bawn Lodge Hotel. The bar leads to intimate alcove seating and then to a large side lounge. Three handpumps serve a changing range of ales at competitive prices. Good-value food is available all day. The large beer garden is popular in the summer. Two large screens show BT Sport. One of very few pubs where traditional bagatelle is played.
⏰🏵️🛏️◗&≒♣P☷🛜

Old Harkers Arms Ⓛ
1 Russell Street, CH3 5AL (down steps off City Rd to canal towpath)

✪ 11.30-11; 12-10.30 Sun ☎ (01244) 344525
⊕ harkersarms-chester.co.uk
Weetwood Cheshire Cat, Eastgate Ale; house beer (by Phoenix); 6 changing beers (sourced nationally; often Derby, Hawkshead) Ⓗ
Upmarket pub converted from the ground floor of a former Victorian canalside warehouse. Timber flooring, traditional wooden furniture and cast iron pillars provide an insight to its former use. Blackboards list real ales with tasting notes – many are from local breweries. Ciders and perries are dispensed direct from the cellar. Food is served all day (booking advised for busy weekend periods). Outside, there is a seating area alongside the canal.
Q✿✪◑&⇌♣●🖵😺🛜

Olde Cottage Inn ♈

34-36 Brook Street, CH1 3DZ
✪ 4-11 (midnight Fri); 2-midnight Sat ☎ (01244) 324065
⊕ oldecottagechester.co.uk
4 changing beers (sourced nationally; often Otter, Sharp's) Ⓗ
Welcoming traditional community hostelry on a popular eating and drinking street between the city centre and railway station. To the left is the games room with pool, darts and a bagatelle table (a game rarely seen outside Chester). The main bar has another dartboard, small TV and a real fire for colder weather. They are competitively priced and include one free of tie, with various loyalty and discount schemes offered. ✿⇌♣🖵🛜

Pied Bull Ⓛ

57 Northgate Street, CH1 2HQ
✪ 10-11 (midnight Fri & Sat) ☎ (01244) 325829
⊕ piedbull.co.uk
Adnams Broadside; house beer (by Pied Bull); 2 changing beers (sourced nationally; often Blackjack, Ossett, Waen) Ⓗ
Home to the only microbrewery inside the city walls, this oak-beamed historic pub attracts a lively mix of locals and visitors. Up to three of the six cask ales on offer come from the range of 19 house brews. A loyalty discount is available on the cask ales and brewery tours of the cellar can be booked. High-quality pub food, made with locally sourced ingredients, is available all day. A competitive quiz is hosted every Thursday. Dogs are allowed in the area by the entrance. 🐕🍴◑&●🖵😺🛜

Telford's Warehouse Ⓛ

Canal Basin, Tower Wharf, CH1 4EZ (just off city walls)
✪ 12-1am (11 Mon & Tue; 12.30am Wed & Thu)
☎ (01244) 390090 ⊕ telfordswarehousechester.com
Salopian Oracle; Thwaites Original; Weetwood Cheshire Cat; 3 changing beers (sourced nationally; often Derby, Tatton, Three Tuns) Ⓗ
Impressive converted Georgian warehouse located adjacent to the Shropshire Union Canal. The building features a glass frontage overlooking the canal basin and industrial artefacts inside. During the daytime a relaxed atmosphere prevails while evenings are livelier with events such as salsa dance classes and live concerts when an admission charge may apply. The regular ales are complemented by guest ales which are often from local micros. High-quality food is available in the bar and family-friendly upstairs restaurant.
✿◑●🖵(1A)😺🛜

Childer Thornton

White Lion

New Road, CH66 5PU (off A41 between Great Sutton and Hooton)
✪ 11.30-11.30; 11.30-11 Sun ☎ (0151) 339 3402
⊕ whitelionchilderthornton.co.uk
Thwaites Original, Wainwright, Lancaster Bomber; 2 changing beers Ⓗ
Friendly village local which has been an inn since 1724. The main bar features an original inglenook fireplace with logburner where most of the locals gather round on winter evenings. A small snug is located off the bar, there is a separate cosy room across the corridor and a recently added dining room. Home-cooked, good-value meals are available all day until 8pm. Pleasant outdoor drinking areas can be found at both the front and rear of the pub. 🐕✿◑P🖵(1,2)🛜

Congleton

Barley Hops Ⓛ

2 Swan Bank, CW12 1AH
✪ 2-8 (10 Fri); 12-8 Sat; 12-6 Sun; closed Mon
☎ (01260) 270164 ⊕ barleyhops.co.uk
3 changing beers (sourced locally) Ⓗ
This well-stocked bottled beer specialist is also a micropub. Three handpumps dispense predominantly local beers. The bottled beer selection focuses on British beers but there is also a well-chosen selection of foreign beers, plus local cider in bottles. A discount scheme offers a free pint/bottle for every 10 purchased. Occasional Meet the Brewer events are held, and Pie and Pint every Friday and Saturday. Closing time may vary according to demand. Q🐕◑●🖵(38,42)😺🛜

Queen's Head Hotel Ⓛ

Park Lane, CW12 3DE
✪ 12-midnight (1am Fri & Sat) ☎ (01260) 272546
⊕ queensheadhotel.org.uk
Black Sheep Best Bitter; Draught Bass; Greene King Abbot; Joule's Pale Ale; 3 changing beers (sourced locally) Ⓗ
This place is a welcome sight for the thirsty traveller. The real fire in the lounge is particularly welcoming in winter. Food is available every day – pub favourites supplemented by specials. There are two outdoor drinking areas, a child-free patio off the lounge and a garden with children's play area behind the car park. Moorings on Macclesfield canal have direct access. Accommodation in en-suite rooms is adjacent.
🐕✿🛏◑⇌♣●P🖵(94)😺🛜

Crewe

Borough Arms Ⓛ

33 Earle Street, CW1 2BG (on Earle St railway bridge, entrance up steps in adjoining Thomas St)
✪ 5 (12 Fri & Sat)-11; 12-10.30 Sun
12 changing beers (sourced nationally; often Dark Star, Fyne Ales, Oakham) Ⓗ
Popular town pub with 12 changing real ales – mainly golden, one or two dark – plus a wide selection of Belgian beers on tap and in bottles. Real cider is sometimes available. Some beers are discounted on Monday nights. The pub is open plan upstairs with three distinct drinking areas on two levels. Downstairs, a large L-shaped room leads to a beautiful sheltered beer garden. Many TV screens show TV sport. 🐕✿♣●P😺🛜

Hops Ⓛ

Prince Albert Street, CW1 2DF (opp Lifestyle Centre)
✪ 11 (5 Mon)-11.30; 12-11.30 Sun ☎ (01270) 211100
House beer (by Townhouse); 7 changing beers (sourced nationally) Ⓗ

Friendly Belgian-style café-bar in a secluded spot on the edge of the town centre. It has two floors of intimate seating plus a suntrap terrace out front. Six beers are on handpump and one or two on gravity, always including at least one dark beer, sourced from smaller breweries both near and far. An extensive range of Belgian beers is also kept both on tap and bottled. CAMRA members receive a discount on Monday evenings. CAMRA Cheshire Pub of the Year 2015. Q✿⟡⊛◖◗♣●🐾●🐾🖥

Daresbury

Ring o' Bells Ⓛ ✓

Chester Road, WA4 4AJ (just off A56 in centre of village)
✪ 11.30-11; 11.30-10.30 Sun ☎ (01925) 740256
⊕ ringobells-daresbury.co.uk
4 changing beers (sourced locally; often Frodsham, Weetwood) Ⓗ

Once the village courthouse, this 19th-century pub retains many original features including a listed horse trough. Although food oriented, this Chef & Brewer pub has four handpumps which, more often than not, serve local ales from breweries such as Weetwood and Spitting Feathers. Opposite is Daresbury parish church, once officiated over by Rev Charles Dodgson, better known by his pen name Lewis Carroll. ✿⊛◖◗♿P🖥(X30)●

Davenham

Davenham Cricket Club Ⓛ

Butchers' Stile, Hartford Road, CW9 8JG
✪ 4.30-8.30; 4-11 Fri & Sat ☎ (01606) 48922
⊕ davenham.play-cricket.com
4 changing beers (sourced locally; often Beartown, Brimstage, Mobberley) Ⓗ

This is a community facility in an idyllic village. There is a main lounge and sports bar. Four handpumps serve the real ales, mainly from local breweries. Other sporting groups share the club. During the cricket season the opening hours are extended. ✿⊛♿P🖥●🖥

Disley

White Lion Ⓛ ✓

135 Buxton Road, SK12 2HA
✪ 12 (6.30 Mon)-11; 12-12.30am Fri & Sat
☎ (01663) 762800
9 changing beers (often Adnams, Ossett, Purity) Ⓗ

Originally the red house that gave the name to the adjacent side road, this pub is now painted white. Nine ever-changing real ales are on offer, many from micros and all selected from SIBA member breweries. The contemporary interior is open plan apart from a separate dog room. A comprehensive menu is served daily until 9pm (Sun 8pm, no food Mon). On the A6 towards the eastern end of the village, a short walk from Peak Forest Canal (bridge 26). ⊛◖◗P🖥(199)●🖥

Frodsham

Helter Skelter ▼ Ⓛ

31 Church Street, WA6 6PN

✪ 11-11.30 (midnight Fri & Sat); 12-11 Sun
☎ (01928) 733361 ⊕ helterskelter-frodsham.co.uk
Weetwood Best Bitter; 7 changing beers (sourced nationally; often Liverpool Organic, Ossett, Thornbridge) Ⓗ

Regular local CAMRA branch award winner and Pub of the Year 2016, this single-roomed bar offers a budget-priced local bitter and seven handpumps serving a beer range mainly from local and national micros. A guest cider and a selection of imported bottled beers are also available. The relaxed atmosphere attracts friendly conversation among discerning real ale enthusiasts. Excellent home-cooked food is served in the bar and upstairs restaurant. An informal folk band plays music upstairs on Sunday evenings. ◖◗⇌●🚌🖥(48,X30)●🖥

Kash 22 Brew & Chew Ⓛ

22 Church Street, WA6 6QW (near railway bridge)
✪ 4-11; 12-midnight Thu-Sat; 12-10.30 Sun
☎ (01928) 733116
4 changing beers (sourced locally; often Blueball) Ⓗ

A lively neighbourhood bar in the centre of Frodsham. Americana adorns the walls downstairs, while upstairs there is a TV sport lounge and a small adjoining open-air space for summer drinking. Three real ales and three craft beers from local Blueball Brewery are served alongside a changing range of guest beers from local and national microbreweries. With good fresh food, excellent service and live music at weekends, Kash 22 provides a truly vibrant atmosphere. ⊛◖◗⇌🖥(48,X30)●🖥

Gawsworth

Harrington Arms ★ Ⓛ ✓

Church Lane, SK11 9RJ (off A536)
✪ 12-3, 5-11.30 (midnight Fri); 12-11.30 Sat; 12-11 Sun
☎ (01260) 223325
Robinsons Dizzy Blonde, Unicorn; 2 changing beers (sourced locally) Ⓗ

An important community asset in this picturesque village as well as a must-visit for tourists. The multi-room interior features on CAMRA's National Inventory of Historic Pub Interiors. The Robinsons beers are all delivered by handpump, with Unicorn and Dizzy Blonde the mainstays, and seasonal beers added to the range when they are available. Good pub food is available daily. Q✿⊛◖◗♿♣🖥(38)●

Great Barrow

White Horse Ⓛ

Main Street, CH3 7HX (100yds E of B5132)
✪ 4-11.30 (12.30am Fri); 12-12.30am Sat; 12-11.30 Sun
☎ (01829) 741633 ⊕ whitehorsebarrow.co.uk
3 changing beers (sourced regionally; often Big Hand, Purple Moose, Weetwood) Ⓗ

Characterful and welcoming family-run village local. The attractive split-level interior has a small raised front room with a pool table, and a smart bar room. Up to three cask beers are on handpump, at least one from a local micro. Pizzas are served Thursday to Sunday. Sports fans are catered for with satellite TV. High-quality accommodation is available. Tucked away at the back is a pleasant beer garden. ✿⊛🛏◖◗▲♣P●🖥

Hartford

Chime L

279 Chester Road, CW8 1QL
☼ 10-11 (midnight Sat); 10-10.30 Sun ☎ (01606) 872158
⊕ chimehartford.co.uk
3 changing beers (sourced locally; often Merlin, Tatton, Wincle) Ⓗ
Wine bar/restaurant opened in 2014 focusing on food. The three rotating cask ales are from local breweries, sometimes including a house beer which is a rebadged Merlin ale. Both Hartford and Greenbank stations are nearby, making Chime accessible from two railway lines.
🛲⑪க≢🖥(46,82)🛜

Higher Burwardsley

Pheasant Inn L

Barracks Lane, CH3 9PF
☼ 11-11; 12-10.30 Sun ☎ (01829) 770434
⊕ thepheasantinn.co.uk
Weetwood Best Bitter, Cheshire Cat; 2 changing beers (sourced locally) Ⓗ
Charming 300-year-old inn nestled high up the Peckforton Hills with stunning views over the Cheshire plain to the Clwydian Range. It is popular with walkers on the Sandstone Trail and visitors to the nearby candle workshops. Up to three Weetwood beers are on offer supplemented by locally sourced guest ales. High-quality food is served in both the main bar and separate dining room. Accommodation is in 12 en-suite rooms. Well-behaved children and dogs are welcome.
Q🛲🏵🖨⑪க🅿😺🛜

Holmes Chapel

Old Red Lion ✅

19 London Road, CW4 7AQ (next to St Luke's Church)
☼ 11-11 (11.30 Wed & Thu; 1am Fri & Sat)
☎ (01477) 549282
Black Sheep Best Bitter; Brakspear Bitter; Timothy Taylor Landlord; Thwaites Wainwright; 1 changing beer (sourced regionally) Ⓗ
This attractive former coaching inn set next to the stone parish church has served Holmes Chapel for many generations. The interior is modern but tasteful following a refurbishment in 2014. On the bar there are four regular beers plus one guest sourced from the Ember Inns list. Beers are discounted on Mondays. There is a Pay & Display car park with the charge refundable at the bar.
🛲🏵⑪க≢🅿🖥(42,319)🛜

Knutsford

Tap & Bottle

15 Minshull Street, WA16 6HG
☼ 3 (12 Fri & Sat)-midnight; 12-10.30 Sun
☎ (01565) 228269 ⊕ tapandbottle.co.uk
6 changing beers (sourced locally; often Tatton) Ⓗ
A modern independently owned bar that offers six real ales in casks and an extensive range of bottled beers, usually including some that are gluten-free. Belgian fruit beers are often available. Mass branded products are avoided, even for spirits. The upstairs area is spacious, comfortable, light and airy, with a TV showing sporting events. Downstairs is more compact. ≢🖥😺🛜

Little Bollington

Swan with Two Nicks L ✅

Park Lane, WA14 4TJ (signposted off A56)
☼ 12-11; 12-10.30 Sun ☎ (0161) 928 2914
⊕ swanwithtwonicks.co.uk
Timothy Taylor Landlord; house beer (by Coach House); 2 changing beers (sourced locally) Ⓗ
Large, traditional country pub popular with walkers and canal boaters. It comprises several rooms, with a central bar and restaurant area to the rear. The house beer, Swan with Two Nicks, is from Coach House and is typically accompanied by two local beers, and three nationally sourced ales. There is a varied food offering available all day until 9pm (8pm Sun), served in the pub rooms and the restaurant, with gluten-free dishes on the menu.
🛲🏵⑪🅿🖥😺

Little Budworth

Egerton Arms L ✅

Pinfold Lane, CW6 9BS
☼ 12-11; 11-1am Fri & Sat; closed Mon ☎ (01829) 760424
⊕ egerton-arms.co.uk
6 changing beers (sourced locally; often Big Hand, Brimstage, Dunham Massey) Ⓗ
Knowledgeable, enthusiastic and friendly staff contribute to a convivial atmosphere that makes drinking and dining such a pleasant experience at this unspoilt country pub, reopened in 2013 after a four-year closure. A range of continental lagers on draught is available plus a selection of bottled world beers. The pub holds regular live music sessions, themed events and beer festivals. Watch cricket from the beer garden or take a short stroll to nearby Budworth Common or Oulton Park Circuit.
🛲🏵⑪Å♣♠🅿🖥😺🛜

Little Neston

Harp

19 Quayside, CH64 0TB (turn left at bottom of Marshlands Road, pub is 300yds on left overlooking marshes)
☼ 12-11; 12-10.30 Sun ☎ (0151) 336 6980
Holt Bitter; Peerless Triple Blonde; Timothy Taylor Landlord; 2 changing beers (sourced regionally) Ⓗ
A former coal miners' inn near the site of Neston Colliery which closed in 1927. Converted from two cottages, it has a public bar with a real fire in winter and a basic lounge. In a glorious location on the Deeside to Neston part of the national cycle network, the pub overlooks the Dee Marshes and North Wales, with a garden and a drinking area abutting the edge of the marshes. Q🛲🏵🅿😺

Lower Stretton

Ring o' Bells L

Northwich Road, WA4 4NZ (near M56 jct 10)
☼ 5.30-11; 3-10.30 Sun
Lees Manchester Pale Ale; Merlin Dark Magic; Wood Shropshire Lad; 3 changing beers (sourced locally; often Bathams, Brightside, Merlin) Ⓗ
An unspoilt village local, just as pubs used to be – no amplified music or games machines, just conversation and banter. The main room, served by a single bar, leads to two smaller rooms. Three regular and up to three rotating guest beers, including a mild, are on offer, often from local microbreweries. Quiz nights are the first and third

Tuesdays of the month, folk sessions feature monthly, and charity bingo on Saturday evenings.
Q ⌂ ☺ ♣ ● P ⊟ (45,46) ☺

Lymm

Brewery Tap 🅻
18 Bridgewater Street, WA13 0AB
🌣 12-11 (midnight Fri & Sat); 12-10.30 Sun
☎ (01925) 755451 ⊕ lymmbrewing.co.uk
Lymm Bitter, Bridgewater Blonde; 5 changing beers (sourced locally; often Dunham Massey) 🅗
A modern venue in the red-brick former post office near the canal. The well-lit bar is complemented by a tastefully decorated front room with subdued lighting, comfy armchairs and a wood-fired stove. Five guest ales are either from the microbrewery under the pub or nearby Dunham Massey. Two rotating real ciders are also available. Renowned local pies are always on offer or you can bring in sandwiches from the deli next door.
⌂ ☺ & ♣ ● ⊟ (5,35,47) ☺ 🤟

Macclesfield

Park Tavern 🅻 ✔
158 Park Lane, SK11 6UB
🌣 4-11; 12-midnight Fri & Sat; 12-10.30 Sun
☎ (01625) 667846 ⊕ park-tavern.co.uk
Bollington Long Hop, Best; 4 changing beers (sourced locally; often Bollington) 🅗
Just outside Macclesfield town centre, this Bollington Brewing-owned pub is a recommended stop for anyone visiting the area. The core range of two Bollington beers is complemented by a changing range of others from the brewery, often featuring a dark beer. Two real ciders add to the choice. It has a modern interior with separate rooms and drinking areas. There is a quiz on Thursday, a monthly science discussion group – Sci Bar – and it has its own cinema/function room upstairs. Lunches are served Friday and Saturday, while Thursday is burger night.
⌂ ☺ ◑ ≈ ♣ ● ⊟ ☺ 🤟

RedWillow 🅻
32A Park Green, SK11 7NA
🌣 4-11; 12-midnight Fri & Sat; 12-10.30 Sun; closed Mon
☎ (01625) 503253 ⊕ redwillowbar.com
RedWillow Headless; 4 changing beers (sourced regionally) 🅗
A relative newcomer to the Macclesfield real ale scene, this bar, sensitively converted from former shop premises, is now well established with a broad offering of beer types and styles. Five handpumps dispense RedWillow beers alongside a changing range of beers from other micros and one ever-changing real cider. A wide selection of gins is also stocked. Do not expect to find national brand lagers or stouts here. Seating includes comfortable sofas. ⌂ ◑ & ≈ ● ⊟ ☺

Treacle Tap 🅻
43 Sunderland Street, SK11 6JL
🌣 12-11 (midnight Thu-Sat) ☎ (01625) 615938
⊕ thetreacletap.co.uk
3 changing beers (sourced locally) 🅗
This pub packs a lot into a small space, with weekly live music on a Friday, stitch and bitch, a chess club and a weekly quiz on Sunday evening. The food selection is a good choice of locally made pies and cold platters. Likewise the cask beer range is an

interesting ever-changing selection of three beers from some of the best micros, served by friendly, helpful staff. There is also a selection of bottled Belgian, American and world beers.
Q ⌂ ◑ ≈ ⊟ ☺ 🤟

Waters Green Tavern 🅻
96 Waters Green, SK11 6LH
🌣 12-3, 5-11; 12-4, 7-11 Sat; 12-4, 7-10.30 Sun
☎ (01625) 422653
7 changing beers (sourced regionally; often Abbeydale, Acorn, Elland) 🅗
Consistently the main attraction for Macclesfield real ale drinkers for many years, partly due to the knowledge and experience of the landlord and staff. Multi-award winning, a range of seven real ales is maintained, with particular appeal for those seeking pale beers from northern breweries or real cider. Good food is served at lunchtime (no food Sun). Regional Cider Pub of the Year 2015.
⌂ ☺ ◑ ≈ ♣ ● ⊟ ☺ 🤟

Wharf 🅻
107 Brook Street, SK11 7AW
🌣 4 (12 Mon)-11.30; 12-midnight Fri & Sat; 12-11.30 Sun
☎ (01625) 261879 ⊕ thewharfmacc.co.uk
St Austell Cornish Best Bitter; 4 changing beers (sourced locally; often AllGates, Pictish) 🅗
Drinkers thirsty after a walk up the hill from the town centre are rewarded with a friendly welcome at this pub which mixes the traditional – games such as pool, darts and skittles – with the modern. A selection of KeyKeg and bottled beers complements the superb range of changing cask beers from local and regional breweries. The beers can be enjoyed in a cosy fireside area with books and board games. A former Cheshire CAMRA Pub of the Year. ⌂ ☺ ≈ ♣ ● ⊟ (1,58) ☺ 🤟

Middlewich

King's Lock 🅻
1 Booth Lane, CW10 0JJ (cross the canal off A533)
🌣 11-11 ☎ (01606) 836894 ⊕ kingslockinn.com
House beer (by Merlin); 5 changing beers (sourced nationally) 🅗
Great canalside pub by the King's Lock, number 71, on the Trent & Mersey Canal. Access is via the canal road bridge. At one time it had just the tiniest of bars and a very small dining room but in recent years it has been opened out and there is more room than there used to be. Up to five real ales are usually available. Canalside seating outside is pleasant on summer days. Diners are advised to book a table in advance.
⌂ ☺ ◑ ● P ⊟ (37,37E) ☺ 🤟

White Bear Hotel 🅻
Wheelock Street, CW10 9AG
🌣 11-11 (midnight Fri & Sat); 12-10.30 Sun
☎ (01606) 837666 ⊕ thewhitebearmiddlewich.co.uk
4 changing beers (sourced locally) 🅗
Free house dating from 1625, with a wide rotating range of four real ales and a traditional cider on handpump, all at reasonable prices. The interior is tastefully divided into distinctive seating areas, with comfortable furniture. Musical events catering for all tastes are held on a regular basis. The walls are adorned with interesting stone artefacts. All major sporting events are screened.
⌂ ☺ ⊨ ◑ ● P ⊟ (37) ☺ 🤟

Mobberley

Bull's Head 🅛 ⊘
Mill Lane, WA16 7HX
⊘ 12-10.30 (midnight Fri & Sat) ☎ (01565) 873395
⊕ thebullsheadpub.co.uk
Weetwood Cheshire Cat; 7 changing beers (sourced regionally) Ⓗ
Excellent country inn which bills itself as 'a real pub – local and proud' with cobbles outside, three open fires, stone floors, candlelit tables, low beams, exposed brick and an old back-to-back fireplace. Food and ale are often sourced locally, with the house brew supplied by Weetwood. Each beer has tasting notes and tasters are available in tiny pots.
🌣🕸🕭🕩♿♣P🚍(88)🐾🐱📶

Moulton

Lion Hotel 🅛
74 Main Road, CW9 8PB
⊘ 5-11 (midnight Fri); 2-midnight Sat; 2-11 Sun
☎ (01606) 606049
Timothy Taylor Landlord; Wychwood Hobgoblin; 3 changing beers (sourced locally; often Cheshire Brewhouse, RedWillow, Tatton) Ⓗ
An award for local CAMRA Pub of the Year in 2015 is a reflection of the efforts the licensee has made to put this family pub at the heart of the community. Located in the centre of the village, five handpumps dispense quality ales from mainly local breweries. Quiz nights and themed music events are popular. A complimentary cheeseboard is offered on Friday evenings. Two outside seating areas enable customers to take advantage of the warm summer months. 🌣🕸♣♥P🚍🐾📶

Nantwich

Black Lion 🅛
29 Welsh Row, CW5 5ED (opp Cheshire Cat)
⊘ 12-3 (not Mon), 5-11; 12-11 Sat; 12-10.30 Sun
☎ (01270) 628711 ⊕ blacklion-nantwich.co.uk
Weetwood Best Bitter, Cheshire Cat, Old Dog Bitter; 3 changing beers (sourced regionally) Ⓗ
Black-and-white fronted inn dating from the 17th century, standing among the historic buildings of Welsh Row. The beautiful plaster and oak-beamed interior boasts the requisite bowed walls and creaking floorboards. An open fire welcomes you into an open-plan area which in the past would have been three separate rooms. There is a dining area upstairs and a covered beer garden to the side leading to an additional small room with a pot-bellied stove for heating. Local beers are from Weetwood. Q🕸🕩🚲♣🚍(84)🐾📶

Crown 🅛
High Street, CW5 5AS (on High Street between NatWest and Café Nero)
⊘ 10-midnight (11 Mon & Tue); 11.30 Wed & Thu)
☎ (01270) 625283 ⊕ crownhotelnantwich.com
Salopian Shropshire Gold; 3 changing beers (sourced regionally) Ⓗ
Grade II-listed building, with a fascinating history dating from its rebuild in 1585, following its destruction in the Great Fire of Nantwich. It is full of exposed beams, wattle and daub, and the strangest uneven bespoke flooring to be found in Cheshire. The bar is open to non-residents and offers a selection of four real ales, including one regular from the Salopian Brewery, plus three rotating guest ales. 🌣🛏🕩♿🚲P🚍(84)🐾📶

No Mans Heath

Wheatsheaf
Chester Road, SY14 8DY (just off A41, 4 miles N of Whitchurch)
⊘ 12-2.30, 5.15-11 (midnight Fri & Sat); 12-3, 5.15-11 Sun; closed Mon ☎ (01948) 820337 ⊕ pubwheatsheaf.co.uk
Facer's North Star Porter, Sunny Bitter; 1 changing beer Ⓗ
An 18th-century free house handy for walkers on the Sandstone Trail and cyclists on the Cheshire Cycleway. Food is largely home-made with vegetarian, vegan and gluten-free options. Allergies can often be catered for. This is a dining pub but customers just wanting a drink are equally welcome. There are gardens to the side and rear. North Star Porter is suitable for vegans, and gluten-free bottled beers are available. Dogs are permitted outside food service times.
🕸🕩♿♣P🚍(41,41A)

Northwich

Penny Black 🅛 ⊘
110 Witton Street, CW9 5AB
⊘ 8am-midnight (1am Fri & Sat) ☎ (01606) 42029
Greene King Abbot; Ruddles Best Bitter; Sharp's Doom Bar; 9 changing beers (sourced nationally; often Peerless, Phoenix, Weetwood) Ⓗ
Dating from 1914 and once a post office, the building is Grade II-listed and has been transformed into a large and mainly open-plan pub. Cheshire-brewed beers are often to be found on the bar in this former local CAMRA Pub of the Year, and at least one beer will be dark – a mild, stout or porter. The car park is behind the building off Meadow Street immediately after the Royal Mail sorting office.
Q🌣🕸🕩♿🚲♥P🚍(2,46,289)📶

Penketh

Ferry Tavern
Station Road, WA5 2UJ (near yacht marina)
⊘ 12-3 (not Mon), 5.30-11; 12-3, 5.30-midnight Fri; 12-midnight Sat; 12-10.30 Sun ☎ (01925) 791117
⊕ theferrytavern.com
Jennings Cumberland Ale; 5 changing beers (sourced nationally) Ⓗ
One of Warrington's oldest pubs, it has arguably the best setting in the town, nestling on its own island between the River Mersey and the St Helens Canal on the Transpennine Trail, attracting hikers, ramblers, cyclists and horse riders. The Ferry is light and airy in the summer with views over the river from the large beer garden and welcoming in the winter with a roaring stove fire.
🌣🕸♿P🚍(32)🐾📶

Poynton

Cask Tavern 🍺 ⊘
42 Park Lane, SK12 1RE
⊘ 4-11; 12-midnight Fri & Sat; 12-10.30 Sun
☎ (01625) 875157 ⊕ casktavern.co.uk
Bollington Long Hop, Best, Dinner Ale; 2 changing beers (sourced regionally) Ⓗ
One of three Bollington Brewery taps in Cheshire, showcasing its own range of beers and a couple of guests. A mecca for real ale drinkers, national brands are conspicuous by their absence. It also features a locally brewed craft lager – Moravka. The

single-roomed pub has comfortable seating areas including two outside and an upstairs area used for local group meetings. Q❀♿♣●🚌🐾📶

Runcorn

Lion Hotel

100 Greenway Road, WA7 5AG (5 mins walk from station, 10 mins from old town)
4-11 (midnight Thu); 2-midnight Fri & Sat; 12-11 Sun
☎ (01928) 574129
2 changing beers H
Now in its fourth year in the Guide, this old Greenalls boozer shows what can be done to bring pubs up to modern-day standards and give them a new lease of life. What was once a two-roomed keg pub is now a bright, airy place with a horseshoe bar with four handpumps. Beers change regularly. Quiz night is Sunday. ≈🚌(10)

Norton Arms

125-127 Main Street, WA7 2AD
12-11 (midnight Fri & Sat) ☎ (01928) 567642
thenortonarms.co.uk
4 changing beers (sourced nationally) H
A two-roomed, Grade II-listed, oak-beamed venue in the centre of Halton village. Although dominated by football on three screens, this pub is still a nice find. It can get busy at weekends. There are four handpumps and third-pint taster glasses are available. The food is sourced locally. Due to the age of the building, disabled access is difficult. Entertainment includes quiz nights, live music and open mic nights. ❀♿♣P🚌🐾📶

Prospect L

70 Weston Road, WA7 4LD
12-11; 12-10.30 Sun ☎ (01928) 561280
folkattheprospect.co.uk
Adnams Broadside; Timothy Taylor Landlord; 2 changing beers H
This traditional two-roomed pub on the outskirts of Weston village has three ale handpumps and one for cider. The lounge is decorated with local memorabilia. The pub prides itself on sourcing local produce for meals and commits to local businesses whenever possible. It is home to a busy folk club. Situated high above the rivers Mersey and Weaver, it has views reaching from Liverpool to North Wales. Winner of numerous awards including local CAMRA Pub of the Year 2015.
❀♿♣●P🚌(3A,3B,3C)🐾

Sandbach

Old Hall L

High Street, CW11 1AL (opp St Mary's Church)
11.30-11; 12-10.30 Sun ☎ (01270) 758170
oldhall-sandbach.co.uk
House beer (by Phoenix); 5 changing beers (sourced nationally) H
Grade I-listed building dating from 1656. It was allowed to decay by previous owners but brought back to life by Brunning & Price, reopening in 2011. The main entrance leads to a centrally arranged bar to the right. On the left is a wonderful Jacobean carved fireplace, one of two in the pub. Up to six real ales are available. Q❀♿P🚌🐾

Stockton Heath

Costello's Bar L

23 Walton Road, WA4 6NJ
12-11 (midnight Fri & Sat); 12-10.30 Sun
☎ (01925) 600910 costellosbar.co.uk
Dunham Massey Big Tree Bitter; Lymm Bridgewater Blonde; 5 changing beers (sourced locally; often Dunham Massey, Lymm) H
Friendly, welcoming, well-maintained real ale bar owned and run by Dunham Massey Brewing. With a modern, comfortable interior, it has seven handpumps for cask ale, five on rotation and two mainstays, as well as real cider. There is always at least one dark beer, one mild and one strong ale. All cask ale is provided by Dunham Massey and Lymm brewers. Q❀♿♣●🚌🐾📶

Red Lion ✔

60 London Road, WA4 6HN
11-11; 12-1am Fri & Sat; 12-11 Sun ☎ (01925) 861041
Thwaites Nutty Black, Original, Wainwright, Lancaster Bomber; 1 changing beer (sourced nationally) H
A 200-year-old Georgian coaching inn with many rooms, set in the centre of Stockton Heath. It has four permanent Thwaites ales and one rotating guest. It is the proud owner of a floodlit bowling green to the rear and home to several sports teams. The Bridgewater Canal is nearby.
Q❀♣🚌🐾

Thelwall

Little Manor L

Bell Lane, WA4 2SX
10.30-11; 10.30-10.30 Sun ☎ (01925) 212070
littlemanor-thelwall.co.uk
Coach House Cromwells Best Bitter; Tatton Blonde; house beer (by Phoenix); 5 changing beers (sourced locally) H
A large upmarket food-based pub with an interesting and changing range of local cask beers. The building is tastefully furnished and has attractive garden areas for dining alfresco in summer. The staff are efficient, knowledgeable and helpful. The building has graced Thelwall since 1660 and the pub sign uses the crest of the Percival family, the original owners. A range of country walks is based around the pub – ask at the bar for details. Q❀♿♣P🚌(5,6)🐾📶

Warrington

Looking Glass L ✔

41-43 Buttermarket Street, WA1 2LY
8am-midnight (1am Fri & Sat) ☎ (01925) 405030
Greene King Abbot; Ruddles Best Bitter; Theakston Old Peculier; house beer (by Coach House); 5 changing beers (sourced nationally; often Kelham Island, Peerless, Thornbridge) H
On the edge of the town centre and originally converted from a cinema, this Wetherspoon is on two levels with a small bar upstairs. You will always find an interesting selection of guest ales, chosen by the real ale enthusiast manager. Jabberwocky is brewed specially for the pub by local brewery Coach House.
Q❀♿≈(Central)●🚌📶

Lower Angel L

27 Buttermarket Street, WA1 2LY (in pedestrianised town centre)

🌣 11-11 (midnight Fri); 11-12.30am Sat; 12-10 Sun
☎ (01925) 653326
Dunham Massey Dunham Dark; Weetwood Bitter; 6 changing beers (sourced nationally) ⊞
A step back in time in the traffic-free area of the town centre's heart, with a traditional vault and lounge layout and rear beer garden. Memorabilia from the former Walkers Brewery and stained-glass windows remain. The six changing beers are mainly from independent breweries. Real cider is available in spring and summer. There are plans to relaunch the mothballed brewery behind the pub in the future. ❀≷(Central)●🖳😺🛜

Tavern 🗓
25 Church Street, WA1 2SS
🌣 12 (4 Mon & Tue; 3 Wed & Thu)-midnight ☎ 07747 668817
4T's Pale Ale; 7 changing beers (sourced nationally) ⊞
A friendly single-roomed pub featuring a regular from 4T's and up to seven cask ales, all of which are colour-coded by beer style. Two real cider/ perries are added in summer. Sporting events including rugby and football feature on multiple TV screens. A covered rear area also has TV screens and plentiful seating. The pub gets very busy when Rugby League matches are being shown or when Warrington Wolves are at home.
❀≷(Central)♣●🖳😺🛜

Widnes

Eight Towers 🍷 🗓
Weates Close, WA8 3RH
🌣 11-11 (midnight Fri & Sat) ☎ (0151) 424 8063
Banks's Sunbeam; Ringwood Boondoggle; Wychwood Hobgoblin Gold, Hobgoblin; 2 changing beers ⊞
A first time in the Guide for this spacious, open-plan Marston's pub on the outskirts of Widnes, offering beers from the Marston's group. Family-friendly with a large beer garden and heated patio area, Sky Sports TV is the main attraction. The pub gets its name from the cooling towers of Fiddler's Ferry energy plant, situated a mile away.
🕭❀🕪P🖳(27)

Willey Moor Lock

Willey Moor Lock Tavern
Tarporley Road, SY13 4HF
🌣 12-2.30, 6-11 (10.30 Sun) ☎ (01948) 663274
🌐 willeymoorlock.co.uk
6 changing beers (sourced nationally) ⊞
This family-run free house is a former lock-keeper's cottage, reached from the car park by a footbridge over the Llangollen Canal. The pub is popular with boaters and walkers on the Sandstone Trail, especially in summer. Good-value meals are served lunchtimes and evenings. Three changing beers increase to six in summer, with at least one from a local micro. Outside seating is available by the canal and in the attractive beer garden. There is a campsite close by. Q🕭❀🕪♠P😺🛜

Wilmslow

Coach & Four 🗓 🗓
69-71 Alderley Road, SK9 1PA
🌣 11.30-11 (midnight Thu-Sat); 12-11 Sun
☎ (01625) 525046 🌐 thecoachandfour.co.uk
Hydes Original; 7 changing beers (sourced locally; often Hydes) ⊞

Large, comfortable old coaching house close to the centre of Wilmslow catering to a mixed clientele. The spacious single room is divided into secluded alcoves, with a space for dining. Food is served all day in the restaurant and bar area. Three Hydes and Beer Studio beers are on handpump plus up to two rotating guests and a real cider. Quiz nights, music and comedy feature as well as charity and community events and an annual beer festival. A covered and heated patio is available for smokers. Lodge-style accommodation is attached.
🕭❀🚐🕪🕭≷●P🖳(88,130)🛜

Old Dancer 🍷 🗓
16 Grove Street, SK9 1DR (on main pedestrianised shopping street)
🌣 12-midnight (1am Fri & Sat) ☎ (01625) 530775
🌐 theolddancer.co.uk
5 changing beers (sourced locally) ⊞
Lively café-bar furnished mainly with simple wooden tables set on boarded floors; the walls are decorated with striking handpainted murals with a dance theme. Six handpumps serve an interesting range of beers including LocAles plus a cask cider. Tea, coffee and food are available until 10pm. There are weekly live music, film and quiz nights and monthly Spanish conversation, writers group, book club and science nights.
🕭❀🕪🕭≷♠●🖳😺🛜

Winsford

No. 4 Bar
Over Square, CW7 2LS (on roundabout at S end of Delamere St)
🌣 4-11; 12-midnight Fri & Sat; 12-11 Sun ☎ (01606) 550835
🌐 no4pub.com
4 changing beers (sourced regionally) ⊞
A unique bar in Winsford, No. 4 prides itself on its four cask beers from different regional and microbreweries throughout the country. Victorian awnings to the front provide shelter over a pavement area that is popular all year. An upstairs seating area provides a quieter environment when there is live music downstairs (most weekends). Complimentary bar snacks for both customers and dogs are standard. Quality beer, friendly staff and good music help to create a welcoming atmosphere. ❀🕭(31)😺🛜

Queen's Arms 🗓
Dene Drive, CW7 1AT (opp Winsford Cross shopping centre)
🌣 8am-midnight (1am Fri & Sat); 9am-11 Sun
☎ (01606) 595350
Greene King Abbot; Ruddles Best Bitter; 4 changing beers (sourced regionally) ⊞
Open-plan Wetherspoon pub in Winsford town centre, close to the bus stop and taxi rank. The pub has a large number of local regulars and can get very busy. There are muted TV screens at both ends, and a patio area with decking at the front which is popular in summer. In addition to the Wetherspoon national beer festivals, Queen's hosts monthly Meet the Brewer sessions and an annual Battle of the Brewers challenge. A good range of ever-changing guest beers is on offer, both local and national. Q🕭❀🕪🕭≷●P🖳(31,31A,37)🛜

CORNWALL

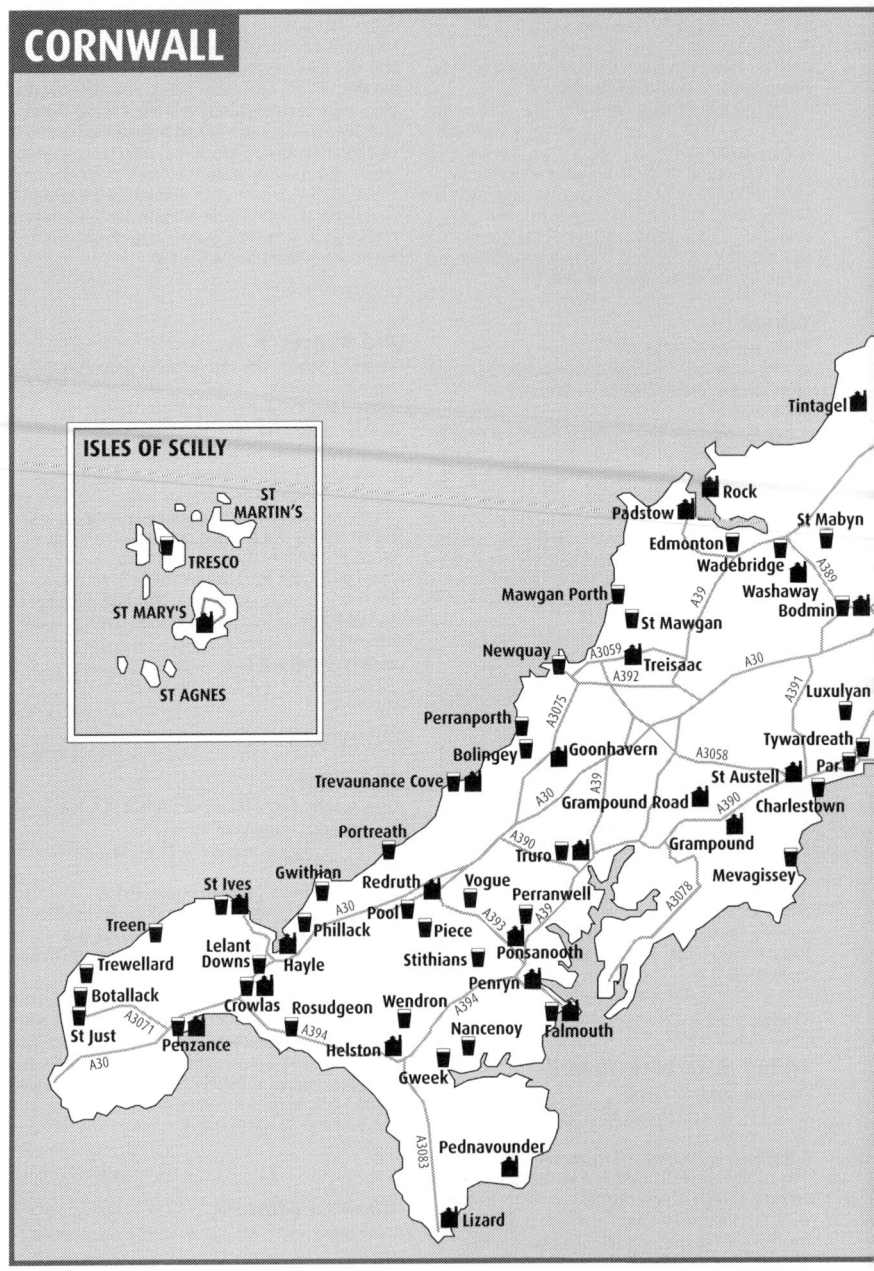

ISLES OF SCILLY

ST MARTIN'S

TRESCO

ST MARY'S

ST AGNES

Tintagel

Rock

Padstow
St Mabyn
Edmonton
Wadebridge
Washaway
Mawgan Porth
Bodmin
St Mawgan

Newquay
Treisaac
Luxulyan
Perranporth
Tywardreath
Bolingey
Goonhavern
Par
Trevaunance Cove
St Austell
Portreath
Grampound Road
Charlestown
Truro
Grampound
Gwithian
Redruth
Vogue
Mevagissey
St Ives
Perranwell
Treen
Pool
Piece
Phillack
Ponsanooth
Penryn
Trewellard
Lelant
Downs
Hayle
Stithians
Botallack
Crowlas
Rosudgeon
Wendron
Falmouth
St Just
Penzance
Nancenoy
Helston
Gweek
Pednavounder
Lizard

Altarnun

Rising Sun ⬡

PL15 7SN (off A30, 2 miles NW of Five Lanes village)
SX215825

☼ 12-2.30, 5.30-11; 12-11 Sat; 12-10.30 Sun
☎ (01566) 86636 ⊕ therisingsuninn.co.uk

**Penpont St Nonna's, Shipwreck Coast; Skinner's
Lushingtons; 2 changing beers (sourced regionally)** Ⓗ
A pub for 150 years, this characterful building on
the outskirts of Altarnun is a thriving community
pub and tap for nearby Penpont Brewery. The
interior is cosy and warm with beamed ceilings, an
open fireplace, and antique guns and various
pictures on the walls. Deceptively spacious, the
pub offers ample seating in the bar, two small
annexes for pool and drinkers, and a separate
restaurant. There is a large patio and grassed area
for games. Food is made with locally sourced
ingredients. Q⟲❄⎈◑⭓&A♣♠P⬚❀🛜

Blisland

Blisland Inn ⬡
The Green, PL30 4JF (off A30 NE of Bodmin) SX100732
☼ 11.30-11; 12-10.30 Sun ☎ (01208) 850739

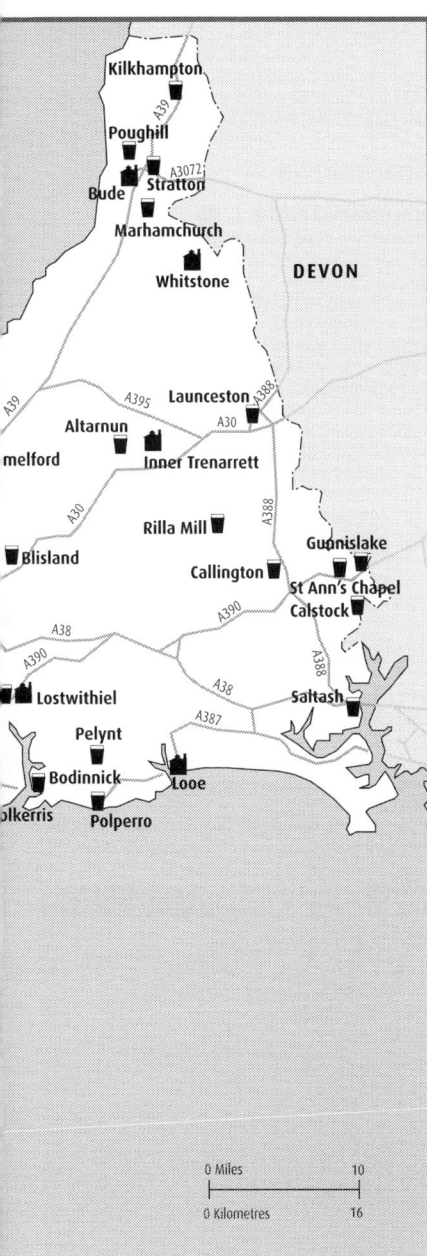

Bodinnick

Old Ferry Inn
PL23 1LX

✪ 10-midnight ☎ (01726) 870237 ⊕ oldferryinn.co.uk

Sharp's Cornish Coaster, Original; 2 changing beers (sourced locally; often Sharp's, Tintagel) ⊞

Unspoilt 400-year-old pub in a scenic village location, overlooking the Fowey River and next to Bodinnick Ferry. The lounge has a slate floor and is full of nautical artefacts and memorabilia, and antique pictures of the area. A separate family room has one wall of the bedrock into which the inn is built, while the upstairs terrace and dining room afford great views over the river. Parking is up the hill through an archway. Draught cider is from Haye Farm. Q ⏰ ✿ 🛏 🜋 ◑ ⚓ ♣ ➔ ⛁ (24) ✿ 🗢

Bodmin

Chapel an Gansblydhen ⌊ ✪
Fore Street, PL31 2HR (near top of main street)

✪ 8am-midnight; 8am-10.30 Sun ☎ (01208) 261730

Greene King Abbot; Ruddles Best Bitter; Sharp's Doom Bar; 4 changing beers (often Cornish Crown, Harbour, Tintagel) ⊞

This busy town-centre pub has been beautifully converted from a former Methodist chapel, with many original features restored or retained. Four real ales are on offer, mostly from Cornish microbreweries, with two draught ciders also available. The pub supports the CAMRA pub guide that covers the Bodmin district, and outings to local breweries are held from time to time. Two beer festivals and a real cider festival are held annually, and a popular quiz night each Sunday.
Q ⏰ ✿ ◑ 🜋 ♣ ➔ ⛁ (11A,27) 🗢

Hole in the Wall ❢ ⌊ ✪
16 Crockwell Street, PL31 2DS (entrance from town car park)

✪ 12-11; 12-10.30 Sun ☎ (01208) 72397

Butcombe Bitter; Sharp's Doom Bar; Skinner's Porthleven; 1 changing beer (sourced nationally) ⊞

Popular locals' pub built in the 18th century as a debtors' prison. The building can be accessed direct from the public car park or through a secluded, leafy garden containing its own hop bine, stream and stuffed lion. The single bar, which is subdivided by archways, displays a large and eclectic collection of antiques and military memorabilia, while a comfortable adjacent conservatory houses the TV. Upstairs is a separate function room. Cornwall CAMRA Pub of the Year 2015.
Q ⏰ ✿ ⚅ 🜋 ♣ ➔ ⛁ (11A,27) ✿ 🗢

Bolingey

Bolingey Inn ⌊ ✪
Penwartha Road, TR6 0DH (near B3284) SW763532

✪ 11-midnight; 12-11 Sun ☎ (01872) 571626

Sharp's Doom Bar; 3 changing beers (sourced regionally) ⊞

Warm and cosy pub delightfully located in a small village within reasonable walking distance of Perranporth and its hotels, caravan sites and sandy beach. The bar is wood-floored with low ceilings and an open fire. The carpeted L-shaped lounge is furnished with tables set for dining – food is home-cooked using local produce. Four beers are offered throughout the year, boosted by occasional beer festivals. You will be welcomed by the locals, who love to chat. Q ✿ ◑ 🜋 ♣ P ✿ 🗢

---

6 changing beers ⊞ / Ⓖ

Friendly rural community pub by the village green and a former CAMRA National Pub of the Year, this establishment retains its reputation as a real ale centre of excellence on the edge of Bodmin Moor. It has served over 3,000 different real ales and usually has six or seven beers available, at least two brewed locally. Frequently changing draught ciders include more unusual varieties. Freshly-prepared food uses locally sourced produce (book ahead). Popular with walkers and cyclists, well-behaved children and dogs are welcome too.
Q ⏰ ✿ ◑ ♣ ➔ 🖫 ✿

Botallack

Queen's Arms �revL

Botallack, TR19 7QG (just off Lands End-St Ives road, near St Just)
✪ 12-11 ☎ (01736) 788318 ⏚ queensarms-botallack.co.uk
Sharp's Doom Bar; Skinner's Heligan Honey; 2 changing beers (sourced locally; often Dynamite Valley, Tintagel) Ⓗ
Popular with coast path walkers, this charming family-friendly free house offers a warm welcome to all. Situated in the heart of tin mining country, its cosy single bar interior features an open fire and several distinct drinking and dining areas, with a family room at the rear. Its homely decor depicts old local mining scenes. Up to four ales are offered, usually from Cornish breweries. Imaginative meals served daily. A popular August beer festival is held annually in the rear beer garden.
Q⏝⏣⏚◑▲⏛P⏟(10,300)⏦☀

Callington

Bull's Head

38 Fore Street, PL17 7AQ
✪ 10-midnight; 11-11 Sun ☎ (01579) 383387
Sharp's Doom Bar; 2 changing beers (sourced locally; often Dartmoor, St Austell) Ⓗ
Friendly and sociable locals' drinking house dating from the 15th century. The comfortable lounge has a vast stone fireplace, oak beams, latticed windows and a profusion of brass. The pub supports darts teams and there is live music every Friday. Meals are to a traditional pub food format and home cooked – a barbecue may be held outside in the summer months. Occasional beer festivals are hosted. There is disabled access but no facilities. Parking is limited.
⏝⏣◑⏛P⏟(12,79,76)⏦☀

Calstock

Tamar Inn

The Quay, PL18 9QA SX436686
✪ 12-midnight; 12-2.30, 5-midnight Mon-Thu winter
☎ (01822) 832487
Sharp's Doom Bar; 4 changing beers (sourced regionally; often Exeter, Tintagel) Ⓗ
Split-level village pub beside the River Tamar, built in granite and other materials. The beamed interior is divided into distinct drinking areas with well-worn floorboards and slate flagstones underfoot, and decorated with a few framed paintings. A small bookshelf provides an additional service for the locals. The rear bar is airy and leads to the courtyard. Beers are usually from Cornwall and Devon, the cider is Westons Old Rosie. Live entertainment plays on Friday or Saturday evenings. ⏝⏣◑▲⇌⏛⏟(79)⏦

Camelford

Masons Arms

11 Market Place, PL32 9PB (on A39)
✪ 11-midnight ☎ (01840) 213309
St Austell Cornish Best Bitter, Tribute, Proper Job Ⓗ
Unpretentious two-room town-centre pub with open stone walls and low beamed ceilings. The public bar has a wood and tile floor, the separate lounge flagstones, and both are adorned with an eclectic collection of artefacts including old toys, long-vanished domestic products, bottles,

banknotes and sheet music. The garden overlooks an early stage of the River Camel. Home-cooked meals include a selection of fresh fish. The beer choice reduces to two in winter. A proper locals' pub. Q⏝⏣◑▲⏛⏟(55,584,595)⏦☀

Charlestown

Harbourside Inn ⏕L ✓

Charlestown Road, PL25 3NJ (on harbour front)
✪ 11-11 (midnight Fri & Sat); 12-11 Sun ☎ (01726) 68051
⏚ pierhousehotel.com
Draught Bass; St Austell Tribute; Sharp's Doom Bar; Skinner's Betty Stogs; 2 changing beers (sourced locally; often Skinner's) Ⓗ
Harbourside watering-hole popular with film crews on location at this historic port, drawn by the choice of ales available. A former waterfront warehouse, its expansive glass frontage affords views of the tall ships moored nearby. A lively, sports-oriented pub, its single-bar split-level interior features exposed stonework with mixed slate and wood flooring, and wooden furnishings throughout. All popular sporting events are screened, and there is live music Saturday evenings. One of the changing ales is normally from Skinner's Brewery. ⏣⇌◑⏟(24,25)☀

Crowlas

Star Inn ⏕L

TR20 8DX (on A30, 3 miles E of Penzance)
✪ 11.30-11; 12-10.30 Sun ☎ (01736) 740375
Penzance Mild, Crowlas Bitter, Potion No 9, Brisons Bitter; 2 changing beers (sourced nationally; often Coastal) Ⓗ
Roadside free house and former Cornwall CAMRA Pub of the Year, home to the Penzance Brewery.

REAL ALE BREWERIES

Ales of Scilly St Mary's
Atlantic Treisaac
Black Flag Goonhavern
Black Rock Falmouth
Blue Anchor ⚑ Helston
Bude Bude
Castle Lostwithiel
Coastal Redruth
Cornish Chough Lizard
Cornish Crown Penzance
Driftwood ⚑ Trevaunance Cove
Dynamite Valley Ponsanooth (NEW)
Fish Key Looe (NEW)
Granite Rock Penryn
Harbour Bodmin
Keltek Redruth
Leafy Hollow Washaway (NEW)
Lizard Pednavounder
Longhill Whitstone
Padstow Padstow
Paradise ⚑ Hayle
Penpont Inner Trenarrett
Penzance ⚑ Crowlas
Rebel Penryn
Sharp's Rock
Skinner's Truro
St Austell St Austell
St Ives St Ives (NEW)
Tintagel Tintagel
Tremethick Grampound (NEW)
Wooden Hand Grampound Road

The long U-shaped bar features real ales from the pub's own brewhouse and one or two from other microbreweries. There is a pool table to the right, a comfy raised seating area, a cosy lounge area with leather sofas and chairs, and an adjacent meeting room. This is essentially a beer-drinkers' local where conversation is the main entertainment, with no noisy machines to distract. Q✿▲♣♥P🖵(17,18,404)♣

Edmonton

Quarryman Inn 🄻
Edmonton, PL27 7JA (just off A39 near Royal Cornwall showground)
✿ 12-11; 12-10.30 Sun ☎ (01208) 816444
🌐 thequarryman.co.uk
Otter Bitter; Skinner's Lushingtons; 2 changing beers (sourced locally; often Padstow) 🄷
Near the county showground, a diversion to this popular pub rewards the effort. A comfortable family-friendly free house, it is set in an old schoolhouse and quarrymen's housing complex. Its traditional interior divides into a slate-floored public bar, a carpeted lounge and a separate dining area. Eclectic decor includes local art. The beer menu always features one each from Otter and Skinner's breweries, which may vary. Excellent cuisine is made with locally sourced produce. Dogs are allowed in the bar. Mobile phones are prohibited here. Q☎✿⑩▲♣P🖵(11A,94)♣ 🛜

Falmouth

'Front 🄻
Custom House Quay, TR11 3JT
✿ 11-11 (midnight Fri & Sat); 11-10.30 Sun ☎ 07977 813494
Sharp's Special 🄷**; 9 changing beers (sourced regionally; often Atlantic, Skinner's, Tintagel)** 🄷/🄶
A warm welcome awaits at this quayside cellar-style bar. Friendly, knowledgeable staff are on hand to serve from 14 handpumps arranged along the bar, 10 dedicated to real ales and four to ciders. Cornish breweries are well represented, and there are regular brewery showcase sessions which can be local or regional. A popular Sunday quiz is hosted and other evening entertainment. No food is available but you may bring your own. The pub offers a 10 per cent discount on real ales and ciders before 6pm. Q☎✿&≠●♣

Boathouse 🄻
Trevethan Hill, TR11 2AG (top of High St)
✿ 12-11 (midnight Thu-Sat) ☎ (01326) 315425
4 changing beers (often Black Rock, Rebel, Skinner's) 🄷
Multi-level, locally-oriented pub on the corner of two steep hills on the edge of the town centre. Bare wooden floors, a decked balcony and porthole windows give the impression of being on board a boat, with fine views over Falmouth inner harbour. The real ales vary frequently, at least two being locally brewed. An interesting freshly cooked food menu features as much locally sourced produce as possible (booking advised for Sunday lunch). Live entertainment is hosted most weekends.
☎✿⑩♣●🖵♣

Seven Stars ★ 🄻
The Moor, TR11 3QA
✿ 11-11; 12-10.30 Sun ☎ (01326) 312111

Draught Bass; Sharp's Special; Skinner's Porthleven; 1 changing beer (sourced locally) 🄶
Grade II-listed and on CAMRA's National Inventory of Historic Pub Interiors, the pub's taproom at the front links via a corridor with the original bottle and jug hatch to a snug at the rear. Beers are drawn straight from the cask. Popular with locals, conversation is the entertainment. No food is available but you may consume your own on the benches outside. Q✿♣●🖵♣

Gunnislake

Rising Sun Inn
Calstock Road, PL18 9BX (off A390) SX432711
✿ 12-11 (midnight Fri & Sat) ☎ (01822) 832201
6 changing beers (sourced regionally) 🄷
Friendly, oak-beamed country inn dating from the 17th century, lying in a conservation area in a rural setting off the beaten track. It has much charm and character, with exposed stone walls and wooden beams home to an extensive display of chinaware. A good choice of up to six ever-changing real ales is served, normally from Cornish or other West Country breweries. The beautiful terraced garden affords views of the Tamar Valley. Food is available daily except Sunday evenings. A true community pub. Q☎✿⑩▶≠♣●P🖵(79)♣ 🛜

Gweek

Black Swan ✅
TR12 6TU
✿ 11-11.30 (midnight Fri & Sat); 12-11.30 Sun ☎ (01326) 221502 🌐 blackswangweek.co.uk
St Austell Tribute; Sharp's Doom Bar, Atlantic; Skinner's Lushingtons; 2 changing beers (sourced nationally; often Draught Bass) 🄷
Welcoming and lively pub in the heart of Gweek village. The large L-shaped bar, with wooden floor and wooden and exposed stone walls, is warmed by a stove in winter. To the left and up some steps is a slate-floored dining room enjoying views to the harbour. The rightward end of the spacious bar room hosts a pool table. Entry from the car park is down flights of steps, with more level access gained from the main road.
☎✿⑩▶♣P🖵(35)♣ 🛜

Gwithian

Red River Inn 🄻
1 Prosper Hill, TR27 5BW
✿ 12-11 summer; 12-2, 5.30-11; 12-11 Sat & Sun; closed Mon winter ☎ (01736) 753223 🌐 red-river-inn.com
5 changing beers (sourced locally; often Sharp's, Skinner's) 🄷
Named after the nearby river and close to the dunes of Hayle Towans, this community-oriented, family-friendly free house is well worth a visit. Its pleasant single-bar interior is dominated by wood furnishings, and accommodates both drinking and dining; a wood-burning stove adds winter warmth. A quiet, relaxing ambience allows conversation to thrive. Up to five ales are available, three often from Cornish breweries. Meals using local produce are served daily. Entertainment includes live music on Saturday evenings. The Easter beer festival is always popular. ☎✿⑩▶&▲♣P🖵(57,515)♣ 🛜

Kilkhampton

New Inn

EX23 9QN

✪ 11-11 ☎ (01288) 321488 ⊕ newinncornwall.com

Dartmoor Legend; Sharp's Original; 1 changing beer (sourced locally) Ⓗ

Spacious 15th-century village pub on three levels – a quiet front bar where conversation dominates, a busy middle bar with dartboard and TV, and an old skittle alley deep in the back. The interior makes extensive use of recycled materials and is furnished with wooden tables, settles and other pew-style seating. The bar itself is constructed of old bricks and timber beams with a polished wooden top. A guest beer from a local brewery is added in summer; cider sources vary.

Q ⚲ ⊛ 🛏 🕪 🅰 ♣ ♠ P 🖵 (219,319) 🛜

Launceston

Bell Inn

1 Tower Street, PL15 8BQ

✪ 12-11 (10.30 Sun) summer; 4 (12 Fri & Sat)-11; 12-4 Sun winter ☎ (01566) 779970

6 changing beers Ⓗ

Cosy 14th-century town pub originally built to house stonemasons erecting the nearby church. Conversation rules at this locals' pub, with a varied range of mostly local beers and two ciders, although the selection may be reduced out of season. A separate family room, available for local groups to use, has some ancient frescoes uncovered when previous owners stripped away decades of modernisation. Pub games include chess and other board games. Food is limited to a pasty or pork pie. Q ⚲ ⊛ 🛏 🕹 ♣ ♠ 🖵 (6,12,76) 🛜

Lelant Downs

Watermill Inn Ⓛ

Old Coach Road, TR27 6LQ (off A3074, on secondary St Ives road)

✪ 12-11 ☎ (01736) 757912 ⊕ watermillincornwall.co.uk

Sharp's Doom Bar; Skinner's Betty Stogs; 2 changing beers Ⓗ

In attractive surroundings near Lelant Saltings station, this former 18th-century mill house is now a family-friendly two-storey free house. The comfortable traditional-style single bar incorporates part of the original watermill complete with millstones, and is divided into drinking and dining areas. Up to four real ales and a creative menu are served. A stylish evening-only restaurant is upstairs in the former mill loft. Annual June and November beer festivals are staged in the beer garden. Live music plays on Friday nights.

Q ⚲ ⊛ 🕪 ⇌ P 🖵 (14,17) 🛜

Lostwithiel

Globe Inn Ⓛ

3 North Street, PL22 0EG (near railway station, town side of river bridge)

✪ 12-11 (midnight Fri & Sat) ☎ (01208) 872501 ⊕ globeinn.com

Sharp's Original; Skinner's Betty Stogs; 1 changing beer (sourced regionally; often Exmoor) Ⓗ

Nestling in the streets of an old stannary town near the railway station, this cosy 13th-century free house is definitely worth visiting. Its rather rambling interior accommodates a single bar with several drinking and dining areas, to the rear an intimate stylish restaurant, and a sheltered suntrap patio. The changing beer is generally from a regional microbrewery and varies frequently. An imaginative cuisine prepared from local seasonal produce features daily specials including game. All accommodation is en suite.

Q ⚲ ⊛ 🛏 🕪 🅰 ⇌ ♠ 🛏 🐾 🛜

Luxulyan

King's Arms ✔

Bridges, PL30 5EF SX048580

✪ 11-11 (midnight Fri & Sat) ☎ (01726) 850202

St Austell Trelawny, Tribute, Proper Job, HSD; 1 changing beer (sourced locally; often St Austell) Ⓗ

Typical Cornish granite community pub, locally known as Bridges, offering a friendly welcome to both locals and visitors. Its single large L-shaped room hosts both drinking and dining – the pub offers Sunday roasts and a take-away service. More unusual services include a cashpoint and a defibrillator. The King's can be reached via the beautiful Luxulyan Valley, which still shows many remnants of the area's industrial past. The nearby railway station is on the local Rail Ale Trail.

⚲ ⊛ 🕪 🕹 🅰 ⇌ ♣ P 🖵 (101) 🐾 🛜

Marhamchurch

Buller's Arms Hotel

Helebridge Road, EX23 0HB (off A39 south of Bude)

✪ 12-11 summer; 12-2 (11 Fri-Sun); closed Mon winter ☎ (01288) 361277 ⊕ thebullersarmshotel.com

Greene King Abbot; St Austell Cornish Best Bitter; Sharp's Atlantic; Tintagel Arthur's Ale; house beer (by Tintagel); 1 changing beer (sourced locally; often Longhill) Ⓗ

Large, community-oriented village pub/hotel with a spacious beamed and slate-flagged bar room. Decorative bric-a-brac includes buffalo horns and a stuffed fox and badger at one end of the room; the other end is home to a dartboard, pool table and an upright piano 'for adult use only'. The beers may vary occasionally but are generally from local breweries. The pub holds quiz nights and monthly live weekend entertainment. Families are offered an under-fives soft play area most afternoons.

Q ⚲ ⊛ 🛏 🕪 🕹 🅰 ♣ P 🖵 (218) 🐾 🛜

Mawgan Porth

Merrymoor Ⓛ ✔

TR8 4BA (beside B3276 coast road, opp beach)

✪ 10-midnight; 10-11 Sun ☎ (01637) 860258 ⊕ merrymoorinn.com

St Austell Tribute; Sharp's Doom Bar, Original; 1 changing beer Ⓗ

Family-run pub on the coast road, overlooking the beach and coastal path a short distance away. It has a contemporary interior with picture windows, a separate family room and a large garden which hosts an annual beer festival. Cuisine features locally sourced produce and includes a Sunday carvery and steak and mussel nights. The pub is community orientated and raises large sums for charity every year. It has a beauty salon and offers B&B in seven en-suite rooms.

⚲ ⊛ 🛏 🕪 🕹 🅰 P 🖵 (55,171) 🐾 🛜

Mevagissey

Fountain Inn
3 Cliff Street, PL26 6QH
🌀 11-midnight; 11-11.30 Sun ☎ (01726) 842320
St Austell Cornish Best Bitter, Tribute, HSD; 1 changing beer (often St Austell) Ⓗ
Friendly two-bar 15th-century inn near the harbour, with slate-flagged floors, exposed stone walls and low beamed ceilings. The decor includes historic photographs and paintings of old Mevagissey. The back Smugglers Bar once housed a pilchard press – a glass plate in the floor covers the former fish-oil sump, which also served as a store for contraband. The menu offers a range of home-cooked dishes wherever possible. Nearby buses connect with St Austell and the Lost Gardens of Heligan. Q ⚲ 🖧 🌐 ᕕ 🍴 🚌 (24,471) ⚘ 🌐

Nancenoy

Trengilly Wartha Inn Ⓛ
TR11 5RP (off B3291 near Constantine) SW732283
🌀 11-3.15, 6-11; 12-midnight Sat summer
☎ (01326) 340332 🌐 trengilly.co.uk
Penzance Potion No 9; 3 changing beers Ⓗ
Versatile inn in extensive grounds including a lake, set in an isolated steeply wooded valley – the pub's name means 'settlement above the trees'. Originally a farmhouse, it has a variety of furniture and rooms, the wood-beamed bar displaying pictures by local artists. A conservatory extension serves as the family room. The real ales are mainly from local microbreweries, with cider appearing in summer. The Trengilly offers a wide-ranging and imaginative food menu using mostly fresh local produce. Q ⚲ 🖧 🌐 ᕕ 🍴 🅿 ⚘ 🌐

Newquay

Red Lion Ⓥ
North Quay Hill, TR7 1HE (NW side of town centre near The Beacon)
🌀 11-11 (midnight Fri & Sat) ☎ (01637) 872195
🌐 redlionnewquay.co.uk
Sharp's Doom Bar, Atlantic, Special; Skinner's Betty Stogs, Cornish Knocker, Porthleven; 2 changing beers (sourced nationally; often Marston's, Ringwood) Ⓗ
Warm, welcoming open-plan pub with a mixture of bare boards and granite flooring, five minutes' walk from the town centre and 10 from the famous Fistral surfing beach. Picture windows at the front overlook the harbour and coastline. The pub offers a central log fire, pool table, dartboard and TV screens showing surfing videos, plus live bands Friday and Saturday evenings. There is a separate seating area for diners and a secluded beer garden. CAMRA members receive a discount on ales and ciders. ⚲ 🌐 ᕕ 🍴 🚌 🅿 🚌 ⚘ 🌐

Towan Blystra Ⓛ Ⓥ
Cliff Road, TR7 1SG
🌀 8am-midnight (1am Fri & Sat) ☎ (01637) 852970
Greene King Abbot; Ruddles Best Bitter; Sharp's Doom Bar; 4 changing beers (sourced locally; often Bude, Cornish Crown, Tintagel) Ⓗ
A short walk from the railway station, hotels and beaches, this Wetherspoon shop conversion is constructed on one level but divided by partitions, offering some privacy to drinkers and diners. The walls are decorated with a surfing mural and pictures of old Newquay. Towan Blystra was the town's former name before the arrival of the

railway and tourism. A narrow drinking terrace overlooks the main street. Disabled access is via an alley off Springfield Road at the rear. Q ⚲ 🌐 ᕕ 🌐 ᕕ 🍴 🚌 🅿 🚌 🌐

Par

Royal Inn
66 Eastcliff Road, PL24 2AJ (outside Par station, by bridge)
🌀 11-11 (midnight Fri & Sat) ☎ (01726) 815601
🌐 royal-inn.co.uk
Sharp's Doom Bar, Original; 2 changing beers (sourced regionally) Ⓗ
Large one-bar pub with a separate restaurant outside Par railway station. A family pub, it is popular for eating out. As well as bar food, full meals are available in the separate raised dining room and alfresco dining and drinking on the large patio. The pub acquired its Royal tag when the then Prince of Wales's train broke down nearby in the late 19th century. Quiz night is Wednesday and there is live entertainment on Saturday evenings. Accommodation is in 15 en-suite rooms. Q ⚲ 🌐 🖧 ᕕ ᕕ 🍴 🅿 (24,25) ⚘ 🌐

Pelynt

Jubilee Inn Ⓥ
Jubilee Hill, PL13 2JZ (on B3359)
🌀 12-11 ☎ (01503) 220312 🌐 jubilee-inn.co.uk
St Austell Trelawny, Tribute, Proper Job, HSD; 1 changing beer (sourced locally; often St Austell) Ⓗ
Welcoming 17th-century village inn in a former farmhouse, originally called the Axe, but renamed in 1887 at Queen Victoria's Golden Jubilee. Inside are oak-beamed ceilings, antique furniture, a Delabole slate floor, a wood-panelled bar with a huge burnished copper hood, plus a collection of jubilee and other royalty-related memorabilia. An extensive menu features locally sourced produce. The beer range may reduce to two in winter and one of the regular brews may be replaced by a St Austell seasonal beer. Q ⚲ 🌐 🖧 ᕕ ᕕ 🅿 (72,73) ⚘ 🌐

Penzance

Crown Ⓛ
Victoria Square, TR18 2EP
🌀 12-11.30 ☎ (01736) 351070 🌐 thecrownpenzance.co.uk
Cornish Crown Mousehole, Causeway, SPA Ⓗ
Cosy town pub with a friendly local atmosphere, tucked away in a small square behind Market Jew Street. The brewery tap for Cornish Crown, the small bar has three handpumps, usually offering its own beers. The wood-floored bar has a seating and dining area including window seats, with another small snug through the arch. No food is available but you are welcome to bring your own and the pub will provide cutlery and plates. There is a small patio outside. Q 🌐 Ⓐ 🚌 🚌 ⚘ 🌐

Perranporth

Seiners Arms
Beach Road, TR6 0JL
🌀 11-midnight (11 Sun) summer; 11-11 (midnight Fri & Sat) winter ☎ (01872) 573118 🌐 seiners.co.uk
House beer (by Black Flag); 3 changing beers (sourced locally; often Sharp's, Skinner's, St Austell) Ⓗ

Wood-beamed split-level bar, part of a beach-side hotel in a superb location. A large terrace offers panoramic views across Perranporth beach. Two of the three levels are restaurant areas and there is subtle wood partitioning further dividing the dining/drinking spaces. The Seiners hosts traditional Cornish music nights weekly and mini beer festivals throughout the year, as well as a range of activities including quizzes, film screenings and hog roasts. Real ales and food are sourced locally. ❧🏠🐾🛏🄌🅓🕭☕⚓♣️👜P🚋(87)🐾🛜

Perranwell

Royal Oak 🅛

TR3 7PX
🕚 11-3, 6-11; 11-11 Sat & Sun ☎ (01872) 863175
⊕ theroyaloakperranwellstation.co.uk
Sharp's Doom Bar; 3 changing beers (sourced locally; often St Austell, Skinner's) 🄷
Small, sociable 18th-century cottage-style village community pub with an emphasis on good food most of the tables are set for meals but drinkers are equally welcome. Booking for meals is advisable, however, especially in the evening. The beers listed may vary occasionally – the third changing ale is often from outside the region. Bus services stop close by, and the railway station is about 15 minutes' walk away. Q❧🐾🛏🄌🚆🕭👜P🚋(36,46)🐾🛜

Phillack

Bucket of Blood ✅

14 Churchtown Road, TR27 5AE
🕚 12-2.30, 5.30-11; 11.30-3, 5.30-midnight Fri & Sat; 12-4, 5.30-11 Sun summer; 12-2 (not Mon-Wed), 6-11; 12-2.30, 6-11 Sat; 12-2, 7-11 Sun winter ☎ (01736) 752378
⊕ bucketofblood.co.uk
St Austell Tribute, Proper Job, HSD; 1 changing beer (sourced locally; often St Austell) 🄷
Cottage-style pub nestled in the pretty village of Phillack and named after a grisly event in the past – details are displayed in the pub. Look out for the low beams – 'mind the beams, duck or grouse' appears on one of them. Seating and tables are arrayed around a pool table just inside the door, with a dining area to the right of the bar. The decor includes a mural depicting St Ives Bay. The fourth beer is added in summer. Q❧🐾🛏🄌⚓P🐾

Piece

Countryman Inn

TR16 6SG (on Four Lanes-Pool road) SW679398
🕚 11-11 (midnight Sat); 12-11 Sun ☎ (01209) 215960
Courage Best Bitter, Directors; Sharp's Doom Bar, Original; Skinner's Heligan Honey; Theakston Old Peculier; 1 changing beer 🄷
Once a grocery shop for miners, this is now a lively community pub set high among old copper mines near the distinctive landmark of Carn Brea. The larger of the two bars is dominated by a granite fireplace and massive cast-iron coal-fired cooking range; the smaller room is more public bar in style and welcomes families. The pub hosts entertainment most nights, and a raffle in support of local charities on Sunday lunchtime. ❧🐾🄌⚓♣️P🚋(442)🐾

Polkerris

Rashleigh Inn 🅛

PL24 2TL (off A3082 Par-Fowey road) SX093521
🕚 11-11 ☎ (01726) 813991
⊕ therashleighinnpolkerris.co.uk
Otter Bitter; Skinner's Betty Stogs; Timothy Taylor Landlord; 3 changing beers (sourced regionally) 🄷
Known as the 'inn on the beach', this former 18th-century pilchard boathouse is now an excellent family-run free house beside a sheltered beach near the Saints' Way footpath, and on the South West Coastal Path. The atmospheric interior features exposed stonework, wooden flooring, a beamed ceiling, open fires and a splendid slate-topped bar. Up to six ales are available and quality meals are served in the bar and restaurant. The bar bay windows and sheltered terrace offer panoramic views of St Austell Bay. Q❧🐾🛏🄌♣️P🐾🛜

Polperro

Crumplehorn Inn 🅛

The Old Mill, Crumplehorn, PL13 2RJ (on A387, top of town near coach park)
🕚 11-11; 12-10.30 Sun ☎ (01503) 272348
⊕ crumplehorn-inn.co.uk
St Austell Tribute; Sharp's Doom Bar; Tintagel Castle Gold, Harbour Special 🄷
Once a mill and mentioned in the Domesday Book, this 14th-century inn at the entrance to the village still has a working waterwheel outside. The split-level bar has three comfortable areas with low ceilings and flagstone floors, and a spacious patio by the millstream offers large umbrellas as sunshades. A varied menu includes locally sourced food and fish. Accommodation is B&B or self-catering. In summer catch the milk float 'tram' down to the harbour from the nearby public car park. Q❧🐾🛏🄌⚓♣️P🚋🐾

Pool

Plume of Feathers ✅

Fore Street, TR15 3PF (on A3047)
🕚 11.30-11.30; 12-midnight Sat; 12-10.30 Sun ☎ (01209) 713513
3 changing beers (sourced nationally; often Adnams, Sharp's, Tintagel) 🄷
Cosy old granite inn with low beams and several drinking areas around a central bar. There is a separate restaurant and a sandwich takeaway bar. The ever-changing beer range comes mainly from Cornish and South-west microbreweries, with three brews always available, and occasional cider. Family friendly, with an outdoor play area, it is also a meeting place for clubs. Once used as a mortuary for a local mining disaster, the pub is home to two ghosts. No food on Tuesday or Sunday evenings. Q❧🐾🛏🄌♣️👜P🚋(14,18)🐾🛜

Portreath

Basset Arms

Tregea Terrace, TR16 4NG
🕚 11-11 (midnight Fri-Sun) ☎ (01209) 842077
⊕ bassetarms.com
Dartmoor Legend; St Austell Tribute; 1 changing beer (sourced locally; often Skinner's) 🄷
Cosy community pub near the beach. It caters for all with a large bar, sun-lounge restaurant and

conservatory together with a garden and play area for children. The pub features quiz nights, live entertainment and a variety of special events. There are bicycle racks outside, useful for the cycle trail starting here. The adjacent pub cellar has formerly served as a café, fish and chip shop and mortuary for shipwrecked mariners. There is disabled access but no facilities.

Q☎✿◑▶P⎕(47,57)❤🐾📶

Poughill

Preston Gate Inn

Poughill Road, EX23 9ET (just outside Bude, on Sandymouth Bay road) SS224077

✪ 11-11 (midnight Fri & Sat) ☎ (01288) 354017
🌐 prestongateinn.co.uk

4 changing beers (sourced locally; often Holsworthy, Sharp's, Tintagel) Ⓗ

Originally two cottages, this cosy 16th-century building became the village pub in 1983. The spacious U-shaped room hosts the dartboard at one end of the bar; the other, roomier end has more seating and a roaring log fire in winter. Conversation rules here, and the pub supports darts and quiz teams. Meals include monthly themed nights (booking is advised). The beer range may reduce in winter; the cider varies. The name Preston comes from the Cornish word for priest.

Q☎✿◑▶A♣🌸P⎕(128)❤📶

Rilla Mill

Manor House Inn

PL17 7NT (NE of Liskeard on B3254)

✪ 12-3, 5-11; 12-11 Sat & Sun ☎ (01579) 362354
🌐 manorhouserilla.co.uk

Draught Bass; Sharp's Doom Bar; 1 changing beer Ⓗ

Comfortable, traditional 17th-century inn and restaurant in the Lynher Valley, on the edge of Bodmin Moor, allegedly haunted by three ghosts. There are three main rooms, one with a slated and carpeted floor, the other two comprising the restaurant areas. The changing beer varies frequently and the cider is Old Rosie from Westons. Meals generally use local produce. The pub is situated near the Sterts open-air theatre and the dairy which makes Cornish Yarg cheese.

Q☎✿🏨◑♣🌸P⎕(236)❤

Rosudgeon

Falmouth Packet ⌊

TR20 9QE (on A394 Penzance-Helston road)

✪ 12-11 summer; 12-3, 5.30-11; 12-7 Sun winter
☎ (01736) 762240 🌐 falmouthpacketinn.co.uk

Penzance Potion No 9; 3 changing beers (often Penzance) Ⓗ

A light and airy family-run free house enjoying a reputation for fine beers and excellent food. A single L-shaped bar divides the pub into two distinct drinking and dining areas characterised by traditional exposed stonework, slate floors and wooden furnishings. The rear conservatory offers additional drinking and dining space and houses a pool table in winter. One guest ale is usually from the local Penzance Brewing. Food ingredients are sourced locally – booking ahead for meals is wise.

Q☎✿🏨◑👌A♣🌸P⎕(2)❤📶

St Ann's Chapel

Rifle Volunteer Inn

PL18 9HL (on A390)

✪ 11.30-11 ☎ (01822) 833038 🌐 theriflevolunteer.co.uk

St Austell Tribute; Sharp's Doom Bar; 1 changing beer (often Dartmoor) Ⓗ

Former mine captain's house, converted to a coaching inn during the mid-19th century. The main bar has been extended to accommodate a conservatory, popular with diners for the view over the garden. Meals are made with locally sourced ingredients. A separate public bar caters for more dedicated drinkers and houses a pool table and dartboard. The changing beer is usually from a local brewery. The pub offers panoramic views across the Tamar Valley and is in good walking country.

Q☎✿◑👌♣P⎕(79)📶

St Ives

Castle Inn

16 Fore Street, TR26 1AB

✪ 11-11; 12-11 Sun ☎ (01736) 796833
🌐 castleinn-stives.co.uk

Sharp's Original Ⓗ**; 6 changing beers (sourced nationally)** Ⓗ/Ⓖ

Reputedly once the offices of the Union Castle shipping line, this popular and busy town-centre pub draws custom from locals and tourists alike. The numerous nautical artefacts displayed in its quiet, relaxing single bar reflect the pub's maritime history. The emphasis here is on quality beers, with up to seven ales stocked from both local and national breweries, plus a varying cider menu. Good pub grub is served daily. A warm welcome is assured here. Q☎◑A⇌♣🌸🍴❤📶

St Just

Star Inn ⊘

1 Fore Street, TR19 7LL

✪ 11.30-midnight; 11.30-11.30 Sun ☎ (01736) 788767
🌐 thestarinn-stjust.co.uk

St Austell Cornish Best Bitter, Tribute, Proper Job; 2 changing beers (sourced locally; often St Austell) Ⓗ

A proper drinkers' pub, this 18th-century inn is a timeless place where the emphasis is on good ale and conversation. Wooden furnishings and an open fire in the atmospheric single bar enhance the traditional ambience. The decor reflects a long association with mining and maritime activities. Celtic flags adorn the beamed ceiling. A separate snug functions as a meeting and family room. Up to five St Austell ales are offered, but no food. Live music plays three times a week.

Q☎✿👌A♣⎕(10,300)❤

St Mabyn

St Mabyn Inn

Churchtown, PL30 3BA

✪ 12-midnight; 12-11 Sun ☎ (01208) 841266

Sharp's Doom Bar, Special; 2 changing beers (sourced locally) Ⓗ

Welcoming, traditional village-centre local near the church. It has a single bar and adjoining snug, games room and a stylish well-appointed restaurant. At the rear is an attractive beer garden. The comfortable interior features open fires, wooden furnishings including settles, stained-glass windows and partitions, plus an interesting collection of Toby jugs and horse brasses. An excellent ever-changing food menu specialises in local produce. With four real ales on offer and conversation the main entertainment, this pub is well worth a visit. Q♘❀◐♿⛺♣🍎P🐾

St Mawgan

Falcon Inn 🄻 ✔

TR8 4EP

🕒 11-11 (midnight Fri & Sat); 12-11 Sun summer; 11-3, 5.30-11 (midnight Fri); 12-11 Sat & Sun winter

☎ (01637) 860225 🌐 thefalconinnstmawgan.co.uk

4 changing beers (sourced locally) 🄷

Located in the Lanherne Valley near Newquay airport, this picturesque and charming 16th-century free house is worth seeking out. Its cosy, relaxed interior features a single bar with a large open hearth and an adjoining stylish restaurant. The extensive well-kept garden is ideal for alfresco drinking and dining, and hosts an annual July beer festival. Four ales, at least one from a local brewery, are available from a changing range; real cider also varies regularly. Home-cooked food is served daily. Q♘❀🛏◐⛺♣🍎P🚌(56)🐾📶

Saltash

Union Inn

Tamar Street, PL12 4EL (on waterfront, beneath bridges)

🕒 11-11; 12-10.30 Sun ☎ (01752) 844770

Dartmoor Legend, Jail Ale; Sharp's Doom Bar 🄷**; 1 changing beer (sourced locally; often Bays)** 🄶

The frontage of this riverside local, overlooked by the Tamar bridges, is strikingly painted as a union flag. The single bar offers a selection of real ales and a varying guest beer, usually on gravity in the cellar. The draught cider is Sam's Devon Dry. Tables outside overlook the river. Live music features on Tuesday and weekend evenings. Tamar Street, the pub's location, used to be known as Pickle Cock Alley, as shellfish were sold through open windows. Q❀🚆♣🍎P🚌🐾

Stithians

Seven Stars Inn ✔

Church Road, TR3 7DH

🕒 12-11 (midnight Fri & Sat) ☎ (01209) 860003

St Austell Cornish Best Bitter, Tribute; 1 changing beer (sourced nationally; often Bristol Beer Factory) 🄷

Lively cottage-style village local, used by a broad cross-section of the community and supportive of local events and sports teams. The pub was purpose built as a farmhouse extension to serve the drinking needs of tin miners at the end of the 19th century. The original bar and lounge (note the adjacent twin front doors) have been merged into one L-shaped drinking/dining area, with a later extension added towards the rear. The ever-changing guest beer is usually from a microbrewery. Q♘❀◐♣🚌(36,442)🐾📶

Stratton

King's Arms 🄻 ✔

Howells Road, EX23 9BX (on A3072)

🕒 12-11 ☎ (01288) 352396

Sharp's Atlantic; Tintagel Cornwall's Pride; 2 changing beers (often Forge, Tintagel) 🄷

Popular locals' local in the heart of this ancient market town, a 17th-century former coaching inn whose name reflects the town's loyalties after the Civil War. The pub has many original features including two simply furnished bars, with well-worn Delabole slate flagstone and wooden floors. During renovation work, a small bread oven was exposed in the lounge. The two changing beers usually include one from a Cornish brewery and one from Devon. Four letting rooms are available, one of them en-suite. Q❀🛏◐♿⛺♣🍎P🚌🐾

Treen

Gurnard's Head Hotel 🄻

TR26 3DE (on B3306, Lands End-St Ives coast road, and near Zennor)

🕒 10-11.30 ☎ (01736) 796928 🌐 gurnardshead.co.uk

St Austell Tribute; 3 changing beers (sourced locally; often Skinner's) 🄷

Named after the nearby headland, this impressive and characterful free house, with a well-deserved reputation for good ale and cuisine, draws custom from near and far. An expansive wood-floored interior accommodates a single bar, cosy snug and stylish dining room. Open fires, attractive decor, wood furnishings and comfy sofas create a relaxed atmosphere. Most of the changing ales are from Cornish microbreweries; a third is added in summer. An extensive menu changes daily, reflecting the availability of local produce. Q♘❀🛏◐♿⛺🍎P🚌(7,16A)🐾📶

Tresco: Isles of Scilly

New Inn

Townshill, TR24 0QG

🕒 11-11 summer; 11-3, 6-11 winter ☎ (01720) 422844

Sharp's Doom Bar; 3 changing beers (sourced locally; often Ales of Scilly, St Austell, Skinner's) 🄷

Excellent old pub near New Grimsby harbour, a haven between demanding coastal walks and the boat to St Mary's. Extensions to the garden and provision of a covered pavilion have added to the attractions of this popular real ale outlet. The varying beers are mostly from Cornish breweries, usually including a brew from Skinner's and St Austell, with local brewer Ales of Scilly often represented. Beer festivals are held over the spring and late summer bank holidays. Q♘❀🛏◐♣🍎🐾📶

Trevaunance Cove

Driftwood Spars 🄻 ✔

Quay Road, TR5 0RT

🕒 11-11 (midnight Fri & Sat) ☎ (01872) 552428

🌐 driftwoodspars.co.uk

Sharp's Doom Bar; 4 changing beers (sourced locally; often Driftwood) 🄷

This vibrant coastal free house is a magnet for ale drinkers and should not be missed. It has three bars, a sea-view fish restaurant with sun terrace, two separate beer gardens and ample parking. The decor is on a nautical theme. The brewpub is the Driftwood Brewery tap and its ales dominate the changing beer menu. Live musicians and occasional theatre perform in one of the bars. March and May beer festivals include tutored tasting sessions. The pub has become a popular wedding venue. Q♘❀🛏◐♿🍎P🚌(57,87)🐾📶

Trewellard

Trewellard Arms 🅛

Trewellard Road, TR19 7TA (on B3318/B3306 jct)
✪ 12-11 (midnight Sat) ☎ (01736) 788634
6 changing beers (sourced regionally; often Bays, Tintagel) 🅗
Formerly the nearby Geevor mine-owner's residence, this pub is now a thriving, award-winning free house. Welcoming and family friendly, its cosy interior accommodates a spacious open-beamed single bar, a pleasant restaurant serving home-cooked food, a secluded cellar space and a patio area outside. Open fires contribute to the homely atmosphere. A diverse beer menu features up to six local ales and there is a beer festival each May. The pub is easily accessed by bus and has ample parking.
🔄❀◑♣👜P🚲(7,10,10A)🐾🍴

Truro

Old Ale House 🧲

7 Quay Street, TR1 2HD
✪ 11-11 (midnight Mon & Fri; 1am Sat); 12-10.30 Sun
☎ (01872) 271122 ⊕ old-ale-house.co.uk
Skinner's Betty Stogs, River Cottage EPA, Lushingtons, Cornish Knocker, Porthleven 🅗**; 7 changing beers (sourced regionally; often Skinner's)** 🅗/🅖
This lively two-storey city-centre pub is Skinner's brewery tap. Located near the bus station, the atmospheric main bar is on the lower floor, with wooden flooring, furnishings, pillars, beamed ceilings and old artefacts creating character. Up to 13 ales and eight ciders may be available. Bar meals are served plus free monkey nuts. Upstairs, the intimate, stylish Hop Store restaurant serves an interesting menu created with the River Cottage organisation. Live music plays on Friday and Saturday evenings. Q◑♣👜🐾🍴

Rising Sun 🧲

Mitchell Hill, TR1 1ED
✪ 11.30-11.30 (12.30am Fri & Sat); closed Mon
☎ (01872) 240003 ⊕ risingsuntruro.co.uk
Fuller's London Pride; Skinner's Betty Stogs; 2 changing beers (sourced locally; often Skinner's) 🅖
Small pub up a short but rather steep hill about 15 minutes' walk from the bus station. Frequented by locals, it has a substantial food offering. A small bar inside the door leads to a slightly larger one beyond, then a stylish restaurant area on a higher level and a patio at the rear. The decor includes old Truro scenes. Despite the bar-mounted handpumps, ales are dispensed straight from casks – the changing beers are generally local.
🔄❀◑P🚲🐾🍴

Tywardreath

New Inn 🅛

Fore Street, PL24 2QP
✪ 12-11 ☎ (01726) 813901
Draught Bass 🅖**; St Austell Trelawny, Tribute, Proper Job; 1 changing beer** 🅗
This classic village pub is a perfect example of a community local, built in the mid-18th century by mine owners. Although tied to a brewery, the

landlord serves a guest beer, as well as Draught Bass, which the pub is covenanted to sell in perpetuity. Pub games, good conversation and regular live music provide the entertainment. Groups meet here regularly and fêtes are held in the extensive gardens. The pub was Cornwall CAMRA Village Pub of the Year in 2014 and 2015.
Q🔄❀◑♣P🚲(24)🐾🍴

Vogue

Star Inn 🧲

TR16 5NP (on Redruth-St Day road)
✪ 11-11 (1am Fri & Sat) ☎ (01209) 820242
⊕ starinnvogue.biz
4 changing beers 🅗
Enterprising licensees maintain an imaginative beer range for a diverse range of customers, encouraging a strong community focus by hosting a county library, hairdressing salon and meeting place for village events. The pub's homely interior includes a bar for drinking and dining, a quiet lounge and restaurant. Good home-cooked food is available during the day, including roasts on Sunday (booking advisable), with an evening menu prepared by a professional chef. A charity beer and music festival is held every June.
🔄❀◑♿♣👜P🚲(47)🐾🍴

Wadebridge

Ship Inn

Gonvena Hill, PL27 6DF (across the bridge from town centre)
✪ 12-2, 5-11; 12-10 Sun ☎ (01208) 813845
⊕ shipinnwadebridge.co.uk
Sharp's Doom Bar, Atlantic; 2 changing beers (sourced locally; often Harbour, Padstow) 🅗
Traditional 16th-century coaching inn across the river from the town centre. Recently refurbished, this award-winning pub has a beamed ceiling, wooden floor and fine leaded front window, and offers a welcoming, relaxing atmosphere. On three levels, it is surprisingly extensive inside – the main bar at the lowest end adjoins the split-level, well-appointed restaurant leading to a suntrap deck and courtyard seating. The changing ales are generally from local microbreweries and the food is locally sourced. Q🔄❀◑♣👜P🚲(94,595)🍴

Wendron

New Inn 🅛

Redruth Road, TR13 0EA (on B3297)
✪ 12-3, 6-11; 12-3, 6-10.30 Sun ☎ (01326) 572683
3 changing beers 🅗
Sitting opposite the village church, this cosy, welcoming country pub caters for locals and visitors alike. Paintings of hunting scenes and horses adorn the Cornish stone walls, while a lovely wood carving of the four horsemen of the apocalypse resides above the fireplace. The restaurant is accessed through the bar, with food prepared by the landlady and her daughter. The wooden bar sports three handpumps, dispensing a Skinner's beer and other local brews. Real cider is occasionally available.
Q🔄❀🚪◑P🚲(36,37)🐾🍴

Keep your Good Beer Guide up to date by visiting the CAMRA website **camra.org.uk**, then Good Beer Guide, then Updates.

89

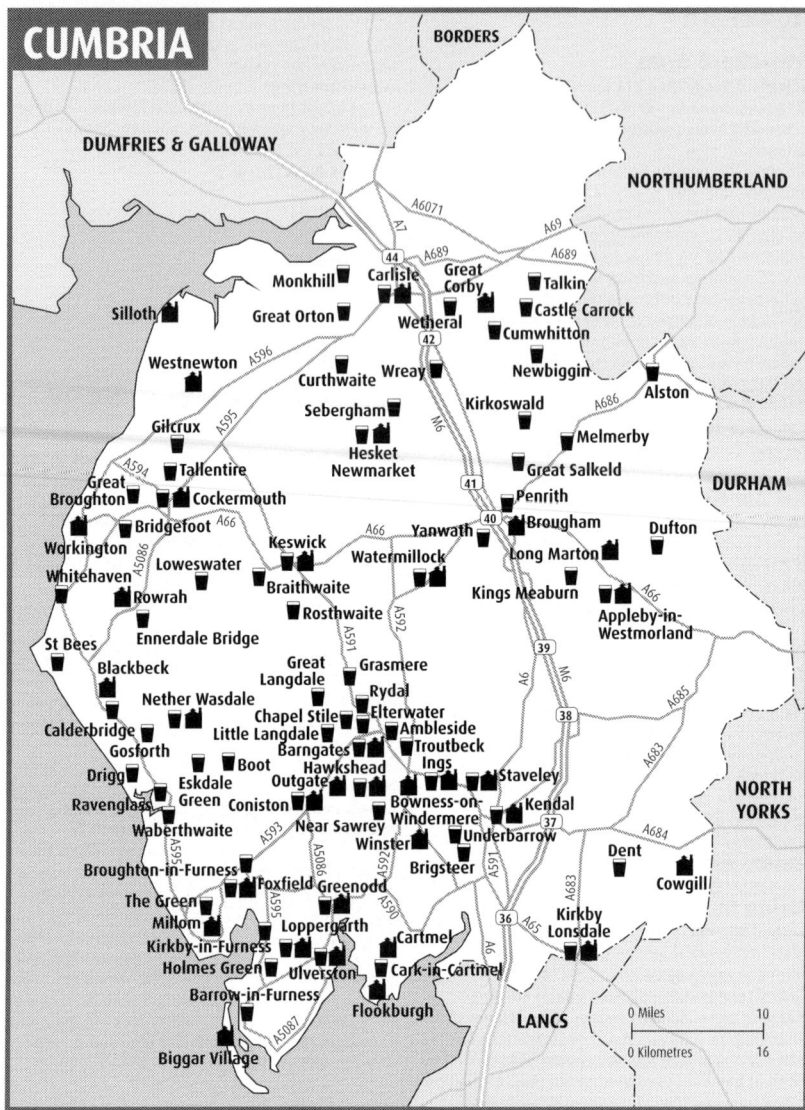

CUMBRIA

BORDERS

DUMFRIES & GALLOWAY

NORTHUMBERLAND

Monkhill
Carlisle
Great Corby
Talkin
Silloth
Great Orton
Castle Carrock
Wetheral
Cumwhitton
Westnewton
Curthwaite
Wreay
Newbiggin
Alston
Kirkoswald
Sebergham
Melmerby
Gilcrux
Hesket Newmarket
Great
Tallentire
Great Salkeld
DURHAM
Broughton
Cockermouth
Penrith
Bridgefoot
Yanwath
Brougham
Dufton
Workington
Keswick
Watermillock
Long Marton
Loweswater
Whitehaven
Braithwaite
Kings Meaburn
Rowrah
Rosthwaite
Appleby-in-Westmorland
St Bees
Ennerdale Bridge
Grasmere
Great
Langdale
Blackbeck
Rydal
Nether Wasdale
Chapel Stile
Elterwater
Calderbridge
Little Langdale
Ambleside
Gosforth
Barngates
Troutbeck
Drigg
Boot
Hawkshead
Ings
Eskdale
Outgate
Staveley
Ravenglass
Green
Coniston
Bowness-on-Windermere
Kendal
NORTH YORKS
Waberthwaite
Near Sawrey
Underbarrow
Winster
Broughton-in-Furness
Brigsteer
Dent
Foxfield
Greenodd
Cowgill
The Green
Millom
Loppergarth
Kirkby Lonsdale
Kirkby-in-Furness
Cartmel
Holmes Green
Ulverston
Cark-in-Cartmel
Barrow-in-Furness
Flookburgh
LANCS
Biggar Village

0 Miles 10
0 Kilometres 16

Alston

Cumberland Inn L
Townfoot, CA9 3HX
☎ 12-11 ☎ (01434) 381875 ⊕ alstoncumberlandhotel.co.uk
Yates Bitter; 3 changing beers ⊞
A family-run 19th-century hotel overlooking the South Tyne river. Close to the Coast-to-Coast cycle route and Pennine Way, it is an ideal base to explore the highest market town in England. The house beer is Yates Bitter, with guest beers from Hesket Newmarket, Allendale, High House Farm, Mordue breweries and further afield. Old Rosie and occasional Cumbrian ciders and perry are stocked. Bar meals are prepared with locally sourced ingredients where possible, attracting both visitors and locals. Local CAMRA Cider Pub of the Year 2014. Q ⦿ ⏧ ❀ ⏧ ◑ ❀ P ⏧ ❀

Ambleside

Queen's Hotel L ✓
Market Place, LA22 9BU
☎ 10-11 (1am Fri & Sat); 10-11.30 Sun ☎ (015394) 32206
⊕ queenshotelambleside.com
Beckstones Black Dog Freddy Mild; Coniston Bluebird Bitter; Cumbrian Legendary Ales Loweswater Gold, Langdale; Hawkshead Windermere Pale; Yates Bitter; 1 changing beer (sourced nationally) ⊞
Town-centre hotel with a large bar and dining area, and the separate Victoria's Restaurant on the ground floor, as well as a cellar bar beneath. It is popular with locals and visitors for the quality and range of the local beers and its location in the centre of the Lake District. Buses run to several villages and towns with tourist attractions and fine walking opportunities. ⏧ ❀ ◑ ❀ ⏧ ❀ 🛜

Appleby-in-Westmorland

Midland Hotel L

25 Clifford Street, CA16 6TS

✪ 11.30 (5.30 Tue)-11; closed Mon ☎ (017683) 51524
⊕ themidlandhotelappleby.co.uk

3 changing beers (sourced nationally) Ⓗ

Set in the beautiful Eden Valley between the Lake District National Park and the Yorkshire Dales National Park, the Midland is adjacent to the town station on the Settle-Carlisle Railway. It has been extensively refurbished and much improved, now having a light, modern feel. Three handpumps offer beers from microbreweries, often Appleby and Eden. Real cider and perry are frequently available. ✿🏠🍴🚲⇌P🖿 (563)🌸♣ 🛜

Barngates

Drunken Duck Inn L

LA22 0NG (signed off B5286 Hawkshead to Ambleside road)

✪ 11.30-11; 12-10.30 Sun ☎ (015394) 36347
⊕ drunkenduckinn.co.uk

Barngates Cat Nap, Cracker, Tag Lag; 1 changing beer (sourced nationally) Ⓗ

Home of Barngates Brewery, the Duck always serves seven of the nine beers brewed here. The bar has been extensively renovated to create a pleasing mix of local and modern styles. Lunchtime bar meals, and the à la carte menu available in the dining room in the evening, are of an exceptionally high standard. The seating area outside at the front offers magnificent views of the fells to the north-east. Dogs are allowed except in the dining room. Q🕭🖘🏠🍴🚲♣P🌸♣ 🛜

Barrow-in-Furness

Furness Railway L ✓

76-80 Abbey Road, LA14 1PQ

✪ 8am-midnight (1am Fri & Sat) ☎ (01229) 820818

Courage Directors; Fuller's London Pride; Greene King Abbot; Ruddles Best Bitter; Sharp's Doom Bar; 5 changing beers (sourced nationally) Ⓗ

A Wetherspoon pub on the ground floor of the old Co-op department store, divided into drinking and dining areas. The place is a fine example of early 20th-century commercial architecture. It has recently been refurbished, with the addition of 50 bedrooms. The pub can be busy, especially at weekends, when it is a popular starting point for the town-centre circuit. Good-value food is served all day. 🖘🍴🚲♣🖿 🛜

King's Arms L

Quarry Brow, Hawcoat, LA14 4HY

✪ 5.30-11; 4-midnight Fri; 12.30-midnight Sat; 1-11 Sun
☎ (01229) 828137

Barngates Cracker; Copper Dragon Best Bitter; Cumbrian Legendary Ales Loweswater Gold; 6 changing beers (sourced nationally) Ⓗ

Popular local pub selling mainly from local micros, including Barngates, Bowness Bay, Copper Dragon, Cumberland Breweries, Cumbrian Legendary Ales and Kirkby Lonsdale. A beer menu on a chalkboard lists forthcoming attractions. The pub, which has been on these premises since the 1860s, has just been extensively extended and renovated, and features an open bar with adjacent separate rooms. Friendly staff offer a warm welcome. Well-behaved dogs are allowed in one of the rooms. Q🕭♣🖿 (1,6,X6)🌸 🛜

Boot

Brook House Inn L

CA19 1TG (200yds from Dalegarth Station)

✪ 9am-11 ☎ (019467) 23288 ⊕ brookhouseinn.co.uk

Cumbrian Legendary Ales Langdale; 6 changing beers (sourced nationally) Ⓗ

In the heart of the western Lake District in the beautiful Eskdale valley, close to the terminus of the Ravenglass & Eskdale narrow-gauge railway, this popular family-run tourist pub is renowned for good food and a wide range of cask ales. Together with other nearby pubs in the Eskdale valley, the Brook House Inn provides the focal point for an annual beer festival held in June. Local CAMRA Pub of the Year 2014. Q🕭✿🏠🍴🚲🅰⇌(Dalegarth)♣P🌸 🛜

Hardknott Bar & Café at the Woolpack Inn L

CA19 1TH (¾ mile E of Boot village on approach to Hardknott Pass) OL191010

✪ 9am-11 ☎ (019467) 2328 ⊕ woolpack.co.uk

Barngates Goodhew's Dry Stout; Ennerdale Blonde; 4 changing beers (sourced nationally) Ⓗ

Iconic Lakeland inn on the approach to Hardknott Pass and surrounded by the stunning scenery of Eskdale valley. This popular tourist pub serves food,

REAL ALE BREWERIES

Appleby Appleby-in-Westmorland
Barngates Barngates
Beckstones Millom
Biggar Biggar Village (NEW)
Blackbeck ⬛ Blackbeck
Bowness Bay Kendal
Brack'N'Brew ⬛ Watermillock (NEW)
Brewshine Kendal
Carlisle Carlisle
Chadwick's Kendal
Coniston Coniston
Cumberland Great Corby
Cumbrian Legendary Hawkshead
Dent Cowgill
Derwent Silloth
Eden Brougham
Ennerdale Rowrah
Fell Flookburgh
Foxfield ⬛ Foxfield
Greenodd ⬛ Greenodd
Hardknott Millom
Hawkshead Staveley
Healey's ⬛ Loppergarth
Helm Bar Appleby-in-Westmorland (NEW)
Hesket Newmarket Hesket Newmarket
Jennings Cockermouth
Kendal ⬛ Kendal
Keswick Keswick
Kirkby Lonsdale Kirkby Lonsdale
South Lakes Ulverston (NEW)
Strands ⬛ Nether Wasdale
Stringer's Ulverston
Tarn Hows Outgate
Tirril Long Marton
Tractor Shed Workington
Ulverston Ulverston
Unsworth's Yard Cartmel
Watermill ⬛ Ings
Westmorland Kendal (NEW)
Wild Boar ⬛ Bowness-on-Windermere
Winster Valley ⬛ Winster
Yates Westnewton

cask ales and draught ciders. The lounge and walkers' bar offer an attractive mix of traditional and modern styles, with woodburning stoves in both areas. The pub participates in the annual Boot Beer Festival in June as well as staging its own cider festival in April. Q ☕ ❀ ⏰ ◁▷ Å ♠ P ❀ 🐾 ⬢

Braithwaite

Middle Ruddings Country Inn 🛈

CA12 5RY (W end of village)
✪ 10.30-11 ☎ (017687) 78436 ⊕ middle-ruddings.co.uk
3 changing beers (sourced nationally) ⊞
Traditional country inn, in a great location close to Keswick, which offers an attractive garden and views of Skiddaw. In addition to a range of Cumbrian beers there are also up to two ciders and a perry. Non-residents are always welcome. It serves meals with ingredients that are sourced locally and holds an annual beer lovers' dinner and a Burns Night celebration. Previous winner of CAMRA West Cumbria Pub of the Year.
Q ☕ ❀ ⏰ ◁▷ ♿ Å ♠ P ❺ ⌨ (X5) 🐾 ⬢

Bridgefoot

Duke of Cumberland 🛈 ✅

CA14 1YF
✪ 7-11; 4-midnight Sat; 4-11 Sun; closed Mon
☎ (01900) 606105 ⊕ doci2014.com
Keswick Thirst Gold; 1 changing beer (sourced nationally) ⊞
Extensively modernised and now bright, cheerful and comfortable, with many homely touches and a warm welcome from the licensees, this previously run-down Robinsons pub is now a free house and is once again functioning as a village focal point. Children are permitted until 7pm. It has easy parking outside. There is live music, a monthly quiz night, and a folk session on the first Wednesday of each month. Q ☕ 🐾

Brigsteer

Wheatsheaf Inn ✅

LA8 8AN
✪ 10-11; 10-10.30 Sun ☎ (015395) 68254
⊕ thewheatsheafbrigsteer.co.uk
Bowness Bay Swan Blonde; Hawkshead Bitter; Thwaites Wainwright; 1 changing beer (sourced nationally) ⊞
Delightful village inn, recently restored inside and out to a very high standard sympathetic with its surroundings. Patios and terraced gardens give stunning streamside views. Inside, several small rooms, the main bar area and a conservatory all maintain a tasteful rural appeal. The pub is on popular cycling routes and walkers and dogs are welcome. Great dining is offered to suit all tastes.
Q ☕ ❀ ◁▷ ♿ 🐾 ⬢

Broughton-in-Furness

Manor Arms 🛈

The Square, LA20 6HY
✪ 12-11.30 (midnight Fri & Sat); 12-11 Sun
☎ (01229) 716286 ⊕ manorarmsthesquare.co.uk
Cumberland Corby Blonde; Hawkshead Windermere Pale; Yates Bitter; 5 changing beers (sourced nationally) ⊞
An outstanding free house owned by the Varty family for more than 27 years. It is the winner of

numerous CAMRA awards, including local CAMRA Pub of the Year 2015. A comprehensive, frequently changing choice of up to eight real ales is served, with a range to suit all tastes. Six traditional ciders and perries are available. A mini beer festival is held every day. Q ☕ ❀ ♣ ♠ ❺ ⌨ 🐾 ⬢

Calderbridge

Stanley Arms Hotel

CA20 1DN (on A595)
✪ 12-11.30 ☎ (01946) 841235 ⊕ stanleyarmshotel.com
Bowness Bay Swan Blonde; 3 changing beers (sourced nationally) ⊞
A family-run hotel in this small village on the edge of the Lake District National Park, with its delightful beer garden beside the Calder River, on which it has full fishing rights. On the A595, it gives easy access to the Western lakes, coasts and valleys. Hearty meals featuring locally sourced produce are available in the two-room bar and restaurant. Local attractions include a riverside walk past the ruins of 12th-century Calder Abbey.
Q ☕ ❀ ❀ ◁▷ ♠ P ⌨ (X6) 🐾 ⬢

Cark-in-Cartmel

Engine Inn 🛈

LA11 7NZ
✪ 11.30-1am; 11.30-midnight Sun ☎ (015395) 58341
⊕ engineinn.co.uk
Unsworth's Yard Sir Edgar Harrington's Last Wolf; 3 changing beers (sourced nationally) ⊞
A 17th-century inn, refurbished in 2010, a short stroll from the station and one that makes an excellent end to the walk from Grange described in CAMRA's Lake District Pub Walks book. Beers from the Punch range are supplemented by ales from local breweries Fell and Unsworth's Yard, and breweries in Ulverston. There is an open bar area with a cosy fire, separate rooms away from the bar, and a riverside beer garden. Check hours in winter. ☕ ❀ ◁▷ ♿ Å ⇌ ♠ P ⌨ 🐾 ⬢

Carlisle

Crown & Thistle

53 Church Street, CA3 9DS
✪ 10-midnight ☎ (01228) 532965
Sharp's Atlantic; 1 changing beer (sourced nationally) ⊞
A popular community local at the centre of Stanwix village and close to the route of Hadrian's Wall. This friendly venue consists of a bar, lounge and outdoor drinking area. There is a popular quiz night every Thursday. It serves Sharp's Atlantic and one changing real ale. This is a pub of great character and great characters. ☕ ❀ ♠ P ⌨ 🐾 ⬢

King's Head Inn 🛈

Fisher Street, CA3 8RF
✪ 10-11; 11-midnight Sat; 12-11 Sun
⊕ kingsheadcarlisle.co.uk
Yates Bitter; 3 changing beers ⊞
An excellent city-centre pub, winner of many CAMRA awards. It serves Yates Bitter and a range of guest ales from four handpumps. Pictures of old Carlisle adorn the internal walls and outside is an explanation of why the city is not in the Domesday Book. Good-value meals are served at lunchtime. The covered courtyard has a large-screen TV and regularly features live music. ❀ ◁▷ ⇌ ♣ ♠ ⌨ 🐾 ⬢

Moo Bar 🅛

5 Devonshire Street, CA3 8LG
✪ 12-midnight ☎ (01228) 317273
Changing beers 🅗

Opened in November 2014 in central Carlisle, this bar has rapidly established itself as a beer-lover's heaven. Eighteen handpumps and 16 keg taps await the drinker's pleasure, featuring a varied range of beers heavily biased towards Cumbrian breweries, as well as regional, national and international ales. There is also an extensive range of interesting world bottled beers. Although generally a quiet pub, it does have live music every Monday evening, with other occasional music nights. Q ➷ ⬱ ♣ 🖶 🖵 😼 🛜

Spinners Arms 🅛

Cummersdale, CA2 6BD
✪ 6 (5 Fri; 12 Sat & Sun)-midnight ☎ (01228) 532928
⊕ thespinnersarms.org.uk
Carlisle Spun Gold, Flaxen, Magic Number, Oatmeal Stout; 1 changing beer (sourced locally; often Carlisle) 🅗

Cosy family-friendly hostelry, an original Redfern pub with unique and original features. Less than half a mile from Carlisle's south-western boundary, it is close to the Cumbrian Way and National Cycle Route 7, which run alongside the picturesque River Caldew. There is regular live music, with Irish music sessions every first and third Wednesday. Children are welcome until 9pm. The pub is the brewery tap for Carlisle Brewing Co, showcasing its beers on five pumps. ➷ ⊛ ⅙ ♣ P 🖵 (75) 😼

Woodrow Wilson 🅛 ✪

48 Botchergate, CA1 1QS
✪ 8am-midnight (1am Thu-Sat) ☎ (01228) 819942
Cumberland Corby Ale; Greene King Abbot; Jennings Sneck Lifter; Marston's Old Empire; Ruddles Best Bitter; Sharp's Doom Bar; 6 changing beers (sourced nationally) 🅗

Wetherspoon pub in a refurbished Co-op building named after the former US president, whose mother was born in Carlisle. Up to 12 handpumps offer the largest range of real ales to be found in Carlisle, usually including many LocAle beers. Food is available all day till 10pm. At the rear there is a spacious outdoor seating area, heated patio and smokers' area. Children are welcome in some parts until 8pm. ➷ ⅅ ⅙ ⬱ 🍴 P 🖵 🛜

Castle Carrock

Duke of Cumberland 🅛

CA8 9LU
✪ 12-11.30 (midnight Fri & Sat) ☎ (01228) 670341
⊕ thedukeofcumberlandinn.com
2 changing beers (often Derwent, Hesket Newmarket) 🅗

At the heart of this charming village, the Duke reopened in 2009 and is now successfully re-established. A local following also sees it as the centre for the annual Marr Folk Festival in July. At the foot of the northern Pennines, it is ideally located for outdoor activity enthusiasts, who can enjoy real ale and sample the home-made food, which has a growing reputation. The layout separates the games/TV area from the dining area. ➷ ⊛ ⅅ ⅙ ♣ 🍴 P 🛜

Chapel Stile

Wainwrights' Inn ✪

LA22 9JH
✪ 11.30-11; 12-11 Sun ☎ (015394) 38088
⊕ langdale.co.uk/dine/wainwrights
Jennings Cumberland Ale, Sneck Lifter; Thwaites Wainwright; 4 changing beers (sourced nationally) 🅗

This was originally a farmhouse near the former gunpowder works before becoming a hotel. It was converted in the late '80s to a pub, and is well known for its location in one of the most popular Lakeland valleys and for its quality of service and variety of real ales. The stone-flagged bar area has the regular beers plus four guests, usually from Cumbrian or small northern breweries. ➷ ⊛ ⅅ ⅙ Å P 🖵 (516) 😼 🛜

Cockermouth

Castle Bar

14 Market Place, CA13 9NQ
✪ 11-11 (midnight Fri & Sat); 12-10.30 Sun
☎ (01900) 829904 ⊕ cockermouth.org.uk/castlebar
Cumbrian Legendary Ales Loweswater Gold; Jennings Bitter, Cumberland Ale; 2 changing beers (sourced nationally) 🅗

Gastro-pub in the town's marketplace with a modern interior that retains many historic features of this fine old building. The ground floor has a bar with five handpumps serving mainly Cumbrian ales. It has a restaurant on the first floor and a relaxing second-floor room with comfy leather sofas. The terraced beer garden at the rear is popular in summer. TV screens show sport. The bar gets busy at weekends, and can be booked for private functions. ➷ ⊛ ⅅ 🍴 🖵 (X4,X5,600) 😼

Swan Inn 🅛

52-56 Kirkgate, CA13 9PH
✪ 5.30-11.30 (midnight Fri); 12-midnight Sat; 12-11 Sun
☎ (01900) 822425 ⊕ swaninncockermouth.com
Jennings Bitter, Cumberland Ale, Cocker Hoop; 2 changing beers (sourced nationally) 🅗

Voted CAMRA West Cumbria Pub of the Year 2015, this place is well supported by locals. Dating back to the 17th century and mentioned in the churchwarden's account books of 1668, the pub has flagged floors, exposed beams and a real fire. It is used as a meeting venue by various local groups and hosts two quiz teams and a monthly folk music session. Three Jennings beers are usually on plus two guests. Q ➷ ♣ 🖵 (X4,X5,600) 😼 🛜

Coniston

Black Bull Inn & Hotel 🅛

The Lake District, LA21 8DU
✪ 8.30am-11 ☎ (015394) 41335 ⊕ blackbullconiston.co.uk
Coniston Oliver's Light Ale, Bluebird Bitter, Bluebird Premium XB, Old Man Ale, Special Oatmeal Stout, No. 9 Barley Wine 🅗

A 16th-century coaching inn serving good food in traditional and comfortable surroundings and the tap house for the on-site Coniston Brewing Company. The six regular beers (available from 11am) are supplemented by other beers from the brewery on a rotation basis. The spacious bar and lounge are always well frequented by tourists in this hugely popular area. The outside seating area is perfect for the summer months, in a spectacular location near Coniston Old Man. Q ➷ ⊛ 🛏 ⅅ Å 🍴 P 🖵 (X12,505) 😼 🛜

Sun ⓛ
LA21 8HQ
✪ 11-11 ☎ (015394) 41248 ⊕ thesunconiston.com
Barngates Red Bull Terrier; Coniston Bluebird Premium XB; Cumbrian Legendary Ales Loweswater Gold; 4 changing beers (sourced nationally) Ⓗ
Take the Walna Scar road up from Coniston village, or down from Coniston Old Man, to visit this 16th-century inn. The unmodernised dual-level bar area has atmosphere and character, with slate flooring and abundant exposed beams and stone walls, heated by a large open range. The slate-topped bar offers up to eight cask ales, mostly from local brewers. The conservatory and terrace complete the picture, with delightful views over the garden. Q❄☀⇔◑☕♣P🖵🐾🐕‍🦺🍽

Yewdale Inn ⓛ
2 Yewdale Road, LA21 8DU
✪ 12-11 ☎ (015394) 41280 ⊕ yewdaleinn.com
Cumbrian Legendary Ales Loweswater Gold; Theakston Best Bitter; 3 changing beers (sourced nationally) Ⓗ
A welcoming village inn in the centre of Coniston for locals and visitors alike. In winter, a cosy fire and jovial atmosphere prevail; in summer, enjoy a drink on the terrace with stunning views of the Old Man of Coniston and surrounding fells and Church Beck, a babbling brook that runs through the village. Opening hours and food service are reduced in winter. ❄☀⇔◑☕♣🐾🍽

Cumwhitton
Pheasant Inn ⓛ ✔
CA8 9EX
✪ 6-11; 1-3, 6-9 Sun; closed Mon ☎ (01228) 560102
⊕ pheasantinncumwhitton.co.uk
3 changing beers (often Ennerdale) Ⓗ
Partly dating from the 17th century, this pub has a well-deserved reputation for excellent food using fresh local ingredients, but retains that good pub welcome for the thirsty visitor in for a pint. There are three handpumps with a changing range of real ales. The venue has won several CAMRA awards, proudly displayed in the bar alongside a water jug collection. A quiz night is held every second week. Closed Mondays, and open evenings-only other days except Sunday. Q❄☀◑☕♣P

Curthwaite
Royal Oak ⓛ
CA7 8BG
✪ 12-2, 5-11; 12-2, 5-10.30 Sun ☎ (01228) 710219
3 changing beers Ⓗ
The Royal Oak is a popular, welcoming, traditional country inn less than a mile south of Thursby, which is fairly well served by public transport. The pub has a justified reputation for excellent food with an emphasis on local produce. Three changing real ales are sold and these are usually from local breweries, including Carlisle, Cumberland, Eden, Hesket Newmarket and Jennings. Local CAMRA Highly Commended award 2014. ❄☀◑☕♣P

Dent
Sun Inn ⓛ
Main Street, LA10 5QL
✪ 11-11; 12-10.30 Sun ☎ (015396) 25208
⊕ suninndent.co.uk

Kirkby Lonsdale Monumental Blonde, Tiffin Gold; 2 changing beers (sourced nationally) Ⓗ
A traditional, unspoilt 16th-century inn at the heart of this attractive village in the Yorkshire Dales National Park. The main bar is oak beamed with an open fire and a fascinating collection of local photographs. Two smaller rooms lead off the bar, one displaying more old photographs. Good home-made bar meals are served. Popular with walkers and all outdoors enthusiasts and dog-friendly. Q❄☀⇔◑☕A♣P🐾

Drigg
Victoria Hotel ⓛ
Station Road, CA19 1XQ (next to railway station)
✪ 12-2 (not Mon), 5.30-11.30; 12-midnight Sat; 12-11.30 Sun ☎ (019467) 24231 ⊕ thevicatdrigg.co.uk
Jennings Bitter, Cumberland Ale; 4 changing beers (sourced nationally) Ⓗ
A small village pub with a welcoming and friendly atmosphere, open plan and L-shaped, with a cosy fire in colder weather. As it is popular for meals it is wise to book ahead. Frequent charity quizzes support Mountain Rescue, Air Ambulance and MLI charities. It is one mile from Drigg seashore and nature reserve, and adjacent to Drigg railway station (to request the stop stick your hand out!). Has a well-stocked crafts shop. Q❄☀⇔◑☕A⇌P🐾

Dufton
Stag Inn ⓛ
CA16 6DB
✪ 12-3 (not Mon & Tue), 6-11; 12-3, 6-midnight Fri; 12-11 Sat & Sun ☎ (017683) 51608 ⊕ thestagdufton.co.uk
4 changing beers (sourced nationally) Ⓗ
Lovely old pub on the green in this beautiful fellside village on the Pennine Way. A beamed bar with an old range and a side room with a wood-burning stove ensure a warm welcome all year round. The dining room leads to a sunny beer garden with views over the Pike; great walking can be enjoyed before trying one of the four local ales of all styles. Fine home-made food and banter with the locals complete the picture. Q❄☀◑AP🐾

Elterwater
Britannia Inn ✔
LA22 9HP
✪ 10-11 ☎ (015394) 37210 ⊕ britinn.co.uk
Coniston Bluebird Bitter; Eden Gold; 5 changing beers (sourced nationally) Ⓗ
A traditional Lakeland pub overlooking the village green. The small bar is to the right of the hallway, with the dining room off to the left, and the flagged back bar to the rear. Seven handpulls dispense the permanent beers, plus the house beer brewed in the style of Taylor's Landlord by Coniston Brewery, and the mainly Cumbrian guest ales. Dogs, children, muddy boots and dripping waterproofs are always welcome here. Q❄☀⇔◑AP🐾(516)

Ennerdale Bridge
Fox & Hounds Inn ⓛ
CA23 3AR
✪ 12-11 (11.30 Fri & Sat) ☎ (01946) 861373
⊕ foxandhoundsinn.org

Ennerdale Blonde, Darkest, Wild Ennerdale; 1 changing beer (sourced nationally) Ⓗ
A popular destination on Wainwright's coast-to-coast walk, with ready access to the heart of wild Ennerdale, this community-run traditional Lakeland inn, with one bus per week and no mobile phone signal, enjoys a sense of remoteness. Up to five local beers are offered, mostly from Ennerdale Brewery. The cosy bars have welcoming log fires, and quality freshly prepared dishes are sourced locally and provide hearty fare. Winter opening hours vary. Walkers, cyclists and dogs are welcome. Q★🌟🚲◐⬥▲♣🌢P🏠👪🛜

Eskdale Green

George IV Inn Ⓛ
CA19 1TS (400yds E of Outward Bound Centre)
✪ 11-midnight (1am Fri & Sat) ☎ (019467) 23470
🌐 kinggeorge-eskdale.co.uk
4 changing beers (sourced nationally) Ⓗ
Traditional Lakeland pub with oak beams, flagged floors and open fires in winter. Set at the entrance to the glorious Eskdale valley, this pub is renowned for its food and cask ales. It is popular with tourists and locals alike. Up to nine beers can be on offer at the busiest times of year. Mountain Goat buses run past in high season. Q★🌟🚲◐▲⬥P🏠🛜

Foxfield

Prince of Wales ♈ Ⓛ ✪
LA20 6BX
✪ 2.45-11; 11.45-11 Fri & Sat; 12-10.30 Sun; closed Mon & Tue ☎ (01229) 716238
6 changing beers (sourced nationally) Ⓗ
Stuart and Lynda are testament to what is achievable through passion and hard work at this splendid pub, voted CAMRA West Pennines Pub of the Year 2014. The guest ales come from the pub's two house breweries, Foxfield and Tigertops, plus others nationwide. Beers will always include a mild. Beer and cider festivals twice a year are an added bonus. Excellent accommodation includes superb breakfasts. Bus and rail stops are outside.
Q★🌟🚲◐⬥♣🌢P🏠👪🛜

Gilcrux

Barn Bistro Ⓛ
CA7 2QX (4 miles S of Aspatria via A596) NY114380
✪ 12 (5 Tue)-11; closed Mon ☎ (016973) 23289
🌐 barnbistro.co.uk
Jennings Bitter; 2 changing beers (sourced nationally) Ⓗ
Next to the Beeches Caravan Park in the village of Gilcrux, this restaurant-bar was formerly known as the Beeches. Renamed and reopened in 2010, the always-on Jennings Bitter (brewed five miles away in Cockermouth) is the landlord's favourite. The two other handpumps showcase Cumbria's many other breweries, with over 200 different local brews having being served in the Barn's six years. It also offers 35 malt whiskies plus a gin menu, and has a great reputation for its locally sourced food.
Q★🌟◐P👪

Gosforth

Gosforth Hall Inn Ⓛ
Wasdale Road, CA20 1AZ (next to St Mary's church)
✪ 12-11 ☎ (019467) 25322 🌐 gosforthhall.co.uk

Yates Golden Ale; 3 changing beers (sourced nationally) Ⓗ
Mid 17th-century Grade II-listed building set in attractive surroundings at the edge of this west Lakeland village close to Wasdale. The lounge reputedly has the widest spanning hearth in England. In winter there are real fires in both bar and lounge. Accommodation in the main building has recently been extensively refurbished. The menu always features a selection of the landlord's home-made pies. Q★🌟🚲◐⬥≢♣🌢P🏠👪🛜

Grasmere

Tweedies Bar (Dale Lodge Hotel) ✪
Langdale Road, LA22 9SW
✪ 12-11 (midnight Fri & Sat) ☎ (015394) 35300
🌐 dalelodgehotel.co.uk
8 changing beers (sourced nationally) Ⓗ
Popular hotel bar in the heart of Grasmere. The main bar, with a stone-flagged floor and welcoming wood-burning stove, has a side room leading off. The varied selection of beers always includes several local beers along with two changing ciders. A quiz night is held on Thursdays and there is live music at weekends, and an annual beer festival is staged in September in a marquee in the garden. ★🌟🚲◐🌢P🏠(555,599)👪🛜

Great Broughton

Punch Bowl Inn
19 Main Street, CA13 0YJ
✪ 8-11 Thu; 6-11 Fri; 3-11 Sat; 12-3, 6-11 Sun; closed Mon-Wed ☎ (01900) 267070
2 changing beers (sourced nationally) Ⓗ
Originally a coaching inn, this 17th-century hostelry is now a community pub, very much a drinkers' venue and run by a committee that includes a number of CAMRA members. It has two handpumps serving beer from a choice of Cumbrian breweries. The bar is adorned with sporting memorabilia and a selection of water jugs. The inn has darts, dominoes and a quiz team. The choice of beer is usually one light and one dark.
Q★P🏠🛜

Great Langdale

Old Dungeon Ghyll Hotel Ⓛ
LA22 9JY
✪ 11-11; 11-10.30 Sun ☎ (015394) 37272 🌐 odg.co.uk
Cumbrian Legendary Ales Esthwaite Bitter; Jennings Cumberland Ale; Theakston Old Peculier; Yates Bitter; 3 changing beers (sourced nationally) Ⓗ
Traditional walkers' and climbers' bar set in the magnificent Langdale valley, part of the hotel with a separate residents' bar. An old range in the main area always has a welcoming real fire, much needed after a long day on the fells in winter. There is always a good selection of local ales, with several guest beers in the summer months. The two charity folk festivals are popular.
Q★🌟🚲◐▲🌢P🏠(516)👪🛜

Great Orton

Wellington Inn
CA5 6LZ
✪ 12-2, 6-11; 12-3, 6-11.30 Sun; closed Mon & Tue ☎ (01228) 710775
Robinsons Dizzy Blonde, Trooper Ⓗ

Set in a quiet village a couple of miles north of Carlisle, this is an attractive country inn. Good-value meals using ingredients sourced locally are served, including meat from the renowned butcher. Two handpumps dispense ales from the Robinsons beer range as well as seasonal beers. Live music is being reintroduced here, with open mic nights on an occasional basis. There is space for 10 touring caravans on the adjacent campsite.
Q🐴❀🍴♿♣**P**

Great Salkeld

Highland Drove [L]

CA11 9NA
🕘 12-2.30 (not Mon), 6-11; 12-midnight Sat
☎ (01768) 898349 🌐 highland-drove.co.uk
Theakston Black Bull Bitter; house beer (by Eden); 1 changing beer [H]
Just off the main road through this attractive village, everything here is of a high standard. Entering the exceptionally well-stocked bar there is a lounge and a games room either side, with the award-winning Kyloes restaurant upstairs, all with carefully chosen decor, featuring exposed timber and brickwork embellished with Highland-style soft furnishings, brass and copper ornaments. Excellent food is served every day (no food Mon lunchtime) and themed nights have recently been introduced. Watch out for the Highland cows!
🐴❀🛏🍴♿⛺♣🐾📶

Greenodd

Ship [L]

Main Street, LA12 7QZ
🕘 5-11 (midnight Fri); 12-midnight Sat; 12-10.30 Sun; closed Mon ☎ 07782 655294
Greenodd Best Bitter, Citra, Coal Wharf, Roundabout; 1 changing beer (sourced nationally) [H]
A traditional village inn attracting a good mix of locals and visitors. Five handpumps deliver beers selected from a range of 20 or more brewed by Greenodd Brewery at the back of the building. The open-plan interior features slate floors, stone walls, exposed beams and open fires, with a separate quiet room to the rear. An authentic range of pizzas and Italian specials is served Wednesday to Sunday. 🐴🍴♣**P**🚌(X6)🐾📶

Hawkshead

King's Arms Hotel [L]

The Square, LA22 0NZ
🕘 11-midnight ☎ (015394) 36372
🌐 kingsarmshawkhead.co.uk
Cumbrian Legendary Ales Loweswater Gold; Hawkshead Bitter; 2 changing beers (sourced nationally) [H]
Characterful 500-year-old village inn on the square of this historic settlement. The traditional interior features beamed ceilings, an open fire and a hand-carved king in the bar supporting the floor above. Good food is available in the bar and dining area. The patio area is south-facing on the edge of the square. Frequent live music and twice-yearly beer festivals take place. The pub is family-friendly and dogs are welcome in the bar area. There are plenty of places to park in the village.
Q❀🛏🍴♣🚌(505)🐾

Red Lion [L]

Main Street, LA22 0NS
🕘 12-11; 12-10 Sun ☎ (015394) 36213
🌐 redlionhawkshead.co.uk
Cumbrian Legendary Ales Esthwaite Bitter; Hawkshead Bitter; Tarn Hows Pigling Blonde; 2 changing beers (sourced nationally) [H]
A 15th-century coaching inn set in one of the prettiest villages in the Lake District, with links to Wordsworth and Beatrix Potter. Food is honestly priced, sourced locally and available all day. There is a warm and friendly informal atmosphere; dogs and wet boots are welcome, and it is a great place to relax. The attractive paved patio area has plenty of tables for summer eating and drinking.
🐴❀🛏🍴♣**P**🚌(505,525)🐾📶

Hesket Newmarket

Old Crown Inn [L] ✔

CA7 8JG
🕘 5-11; 12-11 Fri & Sat; 12-10.30 Sun ☎ (016974) 78288
Hesket Newmarket Haystacks, Black Sail, Helvellyn Gold, High Pike, Doris' 90th Birthday Ale, Brim Fell [H]
Sitting in the heart of this lovely fell-side village, the Old Crown is a showcase for the Hesket Newmarket Brewery, which is immediately behind the pub. It is well known as the first co-operatively owned pub in the country and is popular with locals and visitors alike, with Prince Charles and Sir Chris Bonington among its supporters. Closed Monday to Thursday afternoons in winter, with no meals on winter Mondays. **Q**🐴❀🍴♣🍎🐾📶

Holmes Green

Black Dog Inn [L]

Broughton Road, LA15 8JP (from Dalton 1 mile past South Lakes Safari Zoo) SD233761
🕘 4 (3 Fri & Sat)-midnight; 12-9 Sun; closed Mon
☎ (01229) 462975
Abbeydale Moonshine; Cumbrian Legendary Ales Loweswater Gold; Hawkshead Windermere Pale; 3 changing beers (sourced nationally) [H]
A warm welcome awaits at the Black Dog from the landlord and locals alike. The former coaching inn, with two real fires, quarry-tiled floor and rustic beams, has plenty of character. Five real ales are on offer, with local microbreweries well supported. Live music features most Saturdays, plus open mic nights and music festivals (Dog Fest!). Quality food is served on Thursdays, Saturday evenings and Sunday lunchtimes. **Q**🐴❀🍴**P**🐾📶

Ings

Watermill Inn [L]

LA8 9PY
🕘 11-11; 11-10.30 Sun ☎ (01539) 821309
🌐 watermillinn.co.uk
Watermill A Bit'er Ruff, Collie Wobbles, Dogth Vader, Isle of Dogs, Windermere Blonde, Wruff Night; 8 changing beers (sourced nationally) [H]
An award-winning family-owned pub and brewery with a relaxed and friendly atmosphere, serving up to 16 real ales, including those brewed on site. The two recently refurbished bars are a mecca for real ale. The bottom bar has viewing windows into both the cellar and the on-site brewery. A wide selection of meals is served daily until 9pm, while dogs are provided with biscuits and water.
Q🐴❀🛏🍴♿♣🍎**P**🚆🚌(555)🐾📶

Kendal

Castle Inn

Castle Street, LA9 7AA

🔆 11.30-midnight (1am Fri & Sat); 12.30-11.30 Sun
☎ (01539) 729983 ⊕ castleinnkendal.webs.com

Cumbrian Legendary Ales Loweswater Gold; Hawkshead Bitter; Sharp's Doom Bar; Tetley Bitter; Timothy Taylor Landlord; 1 changing beer (sourced nationally) 🅗

A popular local pub which is also welcoming to visitors. The central bar serves several areas, the lounge to the left has a fine fish tank set into the side wall, and the bar area to the right has a dartboard. Up a step is the adjoining games area with pool table. Good-value, quickly served lunches, especially the Sunday roast, are a popular feature. Close to the town centre and the ruins of Kendal Castle. 🛏🕽🍴🕭➔♣🖵(43)🐾🛜

Rifleman's Arms 🅛 ✅

4 Greenside, LA9 4LD

🔆 6.30-midnight; 12-midnight Sat & Sun ☎ (01539) 723224

Greene King Abbot; 4 changing beers (sourced nationally) 🅗

A true community pub on the edge of town, with the Vaux motif still etched on the windows. Numerous local groups meet here, with a popular live folk music session on Thursdays. It has a quiet atmosphere, with a Sunday quiz and traditional pub games. There are always five real ales on tap, including local beers. The pub looks out onto a pleasant green and is often involved with events taking place there. Q🛏♣🖵(44,48)🐾

Keswick

Dog & Gun 🅛 ✅

2 Lake Road, CA12 5BT

🔆 11-11 (midnight Fri & Sat); 12-11 Sun ☎ (017687) 73463
⊕ thedogandgunkeswick.co.uk

Theakston Old Peculier; 4 changing beers (sourced nationally) 🅗

The pub has been completely refurbished, with a change in design that has created more seating and space. The menu has been updated but has kept the goulash, which is its signature dish. A large range of beers is offered, with the pub acting as brewery tap for Keswick Brewery, situated 500 yards away – Woof & Bang is brewed especially for them. A very popular venue with locals and tourists alike. 🛏🕽🕭♣🖵(X4,X5,555)🐾🛜

Wainwright

Lake Road, CA12 5BZ

🔆 11.30-11.30 (midnight Fri & Sat) ☎ (017687) 44927
⊕ thewainwright.pub

Thwaites Wainwright; 6 changing beers (sourced nationally) 🅗

A recent refurbishment has created a dining area in the front and a large open bar to the rear, where food is also served. The Wainwright theme has been incorporated into the decor, with a pictorial guide to where in the county beers are from. There are large-screen TVs, with the sound turned off, showing Wainwright walks. The beers served are from all over Cumbria with the exception of Thwaites Wainwright. Q🛏🕽🖵(X4,X5,555)🐾

Kings Meaburn

White Horse Inn

CA10 3BU

🔆 5-11; 12-11 Sat; 12-10.30 Sun ☎ (01931) 714256

Cumberland Corby Ale; 3 changing beers (sourced nationally) 🅗

A 400-year-old whitewashed pub set in the picturesque Lyvennet Valley, a real locals' place with good craic, friendly patrons, a roaring fire and well-kept local ales. Numerous community events are supported throughout the year including the summer beer and music festival each July. Great home-cooked meals include Jess's famous pies. Superb cycling and walking are at hand in the lovely quiet surrounds of the Eden Valley. Q🛏🕽🕭♣🐾

Kirkby Lonsdale

Orange Tree 🅛 ✅

9 Fairbank, LA6 2BD

🔆 11-11 (midnight Fri & Sat) ☎ (015242) 71716
⊕ theorangetreehotel.co.uk

Kirkby Lonsdale Tiffin Gold, Ruskins Bitter, Singletrack, Monumental Blonde, Jubilee Stout; 3 changing beers (sourced nationally) 🅗

This local pub, formerly the Fleece, was renamed after a pub near Twickenham, and the walls are adorned with rugby memorabilia. It is the brewery tap of Kirkby Lonsdale Brewery, so always has five of its beers available plus a guest beer and a real cider. It has been a worthy former local CAMRA Pub of the Year on several occasions. There is a separate dining area to the rear serving good wholesome food. 🛏🚪🕽♣🖵(567)🐾🛜

Kirkby-in-Furness

Burlington Inn 🅛

Askew Gate Brow, LA17 7TF

🔆 4-midnight (1am Fri); 2-1am Sat; 12-midnight Sun
☎ (01229) 889039

Beckstones Black Dog Freddy Mild; 4 changing beers (sourced nationally) 🅗

Busy roadside inn on a crossroads at the centre of the village, named after the slate quarry situated on the hills above and the reason for the village's existence. Four handpumps dispense a varied selection of local and other ales. Food is served Wednesday to Saturday evenings and Sunday lunchtime only. Several separate drinking areas make this a cosy, atmospheric pub. The dining room at the rear has pleasant views over the Duddon Estuary to the fells. No trains on Sunday. 🛏🕭🕽≠P🐾

Kirkoswald

Fetherston Arms

The Square, CA10 1DQ

🔆 4-11; 12-midnight Sat & Sun ☎ (01768) 898284
⊕ fetherston-arms.co.uk

Theakston Best Bitter; 3 changing beers (often Allendale, Hesket Newmarket) 🅗

The Fethers is situated in the centre of this historic village. Extensive alterations and the friendly enthusiasm of the family owners have helped convert it into a truly outstanding pub. It has a well-deserved excellent reputation for its food. Three changing real ales come from breweries such as Allendale and Hesket Newmarket. Although the village is not on a bus route, it is 20 minutes' stroll from Lazonby station on the Carlisle-Settle line. Check hours in winter. Q🛏🕭🕽🐾🐾🛜

Little Langdale

Three Shires Hotel ✅

LA22 9NZ

🌣 11-11; 12-10.30 Sun ☎ (015394) 37215

⊕ threeshiresinn.co.uk

Coniston Old Man Ale; Cumbrian Legendary Ales Loweswater Gold; Hawkshead Windermere Pale; Jennings Cumberland Ale Ⓗ

A family-run village hostelry popular with tourists and the local population of this Lakeland valley. The main bar has a slate-flagged floor with a small snug to the side, which was the original bar. A good selection of malt whiskies and home-made food is available. There are superb views of the Southern Fells from the front of the pub, and the much photographed Slater's bridge is a short walk away. Closed early January. Q🍽🛏🕿⊄🕪⑀ᵱ❅

Loppergarth

Wellington Inn ⑃

Main Street, LA12 0JL

🌣 6-11 (10 Mon; 1am Fri & Sat); closed Sun

☎ (01229) 582388

Healey's Best, Blonde; 3 changing beers (sourced nationally) Ⓗ

Superb village local with its own microbrewery – Healey's – a custom-made stainless steel plant which is viewable from the games room. Four handpumps, occasionally five, primarily dispense Healey's beers. These include an award-winning blonde, a golden bitter, a traditional darker best bitter, a superb mild and occasional specials. Wood-burning stoves make this a cosy pub, with games, books and good conversation. There is a quiz on alternate Saturdays. 🍽❅♣●🕈❅≋

Loweswater

Kirkstile Inn ⑃

CA13 0RU (off B5289, 7 miles S from Cockermouth) NY140210

🌣 11-11; 11-10.30 Sun ☎ (01900) 85219 ⊕ kirkstile.com

Cumbrian Legendary Ales Esthwaite Bitter, Langdale, Grasmoor Dark Ale, Loweswater Gold; 1 changing beer (sourced nationally) Ⓗ

The brewery tap for Cumbrian Legendary Ales, creator of the 2011 Champion Golden Ale of Britain, Loweswater Gold, originally brewed in the pub, but now in bigger premises near Hawkshead. A short stroll from the waters of Loweswater and Crummock, this 16th-century pub has six handpumps, two seating areas and a reputation for food (but take note, it will be busy at mealtimes). Consistent winner and finalist for local CAMRA branch Pub of the Year since the early 2000s. Q🍽❅🛏⊄🕪⑀ᵱ❅

Melmerby

Shepherds Inn ⑃

CA10 1HF

🌣 12-11 ☎ (01768) 889064

6 changing beers Ⓗ

Built in 1789, this fine pub has a seating area at one end complete with easy chairs and, at the other end, an attached barn that has been converted into an airy dining area. Both rooms create a relaxed atmosphere, with fine oak beams in the barn and stone-flagged floors throughout. The good beer is complemented by excellent food.

The changing guest ales usually include a good representation from Cumbrian breweries. Hours vary depending on the time of year. 🍽⊄🕪ᕤᵱᕕ❅≋

Monkhill

Drovers Rest ⑂

CA5 6DB

🌣 12-11 ☎ (01228) 576141

4 changing beers Ⓗ

A traditional country pub close to the popular Hadrian's Wall path, with a strong community focus. Although opened up, the interior still has the feel of three distinct rooms. The bar area is cosy and welcoming, with a roaring fire in winter. Some interesting historical State Management Scheme documents adorn the walls. The Drovers is an oasis for different and sometimes obscure (for the area) real ales. Winner of the CAMRA Super Regional Pub of the Year award. 🍽❅⊄ᕤ♣ᵱ🕮(93)❅

Near Sawrey

Tower Bank Arms ⑃

LA22 0LF (on B5285 2 miles S of Hawkshead)

🌣 12-11; 12-10.30 Sun ☎ (015394) 36334

⊕ towerbankarms.co.uk

Cumbrian Legendary Ales Loweswater Gold; Hawkshead Bitter, Brodie's Prime; 2 changing beers (sourced nationally) Ⓗ

A 17th-century Lakeland inn with slate floors, oak beams and a cast-iron range with open fire. It is next to the National Trust Hill Top (Beatrix Potter's home), and delivers great local flavours in food, beer and atmosphere. Five handpumps serve local beer, and cider and perry are available. Families and dogs are welcomed. There is a seasonal bus service connecting to the Windermere ferry and Hawkshead. Phone to check winter hours. Q🍽❅🛏⊄🕪♣●ᵱ🕮❅

Nether Wasdale

Strands Inn ⑂ ⑃

CA20 1ET

🌣 11-11; 11-10.30 Sun ☎ (019467) 26237

⊕ thestrandsinn.com

Strands Pied Piper, Green Bullet, Brown Bitter, Low Flyer, Irresponsibly, T'errmmm-inator; 6 changing beers (sourced nationally) Ⓗ

Along winding, wooded and gently hilly lanes, this picturesque village is a delightful surprise, with its view of the highest mountains in England just a few miles away. One of three real ale pubs in the locality, Strands has its own brewery, with any six of around 30 beers on the bar (and more in bottles). Try them all in May at the festival of beers. There is no mobile phone reception in the valley, but there is free Wi-Fi here. Local CAMRA branch Pub of the Year for 2016. Q🍽❅🛏⊄🕪♣ᵱ❅≋

Newbiggin

Blue Bell Inn ⑃

Heads Nook, CA8 9DH

🌣 6 (7 Mon)-midnight; 6-1am Fri; 12-3, 6-1am Sat; 12-3, 6-midnight Sun ☎ (01768) 896615

⊕ bluebellinnnewbiggin.co.uk

1 changing beer (sourced locally; often Cumberland, Eden, Tirril) Ⓗ

Nestled in the North Pennines Area of Outstanding Natural Beauty, this small country pub is popular with the locals. It also attracts holidaymakers and walkers needing refreshment, with food served every evening and lunchtimes at weekends. Try the renowned home-made chips. Traditional pub games, darts and pool can be enjoyed. It stocks one real ale from a local brewery. Winter hours may vary. Look out for the naughty gnomes! ❀❀◑&♣P

Penrith

Moo Bar ℒ
52 King Street, CA11 7AY
✪ 12-12.30am ☎ 07832 475910
6 changing beers ⊞
A small and intimate venue in the centre of Penrith on three floors, which only became a pub in 2012. Since then it has rapidly built up a reputation for offering a wide range of beers. There is always a mix of ales sourced locally and from further afield. Small brewery keg beers are also kept and real cider is often available. There is a large choice of bottled beers from around the world. ➳≠◲❀⬠

Ravenglass

Inn at Ravenglass ℒ
Main Street, CA18 1SQ (N end, overlooking Irish Sea)
✪ 12-11; 12-8 Sun ☎ (01229) 717230
⊕ theinnatravenglass.co.uk
Bowness Bay Swan Blonde; Ulverston Laughing Gravy; 2 changing beers (sourced nationally) ⊞
A 17th-century inn in this national park coastal hamlet that was once a Roman port. The dining room has a reputation for seafood, fresh from the local catch of the day. A good range of real ales is particularly enjoyable after a day in the fells, or messing about in boats. You can enjoy great sunset views over the estuary. Close to Ravenglass stations for mainline and Ravenglass & Eskdale valley railways (La'al Ratty), it gives easy access to the Western Lakes valleys.
Q❀➳❀◑⬠▲≠♣●P◲(6)❀⬠

Rosthwaite

Scafell Hotel
Borrowdale, CA12 5XB (on B5289)
✪ 12-11; 12-10.30 Sun ☎ (017687) 77208 ⊕ scafell.co.uk
Jennings Bitter, Cumberland Ale; 4 changing beers (sourced nationally) ⊞
Open all year round, the Riverside Bar is positioned to the left of the main hotel building, which sits six miles south of Keswick, on the Borrowdale road. In good weather, enjoy the garden and its mountain views. For the rest of the time a roaring coal fire helps welcome walkers, cyclists (it is on the Coast-to-Coast and Cumbrian Way routes), fell runners and drinkers. There are six handpumps on the long slate-fronted bar, offering mainly Cumbrian beers. ➳❀◲◑&▲♣●P◲(78)❀

Rydal

Badger Bar (Glen Rothay Hotel) ℒ
LA22 9LR
✪ 10-11; 10-10.30 Sun ☎ (015394) 34500
⊕ theglenrothay.co.uk
Barngates Goodhew's Dry Stout; 4 changing beers (sourced nationally) ⊞

Situated opposite the beautiful Rydal Water and close to Rydal Mount, there are ample opportunities for the keen walker in the area. Several rooms off the main bar offer a cosy and welcoming atmosphere, and the refurbished toilets feature local stone. All the beers are from Cumbria or close by – the house beer is brewed by Old School Brewery. Reasonably priced food is locally sourced. Local photographs and artefacts adorn the walls. Q➳❀◲◑▲P◲(555,599)❀⬠

St Bees

Manor ✪
Main Street, CA27 0DE
✪ 12-11 ☎ (01946) 820587
St Austell Tribute; 3 changing beers (sourced nationally) ⊞
One hundred yards from the railway station, this Grade I-listed hotel, one of four pubs on the main street offering real ale, is popular with tourists and locals alike for its food and the three changing beers. The pub boasts a sports bar, lounge bar, dining areas, garden and a pleasant outside drinking area. It is on the picturesque Carlisle to Barrow train line and near the start of the Coast-to-Coast walk. ➳❀◲◑≠●P◲(6)❀⬠

Sebergham

Sour Nook Inn
Sour Nook, CA5 7DY
✪ 5-11 Mon & Tue; closed Wed; 11.30-11 (midnight Fri & Sat); 12-11 Sun ☎ (016974) 76242 ⊕ sournookinn.co.uk
House beer (by Tetley); 2 changing beers (often Hesket Newmarket) ⊞
On the B5305 on the southern edge of the village, this pub has a Tack Room bar, a pool/darts room, a function room and restaurant. Meals are locally sourced and reasonably priced (no food Wed). The area tractor group meets here on a regular basis, and the local fells pensioner group meets fortnightly for a specially produced lunch. It usually serves at least one guest ale from the local Hesket Newmarket Brewery in addition to Sour Nook (Tetley Bitter). ➳❀◑&♣●P❀

Staveley

Beer Hall ▼ ℒ ✪
Mill Yard, LA8 9LR
✪ 12-6 (5 Mon; 11 Fri & Sat); 12-8 Sun ☎ (01539) 825260
⊕ hawksheadbrewery.co.uk
Hawkshead Windermere Pale, Bitter, Red, Lakeland Gold, Brodie's Prime, Cumbrian Five Hop ⊞
The brewery tap next door to the brewery, on two storeys; on both floors there is a mix of comfy sofas and solid wooden furniture. The food menu now includes a good selection of tapas to complement the Hawkshead beers. Spring (March) and summer (July) beer festivals are held, with up to 60 beers to sample. The beer shop has a range of bottled Hawkshead and foreign beers.
Q➳❀◑&▲≠♣●P◲(555)❀⬠

Eagle & Child Hotel
Kendal Road, LA8 9LP
✪ 11-11; 12-10.30 Sun ☎ (01539) 821320
⊕ eaglechildinn.co.uk
5 changing beers (sourced nationally) ⊞
In winter there are log fires to keep you warm and in summer riverside tables and the garden to

enjoy. The five changing beers are mainly from Cumbria or north Lancashire, often including a Yates ale. The pub has an interesting arrangement of artefacts around the walls. There are great lunchtime meal deals including a two-course Sunday lunch. An entertaining Thursday night quiz is held, popular both with locals and visitors.
Q ≿ ✿⌂◑≈➸P🖵 (555)😺 🤶

Talkin

Blacksmiths Arms Ⓛ
CA8 1LE
✿ 12-3, 6-11 ☎ (016977) 3452 ⊕ blacksmithstalkin.co.uk
Black Sheep Ale; Yates Bitter; 2 changing beers Ⓗ
Since taking over in 1997, the present owners have made this probably the most popular pub in the vicinity. The winning formula includes four real ales, a superbly stocked bar, friendly, efficient staff, no TV, and meticulous attention to detail. Set on the edge of an Area of Outstanding Natural Beauty, with a golf course and country park within two miles and plenty of other outdoor activities available locally, it attracts visitors from far outside the north Cumbria area. Q ≿ ✿⌂◑ ᵬ♣P 🤶

Tallentire

Bush Inn
Tallentire, CA13 0PT
✿ 5.30-midnight; closed Mon ☎ (01900) 823707
3 changing beers (sourced nationally) Ⓗ
An old-fashioned pub that often serves at least one ale from a Cumbrian brewery. The hub of the community and home of the cricket team, it hosts a traditional music session on the last Wednesday of the month. In addition to its exposed beams, stone floor and wood-burning stove, the pub also has an exterior sensitive to the character of the village. Food is served in a separate restaurant Thursday to Saturday evenings. Q◑➸😺🤶

The Green

Punch Bowl Ⓛ
The Green, LA18 5HJ
✿ 5.30-11; 5.30-10.30 Sun ☎ (01229) 774457
⊕ the-punch-bowl.co.uk
6 changing beers (sourced nationally) Ⓗ
Sitting on the A5093, the Punch Bowl is a thriving community pub, with up to six handpumps serving local beers from Beckstones and Barngates breweries alongside other ales both local and from further afield. It is one of the venues for the popular Broughton Festival of Beer which is held each autumn. The open-plan bar area has real fires. Food is served on Wednesday and Friday evenings, and at other times by arrangement. Closed Monday in winter (ring to check). Q≿✿⌂◑ᵬ♣P😺🤶

Troutbeck

Mortal Man Ⓛ
LA23 1PL (nr Windermere)
✿ 10.30-midnight ☎ (015394) 33193
⊕ themortalman.co.uk
Coniston Bluebird Bitter; Cumbrian Legendary Ales Loweswater Gold; Hawkshead Bitter; Hesket Newmarket Haystacks; 1 changing beer (sourced nationally) Ⓗ
An unspoilt pub within the hotel which is popular with locals and walkers, comprising a main bar and

several smaller dining areas and a large well-appointed garden. The bar and garden have spectacular views of the Troutbeck valley down to Windermere and the surrounding fells. A range of local ales is available all year round, with guest beers in summer. ≿✿⌂◑ᵬ➸P🖵 (517)😺 🤶

Ulverston

Devonshire Arms Ⓛ
Braddyll Terrace, Victoria Road, LA12 0DH
✿ 4 (3 Fri)-11; 12-midnight Sat; 12-11 Sun
☎ (01229) 582537
Abbeydale Absolution; Copper Dragon Golden Pippin; Cumbrian Legendary Ales Loweswater Gold; 5 changing beers (sourced nationally) Ⓗ
Conveniently situated between the bus and train station, the Dev is a real locals' pub with a welcoming atmosphere. Four TVs provide comprehensive sports coverage, while there is plenty of room for banter around the bar or more intimate conversation in the comfortable seating areas. Outside tables are popular especially in summer, and solar panels provide supplementary power. An informal quiz is held every other Sunday and a pool table and two dartboards add to the entertainment. ≿✿ᵬ Å≈♣P🖵😺 🤶

Mill Ⓛ
Mill Street, LA12 7EB
✿ 11-11 (midnight Fri & Sat); 11-10.30 Sun
☎ (01229) 581384 ⊕ mill-at-ulverston.co.uk
Lancaster Amber, Blonde, Black, Red; 6 changing beers (sourced nationally) Ⓗ
Town-centre converted flour mill with an interesting layout. The original waterwheel is central to the ground floor, fed from the stream channelled alongside the first-floor outdoor terrace. Food is served in both the bar and, on weekends, in the upstairs restaurant (booking recommended). Tuesday is quiz night and open mic session is Wednesday, while a loft bar/ function suite serves wine and cocktails on Friday and Saturday evenings. ≿✿◑ᵬ Å≈🖵😺 🤶

Old Friends Ⓛ
49 Soutergate, LA12 7ES
✿ 4-11; 2-midnight Fri; 12-midnight Sat; 12-10.30 Sun
☎ (01229) 208195
Old School Blackboard; Stringers Plan B; 6 changing beers (sourced nationally) Ⓗ
Welcoming old-fashioned locals' pub about 200 yards uphill from the town centre. There is a cosy snug in front of the bar with an open fire; another seating area with TV is separated by a passageway with a hatch to the bar. Beers are mostly from local brewers. A popular quiz night is held every Tuesday and there is a wonderful beer garden at the back.
≿✿Å≈➸🖵😺 🤶

Stan Laurel Inn Ⓛ
31 The Ellers, LA12 0AB
✿ 7-11 Mon; 12-2.30, 6-11 (midnight Fri & Sat); 12-11.30 Sun
☎ (01229) 582814 ⊕ thestanlaurel.co.uk
Thwaites Original; 5 changing beers (sourced nationally) Ⓗ
Just off the centre of Stan Laurel's home town, the Stan offers a warm welcome to locals and visitors alike. Six handpulls serve a variety of mainly locally brewed beers. Excellent-value quality food is available throughout the week (no food Mon). Adjacent to the bar is a large room with pool and darts, and a smaller room primarily used by diners.

In winter a log-burning stove adds to the pub's comfortable ambience. Well-behaved dogs are welcome. Q✿☎🛏🕔🍴🎵♣P🚆(6,6A)🐾 🛜

Swan Inn 🅛
Swan Street, LA12 7JX
✪ 3.30-11; 12-midnight Fri-Sun ☎ (01229) 582519
9 changing beers (sourced nationally) Ⓗ
On the edge of the town centre overlooking the A590, the pub has an open-plan feel, yet there are three distinct drinking areas for darts, TV or just good conversation by the fire. Live music features occasionally, while a jukebox allows all genres of music to be played. All Premier League football and major sports events are screened, and a Sunday night quiz rounds off the entertainment. A large beer garden behind the pub is popular in summer. ✿♿🍴♣🚲🚆(6,X6)🐾 🛜

Underbarrow

Punch Bowl Inn 🅛
LA8 8HQ
✪ 12-3, 6-11; closed Tue; 12-11 Sat & Sun
☎ (015395) 68234 ⊕ punch-bowl-inn.co.uk
3 changing beers (sourced nationally) Ⓗ
Traditional village inn on a scenic route between Kendal and Windermere. The flagstone-floored main bar includes large leather sofas around an inglenook fireplace. The pub is popular with locals, walkers and their dogs, and those who love good beer and food. There are separate dining and function rooms. Happy hour is 4-6pm on Wednesday and 5-6pm on Friday. There is free local-radius transport home for diners. Q✿☎🕔♿♣🐾 🛜

Waberthwaite

Brown Cow Inn 🅛
LA19 5YJ (on A595)
✪ 4-11.30; 12-11.30 Fri-Sun ☎ (01229) 717243
⊕ thebrowncowinn.com
Ennerdale Blonde; Hawkshead Bitter; 7 changing beers (sourced nationally) Ⓗ
This 100-year-old pub is the centre of activity in a lively village. Beers are from Cumbrian and north Lancashire breweries – the local ale tasting society helps to choose the guest ales. An annual beer festival is held in June. Cider is available in summer. Home-cooked food uses local produce. Quiz nights are held regularly and live music features occasionally at weekends. The pub is close to the Western Fells, the coast and Eskmeals Nature Reserve. A recent winner of local CAMRA branch awards. Q✿☎🛏🕔♣🍴♠P🚆🐾 🛜

Watermillock

Brackenrigg Inn 🅛
CA11 0LP (on A592)
✪ 12-11; 12-10.30 Sun ☎ (017684) 86206
⊕ brackenrigginn.co.uk
Black Sheep Best Bitter; Brack 'n' Brew Ullswater Gold, Blonde; 5 changing beers (sourced nationally) Ⓗ
A large, welcoming roadside inn with outstanding views of Ullswater and the north-eastern Lake District fells which attracts locals and tourists with a friendly atmosphere and real fires. The landlord keeps up to three guest ales in winter and seven in the summer. The Brack 'n' Brew Brewery is at the

rear of the pub. There is a great range of locally sourced food and cheeses. Q✿☎🛏🕔♿🍴♠P🚆(108)🐾 🛜

Wetheral

Wheatsheaf Inn 🅛 ✅
CA4 8HD
✪ 12-11 (midnight Fri & Sat); 12-11.30 Sun
☎ (01228) 560686
Cumberland Corby Ale; 2 changing beers Ⓗ
An early 19th-century village pub, just a few minutes' walk from the village green and railway station, deservedly popular with locals and visitors. Along with Corby Ale from the local Cumberland Brewery, there are two changing ales from both local and national breweries. Good-value bar meals are served Wednesday to Sunday. Booking is advisable at weekends. The regular Tuesday quiz nights are well supported. A former local CAMRA award winner. ✿☎🕔🍴♣P🚆(75)🐾 🛜

Whitehaven

Vagabond 🅛
9 Marlborough Street, Harbourside, CA28 7LL
✪ 7-11; 4-midnight Fri; 12-midnight Sat; closed Sun
☎ (01946) 66653 ⊕ thevagabondpub.co.uk
4 changing beers (sourced nationally) Ⓗ
A two-storey pub with wooden floors, close to the harbour. It serves four beers in the downstairs bar, which is used to host regular popular musical entertainment; the upstairs area is generally used for dining, parties and meetings. Lunchtime food is served at weekends only, but at all times is locally sourced. Q✿🕔♿🍴🚆 🛜

Wreay

Plough Inn 🅛
CA4 0RL
✪ 7-11 Mon; 5.30-11 Tue; 12-3, 5.30-11 ☎ (016974) 75770
⊕ theploughwreay.co.uk
Hawkshead Lakeland Gold; 2 changing beers (sourced locally) Ⓗ
Tastefully modernised pub dating back to 1786, set in the heart of this picturesque village, just five miles south of Carlisle. Locally sourced, excellent food is served in the split-level bar and dining area, with two cask ales from Cumbrian breweries usually available. The village guardians continue to use it as a meeting place – their display of clay pipes can be seen inside. Quiz night is Monday at 8pm and acoustic night is Tuesday. Q✿☎🕔P🐾

Yanwath

Gate Inn
CA10 2LF
✪ 12-11 ☎ (01768) 862316 ⊕ yanwathgate.com
Yates Bitter; 3 changing beers (sourced nationally) Ⓗ
Lovely old hostelry in a quiet village close to the M6 and the northern fells. Friendly staff, a roaring fire and low beams await. A separate dining room affords a pleasant atmosphere in which to enjoy award-winning fare, along with an imaginative wine list. The pub only serves ales – there is no keg lager. Q✿☎🕔♣♠P🚆(108)🐾

DERBYSHIRE

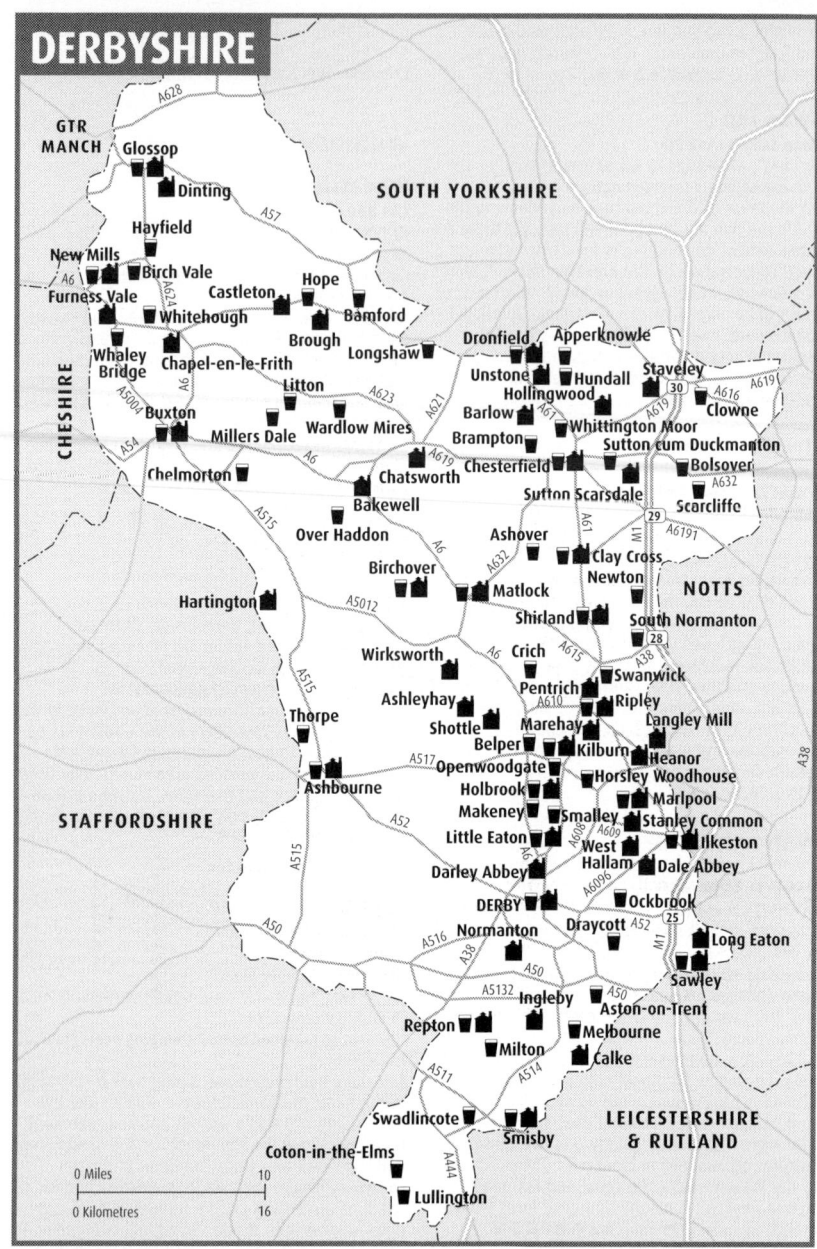

GTR MANCH
Glossop
Dinting
Hayfield
New Mills
Birch Vale
Furness Vale
Castleton
Hope
Whitehough
Bamford
Brough
Whaley Bridge
Chapel-en-le-Frith
Longshaw
Litton
Buxton
Millers Dale
Wardlow Mires
Chelmorton
Chatsworth
Bakewell
Over Haddon
Birchover
Hartington
Matlock
Shirland
Wirksworth
Crich
Ashleyhay
Pentrich
Thorpe
Shottle
Marehay
Belper
Ashbourne
Openwoodgate
Holbrook
Makeney
Little Eaton
Darley Abbey
DERBY
Normanton
Ingleby
Repton
Milton
Swadlincote
Coton-in-the-Elms
Smisby
Lullington

SOUTH YORKSHIRE
Dronfield
Apperknowle
Unstone
Hundall
Staveley
Hollingwood
Barlow
Clowne
Brampton
Whittington Moor
Sutton cum Duckmanton
Chesterfield
Bolsover
Scarcliffe
Sutton Scarsdale
Ashover
Clay Cross
Newton
NOTTS
South Normanton
Swanwick
Ripley
Langley Mill
Kilburn
Heanor
Horsley Woodhouse
Marlpool
Smalley
Stanley Common
West Hallam
Ilkeston
Dale Abbey
Ockbrook
Draycott
Long Eaton
Sawley
Aston-on-Trent
Melbourne
Calke
LEICESTERSHIRE & RUTLAND

CHESHIRE
STAFFORDSHIRE
GTR MANCH

0 Miles 10
0 Kilometres 16

Apperknowle

Traveller's Rest

High Street, S18 4BD SK384782

🕐 12-11 ☎ (01246) 460169

🌐 travellersrestapperknowle.co.uk

Abbeydale Moonshine; John Smith's Bitter; Timothy Taylor Landlord ⊞; 3 changing beers (sourced nationally; often Church End, Oldershaw, Welbeck Abbey) ⊞/Ⓖ

The Traveller's Rest is a regular winner of branch awards, including local CAMRA Pub of the Year for 2014 and 2015. It is a traditional country hostelry at the edge of the village, serving a good range of

beers, cider and perries. The outdoor drinking area provides sweeping views over the Drone Valley – one of the best views in Derbyshire. Good-quality food is available at all times, with the cheese platters and pork pies being particularly popular. Live music features strongly, with jazz every Monday night. Q☎✿🐕◗Å♣🌳P🚌☕🛜

Ashbourne

Smith's Tavern ✅

36 St John Street, DE6 1GH

🕐 12-11 (midnight Fri & Sat) ☎ (01335) 300809

Banks's Sunbeam; Jennings Bitter; Marston's Pedigree; Ringwood Fortyniner; 4 changing beers (often Jennings, Marston's) Ⓗ
Small, highly traditional town-centre pub, with as many as seven real ales. The landlord selects the widest possible choice of beers from the Marston's portfolio. He is also allowed one free choice guest ale, served at weekends, always from a local brewery. A local CAMRA Pub of the Year three times in succession in recent years. **Q♣🚌🐾📶**

Ashover

Old Poets' Corner Ⓛ

Butts Road, S45 0EW (downhill from church)
⏲ 12-11 ☎ (01246) 590888 🌐 oldpoets.co.uk
Ashover Poets Tipple, Butts Pale Ale; changing beers Ⓗ
Home of the award-winning Ashover Brewery, this large Brewers' Tudor pub is a frequent CAMRA award winner, the most recent being East Midlands Pub of the Year 2015. The staff welcome walkers and dogs and provide excellent food and beer. Choose from up to 10 beers, including several from Ashover, along with a range of guest ales, traditional ciders, bottled Belgian beers and country wines. The pub hosts three beer festivals a year, weekly quizzes and live music.
Q❀🛏◐♿♣●P🚌(63,64)**🐾📶**

Aston-on-Trent

Malt Ⓛ ✔

14 The Green, DE72 2AA
⏲ 12-11 (midnight Fri & Sat) ☎ (01332) 792256
🌐 themaltpubaston.co.uk
Draught Bass; Marston's Pedigree; Sharp's Doom Bar; 3 changing beers (often Dancing Duck) Ⓗ
The Tudor exterior makes this pub stand out from the other properties just off the main road in the centre of Aston-on-Trent. A traditional two-room village pub, it has oak panelling in one room and beams throughout, adding to a cosy and stylish atmosphere. A cheery welcome awaits families, dogs and walkers. It is popular for meals, and there is a choice of six beers, with an emphasis on local brews from the Derby and Nottingham areas.
Q🔥❀◐♣P🚌🐾📶

Bamford

Anglers Rest Ⓛ

Main Road, S33 0DY
⏲ 11-11 (midnight Sat); 12-11 Sun ☎ (01433) 659317
🌐 bcs.anglers.rest
Black Sheep Best Bitter; Intrepid Explorer; 3 changing beers (sourced locally; often Abbeydale, Bradfield, Intrepid) Ⓗ
At the heart of Bamford and not far from Ladybower Reservoir, this is a community hub in every sense, where the locals have been running the pub (and associated Post Office and café) since 2013. The main bar is the focal point and is extremely popular with families, walkers and, particularly, cyclists, who have access to dedicated cycle parking and a DIY repair shop. There is also a quieter snug. Good-value, rustic bar food is served Wednesday to Sunday.
Q🔥❀◐♿⛺⇌♣P🚌(273,274)**🐾📶**

Belper

Arkwright's Real Ale Bar Ⓛ

5 Campbell Street, DE56 1AP
⏲ 4-11; 12-11 Sat & Sun ☎ (01773) 823117
🌐 arkwrightsbar.com
Marston's Pedigree; 6 changing beers Ⓗ

REAL ALE BREWERIES

Abstract Jungle Langley Mill (NEW)
Amber Ripley
Ashleyhay Ashleyhay
Ashover ▪ Clay Cross
Barlow Barlow
Birchover ▪ Birchover (NEW)
Boot ▪ Repton (NEW)
Bottle Brook Kilburn
Brampton Chesterfield
Brunswick ▪ Derby
Bumpmill Shirland
Buxton Buxton
Dancing Duck Derby
Derby Derby
Derventio Darley Abbey
Draycott Dale Abbey
Drone Valley Unstone (NEW)
Falstaff ▪ Derby: Normanton
Gaol Wirksworth (NEW)
Globe ▪ Glossop
Hairy Brewers Holbrook (NEW)
Hartshorns Derby
Haywood Bad Ram Ashbourne
High Peak Chapel-en-le-Frith (NEW)
Hope Valley Castleton
Hopjacker ▪ Dronfield (NEW)
Howard Town Glossop
Instant Karma ▪ Clay Cross
Intrepid Brough
John Thompson ▪ Ingleby
Landlocked ▪ Ripley
Leadmill Heanor
Leatherbritches ▪ Smisby
Little Bush ▪ Marehay
Littleover Derby (NEW)
Marlpool Marlpool
Matlock Wolds Farm Matlock
Middle Earth Derby
Mouselow Farm Dinting
Mr Grundy's ▪ Derby
Muirhouse Ilkeston
Nutbrook Stanley Common/West Hallam
Old Sawley ▪ Sawley
Peak Chatsworth
Pentrich Pentrich
Pigeon Fishers Hollingwood
Raw Staveley
Rock Mill New Mills (NEW)
Rowditch ▪ Derby
Shiny Little Eaton
Shottle Farm Shottle
Songbird ▪ Long Eaton
Spire Sutton Scarsdale
Taddington Buxton
Tap House ▪ Smisby
Thorley & Sons Ilkeston (NEW)
Thornbridge Bakewell
Tollgate Calke
Torrside New Mills (NEW)
Townes ▪ Staveley
Wentwell Derby
Whaley Bridge Furness Vale
Whim Hartington

Situated below the Strutt Club in the centre of the town and popular with local drinkers, Arkwright's is a modern, friendly one-roomed bar regularly serving six real ales, ciders and perry. Good-quality snacks are available during the day and evening. Only major sporting events are shown on TV which, coupled with a no under-14s rule, helps to ensure a quiet and relaxing environment for adults to enjoy a pint or two. Q❀🚲🎵♣🍴🖪🐾🎅🛜

Birch Vale

Printers Arms
Thornsett Road, SK22 1AZ (in village of Thornsett)
🕐 4.30-11.30 (midnight Fri & Sat); 12-9 Sun
☎ (01663) 744650
5 changing beers (sourced regionally; often Cottage, Holt, Storm) 🅗
Refurbished and modernised friendly village local, with accommodation and a well-maintained children's play area, overlooking the Sett Valley. A free house, it has a changing range of five ales offered at competitive pricing for the area, normally including one from the Storm Brewery, and is well known for the excellent-value early evening meal plus a pint deals Wednesday to Friday. The pub is the centre of the local community, with a popular pool table and dartboard. 🛏❀🍴🎵♣🖪🐾🛜

Birchover

Druid Inn 🅛
Main Street, DE4 2BL
🕐 12-midnight; 12-10.30 Sun; closed Mon
☎ (01629) 653836 🌐 druidinnbirchover.co.uk
5 changing beers (sourced regionally; often Abbeydale, Oakham, Sarah Hughes) 🅗
Traditional country free house with a main room featuring open fires at both ends. The landlord and landlady are passionate about beer, with the central bar offering five real ales, usually from breweries including Abbeydale, Blue Monkey, Oakham and Sarah Hughes. The pub has a mixed clientele of locals and tourists visiting the Peak District National Park. Excellent home-cooked food is served in the bar and separate restaurant.
Q🛏❀🍴🅗&A P🐾🛜

Bolsover

Fidlers Rest 🅛
Craggs Road, S44 6BQ (just off A632, Bolsover Hill)
🕐 5-11; 12-11 Sat & Sun ☎ (01246) 828300
2 changing beers (often Dukeries, Welbeck Abbey) 🅗
A pub with a modern interior, with a view through the floor into the original cellar. Panoramic views from the seating area outside include Bolsover Castle, extending across to the Peak District. Originally called the Castle Inn, it is now named after Peter Fidler, the Bolsover-born explorer who mapped the Canadian wilderness for the Hudson Bay Company. Occasional live artists make an appearance. 🛏❀♣🍴🖪🐾🛜

Brampton

Real Ale Corner 🅛
415 Chatsworth Road, S40 3AD
🕐 3 (1 Wed & Thu)-7; 11-10 Fri & Sat; 1-5 Sun; closed Mon
☎ (01246) 202111
2 changing beers 🅗

A bottle shop with two real ales to drink while browsing the 150 bottles of beer, especially beers that you cannot buy from the supermarket, plus nine ciders and wines. A seating area is extended to the outside, giving it the feel of a small local. It offers a CAMRA-friendly home delivery service within five miles. Gift vouchers and gift packs can be purchased, or you can just enjoy a pint in a pleasant atmosphere. Q❀🍴🖪🐾🛜

Rose & Crown 🅛 ✅
104 Old Road, S40 2QT
🕐 12-11 (midnight Fri & Sat) ☎ (01246) 563750
🌐 roseandcrownbrampton.co.uk
Brampton Golden Bud; Everards Tiger; 6 changing beers 🅗
Everards' Project William renovation of a run-down local enabled the Brampton Brewery to open its first tied house. A compact snug provides room for group meetings, while the main room has plenty of quiet corners. Memorabilia from the original Brampton Brewery festoon the walls. Quiz night is Tuesday. Outdoor drinking areas are to the front and rear, with a lawn. Sunday lunches and cold platters can be had during the week, and an annual beer festival is held to mark St George's Day, with a second in September. 🛏❀🍴♣🖪P🚌(170)🐾🛜

Tramway Tavern 🅛 ✅
192 Chatsworth Road, S40 2AT
🕐 4-11; 12-midnight Fri & Sat; 12-11 Sun ☎ (01246) 200111
🌐 tramwaytavern.co.uk
Brampton Golden Bud, Best; Everards Tiger; 5 changing beers 🅗
This is the second tied house for Brampton Brewery and also the tap – the brewery is only two minutes' walk away. There are eight ales on handpump on the bar, four Brampton, one Everards and three guests. A selection of world beers is available, along with traditional ciders and perries. Regular themed nights are held. An area is dedicated to pictures and history of the old Chesterfield tram service that once passed by. There is an outdoor courtyard to the rear. ❀🍴🖪🛜

Buxton

53 Degrees North
8a Hall Bank, SK17 6EW (near town hall)
🕐 11-11 (1am Fri & Sat) ☎ (01298) 79119
Thornbridge Jaipur IPA; 3 changing beers (sourced regionally; often Marston's, Wincle) 🅗
A café/bar in a late 18th-century terrace close to the opera house, Pavilion Gardens and Crescent, up a steep hill towards the market square. The front area is laid out in café style, with the bar to the rear. Four handpulls offer both local and national ales, while food focuses on quality local produce, and there are Sunday roasts. An excellent addition to the social scene in Buxton, with friendly staff ensuring a warm welcome. 🛏🍴🚲🖪P🐾🛜

Ale Stop
Chapel Street, SK17 6HX
🕐 11 (12 Mon)-10; 11-midnight Fri; 12-9 Sun ☎ 07403 528605
3 changing beers (sourced nationally) 🅗
The first micropub in the High Peak, this is a former wine shop off Buxton market square converted to a two-room venue. Beer is the thing here, with three changing ales from microbreweries up and down the country, as well as two real ciders from Sandford Orchards. The objective is to bring to

Buxton beers that are rarely, if ever, seen in the town. The knowledgeable owner and staff offer a warm and friendly welcome. An eclectic choice of background music on vinyl is played.
🐴♿♣🍎🚌🐾📶

Cheshire Cheese

37-39 High Street, SK17 6HA
🕘 12-11 (midnight Fri & Sat) ☎ (01298) 212453
Everards Tiger; Titanic Steerage, Iceberg, White Star, Plum Porter, Captain Smith's; 3 changing beers (often Titanic) 🄷
A double-fronted building of considerable age; following refurbishment, it reopened under the management of Titanic in 2013. The pub is essentially open plan, but split into several distinct areas. Low ceilings with original beams add to the cosy atmosphere. There is a quiet area at one end which features an open fire. The bar boasts an impressive array of 10 handpulls serving a range of Titanic beers and guests. Thursday is pie night.
Q🐴❀◐♿⛺♣🍎P🚌(199)🐾📶

Chelmorton

Church Inn

Main Street, SK17 9SL
🕘 12-3, 6-11; 12-11 Fri-Sun ☎ (01298) 85319
🌐 thechurchinn.co.uk
Adnams Southwold Bitter; Marston's Burton Bitter, Pedigree; 3 changing beers (often Abbeydale, Storm, Thornbridge) 🄷
Set in beautiful surroundings opposite the local church, this traditional village pub caters both for locals and walkers. The main room is laid out for dining and good home-cooked food is on offer; however, a cosy pub atmosphere is maintained, with a low ceiling and real fire. Guest beers are usually from local micros. There is an excellent patio area outside. Parking is available at the end of the road. Monday is quiz night. Q❀🛏◐⛺🐾📶

Chesterfield

Chesterfield Alehouse 🄻

37 West Bars, S40 1AG
🕘 12-10 🌐 chesterfieldalehouse.co.uk
6 changing beers (often Abbeydale, Ashover, Raw) 🄷
Chesterfield's first micropub is a few minutes' walk from the historic marketplace. Previously a furniture shop, the split-level bar has a small seating area leading up a few steps to the serving area, where you will find six varying beers, always including a stout or a porter. It also has a growing range of bottled world beers, ciders and wines. Traditional pub snacks including local pork pies are available, and a popular free cheese night is held every Tuesday. Q♿♣🍎▯🚌🐾📶

Chesterfield Arms 🄻

Newbold Road, S41 7PH
🕘 4 (12 Thu)-11; 12-11.30 Fri & Sat; 12-11 Sun
☎ (01246) 236634
Everards Tiger; house beer (by Ashover); changing beers (often Abbeydale, Thornbridge) 🄷
Oak-clad walls, open fires and hop-strewn bars create a relaxing and welcoming ambience in this former local CAMRA Pub of the Year. Ten real ales are on tap, often from microbreweries and including two house ales. A log-burning stove heats the barn, which opens at weekends with additional beers and hosts beer festivals.
Conservatory doors open up on a warm evening, extending the outdoor seating area.
Q🐴❀♿🍎🚌(10)🐾

Market Pub 🄻

95 New Square, S40 1AH
🕘 11-11 (midnight Fri & Sat); 12-11 Sun ☎ (01246) 273641
🌐 themarketpub.co.uk
Greene King Abbot; Kelham Island Easy Rider; Timothy Taylor Landlord; 5 changing beers 🄷
Popular, friendly town-centre pub in the historic market square. Eight handpulls serve real ales and ciders, and there is an extensive wine list and 100-plus whiskies. Quality home-cooked food is served, made with locally sourced produce. Regular events such as murder mysteries, gourmet food nights, wine, whisky and spirit tastings take place, and there is a general knowledge quiz on Thursdays, and a film and music quiz on Sundays. Live music features occasionally. ❀◐⇌♣🍎🚌

Rutland Arms 🄻

23 Stephenson Place, S40 1XL
🕘 12-11.30 (12.30am Thu-Sat); 12-11 Sun
☎ (01246) 205857
Greene King Abbot; Thornbridge Jaipur IPA; 5 changing beers (often Bradfield, Exmoor, Oakham) 🄷
Popular town-centre pub under the famous Crooked Spire parish church. It has the appearance of two buildings joined together, with a partly castellated roof line. Inside, there are two areas divided by steps. The beers come from far and wide, and there are two guest ciders. The food, especially the roasts, is recommended and good value. There are occasional beer festivals, a screen for sport and piped music. 🐴❀◐⇌🍎🚌📶

White Swan 🄻

16 St Mary's Gate, S41 7TJ
🕘 12-11 (12.30am Fri; 1am Sat) ☎ (01246) 229570
🌐 rawbrew.com/whiteswan
Greene King Abbot; house beer (by Raw); 9 changing beers (often Raw) 🄷
Affectionately known as the Mucky Duck, this popular pub is in sight of the famous Crooked Spire parish church. A spacious all-in-one room, it is the Raw Brewing Company's tied house. Continually changing guest beers are stocked, and there is an impressive selection of bottled beers and real ciders. Home-made food is served all day, including light bites (12-3pm) and Sunday lunches. An upstairs function room is available for hire.
❀◐♿⇌🍎P🚌📶

Clay Cross

Rykneld Turnpyke 🏆 🄻

4 John Street, S45 9NQ
🕘 2-11.30 (midnight Fri); 12-midnight Sat; 12-11.30 Sun
☎ (01246) 250366
Changing beers 🄷
A venue that returns to the Guide after being refitted following a devastating fire. Formerly the Egstow Working Men's Club, the Rykneld Turnpyke (named after Rykneld Street, the old road between Chesterfield and Derby) has one large room divided into different areas, with comfortable seating. There is an excellent choice of up to 12 reasonably priced beers from mostly local brewers. Cribbage and dominoes are always available. The on-site Instant Karma Brewery can be seen through a viewing panel at the rear. ♣🍎🚌🐾

Clowne

Centre 🄻
Recreation Close, S43 4PL
⏲ 7-11 ☎ (01246) 819546
House beer (by Timothy Taylor); 3 changing beers 🄷
A council-run community centre widely used by the locals for functions. The Rock & Blues Club has live bands every Sunday and there is a popular quiz night on Tuesday with free food. The venue is well cared for, with a relaxed and friendly atmosphere, and it holds a beer festival in May. Ample car parking is available. ♞❀♿P▯🚌(53,77,79)

Coton-in-the-Elms

Black Horse
17 Burton Road, DE12 8HJ (centre of village)
⏲ 4-11 (midnight Fri); 1-midnight Sat; 12-10.30 Sun
☎ (01283) 762947 🌐 theblackhorsederbyshire.co.uk
Draught Bass; Joule's Pale Ale; Marston's Pedigree; 1 changing beer (sourced regionally, often Burton Bridge, Gates Burton, Tollgate) 🄷
Lively and popular free house, owned by the licensee, with a bright and airy main room divided into bar and lounge areas by glass-topped wood partitions. A small snug, served through a hatch, features a bar billiards table. Guest beers are often from a local microbrewery. Up to six ciders/perries are available (the source varies). A free cheeseboard is offered weekday evenings and weekend lunchtimes. Quiz night is Tuesday and occasional live music is played on Sunday. Accommodation is in a two-person self-catering holiday flat. Q❀🛏⛺♣●P🚌(22)🐾📶

Crich

Cliff Inn 🄻
Town End, DE4 5DP (150yds from Crich Tramway Village)
⏲ 5 (7 Mon)-11; 12-midnight Sat & Sun ☎ (01773) 852444
Dancing Duck Ay Up; Sharp's Doom Bar; Whim Arbor Light; 2 changing beers (sourced locally) 🄷
Traditional gritstone free house at the top of the village just below the National Tramway Museum. Built about 1800, the two rooms are largely unchanged since the 1960s. There are logburners in both rooms and a quarry-tiled floor in the taproom. Five handpumps operate, of which four normally dispense LocAles. Home-made food is served Tuesday to Friday evenings and weekend lunchtimes. Q♞❀◐◑⛺♣P▯🚌(140,142)🐾📶

Derby

Alexandra Hotel 🄻
203 Siddals Road, DE1 2QE
⏲ 12-11 (midnight Fri); 11-midnight Sat ☎ (01332) 293993
🌐 alexandrahotelderby.co.uk
Castle Rock Harvest Pale; 6 changing beers 🄷
The Alex is a Castle Rock pub serving two or three of the brewery's beers and up to five guest ales, including a mild and a stout/porter. There are also more than 50 UK and continental bottled beers of varying styles. The bar is adorned with railway memorabilia, and the lounge with breweriana. A Class 37 locomotive cab resides in the car park. This pub was the birthplace of Derby CAMRA in 1974 and was voted local CAMRA Pub of the Year in 2015. Q♞❀🛏♿≠♣●P🚌🐾📶

Babington Arms 🄻 ✔
11-13 Babington Lane, DE1 1TA
⏲ 8am-midnight (1am Fri & Sat) ☎ (01332) 383647
Greene King Abbot; Marston's Burton Bitter, Pedigree; Small World Long Moor Pale, Thunderbridge Stout, Twin Falls; 9 changing beers 🄷
This Wetherspoon pub is a converted furniture showroom close to the city centre. It boasts a huge range of real ales, many from local microbreweries, and typically has five ciders on handpump/gravity dispense. The back end of the large bar has some half-partitioned banquette seating and caters for family dining. At the front of the pub there is a small fenced-off area where outdoor drinkers can have a smoke and watch the hustle and bustle of Babington Lane.
Q♞◐◑♿●🚌📶

Brunswick Inn 🏆 🄻
1 Railway Terrace, DE1 2RU
⏲ 11-11 (11.30 Fri & Sat); 12-10.30 Sun ☎ (01332) 290677
🌐 brunswickderby.co.uk
Everards Beacon Bitter, Tiger; Timothy Taylor Landlord; 13 changing beers (often Brunswick) 🄷
Originally part of the railway village, the pub was closed in 1974 and fell into disrepair. Rescued and restored, it opened as Derby's first multiple-choice real ale house in 1987. A purpose-built brewery was added in 1991 and the place has since become one of the best-known free houses in the country. Although owned by Everards, its range of up to 16 real ales includes at least six from the in-house brewery. Local CAMRA Pub of the Year 2016.
Q♞❀◐♿≠♣●P🚌🐾📶

Exeter Arms 🄻 ✔
13 Exeter Place, DE1 2EU
⏲ 12-11 (11.30 Wed & Thu; midnight Fri & Sat); 12-10.30 Sun
☎ (01332) 605323 🌐 exeterarms.co.uk
Dancing Duck Ay Up, Dark Drake; Marston's Pedigree; 4 changing beers 🄷
Thanks to a remarkable transformation in recent times by the licensees and Dancing Duck Brewery, the Ex simply oozes old-world charm, featuring a small bar with open fire, partitioned lounges and a wooden-settled snug with an old-fashioned range. The adjoining atmospheric cottage dating from about 1815 has been incorporated into the pub. A quiz takes place on Monday evening and live music is played every Saturday evening in summer.
♞❀◐◑♣●P🐾📶

Falstaff 🄻
74 Silverhill Road, DE23 6UJ
⏲ 12-11 (midnight Fri & Sat) ☎ (01332) 342902
🌐 falstaffbrewery.co.uk
Falstaff Fist Full of Hops, Phoenix, Smiling Assassin; 1 changing beer 🄷
A 20-minute walk from the city centre rewards you with this atmospheric and reputedly haunted free house. Originally a coaching inn before the neighbourhood was built up, it is now the Falstaff Brewery tap and has long been the best real ale house in the Normanton area of Derby. The rear lounge is a shrine to Offilers' Brewery, with a display of memorabilia. Other collectables can be viewed throughout the games room and second bar room. Q♞❀♣●🚌🐾

Five Lamps 🄻 ✔
25 Duffield Road, DE1 3BH
⏲ 12-11 (midnight Fri & Sat) ☎ (01332) 348730
🌐 fivelampsderby.co.uk

Everards Tiger; Oakham Citra; Peak Ales Chatsworth Gold; Thornbridge Jaipur IPA; Whim Hartington IPA; 8 changing beers ⓗ
Since it reopened in 2010 the pub has gone from strength to strength, thanks to the dedication of the licensees and staff. Fourteen handpumps showcase many local ales from breweries such as Derby, Buxton, Peak and Whim. The Lamps is essentially open plan, but has many little nooks and crannies, giving it a homely feel. It has been tastefully refurbished with wood panelling and leather seating in a traditional style. ⓐⓓ&⬤Pᵭ🐱🔊

Flowerpot ⓛ
23-25 King Street, DE1 3DZ
❀ 12-11 (11.30 Wed & Thu; 12.30am Fri & Sat)
☎ (01332) 204955 ⊕ flowerpotderby.co.uk
Frontier Gold Rush; Oakham Bishops Farewell; Whim Hartington IPA; 4 changing beers ⓗ/ⓖ
Dating from around 1800 but much expanded from its original premises, this vibrant pub reaches back from the roadside frontage and divides into several interlinking rooms. One room provides the stage for regular live bands; another has a glass cellar wall revealing rows of stillaged firkins, which can be seen from the bar and from the road outside. At least eight real ales are offered and it is now the home of the Frontier Brewery. Good en-suite accommodation is available. Qⓐ⊕⌂&⬤ᵭ🐱🔊

Furnace Inn ⓛ
Duke Street, DE1 3BX
❀ 2-11; 11-midnight Fri & Sat; 11-11 Sun ☎ (01332) 385981
6 changing beers ⓗ
Since it reopened in 2012, the pub has been transformed into a real ale mecca, culminating in being voted CAMRA Derbyshire Pub of the Year in 2014. A former Hardys & Hansons hostelry, it is now the tap for Shiny Brewing Company. Up to eight real ales and three ciders/perries are served plus guest beers from all over. There are two distinct open-plan rooms with a central bar. Open mic, poker and cheese nights feature, with regular beer festivals held throughout the year. Qⓑ🐱&♣⬤🐱🔊

Golden Eagle ⓛ
55 Agard Street, DE1 1DZ
❀ 12-midnight; 12-11.30 Sun
Morland Old Golden Hen; 5 changing beers ⓗ
Completely refurbished by the Titan Brewery, this is now the brewery tap. The pub's original name has also been restored after many changes. A mural on the outside pays homage to Derby history. Inside, the single room is comfortable and welcoming, with a wooden floor throughout, and a table next to the bar for newspapers and local interest books. The upstairs function room hosts a poker night on Sunday and there is live acoustic music every Thursday evening. ⓑⓐ♣⬤Pᵭ🐱🔊

Greyhound ⓛ
76 Friar Gate, DE1 1FN
❀ 12-11 (midnight Thu; 1am Fri); 11-1am Sat; 11-11 Sun
☎ (01332) 344155 ⊕ greyhound-dbc.co.uk
Derby Business As Usual; 8 changing beers ⓗ
An old coaching inn that has been restored to a high standard by Derby Brewing Company, the Greyhound has a roof terrace (open in summer) and a walled beer garden which are a boon in fine weather. Modern art adorns the walls in this vibrant establishment that caters for a mixed clientele. Up to seven beers from the Derby Brewing range and up to three guests are on offer, as well as a real cider. ⓑⓐⓓ&⬤ᵭ🐱🔊

Horse & Groom
48 Elms Street, DE1 3HN
❀ 12-11 ⊕ horseandgroomderby.co.uk
Draught Bass; 3 changing beers ⓗ
A traditional community pub that has morphed from a small corner house into a larger establishment by knocking through into two adjoining properties. In the heart of Derby's West End, this family-owned and run free house is noted for its regular Draught Bass and interesting range of three guest beers. Free live music takes place at the weekend, open mic Thursday evening, and jazz on the last Wednesday of the month. ⓐ♣ᵭ🐱🔊

New Zealand Arms ⓛ
2 Langley Street, New Zealand, DE22 3GL
❀ 12-midnight; 12-11 Sun ☎ (01332) 384945
⊕ newzealandarms.com
7 changing beers (often Dancing Duck) ⓗ
Popular local brewery Dancing Duck has taken on another pub near the city centre, where six of its ales plus guests and draught ciders are on offer. Comfortable surroundings, pleasant staff and a good choice of home-cooked food have helped to re-establish it as a pub to visit in this part of the city after a period of closure. Wednesday is quiz night, while Monday, Thursday and Saturday are music nights. Food is served Wednesday to Friday evenings and Saturday and Sunday lunchtimes. ◑♣⬤ᵭ(28,29)🔊

Old Bell Hotel ⓛ
Sadler Gate, DE1 3NQ
❀ 12-11 (1am Fri); 11-1am Sat ☎ (01332) 723090
Draught Bass; 8 changing beers ⓗ
One of Derby's best-loved pubs continues to be restored to its former magnificence. The front Tavern Bar features a range of kegs but discerning drinkers should seek out the Tudor Bar to the rear, which only ceased being a men-only bar in 1975. This 18th-century coaching inn is a welcome oasis in Sadler Gate, a premier shopping street in the Cathedral Quarter. The exterior Tudor-style half-timbering was added only in 1929. ⓑⓐ◑🐱

Peacock Inn ⓛ
87 Nottingham Road, DE1 3QS
❀ 11-11 (midnight Fri & Sat); 12-10.30 Sun
☎ (01332) 583308
Draught Bass ⓖ; Marston's Pedigree; Whim Arbor Light; 6 changing beers ⓗ
Attractive 18th-century stone-built roadside pub that was once a staging post on the main coach road out of Derby, which ran alongside the old Derby Canal. Two rooms on different levels are divided by a central bar, featuring wooden floors, stove burners, photos of old Derby and Derby County memorabilia. Up to nine real ales and two ciders and/or perries are stocked; beer festivals are held in the large, covered garden area to the rear. Qⓑⓐ&⬤🐱

Rowditch Inn
246 Uttoxeter New Road, DE22 3LL
❀ 7-11; 12-2, 7-11 Sat & Sun ☎ (01332) 343123
Marston's Pedigree; 2 changing beers (often Rowditch) ⓗ
Welcoming roadside hostelry with an unexpectedly deep interior which divides into two bar areas and

a small snug. There is a display cabinet of pub memorabilia, and the pumpclips adorning the walls testify to myriad guest ales. Downstairs, at the rear, the garden is a peaceful haven in warmer weather. The output of the pub's brewery is almost exclusively consumed on the premises. Well worth the walk or five-minute bus ride from the city centre. Q❀♣●🖾❀🎵🛜

Silk Mill Cider & Ale House 🅛 ✅

19 Full Street, DE1 3AF
✪ 12-11 (midnight Fri & Sat); 12-10.30 Sun
☎ (01332) 349160 ⊕ thesilkmillderby.co.uk
Dancing Duck Ay Up; Draught Bass; 5 changing beers 🅗
Handsome stone-faced building named after the historic silk mill nearby, which marks the start of the Derwent Valley World Heritage Trail. To the right of the entrance is the Offilers' Lounge with a cosy real fire, ideal for drinkers. There is a dedicated dining area to the rear of pub – booking is recommended at peak times. The central bar has nine handpumps shared between real ales and ciders. Quirky decorative ornaments and fittings are used throughout. 🛏❀❸🍴●🛜

Draycott

Coach & Horses

Victoria Road, DE72 3PS
✪ 4-7 Mon; 4-11 Tue & Wed; 2-11.30 Thu & Fri; 12-11.30 Sat; 12-11 Sun ☎ (01332) 874636
Blue Monkey BG Sips; Greene King Abbot; 1 changing beer (sourced locally) 🅗
Large two-roomed friendly and informal village pub, part of the local Draycott heritage area. An ideal choice for a quiet, well-kept pint, with periodic entertainment in the large bar area. There is ample parking and a large smoking outside area at the rear. Entertainment at weekends includes karaoke on Saturday nights and occasional gigs. Q🛏❀♿♣P🖾❀🛜

Dronfield

Coach & Horses 🅛

Sheffield Road, S18 2GD
✪ 4-10.30 Mon; 12-11 (midnight Fri & Sat); 12-10.30 Sun
☎ (01246) 413269 ⊕ mycoachandhorses.co.uk/home.html
5 changing beers 🅗
The pub is located next to Sheffield FC (the world's oldest football club), on the northern edge of Dronfield. It is operated by Thornbridge Brewery and showcases a good range of its beers and occasional guests across a wide selection of beer styles. The large outdoor drinking area is particularly popular when Sheffield FC have a home fixture, or when live music is being played. Good-value meals are available (no food Sun or Mon). The pub hosts a quiz night on Sunday and an open mic session. Acoustic night is Monday.
Q🛏❀❸●P🖾(43)❀

Dronfield Arms

Chesterfield Road, S18 2XE
✪ 4-11; 3-midnight Fri; 12-midnight Sat; 12-10.30 Sun
☎ (01246) 414413 ⊕ dronfield-arms.co.uk
Abbeydale Moonshine; Bradfield Farmers Blonde; Hopjacker The Mark, The Grifter; 3 changing beers (sourced nationally; often Drone Valley, Magic Rock, RedWillow) 🅗

The Dronfield Arms became Dronfield's first brewpub when the Hopjacker Brewery was opened in 2015. The brewery is downstairs in the former restaurant, and is on display to customers through a glass panel in the floor of the main bar. Regular customers may buy a Dronfield Arms loyalty card (£1) to benefit from a free pint for every seven bought. An additional handpump installed towards the end of 2015 raised the available real ales to seven. Quiz night is Tuesday. 🛏➽●P🖾❀🛜

Glossop

Crown Inn ★

142 Victoria Street, SK13 8JF (on Hayfield road out of town centre)
✪ 5-11; 12-11 Fri & Sat; 12-10.30 Sun ☎ (01457) 862824
Samuel Smith Old Brewery Bitter 🅗
End-of-terrace community pub, a few minutes from the town centre and railway station, built in 1846 and acquired by the brewery in 1977. The interior of the pub has been identified by CAMRA as of Outstanding National Historic Importance. A curved bar serves two snugs, each with real fires in winter, and a pool/games room. Pictures of bygone Glossop add to the traditional character. Prices are keen. An enclosed outdoor drinking area is provided in the rear yard. Q❀♿➽♣🖾(390)❀

Queen's Arms

1 Shepley Street, SK13 7RZ
✪ 9.30am-midnight ☎ (01457) 853005
⊕ queens-arms-hotel-old-glossop.co.uk
Holt Bitter; Morland Old Speckled Hen; Robinsons Unicorn; Thornbridge Jaipur IPA; Thwaites Wainwright; 3 changing beers (sourced locally) 🅗
Located in the Old Glossop part of the town, below the Bleaklow hills, this place is a pleasant 15-minute walk from Glossop centre through Manor Park. It is popular with locals, visitors and hikers. It now serves breakfasts from 9.30am. A standard pub menu is available downstairs, while the Queen Spice Indian restaurant is on the first floor. Live entertainment features on Tuesdays and Saturdays, Thursday is quiz night. 🛏❀➽❸♿🖾(390)❀🛜

Star Inn ✅

2 Howard Street, SK13 7DD (next to railway station)
✪ 4-11; 2-midnight Fri; 12-midnight Sat; 12-10.30 Sun
☎ (01457) 853072
Timothy Taylor Landlord; 4 changing beers (sourced regionally; often Abbeydale, Howard Town, Pictish) 🅗
A highly popular town-centre pub, run by a dedicated CAMRA member. A large, comfortable main room, where conversation predominates, features wood panelling and is complemented by a smaller room to the rear. Guest beers are sourced mainly from local microbreweries and real draught cider is available. Regular beer and cider festivals are held throughout the year. Situated close to the railway station, the pub is an ideal starting/finishing point for walking within the Dark Peak area. Q⚠➽●P🖾❀🛜

Hayfield

George Hotel

14 Church Street, SK22 2JE
✪ 11.45-11 (11.30 Fri & Sat); 12-11 Sun ☎ (01663) 743691
⊕ georgehotelhayfield.co.uk

Banks's Bitter; 3 changing beers (sourced regionally) Ⓗ
Rambling stone-built 16th-century pub in the centre of the village, originally a mail house. The Derby militia was formed here in 1808. In addition to the handpulled ales, Thatchers Heritage cider is available. The interior includes stained-glass mullioned windows and a magnificent cast-iron range fireplace incorporating a real fire in winter. Two comfortable lounges, a cosy bar area and a separate dining room are complemented by a function room. Hikers and cyclists are welcome. Close to Hayfield bus station. ❀✿◖◗▲🍴P🚗🛜

Royal Hotel
Market Street, SK22 2EP
✪ 11-11 ☎ (01663) 742721 ⊕ theroyalhayfield.co.uk
Thwaites Lancaster Bomber; house beer (by Happy Valley); 2 changing beers (sourced locally) Ⓗ
An imposing stone pub, built as a coaching inn in the 18th century, close to the church, cricket ground and River Sett. The interior boasts oak panels and pews, creating a relaxing atmosphere, and there are real fires in winter. Guest beers from local micros are always available. A restaurant and function room complete the facilities (food is served all day in summer). The village is the base for many leisure activities in the Dark Peak and was the birthplace of actor Arthur Lowe.
Q🕏❀✿◖◗&▲P🚗 (61,358)🛜🐾

Holbrook

Dead Poets Inn
38 Chapel Street, DE56 0TQ
✪ 12-2.30, 5-11; 12-11 Fri-Sun ☎ (01332) 780301
⊕ socialserenity.co.uk
Draught Bass; Greene King Abbot; Marston's Pedigree; Oakham Citra; 5 changing beers Ⓗ
Stone village pub built in 1800 and formerly known as the Cross Keys. It has a delightful, old-world atmosphere and is popular with locals. There is a delightful snug and the main bar has high-backed pews, low ceilings, stone-flagged floors, a real fire in the winter and an inglenook. There is a welcoming, recently refurbished, conservatory to the rear which is bright in summer and warm in winter. Q🕏❀✿◖&🍴P🚗 (138,71)🐾

Hope

Cheshire Cheese Inn ✪
Edale Road, S33 6ZF
✪ 12-3, 6-11; 12-11 Sat; 12-9 Sun; closed Mon
☎ (01433) 620381 ⊕ thecheshirecheeseinn.co.uk
Bradfield Farmers Blonde; Peak Ales Bakewell Best Bitter; 3 changing beers (sourced locally; often Bradfield, Peak Ales) Ⓗ
A cosy country inn dating from 1578 with an open-plan bar area and a smaller room at a lower level that was probably originally used to house animals, but now is mainly used as a dining area. Home-cooked meals using local produce are served lunchtimes and evenings. The pub is in good walking country but the parking is limited as the road outside is narrow. Q🕏❀✿◖◗P🐾🛜

Horsley Woodhouse

Old Oak Inn �btrophy
176 Main Street, DE7 6AW (on A609)
✪ 4 (3 Thu & Fri; 12 Sat)-11; 12-10.30 Sun ☎ (01332) 881299

Changing beers (often Bottle Brook, Salamander, Welbeck Abbey) Ⓗ
Taphouse for the Leadmill Brewery, the Old Oak features an extensive variety of Leadmill beers plus a couple of guests. This traditional pub boasts four rooms of differing character, some with open fires. At weekends drinkers can enjoy the RuRAD bar which is effectively a mini beer festival offering gravity-dispensed ales from the local Leadmill and Bottle Brook breweries. Homely, welcoming and excellent value for money. CAMRA Derbyshire South Pub of the Year 2016. 🕏❀✿◖P🚗🚗🐾

Hundall

Miners Arms ♟trophy
Hundall Lane, S18 4BP
✪ 12-midnight ☎ (01246) 414505
Abbeydale Moonshine; 4 changing beers (sourced nationally; often Church End, Drone Valley, Exit 33) Ⓗ
Situated on the high ridge above Unstone, this is a traditional village local that has thrived since a change of ownership in 2015. The beer garden to the rear provides an excellent space in which to enjoy the wide range of beers and ciders that are always available. The Miners operates a Monday Club, when real ales are £2 a pint. Local CAMRA Cider Pub of the Year 2015 and Derbyshire North Pub of the Year 2016. Q🕏❀✿◖▲♣◗P🚗🚗🐾🛜

Ilkeston

Burnt Pig Ⓛ
53 Market Street, DE7 5RB
✪ 11-11; closed Mon-Wed ☎ 07709 990895
5 changing beers Ⓗ/🄖
A short walk from the marketplace will bring you to what was a long-closed corner shop. It is now a busy and popular micropub run by its enthusiastic owner, Simon. It dispenses five varying beers and a good selection of real ciders and continental bottled beers. With its multi-roomed, cosy interior, it is also famous for its pork scratchings. This is a pub not to be missed. Q♣◗🚗🐾

Dewdrop ♟trophy Ⓛ
24 Station Road, DE7 5TE
✪ 4 (3 Fri: 12 Sat)-11; 12-10.30 Sun ☎ (0115) 932 9684
Bob's White Lion; Oakham Bishops Farewell, Green Devil IPA; changing beers (often Acorn, Blue Monkey, Castle Rock) Ⓗ
Award-winning Victorian pub on the outskirts of town. The large lobby features a plaque commemorating the wartime visit of bouncing bomb inventor Barnes Wallis. Conversation thrives in the friendly lounge, warmed by a large woodburner, and a pool table and classics jukebox dominate the bar. Lastly, there is a quiet family room. A dark beer is usually served. Westons Old Rosie and Wyld Wood are the permanent ciders. Hearty cobs are made to order. Outside is a covered, heated smoking area.
Q🕏❀✿◗♣◗🚗 (27)🐾

Observatory ✪
14A Market Place, DE7 5QA
✪ 8am-11 (midnight Fri & Sat) ☎ (0115) 932 8040
Greene King Abbot; Ruddles Best Bitter; Sharp's Doom Bar; 4 changing beers (often Exmoor) Ⓗ
A glass-fronted edifice with an astronomical theme, commemorating John Flamsteed, the first Astronomer Royal. It is on the east side of the

marketplace, with a ground floor drinking area, a smaller dining and drinking area upstairs and an outside terrace. A large bar dispenses seven cask beers. This pub gets quite busy at times and is a short walk to Wharncliffe Road for all bus routes. The toilets are on the ground floor. Q✿❀➊◗ö♿☀♋ᾣ令

Kilburn

Hunter Arms
Church Street, DE56 0LU
✪ 2-11; 12-midnight Fri-Sun ☎ (01332) 781518
Marston's Pedigree; Oakham Bishops Farewell; Timothy Taylor Landlord; 6 changing beers (often Blue Monkey, Dancing Duck, Thornbridge) ⑭
Built in 1879 and named after the owners of nearby Kilburn Hall, the pub is a popular, friendly local serving good beer. The main bar has a pleasant, open-plan, carpeted interior, TV and a welcoming fire in winter. Six guest beers are sourced mainly from local breweries, often Thornbridge, Blue Monkey and Dancing Duck. The separate Old Slaughterhouse cider bar is open all week and features up to 14 ciders and perries. A large function room is available upstairs. Snacks are served Tuesday to Saturday. Q✿❀♿♋P⧄

Little Eaton

Queen's Head 🅛
131 Alfreton Road, DE21 5DF
✪ 12-11; 11-midnight Fri & Sat; 11-11 Sun
☎ (01332) 986065 ⊕ queenshead-dbc.co.uk
Derby Business As Usual, Dashingly Dark; Everards Tiger, Original; 6 changing beers ⑭
Historic Derbyshire stone inn situated in Little Eaton village boasting some original features including low-beamed ceilings. The original main entrance has been renovated and the bar relocated to create a welcoming and stylish interior. There is an attractive patio garden to one side for warmer summer days. There are normally nine real ales, five of which are from Derby Brewing Company. The menu selection includes home-made locally sourced food, all prepared and cooked on-site. ✿❀➊◗ö♋P⧄♣ᾣ令

Litton

Red Lion 🅛 ✔
Main Street, SK17 8QU
✪ 12-11 (midnight Fri & Sat); 12-10.30 Sun
☎ (01298) 871458 ⊕ theredlionlitton.co.uk
Abbeydale Absolution; Peak Ales Bakewell Best Bitter; 1 changing beer (sourced locally) ⑭
Nestling on the green and the only pub in the village, the Red Lion is a welcome refuge for locals and visitors alike. There is a large fireplace serving several rooms off a central passageway. Not to be missed, the annual wakes week is at the end of June, during which the pub holds a beer festival, and events include a well dressing on the village green. Fresh food is served all day, every day. ❀♨➊◗♣♋(65,173)❀令

Longshaw

Grouse
S11 7TZ
✪ 12-3, 6-11; 12-11 Sat & Sun ☎ (01433) 630423
⊕ thegrouseinn-derbyshire.co.uk

Banks's Bitter; Marston's EPA, Pedigree; 1 changing beer (often Banks's) ⑭
In the same family for the past 52 years, this free house stands in isolation on bleak moorland south-west of Sheffield, and is a welcome refuge for walkers as well as climbers from the nearby Froggatt Edge. The comfortable lounge and bar are at the front, with a room at the rear reached through the conservatory in which vines grow. A self-catering holiday flat is available. No food Monday evenings. Q✿❀♨➊◗ö♿P❀令

Lullington

Colvile Arms
Main Street, DE12 8EG (centre of village)
✪ 6-11; 12-3, 7-11 Sun ☎ (01827) 373212
⊕ colvilearms.co.uk
Draught Bass; Marston's Pedigree; 1 changing beer (sourced regionally; often Church End, Holden's, Oakham) ⑭
Leased from the Lullington Estate, the seat of the Colvile family since the early 1900s, this popular 19th-century free house is at the heart of an attractive hamlet at the southern tip of the county. The public bar comprises an adjoining hallway and snug, each featuring high-backed settles with wood panelling. The bar and a comfortable lounge are on opposite sides of a central serving area. A second lounge/function room overlooks the beer garden and lawn. Q❀♣P❀令

Makeney

Holly Bush ★
Holly Bush Lane, DE56 0RX
✪ 12-11; 12-10.30 Sun ☎ (01332) 841729
⊕ hollybushinnmakeney.co.uk
Fuller's London Pride; Greene King Abbot; Marston's Pedigree ⑭; Ruddles County Ⓖ; Timothy Taylor Landlord; 3 changing beers ⑭
Local CAMRA 2015 Pub of the Year, the Holly Bush is an excellent late 17th-century Grade II-listed pub with character. Once a farmhouse and brewery on the Strutt Estate, this inn stood on the main Derby turnpike before the new road opened in 1818. Dick Turpin reputedly drank here. The pub has a nationally important historic pub interior, featuring various hideaway, stone-flagged rooms, with welcoming fires in winter. Bar snacks are available all day, every day. Q✿❀➊◗ö♣♋P⧄❀令

Marlpool

Marlpool Ale House 🅛
5 Breach Road, DE75 7NJ
✪ 2-11 Fri; 12-11 Sat; 12-10 Sun; closed Mon-Thu
☎ (01773) 711285 ⊕ marlpoolbrewing.co.uk
Marlpool Blind Boris, Otters Pocket, Scratty Ratty ⑭; 5 changing beers (sourced regionally; often Marlpool) ⑭/Ⓖ
Originally a butcher's, this is one of the smallest alehouses in Derbyshire. It is now a friendly and cosy place to meet up with friends and strangers, where staff are welcoming and informative. The bar is an old Methodist chapel pulpit, and beers are delivered by handpump or from the cellar. Divided into two main rooms, the rear room has a wood-burning stove, while a two-barrel brewery is in the rear yard. Impromptu acoustic sessions and beer festivals take place during the year. Q❀♣⧄❀

Matlock

MoCa Bar ⓛ
77 Dale Road, DE4 3LT
✪ 11-11 (1am Fri & Sat) ☎ (01629) 583973
7 changing beers (sourced locally; often Thornbridge, Abbeydale, Blue Monkey) Ⓗ
A single-room modern bar that has a sophisticated big-city-café feel, with wooden floors and chunky pine furniture. Comfortable seating includes a large window area and a decked terrace at the rear. Open plan and urbane, with music memorabilia adorning the walls, the MoCa Bar has seven handpulls featuring ales from dedicated breweries Abbeydale, Blue Monkey, Brampton, Dancing Duck, Kelham Island, Oakham and Thornbridge. There is a reduction in the price of real ales (except premium ales) Monday-Wednesday. ᗡ❀Ⓓ☀⇌🖥😺🐾

Stanley's Alehouse ♈ ⓛ
76 Smedley Street, DE4 3JJ
✪ 2 (5 Thu)-11; closed Mon-Wed ☎ (01629) 583350
5 changing beers (often Ashover, Bumpmill) Ⓗ
Small in size but big on atmosphere, this cosy micropub sits opposite County Hall in Matlock. The five cask ales on offer always change, but usually include three from Derbyshire breweries, often including Bumpmill, where the landlord is the brewer. As well as the excellent variety of microbrewery ales, there are also two real ciders on draught. The pub hosts live acoustic music on Thursdays, and a fun quiz on Sunday evenings, with complimentary cheese and crackers.
Q♣❀😺🐾

Thorn Tree Inn ✅
48 Jackson Road, DE4 3JQ
✪ 12-2 (not Mon), 5-11.30; 12-midnight Fri & Sat; 12-11.30 Sun ☎ (01629) 580295 ⊕ thorntreeatmatlock.co.uk
Draught Bass; Nottingham Extra Pale Ale; Timothy Taylor Landlord; 4 changing beers (sourced nationally; often Castle Rock, Oakham, Thornbridge) Ⓗ
Perched high above Matlock town, this two-roomed traditional pub enjoys beautiful views from the heated patio area. Children and dogs are welcome although cat-swinging is not recommended due to the compact nature of the establishment. Reputedly, a haunted wall clock hangs in the lounge where regulars, ramblers and real ale enthusiasts convene to enjoy the atmosphere. Three permanent real ales are complemented by four changing guest beers. Home-made food is served Tuesday-Friday lunchtimes, pie night is Wednesday, and Sunday lunch is served from 5pm. Q❀Ⓓ♣🖥🚃😺🐾

Twenty Ten ⓛ
16 Dale Road, DE4 3LT
✪ 12-10 (midnight Fri; 1am Sat); closed Mon ☎ 07710 427442
3 changing beers (often Matlock Wolds Farm) Ⓗ
A stone's throw from the railway station, Twenty Ten nestles among the antique shops on Matlock's historic Dale Road. Bare floorboards and French chic furnishing lend the place a style not often encountered in the area. Focusing on LocAle, the bar is the only dedicated outlet for Matlock Wolds Farm ales. Children and dogs are welcome, and food is available throughout the day. Often quiet early doors, things liven up considerably on Friday and Saturday evenings, with live music laid on. ᗡ❀Ⓓ⇌🖥😺🐾

Melbourne

Chip & Pin ⓛ
8-10 High Street, DE73 8GN
✪ 4.30-9.30; 12-9.30 Fri & Sat; 12-2.30 Sun; closed Mon ☎ 07957 806454 ⊕ chipandpinpub.com
4 changing beers Ⓖ
Centrally located in Melbourne's old Midland Bank premises, this micropub is owned by a group of local real ale enthusiasts who serve you at your table. The building has been sympathetically restored and comprises two rooms, a main drinking area and a meeting room for local groups. It is south Derbyshire's first micropub and usually has four gravity-dispensed beers, real cider, wine and soft drinks on sale. Beers can be served in third-pint taster racks. No under-18s permitted. Q♿🖥😺

Millers Dale

Angler's Rest ⓛ
SK17 8SN
✪ 12-3, 6.30-11; 12-midnight Sat; 12-5 Sun
☎ (01298) 871323 ⊕ theanglersrest.co.uk
Adnams Southwold Bitter; Storm Silk of Amnesia; 2 changing beers (sourced locally; often Intrepid) Ⓗ
Ivy-clad inn dating from 1753 on the banks of the River Wye, handy for the spectacular walk along the Monsal Trail. It is a multi-room establishment including a cosy lounge with a real fire and a comfortable dining area. Walking boots and dogs are welcome in the hikers' bar. Good, traditional pub food is served daily and the guest beers are mostly LocAle. Accommodation is a self-catering apartment. Q🛏❀♿🛏Ⓓ♣Ⓟ🖥(65)😺

Milton

Swan Inn
49 Main Street, DE65 6EF
✪ 11-4 (not Mon; 3 Wed), 6-11; 11-4, 6-midnight Fri & Sat; 11-10.30 Sun ☎ (01283) 703188 ⊕ theswaninnmilton.co.uk
Draught Bass; 2 changing beers Ⓗ
This free house serves highly praised ale including at least one guest beer, often from a local microbrewery, and hosts regular mini beer festivals. There is a fine display of railway memorabilia in the bar. The restaurant, which operates as the Cygnets Tearoom during the day, serves excellent home-cooked food. Located in a small village just over a mile from the nearest bus route through Repton, the Swan is well worth a visit. ❀Ⓓ♿🖥Ⓟ😺🐾

New Mills

Beehive
67 Albion Road, SK22 2EY
✪ 5-midnight; 4-1am Fri; 2-1am Sat; 3-midnight Sun
☎ (01663) 742087
3 changing beers (sourced nationally) Ⓗ
In an interesting triangular building, this friendly free house features three changing guest beers from local micros and national breweries. A selection of bottled beers, mainly from local microbreweries, is also available. Upstairs is a well-furnished cocktail and whisky bar with a single handpump. Recently renovated, the pub features a logburner and hosts community events and live music. A beer festival is held during the late spring bank holiday weekend. ᗡ❀♿⇌♣🖥😺🐾

Newton

New Inn Ⓛ
80 Main Street, DE55 5TE
✪ 4 (12 Sat)-1am; 12-midnight Sun; closed Mon
☎ (01773) 873944
Dukeries A Ray of Sunshine; 2 changing beers (sourced locally; often Dukeries) Ⓗ
Fully refurbished in 2014, four handpulls offer two beers from the Dukeries range and one guest, as well as one real rotating cider. Traditional Sunday lunch is served noon-4pm, Tuesday is pool night, Wednesday is poker, Thursday is steak night followed by a quiz and bingo, and karaoke is every other Friday. Live music plays most Saturdays. Third-pint taster batons are available for the price of a pint. Pool and darts are played in an upstairs games room. Q☺🛏️🕪🕭♣💷P🖵🐾

Ockbrook

Cross Keys ⚫
Green Lane, DE72 3SE
✪ 12-midnight (11.30 Sun) ☎ (01332) 662308
⊕ crosskeys-ockbrook.co.uk
Marston's Pedigree; Sharp's Doom Bar; Tetley Mild; 2 changing beers Ⓗ
A traditional village pub with a quirky character, a selection of five real ales and one real cider. The bar has a low-beamed ceiling, darts area, several screens for TV sport and a woodburner for the winter months. Events include karaoke and theme nights. Home-made food features stone-baked pizza. Outside, there is a small terrace with seating at the front and a small enclosed garden and play area to the side. 🛏️🕭🕪♣💷P🖵🐾

Royal Oak Ⓛ
55 Green Lane, DE72 3SE
✪ 11.30-3, 5-11.30; 11.30-11.30 Sat; 12-11.30 Sun
☎ (01332) 662378 ⊕ royaloakockbrook.com
Draught Bass; 4 changing beers Ⓗ
Attractive 18th-century pub with a number of small rooms. Run by the Wilson family since Coronation year, they have brought about many improvements while retaining the original character and features. Excellent home-cooked food is served every lunchtime and Monday to Friday evenings. A large function room allows the pub to host community and public events including live music nights. Outside there are two pleasant gardens, one with an enclosed play area for children. Q☺🕭🕪🕭♣💷P🖵🐾

Openwoodgate

Black Bull's Head
2 Kilburn Lane, DE56 0SF
✪ 12-11; 12-10.30 Sun ☎ 07860 757741
⊕ blackbullshead.com
Draught Bass; Greene King Abbot; Oakham Bishops Farewell; 6 changing beers (often Blue Monkey, Castle Rock, Dancing Duck) Ⓗ
Two-roomed former Greene King pub, now a free house, offering a warm welcome in comfortable surroundings and with real fires in winter. Walls are adorned with historic photographs and newspaper clippings of local and national interest, with one wall dedicated to the RAF. The pub serves many real ales and ciders, with more available in the separate, rustic, Bedlam Bar, open Friday to Sunday. Local CAMRA Pub of the Year 2014. Q🕭♣💷P🖵🐾

Over Haddon

Lathkil Hotel Ⓛ
School Lane, DE45 1JE
✪ 11-11; 12-10.30 Sun ☎ (01629) 812501 ⊕ lathkil.co.uk
Everards Tiger; 4 changing beers Ⓗ
This pub overlooks a masterpiece of Peak District scenery, marvellous in any weather. Walking in, one side is an old-fashioned bar room with a real fire and oak beams, while the larger room opposite is where diners enjoy superb home-cooked meals, again with a log-burning fire. The outside covered beer garden is the perfect place to while away summer evenings with a pint. Dogs are welcome in the bar, but walkers should remove their boots at the door. Q🛏️🕭🕪🕭🕪AP🖵🐾

Repton

Boot Inn Ⓛ ⚫
12 Boot Hill, DE65 6FT
✪ 11-11.45pm ☎ (01283) 346047 ⊕ thebootatrepton.co.uk
House beer (by Boot); 6 changing beers Ⓗ
Close to the Repton Cross at the centre of the village, this pub has been brought back to life by the local Bespoke pub company with a recent refurbishment and the addition of an on-site microbrewery supplying all six of the real ales on the bar. Boot Brewery beers are to be found in Bespoke sister pubs in the neighbouring villages of Willington and Melbourne – the Dragon and Harpurs respectively. Food and accommodation are catered for. 🛏️🕭🕪🕭💷P🖵(V3)🐾

Ripley

Beehive Inn
151 Peasehill, DE5 3JN
✪ 5-midnight (1am Fri); 3-1am Sat; 4-midnight Sun
☎ (01773) 749593
9 changing beers (often Batemans, Landlocked) Ⓗ
Three-roomed free house half a mile from the town centre, a hub for local rugby and pub league teams. The pub has low prices, welcoming fires in winter, Sky TV in the public bar and a large, pleasant beer garden. It is also the home of Landlocked brewing company. The Honeypot Bar, in a building at the top of the garden, is popular, with up to four real ales and several ciders always available. Q🛏️🕭🕪♣💷P🖵🐾

Red Lion
Market Place, DE5 3BS
✪ 8am-midnight (1am Fri & Sat) ☎ (01773) 512875
Adnams Broadside; Greene King Abbot; Ruddles Best Bitter; 6 changing beers (often Exmoor, Thornbridge) Ⓗ
Former Home Brewery pub built in the 1960s and easily identified by the large red lion rampant on the pub frontage. It faces the Victorian Ripley town hall and marketplace, and is at the centre of a vibrant, well-pubbed market town. A busy Wetherspoon outlet, the venue serves a large selection of guest beers and good-quality wines. Food is available all day. Q🛏️🕪🕭💷P🖵🐾

Talbot Taphouse
1 Butterley Hill, DE5 3LT
✪ 5-11; 3-11.30 Fri; 2-midnight Sat; 12-11 Sun
☎ (01773) 742626 ⊕ amberales.co.uk/brewerytap
Amber Derbyshire Gold, Original Black Stout, Barnes Wallis; 3 changing beers (often Amber) Ⓗ

The eye-catching Amber Ales brewery tap occupies a flat-iron site and is handily situated between Ripley town centre and Midland Railway Heritage Centre. This Victorian former Shipstone's house is blissfully free of music and TV, instead the sounds of conversation, laughter and the traditional games of bar billiards and table skittles are preferred. Recognised for innovation in brewing, Amber Ales regularly tests experimental brews as well as serving local favourites. There is always at least one guest beer. Q♣🕑🅿🚪(91,92)🌣

Sawley

Nag's Head Inn ✅
Wilne Road, NG10 3AL
🌀 11-11 (midnight Fri & Sat); 12-11 Sun ☎ (0115) 973 2983
🌐 sawleypub.wix.com/nagshead
Marston's Burton Bitter, Pedigree; 1 changing beer ⊞
Early 19th-century inn close to the River Trent and Sawley Marina. This is a traditional Marston's local with a good community spirit. The bar, with a flagstoned floor and wood-burning stove, is often lively. The low-beamed ceiling provides a homely, intimate feel. Good-value home-cooked food is available lunchtimes and early evenings (no food Sun). 🚌🕑🅑🕑🅿🚪🌣

Railway Inn ✅
29 Wilne Road, NG10 3AP
🌀 12-11 (midnight Fri); 11-midnight Sat; 11-11 Sun
☎ (0115) 973 4728
Marston's Pedigree; Wychwood Hobgoblin; 2 changing beers ⊞
Brick-built corner house from around the early 1900s. Although open plan, the pub is split into four distinct areas, with a central bar. As you enter from the road there is a lounge to the left and a smaller snug to the right. Further forward you will come to the bar on the right with a pool room to the left. Although called the Railway Inn, the local station and line closed in the early 1930s. Guest beers come from the Marston's portfolio. 🕑🅑🚪

Scarcliffe

Horse & Groom
Mansfield Road, S44 6SU
🌀 12-11 ☎ (01246) 823152
Black Sheep Best Bitter; Greene King Abbot; Morland Old Golden Hen; Sharp's Doom Bar; 2 changing beers ⊞
Charming two-room rural pub, over 500 years old, with a large car park to the front and a mobile-phone-free main bar. Owned by generations of the same family for the last 17 years, it is run to high standards. Accommodation is available on-site in a couple of cottages. Locally made pork pies should be tried. A bus stop is right outside the pub. Q🕑🛏🅿🚪(53)

Shirland

Shoulder of Mutton Ⓛ
Hallfieldgate Lane, DE55 6AA
🌀 5-11 Mon, Wed & Thu (closed Tue); 12-11 Fri & Sat; 12-10.30 Sun ☎ (01773) 834992
3 changing beers ⊞
Eclectic, 16th-century traditional drinking den, nestling on the edge of Amber Valley. The beer garden offers spectacular views and sunsets. It is a true free house where real people enjoy real ale

from small breweries; there is no beer list on the wall because the ales change daily. The regular customers are drawn from far and wide, fuelling the unique, easy atmosphere created by the irrepressible landlord and landlady. Check out the teacups. Q🕑🛏♣🅿🌣🌣🛜

Smalley

Bell Ⓛ ✅
35 Main Road, DE7 6EF (on A608)
🌀 12-2.30, 5-11; 11.30-11 Fri-Sun ☎ (01332) 880635
🌐 thebellsmalley.co.uk
Abbeydale Moonshine; Marston's Pedigree; Sharp's Doom Bar; 2 changing beers ⊞
Situated near Shipley Country Park, this mid-19th-century inn has three rooms in which breweriana and other memorabilia adorn the walls. A drinkers' pub, it serves three regular beers plus guests, but is also renowned for food, with a good and varied menu including daily home-made specials (no food Sun eves). Accommodation is in three self-catering apartments in converted stables, and there is a large attractive garden. Weekday opening hours may be extended in the summer. Quiz night is Wednesday. Q🕑🛏🕑🅿🚪🛜

Smisby

Tap House
Annwell Lane, LE65 2TA
🌀 11-11 (midnight Fri & Sat) ☎ (01530) 413604
🌐 taphousesmisby.co.uk
Marston's Pedigree; 5 changing beers (sourced locally; often Tap House) ⊞
Friendly 19th-century local and tap for the nearby Tap House Brewery. The main bar, with its beamed ceiling, is at the front, beyond which is a restaurant featuring a popular carvery. While the changing beers are usually from Tap House, one may be replaced by a beer from another microbrewery. Quiz night is Monday, pie night is Wednesday, open mic night is alternate Thursdays and live music plays on Friday evening. The enclosed garden to the rear includes a children's play area. 🚌🕑🛏🕑🅑♣🅿🚪(9)🌣🛜

South Normanton

Devonshire Arms 🍷
137 Market Street, DE55 2AA
🌀 12-midnight ☎ (01773) 810748
5 changing beers ⊞
Genuine free house offering up to five real ales and three real ciders or perries. Home-cooked food is served until 9pm every day except Sunday, when a popular carvery is offered. Vegetarians, vegans and coeliacs are all catered for. Sky Sports and BT Sport are shown on three big screens. Local CAMRA Pub of the Year for an impressive nine years running, 2008-2016. 🕑🅑♣🕑🅿🚪🌣🛜

Sutton cum Duckmanton

Arkwright Arms Ⓛ
Chesterfield Road, S44 5JG
🌀 11-11 (midnight Fri & Sat); 11-10.30 Sun
☎ (01246) 232053 🌐 arkwrightarms.co.uk
Greene King Abbot; Whim Arbor Light; changing beers ⊞
Brewers' Tudor-fronted free house. A changing range of 10 guest ales, many from local micros, is

complemented by 12 ciders and four perries. Beer festivals are held at Easter and bank holidays, with mini events throughout the year. Quality food is served daily. The spacious beer garden has play equipment for children. A winner of numerous CAMRA awards, including East Midlands Cider Pub of the Year and local Pub of the Year. ✿✿◑▲♣♠P🖪(81,82,83)✿

Swadlincote

Sir Nigel Gresley ✅
Market Street, DE11 9DA
✿ 8am-11 (midnight Fri & Sat) ☎ (01283) 227560
Greene King Abbot; Marston's Pedigree; Ruddles Best Bitter; 5 changing beers (sourced regionally; often Burton Bridge, Milestone, Shepherd Neame) Ⓗ
Popular town-centre Wetherspoon's pub, created in 2001 from the semi-derelict former Granville Arms and named after the railway engine designer, scion of a local family. The large, open-plan, main drinking area has low ceilings and features memorabilia with a railway theme. The airy conservatory at the side is used mainly for dining. Guest beers are often from local microbreweries. The bus station and free public car parks are nearby. Q✿✿◑◗🅟♣♠🖪🛜

Swanwick

Steampacket Inn
Derby Road, DE55 1AB
✿ 2.30-11; 2-midnight Fri; 12-midnight Sat; 12-11 Sun
☎ (01773) 607771
5 changing beers (often Blue Monkey, Derby, Nottingham) Ⓗ
A friendly and welcoming ex-Shipstone's pub in the centre of Swanwick. Popular with locals, the Steampacket boasts an excellent and constantly changing range of well-kept real ales and ciders, many of them from local microbreweries. It is a lively pub at the weekends with regular live music, and hosts quiz nights during the week. It has a welcoming fire in winter, and outdoor tables in summer. Local CAMRA branch Cider Pub of the Year in 2014 and 2015. ✿♠♣♠P🖪(9.1,9.2,9.3)✿🛜

Thorpe

Old Dog ♗
Spend Lane, DE6 2AT
✿ 11-10.30 (midnight Fri & Sat); closed Mon
☎ (01335) 350990 🌐 theolddog.co.uk
4 changing beers (sourced locally; often Dancing Duck, Derby, Titanic) Ⓗ
Brilliant pub revived in 2014 after a lengthy closure. Four real ales are permanently available, usually from local breweries, always including a dark ale. Excellent food is served at most times. Set alone outside the village, it is within easy walking distance of the Tissington Trail and Dovedale. Local CAMRA Pub of the Year 2016. ✿✿◑◗♠P✿

Wardlow Mires

Three Stags' Heads ★
SK17 8RW (jct A623/B6465)

✿ 7-11 Fri; 11-11 Sat; 12-10.30 Sun; closed Mon-Thu
☎ (01298) 872268
Abbeydale Brimstone, Absolution; house beer (by Abbeydale); 2 changing beers (sourced regionally; often Abbeydale) Ⓗ
A quaint 300 year old pub with two small rooms, stone-flagged floors and low ceilings. Unspoilt, it is one of the few pubs in the area on CAMRA's National Inventory of Historic Pub Interiors. An ancient range warms the bar and the house dogs, one of which gave the name to the house beer – Black Lurcher. The food is locally sourced, with game a speciality in season. Traditional cider is only available in summer. Q✿▲♠P🖪(173)✿🛜

Whaley Bridge

Shepherds Arms
7 Old Road, SK23 7HR
✿ 3 (2 Sat)-midnight; 2-11.30 Sun ☎ (01663) 732840
Marston's Burton Bitter, Pedigree; 3 changing beers Ⓗ
A little gem of a pub nestling close to the centre of the village. This attractive, whitewashed, stone building has been preserved unspoilt, conveying the feel of the farmhouse it once was. The unchanged taproom is a delight, with open fire, flagged floor and scrubbed table tops. Additionally, there is a comfortable lounge with an open fire in winter. The changing guest beers are selected from the Marston's range. In attractive walking country, hikers are welcome. Q✿≓♣P🖪(199,61)

Whitehough

Old Hall Inn Ⓛ ✅
Chinley, SK23 6EJ (in village)
✿ 12-11 ☎ (01663) 750529 🌐 old-hall-inn.co.uk
Marston's Burton Bitter; changing beers Ⓗ
The 14th-century Whitehough Hall forms part of this quintessential country inn, which has won the Great British Pub award for best cask pub in the region for several years and is a regular entry in this Guide. Eight ales, including seven changing guests from quality local micros, complement those available at the adjacent Paper Mill Inn (under the same ownership). A popular menu features dishes using local produce. ✿✿🛏◑▲≓♠P🖪(189,190)✿🛜

Whittington Moor

Beer Parlour Ⓛ
1 King Street North, S41 9BA
✿ 4-11; 12-midnight Sat; 1-10 Sun ☎ 07870 693411
🌐 the-beer-parlour.co.uk
8 changing beers (often Double Top, Thornbridge, Timothy Taylor) Ⓗ
Originally a bottle beer shop with a few handpumps, now in larger premises. The rustic one-roomed bar has a warm, friendly feel, with comfortable seating giving it a real micropub feel. A choice of eight real ales is offered along with cider and Belgian and continental beers. Winner of a CAMRA award, you can opt to take a beer home too. Q✿♠🖵🖪✿

When you have lost your inns, drown your empty selves, for you will have lost the last of England. **Hilaire Belloc, The Four Men, 1912**

Many entries in the Guide refer to pubs' support for CAMRA's LocAle scheme. The ℓ symbol is used where a pub has LocAle accreditation. The aim of the scheme is to get publicans to stock at least one cask beer that comes from a local brewery no further than 20 miles away. It also encourages publicans to use the Beerflex scheme run by SIBA, the Society of Independent Brewers (see p971). SIBA members deliver direct to pubs in their localities instead of going through the central warehouses of pub-owning companies.

The aim is a simple one: to cut down on 'beer miles'. Research by CAMRA shows that food and drink transport accounts for 25 per cent of all HGV vehicle miles in Britain. Taking into account the miles that ingredients have travelled on top of distribution journeys, an imported lager produced by a multi-national brewery could have notched up more than 24,000 'beer miles' by the time it reaches a pub.

Supporters of LocAle point out that £10 spent on locally-supplied goods generates £25 for the local economy. Keeping trade local helps enterprises, creates more economic activity and jobs, and makes other services more viable. The scheme also generates consumer support for local breweries.

Support for LocAle has grown at a rapid pace since it was created in 2007. It's been embraced by pubs and CAMRA branches throughout England and has now crossed the borders into Scotland and Wales.

For more information, see the CAMRA website www.camra.org.uk and type 'locale' into the search window.

What is CAMRA LocAle?

- An initiative that promotes pubs which sell locally-brewed real ale.
- The scheme builds on a growing consumer demand for quality local produce and an increased awareness of 'green' issues.

Everyone benefits from local pubs stocking locally brewed real ale...

- Public houses, as stocking local real ales can increase pub visits
- Consumers, who enjoy greater beer choice and locally brewed beer
- Local brewers, who gain from increased sales and get better feedback from consumers
- The local economy, because more money is spent and retained in the local economy
- The environment, due to fewer 'beer miles' resulting in less road congestion and pollution
- Tourism, due to an increased sense of local identity and pride – let's celebrate what makes our locality different.

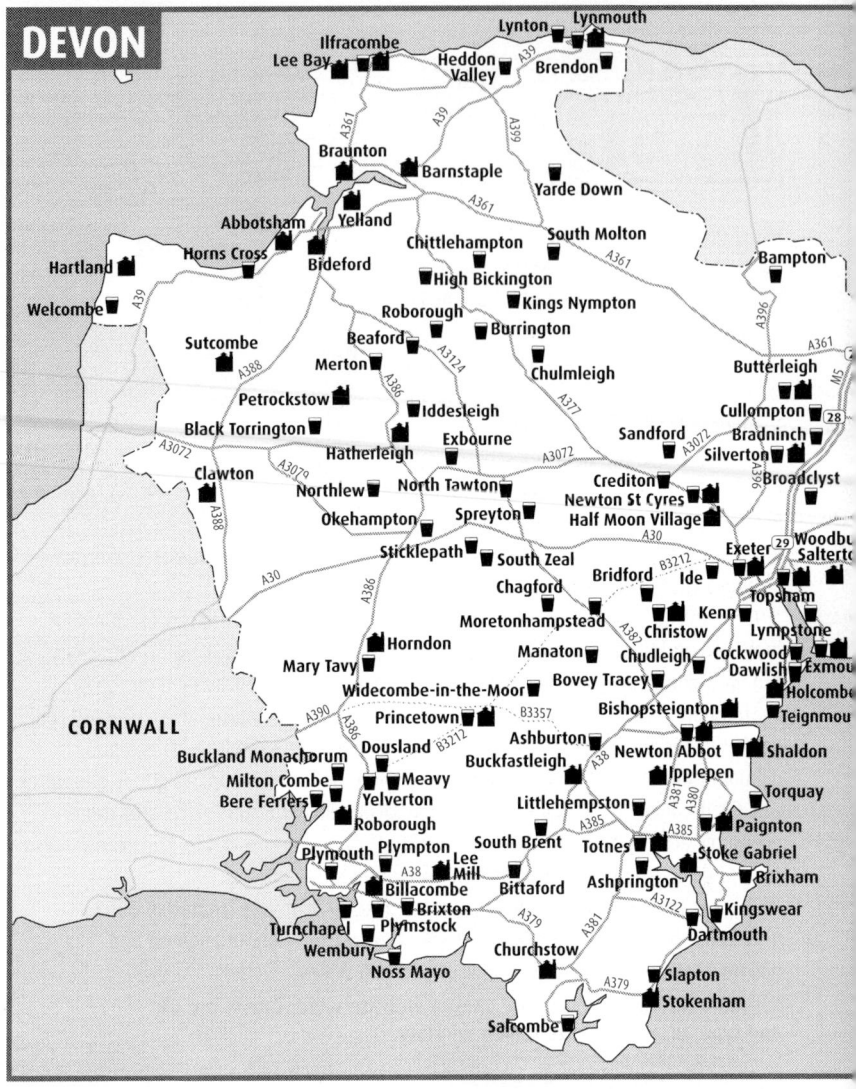

DEVON

Lynton
Lynmouth
Ilfracombe
Lee Bay
Heddon Valley
Brendon
Braunton
Barnstaple
Yarde Down
Abbotsham
Yelland
Chittlehampton
South Molton
Bampton
Horns Cross
Hartland
Bideford
High Bickington
Welcombe
Roborough
Kings Nympton
Sutcombe
Beaford
Burrington
Merton
Chulmleigh
Butterleigh
Petrockstow
Iddesleigh
Cullompton
Black Torrington
Exbourne
Sandford
Bradninch
Hatherleigh
Crediton
Silverton
Clawton
Northlew
North Tawton
Newton St Cyres
Broadclyst
Okehampton
Spreyton
Half Moon Village
Sticklepath
South Zeal
Exeter
Woodbu
Chagford
Bridford
Ide
Salterto
Moretonhampstead
Christow
Topsham
Horndon
Manaton
Chudleigh
Kenn
Lympstone
Mary Tavy
Bovey Tracey
Cockwood
Exmou
Widecombe-in-the-Moor
Dawlish
Holcombe
CORNWALL
Princetown
Bishopsteignton
Teignmou
Dousland
Ashburton
Shaldon
Buckland Monachorum
Buckfastleigh
Newton Abbot
Milton Combe
Meavy
Ipplepen
Torquay
Bere Ferrers
Yelverton
Littlehempston
Roborough
South Brent
Totnes
Paignton
Plymouth
Plympton
Stoke Gabriel
Lee Mill
Billacombe
Bittaford
Ashprington
Brixham
Turnchapel
Brixton
Kingswear
Wembury
Plymstock
Churchstow
Dartmouth
Noss Mayo
Slapton
Stokenham
Salcombe

Appledore

Champ L ✔

Meeting Street, EX39 1RJ (just off Appledore Quay)
🕐 5-midnight (11 Tue & Wed); 5-11 Sun ☎ (01237) 421662
🌐 champappledore.co.uk
Clearwater Devon Darter, Real Smiler, Submariner; 3 changing beers (sourced nationally) Ⓗ
Set in a charming coastal village, the Champ is a cosy, traditional evening venue renowned for live music. The brewery tap for nearby Clearwater, it keeps real ale on four pumps, with three Clearwater ales joined by a guest. Real cider is also available, together with a selection of Belgian beers. Informal soul food including pizzas, ribs and tacos is served 6-9pm. Live bands feature on Fridays and Saturdays and popular open mic sessions Monday to Thursday. Quiz nights are held fortnightly on a Sunday. ⛴🅿♿♣🌭🚌🐾🛜

Ashburton

Exeter Inn L

26 West Street, TQ13 7DU (on main road through centre of Ashburton opp church)
🕐 11-2.30, 5-11 (midnight Fri & Sat); 12-3, 7-10.30 Sun
☎ (01364) 652013
Dartmoor IPA, Legend Ⓗ
The oldest pub in Ashburton, this friendly local was built in 1131, with additions in the 17th century. It originally housed the workers constructing the nearby church. There are seated drinking areas either side of the entrance hallway, with the main bar to the right, which is L-shaped, rustic and wood panelled, with a canopy. A smaller seated bar area at the rear is served via a small counter. There is a lovely secluded walled garden outside at the back. Local Thompstone's cider is on sale.
Q🅿🐕🍴🐾🌭🚌🐾🛜

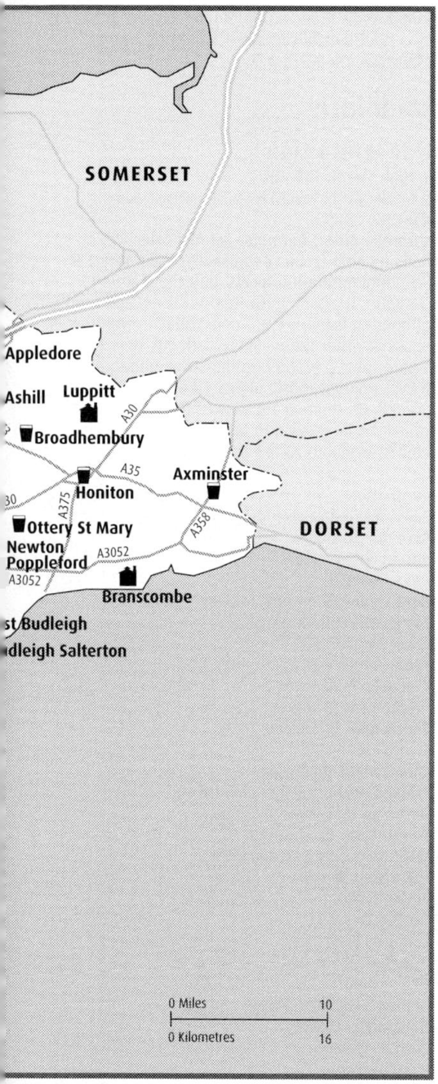
SOMERSET
Appledore
Ashill
Luppitt
A30
Broadhembury
A35
Axminster
A375
Honiton
30
Ottery St Mary
A358
DORSET
Newton Poppleford
A3052
A3052
Branscombe
st Budleigh
dleigh Salterton
0 Miles
10
0 Kilometres
16

Ashill

Ashill Inn

EX15 3NL ST086113

12-2.30 (not Mon), 5.30-11.30; 12-4, 6.30-10.30 Sun

(01884) 840506 ashillinndevon.co.uk

Otter Bitter; 2 changing beers (sourced regionally) [H]

Small Grade II-listed pub, built in 1835. It is a charming venue with a cosy bar and a recently extended restaurant area to one side, with large windows which look out onto the beer garden. The comfortable bar serves local ales. Good-value food is available, with produce mainly from local farms. Live music and special events are often featured. Sandford Orchard Old Kirton real cider is served. **Q P**

Ashprington

Durant Arms

TQ9 7UP

12-3, 6-10 (11 Thu); 12-3, 5-11 Fri; 12-11 Sat; 12-5 Sun; closed Mon (01803) 732240 durantarms.co.uk

Noss Beer Works Church Ledge [H]**; 2 changing beers (sourced regionally)** [H]/[G]

On the war memorial roundabout in the heart of the village, three miles from Totnes, this is a traditional family-run inn serving up to three ales and a varying cider. The bar has slate floors, open fire and a good reputation for home-cooked food, with two adjoined areas for diners. It is popular with walkers and cyclists, and dogs are welcome in the bar and in the accommodation. There is pleasant seating at the front and a secluded rear courtyard. **Q P**

Axminster

Axminster Inn

Silver Street, EX13 5AH

10.30-1am (midnight Mon); 10-1am Thu; 10.30-midnight Sun (01297) 34947 axminsterinn.pub

Palmers Copper Ale, Best Bitter, Dorset Gold, 200, Tally Ho! [H]

A friendly, traditional pub, lying just off the town centre, with a real log fire, and a lovely enclosed beer garden. It offers a good range of Palmers ales as well as Sheppy's real cider. Good-value home-cooked food, often locally sourced, is served lunchtimes, including roast on Sundays. Breakfast is available Monday to Thursday, 8.30-11am. Free Wi-Fi is provided, and there is a skittle alley and dartboard. Children are welcome and the pub is dog-friendly. Live music is featured (see website). **P**

Bampton

Swan

Station Road, EX16 9NG

12-11 (midnight Fri & Sat); 12-10.30 Sun

(01398) 332248 theswan.co

Changing beers [H]

The oldest pub in Bampton and the original lodgings for the masons and craftsmen who were hired to enlarge the nearby church. The pub has recently been renovated, with solid oak fittings, polished wood tables and boarded flooring, to give it a wine-bar feel. The large fireplace contains the original bread oven from 1450. A large public car park, on the site of the old railway station, is close by. The Swan has won numerous food awards. **Q P** (398)

Beaford

Globe Inn

Exeter Road, EX19 8LR (on main road in centre of village)

12.30-midnight Mon; 12-3, 5.30-11; 12-4 Sun

(01805) 603358 globeinnbeaford.co.uk

3 changing beers (sourced nationally) [H]

Village pub with a single L-shaped bar and dining area, a pleasant beer garden and a car park to the rear. A 300-year-old Grade II-listed former coaching house, the Globe reopened in 2014 and has since gained a reputation for excellent locally sourced pub food and good beer. Three real ales are kept, with one invariably from a north Devon brewery, together with a local cider. Children and dogs are all welcome. **Q P**

Bere Ferrers

Olde Plough Inn ⬡

Fore Street, PL20 7JG (close to church and river)
🕐 11-3, 5-11; 11-11 Sat; 12-11 Sun ☎ (01822) 840358
⊕ theoldeploughinn.co.uk

Sharp's Doom Bar; 3 changing beers (sourced locally; often Dartmoor, Noss Beer Works, Summerskills) H
Friendly 16th-century pub, just a 15-minute walk from the station, and only 18 minutes from Plymouth on the Tamar Valley line. Up to four real ales are sold, and a real cider in summer. Inside, there are real fires, exposed stonework, flagstone floors and a warm welcome. From the beer garden, there are spectacular views over the River Tavy. Food is served to suit all ages, tastes and appetites, including vegetarian. Q ⬠ ❀ ⬤ ➾ ♣ ● 🖵 (87) ❀ 🛜

Bittaford

Horse & Groom ⬡

Exeter Road, PL21 0EL
🕐 12-11 (midnight Fri & Sat) ☎ (01752) 892358
Dartmoor Jail Ale; house beer (by Hunters); 4 changing beers (sourced locally; often Dartmoor, Hunters) H
A family-owned pub with Oliver, a keen real ale enthusiast, as landlord, serving good home-cooked food and boasting six pumps, one dedicated to real cider. The other pumps offer predominantly local ales from breweries in south Devon and Cornwall. It has a long bar and separate dining area, with pictures of the former Moorhaven Hospital on the wall. A monthly quiz night is held. One beer festival, and a cider and sausage festival, are hosted, supporting local charities. Third-pint tapas available. Q ⬠ ❀ ⬤ Å ♣ ● P 🖵 (X38) ❀

Black Torrington

Torridge Inn

Broad Street, EX21 5PT SS465056
🕐 12-3 (not Tue-Thu), 6-11; 12-3, 6-10.30 Sun; closed Mon
☎ (01409) 231243 ⊕ thetorridgeinn.co.uk
Otter Amber; 1 changing beer (sourced nationally) H
Convivial village local dating from the 18th century and close to both the Tarka Trail and the Ruby Way. A large log fire welcomes in winter, while in summer the pleasant beer garden affords attractive views of the Torridge Valley. At least two real ales are always available, together with a local cider. A good selection of home-cooked, locally sourced food is served and the pub operates a CAMRA discount scheme on ales. Closed winter Mondays. Q ⬠ ❀ ⬤ Å ♣ ● P 🖵 (639,642) ❀ 🛜

Bovey Tracey

Cromwell Arms ✅

Fore Street, TQ13 9AE
🕐 11-11 (11.30 Fri & Sat); 12-11 Sun ☎ (01626) 833473
⊕ thecromwellarms.co.uk
St Austell Tribute; house beer (by St Austell); 2 changing beers H
Centrally located 17th-century town pub with easy access to Dartmoor and only yards from the bus stops. Up to five real ales are in constant rotation from St Austell, with seasonal brews well represented. There are two drinking areas around a central bar, with an adjoining dining area and separate restaurant, both of which permit children. To the rear an enclosed wisteria-covered smokers'

retreat leads to an excellent garden next to the car park. Additionally there are 14 letting rooms.
Q ⬠ ❀ ⬅ ⬤ ⬥ ♣ P 🖵 ❀ 🛜

Bradninch

Olde White Lion

26 High Street, EX5 4QL
🕐 4-midnight; 12-1am Fri & Sat; 12-midnight Sun
☎ (01392) 881263
Butcombe Bitter; Dartmoor Jail Ale; Otter Ale; 1 changing beer (sourced regionally; often Otter) H
A friendly family-run locals' pub that caters for everyone. It offers up to four real ales, and food is confined to fish and chips on a Friday evening, with snacks at other times. Many dark oak beams are a feature, plus a wood-burning stove under a stone alcove. Popular music nights take place; there is a folk club on the first Tuesday of the month, and an annual music festival in June. Westons Old Rosie cider is available. Q ⬠ ● ♣ ● P 🖵 ❀ 🛜

Brendon

Staghunters Inn Ⓛ

Brendon, EX35 6PS SS767481
🌐 12-11 ☎ (01598) 741222 ⊕ staghunters.com
Exmoor Ale; St Austell Proper Job; 2 changing beers (sourced nationally) Ⓖ
Owned and run by a family, set deep in the valley at Brendon, this inn nestles on the banks of the River Lyn. All beer is served direct from the cask, with the regular Exmoor and St Austell ales often joined by guests from other local breweries. A wide range of locally sourced food can be enjoyed in the attractive restaurant. There are 14 well-appointed rooms and walkers can also keep their dogs here overnight for a nominal charge.
Q ☎ ⊛ ⊟ ◑ Å ♣ ● P ❀ 🤶

Bridford

Bridford Inn Ⓛ

EX6 7HT
🌐 12-11 (midnight Fri & Sat) ☎ (01647) 252250
⊕ bridfordinn.co.uk
Dartmoor Jail Ale; 3 changing beers (sourced regionally) Ⓗ
A 17th-century Devon longhouse within the Dartmoor National Park that was converted to a pub in 1968, and now houses a village shop. It has a spacious open-plan interior for both drinkers and diners, with old oak beams, and an inglenook fireplace complete with old bread oven and a woodburner. Freshly home-cooked quality food is served to order. Outside there is a beer garden with picnic tables and stunning views. Traditional ciders from Devon and Somerset producers are always available.
Q ☎ ⊛ ◑ ♿ ♣ ● P ❏ (360,361) ❀ 🤶

Brixham

Queen's Arms 🍷 Ⓛ ✅

31 Station Hill, TQ5 8BN (from Brixham Library go up Church Hill East, then Station Hill)
🌐 4-11; 2-midnight Fri; 12-midnight Sat; 12-11 Sun
☎ (01803) 852074 ⊕ thequeensarmsbrixham.co.uk
6 changing beers (sourced nationally; often Hunters, Oakham, Teignworthy) Ⓗ
Up a short hill just outside the town, next to where Brixham station used to be, is this single-bar, end-of-terrace pub. It is a friendly, community-oriented venue with six constantly changing ales, mainly from Devon and Cornwall, but with guest ales from up country. There is always one at £2.60 and a selection of up to three real ciders. It does great-value Sunday lunch, there is a Monday supper club, and it serves basic meals on request. Local CAMRA Pub of the Year 2014 and 2016. ☎ ⊛ ◑ ♣ ● ❏

Brixton

Foxhound Inn 🍷 Ⓛ

PL8 2AH
🌐 11-11 (midnight Fri & Sat); 12-11 Sun ☎ (01752) 880271
⊕ foxhoundinn.co.uk
Courage Best Bitter; house beer (by Summerskills); 3 changing beers (sourced nationally; often Cottage, Dartmoor, Summerskills) Ⓗ
This 18th-century former coaching house is situated in a rural village just east of Plymouth, well served by a frequent daytime bus service. The pub has two separate bars and a small restaurant. Traditional English meals are served daily, made with locally sourced ingredients. Look out for Red Coat, an ale crafted by the landlord, among four guest ales. A monthly charity quiz night is held. Local CAMRA branch Country Pub of the Year 2016.
Q ☎ ⊛ ◑ Å ♣ ● P ❏ (3,91,875) ❀

Broadclyst

New Inn Ⓛ

Whimple Road, EX5 3BX (½ mile E of village)
🌐 11-11 ☎ (01392) 461312 ⊕ newinn-exeter.co.uk
Dartmoor Jail Ale; Hanlons Yellowhammer; Otter Bitter; Sharp's Doom Bar Ⓗ
Large, traditional 17th-century inn located to the east of the main village, with a recently extended car park to the rear, and a two-acre beer garden and play area. The large grounds host the village Year Seven football club. Freshly cooked food is available lunchtimes and evenings. There are three secluded rooms and the skittle alley can double as a function room. Regular events are held, plus an annual bonfire night. Q ☎ ⊛ ◑ ♣ ● P 🤶

Broadhembury

Drewe Arms

EX14 3NF
🌐 12-11; 12-10.30 Sun ☎ (01404) 841267
⊕ drewearmsinn.co.uk
Bays Topsail; Branscombe Vale Summa That; Exeter Avocet; Otter Ale; 2 changing beers (sourced locally) Ⓗ
A Grade II-listed 16th-century thatched pub with a secluded garden, set in a picturesque estate village within the Blackdown Hills. This is a friendly and welcoming family-run venue, with the emphasis on local real ales and produce. Good-value food is served lunchtimes and evenings Monday to Saturday, and lunchtimes on Sunday. A takeaway menu is always available. The pub holds an annual beer festival over the Easter weekend.
Q ☎ ⊛ ◑ Å ● P ❀ 🤶

Buckland Monachorum

Drake Manor Inn Ⓛ ✅

The Village, PL20 7NA
🌐 11.30-2.30, 6.30-11; 11.30-11.30 Fri & Sat; 12-11 Sun
☎ (01822) 853892 ⊕ drakemanorinn.co.uk
Dartmoor Jail Ale; Sharp's Doom Bar; 1 changing beer (sourced regionally; often Otter) Ⓗ
Cosy and friendly pub, dating from the 16th century, in a pleasant village on the edge of Dartmoor. It attracts a regular clientele who are happy to be assisted with the daily crossword. The inviting traditional interior features an intimate meeting area, a public bar and a restaurant area in which to sample the good food. The garden, with a stream, is an enjoyable suntrap. Good-value food is served lunchtimes and evenings.
Q ☎ ⊛ ◑ ♣ ● ❏ (55) ❀ 🤶

Budleigh Salterton

Salterton Arms Ⓛ ✅

22 Chapel Street, EX9 6LX
🌐 11-11.30; 12-11 Sun ☎ (01395) 445008
Dartmoor Jail Ale; Otter Ale; Sharp's Doom Bar; 1 changing beer Ⓗ

A local pub with Cotswold stone and bare wood floors. The walls are painted in terracotta, pastel yellows and greens in keeping with the local seaside tradition. A small TV at the back of the bar is mainly used to show major sporting events. A large variety of meals is available and can be eaten in the bar or in the upstairs mezzanine area. Euchre is played and there are the occasional live music events. ◑&♣🖥😺🛜

Burrington

Portsmouth Arms

EX37 9ND (on A377 approx 4 miles S of Umberleigh)
✿ 4-11; 12-11 Fri-Sun ☎ (01769) 561117
Otter Bitter Ⓗ; **1 changing beer (sourced nationally)** Ⓖ
Welcoming former coaching inn in the heart of the Taw Valley, an ideal base for walkers, fishermen and those exploring the local area. Featuring a cob structure some 600 years old at the entrance to the front bar area, there are also original oak beams and a log fire. In summer attractive views across the river from the peaceful, decked rear veranda can also be enjoyed. The pub serves well-sourced local food every day until 9pm.
Q🌳😺◑⇌♣P😺🛜

Butterleigh

Butterleigh Inn Ⓛ

The Green, **EX15 1PN** (opp church) SS9746108212
✿ 12-2.30 (not Mon), 6-11; 12-2.30, 6-midnight Fri & Sat; 12-3 Sun ☎ (01884) 855433 ⊕ butterleighinn.co.uk
Cotleigh Tawny Owl; Dartmoor Jail Ale; Otter Ale; 1 changing beer Ⓗ
Situated in this small, quaint village, the Butterleigh is an excellent country pub with a mixed clientele creating a great atmosphere with diverse conversation. Good-value home-cooked food is served lunchtimes and evenings Tuesday to Saturday, with a carvery Sunday lunchtime. There is always a choice of four real ales, one a LocAle, plus Sandford Orchards Devon Scrumpy, Winkleigh Sam's Medium and a rotating guest cider. There is a main bar, lounge and a modern dining room.
Q🌳😺⇌◑&♣P😺🛜

Chagford

Globe Inn Ⓛ ✅

9 High Street, **TQ13 8AJ**
✿ 11-11.30 (midnight Fri & Sat); 12-10.30 Sun
☎ (01647) 433485 ⊕ theglobeinnchagford.co.uk
Dartmoor IPA; Exeter Ferryman; Otter Bitter Ⓗ
Formerly a coaching inn and coopery, the Globe overlooks the parish church in this historic stannary town. It is a focal point, providing good food, music evenings, a cinema club and numerous other events. There is a splendid public bar and a separate bar and restaurant, both with big open fires. A small courtyard is at the rear and car parking is nearby. The ciders are Westons Old Rosie and Winkleigh. 🌳😺⇌◑●🖥(173,178)😺🛜

Sandy Park Inn Ⓛ

Sandy Park, **TQ13 8JW** (on A382 Moretonhampstead-Whiddon Down road)
✿ 12 (4 Tue)-11; 12-10.30 Sun summer; 4 (12 Sat)-11; 12-10.30 Sun winter; closed Mon ☎ (01647) 433267
⊕ sandyparkinn.co.uk

Otter Bitter; St Austell Tribute; 1 changing beer (sourced locally) Ⓗ
Thatched free house, thought to be 17th century. The small wood-panelled bar has ancient beams and a large open fireplace. Beyond is a small snug set around a large table, and a further room is beyond the front door. Good home-cooked meals are served lunchtimes (not Tue) and Friday and Saturday evenings. There is a small front car park with steps up to the garden. Castle Drogo (NT), Fingle Bridge and Chagford are nearby. The cider is Westons Old Rosie. A third beer is added in summer. 🌳😺◑♣●P🖥(173,178)😺🛜

Chittlehampton

Bell Inn Ⓛ

The Square, **EX37 9QL** (opp St Hieritha's parish church) SS636254
✿ 11-3, 6-midnight; 11-midnight Fri & Sat; 12-11 Sun
☎ (01769) 540368 ⊕ thebellatchittlehampton.co.uk
Exmoor Ale; Otter Ale; 5 changing beers (sourced nationally) Ⓗ
Owned and run by the same family for more than 30 years, the Bell has been a regular in the Guide for most of that time. It offers a fine selection of real ales, with four on handpump and up to four more usually available on gravity. The bar area contains some interesting sporting memorabilia. Good-value home-cooked food is served both here and in the adjoining restaurant. Well-behaved children and dogs are welcome.
🌳😺⇌◑&▲♣●P🖥(658,859)😺🛜

Christow

Teign House Inn Ⓛ

Teign Valley Road, **EX6 7PL**
✿ 12-3, 5-11; 12-11 Sat & Sun ☎ (01647) 252286
⊕ teignhouseinn.co.uk
Exeter 'fraidNot; Otter Ale; 2 changing beers (sourced regionally; often Black Tor, Hunters) Ⓗ
A welcoming atmospheric country pub with beams and a warming log fire, situated on the edge of Dartmoor. The pub enjoys strong local support – the sizeable garden attracts families and locals alike, while the adjoining field has space for caravans, camper vans and campers. An annual beer festival with up to 30 beers is held on the second weekend in July. Great pub food, all home cooked, includes a gluten-free menu.
Q🌳😺◑&▲♣●P🖥(360,361)😺🛜

Chudleigh

Bishop Lacy Inn Ⓛ

Fore Street, **TQ13 0HY**
✿ 12-midnight (1am Fri & Sat) ☎ (01626) 854585
3 changing beers (sourced regionally) Ⓗ
You will get a warm welcome from an ebullient landlady at this Grade II-listed building opposite the church and named after the Bishop of Exeter (1420-1455). Beers are predominantly from the West Country and often local, from Exeter, Hunters or Black Tor. The left-hand bar is dominated by a magnificent fireplace which was once used for hanging hams, and witch dolls are suspended above the bar. Excellent home cooking is on the menu and the interior is child- and dog-friendly throughout, as Sambuca the pub dog will testify.
🌳◑▲♣🖥(39,182)😺🛜

Chulmleigh

Old Court House

South Molton Street, EX18 7BW
🕓 11-11; 12-11 Sun ☎ (01769) 580045
⊕ oldcourthouseinn.co.uk
Butcombe Bitter; Dartmoor IPA; Exmoor Ale Ⓗ
Traditional thatched country inn dating from 1633.
Charles I stayed here in 1634 on his first tour of the
West Country and a bedroom contains an original
Royal House of Stuart coat of arms. Today this
welcoming local usually has three real ales on
offer, together with a local cider. Good home-
cooked food is served in the separate restaurant
and a CAMRA discount of 10p per pint is available
to members. 🌣🕮✿🕦🕭🕭🚍(377)🌣 🛜

Cockwood

Anchor Inn Ⓛ ✅

EX6 8RA (just off A379, outside Starcross, next to
harbour) SX9756480692
🕓 11-11; 11.30-10.30 Sun ☎ (01626) 890203
⊕ anchorinncockwood.com
**Otter Ale; St Austell Trelawny; Tintagel Castle Gold; 2
changing beers (sourced nationally)** Ⓗ
On picturesque Cockwood harbour, this 450-year-
old inn and former seaman's mission has many old
settles, timber panelling, low beams and snugs,
with an impressive display of old nautical
memorabilia. It has an extensive award-winning
seafood menu. Up to five ales are usually offered.
Haunted by a friendly ghost and his dog, this is an
atmospheric Devon gem. Close to the main GWR
line, it is a steam train spotters' paradise. Parking is
limited; the bus stop is over the bridge.
Q🌣🕮🕦✿🕭♣🅿🚍(2)🌣

Ship Inn ✅

Church Road, EX6 8NU (just off A379, outside Starcross,
close to harbour)
🕓 11-11; 12-10.30 Sun ☎ (01626) 890373
⊕ shipinncockwood.co.uk
**Dartmoor Jail Ale; St Austell Tribute; 3 changing beers
(sourced nationally)** Ⓗ
A busy family-run pub, close to the harbour at
Cockwood, with a large beer garden that has views
of the estuary, and a log fire in winter. Popular
with drinkers and diners, it offers a choice of three
regular ales and usually two rotating guests, and
has an excellent food menu. Meals are prepared
with local produce where possible including a
varied choice of locally caught fish. The bus stop is
across the bridge. Q🌣🕮🕦🅰🅿🚍(2)🌣 🛜

Crediton

Crediton Inn Ⓛ

28a Mill Street, EX17 1EZ (opp Mole Avon)
🕓 10-11; 12-3, 7-10.30 Sun ☎ (01363) 772882
⊕ crediton-inn.co.uk
**Branscombe Vale Best Bitter; 4 changing beers
(sourced regionally)** Ⓗ
The framed deeds date this inn to 1878, with
windows etched with the ancient town seal. It is a
genuine free house, well supported by the locals.
The handpumps have increased to 10, served by
local breweries, with an ale festival in November.
The skittle alley doubles as a function room. Good
home-cooked food is available at weekends, with
snacks and renowned Scotch eggs at other times.
The welcoming owner is the longest-serving
landlady in Crediton. 🌣🕮🕦🕭✿♣🅿🚍🌣 🛜

Cullompton

Pony & Trap Ⓛ ✅

10 Exeter Hill, EX15 1DJ (on B3181 S of town)
🕓 12-2, 5-11.30; 12-5, 8-11 Sun ☎ (01884) 34182
⊕ ponyandtrapcullompton.co.uk
**Dartmoor Jail Ale; Draught Bass; Otter Bitter; 4
changing beers** Ⓗ
A traditional local with good atmosphere and a
mixed clientele. It has a smart interior featuring a
logburner, making it cosy in winter; flowers and
ornaments give it a homely feel. Up to eight real
ales are on offer. Home-cooked food is served
Friday, Saturday and Sunday lunchtimes only. There
is a garden and seating area. Live music features
once a month and pub games are played. Local
CAMRA branch Pub of the Year 2014.
Q🕮🕦♣🚍(1)🌣

Dartmouth

Cherub Inn ✅

13 Higher Street, TQ6 9RB
🕓 11-11; 12-10.30 Sun ☎ (01803) 832571
⊕ the-cherub.co.uk
**Exeter Ferryman; St Austell Proper Job; South Hams
Devon Pride; house beer (by St Austell); 1 changing
beer (sourced locally)** Ⓗ
Probably the oldest house in Dartmouth, this
belonged to a merchant in the 14th century and is
Grade II-listed. Behind the Tudor façade, the small
bar has dark wooden seating and a comfortable
atmosphere. It has beams made from ships'
timbers and a spiral wooden staircase to the
restaurant and rest rooms. Locally sourced fish and
steaks are among the choices on lunchtime and
evening menus – food is served in the bar area and
first floor restaurant. Q🌣🕦🅰✿🅿🚍(90,X64)🌣

Dawlish

Gresham House Inn Ⓛ

1 Commercial Road, EX7 9HU
🕓 12-11.30 (midnight Fri & Sat) ☎ (01626) 864061
⊕ greshamhouseinn.co.uk
3 changing beers (often Teignworthy) Ⓗ
Formerly the Laffin Pig, the pub changed to the
Gresham House Inn, its original name, when it was
taken over in 2011. It is a four-storey property built
circa 1850. It is now family run, and has two double
en-suite B&B guest rooms on the first floor. There
are usually two real ales on tap, sometimes three,
one always from Teignworthy Brewery, plus a real
cider. Q🌣🕮🕦🛶♣✿🚍🌣 🛜

Dousland

Burrator Inn Ⓛ

PL20 6NP
🕓 12-11 (12.30am Sat) ☎ (01822) 853121
⊕ theburratorinn.com
**Dartmoor Jail Ale; Otter Amber; St Austell Tribute;
Sharp's Doom Bar** Ⓗ
Substantial pub on the road between Yelverton and
Princetown, close to the picturesque Burrator
Reservoir. It has several rooms including a separate
dining room, plus a pool table and two dartboards.
Home-made food and pies use ingredients from
local suppliers and are served throughout the day.
There is ample parking and a large enclosed beer
garden incorporating a children's play area. A beer
festival is held annually in September; a Sunday

quiz night, live music and other entertainment feature regularly.

Q❄☕🛏🍴🕭&♣P🚪(55,56,98)🐾❤🌱

East Budleigh

Sir Walter Raleigh Inn Ⓛ

22 High Street, EX9 7ED (off B3178 opp Hayes Lane)
❂ 12-2.30, 6-11; 12-2.30, 7-10.30 Sun ☎ (01395) 442510
4 changing beers (sourced regionally) Ⓗ
Set in the middle of the delightful village of East Budleigh, the birthplace of Sir Walter Raleigh, this free house is a truly welcoming 16th-century country inn. Good-quality pub food is served lunchtimes and evenings, and four real ales, and a real cider, are usually available. Originally two cottages, it was then converted into a Jacobean-style pub, retaining the original wooden beams throughout. Q❄☕🕭🍴🚪(157)🐾

Exbourne

Red Lion Ⓛ ✅

High Street, EX20 3RY SS602018
❂ 12-11 ☎ (01837) 851551 🌐 theredlionexbourne.co.uk
Bays Topsail; Sharp's Special; 1 changing beer (sourced nationally) Ⓖ
Dating from the 16th century, this village pub was local CAMRA branch Pub of the Year in both 2014 and 2015. All ales, as well as the cider from nearby Sam's, are served on gravity. The bar has no handpumps of any description, as the landlord refuses to serve draught lager. Food, much of which is supplied by local farmers, is served throughout the day. Regular beer festivals are held and live music features monthly.
Q❄☕🕭🍴🚪P🚪(318,631,648)🐾🌱

Exeter

Beer Cellar

2 South Street, EX1 1DZ
❂ 11-11 (midnight Fri & Sat) ☎ (01392) 757570
🌐 beercellarexeter.co.uk
5 changing beers (sourced nationally; often Bristol Beer Factory, Hanlons) Ⓗ
A small city-centre pub specialising in traditional beers from across the UK. Five ales plus one cider are on handpump, with a wide range of continental and American beers in bottles. With a friendly atmosphere, it is a good place to meet people who love to talk about beer, and has an outside seating area right next to Exeter Cathedral. The selection of beers is constantly changing, with established and new breweries from across the country represented. 🕭🍴♣🍴🚪🐾🌱

Fat Pig Ⓛ

2 John Street, EX1 1BL (behind Fore St)
❂ 5 (12 Sat)-11; 12-5 Sun ☎ (01392) 437217
🌐 fatpig-exeter.co.uk
3 changing beers (sourced locally) Ⓗ
Formerly the Coachmakers Arms, this Victorian corner local has been brought back to life as a traditional pub, featuring a range of locally sourced food, including the pub's own pork and sausages from its herd of rare-breed pigs. In addition to making its own cider, it is also a brewpub producing a wide range of styles for its three pubs. There are malt whisky evenings, a Monday quiz night and home-brew competitions. It is now making its own whisky and gin. Q🍴≈♣🍴🚪🌱

George's Meeting House ✅

38 South Street, EX1 1ED
❂ 8-midnight (1am Fri & Sat) ☎ (01392) 454250
Dartmoor Jail Ale; Greene King Abbot; Sharp's Doom Bar; 5 changing beers (sourced nationally) Ⓗ
This building was originally a Unitarian chapel dating from 1760, and many of the original features remain unaltered, with stained-glass windows, a pulpit and upstairs galleries. It is now a Wetherspoon pub and was sympathetically converted and reopened in 2005. Food is available all day, and a range of real ales and ciders is offered. There is outside seating which may be accessed via a newer extension to the rear of the main building. Q❄☕🕭&≈🍴🚪🌱

Hour Glass Inn

21 Melbourne Street, St Leonard's, EX2 4AU (approx 300yds from Exeter quayside)
❂ 5-11; 12-midnight Sat; 12-10.30 Sun ☎ (01392) 258722
Changing beers Ⓗ
An old-fashioned pub in the back streets of Exeter, in the hub of the local area close to the quay and about five minutes' walk from the main city centre. The pub has two restaurants and a bar, serving contemporary and continental food. It is very traditional in its features, with a mixture of live entertainment including light theatre and music, which has proved popular with its eclectic group of customers. Q🕭♣🚪

Imperial Ⓛ ✅

New North Road, St David's, EX4 4AH
❂ 9am-midnight (1am Fri & Sat) ☎ (01392) 434050
Greene King Abbot Ⓗ**; Ruddles Best Bitter** Ⓗ/Ⓖ**; changing beers** Ⓗ
You will find a range of beers from local and national breweries here. Starting out in 1810 as a private house, the building was converted to a hotel and opened as a Wetherspoon pub in 1996. It has an orangery and a large beer garden. Located close to the university, there is a bus stop directly outside the premises. Regular beer festivals are held, featuring local, national and international breweries. Food is served all day. St David's railway station is nearby. Q❄☕🕭&≈🍴P🚪🌱

Mill on the Exe ✅

Bonhay Road, St David's, EX4 3AB
❂ 10.30-11 ☎ (01392) 214464 🌐 millontheexe.co.uk
St Austell Tribute, Proper Job; 2 changing beers (sourced regionally) Ⓗ
A beautiful riverside pub, formerly a paper mill, with a welcoming and vibrant atmosphere. It has two floors with a bar on each, serving two regular St Austell ales and usually two guests, one of which may not be a St Austell beer, plus a range of bottled beers. Quality home-cooked food is served 12-9pm daily. The large garden has stunning views of Blackaller Weir. Children and dogs are welcome, and there are three log fires. 🕭🍴&≈P🚪🐾🌱

New Inn Ⓛ

Cowley Bridge Hill, Cowley Bridge, EX4 5BX
❂ 11-11 ☎ (01392) 431010
🌐 thenewinncowleybridge.co.uk
Brains Rev James; Exeter Avocet; Hanlons Yellowhammer Ⓗ**; 1 changing beer (sourced nationally)** Ⓖ
This friendly free house is found on the outskirts of Exeter beside the railway and the junction of the A377 and A396. Formerly the Cowley Bridge Inn, the pub reopened in 2014 after several years as a

Chinese restaurant. Delicious home-cooked food (including gluten-free and vegetarian dishes) is served all week (no food Sun and Mon eves). A games room with a free pool table leads to a pleasant garden, where barbecues and beer with music festivals are held. ⌂⊛⊕◑♿♣♠♣P🚃🐾🐱🛜

Oddfellows ✓

60 New North Road, EX4 4EP (just off High St)
🕰 12-3 (not Mon-Wed), 5-11; 12-1am Fri & Sat; 12-8 Sun
☎ (01392) 209050 ⊕ theoddfellowsbar.co.uk
St Austell Tribute, Proper Job Ⓗ; **1 changing beer** Ⓗ/Ⓖ
The narrow frontage at the end of a Victorian terrace belies a deep interior and features the original Victorian conservatory. Its cellar benefits from backing onto the old Roman city wall. A friendly gastro-style bar with a varied clientele, it is divided into small areas and alcoves, with sofas and rustic furniture. It has weekly acoustic music and open mic evenings. The open kitchen allows you to watch your food being cooked.
Q⌂◑≉ꗃ🚃🐱🛜

Pig & Pickle Taphouse

38a Fore Sreet, Heavitree, EX2 5PE
🕰 5-11; 12-11 Fri & Sat; closed Sun & Mon
3 changing beers (sourced locally; often Fat Pig) Ⓗ
Small micropub in the Fat Pig mini estate. It has been converted from the old post office, with the original signs and old counter, and is a friendly and welcoming venue, with a quiz every Tuesday evening. Food is restricted to platters of ham and various pickles. Also featured is the Fat Pig range of whiskies and gin. The three changing beers are all from the Fat Pig range. Old-style dimpled mugs are used. ♣🚃🐱

Royal Oak Ⓛ ✓

79-81 Fore Street, Heavitree, EX1 2RN
🕰 11.30-11 (10.30 Tue; midnight Fri & Sat); 12-4, 7-11 Sun
☎ (01392) 254121 ⊕ heavitreeroyaloak.co.uk
Otter Amber, Ale; Young's Bitter; 3 changing beers Ⓗ
Traditional family-run pub on several bus routes, with ample parking nearby. Three regular ales plus three guests are usually on offer. Good-value pub food is served lunchtimes, with a traditional roast on Sunday; no food is served evenings, except for a steak/fish night on Thursday. With a large comfortable main bar and smaller side room, the pub has a real community feel, while remaining welcoming to visitors. It has front and rear beer gardens with a covered smoking area.
⌂⊛◑♣🚃🐱

Exmouth

Bicton Inn Ⓛ

5 Bicton Street, EX8 2RU
🕰 11-midnight ☎ (01395) 272589 ⊕ bictoninn.co.uk
Branscombe Vale Branoc; Dartmoor Jail Ale; Hanlons Port Stout; Wadworth 6X; 4 changing beers Ⓗ
A friendly and popular back-street local, offering good beer and chat. Traditional games are played such as darts, pool and euchre, and regular live music events are featured (see website for details). Up to eight real ales and one cider are normally on offer, usually including several LocAles. The snug is available for small gatherings and meetings. There is a logburner in the main bar. Three beer festivals are held every year. ⌂≉♣🚃🐱🛜

First & Last Inn Ⓛ

10 Church Street, EX8 1PE (off B3178 Rolle St)
🕰 11-11 (11.30 Sat); 12-10.30 Sun ☎ (01395) 263275
Courage Directors; Otter Ale; Teignworthy Neap Tide Ⓗ; **1 changing beer** Ⓖ
Victorian pub near the town centre with a public car park opposite. It is a genuine free house, with three distinct drinking areas and an outside patio with heated awnings. Games include pool and darts, and there is a skittle alley. Televised sport is prominent. Two or three guest beers are sold, usually from the West Country, and Green Valley, Old Rosie and Thatchers Dry ciders. Well-behaved dogs are welcome. ⊛♿≉♣🐾🚃🐱

Grapevine

2 Victoria Road, EX8 1DL
🕰 4-11; 12-midnight Thu-Sat; 12-11 Sun ☎ (01395) 222208
⊕ thegrapevineexmouth.com
6 changing beers Ⓗ
A stylish free house with a continental café ambience which stocks a changing range of real British beers – over 100 different ales ales feaured last year – along with continental lagers and bottled beers. Green Valley Cyder is also sold. The excellent food, with a regularly changing plat du jour, makes the pub the ideal place for people looking for something special. Monday is quiz night, Friday features live music, and an informal chess club has started on Tuesday. The Grapevine started brewing its own beer in 2016, under Crossed Anchors Brewery. ⊛◑♿≉♣🐾🚃🐱🛜

Heddon Valley

Hunters Inn Ⓛ

EX31 4PY (signed from A39 N of Parracombe; continue down this country lane for a few miles; keep going but worth the effort) SS655481
🕰 10-11 ☎ (01598) 763230 ⊕ thehuntersinnexmoor.co.uk
Exmoor Ale, Beast, Gold, Stag; 3 changing beers (sourced nationally) Ⓗ
Among landscaped gardens and a deep valley, with the sea nearby at Heddons Mouth, this is a country inn popular with everyone, especially walkers. Following major refurbishments in 2015 there are now two bars in which to enjoy the complete range of Exmoor beers, together with the Heddon Ales brewed especially for the Hunters. Both light bites and an extensive à la carte menu are available. The September beer and music festival is a must-visit. Q⌂⊛⌸◑♿♠♣🐾P🐱🛜

High Bickington

Golden Lion Ⓛ

North Road, EX37 9BB (on B3217) SS600205
🕰 4.30 (12 Wed & Thu; 11 Fri & Sat)-11; 12-10.30 Sun
☎ (01769) 561006
Forge Lite House; 2 changing beers (sourced nationally) Ⓗ
Traditional Devon village pub dating from the 19th century. There is a single bar with an adjacent skittle alley which converts into a pleasant dining area. Good-value home-cooked food is served all day. Three local real ales are usually on the bar and the pub participates in the CAMRA discount scheme, with a 20p per pint reduction offered to card-carrying members. Well-behaved children and dogs are welcome. ⌂⊛◑♣P🚃(377)🐱🛜

Honiton

Holt 🟦

178 High Street, EX14 1LA
⚙ 11-3, 5.30-11; closed Sun & Mon ☎ (01404) 47707
⊕ theholt-honiton.com
Otter Bitter, Amber, Bright, Ale, Head; 1 changing beer (sourced locally) Ⓗ

A former wine bar that was converted 10 years ago. It has a cosy bar at street level with a restaurant upstairs. The kitchen is in full view of the clientele. A lunch menu of tapas and home-smoked food is available in the bar. A family business, the Holt has won Gastro-Pub of the Year, and is a past winner of Taste of the West. Seasonal music festivals are held. It could be considered the Otter Brewery tap. ⏱◑👤♿⇆♣🚃❀

Horns Cross

Coach & Horses 🟦

EX39 5DH (on A39 between Bideford and Clovelly)
⚙ 11-2.30 (not Mon), 5-11; 11-11 Sat; 12-9.30 Sun
☎ (01237) 451214 ⊕ thebestpubindevon.co.uk
Forge Rev Hawker; Sharp's Doom Bar; 2 changing beers (sourced nationally) Ⓗ

A cosy 17th-century roadside inn, handily situated for exploring the local north Devon coast, with a single bar and eating area, a separate pool room, and three en-suite B&B rooms. Up to five real ales are usually on, together with a cider from Sam's. Good-quality food is sourced from local suppliers and a very good-value lunchtime menu is offered during the week. Thursday is steak night.
Q⏱❀🍴◑♣🚶P🚃(319)🛜

Iddesleigh

Duke of York

EX19 8BG (off B3217 next to church) SS570083
⚙ 11-11; 12-10.30 Sun ☎ (01837) 810253
⊕ dukeofyorkdevon.co.uk
Adnams Broadside; Bays Topsail; 1 changing beer (sourced nationally) Ⓖ

Dating from the 15th century and built of stone and cob, this traditional, thatched village inn has old beams, inglenook fires and a friendly, homely atmosphere. Close to the Tarka Trail, River Torridge and Stafford Moor fishery, there are eight en-suite rooms for visitors. It was here that village resident Michael Morpurgo was inspired to write his famous book, War Horse. A courtesy bus services local B&Bs and nearby villages. In August a popular beer festival is held. Q⏱❀🍴◑👤♣🚶🚃❀🛜

Ide

Poachers Inn 🟦

55 High Street, EX2 9RW (3 miles from M5 jct 31, via A30)
⚙ 12-midnight (1am Fri & Sat) ☎ (01392) 273847
⊕ poachersinn.co.uk
Exeter Lighterman; 5 changing beers (sourced regionally; often Exeter, Palmers, Sharp's) Ⓗ

A busy, friendly local at the top of the village street, with a history of serving beer since the 18th century. Five ales are usually on tap, and a varied, locally sourced menu is available all day, plus excellent-value fish and chips on Wednesday evenings. The bar is comfortably furnished with old sofas and chairs, heated by a log fire, and decorated with an interesting collection of hats and

ties. There is a lovely garden with beautiful countryside views over the Devon hills.
Q⏱❀🍴◑👤AP🚃(360)❀🛜

Ilfracombe

Wellington Arms ✔

66-67 High Street, EX34 9QE
⚙ 11-midnight ☎ 07809 434194
Courage Best Bitter; St Austell Tribute; Sharp's Doom Bar; Wychwood Hobgoblin; 2 changing beers (sourced nationally) Ⓗ

This traditional, friendly town pub keeps up to seven real ales, all at very competitive prices, and also operates a CAMRA discount scheme. Originally two pubs, it now has public and lounge bars, a function room which can accommodate up to 70 people, and an attractive beer terrace at the rear. The L-shaped public bar features TV sport and an extensive jukebox, while the cosy lounge has an original beamed ceiling and large open fire.
⏱❀🍴◑A♣P🚃❀🛜

Kenn

Ley Arms

EX6 7UW
⚙ 11-11; 12-10.30 Sun ☎ (01392) 832341
⊕ theleyarmskenn.co.uk
Dartmoor Legend; St Austell Tribute; 3 changing beers (sourced regionally; often Otter, Teignworthy) Ⓗ

A large 12th-century thatched building on the fringes of the villages of Kenn and Kennford, just off the A38 near Exeter. It serves good-quality food (a blackboard displays the local shops and farm sources), with a varied and changing menu, plus a popular Sunday roast. Two regular ales and up to three guests are enthusiastically cared for by the landlord. A lovely beer garden, spacious car park and warming log fires are attractive features. A true village pub maintained to modern standards.
Q⏱❀🍴◑A♣P❀

Kings Nympton

Grove Inn 🍷 🟦

EX37 9ST (in centre of village) SS683194
⚙ 12-3, 6-11; 12-4, 7-10 Sun; closed Mon ☎ (01769) 580406
⊕ thegroveinn.co.uk
Exmoor Ale Ⓖ**; 3 changing beers (sourced nationally)** Ⓗ

A 17th-century, Grade II-listed thatched pub, with flagstone floor and bare stone walls, attracting locals and visitors alike. Four real ales are kept, two of which are on stillage, together with a local cider. A CAMRA discount scheme operates. Award-winning food is served in the dining area, which is adjacent to the bar. The Grove also has a collection of over 65 single malts, together with an extensive wine list. Local CAMRA Pub of the Year 2016.
Q⏱❀🍴◑♣P❀🛜

Kingswear

Ship Inn 🟦 ✔

Higher Street, TQ6 0AG
⚙ 12-3, 6-midnight; 12-midnight Sat & Sun
☎ (01803) 752348
Adnams Southwold Bitter; Otter Ale; St Austell Trelawny; 3 changing beers (sourced regionally; often Otter) Ⓗ

A 15th-century village pub with a well-deserved reputation for fish and seafood. There are four beers in winter, increasing to six in summer. A family-run pub, it has appeared in this Guide for over 11 years. The horseshoe-shaped bar with a nautical theme has two open fires, and the adjoining dining room has extensive views of Dartmouth and the River Dart, as does the patio at the front. Beer festivals are held during Dartmouth food and sailing festivals. Q ☼ ⊛ ❻ ❶ ≈ ♣ 🖥 ☘ 🛜

Littlehempston

Tally Ho 🅛

TQ9 6LY SX813627

✪ 11-3, 5.30-11; 12-10.30 Sun; closed Mon

☎ (01803) 862316 ⊕ tallyhoinn.co.uk

Dartmoor Legend; 2 changing beers (sourced locally) Ⓗ

A charming 14th-century stone-built pub saved by the local community from closure in 2014. The timber-beamed single-roomed bar, furnished with pews and wooden settles, has a cosy feel that is enhanced by two woodburners. The pub hosts numerous events including an annual beer festival, occasional local live music and a regular Sunday night quiz. Guest beers are from local breweries including Hunters and New Lion. The enclosed beer garden is to the rear of the building.
Q ☼ ⊛ ❶ Å P 🖥 ☘ 🛜

Lympstone

Redwing Bar & Dining

Church Road, EX8 5JT

✪ 11.30-3, 5.30-11; 11.30-11 Fri-Sun ☎ (01395) 222156

⊕ redwingbar-dining.co.uk

Branscombe Vale Summa This; Hanlons Firefly; St Austell Proper Job; 1 changing beer Ⓗ

Formerly the Redwing, this delightful pub is set in the charming village of Lympstone. Recently refurbished, it now has a long bar with soft furnishings and a large conservatory. Fresh food is served lunchtimes and evenings. A large garden is to the rear, along with parking. A separate lunch menu is available Monday to Friday, and it has a function room. Q ☼ ⊛ ❶ & ≈ P ☘ 🛜

Lynmouth

Blue Ball Inn 🅛 ✅

Countisbury Hill, Countisbury, EX35 6NE (on A39, 1 mile E of Lynmouth) SS747496

✪ 11-11 ☎ (01598) 741263 ⊕ blueballinn.com

Exmoor Gold; St Austell Tribute; 2 changing beers (sourced nationally) Ⓗ

Privately owned and run historic inn, on the old coaching route from Porlock to Lynmouth. The unspoilt interior has blackened beams and a large 13th-century inglenook fire near the bar. Four real ales are usually sold, including a good house beer and at least one guest. Food is served all day from an extensive menu, either in the bar or the large dining area. This dog-friendly pub is particularly popular with walkers and hikers.
Q ☼ ⊛ ⊠ ❶ Å ♣ P 🖥 (300) ☘ 🛜

Lynton

Sandrock Hotel 🅛

Longmead, EX35 6DH

✪ 11-11 (midnight Fri & Sat); 12-11 Sun ☎ (01598) 752000

⊕ sandrockhotel.co.uk

Draught Bass; Exmoor Ale, Stag; 2 changing beers (sourced nationally) Ⓗ

An excellent selection of local beers and ciders is available in this friendly Edwardian hotel and pub. Many of the original features have been retained and the large wood-burning stove adds to the atmosphere in the bar. There is also a pleasant beer garden to enjoy in summer. Not far from the Valley of the Rocks, it provides a great base from which to explore the local area. Good-value pub food is served. Q ☼ ⊛ ⊠ ❶ & ♣ ♥ P 🖥 ☘ 🛜

Manaton

Kestor Inn 🅛

TQ13 9UF (on main road through village)

✪ 11-11 ☎ (01647) 221626 ⊕ kestorinn.com

Dartmoor Legend Ⓗ**; Otter Bitter** Ⓗ**/**Ⓖ**; 1 changing beer (sourced locally)** Ⓗ

Spacious local village inn with a warm welcome and friendly atmosphere. Located within Dartmoor National Park, the pub has a large open-plan L-shaped bar with plenty of seating, including alcoves. There is a separate long dining room, which can also be used for functions. It has a selection of local real ales on offer. The lobby area of the pub has become a small shop selling basic items, and a book exchange scheme is in operation. Sam's Medium Cider is sold.
Q ☼ ⊛ ⊠ ❶ ♣ ♥ P 🖥 (271,671) ☘ 🛜

Mary Tavy

Mary Tavy Inn 🅛

Lane Head, PL19 9PN

✪ 12-2.30, 6-11 (5-midnight Fri); 12-11 Sat & Sun

☎ (01822) 810326 ⊕ themarytavyinn.com

Dartmoor IPA, Jail Ale; St Austell Proper Job; 1 changing beer (sourced nationally) Ⓗ

A traditional roadside inn where families, visitors and locals are welcome. The popular bar area accommodates pool, darts, TV, a large fire and up to four real ales. This is complemented by a spacious restaurant and garden with views to Dartmoor. Music nights, charity events, a Sunday carvery and a bank holiday beer festival feature in the pub's calendar. Modern B&B accommodation is available in an adjacent building. The pub closes on Mondays and weekend afternoons in the winter.
Q ☼ ⊛ ⊠ ❶ ♣ P 🖥 (46) ☘ 🛜

Meavy

Royal Oak Inn 🅛

Meavy, PL20 6PJ (on village green)

✪ 11-11; 11-10.30 Sun ☎ (01822) 852944

⊕ royaloakinn.org.uk

Dartmoor IPA, Jail Ale; house beer (by Dartmoor); 1 changing beer (sourced regionally) Ⓗ

An iconic English village inn, dating from the 16th century, next to the church and overlooking the green, where the eponymous tree stands. The lounge has a restaurant serving home-cooked food, complemented by an eclectic wine list. Up to four local ales figure prominently. The public bar provides a return to its history and agricultural roots – flagstone floor, large open fire and photos of times past. It has a good cider range. Local CAMRA branch Country Pub of the Year runner-up 2016.
Q ☼ ⊛ ❶ Å ♥ 🖥 (56) ☘ 🛜

Merton

Malt Scoop Inn

EX20 3EA (on A386, 7 miles S of Great Torrington)
SS527121
☼ 12-3, 6-midnight; 12-1am Fri & Sat; 12-10.30 Sun
☎ (01805) 603924 ⊕ themaltscoop.co.uk
St Austell Cornish Best Bitter, HSD, Tribute Ⓗ
A friendly local that was originally part of a farm
dating from the 1700s and which became a
coaching inn during the 19th century. The
horseshoe-shaped bar, with inglenook fireplace,
leads through to an adjoining restaurant where
locally sourced food is served. A good range of
beers from St Austell is always on the bar, together
with a local cider in summer. Popular both with
cyclists and walkers, the pub lies just one mile from
the Tarka Trail. Q ⅀ 器 ⇔ ❶ ♣ P 🖵 (118) ✿ 🛜

Milton Combe

Who'd Have Thought It Inn Ⓛ

PL20 6HP
☼ 12-10.30 (11 Fri & Sat) ☎ (01822) 853313
⊕ whodhavethoughtitdevon.co.uk
**4 changing beers (sourced regionally; often
Dartmoor, Skinner's, Teignworthy)**
An ancient, multi-roomed pub nestling in a small
village near Buckland Abbey. It has been extended
and improved by the current owners, with a decor
consisting of flagstones, beams, stone walls and
dark wooden panelling. The low-level lighting adds
to the ambience. One ale from Dartmoor, Sharp's
and St Austell usually feature, supplemented by
one other South-west ale and up to three ciders. A
beer festival features at Easter and a cider festival
in late summer. Q 器 ⇔ ❶ Å ♣ ● P 🖵 (55) ✿

Moretonhampstead

Union Inn Ⓛ

10 Ford Street, TQ13 8LN (on A382 heading out of town
toward Chagford)
☼ 11-11; 12-10.30 Sun ☎ (01647) 440199
⊕ theunioninn.co.uk
**Red Rock Lighthouse IPA, Red Rock, Break Water; St
Austell Tribute** Ⓗ
Traditional 16th-century free house in the village
centre. The beamed and panelled bar and
adjoining pool room feature old photographs of the
village. The function room, with its own bar and
skittle alley, is reached via a corridor displaying
artefacts relating to the inn's history. Good-value
home-cooked food is served, with a carvery
Sunday lunchtime. There is outside seating on the
decking next to the small car park. The Red Rock
beers are given house names and the cider is from
Sampford Courtenay.
⅀ 器 ❶ ♿ ♣ ● P 🖵 (173,178,359) ✿ 🛜

Newton Abbot

Teign Cellars Ⓛ

67 East Street, TQ12 2JR
☼ 10.30-11 (midnight Fri & Sat); 11-11 Sun
☎ (01626) 332991 ⊕ teigncellars.co.uk
4 changing beers (sourced nationally) Ⓗ/Ⓖ
This pub was previously the Greene Man and, even
further back, an annexe of the 1836 workhouse
that stood opposite. It has one bar with a
combination of high stools and soft furnishings,
plus a small area to the rear incorporating a shop

selling 170 bottled beers. Draught beers are
generally unusual for the area and one will be local
at a reduced price; there is also a good and varying
range of real ciders. Note the unusual beer periodic
table. Food is excellent and the pub can be
extremely busy at weekends. Q 器 ❶ ⇔ ● 🖵 ✿ 🛜

Newton Poppleford

Cannon Inn ✪

High Street, EX10 0DW
☼ 11-2.30, 5.30-11 (midnight Thu & Fri); 11-midnight Sat;
12-11 Sun ☎ (01395) 568266 ⊕ pubindevon.com
**Exmoor Gold; 2 changing beers (sourced
nationally)** Ⓖ
Cheery, welcoming two-bar pub, with tables for
dining in the lounge bar and restaurant area. Real
ales are served by gravity from stillage behind the
bar. This is a friendly locals' pub with busy passing
trade. Good-value home-cooked food, served
lunchtimes and evenings, covers most traditional
pub favourites and, locals say, is of a very tasty
standard. Well-behaved dogs are allowed. There
are two large gardens and a skittle alley. The only
pub in the village, it is a community hub.
Q ⅀ 器 ⇔ ❶ ♿ Å ♣ P 🖵 (52,157) ✿ 🛜

Newton St Cyres

Beer Engine Ⓛ

EX5 5AX (beside railway station ½ mile N of A377)
☼ 11-11; 12-10.30 Sun ☎ (01392) 851282
⊕ thebeerengine.co.uk
**Beer Engine Rail Ale, Silver Bullet, Piston Bitter,
Sleeper Heavy** Ⓗ
Victorian pub, built in 1850, on the Exeter to
Barnstaple Tarka Line. Popular with drinkers and
diners alike, it is well frequented by locals, visitors
and its own cricket team. Home-cooked food is
served lunchtimes and evenings using locally
sourced produce. The pub brews its own ales,
including four regulars and a seasonal ale which,
like the village pictures and old pub signs, reflect a
railway theme. Q ⅀ 器 ❶ ♿ ⇔ P 🍺 ✿

North Tawton

Railway Inn Ⓛ

Whiddon Down Road, EX20 2BE (1 mile S of town, just
off A3124 and next to old North Tawton railway station)
SS666000
☼ 12-3, 6-11; 12-3, 7-10.30 Sun ☎ (01837) 82789
⊕ therailwaynorthtawton.co.uk
**Teignworthy Reel Ale; 1 changing beer (sourced
nationally)** Ⓗ
A warm Devonian welcome awaits you at this
farming and railway oriented pub. Adjacent to the
former North Tawton railway station (closed in
1971), it is not near to any settlement, but
nevertheless has a friendly local atmosphere. Reel
Ale is joined by a guest ale from another West Country brewery, together with a
real cider in summer. The dining room is popular in
the evening (no food Thu), with light meals served
at lunchtime. Guide dogs only.
Q ⅀ 器 ❶ ♣ ● P 🖵 (51,315,318) 🛜

Northlew

Green Dragon Ⓛ

EX20 3NN

⏰ 12-2, 6-11.30 (2am Fri & Sat); 12-2, 6-11 Sun
☎ (01409) 221228

Bays Gold; Holsworthy Ales Muck 'n' Straw; 1 changing beer (sourced nationally) ⊞
This historic 18th-century inn is at the heart of Northlew. The Green Dragon offers three regular real ales from Devon breweries and an occasional guest. The extensive menu is complemented by frequent themed food nights and periodic beer festivals. The wooden beams, snug interior and blazing fire in winter all help to ensure a warm welcome in this classic village pub.
🛏️🕷️🍴◀🅙♣🅿🍽️♿🛜

Noss Mayo

Ship Inn 🅛
Noss Mayo, PL8 1EW
⏰ 10-11; 10.30-10.30 Sun ☎ (01752) 872387
⊕ nossmayo.com

Dartmoor Jail Ale; Noss Beer Works Church Ledge; St Austell Tribute; 1 changing beer (sourced locally) ⊞
Popular with ramblers and seafarers alike, this fine pub is situated on an inlet of the Yealm estuary. Like the four ales, excellent food is available daily. A former CAMRA branch Pub of the Year, it is an ideal start and finish point for a walk to sample the breathtaking river and sea views along the route of Lord Revelstoke's Drive. If sailing, ring ahead to ascertain the tide times and mooring availability. There is no bus service in the evenings or on Sundays. Q🅠🛏️🕷️🅙⬤🏕️Å♣🅿🚃(3)♿

Okehampton

Plymouth Inn 🅛
26 West Street, EX20 1HH (W end of town nr West Okement Bridge)
⏰ 11-11 (midnight Fri & Sat) ☎ (01837) 53633

Black Tor Pride of Dartmoor; 2 changing beers (sourced nationally) ⊞
A 17th-century former coaching inn standing at the western end of Okehampton near the bridge over the West Okement River. A friendly pub, it brings the welcome and atmosphere of a village local to an old market town. The ales are usually from West Country brewers, at least one local cider is kept, and reasonably priced locally sourced food is served. Two popular beer festivals take place each May and October. 🛏️🕷️🅙♣⬤🅿🚃(X9,510)♿

Ottery St Mary

London Inn 🅛
4 Gold Street, EX11 1DG
⏰ 12 (4 Mon)-11; 12-midnight Fri & Sat; 12-10 Sun
☎ (01404) 812045 ⊕ londoninn.net

Sharp's Doom Bar; 5 changing beers (sourced regionally) ⊞
Coaching inn dating back to the 12th-century and close to the historic 14th-century parish church. Good-value home-cooked food, using local ingredients where possible, is served lunchtimes and evenings, plus a traditional roast on Sunday. It is a typical locals' pub, offering one regional real ale and up to five guests. Four B&B rooms are available. Dogs are allowed in the bottom bar.
Q🅠🛏️🕷️🛏️🅙🅙♿🅿🚃(4)♿🛜

Paignton

Henry's Bar 🅛 ✅
53 Torbay Road, TQ4 6AJ
⏰ 11-11 (midnight Fri & Sat) ☎ (01803) 551190
⊕ henrysbarpaignton.co.uk

Dartmoor IPA; Sharp's Doom Bar; 2 changing beers (sourced nationally; often Exmoor) ⊞
Traditional-style pub located on the street running from the bus and railway stations to the beach, nestled between gift shops and arcades. The welcoming, warm venue boasts excellent beers that are very reasonably priced. On handpump there are three regular and one guest beer, Sam's traditional cider plus various polyboxes and bottles. Wholesome, fairly priced home-cooked food is served throughout the day until 9pm, and there is a highly rated roast on Sundays. Families are welcome until 10pm. 🛏️🅙⮀⬤🏕️♿🛜

Isaac Merritt 🅛 ✅
54-58 Torquay Road, TQ3 3AA
⏰ 8am-midnight ☎ (01803) 556066

Dartmoor Jail Ale; Greene King Abbot; Ruddles Best Bitter; Sharp's Doom Bar; changing beers (often Hanlons, Hunters, Teignworthy) ⊞
Community-oriented Wetherspoon pub just five minutes' walk from both the bus and railway stations, popular with locals and visitors alike. The place boasts a well-deserved reputation for the quality and extensive range of ales plus various ciders, both bottled and polyboxed. The decor is themed around Isaac Merritt Singer, the inventor of the Singer sewing machine. There are seated alcoves, separate family dining, a covered and heated smokers' area, and disabled access for both pub and toilets. Q🅠🛏️🕷️🅙⬤⮀⬤🚃🛜

Plymouth

Artillery Arms 🅛
6 Pound Street, Stonehouse, PL1 3RH (behind Stonehouse Barracks and Millbay Docks)
⏰ 12 (4 Mon & Tue)-midnight ☎ (01752) 262515

Draught Bass; 2 changing beers (sourced locally; often Dartmoor, Summerskills) ⊞
Cracking back-street local tucked away in the old quarter of Stonehouse, close to the magnificent Grade I-listed Royal William Yard, which maintains the area's military connections. Good home-cooked food is served (but no food Mon or Tue). Two South-west guest beers and Thatchers Heritage cider are normally available. An out-of-season beach party takes place on the last weekend of February, and charity monkey racing also features. This place is a real find and is popular with local hockey teams. 🕷️🅙⬤🚃(34,34A)♿🛜

Britannia Inn 🅛 ✅
2 Wolesely Road, Milehouse, PL2 3BH
⏰ 8am-midnight (1am Fri & Sat) ☎ (01752) 607596

Dartmoor Jail Ale; Greene King Abbot; Ruddles Best Bitter; Sharp's Doom Bar; changing beers (sourced nationally; often Bays, Fuller's, Summerskills) ⊞
A large vibrant pub built in the 1830s which retained its name when it became a Wetherspoon in 1999. Close to the football ground, it can get busy on match days. There are 10 pumps, one of which always dispenses a real cider; others are available. Opposite the main bus depot, it is on numerous bus routes from the train station and city centre. This is a community-oriented pub.
🛏️🕷️🅙⬤♿⬤🚃🛜

Dolphin Hotel ✪

14 The Barbican, PL1 2LS

✪ 10-11 (midnight Thu-Sat); 11-11 Sun ☎ (01752) 660876

Dartmoor Jail Ale; Draught Bass; Otter Ale; St Austell Tribute; Sharp's Doom Bar; Skinner's Betty Stogs; 2 changing beers (sourced regionally; often St Austell, Sharp's) Ⓖ

A Plymouth institution, this unpretentious hostelry is steeped in history. Its character is charming, with tiled floors, well-used wooden benches and a traditional open fire, all creating the perfect ambience. The walls are adorned with works by a local artist, the late Beryl Cook, who painted many of the characters she encountered in the Dolphin. Up to eight ales are all dispensed by gravity from the cask. Local CAMRA City Pub of the Year runner-up 2016. ●🚃(25)❀

Fawn Private Members Club Ⓛ

39 Prospect Street, Greenbank, PL4 8NY

✪ 3 (2 Fri)-11; 12-11 Sat & Sun ☎ (01752) 226385

Bays Topsail; 4 changing beers (sourced regionally; often Cotleigh, St Austell, Teignworthy) Ⓗ

A mid 19th-century establishment that was originally the Fawn Inn/Hotel, prior to converting to a club. CAMRA members are welcome with a valid membership card; regular visitors will be required to join. Four guest ales from the local area are generally on sale, as well as a rotating range of local cider from Countryman. The club is popular for rugby and other televised sport, and supports multiple darts and euchre teams. Local CAMRA branch Club of the Year 2016 and regional Club of the Year runner-up 2015. ≈♣●🚃❀

Ferry House Inn

888 Wolesley Road, Saltash Passage, PL5 1LA

✪ 12-midnight ☎ (01752) 361063 ● ferryhouseinn.com

Dartmoor Jail Ale; Sharp's Doom Bar, Atlantic; 1 changing beer (sourced regionally) Ⓗ

Picturesque riverside pub on the River Tamar, which separates Devon from Cornwall. Three regular West Country ales are served, as well as good home-cooked food. A decking area on the edge of the river gives spectacular views of Brunel's iconic 1859 railway bridge, and the bars display photos of the bridge dating from the turn of the 20th century, as well as photos of the pub and the Saltash foot ferry. There are seven en-suite rooms on the new third floor. ▷🚗🚄◀Ⓓ♿≈(St Budeaux)●🚃(13)❀

Fisherman's Arms Ⓛ

31 Lambhay Street, Barbican, PL1 2NN

✪ 11-midnight (1am Fri & Sat) ☎ (01752) 268243

● fishermansarms.co.uk

St Austell Tribute; Sharp's Doom Bar; Summerskills Devon Dew Ⓗ

Owner Donna, her partner Lee, and his family, have returned this former St Austell pub into a traditional free house. The interior is welcoming, with several distinctly decorated areas. The dartboard has returned and a variety of games and puzzles is available. Ale and cider festivals are held twice a year. Traditional pub grub at affordable prices is supplemented by specials – only the famous roast is available on Sundays. Close to the Royal Citadel and the Barbican. ▷◀♣●🚃(25)❀🛜

Fortescue Hotel ▼ Ⓛ ✪

37 Mutley Plain, PL4 6JQ

✪ 11-midnight; 12-11 Sun ☎ (01752) 660673

Bays Devon Dumpling; St Austell Proper Job; Skinner's Betty Stogs; 5 changing beers (sourced nationally; often Cornish Crown, Hunters, South Hams) Ⓗ

The landlord is a real ale enthusiast and the bar has nine handpumps, with one dedicated to a real cider. The rest serve a varying range of ales. There are several local beers always available, and up to seven real ciders/perries. There is a long main bar, a cellar bar, and a beer garden which is covered. Traditional roasts are served on Sundays only, washed down with Spingo beer. Local CAMRA branch Pub of the Year 2014, 2015 and 2016. ▷🚗◀◁≈♣●🚃❀🛜

Lord High Admiral ✪

33 Stonehouse Street, Stonehouse, PL1 3PE

✪ 11-11; 12-10.30 Sun ☎ (01752) 256881

St Austell Tribute, HSD; 1 changing beer (sourced regionally) Ⓗ

Friendly community pub not far off Union Street in an area undergoing regeneration. It is close to Millbay Ferry port, not far from Plymouth Albion's Brickfields rugby ground, and across the road from a highly rated restaurant. Diners having a drink before or after their meal mix happily with locals. On entering, customers are offered free tapas. It is advisable to book for Sunday lunch. Large-screen TVs show major sport. A woodburner keeps you warm in winter. ▷🚗◁♣🚃

Lounge

7 Stopford Place, Devonport, PL1 4QT

✪ 11.30-3 (not Mon), 6-11; 11.30-3, 5.30-midnight Fri; 11.30-11 Sat; 12-11 Sun ☎ (01752) 561330

Draught Bass; 2 changing beers (sourced regionally; often Cotleigh, Hunters, Skinner's) Ⓗ

In a quiet residential area, this street-corner local is near to Devonport Park, and offers you a very warm welcome. The wood-panelled bar is comfortable and relaxing, although it may be busy at times with Plymouth Albion RFC's ground nearby. One weaker, one stronger than the regular Bass is the rule for guest beers, with lighter and darker brews also alternating. A secluded garden at the front offers a retreat for smokers. Food is only served lunchtimes (no food Mon). Q▷🚗◀◁≈♣●🚃(32,34)❀

Minerva Inn Ⓛ

31 Looe Street, Barbican, PL4 0EA

✪ 11.30-11.30 (midnight Wed; 12.30am Thu & Fri); 12-12.30am Sat; 1-10.30 Sun ☎ (01752) 223047

● minervainn.co.uk

St Austell Trelawny, Tribute; 2 changing beers (sourced nationally) Ⓗ

Plymouth's oldest pub, dating from about 1540, and within easy walking distance of the city centre and the historic Barbican. There is a long and narrow bar leading through to a cosy seating area at the rear. Two guest beers are supplemented by spring and autumn beer festivals, where beer could, and does, come from all over the country. Live music takes place Thursday to Sunday evenings and Sunday lunchtimes. The pub benefits from a varied clientele. ▷🚗♣●🚃❀🛜

Nowhere Inn Ⓛ

21 Gilwell Street, PL4 8BU

✪ 4 (6 Sat)-3am; 7-midnight Sun ☎ (01752) 670592

House beer (by Noss Beer Works); 4 changing beers (sourced locally; often Noss Beer Works, Summerskills, Tavy Ales) Ⓗ

Old-fashioned back-street pub tucked away in the midst of the student campus, near to the city centre. There is usually one mainstream beer, supplemented by three changing guest beers, one of which is always LocAle-qualified, plus a cider. The house beer is brewed by Noss Beer Works. The bar is frequented by an eclectic variety of patrons, from students to elderly locals. Quiz nights are held on Mondays and live music plays on Thursdays. Beer festivals take place twice annually.
≠♣♠💂🖢

Prince Maurice ⓛ ⊘
3 Church Hill, Eggbuckland, PL6 5RJ
✪ 11-3, 6-11; 11-11 Fri & Sat; 12-10.30 Sun
☎ (01752) 771515
Dartmoor Jail Ale; Hanlons Stormstay; St Austell Tribute, Proper Job; Sharp's Doom Bar; Summerskills Best Bitter; 2 changing beers (sourced locally; often St Austell, Teignworthy) Ⓗ

There is very much a village feel to this four-times local CAMRA Pub of the Year, which sits between the church and village green. The seven regular ales are supplemented by a changing guest ale. It is named after the Royalist General, the King's nephew, who had his headquarters nearby during the siege of Plymouth in the Civil War. The two log fires keep you warm in winter, adding to the ambience. Food is not available at weekends.
🕭🏵🕽♣♠P💂(28)🐾

Stoke Inn ⓛ ⊘
43 Devonport Road, Stoke, PL3 4DL
✪ 12-midnight (1am Fri & Sat) ☎ (01752) 515749
⊕ stokeinnplymouth.co.uk
Skinner's Betty Stogs; 5 changing beers (sourced nationally; often Bays, Wadworth) Ⓗ

Traditional family-friendly pub in the village suburb of Stoke. It is close to the city centre and has a large garden. Six beers are on the bar, with the range being chosen from the national pubco list. Good-value food is served (no food Sun, Mon or Tue evenings). Live sport is shown on TV, with occasional live music events held in the garden. Two function rooms are available for hire, with parking for motorhomes by prior arrangement.
🏵🕽≠♣♠P💂(32,34)🐾🛜

West Hoe ⓛ
24 Bishop's Place, West Hoe, PL1 3BW
✪ 12-11 (midnight Fri & Sat) ☎ (01752) 216388
Dartmoor Jail Ale; Sharp's Doom Bar; 1 changing beer (sourced locally; often Draught Bass, Hunters, Otter) Ⓗ

The pub was refurbished in 2015 and has quickly become a popular and friendly place to visit, and is well supported by the local community. The two regular ales are supplemented by a third which could be sourced from anywhere, but is usually local. Regular open mic nights, quiz nights and a monthly comedy night are held. The history of the pub is displayed on boards around the walls. Well worth seeking out. 🕭🏵🕽♣♠P💂(25)🐾🛜

Plympton

Union Inn ⓛ
17 Underwood Road, PL7 1SY
✪ 4-11 (11.30 Fri); 2-midnight Sat; 12-11 Sun
☎ (01752) 336756 ⊕ unioninnplympton.com
4 changing beers (sourced nationally; often Exeter, Summerskills, Tintagel) Ⓗ

Family-run community pub that offers a warm welcome to all who enter this traditional, cosy, 19th-century venue. The landlord's passion for ale is evident, with up to four varying beers providing a year-round beer festival. There are also four real ciders served on gravity. All meals are freshly prepared using local produce, and booking is advisable. Lunchtime meals are only available on Sundays. Dogs on leads are welcome.
Q🕭🏵🕽♣♠P💂🐾🛜

Plymstock

Morley Arms
4 Billacombe Road, PL9 7HP (E end of Laira Bridge)
✪ 11.30-2.30, 5-11; 12-9 Sun ☎ (01752) 401191
⊕ morleyarms.co.uk
Dartmoor Jail Ale; Sharp's Doom Bar; 2 changing beers (sourced nationally; often Brains, Fuller's, Wychwood) Ⓗ

The building was constructed in 1824 to house the workers who built the original Laira Bridge. Most of the rooms have been opened out but retain the wall beams, giving a cosy feel to a visually open area. Two regular ales and one real cider are supplemented by up to two guest beers which could come from breweries nationally. Home-cooked food has an excellent local reputation. Live acoustic music features most Sundays, and morris men visit occasionally. 🕭🏵🕽🕭P💂🐾

Princetown

Plume of Feathers Inn ⓛ ⊘
Plymouth Hill, PL20 6QQ
✪ 10.30-11 (midnight Fri & Sat) ☎ (01822) 890240
⊕ theplumeoffeathersdartmoor.co.uk
Dartmoor Jail Ale; St Austell Tribute; Sharp's Doom Bar; 3 changing beers (sourced regionally; often Bays, Otter, Tavy Ales) Ⓗ

Three local Devon ales supplement the regular beers, and two guest ciders are available alongside Old Rosie. Two beer festivals are held in spring and December. It is Princetown's oldest building (1785) and features granite walls, slate floors and slate-topped tables. A later addition is the large function/family room. Food is served all day, with a carvery on Sundays. Outside there is ample seating on the spacious patio, a large car park, children's play area, campsite and bunkhouse. The bus service is infrequent.
Q🕭🏵🕽🕭♣A♠P💂(98)🐾

Roborough

New Inn ⓛ
West Road, EX19 8SY (100yds W of parish church)
SS575170
✪ 12-3 (not Mon & Tue), 5-11; 12-11 Fri-Sun
☎ (01805) 603247 ⊕ thenewinnroborough.co.uk
Teignworthy Gun Dog; 2 changing beers (sourced nationally) Ⓗ

A 16th-century thatched inn with a warm friendly atmosphere, a lovely fire in colder months and a superb south-facing patio with views of the countryside to enjoy in the summer. Dogs are made very welcome. There are three real ales available and the interesting menu, based on locally sourced food, includes home-made ice cream and bread. The range of ciders and perries is outstanding. Local CAMRA Cider Pub of the Year 2015 and 2016. Q🕭🏵🕽♣♠P💂🐾🛜

Salcombe

Victoria Inn ✪

Fore Street, TQ8 8BU

☼ 11-11 ☎ (01548) 842604 ⊕ victoriainn-salcombe.co.uk

St Austell Tribute, Proper Job; house beer (by St Austell); 1 changing beer (sourced nationally) ⒣

With many awards from prestigious bodies, this pub and its staff members are welcoming and friendly. There is a slate-floored bar with open fire, a traditionally furnished restaurant downstairs and a bright and modern restaurant upstairs. The pub is extremely popular for food. Outside, at the back, a large terraced garden has a children's play area, while dogs are welcome in the pub and well catered for with their own menu (profits going to a hearing dog charity).

Q ⅏ 🐕 ⊛ 🛏 ◀) ▲ 🚃 (606,X64) 🐾 ☂

Sandford

Lamb Inn

The Square, EX17 4LW

☼ 10.30-11 ☎ (01363) 773676 ⊕ lambinnsandford.co.uk

Otter Bitter; changing beers ⒣

A traditional 16th-century free house in the village centre with a warm, welcoming atmosphere. It is well supported by locals and visitors alike, offering award-winning food, West Country ales and Sandford Orchards cider. Skittles is played four nights a week in the alley-cum-cinema-cum-conference venue. There are open mic music and comedy evenings. Accommodation is available and children and dogs are welcome. It is frequented by the village football, squash and cricket teams.

Q ⅏ 🐕 ⊛ 🛏 ◀) 🕭 ♣ ● P 🚃 (369) 🐾 ☂

Shaldon

Clifford Arms 🅛

34 Fore Street, TQ14 0DE

☼ 11-2.30, 5-11 (11.30 Fri & Sat); 11.30-3, 5.30-10.30 Sun ☎ (01626) 872311

Black Tor Devonshire Pale Ale; Dartmoor Jail Ale; 1 changing beer (sourced nationally) ⒣

Beautifully restored and refurbished, this village pub is popular with drinkers and diners. Set on the village's main street, steps lead up to the open-plan modern bar and restaurant areas where a log fire burns in winter. Outdoor seating is available to the front and rear. Good-quality food is served lunchtimes and evenings, plus there is a regular Monday night jazz café. Dogs and families with children over five are welcome. Real cider is Tolchards Ernie Boy's Scrumpy.

Q ⅏ 🐕 ⊛ ◀) ● 🚃 (11) 🐾

Shaldon Conservative Club 🅛

Dagmar Street, TQ14 0DU

☼ 12-3, 5-11; 12-11 Sat & Sun ☎ (01626) 873667

Teignworthy Reel Ale; 2 changing beers (sourced nationally) ⒣

A real hub of the community, the club is located in the centre of the village and offers three real ales and a cider at reasonable prices. The comfortable single-bar venue is home to snooker, darts and euchre teams, and also offers regular live music on Saturday nights. Televised rugby is popular, as is the mini annual beer festival held in August. Card-carrying CAMRA members are welcome.

ⴜ ♣ 🖨 🚃 (11) ☂

Silverton

Lamb Inn 🅛 ✪

Fore Street, EX5 4HZ

☼ 11.30-2.30, 6-midnight; 11.30-midnight Sat; 12-11 Sun ☎ (01392) 860272 ⊕ thelambinnsilverton.co.uk

Exe Valley Dob's Best Bitter; Otter Ale; 1 changing beer (sourced regionally) ⒢

Popular family-run village pub with stone floors, stripped timber, old pine furniture and a large, open real fire. A fine display of old pumpclips is a reminder of the long list of previous guest beers. Three ales are served by gravity from a temperature-controlled stillage behind the bar, at competitive prices. There is a function room and skittle alley. Good-value home-cooked food is served lunchtimes and evenings, plus a popular Sunday roast. Q ⅏ 🐕 ⊛ ◀) ⴜ ♣ ● 🚃 (55B) 🐾 ☂

Slapton

Queen's Arms 🅛

TQ7 2PN

☼ 12-3, 5.30-11; 12-3, 6-10.30 Sun ☎ (01548) 580800 ⊕ queensarmsslapton.co.uk

Dartmoor Jail Ale; Otter Bright, Ale; 1 changing beer (sourced regionally) ⒣

Splendid 14th-century village pub at the heart of the community, boasting a flower-filled garden in the summer months with patios to the rear, and an open fire in the winter. Numerous WWII evacuation photographs adorn the walls depicting local life and history. An extensive menu is available, with daily specials; the chef is known for his home-made pies, in winter, and Sunday roasts are popular (booking advisable). A takeaway food service is available. Children and dogs are welcome. Q ⅏ 🐕 ⊛ ◀) ▲ ♣ ● P 🚃 (3) 🐾 ☂

South Brent

Oak

Station Road, TQ10 9BE

☼ 12-2 (not Mon & Tue), 4-11; 12-2, 4-midnight Fri; 12-midnight Sat; 12-10.30 Sun ☎ (01364) 72133 ⊕ oakonline.net

Dartmoor IPA; Teignworthy Gun Dog; 2 changing beers (sourced locally) ⒣

Village-centre pub on the edge of Dartmoor. The wood-panelled L-shaped bar is surrounded by a large open-plan area on both sides with plenty of seating. An excellent range of real ales is available in a friendly atmosphere. At the rear a restaurant serves good-quality food, and a new function room can be found upstairs, which is available for meetings. There is a no-smoking courtyard outside and good-quality accommodation is offered.

Q ⅏ 🐕 ⊛ 🛏 P 🚃 (X38,X80) 🐾 ☂

South Molton

Town Arms Hotel 🅛 ✪

124 East Street, EX36 3BU (100yds E of town square)

☼ 11-midnight (1am Fri) ☎ (01769) 572531

Exmoor Ale; Sharp's Doom Bar; 1 changing beer (sourced nationally) ⒣

A good example of a north Devon market-town pub. Popular with locals, there is a strong commitment to real ale, and a long-established CAMRA discount scheme operates. Although no cooked food is served, good-value filled rolls are usually on offer. An ideal base for exploring

Exmoor, there are four letting rooms and a quieter back room for families. Well-behaved dogs are also welcome. The pub can be particularly busy on market day (Thursday).
🏠🛏️👪♿♣♠Pᴿ(X7,155)🐾📶

South Zeal

King's Arms ⓛ

EX20 2JP SX649936
🌀 12-11 ☎ (01837) 840300 ⊕ thekingsarmssouthzeal.com
Dartmoor IPA, Legend; 2 changing beers (sourced nationally) Ⓗ
Set in the northern foothills of Dartmoor on the Trafalgar Way, this thatched 14th-century village local, once a cider house, is the hub of the village community. The long single bar has two regular Dartmoor beers, together with two changing guest ales from other local brewers. Good food is served 12-2.30pm and 6-9pm every day. The pub is a popular meeting place, particularly during the Dartmoor Folk Festival in August.
Q🏠🐕🏠♿👪♣♠Pᴿ🐾📶

Oxenham Arms ⓛ

EX20 2JT (on main road through village at lower end)
🌀 11-11 ☎ (01837) 840244 ⊕ theoxenhamarms.co.uk
4 changing beers (sourced nationally) Ⓗ
Home of the Neolithic South Zeal menhir, this 13th-century former Benedictine monastery is said to be the oldest heritage pub in Devon and Cornwall. Steeped in history, the largely untouched interior has to be seen. Two beers are brewed specially for the pub, which are served alongside two changing guest ales, together with a local cider. Accommodation comprises seven rooms, all with four-poster beds. During January and February the pub closes 3-6pm.
Q🐕🏠🛏️◑♿👪♣♠Pᴿ(178)🐾📶

Spreyton

Tom Cobley Tavern ⓛ

EX17 5AL (off A3124 in village) SX6986096761
🌀 6.30-11 Mon; 12-3, 6-11 (1am Fri & Sat); 12-4, 7-11 Sun
☎ (01647) 231314 ⊕ tomcobleytavern.co.uk
Changing beers (sourced locally) Ⓗ/Ⓖ
You will find a choice of up to 14 real ales here, depending on the season, all from West Country brewers, plus 16 real ciders and perries. It also does a wide range of bar snacks, plus an extensive full menu. Admire the eye-catching display of 15 CAMRA certificates from National Pub of the Year 2006 onwards, covering local, regional and national awards. It is a true village community pub, with darts, quizzes and social events, and you will always get a cheery welcome from the family and staff. Dogs and children are welcome. There is a delightful garden and five en-suite guest rooms.
Q🏠🛏️◑♣♠P🐾

Sticklepath

Taw River Inn ⓛ

Sticklepath, EX20 2NW (on main road – old A30 – going through village) SX642941
🌀 12-midnight; 12-11 Sun ☎ (01837) 840377
⊕ tawriver.co.uk
Dartmoor Jail Ale; St Austell Tribute; Sharp's Doom Bar; 1 changing beer (sourced nationally) Ⓗ
Set in the northern foothills of Dartmoor on the Trafalgar Way and dating from the 17th century,

this friendly and relaxed pub is popular with locals and visitors alike. It is ideally situated for exploring the area or visiting the Finch Foundry Museum opposite. Real ales are attractively priced, the cider is made in the village, and good-value pub food is served in both the bar area and adjacent dining room. Well-behaved children and dogs are welcome. 🐕🏠◑♣♠Pᴿ(X9)🐾📶

Teignmouth

Blue Anchor Inn ⓛ

Teign Street, TQ14 8EG
🌀 12-midnight (11 Mon-Wed) ☎ (01626) 772741
6 changing beers (sourced nationally; often Bays, Teignworthy) Ⓗ
Friendly Grade II-listed pub in the town's Teign Street conservation area and opposite the entrance to the docks. Billed as Teignmouth's real ale pub, the eight handpumps sell six changing beers and two ciders. Mini beer and cider festivals are held over the Easter and August bank holiday weekends. The pub supports a pool and darts team, as well as showing major televised sports events. It has an outside drinking area to the side and rear. Q🏠♿🚃♣♠🚌(2,11)🐾

Brass Monkey ⓛ ✅

Hollands Road, TQ14 8SR
🌀 11-midnight; 12-11 Sun ☎ (01626) 773961
St Austell Tribute, HSD Ⓗ
Formerly the Half Moon, you can expect a friendly welcome at this community-oriented pub. It is capable of being quiet, or else very busy on Friday and Saturday nights with the entertaining karaoke, and there is a Tuesday night quiz. Between the railway station and town-centre bus bays, it acts as the waiting room and is also a welcome retreat from some of the more brash establishments close by. The layout is simplicity itself, being a single bar with a pool area and two TV screens.
Q♿🚃♣🚌(2,11)🐾

Topsham

Bridge Inn ★ ⓛ

Bridge Hill, EX3 0QQ
🌀 12-2, 6-10.30 (11 Fri & Sat); 12-2, 7-10.30 Sun
☎ (01392) 873862 ⊕ cheffers.co.uk
Branscombe Vale Branoc; changing beers Ⓖ
Historic, cosy, 16th-century inn that has been run by six generations of the same family since 1897, with a varying range of ales from local breweries and further afield. This hostelry is a delight for fans of real ale, in a traditional setting overlooking the banks of the River Clyst. The inn was visited by the Queen in 1998. Nine beers are usually on tap, all dispensed by gravity straight from the cellar. Wholesome traditional pub lunches, such as ploughmans, sandwiches and pasties, are served.
Q🏠◑🚃Pᴿ(57,T)🐾

Exeter Inn ⓛ

68 High Street, EX3 0DY
🌀 11-11 (midnight Fri & Sat); 12-10.30 Sun
☎ (01392) 873131
Teignworthy Beachcomber; 2 changing beers (sourced regionally; often Bays, Dartmoor, Sharp's) Ⓗ
A pub since at least 1860, some of this partially thatched building dates from the 17th century, when it was part of a farm. The Exeter is a friendly local serving three real ales and two ciders, plus

snacks such as rolls. Three TVs show various sports, while the front area is devoted to pool and darts. There is a small, sheltered garden and smoking area at the side. Dogs are welcome, and there is occasional live music. ⏰👪✦♣👜🚆🐾📶

Passage House Inn ✦
Ferry Road, EX3 0JN
⏰ 10-11; 10-10.30 Sun ☎ (01392) 873653
🌐 passagehouseinntopsham.co.uk
Dartmoor Jail Ale; Otter Bitter, Amber; St Austell Tribute; 1 changing beer (sourced nationally) 🅗
This picturesque building in the historic port of Topsham has a plaque dated 1788, and sits above the River Exe opposite the ferry point. The cosy interior is divided into three areas with a central fireplace. Good-value food using local produce, with an ever-changing menu, is served all day every day. Theme nights, such as fish and chips with a pint, are a feature. The garden by the river is a popular suntrap in summer. ⏰👪🌓🍴≠♣👜🚆🐾📶

Torquay

Crown & Sceptre
2 Petitor Road, St Marychurch, TQ1 4QA
⏰ 12-4, 5.30-11; 12-midnight Fri & Sat; 12-11 Sun
☎ (01803) 328290
Bath Ales Gem; Butcombe Gold; Courage Best Bitter, Directors; Dartmoor Jail Ale; Otter Ale; 2 changing beers (sourced nationally) 🅗
Popular local, run by the same family for many years, close to St Marychurch shopping precinct. The interior decor is traditional wood and stone, with the ceiling adorned with chamber pots, pennants and other interesting paraphernalia. Tuesdays are jazz nights and Fridays are folk, with a regular music night featuring well-known acts. Dogs and families are welcome and there are two enclosed gardens. Food is home-made pies and bar meals at lunchtimes, with roast lunches served on Sundays. ⏰👪🐾♣👜🚆(32,11,34)🐾📶

Hole in the Wall 🅛
6 Park Lane, TQ1 2AU
⏰ 12-midnight ☎ (01803) 200755
🌐 holeinthewalltorquay.co.uk
Butcombe Bitter; Dartmoor Jail Ale; Otter Bitter; Sharp's Doom Bar; 3 changing beers (sourced regionally) 🅗
Close to the harbour, this is Torquay's oldest pub (circa 1540). Its cobbled floors and low ceilings provide an intimate atmosphere that is popular with tourists and locals alike, and the flower-bedecked outside passageway serves as a pretty drinking area. An attractive restaurant offering good-quality meals complements the separate bar with a fine choice of ales. Dogs on leads are welcome and there is live music on Tuesdays, Thursdays, Saturdays and Sundays. ⏰👪🌓🍴♣👜🚆🐾📶

Kents
1 Ilsham Road, TQ1 2JG
⏰ 11-11 (midnight Fri) ☎ (01803) 292522
🌐 thekentstorquay.co.uk
Dartmoor Jail Ale; Otter Ale; St Austell Tribute; Sharp's Doom Bar; 1 changing beer (sourced regionally) 🅗
Located in the leafy village of Wellswood, 400 yards from Kents Cavern and just over a mile from Torquay Harbour, this popular traditional inn has a large comfortable bar, separate restaurant and pleasant garden. In addition to its five real ales and

35 gins, this family- and dog-friendly pub has a reputation for excellent food. It has a smokery and produces its own sausages. A lively open quiz is held every Sunday evening. Q⏰👪🌓🍴👤♣👜🚆🐾📶

Totnes

Bay Horse Inn 🅛
8 Cistern Street, TQ9 5SP
⏰ 12-midnight ☎ (01803) 862088 🌐 bayhorsetotnes.com
Dartmoor Jail Ale; New Lion Mane Event, Pandit IPA; Otter Bitter; Teignworthy Reel Ale; 3 changing beers 🅗
At the top of the town is this 15th-century coaching inn with a large courtyard garden to the rear. The interior comprises three interconnected rooms, with the middle one popular for live music (jazz, folk and acoustic). The front bar has slate floors and a woodburner, and the back bar is more of a snug. Successful beer festivals are held on the Easter and August bank holidays and the pub is the brewery tap for the New Lion Brewery.
Q⏰👪🌓🍴👤♣👜🚆🐾📶

Turnchapel

Clovelly Bay Inn 🅛
1 Boringdon Road, PL9 9TB
⏰ 6-11; 12-3, 6-11 Fri & Sat; 12-3, 7-10.30 Sun
☎ (01752) 402765 🌐 clovellybayinn.co.uk
5 changing beers (sourced nationally; often Bays, Skinner's) 🅗/🅖
Family-run free house nestled in a picturesque village on the South-West Coast Path. It has an enthusiastic landlord with a passion for real ales and ciders, with up to five available. Guest ales and ciders are usually local, but can come from further afield. It holds a variety of festivals throughout the year, with an emphasis on local produce and a willingness to source beers and ciders from anywhere. It is also renowned for its wonderful food. ⏰🌓👤♣👜🚆(2,2A)🐾

Welcombe

Old Smithy Inn 🅛
EX39 6HG (turn off A39 Bideford to Kilkhampton road at Welcombe Cross and follow signs to Welcombe and then to pub)
⏰ 12-midnight; 12-11.30 Sun ☎ (01288) 331305
🌐 theoldsmithyinn.co.uk
3 changing beers (sourced nationally) 🅗
Although fairly remote, this 17th-century country inn is in fact only 20 minutes from Bude, Bideford and Holsworthy. Set in stunning countryside, and just a mile from the sea, it has an L-shaped slate bar and a cosy eating area with open fire. Three ales are available and cider also figures strongly here. Regular folk, jam and quiz evenings are held and a 16th-century function room also serves as an extra restaurant. The pub is dog-friendly. ⏰👪🌓🍴👤♣👜🚆🐾📶

Wembury

Odd Wheel 🅛
Knighton Road, PL9 0JD
⏰ 12-3, 5-midnight; 12-midnight Sat & Sun
☎ (01752) 863052 🌐 theoddwheel.co.uk
Dartmoor Jail Ale; St Austell Tribute; Sharp's Doom Bar; 3 changing beers (sourced regionally) 🅗

Friendly country pub which was tastefully refurbished several years ago, and is at the northern end of this picturesque village. The three regular beers are supplemented by up to three guest beers, mainly from Devon and Cornwall. Regular beer festivals are held. It is only a short distance from many walking routes, including the South-West Coast Path. Food is served daily, with ingredients from local suppliers. Outside, there is a terraced garden and play area for children. ७★⌂◑♿♣P🚃(48)🐾🐱🛜

Widecombe-in-the-Moor

Rugglestone Inn 🅛

TQ13 7TF (¼ mile from centre of village)
✪ 11.30-3, 6-11.30 (5-midnight Fri); 11.30-midnight Sat; 12-11 Sun ☎ (01364) 621327 ⊕ rugglestoneinn.co.uk
Dartmoor Legend; house beer (by Teignworthy); 2 changing beers (sourced regionally) 🅖

Grade II-listed unspoilt Dartmoor building converted to an inn in 1832 and named after a local logan stone. There is a cosy bar with a woodburner and two further rooms, one with an open fire, and beer is also served through a hatch in the passageway. A wide selection of home-cooked food is available. Across the stream is a large grassed seating area. Local farm Ashridge cider is sold. The pub's car park is just down the road. Q★⌂◑♣●P🐱

Yarde Down

Poltimore Arms 🅛

EX36 3HA (2 miles E of Brayford on jct with unclassified road from South Molton to Simonsbath) SS725356

✪ 7-11 ☎ (01598) 710381 ⊕ poltimorearms.co.uk
Exmoor Ale; Otter Bitter; 1 changing beer (sourced nationally) 🅖

An old coaching inn dating from the 13th century, this remote pub is set in glorious Exmoor countryside and well worth seeking out. The Poltimore retains many original features, together with a friendly ghost who is said to haunt the pub. Three real ales are usually sold, and it is beer that the engaging landlord concentrates on. Dogs are welcome in the bar area, and there is a large beer garden. The atmospheric restaurant operates as a franchise and an attractive, independently run shop and gallery also trades from the premises. Q★⌂◑Å♣P🐱🛜

Yelverton

Rock Inn

Yelverton, PL20 6DS
✪ 11-11 (midnight Fri & Sat); 11-10.30 Sun
☎ (01822) 852022 ⊕ therockinnyelverton.pub
Dartmoor Jail Ale; St Austell Tribute; Sharp's Doom Bar; 1 changing beer (sourced regionally; often Dartmoor, St Austell) 🅗

Ideally located by the Plymouth to Princetown road, this is a pub with something for everyone. The popular lounge bar caters for tourists and diners, the farmers bar offers a lovely fire and convivial chat, and the back bar caters for the younger element and those interested in sport and music. In recent times, live music and the occasional beer festival have come to the fore. Food is served all day in summer. Q★⌂◑♿♣P🚃🐱🛜

Hunters Inn, Heddon Valley (Photo: Russell Taverner)

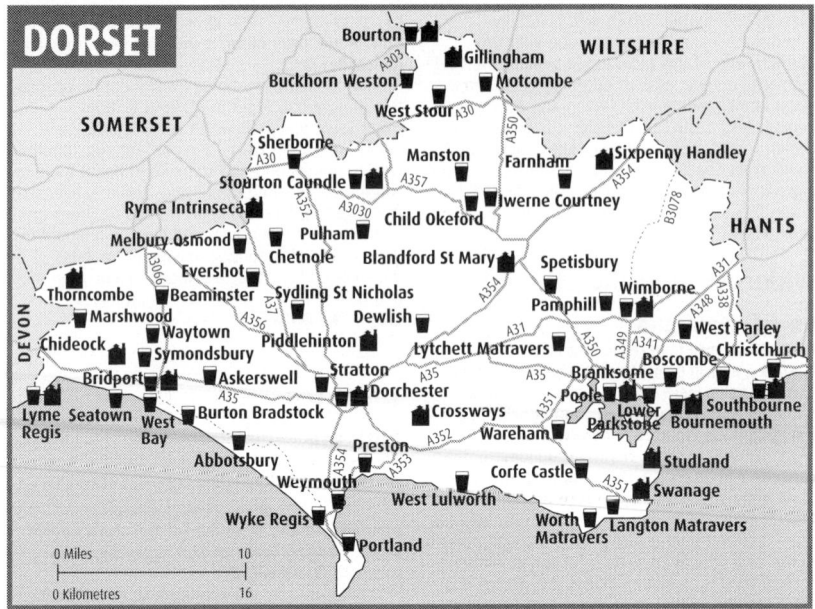

DORSET

SOMERSET

WILTSHIRE

Bourton
Gillingham
Buckhorn Weston
Motcombe
West Stour
Sherborne
Manston
Farnham
Sixpenny Handley
Stourton Caundle
Iwerne Courtney
Ryme Intrinseca
Child Okeford
HANTS
Melbury Osmond
Pulham
Evershot
Chetnole
Blandford St Mary
Spetisbury
Thorncombe
Beaminster
Sydling St Nicholas
Pamphill
Wimborne
Marshwood
Waytown
Dewlish
West Parley
Chideock
Symondsbury
Piddlehinton
Lytchett Matravers
Boscombe
Christchurch
Bridport
Askerswell
Stratton
Branksome
Dorchester
Poole
Lyme Regis
Seatown
West Bay
Burton Bradstock
Crossways
Lower Parkstone
Southbourne
Bournemouth
Abbotsbury
Preston
Wareham
Weymouth
Corfe Castle
Studland
West Lulworth
Swanage
Wyke Regis
Worth Matravers
Langton Matravers
Portland

DEVON

0 Miles 10
0 Kilometres 16

Abbotsbury

Swan Inn
Rodden Row, DT3 4JL
✪ 11-11 ☎ (01305) 871249 ⊕ swan-inn.net
Caledonian Flying Scotsman, Edinburgh Castle 80/-;
house beer (by Caledonian) Ⓗ
Deceptively large pub with a single-bar room,
separate games/family room with a skittle alley
and pool table, and beer garden. Accommodation
is opposite in the Swan Lodge B&B. A varied food
menu is served lunchtimes and evenings. The
licensee has served here for over 40 years. The
village is popular with tourists who come to visit
the Swannery, Children's Farm and Subtropical
Gardens. The Flying Scotsman is badged as Swan.
Q ⑃ ♿ ⚑ ◀❶ ♿ ♣ P ⊟ (X53) ♣ ☞

Askerswell

Spyway Inn Ⓛ
DT2 9EP
✪ 12-3, 6-11 ☎ (01308) 485250 ⊕ spyway-inn.co.uk
Otter Bitter, Ale Ⓖ
Family-friendly 16th-century smugglers' inn
perched on a hill outside Askerswell on the road to
Eggardon Hill fort. There is a selection of local
ciders as well as the Otter beers on gravity. The
lounge bar has beams and a woodburner; a further
bar has tables for dining. The menu features dishes
made with locally produced ingredients. The
garden is popular with locals, walkers and dog
owners, and has a play area for families.
Q ⑃ ♿ ⚑ ◀❶ ♿ P ☞

Beaminster

Greyhound Ⓛ ✅
11 The Square, DT8 3AW
✪ 12-11.30 ☎ (01308) 862496
⊕ thegreyhoundbeaminster.co.uk
Palmers Copper Ale, Best Bitter; 1 changing beer
(sourced locally; often Palmers) Ⓗ

Small friendly pub on the square with plenty of
character. The single bar offers lunchtime snacks
and an extensive lunchtime and evening menu
using locally sourced ingredients, including
vegetarian options plus Sunday roasts (no food Sun
eves). The 18th-century bar has a real fire and the
floor is half carpeted and half stone. The changing
beer may be a Palmers seasonal ale.
⑃ ◀❶ ♿ ⚑ ⊟ (40,53) ♣ ☞

Boscombe

Chaplin's & The Cellar Bar Ⓛ
529 Christchurch Road, BH1 4AG
✪ 11.30-1am; 12-1am Sun ☎ (01202) 251953
⊕ chaplins-bar.co.uk
Dorset Jurassic Ⓗ; 5 changing beers (sourced
nationally; often Dorset, Sunny Republic, Vibrant
Forest) Ⓗ/Ⓖ
This multi award-winning community-focused
establishment is split into two distinct bars. The
upstairs bar is Charlie Chaplin-themed with
memorabilia and hand-painted murals, and serves
excellent food. Downstairs is the Cellar Bar which
hosts live music and has a cosy, quirky feel. The
jewel in the crown is the fabulous rear garden
which hosts regular beer festivals on the solstices
and is a great place to relax and admire the
amusing, surreal and downright brilliant artwork.
The cider changes and is often local.
⑃ ❀ ◀❶ ♣ ♦ ⊟ ☞

Bournemouth

Cricketers Arms ✅
41 Windham Road, BH1 4RN
✪ 11-11; 12-10.30 Sun ☎ (01202) 551589
Fuller's London Pride; 2 changing beers (sourced
nationally) Ⓗ
Bournemouth's oldest public house, dating from
1847. The main bar area retains many original
features including traditional wood panelling and
stained-glass windows from its time as a boxing

gym used by former world champion Freddie Mills. This pub, at the heart of the community, offers two varying guest beers, real cider straight from the box and hosts an annual October beer festival. There is occasional live entertainment, a quiz night on Tuesday, games on Thursday and lunches served at weekends. ♉❀◑♣●P🚌🐾📶

Firkin Shed 🏆

279 Holdenhurst Road, BH8 8BZ
⌚ 4-11; 12-midnight Fri & Sat; 12-9 Sun; closed Mon
☎ (01202) 302340
6 changing beers (sourced nationally; often Cerne Abbas, Siren, Vibrant Forest) Ⓖ
Award-winning, friendly, family-run micropub in what was once a video store. Tables and benches hug the walls here and a shed is used as the bar. Six changing beers are complemented by 20 or more ciders from around the country. Beers are served straight from the cellar which can be viewed through the window in the rear corridor. There is occasional spontaneous acoustic music with instruments provided by the landlord. The pub is a mobile-free zone with a fine for improper use payable to charity. ❀⇌●🚌(2)🐾

Bourton

White Lion

High Street, SP8 5AT
⌚ 11.30-11; 12-10.30 Sun ☎ (01747) 840866
🌐 whitelionbourton.co.uk
Otter Amber; 1 changing beer (sourced nationally; often Ruddles, Timothy Taylor) Ⓗ
The White Lion is a traditional inn dating from 1763. Originally separate rooms, the small bar with stone-flagged floor has been opened out but there is always a quiet corner to be found. There is a cosy, intimate restaurant and a large beer garden. Either Thatchers Original or Rich's Cider is served on the cider handpump. The pub is set back from the B3081 with parking opposite as well as in the car park. Q❀🛏◑●P🚌(158)📶

Branksome

Branksome Railway Hotel

429 Poole Road, BH12 1DQ
⌚ 12-11 ☎ (01202) 769555
Hop Back Summer Lightning; Timothy Taylor Landlord; 2 changing beers (sourced regionally; often Dark Star) Ⓗ
Award-winning Victorian railway hotel dating from 1894 opposite Branksome station on the Waterloo to Weymouth line, and on the main bus routes between Poole and Bournemouth. The large, open-plan interior is divided into three areas with a log fire between two of them. Up to two guest beers are available, often from the Dark Star range, to complement the two permanent beers. Live major sporting events are shown and there is occasional live music and open mic sessions at weekends. ♉⇌P▯🚌🐾📶

Bridport

Crown Inn Ⓛ ✔

56 West Bay Road, DT6 4AX
⌚ 11.30-11 (1am Fri & Sat) ☎ (01308) 422037
Palmers Copper Ale, Best Bitter, Dorset Gold, 200, Tally Ho!; 1 changing beer (often Palmers) Ⓗ
Welcoming traditional single-bar hostelry on the A35 Crown roundabout between Bridport and West Bay. A popular locals' pub but families, parties and tourists are also made to feel at home. Good food is served daily until 9pm. Large TV screens show sport and there is a great live music scene at weekends. The full range of Palmers beers is served and Dorset Orchards First Press cider. The pub has a beer garden and a large car park. ♉❀◑♣●P🚌🐾📶

Ropemakers Arms Ⓛ ✔

36 West Street, DT6 3QP
⌚ 10-11 (12.30am Fri & Sat); 12-4 Sun ☎ (01308) 421255
🌐 theropemakers.com
Palmers Copper Ale, Best Bitter, Dorset Gold, 200, Tally Ho!; 1 changing beer (often Palmers) Ⓗ
Deceptively large pub in the centre of town serving the full Palmers range of ales and seasonal beers plus Dorset Orchards First Press cider. The interior is divided into lots of separate themed areas decorated with memorabilia and local history. There is a large partially covered courtyard at the rear and disabled access via the back door. Quality home-cooked food is from local suppliers. Live music plays on Friday and Saturday evenings. The pub closes around 4pm on Sundays in winter (later if there is live music). ♉❀◑⛺♣●🚌🐾📶

Buckhorn Weston

Stapleton Arms

Church Hill, SP8 5HS (between A303 and A30)
ST75652462
⌚ 11-3, 6-11; 11-11 Sat & Sun ☎ (01963) 370396
🌐 thestapletonarms.com
Butcombe Bitter; 3 changing beers (sourced locally; often Plain, Wriggle Valley) Ⓗ
Imposing village pub with a large car park and secluded garden. Children, dogs and muddy boots are welcome. The three guest beers often reflect the seasons and are frequently sourced from local breweries. The cider is Thatchers Cheddar Valley. Excellent food is served as well as classic bar snacks such as hand-made pork pies, Scotch eggs and chutney. Four individually designed bedrooms complete the Drink, Eat, Sleep motto. Q♉❀🛏◑●P🐾📶

REAL ALE BREWERIES

Blackmore ▮ Stourton Caundle
Bournemouth Poole
Brew Shack Wimborne Minster (NEW)
Brewhouse & Kitchen ▮ Dorchester
Brewhouse & Kitchen ▮ Poole
Brewhouse & Kitchen ▮ Southbourne (NEW)
Cerne Abbas Chideock
Dorset Crossways
Eight Arch Wimborne
Gyle 59 Thorncombe
Hall & Woodhouse (Badger) Blandford St Mary
Hattie Brown's Swanage (NEW)
Isle of Purbeck ▮ Studland
King Alfred Bourton
Lyme Regis Lyme Regis
Palmers Bridport
Piddle Piddlehinton
Sixpenny Sixpenny Handley
Small Paul's Gillingham
Southbourne Bournemouth
Wriggle Valley Ryme Intrinseca

Burton Bradstock

Three Horseshoes L ✓

Mill Street, DT6 4QZ

✪ 12-3, 5-11; 12-11 Sat; 12-10.30 Sun ☎ (01308) 897259

⏣ threehorseshoesburtonbradstock.co.uk

Palmers Copper Ale, Best Bitter, Dorset Gold, 200, Tally Ho!; 1 changing beer (often Palmers) H

Three-hundred-year-old thatched pub and restaurant with suntrap seating at the front and in the beer garden. It serves very good home-cooked food and is popular with families using the beach. The full Palmers ale range is available plus a Palmers seasonal beer or Dorset Orchards First Press cider. Open all day April to September, Easter and summer school holidays and bank holidays. ㋡❀◑❀☖▲♣♠P⎚(X53)❀❧

Chetnole

Chetnole Inn L ✓

DT9 6NU

✪ 11.30-3, 6-11; 12-4 Sun ☎ (01935) 872337

⏣ thechetnoleinn.co.uk

Wriggle Valley Valley Gold; Yeovil Lynx Wildcat; 2 changing beers (sourced regionally; often Butcombe, Cerne Abbas, St Austell) H

Flagstone floors and a wood-burning stove help this inn blend the modern with the traditional. There are three bar areas and a beautiful garden. Two regular beers are served and one or two guest ales, the selection often led by customer recommendation. The cider is Burrow Hill. B&B accommodation comprises three large rooms. Award-winning food is served 12-2pm and 6.30-9pm. Q㋡❀❀✿◑☖♣♠P⎚⎚(212)❀❧

Child Okeford

Saxon Inn

Gold Hill, DT11 8HD

✪ 12-3, 6-11 ☎ (01258) 860310 ⏣ saxoninn.co.uk

Butcombe Bitter; Otter Bitter; 3 changing beers (sourced regionally; often Palmers) H

Local CAMRA Rural Pub of the Year 2015, this 300-year-old inn retains its rustic charm despite significant extension following conversion from cottages in the 1950s. There are two distinct dining areas and a garden for alfresco refreshment. The bar area is cosy with tables and chairs around a log fire. A varied menu of quality home-cooked food is available. A beer festival is held in September. The pub offers B&B and is an ideal base for exploring rural Dorset. Q㋡❀✿◑☖♣P❀❧

Christchurch

Thomas Tripp ✓

10 Wick Lane, BH23 1HX

✪ 11-11.30 (midnight Fri & Sat); 12-11.30 Sun

☎ (01202) 490498 ⏣ thomastripp.co.uk

Ringwood Best Bitter, Fortyniner; 2 changing beers (sourced nationally; often Vibrant Forest) H

Popular town-centre pub named after a legendary local smuggler. The Tripp is located close to the historic Priory and Quay, with one of the few preserved trolleybus turntables nearby. Live music features several nights a week and good food is available lunchtimes and evenings. There is a barbecue on the patio in summer. A covered area for smokers is provided. ㋡❀◑☖♠❀❧

Corfe Castle

Royal British Legion Club

70 East Street, BH20 5EQ (off A351)

✪ 12-2.30, 6-11; 12-11 Sat & Sun ☎ (01929) 480591

Ringwood Best Bitter; Timothy Taylor Landlord; 1 changing beer (sourced nationally) H

A small friendly club housed in a national school building dating from 1834, constructed from local Purbeck stone. Alongside ales, filled rolls are available daily. Major sporting events are shown on TV and darts, shove-ha'penny and occasional live music are played. The garden has a boules court and views over the Purbeck countryside. Convenient for the castle and steam railway, visitors can show a CAMRA membership card or a copy of this Guide for entry. ❀⇌P⎚(40)

Dewlish

Oak at Dewlish

DT2 7ND

✪ 11.30-2.30, 6-11; 12-2.30, 7-11 Sun ☎ (01258) 837352

⏣ oakpub.co.uk

3 changing beers (sourced regionally; often Butcombe, Cotleigh, Dartmoor) H

Unpretentious village inn with three ever-changing ales sourced mainly from the West Country. Local Cider with Rosie also features. The horseshoe-shaped bar has a dining area and opens onto a patio and large garden. To the rear is a separate room with a pool table. A varied food menu offers good home-cooked dishes made using local produce. Two B&B rooms and self-catering accommodation are available in an adjacent converted coach house. Dogs and children are welcome. Q㋡❀✿◑♣♠⎚(311)❀

Dorchester

Blue Raddle

9 Church Street, DT1 1JN

✪ 11.30-3 (not Mon), 6.30-11; 12-3, 7-10.30 Sun

☎ (01305) 267762 ⏣ blueraddle.co.uk

Butcombe Adam Henson's Rare Breed; Fuller's London Pride; St Austell Tribute; 1 changing beer (sourced locally; often 8 Arch, Cerne Abbas) H

Popular, genuine, town-centre free house with friendly staff and an enthusiastic landlord. In addition to the regular beers, a guest ale and local ciders are also on offer. Good locally sourced food is served lunchtimes (Wed-Sat) and evenings (Thu-Sat). The pub takes part in local events and hosts regular folk music sessions. No children, but dogs are welcomed. ◑⇌(West)♠⎚❀❧

Brewhouse & Kitchen L ✓

27 Weymouth Avenue, DT1 1QY

✪ 11-11 (12.30am Fri & Sat); 12-10.30 Sun

☎ (01305) 265551 ⏣ brewhouseandkitchen.com

Brewhouse & Kitchen Station Masters Ale, Nine Stones, Crickmay, Judge Jeffreys, Cerne Abbas Giant; 2 changing beers H

Brewpub in the former stationmaster's house, tastefully refurbished and extended in 2014, with bar, lounge and restaurant areas. The microbrewery is fully on display in the bar and provides a large range of its own ales on eight handpumps, complemented by a local cider. Food is served seven days a week. The pub hosts occasional live music on Fridays and offers brewing experience days. Dogs are welcome, except in the restaurant area. ㋡❀◑☖♣♠P❀❧

Royal Oak ✪

20 High West Street, DT1 1UW
✪ 8am-midnight (1am Fri & Sat); 8am-11 Sun
☎ (01305) 755910
Greene King Abbot; Ruddles Best Bitter; Sharp's Doom Bar; 5 changing beers (sourced nationally; often Butcombe, Dorset, Otter) Ⓗ

A busy town-centre JD Wetherspoon offering a wide selection of local and national ales on handpump, frequently changing with regular beer festival selections to add to the usual range. The pub also offers a full food menu and is open for breakfast daily, welcoming children and families. To the rear is a sunny external patio area with disabled access to the main area of the pub.
Q ⏷ ⊛ ◖ & ⇆ ● 🖨 🛜

Evershot

Acorn Inn Hotel Ⅼ ✪

28 Fore Street, DT2 0JW
✪ 11-11; 12-10.30 Sun ☎ (01935) 83228 ⊕ acorn-inn.co.uk
3 changing beers (sourced regionally; often Dorset, Otter, Yeovil) Ⓗ

Small, attractive 16th-century inn mentioned in Thomas Hardy's Tess of the d'Urbervilles as the Sow and Acorn. The large flagstoned village bar at the back has a wood-burning stove. A smaller bar and restaurant are at the front. Two ales are always available, usually from Dartmoor, Dorset Brewing Co, Otter or Yeovil Ales. A third ale is added in the summer. The skittle alley can be hired for functions. Winner of Taste of the West Gold Awards in 2014 and 2015. ⏷ ⊛ ◖ ◖ & ♣ P 🖨 (212) ❀ 🛜

Farnham

Museum Ⅼ ✪

DT11 8DE (off A354)
✪ 12-11 ☎ (01725) 516261 ⊕ museuminn.co.uk
Sixpenny 6d Best Bitter; 2 changing beers (sourced locally) Ⓗ

Set in tranquil Dorset countryside, this 17th-century part-thatched country inn has a cosy, intimate feel. Some original features have been retained including the flagstone floor in the bar area, large inglenook and window seat. The pub is predominately food oriented but also welcomes ale drinkers. Excellent, locally sourced food is served all day. Beers tend to be from the local Sixpenny Handley Brewery. Q ⏷ ⊛ ◖ ◖ P ❀

Iwerne Courtney

Cricketers

Main Street, DT11 8QD (also known as Shroton; off A350 N of Stourpaine)
✪ 12-3, 6-11; 12-10.30 Sun ☎ (01258) 860421
⊕ thecricketersshroton.co.uk
Butcombe Bitter; 3 changing beers (sourced nationally; often Butcombe, Otter) Ⓗ

A spacious pub in this picturesque village, with the imposing fort of Hambledon Hill nearby, which is well used by locals, tourists and walkers. A bustling central bar serves an extensive drinking area and large rear dining area. The menu offers local specialities and traditional pub food; Thursday is pie night. In the summer the tranquil garden is popular, while a cosy woodburner inside warms you in the winter months. Q ⏷ ⊛ ◖ & ● P 🛜

Langton Matravers

King's Arms Hotel ✪

27 High Street, BH19 3HA
✪ 12-11 ☎ (01929) 422979
Ringwood Best Bitter, Fortyniner; 2 changing beers (sourced nationally) Ⓗ

Purbeck stone-built village pub with many small nooks and crannies. Dating back to 1743, with the original flagstone floors, the walls are adorned with paintings and photographs recording the pub's local history. Marston's Ringwood beers are permanent alongside two well-chosen guest ales. Entertainment features occasionally, there is camping nearby and the local steam railway is close. The large suntrap garden hosts barbecues in summer. Q ⏷ ⊛ ◖ ◖ ⋏ ♣ 🖨 (40) ❀ 🛜

Lower Parkstone

Bermuda Triangle

10 Parr Street, BH14 0JY
✪ 12-3, 5-11; 12-midnight Fri & Sat; 12-11 Sun
☎ (01202) 748047
4 changing beers (sourced nationally; often Dark Star, Goddards, Sharp's) Ⓗ

This busy pub is decorated to reflect the Bermuda Triangle story. The single-room bar is on three levels. The walls and ceiling display a range of artefacts relating to ships and planes including maps, newspaper cuttings and ship and aircraft fittings. Run by the same owner for 25 years, the bar has four handpumps offering a variety of ales sourced locally and throughout the UK as well as speciality lagers and foreign beers. ⊛ ⇆ ● P 🖨

Poole Ex Servicemen's (RBL) Club

66 North Road, BH14 0LY
✪ 6-11 Mon & Tue; 12-3, 6-midnight Wed & Thu; 12-midnight Fri-Sun ☎ (01202) 744515
4 changing beers (sourced nationally) Ⓗ

National finalist in the CAMRA Club of the Year competition in 2014, this friendly RBL-affiliated club stocks four different ales from around the country and two real ciders. The club boasts facilities for pool, darts and other traditional games, plus a weekly entertainment schedule. There is a function/meeting room available. Three beer festivals are held annually in May, August and November and are well worth a visit. Visitors are welcome with a CAMRA membership card or a copy of this Guide. ⏷ ⊛ ◖ & ⇆ ♣ ● P 🖨 (M2,1B,1C) 🛜

Lyme Regis

Lyme Regis Brewery Tap Ⅼ

Mill Lane, DT7 3PU
✪ 10 (11 Sat & Sun)-5 ☎ (01297) 444354
⊕ lymeregisbrewery.com
3 changing beers (sourced locally; often Lyme Regis) Ⓗ /Ⓖ

Formerly named the Town Mill Brewery, the compact shop sells its beer in an outside courtyard in the Town Mill complex. There is limited seating available. The brewing equipment for this four-barrel plant is on display, with the brewing process explained on information boards. Increased demand has now led to some beers being brewed off-site. A local real cider is sold in the summer and bottles are stocked all year. Closes at 4pm at weekends in the winter. Q ⊛ ● 🖨 (X31,X53)

Volunteer Ⓛ

31 Broad Street, DT7 3QE
⊙ 11-11; 11-10.30 Sun ☎ (01297) 442214 ⊕ thevoli.co.uk
St Austell Tribute Ⓗ; house beer (by Branscombe
Vale) Ⓖ; 2 changing beers (sourced regionally; often
Exmoor, Otter, Sharp's) Ⓗ
Old two-room pub in the heart of this historic town,
close to the seafront and popular with locals. Dogs
are welcome in the main bar and children in the
refurbished left-hand room – both these rooms are
warmed by real fires in the colder months. Food is
served at weekends only in the winter. Buses
heading easterly stop right outside the door.
Q🞭🖐ⓓ🖳(X31,X53)🐾🛜

Lytchett Matravers

Rose & Crown ✔

178 Wareham Road, BH16 6DT
⊙ 12 11 (midnight Fri & Sat); 12-10.30 Sun
☎ (01202) 625325 ⊕ roseandcrownlytchett.co.uk
3 changing beers (sourced nationally) Ⓗ
The Rose & Crown is a welcoming, friendly, two-
bar free house. Three beers range from local brews
to popular national ales, and real cider is also on
handpump. The public bar has an open fire and a
dartboard. Excellent home-cooked food is
available. The lawned garden displays hanging
baskets and has a covered archway for smokers.
The pub regularly holds comedy and live music
evenings, and hosts beer and cider festivals in the
village hall in the summer.
🞭🞛ⓓ🖐🗚🌢🖳🖳(X8)🐾🛜

Manston

Plough Inn

Shaftesbury Road, DT10 1HB (on B3091 2 miles NE of
Sturminster Newton) ST81351611
⊙ 11.30-2.30, 6-11; 12-3 Sun ☎ (01258) 472484
Fuller's London Pride; Palmers Copper Ale; Sharp's
Doom Bar; Timothy Taylor Landlord; 1 changing beer
(sourced regionally; often Butcombe) Ⓗ
This 450-year-old stone-built country inn has a
single large bar with oak beams and unique plaster
decorations to the ceiling and bar front, thought to
be harvest fertility symbols. There is a large
conservatory dining area, a covered patio, a large
garden complete with pétanque rink and a
campsite. Live music plays every Saturday night. An
annual beer festival is held in May.
🞭🞛ⓓ🖐🗚🌢🖳🖳(309)🐾

Marshwood

Bottle Inn ☗

DT6 5QJ (on B3165 near Dorset/Devon border)
⊙ 12-11 ☎ (01297) 678484 ⊕ bottle-inn.net
6 changing beers (sourced nationally) Ⓗ
Sixteenth-century thatched pub where a single bar
serves two rooms, with a secondary bar adjacent to
the family room and skittle alley at the rear. The six
continuously changing ales come from a mix of
local and national beers. There is also a range
of ciders, perries and foreign bottled beers. A large
garden overlooks Marshwood Vale. The pub holds a
nettle-eating competition in June incorporating a
beer festival. Local CAMRA Pub of the Year 2014
and 2016. Q🞭🞛ⓓ🗚🌢🖳🐾🛜

Melbury Osmond

Rest & Welcome Ⓛ

Yeovil Road, DT2 0NF (on A37 Yeovil-Dorchester road)
⊙ 11-11; 12-10 Sun ☎ (01935) 83248
3 changing beers (sourced locally; often Cerne Abbas,
Plain, Wriggle Valley) Ⓗ/Ⓖ
Split-level, two-roomed roadside pub on a main
Dorset artery offering a welcome break to all
visitors. There is a choice of two or three changing
local or regional guest beers with at least one
served direct from the cask, and one or two real
ciders. The home-cooked food is locally sourced.
TVs show rugby and Formula 1. The skittle alley
doubles as a function room.
🞭🞛ⓓ🗚🌢🖳🖳(212)🐾🛜

Motcombe

Coppleridge Inn ✔

Elm Hill, SP7 9HW
⊙ 10-11; 12-11 Sun ☎ (01747) 851980 ⊕ coppleridge.com
Butcombe Bitter; 2 changing beers (often Wadworth,
Yeovil) Ⓗ
Family-run country inn and restaurant, originally a
farmhouse, set in 15 acres of woodland, meadow
and gardens. It has a cosy wood-panelled bar and a
number of separate dining areas. Local produce
features on the menu, and there are occasional
themed nights. Two guest beers are offered, often
unusual for the area. Accommodation is provided
in converted stables around a courtyard. Function
and conference facilities are available and the pub
is licensed for weddings. Q🞭🞛🖾ⓓ🗚🖳🐾🛜

Pamphill

Vine Inn ★ Ⓛ

Vine Hill, BH21 4EE (off B3082)
⊙ 11-3, 7-10.30 (11 Thu-Sat); 12-3, 7-10.30 Sun
☎ (01202) 882259
2 changing beers (sourced regionally) Ⓗ/Ⓖ
Former bakery, now owned by the National Trust
and run by the same family for 116 years – the
current landlady has been here 30 years. The pub
has two small bars plus an upstairs room; outside
there is a large suntrap patio and garden. Two
changing beers are available from local and
regional breweries alongside a changing cider. At
lunchtimes there is a choice of ploughman's or
toasties. Popular with walkers and cyclists, this
rural gem has won many local CAMRA awards and
is listed on the National Inventory of Historic Pub
Interiors. Q🞭🞛🌢🖳🖳🐾

Poole

Brewhouse

68 High Street, BH15 1DA
⊙ 11-11; 11.30-11 Sun ☎ (01202) 685288
Milk Street The Usual, Beer; 2 changing beers
(sourced nationally; often Dark Star, Milk Street,
Oakham) Ⓗ
This multi award-winning pub is a long-established
feature of Poole High Street and a reliable source of
interesting ales from Milk Street Brewery and well-
chosen nationally sourced ales from
microbreweries. The real cider varies. A no-frills,
traditional community pub, it has table seating in
the window and through the busy bar area there is
a space for pool and darts. A warm welcome for
locals and visitors alike is assured. 🞛🛒🌢🖳🐾🛜

Brewhouse & Kitchen ⓛ ◉
3 Dear Hay Lane, BH15 1NZ
☼ 11-11 (midnight Fri & Sat); 12-10.30 Sun
☎ (01202) 771246 ⊕ brewhouseandkitchen.com/poole
Brewhouse & Kitchen Brewers House, Brownsea Boy, Squirrel Island, Code Name, Rhodes Test, Telemark Extra; 2 changing beers Ⓗ
Opened in 2015, this brewpub is one of the growing Brewhouse & Kitchen chain. An old Poole pub tastefully modernised and expanded, the working brewery is on view in the bar area. An extensive food menu is available all day, with beer and food pairings suggested. Five regular beers are available, brewed on-site in English and American styles, as well as two seasonal brews. The pub is conveniently sited for the railway and bus stations, town centre and quay. Q ⓢ ⓥ ⓞ ≠ ⓔ ⓡ ⓦ ⓕ

Drift ⓛ
9 The Quay, BH15 1HJ
☼ 12-11 (1am Fri & Sat)
4 changing beers (sourced nationally; often 8 Arch, Siren, Vibrant Forest) Ⓗ
This quayside microbar was formerly part of the adjoining Italian restaurant, and shares the same tiling at the entrance. Lively at weekends, modern styles of ale predominate including craft keg. The bar top and some decor are made from driftwood, and the two tables are two halves of a surfboard. Live sport or music videos are screened and live music features on some weekends. The upstairs bar has a commanding view over the dock and serves specialist gins. There is harbourside seating outside. ⓥ ≠ ⓡ

King Charles Inn ⓛ ◉
Thames Street, BH15 1JN
☼ 11-11 (midnight Thu-Sat) ☎ (01202) 672518
⊕ kingcharlespoole.co.uk
Timothy Taylor Landlord; Young's Bitter Ⓗ**; 2 changing beers (sourced locally; often 8 Arch)** Ⓗ/Ⓖ
Allegedly haunted 14th-century pub just off Poole Quay. The long main bar area offers comfortable seating, darts and bar billiards, and shows live sports. The unique adjoining medieval King's Banquet Hall is constructed from original oak ship beams and hosts live music every weekend. There is an excellent menu of home-cooked food and a carvery on Sunday. Two regular beers are complemented by two well-chosen guests usually sourced from local breweries. ⓞ ≠ ⓔ ⓡ ⓦ ⓕ

Rope & Anchor ◉
4 Sarum Street, BH15 1JW
☼ 12-11 (midnight Fri & Sat) ☎ (01202) 675677
⊕ ropeandanchorpoole.co.uk
Wadworth IPA Ⓐ**, Horizon** Ⓗ/Ⓖ**, 6X, Swordfish; 2 changing beers (sourced nationally)** Ⓗ
In an old cobbled alley off historic Poole Quay, this Wadworth house offers up to six real ales and an extensive home-cooked food menu with locally caught fish a speciality. There is a comfortable bar-side seating area perfect for conversation and a tabled area for dining. Outside, the rear patio is a real suntrap. Live music plays every Friday. This friendly pub is the perfect place to relax and escape the bustle on the quay. ⓢ ⓥ ⓞ ⓑ ≠ ⓡ ⓦ ⓕ

Smuggler's Run ⓛ
184 Ashley Road, Parkstone, BH14 9BY
☼ 12 (5 Mon)-11 ☎ (01202) 385399 ⊕ smugglerspubs.co.uk
8 changing beers (sourced nationally; often Bournemouth, Oakham, Vibrant Forest) Ⓗ

Award-winning Artisan Ale House offering an interesting range of beers from local and national microbreweries. Bournemouth Brewery beers always feature alongside numerous well-chosen guests, real ciders and keg beers. The bustling open-plan main bar offers comfortable seating for conversation and Monday night quizgoers, and hosts occasional live music. A rear games room doubles as a function room (available to book). Customers are welcome to bring in a takeaway from the Chinese restaurant next door. ⓢ ≠ ⓐ ⓔ ⓡ ⓦ ⓕ

Portland

New Inn ◉
35 Easton Street, Easton, DT5 1BS
☼ 12-10 (11 Fri & Sat); 12-6 Sun; closed Mon
☎ (01305) 821232 ⊕ newinnportland.co.uk
House beer (by Ringwood); 5 changing beers (sourced locally; often Cerne Abbas, Dorset, Ringwood) Ⓗ
A friendly family-oriented local conveniently situated on the bus route from Weymouth. To the front is a cosy bar area with woodburner. Behind is a dining area where local seafood is the speciality. The large enclosed garden hosts popular cocktail and pizza nights in summer. The regular beer is Shipyard IPA, brewed in collaboration with Ringwood Brewery. Quality B&B accommodation is available. ⓢ ⓥ ⓐ ⓞ ⓑ ⓐ ⓡ (1) ⓕ

Royal British Legion
3 High Street, Fortuneswell, DT5 1JQ
☼ 12-3, 7.30-11 Mon; 12.30-3, 7-11 Tue-Thu; 11.30-3, 6.30-11.15 Fri; 11-11.30 Sat; 12-4, 7.30-11 Sun
☎ (01305) 821207
Exmoor Ale; 2 changing beers (sourced regionally; often Dartmoor, Piddle, St Austell) Ⓗ
Popular members' club with a large downstairs bar serving three ales on handpump. There is a pool table, snooker table and skittle alley. Sky and BT sport are screened, showing all major events. The upstairs function room is available for hire. Live music features most weekends, and meat and alcohol raffles Sunday lunchtime. Show your CAMRA membership card to be signed in as a guest. ⓐ Pⓡ (1) ⓕ

Preston

Spiceship Inn ◉
240 Preston Road, DT3 6BJ
☼ 11.30 (12 winter)-11 ☎ (01305) 834651
⊕ spiceship.co.uk
Ringwood Best Bitter; Sharp's Doom Bar; Timothy Taylor Landlord; 1 changing beer (sourced regionally; often Butcombe, St Austell, Sharp's) Ⓗ
Family-friendly Grade II-listed coaching house with wood panelling, low beams and a central bar separating the restaurant from the dog-friendly bar, where screens show televised sport. The restaurant, which serves good-quality food from an à la carte menu, adjoins a covered, elevated patio overlooking a large beer garden with children's play area. Thursday is curry night and live music plays most Fridays. Wheelchair access is available using the road entrance to the bar and restaurant, and a new toilet with access has been installed. Q ⓢ ⓥ ⓐ ⓞ ⓐ ⓐ Pⓡ (4A,X53) ⓦ ⓕ

Pulham

Halsey Arms

DT2 7DZ

☼ 11.30 (12 Sat)-2, 6-11; 11.30-4 Sun; closed Mon

☎ (01258) 817344

Ringwood Best Bitter; 2 changing beers (sourced nationally; often Purity, St Austell, West Berkshire) Ⓗ
Family-friendly pub with a snug and main bar. Home-cooked and locally sourced food is served in the restaurant, where vegan and vegetarian diets can be catered for, including popular Sunday lunches. Bar snacks are also available. A range of ciders is on offer. The pub is home to four skittles teams, and live music and quizzes are hosted regularly, and it has a function room.
Q ⛴ ❀ ⅅ & ♣ ♠ ♦ 🅿 🚌 (307) ♥ 🛜

Seatown

Anchor Inn Ⓛ ✔

DT6 6JU

☼ 11-11; 11.30-10.30 Sun ☎ (01297) 489215

⊕ theanchorinnseatown.co.uk

Palmers Copper Ale, Best Bitter, Dorset Gold, 200, Tally Ho! Ⓗ
A traditional country pub on the Jurassic Coast, family- and dog-friendly, serving Palmers ales and fantastic food featuring locally sourced ingredients. There are plenty of coastal walks to build up an appetite. Warm up by the open fires or enjoy the sea views towards West Bay or Golden Cap from the large terraces. Accommodation is in three boutique rooms. Q ⛴ ❀ ✿ 🛏 ⅅ ♣ 🅿 ♥ 🛜

Sherborne

Crown

Greenhill, DT9 4EP (on A30)

☼ 12-2.30, 5.30-11; 12-3, 7-11 Sun ☎ (01935) 816115

3 changing beers (sourced regionally; often Cerne Abbas, St Austell, Yeovil) Ⓗ
A large, roadside free house offering visitors a warm welcome and good-value beer and food. There are three varying real ales – one from St Austell and the others mainly from West Country breweries. The pub runs themed food nights and hosts live music of various genres. The real cider is from Lawrence's just down the road in Corton Denham. ⛴ ❀ ⅅ ♣ ♦ 🚌 (57,58/58A) ♥ 🛜

Digby Tap ✔

Cooks Lane, DT9 3NS

☼ 11-11; 12-11 Sun ☎ (01935) 813148 ⊕ digbytap.co.uk

4 changing beers (sourced regionally; often Bath Ales, Otter, Teignworthy) Ⓗ
The Digby Tap is an institution in west Dorset. Hidden away between the railway station and the beautiful abbey church, it is well worth seeking out. The owners of 18 years have retained the old character and atmosphere, with four separate drinking areas, pine panelling, flagstone floors, old beams, settles and three fireplaces. Two or three regional ales, often accompanied by an interesting national ale, offer superb value, as does the excellent lunchtime pub food. Q ❀ ⅅ & ≠ ♣ 🚌 ♥

Southbourne

Wight Bear Ale House

65 Southbourne Grove, BH6 3QU

☼ 12 (4 Tue & Wed)-11; 12-10.30 Sun; closed Mon

☎ (01202) 433733 ⊕ thewightbear.co.uk

6 changing beers (sourced nationally) Ⓖ
This popular bear-themed, high-street micropub opened in a former card shop in 2015. There is no bar; instead knowledgeable beer handlers serve you at high benches and tables that surround the open-plan room. A blackboard details six ever-changing ales, of varying styles from across the country, which are dispensed straight from the cask in the windowed cellar along with five ciders or perries. Traditional bar snacks are available. Convivial conversation is the entertainment here.
Q ♦ 🚌 ♥

Spetisbury

Woodpecker Ⓛ

High Street, DT11 9DJ (A350)

☼ 12-3, 6-11; 12-3, 7-10.30 Sun ☎ (01258) 452658

⊕ woodpeckerspetisbury.co.uk

4 changing beers (sourced regionally; often Hop Back, Isle of Purbeck, Palmers) Ⓗ
Busy community free house with beer from local breweries dominating the four handpumps. Bar billiards and shove-ha'penny are played in the cosy main bar area. Excellent food can be enjoyed in the comfortable seating area or in the spacious gardens when weather permits (no food Sun eve and Mon). A good selection of ciders is always available, with a wider choice during the annual cider festival held in May. ⛴ ❀ ⅅ ♣ ♦ 🅿 🚌 (X8) ♥

Stourton Caundle

Trooper

Golden Hill, DT10 2JW (1½ miles E of A357) ST71491495

☼ 12-2 (2.30 Sat), 7-11; 12-3.30, 7-11 Sun; closed Mon

☎ (01963) 362405 ⊕ thetrooperinn.co.uk

2 changing beers (sourced locally; often St Austell, Sharp's, Yeovil) Ⓗ
Stone-built, single-room community pub with a separate function room/skittle alley. There is an attached camping and caravan site and children's play area next to the beer garden. Good food is served lunchtimes and early evenings including a popular Friday fish and chips night. There are two guest ales and a farmhouse cider, with a beer from the on-site microbrewery occasionally available. An annual beer festival is held in the spring. Dogs and walkers are welcome. Q ❀ ⅅ ♣ ♦ 🅿 ♥

Stratton

Saxon Arms

20 The Square, DT2 9WG

☼ 11-2.30, 5.30-11; 11-midnight Fri & Sat; 12-midnight Sun

☎ (01305) 260020 ⊕ thesaxon-stratton.co.uk

Butcombe Bitter; Timothy Taylor Landlord; 2 changing beers (sourced nationally; often Fuller's, Otter, St Austell) Ⓗ
A thatched, stone and flint country pub built in 2001 overlooking the village hall and green. This welcoming and homely free house offers four real ales and a changing cider, and serves good locally sourced food (booking recommended). Staff are friendly and knowledgeable. Dogs are welcome, but not in the main restaurant area.
Q ⛴ ❀ ⅅ & ♣ ♠ ♦ 🅿 🚌 (212) ♥ 🛜

Sydling St Nicholas

Greyhound Inn
26 High Street, DT2 9PD
☼ 11-3, 5.30-11.30; 11-11.30 Sat; 12-10 Sun
☎ (01300) 341303 ⊕ dorsetgreyhound.co.uk
Bath Ales Gem; 2 changing beers (sourced nationally; often Cerne Abbas, St Austell, Timothy Taylor) ⊞
Large refurbished pub in a picturesque village with a separate restaurant serving food to a high standard. The flagstoned bar has a woodburner; an adjoining carpeted area with tables has a small open fire. As well as the permanent beer there is a changing guest, often from a local brewery such as Dorset Brewing Company and Piddle. There is also a changing cider, usually from Harry's or Purbeck Cider. The pub is popular with locals, and dogs are welcome in the bar areas. ⊁✿🍴◑&⚘🅿🐾🛜

Symondsbury

Ilchester Arms ⓛ ✔
DT6 6HD
☼ 11.45 (12 Mon)-3, 6-11; 12-4 Sun ☎ (01308) 422600
⊕ ilchesterarmssymondsbury.co.uk
Palmers Copper Ale, Best Bitter; 1 changing beer (often Palmers) ⊞
Family-run former Devenish pub dating back to the 16th century, with oak beams, a tiled floor and inglenook fireplace. Horse brasses and copper pots are on display. The full food menu is available 12-2pm and 6-9pm, with bar food served Monday to Saturday lunchtimes. One handpump rotates between Palmers Dorset Gold, 200 and a seasonal ale. Opening times can vary. Q⊁✿🍴◑⚘🅿🐾

Wareham

King's Arms ✔
41 North Street, BH20 4AD
☼ 11.30-11 ☎ (01929) 552503 ⊕ kingsarmswareham.co.uk
5 changing beers (sourced regionally; often Otter, St Austell, Skinner's) ⊞
This award-winning traditional thatched inn has its roots in the 1500s and survived the great fire of 1762. The multi-roomed establishment has a flagstone-floored public bar, real fire, drinking corridor and one room exclusively for dining, with an excellent range of home-cooked food on offer. To the rear is a large garden with a covered area for smokers. The five different guest beers are usually from the West Country, and a changing cider is always available. Live music occasionally features at weekends. Q✿◑➔⚘🅿🚍(40,X53)🐾

Waytown

Hare & Hounds ⓛ ✔
DT6 5LQ
☼ 12-3, 6-11; 12-3, 7-11 Sun ☎ (01308) 488203
Palmers Copper Ale, Best Bitter; 1 changing beer (often Palmers) ⊞
An unspoilt gem well worth seeking out. The garden, with stunning views, has a play area. A good food menu features home-cooked meals. Palmers Dorset Gold or seasonal beers are on offer in the summer and Tally Ho! in the winter. At least two real ciders are available in summer. A monthly quiz replaces food on some Sunday evenings in winter. The pub may close earlier on quiet nights or stay open later if busy (closed Mon and Tue winter). Q⊁✿◑&⚘🅿🐾🛜

West Bay

West Bay Hotel ⓛ ✔
Station Road, DT6 4EW
☼ 12-3, 6-11; 12-midnight Fri & Sat; 12-6 Sun
☎ (01308) 422157 ⊕ thewestbayhotel.co.uk
Palmers Copper Ale, Best Bitter, Dorset Gold, 200; 1 changing beer (often Palmers) ⊞
Fine dining pub with a menu specialising in locally sourced shellfish and seafood. The pub has a central bar and features wooden beams, a wood floor and panelling. Situated adjacent to Chesil Beach and handy for the coastal path, it gets very busy during the summer months. Accommodation is in four rooms. Open all day and until 10pm on Sundays in summer.
Q⊁✿🛏◑&⚓⚘🅿🚍(31,X53)🐾🛜

West Lulworth

Castle Inn ⓛ
Main Road, BH20 5RN
☼ 12-10 ☎ (01929) 400311
⊕ thecastleinn-lulworthcove.co.uk
Palmers Best Bitter ⊞; **4 changing beers (sourced regionally)** ⊞/Ⓖ
This enchanting 16th-century thatched inn close to Lulworth Cove has two comfortable bars, one with a low ceiling and both beamed. Up to six mostly local ales and over 45 ciders and perries are served alongside an extensive menu of good-value home-made dishes in generous portions. At the rear is a tiered garden with giant chess set; board games are available inside. The inn has 15 bedrooms, 14 en-suite, and is dog-friendly. CAMRA Cider Pub of the Year 2014 and 2015. Q✿🛏◑⚓⚘🅿🐾🛜

West Parley

Owls Nest ⓛ
196 Christchuch Road, BH22 8SS
☼ 12-3 (not Mon), 5-11; 11.30-3, 6-midnight Sat; 12-3, 6-10 Sun ☎ (01202) 572793 ⊕ theowlsnest-westparley.com
Otter Bitter; 3 changing beers (sourced regionally; often 8 Arch, Flack Manor, Hop Back) ⊞
Charming and welcoming, this Tudor-style building with beamed ceilings and a woodburner has a comfortable ambience. Decorated with numerous adornments, owls feature heavily among miniatures, jugs and plates. Four handpumps dispense well-chosen local and regional ales. A beer and home-made pie festival has become an early year favourite. Live music features occasionally, with an Irish session on the first Thursday of the month. Excellent home-made food is very popular (booking recommended for diners). Q⊁◑&⚘🅿🚍🐾🛜

West Stour

Ship Inn
SP8 5RP
☼ 12-3, 6-11; 12-11 Sun ☎ (01747) 838640
⊕ shipinn-dorset.com
3 changing beers (sourced regionally; often Plain, St Austell, Small Paul's) ⊞
Once a coaching inn, this popular roadside pub has views across the Blackmore Vale. The public bar features a flagstone floor; the separate light and airy restaurant area has stripped oak floorboards. There is a patio and large garden at the rear. This friendly pub is renowned for superb home-cooked

food (no meals Sun eve) and comfortable accommodation. A choice of six local ciders usually accompanies the three ales. Dogs are welcome in the bar. A beer festival is held annually in July. Q❄️🏠◑♣🐾P🐾

Weymouth

Boot Inn ✅
High West Street, DT4 8JH
☼ 11-11 (midnight Fri & Sat); 12-11 Sun ☎ (01305) 770327
⊕ bootweymouth.co.uk
Marston's Old Empire; Ringwood Best Bitter, Fortyniner; 7 changing beers (sourced nationally; often Banks's, Jennings, Wychwood) ℍ
Weymouth's oldest pub has a single bar area with rooms at each end and two roaring fires in winter. Ten beers are served, the regulars supplemented with guests, mainly from Marstons. Cheddar Valley cider is also available. Only large pork pies are served, however at Sunday lunch a free banquet is provided, with both landlord and customers contributing. A conversation dominated venue, no television or background music. Live music Tuesdays, with quizzes on Wednesdays.
Q❄️♣🐾🚃(1,3,8)

Globe Inn
24 East Street, DT4 8BN
☼ 11-1am; 11-midnight Sun ☎ (01305) 786461
Dartmoor Jail Ale; St Austell Cornish Best Bitter, Proper Job; Sharp's Doom Bar; 2 changing beers (sourced regionally; often Cerne Abbas, Clearwater, Flack Manor) ℍ
Free house with a friendly welcome, tucked away on a street corner, just 30 yards from the iconic harbourside. The Globe is only a short distance from the town centre, the beach and the esplanade, and offers a distinct change from the packed waterside. There is a jukebox and a separate games room with pool table, darts and pub games. A fun quiz is held on Sunday afternoons. Guest ales are not always available in the low season. The cider is Thatchers Cheddar Valley. 🛏️♣🐾🚃🐾🛜

Wimborne

Greenman
1 Victoria Road, BH21 1EN
☼ 10-11.30 (1.30am Fri & Sat) ☎ (01202) 881021
⊕ greenmanwimborne.com
Wadworth IPA, 6X, Swordfish; 1 changing beer (often Wadworth) ℍ
An 18th-century one-bar inn with four small open-plan drinking areas and a patio where games are played. The interior is wood panelled with ubiquitous brasses adorning the walls. The exterior is noted for its award-winning summer floral displays, watched over by a red telephone box and a plaque marking the spot of the former town pond. Excellent food is served lunchtimes only. Live music features at weekends. Watch you do not step on the green man as you enter the pub.
Q🛏️❄️◑♣🐾P🚃(3,4,13)🐾🛜

Man in the Wall 🅛 ✅
10 West Borough, BH21 1NF
☼ 8am-midnight (1am Fri & Sat) ☎ (01202) 639800
Greene King Abbot; Ringwood Boondoggle; Ruddles Best Bitter; Sharp's Doom Bar; house beer (by Sixpenny); 4 changing beers (sourced nationally) ℍ

This listed building is an excellent refurbishment of a former Conservative Club, located near the town centre and handy for the Tivoli Theatre. It has three separate rooms – the two side rooms decorated with antique books, pictures of Kingston Lacy, a map of the Wessex region and Thomas Hardy quotes. Wetherspoon's regular beers feature plus three guests and a house beer from Sixpenny. Do look for the man in the wall.
Q🛏️❄️◑🅑🐾🚃(3,4,13)🛜

Taphouse ✅
11 West Borough, BH21 1LT
☼ 11-11.30 ☎ (01202) 911200
⊕ thetaphousewimborne.co.uk
8 changing beers (sourced nationally; often 8 Arch, Butcombe, Sixpenny) ⅾ
Opened in 2013, the Taphouse instantly gained a following and won local CAMRA Pub of the Year in 2014. Close to the town centre, it features a long hardwood bar, with beers displayed on a stillage behind. Eight well-chosen real ales are on offer including some from local and national microbreweries as well as some popular favourites. The cider changes hour by hour. Always a bustling community pub full of atmosphere, conversation rules, although there is live acoustic music some weekends. Q❄️🅑♣🐾🚃(3,4,13)🐾

Worth Matravers

Square & Compass ★
Weston Road, BH19 3LF (off B3069)
☼ 12-11 ☎ (01929) 439229 ⊕ squareandcompasspub.co.uk
Palmers Copper Ale; 4 changing beers (sourced regionally; often Hattie Brown's) ⅾ
A real gem, this multi award-winning pub with a nationally important historic interior has appeared in every edition of the Guide and has been in the same family since 1907. Two rooms either side of a serving hatch convey the impression that little has changed over the years. The sea-facing garden offers fantastic views across the Purbecks, and fossils are displayed in the small adjacent museum. Pasties are available along with home-made cider. Beer and cider festivals are held in October and November respectively. In the winter the pub closes 3-6pm. Q❄️🅑🐾🚃(44)🐾

Wyke Regis

Wyke Smugglers ✅
76 Portland Road, DT4 9AB
☼ 11-11 Mon-Wed; 12-midnight Thu; 12-1am Fri & Sat; 12-midnight Sun ☎ (01305) 760010
⊕ thewykesmugglers.com
St Austell Proper Job; 2 changing beers (sourced regionally) ℍ
A large, lively local hosting many community pastimes. Live music features on most Friday and Saturday nights, when it can be busy. The menu offers good-quality locally sourced pub food, served in the main dining area which is warmed by a woodburner. Guest beers are mainly from the Punch Cask range. The large skittle alley doubles as a function room, and is home to a pool table. A beer and cider festival is held in July.
🛏️❄️◑🅑P🚃(1)🐾🛜

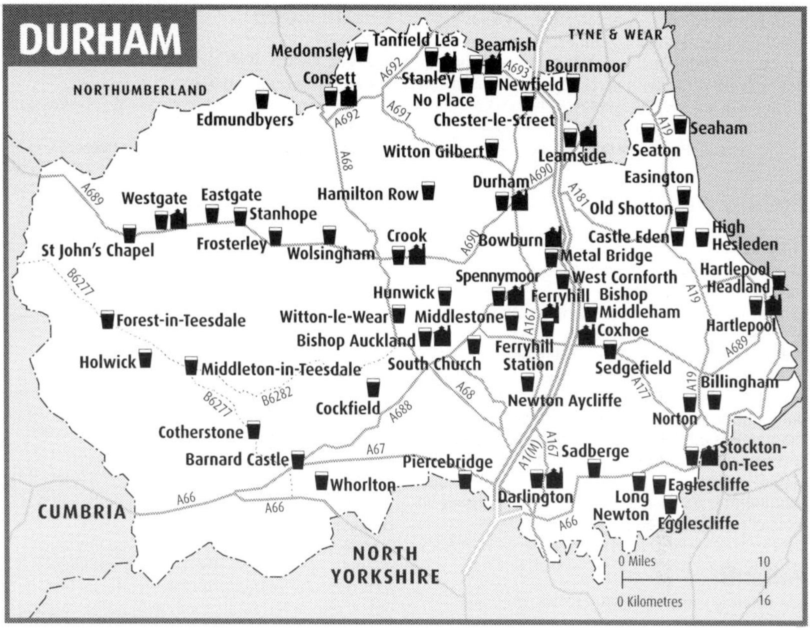

Co Durham incorporates part of the former county of Cleveland

Barnard Castle

Golden Lion ✓

30 Market Place, DL12 8NB

12-11 (midnight Fri & Sat) ☎ (01833) 690295

Marston's New World Pale Ale, Pedigree; Wychwood Hobgoblin; 3 changing beers H

Friendly and welcoming pub in the centre of Barnard Castle – the tall chequered-front hostelry is built partly into the castle ditch. Dating back to 1679, it is the town's oldest pub. It has a quirky layout with a central bar serving two rooms, one with an open fire. Run by CAMRA members, it offers good-value food. Real ale and real cider are £2.50 a pint to CAMRA members. An annual beer and sausage festival is hosted.

❀ ♿ (75,76)

Old Well Inn L

21 The Bank, DL12 8PH

12-11 ☎ (01833) 690130 theoldwellinn.co.uk

Timothy Taylor Landlord; 4 changing beers H

The boundary of this 17th-century town-centre inn incorporates part of the medieval castle wall. The pub has a cosy front bar and a comfortable lounge, a separate restaurant and an airy conservatory, plus an enclosed beer garden. At least five well-kept beers are available including four guests from local micros. Excellent food is served daily and there is accommodation in 10 rooms. Two five-day beer festivals are held at Easter and in October. The Castle Players meet here.

Q ❀ ♿ (75,76)

Beamish

Stables Bar & Restaurant L

Beamish Hall Country House Hotel, DH9 0YB

11-11 (midnight Fri & Sat); 11-10.30 Sun

☎ (01207) 288750 beamish-hall.co.uk/stables

Stables Beamish Hall Best Bitter, Old Miner Tommy, Bobby Dazzler, Silver Buckles, Beamish Burn, Bell Tower H

The Stables is attached to Beamish Hall Country House Hotel, and has its own microbrewery. Stone floors, old beams, solid furniture and crackling log fires in winter help to create a relaxing environment. Outside is a courtyard seating area and, behind the pub, an extended play area for children. Beer festivals are hosted in September and January. The pub is also a popular live music venue. An extensive menu of locally produced food is served. **Q** ❀ ♿**P**

Billingham

Green Hops Real Ale Bar L

55 The Green, TS23 1EW (on village green in old Billingham)

12-midnight (12.30am Fri & Sat) ☎ (01642) 205025

4 changing beers (sourced nationally) H

The town's first micropub, opened by two enthusiasts who noticed a gap in the market. Four ales are on handpump, usually including one from either Camerons or Maxim. Four ciders and two perries are also on offer, providing an eclectic mix – some well known, some more uncommon, and some quite strong. Third-pint beer/cider bats are available. Local CAMRA Cider Pub of the Year 2016.

♣ (36,X9)

Greenholme Catholic Club L

37 Wolviston Road, TS23 2RU (on E side of old A19, just S of Roseberry Road roundabout, next to bus stop)

7-midnight (12.30am Fri); 12.30-1am Sat; 12-midnight Sun

☎ (01642) 901143 billinghamcatholicclub.webs.com

3 changing beers (sourced nationally) H

This Victorian mansion and former school is a friendly private members' club, renowned locally for its vibrant R&B/rock scene, where a genuine welcome awaits CAMRA members. Dedicated and enthusiastic volunteers ensure that the club's reputation for serving 150 different beers annually continues. Three ales, two ciders and a perry are normally on offer, with up to eight beers available during regular beer/music festivals, held during bank holiday weekends. Local CAMRA branch Club of the Year 2016. ⏾&♣♥P🚺🖳(35,36)🌼

Bishop Auckland

Bay Horse
38-40 Fore Bondgate, DL14 7PE (50yds N of bus station)
⏾ 11-11 (1am Fri & Sat); 12-11 Sun ☎ (01388) 609765
⊕ bayhorse-pub.co.uk
Timothy Taylor Landlord; 1 changing beer Ⓗ
At the heart of Bishop's pub scene since 1530, the open-plan L-shaped bar is a haven from the shops during the week, and a joyfully boisterous place at the weekend. It is popular for televised sport, as well as buskers' night on Thursday, live bands on Friday, and karaoke on Saturday. It retains its roots as a long-established, proper pub, and is home to various pub games teams. ⏾&♣♥🖳

Pollards
104 Etherley Lane, DL14 6TU (400yds W of railway station)
⏾ 12-2, 5.30-11; 12-3, 6-11 Sun ☎ (01388) 603539
⊕ thepollardsinn.co.uk
Jennings Cumberland Ale; Marston's Pedigree; 5 changing beers Ⓗ
Towards the western edge of town, this busy pub is a great combination of traditional pub and pleasant eatery. Open fires feature in two of the four original areas, while a spacious restaurant lies to the rear, where the famous Sunday carvery can be enjoyed. There is a quiz on Sunday evenings, while good conversation and seven well-kept ales top things off. Q⏾🌼🕪&≉♣P

Bishop Middleham

Cross Keys Ⓛ
9 High Street, DL17 9AR (1 mile from A177)
⏾ 12 (2.30 Mon)-11 ☎ (01740) 651231 ⊕ crosskeyspub.net
3 changing beers Ⓗ
A busy family-run village pub with a good reputation for food. It has a bar with a real fire, a lounge and a large restaurant at the back. The place is opposite the remains of Fosters Brewery which closed in 1913 and may well have been its tap house. The village has a series of walks through beautiful countryside and to the ruins of Bishop Middleham Castle. Q⏾🌼🕪♣🖳🌼

Bournmoor

Dun Cow Ⓛ
Primrose Hill, DH4 6DY
⏾ 12-11 ☎ (0191) 385 2631 ⊕ theduncowbournmoor.co.uk
3 changing beers Ⓗ
Welcoming 18th-century pub, reputedly haunted by an oft-seen Grey Lady ghost. It offers a varying beer range, good-value pub food served in the lounge and bar, and an à la carte menu in the Lambton restaurant. There is also a large function room. The pub is family-friendly, with extensive gardens. A beer festival is held in October offering local ales. Music festivals in June and September feature local folk and rock bands. ⏾🌼🕪P🌼📶

Castle Eden

Castle Eden Inn Ⓛ
Stockton Road, TS27 4SD
⏾ 11-11 (midnight Fri & Sat); 12-11 Sun ☎ (01429) 835137
⊕ castleedeninn.com
Timothy Taylor Landlord; 3 changing beers Ⓗ
Castle Eden village is famous for the former Castle Eden Brewery. This refurbished old coaching inn has a large bar offering a good selection of ales. The lounge has a spacious and comfortable seating area. Quality food featuring local produce is served in the bar, lounge or the more formal restaurant. There is also a private function room which can comfortably seat 60 people. ⏾🌼🕪P

Chester-le-Street

Butchers Arms
Middle Chare, DH3 3QD
⏾ 11-11 (midnight Fri & Sat) ☎ (0191) 388 3605
⊕ butchersarms.org.uk
Jennings Cumberland Ale; Marston's Pedigree; 5 changing beers Ⓗ
A cosy pub acknowledged for the quality and quantity of its beers – the landlady has now increased the number of cask ales to seven. The pub is also noted for its food, with home cooking a speciality – Sunday lunches are popular and good value. Teas and coffees are also served. Convenient for the railway station and all buses through the town. Quiz night is Tuesday. Q⏾🌼🕪&≉♣🖳(21)🌼

Lambton Worm Ⓛ ✔
North Road, DH3 4AJ
⏾ 11.30-11 (midnight Fri & Sat); 12-10.30 Sun
☎ (0191) 387 1162 ⊕ thelambton.com
Sonnet 43 Abolition, Seraphim, The Raven, The Aurora, Impressment; 2 changing beers Ⓗ
Sonnet 43 pub with a bar at the front and gastro restaurant at the back matching traditional English food with its beers. Experimental and limited edition beers are offered alongside the core range, complemented by ales from regional breweries. A relaxed ambience, friendly staff, spacious bar area and plenty of tucked-away areas for seating add to the enjoyment. Accommodation is in 14 boutique B&B rooms. There is a patio drinking area to the rear, a weekly quiz and live music on Fridays. ⏾🌼🕪P🖳(21)📶

REAL ALE BREWERIES

Black Paw Bishop Auckland
Blackhill Stanley
Camerons Hartlepool
Consett Ale Works 🍺 Consett
Crafty Pint 🍺 Darlington
Durham Bowburn
Fat Crook (NEW)
George Samuel Spennymoor
Hill Island Durham
Leamside 🍺 Leamside
Rocket Town Darlington (NEW)
Schoolhouse Darlington
Sonnet 43 Coxhoe
Stables 🍺 Beamish
Stockton Stockton on Tees
Village Brewer: Brew 22 🍺 Darlington
Weard'ALE 🍺 Westgate
Yard of Ale 🍺 Ferryhill

Smiths Arms ⅃
Forge Lane, Castle Dene, DH3 4HE NZ299507
☼ 4-11; 12-midnight Fri & Sat; 12-11 Sun ☎ (0191) 385 7559
8 changing beers Ⓗ
Somewhat off the beaten track, this traditional pub has a small cosy bar with an open fire, a room for pool and darts and a larger lounge also with an open fire. The beers are sourced by the landlord, including up to eight real ales, with LocAle always featured. The Castle Dene restaurant is on the first floor. The pub is reputed to be haunted. Beer festivals are held in May and December.
🛏️❶♿♣Ⓟ🚍(71,78)❀🐕🛜

Cockfield

Queen's Head
106 Front Street, DL13 5AA
☼ 5 (11 Sat)-11; 12-11 Sun ☎ (01388) 710981
2 changing beers Ⓗ
This cosy, welcoming and popular pub is right next to the bus stop at the north end of the village, and serves two changing beers from the Marston's range. It is open plan but with various seating areas, as well as tables outside at the front of the building. Bar staff will happily ask your opinion of the beers and chat about which ones have been popular. A proper community local, handy for the historic Cockfield Fell and associated industrial archaeology. Q❀♣Ⓟ🚍(6,8)

Consett

Company Row ⅃ ✅
Victoria Road, DH8 5BQ
☼ 8am-11 ☎ (01207) 585600
Greene King Abbot; Ruddles Best Bitter; 5 changing beers Ⓗ
Modern pub named after the rows of houses built by the Derwent Iron Company for its workers which were mostly demolished in the mid-1920s. This spacious and well-decorated Wetherspoon establishment is a real asset to Consett town centre. An excellent beer selection and good food make this social pub popular with a wide clientele of all ages. Alcohol is served from 9am.
🛏️❀❶♿♣🍴🚍🛜

Grey Horse ⅃ ✅
115 Sherburn Terrace, DH8 6NE
☼ 12-12.30am (midnight Mon & Tue); 12-midnight Sun
☎ (01207) 502585 ⊕ thegreyhorse.co.uk
Consett Red Dust; Steel Town Bitter; White Hot; 4 changing beers Ⓗ
Traditional pub dating back to 1848. The interior comprises a lounge and L-shaped bar, with a wood-beamed ceiling. Consett Ale Works Brewery is located at the rear. Beer festivals are held twice a year, live entertainment is hosted on Thursday and a quiz on Wednesday. The coast-to-coast cycle route is close by. There is some bench seating outside at the front of the pub. ❀♿🍴🚍🐕🛜

Cotherstone

Red Lion ⅃
Main Street, DL12 9QE
☼ 12-3 (not Mon-Fri), 7-11; 12-4, 7-10.30 Sun
☎ (01833) 650236 ⊕ theredlionhotel.blogspot.com
3 changing beers Ⓗ
An 18th-century Grade II-listed coaching inn, built in stone and set in an idyllic village. Simply

furnished, this homely local with two open fires has changed little since the '60s. There is no TV, jukebox or one-armed bandit, just good beer and conversation. Children, dogs and clean boots are welcome. Local CAMRA Community Pub of the Year, the venue is used by various local clubs, and the small garden is a suntrap. The house beer is by Yorkshire Dales and guest beers regularly come from Mithril Ales. 🛏️❀♣🐕🛜

Crook

Horse Shoe ⅃ ✅
4 Church Street, DL15 9BG
☼ 8am-midnight ☎ (01388) 744980
Greene King Abbot; Ruddles Best Bitter; 6 changing beers Ⓗ
Formerly a pub and butcher's shop, with a nod to its previous use in the metal bar top. This Wetherspoon refurbishment has four interlinked drinking areas making up the main part of the pub, with a pleasant patio to the side. Local history is reflected in the decor, with a surprise at the top of the stairs in the shape of old mining equipment.
🛏️❀❶♿🍴🚍(1)🛜

Darlington

Britannia ⅃ ✅
1 Archer Street, DL3 6LR (next to ring road W of town centre)
☼ 12-11; 12-9 Sun ☎ (01325) 463787
Camerons Strongarm; John Smith's Bitter; 3 changing beers Ⓗ
Warm, friendly, popular local CAMRA award-winning inn – a bastion of cask beer since 1859. The comfortable, traditional pub retains much of the appearance and layout of the private house it once was, with a modestly enlarged bar and small parlour either side of a central corridor. Listed for its historic associations, it was the birthplace of teetotal 19th-century publisher JM Dent. Three guest ales, two regular ales and a real cider are available. Q🚌♣🍴🐕🛜

Darlington Snooker Club ⅃
1 Corporation Road, DL3 6AE (corner of Northgate)
☼ 12-11; 11-1am Sat; 11-11 Sun ☎ (01325) 241388
4 changing beers Ⓗ
A warm welcome is assured at this first-floor, family-run and family-oriented private snooker club which in 2015 celebrated its centenary. Four guest beers from micros countrywide are stocked. A cosy, comfortable TV lounge is available for those not playing on one of the 10 top-quality snooker tables. Twice-yearly, the club plays host to a professional celebrity, and two beer festivals are held annually. Frequently voted CAMRA Regional Club of the Year, and a finalist for National Club in 2014, it welcomes CAMRA members on production of a membership card or copy of this Guide.
🛏️❶🚌🍴

Half Moon ⅃
130 Northgate, DL1 1QS
☼ 12 (5 Wed)-11 ☎ (01325) 469965 ⊕ thecraftypint.co.uk
7 changing beers Ⓗ
Across the ring road from the town centre, this relaxed and welcoming local reopened in 2013 as a real ale pub following a long period of closure. Seven guest beers occasionally include some from the on-site Crafty Pint nano brewery as well as

micros unusual for the area. There is a choice of two ciders. The Crafty Pint bottled beer shop is also incorporated here, offering a selection of bottled beers from regional micros. ▲⌂&♣●♨︎⚲

Number Twenty 2 ℄ ⦿
22 Coniscliffe Road, DL3 7RG
☼ 12-11 (9 Mon); closed Sun ☎ (01325) 354590
⊕ villagebrewer.co.uk/our-pubs/number-twenty-2
Village Bull, Old Raby, White Boar; 10 changing beers ⊞
Town-centre ale house with a passion for cask beer and winner of many CAMRA awards. Ales are dispensed from 16 handpumps, including a stout or porter alongside two real ciders and 10 draught European beers. Huge curved windows, stained-glass panels and a high ceiling give the interior an airy, spacious feel. To the rear is the in-house nano distillery and microbrewery producing gin, vodka and fine ale. Sandwiches and snacks are available throughout the day. Home of Village Brewer beers, commissioned from Hambleton by the licensee.
Q⌂⟐&♨︎⚲

Old Vic ℄
95a Victoria Road, DL1 5JQ (200yds from Victoria Rd train station entrance)
☼ 11.30-11; 1-11 Sun ☎ 07984 574332
⊕ theoldvicdarlington.co.uk
4 changing beers ⊞
This upstairs pub, formerly the Victoria Social Club, is situated on the corner of Victoria Road and Backhouse Street – perfect for a pint on the way to or from the train station. Once you have negotiated the stairs you are welcomed by an enthusiastic landlady. Up to four real ales are on offer in a good range of styles, sourced from local breweries including Mithril – the house beer is Mithril The Quaker – and occasionally Truefit. Up to four real ciders are also available. CAMRA branch Town Cider Pub winner 2015 and 2016.
⇌♣●☷(14,14A)♨︎⚲

Old Yard Tapas Bar
98 Bondgate, DL3 7JY
☼ 11-11; 12-10.30 Sun ☎ (01325) 467385 ⊕ tapasbar.co.uk
Theakston Old Peculier; 5 changing beers ⊞
Interesting mixture of a bar and Mediterranean taverna offering real ales alongside a fascinating blend of international wines and spirits in a friendly setting. Five guest beers are sourced anywhere from local micros to brewers countrywide, with an extra two from Thursday onwards. Although this is a thriving restaurant you are more than welcome to pop in for a pint and tapas. Food is served lunchtimes and evenings Friday to Sunday and all day Saturday. The pavement café is popular in good weather. TV is for sport only. Q⌂⟐&♨︎⚲

Quakerhouse ⚲ ℄
2 Mechanics Yard, DL3 7QF (off High Row)
☼ 11-11 (midnight Fri & Sat) ☎ (01325) 245052
⊕ quakerhouse.co.uk
10 changing beers ⊞
Fifteen times local CAMRA Town Pub of the Year and North-East Pub of the Year 2015, this gem of a hostelry is located in one of the town's historic Yards. The lively bar offers 10 handpulled guest beers from local and regional breweries and three ciders. A popular music venue, it caters for all tastes from acoustic to rock, with live music every Wednesday and other nights too. Entry is free to all music events. ⌂&♣●P☷♨︎⚲

Tanners Hall ⦿
63-64 Skinnergate, DL3 7LL
☼ 8am-midnight (1am Sat) ☎ (01325) 369939
Greene King Abbot; Ruddles Best Bitter; 7 changing beers ⊞
A popular Wetherspoon town pub named after the local leather trade that dominated the town in the 18th century. Its 12 handpumps provide a good selection of real ales including up to nine guests, often from local micros. A large interior provides plenty of space for holding its own beer festivals and Meet The Brewer nights as well as the chain's national events. Reasonably priced food is served until 11pm, with a 20 per cent discount for CAMRA members. Q⌂⏾⟐●⚲

Durham

Bishop Langley ℄
Framwellgate Bridge, North Road, DH1 4PW
☼ 12-11 (midnight Fri & Sat) ☎ (0191) 386 4779
⊕ bishoplangleydurham.co.uk
Sharp's Doom Bar; 4 changing beers ⊞
This is a popular city-centre venue with a large roof terrace overlooking the River Wear and providing stunning views of the cathedral. There is a good selection of changing cask ales alongside the regular Doom Bar, and a large selection of bottled beers. The pub is open until late each evening and acoustic singers perform on Fridays or Saturdays. The food menu is excellent. ⌂⟐⟐⇌☷⚲

Colpitts Hotel
Colpitts Terrace, DH1 4EG
☼ 2 (12 Thu-Sat)-11; 12-10.30 Sun ☎ (0191) 386 9913
Samuel Smith Old Brewery Bitter ⊞
Step back in time and you will find this late-Victorian pub which has changed very little since it was first built. Like all Samuel Smith pubs, the noise comes from the chatter of conversation rather than from a jukebox or TV. The unusual A-shaped building comprises a cosy snug, a pool room and the main bar area partially divided by the fireplace. A quiz is hosted on Tuesday evenings. This is a traditional hostelry not to be missed if you appreciate pubs as they used to be. Q⌂⇌♣☷♨︎

Court Inn ℄ ⦿
Court Lane, DH1 3AW
☼ 11-11 (midnight Fri & Sat) ☎ (0191) 384 7350
⊕ courtinn.co.uk
Timothy Taylor Landlord; 5 changing beers ⊞
This is a lively pub with a decor reflecting its location near the city's Crown Courts, with exposed brickwork. Up to six real ales are on offer at any one time as well as two real ciders. A wide selection of food is served until 10.15pm daily. The pub is popular with students and prison staff, and offers a warm welcome to all visitors to the area. ⌂⟐⟐●☷(6)♨︎⚲

Duke of Wellington ℄ ⦿
Darlington Road, Neville's Cross, DH1 3QN
☼ 11 (10 Sat & Sun)-midnight ☎ (0191) 375 7651
Black Sheep Best Bitter; Brakspear Bitter; Durham White Gold; 2 changing beers ⊞
A popular roadside hostelry, frequented by diners and real ale drinkers, retaining the atmosphere of a local pub. Durham White Gold, Brakspear Bitter and Black Sheep Bitter are always available plus two guest ales. There is a cask ale club on Mondays, and quizzes are held on Monday and Wednesday

nights. It is a friendly, relaxed pub with an emphasis on classic pub food, value-for-money set menus and good beer. ৬❀◑&P⊟(7,X21)❖

Half Moon Inn ⭘ ✔

86 New Elvet, DH1 3AQ
✪ 11-11 (midnight Fri & Sat); 12-11 Sun ☎ (0191) 374 1918
⊕ thehalfmooninndurham.co.uk
Draught Bass; Durham White Gold; Greene King IPA; Timothy Taylor Landlord; 2 changing beers �H
Popular city-centre pub named after the crescent-shaped bar that runs from the front room through to the lounge area. With traditional decor throughout, it features interesting photos of the pub at the beginning of the 20th century, including many from the Miners' Gala. It has a large beer garden next to the river and is a friendly venue with a relaxed atmosphere, offering a good selection of real ales to locals and visitors to the city. ❀&⊟(6)❖❖

Head of Steam ⭘

Reform Place, DH1 4RZ (through archway from North Rd)
✪ 12-11 (midnight Fri & Sat) ☎ (0191) 383 2173
4 changing beers �H
This is a popular pub which attracts beer lovers of all ages. As well as the four changing real ales, it offers an extensive choice of bottled beers from around the world and a range of real ciders. Excellent, good-value food is prepared on the premises, and the pub often holds special tasting events featuring a wide choice of ales and ciders. During the day the pub is family-friendly, and at weekends it gets very busy. Local CAMRA Town Cider Pub of the Year runner-up 2016.
৬❀◑&≠●⊟❖

Market Tavern ⭘ ✔

27 Market Place, DH1 3NJ
✪ 11-midnight (12.30am Sat); 11-11 Sun ☎ (0191) 386 2069
5 changing beers �H
Occupying a central location in Durham's historic market place, this single-roomed, L-shaped bar offers a good selection of five local and national cask ales and one real cider. Despite recent refurbishments, the pub has managed to keep its traditional wooden ale house appearance and offers a warm welcome to locals and visitors to the city. Good food based on pub classics is served until 9.30pm and there is a quiz on Thursday evenings. ৬❀◑≠●⊟(64,204,265)❖

New Inn ⭘ ✔

29 Church Street, DH1 3DN (corner of A177 and Church St)
✪ 11-11 (midnight Sat); 12-11 Sun ☎ (0191) 384 7308
3 changing beers �H
Situated opposite the Bill Bryson University Library, this pub is popular with locals and university students alike. It is open until midnight on weekdays during term time. Darts, dominoes and shove-ha'penny are played, and all major sporting events are shown on TV. Good pub grub is served until 8pm. Look out for the jazz nights on Tuesdays, the Thursday quiz in term time and the popular annual beer festival in March. The pub offers three ales including its own New Inn Ale, brewed by Camerons. ৬❀◑&♣P⊟(6,X12)❖

Old Elm Tree ♥ ⭘

12 Crossgate, DH1 4PS
✪ 11.30-11 (midnight Fri & Sat) ☎ (0191) 386 4621

Wychwood Hobgoblin; 5 changing beers �H
This is one of Durham's oldest inns, dating back to at least 1600, and is reputed to have two ghosts. The interior comprises an L-shaped bar and a top room linked by stairs. A friendly pub, it attracts a good mix including locals, students and visitors to the city. Enjoy a wide range of excellent home-cooked food, the Wednesday quiz (arrive early), and a folk group on Mondays and Tuesdays. Local CAMRA branch Town Pub of the Year 2015 and 2016. ৬❀◑≠●P⊟❖❖

Tap & Spile ⭘

Front Street, Framwellgate Moor, DH1 5EE
✪ 12-3 (not Mon-Fri), 6-11; 12-3, 7-10.30 Sun
☎ (0191) 386 5451
8 changing beers (sourced nationally) �H
A local CAMRA award winner and runner-up in 2016, this popular drinkers' pub offers a wide range of eight varying real ales. There are two bars at one side while the other side can be partitioned into two – families are welcome in the side room until 9pm. Thursday is folk music night and Wednesday is quiz night. The atmosphere is very relaxed with a warm welcome for locals and visitors from further afield. ৬●P⊟(21)❖

Victoria Inn ★ ⭘

86 Hallgarth Street, DH1 3AS
✪ 11.45-11; 12-2, 7-10.30 Sun ☎ (0191) 386 5269
⊕ victoriainn-durhamcity.co.uk
Wylam Gold Tankard; Big Lamp Bitter; 3 changing beers �H
This Grade II-listed Victorian pub remains almost unaltered since it was built in 1899. The quaint decor, coal fires, cosy snug and genuine Victorian cash drawer help create an olde-worlde feel. Ales are mainly from local breweries and a wide selection of single malt whiskies and whiskeys is on offer. No meals are served but toasties are available. Voted local CAMRA Pub of the Year for the eighth time in 2014, it is popular with locals, students and visitors to the city.
Q৬⊭♣●⊟(6,PR2)❖❖

Woodman Inn

23 Gilesgate, DH1 1QW
✪ 12-11.30 (12.30am Fri & Sat); 12-11 Sun
☎ (0191) 680 8317 ⊕ woodmaninn.co.uk
3 changing beers �H
A traditional-style pub, refurbished in 2015, serving three real ales. It also has a great choice of spirits including gins and malt whiskies. The pub has a pool table, dartboard and various other games, and karaoke on Saturday evenings. There is a large beer garden with children's play area. Bar food is available throughout the day. A friendly family-run pub offering a warm welcome to all its visitors. ৬❀◑♣⊟(64,204,PR1)❖❖

Eaglescliffe

Cleveland Bay ⭘

718 Yarm Road, TS16 0JE (jct of A67 and A135, N of Tees bridge)
✪ 11-1am ☎ (01642) 780275 ⊕ clevelandbay.co.uk
Timothy Taylor Landlord; 3 changing beers (sourced nationally) �H
This popular locals' pub is under the stewardship of an enthusiastic licensee who has established an enviable reputation for serving a fine range of premium bitters, in oversized glasses, as well as a free Sunday lunch. The main bar, with four

handpumps, has two sports TVs. There is also a lounge and a function room where live bands play on Friday evenings. Third-pint glasses and tasting notes are available. A former CAMRA branch Community Pub of the Year.
Q❀♿⌖♣🅿🚪🚃(7,17)❀🛜

Easington

Half Moon

The Green, SR8 3AZ (at top of village green)
🟢 11-3, 5-11; 11-midnight Fri & Sat; 11.30-midnight Sun
☎ (0191) 527 0203 ⊕ halfmoonuk.com
Sharp's Doom Bar; 1 changing beer Ⓗ
A good-sized welcoming former Vaux hostelry in a prominent position at the head of the village green. Meals can be enjoyed in the bar or the restaurant lounge. Two well-kept beers are always on offer. The pub's history can be traced back to the early 19th century when it was an inn owned by the church until 1866.
🚃❀🍴♿♣🅿🚃(208)❀🛜

Eastgate

Cross Keys Ⓛ

A689, DL13 2HW
🟢 5 (12 Sat & Sun)-midnight; closed Mon winter
☎ (01388) 517234 ⊕ crosskeyseastgate.co.uk
Allendale Wagtail Best Bitter; 1 changing beer Ⓗ
Ancient building with a pleasant interior right next to the main road to Weardale. Popular with holidaymakers and locals, a restaurant provides relaxed dining while the bar is comfortable and welcoming. The ceiling is adorned with tankards and there are tables to the front of the pub. A second Allendale beer is occasionally sold.
Q🚃❀🍴♿🅰♣🚃(101)❀

Edmundbyers

Punch Bowl Ⓛ

DH8 9NL (2½ miles W of A68)
🟢 11-11; 12-10.30 Sun ☎ (01207) 255545
⊕ thepunchbowlinn.info
3 changing beers Ⓗ
In a lovely rural location close to Derwent reservoir – fishing permits can be arranged. Three handpumps dispense a wide range of local ales. The three comfortable rooms are smartly furnished with roaring log fires in the winter months. The pub has a separate room that serves as a comfortable and attractive tea room as well as a delicatessen and shop. Quiz night is Thursday.
Q🚃❀🍴♿🅿🚃(773)❀🛜

Egglescliffe

Pot & Glass Ⓛ 🏅

Church Road, TS16 9DQ (300yds E of A167, opp parish church)
🟢 12-2.30 (not Mon), 6-11; 12-2.30, 5.30-midnight Fri; 12-midnight Sat; 12-11 Sun ☎ (01642) 651009
Black Sheep Best Bitter; Caledonian Deuchars IPA; 5 changing beers (sourced nationally) Ⓗ
A previous local CAMRA branch award winner, this cosy, multi-roomed 17th-century village local is in a quiet cul-de-sac opposite the parish church. Former licensee and cabinet maker Charlie Abbey, whose last resting place overlooks the pub, fashioned the ornate bar fronts from old country furniture. Tasting notes are available for the range

of seven ales, which includes five guests. Themed food evenings complement the good-value home-cooked food. Outside is a large south-facing garden. Q🚃❀🍴♿⌖🚃♣🅿🚃(7,17)

Ferryhill Station

Surtees Arms Ⓛ 🏅

Chilton Lane, DL17 0DH
🟢 4-11; 12-midnight Sat; 12-11 Sun; closed Mon
☎ (01740) 655724 ⊕ thesurteesarms.co.uk
Yard of Ale Surtees Gold, One Foot in the Yard, Black As Owt Stout; 2 changing beers Ⓗ
Traditional pub serving locally and nationally sourced ales and ciders as well as beers from the on-site Yard of Ale Brewery (est 2008). Annual beer festivals are held in the summer and at Halloween. Live music and charity nights are regular events. Lunches are served on Sunday only. A 60-seat function room is available. A former regional CAMRA Pub of the Year and local branch Country Pub of the Year 2015.
Q🚃❀🍴♿🚃(2b,8,35A)❀🛜

Forest-in-Teesdale

Langdon Beck Hotel 🏅

DL12 0XP (on B6277, 8 miles NW of Middleton in Teesdale)
🟢 11-10.30; 12-10.30 Sun; closed Mon winter
☎ (01833) 622267 ⊕ langdonbeckhotel.com
Ringwood Best Bitter; 1 changing beer Ⓗ
Known as the Sportsman's Rest in the early 1800s, this pub is situated in the North Pennines, three miles from the spectacular High Force and Cauldron Snout waterfalls and close to the Pennine Way. The welcoming inn has long been a destination for walkers, fishermen and those seeking hospitality in scenic and peaceful surroundings, whether staying overnight or just long enough to enjoy the excellent food and drink. A beer festival is held over the late-May bank holiday weekend.
Q🚃❀🍴🍴♿🅰♣🅿❀

Frosterley

Black Bull Ⓛ

Bridge End, DL13 2SL
🟢 11-11 (5 Sun); closed Mon-Wed ☎ (01388) 527784
⊕ blackbullfrosterley.com
4 changing beers Ⓗ
A truly unique, family-run pub next to the Weardale Railway and river, with four guest ales usually from local brewers, and up to four ciders and perries. Bare boards, stone flags featuring Frosterley marble, all manner of artefacts and antique furniture create a wonderful ambience. It offers high-quality, locally sourced food, and music, plays and story-telling. The outbuilding houses a peal of bells, visited by enthusiasts from far and wide. Branch CAMRA Country Cider Pub of the Year runner-up 2015 and 2016.
Q❀🍴♿♣🚃🅿🚃(101)❀

Hamilton Row

Black Horse Ⓛ

DH7 9AU
🟢 2-11.30; 12-midnight Sat; 12-11.30 Sun
☎ (0191) 373 4576
3 changing beers Ⓗ

A friendly local with an open fire at one end and a glass-fronted fire at the other helping to create a warm, cosy atmosphere. Three well-kept real ales are available, one of which is invariably from a local brewery. Good-value Sunday lunches are served. There is a pool table. Handily situated adjacent to the Deerness Valley Way. Q✿⌂◗♣P⌷(52,725)✿♠

Hartlepool

Brewery Tap ⓛ
Stockton Street, TS24 7QY (on A689, in front of Camerons Brewery)
✪ 11-4; closed Sun ☎ (01429) 852000
⊕ cameronsbrewery.com
Camerons Strongarm; 2 changing beers (often Camerons) Ⓗ
When Camerons Brewery discovered it owned a derelict pub, the former Stranton's future was secured – it was converted into the brewery tap, now in its 13th successful year. A strengthened marketing department has resulted in there now being 16 'monthly' specials, one of which is always available, together with Strongarm and another of its regular beers – IPA or Gold Bullion. Brewery tours start from here. Meetings and conferences, evening opening and other social events, as well as superb buffets, can all be arranged.
&≈P⌷⌷(1,36)✿

Causeway ⓛ
Vicarage Gardens, Stranton, TS24 7QT (beside Camerons Brewery)
✪ 11.30-11 (11.30 Thu; midnight Fri & Sat); 11-11 Sun ☎ (01429) 273954
Banks's Bitter; Camerons Strongarm; 3 changing beers (often Marston's) Ⓗ
Marvellous multi-roomed, red-brick Victorian building, dating from 1862, and Camerons' unofficial brewery tap for more than a century. The Causeway is now owned by Marston's, though the sales of banked Strongarm remain huge and which even gets a mention in Hansard for its quality. The licensee hosts an eclectic mix of live music most evenings, while Tuesday is quiz night. Guest beers are from the Marston's stable. Good-value bar snacks are available. A CAMRA branch multi award winner. ✿&≈⌷⌷(1,36)✿

King John's Tavern ✪
1 South Road, TS26 9HD (at NW corner of market)
✪ 8am-midnight (1am Fri & Sat) ☎ (01429) 274388
7 changing beers (sourced nationally) Ⓗ
Converted from a marketplace furniture shop, this Wetherspoon outlet is named after King John who, in 1201, granted the town the right to hold markets. The pub offers the chain's nationally contracted beers and ciders, alongside locally sourced guest beers. Beer festivals, Meet the Brewer, a January sale and celebrations of saints' days are hosted. There is a large sunny patio, however, with onshore north-easterly winds, it is advisable to wrap up well, even in the middle of summer. ✿❀◗&≈⌷⌷令

Rat Race Ale House ✪
Hartlepool Railway Station, Station Approach, TS24 7ED (on Platform 1)
✪ 12.02-2.15, 4.02-8.15; 12.02-9 Sat; closed Sun & Mon ☎ 07903 479378 ⊕ ratracealehouse.co.uk
4 changing beers (sourced nationally) Ⓗ

Recent CAMRA Regional Cider Pub of the Year and branch multi award winner, the station's newsagent's is now a drinkers' paradise, with 200 beers, cider and perry, and half a dozen bottled Belgian beers served annually. Its opening/closing times coincide with the arrival/departure of the coast trains. No fizzy lager/beer, no spirits/alcopops, no TV/jukebox, no one-arm bandit, no bar! During the last eight years, more than 1,300 different beers have been served direct to the table by the licensee himself. Perfect! Q&≈♣●⌷⌷

Hartlepool Headland

Fishermans Arms ⓛ ✪
Southgate, TS24 0JJ (close to Fish Quay in Old Hartlepool)
✪ 6 (5 Sat)-midnight; 12-11 Sun ☎ 07464 953667
York Guzzler; 4 changing beers (sourced nationally) Ⓗ
The Fish, a recent local CAMRA branch Community Pub of the Year and branch multi award winner, is a typical, friendly, family-run establishment close to the Fish Quay. Now free of tie, five locally sourced beers and Westons Rosie's Pig are available, served in three third-of-a-pint tasters on request. Music nights are well supported on Friday and Saturday, while a popular quiz is held on Sunday. Two beer festivals are hosted annually.
Q●⌷⌷(7)✿令

High Hesleden

Ship Inn ⓛ
Mickle Hill Road, TS27 4QD (signed from B1281, between A19 and Blackhall)
✪ 12-3 (not Mon-Fri), 6-11; 12-9 Sun; closed Mon ☎ (01429) 836453 ⊕ theshipinn.net
7 changing beers (sourced locally) Ⓗ
Now in its 16th year of family ownership, complete satisfaction is guaranteed at this rural gem. The landlord serves seven locally sourced real beers, as well as real cider. His wife runs the superb restaurant offering top-quality food at reasonable prices, including mid-week early-doors two-course specials. Six motel-style chalets provide good-value accommodation. There are stupendous coastal views from the well-kept gardens. It is closed during the owners' annual holidays, so check before making a long journey. A recent CAMRA Regional Pub of the Year.
Q✿❀⌂◗&●P⌷(206)

Holwick

Strathmore Arms ⓛ
DL12 0NJ (just outside Middleton-in-Teesdale)
✪ 12-midnight; closed Tue ☎ (01833) 640362 ⊕ strathmoregold.co.uk
Mithril A66; Thwaites Wainwright; 3 changing beers Ⓗ
Three miles off the B6277 at Middleton-in-Teesdale, this 17th-century stone and buttressed roadside pub has a welcoming bar with a stone flag floor, beams and real fire, a separate lounge with tiled floor and pool table, and a beer garden. It offers a house beer from Mithril, four guest ales (six in summer) and six ciders. A beer festival is held at the end of July. Food is served during all sessions. Live music plays on Fridays. Four en-suite letting rooms are available. CAMRA Country Cider Pub 2016. ✿❀⌂♣●P✿令

Hunwick

Joiners Arms ⅃
13 South View, DL15 0JW
✪ 5 (12 Sat)-11; 11.30-11 Sun ☎ (01388) 605131
⊕ thejoinersarms.webnode.com
Theakston Best Bitter; 2 changing beers ⊞
Good village local with a friendly bar where you can expect proper pub talk. It also has a restaurant, small snug and covered yard/pool room. Three handpumps feature a varied selection, occasionally including cider or perry. Quality locally sourced food is offered Tuesday to Saturday evenings and Sunday lunchtimes in the restaurant. On Monday evenings it is special cheese night in the bar.
⊛⊕▶♣️P🖵(108,109)🛜

Leamside

Three Horseshoes ⅃
Pit House Lane, DH4 6QQ (about half a mile N of A690)
✪ 11-11 ☎ (0191) 584 2394
⊕ threehorseshoesleamside.co.uk
Leamside Adventure, Alexandrina, Brockwell; Timothy Taylor Landlord; 4 changing beers ⊞
A country pub with an excellent restaurant (the Back Room – booking advisable). The traditional bar has open fires in winter and a large TV for sport. The attached Leamside Brewery provides up to five real ales, with Timothy Taylor Landlord always available. The Leamside beers are named after local geographical features, with a map in the corner of the room pointing out their location. The pub is home to local cycle and clay pigeon clubs.
Q🌣⊛⊕&♣️P🐾🛜

Long Newton

Vane Arms ⅃ ✔
Darlington Road, TS21 1DB (at W end of village, close to A66 jct)
✪ 12-2 (not Mon), 5-11; 12-2, 5-midnight Fri & Sat; 12-11 Sun
☎ (01642) 580401 ⊕ thevaneatlongnewton.com
Black Sheep Best Bitter; 2 changing beers (sourced nationally) ⊞
This picturesque village inn is fast becoming the benchmark for country pubs – offering a warm welcome, real beer, real food and B&B. Its reputation for serving interesting guest beers in the bar, together with home-made, reasonably priced, top-quality restaurant meals, is now spreading far and wide. Accommodation is in four en-suite bedrooms. The sunny south-facing outdoor drinking space enhances the experience.
Q🌣⊛⊯⊕&♣️P🖵(88)🛜

Medomsley

Royal Oak ⅃
7 Manor Road, DH8 6QN
✪ 11.30-3, 5.30-11; 11-11 Sat; 12-11 Sun ☎ (01207) 560336
⊕ homeeditor.wix.com/the-royal-oak
Hadrian Border Tyneside Blonde; 2 changing beers ⊞
The Royal Oak is a traditional country-style pub which has been refurbished to create a warm, welcoming country feel. It has a large bar with a selection of seating including soft sofas and leather chairs, and plenty of dining space. Outside, there is a large, attractive garden at the back and ample parking to the front. An excellent, friendly local, it offers a rotation of quality beers as well as good food. Quiz night is Sunday. Q🌣⊛⊕&P🐾🛜

Metal Bridge

Old Mill Hotel ⅃
Thinford Road, DH6 5NX (off A1M jct 61, follow signs on A177)
✪ 12-11 (10.30 Sun) ☎ (01740) 652928
⊕ oldmilldurham.co.uk
4 changing beers ⊞
Originally built as a paper mill in 1813, this spacious inn is now the venue of choice for discerning locals and visitors alike. It offers good-quality food and well-kept ales – four handpumps serve a diverse range, with the nearby Durham Brewery often supplying one of the beers. The food menu is extensive, with daily specials written on a board above the bar. Larger groups are welcome in the conservatory. Accommodation is of a high standard, with all rooms en-suite. Q🌣⊯⊕P

Middlestone

Ship Inn ⅃
Low Road, DL14 8AB (between Coundon and Kirk Merrington)
✪ 4-11.30 (10 Tue); 12-11.30 Fri & Sat; 12-10 Sun
☎ (01388) 810904
6 changing beers ⊞
Regular drinkers come from far and wide to the Ship. It has a bar room divided into three areas with an open fire, and a large function room upstairs which is the location for twice-yearly beer festivals. The rooftop patio has spectacular views, and there is always an event either in the offing or taking place. Various pieces of Vaux memorabilia are on display. Sunday lunches are popular. Local CAMRA Country Pub winner 2014.
Q🌣⊛⊕&♣️P🐾

Middleton-in-Teesdale

Cafe 1618
16 Market Place, DL12 0QG
✪ 11-midnight; closed Mon ☎ (01833) 640300
⊕ cafe1618.com
2 changing beers ⊞
Cafe 1618 is in the marketplace in this small Dales town in the North Pennines countryside. The area, one of natural beauty, attracts walkers, cyclists and many bikers. The bistro/restaurant serves visitors and locals with a wide range of freshly cooked local food, which can also be enjoyed at street tables or in the extensive beer garden. Two beers come from near and far, and beer festivals feature on the May and August bank holidays and Carnival (first weekend in August). A Northumberland in Bloom winner. 🌣⊛⊯⊕&🖵(95)🐾🛜

Newfield

Newfield Inn ⅃
Front Street, DH2 2SP
✪ 4 (12 Sat & Sun)-11.30 ☎ (0191) 370 0565
Maxim Ward's Best Bitter; 2 changing beers ⊞
A friendly two-roomed pub in the centre of the village, known locally simply as the Inn, now owned by Maxim Brewery from nearby Houghton-le-Spring, with two of its beers and a guest on the bar. The pub offers accommodation, fortnightly live music entertainment, quiz nights and televised football. Families are welcome and there is a pleasant beer garden. Occasional beer festivals are held here. 🌣⊯&♣️P🖵(78)

Newton Aycliffe

Turbinia
Parsons Centre, Sid Chaplin Drive, DL5 7PA
☼ 12.30-midnight (1am Fri & Sat) ☎ (01325) 313034
⊕ turbiniapub.co.uk
4 changing beers Ⓗ
Named after the famous Tyneside ship, this
friendly free house comprises a large lounge and
function room with traditional pub decor, featuring
a pictorial history of the Turbinia ship throughout.
This local favourite serves a rotating variety of light
and dark beers sourced locally and nationally. It
hosts its own beer and cider festival twice yearly.
In the main bar, darts, dominoes and pool can be
found during the week and live music at the
weekend. ⭑&♣P☐(7)❤♠

No Place

Beamish Mary Inn Ⓛ
DH9 0QH (follow signs to No Place off A693 from
Chester-le-Street to Stanley)
☼ 12-11 (10.30 Sun) ☎ (0191) 370 0237
⊕ beamishmaryinn.co.uk
**Big Lamp Sunny Daze, Lamplight Bitter; Consett White
Hot, Red Dust; 5 changing beers** Ⓗ
This pub, full of character, is widely respected for
its warm welcome, generously portioned pub grub
and ample choices of well-kept real ale.
Accommodation is available including twin, double
and family rooms. The location is handy for visitors
to the nearby world-renowned Beamish Open Air
Museum. Owned by the owner of the Consett Ale
Works, its beers are now included among the range
of LocAles available. Q⭑&❤●Ⓓ&P☐(8,78)❤♠

Norton

George & Dragon
109 High Street, TS20 1AA (80yds S of duck pond)
☼ 3-11; 12-midnight Fri & Sat; 12-11 Sun ☎ (01642) 554150
**Jennings Sneck Lifter; 2 changing beers (sourced
nationally)** Ⓗ
Traditional, ornate and unobtrusive, this three-
roomed locals' pub has been described as 'how
pubs used to be and how pubs ought to be'. It
comprises a bar, where locals sit on leather
benches and muse over wise quotations and
photographs of yesteryear, together with two
lounges, a pool room and a sheltered outdoor
drinking/smoking area. The three ales are always
stronger premium bitters and include a dark beer,
all chosen by the regulars themselves. Recent
CAMRA branch Community Pub of the Year.
⭑&♣☐(35,37)♠

Unicorn
147 High Street, TS20 1AA (next to duck pond at N end
of village)
☼ 12-11 (midnight Fri & Sat) ☎ (01642) 643364
3 changing beers (sourced nationally) Ⓗ
A warm welcome is assured from the enthusiastic
licensee and friendly bar staff at this unspoilt three-
roomed local, comprising a bar, front and back
lounges, and a sheltered outdoor area. The 'top
house' is the last of four traditional pubs that were
dotted around The Green. The pub is also still
known affectionately by some as Nellie's, a
popular long-standing barmaid and daughter of a
previous licensee, sadly both long-since departed.
The beers come from Enterprise's list.
Q⭑&❤☐(35,37)❤♠

Old Shotton

Royal George Ⓛ
The Village, SR8 2ND
☼ 11-11 (midnight Fri & Sat); 11-10.30 Sun
☎ (0191) 586 6500 ⊕ royalgeorgeoldshotton.co.uk
**Leamside Adventure, Alexandrina; Timothy Taylor
Landlord; 2 changing beers** Ⓗ
Pub and restaurant situated on the old village
green reopened after a major refurbishment of a
virtually derelict establishment in 2014. The bar
has been reinstated as well as a larger lounge and
restaurant area. Owned by the Leamside Ale
Company, at least two of its beers are on
handpump. Traditional pub grub and bar snacks are
available. Q⭑&●Ⓓ P❤♠

Piercebridge

Fox Hole Ⓛ
Carlbury, DL2 3SJ (on B6275)
☼ 11-11; 12-10.30 Sun ☎ (01325) 374286
⊕ the-foxhole.co.uk
3 changing beers Ⓗ
Set in this Roman village, the Fox Hole sits almost
centrally between the towns of Darlington, Barnard
Castle, Bishop Auckland and Richmond. From the
welcoming Wellie bar through to the relaxed yet
elegant dining room and alfresco dining terrace,
the emphasis is on high-quality, carefully locally
sourced food and drink, combined with traditional
pub values. A warm welcome and friendly service,
along with three beers from local micros, including
Mithril three miles away, make this pub a must-
visit. ❤●Ⓓ&P☐(75,76)❤♠

Sadberge

Buck Inn Ⓛ
Middleton Road, DL2 1RR
☼ 12-11 (10 Sun winter) ☎ (01325) 335307
⊕ thebuckinnsadberge.co.uk
3 changing beers Ⓗ
Friendly traditional English pub overlooking the
village green in an attractive village setting, named
after George Buck, a benevolent 18th-century
landowner. It has two bars, one mainly for dining.
There is a beer garden at the rear (with an outside
bar in summer) and benches and tables in front. A
supporter of local micros, it usually has two beers
from Sonnet 43 and one other, often from Mithril,
George Samuel or Pennine. A variety of good food
is served lunchtimes and evenings. The village sits
atop a hill and is in a popular walking area.
❤●Ⓓ P☐(20)♠

St John's Chapel

Blue Bell Inn Ⓛ ✓
Hood Street, DL13 1QJ
☼ 5 (12 Sat & Sun)-1am ☎ (01388) 537256
2 changing beers Ⓗ
Originally a pair of terraced cottages, the Blue Bell
is a friendly and cosy pub with a bar across the
front of the building leading to a small pool room,
and a garden to the rear. Situated right on the
A689, it serves the local community and those who
holiday in Upper Weardale. Pub games are popular
and there are plenty of books to choose from.
Q⭑&❤♣☐(101)♠

Seaham

Crow's Nest ✪

Featherbed, East Shore Village, North Road, SR7 7XR

✪ 11.30-11; 9am-11 Sat; 9am-10.30 Sun ☎ (0191) 581 4927
⊕ crowsnestpub.co.uk

Banks's Bitter; Marston's Pedigree; Wychwood Hobgoblin; 3 changing beers Ⓗ

A light and airy pub from the Marston's group with an excellent position on Seaham seafront at the head of East Shore Village. The site was originally part of Vane Tempest pit. The pub reopened in 2013 after major refurbishment, with six handpumps. A cask platter can be ordered with three one-third pints. It offers an extensive menu including a weekend carvery and opens at 9am at weekends for breakfast (no alcohol sold until 11am). ⤳❀⊕♪⅄♣P🖿(202,238)🛜

Seaton

Dun Cow 🍸 Ⓛ

The Village, SR7 0NA

✪ 4 (5 winter)-midnight; 12-midnight Fri-Sun
☎ (0191) 513 1133

4 changing beers Ⓗ

Excellent, friendly, unspoilt inn on the village green comprising public bar and lounge areas. A pub for good conversation or a game of darts, the TV is only turned on for special events. No meals are served but toasties are always available. The guest beer selection changes but usually comprises two light and two dark beers to satisfy all tastes. Regular busker and acoustic music nights feature. CAMRA branch Country Pub of the Year 2016. ⤳❀⅄♣P🖿(238)🐾

Sedgefield

Dun Cow Ⓛ

43 Front Street, TS21 3AT

✪ 11-3, 6-11; 11-11 Sat; 12-10.30 Sun ☎ (01740) 620894
⊕ duncowinn.co.uk

Black Sheep Best Bitter; Theakston Best Bitter; 2 changing beers Ⓗ

Run by the same landlord for 40 years, this large and comfortable 18th-century inn has an excellent county-wide reputation for good food using locally sourced produce as much as possible. It was the scene of a historic George Bush and Tony Blair lunch in 2003. There are three bars including a farmers' bar-cum-snug and restaurant. Four real ales are always available including at least one local beer. Q⤳❀🚍⊕P🖿

South Church

Red Alligator

Auckland Road, DL14 6SP

✪ 12-2.30, 5.30-10.30 (11.30 Sat); 11.30-3 Sun
☎ (01388) 605644

2 changing beers Ⓗ

A mile from the centre of Bishop Auckland, and in the shadow of St Andrew's Church, this smart local has a bright feel and a good reputation for food. There is a spacious L-shaped bar across the front and a small dining room/snug to the rear. The eponymous Grand National winner was trained just across the road. Two beers are generally on offer. Q⊕⅄P🖿(1,5)

Spennymoor

Grand Electric Hall Ⓛ ✪

Cheapside, DL16 6DJ

✪ 8am-midnight (1am Fri & Sat) ☎ (01388) 825470

Greene King Abbot; Ruddles Best Bitter; 6 changing beers Ⓗ

Formerly a cinema and bingo hall, this is a bright, spacious Wetherspoon conversion, with film-themed decor and fittings. The main area is high-ceilinged, and there is a smaller room on a lower level. It is in the centre of town and boasts a large patio drinking area to the front which can be quite a suntrap in the summer months. Alcohol is served from 9am. ⤳❀⊕⅄P🖿(6,21)🛜

Stanhope

Bonny Moorhen

Market Place, DL13 2TS

✪ 11-11.30 ☎ (01388) 528214
⊕ thebonnymoorhenstanhope.co.uk

4 changing beers Ⓗ

Busy pub next to the church in the marketplace, with a lively bar that has a pool table, a separate lounge, and beer garden to the rear. Convenient for the coast-to-coast cycleway, it is popular with locals and holidaymakers – families and dogs are welcome. TVs screen sport and there is live music at weekends plus occasional beer festivals. ⤳❀🚍⊕♣🖿(101)🐾

Stockton-on-Tees

Golden Smog 🍸

1 Hambletonian Yard, TS18 1DS (in a ginnel between High St and West Row)

✪ 2-10 ☎ (01642) 385022

4 changing beers (sourced nationally) Ⓗ

The town's first micropub is located in a narrow ginnel leading west off the main road, and named after the environmental conditions that recently prevailed on Teesside. Four real beers and two real ciders (or one cider/one perry) are served alongside a hugely impressive range of Belgian beers, some familiar, most not so familiar, served in matching glasses in the continental way. Third-of-a-pint glasses and tasting tables are available. Local CAMRA Pub of the Year 2016. Q⇌(Stockton/Thornaby)🍴🖿🐾

Sun Inn ✪

2 Knowles Street, TS18 1SU (off High St in centre of town)

✪ 11-11; 12-10.30 Sun ☎ (01642) 611461

Draught Bass Ⓗ

This popular traditional town-centre drinkers' pub is reputed to sell more banked Draught Bass than any other pub in the country – a gallon of Bass is pulled for each pint of lager. The pub supports darts, football teams and various charitable causes. At weekends, R&B bands feature in the back lounge, while on Mondays it has hosted the famous Stockton Folk Club for the last 46 years. The clock in the bar deliberately runs fast. ❀⇌(Stockton/Thornaby)🍴🖿🐾

Tanfield Lea

Tanfield Lea Working Men's Club Ⓛ

West Street, DH9 9NA

✪ 2-4, 7-11; 12-11.30 Fri & Sat; 12-2, 7-11 Sun
☎ (01207) 238783
2 changing beers Ⓗ
The village has no pub, reflecting its strong Methodist history, but guests are most welcome in this CIU-affiliated club, which has become something of a flagship for real ale in the area after a diet of keg beer for many years. TV sport is shown in the bar and there is a comfortable quiet lounge. Traditional club activities such as bingo take place and there is usually a live act on Sundays when nibbles are provided on the bar. Local CAMRA Club of the Year 2016. Ⓢ&♣P🚪(706,707)🛜

West Cornforth

Square & Compass Ⓛ

7 The Green, DL17 9JQ (off Coxhoe-W Cornforth rd)
✪ 7 (5 Fri; 11.30 Sat & Sun)-midnight ☎ (01740) 653050
3 changing beers Ⓗ
A proper drinking pub and friendly local on the village green in the old part of Doggy (the village's local nickname). It has sold real ale for over 30 years and always offers at least one local beer among its three guests. It hosts darts, dominoes and chess clubs. The pub has good views over to Wear Valley and Durham City. Q🟢🌭♣P🚪(56)🐾

Westgate

Hare & Hounds Ⓛ

24 Front Street, DL13 1RX
✪ 6.30 (5.30 Fri; 3 Sat)-11; 12-3, 6.30-9.30 Sun; closed Mon
☎ (01388) 517212
🌐 hareandhoundswestgate.blogspot.co.uk
Weard'ALE Challenger, Gold, Fell Over, Dark Nights, Chilled Nights; 1 changing beer Ⓗ
Situated on the main road up Weardale, with the river at the bottom of the garden. The spacious stone-flagged bar is partially fitted out with furniture and other items salvaged from the former village chapel, and the restaurant has a patio overlooking the Wear. Catch up on the local news over a pint brewed only a few feet below you, while watching the pub's poultry in the rear garden. Food, including the famous Sunday carvery, is locally sourced. Local CAMRA Country Pub of the Year runner-up in 2015.
Q🟢🌭🌙&▲♣P🚪(101)

Whorlton

Fernaville's Rest Ⓛ

The Green, DL12 8XD (1 mile S of A67)
✪ 12-10 (11 Fri & Sat); 12-5 Sun ☎ (01833) 627341
🌐 fernavilles.com
Mithril Flower Power; Timothy Taylor Landlord; 3 changing beers Ⓗ
Grade II-listed country inn in Teesdale that retains its traditional features and charm. Set in a quintessential English village surrounded by

riverside walks, it is a welcome stop for ramblers. Whether you are treating yourself to a break, sampling some of the country fare or simply popping in to try the excellent cask ales, you will be warmly welcomed and looked after. The house beer, Fernaville's Best, is from Mithril. Stay in the pub in three rooms. ⓈⓈ🌭🍴🌙♣P🐾🛜

Witton Gilbert

Travellers Rest ✓

Front Street, DH7 6TQ (off A691 bypass 3 miles from city centre)
✪ 12-11 ☎ (0191) 371 0458
🌐 travellersrest-wittongilbert.co.uk
Theakston Best Bitter; 3 changing beers Ⓗ
A bright open-plan pub completely refurbished in 2014 and popular with diners. The bar area is divided into three sections with a conservatory off to the side which can be booked for private functions. Four handpulled beers are on tap including changing guest beers. The pub is family-friendly, with a dedicated children's menu.
QⓈ🌭🍴&P

Witton-le-Wear

Dun Cow

19 High Street, DL14 0AY
✪ 6 (1 Sat)-11; 12-11 Sun ☎ (01388) 488294
3 changing beers Ⓗ
Dating from 1799, this comfortable and welcoming pub is set back from the road through the village. The single room has an open fire at both ends, one guarded by a sleeping fox who always seems to have just closed his eyes, and the other by an impressive set of horns. There are benches to the left of the bar, and seating outside offering pleasant views. The decor is completed by some interesting football memorabilia. Q🌭♣P

Wolsingham

Black Lion Ⓛ

21 Meadhope Street, DL13 3EN (50yds N of marketplace)
✪ 6.30 (6 Fri; 12 Sat)-11; 12-10.30 Sun ☎ (01388) 527772
4 changing beers Ⓗ
Hidden away a minute from the Market Place, this is a friendly, comfortable gem. An open fire features in the single open-plan room, with a pool table to the rear and a bar with TV sport to the front. Regular beer festivals are held in the suntrap garden at the rear, and local charities benefit from the efforts of the pub. Six or more ciders can be on offer. Local CAMRA Country Cider Pub of the Year 2014-2016. Q🌭&🍺🚪(101)🐾🛜

A quart a day keeps the doctor away

A judicious labourer would probably always have some ale in his house, and have small beer for the general drink. There is no reason why he should not keep Christmas as well as the farmer; and when he is mowing, reaping, or is at any other hard work, a quart, or three pints, of really good fat ale a-day is by no means too much.

William Cobbett, Cottage Economy, 1822

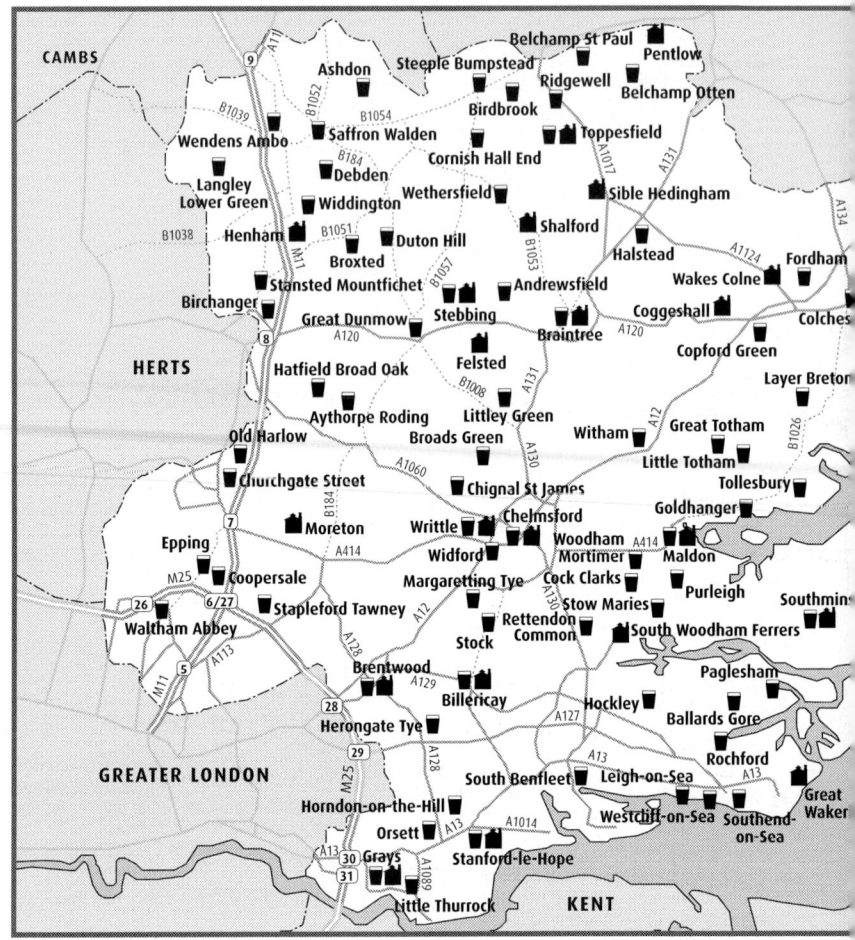

Andrewsfield Airfield

Milli-bar 🄻
Saling Road, CM6 3TH (accessed by track beside runway, near Stebbing Green) TL689248
🕘 8.30am-9 ☎ (01371) 981900 🌐 andrewsfield.com/bar
Bishop Nick Ridley's Rite 🄷

Local private pilots' airfield with a small grass strip and clubhouse. Also a flying school, it offers trial lessons up to a commercial pilot's licence, and is dominated by single-engined Cessna aircraft, a Mustang III and B17 Meteor IIIs. The bar manager is keen on local supply and has installed Ridley's Rite from Bishop Nick Brewery as his sole ale. There is also a range of bottled beers from Bishop Nick. The public are welcome in the café/bar. Q⊱🄲P🐾📶

Ashdon

Rose & Crown
Crown Hill, CB10 2HA
🕘 12-2.30, 5.30 (5 Fri)-11; 12-11 Sat; 12-7 Sun; closed Mon
☎ (01799) 584337
Woodforde's Wherry; 4 changing beers (sourced nationally) 🄷

The last remaining pub in this village, where there were once six. It has an unusual layout and a room named after Oliver Cromwell, where he is reputed to have kept prisoners, who illustrated the walls with their feelings at the time. These are now hidden behind removable panels. Guest beers often come from Nethergate and Lacons. ⊱🏠🄲P🐾

Aythorpe Roding

Axe & Compasses 🄻
Dunmow Road, CM6 1PP (on B1845) TL594154
🕘 9am-11 (midnight Sat) ☎ (01279) 876648
🌐 theaxeandcompasses.co.uk
Adnams Broadside; Sharp's Doom Bar 🄷; 3 changing beers (sourced regionally) 🄶

Surrounded by beautiful countryside, the Axe is an 18th-century building. While drinkers are welcome, it has won awards for being the best Essex pub-restaurant. A mixed clientele of locals and farming folk enjoys the selection of beers and ciders. The food menu offers pub classics with a modern twist, all locally sourced, and the service is efficient and friendly. The pub hosts quizzes and food-themed nights. Q🏠🄲🏠P🚌(17,18)🐾📶

Ballards Gore

Shepherd & Dog
Gore Road, Stambridge, SS4 2DA

nningtree
Great Bromley
Wix
Harwich
Wivenhoe
Rowhedge
Kirkby-le-Soken
Weeley Heath
Brightlingsea
Great Clacton
Clacton-on-Sea
East
ersea

0 Miles 10
0 Kilometres 16

evenings and to take away too (no food Mon and Tue). There are excellent views, good walks and cycle rides from here. This pub often runs brewery-based festivals where most of the chosen brewery's ales will be available together.
Q ⚫ ☸ ◑ ♣ ⬤ P ✿ 📶

Belchamp St Paul

Half Moon ⊘

Cole Green, CO10 7DP TL792423
⚙ 12-3, 6-11; 12-11 Sat & Sun ☎ (01787) 277402
⊕ halfmoonbelchamp.co.uk
Greene King IPA; 2 changing beers (sourced nationally) Ⓗ
Beautiful and friendly thatched rural pub, dating from about 1685, opposite the village green. Three beers are available and guest beers change regularly. The place is popular with locals and has an excellent choice of bar and restaurant meals (no food Sun eves or Mon). In the past the pub provided one of the locations for the first Lovejoy TV series. Outside there is a separate smoking area.
Q ⚫ ☸ ◑ P 📶

Billericay

Billericay Brewing Co Shop & Micropub

52 Chapel Street, CM12 9LS
⚙ 10-9 (5 Tue & Wed); closed Sun & Mon ☎ (01277) 500121
⊕ billericaybrewing.co.uk
Billericay Zeppelin, Blonde, Dickie; 3 changing beers (sourced locally; often Billericay) Ⓖ
Brewery tap micropub next door to the Billericay Brewery, which can be viewed while drinking. It serves up to six ales, five from Billericay, with usually one gold, amber, dark and strong ale served on gravity. There are seasonal extensions to the opening hours. The micropub is also a beer shop where bottle-conditioned ales from Billericay,

⚙ 12-11; 12-10.30 Sun ☎ (01702) 258658
⊕ sdpub.wordpress.com
4 changing beers (sourced locally; often George's) Ⓗ
Following 15 months' closure, the Shepherd & Dog reopened in early 2015 with new owners. It is a traditional country pub, L-shaped, with oak beams throughout and a real fire. The bar at the front serves four changing real ales, with two from the local George's Brewery, and a range of real ciders. Towards the back is the restaurant serving home-cooked food made with local produce. There is seating outside at the front and a beer garden to the rear. ☸ ☸ ◑ ⬤ P 🚪 (60) ✿

Belchamp Otten

Red Lion Ⓛ

Fowes Lane, CO10 7BQ (on very small single track lane, signed by duckpond) TL799415
⚙ 12-3, 5.30-11 Mon, Wed & Thu; 12-11 Fri & Sat; 12-6 Sun; closed Tue ☎ (01787) 278301 ⊕ ottenredlion.co.uk
Adnams Southwold Bitter; 3 changing beers (sourced nationally) Ⓗ
Lovely local hostelry, hidden away in the smallest of the Belchamps. The owners provide a warm welcome, with an open fire in winter. The pub has darts and runs occasional events. Wholesome home-cooked food is served at lunchtimes,

Essex and London breweries are on sale, plus foreign beers. Beer festivals are held in March, autumn and at Christmas.
Q🍴🐕✿♿♣🅿🚃(100,222)👹

Coach & Horses Ⓛ
36 Chapel Street, CM12 9LU
✪ 11-11; 10-11 Sat; 12-10 Sun ☎ (01277) 622873
⊕ thecoachandhorses.org
Sharp's Doom Bar; Skinner's Betty Stogs; Wibblers Dengie IPA; 2 changing beers (sourced nationally) Ⓗ
Close to the high street, this welcoming one-bar pub with an inviting atmosphere is now in its 20th consecutive year in the Guide. Two guest beers from the Gray's portfolio change weekly, along with three regular ales. Good-quality home-made food is available lunchtimes and evenings, with curry night on Wednesday. The walls are adorned with prints and decorative plates, and a collection of jugs and tankards hangs from the ceiling. It has BT Sport for rugby and football matches.
Q✿⬤♿✈♣🅿🚃(100)👹🐈📶

Railway
1 High Street, CM12 9BE
✪ 12-11 (midnight Fri & Sat) ☎ (01277) 652173
Greene King IPA; Woodforde's Wherry; 3 changing beers (sourced nationally) Ⓗ
Friendly, old-fashioned pub with a welcoming atmosphere and the tag line 'No.1 in the High Street' (see address above). The guest beers are updated regularly on Facebook. Live music features twice a month and on bank holidays, and charity events are held in this community-oriented pub which has three darts teams and sponsors a local rugby team. It has traditional bar games including shove-ha'penny with real ha'pennies. Outside is a small beer garden. 🐕✿♿✈♣🅿🚃👹📶

Birchanger

Birchanger Sports & Social Club
229 Birchanger Lane, CM23 5QJ
✪ 7-11 Mon, Tue & Thu; 11.30-2.30, 6-11 Wed; 11.30-11 Fri & Sat; 12-10.30 Sun ☎ (01279) 813441 ⊕ birchangerclub.com
3 changing beers (sourced nationally) Ⓗ
A friendly local social club, where it is possible for CAMRA members to drink as guests. Many matches and events are held here, so the club can get busy. It was the local CAMRA Club of the Year 2014 and 2015 and East Anglian Club of the Year 2014 and 2015. Beers change frequently as the turnover is high. The club has football, cricket, bowls, darts, crib and snooker teams, regular quizzes, bingo and bottle draws. 🐕✿⬤♿♣⬤🅿🚃(7,7A)👹

Birdbrook

Plough Ⓛ
The Street, CO9 4BJ
✪ 5-11; 4-midnight Fri; 12-midnight Sat; 12-10.30 Sun
☎ (01440) 788066
Greene King IPA; 2 changing beers (sourced locally) Ⓗ
Low-ceilinged inn that is the central focus of the village. It has been divided into three rooms: a games room, the bar area and a restaurant. The owners have extended the building, adding new toilets at the back that replaced the outside loos. The roof has been re-thatched and the pub has been restored into a flourishing, successful business. ✿⬤♣🅿🐈📶

Braintree

King William IV Ⓛ
114 London Road, CM77 7PU
✪ 3-11; 12-midnight Fri-Sun ☎ (01376) 567755
⊕ kingwilliamiv.co.uk
4 changing beers (sourced nationally) Ⓖ
Warm and friendly free house serving a changing range of four to five real ales, usually featuring Essex microbreweries and at least one from the Moody Goose Brewery, located in the grounds of the pub. It also serves an interesting selection of three or four ciders. There is a main bar and a small back bar with a dartboard. A large patio area and extensive gardens are used to host beer festivals and other events. Q✿♣⬤🅿🚃(70,352)👹📶

Brentwood

Rising Sun Ⓛ ✅
144 Ongar Road, CM15 9DJ (on A178, at Western Rd jct)
✪ 3-11.30 (midnight Fri); 12-midnight Sat; 12-10.30 Sun ☎ 07828 738549 ⊕ rising-sun-brentwood.co.uk
Fuller's London Pride; Sharp's Cornish Coaster; Timothy Taylor Landlord; 2 changing beers Ⓗ
A brilliant little locals' pub just out of the town centre, with a landlord who is a real ale lover and a CAMRA member. The pub has a good beer selection, with five handpumps in the saloon bar dispensing three regular ales plus one or two beers from Brentwood Brewery and sometimes a guest beer from anywhere. There are three dartboards, a chess club, and quiz nights are held regularly. 🐕✿♿♣🅿🚃(21,71,72)👹

Spread Eagle
88 Queens Road, CM14 4HD
✪ 11-11 (midnight Fri & Sat) ☎ (01277) 232485
⊕ spreadeaglebrentwood.co.uk
Adnams Broadside Ⓗ**; Draught Bass** Ⓖ**; Sharp's Doom Bar** Ⓗ
Much-improved and refurbished, this wedge-shaped community pub has a strong focus on real ale. Southern States pit-barbecue-style food is served; the pub has a food smoker. Live music features open mic on Sunday evenings and acoustic bands. Events include charity rock and roll bingo and Elvis nights. There is a courtyard patio. 🐕✿⬤♿⊖♣⬤(498)👹📶

Brightlingsea

Railway Tavern Ⓛ
58 Station Road, CO7 0DT
✪ 4 (5 winter)-10; 12-11 Fri & Sat; 12-3, 7-10.30 Sun
Crouch Vale Essex Boys Best Bitter; 2 changing beers (sourced regionally) Ⓗ
The Railway Tavern is a basic but friendly brewpub in an historic Cinque Port town. It always has real cider and often has beers from its own brewery (dark and vegetarian). It was one of the first pubs in the area to hold a regular cider festival (the first weekend in May). Music events are staged throughout the year, frequently featuring local bands, including the pub's own group, The Railwailers. Children are not allowed.
Q⬤🚃(78,79,87)

Broads Green

Walnut Tree L ✓

CM3 1DT (turn off B1008 at Ash Tree corner, signposted Great Waltham; after ¼ mile turn left into Larks Lane and continue for ¾ mile) TL694125

☼ 12-11 ☎ (01245) 360222

Adnams Southwold Bitter; Timothy Taylor Landlord; 1 changing beer (sourced locally) Ⓖ

Handsome Victorian pub overlooking the green. The front door opens into what was the bottle and jug, now a small snug. To the left is the wood-panelled public bar, little changed since 1888. To the right is the more modern saloon bar. Outside is seating in front of the pub, a children's play area and a large garden. There is no food, the landlord preferring to focus on his beers and maintain a traditional atmosphere. Q➼❄♠♣♠P♠🐾 🗢

Broxted

Prince of Wales L ✓

Brick End, CM6 2BJ

☼ 11.30-11 (midnight Fri & Sat); 12-11 Sun; closed Mon ☎ (01279) 850256 ⊕ princeofwalesbroxted.co.uk

Greene King IPA; 5 changing beers (sourced nationally) Ⓗ

Former Charrington's pub that has been transformed into a welcoming community venue since the current landlords took over in late 2011. It has a comfortable split-level bar, an adjoining room with two woodburners and a conservatory seating up to 50. Generously portioned pub food, mostly locally sourced, will satisfy the most demanding appetite. A small garden is to the rear. Up to five guest beers are available, with LocAle from Bishop Nick. Local CAMRA Pub of the Year 2014. ➼❄◑P🖨(5)🐾 🗢

Chelmsford

Ale House L

24-26 Viaduct Road, CM1 1TS

☼ 11-11 (midnight Fri & Sat); 12-10.30 Sun ☎ (01245) 260535 ⊕ the-ale-house-chelmsford.co.uk

12 changing beers (sourced nationally) Ⓗ

In the style of a continental ale house, this pub is in three railway arches beneath Chelmsford station. There are 12 real ales, with the continuously changing range always including dark and stronger beers, and 12 real ciders. There are also imported German lagers on tap and a wide range of bottled beers from around the world. No food is served but customers are welcome to bring their own. Mini beer festivals are held often. ♿≢♠🖨 🗢

Endeavour L

351 Springfield Road, CM2 6AW

☼ 11-11; 12-11 Sun ☎ (01245) 257717

Adnams Southwold Bitter; Mighty Oak Maldon Gold; Skinner's Betty Stogs; Wibblers Dengie IPA; 2 changing beers (sourced nationally) Ⓗ

Busy and friendly pub with three rooms, one used for early evening dining on Friday (fish night) and Saturday (steak night); bookings are required for these and Sunday lunch. There are no evening meals on other days. All food is locally sourced and home cooked. Mainly light meals are available at lunchtimes, with sandwiches served at all times. A true community pub with a darts team, weekly poker nights and charity events. The pub also shows BT Sport. ➼◑♣♠🖨(54,71c)🐾 🗢

Hop Beer Shop ♥ L

173 Moulsham Street, CM2 0LD

☼ 12-9; closed Sun & Mon ☎ (01245) 353570 ⊕ thehopbeershop.co.uk

4 changing beers (sourced nationally) Ⓖ

Essex's first micropub, with the atmosphere of a traditional pub where people can meet and talk. Four or five beers are served by gravity, always including local brews as well as interesting beers from around the country, often a stout or porter and a golden beer. In addition, there are around 100 bottled beers from local and international breweries, which may be drunk here or purchased to take home. You can also buy draught cider, wine or soft drinks. CAMRA branch Pub of the Year 2016. Q♠🖨(42,100,351)

Orange Tree L

Lower Anchor Street, CM2 0AS

☼ 12-11 (11.30 Fri & Sat) ☎ (01245) 262664 ⊕ the-ot.com

Dark Star Hophead; Harveys Sussex Best Bitter; Mighty Oak Oscar Wilde; Plain Sheep Dip; Skinner's Betty Stogs; 3 changing beers (sourced nationally) Ⓗ

The Orange Tree is one of the best real ale pubs in Chelmsford and was voted local CAMRA Pub of the Year 2014 and 2015. It is a place for conversation and meeting friends. A refurbishment in 2015 has made the separate public and saloon bars both much larger. If rugby is your sport, this is the pub for you, as the landlord loves the game. Lunchtime food is served including Sunday roasts, plus a steak and curry night on Thursday evening. Q➼❄◑♿♠P🖨(42,100,351)🐾 🗢

Railway Tavern L

63 Duke Street, CM1 1LW

☼ 10-11 (11.30 Fri & Sat); 12-6 Sun ☎ (01245) 280679

Adnams Broadside; Greene King Abbot; Red Fox IPA; Woodforde's Wherry; 4 changing beers (sourced nationally) Ⓗ

A Tardis-like corner pub right outside Chelmsford station, more visible now due to nearby development. Not surprisingly, a railway theme dominates. It is long and narrow, with banks of handpumps at opposite ends of the central bar counter and seating towards the rear, laid out like a railway carriage. There is even a small garden where you can listen to the station announcements and marvel at the ever-changing mural. Meet the Brewer events take place on the first Wednesday of alternate months. ❄◑≢♣♠🖨🐾🐾

Ship ✓

18 Broomfield Road, CM1 1SW

☼ 10-11 (1am Fri & Sat); 12-11 Sun ☎ (01245) 265961 ⊕ theshipchelmsford.co.uk

Greene King IPA, Abbot; 4 changing beers (sourced nationally) Ⓗ

Traditional medium-sized pub with a comfortable interior and some outside seating in front. The decor is nautical, with dark brown panelling, portholes, masts, rope, rigging and other maritime artefacts. It is close to the rail and bus stations and has a public car park at the rear. A wide range of food is offered with daily specials. There is a jukebox but no live music on a regular basis. Sport is shown on the TV. 🛏◑≢🖨 🗢

Thomas Mildmay L ✓

7 Grays Brewery Yard, CM2 6QR

☼ 8am-midnight (2am Fri & Sat) ☎ (01245) 293700

5 changing beers (sourced nationally) Ⓗ

Modern, family-friendly Lloyds No.1 bar with music in a pedestrianised area of the city centre. It is named after the Sheriff of Essex of 1557 who had manors at Moulsham and Bishops Hall in Chelmsford. It is ideal for those who are shopping or indeed escaping shopping. An upstairs room provides additional seating and can be reserved. You will find the regular Wetherspoon food offering, plus its beer and cider festivals. ♿🛇♿🌿➡️🚌(54,71c)🛜

Chignal St James

Three Elms 🍺

CM1 4TZ
🕛 12-3, 6-11 Mon, Wed & Thu; 5-11 Tue; 12-midnight Fri-Sun ☎ (01245) 443151 ⊕ the-three-elms.com
4 changing beers (sourced regionally) Ⓗ
Traditional single room village pub with a piano in one corner and open fires at each end. TV, darts and bar billiards are tucked away in a small annexe. Outside, there is a beer garden and pétanque piste at the rear, and wooden benches in front. Food is from local suppliers, with home-made pork pies and Scotch eggs. Beer and cider festivals are held in May, August and October. Essex CAMRA Cider Pub of the Year 2016, it offers 16 or more ciders. 🛇🛇🌿♿🅿🐾

Churchgate Street

Queen's Head Ⓛ

26 Churchgate Street, Old Harlow, CM17 0JT
🕛 12-11.30; 12-9 Sun ☎ (01279) 427266
⊕ tqhchurchgatest.co.uk
Adnams Southwold Bitter, Broadside; Crouch Vale Essex Boys Best Bitter, Brewers Gold; Woodforde's Wherry Ⓗ; **1 changing beer** Ⓗ/Ⓖ
Originally a Tudor building, with wooden beams spanning a spacious interior, the Queen's Head is believed to have been a pub since 1750. It is situated in a pleasant village street on the outskirts of Harlow. The smaller side bar has a fire in winter and there is a garden bar and barbecue in the summer. Good home-made food is known for its fresh ingredients. There are regular quizzes, special events and cocktail evenings. Q🛇🛇🌿🅿🚇(7)🐾🛜

Clacton-on-Sea

Moon & Starfish ✅

1 Marine Parade East, CO15 1PT
🕛 8am-11 (12.30am Fri & Sat) ☎ (01255) 222998
Fuller's London Pride; Greene King Abbot; Sharp's Doom Bar; 6 changing beers (sourced nationally) Ⓗ
The first Wetherspoon pub in the Tendring district, and a regular Guide entrant in recent years. In common with the chain's other outlets, it holds two beer festivals and one cider festival each year. The pub is opposite Clacton's famous pier and the outside area offers excellent views of the August air show and the carnival street procession which the pub supports, as well as the local branch's beer festival. Food is available daily. Q🛇🛇🛇♿🌿➡️🚇🛜

Old Lifeboat House

39 Marine Parade East, CO15 6AD
🕛 12-10 ☎ (01255) 476799
5 changing beers Ⓗ
Local CAMRA Pub of the Year 2012-2014 and Cider Pub of the Year 2015, this is a friendly family-run

venue which is popular with local CAMRA members. The landlord provides excellent home-made food on Wednesdays, when all the ales are discounted by 50p. The Old Lifeboat House hosts four darts teams – two play on Mondays and two on Thursdays. The varied beer range makes it a popular pub for the away teams. 🛇🛇🌿♣️♿🅿🚌🐾🛜

Cock Clarks

Fox & Hounds

Birchwood Road, CM3 6RF TL814028
🕛 12-3 (not Mon, Tue & Wed), 5-11; 12-11 Fri & Sat; 12-8 Sun; 12-8 Sun ☎ (01621) 829662
Fuller's London Pride; Harveys Sussex Best Bitter; 1 changing beer (sourced nationally) Ⓗ
Dating from 1874 and with handsome red brickwork, this pub was released from the Ridley's estate in 2005. Following a recent period of closure, it is now a family-friendly village pub mainly serving the local trade, although it also attracts passing motorists, bikers, cyclists and walkers. There are normally two premium bitters on offer with possibly a third available at weekends. Good home-cooked food is served Wednesday to Saturday (not Thu lunch) and until 4pm Sunday. 🛇🛇🛇🌿🅿🐾🛜

Colchester

Ale House Ⓛ

82 Butt Road, CO3 3DA
🕛 3-11; 12-midnight Fri; 12-11 Sat; 12-9.30 Sun ☎ (01206) 573464 ⊕ thealehousecolchester.co.uk
8 changing beers (sourced nationally) Ⓗ
You will find a changing range of ales in this free house, normally including a dark beer, served on both gravity and handpump. A lovely walled garden is to the rear. Quiz night is every third Wednesday, while both darts and bar billiards are popular. BT Sport is screened and there is a public car park nearby. Highly commended in the local CAMRA Pub of the Year competition, it has a friendly landlady and staff. 🛇🛇➡️♣️♿🐾🛜

Bricklayers

27 Bergholt Road, CO4 5AA
🕛 11-3, 5.30-11; 11-midnight Fri; 11-11 Sat; 12-7 Sun ☎ (01206) 852008
Adnams Southwold Bitter, Broadside; 7 changing beers (sourced nationally) Ⓗ
Large Adnams flagship pub, very close to the station, with up to eight ales from the Adnams regular and seasonal range, as well as a wide variety of guests. Up to six real ciders are kept, with Crones always on. The pub has a traditional public bar with a pool table and dartboard, and a large lounge bar. The spacious beer garden has cycle racks. Excellent home-cooked food is available at lunchtimes (no food Sat), with a great-value roast on Sunday. Q🛇➡️(North)♣️♿🅿🚇

Britannia Gurkha Restaurant & Bar Ⓛ

42 Meyrick Crescent, CO2 7QY
🕛 3.30-11; 2-11 Fri; 12-11 Sat; 12-10.30 Sun ☎ (01206) 761003 ⊕ britanniagurkharestaurant.co.uk
Colchester Metropolis, No. 1; Skinner's Cornish Knocker; 1 changing beer (sourced nationally) Ⓗ
Large corner pub and restaurant, owned and run by a Gurkha family. The bar has various seating areas

with a pool table and darts at the far end. A large-screen TV shows major sporting events. There is much Gurkha memorabilia on display, including clocks showing times in various cities. Delicious and popular home-cooked Nepalese cuisine is served in a separate cosy and relaxing dining area (every evening except Tue). Takeaways are also available. ⏰🍴◑♿≈♣P🖵☺🛜

British Grenadier L
67 Military Road, CO1 2AP
🕒 5-11.45; 12-midnight Fri & Sat; 12-3, 7-11.45 Sun ☎ 07832 215118
4 changing beers (sourced nationally) Ⓗ
Former Adnams-tied LocAle and Apple-accredited venue which has been a regular in the Guide for more than 10 years and has won numerous awards during this time. This two-bar Victorian pub offers a changing range of local, regional and national beers served from four handpumps. The small back bar is dominated by a pool table, while the larger main bar is heated by an open fire in the colder months. 🍴♿≈♣●🖵(6,61,66)🛜

Live & Let Live L
12 Millers Lane, Stanway, CO3 0PS
🕒 12-11 (midnight Fri & Sat) ☎ (01206) 574071
5 changing beers (sourced nationally) Ⓗ
Traditional, welcoming local pub with a quiet, homely saloon bar and a public bar offering TV sport, darts, pool and a comprehensive jukebox. The publicans are keen to support local breweries and take great pride in the quality of their real ales. The beers are very competitively priced and also available in take-out containers. The pub offers a good-value menu of traditional home-cooked food and bar snacks and is internationally famous for its winter and summer beer and sausage festivals. ⏰🍴◑♿♣P🖵(65,70,71)☺🛜

New Inn L
36 Chapel Street South, CO2 7AX
🕒 12 (4 Mon)-11; 12-midnight Fri & Sat ☎ (01206) 575277
🌐 theoldnewinnpub.co.uk
Bishop Nick Ridley's Rite; 4 changing beers (sourced nationally) Ⓗ
Classic community-focused pub with separate saloon and public bars, both warm and welcoming. It has comfy seats, an open fire in the saloon, and wooden seating plus TV in the public bar. A large, free-to-hire function room with a woodburner is available to the rear, together with a large, covered smoking area. The enthusiastic young licensees are keen to introduce regular beer festivals. Both Sky and BT Sport are shown in the public bar and function room. Q⏰🍴♿≈♣P☺🛜

Odd One Out L
28 Mersea Road, CO2 7ET
🕒 4.30-11; 12-11 Fri & Sat; 12-10.30 Sun ☎ (01206) 513958
7 changing beers (sourced nationally) Ⓗ
Traditional local pub with 31 years under the same landlord, serving a varied selection of at least five real ales including one dark, and three or four ciders (it has repeatedly been a CAMRA Cider Pub of the Year winner). The bar also displays a fine selection of over 50 malt whiskies plus a range of wines. Open fires are in each room, with lounge, bench or bar seating. Pub snacks are on tap at all times, and there is the occasional barbecue. Q🍴≈●🖵(8,67,175)☺

Purple Dog L ✅
42 Eld Lane, CO1 1LS
🕒 11-11 (1am Thu); 10-1am Fri; 10-2am Sat; 11.30-10.30 Sun ☎ (01206) 564995
Crouch Vale Brewers Gold; Woodforde's Wherry; 4 changing beers (sourced nationally) Ⓗ
A place of refreshment since 1687 and still popular with younger folk, shoppers and ale enthusiasts. A single bar serves various drinking and dining areas and a sunny courtyard. Up to six ales on handpump and a guest on gravity are available, alongside excellent food. Seasonal beer festivals, monthly music nights and quizzes complete the experience. A fine modern pub in an historic building, right in the heart of Britain's oldest recorded town. ⏰🍴◑≈🛜

Victoria Inn 🏆 L
10 North Station Road, CO1 1RB
🕒 12-11 (midnight Fri & Sat); 2-11 Sun ☎ (01206) 514510
🌐 victoriainncolchester.co.uk
5 changing beers (sourced nationally) Ⓗ
Yorkshire hospitality in the heart of Essex, this calls itself a proper pub, serving five real ales including a house beer brewed by Colchester Brewery. A selection of bottled beers and up to nine real ciders are also available. Live music plays on Sundays, often accompanied by Yorkshire puddings and roast tatties. The courtyard garden and outbuilding host a themed annual beer festival. Local CAMRA Pub of the Year 2016, and previously county and regional winner. 🍴≈♣●🖵☺🛜

Coopersale

Theydon Oak L ✅
9 Coopersale Street, CM16 7QJ
🕒 12-11 (9 Fri; midnight Sat); 12-8.30 Sun ☎ (01992) 572618 🌐 thetheydonoak.co.uk
Dominion Woodbine Racer; Fuller's London Pride; Greene King IPA; 3 changing beers (often Brentwood) Ⓗ
An ancient pub with an open inglenook fireplace and comfortable seating, lots of exposed beams, horse brasses and antiques. A fire is lit in the cold winter months. Parts date back 400 years and there is reputed to be a ghost. A wide assortment of home-cooked food is served, for which the pub has a good reputation. Set in beautiful countryside, not far from Epping. Q⏰🍴◑●P🖵(381)☺🛜

Copford Green

Alma L ✅
School Road, CO6 1BZ
🕒 12-3, 5-11 (midnight Fri); 12-midnight Sat; 12-11 Sun ☎ (01206) 210607 🌐 thealma.org.uk
Greene King IPA, Abbot; Red Fox Hunter's Gold; 1 changing beer (sourced nationally) Ⓗ
This is the sixth consecutive year in the Guide for this picturesque 16th-century village pub, which recently received a rural top three Pub of the Year award from the local CAMRA branch. The spring bank holiday festival offers over 20 beers. Lunchtime and evening home-cooked meals are available daily. There is an open fire, TV sport, darts and pool, which complement classic motor vehicle meetings and quiz nights on every first Thursday. Q🍴⏰◑♿♣P☺🛜

Cornish Hall End

Horse & Groom L ✓

B1057, CM7 4HF TL683366
☼ 12-11; closed Mon ☎ (01799) 586306
⊕ thehorseandgroom.org
Greene King IPA; 4 changing beers (sourced nationally) ⊞

A pleasant village pub opposite the parish church, with a restaurant and garden. It runs beer festivals and events and is a warm and friendly place, with beers that change frequently. It offers good food and is the social centre of this village, supporting many charities. Special lunches, carveries and fish and chips nights are held regularly and always popular. Local CAMRA Pub of the Year 2015.
Q ➲ 🏠 🕪 ♣ P 🐾 🕏

Debden

Plough L

High Street, CB11 3LE
☼ 12-3 (not Tue), 5-11; 12-midnight Fri & Sat; 12-10 Sun; closed Mon ☎ (01799) 541899
Greene King IPA; 3 changing beers (sourced locally) ⊞

The sole remaining village inn, which is under new ownership. A warm and friendly pub, it has a restaurant with an extensive menu, and a garden. It offers an interesting and varied range of local beers and is now a very important social centre for the village, as well as for the surrounding area. Beer festivals and local celebrations feature regularly. A good base for walkers and cyclists too.
Q ➲ 🏠 🕪 ♣ P 🖳 (6,313)

Duton Hill

Three Horseshoes L

CM6 2DX (1 mile W of B184) TL606268
☼ 12-2.30 (not Mon-Thu), 6-11; 12-3, 6-11 Sat; 12-3, 7-10.30 Sun ☎ (01371) 870681
Mighty Oak Captain Bob; 2 changing beers (sourced nationally) ⊞

Outstanding village local with a garden, wildlife pond and terrace overlooking the Chelmer Valley and farmland. The landlord often hosts a weekend of open-air theatre in July. A millennium beacon in the garden, breweriana and a remarkable collection of Butlin's memorabilia are pub features. A beer festival is held on the spring bank holiday in the Duton Hill Den. Look for the pub sign depicting a famous painting, Our Blacksmith, by a former local resident Sir George Clausen.
➲ 🏠 ♿ ♣ P 🖳 (313) 🐾

Epping

Forest Gate Inn

111 Bell Common, CM16 4DZ
☼ 10-2.30, 5-11; 12-3.30, 6.30-10.30 Sun ☎ (01992) 572312
Adnams Southwold Bitter, Broadside; Bishop Nick Ridley's Rite ⊞; 2 changing beers ⊞/ⓖ

On the edge of Epping Forest, the pub is in a 17th-century building, with low ceilings and flag floors, run by the same family for 50 years. It is popular with locals, walkers and their dogs. Hot pub meals and soups are served in the bar, as well as in Haywards Restaurant next door. There is a large grassed seating area.
Q ➲ 🏠 🛏 🕪 ♣ P 🖳 (213,541) 🐾 🕏

Fordham

Three Horseshoes L

Church Road, CO6 3NJ
☼ 12-3, 5-11; 12-midnight Sat; 12-8 Sun; closed Mon
☎ (01206) 240195 ⊕ threehorseshoes-fordham.co.uk
3 changing beers (sourced nationally) ⊞

A traditional, welcoming 16th-century village local with a heavily timbered interior, lovely red-brick fireplace and comfy sofas. The separate dining area offers a reasonably priced menu of local home-cooked food at lunchtimes and evenings, with a monthly themed night. There is a folk night every second Tuesday, a crib night every first Thursday and a beer festival in October. Q ➲ 🏠 🕪 P 🖳 🐾

Goldhanger

Chequers ✓

The Square, CM9 8AS
☼ 11-11; 12-10.30 Sun ☎ (01621) 788203
⊕ thechequersgoldhanger.co.uk
Adnams Ghost Ship; Crouch Vale Brewers Gold; St Austell Proper Job; Sharp's Doom Bar; Young's Bitter; 1 changing beer (sourced nationally) ⊞

A quintessential 15th-century timbered inn with many rooms including a snug and games room with bar billiards. Cosy real fires burn in winter, and in summer the courtyard provides a sunny, relaxed drinking area which also hosts beer festivals in March and September. A large, varied selection of locally sourced food complements the excellent beers and ciders. Goldhanger is an ideal centre for walks along the Blackwater Estuary sea wall.
Q ➲ 🏠 🕪 ♣ 🍴 P 🖳 (95) 🐾 🕏

Grays

Theobald Arms ♟

141 Argent Street, RM17 6HR
☼ 11-11 (midnight Fri & Sat); 12-11 Sun ☎ (01375) 372253
4 changing beers ⊞

Genuine, traditional pub with a public bar that has an unusual hexagonal pool table. The changing selection of four guest beers showcases local independent breweries, and a range of British bottled beers is also stocked. Regular St George's weekend and summer beer festivals are held in the old stables and on the rear enclosed patio. Lunchtime meals are served Monday to Friday. Darts and cards are played. Local CAMRA Pub of the Year 2016. 🏠 🕪 ♿ ⇌ ♣ P 🖳

White Hart L

Kings Walk, RM17 6HR
☼ 12-11.30 (midnight Fri & Sat); 12-11 Sun
☎ (01375) 373319 ⊕ whitehartgrays.co.uk
Crouch Vale Brewers Gold; 4 changing beers (often Sharp's) ⊞

Situated just outside the town centre, this local has been rejuvenated since it was taken over in 2006. Two regular ales including the house beer, White Hart Ale, are supplemented by three guests (usually one dark) and a selection of over 30 bottled Belgian beers. Good-value meals are served weekday lunchtimes. Live music features on Saturdays. The pub supports pool and darts teams, and sport is screened. There is a secluded beer garden. Local CAMRA Pub of the Year 2015.
🏠 🛏 🕪 ♿ ⇌ ♣ P 🖳 🐾 🕏

Great Clacton

Ship ✅
2 Valley Road, CO15 4AR
✪ 12-midnight (1am Sat); 12-10.30 Sun summer; 12 (3 Mon)-midnight; 12-1am Sat; 12-10.30 Sun winter
☎ (01255) 475889
Adnams Ghost Ship; Sharp's Doom Bar; 1 changing beer (sourced nationally) Ⓗ
A traditional local dating back to the 16th century, which has been renovated in the past few years, creating a fresh, modern appearance while still retaining character. Although half the pub is allocated for dining during mealtimes, plenty of room is still available for those just after a pint (or two). It regularly has entertainment at weekends. There is also a large garden with a terrace and a secure children's play area. ⓢ☆◑⅁P🖳❀🐾🛜

Great Dunmow

Boar's Head
37 High Street, CM6 1AB
✪ 11-11 (1am Fri & Sat); 12-11 Sun ☎ (01371) 873630
Adnams Southwold Bitter; Fuller's London Pride; 1 changing beer (sourced nationally) Ⓗ
Four-hundred-year-old traditional town-centre pub on the corner of the main public car park. This is a timber-framed lath and plaster building with beamed low ceilings and three large-screen TVs for sport. Live music is performed on Saturday evenings. A large decking area at the rear includes covered seating for smokers. No food is served, so you can enjoy visiting here for social drinking. ☆P🖳(33,133)🛜

Great Totham

Compasses ♟ ✅
12 Colchester Road, CM9 8BZ
✪ 12 (3.30 Mon)-11 ☎ (01621) 332587
⊕ tothamcompasses.com
Crouch Vale Essex Boys Best Bitter; Mighty Oak Captain Bob; Wibblers Apprentice; 3 changing beers (sourced regionally; often Theakston) Ⓗ
Reopened in 2015, this friendly village pub, built in the 16th century, has quickly established a reputation for its range of local ales, including difficult-to-find specials. Three traditional ciders are available. There is an open fire, cosy armchairs and a light, airy feel to the public bar. Good food is served lunchtimes and evenings Tuesday to Saturday and until 6pm Sunday. There is a separate restaurant. Awarded CAMRA branch Pub of the Year for 2016. ⓢ☆◑♣🍴P🖳(75,505)❀🛜

Halstead

Bird in Hand ✅
54 Chapel Hill, CO9 1JP
✪ 12-11; 11-7 Sun ☎ (01787) 274993
⊕ thebirdinhandhalstead.co.uk
3 changing beers (sourced nationally) Ⓗ
Single-bar pub serving a drinking area and comfortable lounge, with a separate restaurant area. The changing beer selection comes from around the country. There is a good-value menu of home-cooked food with traditional and unusual dishes, including light snacks and cakes, and a Sunday carvery. The pub hosts an occasional quiz for charity and is also home to the local rugby club. Q ⓢ☆◑P🖳🛜

Griffin Ⓛ
Parsonage Street, CO9 2JT
✪ 12-11 (midnight Fri & Sat); 12-10.30 Sun
☎ (01787) 476569 ⊕ griffinhalstead.co.uk
5 changing beers (sourced nationally) Ⓗ
Set in a back street, the Griffin is a modernised and pleasant local. The interior has polished wooden floors with various light and airy drinking spaces, including an area with a pool table, and there is a pleasant space outside. Most beers are served on gravity dispense. On the third Tuesday of the month there is a beer tasting session for a small fee. Look out for the clocks made from pumpclips, available to buy. Q ⓢ☆❀♣🍴P🖳(88)❀🛜

Three Pigeons Ⓛ
6 Mount Hill, CO9 1AA
✪ 4.30-11.30; 12-midnight Fri & Sat; 12.30-midnight Sun
☎ (01787) 274392
3 changing beers (sourced nationally) Ⓗ
Friendly and welcoming pub with a real fire and separate drinking areas. There is a pleasant outdoor space where an annual beer festival takes place. Live music and a quiz night are regular features. The ales on offer change frequently, and come from local breweries as well as from much further afield. A meat raffle is held every Sunday. Q ⓢ☆❀♣P🖳(88)❀🛜

Harwich

Alma Inn ♟ Ⓛ ✅
25 Kings Head Street, CO12 3EE
✪ 12-11 (midnight Fri & Sat) ☎ (01255) 318681
⊕ almaharwich.co.uk
Adnams Southwold Bitter; 4 changing beers (sourced regionally) Ⓗ
This vibrant community inn occupies an historic building, welcoming both locals and travellers alike, with an ever-changing selection of real ales and an extensive menu, using local ingredients, with an emphasis on seafood. There is a large main bar area, two back rooms and a courtyard garden for eating and drinking, plus six B&B rooms to choose from, making an excellent base to explore the area. Local CAMRA Pub of the Year 2016 and Cider Pub of the Year 2014. ⓢ☆🛏◑≈🍴🖳❀

Hatfield Broad Oak

Cock Inn
High Street, CM22 7HF
✪ 12-11 (midnight Fri & Sat); 12-10.30 Sun
☎ (01279) 718306 ⊕ thecockinn-hatfieldbroadoak.co.uk
Adnams Southwold Bitter; Wells Eagle IPA; Woodforde's Wherry; 1 changing beer (sourced regionally) Ⓗ
Close to Hatfield Forest and popular with walkers, this is a real village local in a picturesque location. The building is a 16th-century coaching inn, decorated in a rustic yet elegant style. It offers freshly made food with good-quality ingredients, locally sourced, where possible, and sensibly priced. A second bar has a dartboard and satellite TV; a third room is a quiet area except when used by groups on occasion. Q ⓢ◑P🖳(5,347,7)🛜

Herongate Tye

Olde Dog Inn Ⓛ
129 Billericay Road, CM13 3SD (1 mile E of A128)
TQ641909

✪ 11.30-11; 12-11 Sat; 12-10.30 Sun ☎ (01277) 810337
⊕ theoldedoginn.co.uk
Crouch Vale Brewers Gold; Greene King Abbot ⊞; 3 changing beers Ⓖ
This 17th-century weatherboarded inn is a family-owned and run free house with traditional decor. It offers a variety of real ales, with three changing guest beers from microbreweries, along with more established national brands and its own Olde Dog IPA, brewed locally. A traditional cider is also sold. Food is available at the bar or in the restaurant area. You can order fish and chips to take away. Dogs are welcome in an area known as the Dog House. ✿⊕&♣P❀❞

Hockley

White Hart
274 Main Road, SS5 4NS
✪ 11-11; 12-10.30 Sun ☎ (01702) 203438
⊕ whiteharthockley.co.uk
House beer (by Caledonian), 2 changing beers (sourced nationally) ⊞
Friendly coaching inn facing Hawkwell village green, with a modern, comfortable interior. It runs a popular quiz night on the first Monday of the month. Housing surrounding this hostelry has made it the centre of village life for over 200 years. It still retains original sash windows, a central open fire and horse brasses. One house beer and two changing guest ales are served. There is a large rear garden with seating and a patio area, plus picnic tables at the front. ✿✿⊕&⇌♣P🖬(7,8)❞

Horndon-on-the-Hill

Bell Inn
High Road, SS17 8LD
✪ 11-11; 12-10.30 Sun ☎ (01375) 642463 ⊕ bell-inn.co.uk
Crouch Vale Brewers Gold; Greene King IPA; Sharp's Doom Bar; 3 changing beers ⊞
Popular 15th-century coaching inn, where beamed bars feature wood panelling and carvings, that has been run by the same family since 1938. Note the hot cross bun collection; a bun has been added every Good Friday for more than 100 years. Two regular beers plus three guests, including ales from Essex breweries, are on the bar. The award-winning restaurant is open daily, lunchtimes and evenings (booking advisable), and hosts gourmet nights. Accommodation is available in 27 bedrooms. Q✿➤⊕&P🖬(265)❀❞

Kirby-le-Soken

Red Lion ✅
32 The Street, CO13 0EF
✪ 11-11; 12-10.30 Sun ☎ (01255) 674832
⊕ redlionkirby.com
Colchester No. 1; Fuller's ESB; Sharp's Doom Bar; 1 changing beer ⊞
This 14th-century pub acquired a scaffolding cocoon prior to a regeneration, and three fluorescent logos have appeared outside. Inside is an experienced landlord, and a brighter, warmer feel in drinking areas. Food signs promise an eclectic menu (booking advised). The real ale board is highly informative, including details such as beer miles. The beer garden has also been transformed and is a pleasant place to sit in summer months, with a children's play area to the rear. ✿✿⊕P🖬(8,107)

Langley Lower Green

Bull
Park Lane, CB11 4SB (from Clavering take road past windmills – it is a long way) TL437345
✪ 5-11; 12-2, 4-11 Fri; 12-11 Sat & Sun ☎ (01279) 777307
Adnams Southwold Bitter; Greene King IPA; 2 changing beers (sourced regionally) ⊞
Classic Victorian village local with original cast-iron lattice windows and fireplaces, located in a tiny isolated hamlet. The pub has a devoted band of local regulars, including cricket and football teams. Unusually, there is an aquarium and a penny-in-the-hole game in the lounge bar. Open mic and quiz nights are held regularly with an annual beer festival in September. If you can plan in advance, a party can pre-book meals outside usual food service hours. ✿✿⊕♣P❀❞

Layer Breton

Hare & Hounds
Crayes Green, CO2 0PN
✪ 9am-midnight (1am Fri & Sat); 9am-11 Sun
☎ (01206) 330459 ⊕ thehareandhound.co.uk
Greene King IPA, Abbot; 3 changing beers (sourced nationally) ⊞
Pleasant community pub with a welcoming real fire. There is a separate room set aside for dining, which includes pub classics and a varying menu of quality food. Three beer festivals are held each year, including one for St George's Day. A quiz night is held on the first Wednesday of each month, and there are occasional themed evenings and live music. A post office is available Tuesday morning and Thursday afternoon. Winner of Morning Advertiser's Community Pub of the Year. ✿✿➤⊕&▲♣♥P🖬(92)❀❞

Leigh-on-Sea

Crooked Billet ✅
51 High Street, Old Leigh, SS9 2EP
✪ 12-11; 12-10.30 Sun ☎ (01702) 480289
Adnams Southwold Bitter; Sharp's Doom Bar; St Austell Nicholson's Pale Ale; 3 changing beers (sourced nationally) ⊞
In Old Leigh fishing village overlooking the Thames estuary, this 16th-century pub has two small bars with bare floorboards and beamed ceilings. The walls are decorated with local village and fishing pictures. Beer sampling evenings take place monthly and a charity beer festival is held yearly. It has a small garden to one side and a larger seating area to the front, which is shared with a seafood merchant. Ten minutes' walk from Leigh-on-Sea station. ✿✿⊕⇌🖬(21,26)❞

Elms ⓛ ✅
1060 London Road, SS9 3ND (on A13)
✪ 8am-midnight (1am Fri & Sat) ☎ (01702) 474687
Greene King Abbot; Ruddles Best Bitter; Sharp's Doom Bar; 4 changing beers (sourced nationally) ⊞
Old coaching inn converted by Wetherspoon into a large open pub, decorated with old photos of the local area. Breakfast is available until noon, with main meals and snacks until 11pm. Three regular beers, four changing guest ales and up to three real ciders are served. There is no music but there are fruit machines and muted TVs. Outside is a paved, heated and covered area for smokers and the pub also has a hedged front garden, popular in summer. ✿✿⊕&♥P🖬(1,27,28)

Mayflower 🍸

5-6 High Street, Old Leigh, SS9 2EN

✪ 11-11; 12-11 Sun ☎ (01702) 478535

⊕ mayfloweroldleigh.com

Crouch Vale Yakima Gold; George's Cockleboats; 3 changing beers (sourced regionally) ⊞

Local CAMRA Pub of the Year 2014-2016. This single-bar hostelry is unusual in that it adjoins a fish and chip restaurant. The menu, unsurprisingly, consists mainly of fish dishes. Two permanent Essex ales, one from local brewer George's, are served, with up to three guest ales, usually from East Anglia. One wall depicts the passenger manifest of the Pilgrim Fathers who sailed on the Mayflower. There is a terrace with views across the estuary. ⏃❀◑▶≉P🖵(26)❀

Little Thurrock

Traitors' Gate Ⓛ

40-42 Broadway, RM17 6EW (on A126)

✪ 12-11 (midnight Fri-Sun)

Greene King Abbot; 5 changing beers ⊞

Since being taken over in 2013, this pub has become the tap for Deverell's Brewery. There are six handpumps with a rotating selection of Deverell's beers, plus other guests, with an emphasis on Essex breweries. Look for the chalkboard above the bar listing current and forthcoming beers. Live music plays on alternate Thursdays and live bands most Fridays and Saturdays. ⏃❀♣🖵(22A,66)❀ 🛜

Little Totham

Swan

School Road, CM9 8LB

✪ 12-11; 12-10.30 Sun ☎ (01621) 331713

Crouch Vale Brewers Gold; Mighty Oak Oscar Wilde, Captain Bob; Sharp's Doom Bar; house beer (by Red Fox); 3 changing beers (sourced nationally; often Adnams, Dark Star) Ⓖ

Cosy three-room cottage-style pub including a separate restaurant area and a public bar with dartboard. There is a good log fire in the historic inglenook fireplace in winter in the front bar. The pub was recently refurbished to its former glory, and with additions including a pizza oven and a summerhouse, the garden now provides an attractive area for outdoor socialising. Several ciders, usually from Westons, complement the beer range. Beer and cider festivals are held in June and December. Q⏃❀◑♣▶P🖵❀🛜

Littley Green

Compasses Ⓛ ✅

CM3 1BU

✪ 12-3, 5.30-11.30; 12-11.30 Thu-Sun ☎ (01245) 362308

⊕ compasseslittleygreen.co.uk

Bishop Nick Ridley's Rite; 3 changing beers (sourced nationally) Ⓖ

Formerly Ridley's Brewery tap, this is a Victorian country pub in a quiet hamlet. A wood-panelled bar has benches around the walls and a tiled floor. Beers are drawn directly from casks in the half-cellar. A range of three ciders and a perry is offered. Renowned filled huffers (giant baps) are available, plus other traditional dishes. There are seats and tables outside and in the large gardens. Accommodation is in five high-quality rooms. Q⏃❀🚲◑♣▶P🖵❀🛜

Maldon

Carpenters' Arms

33 Gate Street, CM9 5QF

✪ 11-11 ☎ (01621) 859896

Adnams Southwold Bitter; Sharp's Special; 4 changing beers (sourced nationally) ⊞

A popular, welcoming pub away from the high-street bustle in a quiet back street. Voted CAMRA branch Cider Pub of the Year in 2016 for the second year running, there are usually four real ciders and a perry available. Beer and cider festivals are held annually. The pub hosts men's and women's darts teams, a dominoes team and a local golf society. Fresh crusty rolls are available lunchtimes. Live music features on Sunday afternoons most months. ⏃❀◑🚲♣▶🖵❀🛜

Farmers Yard

140 High Street, CM9 5BX

✪ 11-2, 5-9; 11-9 Sat; 12-9 Sun ☎ (01621) 854202

⊕ maldonbrewing.co.uk

5 changing beers (sourced locally; often Maldon) Ⓖ

Maldon's first micropub and bottle shop, in a 400-year-old listed building. The 12-foot square bar seats 12 on high benches, enabling eye-level conversation with up to 12 standing customers. There is a convivial atmosphere where conversation flows, uninterrupted by TV. A full range of Maldon Brewing Company's gravity cask ales and bottled beers are on offer, as well as one guest beer from a local/regional microbrewery and guest bottled beers. Draught cider, wine, soft drinks and snacks are also available. Q⏃▶🖵❀

Manningtree

Red Lion

42 South Street, CO11 1BG

✪ 12-11 (midnight Fri & Sat) ☎ (01206) 391880

⊕ redlionmanningtree.co.uk

Adnams Southwold Bitter; 2 changing beers (sourced regionally) ⊞

Newly refurbished and extended for 2016, of particular note are the furnishings in the gents' toilets. It is the oldest pub in Manningtree and appears in the Guide for the third consecutive year. Food is not available, but crockery and cutlery are provided for use with food ordered from local takeaways (menus provided). Runner-up in the Observer Food monthly awards Place To Drink in 2014. ⏃❀♣▶🖵❀🛜

Margaretting Tye

White Hart Inn Ⓛ ✅

The Tye, CM4 9JX

✪ 11.30-3, 6-11; 11.30-midnight Sat; 12-midnight Sun; closed Mon ☎ (01277) 840478 ⊕ thewhitehart.uk.com

Adnams Southwold Bitter, Broadside; Mighty Oak Oscar Wilde, IPA ⊞**; 2 changing beers (sourced nationally)** Ⓖ

Slightly off the beaten track, this fine pub has origins in the 17th century. Known for good traditional home-cooked food and fine ale, it generally offers two or three guest beers, all on gravity. Regular club meetings are held here for cyclists, car owners, ramblers and the Young Farmers. Very much community-focused, a book stall raises money for charities, and beer festivals are held in July and November. Children are confined to the conservatory. Q⏃❀🚲◑🚲P❀🛜

Old Harlow

Crown L ✅
40 Market Street, CM17 0AQ
☼ 12-11 (midnight Fri & Sat); 12-10.30 Sun
☎ (01279) 301380
Greene King IPA, Abbot; 4 changing beers (sourced locally; often Greene King) Ⓗ
A 16th-century building housing the former coaching inn, with many original beams. The smaller part of the pub was a grocer's shop until about 20 years ago. When removing the connecting wall, a 17th-century floral wall painting was discovered, and is preserved in the side room. The large garden is very popular in summer. The pub is a favourite meeting place for a varied clientele. The tenants pride themselves on having no TV and host occasional acoustic afternoons.
◖&≠日🏠😺🎅🛜

Orsett

Foxhound
18 High Road, RM16 3ER (on B188)
☼ 11-11 ☎ (01375) 891295
Sharp's Doom Bar; Timothy Taylor Landlord; 2 changing beers Ⓗ
A traditional two-bar village pub with a separate Fox's Den restaurant, which may be reserved for private functions. There is also a small seating area in-between the saloon bar and the outside rear patio which can double as a meeting room. There are monthly quizzes which raise money for the Guide Dogs for the Blind Association. Two regular beers are generally on, with an ever-changing guest. Always a friendly welcome, whichever bar you choose to be in. 🏠◑♣P😺

Paglesham

Punch Bowl
Church End, SS4 2DP
☼ 11.30-11 (10 Mon); 12-10 Sun ☎ (01702) 258376
Adnams Southwold Bitter; 3 changing beers Ⓗ
A 16th-century building clad in white Essex board with a single low-beamed bar. It has been a pub since the 1800s and is said to have been used by the notorious local smuggler William Blyth. His reputed exploits include drinking two glasses of wine in the Punch Bowl, then eating the glasses (not allowed now!). A small cosy restaurant next to the bar serves excellent, reasonably priced food. Picnic tables are to the front of the pub. Four ales are served. Q👶🏠◑P

Purleigh

Bell
The Street, CM3 6QJ
☼ 11.30-3 (12-4 Sat), 6-11; 12-5 Sun; closed Mon
☎ (01621) 828348 ⊕ purleighbell.co.uk
Adnams Southwold Bitter; Mighty Oak Captain Bob; 2 changing beers (sourced regionally; often Crouch Vale) Ⓗ
A 14th-century village pub providing a warm welcome and offering commanding views of the Blackwater Estuary from its hilltop garden. There is a large inglenook fireplace with an open fire, two heavily beamed seating areas and a hop-decorated bar. There is an emphasis on high-quality food, but beer drinkers are well catered for. The pub hosts a wide range of activities, including movie nights

and art exhibitions. Incredibly popular with walkers, as it is on the St Peter's Way footpath. Q🏠◑♣P😺🛜

Rettendon Common

Bell L
Main Road, CM3 8DY
☼ 11.30-11; 12-10.30 Sun ☎ (01245) 400616
⊕ bellandchimesrettendon.co.uk
Crouch Vale Brewers Gold; Greene King IPA; 1 changing beer (sourced nationally) Ⓗ
Traditional pub, built in the 18th century, with a beamed ceiling supported on brick pillars and the bar running along the length of the large rectangular room. Alcove seating bays are around the perimeter, with a brick fireplace at one end. Historic pictures of the locality decorate the walls. Outside at the front of the pub there are plenty of tables with large parasols. Harley-Davidson, BAC Phantoms, Southend Motor Cycle Club and a Steam Engine Club meet here regularly.
Q👶🏠◑P🚃(1,3)🛜

Ridgewell

White Horse Inn L
Mill Road, CO9 4SG (on A1017) TL735408
☼ 12 (5 Mon)-11; 12-10.30 Sun ☎ (01440) 785532
⊕ ridgewellwhitehorse.com
Mighty Oak Oscar Wilde; 3 changing beers (sourced nationally) Ⓖ
Set in a pretty village which was home to the American 381st Heavy Bomb Group during WWII. At least one dark beer is always available here. Annual beer festivals are held in early March and early August, on the patio behind the pub. Besides a choice of excellent real ale and food, this pub offers 4-star accommodation and an interesting selection of good-quality wines to suit a variety of different tastes. Q👶🏠🛏◑&♣P日🚃🛜

Rochford

Golden Lion L
35 North Street, SS4 1AB
☼ 11-midnight (1am Fri & Sat) ☎ (01702) 545487
⊕ goldenlionrochford.co.uk
Adnams Southwold Bitter; Greene King Abbot; Mighty Oak Maldon Gold; Shalford Levelly Gold; 3 changing beers Ⓗ
Long-standing Guide entry within the town centre conservation area. This is a small 16th-century free house with stained-glass windows and a fireplace with a traditional logburner. Seven ales are always available, including three changing guests (one usually a dark beer) from local micros. Three ciders are also served including one from Essex. This traditional Essex weatherboarded pub has a pretty patio garden to the rear with a vintage petrol pump water feature. There are two beer festivals each year. 🏠≠♣🍺P日(7,8,60)😺

Miley
1 Union Lane, SS4 1AP (behind Sainsbury's Local)
☼ 12-midnight (1am Fri & Sat) ☎ (01702) 544229
4 changing beers (sourced nationally) Ⓗ
True community local with a genuinely warm welcome which has only ever been in one family in its 23 years of opening. It is a live music venue all year round, with a piano inside and an outside stage in the courtyard for the summer months.

Annual beer festivals are held on the spring and August bank holidays. It is two minutes' walk from the train station or the historic town centre. There is a happy hour all day on Mondays. Current local CAMRA Most Improved Pub of the Year.
❀♿⇌♣●P🚌(7,8,60)🐾📶

Rowhedge

Olde Albion

High Street, CO5 7ES
12-3 (not Mon), 5-11; 12-11 Thu-Sat; 12-10.30 Sun
☎ (01206) 728972
4 changing beers (sourced nationally) Ⓗ
Friendly, split-level pub on Rowhedge waterfront which has offered a choice of 560 ales in the past year. There are normally four guest real ales and one guest real cider. The lower seating area has benches, a logburner in winter and views over the river, while the upper bar area has high-level seating and tables. The pub hosts annual beer festivals on St George's Day, Halloween and one coinciding with Rowhedge Regatta. The riverside beer garden offers picturesque views along the River Colne and over the nature reserve opposite.
❀♣●🚌(66)🐾

Saffron Walden

King's Arms ✔

10 Market Hill, CB10 1HQ
12-midnight (11 Mon; 12.30am Fri & Sat); 12-11 Sun
☎ (01799) 522768 🌐 thekingsarmssaffronwalden.co.uk
Adnams Southwold Bitter; Sharp's Doom Bar; Woodforde's Wherry; 1 changing beer (sourced nationally) Ⓗ
Venerable multi-roomed pub, just off the market square – market days are Tuesday and Saturday. Five handpumps feature four regular beers and one guest, often a mild in winter. There is live music at weekends, acoustic music on Thursdays and a monthly quiz. Welcoming log fires in the winter and a pleasant patio for alfresco eating and drinking are particular features. Food is served at lunchtimes and on some evenings.
Q🛋❀◐●P🚌🐾📶

Old English Gentleman ✔

11 Gold Street, CB10 1EJ (E of B184/B1052 jct)
11-midnight (11 Mon; 1am Fri & Sat); 11-11 Sun
☎ (01799) 523595 🌐 oldenglishgentleman.com
Adnams Southwold Bitter; Woodforde's Wherry; 2 changing beers (sourced regionally) Ⓗ
An 18th-century town-centre pub, with log fires and a welcoming atmosphere, serving a selection of guest ales and an extensive menu of bar food and sandwiches that changes regularly. Traditional roasts and chef's specials are available on Sunday in the bar or dining area, where a variety of works of art are displayed. Saffron Walden is busy on Tuesday and Saturday market days. There is a heated patio at the rear and a wood-burning stove too. 🛋❀◐🚌🐾📶

South Benfleet

South Benfleet Social Club Ⓛ

8 Vicarage Hill, SS7 1PB
12-11 (midnight Fri & Sat) ☎ (01268) 206159
3 changing beers Ⓗ
Three times local CAMRA Club of the Year, all the family are welcome here at this friendly, spacious club, as are CAMRA members (show a membership card or a copy of this Guide). The changing beers are updated on Facebook. Two beer festivals are held each year, and other events include a family day and barbecues in summer. Quiz night is on Thursday and pool on Tuesday. It has a separate function room, and live music plays most Saturday evenings. BT/Sky TV sports are shown, and there are bar snacks all day. 🛋❀◐♿⇌●P🚌📶

Southend-on-Sea

Olde Trout Tavern

56 London Road, SS1 1NX
11-11; 12-11 Sun ☎ (01702) 337000
🌐 theoldtrout.webs.com
House beer (by Brentwood); 3 changing beers Ⓗ
Modern town hostelry within walking distance of Southend High Street and both mainline railway stations. Trout Ale, the house beer, is from the local Brentwood Brewery. Two guest ales are served (three at weekends and on Southend United match days), together with Westons Rosie's Pig cider. Hot meals and snacks are served 12-3pm. A quiz night is held fortnightly on Sundays.
◐⇌(Victoria/Central)♣●🚌📶

Railway Hotel Ⓛ

32 Clifftown Road, SS1 1AJ
5-11 Mon; 11-11 (1am Fri & Sat); 11-11 Sun
☎ (01702) 343194 🌐 railwayhotelsouthend.co.uk
Adnams Southwold Bitter, Ghost Ship, Broadside; Crouch Vale Brewers Gold; Sharp's Doom Bar; 1 changing beer (often Adnams) Ⓗ
This three-storey Victorian building is a CAMRA heritage pub. Original features include the counter, bar-back, panelled walls and parquet floor. The Nelson Street entrance has stained glass windows and mosaic floors. Live bands feature most nights, with Blues Tuesdays and Jazz Wednesdays. The food is vegan or vegetarian – the pub is in the top ten vegan pubs in the country. Community projects range from gardening to local radio. Up to six ales are served and one cider.
🛋❀◐◑♿⇌(Central)●🚌📶

Southminster

Station Arms

39 Station Road, CM0 7EW
12-2.30, 6-11 (5.30-11 Fri); 2-11 Sat; 12-4, 7-10.30 Sun
☎ (01621) 772225 🌐 thestationarms.co.uk
Adnams Southwold Bitter; 4 changing beers (sourced locally) Ⓗ
A short walk from Southminster railway station, this is a friendly, traditional weatherboarded pub with an open fire in winter and a pleasant courtyard for the warmer months. It has appeared in every edition of the Guide for the past 26 years. Community activities include a darts team, dominoes and a weekly charity meat raffle. Folk features every fourth Thursday. The courtyard hosts occasional events such as live music and barbecues. Q❀⇌♣●🚌

Stanford-le-Hope

Rising Sun Ⓛ

Church Hill, SS17 0EU (opp church and near A1014)
3-10.30 Mon; 12-midnight (10.30 Tue; 11 Wed; 11.30 Thu); 11-10.30 Sun ☎ (01375) 671097
5 changing beers Ⓗ

Much-improved two-bar traditional town pub in the shadow of the church. The five guest beers are mainly from independent breweries, including LocAle beers, and up to three ciders or perries are stocked. Monthly live music takes place. Beer festivals are held in spring, summer and winter, with the summer festival staged in the pub's large rear garden. A back bar is available for private functions. Local CAMRA Pub of the Year runner-up in 2015. ❀≈♣●P🖵(100,200,374)😸🛜

Stansted Mountfitchet

Rose & Crown Ⓛ
31 Bentfield Green, CM24 8HX TL505256
✪ 12-3 (not Tue), 6-11; 12-11 Fri & Sat; 12-9 Sun; closed Mon
☎ (01279) 812107
3 changing beers (sourced regionally) Ⓗ
Family-run Victorian pub near a duck pond, on the edge of a small hamlet. This free house has been modernised to provide one large bar but retains the atmosphere of a village inn and is well used by locals. Food is home cooked and made from locally sourced produce (no meals Sun eve). Guest beers are often from local breweries. A large variety of gins is kept. The pub has an old seven-inch singles jukebox. ⭓❀◑P🖵(7,7a)😸🛜

Stapleford Tawney

Moletrap
Tawney Common, CM16 7PU (3 miles E of Epping, in the middle of nowhere!) TL500013
✪ 11.30-2.30, 6-11; 12-4 Sun ☎ (01992) 522394
⊕ themoletrap.co.uk
Fuller's London Pride; 3 changing beers Ⓗ
A 200-year-old inn in beautiful countryside, offering a good selection of guest ales, normally including one dark one. Good-value, home-cooked food is served (no food Sun and Mon eves). There is a cosy bar with a real fire; well-behaved children and dogs are allowed at the landlord's discretion. Extensive outdoor seating provides amazing views. The pub is difficult to locate without sat nav, but is well worth it! Q⭓❀◑P😸🛜

Stebbing

White Hart Ⓛ
High Street, CM6 3SQ
✪ 11-3, 4.30-11; 11-11 Sat; 12-10.30 Sun ☎ (01371) 856383
Hart of Stebbing IPA; 1 changing beer (sourced nationally) Ⓗ
A 15th-century timbered inn in a picturesque village, featuring exposed beams, an open fire, eclectic collections from chamber pots to cigarette cards, an old red post box on an interior wall, and a section of exposed lath and plaster wall behind a glass screen. The Hart of Stebbing microbrewery is in the garage, producing beers that are currently only available here and at beer festivals. Good-value food is served daily. There is a patio and a covered, heated gazebo. Q⭓❀◑♣P🖵(16)😸🛜

Steeple Bumpstead

Fox & Hounds ♍ Ⓛ ✔
3 Chapel Street, CB9 7DQ
✪ 12-3, 5-11; 12-midnight Fri & Sat; 12-11 Sun
☎ (01440) 731810 ⊕ foxinsteeple.co.uk
Greene King IPA; 3 changing beers (sourced nationally) Ⓗ

A 500-year-old pub with a main bar warmed by an open fire and two rooms used mainly for dining. To the rear is a courtyard garden. The four beers are from local and national breweries. Locally sourced food ranges from bar snacks to a full à la carte menu. Live music plays on occasional Friday evenings, and some Sundays have quiz nights. Reduced-price beer, wine and free cheese are on offer on Wednesday evenings, with steak nights on Thursdays. Local CAMRA Pub of the Year 2016. Q⭓❀◑♣P🖵(18)😸🛜

Stock

Hoop ✔
High Street, CM4 9BD
✪ 11-11 (midnight Fri & Sat); 12-10.30 Sun
☎ (01277) 841137 ⊕ thehoop.co.uk
Adnams Southwold Bitter Ⓗ**; 4 changing beers (sourced regionally)** Ⓗ/Ⓖ
A 450-year-old weatherboarded pub which has been welcoming drinkers and diners alike for centuries, and a regular in this Guide for over 20 years. It is heavily beamed, with two fires and lots of character. Up to four guest ales and three real ciders are on handpump or gravity, often from local suppliers. Home-made food is served lunchtimes and evenings, 12-5pm on Sundays. A quiz is held monthly and a popular beer festival is staged over the May bank holiday. Q❀◑♿♣🖵(100)😸

Stow Maries

Prince of Wales
Woodham Road, CM3 6SA
✪ 11-11 (midnight Fri & Sat); 12-10.30 Sun
☎ (01621) 828971 ⊕ prince-stowmaries.net
Mighty Oak Oscar Wilde, Captain Bob; 3 changing beers (sourced nationally) Ⓗ
Attractive 17th-century weatherboarded pub with cosy drinking areas inside, all with real fires, and plenty of seating outside for the better weather. Interesting breweriana adorns the walls. Many special events are held, including Burns' supper, live music, comedy, summer barbecues and fireworks. There are pizza nights on Thursdays in winter, using the old baker's wood-fired oven. Good food using local produce is prepared and cooked in-house. An excellent selection of Belgian beers in bottle and on draught is available. Q⭓❀🍴◑♿P🖵(593)😸🛜

Tollesbury

King's Head
1 High Street, CM9 8RG
✪ 12-11 (midnight Fri & Sat); 12-10.30 Sun
☎ (01621) 869203
Bishop Nick Ridley's Rite; house beer (by Colchester); 3 changing beers (sourced nationally) Ⓗ
The only pub left in this village, with a long yachting heritage, it was traditionally the seafarers' public house. The maritime connection survives, with the pub providing hospitality for the Tollesbury v East Coast Old Gaffers' small boat event every year. The public bar has pool and darts. Home-cooked food is available Friday lunchtimes only. During the week, bring in pies, pasties or sandwiches from the baker's opposite. Q⭓❀◑♣●P🖵😸

Toppesfield

Green Man 🅛
Church Lane, CO9 4DR
☼ 5-midnight; 12-1am Sat; 12-midnight Sun
☎ (01787) 237418 ⊕ thegreenmantoppesfield.co.uk
Pumphouse Toppesfield Tap, Black, Gold; 2 changing beers (sourced regionally) 🖽
Community-owned pub and brewery (the Pumphouse), purchased by the village, with the same landlord in place during all the changes. There are beer festivals and events throughout the year. Darts and pool are available in the public bar. This village is the only place in the UK to have a pub, brewery and shop all owned by the community. Q❀☻❀⬧⬧♣⬧P❀☀🎵

Waltham Abbey

Woodbine Inn 🅛 ✅
Honey Lane, EN9 3QT
☼ 11.30-11 (2am Fri & Sat); 11.30-10.30 Sun
☎ (01992) 713050 ⊕ thewoodbine.co.uk
Dominion Woodbine Racer; 5 changing beers (sourced regionally) 🖽
Local CAMRA branch Pub of the Year 2015, situated in Epping Forest and close to Junction 26 of the M25. It is popular with walkers, locals and motorists. The pub has a separate restaurant, but concentrates on real ales and over 20 small-producer ciders. Food is home made, locally sourced and hearty, with sausages, ham and steak as specialities. The Ale Sampling Society meets monthly. CAMRA branch Cider Pub of the Year 2016. ❀◑♣⬧P⊟(250,251)❀🎵

Weeley Heath

White Hart
Clacton Road, CO16 9ED (on B1441) TM153208
☼ 12-2.30, 4-11 (10 Mon); 12-11 Fri & Sat; 12-8 Sun
☎ (01255) 830384
2 changing beers 🖽
Typical village community local and a regular Guide entry. The pub hosts pool and darts teams. A recently added large conservatory now houses the pool table. The garden has a covered patio for smokers. A great sportsman's venue, it has Sky TV and BT Sport, with different events on various TV screens. Local CAMRA Pub of the Year 2015 and Cider Pub of the Year 2016, it runs a real ale club. ❀▲♣⬧P⊟(2,76)🎵

Wendens Ambo

Fighting Cocks
London Road, CB11 4JN (on B1383, at village edge)
☼ 12-11 ☎ (01799) 541279 ⊕ thefightingcocks.biz
Colchester Jack Spitty's Ale; Marston's Pedigree; house beer (by Camerons); 1 changing beer (sourced nationally) 🖽
Formerly a local bikers' haunt, this is now an after-work pub, with a large garden and car park that serves Audley End station. An excellent and interesting food menu is offered here, including Sunday roasts. Meal deals are available for station-users who park regularly here. Unusually, this pub has some national beers that are not available elsewhere locally. ❀◑⇌♣⬧P⊟(59,301)❀

Westcliff-on-Sea

Cricketers
228 London Road, SS0 7JG (on A13 London Rd)
☼ 12-midnight (2am Fri & Sat); 12-11 Sun ☎ (01702) 345053
Dark Star Hophead; Greene King Abbot; Mighty Oak Maldon Gold; Sharp's Doom Bar; 1 changing beer (sourced locally) 🖽
A large family-run, street-corner Gray & Sons hostelry close to Southend. Up to five ales can be found here, four regulars and one guest. The pub has been split into bar and restaurant areas, with home-made food served until 9.30pm and roast dinners available on Sundays. The Venue adjoins the premises, so this popular pub can get busy on music nights. Jazz nights are every second Wednesday of the month, featuring Digby Fairweather. ❀☻◑⬧⇌⊟❀🎵

Wethersfield

Wethersfield Village Club
Old Mill Chase, CM7 4EB
☼ 5-11; 1-midnight Sat; 1-7 Sun ☎ (01371) 850598
Wells Eagle IPA; 2 changing beers (sourced nationally) 🖽
Friendly and hospitable club in a village where there are no pubs. It was dug out of the ground by villagers after the First World War. Facilities include two full-size snooker tables, pool, darts, table tennis and a dance floor. To get into the club take the cul-de-sac to the right of the village hall and the door is down the alleyway at the end. Visiting CAMRA members are welcome. Local CAMRA Club of the Year 2016. ❀♣❀🎵

Widdington

Fleur de Lys
High Street, CB11 3SG TL538316
☼ 12-3 (not Mon), 6-11; 12-11.30 Fri & Sat; 12-10.30 Sun
☎ (01799) 543280 ⊕ thefleurdelys.co.uk
Adnams Southwold Bitter; Woodforde's Wherry; 2 changing beers (sourced nationally) 🖽
Rumours of a ghost abound at this welcoming 400-year-old village local, which boasts a large open fireplace and beams. The games room has a full-sized pool table, football table and dartboard. This was the first pub to be saved from closure by the local branch of CAMRA after its formation. Quality meals are offered with fresh local ingredients. The source of the River Cam and Prior's Hall Barn, an English heritage site, are both nearby. Q☻◑⬧♣P⊟(301)❀

Widford

Sir Evelyn Wood 🅛
56 Widford Road, CM2 8SY
☼ 12-midnight ☎ (01245) 269239
Adnams Southwold Bitter; Mighty Oak IPA; 1 changing beer (sourced nationally) 🖽
This pub is named after the British Army Field Marshall who won the VC in 1858 during the Indian Mutiny. It has two connected bars and a games room in traditional style, including bench window seats, a covered patio area and a largish garden. An extraordinary collection of salt and pepper pots is on display on shelves and in cabinets. There is a pin table, a pool table and dartboard in the games room. A selection of secondhand books is on sale for charity. Q❀☻☻⬧♣P⊟(351)❀

Witham

Battesford Court 🅻 ✓
100-102 Newland Street, CM8 1AH
🕗 8am-midnight (1am Fri & Sat); 8am-11 Sun
☎ (01376) 504080
Greene King Abbot; Ruddles Best Bitter; Sharp's Doom Bar; 5 changing beers (sourced nationally) ⓗ
Large Wetherspoon conversion of a former hotel of the same name. The 16th-century building was previously the courthouse of the manor of Battesford. It has distinct areas with wood panelling and oak beams. There is a family area. Up to five regional beers are served, including something local, usually from Nethergate or Wibblers, plus up to two ciders and perries, usually from Westons and Gwynt y Ddraig. The standard Wetherspoon food offering is available.
Q❄☺◑&♠🖵(38,71,90)🎶

Woolpack Inn 🅻
7 Church Street, CM8 2JP
🕗 11.30-11.30 (midnight Fri & Sat); 12-10.30 Sun
☎ (01376) 511195
Greene King IPA; Witham Brewery No Name; 2 changing beers (sourced locally) ⓗ
A traditional local pub, it is the only regular outlet for the Witham Brewery, which is now based in Coggeshall. Set in the conservation area, the building probably dates from the 15th century. It has two rooms with low wooden beams and a real log fire during the winter. Up to two guest beers are served, always from the local area, and real cider in summer. Note the extensive collection of glass soda syphon bottles. ⇌♣🖛🖵(40)🎶🎶

Wivenhoe

Black Buoy
Black Buoy Hill, CO7 9BS
🕗 11-11; 12-10.30 Sun ☎ (01206) 822425
🌐 blackbuoy.co.uk/index.html
6 changing beers (sourced nationally) ⓗ
Popular, community-owned pub, now twice CAMRA Rural Pub of the Year. It has a bustling main bar with open log fire, high-level seating and a range of six real ales from local and national breweries. Further into the pub there is a second bar, restaurant area and the beer garden which hosts the twice-annual beer festival. Two B&B rooms are available. The pub also stages nights for local musicians and an open mic night, is dog and family friendly, and has secure cycle racks.
❄☺◻◑⇌🖵🎶🎶

Horse & Groom ✓
55 The Cross, CO7 9QL
🕗 10.30-3, 5.30 (6 Sat)-11; 12-4.30, 7-11 Sun
☎ (01206) 824928
Adnams Southwold Bitter, Broadside; 2 changing beers (sourced nationally) ⓗ
Local pub at the top of this popular village, hosting a mix of regulars, families and students. There are lounge and public bars serving a good range of ales – Adnams is often featured alongside locally

sourced guests. Children and dogs are welcome throughout, and there is a small play area in the beer garden at the rear. Pub games include darts and dominoes. It offers a home-cooked menu, with roast lunch on Thursdays and a regular curry club.
Q❄☺◑♠P🖵🎶

Wix

Waggon
Clacton Road, CO11 2RU
🕗 12-11 (midnight Sat) ☎ (01255) 870279
Wells Bombardier; 2 changing beers (sourced regionally) ⓗ
Free house on the crossroads in Wix, with a pool and darts room and regular live music and event nights, serving very reasonably priced beers. The earliest known reference to the pub was in 1810, although the current landlord has only been here since April 1987. The pub helps organise the annual village fair and provides a well stocked beer tent for the occasion. The pool room is occasionally used as a function room. ❄☺&♠P🖵(102,104)🎶🎶

Woodham Mortimer

Hurdlemakers Arms
Post Office Road, CM9 6ST
🕗 12-11; 12-9 Sun ☎ (01245) 225169
🌐 hurdlemakersarms.co.uk
5 changing beers (sourced locally) ⓗ
A family-friendly Gray's pub in an old farmhouse which dates back 400 years. A large garden includes a play area, purpose-built barbecue, barn and marquee for hire. It always has a good range of ciders and beers (many from local breweries). First-class, locally sourced food is served daily. Community events include a monthly quiz night. An annual beer festival is held on the last weekend in June. The pub is popular with walkers.
Q❄☺◑&♣🖛P🖩🖵🎶🎶

Writtle

Wheatsheaf 🅻
70 The Green, CM1 3DU
🕗 11-11.30 (midnight Fri & Sat); 12-11 Sun
☎ (01245) 420672 🌐 thewheatsheafwrittle.co.uk
Adnams Southwold Bitter; Camerons Strongarm; Maldon Drop of Nelson's Blood ⓗ**; Mighty Oak Oscar Wilde** ⓖ**, Maldon Gold; Wibblers Dengie IPA** ⓗ**; 2 changing beers (sourced nationally)** ⓖ
Traditional village pub built in 1813 with a small public bar, an equally compact lounge and a covered patio by the road. The Wheatsheaf is a long-time favourite of the local CAMRA branch. The atmosphere is generally quiet, with the TV switched on only for occasional sporting events. Traditional pub food is served Tuesday to Saturday lunchtimes. Note the old Gray's sign in the public bar. Q◑♣P🖵(45)

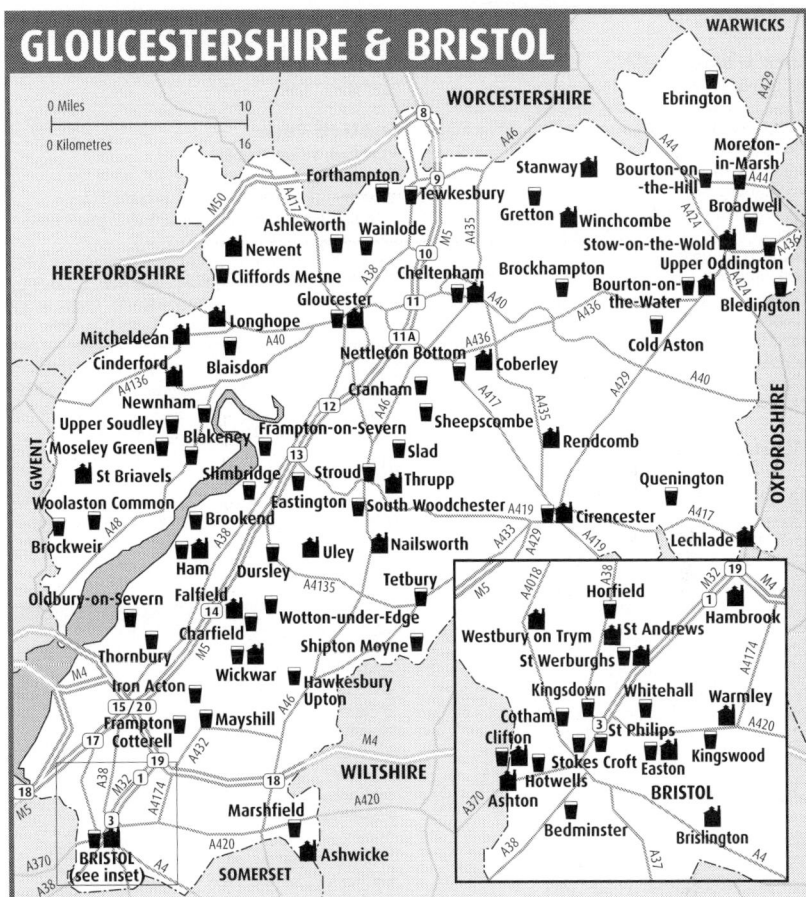

GLOUCESTERSHIRE & BRISTOL

0 Miles 10
0 Kilometres 16

WARWICKS

WORCESTERSHIRE

Ebrington

Moreton-in-Marsh

Forthampton
Tewkesbury
Stanway
Bourton-on-the-Hill
Broadwell

Ashleworth Wainlode
Gretton Winchcombe
Newent
Stow-on-the-Wold
Cliffords Mesne Cheltenham Brockhampton Upper Oddington
HEREFORDSHIRE
Gloucester
Bourton-on-the-Water Bledington
Longhope
Mitcheldean
Nettleton Bottom Coberley Cold Aston
Cinderford Blaisdon
Cranham
Newnham
Sheepscombe
Upper Soudley Blakeney Frampton-on-Severn
Moseley Green Slad Rendcomb
St Briavels Slimbridge Stroud Thrupp Quenington
Woolaston Common Eastington South Woodchester
Brookend Cirencester Lechlade
Brockweir Uley Nailsworth
Ham Dursley Tetbury
Oldbury-on-Severn Falfield
Horfield
Thornbury Wotton-under-Edge
Charfield Shipton Moyne Westbury on Trym St Andrews
Iron Acton Wickwar St Werburghs
Frampton Mayshill Hawkesbury Kingsdown Whitehall Warmley
Cotterell Upton Cotham
Clifton St Philips Kingswood
WILTSHIRE Stokes Croft Easton
Hotwells
Marshfield Bedminster BRISTOL
BRISTOL Ashton Brislington
(see inset) SOMERSET Ashwicke

Ashleworth

Boat Inn L

The Quay, GL19 4HZ (beyond tithe barn on road to quay)
SO8187025073
☼ 12-3 (not Wed), 6-11; 12-midnight Fri; 12-11 Sat & Sun;
closed Mon ☎ (01452) 700272 ⊕ boatinn.wordpress.com
4 changing beers G
This tranquil haven on the banks of the River
Severn is a real gem. Owned by the same family
for over 450 years, it serves up to 10 regional
microbrewery beers by gravity along with 11
ciders. There is a covered courtyard with tables,
and a grass area on the river edge also with tables.
Soup and rolls are available lunchtimes. The pub
has its own moorings and is popular in the
summer. Winter opening times vary.
Q ⏰ ❀ ◑ ▲ ♣ ● P ➡ (351) ❀ 🔊

Blaisdon

Red Hart L

GL17 0AH (centre of village, signed from A4136 E of
Longhope or N of A48)
☼ 12-3, 6-11; 12-3, 7-11 Sun ☎ (01452) 830477
⊕ redhartinn.co.uk
**4 changing beers (sourced nationally; often Bespoke,
Young's)** H

Local CAMRA Pub of the Year, this lovely old
building has flagstones in the bar, a welcoming
fireplace, and a plethora of memorabilia. Guest
ales are usually LocAle, alongside a local cider or
perry from Severn Cider. The pub has a popular
restaurant and is often busy, so be prepared to mix
it with a rack of lamb, not to mention free-range
children, if the meals encroach into the bar area.
Families are welcome to use the well-tended
garden. ⏰ ❀ ◑ ⅃ ▲ ♣ ● P ❀

Blakeney

Cock Inn ⊘

Nibley Hill, GL15 4DB (bottom of Nibley Hill on main
road S of Blakeney)
☼ 5-10.30; 12-11 Fri & Sat; 12-8 Sun; closed Mon
☎ (01594) 510239 ⊕ thecockinnblakeney.com
3 changing beers (sourced regionally) H
Over 200 years old, this attractive roadside pub
retains many original features, including natural
stone walling and old beams. A blazing fire in
winter adds to the welcoming atmosphere in the
low, L-shaped bar. The chef takes great pride in
adding a modern twist to the excellent food menu.
The three ales usually come from a mixture of local
and regional breweries, and two ciders are kept. A
large garden with children's play equipment offers
great views. ⏰ ❀ 🛏 ◑ ▲ ♣ ● P ➡ (73)

Bledington

King's Head L ✅
The Green, OX7 6XQ (off B4450)
✪ 12-3, 6-11 ☎ (01608) 658365 ∰ kingsheadinn.net
Brakspear Oxford Gold; Butcombe Bitter; Hook Norton Hooky; 2 changing beers Ⓗ
Delightful 16th-century stone-built inn overlooking the village green. The pub has original old beams and an open inglenook log fire with high-back settles. This free house, with 12 comfortable letting rooms, is renowned for its wide range of ale and food. Bledington is about four miles from Stow-on-the-Wold. There are good local walks to nearby villages, with Kingham station close by. The two guest beers are selected from local brewers in Gloucestershire and Oxfordshire. CAMRA award winner and finalist in 2015 Pub of the Year.
Q ➢ ❀ ⇦ ◖ ◗ ♣ P

Bourton-on-the-Hill

Horse & Groom L ✅
Moreton-in-Marsh, GL56 9AQ (on A44, at top of hill)
✪ 12-2.30, 6.30-11 ☎ (01386) 700413
∰ horseandgroom.info
Goff's Jouster; 2 changing beers (sourced locally) Ⓗ
This Grade II-listed Georgian stone inn has been successfully family run since 2005. Friendly service will provide you with three local real ales - Goff's and two guests - and award-winning contemporary food in an attractive dining area. The light and airy bar has been tastefully refurbished, with bar stools and an open fire. Ideal for visits to nearby Moreton-in-Marsh and the Batsford Arboretum, the pub has five en-suite rooms. The delightful sheltered garden has plenty of seating, with stunning views over the Cotswold countryside. ❀ ⇦ ◖ ◗ P ⊟

Bourton-on-the-Water

Mousetrap Inn L
Lansdowne, GL54 2AR (300yds W of village centre)
✪ 11.30-3, 6-11; 12-3, 6-11 Sun ☎ (01451) 820579
∰ mousetrap-inn.co.uk
Hook Norton Old Hooky; Stroud Budding; 1 changing beer Ⓗ
Traditional Cotswold stone free house run by the same family for 11 years. The dining area, refurbished in 2016, has a feature fireplace. This consistent Guide entry has 10 en-suite rooms, and offers two regular local beers plus a guest beer. Friendly service and good-value home-cooked meals can be enjoyed here. A patio area in front of the pub with tables and hanging baskets provides a suntrap in the summer.
Q ➢ ⇦ ◖ ◗ ♣ P ⊟ (801,855) 🛜

Bristol: Bedminster

Hare
51 North Street, BS3 1EN
✪ 4-11; 2-midnight Fri & Sat; 3-11 Sun ☎ (0117) 966 5740
∰ theharepub.co.uk
3 changing beers (often Twisted Oak) Ⓗ
Formerly the Full Moon, this building has been a pub since at least 1822. Three changing guest beers are served, often from Twisted Oak Brewery. The bar area has recently been expanded to give much more indoor seating. A steep flight of stairs leads to a rear garden/patio area above the pub

which is used for barbecues in the summer. Pork pies are available at the weekend. It has no connection with Bath Ales, despite the name.
❀ ≈ ◖ ⊟ (24) ☙

Spotted Cow
139 North Street, BS3 1EZ
✪ 12-midnight (11 Mon; 1am Fri & Sat); 12-11 Sun
☎ (0117) 963 4433 ∰ thespottedcowbristol.com
Bath Ales Gem; Butcombe Gold; 3 changing beers (often Arbor, Tiny Rebel) Ⓗ
An original Georges & Co Ltd sign is still prominent over the entrance to this single-bar pub, which was for a while called 139 Degrees North. Guest beers usually come from independents such as Tiny Rebel and Arbor Ales. A pleasant refurbishment has given it a chilled atmosphere, with mood music played at a non-intrusive volume. Quality food is sourced mainly from local suppliers. The pub has a sizeable garden. ➢ ❀ ◖ ♿ ⊟ (24) ☙ 🛜

Victoria Park
66 Raymend Road, BS3 4QW (250yds off St Johns Lane)
✪ 11-11 (11.30 Fri & Sat); 11-10.30 Sun ☎ (0117) 330 6043
∰ thevictoriapark.co.uk
Wye Valley Butty Bach; 2 changing beers Ⓗ

REAL ALE BREWERIES

Arbor Ales Ltd Bristol
Ashley Down Bristol: St Andrews
Bath Bristol: Warmley
Battledown Cheltenham
Beer Bores Ashwicke (NEW)
Bespoke Mitcheldean
Bolthole Bristol: Westbury on Trym (NEW)
Brewhouse & Kitchen 🍺 Bristol: Clifton
Brewhouse & Kitchen 🍺 Cheltenham (NEW)
Brewhouse & Kitchen 🍺 Gloucester (NEW)
Bristol Beer Factory Bristol: Ashton
Brythonic St Briavels (NEW – brewing suspended)
Ciren 🍺 Cirencester
Combined Brewers Falfield
Corinium Cirencester
Cotswold Bourton-on-the-Water
Cotswold Lion Coberley
Crane Bristol (NEW)
Dawkins Bristol: Easton
Donnington Stow-on-the-Wold
Force Cirencester
Freeminer Cinderford (brewing suspended)
Gloucester Gloucester
Goff's Winchcombe
Good Chemistry Bristol: Clifton (NEW)
Great Western 🍺 Bristol: Hambrook
Halfpenny 🍺 Lechlade
Hillside Longhope
Incredible Bristol: Brislington
King Street 🍺 Bristol (NEW)
Moor Bristol
Nailsworth 🍺 Nailsworth
New Bristol Bristol
Prescott Cheltenham
Stanway Stanway
Stroud Thrupp
TAP Rendcomb (NEW)
Tiley's 🍺 Ham
Towles' Bristol: Easton
Uley Uley
Whittington's Newent
Wickwar Wessex Wickwar
Wiper & True Bristol: St Werburghs
Zerodegrees 🍺 Bristol

A thriving red-brick pub in a residential area. The interior has something of a gastro-pub feel but drinkers are most welcome. There is a large garden/patio area to the rear which features a wood-fired pizza oven. Three handpumps dispense quality beers, usually including a dark offering. The interesting all-day menu is displayed on a chalkboard, and a large drop-down screen shows some major sports matches. Other events take place throughout the week including films, a book club and a quiz. ⓢ🏠🄾➤♣🖵(90,91)🐾🔊

Windmill

14 Windmill Hill, BS3 4LU (100yds uphill from Bedminster station)
⊕ 12-11 (midnight Sat); 12-10.30 Sun ☎ (0117) 963 5440
⊕ thewindmillbristol.com
Bath Ales Gem; Purity Pure Gold; 1 changing beer ⊞
With pastel colours and wooden flooring throughout, the pub is on two levels, with a family room on the lower area where children are welcome until 8pm. There are two regular ales and one guest, as well as real cider and foreign bottled beers. An old 1970s jukebox features. Outside to the front is a small patio area. The pub has level access, with the ladies' toilet on the lower level, but there is no toilet accessible by wheelchair. ⓢ🏠🄾➤●🖵(75,76,77)🐾🔊

Bristol: City Centre

Bank Tavern ✓

8 John Street, BS1 2HR (take lane next to arcade on All Saints St)
⊕ 12-midnight (1am Thu-Sat) ☎ (0117) 930 4691
⊕ banktavern.com
4 changing beers ⊞
Popular, compact, one-bar pub, in the city centre yet well hidden away. The four beers are often from microbrewers from the South-west and can be of any style. Two real ciders change constantly. Quirky humour and many varied events define the pub, and it is a great alternative to the more predictable establishments all around. Live music is performed Wednesdays and Thursdays. Look out for the summer fête and Christmas party. Quality food is served 12-4pm (booking advisable Sun). ⓢ🏠🄾♣●🖵(1,2,3)🐾🔊

Beer Emporium

13-15 King Street, BS1 4EF
⊕ 12-2am; 2-midnight Sun ☎ (0117) 379 0333
⊕ thebeeremporium.net
12 changing beers ⊞
A beer cellar bar opened in 2013, set in three tunnels – one containing the bar and seating, one for seating only, and the third housing the kitchens. A lift makes it all accessible. Up to 12 changing real ales are served and a wide range of world bottled beers. There is also a bottle shop just inside the entrance. Regular beer-related events feature plus an open mic night every Monday. 🄾&●🖵🔊

Bridge Inn

16 Passage Street, BS2 0JF
⊕ 12-11 (1am Fri & Sat); 2-11 Sun ☎ (0117) 929 0942
⊕ bridgeinnbristol.co.uk
Dark Star Hophead; 3 changing beers ⊞
Tiny pub by the river bridge and not too far from the station, yet only a short walk from the city centre. Music industry souvenirs feature, along with a selection of board games and free Wi-Fi. Guest beers are adventurous and usually hoppy,

with two from high-quality microbreweries. Lunch is served 12-3pm weekdays only. Outside tables increase capacity in good weather. It now stocks a range of UK and US bottled beers, plus around 50 Scottish single malt whiskies. 🅿🄾➤♣🖵🐾🔊

Commercial Rooms ✓

43-45 Corn Street, BS1 1HT
⊕ 9am-midnight; 8am-1am Fri & Sat ☎ (0117) 927 9681
Greene King Abbot; Ruddles Best Bitter; changing beers ⊞
Grade II-listed building dating from 1810 and impressively converted to Bristol's first Wetherspoon pub in 1995, offering up to 10 guest beers. The interior features Greek revival-style decor, a stunning ceiling with dome, and portraits and memorabilia from its days as a businessmen's club. The main bar can be busy at peak times, although there is a quieter galleried room. Disabled access is via the side entrance in Small Street. It always gets fully involved with Wetherspoon festivals. Q ⓢ🄾&●🖵🔊

Cornubia

142 Temple Street, BS1 6EN
⊕ 12-11; 12-6 Sun ☎ (0117) 925 4415 ⊕ thecornubia.co.uk
8 changing beers ⊞
A small, cosy pub with two linked rooms adorned with much patriotic memorabilia as well as countless pumpclips. Eight real ales are served, plus changing ciders in spring and summer. Pork pies and pasties are usually available. You can enjoy a wide range of board games and books here. Live blues takes place on Thursday evenings, when anyone can come along and jam, and live bands some Saturdays. The outside area with a boules piste has been enclosed, developed and expanded. 🅿➤♣●🖵(1,2,50)🐾🔊

Gryphon

41 Colston Street, BS1 5AP
⊕ 1 (3 Mon)-11; 1-1am Fri & Sat; 6-11 Sun ☎ 07894 239567
6 changing beers ⊞
A shrine to dark beer and great rock/heavy metal music in which posters, guitars and many pumpclips adorn the walls. Triangular in shape due to its corner plot, and just a few yards uphill from the Colston Hall, it has six handpumps dispensing changing brews, many dark and often strong. Live bands sometimes play upstairs and beer festivals are in March and September. Food is served evenings Tuesday-Saturday. It may open earlier on Sundays. Children and dogs are admitted at the licensee's discretion. 🄾🖵🐾🔊

King's Head ★

60 Victoria Street, BS1 6DE
⊕ 11-midnight; 12-midnight Sun & Sun ☎ (0117) 929 2338
Castle Rock Harvest Pale; Harveys Sussex Best Bitter; Sharp's Doom Bar, Atlantic; 1 changing beer (sourced nationally) ⊞
Classic small pub, dating from around 1660 and identified by CAMRA as having a nationally important historic interior. A narrow area around the bar leads to the tramcar snug at the rear. Pictures of old Bristol make fascinating viewing. An earlier landlady is reputed to haunt the pub. Popular food is served on weekday lunchtimes only. There are tables for outside drinking in summer. Quiz night is the third Thursday of the month. Handy for Temple Meads station and buses. Q🅿🄾➤🖵(1,2,51)🔊

Lime Kiln

17 St Georges Road, BS1 5UU (behind City Hall – formerly Council House)

✪ 12-11; 12-10.30 Sun ☎ 07903 068256

6 changing beers Ⓗ

Cosy city-centre free house reopened in 2015 directly behind the City Hall on College Green. The six handpumps dispense beers of a variety of styles. The intention is mostly to stock ales which are seldom seen in Bristol, either new or generally from a bit further afield, with only the best local breweries taking their place on the bar. Traditional cider also features prominently, with at least two kept. You are welcome to bring your own food. ●P🚆(1,2,3)☻♥

No.1 Harbourside

1 Canons Road, BS1 5UH

✪ 10-midnight (11 Mon; 1am Fri & Sat); 10-11 Sun

☎ (0117) 929 1100 ⊕ no1harbourside.co.uk

8 changing beers (often Arbor, Bristol Beer Factory) Ⓗ

Refurbished pub/diner on the covered walkway on the quayside of the floating harbour. With early opening it is ideal for morning coffee, snacking or a cheeky early beer. Five handpumps usually feature two Bristol Beer Factory products and three guests, many from Arbor, supplemented by a good selection of bottled beers and changing ciders. Food is served all day and there are some tables outside. Free live music takes place late evenings Wednesday to Saturday. ✿◑♿●🚆☻♥

Seven Stars

1 Thomas Lane, BS1 6JG (just off Victoria St)

✪ 12-11; 12-10.30 Sun ☎ (0117) 927 2845 ⊕ 7stars.co.uk

8 changing beers Ⓗ

Many who live miles away call this small free house their local. It has a pool table, a rock-oriented jukebox and outdoor seating. Eight pumps dispense a full range of styles and strengths, plus ciders and perries. Quality acoustic acts play on weekend afternoons. Beeriodicals are held on the first Monday to Thursday of every month, with 20 beers from a different county each time. Anti-slavery campaigner Thomas Clarkson used this pub as a base during his research into the trade. ✿➥♣●🚆(1,2,51)☻♥

Small Bar

31 King Street, BS1 4DZ

✪ 12-12.30am (1am Fri & Sat); 12-midnight Sun

⊕ thebigbeerco.com/small-bar

8 changing beers Ⓗ

Opened in late 2013, this bar specialises in great beer - up to eight on cask and a huge bottle list. Not really small, it has three rooms - the upstairs one features comfy sofas and a small library. The small brew kit on-site is used to test recipes for Left Hand Giant Brewery, which are then brewed elsewhere. Quality food is available most times when open. Unusually, the beer is served in third, half or two-thirds of a pint measure only. Q✿◑●🚆☻♥

Three Tuns

78 St George's Road, BS1 5UR (300yds from Bristol Cathedral towards Hotwells)

✪ 12-11 (midnight Thu-Sat); 12-10.30 Sun

☎ (0117) 907 0690 ⊕ the3tuns.com

9 changing beers (often Arbor) Ⓗ

Though no longer in the direct control of Arbor Ales, the pub still showcases many of its beers. There are seven pumps dispensing the full range of

beer styles, with two or three from Arbor and the rest from top-rated British brewers, plus many unusual bottled beers and several ciders. The L-shaped interior has scrubbed wooden tables and mixed seating, plus a covered, heated rear patio. A small range of high-quality bar food is served. It hosts occasional beer festivals. ✿◑●🚆☻♥

Volunteer Tavern 🏆

9 New Street, BS2 9DX (close to main Cabot Circus car park across carriageway from shops)

✪ 12-11 (midnight Fri & Sat) ☎ (0117) 955 8498

⊕ volunteertavern.co.uk

6 changing beers Ⓗ

Dating from 1670 and listed, the Volunteer is tucked away in a side street close to Cabot Circus shops and Old Market bus interchange. It reopened in 2011 and has quickly become popular on the local scene. Six changing beers including dark brews are served, plus two changing ciders. Regular beer festivals, with 25-plus ales, take place, as do live music events. It has a large, fully enclosed paved garden. Food is served every day and is hugely popular on Sundays (book ahead). CAMRA branch Pub of the Year 2016. ✿◑●🚆☻♥

Bristol: Clifton

Eldon House

6 Lower Clifton Hill, BS8 1BT (off top of Jacobs Wells Rd)

✪ 12-2.30 (not Mon-Wed), 5-11.30; 12-1am Fri & Sat; 12-11 Sun ☎ (0117) 922 1271 ⊕ theeldonhouse.com

Bath Ales Prophecy, Gem; 3 changing beers (often Bristol Beer Factory) Ⓗ

A tasteful extension in 2009 has not detracted from the traditional look and feel of this cosy end-of-terrace pub, which lies close to the busy Clifton Triangle area. Get off a bus near the top of Park Street and head a short way down Jacobs Wells Road. The four or five beers include guests from well-chosen independent brewers, often local, and occasionally from further afield. Good-quality food is served daily and Sunday roasts are popular. Many events are hosted. ◑🚆(1,2,3)☻♥

Hope & Anchor

38 Jacobs Wells Road, BS8 1DR (between Anchor Rd and top of Park St)

✪ 12-11 ☎ (0117) 929 2987 ⊕ hopebristol.com

6 changing beers Ⓗ

Popular and friendly pub offering up to six changing microbrewery real ales in a range of strengths and styles, generally including a dark ale. Food is served all day every day until 9.30pm. On summer days the secluded terraced garden up some steep steps at the rear can be pleasant. Expect beer festivals, usually three a year, tying in with those of its sister pub, the Volunteer Tavern in St Judes, or with other nearby pubs. Street parking is limited. ⏃✿◑●🚆☻♥

Portcullis

3 Wellington Terrace, BS8 4LE (close to Clifton side of suspension bridge)

✪ 4-11; 12-11 Sat; 12-10.30 Sun ☎ (0117) 973 0270

Dawkins Ales Bristol Blonde, Bristol Best; 4 changing beers Ⓗ

A pub since 1821, rescued by Dawkins in 2008, with a downstairs bar and an upstairs lounge (also used for functions). It has a beautiful, strange design and sits in a Georgian terrace. Seven handpumps dispense two or more Dawkins beers and a range of guests, usually from other micros, and a traditional cider. More formal pub food has started to appear (no food Wed) since a change of management in 2015. The rear garden is accessed from upstairs. ✿☼♪●🖥(8,9,505)🐾 ᜑ

Bristol: Cotham

Brewhouse & Kitchen ✅
31-35 Cotham Hill, BS6 6JY
✿ 11-11 ☎ (0117) 973 3793
Brewhouse & Kitchen Crockers, Hornigold, Yankee Cabot; 1 changing beer (often Brewhouse & Kitchen) Ⓗ
Popular brewpub and dining spot within 100 yards of Clifton Down station on the other side of Whiteladies Road, opened in 2015 and formerly called Crockers. The brewery is at one end of the large room and the kitchen to one side. There is imaginative cooking and even more imaginative brewing on-site. The bar upstairs is being refurbished for 2016 and a patio area is located just across the road from the pub.
🛏✿♪≠●🖥(1,2,3)🐾 ᜑ

Bristol: Easton

Plough
223 Easton Road, BS5 0EG
✿ 4-midnight; 2-2am Fri; 12-2am Sat; 12-midnight Sun
☎ (0117) 955 8556
4 changing beers (sourced locally) Ⓗ
Lively street-corner pub with a young and cosmopolitan clientele. There is a pool table, several large screens for TV sport, and a stage for live acts in the back room. An easy-to-miss door leads to a rear patio/smoking area that tends to be extremely busy and has two further screens on which to watch sport. Four handpumps dispense a varied range of interesting beers, mainly from local brewers. Food is served on Sundays only, with roasts from 12.30pm. ✿≠♣🖥(6,7,506)ᜑ

Bristol: Horfield

Annexe
Seymour Road, BS7 9EQ (behind Sportsman pub)
✿ 11.30-3, 5-11.30; 11.30-11.30 Sat; 12-11 Sun
☎ (0117) 949 3931 ⊕ the-annexe.co.uk
Otter Amber; St Austell Tribute; Sharp's Doom Bar; Timothy Taylor Landlord; Wye Valley HPA; 2 changing beers Ⓗ
Community pub close to the county cricket ground and not far from the Memorial Stadium, which means it can be busy on match days. Inside is a converted skittle alley and a large conservatory/family room. Several TVs show live sport, including one on the partially covered patio outside. Good wholesome food is served, including quality pizzas, available until 10pm. No dogs are allowed, even on the patio. One or two of the guest beers can be fairly adventurous. 🛏✿♪🖥(19,71,72)ᜑ

Drapers Arms
447 Gloucester Road, BS7 8TZ
✿ 5-9.30; 12-9.30 Sat ⊕ thedrapersarms.co.uk
4 changing beers (often Ashley Down) Ⓖ
Close to the Memorial Stadium, this is Bristol's first micropub. It has close links to Ashley Down Brewery and all beers are from local breweries. The emphasis is on real ale, served by gravity, and conversation. There is no music, TV or gaming machines, and mobile phones should be used with

discretion. Traditional cider, wine and bar snacks are sold, but no keg beers, lagers or spirits. There is disabled access to the pub but no disabled toilet.
Q●🖥(19,71,72)🐾

Bristol: Hotwells

Bag of Nails
141 St Georges Road, BS1 5UW
✿ 12-11; 12-10.30 Sun
8 changing beers Ⓗ
Small, gas-lit terraced free house dating from the 1860s, serving up to eight changing beers from small or new brewers from all over, including local micros. It also has over 100 bottled beers, a real cider, occasional beer festivals and a policy of no children or 'idiot pub crawls'. The interior features terracotta colours, sultry wallpaper, portholes in the floor, many pub cats roaming free, eclectic music from a proper record player, plus board games and toys for the incurably playful.
●🖥(55,352,354)

Merchants Arms
5 Merchants Road, BS8 4PZ
✿ 4-11; 12-11 Fri-Sun ☎ (0117) 907 3047
Bath Ales Special Pale Ale, Gem; 2 changing beers Ⓗ
One of the earliest Bath Ales tied houses, but now a free house, it still usually has two Bath Ales beers on, but also two guest beers, usually from South-west brewers. Pies and rolls are available at most times. Both rooms are furnished with dark wood seating. In the small back bar chess, draughts, Othello, cribbage, dominoes and other games can be played. There is a small free car park 50 yards behind the pub. **Q**🛏♣🖥🐾ᜑ

Bristol: Kingsdown

Hillgrove Porter Stores
53 Hillgrove Street North, BS2 8LT
✿ 4-midnight (1am Fri); 2-1am Sat; 2-midnight Sun
☎ (0117) 924 9818
Dawkins Ales Bristol Blonde, Bristol Best; 10 changing beers (often Dawkins Ales) Ⓗ
The first of the Dawkins Taverns, this is the brainchild of a local entrepreneur who also owns the Dawkins Brewery. The interior is horseshoe-shaped, with a lounge area hidden behind the bar, and a pleasant patio. An excellent community pub, it usually dispenses up to eight guest ales, including dark beers and rare styles, plus up to two changing traditional ciders. Guest beers are sourced regionally and there are occasional beer festivals. Booking is advised for the popular Sunday carvery.
✿♪≠●🖥(5,70,71)🐾

Bristol: St Philips

Barley Mow
39 Barton Road, BS2 0LF (400yds from rear exit of Temple Meads station over footbridge)
✿ 12-11 (11.30 Fri & Sat); 12-10 Sun ☎ (0117) 930 4709
⊕ barleymowbristol.com
Bristol Beer Factory Seven; 6 changing beers Ⓗ
Completely refurbished in early 2013 and relaunched as Bristol Beer Factory's flagship pub. Eight handpulls offer two beers from the brewery plus six changing guests from only the highest-quality UK breweries. There is also an extensive bottled beer list, and regular beer-related events are hosted. A small varying range of quality meals

is available lunchtimes and evenings, with Sunday roasts 12-5pm. A short walk from Temple Meads station and the Old Market bus interchange.
🏂🅰🍴🕱🛉🖿(506)🐾🛜

Bristol: St Werburghs

Miners Arms

136 Mina Road, BS2 9YQ (400yds from M32 jct 3)
🅒 4-11 (midnight Fri); 2-midnight Sat; 2-11 Sun
☎ (0117) 907 9874
Dawkins Ales Bristol Blonde; house beer (by Dawkins Ales); 4 changing beers Ⓗ
Located close to St Werburghs City Farm, this is an excellent street-corner local, part of the Dawkins chain. There are usually four guest beers and two from Dawkins, along with Westons cider. A small, quiet bar lies to the side of the main bar, with a larger pool room to the rear and an upstairs room which can be booked for functions and private parties. Roasts are served Sundays from 2pm and Mondays from 4pm. Thursday is quiz night.
🏂🅰♣🛉🖿(5)🐾🛜

Bristol: Stokes Croft

Canteen

80 Stokes Croft, BS1 3QY
🅒 11-midnight (1am Fri & Sat); 11-11 Sun
☎ (0117) 923 2017 ⊕ canteenbristol.co.uk
5 changing beers Ⓗ
On the ground floor of a 1970s office block, now a cultural/community centre, this café-style bar has a fitting name as it comprises a large open-plan area with plywood tables and steel tube chairs. The long bar serves up to five real ales, usually local ones, of varying strengths and styles. An open kitchen offers a range of good-value locally sourced food. At the other end of the room is a stage, with nightly live music.
🅰🍴🚻♣🛉🖿(5,25,11)🛜

Bristol: Whitehall

Red Lion

206 Whitehall Road, BS5 9BP
🅒 2-12.30am (3am Fri); 12-3am Sat; 12-midnight Sun
☎ (0117) 329 1316
4 changing beers Ⓗ
Built at the beginning of the 20th century and rescued from closure in 2012, this basic pub has a bar, lounge, pool table and darts. There is a log-burning fire, and a beer garden to the rear. The real ales change regularly, with a minimum of three on at any time, often from local microbreweries. At least one dark beer is usually served, plus two real ciders, Black Dragon and the locally made Lucifer Dry. There is regular live music.
🏂🅰🕱♣🛉🖿(6,7)🐾🛜

Broadwell

Fox Inn Ⓛ

The Green, GL56 0UF (off A429 Fosse Way)
🅒 11-2.30, 6-11; 12-3, 7-10.30 Sun ☎ (01451) 870909
Donnington BB, Gold, SBA; 1 changing beer (sourced locally) Ⓗ
Attractive stone-built hostelry overlooking the village green. The good-value local Donnington beers are brewed only a few miles away, and are popular with visitors. A family-run regular Guide local, it offers good company and quality home-

cooked food. There are flagstoned floors in the bar area, jugs hanging from the beams, darts in the bar and games of Aunt Sally in the garden. Nearby are some great local walks, and it is handy for Stow-on-the-Wold and Moreton-in-Marsh.
Q🏂🅰🅓Å♣🛉P🖿🐾

Brockhampton

Craven Arms 🍺 Ⓛ

Kingsbury Street, GL54 5XQ (off A436)
🅒 12-3, 6-11 ☎ (01242) 820410 ⊕ thecravenarms.co.uk
Butcombe Bitter; Otter Bitter; 2 changing beers Ⓗ
A 17th-century free house set in an attractive hillside village with outstanding views and walks. It has a cosy bar area with an open fire and a dining room separated by stone windows. Four carefully selected beers are well kept by the owner-chef. A regular in the Guide, it is well managed by a friendly family who organise functions for locals each month and a summer beer festival. Local CAMRA Pub of the Year runner-up 2015 and finalist in 2016. Q🏂🅰🍴🅓Å♣P🐾🛜

Brockweir

Brockweir Inn Ⓛ

Mill Hill, NP16 7NG (off A466, over bridge)
🅒 12-2.30, 6-11; 12-11 Sat & Sun ☎ (01291) 689548
⊕ thebrockweirinn.co.uk
Kingstone Tewdric's Tipple; 3 changing beers (sourced regionally; often Butcombe, Kingstone) Ⓗ
A veritable gem of the Wye Valley, this cracking hostelry is blessed with two bars of differing character, both a symphony of stone. This much-loved and quirky pub generates a convivial, warm and calming atmosphere. There is a small dining area to the rear, while upstairs is a popular community games room (also available for meetings). Outside is an intriguing walled garden complete with clay oven; a beautiful suntrap for those wanting to relax away from hectic modernity. Q🏂🅰🍴Å♣P

Brookend

Lammastide Inn Ⓛ

Old Brookend, GL13 9SF (off B4066, near Berkeley)
SO6842202062
🅒 12-3, 6-midnight; 12-midnight Sat & Sun
☎ (01453) 811337 ⊕ lammastideinn.co.uk
Draught Bass; Wye Valley Bitter; 2 changing beers (sourced nationally) Ⓗ
An attractive, popular pub built in 1932. The imposing main bar has a lovely bay window, and the comfortable lounge is warmed by a real fire. The bar, garden and toilets are accessible by wheelchair. The large dining area serves some great food all week (including takeaway fish and chips Mon and Tue). The extensive garden is equipped with children's play equipment and offers great views towards the River Severn and Forest of Dean. Well-behaved dogs are welcome.
Q🏂🅰🍴🛉P🐾🛜

Charfield

Pear Tree Micropub Ⓛ

6 Wotton Road, GL12 8TP (1½ miles from M4 jct 14)
🅒 2-9.30; 12-10.30 Sat; 12-9.30 Sun ☎ (01454) 260663
4 changing beers (sourced regionally) Ⓖ

Reinvented as a lively micropub, this cosy one-roomed wonder is a joy to behold, from the attractively tiled flooring, the small wooden bar, the way the ales are served (through casks mounted in an old fireplace), to the myriad humorous details among the wonderful murals covering most of the vertical surfaces. Up to four beers are offered at busy times, usually from local and regional microbreweries. Some raised decking provides outdoor seating at the front. Q♣●P🚲

Cheltenham

Beehive Inn 🅛 ✅
1-3 Montpellier Villas, GL50 2XE
🕒 12-midnight (1am Fri & Sat) ☎ (01242) 702270
🌐 thebeehivemontpellier.com
6 changing beers (often Great Western, Hop Back, Timothy Taylor) 🅗
Bustling, popular local in the Suffolks residential area of town serving up to six ales. It has a separate first-floor restaurant/function room with a good range of food, including a popular bar menu. The pub was transformed by Steve, the former landlord of the Old Spot in Dursley, when it was a recent national CAMRA Pub of the Year. It continues to thrive under the same team, with plans for further improvements including going free of tie. 🌞😺🕙♣●🚲(61,51)🐾🎵

Charlton Kings Club
21 Church Street, Charlton Kings, GL53 8AP
🕒 12-3, 6-11; 11.30-3, 6-midnight Fri; 12-midnight Sat; 12-11 Sun ☎ (01242) 525511 🌐 charltonkingsclub.co.uk
Butcombe Bitter; 3 changing beers (often Butcombe, Hop Kettle, Oakham) 🅗
Popular village club in the heart of Charlton Kings, with a large lounge, separate sports bar and a skittle alley on the ground floor, plus a large function room and snooker room upstairs. Regular live music is played upstairs (Vonnies Blues Club) and also in the main lounge. Four regularly changing beers are sold, generally at least one from Butcombe, with guests sourced nationally. A beer festival is held annually in November. Card-carrying CAMRA members are admitted free for occasional visits (for others there is a small fee). Bar snacks available. 🌞😺♣P🚲(B,P,Q)🎵

Cheltenham Motor Club 🅛
Upper Park Street, GL52 6SA (first right off Hales Rd from London Rd lights, 100yds on right; pedestrian access from A40 via Crown Passage opp Sandford Mill Rd jct)
🕒 6-midnight (1am Fri); 12-1am Sat; 7-midnight Sun ☎ (01242) 522590 🌐 cheltmc.com
Stroud Tom Long; 4 changing beers (often Moor Beer) 🅗
Visitors are welcome at this friendly club just off London Road which has recently been refurbished with new bars, furnishings, and a new snug. It has won many awards. Four changing ales from across the country are on the bar, plus the regular Stroud Tom Long, at least one KeyKeg, and four ciders. Two or more beer festivals are held annually, plus regular Meet the Brewer evenings. Home to quiz, darts and pool teams. Q🌞♣●P🚲(B,51)🐾🎵

Jolly Brewmaster 🅛
39 Painswick Road, GL50 2EZ
🕒 2.30-11; 12-11 Sat; 12-10.30 Sun ☎ (01242) 772121
7 changing beers (often Bespoke, Moor Beer, Severn Vale) 🅗

Frequent local CAMRA Pub of the Year, with seven handpumps featuring a changing range of ales sourced nationally, and at least six ciders including Black Rat perry and cider and Gwynt y Ddraig Black Dragon. This busy and friendly community hub features original etched windows, a horseshoe bar and open fire. The attractive courtyard garden is popular in the summer and holds regular barbecues. Bar snacks are available. Quiz nights are Monday and Wednesday. Q🌞😺●🚲(10,94)🐾🎵

Kemble Brewery Inn 🅛 ✅
27 Fairview Street, GL52 2JF (off northern inner ring road jct Fairview Rd/St Johns Ave, look for Fairview St beside Machine Mart, and pub is approx 100yds on right)
🕒 11-11 (midnight Fri & Sat); 12-11 Sun ☎ (01242) 243446
Bath Ales Gem; Wye Valley Butty Bach; 4 changing beers 🅗
Small, popular back-street local, hard to find but well worth the effort. Originally a butcher's shop in 1845, it became a pub in 1847, and was fully refurbished in 2016. Six ales from near and far are dispensed alongside Westons Traditional Scrumpy. There is a small attractive walled garden where smoking is permitted. It stages a guest chef night Mondays 7-9pm for charity. Q🌞😺🕙♣●🐾

Moran's Eating House
123-129 Bath Road, GL53 7LS
🕒 10-11, closed Sun ☎ (01242) 581481
🌐 moranseatinghouse.co.uk
2 changing beers (often Purity, Timothy Taylor, Wye Valley) 🅗
Highly regarded as a restaurant, but the separate attractive ale and wine bar is popular for socialising and currently serves two ales. The beer range varies daily and features interesting ales, generally from the region, although Timothy Taylor beers are frequent guests. The bar menu includes tapas and platters, and speciality sandwiches and home-made cakes are served in the afternoon. There is a pleasant conservatory to the rear and covered outdoor seating to the front. Q🌞😺🕙🚲(F,46)🎵

Sandford Park Alehouse 🅛
20 High Street, GL50 1DZ (E end of High St, past Strand on right)
🕒 12-midnight (11 Mon & Tue); 12-11 Sun
☎ (01242) 574517 🌐 spalehouse.co.uk
Oakham Citra; Purity Mad Goose; Wye Valley Butty Bach; 6 changing beers 🅗
Local CAMRA Pub of the Year 2014 and National Pub of the Year 2015, this smart, contemporary alehouse has a U-shaped main bar area complete with bar billiards table, a cosy front snug with wood-burning stove, and a large south-facing patio/garden. A function room/lounge with TV sport is on the first floor. Ten handpumps feature different ales from microbreweries sourced nationally and locally, plus a cider (the website keeps you up to date). There are also 16 speciality lagers. Q🌞😺🕙●♣🚲(B,P,Q)🐾🎵

Strand 🅛
40-42 High Street, GL50 1EE
🕒 12-11 (midnight Fri); 10-midnight Sat; 12-10.30 Sun
☎ (01242) 511848 🌐 strandpub.co.uk
5 changing beers (often Bespoke, Otter, Stroud) 🅗
Modern wine bar-style pub at the east end of the High Street, offering five beers mainly from the region (at least one from the featured brewery of the month) and a cider. Good-value food is served daily (12-2.30pm, 6-9pm Mon-Fri; 12-9pm Sat; 12-

5pm Sun), including gourmet burger night on Wednesday. An upstairs function room is available for hire, along with a cellar bar that is home to live comedy and music nights. The large south-facing patio/garden provides a pleasant outdoor drinking area. ⊛◑●🖳🐾≋

Cirencester

Drillman's Arms
34 Gloucester Road, GL7 2JY (on old A417)
✪ 11-2.30, 5.30-11; 11-midnight Sat; 12-4, 7-10.30 Sun
☎ (01285) 653892
Sharp's Doom Bar; 3 changing beers (sourced nationally) Ⓗ
Local CAMRA Pub of the Year, this lively Georgian free house, perched beside a busy road, has a convivial lounge with woodburner, a pub games-dominated public bar and a popular skittle alley. Run by the same landlady for over 25 years, the lovely interior features low beamed ceilings, horse brasses and brewery pictures. Fresh flowers grace the immaculate toilets. Well-priced pub food is served, lunchtimes only. A summer beer festival is hosted in the small car park at the front.
⊛◑▲♣P🐾≋

Marlborough Arms Ⓛ
1 Sheep Street, GL7 1QW
✪ 12-midnight
Box Steam Piston Broke; North Cotswold Windrush Ale; 6 changing beers (sourced nationally) Ⓗ
Local CAMRA Cider Pub of the Year again, this lively, wooden-floored pub lies opposite the old GWR Station. A real ale haven, it offers eight beers from regionals and microbreweries (look for Corinium Ales), and a plethora of interesting boxed ciders. Brewery memorabilia adorn the walls, with pews and a deep-set fireplace adding character. The ceiling is disappearing behind the encroaching pumpclip collection. The patio at the rear is used for barbecues during the beer and cider festivals.
⊛♣●🐾≋

Cliffords Mesne

Yew Tree Ⓛ
GL18 1JS (just S of village)
✪ 12-10.30 (11.30 Fri & Sat); 12-6.30 Sun; closed Mon
☎ (01531) 820719 ⊕ yewtreeinn.com
Sharp's Doom Bar; Wye Valley HPA, Butty Bach; 1 changing beer (sourced locally; often Bespoke) Ⓗ
Stone pub in an attractive village near to Newent Woods. With good views to the Malverns, it is a starting point for keen walkers doing a climb up May Hill. Up to four ales are served, with an in-house brewery due to come on stream soon. The restaurant has an excellent range of food (booking strongly advised). Popular regular quiz nights with food take place every second Friday of the month.
🌜⊛◑&▲♣P

Cold Aston

Plough Inn Ⓛ
Cheltenham, GL54 3BN (centre of village)
✪ 12-3 (not Mon), 6-11; 12-11 Fri-Sun ☎ (01451) 822602
⊕ coldastonplough.com
3 changing beers (sourced nationally) Ⓗ/Ⓖ
A transformed stone-flagged country pub high in the Cotswolds. The attractive village went by the name of Aston Blank in the Domesday Book.

Reopened in 2013 by young owners and their team, it has three letting luxury bedrooms within the innovative internal extension of the 17th-century cottage. The emphasis is on real ale and serving good, interesting food. Look out for three changing beers from award-winning brewers, two served directly from the cask. Local CAMRA Pub of the Year 2014/2015 and finalist 2016. Q🌜⊛🛏◑&▲♣P🖳🐾

Cranham

Black Horse Inn Ⓛ
GL4 8HP (off A46 or B4070)
✪ 12-2.30, 6.30-11; 12-11 Sat; 12-5 Sun; closed Mon
☎ (01452) 812217
4 changing beers (sourced regionally; often Wye Valley) Ⓗ
A 17th-century, stone-built free house almost hidden up a side lane in the village. A quiet idyll with a proper fire and no jukebox, TV or fruit machines, the lack of a reliable mobile phone signal in the village means that patrons here indulge in the traditional pursuit of conversation with friends, strangers and the walkers who have explored the myriad woodland paths nearby. A menu of hearty pub food is served. Q🌜◑♣●P🐾

Dursley

New Inn Ⓛ
82-84 Woodmancote, GL11 4AJ (on A4135)
✪ 2.30 (5 Thu)-11; closed Mon-Wed ☎ (01453) 519288
⊕ newinnwoodmancote.co.uk
4 changing beers (sourced nationally; often Cotswold Spring, Wye Valley) Ⓗ
Known as a dog-friendly establishment, with a greeting assured from the pub labrador, this comfortable inn features a large L-shaped public bar with tiled floor and a smaller lounge. A range of fine beers is sourced from smaller, local and regional brewers where possible, dependent upon which ales the regulars request. There is a spacious suntrap of a garden at the rear, which is popular on sunny days. Freshly made rolls are often available.
🌜⊛♣●P🐾

Old Spot Inn Ⓛ
2 Hill Road, GL11 4JQ (by bus station and free car park)
✪ 11-11; 12-11 Sun ☎ (01453) 542870 ⊕ oldspotinn.co.uk
Uley Old Ric; 7 changing beers (sourced nationally) Ⓗ
Cracking free house dating from 1776, serving up to seven independent ales. Named after the Gloucestershire Old Spot pig, a porcine theme blends with extensive brewery memorabilia, low ceilings and log fires to create a convivial atmosphere, enhanced by welcoming staff. The attractive garden has a heated, covered area. Wholesome, freshly prepared food, which complements the pub's enthusiasm for real ale, is served 12-6pm. On the Cotswold Way, it is popular with walkers. Regular Meet the Brewer evenings are hosted. Q🌜⊛◑&●🖳🐾≋

Eastington

Old Badger Inn Ⓛ ✔
Alkerton Road, GL10 3AT (near Spring Hill)
✪ 12-11; 12-10.30 Sun ☎ (01453) 822892
⊕ oldbadgerinn.co.uk
Stroud Budding; Uley Bitter; Wye Valley Butty Bach; 4 changing beers (sourced regionally) Ⓗ

Formerly the Victoria – closed by Punch Taverns in 2010 – the pub was reopened as a free house after being sympathetically renovated, modernised and extended. The large single bar features a wood-burning stove, with smaller rooms on either side plus a restaurant area. The walls are covered with brewery and other memorabilia. Outside there is a covered and heated patio and a pleasant, well-tended garden. Local CAMRA Cider Pub of the Year. Q☺☆☺◑♿♣☕P🚃 (61,401)🐾☕📶

Ebrington

Ebrington Arms 🅛

Chipping Campden, GL55 6NH (by village green)
✪ 12-11 ☎ (01386) 593223 ⊕ theebringtonarms.co.uk
2 changing beers

A 17th-century Cotswold stone-built inn in a beautiful village with excellent walks close by. The cosy bar holds a lovely open fireplace and six handpumps, with three dispensing the pub's own Yubby ales and two changing guests. It offers an excellent range of food from local suppliers. A regular Guide entry, it also owns the Killingworth Castle in Wotton, in Oxfordshire. Five en-suite rooms are available. A class-leading family-run pub with enthusiastic staff, it is a former CAMRA Pub of the Year finalist. ☎☆🛏◑♿♣☕P

Forthampton

Lower Lode Inn 🅛

GL19 4RE (follow sign to Forthampton from A438 Tewkesbury to Ledbury road) SO8788231809
✪ 12-midnight (2am Fri & Sat); 12-11 Sun
☎ (01684) 293224 ⊕ lowerlodeinn.co.uk
Sharp's Doom Bar; 4 changing beers 🅷

Blessed with views across the River Severn to Tewkesbury Abbey, this 15th-century inn, with its three acres of lawns, is a popular stopover for boats and is a Camping and Caravanning Club hideaway site. Some stained glass is noteworthy, although the fireplace dominates if you have battled flooded approach roads in winter. A beer festival is hosted in September, and a small ferry operates from the Tewkesbury side from Easter to mid-September. Day fishing is available, plus en-suite accommodation. Q☺☆🛏◑♣P🐾

Frampton Cotterell

Globe Inn

366 Church Road, BS36 2AB
✪ 12-11; 12-10.30 Sun ☎ (01454) 778286
⊕ theglobeframptoncotterell.co.uk
Butcombe Bitter; Fuller's London Pride; 3 changing beers 🅷

Independent free house on the Frome Valley walkway, which links the Cotswolds with the Avon Valley walkway. An open-plan pub with a separate pavilion which can be hired for functions, it has an active golf society, a Tuesday quiz and caters for children with an excellent play area. Home-made food using local produce is its speciality. Three guest beers are normally available and include many local brews. Moles Black Rat cider is served. ☆☆◑♣P🚃 (222,46,81)📶

Rising Sun

43 Ryecroft Road, BS36 2HN
✪ 11.30-11.30 (midnight Fri & Sat); 12-11 Sun
☎ (01454) 772330

Draught Bass; Great Western Maiden Voyage, Classic Gold; 2 changing beers (often Great Western) 🅷

Brewery tap for the Great Western Brewery, this is an excellent free house owned by the same family for many years. At least two Great Western beers and at least one guest are on tap. The three-roomed interior comprises the main bar, a small snug, and a conservatory/restaurant. Food is served all day (until 8pm Sun). There is also a skittle alley and function room, and an enclosed child-safe beer garden. The pub has featured in almost every edition of this Guide. Q☺◑♣P🚃 (46,81,82)🐾📶

Frampton-on-Severn

Three Horseshoes 🅛

The Green, GL2 7DY (off B4071)
✪ 11.30-2, 5.30-11 (1am Fri); 11.30-1am Sat; 11.30-10 Sun
☎ (01452) 742100 ⊕ threehorseshoespub.co.uk
Sharp's Doom Bar; Timothy Taylor Landlord; Uley Bitter 🅷

Atmospheric 19th-century two-bar rural community pub originally built by a farrier at the south end of England's longest village green. The food is home-cooked, especially its unique 3-Shu pie, which is freshly baked to order. Both bars have coal fires, and dogs are welcome in the flagstoned public bar. Evening jamming sessions are popular (largely biased towards folk music), as are pasty baking competitions, conker contests and veggie Olympics. A double boules court hosts annual championships. Q☺☆☺◑♿Å♣☕🐾

Gloucester

King Edward VII 🔵

47 Old Cheltenham Road, Longlevens, GL2 0AN
✪ 11.30-11 (midnight Thu-Sat) ☎ (01452) 381273
Bath Ales Gem; Butcombe Bitter; Wadworth 6X; 2 changing beers (sourced nationally) 🅷

Red-brick pub built in 1907 by Mitchells & Butlers, renamed after Edward VII's visit to Gloucester in 1909. This large, popular community asset was given a total refit in 2001, featuring some practical modern styling and a large, central bar layout, while keeping the real fire. The menu choices go down well with the locals, and the changing guest ales are from the Ember Inns cask list. An attractive garden graces the front. ☆◑♿P🚃 (94)🐾📶

Pelican Inn 🅛 🔵

4 St Mary's Street, GL1 2QR (WNW of cathedral)
✪ 11-11.30 ☎ (01452) 387877
Wye Valley Bitter 🅷, HPA 🅷/🅖, Butty Bach, Dorothy Goodbody's Wholesome Stout; 4 changing beers (sourced regionally; often Wye Valley) 🅷

Local CAMRA Pub of the Year again. It was licensed as an alehouse in the 17th century – people believe some of its beams are from Drake's ship, the Golden Hind, which began life as the Pelican. Rescued and refurbished by Wye Valley Brewery in 2012, its popularity has grown steadily, with the single bar dominated by conversation; there is a smaller room to the side and an attractive outdoor drinking area. The growing range of cider and perry increases during the summer. Q☺♿♣☕🚃🐾

Tank 🅛 🔵

12-14 Llanthony Road, GL1 2EH
✪ 12-11 ☎ (01452) 690541 ⊕ tankgloucester.com

**Gloucester Priory Pale, Mariner, Citra, Dockside Dark;
4 changing beers (sourced nationally)** H
A welcoming, urban warehouse-style bar with a
contemporary feel, in the heart of the Gloucester
Docks redevelopment that opened in 2015. The
decor utilises the building's strengths, and is well
worth a look. Though primarily the brewery tap for
Gloucester beers, it offers a wide range of guest
ales, bottled beers and ciders. Food is available in
the shape of local meats and cheeses served on
platters, along with a selection of hand-made
pizzas. ⫷▶⅋♿P🚌(10)🛜

Gretton

Royal Oak 🅛 ✅
Gretton Road, GL54 5EP (E end of village)
✪ 11-11; 12-10.30 Sun ☎ (01242) 604999
⊕ royaloakgretton.co.uk
**Marston's EPA; Ramsbury Gold; Wye Valley HPA; 3
changing beers** H
A warm welcome is assured from the local owners
of this popular Cotswold pub set in two acres. All
the regular beers are from local breweries or
Marston's. The home-cooked food can be eaten in
the L-shaped bar or in the conservatory with its
outstanding views across the Vale of Evesham. The
Royal Oak dates from about 1830 and the large
garden includes a children's play area and a tennis
court. The Gloucestershire-Warwickshire railway
runs past the garden. 🚶🐕🏠⫷♿♣P🐾

Ham

Salutation Inn 🏆 🅛
Ham Green, GL13 9QH (from Berkeley take road
signposted to Jenner Museum)
✪ 12-2.30 (not Mon), 5-11; 12-11 Sat; 12-10.30 Sun
☎ (01453) 810284 ⊕ the-sally-at-ham.com
**Butcombe Bitter; 4 changing beers (sourced
nationally; often Tiley's)** H
Branch CAMRA Pub of the Year again, this cracking
rural free house/brewpub is within walking
distance of the Jenner Museum and Berkeley
Castle. The enthusiastic landlord has turned brewer
(Tiley's), keeping an inspired selection of ales and
eight real ciders and perries. The pub has two cosy
bars, a lovely woodburner and a skittles alley/
function room. Food is served lunchtimes and
occasional evenings only. Live folk music and piano
singalongs occur fairly regularly – see the website.
Q🚶🐕🏠⫷♣♿P🐾🛜

Hawkesbury Upton

Beaufort Arms 🅛
High Street, GL9 1AU (off A46, 6 miles N of M4 jct 18)
✪ 12-11; 12-10.30 Sun ☎ (01454) 238217
⊕ beaufortarms.com
**Bath Ales Special Pale Ale; Bristol Beer Factory Seven;
3 changing beers (sourced regionally)** H
A wonderful Grade II-listed Cotswold stone free
house, built in 1602 and close to the historic
Somerset Monument. It features separate public
and lounge bars, a dining room and skittle alley/
function room, which are all required to house a
veritable plethora of ancient brewery and local
memorabilia. Up to five ales and a traditional cider
are on handpump. It has an attractive garden with
a barbecue used for local community activities. A
great bunch of regulars assure a warm welcome.
Q🚶🐕🏠⫷♿♣♿P🐾🛜

Iron Acton

Lamb Inn 🅛
Wotton Road, BS37 9UZ (opp school)
✪ 11-midnight (1.30am Fri & Sat); 12-11 Sun
☎ (01454) 228265 ⊕ thelambinnironacton.com
**Butcombe Bitter; Courage Best Bitter; 2 changing
beers (sourced locally; often Cotswold Spring)** H
A coaching house since 1690 and a listed building,
it is claimed that William of Orange stayed here.
The central bar is the hub. There is a skittle alley
and function room, and a room upstairs has pool,
darts and TV. Children's swings, a stream and a
covered veranda feature in the garden to the rear.
Look out for great-value offers on meals. The two
guest beers are usually from the local Cotswold
Spring Brewery. Real cider is sold during the
summer. Q🚶🐕🏠⫷♣♿P🚌(X46)🐾🛜

Kingswood

King's Arms 🅛
16 High Street, BS15 4AB
✪ 12-11; 10-midnight Sat & Sun ☎ 07737 794115
Cheddar Ales Gorge Best; 2 changing beers H
A Grade II-listed building that was formerly a
coaching inn, this traditional pub is now a free
house in an area short of real ale-friendly outlets.
There is a recessed games area and a large patio
and garden area to the rear. The young owner/
landlord is a real ale enthusiast and tries to offer
interesting guest beers of all styles – one or two at
a time, plus bottle-conditioned beers, often from
local breweries. 🚶🐕🏠♣♿🚌🚌(6,17,19)🐾🛜

Marshfield

Catherine Wheel
39 High Street, SN14 8LR
✪ 12-11 ☎ (01225) 892220 ⊕ thecatherinewheel.co.uk
**Butcombe Bitter; Cotswold Spring Stunner; Sharp's
Doom Bar; 1 changing beer (sourced locally)** H
Impressive mainly 17th-century building in a large
yet quiet village on the edge of the Cotswolds, but
close to Georgian Bath, ideally situated for a
number of tourist attractions in three counties and
also the city of Bristol. It is an owner-operated free
house. There are several dining areas in addition to
the bar, including a snug. There are also three
letting rooms available. The large fire creates a
cosy atmosphere in the winter months.
Q🚶🛏⫷♿♿P🚌🐾🛜

Mayshill

New Inn ✅
Badminton Road, BS36 2NT (on A432 between Coalpit
Heath and Nibley)
✪ 11.45-2.30, 5.30-10.30; 11.45-11 Fri & Sat; 11.45-10 Sun
☎ (01454) 773161 ⊕ newinn-mayshill.co.uk
3 changing beers (sourced nationally) H
A 17th-century inn hugely popular for its food,
including gluten-free options (booking is advised).
The three guest beers are from far and wide – one
of them usually dark – and a traditional cider is also
kept. The main bar is warmed by a real fire in
winter, and the rear area serves as a restaurant.
Children are welcome until 8.45pm. The garden,
with a play area, is pleasant in summer.
Q🚶🐕🏠⫷♣♿P🚌(46,47,81)🐾🛜

Moreton-in-Marsh

Inn on the Marsh ✔

Stow Road, GL56 0DW (on A429, at S end of town)
⏲ 12-2.30, 7-11 ☎ (01608) 650709
Marston's Pedigree; Ringwood Best Bitter; 2 changing beers (sourced nationally; often Ringwood) [H]
Charming former bakery featuring woven hanging baskets, with a comfortable locals' bar and a large, attractive conservatory and dining area suitable for parties. The pub is a rare outlet in the area for Marston's beers and guest ales such as Ringwood. It has a secluded garden area with nesting sites for the resident ducks who swim on the pond next door. One of the best pubs in Moreton, with an attentive landlord and an annual beer festival. Q🐎❀◐◑♿⛺⇌♣●P🚌🐾

Moseley Green

Rising Sun L

GL15 4HN (off A48 at Blakeney towards Parkend then first left)
⏲ 12-11 (midnight Fri & Sat) ☎ (01594) 562008
🌐 therisingsuninn.biz
Wickwar BOB; 3 changing beers (sourced nationally) [H]
Enjoying panoramic views from its isolated position amid defunct coal mines, this extended pub was built for miners in the early 1800s. Popular with cyclists, hikers, cavers and families, there are several patios, large gardens and a pond. It is hard to believe that trams and trains ran only yards from the pub doors. There are bars on both floors (when busy), a games room and a special children's menu in the dining areas. A local music ensemble rehearses here. 🐎❀🛏◐◑♣●P🚏

Nettleton Bottom

Golden Heart

Birdlip, GL4 8LA (on A417)
⏲ 10.30-11 ☎ (01242) 870261 🌐 thegoldenheart.co.uk
Brakspear Bitter; 3 changing beers (sourced nationally; often Marston's) [H]
A welcome oasis of tranquillity beside the single-carriageway section of the Gloucester to Swindon road, this 400 year-old Cotswold free house retains most of its original features, although adjoining cottages have been absorbed to create extra rooms. The small bar, almost hidden beyond a huge open fireplace, overlooks a stone-paved patio and garden abutting a cow pasture. The food menu offers the finest award-winning meats and local produce at reasonable prices. There are two en-suite guest bedrooms. Q🐎❀🛏◐◑P🐾📶

Newnham

Black Pig Ale House ✔

High Street, GL14 1BY (up alleyway to side of Ship Inn)
⏲ 3.30-11; 3.30-10.30 Sun ☎ (01594) 516283
🌐 blackpigale.co.uk
4 changing beers (sourced nationally; often St Austell, Wickwar) [G]
This wonderful new venture is within a 16th-century Grade II-listed horse stable, set in the grounds of the Ship Inn. Effectively a micropub, an impressive wooden bar sits opposite a huge fireplace, with the drinks stillaged behind, against the thick stone walls. The changing ales are served direct from the barrel, and there is an upstairs mezzanine area for darts, space invaders and conversation. The winsome garden and courtyard are an enjoyable spot on warmer evenings. ❀♣🚌🐾

Railway Inn

Station Road, GL14 1DA (turn off A48 at clock tower)
⏲ 1-midnight; 12-midnight Sat & Sun ☎ (01594) 516317
3 changing beers (sourced nationally) [H]
County CAMRA Cider Pub of the Year again, this friendly community hub is a joy to visit, with its railway memorabilia adorning the walls, flagstoned floors, warm fires, a beer garden, and an Indian restaurant upstairs. It offers 15 ciders and perries and 30-plus bottled real ciders. Several local cider producers drink here and love explaining their craft to visitors – everyone wants you to find a cider or perry that you genuinely enjoy. Lively music acts are hosted most weekends. ❀◑⛺♣●🐾📶

Oldbury-on-Severn

Anchor Inn

Church Road, BS35 1QA
⏲ 11.30-3, 6-10.30; 11.30-11 Fri & Sat; 12-10 Sun
☎ (01454) 413331 🌐 anchor-inn-oldbury.co.uk
Butcombe Bitter; Draught Bass; St Austell Trelawny; 1 changing beer [H]
A lovely village local set by a tributary of the River Severn. There is a traditional public bar to the right, and a comfortable lounge through the main entrance. A bright restaurant sits at the rear, and the extensive garden has mature trees for shelter, with a pétanque piste at the far end. The guest beer is served from Thursday until it runs out. Three rooms have recently become available for B&B accommodation. Q❀🛏◐◑♿●P🐾📶

Quenington

Keepers Arms

Church Road, GL7 5BL (from Fairford turn right at village green)
⏲ 12-3 (not Mon & Tue), 6-11; 12-3, 7-11 Sun
☎ (01285) 750349 🌐 thekeepersarms.co.uk
4 changing beers (sourced nationally; often Butcombe, Otter, St Austell) [H]
Hosted by a delightfully idiosyncratic landlord, this wonderful community local has been transformed into a cracking modern hostelry by the enthusiastic owner. Dogs, children, cricketers, cyclists, art lovers and ramblers are welcome in both the refurbished oak bar and the petite front garden. The unpretentious menus help fill both dining areas (no food Mon or Tue), with regular theme nights and quizzes also proving popular. Two fireplaces give a pleasant glow in winter. Four swish en-suite rooms have garnered great status. 🐎❀🛏◐◑P🐾📶

Sheepscombe

Butchers Arms L ✔

GL6 7RH (signed off A46 N of Painswick and B4070 N of Slad) SO8911610434
⏲ 11.30-3, 6.30 (6 Fri)-11; 11.30-11 Sat; 12-10.30 Sun
☎ (01452) 812113 🌐 butchers-arms.co.uk
Prescott Hill Climb; 2 changing beers (sourced regionally; often Butcombe, Otter, Wye Valley) [H]
Handsome 17th-century Cotswold-stone pub overlooking a wooded valley. Its inn sign, a painted three-dimensional carving of a butcher quaffing ale

while tethered to a pig, is world famous. In 2014 the lean-to outdoor toilets metamorphosed into a new bar, seamlessly executed in reclaimed stone and Welsh oak. This complements a quality inter-war refurbishment that added the generous bay windows and porch. A wood-burning stove offers warmth in winter while the forecourt tables and sloping side garden are suntraps in summer.
Q✤🐕🎂🍴👶🦽♣👜P🅿🔌🐾📶

Shipton Moyne

Cat & Custard Pot 🅛

The Street, GL8 8PN (centre of village, on Tetbury Rd)
✪ 11-3, 6-11 Mon; 11-11 ☎ (01666) 880249
Flying Monk Elmers; Hook Norton Hooky; Wickwar BOB; 1 changing beer (sourced nationally) 🅗
Owned by five local families, this vibrant village pub has a unique pub sign (see the plaque inside) and equestrian memorabilia on the walls. This lovely establishment has recently been updated with disabled toilets and extended dining areas (its food is popular). While the quieter snug is a favourite with families, the busy main bar and attractive front garden can, at times, appear to be the hub of the local dog-walking society.
Q✤🐕🎂🍴♣🐾📶

Slad

Woolpack 🅛

GL6 7QA (on B4070)
✪ 12-midnight ☎ (01452) 813429 ⊕ thewoolpackslad.com
Stroud Budding; Uley Bitter, Old Spot Prize Strong Ale, Pig's Ear Strong Beer; 1 changing beer (sourced regionally; often Gloucester) 🅗
Popular 17th-century inn made famous by Cider with Rosie – its author, Laurie Lee, was a regular all his life. Only one room deep, the pub offers superb views over the Slad Valley, and has been thoughtfully restored – the built-in dark wooden settles in the end rooms are modern. The bar runs the length of the building, extending into all four rooms. Monday is pizza night – prepared on the hob in the revolutionary oven designed by the pub's owner, Daniel Chadwick. Q✤🐕🎂🍴♣👜🐾📶

Slimbridge

Tudor Arms 🅛 ✅

Shepherd's Patch, GL2 7BP (from A38 1 mile beyond Slimbridge village)
✪ 11-11 ☎ (01453) 890306 ⊕ thetudorarms.co.uk
Palmers Dorset Gold; Uley Bitter, Pig's Ear Strong Beer; Wadworth 6X; Wye Valley HPA; 1 changing beer (sourced regionally) 🅗
Licensed since the early 1800s when the Gloucester-Sharpness canal was being dug, this large, family-owned and operated free house has two bars and five dining areas plus a skittle alley and games room. A modern lodge alongside offers accommodation for visitors to the Wildfowl and Wetlands Trust site. Known for good food and a great range of up to 10 ciders and perries, this is a popular spot, with a separate caravan and camping site at the back. Q✤🐕🎂🛏🍴🏕♣🅿🐾📶

South Woodchester

Ram Inn 🅛

Station Road, GL5 5EL (signed off A46) SO8395202189
✪ 11-11; 12-11 Sat & Sun ☎ (01453) 873329

Butcombe Adam Henson's Rare Breed; Flying Monk Elmers; Otter Amber; St Austell Tribute; 2 changing beers (sourced regionally; often St Austell, Sharp's) 🅗
Sensitively altered and extended 400-year-old Cotswold-stone inn tucked into the west flank of the Nailsworth Valley. It commands fine views towards Amberley and Minchinhampton Common on the opposite side of the valley from a suntrap front terrace. Inside, three interconnecting rooms (one with a log fire) are grouped around a long stone-built bar. Popular with locals and visitors alike, it is situated in superb walking country near Woodchester Mansion. Car parking at the front is on two levels. Q✤🐕🎂🍴👶🦽♣👜P🅿(40,63)🐾📶

Stroud

Ale House 🅛

9 John Street, GL5 2HA (opp Cornhill farmers' market)
✪ 12-3, 5-11; 12-midnight Fri; 10.30-midnight Sat; 12-11 Sun ☎ (01453) 755447
Cotswold Lion Golden Fleece; Dark Star Hophead; Stroud Budding; 6 changing beers (sourced nationally; often Brass Castle, Burning Sky, Tiny Rebel) 🅗
Built in 1837 for the Poor Law Guardians, this Grade II-listed building is a mecca for ale lovers. The bar occupies the double-height top-lit former boardroom, where an all-year-round beer festival showcases beers from the likes of Black Rock, Brass Castle, Burning Sky, Fyne Ales, Marble, Salopian, Saltaire and Tiny Rebel – plus a cider and perry – dispensed from 12 handpumps. Opposite is a blazing log fire and adjoining are two smaller rooms. Home-made curries are a speciality. Local CAMRA Pub of the Year. Q✤🐕🎂🍴👶🦽♣🍴👜📻🐾📶

Crown & Sceptre 🅛

98 Horns Road, GL5 1EG
✪ 3-11; 12-11 Fri & Sat; 12-10.30 Sun ☎ (01453) 762588 ⊕ crownandsceptrestroud.com
Stroud Budding; Uley Bitter, Pig's Ear Strong Beer; 1 changing beer (sourced regionally; often Brains) 🅗
Lively back-street local set at the heart of its community – a genuine free house where Blue Anchor Spingo beers are regular guests. The walls display an eclectic mix of framed prints and posters. A large oak table in a side room is popular with local groups, including Knit and Natter. The pub also has its own motorcycle society. Football, rugby and cricket are screened in the back bar. A terrace to the rear offers panoramic views over Stroud. 🐕🎂♣🅿(8,227)🐾📶

Prince Albert 🅛 ✅

Rodborough Hill, GL5 3SS (corner of Walkley Hill)
✪ 4-11.30 (12.30am Fri); 12-12.30am Sat; 12-10.30 Sun ☎ (01453) 755600 ⊕ theprincealbertstroud.co.uk
Otter Bitter; Stroud Budding; Timothy Taylor Landlord; 4 changing beers (sourced nationally; often Bath Ales, Bristol Beer Factory, Church End) 🅗
Simultaneously bohemian, homely and welcoming, this lively, cosmopolitan, Cotswold-stone pub below Rodborough Common has a big reputation for live music. The L-shaped bar boasts an eclectic mix of furniture, fittings and memorabilia – the walls are covered with film and music posters – and a log fire. The pub hosts a May beer festival, exhibitions and open mic nights. Some events are ticketed (phone or check website). Friday night is street food from Bison Kitchen, at other times bring your own. 🐕🎂📻♣👜📻🐾📶

Tetbury

Royal Oak L ✓

1 Cirencester Road, GL8 8EY (on B4067)
☼ 11-11 (11.30 Fri & Sat); 12-11 Sun ☎ (01666) 500021
⊕ theroyaloaktetbury.co.uk
Bath Ales Barnsey; Stroud Tom Long; 3 changing beers (sourced regionally; often Left Handed Giant, Moor Beer) Ⓗ
Multi award-winning pub that uses clever design options to make this totally renovated establishment feel so modern it is almost traditional! The expanse of wooden surfaces provides a welcoming feel, with a small fireplace adding warmth. Six handpumps include Severn Cider and a vegan ale from Moor – chosen to match the vegan menu option. The one-pot meal is popular, especially on quiz nights. Upstairs dining rooms and six letting rooms are available, with acoustic music most Sunday evenings.
🛏️❀🛲🌙&♣🕯️P🐾🐕🛜

Tewkesbury

Berkeley Arms

8 Church Street, GL20 5PA (between Tewkesbury Cross and Abbey on old A38)
☼ 10-11 ☎ (01684) 290555
Wadworth IPA, 6X, Swordfish; 2 changing beers (often Wadworth) Ⓗ
Popular 15th-century half-timbered venue, just off Tewkesbury Cross. At the rear of this Grade II-listed two-bar pub is a barn, believed to be the oldest non-ecclesiastical building in this historic town, which is used for dining in the summer and serves as a meeting room year round. Good-value food is available daily – of particular note are the landlord's home-baked steak and ale pies. Live music is performed on Saturday evenings. Buses to Cheltenham and Gloucester stop close by.
Q🛏️❀🛲🌙&🛡️♣🕯️🚌(41)🐾🛜

Nottingham Arms L ✓

129 High Street, GL20 5JU (A38, in town centre)
☼ 11-11 ☎ (01684) 276346
St Austell Tribute; Sharp's Doom Bar; Wye Valley HPA, Butty Bach Ⓗ
A fourteenth-century town-centre hostelry with two welcoming rooms - a public bar at the front and the restaurant behind - with timber predominating. Framed photographs of old Tewkesbury adorn the walls. The pub is getting noticed for its excellent, well-priced food, served lunchtimes and evenings. Knowledgeable staff will happily tell you about the resident ghosts. Live music takes place most Sunday evenings and Thursday is quiz night. Westons Old Rosie cider is on the bar. 🛏️🌙🛡️♣🕯️🚌🐾

Royal Hop Pole Hotel L ✓

94 Church Street, GL20 5RS
☼ 7am-11 ☎ (01684) 274039
Great Western Old Higby; Greene King IPA; Hook Norton Old Hooky; Ruddles County; 4 changing beers (sourced locally; often Battledown, Prescott) Ⓗ
Well-known landmark that is an amalgamation of historic buildings from the 15th and 18th centuries. It has been known as the Royal Hop Pole since a visit in September 1891 from Princess Mary of Teck (Queen Mary, Royal Consort of George V). The pub is mentioned in The Pickwick Papers. Purchased by Wetherspoon, it reopened in 2008. There is wood panelling on almost every wall of the spacious,

multi-roomed drinking establishment, with a large patio and garden at the rear.
Q🛏️❀🛲🌙&🛡️P🚌(41,42,72)🛜

Tudor House Hotel L

51 High Street, GL20 5BH
☼ 11-11; 12-10 Sun ☎ (01684) 297755
⊕ tudorhouse.relaxinnz.co.uk
Butcombe Bitter; 7 changing beers (often Butcombe, Exmoor, Titanic) Ⓗ
Situated on the High Street, this delightful Tudor building oozes charm and dignity. The bar offers a selection of eight ales, seven constantly changing. Pub meals are served in the bar and adjoining dining areas. Two outdoor spaces provide a relaxing place to watch the boats on the river behind the pub, or you can enjoy a quiet drink in the Secret Garden. Q🛏️❀🛲🌙&🛡️P🚌🛜

White Bear L

Bredon Road, GL20 5BU (off N end of High St)
☼ 10-midnight ☎ (01684) 296614
⊕ famouswhitebear.co.uk
7 changing beers (sourced nationally; often Bristol Beer Factory, Sadler's, Salopian) Ⓗ
On the north-western edge of the town, this good-value, family-run pub attracts ale and cider drinkers from far and wide. The open-plan L-shaped bar offers room to play pool and darts; there is also a skittle alley. Live music features every Sunday afternoon. The seven ales change frequently and include offerings from local and national award-winning breweries. At least five traditional perries and ciders are always stocked and there is a cider and cheese festival in May. 🛏️❀🛡️♣🕯️P🚌🐾🛜

Thornbury

Anchor Inn L ✓

Gloucester Road, Lower Morton, BS35 1JY
☼ 11-11 ☎ (01454) 281375 ⊕ theanchorthornbury.co.uk
Draught Bass; 5 changing beers Ⓗ
Licensed since 1695 and the second-oldest pub in Thornbury, this friendly, traditional inn has one regular beer and five changing guests, mostly of low to medium strength, with occasional milds, plus a real cider. Good home-cooked food is served daily. There are two large rooms, one with a central fireplace. The pub has its own darts, crib, dominoes and cricket teams and an angling syndicate. The garden includes a boules piste and children's play area. 🛏️❀🌙♣🕯️P🚌🐾🛜

Wheatsheaf ✓

Chapel Street, BS35 2BJ
☼ 11-11 (midnight Fri & Sat); 12-10.30 Sun
☎ (01454) 412356 ⊕ wheatsheafthornbury.co.uk
Draught Bass; St Austell Tribute; Sharp's Doom Bar; 1 changing beer Ⓗ
A two-bar local close to the town centre. The right-hand bar is popular with local residents and the left-hand lounge is more plushly furnished. There is also a skittle alley at the rear, adjacent to a small room with a pool table. Vegans and vegetarians are catered for. There is a large free car park directly opposite and space for about eight cars in front of the pub. The garden has a pet's corner, with rabbits and guinea pigs. 🛏️❀🌙♣🕯️P🚌🐾🛜

Upper Oddington

Horse & Groom ⃝L

Upper Oddington, GL56 0XH (top of village signed off A436 E of Stow)

✪ 12-3, 5.30-11 ☎ (01451) 830584

⊕ horseandgroom.uk.com

Otter Ale; Wye Valley Bitter; 2 changing beers Ⓗ

You are assured of a warm welcome at this privately owned, 16th-century inn run by friendly licensees, runner-up local CAMRA Pub of the Year in 2015 and a finalist in 2016. It has an extended bar area for locals with its own sitting room, linked by a real open log fire in an inglenook setting. Wye Valley beers feature, with a weekly changing guest usually coming from a Gloucestershire brewer. There is a large car park and attractive garden and patio area. It is in good walking country close to Stow, and has eight letting bedrooms.

Q⭗⭐⌂◗▣⍾

Upper Soudley

White Horse Inn

Church Road, GL14 2UA (on B4227)

✪ 7-11 (midnight Fri); 3-midnight Sat; 12-6 Sun

☎ (01594) 825968

2 changing beers (sourced nationally) Ⓗ

Built as a railway hotel, next to the now defunct Soudley Halt, this pub has great views across the valley from the garden. It is an interesting venue for geologists and walkers, with the Blue Rock Trail and Soudley Ponds nearby. Run by an enthusiastic couple, this lovely old inn has a small main bar with a welcoming fireplace and two regularly changing guest ales. The old dining room down the passageway is used for functions, and leads through to a much-loved skittle alley.

⭗⭐⅙♣◗▣(717)⭐

Wainlode

Red Lion Inn ⃝L

Wainlode Hill, GL2 9LW

✪ 6-11 Mon; 12-3, 5-11; 12-11 Sat & Sun ☎ (01452) 730935

⊕ redlionwainlode.co.uk

Wickwar BOB; Wye Valley HPA; 1 changing beer (sourced regionally) Ⓗ

On a picturesque stretch of the River Severn, this iconic riverside pub has been a popular stopping-off point since the mid-1800s. Refurbished in 2015, there is lots of exposed red brickwork and wooden floors on show in its well-tended rooms. Often busy in good weather, it is well regarded for both food and drink. An ideal port of call for cyclists and walkers alike, there is a Caravan Club site adjacent.

⭗⭐◗▲♣◗⭐

Wickwar

Buthay ⃝L

15 High Street, GL12 8NE (close to traffic lights)

✪ 12-11 (midnight Fri & Sat); 12-9 Sun; closed Mon

☎ (01454) 299083 ⊕ thebuthay.co.uk

3 changing beers (sourced regionally; often Wickwar) Ⓗ

Family-run 16th-century coaching inn attracting a varied clientele into its welcoming single-bar

drinking area, complete with log fire. Some lovely internal glazing enhances a large dining room which specialises in authentic Italian food, cooked fresh to order by Roberto. There is a skittles alley/function room and to the rear a large enclosed garden with a well-equipped children's play area.

⭗⭐⌂◗⅙♣◗▣⭐⭐ 📶

Woolaston Common

Rising Sun

The Common, GL15 6NU (1 mile off A48 at Woolaston) SO5901500924

✪ 12-2.30, 6.30-11; 12-3, 6.30-midnight Sat

☎ (01594) 529282

Butcombe Bitter; Wye Valley Bitter; 1 changing beer (sourced regionally) Ⓗ

Off the beaten track, this comfortable 350 year-old stone-built pub enjoys gorgeous views over the Forest of Dean. There is a welcoming main bar with an open fire, and a small snug, both of which display part of the landlord's large collection of framed banknotes. Featured in guides to circular pub walks of the forest, its varied menu of good home-cooked food is popular with ramblers (no food Mon and Tue lunchtimes). Friendly locals help make for a convivial atmosphere. Q⭐◗♣P

Wotton-under-Edge

Falcon Inn ⃝L

20 Church Street, GL12 7HB

✪ 12-11.30; 12-11 Sun ☎ (01453) 521894

Great Western Maiden Voyage Ⓖ; Stroud Tom Long; 2 changing beers (sourced locally) Ⓗ

A free house built in 1659, the quirky layout of the interior has rooms on differing levels. The cosy single bar has an open fire and leads to a snug with a flagstone floor. The dining room specialises in steaks from the family farm and uses locally sourced ingredients. Competitively priced beers are selected by customer vote from brewers within a 25-mile radius. A popular stop-off for walkers traversing the Cotswold Way. Q⭗◗♣◗▣⭐ 📶

Royal Oak Inn ⃝L

3-5 Haw Street, GL12 7AG (top end of town)

✪ 12-midnight ☎ (01453) 844366

⊕ theroyaloakwotton.com

Cotswold Spring Codger; Fuller's London Pride; Wye Valley HPA; 1 changing beer (sourced nationally) Ⓗ

A large coaching inn with a friendly atmosphere, complete with two comfortable bars, both with open fires, plus a large 50-seat dining room with wooden beams. There is a full-size snooker table upstairs which is popular. This lively establishment supports the local community and welcomes walkers using the Cotswold Way. At the rear is a car park and enclosed garden containing a well-equipped children's play area, a site originally occupied by stables, pigsty and poultry house.

Q⭗⭐◗P▣⭐ 📶

Good ale is the true and proper drink of Englishmen. He is not deserving of the name of Englishman who speaketh against ale, that is good ale. **George Borrow, Lavengro**

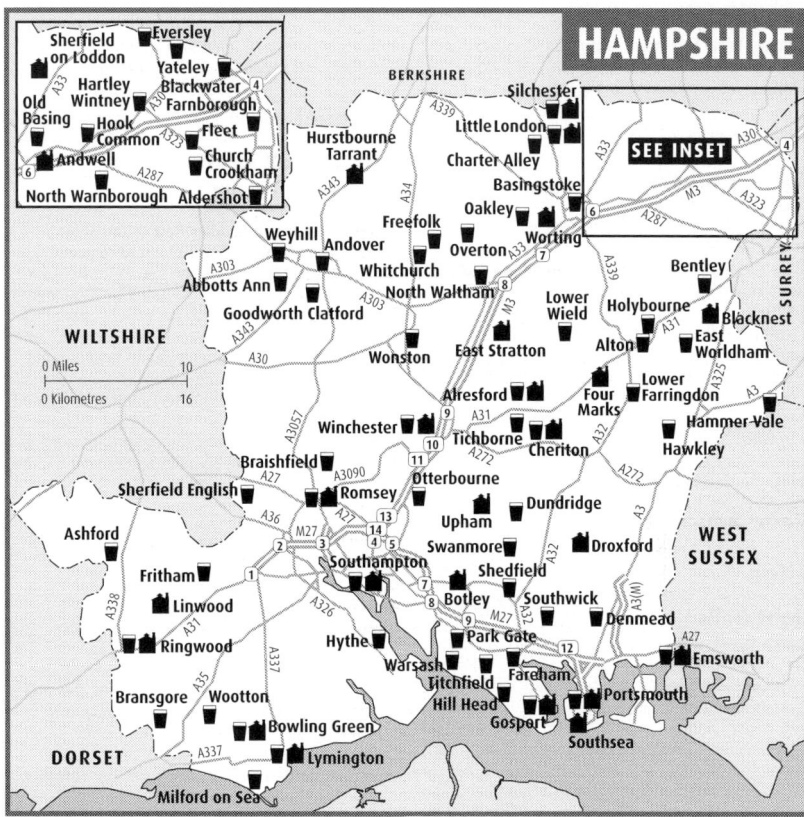

HAMPSHIRE

Abbotts Ann

Eagle Inn 🗓
Duck Street, SP11 7BG
☼ 11.30-11; 12-10.30 Sun ☎ (01264) 710339
🌐 theeagleinn.wordpress.com
Bowman Meon Valley Bitter; 3 changing beers (sourced locally) Ⓗ
In a picturesque village just two miles south-west of Andover, this pub is at the heart of the community. Friendly conversation rules the house. The regular Meon Valley Bitter is supplemented by three changing beers, often from local breweries. A beer and cider festival is held over the second weekend of June. The public bar features pool and there is a skittle alley at the rear. Locally sourced food is available (no food Tue and Sun eves).
😊🍽♣♿P🚭(87)🐾🎵🛜

Aldershot

Garden Gate 🗓
4 Church Lane East, GU11 3BT
☼ 5-11 (midnight Thu; 1am Fri); 12-1am Sat; 12-10.30 Sun ☎ (01252) 219717
Greene King IPA; St Austell Tribute; Surrey Hills Ranmore; 1 changing beer (often Ascot Ales, Timothy Taylor, West Berkshire) Ⓗ
An old-fashioned community pub reinvigorated by an experienced management team. They tweaked the range, introducing Ranmore Ale and usually a dark beer in winter. Originally used by Prussian mercenaries based nearby, the Garden Gate is now a focal point for the local community, who won it

Asset of Community Value status when it was threatened. Four-legged locals appreciate the free dog treats policy. Background music and conversation fill this pub, with occasional live music, and quizzes on Thursdays. There is limited parking. 😊🚃♣P🚭🐾🛜

Imperial Standard
25 Western Road, GU11 3PL
☼ 1-11 (midnight Fri & Sat); 12-11 Sun ☎ (01252) 322517
Ringwood Best Bitter, Fortyniner Ⓗ
A dog-friendly community local, holding Asset of Community Value status as one of the last surviving pubs in West End Aldershot. It is a welcome new entry to the Guide and is worth seeking out. The unusually shaped Edwardian pub (though there was previously an inn on this site) has a pool table, board games and dartboard. It serves no food but you may bring your own and takeaway menus are supplied. Occasional events and live music take place on Saturdays. Children are welcome until 8pm. 🛏♣🚭(5)🐾🛜

White Lion 🗓
20 Lower Farnham Road, GU12 4EA
☼ 1-11 (10.30 Mon; midnight Fri); 12-midnight Sat; 12-10.30 Sun ☎ (01252) 323832
Triple fff Alton's Pride, Moondance; 3 changing beers (often Cottage, Triple fff, Weltons) Ⓗ
One of the oldest surviving pubs in Aldershot, the White Lion retains two rooms. The back room tends to be the quieter. A rare Triple fff-run pub, most beers are from its range. This dog-friendly venue is second home to Aldershot A5 Scooter Club.

Unusually for the area, the pub owns a piano. Good hanging basket displays feature at the back in summer. A pub quiz and rock and roll bingo alternate on Thursdays. ♣♠🚲😋

Alresford

Horse & Groom
2 Broad Street, SO24 9AQ
✪ 10.30-11; 11.30-10.30 Sun ☎ (01962) 734809
⊕ horse-and-groom-alresford.co.uk
Fuller's London Pride, Oliver's Island; Gale's Seafarers Ale; 3 changing beers (sourced nationally) ⊞
A 17th-century coaching inn in the centre of Alresford. Following a renovation it now features pale wooden beams, flagstones and log fires. The deceptively spacious interior has been divided into a number of smaller, more intimate areas. To the rear is a courtyard garden with plenty of seating. Four Fuller's beers are always on sale, including the current seasonal. Like the interior, the menu is stylish and upmarket. Board games, newspapers and Wi-Fi are freely available.
🛏🏠🕽🍴🚲(64,67,C41)😋🛜

Alton

Eight Bells
Church Street, GU34 2DA (opp St Lawrence church)
✪ 11-11; 12-10.30 Sun ☎ (01420) 82417
Bowman Swift One; Sharp's Doom Bar; 3 changing beers (sourced nationally) ⊞
Free house, dating from circa 1640, near the town centre, with St Lawrence Church, site of the Civil War Battle of Alton, just across the road. It has an original oak-beamed interior with a main bar and a smaller drinking area, plus a restored listed smoking shelter incorporating a 17th-century well in a secluded paved garden. Sandwiches are available Monday to Saturday from 12.30pm. Look out for Nigel's not-so-secret beer festival following the late summer holiday. Q🏠🚲😋

George ✪
Butts Road, GU34 1LH
✪ 11-11 (midnight Thu-Sat); 11-10.30 Sun ☎ (01420) 82331
⊕ thegeorgealton.co.uk
5 changing beers (sourced nationally; often St Austell, Sharp's) ⊞
Grade II-listed pub dating from 1745, which was the courthouse famed for the trial of the murderer of Sweet Fanny Adams. Previously the Duke's Head, it is back under Jason and Suzie's stewardship, who run a friendly local, with one West Country beer and up to four guest ales from the SIBA list. Excellent snacks and main meals to suit all tastes are served. There are regular open mic sessions, visiting bands and performers. Look out for the July beer festival. 🛏🏠🕽P🚲(64)😋🛜

Railway Arms L
26 Anstey Road, GU34 2RB (opp Station Rd)
✪ 12-11; 11-midnight Fri & Sat ☎ (01420) 82218
Triple fff Alton's Pride, Moondance, Comfortably Numb; 2 changing beers (sourced nationally) ⊞
Friendly pub close to the Watercress Line and mainline station. Owned by Triple fff Brewery, its beers are supplemented by ales from a host of micros. Bottled cider is from Mr Whitehead's. A rear function room, with its own bar, is available for hire. The patio area, designed with a traditional railway theme, incorporates a covered smoking

area. There are tables outside at the front under a striking sculpture of a steam locomotive. CAMRA members are welcome. 🏠🚲♣🚲😋

Andover

John Russell Fox ✪
10 High Street, SP10 1NY
✪ 7am-midnight (1am Fri & Sat) ☎ (01264) 320920
Greene King Abbot; Ruddles Best Bitter; Sharp's Doom Bar; 7 changing beers (sourced regionally) ⊞
A high-street JD Wetherspoon pub in former offices of the Andover Advertiser, founded by John Russell Fox. The first edition of the paper was produced here in 1858. A large entrance area leads to a bar with 10 handpumps. References to printing and newspapers adorn the pub; there is even a small printing press. A separate raised seating and dining area is to the rear, where families are welcomed. Note the Time Ring set in the pavement outside. There is a large public car park to the rear.
🛏🕽🍴P🚲🛜

Lunar Hare ✪
71 Weyhill Road, SP10 3AN
✪ 9am-11; 10-10 Sun ☎ (01264) 336638
⊕ thelunarhare.co.uk
Otter Amber; Sharp's Atlantic; Timothy Taylor Landlord; West Berkshire Good Old Boy ⊞
Recently refurbished, this pub is an eclectic mix, with something for everyone. Four real ales and a real cider are served alongside speciality coffees, teas and cakes. The large restaurant offers meals ranging from pub classics to à la carte. An extensive garden is very popular in the summer.

REAL ALE BREWERIES
Alfred's Winchester
Andwell Andwell
Betteridge's Hurstbourne Tarrant
Botley Botley
Bowman Droxford
Brewhouse & Kitchen 🍴 Portsmouth
Brewhouse & Kitchen 🍴 Southampton (NEW)
CrackleRock Botley
Dancing Cows Lymington (NEW)
Dancing Man 🍴 Southampton
Emsworth Brewery Emsworth
Emsworth Brewhouse Emsworth (NEW)
Flack Manor Romsey
Flowerpots 🍴 Cheriton
Fulflood Arms 🍴 Winchester (brewing suspended)
Hop Art Blacknest
Irving Portsmouth
Itchen Valley Alresford
Little London Little London (NEW)
Longdog Worting
MASH East Stratton
Oakleaf Gosport
Queen Inn 🍴 Winchester
Red Cat Winchester
Red Shoot 🍴 Linwood
Ringwood Ringwood
Sherfield Village Sherfield on Loddon
Southsea Southsea (NEW)
Staggeringly Good Southsea
Triple fff Four Marks
Upham Upham
Urban Island Portsmouth (NEW)
Vibrant Forest Bowling Green
Wild Weather Silchester

Sunday Night Social can include live music or a quiz, highlighting the pub's community focus. The portcullis on the snug fireplace is a reminder that this was once a Strong's Brewery house. ⏰✪🍴♿⇄🍺P🚃🐾🐕📶

Town Mills
20 Bridge Street, SP10 1BL
✪ 11-12.30am ☎ (01264) 332540 ⊕ thetownmills.co.uk
Wadworth IPA, 6X; 2 changing beers (sourced regionally; often Wadworth) Ⓗ
Although in the town centre, this pub is situated in an historic mill with a working water wheel. There are several separate areas for dining and drinking, including a comfy lounge upstairs. Pub games are played upstairs and a well-supported quiz is held on Wednesday evenings. The riverside garden is popular in summer months. Usually three to four beers are available from Wadworth's guest list. ⏰✪🍴♿🍺P🚃🐾📶

Ashford

Augustus John ✓
116 Station Road, SP6 1DG (½ mile W of Fordingbridge on road to Sandleheath)
✪ 12-2.30, 6-10.30 (5-11.30 Fri & Sat); 12-3, 7-10 Sun
☎ (01425) 652098 ⊕ augustusjohnfordingbridge.co.uk
Ringwood Best Bitter, Fortyniner; 1 changing beer (sourced nationally) Ⓗ
Quirky community pub befitting the artist Augustus John, who resided in the village and whose artwork adorns the walls. Diverse, regular weekly events take place, from classic film nights to quizzes and themed food nights. Sensibly priced, high-quality food is supplemented by snacks, from jelly babies to olives and Scotch eggs. Motorcyclists, classic car owners, walkers and cyclists are all catered for and local artists' work is displayed. Guest ales come from the Marston's list and real cider is sold in the summer. Q⏰✪🚲🍴♣🐾📶

Basingstoke

Angel ✓
Unit R6, Lower Ground, Festival Place, RG21 7BB
✪ 8am-12.30am (2am Fri & Sat) ☎ (01256) 854800
Greene King IPA, Abbot; Sharp's Doom Bar; 3 changing beers Ⓗ
Formerly a Lloyds No.1 Bar, this spacious one-bar modern pub is at the edge of the restaurant quarter in the town's Festival Place shopping centre, handy for the nearby bus station and five minutes' walk from the rail station. Popular with younger people, the pub can get very busy and often noisy in the evenings, especially at weekends. Lunchtimes attract a wider age range and tend to be quieter. The walls are adorned with TVs, all in silent mode. ⏰✪🍴♿⇄🚃📶

Basingstoke Sports & Social Club ✓
Fairfields Road, RG21 3DR (S end of town)
✪ 12-3, 5-11; 12-11 Fri & Sat; 12-10.30 Sun
☎ (01256) 331646 ⊕ basingstoke-sports-club.co.uk
Fuller's Oliver's Island, London Pride; Gale's Seafarers Ale; 2 changing beers (sourced nationally; often Andwells, Little London, Longdog) Ⓗ
While technically a club, the public have access as if it were a public house. Founded in 1865 by local brewery owner and entrepreneur Col. John May, this fine venue is home to cricket, rugby, football and squash. Wide-screen TV in the bar is dedicated

to sports events. A full programme of social activities is held throughout the year, and the grounds are currently home to the annual Hampshire OctoberFest. Opening hours are flexible when sporting fixtures are held. ⏰✪🍴♣🐾P🚃🐕📶

Maidenhead Inn ✓
17 Winchester Street, RG21 7ED (at top of town)
✪ 8am-midnight (1am Fri & Sat) ☎ (01256) 316030
Greene King Abbot; Loddon Forbury Lion; Ruddles Best Bitter; Sharp's Doom Bar; 3 changing beers (sourced nationally) Ⓗ
Formerly home to a building society and on the site of an inn of the same name, this JD Wetherspoon pub is in the sometimes lively Top of Town area, with a range of local and guest ales. Beers from breweries such as Andwell's, Longdog, Wild Weather and Loddon regularly feature. A dining area at the front leads to the compact bar, with further seating to the rear over two levels, complemented by a courtyard beer garden at the back. ⏰✪🍴♿⇄🐾P🚃📶

Queen's Arms
Bunnian Place, RG21 7JE
✪ 11-11 (midnight Fri & Sat) ☎ (01256) 465488
Courage Best Bitter; Sharp's Doom Bar; 3 changing beers (sourced nationally) Ⓗ
Just outside the main shopping area, this cosy pub is handy for all transport links. It attracts a wide-ranging clientele of all ages from all walks of life, and is a regular port of call for rail commuters. The choice of up to four guest beers is imaginative and the turnaround can be swift. Good-value home-cooked food is served lunchtimes and evenings. During warmer weather the shady courtyard garden at the rear is a popular attraction. Q✪🍴⇄P🚃📶

Soldier's Return ✓
80 Upper Sherborne Road, RG21 5RP
✪ 11-11; 12-10.30 Sun ☎ (01256) 842542
Fuller's London Pride; 2 changing beers (sourced regionally) Ⓗ
Some 160 years old, the pub is on the north side of town, near the A339 ring road. After a period of being closed and looking likely never to reopen, the Soldier's has a new lease of life, becoming a focal point for the local community. Good-value food and themed evenings balance nicely with discos and music quiz nights. The front of the pub overlooks the playing fields opposite. There are usually two guest ales alongside the London Pride, often from local Basingstoke brewery Longdog. 🍴♣P🚃(5)📶

Bentley

Star Inn 🄻
Main Road, GU10 5LW
✪ 9am-midnight; 10.30-11 Sun ☎ (01420) 23184
⊕ thestarinnbentley.co.uk
Sharp's Doom Bar; 3 changing beers (sourced locally; often Triple fff) Ⓗ
Following an extensive refurbishment, this pub now has a pleasant imbibers' environment. From the station follow signs to Bentley Village or local footpaths. The 65 bus stops nearby (outside from the Alton direction). It opens at 9am for breakfast and is licensed from 11am. There is a premium for half pints – check the price board above the bar. It does excellent food, much of which is locally

sourced – the licensee is also a local farmer. The varying beer range is mainly from local breweries. Q⬆🐾⏱◐●P🖵(65)🐾🌼📶

Blackwater

Mr Bumble 🅛
19 London Road, GU17 9AP
✪ 12-11 (midnight Fri); 11-midnight Sat; 12-10.30 Sun
☎ (01276) 32691
Fuller's London Pride; 3 changing beers (sourced regionally; often Ascot Ales) 🅗
Busy pub in the centre of Blackwater, near the station, a bus route and local shops. London Pride is the regular beer, plus up to three other real ales, including LocAles; stout and porter are popular in the winter months. There is a large bar for drinking and conversation, a smaller bar with three tables leading to the pool room, which in turn leads out to the patio and smoking area. Live music plays on Thursday and Saturday. ⬌♣P🖵(3)📶

Bowling Green

Wheel Inn 🅛
Sway Road, SO41 8LJ (2 miles NW of Lymington)
✪ 12-midnight (1am Fri & Sat) ☎ (01590) 676122
🌐 thewheelinnpub.co.uk
Ringwood Best Bitter; 1 changing beer (sourced locally; often Dancing Cows, Downton, Vibrant Forest) 🅗
Friendly pub with a rare two-bar arrangement, supporting local breweries by regularly changing guest ales. It is always good for conversation with a considerable loyal and varied customer base, or for quiet reading on comfortable settees. The public bar has a TV used sparingly for important sporting and news events. Musical entertainment equipment is available when needed. The lounge bar has a real fire for colder times. It has a good reputation for authentic international cuisine. A short walk from Vibrant Forest Brewery. Q⬆🐾⏱◐●♿▲♣P🖵(X2)🐾📶

Braishfield

Dog & Crook 🅛
Crook Hill, SO51 0QB (S edge of village)
✪ 11.30-11; 12-9 Sun ☎ (01794) 368530
🌐 dogandcrook.co.uk
Ringwood Best Bitter; Sharp's Doom Bar; 1 changing beer (sourced locally; often Bowman, Itchen Valley, Triple fff) 🅗
Well-established village pub with a restaurant, real fire and large garden, refurbished in 2016. Three handpumped beers are on sale, at least one from a local brewery. Excellent home-cooked food and bar snacks are served every day, lunchtimes and evenings (no food Sun). There is no jukebox or sport TV, but sport is sometimes shown on terrestrial TV. Cribbage and darts are played and alternate Tuesdays are quiz nights. Dogs and ramblers are welcome (please remove muddy boots). A Pubs In Bloom award winner. Q⬆🐾⏱◐●♣P🖵(35)🐾📶

Wheatsheaf 🅛
Braishfield Road, SO51 0QE
✪ 11.30-11; 12-10.30 Sun ☎ (01794) 368652
🌐 thewheatsheafbraishfield.co.uk

Flack Manor Flack's Double Drop; St Austell Tribute; Sharp's Doom Bar; 1 changing beer (sourced nationally) 🅗
The Wheatsheaf, close to the world-famous Hillier Arboretum, offers views of surrounding hills and farmland from a large garden containing a children's mini assault course. Its interior comprises several discrete areas, each with a selection of not-quite-matching furniture, including an extension principally used by diners, and a non-intrusive games annexe. Quality food is on offer. Events include live music, occasional pie nights and quizzes, and an annual carol service. A loyalty card scheme operates. 🐾⏱◐●♿♣P🖵(35)🐾📶

Bransgore

Three Tuns ✅
Ringwood Road, BH23 8JH
✪ 11-11; 11.30-11 Sat; 12-10.30 Sun ☎ (01425) 672232
🌐 threetunsinn.com
Otter Bright; Ringwood Best Bitter, Fortyniner; 2 changing beers 🅗
The Three Tuns is an award-winning 17th-century thatched inn. The main entrance opens into the bar area, leading to a large dining room and a separate snug. Staff are friendly and helpful. Tasting notes feature over the bar, and newspapers are provided. The creative menus, based around fresh local produce, offer daily specials. A large terrace and gardens give views over open countryside. The barn is available for events. A pétanque league plays here. Q⬆🐾⏱◐●♿▲P🖵(125)🐾📶

Charter Alley

White Hart 🅛
White Hart Lane, RG26 5QA
✪ 7-11 Mon; 12-2.30, 5.30 (7 Tue)-11; 12-3, 6.30-11 Sat; 12-4 Sun ☎ (01256) 850048 🌐 whitehartcharteralley.com
Triple fff Moondance; 3 changing beers 🅗
Cosy inn, built in 1819, the epicentre of this rural village, where allcomers are assured of a friendly greeting. Welcoming features include log fires, oak beams and a capacious dining area, serving a variety of quality food and home-made pies. The breweriana-decorated main bar dispenses an array of ales that changes frequently. The pub has been a stalwart Guide entry for the past 26 years. The website shows which beers are on and what is in the cellar. Q⬆🏠◐●P🐾📶

Cheriton

Flowerpots Inn 🅛
Brandy Mount, SO24 0QQ (½ mile N of A272 Cheriton/Beauworth crossroads) SU581283
✪ 12-2.30, 6-11; 12-3, 7-10.30 Sun ☎ (01962) 771318
🌐 flowerpotscheriton.co.uk
Flowerpots Perridge Pale, Bitter, Goodens Gold; 1 changing beer (often Flowerpots) 🅖
A two-bar village pub dating from the early 1800s. The public bar has a glass-covered well and large fireplace, which is especially welcoming on a winter's day. The lounge is smaller and cosy. The garden is well kept and has plenty of seating in summer. Home-cooked food is available every day (no food Sun eve); Wednesday is curry night. The gravity-dispensed beer comes from the on-site Flowerpots Brewery, which is now Hampshire's oldest independent brewery. The cider is Westons Old Rosie. Q⬆🏠◐●🌼P🖵(67)🐾

Church Crookham

Fox & Hounds ✪
71 Crookham Road, GU51 5NP
🕓 12-11 (midnight Fri) ☎ (01252) 663686
🌐 foxandhoundscc.co.uk
Caledonian Flying Scotsman; Courage Best Bitter; Fuller's London Pride; house beer (by Caledonian); 1 changing beer (sourced nationally; often Caledonian) Ⓗ
A welcoming old-style community pub, alongside a picturesque section of the Basingstoke Canal, with three separate seating areas. Traditional home-cooked pub food is served daily, with a section of the dining area available for dog walkers. Four cask ales are on tap, including the Fox & Hounds' own ale. The garden and children's play area are always busy on warmer days. Panelled walls are adorned with historic pub photos. Live music is a feature every Friday and a pub quiz is held every fortnight on Tuesdays. Q🏠🐕🛏️◑🗐🅿️🚲(10)👶🌐

Denmead

Fox & Hounds ✪
School Lane, PO7 6NA
🕓 12-11 (midnight Fri & Sat) ☎ (023) 9226 5984
🌐 foxandhounds-pub.co.uk
Greene King Abbot; Sharp's Doom Bar; 2 changing beers (sourced regionally; often Bowman, Dark Star, Langham) Ⓗ
Community-owned free house at the edge of the village, offering great views and a good base for exploring the countryside. It has a single low-ceilinged bar at the front and a large dining area to the rear. Inside, the decor is unpretentious country vintage kitsch, light and airy throughout, encouraging a casual, relaxed atmosphere. Chess, cribbage and dominoes are popular. Locally-brewed real ales are often sold, and home-cooked food is served every day using fresh, seasonal produce, often from the kitchen garden.
Q🏠🐕◑♣🅿️👶🌐

Dundridge

Hampshire Bowman Ⓛ
Dundridge Lane, SO32 1GD SU578184
🕓 12-11 (midnight Fri); 12-10.30 Sun ☎ (01489) 892940
🌐 hampshirebowman.com
Bowman Swift One; Oakleaf Quercus Folium; 3 changing beers Ⓖ
An isolated free house typically offering five beers (mostly local) served directly from the cask, 10 real ciders, and a wide selection of bottled beers. It serves freshly prepared food ranging from sandwiches and traditional pub food to an interesting specials menu. Outside is a large garden and patio with plenty of seating, which can be busy at weekends. It is an ideal location for walks, with the pub welcoming dogs. A beer festival is held on the last weekend in July. Q🏠🐕◑🗐♣🍺🅿️👶🌐

East Worldham

Three Horseshoes ✪
Cakers Lane, GU34 3AE
🕓 11.30-2.30 (not Mon), 5.30-10.30; 12-11 Sat; 12-5 Sun
☎ (01420) 83211 🌐 threehorseshoesalton.co.uk
Fuller's London Pride; Gale's Seafarers Ale, HSB; 1 changing beer (sourced nationally; often Fuller's) Ⓗ

Once a Gale's house and former coaching inn, part of the building dates back over 300 years and is allegedly haunted. John and Gill have rapidly gained an excellent reputation for their high-quality locally sourced food as well as their ales. Very much a community pub, it is the place to go to for information about local events. Quiz night is the last Thursday of the month and other entertainment, including live bands, features regularly. Q🏠🐕🛏️◑🗐🅿️🚲(13)👶🌐

Emsworth

Coal Exchange ✪
21 South Street, PO10 7EG
🕓 10.30-3, 5.30-11; 10.30-midnight Fri & Sat; 12-11 Sun
☎ (01243) 375866 🌐 thecoalexchange.co.uk
Fuller's London Pride; Gale's HSB, Seafarers Ale; 3 changing beers (sourced nationally; often Brains, Butcombe) Ⓗ
A cosy pub at the south of the town centre and close to the harbour. It has a single L-shaped bar with an attractive walled garden to the rear. The building was originally a pork butchery and ale house and then, as the name suggests, a place where local produce was traded for coal delivered by sea. In addition to award-winning lunchtime food there are a number of themed evening dining options available. 🐕🅑◑🍺🚲(700)👶

Eversley

Golden Pot Ⓛ
Reading Road, RG27 0NB
🕓 12-11 ☎ (0118) 973 2104 🌐 golden-pot.co.uk
3 changing beers (sourced regionally) Ⓗ
A picture-postcard village free house dating back to the 18th century. The pub is supplied by 14 different microbreweries on rotation. The restaurant specialises in serving fresh fish and Angus steak. Seating includes tables and chairs as well as comfortable sofa areas. There is a covered outdoor space at the front of the pub and a delightful garden to the rear. The bus service is very limited. Q🏠🐕◑🅿️🚲(8)👶🌐

Fareham

Crown Ⓛ ✪
40 West Street, PO16 0JW
🕓 8am-midnight (1am Fri & Sat) ☎ (01329) 241750
Greene King Abbot; Ruddles Best Bitter; Sharp's Doom Bar; 2 changing beers Ⓗ
A snug and cosy Wetherspoon pub with an interesting history, and home of the Crown Brewery from 1841 to 1911. With the closure of the brewery the building became the Crown Inn. Three regular ales are offered with two changing guest ales, often from local independents. The usual range of Wetherspoon food is available all day. Near each handpump is a mini Kilner jar showing the beer colour. Real cider is available occasionally. Near the bus station and shopping centre.
Q🏠🐕◑🅑🍺🚲🌐

Lord Arthur Lee ✪
100-108 West Street, PO16 0EP
🕓 8am-11 ☎ (01329) 280447
Greene King Abbot; Ruddles Best Bitter; Sharp's Doom Bar; 5 changing beers Ⓗ
This spacious Wetherspoon pub is always busy with shoppers and popular with office workers, and is

close to bus and rail stations. A separate dining area makes this attractive for family lunches. The walls are adorned with photographs and historic details of the pub's namesake and other locals. Three regular ales and five guest ales, often from small independent breweries, are offered. The usual Wetherspoon food is available all day, including breakfast. ♿🕴🍴♿🚾♿🚗🛜

Farnborough

Prince of Wales ♥ Ⓛ ✅
184 Rectory Road, GU14 8AL
🕐 11.30-2.30, 5.30-11; 11.30-11 Fri & Sat; 12-10.30 Sun
☎ (01252) 545578 ⊕ theprinceinfarnborough.co.uk
Dark Star Hophead; Fuller's London Pride; Hop Back Summer Lightning; Ringwood Fortyniner; Young's Bitter; 5 changing beers (sourced nationally) Ⓗ
Award-winning pub in the heart of Farnborough featuring 10 beers, one always a lower-priced (but never low quality) session ale. Reasonably priced pub grub makes it a lunchtime favourite, with roasts on Sundays. In the evenings, Monday is pie night, Friday is fish and chips (no other evening meals). Quiz night is the first Sunday of the month and in October there is an almost too popular beer festival. Farnborough North station is nearby. CAMRA branch Pub of the Year 2016.
🕴🍴🚾(North)🅿🚗(41)🐾🛜

Tilly Shilling Ⓛ ✅
Unit 2-5 Victoria Road, GU14 7PG
🕐 7am-midnight (1am Fri & Sat) ☎ (01252) 893560
Greene King Abbot; Ruddles Best Bitter; Sharp's Doom Bar; 5 changing beers (often Binghams, Hogs Back, Langham) Ⓗ
Modern town-centre aviation-themed pub named after an engineer at the nearby Royal Aircraft Establishment who designed a major improvement to the Merlin engines that powered many RAF aircraft during WWII. The large rectangular open-plan lounge features a glass frontage that opens in good weather, extending the pub onto the pavement. Ten handpumps leave plenty of space for regular and changing guest beers. Real cider is available from polypins at the end of the bar. Alcohol goes on sale from 9am. ♿🍴♿🚾♿🚗🛜

Fleet

Prince Arthur Ⓛ ✅
238 Fleet Road, GU51 4BX
🕐 8am-midnight (1am Fri & Sat) ☎ (01252) 622660
Greene King Abbot; Ruddles Best Bitter; 5 changing beers (sourced nationally; often Dark Star, Hop Art, Twickenham) Ⓗ
Wetherspoon pub with rustic charm located in a 100-year-old former grocery store, named after Prince Arthur, son of Queen Victoria, who lived in Fleet in the 1890s when Commander of the nearby Aldershot Garrison. Eight different cask ales, including those from Dark Star, Twickenham and 15 local breweries, appear regularly, and a real cider is on handpump. Ale festivals twice a year, featuring LocAles and beers from further afield, are in addition to the two Wetherspoon festivals.
Q♿🕴🍴♿🚗🚗(7,10)🛜

Freefolk

Watership Down Inn Ⓛ
Freefolk Priors, RG28 7NJ (just off B3400)

🕐 12-3, 6.30-11; 12-11.30 Fri & Sat; 12-9.30 Sun
☎ (01256) 892254 ⊕ watershipdowninn.com
5 changing beers (sourced locally) Ⓗ
Built in 1840, in the Upper Test Valley, and still affectionately known locally as the Jerry, the pub has been named in honour of local author Richard Adams' book Watership Down, set in the downland to the north of the pub. Outside there is an extensive garden, patio and family area. Each May a beer festival is held and occasional live music evenings arranged. It is close to the Laverstoke gin distillery. Local CAMRA Pub of the Year 2015.
Q♿🕴🍴🕴🅿🚗(76,86)🐾🛜

Fritham

Royal Oak ♥ Ⓛ ✅
SO43 7HJ (W end of village – no through road)
🕐 11-3, 6-11; 11-11 Sat; 12-10.30 Sun ☎ (023) 8081 2606
Flack Manor Flack's Double Drop; Ringwood Best Bitter; house beer (by Bowman); 4 changing beers (sourced locally; often Dancing Cows, Keystone, Stonehenge) Ⓖ
A New Forest institution. The front bar leads through to two interconnected back rooms. Throughout, bare boards, beams, log fires and wainscotted colourwashed walls epitomise a rural inn. It is a welcoming haven for walkers, cyclists, equestrians (facilities provided) and dog lovers. Local breweries provide most of the seven gravity-dispensed ales; by 2017 perhaps some even brewed in Fritham. Excellent, simple lunches utilise much local produce. A vast tabled garden area also houses three high-grade rentable shepherd's bothies (adults only). Q♿🕴🍴🕴🐾

Goodworth Clatford

Clatford Arms ✅
Village Street, SP11 7RN
🕐 11.30-11 (11.30 Thu; midnight Fri & Sat)
☎ (01264) 363298
Flack Manor Flack's Double Drop; 3 changing beers (sourced regionally; often Otter, Red Cat, Stonehenge) Ⓗ
Popular village local in this pretty village. There is a dining room at one end where good-value home-cooked food is served. The other end is known as the sports area, with a pool table, darts and TV. Four beers are served, mostly from local breweries, alongside traditional favourites. There is a large garden to the rear where it is possible to enjoy a game of boules. Q♿🕴🍴♿♣🅿🚗(15)🐾🛜

Gosport

Brewpot Ⓛ
11A/B North Cross Street, PO12 1BE
🕐 12-5 (6 Wed & Thu; 7 Fri); 11-7 Sat; closed Sun & Mon
☎ (023) 9252 2746 ⊕ oakleafbrewing.co.uk/brewpot.html
Oakleaf Hole Hearted Ⓖ, **I Can't Believe It's Not Bitter** Ⓗ, **Pompey Royal** Ⓖ, **Piston Porter** Ⓗ; **2 changing beers (sourced locally; often Oakleaf)** Ⓖ
Brewpot is the Oakleaf Brewery outlet and is located around the corner from the brewery. Its ales are available to drink on site but there is also a large bottle shop selling Oakleaf and other local brewery ales. The bar is also used to launch the brewery's seasonal beers on a Friday. A limited range of bar snacks, including savoury pies, is sold. Q♿♣🚗🛜

Queen's Hotel

143 Queens Road, Forton, PO12 1LG

☎ 5-11; 11.30-2.30, 5-11.30 Fri; 11.30-11.30 Sat; 12-3, 7-11 Sun ☎ 07974 031671 ⊕ queenshotelgosport.co.uk

Castle Rock Harvest Pale; Ringwood Fortyniner; 4 changing beers (sourced nationally; often Oakleaf, Titanic, White Horse) Ⓗ

Award-winning free house with over 30 years in this Guide, which is sought out by locals and visitors from all over the country. The focal point of the bar is a real fire with a carved wood surround. Beers from local breweries appear from time to time and JJ's Suicider is the regular cider. An annual beer festival takes place in October. Snacks are served on Friday lunchtimes. ✿♣♠🖵

Hammer Vale

Prince of Wales

Hammer Lane, GU27 1QH (enter Hammer Lane from Haslemere end, due to width restriction at Liphook end)

☎ 11-11; 12-11 Sun ☎ (01428) 652600

Fuller's London Pride; Gale's HSB; 1 changing beer (sourced nationally; often Fuller's) Ⓗ

Although tucked away, this pub is well worth a visit to sample the Pride, HSB and occasional Fuller's guest. With a huge outside seating area it is well sited for walkers and campers. Nick and Heidi do excellent meals and the lunchtime baguettes will hit the spot. There are many stories (mostly apocryphal) as to how such a large 1927 roadhouse was sited away from the main road. Check the stained glass windows, one for Amey's of Petersfield. Q☎✿◑◐ᗒ▲♣P✿🤶

Hartley Wintney

Waggon & Horses

High Street, RG27 8NY

☎ 11-11 (midnight Fri & Sat); 12-11 Sun ☎ (01252) 842119

Courage Best Bitter; Gale's HSB; 2 changing beers (sourced locally) Ⓗ

A village pub whose landlord of 30 years has won several local CAMRA awards. HSB and Courage Best are regularly served alongside changing guest beers. The pub's lively public bar contrasts with a quieter lounge. Tables outside on the pavement enable guests to enjoy the atmosphere of the village, renowned for its antique shops. At the rear is a pleasant courtyard garden and a heated, covered smokers' area. Food is served lunchtimes only, but not on Sundays. Q✿◐ᗒ♠🖵(7)✿

Hawkley

Hawkley Inn

Pococks Lane, GU33 6NE

☎ 12-3, 5.30-11; 12-11 Sat; 12-10.30 Sun ☎ (01730) 827205 ⊕ hawkleyinn.co.uk

Dark Star Hophead; Hop Back Summer Lightning; Sharp's Doom Bar; 5 changing beers (often Flack Manor, Red Cat, Triple fff) Ⓗ

A country, two-bar free house popular with locals, walkers and visitors. A warm welcome awaits all, including their dogs, helped by a real fire on winter's days. A good range of real ales, served from eight handpumps, is at the heart of the pub, supplemented by excellent food. There is a small verandah to the front and a large garden to the rear. A beer festival is in May. Accommodation is available all year round. ᗒ✿🛏◑◐✿

Hill Head

Crofton Ⓛ ✅

48 Crofton Lane, PO14 3QF

☎ 11-11; 12-10.30 Sun ☎ (01329) 314222 ⊕ thecrofton.co.uk

Oakleaf Hole Hearted; Sharp's Doom Bar; 4 changing beers (sourced nationally) Ⓗ

Close to the Solent, this popular and successful Punch Tavern, which was extended in 2012, offers a warm welcome to allcomers. Four changing ales plus two permanents, supplemented by Old Rosie cider, make a visit always worthwhile. Home-cooked food is available all day, with a beer festival on St George's Day and a larger festival in November. A separate function room with skittle alley can be booked. ᗒ✿◑ᗒ♣♠P🖵(21)✿

Holybourne

Queen's Head ✅

20 London Road, GU34 4EG

☎ 12-11.30 (1am Fri; midnight Sat); 12-11 Sun

☎ (01420) 86331 ⊕ queensheadalton.co.uk

Hardys & Hansons Olde Trip; 3 changing beers (sourced locally; often Triple fff) Ⓗ

A friendly, traditional and unpretentious English pub run by the same landlord and landlady for over 12 years – many as a Guide regular. The pub hosts a number of activities including a quiz night, darts and pool leagues, and an established and popular charity music and beer festival, Altonbury, every July. The Queen's comprises three refurbished rooms, a covered and heated smoking area, plus a large family-friendly garden. Q ᗒ✿◑♣P🖵(65)✿🤶

Hook Common

Crooked Billet ✅

London Road, RG27 9EH

☎ 11.30-3, 6-midnight; 11.30-midnight Sat; 12-11 Sun

☎ (01256) 762118 ⊕ thecrookedbilletpub.co.uk

Courage Best Bitter; Sharp's Doom Bar; 2 changing beers Ⓗ

The Crooked Billet is situated on the London Road just outside Hook, and has been a free house under the same ownership for 28 years. In the summer you can enjoy the pleasant riverside garden or the air-conditioned bars, restaurant or snug. In winter, warm up around one of the traditional log fires. A fine selection of good food and real ales is always available here. An annual beer and music festival is held over August bank holiday weekend. Q✿◑P✿

Hythe

Ebenezers Ⓛ

18A Pylewell Road, SO45 6AR

☎ 11.30-2.40, 5.30-11; 11.30-11 Fri & Sat; 12-10.30 Sun ☎ (023) 8020 7799

Flack Manor Flack's Double Drop; Greene King Abbot; 2 changing beers (sourced locally; often Bowman, Flowerpots, Vibrant Forest) Ⓗ

A Baptist chapel in 1845 then, successively, a school, flour store, and furniture store, before becoming a pub in 1998. The open-plan bar serves four real ales and cider from JJ's and 146 – the warm friendly atmosphere encouraging good conversation. Home-made food is available lunchtime and evenings, and you are assured of a friendly welcome from the very efficient bar staff. Outside is a large, partly covered eating/smoking area. Four hundred yards away is the world's oldest working pier railway, connecting Hythe to the Southampton ferry. Q✿◑▣ᵭ♠▣(8,9,H1/H2)☞

Little London

Plough Inn
Silchester Road, RG26 5EP
✿ 12-3, 5.30 (6 Fri & Sat)-11; 12-3, 7-10.30 Sun
☎ (01256) 850628
Palmers Dorset Gold; Ringwood Best Bitter Ⓖ; 2 changing beers (sourced regionally; often Andwells, Branscombe Vale, Stonehenge) Ⓗ
Excellent traditional village pub and recent CAMRA Regional Pub of the Year. Enjoy beer gravity-fed from casks behind the bar and sit in front of a log fire or in the peaceful garden. A good range of baguettes is available (no food Sun eve). It is popular with locals and also visitors to Pamper Forest and the nearby Roman remains in Silchester. Wessex CAMRA Pub of the Year 2015.
Q☎✿♣▣(14)✿

Lower Farringdon

Golden Pheasant Ⓛ
Fareham Road, GU34 3DJ
✿ 12-11; 12-10.30 Sun ☎ (01420) 588255
Sharp's Doom Bar, Atlantic; house beer (by Sharp's); 3 changing beers (sourced locally; often Bowman, Flowerpots, Hogs Back) Ⓗ
The owners have run pubs in the area for over 10 years, and five years ago brought their expertise to this delightful privately owned free house. The beers are well kept, with six handpumps serving three fixed and three guest beers. The food is freshly cooked, with vegetarian options; the fish and chips warrants special mention due to the secret recipe batter used. Easily accessible down the A32 four miles from Alton, this is a pub not to be missed. Q☎✿◑♣▣✿☞

Lower Wield

Yew Tree Ⓛ
SO24 9RX SU636398
✿ 12-3, 6-11; 12-10.30 Sun; closed Mon ☎ (01256) 389224
⊕ the-yewtree.org.uk
House beer (by Triple fff); 1 changing beer (sourced locally; often Itchen Valley, Stonehenge) Ⓗ
Out-of-the-way rural local set in picturesque rolling Hampshire countryside, on a quiet lane opposite the local cricket pitch, with an old yew tree growing outside (hence the name). The house beer is Triple fff Alton's Pride and the guest normally comes from a local brewery. All real ales are sold at a very reasonable price. The pub has a separate dining area where locally renowned, reasonably priced food is served. Cyclists, ramblers and dog walkers welcome. Q☎✿◑P✿☞

Lymington

Monkey House Ⓛ
167 Southampton Road, SO41 9HA (N of town)
✿ 11-11; 12-10.30 Sun ☎ (01590) 676754
⊕ themonkeyhouse.co.uk
Dancing Cows Pony; Flack Manor Flack's Double Drop; 1 changing beer (sourced locally; often Bowman, Goddards, Vibrant Forest) Ⓗ

This venue has been transformed into a thriving community free house under private ownership, after years of failure under a major pub company. It is a strong supporter of local breweries, serving good-value, traditional pub food and creative daily menu specials (booking recommended for busy periods). It is also very supportive of all things rugby and maritime, but not to the detriment of a warm welcome for all. Monkey business and décor abound, and the pub is tastefully decorated throughout. The large car park can get busy.
Q☎✿✿◑▣ᵭP▣(6)✿☞

Six Bells Ⓛ ✔
48 St Thomas Street, SO41 9ND (top of High Street)
✿ 8am-11 (midnight Fri & Sat) ☎ (01590) 689990
Greene King Abbot; Ringwood Best Bitter; Sharp's Doom Bar; house beer (by Vibrant Forest); 2 changing beers (sourced nationally; often Vibrant Forest) Ⓗ
Previously a large furniture/houseware store, tastefully converted; it is on three levels, two of which have seating. A pub with this name once stood nearby – historic details and local photographs are displayed around the walls. Entering from the High Street, the lower seating area has a flame-effect gas fire, disabled toilet, and lift to the middle floor area with the bar and servery. The pleasant walled garden and smoking area is accessed from this floor via a back door.
Q☎✿◑ᵭ☀▣▣✿☞

Milford on Sea

Red Lion ✔
32 High Street, SO41 0QD
✿ 11.30-2.30, 6-11 (11.30 Fri); 11.30-11.30 Sat; 12-7 Sun
☎ (01590) 642236 ⊕ theredlionmilford.co.uk
House beer (by Ringwood); 2 changing beers (sourced locally; often Bowman, Dancing Cows, Itchen Valley) Ⓗ
Popular, homely, community pub in a vibrant village. It has a partial tie on ales but guest ales are always supported and usually sourced locally. One real cider should always be available. Good-value, traditional pub food is served and entertainment from local musicians is well supported. The pub is within easy reach of the beach, Sturt Pond Nature Reserve and Danestream woodland walks. There are three double en-suite rooms but, unlike the pub itself, they are not suitable for families. Dogs and walkers are welcome.
Q☎✿✿◑ᵭ▲♣♠P▣(X1)✿☞

North Waltham

Fox Ⓛ ✔
Popham Lane, RG25 2BE (off Frog Lane, between village and A30, M3 jct 7)
✿ 11-11 (midnight Fri & Sat); 12-10.30 Sun
☎ (01256) 397288 ⊕ thefox.org
Brakspear Bitter; Sharp's Doom Bar; West Berkshire Good Old Boy; 1 changing beer (sourced locally) Ⓗ
Lovely traditional country pub on the edge of the village and overlooking extensive farmland. The venue is divided into two – a popular restaurant, and a public bar where food is also served (booking advisable). Local seasonal produce is featured where possible. Outside there is an extensive beer garden and a children's adventure play area. The Ushers signage remains on the rear of the pub.
Q☎✿◑ᵭP▣✿☞

North Warnborough

Mill House 🅛

Hook Road, RG29 1ET (M3 jct 5; head towards Odiham)
🌣 11-11 ☎ (01256) 702953 🌐 millhouse-hook.co.uk
Hogs Back TEA; house beer (by Phoenix); 4 changing beers (sourced regionally; often Frensham, Itchen Valley, West Berkshire) 🅗
Listed as one of eight mills of Odiham in the Domesday Book, the current sections are 17th-century additions, and it was last used as a corn mill in 1895. Most recently a restaurant, it is now under Brunning & Price ownership. It has a pleasant central bar area, separate tabled dining spaces and a lower level view of the waterwheel and restaurant. The area surrounding the millpond fed from the Whitewater provides a pleasant outdoor seating area linking the function barn and parking. Q🕽🖾🛈🕽&P🚃(13)🦮🛜

Oakley

Barley Mow 🅛 ✅

19 Oakley Lane, RG23 7JZ
🌣 12-11; 12-10.30 Sun ☎ (01256) 782591
🌐 barleymowatoakley.com
Flowerpots Goodens Gold; Sharp's Doom Bar; 2 changing beers 🅗
A classic local English pub in the heart of a picturesque village, serving well-kept ales including one from a local brewer. Tasty, traditional pub food is on offer and cooked to order, including daily specials. It is a warm and family-oriented pub with a large garden with climbing frame and swings. The garden also includes a pizza oven and barbecue station. The place is dog-friendly and often used as a refreshment point for ramblers and walkers. A function room is available for dining or events. Q🕽🖾🛈P🚃(11)🦮🛜

Old Basing

Millstone

Bartons Lane, RG24 8AE (follow signs from Bartons Lane to Basing House and car park)
🌣 11-11; 12-10.30 Sun ☎ (01256) 331153
🌐 millstoneoldbasing.co.uk
Wadworth Henry's IPA, Horizon, 6X, Bishops Tipple; 1 changing beer 🅗
An attractively situated Wadworth house, once part of a still-existing water mill that overlooks the River Loddon and a water meadow. The pub is a short walk from the historic and picturesque ruins of Basing House and a large medieval tithe barn. The Millstone features traditional pub food and six Wadworth cask ales, plus one rotating guest ale, served seven days a week by friendly staff. Children are welcome, as is the occasional duck from the river! 🖾🛈&♣P🦮🛜

Otterbourne

Otter

Boyatt Lane, SO21 2HW (on hilltop village green)
🌣 11-11; 12-10.30 Sun ☎ (023) 8025 2685
🌐 theotterpub.co.uk
Otter Ale; Ringwood Best Bitter; Sharp's Doom Bar; Timothy Taylor Landlord; 1 changing beer (sourced nationally) 🅗
The Otter is a busy village pub serving a mix of locals and visitors. It looks out across a grassed village green. The bar serves up to five real ales

including one guest. The separate restaurant area offers an extensive menu and bar snacks are available. There are regular events such as the Monday quiz, food nights and a meat draw. The garden is pleasant in warmer weather. Legend says the pub has a smuggling history.
Q🖾🛈♣P🚃(1,E2)🦮🛜

Overton

Red Lion 🅛

37 High Street, RG25 3HQ
🌣 12-3, 6-11 (midnight Fri & Sat); 12-10.30 Sun
☎ (01256) 773363 🌐 redlion-overton.co.uk
Flowerpots Bitter; Sharp's Doom Bar; 1 changing beer (sourced locally) 🅗
Popular village pub that prides itself on well-kept local real ales and high-quality, freshly cooked food every day, including a range of speciality steaks. It is divided into three areas including a restaurant, main bar and snug with wood-burning stove. Located near the new Bombay Sapphire Distillery, the pub also offers an extensive gin menu. Outside there is a pleasant beer garden, partially covered patio area, separate function room with skittle alley available for hire, and a car park.
Q🕽🖾🛈&♣P🚃(76,86)🦮🛜

Park Gate

Village Inn ✅

67 Botley Road, SO31 1AZ
🌣 11.30-11 (midnight Fri & Sat) ☎ (01489) 573223
Sharp's Doom Bar; 3 changing beers (often Bays, Harviestoun, Oakham) 🅗
The Village Inn is a cosy atmospheric pub and part of Ember Inns. It serves great food alongside a selection of ales on six handpumps, three of which are rotating guest beers. The pub is less than five minutes' walk from Swanwick train station, and has ticket metered car parking Monday to Friday until 5pm. Parking charges are refundable on bar purchases. 🖾🛈&➔(Swanwick)P🚃(28,28A)🦮🛜

Portsmouth

Artillery Arms 🅛

Hester Road, Milton, PO4 8HB
🌣 12-11.30 (midnight Fri & Sat) ☎ (023) 9273 3610
Ringwood Fortyniner; Triple fff Alton's Pride, Moondance, Pressed Rat & Warthog; 3 changing beers 🅗
Tucked away in the back streets of Portsmouth, close to Fratton Park football ground, this pub is a real find and one to tick off on a visit to the city. There are two different bar areas and a large garden at the rear with plenty of seating. Pool and darts teams compete weekly. A good selection of regional ales is to be found all year round.
🖾🛈♣P🚃🦮🛜

Barley Mow 🅛 ✅

39 Castle Road, Southsea, PO5 3DE
🌣 12-midnight; 11-midnight Sat; 12-11 Sun
☎ (023) 9282 3492 🌐 barleymowsouthsea.com
Fuller's London Pride; Gale's HSB; 6 changing beers (sourced nationally) 🅗
Friendly two-bar community pub offering a selection of eight ales including a mild, stout or porter, and Westons Old Rosie cider. There is an impressive array of events including live music,

meat raffles, quizzes, pool, darts, and golf teams, bar billiards, chess league, and monthly druid moots, all listed on the pub's website. The garden is a real gem, with some hidden treasures, and has won awards in its own right. Children are welcome until 8pm. 🏮♣♠🚲🍴😺🐾🛜

Brewhouse & Kitchen 🅻 ⊘

26 Guildhall Walk, Landport, PO1 2DD

🕐 10-11 (10.30 Sun) ☎ (023) 9289 1340

Brewhouse & Kitchen Sexton, Mucky Duck, Black Swan; 2 changing beers Ⓗ

Recently refurbished hostelry in an accessible location close to Portsmouth and Southsea rail station. The ales are all brewed on site by their 2.5 barrel plant that greets you as you walk in. There is a choice of real ciders. Food is from 10am until 9pm, served from an open kitchen. A true LocAle pub in the city centre.
🚆🏮🕐🖣🚲⟶(Portsmouth & Southsea)🍴🚌😺🛜

Bridge Tavern

54 East Street, Old Portsmouth, PO1 2JJ

🕐 11-11; 12-10.30 Sun ☎ (023) 9275 2992

🌐 bridge-tavern-portsmouth.co.uk

Fuller's London Pride; Gale's HSB, Seafarers Ale; 1 changing beer Ⓗ

Situated in the heart of the Camber docks, this is the only surviving pub in East Street. The single downstairs bar is welcoming and divided into several areas. There is an old ship's telegraph attached to one wall (but be careful about trying it). Upstairs is another bar and function room. The outside seating allows you to enjoy the sea air and the bustle of a small fishing port. Not surprisingly, fish features heavily on the menu.
🏮🕐🖣🚌(16,19)🛜

Florist 🅻

324 Fratton Road, Fratton, PO1 5JX

🕐 3-11; 12-11 Fri & Sat; 12-10.30 Sun ☎ (023) 9281 4994

🌐 oakleafbrewing.co.uk/florist.html

Oakleaf Hole Hearted; 5 changing beers (often Oakleaf) Ⓗ

Now operated by Oakleaf Brewery of Gosport, and currently the only brewery-owned, independent pub in Portsmouth, this former Brickwood's Brewery establishment is also one of the only remaining in the city to feature the distinctive witch's hat tower design. The brewery's own ales are on constant rotation, as well as at least one guest and real cider. A popular pub with locals and visitors from further afield. 🚆🏮♣🖣🚌😺🛜

Golden Eagle

1 Delamere Road, Southsea, PO4 0JA

🕐 12-12; 12-11 Sun ☎ (023) 9282 1658

Fuller's London Pride; Gale's Seafarers Ale, HSB; 2 changing beers Ⓗ

A large two-bar street-corner local with a small garden about halfway between Fratton Station and Albert Road, a good stop-off on the way. It is well known as one of the top live music venues in the area, with bands performing most weekends – and classic rock music on vinyl once a month. In 2015 the pub was one of the seven finalists in the Fuller's Master Cellarman competition and won the Pride & Passion award. 🏮🚲(Fratton)♣🖣🛜

Hole in the Wall 🍸 🅻

Great Southsea Street, Southsea, PO5 3BY

🕐 4-11; 12-midnight Fri; 2-11 Sat & Sun ☎ (023) 9229 8085

🌐 theholeinthewallpub.co.uk

Langham Arapaho; Oakleaf Hole Hearted Ⓖ; 9 changing beers (sourced nationally) Ⓗ

The Hole is one of the smallest pubs in Portsmouth but, as a genuine free house, it offers a wide range of beers from a changing selection of local and national breweries (check website for current beer range). Oakleaf Hole Hearted, originally brewed for this pub, is generally available on gravity, but other local brewery beers are sometimes on sale instead. There are always real ciders. Local CAMRA Pub of the Year 2016. 🕐🖣🚌(7,15)😺🛜

John Jacques 🅻 ⊘

78-82 Fratton Road, Fratton, PO1 5BZ

🕐 8am-11 (midnight Fri & Sat) ☎ (023) 9277 9742

Greene King Abbot; Ruddles Best Bitter; Sharp's Doom Bar; 6 changing beers (sourced nationally; often Irving, Itchen Valley, Oakleaf) Ⓗ

A large Wetherspoon pub in the old Portsea Island Mutual Co-operative Society head offices. It is convenient for Fratton Road and Bridge Centre shops and close to Fratton rail station. Six guest real ales are on the bar at all times, while the real cider is usually from Westons or Gwynt y Ddraig. Children are welcome until 9pm. It is Cask Marque accredited and there is free cloud Wi-Fi. 🚆🖣🚲⟶(Fratton)🖣🚌(18,13)🛜

Lawrence Arms 🅻 ⊘

63 Lawrence Road, Southsea, PO5 1NU

🕐 2-11.30 (12.30am Fri); 11-12.30am Sat; 11-11 Sun ☎ (023) 9282 1280 🌐 lawrence-arms-portsmouth.co.uk

Sharp's Doom Bar; 5 changing beers (sourced nationally; often Irving) Ⓗ

Dating back to 1887, this street-corner pub's exterior retains some traditional tiles and lanterns. Inside, the L-shaped bar faces a large lounge area. Very much a friendly community pub, there are darts, pool and football teams, weekly meat raffles, quizzes and themed days. Guest ales are Irving seasonals, another local beer, and three others. The good cider selection offers Westons, plus boxed and bottled ciders – up to 20 in the summer. Food includes tasty gourmet toasties. 🏮🚲⟶(Fratton)♣🖣🚌(2,18,20)🛜

Leopold Tavern 🅻

154 Albert Road, Southsea, PO4 0JT

🕐 12-midnight; 12-11 Sun ☎ (023) 9282 9748

🌐 leopoldtavern.co.uk

Dark Star American Pale Ale, Hophead; 8 changing beers (sourced nationally; often Irving, Oakleaf, Vibrant Forest) Ⓗ

A corner local in vibrant Albert Road, popular with locals and students alike. Ten handpumps face you as you come in, with eight guest ales on at all times. Gravity-dispensed real cider is sold, with at least four varieties at any one time. Rolling muted Sky News can be seen on the big screen in the corner, and there is a pub quiz on Monday night. Q🏮🖣🚌(2,19)🛜

Lord Palmerston 🅻 ⊘

84-90 Palmerston Road, Southsea, PO5 3PT

🕐 8am-midnight (1.30am Fri & Sat) ☎ (023) 9272 8000

Fuller's London Pride; 9 changing beers (sourced nationally) Ⓗ

Large Lloyds No.1 bar in a busy shopping area. The landlord is a firm supporter of LocAle, with as many as six on the bar at any time, served on a rota basis; he also sells a range of ciders. Food is available all day from 8am. Close to many bus routes and just yards from Southsea Common and the beach, the pub is popular with families throughout the day. A DJ plays on Friday and Saturday nights, when it can get noisy. ☕🕦🍴🚪♻

Northcote Hotel L

35 Francis Avenue, Southsea, PO4 0HL
☀ 12-midnight (1.30am Fri & Sat) ☎ (023) 9278 9888
Irving Invincible; Long Man Brewery Pale Ale; Timothy Taylor Landlord; Wadworth 6X; 1 changing beer (sourced locally; often Irving) H
A large back-street local with two bars and a sizable heated patio garden. The lounge bar is decorated with film memorabilia going back to the comedians of the silent era and the most famous of all fictional detectives, Sherlock Holmes. The bar-back is somewhat unusual, having glass instead of mirrors, allowing you to watch a game of darts in the public bar from the comfort of the lounge. The choice of cider varies. ⛲♣🚪 (2,19)

Phoenix

13 Duncan Road, Southsea, PO5 2QU
☀ 10-midnight (1am Fri & Sat); 12-midnight Sun
☎ (023) 9278 1055
Ringwood Fortyniner; 2 changing beers (sourced regionally; often Exmoor, Goldmark, Irving) H
This hidden gem is a popular two-bar community local just off Albert Road. The lounge is adorned with photos of many celebrities who have appeared at the nearby Kings Theatre (including three Goons). The separate games room (part of the former Dock End Brewery) is separated from the rest of the pub by a quirky patio garden. There is even a Space Invaders machine among other games, should you wish to try your skill. The cider choice changes. ⛲♣🚪 (2,20)♻

Rose in June L ✓

102 Milton Road, Milton, PO3 6AR
☀ 12-midnight (1am Fri & Sat) ☎ (023) 9282 4191
⊕ theroseinjune.co.uk
Ballard's Midhurst Mild; Gale's HSB; Irving Frigate; Thwaites Lancaster Bomber; Upham Punter; 2 changing beers H
A two-bar pub with plenty of events such as the Thursday quiz, pool and darts matches, occasional comedy nights and a curry night on the first Wednesday of the month. The extensive garden has a play area and is made use of for barbecues and a popular summer beer festival – there is also an annual winter festival. Real ciders are available. ☕⛲🚪 (2,17,21)♻🌐

Rutland Arms L

205 Francis Avenue, Southsea, PO4 0AH
☀ 4-11; 2-midnight Fri; 11-midnight Sat; 12-10 Sun
☎ (023) 9275 1221
Butcombe Bitter; 2 changing beers (sourced locally; often Bowman, Irving, Oakleaf) H
About a five-minute walk from Fratton Park, this two-bar pub is often thronged with football fans; drinks are served in plastic glasses on match days before and after the game. Thursday is quiz night and darts is played. The extensive garden is popular and a beer festival is held in summer. ☕⛲🕦🚆(Fratton)♣🚪(1,15)🌐

Sir Loin of Beef

152 Highland Road, Eastney, PO4 9NH
☀ 11-midnight; 12-midnight Sun ☎ (023) 9282 0115
Gale's HSB; Titanic Plum Porter; 6 changing beers (sourced nationally) H

From the moment you approach and see the unique pub sign, made by the local blacksmith, you know that you will be in for a treat. You will be greeted by a bank of eight handpumps, serving ales from near and far, supplemented by an interesting range of keg, English bottled beers and changing real cider. A warm welcome is assured; the pub is decked out with, mainly, submarine memorabilia. Features are live music and a popular raffle on a Sunday lunchtime. ♿♣🚪 (1,2,17)

Wave Maiden L

36 Osborne Road, Southsea, PO5 3LT
☀ 6-11; 12-midnight Fri & Sat; 12-10 Sun ☎ (023) 9217 8878
3 changing beers (often Goldmark, Staggeringly Good, Vibrant Forest) G
An independent, family-owned establishment, focusing on artisanal produced beer and cheese. Go to this pub for beer brewed for taste, not mass consumption, alongside a menu that offers delicious home-made cheese-based dishes. It is one of the only gravity stillages in the area, with a constant rotation of local and national ales and a changing cider choice. It offers a welcoming atmosphere for beer lovers from 18 to 80. ☕🕦♿🍴🚪(1,23)♻🌐

Winchester Arms L

99 Winchester Road, Buckland, PO2 7PS
☀ 4-11; 3-midnight Fri; 12-11 Sat & Sun ☎ (023) 9266 2443
Oakleaf Hole Hearted; 3 changing beers (sourced regionally) H
The Winch is a proper back-street local, offering one regular beer and two or three varying guests. Ciders are available during the summer. Every third Sunday evening of the month is open mic night with music and comedy, and there is live music on the other Sundays, plus music one Saturday a month. A beer festival is held over the Spring Bank Holiday weekend. It has a covered smoking shelter outside, and may stay open until midnight Saturday if busy. Dogs welcome, but beware of the cat! ⛲🚪♻

Wine Vaults L

41-47 Albert Road, Southsea, PO5 2SF
☀ 12-11 (12.30am Fri & Sat); 12-10.30 Sun
☎ (023) 9286 4712 ⊕ wine-vaults-southsea.co.uk
Fuller's London Pride, ESB; Gale's Seafarers Ale, HSB; 3 changing beers (sourced locally; often Dark Star, Oakleaf) H
On the bustling Albert Road, this sprawling establishment offers five bars over three floors. Up to eight real ales are on offer at any time. Food is served until 9.30pm Monday to Saturday (8pm Sunday), with pizzas, scrumptious bar boards and Sunday roasts particular highlights. Live music on Thursdays, and jazz alternate Tuesdays, make this a destination for partygoers or serious beer drinkers. ☕⛲🕦♿🚪(2)♻🌐

Ringwood

Inn on the Furlong ✓

12 Meeting House Lane, BH24 1EY (by bus terminus)
☀ 9.30am-11 (midnight Fri & Sat); 10-11 Sun
☎ (01425) 475139 ⊕ innonthefurlong.co.uk
Ringwood Best Bitter, Boondoggle, Fortyniner; 2 changing beers (sourced nationally; often Marston's, Ringwood) H
The Inn on the Furlong sits conveniently between the bus station and the town centre, making it an ideal place to meet. Friendly, helpful staff open

from 9.30am for breakfast, and serve a good range of food through until 8pm. It is a tied Marston's pub stocking Ringwood Brewery beers. Live music features on Saturday evenings, and sporting events are shown on two TV screens. There are three good outside patio areas. Dogs permitted, but not in dining areas. 🐕🏵🌓🅿🚬🏨🐾🛜

Railway Hotel ⑃
35 Hightown Road, BH24 1NQ (turn E off Christchurch Rd at Lamb Inn) SU152048
✪ 11.30-11; 12-10 Sun ☎ (01425) 473701 ⊕ therailway.co
Ringwood Best Bitter; 4 changing beers (often Downton, Vibrant Forest) Ⓗ
Friendly two-bar traditional pub with a cosy snug at the rear, leading to a tidy child-friendly enclosed beer garden. The pub derives its name from the nearby station (now demolished) which is reflected in the railwayana, pictures, maps and photos adorning the public bar. The lounge has interesting old pews and chairs, with more photographs. Home-cooked traditional food is served, including Sunday roast. Four changing ales are available, two of them generally local beers. Q🐕🏵🌓◗🅿🚶♣🅿🚬🐾🛜

Romsey

Luzborough ⑃ ✅
Luzborough Lane, SO51 9AA
✪ 11-11 ☎ (01794) 523816
Greene King IPA, Abbot; 2 changing beers (sourced locally) Ⓗ
First time in the Guide for this quaint Grade II*-listed pub in the eastern outskirts of Romsey, just off the A27. The Luzborough is a Greene King Old English Inn, providing an extensive menu all day. It was originally a 16th-century house, refurbished and extended, yet a couple of the rooms still seem completely genuine. Some interesting architectural features can be seen from a second, small secret garden. Westons cider is available in the summer. Q🐕🏵🌓◗♿♣🅿🚬(4,5,W1)🐾🛜

Old House at Home
62 Love Lane, SO51 8DE (NE of town centre, adjoining Waitrose car park)
✪ 11-11 (11.30 Fri & Sat); 12-10.30 Sun ☎ (01794) 513175 ⊕ theoldhouseathomeromsey.co.uk
Fuller's London Pride; Gale's Seafarers Ale, HSB; 2 changing beers (often Fuller's) Ⓗ
Popular thatched pub in the centre of Romsey that has appeared in every edition of the Guide since 2005 and has been recognised in Fuller's national awards. Step down into the pub from outside and you will find a single L-shaped bar on two levels. Food is served in the bar and in a separate dining area. Booths, wooden beams and woodburners make for cosy drinking in the winter, while the courtyard garden is a relaxing retreat in the summer months. 🏵🌓🚶♣🅿🚬🛜

Star Inn ⑃
13 Horsefair, SO51 8EZ (N of town centre)
✪ 12-11 (midnight Fri & Sat) ☎ (01794) 511165
3 changing beers (sourced locally; often Bowman, Flack Manor, Red Cat) Ⓗ
A free house for over a year, the Star is welcoming and comfortable, offering a choice of at least three beers from local breweries. Draught cider is available in summer. A TV is on quietly, and there is live music every Saturday evening, and a long-established folk session on Wednesday evening –

all musicians welcome. Old photos and documents on display show that masonic lodge meetings once took place here. The accommodation comprises two double and two family rooms. Reputedly, the building is haunted. 🐕🏵🛏🚆🅿🏨🐾🛜

Shedfield

Wheatsheaf Inn ⑃
Botley Road, SO32 2JG (on A334)
✪ 12-11; 12-10.30 Sun ☎ (01329) 833024
Flowerpots Perridge Pale, Bitter, Goodens Gold; 3 changing beers (sourced locally; often CrackleRock, Goddards, Palmers) Ⓖ
This popular, award-winning pub has a lively public bar, warmed by a wood-burning stove in winter. The home-cooked food is excellent (no food Tue and Wed lunchtimes). Beers are served on gravity and come mainly from the owners' Flowerpots Brewery, and there are two real ciders from Thatchers. Blues, jazz or folk music is played live most Saturday evenings. A beer festival is held over the late Spring Bank Holiday weekend. The garden's flowers are delightful in summer. Q🏵🌓♣🍴🅿🚬(69)🐾🛜

Sherfield English

Hatchet Inn ✅
Salisbury Road, SO51 6FP (on A27)
✪ 12-3, 5-11.30 (1am Thu-Sat) ☎ (01794) 322487 ⊕ hatchetinn.com
Dartmoor Jail Ale; Sharp's Doom Bar; 2 changing beers (sourced nationally) Ⓗ
The first time in the Guide for this three-generation family-run pub at the very edge of Hampshire. To the right on entering is a comfortable public bar, to the left is a long saloon bar/dining room. The same chef has been cooking here since 1990 – an extensive menu, with large portions, often home-made, is a popular attraction for diners from near and far. Occasionally Adnams or Wells beers replace the West Country ales. There is a beer festival every August bank holiday. Q🐕🏵🌓◗🚶♣🅿🚬(X7R)🐾🛜

Silchester

Calleva Arms
The Common, RG7 2PH
✪ 11-11 (11.30 Fri & Sat); 12-11 Sun ☎ (0118) 970 0305 ⊕ callevaarms.co.uk
Fuller's Oliver's Island, London Pride; Gale's Seafarers Ale, HSB; 1 changing beer (sourced nationally) Ⓗ
An attractive village pub opposite the common, named after the local Roman settlement, Calleva Atrebatum. A Fuller's pub, it has five handpumps serving four of the brewery's regular ales plus one guest, which is often a seasonal beer or a local real ale. There is a welcoming bar with a separate comfortable dining area; an excellent choice of bar and restaurant food is also served in the conservatory, and in the large garden in the summer months. 🐕🏵🌓◗🚶♣🅿🚬(14)🐾🛜

Southampton

Bitter Virtue ⑃
70 Cambridge Road, SO14 6US (jct with Alma Road)
✪ 10.30-8.30; 10.30-2 Sun; closed Mon ☎ (023) 8055 4881 ⊕ bittervirtue.co.uk

2 changing beers (sourced regionally; often Red Cat, Siren, Vibrant Forest) G

Corner shop off-licence that is a treasure trove both for beer aficionados and those who just want something good to drink at home. Over 900 bottled and canned beers and ciders are offered, from local staples to rare imports. Two draught ales are usually available, at least one of which is from a local brewery, and two draught ciders, often Purbeck and 146. Enthusiastic staff are always willing to offer advice. The shop also sells books on beer and brewing and brewery merchandise. ●🖳♣

Butcher's Hook
7 Manor Farm Road, SO18 1NN (hidden by Bitterne Triangle monument)

🕭 6-11 Wed & Thu; 4-11 Fri; 1-11 Sat; 2-10 Sun; closed Mon & Tue ☎ 07912 092928

4 changing beers (sourced nationally) G

Micropub opened in 2014 and formerly a butcher's shop. Look for its scaffold benches outside to avoid walking past. It serves four varying cask ales, real ciders, plus a number of bottled ales. The small interior makes for a lively and sociable drinking atmosphere. With no bar, approach one of the staff to place your order before sitting at one of the few tables – there is seating inside for around 25 people. Closed on the last Sunday of the month for ticket-only music events. Q🕭🕭♿⊷●🖳(7)♣

Dancing Man L ✦
Wool House, Town Quay, SO14 2AR

🕭 12-11 (midnight Thu-Sat) ☎ (023) 8083 6666
⊕ dancingmanbrewery.co.uk

8 changing beers (often Dancing Man) H

The historic Grade I-listed medieval building, transformed in 2015, now houses the bar and brewery. The downstairs bar, with eight handpumps, offers a range of six Dancing Man beers (brewed on site, with pale ales suitable for vegans) and two guest beers. A central spiral staircase leads up to the open-plan restaurant, with four handpumps, sometimes used as a function room. The website includes a history of the building and brewery tour details. Situated opposite the Isle of Wight ferry. ◑♿●♣🖳♣

Dolphin
30 Osborne Road South, SO17 2EZ (W side of St Denys station)

🕭 1 (10 Thu-Sat)-12.30am; 11-12.30am Sun
☎ (023) 8055 0277 ⊕ thedolphinpubstdenys.co.uk

7 changing beers (sourced nationally) H

One-bar pub close to St Denys station, accessible via footbridge next to the pub. The interior features bare boards and brickwork, many tables and chairs, and inviting sofas. A small wood-clad snug adjacent to the bar area can be booked for private use. Traditional home-cooked food is available as well as several real ciders. The large outdoor area includes a separate bar with one cask ale available Easter to October. Live music plays most days. 🕭♣◑⊷♣●P🖳(7)♣

Freemantle Arms ✦
31 Albany Road, SO15 3EF

🕭 12-2.30, 5-8 (11 Tue & Wed); 12-11 Thu & Sat; 12-midnight Fri; 12-10 Sun ☎ (023) 8077 2536
⊕ thefreemantlearms.co.uk

Sharp's Doom Bar; house beer (by Hardys & Hansons); 2 changing beers (sourced regionally) H

Hidden oasis in a quiet no through road in the heart of Freemantle. The single bar has comfortable seating, tastefully decorated with pictures of old Southampton and with the walls displaying old, interesting tools. Four real ales are on the bar, two of which change regularly due to demand. A beautiful enclosed summer garden with wooden trestle seating is outside, ideal for children to play. Polite, friendly staff and locals will always make you feel welcome. Quiz night, darts, two crib teams and regular events take place. 🕭♣≠(Millbrook)♣🖳♣♠

Giddy Bridge L
10-16A London Road, SO15 2AF

🕭 8am-11.30 ☎ (023) 8033 6346

Greene King Abbot; Ruddles Best Bitter; Sharp's Doom Bar; 5 changing beers (sourced nationally) H

Popular Wetherspoon pub on the edge of the city centre, previously a furniture shop. It has a large single bar on the ground floor with additional seating upstairs, and an unusual secluded roof terrace for when it is sunny. Tables and chairs are under cover outside on the pavement. Food is served all day, alcohol from 9am. The large range of guest beers often includes some from local breweries, and there are two draught ciders, Old Rosie and Cheddar Valley. Q🕭♣◑♿●🖳♣

Guide Dog L
38 Earl's Road, SO14 6SF (corner with Ancasta Rd)

🕭 12-11; 12-10.30 Sun ☎ (023) 8063 8947

Dark Star American Pale Ale, Hophead; Flowerpots Goodens Gold; Red Cat Prowler Pale; 7 changing beers (sourced nationally); often Dancing Cows, Fuller's, Longdog) H

Set in a side road, out of sight of the main road, this single-roomed pub concentrates on a wide range of real ales from local and national breweries – currently on 11 handpumps. Despite a change of ownership in 2015, the excellent beer quality remains. The bar area is small and enjoys a friendly atmosphere. The pub becomes crowded at peak times and when Southampton are playing at home. St Mary's Stadium is a 20-minute walk away. 🖳(7,U6)♣♠

Hop Inn L
Woodmill Lane, SO18 2PH

🕭 12-11; 11-midnight Sat; 12-10.30 Sun ☎ (023) 8055 7723

Bowman Swift One; Gale's HSB; Sharp's Doom Bar; Wychwood Hobgoblin H

This 1930s pub is in a mature residential area and retains two bars. The homely lounge is divided by a central fireplace and leads to an outside area alongside the pub. The public bar is more modern, with bar games, jukebox and a rear covered courtyard. In summer the pub is adorned with award-winning flower boxes. A quiz is held on the first Sunday of the month, Wednesday is curry night and live music occasionally features on a Saturday. ♣◑♣P🖳(16,7)♣

Platform Tavern L ✦
Town Quay, SO14 2NY

🕭 12-11 (midnight Thu-Sat) ☎ (023) 8033 7232
⊕ platformtavern.com

Fuller's London Pride; Gale's Seafarers Ale; 4 changing beers (sourced locally; often Dancing Man) H

Original home of the Dancing Man Brewery, the Platform Tavern is a welcoming pub opposite the town quay, with an interior that includes part of the old city wall. African art, batik and musical instruments on the walls give a bohemian atmosphere. The pub offers good, freshly cooked food, and live music is a regular feature. Three beer festivals are held annually, at Easter, August bank holiday and the third weekend in November; a cider festival is at Whitsun weekend. ◖❶♣♠❫♣❀❄

Rockstone ⓛ ✔
63 Onslow Road, SO14 0JL
❀ 11-midnight (1am Fri & Sat) ☎ (023) 8063 7256
⊕ therockstone.co.uk
7 changing beers (sourced regionally; often Dark Star, Flack Manor, Vibrant Forest) Ⓗ
The horseshoe-shaped bar of this free house has a welcoming counter with signs above detailing a changing range of seven guest beers, mainly from the region, alongside two real ciders. To the right, more blackboards list some of the vast selection of premium and rare rums, whiskies, gins and bourbons on offer from around the world. The pub is renowned for its home-cooked food, especially burgers – portion sizes are large. Occasional beer festivals are held and themed nights are frequent. ➤◖♠❫(7,U6)♣❄

South Western Arms ⓛ ✔
38-40 Adelaide Road, SO17 2HW (E side of St Denys station)
❀ 12-11 (midnight Fri & Sat) ☎ (023) 8032 4542
Bowman Swift One; 8 changing beers (sourced nationally) Ⓗ
Single-bar corner pub with one seating area on the ground floor and more seating, a pool table and table football on an upstairs gallery. It is so close to St Denys station that it is almost on the platform. The walled garden, with covered smoking area, is a suntrap in summer. Nine ales are usually offered, many of them local, plus one or two ciders and up to 20 foreign bottled beers. Several beer festivals are held each year. A pizza van serves outside Wednesday to Saturday. Q➤❀≉♣♠❫P❫(7)♣❄

Waterloo Arms ⓛ
101 Waterloo Road, SO15 3BS
❀ 12-11 (midnight Fri & Sat) ☎ (023) 8022 0022
Downton New Forest Ale, IPA; Hop Back GFB, Crop Circle, Entire Stout, Summer Lightning; 3 changing beers (sourced nationally) Ⓗ
A 1930s 'improved' public house, the Waterloo has been a Hop Back pub for more than 25 years. It enjoys a deserved reputation for the quality and range of its ales. The principal public area is of T-shape, with perimeter seating and stools, and is graced by two Roman-brick fireplaces; there is also a large, modern conservatory (available for functions), beyond which is a paved garden. Food options may occasionally include home-made Scotch eggs. Three or four beer festivals are held each year. ❀◖❀(Millbrook)♣❫♣❄

Wellington Arms ⓛ
56 Park Road, SO15 3DE (corner with Mansion Rd)
❀ 12-11.30 (12.30am Fri & Sat) ☎ (023) 8022 0356
⊕ thewellingtonarmssouthampton.co.uk
Fuller's London Pride, ESB; 9 changing beers (sourced locally; often Bowman, Flowerpots, Triple fff) Ⓗ
The Welly, an old Victorian beer house dating from around 1860, has two bars full of character, serving 11 real ales. It has lots of Iron Duke memorabilia, and quirky bar counters decorated with pre-decimalisation coins. A roaring fire in the front bar in winter makes this a popular place to enjoy a pint

and chat with friendly locals. The rear bar leads through to a paved garden. A quiz is held on Thursdays and a ukulele group meets on Tuesdays. ❀♣♠❄

Southwick

Golden Lion ⓛ
High Street, PO17 6EB
❀ 12-3, 5.30-11; 12-midnight Sat; 12-7 Sun
☎ (023) 9221 0437 ⊕ thegoldenlionsouthwick.co.uk
Suthwyk Old Dick, Skew Sunshine Ale; 4 changing beers (sourced locally; often Bowman, Langham, Urban Island) Ⓗ
Warm, welcoming free house with a modern feel, although military crests and wartime adornments reflect its historic past (Montgomery and Eisenhower partially planned the D-Day landings here). The rear car park houses the old brewhouse museum, well worth a visit. Inside the pub is a large rambling bar and a smaller, quiet bar, both tastefully furnished and with locally brewed real ales on offer, plus real cider. The separate dining area is the perfect place to enjoy the award-winning food. Q➤❀◖♣♠P♣

Swanmore

Rising Sun ⓛ
Droxford Road, SO32 2PS
❀ 11.30-3, 6-11; 12-3, 6-9.30 Sun ☎ (01489) 896663
⊕ risingsunswanmore.co.uk
4 changing beers (sourced locally; often Andwells, Ringwood, Triple fff) Ⓗ
A charming 17th-century coaching inn with large fireplaces, oak beams and various seating/dining spaces, including an unusual large alcove area with an arched bricked ceiling. This family-run free house always serves one Ringwood beer plus three other ales from Hampshire. Quality food is provided from a classic pub menu and is supplemented by a varied specials board. Outside is a large garden and plenty of parking. Q➤❀◖P❫♣

Tichborne

Tichborne Arms Ⓗ
SO24 0NA (1¼ miles S from B3047 Alresford Rd jct) SU571304
❀ 11.45-3, 6-10.30 (11 Wed & Thu; 11.30 Fri); 12-11.30 Sat; 12-7.30 Sun ☎ (01962) 733760 ⊕ tichbornearms.co.uk
Palmers Copper Ale; 2 changing beers (sourced locally) Ⓖ
Village pub with an old-fashioned antique-finished interior, popular with local drinkers and walkers. The guest beers tend to be from Dorset or Somerset and draught cider is usually on sale. A beer and cider festival is held over the August bank holiday. Upmarket pub food is served but drinkers are welcome in both bars. The main bar has a piano and a logburner and there is an open fire in the small panelled bar. Dogs and children welcome. Q➤❀◖♣♠P♣❄

Titchfield

Queen's Head ⓛ ✔
13 High Street, PO14 4AQ
❀ 12-11 (11.30 Fri); 11-11.30 Sat; 11-11 Sun
☎ (01329) 842154 ⊕ queenshead-titchfield.co.uk
4 changing beers (sourced locally; often Bowman, Goddards, Irving) Ⓗ

Imposing 17th-century pub, offering four changing ales, usually from local breweries. An open fire is the central feature of the bar. Home-made locally sourced food, including sausages from a nearby butcher, and a gluten-free menu, is available every lunchtime and evening (no food Sun eve). A separate restaurant opens Friday and Saturday evenings and Sunday lunchtimes. An upstairs function room caters for weddings, theme nights and discos. Quizzes and meat raffles are held on Sunday evenings. Q ⌂ ⊛ ◑ ▯ ▭ (X4) ✿ 🛜

Wheatsheaf 🅛
1 East Street, PO14 4AD
✪ 12-11 (midnight Fri & Sat) ☎ (01329) 842965
⊕ wheatsheaftitchfield.co.uk
Flowerpots Bitter; Palmers Best Bitter; 3 changing beers (sourced regionally; often Island, Oakleaf, Red Cat) ℍ
The only free house in Titchfield, with a growing reputation for its fine selection of ales and gastro-style food. The intimate bar with real fire and cosy snug is always popular with locals and a great place to catch up with village gossip. Food is served daily in the bar and separate restaurant, with à la carte and fish specials available Wednesday to Saturday. Steaks headline on Tuesdays and roasts on Sundays. Beer festivals are held every summer and winter. Q ⌂ ⊛ ◑ & ◐ ▯ (X4) ✿

Warsash

Ferryman
2 Warsash Road, SO31 9HX
✪ 12-11 (11.30 Fri & Sat); 12-10.30 Sun ☎ (01489) 573088
Adnams Lighthouse; 4 changing beers (sourced locally; often Adnams, Milk Street, Triple fff) ℍ
At the heart of the village, this spacious pub boasts four different real ales, changing cider and good food. It has a single bar with an additional function room to the rear. A warm welcome awaits, especially for dogs. There is a restaurant area to one side of the bar and a decked area at the front. Occasional beer festivals are held. Buses from Fareham to Southampton stop outside the pub, and the River Hamble is just 600 yards away. ⌂ ⊛ ◑ & ♣ ◐ ▭ (X5) ✿ 🛜

Weyhill

Weyhill Fair
Weyhill Road, SP11 0PP
✪ 11.30-3, 5.30-11; 11.30-11 Fri & Sat; 12-6 Sun
☎ (01264) 773631 ⊕ weyhillfair.com
Fuller's London Pride; Gale's Seafarers Ale, HSB; 2 changing beers ℍ
Country-style pub three miles west of Andover, standing on the site of the historic Weyhill fairground. It serves meals at every session, using locally sourced ingredients where possible. The three regular beers are usually supplemented by both a seasonal and a guest beer from the Fuller's portfolio. A popular outdoor music and beer festival is held in July, featuring local bands and musicians. ⌂ ⊛ ◑ ⏛ ▯ ▭ (Activ8) ✿ 🛜

Whitchurch

Whitchurch Sports & Social Club
Winchester Road, RG28 7RB (S edge of town, by football ground)
✪ 7-11.30; 12-11.30 Sun ☎ (01256) 892493

Fuller's London Pride; Red Cat TomCat; 1 changing beer ℍ
Tucked away opposite the tranquil Millennium Meadow, this club features two large bars which are open in the evenings and at weekends. Two real ales are served, sometimes from local breweries. As well as being home to Whitchurch United Football Club, the venue is shared by the indoor bowling club, whose impressive green can be viewed from the comfortable lounge bar. It also has two squash courts. Regular events include quizzes, parties, cabarets, discos and live bands, and it is the venue for Rockus Music Festival. Open at 1pm on Saturdays when Whitchurch United are at home. ⌂ ⊛ & ▯ ▭ (86) 🛜

Winchester

Albion 🅛
2 Stockbridge Road, SO23 7BZ (just E of station)
✪ 12-11 (11.30 Fri & Sat); 12-10.30 Sun ☎ (01962) 867991
Flowerpots Perridge Pale, Bitter, Goodens Gold; 1 changing beer (sourced locally; often Alfred's, Flowerpots, Longdog) ℍ
Small, cosy pub opposite the bottom of Station Hill, the closest pub to Winchester rail station. The acute street-corner location at a busy junction gives it an unusual shape, and makes it an ideal place to watch the world go by while having a drink and a chat with friends. Now owned by Cheriton's Flowerpots Brewery (its third pub), the Albion serves excellently kept Flowerpots beers. Well worth breaking a rail journey just to sample its wares. Q ⇌ ▭ ✿ 🛜

Alfie's 🅛 ⊘
157 High Street, SO23 9BA (opp Guildhall)
✪ 11.30-2am ☎ (01962) 852985 ⊕ alfieswinchester.com
5 changing beers (sourced locally; often Flowerpots, Red Cat, Upham) ℍ
Alehouse-style single-bar pub situated yards from Winchester bus station, offering a friendly and informal atmosphere. Children are welcome in the bar until 8pm. There is plenty of standing room, and the pub can get busy on Friday and Saturday evenings. A converted double garage forms part of the outside eating/drinking/smoking area, which is heated by a huge logburner. Five real ales are always on, including a regular from Upham Brewery. Cider is from Westons. Food is served until 8pm (6pm Sun). ⌂ ⊛ ◑ & ♣ ◐ ▭ 🛜

Black Boy 🅛
1 Wharf Hill, SO23 9NQ (just off Chesil St, B3404)
✪ 12-11 (midnight Fri & Sat); 12-10.30 Sun
☎ (01962) 861754 ⊕ theblackboypub.com
Alfred's Saxon Bronze; Flowerpots Bitter; 3 changing beers (sourced locally; often Hop Back, Itchen Valley, Ringwood) ℍ
An ancient, multi-level, rambling collection of interconnected rooms surround an island bar. Eclectic, eccentric bric-a-brac decor abounds – more than can be appreciated on one visit. Surprises lie everywhere: tradesmen's tools, a complete farmhouse kitchen, serious taxidermy, and so on. The beer range emphasises local breweries and the cider changes. Lunches are served daily except Mondays, evening food Tuesday-Saturday; for more formal dining the co-owned Black Rat restaurant is opposite, while 10 double en-suite rooms are available in the attached Black Hole B&B. Q ⌂ ⊛ ⛉ ◑ ◐ ♣ ◐ ▭ (4) ✿ 🛜

Eclipse Inn

25 The Square, SO23 9EX
⏰ 11-11 (midnight Thu; 1am Fri & Sat) ☎ (01962) 865676
⊕ eclipseinnwinchester.co.uk
Sharp's Doom Bar; 3 changing beers (sourced nationally) Ⓗ
Enviably located between the High Street and the cathedral, the Eclipse is a tiny pub, originally 16th century. The slightly sloping frontage was part of a 1925 modernisation. Inside, a timeless lounge, with a fine wood ceiling and doorway, leads to a smaller back room. The pub's history includes the death of Lady Alice Lisle, her ghost, and much else. The appealing lunchtime menu, including Sunday roasts, is recommended. Outside are benches, tables and chairs on the broad pavement area.
Q🕏🞨⌸🍴❀🕸

Hyde Tavern Ⓛ

57 Hyde Street, SO23 7DY
⏰ 12.30-2 (not Mon-Wed), 5-11; 5-midnight Fri; 12-midnight Sat; 12-11 Sun ☎ (01962) 862592 ⊕ hydetavern.co.uk
Flowerpots Bitter; Harveys Sussex Best Bitter Ⓗ**; 4 changing beers (sourced locally)** Ⓖ
Twin-gabled building, lying below street level – beware of low ceilings – though larger than it appears from the street, with an attractive garden. The main bar leads through to another cosy area and there is a cellar bar hosting events such as storytelling evenings. Live folk music features on Saturday evenings (and other times). Up to six beers, mostly local, always include a dark beer, and there is Westons Old Rosie cider. No food is served, but customers are welcome to order takeaways.
Q🞨🞬♣🍴⌸❀🕸

Old Vine Ⓛ ✅

8 Great Minster Street, SO23 9HA (adjacent to and facing cathedral)
⏰ 11-11; 11-10.30 Sun ☎ (01962) 854616
⊕ oldvinewinchester.com
Alfred's Saxon Bronze; Timothy Taylor Landlord; 2 changing beers (sourced locally; often Andwells, Bowman, Hop Back) Ⓗ
Grade II-listed and comfortable 18th-century inn; the entrance from the square is opposite the City Museum and the Cathedral Green, and there is a second entrance in Little Minster Street. The restaurant serves award-winning food, often from local produce, and high-quality accommodation is available. Children are welcome in the family room at the rear of the building, which also serves as a small function room. Four handpumps display a selection of mainly local ales.
Q🞨⌸🞬♣🍴⌸(1,69)❀🕸

Wykeham Arms

75 Kingsgate Street, SO23 9PE (just outside city's ancient Kingsgate)
⏰ 11-11 ☎ (01962) 853834
⊕ wykehamarmswinchester.co.uk
Flowerpots Goodens Gold; Fuller's London Pride; Gale's Seafarers Ale, HSB; 1 changing beer Ⓗ
Georgian inn dating from 1755, in the city's most historic area between the cathedral and the college. Several interlinked rooms, crammed with memorabilia, are served from a central bar. Furnishings include old school desks, and

Nelsoniana abounds. Although a Fuller's pub, a Flowerpots beer is nearly always present. This civilised hostelry for conversationalists features in almost every known guide book and also offers 14 highly rated rooms, an extensive food service and over 20 wines by the glass. Q🞨⌸🞬⌸(1,69)❀🕸

Wonston

Wonston Arms 🍷 Ⓛ

Stoke Charity Road, SO21 3LS
⏰ 6-10 (10.30 Fri); 12-10 Sat; 12-8 Sun; closed Mon
☎ (01962) 760288
3 changing beers (sourced locally; often Bowman, Red Cat, Triple fff) Ⓗ
This recently renovated village pub serves well-kept ales, mainly from local breweries such as Bowman, Red Cat and Alfreds. It is around a 15-minute walk from Sutton Scotney and the nearest bus stop. Tuesday is fish and chips night at the Wonston – a local van parks up and serves food direct to pubgoers to eat with their real ale. Curry nights are also held, with meals delivered to the pub. Various themed events are arranged. CAMRA branch Pub of the Year 2016. Q🞨♣P❀🕸

Wootton

Rising Sun Ⓛ

Bashley Common Road, BH25 5SF (on B3058, 1½ miles SE of A35)
⏰ 10-11; 10-10.30 Sun ☎ (01425) 610360
⊕ therisingsunbashley.co.uk
Flack Manor Flack's Double Drop; Morland Old Speckled Hen; 2 changing beers (sourced locally; often Dancing Cows, Downton, Vibrant Forest) Ⓗ
Large 1900s roadside pub facing the open forest, with much seating and an impressive food choice. Up to five ales are dispensed in summer and busy times (look for sealed sample bottles showing a beer's availability and colour). Now tastefully redecorated, with a refurbished kitchen and toilets, the wonderful stained glass windows and original artefacts have been left intact. The pub is popular with families, with a separate room leading to a huge, enclosed adventure playground. It has a large car park and is close to the A35 main road.
Q🕏🞨⌸♿P⌸(C32,C33)❀🕸

Yateley

Dog & Partridge ✅

105 Reading Road, GU46 7LR
⏰ 12-11 (midnight Fri & Sat); 12-10.30 Sun
☎ (01252) 870648 ⊕ dogandpartridgeyateley.co.uk
Caledonian Golden XPA; Theakston Best Bitter; house beer (by Caledonian); 1 changing beer (sourced nationally; often Wychwood) Ⓗ
Spacious, modern one-bar pub with a central area for standing or sitting. There is TV sport, pool and darts at one end of the bar and an open-plan dining area at the other. Live music is played each Saturday evening, and Sunday lunches are popular (booking essential). Attractive local photographs, prints and maps adorn the walls. It was once the home of the Official Monster Raving Loony Party, whose leader was the landlord, and is now home for Yateley Morris. 🕏🞨⌸♿P⌸(3,8)❀🕸

Keep your Good Beer Guide up to date by visiting the CAMRA website **www.camra.org.uk**, then Good Beer Guide, then Updates.

198

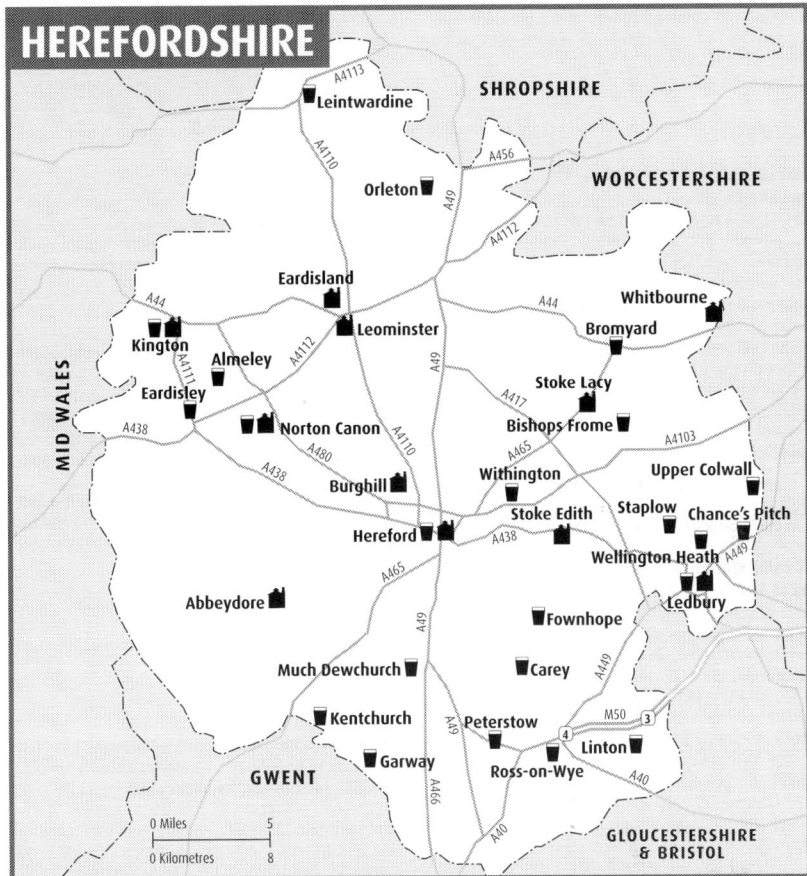

Almeley

Bells Inn L

HR3 6LF

🌐 9am-midnight ☎ (01544) 327216

2 changing beers (sourced locally; often Goff's, Mulberry Duck, Three Tuns) Ⓗ

An unpretentious stone-built village pub that is entered through the erstwhile jug and bottle. Popular with the locals, it has a large low-ceilinged bar and a second room for dining or pool. Outside is a double pétanque piste. Traditional home-prepared lunches are served, with a pensioners' special on the first Tuesday of the month. Live music plays on occasional Saturday evenings. The pub now runs a village shop.

ᄅ🕭🅑🕭♣🅿🖵(446,462)🐱🛜

Bishops Frome

Green Dragon L

WR6 5BP (just off B4214)

🌐 4.30-11; 4-11.30 Fri; 12-11.30 Sat; 12-6 Sun

☎ (01885) 490607 🌐 thegreendragoninn.com

Ledbury Bitter; Otter Bright; Purple Moose Snowdonia Ale; Timothy Taylor Golden Best; Wye Valley Bitter; 1 changing beer (sourced locally) Ⓗ

A warren of flagstone-floored rooms, low beams and an inglenook fireplace are a treat for visitors to this 17th-century village inn. Six handpumps offer a range of local and regional beers alongside five local ciders and perries. Bar meals are served (Tue-Sat evenings, Sat-Sun lunchtimes). A regular CAMRA award winner including Herefordshire Cider Pub of the Year 2014. Q ᄅ🕭🅑♣🅿🐱🛜

Bromyard

Rose & Lion L ✓

5 New Road, HR7 4AJ

🌐 11-11 ☎ (01885) 482381

Wye Valley Bitter, HPA, Butty Bach Ⓗ

The Rosie is very much a traditional town pub. Two small original rooms are complemented by a further bar to the rear, plus a more contemporary

REAL ALE BREWERIES

Arrow Kington
Golden Valley Abbeydore
Hereford 🍺 Hereford
Ledbury Ledbury
Mulberry Duck Burghill
Odyssey 🍺 Whitbourne
Saxon City Stoke Edith (brewing suspended)
Shoes 🍺 Norton Canon
Simpsons Eardisland
Swan Leominster (NEW)
Wobbly Hereford
Wye Valley Stoke Lacy

annexe with disabled toilets and a pleasant garden. Furnished throughout in a modern style, it still retains traditional elements.
Q ⑤ ❀ 㐤 ♣ P ⬚ ⬚ (420) ❀

Carey

Cottage of Content 𝕃 ✓
HR2 6NG (in village)
✪ 12-3, 6-10.30; 12-2, 6-11 Fri & Sat; 12-3 Sun; closed Mon summer; 12-3, 6.30-10.30 Wed & Thu; 12-3, 6-11 Fri & Sat; 12-4 Sun; closed Mon & Tue winter ☎ (01432) 840242
⬚ cottageofcontent.co.uk
Hobsons Best; Wye Valley Butty Bach ⊞
A classic country pub with parts dating from 1485. There are two bars and a separate restaurant. Although the focus is on high-quality food, drinkers are welcome. Booking is advised at most times for the freshly-prepared bar meals at lunchtimes and à la carte menu in the evenings. There is a large garden to the rear. Local cider comes from Ross-on-Wye and Carey Organics. Q ⑤ ❀ 🚲 ⬚ ❶ ❶ P ❀

Chance's Pitch

Wellington Inn 𝕃
WR13 6HW (on A449, near B4218 jct)
✪ 12-3, 6.30-11; 12-3.30 Sun ☎ (01684) 540269
⬚ thewellingtoninnmalvern.co.uk
Goff's Tournament; 2 changing beers (often Gloucester) ⊞
A landmark venue standing alone on the main Ledbury to Malvern road, this is a much-extended, multi-level pub that, while majoring on food, also caters for the drinking trade. The comfortable and plainly decorated drinkers-only bar area has a traditional feel, with a lounge on the lower level offering views across open country. Two restaurant areas to the rear serve a wide range of often locally sourced meals – from sandwiches to full à la carte. Q ⑤ ❀ ❶ ❶ P ❀

Eardisley

Tram Inn 𝕃
HR3 6PG (on A4111)
✪ 12-3, 6-11.30 (12.30am Fri & Sat); 12-3, 7-10.30 Sun; closed Mon ☎ (01544) 327251 ⬚ thetraminn.co.uk
Hobsons Best; Wye Valley Butty Bach; 1 changing beer ⊞
This Grade II-listed black-and-white half-timbered inn takes its name from a long-gone horse-drawn tramway. A cosy bar complete with original floor tiles and woodwork contrasts with a larger bar with panelled walls and grand bay window, and a simple games room to the rear. Traditional locally sourced pub meals are served including Sunday roasts (no food Sun eve). Bottled Orgasmic and Gwatkins ciders are stocked. Q ❀ ❶ Ⓐ ♣ ❶ P ⬚ (446/462) ❀ ☎

Fownhope

New Inn 𝕃
HR1 4PE (on B4224)
✪ 12-3, 6-midnight; 11-midnight Sat; 12-midnight Sun ☎ (01432) 860350 ⬚ thenewinnfownhope.co.uk
Hobsons Best; house beer (by Wye Valley); 1 changing beer (often Hobsons) ⊞
A single room with exposed beams and light decor is divided into more discreet spaces by a central, bare-brick fireplace. Typical pub food is served

Monday to Saturday lunchtimes, with fish and chips, pies, steaks and curry specials in the evenings. A Sunday roast is served monthly. Jam sessions and quiz evenings are held regularly. Fownhope Football Club uses the pub as a base.
⑤ ❀ ❶ Ⓐ ♣ P ⬚ (454) ❀ ☎

Garway

Garway Moon 𝕃 ✓
Garway Common, HR2 8RQ SO465227
✪ 6-11 Mon & Tue; 12-2.30, 5-11 Wed-Fri; 12-11 Sat & Sun ☎ (01600) 750270 ⬚ garwaymooninn.co.uk
2 changing beers (sourced locally) ⊞
A remote but popular and welcoming pub overlooking the delightful village green and cricket pitch, with a lounge and public bar plus a separate snug/family room and garden. A British pub food menu features specials inspired by local growers and farmers, all freshly prepared, including vegetarian options. Food evenings include Italian on Tuesday, curry on Wednesday and steak on Thursday, and roasts feature on Sundays. The last Friday of the month is open mic night and the last Sunday is quiz night. Four local ciders are available.
⑤ ❀ 🚲 ❶ Ⓐ ♣ ❶ P ⬚ (412) ❀ ☎

Hereford

Barrels 𝕃 ✓
69 St Owen Street, HR1 2JQ
✪ 11-11.30 (midnight Fri & Sat); 12-11.30 Sun ☎ (01432) 274968
Wye Valley Bitter, HPA, Dorothy Goodbody's Golden Ale, Dorothy Goodbody's Wholesome Stout; 1 changing beer (often Wye Valley) ⊞
The Barrels enjoys a cult following. Winner of Herefordshire CAMRA Pub of the Year six times, it is first and foremost a community pub. No food, no gimmicks, but tons of character across five different bars. The cobbled courtyard to the rear hosts a charity beer and music festival each August bank holiday weekend. The TV is only on for major sporting events. ⑤ ❀ ≈ ♣ ❶ ⬚ ❀ ☎

Beer in Hand 𝕃
136 Eign Street, HR4 0AP
✪ 5-10.30 Mon; 4-11 Tue-Thu; 12-11 Fri & Sat; 12-10.30 Sun ☎ 07443 487124 ⬚ beerinhand.co.uk
12 changing beers (often Odyssey, Purity) Ⓖ
Herefordshire's first micropub, converted from a launderette in 2013. In 2014 it was named Herefordshire CAMRA Pub of the Year and in 2015 Herefordshire Cider Pub of the Year. With an impressive chilled racking system, it typically sells up to a dozen ales, always one from Odyssey Brewing Co, and 10 mainly local ciders and perries. Meals are served Thursday to Saturday evenings. A quiz is held the first Wednesday and jam session the last Tuesday of the month. Q ⑤ ❀ ❶ 㐤 ♣ ❶ ⬚ ❀

Lichfield Vaults 𝕃
11 Church Street, HR1 2LR
✪ 11-midnight (2am Fri & Sat) ☎ (01432) 266821 ⬚ lichfieldvaultshereford.co.uk
Adnams Broadside; Caledonian Deuchars IPA, Golden XPA; Fuller's London Pride; Sharp's Doom Bar; 1 changing beer (sourced regionally) ⊞
An 18th-century city-centre venue in a charming cobbled alley. Although opened out into a single bar area, the pleasant wood-panelled interior gives an intimate feel, and the secluded, decked beer

garden extends some way back. Speciality Greek-Cypriot dishes feature on the lunchtime menu, and a traditional roast on Sundays. Evening meals are available by arrangement for groups of 15 or more. Live blues plays 4-6pm on the last Sunday of every month. Quiz night is Sunday. 🐕🍴◗&≈♣🚲😊🛜

Kentchurch

Bridge Inn L
HR2 0BY (on B4347)
❂ 12-2 (not Mon), 6-10; 12-2, 6-11 Fri & Sat; 12-4 Sun; closed Tue ☎ (01981) 240408 ⊕ bridgeinnkentchurch.co.uk
Ruddles Best Bitter; 2 changing beers (often Wye Valley) 🅗
On the banks of the River Monnow, the building probably dates from the 14th century. It comprises a welcoming single front bar plus a restaurant with excellent views, and boasts riverside gardens and a pétanque piste. The freshly prepared food ranges from bar snacks to full meals. Guest beers are from regional and local breweries, with local Apple County cider in summer. Opening hours are extended in the summer. Herefordshire CAMRA Country Pub of the Year 2014. Q🏵◗&⚓♣P🛜

Kington

Olde Tavern ★ L
22 Victoria Road, HR5 3BX
❂ 6.30-10.30 (midnight Wed & Thu); 3.30-midnight Fri; 12-midnight Sat & Sun ☎ 07582 235765
Hobsons Mild; 3 changing beers 🅗
Once called the Railway Inn, unlike the now closed railway, this is a real survivor. Behind a delightfully understated Victorian red-brick façade lies a diminutive two-bar gem, with its original entrance lobby, serving hatches, flagstone floor and bench seating intact – plus a treasure trove of interesting keepsakes. Games and pub teams root it firmly in the local community and, in 2016, a hot meals service commenced in a small room to the rear. Q🐕🏵◗♣🚲🚌(41,461,462)😊

Ledbury

Horseshoe Inn L
The Homend, HR8 1BP
❂ 11-11 (midnight Fri & Sat); 11-10.30 Sun
☎ (01531) 632770
Wye Valley HPA; Butty Bach 🅗
Historic town pub with a grand set of stone steps and an attractive façade. Many original features have survived past refurbishments, adding cosiness and much character. Families are welcome. Pizzas feature strongly on the menu, with a pizza oven prominent in the bar, supplemented by tapas, burgers and salads. Q🐕🏵◗≈♣🚲😊🛜

Prince of Wales L ✪
Church Lane, HR8 1DL
❂ 11-11; 11-10.30 Sun ☎ (01531) 632250
⊕ powledbury.com
Hobsons Best; Ledbury Dark; Wells Eagle IPA; Wye Valley HPA; Butty Bach; 2 changing beers 🅗
Hidden away near the imposing parish church, this 16th-century timber-framed pub boasts two bars plus a more private alcove where a folk jam

Bread is the staff of life, but beer is life itself. **Traditional**

session is held each Wednesday evening. It is always bustling with locals and visitors alike. Westons draught cider is stocked, together with an extensive range of foreign beers. The bar meals are excellent value and booking is advisable for the popular Sunday roasts. Herefordshire CAMRA Town Pub of the Year for 2015. 🐕🏵◗♣🚲😊🛜

Leintwardine

Sun Inn ★ L
Rosemary Lane, SY7 0LP (off A4113)
❂ 11-11; 11-10.30 Sun ☎ (01547) 540705
⊕ suninn-leintwardine.co.uk
Hobsons Best; 3 changing beers (sourced locally; often Three Tuns, Wye Valley) 🅗
A national treasure and one of the last parlour pubs, the building was saved in 2009 following a CAMRA-led 'Save the Sun' campaign. A red brick-tiled public bar features bench furniture and a simple fireplace. To the rear is a stylish pavilion-style extension overlooking the garden – the venue for the August bank holiday Sunday beer festival. Basic, hearty meals are served or you can bring in fish and chips from the shop next door. Q🐕🏵◗&⚓♣🚲🚌(738,740)😊🛜

Linton

Alma Inn L
HR9 7RY (off B4221, W of M50 jct 3) SO659255
❂ 12-3 (not Mon), 6-11; 12-3, 7-10.30 Sun
☎ (01989) 720355 ⊕ almainnlinton.co.uk
Butcombe Bitter; Ludlow Gold; Malvern Hills Black Pear; Oakham JHB; 1 changing beer (often Bespoke, Bristol Beer Factory, Untapped) 🅗
A welcome return for this multi award-winner, under sympathetic and dynamic new ownership. It now offers meals. A convivial and cosy front bar, complete with a real fire, contrasts with a rear pool room and a separate wood-panelled restaurant. The food is hearty, freshly prepared pub classics, with seasonal specials, light bites and bar snacks. Events include the major Linton Music Festival in June and Summer Acoustic Sessions in August – both held in the extensive grounds and accompanied by beer festivals. Q🐕🏵◗♣P😊

Much Dewchurch

Black Swan
HR2 8DJ (on B4348)
❂ 12 (11.30 Sat)-3, 5.30-11; 12-4, 6-11 Sun
☎ (01981) 540295
Timothy Taylor Landlord; 2 changing beers (often Butcombe, Slater's, Three Tuns) 🅗
Possibly the oldest pub in Herefordshire, where a small lounge leads to a dining room with open fire, and a separate public bar with flagstone floors leads to a pool and darts room. Home-prepared, mainly locally sourced food is served every session. The guest beers are typically from regional breweries. Draught Westons cider and perry are available, together with bottles from other local cider makers. Thursday is folk night. 🐕🏵◗♣🚲P🏵😊🛜

Norton Canon

Three Horseshoes L
HR4 7BH (on A480)

✪ 12-3 Wed; 7-11 Thu-Sat; 12-3, 7-11 Sun; closed Mon & Tue
☎ (01544) 318375
Shoes Farrier's Ale, Norton Ale, Canon Bitter, Peploe's Tipple ⊞
Utterly unspoilt early-Victorian roadside pub of timeless rural character, home to the Shoes Brewery located at the rear of the premises. A friendly welcome is assured from the small but loyal following. The cosy and comfortable lounge, furnished with an eclectic collection of old chairs and sofas, contrasts with a more traditional public bar with many games and a roaring fire.
Q✿☎☻Å♣P⊟☻

Orleton

Boot Inn 𝕃
SY8 4HN (off B4361)
✪ 12-3, 5.30-11; 12-11.30 Sat; 12-11 Sun ☎ (01568) 780228
⊕ thebootinnorleton.co.uk
Hobsons Best; Wye Valley Butty Bach; 1 changing beer (often Ludlow, Monty's, Three Tuns) ⊞
A comfortable and welcoming village pub. A charity quiz is held monthly on each second Tuesday in winter and a beer and cider festival in July in the large beer garden. The home-prepared food ranges from bar snacks to interesting gourmet meals. With the Mortimer Trail passing about a mile away, walkers are welcome, and the bus stops right outside. Wye Valley Butty Bach may alternate with HPA. Q✿☎☻◑Å♣P⊟(490)☻≋

Peterstow

Red Lion 𝕃
Winters Cross, HR9 6LH (on A49, just NW of village)
✪ 12 (4 Mon)-11 ☎ (01989) 730546
⊕ redlionpeterstow.co.uk
Hobsons Best; Wye Valley Bitter, Butty Bach; 1 changing beer (often Butcombe, Otter, Timothy Taylor) ⊞
A single bar serves extensive drinking and dining areas, including a large roadside conservatory. Home-prepared food ranges from bar snacks to full meals. Guest beers come from local micros or regional breweries. A charity quiz is held on the first Monday of the month. Outside, there is an adventure playground for children. The regular Hereford-Gloucester bus service stops close by.
☎☻◑�&Å♣♠P⊟(32)☻≋

Ross-on-Wye

Mail Rooms ✅
Gloucester Road, HR9 5BS
✪ 8am-midnight (1am Fri & Sat) ☎ (01989) 760920
Greene King Abbot; Ruddles Best Bitter; Sharp's Doom Bar; 2 changing beers (often Bespoke, Oakham) ⊞
Behind the fine red-brick and stone façade of what was once the town's main post office is a well-executed and surprisingly atmospheric Wetherspoon conversion. Good-value food is served all day, including a children's menu. Three regular beers are complemented by up to two guest beers from a diverse range of breweries, plus two Westons ciders. Local beer and cider festivals feature regularly. Alcohol is available from 9am.
Q✿☎☻◑ᴅ♠P⊟(32,33)≋

Staplow

Oak Inn 𝕃
HR8 1NP (on B4214)
✪ 12-11; 12-10.30 Sun ☎ (01531) 640954
⊕ oakinnstaplow.co.uk
Bathams Best Bitter; Ledbury Gold; Wye Valley Bitter; 1 changing beer ⊞
A stylishly renovated and well-run roadside country inn offering exceptional food, good beer and quality accommodation overlooking nearby hop yards (booking essential). A contemporary public area neatly divides into three – a reception bar area with modern sofas and low tables, a snug and a dining area featuring an open kitchen. At the rear is a further room with scrubbed tables.
Q✿☎☻◖◑ᴅP⊟(417)☻≋

Upper Colwall

Chase Inn ♈ 𝕃
Chase Road, WR13 6DJ (off B4218, turn at upper hairpin bend signed British Camp) SO766431
✪ 12-3, 5-11; 12-11 Sat; 12-10.30 Sun ☎ (01684) 540276
⊕ thechaseinnmalvern.co.uk
Bathams Best Bitter; 3 changing beers (often Ledbury, Malvern Hills, Wood) ⊞
Two-bar free house with a genteel atmosphere secreted away in a quiet wooded backwater. It comprises a small lounge for dining (booking advised at weekends) and a long narrow public bar, both adorned with many curios. A delightful manicured rear beer garden commands panoramic views across Herefordshire to the Welsh Hills. A beer festival is held each June and a cider festival in October. Herefordshire CAMRA Pub of the Year 2015. Q✿☎☻◑♣♠P⊟(675)☻≋

Wellington Heath

Farmers Arms 𝕃
Horse Road, HR8 1LS (E of B4214)
✪ 12-3 (not Tue), 5.30-11; 12-11 Sat; 12-10 Sun; closed Mon
☎ (01531) 634776 ⊕ farmersarmswellingtonheath.co.uk
Otter Amber; Wye Valley Butty Bach; 3 changing beers ⊞
The bar and main dining area are in the original 18th-century building, and on either side are more modern extensions housing a games room with pool table and a restaurant. The food covers a wide range, from burgers and pub classics to steaks and speciality dishes, locally sourced where possible. Guest beers usually include one from Hillside Brewery, alongside eight local draught ciders.
☎☻◑ᴅ♣♠P⊟(675)☻≋

Withington

Cross Keys 𝕃
HR1 3NN (on A465 in Withington Marsh)
✪ 5 (12 Sat)-11; 12-10.30 Sun ☎ (01432) 820616
Otter Ale; Wye Valley Butty Bach; house beer (by Wye Valley); 1 changing beer ⊞
Run by the same landlord for over 40 years, this is drinking in the slow lane Herefordshire style. A long single bar divides either side of a central servery into two drinking areas, with original beams, exposed stonework and comfortable bench seating along each wall, both book-ended by two woodburners. A folk jam session is held on the last Thursday of each month. Filled rolls are available on Saturdays. Q✿☎☻Å♣♠P⊟(420)☻

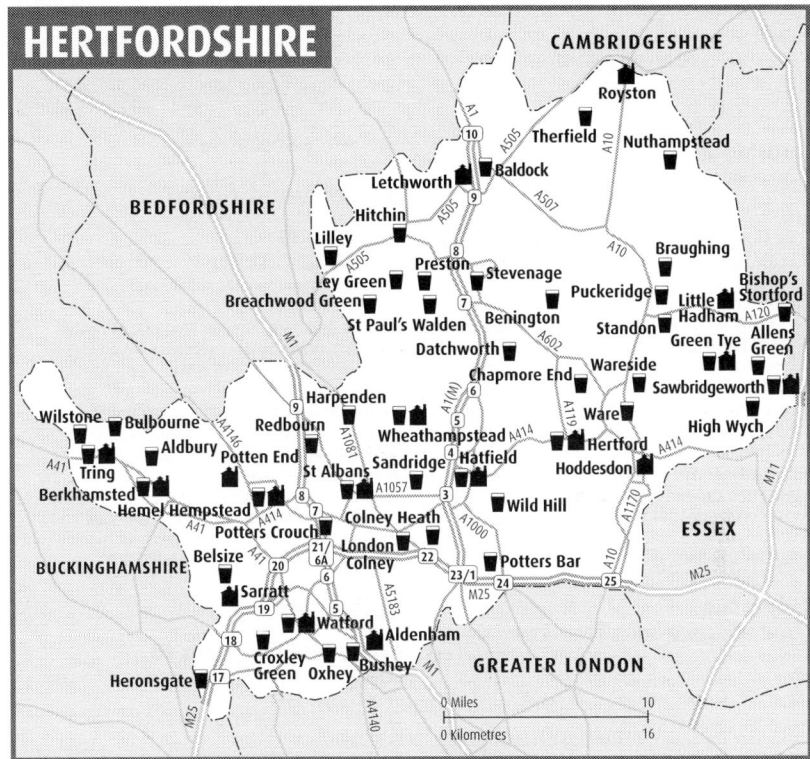

HERTFORDSHIRE

CAMBRIDGESHIRE

BEDFORDSHIRE

BUCKINGHAMSHIRE

ESSEX

GREATER LONDON

Royston
Therfield
Nuthampstead
Baldock
Letchworth
Hitchin
Lilley
Preston
Braughing
Ley Green
Stevenage
Puckeridge
Bishop's Stortford
Breachwood Green
Benington
Little Hadham
St Paul's Walden
Standon
Allens Green
Datchworth
Green Tye
Wareside
Sawbridgeworth
Harpenden
Chapmore End
Ware
High Wych
Wilstone
Bulbourne
Redbourn
Wheathampstead
Hertford
Aldbury
Potten End
Sandridge
Hatfield
Hoddesdon
Tring
St Albans
Berkhamsted
Wild Hill
Hemel Hempstead
Colney Heath
Potters Crouch
London
Belsize
Colney
Potters Bar
Sarratt
Watford
Heronsgate
Croxley Green
Oxhey
Aldenham
Bushey

0 Miles 10
0 Kilometres 16

Aldbury

Valiant Trooper 🅛
Trooper Road, HP23 5RW
🕐 11 (10 Sat)-11; 10-10.30 Sun ☎ (01442) 851203
🌐 valianttrooper.co.uk
Chiltern Beechwood Bitter; Tring Side Pocket for a
Toad; 3 changing beers (sourced locally; often XT) 🅗
The Trooper is situated in an area of outstanding
national beauty. It is a stunning 17th-century pub
retaining much of the charm from that era. A must-
visit, it offers an outstanding beer selection and
separate restaurant for food. The menu features a
good choice of British pub fare to appeal to all
customers. The staff are welcoming. There is a log-
burning fire in the winter and a beer garden for the
summer. Runner-up for local CAMRA Pub of the
Year 2016. Q🏵🌄🕭🕪👌≒♣🍴P🚪🚌(30,31)🐾🐾🛜

Allens Green

Queen's Head 🍷 🅛
CM21 0LS TL455170
🕐 12-2.30 (not Mon & Tue), 5-11; 12-10.30 Sun
☎ (01279) 723393 🌐 shirevillageinns.co.uk
Fuller's London Pride; Mighty Oak Maldon Gold 🅗; 2
changing beers (sourced locally) 🅗/🅖
Popular village inn, well worth seeking out for the
changing range of up to four beers. On the third
weekend of every month and over bank holiday
weekends mini beer festivals are held that use
gravity stillage to bring up the number of beers to
10 or 12. Hot snacks are available unless the pub is
very busy. CAMRA branch Pub of the Year in six of
the past 10 years, and Hertfordshire Cider Pub of
the Year 2014. Q🏵👌🍴P🐾🐾🛜

Baldock

Orange Tree 🅛 ✅
Norton Road, SG7 5AW
🕐 12-2.30, 4.30-11 Mon-Wed; 12-midnight Thu-Sat; 12-10.30
Sun ☎ (01462) 892341 🌐 theorangetreebaldock.com
Greene King XX Mild, IPA, Abbot; 10 changing beers
(sourced nationally) 🅗
Local and County Pub of the Year and Cider Pub of
the Year 2015. Three regular beers include XX Mild,
and there are 10 guests from small brewers
including two from the award-winning Buntingford
Brewery. Add to this five real ciders from East
Anglia Regional Cider Producer of the Year, Apple
Cottage. Entertainment includes a quiz night on
Tuesday, folk music on Wednesday, and a comedy
club. Good home-made locally sourced food is
served. Six Nations Rugby is shown.
🏵🌄🕭🕪👌≒♣🍴P🚪(91,98)🐾🐾🛜

Belsize

Plough
Dunny Lane, WD3 4NP
🕐 12-11; 12-10.30 Sun ☎ (01923) 262261
🌐 theploughatbelsize.co.uk
Greene King IPA; St Austell Tribute; 1 changing beer
(sourced nationally; often Paradigm, Tring, Vale) 🅗
This free house was purpose built for the Kings
Langley Brewery in the 1840s. Located in the
hamlet of Belsize between Chipperfield and Sarratt,
it is a traditional English country pub with oak-
beamed ceilings, open log fires, comfy settees, a
pleasant garden, a restaurant and a large rear car
park. Food is served Tuesday to Sunday lunchtimes
and Wednesday to Saturday evenings, offering

snacks and a regularly changing chalkboard menu. There is a convenient bus stop, but no evening or Sunday service. Q🌣🛏❋◑♿💧♣P🚬(352)🌺🕏

Benington

Lordship Arms
42 Whempstead Road, SG2 7BX
✪ 12-3, 6-11 (not Mon eve); 12-3, 7-11 Sun
☎ (01438) 869665 ⊕ lordshiparms.com
Black Sheep Best Bitter; Crouch Vale Brewers Gold; Timothy Taylor Landlord; 6 changing beers (sourced nationally) ⓗ
Single-room pub situated at the southern end of the village with over two decades in this Guide. The tidy bar is decorated with telephone memorabilia – even some of the handpumps are modelled on telephones. A well-maintained garden sports superb floral displays in the summer. Good-quality sandwiches and snacks are available at lunchtimes. Wednesday is curry night. Classic car club meetings are held in the summer. A repeat winner of local and county CAMRA Pub of the Year awards. Q🌣◑♥P🚬🕏

Berkhamsted

Rising Sun Ⓛ
1 Canal Side, George Street, HP4 2EG (from train station follow the canal towards Hemel Hempstead and pub is at lock 55 on Grand Union Canal)
✪ 12-11.30 (12.30am Thu-Sat); 12-10.30 Sun
☎ (01442) 864913 ⊕ theriserberko.net
House beer (by Tring); 4 changing beers (sourced nationally) ⓗ
The Riser boasts many well-deserved CAMRA awards. The bar has six handpumps and around 17 guest ciders in the cellar. It also stocks a wide range of cigars, snuffs and interesting liqueurs. The excellent ploughman's is renowned. Terrific events are held here throughout the year including a regular cheese club and gastro nights. Real ale festivals are frequent and CAMRA members receive a generous discount. Dog treats are available.
🌣🛏❋⇌♣💧🚬(500,501)🌺🕏

Bishop's Stortford

Star Ⓛ ✅
7 Bridge Street, CM23 2JU
✪ 11-midnight (2am Fri); 12-2am Sat; 12-6 Sun
☎ (01279) 654211 ⊕ thestar-bishopsstortford.co.uk
3 changing beers (sourced regionally; often Adnams) ⓗ
A 17th-century town-centre pub catering for all ages. It is busy on Friday and Saturday evenings with a young crowd. Tuesday is quiz night. A quiet pint can be enjoyed on other evenings and at lunchtimes. Reasonably priced traditional pub food is freshly prepared throughout the day. Additionally pizzas are made to order at any time. 🌣◑⇌🚬🕏

Braughing

Brown Bear Ⓛ
14 The Street, SG11 2QF
✪ 3-6 Mon; 3-11 Tue; 12-11.30; 12-6 Sun ☎ (01920) 82215
⊕ brownbearbraughing.co.uk
Buntingford Twitchell; 3 changing beers (sourced nationally) ⓗ
A pub since at least 1740, the Brown Bear has a public bar and restaurant, both with impressive

fireplaces. At least one beer comes from the nearby Buntingford Brewery. Tuesday is pizza night and Thursday is quiz night. Darts and pétanque are played. The large garden sports an occasional outside bar. Monthly live music offers something for everyone. Summer and winter opening times vary. 🌣◑♣P🚬(331)🌺🕏

Breachwood Green

Red Lion ✅
16 Chapel Road, SG4 8NU
✪ 12-11 (midnight Sat) ☎ (01438) 833123
⊕ redlionbreachwoodgreen.co.uk
Adnams Broadside; Greene King IPA; St Austell Tribute; 1 changing beer (sourced nationally) ⓗ
Friendly locals' pub with a well-kept interior and bright decor. The outdoor seating area and patio provide fine views of rolling countryside and are a good vantage point to view the aircraft approaching Luton Airport runway. The seasonal and guest beers are varied and unusual for the area. Good home-made food is available daily. The pub is home to darts, dominoes, football and cricket teams, and holds a number of music events throughout the year. 🌣◑♣P🚬🌺🕏

Bulbourne

Grand Junction Arms ✅
Bulbourne Road, HP23 5QE (adjacent to Grand Union Canal bridge 138)
✪ 12-11; 12-10.30 Sun ☎ (01442) 891400
⊕ grandjunctionarms.co.uk
Tring Side Pocket for a Toad; Sharp's Doom Bar; 1 changing beer (sourced locally; often Chiltern, Loose Cannon) ⓗ
Popular canalside pub on the outskirts of Tring, with works of art by local artists adorning the walls (and for sale). There is a raised restaurant area away from the bar for diners and a large beer garden with a children's play area. Traditional and interesting fresh food is available lunchtimes and evenings. Dogs and horses are welcome in the garden. Q🌣🛏◑♿♣P🚬(61)🕏

Bushey

Swan
25 Park Road, WD23 3EE

11-11; 12-10.30 Sun ☎ (020) 8950 2256
🌐 swanpubbushey.co.uk
Greene King Abbot; Sharp's Doom Bar; Timothy Taylor Landlord; Young's Bitter Ⓗ
Making yet another appearance in the Guide, this genuine one-bar local pub in a side street off Bushey High Street offers four regular well-kept ales. Bar snacks such as toasties and pies are available all day. There is a cosy feel in winter with two real fires. The walls are adorned with photos of village life and sporting achievements. There are good links with local rugby clubs. Access to the rear garden (and the Ladies') is via a side gate.
🏵️🗢🖥️(142,258)🐾🛜

Chapmore End

Woodman ⓛ

30 Chapmore End, SG12 0HF (turn off B158 between Bengeo and A602 roundabout) TL328164
12 (5 Mon)-11; 12-10.30 Sun ☎ (01920) 463339
🌐 thewoodmanpub-chapmore.com
Greene King IPA, Abbot; 2 changing beers (sourced nationally) Ⓖ
A classic two-bar country pub situated in a quintessential English hamlet off the B158, popular with walkers and the local shoot. The beer is served straight from cooled casks in the cellar behind the bar. In the extensive gardens pétanque can bc played and there is a children's play area. A conservatory with bar and accessible toilets has been added at the rear. A beer/music festival is held annually in the summer. Food is available only in the warmer months. An unspoilt gem.
Q🕭🏵️🐙🖑🗢P🏵️🛜

Colney Heath

Crooked Billet ⓛ

88 High Street, AL4 0NP
11-2.30, 4.30-11; 11-11 Fri; 12-11 Sat; 12-10.30 Sun
☎ (01727) 822128
Tring Side Pocket for a Toad; 3 changing beers (sourced nationally) Ⓗ
Popular and friendly cottage-style village pub dating back over 200 years. A genuine free house, it stocks three to five guest beers from national, regional and microbreweries. A wide selection of good-value home-made food is served lunchtimes and Friday and Saturday evenings. Summer barbecues and Saturday events are held occasionally. This is a favourite stop-off for walkers on the many local footpaths. Families are welcome in the bar until 9pm and in the large garden, where there is play equipment. 🕭🏵️🐙🗢P🖥️(304)🐾

Croxley Green

Sportsman ⓛ

2 Scots Hill, WD3 3AD (at A412 jct with the Green)
2 (12 Fri & Sat)-11; 12-10.30 Sun ☎ (01923) 443360
Fuller's ESB; Sharp's Doom Bar; 6 changing beers (sourced nationally; often Aylesbury, Haresfoot, RedWillow) Ⓗ
Welcoming, family-run community pub with up to eight real ales. Beers are varied and usually include a dark beer, with an emphasis on microbreweries. Tasting trays are available. Pub games include darts, pool and ringing the bull. The pub hosts a popular weekly quiz and a monthly music jam on the last Sunday afternoon of the month. Community activities include a book group, ladies'

darts team and a jazz club. Croxley underground station is a 15-minute walk away.
🏵️🗢P🖥️🖥️(320,324)

Datchworth

Plough ⓛ

5 Datchworth Green, SG3 6TL (on crossroads)
12-11; 12-10 Sun ☎ (01438) 813000
3 changing beers (sourced nationally) Ⓗ
This small single-bar pub just on the edge of Datchworth Green became a free house in 2014 and now sports three varying real ales. At least one pump serves a LocAle. This is a real locals' pub and is the hub of the village but all are made welcome. The secret garden is a real suntrap in the summer months and features a pétanque piste.
🏵️🗢🖤P🖥️(379)🐾🛜

Green Tye

Prince of Wales ⓛ

SG10 6JP (sat nav recommended) TL444184
12-3, 5.30-11; 12-11 Sat; 12-9.30 Sun ☎ (01279) 842139
🌐 thepow.co.uk
Ash Valley Prince of Wales IPA; Wadworth Henry's IPA; 3 changing beers (sourced locally; often Ash Valley) Ⓗ
A traditional and friendly village local, whether you are a walker, cyclist, dog owner or just plain thirsty. Landlord/owner Rob has recently established the Ash Valley Brewery at the back of the pub, making the Prince of Wales its brewery tap. The food offering is sandwiches and great-value traditional pub grub. There is a small garden for smoking and for fine weather. Beer festivals with a barbecue and entertainment are held in May and September.
Q🕭🏵️🖑🖤P🐾🛜

Harpenden

Cross Keys ⓛ ✅

39 High Street, AL5 2SD (opp War Memorial)
11.30-11; 12-10.30 Sun ☎ (01582) 763989
🌐 cross-keys-harpenden.co.uk
Rebellion IPA; Timothy Taylor Landlord; Tring Ridgeway Ⓗ
Tucked in among the shops in the town centre, this two-bar pub has retained its traditional charm with a rare fine pewter bar top and flagstone floors. The original oak-beamed ceiling has tankards from past and present customers hanging from it. In spring and summer enjoy your pint in the secluded, attractive rear garden, and in autumn or winter relax in front of the saloon bar's fire. Traditional home-cooked lunches are served Monday to Saturday. Q🕭🏵️🖑⇌🗢🖥️🐾🛜

Hatfield

Horse & Groom

21 Park Street, AL9 5AT
11.30-11; 11.30-midnight Fri & Sat; 12-10.30 Sun
☎ (01707) 264765
Black Sheep Best Bitter; Greene King Abbot; 3 changing beers (sourced nationally) Ⓗ
In the heart of Old Hatfield, this allegedly haunted, 16th-century, Grade II-listed building is also thought to house a priest hole. The former timber-framed and later brick-clad pub serves up to five real ales and hosts three to four beer festivals every year. Tuesday is bangers and mash night and

Saturday is chilli and rice night – purchase an ale for a free portion. Hatfield railway and bus stations are just a few minutes' walk away.
Q ☜ ⚑ ◗ ⟟ ⚑ ⭠ ♣ ☷ (300,301,724) ✜

Hemel Hempstead

Full House ✔
128 Marlowes, HP1 1EZ (close to bus station)
✪ 8am-midnight (1am Fri & Sat) ☎ (01442) 265512
Greene King IPA, Abbot; Sharp's Doom Bar; 6 changing beers (sourced nationally) ⓗ
Former cinema and bingo hall (hence the name), which is spacious with plenty of seating, and a decor reminiscent of its past. Consistent beer quality and a wide range of changing beers ensure this pub remains in the Guide. The changing beers are often local (Chiltern, Red Squirrel, Tring, Vale) but can vary. The cider is Old Rosie from the box, and one other in season. Food is served all day. Regular beer festivals, occasional Meet the Brewer events and brewery trips all feature.
Q ☜ ⚑ ◗ ⟟ ⚑ ♣ ☷ ⚑

Heronsgate

Land of Liberty, Peace & Plenty ⚑ ⓛ
Long Lane, WD3 5BS (just off jct 17 M25) TQ023949
✪ 12-11 (midnight Fri & Sat); 12-10.30 Sun
☎ (01923) 282226 ⊕ landoflibertypub.com
Downton New Forest Ale; 6 changing beers (sourced nationally; often Dark Star, Downton, XT) ⓗ
Welcoming award-winning pub close to the M25 with historic connections to the Chartists who had a short-lived rural community nearby. Popular with walkers, cyclists, locals and real ale enthusiasts, up to 10 microbrewery beers are offered in a range of styles and strengths. Real ciders, a perry and a wide choice of whiskies are also available. Beer festivals, tastings and regular events are held throughout the year. Bar snacks are served all day. There is a large pavilion outside for families.
⚑ ♣ ♠ P ⛺ ☷ (R2) ✜ ⚑

Hertford

Black Horse ⓛ ✔
29-31 West Street, SG13 8EZ
✪ 12-11 (midnight Fri & Sat); 12-10.30 Sun
☎ (01992) 583630 ⊕ theblackhorse.biz
6 changing beers (sourced nationally) ⓗ
A community-focused timbered free house, dating from 1642 and situated in one of Hertford's most attractive streets, near the start of the Cole Green Way. The well-kept garden includes a separate and safe childrens' area. The interesting food menu features game and the pub has its own bakery. Handy for Hertford Town FC supporters, the pub has a rugby team affiliated to the RFU. Runner-up local CAMRA Pub of the Year 2015.
☜ ⚑ ◗ ⟟ ⭠ (East/North) ♣ ⚑ ☷ ✜ ⚑

Hertford Club
Lombard House, Bull Plain, SG14 1DT
✪ 12 (11 Sat)-11; 12-8 Sun ☎ (01992) 421422
⊕ thehertford.club
4 changing beers (sourced nationally) ⓗ
Dating from the 15th century with later additions, Lombard House, on the River Lea, was built as an English Hall House and is one of the oldest buildings in Hertford. It has been the home of this private club since 1897. CAMRA members are welcome and may be signed in on production of a membership card. You will find a varied choice of three or four beers and real cider, which in summer can be enjoyed in the delightful walled garden. Winner local CAMRA Club of the Year 2015.
☜ ⚑ ◗ ⟟ ⭠ (East) ♣ ⚑ ☷ ⚑

Old Barge ✔
2 The Folly, SG14 1QD (ask for Folly Island and you will find it)
✪ 11-11; 4-11 Fri (midnight Sat); 12-11 Sun
☎ (01992) 581871 ⊕ theoldbarge.com
Sharp's Doom Bar; Woodforde's Wherry; 4 changing beers (sourced nationally) ⓗ
A free house on Folly Island pleasantly situated canalside on the River Lea, offering not only a good selection of beers – often including a dark mild, stout or porter – but also a range of ciders and perries. Locally sourced home-cooked food is served all day. The pub hosts occasional beer festivals, a popular Sunday quiz night and open mic on the last Saturday of the month. Look out for the annual duck race and the children's crayfish festival held in August. ☜ ⚑ ◗ ⟟ ⭠ (East) ♣ ⚑ ☷ ⚑

Old Cross Tavern ⓛ
8 St Andrew Street, SG14 1JA
✪ 4.30-11 (midnight Fri); 12-midnight Sat; 12-10.30 Sun
☎ (01992) 583133
Adnams Southwold Bitter; Old Cross Gertcha!; Timothy Taylor Landlord; 4 changing beers (sourced nationally) ⓗ
Superb town free house offering a friendly welcome. Up to six real ales, usually including a dark beer of some distinction, come from brewers large and small, including the pub's own microbrewery, and there is a fine choice of Belgian bottle-conditioned beers. Two beer festivals are held each year – one over the Spring Bank Holiday, the other in October. No TV or music here, just good old-fashioned conversation. Home-made pork pies are available. Q ⭠ (East or North) ♣ ☷ ✜

High Wych

Rising Sun
High Wych Road, CM21 0HZ
✪ 12-2.30 (not Tue or Thu), 5.30-11; 12-3, 6-11 Sat; 12-3, 7-10.30 Sun ☎ (01279) 724099
Courage Best Bitter; 4 changing beers (often Mighty Oak, Oakham) ⓖ
Friendly village local that has never used handpumps – a range of four or five beers is served on gravity, often from East Anglian breweries. Although recently refurbished, the original character has been preserved by means of a stone floor, attractive fireplace and wood panelling. Popular with locals and walkers, it holds a monthly quiz and an annual vegetable competition. Parking is in the village hall car park opposite.
Q ⚑ ♣ P ☷ (347) ✜

Hitchin

Half Moon ⚑ ⓛ
57 Queen Street, SG4 9TZ
✪ 12-midnight (1am Fri & Sat); 12-11 Sun
☎ (01462) 452448 ⊕ thehalfmoonhitchin.co.uk
Adnams Southwold Bitter; Young's Bitter; 6 changing beers (sourced nationally) ⓗ
This split-level, one-bar pub dates from 1748 and was once owned by Hitchin brewer W&S Lucas. It

sells two regular and six guest beers, often from local breweries, as well as two ciders, a perry and four guests. Home-prepared food and tapas is served daily. Monthly quiz and speciality food nights are popular in this friendly community pub. Cribbage is played during the summer in this local CAMRA Pub of the Year 2016. ✿❂◐⇥♣●P❂❀☂

Highlander ㏒

45 Upper Tilehouse Street, SG5 2EF
✿ 12-2.30, 6-11; 12-11 Fri & Sat; 12-2.30, 7-10.30 Sun
☎ (01462) 454612 ⊕ highlanderpubhitchin.co.uk
Greene King IPA; 3 changing beers (sourced nationally) Ⓗ
This Grade II-listed free house is situated just outside the town centre on the Luton road. It has been run by multiple generations of the same family for the past 43 years. A fusion of traditional English inn and charming French bistro, reasonably priced home-made food featuring locally sourced ingredients is prepared by the pub's French chef. Monthly jazz nights are hosted.
Q✿❂◐&⇥P➡(100,101,102)❀☂

Ley Green

Plough

Plough Lane, SG4 8LA (look for brown pub signs at each end of Plough Lane) TL162243
✿ 4 (12 Wed)-11; 12-midnight Thu-Sat; 12-10.30 Sun
☎ (01438) 871394
Greene King IPA, Abbot; 1 changing beer (sourced nationally) Ⓗ
The Plough has been an ale house as far back as 1846. A warm and friendly traditional pub with spectacular views across the Hertfordshire countryside, it is a popular stop for walkers and cyclists. It has a large patio and children's play area outside. Hot and cold bar snacks are available. The acoustic sessions on Tuesday evenings are open to all. Campervan and tent camping are available; please ring to confirm availability.
✿❂◐▲♣P➡❀☂

Lilley

Lilley Arms ㏒

41 West Street, LU2 8LN (West St is on left by village green) TL117264
✿ 12-11; 12-10.30 Sun ☎ (01462) 768371
⊕ lilleyarms-lilley.co.uk
Greene King Abbot, IPA; 3 changing beers (sourced nationally) Ⓗ
Built in 1705, the Lilley Arms Freehouse is a former coaching inn offering traditional pub food and real ale. It is located just off the A505, handy for Luton and the historic town of Hitchin. For horse riding, cycling or walking, this country pub is the perfect base to start, finish or stop off en-route and close to the Icknield Way path. It is surrounded by beautiful countryside and has a hitching rail for horses.
Q✿❂◑⇥◐⇥P➡❀☂

London Colney

Bull ✓

Barnet Road, AL2 1QU
✿ 12-11 (midnight Thu-Sat) ☎ (01727) 823160
⊕ thebullatlondoncolney.co.uk
Fuller's London Pride; Woodforde's Wherry; 2 changing beers (sourced nationally) Ⓗ

Lovely old 17th-century timbered building near the River Colne with a cosy lounge and original fireplace, offering a range of real ales. The large public bar features darts, pool and TV. Evening events include live music on Saturday and a quiz on Sunday. Good-value home-made meals are served Monday-Saturday lunchtimes. Wednesday is food night, with curry evenings held monthly. There is a children's play area outside. ✿◐♣●P➡❀☂

Nuthampstead

Woodman ㏒ ✓

Stocking Lane, SG8 8NB
✿ 10-11; 10-7 Sun; closed Mon ☎ (01763) 848328
⊕ thewoodman-inn.co.uk
Buntingford Twitchell; Greene King IPA; 1 changing beer (sourced nationally) Ⓖ
Seventeenth-century free house with two bars and a wonderful open fire. The restaurant offers à la carte meals, house specials, snacks, coffee and breakfast from 10am daily (no food Sun eves). Beer is dispensed under gravity from casks behind the bar. The TV is restricted to major sporting events. During WWII the USAF 398th Bomber Group was based nearby and much memorabilia is displayed here. The pub hosts regular events including quarterly comedy nights, monthly quizzes and aviation lectures. Accommodation is 3-star. Q✿❂❂◐♣P❀☂

Oxhey

Railway Arms ✓

1 Aldenham Road, WD19 4AB
✿ 12-midnight (1am Fri & Sat); 12-10.30 Sun ☎ 07976 647569
Greene King IPA, Abbot; 2 changing beers (sourced nationally) Ⓗ
Friendly two-bar pub opposite Bushey station. Sport, including Irish games, is regularly shown on three screens throughout the pub. There is a jukebox and a pool table in one bar and newspapers are available. A Masons' coat of arms marking the Pinner Road side of the building commemorates that it was once a Masonic lodge. As befits the name, there is also some railway memorabilia. ✿❂&⇥➡♣P➡(142,258)❀☂

Potters Bar

Old Manor ✓

Wyllyotts Place, Darkes Lane, EN6 2JD (opp Wyllyotts Centre)
✿ 11-11 (1am Fri & Sat); 12-10.30 Sun ☎ (01707) 650674
⊕ the-old-manor.co.uk
Courage Directors; Fuller's London Pride; 3 changing beers (sourced nationally) Ⓗ
Popular dining and drinking venue close to the railway station, frequented by all age groups. Dating back to the 13th century, the building is the surviving part of an old manor house and opened as a pub in its present form in 2000. The large adjoining galleried restaurant offers an extensive menu. The pub is busy before and after events at the theatre/leisure centre opposite. The walls display a collection of photos of bygone Potters Bar. ✿❂◐&⇥➡P➡❀☂

Potters Crouch

Holly Bush ✔

Bedmond Lane, AL2 3NN (off B5183 at jct of Potters Crouch Lane and Ragged Hall Lane) TL116052
☼ 12-2.30, 6-11; 12-3, 7-10.30 Sun ☎ (01727) 851792
⊕ thehollybushpub.co.uk

Fuller's London Pride, ESB; Gale's Seafarers Ale; 1 changing beer (sourced nationally) Ⓗ

This wisteria-covered and early 17th-century pub sits in rural surroundings. Tastefully furnished throughout, it boasts large oak tables and period chairs. Spotless, there are no jukeboxes, slot machines or TVs to disturb the drinker in any of the three drinking areas. The food menu is not extensive but is of high quality. Well-behaved children are welcome. The garden is ideal in summer. Q ☜ ❀ ◖ ఈ P ♿ (300,301)

Preston

Red Lion Ⓛ

The Green, SG4 7UD (by the green at the crossroads)
☼ 12-2.30 (3.30 Sat), 5.30-11; 12-3.30, 7-10.30 Sun
☎ (01462) 459585 ⊕ theredlionpreston.co.uk

Fuller's London Pride; Young's Bitter; 3 changing beers (sourced nationally) Ⓗ

Attractive free house standing on the village green which was the first community-owned pub in Great Britain. It offers a wide list of beers, including many from small breweries. Ray and Jo prepare the fresh home-made food and many of the ingredients are sourced locally (no food Sun eve and Mon). The pub hosts the village cricket teams and raises funds for charity. Q ☜ ❀ ◖ ♣ ♿ P ♿ 🐾 ☂

Puckeridge

Crown & Falcon

33 High Street, SG11 1RN
☼ 12-3, 5.30-11 (midnight Fri); 12-4, 6.30-midnight Sat; 12-5, 7-11 Sun ☎ (01920) 821561
⊕ crown-falcon.demon.co.uk

Adnams Southwold Bitter; 3 changing beers (sourced nationally) Ⓗ

A public house since 1530, with the Crown part of the name adopted much later from a former pub in the village. Changes to the interior layout can be traced on plans displayed in the bar. It is now one large open-plan room with a separate restaurant. A collection of Allied Breweries memorabilia is on display. The guest beers change weekly. Darts is popular, and a free computer is available in the bar for customers' use. The Falcon is mentioned in Samuel Pepys's diary of 1662 – he bought the landlord's shoes for four shillings.
☜ ❀ ◖ ఈ ♣ P ♿ (331,386)

Redbourn

Cricketers Ⓛ

East Common, AL3 7ND
☼ 12-11 (midnight Fri & Sat); 12-10.30 Sun
☎ (01582) 620612 ⊕ thecricketersofredbourn.co.uk

Sharp's Doom Bar; Tring Side Pocket for a Toad; 3 changing beers (sourced nationally) Ⓗ

Dating back to 1725, the pub is opposite Redbourn's village common and its historic cricket pitch, making it the perfect setting for a drink on a sunny summer's day. In winter a wood-burning stove creates a cosy atmosphere. Serving five real ales and a traditional cider, there are also summer

beer festivals showcasing local beers, held in marquees erected in the car park. Food is excellent. Quiz nights feature regularly, raising funds for local organisations. Q ☜ ❀ ◖ ◖ ఈ ♿ P ♿ (34,46,307) ❀ ☂

St Albans

Boot Inn ✔

4 Market Place, AL3 5DG
☼ 12-midnight (12.30am Fri & Sat) ☎ (01727) 857533
⊕ thebootstalbans.com

Adnams Broadside; Sharp's Doom Bar; Young's Bitter; 4 changing beers (sourced nationally) Ⓗ

A city-centre, Grade I-listed, one-bar pub dating from 1422 featuring low ceilings, exposed beams, wood flooring and a real fire. With a welcoming and warm atmosphere the pub can become busy on weekend evenings and during Wednesday and Saturday market days. The Clock Tower and abbey are nearby and Verulamium Park is a short walk. Families are welcome until 6pm. Real ciders sit alongside a changing range of ales and fresh food comes from local sources. Live music plays on Wednesday and Sunday evenings.
☜ ◖ ➤ (Abbey/City) ♿ 🚲 ♿ ❀ ☂

Farriers Arms Ⓛ

32-34 Lower Dagnall Street, AL3 4PT (off A5183 Verulam Rd)
☼ 12-2.30 (not Mon & Tue), 5.30-11; 12-11 Sat; 12-10.30 Sun
☎ (01727) 851025

McMullen Country Bitter; St Austell Tribute; Skinner's Betty Stogs; 1 changing beer (sourced nationally) Ⓗ

Originally a grocer's and butcher's shop, the building was converted to a pub in the 1920s. Now a free house, this classic back-street local is the only pub in the city never to have forsaken real ale. A plaque outside commemorates the first meeting of the Hertfordshire branch of CAMRA. The split-level interior has an area fronting the bar for stand-up drinking, darts and cards, and a back room with comfortable seating. Sport is shown on TV. Parking can be difficult. Q ☜ ❀ ◖ ఈ ➤ (Abbey/City) ♣ ❀ ☂

Garibaldi ✔

61 Albert Street, AL1 1RT
☼ 2.30 (12 Tue & Wed)-11; 12-11.30 Thu; 12-midnight Fri & Sat; 12-10 Sun ☎ (01727) 894745 ⊕ garibaldistalbans.co.uk

Fuller's London Pride, ESB; Gale's Seafarers Ale, HSB; 2 changing beers (sourced nationally) Ⓗ

Larger inside than its frontage suggests, this is a classic example of a quality back-street community local near the abbey. Named after the 19th century Italian patriot, the Garibaldi offers an extensive range of Fuller's ales and serves excellent home-cooked meals using locally sourced produce, including a fine Sunday roast (booking advisable). Regular live music on Saturdays, quizzes, darts, food nights and charity events give the place a homely feel. Awarded Most Improved Pub by the local CAMRA branch in 2014.
☜ ❀ ◖ ➤ (Abbey/City) ♣ 🐾 ☂

Lower Red Lion Ⓛ

34-36 Fishpool Street, AL3 4RX
☼ 12-11; 12-10 Sun ☎ (01727) 855669
⊕ thelowerredlion.co.uk

Dark Star Hophead; 5 changing beers (sourced nationally) Ⓗ

Both bars in this classic Grade II-listed pub have plenty of character and history. Located in a conservation area between the city centre and the site of Roman Verulamium, the pub stands in one

of St Albans' most picturesque streets. The Lower Red was an early champion of CAMRA's values in the real ale revival movement, and continues to stock quality real ales. Home-made food is served lunchtimes and evenings throughout the week (no food Sun eve). Quiz night is Wednesday.
Q✿⊗☎◑♠●P⊟❅♥ 🛜

Mermaid
98 Hatfield Road, AL1 3RL
✪ 12-midnight (11 Mon & Tue); 12-10.30 Sun
☎ (01727) 568912
Oakham Citra; 5 changing beers (sourced nationally) Ⓗ
This friendly free house is one of the few remaining bare-boards pubs in St Albans. Customers can choose from the award-winning Oakham Citra and five regularly changing ales, over a dozen ciders/perries and a range of Belgian beers. Try the six mixed thirds of cider, perry or ale. Entertainment includes music nights on Wednesdays, regular quizzes and outside events in the garden (and new covered area) during the spring/summer. Winner of local CAMRA Cider Pub of the Year award in 2014 and 2015.
⏃✿⊗◑&≉(City)♣●P⊟🚌(601,602,655)♥ 🛜

Olde Fighting Cocks ✅
16 Abbey Mill Lane, AL3 4HE
✪ 12-10.30; 12-midnight Fri & Sat ☎ (01727) 869152
⊕ yeoldefightingcocks.co.uk
Harviestoun Bitter & Twisted; Purity Pure Ubu; 6 changing beers (sourced nationally) Ⓗ
The pub stakes a claim to be the oldest in the country, dating from the late-8th century, though the current building was completed in 1485. Original features include timbers, low ceilings, interesting nooks and crannies and a bread oven next to one of the fireplaces. Today the pub especially caters for tourists visiting the abbey and the nearby Roman remains in Verulamium Park, offering real ales from across Britain. Parking nearby is a challenge – perhaps take a pleasant walk through the park. ⏃✿◑♣♣⊟♥ 🛜

Six Bells ⓛ
16-18 St Michael's Street, AL3 4SH
✪ 11.30-11; 11.30-midnight Fri-Sun ☎ (01727) 856945
⊕ the-six-bells.com
Oakham JHB; Timothy Taylor Landlord; Tring Ridgeway; 3 changing beers (sourced nationally) Ⓗ
A 16th-century timbered free house with three regular beers and three changing guests, one of which is always from a Hertfordshire brewer. The pub is the only licensed premises within the walls of Roman Verulamium and is within walking distance of the city centre, abbey, Verulamium Park and Museum. Quiz nights and live music sometimes feature. Good home-cooked food is served lunchtimes and evenings (no food Sun eve). Outside is a pleasant patio area. Real cider is available during the summer.
⏃✿◑♣●P⊟(300,301)♥ 🛜

White Hart Tap ⓛ ✅
4 Keyfield Terrace, AL1 1QJ
✪ 12-11 ☎ (01727) 860974 ⊕ whitehartap.co.uk
Castle Rock Harvest Pale; St Austell Proper Job; Sharp's Doom Bar; Timothy Taylor Landlord; 3 changing beers (sourced nationally) Ⓗ
Welcoming one-bar, back-street local with four regular beers and three guests, now brewing beers on the premises with a weekly offering in a varying

brewing style. Several beer festivals are held during the year. Good-value, home-prepared food is served every lunchtime and Monday-Saturday evenings, with fish and chips on Friday and roasts on Sunday. Barbecues are held in summer. Quiz night is Wednesday. Outside is a large garden and a separate heated and covered smoking area. A public car park is opposite. Runner-up local CAMRA Pub of the Year 2015.
⏃✿◑➤≉(Abbey/City)♣●⊟🚌♥ 🛜

St Pauls Walden

Strathmore Arms ⓛ
London Road, SG4 8BT TL193222
✪ 6-11 Mon; 12-2.30, 5-11 Tue-Thu; 12-11 Fri & Sat; 12-10.30 Sun ☎ (01438) 871654 ⊕ thestrathmorearms.co.uk
Buntingford Twitchell; 4 changing beers (sourced nationally) Ⓗ
This pub on the Bowes-Lyon estate caters for drinkers and lunchtime diners. Beers from obscure breweries are a speciality on the constantly changing rota of guest beers. Unusual bottled beers are also available along with a real cider and perry. The pub boasts a full collection of Good Beer Guides from 1976 onwards, in which it has often featured in recent years. It has a separate snug area. Pizza and pasta evenings are held on Wednesdays and occasional wild food nights (booking essential). A renowned local fundraiser. Local CAMRA Cider Pub of the Year 2016. Q⏃✿◑&🅰♣●P⊟♥ 🛜

Sandridge

Green Man ✅
31 High Street, AL4 9DD
✪ 11-midnight; 11-11.30 Sun ☎ (01727) 854845
Cotswold Cask; Greene King Abbot; Sharp's Doom Bar Ⓖ
This family-run pub extends a warm welcome to ale and cider drinkers alike. The landlord has been in residence for over 25 years. All ales are available straight from the cask, and up to six real ciders are served. On the doorstep of the newly established 850-acre Heartwood Forest, the pub is an ideal stop-off for refreshment after a stroll in the woods. Dogs are welcome in the conservatory and the garden which has a small aviary.
Q⏃✿◑●♣●P⊟(304,305,657)♥ 🛜

Rose & Crown ⓛ ✅
24 High Street, AL4 9DA
✪ 11-11; 12-10.30 Sun ☎ (01727) 859739
⊕ roseandcrownpubsandridge.co.uk
Tring Ridgeway; Young's Special; 2 changing beers (sourced nationally) Ⓗ
A 17th-century inn with oak beams, an inglenook fireplace and several areas for drinking and dining. The pub has been tastefully modernised following renovation work, augmenting the building's traditional features with additional seating and dining areas. There is a large car park to the rear and a garden where barbecues are regularly held. The pub hosts a popular summer beer festival.
Q⏃✿◑&♣P⊟(304,305,657)♥ 🛜

Sawbridgeworth

Gate ⓛ
81 London Road, CM21 9JJ

🕏 11.30-2.30, 5.30-11 Mon; 11.30-2.30 Tue & Thu; 11.30-2 Wed; 11.30-11 Fri & Sat; 12-11 Sun ☎ (01279) 722313
⊕ thegatepub.com

Sawbridgeworth Gold; 6 changing beers (often Sawbridgeworth) Ⓗ

A lively pub with a huge collection of pumpclips adorning the beams. It is sports-oriented with several satellite TV screens, and is home to numerous darts and other teams. A range of around six beers is offered, typically three from the small Sawbridgeworth Brewery at the back of the pub and three guest beers from near or far. Beer festivals are held over the Easter and August bank holiday weekends. No dogs are allowed.
⍟◑&♣P🚌 (509,510,511)

Old Bell

38 Bell Street, CM21 9AN

🕏 11-11 (1am Fri & Sat); 12-11 Sun ☎ (01279) 721050

Adnams Broadside; Woodforde's Wherry; 1 changing beer (sourced nationally; often Thwaites) Ⓗ

This 16th-century timber-framed pub boasts many exposed beams in the main bar. Situated among Bell Street's traditional village shops, it is cosy and friendly. There is a side bar where food is served and a popular courtyard and sunny garden with a children's play area. A quiz is held on Sunday evening and a ukulele jam session on Tuesday evening. Real cider and perry are always available.
🛌⍟◑&♣P🚌 (509,510,511)🐾🛜

Standon

Star ✓

62 High Street, SG11 1LB

🕏 12-3, 5-11; 12-11.30 Fri & Sat; 12-11 Sun
☎ (01920) 823725 ⊕ star-standon.co.uk

Greene King IPA, Abbot; 2 changing beers Ⓗ

Traditional 17th-century pub on the picturesque High Street with exposed wooden beams. It has a separate public bar and a quiet and comfortable saloon/restaurant. Food is classic home-made pub grub, with roasts on a Sunday. Two guest beers are on offer, at least one sourced independently of Greene King, normally from a small independent local brewer. 🛌⍟◑♣P🚌 (331,386)🐾🛜

Stevenage

Chequers ✓

164 High Street, SG1 3LL

🕏 12-midnight (1am Fri & Sat); 12-10.30 Sun
☎ (01438) 488692

Greene King XX Mild, IPA, IPA Gold, IPA Reserve; 4 changing beers (sourced nationally) Ⓗ

Friendly locals' pub situated between the old and new towns. There is an interesting old map of Stevenage on the wall and a newly refurbished beer garden. It hosts a quiz night on Wednesday and is home to a scrabble team, a book club and a motorbike club. There is a carvery on Sunday. Rugby is screened on TV as well as selected other sports. Winner of CAMRA Most Improved Pub of the Year award in 2014. Q🛌⍟◑&≠♣👜🛜

Our Mutual Friend ✓

Broadwater Crescent, SG2 8EH

🕏 12-11 (11.30 Fri & Sat) ☎ (01438) 312282
⊕ omfpub.co.uk

6 changing beers (sourced nationally) Ⓗ

Thriving community pub on the southern side of Stevenage serving an ever-changing selection of cask beer and real cider. It has featured in every edition of the Guide since being rescued from the cask ale graveyard back in 2002. At least a dozen real ciders and perries are typically available – many more during mini festivals. The pub is busy when Stevenage Football Club has a home match. Winner of many local CAMRA awards.
Q🛌◑≠♣👜P🖵🚌 (4,5)🐾🛜

Therfield

Fox & Duck

Village Green, SG8 9PN

🕏 12-3, 5.30-midnight; 12-midnight Sat; 12-11 Sun; closed Mon ☎ (01763) 287246 ⊕ thefoxandduck.co.uk

Greene King IPA, Abbot; 2 changing beers (sourced nationally) Ⓗ

Charming country pub-restaurant rebuilt in the 19th century. Food is available from the à la carte, bar or children's menus. The first Sunday of the month is quiz night. On bank holiday Sundays the pub hosts live music, barbecue and bouncy castle. Children's play equipment can be found in the garden and there are tables on the village green. Next to the Hertfordshire Way and Icknield Way long-distance footpaths.
🛌⍟◑&♣P🚌 (23,24,25)🐾🛜

Tring

Castle Ⓛ

Park Road, HP23 6BN (around corner from Natural History Museum)

🕏 3-11; 12-11.30 Fri & Sat; 12-10.30 Sun ☎ (01442) 823552

Vale Wychert Ale, Red Kite; 2 changing beers (sourced locally; often Tring) Ⓗ

A genuine, single-roomed Victorian back-street local serving Vale and Tring beers. Popular with the local rugby club, it hosts two darts teams and has TVs for sports viewing. The front aspect has views of open fields while the back has a courtyard with a covered smoking area. The interior includes a busy bar area with stripped floors and lined with bar stools. There is comfortable, upholstered banquette seating around the half-panelled walls.
🛌⍟♣👜🛜

King's Arms Ⓛ

King Street, HP23 6BE (corner of Queen St and King St) SP921111

🕏 12-2.30, 5.30-11.30; 12-3, 5-11.30 Fri; 12-11.30 Sat & Sun ☎ (01442) 823318 ⊕ kingsarmstring.co.uk

Tring Moongazing; 4 changing beers (sourced regionally; often Leighton Buzzard Brewing Company, Vale, XT) Ⓗ

In the heart of the Tring Triangle, this outstanding free house serves five real ales and one real cider. Popular with young and old alike, the atmosphere is bustling. Two fireplaces provide warmth in winter while outside there is plenty of space and a serving window. Excellent home-made food from posh pub grub to international favourites is available lunchtimes and evenings (no food Sun eve). A beer festival is held over the August bank holiday and a cider festival coincides with the October Apple Fayre.
Q🛌⍟◑♣👜🚌 (64,500,501)🛜

Robin Hood Ⓛ ✓

1 Brook Street, HP23 5ED (B4635/B486 jct)

🕏 11.30-11 (11.30 Fri); 12-11.30 Sat; 12-11 Sun ☎ (01442) 824912 ⊕ therobinhoodtring.co.uk

Fuller's Oliver's Island, London Pride, ESB; Gale's Seafarers Ale; 2 changing beers (sourced nationally; often Butcombe, Liberation, York) ⊞
Situated on the edge of town, this fine 17th-century Fuller's pub offers four well-kept real ales from Fuller's and Gale's plus one seasonal and one guest ale. Wood-burning stoves provide a warm glow on winter days while the courtyard garden is pleasant for summer evenings. A heated, covered area is provided for smokers. Good food including gourmet burgers and pub classics is served all week, with a pop-up Thai on Sunday evenings, speciality sausage nights on Tuesdays and Thursdays and roasts on Sundays.
Q ⏰🚲😻🍴🕪🍽️(61,164,500)🐾🛜

Ware

Crooked Billet ✔

140 Musley Hill, SG12 7NL (via New Rd from High St)
✦ 5.30-11.30 (midnight Fri); 12-midnight Sat; 12-11.30 Sun
☎ (01920) 462516
4 changing beers (sourced nationally) ⊞
Stuart and Sue have presided over the Billet for over 20 years, stocking more than 500 different ales since the pub was acquired by Admiral Taverns. Fully utilising the local SIBA Direct Delivery Scheme, there is a varying range of four or five ales, always including a mild, porter or stout. Two beer and cider festivals are held each year. This gem of a community pub has two small bars featuring TV sport, pool and darts. Carlisle United and Ware FC fans are assured of a warm welcome.
🚲😻🍴🕪🍽️(395)🐾🛜

Maltings

35 Watton Road, SG12 0AD
✦ 4.30-11 (11.30 Thu); 12.30-11.30 Fri & Sat; 12-11 Sun
☎ (01920) 487610
Greene King Abbot, IPA; 1 changing beer (sourced nationally) ⊞
Formerly named after the builder who erected it in the 19th century, the pub is just west of the town centre. It is a small, cosy and friendly community venue, very popular with locals. Your amiable hosts serve Greene King ales and a guest beer. There are occasional live music or theme nights on Friday or Saturday evenings. 🍴🕪🍽️(331)🐾🛜

Wareside

Chequers

Ware Road, SG12 7QY (on B1004)
✦ 12-3, 6-11; 12-4, 6.30-10.30 Sun ☎ (01920) 467010
Buntingford Highwayman; 2 changing beers (sourced regionally; often Adnams) ⊞
A rural free house dating from the 15th century, the Chequers was originally a coaching inn and has three distinct bars plus a restaurant. All the food is home made and reasonably priced, and includes vegetarian options. Walkers and cyclists are welcome, making this a popular base for a ramble. No machines, no music, and there is a ban on swearing. Q😻🕪🍴🍽️P🍽️(M3,M4)🐾

Watford

West Herts Sports Club

8 Park Avenue, WD18 7HP (S of A412, near town hall)
✦ 4-11 (11.30 Fri); 10-11 Sat; 10-10.30 Sun
☎ (01923) 229239 ⊕ westhertssports.co.uk

Young's Bitter; 4 changing beers (sourced nationally; often 3 Brewers, Haresfoot, Shepherd Neame) ⊞
This comfortable members' bar is a multiple winner of CAMRA's East Anglian Club of the Year. Two real ciders are regularly on offer. The bar is tastefully decorated with sporting memorabilia, and major sporting events are screened. A separate function room, home of the Watford Beer Festival, is available to hire. Show a CAMRA membership card or a copy of this Guide to gain entry up to four times a year. Often busy on Watford FC match days.
🐾🍴➰🍴P🍽️🛜

Wheathampstead

Swan ✔

56 High Street, AL4 8AR
✦ 11-midnight; 11-11.30 Sun ☎ (01582) 833110
⊕ theswanwheathampstead.co.uk
Greene King IPA; St Austell Tribute; 3 changing beers (sourced nationally) ⊞
Built around 1500, this traditional inn has retained many interesting features including exposed beams and an inglenook fireplace. It is a thriving and friendly village community pub, popular with walkers and workers. Lunches are available every day and evening meals on Monday and Friday. The three guest ales include beers from the SIBA range. A large and quiet function room at the rear is available for bookings. The upper bar has a darts area and Sky TVs. 🍴🕪🍴P🍽️🐾🛜

Wild Hill

Woodman ♜

45 Wildhill Road, AL9 6EA (between A1000 and B158)
TL264068
✦ 11.30-2.30, 5.30-11; 12-2.30, 7-10.30 Sun
☎ (01707) 642618
Greene King IPA, Abbot; 4 changing beers (sourced nationally) ⊞
Winner of local CAMRA Pub of the Year 10 times and Hertfordshire Pub of the Year three times, this excellent, unpretentious village hostelry extends a warm welcome to a loyal and varied clientele of all ages. Six beers are available including four guests from regional and microbreweries, usually one from Hertfordshire. Food is served lunchtimes Monday-Saturday. The large garden is ideal in summer. An all-round superb pub, but look out for God's Waiting Room! Local CAMRA Pub of the Year 2015. 🍴🕪🍴P🐾🛜

Wilstone

Half Moon 🅛

60 Tring Road, HP23 4PD
✦ 12-11 ☎ (01442) 826410
Sharp's Doom Bar; Tring Side Pocket for a Toad; 2 changing beers (sourced locally; often Malt the Brewery, Tring, XT) ⊞
A lovely traditional pub in the centre of the village. It has a real fire, original beams and lots of horse brasses, and old pictures of the pub and village adorn the main bar area. A varied menu is available at good-value prices. Three to four beers are on offer, mostly local. The pub is home to cribbage and dominoes teams, and other traditional pub games are played. Scrabble night is held on the fourth Sunday of the month.
Q🍴🕪🍴P🍽️(164)🐾🛜

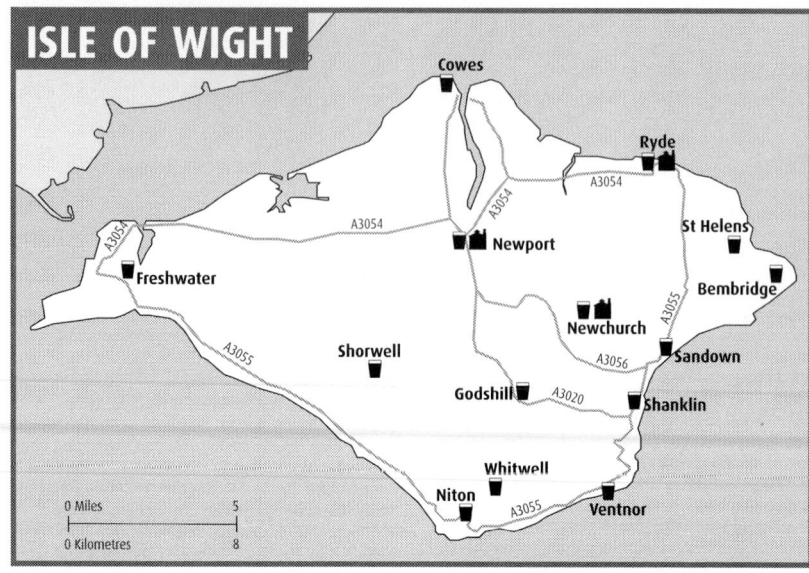

ISLE OF WIGHT

Bembridge

Old Village Inn ✓

61 High Street, PO35 5SF
🕐 12-11 (midnight Fri & Sat); 12-10.30 Sun
☎ (01983) 872616 🌐 yeoldevillageinn.co.uk
Courage Directors; Greene King Abbot; 2 changing beers (often Black Sheep, Thwaites, West Berkshire) Ⓗ
The Old Village Steak & Ale House is a popular addition to the Bembridge scene, specialising in local meat and fish dishes. A fine choice of real ales and selected wines is offered in a refined and relaxed atmosphere. Food is served 12-3pm and 5-9pm. Live music plays on occasional Fridays and a quiz is held on the first Monday of the month. There is a patio area to the rear and a pétanque terrain. Q🕏🏵🕪♣️🍴P🚃(8)🐾🛜

Cowes

Anchor Inn Ⓛ

1 High Street, PO31 7SA (opp Sainsbury's)
🕐 11-11 (midnight Fri & Sat); 12-10.30 Sun
☎ (01983) 292823 🌐 theanchorcowes.co.uk
Fuller's London Pride; Goddards Fuggle-Dee-Dum; 3 changing beers (sourced nationally; often St Austell, Timothy Taylor, West Berkshire) Ⓗ
This High Street pub, originally the Trumpeters back in 1704, is close to the Marina, tempting visiting yachtsman for their first pint ashore. The bar boasts a good selection of beer, with one Island ale and two guests always available. A varied choice of food is on offer, served in prodigious quantities. Live entertainment showcasing the Island's top bands is a regular feature. Outside is a pleasant beer garden and there is accommodation in seven comfortable rooms. 🛏🏵🕭🕪(1)🐾🛜

Union Inn ✓

Watch House Lane, PO31 7QH (just off the Parade)
🕐 11-midnight; 12-10.30 Sun ☎ (01983) 293163
🌐 unioninncowes.co.uk
Fuller's London Pride; Gale's Seafarers Ale, HSB; 1 changing beer (often Fuller's) Ⓗ

A haven for yachting enthusiasts, locals and holidaymakers, one three-sided bar serves the lounge, snug, dining area and airy conservatory. A roaring fire in winter adds to the cosy atmosphere. Delicious family meals are available with portions for children and ingredients sourced from local suppliers. The pub may close at 11pm but frequently stays open later. A popular quiz evening is hosted on Wednesdays. There is pay parking on the Parade 25 yards away, free later in the day. A new sister pub, the Globe, is nearby.
Q🛏🏵🕪🚃(1)🐾🛜

Freshwater

Red Lion Ⓛ

Church Place, PO40 9BP SZ34508738
🕐 11-11 ☎ (01983) 754925 🌐 redlion-freshwater.co.uk
Sharp's Doom Bar; 3 changing beers (often Adnams, St Austell, West Berkshire) Ⓗ
Former three-room coaching inn dating back to the 11th century, now converted to one large bar but still retaining much of its original character. This traditional country pub is in the most picture postcard-like area of Freshwater in the church square and by the Causeway. From here, there are splendid views of the River Yar towards Yarmouth. Q🏵🕪P🚃(7,12)🐾

Godshill

Taverners Ⓛ ✓

High Street, PO38 3HZ
🕐 11-11; 11-5 Sun ☎ (01983) 840707
🌐 thetavernersgodshill.co.uk
Sharp's Doom Bar; house beer (by Yates'); 2 changing beers (often Brains, Butcombe, Goddards) Ⓗ
Tasteful and sympathetic conversion and expansion of an old cottage, full of character with beams and

flagstones. It is difficult to see the join between the old and the new. The accent is on locally sourced food – the comfortable bar is sandwiched between restaurant areas – but is none the worse for that. Outside is an excellent large play area for children. The cider is Godshill Rumpy Pumpy.

Q❄☺❶◗&♿P⌷(2,3)☙

Newchurch

Pointer Inn
High Street, PO36 0NN (next to church)
✪ 11-11; 12-10.30 Sun ☎ (01983) 865202
⊕ pointernewchurch.co.uk
Fuller's London Pride; Gale's HSB; 2 changing beers (often Fuller's) Ⓗ
Ancient village hostelry where locals, visitors and families are all welcome. The home-cooked food features local produce, prepared by a chef with a vast experience of Island trade (booking is essential). Food is served until 9.30pm (9pm Sun). Highchairs and toys are available for children. The large garden has a pétanque terrain and a covered area for smokers. Awards include Fuller's Best Country/Village Pub and a Certificate of Excellence by Trip Advisor. Q❄☺❶◗Å♣P⌷(22)☙♿☞

Newport

Bargeman's Rest Ⓛ
Little London Quay, PO30 5BS (signed from dual carriageway)
✪ 10.30-11; 10.30-10.30 Sun ☎ (01983) 525828
⊕ bargemansrest.com
Goddards Fuggle-Dee-Dum; Ringwood Best Bitter, Fortyniner; 4 changing beers (sourced nationally; often Brakspear, Jennings, Marston's) Ⓗ
Massive, locally owned pub that has been an animal feed store and a sail and rigging loft for the barge fleet that used to ply the river. The spacious interior is divided into intimate drinking areas and the nautical memorabilia, decor and ambience are all you could hope for in a traditional, well-seasoned pub. The outdoor drinking area is only a few feet from the bustling River Medina. Beer and food are consistently good and the range varied. Live entertainment is hosted most nights.
❄☺❶◗&P⌷☙☞

Prince of Wales ✪
36 South Street, PO30 1JE (opp bus station)
✪ 10.30-11; 12-10.30 Sun ☎ (01983) 525026
3 changing beers (sourced nationally; often Adnams, Fuller's, Wadworth) Ⓗ
This excellent mock-Tudor single-bar local in the middle of town has gained a fine reputation for well-kept ale, with up to three beers from the Punch list, usually Finest Cask. Located opposite the bus station and Morrisons, this street-corner venue is very much a locals' pub and retains the feel of a public bar, with a good games following. Food is restricted to good wholesome sandwiches, pies and mother's home-baked specials. A real gem.
❄♣♿☙☞

Niton

Buddle Ⓛ
St Catherine's Road, Niton Undercliff, PO38 2NE (follow signs to St Catherine's Lighthouse) SZ50207580
✪ 12-10.30 (11 Wed & Thu; 11.30 Fri & Sat)
☎ (01983) 730243 ⊕ buddleinn.co.uk

Sharp's Doom Bar; house beer (by Yates'); 3 changing beers (sourced nationally; often Fuller's, Timothy Taylor, Yates') Ⓗ
A 16th-century inn that was built as a farmhouse and reputedly became a smugglers' inn during the 18th century. Extensively refurbished, it retains the ancient flagstones and beams, inglenook fireplace and many interesting photographs. A popular destination dining pub, offering good locally sourced food, it also has a strong real ale following with six ales on handpump. A choice of ciders is also available. Situated near the lighthouse, the pub has many links to Trinity House.
Q❄☺❶♣♿P⌷(6)☙

Ryde

High Park Tavern Ⓛ
84 Marlborough Road, PO33 1AF (out of Ryde towards Tesco)
✪ 12-11.30; 12-12.30am Fri & Sat ☎ (01983) 562841
Sharp's Doom Bar; 3 changing beers (often Dorset, Island, Wychwood) Ⓗ
Corner pub on a busy main road on the outskirts of Ryde which, as a result of a several makeovers in recent years, is now a comfortable local. The beer range varies but often includes at least one local ale and one dark ale. Live music features on Friday, Saturday and Sunday afternoons. A large function room with good access can be used for functions and celebrations. Breakfast is available 9-11am, Thursday night dining is a highlight and a roast is served Sunday 12-3pm. ❄☺❶♣♿⌷(3)☙☞

S. Fowler & Co Ⓛ ✪
41-43 Union Street, PO33 2LF (top of Union St)
✪ 7am-midnight; 7am-1am Fri & Sat ☎ (01983) 812112
Adnams Broadside; Fuller's London Pride; 8 changing beers (sourced nationally) Ⓗ
Although not the most charismatic pub in the Wetherspoon chain, this converted drapery store offers a varied range of well-kept beers. The name was suggested by the local CAMRA branch – not only is it the name of the former store but also that of the first local CAMRA chairman and revered early campaigner. There is an upstairs restaurant which is family-friendly. Set in the centre of town with a bus stop conveniently outside. Q❄◗&⇄⌷☞

Simeon Arms Ⓛ
21 Simeon Street, PO33 1JG (short walk from Canoe Lake)
✪ 11-11 (11.30 Mon & Thu; midnight Fri & Sat); 12-11.30 Sun
☎ (01983) 614954
Courage Directors; Goddards Ale of Wight, Fuggle-Dee-Dum Ⓗ
Thriving yet unlikely gem tucked away in a Ryde back street with a Tardis-like interior and annexed function hall. The pub is immensely popular with the local community who come to participate in various leagues including shove-ha'penny, darts, crib and pool, and pétanque on the enormous floodlit terrain in summer. You can always expect to find a local ale. Live music plays on Saturday and Sunday nights. The smoking area outside is heated and covered. ❄☺⇄♣⌷☞

St Helens

Vine Inn Ⓛ
Upper Green Road, PO33 1UJ (overlooking the Green)
SZ62708915

✪ 12-midnight ☎ (01983) 872337 ⊕ thevinesthelens.co.uk
Sharp's Doom Bar; 2 changing beers (often Courage, Gale's, Ringwood) Ⓗ
The front of the pub overlooks what is possibly the biggest village green in the kingdom, known locally as Goose Island. An eclectic selection of memorabilia reflecting local history, from railways to hunting to breweries to maritime, decorates the walls. From Easter to late summer there is an additional tented area outside. The three beers include one from an Island brewery. A public car park is nearby. Check ahead for food service in winter. ☭⌂✿●Ⓓ♿▲♣●☷(8)☙❀

Sandown

Castle Inn Ⓛ

12-14 Fitzroy Street, PO36 8HY (off High St)
✪ 11-11 (midnight Fri); 10.30-midnight Sat & Sun
☎ (01983) 403169 ⊕ sandowncastle.co.uk
Wychwood Hobgoblin Gold, Hobgoblin; Young's Special; 3 changing beers (often Theakston, Wadworth, Yates') Ⓗ
The Castle is an excellent town free house and locals' pub with crib and two darts teams. Six real ales are on offer including the best from local breweries, plus two ciders. There is a children's room at the back and a patio for warm weather. The TV is not allowed to intrude, but is turned on for special occasions. Happy hour (5-7pm) is popular, as is the Sunday quiz. Beer festivals are held several times a year, usually featuring local ales and cider. Q☭⌂✿&♿⇋♣●☷(2,3,8)☙❀

Culver Haven Inn Ⓛ

Culver Down, PO36 8QT (top of Culver Down by Monument) SZ63258565
✪ 10.30 (4 Mon)-11; closed Tue ☎ (01983) 406107
⊕ culverhaven.com
3 changing beers (often Goddards, Timothy Taylor, Wadworth) Ⓗ
Overlooking Sandown Bay and Bembridge Harbour, the Culver Haven offers surely one of the most spectacular pub views in the whole of Great Britain. Nearby is the Culver Battery, an impressive remnant of the Napoleonic Wars and built to protect Portsmouth (opened regularly by the National Trust). An excellent and varied menu, from snacks to full meals, is served in the cosy bar and restaurant. Q☭⌂✿Ⓓ♿▲P❀❀

Shanklin

Chine Inn Ⓛ

1 Chine Hill, PO37 6BW (up hill at end of Esplanade)
✪ 12-11; 10-10.30 Sun; closed Mon; opening hours vary in winter ☎ (01983) 865880
Sharp's Doom Bar Ⓗ; Timothy Taylor Landlord Ⓖ; Yates' Golden Bitter; 1 changing beer (sourced nationally; often Draught Bass, Towcester Mill) Ⓗ
The building, which has stood since 1621, must be one of the oldest pubs with a licence on the Island. It overlooks the bay with magnificent views. Live music is hosted on Saturday night and Sunday afternoon. The Chine Inn ghosts – a girl in blue and an old man in the corner – have been seen by small children. Ask to see the opening hours notice. Q☭⌂✿Ⓓ☷(2,3)❀

King Harry's Bar ♟

6 Church Road, PO37 6NU (on edge of Old Village towards Ventnor)

✪ 11-midnight summer; 2 (4 Mon)-11; 12-11 Sat & Sun winter ☎ (01983) 863119 ⊕ kingharrysbar.co.uk
Fuller's ESB; 3 changing beers (often Goddards, Shepherd Neame, Young's) Ⓗ
Charming 19th-century thatched property with two established Tudor bars, restaurants, decked gardens and the Chine walk, plus car parking front and rear. Up to three guest beers are offered, chosen for their originality. Food is served in the summer months commencing Easter – the long-established Henry VIII kitchen specialises in steaks to die for. Function facilities and entertainment are also provided, and accommodation is available. Branch Pub of the Year 2016.
Q☭⌂✿⇋Ⓓ▲♣●P⍟☷(2,3)❀

Shorwell

Crown Inn Ⓛ ✿

Walkers Lane, PO30 3JZ
✪ 10.30-11; 11.30-11 Sun ☎ (01983) 740293
⊕ crowninnshorwell.co.uk
Adnams Broadside; Sharp's Doom Bar; Timothy Taylor Landlord; 3 changing beers (often Fuller's, Robinsons, St Austell) Ⓗ
Expansive 300-year-old hostelry in the picturesque village of Shorwell with a central multi-sided bar and traditional bar areas. It offers a range of four to six beers and a good home-cooked pub menu all day. There is a trout stream running through the garden, ducks in abundance to keep the children amused, and plenty of car parking. During the winter months only four real ales are available and the pub may close earlier. Q☭⌂✿Ⓓ♿♣●P☷(12)❀❀

Ventnor

Perks

46 High Street, PO38 1LT (next to Tesco Express)
✪ 9am-midnight; 10-midnight Sun ☎ (01983) 857446
⊕ perksofventnor.com
Draught Bass; 1 changing beer (sourced regionally; often Yates') Ⓗ
Perks is one of those gems that happen infrequently, offering one beer, plenty of wine, good service and sensible prices. A great collection of memorabilia echoes the pub's Best of British theme. Owner Graham Perks has spent over 25 years running a succession of bars in Ventnor and knows what the customer wants – good company and a tipple to suit the most discerning palate. There may be a second beer from Yates' Brewery at the weekends. Q☭✿Ⓓ♿●☷(3,6)❀

Spyglass Inn Ⓛ

The Esplanade, PO38 1JX (far end of Esplanade)
✪ 10.30-11 ☎ (01983) 855338 ⊕ thespyglass.co.uk
Ringwood Best Bitter, Fortyniner; 3 changing beers (often Goddards, Marston's, Yates') Ⓗ
A 19th-century former guest house at the western end of the Esplanade in a superb position overlooking the English Channel. Wisely, the temptation was avoided to knock all the rooms into one; instead they have been skilfully incorporated into the overall layout. The inn has considerable character and boasts a large collection of seafaring memorabilia. Local seafood is a speciality and there is a small beer festival every year. Five ales are always available. Families are welcome and entertainment features most evenings and Sunday lunchtimes. ☭⌂✿⇋Ⓓ♟P❀❀❀

Volunteer ⓁL

30 Victoria Street, PO38 1ES (50yds from bus terminal)
☼ 11-11.30; 11-midnight Fri & Sat; 12-10.30 Sun
☎ (01983) 852537
Courage Best Bitter; 4 changing beers (often Brains, Island) Ⓗ

Built in 1866, the Volunteer is one of the smallest pubs on the Island. Up to six beers are available including an occasional local brew. No chips, no children, no fruit machines, no video games – just a pure adult drinking house and one of the few places where you can still play rings and enjoy a traditional games night. It is popular with locals but welcomes visitors. Live music plays on Sunday afternoon. Westons Old Rosie cider is available. A past winner of local CAMRA Pub of the Year.
Q ☞ ♣ ♨ ⎕ (3,6) ☙

Whitwell

White Horse Inn ⓁL

High Street, PO38 2PY SZ52007800
☼ 10-11; 10-10.30 Sun ☎ (01983) 730375
⊕ whitehorseiow.co.uk
Goddards Fuggle-Dee-Dum; Sharp's Doom Bar; 2 changing beers Ⓗ

Built in 1454, this old stone building is considered to be the oldest established inn on the Isle of Wight. An extension to the side adds a family area and additional dining space. The remainder of the building is traditional with intimate areas to the rear. Four handpumps serve a changing range of beers and the excellent food menu is extensive. A large garden is fine for children on warmer days. Breakfast is served 10am-midday.
Q ☞ 愈 ⊙◑ ♨ ⎕ (6) ☙ ☎

King Harry's Bar, Shanklin

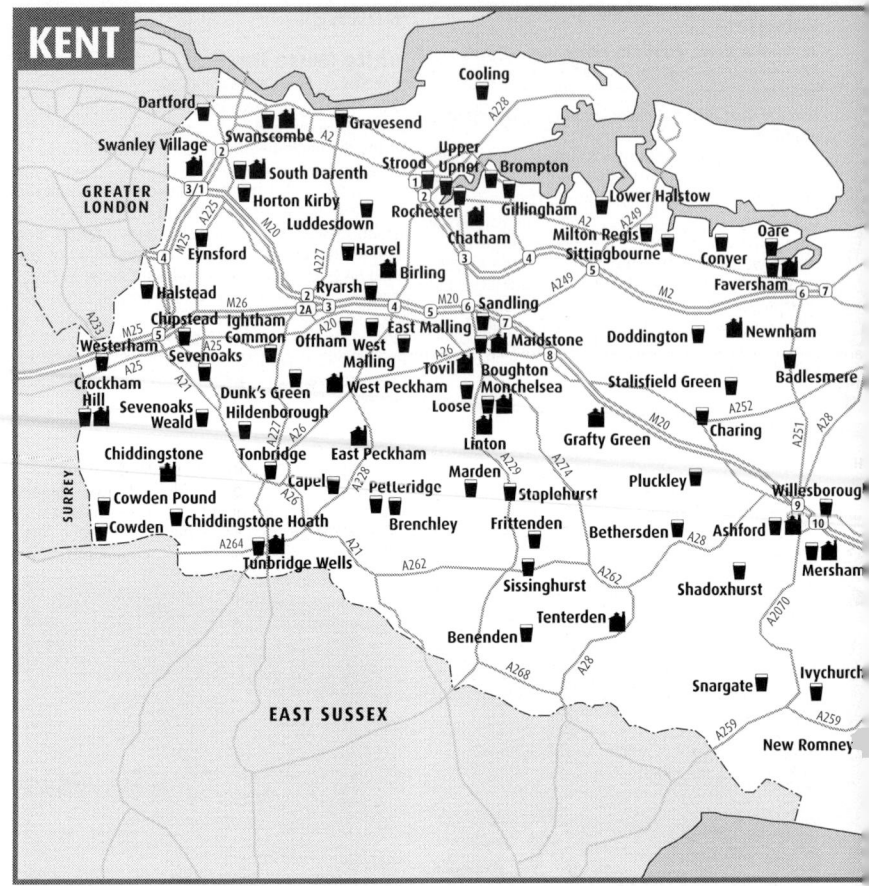

KENT

Cooling

Dartford
Gravesend
Swanley Village
Swanscombe A2
Upper
Strood Upnot Brompton
South Darenth
GREATER
LONDON 3/1
Horton Kirby
Rochester Gillingham
Lower Halstow
Luddesdown
Chatham
Milton Regis
Oare
Eynsford
Harvel
Sittingbourne Conyer
Halstead
Ryarsh
Birling
Faversham
Chipstead Ightham
Sandling
Newnham
Common Offham West
East Malling
Westerham
Malling
Maidstone
Doddington
Sevenoaks
Tovil Boughton
Crockham
West Peckham
Monchelsea
Stalisfield Green
Badlesmere
Hill
Dunk's Green
Loose
Charing
Sevenoaks
Hildenborough
Weald
Linton
Grafty Green
Chiddingstone
Tonbridge East Peckham
Capel
Marden
Pluckley
Willesborough
Cowden Pound
Petteridge
Staplehurst
Cowden Chiddingstone Hoath
Brenchley Frittenden
Bethersden Ashford
Tunbridge Wells
Mersham
Sissinghurst
Shadoxhurst
Tenterden
Benenden
Snargate
Ivychurch
EAST SUSSEX
New Romney

Ashford

County Hotel ⚫
10 High Street, TN24 8TD (at lower end of High Street)
⏰ 8am-midnight (1am Fri & Sat) ☎ (01233) 646891
Adnams Broadside; Greene King Abbot; Ruddles Best Bitter; Sharp's Doom Bar; 3 changing beers (sourced nationally) Ⓗ
A spacious Wetherspoon pub in an 18th-century building in the centre of Ashford. Originally red brick, the top floor and the parapet are now tile hung. It has one bar with three separate seating areas. Up to two real ciders are available, dispensed from polypins in the fridge. Food is served all day every day 8am-11pm. Children are allowed in the dining area until 9pm. There are summer and autumn national and international beer festivals, plus a regional beer festival and a summer cider festival. Q☕⛲⚫❙Ⓚ❄➔♿P🚃🛜

Badlesmere

Red Lion
Ashford Road, ME13 0NX (on A251)
⏰ 12-11; 12-6 Sun; closed Mon ☎ (01233) 740320
🌐 redlionbadlesmere.co.uk
Shepherd Neame Master Brew; 3 changing beers (sourced locally; often Hopdaemon, Millis, Ramsgate) Ⓗ

Traditional country pub built in 1546 with many public bridleways and public footpaths in its vicinity. The selection of ales usually includes several local beers, often including Gadds' and Millis. The pub offers a selection of home-cooked food and can cater for functions and parties. There is regular live music from local bands. There are camping facilities in the pub's own paddock.
☕⛲⚫❙ Å♣P🚃(666)🐾🛜

Barfrestone

Wrong Turn 🍺 Ⓛ
Pie Factory Road, CT15 7JG (2½ miles from Barfrestone jct off A2) TR261503
⏰ 3-9 Wed; 3-8 Thu; 3-9 Fri; 12-9 Sat; 12-8 Sun; closed Mon & Tue ☎ 07522 554118
3 changing beers Ⓖ
Rural pub with a comfortable, country-kitchen style interior with wooden tables, chairs, sideboard and a wood-burning stove. Usually three real ales, which includes a mild, feature, mainly from Kent microbreweries, alongside real ciders from Kentish Pip and Westons. Snacks include pork pies, Scotch eggs and cheeseboards. Opening times may vary during the seasons and the pub may close early if quiet. Outside, there is a sheltered patio and garden. It is a pleasant 1½-mile walk from Shepherds Well railway station. CAMRA branch Pub of the Year 2016. Q⛲⚫♿Å♣♿P🐾🛜

Two-bar free house in a pretty Kentish village, decorated with pictures of local life. The public bar, a survivor of what proper village inns used to be like, has wood panelling, hops over the bar, a wood-burning stove, pub games, a jukebox, and good conversation. The former saloon now doubles as a restaurant. Food is served daily except Monday lunchtime and Sunday evening, with carveries on Wednesday evening and Sunday lunchtime. A beer festival is held around St George's Day. Buses from Ashford and Tenterden stop outside. ⮑❄️◑♣♠P🚌(2)😺🛜

Birchington-on-Sea

Wheel Alehouse
60 Station Road, CT7 9RA
☼ 12-2, 5-9; 12-2 Sun ☎ 07826 130927
🌐 thewheelalehouse.co.uk
5 changing beers 🄶
This nautical-themed micropub converted from a shop has been a welcome addition to the village's beer scene since opening in 2013. The ales are served direct from the cask along with real ciders from a temperature-controlled stillage room behind the small bar counter. At the rear is a steep flight of stairs leading to the Upper Deck where the toilets and further seating can be found. The pub hosts regular quizzes and is an active supporter of the Royal National Lifeboat Institute.
Q🌿♠🚌(33,34)😺

Benenden

Bull 🅛
The Street, TN17 4DE
☼ 12-midnight ☎ (01580) 240054
🌐 thebullatbenenden.co.uk
Dark Star Hophead; Harveys Sussex Best Bitter; Larkins Traditional Ale; 1 changing beer (sourced locally; often Old Dairy, Shepherd Neame) 🄷
Imposing free house dating back to the 17th century, by the picturesque village green where in summer you can watch the local cricket team. The comfortable interior features wooden floors, exposed oak beams and a large inglenook fireplace. Food is served in the public bar as well as in the separate restaurant. Booking is advisable for fish and chips on Friday and the Sunday lunchtime carvery. Meals are prepared using locally grown produce. Q⮑❄️◑♣♠P🚌(297)😺🛜

Bethersden

George
The Street, TN26 3AG (off A28 between Ashford and Tenterden in centre of village)
☼ 12-midnight ☎ (01233) 820235
Brakspear Bitter; Harveys Sussex Best Bitter; Morland Old Speckled Hen; 1 changing beer (sourced nationally) 🄷

REAL ALE BREWERIES

Amazing 🍺 Sandgate (NEW)
Attwell's St Nicholas at Wade (NEW)
Brew Buddies Swanley Village (NEW)
Canterbury Ales Chartham
Canterbury Brewers 🍺 Canterbury
Caveman Swanscombe
Farriers Arms 🍺 Mersham
Four Candles 🍺 St Peters
G2 Ashford
Goacher's Tovil
Goody Herne
Hop Fuzz West Hythe
Hopdaemon Newnham
Isla Vale Margate
Kent Birling
Larkins Chiddingstone
Mad Cat Faversham
Maidstone Maidstone
Millis (Dartford Wobbler) South Darenth
Musket Linton
Nelson Chatham
Old Dairy Tenterden
Pig & Porter Tunbridge Wells
Ramsgate (Gadds') Broadstairs
Range Lympne (NEW)
Ripple Steam Sutton
Rockin' Robin Boughton Monchelsea
Romney Marsh New Romney
Shepherd Neame Faversham
Swan on the Green 🍺 West Peckham
Tír Dhá Ghlas 🍺 Dover
Tonbridge East Peckham
Turnstone Ales Whitstable
Wantsum Hersden
Westerham Crockham Hill
Whitstable Grafty Green

Boughton Monchelsea

Cock Inn 🇱 ✅
Heath Road, ME17 4JD TQ776512
🌣 11-11; 12-10.30 Sun ☎ (01622) 743166
🌐 cockinnmaidstone.co.uk
Shepherd Neame Master Brew; 3 changing beers (often St Austell, Shepherd Neame) Ⓗ
A 16th-century coaching inn built to provide lodgings for Canterbury pilgrims, full of character, with oak beams and an inglenook fireplace. A varied menu complemented by real ales is served in both the bar and restaurant (no food Sun eves). There is a large patio area. Darts and board games are available. Situated near the Greensand Way, walkers are always welcome. Q🕏🕼🌓♣P🐾

Bramling

Haywain 🇱
Canterbury Road, CT3 1NB
🌣 7-11 Mon; 12-3, 6-11; 12-4 Sun ☎ (01227) 720676
🌐 thehaywainbramling.co.uk
Fuller's London Pride; Wells Bombardier; 2 changing beers (sourced locally; often Goacher's, Ramsgate, Whitstable) Ⓗ
Classic and friendly country pub with a cosy snug, adorned with hanging hop bines. Traditional games include darts and bat and trap. There is a Monday quiz night, a Wednesday crib night, a cheese club on the last Sunday of the month, and jazz on the last Tuesday. Guest beers are usually from Kent breweries, and an annual beer festival is hosted over the Spring Bank Holiday weekend in a marquee in the attractive garden. Excellent home-cooked food, using local produce, is served.
Q🕏🕼🌓♣P🖵(13,14)🐾

Brenchley

Halfway House 🇱 ✅
Horsmonden Road, TN12 7AX (½ mile SE of village)
🌣 12-11 ☎ (01892) 722526
🌐 halfwayhousebrenchley.co.uk
Goacher's Fine Light Ale; Old Dairy Gold Top; Skinner's Betty Stogs; Tonbridge Rustic; Westerham 1965 – Special Bitter Ale; house beer (by Goacher's); 4 changing beers (sourced locally; often Dark Star, Larkins, Whitstable) Ⓖ
Just outside Brenchley village, this iconic ale house offers excellent beers, wholesome food and a warm welcome. Hanging hops on exposed beams and chalkboards around the open fire provide that authentic rustic feel. Landlord Sam Allen, recently acquiring the helm from father Richard, continues with gravity-fed cask ales and family food while making subtle improvements – evolution not revolution. Festivals featuring over 50 beers are held Whitsun and August bank holidays in the extensive gardens which incorporate a separate family section and covered seating.
Q🕏🕼🌓♣P🖵(297)🐾🛜

Broadstairs

Thirty-Nine Steps Alehouse
5 Charlotte Street, CT10 1LR
🌣 12-11 🌐 thethirty-ninesteps.co.uk
4 changing beers Ⓖ

This former shop, now operating as one of Thanet's many micropubs, has been tastefully converted, with heavy wooden high tables and bench seating. Changing beers are dispensed from a glass-fronted cooled stillage cabinet behind the bar. The knowledgeable landlord is keen to vary the offering and favours interesting and hard-to-find beers among his selection. The ceiling is decorated with pumpclips of every beer served, adding to the cosy feel of the pub. 🕏🚲🖵(56)🐾

Brompton

King George V 🇱 ✅
1 Prospect Row, ME7 5AL
🌣 12-11; 12-10.30 Sun ☎ (01634) 842418
🌐 kinggeorgevpub.co.uk
Old Dairy Red Top; 3 changing beers (sourced locally; often Canterbury Brewers, Caveman) Ⓗ
Historic 17th-century free house on the Saxon Shore Way featuring naval memorabilia. It has three connected areas, and outside a covered and heated area for smokers in the garden. Guest ales come from Kent breweries and microbreweries, alongside a varied selection of Belgian bottled beers, malt whiskies, rums and ciders. Food is served, with daily specials plus themed pizza and steak nights. Sunday roasts are popular. Three guest rooms are available.
🕏🕏🛏🌓♣🖵(101,182)🛜

Canterbury

Bottle Shop
The Goods Shed, Station Road West, CT2 8AN (next to Canterbury West station)
🌣 12-10; 12-4 Sun; closed Mon ☎ (01227) 656280
🌐 bottleshop.bar
Changing beers (often Beavertown, Magic Rock, Pig & Porter)
Located in the Goods Shed, an acclaimed permanent farmers' market and food hall, the Bottle Shop is a beer emporium serving KeyKeg beers and 150 bottled beers. The products can be enjoyed on the premises at the seating areas between the other stalls, or on the covered terrace. Beers can also be taken away, and mail order is available. The monthly tutored themed tastings are great fun, and the beermongers are very knowledgeable. Personal tastings can be arranged to suit your budget and tastes.
Q🕏🕏🕼🚲(West)P🖵(4,6)🐾🛜

Dolphin 🇱
17 St Radigund's Street, CT1 2AA
🌣 12-11 (midnight Thu-Sat) ☎ (01227) 455963
🌐 thedolphincanterbury.co.uk
Sharp's Doom Bar; 2 changing beers (often Castle Rock, Hopdaemon, Timothy Taylor) Ⓗ
Friendly local decorated with 1950s-1970s memorabilia and free of TV screens. Good pub food in generous portions is served daily, with roasts on Sundays. There is a comprehensive collection of board games. The attractive verandah is popular with diners, and there is a large suntrap garden. Two of the handpumps serve cider, and there is a range of local and regional beers on other pumps. Opening hours vary from month to month (see website). May close on Mondays.
🕏🕼🌓🚲(West)🐾🛜

Eight Bells ✆

34 London Road, CT2 8LN
✪ 3-11; 12-midnight Fri & Sat; 12-10.30 Sun
☎ (01227) 454794
Young's Bitter, Special Ⓗ
Small, traditional local dating from 1708 and rebuilt in 1902, retaining original embossed windows and decorated with memorabilia. There is live music fortnightly on Fridays, and a quiz, usually on the last Wednesday of the month. Five darts teams play every week and their trophies are on display. Food is served only on Sunday lunchtimes. There is an attractive small walled garden and a comfortable heated smoking area.
❀◖≷(West)♣☒(3,6)✿≷

Foundry Brew Pub Ⓛ

White Horse Lane, CT1 2RU (just off High Street)
✪ 12-midnight (3am Fri & Sat); 12-11 Sun
☎ (01227) 455899 ⊕ thefoundrycanterbury.co.uk
Canterbury Brewers Foundryman's Gold, Foundry Torpedo, Streetlight Porter; 4 changing beers (often Canterbury Brewers) Ⓗ
The home of Canterbury Brewers, this 19th-century foundry is on two floors. There are usually six ales, brewed on the premises, and it is now producing its own ciders. Look out for interesting experimental brews. The brewery's own bottled ale can be bought to take away. Good-value pub food is sold 12-8pm Wednesday and Thursday, 12-9pm Friday and Saturday. A DJ plays upstairs on Friday and Saturday nights. CAMRA members receive a 10 per cent discount on food and beer (also at nearby sister pub, the City Arms). There is a pleasant patio. ☎❀◖&≷●☒≷

New Inn

19 Havelock Street, CT1 1NP (off ring road near St Augustine's Abbey)
✪ 12-3, 5.30-11; 12-midnight Fri & Sat; 12-2.30, 6-11 Sun
☎ (01227) 464584 ⊕ newinncanterbury.co.uk
6 changing beers (often Adnams, Dark Star, Kent) Ⓗ
Victorian back-street terraced house only a few minutes' walk from the cathedral, St Augustine's Abbey and the bus station. The main bar has a cosy woodburner, a wooden floor and a jukebox. At the back is a long, bright conservatory where there are newspapers to browse over your pint, and a range of board games. Beer festivals are held on the Whitsun and August bank holiday weekends. Disabled access is through the attractive garden via Old Ruttington Lane. ☎❀&♣●☒✿

Unicorn Ⓛ ✆

61 St Dunstan's Street, CT2 8BS
✪ 11.30-11; 11.30-midnight Fri & Sat ☎ (01227) 463187
⊕ unicorninn.com
Sharp's Doom Bar; Shepherd Neame Master Brew; 2 changing beers (often Hopdaemon, Ramsgate, Timothy Taylor) Ⓗ
Comfortable 1604 pub near the historic Westgate, with an attractive suntrap garden. Bar billiards is played and a quiz, set by regular customers, is held weekly on Sunday evening. One of the guest beers is usually from one of several Kent microbreweries, and beer updates are posted on Twitter. Food is good value, with a two-for-£11 special offer on selected meals (no food Sun eve). Sporting events (not Sky) are televised unobtrusively.
Q☎❀◖≷(West)♣●☒(3,4,6)✿≷

Capel

Dovecote Inn

Alders Road, TN12 6SU (½ mile W of A228 towards Tudeley)
✪ 12-3 (not Mon), 5.30-11; 12-10.30 Sun ☎ (01892) 835966
⊕ dovecote-capel.co.uk
Gale's HSB; Harveys Sussex Best Bitter; 3 changing beers (sourced nationally; often Loddon, Long Man, Wye Valley) Ⓖ
Easily accessible from surrounding towns, the Dovecote is ideal for those seeking a peaceful, cosy, cottage-style destination. The homely carpeted interior is hung with hops and includes comfortable bar seating, a snug and charming restaurant. Outside there is a shaded summertime patio and an extensive garden. Four to five ales are served direct from the cask, along with Westons Old Rosie cider and good pub meals (no food Sun and Mon eves). The informative website details news of forthcoming beers and events such as music and quizzes. Q☎❀◖&♣●P☒(6A)≷

Charing

Bowl Inn

Egg Hill Road, TN27 0HG (signposted from A20 and A251)
✪ 12-11 (midnight Fri & Sat) ☎ (01233) 712256
⊕ bowlinn.co.uk
Sharp's Doom Bar; 3 changing beers (sourced locally; often Hopdaemon, Wantsum, Whitstable) Ⓗ
A 16th-century free house on the top of the North Downs in an Area of Outstanding Natural Beauty. A large inglenook fire warms the bar and there is a large garden with heated patio area. The pub is a popular stop-off point for walkers and cyclists and offers five rooms. Camping is also available. An annual beer festival is held. Opening hours in winter may vary. ☎❀➤◖&AP✿≷

Chiddingstone Hoath

Rock Ⓛ

Hoath Corner, TN8 7BS (1½ miles S of Chiddingstone)
✪ 12-11; 12-10.30 Sun ☎ (01892) 870296
Larkins Traditional Ale, Pale; 1 changing beer (sourced locally; often Larkins) Ⓗ
Named after nearby rocky outcrops, this cosy Grade II-listed pub was built in 1520 and retains its wonderfully rustic atmosphere. The tile-hung exterior, extensively beamed ceiling, worn brick floor and large open fireplace entice the visitor in to sample a selection of Larkins ales, brewed just down the road. Try your hand at ringing the bull. Bench seating by the entrance and a quiet rear garden enable ramblers and locals to enjoy their refreshments in tranquillity, away from the hubbub of modern life. Q❀♣P☒✿

Chipstead

Bricklayers Arms ✆

39-41 Chevening Road, TN13 2RZ (by entrance to sailing club)
✪ 11-11.30 (midnight Fri & Sat); 11-10.30 Sun
☎ (01732) 743424 ⊕ the-bricklayers-arms.co.uk
Harveys Sussex Best Bitter Ⓖ; **3 changing beers (sourced locally; often Harveys)** Ⓗ

Warm, friendly terraced local resting at the foot of the North Downs and overlooking the green and Longford Lake. The pub and adjoining restaurant have a strong following attracted by the quality and range of food, themed food nights and excellent Harveys ales. Sussex Best is served direct from the cask while handpumps dispense the brewery's range of seasonal brews. The front bar includes a large log fire and stone-flagged floor where dogs are welcome, and pictures of village history adorn the walls. **Q🐴❀◑◐♣P🚌**(401)🐾📶

Coldred

Carpenters Arms [L]

The Green, CT15 5AJ

🕓 5-9; 6-11 Fri & Sat; 7-11 Sun ☎ (01304) 830190

2 changing beers [H]/[G]

Overlooking the village green and duck pond, this 18th-century two-roomed pub is a real gem and well worth seeking out. It has been in the Fagg family for over a century, and largely unchanged in the last 50 years. The pub is the centre of the community and conversation is king. At least two real ales are served alongside two real ciders from Kentish Pip. The pub hosts regular community events including quizzes and vegetable competitions. A beer festival is held in June. **Q🐴❀♣🍎P**🐾📶

Conyer

Ship ✔

Conyer Quay, ME9 9HR

🕓 12-3, 6-11 (midnight Fri); 10-11.30 Sat; 10-9.30 Sun ☎ (01795) 520881 🌐 shipinnconyer.co.uk

Shepherd Neame Master Brew; 3 changing beers (sourced regionally; often Adnams, Old Dairy) [H]

An 18th-century creekside inn with a nautically themed interior. Bare floorboards and scrubbed pine tables add rustic charm, and a real fire adds character. Situated on the Saxon Shore Way and a 20-minute walk from Teynham train station, the pub is popular with walkers and cyclists. Food is served in the main area and in an upstairs dining room. It has a small courtyard garden overlooking the creek. **Q🐴❀◑◐♣P🚌**(344,345,346)🐾📶

Cooling

Horseshoe & Castle [L]

Main Road, The Street, ME3 8DJ

🕓 6-11 Mon; 12-3, 6-11 Tue; 12-11; 12-10.30 Sun ☎ (01634) 221691 🌐 horseshoeandcastle.com

Shepherd Neame Master Brew; 1 changing beer (sourced locally) [H]

A friendly free house which has had the same owners for over 25 years. It lies six miles north of Rochester in a village near the north Kent marshes. The restaurant offers good-value Sunday lunches and specialises in seafood (closed Mon). The guest ale always comes from a local microbrewery. Accommodation of a high standard is available. Nearby are castle ruins and a churchyard widely considered to feature in Charles Dickens' Great Expectations. **Q❀🛏◑◐♿♣P**🐾

Cowden

Fountain ✔

30 High Street, TN8 7JG (1 mile W of B2026)

🕓 12-3, 6-midnight (11 Tue); 12-midnight Sun ☎ (01342) 850528 🌐 fountain-cowden.com

Harveys IPA, Sussex Best Bitter; 1 changing beer (sourced locally; often Harveys) [H]

In a quaint village surrounded by lovely countryside perfect for walking and cycling, this is a lively local popular with drinkers and diners alike. This Harveys pub draws folk from miles around, while also forming the centre of village life by hosting many local events and groups. One room is reserved for drinkers. Traditional English fare is served in three dining areas including a conservatory. Close to Hever Castle, Penshurst Place and Gardens and three nearby golf courses. **Q🐴❀◑◐♣P🚌**(234)🐾📶

Cowden Pound

Queen's Arms ★ [L]

Hartfield Road, TN8 5NP (on B2026 halfway between Edenbridge and A264)

🕓 5-7.30 (10.30 Mon & Tue); 5-9 Fri; 12-3 Sun

Larkins Traditional Ale [H]; 1 changing beer (sourced locally; often Larkins) [G]

Rare example of a largely unaltered and unspoilt Victorian inn thankfully saved from the threat of closure by a local family operating it with limited opening hours. Open log fires in winter in both bars together with friendly, chatty locals add to the charm of a visit. A cask of seasonal ale from nearby brewery Larkins is often to be found on the bar alongside produce from the surrounding area brought in by customers – contributions accepted. Monthly live music is advertised locally. **Q♣P🍺**🐾

Crockham Hill

Royal Oak [L]

Main Road, TN8 6RD (on B2026 jct with B269)

🕓 11-3, 5-11; 11-11 Sat; 12-10.30 Sun ☎ (01732) 866335 🌐 royaloakcrockhamhill.co.uk

Westerham Finchcocks Original; 3 changing beers (sourced locally; often Westerham) [H]

Perched on the Greensand Ridge in an Area of Outstanding Natural Beauty, this smart pub is sought out by walkers, cyclists and car-borne visitors for excellent home-cooked food. The changing selection of local Westerham ales can also be sampled in three third-pint taster glasses, served by friendly staff. The homely public bar has a log fire and the comfortable furnishings are enhanced by the amusing Tottering cartoons donated by Country Life artist Annie Tempest, which adorn the walls. **Q🐴❀◑◐♣P🚌**(236)🐾📶

Dartford

Dartford Working Men's Club [L] ✔

Essex Road, DA1 2AU

🕓 11-11; 12-10.30 Sun ☎ (01322) 223646 🌐 dartfordwm.club

Courage Best Bitter [H]; 14 changing beers (sourced regionally; often Caveman, Leatherbritches, Oakham) [H]/[G]

Modern CIU club boasting a selection of 15 real ales on handpump, plus ciders on gravity. The ales come from various micro and regional breweries, with over 500 different beers served each year. The club is home to the BBC award-winning Dartford Folk Club meeting on Tuesday evenings. There is live music every Saturday night and a popular quiz takes place on the first Wednesday evening of each month. Up to four beer festivals are held each year. CAMRA members are welcome as guests. ⏵🅰🆀🅳🅶♿⇌🚲🚪🚽🛜

Foresters ✓

15/16 Great Queen Street, DA1 1TJ
🟢 12-11.30; 12-11 Sun ☎ (01322) 223087

Adnams Ghost Ship; Harveys Sussex Best Bitter; 1 changing beer (sourced regionally; often Skinner's) Ⓗ

This pleasant back-street local dates from 1869 and is a five-minute walk up East Hill from the town centre. It has an L-shaped bar with an open wood-burning fireplace, and serves two real ales plus a guest. The car park holds about 15 vehicles and there is a large paved beer garden with a covered heated smoking area. Opposite is a graveyard which contains the unmarked pauper's grave of famed steam pioneer Richard Trevithick, a rough location given by a plaque on the north wall. ⏵🅰⇌🚲🅿🚪🚽🛜

Ivy Leaf Ⓛ ✓

72 Darenth Road, DA1 1LS
🟢 12-11; 12-10.30 Sun ☎ (01322) 220993

Sharp's Doom Bar; Wells Bombardier; 4 changing beers (sourced regionally) Ⓗ

About 10 minutes' walk from the town centre and even nearer to Dartford football ground, this long single-bar pub offers two regular real ales and up to four guests, including at least one from a local brewery. There are wood-burning fires at either end of the bar, and a covered smoking area to the right of the pub with steps leading up to a beer garden. Live music is played on Thursday and Saturday nights and an open quiz takes place on Sunday evenings. The Fastrack B bus stops nearby. 🅰🅳⇌🅿🚪

Malt Shovel

3 Darenth Road, DA1 1LP
🟢 3 (12 Thu)-11; 12-midnight Fri; 12-11 Sat & Sun ☎ (01322) 224381

St Austell Tribute; Young's Bitter, Special; 2 changing beers (sourced nationally) Ⓗ

A Young's-owned pub dating from 1673, near the town centre. It has two bars – a low-ceilinged taproom featuring an 1880 Dartford Brewery mirror, and a larger bar leading to a conservatory where meals are served Wednesday to Sunday lunchtimes and Thursday to Saturday evenings. A large beer garden leads off the conservatory. The Fastrack B bus stops just across the road to the rear of the garden, where barbecues are hosted in the summer. There is a thriving open quiz on Monday evenings. 🅰🅳⇌🅿🚪

Deal

Just Reproach Ⓛ

14 King Street, CT14 6HX
🟢 12-3, 5-8 Mon; 12-2, 5-9 (11 Fri); 12-11 Sat; 12-4 Sun

4 changing beers Ⓖ

One of Kent's first micropubs, located in the town centre. The welcoming ambience, high benches

and table service make for a friendly, convivial atmosphere. Up to five real ales are served, usually from Kent breweries. Ciders are from Kent makers, typically Kent Cider Company. Wines from the local Barnsole Vineyard and quality soft drinks are also available. Snacks include pork pies and local cheese. No keg, no spirits, no fruit machines, no music, and do not let your mobile phone ring. 🆀⇌🅰🚲🅿🚪😺

Ship Inn Ⓛ

141 Middle Street, CT14 6JZ
🟢 11-midnight; 12-midnight Sun ☎ (01304) 372222

Dark Star Hophead; Ramsgate Gadds' No.7 Bitter Ale; 3 changing beers (often Dark Star, Ramsgate) Ⓗ

Only 10 minutes' walk from the town centre, this unspoilt, traditional pub is located in Deal's historic conservation area. Dark wooden floors and subdued lighting create a warm and comfortable atmosphere, complemented by the nautical theme. A wide variety of drinkers enjoys the good range of beers dispensed from the five handpumps, including ales from Ramsgate and Dark Star. The pub has a small cosy rear bar overlooking a large patio garden, accessed by a staircase, with a covered smoking area. ⏵🅰🚲🚪😺🛜

Doddington

Chequers

The Street, ME9 0BG (6 miles W of Faversham)
🟢 12-11 Mon; 12-3, 5-11; 12-midnight Fri & Sat; 12-8 Sun ☎ (01795) 886366

Shepherd Neame Master Brew; 1 changing beer (often Shepherd Neame) Ⓗ

With two ghosts, oak timbers, mullion windows and an inglenook fireplace, the Chequers has great character. The welcoming landlord and landlady use locally sourced food for their home-cooked meals. This dog-friendly pub has a large garden and is popular with walkers, ramblers and cyclists. It host darts and pool teams and acts as the local post office on Tuesdays. ⏵🅰🅳🚲🅿😺🛜

Dover

Eight Bells Ⓛ ✓

19 Cannon Street, CT16 1BZ
🟢 8am-midnight (1am Fri & Sat) ☎ (01304) 205030

Adnams Broadside; Sharp's Doom Bar; 9 changing beers Ⓗ

The name of this popular and bustling Wetherspoon pub, situated on the precinct, is linked to the church opposite. Inside, there is a large open-plan room with a long bar and a raised restaurant area. At the front an enclosed seating area looks out onto the precinct. Twelve handpumps dispense a range of regular and guest ales, with at least one beer from a Kent microbrewery. There are real ale offers on Monday. The pub is close to public transport services. 🆀⏵🅰🅳🅶⇌🚲🚪🛜

Lanes Ⓛ

15 Worthington Street, CT17 9AQ
🟢 12-11 (6 Mon); 1-11 Sun ☎ 07504 258331

5 changing beers Ⓖ

A micropub, near the pedestrian precinct, that is comfortably furnished and carpeted. Real ales, ciders, wines, a mead and soft drinks are from Kent

producers. Five real ales, two from Kent, and at least 10 ciders, are served on gravity dispense from the temperature-controlled cellar room. There is no keg beer, lager, spirits or piped music. Snacks can be brought in from the local deli and a feasting board is available with 48 hours' notice. Dogs on a lead are allowed, but no children.
Q🅫♿🕿♣🍴⏰🖪🐾🛜

Louis Armstrong 🅛
58 Maison Dieu Road, CT16 1RA
🕙 2-11; 7-11 Sun ☎ (01304) 204759
Hopdaemon Skrimshander IPA; 3 changing beers Ⓗ
Down-to-earth pub and music venue that has featured live music for over 50 years. The large L-shaped bar and stage is surrounded by music posters, a large mirror and long bench seating. Up to four real ales are on offer, principally from Kent microbreweries, and the occasional real cider. Two beer festivals are usually held. On Wednesday, good-value food and real ales for £2.50 are served in the evening, and there is a monthly charity quiz night. It has a pleasant beer garden and is easily accessible by bus. A public car park is opposite.
🕿♣🖪🐾🛜

Mash Tun 🅛
3 Bench Street, CT16 1JH
🕙 12-10; 12-4 Sun; closed Mon & Tue ☎ (01304) 219590
House beer (by Hopdaemon); 3 changing beers Ⓖ
Comfortable micropub on the southern edge of Dover's shopping precinct. Cosy armchairs, a sofa, tables and chairs give the bar a homely feel. A 200-year-old church pulpit forms the bar. On offer is a varying list of ales including a house beer from Hopdaemon, and a large choice of ciders from rare and smaller cider makers including Kent makers. There is no food, but customers are welcome to bring their own or order a takeaway. Can open Monday and Tuesday by arrangement.
🛒🕿◑🕿♣🍴🖪🐾🛜

Rack of Ale 🅛
7 Park Place, CT16 1DF
🕙 12-10.30; 1-10.30 Sun ☎ 07703 059201 ⊕ rackofale.co.uk
5 changing beers Ⓗ/Ⓖ
Modern two-roomed pub with simple but quirky decor. It encourages conversation, reading a paper or a book, or playing a game or two, but frowns upon the use of mobile phones. Typically five real ales, with beers from Kent microbreweries, and cider from Kentish Pip, are served, on a tasting rack if requested. Occasional beer festivals are held. Food is not available but you can bring your own. Opening hours are flexible, depending on how busy the pub is. There is a loyalty card scheme.
♿🕿♣🍴🖪🐾

Dunk's Green

Kentish Rifleman 🅛
Roughway Lane, TN11 9RU (jct with Dunks Green Rd, 4 miles N of Tonbridge, off A227)
🕙 11.30-3, 6-11; 11.30-11 Fri-Sun ☎ (01732) 810727
⊕ thekentishrifleman.co.uk
Harveys Sussex Best Bitter; Whitstable Native Bitter; 2 changing beers (sourced locally; often Tonbridge, Westerham) Ⓗ
Cosy, friendly and justifiably popular 16th-century inn attracting a variety of clientele from farmers to diners. It has low-beamed ceilings throughout, with the wooden-floored drinkers' (and dogs') bar

featuring wall-mounted rifles, leading through to a carpeted dining area, with real fires in both. Wooden benches are provided at the front and a secluded garden to the rear. It is a haven for local beers, mostly Kentish. Food is also a draw, with booking often advisable. A twin room is available for those wishing to linger longer.
Q🅫🛏◑P🖪(222)🐾🛜

East Malling

King & Queen 🅛 ✓
1 New Road, ME19 6DD
🕙 11 (12 Sat)-11; 12-6 Sun ☎ (01732) 842752
⊕ kingandqueeneastmalling.co.uk
Harveys Sussex Best Bitter; Kent Pale; Musket Fife and Drum; 1 changing beer (often Black Sheep, Hook Norton) Ⓗ
A 16th-century Grade II-listed inn noted for the quality of its restaurant food and traditional bar snacks that are available all day. The garden is pleasant in the summer and dogs are welcome there, but not in the bar. Quiz nights and occasional music or comedy nights take place on Sunday evenings, for which the pub stays open later. Accommodation is at the rear with three well-appointed rooms. Handy for the station.
Q🛒🅫🛏◑🕿P🖪(58)🛜

Eastry

Five Bells ✓
The Cross, CT13 0HX
🕙 11-11.30 (1am Fri & Sat) ☎ (01304) 611188
⊕ thefivebellseastry.com
Greene King IPA; 1 changing beer Ⓗ
Traditional community pub in the heart of the village, well served by local buses, including in the evenings. There is a comfortable lounge bar and a public bar with pool, darts and TV sport. The old fire station, with historic memorabilia, serves as a restaurant/function room. The busy calendar features live music, quiz nights, poker evenings and an Easter beer festival. Home-made food is served all day, plus an excellent-value two-course lunchtime menu Monday to Friday. The suntrap patio has a children's play area and pétanque pitch.
🛒🅫🛏◑Å♣P🖪(14,87,88)🛜

Eynsford

Five Bells
High Street, DA4 0AB
🕙 4 (12 Sat)-11; 12-10.30 Sun ☎ (01322) 863135
Dark Star Hophead; Harveys Sussex Best Bitter; Sharp's Doom Bar; 1 changing beer (sourced regionally; often Long Man) Ⓗ
Traditional community pub in the heart of an attractive village. The public bar retains a homely atmosphere, with wooden tables and a wood-burning fire in winter. It also has a comfortable separate saloon bar. The changing guest beer comes from an independent brewery. Quiz night is the third Thursday of each month. There is a pleasant garden to the rear and a small car park. Dogs are welcome in the public bar. Food is not served here but try its larger sister pub, the Malt Shovel, nearby. Q🅫P🖪🐾🛜

Faversham

Bear Inn
3 Market Place, ME13 7AG

🌣 10.30-11; 11.30-11 Sun ☎ (01795) 532668

Shepherd Neame Master Brew; 1 changing beer (sourced locally; often Shepherd Neame) Ⓗ

A 16th-century pub in Faversham's historic market square. The traditional interior has three separate bar areas running the length of the building. The lunchtime menu is popular, and a general knowledge quiz is held on the last Monday of the month. The venue often features the seasonal Shepherd Neame beer and is frequented by visitors to Faversham and locals alike. A small number of tables at the front of the pub come into their own in summer. Q◖╈♣🖳😺🤶

Elephant Ⓛ ✅
31 The Mall, ME13 8JN

🌣 3-11; 12-11 Sat; 12-7 Sun; closed Mon ☎ (01795) 590157

5 changing beers (sourced regionally; often Dark Star, Mad Cat, Rother Valley) Ⓗ

The Elephant is an awarding-winning pub close to Faversham railway station. The five changing beers often include rarer styles such as mild, and they come mainly from microbreweries. Local real cider, frequently from Kent Cider or Dudda's Tun, is available on handpump. The pub has a log fire and a large enclosed garden. Regular music nights feature and dogs and children are welcome. A house beer is brewed by Hopdaemon or Mad Cat. 🏵️😺♣🖳😺🤶

Furlongs Ale House
6 Preston Street, ME13 8NS

🌣 4 (2 Fri; 12 Sat)-10; 12-8 Sun ☎ 07747 776200

4 changing beers (sourced locally; often Ramsgate, Tonbridge, Wantsum) Ⓗ

Faversham's first micropub, opened in late 2014, with bench-style seating and solid wooden tables. The beers, drawn by handpump from the cellar to a small bar, are mainly from Kent microbreweries, although some, such as Dark Star, come from across the border. Kent wines and ciders are also served. It now offers a CAMRA discount on ale and cider. Q🏵️╈♣🖳(333)😺

Phoenix Tavern ✅
98/99 Abbey Street, ME13 7BH

🌣 12-11 (midnight Fri & Sat) ☎ (01795) 591462

⊕ thephoenixtavernfaversham.co.uk

Harveys Sussex Best Bitter; Timothy Taylor Landlord; 3 changing beers Ⓗ

A 14th-century traditional English pub set in the heart of Faversham and close to Faversham Creek. The range of ales usually includes well-known national brands such as Timothy Taylor, Harveys and Otter. A separate restaurant serves a varied menu, and a bar menu of West Country pies is on offer. The pub boasts two open fires and hosts regular meetings of the Timothy Taylor Appreciation Society, as well as other events. Q🏵️😺╈♣P🖳😺🤶

Shipwright's Arms Ⓛ
Hollowshore, ME13 7TU (over 1 mile N of Faversham at confluence of Faversham and Oare creeks) TR017636

🌣 11-3 , 6-10 (not Tue & Wed eve); 11-11 Sat; 12-9 Sun; closed Mon ☎ (01795) 590088

⊕ theshipwrightsathollowshore.co.uk

Goacher's Real Mild Ale, Special House Ale; 3 changing beers (sourced locally; often Goacher's, Kent) Ⓖ

Remote 300-year-old family-run free house with a welcoming old-style landlord, a good pub to relax in after a 45-minute walk across the marshes from Faversham. The wooden-clad building's interior reflects its nautical heritage, with many associated ornaments and pictures on display or tucked into nooks and crannies. The large garden at the rear is open spring to autumn, with outside seating at the front all year round. It has extended opening hours in the summer, but in severe winter weather telephone to check opening times. Q🏵️😺◖♣P😺

Vaults Cask & Kitchen Ⓛ
75 Preston Street, ME13 8PA

🌣 11-11 ☎ (01795) 591817 ⊕ theoldwinevaults.com

4 changing beers (sourced nationally; often Cottage, Mad Cat, Otter) Ⓗ

A 16th-century town-centre pub with two bars. The small front bar has traditional pub games such as skittles, bar billiards and darts; the large back bar has an area that can accommodate private parties. Good-quality food is served. The pub has a large beer garden and holds regular events including a beer festival and a cider festival. Four beers, always including a local ale, are on sale along with at least two ciders, such as Dudda's Tun. 🏵️😺◖╈♣🖳(333)😺🤶

Finglesham

Crown Inn Ⓛ
The Street, CT14 0NA

🌣 12-11; 12-10 (9 winter) Sun ☎ (01304) 612555

⊕ thecrownatfinglesham.co.uk

Dark Star Hophead; 2 changing beers Ⓗ

Traditional village pub with a warm welcome and friendly atmosphere. Three to four real ales, one usually from a local microbrewery, are served, and you can get quality home-made food lunchtimes and evenings, including a roast on Sunday. Eat in the bar or the restaurant, which opens onto the pleasant garden. Occasional live music events take place, bat and trap is played in summer, and there is a children's play area. Buses are a 5-15 minutes' walk, depending on the day and time. The magnificent Kentish barn is available for functions and weddings. 🏵️😺◖Å♣P😺🤶

Folkestone

Chambers Ⓛ
Radnor Chambers, Cheriton Place, CT20 2BB (off Hythe end of Sandgate Rd)

🌣 12-11 (1am Fri & Sat); closed Sun ☎ (01303) 223333

⊕ pubfolkestone.co.uk

Adnams Lighthouse; 4 changing beers Ⓗ

A spacious cellar bar beneath a licensed coffee shop with six handpumps. Beers include some from local breweries and at least two real ciders. A beer festival is held over the Easter weekend. Food, including Mexican, European and daily specials, is served daily except Mondays and Friday evenings. There is a disco on Fridays, a quiz on the first Sunday of the month (closed on other Sundays), and live music on Thursday, usually with free admission. 🏵️◖╈♣🖳😺🤶

East Cliff Tavern

13-15 East Cliff, CT19 6BU

✪ 5-11; 12-11 Sat & Sun ☎ (01303) 251132

2 changing beers (sourced regionally) Ⓗ

Friendly terraced back-street pub, near a footpath across the railway line, a short walk from the harbour. The main bar is to the right and there are usually two beers, often from local breweries, with cider on gravity behind the bar. Old photographs of Folkestone decorate the walls, and community events include weekly raffles. The TV is in the saloon bar. Opening hours may vary – check if making a special visit. Q✿♣●🖵❀

Firkin Alehouse

18 Cheriton Place, CT20 2AZ

✪ 12-9 (10 Fri & Sat); 12-4 Sun ☎ 07894 068432

⊕ firkinalehouse.co.uk

3 changing beers Ⓖ

Folkestone's first micropub, selling up to four cask beers, normally with one from a Kent microbrewery. No lager, alcopops or spirits are sold, but a limited wine selection is kept, and five ciders are always available. Food consists of Kentish cheeses and basic bar snacks. You will not find music or pub games here, only pleasant company and conversation, making the Firkin an ideal place to enjoy a good drink and relax with friends. Mobile phones are prohibited and their usage incurs a minimum donation of £1 to charity. CAMRA branch Pub of the Year for 2014. Q⇌●🖵

Kipps' Alehouse Ⓛ

11-15 Old High Street, CT20 1RL

✪ 12-10 (11 Fri & Sat) ☎ (01303) 246766

3 changing beers (sourced regionally; often Mad Cat) Ⓖ

Real ale is on gravity dispense from casks racked in a glass-enclosed, cooled stillage. The Alehouse usually keeps a local Kentish ale, an award-winning guest, plus another unusual beer from around the country; when practical, a fourth beer will be tapped to add variety. All ales are sourced from small independent microbreweries. Several ciders are on sale from boxes on the bar counter. Vegetarian food is served most times.
🏠⬤🖕●🖵❀☎

Fordwich

Fordwich Arms Ⓛ

King Street, CT2 0DB

✪ 11-11; 12-11 Sun ☎ (01227) 710444

⊕ fordwicharms.co.uk

Otter Ale; Sharp's Doom Bar; Shepherd Neame Master Brew; 1 changing beer (sourced nationally) Ⓗ

Classic 1930s building opposite the ancient town hall in England's smallest town and overlooking the River Stour. The large bar has a lovely open fireplace and there is a separate oak-panelled dining room. Home-cooked food is served in both areas (no food Sun eve). There are regular themed food evenings including a popular pudding night, which is usually on the second Wednesday of the month – advance booking is essential. A folk club meets every second and fourth Sunday night, and there is live jazz once a month on a summer Sunday afternoon. Q✿⬤⬤🖕⇌P🖵(7,8,9)❀☎

Frittenden

Bell & Jorrocks

Biddenden Road, TN17 2EJ TQ815412

✪ 12 (3 Mon & Tue)-11; 11-11 Sat; 12-10.30 Sun

☎ (01580) 852415 ⊕ thebellandjorrocks.co.uk

Harveys Sussex Best Bitter; Woodforde's Wherry; 2 changing beers (often Dark Star, Rother Valley, Tonbridge) Ⓗ

Originally the Bell, it gained its current name when the other village pub, the John Jorrocks, closed in 1969. The pub sign celebrates both its Whitbread and Fremlins antecedents – one on each side. It serves excellent food and is very much the social centre of the village. A coaching inn dating from the early 18th century, its stables are used for a mid-April beer festival, and it acts as a good base for circular walks in the picturesque Low Weald countryside surrounding the village and for exploring the Frittenden Treacle Mines.
🏠✿⬤Å♣❀☎

Gillingham

Frog & Toad Ø

38 Burnt Oak Terrace, ME7 1DR

✪ 2-11; 12-11 Fri-Sun ☎ (01634) 852231

Fuller's London Pride; 1 changing beer (sourced nationally) Ⓗ

A typical back-street pub with the name reflected in the pub's carpet-patterned motifs. A multitude of beer bottles sit on shelves on the walls of this one-bar local. Outside is a large rear patio area and garden with covered tables and bench seating, ideal for the beer festivals held at various times of the year. Two ales are on offer, with the guest usually from either Cottage or Elgood's breweries. Q✿⇌♣●🖵❀☎

Past & Present Ⓛ

2 Skinner Street, ME7 1HD

✪ 12-7 Mon & Tue (6 Wed; 9 Thu; 11 Fri & Sat); 12-4 Sun ☎ 07725 072293

3 changing beers (sourced nationally) Ⓖ

With a friendly atmosphere, Medway's first micropub goes from strength to strength, and was voted local CAMRA Cider Pub of the Year for 2016. A minimum of three ales and five ciders are served by gravity from a temperature-controlled room, and three third-pint taster boards are available. The pub opens to 6pm on a Sunday in the summer months to take advantage of the enclosed decked rear area, which is a suntrap. Regular beer and cider festivals are held. There is no admittance after 10pm Friday or Saturday. Q🏠✿⇌♣●🖵❀

Will Adams

73 Saxton Street, ME7 5EG

✪ 12.30-4 (not Mon-Fri), 7-11; 12.30-3, 8-11 Sun ☎ (01634) 575902

3 changing beers (sourced regionally; often Dark Star, Oakham, St Austell) Ⓗ

A single-bar local near the high street and railway station – the walls are decorated with painted murals celebrating the adventurer and samurai warrior born in Gillingham. The pub will usually have three ales on handpump from breweries regionally, plus up to four ciders and a perry. It gets especially busy during Gillingham Football Club home games, welcoming away supporters from up and down the country. ✿⬤⇌♣●🖵(116,176)❀☎

Gravesend

Compass Alehouse [L]

7 Manor Road, DA12 1AA

🕐 12-2 (not Tue & Wed), 5-9; 12-2, 5-10 Fri; 12-10 Sat; 1-4 Sun; closed Mon ☎ 07873 918545

4 changing beers (sourced locally; often Goacher's, Kent, Ramsgate) [H]/[G]

Micropub opened in autumn 2014 in a former estate agents' showroom, seating 18 in a small front room, plus standing in an overflow area and a small courtyard to the rear. Up to four real ales are sold, at least one from a Kentish brewery, and four ciders are available from Kent producers. A convivial atmosphere and conversation are paramount, but talking on mobile phones is outlawed, with a fine for charity. Water is always available for our canine friends.
Q🐎❀♿🚆🍎🥛🚌🐾

Jolly Drayman

1 Love Lane, Wellington Street, DA12 1JA

🕐 12-11.30 (midnight Fri & Sat); 12-11 Sun
☎ (01474) 352355 🌐 jollydrayman.com

Dark Star Hophead; St Austell Trelawny; 3 changing beers (sourced nationally; often Skinner's) [H]

Comfortable and cosy pub with a friendly, intimate atmosphere and consistently good ale, to the east end of the town on the site of the former Wellington Brewery. At least four pumps deliver beers, including two regulars. It has quirky low ceilings and feels relaxed, with no gaming machines and a TV that is muted. Daddlums (Kentish skittles) is played on Sundays, as well as regular men's and women's darts matches. Annual beer festivals take place. There is a large outdoor area and a small car park at the front of the pub.
Q🐎❀🛏♿🚆♣P🚌🐾📶

Robert Pocock [L] ✔

181-183 Windmill Street, DA12 1AH

🕐 8am-midnight (1am Fri & Sat) ☎ (01474) 352765

Adnams Ghost Ship, Broadside; Greene King Abbot; Ruddles Best Bitter; Sharp's Doom Bar; 6 changing beers (sourced nationally; often Kent, Long Man, Rockin' Robin) [H]

A large town-centre Wetherspoon outlet, converted from a furniture shop. Robert Pocock brought the first printing press to Gravesend in 1786 and published the History of Gravesend and Milton in 1797 – the first history book of the area. There is seating on two levels, with a balcony above the ground floor. The TVs are muted, showing news. A changing range of well-kept guest beers is served, including local ales, plus two ciders. 🐎◐◑♿🚆🍎🚌🐾📶

Rum Puncheon [L]

87 West Street, DA11 0BL (on one-way system, next to Tilbury ferry)

🕐 11-11; 11-10.30 Sun ☎ (01474) 353434
🌐 rumpuncheon.co.uk

7 changing beers (sourced nationally; often Adnams, Fuller's, Skinner's) [H]

Historic riverside pub within easy reach of the ferry to Tilbury. Real ales from Kentish breweries are strongly featured. TV and gaming machines are absent, there is just background music and conversation. The rear terrace offers a view of the River Thames. In the main bar are a log fire, chandeliers and local and river-related photographs. Home-cooked meals are served at lunchtimes, with light bites on Friday and Saturday evenings. Dog-friendly, but not when food is served. Q🐎❀◐🚆♣P🚌🐾📶

Three Daws [L]

7 Town Pier, DA11 0BJ

🕐 11-11; 12-11 Sun ☎ (01474) 566869 🌐 threedaws.co.uk

6 changing beers (sourced locally; often Millis, Truman's) [H]

The building, formerly a hotel, dates from 1488. The back room and patio provide spectacular views of the town pier and passing river traffic. It was rescued from closure and semi-dereliction by the current owner following years of neglect by Truman's/Grand Met. Once a haven for smugglers, the tastefully restored bar area features a variety of nooks and crannies, behind which there is a network of secret passages and tunnels. The range of six cask ales varies constantly and often features Kent microbreweries. A good selection of value-for-money food is served daily. Quiz night is Sunday. 🐎❀◐◑🚆♣🚌📶

Halstead

Rose & Crown

Otford Lane, TN14 7EA

🕐 12-11.30; 12-10.30 Sun ☎ (01959) 533120

6 changing beers (sourced regionally; often Larkins, Sharp's, Westerham) [H]

Grade II-listed two-bar pub with an attractive flint façade and a restaurant annexe to the side. The bar menu featuring home-cooked food is well priced and booking is recommended for Sunday lunch (no food Mon). The lively front bar has a dartboard, TVs showing sporting events and board games, while the more sedate lounge features a log fire. A secluded rear garden has a children's play area, covered patio and barbecue.
🐎❀◐◑♣P🚌(402,R5)🐾📶

Harvel

Amazon & Tiger [L]

Harvel Street, DA13 0DE

🕐 4 (6 Mon)-11; 12-11 Fri & Sat; 12-10.30 Sun
☎ (01474) 814705
🌐 amazonandtiger-harvel.webeden.co.uk

Kent Session Pale; 3 changing beers (sourced locally; often Hogs Back, Tonbridge, Westerham) [H]

Situated in a remote village close to the North Downs Way and Pilgrims Way, and popular with walkers. Built in 1914, it is on the opposite side of the road to the original pub and was designed to blend in with the village houses. It has two distinct bar areas where modern furnishings combine with flagstones and wood floors, a bar billiards table and a separate TV area. The good range of ales comes mainly from West Kent and East Sussex. The village cricket team can be watched from the garden.
Q🐎❀🛏◐◑⛺♣P🐾📶

Hastingleigh

Bowl Inn [L]

The Street, TN25 5HU TR095449

🕐 5-9 (10 Thu & Fri); 12-10 Sat; 12-9 Sun; closed Mon
☎ (01233) 750354 🌐 thebowlonline.co.uk

3 changing beers (sourced locally) [H]

This lovingly restored, listed village building retains many period features, including a taproom used for playing pool and decorated with vintage advertising material. The lovely garden has a tame European eagle owl. Sandwiches and baguettes are available weekends, and a beer festival is held on August bank holiday Monday. The pub will stay open if custom warrants it or if you phone ahead. The adjacent barn is used for blues and folk music and open mic evenings. Q👶❀◐♣🍏P📶

Herne

Butcher's Arms [L]

29A Herne Street, CT6 7HL (opp church)

🕒 12-1.30, 6-9; 12-2 Sun; closed Mon ☎ (01227) 371000

🌐 micropub.co.uk

Adnams Broadside; Dark Star Hophead; Old Dairy Copper Top; 2 changing beers (sourced locally; often Adnams, Ramsgate) [G]

Britain's first micropub, opened in 2005, is a real ale gem and the inspiration for other micropubs. Once a butcher's shop, it still has the original chopping tables. There is seating for 10 customers and standing room for 20 – the compact drinking area ensuring lively banter. Customers can also buy beer to drink at home. Snack food includes local Ashmore cheeses. The pub has won many CAMRA awards and the landlord was voted one of CAMRA's top 40 campaigners. Q🚌(4,6)🐾

Herne Bay

Bouncing Barrel [L]

20 Bank Street, CT6 5EA

🕒 12-2, 6-9; 12-11 Sat; 12-2 Sun; closed Mon ☎ 07777 630685

4 changing beers (often Goody Ales, Old Dairy, Ramsgate) [G]

Friendly, welcoming micropub with bench seating for 20 customers around old workshop tables. The beer range changes regularly and normally includes up to five beers; there is generally at least one from a Kent brewery. Local snacks are available. The pub is named after the bombs used in the Dam Buster raids, which were tested off the coast nearby. The pub has a mural of a bomber flying past the Reculver Towers. Q👶♿♣🍏🚌🐾

Hildenborough

Plough [L]

Leigh Road, TN11 9AJ (½ mile S of Hildenborough at Powdermills)

🕒 closed Mon-Wed; 12-11; 12-3, 6-11 Sat; 12-9 Sun

☎ (01732) 832149 🌐 theploughatleigh.com

Tonbridge Coppernob; 2 changing beers (sourced locally; often Old Dairy, Rockin' Robin) [H]

Near busy population centres, but a peaceful rural oasis worth the detour. A rustic brick exterior leads to an archetypical olde English pub interior with a low-beamed ceiling liberally decorated with Kentish hops, wooden and flag flooring and an impressive open-sided fireplace. There is an extensive tranquil garden with willows clustered around a stream. The Plough is proud to support local brewers with offerings changing regularly. The stunning Great Barn is popular for weddings and celebrations. Open Wednesdays during spring and summer. Q👶❀◐◑♣P🚌(210)🐾📶

Horton Kirby

Bull [L] ✔

Lombard Street, DA4 9DF

🕒 12-11; 12-10.30 Sun ☎ (01322) 860341

🌐 thebullhortonkirby.co.uk

Dark Star Hophead; Kent Pale; Oakham Citra; 3 changing beers (sourced regionally; often Rockin' Robin, Rudgate) [H]

Comfortable one-bar village local with a large garden affording views across the Darent Valley, 15 minutes' walk from Farningham Road railway station and close to the daytime 414 bus route. This friendly pub has six handpumps with three regular and three rotating guest ales. There are live bands every Saturday night and open mic on the first Friday night of each month.
👶❀◐◑🚆♣🍏🚌(414)🐾📶

Hythe

Potting Shed [L]

160A High Street, CT21 5JR

🕒 12-6 (7 Wed & Thu; 9 Fri & Sat); 12-4 Sun; closed Mon ☎ 07780 877226

4 changing beers (sourced regionally) [G]

A former café which has been converted into a micro-alehouse, retaining the original high service counter. At the Folkestone end of Hythe High Street, it serves an interesting range of ales from around the country including at least one local Kentish beer, usually from Hop Fuzz. Ciders and ales are on gravity except for one ale which is sometimes pulled through a handpump. Limited bar snacks are available. A good place to enjoy a drink and interesting conversation. ❀🍏🚌📶

Three Mariners [L]

37 Windmill Street, CT21 6BH

🕒 4-10 Mon; 12-11 (midnight Fri & Sat); 12-10.30 Sun

☎ (01303) 260406

Young's Bitter; 4 changing beers [H]

Hidden away in a side street not far from the Royal Military Canal, this traditional pub is well worth visiting and an ideal destination after a trip on the narrow gauge Romney Hythe & Dymchurch Railway. Friendly staff and local customers are always happy to have a chat with you. With no food available, it attracts customers due to the quality and selection of real ales and cider; these can be enjoyed in one of the two bars or the outside area that is partly heated. 👶❀🚆♣🍏🚌🐾

Ightham Common

Old House ★

Redwell Lane, Redwell, TN15 9EE (½ mile SW of Ightham village, between A25 and A227) TQ590558

🕒 7-11 (9 Mon & Tue); 12-3, 7-11 Sat & Sun

☎ (01732) 886077

Changing beers (sourced regionally; often Bespoke, Dark Star) [G]

Kentish red-brick, tile-hung cottage, with no pub sign, located in a narrow isolated country lane. The public bar features a Victorian wood-panelled counter, parquet flooring and an imposing inglenook fireplace. The parlour bar is a quiet haven. Up to six rotating beers are dispensed by gravity from the chilled taproom, always including at least one bitter, a golden ale and a dark beer, from a large range of regional breweries. It has a CAMRA designated Nationally Important Historic Interior. Q✿🅰♣🌢P😋 🛜

Ivychurch

Bell Inn 🍷 ⊘

Ashford Road, TN29 0AL (signposted from A2070 between Brenzett and Hamstreet, 1 mile from A259/A2070 roundabout at Brenzett) TR028275
🌍 12-11; 12-10.30 Sun ☎ (01797) 344355
🌐 thebellinnromneymarsh.co.uk
St Austell Trelawny; Sharp's Doom Bar, Atlantic; 2 changing beers 🅷
A warm welcome awaits everyone who visits this pretty 16th-century free house adjacent to St George's Church. Its real ales and beers have won many awards. During the colder months a wood-burning stove adds to the comfortable atmosphere. The Bell Inn is well worth finding and is steeped in marshland history, as it was once the centre of smugglers known as the Romney Marsh Owlers. Local CAMRA Pub of the Year 2016.
🌢✿🕙♣🌢P😋 🛜

Loose

Chequers 🅛

Old Loose Hill, ME15 0BL
🌍 12-11 (11.30 Fri & Sat); 12-10.30 Sun ☎ (01622) 743125
🌐 theloosechequers.com
Fuller's London Pride; Harveys Sussex Best Bitter; Rockin' Robin Reliant Robin; Sharp's Doom Bar; Shepherd Neame Master Brew; 1 changing beer (often Rockin' Robin, Timothy Taylor) 🅷
A former 17th-century coaching inn on the old road to Hastings, tastefully decorated to emphasise original oak beams. It lies snuggled in Loose Valley by the side of a trout stream and in the shadow of a Brunel road bridge. Traditional home-cooked food is served including vegetarian options. Live music is played monthly and there is an annual duck race on the river. 🌢✿🕙♿P🚌(5,89)😋

Lower Halstow

Three Tuns 🅛

The Street, ME9 7DY
🌍 12-11 (midnight Fri & Sat); 12-10.30 Sun
☎ (01795) 842840 🌐 thethreetunsrestaurant.co.uk
Goacher's Real Mild Ale; 3 changing beers (sourced locally; often Caveman, Hop Fuzz, Wantsum) 🅷
True family village pub with a friendly, cheerful atmosphere and lively conversation. The owners actively support real ale, offering mainly Kentish ales and several local ciders, including Dudda's Tun. It has a good reputation for food and has won many awards. Two beer festivals are held each year during the summer bank holiday and in December. A log fire, sofa seating, brick walls and beams add character. It has a large garden with stream-side decking. 🌢✿🕙♿♣🌢P🚌😋🛜

Luddesdown

Cock Inn 🍷 🅛 ⊘

Henley Street, DA13 0XB (1 mile SE of Sole Street station) TQ664672

🌍 12-11; 12-10.30 Sun ☎ (01474) 814208
🌐 cockluddesdowne.com
Adnams Lighthouse, Southwold Bitter, Broadside; Goacher's Real Mild Ale; St Austell Trelawny; Young's Bitter; 2 changing beers (sourced regionally; often Musket) 🅷
Traditional rural free house dating from 1713, under the same ownership since 1984, with two separate bars, a large conservatory, function room and a comfortable heated smoking area. It is used as a meeting place for many local clubs and societies. Traditional pub games are played including pétanque, bar billiards and several forms of darts. There is a free quiz on Tuesday evenings devised and hosted by the landlord. No children are allowed in the bars or garden. Local CAMRA branch Pub of the Year 2015, and now 2016.
Q✿🕙♣P🛢😋

Maidstone

Flower Pot 🅛

96 Sandling Road, ME14 2RJ
🌍 12-11; 11-11 Sat; 12-10.30 Sun ☎ (01622) 757705
🌐 flowerpotpub.com
Goacher's Gold Star Strong Ale; 9 changing beers (sourced nationally; often Dark Star, Maidstone, Oakham) 🅷
Split-level street-corner free house, a must-visit when in Maidstone. The upper bar has 10 handpumps, with the ales coming mainly from microbreweries. Up to four ciders and perries are served directly from the container. The lower bar has a pool table and there are video screens showing the beers on offer and the price. The football ground is nearby. There are music nights every other Saturday and jam nights on Tuesdays. A beer festival is held in June.
✿🕙🚉(East)♣🌢🛢🚌(101,155)😋🛜

Olde Thirsty Pig 🅛 ⊘

4a Knightrider Street, ME15 6LP
🌍 12-1am (2am Fri; 3am Sat) ☎ (01622) 299283
🌐 thethirstypig.co.uk
4 changing beers (sourced locally; often Mad Cat, Musket, Rockin' Robin) 🅷
A 15th-century street-corner pub that is Grade II-listed, with original beams, low ceilings and tucked-away rooms throughout. Outside, there is a heated and covered courtyard area. The bar contains four handpumps dispensing ales mainly from Kent microbreweries. Draught local cider is also served. There is an array of bottled beers to choose from, including several foreign ones. Keep your eyes open for unusual gaming tournaments.
✿♣🛢🚌😋🛜

Rifle Volunteers 🍷 🅛

28 Wyatt Street, ME14 1EU
🌍 12-3 (not Mon), 6-11; 12-6 Sun ☎ (01622) 758891
Goacher's Real Mild Ale, Fine Light Ale, Gold Star Strong Ale; 1 changing beer (sourced locally; often Goacher's) 🅷
New management has vowed to maintain the stone-built street-corner pub's distinctive charms, where conversation still rules, and it is current CAMRA branch Pub of the Year. It is a tied house, and has been identified by CAMRA as having a regionally important historic pub interior. The addition of a fourth pump in the single-bar venue allows a wider range of Goacher's brews. A popular fun quiz is run fortnightly, alternating in winter

with a local quiz league. Toy Greek soldiers or regulars' own figures mark one in the wood for prepaid drinks. Snacks are made to order. Q❀⇌(East)♣●🚌📶

Society Rooms ✔

Brenchley House, Week Street, ME14 1RF

7am-midnight (1am Fri & Sat) ☎ (01622) 350910

Greene King Abbot; Ruddles Best Bitter; Sharp's Doom Bar; 7 changing beers (sourced nationally; often Old Dairy, Rockin' Robin, Wantsum) H

A spacious Wetherspoon pub on the site of a former local newspaper printing works, situated on the ground floor of a five-storey office block. The mainly glass external walls allow panoramic views of the pedestrian shopping street alongside. A large covered outside space is split into smoking and non-smoking areas. The name is taken from William Shipley, founder of the Royal Society of Arts and the Maidstone Society for Promoting Useful Knowledge, who is buried nearby. Food is served 7am-11pm.
Q❀◐◑♿⇌(East)♣●🚌(101,155)📶

Marden

Marden Village Club L

Albion Road, TN12 9DT

6 (5 Fri)-11; 12-3, 7-11 Sat & Sun ☎ (01622) 831427

mardenvillageclub.co.uk

3 changing beers (sourced regionally) H

Four real ales are offered at this club; three change regularly and are generally from local microbreweries. The club is the community hub, with regular entertainment on Saturday evenings. Many members are followers of football and rugby on the TV and are also involved in the club's snooker and darts teams; others simply enjoy the friendly ambience. Voted CAMRA branch Club of the Year 2015. Card-carrying CAMRA members are welcome but regular visitors will be required to join. ♿♣●🐾📶

Stile Bridge L ✔

Staplehurst Road, TN12 9BH (on A229 just before jct with B2079)

11-11; 12-8 Sun ☎ (01622) 831236

thestilebridge.co.uk

Goacher's Special House Ale; 4 changing beers (often Dark Star, Musket, Rockin' Robin) H

A friendly free house with an impressive array of cask ale plus an extensive bottle selection. It has a good mixture of drinking and dining areas decorated with pub memorabilia, plus a refurbished restaurant which is fine for private functions and parties. The food is popular, as are the live music and comedy nights which feature several times a year. A large paved area at the rear is pleasant in warmer weather. Voted local CAMRA Pub of the Year 2014. ❀◐◑●P🚌(5)

Margate

Harbour Arms

Margate Harbour Arm, Stone Pier, CT9 1AP

12-10 (11 Fri & Sat); 12-9.30 Sun ☎ 07776 183273

harbourarmsmargate.co.uk

4 changing beers G

This pub moved into a larger unit on the stone pier in 2015, having previously been located in two fishermen's net stores knocked into one. Its walls are adorned with a variety of nautically themed items, with a fishing net hanging from the ceiling. The beers, served direct from the cask, are housed in a cool room at the side of the building. The pub does not have a toilet and patrons are asked to use the public ones next door. Q⇌♣●P🚌(56)🐾

Two Halves

2 Marine Drive, CT9 1DH

3-10.30; 12-10.30 Fri-Sun ☎ 07538 771904

3 changing beers G

Small and welcoming micropub in a superb location on Margate's seafront. The beers supplied are from all regions of the country and are regularly changed, under the watchful eye of a landlord who knows his ale. No matter what the weather, this micropub has a great aspect; admire sunsets out of the window or just watch the world go by. The beer and cider are kept in immaculate condition in a large stillage room. Look out for the old-fashioned postcards in the loo. Q⇌●🚌(56)🐾

Mersham

Farriers Arms L

The Forstal, TN25 6NU (through Mersham village turn right into Church Rd; pub is on left after approx ½ mile)

12-midnight; 11-1am Fri & Sat; 11-11.30 Sun

☎ (01233) 720444 thefarriersarms.com

Farriers Arms Farriers 1606; 3 changing beers H

Community-owned Grade II-listed free house and restaurant which dates back to 1606, providing a warm village welcome and offering a wide selection of real ales. These include those brewed in its own five-barrel microbrewery. The house beer is Farriers 1606 and seasonal ales are regularly on offer. The annual beer festival is usually held in late May, and many other events take place throughout the year, from murder mysteries to firework displays and vintage vehicle meets. Food is available at the Barn in Anvil restaurant. ❀◐◑♿♣P🚌(125)🐾📶

Milton Regis

Three Hats ✔

93 High Street, ME10 2AR

12-11; 12-10.30 Sun ☎ (01795) 427645

4 changing beers (sourced nationally; often Dartmoor, Purity, St Austell) H

Popular and friendly local in historic Milton Regis. The open-plan interior has low beams and a large rear lounge bar area. The landlord serves a selection of national beers from the Enterprise range, including ales rarely available in this part of Kent from breweries such as Dartmoor and Windsor & Eton. The pub hosts a number of darts teams and holds regular charity events. Pub food is available at lunchtimes. Local CAMRA Pub of the Year 2014. ❀◐●🚌(347)🐾📶

Minster-in-Thanet

Hair of the Dog

73 High Street, CT12 4AB

12-9; 12-3 Sun ☎ 07885 362326 hairofthedogpub.co.uk

3 changing beers G

This micropub, previously a dog groomer's, offers a warm welcome on a village high street. It usually has three real ales and at least three ciders, all served from the cask in a cool room directly off the bar. The furniture is rustic, with a mix of high and low seating and tables, where you can play old games such as shove-ha'penny or try and crack some of the puzzles left out. Dogs are still welcome. Q ⚲ ⇆ ♣ ● ᗌ (11,42)❀

Oare

Castle
2 The Street, ME13 0PY
⚙ 11-3, 6.30-11; 11-11 Fri & Sat; 12-8 Sun
☎ (01795) 533674
Shepherd Neame Master Brew; 2 changing beers (sourced nationally; often Brains, Greene King, Harveys) Ⓗ
Large free house on a corner of the main street next to Oare Creek, near Faversham. The pub dates from the 17th century and has been licensed since 1698. It has a restaurant area and a pleasant garden. It also has a bat and trap pitch and is home to four darts teams. ⚲❀◑♣Pᗌ❀

Offham

Kings Arms Ⓛ
Teston Road, ME19 5NR
⚙ 12-midnight ☎ (01732) 845208
⊕ kingsarmsoffham.co.uk
6 changing beers (often Kent, Musket, Tonbridge) Ⓗ
Originally two 16th-century farm cottages, the pub has two areas for drinking and another for the restaurant. The left bar area is used as a sports bar with a variety of games, while the main area enjoys a warm atmosphere and serves ales from many Kent microbreweries. The pub holds beer festivals periodically and has live music monthly. Home-made pies are a speciality, with Thai food served on Friday and Saturday evenings plus roasts every Sunday. Jam nights are held on a Thursday. Q ⚲❀◑♣Pᗌ(70)❀ 🛜

Petham

Chequers Ⓛ
Stone Street, CT4 5PW
⚙ 12-3 (not Mon), 6-11; 12-4, 7-10.30 Sun
☎ (01227) 700734 ⊕ thechequersinn.wordpress.com
Dark Star Hophead; Oakham Citra; 1 changing beer (often Old Dairy, St Austell, Sharp's) Ⓖ
On the Roman road from Canterbury to Hythe, the Chequers was built in 1898. The bar has comfortable leather sofas. A spacious dining area and restaurant is at the back, with a tempting menu including a popular carvery on Sunday lunchtime and Wednesday evening. Darts and bar billiards are played. Up to six beers are served at busy times. Mini beer festivals featuring Kent microbreweries are planned.
⚲❀◑ ♣ ● P ᗌ (620,18)

Petteridge

Hopbine
Petteridge Lane, TN12 7NE (1 mile W of Brenchley)
⚙ 12-2.30, 5-11; 12-11 Fri-Sun ☎ (01892) 722561
⊕ thehopbine.pub

Long Man Best Bitter; Tonbridge Traditional Ale; 2 changing beers (sourced locally; often Dark Star, Isfield) Ⓗ
A unique and compact country pub in this hamlet, serving four ales and one real cider and well worth a visit. It is accessible by car, bus, or on foot as a walking destination. The food offering is mainly home-cooked wood-fired pizzas, but ploughman's and hot bar snacks are also available. The recently extended patio, decking and lawn serve as an attractive and inviting area for alfresco drinking and dining in quiet rural surroundings.
Q ⚲❀◑ ♣ ● P ᗌ (297)❀ 🛜

Pluckley

Rose & Crown ✅
Mundy Bois Road, Mundy Bois, TN27 0ST (off the beaten track between Pluckley, Egerton and Smarden) TQ908455
⚙ 12-11; 12-10.30 Sun ☎ (01233) 840048
⊕ theroseandcrownpluckley.co.uk
Harveys Sussex Best Bitter; Whitstable Native Bitter; 1 changing beer Ⓗ
Tile-hung 17th-century pub combining the warmth of a traditional Kentish country free house with a first-class restaurant, lying in farmland in the heart of the Weald of Kent; there are many good walks to be enjoyed nearby. The Village Bar is hop-entwined and has a welcoming fire; the saloon also features an open fire. The 1989 Guinness World Records names Pluckley the most haunted village in England, with 12 ghosts. ⚲❀◑P❀ 🛜

Ramsgate

Artillery Arms
36 Westcliff Road, CT11 9JS
⚙ 12-11 (midnight Fri-Sun) ☎ (01843) 853202
5 changing beers Ⓗ
Celebrated alehouse a short walk from the town, attracting a diverse clientele. The lower bar area with stairs leads to an upper area with more seating. The landlord maintains a long tradition of stocking a carefully considered range of real ales. Handpumps serve a selection of beers from Kent and around the country. Interesting old painted windows depict battle scenes and the theme is continued with displays of other militaria. ♣ᗌ❀

Conqueror Alehouse
4c Grange Road, CT11 9LR (on corner of St Mildred's Road)
⚙ 11.30-2.30, 5.30-9.30; 12-3 Sun; closed
Mon ☎ 07890 203282 ⊕ conqueror-alehouse.co.uk
3 changing beers Ⓖ
Welcoming award-winning micropub with room for about 20 customers and offering a cosy and pleasant environment. Seating is at high tables and along a wall counter. Three changing real ales are mainly local, and are served straight from the cask, as is a local cider. It is named after a two-funnelled paddle steamer that operated excursions from the town in the early 1900s, pictures of which adorn the walls. Q ⬥ ♣ ● ᗌ (34,9)❀

Hovelling Boat Inn
12 York Street, CT11 9DS
⚙ 11.30-7 (9 Wed & Thu; 10 Fri & Sat); 12-4 Sun; 11.30-9 (10 Fri & Sat); 12-4 Sun summer ☎ 07974 613030
⊕ hovellingboatinn.co.uk

4 changing beers G

Sympathetic conversion from a shop to micropub in a handy town-centre location; it was to have had another name until the landlord discovered it had originally been the Hovelling Boat pub that ceased trading in 1909. With exposed brickwork displaying breweriana, it offers up to four different beers from Kent and beyond served at customers' tables by friendly staff. Local cider along with wine, cold snacks, tea and coffee are also sold. Q ⏳ ⊛ ♠ ⊟ ♣

Montefiore Arms

1 Trinity Place, CT11 7HJ

🕒 12-2.30 (not Wed), 5.30-11; 12-11 Sat; 12-3, 7-10.30 Sun
☎ (01843) 593265 ⊕ montefiorearms.co.uk
Ramsgate Gadds' No.7 Bitter Ale; 4 changing beers H

Award-winning traditional back-street local enjoying a good reputation with real ale drinkers in the Thanet area. The pub's name and sign are unique, honouring the great Jewish financier and philanthropist Sir Moses Montefiore, who lived locally for many years. Now under the personal control of Eddie Gadd of nearby Ramsgate Brewery, the pub showcases its beers along with changing guest ales and Biddenden cider. ♣ ♠ ⊟ (38,39) 🔊

Rochester

Britannia Bar Café L

376 High Street, ME1 1DJ (midway between Chatham town centre and Rochester Star Hill)

🕒 10-11 (9 Mon); 12-9 Sun ☎ (01634) 815204
⊕ britannia-bar-cafe.co.uk
Goacher's Fine Light Ale; 2 changing beers (sourced nationally; often Caledonian) H

Within reasonable walking distance of both Rochester and Chatham town centres, in what is turning into the creative and cultural hub of Medway, this stylish corner establishment successfully mixes a traditional pub bar with a vibrant and popular eatery. Late breakfasts start at 10am and the extensive menu continues through to evening, via lunchtime specials and bar snacks. Occasional special food evenings are held and it does popular Sunday roasts. There is a small walled garden at the rear. Q ⏳ ⊛ ⏲ ⇌ ⊟ (145) ♣

Coopers Arms

10 St Margaret Street, ME1 1TL

🕒 12-11 (midnight Fri & Sat) ☎ (01634) 404298
⊕ thecoopersarms.co.uk
Courage Best Bitter; house beer (by Tonbridge); 5 changing beers (sourced regionally) H

Promoting itself as the oldest pub in Kent, this two-bar town house, a couple of minutes from the busy High Street, is a thriving outlet for regional ales and quality food. Meals are served only at lunchtimes, with Sunday roasts ever popular. Under-fives are not allowed unless with adults eating. It has a well-kept small garden with limited parking at the rear of the building. ⊛ ⏲ ⇌ ⊟ ♣ 🔊

Eagle Tavern ✓

124 High Street, ME1 1JT

🕒 12-midnight (9 Mon; 11 Tue); 12-8 Sun ☎ (01634) 409040
⊕ theeagletavern.org.uk
St Austell Tribute, Proper Job; Sharp's Doom Bar, Atlantic; 4 changing beers (sourced nationally) H

Seen as Rochester's premier music pub venue, the Eagle hosts jam nights on a Wednesday, bands on Thursday evenings and jazz on Sunday lunchtimes. In the heart of historic Rochester High Street, it is a

lot quieter during the day. The single-room hostelry is situated opposite a large public car park and the garden at the rear gives splendid views of the old city wall. Food is available lunchtimes (not Sun). ⊛ ⏲ ♿ ⇌ ⊟

Good Intent

3 John Street, ME1 1YL

🕒 12-midnight ☎ (01634) 843118
3 changing beers (sourced nationally) G

Regular beer festivals are held in this two-bar, back-street town house. Up to three ales are served by gravity from racking in the main bar. Entrance to the small back bar is via the garden. There is a lively, friendly atmosphere, with music events held a minimum of once a month. The monthly quiz is also popular. A lively free house, worth seeking out. Q ⊛ ♣ ♠ ⊟ ♣ 🔊

Man of Kent Ale House L

6-8 John Street, ME1 1YN (200yds off A2 from bottom of Star Hill)

🕒 2 (3 Mon)-11; 12-11 Sat & Sun ☎ 07772 214315
Goacher's Gold Star Strong Ale; 10 changing beers (sourced locally) H

This wonderful outlet keeps evolving, getting better all the time. It is renowned for the Kentish theme to its ales, ciders and wines, and has now added Kent gin and vodka to the range. Pizzas are occasionally available as a bar snack. As a live music venue it can get very busy. There is a small enclosed garden area for smokers which is a suntrap for the summer. ⊛ ⇌ ♣ ♠ ⏲ ⊟

Two Brewers

113 High Street, ME1 1JS

🕒 11-11 (midnight Fri & Sat); 12-7.30 Sun
☎ (01634) 812448 ⊕ twobrewersrochester.com
Shepherd Neame Master Brew, Whitstable Bay Pale Ale, Spitfire; 1 changing beer (sourced regionally) H

Sited in the tourist heart of Rochester High Street, this outlet is a small back-street pub frequented by local residents. There has been an inn on this site since 1683 during the reign of Charles II. It is convenient for the castle and cathedral, Huguenot Museum and other attractions. It has background piped music and occasional TV (for major sporting events only). Despite its size, live music is staged every Sunday at 4pm. ⇌ ⊟ ♣

Who'd Ha' Thought It

9 Baker Street, ME1 3DN

🕒 12-11 (9 Tue); 12.30-11 Sun ☎ (01634) 830144
⊕ whodha.co.uk
3 changing beers (sourced nationally) H

A friendly back-street local off Rochester's Maidstone road, this outlet offers three rotating ales. It has a wood-panelled bar with a traditional bell for last orders. A log fire keeps it cosy, alongside a large satellite TV for showing sporting events. A small snug bar is to the rear of the pub. The range of events held includes regular quiz nights, comedy club and curry evenings. There is a well-maintained garden where regular beer festivals are held. ⏳ ⊛ ♣ ⊟ (134,155) ♣ 🔊

Ryarsh

Duke of Wellington L ✓

The Street, ME19 5LS

🕒 11-11; 12-10.30 Sun ☎ (01732) 842318
⊕ dukeofwellingtonryarsh.com

Harveys Sussex Best Bitter; Westerham Grasshopper Kentish Bitter; 2 changing beers (often Kent, Portobello) Ⓗ
A 16th-century pub in the village centre, welcoming to ramblers. The main bar is to the left while the restaurant to the right features a varied menu plus Sunday roasts. Fireplaces in both bars provide winter warmth. A covered and heated patio with tables opens onto the garden and overlooks the pétanque piste. In front, an area with tables provides additional space. A popular jazz evening is held the first Thursday of each month, and every other Sunday evening is quiz night.
Q🕏🏵🕽🕽♣Pᗡ(58)🐾🕏

St Peter's

Four Candles Alehouse
1 Sowell Street, CT10 2AT
✪ 5-10.30 (11.30 Fri); 12-3.30, 5-11.30 Sat; 12-3.30, 5-10.30 Sun ☎ 07947 062063 ⊕ thefourcandles.co.uk
3 changing beers Ⓖ
A former shop now firmly cemented on the local micropub scene and renowned for its friendly atmosphere. Seating is provided at high bench tables, while the beer is served from a cooled cabinet in an adjacent room. The pub has its own microbrewery in the cellar, which supplies excellent one-off beers to complement the offerings from other brewers. In the warmer weather benches bask in the sunshine.
Q≅🕽ᗡ(56)🐾

Yard of Ale 🏆
61 Church Street, CT10 2TU
✪ 5-11; 12-11 Sat & Sun ☎ 07790 730205
3 changing beers Ⓖ
Attractive rustic stable converted into a unique micropub in a village location. It is adorned with hops and old riding equipment; seating varies from high stools to straw bales, and there is a wood-burning stove for the colder months. It is family- and dog-friendly and has a strong link to the community. The outside yard is a suntrap, with a large seating area; a canopy and heaters are available for inclement weather. It offers a wide-ranging selection of ales and cider. Finalist for 2016 CAMRA National Pub of the Year. Q🕏🏵♣🕽ᗡ🐾

Sandgate

Ship Inn Ⓛ
65 Sandgate High Street, CT20 3AH (on A259)
✪ 11.30-11.30 (12.30am Fri & Sat) ☎ (01303) 248525
Dark Star Hophead, American Pale Ale; Greene King IPA, Abbot; Hop Back Summer Lightning; Hopdaemon Incubus Ⓗ; 2 changing beers Ⓖ
Narrow corner pub incorporating the Amazing Brewery, fronting onto the High Street and backing onto the beach. In part dating from 1798, it has a front bar and a back room, plus a restaurant with sea views. Upstairs, there is a top deck for drinkers. Nautical maps and pictures featured on the walls reflect the landlord's naval and military interests. Biddenden and guest ciders are always available and an August bank holiday beer festival is held.
🛏🕽🕽ᗡ

Sandling

Yew Tree
Grange Lane, ME14 3DB (down Boarley Lane, bear right, continue; on right just before going under M20)
TQ757584
✪ 12-11 (12-3, 5.30-11 winter); 12-midnight Fri & Sat; 12-6 Sun; closed Mon ☎ (01622) 752882
⊕ theyewtreesandling.co.uk
Dark Star Hophead; St Austell Tribute, Proper Job; Young's Bitter; 1 changing beer Ⓗ
A former cottage dating from 1782 that lies in the shadow of the M20 and is accessed via a narrow lane. The nearest bus stop, at Ringlestone, is an easy 15-minute walk. The homely bar has red quarry tiles on the floor while the popular restaurant is carpeted. Bar food is available throughout the day on Friday and Saturday. Bookings for the restaurant are advisable. Open all day in the summer months. 🕏🏵🕽🕽♣P🐾🕏

Sandwich

Crispin Inn Ⓛ ✅
4 High Street, CT13 9EA
✪ 11-11; 12-10.30 Sun ☎ (01304) 621967
⊕ sandwichpubs.co.uk
Adnams Broadside; Sharp's Doom Bar; house beer (by Mad Cat); 1 changing beer Ⓗ
Ancient public house by the medieval barbican and toll bridge. Low ceilings, wooden beams and brick walls create a congenial ambience. Relax by the window and watch the world go by, or sit in the back courtyard overlooking the river. Two or three real ales feature alongside its house ale from the Mad Cat Brewery. Real cider is from Westons or Thatchers. A good range of home-made food and snacks usually includes Caribbean specialities, for example goat curry. Regular live music events are held. 🕏🏵🕽🕽♿▲≅♣🕽🐾🕏

George & Dragon Ⓛ ✅
24 Fisher Street, CT13 9EJ
✪ 11-11; 11-4.30 Sun ☎ (01304) 613106
⊕ georgeanddragon-sandwich.co.uk
Otter Amber; 3 changing beers (often Butcombe, Wantsum) Ⓗ
A 15th-century pub and restaurant tucked away in the back streets of this Cinque Port, just a few minutes' walk from the town centre, bus and railway services. Inside, the wood-floored bar area with its beamed ceilings and real fire provide a welcoming and relaxed atmosphere. Wantsum Brewery features in the selection of real ales. The restaurant's varied menu is complemented by home-made bar snacks. A small rear courtyard offers a pleasant place to sit in summer.
🕏🏵🕽🕽▲≅🕽🐾🕏

King's Arms Hotel
63 Strand Street, CT13 9HN
✪ 11.30-11 ☎ (01304) 617330 ⊕ kingsarms-sandwich.co.uk
Harveys Sussex Best Bitter; 1 changing beer (sourced nationally; often Greene King, Sharp's) Ⓗ
A 16th-century Grade II-listed inn providing a warm welcome and great service. Although refurbished over the centuries, it still retains its original charm and character. The main lounge bar has an open fire with hops hanging from the ceiling. While popular with diners, drinkers are made welcome. The extensive menu features home-made food

cooked with locally sourced ingredients, including fresh fish. Occasional live music events are held in summer. The paved patio and walled garden provide a pleasant place to sit in the summer. ⛲❀✿❍⊕▲P➱☺✿

Red Cow ⒧
12 Moat Sole, CT13 9AU
✪ 11-11 ☎ (01304) 613399
Sharp's Doom Bar; 5 changing beers ℍ
You cannot miss the large red cow on the front of this timber-framed building which was used by market traders in years gone by. Its tiled floors and exposed beams give it a comfortable and traditional country-pub ambience. Up to six ales are on the bar including one usually from the Ramsgate Brewery, and cider is from Broomfield. There are areas for drinkers, diners and bar billiards players, and there is a pleasant suntrap garden. Quiz night is every Sunday and there is a TV for major sporting events. ⛲❀❍⊕▲♣●P➱☺✿

Sevenoaks

Anchor
32 London Road, TN13 1AS
✪ 11-3, 6-11; 10.30-11 Fri; 10.30-4.30, 7-11 Sat; 12-11 Sun
☎ (01732) 454898 ⊕ anchorsevenoaks.co.uk
Harveys Sussex Best Bitter; house beer (by Turners); 1 changing beer (sourced nationally; often Dark Star) ℍ
This lively town-centre community pub is presided over by cheerful Barry, who has been the landlord for 37 years. High-quality real ales, which now include the house beer, Pride of Sevenoaks, are complemented by good, keenly priced traditional pub food, which is now served every day. The loyal customer base is supplemented by local shoppers and patrons of the nearby Stag Theatre and cinema. Other draws include quiz and poker evenings and live blues and open mic events most Wednesday nights. ⊕♣➱☺

White Hart ⒧
Tonbridge Road, TN13 1SG (1 mile S of town centre)
✪ 11.30 (11 Sat)-11; 11-10.30 Sun ☎ (01732) 452022
⊕ whitehart-sevenoaks.co.uk
Harveys Sussex Best Bitter; Old Dairy Blue Top; house beer (by Phoenix); 4 changing beers (sourced nationally; often Timothy Taylor, Titanic, Westerham) ℍ
Bustling, extensive coaching inn with dining predominant but nevertheless welcoming to drinkers. The large menu applies to food and beer choice, with three regular ales plus four to five guests, often from UK microbreweries – third-pint taster boards are available for the indecisive. Food and drink festivals are organised through the year, where beer and cider feature prominently. Low ceilings and subdued lighting create a cosy atmosphere in which to find a quiet nook to read, play board games or warm by the four real fires. Q⛲❀❍⊕♣P➱(402)☺✿

Sevenoaks Weald

Windmill ⚑ ⒧
1 Windmill Road, TN14 6PN
✪ 12 (5 Mon)-11; 12-9 Sun ☎ (01732) 463330
Larkins Traditional Ale; 5 changing beers (sourced nationally; often Brewsters, Rockin' Robin, Sambrook's) ℍ

One of the best pubs in Kent and recently a finalist for the national CAMRA Pub of the Year award. Matthew takes pride in sourcing a varying range of six beers of different styles and strengths alongside three Kentish ciders, imported draught lager and international bottled beer. Renowned for the quality of food served in a traditional pub atmosphere, it is often advisable to book (no food Mon). The adjoining patio garden, adorned with floral displays, is an enticing space to enjoy your drinks in warm weather. Q⛲❀❍⊕▲♣●➱(401,402)✿✿

Shadoxhurst

King's Head ⒧ ✓
Woodchurch Road, TN26 1LQ
✪ 11.30-3, 6-11; 11.30-4, 6-11 Sun; closed Mon
☎ (01233) 732243
Shepherd Neame Master Brew, Spitfire; 3 changing beers (often Shepherd Neame) ℍ
Shadoxhurst dates from the 13th century and has a parish church with lancet windows. The many footpaths and woods around the area offer many interesting walks. The pub building dates back in part to 1580 and retains some fine architectural features, notably the old porch with the family crest of the original owners. It is a spacious, typical country inn with historic charm, catering for the local community and visitors. Closed on Mondays except bank holidays. ⛲❀❍⊕♿▲♣P➱(2A)☺

Sissinghurst

Milk House ⒧
The Street, TN17 2JG
✪ 9am-11 (midnight Fri & Sat) ☎ (01580) 720200
⊕ themilkhouse.co.uk
Harveys Sussex Best Bitter; 1 changing beer (sourced regionally; often Dark Star, Old Dairy) ℍ
Large, light and airy inn with accommodation available, close to the National Trust gardens at Sissinghurst (formerly Mylkehouse Street) Castle. The building is open plan and wheelchair friendly with wooden floors throughout. The bar to the right has a frontage of woven hurdles. Food features significantly, with classic pub fare served in the bar and restaurant and fine dining in the restaurant only. A grazing menu is available at any time to enjoy in front of the Tudor fireplace in winter or on the terrace in summer. ⛲❀❍⊕♿P➱(5)☺✿

Sittingbourne

Golden Hope ✓
The Court House, 1 Park Road, ME10 1DR
✪ 8am-midnight (1am Fri & Sat) ☎ (01795) 476791
Greene King Abbot; Ruddles Best Bitter; Sharp's Doom Bar; 5 changing beers (sourced nationally; often Batemans, Shepherd Neame, Wantsum) ℍ
Opened in 2015, this Wetherspoon has been converted from the old magistrates' court and police station. Some original features remain, including the old cells, which have been converted into small dining areas. The pub's name derives from a Thames sailing barge built on the nearby creek. It has one main bar area and several smaller seating areas. There are front and rear patios; smoking is allowed on the rear one. Disabled access is via Park Road. Q⛲❀❍⊕♿●➱☺✿

Paper Mill 🍷 Ⓛ

2 Charlotte Street, ME10 2JN (N of Sittingbourne station, almost in Milton Regis, at corner of Church St and Charlotte St)
🕒 12-2 (not Mon-Thu), 5-9; 12-9 Sat; 12-6 Sun ☎ 07927 073584 🌐 thepapermillmicropub.co.uk
Goacher's Real Mild Ale; 3 changing beers (sourced locally; often Goacher's, Kent, Wantsum) Ⓖ
The first micropub to open in Swale is located close to Sittingbourne town centre and railway station. The Paper Mill is a one-room pub with bench seating around four large wooden tables. Local beers feature alongside national beers such as Blue Monkey and Redwillow, and there is a range of Dudda's Tun ciders available. Occasional events such as food tasting and pub quizzes take place. Opening hours are flexible with advance notice. Local CAMRA Pub of the Year 2015 and now 2016.
Q♿🚲&♿🚆♣♿🍴🚆(334,347)♨

Snargate

Red Lion ★ Ⓛ

TN29 9UQ (on B2080, 1 mile NW of Brenzett) TQ990285
🕒 12-3, 7-11; 12-3, 7-10.30 Sun; closed Mon
☎ (01797) 344648
4 changing beers Ⓖ
Superb multi-room 16th-century smugglers' pub which has been in the same family for over 100 years and is universally known as Doris's. Decorated with posters from the 1940s and the Women's Land Army, it has a nationally important historic pub interior. It serves four or five guest beers, at least one of which is from Goacher's. Food is limited to basic bar snacks. A beer festival is held in June, with a mini festival in October.
Q🏡♣♿🍴🚆(11B)♨

South Darenth

Queen Ⓛ

58-62 New Road, DA4 9AR
🕒 2-11; 12-11.30 Sat; 12-10.30 Sun ☎ (01322) 862430
Greene King Abbot; Kent Session Pale; 2 changing beers (sourced nationally; often Dark Star, Hook Norton, Kent) Ⓗ
Friendly community back-street local within walking distance of Farningham Road railway station. Extended in 1998 to incorporate a former shop, it has two separate bars, one a sports bar adorned with memorabilia of London football teams, the other a traditional, quieter saloon bar. It is a genuine free house, promoting beers from Kent Brewery and other independent suppliers. Free bar food is available Sunday lunchtimes. Children are welcome until 8.30pm. The pub has a garden/patio area. 🏡🍴♣♿🍴🚆(414)♨🌐

Stalisfield Green

Plough Inn Ⓛ

Stalisfield Road, ME13 0HY
🕒 12-3, 6 (5 Fri)-11; 12-11 Sat; 12-6 Sun; closed Mon
☎ (01795) 890256 🌐 theploughinnstalisfield.co.uk
House beer (by Musket); 3 changing beers (sourced locally; often Musket, Old Dairy, Whitstable) Ⓗ
Grade II-listed family-run country pub serving local beers, wines and cider and located high on the North Downs. Two miles from Charing and close to the A20, the Plough has wonderful views over

farmland. It offers a seasonal and changing food menu, sourcing ingredients locally whenever possible. Biddenden's Bushels cider is available on handpump. The pub is frequented by walkers and cyclists. A family-friendly garden is popular in the summer and a real fire adds character.
Q♿🏡🍴♿&▲♿P🚆(660)♨

Staplehurst

Lord Raglan Ⓛ

Chart Hill Road, TN12 0DE (½ mile N of A229 at Cross at Hand) TQ786472
🕒 12-3, 6.30-11; closed Sun ☎ (01622) 843747
Goacher's Fine Light Ale; Harveys Sussex Best Bitter; 1 changing beer (sourced locally; often Musket, Tonbridge, Westerham) Ⓗ
A long-standing entry, this popular and unspoilt free house retains the atmosphere of a country pub from bygone days. The bar is hung with hops and warmed by two log fires and a stove. The large orchard garden catches the evening sun. Excellent snacks and full meals are always available. The guest beer changes regularly and Westons perry and local Double Vision cider are sold. Well-behaved children and dogs are welcome. A short walk from the No.5 bus stop on the A229.
Q🏡🍴♿P♨🌐

Strood

10:50 From Victoria

Rear of 37 North Street, ME2 4SJ
🕒 4-9; 1-10.30 Fri & Sat; closed Sun ☎ 07941 449137
🌐 1050fromvictoria.co.uk
Grainstore Ten Fifty Ⓖ**; 6 changing beers (sourced nationally)** Ⓗ/Ⓖ
Justly popular micropub opened in 2015 in a railway arch at the rear of the ASDA car park. The name relates to the Network Rail arch number, rather than a real or imagined train time, and the place is full of railway memorabilia and bric-a-brac. It has wall-mounted internal bench seating plus a large outside decked area which is very pleasant on nice summer days, and a log-burning stove to keep warm in winter. No children permitted either in the pub or outside area. Q🏡&🚆♿P🚆(191)♨

Swanscombe

George & Dragon Ⓛ

1 London Road, DA10 0LQ
🕒 12 (4 Mon & Tue)-11; 12-10.30 Sun ☎ (01322) 386440
🌐 georgedragonswanscombe.co.uk
Wells Bombardier; 5 changing beers (sourced nationally; often Caveman, Magic Rock, Tiny Rebel) Ⓗ
Enterprising Victorian coaching inn, now a destination visit for quality real ales and good food. A horseshoe-shaped bar supports six handpumps with different beers, three local ciders and a cabinet with whiskies and bottled beers from UK and international brewers. The restaurant is open Wednesday to Saturday lunchtimes and evenings, plus Sunday lunchtime for recommended roasts. Caveman Brewery is located in the pub cellar and at least one Caveman beer is always available. A CAMRA members' discount is offered on pints.
🏡🛏🍴🚆♣♿P🚆♨🌐

Tankerton

Tankerton Arms ▼ 🗓

139B Tankerton Road, CT5 2AW

✪ 12-2, 5-9.30 (11 Fri); 12-11 Sat; 12-3 Sun; closed
Mon ☎ 07532 025626 ⊕ thetankertonarms.co.uk

**4 changing beers (sourced locally; often Kent, Ripple
Steam, Tonbridge)** Ⓖ

A friendly micropub, voted CAMRA branch Pub of
the Year 2016, with a firm policy of supporting Kent
microbreweries, situated among Tankerton's small
shops. The pleasant, airy room is lined with high
wooden tables which encourage conversation
among customers. The walls are adorned with hop
bines, bunting and pictures featuring Thames
sailing barges and the sea forts. Food is restricted
to local Ashmore cheeses and Scotch eggs from the
butcher's shop opposite. There is some seating
outdoors on the tree-shaded pavement.

Q 🕸 ♣ 🍴 � (4,6) 🐾

Temple Ewell

Fox 🗓

14 High Street, CT16 3DU

✪ 11.30-3.30, 6-11.30; 12-4, 7-11 Sun ☎ (01304) 823598

**Butcombe Bitter; Kelham Island Pride of Sheffield;
Shepherd Neame Spitfire Gold; 1 changing beer** Ⓗ

A traditional village pub that offers a warm
welcome to locals and visitors. A good range of
styles and strengths of real ales is on offer,
including a regular from Shepherd Neame. A
variety of events, quiz nights, curry nights and
occasional music evenings keep the pub busy. In
May a charity beer festival is organised by the local
Rotary Club. There is an attractive stream-side
garden with skittle alley. The pub is close to
Kearsney Abbey gardens and public transport.

🕸 🗓 ♦ ≠ ♣ P �Ⅵ 🐾 🎧

Tonbridge

Humphrey Bean ✅

94 High Street, TN9 1AP (near castle and river)

✪ 7am-midnight (1am Fri & Sat) ☎ (01732) 773850

**Adnams Broadside; Greene King Abbot; Ruddles Best
Bitter; Sharp's Doom Bar; 6 changing beers (sourced
locally; often Dark Star, Long Man, Whitstable)** Ⓗ

A real ale showcase in the heart of town, the pub is
welcoming and spacious, occupying the former
post office building. Ample seating both inside and
out make this Wetherspoon outlet a comfortable
place in which to eat and drink. It has a good
reputation for well-conditioned ales, beer festivals
and brewery promotion weeks. Ask at the bar for
the current real ciders supplementing Old Rosie.
The garden is colourful and inviting in summer,
with views of the River Medway and Tonbridge
castle. Q 🕸 🗓 ♦ ≠ 🍴 P �Ⅵ 🎧

Tunbridge Wells

Bedford 🗓 ✅

2 High Street, TN1 1UX

✪ 11-11; 12-8 Sun ☎ (01892) 510133
⊕ thebedfordtw.co.uk

**Greene King IPA, Abbot; Morland Old Speckled Hen; 7
changing beers (sourced locally; often Kent, Old
Dairy, Pig & Porter)** Ⓗ

Often lively pub opposite the railway station,
dating from Georgian times. An extensive range of
changing beers supplements the Greene King
regulars and a Kentish cider, including strong IPAs,
stouts and porters, while a beer cave in the cellar is
available for takeaways. Popular quiz nights are
held on Mondays, live music Saturday evenings,
and the TV shows mainly rugby and football
matches. A Wednesday price promotion (5-8pm)
tempts commuters to break their journey home.
You will find friendly, helpful staff and a
welcoming atmosphere. 🕸 🗓 ≠ ♣ 🍴 �Ⅵ 🐾 🎧

Fuggles Beer Café ✅

28 Grosvenor Road, TN1 2AP

✪ 11.30-11; 12-9.30 Sun ☎ (01892) 457739
⊕ fugglesbeercafe.co.uk

**Tonbridge Coppernob; 4 changing beers (sourced
nationally; often Burning Sky, Oakham, Otley)** Ⓗ

Enthusiastically welcomed by town residents,
Fuggles has become a firm favourite since opening
in late 2013. Five real ales from small breweries
across the UK along with 13 keg beers, a cider and
around 100 bottles showcasing British, Belgian and
Dutch brews, are served by knowledgeable and
friendly staff. There is always something new to
try, perhaps using third-pint tasting racks, in
relaxed surroundings featuring wooden flooring,
candlelit tables and comfy sofas. Charcuterie and
cheeses complement the beer. Children are
welcome until 7pm. 🕸 🗓 ≠ ♣ 🍴 �Ⅵ 🐾 🎧

Grove Tavern 🗓 ✅

19 Berkeley Road, TN1 1YR

✪ 12-midnight ☎ (01892) 526549 ⊕ grovetavern.co.uk

**Harveys Sussex Best Bitter; Timothy Taylor Landlord;
2 changing beers (sourced nationally; often Dark Star,
Otter)** Ⓗ

A traditional local single-bar pub dating from the
17th century at the top of a cobbled lane in the
Grove Village area of the town. Conveniently
located a few minutes' walk from the railway
station and various bus routes, it sits between the
Pantiles and the main shopping area. This busy
local hosts a pool table and dartboard, and a cosy
fire in winter. A venue for lively and topical
conversation while enjoying guest ales sourced
from near and far. 🕸 ≠ ♣ �Ⅵ 🐾 🎧

Mount Edgcumbe

The Common, TN4 8BX

✪ 11-11 (11.30 Thu-Sat); 12-10.30 Sun ☎ (01892) 618854
⊕ themountedgcumbe.com

**Harveys Sussex Best Bitter; 3 changing beers (sourced
locally; often Pig & Porter, Rockin' Robin,
Westerham)** Ⓗ

An interesting 18th-century building with a unique
eighth-century cave inside the bar area. Half of the
reception area is furnished if you just want to relax
with a drink, while the other half is a superb
restaurant extending to a beer garden that
overlooks the common and town. Friendly staff,
real fires, a choice of beer from Kent and Sussex
breweries and soft background music are to be
found at this Georgian gem. 🕸 🗓 🗓 ≠ ♣ P �Ⅵ 🐾 🎧

Ragged Trousers

44 The Pantiles, TN2 5TN

✪ 12-11; 10-11 Sun ☎ (01892) 542715 ⊕ theragged.co.uk

**Long Man Best Bitter; 2 changing beers (sourced
locally; often Larkins, Ramsgate, Tonbridge)** Ⓗ

This is a friendly, vibrant pub situated in the
Pantiles, the historic Georgian heart of Tunbridge

Wells. As a free house, three real ales, all locally sourced from favourite Kent and Sussex brewers, and one real cider from Seacider, are served. French brasserie-style food is served up to 3pm (4pm at weekends); the area is then given over to drinkers. Seating extends directly outside under the covered colonnade where music is often heard from the bandstand nearby. 🌳🕸️◗🍺🍴🚃🐾☀️🐾

Sussex Arms ✓
Sussex Mews, TN2 5TE
🕐 12-11 (midnight Thu; 1am Fri & Sat) ☎ (01892) 549579
🌐 thesussextw.co.uk
Long Man American Pale Ale; Timothy Taylor Landlord; 4 changing beers (sourced regionally; often Hepworth, King Beer, Tonbridge) Ⓗ
Quirky pub that is well worth a visit and is something of a hidden gem, being tucked away behind the Corn Exchange, just off the bustling Pantiles, and only yards from sister pub the Ragged Trousers. Good food is served, especially Sunday lunches, but please check availability. Events (some unusual) include live music, DJs, Pink Nights, film club, bad movie club, Thursday quiz nights (winter only) and video games nights. It is welcoming and appealing to all ages. Suntrap patios are an added attraction. 🌳🕸️◗🍺🚃☀️🐾🛜

Upper Upnor

King's Arms 🏆
2 High Street, ME2 4XG
🕐 11.30-midnight; 12-midnight Sun ☎ (01634) 717490
🌐 kingsarmsupnor.co.uk
Adnams Southwold Bitter; 4 changing beers (sourced regionally) Ⓗ
Near the village car park, this outlet is at one end of a scenic cobbled High Street which leads to lovely views of the River Medway and Upnor Castle. A frequent winner of the local CAMRA Pub of the Year award, it serves four guest beers alongside a good range of ciders plus a range of European bottled ales. The restaurant has an excellent reputation for quality food.
Q🌳🕸️◗🍴P🚃(197)☀️

Walmer

Berry Ⓛ
23 Canada Road, CT14 7EQ
🕐 11 (2 Tue)-11; 12-11 Thu; 11.30-11 Sun
☎ (01304) 362411 🌐 theberrywalmer.co.uk
Dark Star Hophead, American Pale Ale; Harveys Sussex Best Bitter; 9 changing beers Ⓗ
This multi-award winning alehouse (including CAMRA Kent Cider Pub of the Year 2016) is located off Walmer seafront. The bar has a light and airy feel to it and outside at the back is a pleasant patio. The welcome, service and quality of the ales and ciders reflect the landlord's enthusiasm. There is plenty of choice, with up to 11 cask ales, six KeyKeg ales (many from Time & Tide) and six ciders. Three ale festivals and a cider festival are hosted annually. Entertainment includes darts, pool, a monthly quiz and live music. 🕸️🍺🍴🚃☀️

West Malling

Bull Ⓛ
1 High Street, ME19 6QH

🕐 12-2.30, 4-11; 12-11 Fri & Sat; 12-10.30 Sun
☎ (01732) 842753 🌐 thebullinnwestmalling.com
Timothy Taylor Landlord; Young's Bitter; 6 changing beers (sourced nationally; often Goacher's, Harveys, Musket) Ⓗ
A welcoming village pub with wood panelling, hops on the beams and a log fire. There is a focus on local beer and cider, with the cider on handpump. A terrace at the rear offers alfresco drinking. A quiz is held on Monday evenings and live music is provided twice-monthly on Saturdays. Good pub meals are served throughout but the left-hand bar is mainly for diners.
Q🌳🕸️◗🍺🍴🚃(72,151)☀️🛜

Westerham

General Wolfe ✓
High Street, TN16 1RQ (W end of town on A25)
🕐 12-11 ☎ (01959) 562104
🌐 generalwolfepubwesterham.co.uk
Greene King IPA, Abbot; house beer (by Greene King); 1 changing beer (sourced locally; often Whitstable) Ⓗ
Small, friendly, white-weatherboarded local dating mainly from the 16th century and at the far western end of the High Street. The cosy interior has a wood-burning stove, while a large decking area to the rear is available for drinking and dining in warmer conditions. The pub is well regarded for good-value home-cooked food (it is advisable to book for Saturday evening) including Friday curries and Sunday lunches (served until 5pm). Live music is performed monthly and Wednesday is quiz night. 🕸️◗P🚃(401,246)☀️🛜

Whitstable

Black Dog Ⓛ
66 High Street, CT5 1BB
🕐 12-11.30 (midnight Thu-Sat)
Dark Star Hophead; 4 changing beers (sourced regionally; often Kent, Oakham, Triple fff) Ⓖ
This attractive town-centre micropub has Victorian decor with a twist. There are five changing real ales from local and regional microbreweries, and six local ciders and perries. The five handpumps on the bar counter are for decoration only, though they do show the beers available, which are dispensed by gravity from the cooled cellar room. Food is limited to Scotch eggs and pies from local producers. There is occasional live music from local folk singers, and morris dancing. Q🍺🚃(4,5,6)☀️

New Inn Ⓛ
30 Woodlawn Street, CT5 1HG
🕐 3-11 (midnight Fri); 12-midnight Sat; 12-10 Sun
☎ (01227) 264746 🌐 newinnwhitstable.co.uk
Shepherd Neame Master Brew; 1 changing beer (sourced locally; often Shepherd Neame) Ⓗ
Dating from 1860, this is a typical Whitstable back-street pub not from the harbour and shopping area. The etched windows hint at the original layout of several small bars; there is now a long narrow bar and a cosy area further back with pool, darts and a collection of board games. It also has a good selection of gins and malt whiskies. A quiz is held on the first Tuesday of the month, and a jazz jam session on the last Thursday. See the website for occasional music events. 🌳🍺🚃☀️🛜

Ship Centurion 🅛
111 High Street, CT5 1AY
✪ 11-11; 12-7 Sun ☎ (01227) 264740
Adnams Southwold Bitter; 4 changing beers (often Canterbury Ales, Old Dairy, Pig & Porter) Ⓗ

A friendly and traditional town-centre pub, CAMRA branch Pub of the Year for 2015. Colourful hanging baskets add to its charm in summer, while pictures of Whitstable decorate the bar room. A dark mild and a Kentish beer are always available, often alongside other Essex beers. Home-cooked bar food frequently includes authentic German dishes, and there is a schnitzel on Saturdays (no food Sun). Live music plays on Thursday evenings (except in Jan) and Friday lunchtimes. There is a summer cider festival and an October beer festival.
◑ ⇌ 🖵 (4,5,6) ♣ 🛜

Wickhambreaux

Rose Inn ✅
The Green, CT3 1RQ
✪ 12-11; 12-10.30 Sun ☎ (01227) 721763
⊕ theroseinnwickhambreaux.co.uk
Greene King IPA; 2 changing beers (often Wells) Ⓗ

Situated in a lovely village, the Rose dates back around 700 years. It has oak beams and hanging hops. The friendly bar has an open fire, and the dining area has a huge inglenook fireplace. One guest beer is often from a Kent brewery. Events include a quiz night on the second Wednesday of each month, a steak night on Thursday, and various beer festivals. There is a bar in the garden on summer weekends. Q ᕦ 🕸 ◑ ♣ 🖵 (11) ♣ 🛜

Willesborough

Blacksmiths Arms ✅
84 The Street, TN24 0NA
✪ 12-11 (midnight Fri & Sat); 12-11.30 Sun
☎ (01233) 623975 ⊕ blacksmithsarmsashford.co.uk
Fuller's London Pride; 3 changing beers (sourced nationally) Ⓗ

An 18th-century Grade II-listed family-friendly pub on the outskirts of Ashford, offering a range of cask ales, wines and a changing food menu. There is a large terraced garden and children's play area. Situated just off junction 10 of the M20, it is ideal for a break on the way to or from the channel ports, or for unwinding after visiting the nearby superstore or the William Harvey Hospital. ᕦ 🕸 ◑ ♿ ♣ 🖵 ♣ 🛜

Rock, Chiddingstone Hoath (Photo: Bob Steel)

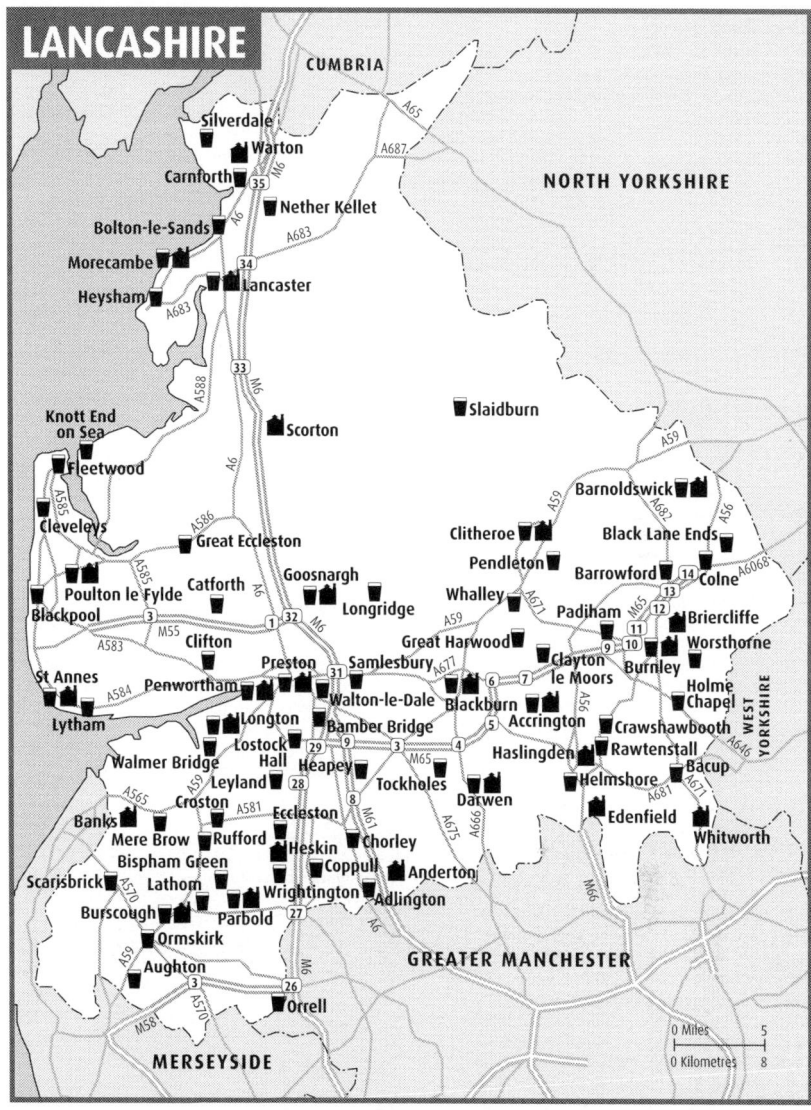

LANCASHIRE

Please note that Thwaites of Blackburn sold its beer brands and brewing rights to the Marston's group in 2015. With the exception of small-run beers brewed on Thwaites's micro plant, all the main Thwaites beers are now brewed and supplied by Marston's. See Breweries section, p701.

Accrington

Commercial Hotel Ⓛ ✓
1 Church Street, BB5 2EN
🕓 8am-midnight (1am Fri & Sat) ☎ (01254) 300140
Greene King Abbot; Ruddles Best Bitter; 8 changing beers Ⓗ
Large open-plan pub including many local features, with more than a nod to the Tiffany glass collection. It is adjacent to the bus station and markets and a short walk from the railway station. A strong supporter of regional breweries, it was also local CAMRA Cider Pub of the Year 2016, with a good variety including Westons and Gwynt y Ddraig. The large, pleasant beer garden provides a quiet refuge from the town-centre bustle.
Q ➦ ☎ ◑ ♿ ≈ ₩ ᵫ 🛜

Grants Ⓛ
1 Manchester Road, BB5 2BQ
🕓 12-11 (midnight Fri & Sat) ☎ (01254) 393938
🌐 grantsbar.co.uk
Big Clock Pals, Dirty Blonde, Dark Knight; 8 changing beers Ⓗ
An imposing building on the southern edge of the town centre. Thoroughly modern on the inside, it is something of a place to be seen at weekends, attracting a wide range of customers. Grants is home to the Big Clock Brewery, which can be viewed from the main bar. Up to eight beers from Big Clock are sold alongside a cider, usually Old Rosie. There is a separate smart function room upstairs for hire (no disabled access). Weekly acoustic music nights take place. ➦ ❀ ≈ ₩ P ᵫ

Peel Park Hotel ⓛ
Turkey Street, BB5 6EW
✪ 12-11.30 ☎ (01254) 235830
Tetley Bitter; 5 changing beers 🅗
A true free house opposite the site of the old Accrington Stanley football ground, still used by Peel Park FC. Six beers are sold, mainly from smaller breweries. The warm and welcoming main bar is divided into split-level front and rear sections. There is a separate small pool room and a smart rear room used for functions and meetings. Outside there is a pleasant garden area to the side of the pub. ➽✿☸◑Pⓗ (23)✿

Adlington

Spinners Arms ⓛ
23 Church Street, PR7 4EX
✪ 12-midnight ☎ (01257) 483331
Castle Rock Black Gold; Moorhouse's Pride of Pendle; 5 changing beers (sourced regionally; often Abbeydale, Moorhouse's, Prospect) 🅗
The pub is known as the Bottom Spinners to differentiate it from the other Spinners Arms in the village. Welcoming and friendly, a single bar serves three seating areas, one of which has a large log fire. There is a pleasant outdoor drinking area to the front. The bar menu offers home-cooked food, with Sunday specials. Five alternating guest beers are sold, often from local breweries. Small functions can be catered for. Quiz night is Tuesday, bingo on Wednesday. ➽◑≉P🖰 (3)✿ ☞

Aughton

Derby Arms ⓛ ✅
Prescot Road, L39 6TA (on B3197 at Bowkers Green between Ormskirk and Kirby)
✪ 12-11 (1am Fri); 9am-1am Sat ☎ (01695) 422237
Tetley Mild, Bitter; 3 changing beers (often Burscough, Moorhouse's, Problem Child) 🅗
Friendly country pub with a long CAMRA award-winning heritage. The interior is intimate, with many small nooks and crannies, and there is a varying choice of beers on the three guest handpumps that could come from any local or national brewery. The pub holds quiz nights on Tuesdays and Thursdays and regular charity events. Excellent-value food is available, with breakfast served on Saturdays from 9am. Q➽✿◑♣P✿ ☞

Bacup

Crown Inn ⓛ ✅
19 Greave Road, OL13 9HQ
✪ 5-midnight; 12-midnight Sat & Sun ☎ (01706) 873982
Pictish Brewers Gold; 3 changing beers 🅗
Cosy traditional country pub with an L-shaped bar and stone-flagged floors throughout. A welcoming coal fire warms the atmosphere in the cooler months. There are always three beers on, usually sourced locally. Food is available most evenings, and quiz nights are held on Wednesday and Sunday. On the second floor is a function room accommodating up to 35 guests. There is a patio beer garden to the front of the pub, and beer festivals are held in July and October. ➽✿◑♿♣P🖰✿

Bamber Bridge

Withy Arms ✅
Station Road, PR5 6QP
✪ 11-midnight (1am Fri); 10.30-1am Sat; 10.30-midnight Sun
☎ (01772) 697706 ⊕ withyarms.com
Ribble WA Bitter, Odd Job; 3 changing beers (sourced nationally) 🅗
There is a small taproom to the right of the entrance, while the open-plan main bar area has a slightly continental feel. The impressive bar counter features six handpumps. Two house beers from Ribble Brewery are brewed under contract by an unnamed brewery to the pub's own recipe. The changing guest ales tend to be below 4.5% ABV and from microbreweries. Outdoor seating on decking is at the front and rear of the pub. ➽✿◑≉●🖰 ☞

Barnoldswick

Barlick Tap Ale House ⓛ
8 Newtown, BB18 5UQ
✪ 4-9; 2-10 Fri & Sat; 2-8 Sun; closed Mon & Tue ☎ 07739 088846
5 changing beers 🅗
A warm welcome from Hazel and Steve is assured at this friendly micropub just off the town square and two minutes from the main bus stop. There is a choice of five constantly changing cask beers with one dark beer, plus a selection of American and European bottled beers and lagers, bottled cider and wines. A place to meet and chat over a glass or two without the intrusion of loud music. Q🖰✿

ENGLAND

Fountain Inn

14 Church Street, BB18 5UT
🕐 12-midnight ☎ (01282) 813412
🌐 fountaininnbarnoldswick.com
Dark Horse Hetton Pale Ale; Goose Eye Bitter; Thwaites Wainwright; 2 changing beers [H]
A pub with a friendly feel and a mix of traditional features such as the stone floor combined with quirky elements including cow wallpaper and artificial grass on the floor. There is a cosy restaurant serving good locally sourced food at reasonable prices, with a daily specials board; there is also an outside smoking area and beer garden. Live music features on Thursday night and some Sundays. Accommodation consists of eight en-suite rooms. It is a five-minute walk from the main bus stop. 🐴❀🛏◑🍎🚌🐾

Barrowford

Bankers Draft

143 Gisburn Road, BB9 6HQ
🕐 4-9 (10 Fri); 2-10.30 Sat; 2-9 Sun; closed Mon & Tue ☎ 07739 870880
5 changing beers [H]
Imposing detached former bank that is now a small and friendly micropub specialising in real ale and conversation, with no loud music or TVs. The five handpumps dispense different cask ales from national small brewers, offering a great variety of styles from hoppy blondes and traditional bitters to dark beers. There is also a good selection of wines and bottled wheat beers, with at least one real cider normally available. Q🐴🍎P🚌🐾

Bispham Green

Eagle & Child

Malt Kiln Lane, L40 3SG
🕐 12-11; 12-10.30 Sun ☎ (01257) 462297
Southport Carousel; Thwaites Original, Wainwright; 5 changing beers [H]
An 18th-century inn with eight handpumps showcasing local ales – Southport Carousel is always available alongside a variety of guest ales from AllGates, Prospect and Moorhouse's. This busy country pub is the Lancashire Dining Pub of the Year for the fifth time (diners are advised to book early for a table). The huge beer garden, with its wildlife area and great views, hosts a beer festival on the May bank holiday. Quiz night is Monday. 🐴❀◑🍎P🐾📶

Black Lane Ends

Black Lane Ends [L]

Skipton Old Road, BB8 7EP (off A56 2 miles E of Colne golf club)
🕐 12-11; 12-10.30 Sun ☎ (01282) 863070
Lancaster Blonde; Timothy Taylor Golden Best, Landlord; 2 changing beers [H]
Called the Hare & Hounds until recently, it changed its name due to there being pubs of the same name in the two nearest local villages. It lies on the old road from Colne to Skipton, close to the border with North Yorkshire and overlooking the Pennine Moors. It is an independent free house with an excellent reputation for food, which is served daily 12-9pm in the two rooms either side of the bar. There is no nearby public transport. Not far from the Pendle Way footpath. Q🐴❀◑P

Blackburn

Black Bull [L]

Brokenstone Road, BB3 0LL (corner of Brokenstone Rd and Heys Lane)
🕐 4-11 (midnight Fri); 12-midnight Sat; 12-10.30 Sun; closed Mon & Tue ☎ (01254) 581381 🌐 threebsbrewery.co.uk
10 changing beers [H]
Brewpub on a crossroads in the hills above Blackburn, two miles from the town centre. Formerly a Thwaites house, it now houses the 3Bs brewery and sells the full range, including the house beer, Black Bull Bitter, and a cider, usually Ribble Valley Gold. This place is popular with walkers, cyclists and beer connoisseurs, and has magnificent views over the hills and out towards the coast. It is an uphill walk from Golden Cup, Mill Hill and Leyburn Road bus stops.
Q🐴❀♿♣🍎P🚌🐾

Hare & Hounds [L]

78 Lammack Road, BB1 8LA
🕐 4-11; 12.30-midnight Sat; 12.30-11 Sun
☎ (01254) 676724
Thwaites Original; Worsthorne Redman; 4 changing beers [H]
Rescued from the jaws of oblivion by the current landlord and backed by a passionate local community, this is the last remaining purpose-built Dalton's pub in the country. It is adjacent to Pleckgate and Lammack playing fields, the meeting place for local sports teams, including women's netball and hockey. It has been restored to a two-storey facility, with the number of handpumps increased from one to five. Live music is played Fridays and Saturdays. 🐴❀♿♣P🚌(5)🐾

Blackpool

Auctioneer ✔

235-237 Lytham Road, FY1 6ET
🕐 8am-midnight ☎ (01253) 346412
Greene King Abbot; Ruddles Best Bitter; 8 changing beers [H]
A large single-room Wetherspoon pub based close to the Waterloo Road shopping area, Blackpool South station and Bloomfield Road football ground. It has a cosy, community-pub feel with a pleasant suntrap of a rear outdoor drinking area. It can get busy in the summer months with trade from the local hotels. Up to eight guest beers are available and normally two ciders, sold in polypins. Food is served until 11pm daily.
🐴❀◑♿🚆🚊🍎🚌(10,11,68)📶

Blackpool Cricket Club ✔

Barlow Crescent, West Park Drive, FY3 9EQ (follow signs to Stanley Park)
🕐 4.30-10.30 Mon & Wed; 4.30-11.30 Tue; 4.30-midnight Thu; 2.30-midnight Fri; 12-midnight Sat; 12-10.30 Sun
☎ (01253) 393347 🌐 blackpoolcricket.co.uk
Thwaites Wainwright; 4 changing beers (sourced nationally) [H]
On the western edge of Stanley Park, within the cricket pavilion, the club is host to many sports teams, while several TVs show major sports fixtures and an upstairs room is available for social events. The club has its own squash courts and holds quiz and entertainment nights. It is the many-time local CAMRA branch Club of the Year and holds an annual beer festival. Free entry to all cricket games except Lancashire's.
🐴❀◑♿🍎P🚌(15,16)🐾📶

Layton Rakes ✅
17-25 Market Street, FY1 1ET
🕙 8am-midnight (1am Fri & Sat) ☎ (01253) 743710
Greene King Abbot; Ruddles Best Bitter; changing beers Ⓗ
Multi-floored town-centre pub, just off the Prom opposite the eccentrically shaped Wedding Chapel. With bars on each of its three floors, it offers a wide range of beers, changing on a regular basis. Music is played on the ground floor on a Friday and Saturday evening, although the middle floor remains fairly quiet. An open-air roof terrace tops the building. Coulrophobiacs should note, the ground floor has a large illuminated feature of Tower Circus legend Charlie Carolli.
🏷️⚙️◐&♿🅡🍴�"🛏�"

Pump & Truncheon
13 Bonny Street, FY1 5AR
🕙 11 (10 Fri & Sat)-midnight; 12-11.30 Sun
☎ (01253) 624099
6 changing beers (sourced nationally; often Acorn, Clark's, Cross Bay) Ⓗ
Behind Madame Tussauds on Blackpool's Golden Mile and close to Central Pier, this delightfully old-fashioned pub boasts up to six different ales from near and far and a range of ciders/perries. The licensee is a keen cask enthusiast and this shows in the quality of his ales. The wood-panelled decor has a strong police theme, doubtless inspired by the pub's proximity to the local nick.
🏷️◐🅡♣🍴�" 🛏�"

Saddle Inn ✅
286 Whitegate Drive, FY3 9PH
🕙 10.30-11 (midnight Thu-Sat); 11-midnight Sun
☎ (01253) 767827 ⊕ thesaddleblackpool.co.uk
Draught Bass; Thwaites Wainwright; 4 changing beers (sourced nationally; often Lytham) Ⓗ
Continuously licensed since approximately 1776 and one of the oldest remaining buildings in the borough of Blackpool, this suburban pub offers a range of well-kept beers and a couple of ciders. The two long thin rooms run off the central bar area. A large outdoor decking space provides a pleasant alternative if weather permits. Food is served daily until 9pm. 🏷️⚙️◐🍴🅿🛏�"

Washington ✅
Topping Street, FY1 3AF
🕙 10.30-11 (midnight Fri & Sat); 11-11 Sun
☎ (01253) 620885
Greene King IPA; Morland Old Speckled Hen; 6 changing beers (sourced nationally) Ⓗ
Large, bustling street-corner pub, built in 1875, between the town centre and Bickerstaff Square development. Handy for the railway station and most bus routes, this mainly single-roomed pub offers a changing range of beers from all over the country, although there is a bias towards the North-west. Food is served all day. Several TVs show sporting events. 🏷️◐&♿🅡♣🛏�"

Bolton-le-Sands

Royal
Main Road, LA5 8DQ (on A6; waterbus stops near garden gate)
🕙 12-11 (midnight Fri & Sat) ☎ (01524) 732057
⊕ royalhotelbls.co.uk
7 changing beers (often Oakham, York) Ⓗ

Spacious, open-plan pub with a central bar. Games are played in the area towards the rear; the rest of the main room consists of comfortable seating and some dining (there is also a separate dining room). The large garden, with tables and seating, has steps leading up to the canal and is popular in the summer. A quiz is on Thursday, pool Tuesday, darts Thursday and entertainment Saturday. The food schedule is pies on Tuesday, steak Wednesday, curry Thursday and fish Friday.
⚙️🏷️◐&♿▲♣🍴🅿�" (5,55,555) 🛏

Burnley

Bridge Bier Huis Ⓛ
2 Bank Parade, BB11 1UH
🕙 12-midnight (1am Fri & Sat); 12-11 Sun; closed Mon & Tue
☎ (01282) 411304 ⊕ thebridgebierhuis.co.uk
Moorhouse's Premier Bitter; 4 changing beers Ⓗ
An award-winning true free house with a large open-plan bar that has a logburner and a small snug to one side. It offers mainly microbrewery beers alongside a changing real cider. More than 60 foreign bottled beers are sold plus seven foreign beers on tap, including rare German brews. Wednesday is quiz night and live music is hosted on occasional weekends. This welcoming pub opens 5pm Monday or Tuesday if Burnley FC are at home. 🏷️⚙️◐⮝(Central)🍴🛏🚺

KSC 110 Club Ⓛ
1 Albert Street, BB11 3BY
🕙 7-midnight (11.30 Mon & Wed; 11 Tue); 1-midnight Sun
☎ (01282) 422571
4 changing beers Ⓗ
Award-winning three-storey club on the road to Turf Moor, home of Burnley FC. Thursday is quiz night, while live music features on Friday and Saturday nights plus Sunday afternoon. A games room and function rooms are on the upper floors, and an annual beer festival is held in the main bar. The club does get busy before and after Burnley home matches. 🏷️⮝(Central)♣🛏(592)

New Brew-m Ⓛ
St James Row, BB11 1DR
🕙 12-8 Mon & Wed; 12-10; 12-6 Sun; closed Tue ☎ 07902 961426
6 changing beers Ⓗ
Smart micropub in the centre of town run as the Reedley Hallows brewery tap. At least one of its own beers is always on the bar, alongside five others sourced nationwide using the head brewer's contacts from years in the trade. A limited range of foreign bottled beers and bottled ciders is available. Comfortable seating around wooden hogsheads on a raised area complements bench seating opposite the bar. The pub will open Tuesday night if Burnley FC are at home.
Q⮝(Manchester Rd)♣🛏🚺

Rifle Volunteer Ⓛ ✅
1 Smalley Street, BB11 3HH
🕙 2 (12 Sat)-11; 12-10.30 Sun ☎ (01282) 453839
Draught Bass; 2 changing beers Ⓗ
The Vols is an award-winning pub and a rare outlet in the area for the iconic Draught Bass. This free house is a supreme example of the street-corner local. There is no jukebox to disturb the quiet ambience of this friendly pub, where the emphasis is on good beer and conversation. Check out the Gents for a rare example of Burnley-manufactured Ducketts urinals. Q♣🅿🛏(483)🚺

Talbot 🏠 ✓
65 Church Street, BB11 2RU
⏰ 5-midnight; 4-1am Fri; 12-1am Sat; 12-midnight Sun
☎ (01282) 412074
Holt Bitter; Timothy Taylor Boltmaker; 6 changing beers Ⓗ
A warm welcome awaits you at this large free house situated just off the town centre and dating back to the 1800s. The licensee is a real ale enthusiast and keen supporter of local breweries. Live music features every weekend. There are two pool tables plus large-screen TVs for sports fans. Four well-appointed en-suite rooms are available for guests, with use of the private car park.
❀🛏♿(Central)♣P🚋(4,5,X43)🌾

Burscough

Hop Vine
Liverpool Road North, L40 4BY (village centre, A59)
⏰ 10.30-midnight (12.30am Fri & Sat); 10.30-11 Sun
☎ (01704) 893799 🌐 thehopvine.co.uk
Burscough Mere Blonde; house beer (by Burscough); 7 changing beers (often George Wright, Phoenix, Timothy Taylor) Ⓗ
Spacious former coaching house that is now a thriving community brewpub renowned for its friendly atmosphere and popular for its exceptional ale and food. The classic country pub interior has wood panelling and characterful wood flooring throughout, and is decorated with historic local maps, photographs and vintage bottled ales. The award-winning Burscough Brewery operates from the attractive floral courtyard at the rear. Catering for all age groups, it offers great-value meals, live music and twice-yearly beer festivals.
🕿❀🕼♿🛏P🚋🛜

Carnforth

Snug
Unit 6, Carnforth Gateway Building, LA5 9TR (at the N end of former mainline up platform)
⏰ 12-2, 5-9; 12.30-3 Sun; closed Mon ☎ (01524) 735677
🌐 thesnugmicropub.blogspot.co.uk
5 changing beers Ⓗ
Described as a micropub, both in the sense of being very small (which it is) and also of being a minimalist concept: the only beverages are ale, cider, wine and a few soft drinks, while the only food is a few light snacks. The only sounds are conversation and the roar of the passing trains. The decor is similarly stripped back: painted walls, bare floorboards and chunky tall tables. The eye is naturally drawn to a beautiful glazed wooden cabinet where all the drinks are stored. Parking is on the station car park (a charge applies). A former local CAMRA Pub of the Year.
Q❀♿🛏♣●🚋(5,55,555)🌾

Catforth

Running Pump
Catforth Road, PR4 0HH
⏰ 12 (4 Mon)-11 ☎ (01772) 690265 🌐 runningpump.co.uk
Thwaites Original, Wainwright; 3 changing beers Ⓗ
After it was closed by Robinsons, this traditional country pub reopened in the spring of 2015 following refurbishment and sympathetic enlargement as a free house. A range of five ales is available, mainly from local microbreweries. Good-quality, home-made and locally sourced food is served, both in the bar and the separate restaurant. It has stunning views of the Pennine fells.
🕿❀🕼♿P🚋(80)

Chorley

Bob Inn
24 Market Place, PR7 1DA
⏰ 10-6; closed Wed & Sun
3 changing beers (sourced nationally) Ⓗ
A tiny bar housed in a market stall, with an adjacent unit now used as a lounge area, this is the smallest pub in the local CAMRA branch area. Outside seating is available during the summer and drinkers often spill over into the market area. With three changing cask beers from smaller breweries, at least two ciders and a good selection of bottled beers, there is something for every taste. No food, but you are welcome to bring your own.
Q🛏●🚋🌾

Crown 🏠
46-48 Chapel Street, PR7 1BW
⏰ 11-midnight; 12-11 Sun ☎ 07552 092176
House beer (by Fuzzy Duck); 4 changing beers (sourced locally; often AllGates, Lancaster, Reedley Hallows) Ⓗ
Newly refurbished and reopened in 2014 following two years of closure, there is an impressive bar counter and bar-back here, together with contemporary seating in a mainly open-plan layout. A small area to the side of the bar and a cosy lounge offer more privacy. Five handpumps provide a changing array of beers sourced mainly from local microbreweries. Live music features every Friday evening from 9.30pm. 🕿♿🛏🚋🌾🛜

Malt 'n' Hops
50-52 Friday Street, PR6 0AH
⏰ 12-11 ☎ (01257) 260074
9 changing beers (sourced nationally) Ⓗ
Converted from an old shop in 1989, the pub is handily situated for both the railway and bus stations. It has a single L-shaped bar on two levels, recently redecorated and with a bright and modern feel. A genuine free house, there are up to nine guest ales, usually from Lancashire and Yorkshire micros, with Rat, Ossett, Elland, Lancaster and Blackedge often featuring. At least one dark beer is usually among the range, and filled rolls and pork pies are available. 🕿❀🛏🚋🌾🛜

Potters Arms 🏠
42 Brooke Street, PR7 3BY (next to Morrisons)
⏰ 3-11.30 (midnight Fri); 12-4, 7-midnight Sat; 12-11 Sun
☎ (01257) 267954
Black Sheep Best Bitter; Three B's Doff Cocker; 1 changing beer Ⓗ
Small, friendly free house named after the owners, at the bottom of Brooke Street alongside the railway bridge. The central bar serves two games areas, while two comfortable lounges are popular with locals and visitors alike. The pub displays a fine selection of photographs from the world of music, as well as vintage local scenes. Regular darts and dominoes nights are well attended and the chip butties go down a treat. The smoking area is covered. 🛏♣P🚋(109A)

Railway ✓
20 Steeley Lane, PR6 0RD (under subway from train station)

✪ 12-midnight (11 Tue & Wed); 12-1am Fri & Sat
☎ (01257) 671541
Jennings Cumberland Ale; Wychwood Hobgoblin Gold, Hobgoblin; 2 changing beers Ⓗ
Adjacent to the railway station and 100 yards from the bus station, this community local offers a changing range of up to five real ales from the Marston's portfolio. A single corner bar serves different drinking areas and a separate pool alcove. Darts, dominoes and pool are popular with the locals, along with seasonal music festivals. Live music (rock and blues) features on Saturday nights and the occasional Friday. ✿≢♣☗✿

Shepherds Hall Ale House ♈ Ⓛ
67 Chapel Street, PR7 1BS
✪ 2-10 (11 Fri); 12-11 Sat; 2-9 Sun; closed Mon ☎ 07412 584907
⊕ shepherdshallalehouse.wordpress.com
5 changing beers (sourced nationally) Ⓗ
Formerly a shop, the building has been tastefully converted and utilises fittings from other closed pubs in the town, the bar coming from Harry's Bar and the tables from the Tut 'n' Shive. Like most micropubs, there is no food, TV or music and the drinks range is limited to real ale, cider, bottled beers, wine and soft drinks. The beers come mainly from microbreweries across the country, although a LocAle or two should normally be expected.
Q≢☗🖬☗✿

Clayton le Moors

Forts Arms Ⓛ
1 Lower Barnes Street, BB5 5TA
✪ 4-midnight; 2-2am Fri & Sat; 2-11 Sun ☎ (01254) 433713
4 changing beers Ⓗ
Partially opened out in a modern style, the pub boasts a large rear beer garden and second-floor function suite. There is always one beer from each of Snaggletooth and Bowland alongside a couple of guest beers, normally from local breweries. It has a small library and a few games, including some for children. Folk music sessions take place weekly and music and beer festivals are held twice a year.
Q☗✿♣P🖬✿

Wellington
Barnes Square, BB5 5NX
✪ 2 (12 Sat)-midnight; 12-11 Sun ☎ (01254) 235762
3 changing beers Ⓗ
Excellent community local on the main square in the centre of town. This imposing building has a traditional vault, a small corridor drinking area and a comfortable lounge with a log fire in winter. The separate function room plays host to craft and walking groups during the week and live music some weekends. Handy for the Leeds-Liverpool Canal, being 200 yards from bridge 114B. Buses to Accrington, Blackburn and Clitheroe stop nearby.
☗♣🖬(6,7)

Cleveleys

Jolly Tars ✪
154-158 Victoria Road, FY5 3NE
✪ 8am-11 (12.30am Thu-Sat); 8am-midnight Sun
☎ (01253) 856042
Greene King Abbot; Ruddles Best Bitter; 8 changing beers (sourced nationally) Ⓗ
Close to the centre of Cleveleys, this conversion of a former supermarket provides a pleasant and airy

environment in which to enjoy a drink. In summer, it opens out onto an open-air drinking area at the front of the pub. Regional and national beers are generally dispensed from a range of ever-changing guest ales along with at least one cider.
☗✿🕪👌🔔☗🖬✿

Clifton

Windmill Tavern Ⓛ
Clifton Lane, PR4 0YE
✪ 12-3, 5-11; 12-11 Fri; 12-midnight Sat; 12-10.30 Sun; closed Mon ☎ (01772) 687203
York Yorkshire Terrier; 4 changing beers Ⓗ
Just outside Clifton and five minutes off the main Blackpool-Preston road, the Windmill is built around the Clifton windmill, constructed in 1778 and believed to be the second tallest windmill of its type in England. The lower bar serves a range of up to five well-kept ales. The raised restaurant has a reputation for fine food. An outside drinking area is available should the weather allow.
☗✿🕪👌≢P✿☗

Clitheroe

New Inn
22 Parson Lane, BB7 2JN
✪ 11-11; 12-11 Sun ☎ (01200) 423312
Coach House Gunpowder Mild, Farrier's Best Bitter; Moorhouse's Premier Bitter, Pride of Pendle; 7 changing beers Ⓗ
Gem of a pub found just off the main street, beneath the 12th-century castle. It has several snug rooms and a cosy bar area, plus a large partly covered beer garden at the rear and seating out the front. The remarkable choice of guest ales frequently includes favourites from Coach House, Worsthorne and Elland. The back room hosts traditional Irish music sessions every second Sunday afternoon and a number of associations meet here regularly. Q✿🅰≢🖬✿

Colne

Admiral Lord Rodney Ⓛ
Mill Green, BB8 0TA
✪ 4-midnight (2am Fri); 1-2am Sat; 1-midnight Sun
☎ (01282) 219759 ⊕ thelordrodney.co.uk
9 changing beers Ⓗ
A much-loved community pub in Colne's old South Valley area, the old industrial heart of the town. The stone floor includes mosaics and there are beautiful tiles up the inner staircase. Arranged over three rooms, the pub has become the meeting place for a number of clubs. Regular live entertainment features during the evenings, plus local history and art displays. It has enjoyed a recent refurbishment, with open fires and flagged floors, plus much-improved outdoor seating and a separate smokers' area. Q☗✿🕪≢♣✿☗

Boyce's Barrel
7 Newmarket Street, BB8 9BJ
✪ 4-9; 1-9 Sat; closed Mon ☎ 07736 900111
5 changing beers Ⓗ
The first micropub in Colne, offering five real ales, no music, no lager, just a great atmosphere and plenty of banter. Tastefully styled with tall polished wooden sleeper tables, it is reminiscent of a rail staging post. Ales are rotated often, always including one mild and one porter or stout, with

new beers put on the bar almost as soon as a cask runs dry (all ales are from non-local breweries). A place that is sure to suit any real ale fan's taste. Q&⇌🍴🐾♿

Coppull

Red Herring
Mill Lane, PR7 5AN
🕏 3-11; 12-11.30 Fri & Sat; 12-11 Sun ☎ (01257) 470130
5 changing beers Ⓗ
Real ale pub in the former offices of the next-door mill. It was converted to a pub some years ago; the bar area comprises a large single room plus an extension. Up to five beers, mainly from micros, are usually served. TV sports fans are catered for, as are anglers who use the pond opposite. The pub hosts regular music nights and barbecues, and has a large first-floor function room.
🏠🏡&♣P🚌(362)🐾🛜

Crawshawbooth

Masons Arms Ⓛ ⊘
6 Co-operation Street, BB4 8AG
🕏 2-11; 12-11 Sat & Sun ☎ 07957 855012
Moorhouse's Pride of Pendle; Thwaites Wainwright; 1 changing beer Ⓗ
Hidden away in the village centre, this is an old stone pub at the end of a row of terraced cottages, close to an interesting Quaker meeting house. It consists of three small rooms, with the bar and its three handpumps being in the main room. The other rooms show TV sport and there are pool and darts teams. Popular with locals. 🏠&♣🚌(X43)🐾

Croston

Wheatsheaf ⊘
Town Road, PR26 9RA
🕏 12-11 (midnight Fri); 10-midnight Sat; 10-11 Sun
☎ (01772) 600370 🌐 wheatsheaf-croston.com
5 changing beers (often Hawkshead, Robinsons) Ⓗ
On the main road and overlooking the village green, this recently refurbished pub has a contemporary feel. It has a distinct space for dining as well as a comfortable drinking area with sofas and chairs. The large patio to the front is also used to hold an annual beer festival during October. Up to five changing ales are served, sourced from the SIBA list. Live music features on either Friday or Saturday nights twice a month.
🏠🏡🕽&⇌P🚌(7,112)🐾🛜

Darwen

Number 39 Ⓛ
39-41 Bridge Street, BB3 2AA
🕏 12-midnight ☎ 07849 369798 🌐 hopstarbrewery.co.uk
Hopstar Dizzy Danny Ale, Dark Knight; 4 changing beers Ⓗ
A continental-style bar in the centre of Darwen, the Hopstar Brewery tap now covers two floors. It has won awards for both beer and cider (local CAMRA Cider Pub of the Year), with new brews tried out here first. There is a large variety of bottled continental and world beers and draught Timmermans. Regular live music is staged weekly. Sunday afternoon is apple, cheese and perry time.
Q🏠🕽⇌♣🍴🐾🛜

Eccleston

Original Farmers Arms
Towngate, PR7 5QS
🕏 12-midnight (1am Fri & Sat) ☎ (01257) 451594
🌐 originalfarmersarms.co.uk
Black Sheep Best Bitter; Sharp's Doom Bar; Thwaites Wainwright; 3 changing beers (sourced nationally; often Moorhouse's) Ⓗ
A white-painted village pub which has expanded over the years into the cottage next door, adding a substantial dining area. However, the original part of the pub is still used mainly for drinking. Meals are served throughout the day, seven days a week, and there is accommodation in four good-value guest rooms. There are currently four standard beers – the Moorhouse's usually being White Witch. Two other pumps dispense changing guests, one of which is free of tie. 🏠🏡🕽P🚌(113,347)🛜

Fleetwood

Royal Oak Hotel
171 Lord Street, FY7 6SR
🕏 12-midnight (1am Fri & Sat) ☎ (01253) 873486
Banks's Sunbeam; house beer (by Reedley Hallows); 6 changing beers (sourced regionally; often Bank Top, Blackedge) Ⓗ
Since reopening in 2013, Dead 'Uns, as it is locally known, has gone from strength to strength. It is still basically a multi-roomed pub, although slightly opened out and with many original features remaining. A range of eight beers, many from brewers within a 50-mile radius, are served along with a cider. A comfortable upstairs function room is available for hire. If you have a spare hour or two, ask why it is called Dead 'Uns!
🏠&🚪♣🍴🐾🛜

Thomas Drummond ⊘
London Street, FY7 6JE
🕏 8am-11 (midnight Thu-Sat) ☎ (01253) 775020
Greene King Abbot; Ruddles Best Bitter; 8 changing beers Ⓗ
Named after the builder who helped construct the town, this conversion of a former Sunday school also displays details of the town's founder, Sir Peter Hesketh-Fleetwood, and architect Decimus Burton. A small, pleasant suntrap garden is at the rear. Eight guest beers, which come from an extensive list and are always changing, are on the bar. A number of ciders are dispensed and these are also rotated. Three beer festivals and two cider festivals are run each year. 🏠🏡&🚪🍴🚌🛜

Goosnargh

Horn's Inn ★ Ⓛ
Horns Lane, PR3 2FJ (corner of Inglewhite Rd, 2 miles NE of village)
🕏 11.30-3 (not Mon), 6-11; 12-9 Sun ☎ (01772) 865230
🌐 hornsinn.co.uk
Goosnargh Red, Bit o' Blonde, Gold Ⓗ
Country pub dating from 1782 close to the Forest of Bowland, with five rooms including a rare snug, one of only three in the country, where customers sit behind a bar counter while staff serve from the same area. The beers are brewed by the landlord in a small outbuilding, and two or three changing Goosnargh beers are available, plus occasional guests. It serves good food using locally sourced ingredients. Accommodation is in a converted barn at the rear. Q🏡🚪🕽🅿P🛜

Great Eccleston

White Bull Hotel
The Square, PR3 0ZB
✪ 11-midnight; 12-11.30 Sun ☎ (01995) 670203
Everards Tiger; Theakston Best Bitter; 3 changing beers Ⓗ
Historic coaching inn in the heart of the village. A family-friendly, welcoming pub with flagged floors and an unspoilt atmosphere, this is a real local, with a games room including pool, darts and TV. The medium-sized room to the right extends to the back, with ample tables to enjoy locally sourced home-cooked food. The smaller room at the front has a real fire to relax in front of. Five real ales are on tap, two permanent and three rotating guests. There is free public parking at the front.
🛏❀◑&♣P☐(42,76,80)🐾 ᚛

Great Harwood

Victoria ★ Ⓛ ✓
St Johns Street, BB6 7EP
✪ 2-11; 12-11 Sat & Sun ☎ (01254) 885210
8 changing beers Ⓗ
A fine Edwardian multi-roomed gem featuring much original woodwork and tiling. Note the sash windows around the central horseshoe bar, the small separate snug and the darts room with latticed seating. The large outdoor area to the rear has moorland views. Lancashire, Yorkshire and Lakeland beers dominate, with at least one dark beer on offer. The pub serves as a meeting place for numerous local groups, from running and cycling to chess and vegetable growing. A varying cider is sold in the summer months.
Q🛏❀♣●☐(6,7)🐾

Heapey

Top Lock
Copthurst Lane, PR6 8LT (by Leeds-Liverpool Canal at Johnson's Hillock)
✪ 12-11; 12-10.30 Sun ☎ (01257) 263376
9 changing beers (sourced nationally) Ⓗ
Popular canalside pub with a large single room at the top of the Johnson's Hillock locks. Nine real ales are served, mainly from micros. Always available are beers from Coniston and Timothy Taylor, a mild and a stout or porter, plus up to three ciders on gravity. Curry night is on Tuesday, fish and chips on Wednesday, Monday is quiz night, and live music plays most Thursdays. An annual beer festival is held in October with up to 100 real ales.
Q🛏❀◑●P☐☐(24)

Helmshore

Robin Hood Inn Ⓛ ✓
280 Holcombe Road, BB4 4NP
✪ 4-11; 12-11 Fri-Sun ☎ (01706) 213180
Hydes Original; 4 changing beers Ⓗ
Traditional stone-built village pub which, although opened up, still retains the impression of having three separate rooms, with two open fires. The original Glen Top Brewery windows are a feature. A selection from the seasonal ranges of Hydes and Beer Studio dominates the guest beers. Quiz night is Thursday. A small beer garden overlooking Helmshore Textile Museum and lodge can be reached by steps to the side of the pub.
Q🛏❀&♣☐🐾

Heysham

Royal Ⓛ ✓
7 Main Street, LA3 2RN (70yds towards St Patrick's Chapel from Heysham Village bus stop)
✪ 12-11 (midnight Fri & Sat) ☎ (01524) 859298
⊕ theroyalheysham.co.uk
Thwaites Wainwright, Lancaster Bomber; house beer (by Thwaites); 3 changing beers (often Marston's, Thwaites) Ⓗ
A 15th-century inn in the heart of the village. As you enter, a tiny locals' bar is on the right and a restaurant is on the left; the main bar is accessed via a winding passage and opens onto a large landscaped garden. Outside is a covered and heated smoking area. A general quiz is on Tuesday, with a music quiz on Thursday. Bands play on bank holidays and the last Sunday of each month from March to August. Plans for B&B accommodation are underway. Q🛏❀◑●P☐(4,5)᚛

Holme Chapel

Queen Ⓛ ✓
412 Burnley Road, BB10 4SU
✪ 5-11; 12-midnight Sat & Sun; closed Mon
☎ (01282) 436712
Thwaites Original; 4 changing beers Ⓗ
A roadside free house in the spectacular Cliviger Gorge on the A671 between Burnley and Todmorden. The pub has recently undergone a major refurbishment without altering the original two-roomed layout. Food is served early evenings weekdays, and afternoons and evenings at weekends. Thursday is quiz night and a beer draw is held on Sunday. The pleasant beer garden is up steps at the back of the pub. 🛏❀◑&☐(592)🐾᚛

Knott End on Sea

Knott End Working Men's Club
Salisbury Avenue, FY6 0BP
✪ 11-midnight; 12-11 Sun ☎ (01253) 812226
⊕ knottendwmc.co.uk
Thwaites Original; 2 changing beers (often Bank Top, Cross Bay) Ⓗ
Private members' club which allows CAMRA members free entry on production of a membership card, otherwise entry is £1. It has a large games room including two snooker tables and a pool table, a comfortable bar lounge with TV to relax in, and a function/concert room for private parties and live music. One bar, central to all three rooms, has three handpumps with two changing guest beers, mostly from fairly local breweries. 🛏❀◑&♣P☐(2C)᚛

Lancaster

Borough Ⓛ
3 Dalton Square, LA1 1PP (near town hall)
✪ 12-11.30 (12.30am Fri); 11-12.30am Sat; 11-11.30 Sun
☎ (01524) 64170 ⊕ theboroughlancaster.co.uk
Borough Pale, Bitter, Wintermere Dark; 4 changing beers (sourced regionally; often 4Ts, Borough, Wells) Ⓗ
An upmarket town house built in 1824 but with a Victorian frontage, now a pub that succeeds in appealing both to food lovers and ale aficionados. The front area resembles a gentlemen's club with deep-buttoned chairs and chandeliers, the large back room is a restaurant, and the bar is in a

passage between them. Outside is a sheltered patio with covered smoking area, and there is a brewery in the cellar. A comedy club features on Sunday evening. Wintertime Dark is replaced by Summertime Dark in the summer.
🏠🛏🏮🌙🚱🍴🐾🌳🛜

Lancaster Brewery ✪

LA1 3LA (on edge of town in Trough of Bowland direction)
🌀 10-5 ☎ (01524) 848537 🌐 lancasterbrewery.co.uk
Lancaster Amber, Blonde, Black, Red; 3 changing beers (often Lancaster) Ⓗ
The brewery visitor centre is in a capacious steel shed on a leafy leisure park with shops, open to the public at the times above (closed Mon-Wed in winter), and available for functions at other times. It is mainly furnished with dining tables and benches, also a few sofas. Brewery tours are at 11am and 3pm, for a £10 charge, and it has a retail shop with ale, clothing and souvenirs.
🏠👍🅿🚱(18)🐾🛜

Merchant's ✪

29 Castle Hill, LA1 1YN
🌀 11.30-11 (12.30am Fri); 11-12.30am Sat ☎ (01524) 66466 🌐 merchants1688.co.uk
House beer (by Old School); 8 changing beers (sourced regionally; often Kirkby Lonsdale, Tirril) Ⓗ
Converted wine merchants' cellars built in 1688 with an extensive outdoor drinking area creating a peaceful haven away from the hubbub of the city centre. The main drinking areas are in three separate tunnels, with a fourth forming the entrance and bar area. Look for the stoneware bottles used in the construction of the cellar walls. One tunnel is now a restaurant, another is used for functions as required. Quiz night is Sunday. The house beer, Castle Blonde, is produced by Old School Brewery. Many board games are available, and there is live music every Saturday evening.
🏠🏮🚱🍴🛜

Pub

China Street, LA1 1EX
🌀 3-midnight; 1-1am Fri; 1-1am Sat; closed Sun ☎ (01524) 848002 🌐 thepub.gb.net
Robinsons Trooper; 2 changing beers (often Bank Top, Robinsons) Ⓗ
The biker/metal pub for the area. It has two rooms with basic decor, one with a pool table, the other with a stage. This venue, originally called the Castle Hotel (although it has never been the nearest pub to the castle), opened in in 1901 when China Street was widened. Poker is played on Tuesday evening, open mic night is Thursday, and live music, invariably loud, is performed on Friday and Saturday nights. 🏠🚱♣🚪🛜

Robert Gillow

64 Market Street, LA1 1HP
🌀 8am-1am; 10-midnight Sun ☎ (01524) 36092 🌐 pubfoodlancaster.co.uk
Hydes Original; 2 changing beers (often Hydes) Ⓗ
This venue was converted from retail premises in 2007, retaining the façade with its huge curved windows. The interior is standard 21st-century pub, with wooden screens to break the area up and furniture of varying height. Old prints hang on the walls, some making a nod to the eponymous Robert, who started his furniture business nearby. An upstairs room is also open to the public (and available to hire). Music is played nearly every day.

There is a collection of bottled beer, some quite rare, strong and expensive. It's Lancaster's only oyster bar. Q🍴🐟♣🍴🚱🐾🛜

Sun ✪

63 Church Street, LA1 1ET
🌀 11-midnight; 11.30-1am Fri; 11-1am Sat; 11-11.30 Sun ☎ (01524) 66006 🌐 thesunhotelbar.co.uk
Lancaster Amber, Blonde, Black, Red; Thwaites Wainwright; 4 changing beers Ⓗ
Completely altered in 2004 and extended next door in early 2005, the decor here combines a mixture of exposed stonework, wood panelling and solid furniture, with ambient candlelight in the evenings. The original pub has open space for vertical drinking; the extension is mostly furnished with old dining tables. Some original features remain, including stone fireplaces (one with a wood-burning stove) and a well. The pub is the primary outlet for Lancaster Brewery in the city. Outside is a peaceful courtyard with a heated and covered smoking area. Open for breakfast 7.30-10.30am, alcohol served from 11am.
🛏🏠🏮🌙👍🚱🐾🛜

Tap House Ⓛ

2 Gage Street, LA1 1UH
🌀 12-midnight (1am Fri & Sat); 12-11 Sun ☎ (01524) 842232 🌐 taphouselancasterbar.com
Hawkshead Windermere Pale; 3 changing beers (often Fell) Ⓗ
This pub describes itself as a world beer shrine, but sells plenty of British beer alongside the imports. It is a small 19th-century street-corner building completely refurbished in 2012, with some bare brickwork, a lot of visible wood (including old beer casks incorporated into the furnishings), high, chunky tables, and a decor that is white and grey. It has a small beer library, and runs weekly tastings/Meet the Brewer events on Wednesdays. The quiz is on Monday. 👍🚱🐾🛜

White Cross Ⓛ ✪

Quarry Road, LA1 4XT (behind town hall, on canal towpath)
🌀 11.30-11 (12.30am Fri & Sat); 12-11 Sun ☎ (01524) 33999 🌐 thewhitecross.co.uk
Copper Dragon Golden Pippin; Sharp's Doom Bar; Theakston Old Peculier; Timothy Taylor Landlord; 10 changing beers (sourced regionally; often Allendale, Hardknott, Tirril) Ⓗ
A modern (1988) renovation of an old canalside warehouse with an open-plan interior and a light, airy feel. French windows open onto extensive canalside seating. There is a Tuesday quiz, and a beer and pie festival each April. It stands in the corner of an extensive complex of Victorian textile mills, now converted to other uses. The wide open spaces and decor makes it look like a circuit pub, but in fact much of the custom comes either from the residential areas up the hill or from the nearby workplaces (including the adult college).
🏠🏮👍♣🍴🚱🛜

Lathom

Ship Inn ✪

4 Wheat Lane, L40 4BX (take School Lane from Burscough, turn left after humpback bridge) SD452116
🌀 12-midnight (1am Fri & Sat); 12-11.30 Sun ☎ (01704) 893117 🌐 shipatlathom.co.uk
Prospect Nutty Slack; Thwaites Wainwright, Lancaster Bomber; changing beers Ⓗ

A traditional country pub in an idyllic canalside location. The cosy central bar features a real fire and separates the two dining areas, which serve pub classics complemented by interesting and ever-changing specials. There is a dog-friendly boot room complete with logburner. The pub is exceptionally popular in summer, with the large beer garden often packed out. A highlight of the year is the September beer, pie and sausage festival, with over 40 handpulled ales.
🏡◑🍴⇌🖳(337,3A)🐾

Leyland

Leyland Lion 🗓 ✅
60 Hough Lane, PR25 2SA
🕐 8am-11.30 (12.30am Fri & Sat) ☎ (01772) 643990
Hawkshead Windermere Pale; Ruddles Best Bitter; Sharp's Doom Bar; house beer (by Moorhouse's); 6 changing beers 🖽
Opened in 2011, this conversion of a town-centre post office is smaller than most Wetherspoon pubs. A central log fire is also unusual for this operator. The pub's name commemorates one of the buses which made the town famous and which were built a few yards up the road. Ten beers are usually on tap, often coming from local breweries, plus a real cider. Handy for the Commercial Vehicle Museum. Alcohol is served from 9am.
🛏🏡◑ᴋ⇌🖳(109,111,113)🛜

Market Ale House 🗓
33 Hough Lane, PR25 2SB
🕐 2-10; 12-11 Fri & Sat; 2-8 Sun; closed Mon
☎ (01772) 623363
6 changing beers (sourced locally) 🖽
Leyland's smallest pub opened in 2013 in former shop premises. It is the area's first micropub and is at the entrance to the former Leyland Motors North Works, which now serves as the town's market hall. Six changing real ales come predominantly from local breweries. Changing ciders, wine and a few spirits are also served. Food is limited to Lancashire cheeses and pork pies. In summer, tables are put on the wide pavement to create an outside drinking area.
Q⇌🍴🖳(109,111,113)🐾🛜

Withy Arms 🗓 ✅
3 Worden Lane, PR25 3EL (opp Fox & Lion near Tesco)
🕐 11-11.45 ☎ (01772) 301969 ⊕ withyarms.com/leyland
Ribble WA Bitter; 5 changing beers 🖽
Previously known as the Roebuck, this inn reopened in 2013 as the Withy Arms. Closely modelled on its sister pub in Bamber Bridge, the interior is attractive and open plan with a wine-bar feel. The five changing guest beers often come from local breweries. There is a surprisingly large beer garden at the rear with open and covered areas which hosts three annual beer festivals. A microbrewery at the rear of the pub is planned.
🛏🏡◑🖳(109,111,113)🐾🛜

Longridge

Corporation Arms
Lower Road, PR3 2YJ (near B5243/B6245 jct)
🕐 11-midnight (Fri & Sat); 12-10.30 Sun ☎ (01772) 782644
⊕ corporationarms.com
4 changing beers 🖽
A substantial 18th-century stone-built inn close to the Longridge Reservoirs on the road to Ribchester,

handy for local walks. This free house has a reputation for excellent ale, food, service and accommodation. Four handpumps serve beers from local breweries, with Bowland, Copper Dragon and Moorhouse's among the favourites. Real cider is normally only available during summer months. There is an annual beer festival on the spring bank holiday weekend. Q🛏🏡🛌◑ᴋ🏕🌸P🖳(5A,5B)🛜

Longton

Dolphin 🗓
Marsh Lane, PR4 5JY
🕐 12-11 ☎ (01772) 612032
4 changing beers (sourced locally) 🖽
Isolated country pub at the end of a lane on Longton Marsh. The handpumps are in the wood-floored public bar, and there is a comfortable lounge and a restaurant in the rear conservatory. A large and varied menu covers everything from sandwiches to man-versus-food challenges. Up to four real ales and a cider are available, in a changing selection with an emphasis on local micros, often including a mild or dark beer. Evening closing is flexible dependent on trade.
🛏🏡◑ᴋ🌸P🐾

Lostock Hall

Anchor ✅
Croston Road, PR5 5LA (300yds from B5254 alongside Preston-Blackburn railway line)
🕐 4.30-11.30; 4-midnight Fri; 12-midnight Sat; 1-11.30 Sun
☎ (01772) 335637 ⊕ theanchorinnlostockhall.co.uk
5 changing beers (sourced nationally) 🖽
Just a short distance from the Tardy Gate shopping area, this friendly community pub offers five changing cask ales from the Heineken Discover Cask range, with LocAle beers often available. In May and September it holds a beer festival in marquees on a large grassy area adjacent to the pub. A traditional roast is served on Sundays only, 3-5pm. Q🛏🏡ᴋ⇌🌸P🖳

Lytham

Railway Hotel ✅
Station Road, FY8 5DH (next to fire station on B5259)
🕐 8am-midnight ☎ (01253) 797250
Ruddles Best Bitter; Sharp's Doom Bar; house beer (by Moorhouse's); 5 changing beers (sourced nationally) 🖽
When Wetherspoon acquired this pub it revived its original Victorian name. It has a bright, new-look interior on different levels, with four distinct themed areas featuring golf, railways and old photos of Lytham's halcyon days as a tourist resort. There is a small beer garden at the front with a separate smoking area, and another small drinking area at the side. The C&S Ale harks back to a long-defunct local brewery. There is limited parking at the rear. Q🛏🏡◑ᴋ⇌🌸🖳🛜

Taps 🗓 ✅
12 Henry Street, FY8 5LE
🕐 11-11 (midnight Fri & Sat) ☎ (01253) 736226
⊕ thetaps.net
Greene King IPA; Morland Old Speckled Hen; Robinsons Dizzy Blonde; 7 changing beers (sourced regionally; often Lytham) 🖽
Traditional wooden-floored, bare-walled pub, refurbished in 2015, with an enthusiastic national

following. Ten beers including guests from independent and local brewers, one always a dark mild, alongside two ciders, are served by friendly and knowledgeable staff. The pub hosts darts and dominoes teams and supports the RNLI. Home-cooked and locally sourced food is served at lunchtime. There is an outside heated seating area and a real fire in winter. A multiple CAMRA award-winner, former branch and Lancashire Pub of the Year, and winner of Greene King Best Development Award 2015. Q🏠🕪🕭&⇌♣🚌🖵🛜

Mere Brow

Legh Arms
82 The Gravel, PR4 6JX
🕓 12-11 (midnight Fri & Sat); 12-10.30 Sun
☎ (01772) 933958
Burscough Mere Blonde; house beer (by Burscough); 1 changing beer (often Moorhouse's) Ⓗ
This village local used to be a regular in the Guide years ago but fell on hard times as a Punch pub, until it was bought by Mike McCombe of the Hop Vine, Burscough, in 2014, who did his magic with it to make it a thriving local pub and restaurant. The X2 Liverpool to Preston bus stops on the A565 near the roundabout into Mere Brow.
Q🛏🏠🕪&P🖵🐾🛜

Morecambe

Eric Bartholomew ✅
10 Euston Road, LA4 5DD
🕓 9am-11 (midnight Fri & Sat) ☎ (01524) 405860
Greene King Abbot; Ruddles Best Bitter; 4 changing beers Ⓗ
Opened in 2004, this Wetherspoon pub is dedicated to Eric Morecambe (born Eric Bartholomew). The venue near the seafront is on two levels, with an upstairs lounge and dinner area. The long bar services an open-plan interior with pictures of 19th-century Morecambe and some artwork with a Morecambe and Wise theme. There is outside seating at the front for smokers but no drinking allowed. Close to shops and a public car park. Q🏠🕪&⇌♿🖵🛜

Morecambe ✅
25 Lord Street, LA4 5HX
🕓 12-11 ☎ (01524) 415239 🌐 themorecambehotel.co.uk
Cross Bay Halo, Sunset Blonde, Zenith; Tetley Bitter Ⓗ
Reopened in 2015 after renovation in a contemporary style, the pub is light and airy, with flagged floors and a variety of seating and tables. The bar is faced with unplaned wood. There are four rooms dotted around the bar, and a surprisingly spacious garden. Screens show videos of 20th-century Morecambe. The name is not hubris: this was a coaching inn built long before there was a town called Morecambe.
🏠🛏🕪&⇌🖵🐾

Palatine
The Crescent, LA4 5BZ (overlooking prom opp clock tower)
🕓 12-11 (midnight Fri & Sat) ☎ (01524) 410503
Lancaster Amber, Blonde, Black, Red; 2 changing beers (often Lancaster) Ⓗ
An Edwardian seafront mid-terraced pub. The ground floor was completely transformed in late-2008 with much bare stone and woodwork. The bar room is quite small, with some intimate

corners. An upstairs room is rather different. Cosy and carpeted, many of the fittings – leaded lights, shelving, fireplace – appear to be original. Enjoy the spectacular views across the bay, especially at sunset. There are seats on the pavement in front. 🏠🕪&⇌🖵🛜

Royal Ⓛ
257 Marine Road Central, LA4 4BJ
🕓 12-11 ☎ (01524) 416668
Exmoor Gold; Sharp's Doom Bar; 3 changing beers Ⓗ
A survival from Edwardian Morecambe, built around 1850, although far from intact; however, renovation in 2012 respected the remaining features and blends with them. A single bar room stretching from the handsome bay window (overlooking the bay and the Eric Morecambe statue) to the back windows is complemented by an upstairs room variously used for dining or functions. Steak night is Thursday, and live music takes place on Thursday (acoustic), Friday, Saturday and Sunday. The house beer is from Cross Bay.
🏠🛏🕪⇌🖵(4,6)🛜

Nether Kellet

Limeburners Arms 🍺
32 Main Road, LA6 1EP
🕓 7.45-11; 4-11 Sun; closed Mon
1 changing beer Ⓗ
The building here dates from the early-19th century. Once – within living memory – most country pubs were like this: no food, no jukebox, plain and simply furnished. Minor improvements have not changed its character. Unsurprisingly, most of the customers are locals, and the landlord himself is a local farmer. His family have run the place for 80 years. The old photos in the bar are a rewarding study. Q🏠🅰♣P🖵(51)🐾

Ormskirk

Court Leet ✅
4 Wheatsheaf Walk, L39 2XA
🕓 8am-12.30am (1am Thu-Sat) ☎ (01695) 579803
Greene King 1799; Ruddles Best Bitter; 10 changing beers (often Cross Bay, Moorhouse's, Weetwood) Ⓗ
Opened in 2014, this Wetherspoon pub is in the centre of Ormskirk in a small courtyard area off Burscough Street. It has a large open-plan main bar area fitted out in a modern and contemporary style. Virtually the entire upper floor is taken up by a fully exposed terrace which includes a no-smoking section. It is thought the pub occupies the site where the court leet met, which was responsible for running the town's affairs until 1876. A lift is available. 🛏🏠🕪&⇌🖵🛜

Cricketers Ⓛ
24 Chapel Street, L39 4QF
🕓 12-midnight; 12-11 Sun ☎ (01695) 571123
🌐 thecricketers-ormskirk.co.uk
Thwaites Nutty Black, Wainwright; 4 changing beers (often George Wright, Old School, Prospect) Ⓗ
Offering an extensive range of real ales from a selection of local breweries, the Cricketers provides a warm and cosy bar area as well as a stunning beer garden as well as a private dining area for up to 10 people. Positioned close to Ormskirk Cricket Club, the walls are adorned with memorabilia including team photos from the local club that date back to the early-1900s. Quality home-cooked food

featuring local suppliers is served daily, with exclusive food and drink offers Monday-Saturday 12-6pm. ◑&≢🖳(375,385)

Hop Inn Bier Shop 🅛
12 Burscough Street, L39 2ER
✪ 11-11 ☎ (01695) 575907
House beer (by Burscough); 3 changing beers (often Burscough, First Chop Brewing Arm, George Wright) 🅗
This former shop has been custom-converted into a plush Belgian-style single-room bar. It features an extensive range of foreign bottled beers (lambic, Trappist, fruit beers) which can be perused on the beautiful menus or in tasteful wall-mounted cabinets. The bar serves authentic foreign lagers and four real ales, including beers from nearby Burscough Brewery. A Bavarian night, a quiz during the week and live music at weekends make this a popular venue. No TV or games. Q≢●🖵🖳🛜

Orrell

Delph Tavern
Tontine Road, WN5 8UJ
✪ 11.30-1am (2am Fri & Sat) ☎ (01695) 622239
Thwaites Wainwright; house beer (by AllGates); 3 changing beers 🅗
A real community pub frequented by a mixed regular clientele and occasional visitors, taking advantage of the varied tasty pub grub on offer served in a pleasant separate dining area. Evening activities cover a broad range including pool, darts, TV sport on several large screens, a quiz and live music. A wide range of local ales is served and the bar area can get quite busy. There is a small outside seating space. 🛏🏵◑&≢♣P🛜

Padiham

Hare & Hounds 🅛 ✅
58 West Street, BB12 8JD
✪ 4-11; 12-midnight Sat; 12-10.30 Sun ☎ (01282) 545308
Coach House Gunpowder Mild; 6 changing beers 🅗
An award-winning true free house rescued from pub company mismanagement, now thriving and selling an excellent choice of beers alongside a changing real cider. Two rooms front the large bar, with a large separate room to one side where beer festivals are held. There are real fires in all rooms. A large beer garden to the rear and a small seating area to the front complete this warm, friendly pub. Adjacent to Padiham FC and cricket club.
🛏🏵&♣●P🖳(27,152)❀

Parbold

Railway Hotel 🅛 ✅
1 Station Road, WN8 7NU
✪ 5-11; 12-11.30 Fri & Sat; 12-10.30 Sun ☎ (01257) 462917
Tetley Bitter; 4 changing beers (sourced locally; often Hophurst, Problem Child, Prospect) 🅗
A traditional village pub ideally located for walkers and cyclists visiting the area. It has a central drinking area and two separate rooms on either side, with a roaring fire in winter, a large-screen TV, comfy seats and sofas, and pub games. Fresh ground coffee and quality bar snacks are served 12-3pm Tuesday to Sunday. There is a fully fitted disabled WC and baby-changing facilities. Outside is a beer garden and large car park with facilities for camper vans. Q🛏🏵&Å≢♣P🖳❀🛜

Wayfarer Inn 🅛
1-3 Alder Lane, WN8 7NL
✪ 12-midnight (1.30am Fri & Sat) ☎ (01257) 464600
🌐 wayfarerparbold.co.uk
Problem Child Rapscallion, Good Spankin'; 4 changing beers 🅗
At least two Problem Child beers, brewed on site, are always available, alongside a range of locally brewed ales and a real cider. The pub is popular for food – diners can choose from bar, restaurant and Italian menus served in the bar and dining areas. It has low-beamed ceilings with cosy nooks and crannies. Close to the Leeds-Liverpool Canal and Parbold Hill with its panoramic views, it is particularly popular in summer. Outside seating is ideal for enjoying the scenery. Q🛏🏵◑&≢P🖳❀🛜

Pendleton

Swan with Two Necks 🏆 🅛
Main Street, BB7 1PT
✪ 12-2.30 (not Mon), 6-11; 12-11 Sat; 12-8 Sun
☎ (01200) 423112 🌐 swanwithtwonecks.co.uk
5 changing beers 🅗
Dating from 1772 as a licensed farm, the pub sits beside the stream in the heart of the village. The landlords have been in charge for 30 years and are renowned for their welcome and hospitality. National CAMRA Pub of the Year in 2014, you will find five beers here (including a mild) and a changing cider on the bar. CAMRA members receive a discount. Home-cooked, locally sourced food, is served daily; booking is essential at weekends, especially for the Sunday roast. Q🏵◑♣●P❀

Penwortham

Black Bull Inn ✅
83 Pope Lane, PR1 9BA
✪ 11-11 (midnight Fri; 11.30 Sat); 12-11 Sun
☎ (01772) 752953 🌐 blackbull-penwortham.co.uk
Greene King IPA; Theakston Lightfoot; 3 changing beers (sourced nationally) 🅗
Attractive cottage-style inn dating back to the early 1800s, which has managed to retain a village-pub atmosphere despite its location in a well-populated area. On entering, a narrow passageway leads through to a central bar serving a number of drinking areas including a separate public bar. A friendly community hostelry, the many social events include a popular Thursday quiz, while local charities are actively supported. Three guest beers are usually available. Q🏵♣P🖳(12,12A)❀🛜

Fleece 🅛 ✅
39 Liverpool Road, PR1 9XD
✪ 11.30-11 (midnight Fri & Sat); 12-11 Sun
☎ (01772) 745561 🌐 fleecepenwortham.co.uk
Tetley Bitter; house beer (by Hart); 3 changing beers (sourced nationally) 🅗
The Fleece is located next to the old water tower, Penwortham's most distinctive feature. From the front, the pub presents a cosy village inn appearance, but the building has been extensively modernised. The interior has been arranged to include a number of separate drinking and dining areas, while outside there is a large beer garden for use in the summer months. The house ale, Fleeced, is a 3.9% ABV beer produced by Hart Brewery. 🛏🏵◑&P🖳(2,3)

Poulton le Fylde

Old Town Hall ✔

5 Church Street, FY6 7AP

☼ 11-midnight (1am Fri & Sat); 12-11.30 Sun
☎ (01253) 892257

5 changing beers (often Kirkby Lonsdale, Moorhouse's, Saltaire) Ⓗ

Right in the centre of Poulton, overlooked by its historic church, this pub was originally called the Bay Horse before being used, for many years, as the town hall. It is now back as a pub and serving a range of five cask beers, mainly from Lancashire and Yorkshire brewers. Several TVs show live sport, the rear of the pub is decorated with football memorabilia, and the front with old photos of the town. A wine bar on the first floor is open on Fridays and Saturdays. &≠♣🖩🐾🎏🛜

Poulton Elk ✔

22 Hardhorn Road, FY6 7SR

☼ 8am-midnight (1am Fri & Sat) ☎ (01253) 895265

Greene King Abbot; Ruddles Best Bitter; 8 changing beers Ⓗ

A conversion of a large former nightclub just a couple of minutes' walk from the town centre, this pub has a reputation for the quality of its 10 changing ales. Although mostly one large room, it has been split into several distinct smaller areas to give a cosier feeling. French doors open onto a popular terrace at the front of the pub. Its name relates to the discovery nearby of an ancient elk skeleton, a spear point found there providing the earliest evidence of people in north-west England. 🎏🕸🐈‍⬛🌙&≠🖩🛜

Thatched House 🍴 Ⓛ ✔

30 Ball Street, FY6 7BG

☼ 11.30-11 (11.30 Thu); 11-midnight Fri & Sat; 12-11 Sun
☎ (01253) 891063 🌐 thatchedhousepoulton.co.uk

Chapel Street Brain's Best, Brewhouse Blonde, Double Hopped; 7 changing beers Ⓗ

A mock-Tudor pub in the corner of the Norman churchyard that replaced a much older, smaller public house that did have a thatched roof. Ten beers are generally available, usually including five from the range of ales produced in the microbrewery in the former stable area. It was the local CAMRA branch's 2016 Pub of the Year. Many pictures of sporting heroes and historic Poulton decorate the wood-panelled walls. There are two wood-burning stoves and one log fire. Q&≠♣🖩🐾🛜

Preston

Ale Emporium

53 Fylde Road, PR1 2XQ

☼ 12-11.30 (11 Mon; 12.30am Fri & Sat) ☎ (01772) 378290

10 changing beers (sourced nationally) Ⓗ

A genuine free house serving 10 guest beers from microbreweries. It has a comfortable single-room bar set back from Fylde Road adjacent to the unrelated Ferret pub. There is a pool table in the area behind the bar and three large sports screens. Live music plays on Thursday and Saturday evenings, and an upstairs room is available for hire. An annual beer festival takes place in September and occasional Meet the Brewer nights are held. Local CAMRA Pub of the Year 2015. It may close early on quiet nights. 🕸♣🖩🛜

Anderton Arms Ⓛ ✔

Longsands Lane, Fulwood, PR2 9PS

☼ 11.30-11 (11.30 Wed & Thu; midnight Fri & Sat)
☎ (01772) 700104

Moorhouse's Pendle Witches Brew; Thwaites Wainwright; 3 changing beers Ⓗ

Welcoming, warm, friendly pub at the heart of the local community. Up to five real ales come from over 90 breweries from a quarterly changing seasonal cask menu (see website for details). Meals are served all day, with breakfast from 10am on Saturday and Sunday. All cask ales are £2.49 a pint on Monday. Bottles of wine are sold at a discount on Sunday from 5pm. There is a quiz night on Wednesday. 🕸🐈‍⬛🌙&P🖩🛜

Black Horse ★

166 Friargate, PR1 2EJ

☼ 10.30-11 (midnight Fri & Sat); 12-10.30 Sun
☎ (01772) 204855

Robinsons Dizzy Blonde, Cumbria Way, Unicorn, Trooper; 4 changing beers (sourced nationally) Ⓗ

Classic Grade II-listed pub in the main shopping area with a nationally important historic pub interior, featuring a tiled bar, walls and mosaic floor. The two front rooms, with real log fires, are adorned with photos of old Preston; the famous hall of mirrors seating area is to the rear. Up to five Robinsons beers are on tap, with the guest beers coming from various smaller breweries. ≠🍴🖩🐾

Continental

South Meadow Lane, PR1 8JP

☼ 12-11.15 (12.15am Fri & Sat) ☎ (01772) 499425
🌐 newcontinental.net

House beer (by Marble); 5 changing beers (sourced nationally) Ⓗ

The pub is set beside the River Ribble, the main railway line and Miller Park. A two-times winner of local CAMRA Pub of the Year, it has a main bar area plus a lounge with a real fire in winter and a conservatory overlooking the garden. Live music and theatre regularly feature in a separate arts/events space that is also used for beer festivals. Seven microbrewery beers are sold, including the house ale from Marble and a dark beer. Freshly cooked meals are served daily except Monday. Q🎏🕸🐈‍⬛🌙P🐾🛜

Grey Friar ✔

144 Friargate, PR1 2EJ

☼ 8am-midnight (1am Fri & Sat) ☎ (01772) 558542

Greene King Abbot; Ruddles Best Bitter; 8 changing beers (sourced nationally) Ⓗ

Modern open-plan Wetherspoon pub with raised areas to the side and rear. Preston's students and citizens, both young and old, appreciate the range of ales and food at good prices. The social mix creates a bustling atmosphere and the bar can get extremely busy at weekends. Alcohol is served from 9am daily. The guest beers vary in both style and strength, but frequently tend towards the stronger end of the scale. Two beer festivals are held every year. 🎏🕸🐈‍⬛🌙&≠🍴🖩🛜

Moorbrook

370 North Road, PR1 1RU

☼ 12-midnight ☎ (01772) 823302 🌐 themoorbrook.com

Thwaites Original; house beer (by Blackjack); 5 changing beers (sourced nationally) Ⓗ

Now privately owned, this pub is where the West Lancs CAMRA branch was formed over 40 years ago. It comprises a traditional-style wood-panelled bar with two rooms off, complete with William Morris wallpaper. The beer garden to the rear is a suntrap. Up to five guest beers plus a house ale attract people from far and wide. Traditional music is staged on the last Wednesday of the month, plus other live acts on Thursday. Food features speciality pies. ⬧🕸🌓➤♣🖭😋🎵

Old Black Bull ⬡ ✔
35 Friargate, PR1 2AT
🕓 10.30-11 (midnight Fri & Sat); 12-10.30 Sun
☎ (01772) 823397
10 changing beers (sourced nationally; often Moorhouse's) Ⓗ

Mock-Tudor city-centre pub with a tiled exterior. A small front vault, a main bar with distinctive black and white floor tiles, and two comfortable lounge areas combine to make this a popular venue. There is also a patio to the rear. Live music plays on Saturday evenings and all televised sport is shown. The guests beers are mainly from micros. Third-pint tasters and a good range of bottled beers are available. 🕸🌓🖮♣🖭😋🎵

Old Vic ⬡
79 Fishergate, PR1 2UH
🕓 10-midnight; 12-midnight Sat & Sun ☎ (01772) 828519
7 changing beers Ⓗ

Opposite the railway station, this popular pub can get busy at weekends. A number of TVs show sports events and at the rear is an outdoor decked smoking area and a car park (only available Sundays and evenings). Seven handpumps offer the widest range of LocAle beers in the area, with several microbreweries usually represented. Real ale carryouts are available, as are three third-pint taster paddles. ⬧🕸🌓➤♣🖭P🖭🎵

Wellington
124 Tulketh Road, Ashton-on-Ribble, PR2 1AR
🕓 12-11 (12.30am Fri & Sat) ☎ (01772) 726641
🌐 thewellington-tulketh.co.uk
Copper Dragon Golden Pippin; Jennings Cumberland Ale; 4 changing beers (sourced nationally) Ⓗ

Friendly end-of-terrace pub that is both community- and family-oriented. A single main room has six handpumps; three white-handled ones serving pale or blonde beers, and three dark-handled ones serving darker ales, with LocAles often available. A pool and darts room is to the rear. Front entry is by a flight of steps, but there is level access at the side from Waterloo Terrace. Live music features on Friday and Saturday nights, and open mic every other Monday. An annual beer festival is in June. ⬧🕸🌓♣🖭(68)😋🎵

Wheatsheaf
50 Water Lane, Ashton-on-Ribble, PR2 2NL
🕓 11-11 (11.30 Fri & Sat); 12-10.30 Sun ☎ (01772) 725917
5 changing beers (sourced nationally; often Moorhouse's) Ⓗ

Victorian local on the way to Preston marina, a mile from the city centre. Beer prices here are among the lowest in the area. It is big on TV sport, and live music plays Friday and Saturday nights. There is disabled access through the courtyard. Five guest beers include at least one from Moorhouse's, otherwise they come from anywhere in the country. Third-pint tasting racks are available. At least two beer festivals a year are held in a marquee at the rear. 🕸🌓➤🖭(68,35)🎵

Rawtenstall

Shepherds Inn ⬡
225 Haslingden Road, BB4 6RE
🕓 5-midnight (1am Sat); 1-11 Sun ☎ (01706) 213025
Copper Dragon Golden Pippin; Lees Bitter Ⓗ

Situated on the A681, this stone-built free house is in the middle of a row of terraced houses and has been recently refurbished. There is an open-plan bar area with two handpumps, a smaller side room with pool table, and a small outdoor area to the rear. This is a community-oriented pub with pool team, mixed darts, quiz nights and regular country music on Sunday evenings. ⬧🕸🌓♣🖭(464,244)😋🎵

White Lion ✔
72 Burnley Road, BB4 8EW
🕓 4.30-11; 1-11 Sat & Sun ☎ (01706) 213117
Black Sheep Best Bitter; Moorhouse's White Witch; 2 changing beers Ⓗ

There has been a public house on this site since 1816. Formerly a row of cottages, it is now a large pub serving an array of guest beers, from the likes of local brewers Reedley Hallows and Worsthorne to the more distant Acorn and Salamander. A weekly quiz is held on Tuesday, with entertainment on Friday and Saturday. There are pool teams, and football on two screens. Close to Ski Rossendale and the terminus of the East Lancs Railway. ⬧🕸🌓♣🖭P🖭(X43)

Rufford

Hesketh Arms
81 Liverpool Road, L40 1SB (on A59 at jct with B5246)
🕓 12-11 (midnight Fri & Sat) ☎ (01704) 821002
Moorhouse's Pride of Pendle; 7 changing beers Ⓗ

A spacious former Greenall's inn on the A59, the Hesketh is now a free house serving up to six ales, mostly from local microbreweries. Set in the charming village of Rufford, it is near to the National Trust property of Rufford Old Hall, the delightful St Mary's Marina, and the popular Mere Sands nature reserve. A large split-level establishment with several dining areas, the pub serves good-quality food throughout the day. Monthly live entertainment and a Tuesday quiz attract a mixed clientele. Q⬧🕸🌓➤🖮🖭P🖭(2A,347)

St Annes

Fifteens at St Annes ⬡ ✔
42 St Annes Road West, FY8 1RF
🕓 11-11 (midnight Fri & Sat); 12-11 Sun ☎ (01253) 725852
🌐 fifteensstannes.com
House beer (by Hawkshead); 5 changing beers (sourced regionally) Ⓗ

Set in a former Lloyd's Bank, Fifteens is a lively, welcoming pub which is larger than it first appears. Eclectically decorated, it incorporates many traditional features including the original vault which is surprisingly comfortable (and peaceful). Popular with regulars, locals and visitors, there is regular weekend entertainment and a quiz on Sundays. Winner of many CAMRA awards, Fifteens is both a former Cider Pub of the Year and runner-up branch Pub of the Year. Still has great coffee! 🖮➤♣🖭😋🎵

St Annes Cricket Club

Vernon Road, FY8 2RQ (road access from Highbury Rd East)
🕓 4-11 (11.30 Fri); 12-11 Sat; 12-10.30 Sun
☎ (01253) 721849 ⊕ stannescricketclub.org
Lees Bitter; 2 changing beers (sourced regionally; often Moorhouse's) Ⓗ
Spacious modern clubhouse, popular in the local area, with views onto the pitch where Andrew Flintoff made his first team debut at the age of 15. A full social calendar includes ladies' nights, live music, sportsmen's dinner, as well as a summer beer festival where real cider is available. Darts, snooker and dominoes teams play in local leagues. Food is served Saturday until 7pm and Sunday until 6pm. 🌲🍴❀🍺&♿♣P🗐(10,17)🔊

Trawl Boat ✓

36-38 Wood Street, FY8 1QR
🕓 8am-midnight (1am Fri & Sat) ☎ (01253) 783080
Greene King Abbot; Ruddles Best Bitter; Sharp's Doom Bar; 7 changing beers (sourced regionally) Ⓗ
Large Wetherspoon house converted from a former solicitors' office. It experiences many different moods throughout the day, and can get busy especially at weekends. A designated family area at the top of the pub is popular, while the real log fire creates a homely atmosphere. The spacious outdoor seating area is an attraction in the summer. Handy for the shops, buses and railway station. 🌲🍴❀🍺&⇌🍴🗐🔊

Victoria ✓

Church Road, FY8 3NE
🕓 12-11 (midnight Thu-Sat) ☎ (01253) 721041
⊕ victoriahotel-lytham-stannes.co.uk
Draught Bass; Greene King IPA; 4 changing beers (sourced nationally) Ⓗ
First appearing in the Guide in 1974, this large traditional pub goes from strength to strength. The tasteful refurbishment, completed in 2015, with the vault and snooker room now reopened, gives a range of different drinking areas. Sport is shown on two big screens, while darts, pool and a full-sized snooker table are available. It offers a range of world beers, and a summer beer festival with real cider. 🌲🍴❀🍺&⇌♣P🗐(11,68)🐾🔊

Samlesbury

Nabs Head ✓

Nabs Head Lane, PR5 0UQ
🕓 12-3 (not Mon), 5-11; 5-midnight Fri; 12-12.30am; 12-11 Sun ☎ (01254) 851416 ⊕ thenewnabshead.co.uk
Thwaites Original, Best Cask; 2 changing beers Ⓗ
Welcoming and friendly village local in a picturesque setting. The central bar, decorated with dried hops, serves two distinct drinking areas. There is a taproom behind the bar with bare boards. The L-shaped lounge is mainly used by diners; the walls are decorated with pictures from local photographers. An extensive menu is available with food from local suppliers wherever possible. There is a quiz night on Tuesday and occasional live music. Q🌲🍴❀♣P🐾🔊

> I never drink water. I'm afraid it will become habit-forming.
> **W C Fields**

New Hall Tavern Ⓛ

Cuerdale Lane, PR5 0XA (on B6230)
🕓 12-11 (midnight Thu-Sat) ☎ (01772) 877942
6 changing beers Ⓗ
On a crossroads just off junction 31 of the M6, this pub has a large car park and a heated outdoor smoking area. Indoors, it is divided up by wood and glass panels, providing separate areas for dining. Up to six real ales are served, often from local micros. Home-cooked food is, where possible, from local suppliers. Old photos and prints give an insight into the history of the area, which includes nearby Samlesbury Hall. 🌲🍴❀🍺&♣P🐾🔊

Scarisbrick

Heatons Bridge Inn 🍸 ✓

2 Heatons Bridge Road, L40 8JG (on B5242 road by Leeds & Liverpool Canal)
🕓 12-midnight ☎ (01704) 840549
Moorhouse's Black Cat; house beer (by Tetley); 1 changing beer (sourced regionally; often Moorhouse's) Ⓗ
Great canalside pub dating from 1837, when it served as offices for the Leeds and Liverpool freight services. It is a traditional pub, with separate areas and home-cooked food. Pillbox beer is often served as a memorial to WWII; there is a lookout post outside. Twice-yearly military displays and an annual classic bus service feature, with themed beers for the occasion. This is a popular pub with families, walkers and cyclists, in an excellent rural setting, with a garden with a dining area. 🌲🍴❀🍺&♣🗐(375)🐾🔊

Silverdale

Woodlands

Woodlands Drive, LA5 0RU
🕓 5-11.30; 12-midnight Sat; 12-11.30 Sun
☎ (01524) 701655
4 changing beers Ⓗ
Large country house on an elevated site, circa 1878, converted to a pub with only minimal alterations. Most of the trade is provided by locals. The bar has a large fireplace as big as the counter and enjoys great views across Morecambe Bay. Beer pumps are in another room, with a list of the four available ales on the wall facing the bar. Home-made sandwiches are served at weekends. The smoking area is covered and sheltered. A beer festival of 30 ales takes place in October, and there is a quiz on the last Sunday of the month. To telephone the pub you need to ring twice. Q🌲🍴♣🍴P🗐🐾

Slaidburn

Hark to Bounty Ⓛ

Townend, BB7 3EP
🕓 11-11 ☎ (01200) 446246 ⊕ harktobounty.co.uk
Theakston Best Bitter, Old Peculier; 2 changing beers Ⓗ
This family-run, traditional inn has nine en-suite bedrooms and is ideal for exploring the Forest of Bowland Area of National Beauty. Either side of the central bar, with four ales on handpump, are comfortable lounges with real fires. Meals are served at lunchtimes and evenings from a home-cooked menu including daily changing specials. Check food service times before travelling in winter. A 16th-century court room, serving as a

function room, can be viewed by request. The large beer garden is popular in summer.
Q🕏🏚🛏◑🔥♿⚽P🚋(10)🐾🌐

Tockholes

Royal Arms Ⓛ
Tockholes Road, Rydal Fold, BB3 0PA
🕰 4-8 Mon; 12-11 ☎ (01254) 705373
4 changing beers Ⓗ
Traditional free house formed from two cottages knocked together. It is small but has a great atmosphere within its four back-to-back rooms, where the original stone walls, real fires and flagged and wooden floors have all been retained. Beers are from local microbreweries. The pub is in the West Pennine Moors close to Darwen Tower and adjacent to Roddlesworth Visitor Centre, looking over moors, woods and reservoirs. Friendly staff welcome guests, walkers and dogs alike, and offer a good menu. Q🕏🕏◑🐾P🐾🌐

Walmer Bridge

Walmer Bridge ✪
Liverpool Old Road, PR4 5QE
🕰 4 (1 Sat & Sun)-midnight ☎ (01772) 612296
3 changing beers Ⓗ
Village local comprising two rooms, from either of which you have to go through four doors to reach the bar. The comfortable lounge contains photographs of bygone Walmer Bridge and Longton. The vault is popular with the sporting fraternity, while outside there is a large garden with a children's play area. Bingo takes place on Monday and a quiz on Thursday night. Up to three changing beers are available from the Punch portfolio, with an emphasis on pale and golden beer. 🕏🕏🐾P🚋(2,2A)🐾🌐

Walton-le-Dale

White Bull Ⓛ
109 Victoria Road, PR5 4BA
🕰 12-11.30 (midnight Fri & Sat); 12-12.30am Sun
Thwaites Wainwright; 3 changing beers (sourced locally; often Cross Bay, Hopstar, Three B's) Ⓗ
A true community local retaining the original multi-room layout, with a bar area and lounge at the front, a games room with pool table and dartboard, and a small lounge behind the bar. Be warned that the corridor leading to the rear rooms slopes steeply downwards. There is a small seating area on the paving at the front of the building. This cosy pub serves three guest beers, usually from local micros, and can get busy at weekends.
🕏🕏♿🐾P🚋🐾

Whalley

Dog Inn Ⓛ
55 King Street, BB7 9SP
🕰 11-11 (midnight Fri & Sat); 12-11 Sun ☎ (01254) 823009
🌐 dog-innwhalley.co.uk
6 changing beers Ⓗ
The Dog is centrally located and opens onto the main street. The curved main bar provides a convivial drinking area, while there are cosy, partly screened seating spaces giving the pub a homely feel. The backyard offers a quiet spot for outdoor drinking. Bar meals are served 12-2pm. The changing range of six real ales almost always includes a Moorhouse's beer. Popular with locals and visitors, there are regular open mic nights and a good jukebox. 🕏🕏◑≒🚋🐾🌐

Worsthorne

Crooked Billet Ⓛ
1-3 Smith Street, BB10 3NQ
🕰 7 (6 Thu)-midnight; 4.30-1am Fri; 12-1am Sat; 12 12.30am Sun ☎ 07766 230175 🌐 crookedbilletworsthorne.co.uk
Tetley Bitter; Timothy Taylor Boltmaker, Landlord; 4 changing beers Ⓗ
An award-winning true free house, this well-presented village pub has a beautiful wood and glass horseshoe bar serving both the main lounge area and snug. Guest beers are mainly from local microbreweries. Quiz nights are popular, as are Thai nights and soul nights. This pub is dog friendly and has a large covered outdoor drinking area where you can enjoy the flower-bedecked exterior. Q🕏🕏◑♿🐾P🚋(2)🐾🌐

Wrightington

White Lion ✪
117 Mossy Lea Road, WN6 9RE
🕰 10-midnight ☎ (01257) 425977
🌐 thewhitelionlancs.co.uk
Banks's Bitter; Jennings Cumberland Ale; 6 changing beers Ⓗ
Extremely popular country pub which attracts many locals, with an excellent range of food and beers for diners and drinkers. Eight handpumps are in constant use, two for regular beers and six for rotating guests from the Marston's range. The weekly quiz is on Tuesday, a poker league on Thursday. Themed evenings are held in the restaurant. The pub is family friendly, with a large beach hut-themed garden area. It is community oriented, running the village scarecrow festival, snail racing and many seasonal events and brewery trips. It has fully fitted disabled WC facilities. Q🕏🕏◑♿P🚋(113)

Cask breather

Where an entry states that some beers in a pub are served with the aid of cask breathers, this means that demand valves are connected to both casks and cylinders of gas; as beer is drawn off, it is replaced by applied gas (either carbon dioxide, nitrogen or both) to prevent oxidation. The method is not acceptable to CAMRA as it does not allow beer to condition and mature naturally. The Campaign believes brewers and publicans should use the size of casks best suited to the turnover of beer in order to avoid oxidation. If a pub in the Good Beer Guide uses cask breathers, we list only those beers that are free of the device.

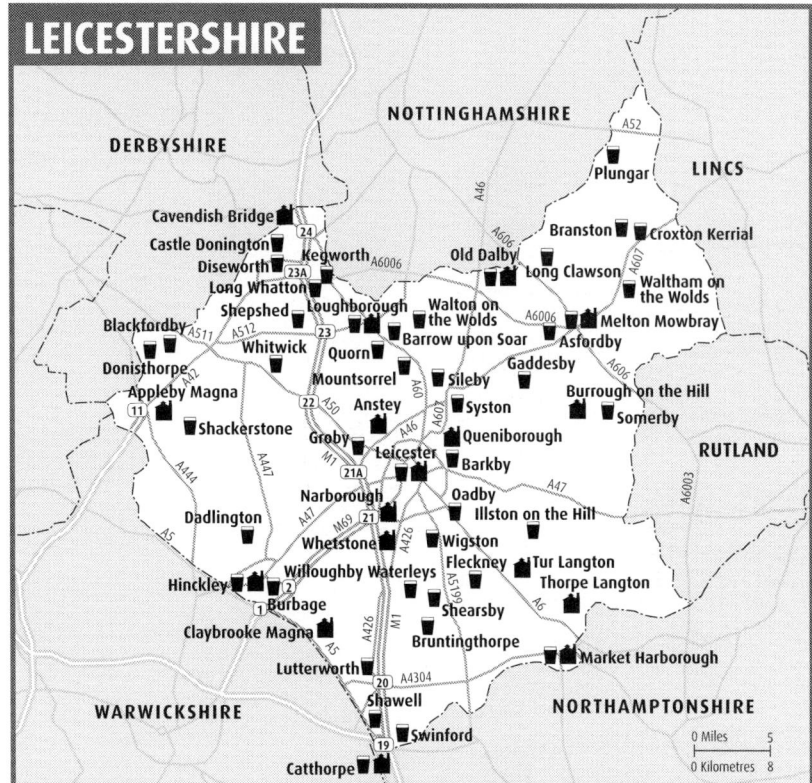

LEICESTERSHIRE

Asfordby

Horse Shoes

128 Main Street, LE14 3SA

⏰ 12-11.30; 12-4.30, 7-11.45 Sat ☎ (01664) 813392

Batemans Gold, XB; 1 changing beer (sourced nationally) Ⓗ

A single-roomed pub at the heart of the village, the Horse Shoes compensates for its plain and simple interior decor with a warm welcome for all. This community inn is home to village darts and dominoes teams and has a skittle alley. This is the only Batemans house within the CAMRA branch area with at least two of the brewery's real ales available and usually a seasonal beer.

🖧🕮♣🖵🐾🛜

Barkby

Malt Shovel

27 Main Street, LE7 3QG

⏰ 11.30-3, 5-11.30; 11.30-11.30 Sat & Sun

☎ (0116) 269 2558

Thwaites Nutty Black, Original, Wainwright, Lancaster Bomber; 3 changing beers (often Hydes, Jennings, Thwaites) Ⓗ

This family-friendly village pub serves good-value home-cooked food in the bar and restaurant. Guest beers are supplied by Thwaites, often from other North-west England breweries. A beer festival is held on the first weekend in August. There is a large garden for the summer months.

🖧🕮🍴🕭♿🖵(100)🐾🛜

Barrow upon Soar

Soar Bridge

29 Bridge Street, LE12 8PN (next to Soar Bridge)

⏰ 12 (4 Mon)-11; 12-10.30 Sun ☎ (01509) 412686

Everards Sunchaser Blonde, Tiger Best Bitter, Original; 3 changing beers Ⓗ

The large single-room interior divides into distinct areas, with a separate restaurant, function room and skittle alley. Outside there is a floodlit pétanque court, beer terrace and garden. Well-behaved dogs and children are welcome. Home-made food is available Tuesday to Sunday with a different theme each evening. Local CAMRA Village Pub of the Year 2015.

Q🖧🕮🍴🕭♿🅰🚆♣♠🖵🐾(K2,CB27)🐾

Blackfordby

Black Lion

3 Main Street, DE11 8AB

⏰ 3-11 (1am Fri); 12-1am Sat; 12-11 Sun ☎ (01283) 337551

🌐 theblacklionblackfordby.com

Draught Bass; 5 changing beers (sourced locally) Ⓗ

Popular local in a quiet village in north-west Leicestershire, bought from Enterprise Inns and reopened in 2013 as a free house following a substantial refurbishment. Grade II-listed with old beams and open fires, it has a lovely courtyard and covered smoking area. Guest beers are often from small local breweries, and up to four ciders are on draught. Cheeseboards and ham and cheese cobs are available. A quiz evening is hosted on the first Sunday of each month and a jam night on the last Wednesday. Q🖧🕮♿♣♠🖵🐾🛜

Branston

Wheel Inn ♥ Ⓛ

Main Street, NG32 1RU

🕓 12-11; 12-8 Sun ☎ (01476) 870376

🌐 thewheelinnbranston.co.uk

Batemans XB; 2 changing beers Ⓗ

This attractive stone-built 18th-century pub houses a small bar with some seating and a larger sympathetically renovated restaurant area. The deceptively spacious outdoor area is quiet and relaxing in the summer months, with traditional outbuildings used to host festivals and regular live music. The Wheel boasts an extensive lunch and evening food menu made with locally sourced ingredients where possible, including produce from the nearby Belvoir Estate. Cask cider is usually available on the bar. Leicestershire CAMRA Pub of the Year 2015 and 2016. Q❀◑&♣🐾P🐾❄🤶

Bruntingthorpe

Plough

Main Street, LE17 5QE

🕓 4-11; 12-midnight Fri & Sat; 12-11 Sun ☎ (0116) 247 8300

🌐 theploughbruntingthorpe.com

Draught Bass; Greene King Abbot; St Austell Tribute; Theakston Best Bitter; 1 changing beer (sourced regionally) Ⓗ

Traditional village pub with a large public bar to the front and a games room to the rear leading to a pretty cottage garden. Pictures on the walls are of the Vulcan Bomber, which has close associations with nearby Bruntingthorpe Aerodrome. It is thought to have originally been a terrace of cottages and, to this day, retains a cottagey character. Q🍴❀&♣🐾❄🤶

Burbage

Anchor Inn ✓

Church Street, LE10 2DA

🕓 12-11 (midnight Fri & Sat) ☎ (01455) 636107

🌐 anchorburbage.com

Marston's Burton Bitter, Pedigree; Thwaites Wainwright; 2 changing beers Ⓗ

Popular village pub that has been comfortably refurbished with a nautical theme and is affectionately known by locals as the Yacht Club. BT Sport attracts a large following of rugby fans. As well as Burton Bitter, Pedigree and Wainwright, two guest ales from the Marston's stable are always served. Live good quality music features every other Saturday night. An attractive well-maintained garden is a delight on warmer days. 🍴❀&♣P🖨❄🤶

Burbage & District Constitutional Club Ⓛ

Church Street, LE10 2DE

🕓 11-2, 6-11; 11-11.30 Fri; 11-11.45 Sat; 12-3, 7-11 Sun ☎ (01455) 615142 🌐 burbageconclub1911.com

Greene King Abbot; Marston's Burton Bitter; 2 changing beers Ⓗ

Grade II-listed building in the heart of the village, offering a comfortable lounge with an open fire, a function room equipped with a skittle alley and a beer garden. Snooker, pool, darts, dominoes, crib, chess and table tennis can be played. Live music is hosted every Saturday night. Sandwiches and cobs are available. Formerly the home of Prime Minister George Canning. ❀&♣🖨🤶

Lime Kilns ♥ ✓

Watling Street, LE10 3ED

🕓 12-3, 5.30-11; 12-11 Sat; 12-10.30 Sun ☎ (01455) 631158

🌐 limekilnsinn.co.uk

Jennings Cocker Hoop; Marston's Burton Bitter, Pedigree; 2 changing beers Ⓗ

Situated alongside the Ashby Canal and the A5, the pub was originally an 18th-century coaching inn. It offers free moorings, a large canalside beer garden and a children's play area. The first-floor lounge has canal views and an open fire in winter. The guest beers change regularly and there are five real ciders, often from Thatchers and Westons. Traditional food is served, with special deals including Monday curry night and pie and a pint on Wednesday. Q🍴❀◑♣🐾P🤶

Castle Donington

Castle Inn

High Street, DE74 2NS

🕓 11-11 (11.30 Fri & Sat); 12-11 Sun ☎ (01332) 391296

🌐 the-castle-inn.co.uk

4 changing beers (often Charnwood, Shardlow) Ⓗ

Eighteenth-century coaching inn, recently refurbished to a high standard and reopened as a family-run free house. This fine new addition to the Castle Donington dining and drinking scene has a wood-burning pizza oven which can be seen in use. The separate bar is welcoming and there is also a comfortable covered outdoor courtyard. Excellent food is served (booking recommended). Local CAMRA branch Most Improved Pub 2015. 🍴◑🚌🖨

Catthorpe

Cherry Tree

Main Street, LE17 6DB (on main road through village ½ mile from A5)

🕓 12-2.30 (not Tue-Thu), 5-11; 12-2.30, 5-12.30am Fri; 12-12.30am Sat; 12-11.30 Sun ☎ (01788) 860430

🌐 cherrytree-pub.co.uk

Marston's Burton Bitter; 3 changing beers (sourced regionally; often Dow Bridge, Jennings, Marston's) Ⓗ

Welcoming two-roomed village free house with an outside drinking area close to the Avon Valley and the Dow Bridge, from which the local brewery takes its name – and whose beers often feature as

REAL ALE BREWERIES

Anstey Anstey (NEW)
Beardy Monkey Melton Mowbray (NEW)
Belvoir Old Dalby
Charnwood Loughborough
Co Pilot Whetstone
D. O'Brien Whetstone (NEW)
Dow Bridge Catthorpe
Elliswood Hinckley
Everards Narborough
Gas Dog ☰ Melton Mowbray
Golden Duck Appleby Magna
Great Central Leicester (NEW)
Langton Thorpe Langton
Market Harborough Market Harborough (NEW)
Parish ☰ Burrough on the Hill
Pig Pub ☰ Claybrooke Magna
Q Queniborough
Shardlow Cavendish Bridge
Très Bien Tur Langton
West End ☰ Leicester (NEW)

guest ales. An excellent bar menu includes locally sourced food and Sunday roasts. This community pub supports local league skittles, draughts and dominoes. A small beer festival is held twice yearly, and there is occasional live music. Camping is available with the landlord's permission. Q❀🕙🅰♣🐾♥🐾🐾

Croxton Kerrial

Geese & Fountain 🅛 ✅
1 School Lane, NG32 1QR
🕙 8.30am (5 Wed)-11; 8.30am-10.30 Sun; closed Tue
☎ (01476) 870350 🌐 thegeeseandfountain.co.uk
5 changing beers Ⓗ
This recently reopened village inn has two wood fires and a quiet, welcoming atmosphere. Dogs, children, cyclists and walkers are all welcome. It has five handpumps with at least one of six local breweries always represented, as well as guest beers from other local microbreweries, alongside locally brewed lagers, usually Brewster's Helles and Nobby's Pilsner, plus three real ciders. Food is served every day, including breakfast. There is no jukebox or fruit machine, but occasional folk nights supplement the hum of conversation.
Q🐾❀♣🐾P🐾🐾

Dadlington

Dog & Hedgehog 🅛
2 The Green, CV13 6JB
🕙 12-11; 12-8 Sun ☎ (01455) 213151
House beer (by Tunnel) Ⓗ
Friendly free house that continues to build on its reputation for quality ales, as well as serving the best in locally produced food in its fine restaurant. In a picturesque location, the terrace and beer garden overlook the Ashby Canal and site of the famous Battle of Bosworth (1485). The bar boasts three LocAles, all rebadged for the pub.
Q🐾❀🕙♿🐾P🐾🐾

Diseworth

Plough ✅
33 Hall Gate, DE74 2QJ
🕙 11.30-11 (midnight Fri & Sat); 12-10.30 Sun
☎ (01332) 810333 🌐 theploughdiseworth.com
Draught Bass; Marston's Pedigree; Timothy Taylor Landlord; 1 changing beer (often Wadworth) Ⓗ
Situated in a village with many half-timbered buildings, this is a cosy, multi-roomed pub with parts dating back to the 13th century. Low-beamed ceilings and exposed brickwork are just some of the original features discovered during renovation work in the 1990s. There is an interesting display of old photographs of the area. Tasty home-made food is served. The spacious, well-presented beer garden is popular in summer. A former local CAMRA Village Pub of the Year. Q❀🕙♿🅰♥P🐾🐾

Donisthorpe

Halfway House
65 Church Street, DE12 7PX
🕙 12-11 (midnight Fri & Sat) ☎ (01530) 588783
🌐 halfwayhousedonisthorpe.com
Draught Bass; Marston's Pedigree; 3 changing beers Ⓗ
Traditional dog-friendly village inn in the heart of Donisthorpe. Recently refurbished to a high

standard, it now comprises a public bar, lounge bar and a separate dining room, with beamed ceilings and a wood-burning fire. Home-made food is available Tuesday to Saturday. Three guest beers, one usually from Burton Bridge, can be served in a taster selection of three third-pint glasses. Local CAMRA Village Pub of the Year in 2014 and branch winner in 2015. Q❀🕙🐾P🐾🐾🐾

Fleckney

Golden Shield 🅛
46 Main Street, LE8 8AN
🕙 4 (12 Wed & Thu)-11; 12-midnight Fri & Sat; 11.30-11 Sun
☎ (0116) 240 2366
Greene King IPA, Abbot; St Austell Tribute; Timothy Taylor Landlord; 2 changing beers (sourced nationally; often Bradfield, Church End, Theakston) Ⓗ
Village pub in the heart of Leicestershire serving six real ales, including a rota of LocAles, microbrewery and regional beers. Home-cooked and à la carte meals are served lunchtimes Wednesday to Sunday and evenings Tuesday to Saturday – Sunday lunches are always popular. A pétanque court is available and BT Sport is screened regularly.
🐾❀🕙♥P🐾(44,49B)🐾🐾

Gaddesby

Cheney Arms 🅛
2 Rearsby Lane, LE7 4XE
🕙 12 (3 Mon)-11 ☎ (01664) 840260
Everards Beacon Bitter, Tiger Best Bitter, Original; 1 changing beer (sourced nationally) Ⓗ
A pleasant and friendly village pub with a bar room on one side of the central servery for those just wanting a pint and a chat, and a popular restaurant room on the other side. Both rooms have a real fire, creating a cosy feel. A garden, patio and pétanque court to the rear make this place an ideal stop-off point for those walking the Leicestershire Round or Midshires Way in the summer months.
Q🐾❀🕙♣🐾P🐾🐾

Groby

Stamford Arms 🅛
2 Leicester Road, LE6 0DJ
🕙 10-11 ☎ (0116) 287 5616 🌐 stamfordarms.co.uk
Everards Beacon Bitter, Tiger Best Bitter, Original; house beer (by Everards); 3 changing beers (sourced nationally; often Brunswick) Ⓗ
At the heart of Groby and home of the Everard family until 1921, the main house has become a comfortable drinking area, while an annexe is now a large restaurant. The menu includes pizzas, pasta, tapas and more traditional fare. The house ale, Lady Jane, is brewed by Everards and complements the Everards cask ales and three guest ales. Beer and cider festivals are held during the year. B&B accommodation is available in a nearby 15th-century cottage. 🐾❀🖾🕙♿♣♥P🐾🐾🐾

Hinckley

New Plough Inn ✅
Leicester Road, LE10 1LS
🕙 4.45-11; 3-midnight Fri; 12-midnight Sat & Sun
☎ (01455) 615037 🌐 thenewploughinn.co.uk
Marston's Burton Bitter, Pedigree; 3 changing beers Ⓗ

A multi award-winning community pub, the Victorian building features original wood settles, comfortable lounge areas and a traditional, cosy ambience, and is decorated with rugby memorabilia. It is home to numerous groups and societies, and darts, dominoes and skittles are played in the games room. A refurbished function room is available to the rear. Outside is a sheltered beer garden and heated smokers' area. The landlady, a CAMRA member, runs a charity pub quiz on the last Thursday of the month and sponsors Hinckley Rugby Football Club.
☺⊛♣⊟(159)✿❀❖

Queen's Head

Upper Bond Street, LE10 1RJ
✪ 5-11 (midnight Fri); 12-midnight Sat; 12-6 Sun ☎ 07887 770038 ⊕ thequeensheadinn.co.uk
4 changing beers ⊞
A warm welcome awaits at this multi award-winning Victorian free house serving four changing real ales. Sympathetically refurbished, open fires and a Victorian range help to make a cosy atmosphere. Voted local CAMRA Pub of the Year 2014 and 2015, and one of CAMRA's top 200 pubs in 2014 and 2015, it has featured in this Guide since 2013. No children or pets. ⊛♣⊟

Illston on the Hill

Fox & Goose

Main Street, LE7 9EG
✪ 6 (11.30 Sat)-11; 11.30-9 Sun ☎ (0116) 259 6340
Everards Beacon Bitter, Tiger Best Bitter; 3 changing beers (sourced nationally; often Everards) ⊞
Unique gem of a pub unscathed by the passage of time, featuring many artefacts including hunting scenes, McLachlan cartoons, farming implements and taxidermy exhibits. Local charities benefit from the proceeds of Onion Sunday, with judging of the annual onion-growing competition held here. The premises comprise a public bar, lounge bar and patio with garden furniture and planters.
Q☺⊛⊕◑⟐♣❀❖❖

Kegworth

Red Lion

24 High Street, DE74 2DA
✪ 11.30-11; 12-10.30 Sun ☎ (01509) 672466
⊕ redlionkegworth.com
Adnams Southwold Bitter; Castle Rock Harvest Pale; Draught Bass; Gale's HSB; Nutbrook The Mild Side; 4 changing beers (sourced locally; often Milestone) ⊞
Georgian building standing on the 19th-century route of the A6, with four rooms served from one bar. There are bench seats and original features including coal fires. Eight cask ales, including Nutbrook The Mild Side, and a real cider are offered plus a good selection of malt whiskies. Food is served every lunchtime and weekday evenings. Outside is a large car park and garden plus a pétanque court and children's play area. En-suite accommodation is available. A frequent winner of local CAMRA awards. Q☺☺⊛⊕◑◐♣❀P⊟❖❖

Leicester

Ale Wagon

27 Rutland Street, LE1 1RE
✪ 11-11; 7-10.30 Sun ☎ (0116) 262 3330 ⊕ alewagon.co.uk

Hoskins Hob Bitter, IPA; 4 changing beers (sourced regionally; often Hoskins) ⊞
Run by the Hoskins family, this city-centre pub with a 1930s interior, including an original oak staircase, has two rooms with tiled and parquet floors and a central bar. There is always a selection of Hoskins Brothers ales and guests available. The place is popular with visiting rugby fans and real ale drinkers. A function room is available to hire. Handy for the nearby Curve Theatre. ❧♣⊛⊟

Babelas

77 Queens Road, LE2 1TT
✪ 5 (4 Fri; 1 Sat)-11; 4-10 Sun ☎ (0116) 270 7744
Castle Rock Harvest Pale; Timothy Taylor Landlord; 1 changing beer (sourced regionally; often Oakham) ⊞
Spread over two floors and decorated with quirky internationally sourced antiques, this converted wine merchant's inhabits an area favoured by academics and urban professionals. Reliable beer quality, fine wines and excellent cheeseboards make for a sophisticated drinking experience. The large front windows open up to create a continental ambience on warmer days. Quiet music does not intrude on conversation. Often busy at weekends but always civilised. ☺◑♣⊟❖

Black Horse

65 Narrow Lane, Aylestone, LE2 8NA
✪ 11-11; 12-midnight Fri & Sat ☎ (0116) 283 7225
⊕ blackhorse-aylestone.co.uk
Everards Beacon Bitter, Tiger Best Bitter, Original; 4 changing beers (sourced nationally; often Brunswick, Everards, Titanic) ⊞
Welcoming traditional Victorian pub with a distinctive bar servery in a village conservation area on the city's edge, sympathetically refurbished in 2015. Up to eight real ales are available and home-cooked food is served noon-8.30pm daily (until 5.30pm on Sun). Coaches are welcome by prior arrangement. The skittle alley and function room can be hired and live music and comedy feature regularly. Beer festivals and community events are hosted. Quiz night is Sunday. There is a large beer garden.
Q⊛⊕◑♣❀⊟❖❖

Black Horse

1 Foxon Street, Braunstone Gate, LE3 5LT
✪ 12-midnight; 12-11 Sun ☎ (0116) 254 0446
Everards Beacon Bitter, Sunchaser Blonde, Tiger Best Bitter, Original; 2 changing beers (sourced nationally) ⊞
The only remaining traditional pub in a street of youth-oriented bars, with two rooms separated by a central bar. Comfortably furnished with practical furniture and wood-panelled walls, this is a genuine community venue. Live music is hosted four nights a week and Wednesday is quiz night. The guest beers are sourced through Everards and the cider is Westons Old Rosie. A roof terrace for alfresco drinking was opened in 2015. ⊛♣❀⊟

Charlotte

8 Oxford Street, LE1 5XZ
✪ 11-11 (midnight Fri & Sat); 11-10 Sun
⊕ thecharlotteleicester.co.uk
6 changing beers (sourced nationally) ⊞
Historic city-centre pub serving six guest ales. The focus here is on quality, variety and friendly service. This pub is considered to have one of the best views in Leicester, overlooking the famous Magazine Gateway through an original Art Deco

window. It is popular with real ale drinkers and fans of the local rugby and football teams. A range of continental bottled beers is available.
Q ⑤ ⬛ ⬤ ⬛ ⬛ ⬛

Criterion

44 Millstone Lane, LE1 5JN

✦ 12-11; closed Sun ☎ (0116) 262 5418

⊕ thecriterion.co.uk

Changing beers (sourced regionally; often Oakham, Sadler's, Shiny) Ⓗ

Two-roomed 1960s pub offering up to 12 ales from microbreweries and regionals. Beer festivals are held regularly and more than 70 international bottled beers are stocked. Italian-style pizzas are available Monday to Saturday. Darts and dominoes are played in the front bar. A general knowledge quiz is hosted on Wednesdays, live music on Thursdays, some Fridays and Saturdays, and special events on occasional Sundays. The pub serves as a venue for the Leicester Comedy Festival.
⑤ ⬛ ⬛ ⬛ ⬛ ⬛ ⬛

High Cross ✪

103-105 High Street, LE1 4JB (400yds from Clock Tower on corner of High St)

✦ 8am-midnight ☎ (0116) 251 9218

Grainstore Ten Fifty; Greene King Abbot; Ruddles Best Bitter; 6 changing beers (sourced nationally; often Grainstore, Nottingham, Oakham) Ⓗ

Named after the cross marking the centre of medieval Leicester which has recently been resited nearby, this is a Wetherspoon conversion of a former shop. The large L-shaped room has some changes of level to create different areas. Guest beers include an Oakham brew and ales from other local breweries. International guest brewers also feature. Beer festivals are held twice yearly as part of national company events. ⑤ ⬛ ⬛ ⬛ ⬛ ⬛ ⬛

King's Head ♛

King Street, LE1 6RL

✦ 12-midnight ☎ (0116) 254 8240

⊕ thekingsleicester.co.uk

Black Country Bradley's Finest Golden, Pig on the Wall, Fireside; 5 changing beers (sourced nationally; often Great Central, Itchen Valley, Mallinson's) Ⓗ

A traditional one-room city-centre local owned by Black Country Ales. Eight handpulls serve five regularly changing guest ales and two varying ciders. Its open fire and roof terrace make it popular at any time of year, attracting real ale and cider enthusiasts as well as visitors to the local football and rugby grounds. Two changing specialist beers and a range of bottles are offered, and seasonal beer festivals are held. Sky and BT sport are screened. Local CAMRA Pub of the Year 2016. ⬛ ⬛ ⬛ ⬛ ⬛ ⬛ ⬛

Old Horse

198 London Road, LE2 1NE

✦ 11-11.30 (midnight Fri & Sat); 11-11 Sun

☎ (0116) 254 8384 ⊕ oldhorseleicester.co.uk

Everards Beacon Bitter, Sunchaser Blonde, Tiger Best Bitter, Original; 4 changing beers (sourced nationally) Ⓗ

Nineteenth-century coaching inn, handy for dog walkers, students and sports supporters. The addition of a cider bar serving eight handpulled ciders earnt the pub the local CAMRA Cider Pub of the Year award in 2015. Tasty and good-value food is served. Behind the building is the largest pub garden in town complete with children's play

equipment and pétanque court. Regular quiz nights, karaoke and special events take place.
⑤ ⬛ ⬛ ⬛ ⬛ ⬛ ⬛ P ⬛ ⬛ ⬛

Rutland & Derby Ⓛ

Millstone Lane, LE1 5JN

✦ 12-11 (1am Fri & Sat); closed Sun ☎ (0116) 262 3299

⊕ therutlandandderby.co.uk

Everards Sunchaser Blonde, Tiger Best Bitter; 2 changing beers (sourced nationally) Ⓗ

This pub has an open-plan interior with a contemporary ambience. The long servery bar directly faces the front entrance while off to the left is a lounge bar which leads to a restaurant area on a raised level. At the back is a block-paved courtyard with a metallic spiral staircase leading to a rooftop terrace. ⑤ ⬛ ⬛ ⬛ ⬛ ⬛ ⬛ ⬛ ⬛ ⬛

Swan & Rushes

19 Infirmary Square, LE1 5WR

✦ 12-11 (midnight Thu-Sat); 12-11.30 Sun

☎ (0116) 233 9167 ⊕ swanandrushes.co.uk

Batemans XB; Oakham JHB, Bishops Farewell; 7 changing beers (sourced regionally; often Blue Monkey, Grainstore, Oakham) Ⓗ

Comfortable, triangular, two-roomed pub in the city centre with a relaxed atmosphere. Up to nine real ales are served plus a changing real cider and bottled beers including international classics. Several food-linked beer festivals are held each year plus cider and cheese events. Thursday is quiz night and open mic the second Wednesday of the month. Home-made pizzas are available.
⬛ ⬛ ⬛ ⬛ ⬛ ⬛ ⬛ ⬛

Western

70 Western Road, LE3 0GA

✦ 12-midnight (1am Fri & Sat) ☎ (0116) 254 5287

Steamin' Billy Tipsy Fisherman, Bitter, Skydiver; 4 changing beers (sourced regionally; often Abbeydale, Charnwood, Leatherbritches) Ⓗ

Traditional local in a residential location close to football and rugby grounds on the edge of the city centre. Sympathetically refurbished in 2015, the bar and lounge are popular with a mixed clientele of all ages. Up to four guest beers are available, mainly from microbreweries. Old pub signs decorate the bar and beer garden. There are regular music and beer festivals and the pub is home to a theatre upstairs. ⬛ ⬛ ⬛ ⬛ ⬛ ⬛ ⬛

Long Clawson

Crown & Plough

3 East End, LE14 4NG

✦ 12-2.30, 5-11.30 (midnight Fri); 12-midnight Sat; 12-6 Sun

☎ (01664) 822322 ⊕ crownandplough.co.uk

4 changing beers Ⓗ

Recently refurbished, the pub is in the centre of a historic village. Now a free house, after a long period as a Marston's pub, it serves up to four real ales, including beers from local breweries Lincoln Green and Belvoir. A popular base for tourists, it offers good-quality rooms and a varied food menu, while retaining its identity as a local village pub.
⑤ ⬛ ⬛ ⬛ ⬛ P ⬛ ⬛ ⬛

Long Whatton

Royal Oak

26 The Green, LE12 5DB

✪ 12-11 (midnight Fri & Sat) ☎ (01509) 843694
⊕ theroyaloaklongwhatton.co.uk
Charnwood Vixen; Draught Bass; St Austell Tribute; 1 changing beer Ⓗ
Tastefully modernised, award-winning gastro-pub welcoming real ale drinkers and diners alike. The owners are passionate about their ales and are strong supporters of local breweries. Local produce also features in an interesting food menu. Convenient for East Midlands airport and Donington race circuit, AA 4-star accommodation is available in a separate building. A former local CAMRA Village Pub of the Year. Q✿⊛✍◑⅃Å♠PⱤ

Loughborough

Generous Briton
85 Ashby Road, LE11 3AB
✪ 12-11 (midnight Fri & Sat) ☎ (01509) 263565
Draught Bass; Nottingham Legend; Oakham JHB; 4 changing beers (often Charnwood) Ⓗ
Reopened in 2011 as a free house, the GB is ideally situated between the town centre and university. The traditional bar has a dartboard and features old local photographs; the lounge has a pool table and jukebox. Satellite sport is shown throughout. A limited food menu is available but customers are welcome to bring their own food. There is an enclosed beer garden to the rear and families are welcome until 7.45pm. ✿♣♠Ⱥ(126)♥

Organ Grinder
4 WoodGate, LE11 2TY
✪ 12-11 (midnight Fri & Sat); 12-10.30 Sun
☎ (01509) 264008
Blue Monkey BG Sips, 99 Red Baboons, Infinity, Guerrilla; 4 changing beers (sourced locally; often Blue Monkey) Ⓗ
Previously known as the Pack Horse and bought by Blue Monkey in 2012, the building has received a top-to-bottom renovation, uncovering lots of interesting original features. The stable bar at the back reflects the pub's past life as a coaching inn. Eight cask ales are always available alongside Belgian bottled beers and a choice of four real ciders and sometimes a perry. Bar snacks include an interesting range of pork pies. ☎✿♠☷Ⱥ♥♥

Tap & Mallet
36 Nottingham Road, LE11 1EU
✪ 7 (5 Tue & Thu)-midnight; 12-midnight Sat; 3.30-midnight Sun
Marston's Pedigree; 4 changing beers (sourced regionally; often Abbeydale, Charnwood, Salopian) Ⓗ
Genuine free house with a regularly changing beer range, mainly seasonal brews from Abbeydale and Salopian. The large single-room interior is divided into two distinct drinking areas – a public bar with pool table, darts and board games, and a quieter lounge area that can be partitioned off for functions. Outside there is a large, secluded lawned garden, patio and pets' corner. Q✿⊛≒♣♠Ⱥ♥

White Hart ♟
27 Churchgate, LE11 1UD
✪ 11-midnight; 12-11 Sun ☎ (01509) 236976
Draught Bass; Timothy Taylor Landlord; 3 changing beers (sourced locally; often Charnwood, Leatherbritches, Sarah Hughes) Ⓗ
Reopened in 2013 as a free house after an extensive refurbishment, the pub has a secluded patio and beer garden to the rear. Regularly changing guest beers are often from local

breweries such as Leatherbritches and Charnwood, and Sarah Hughes Dark Ruby is often available. Live music is hosted on Friday evenings and Sunday afternoons. Local CAMRA branch Town Pub 2014 and Pub of the Year 2016. ✿◑♣♠♥🐾♥

Lutterworth

Fox
34 Rugby Road, LE17 4BN (400yds from Whittle Roundabout)
✪ 12 (5 Mon)-1am ☎ (01455) 550935
⊕ fox-lutterworth.co.uk
Draught Bass; Sharp's Doom Bar; 2 changing beers (sourced nationally) Ⓗ
Situated at the southern end of the town close to the Sir Frank Whittle jet monument, this busy 18th-century pub has an open-plan L-shaped interior warmed by two open fires. Pub food is served lunchtimes, with Thai food available in the evening upstairs in the Sawasdee restaurant. Outside is a large landscaped award-winning garden and drinking area. Weekly quizzes are held on Tuesdays. ✿◑♠PⱤ(84,X44)🐾♥

Unicorn ✓
29 Church Street, LE17 4AE (near church)
✪ 10.30-11 (midnight Fri & Sat); 12-11 Sun
☎ (01455) 552486
Adnams Southwold Bitter; Draught Bass; Greene King IPA; 1 changing beer (sourced nationally) Ⓗ
Traditional town-centre, street-corner local with a black-and-white frontage, built in 1919 on the site of a 19th-century coach house. The large public bar with an open fire offers TV sports coverage and hosts darts, dominoes and skittles teams. A central fireplace divides the comfortable lounge, decorated with historic local photographs, from a small dining area. Lunchtime meals include vegetarian options. ☎◑♠PⱤ(84,X44)

Market Harborough

Admiral Nelson
49 Nelson Street, LE16 9AX
✪ 5-11 (11.30 Wed & Thu); 3-midnight Fri; 9am-midnight Sat; 12-10.30 Sun ☎ (01858) 433173
Wells Eagle IPA, Bombardier; 2 changing beers (sourced regionally) Ⓗ
Welcoming, friendly locals' pub, built in 1900, a short stroll from the centre of the historic market town. Just off the beaten track, this pub is the town's best-kept secret, offering a lounge with TV (where they like their rugby) and a bar with darts, pool, a jukebox and another TV. A function room is also available. Outside is a heated and covered smoking area with seating. ✿◑♣P🐾♥

Beerhouse
76 St Mary's Road, LE16 7DX (behind chip shop)
✪ 6 (12 Thu-Sat)-11; 12-10 Sun ☎ (01858) 465317
⊕ beerhouses.uk
Changing beers (sourced nationally; often Hart Family, Oakham, Tres Bien) Ⓖ
Market Harborough's first micropub, set in a converted furniture shop. The focus is very much on beer – there is no food, gaming machines or loud music. Up to 12 real ales, mostly from local microbreweries, are served by gravity from casks lined up behind the bar. Monday is quiz night and comedy nights and live music feature regularly. ≒♠Ⱥ♥

Melton Mowbray

Boat ✓

57 Burton Street, LE13 1AF

🕓 11-3 (not Mon), 5-11.45; 12-11.45 Fri; 11-11.45 Sat

☎ (01664) 500969

Hook Norton Hooky; Wells Bombardier; 2 changing beers (sourced nationally) Ⓗ

This traditional single-roomed pub takes its name from a canal basin that was once adjacent. The walls are decorated with old pictures of the town and a map of the Melton-Oakham canal. The pub is always busy with mature drinkers and local darts teams, who enjoy good conversation with their pint. An open range gives plenty of warmth and adds to the atmosphere in winter. ⇌♣🖿💥🛜

Kettleby Cross Ⓛ ✓

Wilton Road, LE13 0UJ

🕓 7-midnight ☎ (01664) 485310

Ruddles Best Bitter; Greene King Abbot; 6 changing beers (sourced nationally) Ⓗ

The Kettleby Cross is a Wetherspoon new-build, opened in 2007 as a flagship eco-pub complete with a prominent wind turbine on the roof. The building stands close to the bridge over the nearby River Eye and is named after the cross that once directed travellers in the direction of Ab Kettleby. The large single-room interior is on two levels. Dan the manager has a good commitment to local breweries and hosts an occasional local beer festival. Q🕭🖔🕽&⇌🖿🛜

Noels Arms Ⓛ

31 Burton Street, LE13 1AE

🕓 4-11 (11.45 Fri); 12-11.45 Sat; 12-7 Sun

☎ (01664) 562363

Sharp's Doom Bar; 3 changing beers (sourced nationally) Ⓗ

Popular single-room town pub that became a free house in 2013 and now shows a commendable commitment to real ale, with microbreweries featuring prominently. It has a vibrant live music scene with posters of past and future gigs decorating the walls. Talented individuals are welcome to play the piano. A real fire is prominent in the centre of the room. Always busy and loud on Friday and Saturday evenings. 🖔🕮🕽⇌♣🖿💥🛜

Mountsorrel

Swan

10 Loughborough Road, LE12 7AT

🕓 12-2.30, 5.30-11; 12-11 Sat; 12-10.30 Sun

☎ (0116) 230 2340 ⊕ the-swan-inn.eu

Black Sheep Best Bitter; Castle Rock Harvest Pale; 2 changing beers (often Greene King, Woodforde's) Ⓗ

Traditional 17th-century, Grade II-listed coaching inn entered via a narrow arch into a courtyard. The split-level interior has open fires, stone floors and low ceilings, and includes a small dining area with a polished wood floor. Good-quality, interesting food is cooked to order, with the menu changing weekly, and there are regular themed events. Outside is a long secluded riverside garden with moorings. A beer festival is hosted annually. Q🕭🕽🖿💥

Oadby

Black Dog

23 London Road, LE2 5DL

🕓 4-11 (midnight Fri); 12-midnight Sat; 12-10.30 Sun

☎ (0116) 210 2479

Everards Tiger Best Bitter, Original; 4 changing beers (sourced nationally) Ⓗ

Bought by Everards and refurbished in 2014 to create a specialist ale house, the Black Dog has a single-room interior divided into a number of distinct areas. Tucked away behind the bar area is a restaurant serving pub classics with a twist. There is a covered courtyard at the back and a skittle alley. Guest beers are sourced via Everards.
🖔🕭🕽&♣🖿(31,40)💥🛜

Cow & Plough

Gartree Road, LE2 2FB

🕓 11-11 ☎ (0116) 272 0852

Fuller's London Pride; Steamin' Billy Bitter, Skydiver; 4 changing beers (sourced regionally; often Abbeydale, Belvoir, Charnwood) Ⓗ

Situated in a former farm building with a conservatory, the pub is decked out with breweriana. It is home to Steamin' Billy beers, named after the owner's now departed Jack Russell who features on the logo and pumpclips. A mild is always available and real cider added in the summer months. An annual beer festival is held. Former dairy buildings house a renowned restaurant. Q🖔🕭🕽&♣🖿💥

Old Dalby

Belvoir Alehouse Ⓛ

Station Road, LE14 3NQ

🕓 10-9 (11 Thu-Sat); 12-6 Sun ☎ (01664) 823978

⊕ belvoiralehouse.co.uk

Belvoir Dark Horse, Whippling, Star Bitter, Beaver Bitter, Oatmeal Stout, Old Dalby Ⓗ

The brick-fronted Belvoir Alehouse on the outskirts of the village incorporates a bar, function room and visitors' centre, with brewery tours available by arrangement. A range of regular and seasonal Belvoir Ales is available. The spacious interior is filled with brewing artefacts, and has a traditional bar area, with room for long-alley skittles and a bar billiards table. Large internal windows provide views into the brewery. A full food menu is served daily, with the focus on wholesome meals made with local produce. A former local CAMRA Pub of the Year. 🕭🕽&♣🖿🛜

Plungar

Anchor Ⓛ

Granby Lane, NG13 0JJ

🕓 12-3 (not Mon-Fri), 6-11; 12-10.30 Sun ☎ (01949) 860589

Oldershaw Alchemy; 2 changing beers Ⓗ

This brick building in the middle of a small Leicestershire village dates from 1774 – it was at one time the local courtroom. The pub now houses a large bar and lounge area, a separate restaurant and a pool room. Outside is an attractive beer garden and seating area. The Anchor has developed a reputation for good food, using locally sourced ingredients, and serving quality cask ale – at least one but sometimes all beers are from local breweries. Q🕭🕽&♣🖿💥🛜

Quorn

Manor House

Woodhouse Road, LE12 8AL

🕐 12-11 (midnight Sat); 12-10 Sun ☎ (01509) 413416
🌐 themanorhouseatquorn.co.uk
Charnwood Salvation; Draught Bass; 3 changing beers (often Batemans) Ⓗ
Built in 1899 by the Great Central Railway, the Manor House was designed to serve passengers arriving at Quorn & Woodhouse Station, which it still does today – the preserved steam- and diesel-hauled trains pass by 150 yards from the door. The building has an open-plan bar and award-winning restaurant with a separate function/meeting room available to hire. A free house, two guest beers are available during the week and three at weekends. Q❀◑♿⛺♣P🚉🚌🐾

Royal Oak
2 High Street, LE12 8DT
🕐 5-11; 4.30-11.30 Fri; 2.30-11.30 Sat; 4-10 Sun
☎ (01509) 413506
Charnwood Vixen; Timothy Taylor Landlord; 2 changing beers Ⓗ
Traditional village inn situated in the centre of the village. The building has been an inn for around 160 years. The internal walls were removed long ago to open the pub up while retaining many original features including beamed ceilings, tiled floors and an open log fire. There is a sheltered, covered courtyard to the side. Draught cider is available in the summer. Q⛺🍎🚌🐾

Shackerstone

Rising Sun Ⓛ
Church Road, CV13 6NN
🕐 12-2.30 (not Mon), 5.30-11; 11.30-11 Sat & Sun
☎ (01827) 880215 🌐 risingsunpub.com
Marston's Pedigree; Timothy Taylor Landlord; 2 changing beers Ⓗ
Traditional family-owned free house located in the heart of Shackerstone village near the Ashby Canal and the preserved Battlefield Railway. It has a wood-panelled bar serving traditional ales, a restaurant, pool room with Sky Sports, family-friendly conservatory and an attractive garden. The inn, popular with locals and visitors alike, is renowned for the quality and variety of its ales and serves good pub food – the ideal hub for visiting this rural part of Leicestershire.
Q🧸❀◑♿⚞♣🍎P🚌🐾📶

Shawell

White Swan
Main Street, LE17 6AG (off roundabout on A5/A42)
🕐 11-3, 6-11; 12-6 Sun; closed Mon ☎ (01788) 860357
🌐 whiteswanshawell.co.uk
Wells Bombardier; 3 changing beers (sourced locally; often Church End, Dow Bridge) Ⓗ
A CAMRA design award-winning free house dating from the 17th-century just off the A5 Watling Street. It has been extensively refurbished inside, and has an open-plan feel with two dining areas, a smart bar and a small lounge behind a central fireplace. The White Swan has an excellent reputation for quality food, and in the warmer months there is additional dining space outside.
Q❀◑♿P🐾

Shearsby

Chandlers Arms Ⓛ
Fenny Lane, LE17 6PL
🕐 12-3 (not Tue), 6-11; 12-7 Sun; closed Mon
☎ (0116) 247 8384 🌐 chandlersatshearsby.co.uk
Dow Bridge Acris; 6 changing beers (sourced regionally) Ⓗ
Quintessential village inn with a big reputation – it has won the prestigious local CAMRA Country Pub of the Year award for the past seven years, and was the first pub in the Leicester branch to sign up to CAMRA's LocAle scheme. Microbrewery beers are always on the bar, often locally sourced. The pub's name is a reminder of the building's original use as a tallow candlemaker's business. It has a public bar, dining room and a beer garden overlooking the village green from a high vantage point. ❀◑♣🍎🐾📶

Shepshed

Horse
196 Ashby Road, LE12 9EF (A512)
🕐 12 (4 Mon)-11 ☎ (01509) 502245
Charnwood Salvation; Marston's Pedigree; Sharp's Doom Bar; Shepherd Neame Spitfire; 1 changing beer Ⓗ
Situated on the A512 on the edge of Shepshed, the Horse was reopened in 2014 under new management after a number of years when it seemed more closed than open. Now refurbished, it has a large side extension with a bar area, comfortable seating, TV sport and a wood-burning stove, and a contemporary restaurant offering good food made with locally sourced ingredients. Live music plays occasionally. ◑P🚌(127)

Sileby

Horse & Trumpet
4 Barrow Road, LE12 7LP
🕐 1-11 (midnight Fri & Sat); 12-11 Sun ☎ (01509) 812549
Belvoir Dark Horse; Charnwood Vixen; Steamin' Billy Tipsy Fisherman, Bitter, Skydiver; 2 changing beers Ⓗ
This multi-room pub with open fires has undergone a huge transformation since becoming part of the Steamin' Billy chain. Two guest beers plus a real cider and a perry are on handpump. No hot food is served but cobs are available, and there is a monthly curry club. Open mic nights are held weekly and jazz nights monthly. Well-behaved dogs are welcome in the bar and outside seating area. A function room is available.
Q❀⚞♣🍎P🚌(KB2)

Somerby

Stilton Cheese 🏆 Ⓛ
High Street, LE14 2QB
🕐 12-3, 6-11; 12-3, 7-11 Sun ☎ (01664) 454394
🌐 stiltoncheeseinn.co.uk
Grainstore Ten Fifty; Marston's Burton Bitter; 3 changing beers (sourced nationally) Ⓗ
Late 16th-century family-run pub built in local ironstone, an ideal refreshment stop for walkers on the Leicestershire Round. The cosy bar and adjoining room are decorated with a large collection of objects including a stuffed pike and badger. Tall customers beware the wide range of pumpclips on the low beam above the bar. CAMRA branch Pub of the Year 2015 and 2016.
Q🧸❀🛏◑♣🍎P🚌📶

Swinford

Chequers ✅
High Street, LE17 6BL (near church)
☼ 7-11 Mon; 12-2.30, 6-11; 12-3, 6-11 Sat; 12-3, 7-11 Sun
☎ (01788) 860318 ⊕ chequersswinford.co.uk
Adnams Southwold Bitter; 2 changing beers (sourced nationally; often Sharp's, Timothy Taylor) Ⓗ
A warm welcome is assured at this family-run community local. The food menu caters for all, and includes a vegetarian option. The large garden and play area are popular with families in good weather. A marquee is added in the summer months – this is the venue for the yearly beer festival and is also available for private hire. Pub games include table skittles. Q ⛭ ❁ ⬧ ▲ ♣ P

Syston

Queen Victoria
76 High Street, LE7 1GQ
☼ 4-11; 12-midnight Fri & Sat; 12-10.30 Sun
☎ (0116) 260 5750
Everards Beacon Bitter, Tiger Best Bitter; 3 changing beers (sourced nationally; often Bath Ales, Brunswick, Everards) Ⓗ
A former coach house, the building is 200 years old – Everards has traded here since 1922. The pub has several small rooms and a large garden at the rear. A separate restaurant carvery is accessed via the garden. Entertainment is hosted every other Saturday and a beer festival is held in the summer. Guest beers are sourced through Everards. Opening hours may vary. ⛭ ❁ ⬧ ➡ ♣ P ☍ ❀ 🌐

Syston & District Social Club
36 High Street, LE7 1GP
☼ 6-11; 11.30-midnight Fri & Sat; 11.30-11 Sun
☎ (0116) 260 9086 ⊕ systonsocial.co.uk
Banks's Mild, Bitter; 4 changing beers (sourced regionally; often Blue Monkey, Brewster's, Oakham) Ⓗ
This former pub is home to many local societies and sports clubs including darts, skittles, chess and crib. The large function room is available for hire. The range of six beers includes four regularly rotating guests, and beer festivals are held in February and June. Show a CAMRA membership card or copy of this Guide for entry.
⛭ ❁ ♿ ♣ ☍ (5,6) ❀ 🌐

Waltham on the Wolds

Royal Horseshoes
4 Melton Road, LE14 4AJ
☼ 11.30-3.30, 5-11; 11.30-11 Sun ☎ (01664) 464346
Castle Rock Harvest Pale; Courage Directors; Sharp's Doom Bar; 2 changing beers (sourced nationally) Ⓗ
Fifteenth-century pub and former gin palace with a small bar room and adjacent long lounge. Originally known as the Horseshoes, in 1843 it was visited by Queen Victoria and Prince Albert en-route from Belvoir Castle to Melton Mowbray. The Royal part of its name was added from that day. At the time it was one of 17 ale houses in the village. Five real ales are usually available, at least one from a local brewery. ⛭ ➡ ⬧ P

Walton on the Wolds

Anchor
2 Loughborough Road, LE12 8HT
☼ 12-3, 6-11; 12-10.30 Sun ☎ (01509) 880018
Adnams Southwold Bitter; Fuller's London Pride; Timothy Taylor Landlord; 1 changing beer (often Charnwood) Ⓗ
The Anchor is situated in the centre of a small village within easy reach of Leicester and Nottingham via the A46. It is a popular venue for walkers who stop for a well-earned home-cooked lunch in front of the fire. There is a menu to suit all tastes plus an extensive specials board. Outside is an elevated seating area to the front and a garden and car park to the rear. Q ⛭ ❁ ➡ ⬧ P ☍ ☖ ❀

Whitwick

Three Horseshoes ★
11 Leicester Road, LE67 5GN
☼ 11-3, 6.30-11; 12-2, 7-10.30 Sun ☎ (01530) 837311
Draught Bass; Marston's Pedigree Ⓗ
Identified by CAMRA as having a nationally important historic pub interior, the Three Horseshoes is nicknamed Polly's after a former landlady, Polly Burton. The pub was originally two separate buildings but now has two rooms. To the left is a long bar with a quarry-tiled floor and open fires, wooden bench seating and pre-war fittings; to the right is a small similarly furnished snug. ☖

Wigston

William Wygston ✅
84 Leicester Road, LE18 1DR
☼ 8am-12.15am ☎ (0116) 288 8397
Greene King Abbot; Ruddles Best Bitter; Sharp's Doom Bar; changing beers (sourced nationally) Ⓗ
Classic Wetherspoon establishment named after William Wygston (1456-1536), who was an extremely wealthy wool merchant, philanthropist, MP, and twice mayor of Leicester. This pub opened in 1997 in a former Kwiksave store which was itself part of a redevelopment, many years ago, that replaced terraced housing with retail outlets. The 1911 census records that the house previously on this site was occupied by an elderly widow and her spinster sister. ⛭ ⬧ ♿ ☖ ❀ 🌐

Willoughby Waterleys

General Elliott
Main Street, LE8 6UF
☼ 5.30-10.30 Tue; 11-2, 5.30-11.30 Wed & Thu; 11-2, 4.30-11.30 Fri; 11.30-4, 7-10.30 Sat; 11.30-6 Sun; closed Mon ☎ (0116) 247 8058 ⊕ generalelliott.com
Draught Bass; Marston's Pedigree; 1 changing beer (sourced locally) Ⓗ
Set in a rural village, the pub is named after an 18th-century British Army officer, most noted for his successful defence of the garrison during the Great Siege of Gibraltar. The L-shaped room has skittles and darts at one end, a public/lounge bar space in the middle and a snug area at the other end. It is conveniently situated for passing hikers and cyclists on cycle route 6. ⛭ ⬧ ▲ ♣ ❀

Everard's Project William refers to an arrangement by which the Leicester brewery buys a failing or closed pub, refurbishes it to a high standard and leases it to a smaller brewery that can sell its full range of beer in return for stocking at least one Everard's ale.

LINCOLNSHIRE

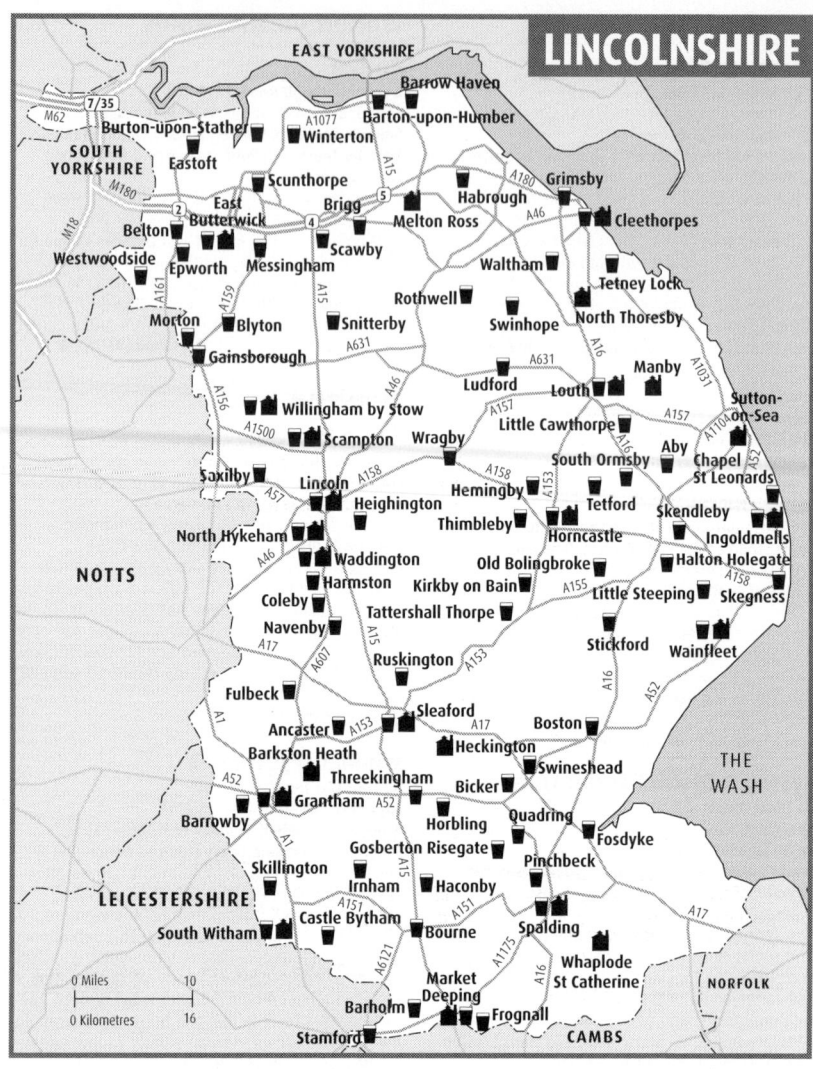

Aby

Railway Tavern
Main Road, LN13 0DR (off A16 via South Thoresby)
🕛 12-11.30 ☎ (01507) 480676
2 changing beers (sourced nationally) Ⓗ
A lovely rural pub which lies just outside the beautiful village of Aby. There is always a good selection of carefully chosen real ales and the pub offers a quality home-cooked food menu. A real fire adds to the homely atmosphere at this welcoming venue. It is closed on Tuesdays during November and between January and Easter.
🛏🍴▶P🐾

Ancaster

Ancaster Social Club
Ermine Street, NG32 3PW
🕛 7-11; 12-10.30 Sun ☎ (01400) 230896
Wells Bombardier; 2 changing beers (often Brewsters, Tom Wood's) Ⓗ

This club is located in the heart of the village and various sporting events take place on its playing fields. These include football, cricket and rounders. In-house darts, pool and live sport are available. It has an airy conservatory and outside seating overlooking the sports field. This excellent club has been voted local CAMRA Club of the Year 2012 to 2016 and Lincolnshire Club of the Year 2012 to 2014. 🛏🌳🐕❤♣P🚌🐾🛜

Barholm

Five Horseshoes Ⓛ
PE9 4RA
🕛 4-11; 1-11 Sat; 12-10.30 Sun ☎ (01778) 560238
Adnams Southwold Bitter; Oakham JHB; 4 changing beers (often Grainstore, Hopshackle, Roosters) Ⓗ
An 18th-century stone-built traditional country pub, comprising two bars, two side rooms and a TV/pool room. A welcoming wood fire burns throughout the winter. Stuffed birds and enamelled adverts adorn the walls. Outside is a garden, kids' play area and car park. Barbecues and

music events are held in the summer. A changing range of beers from local and regional breweries is on the bar, along with real ciders. Pizzas are served Friday and Saturday. The pub supports many charities. Q ℃ ❀ ₺ ● P ❀

Barrow Haven

Haven Inn

Ferry Road, DN19 7EX (approx 1½ miles E of Barrow-upon-Humber)
✪ 11.30-11.30; 12-10 Sun ☎ (01469) 530247
⊕ thehaveninn.co.uk
Timothy Taylor Landlord; Tom Wood's Best Bitter; 1 changing beer (sourced locally; often Great Newsome) ⒣
The Haven has been known as an inn for centuries and is renowned for its hospitality, food and comfortable lodgings. The pub was devastated by the tidal surge of December 2013, but reopened five months later and has retained its style and character, with a traditional beamed ceiling and open fire in the lounge and bar. Good food is served throughout the week including a popular Sunday carvery. ℃ ❀ 🚗 ◑ ₺ ▲ ₹ P 🖳 (252) ❀ �

Barrowby

White Swan ✪

Main Street, NG32 1BH
✪ 12-midnight (1am Fri & Sat) ☎ (01476) 562375
Adnams Southwold Bitter; Sharp's Doom Bar; 2 changing beers (often Castle Rock, Sadler's) ⒣
Popular village pub run by the same landlord for 23 years, who is an enthusiastic CAMRA member. There is a comfortable lounge, separate bar area and a further area where the local darts, cribbage and pool teams play. Offering two regular and two changing guest ales, it also provides locally sourced traditional home-made food Wednesday to Saturday. Outside is a heated smoking area and a secluded garden. First Sunday of the month is quiz night. Q ℃ ❀ ◑ ♣ P 🖳 ❀ �

Barton-upon-Humber

George Inn ✪

George Street, DN18 5ES
✪ 11-11 (midnight Fri & Sat) ☎ (01652) 636303
⊕ thegeorgebarton.co.uk
4 changing beers (sourced regionally; often Black Sheep, St Austell, Tom Wood's) ⒣
Large 17th-century coaching inn occupying a prominent position just off the marketplace and offering town-centre accommodation. Originally called the George & Dragon, it served Barton on the London to Hull route, but has also been used as an excise office, posting house and local government venue. The central bar serves several rooms. There is a quiz on Thursday evenings. A justifiably popular venue. Q ℃ ❀ 🚗 ◑ ♣ P 🖳 ❀ �

White Swan

66 Fleetgate, DN18 5QD (follow signs for railway station)
✪ 11-11; 10-11 Sun; closed Mon ☎ (01652) 661222
2 changing beers (sourced regionally; often Black Sheep, Clark's) ⒣
The White Swan reopened in 2013 and is a large, recently renovated and modernised pub with a separate dining area. It has a spacious, secure beer garden to the rear. It is decorated in contemporary

style while retaining original pub features such as the large bay windows. Friday night activities are supported by numerous groups and societies. Good, locally sourced food is served.
Q ℃ ❀ ◑ ₺ ⚘ ♣ ● P 🖳 ❀ �

Belton

Crown Inn ⓛ

Church Lane, DN9 1PA (300yds off A631 behind church)
✪ 1-midnight; 12-1am Sat; 12-midnight Sun
☎ (01427) 872834
Bradfield Farmers Blonde; Brakspear Bitter; Jennings Cocker Hoop; Thwaites Wainwright; 2 changing beers (sourced nationally; often Glentworth, Ringwood) ⒣
Difficult to find but well worth the effort, this pub is a must for the discerning drinker. The present licensees have carried on a tradition of offering a range of cask beers – six real ales are always available, including a rotating beer from the nearby Glentworth Brewery. Quizzes, live music and occasional beer festivals are features of this lively local. ℃ ❀ ▲ ♣ ● P 🖳 (399) ❀ �

Bicker

Red Lion

Donington Road, PE20 3EF
✪ 12-11; 12-7 Sun; closed Mon & Tue ☎ (01775) 821200
⊕ redlionbicker.co.uk
Adnams Southwold Bitter; Courage Directors; 1 changing beer (often Austendyke Ales) ⒣
A typical country inn with low beams and tiled floor, in a pleasant setting, extensively and tastefully redecorated in 2015 and reopened after a two-year closure. The welcoming multi-roomed pub has a small bar and is a popular dining venue, with a varied, extensive menu. The building is known to date from at least 1665, the time of the Great Plague of London. The Wash would have been in closer proximity years ago.
℃ ❀ ◑ ₺ P 🖳 (59) �

REAL ALE BREWERIES

8 Sail Heckington
Austendyke Spalding
Bacchus ▤ Sutton-on-Sea
Batemans Wainfleet
Black Horse Louth
Blue Bell ▤ Whaplode St Catherine
Blue Cow ▤ South Witham
Brewster's Grantham
Cathedral Heights Lincoln
Cheeky Imp Waddington
DarkTribe ▤ East Butterwick
Firehouse Manby
Fulstow ▤ Louth
Grafters ▤ Willingham by Stow
Greg's ▤ Scampton
Hopshackle Market Deeping
Horncastle ▤ Horncastle
Leila Cottage ▤ Ingoldmells
Lincolnshire Lincoln
Newby Wyke Grantham
Oldershaw Barkston Heath
Poachers North Hykeham
Rowett North Thoresby
Sleaford Sleaford (brewing suspended)
Star Market Deeping
Tom Wood's Melton Ross
Willy's ▤ Cleethorpes

Blyton

Black Horse
93 High Street, DN21 3JX
⊕ 11.45-midnight ☎ (01427) 628277
⊕ blackhorseblyton.co.uk
3 changing beers ⊞
The Black Horse Inn has been a village pub for over 250 years, situated on the A159 in the village of Blyton, around four miles from Gainsborough and some 10 miles from Scunthorpe. In the last few years it has been given a new lease of life thanks to a major building project, where great care has been taken to revitalise the inn and restore it to a traditional public house. ✿⛳◐&♣♦🅿🚍🛜

Boston

Eagle
144 West Street, PE21 8RE
⊕ 11-midnight ☎ (01205) 361116
Castle Rock Black Gold, Harvest Pale, Preservation Fine Ale, Screech Owl; changing beers ⊞
Part of the Castle Rock chain, the Eagle is known as the real ale pub of Boston. This two-roomed, friendly hostelry has an L-shaped bar with a large TV screen for big sport events. The small cosy lounge has an open fire. The pub stocks a wide range of guest ales, and at least one cider. A function room upstairs is home to the Boston Folk Club. Thursday night is quiz night – allegedly the hardest in town. Q✿&≷♣♦🚍🐾🛜

Golden Lion ✪
46 High Street, PE21 8SP
⊕ 7 (6 Mon & Fri)-midnight; 12-1am Sat; 12-midnight Sun
☎ (01205) 353230
Brains Rev James; Theakston Best Bitter; Wells Bombardier Burning Gold ⊞
Low-beamed ceilings, wood panelling and leaded windows mark out this hostelry on the old High Street away from the main shopping thoroughfares. With a keen sports following, this pub has several active traditional games teams. Old fishing boat nameplates hang above the bar as a reminder of the history of Boston as a fishing port. The pub was once owned by Hardys & Hansons and came into private hands in 2010. ✿≷♣🚍

Bourne

Smith's Ⓛ
25 North Street, PE10 9AE
⊕ 10-11 (midnight Fri); 8.30am-midnight Sat; 8.30am-11 Sun
☎ (01778) 426819 ⊕ smithsofbourne.co.uk
Castle Rock Harvest Pale; Fuller's London Pride; 4 changing beers (often Hopshackle, Star, Titanic) ⊞
A successful conversion of an old grocery store into an atmospheric pub with exposed red brick walls throughout, the building is a warren of interconnecting rooms spanning three floors. The main front bar serves six beers, mostly from independent brewers. Two ciders from Westons are usually available. Outside there is a large patio and beer garden with a children's play area. There is an annual beer festival in August and a cider and sausage festival in September.
Q✿◐&♦🚍🐾🛜

Brigg

Nelthorpe Arms
1 Bridge Street, DN20 8LN
⊕ 11-11; 12-11 Sun ☎ (01652) 408088
Batemans XXXB; Greene King IPA, Abbot; 3 changing beers (sourced regionally; often Acorn, Kelham Island, Springhead) ⊞
Town-centre pub with a 1950s interior sitting inside a mid-18th century Grade II-listed building. There is a large, comfortable lounge with a separate snug, both with real fires, and a new function room converted from the old stables. An outside seating area is on the riverside. As well as a varied offering of real ales, there are regularly rotating craft beers and ciders. The pub also holds beer festivals throughout the year. Food is served Wednesday to Sunday. ✿✿◐&≷♣🅿🚍(4)🐾🛜

White Horse ✪
Wrawby Street, DN20 8JR (close to station at E end of Wrawby St)
⊕ 8am-midnight (1am Fri & Sat) ☎ (01652) 659344
Greene King Abbot; Ruddles Best Bitter; 5 changing beers (often Oakham, Roosters, Sharp's) ⊞
New, town-centre Wetherspoon outlet, which is a conversion of an old public house and brewery. Spacious, airy and open plan, it opens onto a large, secure, well-appointed beer garden. The interior is themed on historic Brigg and its people and traditions, and has a calm, quiet atmosphere with no TV screens. There is always a varied selection of beers and ciders, with beer festivals in spring and autumn. Q✿✿◐≷♦🚍(4)🛜

Yarborough Hunt Ⓛ
49 Bridge Street, DN20 8NS (across bridge from marketplace)
⊕ 11-11; 10-midnight Thu; 11-midnight Fri; 10-midnight Sat
☎ (01652) 658333
Tom Wood's Best Bitter, Lincoln Gold, Bomber County; 3 changing beers (sourced nationally; often Greene King, Morland, Timothy Taylor) ⊞
Former Sergeants Brewery tap built in the 1700s and retaining some original rustic features, now extended to include an extra room. It is simply furnished, with open fires in three rooms, has an enclosed beer garden, and offers an extensive range of wines and ciders, and a good selection of quality continental beers on draught. Daily newspapers are available. No food is served, but customers can bring their own sandwiches and other cold food. Q✿✿&♣♦🚍(4)🐾🛜

Burton-upon-Stather

Ferry House Inn ✪
Stather Road, DN15 9DJ (follow campsite signs through village; down hill at church)
⊕ 6-11; 12-11 Sat & Sun ☎ (01724) 721763
⊕ ferryhousepub.co.uk
2 changing beers (sourced locally; often Tom Wood's) ⊞
Friendly village pub on the banks of the River Trent, in the same family for over 55 years. It has its own microbrewery (check ahead for beer availability). Real cider is also sold. An annual beer festival is held over the August bank holiday weekend. It has a large outdoor children's play area and hosts occasional live music events. Food is served all day Friday and Saturday and Sunday lunchtimes. A popular meeting place for local heritage groups.
Q✿✿◐♠♣♦🅿🚍🐾🛜

Castle Bytham

Castle Inn ▼ Ⓛ

High Sreet, NG33 4RZ

❂ 5-11; 6-midnight Sat; 12-3, 6-11 Sun ☎ (01780) 410504

🌐 castleinnbytham.co.uk

3 changing beers (often Black Sheep, Oldershaw, St Austell) Ⓗ

Voted Pub of the Year 2016 and Country Pub of the year 2015 by the local CAMRA branch and one of the original public houses in an historic village, this 17th-century gem has Adnams beers permanently on the bar, with regularly changing guest ales sourced both locally and nationally. A traditional cider is also on offer. An excellent menu of home-made food cooked on a wood-fired stove in the bar is available every evening and Sunday lunchtime. Q🏠❀🕽♣🐾🐾

Chapel St Leonards

Admiral Benbow

The Promenade, PE24 5BQ

❂ 10-7 (10.30 Fri & Sat); 10-8 Sun ☎ (01754) 871847

🌐 admiralbenbowbeachbar.webplus.net

Black Sheep Best Bitter; 2 changing beers Ⓗ

A beach bar on the promenade where the opening times and facilities are dependent on the weather and are limited in winter. Please see the website for current times. Bar snacks and hot food are served. It has an outside seating area on the newly refurbished boat deck (Hispaniola), and provides picnic trays and plastic glasses to take out your favourite food and ale onto the beach. Dogs are welcome on leads. If the flag is flying the pub is open. 🏠❀🕽🐾🛜

Cleethorpes

Coliseum Picture Theatre ⊘

High Street, DN35 8JN

❂ 8am-midnight (1am Fri & Sat) ☎ (01472) 694724

Greene King Abbot; Ruddles Best Bitter; Sharp's Doom Bar; 6 changing beers (sourced regionally; often Black Horse, Tom Wood's) Ⓗ

A Wetherspoon conversion of a former nightclub, although it was originally a cinema. A Roman theme abounds, with Italianate columns and a full-sized model of a centurion standing guard by the bar. It has an impressive ground floor display with a long bar and a viewing area for the beer cellar and forthcoming beers. Stairs lead to more seating and to an enclosed roof terrace. Q🏠❀🕽♿♣�#(3,8,9)🛜

No.1 Pub

Railway Station, DN35 8AX

❂ 12-midnight (7 Mon; 1am Fri & Sat); 12-11 Sun

☎ (01472) 696221

Batemans XXXB; Draught Bass; 6 changing beers (sourced regionally) Ⓗ

Located in part of the original and now listed station building. Railway memorabilia line the walls, along with a sketch of the original 1863 building. It gets lively at weekends when tribute bands and local acts entertain an audience of locals and holidaymakers, although some peace may be found in the rear room. A music weekend is held with a beer festival and an outside stage. Up to eight beers are on the bar. Food is available Sunday lunchtime and Monday, Wednesday and Friday teatime. 🏠❀🕽♣P🚐🐾🛜

No.2 Refreshment Room

Station Approach, DN35 8AX

❂ 7.30am-11 (12.30am Thu-Sat); 9am-11 Sun ☎ 07905 375587

Hancocks HB; Rudgate Ruby Mild; Sharp's Doom Bar; Atlantic; York Guzzler; 2 changing beers (sourced nationally) Ⓗ

This is a little treasure. A small and cosy pub with a reputation for good beer, serving five regular ales plus two guests from both national and independent breweries. Its location on the railway station ensures a flow of customers enjoying a drink before or after their journeys. A free buffet is provided on Sunday evenings. Smokers may use a covered area within the station concourse. 🐾🚆🚐🛜

Nottingham House ⊘

7 Seaview Street, DN35 8EU

❂ 12-11 (midnight Thu; 1am Fri & Sat) ☎ (01472) 505150

🌐 nottinghamhousehotel.com

Oakham Citra; Tetley Mild, Bitter; Timothy Taylor Landlord; 3 changing beers (sourced regionally) Ⓗ

A fabulous example of a real English pub. Converted from two cottages built in 1856, this three-roomed venue comprises a bar, lounge and snug. In winter, open fires add to the atmosphere. Excellent food is served Wednesday to Sunday both in the bars and the upstairs restaurant. It holds an annual beer festival featuring over 20 real ales, and a good selection of permanent and changing beers completes the picture. Q🏠🛏🕽▲🚆♣🐾🚐(8,9,46)🐾🛜

Willy's

17 High Cliff, DN35 8RQ

❂ 11-11 (midnight Thu; 2am Fri & Sat) ☎ (01472) 602145

Draught Bass; Willy's Original; 2 changing beers (sourced nationally) Ⓗ

Willy's has its own microbrewery that can be viewed from inside the pub, and a large open bar downstairs with a function room above, although the latter usually opens at weekends only. This is a place where holidaymakers mix with locals – ideal for a pleasant meal and good ale all year round. Families are welcome when dining until 7pm, but dogs are not admitted at mealtimes. 🏠❀🕽🚆🚐(5,9,10)🐾

Coleby

Tempest Arms

Hill Rise, LN5 0AG

❂ 12-11 (4 Mon; midnight Fri & Sat); 12-10.30 Sun

☎ (01522) 810258 🌐 thetempestcoleby.co.uk

Castle Rock Harvest Pale; St Austell HSD; 4 changing beers (sourced nationally; often Fuller's, Theakston, Thwaites) Ⓗ

With panoramic views across the Trent Valley, this gem, situated on the Viking Way, offers walkers and locals alike the chance to sample some of the fine ales on offer while enjoying friendly conversation in the main bar or relaxing in the aptly named Vista restaurant. An acoustic music evening is held on the second Tuesday of the month, with quizzes every other Thursday. Q🏠❀🕽♣P🚐(1)🐾

East Butterwick

Dog & Gun 🅛

High Street, DN17 3AJ (off A18 at Keadby Bridge, E Bank)

☼ 5-11; 12-11 Sat & Sun ☎ (01724) 782324

DarkTribe Pieces of 8; 2 changing beers (sourced locally; often DarkTribe) 🅗

Traditional old-styled village pub alongside the River Trent, with three rooms, one of which allows in children. Picnic-style bench seating is set out on the riverbank and there is more seating at the rear of the pub. It is home to the DarkTribe microbrewery. Darts is popular and a weekly quiz is held on Tuesday evenings. During the warmer months motorsport meetings are held for motorcycles and vintage cars. ♿❀♿♣♠P🖵(12)♣

Eastoft

River Don Tavern

Sampson Street, DN17 4PQ (on A161 Goole-Gainsborough road)

☼ 3.30-11; 12-11 Sun ☎ (01724) 798040

2 changing beers (sourced regionally; often Acorn, Milestone, Rooster's) 🅗

Friendly local on the main road through the village. It has two distinct drinking areas styled with dark wood ceiling beams, rustic furniture and framed photos showing village life through the ages. One area is also used for dining and there is a separate restaurant where the renowned Sunday carvery is served. Two rotating guest beers are offered, usually including one from Rooster's, plus a real cider in summer. Accommodation is available in three rooms in the pub and four lodges at the rear. ❀🛏♪♿♣♠P🖵(356)♣�🛜

Epworth

Old School Inn

10 Battle Green, DN9 1JT (take first left off Station Rd heading towards Sandtoft)

☼ 12 (4 Mon & Tue)-11 ☎ (01427) 875835

⊕ theoldschoolinnepworth.co.uk

Brains Rev James; Timothy Taylor Landlord; 2 changing beers (sourced nationally; often Sharp's, Tom Wood's, Wychwood) 🅗

Converted from a former village school in the 1980s, this free house was purchased by a local family in 2012. It has been extensively refurbished and boasts an impressive restaurant. Four cask ales are always available, with locally brewed beers often featured as guests. No food on Mondays or Tuesdays – dogs are not permitted inside on days when food is served. ♿❀♿♣♠▲♠P🖵(399)♣🛜

Fosdyke

Ship Inn

Moulton Washway, PE12 6LH

☼ 11.30-10 (11 Fri & Sat) ☎ (01205) 260764

⊕ shipinnfosdyke.co.uk

Adnams Southwold Bitter, Broadside; Batemans XB 🅗

Located just outside Fosdyke when travelling from Boston on the main A17, next to the bridge. As its name suggests, this former Batemans hostelry is dedicated to all things maritime: maps, photographs, charts and model ships of every description are in plentiful supply. The week's tidetable is also detailed on a blackboard. The inn is near to the busy Fosdyke Marina and boaters and

landlubbers are well catered for with excellent home-cooked food and a welcome cheer. Q♿♪♠P♣🛜

Frognall

Goat 🅛

155 Spalding Road, PE6 8SA

☼ 12-3, 6-11.30; 12-11.30 Sat; 12-10.30 Sun

☎ (01778) 347629 ⊕ thegoatfrognall.com

8 changing beers (often Batemans, Hopshackle, Star) 🅗

An attractive food-oriented country pub with five dining areas. There is a drinking area at one end of the bar. Six handpumps serve a range of regional and microbrewery beers, including at least one LocAle and a strong ale. There are two real ciders – sometimes more – on gravity. A large selection of malt whiskies is available. A popular beer festival is held in the summer. The large garden has two separate play areas for children and toddlers. Q♿❀♿♪♣♠P🖵(100)🛜

Fulbeck

Hare & Hounds

The Green, NG32 3JJ

☼ 12-3, 5.30-11; 12-3 Sun ☎ (01400) 273322

⊕ hareandhoundsfulbeck.com

Adnams Broadside; Castle Rock Harvest Pale; Wadworth 6X; Woodforde's Wherry 🅗

This well-presented village pub originating from the 17th century faces the green of the charming cliff village of Fulbeck. It is a picture postcard country inn serving four regular ales. Locally sourced food where possible is used in the restaurant. The pub has accommodation, making it an ideal base for exploring the surrounding picturesque countryside, including the adjacent 10th-century church, Lincoln Cathedral and the Dambusters Museum at Coningsby. A function room is also available for use. ❀🛏♪♠P🖵

Gainsborough

Blues Club

Northolme, North Street, DN21 2QW

☼ 7-midnight; 5-1am Fri; 12-1am Sat; 12-midnight Sun

☎ (01427) 613688

3 changing beers 🅗

The club has a bar area with several TVs showing sport, a quieter lounge and a large function room that hosts regular live entertainment (admission charges may apply). Two changing real ales are usually offered and details of forthcoming beers can be emailed to customers on request. CAMRA guests are always welcome on production of a membership card or a copy of the Guide. ♿≢(Central)♣🖵

Eight Jolly Brewers 🅛

Ship Court, DN21 2DW

☼ 11-midnight; 12-midnight Sun ☎ 07926 797767

Dukeries A Ray of Sunshine; changing beers (often Glentworth) 🅗

The CAMRA branch's flagship real ale haven, in the Guide since 1995, based in a 300-year-old Grade II-listed building. Eight changing beers, at least one at a discounted price, are always on sale, many from northern micros, but new breweries from all areas feature. Real cider and continental bottled beers are also sold. Fortnightly Wednesday quiz nights are a feature and quality live music every Thursday. Customers bring in food to share on Sunday lunchtimes. Q&≠♦P🚯(200)

Elm Cottage ▼ 🄻

138 Church Street, DN21 2JU

🕓 11.30–midnight; 12–11.30 Sun ☎ 07590 806584

Changing beers 🄷

The pub is close to Gainsborough Trinity's football ground and the Blues Club. There are six varying beers, some from the Marston's portfolio, but frequent microbrewery beers can be available. Good value lunchtime food is served from Tuesday to Sunday and early evening meals on Thursday and Friday. The pub is popular with local amateur sports teams. Weekly live music is featured. Q🏃🛈&≠(Central)♦P🚯🐾🛜

Sweyn Forkbeard ✅

22-24 Silver Street, DN21 2DP

🕓 8am–midnight (1am Wed & Thu; 2am Fri & Sat) ☎ (01427) 675000

Ruddles Best Bitter; Sharp's Doom Bar; 3 changing beers 🄷

This town centre Wetherspoon establishment is making itself one of the must-do pubs in town. Three rotating guest beers often include some oddities for this part of the country. Customers can ask for their favourite beer and it often appears. The pub is named after the Danish King of England in 1013, whose son Canute is rumoured to have stopped the Trent Aegir tidal bore near here. Good value food is available until 11pm.
🏃🛈&≠(Central)♦🚯🛜

Gosberton Risegate

Duke of York 🄻

106 Risegate Road, PE11 4EY

🕓 12 (6.30 Mon)-11; 11-3, 7-10.30 Sun ☎ (01775) 840193

Batemans XB; St Austell Tribute; 1 changing beer 🄷

A friendly pub and a long-standing entry in the Guide, with a deserved reputation for value-for-money beers and food. As well as regular ales, guests come from a range of independent brewers. A wide choice of cooked food is available, with portions to suit the largest appetite. Local community life is supported through charities, sports teams and other social events. Visitors can expect an enthusiastic welcome from the two pub dogs. Q🏃🛈🛈&♣P

Grantham

Lord Harrowby 🄻

65 Dudley Road, NG31 9AB

🕓 3-11; 12-11 Sat & Sun ☎ (01476) 563515

Oldershaw Heavenly Blonde; 4 changing beers 🄷

This long-established back-street local comprises a modern lounge and a bar of Victorian style, where traditional pub games are played; it is a real gem in today's world. One regular beer from a local brewery and four different guest ales are served, as well as real cider. The pub was voted Town Pub of the Year by the local CAMRA branch. The landlord is a real ale enthusiast, hosting two beer festivals a year. Q🏃🛈🌾≠♣♦🐾

Nobody Inn 🄻

9 North Street, NG31 6NU (opp Asda car park)

🕓 12-11; 12-10.30 Sun ☎ (01476) 565288

🌐 nobodyinn.com

Blue Monkey BG Sips; Wells Bombardier; 4 changing beers (often Grainstore, Newby Wyke, Oakham) 🄷

Known locally as Eddie's, this pub has been in the Guide for a number of years and is a frequent winner of local CAMRA Pub of the Year. It is a traditional drinkers' pub which caters for customers of all ages. The beers always include a good selection from the local microbrewery Newby Wyke. There are numerous TV screens allowing simultaneous showing of sporting events when fixtures clash. A special feature is the concealed toilet entrance in the bookcase. ♣♦🚯🐾🛜

Tollemache Inn 🄻 ✅

17 St Peters Hill, NG31 6PY

🕓 8am–midnight (1am Fri & Sat) ☎ (01476) 594696

Adnams Broadside; Greene King Abbot; Newby Wyke Bear Island; Ruddles Best Bitter; Sharp's Doom Bar; 5 changing beers (often Brewster's, Newby Wyke, Oldershaw) 🄷

Wetherspoon pub ideally situated in the town centre and next to the Museum and Arts Centre, and in the Guide for the third consecutive year. It always has a large selection of national and guest ales. There is regularly one beer on from one of Grantham's award-winning and renowned microbreweries, either Brewster's, Newby Wyke or Oldershaws. Other guest beers are sourced regionally and nationally. The pub holds two beer festivals every year. 🏃🛈🛈&≠♦🚯🛜

Grimsby

Barge

Riverhead, DN31 1NH

🕓 10-11 (2am Tue, Fri & Sat); 12-11 Sun ☎ (01472) 340911

🌐 thebargegrimsby.co.uk

Wells Bombardier; Wychwood Hobgoblin 🄷

This is an established and popular pub in the town centre. As the name suggests, it is a barge moored at the Riverhead and has two types of custom – those who go for the fantastic menu served each day, and those looking for a night out with a difference. Two regular real ales feature and themed nights such as the Monday quiz and Tuesday student night mean that a visit is a must. Families are welcome until 7pm. 🏃🛈🛈≠🚯

Spiders Web

180 Carr Lane, DN32 8LN

🕓 12-11 (midnight Fri-Sun) ☎ (01472) 692065

🌐 thespiderswebgy.co.uk

John Smith's Bitter; Timothy Taylor Landlord; 2 changing beers (sourced nationally; often Black Sheep, Robinsons) 🄷

A vibrant community pub built in the 1950s with three large rooms, comprising a public bar with pool table and games, a lounge with a real fire and quieter surroundings, and a large function room used most weekends for live music and events. A large, well-kept garden is at the rear with plenty of space for children to run about. 🏃🛈♣P🚯(4)🛜

Habrough

Station Inn

Station Road, DN40 3AP

🕓 11-midnight ☎ (01469) 572896

3 changing beers (sourced regionally; often Horncastle Ales, St Austell) 🄷

Originally a hotel, the Station was built in 1848 as part of the Great Grimsby and Sheffield Junction

Railway. It comprises a single, large room with an open fire and an adjoining pool room. Live bands perform here each Saturday and there are classic car meets and other village events. The pub is slowly being refurbished back to a traditional village local. The house beer, Chuffin Ale, is brewed by Caledonian. ⌂☻🞉◖≒♣P❀

Haconby

Hare & Hounds
2 West Road, PE10 0UZ
✪ 12-2, 6-11 (10.30 Mon); 12-11 Sat; 12-10.30 Sun
☎ (01778) 570521
Marston's EPA; 1 changing beer (often Wychwood) Ⓗ
Low-beamed pub built around 1600, a popular dining hostelry with soft settees in the back room. Walking groups frequent the pub and there is live music on the first and second Sundays as well as on the third Monday in the month. A guest ale is from the Marston's stable and regularly changes. Nearby is the Primitive Baptist Methodist Chapel built in 1867, which must be one of the smallest in the land. Q⌂☻🞉◖&♣P❀

Halton Holegate

Bell Inn
Spilsby Road, PE23 5PA
✪ 6 (5 Thu)-11; 12-3, 5-11 Fri; 12-11 Sat & Sun
☎ (01790) 753242
2 changing beers Ⓗ
A 16th-century country inn with low-beamed ceilings, situated in a quiet village. Pictures of the Dambusters adorn the small, cosy lounge. The friendly, welcoming landlord has a keen interest in beer and the three guests are often from small breweries within the county. There is an annual beer festival on the first weekend in October and an annual Harvest Supper and Festival auction. Check with the pub for food availability.
Q⌂☻🞉♣ ♠P❀

Harmston

Thorold Arms
High Street, LN5 9SN
✪ 6-11; 12-3, 5-11 Fri; 12-3, 6-11 Sat; 12-11 Sun; closed Mon
☎ (01522) 720358
4 changing beers (sourced nationally; often Dark Star, Oldershaw) Ⓗ
A 17th-century stone-built pub in the centre of the village. The bar to the right of the entrance is relaxed and comfortable, with an open fire, sofas, armchairs, and more traditional tables and chairs; the other bar is used as a dining room. A full menu features weekly themed nights such as Wednesday grill night and Thursday pie night. A quiz is held on Sunday evenings. ⌂☻🞉◖P🖵(1)🛜

Heighington

Butcher & Beast
High Street, LN4 1JS
✪ 12-11; 12-10 Sun ☎ (01522) 790386
⊕ butcherandbeast.co.uk
Batemans XXXB; Everards Original; Oakham Citra; 3 changing beers (sourced nationally) Ⓗ
A welcoming, old-stone, village-centre pub on a regular bus route. Award-winning hanging baskets decorate the front and the large garden has a boules lane. Inside is a real fire and historic village

photos. The six handpumps offer Batemans beers and guests from the brewery's monthly list. Real ciders and rare malt whiskies are served. Regular themed nights and charity quizzes feature, plus a grumpy men's club. An extensive menu is available in the refurbished restaurant.
Q⌂☻🞉◖♣ ♠P🖵(2)❀🛜

Hemingby

Coach & Horses Ⓛ
Church Lane, LN9 5QF (1 mile from A158 at Baumber)
✪ 12-2 (Mon & Tue), 6-11; 12-2, 7-11 Sat; 12-3, 7-10.30 Sun
☎ (01507) 578280
3 changing beers (sourced regionally) Ⓗ
This is the 20th consecutive listing in the Guide for this former coaching inn. The village nestles in the rolling Lincolnshire Wolds and the pub is frequented by walkers and cyclists. Very much the hub of the community, the low-beamed bar hosts dominoes, darts and pool teams. There is also a golf society. The three beers always include a mild and a local brew. Home-cooked meals are available. The camping field is busy when there is motorcycle racing at nearby Cadwell Park.
Q⌂☻🞉◖♣♠P❀

Horbling

Plough Inn
4 Spring Lane, NG34 0PF
✪ 11.30-2.30 (not Mon), 6.30-11.30; 11.30-midnight Fri & Sat; 12-10.30 Sun ☎ (01529) 240263
⊕ theploughinnhorblingltd.co.uk
Thwaites Wainwright; 1 changing beer (sourced nationally) Ⓗ
Low-beamed, true community pub, built in 1832 and owned by the parish, set in a quiet village. As well as the lounge and bar it has a snug that is one of the smallest and most intimate of its kind. Beers are often from microbreweries and change regularly. Home-cooked meals are available in the bar and restaurant. Spring wells are a feature just a few yards down the lane. ⌂☻🞉◖&♣ ♠P❀

Horncastle

King's Head
16 Bull Ring, LN9 5HU
✪ 12-midnight (11 Mon; 2am Fri & Sat); 12-1am Sun
☎ (01507) 523360
Batemans XB, XXXB; 1 changing beer (sourced locally; often Batemans) Ⓗ
A comfortable and friendly pub with a single bar/lounge that accommodates two separate drinking areas. Three beers from Batemans are normally on tap. Unusually for this locality, the building has a thatched roof, hence its local name, the Thatch. Reputedly the pub inspired an 00 gauge Hornby model, an example of which is displayed behind the bar. In summer the pub is bedecked with hanging baskets and has won the Batemans Floral Display competition. ⌂☻♠P❀🛜

Old Nicks Tavern
8 North Street, LN9 5DX
✪ 5-midnight (1am Fri); 12-1am Sat; 12-midnight Sun
☎ (01507) 526862 ⊕ oldnickstavern.co.uk
4 changing beers (sourced locally; often Horncastle Ales) Ⓗ
Built in 1752 as a coaching inn, this original building is now a town-centre venue with its own

microbrewery, the home of Horncastle Ales. The place has been refurbished and incorporates the old pub sign and old photos of the pub. There are regular live bands. Of the four handpumps, three are usually from the Horncastle Brewery. The head brewster is the daughter of the landlord.
&◑♣●♞♣

Ingoldmells

Countryman 🔳
Chapel Road, PE25 1ND
✿ 12-midnight ☎ (01754) 872268
Leila Cottage Leila's Lazy Days, Ace Ale, Lincolnshire Life, Leila's One Off Ⓗ
The privately-owned Countryman appears to be a modern building but it incorporates the early 19th-century Leila Cottage, which gives its name to the brewery behind the pub. A notorious smuggler, James Waite, used to reside here when Ingoldmells was a wild and lonely place, but he certainly would not recognise the current holiday coast, with Skegness, Butlin's and Fantasy Island nearby. Information boards give brewery, pub and beer information for visitors. The pub is on northern bus routes from Skegness. ➷&◑♣&▲P🚆🖵

Irnham

Griffin Inn 🔳
15 Bulby Road, NG33 4JG
✿ 11-3, 6-11; 12-3, 6-10.30 Sun; closed Mon & Tue
☎ (01476) 550201 ⊕ thegriffininrnham.co.uk
Oakham JHB; 2 changing beers (often Brewster's, Star) Ⓗ
One of Lincolnshire's best-kept secrets, this fine stone building, set in its own grounds in the heart of the countryside, dates from the 1700s. The newly refurbished interior, with its separate bar and dining areas, creates an atmosphere of ancient and modern. The pub's policy is to source beers and food from local suppliers. It was a finalist for Les Routiers Country Inn of the Year 2015. Classic and vintage car enthusiasts meet on the first Wednesday of the month from April to September.
Q➷&◑♣◑P♣♞🖵

Kirkby on Bain

Ebrington Arms
Main Street, LN10 6YT
✿ 12-2 (not Mon), 6-11 ☎ (01526) 354560
⊕ ebringtonarms.com
Adnams Broadside; Batemans XB; Black Sheep Golden Sheep; Sharp's Doom Bar; 2 changing beers Ⓗ
Attractive country pub close to the River Bain and dating from 1610. World War II airmen used to slot coins into the ceiling beams to pay for beer when they returned from missions over Germany. Sadly, many of these coins are still in situ and make a unique memorial to the dead. The popular restaurant offers good food made with local produce (booking advised). There is a convenient caravan site within a mile of the pub.
Q&◑&▲P🖵(65)♞🖵

Lincoln

Adam & Eve Tavern
25 Lindum Road, LN2 1NT
✿ 12-11 (midnight Fri & Sat) ☎ (01522) 537108
⊕ adamandevelincoln.co.uk

Castle Rock Harvest Pale; Morland Old Speckled Hen; 2 changing beers (sourced nationally) Ⓗ
With low beams and thick walls, this is reputedly the oldest tavern in Lincoln. The main bar has a number of alcoves, one with a dartboard. There is a separate area for pool, and a front room offering views of the medieval Pottergate and the cathedral beyond. There are weekly music gigs and quiz nights, and sports matches are shown on two screens. The guest beers usually include a local brew, and good-value meals are available.
➷&◑P🖵♞🖵

Cardinal's Hat
268 High Street, LN2 1HW
✿ 11-11 (1am Fri & Sat) ☎ (01522) 527084
⊕ cardinalshatlincoln.co.uk
Adnams Mosaic; Bad Comfortably Numb; Tom Wood's Lincoln Gold; house beer (by Tom Wood's); 4 changing beers (sourced regionally) Ⓗ
Atop Lincoln's sloping High Street, this late 15th-century inn quenched thirsts until 1801, and retains its Tudor timber exterior. Recently converted back to a public house, the Hat is now open plan, but with myriad intriguing levels, rooms and snugs, many with old books. The cheese and charcuterie-based menu complements a large range of beers, wines and spirits; there are eight ale and four cider/perry handpulls. Q➷&◑&➷●♞🖵

Dog & Bone
10 John Street, LN2 5BH
✿ 4.30-11; 12-11 Fri-Sun ☎ (01522) 522403
⊕ dogandbonelincoln.co.uk
Batemans Gold, XB; 4 changing beers (sourced nationally) Ⓗ
A traditional, two-roomed pub just a 10-minute walk from the city centre. Features include changing artwork displays, board games and an extensive book-swap library. There is a strong community following, with cook-offs, regular rambles, quizzes, live music and more. A garden room, called the Kennel, is used for monthly Sunday lunches, functions and the annual beer festival. The garden is charming. Lincolnshire CAMRA Pub of the Year in 2015. &♣●🖵(4)♞🖵

Golden Eagle
21 High Street, LN5 8BD
✿ 11-11 (11.30 Fri & Sat); 12-11 Sun ☎ (01522) 521058
Castle Rock Harvest Pale; Fuller's London Pride; house beer (by Castle Rock); 7 changing beers (sourced nationally; often Newby Wyke, Oldershaw, Pheasantry) Ⓗ
Friendy two-roomed old coaching inn with up to nine real ales and at least one real cider. The bar is a pleasant room but can get busy on match days. The lounge is quiet, relaxed and cosy, with old football programmes on display. Occasional beer festivals, live music events and whisky, port or gin tasting nights take place. Friday is quiz night. Outside is a premier beer garden with sheltered seating, lighting and heaters. Q➷&♣●P♞🖵

Joiners Arms
4 Victoria Street, LN1 1HU
✿ 4-11; 2-midnight Fri & Sat; 1-11.30 Sun ☎ 07871 887459
5 changing beers (sourced nationally) Ⓗ
A friendly sanctuary tucked away from the commotion of the city centre. Although appearing small on the outside, the pub is deceptively spacious on the inside, with a large room with a pool table and another room towards the rear. The

decor is in traditional town-pub style, with pictures of bygone Lincoln upon the walls. The bar has an ample choice of changing ales. Regular events include live music, quizzes and more. Upcoming events can be seen on the regularly updated Facebook page. ☎✚♣♠✿

Jolly Brewer 🅛
27 Broadgate, LN2 5AQ
✪ 12-midnight (10 Mon; 11 Tue & Thu); 12-10 Sun
☎ (01522) 528583 ⊕ jollybrewer.org
Welbeck Abbey Henrietta; Portland Black; 4 changing beers (sourced regionally) ⊞
An idiosyncratic pub attracting a diverse clientele. The decoration is Art Deco in style and a side room has reclaimed cinema seating. The colours in the sparkly-topped bar tables reflect in the crystal-clear beers. Music is a major feature, with a jukebox, regular live sessions and quizzes. The large, rear courtyard has seating and a covered barn area where bands perform in summer. There is a dartboard and table football. Good-value meals are served.
☎✪◑≠(Central)♣♠P

Morning Star
11 Greetwell Gate, LN2 4AW
✪ 11-midnight; 12-11 Sun ☎ (01522) 527079
⊕ morningstarlincoln.co.uk
Draught Bass; Ruddles Best Bitter; Timothy Taylor Golden Best; Wells Bombardier; 2 changing beers (sourced regionally; often Brains, Castle Rock, Ossett) ⊞
A regular in the Guide, this long-established real ale pub dates back to the 18th century and is within a few minutes' walk of the cathedral. Customers are greeted with a relaxed atmosphere and the chance to join in with one of the many conversations taking place in the main bar. Quiz night is every Tuesday and there is occasional live music. Q✪◑♣P🖵✿🌺 🛜

Strugglers Inn 🅛 ✓
83 Westgate, LN1 3BG
✪ 12-1am (11 Mon & Tue; midnight Wed); 12-11.30 Sun
☎ (01522) 535023
Greene King Abbot; St Austell Tribute; Timothy Taylor Landlord; 6 changing beers (sourced nationally) ⊞
Known to its locals as the Struggs, this small pub is big on character and conversation, and a warm welcome from the staff is assured. The main bar is adorned with pumpclips of previous ales, which are now appearing on the ceiling as the walls are so full – 608 different guest ales featured over the past year. There is regular live music on Sunday teatimes, and a monthly book club meets in the snug. Q✪🖵(7,8)🌺 🛜

Victoria
6 Union Road, LN1 3BJ
✪ 11-midnight (1am Fri & Sat); 12-midnight Sun
☎ (01522) 541000 ⊕ victoriapub.net
Batemans XB, Gold; Castle Rock Harvest Pale; Timothy Taylor Landlord; 4 changing beers (sourced nationally) ⊞
The Victoria has been a public house as far back as the 1840s. Close to the west gate of the historic Lincoln Castle, this Batemans hostelry is popular with locals and tourists alike. As well as its Good Honest Ales, the pub has quality changing guest ales from around the UK. There is regular live music and fortnightly quizzes in the bar, plus a board games group that meets on Tuesdays in the upstairs room. Q✪◑♥🖵🌺 🛜

Little Cawthorpe

Royal Oak Inn (Splash)
Watery lane, LN11 8LZ (right off main road to Legbourne then left onto Buston Lane, through ford and turn left)
✪ 11-midnight ☎ (01507) 600750 ⊕ royaloaksplash.co.uk
Black Sheep Best Bitter; Greene King IPA; 2 changing beers ⊞
Known locally as the Splash because of the picturesque ford nearby, this 400-year-old inn sits in its own large lawned gardens on the edge of the Lincolnshire Wolds near Louth. Four beers are regularly available, plus often a guest ale from a local brewery. Three restaurants cover most culinary requirements, and themed evenings are popular. The en-suite rooms are often used by visitors to Cadwell Park or explorers of the Wolds. ☎✪🛏◑👤🅰♣P

Little Steeping

Eaves Inn
Main Road, PE23 5BL
✪ 6.30-11; 12-4 Sun; closed Mon-Wed ☎ (01754) 830639
⊕ theeavesinn.com
Batemans XB ⊞
The pub is the only one remaining in the Five Parishes. The restaurant serves good-quality, locally sourced food and attracts visitors from the surrounding area. This inn has maintained a good local feel, and the bar area with a log fire and comfortable chairs is a cosy place to spend time, with the staff often coming in and joining in with the conversation. It also has a camping and caravan site attached. Q☎✪◑👤🅰P🌺

Louth

Brown Cow ✓
133 Newmarket, LN11 9EG (top of Newmarket on jct with Church St)
✪ 5-11; 12-3 Fri; 12-11 Sat & Sun ☎ (01507) 605146
Black Sheep Best Bitter; Castle Rock Harvest Pale; Courage Directors; Fuller's London Pride; 1 changing beer ⊞
Friendly town pub with great atmosphere and, most importantly, great beer. A free quiz is held every Sunday night and the local folk club meets here on a Tuesday evening. The popular bistro serves traditional, home-cooked food, made with locally sourced products. Every Thursday is pie night, with a selection of different pies. Food is available Thursday to Sunday. The pub is a great community meeting place. Q☎✪◑👤♣🖵(51)🛜

Gas Lamp Lounge 🅛
13 Thames Street, LN11 7AD (bottom of Thames St by factories)
✪ 5-11; 12-11 Sat & Sun ☎ (01507) 607661
⊕ fulstowbrewery.com
Fulstow Common, Marsh Mild, Northway IPA; 1 changing beer ⊞
A unique pub, and one of only 22 in the UK lit by gas lamps. You will not find music or bandits, just good pub traditions. It serves four regular beers from the upstairs brewery, plus a guest beer. Benches are set along the canalside for enjoying a drink during the summer, while inside there is a roaring logburner to sit beside in the winter months. Dogs are welcome. Q☎👤♣♥🖵🌺✿🛜

Joseph Morton ✪

Pawnshop Passage, LN11 9EZ (small alleyway off Mercer Row)

🕓 8am-midnight (1am Fri & Sat) ☎ (01507) 353700

Batemans XXXB; Greene King Abbot; Ruddles County; changing beers (sourced regionally; often Black Horse, Milestone) 🅗

A JD Wetherspoon pub which opened in 2011 in Louth town centre. The pub offers good-value food and a large selection of regional and national ales. The former warehouse was built between 1808 and 1834 with cast-iron wall plates bearing the name of the local ironmonger, Joseph Morton. 🌣🕮🌕🅗🚭🍴🚐🛜

Wheatsheaf

62 Westgate, LN11 9YD

🕓 11-11 ☎ (01507) 606262

Batemans XB; Black Sheep Ale; Brains Bitter; Thornbridge Jaipur IPA; 1 changing beer 🅗

Picturesque pub lying close to Louth's historic St James's Church, which boasts the highest single spire of any medieval parish church in England, and is second only to the 19th-century Roman Catholic Church of St Walburge in Preston, Lancashire. It offers a good selection of real ales and a tasty home-made food menu, and has a lovely beer garden. A popular meeting place for walkers and ramblers. 🌣🕮🅗P🌣

Ludford

White Hart 🍷 🅛

Magna Mile, LN8 6AD

🕓 12-2 (not Tue-Thu), 6-11; 11-2, 6-11 Sat; 12-3.30, 7-11 Sun; closed Mon ☎ (01507) 313489

4 changing beers (sourced nationally) 🅗

A flagship ale pub whose licensees do their best to feature as many ales behind the bar as possible. Formerly a coaching house dating from the 18th century, it is now a two-roomed, rural village inn. It is close to the Viking Way, popular with hikers and ramblers. Four different guest beers are offered. The licensees pride themselves on serving real ale from microbreweries. All food is home made using ingredients from local suppliers. Meals are available lunchtimes and evenings. Q🚪🕮P

Market Deeping

Vine Inn 🅛

19 Church Street, PE6 8AN

🕓 4-11; 12-11 Fri-Sun ☎ (01778) 218622

Sharp's Doom Bar; house beer (by Wells); 3 changing beers (often Grainstore, Hopshackle, Star) 🅗

A free house since 2011, this small, friendly pub used to be a Victorian school. The bar features oak beams and stone floors, with many 20th-century prints on the walls. There is a large patio at the rear. Five handpumps dispense two regular beers plus a changing range of mostly LocAle guests. Boxed real cider is available. Free nibbles are provided Sunday lunchtime and early during the week. The TV is only used for major sporting events. 🌣🍴P🚐(101)🌣🛜

Messingham

Pooleys

46 High Street, DN17 3NT

🕓 6-11; 7-11 Sun; closed Mon ☎ 07860 799178

5 changing beers (often Batemans, Everards, Wells) 🅗

Pooleys is a busy and popular bar for locals and visitors alike, only open in the evenings. It has three separate drinking areas with rustic furniture, real fires and wood and flagstone floors. Five handpumps adorn the bar offering constantly rotating real ales, and a large selection of malt whiskies is also available. Updates of current real ales can be found on its Facebook page. Q🚫🚐🌣🛜

Morton

Ship Inn ✪

34 Front Street, DN21 3AE

🕓 4-midnight; 12-midnight Sat & Sun ☎ (01427) 613298

Sharp's Atlantic; Thwaites Wainwright 🅗

In the village of Morton, to the north of Gainsborough, this is a quaint, typical village pub, with weekly darts, dominoes and pool matches and regular quiz evenings. There are two rotating cask ales and food is served six days a week, with Sunday lunches proving to be popular. 🌣🍴🚌🚐

Navenby

Lion & Royal

57 High Street, LN5 0DZ

🕓 12-11 (midnight Fri & Sat); 12-10.30 Sun ☎ (01522) 810368

Greene King Abbot; Tetley Bitter; 2 changing beers (sourced nationally) 🅗

Guy Gibson, commanding officer of RAF 617 Dambusters Squadron, spent his wedding night in this imposing brick and stone building. The bar has a flagged floor and an impressive fireplace. There is a separate area for pool. To the rear is a large, enclosed beer garden. Live music is a regular feature. Walkers on the Viking Way long-distance path often call in for a drink and a good-value meal. 🌣🕮🅗🍴P🚐(1)🌣🛜

North Hykeham

Centurion ✪

Newark Road, LN6 8LB

🕓 11-11 (midnight Thu-Sat) ☎ (01522) 509814

Abbeydale Moonshine; Brakspear Bitter; Wells Bombardier; 5 changing beers (sourced nationally) 🅗

Just a few miles south of Lincoln city centre, this is a modern, family-friendly pub. Part of the Ember Inns chain, it offers an excellent selection of national and international ales and beers. Food is served until 10pm daily. Quiz nights are held three times a week and there are regular food and drink offers to entice customers. Popular with the local community. 🌣🕮🅗🚪P🚐(27,46)🛜

Old Bolingbroke

Black Horse Inn

Moat Lane, PE23 4HH

🕓 7 (8.30 Tue)-11; 12-4, 7-11 Sat; 12-4 Sun; closed Mon ☎ (01790) 763388

Young's Bitter; 3 changing beers (sourced locally; often Tydd Steam, Young's) 🅗

In a splendid walking area, this fine old country inn has 14th-century origins but was largely rebuilt in 1930. Henry IV was born at nearby Bolingbroke Castle, which was also besieged during the Civil War. Still part of the Duchy of Lancaster, the Black

Horse is a great place to visit when exploring the Lincolnshire Wolds. Friday fish night is a speciality and other themed food nights often feature. Lunchtime meals are Saturday and Sunday only.
Q🕷🕮🕭&🗚♣♥P🐾🐾✿

Pinchbeck

Bull Inn
1 Knight Street, PE11 3RA
✪ 12-2.30, 5-11; 12-midnight Fri & Sat; 12-11 Sun
☎ (01775) 723022
John Smith's Bitter; house beer (by Wadworth); 1 changing beer (often Thwaites) Ⓗ
Welcoming, friendly village pub opposite the old stocks. The Bull has two comfortable bars – the public bar with a log fire, and the lounge, used mainly for dining. A carved bull's head features on the long bar front, with the bar rail representing its horns. The pub has a reputation for good food, from bar snacks to meals in the upstairs restaurant, and includes weekend carveries. Guest beers sometimes come from local micros. Quiz night is the second Tuesday of the month.
🕷🕭&P🖩🍴(59,113)✿

Quadring

White Hart
7 Town Drove, PE11 4PU
✪ 12-3 (not Tue-Thu), 6.30-11; 5-11 Fri; 12-3, 6.30-11 Sat & Sun ☎ (01775) 822178
1 changing beer (often Draught Bass) Ⓗ
Friendly low-beamed community pub, popular with locals. One end of the building was previously a small shop and at the rear the large attractive garden once housed a bakery. Just one, occasionally changing, real ale is served at a time, always in excellent condition. Buses from Boston and Spalding stop at the nearby crossroads (not evenings or Sundays). Pool (free of charge) and darts are played in the bar – the landlord often joins in the pool. Q🕸🕷&♣P🖩(59)🐾

Rothwell

Blacksmith's Arms
Wold View, Hill Rise, LN7 6AZ
✪ 12-3, 5-11.30; 12-11.30 Sat; 12-11 Sun; closed Mon
☎ (01472) 371300 ⊕ blacksmiths-rothwell.co.uk
Lees Manchester Pale Ale; Robinsons Dizzy Blonde; Wells Bombardier Burning Gold; 2 changing beers (sourced regionally; often Caledonian, Greene King) Ⓗ
In the centre of a picturesque Lincolnshire Wolds village, this country pub is a Grade II-listed former inn and now a public house that takes its name from the blacksmith's shop that used to stand at the front of the building. A comprehensive menu of locally sourced food is served, with weekly specials on the blackboard. Five handpulls feature beers from independent brewers. Children and dogs are welcome and an open fire adds extra warmth.
Q🕸🕷🕭♣P🐾✿

Ruskington

Shoulder of Mutton
11 Church Street, NG34 9DU
✪ 12-midnight ☎ (01526) 832220
John Smith's Bitter; Sharp's Doom Bar; Wells Bombardier; 1 changing beer (sourced regionally) Ⓗ

A popular and thriving pub in the heart of the village which attracts customers of all ages. With its low wooden ceilings in its two main rooms, it is probably one of the oldest buildings in the village and, reputedly, once housed a butcher's shop, hence the name. Although additions have been made in recent years they have not spoilt the essential character. There is a separate pool room.
🕷&🚲♣P🖩(31)🐾✿

Saxilby

Anglers
65 High Street, LN1 2HA
✪ 11.30-11.30 (12.30am Fri & Sat); 12-11.30 Sun
☎ (01522) 702200 ⊕ anglerspublichouse.com
Theakston Best Bitter; 3 changing beers (sourced nationally; often Adnams, Everards, St Austell) Ⓗ
Convivial village pub near the railway station and at the heart of the local community. Pool, dominoes, darts, crib and two golf societies all feature, and regular poker nights are held. A recent addition is a boules court behind the pub which is much in demand in the summer. The pool table is in a room off the main bar. The lounge is decorated with many old local photographs. Moorings on the Fossdyke Navigation are nearby.
🕷🚲♣P🖩(100,105)🐾✿

Scampton

Dambusters Inn ♥ Ⓛ
23 High Street, LN1 2SD
✪ 12-11 (midnight Fri & Sat); 12-8.30 Sun; closed Mon
☎ (01522) 731333 ⊕ dambustersinn.co.uk
Timothy Taylor Landlord; 6 changing beers (sourced nationally; often Greg's) Ⓗ
Named after the famous RAF 617 Squadron, the Dambusters, the inn is situated in the quiet village of Scampton, adjacent to the Scampton air base, home to the Red Arrows. Medals and RAF memorabilia adorn the multi-roomed interior. Whether a diner or drinker, you can be sure of a warm welcome – you may even be greeted by Bomber the pub's dog. Home to Greg's Brewery and local CAMRA Pub of the Year 2016.
Q🕸🕷🕭🕮♥P🖩(103)🐾✿

Scawby

Sutton Arms
10 West Street, DN20 9AN (on main road through village)
✪ 11.30-midnight; 11.30-11 Sun ☎ (01652) 652430
⊕ suttonarmsscawby.co.uk
Theakston Best Bitter; 3 changing beers (often Axholme, Milestone, Sharp's) Ⓗ
Comfortable, traditionally styled village local with a good reputation for its excellent food. A central bar serves an open-plan dining area and a separate dining room, plus a small snug to one side used mainly for drinking. There is an extensive food menu plus daily specials available lunchtimes and evenings. Theakston Best Bitter is a regular beer, supplemented by three rotating guest ales. Quiz night is Sunday evening. 🕸🕷🕭&P🐾✿

Scunthorpe

Berkeley Hotel ★
Doncaster Road, DN15 7DS (½ mile from end of M181)

◆ 11.30-2.30, 5-11; 12-11 Fri & Sat; 12-10.30 Sun
☎ (01724) 842333 ⊕ theberkeleyscunthorpe.co.uk
Samuel Smith Old Brewery Bitter ⊞
Large 1930s Samuel Smith's pub and hotel,
designated by CAMRA as having a nationally
important historic interior due to its Art Deco
styling. The front entrance leads to three rooms – a
main bar with a real fire, a restaurant lounge and
separate ballroom, plus a large public bar with its
own side entrance, and a beer garden. Eight guest
rooms are available. The landscaped front entrance
has a large car park. The pub is five minutes' walk
from Glanford Park football ground.
Q✿❄◑◖ও♣P☐🖵

Blue Bell ✓
1-7 Oswald Road, DN15 7PU
◆ 8am-midnight (1am Sat) ☎ (01724) 863921
**Greene King Abbot; Ruddles Best Bitter; Sharp's
Doom Bar; 7 changing beers (sourced regionally;
often Acorn, Great Heck, Roosters)** ⊞
Popular Wetherspoon town-centre pub with an
open-plan layout on two levels – the family area is
on the top level. Outside is a patio area with
seating and a heated space for smokers. Beer
festivals are held regularly and the pub celebrates
special events such as Burns Night and St Patrick's
Day. There is a muted TV screen showing sport and
news. Food is served all day until 11pm.
Q❄✿❄◑◖ও♠🖵

Malt Shovel Ⓛ
219 Ashby High Street, DN16 2JP (in Ashby Broadway
shopping area)
◆ 10-11 (midnight Fri & Sat); 12-11 Sun ☎ (01724) 843318
**Exmoor Gold; Tom Wood's Best Bitter; 4 changing
beers (sourced regionally; often Acorn, Mallinson's,
Oakham)** ⊞
Comfortably furnished single-room pub with a
dining/drinking conservatory. It has a loyal, regular
clientele attracted by quality ales served in friendly
surroundings. Oakham beers are a permanent
feature alongside regionally sourced, regularly
changing guest beers and cellar-cool real ciders. It
can get busy lunchtimes and early evenings for
good-value, home-cooked food. Quiz nights are
Tuesdays and Thursdays. Live music features on
alternate Saturdays and a monthly folk night on
Sundays. Members-only snooker facilities are
available. Q❄✿❄◑◖♣♠🖵

Skegness

Vine
Vine Road, PE25 3DB (off Drummond Rd)
◆ 11-11 ☎ (01754) 763018 ⊕ thevinehotel.com
**Batemans XB, XXXB; 1 changing beer (often
Batemans)** ⊞
A delightful building, one of the oldest in Skegness,
dating from the 18th century and set in two acres
of pleasant grounds. Inside are comfortable wood-
panelled bars in which to enjoy a quiet pint or two
after experiencing some of the noisier attractions
and bustle of Skegness. Within striking distance of
the Gibraltar Point National Nature Reserve,
walking trails, beach and golf links, the inn
reputedly has connections with Alfred Lord
Tennyson. ❄✿❄◑◖ও P🖵❄🖵

Skendleby

Blacksmiths Arms Ⓛ
Main Road, PE23 4QE
◆ 12-3 (not Mon), 5.30-11; 12-4 Sun ☎ (01754) 890662
⊕ blacksmithspub.co.uk
**Batemans XB; 2 changing beers (sourced
regionally)** ⊞
A traditional country pub, dating back to the 18th
century, nestling on the south-east edge of the
Lincolnshire Wolds. Ducking beneath the low door
lintel, fortunately well-padded, you discover the
gem of a small quarry-tiled snug, complete with
range and settles, with the cellar visible through a
glass panel behind the bar. The dining room at the
rear incorporates the building's former well. There
is also a separate restaurant and a conservatory. On
the last Sunday of the month the pub opens 7pm-
late for live music. Q❄✿❄◑◖♣P🖵(96)❄🖵

Skillington

Cross Swords
The Square, NG33 5HB
◆ 7-11 Mon; 12-2, 6 (7 Tue & Wed)-11; 12-2 Sun
☎ (01476) 861132 ⊕ thecross-swordsinn.co.uk
Draught Bass; Grainstore Steelback IPA ⊞
Built in the early- to mid-18th century, this
impressive stone-built pub commands a good
position in the centre of the village. The current
hosts have owned the Cross Swords since 1991.
The bar area boasts a real fire. Ales are from
Grainstore and other local breweries, while quality
pub food is served daily; the menu shows allergen
information. There is a patio area with seating, and
three cottages are available to let. Local CAMRA
Country Pub of the Year 2014. Q✿❄◑◖P🖵

Sleaford

Carre Arms Hotel
Mareham Lane, NG34 7JP
◆ 11-11 ☎ (01529) 303156 ⊕ carrearmshotel.co.uk
3 changing beers (sourced nationally) ⊞
A privately run hotel previously owned by Bass,
adjacent to the Bass Sleaford maltings complex
which is now awaiting a regeneration
scheme. There is a comfortable bar area with two
rooms, offering two or three real ales, normally
from larger regional breweries, and they change
regularly. Draught cider is occasionally on
handpump. An extensive food menu is offered,
served in the bar area or restaurant. There is a
pleasant covered courtyard, ideal on inclement
days. ❄✿❄◑◖ও❄P🖵

Packhorse Inn Ⓛ ✓
7 Northgate, NG34 7BH
◆ 8am-midnight ☎ (01529) 308730
**8 Sail Ale; Greene King Abbot; Ruddles Best Bitter;
Sharp's Doom Bar; 3 changing beers (sourced
nationally)** ⊞
An 18th-century coaching inn on the London to
Lincoln road. It has had several names during its
lifetime, reverting to the original name when
taken over by Wetherspoon a few years ago.
Despite being remodelled as partly open-plan, it
retains an intimate atmosphere. As the Lion Hotel it
hosted the opening dinner for the Sleaford
Railway, an event that marked the start of the
decline in coaching trade. Q❄✿❄◑◖ও❄🖵❄🖵

Snitterby

Royal Oak ♈

High Street, DN21 4TP (1½ miles from A15)
✪ 5-midnight; 12-midnight Sat; 12-9 Sun ☎ (01673) 818213
Greene King IPA; Roosters Buckeye Ⓗ; 6 changing beers (sourced regionally; often Adnams, Wold Top) Ⓗ/Ⓖ
Traditional, family-run, community pub in a village setting. It has up to eight real ales with more on bank holidays and special occasions, which are themed, either by region, beer type or event. The comfortable, spacious interior is light and airy, with real fires. Outside, the seating area overlooks a stream and ford. Sky Sports is shown in the snug. Monthly pop-up pizzeria and jazz and jalfrezi nights take place. Local CAMRA Pub of the Year in 2014 and 2016. ⬔❀⚘Å♣⚘P♿❀

South Ormsby

Massingberd Arms

Brinkhill Road, LN11 8QS (1 mile off the A16)
✪ 12-2.30, 6-11; 12-11 Sun; closed Mon ☎ (01507) 480492
Thwaites Original; 1 changing beer Ⓗ
An old, traditional country pub set in the heart of the Lincolnshire Wolds, an Area of Outstanding Natural Beauty. There is home-cooked food and a quiz for charity every Wednesday night. The landlord has recently upgraded the dining room, which now has a wood-burning stove. The pub is closed on Mondays. A proper country pub in a beautiful location – walkers welcome.
Q⬔❀⊕⚘P

South Witham

Angel Inn Ⓛ ✅

13 Church Street, NG33 5PJ
✪ 12-11 ☎ (01522) 768302 ⊕ angelinn.bar
Black Sheep Best Bitter; Wells Bombardier; 1 changing beer (sourced nationally) Ⓗ
A warm welcome awaits you at this recently refurbished Grade II-listed building in a quiet village just off the A1. As well as a choice of fine beers, the pub offers an extensive traditional English pub food menu prepared by a chef who previously worked at Buckingham Palace. BT Sport and Sky Sports are screened in the bar lounge area. ⬔❀⊕&Å♣P♬❀

Spalding

Ivy Wall ✅

18-19 New Road, PE11 1DQ
✪ 8am-midnight (1am Fri & Sat) ☎ (01775) 719770
Greene King Abbot; Ruddles Best Bitter; Sharp's Doom Bar; Wychwood Hobgoblin; 5 changing beers (sourced nationally) Ⓗ
The town-centre site on which this spacious modern pub now stands has had a variety of uses over the years, and used to be on the bank of the former Westlode river. Excavations during the rebuild in 2005 discovered an undercroft and cellar from the late medieval period. There is a guest cider dispensed by gravity. Food is available all day. Photographs and archaeological finds are displayed on the wall. ⬔❀⊕&⚘♬⚘⊛

Priors Oven Ⓛ

1 Sheep Market, PE11 1BH
✪ 12-9 (10 Thu; midnight Fri & Sat); closed Mon

6 changing beers Ⓖ
The first micropub to be opened in Lincolnshire. The building has quite a history and is believed to be 800 years old; it was originally the prison of the local priory. Its more recent use was as a bakery and it became a pub in mid-December 2013. It has a ground-floor bar with a domed ceiling, from where a stone spiral staircase leads up to a comfortable lounge room. Beers can be served in one-third pint measures. Q⇌⚘♬

Stamford

Green Man Ⓛ

29 Scotgate, PE9 2YQ
✪ 11-midnight; 12-midnight Sun ☎ (01780) 753598
Castle Rock Harvest Pale; Sharp's Doom Bar; 6 changing beers (often Blue Monkey, Kelham Island, Sheffield) Ⓗ
Dating from 1796, this stone-built former coaching inn has an L-shaped split-level bar with a real fire. Up to eight ales, complemented by a good range of European bottled beers, are available. As many as seven ciders and perries, often Moonshine and Broad Oak, are on offer. Two beer festivals are held at Easter and September on the secluded patio, which boasts a mounting block from the days of patrons arriving on horseback. The pub has much beer memorabilia adorning the walls. ❀⚌⊕⚘⇌♣⚘♬♬(201)❀♚

Jolly Brewer Ⓛ

1 Foundry Road, PE9 2PP
✪ 11-midnight; 12-11.30 Sun ☎ (01780) 755141
⊕ jollybrewer.com
Brewster's Marquis; Oakham JHB; 4 changing beers (sourced locally; often Baker's Dozen) Ⓗ
A stone-built pub dating from 1830, comprising an L-shaped room around the bar with a smaller adjoining dining room. Outside there is a large patio with tables. The home-cooked food features locally sourced produce. The pub is home to pool, darts, crib and dominoes teams from the local community. Six handpumps dispense a range of LocAles, national ales and its own Baker's Dozen beers. One handpump serves cider, usually Old Rosie. A good range of malt whiskies is available. Q❀⊕⇌♣⚘P♬(9,202)❀♚

Tobie Norris

12 Saint Pauls Street, PE9 2BE
✪ 11-11 (midnight Fri & Sat); 12-10.30 Sun
☎ (01780) 753800 ⊕ tobienorris.com
Castle Rock Harvest Pale Ⓗ; 3 changing beers (sourced regionally; often Adnams, Blue Monkey) Ⓗ/Ⓖ
The building, parts of which date back to 1280, was bought by Tobie Norris in 1617 and used as a bell foundry. A conversion into a pub from the former RAFA Club gained it CAMRA's Conversion to Pub Use Award in 2007. The interior is split into many small rooms with real fires, stone floors and low beams. Five handpumps serve beers from local and countrywide brewers. At least one real cider is always available. Two beer festivals are held each year. Q❀⊕&⇌♣⚘♬(202,203)❀

Stickford

Red Lion Inn Ⓛ

Church Road, PE22 8EP

❄ 7-11; 4-11.30 Fri & Sat; 12-10.30 Sun; closed Mon & Tue
☎ (01205) 480395 ⊕ redlionstickford.co.uk
Batemans XB; 1 changing beer (sourced locally) Ⓗ
The pub name Red Lion, the most common in England, is frequently found hereabouts because it was a heraldic emblem of 14th-century John of Gaunt, Earl of Lancaster and Lord of the Manor at nearby Bolingbroke Castle. This cosy and friendly two-bar pub produces its own range of cider and holds an annual cider festival. Food is served evenings and Sunday lunchtimes using local produce, and all pies are home made. There are two en-suite letting bedrooms.
Q✿❄🍴◑▲♣♿P🚃(113)🐾🛜

Swineshead

Pig & Whistle
Market Place, PE20 3LJ
❄ 5.30-11; 12-11 Sat & Sun ☎ (01205) 821381
Banks's Mild; Fuller's London Pride; 3 changing beers Ⓗ
Years ago the pub was called the Green Dragon. Its fortunes gradually declined; it became run down, and despite a change of name it eventually closed. Now the current owners have brought it back to life as a vibrant and thriving village local, successfully blending old and new to recreate a genuine community pub with an emphasis on beer and traditional pub games. Guest beers come from a wide range of breweries and the food comprises home-made pizzas and bar snacks.
❄◑♣♿P🚃(K59)

Swinhope

Clickem Inn 🏆
Binbrook Road, LN8 6BS (2 miles N of Binbrook on B1203)
❄ 12-3 (not Mon-Wed), 5-11; 12-11.30 Fri & Sat; 12-10.30 Sun ☎ (01472) 398253 ⊕ clickem-inn.co.uk
Batemans XXXB; Timothy Taylor Landlord; house beer (by Batemans); 3 changing beers (sourced regionally; often Horncastle Ales, Rudgate, Springhead) Ⓗ
Country pub set in the picturesque Lincolnshire Wolds and a popular stopping place for walkers and cyclists. The unusual name originates from the counting of sheep passing through a nearby clicking gate. It is renowned for its traditional home-cooked food served in the bar and conservatory. Six handpulls feature both independent and small local brewers; another handpull serves a traditional cider. The house beer, Terry's Tipple, is brewed by Batemans. A covered but unheated area is provided for smokers.
Q❄◑♣♿P🛜

Tattershall Thorpe

Blue Bell Inn
Thorpe Road, LN4 4PE
❄ 12-3, 6-11; 12-4 Sun; closed Mon ☎ (01526) 342206 ⊕ bluebell-inn.com
Thwaites Lancaster Bomber; 2 changing beers (sourced locally; often Horncastle Ales, Springhead) Ⓗ
This ancient building, in a delightful location, has 13th-century origins and is one of Lincolnshire's oldest inns. It has a large open fire and beamed ceilings that are covered in signatures and photographs of airmen from World War II RAF squadrons who used the pub, including the 617

Dambusters and 627 Pathfinders. King Henry VIII reputedly visited the Blue Bell and there is a ghost in residence. Q❄✿❄◑♿▲♣P🛜

Tetford

White Hart Ⓛ
East Street, LN9 6QQ
❄ 12-3 (no Mon), 5-11 ☎ (01507) 533255 ⊕ thewhiteharttetford.co.uk
Brains Rev James Ⓗ; **2 changing beers** Ⓗ/Ⓖ
A historic village pub standing in a beautiful Lincolnshire village where Alfred Lord Tennyson and Dr Johnson have both stayed. It is a traditional English country hostelry and restaurant nestling in the heart of the Lincolnshire Wolds between Horncastle and Louth, ideally positioned for Cadwell Park race track. A selection of real ales and good food is offered in a friendly and relaxed atmosphere. ❄✿❄◑▲♣♿P🐾🛜

Tetney Lock

Crown & Anchor
Lock Road, DN36 5UW
❄ 10-11 ☎ (01472) 388291 ⊕ crownanchor.net
Sharp's Doom Bar; 2 changing beers (sourced nationally) Ⓗ
Overlooking the historic but now defunct Louth Navigation canal, this is a convenient watering hole for lovers of outdoor pursuits. Dogs are welcome in the public bar – the landlord keeps a jar of dog biscuits on the bar for them. There is a pleasant garden at the rear, while at the front is a patio overlooking the canal. Traditional Sunday lunches are served until 6pm. Guest beers are available in the summer months. Q❄✿❄◑P🐾🛜

Thimbleby

Durham Ox
Main Road, LN9 5RB
❄ 12-3, 6-11 ☎ (01507) 527152 ⊕ durhamoxpubthimbleby.co.uk
Batemans XB; Black Sheep Best Bitter; 1 changing beer Ⓗ
Fine country inn over 200 years old and reopened in 2013. The welcoming pub features beamed ceilings, a cowshed bar and RAF corner. Outside is a sunny beer garden and a large field at the rear for caravans and campers. There is an extensive food menu serving freshly cooked local produce. The pub is named after a huge 18th-century ox which toured the country – at its largest it weighed 270 stone. ❄✿❄◑♿▲♣P🚃🐾

Threekingham

Three Kings Inn
Saltersway, NG34 0AU
❄ 12-3, 6-11; 12-3, 6-10.30 Sun; closed Mon ☎ (01529) 240249
Draught Bass; Morland Old Speckled Hen; Timothy Taylor Landlord; 1 changing beer Ⓗ
A classic country inn with charm and character. Its bright and comfortable lounge bar, with attractive rural prints, and the panelled dining room serving locally sourced food, are deservedly popular with locals and visitors. Guest beers are usually from independent brewers. There is a pleasant beer terrace and garden for summer months and a large function room. The pub's name refers to the

slaying, by the Saxons, of three Danish chieftains in battle in 870 at nearby Stow; look for the effigies above the entrance. Q🛏⛱🕪◖▲P☙

Waddington

Three Horseshoes 🅛
High Street, LN5 9RF

✪ 3 (2 Fri)-11; 11-11 Sat; 12-11 Sun ☎ (01522) 720448

John Smith's Bitter; 5 changing beers (sourced locally; often Cathedral Heights, Dukeries, Pheasantry) Ⓗ

A no-nonsense, no-frills village pub with two rooms, both with real fires, which will not disappoint real ale drinkers. The pub has strong links with the local community, hosting many charity and live music events, which adds to the lively atmosphere. The beer range, featuring smaller breweries, changes frequently. Look out for the hook and ring game. Q🛏⛱♣🚃(1,13)☙

Wainfleet

Batemans Brewery Visitors Centre 🅛
Salem Bridge Brewery, Mill Lane, PE24 4JE

✪ 11.30-4 Wed-Sun; 11.30-4 May-Aug; closed Jan; closed Mon & Tue Feb-Apr, Sep-Dec ☎ (01754) 882017

⊕ bateman.co.uk

Batemans XB, Gold, XXXB, Salem Porter; 2 changing beers (sourced locally; often Batemans) Ⓗ

Visiting Batemans Brewery provides the chance to experience the blend of its proud 140-plus years of brewing tradition with its forward-looking outlook. Mr George's Bar, within the attractive windmill, is the ideal venue to sample a range of its beers. Further entertainment is to be found with brewery tours, featuring the Theatre of Beers, and in the pleasant beer garden with its games. A good range of Lincolnshire food is served 12-2pm. Tours are 12.30pm and 2.30pm in summer, 2.30pm in winter. 🛏◖&▲⇌♣P🚃(7)🗢

Waltham

Tilted Barrel
2 Kirkgate, DN37 0LS

✪ 11-11 (midnight Thu-Sat) ☎ (01472) 801817

⊕ tiltedbarrel.co.uk

Morland Old Speckled Hen; Tetley Bitter; Theakston Best Bitter; 1 changing beer (sourced nationally; often Sharp's) Ⓗ

A family-run pub in the heart of Waltham. It has the feel of a village local with seating in the corners, and is a friendly place to drink whether you are from near or far. A stove helps keep those chills away when the weather is cold, while there is a well cared for suntrap garden area for when the sun shines. 🛏⛱🕪◖P🚃(9)☙

Westwoodside

Carpenter's Arms
Newbigg, DN9 2AT (on B1396 in centre of village)

✪ 4-midnight; 2-midnight Sat; 1-midnight Sun

☎ (01427) 752416

Black Sheep Best Bitter; Caledonian Deuchars IPA; Sharp's Atlantic; 2 changing beers (sourced nationally; often Greene King, Wychwood) Ⓗ

This popular village local has been a regular in the Guide for several years under the present licensees. Up to five cask ales are on handpump, with local micros occasionally featured. This is a genuine community venue which raises significant amounts of money for charity and hosts a variety of local events. The pub takes part in the local Haxey Hood game every January. 🛏⛱▲♣P🚃(391)☙ 🗢

Willingham by Stow

Half Moon 🅛
23 High Street, DN21 5JZ

✪ 5-10 Mon; 12-2, 5-11 Tue & Wed (midnight Thu & Fri); 12-midnight Sat; 12-10.30 Sun ☎ (01427) 788340

⊕ graftersbrewery.com

Grafters Moonlight, Traditional, Over the Moon, Darker Side of the Moon; 4 changing beers Ⓗ

Home to Grafters brewery, this popular village pub goes from strength to strength. It offers four changing Grafters beers and four additional pumps serving rotating guests, mainly from micros. Seasonal Grafters beers are also sold when brewed. The renowned home-cooked fish and chips are a must, served lunchtimes and evenings, Tuesday to Friday, all day Saturday and Sunday lunchtimes (booking recommended). Brewery tours, including food and a tasting session, can be arranged by appointment. Q🛏⛱🕪◖&♣🚃☙

Winterton

George Hogg 🅛 ✅
25 Market Street, DN15 9PT

✪ 2-11 (midnight Fri); 9.30am-11 Sat & Sun

☎ (01724) 732270 ⊕ thegeorgehogg.co.uk

Tom Wood's Best Bitter; York Guzzler; 2 changing beers (sourced regionally; often Batemans) Ⓗ

Popular Grade II-listed marketplace pub and local CAMRA award winner. It has a large lounge/dining area and separate public bar, both with real fires. Good-value locally sourced food is available at weekends, plus home-made snacks. It is open for Sunday breakfast from 9.30am. Guest beers change regularly and there is an annual beer festival. The pub is a meeting place for football teams and the local supporters' club. A further dining area is upstairs, as are tea and coffee. Cask Marque accredited. Q🛏⛱🕪◖♣P🚃(350)☙ 🗢

Wragby

Ivy 🅛
Market Place, LN8 5QU

✪ 11.45-midnight ☎ (01673) 858768 ⊕ theivy.vpweb.co.uk

Draught Bass; Batemans XB; 3 changing beers (sourced regionally; often Horncastle Ales, Pheasantry, Tom Wood's) Ⓗ

At the heart of this small market town, nine miles east of Lincoln, the 17th-century Ivy is opposite the free car park. Drinking/dining tables fill the alcoves and edges of a wooden-beamed and panelled bar, off which is a separate dining area. Specialising in gluten-free food, the menu includes sausage and mash, and chunky hand-cut chips. A good range of bottles is available alongside the handpump ales. Sunday is quiz night. Q⇌🕪◖&♠🚃(6,10)🗢

Not all chemicals are bad. Without chemicals such as hydrogen and oxygen, for example, there would be no way to make water, a vital ingredient in beer. **Dave Barry**

London index

*Shown on Inner London map

GREATER LONDON

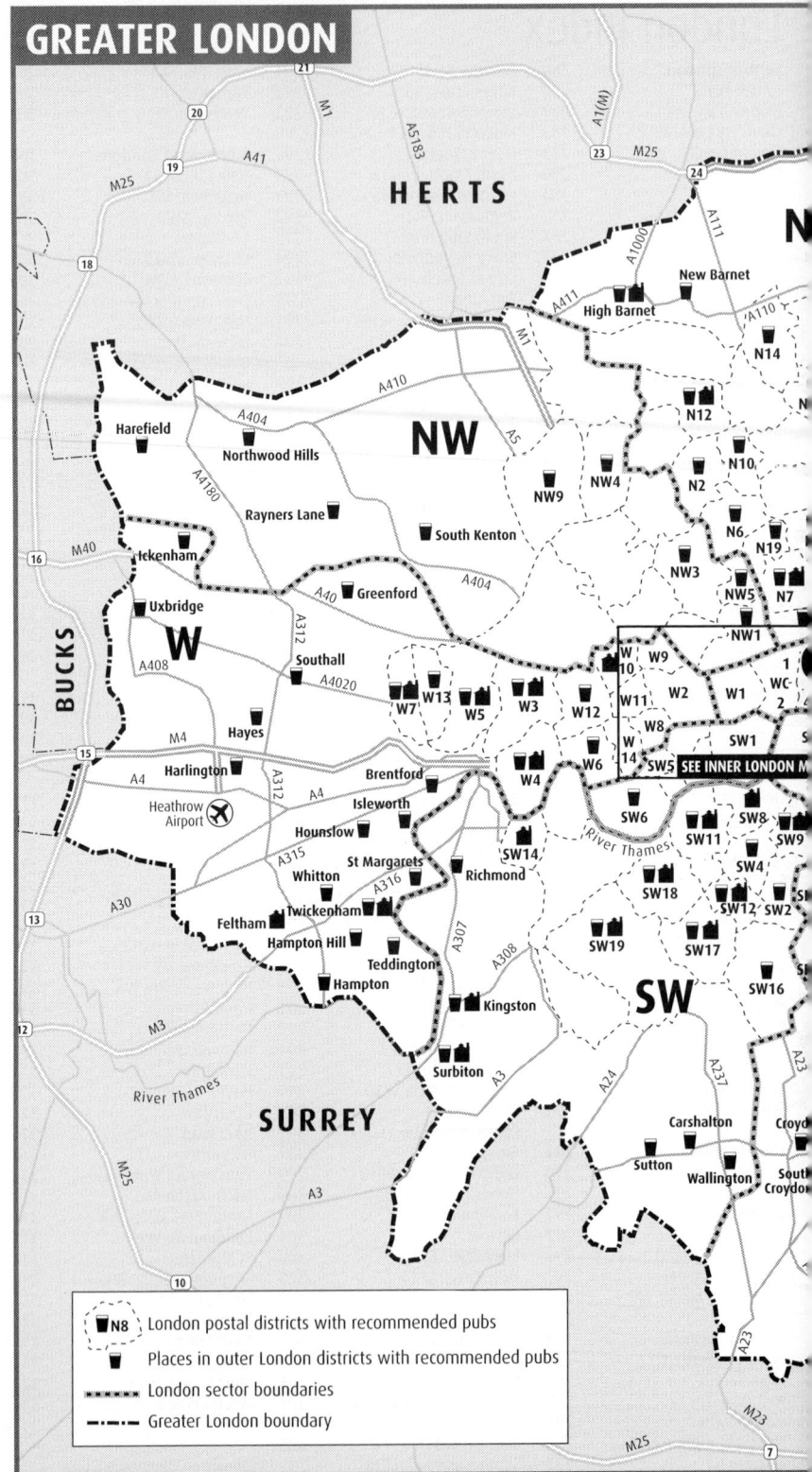

HERTS

21
20
M1
A5183
A1(M)
19
M25
A41
23
M25
24
18
A410
N
A1000
A111
New Barnet
High Barnet
A411
A110
N14
Harefield
A404
A5
NW
N12
Northwood Hills
A4180
N10
Rayners Lane
NW9
NW4
N2
N6
South Kenton
N19
16
M40
A404
NW3
N7
Ickenham
A40
Greenford
A404
NW5
Uxbridge
NW1
W
A312
Southall
W9
A408
A4020
W10
1
Hayes
W7
W13
W5
W3
W12
W11
W2
W1
WC
M4
W8
2
Harlington
A312
Brentford
W14
SW1
Heathrow
Airport
A4
Isleworth
W4
W6
SW5
SEE INNER LONDON M
Hounslow
St Margarets
SW6
A315
SW14
SW11
SW8
Whitton
A316
Richmond
River Thames
SW9
13
A30
Feltham
Twickenham
SW18
SW4
Hampton Hill
A307
SW12
SW2
Teddington
A308
SW19
SW17
Hampton
SW16
12
M3
Kingston
SW
River Thames
Surbiton
A3
SURREY
Carshalton
Croyd
A237
A23
A3
Sutton
Wallington
South
Croydon
10
M25
A23
M23
7

BUCKS

Legend

N8 London postal districts with recommended pubs

Places in outer London districts with recommended pubs

London sector boundaries

Greater London boundary

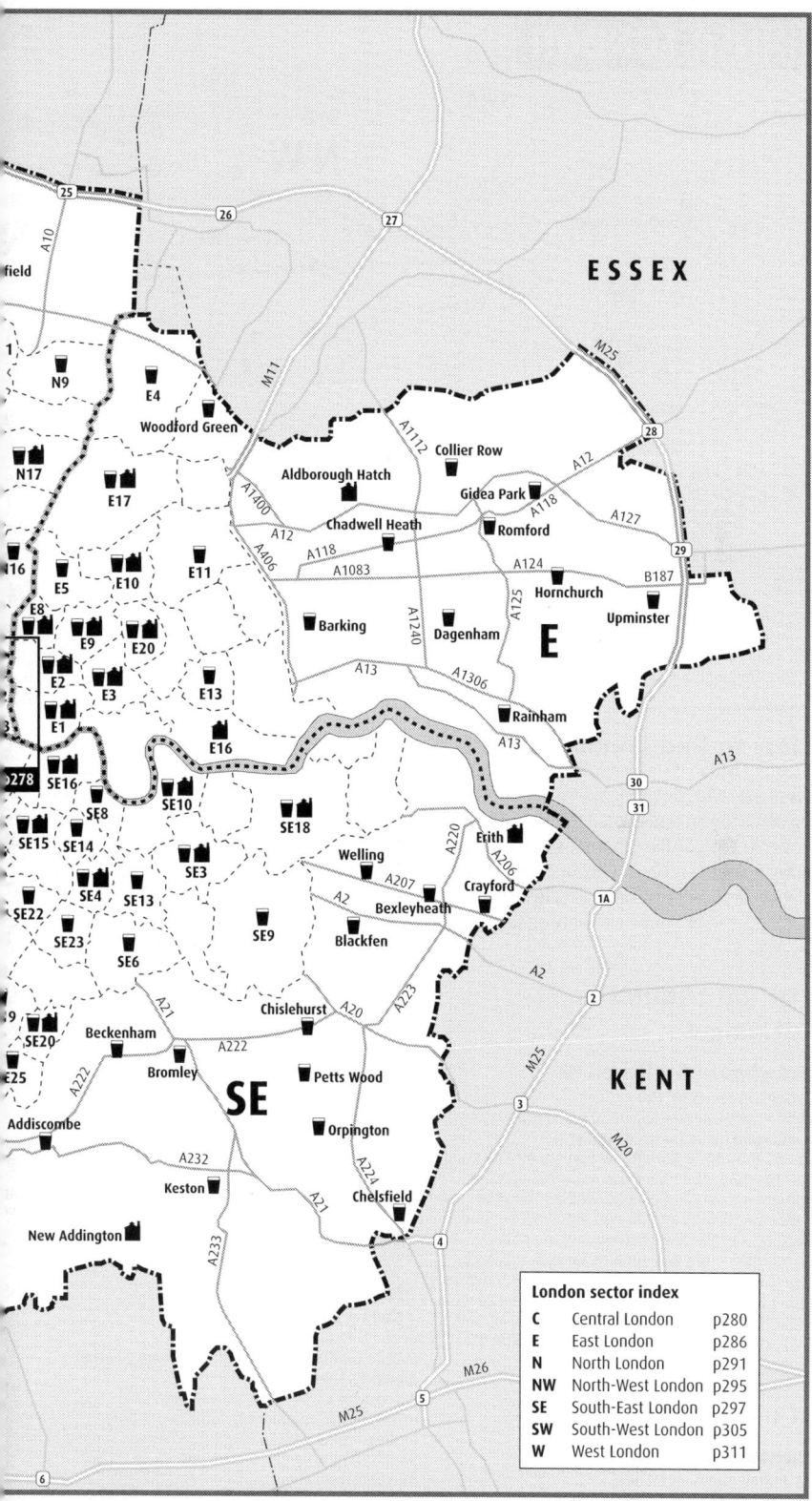

ESSEX

field

N9

E4

Woodford Green

N17

E17

Aldborough Hatch

Collier Row

Gidea Park

Chadwell Heath

Romford

16

E5

E10

E11

Barking

Dagenham

Hornchurch

Upminster

E8

E9

E20

E2

E3

E13

E1

E16

Rainham

278

SE16

SE10

SE8

SE18

Erith

SE15

SE14

SE3

Welling

Crayford

SE4

SE13

Bexleyheath

SE22

SE9

Blackfen

SE23

SE6

KENT

9

SE20

Beckenham

Chislehurst

25

Bromley

SE

Petts Wood

Addiscombe

Orpington

Keston

Chelsfield

New Addington

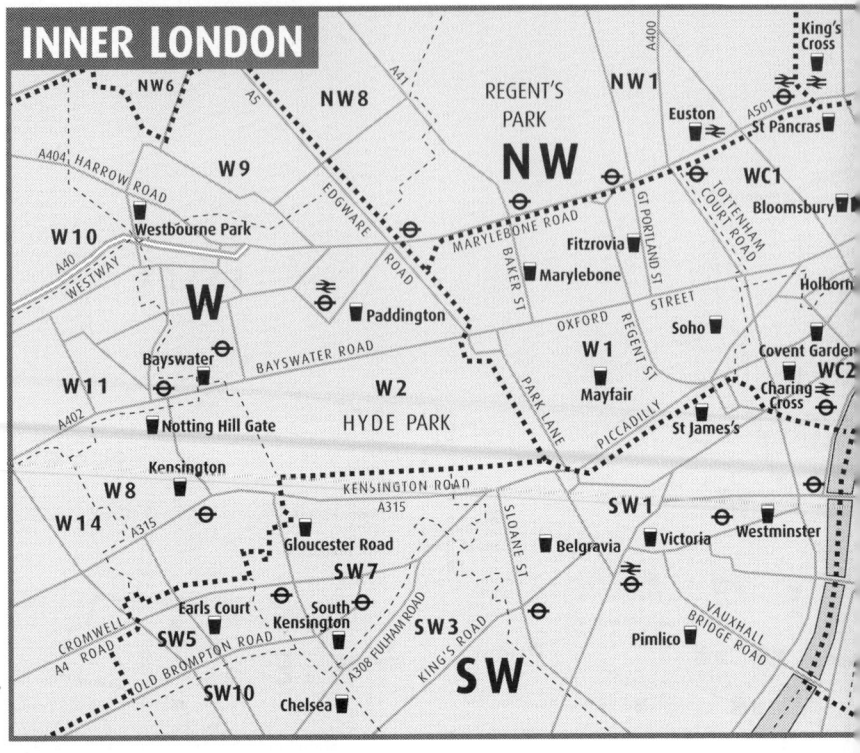

INNER LONDON

How to find London pubs

Greater London is divided into seven sectors: Central, East, North, North-West, South-East, South-West and West, reflecting postal boundaries. The Central sector includes the City (EC1 to EC4) and Holborn, Covent Garden and the Strand (WC1/2) plus W1, where pubs are listed in postal district order. In each of the other six sectors the pubs with London postcodes are listed first in postal district order (E1, E2 etc), followed by those in outer London districts, which are listed in alphabetical order (Barking, Chadwell Heath, etc) – see Greater London map. Postal district numbers can be found on every street name plate in the London postcode area.

CENTRAL LONDON
EC1: Angel
Brewhouse & Kitchen ✪
Torrens Street, EC1V 1NQ
🕐 11-11 (midnight Fri & Sat); 12-10 Sun ☎ (020) 7837 9421
8 changing beers (sourced locally) ⊞
Round the corner from Angel Station, off City Road, this brewpub-restaurant has eight handpumps, usually with seven beers brewed on the premises. Takeaway five-litre minicasks are available and also jars of mustard, chutney and marmalade. The fermenting tanks are open to view at the back, along with display cases of malts, barley and hops. There is also a display of three reasons to choose a glass. The friendly and knowledgeable staff will help you with your choice. ⏰◑♿♨♠➟✿🐶🛜

EC1: Farringdon
Jerusalem Tavern ✪
55 Britton Street, EC1M 5UQ
🕐 11-11; closed Sat & Sun ☎ (020) 7490 4281

St Peter's Best Bitter, Mild, Golden Ale, Organic Best, Organic Ale, Grapefruit Beer Ⓐ
There has been a Jerusalem Tavern in the area since 1692, but this one dates from 1996. The only St Peter's Brewery pub, it dispenses six beers by air pressure from the end of wooden casks on the back wall. The pub is a re-creation of an 18th-century tavern with its worn green-painted settles, dark oak floorboards, old tiles set in the walls and a collection of cartoons in the back room. Check the special seasonal beers. Q⏰◑➟♿♠♨🐶✿🛜

EC1: Old Street
Old Fountain Ⓛ
3 Baldwin Street, EC1V 9NU
🕐 11-11; 12-11 Sun ☎ (020) 7253 2970
Fuller's London Pride; 7 changing beers (sourced regionally) ⊞
A privately owned pub behind Moorfields Eye Hospital. The comfortably furnished interior features an aquarium. Eight handpumps serve a wide range of beers, usually including London microbrewery choices. An informative blackboard lists what is on. Many bottled beers are also

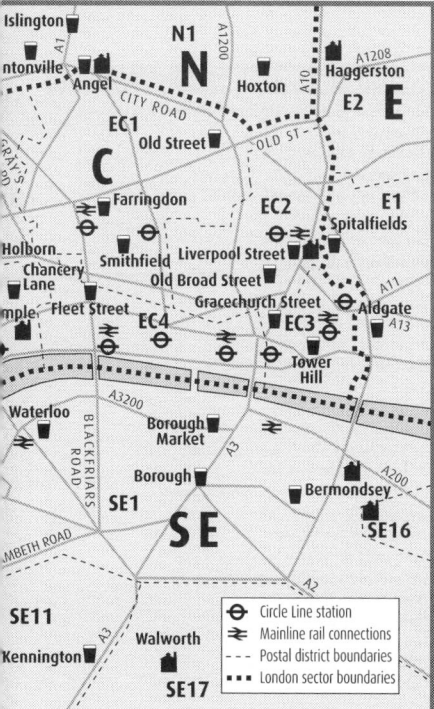

Circle Line station
Mainline rail connections
--- Postal district boundaries
■■■ London sector boundaries

handpumps, with repeated ales. Food is served daily until 10pm. Popular with commuters, the pub has a TV screen downstairs displaying the latest train times. Q⛄◑⟨⟩&⇌Θ●🚃🛜

EC2: Old Broad Street

Phoenix ✅

26 Throgmorton Street, EC2N 2AN
⚙ 11-11; closed Sat & Sun ☎ (020) 7588 7289
⊕ thephoenixec2.co.uk
Greene King IPA; 4 changing beers Ⓗ
A former bank premises, this is a Grade II-listed building. Now a large pub with one bar, it was converted into a Hogshead in 1999 and became the first no-smoking pub in the City in 2003. The following year it became part of Greene King's Metropolitan Pub Company. Four guest beers change weekly, including local brewery offerings. Food is served all day until 9pm. Old photos adorn the walls. ◑⟨⟩&⇌(Liverpool Street)Θ(Bank)🚃🛜

EC3: Gracechurch Street

Counting House ✅

50 Cornhill, EC3V 3PD
⚙ 11-11; closed Sat & Sun ☎ (020) 7283 7123
⊕ the-counting-house.com
Fuller's Oliver's Island, London Pride, ESB; Gale's Seafarers Ale; 1 changing beer (often Fuller's) Ⓗ
Originally built in 1893 as Prescott's Bank, this became part of National Westminster in 1970, this began its life as a pub in 1997. Sitting partly on a north sleeper wall of a 2000-year-old Roman basilica, it is a grand building with an ornate interior, a large dome in the ceiling and an oval central bar. Two upstairs floors and two function rooms at the rear are for hire. Traditional food is served all day, including home-made pies.
Q⛄◑⟨⟩&⇌(Cannon St)Θ(Bank)🚃🛜

Crosse Keys ✅

7-12 Gracechurch Street, EC3V 0DR
⚙ 8am-11 (midnight Fri); 9am-11 Sat; 9am-6.30 Sun
☎ (020) 7623 4824
Fuller's London Pride; Greene King IPA; Sharp's Doom Bar; changing beers Ⓗ
One of the biggest Wetherspoon pubs, this former bank has an oval bar with 24 handpumps dispensing a large choice of ales from national and regional brewers, including microbreweries. Large screens show major sports events. Often busy, it is popular with city office workers and tourists. A spiral staircase leads to downstairs toilets and function rooms are at the rear.
Q⛄◑⟨⟩&⇌(Cannon St)Θ(Bank/Monument)●🚃🛜

EC3: Tower Hill

Draft House Seething ✅

14-15 Seething Lane, EC3N 4AX
⚙ 12-11; closed Sun ☎ (020) 7626 3360
Sambrook's Wandle Ale; 5 changing beers Ⓗ
Featuring tanks of unpasteurised Czech Pilsner Urquell, this is a popular haunt for city workers. The food portions are generous. A wide range of cask and other draught beers is served by an enthusiastic staff who know their products thoroughly. The modern utilitarian layout offers views into the kitchen. A good place to refuel.
◑&⇌(Fenchurch St)Θ(Tower Gateway/Hill)🚃🛜

available. Background music is kept at a reasonable level and major sporting events are shown. Outdoor drinking is on a roof terrace. Food is served lunchtimes and evenings (all day Fri, 1-6pm Sun). 🌟◑⇌Θ♣🚃🐾🛜

EC1: Smithfield

Old Red Cow Ⓛ

71-72 Long Lane, EC1A 9EJ
⚙ 12-11 (midnight Fri & Sat; 10.30 Sun) ☎ (020) 7726 2595
⊕ theoldredcow.com
4 changing beers (often Magic Rock, Redemption) Ⓗ
Part of the local Beerhouse group, with a major interest in food. It is handy for St Bartholomew's, the Smithfield meat market and the Old Bailey. The ground floor has been specially designed for tall clients. The handpumps dispense a variety of changing beers, many of them from London breweries. Food ranges from Scotch eggs, pies and burgers to sharing platters.
◑⇌(Farringdon)Θ(Barbican)♣●🚃🐾🛜

EC2: Liverpool Street

Hamilton Hall ✅

Street-level Concourse, Unit 32, Liverpool Street Station, EC2M 7PY
⚙ 7am-11.30; 9am-11.30 Sun ☎ (020) 7247 3579
Greene King IPA, Abbot; Sharp's Doom Bar; 10 changing beers Ⓗ
An ornate Wetherspoon pub off Bishopsgate in what was once the ballroom of the Great Eastern Hotel, at the south-east corner of Liverpool Street Station, with an entrance outside the station itself. The downstairs bar has 10 handpumps dispensing ale and a cider. The upstairs bar has five

EC4: Fleet Street

Hoop & Grapes ⊘
80 Farringdon Street, EC4A 4BL
⊕ 12-11 ☎ (020) 7353 8088
Shepherd Neame Whitstable Bay, Spitfire Gold,
Spitfire; 1 changing beer (often Shepherd Neame) Ⓗ
Dating from 1721, this cosy, traditional City pub has
a fascinating history. Saved from demolition in the
1990s and now a Grade II-listed building, it has a
friendly, busy atmosphere. Along with the regular
Shepherd Neame choice, seasonal and guest beers
are often available. The heated patio and balcony
are popular throughout the year.
৬⊛❶➠(City Thameslink)⊖(Blackfriars)� ⊛ 🛜

WC1: Bloomsbury

Calthorpe Arms
252 Grays Inn Road, WC1X 8JR
⊕ 11-11.30; 12-10.30 Sun ☎ (020) 7278 4732
Young's Bitter, Special; 2 changing beers (sourced
nationally) Ⓗ
Unusual double doors lead into this single-bar
corner local. With no music and an unobtrusive
corner TV, it is easy either to strike up a
conversation at a bar stool or take one of the tables
along the sides for more privacy. The upstairs
dining room opens for lunch (12-2.30pm) but can
be booked at other times. Evening meals are
served 6-9.30pm. Young's bottle-conditioned beers
are stocked plus a Young's seasonal and a guest
beer. There is pavement seating outside.
⊛❶⊖(Russell Sq)➻🛒⊛

Lamb 🄻
94 Lambs Conduit Street, WC1N 3LZ
⊕ 12-11 (midnight Thu-Sat); 12-10.30 Sun
☎ (020) 7405 0713
Courage Directors; Young's Bitter, London Gold,
Special; 3 changing beers (sourced regionally) Ⓗ
Beautifully preserved, Grade II-listed, and with a
regionally important historic interior, the pub has a
small snug, green upholstery and etched-glass
snob screens above the bar. The Empire Bar and
restaurant are upstairs. The glorious Victorian
history of the pub and area is commemorated by a
working polyphon (predecessor to the
gramophone) and sepia prints of music hall
players. Nine handpumps dispense the beers, with
ciders served from bag-in-a-box. At the back is a
small walled beer garden.
Q⊛❶⊖(Russell Sq)➻🛒 🛜

Swan 🄻 ⊘
7 Cosmo Place, WC1N 3AP
⊕ 12-11 (11.30 Fri); 12-10.30 Sun ☎ (020) 7837 6223
Greene King Taylor Walker 1730, London Glory,
Abbot; 5 changing beers (sourced regionally) Ⓗ
Popular family-oriented pub, close to Great
Ormond Street Children's Hospital. There is a single
long room, and tables in front on a pedestrian
passage. Eight handpumps serve three regular real
ales and five guests, mainly from London
breweries. Real cider is served during summer and
festivals. Pub grub and snacks are available until
10pm (9pm Sun). A large-screen TV shows live
sports events. Q৬⊛❶�& ⊖(Russell Sq)➻🛒⊛ 🛜

WC1: Holborn

Holborn Whippet
25-29 Sicilian Avenue, WC1A 2QH

REAL ALE BREWERIES

Alphabeta ≣ EC2M: Liverpool Street (NEW)
Anspach & Hobday SE1: Bermondsey
Barnet ≣ High Barnet
Beavertown N17: Tottenham Hale
Belleville SW12: Wandsworth Common
Bexley Erith
Big Smoke ≣ Surbiton
Bloomsbury ≣ WC1: Bloomsbury
Brew By Numbers SE16: Bermondsey
Brewhouse & Kitchen ≣ EC1: Angel
Brewhouse & Kitchen ≣ N5: Highbury
Brick SE15: Peckham
Brixton SW9: Brixton
Brockley SE4: Brockley
Brodie's ≣ E10: Leyton
Bullfinch SE24: Herne Hill
By the Horns SW17: Summerstown
Canopy SE24: Herne Hill
Clarkshaws SW9: Loughborough Junction
Crate E9: Hackney Wick
Cronx New Addington
Dragonfly ≣ W3: Acton
East London E10: Leyton
Essex Street ≣ WC2: Temple
Five Points E8: Hackney Downs
Fourpure SE16: Bermondsey
Fuller's W4: Chiswick
Gipsy Hill SE27: West Norwood
Hackney E2: Haggerston
Hammerton N7: Barnsbury
Hop Stuff SE18: Woolwich
Hops & Glory ≣ N1: Islington
Howling Hops ≣ E9: Hackney Wick
Husk E16: West Silvertown (NEW)
Kernel SE16: Bermondsey
Kew SW14: East Sheen
Laine ≣ E9: Victoria Park/SW11: Battersea/W3: Acton
Late Knights SE20: Penge
Left Bank E17: Walthamstow
London Beer Factory SE27: West Norwood
London Brewing ≣ N12: North Finchley
Long Arm ≣ W5: South Ealing (NEW)
Maregade ≣ E8: Hackney (NEW)
Meantime SE10: North Greenwich
Moncada W10: Kensal Town
Mondo SW8: South Lambeth
One Mile End E1: Whitechapel/N17: Tottenham
Orbit SE17: Walworth
Park Kingston
Partizan SE16: South Bermondsey
Portobello W10: North Kensington
Pressure Drop E8: Hackney
Redchurch E2: Bethnal Green
Redemption N17: Tottenham
Reunion Feltham (NEW)
Rocky Head SW18: Southfields
Sambrook's SW11: Battersea
Signature Brew E10: Leyton
Solvay Society Aldborough Hatch
Southwark SE1: Bermondsey
Tap East ≣ E20: Stratford Westfield
Three Sods E2: Bethnal Green
Truman's E3: Hackney Wick
Twickenham Twickenham
Volden Croydon
Weird Beard W7: Hanwell
Wild Card E17: Walthamstow
Wimbledon SW19: Colliers Wood
Zerodegrees ≣ SE3: Blackheath

✪ 12-11 (11.30 Thu-Sat); 12-10.30 Sun ☎ (020) 3137 9937
⊕ holbornwhippet.com
6 changing beers (sourced nationally) ⊞
This pub uses a flow-jet to pump the beer up to the taps, above which a blackboard shows what is on offer. Six guest real ales come from the likes of Adnams, Bristol Beer Factory, Dark Star, Mighty Oak, Oakham, Redemption and other London breweries; many other draught beers are available. It has a simple menu – pizza, bratwurst, burgers, all nicely done. The decor is basic, with bare wooden floors, brown tiles and cream-painted walls. There is outside seating on the attractive Sicilian Avenue.
✪⊄❶⊖⊟

Penderel's Oak ✪
286-288 High Holborn, WC1V 7HJ
✪ 8am-11.30 (midnight Thu; 1am Fri & Sat); 10-11.30 Sun
☎ (020) 7242 5669
Adnams Broadside; Fuller's London Pride; Greene King IPA, Abbot; Sharp's Doom Bar; 6 changing beers (sourced nationally) ⊞
Large, busy Wetherspoon pub offering up to six guest beers. Tables at the front lead to the bar and a raised seating area. There is also a back room, and various settees and high stools; low-key lighting adds to the atmosphere. A cellar bar, popular with younger visitors (with music on screens), opens later than the main bar and is available for hire. Food is served until 11pm; children are welcome until 7pm. Behind is a small walled garden.
Q⛲✪⊄❶⭑⊖(Chancery Lane/Holborn)⊟☎

WC1: St Pancras

Mabel's Tavern ✪
9 Mabledon Place, WC1H 9AZ
✪ 11-11 (midnight Thu-Sat) ☎ (020) 7387 7739
Shepherd Neame Master Brew, Whitstable Bay Pale Ale, Spitfire, Bishops Finger; 1 changing beer (often Shepherd Neame) ⊞
Originally owned by Whitbread and called the Kentish Arms (note the figure high on the outside wall), the pub was renamed for landlady Mabel Macinelly, who is said to haunt these cosy premises. Up to the left of the bar is a snug, and a raised area at the back has a nice fireplace plus a large TV screen. Various prints and old photos adorn the walls. Food is served until 9.30pm. Handy for the British Library.
✪⊄❶⇋⊖(King's Cross/St Pancras)⊟✿☎

Queen's Head 🄻
66 Acton Street, WC1X 9NB
✪ 12-midnight (11 Mon); 12-11 Sun ☎ (020) 7713 5772
⊕ queensheadlondon.com
Redemption Trinity; 3 changing beers (sourced regionally) ⊞
Narrow, late-Georgian premises off the Gray's Inn Road, with a single bar, a smoking patio at the rear and benches in front. The piano is used for jazz and blues on Thursdays. Guest beers from microbreweries usually include a dark one. One handpump serves cider, with three more real ciders and a range of other draught and bottled beers. Sharing platters of snacks are available at this comfortable locals' pub (with occasional tourists), now home to a microbrewery.
✪⊄❶⇋⊖(King's Cross/St Pancras)◐⊟☎

WC2: Chancery Lane

Seven Stars
53-54 Carey Street, WC2A 2JB
✪ 11-11; 12-10.30 Sun ☎ (020) 7242 8521
⊕ thesevenstars1602.co.uk
Adnams Southwold Bitter; 4 changing beers (sourced nationally) ⊞
Dating from 1602 and formerly the League of Seven Stars, this pub has a regionally important historic interior. With its decorative Victorian bar-back, the bar occupies the narrow space between two distinctive drinking areas, one named the Wig Box (the Royal Courts of Justice are nearby). The landlady favours Adnams beers and serves good food. The pub is also home to Ray Brown, the resident cat. Q⊄❶⊖⊟☎

WC2: Charing Cross

Harp 🍷 🄻 ✪
47 Chandos Place, WC2N 4HS
✪ 10-11.30 (midnight Fri & Sat); 12-10.30 Sun
☎ (020) 7836 0291 ⊕ harpcoventgarden.com
Dark Star Hophead, American Pale Ale; Fuller's London Pride; Sambrook's Wandle Ale; 6 changing beers ⊞
Small, friendly Fuller's pub that became a haven for beer choice when it was a free house under the management of the legendary Binnie Walsh. A fine range of real ales and ciders is offered. The narrow bar is adorned with mirrors and portraits. There is no intrusive music or TV, and a cosy upstairs room provides a refuge from the busy throng. Numerous awards include the ultimate accolade, CAMRA National Pub of the Year, in 2010. Q⊄⇋⊖◐⊟☎

Lemon Tree ✪
4 Bedfordbury, WC2N 4BP
✪ 12-11 (10.30 Sun) ☎ (020) 7831 1391
⊕ lemontreecoventgarden.com
Harveys Sussex Best Bitter; Sharp's Doom Bar; 3 changing beers (sourced nationally; often Portobello, Sambrook's, Timothy Taylor) ⊞
A welcome return to the Guide after 16 years, this one-bar pub next to the stage door of the Coliseum is a favourite among locals, musicians and theatregoers. The upstairs Thai restaurant doubles as a function room. The pub's entrance is slightly set back and it could be missed, but it is well worth seeking out. Although guest beers are sourced nationally, there is an emphasis on London brews by popular demand. ⊄❶⇋⊖⊟

WC2: Covent Garden

Coach & Horses
42 Wellington Street, WC2E 7BD
✪ 11-11; 12-10.30 Sun ☎ (020) 7240 0553
Courage Best Bitter; St Austell Tribute ⊞
A small and traditional independent pub with a lot of Irish influence, used very much by locals but also by some tourists; it has a fantastic collection of about 70 Irish whiskeys and Scotch whiskies. Lunchtime food is served Monday to Saturday and may also be available on Sunday. There are photos of Gaelic football teams, and the sport of hurling also features, plus theatre posters. Note the beautiful front windows. Q⊄⭑⇋⊖⊟

Cross Keys 🄻
31 Endell Street, WC2H 9BA
✪ 11-11 ☎ (020) 7836 5185 ⊕ crosskeyscoventgarden.com

Brodie's Bethnal Green Bitter; house beer (by Brodie's); 2 changing beers (often Brodie's) Ⓗ
Built in the mid-1840s when Endell (formerly Belton) Street was widened as part of clearing the St Giles's Rookery, an ornate façade reveals a long, welcoming bar, subdued lighting, comfortable banquette seating and tables and chairs. Copper kettles, pans, street signs, stuffed fish, framed pictures and photos, Beatles memorabilia and a fine Truman, Hanbury, Buxton & Co mirror cover the walls. Families are welcome (over 12s only) until 7pm, unless it is busy, but no dogs. ⬥◗⊖🚲

White Swan ⚫

14 New Row, WC2N 4LF
✪ 10-11 (11.30 Sat); 12-10.30 Sun ☎ (020) 3077 1129
St Austell Nicholson's Pale Ale; Sharp's Doom Bar; Truman's Runner; 4 changing beers Ⓗ
Grade II-listed, once owned by the London banking firm Hoare & Co and formerly an O'Neills, this M&B Nicholson's pub just a stone's throw from Covent Garden is popular with tourists. It has been tastefully refurbished and has a small bar, limited seating in the bar area and more room past a partition. The first-floor dining room can be booked for functions. Breakfast is served until midday (except Sun).
⬥◗⇌(Charing Cross)⊖(Leicester Sq)🚲

WC2: Holborn

Shakespeare's Head ⚫

Africa House, 64-68 Kingsway, WC2B 6BG
✪ 7am-midnight (1am Fri); 8am-1am Sat; 8am-midnight Sun
☎ (020) 7404 8846
Fuller's London Pride; Greene King IPA, Abbot; 6 changing beers Ⓗ
Large Wetherspoon bank conversion from 1998, named after a famous pub located nearby until that entire street (Wych Street) was demolished over 100 years ago. It is nearly always busy with shoppers, tourists, local office workers and students from the nearby London School of Economics during term time. A convenient place for a couple of pints after your cultural sojourn at the British Museum, with up to nine real ales.
⬥◗⊖♣🚲📶

W1: Fitzrovia

Stag's Head

102 New Cavendish Street, W1W 6XW
✪ 11-11; 12-11 Sat; 12-8 Sun ☎ (020) 7580 8313
Fuller's London Pride; Tring Side Pocket for a Toad; 1 changing beer (sourced regionally; often Tring) Ⓗ
A smart, oak-panelled pub, offering a friendly welcome to regulars and visitors alike. Rebuilt in the late 1930s by the brewers William Younger, it has a marvellous Art Deco exterior, sporting a curved corner profile, and a regionally important historic interior in its standard Tudorbethan style. Vertical drinking is assisted by unusual peninsular shelf projections to the bar and elsewhere. Sun-lovers and smokers are catered for by shaded benches outside. Traditional pub food is available lunchtimes only. ⬥❀◗⊖(Gt Portland St)🚲

W1: Marylebone

Carpenters Arms

12 Seymour Place, W1H 7NE
✪ 11-11; 12-10.30 Sun ☎ (020) 7723 1050

Harveys Sussex Best Bitter; 5 changing beers (sourced nationally; often Adnams, Marston's, Portobello) Ⓗ
Sister pub to Southwark's Market Porter, but with a smaller range of beers, this establishment is a welcoming haven for escapees from the bustle of Oxford Street, while the TV sport and dartboard add to the appeal for the regulars. It has benefited from a sensitive refurbishment that preserved the wall tiling and floor mosaics at the main entrance. Elsewhere can be seen a display of woodworking tools. The menu comprises simply pasties, pork pies and Scotch eggs.
❀◗⊖(Marble Arch)♣🚲🐾📶

Golden Eagle

59 Marylebone Lane, W1U 2NY
✪ 12-11 (midnight Fri & Sat); closed Sun ☎ (020) 7935 3228
Fuller's London Pride; St Austell Tribute; 2 changing beers Ⓗ
Take a step back in time. First licensed in 1842 and rebuilt in 1890, this single-bar Victorian pub is traditional in every way, complemented with smart decor. There is a fine etched back-bar mirror, and proper leaded windows. Piano singalongs on Tuesday, Thursday and Friday evenings maintain the timeless atmosphere. Real ales here are quality, not quantity. Q⬥⊖(Bond St)🚲

Gunmakers Ⓛ ⚫

33 Aybrook Street, W1U 4AP
✪ 10-11; 12-10 Sun ☎ (020) 7487 4937
⊕ thegunmakersmarylebone.co.uk
St Austell Tribute; 3 changing beers (sourced locally; often Hackney, London Fields, Sambrook's) Ⓗ
Originally licensed in 1791 and rebuilt some 90 years later, this pub consists of a large, attractively panelled high-ceilinged room with some tables, but also the standing space that its popularity demands. On offer is a wide range of live sport on TV, a pub grub menu, an upstairs function room and a quiz at 8pm each Monday. The resident cat is frequently to be seen in the bar and, like the staff, is friendly. ⬥❀◗⊖(Baker St)🚲🐾📶

Thornbury Castle Ⓛ

29A Enford Street, W1H 1DN
✪ 12-11; closed Sat & Sun ☎ (020) 7402 2189
⊕ thornburycastle.uk.com
6 changing beers (sourced regionally) Ⓗ
Featured in the Guide for the first time is this small, side-street, family-run pub near Marylebone Station, with wood panelling throughout and a raised seating area at the back. There is a strong Rugby Union connection (Wasps) and the pub may open at weekends for big games on TV – check the website. Discerning drinkers will find here a worthwhile alternative to the more mainstream pubs in the area. Q◗⇌⊖♣🚲🐾📶

W1: Mayfair

Clarence ⚫

4 Dover Street, W1S 4LB
✪ 10-11.30 (midnight Fri & Sat); 10-11 Sun
☎ (020) 7491 3607
Fuller's London Pride; St Austell Nicholson's Pale Ale; Sharp's Doom Bar; Windsor & Eton Knight of the Garter; 4 changing beers Ⓗ
Licensed in 1724 as the Coach & Horses, this hostelry was rebuilt in 1892 and 1953. The Duke of Clarence is the person who became King William IV in 1830. A smallish frontage belies a much larger area extending back. It has a convivial atmosphere,

especially since its refurbishment by M&B Nicholson in 2012, with a pleasant, quieter upstairs bar. The pub is located close to the famous Ritz Hotel in Piccadilly. ⬤⬤⬤(Green Park)🚊

Coach & Horses ✪
5 Bruton Street, W1J 6PT
✪ 11.30-11; 12-11 Sat; 12-6 Sun ☎ (020) 7629 4123
Greene King IPA, London Glory, Abbot; 1 changing beer Ⓗ
An excellent refuge from the nearby Bond Street shopping area. First licensed in 1738, it was rebuilt in 1933 and has an imposing mock-Tudor exterior. Inside, the atmosphere is traditional, with wooden beams and panelling. Pictures on the walls feature caricatures of 19th-century politicians and clerics. One of the three handpumps serves a guest ale, albeit often from Greene King. The small dining room with bar upstairs is available for private functions. Q⬤⬤&⬤(Green Park)🚊

Windmill
6-8 Mill Street, W1S 2AZ
✪ 11.45-11; 12-5.30 Sat; closed Sun ☎ (020) 7491 8050
⊕ windmillmayfair.co.uk
Wells Bombardier; Young's Bitter, London Gold, Special; 3 changing beers Ⓗ
In adjoining buildings previously housing a nightclub and an escort agency, this pub has a well-furnished lounge, split into two sections, with wood panelling, decorative ceilings and a frieze. There is a restaurant on the first floor. Pies are a speciality; the Pie Club claims 6,000 members, who enjoy changing monthly specials such as beef and Stilton. A roof terrace is also available.
Q⬤⬤⬤(Oxford Circus)🚊🛜

W1: Soho

Argyll Arms ★ ✪
18 Argyll Street, W1F 7TP
✪ 8am-11.30 (midnight Fri & Sat); 12-10.30 Sun
☎ (020) 7734 6117
Fuller's London Pride; St Austell Nicholson's Pale Ale; Sharp's Doom Bar; 5 changing beers (sourced nationally; often Adnams, Harviestoun, Thwaites) Ⓗ
Victorian Grade II*-listed M&B Nicholson's house with a nationally important historic pub interior. Three snugs are separated by etched glass partitions; note the remarkable Bass mirror. The bar-back is impressive and adjacent is a rare survivor, a manager's office with etched glazing. The magnificent saloon is decorated with ornate mirrors. With eight of the 16 handpumps in regular use, enjoy the range of reliable regular and guest ales. ⬤&⬤(Oxford Circus)🚊🛜

Dog & Duck ★ ✪
18 Bateman Street, W1D 3AJ
✪ 10-11 ☎ (020) 7494 0697
Fuller's London Pride; St Austell Nicholson's Pale Ale; 4 changing beers Ⓗ
In the heart of Soho, this Grade II-listed Nicholson's outlet, built in 1897, has another nationally important historic pub interior. An elaborate mosaic depicts dogs and ducks, and wonderful advertising mirrors adorn the walls. Changing guest beers may include, for example, Sambrook's Wandle and Orkney Dark Island. The upstairs Orwell Bar can be hired for functions. The pub is small and so popular, especially with media people, that it is not just smokers who have to drink outside. ⬤⬤(Tottenham Court Rd)🚊🛜

Lyric Ⓛ
37 Great Windmill Street, W1D 7LU
✪ 11-11.30 (midnight Fri & Sat); 12-10.30 Sun
☎ (020) 7434 0604 ⊕ lyricsoho.co.uk
8 changing beers Ⓗ
A small, independently owned bar just off Shaftesbury Avenue, bay-fronted with a tiled panelled interior, popular with local trade. Originally there were two adjacent taverns, the Windmill and the Ham; these merged in the mid-18th century to form the Windmill & Ham, renamed in 1890 and rebuilt 16 years later. As well as other draught beers including London specialities, cask ales may include Big Smoke, Brodie's, Dark Star, Magic Rock, Marble, RedWillow, Redemption, Tiny Rebel or Thornbridge brews. ⬤⬤(Piccadilly Circus)🚊🛜

Old Coffee House Ⓛ
49 Beak Street, W1F 9SF
✪ 11-11; 12-11 Sun ☎ (020) 7437 2197
Brodie's Bethnal Green Bitter, London Fields Pale, Old Street Pale Ale; 3 changing beers (sourced locally) Ⓗ
A large but cosy pub, close to the buzz of Carnaby Street, with six handpumps offering a range of ales from Brodie's. First licensed as the Silver Street Coffee House, it was rebuilt in 1894 and is now Grade II-listed. The long bar and dark panelling are adorned with Watneys Red Barrel signage, brewery mirrors and an eclectic assortment of prints, posters, pictures and brassware. At lunchtimes you will find good-sized portions of pub grub at reasonable prices. ⬤🐾⬤⬤(Piccadilly Circus)🚊🐾

Queen's Head Ⓛ ✪
15 Denman Street, W1D 7HN
✪ 11-11.30 (midnight Fri & Sat); 12-10.30 Sun
☎ (020) 7437 1540 ⊕ queensheadpiccadilly.com
Fuller's London Pride; Robinsons Trooper; Sambrook's Wandle Ale; 2 changing beers Ⓗ
Dating from 1738, this free house takes its name from its location on what used to be known as Queen's Street, renamed Denman Street in 1862 in honour of a Lord Chief Justice born there. In the 1840s it was known as the Courier's Club, trading in wine, brandy and coal. Later, reduced in size, it became part of the Piccadilly Theatre site. With the main bar on the ground floor and more accommodation upstairs, it is a convenient rendezvous for pre-theatre dining and drinks. ⬤⬤(Piccadilly Circus)🚊🐾

Star & Garter
62 Poland Street, W1F 7NX
✪ 11-11; 12-11 Sat; closed Sun ☎ (020) 7437 9278
Fuller's London Pride; Greene King IPA; Shepherd Neame Spitfire Ⓗ
A pub on one of the earliest sites to be developed in Poland Street; its name appears in 1825 in the Westminster victuallers' records. Formerly a Courage house, it had previously belonged to Style & Winch of Maidstone and the windows advertised Maidstone Ales. It has a small, cosy, wood-panelled bar with matchwood ceiling. There is also an upstairs bar, which is usually open Thursday and Friday nights to cope with the throng. Q&⬤(Oxford Circus)🚊

EAST LONDON
E1: Aldgate

Dispensary

19A Leman Street, E1 8EN

🟢 11-11; closed Sat & Sun ☎ (020) 7977 0486

🌐 thedispensarylondon.co.uk

5 changing beers (sourced regionally) Ⓗ

Built in 1859 as a hospital, this Grade II*-listed building on the edge of the city has been a pub for 15 years. It has one bar with a gallery above it and a room for functions. A genuine free house, three or four changing ales are normally available, including Dark Star and Harveys beers, as well as good food, and it attracts a wide clientele. Local CAMRA Pub of the Year 2014.

Q✿🚲🕼≷(Fenchurch St)⊖(Aldgate/Aldgate East)🚻🐾🛜

E1: Spitalfields

Crown & Shuttle

226 Shoreditch High Street, E1 6PJ

🟢 11-11 (1am Thu-Sat); 11-10.30 Sun ☎ (020) 7375 2905

🌐 crownandshuttle.co.uk

6 changing beers (sourced regionally; often Redemption, Sharp's, Truman's) Ⓗ

Former Truman's pub with bare floorboards which has recently been refurbished. Brick walls are decorated with reclaimed windows and shutters. Six handpumps are spread out on both ends of the bars; check the blackboard for the day's selections. There is a large covered garden with plenty of tables and chairs for eating and drinking. Food is available from a street-food truck.

✿🕼≷(Liverpool St)⊖(Shoreditch High St)🚻🛜

King's Stores ⊘

14 Widegate Street, E1 7HP

🟢 12-11 (midnight Thu-Sat); 12-10 Sun ☎ (020) 7247 4089

🌐 kingsstores.co.uk

Greene King IPA; 4 changing beers (often Hop Stuff, London Beer Factory, Sharp's) Ⓗ

A Greene King Metropolitan pub that gets its name from a previous use of the place; it was a munitions storage site for the English army. Situated on a quiet side street, two minutes' walk from Liverpool Street Station, it has a modern feel. The main bar serves five real ales. There is extra seating space upstairs, along with separate function rooms. Food is available until 10pm (9pm Sun). Large TV screens show sport.

🐕🕼&≷(Liverpool St)⊖(Liverpool St)♣🚻🐾🛜

Pride of Spitalfields

3 Heneage Street, E1 5LJ

🟢 10-1am (2am Fri & Sat); 10-midnight Sun

☎ (020) 7247 8933

Crouch Vale Brewers Gold; Fuller's London Pride, ESB; Sharp's Doom Bar; 1 changing beer (sourced locally; often Truman's) Ⓗ

Small, two-roomed pub just off Brick Lane, famed for numerous curry houses. Comfortably furnished, its walls are adorned with interesting pictures, including some of the original Truman brewery that was nearby and now houses small businesses and exhibitions. At busy times, drinkers spill out onto the pavement. Sport is sometimes shown and background music is usually just that. Monday is vinyl night. Food is served lunchtimes.

🐕🕼≷(Liverpool St)⊖(Aldgate East/Shoreditch High St)🚻🐾

Williams Ale & Cider House Ⓛ ⊘

22-24 Artillery Lane, E1 7LS

🟢 11-11 (midnight Thu-Sat); closed Sun ☎ (020) 7247 5163

🌐 williamsspitalfields.com

House beer (by Greene King); 5 changing beers (sourced locally; often Crouch Vale, Hackney, Truman's) Ⓗ

Tucked away on a narrow street twixt Liverpool Street station and Spitalfields market, this large Greene King Metropolitan pub is divided into two areas, with bare floorboards and brick walls adorned with brewery-related pictures. Thirteen handpumps dispense up to seven beers and six ciders. The beers usually include several from London microbreweries. Food is served all day. Background music is not too loud and major sporting events are shown. Occasionally there is live music. 🐕🕼≷⊖(Liverpool St)♣🚻🐾🛜

E1: Wapping

Town of Ramsgate ⊘

62 Wapping High Street, E1W 2PN

🟢 12-midnight; 12-11 Sun ☎ (020) 7481 8000

🌐 townoframsgate.co.uk

Fuller's London Pride; Sharp's Doom Bar; Young's Bitter; 1 changing beer Ⓗ

Built in 1758 and given its current name in 1811, this originated because Ramsgate fishermen landed their catches to avoid taxes higher up the river. Now that the Thames is devoid of merchant shipping there are many offices and posh flats nearby. The guest beers come from the Enterprise list. The garden, where the Sunday carvery is served, gives a good view of the river.

🐕✿🕼⊖🚌(100,D3)🐾🛜

Turner's Old Star ⊘

14 Watts Street, E1W 2QG

🟢 12-11 (1.30am Thu-Sat) ☎ (020) 7702 9199

🌐 turnersoldstar.co.uk

Fuller's London Pride; Sharp's Doom Bar; 1 changing beer Ⓗ

Bought by JMW Turner (of Fighting Temeraire fame) for his final mistress, hence the name. It was two cottages knocked into a pub, and many original features still survive. The present landlady runs it as a community pub and it has gained Asset of Community Value status. A beer festival is held in June to coincide with the Wapping Shindig on the green outside. 🐕✿🕼♣🚌(100,D3)🐾🛜

E1: Whitechapel

White Hart Ⓛ

1-3 Mile End Road, E1 4TP

🟢 10.30-midnight ☎ (020) 7790 2894

🌐 the-white-hart.co.uk

7 changing beers (sourced locally; often One Mile End) Ⓗ

A large Victorian pub with a modernised interior, bare floorboards and wooden furniture. One Mile End Brewery started in the cellar downstairs before moving to North London, but a small brewery will remain here for experimental and one-off brews. The beer range is eclectic. An upstairs bar is available for hire but has no real ale. Music is played and sport is shown, silent downstairs and with sound upstairs. Food is served afternoons and evenings.

🐕✿🕼&⊖(Bethnal Green/Whitechapel)🚌🚻🐾🛜

E2: Bethnal Green

Camel
277 Globe Road, E2 0JD
🌐 12-11; 12-10.30 Sun ☎ 07535 779229
🌐 thecamelpublichouse.london
Adnams Broadside; Sambrook's Wandle Ale; 2 changing beers Ⓗ
Tucked away behind the Victoria & Albert Museum of Childhood, this small one-bar pub is worth seeking out. There is food until 10pm, with a range of some 10 pies and traditional puddings. It has about 35 seats around the windows and at high and low tables, and it can get crowded. Games are available. The pub has been in the same ownership for many years and has recently returned to direct management. Q🌚🌗⊖🚬😺

Carpenters Arms
73 Cheshire Street, E2 6EG
🌐 4 (12 Thu)-11.30; 12-12.30am Fri & Sat; 12-11.30 Sun
☎ (020) 7739 6342 🌐 carpentersarmsfreehouse.com
Timothy Taylor Landlord; 2 changing beers Ⓗ
Once notoriously associated with the Kray family, this now friendly and inviting East End pub serves a good, mixed clientele, providing a welcome retreat from the hubbub of the nearby Brick Lane and Bethnal Green area. As well as three well-chosen ales on handpumps on the single bar, a good selection of bottled beers is available. The food is recommended, especially the Sunday roasts. A cosy, vibrant atmosphere will ensure your return visits.
🌚🌗⊖(Bethnal Green/Shoreditch High St)
🚬(8,388,D3)

King's Arms
11A Buckfast Street, E2 6EY
🌐 12-11.30 (midnight Fri & Sat) ☎ (020) 7729 2627
🌐 thekingsarmspub.com
6 changing beers (often Buxton, Redemption, Siren) Ⓗ
A back-street corner pub that has a square central bar, with tables and seating around the perimeter as well as at the bar. To the left are six handpumps and at the front are 14 more taps. An unusual feature is the absence of pumpclips; on the wall to the right is a large board listing the beers and cider available, and there are printed lists on the bar to assist your choice. Cheese or charcuterie boards and Scotch eggs are sold.
Q🌚🌗⊖(Bethnal Green/Shoreditch High St)
🚬(8,388)😺

E3: Bow

Eleanor Arms
460 Old Ford Road, E3 5JP
🌐 4-11; 12-11 Fri-Sun ☎ (020) 8980 6992
🌐 eleanorarms.co.uk
Shepherd Neame Whitstable Bay, Kent's Best, Spitfire; 2 changing beers Ⓗ
Built in 1879 and a Shepherd Neame tenancy since 1985, this friendly community pub has become a Guide regular. A popular one-bar back-street local with traditional decor and up to six ales available, its customers come from all over East London. On Friday and Saturday evenings the landlord plays music from his extensive CD collection. Quiz night is the first Thursday of the month, jazz nights are every Sunday evening. When visiting check out the modern and classic pictures on the walls.
🌚🌗⊖(Bow Church/Bow Rd)🚬(8)😺

E4: Chingford

King's Ford Ⓛ ✅
250-252 Chingford Mount Road, E4 8JL
🌐 8am-midnight (1am Fri & Sat); 8am-11 Sun
☎ (020) 8523 9365
Adnams Broadside; Greene King Abbot; Ruddles Best Bitter; Sharp's Doom Bar; 6 changing beers Ⓗ
Located in the busy Chingford Mount shopping area, this large Wetherspoon pub, converted from a furniture store, is now long-established and always busy. It has a number of booths round the side as well as tables in the middle, together with a few tables on the pavement. There are up to 10 ales available, four regulars and up to six guests. Look out for special events and beer nights.
Q🌚🌚🌗👶🚬🔊

E5: Clapton

Anchor & Hope Ⓛ ✅
15 High Hill Ferry, E5 9HG (800yds N of Lea Bridge Rd, along river path)
🌐 1-11; 12-11 Sat; 12-10.30 Sun ☎ (020) 8806 1730
🌐 anchor-and-hope-clapton.co.uk
Fuller's London Pride, ESB; 2 changing beers (often Elgood's, Everards, Fuller's) Ⓗ
Now the only pub on the Clapton Riviera, as the pubs going north have been demolished and rebuilt as flats. It is popular with walkers and cyclists who drink on the River Lea footpath. The ESB is outstanding and the guest beers come from the Fuller's list; the pub was bought by Fuller's from Tolly Cobbold in the 1970s. As a single bar, its food menu consists of rolls. 🌚🌚🌗🚬(393)😺🔊

Clapton Hart Ⓛ ✅
231 Lower Clapton Road, E5 8EG
🌐 4-11 (midnight Thu; 1am Fri); 12-1am Sat; 12-11 Sun
☎ (020) 8985 8124 🌐 claptonhart.com
Volden Session Ale, Pale Ale, Porter; changing beers (often Hackney, Otley, Siren) Ⓗ
There has been a pub on this site since 1722. Now owned by the Antic collective, this welcoming multi-roomed establishment has shabby-chic decor, an extensive food menu and eight handpumps serving beers from Volden, Antic's own brewery in Croydon, and usually from other microbreweries. Quiz nights are on Tuesdays, and DJs play music on Fridays and Saturdays.
🌚🌗👶🚬😺🔊

Crooked Billet Ⓛ
84 Upper Clapton Road, E5 9JP
🌐 4-11; 12-midnight Fri & Sat; 12-11 Sun ☎ (020) 3058 1166
🌐 e5crookedbillet.co.uk
Changing beers (often Dark Star, East London Brewing, Sambrook's) Ⓗ
Reopened in 2013, this friendly pub offers a warm welcome and a good range of beers from five handpumps. Inside is a single U-shaped bar with much wood panelling. The former car park has been transformed into an artificially grassed area, plus booths and an outside bar. Just north of the Lea Bridge roundabout and near Clapton Station, it is popular with viewers of TV sport.
🌚🌚⊖🚬😺🔊

E8: Hackney

Cock Tavern Ⓛ
315 Mare Street, E8 1EJ

✪ 12-11; 12-10.30 Sun ☎ (020) 8533 6369
⊕ thecocktavern.co.uk
8 changing beers (often Howling Hops) Ⓗ
The Howling Hops Brewery has moved to a new site in Hackney Wick and in its place is now Maregade Brewery (gade is Danish for street). There are 16 handpumps dispensing eight real ales and eight real ciders. The ales are usually from Howling Hops and Maregade, with many other London brewers besides. Look out for special food pairing nights. Over the door the eagle sign is a reminder of the pub's Truman origins.
Q✿❀(Downs)⊖(Central/Downs)●🚆❀🛜

Pembury Tavern
90 Amhurst Road, E8 1JH
✪ 12-midnight (1am Fri & Sat); 12-11 Sun
☎ (020) 8986 8597
Milton Minotaur, Pegasus, Nero, Cyclops; changing beers Ⓗ
An open plan pub with bare floorboards and a bar billiards table. On the 16 handpumps you will usually see up to eight Milton beers, varying guest ales, and two ciders. Look out for the regular beer festivals, when they add an extra stillage. Quiz night is Monday night. The cuisine is eclectic during regular kitchen hours, with the addition of pizzas largely throughout opening hours.
Q🏃◑&❀(Downs)⊖(Central/Downs)
♣●🚆❀🛜

E8: Haggerston

Fox
372 Kingsland Road, E8 4DA
✪ 4-midnight; 12-midnight Sat & Sun ☎ (020) 7254 8462
7 changing beers (sourced nationally) Ⓗ
A large Victorian hostelry on the corner of Middleton Road and Kingsland Road, built in 1881. Taken over four years ago, it is now an open-plan pub with five handpumps offering a choice of many beers, mainly from new breweries; Magic Rock features regularly. Food is available in the evenings and Sunday roasts are popular.
🏃✿◑▲⊖♣●🚆❀🛜

E9: Homerton

Adam & Eve Ⓛ
155 Homerton High Street, E9 6AS
✪ 4-11 (midnight Thu); 12-1am Fri & Sat; 12-11 Sun
☎ (020) 8985 1494 ⊕ adamandevepub.com
5 changing beers (sourced locally) Ⓗ
Once a Teddy Boy shrine, this hostelry was sympathetically refurbished in 2014. Behind the attractive blue tiled façade it has a large and interesting interior which, among other eye-catching details, boasts an L-shaped pool table. Food and drinks have a Cornish theme, and there is now a shop selling home-brewing requisites. Several buses pass the door and the pub is a short walk from Homerton Station. 🏃✿◑●♣🚆❀🛜

Chesham Arms
15 Mehetabel Road, E9 6DU
✪ 4.30-11; 1-11 Fri & Sat; 1-10.30 Sun ☎ (020) 8986 6717
⊕ cheshamarms.com
4 changing beers (often Acorn, Dark Star, Salopian) Ⓗ
Built by the couple who owned nearby Sutton House in the late 1800s, this pub was bought by a developer and closed in 2012. Listed as an Asset of Community Value after several failed appeals for

usage change to flats, it was reopened in June 2015, with one bar split into two areas and a leafy beer garden down behind. You will find four beers and a real cider on handpump here, pub snacks and pie and mash. A great reward for successful campaigning. Q✿❀⊖(Hackney Central)●🚆❀🛜

E9: South Hackney

People's Park Tavern
360 Victoria Park Road, E9 7BT
✪ 12-11 (1am Fri; 2am Sat); 11-11 Sun ☎ (020) 8533 0040
⊕ peoplesparktavern.pub
7 changing beers (often Laine) Ⓗ
A large pub with its own brewery, one of three operated in London by Laine brewing company. All the cask ales are brewed on-site. It has a large beer garden overlooking Victoria Park. Upstairs is a bottle shop with over 50 beers from around the world. Traditional pub food is served daily. Comedy, quiz and DJ nights are all part of the entertainment on offer.
🏃✿◑&⊖(Homerton)🚆(388)❀🛜

E10: Leyton

King William IV Ⓛ
816 High Road, E10 6AE
✪ 11-midnight (1am Fri & Sat); 12-midnight Sun
☎ (020) 8556 2460
Changing beers (often Brodie's) Ⓗ
An impressive Victorian edifice and home to Brodie's Brewery, which is housed in the old stables building at the rear. Generally there are up to nine Brodie's and guest beers available. Many more handpumps come into use for the annual Easter Bunny Basher beer festival. Large screens and TVs in both bar areas show major sporting events. 🏃✿🚆◑&⊖(Midland Rd)♣🚆🛜

Leyton Orient Supporters Club Ⓛ
Matchroom Stadium, Oliver Road, E10 5NF
✪ match days from 5.30; 12.30-6 Sat; closed Sun
☎ (020) 8988 8288 ⊕ orientsupporters.org
Mighty Oak Oscar Wilde; 8 changing beers Ⓗ
Winner of many awards, this bar is run by volunteers and a friendly atmosphere prevails. A variety of different styles of ale and four ciders complement the Oscar Wilde mild. The bar is open before and after, but not during, home games. Check the website for details of brewery-themed special evenings. Admission is by club/CAMRA membership card or with a copy of this Guide. &⊖●🚆

Leyton Technical ✅
265B High Road, E10 5QN
✪ 4-11; 12-1am Sat; 12-11 Sun ☎ (020) 8558 4759
⊕ leytontechnical.com
Volden Session Ale; 6 changing beers Ⓗ
Antic conversion of part of the former Leyton Hall that became a technical college. Two main and three smaller rooms feature marble-tiled flooring and chandeliers, with mismatched furniture. Eight handpumps dispense up to seven beers, often from London microbreweries, and one cider, usually Westons. Quiz night is on Wednesday, DJs play on Friday and Saturday nights, and varying live music is performed Sunday afternoons. Comedy nights are staged monthly. Handy for Leyton Orient FC; away supporters are welcome. 🏃◑&⊖●🚆❀🛜

ENGLAND

E11: Leytonstone

North Star
24 Browning Road, E11 3AR
✪ 4-11; 12-10.30 Sun ☎ (020) 8530 3197
Castle Rock Harvest Pale; East London Brewing
Foundation Bitter; 2 changing beers (often Harveys,
Timothy Taylor) ⊞
Set in upper Leytonstone Village, this Victorian pub
welcomes all. Six handpumps on the long bar in
the saloon offer a diverse choice of local and
national brews. A twin hatch servery sustains the
public bar, the separate entrance to which is
sometimes locked. Thai meals and wood-fired
oven pizzas (Thu-Sun) are served. A free quiz is
hosted on Sunday night. ⮕🏮🌑◗🕒♣🚆🐾🎵🛜

Red Lion ⏚ ✅
640 High Road, E11 3AA
✪ 12-11 (midnight Thu; 2am Fri & Sat) ☎ (020) 8988 2929
⊕ theredlionleytonstone.com
Sharp's Atlantic; Volden Session Ale, Pale Ale; 7
changing beers ⊞
Grand Victorian glass-fronted street-corner Antic
pub. A long single bar dispenses ales from 10
handpumps and sells a wide range of other
draught and bottled beers. Live bands and eclectic
DJs entertain (Thu-Sat). A garden at the rear
includes a covered area and screens films one
night a week during the summer. A wide selection
of hot meals and snacks is prepared in the kitchen
behind the bar, which is visible from the entrance.
The Monday night quiz is popular.
⮕🏮🌑◗♿🕒♣🐶🚆🐾🛜

E11: Wanstead

George ⏚ ✅
155-159 High Street, E11 2RL
✪ 8am-midnight (12.30am Fri & Sat) ☎ (020) 8989 2921
Fuller's London Pride; Greene King Abbot; Ruddles
Best Bitter; Sharp's Doom Bar; 8 changing beers
(sourced regionally) ⊞
Large Victorian etched glass fronted pub. Three
doors from the street lead to the main seating
area; two smaller areas are on a raised floor. Extra
seating is available upstairs. The long, single bar is
to the rear. This Wetherspoon pub offers a better
than usual selection of guest beers from the 12
handpumps. Behind are a garden and a car park.
Q⮕🏮🌑◗♿🕒🐶🚆🛜

E13: Plaistow

Black Lion ✅
59-61 High Street, E13 0AD
✪ 11-11; 12-10.30 Sun ☎ (020) 8472 2351
⊕ blacklionplaistow.co.uk
Courage Best Bitter; Mighty Oak Captain Bob; Sharp's
Doom Bar; 3 changing beers ⊞
A pub has occupied this site for 600 years; the
present one dates from 1747. The current landlord
has been here for 30 years and is now the
freeholder, a rare feat in London today. Of seven
handpumps, three are always working; the rest are
used for guest beers and all are on when West Ham
United are at home. Guest beers are mainly from
Mighty Oak. Good home-cooked food is served
lunchtimes and evenings. ⮕🏮🌑◗🕒🚆🐾🛜

E17: Walthamstow

Bell ⏚ ✅
617 Forest Road, E17 4NE
✪ 12-midnight (1am Fri & Sat); 12-11 Sun & Mon
☎ (020) 8523 2277 ⊕ belle17.com
Sharp's Doom Bar; Timothy Taylor Landlord; 6
changing beers ⊞
Grand Victorian pub located at Bell Corner, with
comfortable seating on two levels. Eight
handpumps dispense a varied selection of local,
regional and national brews, with other interesting
draught and bottled beers available. A popular quiz
takes place on Tuesday night, Friday and Saturday
evening entertainment is provided by DJs, and live
jazz is on Sunday evenings. A wide choice of food is
served all day. Children are welcomed until 8pm. It
has an outside smoking area, no TV screens in the
main bar, and a function room at the rear.
⮕🏮🌑◗♿🕒(Central)♣🚆🐾🛜

Nag's Head ⏚
9 Orford Road, E17 9LP
✪ 4-11; 12-11 Sat; 12-10.30 Sun ☎ (020) 8520 9709
⊕ thenagsheade17.com
Mighty Oak Oscar Wilde; St Austell Tribute; Timothy
Taylor Landlord; 5 changing beers (sourced
regionally) ⊞
A 159-year-old former coaching inn, this is a
quirky, cat-loving pub serving the local community,
with up to eight beers, including local brews.
Originally three rooms, it now has one bar. An
annual event is held to celebrate its birthday. The
upstairs function room is named after the
landlady's dad's cat, while dogs are welcome in
the garden. Jazz or occasional blues features on
Sundays, and a quiz every Monday. Food is served
until 10pm. 🏮🌑◗🕒(Central)🚆(W12)🛜

Olde Rose & Crown ⏚ ✅
53-55 Hoe Street, E17 4SA
✪ 10-11 (midnight Fri & Sat); 12-11 Sun ☎ (020) 8509 3880
⊕ yeolderoseandcrowntheatrepub.co.uk
6 changing beers ⊞
A large welcoming community pub, serving
alcoholic drinks from noon. Handpumps supply a
variety of beers from SIBA and local brewers with,
usually, two ciders also available. Sunday
lunchtime roasts are served and Pepe's pizza stall
is to be found just outside most Wednesday, Friday
and Saturday evenings. Many events are held here,
with a theatre upstairs. A folk club and a comedy
club stage regular nights and live music is a
frequent feature in the main bar area.
⮕◗♿🕒(Central)🐶🚆🐾🛜

Wild Card Brewery Tap Bar
Unit 7, Ravenswood Industrial Estate, Shernhall
Street, E17 9HQ
✪ closed Mon-Thu; 5-midnight Fri; 10-midnight Sat; 11-11
Sun ☎ 07890 588991 ⊕ wildcardbrewery.co.uk
Wild Card Pale ⊞/Ⓖ, Jack of Clubs, King of Hearts, Ace
of Spades ⊞; 2 changing beers Ⓖ
Wild Card Brewery moved to these premises in
2014. The Brewery Tap serves four ales, including
occasional guests, and is in the same spacious unit
as the brewery. Wild Card runs three or four beer
festivals a year. Food is available at most opening
times. There is external seating and, when cold,
heating is provided via a woodburner. There is
access from Walthamstow Village via Summit
Road.
⮕🕒(Central/Wood St)🐶P🚆(W12,W16)🐾🛜

E20: Westfield Stratford City

Tap East 🗓️
7 International Square, Montfichet Road, E20 1EE
❂ 11-11; 12-10 Sun ☎ (020) 8555 4467 ⊕ tapeast.co.uk
Tap East Tonic Ale; house beer (by Tap East); 4 changing beers (sourced regionally; often Tap East) �
Is this perhaps the best thing about this Westfield centre for the shop-shy drinker? The on-site brewery helps by providing an exceptionally well-informed staff crew. The range of bottled beers is remarkably in excess of 150. It is an ideal place of welcome for international visitors detraining at the station. The changing range of beers means that there is always something new. Pork pies, pizzas and so forth are served until 9pm.
➳♿≠⊖(Stratford/Stratford Intl)●🖪🛜

Barking

Barking Dog ✅
61 Station Parade, IG11 8TU
❂ 8am-midnight ☎ (020) 8507 9109
Greene King Abbot; Ruddles Best Bitter; Sharp's Doom Bar; 6 changing beers �
Busy town-centre Wetherspoon pub, popular with locals and passing commuters alike. An impressive 12 handpumps serve up to six changing beers of varying types and strengths as well as the three or four regulars, and two or three real ciders including Westons Old Rosie and Gwynt y Ddraig Black Dragon, giving the best choice in the area. Food is available all day until 11pm, alcoholic drinks from 9am. Muted TV screens show rolling news and occasional sport. ➳⏣♿≠⊖●🖪🛜

Chadwell Heath

Eva Hart ✅
1128 High Road, RM6 4AH (on A118)
❂ 9am-midnight ☎ (020) 8597 1069
Adnams Broadside; Greene King Abbot; Morland Old Golden Hen; Ruddles Best Bitter; Sharp's Doom Bar; Wychwood Hobgoblin; 4 changing beers (sourced regionally) ⏱id
Large, comfortable Wetherspoon pub in a building that used to be the local police station. It is named after a local singer and music teacher who was one of the longest living survivors of the Titanic disaster; photographs and memorabilia are on display. A much-improved choice of real ales is now available on handpump. Good-value food is served 8am-10pm. Q➳🕮⏣♿⊖●🖪🛜

Collier Row

Colley Rowe Inn 🏆 ✅
54-56 Collier Row Road, RM5 3PA (on B174)
❂ 9am-midnight (1am Fri & Sat) ☎ (01708) 760633
Fuller's London Pride; Greene King Abbot; Ruddles Best Bitter; Sharp's Doom Bar; 3 changing beers ⏱id
Converted from two shops, this Wetherspoon pub is on three bus routes and near three others, giving easy access to and from Romford. Besides the ales it also serves two ciders on handpump (usually Westons Old Rosie and Gwynt y Ddraig Black Dragon). It is often lively around the bar, but there are quieter alcoves at the rear. Food is served all day, every day, and steak night is particularly popular. Local CAMRA Pub of the Year 2016. Q➳⏣♿●🖪🛜

Dagenham

Eastbrook ★
835 Dagenham Road, RM10 7UP (nr jct with A1112 Rainham Rd South)
❂ 11-11 (midnight Fri & Sat) ☎ (020) 8592 1873
2 changing beers ⏱id
A Grade II*-listed 1937 pub with a nationally important historic interior, this welcoming community local has two bars and a large function room/restaurant. The main bar, the Walnut Room, has extensive panelling; the Oak Room, used for functions, is in Brewers' Tudor and can be visited on request. Beers are from the Brakspear range and change monthly. It is the local for Dagenham & Redbridge football supporters, particularly when their team is at home. Football memorabilia adorn the pub. 🕮🏠⏣♿P🖪(103,174)🐾🛜

Gidea Park

Ship ✅
93 Main Road, RM2 5EL (on A118)
❂ 12-11 (midnight Thu-Sat) ☎ (01708) 741571
⊕ theshipgideapark.co.uk
Adnams Southwold Bitter, Broadside; Courage Best Bitter; Greene King IPA; Sharp's Doom Bar; Timothy Taylor Landlord; 1 changing beer ⏱id
More than 250 years old, this Grade II-listed, split-level pub has extensive dark wood panelling, timber beams and huge fireplaces. The establishment is largely unchanged and is low-ceilinged in places – so duck or grouse. It is a family-run business, with quiz nights held on Thursdays and live music on Saturdays.
Q➳🕮⏣⊖P🖪(174,498,347)🐾🛜

Hornchurch

JJ Moons ✅
48-52 High Street, RM12 4UN (on A124)
❂ 8am-11.30 (12.30am Fri & Sat) ☎ (01708) 478410
Greene King Abbot; Ruddles Best Bitter; Sharp's Doom Bar; 6 changing beers ⏱id
A busy Wetherspoon pub, opened in 1993. It is popular with all age groups, featuring a changing selection of ales with an emphasis on breweries from London and the South-east. Watercolour paintings of local scenes provide the main decoration, with local interest panels to the rear of the pub. Families are welcome until 6pm, and alcoholic drinks are sold from 9am.
Q➳⏣♿⊖(Emerson Park/Hornchurch)●🖪🛜

Rainham

Phoenix
Broadway, RM13 9YW (on B1335)
❂ 11-11; 12-3, 7-11 Sun ☎ (01708) 553700
⊕ the-phoenix-hotel.com
Courage Directors; Greene King Abbot; John Smith's Bitter; Wells Bombardier; 1 changing beer ⏱id
Busy, spacious town pub close to Rainham station and convenient for the RSPB Rainham Marshes nature reserve. It has two bars: a public bar with dartboard, and a saloon for dining. Poker is played on Wednesday, quizzes and live entertainment/ music alternate on Thursday, while entertainment also features on Saturday and Sunday. The large garden has three aviaries, animals and a barbecue area. Family fun days are held every bank holiday Monday. ➳🕮⏣⏱≠♣P🖪🛜

ENGLAND

Romford

Moon & Stars ✔

99-103 South Street, RM1 1NX

🕐 8am-11.30 (midnight Fri & Sat) ☎ (01708) 730117

Adnams Broadside; Greene King Abbot; Ruddles Best Bitter; 5 changing beers (sourced nationally) [H]

A Wetherspoon pub close to Romford station and buses. Children are allowed in the raised area at the back until 6pm Friday and Saturday, later on other days. Real ciders dispensed by gravity from cooled containers behind the bar are usually Old Rosie and Black Dragon. Displays of local history are on the walls and assorted books on the shelves. It can get busy on Thursday and Friday evenings. Food is served until 11pm. Toilets (except disabled) are upstairs. Q🐴◐♿⇌⊖🍎🚌📶

Upminster

Huntsman & Hounds ✔

2 Ockendon Road, Corbets Tey, RM14 2DN (on B1421)

🕐 10-11 (midnight Fri); 11-midnight Sat; 11-11 Sun

☎ (01708) 221672

Adnams Broadside; Brakspear Bitter; Greene King Abbot; 7 changing beers [H]

Newly refurbished and much-extended local with an increased range of real ales, including seasonal guest beer selections from microbreweries. There is a choice of meat, seafood and vegetarian food offerings through the day until 10pm. A set-price buffet is available, as are daily specials. Weekly quiz nights take place on Wednesdays. Outside is a south-facing beer garden and large car park. 🐴✿◐♿P🚌(370)🐾📶

Upminster TapRoom

1b Sunnyside Gardens, RM14 3DT (off B187, St Mary's Lane)

🕐 4-9 Tue & Wed; 4-11 Thu; 12-11 Fri & Sat; 12-9 Sun; closed Mon

Dark Star Hophead; 5 changing beers (sourced locally) [G]

Upminster and East London's first micropub, in a converted office, opened in November 2015 as a snack bar selling real ale, before being granted change of use. There are high tables and chairs, with garlands of hops adorning the walls. Real ales are served straight from the casks in the cool cellar, visible from the bar. Table service is optional. There is no parking available, so please use public transport. Set mobile phones to silent or pay a fee for charity. Q🐴♿⇌⊖🍎▯🚌(248,346,370)🐾

Woodford Green

Travellers Friend ✔

496-498 High Road, Woodford Wells, IG8 0PN (on slip road off A104)

🕐 12-midnight ☎ (020) 8504 2435

🌐 thetravellersfriendwoodford.co.uk

Fuller's London Pride; St Austell Tribute; Wells Bombardier; 3 changing beers [H]

Owned for three years now by two local families, this friendly, comfortable local has a regionally important historic interior, with original oak-panelled walls and rare snob screens. As far as is known, it has never sold keg bitter. Behind is a large heated patio with smoking area, and a small car park. There are picnic tables at the front and in the side beer garden. Perudo, a dice game, is played. Local CAMRA Pub of the Year 2015. Q✿♿♣🍎P🚌(20,179,W13)🐾📶

NORTH LONDON

N1: Canonbury

Hops & Glory [L]

382 Essex Road, N1 3PF

🕐 4-11 (midnight Thu; 2am Fri); 12-2am Sat; 12-10.30 Sun

☎ (020) 7226 2277 🌐 hopsandglory.co.uk

Redemption Big Chief; Weird Beard Mariana Trench; 3 changing beers (sourced regionally) [H]

Popular, privately owned free house offering a fine selection of draught beers, ciders and American bottles. It has an open-plan public area with a high ceiling and the usual Islington mix of unmatched tables, chairs and sofas. With a heated patio garden, it is family friendly and dogs and cyclists are welcome. Live piano music features on Thursdays. The in-house microbrewery produces an IPA and a pale keg beer. The beers listed are likely to change regularly.
🐴✿◐⇌(Essex Rd)⊖🍎P🚌🐾📶

N1: Hoxton

Howl at the Moon [L]

178 Hoxton Street, N1 5LH

🕐 12-11 (1am Fri & Sat) ☎ (020) 7339 9221

🌐 hoxtoncrafthouse.com

Hammerton N1; 2 changing beers (sourced nationally) [H]

Pleasant conversion of a disused pub in a once-run-down but now revived area. Three real ales are served from smaller breweries across the UK, with one real cider on tap plus a cider box behind the bar. A superb selection of music is played. Mixed seating comprises sofas and chairs around the bar, and numerous interesting items adorn the walls. Helpful staff offer tastings. Food, mainly burgers, is served at a reasonable price. Live blues features on Friday. ✿◐⊖♣🍎🚌🐾📶

Wenlock Arms [L]

26 Wenlock Road, N1 7TA

🕐 3-11 (midnight Thu); 12-1am Fri & Sat; 12-11 Sun

☎ (020) 7608 3406 🌐 wenlockarms.com

10 changing beers (sourced nationally) [H]

Saved from closure by a vigorous local campaign, this free house has 10 handpumps featuring beers from all across the UK, concentrating on small and medium-sized breweries, usually including a mild ale and subject to regular change. With up to seven ciders and perries and a small snacks menu of toasties, Scotch eggs, sausage rolls and pickled eggs, this is a truly welcoming street-corner local with an international reputation. Jazz is played in the bar on Thursday nights.
🐴◐♿⇌⊖(Old St)🍎🚌🐾📶

N1: Islington

Charles Lamb

16 Elia Street, N1 8DE

🕐 12 (4 Mon & Tue)-11; 11-11 Sat; 12-10.30 Sun

☎ (020) 7837 5040 🌐 thecharleslambpub.com

Dark Star Hophead; Windsor & Eton Windsor Knot; 2 changing beers (sourced regionally) [H]

Deservedly busy little two-roomed pub serving four real ales, all from independent brewers, and occasional cask cider. Service is fast, friendly and efficient. There is also a worthwhile range of bottle-conditioned ales. Food is a point of pride, but all seating is available to non-diners; bookings

are not taken. The decor is traditional, with bare floorboards. There is some outside seating in a quiet street. Close to Regent's Canal.
🏠❶⊖(Angel)♣🚆🐾🛜

New Rose ⍂ ✅
84-86 Essex Road, N1 8LU
✪ 12-11 (midnight Thu; 2am Fri & Sat); 12-10.30 Sun
☎ (020) 7226 1082
5 changing beers (sourced nationally) Ⓗ
Spacious and friendly pub, traditional but quirky, in the heart of Islington. There is a changing range of five quality real ales, light through dark, many from the surrounding area, as well as American bottled beers and traditional cider. A tempting menu of pub favourites, from locally sourced ingredients, is served; home-cooked pizzas are a speciality and it does impressive Sunday roasts. Enjoy a pint in the small rear garden or on a bench at the front, or catch the big game on TV.
🏠❶⇌(Essex Rd)●🚆🐾🛜

N1: King's Cross

Parcel Yard
Upper Level, King's Cross Station concourse, N1C 4AH
✪ 8am-11; 9am-10.30 Sun ☎ (020) 7713 7258
🌐 parcelyard.co.uk
Adnams Ghost Ship; Fuller's Oliver's Island, London Pride, ESB; Gale's Seafarers Ale, HSB; 3 changing beers (sourced regionally; often Butcombe, Windsor & Eton) Ⓗ
Large pub approached by stairs at the rear of the concourse, converted from the former station parcel office. It is used by local workers, commuters and for meetings; as well as bars on two levels there are bookable semi-private rooms converted from offices and an indoor balcony. It has no music; the decor is minimal and features rescued furniture. Breakfast is served until 11.45am, main meals 12-10pm (9pm Sun). Disabled access is by lift and there are no smoking facilities.
🐀🏠❶♿⇌⊖(King's Cross/St Pancras)♣🚆🛜

N1: Pentonville

Craft Beer Co
55 White Lion Street, N1 9PP
✪ 4-11; 12-1am Fri & Sat; 12-10.30 Sun ☎ (020) 7278 0318
Kent Pale; 9 changing beers (sourced nationally) Ⓗ
Multi-room pub with a wooden bar displaying 10 handpumps, all serving beers from independent brewers. Green curtains and red carpet give some warmth to the main bar, which has two Victorian pillars, a wooden floor and raised tables and stools, all overseen by Winston Churchill. A cosy room, with settees and subtle lighting, is to the right as you enter, and there is a smaller room at the back. To the side is a small garden. 🏠❶⊖(Angel)🍴🚆

N2: East Finchley

Bald Faced Stag ✅
69 High Road, N2 8AB
✪ 12-11 (midnight Fri & Sat) ☎ (020) 8442 1201
🌐 thebaldfacedstagn2.co.uk
Greene King IPA; 3 changing beers (sourced regionally; often Adnams, Sambrook's, Windsor & Eton) Ⓗ
Imposing corner pub just up the road from East Finchley station and near to the Phoenix cinema.

Although part of a Greene King-owned chain, it always offers guest beers from local and regional breweries. Occasional beer festivals are held. English and French cuisine is provided in the dining room and the bar area. Daily newspapers are available and often TV sport on terrestrial channels. A selection of board games can be played.
🐀🐾❶⊖P🚆🐾🛜

N4: Stroud Green

Old Dairy
1-3 Crouch Hill, N4 4AP
✪ 12-11 (midnight Thu; 1am Fri & Sat); 12-10.30 Sun
☎ (020) 7263 3337 🌐 theolddairyn4.co.uk
Greene King IPA; 4 changing beers (sourced locally; often Hop Back, London Fields, Twickenham) Ⓗ
Popular in the evenings, this Greene King Metropolitan outlet was built as a dairy, and murals on Crouch Hill illustrate all of its previous dairy activities. The cavernous space is divided between a sit-down restaurant and two large rooms served by the bar. A menu of British standards is common to both; food is served all day at weekends. Four or five ales include a house beer from Greene King, and a real cider is served in summer.
❶♿⊖(Crouch Hill)♣🚆(210,W3,W7)🐾🛜

N5: Canonbury

Snooty Fox ⍂
75 Grosvenor Avenue, N5 2NN
✪ 4-11 (1am Fri); 12-1am Sat; 12-10.30 Sun
☎ (020) 7354 9532 🌐 snootyfoxlondon.co.uk
Otter Ale; 3 changing beers (sourced nationally) Ⓗ
A vibrant community pub with 1960s icons depicted throughout, serving four real ales and a real cider. The airy bar features a 45rpm jukebox and the patio offers pleasant outside drinking. A function room is available for local groups and private dining. The pub is well known for its ale and cider festivals, which attract people from far and wide. Its kitchen serves quality modern British food and an excellent Sunday roast. Local CAMRA Pub of the Year 2014. 🏠❶⊖🍴🚆

N6: Highgate

Duke's Head ⍂
16 Highgate High Street, N6 5JG
✪ 12-midnight (1am Thu-Sat); 12-11.30 Sun
☎ (020) 8341 1310 🌐 thedukesheadhighgate.co.uk
8 changing beers (sourced regionally) Ⓗ
Former coaching inn with a courtyard, reopened as a specialist beer house offering a large range of real ales and ciders. Local brewer Hammerton is a fairly permanent presence but expect to find beers from around the country, such as Brodie's, Burning Sky, Magic Rock, Moor and Siren – usually at least a mild, a porter or stout, a pale and a best bitter are listed on a board behind the bar.
🐀❶⊖♣🍴🚆(210,271)🐾🛜

N7: Holloway

Coronet ⍂ ✅
338-346 Holloway Road, N7 6PA
✪ 8am-midnight ☎ (020) 7609 5014
Fuller's London Pride; Greene King Abbot; 6 changing beers (sourced nationally) Ⓗ
Impressive Wetherspoon conversion of a cinema, the Savoy, designed by William Glen, that showed

its last film in 1983 and now displays large prints of movie stars and former local entertainers, with an old projector the centrepiece of a raised dais towards the rear. Sometimes there are single brewery festivals. Expect plastic glasses and higher prices when Arsenal are playing at home. Tables (some under cover) are on the pavement and at the rear. Q♿☕🕙🕊️&⬆(Holloway Rd)●🚌🚲?

N9: Lower Edmonton

Beehive ✓
24 Little Bury Street, N9 9JZ
✪ 12-11.30 (1am Fri & Sat); 12-11 Sun ☎ (020) 8360 4358
🌐 thebeehiveedmonton.co.uk
Adnams Southwold Bitter, Ghost Ship; Greene King IPA, Abbot; Timothy Taylor Boltmaker ⊞
Rebuilt in 1929, this pub has been refurbished and retains its friendly community feel. Tucked away in semi-detached suburbia, it has a through bar offering pool and darts at one end and a dining area at the other, and is popular with a good mix of local customers. Quiz night is Tuesday and live music is played most Saturday evenings. The TV shows live football and other sport. Fresh daily specials as well as good pub grub are served lunchtimes and evenings.
♿🕊️🕙&♣P🚲(329,W8)🐾?

N10: Muswell Hill

John Baird 🅛 ✓
122 Fortis Green Road, N10 3HN
✪ 11-11 (midnight Fri & Sat); 12-10.30 Sun
☎ (020) 8444 8830 🌐 thejohnbaird.co.uk
Brakspear Bitter; Sharp's Doom Bar; 4 changing beers (sourced nationally) ⊞
A local mecca for real ale and cider fans, sporting up to six ales and a couple of ciders. One wing of this large pub is home to an excellent Thai restaurant and the other provides ample space for drinkers and those wanting to watch major sporting events in comfort. A sizeable outside smoking and drinking area is provided at the rear. Quiz night is Thursday. Children are allowed in the bar until 7pm and in the restaurant until 9pm.
♿🕊️🕙&●🚲?

N12: North Finchley

Bohemia 🏆 🅛
762-764 High Road, N12 9QH
✪ 12-11 (midnight Thu; 1am Fri & Sat); 12-10.30 Sun
☎ (020) 8446 0294 🌐 thebohemia.co.uk
London Brewing Company Beer Street; 4 changing beers (sourced locally; often London Brewing Company) ⊞
Popular brewpub near Tally Ho Corner, hosting varied community events including salsa classes, quiz nights and Friday and Saturday boogie nights. Its own London Brewing Company real ales are brewed on-site. Take-home growlers are available. With strong emphasis on its own draught beers, it also offers an extensive range of bottled beers, real cider and a varied food menu. Comfortable lounge chairs at the front complement the relaxed air.
♿🕊️🕙&⬆(Woodside Park)♣●🚲(125,263)🐾?

Elephant Inn
283 Ballards Lane, N12 8NR
✪ 11-11 (midnight Fri & Sat); 12-10.30 Sun
☎ (020) 8343 6110 🌐 elephantinnfinchley.co.uk

Fuller's London Pride, ESB; 2 changing beers (sourced locally; often Fuller's) ⊞
Fondly remembered as the Moss Hall Tavern, this fine wood-panelled pub with a U-shaped bar is split into three distinct drinking areas. To the right, TV screens show all live sport, the left bar is TV-free for a more relaxed feel, and the middle bar has raised tables and stools and the daily papers. Thai food from the restaurant upstairs can be ordered at the bar. Note that pumpclips always face forward even though a beer may be temporarily unavailable.
♿🕊️🕙⬆(West Finchley)♣🚲(82,125,460)🐾?

N13: Palmers Green

Alfred Herring ✓
316-322 Green Lanes, N13 5TT
✪ 8am-11 (midnight Thu-Sat) ☎ (020) 3232 1083
Courage Directors; Greene King Abbot; Ruddles Best Bitter; 7 changing beers (sourced nationally; often Adnams, Redemption, Sambrook's) ⊞
A busy Wetherspoon shop conversion in the heart of the Green Lanes shops opened in 2006, comprising a large open drinking and dining area with side booths. Six of the 10 handpumps offer a varying range, with the manager regularly obtaining beers from a wide list of London breweries. There is a resident darts team. The pub is named after a local First World War soldier who was awarded the Victoria Cross for his heroic action in France in 1918. Q♿🕙⇌🚲(121,329,W6)?

N14: Southgate

New Crown ✓
80-84 Chase Side, N14 5PH
✪ 8am-11.30 (12.30am Fri & Sat) ☎ (020) 8882 8758
Greene King IPA, Abbot; Sharp's Doom Bar; 5 changing beers (sourced nationally; often Jennings, Portobello) ⊞
One of the older Wetherspoon pubs, formerly a Sainsbury's store, close to the Underground station and bus stops. It has a large open-plan bar with pictures of Southgate from days gone by hanging on the walls. A superb range of eight real ales, two of which will be from London breweries, is served by keen and enthusiastic staff. Breakfast is served from 8am; you can enjoy a beer from 9am.
Q♿🕙&⬆♣●🚲🐾?

N16: Dalston Kingsland

Railway Tavern Ale House 🅛
2 St Jude Street, N16 8JT
✪ 4-11 (midnight Fri); 12-midnight Sat; 12-10.30 Sun
☎ (020) 0011 1195
Adnams Southwold Bitter; Redemption Pale Ale; 4 changing beers (sourced nationally) ⊞
A gem of a pub well worth visiting, a stone's throw from bustling Dalston. It has six varied and interesting cask ales to suit all tastes, including one from Adnams and a local beer, plus exceptional bottled beers, such as Kernel. A tasty Thai food menu and Sunday roasts complete the offering. It is full of quirky character, friendly, and a perfect venue to relax away from the sports crowd with good beer and good company.
♿🕙&⬆(Dalston Jct/Kingsland)♣●🚲🐾?

N16: Stoke Newington

Jolly Butchers ⓁL
204 Stoke Newington High Street, N16 7HU
✪ 4-midnight (1am Fri); 12-1am Sat; 12-11 Sun
☎ (020) 7241 2185
Five Points Pale Ale; King Beer Horsham Best Bitter; Moor Beer So'Hop; 3 changing beers (sourced nationally) Ⓗ
A classic Art Deco-style bar boasting elaborate ironwork and glass, with a lively modern feel and the enviable status of being a true free house. Nine handpumps offer six different real ales, usually from microbreweries, and three ciders or perries. The beers listed are examples of what might be found but the website provides up to date pouring information. Quality ale is complemented by great food. ✿⏶❶❤▤❀🐾

N17: Tottenham

Beehive ⓁL
Stoneleigh Road, N17 9BQ
✪ 4 (5 Mon)-11; 4-1am Fri; 12-1am Sat; 12-10.30 Sun
☎ (020) 8808 3567 ⊕ beehiven17.com
Redemption Trinity; Sambrook's Junction Ale; Truman's Swift; 4 changing beers (sourced regionally) Ⓗ
Facing the public car park off the High Road, this is a fine Brewers' Tudor pub (1927) with a regionally important historic interior. It has two bars, a games room and a big garden with children's play equipment. Many of the changing beers come from London brewers, and there are numerous others such as local Beavertown ones. Pub food includes Sunday lunches and summer barbecues. Live music and DJs feature at the weekend, and there is a quiz night on Wednesday. A sports TV is in the games room. ➤✿⏶❶♿❤(Bruce Grove)♣❤▤❀🐾

N19: Upper Holloway

Shaftesbury Tavern ⓁL
534 Hornsey Road, N19 3QN (on A103)
✪ 4-11; 12-12.30am Fri & Sat; 12-10.30 Sun
☎ (020) 7272 7950
Dragonfly 2 o'Clock Ordinary, Early Doors; 2 changing beers (often Fuller's) Ⓗ
Comprehensive restoration of a nice old pub, with the former pool room turned into the restaurant area under a fine skylight. Outside seating is available on decking at the front. Operated by Remarkable Restaurants, after a 2014 refurbishment, it now includes beers from the Dragonfly Brewery located at its pub at Acton. There is a Tuesday quiz and occasional live music. ➤✿⏶❶♿❤(Crouch Hill)❤▤(41,91,210)🐾

N21: Winchmore Hill

Dog & Duck ⊘
74 Hoppers Road, N21 3LH
✪ 12-11.30 (12.30am Fri & Sat) ☎ (020) 8886 1987
⊕ doganduckwinchmorehill.co.uk
Fuller's London Pride; Greene King IPA; Timothy Taylor Landlord; Young's Bitter Ⓗ
Small, friendly pub with one bar, popular with locals and welcoming to visitors. A large-screen TV shows sporting events; it can get busy for Spurs or Arsenal games. Local football teams meet here and there is a golf society. The walls are adorned with local history photographs and a Victorian map of the area. The patio-style walled garden at the rear welcomes dogs at quiet times. The pub has been in the Guide for 13 consecutive years, 26 in total. ✿▤(W9)🐾

Orange Tree
18 Highfield Road, N21 3HA
✪ 12-midnight ☎ (020) 8360 4853
⊕ the-orange-tree-pub.co.uk
Greene King IPA; Morland Old Speckled Hen; 2 changing beers (sourced nationally; often Hook Norton, New River, Redemption) Ⓗ
Step back in time when you enter this back-street local just yards from the New River walk. Toby jugs, decorated plates and sporting event posters adorn the walls and shelves. There is a pool table, dartboard and TVs showing news or live sport. Enjoy a summer barbecue or a hearty Sunday lunch. Add all of this to the well-kept ales and you will understand how the landlord has kept this pub in the Guide since 1995. ➤✿⏶❶♣P▤(329)🐾

Enfield

Moon Under Water ⊘
115/117 Chase Side, EN2 6NN
✪ 8am-11 (10.30 Sun) ☎ (020) 8366 9855
Greene King IPA, Abbot; Ruddles Best Bitter; Sharp's Doom Bar; 6 changing beers (sourced nationally; often Adnams, Redemption, Twickenham) Ⓗ
Well-established Wetherspoon pub that used to be a dairy, within easy reach of both Enfield Chase and Gordon Hill stations. The L-shaped bar sports 10 handpumps, with real cider served from polypins. Look up while drinking and you will see exposed roof trusses, stained-glass windows and a mock balcony complete with library. The conservatory at the back adds to the light and airy ambience. The pub attracts all age groups; children are welcome until 8.30pm. ➤✿⏶❶♿❤(Enfield Chase)❤P▤(191,W9)🐾

Wonder ⓁL
1 Batley Road, EN2 0JG
✪ 11-11 (midnight Fri & Sat); 12-11 Sun ☎ (020) 8363 0202
McMullen AK Ⓗ
Traditional two-bar back-street local; a rare survivor for the area. The public bar features a real fire, dartboard and piano while the lounge area is small and cosy. Football-free and with a focus on live music, you can enjoy honky tonk on Saturday evenings and Sunday afternoons, and jam sessions on the last Wednesday of the month. A monthly quiz is held on the first Wednesday. Hot pies are available. Note that a cask breather may be used on beers other than AK. Q➤✿⏶♿❤(Gordon Hill)♣P▤(191,W8)🐾

High Barnet

Lord Nelson
14 West End Lane, EN5 2SA
✪ 12-11 (midnight Fri & Sat); 12-10.30 Sun
☎ (020) 8449 7249
Young's Bitter, Special; 1 changing beer (sourced regionally; often Young's) Ⓗ
A homely community pub on the fringe of High Barnet, close to the hospital and served by several buses. It is full of character, with maritime artefacts that befit its name. There is also a vast collection of cruet sets, some still used for food (served 12-2pm). Autographs of Richard Burton and Elizabeth

Taylor are preserved on a wall. Cribbage, dominoes and scrabble are played; the TV is used sparingly. ⊛🕭♣🖵🐾🛜

Olde Mitre Inne ✅
58 High Street, EN5 5SJ
🕓 12–midnight (1am Fri & Sat) ☎ (020) 8449 5701
Adnams Southwold Bitter; Caledonian Deuchars IPA; Greene King Abbot; Timothy Taylor Landlord; 5 changing beers (sourced nationally; often New River, Red Squirrel, Thwaites) Ⓗ
A 17th-century coaching inn close to Barnet church, now a popular multi-roomed pub with outside drinking. Much of the courtyard can be covered with a retractable roof in winter months; there is even a brick-built chiminea to keep customers warm. Knowledgeable, well-trained bar staff look after a mixed clientele with a good range of beers, often selected from SIBA. It has been a worthy local CAMRA Pub of the Year winner several times over. 🛏⊛🕭Ө♣🖣🖵🐾🛜

New Barnet

Railway Bell ✅
13 East Barnet Road, EN4 8RR
🕓 8am–11 (midnight Fri & Sat) ☎ (020) 8449 1369
Courage Directors; Greene King IPA, Abbot; Ruddles Best Bitter; Sharp's Doom Bar; 6 changing beers (sourced nationally; often Adnams, Blindmans, Hook Norton) Ⓗ
In this open-plan Wetherspoon pub, the large conservatory with open kitchen is bright and may remind you of your school refectory or the works canteen. But do not let that put you off as here you will find quality ales complemented by changing guests, often from London breweries selected by the keen manager. There is a large patio to the side and back of the pub that helpfully offers a no-smoking area. 🛏⊛🕭🖢🚶🖵🛜

NORTH-WEST LONDON
NW1: Camden Town

Constitution 🅛
42 St Pancras Way, NW1 0QT
🕓 11–11 (midnight Fri & Sat); 12–10.30 Sun
☎ (020) 7380 0767 ⊕ conincamden.com
Caledonian Deuchars IPA; Sambrook's Junction Ale; 1 changing beer (sourced locally) Ⓗ
Founded in 1858, this dog- and family-friendly community pub is a welcome haven within bustling Camden and its vibrant market area. Its award-winning patio terraced garden (four times Camden in Bloom finalist) has a pleasant south-facing outlook over the Regent's Canal. The downstairs cellar bar is host to live music and comedy events. Pool and darts are available, and it has a large-screen TV. Weather permitting, there is occasional home-made street food outside.
🛏⊛🖢Ө(Camden Rd/Town)♣🖵🐾

Tapping the Admiral 🅛
77 Castle Road, NW1 8SU
🕓 12–midnight (11 Mon & Tue); 12–11 Sun
☎ (020) 7267 6118
8 changing beers (sourced regionally) Ⓗ
Local CAMRA Pub of the Year in 2015, this is a popular and enjoyable community pub where friendly and knowledgeable staff offer a warm welcome. Eight handpumps deliver guest ales, mainly local. The menu is great British food with

speciality home-made pies. A heated and covered beer garden is well designed and a nice feature. There is a popular Wednesday quiz and live sessions of traditional music on Thursday evenings. Look out for monthly tap takeovers and pop-up events.
Q🛏⊛🕭🖢Ө(Kentish Town West)🖣🖵🐾🛜

NW1: Euston

Bree Louise ♈ 🅛 ✅
69 Cobourg Street, NW1 2HH
🕓 11.30–11; 12–10.30 Sun ☎ (020) 7681 4930
⊕ thebreelouise.com
17 changing beers (sourced nationally) Ⓗ/Ⓖ
One-bar corner pub, busy with locals and Euston commuters. A cooled gravity stillage of up to 11 beers, complemented by six handpumps, offers a wide range from London and across the UK, alongside up to 11 ciders and perries. Regular beer festivals are held. There is no music, just conversation, with occasional TV sport (especially rugby, not football). Outdoor seating is on the pavement. Closing time may be later on weekdays. Local CAMRA Pub of the Year 2016.
⊛🕭🚶Ө(Euston/Euston Sq)🖣🖵🐾🛜

Doric Arch 🅛
Euston Station Colonnade, 1 Eversholt Street, NW1 2DN
🕓 11–11 (10.30 Sun) ☎ (020) 7383 3359 ⊕ doric-arch.co.uk
Fuller's Oliver's Island, London Pride, ESB; 6 changing beers (sourced nationally) Ⓗ
Up a flight of stairs, the pub's large picture windows in a raised area afford a view of the busy urban world below. Right next to Euston Station, it is used extensively by commuters, aided by the train times screen. The excellent staff are helpful and informative about the ales, including guest beers from London and across the UK. Brewery and railway memorabilia adorn the walls, and food is served all day. Toilets are at basement level.
🛏🕭🚶Ө(Euston/Euston Sq)🖣🖵🛜

Euston Tap
West Lodge, 190 Euston Road, NW1 2EF
🕓 12–11.30; 12–10 Sun ☎ (020) 3137 8837
⊕ eustontap.com
8 changing beers (sourced nationally) Ⓗ
Fronting the main station building, this impressive Grade II-listed Portland stone lodge is one of the few relics from the original 1830s station. Up to eight changing beers are pumped up to taps behind the bar. The limited space includes a large heated drinking area outside as well as seating (and the toilets) up a wrought-iron spiral staircase. The Northern Tap opposite will feature northern brewery beers. Food can be ordered from 6pm (Mon-Sat) from Famous Ray's Pizza.
⊛🖢🚶Ө(Euston/Euston Sq)🖵🐾🛜

Royal George 🅛 ✅
8-14 Eversholt Street, NW1 1DG
🕓 11–midnight (1am Fri); 10–1am Sat; 12.30–11.30 Sun
☎ (020) 7387 2431
Greene King IPA, London Glory; Westerham Taylor Walker 1730; 3 changing beers (sourced regionally) Ⓗ
Large pub built in 1939, Grade II-listed, arranged as interconnecting rooms facing the three street frontages with a central bar. One side has an unusual fireplace with marquetry work on the surrounds. Right opposite Euston Station, it is

named after HMS Royal George, a flagship vessel for the Royal Navy in the 1800s. Local London beers are augmented by regional guests or Greene King seasonals. ⚘◑➡⊖🛒🅟

NW3: Hampstead

Duke of Hamilton 🄻 ⊘

23 New End, NW3 1JD

✪ 12-11 ☎ (020) 7794 2068 ⊕ thedukeofhamilton.com

Fuller's London Pride; Sharp's Special; house beer (by Wild Weather Ales); 3 changing beers (sourced nationally) 🄷

A handsome period building up a flight of steps. It has a beautiful, traditional but well-lit interior with a central bar and comfortable and elegant seating. The outside terrace has bench seating. Up to six real ales are served (fewer in winter), some from small independent breweries. The Rabbit Hole, a cellar theatre, is another attraction. Check current opening hours as these vary by season (and closing times displayed at the pub include half-an-hour drinking up time). ⛴⚘◑⊖♣🛒(46)⚘🅟

NW4: Hendon

Greyhound

52 Church End, NW4 4JT

✪ 12-11 (midnight Fri & Sat) ☎ (020) 8457 9730

Young's Bitter, Special; 2 changing beers (sourced regionally; often Twickenham, Wells) 🄷

Near Middlesex University and next door to St Mary's Church, a pub has been on this site since 1675; the current building dates back to 1896. There are three separate comfortable seating areas; one is wood-panelled and is sometimes set out for dining. Check out the photos depicting the pub and village through the years. Quiz nights are Mondays and Thursdays. On a clear day there is an extensive view westward from the pavement seats at the front. Q⛴⚘🛒◑♣🛒🅟⚘🅟

NW5: Kentish Town

Grafton 🄻 ⊘

20 Prince of Wales Road, NW5 3LG

✪ 12-11 (midnight Fri); 11-midnight Sat; 12-10.30 Sun ☎ (020) 7482 4466 ⊕ thegraftonnw5.co.uk

Purity Mad Goose; Sambrook's Wandle Ale; Timothy Taylor Landlord; 4 changing beers (sourced locally) 🄷

Popular pub with beautiful Victorian features, combining a traditional feel with many contemporary touches and specialising in local cask beers. The spacious ground floor horseshoe bar is partly tiled, with ample seating. Upstairs is a bar/ function room (no real ale). It has an elegant, covered roof garden. Knowledgeable and friendly bar staff will serve you. Quiz night is Tuesday; there are also board games and a piano, with occasional open mic evenings. ⛴⚘◑♿➡⊖(Kentish Town West)♣🛒⚘🅟

Junction Tavern 🄻

101 Fortess Road, NW5 1AG

✪ 5-11; 12-midnight Fri & Sat; 12-11 Sun ☎ (020) 7485 9400 ⊕ junctiontavern.co.uk

Adnams Broadside; Sambrook's Junction Ale; Sharp's Doom Bar; 2 changing beers (sourced regionally) 🄷

A real ale and gastro-pub, it appears from the main road as a restaurant with the pub to the rear, boasting two connected drinking areas, conservatory and award-winning beer garden. The

ornate interior has wood panelling and large mirrors. A quality food menu is available; pre-booking is advised for the dining area. Guest beers alternate between other Sambrook's and wider regional offerings. Family- and dog-friendly. There is a seated and covered outside smoking area. Q⛴⚘◑♿➡⊖(Kentish Town/Tufnell Park)🛒🅟🅟

Lion & Unicorn 🄻

42-44 Gaisford Street, NW5 2ED

✪ 12-11; 11-11 Sat; 12-10.30 Sun ☎ (020) 7267 2304

Sharp's Cornish Coaster; Young's Bitter; 3 changing beers (sourced regionally) 🄷

This community venue is a great favourite with its genuine homely feel, open fire and comfortable seating. Run by friendly management and staff as a Geronimo-branded gastro-pub, it offers a good-quality cask ale range featuring several local breweries. It is a winner of local and regional awards for both front and back gardens. There are quizzes on Sunday. Above is the Lion and Unicorn Theatre. Q⛴⚘◑♿➡⊖🛒⚘🅟

Pineapple 🄻

51 Leverton Street, NW5 2NX

✪ 12-11; 12-midnight Fri & Sat; 12-10.30 Sun ☎ (020) 7284 4631

Sharp's Doom Bar; 4 changing beers (sourced nationally) 🄷

An authentic and friendly community pub, saved from closure by the locals, Grade II-listed and with a regionally important historic interior, notable for its mirrors and splendid bar-back. The front bar, with comfortable seating around tables, leads through to an informal conservatory overlooking the patio garden. The food menu is Thai kitchen cuisine. Local beers can come from across London and, the pub being free of tie, the range changes regularly. Q⛴⚘◑➡⊖🛒⚘🅟

Southampton Arms

139 Highgate Road, NW5 1LE

✪ 12-midnight ☎ 07745 939168 ⊕ thesouthamptonarms.co.uk

11 changing beers (sourced nationally) 🄷

A place that does what it says on the sign outside: Ale, Cider, Meat. On and behind the bar, 18 handpumps serve almost equal amounts of cider and different beers from microbreweries across the UK. Snacks include pork pies, cheese and meat baps. Music is played on vinyl only and the piano is in regular use. Down the back is a secluded patio. ⚘◑➡⊖(Gospel Oak/Kentish Town)♣🛒

NW9: Kingsbury

J J Moons 🄻 ⊘

551-553 Kingsbury Road, NW9 9EL

✪ 8am-midnight ☎ (020) 8204 9675

Adnams Broadside; Greene King Abbot; Sharp's Doom Bar; Theakston Old Peculier; 4 changing beers (sourced nationally) 🄷

An early (1988) Wetherspoon shop conversion with silent TV screens. A large, one-room establishment with low ceilings, lots of wood panelling, subdued lighting and a raised section at the rear, here is a rare outlet for real ale in this part of outer London. Children are permitted until 9pm.The name plays on the George Orwell Moon Under Water theme of some of the company's earliest pubs. Q⛴◑♿⊖🛒🅟

Harefield

Old Orchard L

Jacks Lane, UB9 6HJ (off Park Lane) TQ0463190411
✪ 11.30-11; 11.30-10.30 Sun ☎ (01895) 822631
⊕ oldorchard-harefield.co.uk
**Brunning & Price Original; Mighty Oak Oscar Wilde;
Tring Side Pocket for a Toad; 3 changing beers
(sourced locally; often Leighton Buzzard, Oakham,
Tring)** Ⓗ
A Brunning & Price establishment that was once a
country house before becoming a restaurant.
Refurbished in 2010, the pub is lined with
bookcases and pictures and has an unfussy array of
mismatched tables and chairs, and three
welcoming real fires in the colder months. The
Original is brewed by Phoenix. There are
commanding views of the Colne Valley from the
terrace and beer garden. The ciders are Westons
Old Rosie and Thatchers Cheddar Valley.
Q ☼ ⛱ ⍟ ◑ ♿ ♣ ♠ P ⎙ (U9) ❀ 🛜

Northwood Hills

William Jolle L ⊘

The Broadway, 53 Joel Street, HA6 1NZ
✪ 8am-midnight ☎ (01923) 842240
**Greene King Abbot; Ruddles Best Bitter; Sharp's
Doom Bar; changing beers** Ⓗ
A Wetherspoon conversion of a large office
building alongside Northwood Hills station. Twelve
handpumps offer a good range of beers, with local
ale being to the fore. The atmosphere is convivial
and it has recently been nominated as an Asset of
Community Value. There is a small patio area
outside the front of the pub for smokers.
Q ☼ ⛱ ⍟ ◑ ♿ ⊖ ♣ ⎙ (282,H11,H13) 🛜

Rayners Lane

Village Inn ⊘

402-408 Rayners Lane, HA5 5DY
✪ 8am-11 (midnight Thu; 12.30am Fri & Sat)
☎ (020) 8868 8551
Fuller's London Pride Ⓖ; **Greene King Abbot; Ruddles
Best Bitter; Sharp's Doom Bar** Ⓗ/Ⓖ; **changing
beers** Ⓗ
Another split-level, double-fronted shop
conversion. The rear of the pub, accessed down a
few steps, sports the traditional Wetherspoon
booths, with a row of tables down the centre. A
terraced area behind has a variety of large potted
plants among the picnic tables. The front pavement
has a few tables and chairs for that alfresco
moment. The pub has a good cross-section of
custmers who mingle quite happily together.
Alcoholic drinks served from 9am.
Q ☼ ⛱ ⍟ ◑ ♿ ⊖ ♣ ⎙ 🛜

South Kenton

Windermere ★ ⊘

Windermere Avenue, HA9 8QT
✪ 12-11.30 (12.30am Fri); 11-12.30am Sat; 11-11.30 Sun
☎ (020) 3632 0020 ⊕ windermerepub.com
**Courage Best Bitter; 1 changing beer (sourced
nationally; often Fuller's, Young's)** Ⓗ
Built in 1939 and next to South Kenton station, the
Windermere has a nationally important historic
interior. It is a genuine community pub with three
bars, although the public one is now used only for
functions. The saloon and lounge retain many

original features, including the large inner porches,
bar counters, back fittings, wall panelling and
fireplaces. A quiz is held on alternate Thursdays,
and there is sometimes live entertainment.
☼ ⛱ ♿ ⊖ ♣ P ⎙ (223) 🛜

SOUTH-EAST LONDON
SE1: Bermondsey

Simon the Tanner

231 Long Lane, SE1 4PR
✪ 12 (5 Mon)-11; 12-10.30 Sun ☎ (020) 7357 8740
⊕ simonthetanner.co.uk
**Adnams Lighthouse; 3 changing beers (sourced
nationally; often Siren, Southwark)** Ⓗ
In a quiet road just off busy Bermondsey Street, the
Simon is a mid-terrace, modestly sized, Grade II-
listed pub. A former Shepherd Neame outlet is
now a free house. The regularly changing real ales
are often from London breweries, and there is real
and mulled cider. Food is a quality take on standard
dishes such as pies, burgers and soups, plus a roast
on Sundays. A quiz is held on Tuesday evenings
and live piano music features every Wednesday.
⛱ ◑ ⇌ ⊖ (London Bridge) ♠ ⎙ ❀ 🛜

SE1: Borough

Lord Clyde

27 Clennam Street, SE1 1ER
✪ 11-11; 12-11 Sat; 12-6 Sun ☎ (020) 7407 3397
⊕ lordclyde.com
**Adnams Southwold Bitter; Hogs Back TEA; Sharp's
Doom Bar; Young's Bitter; 1 changing beer (sourced
nationally)** Ⓗ
A gem of a street-corner pub that has changed
little since being rebuilt in 1913 and is well worth a
visit to step back in time. The exterior retains its
fine Truman's Brewery tilework and the regionally
important historic interior has traditional decor
with comfortable seating and curtains over the
doors. There is one main bar and also a side room
with its own serving hatch. The pub has been run
by the same family for over 50 years.
◑ ⇌ (London Bridge) ⊖ ⎙ ❀

Royal Oak ⊘

44 Tabard Street, SE1 4JU
✪ 11-11; 12-11 Sat; 12-9 Sun ☎ (020) 7357 7173
**Harveys Sussex XX Mild Ale, IPA, Sussex Best Bitter; 3
changing beers (sourced regionally; often Fuller's,
Harveys)** Ⓗ
A charming back-to-basics drinkers' pub divided in
two by the bar counter and an off-sales hatch.
Although Sussex-based Harveys Brewery's first
London tied house, it also offers a changing guest
Fuller's beer. You will be delighted by the friendly
and attentive service, the extensive range of beers
and the inventive food menu with ingredients
sourced from London markets. The many regulars
come from miles around to spend time here. A rare
regular London outlet for mild.
Q ◑ ⇌ (London Bridge) ⊖ ♣ ♠ ⎙

SE1: Borough Market

Market Porter

9 Stoney Street, SE1 9AA
✪ 11-11; 12-11 Sat; 12-10.30 Sun ☎ (020) 7407 2495
Harveys Sussex Best Bitter Ⓗ; **9 changing beers
(sourced nationally)** Ⓗ/Ⓐ

A classic, rustic market pub adjacent to the famous Borough Market, also retaining its traditional 6-8.30am morning weekday opening hours. A Guide regular, it has up to 10 real ales available plus four ciders, often from Westons. Adorning the walls is a vast array of pumpclips reflecting the huge range of beers offered over the years. Popular with locals and visitors alike, it can get busy, with drinkers spilling out on to the street. An upstairs restaurant serves lunches. ◖≉⊖(London Bridge)●🖰

Old King's Head

King's Head Yard, 45 Borough High Street, SE1 1NA

✪ 11-midnight (1am Fri & Sat); 12-midnight Sun
☎ (020) 7407 1550 ⊕ theoldkingshead.uk.com

Harveys IPA, Sussex Best Bitter; St Austell Tribute, Proper Job; Sharp's Doom Bar; 1 changing beer (sourced nationally) Ⓗ

A traditional pub down a narrow, cobbled road off Borough High Street. Stained glass windows hint at a bygone era and the pictures adorning the walls tell the story of a pub, and an area, that has a rich history. The layout inside is simple, with an L-shaped bar in one corner usually offering six real ales on handpump. The clientele is a mix of tourists, office workers and visitors to the nearby market. ◖&≉⊖(London Bridge)🖰?

Rake

14 Winchester Walk, SE1 9AG

✪ 12 (11 Fri; 10 Sat)-11; 12-8 Sun ☎ (020) 7407 0557
3 changing beers (sourced nationally; often Dark Star, Oakham) Ⓗ

A great, but tiny, destination pub. The walls are covered with handwritten messages left by visiting brewers from around the globe, yet the bar is only 10 feet long. Three real ales are usually on offer, plus several other draught brews and an extensive selection of bottled beers. Light bar snacks are also available and customers may, with permission, bring in food from the nearby Borough Market. The pub can close early in winter months.
Q✿&≉⊖(London Bridge)🖰?

SE1: Waterloo

King's Arms Ⓛ

25 Roupell Street, SE1 8TB

✪ 11-11; 12-10.30 Sun ☎ (020) 7207 0784
⊕ thekingsarmslondon.co.uk

9 changing beers (sourced nationally; often Dark Star, Sharp's, Windsor & Eton) Ⓗ

Tucked away on a back street near Waterloo Station, here is a regionally important historic pub interior worth seeking out, although it gets busy in the early evenings. Seating is at a premium in the two rooms separated by a central bar, though drinking is also allowed outside the front of the pub. The nine real ales usually include two or more from London breweries and at least one dark beer. To the rear is a Thai restaurant.
🏃◖≉(Waterloo/Waterloo East)⊖🖰❀?

SE3: Blackheath

Hare & Billet ✪

1a Eliot Cottages, Hare & Billet Road, SE3 0QJ

✪ 11-11 (midnight Thu-Sat); 12-10.30 Sun
☎ (020) 8852 2352 ⊕ hareandbillet.com

Greene King IPA; house beer (by Greene King); 6 changing beers (sourced nationally; often Kent, Portobello, Sharp's) Ⓗ

Situated on the edge of Blackheath itself, with eight real ales from a variety of breweries and real cider too, this Greene King Metropolitan pub has the largest range in the vicinity. The bare-boarded interior has plenty of natural light, is not chic or trying too hard, and affords a panoramic view of the heath. In summer months plastic glasses are available for outside drinking. The pub is home to the Hare and Billet Pond Volunteers.
🏃◖&≉♣●🖰(380)❀?

SE4: Brockley

Brockley Barge ✪

184 Brockley Road, SE4 2RR

✪ 8am-midnight (1am Fri & Sat) ☎ (020) 8694 7690
Greene King Abbot; Ruddles Best Bitter; Sharp's Doom Bar; 5 changing beers (sourced nationally) Ⓗ

Conveniently located in the heart of Brockley, these premises were reopened in 2000 by Wetherspoon, breathing new life into a pub whose previous incarnation had closed a few years earlier. The name harks back to the old Croydon Canal, replaced in 1836 by the present railway line. The U-shaped interior is spacious, with modern decor and large windows. There is a courtyard garden to one side. It attracts a varied clientele of all ages with a mix reflecting the area.
Q🏃✿◖&≉●🖰(171,172,484)?

Talbot Ⓛ

2-4 Tyrwhitt Road, SE4 1QG

✪ 12-11 (midnight Thu-Sat); 12-10.30 Sun
☎ (020) 8692 2665 ⊕ talbotpublichouse.com

Harveys Sussex Best Bitter; 4 changing beers (sourced regionally; often Brockley) Ⓗ

This fine Victorian suburban local on two floors has recently been redecorated inside and out, with large windows making the interior light and airy. A series of murals, highlighted with gilt, decorates the walls. The guest beers usually include one from the local Brockley Brewery. Popular with all ages, an extensive, upmarket menu caters for vegetarians and vegans, with daily specials and meal deals on Mondays. Regular live music, seasonal events and a weekly quiz all feature.
Q🏃✿◖&≉(St Johns)⊖(Elverson Rd)🖰❀?

SE5: Camberwell

Stormbird

25 Camberwell Church Street, SE5 8TR

✪ 4-midnight ☎ (020) 7708 4460
Dark Star American Pale Ale; 3 changing beers (sourced nationally; often Dark Star, Magic Rock) Ⓗ

The sister pub of the Hermit's Cave across the road and offering a slightly more contemporary feel, attracting a mixed but generally younger crowd. There is a huge range of beers of all types on the bar including four real ales on handpump, up to 10 other beers on tap and an extensive bottled beer selection. This range encompasses brews from the UK, continental Europe and the US. Draught beers are available in third-pint measures.
◖≉⊖(Denmark Hill)🖰?

SE6: Catford

Catford Constitutional Club ✪

Catford Broadway, SE6 4SP

✪ 4-midnight (11 Mon; 1am Fri); 12-midnight Sat; 12-11 Sun
☎ (020) 8613 7188 ⊕ catfordconstitutionalclub.com

Dark Star Partridge Best Bitter; Volden Session Ale, Pale Ale; 2 changing beers (sourced regionally; often Adnams, Rudgate, Weird Beard) ⊞
Tucked away down a short, well-lit alley opposite Canadian Avenue, this Antic pub is in the former Conservative club. It has a single bar and restaurant areas, with a large chandelier hanging from the bare rafters. A quirky assortment of old furniture, pictures, Private Eye covers and mirrors creates a shabby-chic atmosphere. A mix of light and dark beers, plus a cider, is usually sold. The weekly pub quiz, monthly comedy and occasional film nights are held in a separate, smaller room.
⏳❀❶&≈(Catford/Catford Bridge)●🅿🐾🛜

London & Rye ✓
109 Rushey Green, SE6 4AF
✿ 8am-midnight ☎ (020) 8697 5028
Greene King Abbot; Ruddles Best Bitter; Sharp's Doom Bar; 3 changing beers (sourced nationally; often Adnams, Weltons, Westerham) ⊞
A Wetherspoon pub commemorating the nearby former medieval highway to Rye in Sussex. The building dates from the late-1800s and was converted from shop to pub use in 2000. The interior is long and deep, with a relatively short glazed frontage. Displays feature a number of historic figures with local connections, together with various pictures of cats in pub-related poses. There is a covered area at the front for outside drinking.
Q⏳❶&≈(Catford/Catford Bridge)●🅿🛜

SE8: Deptford
Dog & Bell Ⓛ ✓
116 Prince Street, SE8 3JD
✿ 12-11.30 (midnight Fri & Sat) ☎ (020) 8692 5664
Fuller's London Pride; 5 changing beers (sourced nationally; often Clarkshaws, Dent, Old Dairy) ⊞
Traditional and welcoming pub down a side street close to the centre of Deptford, a Guide stalwart offering six real ales plus a selection of Belgian bottled beers, malt whiskies and simple, tasty meals. It has a lively bar, a real fire in winter and a good mix of customers including locals, cyclists and those strolling along the nearby Thames Path. A quiz is held on Sunday evenings and a popular annual pickle festival takes place in November.
Q⏳❀❶≈♣●🅿🐾

Job Centre
120 Deptford High Street, SE8 4NS
✿ 4-11 (midnight Fri); 12-midnight Sat; 12-11 Sun
☎ (020) 8692 6859 ⊕ jobcentredeptford.com
Volden Session Ale; 4 changing beers (sourced regionally; often Brixton, Brockley, Thornbridge) ⊞
A welcome addition to the fairly sparse Deptford real ale scene, opened by Antic in 2014 and named after a former occupier. The spacious rectangular bar area has minimalist decor, including bare concrete flooring and exposed ducts and pipework. Music is often playing from a twin-deck turntable. Kitchen takeovers feature local pop-up street food-style vendors. The beer range has a regional focus in a variety of styles and strengths. The cider is often from Westons.
⏳❀≈⊖(Deptford Bridge)●🅿🐾🛜

SE9: Eltham
Long Pond
110 Westmount Road, SE9 1UT
✿ 5-10 Mon; 11.30-2.30, 5-10 (11 Thu & Fri); 11-3, 6.30-11 Sat; 12-2.30 Sun ☎ (020) 8331 6767 ⊕ thelongpond.co.uk
House beer (by Tonbridge); 5 changing beers (sourced regionally; often Mad Cat, Musket, Wantsum) Ⓖ
A former plumbers' merchants near the long-closed Eltham Park station, this deceptively extensive micropub is named after the pond in nearby Eltham Park North. Four to six real ales, usually local, are served on gravity dispense from a chilled stillage room. In true micropub tradition, no lager or spirits are served but wine and real cider are, along with bar snacks. Seating is mainly high benches and tables, with low tables and chairs in the snug. Q&≈●🅿(B16)

Park Tavern ✓
45 Passey Place, SE9 5DA
✿ 12-11 ☎ (020) 8850 3216 ⊕ parktaverneltham.co.uk
8 changing beers (sourced nationally; often Otter, Sambrook's, Shepherd Neame) ⊞
Traditional Victorian pub with original Truman's Brewery tiled frontage and signage. The compact interior has an L-shaped bar with stylish lamps and chandeliers. The etched windows have elegant drapes, and decorative plates and pictures line the walls. Jazz and light classical background music is played. There is a well-kept, heated rear garden and further seating to the front and side. In addition to the changing range of real ales, an impressive selection of whiskies and wine is available. Q❀❶≈🅿🐾

SE10: East Greenwich
Pelton Arms � ✓
23-25 Pelton Road, SE10 9PQ
✿ 12-midnight (1am Fri & Sat); 12-11 Sun
☎ (020) 8858 0572 ⊕ peltonarms.com
Greene King IPA; St Austell Tribute; 6 changing beers (sourced regionally; often Hop Stuff, Truman's, Westerham) ⊞
Popular and spacious back-street pub just over half a mile from Greenwich town centre. The L-shaped bar is surrounded by an eclectic mix of furnishings and soft lighting, giving the place a cosy and welcoming feel. It is community oriented, with varied live music four nights a week, a quiz on Tuesdays and the Pelton knitters' get-together on Wednesdays. A changing cider on handpump is often from Herefordshire. Five B&B rooms are available. ⏳❀🛏❶&≈(Maze Hill)♣●🅿🐾🛜

SE11: Kennington
Mansion House ✓
48 Kennington Park Road, SE11 4RS
✿ 12-midnight (1am Fri & Sat) ☎ (020) 7582 5599
⊕ oakalondon.com
Oakham JHB, Inferno, Citra, Bishops Farewell; 1 changing beer (sourced regionally; often Gale's, Oakham) ⊞
Oakham Ales' only tied outlet in London, this former cocktail lounge and piano bar was refurbished in 2014. The contemporary design includes a stylish juxtaposition of materials and textures. During the summer, the glass frontage can be opened onto the outside seating area. One guest or seasonal Oakham beer complements the

permanent range. Attentive staff also serve in the attached pan-Asian Oaka restaurant. Discounted cask beers are on the bar between 5pm and 7pm every evening. ⌂ⅅ♿≈(Elephant & Castle)⊖➍🚃🐾🛜

Old Red Lion ✓
42 Kennington Park Road, SE11 4RS
✪ 4-11; 12-1 Fri & Sat; 12-11 Sun ☎ (020) 7735 4312
⊕ theoldredlion.com
4 changing beers (sourced regionally; often Volden) Ⓗ
Grade II-listed twin-bar Antic pub with plenty of character and a fine example of the Brewers' Tudor style, having been rebuilt by Charrington in around 1929. It has a regionally important historic interior with many original features including exposed wooden beams, fireplaces and low doors connecting the bars. In addition to four changing real ales, there are usually two rotating real ciders. Often there is background music. Monthly quiz and folk music nights are held. ⌂☸ⅅ≈(Elephant & Castle)⊖➍🚃🐾🛜

SE13: Hither Green
Station Hotel
14 Staplehurst Road, SE13 5NB
✪ 12-11 (midnight Fri & Sat); 12-10.30 Sun
☎ (020) 8463 0367 ⊕ stationhotelhithergreen.co.uk
11 changing beers (sourced nationally; often Timothy Taylor) Ⓗ
A large and popular 1906 pub and hotel, bright and airy by day but with an ambience of casual elegance in the evening. The bar is pleasantly uncluttered, with a mixture of open and more private spaces. Look for the railway-themed area, complete with luggage racks and old suitcases. A separate dining area serves good-quality food. There is a rear garden and additional summer outdoor seating at the front.
Q⌂☸🍴ⅅ♿≈🚃(273)🐾🛜

SE13: Ladywell
Ravensbourne Arms ✓
323 Lewisham High Street, SE13 6NR
✪ 4-midnight; 12-1am Fri & Sat; 12-midnight Sun
☎ (020) 8613 7070 ⊕ ravensbournearms.com
5 changing beers (sourced regionally; often Hop Stuff, Kent, King Beer) Ⓗ
Spacious Antic pub opposite Lewisham Hospital. The open-plan bar area typifies shabby-chic, with retro furniture, kitsch ornaments and a range of seating areas. Alongside a rotating brew from Volden are three or four guest beers, often from microbreweries, plus a cider on handpump. An extensive range of other draught and bottled beers is also available. Good-quality food, mainly classic British dishes, is served daily until 10pm. A quiz on Wednesdays, DJ on Fridays and live music on Saturdays all feature. ☸ⅅ♿≈♣➍🚃🐾🛜

SE14: New Cross
Royal Albert ✓
460 New Cross Road, SE14 6TJ
✪ 4-midnight (1am Fri); 12-1am Sat; 12-midnight Sun
☎ (020) 8692 3737 ⊕ royalalbertpub.com
Dark Star Hophead; 6 changing beers (sourced regionally; often Brockley, Five Points, Volden) Ⓗ

Grade II-listed early-Victorian pub with original etched glass and bar-back. It has a welcoming, convivial atmosphere and offers up to seven real ales and one real cider on handpump. The cask ales change constantly but usually include one of Antic's Volden brews from Croydon. As is typical of Antic's pubs, furnishings and decor are an eclectic mix, and the food is distinctive and enticing. A quiz features on Monday evenings, a DJ on Fridays and live music on Sundays. ⌂☸ⅅ≈⊖♣➍🚃🐾🛜

SE15: Nunhead
Beer Shop London
40 Nunhead Green, SE15 3QF
✪ 4-11 (11.30 Fri); 12-11.30 Sat; 12-8 Sun; closed Mon
☎ (020) 7732 5555 ⊕ thebeershoplondon.co.uk
3 changing beers (sourced regionally; often Hop Stuff, Moor Beer, Weird Beard) Ⓖ
Former corner shop, haberdashery, and latterly a recording studio, claiming to be on the site of a former brewery. The knowledgeable staff serve a varied selection of three real ales direct from the cask, along with an extensive range of bottled beers, plus wine, spirits and soft drinks. Boxed cider, from various producers, is also available, as are pies and pub snacks. It hosts regular Meet the Brewer evenings. ♿≈➍🚃(78,P12)

Ivy House
40 Stuart Road, SE15 3BE
✪ 12-11 (midnight Fri & Sat); 12-10.30 Sun
☎ (020) 7277 8233 ⊕ ivyhousenunhead.com
Dark Star Hophead; 7 changing beers (sourced regionally; often Brick, Brockley, Truman's) Ⓗ
London's first co-operatively run pub, rescued from closure in 2012 by local community action. Designed by Truman's Brewery and a wonderful example of the 1930s so-called improved public house, it is now Grade II-listed, with a regionally important historic interior. Visit the website for details of its rich 1970s pub rock history. Beers from Brockley and Truman's breweries are usually stocked, with five other guest beers generally from small London breweries. Local CAMRA Pub of the Year 2014. Q⌂☸ⅅ♣➍🚃(343,484)🐾🛜

SE15: Peckham
Beer Rebellion
129 Queens Road, SE15 2ND
✪ 12-11 (12.30am Fri & Sat) ☎ (020) 7732 5552
6 changing beers (sourced locally; often Gipsy Hill, Late Knights, Southwark) Ⓗ
A micropub-style establishment in a former betting shop, one of a small group of bars run by the Late Knights microbrewery. Unlike a true micropub, this one stocks a host of other draught beers, in addition to six real ales and two real ciders on handpump, and has background music. Four of the ales are usually from Late Knights. The somewhat raw interior remains a work in progress and features light fittings made out of recycled Kilner jars. ☸♿≈⊖(Queens Rd)➍🚃

SE16: Rotherhithe
Mayflower
117 Rotherhithe Street, SE16 4NF
✪ 11-11; 12-9.30 Sun ☎ (020) 7237 4088
⊕ mayflowerpub.co.uk

Greene King Abbot; 4 changing beers (often Ossett, St Austell, York) ⊞
A themed pub celebrating the Mayflower ship and its historic journey to New England. The place is bustling and you feel as if you are aboard a ship of old; indeed, the walls are adorned with various nautical objects and documents. Tables and seating are close set and contribute to a communal atmosphere, although upstairs is a more luxurious restaurant with an ambience of fine dining. At the rear is a fantastic wooden jetty above the Thames with wonderful views. Q✿☆❶❺☲(381,C10)

SE18: Plumstead Common

Old Mill

1 Old Mill Road, SE18 1QG
✿ 12-11 (11.30 Fri; midnight Sat); 12-10.30 Sun
☎ (020) 3719 1499
6 changing beers (sourced nationally; often Bexley, Goddards, Hop Stuff) ⊞
Situated on the north side of Plumstead Common, this pub was formerly an 18th-century windmill – the Grade II-listed tower still remains today. The single L-shaped bar is sparsely furnished, including a pool table to the rear, leaving ample space for the frequent live music acts. Real ales change frequently, with those from local and regional independent breweries predominating. Two changing real ciders are also usually sold. Lunchtime and evening meals are served except on Wednesdays. ➽✿❶♣●☲(51,53,291)📶

SE18: Woolwich

Woolwich Equitable

Equitable House, General Gordon Square, SE18 6AB
✿ 4-11 (1am Fri); 12-1am Sat; 12-10.30 Sun
☎ (020) 8309 8126 ∰ woolwichequitable.com
Volden Session Ale, Pale Ale; 4 changing beers (sourced regionally; often Gipsy Hill, Hackney, Sambrook's) ⊞
A spacious Antic pub, occupying the ground floor of the imposing Grade II-listed former headquarters of the Woolwich Equitable Building Society. The open-plan bar area retains a number of original Art Deco features and is furnished with an eclectic range of settees, old theatre seats, varied tables and padded bench seats. There is also a balcony and a separate small snug. Live music is hosted on some weekends and a quiz is held on Thursdays. ➽❶⏎❺(Woolwich Arsenal)☲📶

SE19: Crystal Palace

Westow House ✅

79 Westow Hill, SE19 1TX
✿ 12-midnight (2am Fri & Sat) ☎ (020) 8670 0654
∰ westowhouse.com
Dark Star Hophead; 7 changing beers (sourced nationally; often Clouded Minds, Gipsy Hill, Volden) ⊞
Large Victorian street-corner pub on the edge of the Crystal Palace triangle, with the clientele reflecting the up and coming nature of the area. The Antic style of vintage shabby chic provides a warm ambience and there is a spacious outdoor seating area. Up to eight real ales are complemented by changing ciders on handpump. It hosts regular live music, particularly on Thursdays, DJs on Fridays, and a quiz on Tuesday evenings. ➽✿❶⏎❺♣●☲✿📶

SE19: Gipsy Hill

Beer Rebellion

126 Gipsy Hill, SE19 1PL
✿ 12-11 ☎ (020) 8670 9034
6 changing beers (sourced regionally; often Late Knights) ℗
Conveniently situated opposite the railway station and run by Late Knights Brewery. For a micropub in a parade of shops, this one packs in everything you would expect in a full-sized version. The small ground floor bar is supplemented by additional seating in the basement. Do not be put off by the keg-style taps located in a Welsh dresser; the top row dispenses cask ales and ciders pumped up from a cellar under the pavement. ❶⏎●☲(322)📶

SE20: Penge

Moon & Stars ℗ ✅

164-166 High Street, SE20 7QS
✿ 8am-11 ☎ (020) 8776 5680
Dark Star Hophead; Greene King Abbot; Ruddles Best Bitter; changing beers ⊞
This popular high-street Wetherspoon pub has a large L-shaped bar with a raised seating area at the rear and many small alcoves suitable for small groups. The bar features 17 handpumps, offering a variety of beer styles, normally with some ales from London microbreweries. The pub hosts regular mini festivals and other beer-related events. ➽✿❶⏎⏎❺(Kent House)☲●☲📶

SE22: East Dulwich

East Dulwich Tavern ✅

1 Lordship Lane, SE22 8EW
✿ 12-midnight (1am Fri & Sat) ☎ (020) 8693 1316
∰ eastdulwichtavern.com
Adnams Lighthouse; Dark Star Hophead; Harveys Sussex Best Bitter; Sharp's Doom Bar; 4 changing beers (sourced regionally; often Franklins, Sambrook's, Volden) ⊞
A proper wedge of a pub in a prominent corner position and the home of the Antic pub company. The interior is classic boozer but contemporised and alive with custom. Previously a hotel, the upper storeys are now offices, although the first floor masonic hall with its own bar opens occasionally for music and events, including a monthly film club. There is usually real cider during summer months, and good-quality food is available. ➽✿❶⏎♣●☲✿📶

Flying Pig ℒ

58-60 East Dulwich Road, SE22 9AX
✿ 12-11 ☎ (020) 7732 7575 ∰ theflyingpiglondon.com
4 changing beers (sourced nationally) ⊞
Former restaurant in a shopping parade which, while now a pub, also offers good-quality, mainly barbecue-style food. Six handpumps dispense a changing selection of real ales and ciders in addition to a large range of other draught and bottled beers (many bottle-conditioned). It is a compact venue but definitely not a micropub, as the large selection of spirits behind the bar should make clear. Forecourt seating is available. Table football, board games and a quiz on Wednesday evenings take place. ➽✿❶⏎♣●☲✿📶

SE23: Forest Hill

Blythe Hill Tavern
319 Stanstead Road, SE23 1JB
✪ 11-11 (midnight Thu-Sat); 12-11 Sun ☎ (020) 8690 5176
⊕ blythehilltavern.org.uk
Dark Star Hophead; Harveys Sussex Best Bitter; 2 changing beers (sourced nationally; often Camerons, Sharp's) Ⓗ
A friendly local rooted in the community, this Victorian corner pub has a regionally important historic interior with an interesting three-room layout and 1920s panelling. The bar staff wear traditional collar and tie. TV screens in two of the bars often show sport. The garden includes a children's play area and is abloom with flowers in summer. Quiz nights are held on Mondays from September to April, and traditional Irish music on Thursdays. Local CAMRA Pub of the Year 2015.
🌑❀≉(Catford/Catford Bridge)●🚃❀

Sylvan Post ❷
24-28 Dartmouth Road, SE23 3XU
✪ 4-11 (midnight Fri); 12-midnight Sat; 12-11 Sun
☎ (020) 8291 5712 ⊕ sylvanpost.com
3 changing beers (sourced locally; often Brixton, Gipsy Hill, Volden) Ⓗ
Various types of ambient lighting add to the quirky feel of this Antic pub, set out like a utilitarian café. A former post office, it retains many of the original features. The two strongrooms have been converted into intimate booths and postal memorabilia decorate the walls. Brunch is a feature of the Saturday menu. A quiz is held on Tuesday evenings and a DJ spins on Friday nights. Most of the guest beers are usually from small London breweries. 🌑🍴&≉♦🚃❀≋

SE25: South Norwood

Joiners' Arms ❷
52 Woodside Green, SE25 5EU
✪ 11-11 (midnight Fri & Sat); 12-11 Sun ☎ (020) 8656 8180
Fuller's London Pride; Purity Mad Goose; Sharp's Doom Bar Ⓗ
This traditional local has one bar divided into three drinking areas – a small snug at one end, a bar area and a seating space at the other end. The interior is filled with brassware and other artefacts, giving a rural atmosphere which has remained largely unchanged since the present tenant arrived in 1972 – making her Croydon's longest serving landlady. Several screens provide sports coverage and popular karaoke evenings are regularly held. Sunday roast is served. ❀🍴🚃🚃(130,197,312)

Addiscombe

Claret Free House
5 Bingham Corner, Lower Addiscombe Road, CR0 7AA
✪ 11.30-11 (11.30 Thu; midnight Fri & Sat); 12-11 Sun
☎ (020) 8656 7452
Palmers Best Bitter; 5 changing beers (sourced nationally) Ⓗ
Small, popular, privately owned free house around the corner from the tram stop and 29 years in this Guide. Well over one million pints of Palmers Best Bitter have been sold here over the years. Five changing beers, mainly from microbreweries, come from all over the UK. See the unique board opposite the bar for beers on and coming next. Cider is fetched from the cellar.
🚃●🚃(130,289,367)

Beckenham

Bricklayers Arms
237 High Street, BR3 1BN
✪ 11-11; 12-10.30 Sun ☎ (020) 8402 0007
⊕ bricklayersarms.co
Harveys Sussex Best Bitter; St Austell Tribute, Proper Job; Young's Special; 1 changing beer Ⓗ
A traditional family-friendly local high-street pub attracting a clientele of all ages. There is an open log fire in winter and a covered outdoor seating area with heaters and TV. Good-value home-cooked food is available (no food Mon). The pub is the local CAMRA 2016 Community Pub of the Year, the first winner of this new award.
🌑🍴≉(Junction/Clock House)🚃(Junction)🚃❀≋

Bexleyheath

Furze Wren ❷
6 Market Place, Broadway Square, DA6 7DY
✪ 9am-midnight ☎ (020) 8298 2590
Greene King Abbot; Ruddles Best Bitter; 6 changing beers (sourced nationally) Ⓗ
Spacious Wetherspoon pub named after a local bird, perhaps better known as the Dartford Warbler. It is at the heart of the shopping area, with a full mix of clientele. Plenty of seating and large windows make it a great place to eat, drink and people-watch. The toilets are on the same level, a rarity for this group. Local history panels are displayed throughout the pub. Ciders are Westons and Gwynt y Ddraig Black Dragon.
Q🌑🍴&♦🚃❀≋

Robin Hood & Little John Ⓛ
78 Lion Road, DA6 8PF
✪ 11-3, 5.30-11; 11-3, 7-11 Sat; 12-4, 7-10.30 Sun
☎ (020) 8303 1128 ⊕ robinhoodbexleyheath.co.uk
Adnams Southwold Bitter, Broadside; Bexley BOB; Fuller's London Pride; Harveys Sussex Best Bitter; Sharp's Doom Bar; 2 changing beers (sourced locally; often Bexley, Shepherd Neame, Westerham) Ⓗ
A back-street local dating from the 1830s, when it was surrounded by fields. Eight real ales are on offer, mostly from independent breweries including the Bexley Brewery. It has a good reputation for its home-cooked food at lunchtimes (no food Sun) with Italian specials, which can be eaten at tables made from old Singer sewing machines. Frequent CAMRA branch Pub of the Year and regional winner three times. Over-21s only.
Q❀🚃(B13)❀

Wrong 'Un Ⓛ ❷
234-236 Broadway, DA6 8AS
✪ 9am-midnight ☎ (020) 8298 0439
Greene King Abbot; Ruddles Best Bitter; Sharp's Doom Bar; 5 changing beers (sourced nationally) Ⓗ
Bexleyheath's first Wetherspoon pub, opened in 1994 in a single-storey former furniture store. There are records of cricket being played locally since 1746 and the unusual pub name is an alternative expression for a googly. Westons Old Rosie cider is stocked. Alcoholic drinks are served from 9am and food until 11pm daily. There are comfortable booths to sit in as well as an open-plan area. Q🌑🍴&≉●🚃❀≋

Blackfen

Broken Drum Ⓛ
308 Westwood Lane, DA15 9PT

🕐 3-10; 12-10 Fri & Sat; 1-4 Sun ☎ 07803 131678
🌐 thebrokendrum.co.uk
3 changing beers (sourced nationally) 🅖
The latest addition to Bexley's growing list of micropubs opened in 2015. Named after an inn in a Terry Pratchett novel, it occupies a former nail bar. It sells real ale and cider on gravity from a stillage in a temperature-controlled room at the rear, viewable through its glazed door. Seating is provided by a settee in each of the bay windows and a variety of tables and chairs. Last orders are 30 minutes before closing time.
Q♣🕯🅿🚻🚆(51,132)🐾

George Staples 🛇
273 Blackfen Road, DA15 8PR
🕐 12-11 (midnight Thu-Sat) ☎ (020) 8850 3181
5 changing beers (sourced nationally; often Adnams, Shepherd Neame) 🅗
Originally the Woodman, it was built in 1845 and was one of the first buildings in Blackfen, then demolished and rebuilt in 1931 when large-scale building began in the area. Refurbished in 2007 and renamed after the original landlord, it is now a comfortable and pleasant large, single-roomed pub. There is a buy six, get one free loyalty scheme. Plenty of outside seating is available.
🐾🕯🕻🅿🚆(51,132)🛜

Bromley

Partridge
194 High Street, BR1 1HE
🕐 12-11 (12.30am Fri & Sat); 12-10.30 Sun
☎ (020) 8464 7656 🌐 partridgebromley.co.uk
Fuller's London Pride, ESB; Gale's HSB; 2 changing beers (sourced nationally; often Adnams, York) 🅗
A former NatWest bank, now a Fuller's Ale and Pie House that has retained many of its original features, including the high ceilings and chandeliers. There are two small snug rooms off the main bar. As well as Fuller's regular range, frequently changing guest beers are normally sold. There is also an extensive food menu including vegetarian choices. The pub is popular with shoppers, sports fans watching football and rugby, and for live music on Saturday nights.
🐾🕯🕻🚆(North/South)🚆

Red Lion 🛇
10 North Road, BR1 3LG
🕐 11-11; 12-11 Sun ☎ (020) 8460 2691
Greene King IPA, Abbot; Harveys Sussex Best Bitter; 2 changing beers (sourced nationally; often Black Sheep, Jennings, Oakham) 🅗
A little gem in the quiet back streets north of Bromley town centre which has been a regular Guide entrant for many years and is well worth seeking out. The pub retains many of its original features including tiling, and has an extensive library of books dominating one wall. The five handpumps include two changing guest beers.
Q🕯🕻🚆(North)♣🚆

Shortlands Tavern
5 Station Road, BR2 0EY
🕐 12-11.30 (midnight Fri & Sat); 12-11 Sun
☎ (020) 8466 0202 🌐 theshortlandstavern.com
St Austell Tribute; Timothy Taylor Landlord; 4 changing beers (sourced nationally; often Bexley, Truman's, Westerham) 🅗
A welcoming pub that serves a changing range of well-kept real ales and has friendly and helpful

staff. There is plenty of seating in the extended interior and the large paved pub garden. Good food is served lunchtimes and evenings (no food Mon). Many events take place here including live music, a book club, painting classes and a knitting group.
Q🕯🕯🕻🚆(Shortlands)♣🕯🚆(227,358,367)

Chelsfield

Five Bells 🛇
Church Road, BR6 7RE
🕐 11.30-11; 12-10.30 Sun ☎ (01689) 821044
🌐 thefivebells-chelsfieldvillage.co.uk
Courage Best Bitter; 3 changing beers (often Adnams, Tonbridge, Wells) 🅗
At the centre of this village community and with a rural feel despite being inside the nearby M25, this popular pub still has a traditional public bar. A separate entrance gives access to the saloon and dining areas. Small local breweries often feature among the guest beers, and in the summer there may be an extra cask on the bar. Easily accessible by bus from Orpington, the pub usually holds two annual beer festivals. It has a large garden.
Q🐾🕯🕯🕻♣🅿🚆(R3)🐾🛜

Chislehurst

Imperial Arms 🛇
Old Hill, BR7 5LZ
🕐 12-11 (11.30 Thu; midnight Fri & Sat; 10.30 Sun)
☎ (020) 3605 7899 🌐 imperialarms.co.uk
Fuller's London Pride; Harveys Sussex Best Bitter; Marston's Pedigree; 1 changing beer 🅗
The pub was stylishly refurbished in 2012 and is now cosy, warm and inviting with two bars. The Catherine Bar is named after the mistress of Napoleon III who stayed here when he was exiled to Chislehurst in 1870. Although the management is rightly proud of the food – with lobster a speciality – the pub emphasised its continuing commitment to real ale with the addition of a fourth handpump in early 2016. Casual drinkers are welcome. Q🐾🕯🕯🕻🚆🚆(162,269)🐾🛜

Crayford

Penny Farthing 🍺 🅛
3 Waterside, DA1 4JJ
🕐 12-3, 5-9.30; 12-10.30 Fri & Sat; 12-3 Sun; closed Mon ☎ 07772 866645
4 changing beers 🅖
The local CAMRA branch's second micropub, opened in 2014, a haven of real ale near the banks of the River Cray, where ale and cider are dispensed direct from the cask in a cold room with a viewing window. A charity fine is levied should your mobile phone ring. Cider is usually from Duddas, although Westons is also often sold. Branch Pub of the Year 2015.
Q🐾🚆♣🕯🚆🚆(96,428,492)🐾

Croydon

Builders Arms
65 Leslie Park Road, CR0 6TP
🕐 12-11 (midnight Fri & Sat) ☎ (020) 8654 1803
🌐 buildersarmscroydon.co.uk
Fuller's London Pride, ESB; 1 changing beer (sourced locally) 🅗
A back-street community local opened in the 19th century. The two bars each have their own

character – the smaller public-style bar with dartboard and a large-screen TV shows sport, and the larger saloon bar with comfortable seating leads to a pleasant garden, with outdoor games available during the warmer months. Events include darts on Monday, quizzes on Tuesday and cribbage on Thursday. Food is served daily and the Sunday roasts are recommended. The pub holds Fuller's Master Cellarman accreditation.

🌜🕭🍴👶🕭⇌(East)🍷(Lebanon Rd)🌳🚍🐾🕭

Dog & Bull 🍷

24 Surrey Street, CR0 1RG
🕭 12-11 (11.30 Fri); 11-11 Sat; 12-10.30 Sun
☎ (020) 8667 9718
Young's Bitter, Special; 2 changing beers (sourced nationally) Ⓗ
Historic Grade II-listed pub, with origins back to the 16th century, in the middle of Croydon's daily street market. The interior has a classic layout – an island bar with two adjoining rooms and seating round the sides. It has an unexpected and attractive walled garden at the rear with bedding plants and seasonal baskets. During the summer there are regular barbecues, with beers served from a separate garden bar. An upstairs function room can be hired. Local CAMRA Pub of the Year 2016.

🕭🍷⇌(West)🍷(George St/Reeves Corner)🚍🕭

George Ⓛ ✪

17-21 George Street, CR0 1LA
🕭 8am-midnight (1am Fri & Sat) ☎ (020) 8649 9077
Dark Star Hophead; Fuller's London Pride; Oakham JHB; Ruddles Best Bitter; Sharp's Doom Bar; Thornbridge Jaipur IPA; 9 changing beers (often Surrey Hills, Tillingbourne) Ⓗ
Taking its name from a former coaching inn that was demolished when Croydon was redeveloped, the George is a large pub in the heart of the town. Two bars with a connected drinking area deliver a constantly changing range of local and national beers alongside other Wetherspoon regulars. The rear drinking area has several booths offering some peace and quiet in an otherwise lively pub; however, on quiet evenings service may be available from the front bar only.

🌜🍷👶⇌(West)🍷(George st/Reeves Corner)🐾🚍🕭

Green Dragon Ⓛ ✪

58 High Street, CR0 1NA
🕭 10-midnight (1am Fri & Sat); 12-10.30 Sun
☎ (020) 8667 0684 🌐 thegreendragoncroydon.co.uk
8 changing beers Ⓗ/Ⓖ
Close to Croydon's street market, this former bank offers a unique and friendly atmosphere. Frequented by all age ranges, it provides a place for relaxed drinking and dining during the day and a more lively experience during the evening. Evidence of the wide range of ales across six handpumps and two gravity casks can be seen from the pumpclips adorning the walls. Music and other events take place upstairs and occasional beer and cider festivals are held.

🌜🍷👶⇌(West)🍷(George St/Reeves Corner)🌳🐾🚍🕭

Oval Tavern ✪

131 Oval Road, CR0 6BR
🕭 12-11 (midnight Fri & Sat) ☎ (020) 8686 6023
Robinsons Trooper; 3 changing beers (often St Austell, Twickenham, Wychwood) Ⓗ

A popular back-street family pub with a good reputation for live music, including jam sessions and acoustic. Tasty home-made food is served; the huge Scotch eggs and sausage rolls are especially recommended. Children and dogs are welcome and there is a large garden and barbecue area to the rear. The decor is unusual; the half-timbering creates an interesting interior with a rural atmosphere. Under new management since 2013, the pub continues to improve and boost promotion of cask ale. 🌜🕭🍴⇌🍷(East)🌳🐾🚍🐾🕭

Skylark ✪

34-36 South End, CR0 1DP
🕭 8am-midnight (1am Fri & Sat) ☎ (020) 8649 9909
Dark Star Hophead; Fuller's London Pride; Greene King Abbot; Ruddles Best Bitter; Sharp's Doom Bar; Shepherd Neame Spitfire; 5 changing beers Ⓗ
Wetherspoon pub named after a well-known and widely appreciated poem by former local resident Gerard Manley Hopkins. It is in the restaurant quarter to the south of the town centre. Wood-panelled walls and bookshelves in a raised seating area give a relaxed atmosphere. The internal decoration focuses in part on the history of London's first airport, at Croydon. There is always a good choice of ales, frequently local and from microbreweries. 🌜🕭🍷👶⇌(South)🐾🚍🕭

Spreadeagle

39-41 Katharine Street, CR0 1NX
🕭 11-11 (midnight Fri & Sat); 12-10.30 Sun
☎ (020) 8781 1134 🌐 spreadeaglecroydon.co.uk
Fuller's Oliver's Island, London Pride, ESB; Gale's HSB; 2 changing beers Ⓗ
Large street-corner pub built in 1893 as the Croydon branch of the United Bank of London. Inside it is spacious, with wood panelling, high ceilings, glass mirrors and an imposing staircase leading to two function rooms upstairs, one regularly used as a 50-seater theatre/cinema. As well as beer from six handpumps, a range of Fuller's bottled beers and quality foreign bottled beers is on offer. The pub has Fuller's Master Cellarman accreditation. Quiz night is Sunday.
🍷👶⇌(East)🍷(George St/Reeves Corner)🚍🕭

Keston

Greyhound ✪

Commonside, BR2 6BP TQ413646
🕭 11-11; 12-10.30 Sun ☎ (01689) 856338
🌐 greyhoundkeston.co.uk
St Austell Tribute; Sharp's Doom Bar; Timothy Taylor Landlord; 3 changing beers (sourced regionally) Ⓗ
A popular pub with an enthusiastic and welcoming landlord. It overlooks the common, is on walking routes including the London Outer Orbital Path, but is also easily accessed by bus from Bromley. The pub is at the heart of village life, with a crowded calendar of local events, including pub games and occasional live music. Regular beer festivals are held. 🕭🍷🌳🐾🅿🚍(146,246)🐾

Orpington

Orpington Liberal Club Ⓛ

7 Station Road, BR6 0RZ
🕭 8-11; 6-11 Fri; 12-3, 7-11 Sat; 12-3, 8-10.30 Sun
☎ (01689) 820882 🌐 orpingtonliberalclub.co.uk
4 changing beers Ⓗ

Free-of-tie club that continues to serve an eclectic range of more than 200 different real ales per year, focusing on microbreweries, with twice-yearly beer festivals. A changing range of real ciders and perries is always available. Regular live folk/blues music nights take place in a separate room. The club has won many local and regional CAMRA awards and was a CAMRA National Club of the Year finalist in 2014 and 2016. CAMRA or NULC membership card required for entry.
Q❄✿⚒♣♠P🍴🚱♻🐾☀

Petts Wood

One Inn the Wood 🍷 🅛
209 Petts Wood Road, BR5 1LA
✪ 12-2.30, 5-9.30 (11 Fri); 11.30-11 Sat; 12-8 Sun; closed Mon ☎ 07799 535982 ⊕ oneinnthewood.co.uk
House beer (by Tonbridge); 4 changing beers (often Kent, Old Dairy, Rockin' Robin) 🄶
Micropub that opened in 2014 in a former wine bar. Its wooden floor, bench seating and large woodland scene on one wall give it a rural feel. Beers are served on gravity from a glass-fronted cold room. Carryouts are available and snacks include locally sourced cheeses, sausage rolls, Scotch eggs and crisps. Local CAMRA branch Pub of the Year 2015 and 2016, it was also the Greater London regional winner in 2015. Q❄🚲◑⚒♠🍴☀

Sovereign of the Seas 🅛 ✅
109-111 Queensway, BR5 1DG
✪ 9am-11 (11.30 Fri & Sat) ☎ (01689) 891606
Greene King Abbot; Ruddles Best Bitter; Sharp's Doom Bar; 7 changing beers (sourced regionally; often Kent) 🄷
A popular, large Wetherspoon pub, centrally located in Petts Wood, with 12 handpumps offering a changing range of guest beers plus cider. Seating is of various styles, including alcoves, which gives the pub a cosy feel. Local photographs of historic interest line the walls, including pictures of the ship after which the pub is named and of former local resident William Willett, the daylight saving time campaigner. ❄✿◑♿⚒♠🍴☀

South Croydon

Crown & Sceptre
32 Junction Road, CR2 6RB
✪ 12-11 (midnight Fri & Sat); 12-10.30 Sun
☎ (020) 8688 8037 ⊕ crownandsceptresouthcroydon.co.uk
Fuller's London Pride, ESB; 2 changing beers (sourced locally; often Fuller's, Gale's) 🄷
Quiet, traditional side-street pub, with its name etched into one of the front windows. The single bar has been extended towards a garden at the rear and the walls carry pictures of local scenes and an impressive brewery mirror. The pub participates in local community events such as the summer street carnival, and a cabinet of trophies attests to the local golfing society's successes. Beers come from the Fuller's range and home-cooked food is served. Quiz night is Thursday.
❄✿◑♿⚒♣P🍴☀

Welling

Door Hinge 🅛
11 Welling High Street, DA16 1TR
✪ 3-9 (10 Fri); 12-10 Sat; 12-3 Sun; closed Mon ☎ 07956 845509

3 changing beers (sourced nationally) 🄶
A welcome breath of fresh air on the local pub scene and handy for the football ground, London's first permanent micropub opened in 2013 in part of a former electrical wholesalers. Normally at least three beers are available, dispensed from within a glass-fronted cold room. The cosy bar encourages conversation among previous strangers. Ciders come from various sources. Local CAMRA Pub of the Year and Greater London regional winner in 2014. Q🍴🚲♠

SOUTH-WEST LONDON
SW1: Belgravia

Antelope
22-24 Eaton Terrace, SW1W 8EZ
✪ 12-11 (11.30 Fri & Sat; 10 Sun) ☎ (020) 7824 8512
⊕ antelope-eaton-terrace.co.uk
Fuller's London Pride, Bengal Lancer, ESB; Gale's Seafarers Ale 🄷
Dating back to 1827, this Fuller's venue spent several years as a Nicholson's pub until 2005. Original features are preserved including etched-glass windows, a side room used as a snug, and the central bar. This is an upmarket house and the clientele consists mainly of local professionals. The pub plays cricket matches against the Churchill Arms (Notting Hill). The upstairs bar and side room can be hired for functions. Q❄◑⊖(Sloane Sq)🚲

Star Tavern 🅛
6 Belgrave Mews West, SW1X 8HT
✪ 11-11; 12-11 Sat; 12-10.30 Sun ☎ (020) 7235 3019
⊕ star-tavern-belgravia.co.uk
Fuller's London Pride, ESB; Gale's Seafarers Ale; 2 changing beers (often Fuller's) 🄷
Situated in a mews and near embassies, and rich in the history of the powerful and famous, it is rumoured that the Great Train Robbery was planned here. Now it is a popular Fuller's pub where local residents, business people and embassy staff rub shoulders with casual visitors. Sometimes a special Fuller's beer can be found. The dining room is upstairs, bookable for functions. The Star has featured in every edition of the Guide. Q❄◑⊖(Hyde Park Corner/Knightsbridge)🚲☀

SW1: Pimlico

Cask Pub & Kitchen 🅛
6 Charlwood Street, SW1V 2EE
✪ 12-11 (10.30 Sun) ☎ (020) 7630 7225
⊕ caskpubandkitchen.com
Dark Star Hophead; 9 changing beers 🄷
Formerly the Pimlico Tram, this pub was converted to a beer destination venue by owners who have since taken over several more premises in the South-east. Ten handpumps serve real ales from microbreweries such as Arbor Ales and Dark Star, and a vast range of bottled beers from the UK and around the world complements some unusual draught choices. Burgers feature on the weekday menu, with Sunday roasts until late afternoon. A regular local CAMRA Pub of the Year finalist.
Q◑⚒(Victoria)⊖🍴

SW1: St James's

Red Lion ★ ✅
2 Duke of York Street, SW1Y 6JP

🌀 11.30-11; closed Sun ☎ (020) 7321 0782
🌐 redlionmayfair.co.uk
Fuller's Oliver's Island, London Pride, ESB; Gale's Seafarers Ale, HSB; 1 changing beer (often Fuller's) Ⓗ
Close to the upmarket shops in Jermyn Street, this is a deservedly celebrated little gem, worth visiting just for its nationally important historic pub interior featuring spectacular Victorian etched mirrors and glass. The Grade II-listed building dates from 1821 and was given a new frontage in 1871. With little space inside, visitors often spill onto the pavement. Food is served 12-3pm (4pm Sat).
◑⊖(Green Park/Piccadilly Circus)🚆 🛜

SW1: Victoria

Cask & Glass ✅
39 Palace Street, SW1E 5HN
🌀 11-11; 12-8 Sat; closed Sun ☎ (020) 7834 7630
Shepherd Neame Master Brew, Spitfire; 2 changing beers (often Shepherd Neame) Ⓗ
First licensed in 1862 as the Duke of Cambridge, this attractive, one-room pub on the route between Buckingham Palace and Westminster Cathedral, adorned with flowers in summer, is a haven for tourists, office workers and local residents. The wood-panelled bar has pictures of local scenes and politicians. Look for the bull's-eye windows and the two paintings of the pub on the way to the toilets. A cosy place for a pint after (or instead of) visiting the sights.
Q🌼◑⇌⊖(St James's Park/Victoria)🚆 🛜

Wetherspoon's
Unit 5, Upper Concourse, Victoria Station, Terminus Place, SW1V 1JT
🌀 6am-midnight; 8am-11 Sun ☎ (020) 7931 0445
Fuller's London Pride, ESB; Greene King IPA, Abbot; 8 changing beers Ⓗ
Overlooking the station concourse and accessed mainly by escalators, this pub has a bright café-bar atmosphere. Features include blue and cream tiling, two curved bars with marble-style tops and banquettes along the opposite side. Two sets of six handpumps dispense four regular beers and eight changing guest ales. TV screens show times of train departures. Note that British Transport police sometimes close the bar when football fans are due. Q🏃◑&⇌⊖🌢🚆 🛜

SW1: Westminster

Buckingham Arms
62 Petty France, SW1H 9EU
🌀 11-11 (6 Sat) ☎ (020) 7222 3386
Young's Bitter, Special; 1 changing beer (often London) Ⓗ
Said to have once been a hat shop, this pub opened in the 1720s as the Bell, was renamed the Black Horse in the 1740s, rebuilt in 1898 and renamed again in 1901. Substantially renovated in recent years, it has appeared in every edition of the Guide. A mix of modern and traditional seats and tables, high and low, draws civil servants, visitors and the occasional MP from the Houses of Parliament. Open Sundays (11-6pm) from end March through summer. 🏃◑▶⊖(St James's Park)🚆

Speaker Ⓛ ✅
46 Great Peter Street, SW1P 2HA
🌀 12-11; closed Sat & Sun ☎ (020) 7222 1749

Timothy Taylor Landlord; Young's London Gold; 3 changing beers (sourced nationally) Ⓗ
A comfortable wood-panelled one-bar local decorated with parliamentary caricatures. Dating from at least 1729, first as the Castle, renamed Elephant & Castle around 1800, and the Speaker in 1999, it belongs to the erstwhile Devil's Acre, a notorious slum next to the world's first public gasworks. The pub now welcomes residents from local estates and workers from government and television offices who enjoy the five beers and home-made food. No music, TV or children. Occasional beer festivals are held.
Q◑▶⊖(St James's Park)🚆 🛜

SW2: Streatham Hill

Crown & Sceptre Ⓛ ✅
2A Streatham Hill, SW2 4AH
🌀 9am-midnight (1am Fri & Sat) ☎ (020) 8671 0843
Greene King Abbot; Ruddles Best Bitter; Sharp's Doom Bar; 5 changing beers (often Sambrook's) Ⓗ
A landmark building that retains its original Truman exterior tiling thanks to the local history society. Divided into distinct areas, this spacious pub was the first such Wetherspoon conversion in South-west London, opening in 1990. The manager is in his 10th year here and cask beer is important, with four or five changing guests generally including a wide range of strengths and styles. TVs are silent except for major sporting events. Sunday is quiz night. Q🏃🌼◑▶⇌🌢P🚆 🛜

SW4: Clapham

Craft Beer Co
128 Clapham Manor Street, SW4 6ED
🌀 4-11 (midnight Fri); 12-midnight Sat; 12-11 Sun
☎ (020) 7622 2894
Kent Pale; 9 changing beers Ⓗ
The old Manor Arms became the fifth in the Craft Beer Co pub chain. Ten handpumps serve its regular Kent house beer alongside guest ales selected from reliable microbreweries and an array of other draught offerings. Beer is priced according to its strength. A central square bar has high tables and stools at the front with padded settles, tables and chairs to the sides and rear. The large garden is popular in good weather and for beer festivals.
🌼◑▶⊖(Common/High Street/North)🚌🚆 🛜

King & Co
100 Clapham Park Road, SW4 7BZ
🌀 4-11 (midnight Thu; 1am Fri); 12-1am Sat; 12-11 Sun
☎ (020) 7498 1971 🌐 thekingandco.uk
5 changing beers (sourced nationally) Ⓗ
Lively pub far enough from the centre of Clapham to avoid the bustle. Inside is quirky furniture reminiscent of schooldays and a functional island bar with vibrant neon lighting. The low ceiling and candle lighting add a more intimate feel to the wooden-floored seating areas. Heated decking is provided at the front for smokers and is pleasant on warm evenings. Food is available from pop-up providers in the pub's kitchen, changing monthly.
◑▶⊖(Common)🚆 🛜

Prince of Wales Ⓛ
38 Old Town, SW4 0LB
🌀 4-midnight (1am Fri); 1-1am Sat; 1-11 Sun
☎ (020) 7622 3530 🌐 powsw4.com

Harveys Sussex Best Bitter; Sambrook's Wandle Ale; 1 changing beer Ⓗ
Single-bar corner pub distinguished at night by the neon POW signs and adorned inside by hanging traffic lights, old school desks, stuffed animals and all manner of bric-a-brac. Alongside the Harveys, on draught are a local Sambrook's beer, occasionally Timothy Taylor Landlord, and Millwhites cask cider. An interesting bottled beer selection and real ciders in boxes are also available. A free quiz is held on Thursday evening and pizzas (ordered from a local takeaway) are available in the evenings.
☎🏵️⊖(Common)🍴🚍🐾📶

Rose & Crown ✅
2 The Polygon, SW4 0JG
🕒 3-11 (1am Fri); 12-1am Sat; 12-midnight Sun
☎ (020) 7720 8265
Greene King IPA, St Edmunds, Abbot; 5 changing beers (often Dark Star, Greene King, Purity) Ⓗ
Across the road from the Prince of Wales, this busy, friendly drinkers' pub retains its fine, original tiled Simonds Brewery façade. The compact, L-shaped single bar comprises distinct areas including a snug corner behind pillars. Benches on the ample, recently refurbished pavement at the front provide seating for smokers. Sometimes there may be as many as eight beers on handpump. At quieter times you may get to meet Beyonce and Betty, the resident cats. 🏵️⊖(Common)🚍🐾

SW5: Earls Court

King's Head Ⓛ
17 Hogarth Place, SW5 0QT
🕒 11-11 (10.30 Sun) ☎ (020) 7373 5239
🌐 kingsheadearlscourt.co.uk
Fuller's London Pride, ESB; 1 changing beer (often London Beer Factory, Portobello) Ⓗ
A 1937 rebuild of the oldest (circa 17th century) licensed premises in the area, this is a friendly corner pub off the busy Earl's Court Road, recently refurbished in a modern style with a wooden floor and coloured tiling around the bar. There is comfortable sofa seating, plus high stools around tall tables. Quiz night is Monday and there is live music on special occasions.
☎🌑🚻🛤️≠(West Brompton)⊖🐾📶

SW6: Fulham

Durell Arms Ⓛ ✅
704 Fulham Road, SW6 5SB
🕒 12-11 (1am Fri & Sat) ☎ (020) 7736 3014
🌐 durellarmsfulham.com
Greene King IPA; 3 changing beers (often Portobello, Sambrook's, Truman's) Ⓗ
Making a second consecutive appearance in the Guide is this spacious Greene King Metropolitan corner pub with an L-shaped drinking area. A large rear room, with mouldings and mirrors giving an air of Victorian decadence, can be hired for functions. There is a big screen for sporting events. Attractive local ales complement Greene King and national guests, and it is busy on Sundays for the excellent roast. 🏵️🌑🚻⊖(Parsons Green)♣🚍🐾

SW6: Parsons Green

White Horse Ⓛ ✅
1-3 Parsons Green, SW6 4UL
🕒 9.30am-11.30 (midnight Thu-Sat) ☎ (020) 7736 2115
🌐 whitehorsesw6.com
Adnams Broadside; Oakham JHB; 4 changing beers (often Harveys) Ⓗ
Destination Mitchells & Butlers pub that normally boasts five guest beers on handpump and an international selection of bottled beers. Regular beer and food matching events take place as well as four annual beer festivals, including the not-to-be-missed Old Ale Festival in late November. The pub can get busy when Chelsea FC are playing at home, but the upstairs area is a good place to escape the crowds. Q🏵️🌑⊖🚍(22,424)🐾📶

SW7: Gloucester Road

Queen's Arms ✅
30 Queens Gate Mews, SW7 5QL
🕒 12-11; 12-10.30 Sun ☎ (020) 7823 9293
🌐 thequeensarmskensington.co.uk
Fuller's London Pride; Sharp's Doom Bar; 6 changing beers Ⓗ
Lovely corner mews pub, well worth seeking out for its real ales and its large range of interesting draught and bottled beers. The L-shaped room features wood floors and panelling. The clientele reflects the location – well-heeled locals, students from Imperial College and musicians from, and visitors to, the nearby Albert Hall. The food menu and specials are of superior quality.
Q🌑🚻⊖🍴🚍🐾📶

SW7: South Kensington

Anglesea Arms ✅
15 Selwood Terrace, SW7 3QG
🕒 11-11; 12-10.30 Sun ☎ (020) 7373 7960
🌐 angleseaarms.com
Greene King IPA, Abbot; 4 changing beers (sourced regionally) Ⓗ
A real ale stalwart of CAMRA's early years, this hostelry was built in 1827 and was a Meux tied house for more than a century. Now a Grade II-listed Greene King Metropolitan pub, it has the air of a country inn, with its hanging baskets and terrace. The bar features a large Salt & Co brewery mirror and various paintings, prints, photographs and cartoons. Charles Dickens and Andrew Bonar Law were locals. Q☎🏵️🌑⊖🚍📶

SW9: Brixton

Trinity Arms
45 Trinity Gardens, SW9 8DR
🕒 11-11 (midnight Fri); 12-midnight Sat; 12-11 Sun
☎ (020) 7274 4544 🌐 trinityarms.co.uk
Young's Bitter, London Gold, Special; 1 changing beer (often Young's) Ⓗ
In a quiet square off Brixton High Road and the busy Acre Lane, this traditional, friendly and comfortable pub, with its central horseshoe-shaped bar, was extensively refurbished by Young's in summer 2016 to include additional dining upstairs. The front patio and a rear garden featuring beach huts provide space for outdoor drinking. It is popular in the evening and busy on Brixton Academy nights. Real ale is a big attraction. Families are welcome until 7.30pm; food is available until 10pm. Q☎🏵️🌑≠⊖♣🚍🐾📶

SW10: Chelsea

Sporting Page
6 Camera Place, SW10 0BH
✪ 11-11 (10.30 Sun) ☎ (020) 7349 0455
Sambrook's Wandle Ale; 5 changing beers (often Moncada, Truman's) Ⓗ
A comfortable single-bar gastro-pub with a friendly feel, now one of the small Food & Fuel London chain. It was previously known as the Red Anchor, built in 1974 on the site of the Odell Arms (1856-1971); its current name dates from 1989. Six handpumps serve real ales, often including local brews. An interesting wine selection complements the food offering. Sporting-themed prints and memorabilia adorn the walls. Quiz night is Sunday. Q❶●🖪❀

SW11: Clapham Junction

Beehive ✓
197 St Johns Hill, SW11 1TH
✪ 12-midnight (1am Fri & Sat) ☎ (020) 7450 1756
Fuller's London Pride, ESB; 2 changing beers (often Fuller's) Ⓗ
A recent tasteful and elegant refurbishment, and enthusiastic new management, have revitalised this classic local. Some bench seating has been restored and a big TV screen shows major sporting events. The rear area is now available for functions. The food, although limited, is excellent. Blankets are thoughtfully supplied for guests who wish to sit outside. Look for the wonderful framed housing survey map of SW London dating from 1898 – before the Luftwaffe and town planners altered things somewhat! ⅏❶➤⊖🖪❀☂

Eagle Ale House Ⓛ
104 Chatham Road, SW11 6HG
✪ 4 (3 Fri; 12 Sat)-11; 12-10.30 Sun ☎ (020) 7228 2328
⊕ eaglealehouse.co.uk
Surrey Hills Shere Drop; 7 changing beers (often Downton, Hackney, Pilgrim) Ⓗ
Homely, traditional pub, a short uphill walk from Northcote Road, providing local regulars with a place for lively conversation. Less frequent visitors and dogs also get a friendly welcome. In recent years it has been at the heart of the Fair Deal for Your Local campaign. Twice the local CAMRA Pub of the Year and three times the runner-up, it shows major sporting events on three TV screens and has a heated marquee in the garden.
⅏❀🖪(319,G1)❀☂

Falcon ★ Ⓛ ✓
2 St Johns Hill, SW11 1RU
✪ 11-11.30 (midnight Fri & Sat); 11-11 Sun
☎ (020) 7228 2076
Sharp's Doom Bar; St Austell Nicholson's Pale Ale; changing beers (often Sambrook's, Truman's) Ⓗ
This recently refurbished landmark building dating from 1887 contains a nationally important historic pub interior noteworthy for its island servery, screens, glasswork and the longest bar in the country. The wide range of ales from the Nicholson's list often includes dark beers and choices from London microbreweries. Thatchers or Westons ciders are also served on handpump. The corner closest to Clapham Junction is nearly always busy. The rear seating area is reserved exclusively for diners. ⅏❶⊖●🖪❀☂

Four Thieves
51 Lavender Gardens, SW11 1DJ
✪ 12-midnight (2am Fri & Sat); 12-10.30 Sun
☎ (020) 7223 6927 ⊕ fourthieves.pub
3 changing beers (often Laine) Ⓗ
This pub reopened in 2014 after major refurbishment and the installation of a brewery by Laine Pub Company. The Laine's beers here, for example Light, Best and Porter, are now generally brewed on the premises, where a gin distillery uses lavender grown on-site. The pub comprises a main bar, split over two levels, the Boat House that hosts much of the entertainment, and a gin yard, with heated and covered areas. ❀❶➤⊖🖪☂

Powder Keg Diplomacy
147 St John's Hill, SW11 1TQ
✪ 4-11; 10-midnight Sat; 10-11 Sun ☎ (020) 7450 6457
⊕ powderkegdiplomacy.co.uk
3 changing beers (sourced nationally; often By the Horns, Five Points, Siren) Ⓗ
This gastro pub, kitted out in colonial style, is immensely popular. Three handpumps dispense real ale from innovative microbreweries, often from London. Six draught beers, coming from the likes of Kernel, always include one stout or porter, and about 50 bottled beers are available from around the world. Meet the Brewer events are held from time to time. High-class but reasonably priced restaurant meals include a Sunday brunch. An exemplar for the future of the British pub.
⅏❀❶➤⊖🖪❀☂

SW12: Balham

Nightingale Ⓛ
97 Nightingale Lane, SW12 8NX
✪ 12 (11 Sat)-midnight; 11-11 Sun ☎ (020) 8673 1637
⊕ thenightingalebalham.co.uk
Sambrook's Wandle Ale; Young's Bitter, Special; 1 changing beer (sourced locally) Ⓗ
Built in 1853 by Thomas Wallis and worth going out of your way to find, this friendly community pub serves excellent beers and is a huge contributor to local charities with its well-established annual walk. Long-serving bar staff welcome all customers. The conservatory is child-friendly and the back garden is a summer suntrap. The pub retains a dartboard despite recent refurbishment. A regular local CAMRA Pub of the Year finalist.
Q⅏❀❶♿➤(Wandsworth Common)⊖(Clapham South)🖪(G1)❀☂

SW16: Streatham

Railway Ⓛ ✓
2 Greyhound Lane, SW16 5SD
✪ 12-11 (midnight Thu; 1am Fri & Sat) ☎ (020) 8769 9448
⊕ therailwaysw16.co.uk
Sambrook's Wandle Ale; 4 changing beers (sourced regionally; often Belleville, Redemption, Twickenham) Ⓗ
A busy community pub showcasing London microbreweries, both in cask and in bottle. Often shortlisted for the local CAMRA Pub of the Year competition, it hosts a wide range of activities including a quiz on Tuesdays, a farmers' market on the second and fourth Saturdays of the month, and a comedy night in the back room on the last Sunday. There is outside seating on the pavement in front and in the yard at the rear.
⅏❀❶♿➤(Common)🖪(60,118)❀☂

SW17: Summerstown

By the Horns Brewery Tap

25 Summerstown, SW17 0BQ

✪ 4-10 (11 Thu); 5-11 Fri; 12-10 Sat; 12-9 Sun; closed Mon

☎ (020) 3417 7338 ⊕ bythehorns.co.uk

3 changing beers (sourced locally) Ⓗ

A brewery taproom and adjoining beer hall open Tuesday to Sunday. Three cask beers are usually served from its own range, plus other draught and bottled choices and rotating guests from small breweries. There is plenty of space in the bar and the enclosed car park outside. Major sporting events shown on large projection TVs are popular; it is often advisable to reserve your place in advance. Street food from local suppliers is available. Brewery tours and private event hire are offered. ७※P◻※

SW17: Tooting

Antelope ✓

76 Mitcham Road, SW17 9NG

✪ 4-11 (midnight Thu; 1am Fri); 12-1am Sat; 12-11 Sun

☎ (020) 8672 3888 ⊕ theantelopepub.com

Volden Pale Ale; 7 changing beers Ⓗ

A cavernous Victorian Antic pub featuring a panelled bar at the front and a large dining area at the back, with a huge separate room for TV sport and functions and a walled seating area outside. Friendly staff serve a frequently changing variety of ales including one from Volden, and there is food in the evening. It hosts a weekly quiz, a weekly vinyl night, comedy nights and other special events. ७※❶ㅈ⇌⊖(Broadway)●◻※☞

Wheatsheaf Ⓛ

2 Upper Tooting Road, SW17 7PG

✪ 12-midnight (1am Fri & Sat); 12-11 Sun

☎ (020) 8672 2805 ⊕ thewheatsheafsw17.com

5 changing beers (often Hackney, Truman's, Wimbledon) Ⓗ

A massive late-Victorian coaching house at Tooting Bec crossroads with huge pillars, arches and fireplace, a back room ideal for occasional live music gigs, and a small beer garden to the rear. Now run by Urban Pubs & Bars, it promotes local cask beers along with others from further away. As an Asset of Community Value with two Article 4 Directions, this pub is famously protected from opportunist development activity. ७※❶�⊖(Bec)♣◻

SW18: Wandsworth

Cat's Back ✓

86-88 Point Pleasant, SW18 1NN

✪ 12-midnight (10 Mon); 12-10 Sun ☎ (020) 8617 3448

⊕ thecatsback.com

Harveys Sussex Best Bitter; 3 changing beers (often Harveys) Ⓗ

Harveys' first South-west London pub is an elegant, restrained refurbishment of a wonderful back-street local and a welcome survivor among the mass development of luxury riverside apartments that surround it. The pub offers occasional live music (folk, jazz, classical) and a film show on Thursday and Sunday evenings. The food offering is excellent, with Sunday lunch cited by a major London paper as one of the 10 best in the capital. ७※❶ㅅ♣◻(220,270,485)※☞

Old Sergeant Ⓛ ✓

104 Garratt Lane, SW18 4DJ

✪ 12-11 (midnight Fri & Sat) ☎ (020) 8874 4099

Sambrook's Wandle Ale; Young's Bitter, Special; 2 changing beers (often Sambrook's) Ⓗ

This friendly local has been voted the best place to bring your dog for a drink. Table menus for the excellent food include an informative beer list. The John Young Room upstairs displays treasured memorabilia of the Wandsworth brewery. Quiz night is Monday. The pub achieved a Guinness World Record in 2014 for the longest barbecue marathon. ※❶ㅅ◻(44,270)※☞

SW19: Merton

Trafalgar ☖ Ⓛ

23 High Path, SW19 2JY

✪ 12-11 ☎ (020) 8542 5342 ⊕ trafalgarfreehouse.co.uk

Downton Quadhop; Surrey Hills Shere Drop; 4 changing beers (sourced nationally; often Binghams, By the Horns, Hop Stuff) Ⓗ

A narrow, one-bar, street-corner house, the main part dating from the 1860s. The extension is from 1906, furnished with farmhouse chairs and tables. Alongside the cask choice is a variety of bottled and changing KeyKeg beers (which may be real ale – check with staff) and at least one real cider, often Lilley's. Cold and hot snacks are available until 10pm. There is regular live music. Local CAMRA Pub of the Year 2015. ☖(Morden Rd)⊖(South Wimbledon)♣●◻※☞

SW19: Wimbledon

Crooked Billet

14-15 Crooked Billet, SW19 4RQ

✪ 11-11 (midnight Fri & Sat); 12-10.30 Sun

☎ (020) 8946 4942 ⊕ thecrookedbilletwimbledon.com

Courage Directors; Sharp's Doom Bar; Young's Bitter, Special; 2 changing beers Ⓗ

A homely late 18th-century building, extended in 1969 into an adjacent cottage. The wood-panelled walls are adorned with old prints and photographs and some local painters' works. There are flagstone and wooden floors, a variety of seating and a real fire in winter. Good food is served throughout, including in the intimate restaurant room at the back. Quiz night is Monday. Beer is served in plastic glasses to take outside in the summer. ७※❶◻(200)※☞

Hand in Hand Ⓛ

7 Crooked Billet, SW19 4RQ

✪ 11-11 (midnight Fri & Sat); 12-11 Sun ☎ (020) 8946 5720

⊕ thehandinhandwimbledon.co.uk

Young's Bitter, Special; 3 changing beers (often Sambrook's, Twickenham, Young's) Ⓗ

Celebrated single-bar ale house on the edge of Wimbledon Common with separate drinking areas and a variety of seating. At least three guest beers usually include one or more from each of Sambrook's and Twickenham. Children are welcome in the family room. This is a great place to eat, with beer included in several recipes. There is poker on Mondays, a quiz on Tuesdays and occasional beer tastings. Q७※❶ㅅ♣◻(200)※

Wibbas Down Inn Ⓛ ✓

6-12 Gladstone Road, SW19 1QT

✪ 8am-midnight (1am Fri & Sat) ☎ (020) 8540 6788

Greene King IPA, Abbot; Oakham JHB; Sharp's Doom Bar; changing beers Ⓗ

An enormous two-bar Wetherspoon pub stretching from Gladstone Road to Russell Road, unusual in that it was converted in 1995 from a Tesco supermarket. It is a favourite haunt for drinkers owing to its low prices, and the back bar is handy for Wimbledon Theatre. Fourteen guest beers change frequently, often coming from local breweries, and a Brewery of the Month is showcased. Up to 50 beers are available at the frequent festivals. Q❄☀🕮◑🕭≠♋⊖●🖥🎧≈🛜

Carshalton

Hope ▼ 🄻

48 West Street, SM5 2PR

❄ 12-11; 12-10.30 Sun ☎ (020) 8240 1255

🌐 hopecarshalton.co.uk

Downton New Forest Ale; Windsor & Eton Knight of the Garter; 5 changing beers (often Kent, Magic Rock, Siren) Ⓗ

Popular traditional free house and community hub fully owned by its customers. Five of the handpumps dispense a rapidly changing range of great beers from the country's best breweries, and frequent themed beer festivals offer many more, all in pint, one-third and two-third pint lined glasses. With no music except traditional jam sessions and no machines, beer dominates. Lunches are served until 3pm, pot meals until 10pm. Local CAMRA Pub of the Year 2016. Q❄☀🕮◑≈♣♠P🖥🚃🎧≈

Sun 🄻

4 North Street, SM5 2HU

❄ 12-11 (10 Mon; midnight Fri & Sat); 12-10.30 Sun

☎ (020) 8773 4549 🌐 thesuncarshalton.com

6 changing beers (sourced nationally; often Arbor, Brighton Bier Co, Rooster's) Ⓗ

A handsome and imposing Victorian pub, built as a railway hotel. It was given a tasteful makeover several years ago and has not looked back since. Several distinct areas accommodate diners, with excellent food, and discerning drinkers, with a wide beer choice on six handpumps. In summer the large courtyard garden with its continental-style veranda is popular. Quiz night is Tuesday. ❄☀🕮◑≈♣♠🎧≈

Windsor Castle ✅

378 Carshalton Road, SM5 3PT

❄ 12-11 (11.30 Fri & Sat); 12-10 Sun ☎ (020) 8669 1191

🌐 windsorcastlepub.com

Long Man Best Bitter; Shepherd Neame Kent's Best, Spitfire, Bishops Finger; 2 changing beers Ⓗ

Prominently placed on a busy crossroads, this large pub has a single bar with a restaurant area at one end. At the rear a covered courtyard serves as a smoking area and leads to a separate function room and a garden. Shepherd Neame beers on one bank of handpumps are accompanied by guest ales on another, sourced from local microbreweries. Live music and quiz nights feature regularly. ☀🕮◑≈(Beeches)●P🖥(154,407)🎧≈

Kingston

Boaters Inn 🄻 ✅

Canbury Gardens, Lower Ham Road, KT2 5AU (off A307 via Woodside Rd)

❄ 11-11 ☎ (020) 8541 4672 🌐 boaterskingston.com

Greene King IPA; 4 changing beers (sourced nationally) Ⓗ

Attractive, modern Greene King Metropolitan pub on a towpath in riverside gardens. The L-shaped bar serves two levels – one set out for diners but not exclusively for their use, the other with comfortable seating. Guest beers include local ones. Tables on the veranda and in the patio garden overlook the Thames. It can get busy in summer but the surrounding park tends to be used as an overspill. Phone ahead if you wish to use the pub's moorings. ☀🕮◑🕭🖥(65)🎧≈

King's Tun 🄻 ✅

153-157 Clarence Street, KT1 1QT

❄ 8am-midnight (1am Fri & Sat) ☎ (020) 8547 3827

Greene King IPA, Abbot; Oakham Citra; Sharp's Doom Bar; 8 changing beers (sourced locally) Ⓗ

In a building that was originally the Empire Theatre, this large Wetherspoon pub takes its name from the town where seven Saxon kings were crowned. It attracts all during the day, with a younger crowd in the evenings, particularly on Friday and Saturday nights, when there is a disco from 9pm. A long bar at the rear serves two separate seating areas. There is also a good-sized bar upstairs. Four changing ciders are sold. Alcoholic drinks served from 9am. ☀◑🕭≠♠🎧≈

Willoughby Arms 🄻

47 Willoughby Road, KT2 6LN

❄ 10.30-midnight; 12-midnight Sun ☎ (020) 8546 4236

🌐 thewilloughbyarms.com

Sharp's Doom Bar; Surrey Hills Shere Drop; Twickenham Grandstand Bitter; Upham Punter; 3 changing beers (often Park, Timothy Taylor, Weltons) Ⓗ

Friendly Victorian back-street local, divided into a sports bar with games and large-screen TV, and a quieter lounge area. At least one of the changing beers is locally brewed. The upstairs function room, where the Yardbirds rehearsed in the '60s, can be hired. Pizzas and pies are cooked to order. The spacious garden includes a covered, heated and lit smoking area with large TV screen. Quiz night is Sunday. Q❄☀🕮♠♣●🖥(371,K5)🎧≈

Richmond

Roebuck ✅

130 Richmond Hill, TW10 6RN

❄ 12-11 (midnight Fri & Sat); 12-10.30 Sun

☎ (020) 8948 2329

Greene King IPA; 6 changing beers (often Binghams, Downton, Surrey Hills) Ⓗ

Close to Richmond Park Gate, this 200-year-old pub overlooks the World Heritage view of Petersham Meadows and the River Thames. Air-conditioned and Taylor Walker branded, it has one regular beer, six rotated guest beers and one real cider on tap. There is an upstairs bar (weekends only) and a large function room. The outside terrace across the road can also be used by patrons. Food is served until 10pm. ☀◑🕭≠🖥(65,371)🎧≈

Waterman's Arms ✅

12 Water Lane, TW9 1TJ

❄ 12-11 ☎ (020) 8940 2893

Twickenham Naked Ladies; Young's Bitter, Special; 2 changing beers (often Truman's, Twickenham, Young's) Ⓗ

One of the oldest pubs in Richmond, dating back to at least 1660 and rebuilt in 1898, tucked away

down a side street leading to the Thames. Retaining its Victorian two-bar layout, it is cosy and full of character, wood-panelled throughout and with etched-glass windows. Traditional pub food, Sunday lunches and Thai specials are served daily. A Monday music club meets upstairs.
Q ⛄🕮🍴⊖🖳🌺

Surbiton

Antelope 🅛 ✅
87 Maple Road, KT6 4AW
🕔 12-11 (11.30 Fri & Sat); 12-10.30 Sun ☎ (020) 8399 5565
🌐 theantelope.co.uk
10 changing beers (sourced nationally; often Big Smoke) Ⓗ
The home of the Big Smoke Brewery, located in the yard at the rear, with at least three of its beers usually available. It has a fairly spacious split-level L-shaped interior with a real fire in winter, and a rear covered courtyard. Home-cooked food includes Sunday roasts. Occasional beer festivals and Meet the Brewer events are held. It gets busy at weekends and most evenings, when thirsty commuters invade. Four changing ciders are kept.
🏵🕮🍴🚲🖳🛜

Coronation Hall 🅛 ✅
St Marks Hill, KT6 4LQ (b3370)
🕔 8am-midnight ☎ (020) 8390 6164
Greene King IPA, Abbot; Sharp's Doom Bar; Young's Special; 6 changing beers (often Sambrook's, Surrey Hills, Twickenham) Ⓗ
Popular Wetherspoon pub, handy for homeward-bound commuters, formerly a music hall, cinema, bingo hall and short-lived nudist health club. The decor is themed on a mix of movie stars, film artefacts, the coronation of George V and the planets. Guest beers often come from local microbreweries, and occasional local beer festivals are held. Two or three changing ciders are kept. Alcohol is served from 9am. Q🏵🕮🍴🚲🖳🛜

Lamb 🅛
73 Brighton Road, KT6 5NF (on A243)
🕔 12-11 (midnight Thu-Sat) ☎ (020) 8390 9229
🌐 lambsurbiton.co.uk
Hop Back Summer Lightning; Robinsons Trooper; Surrey Hills Ranmore; 1 changing beer (sourced regionally) Ⓗ
Small family-run free house at the heart of the local community. Built in 1850 and formerly four separate rooms, it retains the original horseshoe-shaped bar. The changing beer is from a micro, sometimes local, and family brewer. Specialist cheeses are available, with cheeseboards all day Friday to Sunday. Live bands play original music Wednesday to Sunday. ⛄🏵🚲🖳🛜

Sutton

Cock & Bull
26-30 High Street, SM1 1HF
🕔 12-11 (midnight Fri & Sat); 12-10.30 Sun
☎ (020) 8652 9910 🌐 thecockandbulluk.co.uk
Fuller's Oliver's Island, London Pride, ESB; 1 changing beer Ⓗ
A warm and friendly Fuller's house at the top of the High Street, just a stone's throw from the station and bus stops. The building, formerly a bank branch, is now a spacious one-bar pub with three separate drinking areas and an outdoor heated

smoking area. Five plasma screens show major sporting events and there is live music on Saturdays. An extensive menu caters for all tastes. ⛄🕮🍴♿➕🖳🌺🛜

Moon on the Hill ✅
5-9 Hill Road, SM1 1DZ
🕔 8am-midnight (1am Fri & Sat) ☎ (020) 8643 1202
Greene King Abbot; Ruddles Best Bitter; Sharp's Doom Bar; 7 changing beers (sourced regionally; often Dark Star, King Beer, Surrey Hills) Ⓗ
Formerly the furniture repository of a department store, this is a popular and well-established Wetherspoon pub, conveniently situated for Sutton's main shopping area. It comprises a single bar with ample seating on three levels and a garden for those preferring to drink and eat alfresco. The guest beers are sourced locally whenever possible and mini beer festivals are held throughout the year. Draught ciders come from different parts of the country. ⛄🏵🕮🍴🚲🖳🛜

Wallington

Wallington Arms 🅛
6-16 Woodcote Road, SM6 0NN
🕔 4-11 (midnight Thu & Fri); 12-midnight Sat; 12-11 Sun
☎ (020) 8773 0404 🌐 wallingtonarms.com
4 changing beers (sourced regionally; often Volden) Ⓗ
Tucked in beside the railway station entrance, this former Marston's pub has been revived by the Antic pub company. The wood-panelled front bar is furnished in an interesting mixture of the plain and the elegant that is Antic's usual style. There is a further drinking and dining area to the rear, and an interesting range of bottled beers is offered. ⛄🕮♿🚲🖳🌺🛜

Whispering Moon ✅
25 Ross Parade, SM6 8QF
🕔 6-11 (midnight Fri & Sat) ☎ (020) 8647 7020
Greene King Abbot; Ruddles Best Bitter; Sharp's Doom Bar; 5 changing beers (sourced regionally) Ⓗ
Wetherspoon house across the road from the station, south of the railway line. Formerly an Odeon cinema premises, the grand entrance remains (see the photograph at the end of the bar). Its movie heritage is reflected in the film star photographs. There is an L-shaped drinking area including a raised dining section. The pub takes part in all the usual promotions and holds two beer festivals each year. ⛄🕮♿🚲🖳🛜

WEST LONDON
W2: Bayswater

Champion
1 Wellington Terrace, W2 4LW
🕔 12-11 (midnight Fri & Sat); 12-10.30 Sun
☎ (020) 7243 6054 🌐 thechampionpub.co.uk
Adnams Broadside; Windsor & Eton Knight of the Garter; 3 changing beers Ⓗ
A Mitchells & Butlers Castle pub, built in 1838, Grade II-listed and refurbished in 2004. In warm weather the front windows are usually opened. A plush basement area, available for functions, leads to a sunken beer garden. Patio heaters are lit in cold weather. Right opposite the security-protected road on the northern side of Kensington Gardens, this pub is the nearest to Kensington Palace. 🏵🕮➡️⊖(Notting Hill Gate/Queensway)🖳🛜

W2: Paddington

Mad Bishop & Bear

Upper Level, Paddington Station, W2 1HB
🟢 8am-11; 10-10.30 Sun ☎ (020) 7402 2441
⊕ madbishopandbear.co.uk
Fuller's Oliver's Island, London Pride, ESB; St Austell Tribute; 4 changing beers (sourced nationally; often Fuller's) Ⓗ
Above the shopping complex just behind the station concourse, the pub's traditional interior features a long bar, mirrors, good prints and a rather grand chandelier, with train information screens and two TVs for sport. The raised area can be hired for events and there are café-style seats outside. It does not get too crowded, even in the rush hour, but the bar may close early if there are football crowds passing through. Local CAMRA Pub of the Year 2015. 🚶🎍👌≠⊖🖫🛈

Victoria ★

10A Strathearn Place, W2 2NH
🟢 11-11; 12-10.30 Sun ☎ (020) 7724 1191
⊕ victoriapaddington.co.uk
Fuller's Oliver's Island, London Pride, ESB; 3 changing beers (sourced nationally; often Adnams, Fuller's, Gale's) Ⓗ
There is plenty to admire in this Grade II-listed mid-Victorian inn. The nationally important historic interior includes ornately gilded mirrors above a crescent-shaped bar, painted tiles in wall niches and numerous portraits of Queen Victoria. The walls display cartoons, paperweights and a Silver Jubilee plate. Upstairs, via a spiral staircase, a library and Theatre Bar are available for public use. Tuesday is quiz night.
Q🚶🎍👌🍺≠⊖(Lancaster Gate/Paddington)🖫🛈

W3: Acton

George & Dragon

183 High Street, W3 9DJ
🟢 4-11; 12-1am Fri & Sat; 12-10.30 Sun ☎ (020) 8992 3712
⊕ dragonflybrewery.co.uk
Dragonfly 2 o'Clock Ordinary, Early Doors; 2 changing beers (often Dragonfly) Ⓗ
At the heart of the historic Acton town centre, this Grade II-listed pub has three bars of real character. An atmospheric front bar, with a list of landlords dating back to 1759, leads through to a heritage bar with exposed original features, and a cavernous and stylish back room includes the Dragonfly Brewery. All Dragonfly's cask beers are served, including seasonal ales, and usually two real ciders. 🚶🎍🍺👌⊖(Central)🍴🖫🛈

Red Lion & Pineapple ✓

281 High Street, W3 9BP
🟢 9am-midnight (1am Fri & Sat) ☎ (020) 8896 2248
Greene King IPA, Abbot; Sharp's Doom Bar; 5 changing beers
A Wetherspoon pub formerly owned by Fuller's, originally two pubs which then combined, hence the unusual name and layout. The larger room is home to the circular bar, surrounded by red and black tiles. The windows are large, with etched and stained tops, and the walls are decorated with photographs of old Acton. The smaller room is mainly for diners and families. There are four guest ales during the week, five at weekends.
Q🚶🎍🍺👌⊖(Town)🍴🖫🛈

West London Trades Union Club

33-35 High Street, W3 6ND
🟢 7-midnight ☎ (020) 8992 4557 ⊕ wltuc.com
2 changing beers (often Nelson) Ⓗ
Small and friendly club, run as a co-operative, which combines excellent real ale with a busy cultural and social life. Two beers are normally served from a variety of small independent breweries, especially from the Nelson Brewery range. The Acton Community Theatre is upstairs, and the club hosts regular special events, including summer barbecues in the courtyard. Show a CAMRA membership card or copy of the Guide for entry. Q🚶🎍🍺⊖(Central)🖫🛈🛈

W3: North Acton

Castle

140 Victoria Road, W3 6UL
🟢 11-11 (midnight Fri); 12-10.30 Sun ☎ (020) 8992 2027
⊕ castlenorthacton.co.uk
Fuller's London Pride; 2 changing beers (sourced locally; often Fuller's) Ⓗ
A 1938 Fuller's pub built for industrial North Acton and Park Royal, but now neighboured by new housing, hotels and student accommodation. The famous BBC rehearsal rooms were next door and are reflected in historic photos in the bar. Often busy with local workers on weekday evenings, the pub is quieter during the day and at weekends. There is a separate family room and a heated paved garden. 🚶🎍🍺👌⊖P🖫(266,440,487)🛈🛈

W4: Chiswick

Fox & Hounds/Mawson Arms

110 Chiswick Lane South, W4 2QA
🟢 9am-8; closed Sat & Sun ☎ (020) 8994 2936
⊕ mawsonarmschiswick.co.uk
Fuller's London Pride, ESB; Gale's Seafarers Ale; 3 changing beers (often Fuller's) Ⓗ
On the corner of the Griffin Brewery and its de facto brewery tap, this Grade II*-listed pub is the start for the Fuller's brewery tour. The two names are a legacy of separate licences for beer and spirits. The emphasis is now on food, which is available until 7pm. Brewery memorabilia on the walls include ancestral portraits of the Fuller, Smith and Turner families. It opens at weekends for functions only.
Q🚶🍺👌⊖(Stamford Brook)🖫(190)🛈🛈

George IV

185 Chiswick High Road, W4 2DR
🟢 12-11 (1am Fri & Sat) ☎ (020) 8994 4624
⊕ georgeiv.co.uk
Fuller's Oliver's Island, London Pride, ESB; 3 changing beers (often Fuller's) Ⓗ
In the heart of Chiswick, there has been an inn here since 1777. The present inter-war pub had a substantial makeover in 2014, but is still reputed to have its own ghost, George. The Boston Room within the pub plays host to a variety of events including a comedy club, and is also available for private hire. The manageress has Master Cellarman status. Enjoy a good pint of Fuller's here.
🚶🎍🍺👌⊖(Turnham Green)🍴🍴🖫🛈🛈

Old Pack Horse

434 Chiswick High Road, W4 5TF
🟢 11-midnight (1am Thu; 2am Fri & Sat); 12-midnight Sun
☎ (020) 8994 2872 ⊕ oldpackhorsechiswick.co.uk

Fuller's Oliver's Island, London Pride, ESB; 1 changing beer (sourced locally) ⊞
A Grade II-listed corner pub last rebuilt in 1910 but claimed to date back to 1747. Refurbished recently, it has a beautiful frontage often featured in local photographs, and a view across Turnham Green. With ornate woodwork and glasswork including some stained-glass panels, it has a regionally important historic pub interior. The walls display theatre memorabilia. Various areas include a snug and a Thai restaurant towards the back.
⊐⊛◖&⊖(Chiswick Park/Gunnersbury)◫⊟⚘⟁

Tabard 🄻 ⊘
2 Bath Road, W4 1LW
⊕ 12-11 (midnight Thu-Sat) ☎ (020) 8994 3492
Greene King London Glory; 8 changing beers (sourced regionally) ⊞
Grade II*-listed establishment, built in 1880 as part of the Bedford Park estate, the first London garden suburb. Notable features include the swing sign painted by TM Rooke, tiling by William de Morgan and Walter Crane, and Arts and Crafts mirrors and pictures; it has a regionally important historic pub interior. Ten handpumps serve a real cider and mainly guest ales – a permanent beer festival always including local beers. There is an intimate first-floor fringe theatre.
⊐⊛◖&⊖(Turnham Green)⬤⊟⚘⟁

W5: Ealing

Grove 🄻 ⊘
1 Ealing Green, W5 5QX
⊕ 11-11 ☎ (020) 8567 2439 ⊕ thegrovew5.co.uk
Greene King IPA; 5 changing beers (sourced locally; often Sambrook's, Southwark, Truman's) ⊞
Large one-room pub owned by Greene King with many semi-private areas. The bar focuses on local microbreweries from London and the Thames Valley such as Truman's, Sambrook's, Southwark and Windsor & Eton. The food offer is broad, and there is a dedicated restaurant area. The large heated front and side garden is popular and overlooks historic Ealing Green.
⊐⊛◖⩥⊖(Broadway)⊟⚘⟁

Questors Grapevine Bar 🄻 ⊘
12 Mattock Lane, W5 5BQ
⊕ 7-11; 12-2.30, 7-10.30 Sun ☎ (020) 8567 0011
⊕ questors.org.uk/grapevine
Fuller's London Pride; 2 changing beers ⊞
A friendly theatre club bar near the centre of Ealing and Walpole Park, run by enthusiastic volunteers. CAMRA members and Questors theatre ticket holders are also welcome. Guest beers include some from local breweries, beer festivals are held twice yearly, and there are malt whisky tastings. Some books and the odd board game are available. Payment is by cash or contactless only.
Q⊐⊛&⩥⊖(Broadway)♣P⊟⟁

Red Lion ⊘
13 St Mary's Road, W5 5RA
⊕ 12-11 (midnight Thu & Fri); 11-midnight Sat
☎ (020) 8567 2541 ⊕ redlionealing.co.uk
Fuller's Oliver's Island, London Pride, ESB; 2 changing beers (sourced nationally; often Fuller's, Gale's) ⊞
A splendid example of a traditional London pub, the earliest record of which is believed to be in local newspapers in the early 1700s. Affectionately known as Stage 6, opposite Ealing Studios, it displays associated black and white photographs of

TV and film stars, with memorabilia of their films. The Lee family have maintained the real character of the pub. Excellent upmarket food is cooked to order and there is a covered patio at the rear.
Q⊐⊛◖⟁⩥(Broadway)⊖(Broadway/South Ealing)⊟(65)⚘⟁

Wheatsheaf
41 Haven Lane, W5 2HZ
⊕ 11-11; 12-10.30 Sun ☎ (020) 8997 5240
⊕ wheatsheaf-ealing.co.uk
Fuller's Oliver's Island, London Pride, ESB; 2 changing beers (often Fuller's) ⊞
Tucked away up a side street just north of Ealing town centre, the interior of this pub is deceptively large and appears to have been constructed almost entirely of wood. The main saloon connects to an open-plan area at the rear; there is also a small space at the front, Rugby Corner, which is frequented by devotees of the oval ball. Several screens show televised sport, and a quiz night is on Monday. ⊐⊛◖⩥⊖(Broadway)♣⊟⚘⟁

W6: Hammersmith

Andover Arms ⊘
57 Aldensley Road, W6 0DL
⊕ 12-11 ☎ (020) 8748 2155 ⊕ theandoverarms.com
Fuller's London Pride; Gale's Seafarers Ale; 2 changing beers (often Fuller's) ⊞
A frequent Guide entry, tucked away in the side streets of Hammersmith, this popular local is an enduring real ale champion. The kitchen offers a wide range of lunchtime and evening meals. There is a terrestrial TV for major sporting events and traditional pub games such as dominoes are available. Regular quiz and live music nights are held. Guest ales are quite a recent innovation; drinkers can enjoy beers from brewers such as Brains or Long Man.
Q⊐◖⊖(Ravenscourt Park)♣⬤⊟⚘⟁

Dove
19 Upper Mall, W6 9TA
⊕ 11-11; 12-10.30 Sun ☎ (020) 8748 9474
⊕ dovehammersmith.co.uk
Fuller's London Pride, ESB; Gale's Seafarers Ale; 1 changing beer (often Fuller's) ⊞
Traditional Fuller's pub, a Grade II-listed building overlooking the Thames and hence often crowded in summer. With a regionally important historic pub interior, it holds the Guinness World Record for the smallest bar area. Classic food with a twist is served every day; meals can take a little time to arrive at busy times but are worth the wait. Dylan Thomas, Ernest Hemingway and Alec Guinness have reputedly enjoyed a pint or two here.
⊐◖⊖(Hammersmith/Ravenscourt Park)⬤⊟⚘⟁

Swan ⊘
46 Hammersmith Broadway, W6 0DZ
⊕ 10-11 (midnight Fri & Sat); 10-10.30 Sun
☎ (020) 8748 1043
Fuller's London Pride; St Austell Nicholson's Pale Ale; Windsor & Eton Knight of the Garter; 4 changing beers ⊞
Claimed to be on the site of the first coaching stop after leaving the City, wood predominates in this bustling M&B Nicholson's pub, handily located opposite Hammersmith Broadway. Ornate stairs lead to a first-floor restaurant and bar (and the toilets). It is well worth breaking your journey here

to or from Heathrow Airport. Guest beers are often from regional brewers such as Adnams, Elgood's and Thornbridge. ⬗⬤⬤⬤➤

W7: Hanwell

Fox ⬥ ⬜
Green Lane, W7 2PJ
🕐 11-11; 12-10.30 Sun ☎ (020) 8567 4021
🌐 thefoxpub.co.uk
Fuller's London Pride; Sharp's Cornish Coaster; Timothy Taylor Landlord; 2 changing beers ⊞
Wonderful back-street free house in the welcoming multicultural town of Hanwell, as popular with walkers, cyclists and other nearby canal users as with locals. A good range of beers, with changing guest ales from independent breweries, is complemented by excellent, inexpensive food, including a popular Sunday lunch (booking recommended). Added to all this are beer festivals and occasional jazz. ⬗⬤⬤⬤⬤➤P⬤(195,E8)⬤➤

Grosvenor ⬜
127 Oaklands Road, W7 2DT
🕐 12 (9 Fri)-11; 12-10.30 Sun ☎ (020) 8840 0007
🌐 thegrosvenorhanwell.co.uk
6 changing beers (sourced locally; often Sharp's, Truman's, Weird Beard) ⊞
A traditional local dating back to 1904, refurbished in 2014 without losing its features and charm. There is a dining room section and a main bar. A good selection of real ales and bottle-conditioned beers is available, plus a wide range of other locally produced beers. Family-friendly, it has a congenial atmosphere and promotes local events. Jazz night is the second Tuesday of every month and there is an open mic night on the fourth Tuesday. ⬗⬤⬤⬤⬤⬤⬤⬤➤

W8: Kensington

Elephant & Castle ⬤
40 Holland Street, W8 4LT
🕐 11-11; 12-10.30 Sun ☎ (020) 7937 6382
St Austell Nicholson's Pale Ale; Sharp's Doom Bar; 3 changing beers (sourced nationally; often Marston's, Truman's) ⊞
Licensed in 1865 as a beer house in what were two adjacent houses tucked away north-east of the town hall, this cosy, wood-panelled M&B Nicholson's pub is a welcome refuge from the hurly-burly of Kensington High Street. There are strong journalistic connections; witness the notable framed newspapers in the back bar. Food is available all day (not between 4-5pm). Note the fine Charrington's bar-back.
⬤⬤⬤(High St Kensington)⬤⬤➤

W8: Notting Hill Gate

Churchill Arms
119 Kensington Church Street, W8 7LN
🕐 11-11 (midnight Thu-Sat); 12-10.30 Sun
☎ (020) 7727 4242 🌐 churchillarmskensington.co.uk
Fuller's Oliver's Island, London Pride, ESB; Gale's Seafarers Ale; 1 changing beer (often Fuller's) ⊞
Long-serving landlord Gerry keeps standards high at this multi-award winning pub with a regionally important historic interior. Churchillian and Irish memorabilia hang from the panelled ceiling. The Thai restaurant in the conservatory was one of the first in a London pub. Often busy, with drinkers

standing on the pavement below the hanging flower baskets, it is a regular local CAMRA Pub of the Year finalist. Q⬤⬤⬤⬤⬤⬤➤

Uxbridge Arms
13 Uxbridge Street, W8 7TQ
🕐 12-11 (10.30 Sun) ☎ (020) 7727 7326
Fuller's London Pride; St Austell Tribute; Wadworth 6X ⊞
A world away from nearby Portobello Road, the manager Linda and her team run a great Enterprise pub, originally dating from 1836 when it opened as a beer house. Carpeted throughout, the bar has a welcoming appeal. The Lieutenant Colonel's tunic has been part of the fabric, together with the plates, for a number of years now.
Q⬗⬤⬤⬤⬤⬤➤

W9: Westbourne Park

Union Tavern ⬜
45 Woodfield Road, W9 2BA
🕐 12-11 (midnight Fri & Sat); 12-10.30 Sun
☎ (020) 7286 1886 🌐 union-tavern.co.uk
Fuller's London Pride, ESB; 3 changing beers ⊞
A radical departure by Fuller's, this beer house offers international draught beers and cask ales produced only within 30 miles and, with only one brewery exception, from London. The mainly young crowd enjoys reduced beer prices on Monday, a weekly quiz, and a Meet the Brewer event on the first Tuesday of the month. Good-value food is another attraction, with traditional Sunday lunches. The canalside terrace comes into its own on a warm, sunny day. ⬗⬤⬤⬤⬤⬤➤

W12: Shepherds Bush

Defector's Weld ⬜
170 Uxbridge Road, W12 8AA
🕐 12-midnight (2am Fri & Sat); 12-11 Sun
☎ (020) 8749 0008 🌐 defectors-weld.co.uk
Young's Bitter, Special; 3 changing beers (sourced locally; often Moncada, Redemption, Sambrook's) ⊞
Since Young's took over this pub, it has continued to rotate local guest beers from those breweries listed or others such as Twickenham. The large horseshoe-shaped main bar has a welcoming mix of sofas, tables and chairs. An upstairs bar is available for hire and DJs play music Thursday to Sunday evenings. Home fans only are admitted on Queens Park Rangers match days, but card-carrying CAMRA members not wearing team colours are welcome.
Q⬤⬤⬤⬤⬤(Shepherd's Bush/Market)⬤⬤⬤➤

W13: West Ealing

Forester ★ ⬜ ⬤
2 Leighton Road, W13 9EP
🕐 11-11.30 (midnight Wed & Thu; 1am Fri & Sat); 11-11 Sun
☎ (020) 8567 1654 🌐 theforesterealing.com
Fuller's London Pride, ESB; 4 changing beers (sourced nationally; often Fuller's, Gale's) ⊞
Built in 1909 from designs by Nowell Parr for the Royal Brewery of Brentford and bought by Fuller's in 2012, this pub has a nationally important historic interior. Thai and English food are available daily, except Sundays when the traditional carvery is served until 6pm. Wednesdays are quiz nights and on Thursdays there are poker tournaments. Two guests beers are supplemented by two additional

beers from Fuller's (often Gale's HSB), and several beer festivals are held annually.
🏴󠁧󠁢󠁥󠁮󠁧󠁿🏠🚲◑🏃⇄⊖(Northfields)♣●🖂(E2,E3)❀ ≈

Brentford

Express Tavern
56 Kew Bridge Road, TW8 0EW
🕐 11-11 (midnight Thu-Sat) ☎ (020) 8560 8484
🌐 expresstavern.co.uk
Draught Bass; Haresfoot Lock Keeper's Launch Ale; 8 changing beers (sourced nationally) Ⓗ
A local landmark since the 1800s, the building still features its illuminated external Bass signage, and Draught Bass remains a fixture on the bar. It has a regionally important historic pub interior. The Chiswick bar has 10 ale handpumps and a playable upright piano (music is also on vinyl LPs), while the Saloon and Lounge bar has five ciders and perries on handpump besides other draught beers. At the rear is a beer garden with a covered and heated area. ❀◑&⇄(Kew Bridge)♣●🖂❀≈

Magpie & Crown Ⓛ
128 High Street, TW8 8EW
🕐 12-midnight (1am Thu-Sat) ☎ (020) 8560 4570
6 changing beers (sourced nationally; often Magic Rock, Marble, Oakham) Ⓗ
This mock-Tudor free house is a cosy haunt for locals and beer lovers. London breweries often feature in the eclectic range of six guest ales. Also on offer are a cider and a perry on handpump, three other draught beers and English, German and Belgian bottled beers, all served by enthusiastic and knowledgeable staff. There are paved areas with tables at front and back, the latter covered. The food is freshly cooked, with roasts on Sunday. ❀◑⇄●🖂❀≈

Greenford

Black Horse
425 Oldfield Lane North, UB6 0AS
🕐 11.30-11 (midnight Thu-Sat); 12-11 Sun
☎ (020) 8578 1384 🌐 blackhorsegreenford.co.uk
Fuller's London Pride, ESB; 1 changing beer (often Fuller's, Gale's) Ⓗ
Tastefully extended canalside pub close to mainline rail, tube and bus routes, with a landscaped garden. Bargees, cyclists and walkers are frequent visitors. Good food includes traditional Sunday roasts and is available lunchtimes and evenings Monday to Thursday and midday-9pm Friday to Sunday. There is TV, a quiz on Thursday and live music on Friday and Saturday.
Q🏠❀◑&⇄⊖♣P🖂(92,395)❀≈

Hare & Hounds
229 Ruislip Road, UB6 9RZ
🕐 11-11 (midnight Fri); 11-10.30 Sun ☎ (020) 8575 7240
🌐 harehoundspub.co.uk
Marston's Pedigree; 2 changing beers (sourced nationally; often Cumberland, Marston's) Ⓗ
A friendly, traditional locals' pub on the busy Ruislip Road. There are two bars with the saloon divided into two areas - the three handpumps are at the rear. The large beer garden is completely enclosed and usually offers a bouncy castle along with picnic tables. A welcome oasis in a real ale desert. 🏠❀&♣P🖂❀≈

Hampton

Jolly Coopers
16 High Street, TW12 2SJ
🕐 11-11 (midnight Fri & Sat); 12-10.30 Sun
☎ (020) 8979 3384 🌐 squiffysrestaurant.co.uk
Caledonian Deuchars IPA; Courage Best Bitter; Hop Back Summer Lightning; 2 changing beers (sourced regionally) Ⓗ
A popular, traditional community pub, proud of its heritage - a wooden wall panel lists landlords from 1727 to the present owners, who took over in 1986. The small horseshoe bar features five handpumps. Walls are adorned with water jugs, old pub photographs and local memorabilia. An extensive menu of tapas and traditional food, including Sunday lunches, is served in the bar, Squiffy's restaurant beyond and, weather permitting, on the sun patio outside. ❀◑⇄♣🖂❀

Hampton Hill

Roebuck
72 Hampton Road, TW12 1JN
🕐 11-11 (11.30 Fri & Sat); 12-4, 7-10.30 Sun
☎ (020) 8255 8133 🌐 roebuck-hamptonhill.co.uk
St Austell Tribute; Sambrook's Junction Ale; Young's Bitter; 2 changing beers (often Itchen Valley, Triple fff, Windsor & Eton) Ⓗ
A comfortable Victorian street-corner pub with screens dividing the single bar into various seating areas. The array of bric-a-brac and other displays (framed banknotes and military memorabilia, fishing rods, model sea planes, cigar store Indian and, of course, a wickerwork Harley-Davidson) is amazing but does not detract from the comfort of the pub. The small, award-winning garden has a gazebo for smokers and there is a garden room (available for hire) for cooler evenings.
Q🏠❀🏠◑⇄(Fulwell)♣P🖂

Harlington

White Hart
158 High Street, UB3 5DP
🕐 11-11 (11.30 Thu; midnight Fri & Sat); 12-11 Sun
☎ (020) 8759 9608 🌐 whitehartharlington.co.uk
Fuller's London Pride, ESB; 1 changing beer (often Fuller's, Gale's) Ⓗ
Large single-room, Grade II-listed Fuller's pub standing proud at the north end of the village. The bar provides access to an open-plan area for sport on large-screen TV, and through to a seated area favoured by diners. The interior was refurbished in 2009 to improve facilities and create the open feel this pub now has, enjoyed by locals and visitors from nearby Heathrow airport. Local history is the theme of the wall displays. Quiz night is Thursday.
🏠❀◑&♣P🖂❀≈

Hayes

Botwell Inn ✅
25-29 Coldharbour Lane, UB3 3EB
🕐 9am-midnight ☎ (020) 8848 3112
Greene King Abbot; Ruddles Best Bitter; Sharp's Doom Bar; 3 changing beers (often Adnams, Hogs Back, Windsor & Eton) Ⓗ
A large Wetherspoon pub opened in 2000 following a shop conversion from furnishers S Moore & Son, with several areas for dining and drinking. There is a fenced paved area to the front

and a patio at the rear with large market-type parasols with heaters. At least one Westons cider is stocked. Several beer festivals are held annually. Q☺⌂❶♿⇒(Hayes & Harlington)♣☗🏠🎵

Hounslow

Moon Under Water ✅

84-88 Staines Road, TW3 3LF (W end of High St)
☼9am-12.30am (1am Fri & Sat) ☎ (020) 8572 7506
Greene King Abbot; Ruddles Best Bitter; Sharp's Doom Bar; 5 changing beers (sourced nationally) Ⓗ
A 1991 Wetherspoon shop conversion in original style, still displaying many local history panels and photos. It is a regular venue for the town's beer lovers, also attracting others from surrounding areas. Up to five guest ales are offered, both nationally and locally sourced, with many more at festival times when 11 handpumps are put to work. The cider is usually Westons Old Rosie, again with others during festivals. Children are welcome until 7pm. Q☺⌂❶♿⇒⊖(Central)♣☗🏠🎵

Ickenham

Tichenham Inn ✅

11 Swakeleys Road, UB10 8DF
☼9am-11 (midnight Fri & Sat) ☎ (01895) 678916
Fuller's London Pride; Greene King Abbot; Ruddles Best Bitter; Sharp's Doom Bar; 6 changing beers (sourced locally; often Twickenham) Ⓗ
Small and friendly Wetherspoon pub converted from a garage, with a strong local following. Food and beers are good value, with the usual chain promotions. The pub has its own occasional festivals with more guest ales, in conjunction with other local Wetherspoon branches. Gwynt y Draig Black Dragon cider is served from the fridge from a bag in a box. Q☺⌂❶♿⊖♣☗(U1,U10)🎵🏠

Isleworth

London Apprentice ✅

62 Church Street, TW7 6BG
☼11-11 (midnight Fri & Sat) ☎ (020) 8560 1915
Adnams Ghost Ship; Greene King IPA, London Glory; 3 changing beers (sourced nationally) Ⓗ
Famous Grade II-listed former Isleworth Brewery riverside pub in old Isleworth, with an interesting history. The interior is classic traditional, although opened out, with an upstairs Riverview Room. The large patio has many tables, with more on the riverbank. Three guest ales are regularly on offer, plus a cider, as well as popular food. With a Thursday pune night, varied music most Friday evenings and a Sunday quiz, it is well worth the walk from the nearest bus stop. ☺⌂❶♿♣☗(H37)

Red Lion Ⓛ

92/94 Linkfield Road, TW7 6QJ
☼12-11.30 (midnight Fri & Sat); 12-11 Sun
☎ (020) 8560 1457 ∰ red-lion.info
Sharp's Cornish Coaster; changing beers (often Belleville, Kew, Twickenham) Ⓗ
Spacious, traditional, two-bar free house with a regionally important historic interior and strong community focus. You will often find an event taking place – a performance by the pub's own theatre group, the Thursday quiz, and live music throughout the week. Up to eight cask beers complement the regular bitter, and up to four

ciders or perries. Dogs on leads are welcome. The pub has now been listed as an Asset of Community Value. ☺⌂❶⇒♣☗🏠🎵

St Margarets

Crown

174 Richmond Road, TW1 2NH
☼11-11 (11.30 Fri & Sat); 11-10.30 Sun ☎ (020) 8892 5896
∰ crowntwickenham.co.uk
Harveys Sussex Best Bitter; Sharp's Cornish Coaster; Surrey Hills Shere Drop; 1 changing beer (often Twickenham, Windsor & Eton) Ⓗ
A spacious pub from about 1730 and Grade II-listed, now refurbished, enhancing the Georgian heritage of the original building. The Victorian hall to the rear has been opened up for dining and the courtyard garden attractively remodelled. Inside are various seating areas and three fireplaces, one with a real fire. Several windows and doors are original and listed. Food is served 12-9.30pm (10pm Fri and Sat). ☺⌂❶♿⇒P🏠🎵🎵

Southall

Southall Conservative & Unionist Club Ⓛ

Fairlawn, High Street, UB1 3HB
☼11.30-2.30, 7-11; 11.30-3, 6-11 Fri & Sat; 12-3, 7-10.30 Sun
☎ (020) 8574 0261
Rebellion IPA; 1 changing beer (often Rebellion) Ⓗ
This is virtually the last real ale outlet in Southall, and is to be found behind the former town hall. Access can be gained by showing this Guide or a CAMRA membership card. It was completely refurbished to a high standard in early 2015. Lunches are served daily except Sundays, but it is a good place to visit either before or after eating in one of the numerous Indian restaurants nearby. ☺⌂❶⇒♣P🏠🎵

Teddington

Masons Arms 🏆

41 Walpole Road, TW11 8PJ
☼12-11 (11.30 Fri & Sat); 12-10.30 Sun ☎ (020) 8977 6521
∰ the-masons-arms.co.uk
Sambrook's Junction Ale; Tillingbourne AONB; 2 changing beers (sourced regionally; often Coastal, Kissingate) Ⓗ
Small back-street community free house with a uniquely friendly atmosphere. It is a beer drinkers' haven, as reflected in the array of bottles, pictures and pub memorabilia on display (including the infamous Watney's Party Seven). Carpeting and comfortable seating create a cosy atmosphere. The digital jukebox is a popular feature. There is a log-burning stove, dartboard and a small secluded rear patio. Guest beers change frequently, coming from a wide range of independent brewers across the UK. ⌂♿⇒♣☗🏠🎵

Twickenham

Prince Blucher

124 The Green, TW2 5AG
☼11-11 (midnight Fri & Sat); 12-11 Sun ☎ (020) 8894 1824
∰ princeblucher.co.uk
Fuller's Oliver's Island, London Pride, ESB; 2 changing beers (often Fuller's, Gale's) Ⓗ
Historic 19th-century inn, the first built on the newly enclosed Twickenham Green and the only

pub remaining in Britain still to pay homage to the Duke of Wellington's left-flanker at Waterloo. Renovated in 2014, it has four separate bar areas, including the bare-boarded main bar, to suit most tastes. Home-cooked food is served all day and, in summertime, there are hog roasts and barbecues in the ample, child-friendly garden. Cornish Orchard cider is on handpump.
ॐ☷❀◐👵≈(Strawberry Hill)♣P🚃☺🛜

Rifleman ✅
7 Fourth Cross Road, TW2 5EL
☼ 12 (2 Mon & Tue)-11; 12-10.30 Sun ☎ (020) 8893 3836
⊕ theriflemantwickenham.co.uk
Butcombe Bitter; Dark Star Hophead; Timothy Taylor Landlord; Twickenham Autumn Red; Young's Bitter; 1 changing beer (often Twickenham) ⊞
Traditional Victorian pub whose name commemorates riflemen billeted nearby in Napoleonic times. It benefits from a small beer garden, front patio and close proximity to seven bus routes. No main meals are served but toasties are available up to 7pm. On Thursday it hosts a lively open mic night. A community hub, with board games and TV sport, it is 15 minutes' walk from Twickenham Stadium and Harlequins rugby club. Local CAMRA Pub of the Year 2014.
❀≈(Strawberry Hill)♣P🚃☺🛜

Sussex Arms ✅
15 Staines Road, TW2 5BG
☼ 12-11 (10.30 Sun) ☎ (020) 8894 7468
⊕ thesussexarmstwickenham.co.uk
Twickenham Grandstand Bitter; changing beers (sourced regionally) ⊞
A traditional pub with two real fires, now a firm favourite with beer lovers. Eighteen handpumps showcase independent UK breweries and six ciders and perries. Acoustic blues and Irish music feature regularly, and recorded music is played from vinyl LPs. Food includes Anthea's famous pies. Every 10th pint of ale is free with the pub's loyalty card. CAMRA Greater London Cider Pub of the Year 2014.
❀◐≈(Strawberry Hill)♣●🚃☺🛜

White Swan ✅
Riverside, TW1 3DN
☼ 11 (10 Sat)-11; 11-10.30 Sun ☎ (020) 8744 2951
⊕ whiteswantwickenham.com
Fuller's London Pride; Sharp's Doom Bar; 3 changing beers (often Portobello, Truman's, Twickenham) ⊞
A Grade II-listed building and award-winning traditional pub, built around 1690. Entry is via steps up to the first floor, with real fires and walls covered with rugby and other memorabilia. A small veranda/balcony and a triclinium (three-sided room with window seats) afford views of the river and Eel Pie Island. Directly opposite there is a larger beer garden, right on the water's edge (tides permitting). Quiz night is Wednesday. A summer beer festival and an annual raft race are held.
Q☷❀◐≈♣☺🛜

William Webb Ellis ✅
24 London Road, TW1 3RR
☼ 9am-11 ☎ (020) 8744 4300
Fuller's London Pride; Greene King IPA, Abbot; Sharp's Doom Bar; 8 changing beers (often Oakham, Twickenham, Windsor & Eton) ⊞
A Wetherspoon pub in the centre of the home of English rugby, named after the alleged inventor of the game. It is spacious inside, with live news and sport on silent screens. Twelve handpumps are in constant use. The rear patio is open until 9pm, food is served all day and children are welcome until 8pm. A Monday ale club offers reduced prices and third-pint glasses. Real cider is available.
ॐ❀◐≈●🚃🛜

Uxbridge

Queen's Head 📏 ✅
54 Windsor Street, UB8 1AB
☼ 11-11 (midnight Fri & Sat); 12-10.30 Sun
☎ (01895) 258750
Greene King IPA; changing beers (often Cotleigh, Twickenham, Windsor & Eton) ⊞
A Grade II-listed, mid-19th century pub that still retains its old feel, opposite the church, a few yards down from the Underground station. The decorations and furnishings are appropriate. It has bay windows, wooden floorboards, low ceilings and walls largely of exposed brick, and an irregularly shaped bar. Local CAMRA Pub of the Year for 2014. ☷◐😋🚃🛜

Whitton

Admiral Nelson
123 Nelson Road, TW2 7BB
☼ 11-11 (midnight Fri & Sat); 12-10.30 Sun
☎ (020) 8894 9998 ⊕ admiralnelsonwhitton.co.uk
Fuller's London Pride, ESB; Gale's Seafarers Ale; 1 changing beer (often Fuller's) ⊞
This large landmark pub, rebuilt in the 1930s, with a small patio area on the side, stands in a prominent position on the crossroads at the end of the high street. Near to Twickenham Stadium and Twickenham Stoop, it is a haven for rugby fans on match days. A comprehensive range of food is available. Sunday is quiz night. There are large TVs for sport, baby-changing facilities and an ATM. Fuller's completed a major refurbishment in 2015.
ॐ❀◐≈🚃☺🛜

Choosing pubs

CAMRA members and branches choose the pubs listed in the Good Beer Guide. There is no payment for entry, and pubs are inspected on a regular basis by personal visits; publicans are not sent a questionnaire once a year, as is the case with some pub guides. CAMRA branches monitor all the pubs in their areas, and the choice of pubs for the guide is often the result of democratic vote at branch meetings. However, recommendations from readers are welcomed and will be passed on to the relevant branch: write to Good Beer Guide, CAMRA, 230 Hatfield Road, St Albans, Hertfordshire, AL1 4LW; or send an email to: **gbgeditor@camra.org.uk**

GREATER MANCHESTER

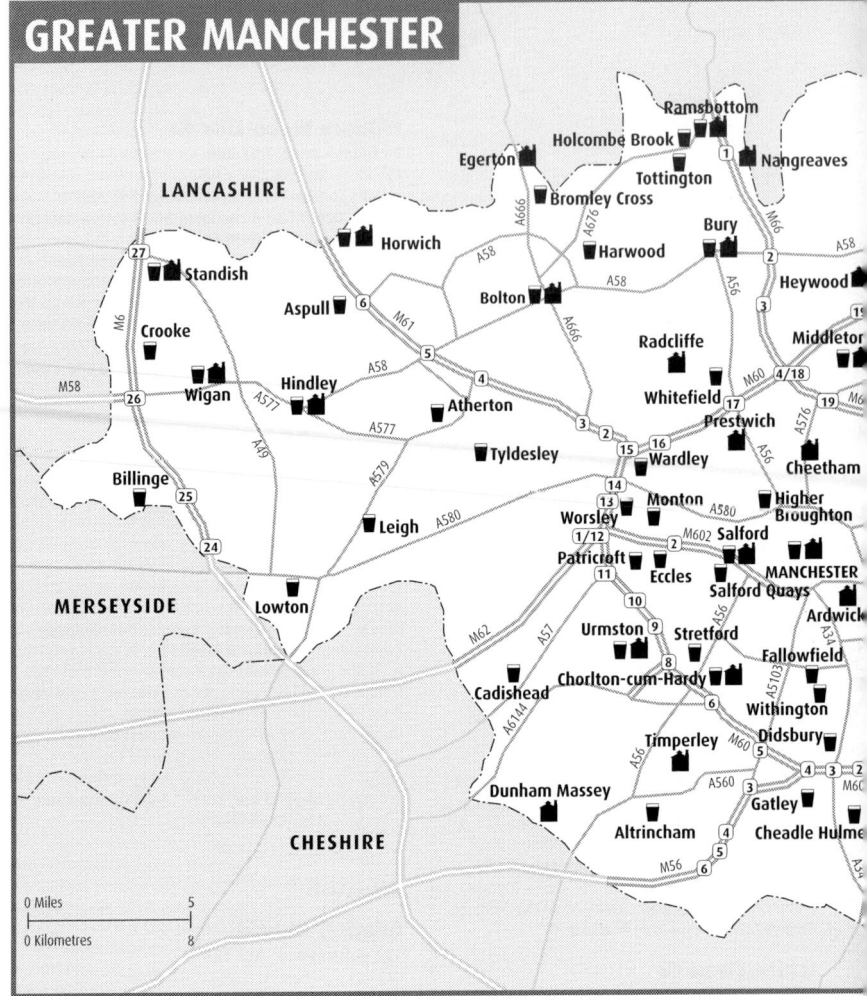

LANCASHIRE

Ramsbottom
Holcombe Brook
Egerton
Nangreaves
Bromley Cross
Tottington
Horwich
Harwood
Bury
Standish
Heywood
Aspull
Bolton
Crooke
Radcliffe
Middleton
Hindley
Atherton
Whitefield
Wigan
Prestwich
Billinge
Tyldesley
Wardley
Cheetham
Leigh
Monton
Higher Broughton
Worsley
Salford
Patricroft
Eccles
Salford Quays
MANCHESTER
Lowton
Urmston
Stretford
Ardwick
MERSEYSIDE
Chorlton-cum-Hardy
Fallowfield
Cadishead
Withington
Timperley
Didsbury
Dunham Massey
Gatley
Altrincham
Cheadle Hulme
CHESHIRE

0 Miles 5
0 Kilometres 8

Altrincham

Costello's Bar ⑴

18 Goose Green, WA14 1DW (down pedestrian road opp jct of Stamford New Rd & Regent Rd)
🕐 12-11 (midnight Fri & Sat); 12-10.30 Sun
☎ (0161) 929 0903 ⊕ costellosbar.co.uk
Dunham Massey Big Tree Bitter; 6 changing beers (sourced locally) Ⓗ
Costello's is Dunham Massey Brewing Company's brewery tap, situated in Altrincham's attractive Goose Green behind the new hospital. The small bar has a modern feel and is popular with locals and visitors alike. The brewery has more than 25 different recipes and showcases them all in the bar over time on seven handpumps. A perry and three real ciders are also available, as well as tea and coffee. ⑱⑲≠Ⓠ●⊟⑲⑲

Jack in the Box

Altrincham Market Hall, Market Street, WA14 1SA
🕐 12-10; 12-6 Sun; closed Mon ☎ 07917 792060
⊕ blackjack-beers.com
Blackjack House Pale; 4 changing beers (sourced nationally) Ⓗ

The first brewery tap from Blackjack Brewery, located inside the renovated Altrincham Market House, part of the town's historic market and a short walk from Altrincham Interchange. There are four handpumps on the bar alongside eight fonts dispensing keg beers. Blackjack beers are always available alongside a wide range of guests sourced from breweries including Marble, Siren, Burning Sky, Weird Beard and Celt. The casks (and kegs) are housed in a glass-fronted chilled cellar located behind the bar. ⑱⑲⑲≠Ⓠ●⊟

Pi ⑲ ⑴

18 Shaws Road, WA14 1QU
🕐 11-11 (midnight Fri & Sat) ☎ (0161) 929 9098
⊕ abarcalledpi.com
Tatton Blonde; 2 changing beers (sourced nationally; often First Chop, RedWillow, Saltaire) Ⓗ
An intimate bar arranged over two floors, four handpumps serve three real ales and a guest cider or perry alongside world beers on draught and an extensive foreign bottle collection. Guest beers are sourced from micros as well as from more established breweries including RedWillow, Saltaire and First Chop. Pieminister pies and mash

Dog & Pheasant ✪
528 Oldham Road, OL7 9PQ
✪ 12-11 (11.30 Fri & Sat) ☎ (0161) 330 4894
Banks's Mild; Marston's Burton Bitter, Pedigree Ⓗ; 3 changing beers Ⓗ/Ⓖ

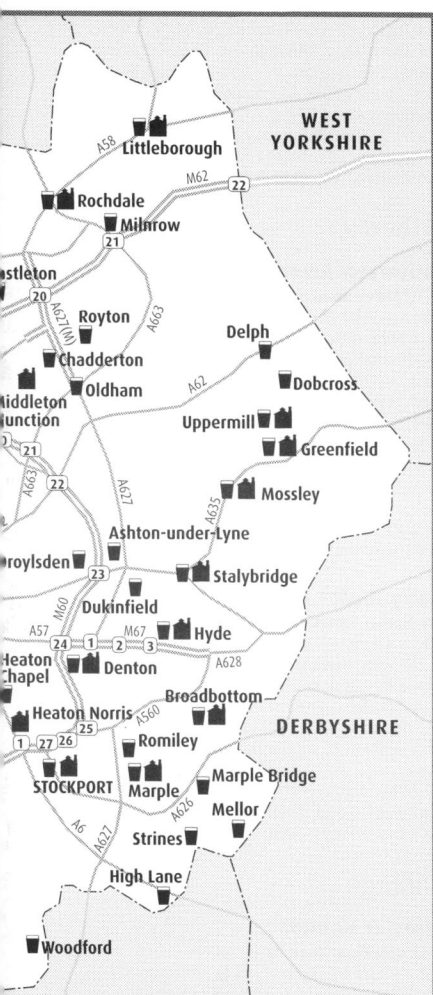

REAL ALE BREWERIES
AllGates Wigan
Alphabet Manchester
Bank Top Bolton
Beer Nouveau Manchester: Ardwick
Blackedge Horwich
Blackjack Manchester
Bootleg 🍺 Chorlton-cum-Hardy
Brewsmith Ramsbottom
Brightside Radcliffe
Carbon Smith Manchester
Chorlton Manchester
Cloudwater Manchester
Cryptic Stockport
Deeply Vale Bury
Drink Up Horwich (NEW)
Dunham Massey Dunham Massey
Dunscar Bridge Bolton
First Chop Salford
Five Oh Prestwich
Fool Hardy 🍺 Stockport: Heaton Norris
Green Mill 🍺 Broadbottom
Greenfield Greenfield
Hay Rake Littleborough
Hexagon Marple (NEW)
Hogarths 🍺 Bolton
Holt Cheetham
Holy Well Egerton
Hophurst Hindley
Hornbeam Denton
Hydes Salford
Irwell Works Ramsbottom
Lees Middleton Junction
Leyden 🍺 Nangreaves
Manchester Manchester (NEW)
Marble Manchester
Martland Mill Wigan
Mayflower 🍺 Wigan
Millstone Mossley
Outstanding Bury
Phoenix Heywood
Pictish Rochdale
Prospect Standish
Quantum Stockport
Ramsbottom Craft Ramsbottom
Remedy 🍺 Stockport (NEW)
Rising Sun 🍺 Mossley (NEW)
Robinsons Stockport
Rtwo Dtoo 🍺 Urmston
Runaway Manchester
Saddleworth 🍺 Uppermill
Serious Rochdale (NEW)
Seven Bro7hers Salford
Silver Street 🍺 Bury
Six O'Clock Manchester
Squawk Manchester: Ardwick
Stockport Stockport
Stubborn Mule Timperley (NEW)
Thirst Class Stockport
Ticketybrew Stalybridge
Track Manchester
Tweed Hyde
Vagrant Manchester
Watts Brewing? 🍺 Stockport
Wilson Potter Middleton

are served until 10pm daily. A sibling to Pi (Chorlton), service is always friendly, with little touches such as complimentary peanuts and blankets for those situated outside.
🏠🍴🌙◗💧🚭🚆🍴🚍🛜

Ashton under Lyne

Ash Tree ✪
9-11 Wellington Road, OL6 6DA
✪ 8am-midnight ☎ (0161) 339 9670
Greene King Abbot; Ruddles Best Bitter; Sharp's Doom Bar; 4 changing beers (sourced regionally) Ⓗ
Directly facing the Victorian Market Hall and square, this pub has become one of the premier real ale destinations in the town centre and is easily accessible by bus and train. Families are welcome in the lower level; above are the bar and lounge/dining area, leading to the rear entrance and outdoor patio/smoking area. Wetherspoon's usual good value applies to the beers and food. Moorhouse's and Greenfield Brewery beers are popular guests. Two real ale festivals are run each year. TVs have the sound turned off.
🏠🍴🌙◗💧🚭🚆🍴🚍🛜

Known as the Top Dog, this popular, friendly local near the Medlock Valley Country Park has been a regular Guide entry since 1992. It has a large bar serving three areas, plus another room at the front. The beer range is supplemented by three guest beers from the Marston's portfolio. A menu of good-value food includes vegetarian options and quiz night is Thursday evenings. The pub is home to a local hiking group known as the Bog Trotters. ✿◖♿P�(409,419)

Witchwood
152 Old Street, OL6 7SQ
✿ 12-midnight (2am Thu & Sat; 3am Fri) ☎ (0161) 344 0321
⊕ thewitchwood.net
Moorhouse's Blond Witch; Wells Bombardier; Wychwood Hobgoblin; 2 changing beers (sourced regionally) Ⓗ
Traditional pub at the west end of Old Street with a well-established separate live music venue to the rear. There is always something going on at this lively venue – quiz night on Monday, free pool on Tuesday, free jukebox on Wednesday and cask ale club on Thursday. Friday features DJs until 3am and on Saturday nights live bands – mostly well-respected tribute acts – perform. A changing cider complements the real ale range. ♿➔ᗡ♠P🖵

Aspull

Crown Hotel Ⓛ
106 Wigan Road, New Springs, WN2 1DP
✿ 7-midnight; 2-1am Sat; 12-11 Sun; closed Mon winter
Prospect Silver Tally, Gold Rush; 1 changing beer (sourced regionally) Ⓗ
Traditional free house just two miles from Wigan centre, close to Haigh Country Park. A real coal fire and woodburner add to the warm, welcoming ambience. The licensee, Kent, offers an excellent range of local beers on up to three handpumps, and high-quality food is served. The pub is renowned for cabaret evenings on Friday and Saturday. Popular in the summer with canal users, which can mean opening hours are variable. This community pub is well-worth a visit. Q❧✿◖♿♠P❀🖵🛜

Gerrard Arms
615 Bolton Road, WN2 1PZ
✿ 11.30 (4 Mon & Tue)-11; 11.30-midnight Fri & Sat
☎ (01942) 832346
Prospect Silver Tally; Tetley Bitter; Thwaites Wainwright; 3 changing beers Ⓗ
One-room, open-plan, cosy pub with a light and airy interior, comfortable seating and a good atmosphere. Original Boddington and Smoke Room windows feature. There are six handpumps, with Tetley and Prospect beers the regulars plus varying guests. Two TV screens show sport. Located on the edge of Borsdane Wood, a local nature reserve, it makes an ideal refreshment stop for walkers. Food is served lunchtimes and evenings, all day at weekends. There is covered seating outside. Over-18s only. No disabled WC. ✿◖♿P🛜

Victoria Ⓛ
50 Haigh Road, Haigh, WN2 1YA
✿ 4-11 (midnight Fri); 3-midnight Sat; 2-midnight Sun ☎ 07962 263974
AllGates Wigan Junction; 5 changing beers Ⓗ
Traditional two-room local and AllGates Brewery's first pub in the now-popular local chain. The smart yet intimate lounge displays photographs depicting the history of Aspull and Haigh. Large screens cater for sports fans, although the TV in the lounge is rarely switched on. The pub is not far from Haigh Hall Country Park and halfway between Bolton Wanderers and Wigan Athletic football grounds. Guest beers come from AllGates and other microbreweries. There is a covered smoking area. No disabled WC. Q❧♣♠P🖵❀🛜

Atherton

Atherton Arms
6 Tyldesley Road, M46 9DD
✿ 12-midnight ☎ (01942) 882885
Holt Mild, Bitter; 2 changing beers Ⓗ
Traditional public house with a great atmosphere and facilities including a full-sized snooker table and function room. The pub is known for its superb beer garden, which has TV screens and heaters. The beer is competitively priced and promotions change on a monthly basis, with happy days Monday to Friday. Mid-week, the pub offers a wide range of entertainment. Fridays and Saturdays feature Steve's Karaoke and there is live entertainment on Sundays. ❧✿♿♠P🖵🛜

Jolly Nailor Inn ✅
20 Market Street, M46 0DN
✿ 12-midnight (11 Mon); 12-1am Fri & Sat
5 changing beers (sourced locally) Ⓗ
The Jolly Nailor is a revitalised local situated on the main Market Street in Atherton. The pub was purchased by AllGates in 2010 and refurbished with the addition of six handpumps offering a range of cask beers plus draught cider. The interior is divided into three areas for live music, TV sport and the weekly quiz. There is still space for the ladies' and men's darts teams. ✿♣♠🖵

Billinge

Hare & Hounds
142 Upholland Road, WN5 7JH
✿ 4 (2 Sat)-midnight; 2-11 Sun ☎ (01744) 892626
Thwaites Wainwright; 3 changing beers Ⓗ
This friendly, welcoming, red-brick pub has a lounge and taproom (once the smoking room), with TVs in both rooms showing live sport, especially rugby. Local league darts is played and entertainment is provided on Saturday evenings. Dementia-friendly activities are held on the first Tuesday of the month 1-3pm. Four handpumps dispense one regular beer and three guests. Local pies are available. The pub has a rural feel to it with great views. Q❧✿◖♿♠P🖵(197,352)

Masons Arms
99 Carr Mill Road, WN5 7TY
✿ 2-11.30; 12-midnight Sat & Sun ☎ (01744) 603572
⊕ masonsarmsbillinge.co.uk
5 changing beers Ⓗ
A regular in the Guide, the pub was built in 1779. Five handpumps offer regularly changing guest beers in top condition, and there are usually four real ciders. Folk and quiz nights feature mid-week. There is Sky Sports TV but usually without the volume, so the pub is just the place for a quiet chat. Outside is a luxurious smoking shelter with a bison's head and logburner, and the beer garden and smoking area overlook fields to the rear. Well-placed for walking or cycling around the local area. ✿♿♠P❀🛜

Bolton

Bank Top Brewery Tap 🗓

68-70 Belmont Road, Astley Bridge, BL1 7AN
✪ 12-11 (11.30 Fri & Sat) ☎ (01204) 302837
⊕ banktopbrewery.com
Bank Top Dark Mild, Flat Cap, Gold Digger, Old
Slapper, Pavilion Pale Ale, Port o' Call; 2 changing
beers (sourced locally) 🖽
The Tap, which has won numerous local CAMRA
awards, is a popular street-corner local. There are
eight handpumps supplying ales from Bank Top
Brewery and a guest is always available. Up to six
real ciders are also on offer. The pub has a pleasant
atmosphere with great service, quiet music and an
absence of distractions from TVs, jukebox and
gaming machines. A dartboard is situated in the
vault and there is a large outdoor drinking area
with a covered smoking shelter.
🏵🐕♿♣🍴🚪(1,534,535)🐾🚲🛜

Bob's Smithy 🗓

1448 Chorley Old Road, Heaton, BL1 7PX
✪ 12 (4.30 Mon & Tue)-11; 12-10.30 Sun ☎ (01204) 842622
⊕ bobs-smithy.com
Bank Top Flat Cap; Thwaites Wainwright; Timothy
Taylor Boltmaker; 3 changing beers (sourced
locally) 🖽
An intimate stone-built hostelry on the edge of the
moors with panoramic views. Now with its own
restaurant, it is handy for walkers and visitors to
Macron Stadium. The inn is some 200 years old and
is named after a local blacksmith who allegedly
spent more time here than he did in his smithy
across the road. This is a genuine free house which
offers guest beers from small independent
breweries. Dogs are welcome and there is a
covered smoking area at the side of the building.
Q🏵◐P🚪(125)🐾

Bolton Ukrainian Social Club 🗓

99 Castle Street, BL2 1JP
✪ 3.30-11; 12-11 Sat & Sun ☎ (01204) 526038
3 changing beers (sourced locally; often Bank Top,
Blackedge) 🖽
Large, imposing building to the east of town with a
comfortable and well-laid-out two-room bar. Two
of the three handpumps usually dispense beers
from Bank Top or Blackedge, and a guest from
another local brewery is on the third one. The
Bolton CAMRA annual beer festival is held here in
April. The club is home to several societies
including brass band, choir, chess and bagpipes.
Local CAMRA Club of the year in 2014.
Q🏵🚲♣P🚪(471,510,544)🛜

Finishers Arms 🗓 ✅

487 Church Road, BL1 5RE
✪ 12 (4 Mon & Tue)-11; 12-midnight Fri & Sat
☎ (01204) 848244 ⊕ finishersarmsbolton.co.uk
Bank Top Bad to the Bone, Flat Cap; Thwaites
Wainwright; 2 changing beers (sourced locally; often
Blackedge) 🖽
Traditional inn dating from the mid-1700s, recently
refurbished. The serving area has moved to the
back wall, opening out the main bar area. A central
raised table provides a focus for locals to meet and
chat. Two rooms have been retained off the side of
the bar and these provide a quieter atmosphere.
Some original features such as the wooden beams
are still visible. The pub has a history of
supernatural events. A real cider is often available
in the summer months. 🏵🏵◐♣🍴🚪(501)🛜

Great Ale at the Market 🍺

Stalls F14 and F15, Ashburner Street Lifestyle Hall,
BL1 1TJ
✪ 9am-6.30; closed Mon, Wed & Sun ☎ 07815 058862
⊕ greataleonline.co.uk
2 changing beers (sourced locally) 🖽
This micro-bar opened as part of the
redevelopment of Bolton's award-winning indoor
market. As well as the handpumped ale you can
also buy from an extensive range of bottled beers
and grab some great food to eat. The bar serves
cold platters or there are nearby takeaway food
stalls from Malaysia and Cameroon, as well as the
sandwich and pasty outlets that all share the large
seating area at the front. Bolton CAMRA Pub of the
Year 2016. ◐♿🚆🚪

Kings Head 🗓

52-54 Junction Road, Deane, BL3 4NA
✪ 3.30-11; 12-11 Sat & Sun ☎ (01204) 62609
Bank Top Flat Cap; Timothy Taylor Landlord 🖽
A late-18th century, Grade II-listed building
extended in the mid-19th century. Located near
Deane parish church in the Deane Village
conservation area, it is set back from the road with
a two-tier car park, and is partially surrounded by
woodland. The pub has three rooms, one with a
cast-iron range and the others with low wood-
beamed ceilings. Outside, there is crown green
bowling and a children's play area.
Q🚲🏵♿♣P🚪(715,540)🐾🛜

Olde Man & Scythe

6-8 Churchgate, BL1 1HL
✪ 11-11 (12.30am Fri & Sat) ☎ (01204) 559060
Bank Top Flat Cap; Hop Back Summer Lightning; 2
changing beers (sourced locally) 🖽
The Olde Man & Scythe was first recorded in 1251
and is reputedly the fourth oldest inn in the
country, situated near the parish church on the
historic Churchgate, site of a famous Civil War
execution. The pub retains some traditional
features such as wooden beams, leaded windows
and stone floors, though there have been recent
modifications to the layout. Nevertheless, it has a
cosy snug and a separate room often used for
jamming and open mic nights. Only the Thatchers
Cider and Broadoak Perry are real. 🏵🚆♣🍴🚪🐾

Broadbottom

Harewood Arms 🗓 ✅

2 Market Street, SK14 6AX
✪ 3-11 (midnight Fri); 2-midnight Sat; 12.30-11 Sun
☎ (01457) 762500
Green Mill Gold, Stellar, Chief, Old Git; 2 changing
beers (sourced regionally) 🖽
Regional CAMRA Pub of the Year, the Harewood
Arms has gone from strength to strength since it
was bought by the current owners in 2013. The
home of the Green Mill Brewery, it offers five
regular Green Mill beers plus seasonals, guests and
a rotating real cider. The bar has various seating
areas and two real fires. For warmer days, there is
a beer garden to the rear. The railway station is five
minutes' walk and buses pass by.
🚲🏵◐♿🅰🚆♣🍴🚪🐾🛜

Bromley Cross

Flag Inn ✅

Arnold Road, BL7 9HL (off B6472 Darwen Rd)

🌣 11-11 (midnight Fri & Sat) ☎ (01204) 598267
Bank Top Flat Cap; Greene King IPA; 6 changing beers (sourced locally; often Hopstar, Nook, Phoenix) ⊞
This popular local is well over 200 years old, and with timber decor, low ceilings and stone-flagged floors it has a very traditional feel. You can call in here after a walk over the local moors or a visit to the nearby Last Drop Village. Beers are dispensed from the viewing cellar adjacent to the bar. The outdoor seating area includes a rather quirky stillaged firkin cask dispensing water for our four-legged friends. ⍟⛲◑🖶(533,538)🐾🍴🛜

Bury

Black Bull ✅

8-10 Lowercroft Road, Starling, BL8 2EY (on B6196 from Bury)
🌣 12-midnight (1am Fri & Sat) ☎ (0161) 761 5961
⊕ theblackbullbury.co.uk
Thwaites Nutty Black, Original, Wainwright, Lancaster Bomber; 1 changing beer ⊞
This family-run local offers a warm and friendly welcome to drinkers and diners alike. Winner of a number of Thwaites' beer and cellar awards, it is also Cask Marque-accredited and takes great pride in serving the perfect pint. Guest beers are from the Thwaites 1807 Cask Club range. Excellent meals are served daily, prepared using locally sourced top-quality produce. Booking is recommended as the pub's reputation creates a high demand for tables. ⍟⛲◑🦽🖶(486,510)🐾🍴

Clarence ⅃

2 Silver Street, BL9 0EX
🌣 11-11; 12-11 Sun ☎ (0161) 464 7404 ⊕ theclarence.co.uk
Silver Street Session, One; 3 changing beers (sourced locally; often Deeply Vale, Silver Street) ⊞
The Clarence is an upmarket brewpub serving real ale and good food. The four-floored building has been lovingly restored, taking care to recreate the pub as it was. The basement houses the Silver Street brewery, the ground floor has the central main bar with original floor tiles (which showed the bar's location), the restaurant is on the first floor, and the second floor has a lounge and cocktail bar. Future plans involve moving the brewing facility into larger premises in Bury while keeping the existing brewery in situ.
⛲⍟◑🦽🚉(Bolton St/ELR)🖶🖶🐾🍴🛜

Lamb ⅃

533 Tottington Road, Woolfold, BL8 1UB (on B6213 from Bury)
🌣 4.30-11; 4-midnight Fri; 1-midnight Sat; 1-10.30 Sun
☎ (0161) 764 2714
2 changing beers (sourced locally; often Deeply Vale, Outstanding, Ramsbottom Craft) ⊞
Originally a coaching house dating back to 1831, this well-run local has an enviable reputation for being a friendly establishment. A warm welcome awaits all – regulars, visitors, young and old alike. An open fire burns in the winter months. The landlord is keen to promote local microbreweries, mainly Deeply Vale, Ramsbottom Craft, Moorhouse's and Outstanding, and others on a less regular basis. Breweries from further afield also feature. A local real cider from Red Bank is available all year. ⍟⛲♣🍴🖶(468,469)🐾🍴🛜

Robert Peel ⅃

10 Market Place, BL9 0LD
🌣 8am-midnight (1am Fri & Sat) ☎ (0161) 764 7287

Greene King Abbot; Ruddles Best Bitter; changing beers (often Brightside) ⊞
Situated in Bury's cultural quarter, the Robert Peel is well-established, popular and has the largest open public area in Bury, with a mixture of tables and booths. This Wetherspoon pub bears the name of the local mill owner and MP whose son became Prime Minister and founded the modern police force. The decor also celebrates other local worthies including Richmal Crompton, the author of the Just William books. Ciders are from Gwynt y Ddraig, Westons and Thatchers.
◑🦽🚉(Bolton St)🍴🍴🖶🛜

Rose & Crown ⅃

36 Manchester Old Road, BL9 0TR
🌣 5-11.30; 5-midnight Fri-Sun ☎ (0161) 959 5146
House beer (by Tetley); changing beers (often Bank Top, Castle Rock, Ramsbottom Craft) ⊞
A traditional, small and welcoming pub just a short walk from the town centre with helpful staff and a relaxed atmosphere. The clientele is varied and friendly. There is an impressive range of real ales and one real cider on handpump. Flights of three third-pints are available for the price of a pint. The pub opens from noon-3pm on Saturdays when Bury FC are at home and is popular with home fans. A live acoustic night is held on the first Thursday of every month. ⍟🚉🍴🍴🖶(92,98,135)

Cadishead

Grocers ▼

152a Liverpool Road, M44 5DD (close to Moss Lane)
🌣 5-10 (10.30 Fri); 2-10 Sat; 2-9 Sun; closed Mon ☎ 07950 522468
3 changing beers (sourced locally; often Brightside, Seven Bro7hers) ⒢
Salford's first true micropub opened in 2016 in a former shop, bringing real ale back to Cadishead. Beers from local micros are stillaged in a separate air-chilled room, served by gravity and brought to the customer by the owner. Three ciders and a perry are also available. Seating in the single room accommodates 20; a corridor provides extra standing room. There is a small yard at the rear with tables and bench seating.
⛲⍟🦽🍴🖶(67,100)🐾

Castleton

Blue Pits Inn

842 Manchester Road, OL11 2SP
🌣 12-midnight ☎ (01706) 632151
Lees Manchester Pale Ale, Bitter; 1 changing beer (sourced locally; often Lees) ⊞
The Blue Pits is a welcoming, friendly local in a former railway building that was once used as a mortuary. The building was fully refurbished by Lees in 2013 and as a result the three distinct drinking areas now offer a much warmer environment. Cards and darts are played in the taproom, and sports fixtures are shown on screen. A regular quiz night is hosted and karaoke on Fridays. Of particular interest is the tiled mosaic of John Willie Lees on the outside wall. Lees seasonal ales are available alongside the regulars.
⍟⛲🦽🚉♣🖶🐾🍴🛜

Chadderton

Crown Inn 🅛
72 Walsh Street, OL9 9LR (off Middleton Rd via Peel St)
🍺 3-11; 12-11 Fri-Sun ☎ (0161) 915 1557
Lees Bitter; 1 changing beer (sourced locally; often Greenfield, Millstone, Wilson Potter) ℍ
A large detached brick-built free house within walking distance of Chadderton town centre and close to the Oldham Metrolink line Freehold stop. The pub hosts darts, football and Rugby League teams. The regular beer is from JW Lees, with Greenfield, Wilson Potter and Millstone beers usually on sale. The landlord is currently in discussion with other local breweries to increase the choice. The pub has been awarded LocAle in recognition of its permanent range of locally produced beers. Live music or karaoke takes place on Saturday evenings 🏆&🍴♣🚌(415)🌟🎵♿

Rose of Lancaster ✪
7 Haigh Lane, OL1 2TQ
🍺 11.30-11 (11.30 Fri & Sat); 12-11 Sun ☎ (0161) 624 3031
🌐 roseoflancaster.co.uk
Lees Brewer's Dark, Manchester Pale Ale, Bitter; 1 changing beer (sourced locally; often Lees) ℍ
Sitting on the bank of the Rochdale Canal with lovely views to the rear and handy for both bus and train links, the Rose attracts a varied and lively clientele. Its conservatory restaurant, lounge bar and thriving separate vault (with screens for sporting events) provide a welcome choice within. Drinkers and diners mix easily in the lounge and the management ensures swift and cheerful service. Look out for the chalkboard detailing the number of pints of real ale sold. Outside, a covered patio is popular in summer.
🏆🍴&♿≠(Mills Hill)♣🅿🚌(59,64)🎵

Cheadle Hulme

Chiverton Tap
8 Mellor Road, SK8 5AU (off Station Rd)
🍺 4-10.30; 12-11 Fri & Sat; 12-10.30 Sun ☎ (0161) 485 4149
🌐 thechivertontap.co.uk
Bollington Long Hop; house beer (by Bollington); 4 changing beers (sourced locally) ℍ
This micropub opened in early 2015 in premises once used by draper Arthur Chiverton – note the mosaic in the entrance. The light and airy premises features a mix of tables and chairs while there are framed displays of drapery tools on the walls and inset into the bar. Six handpumps dispense two beers from Bollington alongside four mainly, but not exclusively, from local microbreweries. Beer tapas is available – three third-pint measures.
Q🏆&≠♿🚌🌟🎵

Chorlton-cum-Hardy

Bar 🅛
533 Wilbraham Road, M21 0UE (opp Morrisons)
🍺 12-11.30 (midnight Thu); 11.30-12.30am Fri & Sat; 11.30-11.30 Sun ☎ (0161) 861 7576 🌐 barchorlton.co.uk
Castle Rock Harvest Pale; 7 changing beers (sourced regionally; often Acorn, Magic Rock, Pictish) ℍ
A Chorlton institution specialising in cask beer for over 15 years and attracting the most diverse clientele in the area. Eight handpumps split over two sections of the bar focus on local breweries and the best micros from further afield. A choice of four ciders and perries is kept in the fridge. A full menu is served until 8.30pm daily with soups,

burgers, sandwiches, pub classics and pies from Lord of the Pies, plus traditional roasts on Sundays. Quiz night is Monday. 🏆&🍴🌟♣♿🚌🎵

Beech Inn ✪
72 Beech Road, M21 9EG
🍺 4-11; 12-midnight Fri & Sat; 12-11 Sun ☎ (0161) 312 0309
Copper Dragon Golden Pippin; Timothy Taylor Golden Best, Landlord; Wychwood Hobgoblin; 5 changing beers (sourced nationally) ℍ
The Beech has a long history in the Guide. The friendly team know their beer and have returned to the pub's roots, focusing on the quality of the ale. Four regular and five guest beers are available. The pub has undergone refurbishment, with a wood fire in the front room and seating outdoors to the rear. At the front, the smaller seating area is great for people-watching on Beech Road. Food is limited to bar snacks and pork pies but staff are happy for you to bring food in. Children are welcome until 7pm. Q🏆&🍴♣♿🚌🌟🎵

Dulcimer 🅛
567 Wilbraham Road, M21 0AE
🍺 4-12.30am (1.30am Fri); 12-1.30am Sat; 12-11.30 Sun ☎ (0161) 860 6444 🌐 dulcimer-bar.co.uk
Thwaites Wainwright; 4 changing beers (sourced nationally; often Blackjack, Oakham, Oud Craft) ℍ
Bar and music venue with five cask ales from local and national micros. House-branded beers are from Outstanding and the bar also has its own cuckoo brewery, Oud Craft Brew. Two or three bag-in-box ciders are available. The first floor regularly hosts live folk music gigs. Monday is quiz night and Tuesday folk jam with the Beech Band. There is a small beer garden/smoking area to the rear.
🏆🌟&♿🚌🌟🎵

Font 🅛
115-117 Manchester Road, M21 9PG
🍺 11-12.30am (1am Fri & Sat) ☎ (0161) 871 2022
🌐 thefontbar.wordpress.com
8 changing beers (sourced nationally; often Mallinson's, RedWillow) ℍ
Vibrant bar in the Font family with eight cask ales and at least four ciders. Featuring breweries such as RedWillow, Magic Rock, Vocation, Siren and Track, a wide range of bottles, and eight rotating craft keg (Cannonball on KeyKeg), there is plenty of choice. All draught beer is available in thirds, halves, two-thirds and pints. A small kitchen serves food including vegan and vegetarian-friendly options until 10pm daily. DJs provide the musical background on Fridays and Saturdays. Regular tap takeovers are hosted. 🏆🌟🍴🚌♿🚌🌟🎵

Marble Beer House 🅛
57 Manchester Road, M21 9PW (close to Chorlton Library)
🍺 12-11 (midnight Thu-Sat) ☎ (0161) 881 9206
🌐 marblebeers.com/beerhouse
Marble Lagonda IPA, Manchester Bitter, Pint; 3 changing beers (sourced locally) ℍ
The Beer House is a stalwart of the Chorlton bar scene and has been a mecca for cask ale lovers since it opened over 16 years ago. The knowledgeable team offers a warm welcome and serves a rotating and varied range of beers from Marble and guest breweries. A good choice of bottled beers (Marble and others) is also available. There are occasional music nights, quiz nights and pop-up food offerings in the front beer garden.
Q🏆🌟♣♿🚌🌟

Parlour

60 Beech Road, M21 9EG

✪ 12-11.30 (1am Fri & Sat); 12-11 Sun ☎ (0161) 881 3871
⊕ theparlour.info

6 changing beers (sourced locally) ⊞

Winner of awards for both food and excellent ale, and with a warm welcome for all, the Parlour has become a favourite. The bar is furnished with comfy sofas and to the front is an extended covered seating area facing the popular leafy Beech Road. The good British food menu features ingredients from local independent suppliers. RedWillow provides the regular beers and there is usually a dark beer among the range. Real cider is available. ➘❀◑⬤➡❀❦❅

Pi ℒ

99 Manchester Road, M21 9GA (500yds from B5217/ A6010 jct, opp Unicorn organic supermarket)

✪ 11-11 (12.30am Fri); 12-12.30am Sat; 12-11 Sun
☎ (0161) 882 0000 ⊕ abarcalledpi.com

Tatton Blonde; 3 changing beers (sourced regionally) ⊞

Small but perfectly formed, Pi is a popular bar on the increasingly crowded northern part of Manchester Road. Four real ales and a guest cider or perry are all on handpump alongside a selection of world beers on draught and an impressive menu of bottled beers from around the world. Food is a changing selection of Pieminister pies (with or without mash/peas and gravy) served until 11pm daily. Coffee, tea and cake are also available. ➘❀◑Ɽ⬤➡❀❅

Sedge Lynn ℒ ✅

21A Manchester Road, M21 9PN (next to Chorlton Library)

✪ 8am-11 (midnight Fri & Sat) ☎ (0161) 860 0141

Greene King Abbot; Moorhouse's Blond Witch; Phoenix Wobbly Bob; Ruddles Best Bitter; Sharp's Doom Bar; 5 changing beers (sourced nationally; often Acorn, Hawkshead, Kelham Island) ⊞

Built by Norman Evans as a billiard hall for the temperance movement, this Grade II-listed building, with a barrelled roof and Art Deco styling, is well-worth a look. This Wetherspoon establishment provides a typical selection of ales – the managers aim to ensure there is a range of light to darker beers always available on the 10 handpumps, including five different guests. Q➘❀◑Ŀ&Ɽ⬤➡❅

Crooke

Crooke Hall Inn ℒ

Crooke Road, WN6 8LR

✪ 12 (5 Mon & Tue)-11 ☎ (01942) 236088

AllGates California; 9 changing beers ⊞

This multi-roomed pub features beers from owners AllGates Brewery and a range of guests. The garden and children's play area at the rear overlook the Leeds-Liverpool Canal. Good food includes an excellent vegetarian selection and children are welcome until 9pm. The refurbished Cellar Bar provides a separate facility, is ideal for clubs and functions, and a ukulele club and folk club perform regularly. Local CAMRA Pub of the Year and Community Pub of the Year 2014 and 2015. ➘❀◑P❀❅

Delph

Royal Oak (Th' Heights) ℒ

Broad Lane, OL3 5TX (via Thame Lane, off main Delph-Denshaw road)

✪ 7 (5 Thu & Fri)-11; 12-6.30 Sun; closed Mon
☎ (01457) 874460

House beer (by Moorhouse's); 3 changing beers (sourced nationally; often Millstone) ⊞

Isolated 250 year-old stone-built pub on a packhorse route overlooking the Tame Valley. In a popular walking area, it benefits from outstanding views. The pub comprises a cosy bar and three rooms, each with an open fire. The refurbished side room boasts a hand-carved stone fireplace, while the comfortable snug has exposed beams and old photos of the inn. The house beer is from Moorhouse's and three changing guests include one from Millstone. A regular in the Guide for 25 consecutive years. Q❀P❀❅

Denton

Lowes Arms

301 Hyde Road, M34 3FF

✪ 12-11 ☎ (0161) 336 3064 ⊕ lowesarms.co.uk

4 changing beers (sourced locally; often Conwy) ⊞

Built in 1824 to serve the new Manchester Road, this thriving local has a reputation for quality beers and good-value food. Unusual for the area, the regular beers are from Conwy, alongside three others, mainly from local micros. To the left is the main food area and to the right is the vault, with wooden floor and pool table. The pub is home to local darts, dominoes and pool teams. Breakfast club is Saturdays and Sundays 10.30am-noon. ➘❀◑&♣P➡(201)❀

Didsbury

Fletcher Moss ✅

1 William Street, M20 6RQ (off Wilmslow Rd, A5145 via Albert Hill St)

✪ 12-11 (11.30 Thu; midnight Fri & Sat) ☎ (0161) 438 0073

Hydes Original; 5 changing beers (sourced nationally; often Hydes) ⊞

Named after the alderman who donated the nearby botanical gardens, this thriving community local attracts people of all ages and drinking tastes, all engaged in lively conversation. The front encompasses three traditional snugs, full of Hydes memorabilia and an extensive collection of porcelain teapots, while the rear opens up into a bright conservatory. Beyond that is a neat garden. A quiz features every Tuesday, acoustic music on alternate Mondays and an acoustic band monthly on a Saturday. Q❀◑&Ɽ⬤➡❅

Gateway ✅

882 Wilmslow Road, M20 5PG (jct Kingsway)

✪ 8am-11.30 (midnight Fri & Sat); 9am-11.30 Sun
☎ (0161) 438 1700

Ruddles Best Bitter; Sharp's Doom Bar; house beer (by Brightside); 5 changing beers (sourced nationally) ⊞

Large, comfortable and extremely popular late-1930s roadhouse conveniently located opposite the Parrs Wood Entertainment Centre and its public transport hub. It has a central island bar surrounded by various drinking areas, including quieter spaces to the rear, giving customers real choice. What makes this Wetherspoon such a deserved success however is the enthusiastic manager and staff who have successfully striven to create a real pub atmosphere and to provide excellent beer – long may it continue. Q♥♨✿❶♦☕♦P☐♠

Dobcross

Navigation Inn Ⓛ
21-23 Wool Road, OL3 5NS
✪ 12-3, 5-11 (midnight Fri); 12-11 Sat; 12-10.30 Sun
☎ (01457) 872418
Millstone Tiger Rut; Thwaites Wainwright; 2 changing beers Ⓗ
A busy family-run watering hole for boaters and walkers, next to the Huddersfield Narrow Canal, this stone pub of 1806 was built to slake the thirst of navvies cutting the Standedge Tunnel. It comprises an open-plan bar and L-shaped interior, with four handpumps offering a variety of guest beers. Freshly prepared food is popular, with special offers Monday to Saturday and occasional themed evenings. Food events raise funds for local charities. It is a venue for the popular Saddleworth Rushcart Festival in August. Families are welcome at all times. Q♥♨✿❶♦P☐(184,350)♣♠

Swan Inn (Top House) ✓
The Square, OL3 5AA
✪ 5-10.30 Mon; 12-3, 5-11 Tue-Thu; 12-3, 5-midnight Fri; 12-midnight Sat; 12-10.30 Sun ☎ (01457) 873451
⊕ theswandobcross.com
Banks's Sunbeam; Jennings Cumberland Ale; Marston's Pedigree; Thwaites Wainwright; 1 changing beer Ⓗ
A focal point for the local community, this rejuvenated stone pub and theatre venue overlooks the attractive village square. Built in 1765, the building has been tastefully renovated with three separate rooms, each with an open fire. The function room upstairs plays host to an astonishing array of frolics, fun and more serious stuff. A home-cooked menu features dishes from around the world. On Happy Mondays there are special offers on real ale, wine and coffee. A former Marston's National Pub of the Year and Best Illuminated Pub in Saddleworth 2014-15.
Q♥♨✿❶P☐(184,353,354)♣♠

Droylsden

Beehive
145 Market Street, M43 7AR
✪ 12-11 (midnight Fri & Sat); 12-10 Sun ☎ (0161) 971 8579
2 changing beers (sourced regionally) Ⓗ
Welcoming town-centre local, close to Droylsden FC, offering two real ales, often from local micros. It is a traditional two-roomed pub with a taproom with dartboard and TV and a lounge with a free jukebox. The lounge features old photographs of the town and many brass ornaments. Pub lunches are served daily. Live music plays most Fridays and some Saturdays, with a singalong on Monday afternoons. This former Wilsons pub features the old Manchester brewer's logo in tiling in the Gents.
♥✿❶♦♣♦P☐☐

Dukinfield

Angel
197 King Street, SK16 4TH
✪ 4-11; 3-midnight Fri; 12-midnight Sat; 12-11 Sun
☎ (0161) 830 0223
4 changing beers (sourced nationally) Ⓗ

A large red-brick pub on the main road close to the centre of Dukinfield, it is something of an oasis for real ale in the area. The pub features four regularly changing beers, nearly always from national microbreweries. There is a large, comfortable lounge, a good taproom and a function room available to hire. This is a pub to suit all tastes and age ranges - it can get busy when one of the local Premier League football sides is on TV.
♥✿❶♦♿♣P☐(330)♠

Eccles

Lamb Hotel ★
33 Regent Street, M30 0BP (opp Metrolink station)
✪ 11.30-11 (11.30 Sat); 12-11 Sun ☎ 07702 400292
Holt Mild, Bitter; 1 changing beer (sourced nationally; often Fuller's, Greene King, Thwaites) Ⓗ
A Grade II listed, red brick and terracotta Edwardian pub from 1906. The central bar serves an L-shaped vault and a lobby that leads to two comfortable lounges and the still-used billiards room with full-sized table. With traditional woodwork, half-tiled walls and etched glass, CAMRA recognises this pub as having a nationally important historic interior. The curved glass windows are typical of Holt's pubs of this era. A guest reciprocal beer may be available. ✿❶♣P☐♣♠

Fallowfield

Friendship ✓
353 Wilmslow Road, M14 6XS (on B5093, jct Egerton Rd)
✪ 12-11 (midnight Fri & Sat) ☎ (0161) 224 5758
Hydes 1863, Hydes Original; 7 changing beers (sourced nationally; often Hydes) Ⓗ
Impressive Victorian mansion in a busy student area. Although it mainly caters for a younger crowd, it does attract a good mix of folk, especially when live sport is shown on the many TV screens. A large horseshoe bar serves a snug, lounge and the large rear extension – this latter area has created more space for the provision of popular pizzas and Italian food. Nine handpumps offer the Hydes range, as well as varying guest ales and ciders. A quiz is held twice weekly. ✿❶♦♿♦P☐♠

Gatley

Horse & Farrier ✓
144 Gatley Road, SK8 4AB (jct Church Rd)
✪ 11-11 (midnight Fri & Sat); 12-10.30 Sun
☎ (0161) 428 2080
Hydes 1863, Original; 6 changing beers (sourced nationally; often Hydes) Ⓗ
Originally three cottages, this former coaching inn is a Tudor-style, low-ceilinged, Hydes heritage house with a central bar that serves several rooms. Refurbished in early 2016, a new dining room in the style of an orangery and a beer garden to the front of the pub were added. The beer range has been extended to include four Hydes/Beer Studio beers plus four guests, and quarterly beer festivals are held. The cider varies. Live bands play at weekends. Q✿❶♿♦P☐(11,11A,44)♠

Greenfield

King William IV Ⓛ ✓
134 Chew Valley Road, OL3 7DD
✪ 12 (2 Mon & Tue Jan-Mar)-midnight ☎ (01457) 873933

Black Sheep Best Bitter; Tetley Bitter; **4 changing beers (sourced locally; often Greenfield, Millstone)** ⓗ
Stone-built pub comprising a central bar and two rooms, one with a wood-burning stove. A benched, cobbled forecourt at the front is used for drinking and smoking. Six handpumps serve three LocAles including Greenfield and Millstone. Home-cooked food is served Wednesday to Sunday. The King Bill is the centre of village life, featuring in the annual August Rushcart Festival and Whit Friday brass band contest. It can get busy when live football is shown. Children and dogs are welcome.
👸⛲🌙◑▲♣⯑🏠(180,350)🐾🐕📶

Railway Inn ⓛ
11 Shaw Hall Bank Road, OL3 7JZ (opp station)
🕐 12-midnight (12.30am Thu & Fri); 11.30-12.30am Sat
☎ (01457) 872307 ⊕ therailwaygreenfield.com
Adnams Lighthouse; Copper Dragon Golden Pippin; Millstone Tiger Rut; Theakston Old Peculier; 2 changing beers ⓗ
Unspoilt pub comprising a central bar, lounge, games area and taproom with a log fire and old photos of Saddleworth. The Railway is a popular venue for all styles of live music on Thursday, Friday (unplugged night) and Sunday. It is also a stop-off on the Transpennine Real Ale Trail. In a picturesque area, the pub affords beautiful views across Chew Valley from the beer garden and is a great base for outdoor pursuits. Various ciders are served on gravity.
Q⛲▲⯑♣⯑🏠(180,184,350)🐾📶

Wellington Inn ⓛ
29 Chew Valley Road, OL3 7AF (near Tesco)
🕐 3-9 Mon; 12 (3 Tue)-11; 12-9 Sun
Nook Blond; Phoenix Arizona; Salopian Lemon Dream; Thwaites Nutty Black, Original, Wainwright; 1 changing beer ⓗ
Friendly village local which became a privately owned free house in 2011. On the end of a terrace, it has a small bar area, an open-plan room catering for diners and a separate function/sports room with dominoes, cribbage and a dartboard. Good-value home-made food features pies, puddings and real chips, served all day Wednesday to Sunday, with fish specials on Friday. A guest beer is sometimes available and real cider in summer.
👸◑▲⯑♣⯑🏠(180,350,353)🐾📶

Harwood

House Without a Name ⓛ
75 Lea Gate, BL2 3ET
🕐 12-midnight (1am Fri & Sat) ☎ (01204) 433568
⊕ housewithoutaname.co.uk
Holt Bitter; 5 changing beers (sourced locally; often Lancaster, Moorhouse's, Outstanding) ⓗ
Locally known as the No Name, this cosy terraced pub was originally two cottages built in the 1830s. It has been sensitively modernised and refurbished, and has a main lounge with the bar, blackboard beer listings, a big-screen TV and a real fire, and a small bar to the left with a dartboard and TV. Simple bar food is available throughout opening hours. All premium TV sports channels are screened. 👸⛲◑♣⯑🏠(480,507)🐾📶

Heaton Chapel

Heaton Hops
7 School Lane, SK4 5DE (jct Manchester Rd)

🕐 4.30-10 Tue; 1.30-10 Wed & Sun; 1.30-11 Thu-Sat; closed Mon ☎ (0161) 442 3541 ⊕ heatonhops.co.uk
2 changing beers (sourced regionally) ⓗ
Cosy, friendly micropub with two small rooms (one downstairs), bench seating and high stools. It has made a huge impact in the relatively short time it has been open, winning the CityLife Awards 2015 Best Pub in Greater Manchester. As well as cask beers, mostly from local micros, and ciders, it sells a large range of bottle-conditioned beers from the UK and around the world. Beers are available to take away, too. ⛲🚆⯑🏠🐕

High Lane

Royal Oak
Buxton Road, SK6 8AY
🕐 12-midnight ☎ (01663) 766827
Marston's Burton Bitter, Pedigree; 4 changing beers ⓗ
Traditional inn on the main A6 as it ascends from Stockport towards the Peak District and Lyme Park. It offers four guest beers from the Marston's portfolio in addition to the two regular Marston's beers. Food is served lunchtimes and evenings during the week and 12-6pm at weekends. Families are welcome and a dog-friendly room is available. The pub is home to crib, darts and pool league teams. Q👸⛲🌙◑🚆♣⯑🏠🐕

Higher Broughton

Duke of York
97 Marlborough Road, M7 4SP (opp Inghamwood Close)
🕐 11-11 (midnight Fri & Sat); 11-10.30 Sun
☎ (0161) 792 6941
Holt Mild, Bitter ⓗ
Dating back to 1899, this imposing Victorian gothic building has all the hallmarks of a truly great Holt's establishment. It is multi-roomed with a central drinking area incorporating a large horseshoe bar and exquisite etched-glass panels. A much-cherished survivor in an area decimated by pub closures in the Hightown clearances of the early '70s, a true sense of community makes this a most welcoming pub. Live music features at weekends. ⛲♣🏠(52,149)📶

Hindley

Hare & Hounds
31 Ladies Lane, WN2 2QA
🕐 2 (3 Mon)-midnight; 12-midnight Sat & Sun
☎ (01942) 516657
AllGates Wigan Junction; 3 changing beers ⓗ
This small but traditional pub located between the railway station and town centre has a large cosy lounge and a distinct bar/vault area. The lounge displays pictures from bygone Hindley and has a large-screen TV for sport. This is an AllGates pub serving its own beers and a range of guests. The pub has a darts team playing in the local league. Quiz night is Thursday. Q👸⛲🚆♣🏠(559)📶

Holcombe Brook

Hare & Hounds ⓛ ✓
400 Bolton Road West, BL0 9RY (on A676 at jct with Longsight Rd)
🕐 12-11 (midnight Thu-Sat) ☎ (01706) 822107
⊕ hare-and-hounds-bury.co.uk

10 changing beers ⊞
There has been an inn on this site for over 100 years and the multi award-winning venue has recently had a major refurbishment. Beer festivals are held throughout the year – the landlord sources ales from around the country, especially from new breweries. The pub has its own quiz team. Excellent food is served until 10pm. Sports events are screened on TV and the function room is free to hire. ⏣⏣⏣⏣⏣🅿🚃(472,474)⏣🔊

Horwich

Bank Top Brewery Ale House ⃝L
36 Church Street, BL6 6AD
✪ 12-11 (11.30 Fri & Sat) ☎ (01204) 693793
Bank Top Bad to the Bone, Dark Mild, Flat Cap, Gold Digger, Old Slapper, Port o' Call; 3 changing beers (sourced locally) ⊞
This is Bank Top Brewery's second tied pub and has been refurbished to a high standard. It is situated opposite Horwich Parish Church with excellent views of Rivington Pike. A welcome addition to the Horwich real ale scene and a popular starting point for a pub crawl around the town, it offers eight competitively priced beers from the Bank Top range plus one ever-changing guest alongside six varying real ciders or perries. Walkers and their dogs are welcome. ⏣⏣🚃(125)⏣

Brewery Bar ⃝L
Moreton Mill, Hampson Street, BL6 7JH
✪ 4-11 Thu & Fri; 2-11 Sat; 2-7.30 Sun; closed Mon-Wed
☎ (01204) 692976 ⊕ blackedgebrewery.co.uk
Blackedge Hop, Black, Pike, Platinum, IPA, Black Port; 1 changing beer (sourced locally) ⊞
Newly opened bar above Blackedge Brewery offering a changing range of seven of the brewery's beers. The bar and drinking area are on the first floor up a flight of stairs, with the brewery visible through large glass windows. Comfortable settees and barrel tables with stools are spread throughout the large drinking area. On Saturday match days the bar opens at noon. ⏣⏣🅿🚃(125,517)🔊

Crown ⃝L
1 Chorley New Road, BL6 7QJ (on B6226)
✪ 11-11 (midnight Fri & Sat); 12-11.30 Sun
☎ (01204) 693109
Holt Mild, IPA, Bitter, Two Hoots; 4 changing beers (sourced locally; often Bootleg) ⊞
A grand local landmark near Lever Park and the West Pennine Moors. The spacious pub has been recently refurbished while retaining its high ceilings and original features. It has a separate pool and games room with its own bar where darts, dominoes and pool teams play. All sports are screened in the games room and other side rooms. Various artists provide entertainment on Sunday evenings. An ideal spot for a refreshing pint after a walk to Rivington Pike or around the nearby reservoirs. Q⏣⏣⏣⏣🅿🚃🔊

Victoria & Albert ⃝L
114 Lee Lane, BL6 7AF
✪ 4-11 (midnight Fri); 2-midnight Sat; 2-11 Sun
☎ (01204) 770837 ⊕ vicandalbert.co.uk
Holt Bitter; 6 changing beers (sourced locally; often Abbeydale, Elland, Ossett) ⊞
Formerly the Albert Arms, the pub is situated across the road from Horwich Public Hall. Refurbished to a high standard, it is a comfortable lounge-style

venue with three separate seating areas. There are six changing beers – Thornbridge Brewery often features alongside the regulars. The pub is handy for Lever Park and walks up to Rivington Pike. Over-21s only. A frequent local CAMRA Pub of the Year. Q⏣⏣🚃(125,517)

Hyde

Cheshire Ring Hotel ▾ ⃝L
72-74 Manchester Road, SK14 2BJ
✪ 4 (12 Sat)-11; 12-10.30 Sun ☎ 07917 055629
Beartown Kodiak Gold, Bearskinful, Polar Eclipse; 4 changing beers (often Beartown) ⊞
One of the oldest pubs in Hyde, the building was comprehensively overhauled several years ago by Beartown. Seven handpumps offer a range of Beartown ales and guests from micros, in addition to ciders, perries and continental beers. A selection of bottled beers is also stocked. Gentle background music plays. Home-made curries are available on Thursday evenings. Opening hours vary with the season – closing time may be earlier on Mondays and Tuesdays. ⏣⏣⏣⏣🅿🚃(201)⏣

Sportsman Inn ⃝L
57 Mottram Road, SK14 2NN
✪ 12-midnight ☎ (0161) 368 5000
Rossendale Floral Dance, Glen Top Bitter, Ale, Halo Pale, Pitch Porter, Sunshine ⊞
A regular in the Guide, the pub offers a full range of Rossendale Brewery ales plus a mild from Thwaites and real cider on a changing basis. Upstairs is a restaurant specialising in Cuban food and tapas. The pub is home to football, darts and pool teams and hosts matches for the local chess team. The rear patio includes a covered and heated smoking area. A former CAMRA pub of the region, it is popular with locals and retains its character. ⏣⏣⏣⏣⏣🅿🚃(201,202)⏣🔊

Leigh

George & Dragon
7 King Street, WN7 4LP
✪ 11-11 (midnight Fri & Sat); 12-11 Sun ☎ (01942) 605214
Moorhouse's Blond Witch; 2 changing beers ⊞
A pub with a Tudor façade in the centre of Leigh near the bus station serving a changing range of guest beers. Many TV screens show live Rugby League and football matches. There is a large outdoor seating area to the rear. No children are allowed and no food is served. ⏣⏣🅿🚃🔊

Thomas Burke ⃝L ✅
Leigh Road, WN7 1QR
✪ 12-midnight ☎ (01942) 609144
Greene King Abbot; changing beers ⊞
Popular with all ages, this Wetherspoon pub is named after a renowned Leigh tenor, known as the Lancashire Caruso. The pub divides into three areas: the main long bar, a raised dining area and, in what was once a cinema foyer, lounge-style seating. Ten handpumps offer a changing range of beers from local and distant breweries. Q⏣⏣⏣⏣🚃🔊

Waterside Inn ✅
Canal Street, WN7 4DB
✪ 11-11 (3am Thu & Fri) ☎ (01942) 605005
⊕ watersideinn-leigh.co.uk
Greene King IPA; 4 changing beers ⊞

The Waterside Inn is a large converted warehouse, situated next to the canal with waterside seating. With wooden beams and themed coal fires, this is a setting that will suit most people. Shoppers and office workers enjoy a range of pub food at lunchtime and at night it is popular with the 18-25 circuit trade, with DJs and live entertainment. ❀❁❂❃❄❅❆❇

White Lion ♟ 🅛

6A Leigh Road, WN7 1QL
✪ 12 (2 Mon-Wed)-midnight ☎ 07814 575883
AllGates California; 5 changing beers (often AllGates) 🅗
The White Lion is situated opposite Leigh's historic parish church just a few minutes' walk from the town centre. You can choose whether to enjoy the comfort of the main bar, bar games in the vault, or the quiet of the snug at this friendly, welcoming pub. Six handpumps dispense a selection of AllGates real ales plus guests. There are a number of screens for football and rugby. Strictly over-18s only. Q❀❁❂❃❄❅❆(12,582)❀❇

Littleborough

Red Lion 🅛

6 Halifax Road, OL15 0HB
✪ 2-midnight; 12.30-1am Fri & Sat; 1-midnight Sun
☎ (01706) 378195
Lees Bitter; Timothy Taylor Landlord; house beer (by Phoenix); changing beers (often Robinsons) 🅗
Detached stone-built pub nestling between the railway and canal (yet older than both) with four distinct rooms, each different in character. The main room is large and homely while the adjacent snug has comfortable high-backed chairs. Two further rooms are for games and TV sport. Up to six guest beers supplement the two regulars, with a house beer from Phoenix. German and Belgian beers and lagers are available on draught, and traditional ciders from Thatchers and Westons. A jam session features on Wednesday and quiz night is Thursday. Q❀❁❂❃❄❅❆❇

White House 🅛

Blackstone Edge, Halifax Road, OL15 0LG
✪ 12-3, 6.30-midnight; 12.30-10.30 Sun ☎ (01706) 378456
⊕ thewhitehousepub.co.uk
Theakston Best Bitter; 3 changing beers 🅗
Originally built in 1691 and named the Coach & Horses, the White House stands on the Pennine Way. At over 1,300ft it commands outstanding views over the local countryside. A family-run inn for over 30 years, it offers a friendly welcome to all, with two bars warmed by log fires. Four handpumps serve one regular beer and three guests, complemented by a wide range of bottled beers, cider and wine. An excellent food menu is available, served all day on Sunday. Q❀❁❂❃❄❅❆❇

Lowton

Travellers Rest ✓

443 Newton Road, WA3 1NZ
✪ 12-10.30 (midnight Fri & Sat) ☎ (01625) 293222
⊕ travellersrestlowton.com
Theakston Best Bitter; Thwaites Wainwright; 2 changing beers 🅗
Traditionally furnished pub/restaurant between Lowton and Newton-le-Willows, the Travellers Rest

has a number of seating areas and a separate restaurant. There is a bar area to the right for drinkers, serving ales from Thwaites and Theakston. Outside is a large garden and car park. Q❀❁❂❃❄❅❆❇(34)❀

Manchester: City Centre

Angel

6 Angel Street, M4 4BQ (off Rochdale Rd)
✪ 12-midnight; 12-9 Sun ☎ (0161) 833 4786
⊕ theangelmanchester.com
Bob's White Lion; 11 changing beers (sourced regionally; often Hawkshead, Liverpool Organic, Pictish) 🅗
A regular in the Guide, the pub offers a wide range of real ales on 11 handpumps, with two more reserved for real cider. The cosy L-shaped downstairs bar has mismatched furniture, bare wood floorboards, a grand piano and roaring log fire in winter. The restaurant is on the first floor. Quiz night is Monday. At the front, the beer garden overlooks the busy road. ❀❁❂❃❄❅❆❇

Britons Protection ★ 🅛 ✓

50 Great Bridgewater Street, M1 5LE
✪ 12-midnight (1am Fri & Sat); 12-11 Sun
☎ (0161) 236 5895
Jennings Cumberland Ale; Robinsons Unicorn; house beer (by Thwaites); 2 changing beers (sourced locally) 🅗
This Grade II-listed, 200 year-old multi-roomed inn is listed on CAMRA's National Inventory of Historic Pub Interiors and famous for its highly ornate ceilings. It is well known for great storytelling and regularly holds Old Time Music Hall events. It is also the home of the Manchester branch of the World Ship Society. A three times winner of the Best Pub – Pride of Manchester award, it is also a regular in this Guide. ❀❁❂❃❄❅❆❇

Cask

29 Liverpool Road, M3 4NQ
✪ 12-11 (midnight Fri & Sat); 12-10.30 Sun
☎ (0161) 819 2527
4 changing beers (sourced locally; often Pictish, Summer Wine, Track) 🅗
A bar for beer lovers, with knowledgeable staff, Cask specialises in UK and imported beers. It has four handpumps plus 14 keg taps – 10 permanent (including rare Budvar Dark) and four rotating guests, always including a nitro-stout. Fridges have a massive range of bottles from around the world. No food is served but you are welcome to bring your own. Well-behaved dogs permitted. ❀❁❂❃❄❅❆❇

Castle Hotel ✓

66 Oldham Street, M4 1LE (near Warwick St)
✪ 12-1am (2am Fri & Sat); 12-midnight Sun
☎ (0161) 237 9485 ⊕ thecastlehotel.info
Robinsons Dizzy Blonde, Cumbria Way, Unicorn, Trooper; 5 changing beers (sourced regionally; often Robinsons) 🅗
The only Robinsons pub in Manchester city centre is a tenancy run by an enterprising team. The Grade II-listed building has a ceramic frontage. On entering you are greeted by a wonderful tiled bar with an array of handpumps. Four guest ales complement the Robinsons beers, along with Old Rosie cider. There are two rooms along the corridor – the second is used as a music venue and is worth a look for the skylight. ❀❁❂❃(Victoria)❄❅❆❇

City Arms 🄻 ✅

46-48 Kennedy Street, M2 4BQ

✪ 12-11 (midnight Fri & Sat); 12-8 Sun ☎ (0161) 236 4610

Moorhouse's Pride of Pendle; 6 changing beers (sourced regionally; often Moorhouse's, Titanic, Howard Town) Ⓗ

Multi award-winning pub with two traditional rooms and many original features. With six handpumps serving a full range of beer styles in excellent condition, the City Arms has been a regular in the Guide for many years. Saturday evenings are Northern Soul nights but mostly the pub is noisy with the buzz of convivial conversation. Q🅑➳🏠🌓🍴🛇🛤🕗🍴🖥🛆🚌🕿

Crown & Kettle

2 Oldham Road, M4 5FE (corner of Great Ancoats St)

✪ 12-11 (midnight Fri & Sat); 12-10.30 Sun

☎ (0161) 236 2923 ⊕ thecrownandkettle.co.uk

Ossett Silver King; 8 changing beers (sourced locally) Ⓗ

This Grade II-listed, street-corner building with a real ale bar, dedicated cider bar with a notable ornate ceiling and central snug was named CAMRA Regional Pub of the Year in 2015. Regular beer festivals are held, live bands play weekly and there are occasional pie-eating competitions. Beers from far and wide as well as from local micros are served from the nine handpumps and third-pint measures can be bought.

🏠🛤(Victoria)🛆🍴🖥🐾🕿

Knott Bar 🄻

374 Deansgate, M3 4LY

✪ 12-11.30 (midnight Thu; 12.30am Fri & Sat)

☎ (0161) 839 9229 ⊕ knottbar.co.uk

House beer (by Marston's); 4 changing beers (sourced nationally) Ⓗ

A modern bar with a continental feel, famous for its real ales and extensive range of foreign beers alongside British keg. One regular ale is complemented by five guests typically including several from local breweries. Real cider is also always available. Excellent transport links make this an ideal start or end point for a crawl. A selection of meals is available daily with all food cooked fresh including interesting vegetarian and vegan options. 🛇🏠🌓🛆🛤🛆🍴🖥🕿

Marble Arch ★

73 Rochdale Road, Collyhurst, M4 4HY (corner Gould St)

✪ 12-11 (midnight Fri & Sat) ☎ (0161) 832 5914

⊕ marblebeers.com/marble-arch

Marble Pint, Manchester Bitter, Chocolate Marble, Earl Grey IPA; 6 changing beers (sourced nationally; often Blackjack, Magic Rock, RedWillow) Ⓗ

From the tiled walls to the sloping floor, this is a gem of a pub. The atmospheric Arch showcases Marble Beers' range of cask, bottled and KeyKeg ales alongside two or three beers from selected regional breweries. There is an additional handpump for cider. An interesting and changing range of pub food is served. The main bar has an open fire in winter and there is a semi-covered area outside for warmer days. Dogs are welcome, with bowls provided.

Q🛇🏠🌓(Victoria)🛆🍴🖥🐾🕿

Micro Bar

Unit FC16, Arndale Market, M4 3AH (in food market)

✪ 11-7; 12-5 Sun ☎ (0161) 277 9666

⊕ boggart-brewery.co.uk

Boggart Hole Clough Rum Porter; 3 changing beers (sourced nationally) Ⓗ

Incongruously set among the food stalls of the Arndale Market, this original micropub has been trading for 10 years now. Previously run by Paradise and then by Boggart breweries, it is now a free house selling four changing beers from smaller breweries, plus a real cider. A wide range of bottled beers often includes rarities from new breweries. No food is served, but if you are hungry, look around you. Note that hours are limited to market opening times. 🛇🛆🛤🛆🍴🖥🚌🕿

Paramount ✅

33 Oxford Street, M1 4BH (jct Portland St)

✪ 7am-midnight; 7am-1am Fri & Sat ☎ (0161) 233 1820

Moorhouse's Blond Witch; Robinsons Trooper; Thwaites Wainwright; house beer (by Elland); changing beers (sourced nationally) Ⓗ

A classic city-centre Wetherspoon in that it is both large and busy. Run by an enthusiastic and long-serving manager, this outlet has a notably positive attitude to both the range and quality of its cask beers. The pub is named after an old cinema that stood on the site, and a theatrical theme is reflected in the decor. It is well placed for many of the city's entertainment venues like the Palace Theatre and Bridgewater Hall. ◖🛆🛤🛆🍴🖥(1,3)🕿

Pie & Ale

Units 1-2 Northern Quarter Arcade, The Hive, Lever Street, M1 1FN (via entrance on Faraday St)

✪ 12-11 (midnight Fri & Sat) ☎ (0161) 227 1610

⊕ pieandale.com

House beer (by Wells); 5 changing beers (sourced nationally) Ⓗ

This modern bar showcases a range of mostly local micro-brewed ales, plus a low-priced house beer, Yipee Pie Ale, together with a selection of mouth-watering pies from the bakery across the way. Real cider has recently been added. Booth seating is to the left of the bar and an upstairs mezzanine area provides more space. There is outside seating at the front. 🛇🏠◖🛆🛤🛆🍴🖥🕿

Port Street Beer House

39-41 Port Street, M1 2EQ (opp Brewer St)

✪ 4 (12 Fri)-midnight; 12-1am Sun; 12-midnight Sun

☎ (0161) 237 9949 ⊕ portstreetbeerhouse.co.uk

7 changing beers (sourced nationally) Ⓗ

A much-loved prize-winning real ale bar on the edge of the Northern Quarter of the city. A mecca for real ale fans and students alike, the range of tipples is diverse and the staff have a genuine passion for the ales. A good choice of traditional and more experimental beers is available, all in prime condition. The buses of Stevenson Square are close by. 🛇🏠🛤🛆🍴🖥🐾🕿

Rising Sun 🄻 ✅

22 Queen Street, M2 5HX ☎ (0161) 834 1193

7 changing beers (sourced nationally) Ⓗ

Traditional, historic, city-centre pub off Deansgate, with entrances on Queen Street and Lloyd Street. Seven handpumps dispense a range of ever-changing beers, with the recent addition of ales from Salford-based Seven Brothers, alongside a regular real cider. Food is served lunchtimes (Mon-Fri). The pub hosts regular beer festivals and Meet the Brewer evenings. An impressive refurbishment has made a huge difference to the feel of this friendly establishment. ◖🛤🛆🍴🖥🐾

Sandbar

**120-122 Grosvenor Street, Chorlton-on-Medlock,
M1 7HL** (off Oxford Rd A34/B5117 jct)
☼ 12-midnight (1am Thu; 2am Fri & Sat)
⊕ sandbarmanchester.co.uk

Facer's Clwyd Gold; Phoenix Arizona; 5 changing
beers (sourced regionally) Ⓗ

This excellent conversion of two 18th-century
townhouses into a quirky and bohemian bar is now
a long-established feature of the university area
beer scene. Popular with both students and staff,
there are regular exhibitions of photographs,
paintings and curios. The cask beers, often sourced
from local brewers, are complemented by a range
of European and modern British bottled and canned
beers. The cider is a changing guest, often from a
smaller producer. Food at weekends features
home-made pizzas. ⊛◑▶≉●🖾🛜

Sir Ralph Abercromby

35 Bootle Street, M2 5GU
☼ 12-11 (midnight Fri & Sat) ☎ (0161) 222 6467

Copper Dragon Golden Pippin; Moorhouse's Blond
Witch; Timothy Taylor Landlord; 2 changing beers
(sourced locally; often Seven Bro7hers) Ⓗ

A traditional town pub with a great atmosphere.
The large beer garden – rare for the city centre – is
a suntrap in the summer. The beers rotate, with
one pump dedicated to dark brews. The building,
named after the 18th-century British army
commander-in-chief in Ireland, is the only structure
remaining from St Peter's Field, where more than a
dozen people were killed during the 1819 Peterloo
Massacre. ⥁⊛◑▶≉🝙P🐾🛜

Waterhouse Ⓛ ✔

67-71 Princess Street, M2 4EG (opp town hall)
☼ 8am-midnight ☎ (0161) 200 5380

Greene King Abbot; Hawkshead Windermere Pale;
Phoenix Wobbly Bob; Sharp's Doom Bar; 5 changing
beers (sourced nationally) Ⓗ

Standing adjacent to the town hall, this
Wetherspoon outlet is unusual for the chain in that
it has a split interior with several areas for drinking
and dining. The four regular beers are
complemented by a varied range of six guest ales
often from local micros. Meet the Brewer nights
feature regularly and such is the relationship
between the cellar team and local breweries that
the pub often stocks beers that have been
produced in collaboration between the two.
Q⥁⊛◑▶🖕≉●🝙🖾🛜

Wharf Ⓛ

6 Slate Wharf, Castlefield, M15 4ST
☼ 11-11 (midnight Fri & Sat); 11-10.30 Sun
☎ (0161) 220 2960

Brunning & Price Original; Thwaites Wainwright;
Weetwood Cheshire Cat; 9 changing beers (sourced
nationally) Ⓗ

Impressive pub with a large terrace overlooking
the Castlefield Basin where the Bridgewater and
Rochdale canals meet, making this a popular
mooring point for leisure boaters. The bar boasts 12
handpumps, nine serving guest beers including
one dedicated to a stout/porter and one
dispensing a real cider. Food is a major attraction
with meals served in the ground-floor bar area and
the restaurant upstairs. Knowledgeable staff can
advise on a wide range of wines and whiskies and
regular Meet the Brewer/Distiller nights are held.
Q⥁⊛◑▶🖕≉🝙♣●P🖾🛜

Marple

Railway

223 Stockport Road, SK6 6EN
☼ 12-11; 12-10.30 Sun ☎ (0161) 427 2146

Robinsons Wizard, Dizzy Blonde, Unicorn Ⓗ

First opened in 1878, replacing a pub called the
Gun Inn, this impressive hostelry has two airy
rooms and an outside verandah and drinking area.
Located close to Rose Hill Station, it is convenient
for rail commuters, and is also handily positioned
for walkers and cyclists on the nearby Middlewood
Way and Goyt Valley Way. Well-run, with a friendly
atmosphere, this is a pleasant place to while away
some time. ⊛◑🖕≉P🖾(358,383,384)

Marple Bridge

Norfolk Arms

2 Town Street, SK6 5DS
☼ 12-11; 12-10.30 Sun ☎ (0161) 427 8090
⊕ thenorfolkarms.co.uk

4 changing beers (sourced regionally; often
Blackjack, Green Mill, Moorhouse's) Ⓗ

A recently refurbished stone-built pub in an
attractive setting next to the Goyt river bridge. The
atmosphere is warm and friendly, with good-value
food available and four real ales, usually from
microbreweries. Comfortably furnished, it attracts a
wide clientele by catering for all tastes. The beer
range is a good addition to the choice in the area.
Live music plays on Thursdays and occasional beer
festivals are held in the summer.
Q⥁⊛◑▶🖕≉🖾(375,383,384)🐾🛜

Mellor

Oddfellows Arms ✔

73 Moor End Road, SK6 5PT
☼ 4-11 Tue-Thu; 12-11 Fri-Sun; closed Mon
☎ (0161) 449 7826 ⊕ oddfellowsmellor.com

Marston's Pedigree; 3 changing beers (sourced
regionally) Ⓗ

Elegant stone-built pub tucked away in a dip in the
road in the old part of the village. The smart but
traditional interior is enhanced by beams and
flagged floors, with blazing real fires in winter.
Guest beers are often from micros such as Marble,
Howard Town and Thornbridge. Sought-after food
comes from a realistic menu with a gourmet twist.
The 375 bus service passes the door but runs only
infrequently. ⊛◑🖕▲P🖾(375)🐾

Middleton

Ring o' Bells

St Leonards Square, M24 6DJ
☼ 5-midnight; 12-1am Fri & Sat; 12-midnight Sun
☎ (0161) 654 9245 ⊕ ringobellsmiddleton.co.uk

Lees Manchester Pale Ale, Bitter; 1 changing beer
(sourced locally; often Lees) Ⓗ

Situated in the conservation area, the pub enjoys a
fine location opposite the historic parish church and
just above Jubilee Park. Live music, Sunday lunches
and quizzes add to its appeal. Community focused,
it hosts an annual Maypole event on May bank
holiday Monday and a unique Pace Egg play on
Easter Monday. Upstairs, the function room
features an unusual set of old collages made from
butterflies. There is a covered smoking area and
beer garden to the rear. ⊛◑♣P🖾🐾🛜

Tandle Hill Tavern

14 Thornham Lane, M24 2SD (1 mile on unmetalled road from either A664 or A627)

☼ 5-10 (11 Fri); 12-10.30 Sat & Sun; closed Mon & Tue
☎ (0161) 376 4492

Lees Bitter; house beer (by Lees); 1 changing beer (sourced locally; often Lees) ⊞

Set on the top of a hill, up an unmade, potholed lane in the Tandle Country Park, this neat little pub nestles among a number of farms. It comprises a main bar and lounge area with a separate quiet side room. A walled rear beer garden and benches to the front and side provide outdoor seating. Popular with walkers, farmers and locals, dogs are welcome. Food is limited to toasties. The house beer, Bumpy Lane, is dry-hopped Lees Bitter. In adverse weather, or in winter, phone ahead to check opening times. Q❀✿

Milnrow

Waggon Inn

35 Butterworth Hall, OL16 3PE

☼ 11-11 (midnight Fri & Sat); 12-11 Sun; closed Tue & Wed
☎ (01706) 648313

Banks's Bitter; 2 changing beers ⊞

The Waggon, locally known as the Back Waggon, was built in 1782 and retains many of its original features including mullioned windows. A recent refurbishment has sympathetically maintained the traditional ambience. A change in landlord has brought with it an excellent menu, available until 9pm (5pm Sun), with an emphasis on Spanish tapas. The fine food is complemented by three beers supplied by Marston's, two of which change on a monthly basis. The pub is within easy walking distance of the Manchester Metrolink Milnrow stop and local bus services. ➱❀◐♿♨P🗟❖

Monton

Malt Dog

169 Monton Road, M30 9GS (opp Park Hotel)

☼ 5 (4 Wed & Thu; 1 Fri & Sat)-11; 1-10.30
Sun ☎ 07541 553646

3 changing beers (sourced locally) ⊞

A small, friendly community pub converted from what once was a jewellery shop. The ground-floor bar is open plan and there is a spacious upstairs lounge. Occasional live music is hosted as well as Meet the Brewer and beer tasting events. A range of mainly Belgian and German draught foreign beers is available, plus a selection of bottled beers for off-sales. The draught beers can also be purchased as carryouts. Food bought at the deli next door can be eaten in the bar.
Q➱❀🗟(22,33,68)❖🛜

Mossley

Britannia Inn ✓

217 Manchester Road, OL5 9AJ

☼ 2-midnight; 12-1am Fri & Sat; 12-midnight Sun
☎ (01457) 838474

Marston's Burton Bitter; 5 changing beers (sourced locally) ⊞

This fine gritstone building overlooks the station yard and car park. It was bought by Shaw & Bentley's Bardsley Brewery in 1887, passed to Rothwell's of Newton Heath in 1902 and Marston's in 1961. Today the Brit belongs to a pubco. Outside there is a covered seating area for drinkers and smokers. Within, the semi-open plan pub has a games room, bar and cosy dining area. Meals are served until 7.30pm (5pm Sun). ➱❀◐♿♣🗟(343,350)🛜

Commercial Hotel ◪ ✓

58 Manchester Road, OL5 0AA

☼ 12-11 (midnight Fri & Sat) ☎ (01457) 510518

Millstone Tiger Rut, Stout; 3 changing beers (sourced nationally) ⊞

This pub is the closest to the station, though it pre-dates the railway and opened to cater for coach travellers. On several occasions in the 19th century it hosted Coroners' Courts – one concerned a man who had fallen into the canal after visiting the establishment. The Commi is a lively pub with bar areas, a games room and a stage for live acts or discos, usually on a Saturday. The pavement patio is popular in warmer weather.
➱❀♿♣🗟(343,350)❖🛜

Fleece ◪

53 Stamford Street, OL5 0LN

☼ 12-midnight (1am Fri & Sat) ☎ (01457) 835487

Irwell Works Tin Plate, Copper Plate, Iron Plate; Thwaites Original; 4 changing beers (sourced nationally) ⊞

The Fleece is in Brookbottom, less than half a mile from the station, but much higher up. You will deserve a pint after the climb – or you could catch the bus. In 1890 the inn could accommodate three travellers, feed up to 50 and stable one horse. Today the visitor will find a tidy pub with a small vault area, an airy back room and a lounge. Cider or perry is always available. Dogs are welcome but horses perhaps less so.
➱❀♿♣●P🗟(343,350)❖🛜

Oldham

Ashton Arms ◪

28-30 Clegg Street, OL1 1PL (rear of Town Square shopping centre)

☼ 11.30-11 (11.30 Fri & Sat); 11.30-8.30 Sun
☎ (0161) 630 9709

Changing beers ⊞

Extremely popular town-centre free house overlooking the new cinema complex, serving an excellent range of four to seven rotating beers from both new and long-established breweries. It specialises in local micros and LocAles, with themed beer festivals throughout the year. Traditional cider/perry is available all year round and a good selection of Belgian and German bottled beers is stocked. Good-value food is served weekdays until 6pm (3pm Fri), and sandwiches at the weekend. ◐♣●🗟🛜

Carrion Crow ✓

271 Huddersfield Road, OL4 2RJ

☼ 12-midnight ☎ (0161) 633 4490

6 changing beers (often Banks's, Jennings, Marston's) ⊞

Situated on the A62, the Crow is a former 18th-century coaching inn. A popular, friendly local, it serves quality ales from the Marston's range through six handpulls. Inexpensive home-cooked fare features locally sourced produce. The pub runs crib, darts, football and quiz teams. There are quarterly beer festivals, trips to theatres and cricket matches, an annual Christmas fair and a St George's Day walk. The landlord offers discounted cask ales on Monday night and CAMRA discounts are available Tuesday to Thursday. CAMRA Branch Pub of the Year 2014 and Marston's Best Cask Ale Pub West Region 2015. ♿❀◗�↔♣P🚲(350)🐾🛈🎵

Up Steps Inn ⓛ ✔

17-23 High Street, OL1 3AJ (between Spindles shopping centre and Tommyfield Market)
❀ 8am-midnight ☎ (0161) 627 5001
Greene King Abbot; Ruddles Best Bitter; changing beers ⓗ

Traditional town-centre Wetherspoon on the main shopping street near the bus station and market. There are usually two regular beers and six to eight rotating guests on offer, including several from local breweries under the LocAle scheme. The pub hosts beer festivals featuring specialist real ales and traditional ciders. Food is available all day from 8am, alcohol from 9am. Ciders are from Westons and Gwynt y Ddraig, with others at festival times. ◗♿🚲🛈🎵

Patricroft

Queen's Arms

Green Lane, M30 0SH (adjacent to railway station)
❀ 7 (5 Fri)-11; 12-11 Sat & Sun ☎ (0161) 789 2019
Thwaites Original; 1 changing beer (sourced nationally) ⓗ

Built in 1828 as the Patricroft Tavern for the coming of the new-fangled inter-city Liverpool and Manchester Railway, this is a wonderful, unspoilt pub. It was renamed in 1851 when Queen Victoria arrived on the train for the first royal visit to Salford. The vault is on the left as you enter and straight ahead is the lobby leading to a comfy snug and large, pleasant lounge. Winner of CAMRA branch Traditional Pub of the Year in 2016.
Q♿❀↔♣P🚲(67,100)🐾

Ramsbottom

Irwell Works Brewery Tap ⓛ

Irwell Street, BL0 9YQ
❀ 12-11; closed Mon ☎ (01706) 825091
🌐 irwellworksbrewery.co.uk
Irwell Works Tin Plate, Copper Plate, Richard Mason 1888, Steam Plate, Iron Plate; 5 changing beers (often Irwell Works) ⓗ

The Irwell Works Brewery is situated in the former Irwell Steam, Tin, Copper and Iron Works foundry. The building was used as an engineering works until a few years ago. It now houses a six-barrel brewery above the entrance on Strang Street. A balcony was opened in 2015. The bar offers a minimum of seven beers and locally produced Ribble Valley Gold cider. Small plates of food are served at lunchtime. Brewery tours are available on request. ◗↔(ELR)🚶🚲(472,474)🐾

Major Hotel ⓛ ✔

158 Bolton Street, BL0 9JA
❀ 3-11 Mon & Tue; 12-midnight ☎ (01706) 826777
Bank Top Flat Cap; St Austell Tribute; 2 changing beers ⓗ

Now in its ninth year under the current owners, the stone-built Major prides itself on being a traditional local, with a large logburner in the main lounge. The central bar features Sky TV, pool, darts and dominoes. Four real ales are sold, from local brews to those from further afield. Unpretentious and reasonably priced food is available, ranging from snacks to full meals. There is a small beer garden

with bench seating and a heated smoking area. The pub is a short walk from the steam railway and has a large car park adjacent.
♿❀◗↔(ELR)♣P🚲(472,474)🐾🎵

Railway Hotel ✔

2 Bridge Street, BL0 9AQ
❀ 4-10 Mon; 12-11 Tue-Thu; 11-12.30am Fri & Sat; 11-10.30 Sun ☎ (01706) 558284
Jennings Cumberland Ale; 3 changing beers ⓗ

This pub is ideally situated for the East Lancs Railway Rail Ale trail and local shops. The building was refurbished a few years ago to a high standard. Four real ales are available, always in excellent condition. Good wholesome food is sold at reasonable prices, with deals on selected meals and real ale. Quiz night is Tuesday. Friendly, helpful staff help make the pub a welcoming environment. All in all, a good place to relax over a pint of beer. ♿❀◗♿↔(ELR)♣P🐾🎵

Rochdale

Baum 🏆 ⓛ

35 Toad Lane, OL12 0NU
❀ 11.30-11 (midnight Fri & Sat); 11.30-10.30 Sun
☎ (01706) 352186 🌐 thebaum.co.uk
7 changing beers ⓗ

A hidden gem within a conservation area, the Baum occupies part of the Rochdale Pioneer Museum building on an isolated part of Toad Lane, just south of the bypass. A split-level inn with old-world charm, the conservatory at the rear overlooks a large beer garden and smoking area. Friendly staff serve seven real ales, a cider, a large selection of worldwide bottled beers and continental lagers on draught. Good, reasonably priced fresh food is available daily. CAMRA branch Pub of the Year 2015 and 2016. ♿❀◗♿🚶🐾🎵

Cemetery Hotel ★ ✔

470 Bury Road, OL11 5EU (1 mile from Rochdale Centre on B6222)
❀ 12-11 (1am Thu-Sat) ☎ (01706) 645635
5 changing beers (often Phoenix) ⓗ

With its nationally important historic interior this splendid pub is well worth the short journey from Rochdale town centre towards the cemetery and football ground. The colourful tiles and mosaic floor, complemented by some splendid mahogany features, give a genuine Edwardian feel. The parlour, to the left of the front entrance, is the most impressive of the three rooms, with a welcoming real fire in winter and four separate seating areas. The pub has a lively atmosphere, especially on Rochdale AFC match days. Real cider is sold in summer. ♿❀◗♣🚶P🚲(468,469)🐾🎵

Flying Horse Hotel ⓛ

37 Packer Street, OL16 1NJ
❀ 11-midnight (1am Fri & Sat); 12-midnight Sun
☎ (01706) 646412 🌐 theflyinghorsehotel.co.uk
Lees Bitter; changing beers (sourced locally; often Phoenix, Pictish) ⓗ

Built in 1691 and rebuilt in 1926, this impressive Edwardian stone free house is situated in the Town Hall Square, with many original architectural features remaining. The hotel features log fires, live sport on TV plus accommodation. Seven cask ales and four ciders are available. The food menu offers meat from the local butcher and pies made on the premises. Live music plays most Thursdays,

Fridays and Saturdays. A function room is available for hire and there is a heated smoking area outside. Parking is free. ♿◑➠♨⬤P🖵☙❄📶

Healey

172 Shawclough Road, OL12 6LW

✪ 11.30-11.30 (midnight Fri & Sat); 12-11.30 Sun

☎ (01706) 645453

Robinsons Unicorn; 5 changing beers (often Robinsons) Ⓗ

The pub is situated close to Healey Dell Nature Reserve. A major enlargement and refit in 2013 has taken this always excellent venue to a new level, while retaining the original tiling and bar. Three changing guest beers complement the three Robinsons ales and a guest cider. The beer garden now has a decked and covered area, also used for smoking, plus a pétanque piste to the rear. Excellent food is served until 9pm (6pm Sun). Children are welcome if dining.

Q❧☙⬤◑♣⬤🖵(446,466)☙📶

Regal Moon Ⓛ ✅

The Butts, OL16 1HB

✪ 9am-midnight (1am Fri & Sat) ☎ (01706) 657434

Ruddles Best Bitter; Thwaites Wainwright; changing beers Ⓗ

A large and imposing former cinema in the town centre, handy for the tram and bus interchange. The pub divides into discrete drinking areas in an open-plan room. Eighteen handpumps dispense a wide variety of ales and ciders, with local and West Yorkshire microbreweries featured. The cider is usually from Westons, with three rotating guests. The interior has been refurbished, but the mannequin organist remains on his perch above the bar. A patio to the rear is available for smokers.

Q☙◑♿♨⬤🖵📶

Romiley

Platform One

6 Stockport Road, SK6 4BN

✪ 12-11 (10.30 Mon; midnight Fri & Sat); 12-10.30 Sun

☎ (0161) 406 8686

Changing beers Ⓗ

The pub is situated adjacent to Romiley railway station within a conservation area close to the village centre. It opened in 2012 as a free house and wine bar following complete refurbishment. Six real ales are on offer, usually including beers from local micros such as Hornbeam and RedWillow, served from a large bar situated down the side of the mainly open-plan lower floor. A separate restaurant area is on the first floor (named Platform 2) where food is served until 8pm. ☙◑➠🖵📶

Royton

Bull's Head Hotel

152 Heyside, OL2 6NB

✪ 4-midnight; 12-midnight Fri-Sun ☎ (01706) 881409

4 changing beers Ⓗ

A friendly two-roomed local adjacent to Bullcote Park offering a variety of real ales from breweries around the country on four handpulls. The main bar area is a relaxing meeting place for locals and visitors alike. A second room offers traditional pub games such as darts and pool. At the rear is a large timber decked area with picnic benches. Food is served on Friday evenings and Sunday lunchtimes.

The pub is conveniently placed on several bus routes between Oldham, Royton and Shaw. ♿❀♿♣P🖵☙📶

Salford

Eagle Inn

18 Collier Street, M3 7DW (opp Rolla St)

✪ 3-11 (1am Fri); 1-1am Sat; 1-11 Sun ☎ (0161) 819 5002

Bootleg Chorlton Pale Ale; Holt Bitter, Two Hoots; 2 changing beers (sourced locally) Ⓗ

Also known as the Lamp Oil, this Grade II-listed, 1902-built, three-roomed gem is hard to find, tucked away in an industrial estate adjacent to Trinity Way. A beautifully tiled lobby and many etched windows and panels make for a truly delightful drinking experience. A neighbouring cottage has been converted into a performance venue. Note the terracotta eagle above the entrance. Handy for Manchester Arena.

☙❀➠♨♣⬤🖵☙📶

New Oxford

11 Bexley Square, M3 6DB (corner of Browning St)

✪ 12-midnight ☎ (0161) 832 7082 🌐 thenewoxford.com

18 changing beers (sourced nationally) Ⓗ

This multi award-winning two-room pub is an 1830 building with a modern interior. The highlight is the bar with its 20 handpumps, 17 for cask ales and three for cider. Add to this draught European beers and a selection of bottled Belgian beers and you have a beer drinkers' utopia. Ales change regularly but usually include at least one from Ossett, and frequent beer festivals are held. Excellent home-cooked lunches are available noon-4pm Monday to Friday. ❀◑➠⬤🖵☙📶

Salford Quays

Craftbrew

Unit 1, Digital World Centre, 1 Lowry Plaza, The Quays, M50 3UB (opp Lowry Theatre and Gallery)

✪ 8am-11 (midnight Fri); 10-midnight Sat; 10-11 Sun

🌐 craftbrew-uk.com

3 changing beers (sourced regionally; often Brightside, Copper Dragon, Hawkshead) Ⓗ

Smart modern bar in a 1990s office block boasting a contemporary pastiche mural based on LS Lowry's work. Note the ground-level cellar illuminated and cooled behind glass. Furnishings include a mix of low seating and high tables with stools. Good food is available all day. The bar is frequented by orchestra members and concertgoers from the Lowry Theatre opposite.

☙❀◑♿🖵🖵(50,53)📶

Stalybridge

Old Hunters Tavern ✅

51 Acres Lane, SK15 2JR

✪ 12-midnight ☎ (0161) 303 9477

Robinsons Unicorn; 3 changing beers (often Robinsons) Ⓗ

Originally opened as a beer house in 1837, the pub became part of the Robinsons estate in 1935 but did not become a fully licensed public house until 1962. The characterful two-roomed community venue was refurbished in 2015. Quiz night is Thursday. Regular football matches are shown in both main rooms. There is a covered, heated area outside for smokers. No food at weekends.

☙❀◑P🖵🖵📶

Q Inn ✪

3 Market Street, SK15 2AL
🕒 12-11 (midnight Wed & Thu; 1.30am Fri & Sat)
☎ (0161) 338 5280
Hydes 1863, Hydes Original; 2 changing beers (often Jennings) Ⓗ

The Q Inn holds the title of the shortest name of a pub in the Guinness Book of Records. This traditional two-level tavern has a warm and friendly ambience. A busy music venue, it currently offers four nights of live music including open mic on Thursdays. The large beer garden is home to occasional live music festivals as well as seasonal beer festivals. The pub is close to Stalybridge railway station. ⬛🕸🕪⬠≈⬛🛜

Society Rooms ✪

49-51 Grosvenor Street, SK15 2JN
🕒 8am-midnight (1am Fri & Sat) ☎ (0161) 338 9740
Greene King Abbot; Ruddles Best Bitter; Sharp's Doom Bar; changing beers (sourced nationally) Ⓗ

Wetherspoon pub named after the former Co-op store premises it occupies within the town centre. It features two elevated sections either side of the entrance and a typically large main area. Enthusiastic management and a strong focus on real ales (using 10 handpumps) have made this a favourite destination for local drinkers. Beer-oriented events such as Meet the Brewer nights, and beer requests by customers, have helped to boost this pub's reputation. Real ciders are always available. ⬛🕸🕪⬠≈⬛🛜

Station Buffet Bar ★ ✪

Stalybridge Railway Station, Platform 4, Rassbottom Street, SK15 1RF (access from station Platform 4)
🕒 11 (12 Mon)-11; 11-midnight Fri; 10-midnight Sat
☎ (0161) 303 0007
Changing beers (sourced regionally) Ⓗ

One of the few Victorian station buffet bars remaining, this gem is worth missing a train for. Sympathetic refurbishment has allowed expansion of the food menu including home-cooked meals. Nine handpumps dispense a variety of beers, most locally sourced, plus at least one real cider or perry. A good range of bottled beers is also available. Events include live music, Meet the Brewer nights and Monday quiz night. On the Transpennine Real Ale Trail. Q🕪⬠≈⬛P⬛

White House ✪

1 Water Street, SK15 2AG
🕒 12-11.30 (1am Fri & Sat); 12-11 Sun ☎ (0161) 303 2154
Hydes Original; 5 changing beers Ⓗ

Previously the Laughing Cavalier, this popular pub close to both bus and rail stations is semi-open plan but retains four distinct drinking areas. Up to five ever-changing guest beers from micros and Hydes Studio complement the regular Old Original, and up to three real ciders are offered. A popular live music venue, folk night is every Thursday and bands play on most Fridays and Saturdays. Quiz night is Sunday. Food is available 12-6pm on Sunday. 🕪≈♣⬠P⬛🕸

Standish

Albion Ale House Ⓛ ✪

12 High Street, WN6 0HL
🕒 2-10 (8 Mon); 2-11 Fri & Sat; 2-8 Sun ☎ (01257) 367897
🌐 albionalehouse.co.uk
House beer (by Bank Top); 7 changing beers Ⓗ

Now sporting Cask Marque and LocAle accreditation, this high-street microbar has a narrow frontage and a deceptively large interior. The room is bright and airy with a heavy pine bar dominating the rear, an attractive stone-style tiled floor and comfortable modern furniture. This is a pleasant place to while away the hours with a pint and friends, with a nice garden area. Light bites are usually available. The pub is well-served by local bus services though nearby parking can be limited. Equipped with a fully fitted disabled WC. Q⬛🕸⬠♣⬛🛜

Silver Tally Ⓛ

41 Shevington Moor, WN6 0SQ
🕒 12-11.30; 12-10 Sun ☎ (01257) 472733
🌐 silvertally.co.uk
Prospect Silver Tally; Thwaites Wainwright; 6 changing beers Ⓗ

The Silver Tally is the first pub to be run by Prospect Brewery and offers its own beers, a regular from Thwaites and real cider. The interior divides into three distinct areas – for games, dining and drinking. It has a traditional feel about it while being contemporarily furnished. Pub food favourites are of a high standard. Mini beer festivals are hosted a couple of times a year. Folk music often features on Fridays and a quiz on Tuesdays. No disabled WC. Q⬛🕸🕪⬠♣⬠P⬛(113)🕸🛜

Standish Unity Club Ⓛ

Cross Street, WN6 0HQ
🕒 7.30-11 (midnight Fri & Sat) ☎ (01257) 424007
🌐 standishunityclub.com
Sharp's Doom Bar; 4 changing beers Ⓗ

Established over a decade ago, this is an independent, non-profit-making club open to all. It has a comfortably furnished bar and function room with a separate pool/snooker room. The busy club hosts popular quizzes and is also a music venue and available for private functions. Prospect Unity Gold is a regular along with ales from many local breweries. The club hosts an annual beer festival and CAMRA members are welcome at all times. A regular local CAMRA Club of the Year. Q⬛⬠♣P⬛

Stockport

Arden Arms ★

23 Millgate, SK1 2LX (jct Corporation St)
🕒 12-midnight ☎ (0161) 480 2185 🌐 ardenarms.com
Robinsons Unicorn, Double Hop Ⓗ, Old Tom Ⓖ, Dizzy Blonde, Wizard; 1 changing beer (often Robinsons) Ⓗ

This Grade II-listed building close to Stockport market is on CAMRA's National Inventory of Historic Pub Interiors. The multi-roomed interior centres around one main serving area; to reach the snug you must walk through the bar. Many Victorian features remain and it is said that the cellar once served as a mortuary and still retains body niches in its walls. Evening meals are served Thursday to Saturday 6-9pm. NB Seating preference is given to diners. Live music plays on Monday and Saturday. This is an unmissable gem. ⬛🕸🕪⬠♣⬛(300,384)🕸🛜

Armoury

31 Shaw Heath, Edgeley, SK3 8BD (on B5465, jct Greek St)
🕒 1-midnight; 11-11am Fri & Sat; 11-midnight Sun ☎ 07931 621220

Robinsons Unicorn, Trooper, Dizzy Blonde, Wizard; 1 changing beer (often Robinsons) [H]
Comfortable, recently refurbished multi-roomed local with efficient, friendly service and a strong community involvement. It caters for a varied clientele from TV sports fans to darts teams to quiet bookworms alike. The lounge walls feature memorabilia of the Cheshire Regiment. Outside there is a pleasant beer garden, quite a suntrap in the summer months. Handy for the train station and football ground, the pub opens at 11am if Stockport County FC are at home.
Q🐴❀♿🚆♣🚌📶

Bakers Vaults ✔

Market Place, SK1 1ES (jct Vernon St)
🕐 12-11 (1am Fri & Sat) ☎ (0161) 480 9448
Robinsons Unicorn, Dizzy Blonde, Trooper; 5 changing beers (sourced nationally; often Robinsons) [H]
Relaxed yet lively market house that is an architecturally impressive space. Grade II- listed, it has a bohemian feel enhanced by high ceilings and arched windows, the decor a muted grey and dark blue. The spacious interior has the bar located towards the back and behind that a small lounge space with low leather sofas for those wishing to escape the bustle of the main area. One of the few Robinsons houses to offer guest beers.
🐴❀◑◐🚆♣🍎🐾📶

Boar's Head 🏆

2 Vernon Street, Market Place, SK1 1TY (jct Market Place)
🕐 11-11; 12-6.30 Sun ☎ (0161) 480 3978
Samuel Smith Old Brewery Bitter [H]
A town-centre multi-roomed pub with a genuine, cosy feel. Owners Samuel Smith spent a fair sum restoring this pub to how it may have once have looked. On entering, the bar runs to the left in the lobby, an open area to the right leads to a corner room, and two small rooms face the bar. Beyond this is a large function room with its own bar. Outside is a small, decked drinking area. Coal fires on winter days add warmth and ambience.
Q❀🚆🐾

Cocked Hat

2 Market Place, SK1 1EW (jct Churchgate, opp St Mary's church)
🕐 11-11 (1am Fri & Sat); 12-11 Sun ☎ (0161) 480 4446
6 changing beers (sourced regionally) [H]
The former Pack Horse, rejuvenated in 2013 by new owners AtWill Pubs. It now enjoys a healthy and buoyant trade with six changing guest ales available, typically from micros within a 30-mile radius of Chester where AtWill is based. Tasting notes on blackboards help you pick the right ale. Two neatly decorated rooms display images of old Stockport. Live music features every Friday and Saturday. 🐴🚆🚌(300)🐾📶

Crown Inn

154 Heaton Lane, SK4 1AR (jct King St W under viaduct)
🕐 12-11; 12-10.30 Sun ☎ (0161) 480 5850
Stockport Stock Porter; 9 changing beers (sourced nationally) [H]
Situated in a dramatic location beneath Stockport's famous viaduct, the Crown continues to be one of the town's leading real ale destinations. Up to 16 guest beers feature, often including those from Stockport Brewing Co across the road. A mild, stout and/or porter and up to four guest ciders are always available. Four rooms with many original features radiate from the busy bar. Food is served until 3pm on weekdays, with pork pies usually available. Q❀◑🚆🍎P🚌(192)🐾📶

Fairway

137 Higher Hillgate, Heaviley, SK1 3HR (jct Longshut Lane)
🕐 12-11 (midnight Fri & Sat); 12-9 Sun ☎ (0161) 474 1082
8 changing beers (sourced nationally) [H]
A single entrance from the street positions you in the centre of the pub between a small games room with trophy cabinet and the light and airy lounge with modern decor. The back-wall bar features up to eight ever-changing local beers, always including a mild/stout, and two real ciders in summer. Recent alterations added a vault to the rear which gives access to the covered beer garden and smoking area. Karaoke features on Saturdays. Over-21s only on Friday and Saturday evenings.
Q🐴❀◑🚆♣🍎🚌

Hope Inn

118 Wellington Road North, Heaton Norris, SK4 2LL (N of Belmont Way)
🕐 12-11 (midnight Fri & Sat) ☎ (0161) 637 6191
🌐 thehopestockport.co.uk
Fool Hardy Ales Rou Shou, Risky Blond, Reckless Danger, Rash Dash; Outstanding 3.9, IPA; 7 changing beers (sourced nationally; often Fool Hardy Ales) [H]
A thorough refurbishment and installation of the Fool Hardy Ales microbrewery has turned a dead duck into a gem – winning CAMRA branch Pub of the Year in 2014. Comprising two large rooms, to the right is the cask ale side with 12 handpumps serving at least four of the brewery's own beers, two regulars from Outstanding, plus changing guests; the left side is dedicated to foreign beers and real ciders. An extensive bottled beer range and beer festivals also feature.
Q❀♣🍎P🚌(22,192,364)🐾📶

Magnet

51 Wellington Road North, Heaton Norris, SK4 1HJ (jct Duke St)
🕐 4-11; 12-11 Fri-Sun ☎ (0161) 429 6287
🌐 themagnetfreehouse.co.uk
Salopian Oracle; 9 changing beers (sourced nationally) [H]
A family-run, award-winning pub focusing on quality and choice, with 14 handpumped ales, six KeyKeg beers, a draught cider and a large range of foreign bottles. On the left is a bustling vault leading to a lower pool room and a series of rooms separated by arched doorways. Outside, there is a twin-storey beer terrace with seating. An in-house microbrewery opened in 2014. CAMRA local branch Pub of the Year 2015.
Q🐴❀🚆♣🍎P🚌(22,192,364)🐾📶

Olde Vic

1 Chatham Street, Edgeley, SK3 9ED (jct Shaw Heath)
🕐 5-11 🌐 yeoldevic.pub/en
6 changing beers (sourced nationally) [H]
Saved from closure last year by a community buyout, the interior of the Olde Vic resembles a licensed version of the Old Curiosity Shop, containing a huge array of bric-a-brac and memorabilia, all presided over by larger-than-life host Steve. Details of the six varying guest beers are displayed on the 'pumpotron' and the traditional cider is from Westons. A real fire makes this a cosy haven in the winter. Last entry is usually 10.30pm. Q❀🚆♣🍎🚌🐾📶

Railway

1 Avenue Street, Portwood, SK1 2BZ (jct Gt Portwood St)

⌚ 12-11; 12-10.30 Sun ☎ (0161) 429 6062

Moorhouse's Pride of Pendle; Outstanding Blond; Pictish Brewers Gold; Rossendale Floral Dance, Pitch Porter, Sunshine; 6 changing beers (sourced nationally) Ⓗ

Bustling street-corner house showcasing the ranges of Rossendale and other local micros plus guests. A changing mild and real ciders are always stocked, plus a wide selection of Belgian, German and other bottled beers. Occasional beer and cider festivals take place too. Note the model railway atop the bar canopy, alongside much railway-related memorabilia. A bar billiards table is well used, while the outside yard is a suntrap in summer. A former local CAMRA Pub of the Year and Cider Pub of Year. Q❀♣●🚲🍴🐾🅆

Railway

74-76 Wellington Road North, Heaton Norris, SK4 1HF (jct Georges Rd)

⌚ 12-midnight ☎ (0161) 477 3680

Holt Bitter; 4 changing beers (sourced nationally) Ⓗ

Welcoming multi-roomed pub on a busy main road. To the front are two lounges, one with a raised stage area for the frequent, and highly rated, live entertainment – jazz on Sunday and Tuesday, open mic on Friday and rockabilly the last Saturday of the month. The games room to the rear features darts – numerous teams are based here – and pool. The four guest beers are often from microbreweries and rarely seen in other local pubs. ❀♣🚲 (22,192,364)

Red Bull ✓

14 Middle Hillgate, SK1 3AY (between Wellington and Edward streets)

⌚ 12-10 (11 Wed & Thu; midnight Fri & Sat)
☎ (0161) 480 1286

Robinsons Unicorn, Dizzy Blonde, Wizard; 1 changing beer (often Robinsons) Ⓗ

Situated 400 yards uphill from Robinsons Brewery, the Red Bull aims to maintain its flagship operation within the brewery's estate. Refurbished and enlarged in 2008, it has a homely, rustic atmosphere. Numerous dining and drinking areas radiate from a large central bar area, with a wooden and tiled floor. Outside are a cobbled courtyard and small car park. Full menus are provided lunchtime and evening, plus daily specials at competitive prices. Robinsons' seasonal beers are showcased. Q🐾❀🍴◑●🚲🅿🚲 (314,310)🐾🅆

Robinsons Brewery Visitors' Centre ✓

Apsley Street, SK1 1YE (off Wellington St)

⌚ 9am-5 (6 Fri); 10.30-6 Sat; 10.30-4 Sun
☎ (0161) 612 4100 ⊕ robinsonsvisitorscentre.co.uk

Robinsons Dizzy Blonde, Unicorn, Trooper, Wizard; 1 changing beer (often Robinsons) Ⓗ

Since opening in 2013, the Robinsons brewery experience has gone from strength to strength and in 2015 won a gold award from Visit England. The reception area features a huge display of brewery memorabilia tracing Robinsons' history from 1838. Steps lead down to a bar to the right and a café to the left. Seasonal and one-off beers are usually premiered here. Brewery tours are available. Q🐾◑&≉🅿🚲 (314,300)🅆

Swan with Two Necks ★

36 Princes Street, SK1 1RY (jct Hatton St)

⌚ 10.30-7 (11 Fri & Sat); 10.30-6 Sun ☎ (0161) 480 2341

Robinsons Unicorn, Old Tom, Wizard; 1 changing beer (often Robinsons) Ⓗ

Narrow-fronted with mock-Tudor façade, the building was bought by Robinsons in 1924, and rejuvenated in 2008 by young licensees with ideas and vigour. It is impressively panelled in light oak throughout in familiar Robinsons style, with labelled doors to match. The front door leads to a vault, then the bustling bar-corridor, beyond that a cosy snug with an attractive skylight, and at the rear a small lounge and diner. Outside is a compact, walled drinking area. Quality lunchtime meals are served Tuesday-Saturday. Cider is Westons Old Rosie. 🐾❀◑≉●🚲 (300,330)🐾

Stretford

Sip Club Ⓛ

164A Barton Road, M32 8DP

⌚ 6-11; 2-11 Sat & Sun; closed Mon ☎ 07903 310125

2 changing beers (sourced locally) Ⓗ

Small, intimate bar situated above Trading Places estate agents, opened in 2014. A short staircase takes you to the cosy open-plan 'living room with a licence'. The bar is in the room to the rear behind the partition wall. Two cask ales are served on handpump and stillaged on the bar. A range of bottle-conditioned ales from Manchester breweries is also available alongside bottled ciders from Dunham Press and The Moss Cider Project. Snacks – locally sourced cheeses and pork pies – are served. 🐾🚲♣●🐾🅆

Strines

Sportsman Ⓛ

105 Strines Road, SK6 7GE (on B6101 outside Marple)

⌚ 12-3, 5-11; 12-11 Sat & Sun ☎ (0161) 427 2888
⊕ the-sportsman-pub.co.uk

Phoenix Spotland Gold; 4 changing beers Ⓗ

Splendid white pub standing alone overlooking the Goyt Valley, popular with local drinkers and diners. The comfortable lounge has large picture windows giving superb views over the wooded valley to the hills beyond. A monumental fireplace accommodates log fires in winter and there is a separate taproom. Five guest beers, mainly from micros, are available. Outside, a terrace and balcony are popular in summer and the pub is close to the Peak Forest Canal and Goyt Way Trail. Q🐾❀◑&🅰♣🅿🚲 (62,358)🐾

Tottington

Dungeon Inn

9 Turton Road, BL8 4AW

⌚ 5-11 (12.30am Fri); 2-1am Sat; 2-10.30 Sun
☎ (01204) 887068 ⊕ thedungeontottington.co.uk

Thwaites Best Cask, Wainwright, Lancaster Bomber; 3 changing beers Ⓗ

Presumably named after the former Tottington jail, built in 1835, the Dungeon Inn is a traditional Edwardian Thwaites pub with comfortable surroundings and a great ambience. Six handpumps dispense the Thwaites ales and guests. It has a quiet lounge with an open fire and a separate pool room. Live entertainment is hosted at weekends. Quiz night is every Wednesday – not one for eggheads. Sunday is acoustic open mic night, from folk to soft rock, ensuring a great evening's entertainment. Winner of Thwaites Best Pint 2015. Q♥☏♣♠P🖵🐾🐾🛜

Tyldesley

Union Arms
83 Castle Street, M29 8EW
✪ 12-11 (midnight Fri & Sat); 12-10.30 Sun
☎ (01942) 870645
AllGates California; Thwaites Wainwright; 2 changing beers (sourced locally) H
Family-friendly pub with occasional themed nights including live music. The interior is divided into a number of connected but separate areas. On the left is the vault and on the right a lounge used for dining. There are more areas at the back, one with a dartboard. Up to four real ales are complemented by good-value fresh home-cooked food (until 8pm) including traditional lunch on Sundays (until 6pm). Most sporting events are shown on TV.
☏☏❀🌙♣🖵🐾🛜

Uppermill

Cross Keys Inn
Running Hill Gate, OL3 6LW (off A670 up Church Rd)
✪ 12-midnight ☎ (01457) 874626 🌐 crosskeysinn.co.uk
Lees Brewer's Dark, Manchester Pale Ale, Bitter; 2 changing beers (sourced locally; often Lees) H
Overlooking Saddleworth Church, this attractive 18th-century stone building has exposed beams throughout. The public bar features a stone-flagged floor and Yorkshire range. Home-cooked food includes puddings, pies and real chips. Folk music is played on Wednesday and Sunday nights. Outside is a children's play area and a covered, heated smoking area. The Rushcart Festival in August is popular. The pub is the centre for Mountain Rescue and the Saddleworth Runners. A regular in the Guide for over 40 years. Q☏☏❀🌙🌙P🐾🛜

Urmston

Flixton Conservative Club ✔
Abbotsfield, 193 Flixton Road, M41 5DF
✪ 12-3, 6-11; 12-11.30 Fri & Sat; 12-11 Sun
☎ (0161) 748 2846
Theakston Best Bitter; 5 changing beers (sourced nationally; often AllGates, Bank Top, Elland) H
With six handpumps on the main bar, this CAMRA award-winning club displays a genuine commitment to quality real ales. Monthly brewery nights are hosted, making good use of another five pumps upstairs. The club is home to a wide range of sports teams including snooker, bowls, darts, dominoes and chess. Various events are held including a regular quiz night. The club has an interesting history and the late-Victorian premises retains a number of original features.
☏❀➤♣🌙P🖵🛜

Wardley

Morning Star
520 Manchester Road, M27 9QW (opp Bagot St)
✪ 12-11 (11.30 Fri & Sat) ☎ 07827 850258

> What care I how time advances! I am drinking ale today. **Edgar Allan Poe**

Holt Mild, Bitter; 1 changing beer (sourced nationally) H
This Edwardian building is set back from the main road with an outdoor drinking area at the front. Inside, to the left is a traditional vault, to the right is a small lounge that leads through to the larger main lounge. This is a friendly community local where everyone is made welcome. There are men's and ladies' darts teams and live entertainment at weekends. The guest beer is sourced nationally as part of Holt's reciprocal agreement. ❀➤♣P🖵(36,37)🛜

Whitefield

Eagle & Child
Higher Lane, M45 7EY
✪ 12-11 (midnight Fri & Sat) ☎ 07827 850229
Holt Mild, IPA, Bitter, Two Hoots; 1 changing beer H
Traditional black-and-white-timbered double-fronted inn with a spacious lounge and a vault served by a central bar, plus a separate front room, ideal for meetings and private parties. Home to darts, dominoes and cribbage teams, it hosts a quiz-and-curry night on a Thursday and live acts every Friday. The place is family-friendly and dogs are allowed on a lead in outside areas. Live Sky and BT Sport are shown on TV. A large floodlit bowling green is open April to September and is available for hire. Q☏❀➤♣P🖵(98,135)🐾🛜

Wigan

Anvil Ⓛ ✔
Dorning Street, WN1 1ND
✪ 11-11; 12-10.30 Sun
AllGates California; Hydes 1863; Thwaites Wainwright; 6 changing beers (sourced nationally) H
Popular town-centre pub with seven handpumps offering beers from the nearby AllGates Brewery, real cider, six draught continental beers and a range of bottled beers. The small snug features a wall of fame displaying the pub's many awards. Several TV screens show sporting action. Close to bus and railway access for the DW Stadium, the pub can be busy on match days. Over-18s only. No disabled WC facilities.
❀➤(Wallgate/N Western)🌙🖵

Blundell's Café Bar Ⓛ
90 Wigan Lane, WN1 2LF
✪ 6 (4 Wed & Thu)-11; 2-11 Fri & Sat; 1-10 Sun; closed Tue ☎ 07810 396736
Hophurst Flaxen; 3 changing beers H
Situated just off the main road with reasonable parking outside and in side streets, this is a quiet haven for a pint of local ale or a fine coffee with simple snacks. Its cream modern furniture and tables are very comfortable. Often candle-lit in the evenings, this is a perfect place for families or a get-together with pals. One wall has an impressive mural of a Venice canal, the others display interesting posters and pictures. Small functions are usually hosted Monday to Wednesday.
Q☏🌙P🖵🐾🛜

Doc's Symposium Ⓛ
85 Mesnes Street, WN1 1QJ
✪ 12-11 Thu-Sat; 1-10.30 Sun; closed Mon-Wed ☎ 07462 896822
Facer's Dave's Hoppy Beer; Prospect Silver Tally; Weetwood Cheshire Cat; 2 changing beers H

Voted local CAMRA New Cask Outlet 2014, this is the town's first micropub. It offers five real ales including local brews and a variety of European beers. With a light and airy interior and on-street seating outside, the pub has a continental feel. It overlooks the beautiful Mesnes Park. June and Chris are well-respected Wigan landlords and visitors are guaranteed a warm welcome from them and their staff. Q❀✪❍➤(Wallgate)P🅿️🐾🐱🛜

Tap 'n' Barrel L ✓

16 Jaxon's Court, WN1 1LR

❀ 12-10 Mon; 12-10.30 Wed & Thu; 12-12.30am Fri; 12-1am Sat; 1-10 Sun; closed Tue ☎ (01942) 386966

⊕ martlandmillbrewery.co.uk

Martland Mill Spinner's Gold, Clogmaker; 4 changing beers (sourced regionally) 🅷

Wigan town-centre mews-style microbar with a pleasant artificial covered beer garden. The Martland Mill brewery tap, its own beers are available on rotation alongside a wide choice of interesting local and regional beers. Two real ciders and a small range of wines are also stocked. Live music features on occasion; check their website and Facebook page.

Q➤(Wallgate/N Western)🍴🖥️🐱🛜

Wigan Central 🍷 L

Arch No.1, Queen Street, WN3 4DY

❀ 12-11 (midnight Fri); 11-midnight Sat; 12-10.30 Sun

☎ (01942) 246425 ⊕ wigancentral.bar

House beer (by Prospect); 6 changing beers (sourced nationally) 🅷

Customers are assured of a warm welcome at this real ale pub owned by Prospect Brewery. With its cosy railway-themed interior and live departure and arrival boards, it is a delight. The beers are sourced from all over and there is a continental bottled beer library for those wanting something different. Bar snacks are available.

Q➤❀🐱➤🍴🖥️🐱🛜

Withington

Victoria ✓

438 Wilmslow Road, M20 3BW (on B5093, jct Davenport Av)

❀ 11-11 (midnight Thu-Sat); 12-11 Sun ☎ (0161) 434 2600

Hydes Old Indie, Original, 1863; 6 changing beers (sourced nationally; often Hydes) 🅷

This thriving one-roomed pub is divided into distinct areas so you can choose what you want from your visit – whether it be a quiet chat, watching sport on TV, listening to live entertainment or playing pool. The etched-glass windows and tiled floor around the bar add to its

character. However, what makes this community pub so popular is the friendliness of the licensees and staff, plus the excellence of the beers. 🐱♿♣🍴🐱🐾🛜

Woodford

Davenport Arms (Thief's Neck)

550 Chester Road, SK7 1PS (on A5102, jct Church Lane)

❀ 11-11; 12-10.30 Sun ☎ (0161) 439 2435

⊕ davenportarms.co.uk

Robinsons Unicorn, Dizzy Blonde, Old Tom, Wizard; 1 changing beer (often Robinsons) 🅷

This characterful red-brick farmhouse-style hostelry received a smart refurbishment in 2014 but retains a multi-roomed feel with real fires in winter. This is the pub's 30th consecutive year in the Guide, and the licence has now been in the same family for 84 years. Excellent food is mostly home made, with some adventurous specials. Outside, the spacious forecourt and attractive garden, set well-away from the road, are popular in summer, with impressive floral displays.

🐱❀✪❍♣P🅿️(157,X57)🐱🛜

Worsley

Bridgewater Hotel ✓

23 Barton Road, M28 2PD (corner Farm Lane)

❀ 12-11 ☎ (0161) 794 6206

Greene King IPA; 7 changing beers (sourced nationally) 🅷

This is a spacious pub opposite the Bridgewater Canal in the picturesque village of Worsley. It has a long bar serving one large room divided into small sections and alcoves. Meals are available throughout the day and children are welcome if dining. Show your CAMRA membership card for a 10 per cent discount on real ale.

🐱❀✪❍♿P🅿️(33,68)🐱🛜

Worsley Old Hall

Worsley Park, M28 2QT (off Walkden Rd)

❀ 11-11 ☎ (0161) 703 8706

Brunning & Price Original; house beer (by Facer's); 4 changing beers (sourced regionally) 🅷

Seventeenth-century building, recently refurbished to a high standard with a country-house feel. It has spacious dining areas and drinking rooms with comfortable seating, and numerous pictures for added interest. Excellent food is served for all the family to enjoy. Cider is always available on handpump. It has a large beer garden and is set in open woodland adjacent to a golf course.

Q🐱❀✪❍♿🍴P🅿️🐱🛜

Ale conner

The official ale-tester wore leather breeches. He would enter an inn without warning, draw a glass of ale, pour it on a wooden bench, and then sit down in the puddle he had made. He would sit for half an hour and would not change his position. At the end of the half hour, he would make as if to rise, and this was the test of the ale; for if the ale was impure, if it had sugar in it, the tester's leather breeches would stick fast to the bench, but if there was no sugar in the liquor, no impression would be present – in other words, the tester would not stick to the seat.

17th-century description of the work of the ale conner, a public official who inspected inns, taverns and ale houses to test the quality of the beer. William Shakespeare's father was an ale conner.

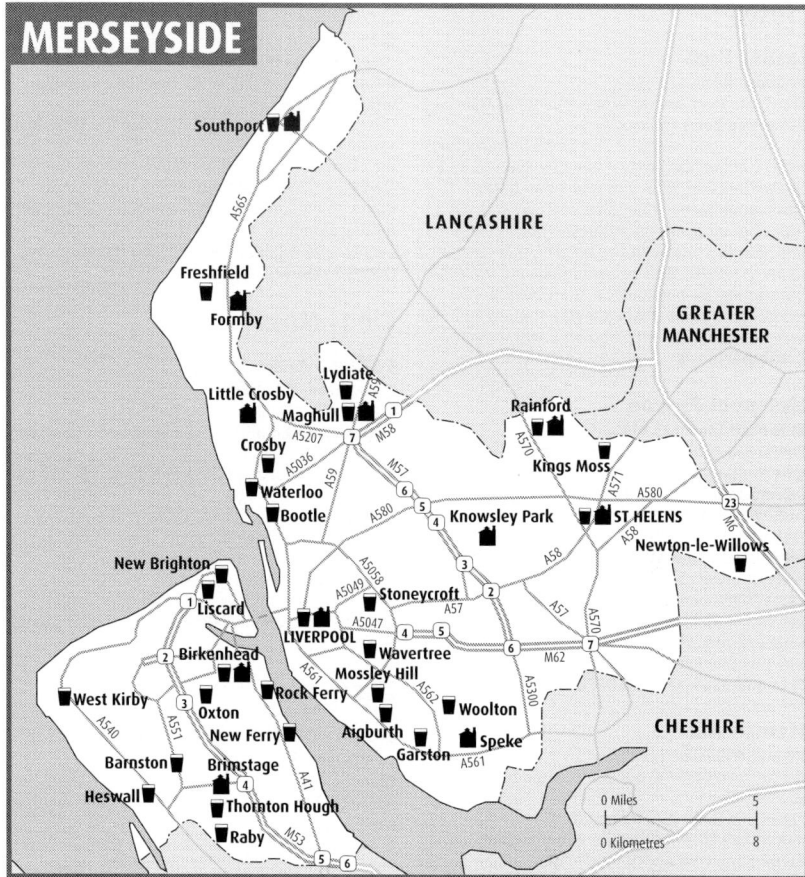

Barnston

Fox & Hounds ✔

107 Barnston Road, CH61 1BW (on A551)
🕐 11-11; 12-10.30 Sun ☎ (0151) 648 7685
🌐 the-fox-hounds.co.uk
Brimstage Trappers Hat Bitter; Theakston Best Bitter, Old Peculier; Timothy Taylor Landlord; 2 changing beers (sourced nationally; often Purple Moose) 🅗
Village pub with a bar, lounge and snug full of bric-a-brac, local photos and other memorabilia. The lounge, converted from tea rooms, is quiet with no music or games machines. The pub retains its character with real fires in the bar and snug. The stone courtyard is a profusion of colour in the summer. Good food includes a fish dish of the day, daily specials and Sunday roasts (no evening meals Mon). The two real ciders are Rosie's Triple D and Black Bart. Q⛱️🐕🍴👪♣🍺P🚌(77)♣🎵🛜

Birkenhead

Gallaghers Pub & Barber's Shop 🍺 🅛

20 Chester Street, CH41 5DQ
🕐 12 (4 Mon)-11; 12-midnight Fri; 11.30-midnight Sat; 12-midnight Sun ☎ (0151) 649 9095
🌐 gallagherspubwirral.com
Brimstage Trappers Hat Bitter; 5 changing beers (sourced regionally; often Hawkshead, Rat, Salopian) 🅗

Multi award-winning genuine free house close to the famous Mersey ferries, resurrected after closure and refurbished in 2010 by a former Irish Guardsman as a unique pub with barber's shop. The interior is decorated with a range of fascinating military memorabilia and a collection of shipping images. The beer garden is popular in the summer. Good-value meals are served lunchtimes and early evenings Friday and Saturday only – no food Sunday or Monday. Several real ciders are always available. 🐕🍴🚆🍺🚌♣🛜

Bootle

Merton Inn 🅛 ✔

42 Merton Road, L20 3BW
🕐 8am-11 (midnight Fri) ☎ (0151) 934 7790
Greene King Abbot; Ruddles Best Bitter; Sharp's Doom Bar; 5 changing beers 🅗
The Merton Inn was once a hotel created when two villas were combined in the 1930s. Used as a hospital during World War II, it was converted to a pub in the 1970s. This spacious multi-level Wetherspoon establishment, with wood panelling and subdued lighting, retains some of the character of its villa origins. The pub boasts some specially commissioned abstract paintings depicting the local landscape. Alcohol is served from 9am. No children after 9pm. ⛱️🍴♿🚆P🚌🛜

Crosby

Corner Post L
25 Bridge Road, L23 6SA
✪ 4 (1 Sat)-9; 1-7 Sun; closed Mon ☎ 07587 177453
4 changing beers (sourced locally) H
Crosby's second micropub, located in a former post office – hence the name – is easily spotted by the postbox outside. Real ales and cider, bottled continental beers, wine, Liverpool gin and soft drinks are all available. Interesting pictures depicting the history of the building and local area adorn the walls. Well-behaved dogs are welcome. Close to the 53 bus route, a short walk from Blundellsands and Crosby railway station, and also near the Iron Men attraction on Crosby beach.
Q ⇌ ♣ ● 🚍 (53) ❀

Liverpool Pigeon L
14 Endbutt Lane, L23 0TR
✪ 4 (12 Sat)-9; 12-5 Sun; closed Mon ☎ 07766 480329
⊕ liverpoolpigeon.co.uk
5 changing beers H
Merseyside's pioneering micropub is a fine example of the type, with real ales, ciders and bottled beers available but no spirits, alcopops, keg beers or music. The cask beers will usually include a local brew and often a dark beer. Locally made pies are available at the bar. The Liverpool Pigeon is named after an extinct bird from Polynesia – long may this one live. Local CAMRA Pub of the Year 2014 and 2015. Q & ♣ ● 🛒🚍 ❀

Stamps Bar L
5 Crown Buildings, L23 5SR
✪ 12-11 (midnight Fri & Sat) ☎ (0151) 286 2662
⊕ stampsbar.co.uk
5 changing beers (often Stamps) H
Stamps is a true community pub attracting a wide mix of people who visit for the great range of real ales, cider, food and live music. The pub supports a range of local and national charities and hosts a number of activities including art classes on Monday, a ukulele band on Tuesday and a quiz night on Wednesday. Come Friday to Sunday for live music. Not sure which beer to try? Get three third-pints for the price of one. 🛒🍴 & ● 🚍 🛜

Freshfield

Freshfield L ✪
1 Massams Lane, L37 7BD
✪ 11-11 (midnight Fri & Sat) ☎ (01704) 874871
⊕ freshfield-liverpool.co.uk
Greene King IPA, Abbot; Ruddles Best Bitter; 11 changing beers (sourced regionally; often Liverpool Organic, Oakham, Red Star) H
At its heart a community pub in Formby, where a welcoming smile awaits the thirsty drinker. The emphasis is on real ale at this Greene King pub. With 14 handpumps, of which only three will be house beers, the choice is from a range of breweries, giving local brewers a chance. The restaurant serves quality food up to 10pm. A multi award-winning pub including CAMRA regional Pub of the Year two years in a row and a national finalist in 2015. 🛒🍴 & ⇌ ♣ ● P🚍 ❀ 🛜

Heswall

Black Horse ✪
School Hill, CH60 0DP

✪ 12-11 (midnight Thu-Sat) ☎ (0151) 325 0248
⊕ theblack.co.uk
Fuller's London Pride; Sharp's Doom Bar; Wychwood Hobgoblin; 2 changing beers (sourced nationally; often Brimstage) H
Down in lower Heswall you will find the large four-storey Black Horse Inn. Built in 1843 and formerly the Heswall Hotel, this attractive building has a stone-built central section with a mock timber frame on the top two floors. The pub is welcoming, hosting meetings for local groups and regular events, and is handy for accessing the Wirral Way. Q 🛒 ✿ & ♣ P🚍 (77,174) ❀ 🛜

Kings Moss

Colliers Arms ✪
Pimbo Road, WA11 8RD
✪ 11-11 (10.30 Sun) ☎ (01744) 89289
Black Sheep Best Bitter; 3 changing beers (sourced nationally) H
In a rural hamlet at the foot of Billinge Hill, the pub is part of a row of what were miners' cottages near the site of the old Hillside Colliery. The interior is made up of four distinct areas served from a central bar. Books, mining memorabilia and photographs decorate the walls and there is a pleasant children's play area and beer garden to the rear. Good-quality home-cooked food is served. 🛒 ✿ 🍴

Liscard

Lazy Landlord Ale House L
56 Mill Lane, CH44 5UG
✪ 2-10; 12-10 Fri-Sun; closed Tue ☎ 07583 135616
House beer (by Wentwell); 4 changing beers (sourced regionally) H
Wirral's first micropub, set in former shop premises, opened in December 2014, run by the Henry brothers who are cask ale enthusiasts. Two small cosy rooms, decorated with large amounts of breweriana, local artworks and a small library, are served from the front bar. Mostly frequented by a more mature, discerning local clientele, the pub is a venue for meetings of local societies. Q 🛒 ♣ ● 🚍 (10A,410,432) ❀

Liverpool: Aigburth

Que Pasa Cantania
94-96 Lark Lane, L17 8UU

REAL ALE BREWERIES

3 Potts Southport (NEW)
Baltic Fleet 🍺 Liverpool
Big Bog Speke
Brimstage Brimstage
Connoisseur St Helens
Craft Southport (NEW)
George Wright Rainford
Liverpool Craft Liverpool
Liverpool Organic Liverpool
Mad Hatter Liverpool
Melwood Knowsley Park
Neptune Maghull (NEW)
Peerless Birkenhead
Red Star Formby (NEW)
Rock the Boat Little Crosby (NEW)
Southport Southport
Stamps Liverpool

✪ 12-11 (midnight Fri & Sat) ☎ (0151) 727 0006
2 changing beers (sourced locally) Ⓗ
Trendy café and bar situated near Sefton Park at the top end of the vibrant Lark Lane alongside many other bars, restaurants and pubs. Despite the name, there is more to this bar than just Mexican food. Beers are normally delivered directly from breweries, usually local, but sometimes from further afield. There is a pleasant outdoor patio to the rear. Q★☆ᐉ◗🖵🖵🛜

Liverpool: City Centre

Abbey Ⓛ
85-89 Hanover Street, L1 3DZ
✪ 11-11; 10-midnight Fri & Sat; 10-11 Sun
☎ (0151) 708 5688
5 changing beers (often Copper Dragon, Lancaster, Peerless) Ⓗ
A large venue with plenty of seating. Most major sporting events are shown live so the pub can get busy, especially in the evening. A private function area is available to book. Good-value food is served and one local beer is usually among the ale range. A discount is available on production of a CAMRA membership card. ᐉ⇌🖵🛜

Augustus John Ⓛ
Peach Street, L3 5TX (off Brownlow Hill)
✪ 11.30-11; closed Sat & Sun ☎ (0151) 794 5507
5 changing beers Ⓗ
Opened in 1901 and run by the University of Liverpool, the Augustus John is an open-plan pub popular with students, lecturers and locals. Up to five guest beers are available alongside a large number of ciders – the pub is a former local and regional CAMRA Cider Pub of the Year. Pizza is served at all times, sport is shown and there is a jukebox. Closed over Christmas and New Year. ᐉ&✦🖵(79)🛜

Baltic Fleet Ⓛ
33 Wapping, L1 8DQ
✪ 12-11; 12-midnight Sat & Sun ☎ (0151) 709 3116
🌐 balticfleetpubliverpool.com
Wapping Summer Ale; 5 changing beers (sourced locally; often Brimstage, Facer's, Melwood) Ⓗ
Liverpool's only brewpub, this Grade II-listed building is located near the Albert Dock. It has a distinctive flat-iron shape and is decorated with a nautical theme. Real ale and cider are dispensed from seven handpumps, including the Wapping Summer Ale brewed below stairs. Pies and home-cooked scouse are available from lunchtime until they run out. The existence of tunnels in the cellar has led to speculation that the pub's history may involve smuggling and press gangs. ☆ᐉ⇌✦🖵🛜

Belvedere Ⓛ ✪
8 Sugnall Street, L7 7EB (off Falkner St)
✪ 12-11 ☎ (0151) 709 0303 🌐 belvedereliverpool.com
4 changing beers (sourced regionally; often Liverpool Organic) Ⓗ
Tucked away in the Georgian area of the city, close to the famous Philharmonic Hall and frequented by its orchestra members, this small two-roomed pub is a free house serving four rotating beers mainly from local microbreweries. This Grade II-listed building retains original fixtures and interesting etched-glass features. It has a mixed local clientele, and is a place where various small cultural groups meet and good conversation thrives. Q✦🖵🖵(86,80A,75)🐾

Blackburne Pub & Eatery Ⓛ
24 Catharine Street, L8 7NL
✪ 9am-midnight ☎ (0151) 709 9159 🌐 theblackburne.co.uk
3 changing beers (sourced locally; often Salopian) Ⓗ
A popular, open-plan, village-style pub in the heart of the Georgian Quarter, with tasteful decor and a relaxed and welcoming atmosphere. There is a strong emphasis on good-quality food, with Friday wine-and-dine offers and Sunday lunches especially good value, but drinkers are also welcome. The four changing real ales usually include one from Salopian Brewery. The pub is a short bus ride or a 15 to 20-minute walk from the city centre. Guest accommodation is available upstairs. Q★🛏ᐉᐉ◗🖵🛜

Dispensary Ⓛ
87 Renshaw Street, L1 2SP
✪ 12-11 (midnight Fri & Sat) ☎ (0151) 709 2160
George Wright Mild; changing beers (often Ossett, Titanic) Ⓗ
The licensee's impeccable attention to beer quality is renowned at this lively city pub, making it a haven for real ale drinkers of all ages. Seven handpumps serve a wide choice of interesting microbrewery beers, offering a good range in terms of both style and strength. A regular local beer, Mark's Mild, commemorates the much-missed barman who died in 2012. The attractive bar area has Victorian features, and there is a raised wood-panelled area to the rear. ⇌🖵

Excelsior ✪
121-123 Dale Street, L2 2JH (close to Birkenhead Tunnel entrance)
✪ 11-11; 12-11 Sun ☎ (0151) 236 0079
Brains Rev James; Robinsons Dizzy Blonde; Timothy Taylor Landlord; 3 changing beers Ⓗ
Large, comfortable corner pub on the edge of the business district. The main room has a three-sided bar with a series of distinct seating areas. There is a large room leading off with a raised seating area, available to hire for meetings or other functions. Three big-screen TVs show sports events, particularly football, but are generally silent otherwise. Tuesday is quiz night, unless Liverpool or Everton are on TV. ᐉ⇌🖵🛜

Fly in the Loaf ✪
13 Hardman Street, L1 9AS
✪ 12-11 (midnight Fri & Sat) ☎ (0151) 708 0817
🌐 flyintheloaf.co.uk
Okells Bitter; 4 changing beers (sourced nationally; often Okells) Ⓗ
A former bakery, the name comes from the slogan 'no flies in the loaf'. Owned by Isle of Man brewer Okells, it serves up to three of its beers alongside a changing range of guests from around the country, many from microbreweries, and a good selection of foreign beers. The spacious interior has a light, airy frontage with contrasting wood-panelled areas towards the rear. There is a small, attractive on-street drinking area at the front and a function room upstairs. ᐉ&⇌🖵(86)🛜

Grapes Ⓛ
60 Roscoe Street, L1 9DW
✪ 12 (2.30 Mon)-12.30am; 12-1.30am Fri & Sat
☎ (0151) 709 3977 🌐 thegrapesliverpool.co.uk
Changing beers Ⓗ
This corner local dates back to 1804 and retains its original Mellors signage outside. There is a total of nine handpumps, with a large number of beers

coming from local microbreweries such as Mad Hatter and Liverpool Craft. The cosy beer garden at the rear is popular with smokers. Live jazz features every Sunday night from 9pm. Home-cooked Thai and Lao food is available. ⊛◑≢♨⚲☞

Lime Kiln 🅛 ✔

Fleet Street, L1 4NR
✪ 9am-midnight (1am Thu; 2am Fri & Sat)
☎ (0151) 702 6810
Ruddles Best Bitter; changing beers (often Peerless) Ⓗ
From first impressions the decor and layout may not appear to offer much for the real ale drinker, but looks can be deceiving. Thanks to significant commitment by the management, real ale is well catered for, with at least one local beer usually available. Situated in the trendy Concert Square area, the pub is a peaceful haven during the day. A Victorian warehouse once occupied the site.
🛏⊛◑♿≢♨⚲☞

Lion Tavern ★ 🅛 ✔

67 Moorfields, L2 2BP
✪ 11-midnight; 12-midnight Sun ☎ (0151) 236 1734
⊕ liontavern.com
Young's Bitter; changing beers (often George Wright) Ⓗ
Named after the locomotive that worked the Liverpool to Manchester railway, the Lion features exquisite artwork plus intricately etched and stained glass which bear testimony to its Grade II-listed status and its entry on CAMRA's National Inventory of Historic Pub Interiors. Regular society meetings and occasional Meet the Brewer events take place. Lunchtime food is served and speciality pork pies are available at all times. The house beer, brewed by George Wright, is the Lion Returns, and the cider is from Westons. ◑≢♨⚲☞

Mackenzie's 🅛

32 Rodney Street, L1 2TQ
✪ 12-11.30 ☎ (07746) 577028 ⊕ mackenziesbar.co.uk
5 changing beers (sourced locally) Ⓗ
Attractive, spacious bar, tastefully converted from a listed ex-HSBC bank in 2015, with up to five changing real ales, many from local breweries. It is renowned for its worldwide collection of over 200 whiskies. Situated in a lively area of the city, with an illuminated beer garden, the bar is popular with a wide-ranging clientele. It is named after a legendary local 19th-century civil engineer whose 15-foot pyramid shaped tombstone is along the street. Food is served daily noon-6pm. Live music plays on Monday and Wednesday evenings and Sunday afternoons. ⊛◑🍴♣☞

North Western 🅛 ✔

7 Lime Street, L1 1RJ
✪ 6am-midnight (1am Fri & Sat) ☎ (0151) 709 6825
Greene King Abbot; Ruddles Best Bitter; Sharp's Doom Bar; 9 changing beers (sourced nationally) Ⓗ
Following a £2million makeover, this Wetherspoon pub was named in honour of the building's original use as the North Western Hotel. It first opened in 1871 and was built by the London and North Western Railway to serve the station. This impressive piece of Liverpool architecture was designed by local architect Alfred Waterhouse. It closed its doors in the early 1930s and reopened in 1996 as student accommodation. The ground floor then became a pub. Alcohol is served from 8am.
🛏⊛◑♿≢♨⚲(14)☞

Pen Factory

13 Hope Street, L1 9BQ
✪ 12-midnight; closed Sun & Mon ☎ (0151) 709 7887
⊕ pen-factory.co.uk
5 changing beers Ⓗ
The Pen Factory opened in 2015, brought to you by innovator of the original Everyman Bistro, entrepreneur Paddy Byrne. A large open-plan bistro with a wood-burning stove and small garden, it is a convivial place to drink and eat. Four handpumps usually include beers from smaller breweries such as Brimstage. The tapas-style food is excellent. The venue can be busy before or after productions at the nearby Everyman Theatre or Philharmonic Hall. ⊛◑♿≢♨⚲(86)☞

Peter Kavanagh's ★

2-6 Egerton Street, L8 7LY (off Catharine St)
✪ 12-midnight (1am Fri & Sat) ☎ (0151) 709 3443
Greene King Abbot; 4 changing beers (sourced locally) Ⓗ
Pub with a nationally important historic interior in the Georgian area of the city. The snugs have murals by Eric Robinson and there are fine stained-glass windows with wooden shutters. The benches have carved armrests thought to be caricatures of Peter Kavanagh, the licensee for 53 years until 1950. These features were not adversely affected when the pub was expanded, firstly in 1964 into next door, then in 1977 into next door but one.
Q⚲

Pumphouse ✔

The Colonnades, Albert Dock, L3 4AN
✪ 11-11 (midnight Fri & Sat) ☎ (0151) 709 2367
⊕ pumphouse-liverpool.co.uk
Greene King IPA; Robinsons Trooper; 8 changing beers (sourced nationally; often Greene King, Liverpool Organic, Robinsons) Ⓗ
Situated within Albert Dock, this establishment opened in 1984. The pub is split over three levels with different seating arrangements to suit individuals, couples and large groups. Real ale now has prominence – guest beers come from the Greene King group, including specials produced in small batches in Bury St Edmunds, plus some from other breweries. The pumphouse itself was built in 1874 and boasts the first steam hydraulic system that served the docks. The bar gets busy on summer weekends. 🛏⊛◑♿≢♨⚲☞

Richard John Blackler 🅛 ✔

Units 1 & 2 Charlotte Row, L1 1HU
✪ 8am-midnight (1am Fri & Sat) ☎ (0151) 709 4802
Greene King Abbot; Ruddles Best Bitter; Sharp's Doom Bar; 7 changing beers Ⓗ
This Wetherspoon pub is the ground floor of the former Blackler's department store which opened in 1908 and finally shut in 1988. The famous rocking horse from that store is in the corner. Close to the bus station, Saint John's shopping centre and Liverpool One, it is always busy, but a good place to take a break. The Beatles' George Harrison served his electrician apprenticeship at Blackler's.
🛏◑♿≢♨⚲☞

Roscoe Head 🅛

24 Roscoe Street, L1 2SX
✪ 11.30-midnight; 12-midnight Sun ☎ (0151) 709 4365
⊕ roscoehead.co.uk
Tetley Bitter; Timothy Taylor Landlord; 4 changing beers (sourced regionally; often Rock the Boat) Ⓗ

One of the Magnificent Five pubs that have been in every edition of the Guide. This is a cosy four-roomed pub where conversation and the appreciation of real ale rule. Run by members of the same family for over 30 years, the name commemorates William Roscoe, a leading campaigner against the slave trade. Six handpumps feature national and local breweries such as Rock the Boat. Home-cooked food is served Monday to Friday lunchtimes. Since its sale by Punch Taverns to New River Retail in 2015 there is concern over the future of this pub, with a Save the Roscoe Head campaign set up by locals.
Q◐⇌♣🚌📶

Ship & Mitre 🄻 ✔

133 Dale Street, L2 2JH (by Birkenhead Tunnel)
🕐 10-11 (midnight Thu); 9am-midnight Fri & Sat
☎ (0151) 236 0859 🌐 theshipandmitre.com
Changing beers 🄷
A 1930s Art Deco pub partly hidden by the Queensway tunnel entrance and the Churchill Way flyover. Fifteen handpulls serve an ever-changing array of beers and real ciders, with the friendly and knowledgeable staff always willing to make a recommendation. There is also an impressive range of world beers. Beer and cider festivals are hosted throughout the year. ◐⇌♣🍎🚌🐾

Thomas Rigby's ✔

23-25 Dale Street, L2 2EZ
🕐 11.30-11; 11.30-10.30 Sun ☎ (0151) 236 3269
Okells Manx Pale Ale, Bitter; 3 changing beers 🄷
This multi-roomed, Grade II-listed building, bearing the name of a wine and spirit dealer, now supplies an extensive world beer range on draught and in bottles. The regular beers on handpump come from the pub's owner, Okells Brewery, the others are frequently changing guests. Good-value food is served until early evening, including specials, with one room offering a friendly and efficient table service. There is a courtyard for outdoor drinking.
❀◐⇌🚌📶

Vernon Arms 🄻

69 Dale Street, L2 2HJ
🕐 11.45-11.30 (12.30am Fri & Sat) ☎ (0151) 236 6132
🌐 vernonarms.co.uk
Boggart Hole Clough Rum Porter; Brains Rev James; 3 changing beers 🄷
Situated close to the business district, the Vernon retains the feel of a street-corner local. The single long-roomed bar serves three drinking areas including a back room with frosted-glass windows advertising the Liverpool Brewing Company which used to serve the pub. The main bar has wood panelling, several large columns and a small snug area. The regular Boggart Rum Porter is popular with many, and real cider on handpull is unusual for the city centre. ◐⇌🍎🚌

Liverpool: Garston

Masonic 🄻

35 Gladstone Road, L19 1RR
🕐 11-midnight (1am Fri & Sat); 12-midnight Sun
6 changing beers (often Liverpool Organic) 🄷
Community pub amid terraced houses with seven handpumps, one usually dispensing a cider. Beers are supplied directly by local breweries and from around the country through brewery swaps. Real ale promotions are offered on Tuesday evenings. A supporter of local sports teams, racing and other sports are shown on TV. Live music plays Thursday to Sunday. There is a drinking area outside in front of the pub and a new covered smoking area to the side. Beer festivals are held in April and September. Accommodation is available for CAMRA members by arrangement. 🛏♣🍎🚌🐾📶

Liverpool: Mossley Hill

Pi

106 Rose Lane, L18 8AG
🕐 11-11 (11.30 Fri & Sat) ☎ (0151) 222 0443
🌐 pi-roselane.co.uk
Tatton Blonde; 2 changing beers (sourced regionally) 🄷
A café-style bar in premises that were previously a shop, near to Mossley Hill railway station. The guest beers are from smaller breweries in the region. A number of foreign beers are also on tap alongside dozens of bottled beers. A simple hot-food menu – real pies with sides – is available all day. The extension into the shop next door has provided more space. ◐⇌🍎🚌(61,80)📶

Liverpool: Stoneycroft

Cask 🏆 🄻

438 Queens Drive, L13 0AR (near jct Queens Drive and Derby Lane)
🕐 4-9.30; 2-9.30 Sat & Sun; closed Mon ☎ 07747 034499
5 changing beers (sourced nationally) 🄷
This comfortable, immaculate, one-roomed micropub opened in July 2015. Located on Queens Drive, a busy dual carriageway that acts like a Liverpool circular road, near the turning to West Derby, some roadside parking is available. An interesting collection of breweriana includes some from Higsons. Four handpumps serve beers from smaller breweries nationwide, plus two for cider and perry. Q♣🍎🗑🚌

Liverpool: Wavertree

Willowbank ✔

329 Smithdown Road, L15 3JA
🕐 12-11 (11.30 Wed & Thu; midnight Fri & Sat)
☎ (0151) 733 5782
Castle Rock Harvest Pale; Greene King IPA, Abbot; Tetley Bitter; 4 changing beers 🄷
Vibrant traditional multi-room pub with the original public bar dating back to when it was a Walkers establishment. Popular with students, it hosts regular events including a quiz night. The food is good value. Up to eight ever-changing guest beers are on offer as well as Westons Old Rosie cider. Real ale night is Tuesday and occasional beer festivals are hosted. The roadside patio has sports TV. 🐴◐🍎P🚌(86)📶

Liverpool: Woolton

White Horse

2 Acrefield Road, L25 5JL
🕐 12-11 (midnight Fri & Sat) ☎ (0151) 428 2255
Fuller's London Pride; 3 changing beers (sourced nationally) 🄷
A small local dating from the time when Woolton was a separate village. There are two cosy drinking areas off the main room. Wood panelling and brasswork help create a traditional atmosphere. A full menu is available to 7.30pm (5pm Sun). Guest beers come from both smaller and larger

breweries. The Quarrymen who became the Beatles were named after Woolton Quarry and played their first gig at St Peter's Church fête. ⦿🍴🚌

Lydiate

Scotch Piper ★ ✅

Southport Road, L31 4HD (800yds N from A5147/Moss Lane jct)

✪ 1-11; 12-11.30 Fri & Sat; 12-11 Sun ☎ (0151) 526 2207

House beer (by Marston's); 2 changing beers 🅗

The medieval, cruck-framed, Grade II*-listed Scotch Piper is a thatched and whitewashed building just north of Lydiate. The entrance opens into a traditional bar with a servery on the left. A passage to the right leads to a further two rooms, the middle one with original woodwork. The end room, added later, is less rustic but retains some upholstered bench seating. The toilets are outside. The house beer is Piper 1320 from Marston's.

Q✿🍴🏛♣P🚌(300)🐾📶

Maghull

Frank Hornby 🅛 ✅

38 Eastway, L31 6BR

✪ 8am-11.30 (midnight Fri & Sat) ☎ (0151) 520 4010

Phoenix Wobbly Bob; 9 changing beers (often Lancaster, Lytham, Moorhouse's) 🅗

This Wetherspoon establishment is named after local man Frank Hornby, famous inventor of the Hornby train set. Unsurprisingly, some samples of his work are on display in the pub including Meccano and Dinky Toys. Situated in a suburban street, the bar is spacious and light with a decked area outside at the front. A selection of guest ales is available including some from local microbreweries. Alcohol is served from 10am. No children after 10pm.

Q✿🍴🏛⦿♿♣P🚌(310,133,231)📶

New Brighton

Stage Door Tap

Queen's Royal, Marine Promenade, CH45 2JT

✪ 11-11; 11-10.30 Sun ☎ (0151) 691 0101

🌐 thequeensroyal.com

Hawkshead Windermere Pale; 5 changing beers (sourced regionally; often Brimstage, Hawkshead, Phoenix) 🅗

A bright, airy, modern bar in the Queen's Royal Hotel, an imposing Victorian building close to the Floral Pavilion Theatre with which it is now associated. In a seafront location overlooking Marine Promenade, Marine Lake and Fort Perch Rock, this free house is popular both with locals and day trippers. The enclosed drinking area outside affords superb views over Liverpool Bay. Good-value bar snacks and meals are served in the bar until 9pm (7pm Sun) and there is an adjoining restaurant. 🏛🍴⦿♿♣🚌🐾📶

Stanley's Cask ✅

212 Rake Lane, CH45 1JP

✪ 11-midnight (11 Mon & Wed); 12-midnight Sun ☎ (0151) 691 1093

5 changing beers (sourced nationally; often Brains, Caledonian, Robinsons) 🅗

This ever-popular local continues to thrive, due in no small part to the landlady. The five guest ales on offer often include seasonal beers from regional breweries. A traditional, single-roomed community

New Ferry

local, it hosts various sports teams, quiz nights and regular live music including rock, blues and folk. 🏛♿♣🚌(410,433)🐾📶

Freddie's Club 🅛

36 Stanley Road, CH62 5AS

✪ 7 (5 Fri & Sat)-11; 12-11 Sun

Brimstage Trappers Hat Bitter; 1 changing beer (sourced locally; often Brimstage) 🅗

A popular social club, formerly a Conservative Club, converted into a comfortable lounge bar with adjoining snooker room with two full-size tables. It is situated in a residential street just a short walk from New Ferry shopping centre. There is regular live entertainment. A former local CAMRA Club of the Year, show a CAMRA membership card or a current copy of the Guide for entry. Q🏛♿♣P🚌

Newton-le-Willows

Firkin Bar

65 High Street, WA12 9SL (on A49)

✪ 5.30-11 Thu; 1-11.30 Fri & Sat; 1-10.30 Sun; closed Mon-Wed ☎ (01925) 225700 🌐 thefirkin.co.uk

6 changing beers (sourced regionally) 🅗

A former shop, this small, friendly, family-run establishment dispenses a selection of six real ales, including at least one dark beer, all sourced from micro or SIBA breweries. Small seating areas are to the front and rear, and pictures of Newton of old adorn the walls. Free of electronic noise, this is a place in which to engage in conversation with like-minded people and to make new friends. Two traditional ciders are available.

Q🔁⦿🚌(22,34)🐾📶

Oxton

Caernarvon Castle ✅

Bidston Road, CH43 2JZ

✪ 11-11.30 (12.30am Fri & Sat) ☎ (0151) 652 2831 🌐 caernarvoncastle-prenton.co.uk

Greene King IPA, Abbot; Morland Old Speckled Hen; 6 changing beers (sourced nationally; often Moorhouse's, Peerless) 🅗

Large, pleasant pub built in 1954 by Birkenhead Brewery on the site of the original Caernarvon Castle pub which was destroyed by bombing in World War II. It is located on a busy road next to St Saviour's Church. The patio area is ideal for alfresco dining and drinking and is popular as it catches the sun for most of the day. Q✿🏛⦿♿P🚌📶

Oxton Bar & Kitchen

2 Claughton Firs, CH43 5TQ

✪ 12-midnight (11 Mon); 1am Fri & Sat); 12-11 Sun ☎ (0151) 651 2535 🌐 oxtonbar.co.uk

3 changing beers (sourced locally; often Brimstage, Liverpool Organic, Mad Hatter) 🅗

Situated in the centre of the attractive Oxton village among shops, bars and restaurants, this former John Smith's pub built in 1969 has been tastefully converted into a smart, comfortable, single-room lounge bar. There is a strong emphasis on quality food, ranging from sandwiches and snacks to full meals, available daily until 9.30pm (9pm Sun). Guest beers are usually all from local microbreweries. ✿🏛⦿🍴P🚌(90,492,495)📶

Raby

Wheatsheaf Inn ⓛ

Raby Mere Road, CH63 4JH

✪ 11.30-11 (midnight Fri & Sat); 12-10.30 Sun

☎ (0151) 336 3416 ⊕ wheatsheaf-cowshed.co.uk

Brimstage Trappers Hat Bitter; Tetley Bitter; Thwaites Original, Wainwright; 5 changing beers (sourced regionally; often Purple Moose) Ⓗ

An inn for 350 years, this is Wirral's oldest pub. The thatched building was rebuilt following a fire in 1611 and is reputed to be haunted by Charlotte, who died here. The walls are decorated with old photographs of Raby. The bar has nine handpumps serving three rooms and a restaurant in a converted cowshed. Lunch is served in the bar until 2pm, then snacks until 5pm. The restaurant is open evenings Tuesday to Saturday.
Q🕏⌚🕯&P🍽(84,85)🐾

Rainford

Junction Inn ⓛ

News Lane, WA11 7JU

✪ 1-11; 11-10.30 Sun ☎ (01744) 882868

3 changing beers (sourced locally; often AllGates, George Wright) Ⓗ

Next to Rainford Junction station, this independent free house concentrates on local ales, often from the nearby George Wright Brewery. There is a games room and small bar at the front of the building and a large comfortable lounge to the right-hand side. Home-cooked food is served. Music features highly throughout the week. During the summer themed beer festivals are staged in a large beer garden overlooking open fields.
⌚🕯♣P

Rock Ferry

Refreshment Rooms

Bedford Road East, CH42 1LS (off B5136, take Rock Lane East, then fourth right and over bridge)

✪ 12-11 (1am Fri & Sat) ☎ (0151) 644 5893

⊕ refreshmentrooms.info

House beer (by Lees); 4 changing beers (sourced locally; often Liverpool Organic, Peerless) Ⓗ

Refurbished and reopened in 2012 under its original name, the pub was built in the 1880s for ferry passengers to Liverpool. Although the ferry terminal is long gone, this off-the-beaten-track establishment is well worth seeking out, with excellent views over the Mersey. One central bar services two rooms. The house beer, HMS Conway, is from Lees and the cider is from Rosie's. Excellent-quality, reasonably priced food is served daily until 9pm. Q🕏⌚🕯&➡♣🌙(1,2)🐾🕯

St Helens

Abbey Hotel ⓛ

Hard Lane, Dentons Green, WA10 6TL

✪ 11-11; 11-10.30 Sun ☎ (01744) 25649

Holt Bitter; 4 changing beers (sourced nationally) Ⓗ

A former coaching inn, just off the A570 to the north of the town, heading towards Rainford, this Joseph Holt pub has been tastefully refurbished retaining many original features. The central bar area serves five rooms, all with their own character. Traditional pub games including dominoes and pool are played in the games room. Private parties can be catered for. 🕯➡♣P🍽

Brown Edge

Nutgrove Road, Nutgrove, WA9 5JR

✪ 1-12.30am ☎ (0151) 426 5078

Banks's Sunbeam; Marston's Pedigree; 2 changing beers Ⓗ

On the main road between St Helens and Rainhill, this is a comfortable suburban pub. It has two main areas – a public bar at the front of the building with pub games such as darts and live sport on TV, and a comfortable lounge at the rear leading to a bowling green. Live bands and beer festivals are hosted at various times of the year.
🕏🕯➡♣P🍽🐾🕯

Cricketers Arms ♈ ⓛ ✅

Peter Street, WA10 2EB

✪ 12-11 (1am Fri & Sat) ☎ (01744) 361846

Changing beers (sourced locally) Ⓗ

The Cricketers has established itself as an excellent cask ale pub. Now with 13 handpumps on the bar, the beers come from newer regional brewers and local microbreweries. There is also an excellent selection of real ciders. This is a friendly local community pub on the edge of the town centre which hosts darts and pool teams. Entertainment is offered at the weekend. Beer festivals are staged several times a year. Local CAMRA Pub of the Year in 2014 and 2015 and regional Pub of the Year 2015. 🕯♣🌙P🍽🐾🕯

News Room ⓛ

Duke Street, WA10 2JG

✪ 5-11; 4-midnight Fri; 1-midnight Sat; 1-11 Sun

☎ (01744) 322129

George Wright Pipe Dream; 2 changing beers (sourced locally) Ⓗ

A small stylish bar in a developing real ale hotspot on Duke Street. With a vibrant and cosy atmosphere it is a recent convert to real ale – three beers are now offered from local microbreweries. It also stocks many different Belgian and foreign bottled beers. Often busy, particularly at weekends. 🍽

Phoenix ⓛ

Canal Street, WA10 3LL

✪ 2-11; 12-1am Fri & Sat; 12-11 Sun ☎ (01744) 751890

Changing beers Ⓗ

Built in 1903, the pub has its name in mosaic tiles on an outer wall, and a mosaic tile floor. A community local, the smallish bar is home to pool, darts and dominoes, and the spacious lounge is comfortable. Up to six beers are available, mostly from local microbreweries. Sky Sports is shown on numerous TVs. Music dominates, with karaoke on Friday night and live bands on Saturday. A yard at the back has been converted into a heated smoking area. ➡♣🌙🕯

Sefton ✅

Baldwin Street, WA10 1QA

✪ 11-11 (3 Fri & Sat) ☎ (01744) 22065

Brains Bitter; 3 changing beers (sourced nationally) Ⓗ

This town-centre local is basically one large room with a long bar down one side offering four beers, usually including one from George Wright Brewery in nearby Rainford. Real ale sales have increased significantly over recent years. There is a large function room upstairs and bands often appear at the pub. Good-value food is offered.
🕯➡(Central)🍽

Talbot Ale House L

Duke Street, WA10 2JG

⚙ 2-midnight (2am Fri); 12-2am Sat; 12-midnight Sun

☎ (01744) 322185

George Wright Drunken Duck, Cheeky Pheasant; 7 changing beers (sourced nationally; often George Wright) Ⓗ

Friendly town-centre pub now with new licensees. It has recently been redecorated and is divided into two areas – a public bar with pool and darts, and a comfortable lounge. Nine handpumps dispense local George Wright beers and quality ales from further afield. Look for the attractive stained-glass windows featuring sporting scenes. ♣♠P🖾🐾🕏

Turk's Head L ⊘

Morley Street, WA10 2DQ

⚙ 2-11; 12-12.30am Sat & Sun ☎ (01744) 751289

Changing beers Ⓗ

A short distance from town, this popular pub was a previous CAMRA National Pub of the Year runner-up. Half-timbered, with etched-glass windows, it was built in the 1870s by Ellis Warde Brewery. It offers a constantly changing beer range, with 12 handpulls in use over the weekend, six at other times. Draught and bottled continental beers are also stocked. Thursday is curry and jazz night, and on Tuesday night there is a free quiz. Darts and dominoes are played. ◖🇩♣♠🗒🐾

Southport

Barons Bar ⊘

239 Lord Street, PR8 1NZ (within Scarisbrick Hotel)

⚙ 11-11 (12.30am Fri & Sat) ☎ (01704) 534000

Moorhouse's Pride of Pendle; Tetley Bitter; house beer (by Moorhouse's); 10 changing beers (sourced regionally; often Cottage, Lytham, Moorhouse's) Ⓗ

An ornate baronial-style bar set within the Scarisbrick Hotel complex, now with a front lounge with chairs, tables and comfy settees overlooking the town's famous Lord Street. The bar has been championing real ale in Southport for many years and offers a varied selection, both local and national. One real cider is also available. Q🏵️🐎🐾🍴🛗♿🌠🖾🐾

Guest House

16 Union Street, PR9 0QE

⚙ 11.30-11 (11.30 Fri & Sat); 12-10.30 Sun

☎ (01704) 537660 ⊕ guesthouse-southport.blogspot.com

Adnams Southwold Bitter; Caledonian Deuchars IPA; Jennings Cumberland Ale; Ruddles Best Bitter; Theakston Traditional Mild, Best Bitter; 4 changing beers (often Moorhouse's) Ⓗ

Close to the station and Lord Street, this listed building has an impressive frontage and interior with three separate wood-panelled drinking rooms. A quiet, traditional pub, attracting a mixed clientele, there is seating outside at the front and a courtyard area to the rear. The bar has 11 handpumps, one serving a local micro beer, and stocks a wide range of malt whiskies. Entertainment includes a Thursday quiz night and acoustic folk club on the first and third Mondays of the month. Q🏵️◖🇩🚲

Inn Beer Shop

657 Lord Street, PR9 0AW

⚙ 12-10.30; 11-11 Fri & Sat ☎ (01704) 533054

Southport Sandgrounder Bitter, Golden Sands; 2 changing beers (sourced locally; often Southport) Ⓗ

Friendly café bar offering a huge selection of local, national and foreign bottled beers for takeaway or consumption on the premises. The bar now sports a second handpump and serves real ciders and draught foreign lagers. The interior is lined with bottles and continental-style seating, leading to a comfy area with games. Snacks and a tea/coffee service with cakes are available throughout the day. Outside seating is on Lord Street. The bar can get busy at weekends. 🚲♣♠🖾🐾🌠🕏

Phoenix ⊘

4-6 Coronation Walk, PR8 1RF (at lower, southern end of Lord St)

⚙ 10-midnight (1am Sat) ☎ (01704) 513233

Sharp's Doom Bar; 2 changing beers Ⓗ

An ideal first stop for drinks before town. Family-run and free of tie, it is a favourite with real ale drinkers and serves good food at reasonable prices. Plenty of traditional games are played, with poker nights on Monday and Wednesday, and darts on Tuesday. Live music features on Friday. All top football games are shown on various plasma TV screens scattered about the pub, and there is a large screen for major fixtures. 🐎♿🚲♣♠🌠🕏

Sir Henry Segrave L ⊘

93-97 Lord Street, PR8 1RH (on A565, S end of Lord St)

⚙ 8am-midnight ☎ (01704) 530217

Greene King Abbot; Moorhouse's Pendle Witches Brew; Phoenix Wobbly Bob; Ruddles Best Bitter; Thwaites Wainwright; changing beers (often Coach House, Lytham, Saltaire) Ⓗ

Named after the former land-speed world record holder who used to race on Southport flats, this is a spacious Wetherspoon pub with an attractive 19th-century exterior. The manager is a strong supporter of real ale and runs regular beer festival trips and occasional Meet the Brewer evenings. The 12 handpumps offer the best all-round choice of microbrewery beers in Southport – regular orders are placed with Phoenix, Saltaire, Titanic and Hawkshead. There is outside seating on Lord Street. 🐎◖🇩♿🐾🍴🖾🕏

Tap & Bottles

19a Cambridge Walk, PR8 1EN

⚙ 12-11 (midnight Fri & Sat); 12-10.30 Sun

☎ (01704) 544322

4 changing beers (often AllGates, George Wright, Southport) Ⓗ

The Tap & Bottles is a micropub situated in the arcade between Chapel Street and Lord Street next to the Atkinson Centre. It offers a choice of four real ales from virtually any brewery, though with a preference for beers from north-west England. A huge bottled selection is also stocked. There is a cosy seating area upstairs with benches and tables. A small tapas menu is available all day. Q🐎🏵️🚲♣♠🌠🕏

Willow Grove L ⊘

387-389 Lord Street, PR9 0AG (on A565)

⚙ 8am-midnight ☎ (01704) 517830

Greene King Abbot Ⓗ/🄶**; Ruddles Best Bitter; Thwaites Wainwright; changing beers (often Moorhouse's, Phoenix, Robinsons)** Ⓗ

The Willow Grove is a Wetherspoon pub with an emphasis on real ale and food. A quiet establishment, it is situated on Lord Street opposite the impressive 1920s war memorial. The interior is L-shaped with a long bar, some cubicles and a mixture of furnishings including comfy settees. Ten handpumps dispense a choice of beers sourced from breweries ranging from the local Parker to other micros to nationals. ⚅⏻&⇌●🚌🛜

Zetland ●
53 Zetland Street, PR9 0RH
⚅ 12-11.30 (midnight Fri & Sat) ☎ (01704) 808404
⊕ zetlandhotelsouthport.co.uk
Jennings Cumberland Ale; 2 changing beers (sourced nationally; often Brakspear, Ringwood, Wychwood) ℍ
Situated in a residential area just 10 minutes from Lord Street, the Zetland is a local community hostelry offering amazingly low-priced home-cooked food in a friendly atmosphere. The pub shows live sport and hosts bowling competitions, with one of the finest crown green facilities in the North-west. A large pub with several side rooms, it offers excellent buffets and can cater for parties of up to 100. ⚅⏚⏻♣P🚌(49)😸🛜

Thornton Hough
Red Fox
Neston Road, CH64 7TL
⚅ 10.30-11; 10.30-10.30 Sun ☎ (0151) 353 2920
⊕ brunningandprice.co.uk/redfox
House beer (by Phoenix); 5 changing beers (sourced locally) ℍ
This imposing building in its own extensive grounds probably dates back to the 1890s. Following an extensive refurbishment it reopened in 2014 as a smart gastro-pub serving quality food and well-kept beers. It has the ambience of a friendly pub with a traditional bar area boasting seven handpumps and a smaller bar space at the back. Up to eight real ciders are available. There is outside seating at the rear and a large lawned garden. ⚅⏚⏻&●P🚌😸🛜

Waterloo
Old Bank ▯ ●
34 South Road, L22 5PE
⚅ 11-11 (midnight Thu-Sun) ☎ (0151) 928 7020
⊕ theoldbankwaterloo.co.uk
4 changing beers ℍ
Four handpumps dispense a range of beers, both local and from across the North-west. A quiet oasis on weekday afternoons, the pub is a hive of activity most evenings and weekends, with a strong commitment to live music and football. Musical instruments hang from the ceiling in a raised area at the front where bands play, and pictures of the Beatles and other musical memorabilia adorn the walls. A book swap library and games are available. A courtyard at the back provides an outdoor drinking area for warmer days, and the marina and beach are nearby. 😸🚌🛜

Queen's Picture House ▯ ●
47-49 South Road, L22 5PE
⚅ 9am-11 (11.30 Thu-Sat) ☎ (0151) 949 2070

Fuller's London Pride; Greene King Abbot; Ruddles Best Bitter; Sharp's Doom Bar; 5 changing beers ℍ
Named after a cinema that once graced this site, this is a typical Wetherspoon refurbishment with decor reflecting local events and people. The main room and bar area offer various seating alternatives. An area to the right of the entrance is a dining space ideal for families and groups. Satellite TV is silent. ⚅⏚⏻&⇌●🚌🛜

Stamps Too ▯
99 South Road, L22 0LR (diagonally opp Waterloo station)
⚅ 12-11 (midnight Thu-Sat) ☎ (0151) 280 0035
5 changing beers (sourced locally; often Liverpool Organic) ℍ
The local CAMRA branch's original accredited LocAle pub. This friendly open-plan venue is the haunt both of real ale enthusiasts and live music fans. Five handpumps serve mainly local beers, from Liverpool Organic, Brimstage, Southport and AllGates in particular, with occasional beers from further afield – a sixth handpump dispenses real cider. Bands and local musicians feature Thursday through to Sunday. &⇌●🚌(53,133)😸🛜

Volunteer Canteen ★ ▯ ●
45 East Street, L22 8QR
⚅ 2-11; 12-midnight Fri & Sat; 12-10.30 Sun ☎ 07891 407464
4 changing beers ℍ
A cosy traditional pub housed in a Grade II-listed terraced building, the Volly, as it is locally known, still provides a table service. Nestling in the back streets of Waterloo, the pub dates back to 1871 and, until the 1980s, was owned by Higsons, evidence of which can be seen etched into its windows. Small breweries around Merseyside and north Wales often supply guest ales. Pies, pâté, olives and a variety of nuts are served at all times. Q😸⇌♣🚌(53)😸🛜

West Kirby
West Kirby Tap ▯
Grange Road, CH48 4DY
⚅ 12-11 (11.30 Fri & Sat) ☎ (0151) 625 0350
⊕ westkirbytap.co.uk
Spitting Feathers Thirstquencher; 7 changing beers (sourced nationally) ℍ
Refurbished and reopened by Spitting Feathers brewery in 2014, this smart, modern bar features wood panelling, bare brick walls and a high ceiling. The single bar has a small raised area and a couple of discrete spaces. It is close to West Kirby's shops and transport connections, a short walk to the beach and convenient for trekkers to Hilbre Island. Eight handpumps dispense a varying range of beers plus a changing real cider. ⚅⏻&⇌●😸🛜

Sick note

Me and some of the fellers decided to cook up a batch of home brew and the instructions on the yeast said 'Add one packet and wait three days' so we added three packets and waited one day. Well, we drank all that brew right up the very next day. Never been sicker in my life. **American home brewer during Prohibition**

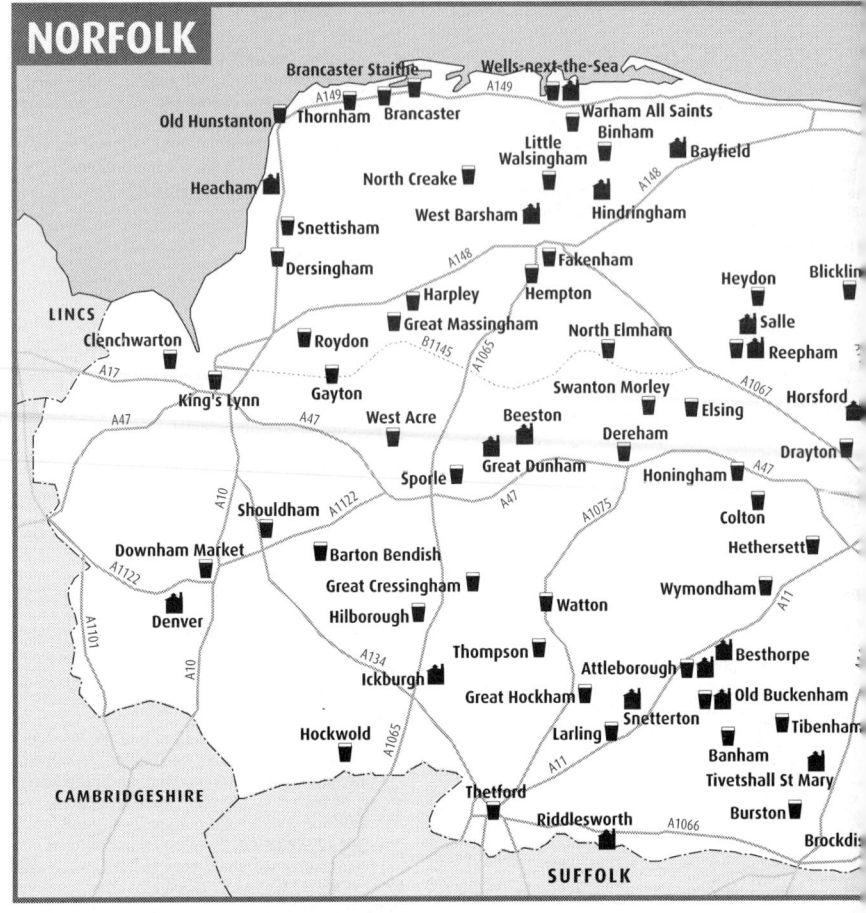

NORFOLK

Map of Norfolk showing: Brancaster Staithe, Wells-next-the-Sea, Old Hunstanton, Thornham, Brancaster, Warham All Saints, Binham, Bayfield, Little Walsingham, Heacham, North Creake, West Barsham, Hindringham, Snettisham, Dersingham, Heydon, Blickling, Harpley, Hempton, Fakenham, LINCS, Clenchwarton, Roydon, Great Massingham, North Elmham, Salle, Reepham, King's Lynn, Gayton, West Acre, Beeston, Swanton Morley, Elsing, Horsford, Dereham, Drayton, Sporle, Great Dunham, Honingham, Shouldham, Colton, Downham Market, Barton Bendish, Hethersett, Great Cressingham, Wymondham, Denver, Hilborough, Watton, Thompson, Besthorpe, Ickburgh, Attleborough, Old Buckenham, Great Hockham, Snetterton, Tibenham, Hockwold, Larling, Banham, Tivetshall St Mary, CAMBRIDGESHIRE, Thetford, Burston, Riddlesworth, Brockdis, SUFFOLK

Attleborough

London Tavern 🄻
Church Street, NR17 2AH
🕒 11-11 (2 Fri & Sat); 11-10.30 Sun ☎ 07871 773206
5 changing beers 🄷
Town centre pub, close to public transport, where families and dogs are welcome. The changing beer range includes up to five real ales, usually including one from the on-site Taylor's of Attleborough Brewery, which commenced brewing in 2014 – the other four come from microbreweries all over the UK. A beer festival takes place over the August bank holiday weekend. The pub has a dining room and serves breakfast and lunch every day.
🌀🕮&🎋P🐾🐾📶

Banham

Garden House (Cider House)
Overcross, NR16 2BY
🕒 12-11; 12-10.30 Sun ☎ (01953) 860437
Adnams Southwold Bitter; Woodforde's Wherry; 2 changing beers (often Grain, Hoxne) 🄷
This recently refurbished pub is under new ownership and usually has four real ales on offer, as well as local real cider. An extensive food menu includes a Man v Food challenge and eclectic American-themed food along with matching decor.

There is a beer festival during the August bank holiday. Located to the north-east of Banham and well worth seeking out. 🌀🕮🕔&🍀🐾🐾📶

Banningham

Crown Inn 🄻 ✔
Colby Road, NR11 7DY (N of B1145 1 mile E of A140)
🕒 12-11 (12.30am Fri & Sat) ☎ (01263) 733534
🌐 banninghamcrown.co.uk
Greene King IPA, Abbot; 3 changing beers 🄷
Traditional 17th-century free house with a welcoming atmosphere, overlooking the village green. The original beamed interior has a log fire in the bar area. The three guest beers (four in summer) are from regional and microbreweries. With a first-class reputation for fine cuisine, using local produce, the superb modern restaurant is open to the kitchen and chefs. The pub has a patio, garden and barbecue areas for summer alfresco dining. Regular events include quiz nights and jazz on Sundays. A warm, friendly and deservedly popular pub. Q🕮🕔&🅰🍀P🄿(18)🐾📶

Barton Bendish

Berney Arms
Church Road, PE33 9GF
🕒 12-11 ☎ (01366) 347995 🌐 theberneyarms.co.uk

reasonable prices. There is an additional specials menu and regular themed evenings. The range of beers is from regional breweries. The owners are knowledgeable and experienced beer enthusiasts. Q⏳🏠🅿🔥⛺♣🅿🚏(46)🐾🛜

Blickling

Buckinghamshire Arms ✪
NR11 6NF (next to Blickling Hall and about a mile from Aylsham)
🕐 10-11; 10-10.30 Sun ☎ (01263) 732133
🌐 bucksarms.co.uk
Woodforde's Wherry; 3 changing beers Ⓗ
Unspoilt 17th-century pub, a former coaching inn, situated a few steps from the even older Blickling Hall, home of Anne Boleyn. Inside, there is a delightful snug and a bar with a real fire, outside, plenty of tables front and rear, with views over the surrounding parkland. The pub does good food from a varied menu. The Weavers Way footpath and Bure Valley Railway are nearby. There are four B&B rooms. Q🏠🛏🍴🅿🐾

Brancaster

Ship Hotel Ⓛ
Main Road, PE31 8AP
🕐 8am-11 ☎ (01485) 210333 🌐 shiphotelnorfolk.co.uk

Adnams Southwold Bitter, Broadside; 2 changing beers Ⓗ
The food in this smart village local is a step above regular pub food, and look out for value-for-money special set menus, or try the afternoon teas 2.30-6pm. The beer mostly comes from Adnams, including its seasonal range, but a guest beer is usually on offer. The decoration in the bar includes some interesting calendars, and there is also a well-appointed dining room and lovely garden as alternatives. The old stable block offers accommodation. Q🏠🛏🍴🅿🐾🛜

Binham

Chequers Inn
Front Street, NR21 0AL
🕐 12-3, 6-11; 12-11 Sat & Sun ☎ (01328) 830297
🌐 binhamchequers.co.uk
Adnams Southwold Bitter; Norfolk Brewhouse Moon Gazer Golden Ale; 3 changing beers Ⓗ
A traditional brick-and-flint village pub, the Chequers is a tremendously popular place with both locals and visitors, a friendly hostelry with strong support from the surrounding community. Ownership changed in 2013, the bar was redecorated, and children and dogs are now welcome. The menu comprises a range of good, wholesome fare (including vegetarian) at

REAL ALE BREWERIES
Aleyard Riddlesworth (NEW)
All Day Salle
Beeston Beeston
Boudicca Hoveton (NEW)
Buffy's Tivetshall St Mary
Bullards Norwich
Chalk Hill ▌ Norwich
Dancing Men ▌ Happisburgh
Elmtree Snetterton
Fat Cat ▌ Norwich
Fox ▌ Heacham
Golden Triangle Norwich
Grain Alburgh
Humpty Dumpty Reedham
Iceni Ickburgh
Jo C's West Barsham
Lacons Great Yarmouth
Neatishead ▌ Neatishead (NEW)
Norfolk Hindringham
Oakwood Wells-next-the-Sea (NEW)
Opa Hay's Aldeby
Panther Reepham
People's Thorpe-next-Haddiscoe
Poppyland Cromer
Redwell Norwich
S&P Horsford
St Andrew's ▌ Norwich (NEW)
Stumptail Great Dunham
Taylors ▌ Attleborough
Tindall Seething
Tipples Salhouse
Tombstone Great Yarmouth
Two Rivers Denver
Wagtail Old Buckenham
Waveney ▌ Earsham
Why Not Norwich
Winter's Norwich
Wolf Besthorpe
Woodforde's Woodbastwick
Yetman's Bayfield

Jo C's Bitter Old Bustard, Knot Just Another IPA, Norfolk Kiwi Ⓗ

A Flying Kiwi inn located on the north Norfolk coast with two bars, serving local ales from Jo C's brewery. There is a large restaurant and beer garden. Accommodation is available in nine en-suite rooms, two of which make a family suite. Takeaway fish and chips can be ordered at the bar seven days a week. Restored in 2010, it has kept much of the original history in its design and decor. ⬢⚫️🏡⚫️🍴P🚲❀🌳

Brancaster Staithe

Jolly Sailors
Main Road, PE31 8BJ
✪ 12-11; 12-10.30 Sun ☎ (01485) 210314
⊕ jollysailorsbrancaster.co.uk
Adnams Broadside; Brancaster Best; Woodforde's Wherry; 1 changing beer Ⓗ

A cosy inn with several small drinking areas and two dining rooms, convenient for the Norfolk coast path and Brancaster Staithe harbour. It has a garden and play area, is family- and dog-friendly and has an ice cream hut. Brancaster beers are produced by a local brewery to the pub's recipes and at least one is always available. Food offerings include local seafood and stone-baked pizza, with the oven visible from the bar. Coasthopper buses stop outside. There is a beer and music festival every June. Closed 3-6pm weekdays in winter. Q⬢⚫️⚫️⚫️♿🅰️♣P🚲❀🌳

Brockdish

Old King's Head
50 The Street, IP21 4JY
✪ 10-10 (11 Fri & Sat); 10-9 Sun; closed Mon
☎ (01379) 668843 ⊕ kingsheadbrockdish.co.uk
Adnams Southwold Bitter, Broadside; 3 changing beers (often Barrell & Sellers, Calvors, Green Jack) Ⓗ

A 16th-century beamed community pub with a friendly atmosphere, reopened in 2015 with a coffee shop serving delicious home-made cakes, plus bread at weekends (open from 10am). There is a family-friendly bar with seating and a bar for drinking, with a woodburner, serving imaginative Italian food from noon. Locally sourced meats and ingredients are used where possible, and gluten-free meals are available. Regular music events feature, usually on a Thursday. A gin club adds to the mix. Local artists display work in the bars and gallery. ⬢⚫️⚫️♣P🚲❀

Burston

Crown Inn
Mill Road, IP22 5TW (by crossroads in middle of village, on the green)
✪ 12-11; 12-10.30 Sun ☎ (01379) 741257
⊕ burstoncrown.com
Adnams Southwold Bitter; 4 changing beers (often Adnams) Ⓗ/Ⓖ

An attractive 16th-century Grade II-listed pub featuring exposed beams, deep sofas, newspapers and a log fire blazing in the inglenook fireplace. There are two bars, one with a pool table and darts. Boules is played in the garden in summer. A small restaurant serves locally sourced freshly cooked food (no food Sun eve or Mon). The cuisine is a mix of styles and booking is advisable. Regular live music features at weekends, and an open mic

night on Thursdays. The village is famous for the Burston School Strike that ran from 1914 to 1939. Q⬢⚫️⚫️⚫️♣P🚲❀🌳

Cantley

Cock Tavern
Manor Road, NR13 3JQ (1½ miles N of village centre)
✪ 11-3, 6-11.30 ☎ (01493) 700895
Adnams Southwold Bitter; 4 changing beers Ⓗ

A roadside pub which serves a large rural catchment area, not just the nearby village of Cantley. Although a popular food venue (booking advisable) it retains the feel and atmosphere of a real pub, helped by the traditional decor. There are several themed food nights weekly, and a quiz night on Mondays. Its wide range of reasonably priced ales make the pub well worth the detour off the usual Broads tourist trail. ⬢⚫️♣P🚲(730)❀

Catfield

Crown Inn Ⓛ ✔
The Street, NR29 5AA (in centre of village, S of A149, E of Stalham)
✪ 12-2.30, 7-11 (5-11 Fri; 7-midnight Sat); 12-3, 7-10.30 Sun
☎ (01692) 580128 ⊕ catfieldcrown.co.uk
Greene King IPA; 3 changing beers Ⓗ

Formerly a Lacons house, this 300-year-old village inn, with its real fire in winter, is a real focus for village life. There is an interesting selection of quality guest beers, mainly from local microbreweries, including Lacons. The food includes traditional pub offerings, with fresh local ingredients used where possible. On Friday, takeaway fish and chips are served. There is a separate function/dining room and a secluded garden for summer. Accommodation is available in an adjoining detached building, once the doctor's surgery. Q⬢🏡⚫️⚫️🍴P🚲❀🌳

Chedgrave

White Horse ✔
5 Norwich Road, NR14 6ND
✪ 12-11.30; 12-10 Sun ☎ (01508) 520250
⊕ whitehorsechedgrave.co.uk
Adnams Southwold Bitter, Ghost Ship; Sharp's Doom Bar; Timothy Taylor Landlord; Young's Bitter; 1 changing beer Ⓗ

Village pub with welcome distinct separate pub and restaurant facilities. Drinkers are well catered for from a range of five real ales sourced from all round the UK, with Timothy Taylor's Landlord often featured as a regular. There is a large pleasant garden for use in summer. Although technically in Chedgrave, the pub is actually within easy walking distance of the nearby holiday moorings in neighbouring Loddon. Beer festivals are held here in April and November, and there is occasional live music. ⬢⚫️⚫️♿🅰️P🚲(X22,146)❀

Clenchwarton

Victory Inn Ⓛ
243 Main Road, PE34 4AQ
✪ 12-11 (midnight Fri & Sat) ☎ (01553) 775668
Elgood's Cambridge Bitter; 3 changing beers Ⓗ

Although an Elgood's house, guest beers are always available to complement the excellent, good-value food. There is a lot going on in this village local, with regular quizzes, classic car meetings and occasional beer festivals among the attractions on offer. There is a pleasant outdoor drinking area in the garden, with a traditional bar and dining area inside. Everything a village local should be. ♿️🕍🍴♣🟎P🚲(505)🐾🎵📶

Coltishall

Red Lion 🅛
77 Church Street, NR12 7DW
☼ 12 (4 Mon)-11 ☎ (01603) 736644
🌐 redlion-coltishall.co.uk
Sharp's Doom Bar; 4 changing beers 🅷
Two bars on two levels plus a separate dining area grace this warm, friendly and comfortable pub which dates from the 16th century. There is a cosy lower bar with a logburner where up to five real ales can be found from mostly local or regional breweries, including microbreweries. The pub also presses and bottles its own cider with apples from local orchards. It has a good menu with specials and theme nights. Beer festivals are held at Easter and in late summer, and the pub even has its own taxi. Q♿️🕍🚲🍴🟎♣🐾📶

Colton

Ugly Bug Inn 🅛
High House Farm Lane, NR9 5DG (2 miles S of A47 Norwich southern bypass)
☼ 12-2.30 (not Tue), 6-11; 12-3, 6-10.30 Sun
☎ (01603) 880794 🌐 uglybuginn.co.uk
Beeston Worth the Wait; 3 changing beers 🅷
Converted fruit barn, well worth finding, eight miles from Norwich. Large, comfortable bar areas are complemented by a restaurant and beer garden, with a friendly and relaxing atmosphere. Good-quality food is on the menu, and there are monthly jazz evenings. The landlord cellars his beers well, and always has four handpumps serving the best of local real ales – or try one of the 60 single malts. Eight en-suite bedrooms are available. Real ales are competitively priced. Q♿️🕍🚲🍴🟎P🐾📶

Dereham

Royal Standard 🅛
86 Baxter Row, NR19 1AY (from Market Place head E down High St; at mini roundabout outside library bear right into Baxter Row; pub is 150yds on right)
☼ 11-midnight (1am Fri & Sat); 12-midnight Sun
☎ (01362) 690948
Batemans XB; 3 changing beers 🅷
A lively, cosy, two-roomed pub with a friendly and welcoming atmosphere. Two beers are usually from Batemans guest beer range from around the country, with the third sourced from a local micro. Traditional pub games feature strongly, with pool, darts and cribbage all played. Live football and music are provided on a regular basis, and good-quality Sunday roasts are served. The pub is 10 minutes' walk from the Mid-Norfolk heritage railway station, which also holds a beer festival in summer. 🕍🍴🟎♣P🚲📶

Dersingham

Coach & Horses ✅
77 Manor Road, PE31 6LN
☼ 12-11 ☎ (01485) 540391 🌐 thecoachpub.com
Woodforde's Wherry; 3 changing beers 🅷

CAMRA Norfolk Pub of the Year 2014 and West Norfolk Pub of the Year 2015, this 19th-century carrstone inn near Sandringham offers one regular beer and three changing guests, and a draught real cider, all at reasonable prices. It is popular for home-made traditional meals. Entertainment includes quiz nights, a piano, a pool table and live music Friday nights and some Sundays. The large garden includes a children's play area. There are three en-suite B&B rooms. An October beer festival offers around 20 real ales plus five real ciders. Q♿️🕍🚲🍴🟎P🚲(11,10,35)🐾📶

Downham Market

Crown Hotel
12 Bridge Street, PE38 9DH
☼ 9.30am-11 ☎ (01366) 382322 🌐 crowncoachinginn.com
Adnams Southwold Bitter; Greene King IPA, Abbot 🅷
An unspoilt 17th-century coaching inn at the heart of the town. Enter through a room with a lovely staircase to discover a good selection of ales served in a bar with a beamed ceiling and large fireplace. There is a restaurant and separate function room that caters for parties and weddings, and plenty of outside seating. Accommodation is in 18 rooms including family suites. Q♿️🚲🍴🟎P📶

Drayton

Red Lion ✅
2 Fakenham Road, NR8 6PW
☼ 11-11 ☎ (01603) 867262 🌐 redlion-drayton.co.uk
Greene King IPA; Woodforde's Wherry, Bure Gold, Nelson's Revenge; 4 changing beers 🅷
A traditional pub dating from 1768. Beers are local with occasional guest ales and promotional events for beers from further afield. Part of Greene King's Spirit Pub Company, the pub is known for its excellent carvery, although it serves bar meals too. It was refurbished in 2014 with a new bar. It has a low-ceilinged bar area and two separate dining areas. Staff are friendly and helpful. Outside is a large garden and car park to the side. 🕍🍴🟎P🚲(28,X29)📶

Earsham

Queen's Head 🅛
Station Road, NR35 2TS (just W of Bungay)
☼ 12-11; 12-10.30 Sun ☎ (01986) 892623
Waveney East Coast Mild, Lightweight, Welterweight; 1 changing beer (sourced locally; often Wolf) 🅷
On the Norfolk-Suffolk border, near Bungay, this 17th-century busy locals' pub has a large front garden overlooking the village green. The main bar has a flagstone floor, wooden beams and a large fireplace with a roaring fire in winter. It is home to the Waveney Brewing Co. There is a separate dining area serving food at lunchtimes (no food Mon and Tue). The landlord has owned the pub since 2000. Usually, four ales and at least one real cider are available. Q♿️🕍🍴♣🟎P🚲(580)🐾📶

Elsing

Mermaid Inn
Church Street, NR20 3EA (opp St Mary's Church in village)
☼ 12-3 (not Mon), 6-11; 12.30-10.30 Sun ☎ (01362) 637640
🌐 elsingmermaidinn.co.uk

Adnams Broadside; Woodforde's Wherry Ⓖ; 2 changing beers Ⓗ
Well-regarded rural pub and restaurant comprising two outdoor seating areas, a large bar and dining room with a log fire at one end and a pool table at the other. A good selection of ales is on offer, dispensed by gravity. The menu includes pies, the chef's celebrated sausage rolls, Indian and Thai curries, and several vegetarian options. Local groups and societies meet here regularly, while ramblers from further afield arrive via the 12-mile Wensum Way. ⏰🏠🍽️♿️👶🅿️😺🛜

Fakenham

Bull Ⓛ
41 Bridge Street, NR21 9AG
⏰ 10-11; 12-11 Sun ☎ (01328) 853410
🌐 thefakenhambull.co.uk
Woodforde's Wherry; 3 changing beers Ⓗ
Close to the marketplace, this modern local offers a warm welcome with its bright decor and open fire. The Bull has a long single bar and a range of comfortable seating options. Meals are served every day, with a roast on Sunday, and Wednesday evening is steak night. As well as Woodforde's Wherry, another Norfolk ale is often available. Accommodation is in four comfortable en-suite bedrooms. ⏰🏠🛏️🍽️👶🚌(X29,29)😺🛜

Fleggburgh

King's Arms ✅
Main Road, NR29 3AG
⏰ 12-10 (midnight Fri & Sat) ☎ (01493) 368333
🌐 kingsarmsfleggburgh.com
Adnams Ghost Ship; Woodforde's Wherry; 2 changing beers Ⓗ
Large two-bar public house which was extended and renovated in 2012 to a high standard. Up to four real ales are offered from around the country, and real cider is sold in summer. There is a traditional pub menu and the separate restaurant offers a fine dining menu. The owner, Mark Dixon, trained as a chef at the Imperial in Yarmouth and was Norfolk Food and Drink Awards Chef of the Year 2013. ⏰🏠🍽️♿️👶🅿️🚌(6,730)😺🛜

Gayton

Crown Inn ✅
Lynn Road, PE32 1PA
⏰ 12-11 (11.30 Fri & Sat) ☎ (01553) 636252
🌐 gaytoncrown.com/index
Greene King XX Mild, IPA, Abbot; Morland Old Speckled Hen; 1 changing beer Ⓗ
Originating from the 13th century, the Crown Inn combines a charming historic feel with a friendly atmosphere. It is a rare outlet for XX Dark Mild and also has an occasional interesting guest beer. There are several drinking areas, and a patio for the summer with attractive flower beds. The restaurant serves locally sourced food including game dishes and there is a popular Sunday carvery.
Q🏠🛏️🍽️♿️👶🅿️🚌(48)😺🛜

Gorleston

Dock Tavern Ⓛ
Dock Tavern Lane, NR31 6PY (opp N side of Morrisons)
⏰ 11-11; 12-11 Sun ☎ (01493) 442255
🌐 thedocktavern.com

Adnams Broadside; 4 changing beers Ⓗ
As its name suggests, the Dock Tavern is close to the river, and not far from the main shopping area. It has been subject to flood damage many times and the various flood levels can be seen by the front door. The outside drinking area at the front has views of the river and docks. There is live music most weekends, and curry and quiz nights monthly, plus an annual charity music day.
⏰🏠🍽️♣️🅿️😺🛜

Great Cressingham

Olde Windmill Inn
Water End, IP25 6NN (off A1065 S of Swaffham)
⏰ 11-11 ☎ (01760) 756232 🌐 oldewindmillinn.co.uk
Adnams Southwold Bitter, Broadside; Greene King IPA; 2 changing beers Ⓗ
The Olde Windmill is a large rural pub that feels like a village pub, despite its size. In the same family since 1956, the Windmill features a rolling range of beers including the house beer, Windy Miller, usually supplied by Purity. Real cider is also a popular feature. The food ranges from value to sophistication and all points in between; the conservatory is a particularly nice place to eat. Modern accommodation is provided in a separate facility behind the pub. Q⏰🏠🛏️🍽️♿️👶♣️🅿️😺🛜

Great Hockham

Eagle Ⓛ ✅
Harling Road, IP24 1NP
⏰ 12-2.30, 6-11; 12-midnight Fri & Sat; 12-10.30 Sun
☎ (01953) 498893 🌐 hockhameagle.co.uk
Adnams Southwold Bitter; Greene King Abbot; Morland Old Speckled Hen; Woodforde's Wherry; 2 changing beers Ⓗ
Dating from the 1850s, this large pub is set in a picturesque village close to Thetford Forest and welcomes families and dogs. Two bars divided by an open fire serve five real ales on handpump; food is available Friday to Sunday. Outdoor seating is provided at the front and in an enclosed brickweave courtyard at the rear. The pub hosts three pool teams and a darts team, in addition to holding a fortnightly quiz and other regular events.
⏰🏠🍽️♣️🅿️🚌🚃😺🛜

Great Massingham

Dabbling Duck Ⓛ
11 Abbey Road, PE32 2HN
⏰ 12-11; 12-10.30 Sun ☎ (01485) 520827
🌐 thedabblingduck.co.uk
Adnams Broadside; Beeston Worth the Wait; Woodforde's Wherry; 1 changing beer Ⓗ
Set between two ponds at the heart of a lovely village, the pub features bar areas with roaring fires in the winter and a garden to enjoy in the summer. With ample room for those wishing to try one of the three or four beers on offer, there is also a popular restaurant (booking is recommended). Accommodation is in nine rooms, and guides featuring details of local walks are available from the bar. ⏰🏠🛏️🍽️♣️🅿️😺🛜

Great Yarmouth

Mariners Ⓛ
69 Howard Street South, NR30 1LN (behind both Palmers and the Star Hotel)

✪ 11-11 ☎ (01493) 332299
8 changing beers ⌂
Traditional two-bar pub in the town centre, this local stocks up to eight ales and eight real ciders/ perries; visitors could be excused for thinking that a beer festival is always in progress, given the range and choice from all over the country. Beer festivals are in fact held throughout the year, including one at Easter, and when the town's maritime festival is held in early September. Most local buses stop nearby. Q✿☎✪≉♣♠P♿📅(1,1a,8)✿

Red Herring ⌶
24-25 Havelock Road, NR30 3HQ (off St Peters St and at the back of the Time & Tide museum)
✪ 12-3, 7-11.30; 12-midnight Sat & Sun ☎ (01493) 853384
3 changing beers ⌂
This back-street corner local is close to the award-winning Time & Tide museum and spectacular sections of medieval town wall. There is a nice relaxed, comfortable atmosphere and the pool table and TV are tucked away in a room separated from the bar by folding doors. There are many photos of Old Yarmouth during the herring fishing days, when the town was invaded by many Scottish herring boats. The cider is Westons Old Rosie. ✿♣♠

Tombstone Saloon
6 George Street, NR30 1HR (on NE corner of Hall Quay)
✪ 4 (12 Thu-Sat)-midnight; 12-11 Sun ☎ 07584 504444
⊕ tombstonebrewery.co.uk
10 changing beers ⌸
Old West-style bar specialising in real ale and cider, operated by the local Tombstone Brewery sited at the rear of the premises. Staff are friendly and knowledgeable about beer, and there are usually up to six Tombstone real ales, plus four others from local breweries. Many buses stop outside the pub. George Street was once one of the main roads into Yarmouth, and in 1870 there were 12 pubs within 100 yards. May close Monday to Wednesday in winter except December.
≉(Yarmouth Vauxhall)♣♠✿

Harpley

Rose & Crown
Nethergate Street, PE31 6TW
✪ 12-3.30 (not Tue), 6.30-10.30; 12-5 Sun; closed Mon ☎ (01485) 521807
Woodforde's Wherry; 2 changing beers ⌂
Just off the A148 King's Lynn to Fakenham road, this attractive 17th-century pub offers guest ales from local breweries. It features open bar areas with a stylish and comfortable feel and has log fires in winter, while outside is an enclosed beer garden for summer drinking. There is an extensive menu serving excellent food, including one of the best Sunday roasts in the area. The unspoilt village provides pleasant walks and is close to Houghton Hall. Q✿✿◑P📅(X8)✿📶

Hempton

Bell
24 The Green, NR21 7LG
✪ 11-2.30 (not Tue), 5-midnight; 11-midnight Sat; 12-midnight Sun ☎ (01328) 864579 ⊕ hemptonbell.co.uk
Sharp's Doom Bar; Woodforde's Wherry; 1 changing beer ⌂

A popular family-run traditional village pub with a relaxed, friendly atmosphere. It retains a two-bar layout little altered since the early 1970s. Pub games including dominoes, cribbage and poker dice are popular – you are welcome to get involved. Changing guest beers are from micros or independent breweries and are typically slightly stronger than the regulars. Open mic folk sessions take place on the second Tuesday of the month and quizzes are held regularly. ♣P✿

Hethersett

King's Head ⌶
36 Old Norwich Road, NR9 3DD
✪ 11-11.30 (12.30am Fri & Sat); 12-11.30 Sun ☎ (01603) 810206 ⊕ kingsheadhethersett.co.uk
Adnams Ghost Ship; Timothy Taylor Landlord; Woodforde's Bure Gold; 1 changing beer ⌂
The pub is one of the oldest in Norfolk, with parts of the building dating back to the 1600s, and is included in CAMRA's Real Heritage Pubs for the gem of a snug bar. The saloon bar is beamed, comfortable and has a real fire in winter in the inglenook fireplace. It also boasts a suit of armour. There is a separate dining room and an outside smoking shelter. Q✿✿◑P📅📶

Heydon

Earle Arms ✅
The Street, NR11 6AD
✪ 12-3, 6 (5 Fri)-11; 12-11 Sun; closed Mon ☎ (01263) 587376 ⊕ theearlearms.com
Adnams Southwold Bitter; 2 changing beers ⌂
This 16th-century former coaching inn – incorporating a bar, busy restaurant, traditional snug, sun-swathed conservatory, and a candle-lit, cushion-filled gazebo – is within a privately owned village (and popular film location). In the equine-themed main bar, also adorned with candles and featuring a log fire in winter, up to four real ciders and three real ales can be enjoyed. There is an extensive food menu, well reviewed by locals and visitors alike. Various community events are hosted on the green opposite. Q✿◑♣♠P✿📶

Hilborough

Swan ⌶
Brandon Road, IP26 5BW
✪ 11-11; 12-10.30 Sun ☎ (01760) 657380 ⊕ hilboroughswan.co.uk
5 changing beers ⌂
If you are visiting ancient Breckland or are en route to the coast, the Swan is ideally placed on the A1065 in the middle of the village. Inside the 17th-century building you will find a changing range of beers on five handpumps, often from local breweries such as Elmtree and Humpty Dumpty, as well as bottled beers. While very much a village pub, it has an interesting food menu including gluten-free meals. There is a popular carvery on Sundays. Quizzes and darts matches feature regularly. Outside is a large garden. Q✿≉◑♣P

Hockwold

Red Lion
114 Main Street, IP26 4NB
✪ 11.30-3, 6 (5 Fri)-11.30; 11.30-11.30 Sat; 12-10.30 Sun ☎ (01842) 829728

3 changing beers Ⓗ
Traditional, friendly village pub set on a green. The Red Lion was refurbished and reopened as a free house in 2012. It has a smart but comfortable interior – see how many Toby jugs you can spot. A good selection of home-made food is served all week, with a carvery on Sunday. There are regular, well supported quizzes and darts matches. Outside is a spacious garden with plenty of seating and a children's play area. **❀◑♣P🐾**

Honingham

Buck 𝕃
29 The Street, NR9 5BL
11.30-11; 11.30-10 Sun ☎ (01603) 880393
thehoninghambuck.co.uk
Lacons Affinity, Encore; 2 changing beers Ⓗ
Dating back to 1789, this traditional one-bar village pub has a separate restaurant area with an emphasis on home-cooked food. It serves four real ales from Lacons – the brewery bought the pub in 2015 and carried out a tasteful makeover, keeping the slate floors and oak beams, and embellishing it with stylish furniture. A large inglenook fireplace adds to the historic venue, popular with US servicemen during WWII. **Q❀◑♿P🐾**

Horstead

Recruiting Sergeant
Norwich Road, NR12 7EE
11-11; 12-11 Sun ☎ (01603) 737077
recruitingsergeant.co.uk
Adnams Southwold Bitter; Greene King Abbot; Timothy Taylor Landlord; 3 changing beers Ⓗ
Popular pub/restaurant mostly given over to dining, but with a welcoming and accommodating bar area. A good selection of three regular and three changing real ales on handpump is mostly sourced regionally. There is a comprehensive food menu including fish and steak dishes, served in the bar area and two separate dining areas. Outside is a good-sized car park and pleasant patio garden. Accommodation is available in five double rooms above the pub. **Q❀◑♿P🐾**

King's Lynn

Live & Let Live 𝕃
18 Windsor Road, PE30 5PL (off London Rd near Catholic church)
11-10.30 (11 Fri & Sat) ☎ (01553) 764990
5 changing beers Ⓗ
A traditional local pub with a small cosy lounge bar and a larger public bar with a TV screen. A range of five beers is sold, including a mild (rare for the area) and something stronger, often featuring local brews. Real cider from Westons and Grainstore is also available. The public bar is occasionally the venue for live music. **🍎**

Stuart House Hotel
35 Goodwins Road, PE30 5QX (up gravel drive off Goodwins Rd)
6-11 ☎ (01553) 772169 stuart-house-hotel.co.uk
3 changing beers Ⓗ
A hotel bar down a gravel drive close to The Walks park and football ground. There are two or three beers from larger regional brewers on offer, and food is served in the evenings. An annual beer festival is held, usually on the last weekend in July, and a variety of other events features through the year. Although closed at lunchtimes, there is often someone around, so arrange a visit in advance, or call if in the area. **❀◑P🐾**

Larling

Angel
NR16 2QU (1 mile SW from Snetterton racetrack, just off A11)
10-midnight; 11-11 Sun ☎ (01953) 717963
angel-larling.co.uk
Adnams Southwold Bitter Ⓗ
The Angel is a must if visiting this part of Norfolk, featuring a well-known and long-established beer festival which averages 70 ales. Even on a normal day you will find five handpumps delivering a constantly changing range of beers, always including a mild, and there is also an enormous range of whiskies. The atmosphere reflects the agricultural nature of the area. The food is home made, with a traditional leaning and what can only be described as farmers' portions. The pub has its own accommodation. **Q❀◑♿▲P**

Lessingham

Star Inn 𝕃
Star Hill, NR12 0DN (just off main B1159, on corner of High Road and Star Hill)
12-3, 6-11; closed Mon ☎ (01692) 580510
thestarlessingham.co.uk
Adnams Southwold Bitter; Buffy's Norfolk Terrier; Woodforde's Once Bittern; 1 changing beer Ⓖ
Excellent local with a welcoming atmosphere, serving well-kept beers to regulars from near and far. It is near the north-east Norfolk coast, and convenient for those visiting nearby East Ruston Old Vicarage garden. The large beer garden is perfect for summer drinking. Three regular and one changing real ale are on sale, plus two or three real ciders. Bar snacks and freshly prepared high-quality lunches and dinners are available daily except Sunday evening. A beer festival is held in August. **Q❀◑▲🍎P🚌(34)🐾**

Little Walsingham

Black Lion Hotel
Friday Market Place, NR22 6DB
11-11; 11-10.30 Sun ☎ (01328) 820235
blacklionhotelnorfolk.co.uk
Adnams Ghost Ship; Woodforde's Wherry; 1 changing beer Ⓗ
Family-friendly pub with rooms, parts of which date back to the 15th century, in the centre of Walsingham, which is a major pilgrimage centre, famed for its religious shrines in honour of the Virgin Mary. The bar is relaxed with a slightly rustic feel, including oak beams, farm implements and old tractor seat stools. The food is all locally sourced, and prepared on site (except the pies). **Q❀◑🚌🐾**

Ludham

Dog Inn 𝕃
Johnsons Street, NR29 5NY (on B1062, 300yds from Ludham Bridge towards Ludham)
12-11; 12-10.30 Sun ☎ (01692) 630321
thedoginnludham.co.uk
2 changing beers Ⓗ

The Dog is a comfortable free house, close to the River Ant, and with its own camping and caravan site. The large pub has been significantly refurbished in the last year, and is both child- and dog-friendly. Food is served lunch and evening, and bar snacks in the afternoon, and the ales are usually from local breweries. Live music features occasionally, especially in summer.
🕮◑♿AP🖵(54)🐾

Martham

King's Arms
15 The Green, NR29 4PL
🌣 12-11 (midnight Fri & Sat); 12-10.30 Sun
☎ (01493) 749156
5 changing beers Ⓗ
Previously owned by Adnams (and well before that by the original incarnation of Lacons), the King's Arms, situated in the centre of the village by the pond, has recently become a free house, serving four or five ales from local and less-local breweries. There is a nice garden at the back and a large car park. A sloe gin competition is held annually.
🕭🕮🚐◑♣♿P🖵🐾📶

Neatishead

White Horse Ⓛ
The Street, NR12 8AD (S of A1151 Wroxham to Stalham road)
🌣 11-11; 11-10.30 Sun ☎ (01692) 630828
🌐 thewhitehorseinnneatishead.com
7 changing beers Ⓗ
A traditional Broadland village pub, tastefully modernised, yet retaining many original features in three drinking areas, and with log fires in winter. The enthusiastic landlord keeps seven frequently changing, mainly microbrewery ales from across the UK including his own, brewed on the premises. Staff are knowledgeable about beer choices. Excellent, reasonably priced food is home prepared using local produce. The restaurant area is split level and cosy. Beer festivals take place in the spring and autumn. It is a short walk from the moorings to this beer lovers' haven.
Q🕮◑♿&A♣P🐾📶

North Creake

Jolly Farmers
1 Burnham Road, NR21 9JW
🌣 12-2.30, 7-11; 12.30-2.30, 7-11 Sat; 12-7 Sun; closed Mon & Tue ☎ (01328) 738185 🌐 jollyfarmersnorfolk.co.uk
Woodforde's Nelson's Revenge, Wherry; 1 changing beer Ⓖ
Comfortable chairs and pine tables, open fires and excellent food from the finest ingredients combine to create a great atmosphere in this unchanging pub. Local artwork hangs on the walls. You are as likely to meet locals as tourists straying from the nearby north Norfolk coast. Dogs and walkers are welcome. The friendly landlords make this a lovely pub – but note that it is closed on Mondays, Tuesdays and Sunday evenings. Q🕭◑♣P🐾

North Elmham

Railway Ⓛ
40 Station Road, NR20 5HH
🌣 11.30-midnight ☎ (01362) 668300
🌐 therailwayfreehouse.co.uk

3 changing beers Ⓗ
Truly a community pub, the Railway regularly hosts meetings for car and bike enthusiasts and the Young Farmers, and sponsors the local cricket club. Its function building, Tracks, is a popular venue for music events, including the Norfolk Blues Society. A rotating choice of ales is available, with the range favouring local brewers, but not exclusively so. Home-cooked meals are on offer, as well as B&B and a campsite at the rear. Restored steam trains run occasionally on the nearby Mid-Norfolk Railway. 🕭🕮◑A♣♿P🖵🐾📶

Norwich

Alexandra Tavern
16 Stafford Street, NR2 3BB (on corner of Stafford St and Gladstone St, off Dereham Rd)
🌣 12-11 (midnight Thu); 10.30-midnight Fri & Sat
☎ (01603) 627772 🌐 alexandratavern.co.uk
Chalk Hill CHB, Gold, Tap Bitter; 2 changing beers Ⓗ
Popular, bustling and friendly, this pub is a little gem found just outside the city centre. The interior is brightly decorated, with the walls featuring pictures and articles about the landlord's charity achievements. The bar normally serves three Chalk Hill Brewery beers as well as guest ales, along with a good variety of food including a soup menu. There is a pool table, dartboard and loads of board games to choose from. Children welcome until 7pm. 🕮◑♣🚼🖵

Angel Gardens Ⓛ
96 Angel Road, NR3 3HT
🌣 11-midnight (1am Sat); 12-11 Sun ☎ (01603) 427490
Elgood's Black Dog; Fuller's London Pride; Oakham JHB; Sharp's Doom Bar; 5 changing beers Ⓗ
Friendly locals' pub with a good selection of four permanent and five changing local and national real ales. Up to six real ciders on gravity are served, depending on the season. The pub offers live entertainment on Saturday evenings, runs darts and crib teams, and has a pool table. There is a covered, heated drinking area at the front and a garden with play equipment at the rear. A small function room is available, with a bar.
🕮◑♿P🖵🐾📶

Beehive Ⓛ
30 Leopold Road, NR4 7PJ
🌣 12-11 (midnight Fri & Sat) ☎ (01603) 451628
🌐 beehivepubnorwich.co.uk
Green Jack Rising Sun; Oakham Bishops Farewell; 4 changing beers Ⓗ
A traditional local with knowledgeable staff, offering two bar areas and a comfortable lounge bar with sofas. There is a function room upstairs with a pool table, and the pub hosts hockey, korfball, golf, darts and pool teams, a regular quiz, folk music nights and wine tasting evenings. A popular beer garden is used all year round and is ideal when summer barbecues are hosted. A beer festival with around 25 ales and ciders is held in June, and the pub was Norfolk CAMRA Pub of the Year in 2015. Q🕮◑♣♿P🖵(25)🐾📶

Coach & Horses
82 Thorpe Road, NR1 1BA
🌣 11-11 (1am Fri & Sat) ☎ (01603) 477077
🌐 thecoachthorperoad.co.uk
Chalk Hill CHB, Gold, Tap Bitter; 3 changing beers Ⓗ
Close to the station, this coaching inn, with its iconic balcony, is the home of the Chalk Hill

Brewery, and serves its full range of beers. A tour of the brewery is available by appointment. Excellent-value food is served along with Burnard's cider. Sport, especially rugby, is shown on big screens, and the large fire is welcome in winter. Not far from the football ground, it gets busy before matches. ✿⏰🕭&♿🍴P🚃🐾🌳📶

Coach & Horses

51 Bethel Street, NR2 1NR
✪ 11.30-11.30 (midnight Fri & Sat); closed Sun
☎ (01603) 618522 ⊕ coachbethelst.co.uk
5 changing beers Ⓗ
Historic city-centre local near the Theatre Royal, the Forum and City Hall. It is a bright, welcoming bar with several separate seating areas, including cosy alcove-style seating, and stocks a great range of local ales including Norfolk Brewhouse, Humpty Dumpty, Golden Triangle and Jo C's. The wholesome food menu is driven by the best of local produce. Ideal for a beer before or after the theatre, or any time of day – try some celeb spotting too! Q🚃✿⏰🕭♣♿🍴🐾🌳📶

Coachmakers Arms

9 St Stephens Road, NR1 3SP
✪ 11-11; 12-10.30 Sun ☎ (01603) 662080
⊕ coachmakers-arms-norwich.co.uk
Greene King Abbot Ⓗ; **Wolf Golden Jackal** Ⓖ; **2 changing beers** Ⓗ
Dating from the 17th century, this allegedly haunted former coaching inn stands on the site of an old asylum. A spacious courtyard converted into a drinking area complements the garden patio. Inside, there is one large L-shaped beamed bar. A function room is also available. Unobtrusive Sky TV combines well with a dartboard and it all adds up to a popular city-centre free house. ✿⏰🕭&♣🌳📶

Duke of Wellington Ⓛ

91-93 Waterloo Road, NR3 1EG
✪ 12-11 (midnight Fri & Sat); 12-10.30 Sun
☎ (01603) 441182 ⊕ dukeofwellingtonnorwich.co.uk
Fuller's London Pride Ⓗ; **Oakham JHB, Bishops Farewell; Wolf Wolf in Sheep's Clothing** Ⓖ, **Golden Jackal** Ⓗ; **15 changing beers** Ⓖ
Over the past year the taproom has been expanded to accommodate even more quality ales, which are obtained from all around the country. A beer festival is held in late August in the attractive enclosed rear garden/patio area, which is also used for barbecues at the weekends in the summer. Customers can bring their own food, and plates and cutlery will be provided, or they may sample the filling and inexpensive pies and sausage rolls. ✿&♣♿P🚃(9A,16)🐾📶

Earlham Arms Ⓛ

41 Earlham Road, NR2 3AD
✪ 11-11 (11.30 Thu); 11.30-midnight Fri & Sat); 9am-10.30 Sun
☎ (01603) 622993 ⊕ theearlhamarms.co.uk
Jo C's Bitter Old Bustard, Knot Just Another IPA, Norfolk Kiwi; 11 changing beers Ⓗ
A lively pub with great food – one of Norwich's best gastro-pubs. Great beers from Jo C's brewery are always available, plus up to 11 guest real ales, either on handpump or gravity from the cellar. The large bar with its dining area works well and diners and drinkers merge seamlessly. Excellent and good-value bar snacks and tapas are served, and in the summer you can make best use of the weather in the large enclosed garden.
Q🚃✿⏰🕭&♣P🚃🐾📶

Eaton Cottage Ⓛ

75 Mount Pleasant, NR2 2DQ
✪ 12-11 (midnight Fri & Sat) ☎ (01603) 453048
Fuller's London Pride; Wolf Golden Jackal; 5 changing beers Ⓗ
A large and friendly local close to the shops in the Golden Triangle, with a number of seating areas inside and out, serving an interesting variety of ales from local breweries such as Elmtree and Wolf, plus beers from other UK breweries large and small. Sport is shown on TV but the screens do not dominate (except in one small area). There is a pleasant pergola-covered patio to one side of the pub. ✿&♣🆓🚃(25)📶

Fat Cat Ⓛ

49 West End Street, NR2 4NA
✪ 11-11 (midnight Fri & Sat); 10.30-11 Sun
☎ (01603) 624364 ⊕ fatcatpub.co.uk
Adnams Southwold Bitter; Crouch Vale Yakima Gold Ⓗ; **Fuller's ESB; Hop Back Summer Lightning** Ⓖ; **Oakham Inferno; Timothy Taylor Landlord** Ⓗ; **20 changing beers** Ⓖ
An outstanding example of what a real ale pub should be, with excellent service, ales from the Fat Cat range, plus about 10 regular and 20 guest beers from all over the UK, and real ciders. The Cat has been voted CAMRA National Pub of the Year twice. Landlord Colin has an amazing range of brewery memorabilia, which is displayed around the walls and alcoves of this traditional-style pub. Food is limited to excellent-value rolls and pies. A beer lover's paradise which no visitor to Norwich should miss. Q✿🕭♣🐾🌳📶

Fat Cat & Canary Ⓛ

101 Thorpe Road, NR1 1TR
✪ 12-11 (midnight Fri); 11-midnight Sat ☎ (01603) 432393
⊕ fatcatcanary.co.uk
Fat Cat Bitter, Hell Cat, Honey Cat, Marmalade Cat, Wild Cat; 7 changing beers Ⓗ
The third member of the Norwich-based Fat Cat mini-chain, about a mile and a half from the centre of the city, serves most of the Fat Cat Brewery's ales, and various guests from around the UK, together with continental beers and real ciders. There is a small TV to the rear of the main bar, a large car park and terraces to the front and rear, the latter being heated. Home-made rolls are available. 🚃✿&♣P🚃(54B,123,124)📶

Fat Cat Tap 🍴 Ⓛ

98-100 Lawson Road, NR3 4LF
✪ 12-11 (midnight Fri); 11-midnight Sat; 11-10.30 Sun
☎ (01603) 413153 ⊕ fatcattap.co.uk
Fat Cat Bitter, Honey Cat Ⓗ, **Marmalade Cat, Wild Cat; Oakham Bishops Farewell, Citra; 14 changing beers** Ⓖ
Home of the Fat Cat Brewery, with a wide-ranging choice of quality ales from near and far. The walls and ceilings are adorned with extensive breweriana; closing time is indicated by a set of traffic lights. Live music features three days a week (Fridays and Sundays, plus jazz on Mondays), and complements the variety of events held at the pub including Brewery Takeovers, Monthly Cycling Club, a fortnightly quiz and a Ladies' Beer Club, to name but a few. No food but cheeseboards can be provided (24-hours' notice).
Q✿&♣♿P🚃(11,11A)🐾📶

Jubilee Ⓛ ✅

26 St Leonards Road, NR1 4BL
✪ 12-11 (midnight Fri & Sat) ☎ (01603) 618734

Greene King IPA; Woodforde's Wherry, Sundew, Nelson's Revenge; 2 changing beers H

An attractive Victorian corner pub with a warm welcome. There is a choice of two bars, plus a comfortable conservatory and an enclosed patio garden. Many of the well-kept ales are local. This popular venue at the heart of the community caters for all tastes, from sports fans to those who enjoy local history talks, and has a village feel while within easy reach of the city centre. Occasional pop-up street food fairs are held.

King's Arms

22 Hall Road, NR1 3HQ

🕓 11-11 (11.30 Fri & Sat); 12-10.30 Sun ☎ (01603) 477888
🌐 kingsarmsnorwich.co.uk

Batemans XB, Gold; 9 changing beers H

A friendly, and recently gently refurbished, Batemans house to the south of the city. It serves an extensive and varied range of guest ales to complement the Batemans beers, usually including a stout or porter, with a mild always available. Between three (in winter) and six (in summer) real ciders are available. Customers can bring their own food from various nearby takeaways (plates and condiments provided). Monthly quiz nights, poker evenings and live music take place here. Busy on football match days. Q🏵️🅾️🍴🍺🍽️🐾🛜

King's Head L

42 Magdalen Street, NR3 1JE

🕓 12-11 (midnight Fri & Sat); 12-10.30 Sun ☎ (01603) 620468
🌐 kingsheadnorwich.co.uk

Woodforde's Nelson's Revenge; 10 changing beers H

Award-winning two-bar pub which offers up to a dozen quality real ales and one cider, but no keg beers at all. The beers are mainly from Norfolk-area microbreweries, but some from favoured breweries around the country may put in an appearance. The house beer, KHB, is brewed by Winter's, and there is a good range of single malt whiskies. Local produce such as fresh eggs and honey is often available. There is no food except pork pies, but the Indian restaurant across the road will deliver to the pub. Q♣️🍴🍺🐾🛜

Leopard L

98-100 Bull Close Road, NR3 1NQ

🕓 12-11 (midnight Fri & Sat); 12-10.30 Sun
☎ (01603) 63111 🌐 theleopardnorwich.co.uk

Lacons Legacy; 4 changing beers H

A classic local, set on a corner, with a variety of changing ales from smaller breweries. The house beer, Leopard Ale, is brewed by Tombstone. The single-bar pub has been completely renovated and renewed since it was sold by Batemans, and has a clean and bright bar area which gives a spacious feel. There is a small patio/garden at the rear of the building which is pleasant and quiet. Q🏵️🅰️♣️🍴🛜

Murderers L

2-8 Timber Hill, NR1 3LB

🕓 10-11.30; 12-10.30 Sun ☎ (01603) 621447
🌐 themurderers.co.uk

Sharp's Doom Bar; Woodforde's Wherry; 8 changing beers H

City-centre free house packed with character, beams and wood panelling. On several levels, with lots of little alcoves, the pub has been family owned for 30 years. Up to 10 real ales are on tap from local micros and from around the country,

including the house ale brewed by Coors. The pub is popular with shoppers, office workers and the evening going-out scene alike. Its real name is the Gardener's Arms, but nobody knows it as that since a 19th-century landlord convicted of murdering his wife gave the pub its alternative name. The case history adorns the walls inside. 🏵️🅾️🍺🐾🛜

Plasterers Arms L

43 Cowgate, NR3 1SZ

🕓 12-midnight (1am Fri & Sat) ☎ (01603) 387525
🌐 theplasterersarms.co.uk

Oakham JHB; 10 changing beers H

This is a friendly corner local with a wide range of local and national microbreweries beers from around the country, with at least one mild and a stout/porter. Golden Triangle and Oakham beers make a regular appearance. Food is provided by Voodoo Daddy pizzas, cooked to order. Occasional themed beer tasting events are held. Live music from local bands takes place on most Tuesdays and Sundays. Q🅰️♣️🍴🛜

Playhouse Bar

42-58 St George Street, NR3 1AB

🕓 10-midnight; 12-midnight Sun ☎ (01603) 612580

4 changing beers H

A bar serving the Norwich Playhouse theatre (so it can be crowded before performances and at the interval), with a large tree-shaded patio by the river. It serves three or four ales including a couple of locals and an eclectic selection of guests. The bar features a 3D cityscape on the ceiling and has comfortable seating. There is also a good-sized lounge across the foyer. Q🏵️🅰️

Plough

58 St Benedict Street, NR2 4AR

🕓 12-11 (midnight Fri & Sat) ☎ (01603) 661384

5 changing beers H

Popular pub in one of the city's oldest areas near the Norwich Arts Centre. One of three Grain Brewery taps, the five ales available are usually all from the brewery. The two-bar interior is fairly small, with wooden chairs and tables, and a roaring log fire in winter. The large Mediterranean-style courtyard garden is a fine place to while away a summer's evening. A Grain-produced lager is also available, along with Vic's special sausage pie, and barbecues in the summer. Q🏵️♣️🍴🛜

Reindeer L

10 Dereham Road, NR2 4AY

🕓 12-11 (midnight Fri & Sat); 12-10 Sun; closed Mon
☎ (01603) 612995 🌐 thereindeerpub.co.uk

Elgood's Cambridge Bitter, Black Dog; 8 changing beers H

A warm pub which manages to feel both modern and traditional at the same time. A large main room connects to a private dining room and an expansive outdoor area. A good number of handpump ales, as well as bottled ales, cider and wines are sold, along with good food, varying by weekday, and excellent Sunday roasts. The chef is keen on using offal and unusual cuts of meat as well as more recognisable dishes. Snacks include home-made pork scratchings. Q🏵️🅾️🍴🐾🛜

Ribs of Beef L ✅

24 Wensum Street, NR3 1HY

🕓 11-11.30 (midnight Fri & Sat); 11-10.30 Sun
☎ (01603) 619517 🌐 ribsofbeef.co.uk

Oakham JHB; 9 changing beers (sourced locally) H

Traditional and well decorated pub overlooking the River Wensum. A welcoming row of nine handpumps dispenses a large selection of local ales, with foreign beers and real cider also available. The pub is popular with visitors and the kitchen offers a great selection of meals made with locally sourced ingredients. The atmosphere is relaxed and friendly, with a room downstairs as well as a big screen that regularly shows major sporting events. Just the place to watch the boats go by. ✿◐♣♠🖵🕾

Rosebery L
94 Rosebery Road, NR3 3AB
🕒 12-midnight (11 Mon); 12-11 Sun ☎ (01603) 414284
⊕ theroseberynorwich.co.uk
6 changing beers Ⓗ
Large corner pub with high ceilings, refurbished in 2015 by Redwell Brewery, with six cask ales on handpump, usually including at least one from Bullards and one from Golden Triangle breweries. The other four are a constantly changing range of local and national ales. There are also four real ciders, with two each on handpump and on gravity. Live music plays on a Sunday evening, food is served Thursday to Sunday, and there are four B&B rooms. ✿🕾🛏◐♿♣♠P🖵🖵(10)🕾🕸

Take 5 L
17 Tombland, NR3 1HF
🕒 11-11 (midnight Fri); closed Sun ☎ (01603) 763099
4 changing beers Ⓗ
Four real ales from Norfolk and Suffolk breweries are always available in this Grade II-listed building, which dates in parts from the 15th century. Situated opposite the 11th-century cathedral in the oldest part of the city, there is a continental feel to the busy bar. Quality home-cooked food is available lunchtimes and evenings, all day Saturday, all sourced locally. A large function room is upstairs, plus a cellar bar downstairs with vaulted ceilings (available to hire). ◐♿♣♠🕸

Trafford Arms L ✿
61 Grove Road, NR1 3RL
🕒 11-11 ☎ (01603) 628466 ⊕ traffordarms.co.uk
Adnams Southwold Bitter, Ghost Ship; Winter's Mild; Woodforde's Wherry; 6 changing beers Ⓗ
This pub stands at the junction of Trafford Road and Grove Road, near the city centre, and continues to be a flagship for real ale in Norwich. The cask beer offering includes both regular and guest beers. High-standard pub food is available and there are special themed food evenings. The Valentine's beer festival continues to be a major attraction, as are the regular pub quizzes. On the pub games front, pool has been replaced by bar billiards. Q✿◐♣🖵(9,17)🕸

Vine L
7 Dove Street, NR2 1DE
🕒 11-11; closed Sun ☎ (01603) 627362 ⊕ vinethai.co.uk
4 changing beers Ⓗ
Just off the marketplace, serving up to four quality ales plus traditional Thai cuisine in an award-winning combination, this is Norwich's smallest pub. Beer festivals held in January and City of Ale week are highlights. The restaurant is upstairs, although customers often eat downstairs in the bar area; functions are catered for outside normal opening hours on demand. Extra tables and chairs are set outside in the pedestrianised street. Q✿◐♣

White Lion
73 Oak Street, NR3 3AQ
🕒 12-11 (11.30 Fri & Sat); 12-10.30 Sun ☎ (01603) 632333
⊕ individualpubs.co.uk/whitelion
Milton Cyclops, Justinian, Marcus Aurelius, Medusa, Nero, Pegasus; 3 changing beers Ⓗ
Award-winning friendly pub, a short walk from the city centre, serving a range of beers from the Milton Brewery and two or three guests from non-local microbreweries. A former CAMRA East Anglian Cider Pub of the Year, it offers over 20 varieties of cider and perry from near and far. Food is varied and of excellent value – check the daily specials menu. An annual beer festival is held in the autumn, and bar billiards and darts are played. Q✿◐♣♠🖵🕸🕾

Wig & Pen L
6 St Martin at Palace Plain, NR3 1RN
🕒 11.30-11 (midnight Fri & Sat); 11.30-6.30 Sun
☎ (01603) 625891 ⊕ thewigandpen.com
Adnams Southwold Bitter; Humpty Dumpty Little Sharpie; Woodforde's Bure Gold; 3 changing beers Ⓗ
Pretty beamed 17th-century free house with a spacious patio immediately opposite the Bishop's Palace, and with an impressive view of Norwich Cathedral spire. Three permanent ales and three guests are always on tap, usually including two local beers. The small back room can be used for meetings. Good-quality food is served lunchtimes and evenings. The pub is a short walk from Tombland, where there are bus stands for several bus routes, and is an ideal starting or stopping place for a walk along the river. Q✿🕾◐♿🖵🕾

Old Buckenham

Ox & Plough
The Green, NR17 1RN (in centre of village overlooking green)
🕒 11-midnight; 12-midnight Sun ☎ 07887 691722
Adnams Southwold Bitter; Sharp's Doom Bar; 3 changing beers (often Oakham) Ⓗ
Family-friendly pub on one of the largest village greens in England, and a community hostelry at the centre of village life. It has two open-plan drinking areas, one being quiet, without TV or electronic game machines. The garden at the front overlooks the green. Real ale is dispensed from three to five handpumps. The pub is a member of Oakham Academy and serves various changing Oakham ales. Bar snacks are available. 🐕✿♿♣P🕸🕾

Old Hunstanton

Ancient Mariner ✿
6 Golf Course Road, PE36 6JJ (within Le Strange Arms Hotel complex)
🕒 11-11 ☎ (01485) 534411
Adnams Southwold Bitter, Broadside; 3 changing beers Ⓗ
Adjoining the Le Strange Arms Hotel, this popular pub consists of old barns and stables and includes a family room and restaurants. At least four real ales are available and live music nights are held occasionally. A large beer garden offers direct access to the beach and as Old Hunstanton is on the east coast facing west, there are superb views of spectacular sunsets over the sea from the decking at the rear. Q🐕✿🕾◐♿P🖵🖵🕸🕾

Poringland

Royal Oak 📖 ✅
44 The Street, NR14 7JT
🌓 11-11 (midnight Fri & Sat); 12-11 Sun ☎ (01508) 493734
🌐 poringlandroyaloak.com
Sharp's Doom Bar; Woodforde's Bure Gold, Wherry; 12 changing beers Ⓗ
A comfortable country pub with welcoming bar staff. The interior is divided into several small seating areas, one of which features memorabilia of the former RAF radar station which was nearby. A good selection of local real ales is stocked, supplemented by others from around the country, plus real ciders from Westons. There is a themed Tea Room from 10-4pm, and at other times customers are welcome to bring in fish and chips from the shop next door. No dogs allowed, even in the garden. Q🕸♣🖤P🖵(87,88)🛜

Reepham

King's Arms 📖
Market Place, NR10 4JJ
🌓 11.30-3, 5.30-11; 11.30-11 Sat; 12-10.30 Sun
☎ (01603) 870345 🌐 kingsarmsreepham.com
Adnams Southwold Bitter, Ghost Ship; Greene King Abbot; Panther Golden Panther; Woodforde's Wherry; 1 changing beer Ⓗ
A former coaching inn dating back to 1667, in the picturesque square of this small market town, with original beams, Norfolk brickwork and open fires. There are several drinking and dining areas and five permanent ales on sale, including at least one from the local Panther Brewery. The comprehensive menu is mostly from nearby suppliers. Jazz bands play in the rear courtyard on summer Sundays, and a bar billiards table is available. Q🕸🤝🕸🖤🖵(42,43,44)🕸

Roydon

Union Jack
30 Station Road, PE32 1AW (off A148)
🌓 4 (2 Mon; 1.30 Fri)-midnight; 12-midnight Sat & Sun ☎ 07771 660439
4 changing beers Ⓗ
Popular with locals, this traditional village inn has twice been local CAMRA Pub of the Year. Four handpumps dispense a variety of ales, and beer festivals held over the Easter and August bank holidays usually feature local breweries. There are occasional food nights, live music each month, regular bingo and quizzes, and weekly support for darts, crib and dominoes. 🕸🤝♣P🖵(48)🕸

Shouldham

King's Arms 🏆
The Green, PE33 0BY
🌓 4.30-10.30 Mon; 12-3, 4.30-11; 12-11.30 Fri; 11.30-11.30 Sat; 12-10.30 Sun ☎ (01366) 347410
🌐 kingsarmsshouldham.co.uk
2 changing beers Ⓖ
Local CAMRA Pub of the Year 2016, this community-owned pub serves two or three beers straight from the cask. There is a volunteer-operated café open from 9.30am each day and, as might be expected, it is the focus of the village, with events ranging from quizzes to Poetry and a Pint nights. Locally brewed beer is usually on tap and cider is often on sale. 🤝🕸🕸🖤P🕸🛜

Snettisham

Rose & Crown
Old Church Road, PE31 7LX (off B1440)
🌓 11-11; 11-10.30 Sun ☎ (01485) 541382
🌐 roseandcrownsnettisham.co.uk
Adnams Broadside; Banks's Bitter; Marston's Pedigree; Woodforde's Wherry; 2 changing beers Ⓗ
A popular traditional village inn with cosy bars, exposed beams, a real fire and a dining room. Head through the narrow passage to find a larger bar and dining areas with a contemporary feel. It is well known for quality traditional and exciting local seasonal fare; the bars also remain popular with local drinkers. The garden and play area make it appealing to families. Accommodation is available for those who wish to remain longer in this beautiful area. Q🤝🕸🕸🤝🕸&♣P🖵(10,11,35)🕸🛜

South Walsham

Ship
18 The Street, NR13 6DQ (in centre of village between post office and church)
🌓 12-3, 5-10; 12-11 Sat; 12-10 Sun; closed Mon
☎ (01603) 270049 🌐 theshipsouthwalsham.co.uk
Woodforde's Wherry; 2 changing beers Ⓗ
The Ship is an ancient listed building, first licensed in 1789, with two rooms, one the bar, the other for dining. There are two regular real ales in good condition, and a pump for one guest, with another on gravity, all usually local. It is owned by a small chain which has established a strong reputation for good food using local ingredients (booking is advisable). A pleasant 20-minute walk from South Walsham Broad. Closed all afternoons in winter. Q🕸🕸P🕸🛜

Southrepps

Vernon Arms ✅
2 Church Street, NR11 8NP (NE of Thorpe Market off A149 Cromer-North Walsham road)
🌓 11-11.30, 12-10.30 Sun ☎ (01263) 833355
🌐 vernonarms.com
Adnams Southwold Bitter; Greene King Abbot; Woodforde's Wherry; 1 changing beer Ⓗ
A popular and welcoming village local, with a traditional brick and flint exterior, at the heart of a vibrant community. Regular ales are augmented by a variety of guest beers, and discerning diners book early for fine food (prepared with locally sourced ingredients where possible), candlelit tables and excellent service. Takeaway fish and chips are available Tuesday to Saturday 6-8pm. There is a log fire in winter, and a heated and covered smoking area. The July beer festival (request your favourite beer in June) features music. 🤝🕸🕸&🜚♣P🖵(33,33A)🕸🛜

Sporle

Peddars Inn 📖
70 The Street, PE32 2DR
🌓 11-3 (not Tue), 6-10.30; 11-3, 6-11 Fri; 2-11 Sat; 12-6 Sun; closed Mon ☎ (01760) 788101 🌐 thepeddarsinn.com
Adnams Southwold Bitter; 2 changing beers Ⓗ
A traditional dog-friendly village local with lots of events such as music and quiz nights. It is close to the Peddars Way long-distance path and so attracts walkers. Food is served in the bar, conservatory and private dining room, but note that the pub is

closed on Monday and food is not available Tuesday. The pub is a member of the LocAle scheme and there is always something interesting on the bar. There is a log fire for winter, and free Wi-Fi. ⌂⊛◑P🐾🛜

Surlingham

Ferry House 🅛 ✅

Ferry Road, NR14 7AR (follow signs to Surlingham Ferry; from Bramerton Rd continue on to Pratts Hill, keeping left at the fork; Pratts Hill turns slightly left and becomes Ferry Rd) TG314067

🕒 11-11 ☎ (01508) 538659 ⊕ surlinghamferry.co.uk

Adnams Broadside; Humpty Dumpty Little Sharpie; Woodforde's Wherry; 1 changing beer Ⓗ

Situated on the banks of the River Yare, this rambling old country inn is popular with boaters and ramblers. The pub provides free mooring for boaters and electrical hook-ups and water are available. The spacious interior has a large brick fireplace in the centre of the room. Three cask ales are always available, plus a guest in summer and at weekends. High-quality home-cooked food is served all day. Live music features occasionally on the first Sunday of the month and a quiz night every Friday. Q⌂⊛◑♿♣P🐾🛜

Swanton Morley

Angel Inn

66 Greengate, NR20 4LX

🕒 12-11; 12-10 Sun ☎ (01362) 637407

⊕ theangelpub.co.uk

Hop Back Summer Lightning; Woodforde's Wherry; 1 changing beer Ⓗ

This charming 400-year-old pub sits in the heart of the village. There is a spacious main bar with a real fire, hop-draped ceilings, and a dining room. At the end of the bar is a darts and pool room, and outside a garden with plenty of seating. A popular beer festival is run each Easter, and there is occasional live music. Food is served lunchtimes and early evenings. The pub closes at 6pm on Sundays during the winter. ⌂⊛◑♣P🚪🐾🛜

Thetford

Black Horse

64 Magdalen Street, IP24 2BP

🕒 11-11; 12-11 Sun ☎ (01842) 762717

Adnams Southwold Bitter; Greene King IPA; Woodforde's Wherry; 2 changing beers Ⓗ

Now in its second year in the Guide under new management, the Horse maintains its high standards, with five handpumps in use and an atmosphere that continues to be friendly in the bar and the darts zone. The food is home made and excellent both in quality and value – the desserts are very inventive – served in a small but pleasant dining area. One feature of the Black Horse you should see is the end wall with its murals. ⊛◑♿

Red Lion 🅛 ✅

Market Place, IP24 2AL

🕒 8am-11 (1am Fri & Sat) ☎ (01842) 757210

Adnams Broadside; Greene King IPA, Abbot; 3 changing beers Ⓗ

The Red Lion has a varied history – it was at one time a Portuguese restaurant before becoming a Wetherspoon pub four years ago. The beer range is the usual fare, but the new cellar manager is keen

to introduce some Norfolk-based mini beer festivals, featuring one brewery at a time. The Lion has a variety of eating and drinking areas plus an outside terrace. The wall outside still retains its Lacons plaque from years gone by. ⌂⊛◑🚆🛜

Thompson

Chequers Inn

Griston Road, IP24 1PX

🕒 12-3, 6.30-11; 11.30-11 Sun ☎ (01953) 483360

⊕ thompsonchequers.co.uk

Greene King IPA, IPA Gold; Woodforde's Wherry Ⓗ

A beautiful 16th-century building featuring a steeply thatched roof and timber-framed interior. As you enter the bar watch out for the beam set at Tudor height level. The Chequers is divided into a small bar area and two different dining areas in which to enjoy the excellent locally sourced food, planned and prepared by the landlord/chef. In the summer a pint outside is the way to go if you are not eating, as the exterior of the building is worth a second look. Guest beers are usually from Wolf. Accommodation is available. ⌂⊛🛏◑♿P

Thornham

Lifeboat Inn

Ship Lane, PE36 6LT (signed from A149 coast road)

🕒 11-11; 12-10.30 Sun ☎ (01485) 512236

⊕ lifeboatinnthornham.com

Adnams Southwold Bitter; Greene King IPA, Abbot; Woodforde's Wherry; 2 changing beers Ⓗ

Busy pub just off the North Norfolk Coastal Path on the edge of the salt marshes, with a wide range of drinking areas, from the dark and cosy bar to the light and airy conservatory. There is an enclosed garden area at the rear. The pub has been tastefully renovated while retaining the atmosphere of the smugglers' inn it undoubtedly was. Food is served in all areas and there is a separate large restaurant. Accommodation is available in 12 rooms. Whatever the season and whatever the weather, this is a comforting place to enjoy a pint. Q⌂⊛🛏◑⛺🐶P🐾🛜

Thorpe Market

Gunton Arms 🅛 ✅

Cromer Road, NR11 8TZ (on W of A149 Cromer to North Walsham road, SE of Thorpe Market; look for hanging sign, lit at night)

🕒 12-11; 12-10.30 Sun ☎ (01263) 832010

⊕ theguntonarms.co.uk

Adnams Southwold Bitter, Broadside; Woodforde's Wherry; 1 changing beer Ⓗ

Popular, national award-winning inn in the beautiful grounds of Gunton Park, with its deer herd. The decor is tasteful, with comfortable furnishings and a log fire in the winter. East Anglian ales predominate, with regular guests. It serves first class cuisine and has two restaurant areas; several dishes are cooked on a range in the vaulted main dining room. Twelve sumptuous bedrooms are available, some overlooking the restored parklands and deer. Interesting art and artefacts abound for the connoisseur. There is a summer beer festival. Q⌂🛏◑♿♣P🚪(4)🐾🛜

Tibenham

Greyhound

The Street, NR16 1PZ (300yds from church)
✪ 12-3, 5-midnight; 12-midnight Sat; 12-11 Sun
☎ (01379) 677676 ⊕ the-greyhound-tibenham.co.uk
Adnams Southwold Bitter, Ghost Ship; 2 changing beers (sourced nationally; often Cottage) Ⓗ
Friendly local community pub in the heart of the south Norfolk countryside, offering beers from Adnams and Fuller's plus rotating guests. The interior has many old beams and comprises a lounge, bar area and a small games room with pool table. There is a large car park, and a four-acre field at the rear which hosts many transport-themed events throughout the summer season. The field provides an ideal base for campers and caravanners, complete with electric hook-ups.
Q⏾❀◑⅃♣P❀ 🛜

Upton

White Horse Ⅼ

17 Chapel Road, NR13 6BT (about 10 mins' walk from moorings at Upton Dyke)
✪ 12-midnight ☎ (01493) 750696 ⊕ whitehorseupton.com
Woodforde's Wherry; 3 changing beers Ⓗ
Traditional broadland pub dating from 1798, a 10-minute walk from Upton Dyke Staithe and moorings, which was renovated in 2012 and is owned by the local community. A community shop has recently been added in converted stables. Four beers are served, mostly from local breweries. As well as the famous fish 'n' chips Fridays (including to take away), there are Curry Tuesdays, Steak Wednesdays and Sunday roasts. Live music takes place every first and third Saturday and on bank holidays. ⏾❀◑⅃♣P❀ 🛜

Warham All Saints

Three Horseshoes

The Street, NR23 1NL (2 miles SE of Wells)
✪ 12-2.30, 6-11; 12-3, 6-11 Sat & Sun ☎ (01328) 710547
⊕ warhamhorseshoes.co.uk
Woodforde's Wherry Ⓖ**; 2 changing beers** Ⓗ
A real pub in every sense of the word, with the perfect atmosphere for a quiet drink and conversation. The interior comprises three connected rooms which are filled with a fascinating collection of antiques and pictures, including the traditional game of Norfolk twister. In winter months customers can warm themselves by a log fire in the main bar, while the beer garden provides a quiet haven in the summer. The pub is renowned for good traditional cooking, featuring soups, pies and puddings. Q⏾❀⊨◑⅃♣♦P❀

Watton

Willow House Ⅼ ✅

2 High Street, IP25 6AE
✪ 10.30-11.30 (midnight Sat); 12-3 Sun ☎ (01953) 881181
⊕ thewillowhouse.co.uk
3 changing beers Ⓗ
The Willow House is unique in Watton as it is the only survivor of the fire of 1679, meaning it is just about the only timber-framed thatched building in this small market town. Its beer range is varying and now dispensed from four handpumps, the dining areas have just received a makeover, and the pub is dog friendly. There are annual

historically themed events and beer tasting nights from local breweries. A full menu is on offer and en-suite accommodation is available. ❀◑P❀ 🛜

Wells-next-the-Sea

Albatros

The Quay, NR23 1AT
✪ 12-11 ☎ 07979 087228 ⊕ albatroswells.co.uk
Woodforde's Wherry, Nelson's Revenge; 1 changing beer Ⓖ
Possibly one of the Guide's most unusual entries, the Albatros is a Dutch North Sea clipper, permanently moored on the quayside of Wells harbour. The bar is in the hold of the ship and is adorned with nautical memorabilia, including many shipping maps. It sells up to four Woodforde's beers on gravity. Dutch pancakes are a speciality, and live bands perform each Friday and Saturday night, as well as Sunday afternoons in high season. As a 19th-century vessel, it is not disabled-friendly. Q⊨◑♣🚌❀

West Acre

Stag Ⅼ

Low Road, PE32 1TR
✪ 12-3, 6.30 (5 Fri)-11; closed Mon ☎ (01760) 755395
⊕ westacrestag.co.uk
3 changing beers Ⓗ
This cosy pub is well worth finding at the east end of picturesque West Acre, and is popular with locals, walkers, cyclists and riders. It is a strong supporter of local ales, maintaining a high standard of three varying beers and hosting excellent beer festivals. There is a popular monthly quiz on Sunday nights. The restaurant serves a variety of great-value freshly prepared meals using locally sourced ingredients. Q❀◑⅃♣P🍴

Woodbastwick

Fur & Feather Inn

Slad Lane, NR13 6HQ
✪ 11-9.30 (9 Mon; 10 Fri); 10-11 Sat; 10-9 Sun
☎ (01603) 720003 ⊕ thefurandfeatherinn.co.uk
8 changing beers Ⓖ
Converted from a row of three cottages, this open-plan pub is largely food-oriented while offering the full range of beers from the adjoining Woodforde's Brewery. A tour of the brewery can be arranged in advance and combined with a meal. In summer the large garden provides an excellent area for a drink. The rare Norfolk Nip is occasionally available, usually as a bottle-conditioned strong ale, which is much prized locally. ⏾❀◑⅃P🛜

Wortwell

Bell ✅

52 Low Road, IP20 0HH
✪ 12 (5 Tue)-11; 12-10.30 Sun ☎ (01986) 788025
Adnams Southwold Bitter; house beer (by Woodforde's); 3 changing beers Ⓗ
A charming village inn just off the A143, where the Adnams bitter is supplemented by one or two guest beers which are often based on customer requests. There are separate dining areas where good home-cooked food is served. The pub welcomes families and dogs, with a room available for small functions. Two campsites are within easy reach. ⏾❀◑⅃♣♦P🅿(80,81)❀ 🛜

Wymondham

Feathers

13 Town Green, NR18 0PN

11-2.30, 7-11.30; 11-2.30, 6-midnight Fri; 11-2.30, 7-midnight Sat; 12-2.30, 7-10.30 Sun ☎ (01953) 605675

Adnams Southwold Bitter; Fuller's London Pride; Greene King Abbot; 2 changing beers H

The Feathers dates from the 18th century. The interior has a single bar serving two main drinking areas with alcoves. The alcoves and walls are adorned with postcard collections, enamel signs and farming and rural memorabilia, including an old bike. There is a large, well-furnished patio garden at the rear, and good-value food is served lunchtimes and evenings. A folk evening takes place on the last Sunday of each month. Feathers Tickler is the popular house beer.
Q❀◐◗⇌♣🚌(14,15)📶

Green Dragon L ✔

6 Church Street, NR18 0PH (between Market St and Wymondham Abbey)

12-11 (midnight Fri & Sat); 12-10.30 Sun

☎ (01953) 607907 🌐 greendragonnorfolk.co.uk

3 changing beers H

Haunted half-timbered inn with an interior of historic interest, formerly a medieval merchant's shop converted in the 16th century. The interior features beamed timbers, carved stone, and medieval carved figures in the mantelpiece over the fireplace. Evidence of medieval construction methods are showcased. One bar serves the downstairs, a snug and restaurant area. An upstairs bar and function room are also available. The rotating real ales are mostly from local or East Anglian breweries. Beer festivals are held twice a year. **Q**❀◐◗⇌♣🚌(14,15)🐾📶

Wig & Pen, Norwich (Photo: Warren Wordsworth)

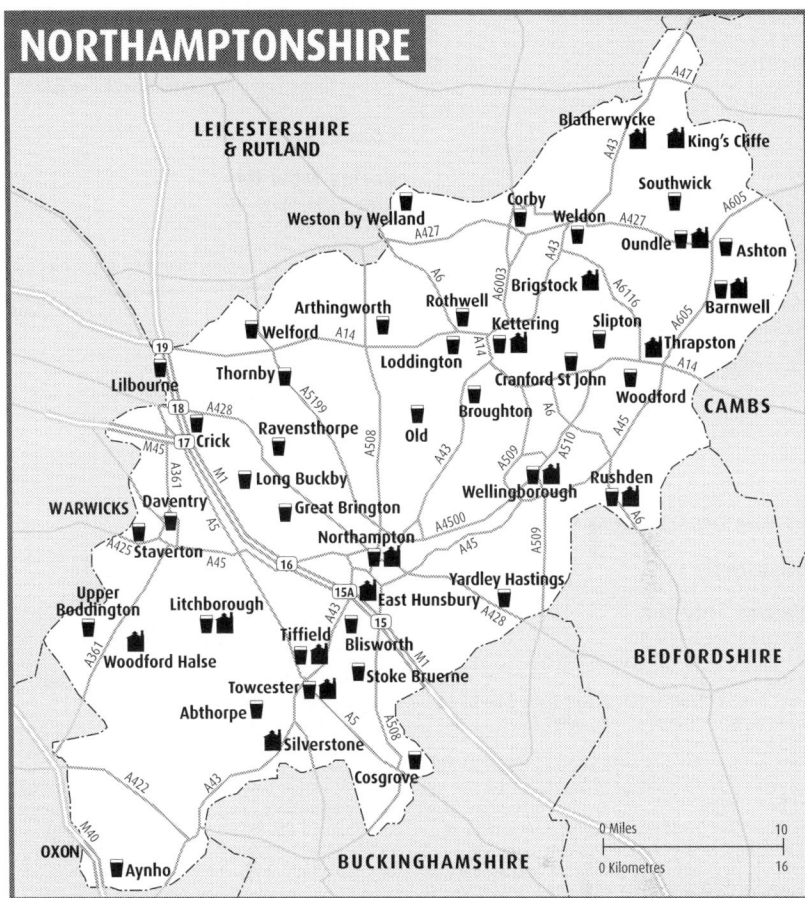

NORTHAMPTONSHIRE

LEICESTERSHIRE
& RUTLAND

Blatherwycke
King's Cliffe
Southwick
Weston by Welland
Corby
Weldon
Oundle
Ashton
Brigstock
Barnwell
Arthingworth
Rothwell
Welford
Kettering
Slipton
Thrapston
Thornby
Loddington
Lilbourne
Cranford St John
Woodford
CAMBS
Ravensthorpe
Old
Broughton
Crick
Long Buckby
Wellingborough
Rushden
WARWICKS
Daventry
Great Brington
Staverton
Northampton
Upper
Boddington
Litchborough
East Hunsbury
Yardley Hastings
BEDFORDSHIRE
Tiffield
Blisworth
Woodford Halse
Stoke Bruerne
Towcester
Abthorpe
Silverstone
Cosgrove
OXON
Aynho
BUCKINGHAMSHIRE

0 Miles 10
0 Kilometres 16

Abthorpe

New Inn Ⓛ ✅
Silver Street, NN12 8QR (off Main St, past church on left)
☼ 12-2.30 (not Mon & Tue), 6-11 ; 12-11.30 Fri & Sat;
12-10.30 Sun ☎ (01327) 857306 ⊕ newinnabthorpe.co.uk
**Hook Norton Hooky, Old Hooky; 2 changing beers
(sourced locally)** Ⓗ
A tranquil country hostelry, hidden up a cul-de-sac
off the corner of the village green. This mellow
sandstone local with its large inglenook fireplace
with seating and low ceilings is well worth a visit.
Welcoming to visitors and locals alike, it offers
high-quality meals cooked to order and served
from the open kitchen, with much of the food
locally sourced, including meat from the owner's
farm. Hook Norton seasonal beers feature as
guests. Q ⛱ 😾 🕪 ♣ P 🖵 🐾 🛜

Arthingworth

Bull's Head Ⓛ
Kelmarsh Road, LE16 8JZ (A14 jct 2, off A508)
☼ 12-2.30, 6-11; 12-11 Sat & Sun ☎ (01858) 525637
⊕ thebullsheadonline.co.uk
**Adnams Southwold Bitter; Everards Original; 1
changing beer (sourced locally)** Ⓗ
A former farmhouse dating from the 19th century
built from red brick. The pub has an opened-up bar
with several cosy drinking areas and a restaurant to

the front serving home-cooked fresh food from
local producers. A beer festival is held over the
Whitsun bank holiday on the suntrap patio.
Sparklers can be removed on request.
Q ⛱ 😾 🕪 🕪 ♿ ♣ P 🖵 🐾 🛜

Ashton

Chequered Skipper Ⓛ
The Green, PE8 5LD
☼ 11.30-3, 6-11; 11.30-11 Sat & Sun ☎ (01832) 273494
⊕ chequeredskipper.co.uk
Brewster's Hophead; 2 changing beers Ⓗ
Named after a rare butterfly, this thatched stone-
built inn was re-arranged internally in 1997
following a fire. It has a main bar area and
passageway with sofas leading to a large function
room, used for the annual beer festival in the
summer. The pub serves traditional food made
with produce sourced locally. Q 😾 🕪 ♿ P 🖵 🐾 🛜

Aynho

Great Western Arms Ⓛ
Station Road, OX17 3BP (on B4031)
☼ 11-11 ☎ (01869) 338288 ⊕ great-westernarms.co.uk
**Hook Norton Hooky, Lion, Old Hooky; 1 changing beer
(sourced regionally)** Ⓗ

Situated on the Northants and Oxfordshire borders and between the former Great Western Railway and Oxford Canal, this traditional ivy-clad pub is full of Great Western Railway memorabilia. The main bar and side restaurant have photos of the railway and the canal adorning the walls. The pub is renowned for excellent food. Outdoor seating alongside the canal is pleasant in the summer. Accommodation is in four individually decorated rooms. ☞🏠🛏🍽🕭♿🅿🚃

Barnwell

Montagu Arms 🅛 ✔

PE8 5PH
🕭 12-3 (not Mon), 6-11; 12-11 Sat & Sun ☎ (01832) 273726
Adnams Southwold Bitter; 3 changing beers 🅗
Overlooking the local river and stone bridge, this 16th-century stone-built inn has a public bar at the front and large restaurant to the rear. The car park is behind the inn and accessed via the village hall entrance. Also at the rear is a large play and camping area, and disabled access to the restaurant only. Q☞🏠🍽♿▲♣🍺🅿🚃❀

Blisworth

Walnut Tree Inn 🅛

21 Station Road, NN7 3DS
🕭 10-11 (1am Fri & Sat) ☎ (01604) 859551
🌐 walnut-tree.co.uk
Great Oakley Wagtail; Phipps NBC India Pale Ale; 2 changing beers (sourced regionally) 🅗
An award-winning family-run hotel and bar offering four ales and fresh cooking. Situated just outside the historic village of Blisworth, it is not too far from Bridge 49 on the Grand Union Canal and overlooks the West Coast mainline. A variety of entertainment is provided monthly including comedy, jazz, folk, bluegrass, rock and acoustic nights, as well as regular quiz nights. ☞🏠🛏🍽♿🅿🚃🛜

Broughton

Red Lion 🅛

7 High Street, NN14 1NF (off A43)
🕭 12-3 (not Mon), 5-11; 12-midnight Fri & Sat; 12-11 Sun
☎ (01536) 790239 🌐 redlionbroughton.co.uk
Black Sheep Riggwelter; 6 changing beers (sourced nationally) 🅗
Large community-focused 18th-century ironstone inn with three main rooms – a bar, lounge and open-plan dining area. Two totem poles list forthcoming beers. The landlady is a dark ale fan and ensures that a mild, porter, or stout is on the bar to accompany the good-value home-cooked food. The pub hosts many unusual social events along with two beer festivals. Local CAMRA Rural Pub of the Year 2014. Q☞🏠🍽♿▲♣🍺🅿(X43)❀

Corby

Saxon Crown 🅛 ✔

Elizabeth Street, NN17 1PF
🕭 7am-midnight (1am Fri & Sat) ☎ (01536) 203672
Adnams Broadside; Caledonian Deuchars IPA; Greene King Abbot; Sharp's Doom Bar; 6 changing beers (often Oakham, Phipps NBC, Star) 🅗
A welcome entry for Corby, this refurbished 1960s landmark building was formerly a Co-op department store and now incorporates a hotel.

The name is a reference to the village's ancient origins. The open-plan bar has high-backed leather booths and stools, with a tiled and wooden floor leading to the rear patio. Q☞🏠🛏🍽♿🚃🍺🅿🛜

Cosgrove

Barley Mow ✔

7 The Stocks, MK19 7JD
🕭 12-11; 12-10.30 Sun ☎ (01908) 562957
🌐 thebarleymowcosgrove.co.uk
Everards Sunchaser Blonde, Tiger Best Bitter, Original; 1 changing beer (sourced nationally) 🅗
A beautiful countryside pub backing onto the Grand Union Canal by Bridge 65. The main bar and adjoining areas of this 17th-century building are full of charm – especially when the log fire is ablaze. Outside is a lovely garden and patio with a large car park. The home-made food menu covers all dietary requirements. Events are staged throughout the year, including murder mystery evenings and a monthly quiz. Q☞🏠🍽♿▲🅿🚃❀🛜

Cranford St John

Red Lion ✔

42 High Street, NN14 4AA (off A14 jct 10 & 11)
🕭 12-3 (not Mon & Tue), 5-11; 12-midnight Fri & Sat; 12-10.30 Sun ☎ (01536) 330724
Woodforde's Wherry; 2 changing beers (sourced nationally; often Adnams, Oakham) 🅗
A listed ivy-clad stone building dating from the 18th century standing on a bank off the beaten track now the village is bypassed by the A14. Inside is a large cosy bar with exposed stone walls and wooden floor, along with an intimate lounge and snug. To the side is a separate restaurant serving locally produced food. The landlord is a long-standing CAMRA member. The two changing beers are from established breweries. Q☞🏠🍽🍺🅿🚃(16)❀🛜

Crick

Wheatsheaf 🅛

15 Main Road, NN6 7TU (on main road through village)

REAL ALE BREWERIES	
Brigstock Brigstock	
Cotton End 🍺 Northampton	
Digfield Barnwell	
Frog Island Northampton	
Great Oakley Tiffield	
Gun Dog Woodford Halse	
Hart Family Wellingborough	
Hunsbury Craft East Hunsbury	
J Church 🍺 Northampton	
King's Cliffe King's Cliffe	
Maule Northampton	
Merrimen Litchborough	
Nene Valley Oundle	
Nobby's 🍺 Thrapston	
Phipps Northampton	
Potbelly Kettering	
Rockingham Blatherwycke	
Silverstone Silverstone	
Tom Smith Kettering (brewing suspended)	
Towcester Mill Towcester	
Weldon Rushden	
Whistling Kite Kettering	

✪ 12-11 (midnight Fri & Sat) ☎ (01788) 823824
⊕ wheatsheafcrick.com
Wells Bombardier; 4 changing beers (often Dow Bridge) Ⓗ
A friendly two-roomed village local that offers a comfortable space to enjoy five different guest beers. This genuine free house sells ales from regional and national breweries. The Wheatsheaf is well known for its locally sourced food, served noon-9pm daily. A pub quiz is held every Tuesday and a variety of events feature throughout the year. A free shuttle service is available from Rugby. ♿🛏◑♣Pⓡ(96)🛜

Daventry

Early Doors Ⓛ
3 Prince William Walk, NN11 4AB
✪ 12-9; closed Sun & Mon ☎ 07707 299959
Phipps NBC India Pale Ale Ⓗ**; 5 changing beers (sourced locally; often Gun Dog Ales, Towcester Mill)** Ⓖ
Opened in February 2015, this was the first micropub in the county, situated in a former mobility shop. Simply decorated with a bare concrete floor, furnishings are mostly created from recycled and reclaimed materials – the bar is made from a weathered scaffolding plank. Hand-made local pork pies are available, and pubgoers are welcome to bring their own food which will be plated up for a small charge donated to charity. Q♿🕭◕Pⓡ🛜

Great Brington

Althorp Coaching Inn (Fox & Hounds) Ⓛ
Main Street, NN7 4JA
✪ 11-midnight; 12-11 Sun ☎ (01604) 770651
⊕ althorp-coaching-inn.co.uk
Greene King IPA; Phipps NBC India Pale Ale; St Austell Tribute; Sharp's Doom Bar; 3 changing beers (sourced locally) Ⓗ
Close to Althorp House, the home of the Spencer family, this lovely thatched country pub dates from 1765. Oak beams and flagstone floors feature throughout, and the lounge area has a large inglenook fireplace. Outside is a courtyard, barn and enclosed garden. Excellent food is served in the bar and separate restaurant. A beer festival is held in August. The pub is often busy, especially on Monday quiz night. Happy hour is 5-7pm every day, with 50p off a pint. Q❀◑♿🅰♣P🐾🛜

Kettering

Piper Ⓛ ✔
Windmill Avenue, NN15 6PS (near Wicksteed Park)
✪ 11-3, 5-11; 11-4, 6-11 Sat; 12-10.30 Sun
☎ (01536) 513870 ⊕ thepiper.net
Copper Dragon Golden Pippin; Woodforde's Wherry; 4 changing beers (sourced regionally; often Brewster's, Cottage) Ⓗ
Popular 1950s two-roomed pub which has been run by an enthusiastic CAMRA member for 25 years. There is a quiet lounge to the left, while to the right is a more lively bar/games room where a quiz is held on Sunday night. A beer festival takes place on the third weekend in August. An outdoor seating area is across the road from the pub. Q❀◑♿🅰♣◕Pⓡ🛜

Three Cocks Ⓛ
48 Lower Street, NN16 8DJ (opp Morrisons)
✪ 12-11.30; 12-11 Sun ☎ 07909 698798
Grainstore Ten Fifty; Mighty Oak Maldon Gold; 5 changing beers Ⓗ
A popular town pub with an L-shaped servery at the centre serving the two main bar areas, furnished with comfortable armchairs and high-backed stools. On an upper level is a games area featuring Northants skittles and darts. A variety of CAMRA branch magazines is available to read. Four beer festivals are held in the rear function room over the Solstice and Equinox weekends. There are well-filled cobs to accompany the great beer choice. Q♿◑♿♣◕🖨🐾

Lilbourne

Head of Steam Ⓛ
10 Station Road, CV23 0SX (just off Rugby Rd)
✪ 5-11.30; 12-3, 5-midnight Fri; 12-midnight Sat; 12-11 Sun
☎ (01788) 860166 ⊕ headofsteam.weebly.com
Dow Bridge Ratae'd; 3 changing beers (sourced regionally; often Bradfield, Phipps NBC, Salopian) Ⓗ
Spacious community free house in a village location with an excellent choice of well-kept beers, including locally brewed ales from Dow Bridge. With a comfortable ambience and free from electronic sources of noise, this is a pub for friendly conversation. Locally sourced cheeseboards and pies are available. Occasional acoustic folk nights are held. The large beer garden is popular on hot summer days. Q♿❀♿🅰♣P🛜

Litchborough

Old Red Lion Ⓛ
4 Banbury Road, NN12 8JF (opp church)
✪ 12-11; 12-10.30 Sun ☎ (01327) 830064
⊕ oldredlionlitchborough.co.uk
Great Oakley Wagtail; house beer (by Grainstore); 1 changing beer (sourced regionally) Ⓗ
A traditional four-roomed stone-built village pub well worth seeking out, popular with walkers and cyclists on the Knightly Way. The bar area has flagstone flooring and seats inside the large inviting inglenook. The snug to the rear of the bar is a comfy casual room with double doors leading to a courtyard. The extension houses a restaurant and shop with local farm produce. A wide range of locally brewed bottled beers is stocked, often from Merrimen Brewery in the village. Q♿❀♿🅰♣Pⓡ🐾🛜

Loddington

Hare at Loddington Ⓛ
5 Main Street, NN14 1LA (on village loop)
✪ 12-3, 5.30-11; 12-midnight Sat & Sun ☎ (01536) 710337
⊕ thehareatloddington.com
Greene King Abbot; Sharp's Doom Bar; Wells Bombardier; 2 changing beers (sourced regionally) Ⓗ
Set in a conservation area, the Hare is a listed building in this picturesque village built from local ironstone. The interior comprises four areas – two spread around the central bar and two for dining, where home-cooked food made from local produce can be enjoyed. The guest beers are often from an established microbrewery and a county brewery. Q♿❀◑♿🅰♣Pⓡ(35)🐾

Long Buckby

Old King's Head Ⓛ

West Street, NN6 7QL

🕑 12 (5 Mon)-11; 12-10.30 Sun ☎ (01327) 842680

🌐 oldkingsheadlongbuckby.co.uk

Everards Beacon Bitter, Sunchaser Blonde, Tiger Best Bitter, Original; 2 changing beers (sourced regionally; often Titanic) Ⓗ

Rescued from almost certain oblivion by Everards in 2014, this thatched pub is now a classic village local with a real commitment to the community. It retains two bars, with the former public bar beautifully restyled into a comfy snug, and an L-shaped main bar with low ceilings leading to a small restaurant. Recently awarded Best Rural Pub in the Northamptonshire Food & Drink Awards. Q🌂🕮🕦🌢♣🐾P🖳(11,96,97)🐾🐾🛜

Northampton

Albion Brewery Bar Ⓛ

54 Kingswell Street, NN1 1PR (bottom of Bridge St)

🕑 12-midnight (4 Mon); 12-1am Fri & Sat; 12-4 Sun

☎ (01604) 946606 🌐 phipps-nbc.co.uk

Hoggleys Northamptonshire Bitter; Phipps NBC Red Star, India Pale Ale, Ratliffe's Celebrated Stout; house beer (by Phipps NBC); 1 changing beer (sourced locally) Ⓗ

Phipps NBC returned to its roots in a Victorian brewery in the heart of Northampton 40 years after Phipps' Bridge Street brewery closed. This brewery bar subsequently opened, with an oak and glass partition between the bar and brewery enabling the brewing process to be viewed. Almost all the bar's fittings are reclaimed, with many coming from former Phipps pubs. Q🌂🕮🕦🕭🌢♣🐾🐾🛜

Lamplighter Ⓛ

66 Overstone Road, The Mounts, NN1 3JS

🕑 12-midnight (1am Fri & Sat); 12-11 Sun

☎ (01604) 631125 🌐 thelamplighter.co.uk

Phipps NBC India Pale Ale; Vale Pale Ale; 4 changing beers (sourced regionally) Ⓗ

A popular traditional street-corner inn just off the town centre attracting young and old alike. There is a roaring fire in the bar, a lovely rear snug and a heated courtyard. Four changing guest beers are from established micros, along with a selection of bottled beers. Home-cooked food is served until 9pm (7pm weekends), with children welcome during mealtimes. The pub hosts open mic, discos, live music and quiz nights each week. 🌂🕮🕦🕭♣🖳

Mail Coach Ⓛ

6 Derngate, NN1 1UB (adjacent to Royal & Derngate theatres)

🕑 10-11 (1am Fri & Sat) ☎ (01604) 376994

🌐 mailcoachpub.co.uk

Fuller's London Pride; Greene King IPA; 4 changing beers (sourced locally) Ⓗ

Large town-centre pub with three rooms that have been opened out to create a J-shaped bar with a wood and tile floor. The middle area has high tables and chairs, while either side is more intimate. The pub is popular with theatregoers, and occasionally actors and musicians after shows, and the walls are decorated with theatre memorabilia. The beer terrace has shelter for all weathers. Under new management, there is a focus on sourcing local ales. 🌂🕮🕦🕭♣🐾🐾🛜

Malt Shovel Tavern Ⓛ

121 Bridge Street, NN1 1QF

🕑 11.30-3, 5-11; 11.30-11 Fri & Sat; 12-10.30 Sun

☎ (01604) 234212 🌐 maltshoveltavern.com

Fuller's London Pride; Greene King XX Mild; Hook Norton Old Hooky; Oakham JHB, Bishops Farewell; 4 changing beers (sourced locally) Ⓗ

Close to the town centre, this popular pub has won many awards over the years including local CAMRA Pub of the Year on numerous occasions. Breweriana features everywhere, with real cider, LocAle and Belgian draught and bottled beers available. Two beer festivals are held each year on bank holidays with live bands. Blues bands play on Wednesday nights. The pub has a strong rugby following. Home-made lunches are served 12-2pm Monday to Saturday. Well worth a visit. 🕮🕦🕭🜚♣🐾🖳

Olde England Ⓛ

199 Kettering Road, The Mounts, NN1 4BP (near racecourse)

🕑 11-11; 12-10 Sun ☎ 07742 069768

🌐 theoldeengland.com

Great Oakley Wagtail Ⓖ, Wot's Occurring; Potbelly Bellowhead Hedonism; St Austell Trelawny; Vale Gravitas; changing beers Ⓗ

A converted end-of-terrace Victorian building on three floors with bars on two floors. The ground and first floors have a medieval theme and solid fuel burners. The cellar bar has a contemporary style and is more intimate. Over 20 beers from local micros and regional breweries are served by gravity and handpump as well as 20 ciders. Various board games, cards and dominoes are provided. Quiz night is Wednesday, live folk music is Thursday. No food on Sunday. Winner of Northants Food & Drink Town Community Pub. Q🌂🕦♣🖳🐾🛜

Pomfret Arms Ⓛ

10 Cotton Road, Far Cotton, NN4 8BS

🕑 4.30 (12.30 Fri-Sun)-11 ☎ (01604) 945201

Great Oakley Wot's Occurring; 5 changing beers (sourced locally; often Hart Family, Great Oakley) Ⓗ

Now with its own microbrewery, this town pub is situated just off the riverbank on the south-west side of the River Nene in Cotton End. Its small central bar has six handpumps serving the front room and rear bar. The brewery and a function room are set in the lovely beer garden. A couple of beers come from the brewery itself or Hart Family sister brewery. 🌂🜚♣♣🖳🐾🛜

Queen Adelaide Ⓛ

50 Manor Road, Kingsthorpe, NN2 6QJ (off A5199)

🕑 11-11.30; 12-10.30 Sun ☎ (01604) 714524

🌐 queenadelaide.com

Adnams Southwold Bitter, Broadside; Nobby's Guilsborough Gold; St Austell Tribute; 2 changing beers Ⓗ

An established pub in Kingsthorpe village, this 18th-century listed stone-built local has a main bar with low beams and an uneven floor, a small snug complete with leather sofas, and a further lounge bar to the rear. Always friendly, it is very popular on rugby match days. The guest beers are often from local microbreweries. The Sunday roasts are exceptional (booking advised). An annual beer festival is held in early September. Local CAMRA Pub of the Year 2014. 🌂🕮🕦🕭♣🐾P🖳🛜

Road to Morocco

Bridgwater Drive, Abington Vale, NN3 3AG

🕭 12-11 (midnight Fri & Sat); 12-10.30 Sun
☎ (01604) 632899

Greene King IPA, Abbot; Theakston Old Peculier; 4 changing beers (sourced regionally) Ⓗ

A popular 1960s brick-built estate pub with a Moorish theme in some of the decor, reflecting its name. There are two connected but distinctly different rooms. The bar area, where darts and pool are played, is quite lively, particularly if there is a sporting event on TV. The homely lounge is generally the quieter part of the pub. Quiz night is Tuesday. Forthcoming beers are posted on Facebook. ➤🏵🕭♿♣🖢P🚃(5,9B)🌸 🤏

Wig & Pen Ⓛ ✅

19 St Giles Street, NN1 1JA

🕭 10-11 (1am Fri & Sat); 12-10.30 Sun ☎ (01604) 622178
🌐 thewigandpennorthampton.com

Adnams Ghost Ship; Black Sheep Best Bitter; Fuller's London Pride; Greene King IPA; St Austell Tribute; 6 changing beers (sourced locally; often Elgood's) Ⓗ

A popular 300-year-old pub close to the town hall, reputedly haunted by a young girl. A long L-shaped bar counter serves up to six guest ales, cider and a wide range of bottled beers. A retractable cover provides shelter in the garden, where jazz bands play on Tuesday nights and live bands on Sunday afternoons. Good home-cooked food features locally sourced ingredients. 🏵🕭🖢🚃 🤏

Old

White Horse Ⓛ

Walgrave Road, NN6 9QX

🕭 12-3, 5-11; 12-11 Sat; 12-7 Sun; closed Mon
☎ (01604) 781297 🌐 whitehorseold.co.uk

3 changing beers (sourced locally; often Phipps NBC, Whistling Kite) Ⓗ

A contemporary country pub comprising two opened out rooms with polished wooden floors and a real fire, and a small snug towards the rear. Upstairs is the recently extended Millstone room which leads to the garden patio. A relatively small food menu offers interesting, quality home-cooked seasonal lunches and evening meals, from pub classics to specials. Monthly live music and quiz nights, and a weekly Tuesday pie night, make this local always worth a visit.
Q➤🏵🕭♣🖢P🚃(38,39,43) 🤏

Oundle

Tap and Kitchen

Oundle Wharf, Station Road, PE8 4DE

🕭 12-11 (midnight Fri & Sat); 12-6 Sun; closed Mon
☎ (01832) 275069 🌐 tapandkitchen.com

8 changing beers (sourced locally) Ⓗ

This spacious venue opened in 2014 in a revamped wharfside warehouse. An extensive menu of home-cooked and locally sourced food is served (open for breakfast 9-11am at weekends). At least six real ales from Nene Valley Brewery are available, plus a range of specialist beers and ciders. There are plans for an outdoor seating area and live music. ➤🕭🖢P🚃🌸 🤏

Ravensthorpe

Chequers Ⓛ

Church Lane, NN6 8ER (off A428 opp church)

🕭 12-3, 6-midnight; 12-midnight Sat & Sun
☎ (01604) 770379 🌐 chequersravensthorpe.co.uk

Black Sheep Best Bitter; Oakham JHB; Thwaites Original; 2 changing beers (sourced locally) Ⓗ

The hosts have enjoyed more than 25 years at this friendly pub which attracts locals, walkers and fishermen alike. A long-standing Guide entry, the brick-built Grade II-listed free house has an L-shaped bar and a restaurant to the rear serving excellent home-cooked food. There is a collection of jugs on the beams, and bank notes on the half-panelled walls. Outside is a children's adventure play area and a separate building for Northants skittles. ➤🏵🕭♿♣🖢P🌸 🤏

Rothwell

Woolpack Ⓛ

Market Hill, NN14 6BW

🕭 2-10; 12-11 Sat & Sun ☎ (01536) 710284

Grainstore Red Kite; Phipps NBC India Pale Ale; Wells Bombardier; 3 changing beers (sourced locally; often Grainstore) Ⓗ

A community focused 17th-century ironstone inn with three low-beamed open-plan rooms, an L-shaped bar and a lounge area to the rear. The pub is believed to be on the site where wool was sold on the medieval market since the granting of the 1204 Charter. The landlady has turned this pub around, increasing the number of changing guest beers to three and winning CAMRA awards for her efforts. Q➤🏵🕭♿♣🖢P🚃(19,43,X43)🌸

Rushden

Rushden Historical Transport Society Ⓛ

Station Approach, NN10 0AW (on ring road)

🕭 7.30 (6 Wed & Thu)-11; 4.30-11 Fri; 12-11 Sat & Sun
☎ (01933) 318988 🌐 rhts.co.uk

Dark Star Hophead; Phipps NBC India Pale Ale; Tring Bring me Sunshine; 4 changing beers (sourced regionally) Ⓗ

The former ladies' waiting room of the Midland Railway Station is now the bar, with gas lighting and walls adorned with enamel advertising panels, railway photos and CAMRA awards. On the platform carriages provide a meeting room, Northants skittles, and a buffet for open days held during the year with steam and diesel train trips. A beerfest is held in September. Day membership is £1 except on open days. Q➤🏵🕭♿♣🖢🚃🌸

Slipton

Samuel Pepys Ⓛ

Slipton Lane, NN14 3AR

🕭 12-3, 6-11; 12-11 Sat; 12-7 Sun ☎ (01832) 731739
🌐 samuel-pepys.com

Digfield Fools Nook Ⓗ**; 3 changing beers (sourced locally; often Nene Valley)** Ⓗ/Ⓖ

Set in a picturesque thatched village, this lovely 16th-century ironstone pub has a low-beamed and brick-floored traditional bar to the front where locals and visitors can chat or relax in cosy armchairs in front of a real fire. The stone-built dining/lounge bar and the conservatory restaurant are decorated and furnished in a smart modern style. Three guest beers often come from local microbreweries, and in summer a real cider is also available. No food Sunday evening.
Q🏵🕭♿🖢P🚃🌸 🤏

Southwick

Shuckburgh Arms 🛏

Main Street, PE8 5BL

☼ 4-10 Mon; 12 (4 Tue)-11; 10-11 Sat; 12-10 Sun
☎ (01832) 272044 ⊕ shuckburghpub.co.uk

Nene Valley Bitter 🗓; house beer (by Grainstore) 🗓/🗓; 3 changing beers (sourced locally) 🗓

Stone-built inn next to the village hall and close to the cricket pitch, serving up to five real ales. The bar area doubles as a restaurant for diners. The pub is run by the local community with shareholders and a small committee. Red Kites are often visible from the large rear garden. The pub hosts the annual World Conker Championship in October. Popular well-priced food is available including breakfasts from 10am by arrangement.
Q❀◑&♿♣♠🅿🚲🐾🛜

Staverton

Countryman 🛏 ✅

Daventry Road, NN11 6JH (on A425 just outside village)
☼ 12-3, 6-11 (10.30 Mon); 12-10 Sun ☎ (01327) 311815
⊕ thecountrymanstaverton.co.uk

3 changing beers (sourced regionally) 🗓

The L-shaped bar, with wood beams throughout, serves four areas, some set aside for diners, and an open-hearth fire between the spaces provides some seclusion. The enthusiastic landlord offers a wide choice of reasonably priced food, sourced locally whenever possible. Three changing guest beers are listed on the website and always include a locally brewed beer. Q❀◑&🅿🚲(66)🛜

Stoke Bruerne

Boat Inn

Shutlanger Road, NN12 7SB
☼ 9am-11 ☎ (01604) 862428 ⊕ boatinn.co.uk

Banks's Bitter; Jennings Cumberland Ale; Marston's Pedigree New World Pale Ale, Old Empire; Wychwood Hobgoblin; 2 changing beers (sourced nationally) 🗓
Situated on the banks of the Grand Union Canal opposite the National Canal Museum and next to the locks, the Boat Inn has been owned by the same family since 1877. The long narrow pub has a wonderful tap bar and interconnecting rooms with canal views, open fires, original stone floors and window seats, while an adjoining room has Northants skittles. A canal boat is available to hire. The cider is Thatchers Heritage. Breakfast is served until 11am. Q❀❀◑&♣♠🅿🚲(86)🐾🛜

Thornby

Red Lion 🛏 ✅

Welford Road, NN6 8SJ (on A5199)
☼ 12-11; 12-10.30 Sun ☎ (01604) 740238
⊕ redlionthornby.co.uk

6 changing beers (sourced regionally; often Dow Bridge, Grainstore, Wadworth) 🗓
An impressive whitewashed village pub whose compact bar has two drinking areas with a wood-burning open fire in the lounge. A motley collection of beer tankards, steins and framed photos is displayed throughout. To the rear is the restaurant, which occupies two linked rooms, one heavily beamed. A beer festival is held in late July. Accommodation has been added in a converted barn. Q❀❀◑&🅿🚲(60)🐾🛜

Tiffield

George at Tiffield 🍽 🛏 ✅

21 High Street North, NN12 8AD
☼ 12-3, 6-11; 7-11 Tue; 12-midnight Sat; 12-7 Sun
☎ (01604) 350587 ⊕ thegeorgeattiffield.co.uk

Great Oakley Wot's Occurring, Tiffield Thunderbolt; Vale Vale Pale Ale; 2 changing beers (sourced regionally) 🗓
A true community inn central to many village activities – the building dates from the 16th century with Victorian additions. It has a cosy bar, games room with Northants skittles and back room restaurant which can be booked for small functions. It is the tap for Great Oakley Brewery, just outside the village. Two annual beer festivals are hosted at Easter and in October. A former Northamptonshire Food & Drink Awards Rural Community Pub of the Year. Q❀❀◑&♣♠🅿🚲🐾

Towcester

Towcester Mill Brewery Tap 🛏

Chantry Lane, NN12 6AD
☼ 5-10.30 (9.30 Mon; 11 Fri); 12-11 Sat; 12-7 Sun
☎ (01327) 437060 ⊕ towcestermillbrewery.co.uk

Towcester Mill Mill Race, Bell Ringer, Black Fire; 5 changing beers (sourced locally; often Towcester Mill) 🗓
Popular and welcoming brewery tap in a historic mill dating from 1794, straddling the old mill race and adjacent to Bury Munt on which the town's fort once stood. The bar retains many original features including beams, stonework and a wooden floor, while a bottle shop is next door. A large garden runs alongside the mill, home to beer festivals in April, June and September. Four rotating guest ales are sourced from other local breweries and eight ciders are available. Q❀❀&♠🅿🚲🐾🛜

Upper Boddington

Plough 🛏

Warwick Road, NN11 6DH
☼ 5.30-11 (midnight Fri); 12-midnight Sat; 12-10.30 Sun
☎ (01327) 260364 ⊕ ploughinnboddington.co.uk

Greene King IPA; Shepherd Neame Spitfire; 2 changing beers (sourced regionally) 🗓
An 18th-century stone-built thatched village inn with a small bar with flagstone floors. The entrance lobby on two levels leads to a small lounge, formerly two small rooms, which has a modern counter and a working Raeburn cooker, and a dining room. Stone and plaster walls and low wood beams feature in more interconnected rooms to the rear, including a snug with leather settees. A quaint and unusual pub. Q❀❀◑♠🅿🚲🐾🛜

Weldon

Shoulder of Mutton 🛏

12 Chapel Road, NN17 3HP
☼ 3-10; 12-midnight Fri-Sun ☎ (01536) 601016
⊕ shoulderofmuttonweldon.co.uk

Shoulder of Mutton Dragline, Rosie's Sweatbox, Weldon Windmill; 3 changing beers (sourced locally; often Shoulder of Mutton) 🗓
Large, friendly pub with two large bar areas, a locals' bar at the front and an events room to the rear. In 2014 a microbrewery was set up in the cellar, and although most of the production is now off-site, it is still in regular use. Home-made

Serbian food is a speciality, with more traditional fish and chips on Friday. Quiz night is Friday. The pub received a local CAMRA branch award in December 2015. ⚙️🍴♿️P�(X4)🐾🐱📶

Welford

Wharf Inn 🅛 ✅
NN6 6JQ (on A5199 by canal basin)
🕐 12-11 ☎ (01858) 575075 ⊕ wharfinn.co.uk
Grainstore Ten Fifty; Marston's Pedigree; Oakham Bishops Farewell; 3 changing beers (sourced locally) 🅗
Originally dating from the 1800s, the Wharf Inn was converted to a pub in the 1980s and is located next to the canal basin where several walks can be started – ask the landlord for a leaflet. It is popular with narrowboaters, walkers and locals alike. Inside is a small bottom bar, while up a couple of steps is the main bar, with an open fire separating the drinking area from the restaurant.
Q🕐⚙️🚪🍴🐾P🚝(60)🐱📶

Wellingborough

Coach & Horses 🍺 🅛 ✅
17 Oxford Street, NN8 4HY (800yds from Market Square)
🕐 12-11 (9 Mon); 12-6 Sun ☎ (01933) 441848
⊕ coachandhorseswellingborough.co.uk
12 changing beers (sourced nationally; often Abbeydale, Great Oakley, Phipps NBC) 🅗
Popular town-centre local with an enthusiastic landlord who operates a constantly changing choice of 12 beers and 12 ciders, including two or more local ales. The central servery looks after three drinking areas adorned with breweriana. Traditional home-cooked food is served including 40 different pies (no food Sun eve, Mon and Tue). A pub quiz is hosted on alternate Wednesdays. A former CAMRA East Midlands Regional Pub of the Year runner-up. 🚪⚙️🍴♿️🐾🐱🚝📶

Golden Lion 🅛 ✅
19 Sheep Street, NN8 1BN
🕐 12-11 (midnight Fri); 11-midnight Sat ☎ (01933) 223206
⊕ thegoldenlionwellingborough.co.uk
Adnams Ghost Ship; St Austell 1913 Cornish Stout; 4 changing beers (sourced nationally; often Langton, Oakham) 🅗
This magnificent Grade II-listed stone Tudor building dates from 1540 and is one of the oldest buildings in the area. Many original features remain, including the restaurant/dining room, known as The Hall, with its vaulted ceiling, exposed beams and minstrels' gallery. Visitors can also relax in the comfortable lounge area with open fires in the winter, and there is seating outside for clement days. 🚪⚙️🍴♿️🐾🚝📶

Little Ale House 🅛
14A High Street, NN8 4JU (close to Jacksons Lane municipal car park)
🕐 12-9 (11 Fri & Sat); 12-4 Sun; closed Mon & Tue ☎ 07787 446460
4 changing beers (sourced nationally) 🅗/🅖
A wonderfully friendly micropub, its size assuring social interaction between visitors and the

landlord. Four rotating real ales are served straight from the cask, plus at least four draught ciders and a small selection of wines and soft drinks. The landlord offers a beer choice system whereby every pint sold is awarded a pea to place in one of three pots to help select beers for the following week. Q🚪⚙️♿️🐾P🚝📶

Weston by Welland

Wheel & Compass 🅛
Valley Road, LE16 8HZ
🕐 12-11; 12-10.30 Sun ☎ (01858) 565864
⊕ thewheelandcompass.co.uk
Black Sheep Best Bitter; Greene King Abbot; Marston's Burton Bitter; Oakham JHB; St Austell Tribute; Sharp's Doom Bar; 1 changing beer (sourced nationally; often Everards, Fuller's) 🅗
A rural pub in the picturesque Welland Valley with a cosy bar/lounge and a large extended dining room. An outside drinking area offers good views across the valley and is an ideal playground for children. The pub is a popular stop-off for walkers on the Jurassic Way which runs close by. Good-value food is available including lunchtime specials. Q🚪⚙️🍴♿️P🚝🐾📶

Woodford

Duke's Arms 🅛
83 High Street, NN14 4HE (off A510)
🕐 12-11 ☎ (01832) 732224
Digfield Fools Nook; Greene King Abbot; 6 changing beers (sourced nationally) 🅗
Originally a 17th-century manor, the Duke's was renamed in honour of the Duke of Wellington who was a frequent visitor to the village. Overlooking the green, it has a split main bar, lounge, rear games room with 3D TV and an upstairs games room. Very much a community-focused pub, it holds a Whitsun bank holiday beer festival and August bank holiday music festival, plus regular open mic, disco, karaoke and acoustic sessions. Traditional pub food is available alongside pizza and chilli. 🚪⚙️🍴♿️🐾🐱P🚝(16)🐾📶

Yardley Hastings

Rose & Crown 🅛
4 Northampton Road, NN7 1EX
🕐 5-10 Mon; 12-11; 12-10 Sun ☎ (01604) 696276
⊕ roseandcrownbistro.co.uk
Greene King IPA, Abbot; Hart Family House Beer; Phipps NBC India Pale Ale; 2 changing beers (sourced locally) 🅗
A lovely ironstone pub extensively refurbished in the 1980s, now a single large room in old-world style. It retains stone-flagged floors and beamed ceilings throughout, and has a small drinking area in the bay window. The emphasis is on traditional home cooking with a daily changing menu. Regular live music ranges from jazz to rock to blues. The landscaped gardens are wonderful in summer. The house beer is from Hart Family. Northamptonshire Food & Drink Awards Food Pub of the Year 2015/16. Q⚙️🍴♿️🐾P🚝(41)🐱

A glass of bitter beer or pale ale, taken with the principal meal of the day, does more good and less harm than any medicine the physician can prescribe. **Dr Carpenter, 1750**

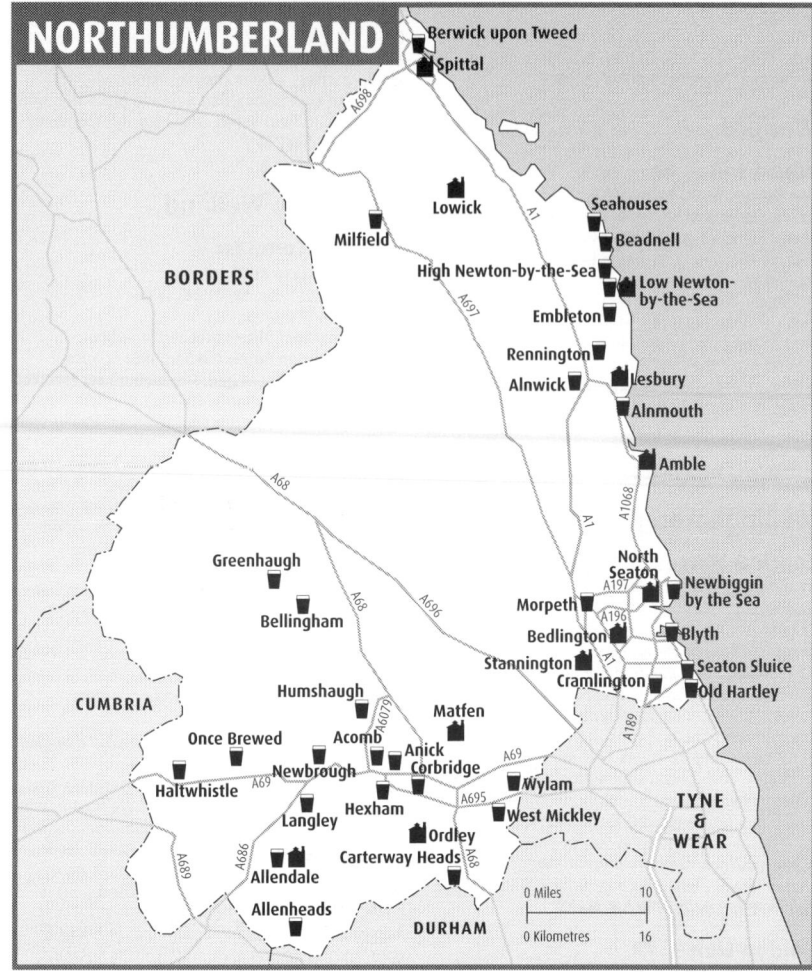

NORTHUMBERLAND

Berwick upon Tweed
Spittal
Lowick
Milfield
Seahouses
Beadnell
High Newton-by-the-Sea
Low Newton-by-the-Sea
Embleton
BORDERS
Rennington
Alnwick
Lesbury
Alnmouth
Amble
Greenhaugh
North Seaton
Newbiggin by the Sea
Morpeth
Bellingham
Bedlington
Blyth
Stannington
Seaton Sluice
Humshaugh
Cramlington
Old Hartley
CUMBRIA
Matfen
Once Brewed
Acomb
Anick
Corbridge
Haltwhistle
Newbrough
Wylam
TYNE & WEAR
Langley
Hexham
West Mickley
Ordley
Carterway Heads
Allendale
Allenheads
DURHAM

0 Miles 10
0 Kilometres 16

Acomb

Miners Arms

Main Street, NE46 4PW (turn off A69 past Hexham roundabout and take A6079)
☼ 5-midnight; 12-midnight Sun ☎ (01434) 603909
⊕ theminersacomb.com
Wylam Gold Tankard; Yates Bitter; 3 changing beers Ⓗ
Superb traditional 1746 inn with an emphasis on real ale, served in oversized lined glasses. The family-run pub hosts regular music and folk nights. The bar has a genuine, cosy feel and is divided by a central staircase – energetic dogs often greet the visitor here. The miners have long gone but this pub is a superb legacy that lives on in this popular hamlet. ☎☼◖◗&♣♿🚌 (880,882)🐾

Allendale

Golden Lion Hotel Ⓛ

Market Place, NE47 9BD
☼ 12-1.30am (1am Wed); 12-2.30am Fri-Sun
☎ (01434) 683225 ⊕ goldenlionhotel.net
Timothy Taylor Landlord; Wylam Gold Tankard; 3 changing beers Ⓗ

Friendly and hospitable pub in the centre of town, patronised by locals and tourists. The walls are adorned with photographs of the annual tar barrel procession, an experience in itself, and local landscapes. Allendale's local choir practise here on Tuesday evening, and live Irish music plays on the last Wednesday of the month. With two regular beers and three guests, there is always plenty of choice of local ales. Home-cooked food is served. The pub has a late licence at weekends.
🐾🛏◖◗🚌 (688)🐾

Allenheads

Allenheads Inn Ⓛ

NE47 9HJ
⏲ 4 (12 Sat)-11; 12-10.30 Sun ☎ (01434) 685200
🌐 allenheadsinn.co.uk
Black Sheep Best Bitter; Mordue Northumbrian Blonde; 4 changing beers Ⓗ
Superb 18th-century rural inn with a public bar with log fire, games room and dining room. On the Coast-to-Coast cycle route, it is popular with cyclists, ramblers and tourists. Good bar meals are available at decent prices. Originally the home of Sir Thomas Wentworth, the premises are bedecked with memorabilia and knick-knacks from a bygone age. The pub will open early on request for coach parties and rambling groups.
🚲🕿❀🛏🌢♣️P🚍 (688) 🐾

Alnmouth

Red Lion Inn Ⓥ

22 Northumberland Street, NE66 2RJ
⏲ 11-midnight ☎ (01665) 830584 🌐 redlionalnmouth.com
Black Sheep Best Bitter; 3 changing beers Ⓗ
Charming family-run, 18th-century coaching inn with a cosy lounge bar with attractive woodwork. Well-patronised by tourists and locals, panoramic views across the Aln Estuary can be enjoyed from the decked area at the bottom of the garden. Occasional live music plays – in the open air in summer. Guest beers usually include one local and two interesting brews from further afield. An annual beer festival is held in October. Open for breakfast from 9am and excellent en-suite B&B accommodation is available.
Q🚲🕿❀🛏🌢●P🚍 (X18) 🐾🛜

Alnwick

John Bull Inn Ⓛ

12 Howick Street, NE66 1UY
⏲ 12-3 (not Mon-Fri), 7-11; 12-3, 7-10.30 Sun
☎ (01665) 602055 🌐 john-bull-inn.co.uk
5 changing beers Ⓗ
Many-time local CAMRA Pub of the Year winner, this 180-year-old inn thrives on its reputation as a back-street boozer. The passionate landlord offers a wide range of cask-conditioned ales at varying ABVs, real cider, the widest range of bottled Belgian beers in the county and over 120 different single malt whiskies. The darts team competes in the local league and the pub upholds the North-east tradition of an annual leek show. There is a cheese club on Saturday night.
Q🕿♣️🚍 (X15,X18) 🐾

Tanners Arms Ⓛ

2-4 Hotspur Place, NE66 1QF
⏲ 5-11 (midnight Fri); 12-midnight Sat; 12-10.30 Sun
☎ (01665) 602553 🌐 tannersarms.com
6 changing beers Ⓗ
Ivy-covered stone-built pub just off Bondgate Without and a short distance from Alnwick Garden. The rustic single room has a flagstone floor, tree beer shelf and a warming real fire in winter. Acoustic music nights feature regularly with open mic on the last Friday of the month. The ever-changing real ales frequently come from North-eastern and Scottish Borders microbreweries.
🚲♿♣️●🚍 (X15,X18) 🐾🛜

Anick

Rat Inn Ⓗ

NE46 4LN (follow sign at Hexham A69 roundabout)
⏲ 12-11.30; 12-10.30 Sun ☎ (01434) 602814
🌐 theratinn.com
4 changing beers Ⓗ
Superb 1750 country inn with spectacular views across Tyne Valley. The pub has a welcoming and friendly feel to it, with an open log fire and chamber pots hanging from the ceiling. It has an excellent local reputation for good food prepared with locally sourced ingredients and appears in several food guides. Half portions are available for children. Bottled beers are stocked to complement the handpumped ales. The first Thursday of the month is singers'/poetry night. Well worth the short taxi ride from Hexham rail station.
Q🚲🕿❀🌢♣️●P🚍

Beadnell

Beadnell Towers Hotel

The Wynding, NE67 5AY
⏲ 12-11 ☎ (01665) 721211
Black Sheep Best Bitter; 2 changing beers Ⓗ
This traditional, family-run inn is only a short walk from some of Britain's most beautiful, unspoilt beaches. Set in the village centre, it boasts a large, comfortable bar and a smaller public bar area with a pool table. There is an outside drinking area to the rear. A large TV shows sporting events.
🕿🛏P🚍 (X18,418)

Bellingham

Cheviot Hotel

Main Street, NE48 2AU
⏲ 10-midnight (1am Fri & Sat) ☎ (01434) 220696
🌐 thecheviothotel.co.uk
4 changing beers Ⓗ
Friendly hotel, recently refurbished, updated and renovated, on Main Street opposite the bus stop. Cask beer is now available all year round including one ale supplied by High House Farm Brewery. A log-burning stove warms the bar area. There is plenty of outside seating at the front. Regular theme nights are hosted. Stay up to date with the monthly newsletter, The Sheep Dip.
🚲🕿🛏🌢♿⚚♣️P🚍 (680,880) 🐾🛜

Berwick upon Tweed

Barrels Ale House

59-61 Bridge Street, TD15 1ES
⏲ 12-midnight; 12-11.30 Sun ☎ (01289) 308013
5 changing beers Ⓗ
There is an Old Curiosity Shop-ambience to this pub, located in the old part of Berwick next to the original road bridge over the Tweed. The excellent real ale no doubt helps customers brave the 'dentist's chair' at the side of the bar. A downstairs bar is used by DJs and bands at weekends. Outside is a unique open drinking area surrounded by high walls. A former winner of CAMRA Pub of the Year.
❀🐾

Curfew 🏆

46a Bridge Street, TD15 1AQ
⏲ 12-9 (10 Fri-Sun) ☎ 07842 912268
4 changing beers Ⓗ

A recent addition to the Berwick pub scene. The town's first micropub is located up a small lane which opens out into a large courtyard off Bridge Street. It has a very small bar area with a bottle fridge to one side. The large courtyard makes a pleasant outdoor drinking area in summer. The cellar is in the shed at the top of the yard. CAMRA Northumberland Pub of the Year 2016 winner.
Q✿❄✿♠

Pilot

31 Low Greens, TD15 1LZ
☼ 12 (11 Sat)-midnight; 12-11 Sun ☎ (01289) 304214
Caledonian Deuchars IPA; 2 changing beers ⊞
This stone-built end-of-terrace hostelry dates from 19th century and has a regionally important historic interior. It retains the original small room layout and boasts several nautical artefacts over 100 years old. It is home to a darts team and hosts music nights. With warm and friendly bar staff, the pub is popular with locals and sought out by train trippers who have found out about this gem.
⏰✿✪◑♿➤♣❀

Blyth

Wallaw ⓛ ✔

14 Union Street, NE24 2DX
☼ 8am-midnight (1am Fri & Sat) ☎ (01670) 356830
Greene King Abbot; Ruddles County; 7 changing beers ⊞
The Wallaw is a former picture house and Wetherspoon has kept the name and Art Deco theme. Note the original projector in the entrance and seating and layout on the balcony (not open to the public). It aims to serve real ale of the highest quality from its 10 handpumps and welcomes suggestions for guest ales. Alcohol is available from 9am. Q⏰✿◑♿♠♣🚲🖤

Carterway Heads

Manor House Inn ✔

DH8 9LX (just off A68 S of Corbridge)
☼ 12-11; 12-10.30 Sun ☎ (01207) 255268
⊕ themanorhouseinn.com
Morland Old Speckled Hen; 3 changing beers ⊞
Warm and hospitable country inn warmed by three open fires. A double-glazed window in the bar wall allows customers to view the well-maintained cellar. Proper home-cooked food is on offer and is popular both with tourists and locals. Excellent accommodation is available. There are superb views over the valley from the rear beer garden. Derwent Reservoir is nearby.
⏰✿✪◑♿♣♠❀🚲

Corbridge

Angel of Corbridge

Main Street, NE45 5LA
☼ 11-11; 12-11 Sun ☎ (01434) 632119
⊕ theangelofcorbridge.com
Cumberland Corby Blonde; Hadrian Border Tyneside Blonde; Wylam Angel; 3 changing beers ⊞
Superb former coaching inn dating from 1726 located on the main road with good transport links. Seven handpulls adorn the bar and a wonderful selection of malt whiskies is also kept. Family-friendly and with a reputation for good food, the pub is popular with tourists, ramblers and locals. A separate lounge area has comfy leather seating

and outside is a relaxed seating area. The town has strong links with the Romans and Hadrian's Wall is nearby. Q⏰✿◑♠P🖤

Cramlington

Plough ⓛ

Middle Farm Buildings, NE23 1DN
☼ 11-11 (midnight Fri & Sat); 12-11 Sun ☎ (01670) 737633
⊕ theploughcramlington.co.uk
Cullercoats Jack the Devil; Harviestoun Bitter & Twisted; 5 changing beers ⊞
Converted farm buildings in the old village make up this Sir John Fitzgerald outlet, which is arranged in the style of a traditional pub with separate bar and lounge areas. Alongside the core range of local beers, an excellent selection of ales from local microbreweries is on continual rotation, backed by a commitment to sourcing the best ales from across the UK. Under-18s are permitted in bar areas daytime only, but families are always welcome in the function room upstairs.
Q⏰✿✪♣♠P🖤(X5,X10,X11)❀⛛

Embleton

Greys Inn ⓛ ✔

Stanley Terrace, NE66 3UZ
☼ 12-11; 12-10.30 Sun ☎ (01665) 576983
6 changing beers ⊞
Pleasant, traditional pub in a lovely seaside hamlet, just a short walk to a wonderful beach. It has three open fires and a framed 1904 grocery list hangs on the wall. The pub is an excellent venue to enjoy a bite to eat washed down with a locally sourced real ale, sitting outside on the superb patio in good weather. It is home to a ladies' darts team, clay pigeon club and golf club.
⏰◑♣♠🖤(418,X18)❀

Greenhaugh

Holly Bush Inn ⓛ

NE48 1PW
☼ 4-11 ☎ (01434) 240391 ⊕ hollybushinn.net
High House Farm Nel's Best; 1 changing beer ⊞
Independently owned pub that is over 300 years old and set in the heart of the Northumberland National Park and the newly defined Dark Sky Park, making it ideal for those with an interest in real ale and real stars. No TV and no mobile reception make for a peaceful drinking experience. The pub is dog-friendly and hosts informal jam sessions – so bring your instrument if you like. Q⏰✿✪◑♿♠P❀⛛

Haltwhistle

Black Bull

Black Bull Lane, Market Square, NE49 0BL
☼ 3.30-11; 12-11 Fri & Sat; 12-10 Sun ☎ (01434) 320463
6 changing beers (sourced nationally) ⊞
Warm, friendly, two-room inn close to Hadrian's Wall and popular with locals and ramblers. An open fire warms the low-beamed interior and horse brasses enhance the traditional ambience. The pub is located down a cobbled lane just off the marketplace in the centre of the town. Beers are available on six handpulls. Regular theme nights are hosted. Ring to check winter hours, and meal times can vary too. Q⏰⏰◑🖤(685)❀

Milecastle Inn ᴸ

North Road, NE49 9NN
✪ 12-11 ☎ (01434) 321372 ⊕ milecastle-inn.co.uk
Big Lamp Sunny Daze, Bitter, Prince Bishop Ale Ⓗ
This 1600s pub adjacent to Hadrian's Wall only sells ale from Newburn-based Big Lamp Brewery. Located a mile and a half north of Haltwhistle, the rural hostelry has a homely feel, popular with ramblers and tourists. Food is locally sourced and attracts customers from as far as Newcastle and Carlisle. There are also two comfy holiday cottages. The Hadrian's Wall bus stops outside April-October. Check ahead for opening times November-Easter.
Q ➓ 💥 🛏 ⊕ P 🖵 ⟨

Hexham

Dipton Mill Inn ᴸ

Dipton Mill Road, NE46 1YA
✪ 12-2.30, 6-11; 12-3 Sun ☎ (01434) 606577
⊕ diptonmill.co.uk
Hexhamshire Devil's Elbow, Shire Bitter, Blackhall English Stout, Devil's Water, Whapweasel, Old Humbug Ⓗ
The tap for Hexhamshire Brewery, soon to be relocated to the rear of the pub, this small inn is run by enthusiasts who brew their own excellent beers. Blackhall English Stout has proved so popular with drinkers that it has ousted Guinness. To complement the ales there is great home-cooked food – Saturday is curry night. A cosy atmosphere and warm welcome make this pub well worth seeking out. The large garden has a stream running through it and there is plenty of countryside to explore. Q ➓ ⊕ ➦ P

Heart of Northumberland ᴸ

5 Market Street, NE46 3NS
✪ 12.30-11 ☎ (01434) 608013
Timothy Taylor Landlord; 4 changing beers Ⓗ
Five handpumps, four selling local ales, adorn the bar in this recently refurbished and reopened, food-led pub. The single large room is divided almost in two near the end of the bar, with wooden floors throughout. A large open fire warms things nicely in the back room and another smaller fire keeps the front room cosy, too. Excellent food is served. ⊕ ⇶ 🖵 ⟨

Tannery ᴸ ⊘

22 Gilesgate, NE46 3QD
✪ 12-midnight ☎ (01434) 605537
6 changing beers Ⓗ
This local hostelry has been taken over by an established landlord from Newcastle with a vision to serve the best beers, ciders, whiskies and gins alongside a menu of meats, cheeses and snacks sourced from small producers in the region. The pub is split into two distinct bars, with the public bar serving six real ales including one LocAle. The lounge offers up to 12 real ciders, six on handpull and six on gravity. ➓ ➓ ⊕ ➦ ⇶ ➦ ➦ 🖵 ⟨

High Newton-by-the-Sea

Joiners Arms

Town Square, NE66 3EA
✪ 11-11; 11-10.30 Sun ☎ (01665) 576112
⊕ joiners-arms.com
Anarchy Blonde Star; 3 changing beers Ⓗ
Eighteenth-century former manor house, tastefully restored and refurbished following closure for two

years. The house ale, St Mary's, reflects the name of the local church and for every pint sold a donation is made towards the church upkeep. Set in a pleasant hamlet off the B1340, the pub's outdoor seating area overlooks the small picturesque green. Five en-suite bedrooms are fitted out to a high standard.
➓ ➓ 💥 🛏 ⊕ ➦ P 🖵 (418) ⟨

Humshaugh

Crown Inn

NE46 4AG
✪ 12-11 ☎ (01434) 681231
High House Farm Nel's Best; 3 changing beers Ⓗ
A traditional village pub located in the centre of the beautiful village of Humshaugh, five miles north of the market town of Hexham. The pub has a homely charm, with a wood-burning stove, cask ales and traditional home-cooked food. Simple guest accommodation is offered in comfortable rooms, ideal for those wishing to explore Hadrian's Wall.
🛏 ⊕ ⟨

Langley

Carts Bog Inn ᴸ

NE47 5NW
✪ 12-2.30, 5-11; 12-11 Sat; 12-10.30 Sun; closed Mon
☎ (01434) 684338 ⊕ cartsbog.co.uk
3 changing beers Ⓗ
Excellent rural pub serving the Langley community and tourists. The building dates from 1730 and was built on the site of an ancient brewery (circa 1521). Carts really did get bogged down here. A large open fire divides the two rooms and the walls proudly display pictures of bygone days. Good locally sourced food including meat from a nearby farm is served (booking essential for Sunday lunch). Three real ales from local breweries are usually available, and a beer festival is held in August. Home to three quoits teams. Winter opening times vary. Q ➓ ➓ ⊕ ⊕ ➦ P 🖵 (688) ⟨ ⟨

Low Newton-by-the-Sea

Ship Inn ᴸ

Newton Square, NE66 3EL
✪ 11-11; 12-11 Sun ☎ (01665) 576262
⊕ shipinnnewton.co.uk
Ship Inn Sandcastles at Dawn, Sea Coal, Sea Dog, Sea Wheat, Ship Hop Ale Ⓗ
Nestling in the corner of a three-sided square of former fishermen's cottages only a few yards from the beach, this small pub is often busy with walkers, diners and beer drinkers seeking ales from the in-house microbrewery. The excellent menu uses fresh local ingredients. The pub is a short walk from the public car park at the top of the hill. Opening times may vary in winter so phone ahead if travelling any distance. Q ➓ ➓ ⊕ ⟨

Milfield

Red Lion Inn

Main Road, NE71 6JD (E of A697)
✪ 12-2, 5-11; 12-11 Sat & Sun ☎ (01668) 216224
⊕ redlionmilfield.co.uk
Black Sheep Best Bitter; 2 changing beers Ⓗ
A true local pub at the heart of the village, just eight miles inside the border, dating back to the mid-1700s. Rescued by the current licensee from

the tight grip of Scottish & Newcastle, the Red Lion is a proper free house, with many varied guest beers served through the third handpump. Freshly prepared food is available, with blackboards proudly displaying where the local produce is sourced. Home to the local leek-growing club. Q⊃✿⊷⊄◐⅊♣⊞⊟(267)♠

Morpeth

Electrical Wizard ✪

11 New Market, NE61 1PS
✪ 8am-11 ☎ (01670) 500640
Greene King Abbot; Ruddles County; 4 changing beers Ⓗ
Formerly a cinema, this pub was refurbished by JD Wetherspoon in 2011 to a high standard. It is named after Dr Walford Bodie, the 'Electrical Wizard' who entertained packed audiences in these premises in the cinema's early years. The long bar is to the right on entering and there is comfortable seating throughout. Interesting electrical sculptures and pictures of old Morpeth adorn the walls. The pub participates in an annual local beer festival along with other Wetherspoons in Northumberland. ⊃◐⅊⟱♠

Office ♟ Ⓛ

The Toll House, Castle Square, NE61 1YL
✪ 5-11; 12-11 Sat & Sun ☎ 07707 703182
5 changing beers Ⓗ
The Office is the brewery tap for Acton Ales. It is a micropub with no music or games machines. It features five handpulls and three keg beers, all of local origin, and three real ciders served on gravity from the glass-fronted fridge opposite the bar. No food is available. Local CAMRA Pub of the Year 2016. Q⇄⊟♣

Newbiggin by the Sea

Queen's Head ✪

7 High Street, NE64 6AT
✪ 10-midnight ☎ (01670) 817293
2 changing beers Ⓗ
Single-room building with the bar, lounge and snug all together. Rebuilt in 1909, some Edwardian features have been retained, including the curved bar counter. The pub sells competitively priced real ales at advantageous opening times and displays an impressive collection of guest beer pumpclips on the walls. One beer is usually available, two on Fridays, varying weekly. This no-nonsense pub is popular with locals and visitors alike. ⊃♣⊟

Newbrough

Red Lion Ⓛ

Stanegate Road, NE47 5AR
✪ 12-11; 12-10.30 Sun ☎ (01434) 674226
⊕ redlionnewbrough.co.uk
3 changing beers Ⓗ
The road outside was first laid down by the Romans in 71AD, long before Hadrian's Wall was built. The building reputedly dates back to the 13th century, featuring many flagstones and beams plus much old stonework. Popular with cyclists, Route 72 of the National Cycle Network runs alongside and the pub operates a pick-up, drop-off luggage service. Opening hours and food service are liable to change in winter. An ale from a local brewery is always available. ✿⊷◐♣⊞⊟(683)♠

Old Hartley

Delaval Arms Ⓛ

NE26 4RL (jct of A193/B1325 S of Seaton Sluice)
✪ 12-11 summer; 12-2.30, 4.30-10.30; 12-11 Fri-Sun winter
☎ (0191) 237 0489 ⊕ thedelavalarms.wordpress.com
4 changing beers Ⓗ
Multi-roomed Grade II-listed building dating from 1748, with a listed WWI water storage tower (part of Roberts Battery) behind the beer garden. It is the first pub in Northumberland for those following the coastal route. Good-quality, affordable meals complement the beer, with guest ales coming from local micros. To the left as you enter there is a room served through a hatch from the bar and to the right a room where children are welcome. Q⊃✿◐⊞⊟(308,309)♣

Once Brewed

Twice Brewed Inn Ⓛ

Miltary Road, Bardon Mill, NE47 7AN
✪ 10-11 ☎ (01434) 344534 ⊕ twicebrewedinn.co.uk
Theakston Best Bitter; 5 changing beers Ⓗ
An excellent remote inn on the Military Road, with Hadrian's Wall nearby, popular with walkers and tourists. Following work at the end of 2015 it now has a fully refurbished bar area, 18 en-suite bedrooms and full disabled access. Theakston Best Bitter, sold as Twice Brewed Bitter, is the house beer, and a wide range of bottled beers from around the world is stocked. A well supplies the pub with water. The inn acts as a rural transport interchange. Q⊃✿⊷◐⅊⊠P⊞♣♠

Rennington

Horseshoes Inn Ⓛ

6 Rennington Village, NE66 3RS (turn off at Alnwick for B1340 and via Denwick for 3 miles)
✪ 12-3, 6.45-11; closed Mon ☎ (01665) 577665
Hadrian Border Farne Island Pale Ale; 1 changing beer Ⓗ
Superb traditional family-run village pub dating from 1841. The bar is warm and friendly without TV or jukebox and with a log fire and dry hops hanging over the serving area. A pleasant beer garden is at the front. The restaurant seats 50 and has an excellent reputation for good home-cooked food. The pub hosts a scarecrow competition every August bank holiday Saturday and is home to two darts teams. Q⊃✿◐⅊♣P⊟

Seahouses

Olde Ship Hotel Ⓛ

7-9 Main Street, NE68 7RD
✪ 11-11; 12-11 Sun ☎ (01665) 720200 ⊕ seahouses.co.uk
Black Sheep Best Bitter; Courage Directors; Hadrian Border Farne Island Pale Ale; Morland Old Speckled Hen; Ruddles County; Theakston Best Bitter; 2 changing beers Ⓗ
This 1745 farmhouse was converted to the licensed trade in 1812 and still has a regionally important historic pub interior. Family-owned since 1910, the pub has three quality bars adorned with a veritable treasure trove of 19th- and 20th-century maritime memorabilia. Fully residential, it offers an interesting menu of fish, fresh crab meals and snacks although, unusually, no chips are served. Q⊃✿⊷◐⅊♣P⊞⊟(501)

Seaton Sluice

Melton Constable

Beresford Road, NE26 4QL

☼ 12-11; 12-10.30 Sun ☎ (0191) 237 7741

⊕ themeltonconstable.co.uk

Caledonian Deuchars IPA; Wells Bombardier; Wychwood Hobgoblin; 3 changing beers Ⓗ

Large roadside pub a few minutes' walk from the beach and local history sights. It is named after the southern seat of Lord Hastings, a member of the Delaval family – Delaval Hall is close by. Tuesday is steak night, Wednesday is quiz night, Sunday evening features live music. The pub hosts a late-night fishing club and the BSA owners' club on the first and third Thursdays of the month.
⏰❀◑♿P🚐(308,309,X7)❀🛜

West Mickley

Blue Bell Inn ✅

17 Mount Pleasant, NE43 7LP

☼ 12-3, 6-11; 12-11.30 Sat; 12-10.30 Sun; closed Mon

☎ (01661) 843146

3 changing beers Ⓗ

Set in the hamlet of West Mickley, on a steep hill above Stocksfield, the Blue Bell is a terraced stone-built country local. Although opened out, it has retained the quite magnificent huge stone fireplace with coal fire in the bar area and highly visible blue star at night. There is also a lounge-dining area and a beer garden to the rear.
❀◑🚐(10)❀

Wylam

Boathouse Inn Ⓛ

Station Road, NE41 8HR

☼ 11-11; 11-midnight Sat; 12-10.30 Sun ☎ (01661) 853431

⊕ theboathousewylam.com

12 changing beers Ⓗ

Superb two-roomed pub with 15 handpulls, three dedicated to cider, with more ciders served from the cellar. Beers are sourced locally and nationwide, and on bank holidays themed beer festivals are held. Toasties and sandwiches are available during the day. The pub is a popular stopping-off point for Whistle Stops II travellers. Fifteen CAMRA awards cover one wall. Alternate Tuesdays are buskers' nights. Q⏰❀≋♣👜P❀🛜

Melton Constable, Seaton Sluice (Photo: Terry Whalebone/flickr)

NOTTINGHAMSHIRE

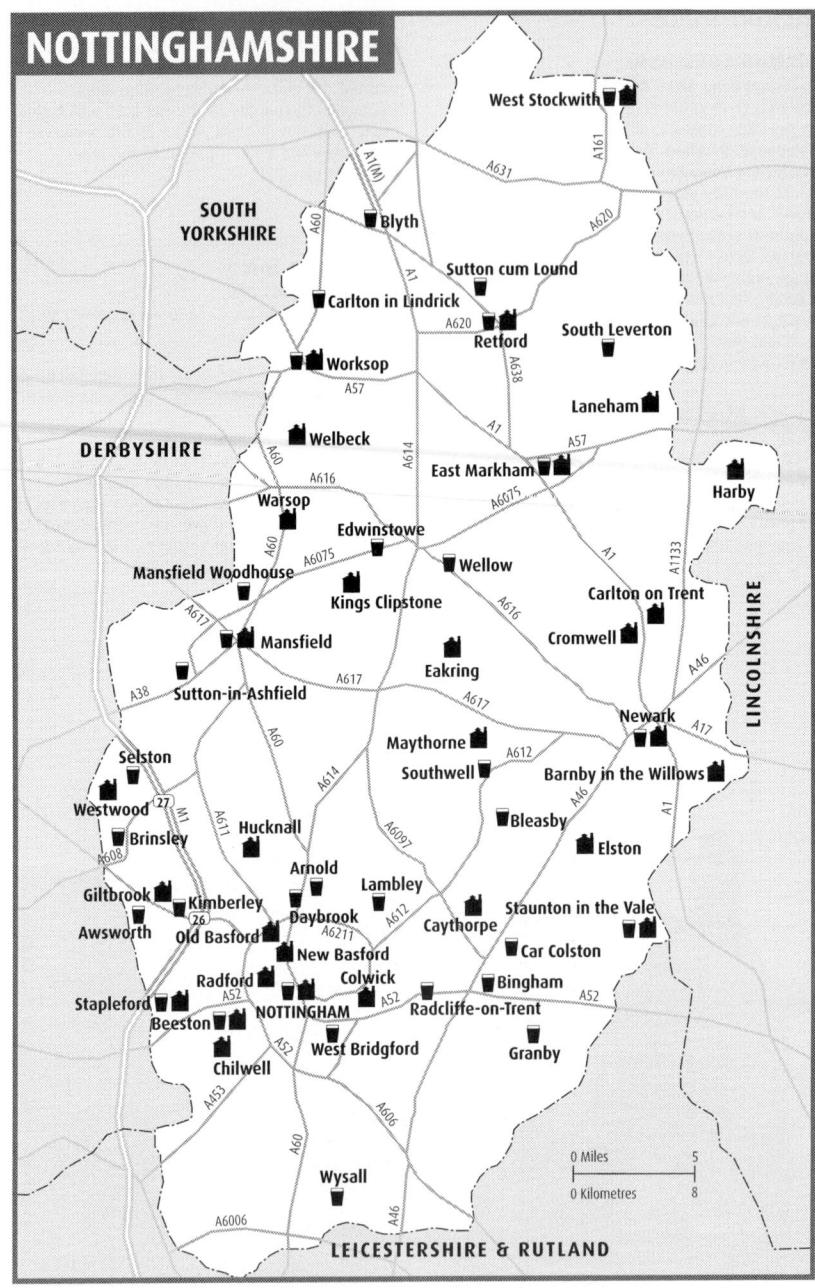

West Stockwith

Blyth

SOUTH YORKSHIRE

Sutton cum Lound

Carlton in Lindrick

Retford

South Leverton

Worksop

Laneham

Welbeck

DERBYSHIRE

East Markham

Harby

Warsop

Edwinstowe

Mansfield Woodhouse

Wellow

Carlton on Trent

Kings Clipstone

Cromwell

Mansfield

Eakring

Sutton-in-Ashfield

Newark

Selston

Maythorne

LINCOLNSHIRE

Westwood

Southwell

Barnby in the Willows

Brinsley

Hucknall

Bleasby

Giltbrook

Arnold

Elston

Kimberley

Lambley

Staunton in the Vale

Awsworth

Daybrook

Old Basford

Caythorpe

Car Colston

Radford

New Basford

Colwick

Bingham

Stapleford

NOTTINGHAM

Radcliffe-on-Trent

Beeston

West Bridgford

Granby

Chilwell

Wysall

0 Miles 5
0 Kilometres 8

LEICESTERSHIRE & RUTLAND

Arnold

Robin Hood & Little John L

1 Church Street, NG5 8FD (on corner of Cross St)
☼ 12-11 (midnight Fri & Sat); 12-10.30 Sun
☎ (0115) 920 1054 ⊕ therobinhoodandlittlejohn.co.uk
Everards Tiger Best Bitter; Lincoln Green Marion, Hood, Sherwood, Tuck; 5 changing beers (often Lincoln Green) ⊞
Two-room Project William refurbishment between Lincoln Green and Everards breweries. The bar features Home Ales memorabilia, while the lounge

has details of the pub's history and the local area. The rear courtyard has outdoor seating and leads to a covered skittle alley. As well as 10 real ale pumps offering microbrewery beers, a real cider wall features eight taps dispensing ciders from small local producers and further afield. National CAMRA Cider Pub of the Year 2015. Q☺♿♣🚆♟🐾♿

Awsworth

Gate Inn L

Main Street, NG16 2RN

❄ 12-midnight ☎ (0115) 932 9821
7 changing beers Ⓗ
Deemed to be unviable and sold by the pub's former owners, the Gate reopened in 2010 as a free house and quickly established itself as a quality real ale outlet. A truly welcoming and friendly local, this late-19th-century inn has a bar, lounge and rooftop terrace. Gradually being renovated throughout, the bar area has recently been refurbished. ♿♣Pꂤ☺

Beeston

Crown Inn ★ Ⓛ

Church Street, NG9 1FY
❄ 12-11.30; 12-11 Sun ☎ (0115) 967 8623
⊕ brownales.co.uk/crown-inn
Draught Bass; Everards Sunchaser Blonde, Tiger Best Bitter; Nottingham Rock Ale Mild Beer; house beer (by Ashover); 8 changing beers Ⓗ
Nineteenth-century Grade II-listed alehouse, acquired and sympathetically refurbished by Everards. Up to 14 ales and several real ciders and perries are served at this former East Midlands CAMRA Pub of the Year. Five distinct drinking areas include a snug and three-seat 'confessional', once used as a hideaway by the local vicar. Although busy, the pub retains a community feel, with a cosy atmosphere throughout. The beer garden regularly hosts events. Substantial snacks are available.
Q❀♿♣ꂤ♠♠Pꂤ☺♿

Star Inn Ⓛ

22 Middle Street, NG9 1FX
❄ 12-11 (midnight Thu-Sat) ☎ (0115) 854 5320
⊕ starbeeston.co.uk
10 changing beers (often Caledonian, Nottingham, Theakston) Ⓗ
Former Shipstone's pub still with the branded windows, restored beyond its former glory. The decor is tasteful and minimal with three separate rooms, complemented by a permanent marquee, sports/games room, spacious garden and patio outside. Visitors may recognise the bar, which featured in Auf Wiedersehen, Pet and Boon. Ten cask ales are on offer alongside a wide selection of whiskies and wines. Meals are served as well as a popular and extensive range of bar snacks. Families are welcome during the day.
Q☕❀▦◖❶♿♣ꂤ♣Pꂤ☺♿

Victoria Hotel Ⓛ

85 Dovecote Lane, NG9 1JG
❄ 10.30-11 (midnight Fri & Sat); 12-11 Sun
☎ (0115) 925 4049 ⊕ victoriabeeston.co.uk
Castle Rock Harvest Pale; Everards Tiger Best Bitter; Timothy Taylor Landlord; 13 changing beers (often Holden's) Ⓗ
Located alongside the platform of Beeston railway station, this restored Victorian masterpiece has mass appeal. Sixteen real ales are joined by real ciders and perries, an extensive whisky and wine list, and a renowned food menu. Taster trays of three third-pints are offered. Two distinct bars are complemented by a dining room and a covered, smoke-free seating area outside. VicFest is hosted in July in addition to beer festivals throughout the year. CAMRA and NUS discounts are available Sunday-Thursday. Q❀◖❶♿♣ꂤ♠Pꂤ☺♿

Bingham

Horse & Plough Ⓛ

Long Acre, NG13 8AF
❄ 11-11 (midnight Fri & Sat) ☎ (01949) 839313
Brains Rev James; Castle Rock Harvest Pale; Wells Bombardier; 7 changing beers Ⓗ
Situated in the heart of a busy market town, this small pub is a former Methodist chapel with a cottage-style interior and flagstone floor. Up to nine cask ales and three ciders are served. Food is available in both the bar and first-floor à la carte restaurant, which offers a varied seasonal menu. Three times local CAMRA Pub of the Year, the pub is a focus for cask ale in Bingham and a recent increase in the range of ales and ciders on offer has enhanced its appeal further. ☎◖❶♿♣♠ꂤ☺♿

White Lion

Nottingham Road, NG13 8AT
❄ 11-11; 11.30-11 Sun ☎ (01949) 875541
Jennings Cumberland Ale; 3 changing beers Ⓗ
The White Lion is your typical local pub, with a loyal following of regulars. It serves up to four cask ales and the landlady involves drinkers in the choice of beers. Good-value meals are available lunchtimes and evenings. The pub is home to pool and darts teams and hosts a quiz night every Sunday. The bar houses a large screen showing all major games on

REAL ALE BREWERIES

Basin City ▤ Nottingham: Old Basford
Beeston Hop Beeston
Black Iris Nottingham: New Basford
Black Market ▤ Warsop (NEW)
Blue Monkey Giltbrook
Castle Rock Nottingham
Caythorpe ▤ Caythorpe
Double Top Worksop
Dukeries Worksop
Flipside Colwick
Full Mash Stapleford
Funfair ▤ Elston
Grafton Worksop
Hale's Worksop
Handley's ▤ Barnby in the Willows
Harby ▤ Harby (NEW)
Idle ▤ West Stockwith
Idle Valley Retford
Kings Clipstone Kings Clipstone
Langwith Mansfield (NEW)
Lenton Lane Nottingham
Lincoln Green Hucknall
Magpie Nottingham
Mallard Maythorne
Maypole Eakring
Milestone Cromwell
Naked Brewer ▤ Westwood
Navigation ▤ Nottingham
Newark Newark
Nottingham Nottingham: Radford
Pheasantry ▤ East Markham
Pickled Pig Staunton in the Vale (NEW)
Prior's Well Mansfield (NEW)
Reality Nottingham: Chilwell
Robin Hood Nottingham: New Basford
Scribbler's Stapleford
Springhead Laneham
Tom Herrick's Carlton on Trent
Totally Brewed Nottingham
Welbeck Abbey Welbeck
Wollaton Nottingham

Sky Sports. There is a large car park plus a decked area for outdoor drinking. Local CAMRA Pub of the Year 2014. ✿❶🕭&≠♣P🖵

Bleasby

Waggon & Horses 🅛
Gipsy Lane, NG14 7GG
✿ 12-2 (not Mon-Wed), 5-11; 12-midnight Sat; 12-11 Sun; closed Thu ☎ (01636) 830283
Blue Monkey BG Sips, Infinity; Sharp's Doom Bar; 3 changing beers (sourced locally; often Blue Monkey) Ⓗ
Thriving village free house overlooking the church and green, and not far from the River Trent. The pub offers six real ales and a cider, featuring award-winning Blue Monkey beers alongside others from micros. This is a true village inn with no gimmicks or electronic games, just good conversation. There is a conservatory to the rear and a small restaurant area (closed Mon-Wed). Walkers with muddy boots and dogs with muddy paws welcome. Q✿❶🕭Å≠♣P🖵🐾🛜

Blyth

Red Hart 🅛
Bawtry Road, S81 8HG (opp church)
✿ 2.30-11.30 Mon; 11.30-midnight ☎ (01909) 591221
⊕ redhart.co.uk
Sharp's Doom Bar; 3 changing beers Ⓗ
An attractive village pub in the centre of Blyth with a reasonably large lounge, traditional taproom and an attractive dining room. The walls in the lounge are decorated with photographs and paintings from nearby locations. Food is served daily in both the lounge and dining room. An annual beer festival is held in May.
Q🐾✿❶🛏❶&♣P🖵(25,29)🐾🛜

Brinsley

White Lion
Hall Lane, NG16 5AH
✿ 4-11; 3-midnight Fri; 1-midnight Sat; 12-11 Sun
☎ (01773) 714328 ⊕ thewhitelion-brinsley.co.uk
Sharp's Doom Bar; 1 changing beer (often Blue Monkey) Ⓗ
An open-plan pub with a large car park to the rear, beer garden and family play area. Two ales are available, one a rotating guest from Blue Monkey, plus a locally produced traditional cider. There is a pool table and dartboard, and TVs show sport or music channels. The walls are adorned with plenty of memorabilia celebrating the achievements of local football teams. 🐾✿❶♣❶P🖵🛜

Car Colston

Royal Oak ✔
The Green, NG13 8JE
✿ 11.30-3, 5.30-11; 11.30-11 Fri & Sat; 12-10.30 Sun
☎ (01949) 20247
Marston's EPA, Burton Bitter; Ringwood Best Bitter; 1 changing beer Ⓗ
This impressive country inn is situated on one of England's largest village greens. The two-room interior includes a lounge and restaurant on one side and a cosy bar with comfortable seating on the other. The bar's vaulted brickwork ceiling is a legacy from the building's life as a hosiery factory. Good-quality, traditional food is served lunchtimes

and evenings. There is a skittle alley to the rear, a beer garden and camping facilities. The landlord maintains his 100 per cent record for entries in the Guide. ✿❶🕭&Å♣P🐾

Carlton in Lindrick

Grey Horses Inn 🅛 ✔
The Cross, S81 9EW (in centre of old village)
✿ 12-11; 11-11 Sun ☎ (01909) 730252
⊕ greyhorsesinn.com
Welbeck Abbey Red Feather; 4 changing beers Ⓗ
The Grey Horses is the brewery tap for Welbeck Brewery and is situated in the heart of the village within the conservation area. It has a front bar accessible from the street where locals gather to play cards and dominoes, and a large lounge bar area where meals are served. You can be sure of a warm welcome here.
Q🐾✿❶&♣❶P🖵(21,22)🐾🛜

Daybrook

Abdication 🅛
89 Mansfield Road, NG5 6BH (opp gates of former Home Brewery)
✿ 4-9.30; 2-6 Sun; closed Mon & Tue ⊕ theabdication.co.uk
4 changing beers Ⓗ
Built in 1936/37, this micropub is part of the Home Brewery Coronation Buildings opposite the former brewery, and was a shop for many years. Four ever-changing beers and two ciders are sourced from microbreweries or small producers, and come in a mix of styles. The pub has a relaxed and friendly atmosphere – an archway divides the single room, giving the appearance of a much larger space. Participants in the monthly quiz are grouped into teams by raffle. Q&♣❶P🖵🐾

East Markham

Queen's Hotel
High Street, NG22 0RE
✿ 12 (2 Mon)-11 ☎ (01777) 870288
Adnams Southwold Bitter; Everards Sunchaser Blonde, Tiger Best Bitter; 2 changing beers (sourced nationally) Ⓗ
The Queen's has recently been refurbished inside with new decor and furniture, and the outside repainted. Situated on the village main street, the cosy pub has a friendly atmosphere. A single bar serves the lounge and dining area, warmed by an open fire in winter. Food ranges from hot and cold snacks to full home-cooked meals. There is a large garden area at the rear where you can enjoy a drink on a warm summer's day.
Q🐾✿❶&❶P🖵(36,37)🐾

Edwinstowe

Forest Lodge ✔
2-4 Church Street, NG21 9QA
✿ 11.30-3, 5.30 (5 Fri)-11; 12-3, 6-10.30 Sun
☎ (01623) 824443
Wells Bombardier; house beer (by Welbeck Abbey); 3 changing beers Ⓗ
Owned and run by the same family for the past 11 years, this 18th-century coaching inn is situated in the heart of Sherwood Forest. A free house, it offers a range of ever-changing guest beers and a house beer from Welbeck Abbey. The high-class restaurant serves a wide choice of daily specials,

and is proud to use local produce wherever possible. Private functions can be catered for. Accommodation is 4-star AA rated.
Q 🕏 🏶 🖐 🕦 P 🖵 (14,15,SA) 📶

Granby

Marquis of Granby
Dragon Street, NG13 9PN
🕏 4-11 (midnight Fri); 12-midnight Sat; 12-11 Sun
☎ (01949) 859517
Brewster's Hophead, Marquis; 4 changing beers Ⓗ
Believed to be the original Marquis of Granby, dating back to 1760 or earlier, this small two-roomed pub is now the brewery tap for Brewster's and four to six cask ales are available. York stone floors complement the yew bar tops and wood-beamed rooms, period wallpaper features throughout and the lounge has a welcoming open fire in winter months. Guest beers served alongside the Brewster's range usually come from micros, and include a mild, stout or porter. Local CAMRA branch Pub of the Year 2015.
Q 🕏 🏶 🕭 🌢 P 🖵 🐾 📶

Kimberley

Stag Inn Ⓛ ✔
67 Nottingham Road, NG16 2NE
🕏 5 (1.30 Sat)-11; 12-10.30 Sun ☎ (0115) 938 3151
🌐 stagkimberley.co.uk
Adnams Southwold Bitter; Timothy Taylor Landlord; 3 changing beers Ⓗ
This wattle and daub Tudor-style house dates from 1737 and is near the town centre. Inside, two rooms are linked by a central bar, with an eclectic mix of seating including wooden settles. Table skittles and dominoes are played, but at most times conversation reigns. The spacious rear garden includes a children's play area and ample seating. A beer festival is held in early summer. The guest beers always include a local brew.
Q 🕏 🏶 🕭 🌢 P 🖵 🐾

White Lion 🍸 Ⓛ ✔
74 Swingate, NG16 2PQ
🕏 4 (2 Fri)-11.30; 12-11.30 Sat & Sun ☎ (0115) 938 3193
🌐 whitelionswingate.co.uk
Sharp's Doom Bar Ⓗ**; 10 changing beers (often Blue Monkey, Castle Rock)** Ⓗ/Ⓖ
Popular two-roomed free house in a residential area, acquired in 2013 and refurbished with a modern decor. Seven cask beers, mainly from local microbreweries, are served via handpump from the central bar. A further selection may be available from a stillage bar adjoining the large rear garden, which is accessed by a central corridor or directly from the car park. Sandwiches are provided on request. Local CAMRA Pub of the Year 2016. Q 🕏 🏶 🕭 🌢 P 🖵 🐾 📶

Lambley

Woodlark Inn Ⓛ
Church Street, NG4 4QB
🕏 12-midnight ☎ (0115) 931 2535 🌐 woodlarkinn.co.uk
Castle Rock Harvest Pale; Samuel Smith Old Brewery Bitter; Timothy Taylor Landlord; 1 changing beer Ⓗ
Tucked away on the edge of the village just past the church, this delightful red-brick local is a quiet, homely pub free of electronic machines, making the art of conversation a delight. A roaring coal fire

greets you on cold winter nights. The bare-brick and beamed bar is welcoming and dog-friendly while the comfortable lounge has a justifiable reputation for home cooking (booking is recommended, even at lunchtime).
Q 🕏 🏶 🕦 🌢 🌢 P 🖵 🐾

Mansfield

Beer Shack
46 White Hart Street, NG18 1DG
🕏 12-10 (10.30 Fri & Sat); closed Sun & Mon ☎ 07810 120805
5 changing beers Ⓗ
Micropub with a single room downstairs that has a full-length bar and two further small rooms upstairs with additional seating. Five handpulled beers and five real ciders are usually available alongside wine, spirits, soft drinks and bar snacks. Well-behaved dogs on leads are welcome. There are no TVs or gambling machines but live music is offered at least once a month. CAMRA branch Cider Pub of the Year 2015. Q 🗟 🌢 🌢 🕭 🖵 🐾

Bold Forester ✔
Botany Avenue, NG18 5NF
🕏 11-11.30 (12.30am Fri & Sat); 12-11.30 Sun
☎ (01623) 623970
Greene King IPA, Abbot; Hardys & Hansons Olde Trip; Morland Old Speckled Hen; 6 changing beers Ⓗ
Hungry Horse-branded split-level pub and restaurant. Up to 12 real ales are available, usually including six from Greene King and up to six guests. Food is served all day until 9pm. The spacious open-plan interior has large-screen TVs showing all major live sport. There is a covered smoking area outside with a TV. The enclosed beer garden is popular with families in the summer months.
🕏 🏶 🕦 🕭 🌢 P 🖵 📶

Brown Cow
31 Ratcliffe Gate, NG18 2JA
🕏 12-11 (midnight Fri & Sat) ☎ (01623) 645854
Everards Tiger Best Bitter; 9 changing beers (often Raw) Ⓗ
Tasteful refurbishment of a former run-down pub by the owners, Everards Brewery, and operated by Raw Brewery under the award-winning Project William scheme. It has two bar areas and a function room upstairs. A range of up to 12 real ales is offered as well a selection of world bottled beers and real ciders. Car parking is available to the side of the building. Q 🕏 🏶 🗟 🌢 P 🖵 🐾 📶

Olde White Lion Ⓛ
White Lion Yard, NG18 1AF (off Church St)
🕏 11-11 ☎ 07449 922821
8 changing beers Ⓖ
Situated in a natural cave in the White Lion Yard development, this venue currently has a real ale and real cider bar in the main cave area with another bar upstairs serving lager and selected spirits. Up to eight real ales are available, all served on gravity dispense. There is a DJ at weekends in a separate cave. Children and dogs are welcome. Because of its setting it can be cool in the evenings. 🕏 🗟 🌢 🖵 🐾 📶

Railway Inn 🍸 Ⓛ
9 Station Street, NG18 1EF
🕏 11-11 ☎ (01623) 623086
4 changing beers Ⓗ

A true community pub close to both the railway and bus stations with a main bar and two quiet rooms popular with diners. Four constantly changing real ales are available, at least one a local ale, and real cider and bottled beer are also on offer. Home-cooked food is served all day at reasonable prices. Music nights are held once a month. Outside there is a small walled garden and smoking area. CAMRA branch Pub of the Year 2015 and 2016. Q🕭🕏🌑🕏🍴🗨🏮😺🛜

Talbot Inn ✅
Nottingham Road, NG18 4AE
🌑 11-11.30 (12.30am Thu-Sat); 12-11.30 Sun
☎ (01623) 623357
Castle Rock Harvest Pale; house beer (by Nottingham); 4 changing beers (often Double Top) ⓗ
Refurbished in 2015 and reopened as part of Golden Oak Inns, this pub now offers six handpulled beers from local and national breweries. Food is available every day. Quiz nights are held on Sunday and Monday and live music every Thursday. There is a beer garden to the rear. Children are welcome up to 9pm; dogs must remain outside. 🕭🌑🕏P🏮🛜

Mansfield Woodhouse
Greyhound Inn
82 High Street, NG19 8BD
🌑 12-11 (midnight Fri & Sat); 12-10.30 Sun
☎ (01623) 464403
Adnams Broadside; Caledonian Deuchars IPA; 3 changing beers ⓗ
This two-room pub has been in the Guide for an impressive 22 out of the last 23 years. Owned by the same licensee for 32 years, the focus is on traditional ales – there is no food, just bar snacks. Weekly activities include open the box, play your cards right, a quiz night and card bingo. Dogs are welcome in the taproom. Pool, darts and dominoes are played in the public bar. The beer garden is to the side. 🌑🕏🕭🍴P🏮😺

Newark
Flying Circus ⓛ
53 Castle Gate, NG24 1BE
🌑 12-11 (midnight Fri-Sun) ☎ (01636) 302444
⊕ flyingcircuspub.com
4 changing beers (often Newark) ⓗ
Reopened in its present incarnation in 2014, the pub walls are decorated with Monty Python quotes and brewery logos, and old aircraft are suspended from the ceiling. A wide range of keg, bottled and canned beers, real cider and perries are available, complementing the four changing cask ales. More beers may be available during special events, including some served by gravity from the Barrel House to the rear of the building.
🌑🕏(Castle)🍴🏮🛜

Just Beer Micropub 🍺 ⓛ
32A Castle Gate, NG24 1BG (in Swan & Salmon Yard)
🌑 1-11; 12-midnight Fri & Sat; 12-10 Sun ☎ (01636) 312047
⊕ justbeermicropub.biz
4 changing beers ⓗ
Micropub concentrating on cask ales, cider and perries. In February 2016 the milestone of 3,000 different beers from 1,000 different breweries was reached. World and unusual UK ales are available from the well-stocked fridge. Food includes locally sourced pork pies, cheeseboards and pork scratchings. Traditional pub games are played, with an annual cribbage tournament contested by regulars. Three beer festivals are held annually. A regular local CAMRA Pub of the Year winner. Q🕭🖑🕏(Castle)🕏🍴🗨🏮😺

Organ Grinder
21 Portland Street, NG24 4XF
🌑 12-11 (midnight Fri & Sat); 12-10.30 Sun
☎ (01636) 671768
Blue Monkey Chimp Chim-in-nee, BG Sips, Sanctuary, Infinity; 3 changing beers (often Blue Monkey) ⓗ
Reopened in 2014 by the Blue Monkey Brewery, this was previously known as the Horse & Gears. A no-nonsense beer-drinking pub, it offers seven real ales from Blue Monkey alongside a range of bottled beers. Bar snacks are available. The Monkey Room is adorned with film and music posters featuring monkey and ape references. An under-cover smoking area is to the rear.
🕏🕭🏮😺🛜

Oscar's Inn
105 Balderton Gate, NG24 1RY
🌑 12-11 (midnight Fri & Sat) ☎ (01636) 918130
5 changing beers (often Thornbridge) ⓗ
Refurbished two-room pub situated close to the town centre, named after the owner's dog. The Oscar Wilde room is open at all times, displaying quotes from the great man, the Oscar Peterson room opens at busier times and hosts live music at the weekend. A lunchtime menu is available but the kitchen specialises in 16-inch pizzas. The house beer, Oscar's Ale, is from the Marston's group.
🌑🕏P🏮(2,3)😺🛜

Prince Rupert ⓛ
46 Stodman Street, NG24 1AW
🌑 11-11 (midnight Wed & Thu; 1am Fri & Sat); 12-11 Sun
☎ (01636) 918121
Brains Rev James; Oakham JHB; 4 changing beers ⓗ
Reopened in 2010, this historic pub dates back to 1452. Multi-roomed on two separate levels, exposed beams are evident and various interesting artefacts and brewery memorabilia decorate the walls and ceilings. The Nelson room has an open fire. An extensive lunchtime and evening food menu is available, with pizzas a speciality. Regular food and drink offers are available throughout the year. Former local CAMRA Pub of the Year.
Q🕭🌑🕏🕏(Castle)🍴🏮😺🛜

Vaults Cider & Ale House
14 North Gate, NG24 1EZ (adjacent to Newark Locksmiths)
🌑 12-3, 5-11 (midnight Thu); 12-midnight Fri & Sat; 12-10 Sun ☎ (01636) 678953 ⊕ thevaultsnewark.co.uk
4 changing beers ⓗ
Situated in one of the historic cellars on Newark's Northgate, the Vaults boasts eight handpumps offering ever-changing cask ales, ciders and perries, with further cider and perry available direct from the box and limited specialist ales in bottles and cans from the fridge. Extensive lunchtime and evening food menus feature local ingredients. Voted local CAMRA Cider Pub of the Year in 2016.
🕏🕏(Northgate)🍴🗨🏮😺🛜

Nottingham: Central
Annie's Burger Shack
5 Broadway, Lace Market, NG1 1PR

✪ 12-11 (midnight Fri & Sat) ☎ (0115) 924 2442
⊕ anniesburgershack.com
10 changing beers ⊞
This 'shack' is a large open and airy building, with a rustic decor throughout, situated in the Lace Market area of Nottingham. It is an authentic slice of Americana, and offers over 30 different burgers. The ground floor restaurant has 10 handpumps dispensing a changing selection of real ales, mainly from microbreweries. Drinkers can sit at the bar but not at the dining tables. The basement bar, Ocean State Tavern, is open from 5pm weekdays and noon at weekends. ☎✪🍴&♿🚲♥🐾🚍

Canalhouse 🅛

48-52 Canal Street, NG1 7EH
✪ 11-11 (midnight Thu); 11-1am Fri & Sat; 11-10.30 Sun
☎ (0115) 955 5060 ⊕ thecanalhouse.co.uk
Castle Rock Harvest Pale; 5 changing beers (often Castle Rock) ⊞
A modern Waterways warehouse conversion. The canal to the rear runs inside the building, where up to two narrowboats are moored. A good selection of real ales, real ciders and perries is complemented by quality world beers both on tap and in bottles. The pub hosts the Champion Beer of Nottinghamshire competition in the first-floor function room in February. Outside is a spacious glass-covered patio overlooking the canal, which is popular on sunny summer days.
✪🍴&♿🚲♥P🚍🐾🚍

Crafty Crow 🅛

102 Friar Lane, NG1 6EB
✪ 12-11; 11-midnight Fri & Sat ☎ (0115) 837 1992
⊕ craftycrownotts.co.uk
10 changing beers (often Magpie) ⊞
This is Magpie Brewery's first pub and has 10 handpulls serving microbrewery beers and a good variety of real ciders. Maintaining a green ethos throughout, the majority of fittings are recycled or home-made – the sinks are made from beer casks with ex-keg fonts as taps. Snacks and light meals are served until 9pm made from locally sourced produce. Situated on two levels, a side entrance leads directly to all facilities. Corvid birds feature strongly. 🍴&♿🚍🐾🚍

Falcon Inn 🅛

1 Alfreton Road, NG7 3JE
✪ 5-11; 12-midnight Fri & Sat; 12-10.30 Sun
☎ (0115) 970 4009 ⊕ thefalconinn.co.uk
8 changing beers ⊞
Established in 1853, this prominently positioned pub in the centre of Canning Circus was acquired and extensively refurbished in 2013. It has two small rooms, with a function room/restaurant area upstairs. Eight handpumps offer a selection of mainly local ales, always including a dark beer, and one real cider. Meals are served on Fridays and Sundays only, although large parties can be catered for at other times by prior arrangement, otherwise bar snacks are available. Q✪🍴♣♥🚍🐾

Hand & Heart 🅛

65 Derby Road, NG1 5BA
✪ 12-11 (midnight Fri & Sat); 12-10.30 Sun
☎ (0115) 958 2456 ⊕ thehandandheart.co.uk
Maypole Little Weed; 7 changing beers (sourced locally; often Dancing Duck) ⊞
The modern frontage and bar area hide the age of this pub – there are sandstone caves to the rear used as a dining space. A high-quality menu of

both food and beer is offered, with eight (mostly local) beers, together with three real ciders or perries. Upstairs is a separate room and bar available for functions, along with a partially covered terrace overlooking the street. Live music features (Sun & Thu). ☎✪🍴♥🚍🐾🚍

Kean's Head 🅛

46 St Mary's Gate, Lace Market, NG1 1QA
✪ 12-11 (midnight Fri & Sat); 12-10.30 Sun
☎ (0115) 947 4052
Castle Rock Harvest Pale; 5 changing beers (often Castle Rock) ⊞
Cosy one-room pub opposite the imposing St Mary's Church in the historic Lace Market district – the building was once a lace factory. Named in honour of the 19th-century actor Edmund Kean, it is popular with a diverse clientele. Owned by Castle Rock, it serves inventive, freshly prepared traditional English and European food from an ever-changing menu. The three guest beers usually include a dark brew. 🍴&♿🚲♥🚍🐾🚍

King William IV 🅛

6 Eyre Street, Sneinton, NG2 4PB
✪ 12 (2 Mon)-11; 12-midnight Thu & Fri; 11-midnight Sat
☎ (0115) 958 9864
Oakham Citra, Bishops Farewell; 5 changing beers ⊞
Nicknamed the King Billy, this cosy Victorian gem nestling on the edge of town is just a stone's throw from the Arena. A family-run free house that oozes charm and character, it is a haven for real ale drinkers, with a choice of seven microbrewery ales from near and far as well as real cider. Occasional live music and televised sport feature. A fine selection of rolls is available. The new pub sign won a national award in 2015. Q✪♣♥🚍🐾🚍

Lincolnshire Poacher 🅛

161-163 Mansfield Road, NG1 3FR
✪ 11-11 (midnight Thu & Fri); 10-midnight Sat; 12-11 Sun
☎ (0115) 941 1584
Castle Rock Harvest Pale, Elsie Mo, Screech Owl; Everards Tiger Best Bitter; 9 changing beers ⊞
Thirteen handpumps offer a wide selection of guest ales, mainly from microbreweries. A mild, stout or porter is always available alongside real ciders and perries, continental bottled beers and a selection of whiskies. Good food features locally sourced ingredients. The walls display artwork celebrating the pub's twinning with In de Wildeman bar in Amsterdam, and various memorabilia of local and international interest. Live music plays on Sundays and Wednesdays. Q✪🍴&♿♣♥🚍🐾🚍

Newshouse 🅛

123 Canal Street, NG1 7HB
✪ 12-11 (midnight Fri & Sat) ☎ (0115) 952 3061
Castle Rock Harvest Pale; Caythorpe Dark Gem; Totally Brewed Papa Jangle's Voodoo Stout, Punch in the Face; 2 changing beers (sourced locally) ⊞
In times past, newspapers would be read out here to inform the illiterate of elections at home and military victories overseas, hence the name. The walls are covered with framed front pages of local newspapers showing headlines stretching back over many years. The public bar has a large TV screen, dartboard, bar billiards and table skittles. The lounge has more comfortable seating. Light lunches are served and snacks at all times. As the brewery tap, beers from the local Totally Brewed Brewery are usually available. ☎✪🍴&♿🚲♣♥🚍🐾🚍

Olde Trip to Jerusalem ★ 🛅 ✅

Brewhouse Yard, NG1 6AD

✪ 11-11 (midnight Fri & Sat) ☎ (0115) 947 3171
⊕ triptojerusalem.com

Greene King IPA; Nottingham Extra Pale Ale; 6 changing beers (often Nottingham) ℍ

Famous pub at the bottom of Castle Road, built into the rock beneath Nottingham Castle. Several rooms on the ground and first floor are open to the public. The Cursed Galleon in the upstairs rock lounge is reputed to have claimed the lives of those who tried to clean it. Play ring the bull at quieter times in the front bar. Beer festivals are held in the enclosed courtyard. A cobblestone area outside is popular on warmer days. Q❀☺◑≠♣⊞❀♿☂

Organ Grinder 🛅

21 Alfreton Road, Canning Circus, NG7 3JE

✪ 12-11 (11.30 Thu; midnight Fri & Sat) ☎ (0115) 970 0630

Blue Monkey BG Sips, 99 Red Baboons, Infinity, Guerrilla; Sharp's Doom Bar; 2 changing beers (sourced locally; often Blue Monkey) ℍ

Previously the Red Lion, this inn was bought and refurbished by Blue Monkey Brewery. The single-room, multi-level pub boasts a wood-burning fire. To the rear is a small courtyard leading to a raised decked area and first-floor function room (where a TV is occasionally in use). The full Blue Monkey range of beers is offered, as well as three real ciders or perries. No meals, but bar snacks such as Scotch eggs and pork pies are sold. ♿☺♣♥⊞♿☂

Sir John Borlase Warren 🛅

1 Ilkeston Road, NG7 3GD

✪ 12-11 (midnight Fri & Sat); 12-10.30 Sun
☎ (0115) 988 1889

Everards Tiger Best Bitter; 11 changing beers ℍ

An Everards Project William pub with Lincoln Green, situated in the centre of Canning Circus. The furnishings are a comfortable mix of chairs and sofas. The lower bar area can be hired for private parties. Outside is a secluded, enclosed pub garden and a large roof patio – a quiet haven in the centre of a busy area. Beers are sourced from breweries country-wide. Bar snacks are available including pork pies. Q♿☺❀◑♣♥⊞♿☂

Vat & Fiddle 🛅

Queens Bridge Road, NG2 1NB

✪ 11-11 (midnight Fri & Sat) ☎ (0115) 985 0611

Castle Rock Sheriff's Tipple, Black Gold, Harvest Pale, Preservation Fine Ale, Elsie Mo, Screech Owl; 6 changing beers ℍ

Brewery tap for the adjacent Castle Rock Brewery, a minute's walk from the station. Twelve handpumps serve the Castle Rock range, with guests from local and new breweries completing the selection. The seated area to the front is the perfect spot to admire the Art Deco frontage and floral displays in summer. Hot food is served all week, with roasts on Sundays. Brewery tours operate Monday to Saturday (book ahead), and end in Golding's Room which opened in 2011. Q♿☺❀◑♿≠⊞♣♥⊞♿☂

Nottingham: East

Bread & Bitter 🛅

153-155 Woodthorpe Drive, Mapperley, NG3 5JL

✪ 10-11 (midnight Thu-Sat); 11-11 Sun ☎ (0115) 960 7541

Castle Rock Black Gold, Harvest Pale, Preservation Fine Ale, Elsie Mo, Screech Owl; Fuller's London Pride; 5 changing beers ℍ

Castle Rock pub converted in 2007 from the premises of the old Judge's Bakery on Mapperley Top. The original baker's oven fronts are still embedded in an inside wall, giving the place a warm and welcoming feel. The pub started a revival of real ale outlets in Mapperley. Twelve beers including a mild and rotating guests are available, along with an extensive foreign bottled beer list. Food is all home-cooked and changes frequently – look for the specials board. Q❀☺◑♿≠♥♿☂

Old Volunteer 🛅 ✅

35 Burton Road, NG4 3DQ

✪ 12-11 (midnight Fri & Sat) ☎ (0115) 987 2299
⊕ oldvolunteer.com

Flipside Sterling Pale, Flipping Best, Russian Rouble; 6 changing beers (often Flipside) ℍ

Refurbished by Flipside Brewery in spring 2014, the pub showcases five of its beers alongside several guests and real cider. The interior is separated into distinct areas by unusual wooden beams, with a raised corner and varied flooring. Outside a decked patio area with parasols, leading to the main entrance. Food choices include speciality burgers with wedges. Snacks are on offer at all times. Two beer festivals are held in a car park marquee annually. Q❀☺◑♿≠♥P♿♿☂

Willowbrook 🛅

13 Main Road, Gedling, NG4 3HQ

✪ 10-11 (midnight Fri); 9am-midnight Sat; 9am-11 Sun
☎ (0115) 987 8596

Castle Rock Sheriff's Tipple, Harvest Pale, Preservation Fine Ale, Elsie Mo, Screech Owl; 5 changing beers ℍ

Formerly a club, the building was refurbished in late 2013 and again in 2015 due to a fire. The 14 handpumps always offer a stout or porter as well as four real ciders and perries. A small side room and entrance lounge lead to the bar which opens to a rear room. Patio doors open onto a secluded smoke-free paved outdoor area. Diners can enjoy a good food menu complemented by daily specials. ♿☺◑♿♥⊞♿☂

Nottingham: North

Doctor's Orders 🛅

351 Mansfield Road, Carrington, NG5 2DA

✪ 5 (4 Fri)-10.30; 12.30-10.30 Sat & Sun ☎ (0115) 960 7985
⊕ doctorsordersmicropub.co.uk

5 changing beers (sourced locally) ℍ

Small beer emporium with two distinct areas, refurbished in 2015. A compact lounge leads to a corridor flanked on one side by a narrow seating area with benches, with a small bar-cum-serving area at the rear where you will find the handpumps. Beer and cider are brought to your table. While now owned by Magpie Brewery, the pub continues its original ethos of providing a range of microbrewery beers in an intimate atmosphere. Q♿♣♥⊟⊞♿☂

Nottingham: West

Johnson Arms 🛅 ✅

59 Abbey Street, Lenton, NG7 2NZ

🕒 12 (4 Sat)-midnight ☎ (0115) 978 6355
🌐 johnsonarms.co.uk
Adnams Southwold Bitter; Sharp's Doom Bar; 4 changing beers Ⓗ
Popular pub close to the University of Nottingham and QMC hospital. This former Shipstone's house retains the original etched windows and has a green-tiled frontage. Beers from local breweries complement the more well-known brands. Traditional home-cooked food includes JA burgers. Events include beer festivals, Johnsonbury and various sporting events on TV, and the pub supports local real ale trails. The beer garden, with a pétanque court, is not to be missed. Note that doors close at 11pm. Q🕮🌐◑▸♣🍴😺🐾🛜

Plough Inn ⒧

17 St Peter's Street, Radford, NG7 3EN
🕒 12-11 (midnight Thu-Sat) ☎ (0115) 970 2615
🌐 nottinghambrewerytaphouse.co.uk
Nottingham Rock Bitter, Rock Mild, Legend, Extra Pale Ale; 3 changing beers (often Nottingham) Ⓗ
Linked with the old Nottingham Brewery since 1887, the Plough is now the brewery tap for the revived company. A range of Nottingham beers is served, four regular and four rotating. The present building, a 1932 two-room house with a central servery, is largely unchanged. Attracting regulars from a wide area, this 'village pub in the city' has retained its local feel in a period of rapid change, offering real fires, a skittle alley and a popular quiz night. Q🕮🌐♣♣🍴P🍽😺🐾🛜

Radcliffe on Trent

Chestnut ⒧ ✅

Main Road, NG12 2BE
🕒 12-11 (11.30 Fri & Sat) ☎ (0115) 933 1994
🌐 horsechestnutradcliffe.com
Castle Rock Harvest Pale; Fuller's London Pride; St Austell Tribute; 4 changing beers (often Brewster's) Ⓗ
Well-regarded, cask beer-led village pub with a smart 1920s-style decor. Originally the Cliffe Inn, following a major refurbishment in 2006 it became the Horse Chestnut and in 2015 simply the Chestnut. Seven reasonably priced real ales are served including ever-changing guests, always including a beer from Brewster's. Quality home-made food, ranging from stone-baked pizzas to classic British dishes, is served in a relaxed, casual atmosphere. 🐾🕮◑♣≈P🍽😺🐾🛜

Retford

BeerHeadZ 🏆

3 Town Hall Yard, DN22 6DU (off Market Square to rear of 10 Green Bottles)
🕒 1 (11 Thu)-11; 11-midnight Fri & Sat; 12-10 Sun
☎ (01777) 949631 🌐 beerheadz.biz
5 changing beers Ⓗ
Friendly pub offering four rotating guest beers and two ciders. The beer is always in excellent condition and served in oversized glasses so you can be sure of a full pint. There are no fonts dispensing lagers and smooth flows. Q♣🍴🍽😺🛜

Brick & Tile Inn ⒧

81 Moorgate, DN22 6RR (above Morrisons garage)
🕒 1-4 (Sun only), 7-11 ☎ (01777) 703681
2 changing beers (sourced locally) Ⓗ

A quiet pub on the main road between Retford and Gainsborough. There is always a choice of two real ales here – one a light beer and the other dark, usually from local breweries Idle, Springhead and Milestone. A separate taproom has games and a TV. B&B is available in two twin and two single rooms. Q🐾🍴♣♣P🍽😺🐾🛜

Galway Arms

Bridgegate, DN22 7UZ
🕒 4 (11 Sat & Sun)-midnight ☎ (01777) 702446
Black Sheep Ale; Copper Dragon Golden Pippin; 1 changing beer Ⓗ
Close to the main Retford Market, this pub has a pleasant atmosphere and friendly service – a fine example of a typical olde-worlde English inn. The interior is divided into three separate areas with two bars – the public bar space has two large TVs showing all major sporting events. The lounge area is screen-free for a more peaceful pint. The quaint snug area has seating for up to 12 people. Live music plays on Fridays and Saturdays. 🐾😺♣P🍽😺🛜

Idle Valley Brewery Tap ⒧

Carolgate, DN22 6AS
🕒 11-11.30 (12.30am Thu-Sat) ☎ (01777) 948586
Idle Valley Jaded Pioneer, Torpid Expression, Indolent Philosopher; 4 changing beers (sourced regionally) Ⓗ
The Idle Valley Brewery tap is a great addition to Retford, providing drinkers with a wider choice of beers. The interior has been tastefully renovated and is now one large single room, with a pool table and dartboard at the far end. The owners are planning to add food to attract a wider clientele. 🐾≈♣🍴🍽

Selston

Horse & Jockey ⒧

Church Lane, NG16 6FB
🕒 12-3.30, 5-midnight; 12-4, 7-1am Sun ☎ (01773) 781012
Greene King Abbot; Timothy Taylor Landlord Ⓗ**; 4 changing beers** Ⓗ/Ⓖ
This rural pub dates from 1664 and features flagstone floors, real fires and plenty of wooden bench seating. Up to six real ales can be available, with two served directly from barrels resting on old stone lintels. A real cider or perry is also always kept. Look out for Selstock beer and music festival held in the car park in July. A winner of CAMRA local branch Pub of the Year in 2014. Q🐾😺♣♣🍴P🍽😺

South Leverton

Olde Plough Inn

Town Street, DN22 0BT (opp village hall)
🕒 5 (4 Sat)-midnight; 2-midnight Sun ☎ (01427) 880323
Draught Bass; 2 changing beers (sourced regionally) Ⓗ
You could drive through South Leverton and not see this pub opposite the village hall, but then you would miss out on a little gem. Some of the seating appears to be old church pews. This small, friendly local is a genuine, old-fashioned hostelry and well worth a visit – visitors are always made welcome. Alongside the Draught Bass there is a rotating guest beer. Q🐾😺♣▲♣P🍽😺🛜

Southwell

Final Whistle
Station Road, NG25 0ET
◑ 12-midnight ☎ (01636) 814953
Draught Bass; Everards Tiger Best Bitter; 6 changing beers (often Oakham) Ⓗ
Adjacent to the Southwell Trail, formerly an old railway line, this comfortable pub has a railway theme and features plenty of memorabilia. The garden is a mock station with a section of track. The bar has 10 handpumps serving two regular beers, six changing ales and two house beers from Ashover Brewery. Quiz nights are Tuesday and Sunday. Bar snacks are available and this is a popular stop-off for walkers and cyclists. Local CAMRA Pub of the Year 2015.
🚫❀&♣●🖛(28,100)✤

Stapleford

Horse & Jockey Ⓛ
20 Nottingham Road, NG9 8AA
◑ 12-11 (midnight Fri & Sat) ☎ (0115) 875 9655
⊕ horseandjockeystapleford.co.uk
Full Mash Horse & Jockey; 9 changing beers Ⓗ
Known locally as the Jockey, it was refurbished in 2012 and has become a real ale destination pub. A choice of 10 cask ales, including five LocAles, is offered, accompanied by local ciders and a range of whiskies. There are two rooms on split levels, each with a different feel. Pictures of local landmarks decorate the pub alongside water jugs for whisky. There is no music, TV (other than for major sporting events) or games machines. CAMRA national Pub of the Year finalist 2013. Q🚫⌂☎&●P🖛✤

Staunton in the Vale

Staunton Arms ☗ Ⓛ ✅
NG13 9PE
◑ 12-11; 11-midnight Fri & Sat; 11-10 Sun
☎ (01400) 281218 ⊕ stauntonarms.co.uk
Castle Rock Harvest Pale; Draught Bass; 1 changing beer Ⓗ
Two-hundred-year-old listed pub in the far north of the Vale of Belvoir, carefully restored to retain its original character. The large bar offers comfortable seating for drinkers and diners, with a further separate raised restaurant area. The venue serves freshly prepared meals lunchtimes and evenings and has built a reputation for good food. Three cask beers, one always a LocAle, are on the bar. Mini festivals are held regularly, with upcoming events publicised on the website. CAMRA branch Pub of the Year 2016. Q🚫❀&⌂◑●P🖛

Sutton cum Lound

Gate Inn
40 Town Street, DN22 8PT
◑ 12-11.30 ☎ (01777) 709408 ⊕ the-gate-inn.co.uk
6 changing beers Ⓗ
Now a country pub and restaurant, this village inn has been completely transformed following a massive refurbishment. It has an attractive rustic-style interior and a friendly, welcoming atmosphere. The beers are well kept and usually include a brew from Welbeck Abbey. Food quality is also excellent. An ideal starting or finishing place for walks around the local countryside.
🚫◑&P🖛✤♠

Sutton-in-Ashfield

Masons Arms
Unwin Road, NG17 4NB
◑ 12-11 ☎ (01623) 610421 ⊕ themasonsarmspub.co.uk
2 changing beers Ⓗ
A thriving community pub with a lounge and public bar served from a central bar dispensing two ever-changing local real ales and a real cider. Darts and dominoes are popular in the bar. A conservatory at the rear leads to the garden and smoking area. Mini beer festivals are held twice a year. On a local bus route. Q🚫❀♣●P🖛✤

Picture House ✅
Forest Street, NG17 1DA
◑ 8am-midnight; 8am-12.30am Sat & Sun
☎ (01623) 554627
Greene King Abbot; Ruddles Best Bitter; changing beers Ⓗ
A popular open-plan Wetherspoon pub near the bus station. Art Deco in style and with a high ceiling, it was originally built as the King's cinema in 1932. It has also been a bingo hall and the Picture House night club. Meals are available until 11pm every day. Sky Sports and BT Sport are shown on several TVs behind the bar, but the main attraction for sports fans is a huge screen projected onto the wall above the front door. Families are welcome. 🚫◑&●🖛✤

Scruffy Dog
Station Road, NG17 5HF
◑ 4-11 (11.30 Thu & Fri); 12-11.30 Sat; 12-10.30 Sun; closed Mon & Tue ☎ (01623) 550826 ⊕ thescruffydog.co.uk
Ringwood Fortyniner; 5 changing beers (often Abbeydale) Ⓗ
This community inn was purchased from a large pub company and refurbished to a high standard by the current owners. The main large open-plan area has a small L-shaped bar and there is a separate room with a real fire and comfy sofas. A free house, it offers up to six beers, often from Abbeydale Brewery, and two ciders. There is a large garden and, as the name suggests, dogs are welcome. Q🚫❀&●P🖛✤

Speed the Plough
Mansfield Road, NG17 4HG
◑ 12-11 (midnight Fri); 12-1am Sat ☎ 07821 331173
3 changing beers (often Falstaff, Lincoln Green) Ⓗ
Small community pub with an intimate enclosed beer garden to the rear. Up to three hand-pulled beers are available including at least one local brew. A popular range of home-made food, including minced beef and onion pies, quarter-pounder burgers and steaks, is available daily, with basket meals at the weekend. The pub gets busy for Saturday night karaoke. There is ample parking. Q🚫❀◑&♣●P🖛✤♠

Wellow

Olde Red Lion Ⓛ
Eakring Road, NG22 0EG (opp maypole)
◑ 12-11 ☎ (01623) 861000
Maypole Wellow Gold; Welbeck Abbey Red Feather; Wells Bombardier; 2 changing beers Ⓗ
This 400-year-old village pub is opposite the village green with its maypole, and participates in a large event on May Day. The traditional wood-beamed interior includes a restaurant, lounge and bar areas with photographs and maps depicting the history

of the village. Three real ales are available and food is good value. Close to both Sherwood Forest and Clumber Park. Q✿⌖☺◑▶P🖿🚃

West Bridgford

Poppy & Pint 🄻
Pierrepont Road, NG2 5DX
✪ 9.30am-11; 10-11 Sun ☎ (0115) 981 9995
Castle Rock Sheriff's Tipple, Black Gold, Harvest Pale, Preservation Fine Ale, Screech Owl; 7 changing beers Ⓗ
Former British Legion Club converted in 2011 to become a Castle Rock pub and café. It has a large main bar with a raised area and a family area with a café bar (children welcome until 9pm). A large upstairs function room features a folk club and the beer garden overlooks a bowling green. Twelve handpumps dispense Castle Rock beers plus guests, often from new breweries. There are usually two real ciders and excellent food is served.
✿☺◑🖐▶P🖿😺🖥

Stratford Haven 🄻
2 Stratford Road, NG2 6BA
✪ 11-11 (midnight Thu & Fri); 10-midnight Sat; 10-11 Sun
☎ (0115) 982 5981
Adnams Broadside; Batemans XB; Castle Rock Harvest Pale, Elsie Mo, Screech Owl; 5 changing beers Ⓗ
A former pet shop, the pub has a single narrow bar with a larger seating area at the back and a secluded snug to one side. Up to 12 cask ales plus a cider are available at any one time, including LocAles from owner Castle Rock's portfolio. A wide food selection includes curry night on Monday and pie night on Tuesday. Sunday is silent quiz night and new brew day is the first Thursday of the month. Q✿☺◑▶🖐♣▶🖿😺🖥

West Stockwith

White Hart 🄻
Main Street, DN10 4EY (opp church and car park)
✪ 11-11 ☎ (01427) 892672
Idle Golden Crown, Bodger, Dog, Black & Tan, Black Abbot, Landlord; 1 changing beer (sourced locally) Ⓗ
Small country pub with a little garden overlooking the River Trent, Chesterfield Canal and West Stockwith Marina. One bar serves the through bar, lounge and dining area. In 2014 a new dining room was added. The Idle Brewery is situated in outbuildings at the side of the pub and the range of five real ales usually includes three from Idle. The area is especially busy during the summer, due to the canal and river traffic.
✿☺◑🖐🅰♣▶P🖿(97)😺

Worksop

Mallard 🄻
Station Approach, S81 7AG (just off railway platform)
✪ 12 (5 Mon; 4.15 Tue)-11; 11.30-11 Fri; 11-11 Sat; 12-10.30 Sun ☎ 07973 521824

Double Top Shanghai Bitter, Adonis; 3 changing beers Ⓗ
Formerly the Worksop station buffet, the Mallard is situated within the railway station buildings, with access from the car park. The pub offers a warm welcome as well as four real ales, usually including one from the Double Top Brewery, a selection of foreign bottled beers and country fruit wines. A further room downstairs is used for special events including four beer festivals each year. Double Top Brewery tours are available by prior arrangement. Nottinghamshire CAMRA Pub of the Year 2015.
Q✿🚃≒♣▶P🖿😺

Station Hotel 🄻
Carlton Road, S80 1PS (opp railway station)
✪ 11-11; 12-11 Sun ☎ (01909) 474108
4 changing beers Ⓗ
Situated opposite Worksop railway station on the edge of the town centre, one long bar serves a large bar area and a separate dining room, and there is a further small room suitable for functions and meetings. Four regularly changing real ales are available. Food is served lunchtimes and evenings. A warm welcome is assured at the Station.
Q✿🚃◑≒♣▶P🖴🖿(5)😺🖥

Unicorn 🄻
37 Bridge Street, S80 1DA (opp Queen's Head)
✪ 10-11.30 (1am Sat); 12-11.30 Sun ☎ (01909) 537011
3 changing beers (sourced locally) Ⓗ
Town-centre pub offering up to three usually local hand-pulled ales and one real cider. Refurbished during the summer of 2013 in a traditional style, its comfortable surroundings attract a more mature clientele. Offering good customer service and value for money, a wide range of drinks is served.
🖐♣▶🖿😺

Wysall

Plough 🄻
Main Street, Keyworth Road, NG12 5QQ
✪ 12-midnight ☎ (01509) 880339
Draught Bass; Greene King Abbot; Timothy Taylor Landlord; 3 changing beers Ⓗ
A busy country pub dating back more than 150 years, and for the past 14 years owned by the same family. This pleasantly updated village free house retains many period features and much original character, with an attractive beer garden at the front. A sensibly priced menu of traditional home-cooked pub favourites is available at lunchtime. Dogs are welcome after 2.30pm when food service is finished. There is a separate area for pool, and a quiz is hosted on Tuesday.
Q✿◑♣P🖿(863)😺🖥

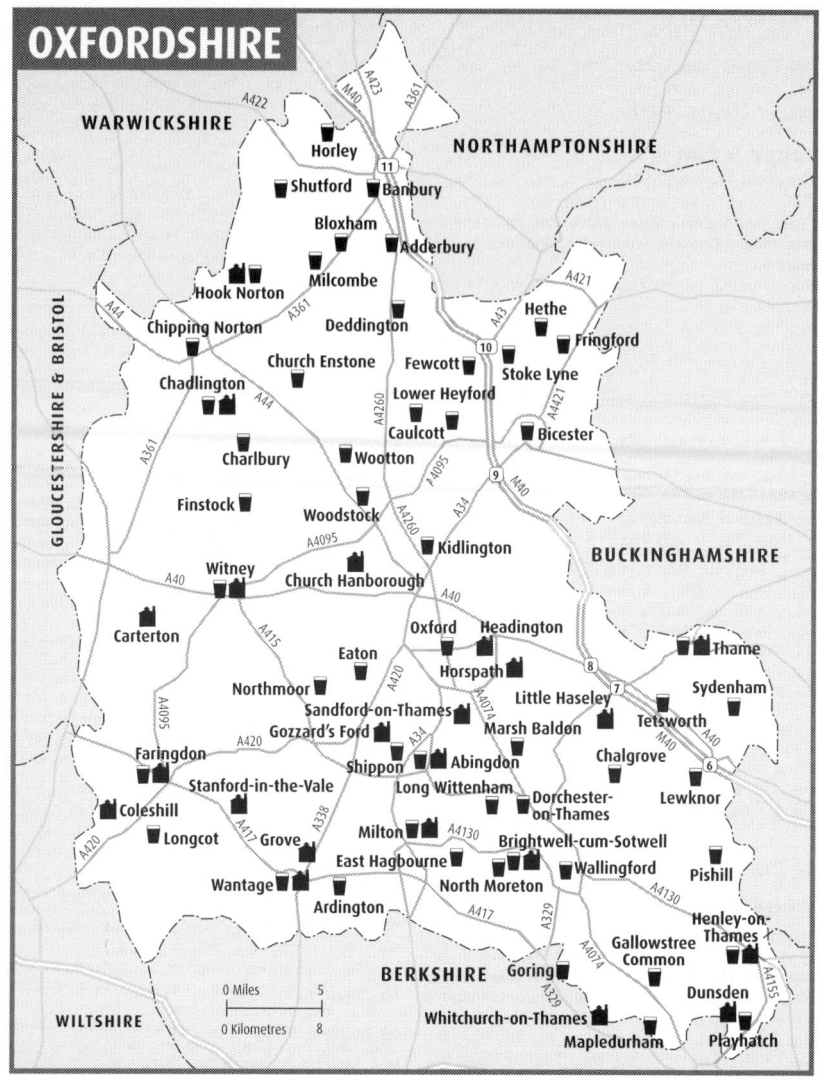

OXFORDSHIRE

WARWICKSHIRE

NORTHAMPTONSHIRE

Horley

Shutford

Banbury

Bloxham

Adderbury

Hook Norton

Milcombe

Chipping Norton

Deddington

Hethe

Fringford

Church Enstone

Fewcott

Stoke Lyne

Chadlington

Lower Heyford

Caulcott

Bicester

Charlbury

Wootton

Finstock

Woodstock

Kidlington

BUCKINGHAMSHIRE

Witney

Church Hanborough

Carterton

Oxford

Headington

Thame

Eaton

Horspath

Sydenham

Northmoor

Little Haseley

Tetsworth

Sandford-on-Thames

Marsh Baldon

Gozzard's Ford

Chalgrove

Faringdon

Shippon

Abingdon

Stanford-in-the-Vale

Long Wittenham

Dorchester-on-Thames

Lewknor

Coleshill

Longcot

Grove

Milton

East Hagbourne

Brightwell-cum-Sotwell

Wantage

North Moreton

Wallingford

Pishill

Ardington

Henley-on-Thames

Gallowstree Common

Dunsden

BERKSHIRE

Goring

WILTSHIRE

Whitchurch-on-Thames

Mapledurham

Playhatch

GLOUCESTERSHIRE & BRISTOL

0 Miles 5
0 Kilometres 8

Abingdon

Brewery Tap 🅛

40-42 Ock Street, OX14 5BZ
🕒 11-11.30 (1am Fri & Sat); 12-11 Sun ☎ (01235) 521655
⦿ thebrewerytap.net

Morland Original Bitter; 5 changing beers (sourced
nationally; often Loose Cannon) 🅗

Morland created a tap for its brewery in 1933 from
three Grade II-listed town houses. The brewery is
no more but the pub, run by the same family since
it openend, has thrived. It has always offered a
diverse beer choice and this is set to stay, with one
Loose Cannon beer among the range. The pub has
three rooms, two of them away from the bar, and
a courtyard outside. It is headquarters for the
Abingdon Traditional Morris Men and hosts three
beer festivals a year. A former local CAMRA Town &
Village Pub of the Year.
Q ☎ 🕸 🍴 🕪 ᴦ ♣ 🍴 P 🖛 🌸 🛜

Nag's Head on the Thames 🅛 ✅

The Bridge, OX14 3HX
🕒 12-10; 11-11 Sat & Sun ☎ (01235) 524516
⦿ thenagsheadonthethames.co.uk

Loddon Ferryman's Gold; Loose Cannon Abingdon
Bridge; Sharp's Doom Bar; house beer (by
Caledonian); 4 changing beers (sourced regionally;
often Plain, Springhead, Two Cocks) 🅗

Set on an island right on Abingdon Bridge, the pub
is split over two levels with a large garden area
next to the river and lovely views of the
countryside and the town's historic buildings. A
free house, it offers eight regularly changing beers,
mostly local, including the house beer Nag's Island
Ale (4.1 % ABV). Good food is available all day. Live
music plays at weekends and some weekdays.
Salter's Steamers cruises from Oxford pass by in
summer. Local CAMRA Town and Village Pub of the
Year 2014-2015. ☎ 🕪 🍴 P 🖛 🌸 🛜

Adderbury

Bell Inn 🄻 ✅
High Street, OX17 3LS (off A4260, nr church)
🕒 12-3, 6-11; 12-midnight Fri & Sat; 12-10.30 Sun
☎ (01295) 810338 ⊕ thebelladderbury.co.uk
Hook Norton Hooky Mild, Hooky, Lion, Old Hooky; 2 changing beers (often Hook Norton) 🄷
Four distinctive rooms are served by six handpumps dispensing a wide range of Hook Norton ales, and the food menu offers home-cooked dishes featuring locally sourced ingredients. A folk club meets monthly on the first Monday and Aunt Sally is played on Thursdays in summer. Two bedrooms are available for visitors wishing to explore this attractive ironstone village and its environs.
Q✿❀☸☕◐▲♣➡(S4,90,81)☘✿🌑

Coach & Horses ✅
The Green, OX17 3ND
🕒 12-2.30 (not Mon), 6-midnight; 12-1.30am Fri & Sat; 12-midnight Sun ☎ (01295) 810422
⊕ coachandhorsesadderbury.co.uk
Wadworth IPA, 6X, Swordfish 🄷
A new entry in the Guide, this early 18th-century Wadworth house was deservedly awarded Community Pub of the Year for 2014. Three handpumps dispense ales from the Wadworth portfolio. Set most favourably of the pubs in this attractive ironstone village, opposite the village green, it almost certainly offers the cheapest dishes locally, with mains from £3.50 and Sunday roast at £4. Aunt Sally, ladies' darts and pool are played and there is a seating area outside overlooking the village green.
Q✿❀◐▲♣P➡(S4,81,90)☘✿🌑

Ardington

Boar's Head 🄻
Church Street, OX12 8QA
🕒 11.30-3, 6-11 ☎ (01235) 835466 ⊕ tbhardington.co.uk
Fuller's London Pride 🄷; Loose Cannon Gunners Gold 🄷/🄶, Abingdon Bridge; 1 changing beer 🄷
The Boar's Head, owned by Lockinge Estates like most of Ardington and Lockinge, is an attractive timbered building set in a side road between Ardington House and the church. The pub was fully refurbished in 2012 and has been converted into one room, subdivided for diners. It is a place to try home-cooked, high-quality food or sample the excellent beer range. Q✿❀◐♿♣P☘✿🌑

Banbury

Exchange 🄻 ✅
49-50 High Street, OX16 5LA
🕒 8am-(1am Fri; 2am Sat) ☎ (01295) 259035
Ruddles Best Bitter; Sharp's Doom Bar; changing beers (sourced nationally) 🄷
One of two Wetherspoon bars in Banbury, it occupies an imposing split-level site in the former post office and telephone exchange close to Banbury Cross. The walls abound with old photos and pictures of the building and surrounding area. Unsurprisingly, it follows the usual Wetherspoon formula with several banks of handpumps offering a changing range of ales (usually including at least one local ale) in addition to the two regulars, real cider, and good value food. ❀◐♿≠●➡🌑

Three Pigeons
3 Southam Road, OX16 2ED
🕒 12-11 (midnight Fri & Sat) ☎ (01295) 275220
⊕ thethreepigeons.com
Purity Pure Gold; Sharp's Doom Bar; 2 changing beers (sourced nationally) 🄷
Beautiful 17th-century thatched coaching inn on the main road through Banbury, close to the town centre. Within recent years it was rescued from pubco neglect by new owners Paul and Tina, and underwent a major renovation to a high standard, reopening in 2012. Four handpumps adorn the bar, serving a selection of ales (two regulars and two changing). There is an interesting menu of high-quality food, and three luxury bedrooms make a good base for a relaxing break.
Q✿❀☸◐♿♣P☘✿🌑

White Horse 🄻
50-52 North Bar Street, OX16 0TH
🕒 2-10.30 Mon; 12-11 Tue-Thu; 12-midnight Fri & Sat; 12-10.30 Sun ☎ (01295) 277484
⊕ thewhitehorsebanbury.co.uk
Everards Tiger Best Bitter; Turpin Golden Citrus; 8 changing beers (sourced nationally; often Charnwood, Cornish Crown, Derby) 🄷
A warm and welcoming ale house, this imposing building is in the heart of Banbury. The White Horse features an extensive range of up to 10 ales and a couple of ciders on its large L-shaped bar. Home-made dishes based on locally sourced ingredients are freshly cooked to order. There is a courtyard area to the rear for alfresco drinking and dining. Regular events such as live music and a weekly pub quiz are organised. Q✿❀◐♿≠♣●➡🌑

Bicester

Bell ✅
84 Sheep Street, OX26 6LP
🕒 12-11 (midnight Thu; 1am Fri & Sat) ☎ (01869) 328893
Wychwood Hobgoblin; 2 changing beers (sourced nationally; often Hook Norton, Vale, XT) 🄷
Traditional 18th-century inn, with stone floors and wooden tables and chairs, standing close to the

REAL ALE BREWERIES
Adkin Wantage
Appleford Brightwell-cum-Sotwell
Barn Owl Gozzard's Ford (NEW)
Bell Street ▤ Henley-on-Thames
Bellinger's Grove
Brakspear Witney
Chadlington Chadlington (NEW)
Church Hanbrewery Church Hanborough (NEW)
Compass Carterton
Faringdon ▤ Faringdon
Hen House Whitchurch-on-Thames
Hook Norton Hook Norton
LAM Sandford-on-Thames
Loddon Dunsden
Loose Cannon Abingdon
LoveBeer Milton
Old Bog ▤ Headington
Old Forge ▤ Coleshill
Philsters Little Haseley (NEW)
Shotover Horspath
Thame ▤ Thame
Turpin Brewery Hook Norton
White Horse Stanford-in-the-Vale
Wychwood Witney

pedestrianised heart of Bicester. There are two rooms – the smaller is mainly used as a games room, the larger houses three handpumps serving a changing selection of beers, many from local breweries. Live music is a big draw at the Bell, with local bands playing every Friday night and most Saturdays. A quiz features every Monday. ⊛☖⇌♣⛁♔

Bloxham

Elephant & Castle ⓛ ✅
Humber Street, OX15 4LZ (off A361)
⏲ 10-3, 6 (5 Fri)-11; 10-11 Sat; 12-11 Sun
☎ (01295) 720383 ⊕ bloxhampub.co.uk
Hook Norton Hooky; 2 changing beers (sourced nationally; often Hook Norton) Ⓗ
Run by the Finch family for over 40 years, this 17th-century coaching inn appears to face the wrong way, as the the turnpike once ran through its carriage entrance and the car park. Inside, a warm welcome awaits, with log fires in each room. Historic features include an old bread oven. Two Hooky beers and one guest are served, plus eight or more ciders and perries. Home-made food is served at lunchtimes (not Sun) and occasional evenings. Live music plays monthly.
⊛⇌◖♣⛁♔(488,489)♛♔

Brightwell-cum-Sotwell

Red Lion ⓛ
Brightwell Street, OX10 0RT (off A4130)
⏲ 12-3, 6-11; 12-9 Sun ☎ (01491) 837373 ⊕ redlion.biz
Loddon Hoppit; West Berkshire Good Old Boy; 2 changing beers (sourced nationally) Ⓗ
A traditional half-timbered thatched inn, dating from the 16th century, with a comfortable bar featuring wood beams and exposed brick leading to a restaurant area to one side. Outside to the rear is a courtyard garden which is a suntrap in summer. The beers and ciders are usually from local breweries, and good-quality reasonably priced pub food is served (no food Mon and Sun eve). Jazz evenings and charity quiz nights are held monthly. A popular pub in a quiet village. Local CAMRA Cider Pub of the Year 2016. ⛳⊛◖☖♣⛁♔(131,X2)♛♔

Caulcott

Horse & Groom ♛
Lower Heyford Road, OX25 4ND
⏲ 12-3, 6-11; 12-3, 7-10.30 Sun; closed Mon
☎ (01869) 343257 ⊕ horseandgroomcaulcott.co.uk
Black Sheep Best Bitter; 3 changing beers (sourced nationally; often Tring, Vale) Ⓗ
An 18th-century thatched stone building, this is a small pub with a big welcome, offering one regular and three guest ales, often from local micros or Cornish brewers. The French landlord and chef serves excellent food and booking is recommended, especially for the Thursday steak night and Sunday lunches (no food Sun eve). The Bastille Day beer festival weekend is not to be missed. A good-sized garden is popular in summer. No dogs are permitted inside. Car parking is available nearby. Local CAMRA Pub of the Year 2016. Q⛳⊛◖P♔

Chadlington

Tite Inn
Mill End, OX7 3NY
⏲ 11.30-11; 11.30-10.30 Sun ☎ (01608) 676910
⊕ thetiteinn.co.uk
Sharp's Doom Bar; 2 changing beers (sourced nationally; often Timothy Taylor, Vale, Wye Valley) Ⓗ
Cosy, welcoming country pub in the picturesque Evenlode valley with one regular and three ever-changing guest ales along with a Westons cider on handpump. The pub name is taken from the old local dialect for 'spring' – water runs under the pub and down the hill to where the famous Great Brook Run takes place each December. Good quality yet reasonably priced meals are served in the comfortable bar and restaurant. Outside, the beautiful hillside garden is an idyllic place for an alfresco pint. ⛳⊛◖Å♣P⛁(S3,X9)♛♔

Chalgrove

Red Lion ⓛ
115 High Street, OX44 7SS
⏲ 11-3, 6-midnight (1.30am Fri & Sat); 12-11 Sun
☎ (01865) 890625 ⊕ redlionchalgrove.co.uk
Butcombe Bitter; Fuller's London Pride; Rebellion Mild; 2 changing beers (sourced nationally; often Rebellion, West Berkshire) Ⓗ
Church-owned village local, run by a friendly husband and wife team, both trained chefs. The two guest beers are usually from small breweries. Good food is a speciality at this picturesque 16th-century inn. The interior is divided into several distinct areas and the pub is used by a wide cross-section of the community. You can drink outside in both front and rear gardens, while a real fire awaits inside in the winter months. Real Hitchcox cider is usually available during the summer in bottles. Q⛳⊛◖☖♣P⛁(125.126,T1)♛♔

Charlbury

Rose & Crown
Market Street, OX7 3PL
⏲ 12-11 (1am Fri); 11-1am Sat ☎ (01608) 810103
⊕ roseandcrown.charlbury.com
Ramsbury Bitter; 7 changing beers (sourced nationally; often Dark Star, Kelham Island, Salopian) Ⓗ
The pub has featured in the Guide for 30 consecutive years. A traditional wet-sales-only alehouse, it boasts one of the best beer selections in the area with eight handpumps serving beers from smaller breweries across the UK plus a good range of traditional ciders and perries. Beers from Turpins, Wye Valley, XT, Vale and Oakham, among others, often complement the regular ale. Live music is held fortnightly featuring international acts, plus an annual beer festival at the end of January. Every Monday a pint of ale is just £2.50. ⛳⊛Å⇌♣♛⛁(S3,X9,C1)♛♔

Chipping Norton

Bitter & Twisted
1a Middle Row, OX7 5NH
⏲ 10-11.30 (midnight Fri & Sat); 10-11 Sun
☎ (01608) 644466
2 changing beers (sourced nationally) Ⓗ
Substantial 17th-century Cotswold-stone pub in the Chipping Norton marketplace. It is a smart

establishment with well-presented, helpful and knowledgeable staff. The eclectic customer mix coupled with high standards of food and drink make this a popular venue with all ages and it is renowned locally for its cocktails. Ale drinkers are kept happy with two handpumps on the bar serving a changing selection. ⊠⊛◑♨☐☀♿

Chequers ✪

Goddards Lane, OX7 5NP (next to theatre, on corner of Spring St)
⊕ 11-11 (midnight Fri & Sat); 11.30-11 Sun
☎ (01608) 644717 ⊕ chequers-pub.com
Fuller's Oliver's Island, London Pride, Black Cab, ESB; Gale's Seafarers Ale, HSB; 5 changing beers (sourced nationally; often Fuller's, Gale's) ⊞
The Chequers is renowned for the range and quality of its ales. An array of handpumps offers the complet Fuller's list plus changing guests. The bar has several seating areas and is free of machines and TV. A spacious and airy restaurant serving quality food lies to the rear, with a function room beyond, often hosting eclectic community and interest groups. The pub is ideal for the adjacent theatre. Look out for the pub badgers, and Indra's legendary home-made Scotch eggs.
Q⊠◑♣●☐☀♿

Church Enstone

Crown Inn ⓛ

Mill Lane, OX7 4NN (off A44, on B4030)
⊕ 12-3, 6-11; 12-4 Sun ☎ (01608) 677262
⊕ crowninnenstone.co.uk
Hook Norton Hooky; 2 changing beers (sourced nationally) ⊞
A warm welcome awaits at this lovely old 17th-century village inn with an inglenook fireplace, wooden beams and stone walls decorated with old photos. Hook Norton Bitter is always on offer alongside two guest ales, one local. Food is served from an award-winning menu featuring locally sourced ingredients. An ideal destination following a walk in the surrounding countryside, this is a quiet pub free from jukebox or games machine and perfect for conversation. Families are welcome in this Cotswold gem. Q⊠⊛◑P☐(S3)♿

Deddington

Unicorn Inn

Market Place, OX15 0SE
⊕ 12-11 (midnight Fri & Sat); 12-10.30 Sun
☎ (01869) 338838 ⊕ unicorndeddington.co.uk
Wells Eagle IPA, Bombardier; 1 changing beer (sourced nationally) ⊞
Set in an attractive village marketplace and full of charm, this 17th-century Charles Wells house boasts three handpumps dispensing two regular beers from its portfolio of brands complemented by a guest ale. There is a central bar area and snug, both with open fires, and a rear garden where Aunt Sally is played in summer. With en-suite accommodation, this is a good base to explore the delights of Banburyshire and its environs.
Q⊠⊛⊠◑♿♣P☐(S4,81,90)♿☀

Dorchester-on-Thames

George Hotel

High Street, OX10 7HH (opp Dorchester Abbey church lychgate)

⊕ 11-midnight ☎ (01865) 340404
⊕ thegeorgedorchester.co.uk
Brakspear Bitter; Sharp's Doom Bar; Wadworth 6X; 1 changing beer (sourced locally; often Loose Cannon, West Berkshire) ⊞
Built in 1495, this coaching inn is one of the oldest in the country. The friendly locals' front bar, lounge and restaurant are complete with oak beams and inglenook fireplaces throughout. Liaan, the landlord, is passionate about serving real ale in perfect condition. Three regular and one guest ale are always available and are discounted by 65p per pint 5-7pm every day. Q⊠⊛⊠◑P☐☀

East Hagbourne

Fleur de Lys ✪

30 Main Road, OX11 9LN
⊕ 11.30-2.30, 6-11 (10 Mon); 11.30-11 Fri & Sat; 12-10 Sun
☎ (01235) 813247 ⊕ thefleurdelyspub.co.uk
Morland Original Bitter; 3 changing beers (sourced nationally) ⊞
The Fleur de Lys is a family- and dog-friendly 17th-century pub situated in the rural village of East Hagbourne. The Greene King tied pub offers two regular beers from Morland and two nationally sourced guests. The large bar and dining area are comfortable and cosy, warmed by a large open fire. Live music evenings feature regularly. Outside is an extensive decked area with a separate beer garden where Aunt Sally is played. No food on Monday or Sunday evenings.
⊠⊛◑♨♣●P☐(94,95,131)♿☀

Eaton

Eight Bells ⓛ

OX13 5PR
⊕ 12-2, 5-11; 12-midnight Sat & Sun; closed Mon
☎ (01865) 862261 ⊕ eightbellseaton.co.uk
Loose Cannon Abingdon Bridge; 3 changing beers (sourced regionally) ⊞
The Eight Bells is a cream-coloured cottage-style brick building in the centre of the hamlet, to which extensions have been added over the years. Inside is a no-frills public bar with wooden benches and tables and a larger, simply furnished lounge bar, which leads to the restaurant/function room. Four beers from local breweries and further afield are available. Q⊠⊛◑♨P☐(66)♿☀

Faringdon

Swan ⓛ ✪

1 Park Road, SN7 7BP
⊕ 4.30-midnight (2am Fri); 12-2am Sat; 12-midnight Sun
☎ (01367) 241480
Faringdon Folly Ale; 5 changing beers (sourced nationally; often Adnams, St Austell, Young's) ⊞
The Swan was completely renovated in 2010. Up to six real ales are always available including a selection from the on-site Faringdon Brewery plus a wide choice sourced locally and further afield. Third-pint glasses are available for the unsure. Live music and folk jamming sessions keep the ever-increasing regular clientele entertained. Pub games include bar billiards, table skittles, bagatelle and many more. Q⊠♣●☐(66)♿☀

Fewcott

White Lion 🍺 ✅

Fritwell Road, OX27 7NZ (1 mile from jct 10 M40)
🕐 11-2 (not Tue & Wed), 4-11; 11-2, 4-midnight Fri;
11-midnight Sat; 12-10 Sun; closed Mon ☎ (01869) 346676
⊕ ardleywithfewcottvillagehall.com/
the-white-lion-fewcott.html
XT Four; 2 changing beers (sourced nationally; often
Black Sheep, Wadworth) Ⓗ
A hub of the community where families are
welcome. A true free house, XT Four is available
alongside two constantly changing ales, sourced
equally from well-known larger brewers and
smaller micros, plus four changing real ciders. The
bar is ideal for enjoying conversation or watching
sport on TV. The spacious garden with a large pirate
ship is popular in summer and Aunt Sally can be
played. A cider and pirate festival is held over the
August bank holiday weekend. Local CAMRA Cider
Pub of the Year for 2016.
🛢️🏮🚃🕎♣️🅿️🚮(81,81A)🐾🛜

Finstock

Plough Inn 🍺

The Bottom, OX7 3BY
🕐 12-3 (not mon), 6-11; 12-11 Sat; 12-6 Sun
☎ (01993) 868333 ⊕ theplough-inn.co.uk
Adnams Broadside; 2 changing beers (sourced
nationally; often Hook Norton, Thwaites,
Wychwood) Ⓗ
Dating from 1772 and originally a house, this
multi-roomed thatched village inn with an
inglenook fireplace offers a warm welcome. The
large garden with patio to the rear is popular for
alfresco dining and drinking. A genuine free house,
it serves one regular and two changing ales, plus a
real cider. There is a good food offering with
ingredients locally sourced as far as possible and
freshly prepared by the chef, who is the owner's
son. Families, walkers and four-legged friends
welcome. Q🏮🕎♣️🅿️🚮(C1,X9)🐾🛜

Fringford

Butchers Arms 🍺 ✅

Main Street, OX27 8EB
🕐 12-11 ☎ (01869) 277363
⊕ thebutchersarmsfringford.com
Black Sheep Best Bitter; Hook Norton Hooky; Sharp's
Doom Bar Ⓗ
A pretty 18th-century country pub adjacent to the
cricket ground in a beautiful village setting. A large,
well-decorated bar area serves three ales from
handpump and there is a separate restaurant
seating up to 40 people which is available for
parties. Excellent traditional food is served daily
and a well-priced, good-quality roast with
generous portions on Sundays; reservations are
advised on all days. To the front there is a large,
paved seating area, which is popular during the
summer. 🛢️🏮🕎♣️🅿️🚮(88,37)🐾

Gallowstree Common

Reformation

Horsepond Road, RG4 9BP
🕐 12-3, 5.30-11; 12-4, 6-11 Sat; 12-5 Sun; closed Mon
☎ (0118) 972 3126 ⊕ therefpub.com

Brakspear Bitter; 2 changing beers (sourced
nationally; often Bell Street, Brakspear,
Wychwood) Ⓗ
A popular local pub with a dining room,
conservatory with extra dining tables, and a
children's play area in the enclosed garden. There
are usually two changing beers from the Brakspear
pubco approved list, often including ales from Bell
Street (Brakspear pubco's own microbrewery).
Home-cooked traditional pub food is often sourced
locally. Events include live music, biannual beer
festivals and vintage tractor runs where tractors do
a tour of local pubs with passengers travelling in
open trailers. Q🛢️🏮🕎🅿️🔺♣️🅿️🚮🐾

Goring

Miller of Mansfield 🍺 ✅

High Street, RG8 9AW (on B4009 in village centre)
🕐 12-11; 12-10.30 Sun ☎ (01491) 872829
⊕ millerofmansfield.com
West Berkshire Good Old Boy; 1 changing beer
(sourced nationally) Ⓗ
The cosy bar area overlooks the village memorial
gardens, and open fires are lit during winter
months. A second guest ale may occasionally be
served from the third handpump. This former
coaching inn is noted for the quality of its food and
there is an attractive and award-winning restaurant
to the rear of the building. Thirteen luxury rooms
are available.
Q🛢️🏮🚃🕎🚉(Goring & Streatley)🚮(134,135)
🐾🛜

Henley-on-Thames

Bird in Hand 🍷

61 Greys Road, RG9 1SB
🕐 12-2, 5-11; 12-11 Sat; 12-10.30 Sun ☎ (01491) 575775
⊕ henleybirdinhand.co.uk
Brakspear Bitter; Fuller's London Pride; Hook Norton
Hooky Mild; 2 changing beers (sourced locally; often
Loddon, Rebellion, West Berkshire) Ⓗ
A Guide regular for more than 20 years, the Bird
has flourished under the stewardship of the same
family throughout. Two ever-changing guest beers,
often sourced locally, complement the three
regulars. The pub is home to darts and cribbage
teams, and hosts regular quiz nights. The family
room leads to a delightful garden boasting a pond
and aviary. TVs show sporting events, snacks are
available all day, and dogs on leads are welcome. A
frequent winner of local CAMRA Pub of the Year,
including 2016.
Q🛢️🏮🔺🚉♣️🚮(145,151,154)🐾🛜

Hethe

Muddy Duck 🍺

Main Street, OX27 8ES
🕐 11-11 ☎ (01869) 278099 ⊕ themuddyduckpub.co.uk
Hook Norton Hooky; St Austell Tribute; Timothy Taylor
Landlord Ⓗ; 2 changing beers (sourced nationally;
often Hook Norton, Skinner's, Timothy Taylor) Ⓗ/Ⓖ
Saved from becoming a house in 2011, the
building was purchased and renovated by a local
businessman. The landlord is a real ale enthusiast
and good quality beers flow from four handpumps
and one gravity-fed cask. The pub has a reputation
for excellent food from seasonal menus, and there
is an extensive wine list. Walkers are welcome.
🛢️🏮🕎♣️🅿️🚮(37,88)🐾🛜

Hook Norton

Pear Tree Inn L ✔
Scotland End, OX15 5NU
☼ 12-11 (midnight Fri & Sat) ☎ (01608) 737482
⊕ thepeartreehooky.com
Hook Norton Hooky Mild, Hooky, Lion, Old Hooky; 1 changing beer (often Hook Norton) H
A warm welcome awaits at this beamed bar, which serves as the brewery tap for Hook Norton's nearby Grade II-listed Victorian brewery. There are always four or more Hook Norton ales available. A large child-friendly beer garden is ideal for summer drinking and Aunt Sally is played in the summer. There are three letting rooms available, making this an ideal place to stay while exploring the local area. Q ᗡ ﷺ ✿ ◑ & Å ♣ P ⊟ (488) ❀ ᗧ

Horley

Red Lion L
Hornton Lane, OX15 6BQ
☼ 6-11; 12-6 Sun; closed Mon ☎ (01295) 730427
⊕ thehorleyviews.com/red-lion-3
Hook Norton Hooky; Purity Pure Ubu; Sharp's Doom Bar H
A traditional wet-sales-only pub, this village local is the focal point of the community and offers a friendly welcome to visitors including walkers and well-behaved dogs. The garden provides a tranquil area for a summer's evening tipple. Three handpumped ales are served, four on special occasions. The annual beer festival for St George's Day has become a must for locals and visitors alike. Aunt Sally, darts and dominoes are played, and a TV shows live sporting events. ✿ ♣ ⊟ (504) ❀

Kidlington

King's Arms ✔
4 The Moors, OX5 2AJ (close to jct of High St and Church Rd)
☼ 11-3, 5.30-11.30; 11-midnight Fri & Sat; 12-11.30 Sun
☎ (01865) 373004
Marston's Burton Bitter; 3 changing beers (sourced nationally; often Hook Norton, Titanic, Wychwood) H
Unspoilt two-room local with a heated, covered patio where occasional beer festivals are held, and a skittle alley. Both bay-fronted rooms are small – the lounge is to the left as you enter and a somewhat cluttered bar is to the right, with a dartboard and a collection of trophies. The pub was built around 1815 and retains some thatched outbuildings which now house the gents' toilets. Good-value traditional lunches are served Monday to Saturday. Friendly dogs are welcome.
Q ᗡ ✿ ◑ ♣ ● P ⊟ ❀ ᗧ

Lewknor

Leathern Bottle
1 High Street, OX49 5TW (off B4009 near M40 jct 6)
☼ 11-2.30 (3.30 Sat), 6-11; 12-3.30, 7-10.30 Sun
☎ (01844) 351482 ⊕ theleathernbottle.co.uk
Brakspear Bitter; Marston's Pedigree; 1 changing beer (sourced nationally) H
Classic 17th-century inn that has featured in all but one edition of the Guide. The pub has a reputation for good home-cooked pub food featuring locally sourced meats, and also offers woodburners, a warm welcome and a family-friendly garden. The guest beer comes from the Brakspear pubco

approved list. Popular with walkers from the nearby Ridgeway, it is a short walk from the Oxford Tube and the airline coach stop.
Q ᗡ ✿ ◑ ◐ & ♣ P ⊟ ❀ ᗧ

Long Wittenham

Plough L
24 High Street, OX14 4QH
☼ 12-11 ☎ (01865) 407738 ⊕ theploughinnlw.co.uk
Butcombe Bitter; 2 changing beers (sourced regionally; often Loose Cannon, West Berkshire) H
The Plough is Grade II-listed and dates back to the 17th century – you may need to duck when you enter the bar to avoid the wooden beams overhead. There are two cosy bars and a restaurant. Beyond the children's play area, the long garden stretches down to the River Thames – a delightful place in summer. Changing guest ales are from breweries and microbreweries in the South-east. On weekdays 5-7pm there is 30p off a pint. ᗡ ✿ ﷺ ◑ Å ♣ P ⊟ (46,97) ❀ ᗧ

Longcot

King & Queen L
Shrivenham Road, SN7 7TL
☼ 12-2 (not Mon), 5-11; 12-2.30, 5-11 Sat; 12-2.30, 5-10.30 Sun ☎ (01793) 784348 ⊕ longcotkingandqueen.com
Loose Cannon Gunners Gold; 2 changing beers (sourced nationally; often Oakham, Ramsbury, XT) H
This pub enjoys one of the best views of White Horse Hill and the famous 3,000-year-old chalk figure on it. The interior comprises an extensive, open-plan drinking area and to one side a restaurant serving organic meat and local produce. The bar offers a good selection of beers from local breweries and two ciders on handpump. In 2014 it was awarded Best Traditional Pub in the Oxfordshire Restaurant Awards.
Q ᗡ ✿ ﷺ ◑ & Å ♣ ● P ⊟ ❀ ᗧ

Lower Heyford

Bell Inn
21 Market Square, OX25 5NY
☼ 12-3, 5-11; 12-11 Fri & Sat; 12-10.30 Sun
☎ (01869) 347176
Salopian Shropshire Gold; 1 changing beer (sourced nationally) H
Large multi-roomed pub in the centre of the village, close to the Oxfordshire Narrowboats wharf on the Oxford Canal and the railway station at Heyford. The regular ale, Salopian Shropshire Gold, is supplemented by an ever-changing guest which could come from near or far. Two changing ciders or perries are always available and good home-cooked food is served lunchtimes and evenings. The large garden is popular in good weather and a beer festival is held in early September.
✿ ◑ ⇌ ♣ ● P ⊟ (25A) ❀ ᗧ

Mapledurham

Packhorse L
Woodcote Road, RG4 7UG (on A4074)
☼ 11.30-11; 12-10.30 Sun ☎ (0118) 972 2140
Loddon Hoppit; 3 changing beers (sourced nationally) H
Originally a farm on the Mapledurham House estate dating from the 1600s, this Brunning & Price establishment is now a cosy pub and restaurant.

The low-beamed bar has ample seating for drinkers and usually features one or two local microbrewery beers. The larger restaurant area is furnished with bookcases and numerous prints and has a wide-ranging good-value menu. A large secluded garden at the rear has a shaded seating area overlooking fields. There is 60p off a pint 5-7pm weekdays. Q❄️🍴🌳♿️🅿️🚃(X39,X40)🐾🛜

Marsh Baldon

Seven Stars on the Green ✓
The Green, OX44 9LP
🕐 12-11 (midnight Fri & Sat); 12-10 Sun ☎ (01865) 343337
🌐 sevenstarsonthegreen.co.uk
Fuller's London Pride; 4 changing beers (sourced locally; often Loddon, Shotover, White Horse) Ⓗ
This establishment reopened as a community-owned pub in 2013 with the main bar room refurbished and a new function room/restaurant. It sits on a village green that claims to be the largest in Europe. Three local ales are always available and food is served all day including extensive gluten-free options. Family- and dog-friendly, it hosts many community events. There is only one bus a day to the village so you need to walk from Nuneham Courtenay. Q❄️🍴🌳♿️🅿️🚃(T2)🐾🛜

Milcombe

Horse & Groom ✓
Main Road, OX15 4RS
🕐 12-3, 6-11; 12-5 Sun ☎ (01295) 722142
🌐 thehorseandgroominn.co.uk
3 changing beers (sourced nationally; often Black Sheep, Brakspear) Ⓗ
Welcoming 17th-century coaching inn constructed from local stone; on entering you are warmed by a log fire in the inglenook fireplace. The bar has a flagstone floor, traditional furnishings and three handpumps serving two or three changing ales. To the rear is a more contemporary dining room serving a regularly changing menu, which is locally sourced. There is an attractive enclosed patio area to the front. An ideal place to end a walk, with both children and dogs welcome.
Q🌳🍴🍝♿️🌳♣🅿️🚃(488)🐾🛜

Milton

Plum Pudding Ⓛ
44 High Street, OX14 4EJ
🕐 11.30-2.30, 5-11; 11.30-11.30 Fri & Sat; 12-10 (4 winter) Sun ☎ (01235) 834443 🌐 theplumpuddingmilton.co.uk
Loose Cannon Abingdon Bridge; house beer (by Ringwood); 2 changing beers (sourced nationally) Ⓗ
Plum Pudding refers to the Oxford Sandy and Black pig, one of the older and rarer British breeds. You wouldn't know it, but it is only a couple of minutes from the busy A34 and close to the thriving Milton Business Park. Regular live music is hosted, and two beer festivals each year. Local CAMRA Pub of the Year 2015. 🌳🍴🌳♣♦🅿️🚃🐾🛜

North Moreton

Bear at Home Ⓛ
High Street, OX11 9AT (off A4130)
🕐 12-3, 6-11; 12-11 Sat; 12-10 Sun ☎ (01235) 811311
🌐 bear-at-home.co.uk
Timothy Taylor Landlord; house beer (by West Berkshire); 2 changing beers (sourced locally) Ⓗ

Friendly village local dating back to the 15th century. There is an open fire and plenty of tables for diners to enjoy the excellent pub food. The four handpumps deliver two regular beers – Landlord and Bear Beer (4% ABV), the latter brewed exclusively for the pub by West Berkshire – together with two changing guests. The Bear adjoins the village cricket ground and a very popular four-day beer and cricket festival is held at the end of July. 🌳🍴♦🅿️🚃(95,131)🐾🛜

Northmoor

Red Lion Ⓛ ✓
Standlake Road, OX29 5SX
🕐 12-3, 5.30-11; 11-11 Sat; 12-4 Sun; closed Mon
☎ (01865) 300301 🌐 theredlionnorthmoor.com
Brakspear Bitter; Cotswold Cask; Wychwood Hobgoblin; 1 changing beer (sourced locally; often Loose Cannon, Ramsbury) Ⓗ
Traditional village inn with whitewashed stone walls, heavy oak beams, real fires and a large garden. Purchased by the local community from Greene King in 2014, the pub has gone from strength to strength ever since. The focus is on local produce, with a changing menu of home-cooked food, some of which is grown in the pub's kitchen garden. A selection of four local beers is available in the small bar, and locally made soft drinks from Samuelsons of Witney are stocked.
Q🌳🍴🌳♣🅿️🚃(18)🐾🛜

Oxford

Chequers Ⓛ
130A High Street, OX1 4DH
🕐 11-11 (11.30 Fri & Sat); 11-10.30 Sun ☎ (01865) 727463
Brakspear Bitter; Hook Norton Hooky; St Austell Nicholson's Pale Ale; Sharp's Doom Bar; changing beers (sourced nationally; often Purity, Red Squirrel, Saltaire) Ⓗ
Down a narrow medieval passageway off the High Street, the Chequers is Grade II-listed, much of it dating back to the early-16th century when it was converted from a moneylender's tenement to a tavern, hence the name. Note the fine carvings, windows and the ceiling in the lower bar. Tasting notes are provided for all real ales including any frequently changing guest beers, and interesting food is available. A cobbled courtyard provides alfresco drinking, dining and smoking facilities.
Q🌳🍴🌳♿️🚃♦🚃🐾🛜

Chester Ⓛ
19 Chester Street, OX4 1SN
🕐 12 (5 Mon)-11; 10-11 Fri & Sat; 12-10 Sun
☎ (01865) 790438 🌐 thechesteroxford.co.uk
4 changing beers (sourced regionally; often Rebellion, XT, Loose Cannon) Ⓗ
A trendy back-street pub, now opened out with boarded floors and powder blue walls, but the star of the show is some original Halls stained and leaded glasswork on the entrance surrounds. There is a large patio garden to the rear. The real ales always include at least two from Loose Cannon. Opens early for breakfast on Friday and Saturday.
🌳🍴🌳♿️🅿️🚃🐾🛜

Gardener's Arms Ⓛ
39 Plantation Road, OX2 6JE
🕐 12-2.30 (not Mon & Tue), 5-midnight; 12-11 Sun
☎ (01865) 559814 🌐 thegarden-oxford.co.uk

Brakspear Bitter; 3 changing beers (sourced nationally; often Jennings, Loose Cannon, White Horse) Ⓗ
Cosy pub down a narrow street off Woodstock Road. The small bar opens up to a spacious dining area, once two rooms, serving some of the finest vegetarian food in the city (with some vegan food available). At the rear is a large and pleasant garden, as well as the outside toilets and another small lounge. A popular and relaxing place to eat and drink. Weekly quiz night is Sunday.
Q❀◐♣●🚌🐾

Lamb & Flag 🏆

12 St Giles, OX1 3JS
12-11; 12-10.30 Sun ☎ (01865) 515787
Palmers Best Bitter; Skinner's Betty Stogs; Theakston Old Peculier; house beer (by Palmers); 3 changing beers (sourced nationally; often Big Hand, Tring, XT) Ⓗ
Grade II-listed building owned by the adjacent St John's College. Some of the profits from the pub support student scholarships. This is a classic city pub with no music, Wi-Fi or other distractions from friendly conversation. Beers from the South-west feature – the house beer Lamb & Flag Gold (4.5% ABV) is brewed by Palmers of Bridport. It is believed to be the setting for the inn in Thomas Hardy's novel Jude the Obscure and has other literary links. Local CAMRA Pub of the Year 2016.
Q◐●🚌

Mason's Arms Ⓛ ✔

2 Quarry School Place, Headington Quarry, OX3 8LH
5 (7 Mon)-11; 12-11 Sat; 12-4, 7-10.30 Sun
☎ (01865) 764579 🌐 themasonsarmshq.co.uk
Dark Star Hophead; Rebellion Mutiny; Timothy Taylor Boltmaker; 2 changing beers (sourced nationally; often Bootleg, Castle Rock, Loose Cannon) Ⓗ
Family-run community pub full of character, hosting many pub games' leagues, including bar billiards and Aunt Sally. The guest ales are varied and regularly come from the Old Bog Brewery (named after the original purpose of the building behind the pub where it was founded). A wide range of bottled beers is stocked. The pub is home to the Headington beer festival in September. A heated decking area and garden lead to the function room. Local CAMRA City Pub of the Year 2014. ❀♣●P🚌(H2)🐾

Rose & Crown Ⓛ

14 North Parade Avenue, OX2 6LX (½ mile N of city centre, off Banbury Rd)
11-midnight (1am Fri & Sat) ☎ (01865) 510551
🌐 roseandcrownoxford.com
Adnams Southwold Bitter; Hook Norton Old Hooky; Shotover Scholar; 1 changing beer (sourced nationally) Ⓗ
Now a free house, this popular Victorian local on a vibrant north Oxford street is a time capsule with two small rooms and many original features. No intrusive music or mobile phones are permitted. Children are welcome until 5pm. Its fame has even spread to Everest – see the photo on the wall. To the rear is a heated, covered patio
Q❀◐♣🚌

Royal Blenheim Ⓛ

13 St Ebbes Street, OX1 1PT
12-11 (11.30 Wed & Thu; midnight Fri & Sat); 11-11 Sun
☎ (01865) 242355 🌐 royalblenheim.co.uk
White Horse Bitter, Village Idiot, Wayland Smithy; 6 changing beers (sourced nationally; often Everards, Isle of Purbeck, Titanic) Ⓗ
Street-corner, single-room, Victorian pub with a bright, airy interior, next to the Museum of Modern Art. Built in 1889 on the site of two earlier pubs, the original Royal Blenheim was a stagecoach. The pub is owned by Everards but leased to the White Horse Brewery. Ten handpumps dispense a full range of White Horse beers, plus guests (including one from Everards) and a real cider. Good food and bar snacks includes vegetarian and gluten-free options. ◐♿≈♣●🚌

St Aldates Tavern Ⓛ ✔

108 St Aldate's, OX1 1BU
11.30-11 (midnight Thu & Fri); 11-midnight Sat; 11.30-midnight Sun ☎ (01865) 241185
🌐 staldatestavernoxford.co.uk
6 changing beers (sourced nationally; often Box Steam, Dark Star, XT) Ⓗ
Refurbished for its reopening in 2012, this friendly pub in the centre of Oxford features up to six well-kept real ales with at least two from local breweries such as XT and Hook Norton. Good-quality, freshly cooked food is served all day using locally sourced ingredients where possible. There is an attractive function room upstairs, available to hire, with its own bar and toilets. Q◐≈🚌🐾

White Hart

12 St Andrews Road, Headington, OX3 9DL (opp church in Old Headington village)
12-11 (midnight Fri & Sat) ☎ (01865) 761737
Everards Sunchaser Blonde, Tiger Best Bitter; 3 changing beers (sourced nationally; often Brunswick, Everards, York) Ⓗ
Terraced, stone-built pub with a good selection of Everards ales that holds a beer festival every year in April or May. There are two rooms including a small bar area and a large garden. Note the poem framed on the wall, 'The Alehouse of Joan of Headington' by William King and written in 1712 about the pub; thankfully now the pub has a much better reputation. The food is traditional and home-made, with pies a speciality. ❀◐●P🚌🐾

White Rabbit Ⓛ

21 Friars Entry, OX1 2BY (off Gloucester Green)
12-midnight ☎ (01865) 241177 🌐 whiterabbitpizza.com
Shotover Scholar; 3 changing beers (sourced regionally; often Loose Cannon, Philsters Ales, Tiny Rebel) Ⓗ
This pub reopened in 2012 as the White Rabbit following the closure of Oxford's 'premier rock pub', the Gloucester Arms. It is brighter and more spacious than before, with a central bar surrounded by three areas. Four real ales are on offer, three changing and often local. Bar snacks and panini are available and a wide range of hand-made pizzas, made with organic gluten-free bases on request.
◐≈♣🚌

Pishill

Crown Inn

RG9 6HH (on B480) SU724900
12-3, 6-11; 12-3.30 Sun ☎ (01491) 638364
🌐 thecrowninnpishill.co.uk
Brakspear Bitter; 1 changing beer (sourced nationally; often Otter, Rebellion, Vale) Ⓗ
This lovely flint-built country pub nestles in the Stonor Valley in the Chilterns. A former coaching

inn dating from the 15th century, it boasts secluded seating, wood beams, exposed brickwork and log fires. The small front bar leads to larger rooms primarily used by diners. Alongside the pub is a beautifully renovated 400-year-old thatched barn used for functions, including a beer festival each September, and an en-suite self-catering cottage, converted from a 200-year-old stable block. Q✿⏰🚪◗ P🐾 🗢

Playhatch

Flowing Spring ✪
Henley Road, RG4 9RB (on A4155)
✪ 12-3, 5-midnight; 12-midnight Sat & Sun; closed Mon
☎ (0118) 969 9878 ⊕ theflowingspringpub.co.uk
Fuller's London Pride, ESB; Gale's Seafarers Ale; 1 changing beer (sourced nationally) Ⓗ
Sociable 18th-century country pub on the edge of the Chilterns featuring Fuller's ales, plus a changing guest from the Fuller's list. It serves home-made food with gluten-free, dairy-free, vegetarian and vegan options. Events include monthly unplugged nights, live jazz nights, stand-up comedy, story-telling, murder mysteries, an annual ferret show and beer and cider festivals in the summer and autumn. The pleasant covered balcony and large riverside garden are ideal for summer.
⏰✿◗ ♣P🚪 (800)🐾 🗢

Shippon

Prince of Wales Ⓛ
60 Barrow Road, OX13 6JQ (off A415, NW of Abingdon)
✪ 5-11 Mon; 11-11.30; 12-11 Sun ☎ (01235) 538546
⊕ princeofwalesshippon.co.uk
Black Sheep Best Bitter; Loose Cannon Abingdon Bridge; Shotover Prospect; Timothy Taylor Landlord; 1 changing beer (sourced nationally; often Loose Cannon) Ⓗ
At the centre of the village, this traditional country pub is rumoured to be haunted. It has two large rooms, both with log fires - one dominating the lounge - and a separate function room. A varied menu of English food is available alongside a large selection of malt whiskies and ciders. The pub hosts regular beer and cider festivals and traditional jazz and folk music evenings. All visitors are welcome including walkers, cyclists and dogs.
Q⏰✿◗ ♣♠P🚪 (4)🐾 🗢

Shutford

George & Dragon Ⓛ
Church Lane, OX15 6PG
✪ 6 (12 Fri & Sat)-11; 12-10.30 Sun; closed Mon
☎ (01295) 780320 ⊕ thegeorgeanddragon.com
4 changing beers (sourced nationally; often CATs, Fuller's, Turpin) Ⓗ
Friendly 13th-century village pub nestling into the hillside beside the church. The welcoming, well-stocked bar, with inglenook fireplace and tiled floor, offers three or four regularly changing ales, usually including at least one local brew. Good home-cooked food made with local ingredients is served. Traditional pub games are played, including darts and Aunt Sally in the beer garden. There is a separate TV room with Sky and BT Sport.
Q⏰✿◗ ♣♠🖥🚪 (269)🐾 🗢

Stoke Lyne

Peyton Arms Ⓛ
OX27 8SD (2 miles from M40 junction 10)
✪ 12-2 (not Wed-Fri), 5-11; 12-7 Sat & Sun; closed Mon ☎ 07546 066160
Hook Norton Hooky, Lion, Old Hooky Ⓖ
Up to three Hooky ales are served through a hatch direct from the casks and simple filled rolls are usually available. This traditional pub is often used by walkers and local shoots looking to wind down and enjoy quality ales with great conversation; however, the bar area is for adults only - children are allowed in the garden but dogs are not permitted. Weekday hours can vary - call ahead to check. Q✿P🚪 (37,81)

Sydenham

Inn at Emmington Ⓛ
Sydenham Road, OX39 4LD
✪ 4 (3 Fri)-11; 12-9 Sun ☎ (01844) 351367
⊕ theinnatemmington.co.uk
Fuller's London Pride; Rebellion IPA; 1 changing beer (sourced locally) Ⓗ
The Inn, renowned for its cask ales, convivial atmosphere and excellent food, is just off junction 6 of the M40, with the proximity of the Chiltern Hills also a big draw. Those looking to explore the area should book a stay in one of the seven guest rooms, some with views over the Oxfordshire countryside. Lunch and evening menus change frequently depending on the fresh local produce available. A 150-year-old English walnut tree presides over the large well-kept garden.
✿⏰◗ ♣♠P🚪 (40)🐾 🗢

Tetsworth

Old Red Lion Ⓛ
40 High Street, OX9 7AS
✪ 10-10 (midnight Fri); 10-6 Sun ☎ (01844) 281274
⊕ theoldredliontetsworth.co.uk
Vale Best IPA; White Horse Bitter; XT Four; 3 changing beers (sourced locally) Ⓗ
The Old Red Lion is situated at the Oxford end of the quiet village of Tetsworth, opposite the village green. It has a warm and friendly atmosphere with a cosy log fire in wintertime. Two well-kept real ales are on offer from various local breweries. Traditional pub food is available all day in the bar and more formal restaurant. The pub also serves as the village shop.
Q⏰✿◗ ♿♣♠P🚪 (124,275)🐾 🗢

Thame

Cross Keys ▾ Ⓛ ✪
East Street, OX9 3JS
✪ 12-2, 5-11; 12-11 Sat; 12-10.30 Sun ☎ (01844) 218202
XT Four; 7 changing beers Ⓗ
Once almost lost forever, this pub was saved by the current tenants, who have transformed it into a drinkers' local. Peter and Trudi always offer a warm welcome to all. Serving an ever-changing range of ales and ciders, local brews feature alongside beers from around the country. At busy times, it is not uncommon for beers to change during the evening. Check Twitter for unusual beers, but be warned, they will go quickly. CAMRA branch Pub of the Year 2015. Q✿♣♠🚪 (280)🐾 🗢

Wallingford

Dolphin ✔

2 St Marys Street, OX10 0EL

🕑 8am-11.30 (1am Fri & Sat); 9am-11.30 Sun

☎ (01491) 837377 ⊕ thedollyinwally.co.uk

Greene King IPA; Morland Original Bitter; house beer (by Greene King); 2 changing beers (sourced nationally) Ⓗ

Situated on a pedestrian street off the main square of the market town, this establishment features live music, karaoke, disco and TV sport. Traditional pub food is served all day until 9pm (no food Sun and Mon eves) and the breakfasts are said to be the best in the area. Alcohol is served from 10am every day. Four handpumps dispense the regular beers and two changing national beers. The house ale is the Dolly (3.9% ABV). Entry on Friday and Saturday is before 11.15pm.

ዼ🏵🖂🅙🕭♣🗛🐾🐾🛜

Wantage

Royal Oak 🍷 Ⓛ

Newbury Street, OX12 8DF (S of Market Square)

🕑 5.30-11; 12-2.30, 7-11 Sat; 12-2, 7-10.30 Sun

☎ (01235) 763129 ⊕ royaloakwantage.co.uk

Wadworth 6X; West Berkshire Maggs' Magnificent Mild, Dr Hexter's Healer; 8 changing beers (sourced nationally; often Flying Monk) Ⓖ

This multi award-winning street-corner pub is a mecca for the discerning drinker and a meeting place for many local clubs. The lounge features wrought-iron trelliswork covered in pumpclips. The pub is the primary outlet for West Berkshire ales in the area – one beer carries landlord Paul Hexter's name – together with 30-plus ciders and perries. All beers are dispensed by gravity. A former national finalist CAMRA Pub of the Year, national CAMRA Cider and Perry Pub of the Year, and local branch Pub of the Year 2016. Q ዼ ♣ 🍴 🗛 🐾 🛜

Shoulder of Mutton

38 Wallingford Street, OX12 8AX (E of Market Square)

🕑 12-11 (midnight Fri & Sat); 12-10.30 Sun

10 changing beers (sourced nationally) Ⓗ

Victorian corner pub close to the town centre with 10 constantly changing beers on handpump to suit all tastes. The sympathetically renovated interior comprises public and lounge bars, a cosy snug and a 'lay-by' leading to the enclosed outdoor patio and function room. Awards include local CAMRA Pub of the Year 2014. Q 🍴 🗛

Swan Ⓛ

28 Market Place, OX12 8AE

🕑 2-midnight (1am Thu; 2am Fri & Sat) ☎ (01235) 767584

Brakspear Oxford Gold; Ramsbury Gold; Sharp's Doom Bar; Wychwood Hobgoblin Ⓗ

Vibrant young people's pub often featuring live music. The long front bar has pleasant views of the local church. Due to some major brewery changes, there are now beverages available here that no other pubs offer in Wantage, including a varied range of cask ales. A happy hour operates 2-8pm daily and all day Sunday on cask beers. At least three draught ciders are served. ዼ🏵🕭🍴🗛🐾🛜

Witney

Eagle Tavern Ⓛ ✔

22 Corn Street, OX28 6BL

🕑 11-3, 5-midnight (2am Fri); 11-2am Sat; 12-midnight Sun

☎ (01993) 700121

Hook Norton Hooky, Lion, Old Hooky; Wychwood Hobgoblin; 1 changing beer (sourced locally; often Hook Norton) Ⓗ

The landlord has been running pubs in Corn Street for 25 years, this one for 10, and has won Hook Norton Pub of the Year and Best Kept Beer and Cellar on several occasions. The wood-panelled and stone-floored building has also been local CAMRA Town and Country Pub of the Year twice. Friendly locals, welcoming staff and quality beer all add up to a must-visit pub. Wychwood Brewery is just around the corner. Q 🏵🕭🕭♣🍴🗛(S1,S2)🛜

New Inn Ⓛ ✔

111 Corn Street, OX28 6AU

🕑 5-midnight; 12-1am Sat; 12-midnight Sun

☎ (01993) 703807

Black Sheep Best Bitter; St Austell Proper Job; Sharp's Doom Bar; Tring Side Pocket for a Toad; 2 changing beers (sourced locally) Ⓗ

Mid-Victorian pub with an older cellar, at the lower end of Corn Street, run by an enthusiastic landlord who serves an excellent choice of real ales. There are seven handpumps, one dispensing a real cider and the other six real ale, including two guests from microbreweries. The pub holds two beer festivals a year in the large room at the rear, and also hosts other fundraising events. It can be noisy when major rugby tournaments are screened. There is live music on some Fridays. Q 🏵♣🍴🗛(S1,S2)🐾

Woodstock

Black Prince

2 Manor Road, OX20 1XJ

🕑 12-11 ☎ (01993) 811530

⊕ theblackprincewoodstock.com

St Austell Trelawny, Tribute; 2 changing beers (often Hook Norton, XT) Ⓗ

Historic and pleasant 16th-century pub with an attractive riverside setting by the River Glyme, opposite Blenheim Palace. There is a terrace with seating for warmer days, from where you can watch the yearly Mock Mayor ceremony or the June Duck Race. Inside, there are ancient fireplaces and even a suit of armour. Ever-changing ales and fresh well-cooked snacks and meals are available at reasonable prices. Aunt Sally is played and families, walkers and well-behaved dogs are welcome. ዼ🏵🕭🕭♣🗛(S3,W12)🐾🛜

Wootton

Killingworth Castle

Glympton Road, OX20 1EJ

🕑 9am-11 ☎ (01993) 811401 ⊕ thekillingworthcastle.com

5 changing beers (sourced locally) Ⓗ

Enter this welcoming former coaching house and enjoy one of three house ales from sister company Yubberton Brewery. One or two guest ales are also usually on tap. The bar is warmed by a wood-burning stove in winter and there is a larger restaurant area to the rear serving award-winning food. Eight letting rooms are now available. Outside, a fine old plaque on the wall highlights the pub's past tie to Morland Brewery. Q 🏵🖂🕭♣🗛(W12)🐾

RUTLAND

LINCOLNSHIRE

LEICESTERSHIRE

Ryhall
Belmesthorpe
Oakham
Ketton
North Luffenham
A606
A47
A6003
CAMBS
Uppingham

0 Miles 5
0 Kilometres 8

NORTHAMPTONSHIRE

Belmesthorpe

Blue Bell 🅛 ✅
Shepherds Walk, PE9 4JG
🕓 12-2.30 (not Mon), 6-11; 12-2.30, 5-11 Fri; 12-11 Sat & Sun
☎ (01780) 753081
Abbeydale Moonshine; Draught Bass; Grainstore Ten Fifty; Greene King IPA; Oakham Bishops Farewell; 1 changing beer (often Abbeydale) ⓗ
Low ceilings, a roaring fire and stone walls are part of the charm of this historic pub. Six handpulls offer a wide range of well-kept guest beers, including at least one LocAle and real cider. Dogs on leads are welcome in the bar area. Good honest home-made pub food is served Tuesday to Sunday lunchtimes (booking advisable). Q�¸⏰◑🕭⅙⚓♣♠P🐾

North Luffenham

Fox 🏆
1 Pinfold Lane, LE15 8LE
🕓 12-2.30 (not Mon & Tue), 5.30-11; 12-11.30 Sat; 11.30-10.30 Sun ☎ (01780) 720991 ⊕ thefoxrutland.co.uk
Grainstore Triple B; Greene King IPA; Oakham JHB; 2 changing beers (often Hopshackle, Langton) ⓗ
Stone-built pub now opened out into one room with restaurant and lounge areas and a modern decor but retaining the rural feel of a country inn, with oak and flagstone flooring, exposed oak beams and an oak bar. Happy hour is 5-7pm Monday to Thursday, with 30p off a pint or glass of wine. Local CAMRA Pub of the Year 2016.
Q➸⏰◑⅙♣♠P🐾🐕📶

Oakham

Grainstore Brewery Tap
Station Approach, LE15 6EA
🕓 11-11 (midnight Fri); 9am-midnight Sat; 9am-11 Sun
☎ (01572) 770065 ⊕ grainstorebrewery.com
Grainstore Rutland Bitter, Rutland Panther, Cooking, Triple B, GB Best, Ten Fifty; 3 changing beers (often Grainstore) ⓗ
A pub and brewery in a small, cleverly converted warehouse over four floors. (Brewery tours need to be booked in advance.) Ten handpumps offer a range of beers, always including a mild. Home-made food is served at lunchtimes. Live bands feature regularly. Dogs and walkers are welcome.

An annual beer festival is held over the August bank holiday. Local CAMRA Pub of the Year runner-up 2015. Q➸⏰◑⅙⚓♣♠P🐕🐾📶

Old Buttercross
Panniers Way, LE15 6US (just off A606 Oakham bypass)
🕓 11-11 ☎ (01572) 842017
⊕ oldbuttercrosspuboakham.co.uk
Marston's Pedigree; Oakham JHB; Wychwood Hobgoblin; 2 changing beers (sourced nationally; often Jennings, Oakham) ⓗ
It has a good reputation as a value-for-money venue with freshly made pizzas a speciality on the food menu. There is plenty of seating and diners and drinkers are made to feel equally welcome. Most of the beers are from within the Marston's group but one or two are usually from Oakham Ales. ➸⏰◑⅙P🐾📶

White Lion
30 Melton Road, LE15 6AY (nr train station)
🕓 12-3 (not Mon), 6-11; 12-3, 7-10.30 Sun
☎ (01572) 724844
Adnams Broadside; Fuller's London Pride; Timothy Taylor Landlord; 1 changing beer ⓗ
Attractive red-brick building with interesting guest beers. A must-visit inn for home-made traditional food – make sure you are hungry as portions are generous. The beer is always top quality and guests change regularly, often from Blue Monkey or Ossett breweries. Old-fashioned standards are upheld, with the landlord in collar and tie.
Q⏰⚓◑≉♣P🖾

Ryhall

Green Dragon
The Square, PE9 4HH
🕓 5-11; 12-11 Fri-Sun ☎ (01780) 751999
⊕ thegreendragonryhall.co.uk
Greene King IPA; 3 changing beers (often Bakers Dozen, Milestone, Oakham) ⓗ
Former Melbourn's stone-built inn in the heart of the village. The main building is Grade II-listed and dates back to the 17th century, with low ceilings and nooks and crannies adding to the cosy feel. Superb home-cooked meals are served including the pub's speciality pizzas cooked in the pizza oven. Local CAMRA Pub of the Year 2015.
Q➸⏰◑♣🖾(202)🐾📶

Uppingham

Crown Inn 🅛
19 High Street East, LE15 9PY
🕓 10-11 (midnight Fri & Sat) ☎ (01572) 822302
Everards Tiger Best Bitter, Original; 2 changing beers ⓗ
The Crown Inn dates back to 1739. It offers up to seven ales, many from Everards, and serves good-quality, home-cooked food in the bar and restaurant. Live music plays regularly. The pub is home to a local dominoes team. En-suite accommodation is available. Winner of many CAMRA awards including local CAMRA Pub of the Year 2014. ⏰⚓◑⅙♠P🖾🐾📶

REAL ALE BREWERIES

Bakers Dozen Ketton (NEW)
Grainstore 🍺 Oakham
Stoney Ford Ryhall (NEW)

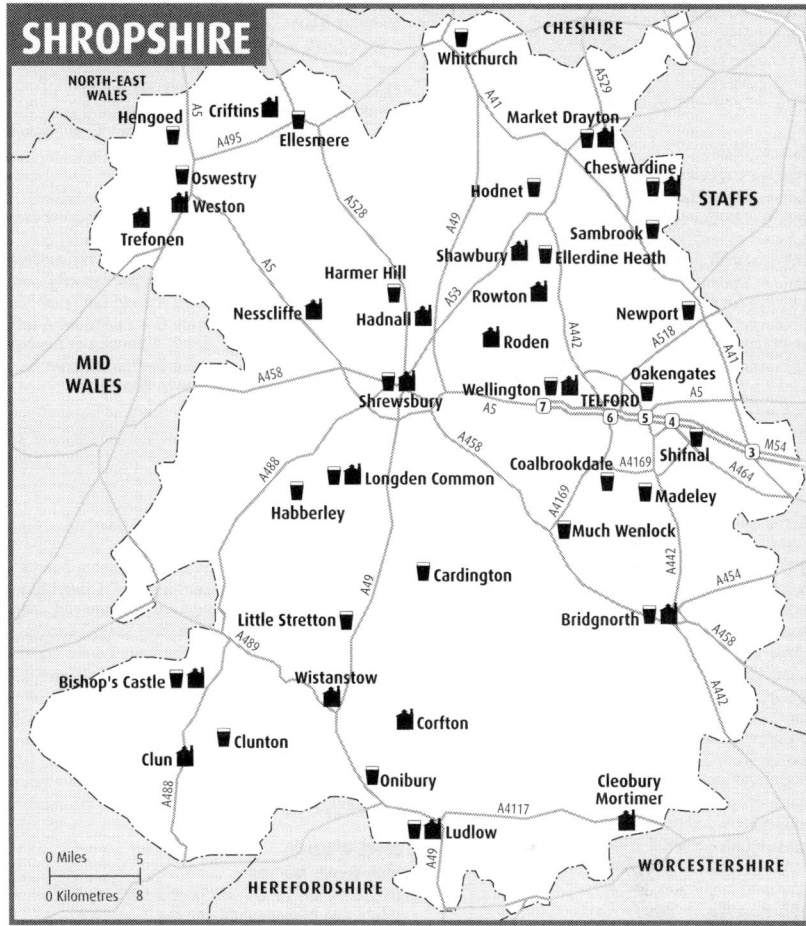

SHROPSHIRE

NORTH-EAST WALES
Hengoed • Criftins
A495 • Ellesmere
A5
Oswestry
Weston
Trefonen
A5
MID WALES
A528
A458
A488
Habberley
Longden Common
A49
Little Stretton
A489
Wistanstow
Bishop's Castle
A488
Clun
Clunton
Corfton
Onibury
A4117
Ludlow
A49
HEREFORDSHIRE

CHESHIRE
Whitchurch
A41
Market Drayton
A529
Hodnet
Cheswardine
STAFFS
A49
Shawbury
Sambrook
Ellerdine Heath
Harmer Hill
Rowton
Newport
A53
Nesscliffe
Hadnall
Roden
A518
A442
Shrewsbury
Wellington
A5
Oakengates
TELFORD
A5
7
6
5
4
M54
3
A464
Coalbrookdale
A4169
Shifnal
A4169
Madeley
Much Wenlock
A442
A454
Cardington
Bridgnorth
A458
A442
Cleobury Mortimer

0 Miles 5
0 Kilometres 8

WORCESTERSHIRE

Bishop's Castle

Six Bells ⃝

Church Street, SY9 5AA

☼ 12-3, 5-11; 12-11 Fri-Sun ☎ (01588) 630144

⊕ sixbellsbrewery.com

Six Bells Ow Do!, Spikey Blonde, Noggin, Cloud Nine; 2 changing beers (sourced locally) Ⓗ

The tap for the re-established Six Bells Brewery, a friendly place and full of character, with a wood-beamed and stone-walled bar. The lounge doubles as a dining room where food is served Thursday to Saturday evenings and Sunday lunchtime. The regular Six Bells ales are complemented by two monthly seasonal beers and cider in summer. The pub participates in the town's beer festival in July, with around 20 ales available. Sunday hours may vary. Q✿☼◑▲♣♠☺

Bridgnorth

Black Boy ♉

58 Cartway, WV16 4BG

☼ 12-11 ☎ (01746) 766497

5 changing beers (sourced nationally; often Greene King, Hobsons, Three Tuns) Ⓗ

This bustling pub with a friendly atmosphere, licensed since 1790, stands on the historic Cartway

linking Low Town with High Town. Open fires in winter make it a welcoming place to enjoy a range of national and local ales. Ten handpumps dispense

REAL ALE BREWERIES

Battlefield Shrewsbury (NEW)
Big Shed Shawbury
Chapel Criftins
Clun ⃠ Clun
Corvedale ⃠ Corfton
Hobsons Cleobury Mortimer
Hop & Stagger ⃠ Bridgnorth
Joule's Market Drayton
Lion's Tale ⃠ Cheswardine
Ludlow Ludlow
Ness ⃠ Nesscliffe (NEW)
Offa's Dyke ⃠ Trefonen
Rowton Rowton
Salopian Hadnall
Shropshire Brewer Longden Common
Six Bells ⃠ Bishop's Castle
Stonehouse Weston
Target Roden
Three Tuns ⃠ Bishop's Castle
Wood Wistanstow
Wrekin ⃠ Telford: Wellington

Black Boy Bitter, five changing beers and one real cider. Snacks are always available. Beer festivals are usually held at Easter and over the August bank holiday weekend. Local CAMRA Pub of the Year 2015. ⏰❀✿≉(SVR)♣🍴🖫✿❤🛜

Black Horse
4 Bridge Street, Low Town, WV15 6AF
❀ 12-1am ☎ (01746) 762415
⏲ theblackhorsebridgnorth.co.uk
Bathams Best Bitter; Hobsons Town Crier; Three Tuns XXX; Wye Valley HPA; 3 changing beers (often Enville, Ludlow, Salopian) 🅷
A lively pub in the centre of Low Town close to the River Severn. The Grade II-listed building has a small bar with a dartboard at the front, a lounge and a conservatory to the rear. The large courtyard drinking area has an awning for smokers. The car park at the back is accessed from Severn Street. There are several TV screens for viewing sporting events. Filled rolls are often available.
❀🍴🚲&≉(Bridgnorth SVR)♣P🖫❤🛜

King's Head 🅻
3 Whitburn Street, High Town, WV16 4QN
❀ 11-11 (midnight Fri & Sat); 12-10.30 Sun
☎ (01746) 762141 ⏲ thekingsheadbridgnorth.co.uk
Hobsons Twisted Spire, Town Crier; Wye Valley HPA; 2 changing beers (sourced nationally; often Kelham Island, Thornbridge, Three Tuns) 🅷
A lovingly restored Grade II-listed 16th-century coaching inn with exposed timber beams, flagstone floor, leaded windows and three roaring log fires in colder weather. Excellent food can be chosen from a modern English menu featuring fresh local ingredients, a selection of daily specials and a delightful choice of desserts. There are three regular local and two changing guest beers, a small but carefully selected wine list and a range of spirits and liqueurs. ⏰❀🍴&≉(SVR)🖫❤🛜

Old Castle 🅻 ✪
10/11 West Castle Street, WV16 4AB (halfway between SVR and town centre)
❀ 11.30-11; 11.30-10.30 Sun ☎ (01746) 711420
⏲ oldcastlebridgnorth.co.uk
Hobsons Town Crier; Sharp's Doom Bar; Thwaites Lancaster Bomber; Wye Valley HPA 🅷
A popular pub dating from the 1600s, a short walk from the Severn Valley Railway. The dining area at the front caters for meals lunchtimes and evenings. The bar in the middle has four handpumps serving local and regional ales. A conservatory/games room at the rear has a pool table and dartboard. There is a small function room and a rear garden offering lovely views, ideal for dining on a beautiful summer's day.
⏰❀🍴&≉(SVR)♣🖫(436,890)❤🛜

Railwayman's Arms 🅻
Severn Valley Railway Station, Hollybush Road, WV16 5DT (follow signs for SVR, pub is on Platform 1)
❀ 11.30 (11 Fri & Sat)-11; 11.30-10.30 Sun
☎ (01746) 764361 ⏲ svr.co.uk
Bathams Best Bitter; Hobsons Mild, Best, Town Crier; 4 changing beers (sourced nationally) 🅷
A unique and popular pub owned by the Severn Valley Railway, licensed since 1861, at Bridgnorth Station, and full of railway memorabilia. There are 10 handpumps, eight serving real ales from near and far, and two for real ciders.
Q⏰❀≉(SVR)🖫P🖫(101,436,890)❤🛜

White Lion 🅻
3 West Castle Street, WV16 4AB (between town centre and SVR)
❀ 11.30-11; 11.30-10.30 Sun ☎ (01746) 763962
⏲ whitelionbridgnorth.co.uk
Hop & Stagger Shropshire Pale Ale, Golden Wander, Bridgnorth Porter, Triple Hop IPA; 3 changing beers (sourced regionally) 🅷
A warm welcome awaits visitors to this 18th-century inn, with eight handpumps serving seven real ales and one cider. Sam and Bob's Hop & Stagger beers are so popular that Bob has moved to a six-barrel brewery, doubling his capacity. Home-made Scotch eggs and a wide range of snacks are available. The pub is a venue for a folk club, quizzes and music nights. The walls in the bar and garden feature murals of Bridgnorth scenes.
Q⏰❀🍴🍴✿≉(SVR)♣🍴🖫(436,890)❤🛜

Cardington

Royal Oak
SY6 7JZ
❀ 12-2.30, 6-11; 12-11 Sat & Sun; closed Mon
☎ (01694) 771266 ⏲ at-the-oak.com
Ludlow Best; Sharp's Doom Bar; 2 changing beers 🅷
Dating back to the 15th century, this is reputedly Shropshire's oldest continuously licensed pub, and is the archetypal country inn. The single room is multi-functional with a bar, lounge and dining area, and has a relaxed ambience. It is low beamed and dominated by an inglenook fireplace which provides a home for various interesting artefacts. A good choice of beers includes a mix of local and regional brews. Q❀🍴🍴▲♣🍴P🖫(540)❤🛜

Cheswardine

Red Lion 🅻
High Street, TF9 2RS
❀ 5 (4 Thu-Sat)-11; 7-10.30 Sun ☎ (01630) 661234
Lion's Tale Blooming Blonde, Chesbrewnette, Lionbru; Marston's Burton Bitter 🅷
Home of the Lion's Tale Brewery, three of its beers are always on sale. It also boasts over 100 whiskies, which the landlord is happy to advise on. A music session is held on the second Tuesday evening of the month showcasing local talent. With its quieter corners and old time charms, the Red Lion is ideal for a relaxing pint. Within walking distance of bridges 52 and 53 of the Shropshire Union Canal. Q⏰❀&♣P❤

Clunton

Crown Inn 🅻
SY7 0HU
❀ 5 (4 Wed & Thu)-11; 12-midnight Fri & Sat; 12-11 Sun
☎ (01588) 660265 ⏲ crowninnclunton.co.uk
Hobsons Best; Ludlow Gold; Stonehouse Station Bitter; 1 changing beer 🅷
Set in AE Housman country, the Clun Valley is a designated Area of Outstanding Natural Beauty. This genuine, community-owned inn, run by a local family, has three rooms including a smart restaurant. It hosts a popular fish and chips night every Wednesday, including takeaways, and an acoustic folk night on the fourth Monday of the month. The Crown takes part in the annual Clun Valley Beer Festival. Ludlow Gold is available in winter, replaced by a changing guest in summer.
Q❀🍴♣🍴P🖫

Ellerdine Heath

Royal Oak 🍽 ⓛ ✅

Hazles Road, TF6 6RL (midway between A442 and A53)
SJ603226

🟢 12-11 ☎ (01939) 250300

Hobsons Best; Tring Side Pocket for a Toad; Wye
Valley HPA; 2 changing beers (sourced nationally) Ⓗ
A gem of a country pub, the Tiddly has been in the
Guide for years. It is frequented by all ages and
hosts a folk group on the third Tuesday of every
month. Real fires warm the rooms in winter and in
summer an extensive outside area hosts summer
activities. A cider festival is held during the last
week of July. Locally sourced food including
vegetarian options is available Wednesday-Sunday.
Q ➰ 🏮 🛏 🍽 ♿ 🅿 ✿ 🐾 ?

Ellesmere

White Hart ⓛ

Birch Road, SY12 0ET

🟢 3-midnight; 1-1am Sat & Sun ☎ (01691) 624653

Salopian Shropshire Gold; 3 changing beers Ⓗ
A Grade II-listed building of the early Jacobean
period. The interior comprises a public bar and a
lounge. Outside, the drinking area to the rear has a
tented gazebo. The three guest beers include
offerings from local breweries. Convenient for
boating folk on the Llangollen Canal as the marina
is close by. 🏮 🅿 🚆 🐾 ?

Habberley

Mytton Arms ⓛ

SY5 0TP

🟢 4-11; 12-11 Fri-Sun ☎ (01743) 792490

Hobsons Best; Three Tuns XXX; 1 changing beer Ⓗ
Situated in a small village on the edge of the South
Shropshire Hills and somewhat off the beaten
track, this popular pub is worth seeking out. There
are four low-beamed rooms and a friendly rustic
atmosphere – beer and conversation predominate.
Outside are seats to the front, and a paved area
with a vine-covered pergola to the side. The South
Shropshire Hills shuttle bus provides transport in
summer. Q 🏮 ♣ 🍽 🅿 🚆 🐾

Harmer Hill

Red Castle

SY4 3EB

🟢 12-4, 6-midnight; 12-midnight Fri-Sun ☎ (01939) 291071

Hobsons Mild, Best; 2 changing beers Ⓗ
A successful village local, under the same
ownership for over 20 years. There are two public
rooms, the larger one very much for dining. The
community aspect is reflected in the stock of
books, jigsaws (including some for children) and
videos, participation in the local darts league, and a
substantial amount of money raised for charity.
Smokers will need to be persistent in seeking out
the smoking area, the route being rather obscure.
Guest beers are from local or national breweries.
➰ 🏮 🛏 ⓓ ♿ 🅿 🚆 (501) 🐾 ?

Hengoed

Last Inn

Brookside, SY10 7EU

🟢 3-11 (midnight Thu & Fri); 12-midnight Sat; 12-10.30 Sun
☎ (01691) 659747 ⊕ thelastinn.co.uk

Oakham Bishops Farewell; 5 changing beers Ⓗ
Large pub in a small village at a rural crossroads. A
former cobbler's workshop, the Last has a games
room, public bar and dining room as well as a
separate, extensive refurbished function room
which hosts music and other entertainment. There
are always six cask ales on offer from regional,
local and micro breweries. The restaurant serves
meals Tuesday to Saturday evenings and Sunday
lunchtimes. Monday hours may vary in winter, so
check first. ➰ 🏮 🛏 🍽 🛏 ♣ 🅿 🚆 (2A) 🐾 ?

Hodnet

Bear

Drayton Road, TF9 3NH

🟢 12-11; 12-10 Sun ☎ (01630) 685214

⊕ bearathodnet.co.uk

Black Sheep Best Bitter; Salopian Shropshire Gold; 2
changing beers (sourced nationally; often Rowton,
Six Bells, Three Tuns) Ⓗ
This old coaching inn dating from the 17th century
once housed bears in the cellar. There are four
logburners, a dedicated room for dogs and a
separate room for meetings and functions. This is
mainly a food pub but drinkers are warmly
welcomed, with plenty of standing and sitting
room. The beer range includes the colourful
regulars and two changing guests sourced
nationwide. The TV shows rugby but not football.
Closes at 7pm on winter Sundays.
➰ 🏮 🍽 🛏 ⓓ ♿ 🅿 🚆 🐾 ?

Little Stretton

Green Dragon

Ludlow Road, SY6 6RE

🟢 11.30-11.30 ☎ (01694) 722925

⊕ greendragonlittlestretton.co.uk

Draught Bass; Hobsons Mild; Ludlow Gold; Wye Valley
Butty Bach; 2 changing beers (sourced locally) Ⓗ
The pub is set in a picturesque location in the
Shropshire Hills Area of Outstanding Natural
Beauty, with an abundance of walks in the district.
The L-shaped bar has a comfortable and welcoming
feel and the pleasant separate dining room is well
used. A collection of wonderfully shaped clay pipes
on the bar wall may well be of interest. The beer is
mostly from local breweries, as is the cider (at the
appropriate time of year).
➰ 🏮 🛏 ⓓ ♣ 🍽 🅿 🚆 (435) 🐾 ?

Longden Common

Red Lion ⓛ

SY5 8AE

🟢 6 (5 Fri)-11; 12-11 Sat; 12-10 Sun ☎ (01743) 718889

⊕ theredlionlongden.co.uk

The Shropshire Brewer The Golden Arrow, Sawn Off,
Spire Dancer Ⓗ
This is the brewery tap for The Shropshire Brewer,
formerly the Longden Brewery, which operates
from a converted stable next door. It is sufficiently
spacious to be able to cater for both diners and
drinkers. There are three public areas – a public bar,
a snug and a conservatory providing dining space.
There is a large garden to the rear. Bottled beers
are available. ➰ 🏮 🛏 🛏 🅿 🚆 (546) 🐾 ?

Ludlow

Queen's 🄻
113 Lower Galdeford, SY8 1RU (just off town centre, opp Co-op)
✪ 12-11 (midnight Fri & Sat); 12-10.30 Sun
☎ (01584) 879177 ⊕ thequeensludlow.com
Hobsons Best; Ludlow Gold; Wye Valley Butty Bach; 1 changing beer (sourced locally; often Hobsons, Ludlow) 🄷
Named after Queen Victoria, this is a popular pub and café bar with a decent range of local ales. Look out for the guest beer offered at a competitive price. The light and airy L-shaped bar has three distinct areas, with dining down a short flight of steps. Bar meals are available with local produce a proud boast. The large enclosed patio garden has views toward Ludford. The monthly quiz is always well attended. 🏵🍴🕽🖘🐾🖪🐾🛜

Railway Shed 🄻
Station Drive, SY8 2PQ
✪ 10-5 (6 Fri); 10-4 Sat; closed Sun ☎ (01584) 873291
⊕ theludlowbrewingcompany.co.uk
Ludlow Best, Blonde, Gold, Black Knight, Boiling Well, Stairway 🄷
The Railway Shed is the brewery tap and visitor centre for the Ludlow Brewing Company, and as the name suggests, the building was once a transit depot for railway goods. An imaginative conversion, it is built on two levels, with two huge brewing vessels on the upper level, and more comfortable seating and tables. On the ground floor there are hand-crafted timber tables and benches, together with a shop. Brewery visits are welcome and the centre is available for hire.
Q🏵🖘🖪🐾🛜

Market Drayton

Hippodrome ✅
Queen Street, TF9 1PS
✪ 8am-midnight; 9am-1am Fri & Sat; 9am-midnight Sun
☎ (01630) 650820
Greene King Abbot; Ruddles Best Bitter; 3 changing beers (sourced locally; often Lymestone, Slater's, Titanic) 🄷
Originally Market Drayton's first cinema, the Hippodrome closed in 1966. After spells as a bingo hall and supermarket, the pub was opened by Wetherspoon in 2007 retaining some unique features. The usual food fare is served, but what makes this pub different is that it actively supports local breweries, regularly showcasing them at the bar. Q🏵🕽🖪🛜

King's Arms
Shropshire Street, TF9 3DA
✪ 4-midnight; 12-1am Fri & Sat; 12-midnight Sun
☎ (01630) 655413
Wadworth 6X; 3 changing beers (sourced nationally) 🄷
Originally an old coaching house built in 1629, this is a friendly every-man-and-his-dog pub. It is a smallish building and maintains the three original rooms, one with a log fire creating a cosy atmosphere. Steeped in history, the walls are decorated with many old photographs depicting Market Drayton. It serves three guest ales and is one of only four free houses in the town.
🕽🏵🖪🛜

Red Lion 🄻
Great Hales Street, TF9 1JP
✪ 11-11 (midnight Fri & Sat) ☎ (01630) 652602
⊕ joulesbrewery.co.uk
Joule's Blonde, Pale Ale, Slumbering Monk; 1 changing beer (sourced locally; often Joule's) 🄷
A previous winner of the CAMRA/English Heritage Pub Design awards, this Joule's brewery tap used to be a coaching inn, built in 1623. Its unique features include an illuminated well in the main bar, and the Mouse Room – a Robert Thompson-inspired function room featuring carved mice. Log fires and oak beams create a comfortable atmosphere where locally sourced food can be enjoyed from an extensive menu, with the Joule's range of beers produced in the adjacent brewery. Q🏵🖥🕽🖪🛜

Sandbrook Vaults 🄻
4 Shropshire Street, TF9 3BY
✪ 5-11 (1am Thu); 11-1am Fri & Sat; 11-11 Sun
☎ (01630) 478405 ⊕ joulesbrewery.co.uk
Joule's Blonde, Pale Ale, Slumbering Monk 🄷
You are guaranteed a warm welcome from the landlord at this Joule's pub, with the familiar easy-on-the-eye Joule's interior and well-kept beers from the brewery 150 yards away. It also offers free hot food at weekends to customers (with an optional donation to charity). The pub holds regular high-quality live acoustic music nights on Thursdays and Sundays, featuring good regional bands. Q🏵🖪🛜

Much Wenlock

George & Dragon ✅
2 High Street, TF13 6AA
✪ 12-11; 12-10.30 Sun ☎ (01952) 727312
⊕ thegeorgedragon.co.uk
Greene King Abbot; Hobsons Best; St Austell Tribute; 2 changing beers (sourced nationally) 🄷
Historic pub, now Punch owned, in a beautiful small market town, close to the Guildhall, parish church, museum and Wenlock Priory, attracting locals and visitors. The bar has settles, a tiled and wooden floor, and open fireplaces with old tile surrounds. Original beams feature, with a collection of jugs hanging from them. There is an attractive, intimate restaurant to the rear. Cider is available in summer only. No evening food Wednesday and Sunday in winter. Q🏵🕽🖪(88,436)🐾🛜

Newport

New Inn 🄻
2 Stafford Street, TF10 7LX
✪ 12-11 (midnight Fri & Sat) ☎ (01952) 812295
⊕ thenewinnnewport.co.uk
Joule's Blonde, Pale Ale, Slumbering Monk; 2 changing beers (sourced locally; often Joule's) 🄷
Originally an old coaching inn dating from 1792, the building has been completely refurbished by Joule's but retains some of the old features such as the latch doors. There is a Yorkist fireplace in the snug area plus a central woodburner for winter comfort and an extensive garden for the summer. A friendly pub catering for all ages, it serves good food including vegetarian options. Live music often plays on Sunday evenings. Q🏵🖥🕽🖪🐾🛜

Onibury

Apple Tree

SY7 9AW (up a short side road from the A49 level crossing)
🕒 5 (12 Fri & Sat)-11; 12-9 Sun; closed Mon
☎ (01584) 856633
Ludlow Gold, Stairway; Monty's MPA Ⓗ
Originally the Griffin Inn in 1877, the building had different uses before becoming a pub again. There are three rooms – the main bar at the front, a smarter room to the side, and a games room with darts and quoits at the back. Car parking is available in the nearby village hall car park.
Q❀♣P☟(435)❁❄

Oswestry

Black Lion Ⓛ

Salop Road, SY11 2RJ (S of town centre on B4579)
🕒 6-11; 4.30-midnight Fri; 12-midnight Sat; 12-11 Sun
☎ (01691) 652745 ⊕ theblacklionoswestry.co.uk
Salopian Oracle; 4 changing beers (sourced locally; often Hobsons, Salopian, Wood) Ⓗ
Just inside the town's conservation area, this is a family-run establishment. It is home to sports teams and social groups, with plenty of TVs for sports fans and tasting boards for beer lovers. The central bar divides the pub into a comfortable lounge at the front and public bar at the rear. Well-kept ales from various local and regional brewers can be enjoyed. Q❧❀♣●P☟❄

Oak Inn Ⓛ

47 Church Street, SY11 2SZ
🕒 12-midnight; 11.30-midnight Sat & Sun ☎ (01691) 659254
Draught Bass; Salopian Shropshire Gold; Stonehouse Station Bitter, Cambrian Gold; 1 changing beer (often The Shropshire Brewer) Ⓗ
Built on a burgage plot typical of the area, the Oak is larger than its frontage suggests. An early 18th-century, Grade II-listed building, this traditional free house is divided into a public bar at the front and a larger comfortable lounge at the rear. A passage at the side leads to the garden. Listed as serving Draught Bass in the 1975 Guide, it is still available alongside the local beers. ❧❀♣☟❄

Sambrook

Three Horseshoes

TF10 8AP (½ mile E of A41, on main road through Sambrook)
🕒 6-11 Mon; 12-2, 5-11; 12-11 Sat & Sun ☎ (01952) 551133
⊕ threehorseshoessambrook.co.uk
Salopian Shropshire Gold; 4 changing beers (sourced regionally; often Hobsons, Rowton, Titanic) Ⓗ
A traditional country pub for over 100 years, it has three rooms including a main bar with a woodburner and a separate restaurant. This welcoming community venue hosts regular quiz nights, music on alternate Fridays, darts and dominoes. A varied menu of home-cooked pub grub is available at all times to suit all tastes and budgets (no food Mon). Families and dogs are welcome throughout the pub, patio and garden, which has a children's play area. Real cider is available in the summer. ❧❀❶♣P☟❄

Shifnal

Plough Inn Ⓛ

26 Broadway, TF11 8AZ
🕒 12 (4.30 Mon)-11; 12-10.30 Sun ☎ (01952) 463118
⊕ theploughinnshifnal.co.uk
Hobsons Mild, Best; house beer (by Broadway Brewery); 5 changing beers (sourced regionally; often Bathams, Sarah Hughes, Wood) Ⓗ
Traditional 17th-century family-run free house with exposed beams and tiled floors, boasting eight ales, mostly from local breweries, and two ciders on handpull. No-nonsense home-cooked food is available (no food Mon). A weekly quiz is held on Wednesdays and there is a free book exchange. Outside is an extensive beer garden and a covered and heated smoking area where dogs are welcome. Local artists exhibit inside the pub. A function room is available to hire. ❧❀❶◗❦♣●☟❄

White Hart Ⓛ ✅

High Street, TF11 8BH
🕒 12-11 ☎ (01952) 461161
Holden's Black Country Mild; Salopian Shropshire Gold; Wye Valley HPA, Butty Bach; 5 changing beers (sourced nationally; often Enville, Greene King) Ⓗ
Historic timber-framed free house with a beer garden and sunny patio off the lounge bar. With 22 years in the Guide, the pub has received many CAMRA awards as well as consistent top marks in Cask Marque inspections. Home-cooked food and fresh baps are available lunchtimes Monday-Saturday. A friendly community local, it supports darts and dominoes teams. Q❀◗❦♣●P☟

Shrewsbury

Admiral Benbow Ⓛ

24 Swan Hill, SY1 1NF (just off Main Square)
🕒 5 (12 Sat)-11; 7-10.30 Sun ☎ (01743) 244423
Ludlow Gold; Salopian Hop Twister; Six Bells Cloud Nine; Slater's Top Totty; The Shropshire Brewer Sawn Off; 2 changing beers (often Wrekin Brewery, Wye Valley) Ⓗ
Spacious free house serving a range of Shropshire and Herefordshire beers plus a selection of ciders from Rosie's including Black Bart, Wicked Wasp and Triple. A good choice of Belgian beers is also offered. A small room off the bar can be used for private functions, and there is a seating and smoking area outside at the rear. Children are not permitted. The Admiral was a notorious 17th-century naval officer who was born in Shrewsbury. Q❀❦♣●☟❄

Coach & Horses Ⓛ ✅

23 Swan Hill, SY1 1NF
🕒 11.30-midnight (12.30am Fri & Sat); 12-11.30 Sun
☎ (01743) 365661 ⊕ odleyinns.co.uk/coach-horses
Salopian Shropshire Gold, Oracle; Stonehouse Station Bitter; 3 changing beers Ⓗ
Set in a quiet street off the main shopping area, it is Victorian in style, and has a wood-panelled bar, a small side snug area and a large lounge where meals are served lunchtimes and evenings. Bar snacks are also available at lunchtimes. Cheddar Valley cider is dispensed on handpull.
Q❶⛰❦♣●☟❄

Montgomery's Tower Ⓛ ✅

Lower Claremont Bank, SY1 1RT
🕒 8am-midnight (1am Wed & Thu; 2am Fri & Sat)
☎ (01743) 239080

Salopian Shropshire Gold; Wood Shropshire Lad; 4 changing beers (often Chapel, Purity, Slater's) ℍ
Close to the Quarry Park and handy for Theatre Severn, this Lloyds No.1 offers a choice of two bars. To the left is a large open area rich in natural light, with a smoking area to the rear. The bar to the right provides quieter surroundings and subdued lighting, except on Fridays and Saturdays when there is a DJ. Food is served 9am-11pm.
🐕🕮🕧🌑🏰🚃🌐🚽🐾🛜

Nag's Head ℒ
22 Wyle Cop, SY1 1XB
✪ 11.30-midnight; 10.30-1am Fri; 12-midnight Sun
☎ (01743) 362455
Hobsons Best; Sharp's Doom Bar; Timothy Taylor Landlord; Wye Valley HPA; 1 changing beer (often Moorhouse's) ℍ
Situated on the historic Wyle Cop, the main features of this Grade II-listed, timber-framed building are best appreciated externally – in particular the upper-storey jettying and, to the rear, the timber remnants of a 14th-century hall house including a screened passage which provided protection from draughts (and now offers shelter for smokers). The pub is said to be haunted and features on the Shrewsbury Ghost Trail.
🕮🚃🍀🚽🐾

Prince of Wales ♈ ℒ
30 Bynner Street, Belle Vue, SY3 7NZ
✪ 5-midnight; 12-midnight Fri-Sun ☎ (01743) 343301
🌐 theprince.pub
Greene King IPA; Hobsons Twisted Spire; St Austell Tribute; Salopian Golden Thread; Three Tuns Mild; Thwaites Wainwright; 1 changing beer (sourced locally; often Big Shed, Rowton, Wood) ℍ
Welcoming two-roomed community pub with a heated smoking shelter and a large suntrap deck adjoining a bowling green. The green is overlooked by a 19th-century maltings. Darts, dominoes and bowls teams abound. Beer festivals take place each year in February and May. Shrewsbury Town FC memorabilia adorn the building both inside and out, with some of the seating from the old Gay Meadow ground skirting the bowling green. Local CAMRA branch Pub of the Year in 2015.
🚽🐕🕮🕧🍀🌑🐾P🐾

Salopian Bar ℒ ✔
Smithfield Road, SY1 1PW
✪ 11-midnight (11 Tue & Wed); 11-11 Sun
☎ (01743) 351505
Oakham Citra; Salopian Oracle; Stonehouse Station Bitter; 5 changing beers (often Oakham, Salopian) ℍ
The bar's dedicated management strives to increase the beer, cider and perry range to satisfy public demand. Regular cider and perry is provided by Westons and Thatchers, and an impressive range of Belgian and American bottled beer is also sold. Coverage of major sporting events is shown on large-screen TVs. Local artwork is on display and for sale. A regular winner of local CAMRA Pub of the Year awards and Town pub winner for 2014.
🕧🚃🌑🐾🚽🐾🛜

Three Fishes ℒ
4 Fish Street, SY1 1UR
✪ 11.30-3, 5-11; 11.30-11.30 Fri & Sat; 12-10.30 Sun
☎ (01743) 344793 🌐 realaleshrewsbury.co.uk
Stonehouse Station Bitter; Three Tuns Stout; Timothy Taylor Landlord; 3 changing beers (often Oakham, Salopian, Three Tuns) ℍ

Fifteenth-century building standing in the shadow of two churches, St Alkmund's and St Julian's, within the maze of streets and passageways in the town's medieval quarter. Freshly prepared food is available at lunchtimes and early evenings Monday to Saturday. The pub offers a range of up to six local and national ales, usually including some dark beers, and a choice of real ciders and perries. A former local CAMRA Pub of the Year.
Q🕧🚃🍀🌑🚽🐾🛜

Woodman ℒ
32 Coton Hill, SY1 2DZ
✪ 4-midnight; 12-midnight Sat & Sun ☎ (01743) 351007
Salopian Shropshire Gold; Wye Valley Butty Bach; 3 changing beers (sourced regionally; often Mallinson's, Ossett, Pictish) ℍ
Half-brick and half-timbered black and white corner pub, originally built in the 1800s, destroyed by fire in 1923, and rebuilt in 1925. The building is reputedly haunted by the ex-landlady who died in the fire. The wonderful oak-panelled lounge has two real log fires and traditional settles, and the separate bar has the original stone-tiled flooring, wooden seating, fire and listed leaded windows. The courtyard has a heated smoking area and seating. Q🕮🐕🚃🍀🌑🚽🐾🛜

Telford: Coalbrookdale

Coalbrookdale Inn
12 Wellington Road, TF8 7DX (opp Enginuity Museum)
✪ 4-11; 12-11 Sat & Sun ☎ (01952) 432166
Hobsons Town Crier; Sarah Hughes Dark Ruby Mild; 5 changing beers (sourced regionally; often Battlefield, Salopian, Wye Valley) ℍ
A Victorian Grade II-listed village local in historic Coalbrookdale, opposite the Enginuity Museum and close to the Iron Bridge and industrial heritage museums which are part of the Ironbridge Gorge World Heritage site. This cosy, welcoming pub has three rooms, two with real fires. A community local, it is home to darts, dominoes, ukulele night on Wednesday, a fortnightly quiz on Tuesday and community eating nights. Simple bar food is available at all times. 🐕🕮🚐🕧🅰🍀🌑P🚽(9)🐾🛜

Telford: Madeley

All Nations ℒ
20 Coalport Road, TF7 5DP (signed off Legges Way, opp Blists Hill Museum)
✪ 12-11.30 ☎ (01952) 585747
Hobsons Twisted Spire; house beer (by Broughs); 3 changing beers (sourced locally; often Kinver, Ludlow, Slater's) ℍ
Historic brewhouse in a secluded location offering a friendly welcome. Four handpulled ales and a cider are available, with Broughs Brewery providing a house beer. A choice of freshly made bar snacks is offered. The pub is warmed by a cosy logburner in winter and there is a pretty beer garden for the warmer months. A TV is brought in for Rugby Union matches. The Monday night quiz is a must. Q🐕🕮🚐🅰🍀🌑P🐾

Telford: Oakengates

Crown Inn ℒ ✔
Market Street, TF2 6EA
✪ 12-11 ☎ (01952) 610888 🌐 crown.oakengates.net

Hobsons Twisted Spire, Best; 10 changing beers (sourced nationally; often Beowulf, Joule's, Rudgate) ⓗ
Vibrant three-roomed 1835 town pub with friendly locals. It has 14 handpumps, increasing to 34 during beer festivals held on the first weekends of May and October, when around 50 ales are served. Real cider, mild and a stout or porter are usually available, plus a range of continental bottled beers. There is a suntrap courtyard to the rear. Entertainment includes the Telford Acoustic Club on Wednesdays, live world music most Thursdays, the Telford Comedy Club on the second Tuesday of the month and a Sunday night quiz.
Q ⃝ 🕭 ⊛ ⓵ ⇌ ♣ ♦ P 🖫 ❀ 🛜

Old Fighting Cocks ⓛ
48 Market Street, TF2 6DU
🕓 12-11 ☎ (01952) 615607
Everards Tiger Best Bitter; Wrekin Pale Ale, Ironbridge Gold; 7 changing beers ⓗ
Four-roomed pub including a cosy snug at the rear, warmed by real fires. Originally a coaching inn, formerly on Watling Street, it retains some of the original windows. Beer festivals are held in May and November in conjunction with the nearby Station Hotel. Bring your own food – plates and cutlery provided. Upstairs a 32-seat cinema is available for hire. A winner of CAMRA branch, county and area Pub of the Year awards.
Q ⃝ 🕭 ⊛ ⓵ ♣ ♦ 🖫 ❀ 🛜

Station Hotel ⓛ
42 Market Street, TF2 6DU
🕓 11-11 (9 Mon); 12-11 Sun ☎ (01952) 612949
Bathams Best Bitter; 8 changing beers (sourced nationally) ⓗ
A basic town pub that has featured in the Guide for many years. The landlord specialises in beers from Yorkshire, but also sources locally and nationally. There is a real fire in the front room where drinkers can enjoy home-made bar snacks and the now legendary Wednesday curry night. Beer festivals are held in May and November along with the Old Fighting Cocks nearby. Do not miss the Belgian beer festival. Cider is available in summer.
Q ⊛ ⇌ ♣ 🖫 ❀

Telford: Wellington
Cock Hotel ⓛ
148 Hollyhead Road, TF1 2DL
🕓 4 (12 Thu)-11.30; 12-11.45 Fri & Sat; 12-11 Sun
☎ (01952) 244954 🌐 cockhotel.co.uk
Hobsons Mild, Best; 5 changing beers (sourced nationally; often Holden's, Ludlow, Salopian) ⓗ
This multi award-winning 18th-century coaching inn has eight handpulls mostly dispensing regional ales, always including a dark beer and a real cider. Continental beers are also kept on draught and in bottles. The two-roomed pub has a main bar decorated with hops and warmed by a fire in winter. Award-winning pork pies are served from the bar at all times. B&B accommodation and a meeting room are available. Q ⊛ 🛏 ♣ ♦ P 🖫 ❀ 🛜

Pheasant Inn ♥ ⓛ
54 Market Street, TF1 1DT
🕓 11-midnight; 12-11.30 Sun ☎ (01952) 260683
Everards Tiger Best Bitter; Wrekin Ironbridge Gold; 5 changing beers (sourced nationally; often Abbeydale, Mallinson's, Rowton) ⓗ

Home of the Wrekin Brewing Company, based in an adjacent outbuilding. The bar has nine handpulls, two used for cider. Gin is also available, produced by the Ironbridge Spirit Company based in the brewery. You can enjoy home-made food Monday to Saturday 11am-4pm. Q ⊛ ⓵ 🕭 ⇌ ♦ P 🖫 ❀

William Withering ⓛ ⊘
43-45 New Street, TF1 1LU
🕓 8am-midnight; 8am-1am Fri & Sat ☎ (01952) 642800
Ruddles Best Bitter; Salopian Shropshire Gold; Sharp's Doom Bar; 5 changing beers (sourced nationally) ⓗ
Named after a local physician who is best remembered for discovering and developing the medical properties of digitalis. The large single open-plan room is styled as an 18th-century study. Three regular beers are complemented by changing ales – local, national and sometimes even international. Good-value food is served 8am-11pm. Ciders include Old Rosie, Black Dragon and up to four others. ⃝ ⊛ ⓵ ◐ 🕭 ⇌ ♦ 🖫 🛜

Whitchurch
Black Bear ⓛ
High Street, SY13 1AZ (opp St Alkmund's church)
🕓 12-3, 6-11; 12-11 Sat; 12-10.30 Sun ☎ (01948) 663800
🌐 blackbearpub.co.uk
6 changing beers (often Big Shed Brewery, Hobsons, Lancaster) ⓗ
Tastefully renovated black and white pub whose ornate bar has six handpulls dispensing a range of guest beers from both local and lesser-known national microbreweries, with pumpclips adorning the walls, ceiling and bar area. Cider is served on gravity. There are two separate dining areas and an upstairs meeting room. Local CAMRA branch Market Town Pub of the Year in 2015.
Q ⊛ ⓵ ◐ ♦ P 🖫 ❀

Cock & Greyhound
20 Bargates, SY13 1LL
🕓 12-11 (midnight Fri); 12-1am Sat ☎ (01948) 665151
Thwaites Wainwright; 4 changing beers (often Salopian) ⓗ
Removal of some internal walls does not detract from the 17th-century feel of the building, resulting in a pleasing single-room interior while retaining distinctive areas within. Six handpulls dispense five regularly changing beers and one cider, almost exclusively from Shropshire/ Cheshire/Staffordshire and North Wales brewers. A centrally positioned real fire enhances the cosy and welcoming atmosphere. ⊛ ⓵ ◐ ♣ ♦ P 🖫 ❀ 🛜

Old Town Hall Vaults ⓛ
St Marys Street, SY13 1QU (just off Whitchurch High St)
🕓 11-11 (midnight Fri & Sat); 12-11 Sun ☎ (01948) 664682
Joule's Blonde, Pale Ale; 3 changing beers (often Hunters, Sarah Hughes, Titanic) ⓗ
Birthplace of composer Sir Edward German in 1862, the pub has undergone a comprehensive restructuring in the Joule's brewery style of stained wood and ornamental glass panelling. Removal of internal walls has provided an open central space, albeit with the retention of two quieter front-facing bays. Beers from the Joule's range are complemented by two regularly changing guests from other Midlands brewers. Q ⊛ ⓵ 🕭 ⇌ 🖫 ❀

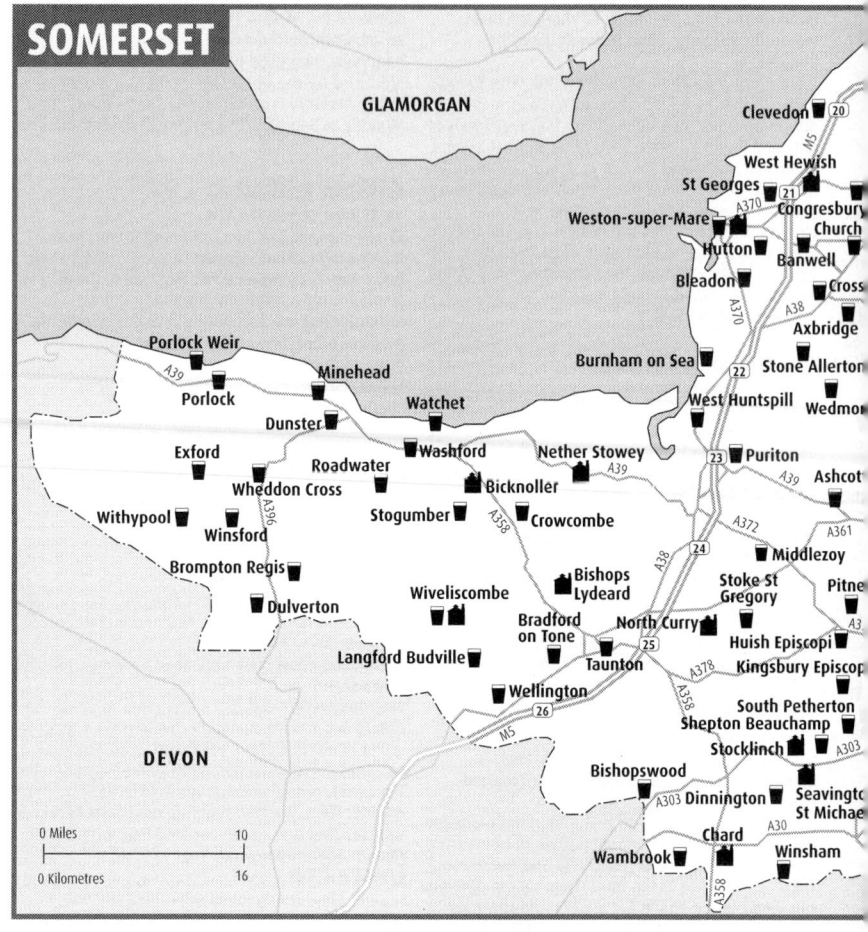

SOMERSET

GLAMORGAN

Clevedon 20
West Hewish
St Georges 21
Congresbury
Weston-super-Mare A370 Church
Hutton Banwell
Bleadon A38 Cross
A370 Axbridge
Porlock Weir Stone Allerton
Minehead Burnham on Sea 22 Wedmor
Porlock West Huntspill
Dunster Watchet
Exford Washford Nether Stowey 23 Puriton
Roadwater A39 Ashcot
Wheddon Cross Bicknoller A372
Withypool Stogumber A358 Crowcombe 24
Winsford Middlezoy
Brompton Regis
Bishops Stoke St Pitne
Dulverton Lydeard Gregory
Wiveliscombe North Curry Huish Episcopi
Bradford 25
Langford Budville on Tone Taunton A378 Kingsbury Episcop
Wellington A358 South Petherton
26 Shepton Beauchamp
DEVON Stocklinch A303
Bishopswood Seavingto
A303 Dinnington St Michae
Chard A30
0 Miles 10 Wambrook Winsham
0 Kilometres 16

Ash

Bell Inn 🄻

3 Main Street, TA12 6NS
🕐 12-11.30 (1am Fri & Sat); 12-10 Sun ☎ (01935) 822727
🌐 thebellinnash.co.uk
4 changing beers (sourced locally) Ⓗ
The Bell continues to be a warm and welcoming traditional pub, with up to four handpumps delivering a wide range of mainly Somerset ales and a real cider. Locally sourced home-cooked meals are served six days a week, with a broad menu choice. Regular live music nights and quiz nights take place. Many unusual old church belfry items adorn the bar walls.
Q🛅🕏🕭◗🕹♣🍴🅿🚌(N9,N9A)🐕

Ashcott

Ring o' Bells

16 High Street, TA7 9PZ (signposted off A39)
🕐 12-2.30, 7-11; 12-2.30, 7-10.30 Sun ☎ (01458) 210232
🌐 ringobells.com
3 changing beers (sourced regionally; often RCH, Teignworthy) Ⓗ
An 18th-century family-run free house in the village, comprising three traditional areas on split levels, with a separate restaurant. Old beams and fireplaces provide a warm ambience. There is a

contrasting modern skittle alley/function room at the rear and an enclosed garden. The pub has been in the Guide for 20 consecutive years. Good home-cooked food is served, with meals and ales available to take away. Close to Ham Wall and Shapwick Heath nature reserves.
🛅🕏🕭◗🕹&🅰♣🍴🅿🚌(19,29)🐕📶

Axbridge

Lamb ✅

The Square, BS26 2AP
🕐 11.30-11 (midnight Fri & Sat); 12-10.30 Sun
☎ (01934) 732253 🌐 lamb.butcombe.com
Butcombe Bitter; 2 changing beers (often Butcombe) Ⓗ
Butcombe-owned Grade II-listed coaching house in the village square. The National Trust's medieval King John's Hunting Lodge is directly opposite. There is a large low-beamed bar area and several smaller, quieter areas leading off it. Outside drinking spaces are to the front and rear. Lunchtime and evening meals are served (not Sun eve). Butcombe seasonals are usually joined by a guest beer and the cider is normally from Thatchers. The Weston to Wells 26 and 126 buses stop nearby during the day.
Q🕏◗♣🍴🚌(26,126)🐕📶

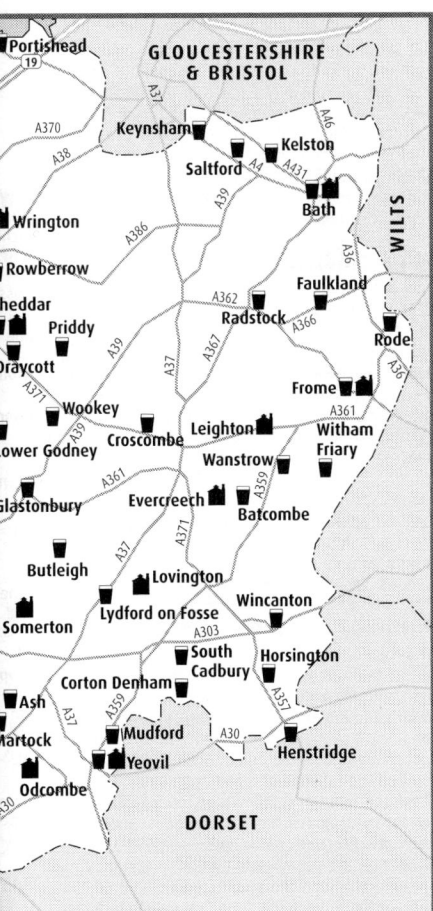

room with a vaulted ceiling, and a lawned garden overlooked by the church tower. The food is from local suppliers. Open to all, it welcomes drinkers, foodies, walkers, children (with colouring books and games to keep them entertained) and dogs. Local cider is from Rich's. Q⛄🏠🚲◁🍴◖👣P

Bath

Bath Brew House ✓

14 James Street West, BA1 2BX
🕓 11-midnight (1am Fri & Sat); 11-11 Sun
☎ (01225) 805609 ⊕ thebathbrewhouse.com

James Street Gladiator, Emperor; 5 changing beers (sourced regionally; often Castle Combe, Milk Street, Yeovil) Ⓗ

Refurbishment in 2013 saw the former Midland Hotel transformed into a City Pub Company brewpub. The on-site James Street Brewery produces two regular beers, the refreshing and malty Gladiator (3.9%) and the hoppy, citrusy Emperor (4.4%), plus rotating seasonal beers. Four guests, usually from nearby micros, are also served. A large L-shaped bar gives out onto a dining area and a good-sized beer garden. The upstairs room hosts TV sport, quizzes, comedy, and so on. 🐈◖&🚲♿🍴♣👣🐾🛜

Bell

103 Walcot Street, BA1 5BW
🕓 11.30-11; 12-10.30 Sun ☎ (01225) 460426
⊕ thebellinnbath.co.uk

Abbey Bellringer; Butcombe Bitter; Hop Back Summer Lightning; Otter Ale; RCH Pitchfork; Stonehenge Danish Dynamite; 2 changing beers (sourced regionally) Ⓗ

The Bell is owned by 536 of its regulars, fans and staff, following a community buy-out in 2013. It serves seven real ales plus two guests from micros near and far. Live music is a mainstay, with bands playing Monday and Wednesday evenings and Sunday lunchtimes. In the separate Love Lounge to

Banwell

Bell Inn

1 The Square, BS29 6BL
🕓 5-11 ☎ (01934) 822330

Butcombe Bitter; 2 changing beers (often St Austell) Ⓗ

This village pub is being slowly and lovingly restored after years of neglect. The guest beer is sometimes joined by a second brew. A real fire warms the front bar and outside is a small patio for alfresco drinking. There is a quiz on Thursdays, occasional live music and board games. Despite the address, the pub is situated on a blind right-angled bend on the busy main road so extra care is needed. Banwell Castle is nearby. 🐈♣🚌(26,126,134)🐾🛜

Batcombe

Three Horseshoes Inn

BA4 6HE (off Back Lane) ST69023908
🕓 11-3, 6-11; 11-11 Sat; 12-10.30 Sun ☎ (01749) 850359
⊕ thethreehorseshoesinn.co.uk

Butcombe Bitter; 3 changing beers (sourced nationally; often Church End, Plain) Ⓗ

The Three Horseshoes is a 400-year-old country pub which has a spacious bar with an inglenook fireplace and beamed ceiling, a stunning dining

REAL ALE BREWERIES

Abbey Bath
Beat North Curry (NEW)
Black Bear 🍺 Wiveliscombe
Blindmans Leighton
Butcombe Wrington
Cheddar Cheddar
Cotleigh Wiveliscombe
Cottage Lovington
Electric Bear Bath (NEW)
Exmoor Wiveliscombe
Glastonbury Somerton
James Street 🍺 Bath
Milk Street 🍺 Frome
North Curry North Curry
Odcombe 🍺 Odcombe
Patriot Bicknoller
Quantock Bishops Lydeard
RCH West Hewish
RPM 🍺 Weston-super-Mare (NEW)
Stocklinch Stocklinch
Stowey Nether Stowey
Tanners 🍺 Wiveliscombe (NEW)
Tapstone Chard
Twisted Oak Wrington
Wild Beer Evercreech
Windy 🍺 Seavington St Michael
Yeovil Yeovil

the rear, open mic nights take place on Thursday evenings. Features include bar billiards, board games and even a tiny launderette. At the rear is a walled garden with covered seating.
🏠🍴♿🅿🐾🛇📶

Garrick's Head
8 St John's Place, Saw Close, BA1 1ET
🕐 12-11 (midnight Fri & Sat); 12-10.30 Sun
☎ (01225) 318368 🌐 garricksheadpub.com
House beer (by Stonehenge); 4 changing beers (sourced regionally; often Flying Monk, Three Daggers, Yeovil) Ⓗ
A theatre pub for over 200 years, this was originally the town house of Richard 'Beau' Nash, Bath's 18th-century Master of Ceremonies. This local is reputedly the most haunted pub in the city. Four guest ales are stocked, mostly from regional micros, including some rarities. Traditional food sourced from local ingredients is served lunchtimes and evenings. Tables in the pedestrianised area outside are ideally placed for watching the world go by. ◑⇌🅿🐾📶

Hop Pole
7 Albion Buildings, Upper Bristol Road, BA1 3AR
🕐 12-11 (midnight Fri & Sat) ☎ (01225) 446327
Bath Ales Special Pale Ale, Gem; 3 changing beers (sourced nationally; often Bath Ales, Beerd, Timothy Taylor) Ⓗ
A Bath Ales pub a half-mile west of the city centre, close to Royal Victoria Park and the River Avon. Four ales from Bath Ales plus an occasional guest are dispensed. The enclosed and spacious beer garden is popular with families. Food is served lunchtimes and evenings Monday to Thursday, all day Saturday, and until 8pm on Sunday. Home-made bar snacks – nuts, pork scratchings and Scotch eggs – are also on offer.
Q🍴🏠◑♿⇌♿🅿🐾📶

Huntsman
1 Terrace Walk, BA1 1LJ
🕐 11-11; 12-10.30 Sun ☎ (01225) 482900
🌐 huntsmanbathpub.co.uk
Fuller's Oliver's Island, London Pride; Gale's HSB; 2 changing beers Ⓗ
Dating back to between 1748 and 1750 and taken over by Fuller's in 2012, this gastro-pub has a long, good-sized bar on the ground floor and an à la carte restaurant with its own bar upstairs. Two guest beers are usually on offer, and live music is played on the second Friday of the month. The pub is popular on the days Bath RFC plays at home.
🏠◑⇌(Spa)🅿🐾📶

King of Wessex ✓
James Street West, BA1 2BX
🕐 7am-11.30 ☎ (01225) 303380
Changing beers Ⓗ
A large new-build Wetherspoon pub at the entrance to a cinema complex, refurbished in January 2016 and now with a brand spanking new carpet. There are up to six, mostly regularly changing, real ales, plus the usual Spoon's regulars. Popular with the younger crowd, it can get very busy in the evenings. 🏠◑⇌♿🅿📶

Old Green Tree ★
12 Green Street, BA1 2JZ
🕐 11-11; 12-4.30 Sun ☎ (01225) 448259
Butcombe Bitter; RCH Pitchfork; house beer (by Blindmans); 2 changing beers (sourced locally) Ⓗ

A classic, unspoilt pub in a 300-year-old building. The three oak-panelled rooms include a superb northern-style drinking lobby. Although it can get crowded, there is often space in the comfortable back bar. Guest beers are generally from local microbreweries, with a stout or porter usually on offer in the winter months. A local farmhouse cider is also available, along with a range of fine wines and malt whiskies. Winter Sunday hours may be longer. Q◑⇌♿🅿

Pig & Fiddle ✓
2 Saracen Street, BA1 5BR
🕐 11-11.30 (midnight Fri & Sat); 12-10.30 Sun
☎ (01225) 460868 🌐 pigandfiddle.butcombe.com
Butcombe Bitter; Fuller's London Pride; 3 changing beers (sourced locally) Ⓗ
A large and busy town-centre pub with a varied clientele and a friendly atmosphere. One end is an old shop front, the other a courtyard with drinking benches and covered heaters. The decor is an esoteric collection of art displays and sports memorabilia. Up to three guest beers come from local breweries. Table football is played, and there are regular live music and open mic nights. The pub is popular with rugby fans and has several large TV screens. 🚲🏠◑⇌♿🅿🐾📶

Pulteney Arms ✓
37 Daniel Street, BA2 6ND
🕐 12-3, 5-11 (midnight Thu); 12-midnight Fri & Sat; 12-10.30 Sun ☎ (01225) 463923 🌐 thepulteneyarms.co.uk
Fuller's London Pride; Otter Bitter; Timothy Taylor Landlord; 3 changing beers (sourced nationally) Ⓗ
Tucked away near the end of Great Pulteney Street, the Pulteney Arms has been open since 1792. There are five gas light fittings (now sadly condemned) above the bar. The decor shows an emphasis on sport, particularly rugby. The cat symbol on the pub sign refers to the Pulteney coat of arms. The food menu is extensive and deservedly popular (no food Sun eves). Two varying guest beers are on offer, usually from national breweries. 🏠◑♿🅿🐾📶

Raven
6-7 Queen Street, BA1 1HE
🕐 11.30-11 (midnight Fri & Sat); 12-10.30 Sun
☎ (01225) 425045 🌐 theravenofbath.co.uk
House beer (by Blindmans); 4 changing beers (sourced regionally; often Cotswold Lion, Moles, Otley) Ⓗ
Busy 18th-century free house in the heart of Bath. Six regular ales include two brewed exclusively by Blindmans. Guest ales come from far and wide, with several mini beer festivals a year. The main bar and the quieter first-floor bar serve the same range of ales. Famous for its sausages and Pieminister pies, the Raven is one of the few pubs in Bath serving food on Sunday evening.
Q◑⇌♿🅿📶

Royal Oak
Lower Bristol Road, Twerton, BA2 3BW
🕐 2-midnight; 12-1am Fri & Sat; 12-midnight Sun
☎ (01225) 481409
Butts Jester, Barbus Barbus; Downton IPA; 5 changing beers Ⓗ
Two regulars from Butts Brewery, one from Downton and up to five guest beers from microbreweries near and far are served here, alongside an interesting range of ciders, perries and bottled British and Belgian beers. There are

Irish and English folk music sessions on Wednesday evenings and live music most weekends. Tuesday is quiz night. Outside is a secluded garden and a small on-site car park. CAMRA members receive a discount on some of the beer range. ❀❦●P🚃(5,15,15A)❀ 🛜

Salamander
3 John Street, BA1 2JL
🕐 11-11 (midnight Fri & Sat); 11-11.30 Sun
☎ (01225) 428889
Bath Ales Special Pale Ale, Gem, Barnsey, Rare Hare; 2 changing beers (sourced locally; often Beerd, Bath Ales) Ⓗ

An 18th-century building, tucked away in a side street, that opened as a coffee bar in 1957 and became a pub five years later. Taken over by Bath Ales in around 2000 and revamped in the company's inimitable style, it looks and feels like a pub that has been here for a century or more. Wooden floorboards, wood panelling and subdued lighting add to the ambience of the ground-floor bar, created from several small rooms. A popular restaurant is upstairs. ◖●🚃 🛜

Star Inn ★ ✅
23 Vineyards, BA1 5NA
🕐 12-2.30, 5.30-midnight; 12-1am Fri & Sat; 12-midnight Sun
☎ (01225) 425072 ⊕ abbeyales.co.uk/star-inn-bath.co.uk
Abbey Bellringer Ⓗ**; Draught Bass** Ⓖ**; 3 changing beers (sourced nationally)** Ⓗ

A main outlet for Abbey Ales, this classic town pub was fitted out by Gaskell and Chambers in 1928. Its four small rooms have benches around the walls, wood panelling and roaring fires. The smallest room has a single bench, called Death Row, while the pub itself, which dates from around 1760, is coffin-shaped. Bass is served from the cask and complimentary snuff is available. Cheese night is every Thursday and live music features on the first Sunday of each month. Q♣●🚃❀ 🛜

Bishopswood

Candlelight Inn
TA20 3RS (½ mile off A303 between Newton and Marsh)
🕐 12-2.30, 6-11; 12-3, 6-11 Sat & Sun; closed Mon
☎ (01460) 234476 ⊕ candlelight-inn.co.uk
Otter Bitter; 3 changing beers (sourced nationally) Ⓖ

A friendly and popular country pub in this pretty village, with flint walls, wooden floors and open fires giving a warm atmosphere. Food is prepared using local ingredients and some of the vegetables are home grown, while ice cream is made in-house and fish is smoked on the premises. Beers come mainly from West Country breweries and there is usually a selection of real ciders available. It also has a lovely garden area. Q❀◖●P❀

Bleadon

Queen's Arms ✅
Celtic Way, BS24 0NF (off A370)
🕐 12-11; 12-10.30 Sun ☎ (01934) 812080
⊕ queensarmsbleadon.com
Butcombe Bitter; 2 changing beers (often Butcombe) Ⓗ

A 17th-century stone-built pub in the centre of the village. Three rooms converge on the bar; the largest is the main dining area. Food sales are strong, but not at the expense of ale drinkers. Two real fires and exposed beams add to the cosy

atmosphere. There is also a garden/patio with a sales hatch. Families are welcome, and there is occasional live music. The 83 bus provides a regular service to the village from Weston. Q❀❦●◖●P🚃(83)❀ 🛜

Bradford on Tone

White Horse Inn Ⓛ
Regent Street, TA4 1HF (off A38)
🕐 12-2.30, 6-11 (5-midnight Fri; 6-midnight Sat); 12-3, 6-11 Sun ☎ (01823) 461239 ⊕ whitehorseinn.co
Otter Bitter; 2 changing beers (sourced locally; often Exeter, Hanlons) Ⓗ

This friendly village pub is very much a local affair, housing the community-run shop in outbuildings. The bar and restaurant are warmed by real fires in winter. Beers and a cider come from nearby. The beautiful large garden hosts barbecues in summer. Excellent food is locally sourced and home-cooked, and themed food nights are held. Regular events include music and quiz nights. On Fridays and weekends in summer the opening hours are extended. ❀◖●&▲♣●P🚃(22)❀ 🛜

Brompton Regis

George Inn Ⓛ
TA22 9NL (on OS map 181; take unclassified road off A396 just S of Dulverton turn)
🕐 12-2.30, 6-11 ☎ (01398) 371273
⊕ thegeorgeonexmoor.co.uk
Exmoor Ale; St Austell Tribute; 2 changing beers (sourced locally) Ⓗ

The George Inn is a 16th-century free house in this pretty village on the eastern side of Exmoor National Park and just west of Wimbleball Lake; the garden has beautiful views over Exmoor. There is en-suite accommodation, and well-behaved children are made welcome. Food is locally sourced and cooked to order. Closed Mondays October to Easter. Q❀❀☙◖▲P❀ 🛜

Burnham on Sea

Dunstan House Inn
8-10 Love Lane, TA8 1EU
🕐 11-11 (midnight Fri & Sat); 12-11 Sun ☎ (01278) 784343
⊕ dunstanhouseinn.co.uk
Courage Directors; St Austell Tribute; Young's Bitter, Special; 2 changing beers (sourced nationally) Ⓗ

Large refurbished and detached Young's pub next to the hospital, with a flagstone floor in the bar, a raised dining area, a family room and two open log fires. Outside there is covered decking, a garden and children's play equipment. Daily themed food specials enhance the food menu. Quiz nights are Wednesday and Sunday. En-suite accommodation is available. ❀❀☙◖&●P🚃❀ 🛜

Butleigh

Rose & Portcullis
Sub Road, BA6 8TQ
🕐 12-2.30, 5.30-11; 12-2.30, 7-10.30 Sun ☎ (01458) 850287
⊕ rose-and-portcullis.co.uk
Otter Bitter; 4 changing beers (sourced regionally; often Butcombe, Cheddar Ales, Hop Back) Ⓗ

A large welcoming hostelry with interesting ales. Although difficult to find, efforts will be rewarded with those time-honoured requirements - good beer, good food and good company - being fully satisfied. The old public bar, now opened into the main area, still has much to remind of its rugby history and has recently been enhanced with the addition of some old pub games; London five board (a darts game), Irish rings and Dutch shuffleboard are all congenial fun. Q ⏰ 🏠 ✿ ⬤ 🌙 ▲ ♣ ● ⬤ 🖿 (667) 🐾 ⬤ 📶

Cheddar

White Hart
The Bays, BS27 3QN
✪ 10-midnight; 10-11 Sun ☎ (01934) 741261
⊕ thewhitehartcheddar.co.uk
Butcombe Bitter; St Austell Tribute; 1 changing beer Ⓗ
A traditional country pub at the bottom of Cheddar Gorge and located in The Bays, a quiet street just off the main road through the gorge. Because it is hidden away from the other pubs in the village it can be more relaxed than other pubs in the village. Good food is served daily from 10am, with a popular carvery on Sundays. There is a large upstairs function room and a pleasant garden to the side of the pub. ⏰ 🏠 ✿ ⬤ 🌙 ● ⬤ 🖿 🐾 ⬤ 📶

Churchill

Crown Inn
The Batch, Skinners Lane, BS25 5PP (off A38)
✪ 11-11; 11-10.30 Sun ☎ (01934) 852995
Bath Ales Gem; Butcombe Adam Henson's Rare Breed; St Austell Tribute; 4 changing beers Ⓖ
Long-time Guide regular and winner of many CAMRA awards. It is tucked away down a small lane yet close to the village centre. Several cosy rooms with stone-flagged floors are warmed by two log fires and offer an assortment of seating. Excellent food is provided at lunchtimes using local ingredients. Up to eight beers, usually local, are served on gravity. Outside drinking areas are to the front and rear. A classic unchanged old pub; cash only, no cards. Q ⏰ 🏠 ✿ ⬤ 🌙 ▲ ● ⬤ 🖿 (121) 🐾

Clevedon

Royal Oak ✓
35 Copse Road, BS21 7QN (behind ice cream parlour)
✪ 12-11 (midnight Fri & Sat) ☎ (01275) 563879
Butcombe Bitter; Fuller's London Pride; Sharp's Doom Bar; 1 changing beer Ⓗ
Lively, friendly, mid-terrace pub close to the seafront and connected via an alley. It has a large front window and a Tardis-like interior of many rooms. This community hub is home to cribbage and cricket teams. The winner of various awards, it hosts many events, including cooking competitions and dancing, ranging from morris men through belly dance to Zulus. There is a quiz on Monday and folk music on Wednesday. Thatchers cider is sold. Q ⏰ ♣ ● ⬤ 🖿 🐾 ⬤ 📶

Congresbury

Plough
High Street, BS49 5JA (off A370 at B3133 jct)
✪ 11.30-2.30, 4.30-11; 12-2.30, 7-10.30 Sun
☎ (01934) 877402 ⊕ the-plough-inn.net
Butcombe Bitter; St Austell Tribute; Twisted Oak Fallen Tree; 5 changing beers (sourced locally) Ⓗ
Characterful village pub with flagstone floors and many original features, decorated with interesting

local artefacts. Five guest beers are delivered from a row of old cask heads behind the bar, sourced mainly from local breweries. Up to 16 ciders are also stocked. Food is served lunchtimes and evenings, except Sunday evening, which is quiz night. The pub has real fires and a large garden. Mendip morris men meet here. Local CAMRA Pub of the Year 2014 and 2015. Q ✿ ⬤ 🌙 ♣ ● ⬤ 🖿 (X1,353) 🐾

Corton Denham

Queen's Arms Ⓛ ✓
DT9 4LR (3 miles S of A303 near Sherborne)
✪ 10-11 (midnight Fri & Sat); 11-11 Sun ☎ (01963) 220317
⊕ thequeensarms.com
Exmoor Ale; Gyle 59 Toujours; 3 changing beers (sourced nationally; often Cheddar Ales, Moor Beer, Timothy Taylor) Ⓗ
A really cosy, friendly pub with real fires in a pretty rural setting overlooking rolling countryside. The place has plenty of letting rooms, popular with walkers, and offers good food from snacks to quality main meals, and numerous food awards have been won. A good selection of real ales is served, which can be sampled in one-third pint glasses if preferred. The pub opens for breakfast at 8am (but not the bar). Q ✿ 🏠 ⬤ 🌙 ♿ ● ⬤ 🖿 🐾 ⬤ 📶

Croscombe

George Inn
Long Street, BA5 3QH (on A371)
✪ 11-3, 6-11 (5-midnight Fri); 11-midnight Sat; 12-11 Sun
☎ (01749) 342306 ⊕ thegeorgeinn.co.uk
House beer (by Blindmans) Ⓗ**; changing beers (often Arbor, Cheddar Ales, Three Daggers)** Ⓗ/Ⓖ
Attractive 17th-century inn refurbished by the owner, serving at least four guest ales from West Country independents and hosting two beer festivals a year. Blindmans King George, and George and Dragon, are brewed exclusively for the pub. Four real ciders are available, with Hecks Kingston Black, Thatchers Cheddar Valley and Orchard Pig being regulars. It has a large main bar, a snug with a fireplace, a family room and a separate dining room. Food is home-cooked using locally sourced ingredients. A skittle alley/meeting room is to the rear, and it has a large garden with a covered terrace. Q ⏰ 🏠 ✿ 🏠 ⬤ 🌙 ♿ ♣ ● ⬤ 🖿 🐾 ⬤ 📶

Cross

New Inn ✓
Old Coach Road, BS26 2EE (on the A38/A361 junction)
✪ 12-11 (midnight Fri & Sat) ☎ (01934) 732455
⊕ newinncross.co.uk
Otter Ale; Sharp's Cornish Coaster; 3 changing beers Ⓗ
Roadside inn on the A38, close to the historic medieval town of Axbridge. Popular for its extensive food menu served all day until 9pm (8pm Sun) and beer festivals at Easter and August bank holiday, it usually has three often adventurous guest beers. There is a function room on the first floor. A large hillside garden with children's play facilities offers a fine view of the Mendip Hills and Somerset Levels. Ale is discounted on Thursdays. ✿ ⬤ 🌙 ♣ ● ⬤ 🖿 (126) 🐾 ⬤ 📶

Crowcombe

Carew Arms 🅛
TA4 4AD (village signed off A358)
🌐 12-3, 5-11 ☎ (01984) 618631 ⊕ thecarewarms.co.uk
Exmoor Ale; Otter Bright; Quantock Wills Neck; 2 changing beers (sourced regionally; often St Austell) 🅗
A classic rural village pub at the foot of the beautiful Quantock Hills. The flagstone public bar has a historic inglenook, and the large garden looking towards the Brendon Hills makes this pub popular with locals, walkers and dogs. Four to five guest ales come from mainly local microbreweries. The bar/restaurant serves locally sourced food, and the skittle alley doubles as a function room. The pub is open all day in the summer.
Q🏴🐕🛏🍴🚶♿🅰♣👜P🚃(28)🐾🛜

Dinnington

Dinnington Docks Inn ✓
TA17 8SX (3 miles E of Ilminster off Crewkerne Rd)
🌐 10.30-3.30, 6-11; 11.30-11 Fri & Sat; 12-10.30 Sun
☎ (01460) 52397
Butcombe Bitter; Teignworthy Gun Dog; 1 changing beer (sourced regionally; often Sharp's, Yeovil) 🅗
Revisit the last century, with much better beer, and find a pub as pubs used to be. Various railway memorabilia abound and the superb illustration of the old rail crossing outside must be seen. Home-cooked comfort food is a feature, so the narrow lanes to be negotiated are a minor irritation when this gem is the objective. Understanding of Somerset-speak is recommended but not essential.
Q🏴🐕🍴♿♣👜P🐾

Draycott

Early Doors Cider & Ale Barn
Latches Lane Crossroads, Draycott Road, BS27 3YB
🌐 12-10.30 ☎ (01934) 741837
2 changing beers 🅗
Quirky, relaxing bar/cafe/takeaway cider and ale barn on the main A371 near Cheddar, where you can also buy coffee/tea and cakes, simple locally sourced home-cooked food and great little snacks (Somerset tapas!). Up to seven real ciders and three real ales are served on gravity (only two ales in summer). There is live music every Saturday evening and every other Sunday afternoon. The bar sometimes stays open until 11pm. 🐕🍴♿👜P🐾

Dulverton

Bridge Inn 🅛 ✓
20 Bridge Street, TA22 9HJ
🌐 12-11 summer; 12-3, 6-11 (not Mon eve); 12-11 Fri-Sun winter ☎ (01398) 324130 ⊕ thebridgeinndulverton.com
Exmoor Ale; 3 changing beers (sourced regionally) 🅗
A warm, welcoming pub dating from 1845. As the name implies, it is close to a bridge, one crossing the River Barle upstream from its confluence with the River Exe. It has a cosy single-room bar with a wood-burning stove. The Bridge Inn holds a Green Tourism Award in recognition of the environmentally friendly way it is run. An annual beer festival coincides with the local folk festival over the Whitsun holiday.
Q🏴🐕🍴🛏♣P🚃(25,198,398)🐾🛜

Dunster

Luttrell Arms Hotel
36 High Street, TA24 6SG
🌐 10-11.30 ☎ (01643) 821555 ⊕ luttrellarms.co.uk
Exmoor Ale; Otter Amber; 2 changing beers (sourced locally) 🅗
The Luttrell Arms, with its 28 unique bedrooms, is on the site of three ancient houses dating back to 1443. The garden offers great views of Dunster Castle. The back bar with its open log fire features some of the oldest glass windows in Somerset and is a gem. And check out some fine plasterwork on the ceiling in the lounge. The hotel also has an à la carte restaurant and private function rooms. Mini beer festivals are held.
Q🏴🐕🛏🍴🛌🍴♣👜🚃(28,198)🐾🛜

Exford

Exmoor White Horse Inn ✓
TA24 7PY (on B3224 W of Wheddon Cross)
🌐 11-11 ☎ (01643) 831229 ⊕ exmoor-whitehorse.co.uk
Exmoor Ale, Gold; 3 changing beers (sourced locally) 🅗
Impressive pub/hotel found in a pretty village in the heart of Exmoor. The long bar features fine ales and a choice of 100 malt whiskies, on shelves and also hanging from the ceiling. Set in a popular walking area, it is also a renowned centre for fishing and other country pursuits. There are 28 en-suite rooms and a honeymoon suite. Tables outside are set on the bank of the River Exe.
Q🏴🐕🛏🍴🚶♣👜P🚃(198)🐾🛜

Faulkland

Tucker's Grave ★
BA3 5XF
🌐 12-3 (not Mon), 6-11; 12-3, 7-10.30 Sun
☎ (01373) 834230
Butcombe Matthew Pale Ale, Bitter 🅖
A gem from a bygone age and with a nationally important historic pub interior, this place was built in the mid-17th century and has changed little since. It was named after Tucker, who hanged himself and was buried at the crossroads outside, and featured in a song by 1970s punk band The Stranglers. There is no bar; the beers and Thatchers cider are served from an alcove. Shove-ha'penny is played and there is a skittle alley. Camping is available in the grounds. Q🌼🅰♣👜P

Frome

Griffin
Milk Street, BA11 3DB
🌐 5-11; 4-1am Fri; 3-1am Sat; 1-9 Sun ☎ (01373) 467766 ⊕ fromegriffin.co.uk
Milk Street Brown Cow, Funky Monkey, The Usual, Beer; 2 changing beers (sourced locally; often Milk Street) 🅗
In the part of Frome known as Trinity or Chinatown, the Griffin is the tap for Milk Street Brewery situated at the back. A wide range of ales is produced along with seasonals and specials. The single bar retains original features such as etched windows, wooden floor and a stained-glass griffin behind the bar. Regular quiz nights and live music take place. The small garden is open all year but food is limited to summer barbecues and Sunday lunches. 🐕🍴P🚃🐾🛜

Three Swans

16-17 King Street, BA11 1BH

☼ 5-11; 12-11 Fri-Sun ☎ (01373) 452009

⊕ threeswans.co.uk

Abbey Bellringer; Butcombe Bitter; 1 changing beer (sourced locally; often Butcombe, Three Daggers) ⊞

A 17th-century Grade II-listed quirky pub in the centre of Frome. Extensively refurbished in 2013, it has a comfortable and inviting feel. The two bars are heated by traditional gas burners, and paintings and various ornaments adorn the wall. The back door leads out to a beautiful secluded courtyard. There is also a function room. The pub does not serve meals but home-made pork pies and Scotch eggs are available on Fridays and at weekends. ⯎⊛♣⊟♨🐾☎

Glastonbury

Hawthorns Hotel

8-12 Northload Street, BA6 9JJ

☼ 12-3 (not Tue & Wed), 6-11; 12-11 Sat; 12-10 Sun; closed Mon ☎ (01458) 831255 ⊕ hawthornshotel.com

2 changing beers (often Cottage, Glastonbury) ⊞

Small family-run hotel with a pub bar and restaurant in the heart of this mystic town. The emphasis is on locally sourced food, ales and cider. Ethnic and vegetarian dishes are popular, as is the Sunday carvery. It is a well-known music venue with an open mic session on Tuesdays and regular music acts on Fridays. In May there is a well-supported beer festival. ⯎⊛🛏◑♣♨P⊟🐾☎

Henstridge

Bird in Hand

Ash Walk, BA8 0QD

☼ 11-2.30, 5.30-11; 11-11 Sat; 12-10.30 Sun
☎ (01963) 362255

Butcombe Bitter; 2 changing beers (sourced nationally; often Butcombe, Sharp's) ⊞

Old stone village pub with low ceilings, beams, a fireplace at each end of an attractive long bar, and a games room housing a TV. There is an adjoining skittle alley. Excellent-quality ales and good-value snacks make a visit to this friendly pub worthwhile. At the heart of most village activities, this really is a true community pub. Thatchers Original cider is on handpump. Q⊛◑♣♨P⊟(58)☎

Horsington

Half Moon Inn ⊘

Duck Lane, BA8 0EF

☼ 12-2.30, 6-11; 12-4 Sun ☎ (01963) 370140

Fuller's London Pride; Wadworth 6X; 4 changing beers (sourced nationally; often Butcombe, Palmers, Shepherd Neame) ⊞

Owned and run by the same couple for over 20 years, this pub is the focal point of a lovely village. There are up to three guest beers; over 1,000 different beers have been served so far. It has gardens to the front and rear, a separate skittle alley, a large function room, an ample car park and 10 letting rooms. Reasonably priced food is available at all sessions. Closed Monday and Tuesday in winter. Q⯎⊛🛏◑♣♨P⊟(58)🐾

Huish Episcopi

Rose & Crown ★ L

TA10 9QT (on A372 in village)

☼ 11.30-3, 5.30-11; 11.30-11.30 Fri-Sun ☎ (01458) 250494

Teignworthy Reel Ale; 2 changing beers (sourced regionally; often Cotleigh, Cottage, Plain) ⊞

Locally known as Eli's, the pub has been in the same family for over 150 years and is revered for its ale, food and occasional music. The serving area is a room with pumps but no bar counter. Leading off are drinking areas, enabling the enjoyment of a relaxed atmosphere almost unheard of in more modern pubs. The local Co-op supplies the excellent food on Friday evenings. Q⯎⊛◑Å♣♨P🐾☎

Hutton

Old Inn

Main Road, BS24 9QQ

☼ 11.30-11 (midnight Fri & Sat); 12-11 Sun
☎ (01934) 812336

Butcombe Gold; Fuller's London Pride; St Austell Tribute; 1 changing beer ⊞

Genuine free house owned by a long-standing Guide landlord and now a thriving local; the Old Inn is right at the heart of the community. The pub is extremely popular for its excellent and great-value food so booking is advised. Dogs are welcome in the bar. The car park to the rear is accessed by narrow one-way lanes either side. Food is available lunchtimes and evenings except Sunday, which is quiz night. Up to two guest beers are served. ⯎⊛◑♣♨P⊟(4)🐾

Kelston

Old Crown ⊘

Bath Road, BA1 9AQ (3 miles from Bath on A431)

☼ 11 (12 Mon & Tue)-11; 12-10 Sun ☎ (01225) 423032

⊕ oldcrownkelston.com

Butcombe Bitter; Draught Bass; 2 changing beers (often Butcombe) ⊞

Attractive multi-roomed 18th-century coaching inn previously owned by Butcombe Brewery. The rare cash register handpumps, flagstone floors, open fires and settles all help create a friendly atmosphere. There are several eating areas, including a small room upstairs which has recently been opened up. One of the guest beers is often dark. In summertime, barbecues and live musical events are occasionally held in the large, attractive garden. Take care crossing the busy road to the car park. Buses stop directly outside. ⊛◑♣♨P⊟(19,37)🐾☎

Keynsham

Lock Keeper

Keynsham Road, BS31 2DD (on A4175)

☼ 11-midnight; 12-11 Sun ☎ (0117) 986 2383

⊕ lockkeeperbristol.com

Bath Ales Gem; Young's Bitter, Special; 1 changing beer (often Young's) ⊞

Multi-roomed Young's pub, noted for its food, by Keynsham lock on the River Avon. The original 17th-century cottage once brewed its own beer and was named the White Hart. It divides into two parts, with the older bar facing the canal, while the large conservatory and heated veranda overlook the river, pétanque pitches and the popular garden.

Families are welcome. Occasional live music features in summer. The pub may stay open later when busy, or close earlier if quiet.
Q ☺ ☆ ⑪ 🅟 ⇄ ♣ 🅟 🚆 (17,17a) ♨ 🛜

Old Bank

20 High Street, BS31 1DQ
✪ 10-11.30 (1am Fri & Sat); 11.30-10.30 Sun
☎ (0117) 904 6356
Otter Ale; 3 changing beers Ⓗ
A free house in the centre of Keynsham, it has one large room for drinking in, with a function room upstairs and a covered, heated outdoor drinking area at the rear where the smokers go. Old pictures of Keynsham adorn the walls. There is a small car park to the rear, reached through a narrow archway. The landlord tries to have at least one dark beer, often strong, on at all times. It can sometimes get lively on late weekend openings.
☆⑪&⇄♣🅟🚆♨🛜

Kingsbury Episcopi

Wyndham Arms Ⓛ ⊘

Folly Road, TA12 6AT (4 miles S of Langport)
✪ 12-midnight (1am Sat & Sun) ☎ (01935) 823239
⊕ wyndhamarms.com
Butcombe Bitter; Cheddar Ales Potholer; 2 changing beers (sourced regionally; often Bays, Cotleigh, Teignworthy) Ⓗ
Most of this pub is 400 years old and is on the edge of the Somerset Levels. Old settles and a log fire can be found in the bar area, with a second log fire in the comfy dining room. Smokers are well catered for, with a smoking area with a pool table and patio heaters. The skittle alley doubles as a meeting/function room and an upstairs room is often used for live music nights. A good place to dine as good quality, home-cooked food is available. Q ☺ ☆ ⑪ & Å ♣ 🅟 ♨ 🛜

Langford Budville

Martlett Inn

TA21 0QZ
✪ 12-3 (not Tue), 7-11; closed Mon ☎ (01823) 400262
⊕ themartletinn.webs.com
Exmoor Ale; 2 changing beers (often Cotleigh, Otter, Sharp's) Ⓗ
A cosy 17th-century village pub with flagstone floor, oak-beam ceiling and inglenook fireplace, and an intimate bar with a woodburner. The village is situated two miles north of the town of Wellington, close to the Brendon Hills. A dining room and conservatory are adjacent to the bar and there is a charming courtyard garden. Food is locally sourced and prepared in house. Private parties are catered for. Q ☺ ☆ ⑪ & 🅟 ♨ 🛜

Lower Godney

Sheppey Inn

Wells, BA5 1RZ
✪ 12-3, 5.30-11; 12-midnight Sat; 12-6.30 Sun
☎ (01458) 831594 ⊕ thesheppey.co.uk
4 changing beers (sourced regionally; often Bristol Beer Factory, Glastonbury, Plain) Ⓗ
Entering this extraordinary pub is like coming into a trendy city bar but set deep in the wilds of the Somerset Levels. It has a good range of different real ales, and up to seven ciders on gravity. Outside the barn-like interior is a lovely terrace overlooking

the pub's eponymous river, where otters have been spotted. The food is highly recommended.
☺ ☆ ⑪ & Å 🅟 ♨ 🛜

Lydford on Fosse

Cross Keys Inn Ⓛ

TA11 7HA (next to A37, at traffic lights in village)
✪ 11.30-3, 5-11; 11.30-midnight Fri; 11.30-3, 5-midnight Sat; 12-4, 7-11 Sun ☎ (01963) 240473 ⊕ crosskeysinn.info
House beer (by Downton); 5 changing beers (sourced regionally; often Cheddar Ales, Hop Back, Milk Street) Ⓖ
Dating from 1759, this is a fine example of a traditional pub with flagstone floors, blue lias stonework and a wealth of beams. There is an open-plan area with two fireplaces at each end and a snug area, also with a fireplace. The owners stage live music, a beer festival and other events, often for charity. Camping is available on-site with facilities. Generally there are six ales on at the weekend and between two and four during the week. Q ☺ ☆ ⑪ 🛏 ⑪ & Å ♣ 🅟 🚆 (667) ♨ 🛜

Martock

White Hart Hotel Ⓛ

East Street, TA12 6JQ
✪ 12-3 (not Mon), 5.30-11; 12-3 Sun ☎ (01935) 822005
⊕ whiteharthotelmartock.co.uk
3 changing beers (sourced regionally; often Otter, Sharp's) Ⓗ
This hamstone Grade II-listed coaching inn dates from 1735 and is a warm and welcoming local. It serves great chef-cooked food, and three real ales are on handpulls, mainly from local breweries. Local groups such as music and film clubs use the pub as a meeting place. There is a main bar for drinks and a cosy restaurant for table service. Ten letting rooms include a family room.
Q ☺ ☆ 🛏 ⑪ & ♣ 🅟 🚆 (N9,N10) ♨ 🛜

Middlezoy

George Inn Ⓛ

42 Main Road, TA7 0NN (off A372)
✪ 12-3, 7-midnight; 12-4, 7-10 Sun; closed Mon
☎ (01823) 698215 ⊕ thegeorgeinnmiddlezoy.co.uk
St Austell Tribute; 3 changing beers (sourced regionally; often Otter, RCH, Teignworthy) Ⓗ
Friendly 17th-century free house with stone-flagged floors, exposed beams and a log fire in the bar and lounge area. Beers are mainly from the South-west, and four local ciders are from Orchard Pig and Farmer Jim's. Excellent locally sourced food is served Wednesday to Saturday only. The landlord holds an annual beer festival over the Easter weekend. This village pub on the Somerset Levels maybe a little remote but is well worth finding, with its history embedded in the Battle of Sedgemoor. Q ☺ ☆ ⑪ Å ♣ 🅟 🚆 (16) ♨ 🛜

Minehead

Kildare Lodge ⊘

Townend Road, TA24 5RQ
✪ 11-3, 6.30-11; 12-5 Sun ☎ (01643) 702009
⊕ kildarelodge.co.uk
St Austell 1913 Cornish Stout; 3 changing beers (sourced regionally) Ⓗ
Grade II-listed building in the arts and crafts style, retaining many interesting features, with a bar,

two lounges and dining room. Close to Minehead town centre, the pub is in local boules and quiz leagues. The food is locally sourced, with daily specials on offer. With 12 en-suite rooms and a bridal suite with four-poster bed, this is a great base for exploring Exmoor, Dunster and the coast. Q❀✿⌂◑Ġ≋♣♠P🚍(28,198)🐾

Old Ship Aground

Quay Street, TA24 5UL (beside Minehead harbour)
🕛 11-11 (midnight Fri & Sat) ☎ (01643) 703516
⊕ oldshipaground.com
Ringwood Boondoggle, Fortyniner; Wychwood Hobgoblin; 2 changing beers (sourced nationally) Ⓗ
Set in the picturesque part of Minehead between the harbour and the lifeboat station, this 1906 pub offers fantastic views over the Bristol Channel. There is locally sourced food, with a Sunday carvery, a sausage festival on Tuesdays, pie and mash on Thursdays and other themed food nights. Exmoor National Park is a 20-minute drive away and it is a short walk to Minehead town centre. Beer festivals are held and there is live music on Fridays. ⍩✿⌂◑Ġ▲♣P🚍(28,198)🐾🛜

Mudford

Half Moon Inn

Main Street, BA21 5TF (on A359)
🕛 11-11; 11-10.30 Sun ☎ (01935) 850289
⊕ thehalfmooninn.co.uk
St Austell Proper Job, HSD Ⓖ
Popular 17th-century roadside inn with a strong regular trade. The real ales and cider are served from a stillage behind the bar. The outside courtyard, in which dogs are allowed (guide dogs only inside the pub) is pleasant on warm days. The extensive menu, which includes light lunches and daily specials, is displayed on a blackboard. The pub has letting rooms in the main building, in the former skittle alley and log store.
Q❀✿⌂◑ĠP🚍(1)🐾🛜

Pitney

Halfway House Ⓛ

Pitney Hill, TA10 9AB (on B3153)
🕛 11.30-3, 5.30-11 (midnight Fri); 11.30-midnight Sat; 12-11 Sun ☎ (01458) 252513 ⊕ thehalfwayhouse.co.uk
Butcombe Adam Henson's Rare Breed; Hop Back Summer Lightning; Otter Bright; Teignworthy Reel Ale Ⓖ; **6 changing beers (often Butcombe, Hop Back, Teignworthy)** Ⓗ
An outstanding pub serving eight to 10 local ales on gravity alongside many bottled beers and a range of real ciders. This basic but busy venue is ever present in the Guide and deserves its many accolades including the ultimate award of CAMRA National Pub of the Year in 1996. It has flagstone floors, a basic assortment of tables, chairs and benches, and three real fires. Superb home-cooked food is served, with a roast lunch on Sundays (no food Sun eve). Q❀◑♣♠P🚍(38,55)🐾

Porlock

Ship Inn Ⓛ ✅

High Street, TA24 8QD
🕛 11-midnight; 12-midnight Sun ☎ (01643) 862507
⊕ shipinnporlock.co.uk
Exmoor Beast; Otter Bitter; 6 changing beers (sourced regionally) Ⓗ

Known locally as the Top Ship, the bar, with its flagstone floor and open fire, has not changed since featuring in RD Blackmore's novel Lorna Doone. The pub dates from the 13th century and sits at the bottom of the notorious Porlock Hill that takes you up to Exmoor. This CAMRA award-winning venue, with its eight ales and local cider, serves good food in its restaurant and three-tiered garden. There is en-suite accommodation and beer festivals are held. Q❀⍩✿⌂◑Ġ▲♣♠P🚍(10)🐾

Porlock Weir

Ship Inn Ⓛ

TA24 8PB (take B3225 from Porlock)
🕛 11-11; 12-10.30 Sun ☎ (01643) 863288
⊕ thebottomship.co.uk
Exmoor Ale, Stag; St Austell Tribute, Proper Job; 2 changing beers Ⓗ
A 400-year-old pub in Exmoor National Park ideal for walkers and close to Porlock village. Next to the harbour, it has possibly some of the best views of any Somerset pub, overlooking the Bristol Channel towards south Wales. Good food is served by friendly staff and it is particularly busy in holiday periods. A beer festival is held in July, with up to 50 ales to choose from. A large Pay & Display car park is opposite. Q❀◑Ġ▲♣♠P🚍(10)🐾

Portishead

Windmill Inn

58 Nore Road, BS20 6JZ (next to municipal golf course)
🕛 11-11; 12-10.30 Sun ☎ (01275) 818483
⊕ thewindmillinn.org
Butcombe Bitter; Fuller's London Pride; 3 changing beers Ⓗ
Large split-level pub with a spacious patio to the rear, plus an extension enjoying panoramic views. It is above the coastal path on the edge of town, and the Severn Estuary and both Severn bridges can be seen on clear days. A varied menu is served all day, with table bookings available. The pub was acquired by Fuller's in 2014 but the three guest ales come from a variety of breweries. Thatchers cider is stocked. Monday is quiz night.
Q⍩❀◑Ġ♠P🚍(X2,X3)🐾🛜

Priddy

Hunters Lodge

Hillgrove Road, BA5 3AR (isolated crossroads 1 mile from A39 close to TV mast) ST549500
🕛 11.30-2.30, 6.30-11; 12-2, 7-11 Sun ☎ (01749) 672275
Butcombe Bitter; Cheddar Ales Potholer; 1 changing beer Ⓖ
Timeless, classic roadside inn near Priddy, the highest village in Somerset, popular with cavers and walkers. The landlord has been in charge for well over 40 years. Three rooms include one with a flagged floor and all beer is served direct from casks behind the bar. Local cider is stocked. The simple home-cooked food is excellent and exceptional value. A folk musicians' drop-in session is held on Tuesday evenings. The garden is pleasant and secluded and mobile phones are not welcome. Q⍩❀◑Ġ♠P🐾

Queen Victoria Inn ✅

Pelting Drove, BA5 3BA
🕛 12-11; 12-10.30 Sun ☎ (01749) 676385
⊕ thequeenvicpriddy.co.uk

Butcombe Bitter; Fuller's London Pride; 2 changing beers (often Butcombe) [H]
Creeper-clad inn, a pub since 1851, with four rooms that feature low ceilings, flagged floors and log fires. A wonderfully warm and relaxing haven on cold winter nights, it is popular during the Priddy Folk Festival in July and the annual fair in August. Reasonably priced, home-cooked food is a speciality. Children are welcome and there is a play area by the car park. Cheddar Valley and Ashton Still ciders are sold. May close briefly on some afternoons. Q🐴❀◐⛺♣🍎P🐾📶

Puriton

37 Club [L]
1 West Approach Road, Woolavington Road, TA7 8AD
🕐 5-11; 11.30-midnight Sat; 12-11 Sun ☎ (01278) 685190
🌐 37club.co.uk
Otter Bitter; St Austell Trelawny, Proper Job; 3 changing beers (often Cottage, Quantock) [H]
On the site of the former Royal Ordnance factory, which was allocated the number 37, this club supplies up to three changing guest beers as well as three regular beers, and also sells real cider from a small local producer. A large two-bar venue, it offers many facilities to members and visitors. The multi-roomed layout incorporates a concert room, two skittle alleys, a dining room and snooker room. Outside is a beer garden and football pitch.
🐴❀◐⛺♣🍎P🚌(73)

Radstock

Fromeway
Frome Road, BA3 3LG
🕐 12-3, 6-11; 12-11 Sun; closed Mon ☎ (01761) 432116
🌐 fromeway.co.uk
Butcombe Bitter [H]**; 2 changing beers (sourced nationally; often Timothy Taylor, Wadworth, Yeovil)** [H]/[A]
Friendly free house which has been in the same family for five generations. The present landlord, who used to run a butcher's shop next door, has been in charge for more than 36 years and still produces his own sausages, faggots and home-cured hams for the excellent bar and restaurant meals. A single bar serves three regular ales, and there are weekly guest beers. The pub organises many functions, quizzes and walks for charity. Three charming bedrooms are available.
Q🐴❀🛏◐🍎P🚌(768,178)🐾📶

Roadwater

Valiant Soldier ✔
TA23 0QZ (off A39 at Washford)
🕐 11.30-2.30, 6-11; 12-3, 6-11 Sun ☎ (01984) 640223
🌐 thevaliantsoldier.co.uk
Exmoor Ale; Sharp's Doom Bar; 1 changing beer [H]
Vibrant locals' hostelry with quiz, pool, darts and nine skittles teams to see it through the winter months. The pub is set by a small river where you can relax and watch the ducks and, if you are lucky, kingfishers. It offers good quality food, locally sourced, and has been run by the same landlord for over 30 years. The building dates back to 1720 and is ideal for country walks and exploring nearby Exmoor and the old Mineral Line.
🐴❀🛏◐♣🍎P📶

Rode

Cross Keys ✔
20 High Street, BA11 6NZ (on main street)
🕐 11.30-2.30, 5.30-11.30; 12-11.30 Sat; 12-10.30 Sun
☎ (01373) 830900 🌐 crosskeysrode.co.uk
Butcombe Bitter; 2 changing beers (sourced nationally; often Bristol Beer Factory, Oakham, Three Daggers) [H]
Reopened in 2004 after 10 years of closure, this was originally the brewery tap for the long-closed Fussell's Brewery, and more latterly was a Bass depot. Sympathetically restored, it has succeeded in bringing back a strong village trade. A passageway featuring a deep well links two bars. There is also a large restaurant. Up to two guest beers can come from almost anywhere and may be major brands, like London Pride, but are more often from breweries rarely seen in the area.
Q🐴❀🛏◐⛺♣🍎P🚌🐾📶

Rowberrow

Swan Inn ✔
Rowberrow Lane, BS25 1QL
🕐 12-11; 12-10.30 Sun ☎ (01934) 852371
🌐 swan.butcombe.com
Butcombe Bitter; 3 changing beers (often Butcombe) [H]
Believed to date from around the late-17th century, this Butcombe Brewery-owned country pub enjoys an attractive setting, nestling beneath the Dolebury Iron Age hill fort. A convenient stop for walkers on the Mendip Hills, the emphasis is on quality home-cooked food, but customers who just want a drink are welcome. There is a collection of artefacts around the walls and a grandfather clock. The large, attractive beer garden and car park are opposite. Q🐴❀◐🍎P🐾📶

St Georges

Woolpack ✔
Shepherds Way, BS22 7XE (close to M5 jct 21)
🕐 11-11; 12-10.30 Sun ☎ (01934) 521670
🌐 woolpack.butcombe.com
Butcombe Bitter, Gold; Fuller's London Pride; 1 changing beer [H]
This 17th-century coaching house was once a packing station that baled wool for local farmers. Owned by Butcombe since 2006, it has two bar areas, a conservatory, and an outside patio area. The pub is in the much-expanded St Georges area just off the M5 at junction 21, and within walking distance of Worle station. Food is served every day from an extensive menu with daily specials, and there is a separate carvery. No table reservations on Sundays. 🐴❀◐♿🚉P🚌(32,X1,85)📶

Saltford

Bird in Hand ✔
58 High Street, BS31 3EJ
🕐 11-11 ☎ (01225) 873335 🌐 birdinhandsaltford.co.uk
Butcombe Bitter; Sharp's Doom Bar; 2 changing beers [H]
Characterful and smart traditional country inn dating from 1869, 400 yards from the A4 and close to the Bristol to Bath cycle path and the River Avon. There is a long L-shaped bar and a pleasant conservatory with fine views across the garden to the hills beyond. Old photographs feature and

there is a small family area. Food is served lunchtimes and evenings, all day at weekends, including gluten-free. It has a pétanque piste.
♿🕭🅿♣🍴🅿🚲(A4,X39,38)🐾🛜

Shepton Beauchamp

Duke of York 🅛
North Street, TA19 0LW
🕒 5-11 Mon; 3.30 (12 Thu & Fri)-11; 12-midnight Sat; 12-10.30 Sun ☎ (01460) 240314 ⊕ thedukeshepton.co.uk
Otter Bright; Teignworthy Reel Ale; 1 changing beer (sourced regionally; often Bays, Cheddar Ales, Sharp's) 🅗
Charming village centred around the school, church, shop and pub. The latter's slightly raised position on a high pavement enables a voyeuristic view of Somerset life. Split levels in the pub itself make an interesting interior, while the recent letting rooms to the rear are increasingly popular with touring visitors. Very much a family-run establishment, it seems naturally to attract families with children, and dogs are welcomed.
♿🕭🅿🍴♣🅿🐾🛜

South Cadbury

Camelot 🅛
Chapel Road, BA22 7EX (just off A303)
🕒 12-3, 6.30-9.30; 11-11 Fri & Sat; 12-10.30 Sun
☎ (01963) 441685 ⊕ camelotpub.com
Sharp's Doom Bar; Yeovil Summerset; 2 changing beers (sourced regionally; often Cotleigh, Exmoor, Otter) 🅗
Beneath the high slopes of Cadbury Castle, the Camelot claims to be just that – the legendary home of King Arthur. An informative display catalogues what is known of the local history, although it fails to have a picture of the King himself. Close to the A303 and signposted from there, it is well worth stopping off en route to or from the West Country. Please try to avoid stepping on the customers' dogs when entering.
Q♿🕭🅿♣🍴🅿(1)🐾🛜

South Petherton

Brewers Arms 🍷 🅛 ✅
18-20 St James Street, TA13 5BW (½ mile off A303)
🕒 11.30-2.30, 6-11; 11.30-midnight Fri & Sat; 12-11 Sun
☎ (01460) 241887 ⊕ the-brewersarms.com
Otter Bitter; 3 changing beers (often Butcombe, Otter, RCH) 🅗
Awarded the Somerset CAMRA branch Pub of the Year in 2016, the pub has been in the Guide for 20 consecutive editions and in the current landlord's capable hands for 22 years. During this time 2,500 different ales have been presented. This establishment is the centre of village life, with its extensive support for local events and charities. A couple of minutes from the A303, travellers have an ideal pit stop to or from the far west.
🕭🅿🅰♣🍴🅿(81)🐾🛜

Stogumber

White Horse Inn
High Street, TA4 3TA (turn left off A358 at Crowcombe)
🕒 6-11 Tue; 12-2.30, 5 (4.30 Mon)-11; 12-11 Sat & Sun
☎ (01984) 656277 ⊕ whitehorsestogumber.co.uk
Otter Bitter; St Austell Proper Job; 2 changing beers (often Otter, Quantock) 🅗

In a picturesque village close to the Brendon Hills, this traditional free house is a Grade II-listed building. The bar has a friendly atmosphere, with a cosy log fire. Beers are from local and South-west breweries. There is a courtyard garden. The separate restaurant, originally the Market Hall, serves Somerset-produced food. The skittle alley doubles as a function room and hosts a music festival in September. ♿🕭🅿🍴♣🅿🐾🛜

Stoke St Gregory

Royal Oak Inn
The Square, TA3 6EH (opp church)
🕒 12-3 (4.30 Sat), 6.30-11.30; 12-5, 7-11.30 Sun; closed Mon
☎ (01823) 490602 ⊕ theroyaloaktaunton.co.uk
Butcombe Adam Henson's Rare Breed; Quantock Wills Neck; St Austell Tribute 🅗
In the centre of the village, this friendly family-run pub offers a warm welcome to all. It has a varied food menu to suit all tastes including home-made stone-baked pizzas. There are facilities for darts, pool and skittles and the pub has a cricket team. A large function room is available. The pub is ideally located for taking a break when walking the Somerset Levels or the long-distance Parrett Trail.
♿🕭🅿♣🍴🅿🅿(51)🐾🛜

Stone Allerton

Wheatsheaf Inn
Notting Hill Way, BS26 2NH
🕒 6-11; 12-2 Sun; closed Mon ☎ (01934) 444333
2 changing beers 🅖
The reopening of this pub in November 2014 is a glorious good news story. Closed and boarded up by Punch Taverns in 2009, it was bought a year later by the owner of the Valley Smokehouse in the Chew Valley. The pub has undergone extensive rebuilding work, including uncovering the original flagstone floors. There are four distinct areas furnished with a modern, yet spartan, feel. The two locally sourced beers are served via gravity from the barrel. Q♿🕭🅿♣🍴🐾

Taunton

Coal Orchard 🅛 ✅
Bridge Street, TA1 1UD
🕒 8am-midnight (1am Fri & Sat) ☎ (01823) 447330
Greene King Abbot; Ruddles Best Bitter; Sharp's Doom Bar; 3 changing beers (often Cotleigh, Exmoor, Quantock) 🅗
North Town Wharf once stood behind this Wetherspoon pub, next to the River Tone. Facing it was the Coal Orchard, which was the site of an orchard which became the landing place for Welsh coal. Latterly the pub was converted from a former hardware store. The pub can be found in the town centre and the frontage has Art Deco styling with one open-plan level and there is a small garden at the rear. Q♿🕭🅿🍴🚲♣🍴🅿🛜

Racehorse Inn ✅
East Reach, TA1 3HT
🕒 12-4, 6-11 (midnight Thu); 12-12.30am Fri & Sat; 12-11 Sun ☎ (01823) 327513
St Austell Trelawny, Tribute, Proper Job; 1 changing beer 🅗
Popular St Austell pub close to the town centre at the top of East Reach. Multi-roomed, it has front and rear bars and a small lounge with comfortable

armchairs. Both skittles and darts are played regularly and there is live music every week. A large walled garden at the rear is ideal for a relaxing drink on those warm summer days. No food is served. 🏚🕯♣🍺🚋😺🎐

Ring of Bells
16-17 St James Street, TA1 1JS
🕐 11-11 (9 Mon; 10 Tue); 11-6 Sun ☎ (01823) 259480
🌐 theringofbellstaunton.co.uk
Tanners Big Horse, Box o' Frogs; 2 changing beers (sourced nationally) 🅗
Town centre pub close to the theatre and Somerset cricket ground, this is a favourite haunt of cricket fans. Wooden floored, there are two bar areas, a downstairs dining area, an upstairs restaurant and a large courtyard. Two handpumps dispense the owners' Tanners Brewery beers, while two more have guest beers sourced from local and national breweries. Excellent locally produced food is served, from light snacks to full meals (booking for meals recommended). Somerset CAMRA Pub of the Year 2014. Q🌜🕯🎵🍴🍺🚋😺🎐

Wyvern Social Club 🅛
Mountfields Road, TA1 3BJ (off South Rd)
🕐 6-11; 2-11 Sat; 12-3, 7-10.30 Sun ☎ (01823) 284591
🌐 wyvernclub.co.uk
Exmoor Ale; 2 changing beers (often Exmoor, Quantock, St Austell) 🅗
Members-only club with a visitors' licence. Show a CAMRA membership card to be signed in as a guest. The club is the hub for squash, rugby and cricket clubs who use the attached playing fields. A former South-west CAMRA Club of the Year, it stages an annual beer festival in October. Lunchtime meals are served on Sunday only. Children are welcome. It has a private function room and a large hall with a stage for hire. Bus timetables are only relevant for Saturday opening. 🌜🕯🎵👤♣P🚋🎐

Wambrook

Cotley Inn
TA20 3EN (from A30 W out of Chard, by toll house, take left fork and almost immediately left again; continue for just over 1 mile on narrow lane)
🕐 12-3 (not Mon), 6-11; 12-3 Sun ☎ (01460) 62348
🌐 cotleyinnwambrook.co.uk
Otter Ale 🅖, **Amber** 🅗; **1 changing beer (often Exmoor)** 🅖
Although called the Cotley Inn, the pub is in Wambrook. It has a skittle alley at one end, with a bar and dining areas on the left. This delightful country inn, although difficult to find, is in a wonderful rural setting where sitting outside is a delight. Excellent food is served. Three well-kept beers are available on gravity and the pub has log fires in winter, making it very cosy. Q🌜🕯🎵♣🍺P😺

Wanstrow

Pub at Wanstrow
Station Road, BA4 4SZ
🕐 6 (6.30 Mon)-11; 12-2.30, 6-11 Sat & Sun
☎ (01749) 850455
Blindmans Golden Spring; Cheddar Ales Bitter Bully; 2 changing beers (sourced regionally; often Abbey, Church End, Stonehenge) 🅗

An absolute gem, this friendly village local has a lounge bar with open fire and flagstone floors, leading to a small restaurant. The pub serves two regular and up to three guest beers, sourced from almost anywhere, along with ciders from Thatchers and Rich's. Games include skittles, bar billiards and ring the bull. A small but imaginative menu is offered by prior arrangement and all food is home cooked. Q🕯🎵♣🍺P😺

Washford

White Horse Inn 🅛
Abbey Road, TA23 0JZ (off A39)
🕐 12-11 ☎ (01984) 640415 🌐 exmoorpubs.co.uk
3 changing beers 🅗
Only 500 yards from the ruins of Cleve Abbey, and close to the Torre cider farm, this riverside free house is an ideal base for visits to the coast, Exmoor National Park or the Quantock Hills. You can relax on the riverside balcony in summer, or by the fire in winter. The food includes locally sourced produce when possible. The inn has a fine skittle alley and is in the local quiz leagues. Q🕯🚐🎵👤♣🍺P🚋(28)😺

Watchet

Esplanade Club 🅛 ✅
5 The Esplanade, TA23 0AJ (opp marina)
🕐 7 (12 Sat)-midnight; 12-3, 7-midnight Sun
☎ (01984) 634518 🌐 esplanade-club.co.uk
4 changing beers (sourced regionally; often Exmoor, Quantock) 🅗
Somerset CAMRA Club of the Year on four occasions, this place has great views over the marina and the Bristol Channel. The club has a great reputation as a music venue, with live acts every weekend and folk nights and open mic held during the week. Built in the 1860s as a sailmaking factory, it displays old photographs and memorabilia, and is home to the boat owners' club. 🌜🕯👤👣🎵♣🍺🚋(28)😺

Pebbles Tavern 🅛
24 Market Street, TA23 0AN (near Watchet Museum)
🕐 10.30-11; 12-10.30 Sun ☎ (01984) 634737
🌐 pebblestavern.co.uk
3 changing beers (often Moles, Otter, Stowey) 🅖
A small tavern that has won CAMRA Somerset Branch and South-West Region Cider Pub of the Year in 2014 and 2015, and was runner-up for National Cider Pub of the Year 2015. The three ales change constantly. You can bring in your fish and chips from the shop next door. It has close links with the national headquarters of folk arts, Halsway Manor, a few miles away. Music nights, with folk, sea shanty, acoustic and jazz, are held regularly. CAMRA Cider Pub of the Year 2016. 🌜🎵♣🍺🍴🚋(18,28)😺🎐

Star Inn 🅛
Mill Lane, TA23 0BZ
🕐 12-3.30, 6.30-11; 12-4, 6.30-11 Sun ☎ (01984) 631367
🌐 starinnwatchet.co.uk
4 changing beers (often Butcombe, Exmoor, Otter) 🅗
This friendly local with four changing real ales has been in the Guide for 15 consecutive years. It is well known for its good-value menu and famous for its cod and chips. It has darts, quiz and boules teams and stages music nights in the summer. It also does port and cheese nights and is home to

the Sunday night Bad Boys club. Mick's beer tours have run over 70 trips from the pub.
🛏🏠🍴💺🅰🎵♣🐾🐾🐱☂🛜

Wedmore

New Inn 🅛

Combe Batch, BS28 4DU
🕐 12-2.30 (not Mon), 5-midnight; 12-2am Fri; 12-1am Sat; 12-10.30 Sun ☎ (01934) 712099 🌐 newinnwedmore.co.uk
Butcombe Bitter; 2 changing beers (sourced regionally; often Bath Ales, Exmoor, Otter) 🅗
A traditional village inn and the centre for many local events including the famous annual turnip prize, conkers, spoof, penny chuffin' and apple bobbin'. The public bar, lounge and dining areas are complemented by beer gardens to the front and rear. A chalkboard lists forthcoming ales, mainly from the West Country, all served from three handpumps. Traditional, good-value home-cooked food is served. There is a skittle alley/function room, and darts and skittles teams meet here in winter. Q🏵🚪🍴🅰♣🐾🚘P🚃(67)🐱☂

Wellington

Dolphin 🅛

37 Waterloo Road, TA21 8JQ
🕐 12 (4 Mon & Tue)-11; 12-10 Sun ☎ (01823) 665889 🌐 thedolphinwellington.co.uk
Otter Amber; Quantock Ale; 2 changing beers (often Bays, Exeter, Kubla) 🅗
Traditional town-centre pub providing great ales and home-cooked food. The frontage has an unusual mural featuring pumpclips from local breweries. Customers are encouraged to request which guest ales they would like to see on the bar. A CAMRA discount of 5% off a pint is given, except on Tuesday when all real ales are £3 from 4pm to closing. Regular live music features on Thursday evenings, and brunch is provided on Saturday from 10am. Q🛏🏠🍴💺♣🐾🚘🚃(22a)🐱☂

West Huntspill

Crossways Inn 🅛

Withy Road, TA9 3RA (on A38)
🕐 12-midnight; 12-10.30 Sun ☎ (01278) 783756 🌐 crosswaysinn.co.uk
Exmoor Gold; RCH PG Steam; 4 changing beers (sourced regionally; often Marston's, Otter, St Austell) 🅗
A past winner of Somerset CAMRA Pub of the Year, this 17th-century inn was runner-up in 2016. It has several bar areas, two fireplaces with log fires during winter and an outside fireplace to keep smokers warm. There is a dining room and a skittle alley/function room. A food menu is available, plus specials boards. Breakfast may be on offer depending on whether guests are staying.
🛏🏠🚪🍴💺🅰♣🐾🚘P🚃(21)🐱☂

Weston-super-Mare

Bear

66 Walliscote Road, BS23 1ED
🕐 1-11.30; 12-midnight Fri & Sat; 12-11.30 Sun ☎ (01934) 641722 🌐 thebearinnweston.co.uk
3 changing beers (sourced regionally) 🅗
Spacious and comfortable pub, formerly called the Balmoral, which reopened in 2012 with a new name after a period of closure. Beers can be

unusual for the area, with a variety of styles usually available. Live music is popular every Saturday evening, as is a student music night one Thursday every month. There is a skittle alley and a refurbished function room at the back with a stage.
🛏🏠🚪🍴💺♣🐾🚘P🚃(5,7)🐱☂

Brit Bar ✅

118 High Street, BS23 1HP
🕐 12-1am ☎ (01934) 632629
3 changing beers (often RPM) 🅗
This town-centre pub has been given a bright, modern makeover while retaining the important traditional elements. Mondays to Wednesdays are gaming nights, with live music at weekends. Two or three changing beers are offered – it is not unusual for all to be dark beers, including stouts and porters. In September 2015 brewing commenced on-site, under the RPM brewery label, and there is usually one RPM beer on the bar.
🛏🏠🐾🚃🐾🐱☂

Cabot Court Hotel ✅

Knightstone Road, BS23 2AH (on seafront)
🕐 7am-midnight (1am Fri; 2am Sat) ☎ (01934) 427930
Greene King Abbot; Ruddles Best Bitter; changing beers 🅗
Large Wetherspoon conversion on the seafront between the Grand Pier and the Winter Gardens. On four levels, each has a distinctive style. There are bars on the ground and second floors with different guest ales in each. The first-floor room is particularly comfortable, with sofas and a real fire in winter – a haven from the TVs and speakers in the other rooms. Local breweries are supported, often Exmoor and GWB. Q🛏🏠🚪🍴💺♣🚘🚃☂

Regency

22-24 Lower Church Road, BS23 2AG
🕐 10-11.30 (midnight Fri & Sat); 10.45-11.30 Sun ☎ (01934) 633406 🌐 theregencyinn.co.uk
Butcombe Bitter; Courage Best Bitter; Draught Bass; Wells Bombardier; 1 changing beer 🅗
Comfortable, friendly town-centre local, attracting a mixed clientele including students at lunchtime. The pub has pool, skittles and crib teams, but also offers a quiet refuge for conversation. The pool room, with TV and jukebox, is separate from the main bar area, and children are welcome here. Keenly priced home-cooked food is served lunchtimes, and there are Wednesday curry and Thursday grill evenings. It has patios to the front and rear. Pub outings feature, plus occasional live bands. 🛏🏠🍴💺♣🚃(4,5,7)

Wheddon Cross

Rest & Be Thankful Inn 🅛

TA24 7DR (on A396 SW of Dunster at jct with B3224)
🕐 11.30-2, 6-midnight ☎ (01643) 841222 🌐 restandbethankful.co.uk
Exmoor Ale; St Austell Tribute; 2 changing beers 🅗
A 19th-century coaching inn at the heart of Exmoor National Park, at the crossroads of Exmoor's highest village, and near to the highest point on Exmoor – Dunkery Beacon (1,687 feet). The renowned Snowdrop Valley is close by and in season is linked by minibus from the pub. It has its own skittle alley, pool table, dartboard and private function room. A lively music venue and a favourite place to stay with cyclists and ramblers.
Q🛏🏠🚪🍴💺🅰♣🐾🚘P🚃(198)🐱☂

Wincanton

Nog Inn

South Street, BA9 9DL

☾ 10.30-11 (midnight Fri & Sat); 12-11 Sun

☎ (01963) 32998 ⊕ thenoginn.com

Otter Bitter; Sharp's Own; 2 changing beers (sourced nationally; often Church End, Cotleigh, Plain) Ⓗ

Attractive listed pub with a striking Georgian façade fronting a long, narrow building, with parts dating back to the 16th century. A secluded sunny garden with covered seating can be found at the far end of the property. The guest ales are often seasonal and an extensive range of continental draught beers is always available, as are real ciders. Home-cooked pub classics are served. Regular events on Thursday evenings include comedy, open mic, and a quiz.

Ꙩ❀❀◐♣♠Pᐰ(58)❀ᕯ

Winsford

Royal Oak Inn Ⓛ

Halse Lane, TA24 7JE

☾ 11-3, 6-11 ☎ (01643) 851455 ⊕ royaloakexmoor.co.uk

Exmoor Ale, Gold; Otter Amber Ⓗ

Picturesque thatched inn in the heart of Winsford, within Exmoor National Park. It has eight en-suite rooms and is a good base from which to explore Exmoor. The village is noted for having been the birthplace of Ernest Bevin, former Foreign Secretary. Well-behaved children and dogs are made welcome in the bar. The Winn brook runs past the pub and over the ford that leads up to Exmoor and Tarr Steps. Summer hours are extended on Saturdays and Sundays.

QꙨ❀❀◐�& Åᐰ♣Pᐰᕯᕯ

Winsham

Bell Inn Ⓛ

Church Street, TA20 4HU

☾ 12-2.30 (not Mon), 7-11; 12-3, 7-11 Sat & Sun

☎ (01460) 30677 ⊕ thebellwinsham.co.uk

Branscombe Vale Branoc; 3 changing beers (sourced regionally; often Cottage, Exmoor, Yeovil) Ⓗ

Popular free house in the centre of the village. The licensees have been running this pub for over 16 years. It has two bars, one with darts, skittles and pool. There is a strong commitment to real ale, with up to three rotating guest ales from the West Country. Monies are raised for village and local charities through a weekly lottery and other events. Good-value food includes a popular Sunday roast. QꙨ❀◐♣Pᐰ(99)❀

Witham Friary

Seymour Arms ★

BA11 5HF

☾ 11-3 (4 Sat), 6-11; 12-11 Sun ☎ (01749) 850742

Cheddar Ales Potholer; 1 changing beer (sourced locally) Ⓖ

A hidden rural gem, this pub has probably changed very little over the past 50 or so years. Built in the 1860s as a hotel to serve the nearby Mid-Somerset GWR branch railway station, it was part of the Duke of Somerset's estate. Sadly, in the 1960s Dr Beeching closed the station, and the hotel became a quiet country pub. Beer and cider are served from a glass-panelled hatch in the central hallway.

QꙨ❀♣♠P❀

Withypool

Royal Oak Inn Ⓛ

TA24 7QP (W of B3223 between Dulverton and Exford)

☾ 12-3 (not Mon), 6-11 ☎ (01643) 831506

⊕ royaloakwithypool.co.uk

Exmoor Ale, Gold; 2 changing beers (sourced locally; often Exmoor) Ⓗ

Set in the remote village of Withypool, for over 300 years this pub has been providing great local ale and food. It has two bars and a dining room, decorated with an interesting array of historic country pursuits memorabilia, and eight en-suite rooms. It offers shooting, riding and fishing. Although remote, there is easy access by car or bicycle to beauty spots such as Tarr Steps, which is only four miles away. QꙨ❀❀◐ Åᐰ♣♠P❀ᕯ

Wiveliscombe

Bear Inn Ⓛ

8-10 North Street, TA4 2JY

☾ 10.30-11 ☎ (01984) 623537

4 changing beers (sourced locally; often Cotleigh, Exmoor, Otter) Ⓗ

Welcoming family-run pub with a large garden, patio and skittle alley. This 17th-century former coaching inn can be found in the centre of the town. An extensive menu offers good-value meals using local produce where possible. There is an on-site microbrewery and you may find one of the Black Bear ales on tap. Real cider features strongly. The emphasis is on conversation at the bar, with customers of all ages.

ꙨꙨ❀❀◐ & ♣♠Pᐰ(25)❀ᕯ

Wookey

Burcott Inn

Wookey Road, BA5 1NJ

☾ 12-2 (not Mon), 6-11; 12-3 Sun ☎ (01749) 673874

⊕ burcottinn.co.uk

Hop Back Summer Lightning; 2 changing beers (sourced regionally; often RCH) Ⓗ

A friendly, well-kept village pub on the B3139 near Wells. One local regular beer and up to two guests (one in the winter months) are stocked, and are also usually local. There are four self-catering cottages attached to the pub, making this a great place to stay for a weekend in Wells. Note that the pub is closed on Sunday evenings and Monday lunchtimes. QꙨ❀❀◐ Åᐰ♣Pᐰ(67)

Yeovil

Quicksilver Mail ⦿

168 Hendford Hill, BA20 2RG (at jct of A30 and A37)

☾ 11-midnight; 10.30-1am Sat; 12-11 Sun

☎ (01935) 424721 ⊕ quicksilvermail.com

Butcombe Bitter; 2 changing beers (sourced nationally; often Adnams, Bath Ales, St Austell) Ⓗ

Friendly, popular community local to the west of the town. The name commemorates a high-speed mail coach service from Exeter to London which used to call here. There is a bar on one level and a restaurant area down a few steps. Historic photos of the pub and sporting and music memorabilia adorn the walls. A skittles alley doubles as a function room, with frequent live music. The food is excellent value, particularly the lunchtime specials. ❀❀◐♣Pᐰ❀ᕯ

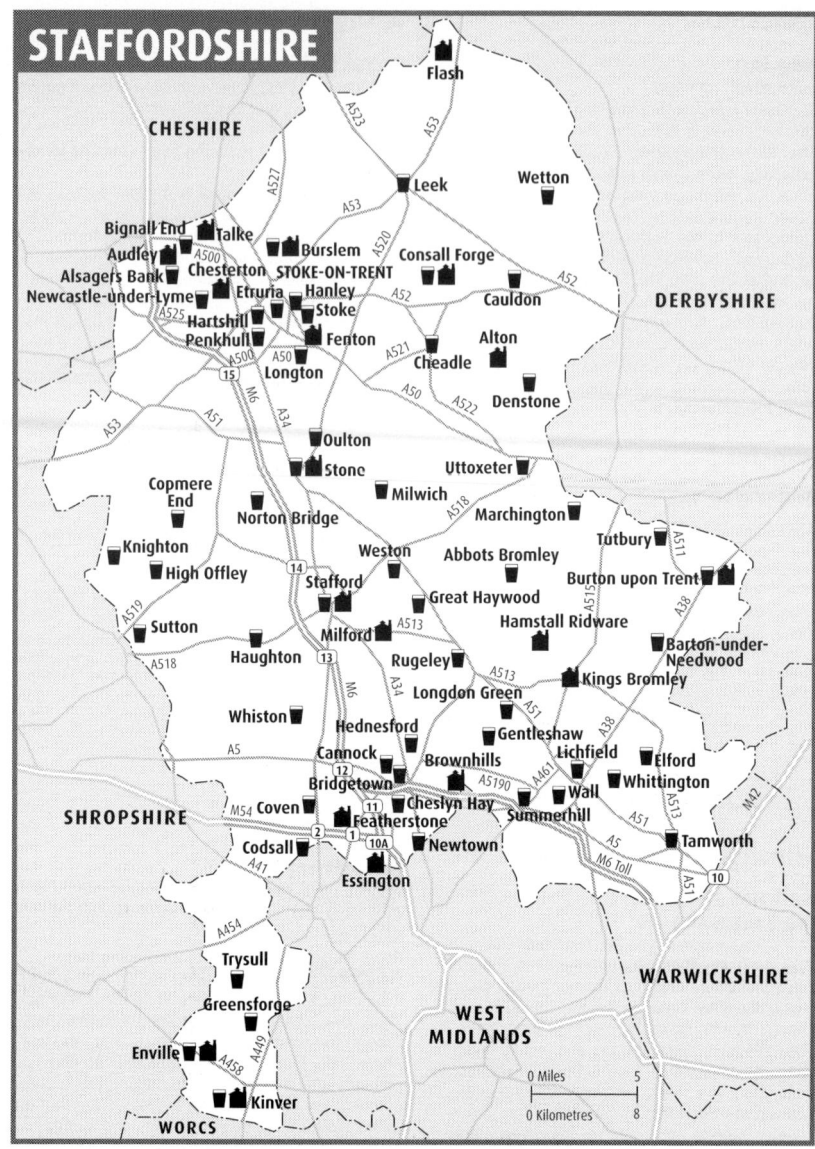

STAFFORDSHIRE

Abbots Bromley

Crown Inn
Market Place, WS15 3BS (opp Butter Cross on B5014)
☼ 12-2.30 (not Mon), 5-midnight Sat & Sun
☎ (01283) 840227 🌐 thecrownatabbotsbromley.co.uk
Draught Bass; Holden's Golden Glow; St Austell Tribute; Thwaites Lancaster Bomber; Timothy Taylor Landlord Ⓗ
Imposing mock-Tudor style village pub overlooking the Butter Cross, believed to have been a series of cottages originally. The public bar features pictures of the world-famous annual Abbots Bromley Horn Dance. The former lounge, comprising two rooms connected through an archway, is now used primarily for dining (no meals Sun eve). A separate large function room to the rear of the pub has its own bar. Quiz night is the first Tuesday of the month. ☕🏮◐♣️P🚲(402A,403)🐾🎴

Alsagers Bank

Gresley Arms Ⓛ
High Street, ST7 8BQ (on B5367 4 miles N of Newcastle-under-Lyme)
☼ 12 (3 Mon-Wed)-11 ☎ (01782) 722469
10 changing beers (often Abbeydale, Marston's, Townhouse) Ⓗ
Sitting at a height of 700 feet above sea level, the Gresley Arms commands views over Cheshire, Shropshire and the Wirral. The pub is also close to two country parks. Ten varied real ales are on offer, plus four real ciders and a huge range of imported bottled beers. Good-value meals are served four nights a week, plus Sunday lunch. A regular folk and blues festival, including a beer festival, takes place in May every year. A gem. ☕🏮◐♿️⛺♣️P🚲(74,74A)🐾🎴

Barton-under-Needwood

Barton Turns

3 Barton Turn, DE13 8EA (off B5016, ½ mile E of village, by Trent & Mersey Canal)
🟢 11-11 ☎ (01283) 480682
Marston's Pedigree; Thwaites Wainwright; 1 changing beer (sourced nationally; often Ringwood, Wychwood) Ⓗ
Friendly traditional Victorian pub with an open-plan single room, close to the Trent & Mersey Canal, still known by locals as the Vine, its former name. The beer garden at the rear has a sheltered decking area and lawn, but outdoor drinking (with picnic tables) is also possible at the front of the pub and across the road by the side of the canal. Bar meals are served every day to 8.30pm. Boaters, cyclists and walkers are welcome. Popular with TV sport fans, especially for Saturday afternoon horse racing. 🏵️🌙▶️P🚲(7,7A,7E)🐾🛜

Royal Oak ✪

74 The Green, DE13 8JD (½ mile from B5016 via Wales Lane)
🟢 12-11.30 (12.30am Fri & Sat); 12-11 Sun
☎ (01283) 713852
Marston's Pedigree; 2 changing beers (sourced nationally; often Brakspear, Jennings, Wychwood) Ⓗ/Ⓖ
Bustling community local on the southern edge of the village, home to many traditional pub games teams and an over-40s football team. While parts of the building date back to the 16th century, the pub has only existed since the mid-1800s. Public bar and lounge customers are served from a central sunken bar, its floor being below the level of the rest of the ground floor. A separate conservatory (accessed from the public bar) overlooks the garden. Beers are available on handpump or by gravity, direct from the cask, on request.
Q🏵️🐕🛗♿♣🌙P🚲(7,7A,7E)🐾🛜

Bignall End

Bignall End Cricket Club

Boon Hill, ST7 8LA (400yds from B5500)
🟢 7-midnight; 12-midnight Fri-Sun ☎ (01782) 720514
🌐 bignallend.play-cricket.com
Draught Bass; 3 changing beers (often Abbeydale, Acorn, Mallinson's) Ⓗ
Welcoming cricket club/pub with great views over the Cheshire Plain, in a semi-rural location. An exceptional beer festival is held in November in the upstairs function room. There is a snooker room and bar with a TV for sports fans. Along with Bass there are three guest ales from breweries local, regional and national. Facing the cricket pitch is a covered outdoor seating area where it is great to sit and watch the sun go down. 🐕♿P🚲(4)

Bridgetown

Stumble Inn

264 Walsall Road, WS11 0JL (200yds from A34/A5/M6 toll jct)
🟢 5-11; 12-midnight Fri-Sun ☎ (01543) 321605
4 changing beers Ⓗ
A split-level one-room pub with a strong musical repertoire, ranging from karaoke to live bands, with discos and jam sessions thrown into the mix. There are also several charity events held from time to time, and a beer festival in September is the highlight of the year for local ale drinkers. A

pool and darts area and a small function room complete the picture for this friendly, vivacious local pub. 🐕🏵️🐕♿♣🌙P🚲(1,2)🐾🛜

Burton upon Trent

Alfred Ale House

51 Derby Street, DE14 2LD (on A5121)
🟢 4-11; 12-midnight Fri & Sat; 12-11 Sun ☎ (01283) 562178
5 changing beers (sourced locally; often Burton Bridge, Everards) Ⓗ
Double-fronted terrace pub which was once the Trumans Brewery tap. A central bar serves two rooms, each featuring wood partitions topped with leaded stained glass, the lounge having a raised seating area, and there is a small snug to the rear. Four changing beers are from Burton Bridge, plus one guest. Traditional cider and English fruit wines, and hot and cold snacks, are also available. Quiz night Wednesday; frequent live entertainment.
Q🐕🏵️🌿♣🌙P🚲🐾🛜

Burton Bridge Inn ♗

24 Bridge Street, DE14 1SY (on A511, at town end of Trent Bridge)
🟢 5-11 Mon; 12-2 (2.30 Thu), 5-11; 11.30-11.30 Fri & Sat; 12-3, 7-11 Sun ☎ (01283) 536596 🌐 burtonbridgeinn.co.uk
Burton Bridge Golden Delicious, Sovereign Gold, Bitter, Porter, Draught Burton Ale, Festival Ale; 1 changing beer (sourced nationally; often Everards, Ossett, York) Ⓗ
This 17th-century pub is the flagship of the Burton Bridge Brewery estate and fronts the brewery itself. It incorporates two rooms served from a central bar: a smaller front room with wooden pews and displaying many awards, brewery memorabilia and framed old maps of Burton, and a back room featuring oak beams and panels. The beer range is supplemented by a selection of malt whiskies and fruit wines. A dining/function room and a skittle alley are upstairs. No lunches Sunday-Wednesday. Q🏵️🌙♣🚲🐾🛜

REAL ALE BREWERIES

Beowulf Brownhills
Black Hole Burton upon Trent
Blythe Hamstall Ridware
Burton Bridge Burton upon Trent
Burton Old Cottage Burton upon Trent
Burton Town Burton on Trent (NEW)
Consall Forge Consall Forge (NEW)
Enville Enville
Flash Flash
Gates Burton Burton upon Trent
Grey Friars Featherstone
Heritage Burton upon Trent (NEW)
Kinver Kinver
Lymestone Stone
Marston's Burton upon Trent
Morton Essington
Otherton Audley
Peakstones Rock Alton
Quartz Kings Bromley
RAN Stoke-on-Trent: Fenton
Shugborough Milford
Slater's Stafford
Talke O' Th' Hill Talke
Titanic Stoke-on-Trent: Burslem
Tower Burton upon Trent
Townhouse Audley
Weal Chesterton

Coopers Tavern ★
43 Cross Street, DE14 1EG (off Station St)
🕙 5-11 Mon; 4-11 Tue & Wed; 12-11 (11.30 Fri & Sat); 12-10 Sun ☎ (01283) 532551 🌐 cooperstavern.co.uk
Draught Bass ⒢; Joule's Blonde, Slumbering Monk ⒣; 6 changing beers (sourced regionally; often Joule's, Nene Valley, Oakham) ⒣/⒢
Classic, unspoilt 19th-century alehouse, once the Bass Brewery tap and now part of the Joule's estate. The intimate inner taproom has barrel tables and bench seating where the beer is served from a small counter by the cask stillage. The more comfortable lounge gives access to a third small room. Up to four ciders/perries (choice varies), plus fruit wines, are also available. There is impromptu folk music on Tuesday evenings and live music Sunday afternoons. A frequent winner of local and regional CAMRA Pub of the Year awards.
Q ☻ ⊛ ⇌ ♣ 🚍 🐾 ❄ 🎵 ≈

Elms Inn
36 Stapenhill Road, DE15 9AE (on A444)
🕙 12-11.30 (midnight Fri & Sat); 12-11 Sun
☎ (01283) 535505 🌐 the-elms-burton.co.uk
Draught Bass; Marston's Pedigree; 2 changing beers (sourced nationally; often Hop Back, Robinsons, Thornbridge) ⒣
Lively local on the opposite bank of the River Trent from the town centre. Built as a private house in the late 19th century, this is one of Burton's original parlour pubs. Sensitively renovated, the small public bar and snug on either side of the bar, plus a side room served through a hatch, are largely unchanged. In contrast, the lounge to the rear has been extended and refurbished in a modern style. Meals are available to 7pm (3pm Sun). Live entertainment is hosted on occasion.
☻ ⊛ ⒟ & ♣ 🐾 ≈

Old Cottage Tavern
36 Byrkley Street, DE14 2EG (off Waterloo St A5121, behind town hall)
🕙 12-11; 11.30-11 Sun ☎ (01283) 619192
Burton Old Cottage Oak Ale, Stout, Halcyon Daze; 3 changing beers (sourced nationally; often Cottage, Milestone) ⒣
No longer owned by the brewery but leased from the Tadcaster Pub Company, this traditional local continues to operate as the Burton Old Cottage Brewery tap. The public bar at the front, with a cosy snug to one side, and the wood-panelled lounge to the rear, are served from a central bar. There is also a games/function room (with demountable skittle alley) upstairs. Guest beers are usually from other SIBA members. It hosts the Brewtown Folk Club and Spoken Word events. Q ☻ ⊛ ⒟ ⇌ ♣ 🚍 🐾 ≈

Roebuck Inn ✅
101 Station Street, DE14 1BT (on corner of jct with Mosley St)
🕙 12-11 (midnight Fri & Sat) ☎ (01283) 511213
🌐 roe-buck-inn.co.uk
Draught Bass; Greene King Abbot; Marston's Pedigree; Theakston Old Peculier; 1 changing beer (sourced regionally; often Gates Burton, Oakham, Sarah Hughes) ⒣
Friendly Victorian corner terrace pub near the railway station, once the Ind Coope Brewery tap, opposite the former brewery. The original classic Draught Burton Ale was launched here in 1976. Inside, there is a long narrow single room with dark wood panelling and the bar counter down one side. A small patio at the rear is available for

outdoor drinking, plus a few tables and chairs outside at the front in summer. Live music is played early Sunday evenings. ⊛ 🖥 ⇌ ♣ 🚍 🐾 ≈

Waterloo Inn ✅
50 Ashby Road, DE15 0LQ (on A511, about ½ mile E from Trent Bridge)
🕙 4-11.30; 12-midnight Fri & Sat; 12-11 Sun
☎ (01283) 354637
Draught Bass; Marston's Pedigree; 2 changing beers (sourced locally; often Gates Burton, Leatherbritches, Tower) ⒣
Traditional two-roomed local, probably Victorian, in the suburb of Winshill, east of the River Trent; there may in fact have been a pub on the site since the 1700s. It was reputedly a halfway point for changing horses on brewery drays delivering to south Derbyshire. Outdoor drinking can be enjoyed on a decking area at the front, accessed via patio doors, creating an alfresco atmosphere in warm weather. Pies and pasties are available at all times, and customers may bring takeaways. Quiz night is Sunday. ☻ ⊛ ♣ P 🚍 (8,9,9A) 🐾 ≈

Cannock

Linford Arms ✅
79 High Green, WS11 1BN
🕙 8am-midnight (1am Fri & Sat) ☎ (01543) 469360
Fuller's London Pride; Greene King Abbot; Ruddles Best Bitter; 5 changing beers (sourced nationally; often Backyard, Beowulf, Salopian) ⒣
Established town-centre Wetherspoon pub serving eight real ales and ciders, with good bus and rail links. Its name originates from the builders' merchants that formerly occupied the premises. Food is served daily 8am-11pm. It has seating areas on two floors, with quieter alcoves and a separate snug. Two ale festivals are held each year and local breweries feature regularly. Local CAMRA Pub of the Year finalist in numerous recent years. Not to be missed if visiting Cannock. ☻ ⒟ & 🍴 🚍 ≈

Cauldon

Yew Tree Inn ⒧
ST10 3EJ (turn left at Cross pub, Cauldon Lowe; approx 1 mile from jct)
🕙 12-3, 6-midnight; 12-midnight Sat & Sun
☎ (01538) 309876
Burton Bridge Bitter; Rudgate Ruby Mild; 1 changing beer (often Blue Monkey, Cottage, Dancing Duck) ⒣
Queen Victoria's stockings anyone? The Yew Tree pub/museum has these and much more – it is a place you must visit at least once and preferably more than once. Your first time will be spent experimenting with the polyphons and checking out the Acme patent dog-carrier and half a zillion other items of interest, all the while sampling the excellent ales, munching a superb pork pie or two and indulging in local craic – no muzak or TV here. Visit! Q ☻ ⊛ ⒟ & ▲ ♣ 🍴 P 🚍 (108) 🐾 ≈

Cheadle

Huntsman ⒧
The Green, ST10 1XS
🕙 12-midnight ☎ (01538) 750502
🌐 thehuntsmancheadle.com
Castle Rock Harvest Pale; Joule's Slumbering Monk; Marston's Pedigree; 3 changing beers (often Peakstones Rock, Sarah Hughes, Wincle) ⒣

Now a regular entry in this Guide, you can expect a warm welcome, with two log fires and friendly bar staff. A good range of beers is on offer for the discerning real ale drinker. Quality traditional pub food is on the menu, with excellent service. The pub plays host to annual beer and cider festivals and also supports other community events. A suntrap beer garden is to the rear, excellent for the summer months. A great pub for families as well as those who just enjoy a quiet pint. ᗧ☺⌂◑➡️ᗧ♣♠P🖩(X51)♣☘

Cheslyn Hay

Colliers Arms ✪
High Street, WS6 7AN
✪ 12-11 (midnight Thu-Sat) ☎ (01922) 415209
Morland Old Speckled Hen; 2 changing beers (often Holden's, Sharp's) ⅢE
Situated on the main Walsall to Cannock bus route in the heart of Cheslyn Hay, this thriving community pub is well worth a visit. A large open-plan room has been tastefully refurbished and divided into distinctive bar and lounge areas displaying local and sporting scenes. Traditional pub games are played and the pub hosts two ladies' darts teams and a local football team, along with a popular weekly quiz. Monday evening, 6-8pm, is curry night. ☺◑&♣P🖩(2)

Codsall

Bull Hotel ⅃
The Square, Wolverhampton Road, WV8 1PU
✪ 11-11 (11.30 Thu-Sat); 11.30-11 Sun ☎ (01902) 842084
⊕ bullhotelpub.co.uk
Banks's Mild, Bitter, Sunbeam; 2 changing beers (sourced nationally) ⅢE
Large historic pub at the heart of Codsall village, originally a farmhouse, comprising a number of rooms that have been knocked together, but retaining distinctive areas including a more basic public bar where darts and dominoes are played. The large fenced garden includes an excellent children's play area and smoking shelters. Note, dogs are excluded from the garden. The pub is popular with the locals at lunchtimes for the reasonably priced bar meals. Guest beers are from the Marston's monthly list.
Q ᗧ☺❁&≈♣P🖩(10B)☘

Codsall Station ⅃
Chapel Lane, WV8 2EJ
✪ 11.30-11 (11.30 Fri & Sat); 12-10.30 Sun
☎ (01902) 847061 ⊕ Holdenscodsallstation.co.uk
Holden's Black Country Mild, Black Country Bitter, Golden Glow, Special; 2 changing beers (sourced regionally; often Holden's) ⅢE
Sensitively converted from the waiting room, offices and stationmaster's house, the Grade II-listed building comprises a bar, lounge, snug and conservatory, and displays worldwide railway memorabilia. Steps lead to the outside drinking area, with tables and benches overlooking the working platforms. Bar meals are served all week except Sunday, with home-made curry on Thursday evenings. Beer festivals are held in May and the weekend after August bank holiday.
Q ❁☺◑≈P🖩(5,10B)♣☘

Firs Club ⅃
16 Wood Road, WV8 1BX (entrance from shared Co-op car park, Station Rd)
✪ 7.30-11 (midnight Fri); 12-midnight Sat; 12-11 Sun
☎ (01902) 844674 ⊕ thefirscodsall.com
Banks's Mild, Bitter ℗; 3 changing beers (sourced regionally; often Hobsons, Ludlow, Wye Valley) ⅢE
Winner of local CAMRA Club of the Year 2016, the Firs has a bar area, a quiet lounge and a sports lounge with pool table, dartboard and card table. Snooker tables are upstairs. Up to three guest ales, some sourced locally, are served. At Sunday lunchtimes there is a popular carvery. A beer festival is held in November. The large function room is available to hire. Show this Guide or a current CAMRA membership card to be signed in. A pedestrian entrance in Wood Road is handy for the bus stop. Q ❁◑&≈♣P🖩(5,10B)☘

Consall Forge

Black Lion ⅃
Wetley Rocks, ST9 0AJ (off A522 follow signs to Consall Gardens, then nature reserve on hairpin bend; go straight on, ignoring No Vehicular Access sign; at bottom of hill, go left along track to car park)
✪ 12-11; 12-10.30 Sun ☎ (01782) 550294
⊕ blacklionpub.co.uk
Peakstones Rock Black Hole; house beer (by Consall Forge); 4 changing beers (often Cottage, Joule's, Kelham Island) ⅢE
A working no-frills pub from a bygone age, set in the picturesque Churnet Valley and adjacent to the Churnet Valley Heritage Railway and the Caldon Canal. Getting there can be an adventure. For people in a wheelchair or with walking difficulties this may present some problems. It is a pub of distinction, selling a wide range of ales, perries and ciders. Three annual beer festivals are held in February, July and December. Whatever form of travel, by car, rail or canal, you are guaranteed a warm welcome. ᗧ☺◑⋏≈♣♠P♣☘

Copmere End

Star Inn ⅃ ✪
ST21 6EW (leave Eccleshall on B5026, turn left at sign for Copmere End, follow road; pub is on crossroads)
✪ 12-3, 6-11; 12-11 Sat & Sun; closed Mon
☎ (01785) 850279 ⊕ thestarinn-eccleshall.co.uk
Draught Bass; Titanic Iceberg; Wells Bombardier; 1 changing beer (sourced regionally; often Joule's) ⅢE
A thriving community pub in the heart of the Staffordshire countryside, adjacent to Copmere Lake and surrounded by numerous walks. The pub has become the community focus for the area; there are charity auctions, events and some music. Food includes an excellent selection of bar meals and an à la carte menu using locally sourced ingredients. The extensive garden has a play area, ideal for families. Q ᗧ☺◑♣P♣☘

Coven

Harrows Inn ℗ ⅃
School Lane, WV9 5AW (by traffic lights on A449 Stafford Rd)
✪ 12-midnight ☎ (01902) 790055 ⊕ theharrowsinn.co.uk
Three Tuns XXX; Titanic Plum Porter; 7 changing beers (sourced regionally; often Broughs, Marston's, Salopian) ⅢE

Privately owned, this attractive pub has been a free house since 2012. A central counter serves two rooms refurbished in a contemporary style; one is for dining and the other is a public bar with piano, dartboard and pool table. Both rooms have wooden floors and logburners. Home-cooked meals are served all day, except Sunday and Monday. Nine real ales and up to 10 real ciders and perries are usually stocked. There is a large beer garden and children's play area.
Q৯✿❀◑&♣●P⊟(76,54)☺🎅

Denstone

Tavern ❢ 🗓
College Road, ST14 5HR
🕓 6-11 Mon; 12-2, 5.30-11; 12-midnight Fri-Sun
☎ (01889) 590847 ⊕ thetaverndenstone.co.uk
Marston's Pedigree; house beer (by Ringwood); 2 changing beers (sourced nationally; often Marston's) 🄷
The Tavern is a 17th-century village inn offering fine food and good beers in pleasant surroundings. There is a bar area with darts, a comfortable lounge area and a conservatory for dining. Quiz night is Monday, when there is no food. Fresh wood-fired stone-baked pizzas are served Friday and Saturday evenings, to eat in or take away (booking a table in advance is advisable). Guest beers come from the Marston's range. Q৯✿❀◑▲♣P⊟(32A)☺🎅

Elford

Crown Inn 🗓
The Square, B79 9DB (600yds E of A513) SK189106
🕓 6-11; 12-midnight Fri-Sun ☎ (01827) 383602
Burton Bridge Sovereign Gold; Draught Bass; 2 changing beers 🄷
Welcoming multi-room village pub. In the 18th century the upstairs rooms were used as a courthouse, and today's dining room once served as the cells. Beamed ceilings feature throughout, with real fires creating a cosy feel. One of the guest beers is a changing mild. Food is served until 9pm Wednesday to Saturday, and until 3.30pm on Sunday. Gourmet evenings feature, while Wednesday has an Italian slant. Bar snacks are available at all times. No evening bus service.
◑♣P⊟☺🎅

Enville

Cat Inn ❢ 🗓
Bridgnorth Road, DY7 5HA (on A458)
🕓 12-2.30 (not Mon), 5-11; 12-11 Fri & Sat; 12-6 Sun
☎ (01384) 872209 ⊕ thecatinn.com
Enville Ale; Ginger Beer; 5 changing beers 🄷
Parts of this traditional country pub date back to the 16th century. It has three oak-beamed rooms, and all have real fires. The Garden Room has been refurbished and there is a function room upstairs. Hanging baskets adorn the beer garden and courtyard during summer months. Regular Enville beers are served, plus three guest ales, usually from local breweries. Home-made dishes and daily specials, using local produce whenever possible, are served. Joint CAMRA branch Pub of the Year 2014, branch South Staffs area Pub of the Year 2015 and 2016, and Cider Pub of the Year 2016.
Q৯✿❀◑●P☺🎅

Gentleshaw

Olde Windmill
Windmill Lane, WS15 4NF SK051118
🕓 12-midnight ☎ (01543) 682468 ⊕ yeoldewindmill.co.uk
Draught Bass; 3 changing beers (sourced regionally; often Burton Bridge, Castle Rock, Springhead)
Welcoming 400-year-old country pub, with smartly attired staff and equally sharp food and drink offerings. Free of tie, the two guest ales are usually interesting microbrews. The cosy bar is dog-friendly, while the wood-panelled lounge offers freshly cooked meals including interesting specials. Both rooms feature old beams (some cleverly fake) and open fires. A number of teams use the crown bowling green. The pub is 100 yards from the stump of an old disused windmill.
Q৯✿❀◑&●P⊟☺🎅

Great Haywood

Clifford Arms ✅
Main Road, ST18 0SR (off A51, 4 miles NW of Rugeley)
🕓 12-11.30 (midnight Fri & Sat); 12-11 Sun
☎ (01889) 881321 ⊕ cliffordarms.co.uk
Adnams Broadside; Draught Bass; Morland Old Speckled Hen; 3 changing beers (sourced nationally) 🄷
Village centre inn with a large bar providing plenty of seating and a restaurant adorned with past photos of the pub. It is a popular local, home to cribbage, dominoes and quiz teams, and to a tug o' war team. It is also popular with walkers, cyclists, boaters and visitors to the nearby Shugborough Estate (National Trust). The Staffordshire Way and bridge 73 of the Trent & Mersey Canal are 200 yards along Trent Lane. The pub is dog friendly.
Q৯✿❀◑▲♣P⊟☺🎅

Greensforge

Navigation
Greensforge Lane, DY6 0AH
🕓 12-midnight ☎ (01384) 273721
Enville Ale; Three Tuns XXX; 2 changing beers (often Holden's, Olde Swan) 🄷
This former Simpkiss pub is popular with locals and walkers alike due to its position adjacent to the Staffordshire & Worcestershire Canal. There is an interesting collection of heritage canal photos on the walls. Up to four real ales are served which are predominantly local. Good food is available at reasonable prices. Occasional light background music plays. Q৯✿❀◑P☺

Haughton

Bell Inn 🗓 ✅
Newport Road, ST18 9EX (on A518)
🕓 12-3, 5-midnight; 12-midnight Fri-Sun ☎ (01785) 780301
⊕ thebellhaughton.co.uk
Marston's Pedigree; Timothy Taylor Landlord; 3 changing beers (sourced nationally) 🄷
The L-shaped interior has a restaurant at the rear that serves really good, locally sourced food. At the front is a small, well-run, friendly bar, with snacks available. As well as running charity events, the pub has six dominoes teams. The beers change regularly and come from the SIBA list, often from local brewers. Booking is recommended for dining. A beer and music festival is held at the end of August. Q৯✿❀◑▲♣P⊟(5,877)🎅

Hednesford

Bridge Inn

387 Cannock Road, WS11 5TD (on jct of Belt Rd and Cannock Rd)

🍺 12-11 (midnight Fri & Sat) ☎ (01543) 423651

Banks's Bitter; Burton Bridge Bitter; Jennings Sneck Lifter; Marston's Burton Bitter; Salopian Lemon Dream; 3 changing beers (sourced locally; often Backyard, Beowulf, Holden's) ⊞

Close to Cannock Chase, this is a real ale-based pub that prides itself on a changing selection of ales, as well as a real cider. Food is served Thursday to Sunday; all meals are produced on site and only fresh local produce is used. The chips are triple cooked and the burgers are made using the chef's own special recipe. Theme nights and live music feature most Saturday nights.

🏆🏵️🕙❧✦♣️🍴🚪(2,T5)😺🎵🛜

Cross Keys Hotel 🍸 🖫

42 Hill Street, WS12 2DN

🍺 12-midnight ☎ (01543) 879534

Brains Rev James; Draught Bass; Holden's Golden Glow; Morland Old Speckled Hen; Salopian Oracle; changing beers (sourced nationally; often Beowulf, Skinner's, Thwaites) ⊞

Serving up to eight real ales including several guests, this former coaching inn dates back to 1746. Hednesford Town Football Club was originally based behind the pub; the licensee is an ex-player and is now assistant manager. Sporting and historic photographs decorate the walls. Monthly quiz nights are held. It is rumoured that the infamous highwayman Dick Turpin stopped here on his famous ride to York. Local CAMRA Pub of the Year. 🏵️🍴♣️P🚪(33A,60,62)😺

High Offley

Anchor Inn ★

Peggs Lane, Old Lea, ST20 0NG (by bridge 42 of Shropshire Union Canal) SJ775256

🍺 12-3, 7-11 ☎ (01785) 284569

Wadworth 6X ⊞

On the Shropshire Union Canal, this Victorian two-bar inn is a rare example of an unspoilt country pub. About two miles from the A519, it is not easily found, but is well worth the journey. It has been run by the same family since 1870, when it was called the Sebastopol. Outside is a lovely award-winning garden. In winter the pub only opens at weekends, and summer lunchtime opening may vary, so it is advisable to check in advance.

Q🏆🏵️🏵️Å♣️✦P😺

Kinver

Cross Inn 🖫

Church Hill, DY7 6HZ

🍺 12-11 (midnight Fri & Sat) ☎ (01384) 878481

Black Country Bradley's Finest Golden, Pig on the Wall, Fireside; 4 changing beers ⊞

Recently refurbished 19th-century pub a few hundred yards from the Staffs & Worcester Canal. It brewed its own beers in the 19th century and still retains a strong community feel. The large L-shaped room has a log-burning fire at one end. A varied range of guest ales and ciders is stocked. Cobs and snacks are served at the bar. The Stourbridge buses stop nearby, but there is no service after 6pm or on Sundays.

🏆♣️✦P🚪(228)😺🛜

Kinver Constitutional Club 🖫

119 High Street, DY7 6HL

🍺 5 (12 Wed & Thu)-11; 12-midnight Fri; 11.30-midnight Sat; 12-10.30 Sun ☎ (01384) 872044

🌐 kinverconstitutionalclub.co.uk

Enville Ale; Hobsons Best, Town Crier; Olde Swan Bumble Hole Bitter; Wye Valley HPA; house beer (by Kinver Brewery); 5 changing beers ⊞

Built in 1902 on the site of an old pub, this converted hotel has three main areas and the bar dispenses up to 18 real ales. The club enjoys an enviable sporting reputation. Card-carrying CAMRA members are welcome but must be signed in, and groups should book ahead. Buses from Stourbridge stop nearby, but there is no service after 6pm or on Sundays. Local CAMRA branch Club of the Year every year since 2007, regional Club of the Year 2013-15, and a former National Club of the Year.

🏵️🕙👍♣️✦P🚪(228)🛜

Knighton

Haberdashers Arms 🖫

ST20 0QH (between Adbaston and Knighton) SJ753275

🍺 12.30 (7 Wed & Thu)-midnight; 12.30-1 Fri & Sat ☎ (01785) 280650 🌐 haberdashersarms.com

Rowton Moonstruck Mild, Bitter; 1 changing beer (sourced locally) ⊞

Built about 1840, this country pub offers a warm and friendly welcome. The four rooms are served from a central bar. The pub hosts a range of events in its large garden including the annual Potato Club Show and music festivals. The collection of oil lamps is not just for decoration; on Lamp Nights electric lights are switched off and the lamps are lit, creating a relaxed atmosphere. Q🏆🏵️🏵️Å♣️😺

Leek

Earl Grey Inn 🍸 🖫

38 Ashbourne Road, ST13 5AT

🍺 3 (5 Mon)-11; 12-11.30 Fri & Sat; 12.30-10.30 Sun ☎ (01538) 372570

Whim Earl Grey Bitter; 4 changing beers (often Blackjack, Great Heck, Marble) ⊞

Small must-visit pub that shot straight to the top, winning local CAMRA Pub of the Year 2015, having reopened in 2014 after a refurbishment following a period of closure. Friendly, knowledgeable and passionate joint licensees sell quality ales not often seen elsewhere locally. Five handpulls serve unusual guests ales, including the house beer by local brewery Whim, plus two real ciders. Uncommon spirits are sold too. Extra seating is available in the rooftop sun terrace. Q🏵️✦🚪😺🛜

Fountain Inn 🖫

14 Fountain Street, ST13 6JR

🍺 12-midnight (1am Fri & Sat); 12-11.30 Sun ☎ (01538) 387205

Greene King IPA; St Austell Tribute; Salopian Oracle; 4 changing beers (often Burton Bridge, Buxton, Sunny Republic) ⊞

The pub is owned by Caldmore Taverns and was refurbished and reopened in 2013. Through the front door there is a spacious bar area which encompasses two real fires either side. To the left of the bar is a small function room and to the right a pool/family room. There is a smoking area and pub garden at the back of the building. The well-stocked bar offers seven traditional ales plus real ciders. 🏆🏵️🍴🕙♣️✦🚪😺🛜

Wilkes Head ⎣

15 St Edward's Street, ST13 5DS
✪ 12 (3 Mon)-midnight; 12-11 Sun ☎ 07976 592787
Whim Arbor Light, Hartington Bitter, Hartington IPA, Flower Power; 2 changing beers (often Broughton, Burton Bridge, Leadmill) ⊞
A Whim tied house, the Wilkes Head is close to the centre of Leek. This ancient pub has featured in the Guide for quite a number of years, and is a traditional drinker's venue, serving beers in excellent condition and a range of real ciders. Well-behaved dogs are admitted but ask the landlord first. Live music is featured regularly and several music festivals occur throughout the summer, utilising the back of the pub as the venue.
Q❀♣●P🐾❀

Lichfield

Beerbohm

19 Tamworth Street, WS13 6JP
✪ 11-11; closed Sun & Mon ☎ (01543) 898252
Salopian Shropshire Gold; house beer (by Whim); 3 changing beers (sourced nationally) ⊞
Elegantly furnished café-bar with a continental feel, looking out onto a busy street. The dark brown decor is enhanced by gilded mirrors and globular chandeliers. The quiet upstairs room offers an unusual view of the three pubs on the opposite side of the street, all cheek by jowl. Four real ales including a house beer, Dandy, brewed by Whim Ales, are complemented by eight upmarket keg beers plus around 50 interesting bottled beers. Customers are permitted to bring their own food. The unisex toilets are situated upstairs.
Q❧≉🚪🐾❀🛜

George & Dragon ✅

28 Beacon Street, WS13 7AJ
✪ 11-midnight (1am Fri & Sat); 12-11.30 Sun
☎ (01543) 254854
Banks's Bitter; Marston's Pedigree; Wychwood Hobgoblin; 4 changing beers ⊞
Friendly traditional local a short distance beyond the historic Erasmus Darwin house. The interior comprises a public bar and cosy lounge, where a small menu of bar snacks is available at all times. Outside in the large beer garden is a plaque marking the spot where an artillery battery was used to bombard the cathedral during the Civil War. Darts, dominoes and board games are played. Guest ales are mostly from the Marston's family.
❀🅰♣P🚪❀🛜

Horse & Jockey ⎣

8-10 Sandford Street, WS13 6QA
✪ 11.30-11 ☎ (01543) 410033
Fuller's London Pride; Holden's Golden Glow; Marston's Pedigree; Timothy Taylor Landlord; Wye Valley HPA; 3 changing beers ⊞
One of the most popular pubs on Lichfield's real ale circuit, this free house complements the regular ales with up to three guests, mainly from small independent breweries. There is a cosy snug and a separate games room at the back of the large open-plan bar. Hot food is served Wednesday to Saturday lunchtimes, and a pork pie/cheeseboard selection is always available. Sport is shown on muted TV screens. Please note there is an over-21 entry policy. ❀🍽≉♣P🚪❀🛜

Whippet Inn ⎣

21 Tamworth Street, WS13 6JP
✪ 12-2.30, 4.30-10; 12-10 Fri & Sat; 12-5 Sun; closed Mon & Tue ☎ 07858 753653
4 changing beers ⊞
Named after a cheeky boozer in a Carry On film, this tiny place holds true to micropub principles – just real ale, real cider, wines and soft drinks. Four interesting ales are offered, often local, and usually collected directly from the breweries by the gaffer, Paul. The two handpulled ciders are always changing. Food is simple snacks like pork pies and Scotch eggs. With seating for around 25 and a maximum capacity of around 40, be prepared to make friends. Q❧≉●🚪❀

Longdon Green

Red Lion ⎣

Hay Lane, WS15 4QF
✪ 10.30-11; 10.30-10.30 Sun ☎ (01543) 490410
Timothy Taylor Boltmaker; 5 changing beers (sourced locally; often Blythe, Brunning & Price, Salopian) ⊞
Having undergone a major restoration, bringing the place up to date but keeping the original fabric, the pub has been refurbished to a high standard. The bar area has comfortable furnishings at one end and traditional seating around the bar itself. It offers the permanent Timothy Taylor Boltmaker and five varying ales, backed up with two ciders. There is a new restaurant with a tremendous food selection and first class views. Plenty of car parking is available, and there is an outside area for drinking. ❧❀🍽&♣●P🚪❀🛜

Marchington

Dog & Partridge

Church Lane, ST14 8LJ (250yds along Church Lane from High St)
✪ 12-3, 6-11 (5-midnight Fri; 6-midnight Sat); 12-11 Sun
☎ (01283) 820394 ⊕ dogandpartridgemarchington.co.uk
Draught Bass; 3 changing beers (sourced locally) ⊞
A gem of a village pub permanently serving Bass and with several handpumps providing a variety of local guest ales. Formerly a restaurant, the pub is split into four main indoor areas with open fires. Food is served lunchtimes and evenings. A pleasant beer garden to the rear is popular in the summer months. It is renowned locally for its weekly live music sessions and the hosting of regular beer festivals. Parking is available to the side of the building. Children are welcome.
Q❧❀🍽 🅰P🚪(402)🛜

Milwich

Green Man 🏆

Sandon Lane, ST18 0EG (on B5027 in centre of village)
✪ 12-2.30 (not Mon-Wed), 5-11; 12-11 Fri & Sat; 12-10.30 Sun ☎ (01889) 505310
Draught Bass; 5 changing beers ⊞
An independent pub at the heart of a vibrant village community, and a more-or-less permanent fixture in the Guide. It celebrated its 200th anniversary in 2015 and the licensee's 25 years in situ. To top it off it was also CAMRA branch Pub of the Year. The Green Man is a two-roomed venue, one of which is set aside for diners. There is a large, verdant garden area where the annual free music festival is not to be missed. A true and lively village pub. ❧❀🍽♣P❀🛜

Newcastle-under-Lyme

Bridge Street Ale House Ⓛ ✪
31 Bridge Street, ST5 2RY
☼ 1 (12 Fri & Sat)-10; 12-4 Sun ☎ 07801 277818
⊕ bridgestreetalehouse.co.uk
Changing beers (often Ramsgate, Raw, Weal Ales) Ⓗ
The first micropub to set up in the local CAMRA branch area opened in 2014. Converted from an antiques shop, the bar is located on the right of the entrance and the cellar is in the window. The front area has high wooden benches, while the back room has more traditional chairs and tables. A success from day one, the pub is now the local Cider Pub of the Year and gained second place in Pub of the Year. Q❤️🚲☼

Castle Mona Ⓛ
4 Victoria Street, ST5 1NT
☼ 4 (12 Sat)-midnight; 12-11.30 Sun ☎ (01782) 257764
⊕ castlemona.co.uk
Joule's Slumbering Monk; Wells Bombardier; 6 changing beers (often Greene King, RAN Ales, Springhead) Ⓗ
Five minutes' walk from Newcastle bus station, the Castle Mona has served the local community since 1787. It is a traditional pub and has a lounge with a woodburner for cold evenings. There is a bar area and a separate room with a pool table and dartboard. Outside is a large beer garden for those hot summer months. The pub serves up to 12 real ciders and hosts an excellent beer festival in November. ❀♣❤️🚲(25,22,10)🌐

Freebird
96 Liverpool Road, ST5 2AX
☼ 5-midnight (1am Fri); 2-1am Sat; 2-11.30
Sun ☎ 07714 782599
12 changing beers (often Falstaff, Ilkley, Salopian) Ⓗ
A biker-friendly pub with a welcoming atmosphere, sporting up to 12 rotating ales of excellent quality from across the whole of the UK, as well as real ciders. The main bar has a pool table and supports local rock DJs on Saturday nights, while the gig room regularly plays host to live bands. Five minutes' walk from the town centre, this is well worth a visit. Occasional barbecues and bike rallies held during the summer add to the fun. 👪♣❤️🅿️🚲(4,4A)☼

Hopinn ▼
102 Albert Street, ST5 1JR
☼ 4-11.30; 12-midnight Sat; 12-11 Sun ☎ (01782) 711121
Black Sheep Best Bitter; Draught Bass; 10 changing beers (often Mallinson's, Northern Monk, Oakham) Ⓗ
Comfortable and friendly family-owned pub on the edge of the town centre, comprising a front bar, lounge and snug with well-preserved original Art Deco features such as wood panelling and a rare stained-glass skylight. Ten guest beers are available, six served by handpull and four from KeyKeg; three real ciders are also available. Local CAMRA Pub of the Year 2015 and a shining star of the local real ale scene. ♣❤️🚲

Lymestone Vaults Ⓛ
Pepper Street, ST5 1PR (in town centre)
☼ 10-11 (midnight Fri & Sat); 11-10.30 Sun
☎ (01782) 615801
Lymestone Stone Cutter, Stone Faced, Foundation Stone, Ein Stein, Stone the Crows; 4 changing beers (often Derventio, Lymestone, Springhead) Ⓗ

This well-run multiple award-winning pub is the first of the Lymestone Brewery taphouses, showcasing its championship beers. Located off the High Street, it provides a relaxed environment in which to sample a wide variety of beverages sourced locally, nationally and internationally. It has traditional yet modern surroundings with a log-burning stove, comfortable seating and pub games, and serves hearty food at lunchtimes. Knowledgeable staff offer a warm welcome to every man and his dog. 🐕🍽️👪❤️🚲☼🌐

Newtown

Ivy House ✪
62 Stafford Road, WS6 6AZ (on A34)
☼ 12-11 ☎ (01922) 476607 ⊕ ivyhousepub.co.uk
Banks's Mild, Bitter; Marston's Pedigree; 2 changing beers Ⓗ
Four times local CAMRA branch Pub of the Year, the Ivy House was first listed as an ale house in 1824. This is a traditional pub with a country feel, backing onto farmland. It comprises four rooms on two levels plus a purpose-built restaurant where quality meals are served. Traditional pub games are played and there is a popular Wednesday quiz night. A visit is highly recommended and a warm welcome assured. Q❀🍽️👪❤️🚲🌐

Norton Bridge

Railway Inn
Station Road, ST15 0NT
☼ 4-11.30; 12-midnight Sat; 12-11 Sun ☎ (01785) 761395
Thwaites Original, Lancaster Bomber; 3 changing beers (sourced nationally) Ⓗ
The pub is at the heart of the village community, hosting events of various types. There is a wide selection of games including darts, crib and dominoes, also a quiz night on Sundays. The North Staffordshire BSA Owners Club meet here once a month, and the pub has a band which practises on Wednesdays. There is a bar and separate rear lounge, both catered for by a small central servery. The building has a number of original features. 🐕❀🅰️♣🅿️🚲(13)☼🌐

Oulton

Brushmakers Arms
8 Kibblestone Road, ST15 8UW (500yds W of A520, 1 mile NE of Stone)
☼ 12-midnight (1am Fri & Sat) ☎ (01785) 812062
Thwaites Original, Lancaster Bomber; 1 changing beer (sourced nationally) Ⓗ
The Brush has won many CAMRA awards over the years for consistently excellent beer. A rare example of a wet-led rural pub, the Brush has no car park (rough parking opposite) but is exceptionally well supported by the local community. It is a two-roomed establishment – as you enter, a small immaculate lounge is to the left and a larger bar to the right. Licensee Mark celebrated 25 years at the helm in 2015 and was duly honoured by the local CAMRA branch. Q❀🅰️♣🅿️🚲(4)☼🌐

Rugeley

Yorkshireman
Colton Road, WS15 3HB (at jct of Colton Rd, B5013, with Blithbury Rd)

🕗 12-2.30, 5.30-11; 12-11 Sat; 12-6 Sun ☎ (01889) 583977
🌐 wine-dine.co.uk
Blythe Bagot's Bitter; Palmers Poison; house beer (by Blythe) Ⓗ
Close to Rugeley Trent Valley railway station, just north of the River Trent, this classic pub reopened as a free house in 2007 after a short period of closure, and has flourished ever since. While much of the pub is set aside for dining, it is known as much for fine ale as fine cuisine, with drinkers welcome in the elegant Oak Room bar. The well-regarded local Blythe Brewery ales have featured for some years. Occasional themed food nights are held. 🕿🕸🕔🅰🚬🅿🐾🛜

Stafford

Greyhound Ⓛ
12 County Road, ST16 2PU (off A34, opp jail)
🕗 4-11.30 (midnight Fri); 3-midnight Sat; 12-11 Sun
☎ (01785) 222432 🌐 greyhoundfreehousestafford.co.uk
Bradfield Farmers Blonde; Wells Bombardier; 6 changing beers (sourced nationally; often Abbeydale, Holden's, Salopian) Ⓗ
A short walk from the centre of Stafford, this two-room free house is well worth a visit. The Greyhound dates from 1831 and a newspaper article from the day it opened can be seen above the bar. Today it offers a range of eight ales, often from breweries in Yorkshire, as well as a selection of bottled ciders. The pub has won a number of CAMRA awards. Q🕿🕸🏵🖤🚌🐾

Market Vaults Ⓛ
4 St Martin's Place, ST16 2LA
🕗 12 (3 Mon)-midnight; 12-1am Sat; 3-midnight Sun
☎ (01785) 256126 🌐 themarketvaults.com
Banks's Sunbeam; Slater's Top Totty; Wychwood Hobgoblin; 3 changing beers (often Marston's, Slater's) Ⓗ
A welcoming pub in the corner of Stafford's Market Square, with a series of rooms and distinct areas rambling around a central bar. It offers a selection of excellent beers alongside a range of gourmet burgers. Music nights include folk and various showcase events; there are also comedy nights, usually on the first Monday of the month. See the pub's Facebook page for the menu, details of the beers available and events. 🖤🚬🚌🐾🛜

Olde Rose & Crown Ⓛ
10 Market Street, ST16 2JZ
🕗 12-11 (12.30am Fri & Sat); 12-10.30 Sun
☎ (01785) 251343
Joule's Blonde, Pale Ale, Slumbering Monk; 1 changing beer (sourced locally; often Joule's) Ⓗ
Comfortable Joule's house right in the heart of Stafford and much larger than it looks from the outside. Four handpumps dispense Joule's ales alongside a cider. Lunches are served Monday to Saturday, and bar snacks using locally sourced ingredients are available all day. Situated next to the Gatehouse Theatre, the pub is a favourite of theatregoers and is frequented by cast members enjoying an after-show pint. An acoustic night is held every Wednesday. Q🕸🕔🖤🚬🐾🛜

Picture House ✅
14 Bridge Street, ST16 2HL
🕗 8am-midnight (1am Fri & Sat) ☎ (01785) 222941
Greene King Abbot; Ruddles Best Bitter; house beer (by Slater's); 4 changing beers (sourced nationally; often Burton Bridge, Slater's, Wood) Ⓗ

A Wetherspoon conversion of a small 1914 provincial cinema, it retains a lot of original and ornate features, including the entrance foyer and projection room. Posters from the golden age of film adorn the walls. On Wednesday nights at 9pm films are shown; it is a cinemagoer's delight. A wide selection of real ales is served to a mixed clientele and it is often busy in the evenings. There is an outdoor drinking area overlooking the River Sow. 🕿🕸🕔🖤🚬🐾🛜

Spittal Brook Ⓛ ✅
106 Lichfield Road, ST17 4LP (1 mile SE of centre off A34 at Queensville Bridge)
🕗 12-3, 5-11; 12-11 Fri & Sat; 12-10.30 Sun
☎ (01785) 245268
Draught Bass; Ludlow Gold; Sharp's Doom Bar; 2 changing beers (sourced locally; often Joule's, Lymestone, Salopian) Ⓗ
A thriving, traditional two-roomed alehouse within walking distance of the town centre. Entertainment includes a folk night on Tuesday, a quiz on Wednesday and a cheese night on the last Sunday of the month - bring your own cheeses to share with others. The pub holds beer and cider festivals in July and October, and a guest real cider is always available. Food is locally sourced wherever possible. Q🕿🕸🍽🕔🖤🚬🅿🚬🐾🛜

Sun Ⓛ
7 Lichfield Road, ST17 4JX
🕗 12-11 (midnight Fri & Sat) ☎ (01785) 248361
🌐 thesunstafford.co.uk
Everards Tiger; Titanic Steerage, Anchor Bitter, Iceberg, White Star, Captain Smith's Strong Ale; 5 changing beers (sourced nationally; often Castle Rock, Wadworth, White Horse) Ⓗ
Titanic Brewery acquired this closed pub in 2010 and reopened it following refurbishment. Twelve handpumps dispense a choice of Titanic ales and changing guest beers. At least one cider is available, usually from Westons. Food is served throughout the day, using locally sourced ingredients. The Sunday menu includes traditional roast, Monday is steak night and Tuesday curry night. Beer festivals are held in spring and late summer in a large marquee at the rear of the pub. Q🕿🕸🕔🚬🖤🚬🅿🚬🐾🛜

Stoke-on-Trent: Burslem

Bull's Head Ⓛ
14 St John's Square, ST6 3AJ
🕗 3-11 (11.30 Wed & Thu); 12-midnight Fri & Sat; 12-11 Sun
☎ (01782) 834153
Titanic Steerage, Iceberg, White Star, Plum Porter; 6 changing beers (often Ashover, Dancing Duck, Holden's) Ⓗ
Titanic's brewery tap in the centre of Burslem, 10 minutes' walk from Port Vale's ground, open at 11am on Vale home Saturdays, and welcoming to all supporters, home and away. A two-roomed pub, it has an island bar with up to 10 real ales on tap and seven or more real ciders and perries served straight from the cellar, alongside draught and bottled Belgian beers. Bar billiards, table skittles and an old jukebox are in the public bar. A multi award-winning cider pub. Q🕿🕸🖤🚬🖤🚌(3,98,92)🐾🛜

Bursley Ale House
Wedgwood Place, ST6 4ED
🕗 1-11; 12.30-10.30 Sat & Sun ☎ (01782) 911393

5 changing beers (often Abbeydale, Blue Monkey, Charnwood) Ⓗ
The Bursley Ale House is a smallish pub with the look and feel of a microbar; there are five handpumps dispensing a wide variety of guest beers from all over the country. Two real ciders are also served by handpull. A function room is available upstairs and the pub is on several major bus routes. A firm bet for a relaxing evening's drinking; the pub also hosts themed food nights, has a sheltered patio area and several log fires.
❀≉♣🍴🚌🖫(3,98)

Duke William Ⓛ

2 St Johns Square, ST6 3AJ
🕓 11.30-11 (midnight Fri & Sat); 12-10.30 Sun
☎ (01782) 814809 ⊕ dukewilliamburslem.com
Draught Bass; Joule's Slumbering Monk; Oakham Citra; Sarah Hughes Dark Ruby Mild; 3 changing beers (often Abbeydale, Acorn, Salopian) Ⓗ
Rebuilt circa 1929 this pub has a regionally important historic interior and was Grade II-listed in 2015. The ground floor comprises a large lounge covering two main rooms and a large public bar. The first floor has been converted into a 48-seater restaurant and a room on the second floor is ideal for meetings. On the bar, there are seven real ales, with three varying ones. Inter-war period features can be seen throughout the pub – it is an ideal place for a pint. ⓆⒹ♿🍴🖫

Post Office Vaults

3 Market Place, ST6 3AA
🕓 11-11 (1am Fri & Sat); 12-11 Sun ☎ (01782) 811027
Greene King Abbot; Oakham Bishops Farewell; Wye Valley Butty Bach; 3 changing beers Ⓗ
The Post Office Vaults is on the main road and on a good bus route. There are eye-catching hanging baskets and the windows have classical engraving. Once you step through the main door - the pub is tiny and has a single bar - you are made to feel at home. The staff are welcoming and attentive, but it can get very busy at the bar at times. The toilets may be cramped but they retain a period feel.
♿🍴🖫(3,29,98)❀

Stoke-on-Trent: Etruria

Holy Inadequate Ⓛ

67 Etruria Old Road, ST1 5PE
🕓 4-11 (midnight Thu); 12-midnight Fri-Sun ☎ 07771 358238
Joule's Pale Ale; 7 changing beers (often Beartown, Burton Bridge, Hawkshead) Ⓗ
A multi CAMRA award-winner, the Holy is firmly established as one of the best pubs in the county, and no surprise, as the commitment to the condition and quality of all its ales is now legendary. Joule's Pale is supported by seven rotating guests (two from KeyKegs), three real ciders, and an extensive range of bottled beers. Popular beer festivals are held every bank holiday providing up to 26 extra ales served from the stillage room. Q❀♣P🖫(4,4A,17)❀🛜

Stoke-on-Trent: Hanley

Coachmakers Arms ★ Ⓛ

65 Lichfield Street, ST1 3EA (off A5008 Potteries Way ring road)
🕓 4-11 (midnight Fri); 12-11 Sat & Sun ☎ (01782) 860438

Draught Bass; Hancocks HB; 4 changing beers (often Lymestone, Titanic, Weal Ales) Ⓗ
The Coach is a regular and well-deserved entry in this Guide; despite the constant shadow of demolition, this gem of the Potteries continues to trade and thrive. A Victorian corridor pub with a nationally important historic interior, this is a must-visit pub when visiting the city centre. In winter a roaring fire welcomes, while in summer there is nothing finer than to sit outside on a bench with a pint and to people-watch in the sunshine. A true classic. Q🛏♣P🖫❀

Victoria Lounge Bar Ⓛ

5 Adventure Place, ST1 3AF (next to Hanley bus station)
🕓 11-11 ☎ (01782) 273530 ⊕ thereardon.com
Draught Bass; 5 changing beers (often Blue Monkey, Brains, Cottage) Ⓗ
A regular in the Guide, this is a popular city-centre watering hole, often referred to as Reardon's because of the well-used snooker hall attached. The Lounge Bar offers a smart, modern, comfortable interior with food, and a choice of six handpumps serving a mixture of local, regional and national breweries. Locals help to suggest the rotating beers. There is a smart, private function room on the first floor with access to the beer.
🛏Ⓓ♿P🖫

Stoke-on-Trent: Hartshill

Greyhound Ⓛ

67 George Street, ST5 1JT
🕓 12-11 (11.30 Wed & Thu; midnight Fri); 11-midnight Sat; 11-11 Sun ☎ (01782) 635814
Everards Tiger; Titanic Steerage, Iceberg, White Star, Plum Porter; 4 changing beers Ⓗ
A warm welcome awaits at this dog-friendly pub on the outskirts of Newcastle. The second pub in the Titanic fleet, the Greyhound boasts nine handpumps showcasing Titanic ales as well as a fantastic and varying range of ales from across the UK. A great selection of bottled beers as well as country wines and real cider make this a pub for everyone. Tasty bar snacks are available. Occasional live music from local groups and a regular pub quiz on Sunday nights take place. Q♣🍴🖫❀🛜

Stoke-on-Trent: Longton

Congress Inn Ⓛ

14 Sutherland Road, ST3 1HJ (¼ mile from Longton bus and rail stations; opp police station)
🕓 12-11 (midnight Fri-Sun) ☎ (01782) 763667
⊕ congressinnlongton.co.uk
Brains Rev James; Castle Rock Sheriff's Tipple; Townhouse Styrian Pale, Gladstone Strong Ale; 5 changing beers (often Acorn, Wadworth, Welbeck Abbey) Ⓗ
A multi award-winning pub and a proper Potteries local. Beer lovers come from all around the area and beyond. A beer festival is held every May, concentrating on a different area of the country each year. Traditional pub games including skittles are played, and local charities are supported. Regular entertainment takes place on Saturday nights. The beer range covers all styles, from stouts and porters to hoppy brews, and there is a large selection of Belgian beers at very good prices.
≉♣🍴🖫(1,2,6)

Stoke-on-Trent: Penkhull

Marquis of Granby
51 St Thomas Place, ST4 7LA
✪ 4 (3 Fri)-midnight; 12-midnight Sat & Sun
☎ (01782) 847025
Marston's Pedigree; Wychwood Hobgoblin; 3 changing beers Ⓗ
A new and welcome addition to the Guide, the Marquis is a large, two-roomed pub in Penkhull Village. A Marston's establishment, Pedigree is always available and kept in superb condition. Boondoggle is also popular among the rotating guest beers, while two ciders are always on handpump. Beers outside the Marston's range are served when allowed. The recently refurbished lounge provides comfortable surroundings for the popular home-cooked meals available throughout opening hours. ⤷❀◑♣♠Pᴽ(41)⛊

Stoke-on-Trent: Stoke

Glebe Ⓛ
35 Glebe Street, ST4 1HG
✪ 12-midnight (11 Mon & Wed); 12-10.30 Sun
☎ (01782) 860670
Joule's Blonde, Pale Ale, Slumbering Monk; 1 changing beer (often Joule's) Ⓗ
A short walk from Stoke rail station, this superb Joule's establishment has justifiably become one of the must-visit pubs in the city. Magnificent features including beautifully restored stained-glass windows, along with candlelit tables, all add to the welcoming atmosphere. The three mainstay Joule's ales are supplemented by one seasonal beer and one handpulled cider. Home-made meals served lunchtime and early evening are of a high standard, with the addition of an extensive cheeseboard. ❀◑▸≉♠♠⛊

Wheatsheaf Ⓛ ✔
84-92 Church Street, ST4 1BU
✪ 8am-midnight (1am Fri & Sat) ☎ (01782) 747462
Greene King Abbot; Ruddles Best Bitter; Sharp's Doom Bar; 9 changing beers (often Lymestone, Summerskills, Titanic) Ⓗ
Unlike a lot of the Wetherspoon chain establishments, the Wheatsheaf has always been a pub, originally an 18th-century coaching house. Proud of its community links, it is often customer-led in its choice of beers via a suggestion box located in the CAMRA Corner. Around nine guest ales are usually available, often from local breweries. It has deservedly been awarded Wetherspoon Regional Real Ale Pub of the Year for the past three years. Popular on match days due to its proximity to the shuttle bus link to the Britannia Stadium. Q⤷◑&≉♣♠ᴽ⛊

Stone

Borehole Ⓛ
Unit 2, Mount Road Industrial Estate, ST15 8LL
✪ 12-10 (11 Fri & Sat) ☎ (01785) 817796
Lymestone Stone Cutter, Stone Faced, Foundation Stone, Ein Stein, Stone the Crows; 3 changing beers Ⓗ
Small and friendly, the Borehole is a pub (not a micro) and has proved a hit with beer and cider fans since its opening in 2015. There are eight handpumps and a nice variety of home-baked cakes, pickled egg of the month, and other snacks, available. A good selection of single malts and Belgian beers add to the craic. Children are

welcome until 8pm and dogs are well provided for. A small meeting room caters for local groups. Q⤷❀⊛≉♣♠Pᴽ(10)⛊

Royal Exchange Ⓛ
Radford Street, ST15 8DA (on corner of Northesk St and Radford St)
✪ 12-11 (midnight Fri & Sat) ☎ (01785) 812685
Everards Tiger; Titanic Steerage, Iceberg, White Star, Plum Porter, Captain Smith's Strong Ale; 6 changing beers Ⓗ
Refurbished sympathetically to a high standard in 2015, the Royal now boasts 12 handpumps. There are three distinct drinking areas with a centrally placed long bar. Alongside the permanent range of beers there are always at least three varying guests, although there can be up to six, which are from anywhere, and the landlady will sometimes offer to add a twist where appropriate. With a large fire at one end of the pub and a logburner at the other, you are assured of a warm and friendly welcome. Q⤷❀◑&≉♣♠⊟ᴽ⛊⛉

Swan Inn Ⓛ
18 Stafford Street, ST15 8QW (on A520 near Trent & Mersey Canal)
✪ 12-1am (11 Mon; midnight Tue & Wed); 12-11 Sun
☎ (01785) 815570 ⊕ swaninnstoke.co.uk
House beer (by Coach House); 8 changing beers (sourced nationally; often Abbeydale, Blythe) Ⓗ
Voted CAMRA branch Town Pub of the Year for 2015, the Swan serves as a permanent mini beer festival in its own right. Beers in the evening are often different from those at lunchtime. The annual themed beer festival attracts beer lovers from far and wide. It is a quiet pub except for music evenings on Fridays and Saturdays, often heavy rock and sometimes nationally known acts. The Swan is strictly adults-only at all times. ❀♣♠(10,12,S1)⛊⛉

Summerhill

Boat
Walsall Road, WS14 0BU
✪ 12-3, 6-11; 12-11 Sun ☎ (01543) 361692
⊕ oddfellowsintheboat.com
3 changing beers (often Cottage) Ⓗ
While largely a dining venue, this free house does have a small bar for drinkers. Diners can peruse the extensive chalkboard menu in the reception area while watching the cooking. A Cottage beer is generally featured, plus two varied ales which are usually interesting and frequently local. There is a large enclosed garden adjacent to the car park. If approaching by car from the north, a U-turn is required after passing the pub on the right. Q❀◑&Pᴽ⛊⛉

Sutton

Red Lion
Newport Road, TF10 8DQ (on A519 near to Newport)
✪ 12-3 (not Mon), 6-11; 12-11 Sun ☎ (01952) 811048
Banks's Bitter; 2 changing beers (sourced nationally; often Castle Rock, Shepherd Neame, Wadworth) Ⓗ
Although the buildings date back to the 17th century, nowadays the Lion is a beautifully kept, old-fashioned pub. The bar has a stone-flagged floor, there is a carpeted lounge area and a small, separate dining room. Food is served 12-3pm and 6-9pm Tuesday to Saturday and 12-3pm Sunday.

The menus are changed every few days and use locally sourced produce wherever possible, with separate children's and vegetarian menus. The licensees celebrated 12 years at the pub in 2016. Q☺☆◑P🖵(350)☻

Tamworth

King's Ditch Ⓛ
51 Lower Gungate, B79 7AS
✿5-9 Tue & Wed; 5-10.30 Thu; 4-10.30 Fri; 12-10.30 Sat & Sun; closed Mon ☎ 07989 805828 ⊕ kingsditch.co.uk
4 changing beers Ⓖ
Specialising mostly in local ales, this is Tamworth's first micropub. Formerly a cycle shop, the interior consists of a single ground-floor room plus a small drinking area upstairs, allowing for around 40 people. Bare brick and wood characterises the simple, modern style of the decor. Three or four gravity-served ales are complemented by a wide range of real ciders. There are occasional mini festivals showcasing a particular brewery. Children are welcome until 7pm. Q☺≈●🛏🖵☻🛜

Market Vaults ♟ ✿
7 Market Street, B79 7LU
✿12-11 ☎ (01827) 66552
Joule's Pale Ale; 7 changing beers Ⓗ
Eight handpulls greet drinkers in this traditional and historic town-centre pub, close to the attractive town hall and Norman castle. One of the changing guest ales is offered at a low beer-of-the-week price, and a wide range of real ciders is available from a chilled cabinet. In winter the pub is cheered by solid fuel stoves, while a picturesque garden provides sanctuary for drinkers on fine days. Hot food is served daily. ☆◑≈●🖵☻🛜

Sir Robert Peel Ⓛ
13-15 Lower Gungate, B79 7BA
✿2 (4 Tue)-11; 12-11 Sat & Sun ☎ (01827) 300910
5 changing beers (often Oakham) Ⓗ
Well-established and popular free house, named after the town's historic 19th-century statesman. Linked with a German pub in Tamworth's twin town of Bad Laasphe, it attracts regular exchange visits. Attentive staff dispense up to five changing ales including a Church End house beer, Apeeling, plus two real ciders and a large selection of foreign bottled beers. It has a small beer terrace to the front, with plans for outdoor drinking to the rear. The up-to-date jukebox ensures a lively atmosphere at the weekend. ≈●🖵☻🛜

Trysull

Bell Inn Ⓛ
Bell Road, WV5 7JB SO852940
✿11.30-3, 5-11 (midnight Fri); 11.30-midnight Sat; 12-11 Sun ☎ (01902) 892871
Bathams Best Bitter; Holden's Black Country Bitter, Golden Glow, Special; 1 changing beer Ⓗ
A fine 18th-century building next to the village church, it comprises a small but cosy bar, pleasant lounge and a large restaurant/dining room. As well as the Holden's range of ales, there is a guest beer which is often from a microbrewery. An extensive food menu is available in the lounge or restaurant. There is a patio area at the front of the pub. Popular with walkers, the Staffordshire and Worcestershire Canal is a 15-minute walk away. Q☺☆◑&P☻

Tutbury

Cask & Pottle
2 High Street, DE13 9LP (close to mini roundabout at centre of village)
✿6-9 Mon; 12-2, 5-9 (10 Fri); 1-10 Sat; 1-4 Sun ☎ 07595 423614
4 changing beers (sourced locally; often Burton Bridge, Dancing Duck, Nene Valley) Ⓖ
East Staffordshire's first micropub, opened in 2013 in a former sweet shop. The small, bright, single room on the ground floor of a Victorian terrace features pine benches with cushions and tables, but no bar counter. One wall is decorated with an aphorism, a mural, and a table of ale measures (a pottle is an archaic name for a half-gallon measure). A window at the rear offers a view of the beer stillage. Two ciders and a perry from varying sources are usually stocked. Q☺&●🖵☻

Uttoxeter

Old Swan Ⓛ ✿
Market Place, ST14 8HN
✿8am-midnight (1am Fri & Sat) ☎ (01889) 598650
Greene King Abbot; Ruddles Best Bitter; Sharp's Doom Bar; 4 changing beers (sourced locally; often Backyard, Hawkshead, Lymestone) Ⓗ
Centrally located close to the town's marketplace, this Wetherspoon pub attracts a mixed clientele throughout the day. Up to six handpumps are in use at any one time, with a varied choice of changing local and national ales. A large open-plan seating area downstairs is supplemented with a quieter upper level to the rear. A small rear outdoor patio and separate smoking area are also provided. Food is served all day. The pub is busy on race days. Q☺☆◑&Å≈●🖵(841,402,32)🛜

Wall

Trooper
Watling Street, WS14 0AN
✿12-11 (11.30 Fri & Sat) ☎ (01543) 480413
⊕ thetrooperwall.co.uk
Holden's Golden Glow; 4 changing beers Ⓗ
Tidy countryside pub, food-focused but welcoming to drinkers. The interior decor is contemporary-rustic – a monochrome colour scheme offset by wood, bare brick and a log-burning stove. An elegant dining room looks out to green views and the multi-level beer terrace, where house martins nest under the eaves. There is a large elevated beer garden to the rear. Two guest beers from nearby Backyard Brewery are usually featured, plus two national guest ales. Wall Roman site is nearby. ☺☆◑&P

Weston

Woolpack Inn Ⓛ ✿
The Green, ST18 0JH (off A518)
✿11-11 (midnight Fri & Sat) ☎ (01889) 270238
⊕ woolpackpubweston.co.uk
Banks's Bitter; Marston's Pedigree; Ringwood Boondoggle; 3 changing beers (sourced nationally; often Banks's, Marston's, Ringwood) Ⓗ
A beautiful village pub set on a tranquil village green in the centre of Weston. It has plenty of character, with low ceiling, oak beams and cosy fireplaces. Four bays inside reflect the pub's origins as a row of cottages and a blacksmith's shop.

Outside, there is a big, attractive beer garden. A refurbishment in 2014 has enhanced the welcoming atmosphere. The property is recorded as being owned by the Bagot family in the 1730s. Q❄☺◑Å♣P🛏☺🛈🕏

Wetton

Royal Oak
DE6 2AF
🕓 12-3, 6-11; 12-11 Sat & Sun; closed Mon & Tue
☎ (01335) 310287 ⊕ royaloakwetton.co.uk
3 changing beers (often Storm, Thornbridge, Wincle) Ⓗ

An attractive building at the heart of a small isolated village in great walking country. Usually there are three real ales available, from local breweries such as Storm, Wincle or Thornbridge. Good and popular food is sold, and there are many theme nights and events throughout the year, including whisky tastings, car and bike rallies, and theatre groups. ❄☺◑Å♣P☺

Whiston

Swan Inn Ⓛ
ST19 5QH (in Penkridge turn W off A449 at roundabout near Texaco garage onto Bungham Lane, cross Cuttlestone Bridge and follow signs to Whiston) SJ895144
🕓 12-3 (not Mon), 5-11; 12-11 Sat; 12-10.30 Sun
☎ (01785) 716200 ⊕ swanwhiston.co.uk

Holden's Black Country Bitter; 4 changing beers (sourced nationally; often Castle Rock, Enville, Wye Valley) Ⓗ

Although remotely situated, this a thriving pub with high-quality, well-kept ales and superb food. Built in 1593, burnt down and rebuilt in 1711, the oldest part today is the small bar housing an inglenook fireplace. The lounge features an intriguing double-sided log fire. Six acres of grounds include a children's obstacle course, aviary and rabbits. A wide range of beers, ciders and perries is usually stocked. Open all day on bank holidays (except Christmas Day). Q❄☺◑&♣●P🛏(878,76)☺🕏

Whittington

Bell Inn ✔
27 Main Street, WS14 9JR
🕓 11-11 (midnight Fri & Sat); 12-10.30 Sun
☎ (01543) 432377 ⊕ bellwhittington.co.uk
Draught Bass; Greene King Abbot; Marston's Pedigree; 1 changing beer Ⓗ

Cosy local at the centre of the village, within walking distance of the canal. Dating from 1834 or possibly earlier, the pub features a wealth of wooden beams, plus two lovely open fires in winter. There is a small bar at the front of the building, a larger bar to the rear, and a large dining room to the side. Sunday carveries are featured. The small beer terrace at the front offers outdoor drinking. ☺◑♣●P🛏(785,786)☺🕏

Coopers Tavern, Burton upon Trent (Photo: Adrian Tierney-Jones)

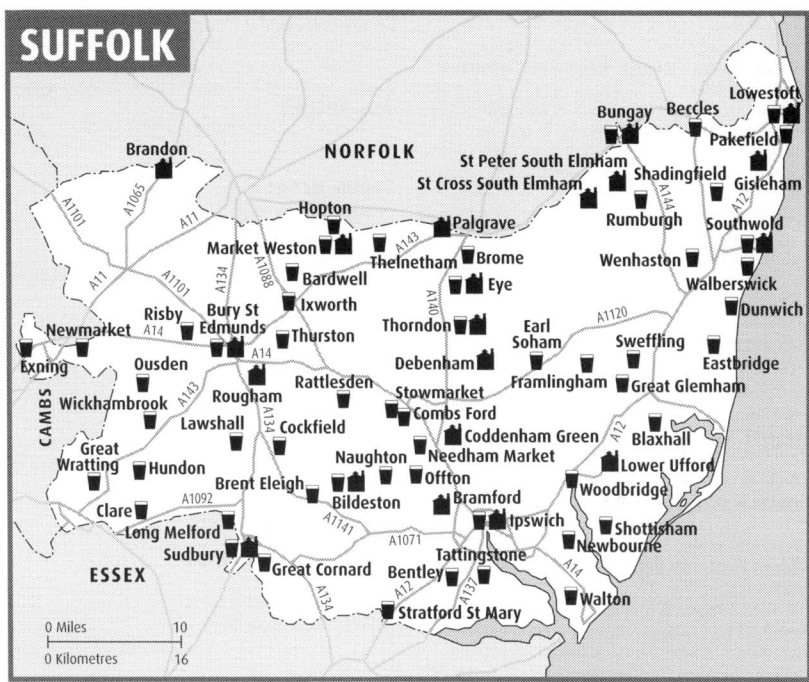

Bardwell

Dun Cow ✓

Up Street, IP31 1AA (approx 1 mile off A143 at Stanton)
☼ 11.30-2.30, 5-midnight; 12-midnight Sat; 12-10.30 Sun
☎ (01359) 250806
Greene King IPA; 3 changing beers ⊞
A traditional pub in a pleasant village set in the Suffolk countryside. The pub has two bars and offers speciality food nights. Six real ales are available at weekends. Outside is a covered smoking area and large family space in the garden. Party bookings and coaches are welcome if booked in advance. The picturesque restored village windmill is worth a visit and has occasional threshing open days. ᏜᏜ֎◑♣P🖵❀

Beccles

Caxton Club ⅃

Gaol Lane, NR34 9SJ
☼ 12-1.30 (not Tue), 7-11; 12-2, 6.30-11 Fri; 12-11 Sat;
12-10.30 Sun ☎ (01502) 712829
4 changing beers (sourced locally; often Green Jack, Woodforde's) ⊞
This large comfortable club welcomes CAMRA members (a small charge is made to cover entertainment on Saturday evenings) and serves four real ales plus a real cider. One side of the central bar and seating area has a function room while the other has a pool table leading to a room with TV and dartboard and a separate snooker room. The garden has a children's play area and bowling green. Guide dogs only are allowed. ᏜᏜ֎&≠♣🍴🖵❖

Bentley

Case is Altered ✓

Capel Road, IP9 2DW

☼ 12-3, 6-11.30; 12-4, 7-10.30 Sun; closed Mon & Tue
☎ (01473) 805575 ⊕ thecasepubbentley.co.uk
Adnams Southwold Bitter; 3 changing beers (sourced locally; often Adnams) ⊞
In January 2014 the Bentley Community Pub Ltd was delighted to announce that it had purchased the freehold from Punch Taverns and this pub reopened at Easter. Since then, with a snug, public bar and garden room, this village local has re-established itself on the local scene. Various music evenings and themed food nights are hosted and traditional pub games are available. A quiz is held every month. Local artists' work is on display. There is plenty of seating in the pretty beer garden.
ᏜᏜ֎◑&♣P🖵❖❀

Bildeston

King's Head ⅃

132 High Street, IP7 7ED
☼ 6-midnight Wed; 6-11 Thu; 4-midnight Fri; 12-midnight Sat; 12-10.30 Sun; closed Mon & Tue ☎ (01449) 741434
⊕ bildestonkingshead.co.uk
Kings Head Bildeston Best, Brettvale Gold; 4 changing beers (sourced locally) ⊞
Home of the King's Head Brewery since 1996, the building's carved timbers indicate its history as part of a larger complex dating from around 1530. Now a single bar with a large inglenook fireplace, a friendly ale house atmosphere has evolved, with food available at the weekends only. There is a fully enclosed rear garden with a covered patio area, lawns and play equipment for children. The late May bank holiday beer festival is long established and popular. ᏜᏜ֎◑&♣🍴🖵❖❀

Blaxhall

Ship ⅃

School Road, IP12 2DY

✪ 12 (11 Mon)-11.30 ☎ (01728) 688316
⊕ blaxhallshipinn.co.uk
Adnams Southwold Bitter; Woodforde's Wherry; 2 changing beers ⊞
A cosy two-roomed 16th-century pub with a reputation for traditional singing in the bar. The menu offers a wide choice of home-made dishes and daily specials using locally sourced ingredients (book for breakfast from 10.30am during the summer months). Live entertainment includes folk music, bands and story-telling every week, and the pub hosts a Folk East stage during the festival weekend. Letting chalets are available beside the pub and camping at the nearby village hall is by arrangement. According to local legend, the pub was supposed to be called the Sheep, but a travelling sign-writer misunderstood the landlord's accent. ➜✿☞◑❍♿♠♣P⊟❀🐾🖥🛜

Brent Eleigh

Cock ★
Lavenham Road, CO10 9PB
✪ 12-4, 6-11; 12-11 Fri & Sat; 12-10.30 Sun
☎ (01787) 247371
Adnams Southwold Bitter; 3 changing beers (sourced locally) ⊞
The Cock remains a real gem and has been identified by CAMRA as having a nationally important historic interior. It has two bars, the smaller one ideal for families. Landlady Deborah provides good food throughout opening times, including popular Sunday lunches, which keeps visiting walkers and cyclists more than happy. Real cider comes from local suppliers. Seating outside is ideal for watching the world go by. The pub has cats but well-behaved dogs are always welcome. Bed & Breakfast accommodation is in a unit at the rear of the pub. Q✿☞◑❍♣♠P⊟(111)🐾🛜

Brome

Swan
Norwich Road, IP23 8AP
✪ 11-2.30, 5 (6 Sat)-11; 12-3, 7-10.30 Sun
☎ (01379) 870749 ⊕ bromeswan.com
Adnams Southwold Bitter, Broadside; 3 changing beers (sourced locally; often Buffy's, Elgood, Hoxne) ⊞
Heavily timbered 17th-century pub with later additions, set on the main A140 equidistant from Norwich and Ipswich. It has had the same owners for more than 30 years. Pictures on the wall in the single bar show how close a WWII bomber came to demolishing the pub in 1944. The spacious restaurant offers an extensive menu and curry specialities on Saturday evenings. The large beer garden has a children's play area. The local cycling club is based here. Q➜✿◑❍♿♠P⊟

Bungay

Chequers ⌊
23 Bridge Street, NR35 1HD
✪ 11-midnight ☎ (01986) 893579
Green Jack Waxwing; 3 changing beers (sourced locally; often Grain, Wolf, Woodforde's) ⊞
Situated close to the town centre, this inn dates from the 17th century. It has been decorated to a high standard but retains the original timber frame, wood panelling and doors. It consists of two rooms separated by an archway with TV screens in both

for sporting events. There is an array of water jugs above the bar. Ample parking is available adjacent to a partially covered area leading to a paved beer garden. Real ales are sourced from local breweries. ✿◑❍♿♣P⊟❀🐾🛜

Green Dragon ⌊
29 Broad Street, NR35 1EE
✪ 11 (12 Sat)-midnight; 12-5 Sun ☎ (01986) 892681
⊕ greendragonbungay.co.uk
Green Dragon Chaucer Ale, Gold, Bridge Street Bitter ⊞, Strong Mild Ⓖ
Originally called the Horse & Groom, this is the home of the Green Dragon brewery and is located on the edge of town. The pub is a regular in the Guide and its ales are brewed in outbuildings next to the car park at the rear – brewery tours are available by appointment. The spacious pub has a public bar and lounge area with a side room where families are welcome. The garden is surrounded by a hop hedge. ➜✿♣P⊟❀🐾🛜

Bury St Edmunds

Beerhouse ⌊
1 Tayfen Road, IP32 6BH
✪ 5 (12 Sat)-11; 12-10 Sun ☎ (01284) 766415
⊕ burybeerhouse.co.uk
Brewshed Best; 7 changing beers (sourced nationally) ⊞
Traditional beer house set in an unusual semi-circular Victorian building (previously called the Ipswich Arms), handy for the railway station, and refurbished with a modern feel. Seven beer engines provide an ever-changing selection of well-kept real ales. It serves its own beers from the Brewshed Brewery which is located in the back yard and also supplies three other local pubs. Three real ciders are also available. Regular beer festivals and an annual cider festival are hosted. Major sporting events are shown on a big screen. ➜✿⇄♠P⊟❀🛜

REAL ALE BREWERIES

Adnams Southwold
Barrell & Sellers St Cross South Elmham
Bartrams Rougham
Brandon Brandon
Brewshed Bury St Edmunds
Briarbank 🍺 Ipswich
Calvors Coddenham Green
Cliff Quay Debenham
Dove Street 🍺 Ipswich
Earl Soham Debenham
Green Dragon 🍺 Bungay
Green Jack Lowestoft
Greene King Bury St Edmunds
Hellhound Bramford
Hoxne Palgrave
Kings Head 🍺 Bildeston
Mauldons Sudbury
Old Cannon 🍺 Bury St Edmunds
Old Chimneys Market Weston
Shortts Farm Thorndon
St Judes 🍺 Ipswich (NEW)
St Peter's St Peter South Elmham
Station 119 Eye
Trinity Ales Gisleham
Uffa 🍺 Lower Ufford

Dove ⓛ

68 Hospital Road, IP33 3JU
✪ 5-11; 12-3, 6-11 Sat; 12-3, 6-10.30 Sun ☎ (01284) 702787
⊕ thedovepub.co.uk
Woodforde's Wherry Ⓗ**; changing beers** Ⓗ/Ⓖ
No lager, TVs or gaming machines here – the Dove is how pubs used to be. This back-street community venue, just five minutes from the town centre, has a traditional, basic main bar and a parlour area. There is an ever-changing range of beers on six handpumps and a good selection of real ciders, and the staff are knowledgeable about the ales. Locally made pies and pasties are also available. A former East Anglian CAMRA Regional Pub of the Year. Q❀♣♠P🖵✿

Oakes Barn 🏆

St Andrews St South, IP33 3PH (opp Waitrose car park)
✪ 11-11.30; 12-5 Sun ☎ (01284) 761592 ⊕ oakesbarn.co.uk
Crouch Vale Brewers Gold; Woodforde's Wherry; 4 changing beers (sourced nationally) Ⓗ
A real ale free house near the town centre with some period features and historic links to the medieval town. It is also a social hub and has a friendly atmosphere. Six real ales are always available including one dark beer alongside craft cider, a selection of lagers and wines. Home-made snacks using locally sourced ingredients are served all day. There is a covered smoking area outside and an open courtyard with seating. Regular events are held in the bar and function room which is available for hire. Local CAMRA branch Pub of the Year 2016. Q🕏❀◑&♣♠🖵✿🔊

Rose & Crown ✅

48 Whiting Street, IP33 1NP (on corner of Whiting St and Westgate)
✪ 11.30-11.30; 11.30-3, 7-11.30 Sat; 12-2.30, 8-11.30 Sun
☎ (01284) 755934
Greene King XX Mild, IPA, Abbot; 3 changing beers (sourced nationally) Ⓗ
In sight of Greene King's Westgate Brewery, this is a traditional pub with two bars and a separate off-sales hatch. The present tenants have run this house for 30 years and it has been in the same family for 40 years. Good-value wholesome food is served lunchtimes Monday to Saturday. Children are not allowed in the bars but are welcome in the garden. The pub is a listed building located within the conservation area of Bury St Edmunds, and has a regionally important historic interior.
Q❀◑♣🖵✿🔊

Clare

Globe

10 Callis Street, CO10 8PX
✪ 5 (4 Fri)-11.30; 11-11.30 Sat; 12-11.30 Sun
☎ (01787) 278122
Young's Bitter; 3 changing beers Ⓗ
A phoenix risen from the ashes, the Globe reopened in 2013 after a two-year closure. Serving one well-kept regular beer and up to three changing guests, it is now a thriving local where beer and conversation dominate. Live music plays every second weekend. It has a separate pool room at the rear and a newly refurbished garden for summer drinking. No food is served.
Q🕏❀P🖵✿

Cockfield

Horseshoes Inn ✅

Stow's Hill, IP30 0JB
✪ 11.30-3, 6-11; 12-4, 6-10.30 Sun; closed Mon
☎ (01284) 828177 ⊕ thehorseshoes-inn.co.uk
Adnams Southwold Bitter, Broadside; Black Sheep Best Bitter; 1 changing beer (sourced nationally) Ⓗ
This thatched 14th-century building on the A1141 road to Lavenham has been sympathetically refurbished. The large long bar room is divided by a chimney breast into two areas, and there is a separate conservatory dining area. The bar area features an exposed crown post and many original beams dating from 1350. Good-value meals are served, with traditional Sunday roasts and speciality food nights. The hilltop beer garden enjoys fabulous views. Q🕏❀◑◖P🖵✿🔊

Combs Ford

Gladstone Arms

2 Combs Road, IP14 2AP
✪ 12-midnight; 12-11 Sun ☎ (01449) 771608
⊕ gladstonearms.co.uk
Adnams Southwold Bitter, Broadside; Crouch Vale Brewers Gold; Fuller's London Pride; Sharp's Doom Bar; Woodforde's Wherry Ⓗ**; 4 changing beers** Ⓗ/Ⓖ
The owners of this refurbished inn also run the Dove Street Inn in Ipswich. The two pubs share a similar beer range, with up to 14 different ales, including house beers brewed in Ipswich. Four or five ciders and a wide range of craft lagers, imported foreign beers and whiskies are also available. Sky Sports and BT Sport are screened, monthly live music is hosted and board games are available. A beer festival features over the Easter weekend. The garden at the rear leads to the river. Q🕏❀◑&♣♠P🖵✿🔊

Dunwich

Ship

St James Street, IP17 3DT
✪ 11-11 ☎ (01728) 648219 ⊕ shipatdunwich.co.uk
Adnams Southwold Bitter; 3 changing beers Ⓗ
Once a haunt of smugglers, this is now a great place to eat, drink, relax and get away from it all. The small public bar is simply furnished with wooden furniture and a woodburner. Comfortable, traditionally furnished rooms have views across the sea or nearby marshes. Beers come from local brewers and bottled local cider is stocked. The enormous garden is dotted with fruit trees including a 300-year-old fig. The beach is just a couple of minutes' walk away. Beer festivals are held in March and September. 🕏❀🛏◑P✿🔊

Earl Soham

Victoria ⓛ

The Street, IP13 7RL
✪ 11.30-3, 5.30-11.30; 12-3, 7-10.30 Sun ☎ (01728) 685758
Earl Soham Victoria Bitter, Sir Roger's Porter, Brandeston Gold; 2 changing beers (often Earl Soham) Ⓗ
Popular, traditional Victorian pub with two small bars and an open fire in winter months, which has changed little over the years – it still has an outside toilet. An ever-changing food menu with daily specials is offered lunchtimes and evenings, all home cooked. The pub gets busy at weekends,

especially on sunny days when even a seat in the garden can be hard to find. Dogs and children are welcome. The Earl Soham Brewery was originally located behind the pub. **Q🐴❀◐◑♣P🚌🐾**

Eastbridge

Eel's Foot [L]

Leiston Road, IP16 4SN (close to entrance to Minsmere nature reserve)

🕒 12-3, 6-11; 11.30-11 Fri-Sun ☎ (01728) 830154

🌐 theeelsfootinn.co.uk

Adnams Southwold Bitter, Ghost Ship, Broadside; 2 changing beers (often Adnams) [H]

Popular with ramblers and birdwatchers, this much-improved pub is adjacent to the famous nature reserve where avocets and otters are local success stories. It has a good reputation for locally sourced home-cooked food, with a small refurbished restaurant area leading to a large terraced seating area for alfresco drinking and dining on summer days, when it can be very busy. There is also an enlarged outdoor play area for children. Traditional music sessions feature on Thursday evenings and live bands monthly. En-suite accommodation is available.

Q🐴❀🛏◐◑♿⛺♣P🐾📶

Exning

White Horse ✔

23 Church Street, CB8 7EH

🕒 12-midnight ☎ (01638) 577323

🌐 whitehorseexning.co.uk

Changing beers [H]

Mentioned in the Domesday Book, this fine free house has been run by the same family since 1923. It comprises a public bar, cosy lounge and separate restaurant offering a good choice of home-cooked food. Beers vary from week to week but often include Bass, Doom Bar and Directors. Happy hour is 5.30-6.30pm, extended to 7pm on Friday. A private room can be hired. **Q❀◐◑♣P🚌🐾**

Eye

Queen's Head

7 Cross Street, IP23 7AB

🕒 11-11; 11-9 Sun ☎ (01379) 870153

🌐 queensheadeye.co.uk

Adnams Southwold Bitter, Broadside; 3 changing beers (often Batemans) [G]

Dating from 1590, this is now the only pub remaining in this delightful north Suffolk town with many buildings of character and historical significance. The main bar has a wood-burning stove, Cross Street bar is a former butcher's shop, and there is also a snug bar. Beers are dispensed direct from the casks (with water-cooling jackets) in the main bar. Traditional pub food and daily specials are served, including breakfasts 8.30-10.30am. Families are welcome. **🐴❀◐◑♿♣P🚌🐾**

Framlingham

Station Hotel [L]

Station Road, IP13 9EE

🕒 12-2.30, 5-11; 12-11 Sat; 11-2.30, 7-10.30 Sun

☎ (01728) 723455 🌐 thestationhotel.net

Earl Soham Gannet Mild, Victoria Bitter, Brandeston Gold; 2 changing beers (often Earl Soham) [H]

Cosy two-bar pub set in a former station buffet (the branch line closed in 1963). It enjoys a good reputation for food, made with locally sourced ingredients and prepared on the premises. An ever-changing menu is displayed on chalkboards. On Sundays, brunch and beers are available from 11am. Beers and a guest cider are dispensed from a set of Edwardian German silver handpumps. A beer festival is held over the third weekend in July. The garden bar has a wood-fired pizza oven. Children and dogs welcome. **Q🐴❀◐◑🍎P🚌🐾📶**

Great Cornard

Five Bells

63 Bures Road, CO10 0HU

🕒 11-midnight; 12-midnight Sun ☎ (01787) 379016

Adnams Southwold Bitter; Greene King XX Mild, IPA; 1 changing beer (sourced regionally) [H]

A friendly community free house situated near the church (home of the five bells) on the main Sudbury to Bures road. The main bar is decorated with philosophical signs and has a library and a piano. There is a separate smaller rear bar. An unusual combination of pub games is available including bar billiards and table football. An open mic session is hosted every third Wednesday as well as other live music. The pies are legendary. A rare outlet for Greene King XX Mild.

Q🐴❀◐◑♿♣P🚌🐾📶

Great Glemham

Crown [L]

The Street, IP17 2DA

🕒 12-3 (not Tue), 6-11; 12-11 Sat; 12-6.30 Sun

☎ (01728) 663693 🌐 thecrowninnglemham.co.uk

6 changing beers (sourced locally) [H]

Closed and threatened with redevelopment in 2012, the building was thankfully saved and fully refurbished. Now an excellent multi-roomed pub, it has woodburners, traditionally tiled floors and many lovely seating areas. Up to 10 beers are on offer during the busy summer months (four or more during quieter periods). All food is cooked on the premises, ranging from bar snacks to à la carte (no food Tue lunchtime). The pub also caters for private parties and a local community lunch once a month. Acoustic music sessions feature regularly.

🐴❀◐◑♿♣🍎P🚌🐾📶

Great Wratting

Red Lion

School Road, CB9 7HA

🕒 11-2.30, 5-11; 11-1.30am Sat; 12-3, 7-10 Sun

☎ (01440) 783237

Adnams Southwold Bitter, Broadside; 1 changing beer [H]

A whale's jawbones frame the doorway to this village local dating from the 17th or 18th century, making an unusual and amusing entrance. Now a free house, this ex-Adnams pub offers good beer, good food and conversation as its mainstay. Locals love this hostelry and are passionate supporters of the activities overseen by an enthusiastic landlord of long experience. Quiz nights and a darts league thrive here. **Q🐴❀◐◑⛺♣🍎P🚌🐾**

Hopton

Vine ▼
High Street, IP22 2QX
☼ 3-11; 12-midnight Sat; 12-10.30 Sun ☎ (01953) 688581
Adnams Southwold Bitter, Broadside; Greene King IPA; 5 changing beers (sourced locally; often Colchester, Lacons, Wolf) Ⓗ
On the main road near the church, this village local has been revitalised by an enthusiastic landlord and friendly staff since it was taken over in 2013. Eight ales including a selection of local and regional guests are currently offered at reasonable prices, with Adnams Southwold, Broadside and Greene King IPA as regulars. The pub has a pool table in one of its three separate areas. Outside is a large play area for children. A welcoming inn, popular with locals and visitors. ➦❀❀♣●P☐(100)❀ 🛜

Hundon

Rose & Crown
20 North Street, CO10 8ED
☼ 6-9 Mon & Tue; 12-2, 6-11 Wed & Thu; 12-midnight Fri & Sat; 12-9 Sun ☎ (01440) 786261 ⊕ hundon-village.co.uk/roseandcrown.html
Sharp's Doom Bar; 3 changing beers (sourced nationally; often Fuller's, St Austell, Timothy Taylor) Ⓗ
Since it became a free house, this refurbished two-roomed pub has developed a reputation for good ale. The three changing beers are dictated by customer demand. A true village atmosphere prevails and the welcome is warm and friendly. Home-cooked food is served Wednesday evening to Sunday lunchtime. A folk evening is held on the third Wednesday of the month and an autumn family festival over the August bank holiday. Weddings can be catered for in a marquee in the extensive garden.
Q➦❀❀♣●P☐(344,346,347)❀

Ipswich

Arcade Street Tavern
Arcade Street, IP1 1EX
☼ 10.30-3 Tue; 10.30-11 Wed & Thu; 10.30-midnight Fri; 10.30-1am Sat; closed Sun & Mon ☎ (01473) 805454 ⊕ arcadetavern.co.uk
2 changing beers Ⓗ
A stylish and quirky multi-roomed café bar with a traditional wooden interior, close to the Corn Exchange. Two handpumps dispense an ever-changing range of beers alongside a selection of around 130 imported bottles. Street food Fridays are hosted in conjunction with various other local traders. There are large heated seating areas outside and two function rooms upstairs – one often used for product launches. Artisan coffee is also available. Q❀☐ 🛜

Briarbank
70 Fore Street, IP4 1LB
☼ 4-10; 12-midnight Fri & Sat; 12-10 Sun ☎ (01473) 284000
Briarbank Perpendicular, Old Spiteful; 4 changing beers (sourced locally; often Briarbank) Ⓗ
A smart and modern first-floor drinking bar that opened in 2013 above the Briarbank Brewery. At one time serving as a bank, the building had been derelict for many years. Many beers from the brewery are also available as keg. Music (usually jazz) features twice-monthly either in the bar or outside when weather permits. The TVs show only

rugby, F1, tennis or golf. Beer festivals are held at Easter and in the summer. The bar may open earlier in the summer months. ❀◑P☐ 🛜

Dove Street Inn Ⓛ ✅
76 St Helen's Street, IP4 2LA
☼ 12-midnight; 12-10.30 Sun ☎ (01473) 211270 ⊕ dovestreetinn.co.uk
Adnams Broadside; Crouch Vale Brewers Gold; Fuller's London Pride; Greene King Abbot Ⓗ; changing beers (often Dove Street) Ⓗ/Ⓖ
Popular multi-roomed inn with a large selection of real ales including milds, plus ciders and continental beers. This is the sister pub to the Gladstone Arms in Combs Ford. Some ales are from the adjacent Dove Street Brewery, and there is a brew shop next door. Home-cooked food and bar snacks are served at all times. The green room, a large covered and heated seating area outside, hosts various events. Well-behaved dogs and children are welcome. Three beer festivals are held annually. There are letting rooms above the brewery. Last admission is 10.45pm.
➦❀🛏◑❀♣●P☐(66)❀ 🛜

Fat Cat Ⓛ
288 Spring Road, IP4 5NL
☼ 12-11 (midnight Fri & Sat) ☎ (01473) 726524 ⊕ fatcatipswich.co.uk
Adnams Southwold Bitter Ⓗ; Crouch Vale Brewers Gold; Fuller's London Pride; Woodforde's Wherry; changing beers Ⓖ
Brewery artefacts adorn the walls in this excellent suburban drinking pub, with no background music or games machines. Up to 16 gravity beers are dispensed from the taproom, and one or two ciders. The secluded garden and patio provide extra space on sunny afternoons, and barbecues feature occasionally. Meals and snacks are available at lunchtimes, and in the evenings customers are welcome to order in takeaways (not Fri or Sat eve). No children under 14. A winner of many local CAMRA Pub of the Year awards over the years.
Q❀◑●☐❀ 🛜

Greyhound
9 Henley Road, IP1 3SE
☼ 11.30-2.30, 5-11; 11.30-midnight Fri; 11.30-11.30 Sat; 10-10.30 Sun ☎ (01473) 252862 ⊕ thegreyhoundipswich.co.uk
Adnams Southwold Bitter, Ghost Ship, Broadside; 3 changing beers (often Adnams) Ⓗ
The Greyhound has a cosy, traditional, small public bar at the front and a larger, more modern drinking and dining room to the side and rear. The outside drinking space can be busy in the summer months and hosts occasional barbecues. Freshly prepared food is served daily, with vegetarian options, and breakfasts 10-11.30am Sunday only. Quiz nights are hosted twice a month on Sunday evenings. The TVs are only used for sporting events.
Q➦❀◑❀♣P☐(116) 🛜

Mulberry Tree ✅
5 Woodbridge Road, IP4 2EA
☼ 12-11 (1am Fri & Sat) ☎ (01473) 225776
Adnams Southwold Bitter Ⓗ; 7 changing beers (often Green Jack, Nethergate) Ⓗ/Ⓖ
An imposing pub on the edge of the town centre, extensively refurbished as a free house by the current owner. A large open fire warms the main bar, and a new kitchen and seating outdoors provide further dining and alfresco drinking

options. Beers are served in oversized glasses. Live music is hosted regularly on Friday and Saturday evenings, and folk sessions fortnightly on Sunday evenings. Dogs and children are welcome. With a choice of seven ciders, it is local CAMRA Cider Pub of the Year once again in 2016. ✪ⓛ&♠P🅿🖩🐾🐕🎵

Spread Eagle
1-3 Fore Street, IP4 1JW
✪ 12-midnight; 12-10.30 Sun; closed Mon
☎ (01473) 256093
Grain Oak, Blonde Ash Wheat Beer, Best Bitter, Slate; 1 changing beer (often Grain) Ⓗ
This distinctive Grade II-listed building is the sole survivor of four pubs that once stood at this junction. Recent refurbishment has restored the building to a high standard and the split-level bar room has been sympathetically furnished throughout. Six real ales are on handpump, all from Grain, plus a selection of specialist beers alongside imported bottles. Some daytime food options and bar snacks are available, and quality, locally roasted coffee. There is seating outside in an enclosed area to the rear. Q✪🖩🐾🐕🎵

Thomas Wolsey
9-13 St Peters Street, IP1 1XF (300yds from bus station)
✪ 4.30-11.30 (1am Fri & Sat); closed Sun ☎ (01473) 210055
Adnams Ghost Ship; Crouch Vale Brewers Gold; Woodforde's Wherry; 1 changing beer Ⓗ
Large single-room lounge bar set in a historic Grade II-listed building. It has a patio area to the side and two well furnished function rooms upstairs, used for a wide variety of events including story-telling nights, charity quizzes and meetings. A range of specialist ales is available on draught plus over 25 bottled beers and 40 quality wines. Games are available including darts. Home supporters only on football match days. ✪🔁♣🖩🎵

Ixworth

Greyhound ✪
49 High Street, IP31 2HJ
✪ 11.30-2.30, 6 (5 Fri & Sat)-11; 12-3, 7-11 Sun
☎ (01359) 230887
Greene King XX Mild, IPA, Abbot; 2 changing beers (sourced nationally) Ⓗ
Situated on the village's pretty high street, this traditional inn has three bars, one a lovely central snug, and families are welcome. The heart of the building dates back to Tudor times. The pub is a rare outlet for Greene King XX Mild. Lunches and early evening meals are served in the restaurant including a good-value daily special. Dominoes, crib, darts and pool are played in leagues and for charity fundraising. Q✪✪⬤▲♣P🐾🐕

Lawshall

Swan
The Street, IP29 4QA
✪ 12-3, 6-11; 12-3, 5-midnight Fri; 12-midnight Sat; 12-10 Sun; closed Tue ☎ (01284) 828477 🌐 swaninnlawshall.com
4 changing beers (sourced nationally; often Adnams, Black Sheep) Ⓗ
Set in the heart of rural Suffolk in the village of Lawshall, the Swan is everything a country pub should be. The beautiful 18th-century thatched building was lovingly restored in 2013 and is crammed full of period features. On the menu you will find all the traditional pub classics and a few

extra culinary delights. A large garden encourages children to play. A real ale festival is held in May. ✪✪⬤♣P🐾🐕🎵

Long Melford

Crown Inn
Hall Street, CO10 9JL
✪ 11.30-11; 12-10.30 Sun ☎ (01787) 377666
🌐 thecrownhotelmelford.co.uk
Adnams Southwold Bitter, Ghost Ship; 2 changing beers (sourced nationally) Ⓗ
This is a busy family-run free house and cosy hotel set in the popular antiques centre of Long Melford. Three regular ales and one changing guest, together with real cider, are on handpump. A high-quality home-cooked menu is served in the large bar and separate restaurant. There is a large attractive patio garden for summer dining and drinking. Twelve comfortable bedrooms are available for those wishing to stay and explore this picturesque area. Q✪✪🛏⬤⬤♠P🖩🐾🎵

Lowestoft

Norman Warrior Ⓛ ✪
Fir Lane, NR32 2RB
✪ 11-11.30 (12.30am Fri & Sat); 12-11.30 Sun
☎ (01502) 561982 🌐 thenormanwarrior.co.uk
Greene King IPA; Morland Old Speckled Hen; 4 changing beers (sourced nationally) Ⓗ
Large estate pub on the northern side of town with ample parking, close to the bus stop and a 20-minute walk from Oulton Broad North railway station. It comprises a public bar where pool and darts are played and a comfortable lounge leading to a spacious restaurant serving home-cooked food daily. Outside is a terrace and garden where a beer and cider festival featuring live music is held over the August bank holiday weekend. A popular quiz takes place weekly. ✪✪⬤&♣P🖩(102)🐾🎵

Stanford Arms 🍷 Ⓛ
Stanford Street, NR32 2DD
✪ 4-midnight (10 Mon); 3-1am Fri; 12-1am Sun; 12-midnight Sun ☎ (01502) 587444 🌐 stanfordarms.co.uk
Bullards No. 1 East Coast Pale Ale; 11 changing beers (sourced locally; often Golden Triangle, Grain, Wolf) Ⓗ
The spacious open-plan bar has a large array of handpumps serving mainly local beers – it is a rare outlet for Redwell brewery. A fine collection of beer trays adorns the walls. To the rear is a courtyard garden with its own wood-fired pizza oven (Friday is pizza night) and a small aviary. A food night is held most Wednesdays (booking required) and a dish of the day is available late Saturday afternoons. Live music features on most Saturday evenings and on Sunday afternoons. ✪✪♣⬤🖩🐾🎵

Triangle Tavern Ⓛ
29 St Peters Street, NR32 1QA
✪ 11-11 (midnight Thu; 1am Fri & Sat); 12-10.30 Sun
☎ (01502) 582711 🌐 green-jack.com
Green Jack Trawlerboys Best Bitter, Orange Wheat Beer, Waxwing, Lurcher Stout, Gone Fishing ESB, Ripper Tripel Ⓗ; 2 changing beers (sourced locally; often Crouch Vale, Oakham) Ⓖ
The flagship for the local Green Jack Brewery, this popular community town hostelry was originally two pubs. The cosy front bar has wood-panelling

surrounds and benches giving the feel of a front parlour, and hosts live music on Friday nights. A corridor leads to an open-plan back bar with a pool table. Both bars are decorated with brewery awards and memorabilia. Quarterly beer festivals are held prior to bank holidays. ≈♣🛏🚐😺

Market Weston

Mill 🅛
Bury Road, IP22 2PD
🌐 11-3 (not Mon), 5-11; 12-3, 7-11 Sun ☎ (01359) 221018
Adnams Southwold Bitter; Greene King IPA; Old Chimneys Military Mild, Golden Pheasant; 3 changing beers (sourced nationally; often Fuller's, Harveys, Marston's) 🅗
Striking white brick and flint-faced inn standing at a crossroads on the main road. It is the closest outlet to the Old Chimneys Brewery, located on the other side of the village. The landlady celebrated 20 years at the Mill in 2015. The pub offers an excellent choice of beers, always including a selection from Old Chimneys, complemented by a good menu of home-cooked meals.
Q🌑😺◑&♣P🖪🚐😺

Naughton

Wheelhouse
Whatfield Road, IP7 7BS
🌐 5-11 (9 Mon); 6-11 Sat; 12-10.30 Sun; closed Tue
☎ (01449) 740496 🌐 thewheelhouseatnaughton.co.uk
2 changing beers 🅗
A picturesque and recently redecorated thatched inn with a low ceiling. The building is reputed to have been a pub since the 12th century and many ancient timbers are in evidence. The main bar has a traditional open fire and the more spacious public bar has a pool table. A varied and changing selection of ales makes this hostelry always worth a visit. The garden to the rear is a pleasant place to relax on sunny days. The bus stop is on the main road. Q😺&♣P🖪(111)😺

Needham Market

Rampant Horse 🅛
Coddenham Road, IP6 8AU
🌐 12-3, 5-11; 12-11 Fri & Sat; 12-10 Sun ☎ (01449) 722044
🌐 therampanthorse.co.uk
Calvors Lodestar Festival Ale, Smooth Hoperator; 1 changing beer 🅗
Calvors Brewery purchased, refurbished and reopened this pub in 2012. It now sells a wide range of locally sourced food and drink including its own high-quality lagers and, more recently, real ale. Beer festivals feature occasionally and live music is hosted. There is a garden and car park to the rear. The pub is close to the railway station which was built in an area previously known as 'camping land', the local pitch for an ancient ball game – a precursor to football – dating back to at least the 17th century. 😺◑≈♣P🖪🚐😺🛜

Newbourne

Fox Inn ✅
The Street, IP12 4NY
🌐 11-11; 12-10.30 Sun ☎ (01473) 736307
🌐 debeninns.co.uk/fox
Adnams Southwold Bitter; 3 changing beers 🅗

Picturesque timber-framed, two-bar village local with a large garden, popular with ramblers and cyclists. A wide range of local food is home cooked and served every day, with an à la carte menu, gluten-free options and daily specials. The garden has a large pond and a shed housing an old skittle alley – the only one active in Suffolk.
Q🌑😺◑&Å♣P🖪(179)😺

Newmarket

Golden Lion ✅
44 High Street, CB8 8LB
🌐 8am-11 ☎ (01638) 672040
Adnams Ghost Ship; Greene King Abbot; Ruddles Best Bitter; 4 changing beers 🅗
This venue is one of Wetherspoon's finest – a large, bustling, 18th-century town pub, situated on the main High Street. Up to seven real ales are available at any one time, including up to four guests, served by knowledgeable and efficient staff. Real cider is also available. The pub's name is thought to have originated from King Henry I – it is also known as the Lion of Justice. Children are welcome until 9pm in the family area. The pub is popular with the local horse racing community.
😺◑&≈🛏P🖪😺🛜

Offton

Limeburners 🅛
Willisham Road, IP8 4SF
🌐 4.30 (1 Fri)-11; 12-11 Sat & Sun ☎ (01473) 658318
🌐 thelimeburners.co.uk
Adnams Lighthouse; Shortts Farm Strummer; 1 changing beer 🅗
A friendly split-level bar with a fish and chip shop attached (eat in or take-away). The pub is named after the chalk pit opposite which used to contain historic limekilns – see the photos on display. A quiz night is held every first Thursday of the month and buskers play on Sunday nights. Guest ales change regularly. Popular Sunday roasts are served 12-2pm (no food Sun eve or Tue). Outside is a large garden and car park. 😺◑&♣P🖪(111)😺

Ousden

Fox
Front Street, CB8 8TR
🌐 11-11; 12-5 Sun ☎ (01638) 500740
🌐 theousdenfox.co.uk
Greene King IPA; Woodforde's Wherry; 2 changing beers (sourced regionally) 🅗
Three distinct areas – a public bar with a piano, dining space and comfy seating area – are all warmed by logburners in winter. Anglo-French food is served and local produce is for sale including home-made cider. A monthly quiz, annual beer festival and car rallies are held here. If you wish to camp there is space but no facilities. Runner-up CAMRA Regional Cider Pub of the Year in 2015. Q🌑😺◑&♣🛏P🖪😺🛜

Pakefield

Oddfellows 🅛
6 Nightingale Road, NR33 7AU
🌐 11-11; 12-10.30 Sun ☎ (01502) 538415
Adnams Southwold Bitter; 4 changing beers (sourced locally; often Green Jack, Lacons, Woodforde's) 🅗

Popular inn situated close to Pakefield's cliffs and coastal path, and just a stone's throw from the sea. A small, cosy pub, it has three open-plan areas including one for diners, with wood flooring and panelling throughout. The walls are festooned with pictures of old Pakefield and sporting events are shown on TV screens. Up to five ales are available from local breweries and, in summer, a popular beer festival is hosted on the green opposite.
❀◑🚌🐾📶

Rattlesden

Five Bells Ⓛ

High Street, IP30 0RA

12-midnight; 12-11 Sun ☎ (01449) 737373

3 changing beers (sourced locally; often Earl Soham, Woodforde's) [H]

Set on the high road through a picturesque village, this is a good old Suffolk drinking house – few of its kind still survive. Three well-chosen ales on the bar are usually sourced direct from the breweries. The cosy single-room interior has a games area on a lower level and there is occasional live music. Pub games include shut-the-box and shove-ha'penny plus pétanque in the garden in summer. A motorcycle show is hosted in May. Q❀♣🚌🐾

Risby

Crown & Castle

South Street, IP28 6QU

12-3, 5 (6.30 Sat)-11; 12-3, 7-10.30 Sun

☎ (01284) 810393 crownandcastle.com

Adnams Southwold Bitter; 2 changing beers (sourced nationally) [H]

This attractive flint-faced building opened as a pub and shop in the late-1800s and was sold by Greene King in 2014. A 120-foot-deep unrecorded well was discovered during alterations in recent times and is now a feature beneath a grille in the entrance lobby. The pub has classic back and front bars, with food served in both. The back bar is the public, dominated by games and conversation – well-behaved dogs are also allowed in here.
Q❀◑♣P🚌🐾

Rumburgh

Buck Ⓛ

Mill Road, IP19 0NT

11.45-3, 6.30-11; 12-3, 7-10.30 Sun ☎ (01986) 785257

Adnams Southwold Bitter; 4 changing beers (sourced locally; often Barrell & Sellers, Green Jack, Lacons) [H]

Originally, this pub and the parish church were part of a Benedictine priory. Extensions have added two dining areas, with a public bar and games room retained around the historic core. The original bar is timber framed with a flagstone floor. Full of character and at the heart of village life, folk music evenings are hosted – the pub is home to both the Rumburgh morris dancers and Old Glory molly dancers. Locally sourced produce features in good-quality meals. Q❀◑⛺♣P🐾📶

Shadingfield

Fox Ⓛ

London Road, NR34 8DD

12-11; closed Mon ☎ (01502) 575100

shadingfieldfox.co.uk

Young's Bitter; 8 changing beers (sourced locally; often Green Jack, Lacons, Wolf) [H]

A charming rural inn on the road from Beccles to Southwold, the pub straddles the boundary of two parishes – Shadingfield and Willingham St Mary. The original inn dates from the 16th century and the arched doors and carved fox heads on the beams have been retained. The interior comprises a bar with comfortable seating plus a restaurant and conservatory. Two beer festivals are held annually, one over Father's Day weekend and the other close to Guy Fawkes Night.
Q❀◑♿♣P🚌(60s)🐾📶

Shottisham

Sorrel Horse

Hollesley Road, IP12 3HD

12-11 (midnight Sat); 12-10.30 Sun ☎ (01394) 411617

thesorrelhorse-shottisham.co.uk

Woodforde's Wherry; 2 changing beers [G]

A former smugglers' inn dating back to the 15th century, this picturesque thatched two-bar pub retains a gravity stillage for beers. Local villagers bought shares in the pub a few years ago. Music nights (folk or jazz) are held on the second and fourth Monday of the month and a quiz on Wednesday evenings. The food menu includes locally sourced dishes prepared in the recently refurbished kitchen. Special themed evenings feature and breakfast on Sundays 9-11am. The main bar has a bar billiards table. Seats in the garden are popular on sunny days.
Q❀◑♿⛺♣P🚌🐾📶

Southwold

Lord Nelson Ⓛ ✔

42 East Street, IP18 6EJ

10.30-11; 12-10.30 Sun ☎ (01502) 722079

thelordnelsonsouthwold.co.uk

Adnams Lighthouse, Southwold Bitter, Ghost Ship, Broadside; 2 changing beers (sourced locally; often Adnams) [H]

A regular entry in the Guide, this pub is situated close to the Sailors' Reading Room museum and enjoys coastal views from the nearby cliff top promenade. A busy and lively pub, it is popular with locals and visitors alike and has a central bar offering the full range of Adnams beers. The walls are adorned with naval memorabilia and photos of old Southwold. Children are welcome in the side room and patio area to the rear. ❀◑⛺🚌🐾

Stowmarket

King's Arms

Station Road, IP14 1RQ

11-11; 10.30-11 Sun ☎ 07852 497412

Woodforde's Wherry; 4 changing beers (often Adnams) [H]

Multi-roomed hostelry, just a short walk from the historic railway station and town centre. Pub games are popular, and occasional live music and barbecues are hosted. Food is available until 4pm including snacks, stews, hotpots, chilli and omelettes. The patio to the rear leads to a smoking room and various other spaces used for live music and private parties. There is a children's play area and dogs are welcome when the pub is not busy. Two or three beer festivals are held each year. The cider is usually Old Rosie. ❀◑🚆♣P🚌🐾📶

Royal William

53 Union Street East, IP14 1HP
🌀 11-11.30 (12.30am Fri & Sat); 12-11 Sun
☎ (01449) 674553
Greene King IPA; Woodforde's Wherry; 10 changing beers Ⓖ

Tucked away down a narrow side street, just a short walk from the town centre and railway station. An end-of-terrace back-street bar, it is well supported by locals and visitors alike. Ales are served by gravity dispense from the cellar behind the bar, with up to 10 guest beers and five ciders. There is a games room, home to regular dominoes, darts and crib matches, and a smoking area in the enclosed garden. Sport is shown on TV. Traditional music features once a month. Home-made bar snacks are offered. 🏆🕏👌⇌♣🚫🚌😺🛜

Stratford St Mary

Swan 🅰

Lower Street, CO7 6JR
🌀 11-11; 11-10.30 Sun; closed Mon & Tue
☎ (01206) 321244 ⊕ stratfordswan.com
3 changing beers Ⓗ

The building is part of a historic former coaching inn dating from about 1520 – the original medieval inn was at least three times larger than the remaining structure. It has a small, friendly bar retaining many historic features, several other wood-panelled rooms mainly used for dining, and a spacious garden to the rear. The pub has its own house brewery – brewing started in summer 2015 – with some beers now available on draught. A wide range of bottled beers is also available and an annual beer festival is hosted. 🏆🕏🍴🍺♣🚫P🛜

Sudbury

Brewery Tap 🅛

21-23 East Street, CO10 2TP (200yds from marketplace)
🌀 11-11 (midnight Fri & Sat); 12-10.30 Sun
☎ (01787) 370876 ⊕ blackaddertap.co.uk
Mauldons Moletrap Bitter, Silver Adder, Suffolk Pride Ⓗ; **3 changing beers** Ⓖ

A mecca for real ale drinkers, the Mauldons Brewery tap is a comfortable, friendly pub in the old traditional style. Soup, rolls, filled baps, occasional chillies, stews and locally made pies are available and takeaways can be ordered in. Events include a Sunday breakfast club, quiz nights, live music and beer festivals in April and October. The pub is home to golf, darts, crib and bar billiards clubs. A must for beer and pub lovers. Q🕏🍴👌⇌♣🚫🛜🚌😺

Waggon & Horses 🅰

Church Walk, Acton Square, CO10 1HJ
🌀 11-11 (midnight Fri & Sat) ☎ (01787) 312147
⊕ thesudburywaggon.co.uk
Nethergate Growler Bitter; 3 changing beers Ⓗ

Originally refurbished by Growler (now Nethergate) Brewery, the pub is currently run by independent owners and is a popular venue on the Sudbury pub scene. One regular and three changing guest beers complement the home-cooked high-quality food. The interior comprises a long main bar with real fire, a small dining area and a snug with a glass floor looking down into the cellar. Regular quiz nights are held and live music plays on the last Sunday of the month. Q🏆🕏🍴👌⇌♣🚫😺

Sweffling

White Horse 🍺 🅛

Low Road, IP17 2BB
🌀 7-11; 12-3, 7-11 Sun; closed Tue-Thu ☎ (01728) 664178
⊕ swefflingwhitehorse.co.uk
3 changing beers Ⓖ

A cosy, traditional two-room pub, warmed by a woodburner and wood-fired range. The current owners have refurbished the building in an environmentally friendly manner. Gravity-dispensed beers from local brewers are served through a taproom door. Fair-trade, organic and locally produced bottled beers are also available, and cider too. Hot and cold bar snacks are sold. Pub games including bar billiards, darts, crib and board games are played, and live music features twice a month. Horse and trap rides are available in summer. CAMRA East Anglian Pub of the Year 2015. Q🏆🕏🚐🅰♣🚫P😺🛜

Tattingstone

Wheatsheaf 🅛

Church Road, IP9 2LY
🌀 12-3, 6-11 Tue-Thu; 12-midnight Fri & Sat; 12-9 Sun; closed Mon ☎ (01473) 805470
2 changing beers (sourced locally) Ⓗ

Comfortable open-plan single bar pub that has been fully refurbished over the past two years by the current owners. It is located on the outskirts of this small village, which was divided by the nearby Alton Water Park reservoir (built 1972-78). Beers are usually from local brewers. Themed food nights and Sunday roasts are popular. Live music and quiz nights feature occasionally. The pub hosts local cribbage league matches and caters for social events and weddings. There is a large garden to the side. 🏆🕏🍴🅰P🚫😺🛜

Thelnetham

White Horse 🅛

Hopton Road, IP22 1JN
🌀 12-3, 5-10.30; 12-10.30 Sat; 12-8 Sun; closed Mon
☎ (01379) 898779 ⊕ whitehorsethelnetham.co.uk
Adnams Southwold Bitter; Woodforde's Wherry; 1 changing beer (often Buffy's, Shortts Farm) Ⓗ

This friendly 1800s-built pub, in a remote location near the windmill, is well worth seeking out. Closed for a couple of years, it reopened at the end of 2012. Dog-, family- and wellie-friendly, it is popular with walkers and cyclists, and welcomes drinkers and diners alike. It has two bar areas and a restaurant offering a monthly changing menu, featuring old favourites and some unusual dishes, using locally sourced ingredients. Wine comes from Thelnetham Vineyard and ciders from local cider makers. Live music plays on Tuesday evenings. Q🏆🕏🍴👌P😺🛜

Thorndon

Black Horse

The Street, IP23 7JR
🌀 12-3, 5 (6 Sat)-11; 12-9 Sun ☎ (01379) 678523
⊕ theblackhorsethorndon.co.uk
Adnams Southwold Bitter; Shortts Farm Strummer; 2 changing beers (sourced regionally; often Grain, Hoxne, Nethergate) Ⓗ

A traditional country pub in the heart of a pretty village. Dating back to the 1600s and full of character, it has many historic photos of the village on display. The central bar has a log fire and two adjoining restaurant areas. Two guest ales are usually on offer, typically local and often from Brandon, Grain or Woodforde's breweries. At lunchtime there is a carvery, and evening meals are served daily. Dogs on leads are welcome in the main bar area. 🚲🏠🍴&🅿🚌🐾🐾📶

Thurston

Fox & Hounds ✅
Barton Road, IP31 3QT
🕐 11.30-11 ☎ (01359) 232228
🌐 thurstonfoxandhounds.co.uk
Adnams Broadside; Greene King IPA; 4 changing beers (sourced nationally; often Cliff Quay, Green Jack, Tring) 🅗
A listed building, this popular village local sits in the middle of the village a short walk from the railway station. The restaurant, serving good home-cooked food, is within the public bar area, separated by uplights from an original wall. There is another bar for pool and darts. On bank holidays and special occasions live music is performed. Regular quiz nights and bingo also feature. A conker competition is held in the autumn. Accommodation is available.
Q🚲🏠🍴🏨🍴&🚂🅿🐾🐾📶

Walberswick

Anchor 🅛 ✅
The Street, IP18 6UA
🕐 11-4, 6-11; 11-11 Sat; 12-11 Sun ☎ (01502) 722112
🌐 anchoratwalberswick.com
Adnams Southwold Bitter, Broadside; 1 changing beer (sourced locally; often Adnams) 🅗
Situated in an idyllic coastal village, this hotel caters for holidaymakers and locals alike. It has two cosy alcove areas heated by a real fire on both sides and a side room for families. Ales from Adnams and a large selection of global craft and bottled beers are on offer. A spacious restaurant to the rear serves high-quality local produce. Accommodation is available in the main building and in chalet rooms in the garden.
Q🚲🏠🍴🏨🍴&🅿🐾🐾📶

Walton

Half Moon 🅛
303 High Street, IP11 9QL
🕐 12-3 (not Mon), 5-11; 12-3, 5-midnight Fri; 12-11 Sat; 12-3, 7-11 Sun ☎ (01394) 285586
Adnams Lighthouse, Southwold Bitter, Broadside; 3 changing beers (often Adnams) 🅗
An excellent two-bar local community pub with wood panelling and an open fire in the public bar in winter. A meeting place for local groups of all kinds, it has quiz nights, darts matches, cribbage and a selection of books to read. There are no gaming machines or music. The secure garden has a children's play area which has proved popular with families. Food is available lunchtimes only. Monthly folk nights are hosted as well as other live music on occasion. 🚲🏠🍴&🐟🅿🐾🐾📶

Wenhaston

Star Inn 🅛
Hall Road, IP19 9HF

🕐 12-3, 6-11; 12-11 Sun ☎ (01502) 478240
🌐 wenhastonstar.co.uk
Adnams Southwold Bitter; 5 changing beers (sourced locally; often Green Jack, Shortts Farm, Wolf) 🅗
Situated on the outskirts of the village with fine views of the Blyth Valley, this free house is popular with walkers and cyclists (dogs and muddy boots also welcome). The interior comprises three small public rooms overlooking a large lawn and garden where beer festivals are held in May and August. The front bar is a gem with old enamel advertising signs and open fires on cold evenings. Good home-cooked food uses locally sourced produce.
Q🚲🏠🍴🏨🍴🚶🚲🅿🚌(88A)🐾🐾📶

Wickhambrook

Greyhound ✅
Meeting Green, CB8 8XS
🕐 12-3, 5 (6 Sat)-11; 12-3, 7-10.30 Sun ☎ (01440) 821017
🌐 greyhoundwickhambrook.co.uk
2 changing beers (sourced nationally) 🅗
The Greyhound opened its doors under its current owners in 2011 after being purchased from Greene King. It has since undergone a thorough refurbishment including the addition of a new building housing a kitchen and restaurant Twenty One. Regular events include an annual beer festival in the large garden. The pub is committed to supporting the local community and was local CAMRA branch Community Pub of the Year in 2015. 🚲🏠🍴🍴🚶🅿

Woodbridge

Angel 🅛
2 Theatre Street, IP12 4NE
🕐 2-11 (midnight Fri & Sat); 12-10.30 Sun
☎ (01394) 383808 🌐 theangelwoodbridge.co.uk
Adnams Southwold Bitter; 5 changing beers 🅗
Dating from the 16th century, this traditional two-bar drinking pub has beams and tiled floors, with an outdoor seating area and former stables at the rear. A regularly changing range of real ales is on offer alongside a selection of over 270 different gins. A new wood-fired pizza oven has been installed in the garden. Live music features regularly, with open mic on the second and fourth Wednesday of the month, and a DJ plays every Saturday evening. 🚲🏠🐟🚶🅿🚌🐾🐾📶

Cherry Tree 🅛
73 Cumberland Street, IP12 4AG
🕐 7.30am-11; 9am-11 Sun ☎ (01394) 384627
🌐 thecherrytreepub.co.uk
Adnams Southwold Bitter, Ghost Ship, Broadside; Elgood's Black Dog; 5 changing beers (often Adnams) 🅗
Spacious lounge bar/diner with a large central counter and several distinct seating areas. Nine beers are usually on offer and an annual summer beer festival is hosted. Food is locally sourced and home cooked, including some gluten-free options, with breakfast 7.30-11am on Sundays. Board games and cards are available to play and a quiz is held on Thursdays. The large recently refurbished garden has children's play equipment. Accommodation is offered in a converted barn. Wheelchair-, child- and dog-friendly. 🚲🏠🍴🏨🍴🐟🚶🅿🐾🐾📶

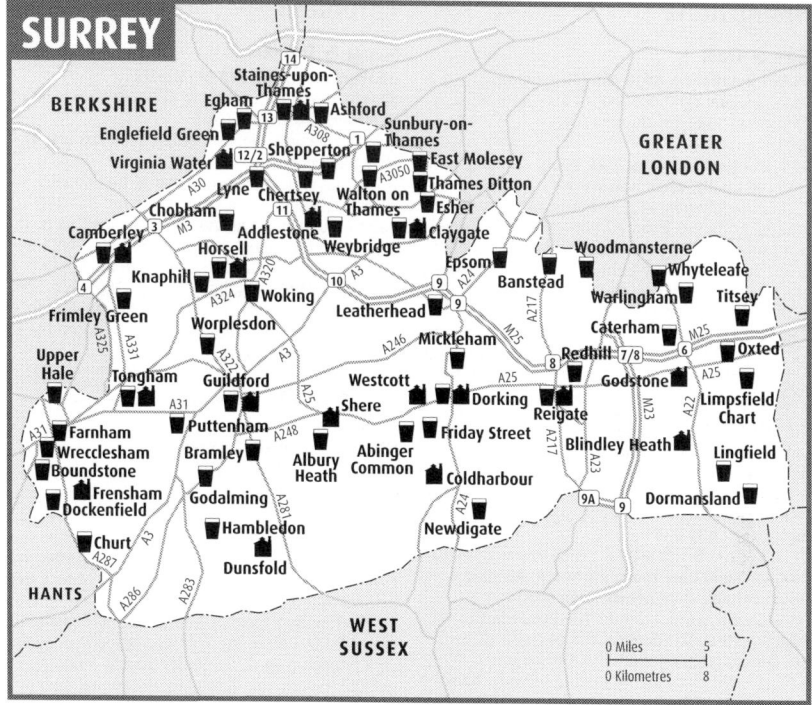

Abinger Common

Abinger Hatch 🅛 ✅
Abinger Lane, RH5 6HZ TQ11574596
🌐 11-11.30; 12-10.30 Sun ☎ (01306) 730737
🌐 theabingerhatch.com
Ringwood Best Bitter; 3 changing beers 🅗
This former Surrey Trust Company inn is situated opposite the village church. The interior of the 17th-century building rambles over three levels. The lowest part has large flagstones on the floor, the other areas have bare boards. The beers, served from a beautiful English oak bar, are mainly from regional brewers but a local ale, often from Tillingbourne, is usually available. Excellent food, served all day, is a feature, with a varied menu on offer. Outside are large gardens.
Q🍽️🕑🌳❄️◐P🖵(22)🐾❄️🛜

Albury Heath

William IV 🅛
Little London, GU5 9DG TQ06554673
🌐 11-3, 5.30-11; 11-11 Sat; 12-11 Sun ☎ (01483) 202685
🌐 williamivalbury.com
Surrey Hills Ranmore, Shere Drop; Young's Bitter; 1 changing beer 🅗
Old-fashioned country pub that has been in the Guide for over 10 years. Set on a quiet lane adjoining extensive woodland and popular with walkers, the part 16th-century building features beams, flagstones and a large fireplace where a welcoming wood fire burns in winter. There are two traditional bars plus a dining room where excellent home-made meals are served (not Sun eve). Dishes include Gloucester Old Spot pork from the pigs kept in the field behind the pub. Shove-ha'penny can be played. Q🌳◐🌿P🐾

Ashford

King's Fairway 🅛 ✅
91 Fordbridge Road, TW15 2SS (on B377)
🌐 11.30-midnight ☎ (01784) 423575
Brakspear Bitter; Fuller's London Pride; Sharp's Doom Bar; 6 changing beers (sourced nationally; often Belhaven, Conwy, Kelburn) 🅗
Popular, rambling, modern pub in a cosy, traditional style. Nine handpumps dispense three regular beers and up to six changing guests. Ale and food are reasonably priced, and families are welcome in the dining area. There is a cask ale discount on Mondays. Two gas fires provide comfort in the winter months. Quiz nights are Wednesday and Sunday. There is a small TV area for sport, and a heated and covered smokers' refuge on the patio. Q🌳❄️◐👶⚃P🖵(290)🛜

Banstead

Woolpack ✅
186 High Street, SM7 2NZ
🌐 11-11; 12-10.30 Sun ☎ (01737) 354560
🌐 thewoolpackbanstead.co.uk
Shepherd Neame Master Brew, Spitfire, Bishops Finger; 2 changing beers 🅗
At the top end of the High Street, a short walk from the town centre, this is a smart pub with a wood-burning stove and sofas. A separate restaurant serves a range of good food, available all day except Sunday evenings. The pub is tied to Shepherd Neame but has two guest beers changing frequently. Live jazz features on the first Tuesday afternoon of each month and a beer festival is held on the last bank holiday in August. ❄️◐👶P🖵🐾🛜

Boundstone

Bat & Ball ℓ

15 Bat & Ball Lane, GU10 4SA (off Sandrock Hill Rd via Upper Bourne Lane) SU833444

☼ 11-11; 12-10.30 Sun ☎ (01252) 792108

⊕ thebatandball.co.uk

Dark Star Hophead; Hogs Back TEA; 5 changing beers (sourced locally; often Bowman) Ⓗ

Popular family-owned free house offering six interesting beers, mainly from adjoining counties, alongside excellent reasonably priced food. Craft lager and cloudy cider from the Hogs Back Brewery are available alongside the real ale. A family-friendly front room complements the beamed, panelled and log-fired bar – a cosy inner sanctum for adults. The garden, with children's playground, hosts an annual beer festival. There is a quiz night every Tuesday and the last Thursday in the month is open mic night. Q ☎ ❀ ◑ ◐ ✦ P ⊟ (16,17) ❄ ☎

Bramley

Jolly Farmer ℓ

High Street, GU5 0HB

☼ 11-11; 12-11 Sun ☎ (01483) 893355 ⊕ jollyfarmer.co.uk

Bowman Swift One; Young's Bitter; 6 changing beers (often Cottage, Hammerpot, Long Man) Ⓗ

Privately owned traditional free house in the village centre. The decor is full of character with oak beams creating a cosy, welcoming atmosphere. High-quality food is served – booking is essential for the Sunday lunchtime carvery. The changing beers are from a rota of 12 small breweries, several from Hampshire and Sussex, and usually include a dark brew. Real cider is added during the summer months. Dogs are welcome in the bar but not the restaurant. Easily accessible by bus at all times. ☎ ❀ ◁ ◑ ◐ ✦ ✿ P ⊟ (24,53,63) ❄ ☎

Camberley

Claude du Vall ℓ ✔

77-81 High Street, GU15 3RB

☼ 8am-midnight (1am Fri & Sat) ☎ (01276) 672910

Greene King Abbot; Ruddles Best Bitter; Sharp's Doom Bar; 5 changing beers (often Ascot Ales, Surrey Hills, Windsor & Eton) Ⓗ

A large, modern Wetherspoon strategically placed at the station (and bus stops) end of the High Street. The competitive price of both food and drinks make this is a popular pub at any time of day, starting with breakfast from 8am. The seating area is imaginatively divided into various large and small spaces, some with lounge furniture. The TVs are muted, and generally show news programmes. ❀ ◑ ◐ & ⇌ ✿ ◉ ☎

Crabtree ✔

220 Frimley Road, GU15 2QJ

☼ 11.30-midnight (11 Mon & Wed); 12-11 Sun

☎ (01276) 24875

Brakspear Bitter; Fuller's London Pride; Purity Pure Ubu; Wadworth 6X; 2 changing beers (sourced nationally) Ⓗ

A spacious modern open-plan pub with a large car park, originally built in the late 1950s but since extended and altered. There is outside seating and a large garden. Six cask ales are always available, four ales are regulars and two change. Good-value food deals are on offer all day every day. Cask Ale Club is every Monday when beers are reduced to £2.49 per pint. ☎ ❀ ◑ ◐ & P ⊟ (1) ☎

Caterham

King & Queen ℓ

34 High Street, CR3 5UA (on B2030)

☼ 11-11 (midnight Fri & Sat); 12-11 Sun ☎ (01883) 345438

⊕ kingandqueencaterham.co.uk

Fuller's London Pride, ESB; Gale's Seafarers Ale; 2 changing beers Ⓗ

A friendly welcome awaits you at this popular community pub. Once three cottages, this 400-year-old building became an inn in the 1840s. It features a traditional public bar together with a beamed room containing an inglenook fireplace. A side room contains a dartboard and there is a patio at the rear. Portraits of King William and Queen Mary, after whom the pub is named, adorn the walls. ☎ ❀ ◑ ◐ ✦ P ⊟ ❄ ☎

Chertsey

Thyme at the Tavern ℓ

20 London Street, KT16 8AA (jct of London St and Heriot Rd)

☼ 12-midnight (1am Fri & Sat) ☎ (01932) 479667

⊕ thymeatthetavern.co.uk

Caledonian Flying Scotsman; Courage Best Bitter; 4 changing beers (sourced locally; often Ascot Ales, Hop Art, Windsor & Eton) Ⓗ

Family-run, dog-friendly free house, and previous local CAMRA Pub of the Year. Alongside the regular cask beers, up to three guests, mostly from local microbreweries, are available. Occasional beer festivals are held, usually on a LocAle or regional theme. An extensive range of food is served, with pie night on Wednesday (no food Sat). Friday is live music night. There is a comfortable marquee for smokers. ☎ ❀ ◁ ◑ ◐ & ⇌ ✦ ✿ ❄ ☎

Chobham

White Hart ℓ

58 High Street, GU24 8AA

☼ 11 (9am Sat)-11; 9am-10.30 Sun ☎ (01276) 857580

Brunning & Price Original; 4 changing beers (sourced locally) Ⓗ

Formerly Bluebeckers, the White Hart was refurbished in 2015 and is now free of tie. Brunning & Price Original is a regular, but other beers can come from any of the many local breweries – the aim is to cover a range of styles and strengths across the five beers on offer. There

REAL ALE BREWERIES

Antoine's Westcott (NEW)
Ascot Camberley
Brightwater Claygate
Crafty Brewing Dunsfold
Decent Addlestone (NEW)
Dorking Dorking
Frensham Frensham
Godstone Blindley Heath (NEW)
Hedgedog Virginia Water (NEW)
Hogs Back Tongham
Leith Hill ⌂ Coldharbour
Little Beer Guildford
Oxted Godstone (NEW)
Pilgrim Reigate
Surrey Hills Dorking
Thames Side Staines-upon-Thames (NEW)
Thurstons Horsell
Tillingbourne Shere

are two restaurant areas and a less formal space for drinkers as you enter the pub. A lovely rambling building with interesting nooks and crannies. Q✿☕❶❺P➂➍(73)☮❀ 🛜

Churt

Crossways Inn Ⓛ
Churt Road, GU10 2JS
✪ 11-3, 5-11; 11-11 Fri & Sat; 12-4, 7-10.30 Sun
☎ (01428) 714323 ⊕ weydonian.net/crossways
Arundel Sussex IPA; Courage Best Bitter; Hop Back Crop Circle Ⓗ; **4 changing beers (sourced locally)** Ⓖ
A friendly, welcoming community local with traditional decor and pub furniture. The current beers are displayed on a blackboard and the guest beers are served direct from the cask in the cellar. Good-value, home-made, locally sourced pub food is served at lunchtimes and on a Wednesday evening (no food Sun). The pub has a lovely ambience and village feel at any time of day and is popular with ramblers and cyclists.
✿❶♣Å♠P➂(19)☮

Claygate

Platform 3 Ⓛ
Claygate Station, The Parade, KT10 0PB
✪ 3-9 Thu-Sat; closed Sun-Wed summer; 4-8 Fri & Sat; closed Sun-Thu winter ☎ (01372) 462374
3 changing beers (sourced locally; often Brightwater) Ⓗ
One of the smallest pubs in the UK, but Platform 3 has already established itself as a focal point for the local community. A former coal office at Claygate Station, this is the outlet for locally brewed Brightwater beers. A guest ale from another brewer may sometimes also be available. All seating is outside on the station forecourt under a gazebo. Call before travelling if the weather is inclement, as it may not open. Extra opening times are advertised on social media.
Q✿☕❺⊖➂(K3)☮🛜

Dockenfield

Bluebell Ⓛ ✔
Batts Corner, GU10 4EX (½ mile N of Dockenfield village) SU820410
✪ 12-3, 5.30-11; 12-11 Fri & Sat; 12-7 Sun
☎ (01252) 792801 ⊕ bluebell-dockenfield.com
Frensham Rambler, Forager; Hogs Back TEA; Triple fff Moondance; 1 changing beer (sourced locally) Ⓗ
This rural pub with a cosy fireplace and four real ales is the perfect place to visit after a walk around Alice Holt forest. A good range of food is served from bar snacks to an à la carte menu. Outside there is plenty of parking and a garden with a children's play area for the warmer weather.
Q✿☕❶❺Å♣P☮🛜

Dorking

Cobbett's Real Ales Ⓛ
23 West Street, RH4 1BY (on A25 one-way system E)
✪ 12 (10 Fri & Sat)-8; 12-6 Sun ☎ (01306) 879877
⊕ cobbettsrealales.com
3 changing beers Ⓖ
This excellent off-licence and micropub is a must-visit when in the area. The pub opens at noon and is situated in a tiny back room complete with garden. The number of cask beers varies from

three early in the week to perhaps six at weekends, including some hop-monsters, plus two KeyKeg beers. Draught ciders are available plus, in summer, perry. A large number of interesting bottled beers and ciders is also stocked. A 10 per cent discount is offered on Tuesdays.
Q✿☕❀⇌●➂☮🛜

Cricketers Ⓛ ✔
81 South Street, RH4 2JU (on A25 one-way system W)
✪ 12-11 (midnight Thu & Sat; 12.30am Fri)
☎ (01306) 889938 ⊕ cricketersdorking.co.uk
Fuller's Oliver's Island, London Pride, ESB; Gale's Seafarers Ale; 1 changing beer Ⓗ
Small bare-brick pub with a good mix of customers. The walls in the single L-shaped room are covered with old photographs and adverts. Rugby is popular and when England are playing it is standing-room only with customers watching the terrestrial TV. At the back there is a walled Georgian garden – this is the scene of the pub's May bank holiday and autumn beer festivals. Basic lunches are available weekdays. On Monday evenings a film is shown. Seafarers Ale and Oliver's Island alternate and the guest beer is supplied by Fuller's. ✿☕❶♣➂🛜

Red Bar & Lounge Ⓛ
45 Dene Street, RH4 2DW (off A25 opp post office)
✪ 12-11 (midnight Fri & Sat); 12-10.30 Sun
☎ (01306) 882222
Surrey Hills Shere Drop; 3 changing beers Ⓗ
A welcoming modern lounge bar in a 1920s building set back from the road. It is brightly lit and features an eclectic mix of modern and traditional decor, with a variety of pub tables, comfy sofas and benches. Locally sourced ingredients play a big part in the menu, and food is popular. There is live music on the first Saturday of the month. The guest beers come from local brewers such as Tillingbourne and Dark Star. Outside is a patio garden. ✿☕❶●P➂☮🛜

Dormansland

Old House at Home
63 West Street, RH7 6QP
✪ 12-midnight (1.30am Fri & Sat) ☎ (01342) 836828
⊕ theoldhousedormansland.com
Shepherd Neame Master Brew Ⓖ, **Kent's Best, Spitfire; 1 changing beer** Ⓗ
Originally a pair of Victorian cottages, this friendly local is hidden away on the west side of the village. It comprises a main bar and a small side room where darts and bagatelle are played. To the rear is a small restaurant where good-value pub fare can be found – pizzas are a speciality, cooked in a traditional stone oven. The guest beer, from either a regional or microbrewer, is available Thursday to Saturday. Live music features on the second Friday and third Sunday of the month.
Q✿☕❶❺⇌♣P➂(281)☮🛜

East Molesey

Albion ✔
34-36 Bridge Road, KT8 9HA (off B3379)
✪ 11-midnight; 11-11 Sun ☎ (020) 783 9342
Brakspear Bitter; Fuller's London Pride; 5 changing beers (sourced nationally) Ⓗ
About 400 years old, this open-plan pub can get busy at times. It has a central bar serving separate drinking and dining areas, with comfortable

seating throughout, and a popular restaurant (booking advised for meals). There is pavement seating at the front. The pub is a short walk from Hampton Court Palace and the River Thames. The five changing beers are sourced from throughout the UK and constantly vary. Westons Old Rosie cider is sold. ⌂⌂⌂⌂⌂⌂⌂⌂⌂⌂

Bell Inn ✪

4 Bell Road, KT8 0SS (off B369)
✪ 12-11 (midnight Fri & Sat); 12-10.30 Sun
☎ (020) 8941 0400 ⊕ bell-pub.co.uk
Courage Directors; Greene King IPA; house beer (by Twickenham); 3 changing beers (sourced nationally; often Twickenham) ⊞
This historic coaching inn dates from 1460 and was later East Molesey's first post office. Known locally as the Crooked House, it has many nooks and crannies, one of which houses the dartboard. The 18th-century highwayman Claude Duvalier hid from the Bow Street Runners here and now has a bar named after him. The large garden has a children's play area. Sport is shown on three TVs. Westons cider is sold in summer.
⌂⌂⌂⌂⌂⌂P⌂(411,514)⌂⌂

Egham

United Services Club Ⓛ

111 Spring Rise, TW20 9PE (close to A30 Egham Hill)
✪ 12-11 (midnight Fri & Sat) ☎ (01784) 435120
⊕ eusc.co.uk
Sixpenny 6d Best Bitter; Surrey Hills Ranmore; 3 changing beers (sourced nationally; often Burning Sky, Red Cat, Thurstons) ⊞
A regular winner of CAMRA branch Club of the Year including in 2016. The ever-changing range of guest ales always includes something dark and a good choice of real ciders is served from the cellar. Three beer festivals a year feature an eclectic range of ales, mostly from the newest micros around. Satellite TV and free Wi-Fi are available and live music is hosted on most Saturday evenings. Show a copy of this Guide or CAMRA membership card for entry. ⌂⌂⌂⌂⌂⌂⌂P⌂⌂(71,441,500)⌂

Englefield Green

Happy Man Ⓛ

12 Harvest Road, TW20 0QS (off A30)
✪ 12-11.30 (midnight Fri & Sat); 12-10.30 Sun
☎ (01784) 433265 ⊕ thehappyman1.weebly.com
Hop Back Summer Lightning; 3 changing beers (sourced nationally; often Crouch Vale, Purity, Twickenham) ⊞
Originally two Victorian cottages, the building was converted to a pub serving workers building nearby Royal Holloway College. Refurbished but virtually unchanged, this is a popular haunt for both students and locals. Four handpumps dispense a rapidly changing range of guest ales, sometimes complemented by additional beers on gravity from the cellar. Darts and quiz nights are hosted and food is available all day. The rear patio has a heated smokers' refuge. Local CAMRA Pub of the Year 2015. ⌂⌂⌂⌂⌂⌂(71,441,500)

Epsom

Barley Mow Ⓛ

12 Pikes Hill, KT17 4EA (off A2022)
✪ 12-11.30 (12.30am Fri & Sat); 12-10.30 Sun
☎ (01372) 721044 ⊕ barley-mow-epsom.co.uk
Fuller's Oliver's Island, London Pride, ESB; 1 changing beer (often Fuller's) ⊞
A pleasant old inn, hidden off Upper High Street. It was converted from three cottages some years ago and is now a highly regarded locals' pub. One bar serves many alcoves and other seating areas, with traditional wooden furnishings and leaded windows giving a rustic feel. The Garden Room is available to hire. A secluded garden at the rear has access from the nearby public car park. The changing beers can be from Fuller's or another brewer. ⌂⌂⌂⌂⌂⌂(166)⌂⌂

Jolly Coopers Ⓛ ✪

84 Wheelers Lane, KT18 7SD (off B280 via Stamford Green Rd)
✪ 12-11; 12-8 Sun ☎ (01372) 723222 ⊕ jollycoopers.co.uk
Fuller's London Pride; 4 changing beers (sourced locally) ⊞
On the edge of Epsom Common and the nearest to the wells that once made Epsom a spa town, this pub is more than 200 years old. The decor is modern, with a carpeted bar area to the left and another larger area with polished parquet flooring to the right used mainly for dining. There is a large paved garden at the rear. Changing beers are mainly from micros in Surrey and slightly further afield. Lilley's cider is sold.
Q⌂⌂⌂⌂⌂⌂P⌂(E9)⌂⌂

Rifleman Ⓛ ✪

5 East Street, KT17 1BB (on A24)
✪ 12-11 (midnight Fri & Sat); 12-10.30 Sun
☎ (01372) 721244 ⊕ therifleman.co.uk
Morland Old Speckled Hen; house beer (by Greene King); 3 changing beers (sourced locally) ⊞
Small corner pub in the shadow of a bridge carrying the railway to and from London. It is decorated in a traditional style with wood panelling and two fireplaces, but also has some modern features such as bare brick and high tables at the front. There is a pleasant garden to the rear, which is an oasis of calm close to central Epsom. Old Speckled Hen is replaced by Old Golden Hen in the summer. Children are welcome until 6pm. ⌂⌂⌂⌂⌂⌂

Esher

Wheatsheaf Ⓛ

40 The Green, KT10 8AG
✪ 11-11 (11.30 Fri & Sat); 11-10.30 Sun ☎ (01372) 464014
⊕ wheatsheafesher.co.uk
Harveys Sussex Best Bitter; Sharp's Cornish Coaster; Surrey Hills Shere Drop; 1 changing beer (sourced locally) ⊞
Imposing inn some 200 years old opposite Esher Green. A smart community pub, diners and drinkers alike are looked after with the same friendly service. Following refurbishment throughout, it is comfortably furnished in a modern style, with an open fire in the bar area, oak flooring, a light and spacious dining area and a private dining room. The guest beer changes twice a month. A bicycle rack is provided at the rear. ⌂⌂⌂⌂⌂P⌂⌂⌂

Farnham

Hop Blossom ✪

50 Long Garden Walk, GU9 7HX (between Waitrose and Castle St) SU838469

12-11.30 (12.30am Fri & Sat); 12-11 Sun
☎ (01252) 710770 ⊕ hopblossom.co.uk
Fuller's London Pride, ESB; Gale's Seafarers Ale; 1 changing beer (often Fuller's) Ⓗ
A traditional quintessentially English pub used and loved by some colourful local characters. The staff are always friendly and helpful. Bare floorboards and hops above the bar create a pleasant ambience and in winter the real log fire is warming and welcoming. The paved conservatory area is charming. The pub can be busy when local events are on such as the food festival and carnival.
Q❄❃♣➡❀🌳

Jolly Sailor Ⓛ ✪
64 West Street, GU9 7EH
12-11 (1am Fri & Sat); 12-10.30 Sun ☎ (01252) 719139
Greene King Abbot; Morland Old Speckled Hen; 6 changing beers (sourced locally; often Thurstons, Tillingbourne, Wild Weather Ales) Ⓗ
Ten minutes' walk from the town centre is sufficient to escape the hurly-burly at this warm, friendly, good-value local. A great choice of beers – usually four from nearby microbreweries and four from the Greene King portfolio – are served by knowledgeable bar staff. The thriving darts club meets on alternate Thursdays and there are weekly quizzes. A decked patio captures the evening sun, great for relaxing in the summer.
❄❃🍴❃♣P➡(65)❀🌳

Nelson Arms Ⓛ ✪
50-52 Castle Street, GU9 7JQ
12-11 (midnight Fri & Sat); 12-10.30 Sun
☎ (01252) 712554 ⊕ nelson-arms.co.uk
Andwells Gold Muddler; Draught Bass; Hogs Back TEA; Timothy Taylor Landlord Ⓗ
Originally three farm cottages belonging to the Bishop of Winchester's Estate, this pub has plenty of history. It is named after Admiral Horatio Nelson, who is reputed to have stayed here while visiting Lady Hamilton, who lived nearby. Nowadays, a friendly welcome awaits in traditional surroundings, with an open fireplace and original wooden beams. Good food is served as well as good beer, and there are regular quiz nights, pudding nights, and even a gin night. ❃❃➡❀

Friday Street

Stephan Langton Inn Ⓛ
RH5 6JR TQ12804559
11-11; 11-7 Sun; closed Mon ☎ (01306) 730775
⊕ stephanlangton.pub
Tillingbourne The Source, AONB, Hop Troll; 1 changing beer Ⓗ
Stephan Langton was a local man who became Archbishop of Canterbury in 1206 and was involved in the writing of Magna Carta. The pub is in a beautiful position, hidden away down narrow country lanes and surrounded by National Trust land. The bar is warmed by a real fire and is popular with walkers and cyclists. Excellent food including local game and fish is served in the bar and restaurant. There is a large and attractive garden to the rear. Q❄❃❃♣♣➡P❀🌳

Frimley Green

Rose & Thistle ✪
1 Sturt Road, GU16 6HT

12-11 (midnight Fri & Sat); 12-10.30 Sun
☎ (01252) 834942 ⊕ theroseandthistlefrimleygreen.co.uk
Sharp's Doom Bar; 2 changing beers Ⓗ
A large open-plan pub, furnished in a modern style and subdivided into separate areas with a more secluded conservatory dining space. The regular beer is Doom Bar, plus usually two guest ales from the Mitchells & Butlers list. Food is served throughout the day until 9pm Monday to Saturday, 5pm Sunday, and includes both pub classics and more inventive dishes. The pub is popular with the local community, with monthly live music and two darts teams. ❄❃❃♣P➡(3,11)❀🌳

Godalming

Jack Phillips Ⓛ ✪
48-56 High Street, GU7 1DY
8am-11 (midnight Thu; 1am Fri & Sat) ☎ (01483) 521750
Greene King IPA, Abbot; Sharp's Doom Bar; 7 changing beers (often Langham, Twickenham, Westerham) Ⓗ
Wetherspoon pub, converted from a shop, with a light, airy interior styled to look like an Art Deco ocean liner passenger saloon. It is named after local hero Jack Phillips who was the radio operator on the Titanic. There is a small patio area to the front, overlooking the pavement. Up to seven guest beers supplement the regulars, usually including at least one from a local brewery. A minimum of two real ciders is available. Alcohol is served from 9am. Q❄❃♣❃➡❀🌳

Star Inn ✪
17 Church Street, GU7 1EL
12-11; 11.30-11.30 Thu; 11.30-midnight Fri & Sat
☎ (01483) 417717
Hardys & Hansons Olde Trip Ⓗ**; 9 changing beers (sourced nationally; often Hardys & Hansons)** Ⓗ/Ⓖ
Dating from the 1830s or earlier, the Star has a small public bar at the front and the main rooms to the side, leading to a separate lounge where dogs are welcome and a patio with a smoking area. Up to 10 real ales are stocked, some from the Greene King range, with beer festivals at Easter and Halloween. The pub regularly wins local and regional CAMRA cider awards, with many ciders and perries on the bar. ❃♣❃➡♣❃❀🌳

Guildford

King's Head
27 King's Road, GU1 4JW (on A320 Stoke Road)
11-11 (1am Fri & Sat); 12-10.30 Sun ☎ (01483) 568957
⊕ kingsheadguildford.co.uk
Fuller's London Pride, Bengal Lancer, ESB; 3 changing beers (sourced locally; often Surrey Hills, Tillingbourne, Fuller's) Ⓗ
Also known as King's Head (Stoke Road) as there is another King's Head in Guildford, this is a mid-Victorian street-corner pub, extended more recently, with many different drinking and dining areas served from a central bar. The subtle Alice in Wonderland theme celebrates Charles Dodgson's association with the town. Alongside Fuller's seasonal beer, the guest ale is from a local brewery, most commonly Surrey Hills or Tillingbourne. A range of Belgian bottled beers is also available. Food is served from opening until 10pm (9pm Sun). Acoustic music features on Tuesdays and open mic on Thursdays.
❄❃❃♣❃(London Rd)♣P➡(3,34,35)❀🌳

Robin Hood Ⓛ

38 Sydenham Road, GU1 3RH
✪ 12-11 (midnight Thu-Sat); 12-10.30 Sun
☎ (01483) 826044
6 changing beers (sourced locally) Ⓗ
Attractive small mid-Victorian street-corner pub which has been left isolated following housing clearance in the late '60s. The L-shaped bar offers a sanctuary from the nearby busy high street. There is an interesting choice of beers, usually sourced from microbreweries within 25 miles. Good-value food is served Monday to Friday lunchtimes and evenings, Saturday all day and Sunday lunchtime. Live music features on occasion.
🌳❶➔≠(London Rd)♣🚆🐾🐾🛜

Rodboro Buildings Ⓛ ✅

1-10 Bridge Street, GU1 4SB (opp Friary Centre)
✪ 8am-midnight (1am Mon; 1.45am Fri & Sat); 9am-10.30 Sun ☎ (01483) 306366
Greene King IPA; Hogs Back TEA; Sharp's Doom Bar; 7 changing beers Ⓗ
This JD Wetherspoon pub is spread over three levels in a Grade II-listed former industrial building that was the original home of the Dennis car, and later truck, company. Branded as a Lloyds No.1, it changes character in the evening, with door staff after 9pm and the downstairs dance floor in use, often with live DJs at the weekend. Choose from a range of up to 10 real ales, often from local breweries. 🌳❶🏃♿≠🐾🚆🛜

Hambledon

Merry Harriers Ⓛ

Hambledon Road, GU8 4DR SU967391
✪ 11-3, 5.15-10.30 (11 Wed & Thu; midnight Sat); 12-10.30 Sun summer; 11-3 (not Tue), 5.30-11; 11-3, 4-midnight Fri; 11-11 Sat; 12-8 Sun; closed Mon winter ☎ (01428) 682883
⊕ merryharriers.com
Surrey Hills Shere Drop; 2 changing beers (sourced regionally; often Firebird, Pilgrim, Ringwood) Ⓗ
A stylish yet traditional establishment with a main bar with inglenook fireplace, a small quiet side room to the left and a restaurant/function room to the right. All food (except fish) is sourced from within a 15-mile radius. Llamas can be admired from the large garden or even walked. Live music features monthly on a Saturday. Accommodation is available either in a converted barn or the camping field. Note the reduced opening times in winter.
Q🌳🐾🚐❶AP🐾🛜

Horsell

Crown Ⓛ

104 High Street, GU21 4ST
✪ 12-11 (midnight Fri); 11-midnight Sat ☎ (01483) 771719
⊕ thecrownhorsell.co.uk
4 changing beers (often Thurstons) Ⓗ
A rare find in the area, this is a traditional two-bar 'wet' pub. Four beers are available, one often from Thurstons Brewery whose beers are brewed next door. At other times a local micro is usually represented. An annual beer festival is held at Easter. The large garden has a pétanque piste. Live music features occasionally. 🌳🐾♣P🚆(48)🐾🛜

Knaphill

Royal Oak Ⓛ

Anchor Hill, GU21 2JH

✪ 12-11 (midnight Fri & Sat); 12-10.30 Sun
☎ (01483) 473330 ⊕ royaloakknaphill.co.uk
5 changing beers (often Exmoor, Ringwood, Wye Valley) Ⓗ
An attractive 17th-century community pub with a single bar and separate restaurant area. The new landlords have already built a strong local reputation for the quality and range of their cask ales and home-made food. There are five ever-changing cask beers, often including LocAles from Thurstons, Surrey Hills and Hop Art breweries. Seven real ciders are also available. Ale festivals are held twice a year and a cider festival in May. The large garden has a barbecue.
🌳🐾❶♣●P🚆(91,48)🐾🛜

Leatherhead

Edmund Tylney ✅

30-34 High Street, KT22 8AW
✪ 8am-midnight (1am Fri & Sat) ☎ (01372) 362715
Greene King IPA; Ruddles Best Bitter; 6 changing beers (often Dark Star, Surrey Hills, Twickenham) Ⓗ
This Wetherspoon pub, a former Woolworths store, lies in the heart of the town, a stone's throw from where the defunct Swan Brewery once stood. Named after a local man who was Master of the Revels to Queen Elizabeth I, the pub is typically open plan though a number of glass partitions create a more intimate ambience. The changing beers frequently include offerings from local suppliers such as Tillingbourne, Dark Star, Twickenham and Sambrook's. A range of ciders is also sold. Q🌳🐾❶♿≠●🚆🛜

Running Horse Ⓛ ✅

38 Bridge Street, KT22 8BZ (off B2122)
✪ 11.30-11; 12-10.30 Sun ☎ (01372) 372081
⊕ running-horse.co.uk
Shepherd Neame Master Brew, Kent's Best, Spitfire; Surrey Hills Ranmore; 1 changing beer (sourced regionally) Ⓗ
Overlooking the River Mole, this Grade II* listed two-room pub, dating from 1403, features a real log fire, home-made food and an outside play area for children. The public bar has TV, a pool table and dartboard, and the rear dining area has a patio. Live blues/rock music sessions are hosted once a month on Saturdays, and live jazz plays Sunday lunchtimes. Quiz night is every Tuesday. The changing beers can be either seasonal offerings from Shepherd Neame or from other brewers.
Q🌳🐾❶♿≠♣P🚆(465,478,479)🐾🛜

Limpsfield Chart

Carpenters Arms Ⓛ

12 Tally Road, RH8 0TG (off B269)
✪ 12-11; 11-midnight Thu-Sat; 12-10.30 Sun
☎ (01883) 722209 ⊕ carpenterslimpsfield.co.uk
Westerham Finchcocks Original, British Bulldog, 1965 Special Bitter Ale; 2 changing beers Ⓗ
Westerham Brewery tied house featuring the full range of its beers. The L-shaped bar has parquet flooring and provides ample room for drinkers and diners. Good home-made food is served daily (no food Sun eve). One side of the bar retains a dartboard and the monthly quiz is very popular. The pub is located adjacent to National Trust land, attracting walkers and horse riders. The locals take great pride in this friendly pub.
🌳🐾❶♣P🚆(594)🐾🛜

Lingfield

Star Inn L

Church Road, RH7 6AH

✪ 10-11.30 (1am Sat); 12-10.30 Sun ☎ (01342) 832364
⊕ thestar-lingfield.co.uk

Harveys Sussex Best Bitter; Sharp's Doom Bar; 2 changing beers Ⓗ

Brick-built pub dating from 1938 situated on the edge of the village with a path leading to the station. The L-shaped bar has wood panelling but gradual refurbishment is exposing the original brickwork. Good food is available noon-9.30pm daily. The guest beers vary, with Long Man and Otter always popular. Acoustic music plays on Saturday night. Dominoes can be played inside, giant Jenga out in the garden. Accommodation comprises 12 en-suite rooms.
🕭🕏🛏🌗♣♠P🖵(281,509)🐾 🛜

Lyne

Royal Marine

Lyne Lane, KT16 0AN (off B386 in village centre)

✪ 12-2.30, 5.30-11; 12-3 Sun; closed Sat ☎ (01932) 873900
⊕ royalmarinelyne.co.uk

Ruddles Best Bitter; 2 changing beers (sourced nationally; often Cotleigh, Goff's) Ⓗ

The name of this former beer house, opened in the mid-1800s, commemorates Queen Victoria's review of her troops nearby on Chobham Common in 1853. Royal Marines memorabilila, a large collection of drinking jugs and other bric-a-brac are on display. Guest beers come mainly from microbreweries. Generous portions of home-cooked food are served. Friday is bingo quiz night. Note that the pub is closed Saturdays.
Q🕭🕏🌗P🐾 🛜

Mickleham

King William IV L

4 Byttom Hill, RH5 6EL (behind Frascati restaurant)

✪ 11-11; 12-10.30 Sun ☎ (01372) 372590
⊕ thekingwilliamiv.com

Hogs Back TEA; Surrey Hills Shere Drop; 2 changing beers (sourced locally; often Fuller's, Surrey Hills) Ⓗ

A welcoming, quaint country pub, nestled on a hillside. The main bar is homely with a log fire and there is a smaller bar to the front. An attractive terrace, with some tables under cover, gives stunning views over the Mole Valley. Good home-made food is popular – book ahead for lunch, especially on summer weekends. Steep steps can make access difficult for some. A shared car park is on the A24 southbound. 🕏🌗P🖵(465)🐾 🛜

Newdigate

Surrey Oaks 🏆 L

Parkgate Road, Parkgate, RH5 5DZ (between Newdigate and Leigh) TQ20524363

✪ 11.30-2.30, 5.30-11; 9am-11 Fri & Sat; 9am-9 Sun
☎ (01306) 631200 ⊕ surreyoaks.co.uk

Surrey Hills Ranmore, Shere Drop; 3 changing beers Ⓗ

This attractive 16th-century inn is renowned for its commitment to real ale and has been awarded numerous CAMRA awards. The guest beers always include one dark ale, alongside four ciders and a perry. The main bar features low beams, flagstones and an inglenook fireplace with a log-burning stove. Excellent food is available including home-

made pizzas and daily specials. Outside is a large garden. The Late Spring and August bank holidays beer festivals are always popular.
🕭🕏🌗♣♠P🖵(22,50)🐾

Oxted

Oxted Inn L ✓

Units 1-4 Hoskins Walk, Station Road West, RH8 9HR

✪ 8am-11 ☎ (01883) 723440

Greene King IPA, Abbot; Sharp's Doom Bar; 3 changing beers Ⓗ

Small purpose-built Wetherspoon pub opened in 1997 and just a one-minute walk from the station. The walls display many photographs of former pubs and other buildings of local historic interest. Oxted is on the Greenwich Meridian and the interior is decorated with more than 20 working clocks showing the time in various parts of the world. Guest beers change frequently and are often from local microbreweries. Food is served all day.
Q🕏🕏🌗🛜🖵🛜

Puttenham

Good Intent ✓

60-62 The Street, GU3 1AR

✪ 12-3, 6-11.30 (11 Mon); 12-11.30 Sat; 12-10.30 Sun
☎ (01483) 810387 ⊕ thegoodintentpub.co.uk

Otter Bitter; Sharp's Doom Bar; Timothy Taylor Landlord; 3 changing beers Ⓗ

A 16th-century inn situated in an attractive village nestled under the Hogs Back. The cosy bar with oak beams and an inglenook fireplace is decorated with hops and hop-growing equipment, which serves as a reminder that the largest remaining hop field in Surrey is just 500 yards along The Street. Food is served daily except Sunday and Monday evenings – pie night is Tuesday, and fish and chips night is Wednesday. Q🕏🕏🌗🔺AP🛗🐾 🛜

Redhill

Garland ✓

5 Brighton Road, RH1 6PP (on A23 S of town)

✪ 12-11 (12.30am Fri & Sat) ☎ (01737) 764612

Harveys Sussex XX Mild Ale, IPA, Sussex Best Bitter, Armada Ale; 2 changing beers Ⓗ

Located just south of the town centre, and Harveys' only tied house in Surrey, the Garland is a classic Victorian street-corner local. Alongside the beers listed there are usually another two or three seasonal beers. Darts is popular here, with two boards, and there is a bar billiards table. Good-value food is sold lunchtimes and Friday evenings. Live music plays on some weekends.
🕭🕏🌗🛜♣♠P🖵🐾

Sun L ✓

17-21 London Road, RH1 1LY (on A25 in town centre)

✪ 8am-midnight (1am Fri & Sat) ☎ (01737) 766886

Adnams Ghost Ship; Greene King Abbot; Ruddles Best Bitter; Sharp's Doom Bar; 5 changing beers Ⓗ

A large, modern town-centre Wetherspoon pub a short walk from the railway and bus stations, named to commemorate local astronomer Richard Carrington who built an observatory at Redhill and studied sunspots. It has one large room with a long bar, a raised dining area, a few sofas and a corner allocated to children (families welcome until 6pm). An extensive menu of reasonably priced food is available all day. TVs show major sporting events

but with the sound turned off. The staff are friendly and attentive. There is no garden, but there is a smoking area outside at the front.
Q ⚭ ◐ ❺ ⬆ ≉ ● ❒ ☞

Reigate

Blue Anchor ⓛ ✅

27 West Street, RH2 9BL (on A25)
✪ 12-11; 12-10.30 Sun ☎ (01737) 669497
⊕ blueanchor-reigate.co.uk
Pilgrim Progress; 2 changing beers Ⓗ
Found just off the town centre and a few doors down from the Pilgrim Brewery (from which one beer is always served), the Blue Anchor has a lot going for it, especially in summer, when the large terrace overlooking the Reigate Priory cricket ground comes into its own. Inside is an oak-beamed L-shaped bar. Good home-cooked food is available, with an outside barbecue in the summer. The pub can get busy at weekends. ⊛ ◐ ➤ ❒ 🐾 ☞

Shepperton

Barley Mow ♟ ⓛ

67 Watersplash Road, TW17 0EE (off B376 in Shepperton Green)
✪ 12-11; 12-10.30 Sun ☎ (01932) 225326 ⊕ themow.co.uk
Hogs Back TEA; Hop Back Summer Lightning; 3 changing beers (sourced locally; often Binghams, Hammerpot, Twickenham) Ⓗ
Friendly community local in Shepperton Green to the west of the main village centre. Five handpumps serve regular ales from Hogs Back and Hop Back, plus three guests, usually from microbreweries. Many pumpclips adorn the bar and beams. Entertainment includes live rock or blues bands on Friday and Saturday nights, jazz on Wednesdays, quiz night on Thursdays and charity meat raffles on Sunday afternoons. Outside is a covered and heated patio area for smokers.
⊛ ♣ ● P ❒ (458) 🐾 ☞

Staines-upon-Thames

Bells

124 Church Street, TW18 4ZB (off B376)
✪ 12-4, 5-11; 12-midnight Fri & Sat; 12-11 Sun
☎ (01784) 454240 ⊕ thebellspub.co.uk
Young's Bitter, Special; 2 changing beers (often Arkell's, St Austell) Ⓗ
Friendly, comfortable, 18th-century pub opposite St Mary's Church in a conservation area. It is close to the Thames Path and within easy walking distance of the town centre. Regular beers and seasonals from Charles Wells are available. The pub is noted locally for the quality of its food. The pleasant rear patio garden, with a large heated smokers' canopy, is especially popular in summer, attracting local workers and shoppers. Q ⊛ ◐ ❺

George ✅

2-8 High Street, TW18 4EE (on A308, opp town hall)
✪ 9am-midnight (1am Fri & Sat) ☎ (01784) 462181
Courage Best Bitter; Greene King Abbot; Ruddles Best Bitter; 5 changing beers (sourced nationally; often Adnams, Hogs Back, King Beer) Ⓗ
Ever-popular, two-storey, town-centre Wetherspoon pub built in the 1990s. The spacious downstairs bar with its mixture of tables and intimate booths is always busy but a quieter bar can be reached via a spiral staircase. Up to six guest

ales are dispensed from one bank of handpumps, with the national brands and two real ciders from Westons on the rear bank. A varied selection of foreign bottled beers and ciders is also stocked. Value-for-money pub food is served all day.
◐ ❺ ≉ ● ❒ ☞

Wheatsheaf & Pigeon ⓛ ✅

Penton Road, TW18 2LL (off B376, corner of Wheatsheaf Lane and Penton Rd)
✪ 12-11; 12-10.30 Sun ☎ (01784) 452922
⊕ thewheatsheafandpigeon.co.uk
Fuller's London Pride; Sharp's Doom Bar; 2 changing beers (sourced nationally; often St Austell, Windsor & Eton) Ⓗ
Welcoming and friendly community local between Staines and Laleham, a short walk signposted from the Thames Path and Staines Town FC. Ales often include local micro or West Country guests and good-value food is served every day (no food Mon and Sun eves). There is outside seating front and back plus a covered smoking area. Quiz night is Sunday. Beer festivals are held occasionally. The local bus stops in Laleham Road.
⭑ ⊛ ◐ ❺ ♣ P ❒ (458) 🐾 ☞

Sunbury-on-Thames

Hare & Hounds ⓛ

132 Vicarage Road, TW16 7QX
✪ 11-11; 12-11 Sat; 12-10.30 Sun ☎ (01932) 761478
⊕ hareandhoundssunbury.co.uk
Fuller's London Pride, ESB; 1 changing beer (sourced locally; often Fuller's) Ⓗ
Traditional spotless Fuller's local, with separate areas featuring TV sport and pub games. The enthusiastic landlord is keen to extend the real ale choice and a wide range of Fuller's bottled beers is available. There is a separate dining area (which also hosts the Monday night quiz) and the Sunday carvery lunch is particularly popular. The pub is handy for nearby Sunbury Cross shops, and close to junction 1 of the M3. The 235 bus stops outside, with many more from around the Cross.
⭑ ⊛ ◐ ❺ ≉ ♣ P ❒ (235) 🐾 ☞

Magpie ⓛ ✅

64 Thames Street, TW16 6AF
✪ 12-11; 11-11 Fri & Sat; 12-10.30 Sun ☎ (01932) 782024
⊕ magpiesunbury.com
Greene King IPA; 4 changing beers (sourced locally; often Southwark, Truman's, Twickenham) Ⓗ
Rambling old pub on two levels with one regular and up to four changing real ales, usually from London and other local microbreweries, available in the downstairs bar. Food is served daily, and the outside drinking area overlooks the Thames. The name relates to a horse called Magpie belonging to a member of the Grand Order of Water Rats; a blue plaque commemorates the founding of the entertainment industry charitable organisation here in 1889. ⭑ ⊛ ◐ ♣ ❒ (216) 🐾 ☞

Thames Ditton

Red Lion

85 High Street, KT7 0SF
✪ 11-11 (midnight Fri); 10-midnight Sat; 10-10.30 Sun
☎ (020) 8398 8662
2 changing beers (sourced locally; often By The Horns, Portobello) Ⓗ

Situated near the church, this eclectically styled pub has an island bar surrounded by quirky decor including odd bits of wooden door panels fronting the bar. There is a wooden floor, two open fireplaces and seating in a wide variety of styles. Original mottled leaded windows have mostly been retained. The restaurant is in the conservatory, where vinyl LPs are used as place mats. Food is served all day. ♿⌂🕮❶&P🚇(514,515)✿🛜

Titsey

Botley Hill Farmhouse 🅛

Limpsfield Road, Botley Hill, CR6 9QH (at top of ridge on B269) TQ39495554
☼ 12-11; 12-8.30 Sun ☎ (01959) 577154
🌐 botleyhill-farmhouse.co.uk

Pilgrim Surrey Bitter, Progress; 2 changing beers Ⓖ
Situated on the crest of the North Downs, at 850 feet this is the highest pub in the South-east. It sits above the Titsey Plantation and has splendid views towards London. Built in 1546 as a farmhouse, it became tea rooms in 1936 and a licensed premises in 1994. The pub is multi-roomed and has low-beamed ceilings, flagstones and a real fire (note the Turkish engraved mantelpiece). High-quality food is served with daily specials among the seasonal offerings. ♿⌂🕮❶&●P🚇(595)✿

Tongham

White Hart ▼ 🅛 ✅

76 The Street, GU10 1DH
☼ 12-11 (10.30 Sun & Mon); 12-midnight Fri & Sat
☎ (01252) 782419 🌐 thewhitetartongham.co.uk

Hogs Back TEA; 5 changing beers (often Ballard's, Surrey Hills) Ⓗ
At the heart of the village, the White Hart is used by a cross-section of the community. A three-roomed pub, the rear games room is the liveliest, the listed older room has village photographs on the walls. The pub serves up to seven real ales and a real cider, with one pump dedicated to rotating milds. Live music regularly plays at the weekend. The pub is conveniently sited for visitors to Hogs Back Brewery. No food on Monday. Local CAMRA Pub of the Year 2016. Q♿⌂🕮❶♣●P🚇(3,20)✿🛜

Upper Hale

Alfred Free House

9 Bishops Road, GU9 0JA
☼ 12-2.30, 5.30-11; 12-10.30 Sun ☎ (01252) 820385
🌐 thealfredfreehouse.co.uk

Bowman Wallops Wood Ⓗ; 3 changing beers (sourced nationally; often B&T) Ⓗ/Ⓖ
This friendly local pub, tucked away in a residential area, has a bar area and a restaurant/function room. Up to three guest ales are on offer including one from B&T Brewery. Fresh home-made food, using locally sourced ingredients, is served every day. Two beer festivals are held a year in May and October, and there is live music every month. Q♿❶&♣P🚇(4,5)✿🛜

> Give my people plenty of beer, good beer and cheap beer, and you will have no revolution among them.
> **Queen Victoria**

Walton on Thames

Regent ▼ 🅛 ✅

19 Church Street, KT12 2QP (on A3050)
☼ 8am-midnight (1am Fri & Sat) ☎ (01932) 243980

Greene King Abbot; Ruddles Best Bitter; Sharp's Doom Bar; 8 changing beers (often Dark Star, Thornbridge, Twickenham) Ⓗ
Characterful Wetherspoon conversion of the former Regent cinema, decorated in Art Deco style with wood-surround panelling under the curved ceiling and period lighting. At the far end, steps lead up to a small seating area for customers seeking a more secluded spot. The walls are hung with photos of old Walton plus relics of local connections with the film industry. The pub gets busy at weekends. Gwynt y Ddraig and Westons ciders are supplemented by guests. Alcohol is served from 9am. Q♿⌂🕮❶&●P(461,564)🛜

Warlingham

White Lion ✅

3 Farleigh Road, CR6 9EG (on B269)
☼ 11.30-midnight ☎ (01883) 625085

Brakspear Bitter; Harveys Sussex Best Bitter; Sharp's Doom Bar; 3 changing beers Ⓗ
A very old building, probably dating from 1467, when it was a farmhouse. It has been a pub since at least 1784, from which date the names of its innkeepers have been recorded. The building has been altered many times over the years resulting in a maze of small rooms, mostly with low ceilings. Food is served all day. Guest beers come from the Ember Inns list and tend to be from regional brewers. ♿⌂🕮❶&♣P🚇(357,403,409)✿🛜

Weybridge

Old Crown

83 Thames Street, KT13 8LP (off A317)
☼ 10-11; 12-10.30 Sun ☎ (01932) 842844
🌐 theoldcrownweybridge.co.uk

Courage Best Bitter, Directors; Young's Bitter; 1 changing beer Ⓗ
A Grade II-listed pub with weatherboarded façade that dates back to at least 1729. There are several distinct bar and lounge areas to meet the needs of drinkers and diners. The two gardens are popular in summer, and mooring for small boats is provided at the waterside, which is at the confluence of the River Wey with the Thames. The changing beer varies in source and can be from microbreweries. Food is served every lunchtime, and in the evenings from Wednesday to Saturday. Q♿⌂🕮❶♣P🚇✿🛜

Whyteleafe

Radius Arms

205 Godstone Road, CR3 0EL (on A22)
☼ 4-9.30; 12-10.30 Fri & Sat; 12-5 Sun; closed Mon ☎ 07514 916172

4 changing beers Ⓖ
A friendly micropub which opened in former commercial premises in 2015. The tables were made from display cabinets and the benches recycled from the Olympic Park in London. An ever-changing selection of beers from around Britain is available, with additional ales added on Friday and Saturday. These are usually served straight from the cask but at busy times handpumps may be

used. Around 12 ciders and perries are also sold.
Q✿(Whyteleafe/Upper Warlingham)
●🖪(407,409,434)👣

Woking

Herbert Wells 🅛 ✅
51-57 Chertsey Road, GU21 5AJ
✿ 8am-midnight (1am Fri & Sat) ☎ (01483) 722818
Courage Best Bitter; Fuller's London Pride; Greene King Abbot; Hogs Back TEA; Sharp's Doom Bar; 7 changing beers (sourced nationally) Ⓗ
A range of up to seven guest beers plus eight ciders and perries are available at this popular town-centre Wetherspoon, which is close both to bus and train stations. The busy pub has a varied clientele – shoppers and office workers by day and drinkers young and old in the evening. Note the nod to HG Wells dotted around the walls and ceiling. Q💺◖👌&♿●🖪🛜

Woking Railway Athletic Club
Goldsworth Road, GU21 6JT (behind offices at E end of Goldsworth Rd) TQ003585
✿ 10.30-11 (11.30 Fri & Sat); 12-10.30 Sun
☎ (01483) 598499
2 changing beers Ⓗ
This friendly club can be hard to find the first time you visit but it is worth searching out. Pool, darts and TV sport are popular, which is obvious as soon as you enter; however once at the bar you can see the quieter area beyond. Two ales are always on and sometimes up to four. The beers constantly change and can be from anywhere, with a greater selection at weekends. Food is limited to rolls on Saturday lunchtimes. For entry show a CAMRA membership card or copy of this Guide.
💺♿♣🖪🛜

Woodmansterne

Woodman ✅
Woodmansterne Street, SM7 3NL (on B278)
✿ 12-11 (midnight Fri & Sat); 12-10.30 Sun
☎ (01737) 371841 ⊕ thewoodmanbanstead.co.uk
Sharp's Doom Bar; 3 changing beers Ⓗ

This attractive brick, flint and tile building also has some late-Gothic flourishes on show. Food is served all day with breakfasts available at weekends. Guest beers come from the Stonegate list and change frequently, including ales both from local microbreweries and regional brewers. Cricket can be viewed from both rear and front gardens, and there is a sandpit for children to play in.
💺✿◖👌♣P🖪(166)👣🛜

Worplesdon

Fox
Fox Corner, GU3 3PP
✿ 4-11 (midnight Fri); 2-midnight Sat; 12-10 Sun
☎ (01483) 234024 ⊕ foxinn.org
3 changing beers (often Tillingbourne) Ⓗ
After a period of closure in 2014, the Fox has reopened as an independently owned free house. The pub provides a convivial atmosphere for a drink, with two separate bars featuring low beams and subdued lighting, and a vinyl record player sitting proudly in the right-hand bar. Quality bar snacks such as pork pies and Scotch eggs from local butchers are available. The substantial garden and patio are popular in the summer.
Q💺✿◖P🖪(28,91)👣🛜

Wrecclesham

Sandrock
Sandrock Hill Road, GU10 4NS
✿ 3.45 (12 Sat)-11; 12-10.30 Sun ☎ (01252) 715865
⊕ thesandrock.com
Exmoor Gold; Fuller's London Pride; Hop Back Summer Lightning; Sharp's Cornish Coaster; Triple fff Moondance; 2 changing beers (often Otter) Ⓗ
The Sandrock has a contemporary feel, with heavy wooden furnishings and a comfy lounge with softer seating. Children are admitted to the small side bar which leads to the attractive and partially covered patio garden. The well-kept beer cellar is complemented by a small but carefully chosen wine list. On weekdays the pub opens evenings only. Q💺✿&●P🖪(16,17)👣🛜

Magpie & Stump

This favoured tavern, sacred to the evening orgies of Mr Lowten and his companions, was what ordinary people would designate a public-house. That the landlord was a man of money-making turn was sufficiently testified by the fact of a small bulkhead beneath the tap-room window, in size and shape not unlike a sedan-chair, being underlet to a mender of shoes; and that he was a being of philanthropic mind was evident from the protection he afforded to a pieman, who vended his delicacies without fear of interruption on the very door-step.

In the lower windows, which were decorated with curtains of a saffron hue, dangled two or three printed cards bearing reference to Devonshire cider and Dantzig [sic] spruce, while a large blackboard announcing in white letters to an enlightened public, that there were 500,000 barrels of double stout in the cellars of the establishment, left the mind in a not unpleasing state of doubt and uncertainty as to the precise direction in the bowels of the earth, in which this mighty cavern might be supposed to extend.

Charles Dickens, The Pickwick Papers, 1837. The Magpie & Stump, London EC4, stands opposite the Old Bailey and featured in the TV series Rumpole. Danzig beer was flavoured with spruce cones and twigs.

The Anchor was built in 1465 as a manor house. By the 1800s it was a workhouse but changed to selling beer in the 1860s. It is located in the centre of this village on the edge of Ashdown Forest. Winnie the Pooh writer AA Milne lived nearby. The front bar contains many interesting old pictures, the rear bar features an inglenook fireplace. Excellent food is served all day. An annual beer festival is held the first weekend in May. Q ♿ 🛏 🍴 ◑ ♿ ♣ ♠ P 🚌 (291) 🐾 📶

Hastings

Crown ℒ
64-66 All Saints Street, Old Town, TN34 3BN
🕐 11-11; 11-10.30 Sun ☎ (01424) 465100
🌐 thecrownhastings.co.uk
4 changing beers Ⓗ
Tastefully furnished by local craftsmen, all customers are made to feel welcome here. Local real ales are always present, and cask cider is served in summer. Home-cooked food uses local ingredients and clipboards detail available food and drink, with its sources. A selection of meals of various sizes and types is on the menu. At the front is a small outdoor seating area. On Sundays the premises open at 11am, but alcohol is not served until midday. Q ♿ ◑ ♣ ♠ 🚌 🐾 📶

Dolphin ✔
11-12 Rock-A-Nore Road, Old Town, TN34 3DW
🕐 11-11 (midnight Fri & Sat) ☎ (01424) 431197
Dark Star Hophead; Harveys Sussex Best Bitter; Young's Special; 3 changing beers (sourced nationally) Ⓗ
In the heart of Old Hastings opposite the Jerwood Gallery and famous net huts, this welcoming pub is popular with locals and tourists. CAMRA branch Pub of the Year in 2014, it serves a variety of local and national ales. Fish and chips on Monday evenings and sausage and mash on Wednesday evenings complement lunchtime meals every day except Sunday. Live music is played on Tuesdays, Fridays and Saturdays, and a quiz night on Thursday provides a lively community atmosphere. Q ♿ 🕐 ◑ 🚌 🐾

First In Last Out ℒ
14-15 High Street, Old Town, TN34 3EY (near Stables Theatre)
🕐 12-11 (midnight Fri & Sat) ☎ (01424) 425079
🌐 thefilo.co.uk
FILO Brewery Mike's Mild, Crofters, Churches Pale Ale, Old Town Tom, Cardinal; 2 changing beers Ⓗ
Birthplace of the FILO Brewery, now located a few hundred yards away, this pub has a large single bar dominated by a central open fire and a restaurant to the rear of the building. Located in the heart of Hastings Old Town, it is popular with locals. Six cask beers are dispensed, four from the FILO range and two nationally sourced. Monday night is tapas and Thursday is thali night. Live music features on Tuesdays, Thursdays and occasional Sundays. Q ♿ ♣ 🍴 🚌 🐾 📶

Jenny Lind ℒ ✔
69 High Street, Old Town, TN34 3EW
🕐 12-11 (midnight Fri & Sat) ☎ (01424) 421392
🌐 jennylindhastings.co.uk
Caledonian Deuchars IPA; Courage Directors; Franklins Mumma Knows Best; Long Man Long Blonde; Theakston Old Peculier; 5 changing beers Ⓗ

Ten handpumps with local and countrywide beers give this pub one of the best real ale choices in the area. Two changing real ciders are served from casks on the bar. There is loud live music at weekends. The pub operates a loyalty scheme from October until the end of March. A separate function room hosts a regular range of events, from music to slot car racing. There is a terraced garden behind the pub which is delightful in warm weather. Q ♿ 🛏 🍴 ◑ ♣ ♠ 🚌 🐾 📶

White Rock Hotel ℒ
White Rock, TN34 1JU (opp pier)
🕐 10-11; 12-11 Sun ☎ (01424) 422240
🌐 thewhiterockhotel.com
4 changing beers Ⓗ
Friendly hotel adjacent to the White Rock Theatre with a modern, spacious bar with plenty of seating, plus a terrace overlooking the seafront and the pier. Open for non-residents, there are four beers on offer from various independent Sussex breweries. A good range of freshly prepared hot and cold food is available until 10pm. Many of the en-suite guest rooms have sea views; the best are on the first floor, complete with balconies. Q ♿ 🛏 ◑ ⇌ ♠ 🚌 🐾 📶

Hove

Neptune Inn ℒ
10 Victoria Terrace, BN3 2WB (on coast road E of King Alfred leisure complex)
🕐 12-1am (2am Fri & Sat); 12-midnight Sun
☎ (01273) 736390 🌐 theneptunelivemusicbar.co.uk
Dark Star Hophead; Greene King Abbot; Harveys Sussex Best Bitter; 2 changing beers (sourced locally) Ⓗ
Five handpumps serve regular favourites plus changing guest ales, always in good condition. This traditional single-bar pub is frequented by a local clientele. Live music is strongly supported, with blues and rock every Friday and jazz on Sunday, together with monthly open mic and vinyl nights on the second and fourth Mondays. This pub is on the Brighton to Shoreham coast road near central Hove. The interior features music-related pictures, posters and other memorabilia. 🚌 (700) 🐾 📶

Sussex Cricketer ✔
Eaton Road, BN3 3AF
🕐 11-midnight ☎ (01273) 771645
Brakspear Bitter; Harveys Sussex Best Bitter; 6 changing beers (sourced regionally) Ⓗ
A stylish single-bar Ember Inn sitting right next to the county cricket ground at Hove. Up to eight real ales are on offer, including beers from Sussex and nationally sourced regional brewers – try before you buy on all ales. Cask Club is all day on Mondays – all real ales at £2.49. Quizzes are held on Tuesdays and Sundays. There is a good selection of food, with various meal deals on different days of the week. ♿ 🕐 ◑ ♿ P 🚌 📶

Watchmaker's Arms
84 Goldstone Villas, BN3 3RU
🕐 12-2, 5-9 (11 Fri); 12-11 Sat; 12-3 Sun; closed Mon
☎ (01273) 776307
5 changing beers (sourced regionally) Ⓖ
A micropub conversion from a former shop. A minimum of five beers are dispensed by gravity from a cool room behind the bar, and there is a microbrewery on site. The main theme, as may be inferred from the name, is clocks; look for the

Captain Scarlet and Thunderbirds ones. Other decorations include hops strung from the ceiling, hunting horns, and so on; that wild boar must have been travelling at a fair speed! Bar snacks, including cold pies, are served. A selection of real ciders is available. Q⇌●🚲🚃(7,21)🐾

Westbourne

90 Portland Road, BN3 5DN
✪ 12-11 (midnight Fri & Sat) ☎ (01273) 823633
⊕ thewestbournehove.co.uk
4 changing beers (sourced locally; often Dark Star, Downlands, Franklins) Ⓗ
Formerly the Aldrington, this large Victorian two-bar pub is at the corner of Portland Road and Westbourne Road. There is covered external seating along the Westbourne Road frontage, together with a patio seating area at the rear. The main bar serves a varied range of local Sussex beers from four handpumps, and there are usually at least six real ciders from the cider shack. Food, cooked to order from the menu, is available, with burgers a speciality. 🚃🌣🍴⇌●🚃(2,46,49)🐾

Icklesham

Queen's Head

Parsonage Lane, TN36 4BL (opp village hall)
✪ 11-11; 12-10.30 Sun ☎ (01424) 814552
⊕ queenshead.com
Greene King IPA, Abbot; Harveys Sussex Best Bitter; 3 changing beers (sourced locally) Ⓗ
Fabulous 17th-century inn tucked away just off the A259. It has been in the Guide for over 30 consecutive years. The three changing ales are from local breweries and at least one real cider is always available. There are open fires in each bar and it has a garden with distant views towards Winchelsea and Rye. Excellent, good-value home-made food is served seven days a week. There is live music on Sunday afternoons and a pub quiz every Wednesday evening. 🚃🌣🍴♣●P🚃(100)🐾☎

Robin Hood Ⓛ

Main Road, TN36 4BD (on A259, W end of village)
✪ 11-3, 6-11; 11-11 Fri & Sat; 12-10.30 Sun
☎ (01424) 814277 ⊕ robinhoodicklesham.co.uk
Greene King IPA; 5 changing beers (sourced nationally) Ⓗ
Multi award-winning locals' pub with a warm, friendly atmosphere and a magnificent open fire. There is an extensive collection of copper and brass built up over 20 years and polished by the landlord. Six ales and at least two ciders are served. A large dining area to the rear offers locally sourced, home-cooked food. The pub hosts league-winning pool and pétanque teams and is the home of the local bonfire society. The large garden includes a children's play area. Q🚃🌣🍴♣●P🚃(100)🐾☎

Isfield

Laughing Fish Ⓛ ✔

Station Road, TN22 5XB (off A26 between Lewes and Uckfield)
✪ 11.30-11 ☎ (01825) 750349 ⊕ laughingfishonline.co.uk
Greene King IPA; Hardys & Hansons Olde Trip; Morland Old Golden Hen; 3 changing beers (sourced locally; often Burning Sky, Gun, Isfield) Ⓗ
Formerly the Half Moon, then the Station Hotel, this 1860s pub is next to the preserved Lavender

Line. World War II brought the custom of Canadian troops, not without incident. In the 1950s it was the HQ of the District Angling Club, the probable origin of the present name. Practically the brewery tap to Isfield Brewing Co, it combines the Greene King portfolio and guest beers from other Sussex breweries. It does good pub food and has a range of games including bar billiards. 🚃🌣🍴👶A♣●P🚃(29, 29B)🐾☎

Lewes

Black Horse ✔

55 Western Road, BN7 1RS
✪ 12-11; 12-10.30 Sun ☎ (01273) 473653
⊕ theblackhorselewes.co.uk
Burning Sky Plateau; Greene King Abbot; Morland Old Speckled Hen; 5 changing beers (sourced regionally; often Greene King) Ⓗ
This spacious pub, with large bay windows, is a great all-rounder and has much to offer visitors. Burning Sky Plateau is one of the four regular ales on tap, together with three guest ales. Biddenden's Bushels Cider is on handpump and there are speciality gins. A wide-ranging menu includes tapas and six flavours of home-made pork scratchings. Quiz nights are held fortnightly on Sundays and there is televised sport. Pub games include toad in the hole, bar billiards and shuffleboard. 🚃🌣🚪🍴👶♣●🚃(28,29)🐾☎

Brewers Arms Ⓛ

91 High Street, BN7 1XN (near Lewes Castle)
✪ 10-11; 12-10.30 Sun ☎ (01273) 475524
⊕ brewersarmslewes.co.uk
Harveys Sussex Best Bitter; 4 changing beers (sourced regionally) Ⓗ
Genuine family-run free house catering for most tastes in its two bars. At the front, the comfortable saloon offers a range of seating with books and games available. The rear bar has a pool table and two TVs show sporting events. It is popular on match days with Lewes FC, Brighton & Hove Albion and away fans. Food, including traditional breakfasts, is served until 8pm. The exterior proclaims the former owners, Page and Overton's, Brewers of Croydon. Q🌣🍴⇌♣●🚃(28,29)🐾☎

Elephant & Castle Ⓛ

White Hill, BN7 2DJ (off Fisher St, near old police station)
✪ 11.30-11 (midnight Fri & Sat); 12-11 Sun
☎ (01273) 473797 ⊕ elephantandcastlelewes.com
Harveys Sussex Best Bitter; 3 changing beers (sourced locally) Ⓗ
Built in 1838 to provide accommodation and stabling for a new road into the town, the Elly is a spacious community-based pub, home to one of the famous Lewes bonfire societies and a Saturday folk club. Major sporting events, including the Rugby Six Nations, are shown on a large-screen TV. The pub has a large function room available for hire. The changing guest beers are usually from a Sussex brewer and the food is locally sourced. 🌣🍴⇌♣●🚃(127,132)☎

Gardener's Arms 🍺 Ⓛ

46 Cliffe High Street, BN7 2AN
✪ 11-11; 12-10.30 Sun ☎ (01273) 474808
Harveys Sussex Best Bitter; 5 changing beers (sourced regionally; often Harveys) Ⓗ
Small, genuine free house in the heart of Lewes, near Harveys brewery. Five changing guest ales are dispensed, generally from small breweries all over

the country. Harveys seasonal ales and one-off brews often feature. Bottled and draught cider is sold. Food consists of locally made pies and pasties. A Guide and ale trail regular, it is popular with Brighton and Lewes FC fans on match days. No children allowed. Local CAMRA Pub of the Year 2014 and 2016. ≈♣🚲🚌(28,29)🐾🛜

John Harvey Tavern 🅛 ✅
Bear Yard, BN7 2AS (opp Harveys Brewery)
🕐 11-11; 12-10.30 Sun ☎ (01273) 479880
🌐 johnharveytavern.co.uk
Harveys Sussex Best Bitter Ⓗ/Ⓖ**, Armada Ale** Ⓗ**; 2 changing beers (sourced locally; often Harveys)** Ⓗ/Ⓖ
Harveys tied house opposite the brewery shop dispensing beers on handpump and gravity. A warm welcome is assured in this modern pub built in a former stable block beside the River Ouse. The venue has three separate areas: a main bar, a quieter room on the same level, and an upstairs restaurant/function room. There is folk music on the second Tuesday of each month. Children are only allowed in the restaurant. The pub is dog-friendly (on leads please). Q🐕🏶🌓≈🚌(28,29)🐾

Lewes Arms ✅
1 Mount Place, BN7 1YH
🕐 11-11 (midnight Fri & Sat); 12-11 Sun ☎ (01273) 473152
🌐 lewesarms.co.uk
Fuller's London Pride; Gale's HSB; Harveys Sussex Best Bitter; 3 changing beers (sourced regionally; often Fuller's) Ⓗ
In the heart of the county town, the pub is a traditional alehouse popular with visitors and locals alike. Fuller's beers are served plus Harveys Best and a guest. It is home to the world pea throwing championship, dwyle flunking matches, spaniel racing and other unusual events. An annual pantomime is held in March in the upstairs function room in aid of a local charity. Home-made food is served every day (times vary).
Q🐕🏶🌓≈♣🚌(28,29)🐾🛜

Rights of Man 🅛 ✅
179 High Street, BN7 1YE
🕐 11-11; 12-10.30 Sun ☎ (01273) 486894
🌐 rightsofmanlewes.com
Harveys IPA, Sussex Best Bitter; 4 changing beers (sourced locally; often Harveys) Ⓗ
Refurbished in 2012, this pub now sports dark oak-panelled walls and etched glass screens on the booths. An entrance from the alley at the side of the pub leads to the Martyr's Bar. The front bar is the place for the highly recommended dining. There is an Astroturf-covered roof terrace to the rear with a view of the castle. Six handpumps dispense a range of Harveys ales, often including mild. 🏶🌓≈🚌(28,29)🐾🛜

Snowdrop Inn 🅛 ✅
119 South Street, BN7 2BU
🕐 12-midnight; 12-11 Sun ☎ (01273) 471018
Burning Sky Plateau; Harveys Sussex Best Bitter; 4 changing beers (sourced locally; often Burning Sky) Ⓗ
On the outer edge of the Cliffe area of this historic town, the Snowdrop is a popular and welcoming free house serving six cask ales, one cider and a selection of bottled beers. With UK and continental beers on tap, the pub has a central bar plus an additional upstairs seating area, where darts and toad in the hole can be played. Serving good home-cooked food using locally sourced produce, it

is family-friendly, with retro sweets for the kids and two outside drinking areas.
🐕🏶🌓≈♣🚲🚌(28,29)🐾🛜

Litlington

Plough & Harrow 🅛
The Street, BN26 5RE
🕐 11-11; 12-11 Sun ☎ (01323) 870632 🌐 thepandh.co.uk
Long Man Long Blonde, Best Bitter, American Pale Ale; 2 changing beers (sourced locally; often Long Man) Ⓗ
Historic, picturesque village free house in the South Downs National Park which acts as the tap for the nearby Long Man Brewery. A spacious main bar, featuring comfortable seating for both drinkers and diners, leads to a small snug with an inglenook fireplace to the front and an attractive garden with seating to the rear. Home-cooked food is available, with an emphasis on local produce; also local are five ales and a cider. A beer festival takes place on the August bank holiday. 🐕🏶🌓◗🐾P🚌🐾🛜

Milton Street

Sussex Ox 🅛
BN26 5RL
🕐 11.30-3, 5.30-11; 11.30-11 Sat; 12-10.30 Sun
☎ (01323) 870840 🌐 thesussexox.co.uk
Harveys Sussex Best Bitter; 2 changing beers Ⓗ
Hidden away above the Cuckmere Valley, this pretty and traditionally decorated pub has a lot to offer walkers and gastronomes alike. The spacious pub, with separate bar, restaurant and function room, has a large garden offering stunning views of the surrounding South Downs. The restaurant has been nominated for several awards, with many of the ingredients sourced from its own farm nearby. Three ales are sold, two of which are usually local; a fourth handpump offers local cider. Q🐕🏶🌓◗♣🐾P🐾🛜

Newhaven

Hope Inn ✅
West Pier, BN9 9DN
🕐 11-10.30 (midnight Wed, Fri & Sat) ☎ (01273) 515389
Harveys Sussex Best Bitter; 2 changing beers (sourced regionally) Ⓗ
Spacious pub at the far end of Newhaven with a covered balcony overlooking the harbour entrance, and close to Newhaven Fort. The interior has a timber-panelled beamed ceiling, a timber-panelled bar, walls and polished timber floors. Look out for the stained-glass panels, the multitude of nautical themed pictures and the flag signals on the ceiling beams. Heed the sign warning you against feeding the pub dog. Quiz night is Wednesday. Home-cooked food is served every day. It has a raised patio smoking area at the front. ◗♣🐾P🚌🐾

Newick

Crown Inn 🅛 ✅
22 Church Road, BN8 4JX
🕐 3-11 Mon; 11-11.30; 12-10.30 Sun ☎ (01825) 723293
🌐 thecrownatnewick.co.uk
Harveys Sussex Best Bitter; 2 changing beers (sourced regionally) Ⓗ
Family-run free house at the southern end of the village, near the post office. The 121 bus stops just round the corner. There is a central bar with two

smaller rooms off to either side and a pleasant garden to the rear. Good-value meals are served using local produce. With two other pubs on the village green, Newick is well worth a whole afternoon's stay, but do not miss the last bus! ⛲🍴🕪♣🖙P🖵(31,121)🐾🛜

Portslade

Stag's Head

35 High Street, Old Portslade, BN41 2LH
�⚙ 12-3, 4.30-11; 12-11.30 Fri & Sat; 12-10.30 Sun
☎ (01273) 417337
Harveys Sussex Best Bitter; Long Man American Pale Ale; 3 changing beers (sourced nationally; often Brains, Goddards) Ⓗ
Originally the Bull, this pub dates from the 16th century. It stands in the shadow of John Dudne's magnificent 1881 brewery to which it was allegedly linked by a tunnel fitted with rails to allow the rolling of barrels. The brewery was closed in 1930. The pub was enlarged in 1959 with the adjacent cottage becoming the saloon bar. The interior shows little sign of the pub's age, but some evidence of Watneyisation remains.
Q⛲🍴♣🖙(1,1A)🐾🛜

Stanley Arms

47 Wolseley Road, BN41 1SS (on corner of Wolseley Rd and Stanley Rd)
�⚙ 3 (4 Mon & Tue)-11; 12-11 Sat; 12-10.30 Sun
☎ (01273) 430234 🌐 thestanley.com
7 changing beers (sourced regionally; often Downlands, Hop Back, St Austell) Ⓗ
Beer festivals feature in spring, summer and autumn at this family-run free house, and reduced price cellar nights with free nibbles are held every second Monday. A changing range of UK beers is served from seven handpumps, and there are UK and imported bottled and real ciders on draught. It has a football team, sport on HD TV, weekly quiz and crib evenings, occasional live music and talks by sporting personalities. A stained-glass tiled canopy hangs over the bar. Named after Henry Morton Stanley of 'Doctor Livingstone, I presume' fame. Q⛲🍴♣🖙🖵(2,46)🐾🛜

Rotherfield

King's Arms Ⓛ

High Street, TN6 3LJ
�⚙ 12-midnight; 12-10.30 Sun ☎ (01892) 853441
Harveys Sussex Best Bitter; 2 changing beers (sourced nationally) Ⓗ
This 17th-century half-timbered building, hung with red tiles, was originally a tithe barn and became a pub in 1731. The cosy interior has two beamed bars – the one at the front has an inglenook fireplace, the rear bar has a dining area. An outside terrace with excellent views of the Sussex Weald is popular in summer. There is disabled access to the front bar and toilets only. ⛲🍴🕪&♣P🖵(252)🐾🛜

Rottingdean

Queen Victoria Ⓛ ✅

54 High Street, BN2 7HF
�⚙ 12-11 (midnight Fri & Sat); 12-10.30 Sun
☎ (01273) 302121 🌐 thequeenvic.co.uk

Harveys Sussex Best Bitter; Long Man Long Blonde; 4 changing beers (sourced locally; often 360 Degree Brewing, Goldstone, Long Man) Ⓗ
Striking mock-Tudor pub built in the 1930s to replace the original opposite. The deep, welcoming single bar is softly lit, with period decor. An old harmonium stands majestically in contrast to gentle jazz background music which goes live on Saturday afternoons. Food is home-cooked and locally sourced where possible and is reasonably priced, with inventive menu choices. A range of great local beers together with three real ciders is dispensed with knowledge and enthusiasm. ⛲🍴🕪♣🖙🖵🐾🛜

Rye

Globe Inn Marsh Ⓛ

10 Military Road, TN31 7NX
�⚙ 8am-11 ☎ (01797) 225220 🌐 globeinnmarshrye.com
Harveys Sussex Best Bitter; house beer (by Tonbridge); 2 changing beers (sourced locally) Ⓗ
A fantastic open fire is the centrepiece of this small, creatively designed and furnished, food-oriented pub, built about 1834. There is a unique open-plan bar offering mainly local beers from five handpumps and a selection of real ciders. Good-quality meals are served including wood-fired oven pizzas and locally sourced meats and fish. Breakfasts are available from 8am. There are unisex toilets and a covered outdoor area decorated with lobster pots and fishing nets. Disabled access is via the entrance from the car park. ⛲🍴🕪&≠🖙🖵(100,344)🐾🛜

Ypres Castle Inn Ⓛ ✅

Gun Gardens, TN31 7HH
�⚙ 12-11 (midnight Fri); 12-10.30 Sun ☎ (01797) 223248
🌐 yprescastleinn.co.uk
Harveys Sussex Best Bitter; 4 changing beers Ⓗ
Known as The Wipers, this attractive weatherboarded pub, built in 1640, is accessible from the steps adjacent to the Ypres Tower. There is one large bar with an open fire. Changing ales are usually from Adnams, Larkins, Old Dairy and Westerham, while the cider is Biddenham Bushels. It has fantastic views across Romney Marsh and a large garden with an outdoor bar and music during Wipers Weekends in August. The excellent menu includes locally sourced seafood. An atmospheric location particularly at night, the outside drinking areas include space on the ramparts at the front. Closed winter Mondays.
Q⛲🍴🕪≠🖙🖵(100,344)🐾🛜

St Leonards on Sea

North Star Inn ✅

Clarence Road, TN37 6SD
�⚙ 11-midnight (1am Fri); 12-midnight Sun
☎ (01424) 436576
Harveys Sussex Best Bitter; Timothy Taylor Landlord; 3 changing beers Ⓗ
Friendly local just off the main Bohemia Road. The changing beers are sourced both locally and nationally. The large U-shaped bar has an open fire and is decorated with railway memorabilia. There is a meat raffle on Sundays, a cheese raffle on Saturdays, a monthly bingo night, a quiz night and occasional live music. Although food is not usually available, there is a popular curry evening on Wednesdays. Q🍴♣🖙🖵(99,100)🐾🛜

Tower 🏆
251 London Road, TN37 6NB
⏲ 11-11.30 (12.30am Fri & Sat); 11-11 Sun
☎ (01424) 721773
Dark Star Hophead, American Pale Ale; 4 changing beers (sourced locally) 🄷
A recipient of several CAMRA branch awards, the Tower is a traditional hostelry, showing football and other live sporting events on HD TV. It has seven handpumps dispensing reasonably priced real ales, including five changing guests, at least one of which is usually a dark beer. The wood-burning stove adds to the cosy atmosphere in winter. The excellent staff are welcoming and one reason this pub was voted Sussex CAMRA Pub of the Year 2015. ♣🍎🥛🚌🐾📶

Salehurst

Salehurst Halt 𝕃
Church Lane, TN32 5PH (by church)
⏲ 12-11; closed Mon ☎ (01580) 880620
🌐 salehursthalt.co.uk
Harveys Sussex Best Bitter; 2 changing beers 🄷
Salehurst Halt is a typical village inn, located next to the church. It has a changing selection of ales, at least one from a local brewery. On summer Wednesday evenings customers can order freshly baked pizza from an outdoor oven. The Halt serves good-quality locally sourced and home-cooked food. The choice of cider varies, usually sourced from Biddenden and East Stour. There is a strong community focus and the pub is popular with locals and walkers. **Q**🐴❀◐◑♿🍎🐾📶

Seaford

Wellington Hotel 𝕃 ✔
33 Steyne Road, BN25 1HT
⏲ 12-11 (midnight Fri & Sat); 12-10 Sun ☎ (01323) 899517
🌐 thewellington-hotel.com
Dark Star Hophead, American Pale Ale; Long Man Best Bitter; 7 changing beers (sourced nationally; often Moorhouse's, Springhead, Timothy Taylor) 🄷
Previously known as the New Inn, this 18th-century pub is built on the site of what used to be the quayside of this former Cinque Port, the port being closed in the 19th century. This fine building is now a well-maintained hotel. The main bar serves 10 ales, with at least four beers conditioning – check the high-tech screen – plus various ciders. Food deals are on offer together with 3-star B&B.
Q🐴🛏◐◑⇌🍎🚌(12,12A)🐾📶

Uckfield

Alma Arms 𝕃 ✔
65 Framfield Road, TN22 5AJ (on B2102)
⏲ 11-11 (11.30 Fri & Sat); 12-10.30 Sun ☎ (01825) 762232
🌐 alma-arms.co.uk
Harveys Sussex XX Mild Ale, Sussex Best Bitter; 2 changing beers (often Harveys) 🄷
Harveys pub about five minutes' walk from the town centre, station and buses. The large main bar has smaller seating areas and there are independent meeting/function rooms. A separate area houses traditional games including toad in the hole. There is no food Monday or Tuesday but on Saturday evening Thai food is a speciality and on Sunday roasts are served 12-4pm. XX Mild is available all year round and the cider is Thatchers Heritage. **Q**❀◐◑♿⇌♣🍎**P**🚌(31)🐾

Upper Hartfield

Gallipot Inn 𝕃
Gallipot Street, TN7 4AJ
⏲ 11-11 ☎ (01892) 770008 🌐 the-gallipot-inn.co.uk
Harveys Sussex Best Bitter; Larkins Traditional Ale; 1 changing beer (sourced locally) 🄷
Traditional 16th-century pub in Winnie the Pooh country. There is a welcoming log fire in winter and an attractive garden in summer. Local cask ales are always available and locally sourced freshly cooked food is served. The pub's name comes from the fact that Gallipots (a type of ointment jar) were made in an adjoining cottage (while the opposite end of the pub housed a clockmaker).
Q❀◐◑⛺♣**P**🚌(291)🐾📶

Westfield

New Inn
Main Road, TN35 4QE
⏲ 12-11 (11.30 Sat); 12-6 Sun ☎ (01424) 752800
🌐 newinnwestfield.com
5 changing beers 🄷
Reopened under new management after a complete renovation in 2015, this village pub serves up to five real ales, often from Harveys and Rother Valley, together with beers from other local, regional and national breweries. Home-cooked, locally sourced food, offered at good prices, is popular with locals and visitors alike (booking advisable). Family run, it is warmed by a log fire on cold days, and has a welcoming, friendly atmosphere. Closed Mondays in January and February. **Q**🐴❀◐◑♿**P**🚌(2,342)🐾📶

Wivelsfield Green

Cock Inn 𝕃
North Common Road, RH17 7RH (900yds E of B2112)
⏲ 12-11; 12-10.30 Sun ☎ (01444) 471668
🌐 cockinn-wivelsfield.co.uk
Harveys Sussex Best Bitter; 2 changing beers (sourced locally; often Harveys) 🄷
A two-bar pub on the eastern edge of the village, popular with walkers, cyclists and locals alike. More frequent buses are available at the other end of the village. Two guest beers supplement the Harveys, and in summer real cider is available. There is a large garden/seating area to the front and a smaller outdoor area to the side. The recently refurbished lounge bar has a timber-panelled bar counter. Look for the cow bell!
Q🐴❀◐◑♣**P**🚌(166,167,168)🐾📶

SUSSEX (WEST)

Amberley

Bridge Inn 𝕃 ✔
Houghton Bridge, BN18 9LR (on B2139 just W of railway bridge at Amberley station)
⏲ 11-11; Sun 12-9 ☎ (01798) 831619
🌐 bridgeinnamberley.com
Harveys Sussex Best Bitter; Timothy Taylor Landlord; 1 changing beer (often Langham) 🄷
Delightful Grade II-listed, family-run venue set in the South Downs National Park, with stunning views across the Arun Valley towards Arundel. The cosy bar has an open fire and offers three well-kept ales. A menu of locally sourced, home-cooked food can be served in the bar or its side room and in the

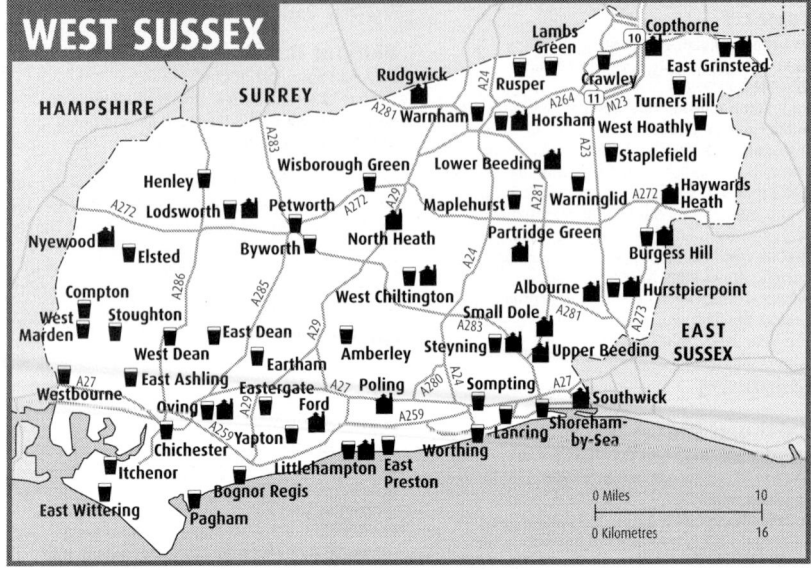

WEST SUSSEX

HAMPSHIRE
SURREY
Lambs Green
Copthorne
Rudgwick
Rusper
Crawley
East Grinstead
Turners Hill
Warnham
Horsham
West Hoathly
Wisborough Green
Lower Beeding
Staplefield
Henley
Lodsworth
Petworth
Maplehurst
Warninglid
Haywards Heath
Nyewood
Elsted
Byworth
North Heath
Partridge Green
Burgess Hill
Compton
Stoughton
West Chiltington
Albourne
Hurstpierpoint
West Marden
East Dean
Small Dole
EAST SUSSEX
West Dean
Eartham
Amberley
Steyning
Upper Beeding
Westbourne
East Ashling
Eastergate
Poling
Sompting
Southwick
Oving
Ford
Shoreham-by-Sea
Chichester
Yapton
Lancing
Itchenor
Littlehampton
East Preston
Worthing
East Wittering
Bognor Regis
Pagham

0 Miles 10
0 Kilometres 16

garden. Access to nearby Amberley Working Museum and Amberley railway station is via a short footpath leading from the garden.
Q ☼ ⊛ ◑ ⇌ ● P ⊟ (73) ❀ ☎

Sportsman L

Rackham Road, BN18 9NR (½ mile E of village, signposted off B2139)
🕐 11-11; Sun 12-10.30 ☎ (01798) 831787
⊕ thesportsmanamberley.com
Harveys Sussex Best Bitter; 3 changing beers (sourced locally; often Greyhound) Ⓗ
This 17th-century inn is worth the walk from Amberley railway station. The Sportsman offers a changing selection of ales on its four handpumps, always including two local beers. There is a central bar serving three separate rooms. From the dining room/conservatory and exterior decking there are stunning views of the Amberley Wild Brooks and Arun Valley flood plain. Binoculars are provided to help spot the wildlife. A warming log fire burns during the colder months.
Q ☼ ⊛ ⊟ ◑ P ⊟ (73) ❀ ☎

Bognor Regis

Hatters L ◉

2-10 Queensway, PO21 1QT (at W end of High St opp Iceland)
🕐 8am-midnight (1am Fri & Sat) ☎ (01243) 840206
Greene King Abbot; Sharp's Doom Bar; changing beers (sourced locally; often Arundel, Langham, Ringwood) Ⓗ
Large town-centre Wetherspoon that was formerly a Sainsbury's store, part of a concrete '60s retail development at one end of the main shopping street. The usual JDW beer range of regulars plus changing guests (usually from local micros) can be found, plus good-value food all day. A small patio garden at the rear has space for drinkers and smokers. Public parking is available in Queensway car park or the adjacent multi-storey.
☼ ⊛ ◑ ♿ ⇌ ● ⊟ ☎

Burgess Hill

Quench Bar & Kitchen L

2-4 Church Road, RH15 9AE
🕐 9am-11 (12.30am Fri; 1am Sat); 10-10.30 Sun
☎ (01444) 253332 ⊕ quenchbar.co.uk
Harveys Sussex Best Bitter; 2 changing beers (sourced locally; often Downlands, Franklins, Kissingate) Ⓗ
Within sight of the railway station, this bar occupies a location at the top end of the town's original shopping street. It comprises a bar area together with a comfortable lounge. Quality local beers prevail, together with a range of bottled beers, spirits, teas and espresso coffees. Occasional live music events and beer festivals are held. A limited number of tables and chairs are provided outside. All buses that serve Burgess Hill pass by the door.
◑ ⇌ ⊟ ☎

Byworth

Black Horse Inn L

The Street, GU28 0HL (head E from Petworth on A283 for about 1 mile, then left into The Street) SU987211
🕐 12-11; 12-8.30 Sun ☎ (01798) 342424
⊕ theblackhorseatbyworth.com
Flowerpots Bitter; Fuller's London Pride; 2 changing beers (sourced locally) Ⓗ
Friendly unspoilt village pub dating from 1791, voted as the local CAMRA branch Pub of the Year for 2015. As well as a choice of beers from four handpumps, locally sourced food, including game and fish, is on offer. One of the old stables has been converted into a letting room. From the main public bar, with its huge fireplace and memorabilia-filled walls, a short corridor leads to the dining rooms and extensive garden. A function room is available for hire.
Q ☼ ⊛ ⊟ ◑ ♣ ● P ⊟ (1) ❀ ☎

Chichester

Bell Inn

3 Broyle Road, PO19 6AT (on A286 just N of Northgate, close to station)

✪ 11.30-2, 5-midnight; 12-3, 7-11 Sun ☎ (01243) 783388
⊕ thebellinnchichester.com
3 changing beers (sourced nationally; often Exmoor, Langham, Suthwyk) 🅷
Cosy and comfortable city local with a traditional ambience enhanced by exposed brickwork, wood panelling and beams. A rear suntrap garden has a covered smoking area heated by a coal stove in winter. The pub tends to become busiest after 10pm, when the nearby Festival Theatre empties out. The beer selection usually comprises two from the Enterprise range and one from a local micro, complemented by an extensive food menu chalked up on the blackboard (no food Sun eve).
Q🛇🏠🕭❀P🗐🚭(60)●🛜

Chichester Inn 🅛

38 West Street, PO19 1RP (at Westgate roundabout)
✪ 12-11.30 (midnight Fri & Sat); 12-10.30 Sun
☎ (01243) 783185 ⊕ chichesterinn.co.uk
Harveys Sussex Best Bitter; 2 changing beers (sourced locally; often Burning Sky, Dark Star, Langham) 🅷
Pleasant two-bar pub with a real fire in the front lounge bar surrounded by comfy chairs, with a mix of seating and table types elsewhere. The larger public bar to the rear features live music on Wednesday, Friday and Saturday evenings. Outside is an attractive walled garden with a heated and covered smoking area. Two changing beers, often from further afield, are put on at weekends. Food includes Sunday lunches. Four B&B rooms are available. January-March the pub closes 2.30-5.30pm Monday-Thursday and at 7pm Sunday.
🏠🛏🕭≠❀🕭P🚭●🛜

Dolphin & Anchor 🅛 ✅

5 West Street, PO19 1QF (opp cathedral)
✪ 8am-midnight (1am Fri & Sat) ☎ (01243) 790280
Greene King Abbot; Langham Saison; Sharp's Doom Bar; 5 changing beers (sourced locally; often Arundel, Dark Star, Goldmark) 🅷
Conversion of part of a historic city-centre hotel opposite the cathedral. Once two separate hotels, combined in 1910, the pub occupies the lower floor of what was the Anchor. This venue has improved remarkably since the current manager arrived in 2013 and is now always popular with young and old alike – it can be crowded at the bar on weekend evenings. The pub champions local microbreweries and hosts Meet the Brewer evenings on one Thursday most months.
🛇🏠🕭ᵫ≠🗐🛜

Eastgate ✅

4 The Hornet, PO19 7JG (500yds E of Market Cross)
✪ 12 (11 Wed)-11; 10-12.30am Sat; 12-11.30 Sun
☎ (01243) 774877 ⊕ eastgatechichester.co.uk
Fuller's London Pride; Gale's Seafarers Ale, HSB; 2 changing beers (sourced nationally; often Adnams, Fuller's, Ossett) 🅷
Welcoming town pub with an open-plan bar and tables for diners. Good-quality traditional pub meals are served daily. There is a heated patio garden to the rear, which is the venue for a beer festival in July. The pub attracts locals, holidaymakers and shoppers from the nearby market, with a warm welcome and traditional pub games such as darts, cribbage and pool. Music is turned up on Friday and Saturday late evenings, while live bands perform once a month.
🏠🕭❀🗐(51,700)●🛜

Compton

Coach & Horses 🅛

The Square, PO18 9HA (on B2146)
✪ 12-3, 6-11; 12-3, 7-10 Sun; closed Mon ☎ (02392) 631228
⊕ coachandhorsescompton.com
Burning Sky Plateau; house beer (by Ballard's); 3 changing beers (sourced locally; often Ballard's, Burning Sky, Dark Star) 🅷
A 16th-century pub in a quiet, pleasant downland village, popular with walkers and cyclists. The front bar, with internal wooden shutters and wooden floors, has a wood-burning stove at one end and an open fire at the other. The oldest part of the building is the rear, which is now the restaurant, where an adventurous menu of high-quality food is served daily. The well-loved owners, David and Christiane, have been here for over 30 years.
Q🏠🕭▲❀🍴🗐(54)●

Crawley

Brewery Shades 🅛

85 High Street, RH10 1BA
✪ 11-11.30 (1am Fri & Sat); 11-10.30 Sun ☎ (01293) 514105
Greene King Abbot; Morland Old Speckled Hen; 8 changing beers 🅷
Arguably the oldest building in Crawley High Street, dating back to the 1400s and complete with two ghosts. The pub is wet-sales led. The licensee has a true passion for the trade, demonstrated by the inspired range of guest ales and ciders which are always in excellent condition. The haunted upstairs room is now available for meetings. Good food is served during the day and evening – check the specials board. 🛇🏠🕭≠🍴🗐🛜

Eartham

George 🅛 ✅

PO18 0LT (turn N off A27 at Crockerhill or W of Fontwell and proceed 2 miles to centre of this tiny village)

REAL ALE BREWERIES	
Adur Steyning	
Arundel Ford	
Ballard's Nyewood	
Bedlam Albourne	
Crooked Brook Copthorne	
Dark Star Partridge Green	
Downlands Small Dole	
Firebird Rudgwick	
Goldmark Poling	
Greyhound West Chiltington	
Gribble 🍺 Oving	
Hammerpot Poling	
Heathen Haywards Heath	
Hepworth North Heath	
High Weald East Grinstead	
Hurst Hurstpierpoint	
Kiln Burgess Hill	
Kissingate Lower Beeding	
Langham Lodsworth	
Lister's Ford	
Littlehampton 🍺 Littlehampton	
Pin-Up Southwick	
Riverside Upper Beeding (NEW)	
Top-Notch Haywards Heath	
Two Tribes Horsham (NEW)	
Weltons Horsham	

✪ 11.30-11; 12-7 Sun; closed Mon ☎ (01243) 814340
⊕ thegeorgeeartham.com
House beer (by Otter); 3 changing beers (often Downlands, Goldmark, Langham) Ⓗ
A tastefully refurbished old village pub run by a landlord whose passion for the best of English, and especially Sussex, extends to the entire drinks and food menu. All changing beers are LocAle and always include one from Langham. Usually one is a hoppy golden ale while another is a porter, old ale or mild. The food menu features locally sourced ingredients. Popular with walkers and cyclists, the pub holds a beer festival in April featuring Sussex ales and live music. Q✿❀⏱◐♿P▣(99)❀🐾🔊

East Ashling

Horse & Groom Ⓛ

PO18 9AX (on B2178 in village) SU820077
✪ 12-11; 12-6 Sun ☎ (01243) 575339
⊕ thehorseandgroomchichester.co.uk
Dark Star Hophead; Hop Back Summer Lightning; Long Man Best Bitter; Young's Bitter; 1 changing beer (sourced regionally; often Red Cat) Ⓗ
Between the South Downs and the sea, and an inn for over 200 years, this fine country free house has a compact bar featuring flagstones, settles, half-panelled walls and a fine old range. Sympathetically extended, it remains unspoilt. The beers are meticulously presented and sold at consistently good-value prices. A blackboard reveals the diverse, high-quality menu of home-made dishes, all sourced locally (no food Sun eve). En-suite accommodation is dog-friendly, some in a converted 17th-century oak-beamed flint barn.
Q✿🛏◐♿▲♣P▣(54)🐾🔊

East Dean

Star & Garter

PO18 0JG (overlooking pond in village centre)
✪ 12-3, 6-11; 11-11 Sat; 12-11 Sun ☎ (01243) 811318
⊕ thestarandgarter.co.uk
Arundel Black Stallion, Castle; 2 changing beers (sourced nationally; often Arundel, Langham) Ⓖ
An 18th-century free house nestled opposite the duckpond in this charming village. The large bar has an area for dining. The pub is renowned for good food, using local seasonal produce, with fresh local fish a speciality (Sunday lunchtime booking is essential). Local Arundel beer is poured straight from the cask from a cold room behind the bar. There is often a guest beer from further afield in the summer, which can be enjoyed in the large walled garden to the rear. Q✿❀🛏◐♿♣🐾🔊

East Grinstead

Old Dunnings Mill

Dunnings Road, RH19 4AT
✪ 9am-11.30 (midnight Fri & Sat); 9am-11 Sun
☎ (01342) 326341 ⊕ olddunningsmill.co.uk
Harveys Sussex Best Bitter, Armada Ale; 1 changing beer (often Harveys) Ⓗ
This large pub on the edge of town is based on an old watermill. Separate bar and restaurant areas are on various levels but the main areas are disabled-friendly. A heated, covered area to the rear has a working water wheel. Two beer festivals a year are planned. It is basically a quiet pub, though music is played on appropriate occasions. Family- and pet-friendly. Q✿❀❀◐♿P▣(84)🐾

East Preston

Clockhouse Bar Ⓛ ✅

103-105 Sea Road, BN16 1NX (through East Preston near sea and beach)
✪ 12-11 (midnight Fri & Sat); 12-10.30 Sun
☎ (01903) 788367 ⊕ theclockhousebaranddeli.co.uk
Skinner's Betty Stogs; 2 changing beers (sourced locally; often Hammerpot) Ⓗ
A warm welcome awaits you in this lovely seaside village pub at the quiet beach end of East Preston. An ex-bank building, it has plenty of character, complete with its own deli next door, serving local produce in both the shop and the pub. The emphasis is on local ales and there are three handpumps in use. It is a modern but comfortable meeting place with an upstairs family room, and dogs are welcome. There is an outside pavement seating area. Q✿❀◐♣(700)🐾🔊

East Wittering

Shore Ⓛ

Shore Road, PO20 8DZ (50yds from sea)
✪ 11-11; 11-10.30 Sun ☎ (01243) 674454
⊕ theshorepub.co.uk
Dark Star Hophead, American Pale Ale; Palmers Copper Ale, Dorset Gold; Sharp's Doom Bar, Atlantic; 1 changing beer (sourced regionally; often Urban Island) Ⓗ
Friendly beachside town pub popular with the locals (particularly dog owners) and the many summer visitors. There are two main bars, a children's room and a fair-sized decked area for outside drinking as well as smoking. The good-quality lunchtime menu can be enjoyed either in the bar or restaurant. Evening meals are Friday only (fish on Fry-day), with an extremely inviting fish menu at fair prices. Live music features occasionally. Q✿❀◐♿♣P▣(52,53)🐾🔊

Eastergate

Wilkes' Head Ⓛ ✅

Church Lane, PO20 3UT (off A29 in old village, 350yds S of B2233 roundabout, 1¼ miles W of Barnham station) SU943053
✪ 12-11 ☎ (01243) 543380 ⊕ wilkesheadeastergate.co.uk
Adnams Southwold Bitter; 5 changing beers (sourced nationally; often Langham, Long Man, Oakleaf) Ⓗ
Small Grade II-listed red-brick pub, built in 1803 and named after the 18th-century radical, John Wilkes. There is a cosy lounge left of the central bar and to the right a larger room with an inglenook fireplace, flagstones and low beams, plus a separate restaurant. At the rear is a permanent marquee with seating plus a heated smokers' shelter and a large garden. There are five well-chosen changing beers, and regular beer festivals are held. Local CAMRA Pub of the Year 2014. Q✿❀◐♿♣P▣(66,85,85A)🐾🔊

Elsted

Three Horseshoes

GU29 0JY (at E end of village)
✪ 11-2.30, 6-11; 12-3, 7-10.30 Sun ☎ (01730) 825746
Bowman Wallops Wood; Flowerpots Bitter; Young's Bitter; 2 changing beers (sourced locally; often Ballard's, Langham) Ⓖ
Old and cosy rural inn divided into small rooms, including one reserved for dining and one with a

blazing log fire in winter. Outside, the large, pleasant garden enjoys superb views of the South Downs. In summer there are five beers (mainly from local micros), and three in winter, all served by gravity from a stillage alongside the bar. Meals are substantial and of high quality. This is a popular and homely pub, which you will be reluctant to leave. Q❀◑♣P❀

Henley

Duke of Cumberland ⌊

GU27 3HQ (off A286, 3 miles N of Midhurst) SU894258
❀ 11-11; 12-10.30 Sun ☎ (01428) 652280
⊕ dukeofcumberland.com
Harveys Sussex Best Bitter; Langham Hip Hop, Best; 1 changing beer (sourced locally; often Langham) Ⓖ
Stunning 15th-century inn nestling against the hillside in over three acres of terraced gardens with extensive views. The rustic front bar has scrubbed-top tables and benches, plus log fires at both ends, while to the rear is a dining extension that blends in perfectly with the original pub and offers much-needed additional space. Outside is a smokers' shelter with its own woodburner. A former local CAMRA Pub of the Year, this is a rural gem. May close winter Sunday evenings. Q❀◑♣P🖵(70)❀

Horsham

Beer Essentials ⌊

30a East Street, RH12 1HL
❀ 10-6 (7 Fri & Sat); closed Sun & Mon ☎ (01403) 218890
⊕ thebeeressentials.co.uk
Arundel Sussex Gold; 7 changing beers (sourced locally) Ⓖ
A mecca for the connoisseur, this shop opened in Horsham following the demise of King & Barnes in 2000. Up to seven cask ales are served on gravity to take away in 2-, 4- and 8-pint containers, along with JB medium cider and occasionally perry. The shop also stocks over 150 bottled beers from near and far. A popular beer festival is organised each September in the nearby Drill Hall. Every town should have a shop like this! ➦&≒●P🖵❀

Lynd Cross ⌊ ✔

1 Springfield Road, RH12 2PJ
❀ 8am-11 (midnight Fri & Sat); 8am-10.30 Sun
☎ (01403) 272393
Greene King Abbot; Ruddles Best Bitter; Shepherd Neame Spitfire; 5 changing beers (sourced locally) Ⓗ
Large Wetherspoon outlet to be found at the end of West Street, opposite Shelley's Fountain. Once the Horsham Pine Shop, it is now a popular, family-friendly, open-plan town pub. The guest ales are usually sourced from independent Sussex breweries. The pub hosts Meet the Brewer sessions and several beer festivals throughout the year. Q➦❀◑&▲●🖵❀≑

Malt Shovel ❢ ⌊

15 Springfield Road, RH12 2PG
❀ 11-midnight (1am Fri & Sat); 12-midnight Sun
☎ (01403) 252302
Robinsons Trooper; Timothy Taylor Landlord; 5 changing beers (often Long Man, Pilgrim, Surrey Hills) Ⓗ
Located close to the centre of Horsham, the pub serves seven real ales and two ciders/perries at all times. There is live music every Saturday night, as well as regular open mic and jam events. The

landlord and his friendly staff take great pride in serving quality real ale. There is good parking for a town-centre pub. ❀◑&♣●P🖵❀≑

Piries Bar ⌊

15 Piries Place, RH12 1NY
❀ 11-midnight (1am Fri-Sun) ☎ (01403) 267846
⊕ piriesbar.co.uk
Dark Star Hophead; 2 changing beers (sourced locally; often Long Man) Ⓗ
In a building dating from the 15th century with exposed original timber beams, the pub is tucked away down a narrow alley adjoining Horsham's Carfax, in the centre of town. It comprises a small downstairs room, an upstairs lounge bar and a small modern extension in character with the building. Regular charity events are organised. Evenings here can be lively, with karaoke on Sunday, quiz night on Tuesday and occasional live music. With two cask ales always on tap, this bar is well worth a visit. ➦◑≒🖵❀≑

Hurstpierpoint

Poacher ⌊

139 High Street, BN6 9PU
❀ 12-11 ☎ 07799 085053
Dark Star Hophead; Harveys Sussex Best Bitter; 2 changing beers (sourced regionally) Ⓗ
A friendly one-bar locals' pub, originally a cottage belonging to the nearby Danny Estate, with four handpumps and Thatchers Heritage cider on draught. It has a lovely large real fireplace, making it cosy in the winter months. Attractively priced home-made food is served at lunchtimes (no food Sat). There is a well-kept, quiet garden to the rear with plenty of seating. Darts is played and most sporting events are shown on two large screens. ❀◑●🖵(33,273)

Itchenor

Ship

The Street, PO20 7AH (on main street, 100yds from waterfront)
❀ 11-11; 11-10.30 Sun ☎ (01243) 512284
⊕ theshipinnitchenor.co.uk
Arundel Castle; Ballard's Best Bitter; Langham Hip Hop; 1 changing beer (sourced locally) Ⓗ
Popular pub in an attractive village on the shore of picturesque Chichester harbour. A cosy bar decorated with yachting memorabilia adds to the pub's character and is complemented by a pleasant patio, a suntrap in summer. A separate restaurant area offers a wide range of traditional meals, including locally landed fish. Accommodation includes a self-contained three-bed cottage, together with separate B&B rooms. Buses 52 and 53 stop on the B2179 over a mile away, but the infrequent 150 stops opposite the building. Q❀⇋◑♣P❀≑

Lambs Green

Lamb Inn ⌊

RH12 4RG (2 miles N of A264)
❀ 11.30-3, 5.30-11; 11-11 Fri & Sat; 12-10.30 Sun
☎ (01293) 871336 ⊕ thelambinn.org
Dark Star Hophead; 3 changing beers Ⓗ
Lovely old pub with a mixture of flagstones and wood floors interspersed with wrought-iron work, low-beamed ceilings and exposed brick walls.

Furnishings include high-backed settles and soft sofas, and a real fire adds warmth in winter. This welcoming venue, with a friendly landlord and staff, is committed to LocAle – all beers come from within 25 miles and customers elect the guest beer. Lunchtime and evening food is served daily, made with quality home-made locally sourced ingredients, and breakfast is available at weekends. Q➳❀✪❐❀♣♠P❄❀♿ 🕏

Lancing

Stanley Ale House L

5 Queensway, BN15 9AY (N of Lancing railway station)
❁ 12 (2 Mon)-10; 2-8 Sun ☎ (01903) 366820
⊕ thestanleyalehouse.com
3 changing beers (sourced locally) Ⓗ/Ⓖ
The Stanley Ale House opened in 2014 and has become a popular meeting place in the community. With at least three varying real ales on at any one time, along with five ciders and perry, there is always plenty of choice. Evenings offer open mic on Monday, quaff and scoff on Tuesday, a quiz on Thursday, and live music on Friday. A warm welcome awaits you from the staff and friendly regulars, so this is one to visit. Q➳♣♠❐❀♿ 🕏

Littlehampton

New Inn ✓

5 Norfolk Road, BN17 5PL (N from Sea Road)
❁ 12-11 (midnight Fri & Sat); 12-10.30 Sun
☎ (01903) 713112 ⊕ newinnla.co.uk
4 changing beers (sourced nationally) Ⓗ
The New Inn is a friendly, traditional pub and just a short walk from the seafront. There are four handpumps serving a range of national ales. One of these is chosen by the locals in a monthly ballot. The main bar has two sofas in front of a real fire, the rear bar has a pool table and dartboard. A courtyard garden provides a small outside drinking area. Weekly quizzes and monthly live music are held. Q➳❀♣P❐❀♿ 🕏

Lodsworth

Hollist Arms

The Street, GU28 9BZ (in village centre, 1 mile N of A272)
❁ 11-midnight; 12-11 Sun ☎ (01798) 861310
⊕ thehollistarms.com
Dark Star Hophead; Langham Hip Hop; Timothy Taylor Landlord Ⓗ
The pub is set in the village centre overlooking the green, complete with a chestnut tree planted in 1897 to mark Queen Victoria's diamond jubilee. The building was formed from two cottages in 1825. A small bar leads to a larger restaurant area and a small snug with an ancient inglenook fireplace. At the rear, the raised beer garden has a barbecue area, and in front there are seats on the green. The car park houses the village's community shop. Home-cooked food is served all week. Q❀❐♣

Maplehurst

White Horse L

Park Lane, RH13 6LL
❁ 12-2.30 (not Mon), 6-11 (11.30 Fri & Sat); 12-3, 7.30-11 Sun ☎ (01403) 891208

Harveys Sussex Best Bitter; Weltons Pride 'n' Joy; 3 changing beers Ⓗ
Under the same ownership for 32 years, this splendid and welcoming country pub has featured in the Guide 29 times. Popular with locals, cyclists and walkers, the cosy interior, with its unusually large wooden bar, boasts real fires and many interesting artefacts and bric-a-bac. While good honest pub fare is provided, the emphasis is on beer and conversation. Many local beers feature including a good selection of dark ales. Local JB cider is also stocked. Q➳❀✪❐♣♠P❄❀ 🕏

Oving

Gribble Inn L

Gribble Lane, PO20 2BP (at W end of village)
❁ 11-11; 12-11 Sun ☎ (01243) 786893 ⊕ gribbleinn.co.uk
Gribble Sussex Quadhopper, Ale, Fuzzy Duck, Reg's Tipple, Plucking Pheasant, Pig's Ear Ⓗ
Once home to a Miss Gribble, this attractive thatched cottage has been a traditional village pub for over 30 years and shares the premises with the Gribble Brewery. It also now houses the village shop. A wide range of Gribble regular beers complemented by seasonals is always on offer. The place is cosy, with log fires in winter, and home-made food is served in the bar/restaurant. In summer, the large attractive garden offers occasional weekend barbecues. The skittle alley is also available for functions.
Q➳❀✪❐♿♣♠P❐(85,85A)❀ 🕏

Pagham

Inglenook ♟

255 Pagham Road, PO21 3QB
❁ 11-11 (midnight Fri & Sat) ☎ (01243) 262495
⊕ the-inglenook.com
Fuller's London Pride; Young's Special; 3 changing beers (sourced nationally; often Dark Star, Magic Rock, Thornbridge) Ⓗ
A 16th-century Grade II-listed hotel, restaurant and free house, owned and run by the Honour family for over 40 years. There is always a selection of excellent well-hopped real ales available from highly regarded microbreweries alongside local real ciders. The cosy bar areas have real fires and there is a large garden to the rear and a patio area at the front. Local CAMRA Pub of the Year 2015 and 2016. ➳❀✪❐♣P❐(60)❀ 🕏

Petworth

Stonemasons Inn L ✓

North Street, GU28 9NL (just N of village on A283)
❁ 12-11; 12-10.30 Sun ☎ (01798) 342510
⊕ thestonemasonsinn.co.uk
Skinner's Betty Stogs; 4 changing beers (sourced nationally) Ⓗ
A 17th-century inn on the northern edge of Petworth, featuring original oak beams and an inglenook. The pub has been sympathetically extended and welcomes both families and dogs. It has a restaurant serving fine local produce and five pumps showcasing largely local ales. Log-burning stoves create a warm winter welcome. It has a beautiful garden and is opposite the National Trust's Petworth House and park. En-suite accommodation is available.
Q➳❀✪❐❀♿♣♠P❐(1,99)❀ 🕏

Rusper

Royal Oak ⓛ

Friday Street, RH12 4QA (on Langhurstwood Rd off A264 N of Horsham)

✪ 12-2.30, 5-9; 1-9 Sat; 12-4 Sun ☎ (01293) 871393

⊕ theroyaloakrusper.webs.com

Surrey Hills Ranmore; 5 changing beers (sourced locally) Ⓗ

This hostelry is situated on a back road between Rusper and Horsham. Seven handpumps dispense real ale from a variety of sources, and usually two ciders and two perries are available; no lager, keg beer or Guinness is served here. The Royal Oak raises considerable sums for charity through hosting community events including pantomime horse racing, chicken and snail races and weed shows. Despite sweets being available for sale, children are not allowed. Q❀⇦◑ ▲♣●P❀ ⬙

Shoreham-by-Sea

Duke of Wellington ⓛ

368 Brighton Road, BN43 6RE (on A259)

✪ 12-11 (1am Fri & Sat) ☎ (01273) 441297

⊕ dukeofwellingtonbrewhouse.co.uk/home

Burning Sky Aurora; Dark Star Hophead, American Pale Ale; 5 changing beers (sourced regionally) Ⓗ

A short walk from the eastern side of the town centre, this genuine free house offers up to eight beers on handpump and a selection of bottled beers. Live music features most weekends and regular beer festivals are held throughout the year, together with a cider fest on Apple Day. The rear patio garden is an ideal place to relax in summer. Of interest are the original Kemp Town Brewery windows. Children are welcome until 8pm. ⬥❀⇌♣●🚇(2,700)❀⬙

Old Star Ale & Cider House

Church Street, BN43 5DQ

✪ 12-9 ☎ 07982 842057 ⊕ oldstarmicropubsussex.co.uk

5 changing beers (sourced locally; often Downlands, Franklins, Goldmark) Ⓖ

Welcoming micropub in part of the historic former Star Inn at the eastern end of the town centre and close to the Norman St Mary's Church. Up to five beers are served straight from the cask, mainly from Sussex microbrewers. An array of up to nine ciders from Cornwall and Kent complements the beer range. A picture of the original Star Inn from about 1900 dominates one wall. Nibbles are free on Saturday evening. Q⇌♣●🍴🚇(2,700)❀⬙

Sompting

Gardeners Arms ⓛ

West Street, BN15 0AR (in Sompting village, on B2222, just S of A27)

✪ 11-11 (midnight Fri & Sat); 12-11 Sun ☎ (01903) 233666

Courage Directors; Harveys Sussex Best Bitter; Sharp's Doom Bar; 2 changing beers (sourced nationally; often Harveys) Ⓗ

A 19th-century family-run free house located in the original village main street. It offers a friendly, old-fashioned experience, and hosts a popular Tuesday night quiz. Two of the five handpumps supply a changing ale. There is a function room that can be hired, with a 1962 British Rail passenger carriage built onto it, which houses toilets and storage space. Outside is a sun terrace and covered smoking area. Traditional cooked food is available. Q⬥◑♿P🚇(7,16)❀

Staplefield

Jolly Tanners ⓛ ✔

Handcross Road, RH17 6EF

✪ 11-3, 5.30-11; 11-11 Fri & Sat; 12-10.30 Sun

☎ (01444) 400335 ⊕ jollytanners.com

Fuller's London Pride; Harveys Sussex Best Bitter; 5 changing beers Ⓗ

Independently run free house on the north corner of the cricket green. The pub takes great pride in providing a wide selection of real ales and ciders, as well as tasty food made using local ingredients where possible. This is a very friendly place and well worth a visit. A roaring fire welcomes you in winter and there are open mic evenings on Tuesdays. Beer festivals are held regularly during the year with an excellent range of beer to be enjoyed. Q⬥❀◑♿▲♣●P🚇(271)❀⬙

Steyning

Chequer Inn ⓛ ✔

41 High Street, BN44 3RE (in centre of village)

✪ 10-11 (midnight Fri & Sat) ☎ (01903) 814437

⊕ chequerinnsteyning.co.uk

Dark Star Hophead; Gale's HSB; 3 changing beers (sourced nationally) Ⓗ

A 15th-century coaching inn retaining many original design features. It has several drinking areas, including a covered courtyard garden and cosy saloon bar with an open log fire. Along with large plasma TVs in the public bar is a 100-year-old three-quarter-size snooker table. Five handpumps serve local and national ales. Home-cooked food utilises locally sourced ingredients, with the breakfast ever-popular. Live music regularly features, mostly at the weekend. There is an hourly bus service from Shoreham-by-Sea. Q⬥❀⇦◑♣●🚇(2,100,106)❀⬙

Norfolk Arms Hotel ⓛ

18 Church Street, BN44 3YB

✪ 12-2, 6-11 (midnight Fri); 12-3, 6-midnight Sat; 12-3, 7-10.30 Sun ☎ (01903) 812215

Harveys Sussex Best Bitter; 3 changing beers Ⓗ

A traditional beer drinkers' pub, set back off the main high street. It is a real gem and feels like stepping into the past. It has been an alehouse since at least 1880, but parts of the building date from 1668; original beams are evident, and there are real open fires. The pub operates both cricket and rugby teams. Four handpumps offer regularly changing ales, which are mostly local. The ambience is welcoming and friendly. Opening times can vary. Q❀🚇(2,100,106)❀

Stoughton

Hare & Hounds ⓛ

PO18 9JQ (off B2146, through Walderton) SU803115

✪ 11-3, 6-11; 11-11 Fri & Sat; 12-10.30 Sun

☎ (023) 9263 1433 ⊕ hareandhoundspub.co.uk

Dark Star Hophead; Flack Manor Flack's Double Drop; Harveys Sussex Best Bitter; Otter Amber; 1 changing beer (sourced locally) Ⓗ

Traditional country pub in a beautiful setting that makes it an ideal base for walkers. The large dining room serves fresh local produce in comfortable surroundings, with an open fire in winter. A separate public bar where the locals congregate has pictures of vintage racing cars and its own open fire. Stone-flagged floors and simple furniture add to a wonderful atmosphere. Outside, the paved patio area complements a rear garden for alfresco dining and drinking. Two ciders are available. Q✿◖◑▲♣●P🔲🛜

Turners Hill

Crown ✪

East Street, RH10 4PT (in town centre)
✿ 11-11; 11.30-10.30 Sun ☎ (01342) 715218
🌐 thecrownturnershill.co.uk
Dark Star Hophead; Harveys Sussex Best Bitter; St Austell Tribute; Shepherd Neame Whitstable Bay Pale Ale Ⓗ
A tastefully decorated 16th-century farmhouse and 17th-century barn with Jacobean oak beams make up this pub, which converted to an inn during 1706. It holds a St George's Day celebration, a beer festival to coincide with the London to Brighton cycle ride, and a 30-ale festival in October. Leather settees surround a large open fire in the bar area, with another open fire in the restaurant, where traditional English dishes are served.
Q✿🛏◖◑&●P🔲🐾🛜

Red Lion Ⓛ ✪

Lion Lane, RH10 4NU
✿ 11-3, 5-11; 11-11 Sat; 12-10.30 Sun ☎ (01342) 715416
🌐 redlionturnershill.com
Harveys Sussex XX Mild Ale, IPA, Sussex Best Bitter, Armada Ale; 2 changing beers (often Harveys) Ⓗ
Still very much a village local, offering a warm welcome to all who enter. It is a split-level pub with a large inglenook fireplace. Good-value and high-quality lunchtime food is served, and it has recently had a tasteful extension to the dining area. Children and dogs are welcome and there is a fortnightly quiz. The local CAMRA branch held its first meeting here in 1974 and a beer festival was staged to celebrate its 40th anniversary in March 2014. Q✿🛏◖◑&♣●P🔲🐾🛜

Warnham

Sussex Oak Ⓛ ✪

2 Church Street, RH12 3QW
✿ 11-11; 11-10.30 Sun ☎ (01403) 265028
🌐 thesussexoak.co.uk
Dark Star Hophead; Fuller's London Pride; Harveys Sussex Best Bitter; Timothy Taylor Landlord; 3 changing beers (sourced locally) Ⓗ
Popular village pub with a separate dining area. Six handpumps dispense three regular beers and up to three guests; LocAle is actively supported. Two handpumps offer real cider and perry in the summer months. An extensive menu of high-quality, reasonably priced food is available. There is a large garden and dogs are welcome. Quiz nights are held fortnightly and jazz nights on the last Thursday of the month, with beer festivals on bank holidays. Q✿🛏◖◑&♣●P🔲🐾🛜

Warninglid

Half Moon Ⓛ

The Street, RH17 5TR
✿ 11.30-3, 5.30-11; 12-8 Sun ☎ (01444) 461227
🌐 thehalfmoonwarninglid.co.uk
Harveys Sussex Best Bitter; Hurst Founders Best Bitter; 2 changing beers Ⓗ
Large village pub dating back in parts to the 16th century. The entrance leads straight into the bar with oak beams, wooden floors and an open fire.

To the right are two further rooms with fires and a large smartly furnished restaurant featuring a covered and illuminated well flush with the floor. The cellar was upgraded in 2014 with auto-tilt stillage. Regular events take place, including a cheesecake charity event each June.
Q✿🛏✿◖◑&P🔲(89)🐾🛜

West Chiltington

Five Bells Ⓛ

Smock Alley, RH20 2QX (approx 1 mile S of West Chiltington old village centre) TQ092171
✿ 12-3, 6-11; 12-4, 7-10.30 Sun ☎ (01798) 812143
🌐 thefivebellsinn.com
5 changing beers (sourced nationally; often Jennings, Palmers) Ⓗ
The current licensees have been at this fine village free house since 1983, initially as King & Barnes tenants. The changing ales include mild, old in winter, and a selection of bitters from far and wide, with Jennings, Palmers, Timothy Taylor, West Berkshire and LocAles popular. The cider is from Hereford. A short menu of excellent freshly prepared pub food is available (no food Sun eves). The long bar features a copper bar top and a large copper-hooded open fire.
Q✿🛏◖◑●P🔲(1,74)🐾🛜

West Dean

Dean Ale & Cider House

Midhurst Road, PO18 0QX (on A286 just S of West Dean College)
✿ 11-11 (midnight Fri & Sat); 12-10.30 Sun
☎ (01243) 811465 🌐 thedeaninn.co.uk
House beer (by Downlands); 3 changing beers (sourced nationally; often Dark Star, Downlands) Ⓗ
Traditional roadside village pub close to the South Downs and Centurion Way cycle route (with an allocated parking area for bicycles). The stylish beamed bar has modern decor with spaciously arranged seating areas, some with sofas. The adjoining high-ceilinged restaurant is similarly styled, with a large conservatory extension. The garden at the rear has decked and grassed areas. A beer festival is held in May. In winter the pub closes on Monday and 6pm on Sunday, and may only have two changing beers.
Q✿🛏✿◖◑&▲♣●P🔲(60)🐾🛜

West Hoathly

Cat

North Lane, RH19 4PP
✿ 12-11; 12-5 Sun ☎ (01342) 810369 🌐 catinn.co.uk
Harveys Sussex Best Bitter; Larkins Traditional Ale; 2 changing beers Ⓗ
A 16th-century free house with four bedrooms in the hilltop village of West Hoathly, ideally situated for walkers. Four beers are served, mainly from local breweries, with real cider sometimes available. The interior comprises a number of timber-beamed rooms with inglenook fireplaces, and interesting features include a well and an antique telephone. Top-quality food is served throughout the pub and restaurant areas.
Q✿🛏✿◖◑&●P🔲(84)🐾🛜

West Marden

Victoria 🖳

PO18 9EN (just W of B2146 in village)
🌣 12-2.30, 6-10.30 (11 Fri); 12-11 Sat; 12-10 Sun; closed Mon
☎ (023) 9263 1330 ⊕ victoriainnwestmarden.co.uk
3 changing beers (sourced locally) 🅷
Comfortable old rural inn at the heart of its tiny
downland community. Cricket and bar billiards
teams plus a golf society help maintain its local
involvement, and all kinds of country pursuits,
including walking, riding and shooting, are
supported. Inside there are several intimate spaces
in which to drink and dine, with a log-burning
stove for cold evenings. The front garden has
splendid views of surrounding hills. Changing beers
usually come from local breweries and occasional
beer festivals celebrate local ales.
Q❀🕪♣P🖵(54)🕏🕏

Westbourne

Stag's Head 🖳

The Square, PO10 8UE (on B2147, in village centre)
🌣 12-midnight; 12-11 Sun ☎ (01243) 372393
**Greene King IPA; Irving Invincible; Oakleaf Hole
Hearted; 1 changing beer (sourced locally; often
Flowerpots, Lister's)** 🅷
This early 19th-century pub was built on the site of
the village market and subsequently extended into
a neighbouring shop. The newer area is mainly
used for dining (no food Sun eves, or Mondays
Sept-Apr), leaving the remainder of the L-shaped
bar, with its real fire, for drinkers. There is an
outside bar in the yard that comes into its own
during beer and cider festivals. The pub is convivial,
friendly and bursting with local character.
🕏❀🕪♣🕭🖵(36,54)🕏🕏

Wisborough Green

Three Crowns ✅

Billingshurst Road, RH14 0DX
🌣 11-11; 12-10.30 Sun ☎ (01403) 700239
⊕ thethreecrownsinn.com
**Harveys Sussex Best Bitter; Shepherd Neame Spitfire
Gold; 4 changing beers (often Downlands, Firebird,
Langham)** 🅷
A warm welcome awaits at this cosy village pub
next to the cricket green. A fireplace with a
woodburner creates an inviting atmosphere. The
pub serves a selection of handpicked local ales
including Three Crowns Crowning Glory Ale by
Downlands, and home-cooked meals from local
produce within a 20-mile radius. Regular music
plays on a Tuesday night and a seven-course food
and beer matching evening was introduced in
2013. Well worth a visit. Q🕏❀🕪♣P🖵🕏🕏

Worthing

Anchored in Worthing 🖳

27 West Buildings, BN11 3BS (close to seafront)
🌣 12-9.30; 12-5.30 Sun; closed Mon ☎ (01903) 529100
⊕ anchoredinworthing.co.uk
3 changing beers (sourced locally) 🅖
Sussex's first micropub is going from strength to
strength. On offer are three local ales, as well as
local ciders and wines. The ceiling is adorned with
pumpclips showing the vast number of ales the
pub has sold since opening. Small wooden anchors
also hang from it. There are high wooden tables in

the bar, while one of the seats is from a B-17. In
the window are ornaments to remind you that you
are near the seaside. Q♣🕭🖵(700)🕏🕏

Brooksteed Alehouse 🍷 🖳

38 South Farm Road, BN14 7AE (N of Worthing railway
level crossing)
🌣 11.30-2 (not Tue), 5-9.30; 11.30-2 Sun; closed
Mon ☎ 07786 084020 ⊕ brooksteedalehouse.co.uk
5 changing beers (sourced nationally) 🅖
Worthing's second micropub opened in 2014. With
up to five different ales and three ciders served
direct from the cask in a purpose-built cool room,
plus an extensive range of bottled beers and
wines, the licensees have established a loyal
following. The decor is bright and airy and, in
keeping with its previous usage as a hairdressing
salon, there are some innovative features.
Traditional snacks include a cheeseboard plus pies
and savouries from The Pantry next door.
Q🕏🕪♣🕭🖵(16)🕏🕏

Egremont Hotel

32 Brighton Road, BN11 3ED (about 5 mins' walk E
from centre of town along Brighton Road)
🌣 12-11 (11.30 Thu; midnight Fri & Sat); 12-11.30 Sun
☎ (01903) 600064
**Dark Star American Pale Ale; Harveys Sussex Best
Bitter; Hop Back Summer Lightning; house beer (by
Goldmark); 1 changing beer (sourced nationally)** 🅷
Near to the seafront, this pub was built in 1835 and
the old building had a brewery next to it. The Eggie
reopened in 2015 following a refurbishment which
was to a high standard, while retaining a lot of its
history. Ale festivals once every two months
offering award-winning ales, regular weekend live
music and twice-weekly quiz nights take place.
There are six handpumps, with two ales brewed
specially for the pub. 🕪♣🖵🕏

Hare & Hounds ✅

79-81 Portland Road, BN11 1QG
🌣 11-11 (11.30 Tue & Thu; midnight Fri & Sat); 12-11 Sun
☎ (01903) 230085 ⊕ hareandhoundsworthing.co.uk
**Fuller's London Pride; Gale's HSB; Sharp's Doom Bar;
2 changing beers (sourced nationally; often
Harveys)** 🅷
Formerly two fishermen's cottages, this 18th-
century flint building became a pub in 1814,
extending into the adjoining property in the 1990s.
The large, wood-panelled U-shaped bar leads to
the rear conservatory and heated patio. Old prints
focusing on hunting hang from the walls. There are
five handpumps serving national ales. Tuesday
evening features live jazz, Wednesday is quiz
night, on Saturday evening live bands play and
Sunday is music quiz night. Q🕏❀🕪♣🖵🕏

North Star ✅

Littlehampton Road, BN13 1QY (on A2032)
🌣 11-11 (midnight Thu-Sat) ☎ (01903) 247973
**Brakspear Bitter; Fuller's London Pride; Harveys
Sussex Best Bitter; Morland Old Speckled Hen; 4
changing beers (sourced nationally)** 🅷
Spacious 1930s roadhouse with a pleasant interior
with a long central bar and various nooks and
crannies. A cosy fire warms up this popular Ember
Inn. The pub has beers on eight handpumps,
including four rotating ales that are sourced
nationally. There is a dedicated dining area but
food is served throughout, including in the south-
west-facing beer garden. Live music is staged
every few weeks. 🕏❀🕪♣P🖵(6)🕏

Parsonage Bar & Restaurant L ✓

10 High Street, BN14 7NN (at S end of Tarring High St)
🕑 12-9 Mon; 11-11; 11-midnight Fri & Sat; 12-9 Sun
☎ (01903) 820140 ⊕ theparsonage.co.uk
Burning Sky Plateau; Dark Star Hophead; Harveys Sussex Best Bitter 田; 3 changing beers (sourced locally) 田/ᴳ
A 15th-century building that was originally three cottages, saved from demolition in 1927. It is Grade II-listed and has been a restaurant since 1987, serving up high-quality food as well as offering ales of similar distinction. At least two guest LocAles are always on tap, served by gravity from an outside cold store. In the warmer weather the courtyard garden offers a great opportunity to drink outside. CAMRA local branch Pub of the Year in 2014 and 2015. Q❀①➡️🚌 (6,16)

Selden Arms

41 Lyndhurst Road, BN11 2DB (about 5 mins from centre of town and 2 mins from Worthing Hospital on Lyndhurst Rd, opp gasometer by Waitrose)
🕑 11-11; 12-10.30 Sun
6 changing beers (sourced nationally; often Downlands Brewery) 田
A regular in the Guide, this 19th-century free house has one bar with six handpumps and offers a warm welcome. There are interesting photos of Worthing pubs, past and present, on the walls. The ales change regularly, but always include a dark brew. The owners stock a selection of over 120 Belgian bottled beers and will discuss them enthusiastically. Pub food is served Monday to Saturday with curry night on Friday. Beer festivals are held in January and October.
①➡️♣🚌 (106)❀🛜

Sir Timothy Shelley L ✓

47 Chapel Road, BN11 1EG
🕑 8-11 ☎ (01903) 228070
Courage Directors; Greene King Abbot; Oakleaf India Pale Ale; Ruddles Best Bitter; Sharp's Doom Bar; 5 changing beers (sourced nationally) 田
This pub stands on land in the town centre once owned by Sir Timothy Shelley, son of the poet Percy Bysshe Shelley. There is one long bar and plenty of seating, offering the usual Wetherspoon fare and a friendly welcome. There are 10 handpumps; half have regular ales, while half have changing guest ales. At least one guest is from a local microbrewery and there is often an ale from an international brewer. A real cider is always available. ⛲①♿➡️🚽🚌🛜

Yapton

Maypole L

Maypole Lane, BN18 0DP (off B2132 1 mile N of village; pedestrian access across railway from Lake Lane, 1¼ miles E of Barnham station) SU978042
🕑 11.30-11 (midnight Fri & Sat); 12-11 Sun
☎ (01243) 551417
Dark Star Hophead; house beer (by Wessex); 3 changing beers (often Arundel, Dark Star) 田
Small flint-built free house hidden away from the village centre, down a narrow lane ending in a pedestrian crossing over the railway. The cosy lounge boasts two open fires and a row of six handpumps, dispensing up to three changing beers and real cider. There is a traditional public bar and a skittle alley/function room. Fresh rolls are served lunchtimes. It now has a new outside seating area. Dogs are welcome. Q❀♿⅄♣🚽P🚌 (66,700)❀

Coach & Horses, Compton (Photo: Bob Steel)

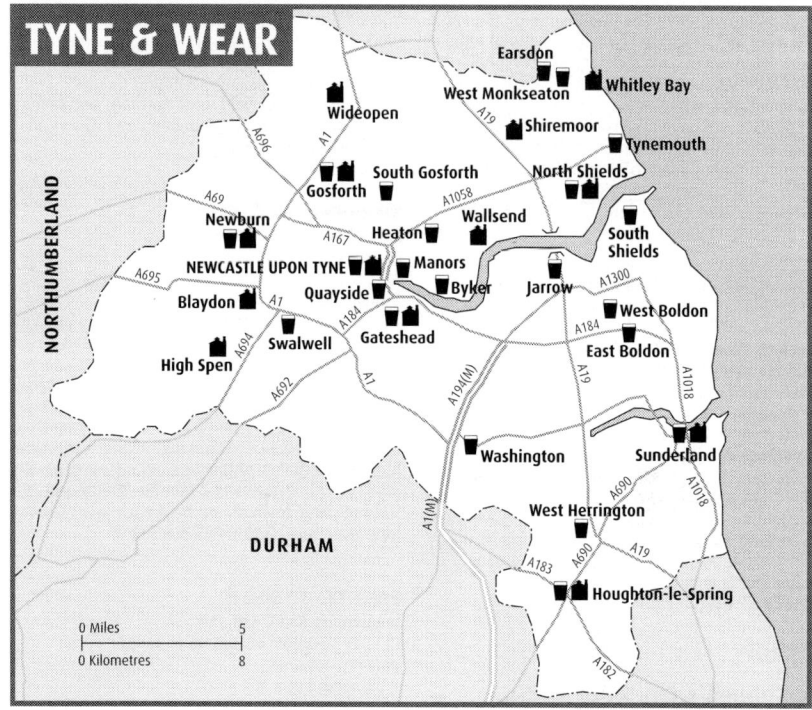

TYNE & WEAR

NORTHUMBERLAND

Earsdon
Whitley Bay
West Monkseaton
Shiremoor
Wideopen
Tynemouth
South Gosforth
North Shields
Gosforth
Newburn
Heaton
Wallsend
South Shields
NEWCASTLE UPON TYNE
Manors
Blaydon
Quayside
Byker
Jarrow
West Boldon
Swalwell
Gateshead
East Boldon
High Spen
Washington
Sunderland
West Herrington
DURHAM
Houghton-le-Spring

0 Miles 5
0 Kilometres 8

Earsdon

Beehive 🗍
Hartley Lane, NE25 0SZ
🕓 12-11; 12-9 Sun ☎ (0191) 252 9352
🌐 beehiveearsdon.co.uk
Mordue Workie Ticket; 2 changing beers Ⓗ
This 18th-century Grade II-listed building has been
an inn since 1896. The superb three-room country
pub is now back to its best, with the owners taking
great pride in the quality of the ale. A choice of
blonde, pale and dark beers is usually available.
Excellent food is served, made with ingredients
sourced from local suppliers. The car park has been
extended and there is a mini goat area, children's
secret garden, a picnic site and extra seating.
🌟🐾🕪🕭🍴P🐾

East Boldon

Grey Horse 🗍
Front Street, NE36 0SJ
🕓 12-11 (midnight Fri) ☎ (0191) 519 1796
6 changing beers Ⓗ
Distinctive mock-Tudor building with separate
lounge and bar areas. There are large-screen TVs in
the bar for football and other sport. A folk club
meets on the first Tuesday of the month and the
Boldon History Society on the last Tuesday. There is
a separate first-floor function room. Guest beers
are mainly from larger independent brewers.
Q🌟🕪🕭P🚊 (9,30)

Gateshead

Central ★ 🗍
Half Moon Lane, NE8 2AN
🕓 10-11; 10-10.30 Sun ☎ (0191) 478 2543

8 changing beers (sourced nationally) Ⓗ
Mid 19th-century, four-storey wedge-shaped
building. It now comprises a revamped public bar,
two function rooms and a rooftop terrace. However
the Central's main attraction is the quite
magnificently restored Buffet Bar (closed when
quiet, ask to view), designated by CAMRA as a
nationally important historic pub interior. The
building itself is Grade II-listed. It is as fitted out
circa 1900 with a carved U-shaped counter and bar-
back, plasterwork frieze and panelling. The pub is
home to regular live music. 🌟🕪🕭🕭🍴🚊🐾🛜

Schooner
South Shore Road, NE8 3AF (just down from jct
between Saltmeadows Rd and Neilson Rd; vehicular
access from E end of South Shore Rd)
🕓 12-11; 12-10.30 Sun ☎ (0191) 477 7404
🌐 theschooner.co.uk
6 changing beers Ⓗ
Following the purchase of the Schooner, husband
and wife team David and Julie have breathed new
life into the pub on South Shore Road. There are
currently six handpulls for cask ales and one for
cask cider – the beer range changes regularly,
showcasing the best local and national ales and
ciders. Great-value home-cooked food is available
throughout the week with a traditional roast on
Sundays. Local and touring bands feature at least
twice-weekly and a buskers' afternoon is on the
first Sunday of the month.
🌟🐾🕭🕭🍴P🚊 (93,94)🐾🛜

Wheat Sheaf 🗍
26 Carlisle Street, Felling, NE10 0HQ
🕓 5 (3 Thu; 12 Fri & Sat)-11; 12-10.30 Sun
☎ (0191) 597 2981
**Big Lamp Bitter, Prince Bishop Ale, Sunny Daze; 1
changing beer** Ⓗ

Welcoming street-corner pub owned by Big Lamp Brewery and patronised by a loyal band of regulars who often travel quite a distance to drink here. The pub features some original details, mismatched furniture and, when needed, real coal fires. The outdoor toilets have original Victorian urinals. There is a fortnightly Monday night quiz, traditional folk music featuring keen local musicians on Tuesday nights and dominoes on Wednesday nights. An original CAMRA clock keeps time behind the bar. Snacks are available. ☎️🚆🏵️♣️●🚐(27,93,94)🐾🤏

Houghton-le-Spring

Copt Hill 🅛
Seaham Road, DH5 8LU (on B1404)
🕚 11-11.30; 11.30-11.30 Sun ☎ (0191) 584 4485
🌐 thecopthill.co.uk
2 changing beers 🅷
With a spectacular vista over the Houghton countryside, this former Vaux pub has six handpulls offering a changing selection of ales, half local and half from a wider area. Excellent food including breakfast is served all day from an extensive menu – booking for the restaurant is advisable as it can get busy at evenings and weekends. A variety of party nights is held in the function room.
Q🏵️◑▲P🍴🚐(20,238)

Jarrow

McConnell's Gin & Ale House
Walter Street, NE32 3PQ (behind town hall)
🕚 12-11 ☎ (0191) 483 6792
5 changing beers 🅷
A well-appointed conversion of the old Crusader, in the traditional ex-Jarrow Brewery style, with an emphasis on wooden panelling, carpets, vintage photographs and pub memorabilia. The pub serves up to five ales and also promotes a dozen or so gins. Take time to examine the ornate tiling on the outside of the building. A quiz is held every Thursday night and a buskers' night on Sunday. 🚐🚐

Newburn

Keelman 🅛
Grange Road, NE15 8NL
🕚 11-11; 12-10.30 Sun ☎ (0191) 267 1689
🌐 keelmanslodge.co.uk
Big Lamp Bitter, Prince Bishop Ale, Summerhill Stout, Sunny Daze; 1 changing beer 🅷
This tastefully converted Grade II-listed former pumping station is now home to the Big Lamp Brewery and the Keelman is the brewery tap. A conservatory restaurant offers excellent food, and quality accommodation is provided in the adjacent Keelman's Lodge and Salmon Cottage. Attractively situated by Tyne Riverside Country Park, the Coast-to-Coast cycleway and Hadrian's Wall National Trail.
🚆🏵️🛏️◑♿P🚐(22)🤏

Newcastle upon Tyne: Byker

Cluny 🅛
36 Lime Street, NE1 2PQ
🕚 12-11; 12-10.30 Sun ☎ (0191) 230 4474
7 changing beers 🅷
Large, former industrial building converted into a pub, art gallery and live music venue. The pub runs frequent themed beer festivals and always has a good selection of British and foreign draught and

bottled products available. The art gallery shows work of all kinds ranging from final degree shows to local independent established artists in all media, with the displays changing monthly. Live music sessions are held most evenings and feature a wide range of British, European and American musicians. Q◑♿🏵️🚐🤏

Cumberland Arms 🅛
James Place Street, NE6 1LD (off Byker Bank)
🕚 3-11 (midnight Fri); 12-midnight Sat; 12-11 Sun
☎ (0191) 265 1725 🌐 thecumberlandarms.co.uk
6 changing beers 🅷
Three-storey venue rebuilt over 100 years ago and relatively little changed since. It stands in a prominent position overlooking the lower Ouseburn Valley. The pub is home to dance and music groups and its house beer, Rapper from Wylam Brewery, is named after the traditional rapper sword dance. A multiple winner of CAMRA regional Cider Pub of the Year awards, it generally offers up to 12 ciders and perries. Winter and summer beer festivals are held each year. Closing time may vary. Q🏵️🛏️♣️●P🐾🤏

Free Trade Inn 🅛
St Lawrence Road, NE6 1AP
🕚 11-11 (midnight Fri & Sat); 12-10.30 Sun
☎ (0191) 265 5764
7 changing beers 🅷
Unique former S&N pub that has wonderful views of the Tyne bridges and the Newcastle and Gateshead quaysides. Up to nine beers and two ciders are available on the bar, with cellar runs willingly offered. Interesting ales come from far and wide including an extensive range of foreign bottled beers. Service is with a smile, friendly and knowledgeable. Tasty sandwiches are supplied by a local delicatessen. The jukebox is classic and free. The beer garden is excellent.
Q🏵️♣️●🚐(Q2,106)🐾🤏

REAL ALE BREWERIES

Almasty Shiremoor
Arcane Bridge Newcastle upon Tyne
Big Lamp Newburn
Box Social Newburn (NEW)
Brinkburn Street Newcastle upon Tyne (NEW)
Cullercoats Wallsend
Darwin Sunderland
Dog & Rabbit Wideopen (NEW)
Errant Newcastle upon Tyne (NEW)
Firebrick Blaydon
George N Porter Whitley Bay (brewing suspended)
Hadrian Border Newburn
Hop & Cleaver 🍴 Newcastle upon Tyne
Leazes Lane 🍴 Newcastle upon Tyne
Maxim Houghton-le-Spring
Mordue North Shields
Northern Alchemy Newcastle upon Tyne
Northern FC 🍴 Gosforth
Olde Potting Shed High Spen
Ouseburn Valley Gosforth
Out There Newcastle upon Tyne
Rail Ale 🍴 Gateshead (brewing suspended)
Tavernale 🍴 Newcastle upon Tyne
Three Kings 🍴 North Shields
Two by Two Wallsend
Tyne Bank Newcastle upon Tyne
Wylam Newcastle upon Tyne

Newcastle upon Tyne: City Centre

Bacchus ⓛ

42-48 High Bridge, NE1 6BX

⏱ 11.30-midnight; 12-11 Sun ☎ (0191) 261 1008

🌐 thebacchusnewcastle.co.uk

6 changing beers ⓗ

CAMRA Tyneside Pub of the Year four years' running, this smart city-centre pub boasts nine handpumps offering a range of changing guest beers, with one pump dedicated to cider and another to beer from Orkney's Highland Brewing Company. A seasonal house beer is brewed by Yorkshire Dales, and a large range of draught and bottled foreign beers is available. Photographs and posters on the walls show the industries in which this region used to lead the world. ⠶⠷⠶⠷♣⠶✿🐾☂

Bodega ⓛ

125 Westgate Road, NE1 4AG

⏱ 12-11 (midnight Fri); 11-midnight Sat; 12-10.30 Sun

☎ (0191) 221 1552 🌐 thebodeganewcastle.co.uk

Big Lamp Prince Bishop Ale; Fyne Ales Jarl; Oakham Citra; 5 changing beers (often Almasty) ⓗ

Two fine stained-glass domes are the architectural highlights of the pub, which is popular with football and music fans. TVs show sporting events and the pub can be busy on match days. The interior offers a number of standing and seating areas with separate booths for more intimate drinking. Several old brewery mirrors adorn the walls. Eight handpumps include beers from Oakham and Fyne Ales, and a good selection of foreign bottled beers is available. ⠷⠶♣🐾✿☂

Bridge Hotel ⓛ

Castle Square, NE1 1RQ

⏱ 11.30-11 (midnight Fri & Sat); 12-10.30 Sun

☎ (0191) 232 6400 🌐 bridgehotelnewcastle.co.uk

Anarchy Blonde Star; Sharp's Doom Bar; Three Kings Castle Keep; 7 changing beers ⓗ

Large Fitzgerald pub situated next to Stephenson's spectacular High Level Bridge – the rear windows and patio have views of the city walls, River Tyne and Gateshead Quays. The main bar area, with many stained-glass windows, is divided into a number of seating areas with a raised section at the rear. Guest beers come from far and wide. Live music, including what is claimed to be the oldest folk club in the country, is hosted in the upstairs function room. ⠶⠷⠶♣⠷🐾

Duke of Wellington ⓛ ✅

High Bridge, NE1 1EN

⏱ 11-11 (midnight Fri & Sat); 12-11 Sun ☎ (0191) 261 4050

7 changing beers ⓗ

This L-shaped bar situated in High Bridge, Newcastle's premier real ale street, has nine handpulls including one for cider. A recent tasteful refurbishment gives a modern look to the pub. The Duke can be busy on match days and during racing festivals. Quiz night is Monday and music night is Thursday. ⠶⠷⠶♣🐾✿☂

Fitzgeralds 🏆 ⓛ

60 Grey Street, NE1 6AF

⏱ 11-midnight; 12-11 Sun ☎ (0191) 230 1350

🌐 fitzgeraldsnewcastle.co.uk

6 changing beers (sourced nationally) ⓗ

Large, open-plan, friendly Sir John Fitzgerald pub, recently refurbished with six handpulls serving local and national beers. The pub is much bigger inside than it appears from the outside owing to its depth, with the bar situated towards the back. There is plenty of seating in various areas as well as a large standing area in front of the bar. The experienced landlord likes to offer an ale selection not found elsewhere locally, including an extensive range of bottled beers. ⠶⠷⠶🚌 (Q1,Q2)☂

Five Swans

14 St Mary's Place, NE1 7PG

⏱ 8am-midnight (1am Fri & Sat) ☎ (0191) 232 3893

Adnams Broadside; Fuller's London Pride; Greene King Abbot; Ruddles Best Bitter; Sharp's Doom Bar; 6 changing beers ⓗ

Multi-roomed Wetherspoon pub opposite Newcastle Civic Centre and close to the main shopping areas. The beer range includes guests from all the local brewers and from further afield. Food is served all day. Outside there is a drinking area to the front and a 'secret' courtyard through the maze of rooms. Children are welcome until 9pm. The pub area can be booked for private functions. Q⠶⠷⠶♣⠷🚌☂

Head of Steam

1 Neville Street, NE1 5EN

⏱ 12-2am (3am Fri & Sat) ☎ (0191) 230 4236

6 changing beers (often Camerons) ⓗ

Facing the central railway station, this is an unusual pub in that there is nothing on the ground floor. Upstairs is the main bar with six cask beers, three real ciders and a good selection of continental draught beers. Downstairs is one of the most popular music venues in the city centre (no draught beers here although there is an extensive range of cans and bottles). ⠶⠷🐾☂

Lady Grey's ⓛ ✅

20 Shakespeare Street, NE1 6AQ

⏱ 11-2am ☎ (0191) 232 3606 🌐 ladygreys.co.uk

Mordue Northumbrian Blonde; 7 changing beers ⓗ

Close to the historic Theatre Royal and busy shopping areas, this pub, formerly the Adelphi, is a welcome addition to the city-centre real ale scene. Beers are mainly from local brewers Mordue, Hadrian Border, Allendale and Wylam, with guests from all over the country. A refurbishment has added two more handpumps for beer and two for real cider. Food is served all day. ⠷⠶⠷🐾☂

Old George ⓛ ✅

Old George Yard, NE1 1EZ

⏱ 11-11 (1am Thu; 2am Fri & Sat); 12-midnight Sun

☎ (0191) 269 3061 🌐 oldgeorgeinnnewcastle.co.uk

Draught Bass; 6 changing beers ⓗ

Built in 1582, this historic pub is alleged to have been frequented by King Charles I and is a welcoming watering hole for customers who like a piece of old England. The corridors and stairs creak and the ambience is mostly original. A cabinet of five handpulls complements the traditional bar area, and a smaller bar has an additional three handpulls. Buskers nights are Thursdays and Sundays. In summer bands play regularly in the yard. ⠶⠷⠶♣⠷☂

Pleased To Meet You ⓛ

High Bridge, NE1 1EW

⏱ 11-1am (2am Fri & Sat) ☎ (0191) 241 4395

🌐 ptmy-newcastle.co.uk

Mordue Five Bridges; 6 changing beers ⓗ

Totally refurbished to a high standard and serving a multitude of drinks, this gin and real ale eatery has a busy mixed clientele. Situated on Newcastle's premier real ale street, it offers six handpulls serving a variety of brews, both local and national, with a trend towards the out of the ordinary. The front of the building features full-height windows which fold away in summer. To the rear are the smoking cabins. ◖▮◗≒ℚ⚡

Split Chimp ℒ
Arch 11, Forth Street, NE1 3NZ
✪ 4-8 (10 Wed); 2-10 Thu; 1-11 Fri & Sat; closed Sun & Mon
3 changing beers (sourced nationally) Ⓗ
Newcastle's first micropub, built into a recently refurbished railway arch behind Central Station opposite the site of the former Federation Brewery. Larger than some micropubs and split over two levels, three handpumps serve an ever-changing selection of real ales. Foreign bottled beers are available from the unusual forward-facing fridge. ℚ≒ℚ

Trent House ℒ
1-2 Leazes Lane, NE1 4QT
✪ 12-11 ☎ (0191) 261 2154
6 changing beers Ⓗ
Friendly and laid back, the Trent is popular with students. It is home to the best jukebox in town, featuring an eclectic mix of classic rock, jazz and electronica. There is an upstairs room with a pool table and board games are available at the bar. The pub has a nightly happy hour 8-9pm, with cask ales priced at £2 per pint, and on the first Sunday of the month ales are just £1 between 5 and 10pm.
ℚ♣ℚ(32,32A)⚡

Tyneside Cinema Bar Café
Pilgrim Street, NE1 6QG
✪ 8am-11 (midnight Fri & Sat); 10-11 Sun ☎ 0845 217 9909
⊕ tynesidecinema.co.uk/food-drink/tyneside-bar-cafe
3 changing beers Ⓗ
Part of Tyneside Cinema, the Bar Café is a large open-plan bar with its own, curtained-off cinema screen. The bar has three handpumps serving a range of locally brewed cask ales including the house beer, 35mm from Wylam Brewery. A tasty selection of cakes and pastries is also available. The cellar is in the vault of a former bank.
◖▮◗&≒ℚ♥⚡

Union Rooms ⊘
Westgate Road, NE1 1TT
✪ 10-midnight (1am Fri & Sat) ☎ (0191) 261 5718
Greene King Abbot; Ruddles County; 6 changing beers Ⓗ
This large multi-floored Wetherspoon pub, not far from Central Station, is an excellent conversion of a listed building. Formerly the Union Club, built in 1877, it was converted after lying empty for many years. There is a glass-roofed, former courtyard area in the centre of the pub. Upper floor opening times may vary. ⛵◖▮◗&≒ℚ⚡

Newcastle upon Tyne: Gosforth

County ℒ ⊘
High Street, NE3 1HB
✪ 11-11; 12-10.30 Sun ☎ (0191) 285 6919
Caledonian Deuchars IPA; Greene King London Glory, IPA; Ruddles County; Wells Bombardier; 6 changing beers Ⓗ

This large L-shaped bar with pleasant stained-glass windows on the main road frontage attracts a variety of visitors, from office workers to students, and can get busy, especially at weekends. A separate quiet room at the back offers respite from the hustle and bustle of the main bar, and also doubles as a small meeting or function room. Several guest beers are available. ⛲Pℚ⚡

Gosforth Hotel ℒ ⊘
High Street, NE3 1HQ
✪ 11-11 (midnight Fri & Sat) ☎ (0191) 285 6617
⊕ gosforthhotelnewcastle.co.uk
Allendale Pennine Pale; Mordue Workie Ticket; 4 changing beers Ⓗ
On the corner of a busy junction at the top of the High Street, this is a stalwart of the Gosforth pub scene. Popular with a wide clientele, from nearby office workers to locals and students, the pub often gets busy. Three ales are regularly available along with the occasional guest beer. A quieter adjoining bar opens occasionally at busier times and also serves as a function room. Another function room is available upstairs. ◖▮◗&ℚℚ⚡

Job Bulman ℒ ⊘
St Nicholas Avenue, NE3 1AA
✪ 8am-11 ☎ (0191) 223 6230
Greene King Abbot; Ruddles Best Bitter; 6 changing beers Ⓗ
Popular Wetherspoon pub located just off the High Street, which strives to serve a wide range of real ales at all times. Aside from the two core beers, up to six guests may be available, often from local established breweries or micros. There is a raised area to the right set aside for families and diners. ⛵⛲◖▮◗&ℚ♥ℚ⚡

Newcastle upon Tyne: Heaton

Chillingham ℒ
Chillingham Road, NE6 5XN
✪ 11-11 (midnight Fri & Sat); 12-11 Sun ☎ (0191) 265 3992
⊕ thechillinghamnewcastle.co.uk
Black Sheep Best Bitter; 6 changing beers Ⓗ
A large two-roomed pub with contrasting styles appealing to the widest possible customer base – the public bar in traditional dark wood with panelling and a historic mirror recalling the past glories of nearby Wallsend, and the lounge with a contemporary feel, flat-screen TVs for sport and excellent artwork depicting the sights of Newcastle. It offers a good choice of local microbrewery beers, as well as bottled beer, whisky and wine. There is a function room upstairs. ◖▮◗♣♥Pℚ(62,63)⚡

Northumberland Hussar ℒ
Sackville Road, NE6 5SY (off Chillingham Rd)
✪ 12-11 (11.30 Mon & Tue); 12-midnight Fri & Sat
☎ (0191) 265 0275 ⊕ northumberlandhussar.co.uk
5 changing beers Ⓗ
Purpose-built in 1955 and named after a local regiment, a major investment in 2013 transformed the pub, with a stylish horseshoe bar and many interesting artefacts on display. Food is made from scratch in the open kitchen. Two banks of five handpulls serve a range of cask-conditioned ales both from local and national microbreweries; a sixth is dedicated to real cider. Beer is available in third-pint measures on request. Quiz night is Thursday. Children are welcome until 7pm.
⛵⛲◖▮◗&♥Pℚ(62,63)❀⚡

Newcastle upon Tyne: Manors

New Bridge ⓛ

2-4 Argyle Street, NE1 6PF

🕐 11-11 (11.30 Thu & Fri); 12-10.30 Sun ☎ (0191) 232 1020
🌐 thenewbridgenewcastle.co.uk

Anarchy Blonde Star; 4 changing beers Ⓗ

Just east of Newcastle city centre, and well served by buses and the metro, this pub has no regular beers but offers a varying choice from independent brewers. It is very much a locals' venue, but all are made welcome. The building is next to a business park and facing a large new extension to Northumbria University, so attracts a mixed lunchtime and early evening crowd enjoying the beer and home-made food. ◁≒◖⬤🖵🛜

Newcastle upon Tyne: Quayside

Bridge Tavern ⓛ

7 Akenside Hill, NE1 3UF

🕐 12-midnight (1am Fri & Sat); 12-11 Sun
☎ (0191) 261 9966 🌐 thebridgetavern.com

7 changing beers Ⓗ

A trendy Newcastle pub with its own microbrewery – the Bridge Tavern's one-barrel plant brews a range of beers under the Tavernale name. Food ranging from bar snacks to buffets and full meals is prepared and cooked by a professional chef. There has been an ale house on this site for over 200 years – the original building was demolished in 1925 and a new premises built following the construction of the town's most famous landmark, the Tyne Bridge. Children are welcome until 7pm. ▸☺◖◗🖓≒◖⬤🖵(Q1,Q2,Q3)🐾🛜

Crown Posada ⓛ

31 Side, NE1 3JE

🕐 12 (11 Thu)-11; 11-midnight Fri; 12-midnight Sat; 12-10.30
Sun ☎ (0191) 232 1269 🌐 crownposadanewcastle.co.uk

Allendale Pennine Pale; Hadrian Border Tyneside Blonde; 4 changing beers (often Hadrian Border) Ⓗ

An architecturally fine pub, identified by CAMRA as having a regionally important historic interior. Behind the narrow street frontage are two impressive stained-glass windows lie a small snug, bar counter and a longer seating area. There is an interesting coffered ceiling, as well as local photographs and cartoons of long-gone customers and staff on the walls. Small brewers are enthusiastically supported, with three regular local ales. Q≒🖵🖓(Q1,Q2,Q3)🛜

Hop & Cleaver ⓛ

40 Sandhill, NE1 3JF

🕐 12-1am ☎ (0191) 261 0921

6 changing beers Ⓗ

Interestingly renovated pub now stripped back to the brickwork throughout. It has its own microbrewery in a room that leads through to the Red House next door. The food majors on smoked American-style meats and burgers, while the Red House features specialist pies, peas and mash. A good range of real ales is served from a bar with an open front. You can also access the Red House via the courtyard, which has covered seating and a smoking area. ◖◗🖓≒🖵🖓(Q1,Q2,Q3)

Newcastle upon Tyne: South Gosforth

Brandling Villa ⓛ ✅

Haddricks Mill Road, NE3 1QL

🕐 12-11 (midnight Fri & Sat) ☎ (0191) 284 0490
🌐 brandlingvilla.co.uk

7 changing beers Ⓗ

Large double-fronted establishment with enthusiastic staff. It offers a changing selection of 10 beers – also available in third-pint tasting glasses – plus two ciders on handpump. The manager organises various well-attended, beer-related events, including brewery takeovers, local sausage and pie festivals, music, cinema and beer festivals. The house beer, Frank & Bird, is from Hadrian Border and is a special brew, not a rebadge. ▸☺◖◗🖓≒🖵⬤🖵(55)🐾🛜

Millstone ⓛ

Haddricks Mill Road, NE3 1QL

🕐 12-11 (midnight Fri & Sat) ☎ (0191) 285 3429

Anarchy Blonde Star; Draught Bass; Sharp's Doom Bar; 5 changing beers Ⓗ

Refurbished by a new entrepreneurial pub company, this is a modern, stylish, two-roomed pub with the lounge to the front and a small public bar to the rear serving beers from local microbreweries as well as national favourites. Bass has been the regulars' favourite for many years. The function room upstairs, also renovated, is available to hire and hosts CAMRA events. ▸☺◖◗🖵🖵(55)🛜

North Shields

Oddfellows ⓛ

7 Albion Road, NE30 2RJ

🕐 11-11; 12-11 Sun ☎ (0191) 435 8450
🌐 oddfellowspub.co.uk

3 changing beers (often Three Kings) Ⓗ

Small, friendly, single-room pub adorned with historic maps and photographs of pre-war North Shields. Three handpumped ales include two changing guests, and up to six real ciders plus real perry are available. The pub is home to active football, darts and cricket teams, and hosts regular folk and blues nights and poker nights. A beer festival is held outside on the patio each year. Free soup is served in the winter months. Q▸☺◖◗🖓≒🖵⬤🖵🐾🛜

South Shields

Alum Ale House ✅

Ferry Street, NE33 1JR

🕐 12-11; 11-midnight Fri & Sat; 12-10.30 Sun
☎ (0191) 427 7245

Jennings Cumberland Ale; Cocker Hoop; Wychwood Hobgoblin; 14 changing beers Ⓗ

Small, traditional pub adjacent to the Market Square, River Tyne and ferry landing. It is popular with local ale drinkers as a haven of good beer. Twelve handpumps offer five permanent beers and seven guests from the Marston's range. The pub has three rooms including a cellar bar, with low ceilings throughout. There is a lively Irish folk session on the first Sunday of each month. A cheese club meets on the last Tuesday of the month. ▸☺🖓⬤⬤

Steamboat ♥ ●

Mill Dam, NE33 1EQ (follow signs for Customs House)
✪ 12-11 (midnight Thu-Sat); 12-11.30 Sun
☎ (0191) 454 0134
6 changing beers Ⓗ

Under the same management for the past 25 years, the Steamboat has one of the largest selections of cask ales in South Shields. Eight handpumps dispense a range of beers from small and family brewers across the country, and Meet the Brewer events and beer festivals take place throughout the year. The split-level bar has a nautical theme. The pub is a short walk from the Shields Ferry and Customs House Theatre. ♫♣♣🐾🛜

Wouldhave ●

16 Mile End Road, NE33 1TA
✪ 8am-midnight ☎ (0191) 427 6014
Greene King Abbot; Ruddles Best Bitter; 3 changing beers Ⓗ

Wetherspoon pub opposite South Shields Metro station rear entrance and close to the main bus stand. The bar is on the ground floor with plenty of seats and tables, and there is more seating upstairs where children are welcome until 7pm. Six handpumps serve two regular beers and four guest beers or ciders. Wetherspoon's popular beer and cider festivals are regular events. Reasonably priced food is available all day from breakfast until late. Q🏴☁️🕭👶🛜

Sunderland

Avenue

Zetland Street, Roker, SR6 0EQ (just off Roker Avenue)
✪ 12.30-11.30; 11-midnight Fri & Sat; 11-11 Sun
☎ (0191) 567 7412
2 changing beers Ⓗ

Close to the Stadium of Light and Roker seafront, this is a popular local hosting entertainment such as live music, quiz nights and bingo evenings. With a ground-floor lounge and bar, and a games room with a full-size snooker table upstairs, there are plenty of options for relaxing with a choice of handpulled ales. A function room provides extra space during busier periods and is available to hire. ♫🛏🚌(E1,E6)🐾🛜

Chesters Ⓛ ●

Chester Road, SR4 7DR
✪ 10-11 (midnight Fri & Sat); 12-10.30 Sun
☎ (0191) 565 9952
6 changing beers Ⓗ

This popular pub just outside the city centre was recently refurbished and has a smart yet comfortable interior, with a large main bar and a more intimate area at the back. There is always at least one ale from Maxim Brewery as well as guest ales from other brewers. Outside is ample car parking and a large beer garden. A function room with private bar is also available. ♿☁️🕭👶🅿🛜

Dun Cow ★ Ⓛ

High Street West, SR1 3HA
✪ 12-12.30am; 12-11.30 Sun ☎ (0191) 567 2984
Camerons Strongarm; 6 changing beers Ⓗ

Dating back to 1900, this architectural gem was reopened in 2014 following a sensitive restoration by Camerons. As part of the Head of Steam chain, it offers seven cask beers from local breweries and from further afield. The beer range is complemented by three real ciders, six specialist keg beers, an extensive range of bottled beers and craft gins. Food is served in the upper floor room from Longhorns Smokehouse. The pub is next to the Empire Theatre and close to Sunderland Minster and city centre restaurants. ☁️🚆🚌👶🛜

Fitzgeralds Ⓛ

12-14 Green Terrace, SR1 3PZ
✪ 11.30-11 (11.30 Fri & Sat); 12-11 Sun ☎ (0191) 567 0852
Fyne Ales Jarl; Timothy Taylor Boltmaker; Titanic Plum Porter; 5 changing beers Ⓗ

Sunderland outpost of the Sir John Fitzgerald chain. This former local and regional CAMRA Pub of the Year has three regular beers complemented by eight guests. There are two separate rooms offering a choice of seating areas, with the smaller nautically themed Chart Room quieter than the main bar. Meet the Brewer evenings are regular events and live music is hosted on Sunday and Tuesday evenings. Q♫☁️🚆🚌👶🅿🚪🛜

Harbour View

Harbour View, SR6 0NU
✪ 10.30-11.30 (midnight Fri & Sat) ☎ (0191) 567 3878
6 changing beers Ⓗ

A modern, open-plan lounge bar close to Roker beach. The first-floor restaurant offers fine views over the nearby River Wear and marina. Six handpumps dispense two regular ales alongside a choice of guests from near and far. The pub can get busy when Sunderland AFC are at home. ♿🅰🚌(E1,18,19)🐾🛜

Ivy House

7A Worcester Terrace, Ashbrooke, SR2 7AW
✪ 12-11 (midnight Fri & Sat) ☎ (0191) 567 3399
5 changing beers Ⓗ

Tucked away but close to the bus and metro interchange, the Ivy House is well worth seeking out. Five ever-changing guest ales are on offer as well as a guest cider. An extensive range of bottled Belgian beers is also kept. Home-made pizzas and burgers are freshly prepared in an open kitchen next to the bar. Quiz night is Wednesday. Note the stag-horn lights. ♿☁️🕭🚆🚌👶🅿🛜

King's Arms Ⓛ

Beach Street, Deptford, SR4 6BU
✪ 4.30 (4 Wed & Thu)-11; 12-midnight Fri & Sat; 12-11 Sun
☎ (0191) 567 9804
Timothy Taylor Landlord; 6 changing beers Ⓗ

Established in the Deptford area of Sunderland in 1834, the King's Arms is a traditional pub with an L-shaped bar featuring eight handpulls, one regularly dispensing Timothy Taylor Landlord and another a real cider. The remaining beers are sourced from local breweries and beyond. There is a small snug and a marquee outside where live music is hosted. A quiz is held every Sunday and curry night is Thursday. Bar snacks are available. ♿🚌👶🅿🚌(10,11)🐾🛜

Poetic License Ⓛ

Roker Terrace, Roker, SR6 9ND
✪ 11-11 (1am Fri & Sat) ☎ (0191) 567 1786
⊕ poeticlicensebar.co.uk
Sonnet 43 American Pale Ale, Blonde Beer, Bourbon Milk Stout, India Pale Ale, Steam Beer; 4 changing beers Ⓗ

Poetic License has fine views of the mouth of the River Wear and seashore. Up to four Sonnet 43 beers are on offer alongside up to four guests. It is also home to the city's first micro-distillery and makes its own spirits. The decor is a blend of modern and traditional, with wood-panelled ceilings and comfortable seating. Meal deals are available Monday to Friday. Disabled access is to the left of the hotel reception. ⌂⬢◖❹❖🅿️�

Port of Call 🅛
1-3 Park Lane, SR1 3NX
✪ 11.30-1am; 11.30-3am Sat & Sun ☎ (0191) 514 5408
⊕ portofcall.co
Thornbridge Jaipur IPA; Maxim Double Maxim Ⓗ
Bar and eatery in a nautical-themed building set over three floors. The two cask ales can be found on the ground floor bar and a selection of international bottled beers is kept on all three floors. There are outside drinking areas on the first and second floors, overlooking Park Lane. Close to most city-centre buses and Park Lane Metro.
⬤🌸◖❹⬆️🈂🅀🛜

Ship Isis 🅛
26 Silksworth Row, SR1 3QJ
✪ 12-11.30 (12.30am Fri & Sat) ☎ (0191) 514 7684
Camerons Strongarm; 7 changing beers Ⓗ
Restored to its original Victorian splendour by Jarrow Brewery and acquired by Camerons, the Isis is now part of the Head of Steam group. Twelve handpumps offer nine cask beers and three real ciders, complemented by an extensive selection of bottled beers and a range of craft gins. The pub has its own beer sommelier and staff are knowledgeable. Wednesday is buskers' night and there is live music on Sundays. Just a short walk from the city centre. ⌂Å🈂🅀🍴🅿️�(10,11)🛜

William Jameson ✓
32 Fawcett Street, SR1 1RH
✪ 8am-midnight ☎ (0191) 514 5016
Greene King Abbot; Ruddles Best Bitter; 4 changing beers Ⓗ
Sunderland's first Wetherspoon is in a former department store under the City Library and Arts Centre and opposite the Winter Gardens. All the usual features associated with the chain can be found is this busy pub at the heart of the city centre. Twelve handpumps offer up to four guest beers to complement the regular range. The pub is a keen supporter of local brewers. Q◖❹Å🈂🅀🛜

Swalwell

Sun Inn ✓
Market Lane, NE16 3AL (just off roundabout at end of Front St)
✪ 11-11; 12-11 Sun ☎ (0191) 488 7783
Marston's Pedigree; 2 changing beers Ⓗ
Situated in the heart of the historic village that spawned many internationally renowned engineers and industrialists, and of course the famous Swalwell cabbage. This truly no-nonsense community pub provides good company for locals and strangers alike. Sword dancers, darts, dominoes handicaps, a monthly pie competition and Saturday buskers' nights all feature. Bar food and snacks are available and are free on Sundays. There is a regular bus service from Newcastle.
🌸🌸❖🍴🚍👟

Tynemouth

Tynemouth Lodge Hotel 🅛
Tynemouth Road, NE30 4AA

✪ 11-11; 12-10.30 Sun ☎ (0191) 257 7565
⊕ tynemouthlodgehotel.co.uk
Caledonian Deuchars IPA; Draught Bass; Mordue Northumbrian Blonde; 1 changing beer Ⓗ
This attractive externally tiled 1799 free house, situated next to a former house of correction, has featured in every issue of the Guide since 1983. The comfortable pub has a U-shaped lounge with the bar on one side and a serving hatch on the other, and is noted in the area for the quality of its Draught Bass. The beer garden, to the rear, is on the fringe of Northumberland Park. A popular stopping-off point for those completing the Coast-to-Coast cycle route. Q🌸🅀🅿️🚍(1,306)🛜

Washington

Courtyard 🅛
Biddick Lane, NE38 8AB
✪ 11-11 (midnight Fri & Sat); 12-11 Sun ☎ (0191) 417 0445
⊕ artscentrewashington.co.uk/courtyard.aspx
Leamside Five quarter, Adventure; Timothy Taylor Landlord; 4 changing beers Ⓗ
Located within the lively arts centre, this light and airy café/bar offers a warm welcome to drinkers and food lovers alike. Eight handpumped beers, one real cider, one perry and a range of bottled Belgian beers are available. An extensive range of food is served throughout the day, with early-evening specials. The pub hosts a weekly quiz and buskers' nights. Outdoor seating is within the courtyard. Popular beer festivals are held annually, on the Easter and August bank holidays.
Q⬤🌸◖❹Å🍴🅿️🍴🚍(2A,4,8)

Sir William de Wessyngton ✓
2-3 Victoria Road, Concord, NE37 2SY
✪ 7am-11 ☎ (0191) 418 0100
Greene King Abbot; Ruddles Best Bitter; 4 changing beers Ⓗ
Large open-plan Wetherspoon pub housed in a former snooker hall and ice cream parlour. It is named after a Norman knight and lord of the manor whose descendants later emigrated to the United States. A real ale oasis, it is the only cask beer outlet in Concord and offers good-value beer and the usual well-priced Wetherspoon menu. The regular ales are complemented by up to four guests, and occasional beer festivals are held.
Q⬤◖❹⬆️🅿️🛜

Steps ✓
47 Spout Lane, NE38 7HP
✪ 3.30 (2.30 Fri)-11; 12-11 Sat; 12-10.30 Sun
☎ (0191) 415 0733
5 changing beers Ⓗ
Opened in 1894 as the Spout Lane Inn, the pub was renamed the Steps in 1976. The small, comfortable, single-room lounge bar is divided into two drinking areas and the walls are decorated with pictures of old Washington. Five beers are on offer, frequently including ales from local microbreweries. Quiz nights are Wednesdays and Thursdays. Opening hours may vary. Q◖🅿️🚍(86)

West Boldon

Black Horse
Rectory Bank, NE36 0QQ (off A184)
✪ 11-11; 11-11.30 Sun ☎ (0191) 536 1814
Jennings Cumberland Ale; 1 changing beer Ⓗ

An old-fashioned pub with unusual bric-a-brac adorning the walls. The photographs on display are by the talented chef, and prints are available to buy. The pub has one small L-shaped bar and, with a popular restaurant serving high-quality food, can get busy in the evenings and at weekends. Live music features on Sunday night. Q♪☐

West Herrington

Stables

DH4 4ND (off B1286)
⊙ 12-11 (midnight Fri & Sat) ☎ (0191) 584 9226
Black Sheep Best Bitter; Timothy Taylor Landlord; 2 changing beers Ⓗ
This conversion from a riding school is well worth a visit and you can be sure of a warm welcome. It oozes farmhouse character with original beams, stonework and a blazing fire. There is a main bar/restaurant and small snug behind the bar. Four handpulls offer two permanent and two guest ales.

An extensive food menu is available daily, with tapas on Friday and Saturday evenings (it is wise to book ahead for a meal). ➷☺◖&P🚍🌼

West Monkseaton

Beacon Hotel ✅

Earsdon Road, NE25 9PT
⊙ 11-midnight ☎ (0191) 253 6911
Brakspear Bitter; Caledonian Deuchars IPA; Durham White Gold; 6 changing beers Ⓗ
Superb modern pub set back from the main road and popular with locals. The manager sources a wide range of ales and there is a quick turnover. Customers can order a wooden paddle of three third-pints for variety. The cellar has dedicated lines so the ale is served at the correct temperature. The food is excellent – there are themed food nights Monday to Thursday and chef's specials Friday and Saturday. Quiz nights are Sunday and Wednesday. Q☺◖&🚍P🚍

Bodega, Newcastle upon Tyne: City Centre (Photo: Cat Button)

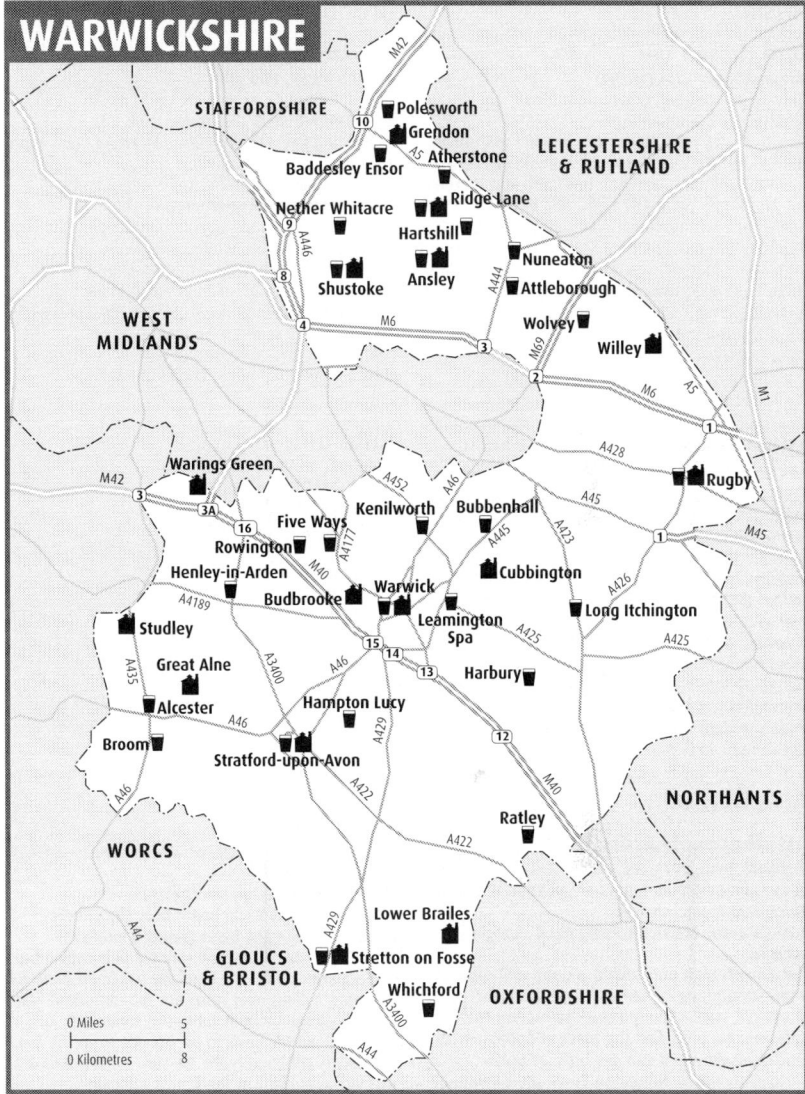

Alcester

Three Tuns

34 High Street, B49 5AB (next to post office)
✪ 12-1am (midnight Sun) summer; 1-midnight; 12-1am Fri &
Sat; 12-midnight Sun winter ☎ (01789) 568255
**Adnams Southwold Bitter; 5 changing beers (sourced
regionally; often Batemans, Hobsons, Titanic)** Ⓗ
An old-fashioned real ale/craft cider/fruit wine
pub, and not forgetting the prosecco on tap! What
a fantastic collection of ales here – with one dark
ale always available. A popular meeting place, the
18th-century building features real beams, original
stone-flagged floors and sections of wattle and
daub walls on display. You are welcome to bring
your own sandwiches or snacks, with plates
provided. A wide range of malt whiskies is also
kept. ✿♣🍴🚌(26,247,X50)🐾🛜

Turk's Head

4 High Street, B49 5AD (near church)
✪ 12-11 (1am Fri); 10-1am Sat; 12-10.30 Sun
☎ (01789) 765948 ⊕ theturkshead.net
**Wye Valley HPA; 3 changing beers (sourced
regionally; often Salopian, Skinner's, Timothy
Taylor)** Ⓗ
A central location helps make this a popular place.
The publican is a real ale enthusiast, staging beer
festivals during the summer months, either from
the garden bar or from the mobile bar outside the
pub during Alcester's popular food festivals. Beers
are sourced from Cornwall, South Wales, Shropshire
and Yorkshire to give a wide range of styles and
flavours. A busy dining pub which sources the best
quality ingredients to deliver classic and modern
pub dishes (booking advisable).
✿◖👌🍴🚌(26,247,X50)🐾🛜

Ansley

Lord Nelson Inn ♈ 🄻 ✅
Birmingham Road, CV10 9PQ
🕓 12-11; 12-10.30 Sun ☎ (024) 7639 2305
⊕ thelordnelsoninnansley.co.uk
Sperrin Ansley Mild, Head Hunter, Band of Brothers, Third Party, Thick as Thieves; 3 changing beers 🄷
This nautically themed pub has been run by the Sperrin family since 1974 and has featured in the Guide for 23 consecutive years. Nine handpulls dispense the family's own Sperrin brews plus ales from other local breweries and some not so local. There is an extensive food menu with meal nights and tribute nights hosted. The suntrap courtyard and garden are a venue for beer festivals and barbecues. ⌂❀🕽P🛒🐾

Atherstone

Angel Ale House ♈ 🄻 ✅
24 Church Street, CV9 1RN
🕓 4-11 (midnight Fri); 12-midnight Sat; 12-10.30
Sun ☎ 07525 183056
Blythe Staffie; Oakham Citra; 4 changing beers 🄷
Attractive establishment with a black and white exterior. Inside, the bar looks out onto the market square and there is a comfortable lounge to the rear. Music in the bar is via customer select-and-play from the large vinyl LP collection. Up to six real ales are offered, often local and usually including a couple of dark beers. Themed beer festivals feature occasionally. If no parking is available on the market square there is a large free council car park to the rear. ⌂❀🚲🚶🛒(48,65)🐾

Attleborough

Attleborough Arms
Highfield Road, CV11 4PL
🕓 11-11 (midnight Fri & Sat); 12-11 Sun ☎ (024) 7638 3231
⊕ attleborougharmspub.co.uk
Banks's Bitter; Marston's Pedigree; 4 changing beers 🄷
Large open-plan pub selling a good and often interesting range of various beers from the Marston's stable. Many value-for-money meal deals are on offer and the place is popular with lunchtime diners. It can get busy at times, particularly when Nuneaton Town are playing at home. Buffets can be catered for on special occasions. 🕽&P🛒🐾📶

Baddesley Ensor

Red Lion
The Common, CV9 2BT (from Grendon roundabout on A5 go S up Boot Hill) SP273983
🕓 7 (4 Fri)-11; 12-3, 7-11 Sat; 12-3, 7-10.30 Sun
☎ (01827) 718186
Everards Tiger Best Bitter; Marston's Pedigree; 4 changing beers 🄷
Busy community local with a landlord who has been at the helm for 20 years. Food does not feature, just ale and conversation. Comfy seating and the log fire are enhanced by a music-free environment. Four guest ales are served, often from major concerns such as Greene King and Everards, but sometimes from small local breweries. The sparkler is willingly removed on request. Off-road parking is available opposite the pub. Q♣🚶🛒(766)🐾

Broom

Broom Tavern 🄻
32 High Street, B50 4HL
🕓 12-3, 5-midnight; 12-midnight Sat; 12-11 Sun
☎ (01789) 778199 ⊕ broomtavern.co.uk
4 changing beers (often Purity, Stratford Upon Avon, Wye Valley) 🄷
A lovely brick and timber multi-room building which retains a great amount of character. It has been tastefully made over, while keeping the cosy snug and log fire in winter. Reopened by two experienced chefs with a good pedigree in the kitchen, it serves great food lunchtimes and evenings, made with local ingredients. Local beers are frequently found here alongside the Cornish contingents and at least one real cider. There is a choice of beer gardens. Q⌂❀🕽P🐾📶

Bubbenhall

Malt Shovel 🄻
Lower End, CV8 3BW
🕓 12-11 ☎ (024) 7630 1141
Church End Fallen Angel; Greene King Abbot; 2 changing beers (sourced locally; often Purity) 🄷
A genuine village pub at the heart of the community, attracting a pleasing mix of locals and visitors. There is a large L-shaped lounge bar and patio area at the front, and a small public bar to the rear. Home-cooked food is available. Behind the spacious car park lies the pleasant walled garden and adjacent bowling green. ❀🕽♣P🛒(539)🐾

Five Ways

Case is Altered 🄻
Case Lane, CV35 7JD (off Five Ways Road near A4141/A4177 jct) SP225701
🕓 12-2.30, 6-11; 12-7.30 Sun ☎ (01926) 484206
Wye Valley Butty Bach; house beer (by Old Pie Factory); 3 changing beers (sourced locally) 🄷
An old-fashioned unspoilt country pub with a bar and separate snug. The landlady has been there for 32 years, taking over from her grandmother. The traditional bar billiards table still takes old sixpences which have to be bought from the bar. Monday is cribbage night. Be sure to take a look at the Victorian print in the bar of a former Leamington brewer plus a clock from another old local brewer. There is also a propeller from a WWI fighter on the ceiling. Q❀&♣P

REAL ALE BREWERIES

Atomic 🍺 Rugby
Blue Bell 🍺 Warings Green
Church End 🍺 Ridge Lane
Church Farm Budbrooke
Clouded Minds Lower Brailes
Griffin 🍺 Shustoke
Kendrick's Willey
Merry Miner Grendon
North Cotswold Stretton-on-Fosse
Old Pie Factory Warwick
Purity Great Alne
Slaughterhouse 🍺 Warwick
Sperrin 🍺 Ansley
Stratford Upon Avon Stratford-upon-Avon
Warwickshire Cubbington
Weatheroak Studley

Hampton Lucy

Boar's Head ⓛ ⓥ

Church Street, CV35 8BE

☼ 12-midnight; 12-10 (8 winter) Sun ☎ (01789) 840533

🌐 theboarsheadhamptonlucy.co.uk

Church End Gravediggers Ale; Ringwood Best Bitter; 4 changing beers (sourced locally; often Church End, Church Farm, Wye Valley) Ⓗ

A friendly, popular village pub dating back to the 17th century. Originally built as a cider house, the present kitchen was once a mortuary. Close to the River Avon, it is frequented by cyclists, walkers and visitors to nearby Charlecote Park. Five or more real ales are served with at least two LocAles. The menu offers fresh, locally sourced home-made food. The sheltered, walled rear garden is popular in good weather. An annual themed beer festival is held in summer. Q�â☼ⓓ▲♣●P🐾🐾 �

Harbury

Old New Inn ⓛ

Farm Sreet, CV33 9LS (SW side of village)

☼ 4.30 (12 Sat & Sun)-midnight; 12-11 Sun
☎ (01926) 614023

Church End Goats Milk; Purity Mad Goose; Slaughterhouse Saddleback Best Bitter; 1 changing beer Ⓗ

A traditional, privately owned village pub where darts, dominoes and pool teams are well supported and major sporting fixtures are screened on TV. Situated on the edge of the village and housed in a former farmhouse and bakery, the building is made of local stone and has two rooms with low ceilings which reflect its age. There is a large family garden situated at the rear. �â☼▲♣P🐾🐾 ♛free

Hartshill

Royal Oak ⓛ ⓥ

Oldbury Road, CV10 0TD

☼ 4-11; 12-midnight Fri-Sun ☎ (024) 7639 6442

🌐 theroyaloakhartshill.co.uk

3 changing beers Ⓗ

This free house has been refurbished to give a village-community, old-fashioned feeling, with many old pictures of Hartshill on display. It offers a constantly changing range of beers from breweries near and far, alongside a cider always on handpull. A good-sized garden at the rear accommodates live music and beer festivals during the summer months. �â☼♣●P🐾🐾 ♛free

Henley-in-Arden

Black Swan ⓥ

23 High Street, B95 5AA

☼ 12-11 (midnight Fri & Sat) ☎ (01564) 795338

🌐 theblackswanhenley.co.uk

Sharp's Doom Bar; Timothy Taylor Landlord; 2 changing beers Ⓗ

A rambling, multi-room, split-level pub on a classic high street in a lovely old market town. The interior is now semi-open plan, featuring a wealth of beams. The beers are exceptionally well kept. Traditional pub games include dominoes, crib and darts. Open mic night is the first Wednesday of the month, karaoke features every Friday, a quiz on Thursday, and occasional live music on Saturday. No food Sunday/Monday evenings.
Q☼â☼ⓓ&🚆♣●P🚇(S20,X20)🐾 ♛free

Kenilworth

Green Man ⓛ

Warwick Road, CV8 1HS

☼ 11-11 (midnight Fri & Sat) ☎ (01296) 863061

Brakspear Bitter; Purity Pure Ubu; 8 changing beers (sourced nationally) Ⓗ

A welcome return to the Guide for this popular Ember Inn. Two banks of five handpulls offer a range of permanent and changing beers, with an often interesting selection of guest ales sourced from throughout the country. The central bar serves several distinct seating areas and a pleasant patio. Good-quality food is available all day until 10pm. There is plentiful parking and dogs are permitted in the outdoor seating area. �â☼ⓓ&P🚇(11,X17)free

Old Bakery 🏆

12 High Street, CV8 1LZ (near A429/A452 jct)

☼ 5.30 (5 Fri & Sat)-11; 5-10.30 Sun ☎ (01926) 864111

🌐 theoldbakery.eu

Wye Valley HPA; 3 changing beers (sourced locally; often Byatt's, Church End, Purity) Ⓗ

Located in a picturesque part of Kenilworth near St Nicholas Church and Abbey Fields, this two-roomed bar has been fashioned out of an oak-beamed 400-year-old building. There are no TV screens, music or noisy games machines, just convivial conversation. Discerning drinkers can enjoy four beers served with friendly efficiency. Home-made Monday night food is always popular. Disabled access is to the rear of the building. En-suite accommodation is available. Q☼🛏&P🚇(11)free

Virgins & Castle

7 High Street, CV8 1LY (A429/A452 jct)

☼ 11-11 (midnight Fri & Sat) ☎ (01926) 853737

🌐 virginsandcastle.co.uk

Everards Beacon Bitter, Sunchaser Blonde, Tiger Best Bitter, Original; 1 changing beer (sourced nationally) Ⓗ

Near Abbey Fields and St Nicholas Church in Kenilworth's old town, this multi-room, split-level pub originally dates from the 16th century. Beers are principally from Everards, with a national guest ale also available. The food is popular, with diners enjoying both English and Filipino cuisine (no food Sun eve). Beer festivals are held twice-yearly in May and October. Street parking is limited but there is a nearby public car park.
Q☼â☼ⓓ&●🚇(11)🐾 free

Leamington Spa

Woodland Tavern ⓛ ⓥ

3 Regent Street, CV32 5HW

☼ 12-midnight (1am Fri & Sat); 12-11.30 Sun
☎ (01926) 425868

Slaughterhouse Saddleback Best Bitter; Wychwood Hobgoblin; 4 changing beers Ⓗ

A traditional Victorian street-corner pub located close to the centre of Leamington Spa and enjoyed by locals and visitors alike. It has a public bar and separate lounge, also used as a function room. The unique partially covered courtyard features murals depicting local references and jokes. On the side of the building is a large colourful mural showing a dray and horses delivering ale to the pub. Real ciders are from Westons and Thatchers.
☼â&🚆♣●🚇🐾 free

Long Itchington

Green Man ✓
Church Road, CV47 9PW
☼ 5-11.30 (midnight Fri); 12-midnight Sat; 12-10.30 Sun
☎ (01926) 812208 ⊕ greenmanlongitchington.co.uk
Black Sheep Best Bitter; Fuller's London Pride; Purity
Mad Goose; St Austell Tribute; 1 changing beer H
Hosts Mark and Sharon run a proper community
pub which has earned a regular place in the Guide.
The building, which dates back some 300 years,
exhibits a number of drinking areas and a function
room. With a garden at the rear and patio at the
front, the outside areas are particularly busy in May
when the annual beer festival attracts drinkers
from miles around. To the rear is a large camping
and caravan site. Q ➸ ✿ & ▲ ♣ ● P ⊟ (64) ❀ ☞

Nether Whitacre

Dog Inn
Dog Lane, B46 2DU SP232930
☼ 12-3, 6-11; 12-11 Sat & Sun ☎ (01675) 481318
5 changing beers H
Well-hidden black-and-white rural classic, with a
peaceful beer garden which includes a pets' corner.
Inside, brass knick-knacks abound, and winter
features two beefy log fires. Easily missed is the
marvellously elaborate carved frontage to the bar,
including two pairs of stuffed jays. There are two
cosy, intimate dining rooms to the side. The four or
five guest ales are generally well-known names
and change slowly – try-before-you-buy is offered.
Complimentary bar nibbles are served on Sunday
lunchtimes. ➸ ✿ ◑ P ❀

Nuneaton

Crown
10 Bond Street, CV11 4BX (between rail and bus
stations)
☼ 12-11 (midnight Fri & Sat) ☎ (024) 7637 3343
6 changing beers H
Close to the railway and bus stations, this regular
Guide entry boasts 10 handpulls offering six real
ales, often from Cottage brewery, and four ciders
or perries. A choice of foreign bottled beers is also
stocked as well as a large selection of malt
whiskies. Live music features on Saturday nights.
There is a large garden to the rear and a function
room available for hire. Beer festivals are held in
June and December. Sunday lunch is served until
4pm. The pub hosts the Nuneaton Folk Club on the
first Wednesday of the month. ✿ ⇌ ● P ⊟ ☞

Felix Holt L ✓
3 Stratford Street, CV11 5BS
☼ 8am-midnight (1am Wed & Thu; 2am Fri & Sat); 8-11 Sun
☎ (024) 7634 7785
Adnams Broadside; Byatt's Regal Blond; Greene King
Abbot; Ruddles Best Bitter; changing beers (often
Oakham, Byatt's) H
Large Wetherspoon outlet situated in the town
centre. Novelist George Eliot was born in Nuneaton
and the pub takes its name from one of her works.
The literary theme is reflected in the décor of books
and pictures of local history. A good range of guest
ales is always on offer. Food is served 8am-10pm.
There is a heated area for smokers.
Q ➸ ◑ & ⇌ ● ⊟ ☞

Horseshoes L
2 Heath End Road, CV10 7JQ (close to George Eliot
Hospital and Coventry Canal)
☼ 11-11 (midnight Fri & Sat); 12-11 Sun ☎ (024) 7767 5066
Everards Beacon Bitter, Tiger Best Bitter, Original; 4
changing beers H
An Everards pub which has been refurbished to
create more room. It sells a large range of the
brewery's own beers alongside a choice of guests
plus cider and perries. The family-friendly venue is
popular with diners and features various themed
food nights. Quiz night is Wednesday. There is an
outside drinking area at the side of the building.
Q ➸ ✿ ◑ & ● P ⊟ ❀ ☞

Lord Hop L
38 Queens Road, CV11 5JX
☼ 12-10 ☎ (024) 7798 1869
4 changing beers H
Town centre micropub run by two local CAMRA
members. It sits on two levels with four or more
real ales available on either handpull or straight
from the cask from both local and far away
breweries plus two cider/perries. Wine and soft
drinks are also stocked. CAMRA magazines from
various branches are available to read. No under-
18s, and guide dogs only. Q ⇌ ● ⊟ ☞

Polesworth

Bull's Head
Tamworth Road, B78 1JH (by canal bridge on B5000)
☼ 11-midnight; 11-11.30 Sun ☎ 07796 538415
Sharp's Doom Bar; 2 changing beers H
Wet-led community local which has a pleasantly
old-fashioned feel, and thrives on a range of
activities including darts and bowls, quizzes, raffles
and sports screenings. When the L-shaped bar is
busy, the small lounge through the archway is
better for a quiet chat. There are two guest
handpumps, though only one may be in action
depending on the time of week. No food, but the
independent Indian restaurant upstairs (open every
evening) will fetch ale for you from downstairs.
♣ P ⊟ ☞

Ratley

Rose & Crown
OX15 6DS
☼ 12-3 (not Mon), 5-11; 12-midnight Fri & Sat; 12-11 Sun
☎ (01295) 678148 ⊕ roseandcrown-ratley.co.uk
Ringwood Best Bitter; St Austell Tribute; Wells
Bombardier; 2 changing beers (sourced regionally;
often Purity, Warwickshire, Wye Valley) H
Tucked away at the bottom of an ancient village,
this 11th-century pub is a real find for the ale
enthusiast, with stone walls, oak beams and open
fires. Situated on the northern tip of the Cotswolds,
the pub is a welcome stop for dogs and their
walkers. Good food includes daily specials, with
fish a speciality. The hidden snug is ideal for groups
and celebrations and the terraced garden is lovely
for sunny days. Reputedly haunted by a Roundhead
soldier found hiding in the inglenook.
Q ➸ ✿ ◑ ▲ ♣ ⊟ (269) ❀ ☞

Ridge Lane

Church End Brewery Tap L
CV10 0RD (2 miles SW of Atherstone)

✪ 6 (12 Fri & Sat)-11; 12-10.30 Sun; closed Mon-Wed
☎ (01827) 713080 ⊕ churchendbrewery.co.uk
Church End Poachers Pocket, Gravediggers Ale, What the Fox's Hat, Fallen Angel; 4 changing beers ⊞
This brewery tap is hidden from the road, with access signposted by a board positioned at the entrance. The brewery can be viewed from the bar area. Eight handpulls serve the bar and vestry. Beers change regularly but always include a mild. The ever-changing ciders are dispensed direct from the barrel. Children are not allowed inside but there is a large meadow garden with ample seating. The pub opens on the third Wednesday of the month for Atherstone Folk Club night.
Q✿&Å♠🚻🅿🗑🐾🐾🛜

Rowington

Rowington Club 🅛

Rowington Green, CV35 7DB (just off B4439 between Rowington and Lapworth; follow signs for Rowington Village Hall) SP1988070150
✪ 2 (12 Sat)-midnight; 12-11 Sun ☎ (01564) 782087
Sharp's Doom Bar; Wye Valley HPA; 2 changing beers ⊞
Busy and thriving community club, popular with locals, also open to visitors, with free entry for card-carrying CAMRA members. Four real ales are on offer at all times plus traditional ciders, usually Lilley's Wild Dog. Darts matches are held on Thursday evenings. Bar snacks are available. The large beer garden overlooks the village cricket ground, and the club is handy for local walking and cycling. Always friendly, it is well-worth seeking out. Q🏰✿&♣♠🅿🐾🛜

Rugby

Alexandra Arms 🅛

72 James Street, CV21 2SL (next to John Barford multi-storey car park)
✪ 11.30-11.30 (midnight Fri & Sat); 12-11.30 Sun
☎ (01788) 578660 ⊕ alexandraarms.co.uk
Atomic Strike, Half life; Fuller's London Pride; 4 changing beers (sourced nationally; often Abbeydale) ⊞
Owned by Atomic Brewery, this town-centre pub has a comfortable recently refurbished lounge bar where good-value pub food is served at lunchtimes. The large bar accommodates a pool table, skittles table and the best rock jukebox in the county. There is a large rear garden which hosts a summer beer festival. The brewery itself is at the back in the garden. Seven times local CAMRA Pub of the Year. Q🏰✿🛢&≒♣♠🛜

Bell ✪

High Street, Hillmorton, CV21 4HD (on A428 2 miles E of Rugby)
✪ 12-midnight; 12-11 Fri-Sun ☎ (01788) 544465
⊕ thebell-hillmorton.co.uk
M&B Brew XI; Sharp's Doom Bar; Wadworth 6X; 1 changing beer ⊞
Popular, recently refurbished, family-friendly pub with a restaurant and spacious bar, offering four excellent real ales. The food comes with beer recommendations, and includes hearty British pub classics, Sunday roasts and breakfasts from 9.30am. Televised sport is shown in the bar area, live music features on Saturday night, and there is a regular quiz night. The large child-friendly garden at the rear is also the scene for regular barbecues in the summer months. 🏰✿🛢♠🅿(3,10,96)🐾🛜

Merchants Inn 🅛

5-6 Little Church Street, CV21 3AW
✪ 12-midnight (1am Fri & Sat); 12-11 Sun
☎ (01788) 571119 ⊕ merchantsinn.co.uk
Batemans XB; Nethergate Suffolk County Best Bitter; Oakham Bishops Farewell; changing beers (sourced nationally) ⊞
Up to nine real ales are available in this flagstoned gem of a pub. Comfortable seating and an open fire make this a welcoming place to enjoy real ales, ciders, perries and foreign beers. Excellent home-cooked food is served at lunchtime. The walls are covered in an impressive range of pub and brewery memorabilia. Rugby and cricket feature on the big screen. There are regular beer festivals, theme nights and quizzes. Situated a mile from the railway station. 🏰✿🛢&♣♠🗑🅿🐾🛜

Raglan Arms

50 Dunchurch Road, CV22 6AD (on A426 near gyratory and town centre)
✪ 4-midnight (1am Fri); 12-1am Sat; 12-11 Sun
☎ (01788) 544441
Abbeydale Moonshine; Greene King Abbot; house beer (by Morland); changing beers (sourced nationally; often Belvoir, Newby Wyke, North Cotswold) ⊞
Up to eight handpumps serving a fine selection of real ales await you at the friendly Raglan Arms. A winner of many CAMRA awards, it was runner-up local CAMRA Pub of the Year for 2015. The pub hosts quiz nights and live music events monthly. It offers tasty locally sourced bar snacks and can cater for corporate and special events. Outside is a heated, covered area. Pop in and see Liz and the team: you will not be disappointed at this characterful little gem.
🏰✿♣♠🅿(12,63,86)🐾🛜

Rugby Tap 🍺 🅛

3 St Matthews Street, CV21 3BY (close to town centre adjacent to A426 gyratory)
✪ 10-6 (10 Fri & Sat); 12-3 Sun ☎ (01788) 576767
⊕ rugbytap.co.uk
Changing beers (sourced locally; often Byatt's, Church End, Purity) 🅖
The Rugby Tap off-licence and Tap Room micropub stock a large selection of draught and bottled ales and ciders, and a large range of imported beers. The Tap Room offers an environment that shuns electronic entertainment, promoting conversation in an intimate setting. Acoustic music features on the first Thursday evening of each month. The Rugby Tap serves up to six LocAles and ciders and has a range of traditional pub snacks. Winner of local CAMRA Pub of the Year 2016.
Q♠🅿(12,63,86)🐾🛜

Seven Stars

40 Albert Street, CV21 2SH
✪ 12-11 (midnight Fri & Sat); 12-10.30 Sun
☎ (01788) 535478 ⊕ sevenstarsrugby.co.uk
Everards Tiger Best Bitter; Grainstore Rutland Panther, Ten Fifty; Oakham JHB; changing beers (sourced nationally) ⊞
Quintessential back-street local tastefully refurbished in 2012. The pub has plenty of charm and character, offering a warm and friendly welcome. Quiet background music makes conversation a delight. The bar boasts 14 handpumps, with mild and two ciders permanently on offer, and guest beers available alongside the Everards, Oakham and Grainstore regular ales. Live

music evenings and charity events feature occasionally. A winner of many CAMRA awards in recent years. Q♿☆🅿🍴🍽🏦🛏📶

Squirrel Inn ⓛ

33 Church Street, CV21 3PU

☼ 12-midnight; 4-11 Sun ☎ (01788) 578527

Marston's Pedigree; 4 changing beers (sourced regionally; often Dow Bridge, Merry Miner) Ⓗ

A small pub with a big welcome. A real fire creates a cosy atmosphere and adds to the Squirrel's genuine charm. Live music is a big part of the pub's culture, and clubs, darts teams and BT Sport add to the lively mix. As well as regular and guest beers from the Marston's range, local breweries including Dow Bridge feature. The railway station is less than a mile away. Occasionally the pub may open later midweek. ♣🍴🛏🐾

Victoria Inn ⓛ

1 Lower Hillmorton Road, CV21 3ST

☼ 12 (4 Mon-Wed)-midnight ☎ (01788) 544374

⊕ downthevic.com

Atomic Strike, Half life; Hook Norton Hooky; 4 changing beers (sourced nationally; often Hop Studio, RCH, Wentworth) Ⓗ

A traditional Victorian real ale pub owned by the Atomic Brewery with 10 handpumps offering rapidly changing ales. Real cider is also on handpull and a selection of foreign beers is available. Friendly, efficient staff serve in the lively, bustling period lounge and the traditional bar which doubles as a games room for darts and pool. TV sport is regularly screened. Themed beer festivals are held twice a year. The railway station is less than a mile away. ♿☆♣🍴🛏🐾📶

Shustoke

Griffin Inn ⓛ

Church Road, B46 2LB (on B4116 on sharp bend)

☼ 12-2.30, 7-11; 12-11 Fri; 12-10.30 Sun ☎ (01675) 481205

⊕ griffininnshustoke.co.uk

Marston's Pedigree; RCH Pitchfork; Theakston Old Peculier; changing beers (often Oakham) Ⓗ

Ever-popular country pub, featuring low beams and inglenook fireplaces with solid fuel stoves. No music or TV intrudes. The seven guest ales always include a mild, and Griffin Inn ales from the on-site brewery feature intermittently. There is always one real cider, up to four in summertime. A large, busy beer festival is the highlight of summer. Children are welcome in the conservatory, beer terrace and meadow-style garden. No food is served on Sundays. Q♿☆🍴Ⓐ🛏🅿🐾📶

Plough

The Green, B46 2AN

☼ 12-3, 5.30-10.30; 12-11 Fri & Sat; 12-10.30 Sun ☎ (01675) 481557

Draught Bass; 3 changing beers Ⓗ

Pretty village-green pub, popular both with locals and visitors. Well regarded for food, the many rooms are often busy with diners. The bar area with a real fire is compact and cosy, with games in a separate room. Three guest ales are usually available, with effort invested to provide the most interesting from the Punch range. There is a feathered-and-furry pets area to the rear, while the front has a tidy beer terrace with greenery. ☆☆🍴👶🅿📶

Stratford-upon-Avon

Bear at the Swan's Nest Hotel ⓛ ✔

Swan's Nest Lane, CV37 7LT (S end of Clopton Bridge)

☼ 12-11 (midnight Fri & Sat) ☎ (01789) 265540

⊕ thebearfreehouse.co.uk

Castle Rock Harvest Pale; Hook Norton Old Hooky; Wye Valley Butty Bach; house beer (by North Cotswold); 4 changing beers (sourced regionally; often Purity, Stratford Upon Avon, Wychwood) Ⓗ

Delightful pub in a waterside location, five minutes' walk from the town centre, serving eight real ales. The focus is on local and regional brewers, with seasonal beers available. The interior has wood panelling and a pewter bar; outside, there are picnic tables for riverside drinking. Excellent home-made meals are served in a warm, friendly, welcoming atmosphere. Board games and newspapers are available. Local CAMRA Pub of the Year 2015. ♿☆☆🍴👶♿🅿🐾📶

Stratford Alehouse ♈ ⓛ

12B Greenhill Street, CV37 6LF

☼ 1-10.30; 1-7 Sun ☎ 07746 807966

⊕ thestratfordalehouse.com

4 changing beers (sourced regionally; often Prescott, Stratford Upon Avon, Uley) Ⓖ

A family-run, one-bar micropub serving the finest real ales, ciders and wines. There is no loud music or gaming machines to distract you here – just a friendly welcome in a relaxing environment for drinking, chatting, making new friends or reading the newspapers. Snacks are served. Since opening in 2013, more than 379 beers from 122 breweries have made an appearance. Home to Stratford Folk Club on the first and third Wednesdays of the month. Q♿🍴🛏🐾

Stretton on Fosse

Plough Inn ⓛ

GL56 9QX (signposted off A429 Fosse Way)

☼ 11-11; 12-10.30 Sun ☎ (01608) 661053

⊕ strettonplough.com

North Cotswold Shagweaver; Wickwar BOB; 2 changing beers (sourced regionally; often Brakspear, Wye Valley) Ⓗ

A beautiful 17th-century stone-built village pub typical of the north Cotswolds, with oak beams and flagstone floors. The bar area is cosy with a large inglenook fireplace adding to the atmosphere. Four real ales and a local cider are available. Home-made food is served. Traditional pub games and quizzes are played in the bar. Q♿☆🍴♣🛏🅿📶

Warwick

Cape of Good Hope ⓛ

66 Lower Cape, CV34 5DP (off Cape Rd)

☼ 12-11; 12-midnight Fri-Sun ☎ (01926) 498138

⊕ thecapeofgoodhopepub.com

Church Farm Harry's Heifer; Hook Norton Hooky; Wye Valley Butty Bach; 3 changing beers Ⓗ

This is a historic 1820s canalside ale house which serves canal users and locals alike. The original building is now the front bar, with a tasteful modern extension to the rear. Internal decorations feature canal memorabilia including interesting maps. The friendly staff are knowledgeable about ale, and proud to serve local beers and foods. Outside, the seating area and garden are adjacent to the Grand Union Canal and the sometimes-busy double lock. ☆☆🍴👶Ⓐ♿🅿🚏(G1)🐾📶

Oak

27 Coten End, CV34 4NT

🌣 1 (3 Mon)-midnight; 12-1am Fri-Sun ☎ (01926) 493774

4 changing beers 🅗

This pub dates back to at least 1874 and is long and narrow, the bar hidden behind a staircase. Beyond the bar are a pool table and dartboard. At the rear is a small patio garden. Two TVs show horse racing and football. The house beer is Oak Bitter, but the brewer is a secret. Real cider is also available. Live music features at the weekend. 🏠🕭≠♣🍴🖪(X17)😋

Old Post Office

12 West Street, CV32 6AN

🌣 12-9; 12-5 Sun; closed Mon ☎ 07765 896155

Slaughterhouse Saddleback Best Bitter; Young's Special 🅗**; 6 changing beers** 🅗/🅖

Located just beyond West Gate and near to Warwick Castle, this small bar is Warwick's first ale house and popular with local residents and real ale enthusiasts. It serves a variety of traditional beers on handpump and straight from the cask, cooled by an ingenious home-made system which keeps the ales in tip-top condition. The interior is adorned with an eclectic collection of pub memorabilia and unusual items including Batman drinking a pint while hanging from the ceiling. 🖳🍴🖪😋

Punch Bowl

1 The Butts, CV34 4SS

🌣 12-11 (11.30 Thu); 12-10 Sun; closed Mon ☎ (01926) 403846 ⊕ punchbowlwarwick.co.uk

Changing beers 🅗

This building is an old coaching inn with a large open bar area on different levels – a raised area acts as a stage for popular music evenings held every Thursday and on special occasions. International sporting events are shown on a large screen. A real ale pub with five changing guest beers available at all times, a blackboard behind the bar shows the number of different beers sold so far. 🖳🕭🕩≠♣P🖪(X17)😋🛜

Tilted Wig ⊘

11 Market Place, CV34 4SA

🌣 11-11 (midnight Fri & Sat) ☎ (01926) 400110 ⊕ tiltedwigwarwick.co.uk

Morland Old Golden Hen; Purity Pure Ubu; Sharp's Doom Bar; 1 changing beer 🅗

Located in Warwick's market square, this Grade II-listed, 17th-century Georgian building was once part of a market hall. The pub has one light airy bar, but the layout and decor divide into three distinct spaces. Seating outside in the square on fine days offers a relaxing continental feel. Real cider is available. Q🖳🕭🕩⚅🍴🖪😋🛜

Wild Boar 🍸 🅛

27 Lakin Road, CV34 5BU

🌣 12-11.30 (12.30am Fri & Sat); 12-10.30 Sun ☎ (01926) 499968 ⊕ thewildboarwarwick.co.uk

Slaughterhouse Saddleback Best Bitter; 10 changing beers (often Everards, Slaughterhouse) 🅗

Award-winning Project William community pub with a bar and snug. This is the tap house for Slaughterhouse Brewery and there are views into the two-barrel microbrewery. Ten handpumps deliver Slaughterhouse, Everards and guest ales alongside two real ciders. A large function room/ beer hall holds many events including the annual Hogtober Fest in October. The attractive patio hop garden provides the hops for Slaughterhouse's The Green Hopper. Q🖳🕭🕩≠♣🍴🖪(X17)😋🛜

Whichford

Norman Knight 🅛

CV36 5PE (2 miles E of A3400, Long Compton, facing village green)

🌣 12-11 summer; 12-3 (not Mon), 6-11; 12-11 Fri & Sat; 12-6 Sun winter ☎ (01608) 684621 ⊕ thenormanknight.co.uk

Stratford Upon Avon Stratford Gold, Malty Pig Bitter; 4 changing beers (sourced locally; often Hook Norton, Purity, Stratford Upon Avon) 🅗

A change of ownership during 2015 saw this pub taken over by Stratford Upon Avon Brewery. Six handpumps showcase the brewery's fine ales alongside local beers and Old Rosie cider. The flagstone-floored pub has two rooms plus a restaurant and a garden with tables overlooking the green. Classic cars gather on the third Thursday of the summer months. Live music features occasionally. Q🖳🕭🕩⚅♣🍴P😋🛜

Wolvey

Blue Pig ⊘

Hall Road, LE10 3LG (set back from village square)

🌣 12-11 (midnight Fri & Sat); 12-10.30 Sun ☎ (01455) 88282 ⊕ bluepigpub.co.uk

Greene King IPA, Abbot; Morland Old Speckled Hen; 1 changing beer 🅗

Picture-postcard village pub in a quiet position near the centre of Wolvey. It has a small outside seating area at the front and garden to the rear. The pub has been sympathetically altered over the years but you can still appreciate its age and history dating back to the 15th century. The long, split-level, L-shaped bar has low ceilings and old settles. It is decorated with traditional farm implements, pitchforks and tankards. The house beer is Blue Pig brewed by Greene King. 🕭🕩P🖪😋🛜

The discreet barman

Over the mahogany, jar followed jorum, gargle, tincture and medium, tailor, scoop, snifter and ball of malt, in a breathless pint-to-pint. Discreet barman, Mr Sugrue thought, turning outside the door and walking in the direction of Stephen's Green. Never give anything away – part of the training. Is Mr so-and-so there, I'll go and see, strict instructions never to say yes in case it might be the wife. Curious now the way the tinge of wickedness hung around the pub, a relic of course of Victorianism, nothing to worry about as long as a man kept himself in hand. **Jack White, The Devil You Know**

WEST MIDLANDS

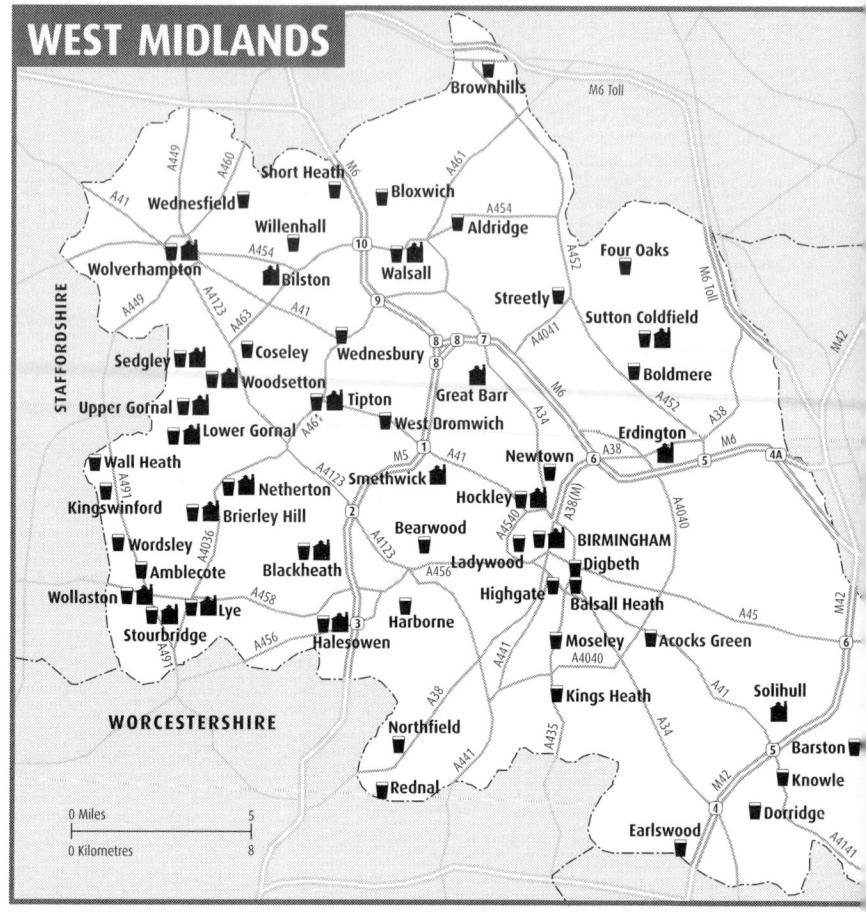

On the map (with markers): Brownhills, M6 Toll, Short Heath, Bloxwich, A454, Wednesfield, Willenhall, Aldridge, A452, Four Oaks, Wolverhampton, Bilston, Walsall, Streetly, Sutton Coldfield, M6 Toll, A42, STAFFORDSHIRE, Sedgley, Coseley, Wednesbury, Great Barr, Boldmere, Woodsetton, Tipton, Upper Gornal, Lower Gornal, West Dromwich, Newtown, Erdington, M6, 4A, Wall Heath, Smethwick, Hockley, Kingswinford, Netherton, Bearwood, BIRMINGHAM, A4040, Brierley Hill, Wordsley, Ladywood, Digbeth, Amblecote, Blackheath, Highgate, Balsall Heath, A45, Wollaston, Lye, Harborne, Moseley, Acocks Green, Stourbridge, Halesowen, Kings Heath, Solihull, WORCESTERSHIRE, Northfield, Barston, Rednal, Knowle, Dorridge, Earlswood

0 Miles 5
0 Kilometres 8

Aldridge

Avion ✓

19 Anchor Road, WS9 8PT
☼ 8am-midnight (1am Fri & Sat) ☎ (01922) 749810
Greene King Abbot; Ruddles Best Bitter; 8 changing beers (sourced nationally; often Backyard, Beowulf) Ⓗ
The former Avion Super Cinema (1938-1967) has been successfully converted into a large single-room Wetherspoon outlet with one long bar. It has a great atmosphere, much loved by families and friends. Some of the original cinema features remain, not least the stained-glass windows. Posters from its former use adorn the walls, including many of George Formby, who opened the cinema in 1938. The pub can accommodate parties of up to 12 if pre-booked. The exterior looks particularly impressive when lit at night.
Q⭢❄🅾⭡🦽♣🚌🛜

Lazy Hill Tavern Ⓛ

196 Walsall Wood Road, WS9 8HB
☼ 6-11; 12-2.30, 7-10.30 Sun ☎ (01922) 457244
Blythe Staffie; Greene King Abbot; Holden's Black Country Mild, Golden Glow; Morland Old Speckled Hen; Wye Valley Butty Bach; 1 changing beer (sourced nationally) Ⓗ
Large and welcoming family-run free house with the same licensee for nearly 40 years. The building

was originally a farmhouse which was converted into a country club, then finally a pub in 1986. Six regular beers are complemented by a changing guest. Four separate rooms are all similarly and comfortably furnished, with logburners in two. The large 160-seater function room is used midweek by local sports/community organisations. A car park is at the rear of pub and there is plenty of off-road parking nearby. P🚌🛜

Amblecote

Maverick Drinking House Ⓛ ✓

1 High Street, DY8 4BX (on jct of A491 and A461)
☼ 12-11.30 (midnight Wed; 12.30am Fri & Sat); 11.30-11 Sun
☎ (01384) 824099
Jennings Cumberland Ale; 3 changing beers Ⓗ
This large corner pub is a former CAMRA branch Pub of the Year. The interior has a Wild West theme and is a live music venue for blues, folk, rock and more. There are always four beers available on handpump including three varying guests – two from local breweries. BT Sport, ESPN and Racing Channel are shown on screens in a separate area when there is no music on, and outside is a covered and heated smoking area and a small garden. Occasional beer festivals are staged, locally advertised. Q❄🦽♣🚌 (256,246,251)

is the place to come to. Cobs are available at lunchtime and there is a varied selection of whiskies to choose from. ✿◁🖳(246)📶

Barston

Bull's Head 🍷 Ⓛ ✅

Barston Lane, B92 0JU (on main street in village, opp church) SP2073378090
✪ 11-2.30, 5.30-11; 11-11 Fri & Sat; 12-11 Sun
☎ (01675) 442830 ⊕ thebullsheadbarston.co.uk
Adnams Southwold Bitter; Purity Mad Goose; 2 changing beers Ⓗ

A true country village local, formerly a 15th-century coaching inn, with two comfortable bars with real fires and a small, intimate restaurant. Racing memorabilia are displayed throughout. A standard food menu is offered plus seasonal home-cooked specials daily (no food Sun eve). Cask Marque and LocAle accredited, it has two regular ales and two guests. Six times local CAMRA Pub of the Year, it has featured in the Guide almost continuously since 1993. The secluded beer garden hosts the annual village fête each August bank holiday. Popular with walkers and dog owners.
Q❄✿◁❶P🐾📶

Bearwood

Bear Tavern ✅

500 Bearwood Road, B66 4BX
✪ 9am-11 (1am Fri; midnight Sat); 10-11 Sun
☎ (0121) 429 1184
Greene King IPA; 6 changing beers (sourced nationally) Ⓗ

Busy community pub at the corner of Sandon Road and Three Shires Road, dominated by a central bar. It is open plan and enjoys a wide customer mix.

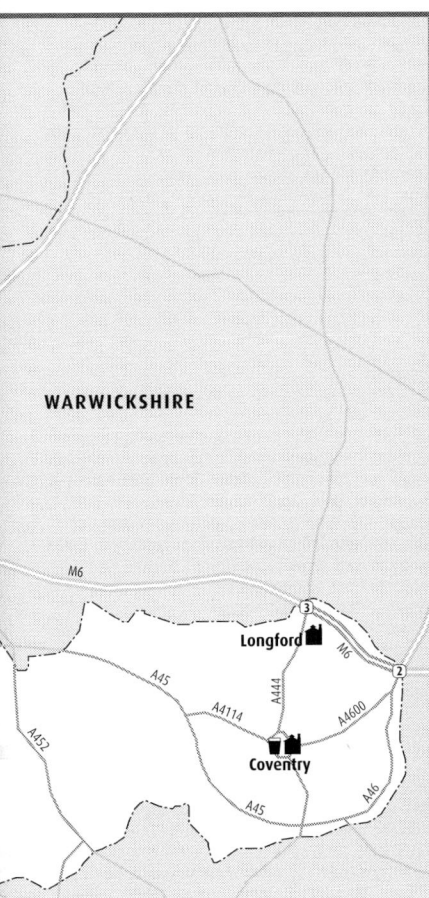

WARWICKSHIRE

M6

Longford 🏭

Coventry 🏭🍺

Robin Hood Ⓛ

196 Collis Street, DY8 4EQ (on A4102, one-way street, off Brettell Lane, A461)
✪ 12 (4 Mon & Tue)-11; 12-midnight Fri & Sat
☎ (01384) 821120
Bathams Best Bitter; Enville Ginger Beer; Holden's Golden Glow; Olde Swan Bumble Hole Bitter; Wye Valley HPA; 5 changing beers Ⓗ

Fine ales, quality food and a warm welcome – a fine traditional Black Country local. Last year saw the pub celebrate 160 years as a licensed house and it was also CAMRA branch Pub of the Year. The front rooms house a wonderful beer bottle collection including international and historic brews. A beer and music festival is hosted in October on the rear patio. The LocAle scheme is emphasised, with more local beers on permanent sale. Real cider is Thatchers Heritage.
Q❄✿◁❶&♿P🖳(246,256,257)📶

Swan

10 Brettell Lane, DY8 4BN (on A461, ½ mile after A491)
✪ 7-11; 12-11 Sat; 12-3, 7-10.30 Sun ☎ (01384) 76932
3 changing beers Ⓗ

This free house is separated into a basic lively public bar and a more sedate, cosy lounge, with a well-kept garden to the rear. Three changing beers are permanently offered. If you want a beer you have never seen before, let alone drunk, then this

REAL ALE BREWERIES

AJ's Walsall
Angel Halesowen
Backyard Walsall
Banks's Wolverhampton
Bathams Brierley Hill
Black Country 🍺 Lower Gornal
Blue Bear Smethwick
Brewhouse & Kitchen 🍺 Sutton Coldfield (NEW)
Broughs Wolverhampton
Byatt's Coventry
Craddock's 🍺 Stourbridge
Dhillon's Longford (production suspended)
Edmunds 🍺 Birmingham (NEW)
Fixed Wheel Blackheath
Fownes Upper Gornal
Froth Blowers Erdington
Green Duck 🍺 Stourbridge
Holden's Woodsetton
Indian Great Barr
Newbridge Bilston
Olde Swan 🍺 Netherton
Pig Iron Brierley Hill
Rock & Roll Birmingham: Hockley
Sacre Brew 🍺 Wolverhampton
Sadler's 🍺 Lye
Sarah Hughes 🍺 Sedgley
Silhill Solihull
Toll End 🍺 Tipton
Twisted Barrel 🍺 Coventry
Two Towers Birmingham
Websters 🍺 Wollaston

Sports screens are available throughout as live matches are often shown. The choice of real ales features breweries from up and down the country, along with local brands such as Enville and Holden's. Food is available all day, every day. There is live entertainment at weekends.
🌣🏠🍴🕭🔥♿🍺🅿🚃🛜

Midland

526-528 Bearwood Road, B66 4BE
✪ 10-11 (midnight Fri & Sat); 12-11 Sun ☎ (0121) 429 6958
Black Country Bradley's Finest Golden, Pig on the Wall, Fireside; changing beers (sourced nationally) 🅗
A former Midland Bank, this is a single-room open-plan pub serving up to 14 real ales and two traditional ciders. Its beer cellar is on the same floor and can be viewed through a glass inspection panel. It can be busy at weekends and is popular with old and young alike. A small selection of continental beers, fruit wines and freshly made cobs is available. Acoustic music is played on Sundays and there is a quiz on Wednesdays.
Q♣🍺🚃(120,82,11)🛜

Birmingham: Acocks Green

Inn on the Green ♈ 🗓

2 Westley Road, B27 7UH
✪ 11-11 (midnight Fri; midnight Sat & Sun)
☎ (0121) 708 0108 ⊕ innonthegreen.pub
6 changing beers (sourced nationally; often Wye Valley) 🅗
Run by a keen and passionate landlord who is an active CAMRA member, with friendly and knowledgeable staff. There is regular entertainment, live sport on screen and live music at the weekend. Excellent beer festivals are held four times a year. The pub was awarded local CAMRA Pub of the Year for 2015. Four handpulls are in use during the week and six at weekends. The same beer is rarely on twice and this is a great place to find ales from new breweries – well worth a visit. 🕭♿🚃🍺🅿🚃🛜

Birmingham: Balsall Heath

Old Moseley Arms 🗓

53 Tindal Street, B12 9QU (400yds off Moseley Road)
✪ 12-11 (midnight Fri & Sat) ☎ (0121) 440 1954
⊕ oldmoseleyarms.co.uk
Enville Ale; Holden's Black Country Bitter; Wye Valley HPA, Butty Bach; 1 changing beer (sourced nationally) 🅗
Traditional 19th-century pub; the left bar has an 80-inch screen for sport, the right bar has the jukebox. Upstairs is used for functions, its pool table and Sunday evening music. Comfy sofas adorn the covered garden/smoking area. A superb tandoori menu is served (6-10.15pm Mon-Thu; 6-10.45pm Fri & Sat; 1-10.45pm Sun). Regular beer festivals feature 16 ales, cider and perry. Live music showcasing local talent is played upstairs every Sunday evening. 🌣🏠🍴♣🚃(50)🛜

Birmingham: City Centre

Old Contemptibles 🗓 ✅

176 Edmund Street, B3 2HB (100yds from Snow Hill station)
✪ 11-11 (midnight Fri); 12-midnight Sat; 12-6 Sun
☎ (0121) 200 3310

Purity Pure Ubu; St Austell Nicholson's Pale Ale; Sharp's Doom Bar; 5 changing beers (sourced nationally) 🅗
Red-bricked corner pub, part of the Nicholson's chain, named after the famous First World War soldiers. The interior resembles a Victorian bar with chandeliers, a wood-panelled bar and a comfortable snug at the rear. Good-quality food is served, with the guest ales coming from the Nicholson's range; there is also an impressive wine list. The venue is popular with local office workers – it has been known to close early if quiet later on.
🍴🚃🍺🚃

Post Office Vaults 🗓

84 New Street, B2 4BA (entrances on New St and Pinfold St)
✪ 11-11 (midnight Fri & Sat); 12-11 Sun ☎ (0121) 643 7354
⊕ postofficevaults.co.uk
Hobsons Mild; Salopian Oracle; 6 changing beers (sourced nationally) 🅗
A two-minute walk from the Stephenson Street entrance to New Street station and close to Victoria Square, this subterranean pub offers a range of eight traditional beers in excellent condition. There are always at least 350 different bottled beers available from all over the world, one of the largest ranges in the country. Serving 14 ciders and perries, the pub was awarded local CAMRA Cider Pub of the Year 2014. The extremely knowledgeable staff will make your visit a pleasure. Q🚃🍺♣🍺🚃🛜

Pure Craft Bar & Kitchen 🗓

30 Waterloo Street, B2 5TJ (5 mins from New St and Snow Hill stations)
✪ 11-11 (midnight Fri & Sat); 12-10 Sun ☎ (0121) 237 5666
⊕ purecraftbars.com
Purity Pure Gold, Mad Goose, Pure Ubu; 4 changing beers (sourced nationally; often Kirkstall, Rooster's, Tiny Rebel) 🅗
Pure Bar & Kitchen is Birmingham's newest real ale outlet, set in a traditional building with an industrial interior on Waterloo Street. Gourmet food is served – all food is made with beer, and the menu has been matched to the beers available. Landlord James describes the bar as a perfect democratic environment where everyone should be able to find their ideal beer. The large chalkboard behind the bar provides details of all beers currently being served. 🌣🍴🚃🍺♣🛜

Queen's Arms ✅

150 Newhall Street, B3 1RY
✪ 12-11 (midnight Thu); 11-1am Fri & Sat; 11-10.30 Sun
☎ (0121) 236 3710 ⊕ queensarmsbar.co.uk
Sharp's Doom Bar; Wye Valley HPA; changing beers 🅗
Classic Grade II Victorian corner pub with outside tiled signage. Its interior is open plan, with a central bar but one that retains its heritage. Comfortable seating is found at either end and there is a sheltered smoking area at the rear. Quality pub food is served alongside a good selection of pizzas. A quiz is held every Thursday and sport shown on screens. It is just outside the city centre, on the edge of the Jewellery Quarter.
🕭🍴🚃🍺♣🐾🛜

Shakespeare 🗓 ✅

31 Summer Row, B3 1JJ (200yds from city end of Broad Street)
✪ 10-11 (midnight Fri & Sat) ☎ (0121) 236 8702

St Austell Nicholson's Pale Ale; Sharp's Doom Bar; 4 changing beers (sourced nationally; often Purity) Ⓗ
Glorious red-bricked Victorian local, part of the Nicholson's brand. It is near the Jewellery Quarter and the new Library of Birmingham. The traditional bar has a small hatch to serve the rear snug, which is normally reserved for diners. There is a decorated patio garden to the rear and seating at the front. It stocks regularly changing guest ales, and has an excellent reputation for good food, with frequent offers such as beer and a burger, and pie and a pint. Families are welcome in food service times, which is normally up to 10pm.
✲❶♿≠ⵗⰍ🤝

Victoria ✅
48 John Bright Street, B1 1BN (next to stage door of Alexandra Theatre)
🕐 12-midnight (1am Thu; 2am Fri & Sat) ☎ (0121) 633 9439
⊕ thevictoriabirmingham.co.uk
Wye Valley Butty Bach; 3 changing beers Ⓗ
The locally based Bitters N' Twisted chain has resurrected this 19th-century theatre bar situated next to the stage door of the Alexandra Theatre. It gets busy before theatre performances and gigs at the nearby O2 Arena. One regular beer and three rotating guests are served alongside food with an American Deep South flavour and a twist on the classic British roast. Quiz night is Tuesday and music plays on Thursday, Friday and Saturday. The pub is reportedly haunted. ❶≠ⵗⰍ🤝

Wellington Ⓛ
37 Bennetts Hill, B2 5SN (5 mins from New St and Snow Hill stations)
🕐 10-midnight ☎ (0121) 200 3115
⊕ thewellingtonrealale.co.uk
Black Country Bradley's Finest Golden, Pig on the Wall, Fireside; Oakham Citra; Purity Mad Goose; Wye Valley HPA; 10 changing beers (sourced nationally; often Froth Blowers, Titanic) Ⓗ
Recently refurbished and extended, with an additional upstairs bar and roof terrace beer garden, this multiple award-winner is a veritable beer festival every day. Sixteen ales and three traditional ciders on handpump, and a wide selection of bottled beers and whiskies, are served to a varied clientele by knowledgeable staff. Regular quizzes, cheese nights and darts competitions are held. There is no food but you are welcome to bring your own – plates, cutlery and condiments provided. Q✲≠ⵗ♣●Ⰽ🤝

Birmingham: Digbeth

Anchor ★ Ⓛ
308 Bradford Street, B5 6ET (adjacent to Digbeth coach station)
🕐 11-midnight (2am Fri & Sat); 12-11.30 Sun
☎ (0121) 622 4516 ⊕ anchorinndigbeth.co.uk
Hobsons Mild; changing beers (sourced nationally) Ⓗ
Grade II-listed and with a nationally important historic pub interior, a four-times winner of the local CAMRA branch Pub of the Year and a 2013 finalist, the Anchor is a must-visit for the ale enthusiast. Run by the Keane family for over 40 years, it brings the local-pub feel to a city-centre location. There is a varied beer range, with new breweries often featuring, along with regular beer festivals. The pub is busy when Birmingham City play at home. Q✲♿≠ⵗ●Ⰽ🤝

Spotted Dog Ⓛ
104 Warwick Street, B12 0NH
🕐 5-11; 3-1am Fri; 12-1am Sat; 12-midnight Sun
☎ (0121) 772 3822 ⊕ spotteddog.co.uk
Castle Rock Harvest Pale; Holden's Black Country Mild; 3 changing beers (sourced nationally) Ⓗ
This is a traditional multi-roomed pub with an Irish feel, off the beaten track but well worth a trip, selling excellent Holden's Mild at a competitive price. It has a large covered garden/smoking area with heaters, and a barbecue area. Live traditional Irish music features on Mondays, jazz nights Tuesdays, and blues nights Thursdays. There is a mixture of sport on the large screen, especially rugby. Excellent Scotch eggs, including vegetarian and gluten-free ones, are served. It can be busy when Birmingham City are at home. ⵗ✲♿♣Ⰽ🤝

White Swan ★ Ⓛ
276 Bradford Street, B12 0QY
🕐 12-2, 4-11; 12-11 Thu; 11-1am Fri & Sat; 12-11 Sun
☎ (0121) 622 2586
Banks's Mild, Bitter; Jennings Bitter, Cumberland Ale; 1 changing beer Ⓗ
Two-roomed unspoilt Victorian red-brick establishment, with a nationally important historic pub interior. The main drinking area has a wooden bar with a large bar-back and etched mirrors, with stools and bench seating around the walls. An impressive ornately tiled hallway leads to a small lounge and smoking area. It gets busy when sporting events are shown on large pull-down TV screens. Sandwiches, pies and cobs are available. Close to Digbeth coach station. Guest beers are from the Marston's portfolio. ⵗ≠♣Ⰽ

Woodman ★ Ⓛ
New Canal Street, B5 5LG (opp old Curzon St by Millennium Point)
🕐 11-11 (midnight Fri); 11-7 Sun ☎ (0121) 643 4960
Castle Rock Black Gold, Harvest Pale; 6 changing beers (sourced nationally) Ⓗ
Environmentally friendly and recently refurbished pub, Grade II-listed and with a nationally important historic pub interior. It has a red-bricked tile and terracotta exterior, with an L-shaped bar tiled above a wooden dado. A tiled lobby on Albert Street leads to an attractive small drinking area, with a hatch to the servery, where there is a real fire. The third plain room on the left now makes a pleasant dividing area. Good food is served daily, and there is an outside seating/dining area. Quiz night is Wednesday. Q✲❶♿≠♣●Ⰽ🤝

Birmingham: Harborne

Green Man Ⓛ ✅
2 High Street, B17 9NE
🕐 11.30-11 (midnight Fri & Sat) ☎ (0121) 428 3581
Brakspear Bitter; Purity Pure Ubu; Wye Valley Butty Bach; 5 changing beers (sourced nationally) Ⓗ
A Mitchells & Butlers community pub furnished like other Ember Inns, which usually has a full range of ales on. Normally busy and bustling due to its convenient situation on the High Street, it boasts a good-value food menu served daily until 10pm. A heated smoking area is in the rear car park. The patio area at the front can be pleasant in summer. A quiz night is held every Tuesday. Ideally placed for the start of a pub crawl. ⵗ✲❶♿♣P Ⰽ✲🤝

Junction ✔

212 High Street, B17 9PT
✿ 11-11 (midnight Thu & Fri); 10-midnight Sat
☎ (0121) 428 2635 ⊕ thejunctionharborne.co.uk

Purity Mad Goose; Sharp's Doom Bar; Timothy Taylor Landlord; 3 changing beers (sourced nationally; often Adnams, Itchen Valley, Woodforde's) Ⓗ
Distinctive Edwardian building dominating the High Street. Inside there is a sophisticated feel to the decor, with a tiled bar area with seating leading to a further main dining area. It has a varying beer range with up to six ales. Quality food is served from an open-plan kitchen, including home-cooked roasts on Sundays. A pleasant, secluded beer garden is at the rear. Quiz nights are every Monday. The pub's original tiles can be viewed in the corridor leading to the toilets.
🍴😋🍽♿🖐🚆🐾❄🚲

Birmingham: Highgate

Lamp Tavern Ⓛ

157 Barford Street, B5 6AH (500yds from A441 Pershore Rd near bottom of Hurst St)
✿ 12.30-11 ☎ (0121) 688 1220

Everards Tiger; Hobsons Mild; Rock & Roll Brew Springsteen; Stanway Stanney Bitter; 2 changing beers (sourced nationally; often Abbeydale, Malvern Hills, Rock & Roll) Ⓗ
A warm welcome awaits from Eddie, a landlord of more than 20 years standing, at this characterful, single-roomed, street-corner local. The Lamp is home to the rooftop Rock & Roll brewery and its only regular outlet, with one beer from the range always stocked. It is also the only Birmingham pub to serve Stanway Stanney Bitter. A Guide regular, it holds a weekly folk club on Friday evenings.
Q♿♣🚆 (35,45,47)

Birmingham: Hockley

Black Eagle Ⓛ

16 Factory Road, B18 5JU (turn right out of Soho Benson Rd metro station, cross road and walk 200yds)
✿ 11.30-3, 5.30-11; 11.30-11 Fri; 12-3, 7-11 Sat; 12-3 Sun
☎ (0121) 523 4008 ⊕ theblackeaglepub.co.uk

Marston's Pedigree; Sadler's Peaky Blinder; Timothy Taylor Landlord; changing beers (often Dark Star, Holden's, Salopian) Ⓗ
Traditional award-winning multi-room pub with a restaurant to the rear. While slightly off the beaten track, this real ale oasis is well worth seeking out for its excellent range of beers and good-value food. Three guest beers are always available and an annual beer festival is held in the summer, as well as occasional barbecues. Real cider and perry usually come from Westons and Gwynt y Ddraig.
😋😋🖐🚆🚆 (74,75,101)🐾❄

Church

22 Great Hampton Street, B18 6AQ
✿ 12-midnight (2am Fri; 1am Sat); 10-11 Sun
☎ (0121) 448 3866 ⊕ churchjq.co.uk

Everards Sunchaser Blonde, Tiger, Original; 1 changing beer Ⓗ
Everards Brewery and Soul Food Project founder Carl Finn have transformed the Church into the headquarters of the Soul Food Project. Three Everards ales are always on tap, with a fourth handpull rotating another of the brewery's real ales. The venue is influenced by the French quarter of New Orleans, without taking away from the

heritage of this British pub. The food focuses on the Cajun and Creole style from the Deep South of the US. Whisky tastings are among the regular events.
😋🖐🚆🚆🚆 (74,79)❄

Red Lion Ⓛ

95 Warstone Lane, B18 6NG
✿ 10-midnight (2am Fri & Sat) ☎ (0121) 233 9144
⊕ theredlionbirmingham.com

Wye Valley Butty Bach; 3 changing beers (sourced nationally; often Bathams) Ⓗ
Traditional two-roomed pub that is rich both in local heritage and modern art. There is a lively front bar and a cosy back lounge. Upstairs is a good-sized clubroom and outside to the rear is a sheltered patio and smoking area. An excellent extensive food menu is served all day, with a Cow Club on Mondays. There are three changing guest beers and two changing ciders. Regular quiz nights are held and large screens show sporting events.
😋🖐🚆🚆🐾🚆❄

Birmingham: Kings Heath

King's Heath Cricket & Sports Club ✔

Charlton House, 247 Alcester Road South, B14 6DT
✿ 12-midnight ☎ (0121) 444 1913

Wye Valley HPA, Butty Bach; 2 changing beers (sourced nationally; often Greene King) Ⓗ
Welcoming sports club where CAMRA members are permitted entry on production of a membership card (maximum 10 visits per year). The club has two rooms: a comfortable lounge for relaxed drinking, and a large room for watching sporting events on big screens, also housing two full-size snooker tables. The beer range always includes two rotating guest ales. Various social events are held throughout the year, including live music.
Q😋😋🖐♿♣🖐🚆 (18,50,X50)❄

Birmingham: Ladywood

Fiddle & Bone

4 Sheepcote Street, B16 8AE
✿ 12-10.30 (midnight Fri & Sat); closed Mon
☎ (0121) 200 2223 ⊕ fiddleandbone.co.uk

Caledonian Deuchars IPA; Purity Mad Goose, Pure Ubu; Sharp's Doom Bar; Theakston Old Peculier Ⓗ
Found on Sheepcote Street in the heart of the city, the Fiddle & Bone reopened in the spring of 2015 boasting a live music venue and restaurant, as well as a full narrowboat service station – it is the very definition of a hidden gem. The venue boasts a sizeable courtyard with ample seating. An open mic night on Tuesdays, evening sessions on Fridays and Saturdays, and an afternoon performance on Sundays make up the regular slots. 😋🖐

Birmingham: Moseley

Prince of Wales Ⓛ ✔

118 Alcester Road, B13 8EE
✿ 12-11.30 (1am Fri & Sat) ☎ (0121) 449 4198
⊕ theprincemoseley.co.uk

Oakham Citra; Purity Mad Goose; Timothy Taylor Landlord; 3 changing beers (often Castle Rock, Holden's) Ⓗ
Serving cask ales since 1861, this three-bar pub is a real community local. The front bar features an authentic Victorian bar-back and there are two further bars at the rear leading to a beer garden

and cigar smoke room boasting the largest selection of Cuban cigars in the country. Two ciders are on sale, alongside a good selection of whiskies and interesting cocktails. There is a TV for sport, a real fire and a quiz night every Tuesday.
✪●🖵(1,35,50)🐾🛜

Birmingham: Newtown

Bartons Arms ★ ✪
144 High Street, B6 4UP
✪ 12-11; 12-10.30 Sun ☎ (0121) 333 5988
🌐 thebartonsarms.com
Oakham JHB, Inferno, Citra, Bishops Farewell; 2 changing beers (sourced nationally; often Oakham) Ⓗ
A stunning red-bricked pub run by Oakham Brewery from Peterborough. The 1901 interior is Grade II-listed and with a nationally important historic pub interior. The Bartons has ornate Minton tiles throughout, including a central tiled staircase, original stained-glass windows and snob screens on the bar. Superb Thai food is served in the lounge. A range of Oakham Ales is available, usually alongside one guest and a cider. Quiz night is Monday and regular music and beer festivals are held. ➳🕽●P🖵🛜

Birmingham: Northfield

Black Horse ★ Ⓛ ✪
Bristol Road South, B31 2QT (opp Sainsbury's)
✪ 8am-11 (1am Fri & Sat); 8am-midnight Sun
☎ (0121) 477 1800
Greene King Abbot; Ruddles Best Bitter; Sharp's Doom Bar; changing beers (sourced nationally; often Adnams, Fuller's, Purity) Ⓗ
Large inter-war mock-Tudor road house offering the only extensive real ale choice in this part of the city. At one time an undesirable local, this is now a popular pub serving consistently high-quality beer. Unusually for a Wetherspoon, it has a multi-room layout and bars on two levels. It still retains the original Baronial Hall entrance but the bar has been tastefully refurbished with an etched-glass entrance door. There is a bowling green with original outbuildings to the rear.
Q➳✪🕽&≉●P🖵🛜

Birmingham: Rednal

Old Hare & Hounds ✪
426 Lickey Road, B45 8UU
✪ 11.30-11 (12.30am Fri); 10-12.30am Sat; 11-10.30 Sun
☎ (0121) 457 9743
Brakspear Bitter; 3 changing beers Ⓗ
A spacious one-roomed Ember Inn pub at the foot of the Lickey Hills, near to buses from the city centre, Halesowen, Bromsgrove and Redditch. There is a discount on the price of real ales on Mondays. Open fires add warmth in winter. Good-quality food is served daily. The pub has a beer garden and a covered smoking area.
➳✪🕽&P🖵(47,98)🛜

Blackheath

Waterfall
132 Waterfall Lane, B64 6RG
✪ 12-11 (midnight Fri & Sat) ☎ (0121) 559 9198

Bathams Best Bitter; Holden's Black Country Bitter, Golden Glow, Special; 4 changing beers (often Enville, Kelham Island) Ⓗ
Recently refurbished in a café style, this is a bustling and popular community pub owned by Holden's. It is a downhill walk from Blackheath town centre or a steep 10-minute walk uphill from Old Hill station. Basic, good-value food is served from Anne's Kitchen daily. Up to four guest beers are served at any time, which tend to be strong and are generally from Olde Swan, Kelham Island and Enville breweries. Due to its popularity the pub can get extremely busy at weekends.
✪🕽≉(Old Hill)♣●P🖵(4M,53)🐾🛜

Bloxwich

Wheatsheaf Ⓛ
35 Field Road, WS3 3JL
✪ 11-11 ☎ (01922) 279799
Banks's Mild, Bitter, Sunbeam; 2 changing beers (sourced locally) Ⓗ
Dating back to the 16th century, the Wheatsheaf is a friendly multi-room pub. Traditional pub games are played, with darts, dominoes, crib and pool teams based here. On Thursdays there are quizzes and a knitting and natter group for real ale drinkers. A cask ale raffle is held every Wednesday, while on Saturday there is live music ranging from rock and Irish to acoustic. It has an enclosed beer garden. Q✪&♣🖵

Boldmere

Bishop Vesey ♗ Ⓛ
63 Boldmere Road, B73 5UY
✪ 8am-11 (midnight Fri & Sat) ☎ (0121) 355 5077
Backyard Blonde; Greene King Abbot; Ruddles Best Bitter; Sharp's Doom Bar; changing beers Ⓗ
Named after the town's Tudor benefactor, this busy Wetherspoon pub has an open-plan layout with upstairs seating and an outside patio and smokers' area. With 16 consecutive years in the Guide, it is a frequent and well-deserved Pub of the Year for the local CAMRA branch. The loyal clientele includes a thriving darts team. Up to eight interesting guest beers, many from local micros, are on the bar. Real cider features occasionally. ➳✪🕽&≉♣🖵🛜

Brierley Hill

Rose & Crown Ⓛ
161 Bank Street, DY5 3DD (on B4179)
✪ 12-11 (midnight Fri & Sat) ☎ (01384) 936166
Holden's Black Country Mild, Black Country Bitter, Golden Glow, Special; 1 changing beer Ⓗ
This traditional pub was originally two terraced properties. The lounge has a cosy, relaxed atmosphere. One end of the bar is dominated by the dartboard. A conservatory extension adds extra space and is used as a separate dining area in the evening. It opens onto a small garden with tables and benches. A large selection of good-value quality food is served. There is a bus stop outside the pub, or it is five minutes' walk from Brierley Hill High Street, which is served by several bus routes.
Q➳✪🕽♣P🖵(222,255)🐾🛜

Vine ♗
10 Delph Road, DY5 2TN
✪ 12-11; 12-10.30 Sun ☎ (01384) 78293
Bathams Mild Ale, Best Bitter Ⓗ

Classic, unspoilt brewery tap with an ornately decorated façade proclaiming the Shakespearian quotation: 'Blessing of your heart, you brew good ale'. Step inside and enter an elongated pub with a labyrinthine feel. The front bar is staunchly traditional, while the larger rear room has its own servery, leather seating and a dartboard. There is a homely lounge which was partly converted from former brewery offices. Well-priced Black Country lunches are served weekdays and great-value rolls and pork pies at other times. There is a car park across the road. Q🛏❀◐♣P🚌(X96)🐾📶

Waterfront Inn ✔

6-7 The Waterfront, Level Street, DY5 1XE (between A461 and A4036)

8am-11.30 (midnight Fri & Sat) ☎ (01384) 262096

Greene King Abbot; Ruddles Best Bitter; 3 changing beers Ⓗ

A welcoming Wetherspoon pub in the Waterfront complex which follows the brand's formula. The offices behind provide the lunchtime trade. A large range of value food from the Wetherspoon menu is served until 11pm. The hostelry is in a pleasant situation overlooking the Dudley No.1 canal basin. This is a dog-friendly pub, with water bowls provided. Q🛏❀◐◑♿🍎P🚌(81,X96)🐾📶

Brownhills

Swan 🄻

Pelsall Road, WS8 7DL

4 (2 Fri)-midnight; 12-midnight Sat & Sun

☎ (01543) 820628

Holden's Golden Glow; 2 changing beers Ⓗ

A traditional pub with two rooms served by a central bar. The main drinking area is the bar to the right of the front entrance, with a lounge area to the left. Beyond the lounge, a separate area houses the pool table. There is an outside drinking area at the front of the pub. The Swan has been refurbished throughout and is a comfortable and welcoming venue both for locals and visitors. Up to two guest beers supplement the regular beer. Local CAMRA branch Pub of the Year 2015. 🛏❀♣P🐾📶

Coseley

Old Chainyard 🄻

63 Castle Street, WV14 9DW

12-11 (11.30 Fri & Sat)

Salopian Oracle; 3 changing beers Ⓗ

Single-roomed community pub full of character in the heart of Roseville village that reopened under new management in 2015. The A4123 Wolverhampton to Birmingham road is close by and the public transport is excellent. Up to three changing real ales sourced from local breweries are served. The board includes one real ale at a weekly special price. 🛏❀⇌♣P🚌(81,82,229)🐾

Coventry

Broomfield Tavern 🏆 🄻

14-16 Broomfield Place, Spon End, CV5 6GY (adjacent to rugby ground but hidden from main road)

4-midnight; 12-1am Fri & Sat; 12-midnight Sun

☎ (024) 7663 0969

9 changing beers (sourced locally; often Byatt's, Church End) Ⓗ

A constantly evolving community free house that was local CAMRA Cider Pub of the Year 2014 and 2015. It boasts an impressive array of handpumps dispensing nine real ales and two ciders, with a further 11 ciders/perries served on gravity. The pub has an L-shaped bar area and a small patio at the front, with a car park opposite. It also has a separate room used for local group meetings and live music at weekends. Q🛏❀🍎🚌(6,6A,10)🐾

City Arms 🄻 ✔

1 Earlsdon Street, Earlsdon, CV5 6EP (on roundabout at centre of Earlsdon)

8am-midnight (1am Fri & Sat) ☎ (024) 7671 8170

Greene King Abbot; Ruddles Best Bitter; 8 changing beers (sourced locally; often Byatt's, Purity) Ⓗ

Large open-plan establishment in the heart of Earlsdon. Built in the 1930s on the site of an earlier pub, it is still often referred to as Ma Cooper's, after an early licensee. Now part of the Wetherspoon chain, it is an enthusiastic promoter of real ale. It attracts a wide-ranging clientele and is particularly popular on Friday and Saturday nights. The community noticeboard is very well used. ❀◐◑♿🍎P🚌(5,12)📶

Drapers 🄻

Earl Street, CV1 5RU

8am-11 (midnight Fri & Sat); 10-6 Sun ☎ (024) 7622 1100

Purity Mad Goose, Saddle Black; 1 changing beer (sourced nationally) Ⓗ

A welcome new entry into the Guide, this retro-style two-floor café bar is conveniently located next to the Herbert Art Gallery and the city's famous cathedrals. Popular with students, university staff and city-centre workers, it features a roof terrace and street-level sliding doors that are opened in fine weather. The bar stocks a wide range of bottled beers, and hosts a variety of popular events such as film screenings and themed evenings. 🛏❀◐◑♿🚌(8,9)📶

Earl of Mercia ✔

18 High Street, CV1 5RE

8am-midnight (1am Fri & Sat) ☎ (024) 7643 3990

Greene King Abbot; Ruddles Best Bitter; 6 changing beers (sourced nationally; often Sadler's) Ⓗ

A new addition to the Guide, this well-established Wetherspoon pub is a conversion of a former bank building. Located opposite the Council House and near the cathedral quarter, it is popular with city-centre workers, shoppers and families during the day and early evening. Seating is available in the ground floor bar area, mezzanine and pavement patio. It gets busy on Friday and Saturday nights, with a mixed crowd. 🛏❀◐◑♿⇌🍎🚌(8,9)📶

Gatehouse Tavern 🄻

46 Hill Street, CV1 4AN (close to Belgrade Theatre and Spon Street, near jct 8 of ring road)

11-11; 12-10 Sun ☎ (024) 7663 0140

gatehousetavern.com

Draught Bass; Fuller's London Pride; 4 changing beers (sourced locally; often Byatt's, Church End, Purity) Ⓗ

Occupying the site of the former Leigh Mills Weaving Company gatehouse, the pub was rebuilt by the current landlord. It has an enthusiastic focus on sport, with up to four screens showing multiple fixtures and events. The pub boasts the largest garden within the city centre and has recently added an outdoor bar with a single handpull. It is popular with shoppers and city-centre workers during the day and hosts a mixed crowd in the evenings. 🛏❀◐◑🍎🚌📶

Greyhound Inn

Sutton Stop, Hawkesbury Junction, CV6 6DF (off Grange Rd at jct of Coventry & Oxford canals)
🕐 11-11; 12-10.30 Sun ☎ (024) 7636 3046
🌐 greyhoundinn.org
Draught Bass; Marston's Pedigree; 4 changing beers (sourced nationally) [H]
This canalside hostelry is popular with locals and visitors alike. It is a four-times winner of the local Godiva award for best pub in Coventry and Warwickshire, and was local CAMRA Pub of the Year for four consecutive years. The pub dates from the 1830s and the terrace to the front overlooks the bustling junction of two canals. An extensive menu of freshly cooked food is offered. Beer festivals are held twice-yearly. Q🎠✿◑◐♣🍎P🐾

Nursery Tavern

38-39 Lord Street, Chapelfields, CV5 8DA (1 mile W of city centre, off Allesley Old Road)
🕐 12-11.30 (midnight Fri & Sat); 12-11 Sun
☎ (024) 7667 4530
Courage Best Bitter; Fuller's London Pride; Hook Norton Hooky Mild; 3 changing beers (sourced nationally) [H]
A regular entry in the Guide, this traditional three-room pub nestles in a Victorian terraced street in the historic watchmaking area. Each room has a distinct feel. The two front rooms are served by a central bar where conversation is king. The rear room is home to monthly quizzes, society and club meetings. Very much part of the community, the pub hosts regular local music, arts and charity nights. Dogs are welcome throughout.
Q🎠✿◑♣🍎🚌(6,6A,10)🐾

Old Windmill ✔

22-23 Spon Street, CV1 3BA (in medieval Spon Street, behind Ikea)
🕐 12 (4 Mon)-11.30; 12-1am Fri & Sat ☎ (024) 7625 1717
Morland Old Speckled Hen; RCH Old Slug Porter; Theakston Old Peculier; Timothy Taylor Landlord; 2 changing beers (sourced locally; often Oakham, Sperrin) [H]
A 15th-century building divided into a number of rooms and areas, one of which was the former brewhouse. Local CAMRA Pub of the Year in 2015, this pub continues to go from strength to strength. Two beer festivals are hosted every year. Live music is played on the first and last Friday of the month, folk on Sunday afternoons and bluegrass once a month. No meals are served, but good-quality pork pies are generally available.
✿♣🍎🚌🐾📶

Town Crier ✔

Corporation Street, CV1 1PB (next to Ikea)
🕐 11-11 (1am Thu & Fri); 10-1am Sat; 11.30-6 Sun
☎ (024) 7663 2317
Jennings Sneck Lifter; Marston's Burton Bitter, Pedigree; 2 changing beers (sourced nationally; often Jennings, Marston's) [H]
A modern but traditional pub built in the late 1980s by Banks's, now branded under the Marston's banner. The landlord has put a lot of effort into turning the pub around, and takes full advantage of the Marston's guest beer list. Being a city-centre pub, it attracts a varied mix of locals, shoppers and workers. There is often live music on Saturday evenings and it has a large screen used occasionally for big sporting events.
🎠✿◑◐♿🍎🚌📶

Town Wall Tavern ✔

Bond Street, CV1 4AH (behind Belgrade Theatre)
🕐 12-11 (midnight Fri & Sat); 12-10 Sun ☎ (024) 7622 0963
🌐 townwalltavern.co.uk
Adnams Southwold Bitter, Broadside; Caledonian Deuchars IPA; Draught Bass; Theakston Old Peculier; 3 changing beers (sourced nationally) [H]
One of the few remaining traditional locals in the city centre, this 200-year-old pub, tucked behind the Belgrade Theatre, is frequented by actors and can become busy during intervals. The bar and lounge are supplemented by the Donkey Box, a small snug at the front which is just big enough to hold a donkey. There is an imaginative, locally sourced food offering (no food Sun or Mon eves).
✿◑◐♿🍎🚌🐾

Twisted Barrel Brewery & Tap House [L]

Unit 5, Fargo Village, Far Gosford Street, CV1 5ED
🕐 5-midnight Fri; 12-midnight Sat; closed Sun-Thu
☎ (024) 7610 1701 🌐 twistedbarrelale.co.uk
Twisted Barrel Beast of a Midlands Mild, God's Twisted Sister, Inspired, Sine Qua Non, The Saison from Another Place, In Amber Clad; 4 changing beers (sourced locally; often Twisted Barrel) [P]
A cavernous room with brewing kit on the left and a bar on the right. There are no handpulls – KeyKegs hold the real ale, which is dispensed through keg fonts. No finings are used which makes the beer suitable for vegans, albeit it is sometimes cloudy. Six regular beers are supplemented by another four from the brewer's comprehensive range. Accompanied children are welcome until 7pm. Visit the website for details of additional opening hours and events.
🎠♿🍎P🚌🐾📶

Whitefriars Olde Ale House

114-115 Gosford Street, CV1 5DL
🕐 12-midnight (1am Fri & Sat) ☎ (024) 7625 1655
North Cotswold Hung, Drawn 'n' Portered; 4 changing beers (sourced nationally) [H]
Atmospheric pub occupying a 14th-century building, formerly part of Whitefriars monastery, serving up to five beers and four ciders. There are two downstairs drinking areas, the smaller of which is a room that was used as a kitchen by the friars. A labyrinth of upstairs rooms features unusual murals, and there is a rear garden for fine-weather drinking. The pub hosts a popular quiz night on Tuesdays and an open mic night on Wednesdays. ✿◑♿🚆♣🍎🚌(8,9)🐾

Dorridge

Forest Hotel

25 Station Approach, B93 8JA
🕐 11-11 (midnight Fri & Sat); 11-10.30 Sun
☎ (01564) 772120 🌐 forest-hotel.com
Wye Valley HPA; 2 changing beers [H]
This Victorian hotel has a bar decorated in a contemporary, eclectic style with polished wooden tables, comfortable armchairs and sofas. The restaurant specialises in fine dining; bar meals are also served. There is a large, partly covered outdoor seating area with several patio heaters. A cider and ale festival is held in July and a real ale festival in November. 12 en suite bedrooms are available.
Q🎠✿🛏◑◐♿🚆P🚌(S2,S3)📶

Railway ⊘

Grange Road, B93 8QA

🕓 11-3, 4.30-11; 11-11 Sat; 12-10.30 Sun ☎ (01564) 773531
🌐 railwaydorridge.com

Draught Bass; Holden's Black Country Mild; M&B Brew XI; Timothy Taylor Landlord; 2 changing beers Ⓗ

This inn dates back to the 1850s and the construction of the Birmingham to London railway, hence the name. Its frontage to the road is Grade II-listed. Run by the Watson family since 1915, up to three guest beers are available as well as a real cider. Good-value pub food is served, including game when in season. The large garden, with children's play area and heated outdoor patio, is busy in summer, while the public bar provides a real fire in the winter. Q⏰✿🕪◑🏃♣🐾P🚃(S3)🐾 📶

Earlswood

Bull's Head ⊘

B94 6BU

🕓 9am-11; 9am-10.30 Sun ☎ (01564) 702335

Thwaites Wainwright, Lancaster Bomber; 4 changing beers Ⓗ

Originally built in 1740 for the navvies constructing the Stratford-upon-Avon canal, this pub is rumoured to be haunted by the ghost of a 17th-century lime kiln worker. It is made up of a collection of late-18th and early-19th century two-storey whitewashed brick buildings, which have been extended and linked. It became a pub in 1832 and was refurbished in the 1990s. Unusual for Solihull, it is now a Thwaites house. Popular with cyclists and walkers. Q⏰✿🕪◑♣P🐾 📶

Four Oaks

Butlers Arms ⊘

444 Lichfield Road, B74 4BL

🕓 12-11 (midnight Fri & Sat); 12-10.30 Sun
☎ (0121) 308 0765 🌐 butlersarms.co.uk

4 changing beers Ⓗ

This attractive, family-run suburban pub has a strong local following and is geared towards dining, though drinkers are always made welcome. The interior decor is a colourful and eclectic mix of styles, with lamps, mirrors and curiosities. The four guest ales vary but usually include a Caledonian beer plus Greene King Abbot. The chalkboard menu features fish specials, with meat and vegetarian alternatives. Two small beer terraces to the front allow for alfresco drinking. Q⏰✿🕪◑♣P 📶

Halesowen

Hawne Tavern Ⓛ

76 Attwood Street, B63 3UG (just off Stourbridge Rd, down Short St opp Tesco Express)

🕓 4.30-11; 12-11 Sat; 12-10.30 Sun ☎ (0121) 602 2601

Bathams Best Bitter; Bob's White Lion; Wye Valley HPA; 6 changing beers Ⓗ

A back-street locals' pub just off the main bus route. It has a large bar with a pool table and TV showing sport (not Sky), with separate seating areas plus a smaller cosy lounge. There are three regular and up to six guest ales, many of which are from microbreweries, specialising in northern beers. Real cider is also sold. Baguettes are available in the evenings, hot sandwiches and chips at weekends. The enclosed rear garden is ideal for smokers and sun-worshippers. Q✿♣🛏🚃(9,002,004)🐾

Swan ♚ Ⓛ

Long Lane, B62 9JY

🕓 12-midnight ☎ (0121) 559 5207

Black Country Bradley's Finest Golden, Pig on the Wall, Fireside; 8 changing beers Ⓗ

Saved from the bulldozers by locals, Stourbridge and Halesowen CAMRA and Black Country Ales, the Swan is a campaigning success story. Eleven real ales and six real ciders are always available. The serving area is a single bar stretching the length of the building. A staircase leads to the toilets and gives access to the garden and smoking area to the rear. Doors close at 11pm with last orders at 11.15pm. Q✿👶♣🐾P🚃(241,140) 📶

Kingswinford

Park Tavern Ⓛ

182 Cot Lane, DY6 9QG (corner of Cot Lane and Broad St)

🕓 11-11 (midnight Thu-Sat) ☎ (01384) 287178

Bathams Best Bitter; Enville Ale, Ginger Beer; 3 changing beers Ⓗ

Popular and lively old pub in the back streets of Kingswinford, currently serving six real ales. Opened as the Brickmakers Arms in 1855, it changed its name to the Park Tavern in 1859. The bar and lounge each have their own feel, but TV does tend to dominate when sporting events are on. For the peckish, try the selection of cobs. There is a patio to the rear for smokers and sports enthusiasts alike. ✿♣P🚃(226)🐾 📶

Knowle

Vaults

St John's Close, B93 0JU

🕓 12-2.30, 5-11 ; 12-11.30 Thu-Sat; 12-11 Sun
☎ (01564) 773656

Salopian Shropshire Gold; Sharp's Doom Bar, Atlantic; Wadworth IPA; 1 changing beer Ⓗ

A wide variety of quality real ales can be found at this traditional pub, as well as real cider from the Westons range. In recent years it has been a regular winner of the local CAMRA branch Pub of the Year, and is a popular meeting place for those visiting the many local restaurants. Major sporting events are shown on Sky Sports TV. Light meals are served 12-2pm Monday to Saturday. ◑♣🚃(S2,S3) 📶

Lower Gornal

Black Bear

86 Deepdale Lane, DY3 2AE

🕓 5-11; 12-11 Fri & Sat; 12-10.30 Sun ☎ (01384) 253333

6 changing beers Ⓗ

Once a farmhouse, this building has been a pub for over 180 years. Subsidence has taken its toll and there is a distinct slope to the split-level interior, and large buttresses support the downhill exterior walls. The views from the garden are stunning. There are up to six ales served, with a house beer, Black Bear, from Kinver Brewery, usually available. Bus stops are close by, or take an uphill walk from the Gornal Wood bus station or downhill from the main number 1 bus route. ✿♣🚃(27,257)🐾

Fountain

8 Temple Street, DY3 2PE (on B4157 5 mins from Gornal Wood bus station)

🕓 12-11; 12-10.30 Sun ☎ (01384) 242777
🌐 fountaininnrealale.co.uk

Greene King Abbot; Hobsons Town Crier; Morland Old Speckled Hen; RCH Pitchfork; 5 changing beers (sourced nationally) Ⓗ

A long-standing Guide entry and twice winner of CAMRA branch Pub of the Year, this excellent free house serves nine real ales accompanied by draught Belgian beers, a real cider and 12 fruit wines. The busy, vibrant bar is complemented by an elevated dining area serving excellent food Monday-Saturday 12-9pm, and Sunday lunches until 5pm. A wide selection of cobs and baguettes is available at lunchtime. During the summer months the rear garden is a suntrap and a pleasant area to while away an hour or two. ⛵☺❀◐♣♠P🚃(27,257)☙🛜

Red Cow Ⓛ

84 Grosvenor Road, DY3 2PR

🕓 4-midnight; 12-midnight Sat & Sun ☎ 07943 189351

Abbeydale Absolution; Holden's Golden Glow; Wye Valley HPA, Butty Bach; 4 changing beers Ⓗ

An early 19th-century hostelry in a cul-de-sac, which is part of Grosvenor Road. This community pub supports numerous pub games teams. The cosy lounge to the right is divided in two by a large chimney breast, which has openings either side to afford passage between them. This is a warm room with a good atmosphere. A large garden is at the rear. Up to eight ales are on offer, often from local breweries. There is a five-minute walk to the bus stop in Corncrake Road. ⛵☺♣P🚃(257)☙🛜

Lye

Sadler's Brewhouse & Bar Ⓛ

Conyers Trading Estate, Station Drive, DY9 8ER

🕓 5-11 Wed & Thu; 12-midnight Fri & Sat; closed Sun-Tue ☎ (01384) 895230 🌐 sadlersales.co.uk

6 changing beers (sourced locally; often Sadler's) Ⓗ

The large bar overlooking Sadler's new brewery opened in 2015. Six changing real ales, all Sadler's, are served along with six kegs, some foreign, and an impressive bottle stock. Sandwiches, burgers, dogs and wings are available until 8pm, Wednesday to Saturday. There is regular entertainment including a monthly home-brew competition, where the winner can produce a batch of their recipe at the nearby Sadler's plant in the Windsor Castle. ◐🚉P🚃(9)☙🛜

Shovel Ⓛ

81 Pedmore Road, DY9 7DZ (on A4036, just S of Lye Cross)

🕓 5.30-11 (midnight Thu & Fri); 2.30-midnight Sat; 12-midnight Sun ☎ (01384) 423998 🌐 theshovelinn.co.uk

Enville Ale, Ginger Beer; Holden's Golden Glow; Ludlow Gold; Morland Old Speckled Hen; Purity Mad Goose; 6 changing beers Ⓗ

Extensive refurbishment by the owner has given this pub a smart feel. A central bar full of handpumps serves three separate areas: a bar area with TV showing sport, a plush lounge, and a rear seating space. Outside is the Mediterranean, a covered and real-fire heated smoking area, with the Real Ale Wall featuring over 1,000 pumpclips. Good-value evening food includes Mexican and balti nights, and on Sundays there is a traditional roast lunch. Opens some lunchtimes during the football season. ☺◐&🚃(9,276)

Netherton

Old Swan ★ Ⓛ

89 Halesowen Road, DY2 9PY (in Netherton centre on A459 Dudley-Old Hill road)

🕓 11-11; 12-11 Sun ☎ (01384) 253075

Olde Swan Original, Dark Swan, Entire, Netherton Pale Ale, Bumble Hole Bitter; 1 changing beer (sourced locally; often Olde Swan) Ⓗ

One of the last four remaining English home-brew pubs from 1974, deservedly on CAMRA's National Inventory of Historic Pub Interiors, featuring an ornate Swan ceiling and stand-alone burner in the bar which is an unspoilt treasure. The premises are home to the Olde Swan Brewery. There is a cosy snug to the rear of the bar, and a two-roomed lounge in which food is available. The upstairs restaurant is highly regarded (open Tue-Sat). Sunday lunches are also served, with booking essential. Q☺◐&♣P🚃(243,244,81)☙🛜

Sedgley

Beacon Hotel ★ Ⓛ

129 Bilston Street, DY3 1JE (on A463)

🕓 12-2.30 (3 Fri), 5.30-11; 12-3, 6-11 Sat; 12-3, 7-10.30 Sun ☎ (01902) 883380

Sarah Hughes Pale Amber, Sedgley Surprise, Dark Ruby Mild; 3 changing beers Ⓗ

In the shadow of the ancient Sedgley beacon, this old hotel has sat virtually unchanged for decades. It is a Grade II-listed building and has a nationally important historic pub interior, where time has stood still. At its heart is a central servery with hatches where you have to bend down to order your drinks, and there are four rooms, including a family room. The Sarah Hughes Brewery lives in a tower at the back and supplies the pub. The Beacon lives up to its name - it shines. CAMRA branch Pub of the Year 2015. Q⛵☺☺P🚃(229,224)

Mount Pleasant

144 High Street, DY3 1RH (on A459)

🕓 6.30 (7 Mon & Tue)-11; 12-3, 7-10.30 Sun ☎ 07950 195652

Oakham Bishops Farewell; 8 changing beers Ⓗ

Known locally as the Stump by its regulars, this friendly, popular free house serves an interesting selection of eight beers. It possesses a Tardis-like interior and a mock-Tudor frontage. The front bar has a convivially warm atmosphere. The lounge has an intimate feel, with two rooms on different levels housing various intimate nooks and crannies and two real coal stoves. Food is limited to ham or cheese cobs. Dog-friendly, it is on the Dudley to Wolverhampton bus route, or five minutes' walk from Sedgley centre. Q☺♣P🚃(1)☙

White Lion

104 Bilston Street, DY3 1JF

🕓 12-3, 6-11; 12-11 Sat & Sun ☎ (01902) 685232

Oakham Bishops Farewell; 3 changing beers (often Dark Star, Oakham) Ⓗ

An old pub, possibly built as early as 1702, with a comfortable modern interior. There is a separate dining room where excellent traditional English-style meals are served – you will not leave hungry. Children under eight are welcome only when dining. The south-facing beer garden makes a lovely suntrap in the right weather. The guest ales are usually pale and hoppy. A five-minute walk from the main number 1 bus route. ⛵☺☺◐&♣P🚃(229,224)🛜

Short Heath

Duke of Cambridge Ⓛ

82 Coltham Road, WV12 5QD

☼ 12-11 ☎ (01922) 712038

Black Country Bradley's Finest Golden, Pig on the Wall, Fireside; 3 changing beers (sourced nationally) Ⓗ

A traditional, homely and welcoming pub converted from 17th-century cottages. The public bar has a solid fuel woodburner and wooden beams. The quieter lounge has been tastefully refurbished. A rear room caters for darts and pool and is also used for functions and beer festivals. A quiz is held every other Wednesday. There is a beer garden at the rear of the pub.

Q ➿ ✿ ♣ ● ☐ (341,369) ❀

Stourbridge

Duke William Ⓛ

25 Coventry Street, DY8 1EP (corner of Coventry St and Duke St)

☼ 12-11; 12-11.30 Fri & Sat ☎ (01384) 440202

⊕ craddocksbrewery.com

Craddock's Saxon Gold, Crazy Sheep, Troll; 6 changing beers (sourced locally; often Craddock's) Ⓗ

Locally listed Edwardian town-centre pub and home of the Craddock's Brewery. There is a main bar with a real fire, an adjacent snug and an upstairs function room with bar. Traditional pie (choice of eight varieties) and mash is served lunchtimes and evenings weekdays, all day until 7pm Friday to Sunday. Cold food is also available. Regular events and brewery tours can be arranged. There is a summer beer and cider festival, with a choice of over 15 ales and ciders. Regular ciders are Dogdancer and Thundering Molly.

Q ✿ ◑ & ⇌ ● ☷ ☐ ❀ ⑨

Royal Exchange Ⓛ

75 Enville Street, DY8 1XW (on A458 just off ring road)

☼ 1-11; 12-11 Sat; 12-10.30 Sun ☎ (01384) 396726

Bathams Mild Ale, Best Bitter Ⓗ

You will find a busy traditional bar to the front and a small cosy lounge to the rear, accessed through a side passage. The bar is decorated with whisky bottles and boxes, pewter tankards and foreign banknotes. The beer is served in handled glasses on request. The large beer garden to the rear includes a heated smoking area and a function room is available upstairs and may be booked for free. Bathams XXX is available in winter. A public car park is directly opposite.

Q ✿ ♣ P ☐ (X96,227,228)

Waggon & Horses Ⓛ

31 Worcester Street, DY8 1AT

☼ 12-11 (midnight Thu-Sat) ☎ (01384) 395398

Enville Ale, Ginger Beer; Holden's Golden Glow; 3 changing beers Ⓗ

A recent refurbishment has created a comfortable, welcoming alehouse. There is a small bar area to the front with a narrow passageway leading to a larger rear bar. To the side is a long bar with a small serving hatchway. Parking can be difficult in the narrow surrounding streets but there is parking in the town centre only a five-minute walk away. Two or more real ciders are usually available.

✿ ◑ & ⇌ ● ☐ (276,125,251) ❀ ⑨

Streetly

Queslett ✅

Queslett Road East, B74 2EY

☼ 11.30-11 (midnight Thu-Sat) ☎ (0121) 580 8123

Brakspear Bitter; Marston's Pedigree; Purity Pure Ubu; 4 changing beers Ⓗ

Comfortable and friendly Ember Inn featuring a large front patio. The open-plan interior is split into a variety of cosily furnished areas, enhanced by flaming gas fires. Well-presented food is served daily until 10pm. Three to four guest beers from the Ember seasonal range are offered, and Cask Ale Monday sees all real ales offered at a special price. Quizzes take place on Tuesdays and Sundays, poker on Mondays, while live music and sports screenings feature occasionally. ➿ ✿ ◑ & ♣ P ☐

Sutton Coldfield

Bottle of Sack ✅

2 Birmingham Road, B72 1QG

☼ 8am-midnight; 8am-11 Sun ☎ (0121) 362 8870

Greene King Abbot; Ruddles Best Bitter; Sharp's Doom Bar; changing beers Ⓗ

Large town-centre Wetherspoon with the usual menu of value food and an interesting range of changing guest ales, often featuring West Midlands breweries. The ground floor includes a bright conservatory area, and outside is a pleasant beer terrace. Upstairs is usually a little quieter, and offers a curved balcony area overlooking the bar downstairs. The pub name refers to a Sutton-related quote in Shakespeare's Henry IV.

➿ ✿ ◑ & ⇌ ● ☐ ⑨

Brewhouse & Kitchen ✅

8 Birmingham Road, B72 1QD

☼ 11-11 (midnight Thu; 1am Fri & Sat) ☎ (0121) 796 6838

⊕ brewhouseandkitchen.com/sutton-coldfield

Brewhouse & Kitchen The Cup, Shoestring, 004 Oaks, Black Belt, Marksman; 2 changing beers (often Brewhouse & Kitchen) Ⓗ

Opened late in 2015, this spacious brewpub is part of a small national chain. The real ales are made in the tidy brewery which is a prominent feature at the entrance. There is also a well-chosen international selection of bottled and keg beers. The decor is rustic wood and bare brick, with a variety of seating areas, and an atmospheric open log fire. It also has a streetside beer terrace – note the ironwork cup sign relating to a former name of the pub. ➿ ✿ ◑ & ☐ ⑨

Station ✅

Station Street, B73 6AT (near Sutton station southbound platform)

☼ 12-11 (midnight Fri & Sat) ☎ (0121) 362 4961

⊕ thestationsuttoncoldfield.co.uk

Holden's Golden Glow; Marston's Pedigree New World Pale Ale; house beer (by Holden's); 1 changing beer Ⓗ

Railway-related decor abounds in this classic pub just a few yards from the station. Two rooms, different in character, are served from a central bar, plus there is an upstairs function room. Monday evening is quiz night, Tuesday live music night and the last Thursday in the month is comedy night. The outdoor drinking area plays host to DJs and live music in summertime. Children are welcome until 6pm. The Holden's house beer is called Station Bitter. ➿ ✿ ◑ & ⇌ ☐ ⑨

Tipton

Fountain ✪

51 Owen Street, DY4 8HE

🌀 11-11 ☎ (0121) 522 3606

Banks's Mild; Wye Valley HPA; 4 changing beers (sourced regionally; often Enville, Hobsons, Wye Valley) Ⓗ

Canalside pub with a central bar and some interesting local photos on the walls. It does a good range of six real ales and a traditional cider. Guest beers are sourced through the Punch Taverns Finest Cask Ales scheme. It is family friendly and serves a range of good-value pub meals and curries lunchtimes and evenings, and roasts on Sunday lunchtimes. ☎❀◑≒♣🌢P🖵(311,229,42)❀❖

Rising Sun ⒧

116 Horseley Road, DY4 7NH (off B4517)

🌀 12-midnight ☎ (0121) 557 1940

Black Country Bradley's Finest Golden, Pig on the Wall, Fireside; 7 changing beers Ⓗ

A former CAMRA National Pub of the Year, reopened in 2013 following a superb refurbishment by Black Country Ales. It is an imposing Victorian hostelry with two distinct rooms warmed by open fires. For the summer there is a tidy yard at the back. There are seven changing guest beers and two traditional ciders, usually including Black Rat. Cobs are available. It is 10 minutes' walk from Great Bridge, which has frequent services to Dudley, West Bromwich and Birmingham. ❀♣🌢🖵(22)❀❖

Upper Gornal

Britannia ★ ⒧

109 Kent Street, DY3 1UX (on A459)

🌀 12-11; 12-10.30 Sun ☎ (01902) 883253

Bathams Mild Ale, Best Bitter Ⓗ

The Britannia has been recognised as having a nationally important historic pub interior for its taproom with wall-mounted handpumps at the rear, named after legendary former landlady Sally Perry. Service can be obtained from the front bar, itself a comfortable place to be, with both areas warmed by a roaring open fire. There is also a family games room with TV. Behind the pub is the former brewhouse and a delightful garden. A selection of bar snacks is available. Bathams XXX is sold in winter. Q☎❀♣🖵(1)❀❖

Jolly Crispin

25 Clarence Street, DY3 1UL (on A459)

🌀 4-11; 12-11 Fri & Sat; 12-10.30 Sun ☎ (01902) 672220

🌐 thejollycrispin.co.uk

Fownes Crispin's Ommer; 8 changing beers Ⓗ

Lively pub on the main route from Dudley to Sedgley. A shoemaker's house in the 18th century, there is a festival of beer here every day. The pub features regular ales from the on-site Fownes Brewery. Crispin Ommer is the house beer and up to eight guests are complemented by a real cider. Oakham Bishops Farewell is usually among the range at weekends. A twice-yearly cider festival is held in the garden and the number 1 bus from Dudley to Wolverhampton stops outside. CAMRA branch Cider Pub of the Year 2014-2016. ❀♣🌢P🖵(1)❀❖

Wall Heath

Wall Heath Tavern ⒧

14 High street, DY6 0HA (on A449)

🌀 12-11 (midnight Fri & Sat); 12-10.30 Sun

☎ (01384) 287319 🌐 thewallheathtavern.co.uk

Enville Ale, Ginger Beer; Holden's Golden Glow; Sharp's Doom Bar; 4 changing beers (often Salopian, Sarah Hughes, Three Tuns) Ⓗ

A bustling pub on the A449 approaching Wall Heath village centre. Serving up to 10 real ales with major emphasis on Enville Ales, it can get busy, particularly at weekends, with a TV showing sport in the bar. The lounge can be predominantly for food, especially in the evenings, where tables can be reserved. The menu features good-value cooking. There is a large patio area at the rear, which is busy in the summer months. ☎❀◑♿🌢P🖵❀❖

Walsall

Black Country Arms ♔ ⒧

High Street, WS1 1QW (in market, opp Asda)

🌀 11-11 (midnight Fri); 12-midnight Sat; 12-11 Sun

☎ (01922) 640588 🌐 blackcountryarms.co.uk

Black Country Bradley's Finest Golden, Pig on the Wall, Fireside; changing beers (sourced nationally) Ⓗ

A large, imposing multi award-winning pub on three levels, part of which was originally the Green Dragon Inn that dated back to the 18th century. The pub lay empty for 70 years until extensive refurbishment saw it reopen in 1987. The impressive bar boasts 16 handpumps serving up to 11 guest ales mainly from microbreweries, with two real ciders always available. Live music features frequently. Booking is recommended for Sunday lunches. ☎❀◑≒♣🌢P🖵❖

Fountain Inn ⒧

49 Lower Forster Street, WS1 1XB (off A4148 ring road)

🌀 12-2.30, 4.30-11; 12-midnight Fri & Sat; 12-11 Sun

☎ (01922) 633307

Backyard The Hoard, Blonde; 5 changing beers (sourced nationally; often Holden's, St Austell) Ⓗ

The brewery tap for Backyard Brewhouse, with up to eight beers on the bar. This is a friendly family-run pub with two rooms and a central bar. Bar snacks consist of freshly made cobs and pork pies. Vinyl night takes place once a month, craft night on a Wednesday, jam night every other Sunday, and a film night every Monday. Q☎◑≒♣🌢🖵(10,977,997)

Longhorn ⒧ ✪

255 Sutton Road, WS5 3AR

🌀 11-midnight (11 Mon); 11-11 Sun ☎ (01922) 625065

Brakspear Bitter; Purity Pure Ubu; Thwaites Wainwright; 5 changing beers (sourced nationally) Ⓗ

Large 1930s roadside inn with a real community feel. The rear of the pub is given over to diners, while drinkers tend to occupy the front section. Many charity events are hosted throughout the year, with quiz nights on Sundays and Wednesdays. Regular food and drinks deals are on offer. There is a function area available free of charge. It will open early (9am) for breakfast parties if given sufficient notice. ☎❀◑♿P❖

Lyndon House Hotel ⒧

9-10 Upper Rushall Street, WS1 2HA (between market and St Matthew's Church)

✪ 11-11 (1am Fri & Sat); 12-11 Sun ☎ (01922) 612511
⊕ lyndonhousehotel.co.uk
**Bathams Best Bitter; Burton Bridge Golden Delicious,
XL Bitter; Caledonian Deuchars IPA; Greene King
Abbot; Holden's Golden Glow** ⊞
Situated at the top of Walsall Market, the New
Royal Exchange pub was incorporated into an
adjoining Salvation Army hostel and leather
factory in 1995. It now forms the luxurious Lyndon
House Hotel. Its comfortable bar has an island
counter, cosy corners, old wood and brick. With its
function room, downstairs Sally Ann bar and
outdoor terraces, the premises are much larger on
the inside than you would expect. Popular with
business people, it is a slice of Walsall life. Live
music is played most Sunday afternoons, with
tribute bands on Saturdays in a separate function
room. Q✿🍴◑♿P🚪(51,377)

Pretty Bricks ⓛ
5 John Street, WS2 8AF (near magistrates court)
✪ 12-11 (midnight Fri & Sat) ☎ (01922) 612553
**Black Country Bradley's Finest Golden, Pig on the
Wall, Fireside; 5 changing beers (sourced
nationally)** ⊞
On the edge of town, this is a real back-street gem
dating from 1845. The pub takes its name from the
ceramic bricks at the front. The Bricks has almost
iconic status among the local CAMRA branch as it
was where their first meeting was held in 1972. A
photograph of the original members still hangs in
the bar. The pub has a front bar with a warm,
convivial atmosphere, while the snug-style lounge
has a more intimate feel. Both rooms feature real
fires. A folk night is held on the second Thursday of
each month. Q✿◑➴♣🚪(301)

St Matthew's Hall ✿
Lichfield Street, WS1 1SX
✪ 8am-midnight (2am Fri & Sat) ☎ (01922) 700820
**Greene King Abbot; Ruddles Best Bitter; Sharp's
Doom Bar; 4 changing beers (sourced regionally;
often AJ's Ales, Burton Bridge, Salopian)** ⊞
A stunning Grade II-listed Wetherspoon pub in the
centre of town, easily accessible by public transport
and with plenty of parking nearby. Monthly beer
festivals feature throughout the year, and live
entertainment every Friday and Saturday evening.
The full food menu is served from 8am till 11pm
each day. The large beer garden at the side has a
no-smoking area. A selection of local and national
guest ales supplements the three regular offerings.
🛏✿◑♿➴🚪🚪🛜

Walsall Cricket Club
Gorway Road, WS1 3BE (off A34, by university campus)
✪ 8-10.30; 6-11 Fri; 12-11 Sat; 12-10.30 Sun; closed Mon
☎ (01922) 622094 ⊕ walsallcricketclub.com
**Castle Rock Harvest Pale; Wye Valley HPA; 1 changing
beer (sourced nationally)** ⊞
On a fine summer evening the click of bat on ball
welcomes you to a green oasis in the heart of
town. The comfortable clubhouse lounge has a
panoramic view of the field, much local cricket
memorabilia and two large sporting screens. There
is occasional entertainment and the venue is
popular for function hire. New building and
improvements are planned. Non-member entry is
by CAMRA membership card. Weekend hours are
reduced in winter to Saturday 5-11pm, and Sunday
12-8.30pm. 🛏✿♿♣P🚪(51)🛜

Wheatsheaf ⓛ ✿
4 Birmingham Road, WS1 2NA
✪ 4-11; 12-1am Fri & Sat; 12-11 Sun ☎ (01922) 636687
⊕ wheatsheafwalsall.com
**Holden's Golden Glow; Oakham Citra; Wye Valley
Dorothy Goodbody's Golden Ale, Butty Bach; 4
changing beers (sourced locally; often Fownes,
Holden's)** ⊞
This friendly community local's once-complex
interior is now open plan, but still retains intimate
drinking areas, and is home to live music every
weekend. Tuesday is jam night and Thursday is the
deservedly popular steak night. Monthly 'tap
takeovers' by different breweries are held. Up to
eight real ales are on tap and a traditional cider. A
pub since at least 1801, formerly in the hands of
historic brewers Allsopps and then Ansells, it
became the Flock & Firkin for a short period in the
'80s before restoration in 2007.
🛏✿◑♿➴♣🚪🚪(51)✿🛜

Wednesbury

Bellwether ✿
3-4 Walsall Street, WS10 9BZ
✪ 7am-midnight (1am Fri & Sat) ☎ (0121) 502 6404
**Greene King Abbot; Oakham JHB; Ruddles Best Bitter;
7 changing beers (sourced nationally)** ⊞
Near the main shopping area and market, the pub
attracts a wide clientele. It has a large L-shaped
room on a split level with open-plan tables and
chairs in front of the bar. More intimate seating at
the rear leads on to a split-level tranquil garden
area. The pub is decorated with details of historic
events and characters associated with the town.
Ten handpumps serve a large selection of guest
ales. Q🛏✿◑♿♿➴♣🚪🛜

Cottage Spring ⓛ
106 Franchise Street, WS10 9RG
✪ 3 (1 Thu)-11.30; 12-midnight Fri & Sat; 12-11.30 Sun
☎ (0121) 531 7191
**Holden's Black Country Mild, Black Country Bitter,
Golden Glow; 1 changing beer (sourced locally; often
Holden's)** ⊞
The front bar has photos of the pub and owners
from yesteryear. There is a dartboard at one end,
the lounge has old-world prints and old-fashioned
manufacturing devices, and there is a stage area in
one corner. The bar features an old red phone box.
Friday is quiz night, and live music features on
Saturday nights and Sunday afternoon. Sunday
lunches are served. Q✿◑♣P🚪

Old Blue Ball ⓛ
19 Hall End, WS10 9ED (just off B4200 Whitley St)
✪ 12-3, 5-11; 12-11 Fri-Sun ☎ (0121) 556 0197
**Brains Rev James; Everards Original; Olde Swan
Original; Wye Valley Butty Bach; 2 changing beers
(sourced nationally)** ⊞
The small front bar has chamber pots, jugs, brasses
and advertising mirrors. Darts is played in the
lounge and a display of trophies adorns the room.
The cosy snug has paintings on the walls and a
sketch of the pub. Artists' impressions of old
Wednesbury, a newspaper story of a local murder,
and this pub's part in cock fighting all feature
throughout the building. A covered back yard with
TV leads out to a large garden and children's play
area. Q🛏✿♣🚪(310,313)✿

Olde Leathern Bottel ✪

40 Vicarage Road, WS10 9DW (just off A461)

🌜 12-2.30 (not Mon), 6-11; 12-3, 6-11.30 Fri; 11-11.30 Sat; 12-4, 7-11 Sun ☎ (0121) 505 0230

🌐 yeoldeleathernbottel.co.uk

3 changing beers (sourced nationally) Ⓗ

The bar and snug at the front of the Bottel are set in cottages dating from 1510, while a later extension contains a comfy lounge. The small snug is often used as a function room. The rooms have many old pictures – the bar displays a photograph of the pub from 1887 and a map of Wednesbury from 1846. At the rear is a pleasant benched patio area with plant pots. There is a quiz on Sunday evenings. The 311 bus from Walsall is five minutes' walk. Q🌜🏵️🕙♣️🅿️🚍(311)🐾🛜

Wednesfield

Vine ★ Ⓛ

35 Lichfield Road, WV11 1TN

🌜 12-11 (midnight Fri & Sat) ☎ (01902) 733529

Black Country Bradley's Finest Golden, Pig on the Wall, Fireside; 6 changing beers (sourced nationally) Ⓗ

Built in 1938, this Grade II-listed community local is a rare intact example of a simple inter-war working-class pub. It has been identified by CAMRA as having a nationally important historic pub interior for retaining its original bar, lounge and snug. Darts and dominoes are played and there are TVs showing live sport. A covered smokers' shelter and a beer garden provide outdoor drinking areas. Cobs and pork pies are available at all times and Sunday lunches are served until 5pm.

🏵️🕙♣️🅿️🚍(59,89)🐾🛜

West Bromwich

Crown & Cushion ✪

2 Lloyd Street, B71 4AT

🌜 12-11 ☎ (0121) 553 4493

St Austell Tribute; 2 changing beers (sourced nationally; often Castle Rock, Harviestoun) Ⓗ

Family-friendly hostelry with a single room L-shaped interior, run by a pleasant and welcoming landlady. The pub is popular in summer with visitors to nearby Dartmouth Park. It is within easy walking distance of West Bromwich Albion's football ground and can therefore get busy on match days However, away supporters are made welcome. 🌜🏵️🕙👍♣️🅿️🚍

Vine

152 Roebuck Street, B70 6RD

🌜 11.30-2, 5-11; 11.30-11 Fri & Sat; 12-10.30 Sun ☎ (0121) 553 2866 🌐 thevine.co.uk

2 changing beers Ⓗ

From the street this appears to be a classic corner pub, but be prepared for a surprise. The traditional interior comprises three small rooms off the corridor. But continue further in and the building opens up into a large dining area where an extensive range of Indian meals is served together with British and vegetarian options, all excellent value. Two guest ales are regularly on tap. This popular establishment gets busy, especially when West Bromwich Albion are at home.

🌜🏵️🕙👍🚆🅿️🚍(74,79)

Willenhall

Falcon

77 Gomer Street West, WV13 2NR (off B4464, behind flats)

🌜 12-11; 12-10.30 Sun ☎ (01902) 633378

Exmoor Gold; Salopian Oracle, Golden Thread; 3 changing beers (sourced nationally; often Backyard, Sadler's) Ⓗ

A two-roomed pub with a lively public bar and quieter lounge at the rear, situated a short walk from the town centre. Dating back to 1936, the Falcon has been in the same family for over 30 years. Old pub memorabilia adorn both rooms, where keenly priced beers are served. There is a beer garden at the rear and plenty of on-street parking nearby. Q🌜🏵️♣️🕙🅿️🚍(525,529)🐾

Robin Hood Ⓛ

54 The Crescent, WV13 2QR (200yds from A462/B4464 jct)

🌜 12-11 (midnight Fri & Sat) ☎ (01902) 635070

Black Country Bradley's Finest Golden, Pig on the Wall Ⓗ**, Fireside** Ⓗ/Ⓖ**; 6 changing beers (sourced nationally)** Ⓗ

Black Country Ales-owned pub with an old-fashioned feel where the friendly staff make you feel welcome. Three permanent beers are supplemented by six changing guest ales from throughout the UK. Two real ciders are also on the bar. Bar snacks, including cobs and pork pies, are available all day. One central bar serves the two drinking areas – a large bar at the front and a more intimate lounge at the rear. 🏵️♣️🕙🅿️🚍(529)

Wollaston

Foresters Arms Ⓛ ✪

Bridgnorth Road, DY8 3PL (on A458 towards Bridgnorth)

🌜 12-2.30 (not Mon), 6-midnight; 12-midnight Fri & Sat; 12-11.30 Sun ☎ (01384) 394476 🌐 foresterswollaston.co.uk

Enville Ale; Wye Valley HPA; 2 changing beers Ⓗ

Located on the ridge, ideal for ramblers, this friendly local is situated on the outskirts of Wollaston close to the countryside. The L-shaped room includes a convenient dining area where customers can sample good-value quality food. Quizzes are usually held on the first and third Sunday of each month. The annual Wollaston Fun Run starts from outside the pub and is followed by a barbecue in the beer garden. There is a heated and covered smoking area.

🏵️🕙▶️🅿️🚍(X96,227,228)🐾

Wolverhampton

Claregate Ⓛ

34 Codsall Road, WV6 9ED

🌜 12-11 (midnight Fri & Sat) ☎ (01902) 754761

Banks's Mild, Bitter, Sunbeam; 3 changing beers (sourced nationally) Ⓗ

The Fieldhouse replaced an earlier pub and was built with a large function room. In the 1970s the name was changed to the Claregate and over time the rooms were amalgamated into two large, but distinct, areas with seating arranged in bays. The dance floor remains beneath the carpet. Although the emphasis is on dining, the bar offers a good selection of Marston's beers for the local community. There is a large car park and the bus stops outside the pub. 🌜🏵️🕙👍♣️🅿️🚍(5,5A)🛜

Combermere Arms

90 Chapel Ash, WV3 0TY (on A41 Tettenhall Rd)
⊕ 12-3 (not Mon winter), 5-11; 12-midnight Fri & Sat;
12-10.30 Sun ☎ (01902) 421880
5 changing beers (sourced nationally; often Greene King) Ⓗ
Grade II-listed building with original sash windows. The three charming rooms have cosy fireplaces and a wealth of pictures depicting the local football team, classic adverts and a comical Guinness series. A pub favourites' menu is served weekday lunchtimes except Monday. Cheese, pie and sausage tasting festivals are held annually and there is live entertainment twice monthly on Saturday evenings. Character features include the tree in the Gents. Beers are from the Greene King portfolio. Q❧❀☕♣P�

Dog & Doublet ⓛ ✅

9 North Street, WV1 1RE
⊕ 12-11 (2am Thu & Fri; 3am Sat); 2-10.30 Sun
☎ (01902) 423805 ⊕ thedoganddoubletinn.co.uk
5 changing beers (sourced nationally) Ⓗ
City-centre pub, located near the Civic and Wulfrun halls, a mix of modern and traditional, with real fires and chesterfield furniture. The outside drinking area includes a cocktail bar. Music features heavily at the pub, with open mic evening on a Thursday, live bands Friday and a DJ on Saturday (admission charges apply after 10pm Sat). Food is not served but you are welcome to bring your own – plates and cutlery provided. Harry's Cider is always on the bar. ❧❀❶≠Ⓠ♣且🛜

Dog & Gun ⓛ ✅

1 Wrottesley Road, Tettenhall, WV6 8SB (off A41 Wergs Road)
⊕ 11.30-11 (midnight Fri & Sat) ☎ (01902) 747943
Brakspear Bitter; St Austell Tribute; Thwaites Wainwright; house beer (by Black Sheep); 4 changing beers (sourced nationally) Ⓗ
Comfortable and welcoming Ember Inns pub with individual seating areas around a large U-shaped bar. It attracts a wide age range, including a local writers' group and a rambling club who meet here regularly. Food quality and an imaginative choice of guest beers, often dark, ensure a busy and friendly atmosphere, particularly on weekend evenings. Monday is Cask Ale Club day, when all ales are sold at a reduced price, and fortnightly open mic sessions are held on a Wednesday. There is a patio for outside drinking. ❧❀❶♿P且(1,891)🛜

Great Western ⓛ

Sun Street, WV10 0DJ (pedestrian access from city centre via subway at station)
⊕ 11-11; 11-10.30 Sun ☎ (01902) 351090
Bathams Best Bitter; Holden's Black Country Mild, Black Country Bitter, Golden Glow, Special; 3 changing beers (sourced regionally) Ⓗ
A previous CAMRA National Pub of the Year, situated near the former low-level railway station. It attracts a varied clientele, including rock climbing, motorbike and railway groups who meet here regularly. Plenty of railway and Wolverhampton Wanderers memorabilia are on display and cosy real fires blaze in the winter. Meals are served at lunchtime and snacks are available until 10pm, except Sundays.
Q❧❀❶≠ⒺP且🐾🛜

Hail to the Ale 🏆 ⓛ

2 Pendeford Avenue, Claregate, WV6 9EF (on Claregate island)
⊕ closed Mon-Wed; 5-10; 12-10 Sat; 12-5 Sun ☎ 07846 562910 ⊕ hailtothealemicropub.co.uk
4 changing beers (sourced regionally; often Morton) Ⓗ
Welcoming one-room beer-focused pub converted from a vacant shop, this is the West Midlands' first micropub and was opened in 2013 by Morton Brewery. A simple formula is followed with no distractions, just good ale and conversation. Four handpulls serve at least one Morton beer and different guests, usually from local microbreweries, while a further two handpulls dispense ciders and/or perries. Locally sourced pies, cheese, sausage rolls, Scotch eggs and fruit wines are also available. CAMRA regional Pub of the Year 2015.
Q❧❀❶♣♿P且(5,6)🐾

Hog's Head ⓛ ✅

186 Stafford Street, WV1 1NA
⊕ 10-midnight (1am Fri & Sat) ☎ (01902) 717955
⊕ hogsheadwolverhampton.co.uk
Broughs Light Pale Ale; Wye Valley HPA; Butty Bach; 6 changing beers (sourced nationally; often Enville, Marston's) Ⓗ
Large 19th-century city-centre pub with an attractive terracotta brick exterior. A stained-glass window above the entrance still displays the original name, the Vine. The large interior single room is divided into separate areas, with widescreen TVs showing sport and music videos throughout the building. It serves a wide range of rotating guest ales, many from local microbreweries, and a varying cider. Popular with all age groups. It stages a quiz on Thursday evenings. ❧❀❶♿≠Ⓠ♣且🛜

Lych Gate Tavern ⓛ

44 Queen Square, WV1 1TX (off Queens Square by St Peter's Church)
⊕ 11-11 (midnight Fri & Sat) ☎ (01902) 399516
⊕ lychgatetavern.co.uk
Black Country Bradley's Finest Golden, Pig on the Wall, Fireside; 6 changing beers (sourced nationally) Ⓗ
Friendly, traditional city-centre pub housed in one of the oldest timber-framed buildings in Wolverhampton. The Georgian frontage dates from 1726, while the timber-framed rear dates from about 1500. The bar area is reached by a short flight of stairs down from street level and there is a function room available for hire upstairs. Cobs are served or you may bring your own food – plates and cutlery are provided. All floors are accessible via a lift. A previous CAMRA branch Pub of the Year.
Q❀♿≠Ⓠ♣且🛜

Moon Under Water ⓛ ✅

53-55 Lichfield Street, WV1 1EQ
⊕ 7am-midnight (1am Fri & Sat) ☎ (01902) 422447
Banks's Sunbeam; Greene King Abbot; Ruddles Best Bitter; Sharp's Doom Bar; 3 changing beers (sourced nationally; often Burton Bridge, Morton, Titanic) Ⓗ
Conveniently located for theatregoers, and for the rail and bus stations. A wide range of food is served from breakfast until 11pm. Wolverhampton memorabilia adorn the walls and the ceiling has some stained glass. The pub attracts a great variety of customers and can be busy match days and before or after theatre performances. A well-balanced choice of beers is always dispensed at

reasonable prices. A music-free zone, it is great for a chat; news and sports programmes are shown silently. Q☺🛇◑🕹️&⇌🅿️🍴📶

Newhampton 🅛 ✅

17 Riches Street, Whitmore Reans, WV6 0DW
✪ 11-11 (midnight Fri & Sat) ☎ (01902) 680766
Caledonian Deuchars IPA; Courage Best Bitter, Directors; Enville Ale; Three Tuns XXX; Timothy Taylor Landlord; 2 changing beers (sourced nationally; often Wye Valley) ⊞
A Victorian street-corner local catering for a cosmopolitan customer base. Hatches service the (former) smoke room and pool room, which has a jukebox. The bar has an additional handpump for Thatchers Heritage cider. An upstairs function room hosts regular music events including folk and jazz, but with no wheelchair access. The large garden includes a popular seating area, children's small adventure playground, a crown green bowls lawn, an occasional pavilion bar and a smoking shelter. 🛇☺◑&♣🅿️🐾📶

Posada 🅛

WV1 1DG
✪ 12-11; 11.30-midnight Fri; 11.30-11.30 Sat; 12-6 Sun
Marston's EPA; Sharp's Doom Bar; 3 changing beers (sourced nationally; often Hobsons, Salopian) ⊞
Victorian Grade II-listed city-centre pub with tiled walls, original bar fittings (including rare snob screens, fabulous tiled walls and an ornate bar back), and little altered since 1900. It attracts a varied clientele and is quiet during the day but busy in the evening and weekends, especially when Wolverhampton Wanderers are at home. There is a courtyard to the rear and a smoking area. Cobs are available and Westons Old Rosie cider is stocked. 🛇☺⇌🅿️📶

Royal Oak 🅛 ✅

70 Compton Road, WV3 9PH
✪ 11.30-11 (midnight Fri & Sat); 12-11 Sun
☎ (01902) 422845 ⊕ royaloakwolverhampton.co.uk
Banks's Mild, Bitter, Sunbeam; Wychwood Hobgoblin Gold; 3 changing beers (sourced nationally; often Jennings, Ringwood, Wychwood) ⊞
Friendly local, a short walk or bus ride from the city centre, serving a wide range of changing real ales from Marston's. The bustling pub, with good sports coverage, hosts open mic evenings on Wednesdays and live bands on Fridays and Saturdays (also Sunday afternoons in summer). Part of the community, the pub raises money for local and national charities, features a book swap library and is the headquarters of Old Wulfrunians Hockey Club. Fresh cobs are available at the bar. 🛇☺&♣🅿️(10,890)🐾📶

Stile Inn 🅛 ✅

3 Harrow Street, Whitmore Reans, WV1 4PB (off Newhampton Rd East/Fawdry St)
✪ 11.30-11 (midnight Fri; 1am Sat) ☎ (01902) 425336
⊕ thestileinn.co.uk
Banks's Mild, Bitter, Sunbeam; 1 changing beer (sourced nationally) ⊞
A typical late-Victorian street-corner pub built in 1900, featuring a public bar, smoke room and snug. It is a true community local with an emphasis on sport – darts and dominoes feature inside, crown green bowls on the unusual L-shaped green outside, and it gets busy with Wolverhampton Wanderers fans on match days. Excellent-value food, including Polish dishes, is served all day (no

food Sun). Friday is open mic night and Saturday is karaoke. Sky Sports is shown in all rooms. 🛇☺◑♣🍴(5,6)🐾📶

Swan 🅛

Bridgnorth Road, Compton, WV6 8AE (at Compton Island, A454)
✪ 12-11 (11.30 Thu; midnight Fri & Sat) ☎ (01902) 754736
Banks's Mild, Bitter, Sunbeam; Jennings Cocker Hoop; Marston's Old Empire; 3 changing beers (sourced nationally; often Brakspear, Jennings, Wychwood) ⊞
Built around 1780, this Grade II-listed building is popular with locals, as well as boaters, ramblers and cyclists, it being close to the Staffordshire & Worcestershire Canal and Smestow Valley Nature Reserve. There are three distinct areas – a games room, a lively bar with local banter and a more sedate snug. It hosts charity dog shows and has a number of beer festivals during the year featuring guest ales from outside the Marston's range. The local pigeon-flyers club meets weekly. Q🛇☺♣🅿️(10,890)🐾📶

Woodsetton

Park Inn 🅛

George Street, DY1 4LW (on A457, 200yds from A4123)
✪ 12-11; 12-10.30 Sun ☎ (01902) 661279
Holden's Black Country Mild, Black Country Bitter, Golden Glow, Special; 1 changing beer ⊞
Vibrant suburban brewery tap, held by the Holden family since 1915. Radiating out from the spacious main bar are a small games room, a raised dining area and a separate conservatory. Functions are catered for and reasonably priced food is served 12-8pm (4.30pm Sun). The pub adjoins the brewery which has been extended and refurbished over the previous year. Note that the new brewery centre is on the right of the car park. 🛇☺◑♣🅿️(81,126,229)🐾

Wordsley

New Inn 🅛

117 High Street, DY8 5QR (on A491)
✪ 12-11; 12-10.30 Sun ☎ (01384) 295614
Bathams Mild Ale, Best Bitter ⊞
On the A491, the building has an imposing three-storey Victorian façade. One of the Bathams 10 and very much a locals' pub, it has become extremely popular and is usually busy. An L-shaped bar serves a single room with a small annexe at one end, with a patio area and newly refurbished garden outside. Children are not allowed in the pub. A variety of cobs is available. The pub has the feel of a proper local. 🛇☺♣🅿️(256,257)🐾📶

Queen's Head 🅛

129 High Street, DY8 5QS (on A491)
✪ 12-11 (midnight Fri & Sat) ☎ (01384) 402967
Black Country Bradley's Finest Golden, Pig on the Wall, Fireside; 6 changing beers ⊞
Comfortable roadside pub on the main A491 Stourbridge to Wolverhampton road. The layout echoes its multi-roomed past although most of the interior walls have gone. The decor is cosy Victorian or Edwardian in style. It sells up to nine real ales, with three from the parent brewery, and a traditional cider. To the right is a bar area which has a large-screen TV and dartboard. The pub now sells food (book ahead for Sunday lunch). 🛇☺◑♣🅿️(256,257)🐾📶

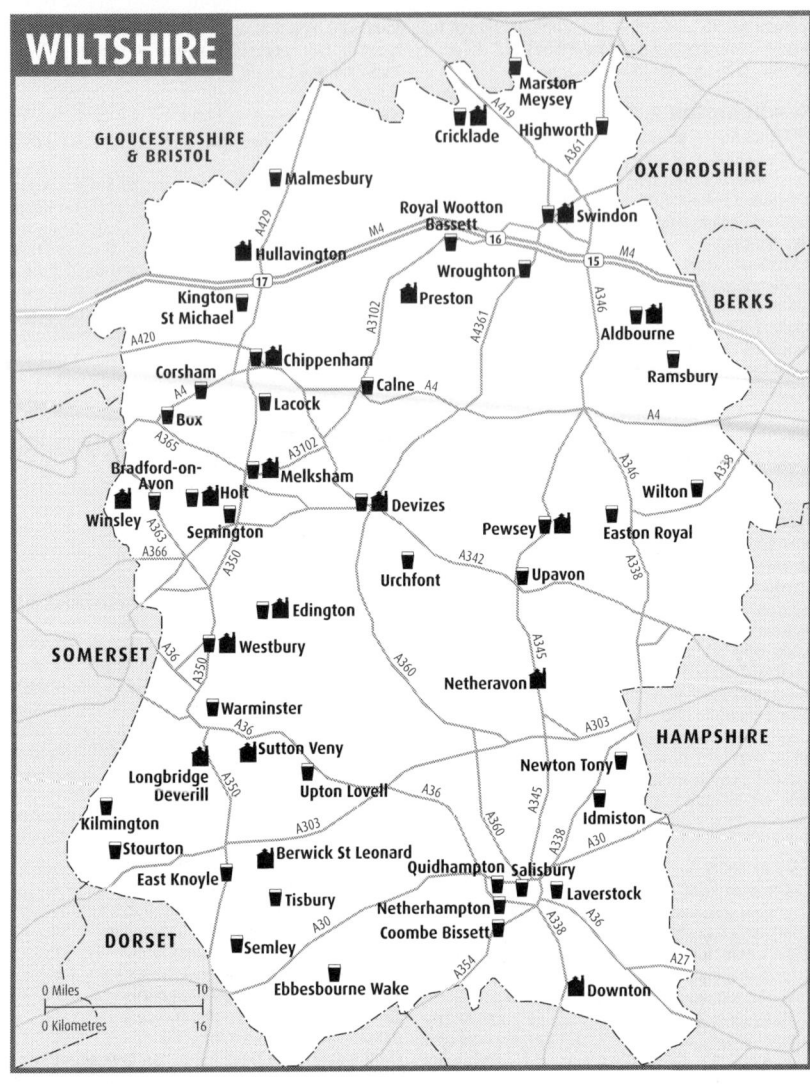

WILTSHIRE

Aldbourne

Blue Boar ⃝L
20 The Green, SN8 2EN
☼ 11.30-3, 5.30-11.30; 11.30-midnight Fri & Sat; 12-10.30
Sun ☎ (01672) 540237 ⊕ thepubonthegreen.com
**Wadworth 6X; 3 changing beers (sourced nationally;
often Wadworth)** Ⓗ
Friendly, comfortable inn by the village green
serving home-cooked food in the bar and dining
room. Beer festivals are held twice a year in June
and December. During World War II it was the
officers' mess for America's 506th Parachute
Infantry Regiment. Easy Company from this
regiment had their story told in TV series Band of
Brothers. The pub also featured in a 1971 episode
of Dr Who. ☜⊛①♦&Å♠₩(46,48)❀ ⟨

Crown Hotel ⃝
The Square, SN8 2DU
☼ 12-midnight; 12-10.30 Sun ☎ (01672) 540214
⊕ thecrownaldbourne.co.uk

**Sharp's Doom Bar; Shepherd Neame Amber Ale; 3
changing beers (sourced nationally; often Castle
Combe)** Ⓗ
The Crown is set in the middle of the village
opposite the duck pond. A Dalek stands guard
outside. It has a relaxed and pleasant atmosphere,
with two bars. The main bar is stylishly refurbished
and has a welcoming fire during the colder
seasons. The smaller bar shows films on a Monday
night. The restaurant serves freshly prepared food
with daily specials until 9.30pm. On Sundays there
is a carvery until it runs out, then the usual menu.
There are four en suite bedrooms.
⊛⇔①♦Å₩(46,48)❀ ⟨

Box

Quarryman's Arms ⃝L
Box Hill, SN13 8HN (off A4 follow signs)
☼ 8am-11 (midnight Fri & Sat) ☎ (01225) 743569
⊕ quarrymans-arms.co.uk

Butcombe Bitter; Moles Best Bitter; Wadworth 6X; 2 changing beers (sourced nationally; often Flying Monk, Kennet & Avon) Ⓗ
The pub is a 300-year-old former miner's cottage – some of the stone for Georgian Bath was mined below Box Hill. It has a separate snug bar with a linked main bar and dining area with a breathtaking view towards Bath and across the valley to Colerne. The walls are decorated with stone-mining paraphernalia and pump labels from the many guest beers served. Food is locally sourced, the cider is Black Rat and there are four B&B rooms. Q☺✿🛏◐🚴♿⚶♠P🏠⏰

Bradford-on-Avon

Castle Inn
Mount Pleasant, BA15 1SJ
❋ 9am-11; 10-10.30 Sun ☎ (01225) 865657
⊕ flatcappers.co.uk/the-castle-inn
Three Castles Barbury Castle, Vale Ale; 4 changing beers Ⓗ
A popular, comfortable pub commanding splendid views across the town towards Salisbury Plain. The recent refurbishment by Flatcappers earned a national CAMRA award. A wide range of handpulled real ales is complemented by excellent food, served all day until 10pm. The three guest beers are usually sourced from micros in Wiltshire and east Somerset. There is a good-sized garden at the front and children are welcome. B&B is available, with four luxury double bedrooms.
☺✿🛏◐♿⚶🚶P🏠⏰

Rising Sun
231 Winsley Road, BA15 1QS
❋ 12 (4 Wed)-11; 12-10.30 Sun ☎ (01225) 862354
Courage Best Bitter; 2 changing beers (sourced regionally) Ⓗ
The Riser is a popular local with two bars – a small, quiet lounge and a more spacious, livelier saloon with TV screens. Behind is a good-sized walled beer garden with patio. The pub is home to darts, quiz, crib, pool and football teams, and hosts regular live music including a Rhythm & Booze beer festival over the August bank holiday. The two guest beers change week by week and the cider is made locally for the pub. ☺✿♠🚶P🏠(265)⏰

Timbrell's Yard
49 St. Margarets Street, BA15 1DE
❋ 9am-11; 9am-10.30 Sun ☎ (01225) 869492
⊕ timbrellsyard.com
Bath Ales Gem; Cheddar Ales Potholer; 2 changing beers (sourced regionally; often Bristol Beer Factory, Electric Bear) Ⓗ
Newly reopened in early 2015, Timbrell's Yard has been beautifully restored and transformed into an upmarket pub with rooms. Originally the home of wealthy local mill owner Mr Timbrell, the building has been returned to its former glory. The beers, two regulars and two guests, are usually locally brewed, while the cider is produced in Winsley, just outside town. The food is excellent and highly recommended. Q☺✿🛏◐♿≢🚶P🏠(265)♣⏰

Calne

White Hart Hotel Ⓛ
London Road, SN11 0AB (on A4 jct with Silver St)
❋ 12-11 (1am Fri & Sat) ☎ (01249) 812413
⊕ whitehartcalne.com

Bath Ales Gem; Box Steam Piston Broke; Sharp's Doom Bar; 1 changing beer (sourced locally; often Castle Combe) Ⓗ
Built in 1659 and formerly a coaching inn, this building has been transformed by the owners into a friendly local pub at the heart of the community. Tuesday night quizzes and live music nights support local charities. The interior features an eclectic decor, including medieval swords and suits of armour, with an open fire adding warmth in the evening. Black Rat cider is occasionally available.
☺🛏◐♿♣P🏠(33)⏰

Chippenham

Buttercross Inn Ⓛ
6 Market Place, SN15 3HD (adjacent to the Buttercross)
❋ 11-11 (midnight Thu; 2am Fri & Sat); 12-10 Sun
☎ (01249) 460662
Box Steam Piston Broke; 6 changing beers (sourced regionally; often Marston's) Ⓗ
Town-centre pub bought from Fuller's and sympathetically refurbished in 2014. Run by an enthusiastic husband and wife team, the pub has three distinct bar areas with plenty of pub and brewery memorabilia. Seven real ales and nine real ciders are available as well as Belgian bottled beers. An annual cider festival is held in September. Popular live music events are hosted on Thursday and Saturday and, although this is not a sports bar, major rugby and football matches are screened. Q☺♿≢♠🚶🐾⏰

Old Road Tavern
Old Road, SN15 1JA (over bridge from railway station)
❋ 11-11.30; 11-12.30am Fri & Sat; 12-11 Sun
☎ (01249) 652094
Bath Ales Gem; Gale's HSB; Hop Back Summer Lightning; Otter Bitter; Wye Valley HPA; 1 changing beer (sourced regionally; often Castle Combe) Ⓗ
Occupying a 140-year-old listed building, this is a traditional community local. It has a large garden with plenty of seating, always popular in summer. The diverse mix of regulars ensures lively and friendly conversation. Five regular beers are complemented by a guest sourced from a local or

REAL ALE BREWERIES
Arkell's Swindon
Box Steam Holt
Castle Combe Preston
Chippenham Chippenham (NEW)
Downton Downton
Flying Monk Hullavington
Hop Back Downton
Hop Kettle 🍺 Cricklade
Kennet & Avon Melksham
Keystone Berwick St Leonard
Moles Melksham
Plain Sutton Veny
Ramsbury Aldbourne
Shed Pewsey
Stonehenge Netheravon
Three Castles Pewsey
Three Daggers Edington
Twisted Westbury
Wadworth Devizes
Weighbridge 🍺 Swindon
Wessex Longbridge Deverill
Willy Good Ale Winsley
World's End 🍺 Pewsey

sometimes more distant brewery. Simple bar food is served Thursday to Saturday lunchtimes. A regular live music and comedy night venue, it is always extremely busy during the Chippenham Folk Festival. ⚜Q♿♨♣🅿🚌😺🛜

Three Crowns 🍷 Ⓛ
18 The Causeway, SN15 3DB (¼ mile S of town centre opp Kwik Fit)
🕐 5 (12 Thu)-11; 12-midnight Fri & Sat; 12-11 Sun
☎ (01249) 449029 ⊕ threecrownschippenham.co.uk
7 changing beers (sourced nationally; often Arbor, Celt Experience, Slater's) Ⓗ
Originally an 18th-century wagon inn on the London to Bath road, this is now a community free house offering seven cask beers from local microbreweries and from further afield. The range always includes two dark beers and one strong brew. CAMRA branch Cider Pub of the Year, it sells three ciders, mainly sourced from Wiltshire producers, and a perry. Four beer festivals are held each year. A popular venue for quiz, poetry and various other ad hoc theme nights.
Q♨♣🅿🖲🚌(55)😺

Coombe Bissett

Fox & Goose Ⓛ
Blandford Road, SP5 4LE
🕐 11-11; 12-10.30 Sun ☎ (01722) 718437
⊕ foxandgoose-coombebissett.co.uk
Sharp's Doom Bar; 2 changing beers (sourced locally) Ⓗ
Eighteenth-century coaching inn on the A354 three miles south of Salisbury. A popular community pub, it has a loyal village clientele and a welcoming atmosphere. It is divided into a bar and restaurant, serving an extensive food menu with ever-changing specials. Outside there is a covered smoking area and gardens to the rear. Two regularly changing ales are sourced mostly from local microbreweries. There is a loyalty card scheme for regular diners.
Q♿⚜◑🅿🚌(X12,29)😺🛜

Corsham

Two Pigs Ⓛ
Pickwick, SN13 0HY
🕐 7-11; 12-2.30, 7-10.30 Sun ☎ (01249) 712515
⊕ thetwopigs.co.uk
Stonehenge Pigswill, Danish Dynamite; 2 changing beers (sourced regionally) Ⓗ
This former CAMRA branch Pub of the Year remains a favourite with a faithful band of loyal regulars and those who come for the Monday evening live blues and rock sessions. Low lighting, stone-flagged floors and background blues music add to the ambience. No food is available but ale fans are treated to two regular and two guest beers. There is plenty of bench seating plus a covered courtyard, aptly named The Sty. Q♣🚌(231)

Cricklade

Red Lion 🍷 Ⓛ
74 High Street, SN6 6DD
🕐 12-11; 12-10.30 Sun ☎ (01793) 750776
⊕ theredlioncricklade.co.uk
Butcombe Bitter; Wadworth 6X; 8 changing beers (often Hop Kettle) Ⓗ

Friendly, popular and comfortable inn, parts of which are quite ancient – the old Saxon town wall passes through the building. It is also home to the Hop Kettle Brewing Co, which started brewing in 2012. Ten real ales – two regular, four from Hop Kettle and four guests – are on handpump, plus cider from Westons. Food is served lunchtimes and evenings Monday-Saturday, lunchtime only on Sunday. There is a large garden at the back and five rooms for B&B. A winter beer festival is held in February, a summer festival in June.
Q⚜🛏◑♿♣🚌(51,53)😺🛜

Devizes

British Lion ⊘
9 Estcourt Street, SN10 1LQ (on A361 London road opp Kwik Fit)
🕐 11-11 (midnight Fri & Sat), 12-11 Sun ☎ (01380) 720665
⊕ britishliondevizes.co.uk
Moles Tap Bitter; Plain Innocence; Ramsbury Gold; Stonehenge Pigswill; 4 changing beers (sourced nationally; often Bath Ales, Hop Back, Palmers) Ⓗ
A Guide regular now for more than 20 years, the Lion is a proper drinkers' pub popular with a variety of friendly locals from builders to office workers. Inside, there are wooden floors, cosy settles and a long bar with plenty of stools; outside is a huge rear beer garden and a covered smoking area. Four varying ales are on the handpumps, mostly from West Country breweries. The cider is Black Rat or Cheddar Valley. The landlord possesses a wealth of brewing industry knowledge and is always happy to advise. ⚜♣🅿🖲🚌(49)🛜

Southgate Inn
Potterne Road, SN10 5BY (on jct of Southbroom Rd & Potterne Rd)
🕐 4-11; 12-midnight Fri & Sat; 12-11 Sun ☎ (01380) 722872
3 changing beers (often Downton, Great Western, Hop Back) Ⓗ
The five-minute walk from the town centre is well worth it for the welcome you will receive here. A cosy and friendly pub, it has three separate bar areas and lots of nooks and crannies. Three handpumps feature a range of ales mainly from West Country breweries. Outside, the large courtyard area hosts an annual Easter beer festival, which is always well attended. Saturdays often feature live music. Well-behaved dogs are positively encouraged. ♿♣♣🅿🚌(49)😺🛜

Vaults
28A St John's Street, SN10 1BN (three mins walk from Market Square, opp town hall)
🕐 12-9; 12-6 Sun ☎ (01380) 721443
⊕ thevaultsdevizes.com
6 changing beers (sourced nationally; often Kennet & Avon) Ⓗ
The Vaults has firmly established itself as the pub offering the largest range of ales in town. The tap for the Kennet & Avon Brewery, it offers up to six real ales and a huge range of bottled beers from around the world at reasonable prices. It has a single, long bar and a vast cellar room often used for tasting evenings. All the fixtures are made from recycled materials. It fills up quickly so get here early. ♣🅿🚌(49)😺🛜

East Knoyle

Fox & Hounds

Wise Lane, The Green, SP3 6BN ST87113135
✪ 11.30-3, 5.30-11 ☎ (01747) 830573
⊕ foxandhounds-eastknoyle.co.uk
3 changing beers (sourced locally; often Butcombe, Hop Back, Plain) Ⓗ

Attractive old thatched black-and-white pub situated high on a hillside with extensive panoramic rural views. Comfortable and cosy inside, the warm welcome is enhanced in winter by a blazing log fire in a huge inglenook fireplace. Three ales are always available encompassing a wide range of strengths and varying continuously, with local beers given prominence. The real cider is Thatchers Cheddar Valley. Food is served at all sessions. An adjacent skittle alley doubles as a function room. Q❀🕭🛏◑🐾P🐾

Easton Royal

Bruce Arms ★ Ⓛ

Easton Road, SN9 5LR
✪ 5-11; 12-11 Sat; 12-7 Sun ☎ (01672) 810216
⊕ thebrucearms.net
Sharp's Atlantic; Stonehenge Pigswill; Wadworth 6X; 1 changing beer (sourced regionally) Ⓗ

Mid-19th-century local that has a nationally important historic pub interior. There is a small cosy bar with furniture that probably goes back to the 1850s, a small lounge with easy chairs and piano, while at the back is a larger dining/function room. The pub exists in splendid isolation, so its campsite with full facilities is welcome and makes it a good venue for meetings and rallies. The pub is home to EROS (Easton Royal Onion Society).
Q❀🕭🛆🐾P🖳(96,19)🐾🛜

Ebbesbourne Wake

Horseshoe

The Cross, SP5 5JF
✪ 12-3, 6.30-11; 12-4 Sun; closed Mon ☎ (01722) 780474
Bowman Wallops Wood; Otter Bitter; Palmers Dorset Gold; 1 changing beer (sourced nationally) Ⓖ

Unspoilt 18th-century pub in a remote rural setting at the foot of an old ox drove. This friendly pub has two small bars that display an impressive collection of old farm implements, tools and lamps, plus a restaurant, conservatory and pleasant garden. Good local food is available Tuesday to Sunday and the beers are served direct from casks stillaged behind the bar. The original serving hatch just inside the front door is still in use. Real cider is usually available – often from Thatchers or Wessex.
Q❀🕭🛆◑🛆🐾P🖳(29)🐾

Edington

Three Daggers

Westbury Road, BA13 4PG
✪ 8am-11; 9am-10.30 Sun ☎ (01380) 830940
⊕ threedaggers.co.uk
Three Daggers Daggers Blonde, Daggers Ale, Daggers Edge; 1 changing beer (often Three Daggers) Ⓗ

This refurbished village pub is now the brewery tap for the eponymous brewery situated in an adjacent farm shop. The pub has a main bar with three distinct drinking areas, leading to a seating area and a dining room. Two mirrors hide TV screens that are occasionally used for sporting events. Dogs are welcomed with free biscuits, and accommodation is available. Regular seasonal beers are brewed, and carryouts and bottles are available from the farm shop.
Q❀🕭🛆◑🛆🐾P🖳(87, 877)🐾🛜

Highworth

Rose & Crown Ⓛ ✅

19 The Green, SN6 7DB
✪ 9am-11 (midnight Fri); 11-midnight Sat; 12-11 Sun ☎ (01793) 764699 ⊕ roseandcrownhighworth.co.uk
5 changing beers (sourced regionally; often Halfpenny, Old Forge) Ⓗ

This is one of the oldest pubs in Highworth. It opened as a free house in 2014 after a major facelift, with a pleasant, welcoming ambience. Cheerful and friendly staff serve a changing range of ales on five handpumps. The lunchtime menu is good quality and great value. There is a boules pitch in the garden. An open mic session is hosted once a month. Q❀🕭🛆◑🛆🐾P🖳(7,64,74)🐾🛜

Holt

Tollgate Inn

Ham Green, BA14 6PX (on B3105 between Bradford-on-Avon and Melksham)
✪ 9am-11.30; 9am-4 Sun ☎ (01225) 782326
⊕ tollgateholt.co.uk
Butcombe Adam Henson's Rare Breed; Fuller's London Pride; 2 changing beers (sourced locally; often Twisted, Box Steam) Ⓗ

A real gem, this old village pub has an upmarket atmosphere with a wood-burning stove, oak floors and comfy sofas to relax in. The local brewery in the village, Box Steam, is usually featured among the range of four or five beers. Beers change daily, with a good selection of local ales alongside many from smaller breweries further afield. A real cider is on handpump during the summer months. The food is recommended, and there is a separate dining room. Q❀🕭🛏◑🛆🐾P🖳(68, 69)🛜

Idmiston

Earl of Normanton 🍴 Ⓛ

Tidworth Road, SP4 0AG
✪ 12-2.30, 6-11; 12-3, 8-10.30 Sun ☎ (01980) 610251
⊕ earlofnormanton.co.uk
Exmoor Gold; Flowerpots Bitter; Hop Back Summer Lightning; 2 changing beers (sourced locally) Ⓗ

Popular roadside inn with a loyal village clientele and a welcoming atmosphere enhanced by two real fires in winter months. Two guest ales, mostly from local breweries, complement a great choice of regular ales. Good-value home-cooked food is served (no food Sun eve). There is a small, pleasant garden on the steep hill behind the pub and a heated, covered smoking area. Live music features occasionally. B&B is available. Local CAMRA Country Pub of the Year 2014 and 2016.
Q❀🕭🛏◑🖳P(66,67)🐾🛜

Kilmington

Red Lion Inn Ⓛ ✅

BA12 6RP (on B3092 between Mere and Frome)
✪ 11-3, 6.30-9 (10 Wed-Sat); 12-3, 7-10.30 Sun
☎ (01985) 844263 ⊕ theredlionkilmington.co.uk

Butcombe Bitter; Wessex Stourton Pale Ale; 1 changing beer (sourced locally; often Butts, Plain Ales) ⊞

A warm and friendly traditional free house which has a low-beamed, flagstoned front bar with cushioned walls and window seats, curved high-backed settle seats and woodburners. There is a larger back bar with more tables to enjoy the home-cooked food sourced from high-quality local food producers (some from the village itself). Thatchers Heritage cider completes the excellent drinks range. Dogs are welcome to join their owners in the front bar or in the large attractive garden which has fine views of White Sheet Hill. Q ❄ 🕮 ◑ ♣ ♠ P ♠ 🕏

Kington St Michael

Jolly Huntsman
SN14 6JB
🕓 11.30-2.30, 6-11 (midnight Fri & Sat); 12-3, 7-10.30 Sun
☎ (01249) 750305 ⊕ jollyhuntsman.com
Moles Gold; Wadworth 6X; 2 changing beers (sourced regionally) ⊞

A former brewery situated on the village high street, this free house offers a warm and friendly welcome, with a large open fire in the winter. A range of locally brewed real ales and ciders is offered along with an excellent food menu available lunchtimes and evenings, featuring a range of traditional fare and chef's specials. Themed evenings are held on occasion. Accommodation is en suite. Q ❄ ⇆ ◑ ◑ ♠ ♠ P ⊟ (99)

Lacock

Bell Inn ⌷
The Wharf, SN15 2PJ (½ mile out of Lacock towards Bowden Hill)
🕓 11-2.30, 5-11; 11.30-11 Sat; 12-10.30 Sun
☎ (01249) 730308 ⊕ thebellatlacock.co.uk
House beer (by Bath Ales); 3 changing beers (sourced regionally; often Box Steam, Cottage, Palmers) ⊞

A friendly welcome is assured at this popular free house on the edge of the National Trust village of Lacock, run by the same family since 2000. A regular local CAMRA Pub of the Year, it has an excellent reputation for quality ale and food. Four ales and a real cider are usually available, and two beer festivals are held each year. The house beer, Red Wharf, is brewed to the pub's own recipe by Bath Ales. This place is on National Cycle Network route 403. Q ❄ 🕮 ◑ ♠ ⚓ ♠ P ⊟ (X34) ♠ 🕏

George Inn ✅
4 West Street, SN15 2LH
🕓 11-3, 6-11; 11-11 Sat; 11-10.30 Sun ☎ (01249) 730263
⊕ georgeinnlacock.co.uk
Wadworth IPA, Horizon, 6X; 2 changing beers (sourced nationally; often Oakham) ⊞

Timber and stone pub near the centre of this idyllic National Trust village, dating from the mid-14th century. Inside, you will find oak beams and a welcoming fire with the original dog-driven spit. Good-quality locally sourced meals are served. There is always a fourth Wadworth offering, as well as an occasional guest ale, alongside a changing range of cider. A summer beer festival is held each year. Q ❄ 🕮 ◑ ⚓ ♠ P ⊟ (X34) ♠ 🕏

Laverstock

Duck ⌷
Duck Lane, SP1 1PU
🕓 12-midnight ☎ (01722) 327678
⊕ theduckatlaverstock.com
Hop Back Crop Circle, GFB, Summer Lightning; 1 changing beer (sourced nationally) ⊞

Large open-plan community pub with a full weekday lunchtime menu and popular Sunday roasts year round as well as themed dinner nights and regular barbecues in summer. Live music is hosted at weekends. There is full disabled access and well-behaved dogs and children are welcome. Outside, there is a garden and large car park. Ideally located for walkers on the Clarendon Way. ❄ 🕮 ◑ ♠ P ⊟ (66,R6) ♠ 🕏

Malmesbury

Whole Hog ⌷
8 Market Cross, SN16 9AS
🕓 11-11 (midnight Fri & Sat); 12-11 Sun ☎ (01666) 825845
Flying Monk Elmers; Stonehenge Pigswill; Wadworth 6X; Young's Bitter; 1 changing beer (sourced nationally) ⊞

Located between the 15th-century market cross and the abbey in the oldest borough in England, this is a popular town-centre pub, serving well-kept ales, Westons Family Reserve cider and freshly prepared food. In a commanding position at the top of the high street, the large front window seating area provides the perfect spot to watch the world go by. A pub central to the community and equally welcoming to visitors. Q ◑ ♣ ♠ ⊟

Marston Meysey

Old Spotted Cow
SN6 6LQ
🕓 11-11; 11-7 Sun ☎ (01285) 810264
⊕ theoldspottedcow.co.uk
Butcombe Gold; Otter Bitter; 1 changing beer (sourced nationally) ⊞

Having large gardens and a cosy interior, with log fires and beamed ceilings, this pub is popular with locals and visitors alike. There is a strong emphasis on good food sourced from local suppliers. In the bar there are three real ale handpumps, and real cider from a range of producers is available during the summer. With the Thames Path nearby, the pub is attractive to hikers, who can enjoy the new accommodation. Q ❄ 🕮 ⇆ ◑ ♣ ♠ P ♠ 🕏

Melksham

Bear ✅
3 Bath Road, SN12 6LL
🕓 8am-midnight ☎ (01225) 792690
Fuller's London Pride; Greene King Abbot; Ruddles Best Bitter; Sharp's Doom Bar; 5 changing beers (sourced nationally; often Box Steam, Moles, Prescott) ⊞

A high-specification Wetherspoon pub with a plethora of local history adorning the walls and a real fire. Friendly and helpful staff serve a range of four regular ales and five guests, often including a local ale. A full range of food is always available, including popular weekly steak, curry and fish nights. The large paved garden area has award-winning floral displays. Frequent buses stop outside the pub. Q ❄ 🕮 ◑ ⚓ ⇆ ♠ P ⊟ (272) 🕏

Pig & Whistle

1 Woodrow Road, SN12 7AU

☼ 12-midnight; 12-11 Sun & Mon ☎ (01225) 705118

Sharp's Doom Bar; Wells Bombardier; 1 changing beer (sourced nationally) ℍ

A friendly and respected community pub selling good-quality ale, just as it should be. This welcoming inn is only a 15-minute walk from the town centre. Its large single room is divided into separate areas – a bar, snug with open fire and curios, and a pool/TV area. There is also a conservatory and great garden. Good simple pub food is served (booking for Sunday lunch is recommended). Local charities are supported.
と❀◑&♣P🖵❀

Netherhampton

Victoria & Albert

SP2 8PU

☼ 11-3, 5.30-11; 12-3, 7-10.30 Sun ☎ (01722) 743174
⊕ victoriaandalbert.org

3 changing beers (sourced nationally) ℍ

Classic thatched inn dating from 1540 in a village setting three miles from Salisbury and close to the race course. A log fire provides winter warmth and for summer there is a large garden and covered patio area. Three changing beers are often from small breweries, alongside Black Rat cider. An established family business, the pub provides quality food ranging from hearty snacks to full meals. Local CAMRA Country Pub of the Year 2015.
Qと❀◑♣●P❀�

Newton Tony

Malet Arms ℒ

SP4 0HF

☼ 11-3, 6-11; 12-3 Sun ☎ (01980) 629279
⊕ maletarms.com

4 changing beers (sourced locally; often Itchen Valley, Ramsbury, Stonehenge) ℍ

Charming and historic pub with a restaurant extension in the conservation area of the village, with the River Bourne flowing past in winter. The window in the larger bar is reputed to come from a galleon. The long-standing landlord is as enthusiastic and proud of his high-quality food as he is of his ales and Old Rosie cider. Four beers change weekly, sourced locally and occasionally from further afield. The pub welcomes walkers and dogs. Qと❀◑●P🖵(67)❀

Pewsey

Coopers Arms ℒ

37-39 Ball Road, SN9 5BL

☼ 5 (12 Sat)-11; 12-10.30 Sun ☎ (01672) 562495

Ramsbury Gold; Wadworth 6X; 2 changing beers (sourced nationally; often Skinner's, Three Castles) ℍ

A lively and friendly down-to-earth thatched pub on the eastern edge of Pewsey. The open-plan bar has a fire in winter and there are two side rooms. Four real ales are served – two local regulars plus two guests usually from the South-west. Live music features on Friday nights every fortnight. There is accommodation in holiday cottages in a separate block at the back. No food, but snacks are available. Q❀🛏♣P🖵(X5)❀�

Quidhampton

White Horse ✓

Lower Road, SP2 9AS

☼ 12-3, 6-10.30; 12-3, 5.30-11 Thu & Fri; 12-11 Sat; 12-5 Sun
☎ (01722) 744448 ⊕ whitehorsequidhampton.co.uk

Exmoor Ale; 2 changing beers (sourced nationally; often Robinsons) ℍ

Nick and Zoe have put this traditional pub back at the heart of village life. Welcoming to regulars and visitors, it offers events including a monthly quiz, whisky tasting and a beer festival in early June. Good-quality, home-cooked favourites make up the menu including a Sunday roast. The separate Loft houses darts, a skittle alley and screens for sports events. とʹ❀◑●♣P🖵(PR3,R3)❀�

Ramsbury

Crown & Anchor

1 Crowood Lane, SN8 2PT

☼ 8am-11; 9am-10.30 Sun ☎ (01672) 520335
⊕ crownandanchorramsbury.co.uk

Wickwar BOB; 3 changing beers (sourced locally; often Ramsbury) ℍ

A welcoming 19th-century country pub with a small bar surrounded by three rooms, two with fireplaces. Interesting bric-a-brac adorns the low ceiling beams including 200-year-old blacksmith's fixings. A Victorian beer engine that was used behind the bar is now on display. Live entertainment features every two weeks, with an acoustic music night on Thursday and a quiz on Sunday evening. Food includes a carvery on Sunday and fish night on Friday. There is a garden area to the rear. Two en-suite B&B rooms are available.
とʹ❀🛏◑P🖵(46,48)❀�

Royal Wootton Bassett

Five Bells ✓

Wood Street, SN4 7BD

☼ 12-3, 5-11.30; 12-midnight Fri-Sun ☎ (01793) 849422

Black Sheep Best Bitter; Fuller's London Pride; 4 changing beers (sourced nationally) ℍ

Dating from before 1841, this is a busy and cosy traditional thatched local with a beamed ceiling and open fires. The bar has seven handpumps for two regular beers, four guests and Westons Old Rosie cider. Food is served lunchtimes and Wednesday and Thursday evenings (booking recommended). The pub has darts and crib teams. Special events are held throughout the year including a beer festival in the summer.
Q❀◑♣●P🖵(55)❀�

Salisbury

Duke of York ℒ

34 York Road, SP2 7AS

☼ 6 (4 Sat)-midnight; 2-11 Sun ☎ (01722) 503872

Hop Back GFB; 4 changing beers (sourced nationally; often Plain Ales) ℍ

Built in 1901 by Ushers and situated down a quiet side street, this small single-bar pub reopened in 2011 after a long closure. Popular with locals, it has a strong community focus with a Sunday night quiz and other occasional events including beer festivals. A true free house, it offers a range of beers – the selection may be reduced mid-week – sometimes accompanied by two real ciders. Conversation thrives. ❀🛬♣🖵(R1)❀�

Rai d'Or 🅛

69 Brown Street, SP1 2AS

🕓 5-10 (11 Thu-Sat); closed Sun ☎ (01722) 327137
⊕ raidor.co.uk

2 changing beers (sourced locally; often Downton, Red Cat) 🅗

Characterful 13th-century free house with a fascinating history. An inglenook fireplace and low ceilings make for an appealing ambience. Excellent, reasonably priced Thai food is complemented by two ever-changing, usually local, beers and a real cider. It can be busy at food times, but drinkers are always welcome. There is a discount on food before 6.30pm. A former local CAMRA Pub of the Year with 12 years in the Guide. 🐶🍽️👜🖪😺

Rugby Club 🅛

Castle Road, SP1 3SA

🕓 7-11; 8-11 Sun; closed Mon summer; 7-11, 12-11 Sat; 12-3, 8-11 Sun; closed Mon Sept-Apr ☎ (01722) 325317
⊕ salisburyrfc.org

Hop Back GFB, Crop Circle, Summer Lightning; 1 changing beer (often Hop Back) 🅗

Occupying a corner of the large club house, this cosy, recently refurbished lounge bar is open to the public. Retaining its sporting roots, the bar features rugby memorabilia. Two TVs generally show rugby or other sport. The function room bar is open at busy times such as match days. The three Hop Back ales are often joined by a Downton or Hop Back seasonal brew. Quiz night is Wednesday. A beer festival is held in May. There are camping facilities close by. 🐶❀🖪(8,PR11,X5)😺🛜

Village Freehouse 🅛

33 Wilton Road, SP2 7EF

🕓 4 (11 Fri)-11; 12-11 Sat & Sun ☎ (01722) 329707

Downton Quadhop; 4 changing beers (sourced nationally) 🅗

Friendly, lively pub close to the railway station with a decor featuring railway memorabilia and books. Microbrewery beers from near and far are core to the spirit of this pub, with requests welcomed. Unique in the area, there is always a dark beer – either mild, porter or stout – available. Major sporting events are screened on terrestrial TV. Hot pastries and filled rolls are available or you are welcome to bring your own food. Local CAMRA Pub of the Year three times in the past decade. ⇌🖪😺🛜

Winchester Gate 🍺 🅛

113-117 Rampart Road, SP1 1JA

🕓 3 (12 Thu-Sat)-11; 12-10 Sun ☎ (01722) 322834
⊕ winchestergate.co.uk

4 changing beers (sourced nationally; often Hop Back, Plain Ales) 🅗

Popular free house, an inn since the 17th century, offering ales from microbreweries across the UK. Real cider is also often served, particularly in summer months. Cider festivals in spring and autumn complement three beer festivals a year. There is live music at weekends and an open mic on the third Wednesday each month. The venue has a pétanque terrain with boules available. Local CAMRA Pub of the year 2016. ❀♣🖪😺🛜

Wyndham Arms 🅛

27 Estcourt Road, SP1 3AS

🕓 4.30 (12 Thu)-11.30; 12-midnight Fri & Sat; 12-11.30 Sun ☎ (01722) 331026

Hop Back GFB, Citra, Crop Circle, Taiphoon, Summer Lightning; 1 changing beer (often Hop Back) 🅗

The birthplace of Hop Back Brewery, now celebrating 30 consecutive years in the Guide. A traditional ale house, it has a single bar with six handpumps serving a selection of Hop Back ales including its seasonal offering. There is also a fine selection of bottled beers and wines. This is a pub for conversation, good-natured banter and fine ales. Local CAMRA Pub of the Year 2015. Q🐶♣🖪(R2)😺

Semington

Somerset Arms

High Street, BA14 6JR

🕓 11-11 ☎ (01380) 870067
⊕ somersetarmssemington.co.uk

4 changing beers (sourced regionally; often Box Steam, Otter, Twisted) 🅗

A coaching inn possibly dating back to the 16th century. It offers four changing beers from micros within 50 miles, and two to four ciders depending on the time of year. The food features local ingredients. The village of Semington is now a quiet cul-de-sac after the bypass was built a few years ago and the pub's proximity to the Kennet & Avon Canal makes it popular with boaters, walkers and cyclists. Accommodation is in three luxury en-suite bedrooms. Q🐶❀🛏️🍽️♿♣👜🖪(234)😺🛜

Semley

Benett Arms 🍺

Village Green, SP7 9AS (1 mile E of A350) ST891270

🕓 12-3, 5-11 ☎ (01747) 830221 ⊕ benettarms.co.uk

Ringwood Best Bitter; 2 changing beers (sourced regionally; often Cotleigh, Keystone, Yeovil) 🅗

A genuine free house sitting by the green and pond in a quiet village, with a single small bar and separate dining areas. The beer choice varies but there are usually three to choose from, either on handpump or direct from the cellar. The cider is from Bridge Farm. Excellent home-cooked food is available at all sessions. A warm welcome is extended to all, including families and dogs, in an area popular with walkers. Local CAMRA branch Pub of the Year 2016. Q🍽️🍴♿♣👜🖪(84,247)😺

Stourton

Spread Eagle

Church Lawn, BA12 6QE

🕓 10-11; 12-10.30 Sun ☎ (01747) 840587
⊕ spreadeagleinn.com

Butcombe Bitter; Wessex Kilmington Best; 1 changing beer (sourced locally; often Butcombe, Wessex) 🅗

Mellow brick and slate pub owned by the National Trust within the Stourhead Estate and adjacent to the famous Stourhead house and gardens. Spacious and comfortable, the inn offers a selection of local ales and bottled ciders. Excellent English cooking features dishes made with locally sourced ingredients. Breakfast is served 8-9am and afternoon refreshments are also available. Q🍽️🛏️🍴♿P

Swindon

Beehive 🅥

55 Prospect Hill, SN1 3JS

✪ 12-midnight (1am Thu-Sat) ☎ (01793) 523187
⊕ bee-hive.co.uk

Hardys & Hansons Olde Trip; house beer (by Hardys & Hansons); 4 changing beers (sourced regionally) Ⓗ
Sympathetically refurbished in 2014 under Greene King's Local Hero initiative, this multi-levelled, four-room pub has retained its quirky charm and layout. The beer range has a local focus supported by Meet the Brewer evenings. A popular live music venue, it hosts performances on most Thursday and Friday evenings. The walls are covered in pictures and other artwork, often for sale. Locally sourced pies are available lunchtime until early evening, with complimentary crisps and snacks from late afternoon. ⓸▶♣🚆(12,49)❀🛜

Glue Pot

5 Emlyn Square, SN1 5BP
✪ 12 (4.30 Mon)-11; 11.30-11 Fri & Sat; 12-10.30 Sun
☎ (01793) 497420

Downton New Forest Ale; Hop Back Citra, Crop Circle, Entire Stout, Summer Lightning; 3 changing beers (sourced regionally; often Downton, Hop Back) Ⓗ
The Glue Pot is part of the historic sandstone Railway Village built in the 1840s in Swindon. It is usually a quiet pub, but gets busy on weekend evenings. There are seven Hop Back or Downton ales, one guest, and at least five real ciders. Real ales are reduced in price on Mondays. There is a pub quiz on Thursday nights. Note the one remaining window with the Allsopp's logo. A beer festival features over the Easter weekend.
❀⇌♣🚆(8,14)❀

Hop Inn Ⓛ

7 Devizes Road, SN1 4BJ
✪ 12-11 (midnight Fri & Sat); 12-10.30 Sun
☎ (01793) 976833 ⊕ hopinnswindon.co.uk

House beer (by Ramsbury); 4 changing beers (sourced regionally) Ⓗ
A genuine free house and a great example of the trend for micropubs, this former shop has become a popular destination for real ale lovers. Five handpumps offer a variety of guest ales sourced from smaller breweries. There are also two real ciders in boxes. The small bar is furnished in an eclectic style with bright plastic chairs and tables made from reclaimed wood. Local CAMRA Pub of the Year 2014. Q🛇ᵫ♣🚆(12,15)❀🛜

Savoy Ⓛ ✓

38-40 Regent Street, SN1 1JL
✪ 8am-midnight (1am Fri & Sat) ☎ (01793) 533970

Adnams Broadside; Greene King Abbot; Ruddles Best Bitter; Wychwood Hobgoblin; changing beers (sourced nationally) Ⓗ
This lively and friendly town-centre pub is the oldest Wetherspoon in Swindon, converted from the foyer and ground floors of a 1930s cinema. Movie photos and information from the 1930s decorate the walls. It has a spacious interior on different levels, divided into separate areas. There is a TV screen in one corner, mainly silent. A large selection of beers is available and food is served all day until 11pm. Handy for the theatre, cinema, restaurants and shopping. Q🛇❀⓸ᵫ♣🚆(1,1A)🛜

Weighbridge Brewhouse Ⓛ ✓

Penzance Drive, SN5 7JL
✪ 12-11; 12-10 Sun ☎ (01793) 881500
⊕ weighbridgebrewhouse.co.uk

Weighbridge Brewhouse Brinkworth Village, Weighbridge Best, Pooley's Golden; 3 changing beers (sourced locally; often Weighbridge Brewhouse) Ⓗ
The Weighbridge Brewhouse is an upmarket brew- and gastro-pub in the former home of Archers brewery. It features a long shiny bar with six handpumps dedicated to the real ales crafted on the premises. Three regular ales are joined by new and seasonal offerings. Seating in the bar is limited, although there is a large lounge upstairs and a bar terrace for the milder season. Live music plays on Thursday, Friday and Saturday evenings. Food is served lunchtimes and evenings.
❀⓸▶P🚆(8,55)

Tisbury

Benett Arms Ⓛ

High Street, SP3 6HD
✪ 12-midnight (1am Thu-Sat) ☎ (01747) 870428
⊕ benetttisbury.co.uk

Keystone Bedrock; house beer (by Keystone); 1 changing beer (sourced regionally) Ⓗ
A warm welcome awaits you at this Keystone Brewery pub. Two Keystone beers – Keystone's Large One is badged as Gordon Benett – are accompanied by another from Wiltshire, Dorset or Somerset, and often a real cider. The front bar is furnished with a range of tables while the rear bar has a pool table. In fine weather you can sit on the front patio and watch the world go by. Hot snacks and light lunches are served daily, including popular Sunday lunches. Curry night is the first Monday of the month. 🛇❀⓸⇌♣🚆(25,26)❀🛜

Boot Inn Ⓛ

High Street, SP3 6PS
✪ 12-2.30 (not Tue & winter Mon), 7-11; 12-3 Sun
☎ (01747) 870363

3 changing beers (sourced regionally) Ⓖ
Fine listed pub built of Chilmark stone, licensed since 1768. It has a relaxed, friendly atmosphere appealing to locals and visitors alike. Run by the same landlord since 1976, it became a free house in 2009 and has three or four ales behind the bar. Excellent food is served and there is a spacious garden. A former local CAMRA Pub of the Year.
Q❀⓸⇌♣P🚆(25,26)

Upavon

Ship Ⓛ

10 High Street, SN9 6EA
✪ 11.30-11.30 (1am Thu-Sat); 12-11 Sun ☎ (01980) 630313
⊕ theshipinnupavon.co.uk

Butcombe Bitter; Wadworth 6X; 4 changing beers (sourced regionally; often Cottage, Plain, Stonehenge) Ⓗ
Parts of this thatched pub date from the 15th century. Inside it combines traditional wooden beams with a light, airy appearance. The decor, including a huge model of the Cutty Sark, is of nautical or local interest. A wood-burning pizza oven in the garden is fired up Thursday to Saturday evenings from 5.30pm. The four guest ales are locally sourced and there are four real ciders and 40 malt whiskies. Tuesday is fish and chips night. ❀⓸ᵫ♣🚆(X5)❀🛜

Upton Lovell

Prince Leopold Inn
54 Upton Lovell, BA12 0JP
✪ 12-3, 6-11; 12-11 Sat & Sun ☎ (01985) 850460
⊕ princeleopold.co.uk
Butcombe Bitter; Plain Sheep Dip; 1 changing beer (sourced locally) ⊞
Hidden away in the beautiful Wylye Valley, the pub is now back to being a proper local as well as catering for visitors. The main bar is reserved for those wishing to enjoy a drink, and there is a small snug with an open fire, books, newspapers and board games. There are several areas dedicated to excellent food, including the large restaurant overlooking the River Wylye. It has a lovely garden which runs right down to the riverbank.
Q ❄ ❁ ✿ ◁ ◐ & ♣ P ✿ ❅

Urchfont

Lamb Inn ✔
The Green, SN10 4QU
✪ 12-3 (not Mon), 6-11; 12-11 Sun ☎ (01380) 848848
⊕ lambinnurchfont.co.uk
Wadworth IPA, 6X; 1 changing beer (often Wadworth) ⊞
The Lamb is a comfortable and friendly pub at the heart of the village. With lots of wooden tables and chairs and a welcoming bar area, it is popular with locals and visitors alike. It features Wadworth's ales plus a varied and good-value no-nonsense restaurant menu. There is a large function room and the pleasant beer garden is a lovely spot to while away a summer's afternoon. Themed entertainment evenings are held regularly.
❄ ◐ ♣ P ❏ (271) ✿

Warminster

Fox & Hounds
6 Deverill Road, BA12 9QP
✪ 11-11 ☎ (01985) 216711
Wessex Warminster Warrior; house beer (by Wessex); 2 changing beers (sourced regionally; often Flack Manor, Otter, Palmers) ⊞
Friendly two-bar inn that is a local CAMRA multiple award-winning pub. The main bar has a pool table and TV for sport at the back; a quiet snug bar is to the right of the entrance. There is also a large skittle alley and function room. Regular ciders are from Thatchers and Rich's, with up to five guests. Guest real ales are usually from local and regional breweries. Closing time may be later than 11pm.
Q ❄ & ♣ ● P ❏ ✿

Organ Inn ✔
49 High Street, BA12 9AQ
✪ 4 (12 Sat)-midnight; 4-11 Sun ☎ (01985) 211777
⊕ theorganinn.co.uk
3 changing beers (sourced regionally; often Cottage, Stonehenge, Twisted) ⊞
An inn until 1913, the Organ reopened as a pub in 2006. The welcoming interior comprises three rooms with a traditional feel, plus a snug games room and a skittle alley. The beer range constantly changes but always includes Organ Bitter (the brewer is a secret). The ciders are mainly Westons and guests. Bar snacks are interesting. There is an art gallery upstairs. A beer festival is held in September. Branch CAMRA Rural Pub of the Year 2014. Q ❄ & ❄ ♣ ● ❏ ✿ ❅

Westbury

Horse & Groom ✔
18 Alfred Street, BA13 3DY
✪ 12-3, 5-10; 12-11 Fri & Sat; 12-6 Sun ☎ (01373) 859433
⊕ horseandgroomwestbury.co.uk
Butcombe Bitter; 1 changing beer (often Twisted) ⊞
A large pub on the north-eastern edge of the town centre, much smartened up in early 2014. There are two separate bars, one of which is essentially a restaurant. At the front is an attractive patio-style drinking area which can be a suntrap in the summer, and there is a large garden with plenty of seating and a good-sized car park. Opposite the pub is a skittle alley which can be used as a function room. ❄ ◐ ♣ P ❏ ✿

Wilton

Swan ⌂
SN8 3SS
✪ 12-3, 6-11; 12-11 Sat; 12-10.30 Sun ☎ (01672) 870274
⊕ theswanwilton.co.uk
5 changing beers (sourced regionally; often Flying Monk, Plain, Ramsbury) ⊞/Ⓖ
This is a pretty red-brick village pub near the Kennet & Avon Canal with an attractive interior. There is an emphasis on good local food and Saturday lunchtimes are busy. Beer dispense is a mixture of handpump and gravity. The five varying beers are mostly local, with the beer board displaying the distance to the brewery. There are also traditional draught ciders. A quiz is held on the second Monday of each month and themed food nights also feature. No evening meals on Sunday.
❄ ◐ ● P ❏ (21,22) ✿ ❅

Wroughton

Carters Rest ⌂ ✔
57 High Street, SN4 9JU
✪ 5-11; 3-midnight Fri; 12-midnight Sat; 12-11 Sun
☎ (01793) 812288
Cotswold Spring Stunner; Marston's Pedigree New World Pale Ale; Otter Amber; Ramsbury Flint Knapper; Sharp's Doom Bar; 6 changing beers ⊞
This inn, first mentioned in 1671, was extensively altered in 1912/13 to give it a Victorian appearance with large gables and high ceilings. It is now a real ale destination with 13 handpumps serving five regular and six guest ales, plus one regular and one varying cider. Quiz night is Thursday and a traditional meat draw is held every Sunday. The pub screens live sport. An annual beer festival is hosted in December.
❄ & ♣ ● P ❏ (49,72) ✿ ❅

The Campaign for Real Ale has been fighting for over 40 years to save Britain's proud heritage of cask-conditioned ales, independent breweries, and pubs that offer a good choice of beer. You can help that fight by joining the campaign: use the form at the back of the guide or see **www.camra.org.uk**

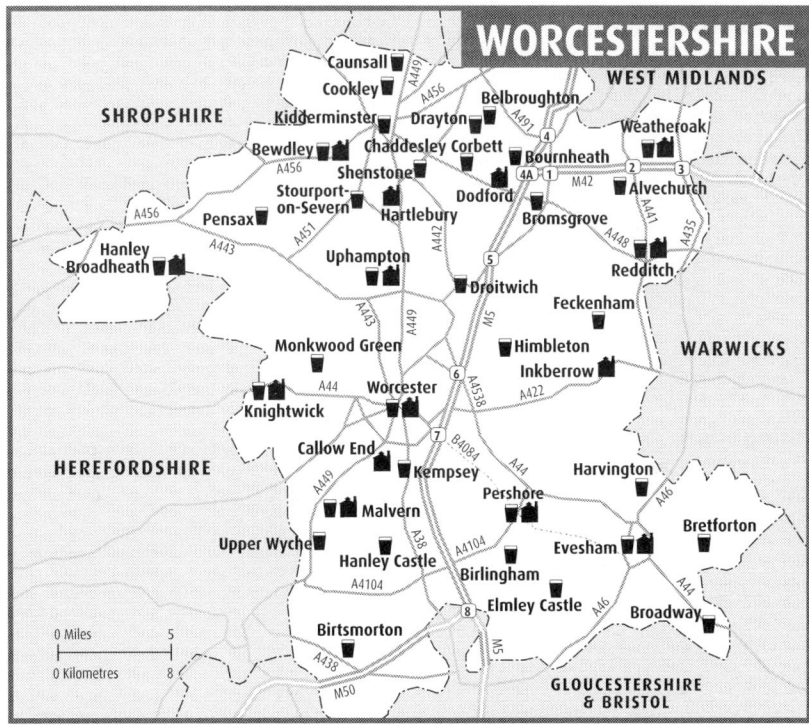

Alvechurch

Weighbridge 🅛

Scarfield Wharf, Scarfield Hill, B48 7SQ (follow signs to marina from village) SP022721

🌞 12-3, 7-11; 12-3, 7-10.30 Sun ☎ (0121) 445 5111

🌐 the-weighbridge.co.uk

House beer (by Weatheroak); 4 changing beers Ⓗ

This cosy canalside pub is a regular local CAMRA Pub of the Year. It has two small lounges, a public bar and a pleasant garden. Spring and autumn beer festivals are held. Good-value home-cooked food is served lunchtimes and evenings (no food Tue and Wed) and excellent Sunday lunches. A covered area outside can be used for functions. House beers are Weatheroak Tillerman's Tipple and Kinver Bargees Bitter. Changing guest beers include a mild, and real cider or perry is available.

Q🕏🌑🌑🍴🚪P🚭(146)🛜

Belbroughton

Holly Bush Inn

Stourbridge Road, DY9 9UG (on A491 Stourbridge Rd)

🌞 11.30-11; 11.30-3, 6-11 Sat; 12-3, 7-10.30 Sun

☎ (01562) 730207

Hobsons Mild, Twisted Spire, Town Crier; 1 changing beer (sourced regionally) Ⓗ

A pub since 1845, this low-level white building was originally a row of terraced cottages. It is set back from the A491 dual carriageway. Full of character, with low ceilings, it has a single bar serving three separate areas including a dining room. Excellent-value traditional home-made meals are available. Thatchers cider is on handpump. It is near to the National Trust Clent Hills. CAMRA branch Pub of the Year 2015.

Q🕏🌑🌑🍴P🚭🛜

Bewdley

Great Western 🅛

Kidderminster Road, DY12 1BY (near SVR station, walk past signal box and under viaduct)

🌞 11.30-11 ☎ (01299) 488828

🌐 thegreatwesternbewdley.co.uk

Bewdley Worcestershire Way, 2857; Greene King IPA; Morland Old Golden Hen; 2 changing beers (sourced nationally; often Belhaven, Bewdley, Greene King) Ⓗ

Conveniently located within a short walk of the Severn Valley Railway station, the pub has a simple yet comfortable railway theme reminiscent of an earlier age. Overlooking the bar is an upper level from which to admire the fine glazed decorative wall tiles. Pub snacks such as pork pies and cobs go with the concept of a traditional pub, and on the bar there are six real ales and Westons cider on handpump. Q🕏🌑🌑🚪≈(SVR)🌑🌑P🚪🛜

Mug House 🅛 ✅

12 Severnside North, DY12 2EE (150yds along Severnside N from river bridge)

🌞 12-11 (11.30 Fri & Sat) ☎ (01299) 402543

🌐 mughousebewdley.co.uk

Bewdley Worcestershire Way; Purity Mad Goose; Timothy Taylor Landlord; Wye Valley HPA; 1 changing beer Ⓗ

Located on the side of the Severn, the Mug House is not to be missed. A friendly pub that welcomes locals and visitors alike, it serves four regular beers, from Bewdley, Purity and Wye Valley, plus a guest. There are cosy settles and a log fire in the lounge bar, and to the rear is a sun terrace with a glass-covered patio with grapevines and wisteria. Fine food is served in the restaurant as well as bar meals at lunchtime.

Q🕏🌑🌑🍴🌑🚪≈(SVR)🌑🚪🛜

Old Waggon & Horses 🅛

91 Kidderminster Road, DY12 1DG (on Bewdley to Kidderminster road, Catchems End)
🌣 12-11; 11.30-1am Fri & Sat ☎ (01299) 403170
🌐 waggonbewdley.co.uk
Banks's Mild, Bitter; Bathams Best Bitter; 2 changing beers (sourced locally; often Hobsons, Ludlow) 🅗
Popular locals' and visitors' pub with a central bar that serves three distinct areas. The small wooden-floored snug has settles, tables and a dartboard; the larger room has a roll-down screen for major sporting events, bench seating and a TV. An old kitchen range in the dining area adds to the cottagey feel. Food is available Tuesday and Thursday evenings with a carvery on Sundays. The attractive terraced garden is on many levels. Guest ales come from local independents.
Q🏠🍴♿🚆(SVR)♣🐾P🚃🐾🐱🛜

Rising Sun 🅛 ✅

139 Kidderminster Road, DY12 1JE (just off Bewdley bypass at Catchems End)
🌣 12-midnight ☎ (01299) 409440
Banks's Mild 🅟, Bitter; Wye Valley HPA; 1 changing beer (sourced locally) 🅗
This lively and welcoming terraced pub dating from 1845 brewed its own ales until 1923. The large, comfortable lounge bar has four beers including some from Banks's and Wye Valley. The cask Banks's Mild is on electric dispense. Cobs are available all day. Crib, darts and a quiz on Tuesdays add to the community atmosphere. On Saturday evenings and occasionally on Sunday afternoons there is live music. To the rear is a pleasant and peaceful flower garden. Q🐾🏠🍴♿♣🚃🐱🛜

Birlingham

Swan

Church Street, WR10 3AQ
🌣 11.30-3, 6-11; 12-7 Sun; closed Mon ☎ (01386) 750485
🌐 theswaninn.co.uk
Purity Mad Goose; 2 changing beers (often Spire) 🅗
A delightful thatched, food-oriented free house tucked away at the end of a lane in a quiet village. The interior has been modernised but retains the exposed wood beams of the black-and-white building. The bar area is set around an open fire and there is a conservatory overlooking the well-kept garden, with food served throughout. Interesting beers from breweries such as Spire and local micros are often available. Q🏠🍴P🚃(382)🛜

Birtsmorton

Farmers Arms

Birts Street, WR13 6AP (off B4208) SO790363
🌣 11-4, 6-midnight; 12-4, 6-midnight Sun
☎ (01684) 833308 🌐 farmersarmsbirtsmorton.co.uk
Hook Norton Hooky, Old Hooky; 2 changing beers (sourced locally) 🅗
Grade II-listed, black-and-white village pub dating from 1480, found down a quiet country lane. The large bar area features an inglenook fireplace while the cosy lounge has old settles and low beams. Good-value, home-made, traditional food is on offer daily (lunch until 2pm, eve meals until 9.30pm weekdays, 9pm Sun). A beer from a small, local independent brewer is often available. A beer festival is held in August. The spacious garden, with swings, provides fine views of the Malvern Hills. A caravan site is nearby. Q🐾🏠🍴♿🚃♣P🚃(577)🐱🛜

Bournheath

Nailers Arms ✅

62 Doctors Hill, B61 9JE
🌣 12-midnight (1am Fri & Sat); 12-11.30 Sun
☎ (01527) 873045 🌐 thenailersarms.co.uk
Morland Old Speckled Hen; Wye Valley HPA; 2 changing beers 🅗
Dating from the late-18th century, this whitewashed three-gabled building was once a nailmakers' workshop-cum-brewery. The bar has a traditional quarry-tiled floor and a real fire. Two guest ales are usually also on handpump alongside the regulars. The restaurant is based around a carvery but other options are available. A beer festival has become a popular attraction in the pub's calendar in May. Valley House, the birthplace of AE Housman, is nearby. 🐾🏠🍴♿♣🐾P🐱🛜

Bretforton

Fleece Inn ★

The Cross, WR11 7JE (near church at centre of village)
🌣 11-11; 12-10.30 Sun ☎ (01386) 831173
🌐 thefleeceinn.co.uk
Uley Pig's Ear Strong Beer; Wye Valley Bitter; 3 changing beers (sourced locally; often Cotswold Lion, Purity, Wye Valley) 🅗
Fifteenth-century timber-framed village pub owned by the National Trust on the edge of the Cotswolds. Sensitively restored in 2005 after a fire, it is recognised by CAMRA as having a nationally important historic pub interior, and houses a world-famous 17th-century pewter collection. Morris dancers and music feature all year round, with entertainment evenings in the medieval barn. Local breweries are represented among the three changing beers, and one of the three or four ciders is made at the Fleece itself. A pub not to be missed. Q🐾🏠🍴🍴♿🅰♣🐾🚃(554)🐱🛜

Broadway

Crown & Trumpet 🅛 ✅

14 Church Street, WR12 7AE (on road to Snowshill, just off Cotswolds Way)
🌣 11-11; 11-10.30 Sun ☎ (01386) 853202
🌐 cotswoldholidays.co.uk

Stanway Broadway Artist's Ale; Stroud Tom Long; Timothy Taylor Landlord; 1 changing beer (sourced locally; often Gloucester, Prescott) H
Picturesque 17th-century Cotswold-stone inn just off the village green. The landlord is a real ale enthusiast and has recently been recognised for over 30 years as a Guide licensee. This hostelry has welcoming and friendly staff and an abundance of character, with oak beams, log fire and plenty of Flowers Brewery memorabilia. Good, honest, well-cooked pub favourites are offered at reasonable prices alongside a range of regular ales and guests plus and ciders and perries. Entertainment includes live jazz and blues nights. Q❀✍◑Å♣♠P⊟❖☎

Bromsgrove

Golden Cross Hotel L ✓
20 High Street, B61 8HH (S end of High St)
✪ 8am-midnight (1am Fri & Sat) ☎ (01527) 870005
Greene King Abbot; Ruddles Best Bitter; Sharp's Doom Bar; 9 changing beers H
This stylish, split-level Wetherspoon pub is located in the town centre, and was previously a coach house. It has 12 individual booths with interesting glass throughout. Seven guest beers are available, many sourced locally. Regular themed beer festivals are held. There is a Pay & Display car park at the rear which is free after 7pm.
Q❀✿◑◆♣♠P⊟(144,147,X3)☎

Little Ale House
21 Worcester Road, B61 7DL (on corner of Station St)
✪ 12 (3 Mon-Wed)-10 ☎ 07773 247179
Malvern Hills Black Pear; 7 changing beers (often Ambridge, Bewdley, Prescott) H
Bromsgrove's first micropub was formerly a hairdresser's salon and has a friendly welcome. It showcases three permanent breweries with a changing selection of their beers alongside four other varying breweries, all ales served from the cask. A selection of real cider and perries is also on offer as well as take-out cartons. A council car park is nearby. Q♣♠♠⊟(144,147,X3)❖☎

Caunsall

Anchor Inn L
DY11 5YL (off A449 Kidderminster-Wolverhampton road)
✪ 11-4, 7-11; 11-3, 7-10.30 Sun ☎ (01562) 850254
⊕ theanchorinncaunsall.co.uk
Hobsons Best, Town Crier; Wye Valley HPA, Butty Bach; 2 changing beers (often Three Tuns) H
Popular village pub run by the same family since 1927, renowned for its six real ales, traditional ciders and especially its well-filled cobs. A central doorway leads into the bar with its original 1920s furniture and horse-racing memorabilia. The friendly staff welcome an impressive mix of customers and it gets especially busy at lunchtimes. Easily reached from the nearby canal, this gem is well worth visiting. Local CAMRA Pub of the Year finalist 2016. Q❀✿◑◆♣♠P⊟❖☎

Chaddesley Corbett

Swan L
The Village, DY10 4SD (along High Street from A448)
SO892737
✪ 11-11; 12-11 Sun ☎ (01562) 777302
⊕ theswanchaddesleycorbett.co.uk
Bathams Mild Ale, Best Bitter H

Dating from 1606, this village pub has a large lounge, snug and public bar. Hot food is served Wednesday to Sunday, with rolls and pork pies at other times. Live jazz plays every Thursday evening. The large garden with children's play area overlooks beautiful countryside. Real cider is available and Bathams XXX is served seasonally. Dogs are welcome in the bar. A popular stop-off for walkers, with the Elizabethan Harvington Hall a mile away. Q❀✿◑◆♣♠P⊟❖☎

Cookley

Cookley Village Hall & Sports Club
Lea Lane, DY10 3RH (near St Peter's Church)
✪ 6-11 Mon; 6.30-11 Tue; 6-11 Wed; 2-11 Thu & Fri; 11-11 Sat & Sun ☎ (01562) 850055 ⊕ cookleyvillagehall.co.uk
Brakspear Oxford Gold; 2 changing beers H
Popular sports club and village hall featuring a comfortable lounge bar, snooker room and two meeting rooms. Outside, the patio affords spectacular views over north Worcestershire. Various sports and leisure clubs are based here and the hall is available for event hire. Access is by membership and visitor passes are available. Well-presented beers are from the Marston's range including two changing guest ales. ✿♣P⊟❖☎

Drayton

Robin Hood ♥
Drayton Road, DY9 0BW (on the Chaddesley Corbett to Belbroughton road) SO905758
✪ 12-11 ☎ (01562) 730526 ⊕ robinhoodinn-drayton.co.uk
Enville Ale; Holden's Golden Glow; Wye Valley HPA; 3 changing beers H
Traditional pub recently refurbished without spoiling the ambience of the cosy rural retreat. The original bar has been extended into the old store room and a small passageway leads to the comfortable lounge. Six real ales plus Thatchers Heritage cider are available and snacks and cooked meals are served. Outside is a paved patio and a large garden with a covered smoking area. Barbecues are held regularly over the summer with drinks served from an outside bar. CAMRA branch Pub of the Year 2016. ✿◑◆♣♠P⊟❖☎

Droitwich

Hop Pole L
40 Friar Street, WR9 8ED (near town centre)
✪ 12-11; 12-10.30 Sun ☎ (01905) 770155
Malvern Hills Black Pear; Wye Valley HPA; Butty Bach; 2 changing beers H
An 18th-century pub in an old part of Droitwich, next to the Norbury Theatre, and popular with locals and visitors alike. A warm welcome is always assured. Pub games are played and there is a separate pool room adjoining the bar. Outside is a heated patio area for smokers and a garden with seating. Guest beers are mostly from local breweries. Good-value home-cooked food is served at lunchtime. Live music plays some weekends. Close by is the restored Droitwich Barge Canal which offers secure moorings. ✿◑≈♣♠❖

Elmley Castle

Queen Elizabeth
Main Street, WR10 3HS

✿ 11-11; 11-7 Sun; closed Mon winter ☎ (01386) 710215
⊕ elmleycastle.com

Goff's White Knight; Purity Mad Goose; Wye Valley Butty Bach; 1 changing beer (sourced locally) ⊞
An old pub with a fresh modern feel inside, it is named after Elizabeth I's visit to the village in August 1575. This is a community-owned pub, thanks to the 26 local residents who rescued it from closure. The bar has a flagstone floor, timber beams and a roaring fire. There is a comfortable lounge and a separate dining room. A range of local real ales and ciders is available. Q✿⬤P

Evesham

Red Lion ⌷

6 Market Place, WR11 4RW
✿ 11-11 (midnight Fri & Sat); 12-10.30 Sun
☎ (01386) 761688

Cannon Royall Hunny Bear, Arrowhead Bitter, Comfortably Stout, Blond Bombshell; 2 changing beers (sourced regionally; often Goff's, Kinver, Three Shires) ⊞
Closed for over 100 years, this basic town-centre pub has been sympathetically refurbished. It has seating areas to the front and side, and to the rear a separate area incorporating the recently discovered inglenook fireplace. It is tucked away in a corner of the marketplace and, with no TV or music, it is a great place for people-watching and conversation. Up to six real ales are served from a central bar including five well-priced Cannon Royall beers, and two ciders. Q✿⬤♣⬤🍴🖳✿🕏

Feckenham

Rose & Crown

High Street, B96 6HS
✿ 11-3, 6-11; 12-11 Sat & Sun ☎ (01527) 892188
⊕ roseandcrownfeckenham.co.uk

Banks's Bitter; Brakspear Oxford Gold; 2 changing beers (often Marston's, Wye Valley) ⊞
A welcoming 19th-century Grade II-listed village pub standing in what was once the historic Forest of Feckenham. Up to four real ales are available, with a changing guest beer selection. An annual beer festival is held over the August bank holiday. There is a large beer garden. Parking is limited, but there is a free car park 200 yards away. The Monarch's Way footpath lies one-and-a-half miles to the east of the village. Q✿⬤⬤♣⬤✿🕏

Hanley Broadheath

Fox Inn ⌷

WR15 8QS SO671652
✿ 5-11; 3-12.30am Fri; 12-12.30am Sat; 12-10 Sun
☎ (01886) 853189

Bathams Best Bitter; Joseph Herbert Smith Foxy Lady; 2 changing beers (often Hogarths) ⊞
The main bar of this 16th-century black-and-white timbered free house is decorated with hops and has a large fireplace with a wood-burning stove. The panelled dining area is separated from the bar by wood beams. The games room has a pool table, TV and darts. Home-made food, including Sunday lunch, is available, with bar snacks at any time. One guest beer is usually from Hogarths Brewery in Bolton. Annual lawnmower racing is held in the adjoining field in August. Q✿⬤⬤A♣P✿🕏

Tally Ho! ⌷

WR15 8QX
✿ 12-midnight (1am Fri & Sat) ☎ (01886) 853241
⊕ tallyhorestaurant.co.uk

Ludlow Blonde, Gold; Wye Valley HPA; 2 changing beers ⊞
An inviting, cosy 14th-century inn with an abundance of beams and stonework, featuring local beers on the bar. Pool and darts are popular. The separate restaurant in the conservatory has grand views of the countryside. The garden enjoys more panoramic views across Worcestershire and the Teme Valley and has a children's playground. Food is served lunchtimes and evenings every day, with a carvery on Wednesday evenings and Sunday lunchtimes. ✿✿⬤⬤⬤&P

Hanley Castle

Three Kings ★ ⌷

Church End, WR8 0BL (signed off B4211) SO838420
✿ 12-3, 7-11; 12-10.30 Sun ☎ (01684) 592686

Butcombe Bitter; Hobsons Best; 3 changing beers ⊞
On CAMRA's National Inventory of Historic Pub Interiors, this unspoilt 15th-century country pub on the village green near the church has been run by the Roberts family since 1911. The three-room interior comprises a small snug with large inglenook, serving hatch and settle wall, a small side room, and Nell's Lounge with another inglenook, beams and its own entrance. Three guest ales are on offer, often from local breweries, plus Westons Old Rosie draught cider. Live music sessions feature regularly and a popular beer festival is held in November. Q✿⬤⬤♣⬤P🖳(363)✿

Harvington

Coach & Horses 🏆 ✅

Station Road, WR11 8NJ
✿ 5 (12 Sat)-midnight; 12-11.30 Sun ☎ (01386) 870249
⊕ coachandhorsesharvington.com

Greene King IPA; 3 changing beers ⊞
Traditional village pub with a separate bar and lounge. The bar has a real fire and the lounge has a logburner in the inglenook. Photos of old Harvington adorn the walls. The pub's real ale drinkers select the guest beers from Finest Cask and SIBA lists. Good-value food is served. A local ukulele group plays on Tuesday and a fun quiz is hosted on Sunday nights. The refurbished skittle alley doubles as a function/training room. An annual beer festival is held in September. Worcestershire Pub of the Year finalist 2014 and local CAMRA branch Pub of the Year 2014 and 2015. ✿⬤⬤A♣⬤P🖳(28,248)✿🕏

Himbleton

Galton Arms ⌷

Harrow Lane, WR9 7LQ
✿ 12-2 (not Mon), 4.30-11; 11-11 Sun ☎ (01905) 391672

Banks's Bitter; Bathams Best Bitter; Wye Valley HPA; 1 changing beer (sourced locally) ⊞
Splendid rural pub, situated on the edge of the village, with a friendly welcome and popular with locals and visitors alike. The unspoilt interior retains the original beams and open fires. The guest beer is often from a local brewery. TV sport is shown in the bar area and a separate restaurant area serves good-value food. Q✿⬤⬤⬤&P✿

Kempsey

Walter de Cantelupe Ⓛ ✅

34 Main Road, WR5 3NA (on A38 next to post office)
🕓 12-2, 6-11; 12-9 Sun; closed Mon ☎ (01905) 820572
⊕ walterdecantelupe.co.uk
Timothy Taylor Landlord; 3 changing beers Ⓗ
Named after a 13th-century Bishop of Worcester, this comfortable pub features a cosy drinking area, a large settle from the 1700s and an imposing inglenook fireplace. It serves traditional but inventive food made with local ingredients where possible. Lighter meals are often available outside restaurant hours. Regular events include a paella party in the attractive walled garden in June. Local beers are served in lined glasses with third-pints available. Opening hours may vary.
Q❄🕭🍴◐❸♿Å♠P🖵🚪(32,362)🐾🐕🛜

Kidderminster

Olde Seven Stars Ⓛ ✅

13-14 Coventry Street, DY10 2BG (upper end of High St facing the Swan Centre)
🕓 11-11 (11.30 Fri & Sat); 12-11 Sun ☎ (01562) 755777
Changing beers Ⓗ
With six varied real ales and one draught cider, this historic town-centre family-friendly pub with friendly atmosphere and excellent ales is well-worth visiting. The front and rear bars display many old features from previous ages. It serves cobs and pork pies, and customers can bring their own food (there are plenty of takeaways nearby), with tableware and condiments provided. It has a quiet rear garden which is popular in summer. Live music plays on Friday evenings. 🕭🕭♿♠🍴🚪🐾🛜

Station Inn Ⓛ ✅

7 Farfield, DY10 1UG
🕓 12-11 ☎ (01562) 569621 ⊕ stationkidderminster.co.uk
Enville Ale; Holden's Golden Glow; Wye Valley HPA; 1 changing beer (sourced locally; often Bewdley, Enville, Hobsons) Ⓗ
A friendly pub just a short walk from the railway station. Two rooms are served from a central bar, warmed by a real fire in winter, and there is a large beer garden to the rear. Up to four ales are available including beers from Enville, Holden's and Wye Valley. Good-value home-cooked food is served during the day, with traditional roast dinners on Sundays. Quiz night is Thursday. The friendly inclusive atmosphere and excellent ales won it local CAMRA Community Pub of the Year 2015 and Pub of the Year finalist in 2016.
Q❄🕭◐♿≈(SVR)♠P🖵🐾🛜

Swan Ⓛ ✅

Vicar Street, DY10 1DE (opp town hall)
🕓 10-8 (10 Thu; 1am Fri & Sat); 12-5 Sun ☎ (01562) 823008
⊕ swankidderminster.co.uk
Bewdley Worcestershire Way, Sir Keith Park, Worcestershire Sway; 3 changing beers (sourced nationally; often Hale's, Purity, Sharp's) Ⓗ
A one-room pub opposite the town hall dating from 1865 and a worthy survivor of town-centre redevelopment. It serves real ciders and up to six real ales, including one from Bewdley Brewery. The single room has a front bar area that gets lively on rugby match days with quiet tables for dining towards the back. Breakfast is available from 10am and bar food Monday to Saturday throughout the day. A beer festival is held over the August bank holiday. 🕭◐♿♠🚪🐾🛜

Weavers at Park Lane Ⓛ

40 Park Lane, DY11 6TG (canalside opp Tesco)
🕓 12-11 summer; 4-10 Mon & Tue; 12-10 Wed & Thu (11 Fri & Sat); 12-6 Sun winter ☎ (01562) 742717
Three Tuns XXX; Wye Valley HPA; 4 changing beers (sourced nationally) Ⓗ
Canalside pub in a listed Georgian building dating from 1804. The beer garden overlooks the canal and moorings are on the towpath side, a short walk over the nearby bridge. It offers cobs, pork pies and an impressive range of real ales, ciders, wines and soft drinks – no spirits or lager. There are six real ales and eight ciders and perries, some from local breweries, and also unusual beers from farther afield. Opening times can vary.
Q❄🕭≈(SVR)♣♠P🖵🛜

Weavers Real Ale House 🍷 Ⓛ

98 Comberton Hill, DY10 1QH (300yds down hill from railway station)
🕓 3 (1 Fri)-10.30; 12-10.30 Sat; 12-10 Sun
☎ (01562) 229413
Three Tuns XXX; Wye Valley HPA; 4 changing beers (often Bewdley) Ⓗ
The single lounge bar is reminiscent of a traditional pub, with old pictures and posters on the walls and a conversational atmosphere. Six real ales are on offer including a dark, a stout and a mild, plus two ciders and a perry. Pub snacks such as pork pies and cobs are always available. Just a short walk from the railway station, this is a place to stop off for a pint and a chat on the way into town. Public parking is nearby. Q♿≈(SVR)♠🖵🐾🛜

Knightwick

Talbot Ⓛ

WR6 5PH (on B4197, 400yds from A44 jct)
🕓 10-11 ☎ (01886) 821235 ⊕ the-talbot.co.uk
Hobsons Best; Teme Valley T'Other, This, That Ⓗ**; changing beers (often Teme Valley)** Ⓖ
Large country pub, originally a 14th-century coaching inn, with a taproom and lounge bar featuring a large fireplace. The attractive conservatory is especially fine in summer. The small wood-panelled restaurant serves an imaginative menu that makes good use of local ingredients. Three or four beers are usually on the bar from the Teme Valley Brewery behind the pub. There is a farmers' market outside on the second Sunday of the month. Beer festivals are held in April, June and early October (for green hop beers). Dog- and walker-friendly.
Q❄🕭🍴◐♿Å♠P🖵(420)🐾🛜

Malvern

Great Malvern Hotel Ⓛ

Graham Road, WR14 2HN (by crossroads with Church St)
🕓 10-11; 11-10.30 Sun ☎ (01684) 563411
⊕ great-malvern-hotel.co.uk
Malvern Hills Black Pear; Wye Valley HPA; 2 changing beers (often Morland, The Friday Beer Co, Timothy Taylor) Ⓗ
Popular hotel public bar a short level walk from the Malvern Theatres complex, ideal for pre- and post-performance refreshment. The beer range usually includes something from Malvern's two breweries. Meals are served in the bar and the adjoining brasserie, including Sunday lunches. There is also a comfortable lounge with lots of sofas, fresh coffee and newspapers. Live music sessions are hosted

weekly. The Great Shakes cellar bar features TV sport and is available for hire. On-site parking is limited but there is plenty of public parking nearby. ᙁ⊛⊜◑▷⊨P₽❀🌐

Morgan L ✓
52 Clarence Road, WR14 3EQ
✪ 12-3.30, 5-11; 12-11 Fri & Sat; 12-10.30 Sun
☎ (01684) 578575
Wye Valley Bitter, HPA, Butty Bach; 2 changing beers (sourced locally) ⊞
This Wye Valley Brewery-owned premises is named after the town's Morgan car factory. The open-plan interior is divided into a games area for darts, a drinking space and a slightly raised seating area with comfy settees. The landscaped patio has ample seating, a fish pond and 'Them Organ' gates. Activities include a monthly book club and weekly quizzes. The pub is muzak-free and the TV is only turned on for major sporting events. Up to two guest beers come from the Wye Valley range. ᙁ⊛◑⊨♣₽(42,43,44)❀🌐

Nag's Head ✓
19-21 Bank Street, WR14 2JG (off Graham Rd at Link Top common)
✪ 11-11.15 (1.30 Fri & Sat); 12-11 Sun ☎ (01684) 574373
🌐 nagsheadmalvern.co.uk
Banks's Bitter; Bathams Best Bitter; St George's Friar Tuck, Charger, Dragons Blood; Wood Shropshire Lad; 2 changing beers (often Otter) ⊞
The permanent beers at this free house, including those from the owner's brewery St George's in nearby Callow End, are joined by up to eight guests from all over the county plus two draught ciders. Mismatched furniture, nooks and crannies, newspapers and foliage create a homely environment. Quality food is served in the bar and restaurant. Outside is a large heated area to the front and a garden to the rear. The car park is small but there is ample on-street parking. Dogs are welcome. ⊛◑♣₽(44)❀🌐

Monkwood Green

Fox
WR2 6NX (S edge of Monkwood Nature Reserve, approx 2 miles from A443) SO803601
✪ 5-11; 12-11 Sat; 12-10.30 Sun ☎ (01886) 889123
Malvern Hills Feelgood; Wye Valley HPA, Butty Bach ⊞
Single-bar village local set on the common near the nature reserve renowned for butterflies and moths. There is seating around the fireplace and hearth at one end, games at the other, and it is a rare outlet for Barker's cider and perry. It is the centre of many events, including skittles and indoor air rifle shooting. Music night is the last Friday of the month. There is no food on general sale but it can be provided by arrangement for groups and parties. There is a very limited bus service. Dog-friendly. Q᙭⊛♠♣₽(308)❀

Pensax

Bell L
WR6 6AE (on Clows Top to Great Witley road S of Pensax)
✪ 12-2.30 (not Mon), 5-11; 12-10.30 Sun ☎ (01299) 896677
Bewdley Worcestershire Way; Exmoor Gold; Hobsons Best; 3 changing beers (sourced locally) ⊞
Local CAMRA Pub of the Year and runner-up West Midlands Pub of the Year in 2015, this friendly

country pub is well-worth making a detour to visit. Seven well-presented real ales plus local cider and perry adorn the bar. There is a separate dining room and a snug where families are welcome. Local seasonal ingredients feature in renowned home-cooked meals. Wooden floors, hanging hops, open fires and some pew seating give a true country feel. Q᙭⊛◑よ♣P❀

Pershore

Brandy Cask L
25 Bridge Street, WR10 1AJ
✪ 11.30-2.30, 7-11 (11.30 Thu); 11.30-3, 7-11.30 Fri & Sat; 12-3, 7-11 Sun ☎ (01386) 552602
Brandy Cask Whistling Joe, Brandysnapper, John Baker's Original; 2 changing beers ⊞
A classic brewpub well-worth a visit. The front entrance leads to a small bar with additional rooms either side. Three house ales are always available plus occasional seasonal brews. Guest beers are from around the country and often unusual for the area. Real cider is also normally kept. Food is good and reasonably priced (no food Mon or Tue in winter). The rear garden runs down to the River Avon and is a delight in summer. Q᙭⊛◑♣₽

Pickled Plum
135 High Street, WR10 1EQ
✪ 12-11 (midnight Fri & Sat) ☎ (01386) 556645
🌐 pickledplum.co.uk
Banks's Sunbeam; Brakspear Bitter; Dark Star Hophead; Wychwood Hobgoblin; 2 changing beers (often Malvern Hills, Pope's, Three Shires) ⊞
Large sympathetically refurbished pub with up to six real ales and six real ciders – the changing beers are usually from local breweries. The interior is divided into several areas, with exposed beams and real fires giving it a cosy old-world charm. A three third-pint tasting option is available. Food is served lunchtimes and evenings. Live jazz plays on Sunday lunchtimes. ⊛◑よ♣P₽

Redditch

Rising Sun L ✓
4 Alcester Street, B98 8AE (opp town hall)
✪ 8am-midnight (1am Fri & Sat) ☎ (01527) 62452
Greene King IPA, Abbot; Sharp's Doom Bar; 9 changing beers ⊞
Large open-plan town-centre pub with a raised seating area and booths. Local histories of Redditch's manufacturing industries adorn the walls, and a large metal horse and rider stands in the centre. Two screens at each end of the pub are usually dedicated to news or sport. The bar gets busy at lunchtimes and weekends. Outside, a glass canopy and café-style seating are ideal for people-watching. The regulars can recommend future beers for sale. ᙁ◑⊨♣♣P₽(55,246,147)🌐

Rocklands Social Club
59 Birchfield Road, Headless Cross, B97 4LB (opp green on Birchfield Rd)
✪ 12 (3 Tue-Thu)-11 ☎ (01527) 544356
🌐 therocklands.co.uk
4 changing beers ⊞
This family club has won multiple CAMRA awards including West Midlands Regional Club of the Year in 2014. Up to four real ales are available from independent brewers, generally including a mild or stout, and up to two real ciders. The club runs a

beer festival and an ale tasting society (RATS). There is a large function room for live entertainment, available to hire. Outside is a sheltered smoking area and landscaped decking. Show this Guide or a CAMRA card for entry. Ale can be bought to take out. ♿🐕❤♣●P🖵(26,47)👜🛜

Shenstone

Plough Ⓛ
DY10 4DL (off A450/A448) SO865735
☼ 12.30-3.30, 6-11; 12-11 Fri-Sun ☎ (01562) 777340
Bathams Mild Ale, Best Bitter Ⓗ
A traditional community pub which has been at the heart of the village since 1840. A long single bar serves both the lounge and public room areas, with a real fire in the lounge. The large enclosed courtyard serves as an overflow area in which children are permitted. Cobs and pork pies are available at lunchtimes. Bathams XXX is served in the winter. Local morris sides dance during the summer months. The Elizabethan Harvington Hall is two miles down the road. Q♿🐕♣P👜🛜

Stourport-on-Severn

Bird in Hand Ⓛ ✅
5 Canal Side, DY13 9BD (off B4193 and Baldwin Rd canalside)
☼ 12-11 ☎ (01299) 871515 ● birdstourport.co.uk
Hobsons Town Crier; 2 changing beers (sourced nationally; often Fuller's, Sharp's, Wells) Ⓗ
Built in 1772 to serve the waterway, a canal theme reflects its location and heritage. The room facing the bar was originally stables. A central bar serves the snug and main lounge. Light meals are served from noon, roasts on Sundays, and main meals in the evenings. In summer it is pleasant to boat, walk or cycle here for a well-deserved pint, enjoyed in the shade of the wisteria by the canal. The pub has one of the few remaining bowling greens in the area. Q♿🐕🅿◐♣P🖵👜🛜

Black Star Ⓛ ✅
Mitton Street, DY13 8YP (just off top end of High St next to canal)
☼ 12-11 (midnight Fri & Sat) ☎ (01299) 488838
Wye Valley HPA, Dorothy Goodbody's Golden Ale, Butty Bach, Dorothy Goodbody's Wholesome Stout; 1 changing beer (often Wye Valley) Ⓗ
Overlooking the canal, the pub was refurbished in 2014 and given a light and airy feel. The main bar has a real fire, low ceilings and cosy corners. At the back is an attractive beer garden with shelter, tables and raised flowerbeds by the canal. Moorings are just through the bridge towards the basins. The varied food menu includes everything from doorstep sandwiches and baguettes to rib-eye steaks and everything in between. Food requests are encouraged. The beers are from Wye Valley. ♿🅿◐●🖵👜🛜

Uphampton

Fruiterer's Arms Ⓛ
Uphampton Lane, WR9 0JW (off A449 by Oldfields of Ombersley, a mile N of Ombersley) SO838648
☼ 12-11.30 (midnight Thu-Sat) ☎ (01905) 620305
Cannon Royall Fruiterers Mild, King's Shilling, Arrowhead Bitter; 2 changing beers (sourced locally; often Wye Valley) Ⓗ

The pub has been in the same family for 162 years and Ted, the licensee, has worked here since 1951. The bar and comfortable beamed lounge serve reasonably priced ales from the Cannon Royall Brewery located at the rear of the pub. Local perry and cider are often available. Filled rolls are on offer Friday to Sunday and a range of home-made pickles, veg and eggs are sold at the bar. Children are welcome until 9pm. Located down a lane off the A449. Q♿♣●P🖵

Upper Wyche

Wyche Inn Ⓛ
Wyche Road, WR14 4EQ (on B4218, follow signs from Malvern to Colwall)
☼ 12-11; 11-11 Sat & Sun ☎ (01684) 575396
● thewycheinn.co.uk
Wye Valley HPA; 3 changing beers (sourced regionally) Ⓗ
The highest pub in Worcestershire, this free house has panoramic views towards the Cotswolds. Ideally situated for hill walkers, it offers two bars – one with pool and darts, the other dedicated to drinking and dining. A range of up to five real ales is available, all sourced from small and micro breweries, including some locals. Home-cooked food is served lunchtimes and evenings. Steak nights on Tuesday and Saturday are especially popular. B&B accommodation is AA 4-star. Q🕸🛏◐♣P🖵👜🛜

Weatheroak

Coach & Horses Ⓛ
Weatheroak Hill, B48 7EA (Alvechurch to Wythall road) SP057740
☼ 11.30-11; 12-10.30 Sun ☎ (01564) 823386
● coachandhorsesinn.co.uk
Hobsons Best; Holden's Golden Glow; Weatheroak Hill Gold, Icknield Pale Ale; Wood Shropshire Lad; 4 changing beers (sourced nationally; often Hook Norton, St Austell, Wood) Ⓗ
Award-winning country free house with a traditional bar with a real fire and quarry-tiled floor, a modern lounge-bar and a restaurant. Formerly a coach house, it has been in the same family for over 40 years. A minimum of 10 real ales are served from breweries across the West Midlands, including the on-site Weatheroak Hill, and takeouts are available. Fresh rolls are always on offer. Outside, the large garden is popular in summer. The building is adjacent to Icknield Street Roman road. Q♿🕸◐♣P👜🛜

Worcester

Bell Ⓛ
35 St Johns, WR2 5AG (W side of Severn off A44)
☼ 10-1am; 11-midnight Sun ☎ (01905) 424570
Fuller's London Pride; 4 changing beers (sourced regionally; often Sharp's, Thwaites, Hobsons) Ⓗ
A community pub dating from the 17th century with a central corridor with two small rooms on one side and the main bar on the other. At the rear is a second bar used at busy times, and a room available for functions. There is also a popular skittle alley. As well as the regular beer there can be up to three guests from local independents or sometimes from more distant breweries. Live music often plays at weekends. ♿🕸♣🖵👜🛜

Bush

4 Bull Ring, St Johns, WR2 5AD

✪ 12-11 (1am Fri & Sat) ☎ (01905) 421086

6 changing beers (sourced regionally; often Cannon Royall) Ⓗ

The main feature of this pub is the public bar which has a Victorian counter with ornate carvings on the front, and etched and stained glass. A smaller room round the back has bench seating. The pub is run by Cannon Royall Brewery and its beers are always available, plus one or two guests. The lined glasses hail from various CAMRA beer festivals. Occasional live music plays at weekends. ◖♠️🚊

Cardinal's Hat

31 Friar Street, WR1 2NA

✪ 12 (4 Mon)-11; 12-11.30 Fri & Sat; 12-10.30 Sun
☎ (01905) 724006 ⊕ the-cardinals-hat.co.uk

4 changing beers (sourced regionally) Ⓗ

A period building set in the heart of the city with a stone-flagged, panelled passageway leading to the small rooms and outdoor patio at the rear. The main bar at the front, with its scrubbed wooden floor, beams and leaded windows, is full of life. The atmospheric back room features wood panelling, a stone-flagged floor, serving hatch and impressive fireplace. A small snug has views of the bustling old street outside. Q🏵️⊛◖≠♣♠😺🏶

Firefly Ⓛ

54 Lowesmoor, WR1 2SE

✪ 12-midnight (1am Thu & Fri); 12-2am Sat; 12-11 Sun
☎ (01905) 616996

4 changing beers Ⓗ

Offering period comfort in a regenerated part of the industrial city, the old vinegar works manager's Georgian residence is now a delightful bar with its own on-site microbrewery (brewing Oct-Mar). The interior has soft furnishings, subtle lighting and an open fire. Downstairs is a cosy snug with bench sofas. The upstairs bar opens at weekends and occasionally during the week for live music. There is a paved partially covered beer garden. Food highlights are a burger deal on Wednesdays and Sunday roasts with all the trimmings. ⊛◖≠♠🚊🏶

Imperial Tavern ♥

St Nicholas Street, WR1 1UW

✪ 12-11 (11.30 Fri); 11-11.30 Sat; 12-10.30 Sun
☎ (01905) 619472

Black Country Bradley's Finest Golden, Pig on the Wall, Fireside; 7 changing beers Ⓗ

This smart city pub is run by the Black Country Brewery. It serves three real ales from the brewery alongside up to seven from small breweries across the country and real cider. Three drinking areas are joined by the bar running front to back. Pictures of old Worcester pubs and street scenes decorate the walls. Voted local CAMRA Pub of the Year in 2016. Q◖≠♣♠🚊

King Charles II

29 New Street, WR1 2DP

✪ 11.30-11 (11.30 Fri & Sat) ☎ (01905) 726100
⊕ thekingcharleshouse.com

Craddock's Saxon Gold, Crazy Sheep, Goat Herder Stout, Troll; house beer (by Bridgnorth); 2 changing beers (sourced locally) Ⓗ

A historically important and listed Tudor black-and-white building featuring a range of beers from Craddock's, Two Thirsty Brewers and Bridgnorth. Barbourne cider on the pumps is occasionally supplemented with its perry. Speciality pies feature large on the menu. Be sure to check out the rollercoaster ride on the first floor and the skeleton in the oubliette. King Charles II escaped from here after the second Battle of Worcester. Q◖≠♣♠🚊😺🏶

Plough Ⓛ

23 Fish Street, WR1 2HN (on Deansway)

✪ 12-11 (11.30 Fri & Sat); 12-10.30 Sun ☎ (01905) 21381

Hobsons Best; Malvern Hills Black Pear; 4 changing beers (sourced regionally; often Salopian) Ⓗ

Grade II-listed pub, near the cathedral, with a short flight of steps leading to a tiny bar with rooms leading off to either side. The beers come from breweries in Worcestershire, surrounding counties and occasionally from further afield. Draught cider and perry are from Barbourne in the city. There is also a wide range of whiskies for the connoisseur. Outside is a small patio area. Rolls are available at weekends and when cricket is on. Hot meals are served Friday and Saturday lunchtimes, roasts on Sundays. 🏵️⊛≠♣♠🚊😺

Postal Order ✔

18 Foregate Street, WR1 1DN

✪ 8am-midnight (1am Fri & Sat) ☎ (01905) 22373

Greene King Abbot; Ruddles Best Bitter; 10 changing beers (sourced nationally; often Pope's) Ⓗ

A classic Wetherspoon pub created from the old Worcester telephone exchange. The Postal Order has one of the largest real ale sales in the chain's West Midlands region and a wide range of beers is served. Mini festivals often showcase ales from local breweries, alongside Wetherspoon's regular beer festivals throughout the year. A cider comes from local producer Barbourne as well as the Westons Old Rosie. Good-value food is served daily 8am-11pm (alcohol from 9am). The volume on the TV may be turned up for important games. Q🏵️⊛◖♿≠♠🚊😺

Learned drinker

He was a learned man, of immense reading, but is much blamed for his unfaithfull quotations. His manner of studie was thus, he wore a long quilt cap, which came two or rather three inches at least over his eies, which served him as an umbrella to defend his eies from the light. About every three houres his man was to bring him a roll and a pot of ale to refocillate (refresh) his wasted spirits so he studied, and dranke, and munched some bread and this maintained him till night, and then he made a good supper.

An Oxford man, William Prynne (1600-69), as described by John Aubrey in Brief Lives, ed. John Buchanan-Brown, 2000

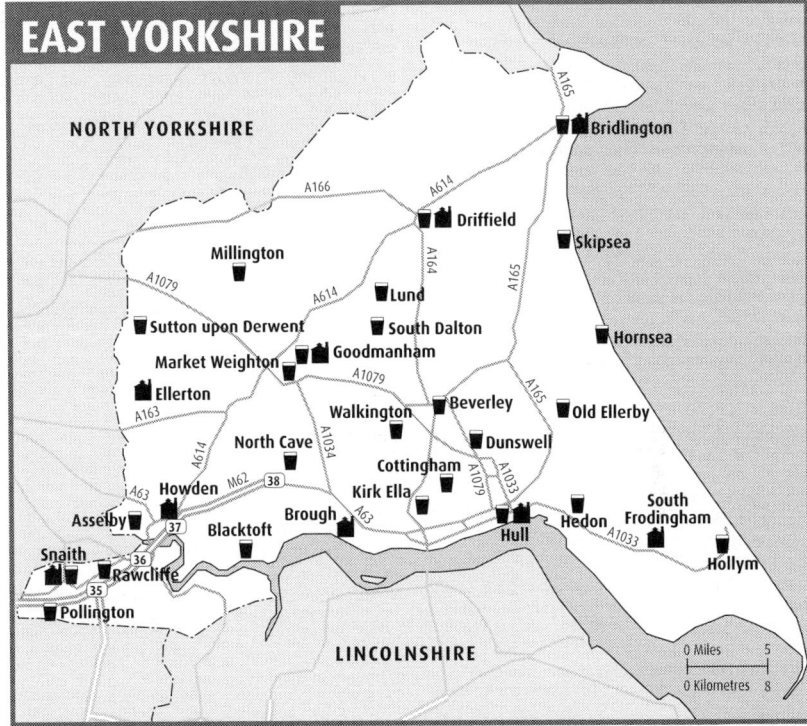

EAST YORKSHIRE

NORTH YORKSHIRE

Bridlington

Driffield

Millington

Skipsea

Lund

Sutton upon Derwent

South Dalton

Hornsea

Market Weighton

Goodmanham

Ellerton

Walkington

Beverley

Old Ellerby

North Cave

Dunswell

Cottingham

Howden

Kirk Ella

Asselby

Brough

Hedon

South Frodingham

Blacktoft

Hull

Snaith

Rawcliffe

Hollym

Pollington

LINCOLNSHIRE

0 Miles 5
0 Kilometres 8

YORKSHIRE (EAST)

Asselby

Black Swan L
Main Street, DN14 7HE
☼ 6-10 Mon & Tue; 5-11; 12-11 Sat & Sun ☎ (01757) 630409
⊕ whelansofasselby.co.uk
John Smith's Bitter; 5 changing beers (sourced locally; often Crystalbrew, Half Moon, Sunbeam) Ⓗ
A most traditional and family-friendly village pub with an interesting array of regional beers. Four rotating guest ales frequently include collaborations with local breweries and there is always a handpulled cider on the bar. A recently refurbished garden room serves as a quiet room and can be used for functions such as the annual beer festival. Grade II-listed, this country pub is on the Transpennine Cycle Trail – which is a good way to visit it as local transport is scarce.
ॐ❀◑◖P❀🗢

Beverley

Chequers Micropub L
15 Swaby's Yard, Dyer Lane, HU17 9BZ (off Saturday Market)
☼ 12-10 (11 Thu-Sat) ☎ 07964 227906
⊕ chequersmicropub.co.uk
5 changing beers (sourced regionally; often Atom, Brass Castle, Half Moon) Ⓗ
Yorkshire's first micropub in a former baker's, near the bus station. Local breweries are always represented on the bar as well as micros from throughout the UK. Eight ciders/perries are sold. The cellar is above the bar. Typically for a micropub, no lager, keg beer or spirits are sold, and there is

no TV or loud music, making Chequers a place for real conversation, like pubs used to be. Former Local CAMRA Town Pub of the Year and Cider Pub of the Year. Q❀ॐ🗢◖🗇🖵❀

Cornerhouse
2 Norwood, HU17 9ET
☼ 5-midnight (1am Fri); 10-1am Sat; 10-11 Sun; closed Mon ☎ (01482) 882652
Abbeydale Deception; Black Sheep Best Bitter; Greene King IPA; Timothy Taylor Landlord; 8 changing beers (sourced nationally; often Abbeydale) Ⓗ
The Cornerhouse looks like a gastro-pub, but the customers are mainly here for the real ale on 12 handpumps and the real cider on two handpumps. Beers from local and regional micros are featured, including mild. A coal fire warms the far end of the bar and there is unusual gallery seating off the bar. Curry night is Tuesday and quiz night Wednesday. Breakfasts, served 10am-1pm, are popular on weekends, and Sunday lunch is served until 8pm.
❀◑&🗢◖P🖵

Dog & Duck

33 Ladygate, HU17 8BH (off Saturday Market)
✪ 11-4, 7-midnight; 11-midnight Fri & Sat; 11.30-3, 7-11 Sun
☎ (01482) 862419 ⊕ bedandbreakfastbeverley.com
**Black Sheep Best Bitter; Copper Dragon Golden
Pippin; John Smith's Bitter; Timothy Taylor Golden
Best; 2 changing beers (sourced nationally)** ⊞
Just off the main Saturday Market, the pub was
built in the 1930s and has been run by the same
family for over 40 years. It comprises three areas: a
bar with a period brick fireplace and bentwood
seating, a front lounge, and a rear snug. The good-
value, home-cooked lunches are popular. Guest
accommodation is in six purpose-built self-
contained rooms to the rear. It is dog-friendly in
the evenings and after food service. Close to
Beverley bus station. 🛏️◗≉♣🛆🚃🚌❀

Sun Inn

1 Flemingate, HU17 0NP (adjacent to Beverley Minster)
✪ 4-11 (12.30am Fri); 12-12.30am Sat; 12-10.30
Sun ☎ 07541 456215 ⊕ suninnbeverley.com
**Black Sheep Best Bitter; Greene King IPA; Morland Old
Speckled Hen; Timothy Taylor Landlord; York Guzzler;
1 changing beer (sourced nationally)** ⊞
The Sun Inn's medieval timber-framed building is
set opposite the eastern front of Beverley's famous
minster, so the view from the courtyard beer
garden should not be missed. Formerly a Tap &
Spile, the pub's stripped-back interior featuring
bare brick walls reflects that style. It is a live music
venue, with blues and rock bands on a weekend
and folk sessions on Saturday teatimes. Quiz night
is Thursday. Sunday lunches are served 12-3pm.
❀◗≉♣🚌(6,246)❀

Tiger Inn ✪

97 Lairgate, HU17 8JG (near Memorial Hall)
✪ 11-11 (midnight Fri & Sat); 12-11 Sun; closed Mon
☎ (01482) 869040 ⊕ tiger-inn-beverley.co.uk
**Timothy Taylor Landlord; Wychwood Hobgoblin; 3
changing beers (sourced nationally; often Great
Newsome, Moorhouse's)** ⊞
Attractive Grade II-listed 18th-century building re-
fronted in 1930s Brewers' Tudor style by the now
defunct Darley & Co, which once owned several
pubs in Beverley. It has a multi-roomed interior
with a public bar, snug, dining room/lounge and
function room. Many local clubs and societies meet
here and folk music sessions are held on Friday
evenings. The large car park to the rear was once
stables and outbuildings. Dogs are welcome in the
public bar. Meals include a Sunday carvery.
Q❀◗≉♣🛆P🚌(X46,X47,180)❀🛜

Woolpack

37 Westwood Road, HU17 8EN (W of Saturday Market)
✪ 4.30-10.30 Mon; 12-3, 4.30-11; 12-11 Sat & Sun
☎ (01482) 867095
**Banks's Sunbeam; Jennings Bitter, Cocker Hoop,
Sneck Lifter; Marston's EPA; Wychwood Hobgoblin; 1
changing beer (sourced nationally)** ⊞
In a Victorian residential street west of the town
centre, the Woolpack started life as pair of cottages
and became a public house around 1831, later
developing its own brewhouse and stables, and is
now owned by Marston's. It retains a quarry-tiled
snug that is dog-friendly; it has an open fire in the
winter, and there is a more recent extension to the
rear. Meals are served at lunchtimes and evenings,
and 12-7pm on Sundays. Quiz night is Thursday.
Q❀◗🐾❀

Blacktoft

Hope & Anchor ⌶

Blacktoft Lane, DN14 7YW (3½ miles S of Gilberdyke rail
station, follow signs to Blacktoft) SE842242
✪ 12 (5 Mon & Tue)-11; 12-10.30 Sun ☎ (01430) 440441
⊕ hopeandanchorblacktoft.co.uk
**Marston's Pedigree; 3 changing beers (sourced
regionally; often Copper Dragon, Great Newsome,
Half Moon)** ⊞
Thriving village hostelry in a superb location on the
bank of the River Ouse; the RSPB's Blacktoft Sands
bird sanctuary is visible on the far bank. Laurel and
Hardy memorabilia is prominent, as is a collection
of jugs suspended from wooden beams. The
conservatory offers fine river views. Popular home-
cooked meals are served lunchtimes and evenings
during the week (no food Mon or Tue) and all day
at weekends, with booking for Sunday
recommended. A mild is often on tap.
🛏️❀◗🛆♣P🛜

Bridlington

Marine Bar ⌶

North Marine Drive, YO15 2LS (1 mile NE of centre)
✪ 11-11 (11.30 Sat) ☎ (01262) 675347 ⊕ marinebar.net
**John Smith's Bitter; Timothy Taylor Landlord; Wold
Top Bitter; 2 changing beers (sourced regionally;
often Daleside, Rooster's)** ⊞
Large open-plan bar, part of the Expanse Hotel.
Take in the spectacular sea views while enjoying
some home-cooked food served daily, including
vegetarian options. Attracting a good mix of
regulars, a warm welcome awaits the influx of
summer visitors. Twice-weekly quizzes and live
music nights are popular. Two regional guest beers
are served. Ample parking is available along the
promenade. A land train operates close by during
the summer. Runner-up local CAMRA Town Pub of
the Year 2015. ❀🛏️◗&🛆♣P🚌(504)

Cottingham

Blue Bell ✪

West Green, HU16 4BH
✪ 11-11 (midnight Fri & Sat); 11-10.30 Sun
☎ (01482) 847113 ⊕ bluebellcottingham.com
**Ringwood Boondoggle, Fortyniner; Wychwood
Hobgoblin; house beer (by Brakspear)** ⊞
In a picturesque setting overlooking a green, this
attractive pub is split into a bar and a recently
extended restaurant with its own secluded garden.
The restaurant has a log fire and enjoys a high
reputation. The modern bar has deep armchairs
and low-level music. To the rear there is a second
garden with a covered smoking area and heaters.
Open mic music night is Wednesday and live jazz
plays on Sunday evening. Dogs are welcome in the
bar. ❀◗&🚌(110,115)❀🛜

King William IV

152 Hallgate, HU16 4DB
✪ 11-11 (midnight Fri & Sat); 12-11 Sun ☎ (01482) 875996
⊕ kingwilliamcottingham.co.uk
**Banks's Sunbeam; Jennings Cumberland Ale;
Marston's Pedigree; 4 changing beers (sourced
nationally; often Brakspear, Ringwood,
Wychwood)** ⊞
Village-centre pub with a traditional bar and quiet
lounge. The pub hosts weekly quiz nights and an
annual music festival. At the rear a former brewery
has been converted into a function room offering

live music and special events. The beer garden and side courtyard have covered smoking areas. Excellent-value meals are served in large and small portions. Thatchers cider is on handpump. Local CAMRA Village Pub of the Year 2014 and runner-up in 2015. Q✪❀❍◗≉♣●🖳(103,105,115)❀ 🛜

Driffield

Butchers Dog 🍸 🅛
24 Middle Street South, YO25 6PS
✪ 12-11 (6 Mon; 10 Tue & Wed); 12-10 Sun
☎ (01377) 254032 ⊕ thebutchersdog.co.uk
5 changing beers (sourced locally; often Brass Castle, Wold Top, Yorkshire) 🅷
One-room micropub but returning to traditional pub values with modern twists. Five real ales from the pub's off-site brewery and other local breweries are served in oversized glasses alongside a wide selection of real ciders (some from local producers), but no spirits. Customers are encouraged to rely on good conversation in the Wi-Fi and music-free environment. Simple bar snacks are provided or customers may bring their own food. Local CAMRA Town and Cider Pub of the Year. Q≉●❍🖳(121)❀

Mariners Arms
47 Eastgate South, YO25 6LR
✪ 3-midnight; 12-midnight Sat & Sun ☎ (01377) 253708
Banks's Sunbeam; Jennings Bitter; Ringwood Boondoggle; 1 changing beer 🅷
A street-corner local well worth seeking out. The beer range is from the Marston's portfolio, as an alternative to the other breweries more commonly available in the town. Formerly part of the Hull Brewery estate, its four small rooms have now become two: a public bar and a more comfortable lounge. Live sport is shown and the pub fields various sports teams. The long-standing licensees enjoy a loyal following among locals and offer a friendly welcome to all visitors. ❀≉♣P🖳(121)

Dunswell

Ship Inn 🅛
Beverley Road, HU6 0AJ
✪ 11.30-11 (11.30 Thu; midnight Fri & Sat); 12-11.30 Sun
☎ (01482) 859160
Great Newsome Frothingham Best; Tetley Bitter; 2 changing beers (sourced regionally) 🅷
Fronting the old Hull-Beverley road, this inn once served traffic on the nearby River Hull, and is decorated with nautical memorabilia including the bell from the shipwrecked Caroline. Log fires warm the convivial interior, which is partly divided to create a separate dining area with church pew seating. Former outbuildings have been developed to create en-suite accommodation in the Ship's Quarters. The large garden has an outside bar and barbecue area for summer events.
❧✪❀❍◗&♣●P🖳(121,122,246)❀ 🛜

Goodmanham

Goodmanham Arms 🍸 🅛
Main Street, YO43 3JA
✪ 11-midnight; 11-11 Sun ☎ (01430) 873849
⊕ goodmanhamarms.co.uk
All Hallows Peg Fyfe Dark Mild, Goodmanham Best, Ragged Robyn, No Notion Porter; Black Dog Whitby Abbey Ale; Hambleton Stallion Premium Bitter; 3

changing beers (sourced regionally; often Great Newsome, Leeds, Yorkshire) 🅷
Close to the Wolds Way footpath, with gardens front and back, this brewery pub makes an ideal resting place for walkers. You can sample nine ales including four from the on-site brewery and seven ciders. A central corridor leading to the bar servery separates two atmospherically lit rooms, both with open fires, one complete with a cooking range. Reclaimed farm tools give the ambience of a farmhouse kitchen. Local CAMRA Village Pub of the Year winner 2015. Q❧✪❀◗●P❀

Hedon

Shakespeare Inn 🅛 ❂
9 Baxtergate, HU12 8JN
✪ 12-11 (11.30 Fri & Sat); 12-10.30 Sun ☎ (01482) 812813
Tetley Bitter; Timothy Taylor Landlord; 3 changing beers (sourced nationally; often Great Newsome, Hardys & Hansons, Jennings) 🅷
A 300-year-old pub in the centre of historic Hedon, largely unaltered for the past 50 years and still with original Darley's wall sconces. Popular with all ages, it stages live music fortnightly on Saturdays during the summer. Rugby League memorabilia, reflecting the landlord's previous career, adorn the walls, and a friendly atmosphere encourages the art of conversation. The menu features freshly cooked local produce alongside popular changing specials. Of the three guest beers, one is usually from a local brewery. ❧✪❍◗♣P🖳🛜

Hollym

Plough Inn
Northside Road, HU19 2RS
✪ 5 (7 winter)-midnight Tue & Wed; 3 (5 winter)-midnight; 12-midnight Sat; 12-11 Sun; closed Mon ☎ (01964) 612049
⊕ theploughinnhollym.co.uk
Greene King IPA; 4 changing beers (sourced nationally; often Great Newsome, Greene King, Hardys & Hansons) 🅷
Family-run free house, parts of which date from the 17th century – see the wattle and daub front wall in the public bar – offering five real ales. Both bars have coal fires bringing warmth and cheer during the winter. Primarily a locals' pub, it is a base for Withernsea rugby club, Withernsea Harriers and Withernsea Pigeon Flyers; it is also a haven for holidaymakers in summer. Former local CAMRA Village Pub of the Year. Open bank holiday Mondays. Q❧✪❀❍◗A♣P🖳(75,76,77)❀ 🛜

Hornsea

Stackhouse Bar 🅛
8a Newbegin, HU18 1AG
✪ 12-midnight summer; 4 (12 Sat & Sun)-midnight winter
☎ (01964) 534407
4 changing beers (sourced regionally; often Atom, Brass Castle, Great Newsome) 🅷
Former shop converted to a micropub in 2014 with an interesting choice of regional ales and a large range of real ciders. Attracting a mixed clientele, customers are encouraged to engage in conversation. A regular folk night is supplemented by piano singalongs and acoustic guitar music. Although no food is provided, customers are allowed to bring their own. Vaping-friendly. Winter opening hours apply January to Easter.
❧♣●❀ 🛜

Hull

Admiral of the Humber ✓

1 Anlaby Road, HU1 2NT

✪ 8am-midnight (1am Fri & Sat) ☎ (01482) 381850

Greene King Abbot; Ruddles Best Bitter; 6 changing beers (sourced nationally) ⊞

A former paint and wallpaper shop; previously, the site was connected to Hull's seafaring past. Now a large single room, mostly on one level, the building is ideally suited to those finding steps or stairs a problem. The pub prides itself on being part of the community, with sport featuring, and away fans are welcome when Hull City are at home. A designated area is set aside for diners during the day, and children are welcome until 6pm. Alcohol is sold from 9am. ⍾⊛⊙&≒♣●⊟≋

George Hotel

Land of Green Ginger, Old Town, HU1 2EA

✪ 12-11 (midnight Fri & Sat) ☎ (01482) 226373

Theakston Old Peculier; Thwaites Wainwright; Timothy Taylor Landlord; 2 changing beers (sourced nationally) ⊞

Situated in the heart of the old town on Hull's most famous street, this one-room pub is of historic interest. The Georgian interior, featuring beamed ceilings, wood-panelled walls and pictures of old Hull, remains virtually unaltered. The fine glazed leaded windows have been retained and it reputedly features the smallest pub window in England, dating from its coaching days with excise searches. Meals are served daily (not Mon). Up to six Westons ciders are available. ⊙♣●⊟

Hop & Vine ⓛ

24 Albion Street, HU1 3TG

✪ 4-11 Tue; 11-11 (11.30 Fri & Sat); closed Sun & Mon ☎ 07500 543199 ⊕ hopandvinehull.co.uk

3 changing beers (sourced nationally; often Great Newsome, Hop Studio, Tom Wood's) ⊞

Atmospheric basement bar free house dispensing three changing guest beers from independent breweries, plus rare farmhouse ciders and perry and a selection of bottled Belgian beers. Oversized lined glasses are used. A selection of freshly prepared food including home-baked bread is served until 9pm, with the owner's home-made chilli notable. Shove-ha'penny, cribbage and shut the box games are available. Former CAMRA National Cider Pub of the Year and four times Yorkshire regional winner, including in 2014. Closed between Christmas and New Year. ⊙≒♣●P⊟☺≋

Larkin's ⓛ

48-52 Newland Avenue, HU5 3AE

✪ 12-11 (11.30 Fri & Sat) ☎ (01482) 440991 ⊕ larkinsbar.co.uk

Wold Top Wold Gold; 3 changing beers (sourced regionally; often Abbeydale, Cottage, Great Newsome) ⊞

One-roomed café-bar, named after poet Philip Larkin, which was once two shops and can still be partitioned for small private functions. A good selection of home-cooked food is on sale, with an excellent Sunday carvery. There is a paved area to the front and a secluded garden at the rear. Regular beer festivals are held, usually over bank holiday weekends, in the adjacent car sales yard, featuring live music from local acts. ⍾⊛⊙&⊟(5,103,115)≋

Minerva Hotel ⓛ

10 Nelson Street, HU1 1XE

✪ 11.30-11.30 ☎ (01482) 210025 ⊕ minerva-hull.co.uk

Tetley Bitter; 5 changing beers (sourced regionally; often Atom, Revolutions, Yorkshire) ⊞

Overlooking the Humber estuary and Victoria Pier, this famous pub, built in 1829, is a great place to watch the ships go by. Photos and memorabilia are a reminder of the area's maritime past. The central bar serves various rooms including a tiny three-seat snug. The former brewhouse now houses Hull's smallest theatre (40 seats) and is available for functions. The Deep visitor attraction can be accessed by a footbridge at the mouth of the River Hull. ⊛⊙◖♣⊟(16)≋

New Adelphi Club ⓛ

89 De Grey Street, HU5 2RU

✪ 8-11 ☎ (01482) 348216 ⊕ theadelphi.com

4 changing beers (sourced locally; often Atom, Great Newsome) ⊞

Hull's justifiably famous music venue has been the launchpad to many an illustrious career and has hosted a veritable Who's Who of popular music since opening in 1984. The main music room is supplemented by a small front bar that accommodates a pool table and features a cut-off bus front as the bar counter. Access to the small bar is free at all times and no membership restrictions apply. Benefit from £1 reduction on ale when no musicians are booked. ♣●P⊟≋

Olde Black Boy ★

150 High Street, Old Town, HU1 1PS

✪ 12 (5 Mon & Tue)-11.30 ⊕ yeoldeblackboy.weebly.com/index.html

6 changing beers (sourced nationally; often Bradfield, Ossett, Timothy Taylor) ⊞

Historic pub, licensed since 1729, with a beamed ceiling and panelled walls, previously a wine merchants' and tobacco dealer's. It has a front snug with an open fire, the main back bar, and a heated rooftop smoking terrace. Black and white photos of past old-town pubs are displayed. Folk music figures monthly on the first Monday. Several museums and England's largest parish church are within five minutes' walk. It sells guest beers of varied styles and Westons Old Rosie cider, as well as bar snacks, and stocks 35-40 single malt whiskies. Q♣●⊟☺≋

Olde White Harte ★

25 Silver Street, HU1 1JG

✪ 11-midnight (1am Fri & Sat); 12-midnight Sun ☎ (01482) 326363 ⊕ yeoldewhiteharte.com

Caledonian Deuchars IPA; Theakston Best Bitter, Old Peculier; 3 changing beers (sourced nationally) ⊞

Historic pub in a 17th-century merchant's house, with strong connections to the English Civil War. The existing ground-floor interior dates back to a major refurbishment in 1881, which was an idealised re-creation of an old English inn, complete with massive inglenook fireplaces and stained-glass windows. The first floor has restaurant facilities, and the Plotting Parlour is available for meetings and functions. There is also a courtyard with heating providing an all-weather outdoor drinking area. ⊛⊙⊟

Pave ⓛ ✓

16-20 Princes Avenue, HU5 3QA

✪ 11-11 (11.30 Fri & Sat) ☎ (01482) 333181 ⊕ pavebar.co.uk

Tetley Gold; Theakston Best Bitter; 3 changing beers (sourced regionally; often Brass Castle, Saltaire, Yorkshire) Ⓗ
A continental-style bar in the Avenues area which attracts a diverse range of customers. As well as the regular ales there are three guest beers, usually regional, and a varied range of European draught and bottled beers. Home-cooked food including vegetarian options is served daily. Complimentary live music is provided on Tuesday evenings and Sunday afternoons. A changing Westons cider is sold. ⏰🕮◑⅃♿🚌 (5,103,105)📶

St John's Hotel ✓
10 Queens Road, HU5 2PY
🕐 12-11.30 (midnight Tue & Thu; 12.30am Fri & Sat)
☎ (01482) 341013 🌐 stjohnshull.com
Marston's EPA, Old Empire; 3 changing beers (sourced nationally) Ⓗ
Grade II-listed, classic street-corner local boasting one of the least-altered interiors in the city. The welcoming front-corner public bar complements a quiet back room, with original bench seating. A more basic larger room accommodates the pool table and is home to the beer festival bar three times a year. It is a community local with two darts teams, a football team and the Oddfellows cricket league which hosts quiz nights in the winter. Open mic night is Tuesday. Local CAMRA City Pub of the Year runner-up 2015. Q⏰🕮♿♣P🚌👺📶

Three John Scotts Ⓛ ✓
Lowgate, HU1 1AA
🕐 8am-midnight (1am Fri & Sat) ☎ (01482) 381910
Greene King Abbot; Ruddles Best Bitter; Sharp's Doom Bar; 7 changing beers (sourced regionally; often Great Heck, Great Newsome, Wold Top) Ⓗ
Originally an Edwardian post office, this open-plan Wetherspoon hostelry features modern decor and works of art. The name derives from three successive 19th-century vicars of St Mary's Church opposite. The pub has established a broad customer base appealing to all types of clientele. Up to 10 real ales and two real ciders are on sale. Children are welcome until 9pm. There is a large rear courtyard seating area which is a great suntrap in the summer. ⏰🕮◑♿🚌📶

Whalebone 🍷 Ⓛ
165 Wincolmlee, HU2 0PA
🕐 12-midnight (11 Tue & Wed) ☎ 07506 868461
Great Newsome Frothingham Best; Rudgate Viking; 5 changing beers (sourced regionally; often Abbeydale, Brass Castle, Elland) Ⓗ
Local CAMRA City Pub of the Year 2014 and 2015, this rare gem sits in an old industrial area associated with the Greenland whaling trade. Continuously licensed since 1791, the current building dates from 1890 though much altered internally. A free house since 2002, the real ales, eight ciders and perries plus continental beers are served in a comfortable saloon bar adorned with photos celebrating the city's sporting heritage and of bygone Hull pubs. Look out for the illuminated M&R brewery sign. ⏰♣👺👺

Kirk Ella

Beech Tree ✓
South Ella Way, HU10 7LY
🕐 11.30-midnight ☎ (01482) 654350
Brakspear Bitter; Tetley Bitter; house beer (by Ember Inns); 5 changing beers (sourced nationally) Ⓗ

Open-plan pub on the western outskirts of Hull, owned by a pub company committed to cask ale. Up to eight real ales are available, including at least one dark beer; try-before-you-buy is encouraged. Food is served 12-10pm every day. Monday and Wednesday are quiz nights. Families with children are welcome throughout and a real fire makes for a hospitable winter feel. Buses stop close to the pub until early evening, and later stop only a 10-minute walk away. ⏰🕮◑♿P🚌 (154,180)📶

Lund

Wellington Inn Ⓛ
19 The Green, YO25 9TE
🕐 7-11 Mon; 12-3, 6.30-11; 12-10.30 Sun ☎ (01377) 217294
🌐 thewellingtoninn.co.uk
John Smith's Bitter; Theakston Best Bitter; Timothy Taylor Landlord; 1 changing beer (sourced locally; often Great Newsome, Wold Top) Ⓗ
Enjoying a prime location on the green in this award-winning Wolds village, most of the pub's trade comes from the local farming community. Renovated by the present licensee, it features stone-flagged floors, beamed ceilings and three real fires. The multi-roomed interior includes a games room and a candlelit restaurant serving evening meals Tuesday-Saturday. Good food can also be enjoyed at lunchtime from the bar menu and specials board. Guest beers are usually sourced locally. ⏰🕮◑♿♣P🚌 (142)

Market Weighton

Carpenters Arms
56 Southgate, YO43 3BQ
🕐 3-midnight; 12-1am Fri & Sat; 12-midnight Sun ☎ 07917 154683
John Smith's Bitter; 5 changing beers (sourced regionally; often Half Moon, Wold Top) Ⓗ
A traditional family-run pub on the outskirts of town, popular with locals and families and a recipient of numerous local media and tourism awards. The saloon design has an open-plan feel, with an area away from the TV to sit and converse while enjoying any of the five changing guest ales (one always a dark beer), or a Westons Old Rosie cider. A beer festival is held over the late May bank holiday weekend. ⏰♣👺🚌 (18,X46,X4)👺📶

Millington

Gait
Main Street, YO42 1TX
🕐 12-3 (not Tue-Thu), 6-11; 12-4, 6-11 Sat; 12-3, 6-11 Sun; closed Mon ☎ (01759) 302045 🌐 gait-inn-millington.co.uk
Black Sheep Best Bitter; Tetley Bitter; Theakston Best Bitter; 2 changing beers (sourced locally; often Half Moon, Wold Top) Ⓗ
This delightful Yorkshire Wolds pub provides a warm welcome (seasonally by means of a wood-burning stove) to both locals and the many walkers enjoying the attractions of Millington woods and pastures. It has an idiosyncratic bar filled with a range of ornaments and local pictures. Sit at kitchen-style tables to enjoy hearty, home-made food served from an extensive menu. The annual beer festival has up to 35 beers. Three regular ales and at least one guest ale, when surveyed, were all from Yorkshire. ⏰🕮◑♣P👺

North Cave

White Hart 🅛 ✅
20 Westgate, HU15 2NJ
❂ 4-11 (midnight Fri & Sat) ☎ (01430) 470940
⊕ whitehartnorthcave.co.uk
**3 changing beers (sourced regionally; often Great
Newsome, Theakston, Wold Top)** Ⓗ
This welcoming traditional village pub is a credit to
the community it serves. There is a long bar to the
side and rear, while the quieter front bar has
comfortable seating and is where the three real
ales are dispensed from. Real fires are lit during
winter months, providing further home-from-
home comfort. Walkers and dogs are welcome. The
Gin Palace now features over 80 gins. Third-pint
taster trays are available. The place is a popular
stopping-off point for Beverley races.
Ω ☎ ❀ ♣ P 🖩 (155) ❀

Old Ellerby

Blue Bell 🅛
Crabtree Lane, HU11 5AJ
❂ 7-11.30 (midnight Fri & Sat); closed Mon & Thu; 12-6, 8-11
Sun ☎ (01964) 562364
**Great Newsome Sleck Dust; Tetley Bitter; 2 changing
beers (sourced regionally; often Great Newsome, Tom
Wood's)** Ⓗ
A 16th-century inn with an L-shaped bar and a
single room divided into distinct areas, including a
snug to the right and a rear pool area where
children are welcome until 8.30pm. The pub has a
strong community feel and is home to several darts
and dominoes teams. Two guest beers in winter
increase to three in the summer months. Outside is
a fish pond and bowling green. Popular with
walkers (wipe your boots, please). Q ☎ ❀ Å ♣ P

Pollington

King's Head 🅛
Main Street, DN14 0DN
❂ 5-11 (midnight Fri); 12-midnight Sat; 12-10 Sun; closed
Mon ☎ (01405) 861507
**Great Heck Navigator; Tetley Bitter; 2 changing beers
(sourced locally; often Great Heck)** Ⓗ
Adam and Diane offer a warm welcome at this
excellent village pub situated conveniently for the
Aire & Calder canal. Popular with regulars, walkers
and visitors alike, the pub is open plan, with a
comfortable lounge area complete with a wood-
burning stove, and another area where darts is
played. Adam is in charge in the kitchen, producing
generous portions of traditional pub food. Guest
beers are often from Great Heck brewery. Quiz
night is Friday. Accommodation is available.
Q ☎ ❀ 🛏 ◑ ♣ P

Rawcliffe

Jemmy Hirst at the Rose & Crown ▼
🅛
26 Riverside, DN14 8RN
❂ 6 (5 Fri)-midnight; 12-midnight Sat & Sun
☎ (01405) 831038 ⊕ jemmyhirst.freeservers.com
**Timothy Taylor Landlord; 4 changing beers (sourced
locally; often Abbeydale, Ossett, Wold Top)** Ⓗ
An outstanding free house that locals say is the
heart of the village. There is always a warm,
friendly welcome from the owners, locals and
Bruno the dog. Book-lined walls and an open fire

provide a haven on a cold winter's day. You can
sample five real ales and a traditional cider here.
The patio or riverbank beckon in warmer weather.
Well known regionally and a winner of numerous
CAMRA branch awards including Pub of the Year
eight times. Q ☎ ❀ ♣ ● P 🖩 (88,401) ❀

Skipsea

Board Inn
Back Street, YO25 8SW (off B1242)
❂ 6-11; 12-midnight Sat; 12-11 Sun ☎ (01262) 468342
**3 changing beers (sourced nationally; often Jennings,
Marston's, Wychwood)**
One mile from the sea in the village conservation
area, this homely pub dating from 1642 is popular
with locals and is a mecca for holidaymakers. It has
a traditional two-roomed bar and lounge,
dispensing three beers (two in winter) from the
Marston's portfolio, plus a 60-cover restaurant
serving home-prepared food using locally sourced
produce. Booking is recommended for Sunday
lunches. Functions are catered for, and walkers and
cyclists are welcome. Closed on Tuesdays in
January and February.
Q ☎ ❀ ◑ & Å ♣ P 🖩 (130) ❀ 🛜

Snaith

Brewers Arms Hotel 🅛
10 Pontefract Road, DN14 9JS
❂ 12-midnight; 12-9.30 Sun ☎ (01405) 862404
⊕ thebrewersarms.co.uk
**Old Mill Traditional Bitter, Blonde Bombshell; 1
changing beer (sourced locally; often Old Mill)** Ⓗ
Fine example of a large village pub, with many
worn oak beams in evidence as well as three
fireplaces. It is split into a large main room and bar,
with four individual side rooms leading off. One of
these is dedicated to 51 Squadron RAF Snaith, a
Halifax bomber station during WWII, with many
photographs and paintings. Another side room has
an angling theme, with fishing rods and stuffed
wildlife. It always has three real ales on handpull,
with an additional one in summer.
Q ☎ ❀ 🛏 ◑ & ⇌ ● P 🖩 🛜

South Dalton

Pipe & Glass 🅛 ✅
West End, HU17 7PN (at end of West End Lane)
❂ 12-11; 12-10.30 Sun; closed Mon ☎ (01430) 810246
⊕ pipeandglass.co.uk
**Black Sheep Best Bitter; house beer (by Great
Yorkshire); 3 changing beers (sourced regionally;
often John Smith's, Wold Top, York)** Ⓗ
Delightful hostelry that stands at the site of the
original gatehouse to Dalton Hall, featuring
exposed beams and custom-made furniture. The
owner and chef holds a Michelin star for the
seventh consecutive year. Three guest ales come
from around Yorkshire, as does the real cider from
Moorlands Farm. Five boutique rooms, with views
of Dalton Hall, are available. Open on bank holiday
Mondays, closed for the first two weeks of January.
Q ☎ ❀ 🛏 ◑ & ● P 🖩 (142)

Sutton upon Derwent

St Vincent Arms 🅛
Main Street, YO41 4BN
❂ 12-3, 6-11; 12-3, 6-10.30 Sun ☎ (01904) 608349

Fuller's London Pride, ESB; Greene King IPA; Theakston Old Peculier; Timothy Taylor Landlord; York Guzzler; 1 changing beer (sourced nationally) ⊞

Former winner of many local CAMRA awards, this pretty white-painted village free house on a bend in the road has been family owned and well run for many years. A long-time supporter of Fuller's beers, it has a consistent and large beer range. The bar, featuring a large Fuller, Smith & Turner mirror, is popular with locals. Another small bar with a serving hatch leads to the dining rooms. Excellent food is available, catering for a variety of tastes. Q⦵⌖❀❄❶P

Walkington

Barrel Inn

35 East End, HU17 8RX

✪ 4.30-midnight; 12-1am Sat; 12-midnight Sun ☎ 07550 078833 ⊕ barrelwalkington.co.uk

Thwaites Wainwright, Lancaster Bomber; 3 changing beers (sourced regionally; often Great Newsome, Leeds, Wold Top) ⊞

Friendly drinkers' local in a quiet three-pub village, and one of only two Thwaites pubs in East Yorkshire. The front bar has a log fire and beamed ceiling; a step leads to a connecting lounge, also with a log fire. Families are welcome. Popular with local sports teams, it is home to a golf society. Up to five real ales are sold, including one free of tie. A secluded cottage-style beer garden is at the rear. Quiz night is Thursday. ⦵❀♣❶P☐(180,61)❀❖

YORKSHIRE (NORTH)

Aldbrough St John

Stanwick ⓛ ✓

High Green, DL11 7SZ (1 mile from B6275)

✪ 12-3, 5.30 (6 Sat)-11; 12-9 Sun ☎ (01325) 374258 ⊕ thestanwick.co.uk

Daleside Bitter; Thwaites Wainwright; 2 changing beers ⊞

In a picturesque North Yorkshire village on one of the country's largest village greens, this multi award-winning and welcoming 19th-century inn has two bars: one for drinkers and one for two excellent restaurants where locally sourced food is served seven days a week (closed Mon in winter). It is the brewery tap for the village's Mithril Ales, and one of its beers is always featured. Cricket, quoits, football and darts are supported. Takeaway fish and chips are served Wednesdays 5.30-8pm, roast baguettes Sundays 2-5pm. Q⦵⌖❶&♣P☐(29)❀❖

Appletreewick

Craven Arms ⓛ

BD23 6DA

✪ 11-11; 11-10.30 Sun ☎ (01756) 720270 ⊕ craven-cruckbarn.co.uk

Dark Horse Craven Bitter, Hetton Pale Ale; Greene King IPA; Saltaire Blonde; Theakston Old Peculier; Wharfedale Blonde; 3 changing beers (sourced regionally; often Dark Horse) ⊞

Dating from 1548, this multi-roomed Dales free house has stone-flagged floors, oak beams and gas lighting. The main bar features an original Yorkshire range while the cosy taproom has an open fire and ring the bull. A snug behind the bar leads to the cruck barn, added in 2006 and built

using traditional techniques, with its minstrels' gallery and large open fireplace. This can be hired for functions. Guest beers are served in summer and usually include a dark beer. Q⦵⌖❶A♣❶P☐(74)❀❖

Arncliffe

Falcon Inn ⓛ

BD23 5QE

✪ 12-3, 7-11 (closed Tue & Thu eve winter); 12-11 Fri & Sat; 12-10.30 Sun ☎ (01756) 770205 ⊕ thefalconinn.com

Timothy Taylor Boltmaker ⊞/Ⓖ**; 1 changing beer (sourced locally)** ⊞

Unspoilt traditional Dales pub-cum-hotel nestled next to the village green and the original Woolpack in Emmerdale Farm. Eschewing modern gimmickry, the last significant changes to the pub interior took place in the 1950s. Timothy Taylor Boltmaker is served from the jug or via a recently installed handpump if you wish. A second handpump offers a changing guest beer from a local brewery. Loved by visitors from near and far, the pub is also well supported by Dales folk. Q⦵⌖🛏❶❀❖

Askrigg

King's Arms ⓛ

Main Street, DL8 3HQ

✪ 11-11.30 (midnight Fri & Sat) ☎ (01969) 650113 ⊕ kingsarmsaskrigg.co.uk

Black Sheep Best Bitter; Theakston Best Bitter; house beer (by Yorkshire Dales); 1 changing beer (sourced locally) ⊞

Historic multi-roomed free house of great character, which starred as the Drover's Arms in TV's All Creatures Great and Small. A painting of the local friendly society and a huge open fireplace dominate the stone-flagged bar, with separate dining room and restaurant, a vaulted games room to the rear and a small outdoor courtyard. No keg beer is sold, and three house beers (one regularly changing) are from the Yorkshire Dales Brewery, a few hundred yards away. ⦵⌖🛏❀❖

Aysgarth

Aysgarth Falls Hotel

DL8 3SR

✪ 11-11 ☎ (01969) 663228 ⊕ aysgarthfallshotel.com

Black Sheep Best Bitter; Theakston Old Peculier; 3 changing beers (sourced regionally) ⊞

Imposing hotel on the main A684 a few hundred yards above the famous torrent of Aysgarth Falls. Completely refurbished in 2013 and renamed (it was formerly the Palmer Flatt Hotel), the public bar here serves up to five real ales from local and regional brewers, and the hotel has its own fishing stretch on the River Ure and a campsite to the rear. Q⦵⌖🛏❶&A♣P☐❀❖

George & Dragon ⓛ

DL8 3AD (on main A684 between Hawes and Leyburn)

✪ 11-midnight ☎ (01969) 663358 ⊕ georgeanddragonaysgarth.co.uk

Black Sheep Best Bitter; Theakston Best Bitter; house beer (by Yorkshire Dales); 1 changing beer (sourced locally) ⊞

Less than a mile from the famous Aysgarth Falls on the River Ure, this 17th-century coaching inn is surrounded by stunning Dales countryside. It caters for drinkers in its cosy wood-panelled bar which

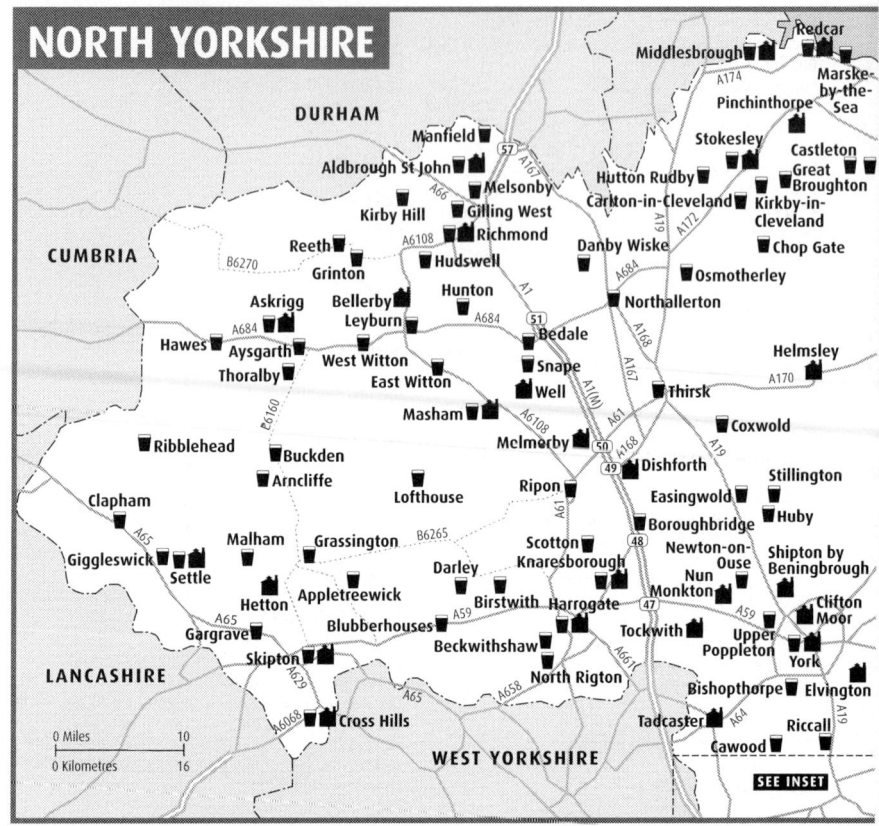

NORTH YORKSHIRE

DURHAM

CUMBRIA

Redcar
Middlesbrough
Marske-by-the-Sea
Pinchinthorpe
Manfield 57
Aldbrough St John
Melsonby
Kirby Hill
Gilling West
Richmond
Reeth
Hudswell
Grinton
Askrigg
Bellerby
Leyburn
Hawes
Aysgarth
Thoralby
West Witton
East Witton
Masham
Ribblehead
Buckden
Arncliffe
Clapham
Gigglewick
Settle
Malham
Grassington
Hetton
Appletreewick
Gargrave
Blubberhouses
Skipton
LANCASHIRE
Cross Hills
WEST YORKSHIRE

Stokesley
Hutton Rudby
Carlton-in-Cleveland
Danby Wiske
Hunton
Bedale
Snape
Well
Melmerby
Lofthouse
Ripon
Scotton
Knaresborough
Darley
Birstwith
Harrogate
Beckwithshaw
North Rigton
Tadcaster
Cawood

Castleton
Great Broughton
Kirkby-in-Cleveland
Chop Gate
Osmotherley
Northallerton
Helmsley
Thirsk
Coxwold
Stillington
Dishforth
Easingwold
Huby
Boroughbridge
Newton-on-Ouse
Shipton by Beningbrough
Nun Monkton
Tockwith
Upper Poppleton
Clifton Moor
York
Bishopthorpe
Elvington
Riccall

0 Miles 10
0 Kilometres 16

SEE INSET

serves up to five real ales, usually including two from the local Yorkshire Dales Brewery. For diners there is a separate restaurant, and en-suite accommodation is offered. An outside drinking area has thatched umbrellas and great views.
Q ☕ 🍴 ◑ ♠ P ☐ 🐾 ✿ 🐕 ♠

Henderson's Bistro 🅛
Westholme Estate, DL8 3SP SE016881
☀ 11-11; 11-10.30 Sun ☎ (01969) 663268
⊕ westholme-estate.co.uk
Black Sheep Best Bitter; 2 changing beers (sourced locally; often Yorkshire Dales) Ⓗ
Situated on a secluded development of 55 eco-lodges in beautiful surroundings just off the main A684, in what was formerly a caravan park and campsite, Henderson's opened in 2009 following a conversion from the campsite reception and bar. It has modern decor and combines a pleasant public bar with a dining area. Henderson's house beer is supplied by the Yorkshire Dales Brewery.
Q ☕ 🍴 ◑ & P 🐾 ✿ 🐕 ♠

Beck Hole

Birch Hall Inn ★ 🅛
YO22 5LE (700yds N of Goathland)
☀ 11-11 ☎ (01947) 896245 ⊕ beckhole.info
Black Sheep Best Bitter; North Yorkshire Beckwatter; 1 changing beer (sourced nationally) Ⓗ
Unspoilt, family-run rural gem resting among a hamlet of nine cottages and run by the same licensee, an accomplished fine artist, for 36 years.

A winner of multiple CAMRA awards, including branch Pub of the Year, it comprises the Big and the Small bars, which sandwich a sweet shop. Outdoor drinking facilities overlook the Murk Esk. The house beer, Beckwatter, is brewed organically by North Yorkshire. Sandwiches, pies, beer cake and traditional sweets are always available. Opening hours change during winter.
Q ☕ 🌳 & ≈ (Goathland) ♠ 🐕 ✿

Beckwithshaw

Smith's Arms 🅛 ✅
Church Row, HG3 1QW
☀ 11-11; 12-10 Sun ☎ (01423) 504871
Black Sheep Best Bitter; Greene King IPA; 2 changing beers Ⓗ
A Chef & Brewer restaurant-cum-pub in an 18th-century inn that, as the name suggests, was formerly a blacksmith's forge. Situated in a quiet hamlet to the south-west of Harrogate, the pub comprises an L-shaped bar area and a separate restaurant. An excellent menu with many seasonal dishes is served throughout the day in both the restaurant and bar. The five handpumps deliver two permanent beers and three widely sourced guest ales. Q ☕ 🌳 ◑ & 🐕 P 🐾 ✿ ♠

Bedale

Green Dragon ✅
16 Market Place, DL8 1EQ

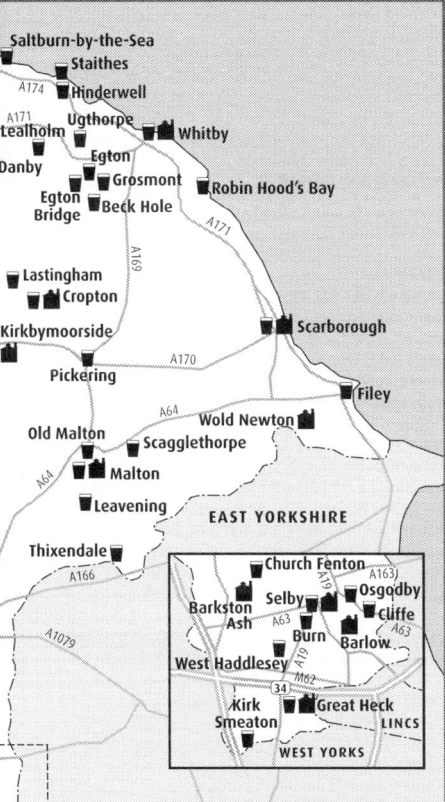

Bishopthorpe

Ebor

46 Main Street, YO23 2RB

⚙ 11-midnight; 12-midnight Sun ☎ (01904) 706190

Samuel Smith Old Brewery Bitter Ⓗ

Officially haunted and with 16th-century origins, this is uniquely the only tenanted Sam Smith's property. Landlord of 35 years, Gordon Watkins, provides a welcoming ambience, well-kept Old Brewery Bitter, and an extensive, home-cooked, hearty menu (with fresh Whitby fish a speciality and vegetarian options) each lunchtime and evening (not Sun). The Ebor is at the heart of the local community, with two separate bars, a family atmosphere and a large beer garden at the rear – children and dogs welcome.

Q ☎ ❀ ◖ ⅃ ⅃ ♣ P ♬ (11) ❀ ☞

Marcia Ⓛ ✪

29 Main Street, YO23 2RA

⚙ 11-midnight; 12-11 Sun ☎ (01904) 706185

⊕ themarciayork.co.uk

Leeds Pale; Ossett Yorkshire Blonde; Rooster's Yankee; Timothy Taylor Landlord; 2 changing beers (sourced locally; often Rudgate, Treboom, York) Ⓗ

Welcoming village local benefitting from a refurbishment in 2013. The landlord is passionate about real ale; six handpumps offer four permanent real ales, mainly LocAle, plus two changing beers. A good range of food is served every day in the bar or large restaurant/ conservatory. A summer beer and cider festival is held in the large rear garden, which has a children's play area. With a friendly atmosphere, there is a weekly quiz night plus regular cheese and wine tasting evenings and occasional live music. Q ☎ ❀ ◖ ⅃ ⅃ ♣ P ♬ (11) ❀ ☞

Blubberhouses

Hopper Lane Hotel

Skipton Road, LS21 2NZ

⚙ 12-11; 12-10.30 Sun; closed Mon ☎ (01943) 880010

⊕ hopperlanehotel.co.uk

Tetley Bitter; 2 changing beers (often Timothy Taylor) Ⓗ

A family-owned establishment on the main A59 Harrogate to Skipton road above Fewston reservoir. Double fronted and stone built, the original three front rooms are pleasantly decorated and furnished; beyond are dining areas set out with tables and chairs. The front rooms have open fires, and the original stone flags remain by the front door. The lounge is furnished with leather settees and chairs and features an old glass-covered well. ☎ ❀ ◖ ⅃ ♣ P ❀

Boroughbridge

Black Bull Inn

6 St James Square, YO51 9AR

⚙ 11-midnight; 12-11 Sun ☎ (01423) 322413

⊕ blackbullboroughbridge.co.uk

John Smith's Bitter; Timothy Taylor Boltmaker; 1 changing beer Ⓗ

Nestling in a corner of the market square, this 13th-century inn is immaculately kept and comfortably furnished, and is popular with locals and tourists alike. A Grade II-listed gem, it has a resident ghost. Three drinking and dining areas include a small cosy snug and a larger bar with open fires and good-value beers. A wide range of

⚙ 11.30-midnight (1am Fri & Sat); 11.30-11 Sun

☎ (01677) 425246

Ringwood Best Bitter, Boondoggle; 2 changing beers (often Marston's) Ⓗ

A comfortable bar on the cobbled High Street of the gateway to the Dales. Up to four beers are on offer, all from the Marston's group. There is live music every Friday night in the front bar, while a conservatory to the rear forms a lounge and dining area. A few hundred yards away, the Wensleydale Railway's Bedale station offers regular heritage trains along the picturesque dale.

☎ ❀ ◖ ⅃ ≈ ♣ ♬ ❀ ☞

Birstwith

Station Hotel ✪

Station Road, HG3 3AG

⚙ 10.30-11; 12-midnight Sat; 12-10 Sun ☎ (01423) 770254

⊕ station-hotel.net

Black Sheep Golden Sheep; Copper Dragon Best Bitter; 2 changing beers Ⓗ

This former station hotel has undergone a high-quality refurbishment and is now a popular drinking and dining pub. It has three open-plan bar spaces and a separate dining area at the rear. There is a large beer garden outside. Five letting rooms are available, one adapted for disabled customers. The pub is noted for its locally sourced food, served all day. The guest beers are usually from local Yorkshire breweries.

☎ ❀ ◖ ⅃ ⅃ P ♬ (24) ❀ ☞

bar meals is available and there is a separate restaurant. A local CAMRA Pub of the Year.
Q⇔◑Ⓐ♣P🚌(142,143)🐾📶

Buckden

Buck Inn L

BD23 5JA

⏲ 12-11 (10.30 Sun) summer; 12-10.30 (11.30 Fri; 11 Sat) winter ☎ (01756) 761401 🌐 buckinnbuckden.co.uk

Theakston Best Bitter, Old Peculier; 6 changing beers (sourced nationally; often Naylor's, Theakston, Wharfedale) H

On the Dales Way National Trail, this Georgian coaching inn sits below Buckden Pike among the stunning scenery of Upper Wharfedale. The main room is split between a stone-flagged bar area and a large comfortable lounge, divided into two distinct areas, with roaring fires in winter. The outside seating area offers a pleasant view of the valley. May close for a short break in early January – check before travelling.
🐴❀⇔◑♣P🚌(72,874)🐾📶

Burn

Wheatsheaf L

Main Road, YO8 8LJ

⏲ 12-11 (midnight Fri & Sat) ☎ (01757) 270614
🌐 wheatsheafburn.co.uk

Copper Dragon Best Bitter; Timothy Taylor Boltmaker; 4 changing beers H

Traditional country pub serving a varied range of guest beers, mainly from Yorkshire breweries. A narrow entrance leads to the bar, a small room to the left and a spacious lounge with an open fire to the right. There is a collection of artefacts from bygone days and memorabilia of 578 and 431 Squadrons stationed at Burn in WWII. Food is served (lunchtimes and Wed-Sat eve). Regular beer festivals, a popular Sunday quiz night and occasional live entertainment take place.
Q❀◑♣P🚌(150,405)🐾

Carlton-in-Cleveland

Blackwell Ox Inn L

TS9 7DJ (800yds E of A172)

⏲ 11-11 ☎ (01642) 712287 🌐 blackwellox.co.uk

Jennings Cumberland Ale; Ringwood Boondoggle; Rooster's Wild Mule; 1 changing beer (sourced nationally) H

Set in a beautiful area on the edge of the North York Moors, with the same licensee for 28 years, this popular multi-roomed village inn is as renowned for its fine beers as it is for its Thai food. Look out for lunchtime and early doors offers, as well as the monthly Monday winter buffets. Four handpumps provide an eclectic range of beer styles. The garden has an extensive children's play area. Q🐴❀◑P🚌(89)

Castleton

Downe Arms 🏆 L ✔

3 High Street, YO21 2EE

⏲ 12-midnight; 12-11 Sun ☎ (01287) 660223
🌐 thedownearms.co.uk

Black Sheep Best Bitter; Camerons Strongarm; 2 changing beers (sourced nationally) H

Overlooking the Esk Valley, this is a family-run country inn under the stewardship of enthusiastic members who serve two regular and two guest beers. Lunchtime and early doors mid-week beat-the-clock specials are available from the menu. The pub features top-class darts exhibitions and also supports charitable causes. Pleasant days are enhanced by superb views over the North York Moors from the south-facing garden. There are four letting bedrooms. Check winter opening hours.
🐴❀⇔◑♿🚆🍎P🚌🐾📶

Cawood

Ferry L

2 King Street, YO8 3TL

⏲ 4-8 Mon; 4-11 Tue; 12-11 (1am Fri & Sat); 10-10 Sun
☎ (01757) 268515 🌐 ferryinncawood.com

Leeds Pale; Timothy Taylor Landlord; 3 changing beers (sourced regionally; often Bradfield, Theakston, Wold Top) H

Wooden-beamed 16th-century inn on the river in this historic village. Cosy, with open fires and numerous rooms, there is a real air of history to the pub. Outside, a pleasant terrace and beer garden are home to Ferry Fest in August, where local crafts, food and beer are celebrated. Five handpumps on the bar provide mainly regional brews and real cider is available. Good food is served daily (no food Mon). 🐴❀◑♿♣P🚌(42)🐾

REAL ALE BREWERIES

BAD Dishforth
Barkston Barkston Ash (brewing suspended)
Black Sheep Masham
Brass Castle Malton
Brown Cow Barlow
Captain Cook 🛢 Stokesley
Copper Dragon Skipton
Daleside Harrogate
Dark Horse Hetton
Great Heck Great Heck
Great Yorkshire 🛢 Cropton
Hambleton Melmerby
Harrogate Harrogate
Helmsley Helmsley
Hop Studio Elvington
Jolly Sailor Selby
Little Brew Clifton Moor
Mithril Aldbrough St John
Naylor's Cross Hills
North Riding (Brewery) Scarborough
North Riding (Brewpub) 🛢 Scarborough
North Yorkshire Pinchinthorpe
Pennine Well
Redscar 🛢 Redcar
Richmond Richmond
Rooster's Knaresborough
Rudgate Tockwith
Ryedale Cross Hills
Samuel Smith Tadcaster
Scarborough Scarborough
Settle Settle
Theakston Masham
Three Peaks Settle
Treboom Shipton-by-Beningbrough
Truefitt Middlesbrough
Wainstones Stokesley
Wensleydale Bellerby
Whitby Whitby
Wold Top Wold Newton
York York
Yorkshire Dales Brewing Co Ltd Askrigg
Yorkshire Heart Ltd Nun Monkton

Chop Gate

Buck Inn Ⓛ

Chop Gate, TS9 7JL (on B1257, between Stokesley and Helmsley)
⏰ 12 (5 Mon-Wed)-9 ☎ (01642) 778334
⏣ the-buck-inn.co.uk
3 changing beers (sourced nationally) Ⓗ
Set amid a walkers' paradise, in the centre of the North York Moors, this picturesque family-run village pub offers a truly Yorkshire experience with a Teutonic twist. Three locally sourced beers, including house brews from Wainstones, and seven draught German lagers, brewed under the 501-year-old German purity law, are served together with real home-made food, half-Yorkshire, half-German. There are six en-suite bedrooms, some designated dog-friendly, while free camping is offered to those campers who also choose to dine.
Q ➰ ☸ 🛏 ◑ ▲ ♣ ♠ 🐾 🛜

Church Fenton

Fenton Flyer Ⓛ ✅

Main Street, LS24 9RF
⏰ 5-11 (midnight Fri); 12-midnight Sat; 12-10.30 Sun
☎ (01937) 558137 ⏣ thefentonflyer.com
Black Sheep Best Bitter; 4 changing beers (sourced regionally; often Hambleton, Ilkley, Ossett) Ⓗ
Friendly village pub with pictures and memorabilia commemorating the nearby WWII airbase, now closed. The pub is in the LocAle scheme with beers, always in good condition, chosen from the SIBA list. There is live music on the first Friday of each month, a monthly Saturday disco with karaoke, and a quiz night on Wednesday which raises money for local charities. It also has a newly opened games room with pool table, Sky Sports TV and darts.
➰ ☸ ◑ ♣ ♠ 🚍 (492) 🛜

Clapham

Clapham Café Bunk & Bar Ⓛ

Church Avenue, LA2 8EQ
⏰ 10-6 (7 Fri & Sat); closed Mon & Tue ☎ (015242) 51144
⏣ claphambunk.com
3 changing beers (often Bowland, Settle, Three Peaks) Ⓗ
In the heart of a major tourist village, this old manor house, dating back to circa 1620, has a café and bar with bare floorboards, bench seats and some books. A huge fireplace (dated 1701) holds a wood-burning stove. Do not overlook the bottled beers and ciders. The café and the bar are in separate but connected rooms. There is also a bunkhouse. Next to the National Park car park.
☸ 🛏 ◑ ▲ ♣ 🚍 (581) 🐾 🛜

Cliffe

New Inn Ⓛ

York Road, YO8 6NN
⏰ 2-11; 12-midnight Fri & Sat; 12-10.30 Sun
☎ (01757) 633888 ⏣ newinncliffe.co.uk/cms
John Smith's Bitter; 5 changing beers (sourced regionally; often Abbeydale, Half Moon, Mallinson's) Ⓗ
Now established as a superb example of how a village local can also be a real ale emporium, this award-winning pub is a delight to visit. Comfortable, two-roomed and serving five guest beers – almost always local and certainly from

Yorkshire – this is a key stop-off point from the nearby A63. Blazing log fires for cosy winter drinking are complemented by a shady beer garden for summer. An annual beer festival is held every August, ramping up the number of ales, alongside live local music and a traditional hog roast. ➰ ☸ ♣ ▲ ♣ 🚍 🛜

Coxwold

Fauconberg Arms Ⓛ

YO61 4AD (from A19, at crossroads in centre of Coxwold village turn left and pub is on right)
⏰ 11-11 ☎ (01347) 868214 ⏣ fauconbergarms.com
John Smith's Bitter; Theakston Best Bitter; 2 changing beers (sourced locally; often Hambleton, Helmsley, Wold Top) Ⓗ
A 17th-century country inn, close to Shandy Hall and Newburgh Priory, with a cosy beamed front bar, a rear bar with pool table, and homely log fires in both bars. It has a separate dining room and a good reputation for both food and accommodation. Guest beers are usually LocAles. In summer, Husthwaite cider is served from a handpump. There are regular quizzes and other events, including music nights with live bands. It is a true village local, but welcomes all.
Q ➰ ☸ 🛏 ◑ ▲ ♣ 🚍 (31X) 🐾 🛜

Cropton

New Inn Ⓛ

Cropton Lane, YO18 8HH
⏰ 11-11 (midnight Fri & Sat) ☎ (01751) 417330
⏣ newinncropton.co.uk
Great Yorkshire Pale, Classic, Golden; 3 changing beers (sourced locally; often Great Yorkshire) Ⓗ
A family-run pub on the edge of the North Yorkshire Moors National Park, the New Inn is the tap for the Great Yorkshire Brewery (formerly Cropton Brewery). A perfect base for walking and cycling, it offers good food in the bars, conservatory or restaurant, and B&B or camping accommodation. Many real ales are on the bar, and a legendary beer festival takes place every November. Other festivals and music events are put on during the year. A positive and chatty pub, where ramblers and dogs are welcome.
Q ➰ ☸ 🛏 ◑ ⅄ ▲ ♣ 🚍 🐾 🛜

Cross Hills

Gallagher's Ale House

1-3 East Keltus, BD20 8TD
⏰ 3-10; 1-11 Fri; 12-11 Sat; 12-10 Sun; closed Mon & Tue ☎ 07834 456134
5 changing beers (sourced nationally) Ⓗ
Popular new micropub, opened in December 2015 by the owners of Skipton's Beer Engine, in what used to be Gallagher's bookmakers. The five changing beers usually include a dark ale, a pale bitter and a strong or speciality beer. No electronic music or TV disturbs the conversation. Parking is available adjacent to the Co-op store round the corner. The phone number given is shared with the Beer Engine. Q ♣ 🚍 (25,66) 🐾

Naylor's Beer Emporium Ⓛ

Midland Mills Station Road, BD20 7DT (in industrial estate on right over railway bridge from Cross Hills)
⏰ 5-10; 3-11 Fri & Sat; closed Sun-Tue ☎ (01535) 637451
⏣ naylorsbrewery.co.uk

Naylor's Aire Valley Bitter, Pinnacle Blonde; 3 changing beers (sourced locally) Ⓗ
In spring 2015, the Emporium, Naylor's brewery tap, expanded upstairs to include the Beer Belly Kitchen serving American diner-style food. The emphasis downstairs is on good company, friendly chatter and the appreciation of good beer. In fine weather customers spill out into the yard outside. The five Naylor's cask beers are all reasonably priced – the three guests are from the brewery's seasonal range and one is usually dark. Brewery souvenir merchandise and bottled beers can also be purchased. Q❀❱♿Ⓟ🚆(66)😺🍺📶

Danby

Duke of Wellington Ⓛ

West Lane, YO21 2LY (300yds N of railway station)
✪ 12-2.30 (not Mon), 7-11; 12-11 Fri & Sat; 12-2.30, 7-10.30 Sun ☎ (01287) 660351 ⊕ dukeofwellingtondanby.co.uk
Daleside Bitter; Copper Dragon Scotts 1816; 1 changing beer (sourced nationally) Ⓗ
This 18th-century inn, and recent CAMRA branch Pub of the Year, is set in idyllic National Park countryside, close to the popular visitor centre and equally popular bakery. It was used as a recruiting post during the Napoleonic Wars. A cast-iron plaque of the first Duke, unearthed during restorations, hangs above the fireplace. All the beers are from Yorkshire, while the menu offers traditional British home-cooked meals at their best, using locally sourced produce. Cider and perry are served Easter-October. Q❧❀⊨◑≈♣🍺🐾😺

Danby Wiske

White Swan Ⓛ

DL7 0NQ (approx 3 miles N of Northallerton off A167)
✪ 12-11 ☎ (01609) 775131
⊕ thewhiteswandanbywiske.co.uk
4 changing beers (sourced locally) Ⓗ
A haven for coast-to-coast walkers with its accommodation and camping, this CAMRA award-winning village hostelry champions local beers. The attractive single-room bar has wood-burning stoves and is home to the local sword dancers. Four changing beers usually include at least one from Wall's of Northallerton, plus Gwynt y Ddraig Happy Daze cider and Westons Perry. Lunchtime snacks and evening meals are available April-October (booking advised), using locally sourced produce. Hours vary at quiet times; between October and March it is closed afternoons, weekday lunchtimes and all day Tuesdays. Q❧❀⊨◑Å♣🍺Ⓟ😺📶

Darley

Wellington Inn

Darley Carr, HG3 2QQ (on B6451 W of village)
✪ 12-11 (midnight Fri & Sat); 12-10.30 Sun
☎ (01423) 780362 ⊕ wellington-inn.co.uk
Black Sheep Ale; Copper Dragon Golden Pippin; Tetley Bitter; Timothy Taylor Landlord Ⓗ
Much-extended popular stone-built pub on the edge of Nidderdale. It is a food-led establishment but with a range of excellent ales. The original building houses a comfortable bar with pool table, and the long extension provides more space, essentially for diners, in a baronial hall-styled room; the fireplace is especially magnificent. Behind is a dining room with spectacular views across Nidderdale. Q❧❀⊨◑♣Ⓟ🚆(24)😺📶

Easingwold

George Hotel Ⓛ ✅

Market Place, YO61 3AD
✪ 11-11 ☎ (01347) 821698 ⊕ the-george-hotel.co.uk
Black Sheep Best Bitter; Timothy Taylor Landlord; 1 changing beer (sourced regionally) Ⓗ
A recorded pub since 1790, this country hotel befits one of the best unspoilt Georgian small towns in the country. Food and accommodation are always of a high standard but it is the beer (with guests from lesser known North Yorkshire breweries) that plays star role. Smart, traditional and always welcoming – Georgian at its best.
Q❧❀⊨◑♿🚆

East Witton

Cover Bridge Inn Ⓛ

DL8 4SQ (½ mile N of village on A6108)
✪ 11-midnight; 12-11.30 Sun ☎ (01969) 623250
⊕ thecoverbridgeinn.co.uk
Black Sheep Best Bitter; John Smith's Bitter; Theakston Best Bitter, Old Peculier; Timothy Taylor Boltmaker; 3 changing beers (sourced locally) Ⓗ
A splendidly traditional Dales inn where numerous CAMRA awards tell their tale. The River Cover runs along the foot of the attractive garden and play area, near its confluence with the River Ure. Fathom out the door latch and enjoy a warm welcome in the unspoilt public bar with its giant hearth, the tiny lounge or pleasant beer garden. Eight handpumps dispense locally brewed beers and guests from further afield; there are two real ciders and perry. Q❧❀⊨◑♿♣🍺Ⓟ🚆(159)😺📶

Egton

Wheatsheaf Inn Ⓛ

YO21 1TZ
✪ 11.30-2.45, 5.30-11; 11.30-11 Sat & Sun; closed Mon
☎ (01947) 895271 ⊕ wheatsheafegton.com
Black Sheep Best Bitter; Timothy Taylor Landlord; 2 changing beers (sourced nationally) Ⓗ
Winner of many CAMRA awards, this Grade II-listed 19th-century pub serves four Yorkshire beers. It is now in its 17th year in the Guide, and remains under the stewardship of a licensee with over 30 years of continuous Guide recognition. Church pews, collectables from auctions and a roaring range add to the ambience. The grassy area to the front and boules to the rear are ideal for summer drinking. The renowned first-class restaurant always features local meat, fish and game.
Q❀⊨◑♿♣Ⓟ🚆(99)😺

Egton Bridge

Horseshoe Hotel Ⓛ

YO21 1XE
✪ 11.30-3, 6-11; 12-11 Sun ☎ (01947) 895245
⊕ egtonbridgehotel.co.uk
Theakston Best Bitter; 3 changing beers (sourced nationally) Ⓗ
Secluded 18th-century gem located in a horseshoe-shaped hollow and accessed either by road, from the railway station, or by walking over the stepping stones across the River Esk. Old-fashioned settles, a large fire and angling memorabilia adorn the bar, while picnic tables on a large raised grassy bank make outdoor drinking a pleasure. Four

handpumps (three in winter) feature some interesting beers. The menu and specials board offer locally sourced, good value food. Accommodation is in six letting bedrooms. Q ☺ ❀ ⌂ ◑ ≒ ♣ P ❒ (99) ⚘

Filey

Bonhommes' Bar

Royal Crescent Court, The Crescent, YO14 9JH
✪ 11-midnight (1am Fri & Sat) ☎ (01723) 515325
⊕ bonhommesbar.co.uk
5 changing beers (sourced nationally; often Wentworth) ⊞
Just off the fine Victorian Royal Crescent Hotel complex, the bar's name celebrates John Paul Jones, father of the American Navy. His ship, the Bonhomme Richard, was involved in a battle off nearby Flamborough Head during the War of Independence. Five handpumps serve rotating guests. Food is served daily (except Tue). A quiz is held on Thursday evening and Saturday afternoon each week. Local CAMRA Rural Pub of the Year runner-up 2015. ☺ ◑ ▲ ≒ ♣ ● ❒ (121) ⚘ 🔊

Star Inn ⚖

23 Mitford Street, YO14 9DX
✪ 12-midnight (1am Fri & Sat) ☎ (01723) 512031
⊕ thestarfiley.co.uk
Black Sheep Ale; Theakston Best Bitter; 2 changing beers (sourced nationally) ⊞
The Star Inn is just off Filey town centre and has a large main room and separate restaurant/function room. Two regular beers and two rotating guests are offered. Freshly cooked meals are served lunchtimes and evenings (no food Mon). Live entertainment features at weekends. Pub teams participate in a local pool league. Smokers are catered for at both the front and rear of the building, while parking is provided behind the pub. ☺ ❀ ◑ ♿ ≒ ♣ P ❒ (121) 🔊

Gargrave

Masons Arms 🄻

Marton Road, BD23 3NL
✪ 12-midnight (11 Wed) ☎ (01756) 749304
⊕ masonsarmsgargrave.co.uk
Tetley Bitter; Thwaites Wainwright; Timothy Taylor Landlord; 1 changing beer ⊞
This attractive, traditional village pub is in a quiet residential location opposite St Andrew's Church, between the railway station and the River Aire. With its low oak-beamed ceilings adorned with horse brasses, it offers a comfortable and relaxing environment both for drinkers and diners. Accommodation is in six en-suite rooms alongside the pub, making it a great base for exploring the Leeds-Liverpool canal, Malhamdale and the nearby market towns of Skipton and Settle. Lockable cycle storage is available for residents. Q ☺ ❀ ⌂ ◑ ▲ ≒ ♣ ● P ❒ ⚘ 🔊

Giggleswick

Hart's Head Hotel 🄻

Belle Hill, BD24 0BA (on B6480 1 mile N of Settle)
✪ 4 (12 Tue-Fri)-11; 11.30-11 Sat; 12-11 Sun summer; 4 (12 Fri; 11.30 Sat)-11; 12-11 Sun winter ☎ (01729) 822086
⊕ hartsheadhotel.co.uk
Tetley Bitter; 4 changing beers (sourced regionally; often Black Sheep, Dent, Kirkby Lonsdale) ⊞

Open-plan 18th-century coaching inn catering for a wide clientele. The bar separates the comfortable lounge from the area where pub games are played and sport is shown on TV. There is a full-sized snooker table in the cellar. Freshly prepared meals from a varied menu are served in the adjacent dining room. The sloping beer garden at the rear is a great place to soak up the sun. A good selection of gins and malt whiskies is available. ☺ ❀ ⌂ ◑ ♿ ▲ ≒ ♣ P ❒ (581) ⚘ 🔊

Gilling West

White Swan 🄻

51 High Street, DL10 5JG (1 mile W of Scotch Corner)
✪ 12 (4 Tue & Wed)-11 ☎ (01748) 825122
⊕ thewhiteswan.co
4 changing beers ⊞
A historic coaching inn with open fires, slate floor and a courtyard garden blending the modern with the traditional, now with three en-suite rooms. Up to four real ales from local microbreweries are dispensed, including a house beer from Mithril. A flagship burger and steak menu showcases the best of the region's produce, featuring 35-day aged beef, local game, artisan bakers and cheesemakers. Quiz nights are fortnightly, there are regular music nights, plus an annual autumnal beer fest. A modern pool and E-sports room is across the courtyard. Q ☺ ❀ ⌂ ◑ ▲ ♣ P ❒ (29) ⚘ 🔊

Grassington

Foresters Arms 🄻 ⚖

20 Main Street, BD23 5AA
✪ 11-midnight (1am Fri & Sat) ☎ (01756) 752349
⊕ forestersarmsgrassington.co.uk
Black Sheep Best Bitter; Riggwelter; Tetley Mild, Bitter; 2 changing beers (sourced locally; often Timothy Taylor, Wharfedale) ⊞
Just off the cobbled town square, the Foresters is a lively pub popular with locals and visitors alike. The main bar and pool/TV area are to the left and further seating to the right leads to a separate dining room. Accommodation is in seven en-suite rooms, and coarse and fly-fishing permits for the local River Wharfe can be bought at the pub. Quizzes are on Mondays. ❀ ⌂ ◑ ♣ ❒ (72,74) ⚘ 🔊

Great Broughton

Bay Horse 🄻

88 High Street, TS9 7HA (at S end of village)
✪ 11.30-3, 5.30-11; 11.30-11 Sat; 12-9 Sun
☎ (01642) 712319 ⊕ thebayhorse-greatbroughton.co.uk
Camerons Strongarm; Jennings Sneck Lifter; 2 changing beers (sourced nationally) ⊞
Everyone enjoys the welcoming hospitality offered by friendly bar staff at this spacious village country inn, situated at one of the northern entrances to the North York Moors. While the emphasis is on good-value, freshly prepared, home-cooked meals, drinkers are also especially well catered for. As well as the two regular beers the pub has been renowned for serving for many years, two changing beers, from the Marston's stable, are also now on the bar. Q ☺ ❀ ◑ P ❒ (89)

Great Heck

Bay Horse 🅛

Main Street, DN14 0BE (between Pontefract and Snaith)
☼ 3-9; 12-midnight Thu-Sat; 12-6 Sun ☎ (01977) 661121
🌐 bayhorsegreatheck.co.uk
Old Mill Traditional Bitter; 1 changing beer (sourced locally; often Old Mill) Ⓗ
In a quiet hamlet close to the Aire & Calder canal, this cosy hostelry is part of the Old Mill Brewery estate. Comprising three former cottages, the pub features Old Mill seasonal beers every month throughout the year. Internally there are several distinct areas, with dining rooms at each end and a central lounge bar with a log-burning fire. Popular with diners, food is served Monday to Saturday evenings and Sunday lunchtime. Quiz night is every Thursday. Q🕿😾🕭🄿🏵️ 🛜

Grinton

Bridge Inn

DL11 6HH (on B6270, 1 mile E of Reeth)
☼ 12-midnight; 12-11 Sun ☎ (01748) 884224
🌐 bridgeinn-grinton.co.uk
Jennings Cumberland Ale; Thwaites Wainwright; 3 changing beers (sourced nationally; often Marston's) Ⓗ
Friendly and well-run country inn close to the River Swale, set beneath the towering hills of Fremington Edge and Harkerside. Its comfortable lounge, wood-panelled bar and two restaurant rooms are a haven for walkers and cyclists on the Coast-to-Coast and Inn Way walks and the Dales Cycle Way. Fresh, home-made food is served all day, along with two or three guest beers from the Marston's range. Q🕿😾🛏️🄳🕭🄰♣🄿🖃🏵️ 🛜

Grosmont

Crossing Club 🅛

Co-operative Building, Front Street, YO22 5QE (opp NYMR car park – ring front door bell)
☼ 8-11 ☎ 07766 197744
5 changing beers (sourced nationally) Ⓗ
Set amid beautiful scenery in the Esk Valley, this CAMRA branch 2016 Club of the Year is located directly opposite the NYMR/Esk Valley railway stations in what was the village's Co-operative store's upstairs delivery bay. Converted by dedicated villagers into a railway-themed private members' club 18 years ago, a warm welcome always awaits CAMRA members. For the railway enthusiast, both steam and diesel memorabilia adorn the walls. Q♣🛏️🏵️

Harrogate

10 Devonshire Place ♟

10 Devonshire Place, HG1 4AA
☼ 3-midnight; 12-midnight Fri-Sun ☎ (01423) 202356
🌐 10devonshireplace.com
Timothy Taylor Boltmaker; 8 changing beers Ⓗ
Restored and renovated in 2014, the original semicircular counter with its stained-glass canopy has been refurbished. Ten handpumps serve local cask ales and a cider. Flights of thirds are offered and a changing style of street food is available afternoons and evenings. To one side at the front is the bottle shop, with a stock of interesting bottled beers and wines which can be drunk on or off the premises. 😾🕭🥗🏵️ 🛜

Coach & Horses

16 West Park, HG1 1BJ
☼ 11-11; 12-10.30 Sun ☎ (01423) 561802
🌐 thecoachandhorses.net
Tetley Bitter; Timothy Taylor Landlord; 4 changing beers (often Daleside, Rooster's) Ⓗ
This community pub located by the Stray has snugs and alcoves all round it, creating a cosy atmosphere inside. Tables and chairs are provided outside for customers in summer, while window boxes create a spectacular display and add year-round colour. Guest beers are available. The pub serves excellent meals at lunchtime and holds reasonably priced themed evenings; many of these, together with a popular Sunday night quiz, have raised a considerable amount of money for a local children's hospice. Q🕭🥗🏵️ 🛜

Hales Bar 🅛 ✅

1-3 Crescent Road, HG1 2RS
☼ 12-midnight (1am Thu-Sat); 12-11.30 Sun
☎ (01423) 725570 🌐 halesbar.co.uk
Daleside Old Leg Over; Draught Bass; Robinsons Dizzy Blonde; Timothy Taylor Landlord; house beer (by Daleside); 1 changing beer (often Belhaven, Thwaites, Wells) Ⓗ
Harrogate's oldest pub and listed on CAMRA's Regional Inventory of Historic Pub Interiors, the lounge has a Victorian-style interior with original gas lighting over the bar; the separate snug is also used as a tea room. There are six handpumps, two serving a changing range of guest beers. Karaoke and occasional party nights are held. The pub is a rare outlet for Draught Bass and a house beer is supplied by Daleside. Food is available lunchtimes and evenings. 🕭👟⬇️🥗🖃🏵️ 🛜

Harrogate Tap

Station Parade, HG1 1TE
☼ 11-11; 10-midnight Fri & Sat ☎ (01423) 501644
🌐 harrogatetap.co.uk
11 changing beers (often Harrogate, Rooster's) Ⓗ
A redundant Victorian railway station refreshment room, closed for 30 years, has been given a new lease of life by the owners of the Tap group of station bars. Twelve handpumps serve a changing range of beers from brewers as diverse as Brass Castle, Harrogate Brewing Company and Rooster's. There is always a real cider. Wood panelling, tiled floors, leather and brass dominate the traditional decor in both the main bar and small snug. Q😾👟⬇️🥗🖃🏵️

Major Tom's Social

The Ginnel, HG1 2RB
☼ 11-11.30 (1am Fri & Sat)
4 changing beers Ⓗ
An unusual café bar housed upstairs in a former antiques emporium. It provides real ale, pizza, music and art in one fun package. Simply furnished and decorated in a mix of styles to suit the eclectic customers, the artwork on display is for sale. Four handpumps dispense a range of ales, usually including some from Rooster's, Kirkstall, and a variety of smaller breweries; it also has interesting bottles from the UK, US and Europe. 🕭⬇️♣🏵️

Old Bell Tavern ✅

6 Royal Parade, HG1 2SZ
☼ 12-11 (midnight Fri & Sat) ☎ (01423) 507930
Hawkshead Windermere Pale; Theakston Best Bitter; Timothy Taylor Boltmaker; 6 changing beers (often Okells, Rooster's) Ⓗ

The building became a pub in 1999 on the site of the Blue Bell Inn. There is a changing range of nine handpumps, six serving different guest beers, usually including one from Okells, a Rooster's and a dark beer. A real cider and a range of UK and foreign bottled beers complete the choice. The side room has a collection of Farrar's Toffee memorabilia and upstairs is a well-regarded restaurant. Q◑⇌●🐾ᯤ

Swan on the Stray ✔

17 Devonshire Place, HG1 4AA

⏲ 11-11; 12-10.30 Sun ☎ (01423) 524587

Daleside Blonde; 8 changing beers (often Black Sheep, Okells, Rooster's) Ⓗ

Formerly known as the Black Swan, this pub was extensively refurbished in a modern style, reopening in early 2010. Eight real ales are served with four changing regularly, most from Yorkshire brewers. A range of foreign beer is on draught, plus a real cider and an added selection in bottles. Allied to a good wine choice and excellent bar meals, the pub appeals to all age groups. There is a beer garden at the rear, and well-behaved children are welcome until 8pm. ❀◑♿⇌P🐾ᯤ

Winter Gardens ✔

4 Royal Baths, HG1 2RR

⏲ 7am-midnight (1am Thu; 2am Fri & Sat)

☎ (01423) 877010

Adnams Broadside; Greene King Abbot; Ruddles Best Bitter; Sharp's Doom Bar; 6 changing beers (sourced regionally; often Daleside) Ⓗ

Converted from part of the Royal Baths complex in 2002, this magnificent building has a large, spacious interior reached from the Parliament Street entrance by a sweeping double stone staircase. Wheelchair access is from the entrance in The Ginnel. In addition to the usual Wetherspoon's core range, a number of locally sourced guests are always available across three sets of handpumps. The pub can get busy due to its location near Harrogate's conference and exhibition centre. ❀◑♿⇌●ᯤ

Hawes

White Hart Country Inn 🄻

Main Street, DL8 3QL (on one-way system, westbound)

⏲ 11-11 ☎ (01969) 667214 🌐 whitehartcountryinn.co.uk

Theakston Best Bitter; Wensleydale Semerwater Summer Ale; 4 changing beers (sourced locally) Ⓗ

Comfortable free house on the town's short one-way system, stylishly refurbished in 2015. A large dining room is popular with visitors and a smaller bar features an attractive stone hearth and mock wood panelling, which works remarkably well. Guest beers are often from the local Yorkshire Dales, Pennine and Wall's breweries. Food is served daily 12-9pm (8pm midweek in winter), including beef and lamb from the family farm. 🛏◑♿▲♣🚌ᯤ

Hinderwell

Brown Cow

55 High Street, TS13 5ET

⏲ 11-midnight (1am Fri); 12-midnight Sun

☎ (01947) 840694

2 changing beers (sourced nationally) Ⓗ

Between the moors and the coast, and reminiscent of walking into someone's front parlour, this family-run pub has a strong local following, as well as attracting holidaying visitors. Two handpumps serve one lighter and one darker beer. The pub supports darts teams, charity nights and dominoes drives, with quiz night on Sunday. Children and dogs are welcome, while smokers are also especially well provided for. In addition to all-day dining, substantial bar snacks are sold. Accommodation is in four bedrooms.
Q❀🛏◑♿♣P🚆🚌(4)🐾

Huby

Mended Drum 🄻

Tollerton Road, YO61 1HT

⏲ 5 (4 Fri)-11; 12-midnight Sat; 12-11 Sun

☎ (01347) 810264

Black Sheep Best Bitter; 4 changing beers (sourced locally; often Atom, Bad, Brass Castle) Ⓗ

You need to make an effort to get to Huby, but once inside this pub it is well rewarded. Bright, lively and dedicated to real ale is a fitting description of both the pub and its staff. With a better beer range than many big city pubs (plus an excellent bottle range to take home if constrained by driving), there is never a dull moment – a destination pub, but what a destination!
❀◑♿▲♣●P🚌(X30)🐾ᯤ

Hudswell

George & Dragon 🏆 🄻

DL11 6BL

⏲ 11-3, 5-11; 11-11 Sat & Sun ☎ (01748) 518373

🌐 georgeanddragonhudswell.com

Copper Dragon Best Bitter; 4 changing beers (sourced locally) Ⓗ

At the heart of the village, this homely multi-roomed country inn has a large beer terrace offering fantastic panoramic views over the Swale Valley. Rescued and refurbished in 2010 after a successful community buy-out, it now offers its own library, shop, allotments and various other community facilities, as well as food and drink. Either Rudgate Ruby Mild or Wall's Northallerton Dark are always available, with other beers mostly from Yorkshire breweries.
Q❀◑▲♣●P🚌(32)🐾ᯤ

Hunton

Countryman's Inn 🄻 ✔

DL8 1PY

⏲ 6-11 (midnight Fri); 12-2.30, 6-midnight Sat; 12-11 Sun

☎ (01677) 450554 🌐 countrymansinn.co.uk

Black Sheep Best Bitter; Theakston Black Bull Bitter; 3 changing beers Ⓗ

A welcoming community free house, slightly off the beaten track but worth searching out. It survived a closure threat a few years ago following a lively campaign by villagers and is now thriving. The comfortable one-room interior has a separate dining area and offers a wide-ranging food menu along with guest beers, usually including LocAles such as Wall's and Wensleydale. A third guest is sold in the summer months.
Q❀🛏◑▲●P🚆🚌🐾ᯤ

Hutton Rudby

King's Head 🄻

36 North Side, TS15 0DA (at W end of village)

✪ 4-11.30; 12-midnight Fri-Sun ☎ (01642) 700342
Banks's Sunbeam; Camerons Strongarm; Jennings Cumberland Ale; 1 changing beer (sourced nationally) Ⓗ
Set in a beautiful village, this previous CAMRA branch award winner is a traditional locals' pub, set in a terrace of houses, where a friendly welcome is always assured. It comprises a comfortable and always-busy main bar, and a snug where children are permitted. Four handpumps include a guest beer from Marston's. Real fires, quiz night on Tuesday, a full menu on Wednesday and Friday, and live music on Saturday, all add to the experience. Outside is a smokers' paradise.
🛏❀➊♣🗑🖳(80)😺🛜

Kirby Hill

Shoulder of Mutton
Kirby Hill, DL11 7JH (2½ miles from A66)
✪ 12-2 (2.30 Sat), 5-11; 12-3, 5-11 Sun ☎ (01748) 822772
⊕ shoulderofmutton.net
Theakston Best Bitter; 3 changing beers Ⓗ
Ivy-fronted country hostelry in a beautiful hillside setting overlooking Lower Teesdale and the ruins of Ravensworth Castle. The pub has an open-front bar that links the lounge with a cosy restaurant to the rear. Three guest beers are chosen by the regulars. On the edge of the Yorkshire Dales, this is a popular venue for walkers. There are five en-suite bedrooms. Excellent food is served all week, although the bar area remains for drinkers.
Q🛏❀➊🚾➊P😺

Kirk Smeaton

Shoulder of Mutton
Main Street, WF8 3JY (follow signs from A1)
✪ 12-midnight; 11.30-midnight Sun ☎ (01977) 620348
Black Sheep Best Bitter; 1 changing beer (sourced regionally; often Theakston, Wharfe Bank) Ⓗ
Fine community pub comprising a spacious lounge and comfortable wood-panelled snug, both with a traditional open fireplace. A beer garden at the rear has a covered and heated shelter for smokers. Ample parking is available. Conveniently situated close to the River Went and the Brockadale nature reserve, it is popular with walkers and visitors alike, and offers a warm and friendly welcome to all. A quiz night is held every Tuesday.
🛏❀♣P🖳(409)😺🛜

Kirkby-in-Cleveland

Black Swan Ⓛ
Busby Lane, TS9 7AW (800yds W of B1257) NZ539060
✪ 12-midnight ☎ (01642) 712512
Black Sheep Best Bitter; Bradfield Farmers Blonde; Timothy Taylor Landlord; Wainstones Amber; 1 changing beer (sourced nationally) Ⓗ
Nestling at the foot of the North York Moors, at the crossroads of an ancient village, this warm and cosy free house, comprising a bar, lounge/restaurant and conservatory, affords a friendly and genuine welcome. Four regular beers, plus a house beer, Kirkby Blonde, brewed by Wainstones, and a guest beer, are served in a convivial atmosphere, where making conversation with the locals always seems a must. Bar snacks and a full menu, including daily specials, represent good value.
🛏❀➊🚹♣P🗑🖳(89)😺🛜

Knaresborough

Blind Jack's Ⓛ
19 Market Place, HG5 8AL
✪ 4 (5 Mon; 3 Fri; 12 Sat)-11; 12-10.30 Sun
☎ (01423) 869148
Bad Comfortably Numb; Black Sheep Best Bitter; 7 changing beers Ⓗ
A multi-roomed pub with bare brick walls, wooden floorboards and panelling. An award-winning ale house, it provides a focal point both for locals and for the many visitors who appreciate the excellent selection of ales, cosy ambience and lively banter. The beer range usually includes several from Bad Company Brewery. Listed in this Guide since 1993, Knaresborough Brewery, which was formerly on the premises, has moved to Bad Company's site at Dishforth and still produces occasional brews.
Q🚂🖳(1)😺

Cross Keys ✪
17 Cheapside, HG5 8AX
✪ 4-11; 12-midnight Fri & Sat; 12-11 Sun ☎ (01423) 863512
Jennings Bitter; Ossett Yorkshire Blonde, Big Red Bitter, Silver King; 2 changing beers (sourced regionally) Ⓗ
A former Tetley's house, refurbished by Ossett Brewery in its trademark style of stone-flagged floors, bare brick walls and stained glass. This traditional pub serves four regular beers and two guests, one of which is usually a dark beer or stout from either a microbrewery or from one of the other breweries within the Ossett company. Thursday is quiz night and a live band plays on most Saturday nights. Lunches are served on Sundays. ➊🚾🚂🖳(1)😺🛜

Half Moon Ⓛ
1 Abbey Road, HG5 8HY
✪ 5 (12 Sat)-11; 12-10.30 Sun ☎ (01423) 313461
4 changing beers (sourced regionally) Ⓗ
Small in size but big in atmosphere, this free house has been sympathetically restored to a high standard by its independent owners. Bare brick walls, reclaimed furniture and real fires give the pub a welcoming atmosphere. Four handpumps dispense a varying range of Yorkshire beers, one of which is usually from nearby Rooster's. A grazing menu of meat and cheese platters complements the beers. The pub hosts a team in the annual tug of war across the adjacent River Nidd.
🛏❀➊➊🚾♣🖳(56,57)😺🛜

Mitre Hotel ✪
4 Station Road, HG5 9AA (opp railway station)
✪ 12-11 ☎ (01423) 868948 ⊕ themitreinn.co.uk
Black Sheep Ale; Okells Manx Pale Ale; 6 changing beers (sourced regionally) Ⓗ
Ideally placed for the railway station, this Market Town Taverns pub serves eight ales, with several from Yorkshire breweries, including a pump dedicated to the town's own Rooster's Brewery. There is a good range of speciality bottled beers. Pumpclips adorn the walls of the modern split-level bar. There are side and downstairs function rooms, and a beer garden with views of the local church. Food is served daily and there is live music on Sunday evenings. 🛏❀🚾➊🚹➊🚂🖳(1)😺🛜

Lastingham

Blacksmiths Arms
Anserdale Lane, YO62 6TN

✪ 11.30-11.30 ☎ (01751) 417247
⊕ blacksmithslastingham.co.uk
Theakston Best Bitter; 2 changing beers (sourced regionally) Ⓗ
Pretty stone inn in a conservation village, opposite St Mary's Church famous for its 11th-century crypt. The interior comprises a cosy bar with York range lit in winter, a snug and two dining rooms. Excellent-quality food, including local game dishes, is served alongside interesting guest beers. A secluded beer garden is to the rear. This remote pub is popular with locals, walkers and shooting parties.
Q ➳ 🏮 ⛺ 🌣 ◑ ▶ ♨

Lealholm

Board Inn Ⓛ
Village Geen, YO21 2AJ
✪ 9am-midnight (2am Fri & Sat) ☎ (01947) 897279
⊕ theboardinn.com
3 changing beers (sourced nationally) Ⓗ
Overlooking the Esk, this family-run traditional 17th-century pub is at the centre of village life. Three beers, four ciders and 60 whiskies are served. It consists of a busy locals' bar, lounge and restaurant, and a riverside patio, where an Easter beer festival is held. The food is virtually all traceable to within a mile of the pub. The licensees air-cure their own hams, keep hens, ducks and livestock, and have local salmon fishing rights. CAMRA branch 2016 Cider Pub of the Year.
Q ➳ ⛺ 🌣 ◑ ▶ ♿ ≠ ♣ ● 🍴🚃 (99) ♨

Leavening

Jolly Farmers Ⓛ
Main Street, YO17 9SA
✪ 5.30-midnight; 5-1am Fri; 12-1am Sat; 12-midnight Sun
☎ (01653) 658276
Timothy Taylor Landlord; York Guzzler; 2 changing beers (sourced locally; often Brass Castle, Half Moon) Ⓗ
Seventeenth-century pub on the edge of the Yorkshire Wolds between York and Malton. The multi-room interior retains old-world cosiness in two small bars, games/family room and separate dining room. It is community focused, with meetings, charity events, darts and quiz leagues, occasional live music and beer festivals. Varied guest beers come from independent breweries. The extensive menu of quality food includes locally caught game dishes in season (no food Mon or Tue eves). Q ➳ ⛺ 🌣 ◑ ▶ ♿ ♣ P 🍴 ♨

Leyburn

Golden Lion Ⓛ
Market Place, DL8 5AS
✪ 11-11 (midnight Fri & Sat) ☎ (01969) 622161
⊕ goldenlionleyburn.co.uk
John Smith's Bitter; Wensleydale Semerwater Summer Ale, Coverdale Gamekeeper; 1 changing beer (sourced locally) Ⓗ
Traditional market town pub facing onto the main square of this busy Dales centre, now served by the revived Wensleydale Railway, with steam trains in summer. The comfortable main bar area is opened out and largely wood panelled, with a real fire at each end. There is also a separate dining room to the rear, particularly popular for the Sunday carvery. Theakston's Old Peculier is sold in summer.
➳ 🏮 ◑ ▶ Å ≠ ♣ 🚃 ♨ 🛜

Lofthouse

Crown Hotel
Thorpe Lane, HG3 5RZ
✪ 12-3, 7-11; 12-3, 7-10.30 Sun ☎ (01423) 755206
Black Sheep Best Bitter; Theakston Best Bitter; 1 changing beer (sourced locally) Ⓗ
A handsome stone building at the far end of beautiful Nidderdale. An unusual panelled entrance corridor leads to a traditionally furnished comfortable bar, with a dining room beyond. Local pictures, maps and brassware decorate the walls. An open fire in winter warms your bones after exploring the surrounding countryside – an Area of Outstanding Natural Beauty – and walking sticks are for sale if needed. In summer there is often a guest ale from a local brewery. 🏮 ◑ ▶ ♨

Malham

Lister Arms Ⓛ ✅
Gordale Scar Road, BD23 4DB
✪ 8am-11 ☎ (01729) 830330 ⊕ listerarms.co.uk
Thwaites Nutty Black, Wainwright, Lancaster Bomber; 3 changing beers (often Dark Horse, Naylor's, Settle) Ⓗ
A 17th-century coaching inn overlooking the village green. The tiled entrance hall opens to the stone-flagged main bar with separate areas to left and right and a dining room/restaurant beyond. The large secluded garden at the rear has ample comfortable seating. Food is served all day, with breakfast/brunch on offer before midday and the main menu available thereafter. Home-made cakes, cream teas and luxury hot chocolate are also available. Check the website for low-season accommodation deals.
➳ ⛺ 🌣 🏮 ◑ ▶ Å ● P 🚃 (75,210,211) ♨ 🛜

Malton

Blue Ball Ⓛ
14 Newbiggin, YO17 7JF
✪ 12-midnight ☎ (01653) 690692
Tetley Bitter; Timothy Taylor Landlord; 1 changing beer (sourced locally; often Great Yorkshire) Ⓗ
Grade II-listed Yorkshire Heritage pub dating from the 16th century and named the Blue Ball in 1823. The low frontage hides a maze-like interior, with the cosy bar, compact servery and linking corridor retaining most of the pub's historical flavour. A smoking area is at the rear of the pub. Home-cooked food is available daily (no food Wed). The Blue Ball Folk Club meets on the second Tuesday of each month. Q ➳ ◑ ▶ ≠ ♣ P 🚃 (843) ♨ 🛜

Crown Hotel
12 Wheelgate, YO17 7HP
✪ 11-11 (11.45 Fri & Sat); 12-11 Sun ☎ (01653) 692038
⊕ suddabys.co.uk
Jennings Cumberland Ale; house beer (by Leeds); 3 changing beers (sourced nationally) Ⓗ
This Grade II-listed market town pub has been in the same family for 135 years and in the Guide for over 25. Double Chance, brewed by Leeds Brewery, is one of two regular beers offered. Beer festivals are held three times annually. The on-site shop stocks more than 200 beers, specialising in Belgian and British microbreweries. A covered smoking patio is at the rear. Accommodation is available (with discounts for CAMRA members staying two nights or more). Q 🏮 ≠ ♣ P 🚃 (843) 🛜

Spotted Cow ✓
Cattle Market, YO17 7JN
✪ 4 (11 Tue & Fri; 12 Sat)-midnight; 12-10.30 Sun
☎ (01653) 697568
**Marston's Pedigree New World Pale Ale; Tetley Bitter;
1 changing beer (sourced nationally)** Ⓗ
Grade II-listed Yorkshire Heritage pub opposite the
livestock market and more than 300 years old, with
traditional cruck-framed construction. It has a
wonderful tile-floored taproom, with wooden
seating and a Rose's Brewery mirror, together with
a main bar area and separate pool room. A covered
smoking area is at the rear. Bar snacks are
available. Q ❧ ⇋ ♣ P ❒ (843) ❀ 🔗

Manfield

Crown Inn Ⓛ
Vicars Lane, DL2 2RF (500yds from B6275)
✪ 11-2 (not Mon & Tue), 4-11.30; 11-11.30 Sat & Sun
☎ (01325) 374243
Village White Boar; 7 changing beers Ⓗ
Local CAMRA Country Pub of the Year 14 times and
previously Yorkshire Pub of the Year, this 18th-
century venue is in a quiet village. It has two bars
and a games room. A mix of locals and visitors
creates a friendly atmosphere, and up to seven
guest beers from microbreweries with occasional
ciders or perry are stocked. Seasonal beer festivals
are planned. Q ❧ ⊛ ◑ ● P ❒ ❒ (29) ❀

Marske-by-the-Sea

Clarendon Ⓛ
88-90 High Street, TS11 7BA
✪ 11-11 (11.30 Fri-Sun) ☎ (01642) 490005
**Black Sheep Best Bitter; Camerons Strongarm; Copper
Dragon Golden Pippin; Theakston Old Peculier, Best
Bitter; 1 changing beer (sourced nationally)** Ⓗ
Recent CAMRA branch award winner, the Middle
House is a family-run, one-room locals' pub, where
the walls are adorned with photographs of
yesteryear. Six beers are served from a mahogany
island bar – a rarity on Teesside. There is no TV or
jukebox, no pool table, no children or teenagers –
just locals indulging in convivial conversation.
There is no catering either, but tea and coffee are
available, together with excellent home-made
scones at lunchtimes, while a free buffet is
provided on Tuesday evenings. Q ⊛ ⇋ P ❒ (3,X4)

Masham

White Bear ✓
Wellgarth, HG4 4EN
✪ 11-midnight ☎ (01765) 689319
⊕ thewhitebearhotel.co.uk
**Caledonian Deuchars IPA; Theakston Best Bitter; Black
Bull Bitter, XB, Old Peculier** Ⓗ
The de facto brewery tap for Theakston's, the
White Bear offers food, drink, accommodation and
conference facilities. There is a large dining area to
one side, and a small cosy taproom to the other
serving almost the full range of Theakston beers.
The pub hosts a popular three-day beer festival in
late June with over 30 beers on offer. During WWII
the pub was a victim of bombing and was left
derelict for many years before being renovated to
a high standard. ⊛ ☎ ◑ ⓓ & ♣ P ❒ (159,144) ❀ 🔗

Melsonby

Black Bull Ⓛ
19 West Road, DL10 5ND (1 mile from A1)
✪ 12-3 (not Mon); 5.30-11; closed Tue ☎ (01325) 718811
3 changing beers Ⓗ
Late 18th-century local pub with a long single room
and seating either end of the central bar. Upstairs
there are two function/dining rooms available for
parties. It has unusual pub games, including ring
the bull. Up to three beers from national and local
micros are on handpump, often from Camerons
and Mithril. It runs men's and women's darts
teams, dominoes on Mondays, and various clubs
hold meetings here. It will open earlier by prior
arrangement with walking groups. Bar meals are
on offer Thursday-Monday evenings and Sunday
lunchtime. ⊛ ◑ ♣ ❒ (29) ❀ 🔗

Middlesbrough

Dr Phil's Real Ale House �
**10 Pilkington Buildings, Roman Road, Linthorpe,
TS5 6DY** (100yds N of Roman Rd and The Crescent jct)
✪ 3-9.30; 1-10 Sat; closed Sun & Mon ☎ 07525 337123
⊕ drphilsrealalehouse.co.uk
4 changing beers (sourced nationally) Ⓗ
Opened in 2013 by an enthusiastic member, this
CAMRA branch 2015 and 2016 Pub of the Year is in
the leafy suburbs of Linthorpe among a terrace of
shops, a mile south of the town. The five-yards-
square micropub manages to accommodate an
eclectic mix of drinkers, who have a choice of four
changing beers, as well as cider/perry. Since
opening, over 600 different beers have been
served. Often, a cask does not even manage to last
the day. Q & ♣ ● ❒ ❒ (11,17)

Infant Hercules
84 Grange Road, TS1 2LS (just S of Cleveland Centre)
✪ 1-10 (11 Fri & Sat) ☎ 07828 039434
3 changing beers (sourced nationally) Ⓗ
One of several new micropubs within the town's
solicitors' quarter, all within a stone's throw of
each other and all located in a series of parallel
streets of Victorian terraced houses, wedged
between the shopping precinct and the university.
It is named after Gladstone's description of the
town in 1862, after he had witnessed the rapid
expansion of the steel and shipbuilding industries –
as explained on a large mural in the pub. Three
interesting beers are served on a try-before-you-
buy basis. Q ⇋ ● ❒

Isaac Wilson ✓
61 Wilson Street, TS1 1SF (N end of town)
✪ 8am-midnight ☎ (01642) 247708
7 changing beers (sourced nationally) Ⓗ
Named after a 19th-century railway industry
magnate and company director of the world's first
public railway, the Stockton & Darlington, the Isaac
is a Wetherspoon conversion of the former law
courts. It comprises one long bar with 12
handpumps, serving a large single room with walls
adorned with photographs of old Middlesbrough.
Alongside the chain's nationally contracted beers
and ciders, guest beers are locally sourced. Beer
festivals, a January sale, Meet the Brewer sessions,
and celebrations of Saints' days are hosted.
❧ ◑ & ⇋ ● ❒ 🔗

Newton-on-Ouse

Dawnay Arms 🍴

Moor Lane, YO30 2BR

🕓 12-2.30, 6-11; 12-11 Sat; 12-7 Sun; closed Mon

☎ (01347) 848345 ⊕ thedawnay.co.uk

Black Sheep Best Bitter; Timothy Taylor Landlord; 2 changing beers (sourced locally; often Rooster's, Rudgate, Treeboom) Ⓗ

Smart, quiet country gastro-pub in a pretty village with a pleasant garden down to the River Ouse. Mooring is available to patrons. Featuring Yorkshire beer and locally sourced food, a modern British menu often includes local game (booking is advisable). The comfortable interior contains a mix of rustic wooden and upholstered furniture and there are open fires in winter. Unobtrusive background music is played. A bus service operates between York and Easingwold. A camping/caravan site is nearby at Linton Lock. 🛏️🅿️◑🚶♿🅿️🚌😸🐾🛜

North Rigton

Square & Compass ✅

Hall Green Hill, LS17 0DJ

🕓 10-11 (midnight Thu-Sat); 10-10 Sun ☎ (01423) 733031

⊕ thesquareandcompass.co.uk

Ilkley Joshua Jane; Leeds Pale; Theakston Best Bitter; 3 changing beers Ⓗ

An elegant dining pub with multiple areas, although the main bar at the front of this large establishment is pleasant for drinking. The bar is furnished with tables and leather armchairs while the dining spaces are more formal. Six handpumps dispense ales from local small breweries and there are well-stocked fridges with a selection of interesting bottled beers. 🛏️🅿️◑♿🅿️🚌(747,X52)🐾🛜

Northallerton

Tickle Toby Inn 🍴

180 High Street, DL7 8JZ

🕓 11.30-11; 11-11 Sun ☎ (01609) 778760

Black Sheep Best Bitter; 3 changing beers (sourced regionally) Ⓗ

Taking its name from a notorious local 18th-century highwayman and pickpocket, this town-centre pub has a long, narrow single bar with several drinking areas. Popular with all age groups, it offers a range of guest beers from local and regional breweries. It can be busy during the weekly Wednesday and Saturday markets which take place outside, and on weekend evenings. 🛏️◑🚲♣🚌🛜

Tithe Bar ✅

2A Friarage Street, DL6 1DP (off High St near hospital)

🕓 12-11 (midnight Fri & Sat) ☎ (01609) 778482

Ilkley Mary Jane; Okells Manx Pale Ale; 5 changing beers Ⓗ

Cosmopolitan town-centre bar just off the busy High Street on the road to the hospital. Part of the Market Town Taverns chain, there is a strong commitment to real ale and numerous continental and speciality bottled beers. The decor is simple, with wooden floors throughout, and there is no music or other electronic entertainment, just conversation. Food is served lunchtimes and early evenings, with a brasserie open upstairs Tuesday to Saturday evenings. Children are welcome during the daytime. Q🛏️◑♿♣🍴🚌🛜

Old Malton

Royal Oak 🍴

47 Town Street, YO17 7HB (off A64 Malton bypass)

🕓 12-midnight (1am Fri & Sat); closed Mon

☎ (01653) 699334 ⊕ royaloakoldmalton.co.uk

Copper Dragon Golden Pippin; Tetley Bitter; York Guzzler; 1 changing beer (sourced regionally) Ⓗ

Historic Grade II-listed inn in a picturesque village off the A64 close to Eden Camp military museum. At the front of the pub is a cosy snug, to the rear is a larger room with original beams (complete with brasses) and a log fire, leading to an extensive beer garden with a large covered smoking area. Four handpumps serve beers mainly from Yorkshire, and traditional home-cooked meals are available. Children and dogs are welcome. The bus stops outside. 🛏️😸◑♣🅿️🚌(840)😸🛜

Osgodby

Wadkin Arms 🍴 ✅

Cliffe Road, YO8 5HU

🕓 12-11 (midnight Fri & Sat) ☎ (01757) 702391

⊕ wadkinarms.co.uk

Brown Cow White Dragon; John Smith's Bitter; Sharp's Doom Bar; 2 changing beers (sourced regionally; often Ilkley, Tetley) Ⓗ

A true community pub at the heart of the village, with five handpumps dispensing ales that are mostly from Yorkshire breweries. The Wadkin has a homely feel, with open fires and a friendly welcome, and is home to locals and visitors alike. The nearby Transpennine Cycle Trail sees cyclist and walkers visiting in the summer months, and a local bus service passes too. You will see much evidence of CAMRA sympathies on display. Bar meals are available throughout the week except Mondays. 🛏️😸◑♣🅿️🚌(4)😸🛜

Osmotherley

Golden Lion 🍴

6 West End, DL6 3AA (in village centre, 1 mile E of A19)

🕓 12-3 (not Mon & Tue), 5-11; 12-midnight Sat; 12-11 Sun

☎ (01609) 883526 ⊕ goldenlionosmotherley.co.uk

Timothy Taylor Landlord; 3 changing beers (sourced locally) Ⓗ

Popular with visitors to the North York Moors, this village on the edge of the National Park is the start of the long-distance Lyke Wake Walk. Hikers and others can enjoy a well-earned rest at the outside drinking tables. There is an emphasis on locally sourced food, which has a fine reputation, but you will also find a warm welcome for drinkers. Regularly changing beers are from Wall's and other local Yorkshire breweries, with a beer festival each November. Q😸🛏️◑🍴🚌(80,89)😸🛜

Pickering

Sun Inn 🍷 🍴

136 Westgate, YO18 8BB (on A171)

🕓 4-11; 12-midnight Fri & Sat; 12-11 Sun ☎ (01751) 473661

⊕ thesuninn-pickering.co.uk

Leeds Best; Tetley Bitter; 4 changing beers (sourced regionally) Ⓗ

Friendly local CAMRA Rural Pub of the Year, close to the town and steam railway. Four guest ales are offered (three from Yorkshire micros). A cosy bar with real fire leads to a separate room, ideal for families and special events, opening onto a large enclosed beer garden. Children, walkers and dogs (on leads) are welcome. Regular events include a bi-weekly acoustic music session, community choir, monthly charity quiz and a vinyl night every third Thursday. ⏰😋🍴🍺♿🚃♣🌳🍴🗪😺

Redcar

Turner's Mill 🆔

Greenstones Road, TS10 2RA (off B1269)
✪ 11.30-midnight ☎ (01642) 496021
10 changing beers (sourced nationally) Ⓗ
This increasingly popular Ember Inn and recent CAMRA branch award winner is close to the town's racecourse. A cosy, relaxing and welcoming ambience prevails. The ever-enthusiastic bar staff serve 10 changing beers on a try-before-you-buy basis. Reasonably priced food is available all day, every day. An email-based newsletter details the pub's latest offers, including seasonal specials. Cask ale club is on Monday, while quiz nights are Wednesdays or Sundays. Children are allowed up to 8pm. ⏰😋🍴♿🌳🗪(22,64)🗪

Reeth

Buck Hotel 🆔

DL11 6SW
✪ 11-midnight ☎ (01748) 884210 🌐 buckhotel.co.uk
Black Sheep Best Bitter, Golden Sheep; Copper Dragon Best Bitter; Ossett Silver King; Timothy Taylor Landlord Ⓗ
Originally an 18th-century Swaledale coaching inn, the pub retains its beamed ceilings, open fire and even an ice house. Also known as the top house, it offers five cask ales and six real ciders along with home-cooked food. Main meals are served 12-2.30pm and 5.30-9pm, with light bites between noon and 10pm. Quoits is popular in the summer, with three teams based here along with two darts teams. ⏰😋🍴🍺♿🅿♣🚃🌳😺🗪

Ribblehead

Station

Ingleton, LA6 3AS (on B6255 near B6479 jct)
✪ 10-11 ☎ (015242) 41274 🌐 thestationinn.net
5 changing beers Ⓗ
Built in 1874 at the same time as the nearby viaduct, this place is a welcome refuge in a bleak spot in the midst of superb walking country. During the day, the main bar room is laid out for diners, while the smaller room has pub games and TV sport. A surprisingly large number of locals frequent the tastefully furnished bar. It benefits from a good train service – times are above the bar counter. There is a bunk barn next door, and wild camping behind. The house ale, Tet, may be any one of a number of different ales according to season. 😋🍴🍺♣🚃🅿🗪(830)🌳😺🗪

Riccall

Greyhound Ⓛ 🆔

82 Main Street, YO19 6TE
✪ 12-midnight; 12-11.30 Sun summer; 3 (12 Sat)-midnight; 12-11.30 Sun winter ☎ (01757) 249101
🌐 thegreyhoundriccall.co.uk
Tetley Mild, Bitter; Theakston Best Bitter; 4 changing beers (sourced regionally; often Acorn, Ossett, Rudgate) Ⓗ

Characterful village pub with seven real ales served at busy times – four rotating guest beers complement the Yorkshire permanent ales on the bar. The pub is popular with cyclists and walkers using the York-Selby cycle path (note the old Cyclists Touring Club emblem on the front of the building) and the large beer garden can get busy in summer. Wholesome food is also available although check opening hours in winter. ⏰😋🍴🍺♣🌳(415,416)😺🗪

Richmond

Ralph Fitz Randal 🆔

6 Queens Road, DL10 4AE (edge of town centre)
✪ 9am-midnight (1am Fri & Sat) ☎ (01748) 828080
Greene King Abbot; Ruddles Best Bitter; 8 changing beers (sourced nationally) Ⓗ
Large single-bar Wetherspoon house converted from Richmond's former post office and telephone exchange, on the edge of the town centre. It is set on three levels, with a large family dining area and an outdoor patio to the rear. It offers several cask beers, usually including a locally brewed ale, and has won numerous CAMRA awards; there are several beer festivals each year. Opens at 8am for breakfast. Q⏰😋🍴♿🍴🗪🗪

Ripon

King William IV 🆔

10 Blossomgate, HG4 2AJ
✪ 4-11 (midnight Fri); 12-midnight Sat; 12-11 Sun
☎ (01765) 608271
Theakston Best Bitter; Village White Boar; 2 changing beers (sourced locally; often Hambleton) Ⓗ
A community-led pub with a large sporting following; five screens show Sky and BT sports channels. The pub hosts many local sports teams and has regular quiz and music nights, including the ever-popular GlastonBilly in August when local musicians play for charity over a full day. The pub is Hambleton Ale's brewery tap but also serves guest beers. There is a hidden beer garden for the summer and roaring fires in winter. 😋♿♣😺🗪

One-Eyed Rat 🆔

51 Allhallowgate, HG4 1LQ
✪ 5-11; 12-11 Fri & Sat; 12-10.30 Sun ☎ (01765) 607704
🌐 oneeyedrat.co.uk
7 changing beers Ⓗ
A premier ale house set within a terrace of 200-year-old houses; the narrow frontage leads to a warm and welcoming family-run hostelry. Seven changing guest beers plus a real cider are served, and there is always a pump dedicated to a mild or stout/porter and another for a stronger beer at around 5% ABV, plus a real cider. The pub hosts regular live music and holds two beer festivals a year. A classic, and continuously in this Guide for over 25 years. Q😋🌳🗪(36)😺🗪

Royal Oak 🆔

36 Kirkgate, HG4 1PB
✪ 11-11 (midnight Fri & Sat) ☎ (01765) 602284
🌐 royaloakripon.co.uk
Timothy Taylor Dark Mild, Golden Best, Boltmaker, Landlord; 2 changing beers (sourced regionally; often Saltaire) Ⓗ
Housed in an 18th-century coaching inn in the centre of historic Ripon, beautifully renovated in a modern idiom, the Royal Oak serves a top quality

range of Timothy Taylor beers alongside regular guests from other Yorkshire breweries. The pub is separated into relaxed dining areas with log-burning stoves and comfortable seating, and offers a first-class locally sourced menu. Accommodation is in six comfortable bedrooms, and includes a hearty English breakfast. 🛏️🏵️�◑♿🅿🚮(36)🐾📶

Water Rat

24 Bondgate Green, HG4 1QW
🌀 11-11 ☎ (01765) 602251 🌐 thewaterrat.co.uk
Theakston Best Bitter; 3 changing beers ⊞
Located by the side of the River Skell with a fine view of Ripon Cathedral from its conservatory and terrace, this is Ripon's only riverside pub. An emphasis on affordable home-cooked traditional English pub food means it tends to get busy at times. There is a small snug at the front of the pub. Black Sheep ales are supplemented by other local ales, typically from Rudgate, Rooster's, Hambleton and Salamander or Copper Dragon.
🛏️🏵️◑♣🐾🐾📶

Robin Hood's Bay

Dolphin 🅛

King Street, YO22 4SH (on a steep pedestrian-only road, down towards bay, from top car park)
🌀 11-11; 12-11 Sun ☎ (01947) 880337
Theakston Best Bitter, Old Peculier; Caledonian Deuchars IPA; 1 changing beer (sourced nationally) ⊞
Olde-worlde pub, full of memorabilia, popular with locals and visitors alike, and where dogs and muddy boots are made equally welcome. It comprises an unspoilt atmospheric public bar, where a real fire burns for most of the year, and a family/dining room. Three regular beers and a guest are served. Quiz night is Sunday, with R&B on Monday and a folk club on Friday. Access to this part of the village is not easy for the less able-bodied. 🛏️◑🚮(X93)🐾

Saltburn-by-the-Sea

Saltburn Cricket, Bowls & Tennis Club

Marske Mill Lane, TS12 1HJ (next to leisure centre)
🌀 8-midnight (1am Fri & Sat); 11.30-3, 8-midnight Sun
☎ (01287) 622761 🌐 saltburn.play-cricket.com
2 changing beers (sourced nationally) ⊞
Visitors are made most welcome at this CAMRA branch multi award-winner. A private sports club, it is run by an enthusiastic steward and is well supported by the local community. It is also the watering hole for the local diving club, as well as other sports. The balcony, ideal for lazy summer afternoons, overlooks the cricket field, and on match-day Saturdays the club opens at 2pm. Two changing beers are served, often not even lasting the night. ♿≉♣🅿🚮(X3,X4)🐾

Scagglethorpe

Ham & Cheese Inn 🅛

Bull Piece Lane, YO17 8DY
🌀 11-11 ☎ (01944) 758249
3 changing beers (sourced regionally; often Brass Castle) ⊞
This village pub is located 50 yards off the A64, some three miles east of Malton. There is a spacious single-roomed bar divided into two main areas, together with a separate restaurant which

doubles as a function room. Three rotating guest ales (from Yorkshire micros and particularly Brass Castle) are offered. Home-cooked meals are served throughout the day. En-suite accommodation is available. To the rear is a drinking/smoking area and large car park. 🛏️🏵️�◑♿Å♣🅿🚮(843)🐾📶

Scarborough

Angel ✪

46 North Street, YO11 1DF
🌀 11-midnight; 12-midnight Sun ☎ (01723) 365504
Copper Dragon Golden Pippin; Tetley Bitter; Timothy Taylor Landlord; 3 changing beers (sourced nationally) ⊞
Friendly town-centre local close to the main shopping area, recently refurbished, with a single-room horseshoe bar. An interest in sport and games is reflected in the impressive array of trophies won by various pub teams and the large-screen TVs for viewing sporting events. It has a surprisingly spacious and well-appointed patio garden at the rear, with two of its boundary walls displaying a superb example of graffiti wall art depicting angels in a misty woodland setting.
🏵️≉♣🚮📶

Hole in the Wall 🅛

26-32 Vernon Road, YO11 2PS
🌀 12-11.30 (12.30am Fri & Sat) ☎ (01723) 325996
4 changing beers (sourced nationally) ⊞
Built in the 1840s, the pub has a split-level interior with three seating areas. This friendly, conversational place is handy for the town centre and spa complex. It has recently been purchased from Marston's by a small family-run pub chain with the intention of resurrecting it to its former glory as a real ale mecca. Four rotating guest beers are offered. TV sport may be enjoyed. There is an outside covered and heated smoking area to the side of the pub. 🛏️🏵️♿≉♣🚮🐾

Lord Rosebery ✪

85-87 Westborough, YO11 1JW
🌀 9am-midnight ☎ (01723) 361191
Greene King Abbot; Ruddles Best Bitter; 8 changing beers (sourced nationally) ⊞
The Lord Rosebery was originally built in 1895 as the Scarborough Liberal headquarters and then acquired by the Co-operative Society after WWII, who opened a walk-round store in the building. This busy pub is on two levels, with a bar located on both. Frequently changing guest beers are on tap and food is served all day every day, with featured club nights. Q🛏️◑♿≉♣🚮📶

North Riding Brewpub 🅛

161-163 North Marine Road, YO12 7HU
🌀 12-midnight (1am Fri & Sat) ☎ (01723) 370004
🌐 northridingbrewpub.com
Timothy Taylor Landlord; York Guzzler; 4 changing beers (sourced nationally; often North Riding Brew Pub, North Riding Brewery) ⊞
Scarborough's only brewpub, serving at least six continually changing beers from local and microbreweries around the UK; there are always one or more North Riding beers available. The pub has a public bar, a quiet lounge and an upstairs dining room serving home-cooked food, all with real fires. Quiz night is Thursday. Local CAMRA Town Pub of the Year 2014.
Q🛏️�◑♣🚮(3)🐾📶

Scholars Bar ⒧

6 Somerset Terrace, YO11 2PA

✪ 4.30-midnight; 12-midnight Fri-Sun ☎ (01723) 372826

7 changing beers (sourced regionally; often North Riding Brewery, Ossett) Ⓗ

A warm, friendly atmosphere prevails at this town-centre pub at the rear of the main shopping centre, voted as CAMRA runner-up Town Pub of the Year 2015. It has a large front bar and a games room. Seven rotating guest beers, usually from Yorkshire microbreweries, are offered, plus numerous ciders and perries. TV screens show major sporting events. Twenty eight pints are the prize for winning the Thursday quiz. ≉♣♠⌂

Stumble Inn Ⓨ ⒧

59 Westborough, YO11 1TS (near railway station)

✪ 12-11; 12-10.30 Sun ☎ 07837 716774

⊕ stumbleinnmicropub.weebly.com/home.html

6 changing beers (sourced nationally) Ⓗ

The first micropub in Scarborough and a welcome addition to the local real ale scene, located a short walk from the railway station and formerly a solicitors' office. This single-roomed pub offers six rotating guest ales, with local breweries always represented. Up to 26 real ciders and perries are also available. It is a quiet establishment which is ideal for a cosy chat and a chill-out. Local CAMRA Town Pub of the Year 2015. Q♿≉♠⌂⏛❀

Valley Bar

51 Valley Road, YO11 2LX

✪ 12-midnight (1am Thu-Sat) ☎ (01723) 372593

⊕ valleybar.co.uk

Dark Star Hophead; 5 changing beers (sourced nationally; often Scarborough, Theakston) Ⓗ

A cellar bar with six handpumps dispensing mainly microbrewery beers, usually including one or more from Scarborough Brewery. Up to eight real ciders and perries are also on tap, Broadoak perry being a regular, together with over 100 bottles of Belgian beers including Cantillon. Further rooms offer additional seating upstairs, which can be used for meetings. There is also a pool table upstairs. ⎌⌂♣♠⌂❒(4)❀ 🛜

Scotton

Guy Fawkes Arms

Main Street, HG5 9HU

✪ 12 (4 Mon)-11 ☎ (01423) 868400

⊕ guyfawkesarms.co.uk

Black Sheep Best Bitter; 3 changing beers Ⓗ

This popular village dining pub was under threat of closure and conversion to housing until rescued by the Peachey and Walker families in 2013. A good balance is struck between the needs of drinkers and diners. The panelled lounge has a mix of traditional and modern furniture, and includes a leather sofa and settles near the counter for drinkers, and more traditional tables and chairs. For serious diners there is a separate area at one end. ⏛♠P❒(58)❀ 🛜

Selby

Giant Bellflower ⒧ ✅

47a Gowthorpe, YO8 4HF

✪ 8am-midnight (1am Fri & Sat) ☎ (01757) 293020

Greene King Abbot; Ruddles Best Bitter; 6 changing beers (sourced nationally; often Adnams, Rudgate, Sharp's) Ⓗ

Named after a local 17th-century botanist and converted from a furniture showroom, this modern and spacious pub is completely different from all the others in Selby. The building is deceptively large given its small frontage, with an enormous stainless steel bar taking pride of place. Artefacts and pictures from Selby's past complement the light and airy interior. Offering a typical Wetherspoon range of keenly priced beers, real ciders and LocAles, it is an important recent addition to the town's pub scene. ⎌❁⏛♿≉♠⌂🛜

Settle

Talbot Arms Ⓨ ⒧ ✅

High Street, BD24 9EX

✪ 12-11 ☎ (01729) 823924 ⊕ talbotsettle.co.uk

Theakston Best Bitter; 3 changing beers (sourced regionally; often Settle, Three Peaks) Ⓗ

Just off the square, this family-run free house offers a welcoming and friendly atmosphere. A stove glows in the large stone feature fireplace to the left of the main entrance, with pool table, dartboard and dominoes tables beyond providing a base for teams in local leagues. A pleasant, terraced beer garden is at the rear. The three to five guest beers and cider are usually from Cumbria, Lancashire or Yorkshire. Good-value food is served until 8pm all week. ⎌❁❁⏛≉♣♠P❒(580,581,11)❀ 🛜

Skipton

Beer Engine ⒧

1 Albert Street, BD23 1JD

✪ 12-10 (11 Fri & Sat); 12-9 Sun; closed Mon & Tue ☎ 07834 456134

5 changing beers (sourced nationally) Ⓗ

Micropub in a tiny street between the town centre and the canal. Five handpumps dispense different beers, stored in refrigerated cabinets behind the bar, at least one being a blonde/pale ale and one a dark beer, plus a character beer alongside a still cider, a fruit cider and a selection of bottled beers and wines. The ambience is friendly and books are available to read or borrow. Well-behaved dogs are welcome. Q≉♠❒❀ 🛜

Narrow Boat ⒧ ✅

38 Victoria Street, BD23 1JE (alleyway off Coach St)

✪ 12-11 ☎ (01756) 797922

Ilkley Mary Jane; Okells Bitter; Timothy Taylor Landlord; 5 changing beers (often Black Sheep) Ⓗ

On a quiet back street between the High Street and the canal, this civilised beer drinkers' emporium is worth seeking out. Bare floorboards, old church pews and international breweriana create an atmosphere in which no piped music, jukebox or gaming machines disturb the conversation. Guest ales, usually including a dark beer, are complemented by continental bottled and draught beers and up to four ciders or perries. There is a quiz on Wednesdays. Well-behaved dogs are welcome. Q⎌❁❁⏛♿≉♠⌂❀ 🛜

Three Links Club

Rectory Lane, BD23 1ER

✪ 7 (5 Fri)-11; 12-3, 7.30-11.30 Sat; 12-5, 7-10.30 Sun

☎ (01756) 798022

Dark Horse Craven Bitter, Hetton Pale Ale Ⓗ

Visitors are welcome at this friendly club with a community spirit, set at the corner of the town-centre car park behind the town hall. It has a large, comfortable and well-appointed lounge bar, with a separate function room for activities and events. There is an annual country & western music weekend as well as a host of regular weekly events. It was a local CAMRA award winner in 2015. Non-members are requested to sign in. ⌂❀♿♣🖥🐎

Snape

Castle Arms
DL8 2TB
✿ 12-3, 5.30-11 (midnight Fri); 12-midnight Sat; 12-5 Sun; closed Mon ☎ (01677) 470270 ⊕ castlearmsinn.uk
Ringwood Best Bitter; 3 changing beers (sourced nationally) Ⓗ
Attractive village lying just off the A1, close to Thorpe Perrow arboretum. The pub takes its name from the nearby former home of Henry VIII's final wife, Catherine Parr. With an excellent reputation for its food and ale, it has a real country-pub feel with church pews, brasses, old pictures of country sports and a splendid fireplace. To the rear is a small Caravanning and Camping Club site. Up to three guest beers from the Marston's range are on tap. Q⌂❀♿🖥🌓Å♣P🖥(144)❀🌐

Staithes

Captain Cook Inn Ⓛ
60 Staithes Lane, TS13 5AD (400yds E of A174)
✿ 11-midnight ☎ (01947) 840200 ⊕ captaincookinn.co.uk
5 changing beers (sourced nationally) Ⓗ
Formerly the Station Hotel, a local CAMRA branch multi award-winner, this venue is on the edge of the national park, sitting high above a pretty fishing village and close to Boulby Cliffs, the highest in England. The pub changed ownership in 2014 and underwent a complete refurbishment, though muddy boots and dogs are still equally welcome. Four handpumps (five in summer) provide an eclectic mix of interesting ales, including the house beer, Northern Navigator, brewed organically by North Yorkshire. Q⌂❀🖥🌓P🖥(4)❀

Cod & Lobster Inn Ⓛ
High Street, TS13 5BH (at end of High St)
✿ 10-11 ☎ (01947) 840330 ⊕ codandlobster.co.uk
4 changing beers (sourced nationally) Ⓗ
Superbly positioned at the seawater's edge in this sleepy, picturesque fishing village, during high tides and easterly winds you are advised to use the roadside door or risk getting very wet. The large open-plan single-room pub offers three national changing beers alongside the house beer, Old Jack, named after a children's TV character. Good-value traditional meals are served. On sunny days, a pleasant patio, directly overlooking the chilly sea, becomes popular. ⌂🌓

Stillington

White Bear Ⓛ
Main Street, YO61 1JU
✿ 12-2.30 (not Mon), 5.30-11 (midnight Sat); 12-11 Sun
☎ (01347) 810338 ⊕ thewhitebearinn-york.co.uk
Leeds Pale; Rudgate Viking; Samuel Smith Old Brewery Bitter; 2 changing beers (sourced regionally) Ⓗ

It was difficult to see how the pub could improve, but it has. There are now three smart self-catering holiday apartments round the back, so in theory you never need to miss a minute of the action. And action it is: three regular and two rotating Yorkshire ales. The temptation to move in is almost irresistible. ⌂🖥🌓♣P🖥(40)

Stokesley

White Swan Ⓛ ✓
1 West End, TS9 5BL (150yds beyond shops)
✿ 11-midnight (1am Fri & Sat); 11-11.30 Sun
☎ (01642) 710263 ⊕ thewhiteswanstokesley.co.uk
Captain Cook Black Porter, Botany Bay, Endeavour, IPA, Slipway, Sunset; 2 changing beers (sourced nationally) Ⓗ
Home of the Captain Cook Brewery, this 18th-century pub, winner of many a local CAMRA branch award, is at the west end of this pretty market town. At least six Captain Cook beers, two guest ales and two ciders are served from 12 handpulls. Beer festivals are held Easter and October. An award-winning and good-value, home-baked pie menu is served Monday-Saturday lunchtimes. Quiz night is Wednesday, music night Thursday. The sheltered outdoor drinking area overlooks the brewery. Over-18s only. ❀♿♣🌭🖥(81,89)❀🌐

Thirsk

Little 3 Ⓛ
13-15 Finkle Street, YO7 1DA
✿ 4-10 (10.30 Wed & Thu); 12-midnight Fri & Sat; 12-10 Sun
☎ (01845) 523782 ⊕ littlethree.co.uk
Black Sheep Ale; Theakston Best Bitter; 4 changing beers Ⓗ
Old low-beamed pub just off Market Place which claims a history as far back as 1214. Inside it is a warren of nooks and crannies, all decorated in mock half-timbered style, and the main bar sports an impressive fireplace and stove. Substantially refurbished yet losing none of its character in 2013, it was formerly Ye Old Three Tuns and then renamed to avoid confusion with the nearby Three Tuns. It has four changing guest beers from local and national brewers plus two regular ales. Food is served in the upstairs bistro and there is live music on Thursdays. 🌓🖥❀🌐

Thixendale

Cross Keys
YO17 9TG
✿ 12-3 (not Mon-Thu), 6-11; 12-3, 7-10.30 Sun
☎ (01377) 288272
Tetley Bitter; 2 changing beers (sourced locally; often Great Newsome, Half Moon, Wold Top) Ⓗ
Evidence of human activity in Thixendale goes back 10,000 years, and this single-room hostelry appears on a map dated 1851. At the heart of five dry valleys, it is popular with walkers, including those on the Wolds Way and, though remote, is well worth seeking out. The two guest beers come from independent breweries and are usually not more than 4% ABV. Children are welcome in the beer garden. Good-value, traditional home-cooked food is served. Accommodation is in the adjoining converted stable. Q❀🖥🌓♣

Thoralby

George Inn �⏣ ✅

DL8 3SU

❄ 12-2 (not Mon-Thu), 6.30-11 ☎ (01969) 663256

⊕ thegeorgeinnthoralby.com

3 changing beers (sourced locally) ⊞

This small, off-the-beaten-track, 18th-century pub lies tucked away in a little village a few hundred yards off the B6160 Bishopsdale Road. The interior has been opened up into a single room but retains two distinct halves; it is cosy and comfortable, with a particularly impressive stone fireplace at one end. Separate apartments offer accommodation. Beers are usually from local Yorkshire brewers. Opens 7pm in the winter. Q ➤ ⏏ ⏐ ◐ ⏏ ♣ P ☶ ❀ ⏛

Ugthorpe

Black Bull Inn ⏣

Postgate Way, YO21 2BQ

❄ 12-2 (not Mon & Tue), 6-11 ☎ (01947) 840286

Theakston Old Peculier; 1 changing beer (sourced nationally) ⊞

A warm welcome is assured at this Grade II-listed traditional pantiled country inn, where photographs of yesteryear adorn the walls. The comfortable family-run establishment comprises a main bar, snug, restaurant and games room. The guest beer, complementing the Old Peculier, changes weekly. Portions of home-cooked food are such that going home hungry is not an option, while diners travel from far and wide for the impressive Sunday carvery. Two letting bedrooms and a holiday cottage are available. Q ➤ ⏏ ⏐ ◐ ⅙ ⏏ ♣ P ⏛

Upper Poppleton

Lord Collingwood

The Green, YO26 6DP

❄ 12-2.30 (not Mon), 5-11.30; 12-midnight Fri & Sat; 12-11.30 Sun ☎ (01904) 787461 ⊕ lordcollingwood.com

Banks's Sunbeam; Marston's Pedigree New World Pale Ale; Ringwood Best Bitter; Thwaites Wainwright; 3 changing beers (sourced nationally; often Jennings, Marston's, Wychwood) ⊞

A fine country pub on the village green housed in a lovely 17th-century, Grade II-listed building, with friendly, welcoming staff. Up to seven ales from the Marston's list are on offer, including seasonals. Good-quality food is served lunchtimes (except Mon) and evenings (except Sun). The comfortable interior features a timber ceiling and pillars, real fires and a 19th-century carved oak bar. It has a beer garden lit by fairy lights, patio, children's play area and car park. Accessible from York by bus or rail. ➤ ❀ ⏐ ◐ ⇌ ♣ P ⏛ (10) ❀ ⏛

West Haddlesey

George & Dragon ⏣

Main Street, YO8 8QA

❄ 5-midnight (1am Fri); 2-1am Sat; 12-10.30 Sun

☎ (01757) 228198 ⊕ thegandd.co.uk

Brown Cow White Dragon; 2 changing beers (sourced regionally) ⊞

Privately owned free house with enthusiastic support for local microbreweries. It has low ceilings, a cosy bar with a real fire, a TV showing sporting events, a separate room for diners and an attractive outside decked area for summer days.

Food is served evenings (not Sun to Tue) as well as Sunday lunch. Beer festivals are held outdoors in April on the weekend closest to St George's Day (23 April) and the end of October, close to Halloween (31 Oct). Q ❀ ⏐ ◐ ⅙ ♣ P ❀ ⏛

West Witton

Fox & Hounds ⏣

DL8 4LP (on A684)

❄ 12-3, 6-midnight; 12-midnight Sat & Sun

☎ (01969) 623650 ⊕ foxwitton.com

Black Sheep Best Bitter; 3 changing beers (sourced locally; often Yorkshire Dales) ⊞

Friendly, family-run free house full of character, with a down-to-earth bar and games room popular with locals and visitors alike. Good-value meals are served all week, with a roast on Sunday. The Grade II-listed pub was a rest house for Jervaulx Abbey monks in the 1400s, and the dining room boasts an inglenook fireplace with quaint stone oven. A pleasant patio at the rear leads onto the quoits pitch. Beware the tight entry to the car park. Q ➤ ❀ ⏐ ◐ ♣ ⏏ P ❀ ⏛

Whitby

Black Horse ✅

91 Church Street, YO22 4BH (on E side of swing bridge on way to abbey steps, close to marketplace)

❄ 11-11; 12-10.30 Sun ☎ (01947) 602906

⊕ the-black-horse.com

5 changing beers (sourced nationally) ⊞

Former CAMRA branch award winner, this little multi-roomed gem, dating from the 1600s, offers a warm welcome. The frontage, with its frosted glass, together with one of Europe's oldest public serving bars, was built in the 1880s and remains largely unchanged. Beer is served from five handpumps. Snuff, tapas, olives, Yorkshire cheeses and hot drinks are always available, while hot lunches are served during the winter months. The cider is Westons Rosie's Pig. Accommodation is in four bedrooms. Q ➤ ❀ ⏐ ◐ ⅙ ⇌ ♣ ● P (X93,840) ❀

Board Inn ⏣

125 Church Street, YO22 4DE (N end of Church St)

❄ 11.30-11; 11-11 Sun ☎ (01947) 602884

⊕ theboardinnwhitby.co.uk

Caledonian Deuchars IPA; Theakston XB, Old Peculier ⊞

The last remaining Board of several that existed during the 1800s on Church Street – traditional shops that sold ale, among other produce, displaying the ales available on chalkboards. Today, three beers are served, allowing the drinker, from the front snug, to admire the 199 steps up to the abbey. There are also fine harbour views to the rear, where the recently refurbished lounge/restaurant serves reasonably priced meals. The famous Fortune's smokehouse can be found nearby. ➤ ❀ ⏐ ◐ ⇌ ♣ (X93,840)

Little Angel Inn ✅

18 Flowergate, YO21 3BA (200yds W of swing bridge)

❄ 12-midnight (1am Fri & Sat) ☎ (01947) 820475

⊕ littleangelwhitby.com

6 changing beers (sourced nationally) ⊞

Just off the main tourist route and up a slight incline, locals and visitors alike are afforded a genuine friendly welcome at this recently refurbished pub where, it is rumoured, the remains of the castle form part of the structure. Pub food, large-screen TVs, live music, outside drinking and even a horse mount, for those requiring this facility, complement the six beers served to three separate rooms from a central bar. CAMRA branch Best Whitby Pub for two years running. ⬛≒♣⬛🅿(X93,840)❀

Station Inn 🅛 ⊘
New Quay Road, YO21 1DH
🕑 10-midnight; 10-11.30 Sun ☎ (01947) 603937
🌐 stationinnwhitby.co.uk
Black Dog Whitby Abbey Ale; Camerons Strongarm; Copper Dragon Scotts 1816; Whitby Platform 3; 4 changing beers (sourced nationally) 🅗
Next to the harbour and marina, this multi-roomed pub and recent CAMRA branch Pub of the Year offers a warm welcome. The enthusiastic licensees ensure that the eight beers, including the house beer, Whitby Platform 3, always encompass a superb range of varying styles, while cider and fruit wines mean there is something for everybody. Opposite the bus station and NYMR/Esk Valley railway station, the pub has become the discerning travellers' waiting room. Live music features three evenings a week. ≒⬛🅿(X93,840)❀

York

Blue Bell ★ 🅛
53 Fossgate, YO1 9TF
🕑 11-11 (midnight Fri & Sat); 12-10.30 Sun
☎ (01904) 654904
Bradfield Farmers Blonde; Timothy Taylor Landlord; 5 changing beers (sourced locally; often Brass Castle, Half Moon, Rooster's) 🅗
Recognised by CAMRA as having a nationally important historic pub interior, it has a central bar supplying two small rooms and, through a servery, the side corridor. This is a small venue and can get busy. It operates a strict no-groups policy and entry may be restricted at busy times or on special occasions. The permanent beers are complemented by fantastic rotating guest beers. Beef and ale stew is served Saturday and Sunday 12.30-5.30pm. Q♣⬛🅿❀

Brigantes 🅛 ⊘
114 Micklegate, YO1 6JX
🕑 12-11 ☎ (01904) 675355 🌐 brigantesyork.co.uk
Okells Manx Pale Ale; 9 changing beers (sourced nationally; often Brass Castle, Great Heck, Leeds) 🅗
Popular, welcoming Market Town Taverns pub in a smart Georgian building just inside the Micklegate Bar. It serves 10 ales, at least one dark, featuring good Yorkshire breweries and interesting guests from across the UK, plus a range of foreign keg and bottled beers. At least one real cider is on the bar, and there is a Wall of Cider festival in October with 25+ ciders and perries. A high-quality food menu is served in the bar or adjoining restaurant. The function room upstairs is available for social group meetings/dining/special events.
Q⬛⬛�≒⬛❀🛜

Duke of York
3-4 King's Square, YO1 8BH
🕑 12-11 (midnight Fri & Sat) ☎ (01904) 676065
🌐 lbdukeofyork.co.uk
Leeds Pale, Yorkshire Gold, Best, Midnight Bell; 4 changing beers (sourced locally) 🅗
Converted to a pub after a failed protest by the Campaign for Real Estate Agents – their loss was

our gain. One of two Leeds Brewery showcases in town, this central hub boasts two contrasting rooms downstairs and two-and-a-half upstairs, one with an excellent minster view. The atmosphere changes with the time of day, but there is something here for all tastes. Enjoy! ⬛🔊db⬛⬛🛜

Falcon Tap 🅛
94 Micklegate, YO1 6JX
🕑 4-midnight; 12-midnight Fri-Sun ☎ (01904) 622225
🌐 thefalcontap.co.uk
Great Heck Chopper; 5 changing beers (sourced locally; often Bad, Brass Castle, Great Heck) 🅗
Originally the Falcon, and dating from the 1770s, the pub had a period when it was called Rumours, and is now refurbished and renamed the Falcon Tap. A small carpeted front bar with two handpumps overlooks busy Micklegate, a spacious back bar has four handpumps and real cider. A large partly covered outdoor area with comfy seating is to the rear. The enthusiastic landlord is keen to offer a wide range of styles and strengths of beers, mostly from local brewers. A local DJ plays vinyl records on Friday nights. ❀db≒⬛❀

Golden Ball ★ 🅛
2 Cromwell Road, YO1 6DU
🕑 5-11.30 (midnight Thu); 4-midnight Fri; 12-midnight Sat; 12-11.30 Sun ☎ (01904) 652211 🌐 goldenballyork.co.uk
Everards Tiger; Timothy Taylor Golden Best; Treboom Yorkshire Sparkle; 4 changing beers (sourced regionally; often Moorhouse's, Treboom) 🅗
Recognised by CAMRA as having a nationally important historic pub interior and Grade II-listed, this friendly local has three rooms, a snug and a beer garden. Becoming York's first community co-operative pub in 2012, its seven handpumps dispense three permanent ales plus a choice of guests. Bread and fresh eggs from local suppliers are on sale in the bar. The pub hosts traditional bar billiards games and community group meetings, as well as open mic, folk and quiz nights and exhibitions by local artists. Q⬛❀db≒♣❀

Hop ⊘
11-12 Fossgate, YO1 9TA
🕑 12-11 (midnight Thu-Sat) ☎ (01924) 261333
🌐 thehopyork.co.uk
Ossett Yorkshire Blonde, Big Red Bitter, Silver King, Excelsior; 5 changing beers (sourced regionally; often Fernandes, Rat) 🅗
Good beer, pizza and live music sum up the Hop. Owned by Ossett Brewery, beers from its family (Rat, Fernandes and occasionally Riverhead Brewery) feature strongly alongside other guests. There is a front bar area leading to a large open area with long tables at the rear and a stage for regular unplugged music acts. A former Italian restaurant, it has original tiling and exposed brickwork throughout. Pizza, cooked in a wood-fired pizza oven, is served lunchtimes and evenings. ⬛db⬛⬛🅿

Maltings 🅛
Tanners Moat, YO1 6HU
🕑 11-11; 12-10.30 Sun ☎ (01904) 655387 🌐 maltings.co.uk
Black Sheep Best Bitter; York Guzzler; 5 changing beers (sourced nationally; often Arbor, Magic Rock, Mallinsons) 🅗
Many a visitor has been tempted into this large black cube while going from the station to the minster and, discovering its delights, has gone no further. Once inside it is cosy, always busy and

packed with choice. That it was a recent local CAMRA branch Pub and Cider Pub of the Year says it all. 🏮🌮🍺🚪♿🐾

Pivni

6 Patrick Pool, YO1 8BB

🕐 11.30-11.30 ☎ (01904) 635464 🌐 pivni.co.uk

5 changing beers (sourced nationally; often Tapped Sheffield) Ⓗ

Founding bar of the expanding group of Pivovar UK beer houses, featuring five regularly changing cask ales from highly regarded breweries throughout the UK. It also keeps an extensive selection of bottled beers. The beautiful timber-framed building dates back to 1190 and drinkers are accommodated on all three floors. Food is restricted to locally sourced artisan pork pies and cheeseboards. ♿🍺🐾

Rook & Gaskill 🍷 Ⓛ

12 Lawrence Street, YO10 3WP

🕐 4-midnight (1am Thu); 2-1am Fri & Sat ☎ (01904) 655450 🌐 rookandgaskillyork.co.uk

Castle Rock Harvest Pale; 7 changing beers (sourced locally; often Great Heck, Rooster's) Ⓗ

This popular local just outside Walmgate Bar focuses on good-quality beer and cider. Eight handpumps dispense a range of changing guest beers (together with the regular beer from Castle Rock), often from local breweries such as Great Heck, Rooster's and Brass Castle. Up to three real ciders are also on handpump. There is a popular (especially with students) quiz on Thursdays. The menu is mainly home-made burgers (including vegetarian). CAMRA branch Pub of the Year 2016. 🏮🍺🚪🐾📶

Slip Inn Ⓛ

Clementhorpe, YO23 1AN

🕐 5-11.30; 4-midnight Fri; 12-midnight Sat; 12-11 Sun ☎ (01904) 621793 🌐 theslipinnyork.co.uk

Leeds Pale; Rudgate Ruby Mild; Timothy Taylor Boltmaker; 2 changing beers (sourced regionally) Ⓗ

Close to York tourist attractions of the city walls, the River Ouse, and the much-acclaimed Bishy Road, this is a friendly pub attracting both the local community and visitors. Drinkers are accommodated in two bars, a snug and a courtyard to the rear of the premises. Three regular beers, including a mild, are complemented by two guests. A wider choice is available at seasonal festivals, including a joint event with the nearby Swan. 🏮♣🍺🚪(11)🐾📶

Swan ★ Ⓛ ✅

16 Bishopgate Street, YO23 1JH

🕐 4-11 (11.30 Thu; midnight Fri); 12-midnight Sat; 12-10.30 Sun ☎ (01904) 634968 🌐 theswanyork.co.uk

Tetley Bitter; Timothy Taylor Landlord; house beer (by Treboom); 3 changing beers (sourced regionally) Ⓗ

A traditional street-corner pub, popular with locals and visitors alike. Grade II-listed, it has has a nationally important historic pub interior, and boasts a 1936 Tetley interior with an impressive West Riding-style drinking lobby, two bars, a snug and a heated beer garden to the rear. Regular Yorkshire beers are complemented by three guests (including one dark beer) from around the country, and two real ciders/perries. An annual beer festival is held jointly with the nearby Slip Inn. 🏮♣🍺🚪(11)🐾

Waggon & Horses

19 Lawrence Street, YO10 3BP

🕐 3-11.30; 12-midnight Fri & Sat; 12-11 Sun ☎ (01904) 637478 🌐 waggonandhorsesyork.com

Batemans Black & White, XB, Gold; Oakham Citra; 3 changing beers (sourced nationally; often Dark Star, Elland, Titanic) Ⓗ

Family-run Batemans venue with multiple rooms. There is a free bar billiards table, dartboard and an array of traditional board games. The bar and front lounge have TVs showing BT Sport while the quieter back rooms are often used by local groups and societies. Food is served in the evenings; the burger-and-pint deal is popular. The pub also offers comfortable en-suite accommodation – book direct for a CAMRA discount. 🏮🛏🍴♿🍺🚪🐾📶

York Tap

Railway Station, Station Road, YO24 1AB

🕐 10-11 (11.45 Fri & Sat); 11-11 Sun ☎ (01904) 659009

18 changing beers (sourced nationally; often Anarchy, Oakham, Thornbridge) Ⓗ

An award-winning conversion of the former Victorian tea rooms on York station, the York Tap opened in 2010. The ornate ceiling, Art Deco stained-glass windows and ceiling domes create a fine backdrop to the central round bar with 20 handpumps, offering 18 cask beers plus two ciders or perries. The beers are sourced by parent company Pivovar from many of Britain's best breweries. Look out for events such as Battle of the Brewers. 🏮♿🍺🚪🐾

YORKSHIRE (SOUTH)

Arksey

Plough Inn Ⓛ

2 High Street, DN5 0SF (behind church)

🕐 7 (6.30 Thu & Fri)-11; 12-3.30, 6.30-11 Sat; 12-3.30, 7-11 Sun ☎ (01302) 872472 🌐 arkseyplough.co.uk

House beer (by Old Mill); 3 changing beers (sourced locally; often Wentworth, White Rose) Ⓗ

A rural gem, this friendly multi-roomed free house features beers from small independent local breweries. A log-burning stove heats the attractive lounge in which brasses and old photographs of the village are displayed. On Thursday, Friday and Saturday evenings reasonably priced bar meals are served and, on Sundays, the excellent lunch is particularly popular. Quiz nights are Thursdays and Sundays. Q🏮🐶🍴♣🚪(64,64A)📶

Auckley

Eagle & Child

24 Main Street, DN9 3HS

🕐 11.30-3, 5-11; 11.30-11.30 Fri & Sat; 12-10.30 Sun ☎ (01302) 770406 🌐 eagleandchildauckley.co.uk

Black Sheep Best Bitter; John Smith's Bitter; Timothy Taylor Landlord; 2 changing beers (sourced regionally; often Bradfield, Ossett, Springhead) Ⓗ

A much-loved pub, on the main road in this village, and a winner of numerous CAMRA awards. Dating from the early-19th century, it has real character. There are two bars, one with TV sport, the other quieter with tables for bar meals. The separate restaurant is decorated with photographs of local historic interest, and the home-cooked meals have a deserved reputation. It's only one mile from Robin Hood airport. Q🏮🐶🍴♣🚪(91)📶

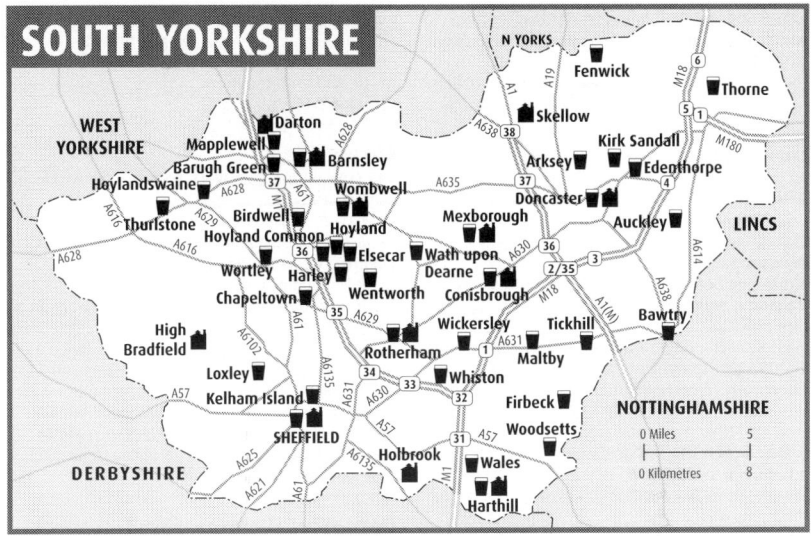

SOUTH YORKSHIRE

Barnsley

Commercial 🗓
74 Summer Lane, S70 2NN
🟢 4.30-11; 12-11 Sat & Sun
Tetley Bitter; 2 changing beers (sourced locally) ⊞
Lively family-owned pub on the edge of the town centre. This attractive one-room hostelry has been extensively refurbished. It offers three real ales, served in lined glasses, and is popular with pool and darts players. There is a Sunday night quiz. To the rear is an appealing enclosed seating area where children and dogs are allowed.
🏠🛱♣🛏🖵(43,44)

Dove Inn
102 Doncaster Road, S70 1TP
🟢 4-midnight; 12-midnight Sat & Sun ☎ (01226) 288351
Old Mill Traditional Bitter; 1 changing beer ⊞
A welcome return to the Guide for this well-loved establishment. Proudly independent, the Dove is owned by Old Mill Brewery and serves only its own real ales. The light wood-panelled interior gives the effect of spaciousness, with a pool area and a lounge/seating area leading off the L-shaped bar. The rear room has an outdoor balcony above a large beer garden and gives views to Oakwell and the Dearne Valley Country Park. 🏠🕽🛱♣🖵🕸

Joseph Bramah 🗓 ✅
Market Hill, S70 2PX
🟢 8am-midnight (1am Fri & Sat) ☎ (01226) 320890
Greene King Abbot; Ruddles Best Bitter; Sharp's Doom Bar; Stancill Barnsley Bitter; 4 changing beers ⊞
The pub is named after the local inventor and locksmith who created unpickable locks, beer engines, and a banknote numbering machine. This Lloyds No.1 Bar offers the core Wetherspoon range of real ales and up to four changing local microbrewery beers. Occasional Meet the Brewer evenings are held here. The pub is set over two levels with quieter spaces upstairs. The beer garden is quite sheltered, with heated areas.
🏠🕽🕭🛱♣🖵🕸

Old No. 7 🗓
7 Market Hill, S70 2PX
🟢 11-midnight (11 Mon & Tue); 11-11 Sun
☎ (01226) 244735 🌐 oldno7barnsley.co.uk
Acorn Barnsley Bitter, Blonde; 6 changing beers ⊞
The recently refurbished CAMRA award-winning hostelry, part-owned by Acorn Brewery, offers eight real ales from Acorn and other micros, real ciders and perries, plus a wide range of continental bottled beers and lagers. Beer festivals are held and live music is staged, including a monthly Celtic music session. This town-centre local is handy for the new Experience Barnsley Museum, the Cooper Gallery and the Civic Theatre. The downstairs bar is also available for functions. 🛱♣🛏🖵🕭🕸

Silkstone Inn 🗓 ✅
64 Market Street, S70 1SN
🟢 8am-midnight ☎ (01226) 320860
Greene King Abbot; Ruddles Best Bitter; Sharp's Doom Bar; 3 changing beers ⊞
Number 700 in Wetherspoon's empire, the Silkstone is now a well-established and family-friendly pub, set in the shopping and pedestrian area of the market town. Named after the local coal seam, the pub's interior reflects the theme with a central fireplace, dark furnishings and even black droplets in the light fittings. The hard-working and helpful staff are customer-focused and keen to promote CAMRA and LocAle beers, often culminating in Meet the Brewer evenings and twice-yearly international beer festivals.
Q🕿🏠🕽🛱🕭🕸

Barugh Green

Crown & Anchor 🗓
Barugh Lane, S75 1LL (on B6428)
🟢 11.30-11.30 (midnight Thu; 1am Fri; 12.30am Sat)
☎ (01226) 387200 🌐 thecrownandanchor.com
6 changing beers ⊞
This pub, once in a real ale desert, has helped transform the local ale scene, serving up to six changing beers (and one cider) from local, regional and national breweries. The pub has two drinking areas and a restaurant. It offers a friendly welcome

to patrons and well-behaved children, both in winter with the log fire or in summer with the extensive garden overlooking the wider countryside. With popular quiz nights and daytime offers, it is a great place to visit. ⊛◑♿♣♠️P🖳 🛜

Bawtry

Ship ✓

Gainsborough Road, DN10 6HT (on A631)
✪ 11.30-10.30 (11.30 Thu-Sat) ☎ (01302) 710275
⊕ theship-bawtry.com
4 changing beers (sourced nationally; often Jennings, Marston's, Wychwood) Ⓗ
One of the local CAMRA area's success stories, this previously run-down roadside pub was taken over in 2007 by the family of the present licensees. Extensively refurbished inside and outside, the Ship has gained an enviable reputation for high-quality food and beer. Four ales are always available, selected from the Marston's range. The pub also holds beer festivals, and is winner of several food awards. ❧⊛◑♿♣♠️P🖳(21,25)🐾🛜

Birdwell

Cock Inn Ⓛ ✓

Pilley Hill, S70 5UD (off The Walk)
✪ 5-10; 12-midnight Thu-Sat; 12-11.30 Sun
☎ (01226) 744227
Tetley Bitter; 4 changing beers Ⓗ
Stone-built village pub that always offers a warm welcome. The main bar area has a slate floor and an inviting open fire, leading into a large lounge area with carpeting and plush seating. The smaller room is ideal for small parties or meetings. Well known for its good food, it is busy for lunches and evening meals (booking for Sunday lunch is advised). Five cask ales are on offer and one real cider. Q⊛◑🅰♣♠️P🖳(7A,67A)

Conisbrough

Hilltop Hotel Ⓛ

Sheffield Road, DN12 2AY
✪ 5-11; 4-midnight Fri; 12-midnight Sat & Sun; closed Mon
☎ (01709) 868811 ⊕ thehilltophotel.co.uk
Welbeck Abbey Cavendish; 3 changing beers (sourced locally; often Acorn, Chantry, Concertina) Ⓗ
A traditional free house on the outskirts of Conisbrough, offering a relaxed and friendly atmosphere and serving up to four real ales, mainly from its own on-site brewery. It is split into a public bar and lounge/dining area, the latter serving an excellent Sunday lunch. Quiz night is on a Wednesday and includes supper, Thursday evenings host panel games. Its own home-made pie shop is open Wednesday to Saturday. Q❧⊛◑♣P🖳(X78)🐾🛜

Doncaster

Cask Corner Ⓛ

3 Cleveland Street, DN1 3EH
✪ 12-2am ☎ (01302) 366277 ⊕ caskcornerbar.co.uk
Thwaites Original, Wainwright; 6 changing beers Ⓗ
The centrally located bar features eight handpumps and four real ciders, and also sells fruit beers and 50 bottled beers. Quirky decor includes pumpclips, old records and a cornucopia of bric-a-brac, some suspended from the ceiling. Upstairs is a quiet cocktail bar and roof patio. Live music features

every night except Monday and Thursday, which are quiz nights. A classic jukebox provides the music at other times. A winner of many awards for music and entertainment.
⊛♿≈♣♠️🖳(76,81)🐾🛜

Corner Pin Ⓛ

145 St Sepulchre Gate West, DN1 3AH (on W side of dual carriageway)
✪ 12-11; 12-10 Sun ☎ (01302) 340670
Leeds Pale; 4 changing beers (sourced locally; often Dukeries, Geeves, Stancill) Ⓗ
Award-winning traditional pub convenient for the town, railway station and bus station. Beers, in a variety of styles, are mainly from local independent breweries. Mini beer festivals are held twice a year. Food is served weekday afternoons and there is a popular Sunday lunch until 2.30pm (later if pre-booked). Inside are both lounge and public bar areas, while outside there is a decked space to the rear. Local CAMRA branch Pub of the Year 2015.
❧⊛◑♿≈♣🍴🖳(71,73A)🛜

Doncaster Brewery Tap 🍴 Ⓛ

7 Young Street, DN1 3EL
✪ 5-10; 12-10 Fri & Sat; 12-4 Sun; closed Mon ☎ 07770 958394 ⊕ doncasterbrewery.co.uk
Doncaster Sand House, Cheswold, Gold Cup, First Aviation Ⓗ
Conveniently situated in the town centre, Doncaster Brewery Tap was opened in 2014. The brewery, originally launched in 2012, was relocated to the rear in 2014. This welcoming pub offers a range of up to six Doncaster beers, a guest beer and six real ciders and perries. A spoken word evening is every second Thursday, and a Phantom Cinema film on the last Friday of the month. Voted local CAMRA Pub of the Year 2016.
Q≈♣♠️P🖳(76)🐾🛜

Leopard ✓

2 West Street, DN1 3AA
✪ 11.30-10 (11 Mon & Fri); 10-11.30 Sat; 12-9 Sun
☎ (01302) 739460 ⊕ leopard-doncaster.co.uk

REAL ALE BREWERIES

Abbeydale Sheffield
Acorn Wombwell
Blue Bee Sheffield
Bradfield High Bradfield
Chantry Rotherham
Concertina 🍺 Mexborough
Doncaster 🍺 Doncaster
Exit 33 Sheffield
Fuggle Bunny Holbrook
Geeves Barnsley
Glentworth Skellow
Harthill Village Harthill
Hilltop 🍺 Conisbrough (NEW)
Imperial 🍺 Mexborough
Kelham Island Sheffield
Lost Industry Sheffield (NEW)
Neepsend Sheffield (NEW)
On the Edge Sheffield
Regather Sheffield (NEW)
Sheffield Sheffield
Stancill Sheffield
Tapped 🍺 Sheffield
Toolmakers Sheffield
Two Roses Darton
White Rose Sheffield

5 changing beers (sourced regionally; often Ossett, Sharp's, York) [H]
A welcome return to the Guide for this street-corner pub that has won many awards over the years. It has a superb tiled frontage recalling its origins as a Warwick and Richardson's house. There are two distinct rooms downstairs, while upstairs a function room hosts regular rock and pop gigs. Five changing real ales are served on handpump.
Q🐴❀◐◑♿🚆🍎P🚌(71)🐾📶

Plough ★ [L]

8 West Laith Gate, DN1 1SF
🕐 11-11 (midnight Fri & Sat); 11-4, 7-11.30 Sun
☎ (01302) 738310 🌐 thelittleplough.co.uk
Acorn Barnsley Bitter; 2 changing beers (often Bradfield, Moorhouse's) [H]
Known as the Little Plough, this is a friendly haven for anyone wishing to escape the town-centre bustle. CAMRA-friendly, it serves a regular LocAle, and hosts mini beer festivals. The interior dates from 1934 and is mentioned in CAMRA's National Inventory of Historic Pub Interiors. There is a public bar at the front and a lounge to the rear. The pub is adorned with pictures of old agricultural scenes. Winner of many local CAMRA awards.
Q❀🚆♣🚌🐾📶

White Swan [L]

34 French Gate, DN1 1QQ
🕐 10-11 (10 Mon; 11.30 Fri & Sat); 11-10 Sun
☎ (01302) 344757
Black Sheep Best Bitter; Glentworth Lightyear; 2 changing beers (sourced locally; often Doncaster) [H]
Town-centre pub with a narrow frontage disguising a roomy interior, serving food, including breakfast. There is a small drinking area inside the front entrance, then a long narrow room beyond the bar where diners can eat in a comfortable setting. It is an outlet for the local Glentworth and Doncaster breweries, with three real ales on handpull. Live jazz is played on the first Saturday of the month, from midday. Many interesting historical photographs of Doncaster adorn the walls.
Q🐴❀◐♿🚆🚌📶

Edenthorpe

Eden Arms ✔

Eden Field Road, DN3 2QR (adjacent to Tesco)
🕐 11.30-midnight; 10-midnight Sat & Sun ☎ (01302) 888682
Abbeydale Moonshine; Brakspear Bitter [H]**; Leeds Pale** [H]/[A]**; 2 changing beers (sourced nationally; often Black Sheep, Brains, York)** [H]
A fine, modern estate pub built in the late-1980s. Attractive and comfortable, it is one of the area's most CAMRA-friendly pubs. On Mondays all cask ales are discounted. Five real ales are usually on offer, with a display at the entrance informing customers about present and future cask beers. Meet the Brewer evenings are popular, and it is notable for good-quality meals.
Q🐴❀◐◑♿P🚌(87)📶

Elsecar

Crown Inn 🏆 [L]

22 Hill Street, S74 8EL
🕐 12 (4 Mon)-midnight ☎ (01226) 743823
3 changing beers (often Acorn, Bradfield, Ossett) [H]
Stone-built roadside pub owned and run by a local family who ran two previous pubs in the village. The well-used front lounge has a community feel, and the lounge/conservatory to the rear is used for meals, meetings and functions. Three changing cask ales are served, one always from Ossett Brewery, while the other two are sourced locally. There are seating areas outside to the front and rear, the latter being a large garden with a play area. 🐴❀◐◑♿🚆♣P🚌(66,N66,72)🐾📶

Market Hotel [L]

2-4 Wentworth Road, S74 8EP
🕐 11.45-11.30 (12.30am Fri & Sat) ☎ (01226) 742240
Acorn Barnsley Gold; 5 changing beers [H]
A traditional hostelry in the cask ale oasis and historic village of Elsecar. Near the Transpennine Trail, Heritage Centre and Heritage Railway, it is popular with locals and visitors. Inside is a traditional multi-room pub. The walls are adorned with old photographs of the area. Look above the front window for the Horse and Gig for Hire sign. The changing beers are from microbreweries, and LocAle is always available. To the rear is an enclosed beer garden.
Q❀🛏🚆♣🚌(66,N66,227)🐾

Fenwick

Baxter Arms

Fenwick Lane, DN6 0HA (between Askern and Moss)
🕐 12 (5.30 Mon)-11 ☎ (01302) 702671
Theakston Best Bitter; 2 changing beers (sourced regionally; often Leeds, Ossett, York) [H]
This wonderful free house is a rural gem and well worth seeking out. Run by the same family for over 25 years, it is a welcoming multi-room pub, including a smaller room complete with snooker table. Fresh food, sourced locally, is served all day; tea and coffee are also available. Beers are from small independent breweries. Outside there is ample parking and seating, with a large garden containing a swing and a slide. Wednesday is quiz night. Q🐴❀◐◑⛺♣P🐾📶

Firbeck

Black Lion [L]

9 New Road, S81 8JY (opp village hall)
🕐 12-3, 5.30-11 (11.30 Sat); 12-5 Sun ☎ (01709) 812575
John Smith's Bitter; 5 changing beers (often Chantry) [H]
This traditional village pub, now a free house, has returned to its former glory under Phil's ownership. It attracts diners, walkers and the local farming community. Four guest beers are offered, usually from local microbrewers. Pictures of old Firbeck adorn the walls of the snug area. The place is a winner of numerous local CAMRA branch awards and is a Guide regular. The food is recommended. The pub is handy for visiting the ruins of Roche Abbey. The no. 20 bus only serves the village every two hours Monday-Saturday daytime.
Q❀🛏◐◑♿♣P🚌(20)🐾

Harley

Horseshoe [L]

9 Harley Road, S62 7UD (off A6135 on B6090)
🕐 4-11 (10 Mon); 2-11 Sat; 12-10.30 Sun ☎ (01226) 742204
🌐 thehorseshoeharley.co.uk
Bradfield Farmers Blonde; 3 changing beers [H]
Village street-corner local that has been in the same family for many years, hosting regular events

and home to football and pool teams. Guest beers change frequently, ensuring their quality, with ales often coming from local breweries. A carvery is held 12-3pm Sunday (book to avoid disappointment). The Horseshoe has been the hub of the local community for well over a century, and is handy for walking around the Wentworth estate and for the Needles Eye and Elsecar Heritage Centre. It can be busy when the pool team has a home fixture. ❀❶◗♣🚌(44)

Harthill

Beehive ❼ 𝕃
16 Union Street, S26 7YH (opp All Hallows church)
🕐 12-2.30, 6-11 (11.30 Fri); 12-3, 6-11.30 Sat; 12-11 Sun; closed Mon ☎ (01909) 770205 🌐 thebeehiveharthill.co.uk
Harthill Village Hart's Desire, Dark Hart; Tetley Bitter; 5 changing beers (often Harthill Village, Welbeck Abbey) 🄷
The Beehive has been welcoming drinkers since 1833. Excellent home-cooked food and up to eight real ales are offered, spread over the bars in the two rooms. Although the Harthill Village Brewery has ceased, the beers are still available but are now brewed in Sheffield. There is a full-size snooker table and a function room with disabled access via a stair lift. A popular beer and music festival is held in the garden in July. There are two outside drinking areas, and folk and morris dancing feature regularly. Local CAMRA Pub of the Year 2014-2016. Q❀❶◗👌♣P🚌(29)

Hoyland

Furnace Inn 𝕃
163 Milton Road, S74 9BG
🕐 11-midnight ☎ 07872 449264
Clark's Traditional; 1 changing beer 🄷
Historic pub, noted on maps in 1890, standing to the side of Milton Pond which served the iron works across the road. It is a great traditional pub at the heart of Hoyland community and appeals to all ages. Two cask ales including a regular and guest are served in superb condition. Popular quiz nights are held Tuesday, Thursday and Sunday. Three plush seating areas are inside plus plenty of seating outside overlooking the pond, where wildlife or fishermen can be observed. Q❀≒♣P🚌(67,67A)

Hoyland Common

Saville Square 𝕃
34 & 36 Sheffield Road, S74 0DQ
🕐 9am-midnight (2am Fri & Sat); 9am-1am Sun
☎ (01226) 747239 🌐 savillesquarebarnsley.co.uk
3 changing beers 🄷
A smart, stylish bar with a good selection of frequently changing real ales from both local and national breweries offered in a friendly atmosphere. This has become a popular place to meet up and share a beer. Food is available, from breakfast and light bites through to main meals. Open just a few years, Saville Square has truly become a great asset to the local community. ❀❶🚌🛜

Hoylandswaine

Rose & Crown 𝕃
Barnsley Road, S36 7JA

🕐 10-11 (midnight Fri & Sat); 10-10.30 Sun
☎ (01226) 762227
Bradfield Farmers Blonde; Timothy Taylor Golden Best; 2 changing beers (sourced locally) 🄷
Small gem of a pub that offers the drinker a choice of up to four real ales, with at least one from the local area. The landlady, who came to the pub in 2013, made small changes, including opening all day and offering tea, coffee, sandwiches and newspapers from 10am, and it has become a true village pub again. ❀❶◗🅰♣P🚌(20,92,92A)🐾

Kirk Sandall

Glasshouse
1 Doncaster Road, DN3 1HP
🕐 11.30-11 (midnight Fri & Sat) ☎ (01302) 884268
🌐 glassh.co.uk
6 changing beers (sourced nationally; often Old Mill, Partners, Tom Wood's) 🄷
The Glasshouse has a long historical connection with the glass industry, being close to the former Pilkington Glass works. The open-plan single-room bar has many large-screen TVs showing sport or news. The pub serves up to six real ales on handpull, and meals are available lunchtimes and evenings. The beer garden has won a local award. ♿❀❶👌≒♣P🍴🚌(84)🛜

Maltby

Queen's Hotel ✅
Tickhill Road, S66 7NQ
🕐 8am-midnight (1am Thu-Sat) ☎ (01709) 812494
Greene King Abbot; Ruddles Best Bitter; 4 changing beers 🄷
Originally a residential hotel, the premises were completely refurbished and opened by Wetherspoon following a lengthy period of closure. Now firmly established, this spacious pub has an attractive family dining area offering typical Wetherspoon value-for-money food and drink. Recent management changes have contributed to a much-needed raising of the profile of real ale in Maltby. ♿❀❶◗👌●P🚌(1,10)🛜

Mapplewell

Talbot Inn 𝕃 ✅
Towngate, S75 6AS
🕐 12-11 (11.30 Wed); 11.30-midnight Fri & Sat; 11.30-11 Sun
☎ (01226) 385629 🌐 thetalbotmapplewell.co.uk
Two Roses Heron Porter; 3 changing beers 🄷
This 17th-century coaching inn has gone through an extensive but sympathetic renovation that has kept the atmosphere but improved the facilities, from its attractive exposed stonework at the front of the building to its warm log fire. The friendly and popular pub supports the local community through its Buy Local policy, and serves beer from the award-winning Two Roses Brewery. Food is available in the bar area or upstairs in the 1776 restaurant. Q♿❀❶◗♣P🚌(1,97)🐾🛜

Mexborough

Concertina Band Club 𝕃
9a Dolcliffe Road, S64 9AZ (off Bank Street, halfway up hill, on left-hand side)
🕐 2-4 (Mon only), 8-11; 2-11 Sat; 1-11 Sun
☎ (01709) 580841

Concertina Club Bitter, Old Dark Attic, Bengal Tiger; John Smith's Bitter Ⓗ
Long-established club and brewery with an interesting history, and a regular in the Guide. The Tina, as it is known locally, was originally home to a concertina band formed in 1887. Pictures and memorabilia, as well as many CAMRA awards, decorate the main room, and there is also a small TV and pool room. The cellar brewery provides three regular ales including the award-winning Bengal Tiger. CAMRA members are welcome; just show the Guide or your membership card.
Q✿✿✲⛶🖵(220,221)✿

Imperial Brewery Tap Ⓛ
Arcadia Hall, Cliff Street, S64 9HU (opp bus station)
✪ 4.30-12.30am; 12-12.30am Sat; 12-10 Sun; closed Mon & Tue ☎ (01709) 584000
Imperial Bitter, Blonde; 2 changing beers (sourced locally; often Great Heck, Ossett, Revolutions) Ⓗ
Friendly brewery tap possessing a large main bar with a cosy lounge area, plus a separate games/function room. Eight handpumps dispense excellent-quality Imperial ales, which may include seasonal specials and one-off brews, as well as guest beers – all served in lined over-measure glasses. A real cider is sometimes available. There is entertainment most nights, with live bands on Friday, Saturday and Sunday evenings, featuring music for a wide range of tastes. Thursday is acoustic open mic night. ♿✿♿✲♣⛶🖵(220)✿🛜

Rotherham

Bluecoat Ⓛ ✅
The Crofts, S60 2DJ (behind town hall)
✪ 8am-midnight (1am Fri & Sat) ☎ (01709) 539500
Greene King Abbot; Ruddles Best Bitter; 8 changing beers Ⓗ
Originally a charity school, opened in 1776, it became a Wetherspoon pub in 2001. The selection of up to 10 beers is listed on a screen at the end of the bar. At least two real ciders or perries are served from bags behind the bar. The pub commissions a specially brewed beer four times a year from a local brewery. It's the winner of local CAMRA Pub of the Year five times. Local breweries feature strongly in the guest beer selection.
♿✿◖♿✲♣♦P🖵🛜

Bridge Inn Ⓛ
1 Greasbrough Road, S60 1RB (alongside Chantry Bridge, between bus and rail stations)
✪ 12-11 (midnight Fri & Sat); 12-9 Sun ☎ (01709) 836818
Old Mill Traditional Bitter, Blonde Bombshell, Bullion; Timothy Taylor Boltmaker; 3 changing beers (often Old Mill) Ⓗ
The original home of Rotherham CAMRA, it reverted to its original name after a spell as Nellie Denes. It is an Old Mill tied house, built in 1930 using stone from the original Bridge Inn, which dated back to the 1700s. Up to three guest beers may come from local, regional and national breweries. There is live music every Saturday evening and most Fridays, with poetry, folk and jazz once a month. Two function rooms upstairs are popular with local groups. The only food served is pie and peas. ◖♿✲♣🖵✿

Cutler's Arms Ⓛ
29 Westgate, S60 1BQ
✪ 12-11 (1am Sat & Sun) ☎ (01709) 382581
⊕ cutlersarms.co.uk

Abbeydale Moonshine; Chantry New York Pale, Iron and Steel Bitter, Diamond Black Stout; house beer (by Chantry); 2 changing beers (often Chantry) Ⓗ
Originally dated 1825, and rebuilt for Stones Brewery in 1907, the pub was restored to its original Edwardian splendour by Chantry Brewery, reopening in 2014. It retains some Art Nouveau windows, tiling and the original curved bar counter with an elegant dividing screen and is recognised by CAMRA as having a regionally important historic pub interior. It offers a full range of Chantry beers, guest ales and two real ciders. Live music plays every Saturday evening, Sunday afternoon and most Fridays. Snacks are offered. It gets busy on Rotherham United home match days.
Q✿✿◖✲♦🖵✿

New York Tavern ▾ Ⓛ
84 Westgate, S60 1BD
✪ 12-midnight ☎ (01709) 375596 ⊕ newyorktavern.co.uk
Chantry New York Pale, Iron and Steel Bitter, Diamond Black Stout; house beer (by Chantry); 3 changing beers (sourced locally; often Chantry) Ⓗ
A pub since 1856 and reopened by a team from Chantry Brewery in 2013, it has been fully refurbished as a real ale led pub. Five Chantry beers are dispensed, with three guest beers and real cider on handpump, all at competitive prices, and there is a large selection of foreign bottled beers. Snuff is available, as well as snack foods. The pub is called after the old name for the area and a long-demolished inn. The pub is near New York football stadium and busy on home match days. Local CAMRA Town Pub of the Year 2014-2016.
◖✲♦🖵(32,33,69)✿

Rhinoceros ✅
35-37 Bridgegate, S60 1PL
✪ 8am-11 (midnight Fri & Sat) ☎ (01709) 361422
Greene King Abbot; Marston's Burton Bitter; 5 changing beers Ⓗ
Busy town-centre pub popular with shoppers and bigger than it looks from the outside. With one long room, there are booths down one side and many local pictures; look out for the one explaining the name. The usual good-value fare is on offer at this Wetherspoon outlet. The beer quality and range has improved recently. Real cider and perry are also available. It can be busy in the afternoon and early evening and on Rotherham United home match days. ◖♿✲♦🖵🛜

Sheffield: Central

Bath Hotel ★
66-68 Victoria Street, S3 7QL
✪ 12-11 (midnight Fri & Sat); closed Sun ☎ (0114) 249 5151
⊕ beerinthebath.co.uk
6 changing beers (sourced regionally; often Thornbridge) Ⓗ
A careful restoration of the 1930s interior gave this two-roomed pub a conservation award and acknowledgement by CAMRA as having a nationally important historic pub interior. The bar lies between the tiled lounge, a small corridor drinking area, and the cosy well-upholstered snug. There are usually three Thornbridge beers and three guests on tap, plus a good choice of malt whiskies. There is regular live music and a weekly quiz on Thursdays. Food is light snacks only.
Q🖵♣♦🖵✿

Devonshire Cat ✅

49 Wellington Street, S1 4HG
🕐 11.30-11 (1am Fri & Sat); 12-10.30 Sun
☎ (0114) 279 6700 ⊕ devonshirecat.co.uk
Abbeydale Moonshine, Absolution; house beer (by Abbeydale); 7 changing beers (often Abbeydale) Ⓗ
With 12 handpumps adorning the bar and over 100 beers from around the world, the Dev Cat is a great place for the discerning drinker. Now operated by Abbeydale Brewery, who brew the eponymous house bitter, there are usually up to six of its beers as well as a number of interesting guests. The menu ranges from light snacks through to hearty meals served all day to 9pm (6pm Sun). An excellent stopping-off point on any visit to the city.
🌡🍴🕐🐕♿🍽🚃

Henry's Café Bar

38 Cambridge Street, S1 4HP
🕐 9am-midnight (1am Fri & Sat) ☎ 0872 107 7077
House beer (by Clark's); 10 changing beers (sourced regionally; often Sheffield) Ⓗ
Former café/bar reopened as a freehouse in 2010. Now thriving again after a thorough refurbishment, it offers one of the largest selections of cask ales in the city centre, with up to 11 on tap. The pub is open plan, with seating at various levels around the long bar. Meals prepared from good locally sourced produce are served daily 11-7pm. Across the beer garden is the in-house Aardvark Brewery with its own bar, the Brewhouse, offering a further eight beers. 🌡🍴🕐🥡🍽🚃

Hop ✅

West One Plaza, Fitzwilliam Street, S1 4JB
🕐 12-midnight (1am Fri & Sat); closed Mon
☎ (0114) 278 1000 ⊕ thehop-sheffield.com
Fernandes Triple O; Ossett Yorkshire Blonde, Silver King; Rat White Rat; 4 changing beers (sourced nationally) Ⓗ
Unusually, this is a pub conversion from former supermarket premises in a modern bar/restaurant/shopping complex. From the entrance there is a small snug area leading to the main bar with 10 handpumps featuring up to four guest beers, often from local breweries, and a real cider. A larger room is used for regular live music sessions, overlooked by a balcony seating area. Quiz night is Tuesday. American barbecue-style food is served all day.
🌡🍴🕐🐕♿🥡🍽🚃(52,95,120)🐾📶

Red Deer Ⓛ ✅

18 Pitt Street, S1 4DD
🕐 12-midnight (1am Fri & Sat); 12-11 Sun
☎ (0114) 272 2890 ⊕ red-deer-sheffield.co.uk
Stancill No. 7; 8 changing beers (sourced regionally; often Kelham Island, Moorhouse's, Salamander) Ⓗ
A genuine, traditional local in the heart of the city. The small frontage of the original three-roomed pub hides an open-plan interior extended to the rear with a gallery seating area. As well as the impressive range of cask beers, including up to five guest ales, there is also a selection of continental bottled beers. Meals are served lunchtimes and evenings daily. The popular quiz is held Tuesday night, and an upstairs function room is available for bookings. Q🌡🍴🕐🥡🍽📶

Rutland Arms Ⓛ

86 Brown Street, S1 2BS
🕐 12-11 (midnight Thu-Sat) ☎ (0114) 272 9003
⊕ therutlandarmssheffield.co.uk

Blue Bee Hillfoot Best Bitter, Reet Pale; 6 changing beers (sourced regionally) Ⓗ
Occupying a corner site in the Cultural Industries Quarter and near Sheffield's main railway station, the pub has operated as a free house since 2009, under the same ownership as Blue Bee Brewery. The comfortable interior provides ample seating either side of the central entrance, and the wall displays include photos of old Sheffield pubs. Most of the guest beers come from local and regional microbreweries together with specials from Blue Bee. Food is served throughout the day to 9pm (6pm Sun). 🌡🍴🕐🥡🍽🍽🚃🐾📶

Sheffield Tap ★ Ⓛ

Platform 1b, Sheffield Station, Sheaf Street, S1 2BP
🕐 11-11; 10-midnight Fri & Sat ☎ (0114) 273 7558
⊕ sheffieldtap.com
Tapped Mojo, Rodeo; Thornbridge Jaipur IPA; 7 changing beers (sourced nationally) Ⓗ
Opened in 2009, this was originally the First Class refreshment room for Sheffield Midland Station, built in 1904. After years of neglect, the main bar area has been the subject of an award-winning restoration retaining many original features. Further seating has been provided in the entrance corridor and to the right of the bar. Usually, three beers are from the on-site Tapped Brewery, opened in 2013 in the impressive former dining room. The brewery can be viewed through a glass screen. Q🌡🌡♿🥡🍽🍽🐾📶

Three Tuns ✅

39 Silver Street Head, S1 2DD
🕐 11.30-11 (midnight Fri); 12-midnight Sat; 12-11 Sun
☎ (0114) 327 6211 ⊕ threetunssheffield.co.uk
Blue Bee Reet Pale; Sharp's Doom Bar; 4 changing beers (sourced locally; often Acorn, Blue Bee, Kelham Island) Ⓗ
A triangular pub on a sharp corner with raised seating areas and lots of wooden and brass features. Now operated by Reet Ale Pubs along with the Closed Shop, Punchbowl and Rutland Arms, it is popular with real ale enthusiasts as well as local office workers. The friendly staff serve six cask beers and provide good-quality traditional pub grub (no food Sun). There is a quiz on Wednesday at 6pm, and occasional live folk music.
Q🍴🥡♣🍽🍽🐾📶

Sheffield: Chapeltown

Commercial Ⓛ

107 Station Road, S35 2XF
🕐 12-11 (midnight Fri & Sat) ☎ (0114) 246 9066
⊕ thecommie.co.uk
Wentworth WPA, Bumble Beer; 6 changing beers (sourced nationally; often Durham, Toolmakers, White Rose) Ⓗ
Built in 1890, this friendly, well-established free house is the tap for the nearby Wentworth Brewery. In addition to six guest beers, including a stout or porter, there is at least one real cider. An island bar serves the lounge, games room and snug. Beer festivals are held in May and November. There is an outdoor area to the rear, and an upstairs function room which hosts regular live folk sessions. Monthly tutored whisky tastings take advantage of the extensive range available. Children are welcome. No meals Sunday evening.
🌡🌡🍴🕐🥡♣🍽P🚃(265,31A)🐾📶

Sheffield: Kelham Island

Fat Cat ⃞
23 Alma Street, S3 8SA
☼ 12-11 (midnight Fri & Sat) ☎ (0114) 249 4801
⊕ thefatcat.co.uk
Kelham Island Best Bitter, Pale Rider; Timothy Taylor Landlord; 8 changing beers (sourced nationally; often Kelham Island) ⃟
Opened in 1981, this is the pub that started the real ale revolution in the area. Beers from around the country are served alongside those from the adjacent Kelham Island Brewery. Vegetarian and gluten-free dishes feature on the menu (food is served 12-3pm, 6-8pm Mon-Fri; 12-7pm Sat; 12-3pm Sun). The walls are covered with many awards presented to the pub and brewery. Beer festivals are held every August and at various other times. Monday is curry and quiz night.
Q ❄ ❀ ⦿ & ▣ ♠ P ▤ ❀

Harlequin ⃞
108 Nursery Street, S3 8GG
☼ 12-11 (11.30 Thu & Fri; midnight Sat) ☎ (0114) 249 4181
⊕ theharlequinpub.wordpress.com
Exit 33 Blonde, New England Best; 8 changing beers (often Exit 33) ⃟
Operated by Exit 33 Brewing, the Harlequin takes its name from another former Ward's pub just round the corner, now demolished. The large open-plan interior features a central bar with seating on two levels. There are two regular and, usually, four other beers from Exit 33, as well as guests from far and wide, with the emphasis on microbreweries. A range of boutique bottled beers is also available. Wednesday is quiz night and there is live music at weekends.
❀ ⦿ ♠ ⦿ ▤ ▣ (47,48,53) ❀

Kelham Island Tavern ▼ ⃞ ⦿
62 Russell Street, S3 8RW
☼ 12-midnight ☎ (0114) 272 2482 ⊕ kelhamtavern.co.uk
Acorn Barnsley Bitter; Bradfield Farmers Blonde; Pictish Brewers Gold; 9 changing beers (sourced nationally; often Abbeydale, Brass Castle, North Riding Brewery) ⃟
Former CAMRA National Pub of the Year and regular regional and local winner, this small gem was rescued from dereliction in 2002. Twelve handpumps dispense an impressive range of beers, always including a mild, a porter and a stout. In the warmer months you can relax in the pub's multi award-winning beer garden. Regular folk music features on Sunday evenings and quiz night is Monday. No meals Sunday. Q ❄ ❀ ⦿ ▣ ♠ ⦿ ▤ ▣ ❀

Shakespeare's Ale & Cider House ⃞
146-148 Gibraltar Street, S3 8UB
☼ 12-midnight (1am Fri & Sat) ☎ (0114) 275 5959
⊕ shakespeares-sheffield.co.uk
9 changing beers (sourced nationally; often Abbeydale, Brass Castle, North Riding Brewery) ⃟
Originally built in 1821, it reopened as a free house in 2011, following a refurbishment including incorporation into the pub of the archway to the rear yard. The central bar serves three rooms as well as the extension and there is a further room across the corridor. Eight handpumps have featured over 4,000 different beers over the last five years, and real cider and over 100 whiskies are also sold. There is regular live music, a quiz on Thursdays, and annual beer festivals. Q ❀ ▣ ♠ ⦿ ▤ ▣ ❀ ☇

Sheffield: Loxley

Nag's Head Inn ⃞
Stacey Bank, S6 6SJ
☼ 11.30-11.30; 10-11.30 Sat & Sun ☎ (0114) 285 1202
Bradfield Farmers Bitter, Farmers Blonde, Farmers Brown Cow, Farmers Pale Ale; 2 changing beers (sourced locally; often Bradfield) ⃟
A friendly two-roomed country pub on the main road towards High Bradfield, it is the tap for the nearby Bradfield Brewery. Six beers from the range, including seasonal beers and one-off specials, are on the bar, all at competitive prices. Good home-cooked food is served (no food Sun eve or Mon and Tue). Excellent views of the Loxley Valley can be enjoyed from the outside drinking area. The games room has a three-quarter-size snooker table. Opens at 10am weekends to cater for anglers and walkers. Q ❄ ❀ ⦿ ♠ P ▤ (61,62) ❀

Sheffield: North

Blake Hotel
53 Blake Street, Walkley, S6 3JQ
☼ 12-11.30 (midnight Fri & Sat) ☎ (0114) 233 9336
Acorn Blonde; 5 changing beers ⃟
At the top of a steep hill (pedestrian handrails provided), this community pub reopened as a free house in 2010 after seven years of closure. Extensively restored, it has retained many traditional Victorian features, original etched windows and mirrors. A large decked garden has been developed to the rear. The five guest beers usually include a stout or porter, the majority from small independent breweries. The pub also has an extensive range of whiskies, with over 200 stocked. Q ❀ ♠ ⦿ ▤ ▣ (31,31a) ❀

Gardeners Rest
105 Neepsend Lane, Neepsend, S3 8AT
☼ 3-11; 12-midnight Fri & Sat; 12-11 Sun ☎ (0114) 272 4978
Sheffield Crucible Best, Five Rivers, Blanco Blonde, Porter; 8 changing beers (sourced nationally) ⃟
Reopened in 2009 after refurbishment following extensive flood damage in June 2007, this friendly and well-run free house acts as the tap for the nearby Sheffield Brewery. The main bar, with its clean, bright interior, houses art exhibitions and a restored bar billiards table. To the rear is a conservatory leading to a beer garden which overlooks the River Don. There is live music at weekends. Up to eight guest beers are sourced nationwide from microbreweries, and at least two real ciders. Q ❀ ▣ & ▣ ♠ ⦿ ▤ ▣ (7,8,8a) ❀

New Barrack Tavern
601 Penistone Road, Hillsborough, S6 2GA
☼ 5 (11 Thu)-11; 11-midnight Fri & Sat; 12-11 Sun ☎ (0114) 234 9148
Acorn Barnsley Bitter; Bradfield Farmers Bitter; Castle Rock Harvest Pale, Screech Owl; 5 changing beers (often Castle Rock) ⃟
Multi-roomed pub with an original 1936 floor plan, a Gilmours-branded doorstep and distinctive colourful exterior tiles. Up to five guest beers include seasonal ales from Castle Rock. Home-cooked food is served daily. There is a snug with a local sporting theme, and the lounge features live bands at weekends and a monthly comedy club on the first Sunday. Outside is an award-winning heated and covered patio garden. The new function room has its own bar.
Q ❄ ❀ ⦿ ▣ ♠ ⦿ ❀ ☇

Sheffield: South

Broadfield
452 Abbeydale Road, Nether Edge, S7 1FR
☼ 12-midnight (1am Fri & Sat); 12-11 Sun
☎ (0114) 255 0200 ⊕ thebroadfield.co.uk
Abbeydale Moonshine; Kelham Island Pale Rider;
Stancill Barnsley Bitter; 6 changing beers (sourced
regionally; often Abbeydale, Stancill) Ⓗ
Dating from 1896, the Broadfield became part of
the Forum Café Bars group in 2011. It has
established a deserved reputation for quality food
(served until 10pm) with an extensive menu
including hearty pies and home-made sausages.
Nine cask ales, usually including beers from the
group's own True North Brewery, are
complemented by a large range of bottled beers
and whiskies. Within the city's antiques quarter,
the Broadfield is now a leading player in the
Abbeydale social scene. ⏣❀◑♿♣P♿🐾📶

Brothers Arms
Well Road, Heeley, S8 9TZ
☼ 12-11 (midnight Fri & Sat) ☎ (0114) 258 9888
Bradfield Farmers Blonde; house beer (by Exit 33); 6
changing beers (sourced locally; often Blue Bee) Ⓗ
A classic, traditional local – although the interior is
open plan, it is designed so the various areas for
seating and games all feel individual and cosy. The
pub's name reflects its association with local
parody ukulele band, The Everly Pregnant Brothers,
and live music is hosted every Monday evening,
supplemented by folk sessions on the last Sunday.
The bar features eight real ales, with two regulars
and six changing beers, together with a real cider.
❀♣♠P♿🐾📶

Mount Pleasant ✓
293 Derbyshire Lane, Norton Woodseats, S8 8SG
☼ 5-midnight (1am Thu); 12-1am Fri; 3-1am Sat; 12-midnight
Sun ☎ (0114) 255 4997
Tetley Bitter, Gold; 4 changing beers (sourced locally;
often Abbeydale, Milestone, Welbeck Abbey) Ⓗ
Small, welcoming, two-roomed pub housed in a
former quarryman's cottage built in 1820, and
largely unspoilt by progress. The public bar is
adorned with a collection of beer bottles from the
1960s and the comfortable quieter lounge features
rare whisky bottles enjoyed by the Whisky Club.
There are two quiz nights weekly, a darts team and
a walking club. The annual beer festival is usually
in August. There have been only 10 licensees since
1841. Q⏣❀♣P♿(18)🐾📶

Sheaf View
25 Gleadless Road, Heeley, S2 3AA
☼ 11.30-11.30 (12.30am Fri & Sat) ☎ (0114) 249 6455
Kelham Island Easy Rider; Neepsend Blonde; 6
changing beers (sourced regionally; often Neepsend,
Pictish, Saltaire) Ⓗ
A 19th-century pub near Heeley City Farm, the
Sheaf experienced a chequered history before
becoming a real ale oasis since reopening as a free
house in 2000. The walls and shelves are adorned
with assorted breweriana and provide an ideal
background for good drinking and conversation. A
wide range of international beers, together with
malt whiskies and a real cider, complement the
eight reasonably priced real ales. A busy pub,
especially on Wednesday quiz night and Sheffield
United match days. Q❀♣♠P♿🐾

White Lion Ⓛ ✓
615 London Road, Heeley, S2 4HT
☼ 4-midnight (1am Fri); 12-1am Sat; 2-midnight Sun
☎ (0114) 255 1500 ⊕ whitelionsheffield.co.uk
Abbeydale Moonshine; Tetley Bitter; Wychwood
Hobgoblin; house beer (by Kelham Island); 7
changing beers (sourced regionally) Ⓗ
Grade II-listed pub, respectfully refurbished over
the years. A tiled central corridor links a number of
delightful small rooms and leads to the larger rear
concert room. There are four regular beers and up
to seven changing guests, and a good selection of
malts. There is always a gluten-free option among
the bottled beers. The pub hosts many community
events along with live music most nights and a
quiz on Wednesdays. ⏣❀♣♠♿🐾📶

Sheffield: West

Beer Engine Ⓛ
17 Cemetery Road, Highfield, S11 8FJ
☼ 4-11; 12-midnight Fri & Sat; 12-11 Sun ☎ (0114) 273 9392
⊕ beerenginesheffield.com
Neepsend Blonde; 5 changing beers (sourced
regionally) Ⓗ
A traditional-style multi-roomed pub reopened in
2015 as a free house following a sympathetic
refurbishment. The changing beer range is mainly
from local and regional microbreweries, and there
is a quality spirits offering. Food is served evenings
(except Sun) and weekend afternoons, and is
mainly tapas-style dishes supplemented by pie and
peas on match days and a roast on Sundays. The
large beer garden has a heated, covered area.
❀◑♠♿🐾📶

Beer House Ⓛ
623 Ecclesall Road, Sharrow, S11 8PT
☼ 12-11
5 changing beers (sourced nationally; often Exit 33,
Stancill) Ⓗ
Sheffield's first micropub opened in a small former
shop unit in late-2014. The front of two rooms has
level access from the street, and contains the bar
with its bank of six handpumps displaying a
changing range of beers, mainly from
microbreweries. Local breweries feature heavily,
particularly Exit 33 and Stancill. The rear room has
seating focused around the fireplace, and there is a
quiz on Wednesday evenings. Q⏣❀♣♿🐾

Closed Shop Ⓛ ✓
52-54 Commonside, S10 1GG
☼ 4-11 (midnight Fri); 12-midnight Sat; 12-11 Sun
☎ (0114) 266 0330 ⊕ theclosedshopsheffield.co.uk
Blue Bee Reet Pale; 7 changing beers (sourced
regionally; often Blue Bee) Ⓗ
Following a significant refurbishment in 2013,
there are now eight handpumps dispensing beers
from Blue Bee, other local breweries and guests,
alongside three real ciders and a perry. Two large
bay window areas at the front provide comfortable
seating. The smaller space at the end of the bar has
photos of the local area, and there is a display of
limited edition prints by a local artist for sale. A
raised area at the rear houses a pool table.
⏣❀◑♣♠P♿(95)🐾📶

Princess Royal Ⓛ
43 Slinn Street, Crookes, S10 1NW
☼ 5-midnight; 1-1am Fri; 12-1am Sat; 12-midnight Sun
☎ (0114) 266 0752

Black Sheep Best Bitter; Tetley Bitter; house beer (by Welbeck Abbey); 2 changing beers (sourced locally; often Bradfield, Welbeck Abbey) [H]
This popular local tucked away on the side streets was a Victorian beer house forming part of a row of cottages. Converted to its present form in the 1920s by Gilmours Brewery, the original etched windows include one for Oatmeal Stout. The central bar serves the open-plan lounge and a snooker room to the rear. There are quiz nights on Mondays and Thursdays, with free sandwiches and chips. The upstairs function room is the venue for the Crookes Folk Club on Thursdays.
Q🐴❀♣🚌🐾📶

Punchbowl ✔
236 Crookes, Crookes, S10 1TH
🕒 11.30-11 (midnight Thu-Sat); 12-11 Sun
☎ (0114) 267 1052 🌐 thepunchbowlsheffield.co.uk
Blue Bee Reet Pale; 7 changing beers (sourced regionally) [H]
Locally known as the Top Shop, this is a modern and open-plan pub with mixed seating areas, booths, high tables and chairs, and a cosy corner. A raised area at one end has views over Sheffield. There is wooden flooring with a tiled area round the bar and kitchen, where freshly baked pizzas are made. Table skittles and Jenga can be played.
🐴❀◑♿♣P🚌(52a,52)🐾📶

Rising Sun ✔
471 Fulwood Road, Nether Green, S10 3QA
🕒 12-11 (11.30 Fri & Sat) ☎ (0114) 230 3855
🌐 risingsunsheffield.co.uk
Abbeydale Daily Bread, Brimstone, Moonshine, Absolution; 9 changing beers (sourced nationally; often Abbeydale) [H]
Operated by local brewer Abbeydale, this is a large suburban roadhouse. There are two comfortably furnished rooms with a log-burning fire between the main bar and the new extension, which has glass panels in the end wall and a lantern roof. A range of Abbeydale beers is always served, with up to six guests, mainly from micros, dispensed from the impressive bank of 13 handpumps. Quizzes are on Sunday and Wednesday evenings. The Sunfest beer festival is in July.
Q🐴❀◑♿♣🍎P🚌(120,83a)🐾📶

University Arms [L]
197 Brook Hill, Broomhall, S3 7HG
🕒 12-11 (midnight Fri & Sat); closed Sun ☎ (0114) 222 8969
Kelham Island Pale Rider [H]**; Welbeck Abbey Red Feather** [H]/[G]**; house beer (by Acorn); 5 changing beers (sourced nationally)** [H]
Owned by the University of Sheffield, this former staff club has an open-plan lounge with a bar at one end adjacent to a small alcove seating area, and a conservatory leading to the large garden. There is additional seating upstairs, with separate rooms for snooker and darts. The guest beers are mostly local and there are regular beer festivals. Entertainment includes a quiz on Tuesdays and live blues or jazz some weekends. No food Saturday.
Q🐴❀◑🍺♣🍎🚌(51,52)🐾

York [L]
243-247 Fulwood Road, Broomhill, S10 3BA
🕒 11.30-11.30; 9.30am-12.30am Fri & Sat; 9.30am-11.30 Sun
☎ (0114) 266 4624 🌐 theyorksheffield.co.uk
8 changing beers (sourced regionally; often Abbeydale) [H]
Occupying a prominent site in the centre of Broomhill, the York was built in the 1830s and was originally a blackmith's and alehouse called the Travellers Inn. Extensively refurbished in 2010, with parquet flooring and wood-panelled walls, it now offers high-quality dining, with its own bakery and smokery. The house beers from True North are complemented by a range of six local and regional guest ales and two real ciders. Beer and food events feature regularly throughout the year.
Q🐴❀◑♿🍎🚌(51,52,120)🐾📶

Thorne

Windmill ✔
19 Queen Street, DN8 5AA
🕒 2-11 (11.30 Fri & Sat); 12-midnight Sun ☎ (01405) 812866
Black Sheep Best Bitter; Kelham Island Easy Rider; 2 changing beers (often Adnams, Sharp's) [H]
Three or four well-kept real ales are on offer in this friendly community pub, where cheerful banter is the order of the day. The pub comprises a smart lounge linked by an archway to a larger public bar, and outside there is a large beer garden with play equipment. It is close to the town centre, convenient for public transport, and has ample car parking. Quiz night is Sunday.
❀⇌♣P🚌(87,88)🐾📶

Thurlstone

Huntsman [L]
136 Manchester Road, S36 9QW (on main A628)
🕒 6 (5 Fri & Sat)-11; 12-10.30 Sun ☎ (01226) 764892
🌐 thehuntsmanthurlstone.co.uk
Black Sheep Best Bitter; Tetley Bitter; Timothy Taylor Landlord; 3 changing beers [H]
A popular pub and a regular in the Guide. It has a fantastic ambience created mainly by a chatty and appreciative clientele, is a hub for many local activity groups, and is a strong supporter of local charities. Food is only available on Sunday lunchtimes. Dogs are especially welcome. The six cask ales are superb. Q🐴❀♣🚌🐾

Tickhill

Scarbrough Arms [L]
Sunderland Street, DN11 9QJ (on A631)
🕒 12-11; 12-10.30 Sun ☎ (01302) 742977
Greene King Abbot; John Smith's Bitter; Timothy Taylor Landlord; Wychwood Hobgoblin; 1 changing beer (sourced locally; often Chantry, Glentworth, Pheasantry) [H]
A deserving Guide entry since 1990, this three-roomed stone-built pub has won several CAMRA awards over the years. Originally a farmhouse, the building dates back to the 16th century, although it has undergone structural changes since then. The snug is a delight with its barrel-shaped furniture and real fire; there is also a rejuvenated front lounge with logburner and a traditional rear bar. An outbuilding doubles as a covered smoking area and an extension for beer festivals.
Q🐴❀🔥♣🍎P🚌(22,205)🐾📶

Wales

Duke of Leeds ✔
16 Church Street, S26 5LQ (off A618 into School Rd)
🕒 12-11 ☎ (01909) 515490

Theakston Old Peculier; Timothy Taylor Landlord; 2 changing beers (sourced locally; often Abbeydale) ⒽReopened in 2015, following substantial refurbishment after a period of closure, it was once the coaching inn of the Duke of Leeds, and is more than 300 years old. The bar area features an old jukebox, and there are three other spaces where drinks and meals can be taken. The food menu is extensive and freshly cooked to order. Outdoor areas afford views of the village and this is a popular area for walkers. Ample parking is provided behind the pub, while buses travel along the main Wales road, a few minutes' walk away. ✿◖ⅅPⓓ

Wath upon Dearne

Church House ⅃ ✅
Montgomery Square, S63 7RZ
✿ 8am-midnight ☎ (01709) 879518
Greene King Abbot; Ruddles Best Bitter; 5 changing beers Ⓗ
Large pub with an impressive frontage set in a pedestrian square in the town centre, with excellent access to local bus services across the square. It was built in 1810 and consecrated by the nearby church in 1912. It became a pub in the 1980s, and then a Wetherspoon outlet in 2000. A wide variety of beers from regional, national and local brewers is offered alongside real ciders or perries on handpull. Handy for exploring the RSPB Old Moor Wetlands Centre and for Manvers Commercial Park. ✿◖ⅅ♿♣Pⓓ (22,220,229)⬢

Wentworth

George & Dragon ⅃
85 Main Street, S62 7TN
✿ 11-11 (11.30 Thu; midnight Fri & Sat) ☎ (01226) 742440
Theakston Old Peculier; 7 changing beers (often Wentworth) Ⓗ
In a picturesque village, this free house offers up to eight ales from local, regional and national brewers. The pub has a car park and patio, and a grassed area at the rear with a children's adventure playground and a craft shop. There is also a marquee in the garden. Home-cooked food is popular here. This local, licensed since 1804, is handy for walking to historic Wentworth Woodhouse and Hoober Stand. It can also be accessed through the rear garden from the parish church. A discount is given for CAMRA members. Q➤✿◖ⅅPⓓ (44,227)❀⬢

Rockingham Arms ⅃ ✅
8 Main Street, S62 7TL
✿ 11-11 (midnight Fri & Sat); 11-10.30 Sun
☎ (01226) 742075
Black Sheep Best Bitter; Theakston Old Peculier; 5 changing beers (sourced regionally; often Wentworth) Ⓗ
Country pub dating from 1814, in the grounds of the Wentworth estate near the Wentworth Brewery and historic Wentworth Woodhouse. An ideal stop-off point for walkers, the pub offers accommodation – across the road in converted cottages – local entertainment and a range of home-cooked meals. A crown green bowling green is attached. The pub is welcoming, warmed by real fires in winter and with a patio and garden for summer drinking. Three rooms plus a large function room are to the rear. Entertainment is staged in the barn. Q➤✿⇋◖ⅅ♣Pⓓ (44,227)❀⬢

Whiston

Chequers Inn ✅
Pleasley Road, S60 4HB (on A618, 1½ miles from M1)
✿ 12 (4 Mon & Tue)-11; 12-11.30 Fri & Sat
☎ (01709) 325676
Abbeydale Moonshine; Castle Rock Harvest Pale; Sharp's Doom Bar; Tetley Bitter; 2 changing beers Ⓗ
Next to a 13th-century thatched barn, this friendly local replaced an old coaching inn when the road was widened in 1933. One side of the bar acts as a taproom, with a split-level lounge to the right. The large garden features a barbecue area. In the heart of Whiston, the pub is a regular local CAMRA award winner. The food is home-cooked by chefs. Features include quiz nights, discos, regular live music and scooter club meets, and it has a dartboard and pool table.
✿◖ⅅ♿♣Pⓓ (25,27,29)⬢

Hind ⅃ ✅
285 East Bawtry Road, S60 4ET (on A631 link road between M1 and M18)
✿ 11.30-midnight ☎ (01709) 532490
Abbeydale Moonshine; Brakspear Bitter; Tetley Bitter; house beer (by Black Sheep); 2 changing beers (sourced nationally) Ⓗ
A large pub, built for Mappins Brewery of Rotherham in 1936. Originally named as King Edward VIII, it was renamed when the king abdicated. Since refurbishment by Ember Inns the interior has been opened out, creating good disabled access. There are extensive gardens and a patio to the rear, with a snooker table upstairs (membership required to play). Daytime, evening and now takeaway food is popular. There is a 20p per pint discount with a CAMRA card and guest beers are cheaper on Mondays. Home to a cask club. Q➤✿◖ⅅ♿Pⓓ (10,10A,19B)⬢

Wickersley

Wickersley Old Village Cricket Club ⅃
Northfield Lane, S66 2HL (opp Wickerley Northfield primary school, down driveway beside pitch)
✿ 5-10 (11 Wed, Fri & Sat); 12-10 Sun ☎ (01709) 700536
Sharp's Doom Bar; 3 changing beers (often Chantry) Ⓗ
Demand for real ale has increased and there are now four handpumps on the go in this comfortably appointed and friendly club. The large lounge offers a more peaceful location for a quality beer than the local pubs. CAMRA members are more than welcome for a good-value pint, and of course you can always watch the cricket. A real ale discount is offered for card-carrying CAMRA members. Opening hours are likely to be extended during home matches. CAMRA branch Club of the Year 2014-16. ✿◖♣Pⓓ

Wombwell

Anglers' Rest ⅃
66 Park Street, S73 0HS
✿ 5-11.30 Mon; 5 (7 Wed)-midnight; 12-midnight Sun
☎ (01226) 345747 ⊕ anglersrestwombwell.co.uk
Geeves Clear Cut; 5 changing beers Ⓗ
This small and friendly pub on the edge of Wombwell town centre is the Geeves Brewery tap, and prides itself on being a traditional community local. The beer is excellent and comes direct from

the brewery, with guest ales from other small independent brewers. It is very much an old-fashioned drinkers' establishment. Tuesday is quiz night. In keeping with pub's character, entertainment is of a come-along-and-join-in style on the second Wednesday of the month. Q❀♣♠P🖰🗑❀🗢

Woodsetts

Butchers Arms 🅛
2 Gildingswell Road, S81 8QA
🕘 12-11; 12-midnight Fri & Sat ☎ (01909) 567700
🌐 rawbrew.com/butchersarms
Courage Best Bitter; Raw Blonde Pale; 5 changing beers (sourced nationally; often Raw) 🄷
A joint venture between Raw Pub Co and Enterprise, the Butchers had a complete refurbishment in a contemporary style and reopened in 2013. Three Raw ales are prominently featured alongside three guest beers, and there is an interesting range of foreign bottle beers to try. Quality home-cooked food is another major attraction at this friendly community pub. Beer festivals and live music are also regular features, with the garden area busy in the summer months. Q🏃🍺🌙♦🖐♠P🖰🗑❀🗢

Wortley

Wortley Men's Club 🅛 ✅
Reading Room Lane, S35 7DB (in centre of village at back of Wortley Arms public house)
🕘 2-11; 12-11 Sat & Sun ☎ (0114) 288 2066
Timothy Taylor Landlord; 2 changing beers 🄷
CAMRA national, regional and branch Club of the Year, set in the pretty rural village of Wortley, near Wortley Hall and gardens. The opulent building features exposed timber frames, ornate ceilings, wooden panelling and a real fire. Guest ales are from local and national breweries, and a guest cider is always available. The club runs an annual beer festival in July. Show your CAMRA membership card or a copy of this Guide on entry. Q🍺♠P🖰(29)

YORKSHIRE (WEST)

Ackworth

Masons Arms
Bell Lane, WF7 7JD (Bell Lane is a turning off A628 by a defunct railway bridge)
🕘 4 (1.30 Fri)-midnight; 12-1am Sat; 12-midnight Sun ☎ 07966 501827
Bradfield Farmers Blonde, Farmers Brown Cow; 4 changing beers (sourced locally) 🄷
A Grade II-listed former coaching house dating from 1682 built of locally quarried stone, one of seven real ale establishments in the village. A central bar serves the main room, pool room and smaller lounge. Log-burning fireplaces in both the main rooms were discovered 15 years ago during a sensitive refurbishment. Live music features Saturday evening and Sunday afternoon, games night is Tuesday and quiz night is Thursday – all well attended by locals and visitors alike. 🍺♣P🖰

Altofts

Robin Hood 🍷 🅛
10 Church Road, WF6 2NJ

🕘 4-11; 3-midnight Fri; 12-midnight Sat; 12-11 Sun
☎ (01924) 892911
Acorn Barnsley Bitter; 5 changing beers (sourced locally) 🄷
Locally owned free house/brewpub at the top end of the village. Crowned local CAMRA Pub of the Year 2015, this village hostelry has a large patio area seating 70 people. Tarn 51 microbrewery is on-site next to the patio. The pub is within easy reach of the Pennine Trail and Aire & Calder Navigation, and only a mile from Stanley Ferry marina. The intention is to have three Tarn 51 brews alongside three guest beers. Q🏃🍺♣♠P🖰❀🗢

Alverthorpe

Alverthorpe WMC 🅛 ✅
111 Flanshaw Lane, WF2 9JG
🕘 2-11; 11.30-11 Fri & Sat; 12-11 Sun ☎ (01924) 374179
Bob's White Lion; Theakston Best Bitter; 3 changing beers (sourced locally) 🄷
Multi-roomed CIU-affiliated club with a very cosy interior with unusual stained-glass features. A wide selection of guest ales is featured, mainly from local micros. The club is a regular winner of local CAMRA awards. Live entertainment takes place on Saturdays and Sundays. Snooker and darts are among the traditional games, with a wide-screen TV for the armchair enthusiasts. It has sporting teams and a floodlit bowling green. Local CAMRA branch Club of the Year 2015.
🏃🍺♦♠P🖰(104,212)

Baildon

Bull's Head Inn ✅
6 Westgate, BD17 5ES
🕘 12-11.30 (midnight Fri & Sat) ☎ (01274) 976416
Goose Eye Chinook Blonde; Saltaire Blonde; Sharp's Doom Bar; Tetley Bitter; 2 changing beers (sourced nationally) 🄷
A popular two-roomed village local where visitors and well-behaved dogs are always welcome. The separate taproom houses darts and dominoes. Log fires give a homely atmosphere and local photos of Baildon adorn the walls. Two independent guest beers complement the four regular real ales. There is a quiz on Sunday nights. Occasional music nights are held and piped background music is often played. 🍺♣P🖰❀🗢

Junction 🅛
1 Baildon Road, BD17 6AB (on A6038)
🕘 12-midnight (1am Fri & Sat) ☎ (01274) 582009
Fuller's ESB; Junction Blonde; Oakham Bishops Farewell; Saltaire Blonde; Tetley Bitter; 2 changing beers (sourced nationally) 🄷
This busy three-roomed local comprises a lounge, public bar and games area. The five regularly available ales, including at least one from the in-house brewery, are complemented by two guest ales. Real cider and foreign bottled beers are also sold. Food is served weekday lunchtimes and other times by arrangement. A quiz night is held on Thursday, an acoustic session on Sunday night and pub games on other evenings. An annual beer festival is staged at the end of July. 🍺🌙♣♠🖰❀

WEST YORKSHIRE

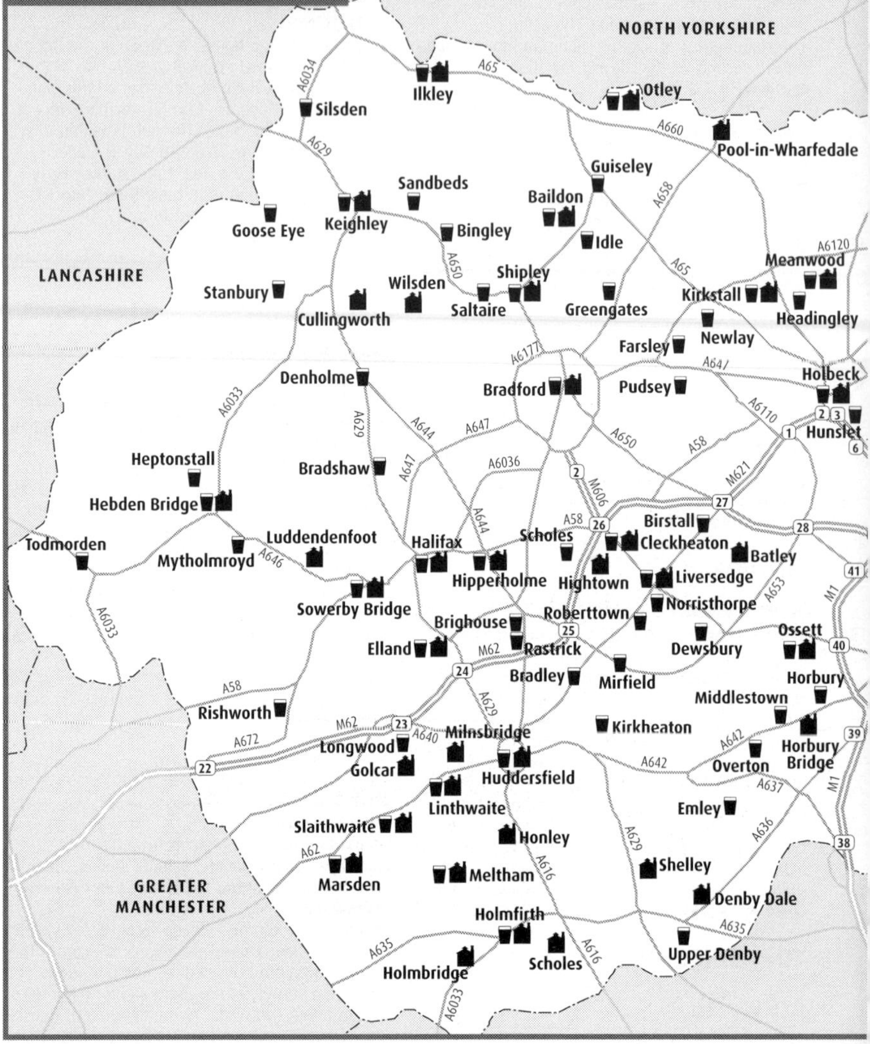

Bingley

Foundry Hill [L]

Wellington Street, BD16 2NB (opp railway station)
🕐 12-midnight (11 Wed); 12-9 Sun; closed Mon & Tue
☎ (01274) 566144 🌐 foundryhillbar.co.uk
4 changing beers (sourced nationally) [H]
Modern basement pub comprising a small bar area and an adjacent larger room for drinking and dining. A changing range of real ales is sold, sourced both locally and nationally, and a real cider is usually available. The pub can get quite busy, especially at weekends. Meals are home-made and popular on Sunday lunchtime, when bookings are advised. Events are occasionally held and are detailed on the website. Q🐴◑🚉🍎🚌📶

Off the Tap [L]

1 Burrage Street, BD16 1GH (close to railway station and off Chapel Lane)
🕐 4 (12 Fri & Sat)-11.30; 2-10.30 Sun; closed Mon ☎ 07960 995267 🌐 offthetap.co.uk
6 changing beers (often Bingley, Elland, Saltaire) [H]/[G]
Single-room café-style pub offering up to six real ales, with the majority served direct from the cask. A range of beer styles and ales from local breweries are featured. At least one real cider and perry is also available, as are bottled beers and wines. Live bands often play on Fridays and there are regular open mic nights mid-week. The pub is closed on Mondays except bank holidays, and is usually closed for the first few weeks in January. 🐴❀♿🚉🍎🚌(760,662)🐾

Birstall

Horse & Jockey [L] ✔

97 Low Lane, WF17 9HB (on A643 near the village centre)

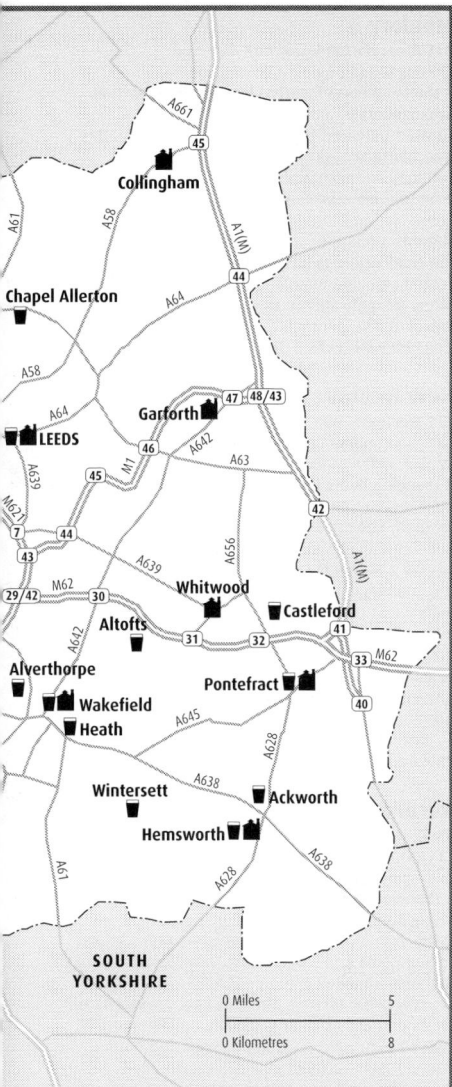

✿ 12 (4 Wed)-midnight; 12-1am Fri & Sat ☎ (01924) 472559
Jennings Cumberland Ale; John Smith's Bitter; Ossett Yorkshire Blonde, Silver King; Sharp's Doom Bar; 1 changing beer (sourced nationally; often Durham, Naylor's, Rudgate) ⊞
A country-style pub first licensed in the 1750s, which lies west of the village centre. The open-plan bar is divided into four areas, with half-panelled walls and beamed ceilings. Darts, dominoes and pool are played, on Thursdays there is a music and knowledge quiz, and on Saturdays karaoke. Guest beers come mainly from independent breweries. Outside is a patio with a beautiful flower display which has won the Birstall in Bloom award for the past three years. Please note pub policy says no hats, no tracksuit bottoms. Last admission is at 11pm.
❀♣P🚐(283,229,220)🛜

Bradford

Castle ⬙

20 Grattan Road, BD1 2LU
✪ 12-11; 1-9 Sun ☎ (01274) 393166
Jennings Cumberland Ale; 3 changing beers (often Empire) ⓗ
A traditional city-centre pub kept alive by an enthusiastic Indian landlord. The imposing stone building, dating from 1898, comprises a large open-plan room with a wraparound bar to one side. Formerly a Webster's house, it now sells a variety of beers of varying strengths in a relaxed atmosphere. Guest ales include at least one from a local brewery. A dartboard and TV are located to one end. Free, live folk music is played on a Friday night and a DJ plays on a Saturday night.
🚲🚶♿⌷♣🚐☺

Corn Dolly ⬙

110 Bolton Road, BD1 4DE
✪ 11.30-11; 12-10.30 Sun ☎ (01274) 720219
🌐 corndolly.pub
Everards Tiger; Moorhouse's Pride of Pendle; Timothy Taylor Boltmaker; 5 changing beers (sourced nationally) ⓗ
Award-winning free house run by the same family for over 25 years, a short distance from the city centre and Forster Square railway station. Previously called the Wharf due to its location near to the former Bradford canal, it first opened its doors in 1834. An open-plan layout incorporates a games area to one end. Good-value food is served weekday lunchtimes. It has a friendly atmosphere and is popular before Bradford City matches. A collection of pumpclips adorns the beams.
⌷≒♣P🚐

Fighting Cock ⬙

21-23 Preston Street, BD7 1JE (close to Grattans, off Thornton Rd)
✪ 11.30-11; 12-10.30 Sun ☎ (01274) 726907
Ilkley Mary Jane; Theakston Old Peculier; Timothy Taylor Golden Best, Boltmaker, Landlord; 7 changing beers (often Dark Star, Glentworth, Pictish) ⓗ
A drinkers' paradise in an industrial area, this multi award-winning pub is 20 minutes' walk from the city centre and close to bus routes along Thornton Road and Legrams Lane. A large beer garden on the opposite side of the street was added in 2015 and summer beer festivals now take place. Twelve real ales are usually on sale, including at least one dark beer. A choice of real ciders and foreign bottled beers is also offered. Good-value lunches are served Monday to Saturday. ☺⌷♣🍴🚐☺

Jacob's Beer House ⬙

14 Kent Street, BD1 5RL (by Jacobs Well roundabout at end of Hall Ings)
✪ 4-11 (10 Mon); 12-11 Sat; closed Sun ☎ (01274) 394479
9 changing beers (sourced nationally; often Salamander, Stancill, Titanic) ⓗ
Refurbished and reopened in 2013, this pub was formerly known as Jacob's Well, dating from about 1830. (If arriving from Interchange bus or railway station, take the Nelson Street exit and cross the council offices' car park.) The layout is open but with a snug to the side of the bar. Nine handpulls offer a changing range of beers from independents, always featuring some darker ales. Sit outside and watch the city's bustle while supping good ale. ☺≒🍴🚐🤫

Monkey ⬙

931 Great Horton Road, BD7 4AQ
✪ 3-11; 12-11 Fri-Sun
3 changing beers (sourced locally; often Junction, Salamander) ⓗ
Located between Bradford and Queensbury, this free house was originally two 17th-century cottages and comprises a games room and lounge with real fire. The real ales are from Junction Brewery plus other locals such as Salamander. There is a range of bottled, imported beers. One of the outdoor areas has a barbecue and a covered, seated smoking area. The other is elevated and offers magnificent views over and beyond Bradford. The pool table, jukebox and Wi-Fi are all free. 🚲🏵♣🚐(576,610,614)☺🤫

New Beehive Inn ★ ⬙

171 Westgate, BD1 3AA (on B6144)
✪ 1.30-11 (midnight Fri); 12-midnight Sat; 6-11 Sun
☎ (01274) 721784 🌐 newbeehive.co.uk
4 changing beers (sourced nationally) ⓗ
Built in 1901 and re-modelled in 1936, the multi-roomed, Edwardian interior of this imposing building will charm you. Recognised by CAMRA as having a nationally important historic pub interior, it comprises a drinking hallway and three rooms with wood panelling. Gas lighting and a real fire add to the warmth. Beers are almost exclusively from local or national microbreweries. Spend time looking at the impressive murals of deceased musicians in the back bar. You can order a curry from next door and have it plated and served here. Seventeen en-suite rooms are available.
🚲🏵🛏⌷《≒♣🍴P🚐🤫

Record Café

45-47 North Parade, BD1 3JH
✪ 11-11 (midnight Fri & Sat) ☎ (01274) 723143
🌐 therecordcafe.co.uk
4 changing beers (sourced regionally; often Half Moon, Sonnet 43, Vocation) ⓗ
Opened in late 2014, this café-style pub's unique selling point is the sale of ale, vinyl and ham. Four real ales are available on handpull with further KeyKeg beers offered. The ales cover a variety of styles and a dark beer is usually on tap. There is also an extensive selection of imported bottled beers. Food is offered in a charcuterie style, specialising in hams and cheeses from Spain. Meanwhile, in the upstairs mezzanine area, it is possible to browse and purchase vinyl records. Occasional live music plays on Sunday evenings.
🏵≒🍴(662,680)☺🤫

Sir Titus Salt ⬙ ✔

Unit B, Windsor Baths, Morley Street, BD7 1AQ (behind Alhambra theatre)
✪ 8am-midnight (1am Fri & Sat) ☎ (01274) 732853
Greene King Abbot; Ruddles Best Bitter; Sharp's Doom Bar; 7 changing beers (sourced nationally; often Baildon, Wychwood) ⓗ
Excellent conversion of a former public baths by Wetherspoon, comprising a large open-plan main room with an additional room to one side and an upper mezzanine area. Ten handpumps serve a variety of real ales. Named in honour of a local mill owner and industrial philanthropist, the interior decoration includes photographs and artefacts relating to his life. Located within Bradford's cultural quarter, the National Media Museum and Alhambra theatre are nearby. Q🚲🏵《♿≒🍴🚐🤫

Sparrow Bier Café L

32 North Parade, BD1 3HZ

🕿 11-11 (midnight Thu-Sat); 12-11 Sun ☎ (01274) 270772
⊕ thesparrowbradford.co.uk

4 changing beers (sourced regionally; often Kirkstall, Summer Wine, Wishbone) Ⓗ

A simply furnished café-style pub which has thrived since opening in 2011 in the city's independent quarter. A large main bar is complemented by additional seating in the basement. Four cask ales are offered plus at least two real ciders and a varied selection of international bottled beers. Deli-style sandwiches and platters are available and free snacks are served on Bradford City FC match days.
❀⇄●🖵(680)🐾🛜

Bradley

White Cross ✓

2 Bradley Road, HD2 1XD (at Leeds Rd/Bradley Rd crossroads)

🕿 11.45-11 (midnight Fri & Sat); 12-10.30 Sun
☎ (01484) 425728

Copper Dragon Golden Pippin; St Austell Tribute; 3 changing beers Ⓗ

Friendly Bradley pub by the Leeds Road roundabout which has been in the Guide for 14 years. It has been serving the community since circa 1806 and still retains its Bentley Yorkshire Breweries green tiled entrance and windows. The dining area and lounge sit either side of the central bar, where two regular beers are supported by up to three varied guests. Home-cooked food is served 12-2pm Monday-Friday, 12-4.30pm Sunday (but no food Sat). ❀◑♣P🖵🛜

Bradshaw

Golden Fleece ✓

1 Bradshaw Lane, HX2 9UZ

🕿 4-11 (midnight Fri); 12-midnight Sat; 12-10.30 Sun ☎ 07522 190990 ⊕ goldenfleecebradshaw.co.uk

Saltaire Blonde; house beer (by Pennine); 2 changing beers Ⓗ

At the heart of Bradshaw, this busy village pub provides the focus for a variety of sporting enthusiasts including pool teams, Sunday footballers, Sky TV viewers and a dominoes team. Two popular quiz nights are held weekly. It also has a Saturday disco night and '60s and '70s theme nights. Barbecues are held in the summer to take advantage of the beer garden, which enjoys excellent views across nearby countryside. There is a free buffet every Friday night.
❀♣P🖵(504,526,521)🛜

Brighouse

Red Rooster

123 Elland Road, Brookfoot, HD6 2QR (on A6025 towards Elland)

🕿 4-11; 12-midnight Fri & Sat; 12-10.30 Sun

Abbeydale Moonshine; Atom Schrodinger's Cat; Saltaire Blonde; Timothy Taylor Boltmaker, Landlord; 4 changing beers Ⓗ

Half a mile from Brighouse town centre, it is well worth the walk to this excellent free house. Formerly known as the Wharf, the Red Rooster was purpose-built around 1900 for the adjacent coal wharf, which served much of western Yorkshire. Three wharfmen's cottages still stand alongside the

pub by the Red Beck. Four hundred yards further on is the Cromwell Bottom Nature Reserve, where you can walk along the canal to Elland or Brighouse. Dark beers are always on tap. ❀♣P🖵(571)🐾🛜

Richard Oastler ✓

Bethel Street, HD6 1JN

🕿 8am-midnight (1am Fri & Sat) ☎ (01484) 401756

Greene King Abbot; Ruddles Best Bitter; Sharp's Doom Bar; 7 changing beers (sourced locally; often Elland, Goose Eye, Naylor's) Ⓗ

Formerly a Methodist chapel dating back to 1878, this Wetherspoon pub has been beautifully restored. The main bar area is lit by two extravagant chandeliers hanging from an unusual ceiling. Look closely to see hymn book numbers, but organ pipes and pews are easily spotted upstairs, which is not open to the public. A room in an extension into a later chapel annexe is available for private functions and meetings.
Q⮆❀◑♿⇄●🖵🛜

Castleford

Junction L

Carlton Street, WF10 1EE (top of town centre)

🕿 2-10.30 (midnight Wed & Thu); 12-11 Fri & Sat; 12-11.30 Sun ☎ (01977) 277750 ⊕ thejunctionpubcastleford.com

6 changing beers (often Elland) Ⓗ

Rejuvenated pub handy for bus and train stations, specialising in beers in the landlord's own wooden casks, which are loaned to enterprising local brewers such as Ridgeside, Elland and Walls. Sam Smith's Old Brewery Bitter and up to six guest beers are sold in the wood. The pub hosts an annual Easter Woodfest beer festival. The large horseshoe-shaped bar is kept warm with open fires, and a stove-heated snug is available for functions. Folk night is the last Sunday of each month, and quiz night is Wednesday.
Q⮆⇄♣●🖵🐾🛜

Cleckheaton

Rose & Crown L

6 Westgate, BD19 5ET (on A643, W off A638)

🕿 12-11; 12-10.30 Sun ☎ (01274) 861530
⊕ rosebrewpub.co.uk

Copper Dragon Best Bitter; 5 changing beers (sourced locally; often Empire, Ossett, Salamander) Ⓗ

A cosy town-centre pub with a five-barrel microbrewery. It is newly refurbished to a high specification with lots of woodwork in the three rooms, plus comfortable seating and attractive features. Great-quality food is served lunchtimes and evenings, with a good choice of mainly local beers including one or two brewed here, dark beers being especially popular. The bus station is a three-minute walk. ⮆◑●🖵🐾🛜

Denholme

New Inn

Keighley Road, BD13 4JT (on A629)

🕿 4-11; 12-11 Sat & Sun ☎ 07887 510354

Tetley Bitter; 3 changing beers (sourced regionally) Ⓗ

A warm welcome is assured at this homely free house on the Keighley-Halifax road in the village of Denholme. The premises have an open-plan layout but still retain a multi-room feel. A conservatory extension houses a pool table. All ales are keenly priced. The pub sits high on the hillside, with stunning views over the Aire Valley. For the energetic, the Great Northern walking/cycling trail is nearby. ⚲🏵♣P🚉(502,696)🦮💥📶

Dewsbury

West Riding Refreshment Rooms 🅛 ✅

Dewsbury Railway Station, Wellington Road, WF13 1HF
🕐 11 (12 Mon)-11; 11-midnight Fri; 10-midnight Sat
☎ (01924) 459193 🌐 beerhouses.co.uk
Timothy Taylor Landlord; 8 changing beers (sourced nationally; often Black Sheep, Magic Rock) 🅷
Multi award-winning pub in a Grade II-listed station building. The excellent range of nine real ales always includes a mild. Real cider is sold, as well as a selection of speciality bottled beers. Live music plays outside in summer, and occasional beer festivals are held. Good food is served daily. The pub is a mainstay of the Transpennine Rail Ale Trail and consequently tends to be busy on Saturdays.
🏵◑🖒🚲♣P🚉📶

Elland

Barge & Barrel

10-20 Park Road, HX5 9HP (on A6025 NE of town centre)
🕐 12-11.30 ☎ (01422) 254604
Abbeydale Moonshine; Black Sheep Best Bitter; Milltown Platinum Blonde; Phoenix Wobbly Bob; Timothy Taylor Landlord; 7 changing beers (sourced regionally) 🅷
A large roadside pub built to serve the former Elland station. A three-sided bar caters for the comfortable lounge, with views over the canal and river to Elland town. Opposite, a games area and a snug with an open fire are separated from the bar by partitions of modern stained glass. Up to seven guest beers are sold, mainly from microbreweries. The smoking shelter is heated and a decking area provides views of the canal. Thursday is quiz night.
Q⚲🏵◑🖒♣P🚉(537,E7,564)🦮📶

Emley

White Horse 🅛 ✅

2 Chapel Lane, HD8 9SP (on main road on Huddersfield side of village)
🕐 4-11; 2-11 Fri; 12-11 Sat & Sun ☎ (01924) 849823
🌐 white-horse-emley.co.uk
Ossett Yorkshire Blonde, Silver King, Excelsior; 4 changing beers (sourced locally; often Fernandes, Great Heck, Jennings) 🅷
Ossett Brewery-managed village pub, with a central bar with a stone floor and range. A second room, accessed via a small flight of stairs, has a stove and is used as a family or function room. Carvery meals are served from the third room, a newly refurbished restaurant area. The regular Ossett group beers are complemented by guests from small local breweries and others from further afield. There is always a mild, stout or porter on handpump, as well as a real cider.
Q⚲🏵◑♣P🚉(232)🦮📶

Farsley

Fleece 🅛 ✅

116 Town Street, LS28 5LF

🕐 12-11 (midnight Fri & Sat); 12-10.30 Sun
☎ (0113) 257 7683
Black Sheep Best Bitter; Leeds Pale; Tetley Bitter; Timothy Taylor Landlord; 4 changing beers (sourced locally) 🅷
The oldest surviving Joshua Tetley public house, the Fleece is located at the north end of Farsley. A central bar, serving eight ales, separates the comfortable front lounge from the darts and pool area to the rear, with hearty pub food served throughout. The terrace to the front and two beer garden areas to the rear provide ample outdoor drinking opportunities. Televised live sport is shown, with live music on some Saturdays and a quiz on Thursdays. ⚲🏵◑♣P🚉📶

Goose Eye

Turkey Inn 🅛

BD22 0PD SE028406
🕐 12-11 (midnight Fri & Sat) ☎ (01535) 681339
🌐 theturkeyinn.com
Goose Eye Bitter, Chinook Blonde; Timothy Taylor Golden Best, Landlord; 3 changing beers 🅷
Friendly historic pub in a tiny hamlet approached by steep roads or a riverside footpath. It has three snugs, each with a real fire to keep out the winter chill, and is a good base for exploring the surrounding countryside. It has a pool table, holds a quiz night on Wednesday, and hosts occasional live music and special theme nights. Food is served every day until 8pm (9pm Fri and Sat). Three to six guest beers are usually available.
⚲🏵◑♣P🚉(916,917,918)🦮📶

Greengates

Albion

25 New Line, BD10 9AS
🕐 12-11
Acorn Barnsley Bitter; Tetley Bitter; 2 changing beers (sourced regionally; often Empire) 🅷
Comfortable, traditional, neighbourhood pub with an L-shaped lounge and a separate public bar where pub games can be played. Previously pubco-owned, this establishment became a free house in 2014. Consistently good beer, including a house ale produced by Acorn Brewery, is served here by dedicated staff. Real cider is also often available. The venue is popular with the local community and is home to a thriving social club. A regular bus service, 760, runs past the pub. ♣P🚉(760)🦮

Guiseley

Guiseley Factory Workers' Club 🅛

6 Town Street, LS20 9DT
🕐 1-11 (midnight Fri); 11.30-midnight Sat; 11-11 Sun
☎ (01943) 874793 🌐 guiseleyfactoryworkersclub.co.uk
Tetley Bitter; 3 changing beers (sourced locally) 🅷
Founded over 100 years ago by the Yeadon and Guiseley Factory Workers' Union, this multi award-winning club serves three varied guest ales from micros and independents. It has three rooms, with a small lounge, concert room and snooker room. Varied musical concerts take place on Friday and Saturday nights. The venue hosts many local clubs and organisations, and an annual beer festival is held in April. CAMRA members are welcome with this Guide or a membership card.
🏵🚲♣P🚉(33A,97,737)🦮📶

Halifax

Barum Top ☐ ✓
17 Rawson Street, HX1 1NX
✪ 8am-midnight (1am Fri & Sat) ☎ (01422) 300488
Greene King Abbot; Marston's Pedigree; Ruddles Best Bitter; 8 changing beers (often Elland, Goose Eye, Springhead) Ⓗ
A popular Wetherspoon pub in the heart of Halifax, this former long-standing garage is in the area once known as Barum Top, so named from the Yorkshire word bouram, meaning a natural watercourse. Before the advent of purpose-built drainage systems, this watercourse descended from Barum Top into Hebble Brook. This is a large, open pub with an upper balcony and a separate area for food (served daily until 10pm) or families. Breakfast is served from 8am until noon.
🛏️🕽️👌♿🕭🖩🛜

Big Six
10 Horsfall Street, Savile Park, HX1 3HG (off A646 Skircoat Moor road at King Cross) SE081241
✪ 4 (3.30 Fri)-11; 12-midnight Sat & Sun ☎ (01422) 350169
⊕ thebig6inn.co.uk
Old Mill Traditional Bitter; 4 changing beers (sourced regionally) Ⓗ
A hidden gem in a row of terraces, adjacent to the Free School Lane recreation ground. The emphasis in this friendly pub is on good beer and conversation. A through corridor separates the bar and the games room from the two lounges, and there is a rear beer garden. The pub's name derives from the mineral water company which operated here a century ago, whose memorabilia adorn the walls. Four rotating guest beers from regional or microbreweries are on the bar, and a house beer. Monday is quiz night. Q✿♣🖩 (577,578)🐾

Cross Keys
3 Whitegate, Siddal, HX3 9AE
✪ 3-11; 12-11 Fri-Sun ☎ (01422) 300348
6 changing beers Ⓗ
This venue reopened with new owners as a true free house at the end of 2012. The cosy three-roomed interior with a real fire is set around a 17th-century core. Ten handpulls serve nine beers from microbreweries, always including a dark beer and a changing real cider. The pub offers pork pies, darts, dominoes and a bull ring with live music on Sunday afternoons. Walkers and cyclists are welcome and two letting rooms are available.
✿🛌♣🕭🖩 (541,542,555)🐾🛜

Gundog
Crown Street, HX1 1JB
✪ 3-9 (11 Wed & Thu); 12-midnight Fri; 12-1am Sat; 1-11 Sun; closed Mon ☎ (01422) 380135
Stod Fold Gold, Amber; 4 changing beers (sourced regionally) Ⓗ
Grade II-listed town-centre pub, an 18th-century inn with an Edwardian frontage dating from 1904. The original tiles in the entrance porch are notable, as are the stairs inside. To the right of the bar, and easily missed, is a separate room facing onto the street with a largely intact Edwardian interior. The room to the left of the bar has a comfy lounge area with sofa seating. Four real ales are currently available. Q🕭🕭🛜

Three Pigeons ★ ✓
1 Sun Fold, HX1 2LX
✪ 4-11; 12-11 Fri-Sun ☎ (01422) 347001

Ossett Pale Gold, Big Red Bitter, Silver King; 5 changing beers (sourced nationally; often Fernandes, Jennings, Rat) Ⓗ
A striking octagonal drinking lobby forms the hub from which five distinctive rooms radiate in this Art Deco pub, built in 1932 by Webster's Brewery. Sensitively refurbished and maintained by Ossett Brewery, the Three Pigeons attracts a variety of local groups and societies together with football and rugby enthusiasts. Up to four guest beers are on offer from regional and national microbreweries as well as those from Ossett's own stable.
Q✿♿♣🕭P🖩 (561,562,563)🐾

Victorian Craft Beer Café
18-22 Powell Street, HX1 1LN
✪ 11-11; 12-10 Sun
10 changing beers Ⓗ
The café opened in 2014 after the complete refurbishment of a once-popular Italian restaurant situated behind the Victoria Theatre. With 10 rotating real ales available from microbreweries, you are spoilt for choice. There are also numerous world bottled beers and 12 keg lines available. On entering you find the main seating and drinking area with wooden floors and a tiled bar. To the left is a more secluded part and steps to an upper level which offers several seating spaces. Q🕭🕭P🖩🛜

Heath

King's Arms ★ ☐ ✓
Heath Common, WF1 5SL (at edge of Heath Village, off A655 Wakefield-Normanton road)
✪ 12-11 (midnight Fri & Sat) ☎ (01924) 377527
⊕ thekingsarmsheath.co.uk
Ossett Yorkshire Blonde, Silver King; house beer (by Ossett); 5 changing beers Ⓗ
The King's Arms, acquired by Clark's Brewery in 1989, is now leased to Ossett Brewery. Built in the early-1700s and converted into a public house in 1841, it consists of three oak-panelled rooms with gas lighting, plus a conservatory and gardens to the rear. In the summer months you can sit outside and relax peacefully amid the acres of common grassland surrounding the area. A quiz takes place on Tuesdays. Time may be called early on quieter evenings. Q🛏️✿🕽️👌♣🕭P🖩 (188)🐾🛜

Hebden Bridge

Calan's Micropub
3 The Courtyard, Bridge Gate, HX7 8EX (from A646 turn into Bridge Gate; at start of pedestrian section turn into yard on right)
✪ 12-9 (10 Fri & Sat); 12-8 Sun; closed Mon & Tue ☎ 07739 565983
5 changing beers (often Great Heck, Mallinson's, Vocation) Ⓗ
Calderdale's first micropub, in a suntrap courtyard just off the main pedestrianised shopping street, is intimate, friendly and welcoming. Five rotating ales, mainly from Northern microbreweries, are complemented by a couple of rotating ciders and perries. No piped music or gaming machines disturb the conversation, but there are books, cards and dominoes to occupy customers. Closed on Mondays (except bank holidays) and Tuesdays.
Q✿🕭♣🕭🖩🐾

Fox & Goose ✓

7 Heptonstall Road, HX7 6AZ (on A646 at bottom of Heptonstall Road; on foot walk through Hebden Bridge W along A646 towards Todmorden; pub is on your right)
🌣 12-midnight (2am Fri & Sat) ☎ (01422) 648052
⊕ foxandgoose.org
6 changing beers (sourced nationally; often Mallinson's, Pictish, Vocation) Ⓗ

West Yorkshire's first community co-operative pub has a small bar serving three flagstone-floored rooms. The main bar has a roaring fire in winter. The left-hand room is frequently used for organised or impromptu live music performances, while the room to the right has a dartboard. A welcoming, inclusive atmosphere and eclectic clientele ensure that customers who enter as strangers will leave as friends. Beer festivals are held in May and November. Quiz night is Monday. Q🌣♣👜🖶♿🖼🗺🛜

Old Gate Bar & Restaurant

1-5 Old Gate, HX7 8JP
🌣 10-midnight; 10-11 Sun ☎ (01422) 843993
⊕ oldgatehebden.co.uk
Magic Rock Ringmaster; Moorhouse's Pride of Pendle; 7 changing beers (sourced nationally; often Abbeydale, Blackjack, RedWillow) Ⓗ

Smart, modern inn and restaurant on two floors with an impressive long copper-topped bar, whose 10 handpumps dispense the biggest selection of real ales in town, plus one rotating cider. Quality food is served all day. An eclectic mix of furniture and the large picture windows make it an ideal spot for relaxing with a pint and observing the comings and goings of Hebden's diverse and colourful population. At least one dark beer is always on. 🛏🌣👜�🌣♣🖶🗺🛜🛜

Hemsworth

Hamelsworde Brewery Tap Ⓛ

41B Kirkby Road, WF9 4DA (on road out of town past marketplace in direction of South Kirkby)
🌣 12-3; 1-11 Fri & Sat; 12-7 Sun; closed Mon & Tue
☎ (01977) 619528 ⊕ hamelsworde.co.uk
Hamelsworde Spanish Stout, Colin Brown Ale, The Bishop; 3 changing beers (sourced locally) Ⓗ

A friendly, quirky, family-run pub with a great community spirit. All Hamelsworde beers are produced on-site on a 2.5-barrel plant. Locally sourced produce is part of the ethos. Six handpulls provide three Hamelsworde beers and three changing guest ales from local microbreweries. Bottled German beers are also sold. It offers a local menu on selected dates. Quiz night is the last Thursday of the month, and Meet the Brewer nights, brewery tours and mini-festivals all feature. Private bookings are available.
🛏🌣👜♿🖼🗺(28,29,48)🛜

Heptonstall

White Lion

58 Towngate, HX7 7NB
🌣 12-midnight ☎ (01422) 842027
Goose Eye Chinook Blonde; Thwaites Wainwright; 3 changing beers (sourced nationally; often Abbeydale, Leeds, Saltaire) Ⓗ

Friendly local in the cobbled main street of a historic conservation village. The single bar serves two distinct drinking areas; that to the left has a real fire in winter, while that to the right has a piano and is used for food service. Three guest beers and three ciders come from far and wide. Do not miss the recently uncovered historic inglenook fireplace in the corridor leading to the beer garden. Irish traditional music sessions take place on Tuesday evenings. Q🌣👜♣🖶🗺(517,596,906)🌣

Hipperholme

Cock o' the North Ⓛ

The Conclave, South Edge Works, Brighouse Road, HX3 8EF (on A644)
🌣 5 (4 Fri)-11.30; 12-11.30 Sat & Sun ☎ 07506 022504
⊕ halifax-steam.co.uk
Halifax Steam Aussie Kiss, Jamaican Ginger, Uncle Jon, Cock o' the North Ⓗ

Set back from and below the main road, the pub is next to a red brick industrial building which houses the brewery. Six changing Halifax Steam beers are available alongside three rotating ciders. The single large room is divided into different areas, with a relaxed atmosphere and a friendly and varied clientele. Wednesday is quiz night, live music features on the first Saturday most months. The ground of Brighouse Town (Evo-Stik League) is less than 10 minutes' walk away.
Q🌣A🖶P🗺(548,549)

Travellers Inn ✓

53 Tanhouse Hill, HX3 8HN (off A58)
🌣 12-11.30 (11 Mon); 12-midnight Thu-Sat; 12-11 Sun
☎ (01422) 202434
Ossett Pale Gold, Yorkshire Blonde, Silver King, Excelsior; 4 changing beers (sourced locally; often Marston's, Rat, Salamander) Ⓗ

Opposite the former railway station, this traditional 18th-century stone-built local has taken in adjoining cottages to create a series of distinct spaces. Well-behaved children and dogs on leads are welcome until 7pm. A covered yard with heating is provided for smokers. Four guest beers are from Ossett group breweries and other microbreweries, always including a dark brew.
🛏🌣♣🖶🗺(265,548,549)🌣🛜

Holmfirth

Nook (Rose & Crown) Ⓛ ✓

7 Victoria Square, HD9 2DN (down alley behind Barclays bank)
🌣 11.30-midnight ☎ (01484) 682373
⊕ thenookbrewhouse.co.uk
Nook Yorks, Baby Blond, Rescue Red, Best, Blond, Oat Stout; 2 changing beers Ⓗ

The Nook (properly, the Rose & Crown) dates from 1754, and is a well-known real ale pub in the village. It serves home-cooked food all day, and has been dispensing beers from its own brewhouse since 2009. Guest beers are also available, and Pure North ciders. There is a popular folk evening every Sunday and real ale festivals on the weekend before Easter and August bank holiday. The log fire is particularly warming on cold winter nights. 🛏🌣�👜♣🖶🗺(313,314,316)🌣🛜

Horbury

Cricketers Arms Ⓛ ✓

22 Cluntergate, WF4 5AG (Cluntergate is a right fork off High Street at lower end)
🌣 4-11; 12-midnight Fri & Sat; 12-11 Sun ☎ (01924) 267032
Bosun's Horbury Blond; Timothy Taylor Landlord; 6 changing beers Ⓗ

This former Tetley's house is now a genuine free house. The pub has had a tasteful refurbishment that has extended the length of the bar. Cheese and meze boards are available all the time. There is a frequent bus service to Wakefield, Ossett and Dewsbury. Poker night is Monday, quiz night Wednesday and open mic night on the second Sunday of each month. Beer festivals take place in late-May (Yankee Fest) and mid-October (Oktoberfest). ✪◗♣▬P🖵😺🛜

Huddersfield

Grove 🄻

2 Spring Grove Street, HD1 4BP
✪ 2-11 (midnight Thu); 12-midnight Fri & Sat; 12-11 Sun
☎ (01484) 430113 🌐 thegrove.pub
Oakham Citra; Thornbridge Jaipur IPA; Timothy Taylor Landlord; Vocation Bread & Butter; changing beers (often Atom, Durham, Hawkshead) 🄷
The Grove Inn has a phenomenal list of 19 cask ales – four permanent, six from rotating breweries and nine from different breweries across the UK. New breweries feature regularly along with stouts and strong ales. In addition there is a superb list of 200-plus bottled beers. This is a friendly pub with quirky, surreal artwork. No food is served, but a unique range of bar snacks is on offer. Real cider is also sold here. Q✪🐾🍴🛍🖵😺🛜

King's Head

St George's Square, HD1 1JF (in station buildings, on left when exiting station)
✪ 11.30-11; 12-11 Sun ☎ (01484) 511058
Bradfield Farmers Blonde; Magic Rock Ringmaster; Timothy Taylor Golden Best, Landlord; 6 changing beers 🄷
A recently restored popular fixture in Huddersfield's real ale scene, conveniently situated at the listed railway station. A warm and friendly atmosphere makes it a necessary stop for the weary traveller. Ten beers are on tap (four regular, six guest), all top-quality and sold at competitive prices. There are always two dark ales, and real cider on handpull is also available. Live bands play on Sunday afternoons. It can get busy at weekends, but it is a real local gem to appreciate. 🐾🍴🐾😺

Rat & Ratchet 🄻 ✅

40 Chapel Hill, HD1 3EB (on A616, just off ring road; car park is at rear)
✪ 3-midnight (11 Mon); 12-midnight Fri & Sat; 12-11 Sun
☎ (01484) 542400
Ossett Yorkshire Blonde, Silver King; Rat White Rat, King Rat; 8 changing beers (often Ossett, Rat) 🄷
The Rat & Ratchet has been part of Huddersfield's real ale scene for many years, regularly winning awards from CAMRA and others. It is a friendly, recently refurbished pub offering 12 handpulled ales: three Rat beers (from the award-winning on-site Rat Brewery), three from Ossett Brewery, and six guests including dedicated mild and stout/porter pumps. A range of ciders and perries is also available. There is a popular pub quiz on a Wednesday, and regular beer festivals are held. 😺🐾P🖵😺🛜

Sportsman 🍺 ★ 🄻 ✅

1 St John's Road, HD1 5AY
✪ 12-11; 11-midnight Fri & Sat ☎ (01484) 421929
Timothy Taylor Boltmaker; 7 changing beers (often Mallinson's) 🄷

This restored 1930s pub has won a CAMRA English Heritage Conservation Pub design award. Eight handpumps include a dedicated pump for a Mallinson's beer. Guest beers often come from local breweries Empire, Golcar and Magic Rock, usually including a stout/porter. The two ciders are usually from Pure North. This pub has established itself as a favourite of the Huddersfield drinking scene. Food times vary – phone to check. 😺✪◗🐾🍴🖵😺🛜

Star 🄻

7 Albert Street, Folly Hall, HD1 3PJ (off A616)
✪ 5-11; 12-11 Sat; 12-10.30 Sun; closed Mon
☎ (01484) 545443 🌐 thestarinn.info
Pictish Brewers Gold; 9 changing beers (often Briggs Signature Ales, Mallinson's, Timothy Taylor) 🄷
Multi award-winning local that has featured in this Guide for many years. It acts as a showcase for new breweries, with different ales sourced countrywide, and has dedicated pumps for Taylors, Mallinson's and a dark beer. No jukebox, pool table or games machine intrude, but there is lively conversation around the bar and a real fire during winter. The ambience is summed up by a sign that reads: Be Nice or Leave. Three beer festivals are held annually, usually in a marquee, featuring only handpulled beers. Q😺✪🐾😺🛜

Idle

Symposium Ale & Wine Bar 🄻 ✅

7 Albion Road, BD10 9PY (nr village green)
✪ 5.30-11; 12-11 Fri & Sat; 12-10.30 Sun ☎ (01274) 616587
Okells Manx Pale Ale; 5 changing beers (sourced nationally) 🄷
Located in a Victorian building with an unusual front that was formerly a grocer's and wine merchant's, this is a popular bar/restaurant in the heart of the village. The bar is raised from the main restaurant and there is a rear snug leading to an elevated terrace outside. The range of six real ales usually includes some rare offerings of impressive strength. Real ciders plus bottled beers from around the world are also kept, along with a wide range of whiskies and gins. Excellent meals from an inventive menu are served until 9pm.
Q😺✪◗🍴🖵😺🛜

Ilkley

Crescent Inn 🄻

Brook Street, LS29 8DG (within Crescent Hotel)
✪ 12-11 (midnight Fri & Sat) ☎ (01943) 811250
🌐 thecrescentinn.co.uk
Copper Dragon Best Bitter; Leeds Pale; Saltaire Blonde; 5 changing beers (sourced regionally; often Ilkley) 🄷
This venue occupies the ground floor of a town-centre building that has been a hotel since 1861. Furnishings are smart, while the original internal finishes are retained. Eight real ales are always on the bar and the guests are usually from local breweries. Bar meals are available until 9.30pm, with meal deals during the week. There is also an adjacent restaurant. It has full disabled facilities but the rear door provides best access. 😺✪🏨◗♿🐾🍴😺🛜

Flying Duck ✅

16 Church Street, LS29 9DS (on A65)
✪ 12-11; 11-12.30am Fri & Sat ☎ (01943) 609587

Wharfedale Black, Blonde, Best; 6 changing beers (sourced regionally; often Dark Horse) Ⓗ
Originally constructed as a farmhouse in 1709, this is reputed to be Ilkley's oldest pub building. Substantially refurbished and reopened in late 2013, the Grade II-listed building retains many original features such as the York stone, oak flooring, beamed ceilings, internal stonework and mullioned windows. Up to nine real ales and two real ciders are offered. Wharfedale Brewery is located to the rear and tours can be arranged. The first-floor function room includes a bar.
🕿🕸◑⇶♠🖳🌐♥🛜

Keighley

Boltmakers Arms Ⓛ ⦿
117 East Parade, BD21 5HX
⏱ 11-midnight (11 Mon); 12-11 Sun ☎ (01535) 661936
⊕ boltmakers.com
Timothy Taylor Dark Mild, Golden Best, Boltmaker, Landlord, Ram Tam; 2 changing beers Ⓗ
Welcoming classic Keighley town-centre pub, the de facto Timothy Taylor Brewery tap and the smallest pub in town. Brewery, whisky and music memorabilia adorn the walls of the single split-level room. The guest beers and handpulled cider are from various suppliers chosen by the licensee, and there is an excellent selection of single malts. An idiosyncratic quiz, with free food, takes place every Tuesday night, and live music most Wednesdays. Dominoes and cards are available on request. 🕸⇶♣♠🖳(662,760)♥🛜

Brown Cow Ⓛ
5 Cross Leeds Street, BD21 2LQ
⏱ 4-11; 12-10.30 Sun ⊕ browncowkeighley.co.uk
Timothy Taylor Golden Best, Boltmaker, Landlord; 4 changing beers Ⓗ
Family-run community local. The ethos of this award-winning free house is quality, beer choice and customer comfort. A no-bad-language policy is in force. The pub is adorned with local breweriana, including the original sign from the entrance to Bradford's now-defunct Trough Brewery. The back room can be booked for meetings. Four guest beers (usually from local micros) always include a dark beer and one beer at a higher strength. The discounted beer on Super Saver Sunday is popular.
🕿🕸♣♠P🖳♥🛜

Cricketers Arms
Coney Lane, BD21 5JE
⏱ 4-11; 12-midnight Fri; 11.30-midnight Sat; 12-11 Sun ☎ (01535) 669912
Yates Bitter, Golden Ale; 3 changing beers (sourced nationally) Ⓗ
Serving four guest beers from far and wide and a range of bottled beers alongside the regular ales, the Cricketers has been a family-owned free house for over 12 years and a regular entry in this Guide since 2006. On the eastern edge of the town centre, it is a short walk from the bus and railway stations. Live music features once a month.
🕸⇶🖳(705,720,708)🛜

Lord Rodney Bar & Kitchen Ⓛ ⦿
Church Street, BD21 5HT
⏱ 11.30-11 (2am Fri & Sat); 12-10 Sun ☎ (01535) 603053
⊕ lordrodney.co.uk
Timothy Taylor Golden Best, Boltmaker, Landlord Ⓗ
On the site of Keighley's oldest pub, the Olde Red Lion, the Rodney is next to the parish church and offers a splendid view along North Street. Timothy Taylor-owned, it underwent extensive rebuilding and is now a bright and modern town-centre pub. A variety of furniture, from tall stools to armchairs, surrounds the bar in the long single room, warmed by a real fire. A separate dining area leads to a heated beer garden at the rear. 🕿🕸◑♣⇶🖳🛜

Kirkheaton

Yeaton Cask
4 Town Road, HD5 0HW
⏱ 4 (12 Wed & Thu)-11; 12-11.30 Fri & Sat; 12-10.30 Sun ☎ 07796 641003
Thwaites Wainwright; 5 changing beers (often Geeves, Rooster's, Salamander) Ⓗ
Formerly the Junction, the pub was bought as a true free house by the current owner in 2010. Beautiful furniture and flooring with a backdrop of striking exposed stonework gives a traditional yet contemporary feel. Two permanent ales are on the bar, including the house beer from a secret West Yorkshire microbrewery. The other four changing guests are sourced countrywide, always including a dark beer. Food is not available but there are complimentary bar snacks daily. A highly rated beer festival is held in October. Q🕿♣🖳(262)♥🛜

Leeds: Chapel Allerton

Further North Ⓛ
194 Harrogate Road, LS7 4NZ (200yds N of centre of Chapel Allerton)
⏱ 5-11 (midnight Thu); 3-midnight Fri; 1-midnight Sat; 1-11 Sun ☎ (0113) 237 0962
3 changing beers (sourced locally) Ⓗ
Small wooden-floored bar, previously a car spares shop, cosy, light and airy with a hint of nostalgia created by vintage lampshades, bare stone walls and a sociable atmosphere. A recently opened upstairs room, which is available for private functions, is testament to the bar's popularity. Two cask ales and a range of global beers are served, and boxed cider is occasionally available. Quality bottled soft drinks are stocked, so the designated driver does not miss out. ♠🖳♥🛜

Leeds: City Centre

Crowd of Favours Ⓛ
4-12 Harper Street, LS2 7EA
⏱ 12-11 (midnight Fri & Sat); 12-10.30 Sun ☎ (0113) 246 9405 ⊕ crowdoffavours.co.uk
Leeds Pale, Yorkshire Gold, Best, Midnight Bell; 4 changing beers (sourced locally) Ⓗ
At the regenerating, bohemian, Market end of Leeds, this relaxed and welcoming many-windowed pub takes up most of the street. Dim and woody inside, the place is replete with candles and quality junk shop furniture. Around the central bar, the wobbly floorboards take you from nook to wood-panelled cranny, with ever-changing murals and proper prints on the walls. Downstairs are whopping sofas, fairy lights and the weekly Cinema Club. Poker nights, comedy and video and board games provide further entertainment.
🕿◑♠⇶♠🖳♥🛜

Duck & Drake Ⓛ ⦿
43 Kirkgate, LS2 7DR
⏱ 10-11 (midnight Fri & Sat); 11-11 Sun ☎ (0113) 245 5432 ⊕ duckndrake.co.uk

Brains Bitter; Rooster's Yankee; Saltaire Blonde; Theakston Old Peculier; Timothy Taylor Landlord; York Centurion's Ghost Ale; 9 changing beers (sourced locally; often Rudgate, Salamander, Two Roses) Ⓗ
Two-roomed pub with the larger one used for the live music which is on most nights. The smaller room is a place full of chat and banter. There is an outdoor drinking area to the side of the building. Nourishment is available in the form of pie and peas. Usually some of the beers come from wooden casks. The front room has a mural on the back wall depicting many blues and rock legends. ✿≠♠♣⏰🍴🛜

Foleys Tap House Ⓛ
159 The Headrow, LS1 5RG
🕐 12-11; 11-1am Fri & Sat; 12-10 Sun ☎ (0113) 242 9674
🌐 mrfoleysleeds.co.uk
York Guzzler, Yorkshire Terrier, Centurion's Ghost Ale; 9 changing beers (sourced locally; often York) Ⓗ
City-centre pub usually with four beers from York Brewery's range plus eight guest beers. Also available is a wide selection of real ciders along with draught and bottled beers from around the world. The building is an impressive edifice built of Portland stone and previously owned by the Pearl Assurance Company. The company was founded by Patrick James Foley, hence the name of the pub. The interior is on several levels with a variety of seating. ♿≠♠🍴♣

Friends of Ham
4-8 New Station Street, LS1 5DL
🕐 12-11 (midnight Thu-Sat); 12-10 Sun ☎ (0113) 242 0275
🌐 friendsofham.co.uk
4 changing beers (sourced locally) Ⓗ
Since opening in 2012, this bar and charcuterie has supported brewers who are not afraid to use their skill to challenge taste buds, with four handpumps dispensing imaginatively chosen real ale. Drinkers and diners share the same space in the modern shabby-chic interior; downstairs is more food-oriented. The bar is rarely quiet but never over-busy as attentive door staff control entry to a comfortable number. ◐≠♠🍴🛜

Head of Steam Ⓛ
13 Mill Hill, LS1 5DQ
🕐 11-midnight (1am Fri & Sat); 12-11 Sun
☎ (0113) 243 6618
9 changing beers (sourced locally; often Camerons, Leeds, Timothy Taylor) Ⓗ
Local CAMRA award-winning pub with a well-kept selection of cask ale, mainly from Yorkshire and the North-east. Complementing this is an extensive selection of international beers on draught and in bottles and cans, especially focusing on Belgium and the United States. There is a wide range of seating in the drinking areas that surround the 360-degree island bar, which is staffed by people passionate about their beer. ≠♠🍴♣🛜

Hop Ⓛ ⊘
Granary Wharf, Dark Neville Street, LS1 4BR
🕐 12-midnight ☎ (0113) 243 9854 🌐 thehop-leeds.co.uk
Ossett Yorkshire Blonde, Big Red Bitter, Silver King, Excelsior; 7 changing beers (sourced locally) Ⓗ
Busy, lively pub beneath the arches of Platform 17 of Leeds station. On the ground floor pictures of rock bands and brewery mirrors adorn the walls. Eleven handpumps serve beers from the Ossett family of brewers together with several guest ales and a real cider. Either side of the bar is

comfortable seating. Two sets of stairs lead to an area which hosts live music at weekends and has colourful murals. ✿◐≠♠🍴🛜

Lamb & Flag Ⓛ
1 Church Row, LS2 7HD
🕐 11-11.30 (midnight Fri & Sat) ☎ (0113) 243 1255
🌐 lambandflagleeds.co.uk
Leeds Pale, Yorkshire Gold, Best, Midnight Bell; 4 changing beers (sourced locally; often Abbeydale, Acorn, Hambleton) Ⓗ
The latest addition to the Leeds Brewery pub estate, opening in 2015, nestling in the shadow of Leeds Minster. Originally a pub in the 19th century, the building has been restored at great expense to rapidly become a jewel in the Leeds pub scene. There is an upstairs bar with two handpumps and a balcony overlooking the suntrap courtyard. The small downstairs bar has eight handpumps. ♿✿◐≠♠🍴♣🛜

North Bar Ⓛ
24 New Briggate, LS1 6NU
🕐 11-2am (1am Mon & Tue); 12-midnight Sun
☎ (0113) 242 4540 🌐 northbar.com/northbar
North Prototype; 4 changing beers (sourced locally) Ⓗ
Small bar with many lightbulbs hanging from the wooden ceiling. The bar along one wall has five handpumps and a large range of beers from around the world both on draught and in bottles. Behind the bar are tankards belonging to staff and regulars. The narrow wooden-floored drinking area has wooden chairs and tables with pictures from local artists on the wall. Bar food such as pork pies and cheese platters is on offer. ◐≠♠🍴

Reliance
76-78 North Street, LS2 7PN
🕐 12-11 (midnight Fri & Sat); 11-10.30 Sun
☎ (0113) 295 6060 🌐 the-reliance.co.uk
House beer (by Acorn); 3 changing beers (sourced locally; often Rooster's) Ⓗ
A relaxed bar at the eastern edge of the city centre with three distinct areas: one behind the bar which is mainly for food, a lounge area with comfy chairs, and a main bar area. The huge bay windows are ideal for people-watching. The food is more than standard pub fare and there are frequently unusual dishes on the menu. A handpump is dedicated to Rooster's beers and one guest real cider is always served. Regular cinema nights are held. ◐♿♠🍴

Scarbrough Hotel Ⓛ ⊘
Bishopgate Street, LS1 5DY
🕐 10-midnight (1am Fri & Sat); 10-10.30 Sun
☎ (0113) 243 4590
St Austell Nicholson's Pale Ale; Tetley Bitter; 6 changing beers (sourced regionally) Ⓗ
The Scarbrough is a busy ale house and convenient for Leeds railway station. The building dates from 1765 and became a pub in 1826. It is named after Henry Scarbrough, the first owner of the pub, though it was then known as the King's Arms. At either end of the long bar are comfortable seating areas. Guest ales are selected from breweries in the area as well as from around the country. ✿◐♿≠♠🍴🛜

Stick or Twist Ⓛ ⊘
Podium Buildings, Merrion Way, LS2 8PD
🕐 8am-midnight (1am Fri & Sat) ☎ (0113) 234 9748

Greene King IPA, Abbot; Sharp's Doom Bar; 9 changing beers (sourced locally) ⊞
A CAMRA award-winning pub and the oldest Wetherspoon in Leeds; the name is a nod to its casino neighbours. As the pub is in the shadow of the Leeds Arena it gets exceptionally busy when an event is on. With 12 handpulls, it offers among the largest selection of real ales in the city centre. Food is served from 8am until 11pm daily. Outdoor seating offers a stunning suntrap in the warm months. Q☺🕭⊛◑♿🖤🅿🛜

Tapped Leeds
51 Boar Lane, LS1 5EL
✪ 11-11 (midnight Thu; 1am Fri & Sat) ☎ (0113) 244 1953
⊕ tappedleeds.co.uk
13 changing beers (sourced regionally; often Tapped Sheffield) ⊞
Modern one-roomed brewpub with the bar and a pizza oven on the right, and the brewing equipment along the opposite wall. In between is a variety of tables and benches. The look is completed by a low ceiling with industrial lighting and silver-coloured pipes. Thirteen cask-conditioned ales are served from the bottom set of beer taps behind the bar. Notices above the bar give details of the beers and method of dispense. ◑♿≒🅿🛜

Templar 🅛 ✪
2 Templar Street, LS2 7NU
✪ 11-11; 12-10.30 Sun ☎ (0113) 243 0318
Greene King IPA; Tetley Bitter; 6 changing beers (sourced locally; often Elland, Goose Eye, Leeds) ⊞
Community local in the city centre which has a fine exterior with green and cream glazed Burmantoft tiles. The bowing courtier logo can be seen in the leaded window panes from when it was a Melbourne Brewery pub. The interior is adorned with wooden panelling, still with the old service bells in place. There are large-screen TVs throughout the pub showing a range of sporting events. Guest beers range from local ales to those from further afield. ◑≒♣🅿

Veritas Ale & Wine Bar 🅛 ✪
43 Great George Street, LS1 3BB
✪ 11-11; 12-10.30 Sun ☎ (0113) 242 8094
Black Sheep Best Bitter; Ilkley Mary Jane; 6 changing beers (sourced locally; often Okells, Timothy Taylor) ⊞
Busy modern bar which is part of the Market Town Taverns local chain of pubs. The single open-plan L-shaped room is on several levels and has four different areas. The six guest beers change regularly and are mainly from local microbreweries. A good range of bottled and draught beers from around the world is also on offer. A deli counter features local produce (open from 9.30am, 10.30am Sun). Q◑♿≒◑🅿🖤

Victoria Family & Commercial Hotel 🅛 ✪
28 Great George Street, LS1 3DL (behind town hall)
✪ 11-11 (midnight Fri & Sat); 12-10 Sun ☎ (0113) 245 1386
Leeds Pale; St Austell Nicholson's Pale Ale; Sharp's Doom Bar; Tetley Bitter; 5 changing beers (sourced locally; often Great Heck, St Austell, Salopian) ⊞
Built by the Victoria Hotel Company in 1865 as a 28-room hotel to accommodate visitors to the Assizes Court in Leeds town hall, the building has an impressive Victorian exterior, and an ornate interior with high ceilings. There is a long main bar

area and two separate rooms, all of which feature much polished wood and shiny brass. The guest beers are a selection of local ales and quality beers from around the country. ◑◑♿🅿🛜

Whitelock's Ale House ★ 🅛 ✪
Turk's Head Yard, LS1 6HB (off Briggate)
✪ 11-midnight (1am Fri & Sat); 11-11 Sun
☎ (0113) 242 3368 ⊕ whitelocksleeds.com
Ilkley Mary Jane; Kirkstall Pale Ale; Theakston Best Bitter, Old Peculier; Timothy Taylor Landlord; 5 changing beers (sourced locally; often Acorn, Great Heck, Saltaire) ⊞
Described by poet Sir John Betjeman as the very heart of Leeds, Whitelock's is steeped in history dating back to 1715, when it was called the Turk's Head. It features 19th-century decor, including a rare copper bar and a feast of Victorian mirrors, stained glass and brass. The pub is free of tie, meaning the ale choice is rich and varied. The sumptuous faience tiling is just one of the many features of historic interest at this must-visit hostelry. Q☺🕭⊛◑≒◑🐾🛜

Leeds: Headingley

Arcadia Ale House 🅛 ✪
34 Arndale Centre, Otley Road, LS6 2UE (corner of Alma Rd)
✪ 12-11 ☎ (0113) 274 5599 ⊕ arcadialeeds.co.uk
Okells Manx Pale Ale; Timothy Taylor Boltmaker; 6 changing beers (sourced locally; often Elland, Ilkley, Rooster's) ⊞
This cleverly converted former bank is now a well-established and multi award-winning pub. The bar has ground-floor rooms plus an upstairs mezzanine level. Framed breweriana adorn the walls and some of the light fittings are made from old beer crates. Eight real ales are offered, along with a wide range of other draught and bottled beers. Up to five real ciders are served from boxes behind the bar. Children, large groups (over eight people) and fancy dress are not permitted. Q♿◑🅿🐾🛜

Leeds: Holbeck

Cross Keys 🅛
107 Water Lane, LS11 5WD
✪ 12-11 (midnight Fri & Sat); 12-10.30 Sun
☎ (0113) 243 3711 ⊕ the-crosskeys.com
North Prototype; 3 changing beers (sourced locally; often Kirkstall, Rooster's) ⊞
The Cross Keys is a cosy pub, owned by the North Bar pub group and with plenty to offer both drinkers and diners. The ground floor has a small foodie area to the left and a larger traditional pub area to the right. Upstairs is a function room which is available to hire and has two handpumps. There is a courtyard drinking area to the rear. It carries a selection of – mainly British – bottled beers and some Trappist-style bottles. ⊛◑♿≒🅿🐾🛜

Grove Inn 🅛
Back Row, LS11 5PL
✪ 12-midnight ☎ (0113) 244 2085
Daleside Blonde; 7 changing beers (sourced locally; often Ridgeside, Timothy Taylor) ⊞
Traditional pub nestled among modern offices, which has four rooms off a corridor. Eight real ales from local and regional breweries are served from the bar, with service both to the public bar and corridor. There are two small side rooms and the

Concert Room to the rear, which hosts an eclectic range of music including, every Friday since 1962, reputedly the oldest folk club in the world. Bands play most Saturday nights and often on Sundays. ✦✦❅♣♠🍴✿🐾📶

Midnight Bell ⓛ

101 Water Lane, LS11 5QN
✪ 11.30-11.30 (midnight Fri & Sat) ☎ (0113) 244 5044
⊕ midnightbell.co.uk
Leeds Pale, Yorkshire Gold, Best, Midnight Bell; 2 changing beers (sourced locally; often Castle Rock, Oakham, Ridgeside) Ⓗ
The development of the Midnight Bell commenced along with regeneration of the Leeds South Bank area, now designated as the Holbeck Urban Village. This award-winning pub caters for office workers and discerning drinkers and diners, who come to enjoy the Leeds Brewery range of beers in a comfortable and relaxed atmosphere. To the rear of the building is a pleasant courtyard area. An upstairs bar is a more food-oriented area. Real cider is served in the summer months.
✦❶&❅♠🍴✿📶

Leeds: Hunslet

Garden Gate ★ ⓛ

3 Whitfield Place, LS10 2QB (400yds from Hunslet – Penny Hill – shopping centre)
✪ 12-11; 11-11 Sat ☎ (0113) 345 1234
⊕ gardengateleeds.co.uk
Leeds Pale, Best; 2 changing beers (sourced locally; often Black Sheep, Leeds) Ⓗ
Now in a modern housing estate in what was the industrial heartland of Leeds, this unaltered pub is recognised by CAMRA as having a nationally important historic pub interior. It is a Grade II*-listed building with some of the finest Burmantofts tiling in the north of England. The walls are adorned with Hunslet Rugby League memorabilia and it hosts regular ex-player reunions – an example of the pub's strong ties to the local community. ✦❶♣♠🍴(12,13)✿📶

Leeds: Kirkstall

Kirkstall Bridge Inn 🍺 ⓛ

Bridge Road, LS5 3BW
✪ 12-midnight (1am Fri & Sat) ☎ (0113) 278 4044
⊕ kirkstallbridge.co.uk
Kirkstall Pale Ale, Three Swords, Dissolution IPA, Black Band Porter; 4 changing beers (sourced locally) Ⓗ
Winner of the joint CAMRA and English Heritage Pub Design Awards 2015, this Kirkstall Brewery tap has been tastefully refurbished to a high standard throughout, with plenty of mirrors, photos and breweriana on display. The main bar upstairs has eight handpumps, which serve beers from the nearby Kirkstall Brewery, along with interesting guest ales. The partially stone-flagged downstairs bar has six handpumps and is open during busy periods. The large beer garden overlooks the River Aire. ✦❶ⓅP🍴✿📶

Leeds: Meanwood

East of Arcadia ⓛ ✓

607 Meanwood Road, LS6 4HQ
✪ 11-11 (11.30 Fri & Sat); 12-11 Sun ☎ (0113) 275 5488

Leeds Pale; Okells Manx Pale Ale; Timothy Taylor Boltmaker; 5 changing beers (sourced locally; often Ilkley, Ridgeside) Ⓗ
Modern bar occupying a prominent corner position in the heart of Meanwood. Open plan and on one level, there is a carpeted area which follows the sweep of tall windows curving around the pub. Closer to the bar there is a bare-boarded area with large casks which have been converted to small tables, complete with foot rails. The light-coloured walls display international breweriana. Beers from Ridgeside and Ilkley breweries are normally available. Quiz night is on Wednesday.
🚲❶&♠🍴✿📶

Leeds: Newlay

Abbey Inn ⓛ

99 Pollard Lane, LS13 1EQ (vehicle access from B6157 only)
✪ 12-11 ☎ (0113) 258 1248
7 changing beers (sourced locally) Ⓗ
The inn is a former farmhouse between the River Aire and the Leeds-Liverpool canal. Tuesday is a traditional folk night, Wednesday is pool league and games night, and Thursday is music quiz night. Free live music always plays on Saturday and a general knowledge quiz takes place on Sunday. The building dates from 1714 and is reputedly haunted. There is plenty of outside seating and a popular beer and music festival is held in July each year. Real cider is on sale during the summer months. 🚲✦❶&♣P✿

Linthwaite

Sair ⓛ ✓

139 Lane Top, HD7 5SG (top of Hoyle Ing, off A62)
✪ 5-11; 12-11 Sat; 12-10.30 Sun ☎ (01484) 842370
Linfit Bitter, Gold Medal, Special, Swift, Autumn Gold, Old Eli Ⓗ
High on the edge of the Colne Valley, the Sair Inn is home to the famous Linfit Brewery, which has now been brewing for over 33 years. The brewpub, steeped in local history, is a traditional multi-roomed stone building with central bar, real fires and a long-suffering landlord. The beer range is as LocAle as it gets, with six beers unique to the pub, and real cider from Pure North. It is a welcome refuge for walkers, musicians and visitors alike. Q✦♣♠🍴(181,183,184)✿📶

Liversedge

Black Bull ⓛ ✓

37 Halifax Road, WF15 6JR (on A649, close to A62)
✪ 12-midnight (1am Fri & Sat) ☎ (01924) 403779
Ossett Pale Gold, Yorkshire Blonde, Big Red Bitter, Silver King, Excelsior; 3 changing beers Ⓗ
Ossett Brewery's first pub. The five rooms have their own styles, including one dubbed the Chapel, with a mix of stained glass and woodwork and a high ceiling. Nine handpumps always offer a mild or dark ale, plus good guest beers from the group and from independents. A regular Guide entry, the Black Bull is a popular, sociable community local with a warm welcome. Quiz night is Tuesday. 🚲✦♣P🍴(220,253,254)✿📶

Longwood

Dusty Miller Inn L ✔

2 Gilead Road, HD3 4XH

☼ 5-11; 4-midnight Fri; 12-midnight Sat; 12-11 Sun ☎ 07946 589645 ⏚ dustymillerlongwood.com

Milltown Platinum Blonde; Timothy Taylor Landlord; 5 changing beers (often Milltown, Phoenix, Scarborough) Ⓗ

Recently refurbished Punch house, now operated by local brewery Milltown as a brewery tap. Local historic photographs adorn the walls and stone floors dominate in this multi-roomed, cosy pub. From its outside benches there are great views of the Colne Valley and it is a haven for walkers. Seven real ales are served, at least two from Milltown, plus Taylor Landlord and guests. A dark beer is usually on offer. You can also get a locally-made pie with chutney. Q ☕ ♣ ⊞ (356)♣ ☎

Marsden

Riverhead Brewery Tap L ✔

Peel Street, HD7 6BR

☼ 12-midnight ☎ (01484) 844324 ⏚ theriverheadmarsden.co.uk

Ossett Yorkshire Blonde, Silver King; Riverhead Butterley Bitter, March Haigh, Redbrook Premium; 5 changing beers Ⓗ

A friendly, welcoming pub at the heart of village life. Up to 10 beers are on offer, usually including four from the on-site brewery, two from Ossett, plus guest beers sourced nationally. A dark beer is almost always on the bar. There is also real cider and a good range of bottled beers. The pub is a popular stop on the Real Ale Rail Trail and Saturdays are often extremely busy. Great food is served in the restaurant and there is a riverside terrace for alfresco drinking. Walkers and their dogs are welcome. Q ☕ ⊛ ◑ ♿ ≠ ♣ P ⊞ (185)♣ ☎

Meltham

Wills o' Nats ✔

Blackmoorfoot Road, HD9 5PS

☼ 12-3, 5-11; 11.30-midnight Sat; 11.30-11 Sun ☎ (01924) 850078 ⏚ willsonats.com

Black Sheep Best Bitter; Bradfield Farmers Blonde; Timothy Taylor Landlord; 3 changing beers Ⓗ

In 1852 William, son of Nathaniel, took over the Spotted Cow, which gradually became Wills o' Nats. Today it is renowned for locally sourced home-cooked food and six or more ales. Live music events are held on the first Saturday of each summer month, when you can camp behind the pub. Close to the Peak District and the Pennines, the views are stunning. A welcome stop for families, walkers and their dogs, and a regular in the Guide. ☕ ⊛ ◑ ▲ P♣ ☎

Middlestown

Little Bull L

72 New Road, WF4 4NR (on A642 at crossroads in centre of village)

☼ 12-11.30; 12-12.30am Thu-Sat; 12-11.30 Sun ☎ (01924) 726142 ⏚ thelittlebull.co.uk

Abbeydale Absolution; Rat White Rat; 3 changing beers (sourced locally) Ⓗ

This pub has been established since 1814 and is free of tie. Beers come from local and regional breweries, alongside a range of world bottled beers. Real cider is also available (summer only). All food is locally sourced and home cooked. A single bar services a number of smaller rooms, with an open fire in colder weather. The National Coal Mining Museum is nearby. Meals are served lunchtimes Monday-Saturday, evenings Wednesday and Thursday, and 12-4pm Sunday. Steak night is the first Friday of the month. A beer festival takes place in mid-July. Q ☕ ⊛ ◑ P ⊞ (232,128)♣ ☎

Mirfield

Flowerpot L ✔

65 Calder Road, WF14 8NN (over river, 400yds S of railway station)

☼ 12-12.30am (1.30am Fri & Sat); 12-midnight Sun ☎ (01924) 496939

Ossett Yorkshire Blonde, Big Red Bitter, Silver King, Excelsior; 4 changing beers Ⓗ

An 1807 pub now run by Ossett Brewery and refurbished to an excellent standard, with interesting features and three real fires. It has three rooms with an impressive central bar and a tiled flowerpot centrepiece, while the garden has good riverside views. Guest beers come from such as the company's Rat, Riverhead and Fernandes breweries, plus independents, changing on a daily basis, including mild or stout. Haigh's pie and peas plus other light meals are served Monday-Saturday daytimes. Q ☕ ⊛ ◑ ≠ ♣ ♣ P ⊞ (262)♣ ☎

Navigation Tavern

6 Station Road, WF14 8NL (next to Mirfield railway station)

☼ 11.30-11; 12-11 Sun ☎ (01924) 492476

Caledonian Flying Scotsman, Deuchars IPA; John Smith's Bitter; Theakston Black Bull Bitter, XB, Old Peculier; 3 changing beers (sourced nationally) Ⓗ

A canalside free house serving eight regular beers including five from Theakston plus up to four guests at weekends, all at keen prices. The pub features on the Transpennine Rail Ale Trail and holds renowned beer festivals three times a year. It hosts Saturday night entertainment and active sports and pool teams. A large function room and en-suite B&B with stairlift are available, and winter heating is aided by a large wood-burning fire. Real cider and perry choices are offered. ☕ ⊛ ⊨ ♿ ≠ ♣ ♣ P ⊞ ☎

Old Colonial

Dunbottle Lane, WF14 9JJ (off A644 up Church Lane, 1 mile NE of station)

☼ 5-11; 12-midnight Fri & Sat; 12-10 Sun ☎ (01924) 496920

Copper Dragon Best Bitter; 3 changing beers Ⓗ

Former club with fascinating colonial memorabilia offering a cosy retreat with sofas around the fire. There is a Royal British Legion memorial in the prize-winning garden and local charities are well supported. The spacious conservatory is popular for functions and meetings. Three to five guests, including a dark ale from such as Thwaite's, Lee's, Marston's and small brewers, are available. Evening meals are served Thursday to Saturday and the excellent-value Sunday lunch is recommended. Mirfield station is one mile away. ☕ ⊛ ◑ P ⊞ (202,205) ☎

Mytholmroyd

Robin Hood

Cragg Road, HX7 5SQ (on B6138 1½ miles S of Mytholmroyd)

✪ 3-11; 12-11 Fri-Sun ☎ (01422) 885899

Timothy Taylor Boltmaker, Landlord; 3 changing beers (sourced regionally; often Ilkley, Small World, Vocation) Ⓗ

Friendly two-roomed split-level local in a beautiful wooded valley popular with walkers and cyclists. On entering, the cosy bar, with a real fire in the winter, is to the right and is dog-friendly. The larger dining room serves food Thursday to Sunday (telephone to check times and book for peak periods). Real cider is sometimes available. Guest ales are usually from West Yorkshire breweries such as Ilkley and Small World, while beers from Vocation, one mile away, are regularly featured. Q❀◑🚍(900,901)🐾🛜

Norristhorpe

Rising Sun Ⓛ

254 Norristhorpe Lane, WF15 7AN (½ mile off A62)

✪ 12-11.30 (12.30am Fri & Sat) ☎ (01924) 400190

🌐 norristhorperisingsun.co.uk

Acorn Barnsley Bitter; Saltaire Blonde; 5 changing beers (sourced locally; often Acorn, Bob's, Bradfield) Ⓗ

Now under family ownership, this village local has been tastefully refurbished inside and out, featuring cosy lounge areas with exposed brickwork and several real fires plus an open, light and spacious bar area. The seven beers on offer are mainly from Yorkshire. There are fine views across the valley from the attractive beer garden and there is a good smoking area with seating. Outdoor music and barbecue events are held in summer. 🐾❀◑♣P🚍🐾🛜

Ossett

Bier Huis Ⓛ

17 Towngate, WF5 9BL (in shopping precinct opp town hall)

✪ 9.30am-6.30 (8 Fri & Sat); 11-3 Sun ☎ (01924) 565121

🌐 bierhuis.co.uk

2 changing beers (often Bradfield, Saltaire) Ⓗ

A beer shop selling bottled beers from many Yorkshire breweries alongside an extensive selection of foreign bottles. Two draught beers usually come from Bradfield and Saltaire breweries and can be drunk on the premises. Meet the Brewer evenings are held at regular intervals and brewery visits are popular. It also holds Thirsty Friday events when more beers are on draught. Q🐾&♣P🚍

Brewers Pride Ⓛ

Low Mill Road, Healey, WF5 8ND (at bottom of Healey Rd, 1½ miles from town centre)

✪ 12-11; 12-10.30 Sun ☎ (01924) 273865

🌐 brewers-pride.co.uk

Bob's White Lion; Rudgate Ruby Mild; 8 changing beers (often Oakham) Ⓗ

An independent free house on the outskirts of Ossett close to the Calder & Hebble canal. Two regular beers plus eight guest ales are offered. Bar meals are served lunchtimes (or you can eat in the linked Miller's Restaurant Monday-Saturday evenings or Sunday 12-7pm). The pub has themed food evenings: Monday pies, Tuesday tapas,

Wednesday and Thursday specials. Monday is quiz night, there is live music on the first Saturday of each month, a beer festival on August bank holiday, and charity events throughout the year. Q🐾❀◑●🚍(102)🐾🛜

Otley

Junction Inn Ⓛ

44 Bondgate, LS21 1AD

✪ 11-11 (11.30 Thu; midnight Fri & Sat); 12-11 Sun ☎ (01943) 463233

St Austell Tribute; Theakston Best Bitter, Old Peculier; Timothy Taylor Boltmaker, Landlord; 6 changing beers (sourced locally) Ⓗ

A solid-looking stone-built pub on a prominent street-corner site on the approach from Leeds. Up to 11 ales are served, along with a real cider and a wide range of malt whiskies. There is a central fireplace, and comfortable fixed seating runs around the walls of the room. Farming implements hang from the ceiling, and on the walls are pictures of old Otley. Several brewery enamel signs complete the decor. To the front, roadside tables allow for outdoor drinking. ❀♣●🚍🐾🛜

Old Cock Ⓛ

11-13 Crossgate, LS21 1AA

✪ 11-11 ☎ (01943) 464424 🌐 theoldcockotley.co.uk

Ilkley Mary Jane; Theakston Best Bitter; 7 changing beers (sourced locally) Ⓗ

Compact and welcoming, this is a genuine free house which only opened in 2010 after being converted from a former café, but it has a traditional pub feel. There are two low-ceilinged rooms downstairs with stone-flagged floors, and a further room upstairs. The guest ales are mostly from local breweries. At least two real ciders are also served plus a range of foreign beers. No admittance to under-18s. Q&●🚍🐾🛜

Overton

Reindeer Inn Ⓛ

204 Old Road, WF4 4RL (signed off A642 near National Coal Mining Museum)

✪ 12 (4 Mon)-midnight; 12-11 Sun ☎ (01924) 848374

Cap House Miners a Pint; 5 changing beers Ⓗ

A traditional, independent free house, once a coaching inn, now the brewery tap for Cap House Brewery, and offering locally sourced guest beers. Home-cooked food is served in the restaurant or conservatory, which leads out into the beer garden overlooking the National Coal Mining Museum. Quiz night is Wednesday. The games room has a pool table, dartboard, dominoes and games machines. Restaurant opening hours are Tuesday-Saturday lunchtimes, Wednesday-Saturday evenings, and 12-6 on Sunday. 🐾❀◑♣●P🚍(232,128)🐾

Pontefract

Carleton Ⓛ 🗸

Hardwick Road, WF8 3PQ (on A639 1 mile S of town centre)

✪ 11-11 (midnight Fri & Sat) ☎ (01977) 703797

Greene King IPA; Leeds Midnight Bell; Timothy Taylor Landlord; house beer (by Greene King); 4 changing beers (often Revolutions, Wharfe Bank) Ⓗ

A popular estate pub which now offers 10 well-kept cask ales and not just from the Greene King

stable. Plenty of outdoor seating is available round the side and to the rear. It gets busy at weekends, with the locals enjoying sport on the many TV screens. It holds beer festivals and Meet the Brewer evenings. The house beer is brewed by Greene King to the landlady's recipe. A carvery is being added after a kitchen refurbishment.
🛏️🕸️🕽️⑥♿P🚃 (29,30,46) 🛜

Robin Hood 🗓

4 Wakefield Road, WF8 4HN (on A645/A639 jct on S side of town)
🕐 5-midnight; 12-1am Fri & Sat; 12-midnight Sun
☎ (01977) 702231
James & Kirkman Little John; 5 changing beers 🖽
Busy locals' pub with a public bar and three other drinking areas. It holds quizzes twice weekly and has darts and dominoes teams in the local charity league. A former winner of several local CAMRA awards, it stages a beer festival over the August bank holiday weekend. The James & Kirkman Brewery is behind the pub. Open mic night takes place once a month.
Q🛏️🕸️♿≠(Tanshelf)♣●🚃♣

Pudsey

Fleece 🍺 🗓 ⊘

100 Fartown, LS28 8LU
🕐 12-11 ☎ (0113) 236 2748 🌐 fleecepudsey.co.uk
Bridgehouse Blonde; Tetley Bitter; Timothy Taylor Golden Best, Landlord; 1 changing beer (sourced locally) 🖽
A traditional, warm and friendly community pub. The lounge room has a theme of Laurel and Hardy and other film stars of the golden age of Hollywood. The games room, where you can play dominoes or watch TV sport, has an open fire. To the back of the pub is an attractive garden. This award-winning venue holds regular quizzes, charity events and a summertime beer festival.
🕸️♣P🚃 (14,X14,205) 🛜

Rastrick

Roundhill Inn ⊘

75 Clough Lane, HD6 3QL (400yds from A643/A6107 jct towards M62 motorway bridge)
🕐 4-11; 12-midnight Sat & Sun ☎ (01484) 713418
🌐 roundhillinn.co.uk
Black Sheep Best Bitter; Timothy Taylor Golden Best, Landlord; 2 changing beers (sourced regionally) 🖽
Two-roomed genuine free house and locals' pub lying on the edge of Rastrick, easily reached by bus from Brighouse or Huddersfield. In daytimes during the week the pub doubles as a private function venue, notably hosting wakes, as the crematorium in neighbouring Kirklees is less than half a mile away. Originally a terrace of three houses, there are plans to extend into an adjoining barn while retaining the two-roomed layout.
QP🚃 (547,549) 🛜

Rishworth

Booth Wood Inn

Oldham Road, HX6 4QU (on A672 towards jct 22 of M62) SE034170
🕐 12-10 (11 Fri & Sat) ☎ (01422) 825600
🌐 boothwoodinn.co.uk
Holt Bitter; 4 changing beers (sourced locally) 🖽

A traditional family country pub and restaurant close to the scenic Yorkshire Moors. It is open plan, with a large central bar and two restaurant areas featuring beams and flagstone floors. All food is freshly prepared each day. In addition to the main menu there are daily specials, classic and retro dishes. There is always a good selection of carefully chosen real ales. 🛏️🕸️🕽️⑥♿P🚃 🛜

Roberttown

New Inn 🍺 🗓 ⊘

Roberttown Lane, WF15 7NP
🕐 3-11; 12-11.30 Fri & Sat; 12-10.30 Sun ☎ (01924) 402069
🌐 thenewinnroberttown.com
Abbeydale Moonshine; Leeds Best; house beer (by Mallinson's); 3 changing beers (sourced nationally) 🖽
A traditional village local, popular with all ages. It is the brewery tap for the New Inn Brewery, with one of the family's beers always on. A seasonal dark beer is also offered. There is a snug with comfy chairs, and a function room. The Wednesday quiz is popular, along with the occasional Sunday race day. An annual beer festival is now well established, featuring rare beers. Guest ales are from local and national sources.
🛏️🕸️♣P🚃 (229,253) ♣

Saltaire

Cap & Collar

4 Queens Road, BD18 4SJ
🕐 5-10; 4-11 Fri; 1-11 Sat; 1-6 Sun; closed Mon
4 changing beers (sourced regionally; often Mallinson's, Saltaire, Wishbone) 🖽
Relatively new micropub, opened in late 2014, with a modern open-plan café-style layout and space for up to 35 people. A beer garden and smoking area are to the rear. Four handpulls serve a varying range of real ales, often from local breweries, alongside a real cider. There is also a selection of bottle-conditioned ales. Food is of the pub-snack variety. There are occasional cheese-tasting nights and live acoustic music evenings.
🛏️🕸️≠●🚃 (760) 🛜

Fanny's Ale & Cider House 🗓 ⊘

63 Saltaire Road, BD18 3JN (on A657, opp fire station)
🕐 12 (5 Mon)-11; 12-midnight Fri & Sat ☎ (01274) 591419
Timothy Taylor Golden Best, Landlord; 6 changing beers (sourced regionally; often Bradfield, Ossett) 🖽
Near the UNESCO World Heritage Site of Saltaire village and the historic Salts Mill, this cosy pub was formerly a beer shop. It is now a free house, serving two regular ales, up to six guests and real ciders. An extension has increased seating capacity downstairs and added disabled access. Upstairs there is a room with comfortable seating. The gas-lit lounge is adorned with breweriana, and real fires add nicely to the welcome.
♿≠●🚃 (760) ♣ 🛜

Hop 🍺 ⊘

199 Bingley Road, BD18 4DH
🕐 12-midnight ☎ (01274) 582111 🌐 thehopsaltaire.co.uk
Ossett Yorkshire Blonde, Big Red Bitter, Silver King, Excelsior; 4 changing beers (sourced regionally; often Fernandes, Rat, Saltaire) 🖽
Adjacent to the main A650 road and built within an old tramshed (which was also the pub's former name), originally constructed in 1904. There is a large open-plan main room, with an upper

mezzanine primarily used for dining. A large outdoor seating area is popular in good weather. Many of the real ales are from the Ossett Brewery range or its associated breweries such as Fernandes and Rat. Wood-fired pizzas can be seen being prepared from the main bar area. Regular live music events take place. ⏰🕭🍴⇌🍺🅿🖵🛜

Sandbeds

Airedale Heifer 🅛
Bradford Road, BD20 5LY
🍺 11.30-11 ☎ (01274) 515870 🌐 theairedaleheifer.co.uk
Bridgehouse Blonde, Yorkshire Ale, Holy Cow; house beer (by Bridgehouse); 2 changing beers (sourced locally; often Bridgehouse) 🅗
Fully refurbished throughout in 2015, this extensive roadside pub has a substantial food presence and is the tap for Bridgehouse Brewery. The pub is named after a famous heifer of the early 1800s, the heaviest cow in the UK (see the sculpture at the front). The open-plan layout revolves around a single L-shaped bar. Many dishes feature the brewery's beers. There is a sizeable south-facing garden with patio heaters. Children are welcome until 8pm, later if dining. ⏰🕭🍴🅿🖵(662,760)🐾🛜

Scholes

Stafford Arms 🅛
192 Scholes Lane, BD19 6LS (A649)
🍺 4-midnight; 12-midnight Sat & Sun ☎ (01274) 873737
Copper Dragon Golden Pippin; Timothy Taylor Golden Best, Landlord; 1 changing beer 🅗
An attractive pub on the edge of Scholes village, popular with locals and offering a warm, friendly welcome to all, including walkers. Rescued from closure when it was bought and refurbished by concerned locals, it has an open-plan, comfortable layout with a large central fireplace and traditional decor, and a large beer garden to the rear. Bus 256 passes by while the 252, 253 and 254 stop a few minutes' walk away. ⏰🕭🅿🖵(256)🐾🛜

Shipley

Fox 🅛
41 Briggate, BD17 7BP
🍺 10.30-11; 10-midnight Fri & Sat; 12-10.30 Sun
☎ (01274) 594826 🌐 thefoxshipley.co.uk
6 changing beers (sourced regionally; often Titanic, BEEspoke) 🅗
Opened in 2013, this is an independent, single-roomed, café-style bar, simply but smartly furnished and featuring recycled church pews. Small, friendly and welcoming, it offers six handpulled ales including its own in-house BEEspoke beers. Real ciders are also sold as well as a wide range of international bottled beers. It is handy for quick refreshment when waiting for trains at Shipley station as the train times appear on a TV monitor. Live music plays every Tuesday evening. ⏰🕭🍴⇌🍺🖵🐾🛜

OddFellows
rear of 16-17 Market Street, BD18 3QD (behind Shipley Bowling Alley)
🍺 12-11 (midnight Sat & Sun) ☎ (01274) 599389
4 changing beers 🅗
Opened in 2014, this was the second of the new micropubs in Shipley. The entrance, at the rear of Shipley Bowling Alley, is in a car park. Behind the unassuming exterior lies a comfortable, inviting interior with a friendly welcome. The place has an open-plan layout and features four varying guest ales including a selection from local breweries. Frequent live music events are held. ⏰🕭⇌🍺🖵🛜

Ring o' Bells 🅛 ✅
3 Bradford Road, BD18 3PR (on A650)
🍺 11-midnight (1am Fri & Sat); 12-11 Sun ☎ (01274) 584386
Leeds Pale; Tetley Bitter; 4 changing beers (often Saltaire) 🅗
Traditional roadhouse-type pub with an impressive frontage and close to the historic village of Saltaire. Sensitively refurbished in 2014, it retains a comfortable, homely feel. Up to four guest ales are mainly sourced regionally. Sports matches are shown on several TV screens and there is occasional live music. A small Edwardian smoke room merits a mention in CAMRA's book, Yorkshire's Real Heritage Pubs, and is a meeting place for activity groups including writers and anglers. 🕭🍺♿⇌🍴🅿🖵🐾🛜

Silsden

King's Arms 🅛 ✅
Bolton Road, BD20 0JY
🍺 12-midnight (11 Mon) ☎ (01535) 653216
Saltaire Blonde; Theakston Best Bitter; 4 changing beers (sourced nationally; often Rudgate, Wishbone) 🅗
Award-winning, bustling community pub, run by the same couple since 2003, with music nights (Tue and Thu), quiz nights (Wed), a pool table and beer festivals, all combining to make it a great place to visit. Partitions divide the main bar into three distinct areas, each with its own feel. Westons cider and at least three guest beers from near and far, including a darker beer, provide something for all tastes. Regular buses between Keighley and Ilkley stop close by. 🕭🍺🍴🍺🅿🖵🐾🛜

Slaithwaite

Swan Inn 🅛 ✅
Carr Lane, Crimble, HD7 5BQ
🍺 4-midnight; 12-midnight Sat & Sun ☎ (01484) 841115
Saltaire Blonde; 4 changing beers (often Empire, Mallinson's, Rat) 🅗
Traditional two-roomed local next to Slaithwaite viaduct. Historic posters from Huddersfield's long-closed Palace Theatre and some interesting old books are features of the lounge, along with an impressive bar and etched glass. A blackboard lists current and forthcoming beers, with six normally on tap. There is also a good selection of bottled beers, and bar snacks are served. The Swan is friendly and welcoming, with a quiz on Wednesdays, disco on Saturdays and occasional live music. Q⏰🕭🕭⇌🍴🍺🅿🖵🐾

Sowerby Bridge

Firehouse 🍷 🅛
1 Town Hall Street, HX6 2QD
🍺 4 (12 Sat)-11.30; 12-10.30 Sun; closed Mon
☎ (01422) 832586 🌐 firehousesowerbybridge.co.uk
Magic Rock Ringmaster; Moorhouse's Pride of Pendle; 4 changing beers (sourced regionally) 🅗

Close to the bridge crossing the River Calder in the centre of Sowerby Bridge, this prominent building, dating from 1874, is a popular venue for those who like to eat out with the option of a traditional pint. The family-run outlet has built a reputation for food and real ale, in particular pizza cooked in an open oven and its tapas menu. Four guest beers are served with at least one from a local or regional brewer. ⏸️≈♿🚌🚲🍴🛜

Jubilee Refreshment Rooms 🅛

Station Road, HX6 3AB (on railway station)
🕒 9.30am (9am Sat)-10; 12-9 Sun ☎ (01422) 648285
🌐 jubileerefreshmentrooms.co.uk
3 changing beers (often Goose Eye, Mallinson's, Small World) 🅗
Located in the only surviving part of the 1876 station building, the bar serves three changing local beers and offers a pleasant place to while away the time or stop off on the real ale trail. Refreshments are available in the morning to benefit rail users, with alcohol served from noon onwards. The walls are adorned with interesting railway and brewery-related memorabilia, and events and talks take place frequently. Trains depart regularly for Leeds and Manchester.
Q🌞♿≈P🚲🛜

Shepherd's Rest ✪

125 Bolton Brow, HX6 2BD (on A58 towards Halifax)
🕒 3-11; 12-11.30 Fri & Sat; 12-11 Sun ☎ (01422) 831937
Ossett Pale Gold, Yorkshire Blonde, Silver King; 5 changing beers 🅗
Built in 1877, this establishment took the name of a previous pub on the other side of the busy main road. It was purchased by Ossett Brewery in 2005 and the available space has been used to good effect. From the entrance steps a triangular area leads to the bar, which faces a cosy and compact lounge with a large brick-arched fireplace. It has comfortable seating and a flagged floor, which in turn leads to an enclosed outside area. Monday is quiz night. Q🌞♿≈♣🚲(560,574,579)🐾

Stanbury

Friendly 🅛

54 Main Street, BD22 0HB
🕒 12-11; 12-10.30 Sun ☎ (01535) 645528
2 changing beers (often Goose Eye, Rat, Stod Fold) 🅗
Popular village local which also attracts those walking the Pennine Way or visiting the ruined farmhouse claimed to be Wuthering Heights. The pub is small and retains a traditional layout, with two small lounges either side of a central bar, plus a separate games room. Stanbury is only two miles from Haworth but a million miles from its tourist hustle and bustle. At least one beer is usually from Goose Eye Brewery. Tea and coffee are available on request. 🌞👤♣P🚲(664,916,917)🐾

Wuthering Heights Inn 🅛 ✪

Main Street, BD22 0HB
🕒 12-midnight ☎ (01535) 643332
🌐 thewutheringheights.co.uk
Theakston Best Bitter; Thwaites Wainwright; 2 changing beers (sourced nationally; often Bradfield) 🅗
A popular, friendly local dating from 1763. Warmed by logburners, the traditional main bar has photographs showing the history of the village and an internet terminal for customers' use. The cosy dining room has a Bronte theme. A third room

hosts regular folk music gatherings and can be booked for parties and meetings. The rear garden has spectacular views down the Worth Valley and a separate camping area (no caravans). Well-behaved dogs and children are welcome. A quiz takes place every Thursday.
🛏️🌞🏮⏸️👤A♣P🚲(916,917,918)🐾🛜

Todmorden

Staff of Life

550 Burnley Road, Knotts Grove, OL14 8JF (on A4646 between Todmorden and Cornholme)
🕒 12-3, 5.30-11; 12-midnight Fri-Sun ☎ (01706) 819033
🌐 staffoflifeinn.org.uk
Timothy Taylor Golden Best, Landlord; 3 changing beers (often Goose Eye, Ilkley, Rooster's) 🅗
Comfortable roadside inn nestling in a deep, narrow gorge beneath the local landmark of Eagle's Crag. Three guest ales come from a variety of northern independents. High-quality food can be enjoyed at a table in one of several cosy nooks and crannies, or on the outside terrace. Unusual artwork on the interior walls alludes to the local legend of the white doe – ask the landlord or landlady to explain the story.
🛏️🌞🏮⏸️P🚲(589,592)🐾🛜

Upper Denby

George Inn 🍺 ✪

114 Denby Lane, HD8 8UE
🕒 5-10.30 (11.30 Fri); 1-11.30 Sat; 11.30-10.30 Sun ☎ (01484) 861347 🌐 thegeorgeinn-upperdenby.co.uk
Tetley Bitter; Timothy Taylor Landlord; 1 changing beer (often Great Heck, Ossett, Small World) 🅗
Family-run village local which is going from strength to strength since becoming a free house in late 2012. The pub has hosted walk and food days, with home-made pie and peas, along with other events. Occasional live music and traditional sings take place. Walkers are welcome, and families until 8.30pm. Local CAMRA Rural Pub of the Year 2016. 🛏️🌞⏸️A♣P🚲🐾🛜

Wakefield

Black Rock ✪

19 Cross Square, WF1 1PQ (between Bull Ring and top of Westgate)
🕒 11-11 (midnight Sat); 12-10.30 Sun ☎ (01924) 375550
Kelham Island Easy Rider; Tetley Bitter; 3 changing beers (sourced regionally) 🅗
An arched, tiled façade leads into this compact city-centre local, with its warm welcome and comfy interior adorned with photographs of old Wakefield. The Rock stands as one of the few proper pubs left in the middle of the clubs and bars of Westgate, and is popular with drinkers of all ages looking for a real pint. Drinkers are encouraged to suggest beers to try, with four changing guest ales on offer. There is a free function room for private use. Q≈🚲

Bull & Fairhouse 🅛

60 George Street, WF1 1DL (turn right out of Westgate Station, left at Westgate, then right at traffic lights, and bear left at bottom of hill; pub is on left after 200yds)
🕒 4-11; 12-midnight Fri & Sat; 12-11 Sun ☎ (01924) 362930
Bad Comfortably Numb; Great Heck Chopper; 4 changing beers 🅗

Brewery tap for the Great Heck Brewery which has reverted to an earlier name alluding to the cattle market and fairground in the area. It is a comfortable multi-roomed premises now enjoying a lighter feel, with a new lounge at the front and the toilets relocated to the rear, improving disabled access via a passageway. Play Your Cards Right is held on Thursdays, with live music at weekends. A changing real cider/perry is served on gravity.
Q♿⇌(Westgate/Kirkgate)♣●🚌(443,444)🐾📶

Fernandes Brewery Tap & Bier Keller L ✔

5 Avison Yard, Kirkgate, WF1 1UA (turn right approx 100yds S of George Street/Kirkgate jct near Scartop Pine)
4-11 (11.30 Thu); 12-midnight Fri & Sat; 12-11 Sun
☎ (01924) 386348
10 changing beers (often Fernandes, Marston's, Ossett) H
Owned by Ossett Brewery, the Fernandes Brewery is based in the cellar. Eleven handpulls are on the bar, with two dedicated to dark beers. There are four Fernandes beers, two Ossett and three guest beers, plus draught cider. The Bier Keller, which opens 6pm-midnight Friday and Saturday, has premier foreign beers on draught plus an Ossett beer and a cider on handpump. There is a quiz on Wednesday evening, plus folk music on the first and open mic on the third Sunday of each month.
Q⇌(Kirkgate)🚌🐾📶

Harry's Bar L ✔

107B Westgate, WF1 1EL (turn right from Westgate station, cross road at traffic lights and pub is at back of car park on right)
5 (4 Sat)-1am ☎ (01924) 373773
Bob's White Lion; Leeds Pale; Ossett Silver King; house beer (by Five Towns); 3 changing beers (often Moorhouse's) H
This small, one-roomed pub is set in an alleyway just off Westgate. A real fire and a bare brick and wood interior plus vintage sporting pictures enhance this cosy venue. There is also a fantastic view of Wakefield's famous 99-arch viaduct: if only steam trains were still a regular feature. A selection of bottled Belgian beers adds to the temptation.
Q❀♿⇌●🚌🐾📶

Hop L ✔

19 Bank Street, WF1 1EH (in cobbled street off Westgate almost opp Theatre Royal)
4-midnight (1am Fri); 12-1am Sat ☎ (01924) 367111
thehopwakefield.co.uk
Ossett Yorkshire Blonde, Silver King, Excelsior; Rat White Rat; 5 changing beers H
Converted into a venue for music, comedy and conversation, this Georgian building retains bare-brick walls, fireplaces and other original features, along with new additions including a VW camper van converted into a bar. The main bar has nine handpumps, one reserved for a dark beer and one for a Fernandes or Riverhead beer, alongside a selection of bottled Belgian and American beers. There is open mic night on Monday, a quiz on Tuesday and live music on Thursday, Friday and Saturday. Rooms are available for hire.
❀♿⇌(Westgate/Kirkgate)●🚌

Inns of Court Hotel

22 King Street, WF1 2SR (on narrow street behind town hall)
11-midnight (1am Fri & Sat) ☎ (01924) 375560
Jennings Bitter; Marston's Old Empire; Wychwood Hobgoblin; 3 changing beers (sourced nationally) H
Named after its proximity to the law courts, the pub is surrounded by offices and solicitors' practices. It has a friendly atmosphere with a clientele that varies depending on the time of visit, and is popular with office staff and students on weekdays. The landlord has recently removed the smooth beer and increased the well-kept range of cask ales, offering a changing choice of beers from Marston's breweries, with the occasional guest brewery making an appearance.
❀🛏☾⇌(Westgate/Kirkgate)🚌📶

Wakefield Labour Club L

18 Vicarage Street, WF1 1QX (at top of Kirkgate, round corner from Wakey Tavern)
7-11 (midnight Fri); 11-midnight Sat; 7-midnight Sun
☎ (01924) 215626
5 changing beers (sourced regionally) H
The Red Shed is a secondhand army hut that has been extensively refurbished. Home to many union, community and charity groups, it has a quiz night on Wednesday, occasional live music on the second Saturday of each month and an open mic folk music night on the last Saturday. There are three rooms, two available to hire for functions. An extensive collection of union plates and badges is displayed over the bar as well as numerous CAMRA awards on the walls.
Q♨♿⇌(Westgate/Kirkgate)♣P🚌🐾📶

Wintersett

Anglers Retreat L

Ferrytop Lane, WF4 2EB (between villages of Crofton and Ryhill; follow signage all over district for nearby Anglers Country Park)
12-3 (not Tue), 7-11; 12-11 Sat; 12-3.30, 7-11 Sun
☎ (01924) 862370
Acorn Barnsley Bitter; 3 changing beers (sourced locally) H
Old-fashioned, no-frills, rural alehouse, a rare example of a cosy, locals' pub, whose owner has just celebrated 20 years in charge. Close to the Anglers Country Park, Haw Wood and the Transpennine Trail, it is frequented by twitchers, cyclists, walkers and bikers. There is a beer garden to the side and seats at the front for fine weather drinking, and a large car park across the road. A frequent bus service passes within three minutes' walk. Q♨❀♿⛺♣P🚌(194,195,196)🐾

Join CAMRA

The Campaign for Real Ale has been fighting for over 40 years to save Britain's proud heritage of cask-conditioned ales, independent breweries, and pubs that offer a good choice of beer. You can help that fight by joining the campaign: use the form at the back of the guide or see **www.camra.org.uk**

CAMRA'S
Beer Anthology

Edited by Roger Protz

'A good local pub has much in common with a church, except that a pub is warmer, and there's more conversation'
William Blake

'A fine beer may be judged with only one sip, but it is better to be thoroughly sure'
Czech proverb

An anthology of excerpts from literature, television, film and music about beer, pubs and drinking. Roger Protz, in themed chapters and using easily digested quotations, demonstrates how deeply beer and pubs are woven into the DNA of British culture. The book runs the gamut of culture, from Eastenders to Dickens, and is ideal for the casual reader looking for beer-based entertainment or for the more studious one who wants to gather a sense of how Britain's national drink – and the consumption of it – have been represented in many media.

£9.99 ISBN: 978-1-85249-333-2 CAMRA members' price: £7.99 136 pages

For this and other books on beer and pubs visit CAMRA's online bookshop at **www.camra.org.uk/books** or call **01727 867201**

NORTHERN
ISLES

SHETLAND

HIGHLANDS
&
WESTERN ISLES

ABERDEEN
& GRAMPIAN

TAYSIDE

LOCH LOMOND,
STIRLING
& THE
TROSSACHS

FIFE

ARGYLL &
THE ISLES

GREATER
GLASGOW
& CLYDE

EDINBURGH & LOTHIANS

AYRSHIRE
& ARRAN

BORDERS

NORTHERN
IRELAND

DUMFRIES &
GALLOWAY

NORTHUMBERLAND

TYNE &
WEAR

CUMBRIA

DURHAM

ISLE OF
MAN

NORTH
YORKSHIRE

LANCASHIRE

WEST
YORKS

EAST
YORKS

MERSEYSIDE

GREATER
MANCHESTER

SOUTH
YORKS

CHESHIRE

DERBYSHIRE

NOTTINGHAM-
SHIRE

LINCOLNSHIRE

NW
WALES

NE
WALES

SHROPSHIRE

STAFFORD-
SHIRE

LEICESTERSHIRE

NORFOLK

MID
WALES

WEST
MIDLANDS

WARWICK-
SHIRE

NORTHAMPTON-
SHIRE

CAMBRIDGE-
SHIRE

SUFFOLK

WORCEST-
ERSHIRE

HEREFORD-
SHIRE

HUNTINGDON

BEDFORD-
SHIRE

WEST
WALES

GLAMORGAN

GWENT

GLOUCS &
BRISTOL

OXFORD-
SHIRE

BUCKINGHAM

HERTFORD-
SHIRE

ESSEX

GREATER
LONDON

BERKSHIRE

WILTSHIRE

SURREY

KENT

SOMERSET

HAMPSHIRE

WEST
SUSSEX

EAST
SUSSEX

CHANNEL
ISLANDS

DEVON

DORSET

ISLE OF
WIGHT

CORNWALL

Wales

GLAMORGAN

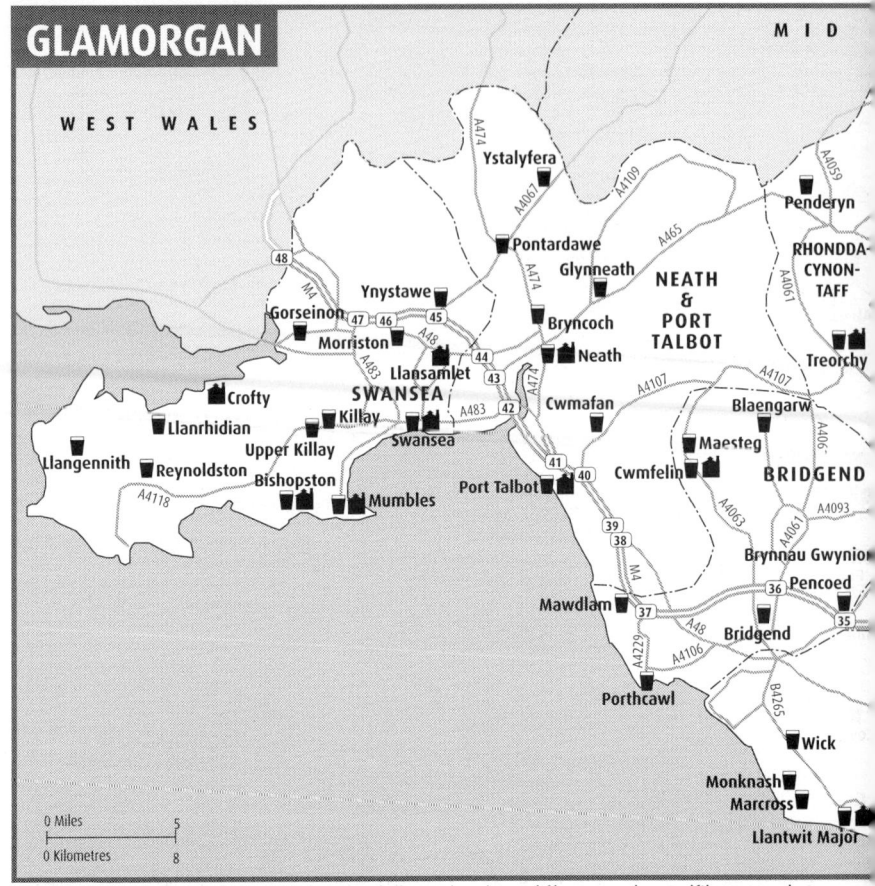

M I D

WEST WALES

Ystalyfera

Penderyn

48

Pontardawe

Ynstawe
Glynneath

**NEATH
&
PORT
TALBOT**

RHONDDA-
CYNON-
TAFF

Gorseinon
47 46 45
Morriston

Bryncoch

Llansamlet
43

Neath

Treorchy

Crofty

SWANSEA

42

Cwmafan

Killay

Llanrhidian

Upper Killay
Swansea

Blaengarw

Maesteg

Llangennith
Reynoldston
Bishopston

41
40

Cwmfelin

BRIDGEND

Mumbles
Port Talbot

39
38

Brynnau Gwynion

Pencoed
36

Mawdlam
37

Bridgend
35

Porthcawl

Wick

Monknash
Marcross

0 Miles 5

0 Kilometres 8

Llantwit Major

Authority areas covered: Bridgend UA, Caerphilly UA (part), Cardiff UA, Merthyr Tydfil UA, Neath &
Port Talbot UA, Rhondda, Cynon & Taff UA, Swansea UA, Vale of Glamorgan UA

Aberdare

Whitcombe Inn
Whitcombe Street, CF44 7DA
☼ 12-midnight; 12-11.30 Sun ☎ (01685) 875106
**Grey Trees Diggers Gold, Drummer Boy; 2 changing
beers (sourced nationally; often Fuller's, Gower,
Sharp's)** Ⓗ
Welcoming and friendly traditional street-corner
local, close to the town centre. Local brewery Grey
Trees features prominently, and other beers from
its range may substitute. The large front bar backs
onto a pool room at the rear. Sport sometimes
plays on TV, with projector screens for major
sporting events, but is rarely intrusive. Live music is
hosted occasionally. ❧♣♠🚐

Aberthin

Hare & Hounds
Aberthin Road, CF71 7LG
☼ 12-midnight (1am Fri & Sat) ☎ (01446) 774892
**Hancocks HB; Wye Valley HPA; 2 changing beers
(sourced regionally; often Evan Evans, Glamorgan)** Ⓗ
A characterful village pub whose cosy public bar
has traditional stone walls, wooden beams and a
log fire. The bar is the focal point, where the locals
gather, and there is a newly furnished dining area

serving high-quality fare, most of the ingredients
freshly bought every day. The chef makes his own
butter and bread. Ales are mainly sourced locally
by the knowledgeable and helpful licensee. The
sun trap beer garden with its own outdoor bar
occasionally hosts live music. There is limited
parking at the front of the building.
Q❧☺❀◐♿♣♠🚐🚌(321)🐾🛜

Barry

Barry West End Club Ⓛ
54 St Nicholas Road, CF62 6QY
☼ 1-midnight; 11-11 Sun ☎ (01446) 735739
⊕ barrywestendclub.webs.com
**Brains Dark; Wychwood Hobgoblin; Wye Valley HPA; 2
changing beers** Ⓗ
Visitors are welcome to sample the keenly priced
ales at this former local CAMRA branch Club of the
Year. Housed in a red-brick building overlooking
Barry Old Harbour, it has a bar, lounge, function
room and snooker room. The club holds beer
festivals during the year and is a hub of local
activity. Home to a cricket club for over 30 years, it
also fields skittles teams, adult and junior football
squads, snooker teams, and is home to chess,
fishing and scuba clubs. Q❧☺❀◐♿❧♣♠🚐🛜

Blaengarw

Blaengarw Hotel

The Strand, CF32 8AA

🕐 11.30-11 (midnight Wed); 11-midnight Fri; 11-1am Sat; 11-10.30 Sun ☎ (01656) 870287

1 changing beer (often Evan Evans, Glamorgan, Rhymney) Ⓗ

Large, recently refurbished, street-corner local at the heart of the community. The public bar is popular for TV sport and hosts pool and darts league teams, and there is a fine jukebox. Just one carefully chosen changing cask beer is on offer along with up to four ciders. Meals are available in the lounge/dining room 12-8pm Tuesday and Thursday, and the Sunday lunches (12-3pm) are always popular. The famous Welsh hymn Calon Lan was written upstairs. ▷☺❶❺♣🚃🚌(16,72,73)🛜

Bridgend

Cabo Roche

Five Bells Road, CF31 3HW

🕐 11-11.30; 12-11.30 Sat ☎ (01656) 663555

Sharp's Doom Bar; 1 changing beer (often Exmoor) Ⓗ

Situated at the southern end of the town centre and close to the college, this establishment has continued to thrive since its conversion from a bathroom showroom to a bar in 2007. A mixed clientele uses the three distinct areas – a café, bar and lounge with comfortable settees. TV sport is available throughout. Real ale is on two handpumps, often including an interesting and well-chosen guest beer. Lunches are served Monday to Friday. ▷☺❶❺⇆♣🚌(303,X2)😺🛜

Coach Inn

37 Cowbridge Road, CF31 3DH

🕐 11.30-11; 12-10.30 Sun

Wye Valley Butty Bach Ⓗ**; 4 changing beers (often Grey Trees, Otley, VOG)** Ⓗ/Ⓖ

Basically furnished free house with a passion for real ale and cider from Wales and beyond. Three guest beers on handpull and two served straight from the cask complement the house ale.

Bishopston

Joiners Arms Ⓛ

50 Bishopston Road, SA3 3EJ

🕐 3-10.30 Mon & Tue; 11.30-11; 12-10.30 Sun
☎ (01792) 232658 🌐 thejoiners.info

Courage Best Bitter; Marston's Pedigree; Swansea Bishopswood Bitter, Three Cliffs Gold, Original Wood; 2 changing beers Ⓗ

Situated in the heart of the village, this 1860s free house remains popular with locals and visitors. Home of the Swansea Brewing Company, the pub has two bars and holds beer festivals and occasional music events, usually around public holidays. Good-value food is served lunchtimes and evenings (no food Mon and Sun eve). There is a small car park. ▷☺❶P🚌(14)😺🛜

Valley

41 Bishopston Road, SA3 3EJ

🕐 12-11 ☎ (01792) 234820

Courage Best Bitter; 3 changing beers Ⓗ

Traditional country pub set in the heart of this attractive Gower village. A large porch area (which doubles as a convenient bus shelter) leads to a split-level bar and dining area, with exposed beams, hearth and open fire. Occasional live music and quiz nights are hosted. A wide variety of home-cooked meals made using local ingredients is served daily, with a takeaway service available on Sunday lunchtimes. ☺❶❺♣🚌P🚌(14)😺🛜

Continental beers are also available. A popular weekend venue, customers enjoy open mic nights, themed evenings, brewery trips, Meet the Brewer and tap takeover events, a spring beer festival and a stout and porter festival in November. See the pub's lively Facebook page for current events. ✿≠♣🚌🚋(303,X2)😸🛜

Wyndham Arms ✅

Dunraven Place, CF31 1JE
🕐 9am-midnight (1am Fri & Sat) ☎ (01656) 673571
Greene King Abbot; Sharp's Doom Bar; 4 changing beers (often Brecon, Bullmastiff, Glamorgan) Ⓗ
Totally refurbished in 2014, this town-centre Wetherspoon hotel features beers from south Wales breweries. The building, named after a centuries-old local family, dates from 1792, and has 25 en-suite bedrooms. Seating ranges from high stools to comfortable settees in three distinct sections, including areas suited to dining. A conference room is available for hire. The pub opens at 7am for breakfast, the bar opens at 9am. Q✿🛏🕽🕽&≠🍴🚋🛜

Bryncoch

Dyffryn Arms

Neath Road, SA10 7YF (on A474)
🕐 12-11 ☎ (01639) 636184 🌐 thedyffrynarms.com
Wadworth 6X; 2 changing beers (sourced nationally) Ⓗ
Popular roadside pub with a large bar/lounge area, cosy nooks and a separate restaurant. A clean and modern interior is enhanced by old local photographs and a real log fire. Outside seating overlooks the large car park and children's play area. Wadworth 6X is always available alongside two changing guest ales, sourced from national and independent breweries. Food is served all day until 9pm (8pm Sun). 🛏✿🕽&🅿🚋(56)🛜

Brynnau Gwynion

Mountain Hare

Brynna Road, CF35 6PG
🕐 4 (5 Mon)-11; 3-midnight Fri; 12-midnight Sat; 12-10.30 Sun ☎ (01656) 860453 🌐 mountainhare.co.uk
Mountain Hare Far Shores IPA; Wickwar BOB; 2 changing beers (often Glamorgan, St Austell) Ⓗ
Self-taught brewer and licensee Paul began brewing on-site in 2014. One of his two Mountain Hare beers is always on sale, along with real cider in summer. A traditional Welsh village local, this proper community pub has been in the same family for over 40 years. It has a public bar and a lovely old stone-walled lounge. Sport is often shown on TV in this rugby-lovers' pub. Families are welcome until 9pm in the lounge.
🛏✿🕽♣🍴🅿🚋(64,404)😸🛜

Caerphilly

Green Lady

Pontygwindy Road, CF83 3HF
🕐 10-11 (midnight Fri); 9am-midnight Sat; 9am-11 Sun ☎ (029) 2085 1510
3 changing beers (sourced nationally; often Marston's, Ringwood, Wychwood) Ⓗ
Open-plan Marston's pub alongside the old main road, north of the town centre. Comfortable and spacious, it has a separate dining/function room. Three handpumps dispense a widely varying selection of ales from the wider Marston's group, including seasonals. Good-value meals are available (no food Sun eves). Live music features most Saturday evenings and there is a quiz night every Sunday. 🛏✿🕽&≠(Energlyn & Churchill Park)🅿🚋(26,50)

Malcolm Uphill ✅

89-91 Cardiff Road, CF83 1FQ
🕐 8am-midnight (1am Fri & Sat) ☎ (029) 2076 0720
Greene King Abbot; Ruddles Best Bitter; Sharp's Doom Bar; 3 changing beers (sourced nationally; often Adnams) Ⓗ
Busy Wetherspoon pub, handy for the rail and bus interchange. Up to five guest beers are usually on sale, plus one or two guest ciders. The usual JDW deals and promotions are offered. This pub can be crowded at weekends and hosts a popular quiz on Sundays. A separate accessible entrance is available if required. Q🛏✿🕽&≠🍴🚋🛜

Cardiff

Andrew Buchan

29 Albany Road, Roath, CF24 3LH
🕐 11-11
Rhymney Hobby Horse, Dark, Best, Export; 1 changing beer Ⓗ
This converted shop offers the full range of Rhymney beers and a variety of real ciders from local producers. It features an open fireplace with the brewery moose head hanging above, and an eclectic collection of modern art on the walls. On an outside wall is an allegoric mural featuring the brewery's hobby horse logo. The pub has a good reputation for live music and hosts a spoken word event. An upstairs meeting room is available, free of charge for community groups.
✿≠(Cathays)🚋🚋🛜

Birchgrove ✅

1-3 Birchgrove Road, CF14 1RR
🕐 12-11 (11.30 Thu); 11.30-11.30 Fri; 12-11.30 Sat; 12-10 Sun ☎ (029) 2031 1319
Brains Dark, Bitter, SA, Rev James Original; St Austell Tribute; 1 changing beer Ⓗ
Busy suburban community pub in a prominent position at a major crossroads. Built in Arts and Crafts style but modernised in recent years, it has retained original features including wood panelling in the public bar and two red-brick fireplaces. A large range of Brains beers is served together with seasonal and guest ales from other breweries. During the summer months a changing guest cider is also available. The pub has a traditional skittle alley, darts and Sunday quiz. 🛏✿🕽&♣🚋😸🛜

Cambrian Tap ✅

51 St Mary Street, CF10 1AD
🕐 11-11 (midnight Fri & Sat); 12-10.30 Sun ☎ (029) 2064 4952
7 changing beers (often Brains) Ⓗ
This historic street-corner city-centre pub has been refurbished and has a light and airy feel. Now a popular specialist beer bar, it showcases the cask and keg products of Brains Craft Brewery, and a mural depicts the various beers, often brewed in collaboration with other breweries or individuals. Guest beers are sourced from UK-wide microbreweries. Pork pies are a speciality here.
🕽≠(Central)🚋🛜

Chapter Arts Centre
Market Road, Canton, CF5 1QE (off Cowbridge Road East behind Iceland store)
🕓 12-11 (12.30am Fri); 12-midnight Sat; 12-10.30 Sun
☎ (029) 2030 4000 ⊕ chapter.org
Ringwood Best Bitter; 5 changing beers (sourced nationally) Ⓗ
Formerly a Victorian school, this arts centre and cinema complex bar retains original features including tilework and fireplaces. Beers are often from the Marston's extended range, but can also be local ales or from anywhere across Britain. Fridges contain a wide selection of continental bottled beers. The interior is open plan with plenty of seating, and there is a large outdoor drinking area. The walls are decorated with interesting changing artwork. ⌂❀❶♿⚲➞(Ninian Park)🅿🚆(17,18) 🛜

City Arms Ⓛ ❂
10-12 Quay Street, CF10 1EA
🕓 12-midnight (2am Fri & Sat); 12-10 Sun
☎ (029) 2064 1913
Brains Bitter, SA, Rev James Original Ⓗ; **7 changing beers** Ⓗ/Ⓖ
Popular pub in the heart of Cardiff's top beer and cider area. It has two rooms served by a central bar featuring 10 handpumped real ales, 10 specialist keg beers and 10 traditional ciders mainly pumped from the cellar using air pressure. Though a Brains house, it offers a large range of guest beers from almost anywhere in the UK. The pub gets extremely busy when events take place at the adjacent Millennium (Principality) Stadium and Arms Park. ❀♿⚲➞(Central)♣🍴🚆🛜

Discovery Ⓛ
Celyn Avenue, Lakeside, CF23 6EH
🕓 12-11.30 (12.30am Fri & Sat); 12-11 Sun
☎ (029) 2075 5015
5 changing beers (often Otley) Ⓗ
A spacious contemporary pub situated close to the north end of Roath Park Lake. The public bar retains a community atmosphere with a large-screen TV, darts and weekly quiz nights. The larger, quieter lounge/restaurant serves a variety of meals including chef's specials. Outside is a paved, covered patio. An impressive function room is available for weddings and other events. There are usually five guest beers including at least one LocAle. ❀❶♿➞(Heath)♣🅿🚆(54)🐾🛜

Gatekeeper ❂
9 Westgate Street, CF10 1DD
🕓 8am-midnight (2am Fri & Sat) ☎ (029) 2064 6020
Greene King Abbot; Ruddles Best Bitter; 5 changing beers Ⓗ
Large Wetherspoon pub spread over three distinct drinking areas. Located near the Millennium (Principality) Stadium, it gets busy on event days and when sporting fixtures are shown on the many TV screens. Up to five handpumps are devoted to real ciders, frequently from the Gwynt y Ddraig range. Bars are situated on the lower and upper floors, but the lower bar offers the greatest choice. ⌂❀❶♿⚲➞(Central)🍴🚆🛜

Hopbunker 🍺
Kingsway, CF10 5AF
🕓 12-11; 11-midnight Fri & Sat; 11-11 Sun
☎ (029) 2039 8889
15 changing beers (sourced regionally) Ⓗ

As the name suggests, this is a basement bar – it is the brewery tap for Hopcraft Brewery, so expect to find some of its ales on sale. Up to 15 handpumps serve a variety of cask beers sourced from throughout the UK, plus 20 craft keg beers and at least six real ciders, providing unparalled choice in the city. The range invariably includes a dark ale. Prices are reasonable for a specialist outlet. Local CAMRA Pub of the Year 2016. ➞(Central/Queen St)🍴🚆

Lansdowne
71 Beda Road, Canton, CF5 1LX
🕓 12-11 (11.30 Fri & Sat) ☎ (029) 2022 1312
⊕ thelansdownecardiff.co.uk
4 changing beers (often Grey Trees, Tiny Rebel, Waen) Ⓗ
A successful example of a conversion of a disused former hotel into a mixed-use development, this venue has become the hub of the local community. The upper storeys have been converted into flats and the ground floor has been refurbished into three drinking/dining areas. The decor is fairly basic but is bright and attractive with plenty of woodwork. Beers are sourced from microbreweries including a few LocAles. A recent local CAMRA Pub of the Year. ⌂❀❶➞(Ninian Park)♣🍴🚆🐾🛜

Mochyn Du
Sophia Close, Pontcanna, CF11 9HW
🕓 12-11 (midnight Fri & Sat); 12-10.30 Sun
☎ (029) 2037 1599 ⊕ ymochyndu.com
5 changing beers (often VOG) Ⓗ
Located near Glamorgan County Cricket Club ground, the pub is a short walk from the city centre. A large, attractive free house, formerly a lodge, it offers a choice of up to five real ales. The house beers from VOG (Vale of Glamorgan) Brewery are rebadges of its normal range. This is a popular meeting place for Welsh speakers. The conservatory provides a comfortable environment in which to enjoy home-cooked food. The large decked areas outside offer pleasant surroundings in fine weather. Q❀❶♿🅿🚆

New Conway
58 Conway Road, Pontcanna, CF11 9NW (off A4119 south of Llandaff Fields)
🕓 12-11 (midnight Fri & Sat); 12-10.30 Sun
☎ (029) 2022 4373
Greene King IPA; VOG South Island; 3 changing beers (often Celt Experience, Grey Trees, VOG) Ⓗ
Set in the leafy urban village of Pontcanna, a mile or so from the city centre, the Conway has a contemporary decor and an upmarket feel. A small front bar (where dogs are welcome) is linked by a corridor to a larger back bar where dining predominates. High-quality food features locally sourced produce. A beer festival is held in mid-summer. ⌂❀❶♿♣🚆🐾🛜

Pen & Wig Ⓛ ❂
1 Park Grove, CF10 3BJ
🕓 11.30-midnight (1am Fri & Sat); 11.30-11.30 Sun
☎ (029) 2037 1217 ⊕ penandwigcardiff.co.uk
8 changing beers (sourced nationally; often Brecon, Celt Experience) Ⓗ
Victorian-built terraced pub, just off the city centre and near the university. The clientele is a mix of students, young professionals and office workers. It offers a varied beer range sourced from local, regional and national breweries. Two ciders are also available. The large garden includes a covered

section and a smokers' area. It can become crowded at peak periods and weekends.
❀❐⇌(Queen St)●⊟

Rummer Tavern ✪
14 Duke Street, CF10 1AY
🌣 11.30-midnight; 12-11 Sun ☎ (029) 2023 5091
🌐 therummertaverncardiff.co.uk
Hancocks HB; Wye Valley HPA; 5 changing beers (sourced regionally) Ⓗ
Opposite Cardiff Castle, this claims to be Cardiff's oldest trading pub, with a history spanning three centuries. Beyond the leaded windows, the interior is narrow but long, comprising a series of simply furnished areas, with dark-wood panelling throughout. A similarly furnished upstairs room is available for hire. The regularly changing guest beers can come from anywhere in the UK. Real cider complements the beer range, and food is served until early evening.
❐Ⓐ⇌(Central/Queen St)●⊟🛜

Urban Tap House
26 Westgate Street, CF10 1DD
🌣 12-2am ☎ (029) 2039 9557 🌐 urbantaphouse.co.uk
8 changing beers (often Tiny Rebel) Ⓗ
Owned by the award-winning Tiny Rebel Brewery, this landmark building opposite the Millennium (Principality) Stadium has several rooms, upstairs and downstairs, decorated in the brewery's unique, quirky style. As well as eight real ales from innovative breweries, there are four handpumped ciders/perries, a range of craft kegs and interesting bottled beers. The pub hosts board game and 'bring your own vinyl' evenings and occasional brewery tap takeovers. Local CAMRA joint Pub of the Year 2015. ❀❐♿Ⓐ⇌(Central)♣●⊟❀🛜

Zerodegrees
27 Westgate Street, CF10 1DD
🌣 12-11 ☎ (029) 2022 9494 🌐 zerodegrees.co.uk/cardiff
Zerodegrees Wheat Ale, Black Lager, Pale Ale, Pilsner; 2 changing beers (sourced locally; often Zerodegrees (Cardiff)) Ⓐ
Brewpub set in a listed former bus garage with an interesting 1930s frontage. The brewery forms a backdrop to the well-stocked bar, and beer storage tanks rise to one side. The decor is contemporary and there are two upstairs areas for diners, one with a small patio. Pizzas are a speciality but other food is also served. Happy hour for pints is 4-7pm Monday-Friday. Closing time may extend to midnight. ❀❐♿Ⓐ⇌(Central)🍴⊟🛜

Cowbridge

Edmondes Arms
Cardiff Road, CF71 7EP
🌣 4 (1 Sat)-11; 4-10.30 Sun ☎ (01446) 773192
Hancocks HB; Wye Valley HPA; 1 changing beer (sourced nationally; often Glamorgan, Sharp's) Ⓗ
This three-roomed pub has a strong local following. The building is of brick and local limestone and a sign dates it to 1899. It has an unspoilt interior with stained-glass panels in the windows, wood panelling and other original features. The main bar and games room have wooden floors and open fires. There is a separate cosy lounge with a piano and a door leading to a small patio outside. Live bands play most Saturday evenings.
Q❀♣⊟(X2,321)🛜

Vale of Glamorgan Inn
51 High Street, CF71 7AE
🌣 11.30-11 (midnight Fri & Sat); 12-11 Sun
☎ (01446) 772252
Draught Bass; Hancocks HB; Robinsons Trooper; Sharp's Atlantic; Wye Valley HPA, Butty Bach; 1 changing beer (sourced nationally; often Borough Arms, Grey Trees, VOG) Ⓗ
Popular single-roomed pub in the centre of town. The wooden-floored bar area has seating beside a warming fire, with more seating in the lounge section. Pumpclips hanging over the bar showcase the many guest beers sold. Outside there is an attractive enclosed beer garden with a separate covered and heated smoking area. The annual beer festival coincides with the town's food and drink festival in May. Good-value home-made food is served lunchtimes (no food Sun). A former local CAMRA Pub of the Year. Q⌚❀❐●⊟(X2,321)❀🛜

Cross Inn

Cross Inn Hotel
Main Road, CF72 8AZ
🌣 12-11 ☎ (01443) 223431
Hancocks HB; Sharp's Doom Bar; Wye Valley HPA; 1 changing beer (sourced nationally) Ⓗ
Delightfully traditional, peaceful pub, blending into the Pennant stone of the surrounding streets. Popular with locals and visitors, the large single room is divided into a bar area with a TV and a spacious lounge/dining area. Beers are excellently kept, and good-value food is served. Wednesday is curry night. Sunday lunches are popular (booking advised). Q❀❐♿♣P⊟🛜

Cwmafan

Brit Pub Ⓛ
London Row, SA12 9AH
🌣 11-11 (midnight Fri & Sat); 11-10.30 Sun
☎ (01639) 680247 🌐 thebrit.wales
Sharp's Atlantic; 4 changing beers (sourced locally) Ⓗ
Established in 1845, this recently refurbished riverside pub is situated in the picturesque Afan Valley, providing a warm welcome for visitors to the area, renowned for its scenery and mountain cycling. With its stone floors and open fire, the pub has a relaxed atmosphere and conversation fills the air. There are up to four guest ales, often sourced locally. Home-made meals are served lunchtimes and evenings. Curry night is Tuesday, quiz night Sunday and acoustic music plays every other Thursday. Q⌚❀❐♿●P⊟(1,23)❀🛜

Cwmfelin

Cross Inn
Masteg Road, CF34 9LB
🌣 11.45-midnight (1am Fri & Sat); 11-midnight Sun
☎ (01656) 732476
Cerddin Solar, Oops, Cascade, Lighter Shade of Pale; 1 changing beer (often Cerddin) Ⓗ
Winner of numerous local CAMRA awards and home to the on-site Cerddin Brewery, five cask beers are on offer alongside the bottle-conditioned range, as well as five real ciders. This is a traditional two-roomed valleys' pub with strong community links. The Tuesday night quiz raises money for the local food bank and 'locals' come from as far away as Australia. A must-visit pub. Q❀⇌(Garth)●🍴⊟(71)❀🛜

Deri

Old Club ✪

93 Bailey Street, CF81 9HX

✪ 5-midnight; 12-midnight Sat & Sun ☎ (01443) 830278

2 changing beers Ⓗ

Independent public house offering a diverse range of widely and locally sourced ales – national brands are rarely seen here. Two beers are always available, occasionally three at weekends. The nearest transport hub is Bargoed, where a bus or taxi to Deri can be found. Alternatively, the former railway path to Deri offers a pleasant 45-minute stroll. Cwm Darran Country Park is nearby.

Å♣🖳(1)♣

Gilfach Fargoed

Real Ale Farm Ⓛ

Gilfach Fargoed Fawr Farm, Cardiff Road, CF81 8NY

✪ 7 (6.30 Fri)-midnight; 12-4, 6.30-midnight Sat; 12-8 Sun; closed Wed

Felinfoel Double Dragon; 4 changing beers (often Celt Experience, Grey Trees) Ⓗ

A remarkable free house with a progressive and varied beer range. The name celebrates Gilfach Fargoed Fawr Farm, built in the 17th century, now the oldest building in Bargoed. Up to four guest ales and two ciders/perries are sourced from local brewers and from further afield. It hosts numerous charity events and also the occasional beer festival. The walk from Gilfach Fargoed railway halt involves a steep climb. Visitors are always welcome but must be signed in. CAMRA Welsh Club of the Year 2015. Q🖒❀➤♣🖳P🖳(50)♣

Glan-y-Llyn

Fagins Ale & Chop House Ⓛ

9 Cardiff Road, CF15 7QD

✪ 3-11 Mon; 12-11.30; 12-10.30 Sun ☎ (029) 2081 1800

Dark Star Hophead Ⓗ, **American Pale Ale; 3 changing beers (sourced nationally)** Ⓖ

Friendly single-bar free house just north of Taffs Well. A rare Dark Star outlet, it features American Pale Ale plus two or more similarly styled guest beers on gravity. Two handpumps offer cider, mostly from Gwynt y Ddraig. A separate restaurant serves excellent food. Eclectic live music plays on Thursdays and some Saturdays, with open mic night on alternate Mondays. The pub is well-served by bus and is 15 minutes' easy walk from Taffs Well railway station. Two time local CAMRA Pub of the Year winner. Q🖒❀◑▶🖳(26,132)♣ 🖥

Glynneath

Dinas Rock Hotel Ⓛ

High Street, SA11 5AP

✪ 5 (3 Fri)-11; 12-midnight Sat; 12-10.30 Sun; closed Mon

☎ (01639) 720105

3 changing beers (sourced regionally) Ⓗ

This traditional town-centre local has been refurbished and now has an open-plan layout. The original stone walls have been revealed and two wood-burning stoves make for a cosy atmosphere in winter. Live rugby features on TV, in particular Six Nations and Ospreys matches, and live music plays most weekends. A warm welcome is assured and CAMRA members get a discount on real ale, in an area where it can be hard to find.

Q🖒❀♣♣🖳(8,X55)♣

Gorseinon

Mardy Inn ✪

117 High Street, SA4 4BR

✪ 8am-midnight (1am Fri & Sat) ☎ (01792) 890600

Fuller's London Pride; Greene King Abbot; Ruddles Best Bitter; 4 changing beers Ⓗ

Formerly a traditional high-street pub, this Wetherspoon establishment opened in 2013 following a major refurbishment. It has a large single bar in a contemporary style with several TVs showing news and sport, and an adjoining airy extension overlooking the furnished patio area. Some interesting pictures of old Gorseinon adorn the walls. A good selection of local and national beers can be enjoyed in the beer garden.

🖒❀◑▶🖒♣♣P🖳🖥

Groeswen

White Cross Inn

CF15 7UT (overlooking the chapel)

✪ 4-midnight; 12-midnight Fri-Sun ☎ (029) 2085 1332

⊕ thewhitecrossinn.co.uk

5 changing beers (sourced nationally) Ⓗ

Close to Caerphilly, this traditional gem is well-worth finding. Six handpumps dispense five changing beers and a cider. A broad range of styles offers something for everyone, always including a dark ale. Prices are keen, and the back room is a popular meeting venue. Many novel events attest to the inclusive and fun nature of the pub. Occasional beer festivals are hosted. Road access is narrow from all directions and frequent local buses stop a mile away. 🖒❀♣♣P♣🖥

Gwaelod-y-Garth

Gwaelod-y-Garth Inn

Main Road, CF15 9HH

✪ 10-11; 12-10.30 Sun ☎ (029) 2081 0408

⊕ gwaelodinn.co.uk

Wye Valley Bitter; 5 changing beers (often Dark Star, Thornbridge, Violet Cottage) Ⓗ

A stone-built multi award-winning village inn. Situated on the slope of Garth Mountain, in the centre of the village, it is popular with locals as well as those who travel some distance to visit. Expect to find at least one beer from the on-site Violet Cottage Brewery, complemented by a varying range of real ales which could originate from anywhere across the UK. There is a separate games room and upstairs restaurant.

Q🖒❀❀◑▶♣♣P🖳(26B)

Hendreforgan

Griffin Inn Ⓛ

Gilfach Goch, CF39 8YL (from Tonyrefail on A4093, turn down lane after Gilfach Goch village sign)

✪ 7 (6 Fri)-11; 12-11 Sat & Sun ☎ (01443) 670379

Brains SA Ⓗ

Listed in CAMRA's Real Heritage Pubs of Wales, the Griffin has been in the same family for over 50 years. It is a little remote, but well-worth the effort to find. There is just the one cask ale served but the SA is always top quality. Period features in the back bar include a splendid Victorian counter with an 1870 till, plus oak furniture and gleaming brasses.

Q🖒❀Å♣P🖳(150,172)♣

Killay

Village Inn
5-6 Swan Court, The Precinct, SA2 7BA
☼ 10.15-11 (11.30 Fri & Sat); 12-11 Sun ☎ (01792) 203311
Fuller's London Pride; Timothy Taylor Landlord; 2 changing beers Ⓗ
Cosy pub with an L-shaped bar and wood panelling, situated in a small shopping precinct. The pub has a strong community focus, with Sunday and Tuesday quiz nights, traditional and electronic community noticeboards, and occasional music and themed food evenings (or challenge the bar manager to a game of chess). Home-made food, including speciality pizzas, is served from a daily-changing menu. Selected sport is shown on TV. This former CAMRA branch Pub of the Year holds an annual beer festival at Easter.
◑&♣P🚭(20,21)🐾🖤

Llangennith

King's Head Ⓛ
SA3 1HX
☼ 11-11; 12-10.30 Sun ☎ (01792) 386212
⊕ kingsheadgower.co.uk
Gower Brew 1, Gower Gold; 3 changing beers (often Gower) Ⓗ
A row of three 17th-century stone-built cottages make up this pub. It lies at the western end of the Gower Peninsula, a short distance from the sandy stretches of Llangennith Beach. Ales from nearby Gower Brewery are available (up to six in summer) plus a cask cider. An impressive variety of home-made food is served with dishes inspired by fresh local produce. An annual beer festival is held in October and a themed fancy dress event over the August bank holiday. Quality 4-star accommodation is available, with some rooms pet-friendly. 🐾🛏️◑▲♣🅿🚭(116)🐾🖤

Llanharry

Fox & Hounds
Llanharan Road, CF72 9LL
☼ 12-11 (midnight Fri & Sat) ☎ (01443) 222124
⊕ fox-and-hounds-inn-llanhari.co.uk
4 changing beers (sourced locally) Ⓗ
Delightful independent pub, tastefully decorated with a thoughtful blend of modern and period furniture and artefacts. The main bar is complemented by a relaxing lounge and a separate restaurant. Guest beers are mainly from local brewers, accompanied sometimes by regional and national beers. There is a large car park beside the pub. Q🐾❀◑&♣🅿🚭(44,244)🐾🖤

Llanrhidian

Dolphin Inn
SA3 1EH (just off B4295 N Gower Road)
☼ 1 (12 Sun)-11 summer; 4.30 (6 Tue)-11; 1-11 Fri & Sat; 12-10.30 Sun winter ☎ (01792) 391069
Fuller's London Pride; St Austell Tribute; 1 changing beer Ⓗ
Cosy village pub dating from the 18th century on the north side of Gower next to a 13th-century church, with stunning views of the estuary from the lovely beer gardens. The characterful single room is warmed by a solid fuel stove. A limited range of cold and hot meals is available. There is a children's play area at the rear with a fenced area for rabbits and poultry to roam. Quiz night is Sunday. Check ahead for afternoon opening times.
🐾❀◑🅿🚭(115,116)🖤

Greyhound Inn Ⓛ
Oldwalls, SA3 1HA (1 mile W of Llanrhidian on B4295)
☼ 11-11 ☎ (01792) 391027
⊕ thegreyhoundinnoldwalls.co.uk
Gower Gold; 5 changing beers (often Gower) Ⓗ
Traditional 19th-century inn with a welcoming atmosphere, home to the Gower Brewery, with a range of its ales on offer at the bar. An extensive home-cooked bar menu is served every day, with Sunday lunches particularly popular. Outside at the rear is a large beer garden with a children's play area and wonderful views over the Gower countryside. The pub hosts the Gower Brewery beer festival in June, with camping available.
🐾❀◑&🅿🚭🐾🖤

Llantwit Major

King's Head
East Street, CF61 1XY
☼ 11.30-11.30 (midnight Fri & Sat); 11.30-11 Sun ☎ (01446) 792697
Brains Bitter; 1 changing beer (often Brains, Draught Bass) Ⓗ
This family-run town-centre local has been in the Guide for 18 consecutive years. A traditional two-bar pub with a strong local following, the stone-floored public bar is popular for darts and pool. The comfortable wood-panelled lounge features an eclectic mix of furnishings, and leads to the patio garden. There is a large-screen TV for sport in both bars. Guest beers come from local and national brewers. Q🐾❀⇌♣🚭(303,321,X91)🐾🖤

Llantwit Major Rugby Club
Boverton Road, CF61 1XZ
☼ 4.30-11 (midnight Fri); 12-midnight Sat; 11-11 Sun ☎ (01446) 792276 ⊕ llantwitmajor.rfc.wales
Morland Old Speckled Hen; Sharp's Doom Bar; 1 changing beer Ⓗ
Friendly, vibrant community club where non-members are welcome, with plans for expansion in the near future. Two staple beers are on offer plus a guest. The local boxing club shares the facility and there are regular pool and darts league matches. Dogs are welcome in the players' bar, the club's equivalent of a public bar. There is also a cosy lounge bar and a large function room (available to hire). ▲⇌🅿🚭(303,321,X91)🐾🖤

Old Swan Inn
Church Street, CF61 1SB
☼ 12-11; 12-10.30 Sun ☎ (01446) 792230
4 changing beers (sourced nationally; often Grey Trees, Springhead, VOG) Ⓗ
Llantwit Major's oldest inn, overlooking the historic St Illtyd's Church and the town hall. It boasts a range of four – sometimes five – ales, frequently from local brewers. There is a popular front bar where excellent food is served and a lively back bar frequented mostly by younger customers. Beer festivals are held in spring and summer featuring live local bands. There is parking nearby in the town car park. Cider is often available, particularly in summer. Q🐾❀◑⇌♣🅿🚭(303,321,X91)🐾🖤

Llanwonno

Brynffynon Hotel

CF37 3PH (opp church) ST030955
☼ 12-11; 12-10.30 Sun; closed Mon ☎ (01443) 790272
⊕ brynffynonhotel.com
3 changing beers (sourced nationally) Ⓗ
Set on top of the ridge between the urban Cynon and Rhondda Fach valleys, this tranquil country inn is well-worth the effort to seek out. The lounge has a timeless atmosphere with its relaxing leather couches and log-burning fire. The dining room serves food of an excellent standard (booking advised), including cream teas. Three guest beers are available, and beer festivals are held throughout the year. A patio offers views of the forest and ancient churchyard. Three en suite rooms are available. Q⅗❀⌂◑ ΔP❀

Maesteg

Federation Bar

26 Commercial Street, CF34 9DH
☼ 10-midnight (1am Fri & Sat) ☎ (01656) 856298
Rhymney Dark, Export Ale; 1 changing beer (sourced locally; often Rhymney) Ⓗ
Rhymney Brewery converted this former florist's shop on the main street in 2015. Decorated in the brewery's typical style, the Fed offers good-value beer in comfortable, basic surroundings. There are many photographs of Maesteg in bygone days, a moose head above the fireplace, TVs with the sound usually turned down and a jukebox playing. Strictly no under-21s are admitted but well-behaved dogs are welcome. No entry after midnight at weekends. ⇌🚌❀🎵

Marcross

Horseshoe Inn

CF61 1ZG
☼ 12 (6 Mon)-11; 12-10.30 Sun ☎ (01656) 890568
⊕ theshoesmarcross.co.uk
Sharp's Atlantic; 2 changing beers (often Gower, Grey Trees, VOG) Ⓗ
Picturesque 19th-century country pub offering a large range of good food and three regularly changing real ales, usually including at least one from Wales. The building is of local limestone and comprises a small, cosy bar and a lounge with a log-burning stove. Close to the Nash Point lighthouse, it is popular with walkers along the coastal path. The beer garden is delightful in the summer months. Q⅗❀◑P🚌(303)

Mawdlam

Angel Inn ⊘

Marlas Road, CF33 4PG
☼ 12-11; 12-10.30 Sun ☎ (01656) 743995
⊕ theangelinnmaudlam.co.uk
Gower Gold Ⓗ**; Sharp's Doom Bar; 2 changing beers (often Boss, Glamorgan, VOG)** Ⓗ
Although the majority of the pub's trade is high-quality locally-sourced food, there is a comfortable bar for drinkers with a TV for sport. The four ales are kept at a perfect temperature, all served straight from the cask. The pub has greatly improved under the current licensee and occasional food theme nights are hosted, as well as a successful summer beer festival. Accommodation comprises three en suite double rooms, one dog-friendly. The inn is

close to the M4 motorway and to Kenfig National Nature Reserve and Margam Country Park.
Q⅗❀⌂◑➕P🚌(63B)❀🛜

Merthyr Tydfil

Aberglais

Pontsarn, CF48 2TS
☼ 10.30-11 ☎ (01685) 377344
Wye Valley Bitter; 1 changing beer (sourced nationally; often Wye Valley) Ⓗ
New-build pub on the site of an old barn next to Pontsticill Reservoir beauty spot with fine views, good food and great beers. A wonderful country inn with a delightful atmosphere, the landlord came here from a nearby pub and has a long association with the area. Walkers and holidaymakers are welcome. There is a children's play area and the car park is across the road. ⅗❀◑♿➕P❀🛜

Monknash

Plough & Harrow

CF71 7QQ
☼ 12-11 (midnight Fri & Sat) ☎ (01656) 890209
⊕ ploughandharrow.org
Draught Bass Ⓖ**; Hancocks HB; Timothy Taylor Golden Best** Ⓗ**; 5 changing beers (often Celt Experience, Grey Trees, Tudor)** Ⓖ
Renowned 14th-century pub, originally a monastic farmhouse, with many original features remaining and an eclectic farmhouse style that is always a surprise to newcomers. Up to eight real ales are available, four on handpump and the others dispensed by gravity, with local breweries well supported. A large selection of ciders and perries is also kept – the pub is a previous branch CAMRA Cider Pub of the Year winner. Good home-cooked food is served. The large beer garden is the setting for festivals and live music in summer.
Q⅗❀◑Δ➕P🚌(303)

Morriston

Red Lion Hotel ⊘

Sway Road, SA6 6JA
☼ 8am-midnight (1am Fri & Sat) ☎ (01792) 761870
Greene King Abbot; Ruddles Best Bitter; 4 changing beers Ⓗ
The Red Lion has a large dining area with an open log fire at the front and high bar stools at the back. On the walls are a number of pictures depicting former local industry, and a community board advertises trips to breweries and other events. Outside is a large patio area with tables and chairs and a smoking area. There are good parking facilities and disabled access. ⅗❀◑♿➕P🚌(4)🛜

Mumbles

Mumbles Ale House 🍸

2 Dunns Lane, SA3 4AA
☼ 4 (12 Fri & Sat)-11; 12-10.30 Sun; closed Mon & Tue ☎ 07437 421963
Wye Valley Butty Bach Ⓗ**; 6 changing beers (often Butcombe, Oakham, Tiny Rebel)** Ⓗ/Ⓖ
This intimate ale house is located on the ground floor of a terraced house and has quickly become popular as a pub for conversation. It offers a regularly changing range of real ales, along with real cider and perry, wine, limited spirits and soft

drinks. All are listed on a regularly updated blackboard and drinks menus on the bar. It is the recipient of an Oakham Ales Oakademy Centre of Excellence award and there is no keg beer. Traditional bar snacks are available. Q❀●🖾🐾

Park Inn 🛈

23 Park Street, SA3 4DA

🕔 4-midnight; 12-midnight Sat & Sun ☎ (01792) 366738
Changing beers (often Mumbles, Otley, Tiny Rebel) 🅷
The convivial atmosphere in this small establishment attracts discerning drinkers of all ages, though the games room is particularly popular with younger people. Five handpumps dispense a range of beers, with special emphasis on independent breweries from Wales and the west of England. Alongside a fine display of pumpclips are pictures of old Mumbles and its pioneering railway. A popular quiz is held on Thursday, with occasional music at weekends.
Q🛏❀♣●🖾(2,3)🐾🛜

Pilot Inn 🛈

726 Mumbles Road, SA3 4EL

🕔 12-11 (midnight Fri & Sat) ☎ 07897 895511
🌐 thepilotofmumbles.co.uk
Draught Bass; 4 changing beers (often Pilot Swansea) 🅷
Welcoming and friendly local on the attractive seafront at Mumbles and home to the Pilot Brewery. This historic pub, built in 1849, is next to the coastal path and popular with lifeboatmen, locals, real ale fans, walkers and cyclists. Six ales are always available plus a wide range of bottled ciders. Hot drinks are also served. Voted Wales CAMRA Pub of the Year 2014. Q🛏🖾(2b)🐾🛜

Neath

Borough Arms 🛈

2 New Henry Street, SA11 1PH (off Briton Ferry road)

🕔 4.30-9 Mon; 4 Thu & Fri (12 Sat)-11; 12-6 Sun
☎ (01639) 644902 🌐 boroughbreweryneath.com
Draught Bass; 5 changing beers (sourced locally) 🅷
A traditional pub, a half-mile walk from the town centre, with a central bar and six handpumps. It is popular with locals and visitors alike. A varying choice of beers comes from the house brewery, Borough, as well as regional and national breweries. An annual beer festival is held in September. The place gets packed when Six Nations and other rugby is televised.
Q❀&≒♣🖾(227,228)🐾🛜

David Protheroe ✅

7 Windsor Road, SA11 1LS

🕔 8am-midnight (1am Fri & Sat) ☎ (01639) 622130
Greene King Abbot; Ruddles Best Bitter; Sharp's Doom Bar; 4 changing beers (sourced nationally) 🅷
Situated opposite Neath railway station, this popular Wetherspoon outlet is easily accessible. It was the former Neath Police Station and is named after the town's first policeman who was appointed in 1836. It has an open-plan interior with a family area at the rear – the four alcoves were once the lock-ups for the town. A wide range of food is available with themed menus throughout the week. The regular beers and guest ales are often complemented by a real cider.
🛏❀🕽&≒●🖾(X4,X55,X63)🛜

Penarth

Golden Lion 🍺 🛈

69 Glebe Street, CF64 1EF

🕔 10-11; 11-midnight Fri & Sat; 12-10.30 Sun
☎ (029) 2070 1574
4 changing beers (often Gower, Otley, VOG) 🅷
JW Bassett pub situated a short walk from the town centre, towards the Cardiff Bay Barrage. It offers good-value food, including a Sunday carvery, and two or three real ales usually from Welsh breweries. TV sport is available throughout, even in the small beer garden, and the jukebox has an impressive 20,000 tracks – it can be lively. Regulars include local sports teams, including football and darts sides. Local CAMRA Pub of the Year 2016.
🛏❀🕽&≒♣🖾🛜

Pilot

67 Queen's Road, CF64 1DJ

🕔 12-11 (midnight Fri & Sat); 12-10.30 Sun
☎ (029) 2071 0615
4 changing beers (often Celt Experience, Otley, Tiny Rebel) 🅷
For many years a Brains pub, the Pilot was refurbished in 2012 and is now operated by Knife & Fork Food, with the emphasis on high-quality food and drink. Five handpumps offer quality beers and occasional real cider. Ales are chosen from all over the country, and some of the best Welsh breweries often feature, including Vale of Glamorgan. There is seating outside at the front for warm weather, and a view across Cardiff Bay at the rear.
Q🛏🕽≒●🖾🐾🛜

Pencoed

Little Penybont Arms

11 Penybont Road, CF35 5PY

🕔 3-11; 12-11 Fri-Sun; closed Tue ☎ 07734 767937
4 changing beers (often Boss, Mumbles, VOG) 🅶
Opened in 2015, this micropub was converted from a former café. Featuring up to four beers and 27 ciders, it quickly picked up a strong local following. Even the malt whisky selection is subject to ongoing expansion. Home to a cask ale club, visitors can pick up a loyalty card to earn a free pint. Excellent bar snacks include home-made scratchings, pork pies, pickles and nuts. Families are welcome until 9pm. A gem.
Q🛏≒♣●🖾(62,64,404)🐾

Penderyn

Red Lion

Church Road, CF44 9JR

🕔 7-11; 12.30-midnight Sat; 12-10.30 Sun
☎ (01685) 811914 🌐 redlionpenderyn.com
Brains Rev James Original; Draught Bass; Fuller's ESB; Tomos Watkin Old Style Bitter; 6 changing beers (often Box Steam, Glamorgan, Rhymney) 🅶
Quaint old pub on the edge of the Brecon Beacons National Park with two log fires to keep it cosy in the colder months. Between six and 10 local and national beers are on gravity, with Fuller's ESB a favourite over the years. Up to five real ciders and perries are also available, often from local producer Bragdy Brodyr. High-quality traditional home-cooked pub food is served and excellent value (booking essential). Q❀🕽&●P🛜

Pontardawe

Pontardawe Inn ▼ 🍴 ✅
123 Herbert Street, SA8 4ED
🌐 12-midnight ☎ (01792) 447562 ⊕ pontardaweinn.co.uk
**Banks's Sunbeam; Marston's Pedigree; Ringwood
Fortyniner; 3 changing beers (sourced nationally;
often Mumbles)** Ⓗ
Originally a drovers' pub on the route to Neath
mart, and well placed on Route 43 of the National
Cycle Network, the Gwachel, as it is known locally,
is worth the short walk from the town centre. Live
music is prominent on Friday and Saturday
evenings, with Welsh language bands playing on
the third Friday of the month. Beer festivals are
held in May, August and November. The
landscaped garden is popular in summer. CAMRA
branch Pub of the Year 2014-2016.
🌇🏵️🕽🍴🚅🅿🚃(X50,X51)♣🌐

Pontypridd

Bunch of Grapes 🍴 ✅
Ynysangharad Road, CF37 4DA (off A4054)
🌐 11-1am; 11-midnight Sun ☎ (01443) 402934
⊕ bunchofgrapes.org.uk
**Otley 02 Croeso; 9 changing beers (often Dark Star,
Otley, Salopian)** Ⓗ
A short stroll from the town centre, this popular
pub has distinct areas around a central bar. Six
guest beers accompany four from Otley Brewery,
plus two ciders/perries. Guest ales are varied and
wide ranging. A separate and acclaimed restaurant
serves locally sourced food with themed nights a
regular feature (booking suggested, especially at
weekends). Events include beer, cider and cheese
festivals and much more. Winner of many awards
including CAMRA Welsh Pub of the Year 2015.
Q🌇🏵️🕽🚅🅿🚃♣

Llanover Arms 🍴
Bridge Street, CF37 4PE (opp N entrance to
Ynysangharad Park, off A470)
🌐 11-midnight; 11-11 Sun ☎ (01443) 403215
3 changing beers Ⓗ
Built around 1794 to serve thirsty boatmen
working the newly opened Glamorganshire Canal,
this historic free house has been in the same family
for over a century. Three rooms are linked by a
central passageway, each room with its own
regulars. Nearby is Ynysangharad Park and the
famous town bridge and museum. The Taff Trail
passes close by. Q🏵️🚅♣🅿🚃

Patriot Bar 🍴
25B Taff Street, CF37 4UA (at N end of main shopping
street)
🌐 12-midnight ☎ (01443) 407915
**Rhymney Hobby Horse, Dark, Bitter, Export Ale; 1
changing beer (often Rhymney)** Ⓗ
A Rhymney Brewery tied house, this is a no-frills
bar offering a range of well-kept beers. Prices are
always reasonable and turnover is rapid. The
central location on the main shopping street is
appreciated by the local clientele. Converted from
a shop unit and affectionately called the Wonky
Bar, it is close to the bus station and a modest stroll
along Taff Street from the train station. Real cider is
sometimes available. ♿🚅♣🚃🌐

Port Talbot

Lord Caradoc ✅
69-73 Station Road, SA13 1NW (5 mins' walk from
Parkway railway station)
🌐 8am-midnight (1am Fri & Sat) ☎ (01639) 896007
**Greene King Abbot; Ruddles Best Bitter; Sharp's
Doom Bar; 8 changing beers (sourced nationally)** Ⓗ
A typical Wetherspoon pub, situated on the high
street, handily placed close to the railway and bus
stations. The pub attracts a varied clientele and is
family-friendly. There is a suntrap patio at the rear.
Twelve handpumps dispense the three regular ales
plus a changing selection of local, national and
international beers. Real cider is available
seasonally. Themed food menus are offered
throughout the week. Q🌇🏵️🕽♿≒♣🅿🚃🌐

Porth

Rheola
Rheola Road, CF39 0LF
🌐 2-midnight; 1-1am Fri; 12-1am Sat; 12-midnight Sun
☎ (01443) 682633
**Rhymney Hobby Horse, Dark, Best, Bevans Bitter,
Export; 4 changing beers (sourced locally; often
Rhymney)** Ⓗ
Acquired by Rhymney Brewery in 2015 and now a
tied house offering a range of competitively priced
Rhymney beers. Situated where the Rhondda
Valley divides, it is easy to reach by bus and train. A
central bar separates the games room (which can
sometimes be loud) and the comfortable lounge.
There are quiz nights, whist nights and live music
nights. The outdoor smoking area is sheltered.
🏵️≒♣🅿🚃

Porthcawl

Lorelei Hotel
36-38 Esplanade Avenue, CF36 3YU
🌐 12 (5 Mon & Tue)-11; 12-10.30 Sun ☎ (01656) 788342
⊕ loreleihotel.co.uk
**Draught Bass Ⓖ; Rhymney Export Ale; 2 changing
beers (often Boss, Tomos Watkin, VOG)** Ⓗ
Situated close to the seafront and the Grand
Pavilion, the Lorelei is in the Guide for the 18th
year and is a multiple award winner. It serves four
draught beers plus cider during the summer. Beer
festivals are held on Grand National and Halloween
weekends. Good-quality and good-value food is
available evenings (except Mon) and Sunday
lunchtime. Built around the end of the 19th
century, during World War I it was two separate
buildings – one used as a hospice for injured
soldiers. Q🌇🏵️🕽♣♣🚃🌐

Quakers Yard

Glantaff Inn 🍴
Cardiff Road, CF46 5AH
🌐 11.30-11.30 (1am Fri & Sat) ☎ (01443) 410822
**3 changing beers (sourced nationally; often Grey
Trees, Rhymney)** Ⓗ
Set above the river, this pub is popular with
walkers and cyclists on the nearby Taff Trail. Its
comfortable bar recalls local history in early
photographs and artefacts. Three beers are usually
available; two tend to change regularly, the third is
often a guest beer back by popular demand. Styles
and breweries vary. Good-value, good-quality food
is served. There is a quiz every Sunday. Q🕽♿🚃🌐

Reynoldston

King Arthur Hotel
Higher Green, SA3 1AD (on village green)
✪ 10-11 ☎ (01792) 390775 ⊕ kingarthurhotel.co.uk
Felinfoel Double Dragon; Sharp's Doom Bar; 3 changing beers (often Gower, Tiny Rebel) Ⓗ
Traditional family-owned hotel and an acclaimed wedding venue. Situated at the foot of Cefn Bryn in beautiful Gower, it overlooks the village green and has covered seating outside by the entrance, as well as a large seating area on the green itself. The cosy, atmospheric main bar is open to drinkers and diners, offering home-cooked food made with local produce. Main meals and snacks are available all day, and breakfasts for non-residents from 9 till 11am. ⓢ⚲⛴Ⓓ🚳♣🍴Ⓟ🚆(116,118)🛜

Swansea

Bank Statement ✪
57/58 Wind Street, SA1 1EP
✪ 8am-midnight (1am Wed & Fri); 8am-2am Sat
☎ (01792) 455477
Greene King Abbot; Ruddles Best Bitter; 4 changing beers Ⓗ
A former Midland Bank, sympathetically transformed by Wetherspoon, while retaining its original ornate interior. Trading as a Lloyds No.1, the pub is at the heart of the city's bar quarter and has a large ground floor with plenty of seating. Popular with all ages, it is busy throughout the week as well as at the weekend. ⓢⒹ🚳♣🍴🚆🛜

Cockett Inn
Waunarlwydd Road, Cockett, SA2 0GB (just off A4216)
✪ 11.30-11 ☎ (01792) 588748
Brains Bitter, SA Gold, Rev James Original; 1 changing beer Ⓗ
Recently refurbished, this single-bar pub has one large room with distinct dining, bar and pub games areas. Sports historians will find several reminders of past generations of local and Welsh celebrities. Quiz night is Sunday and karaoke night the third Wednesday of the month. There is a community focus and charity fundraising events are organised regularly. Take bus 12/13 to Elphin Crescent and walk down the hill. ⚲Ⓓ♣🚆🐾🛜

No Sign Bar
56 Wind Street, SA1 1EG
✪ 11-11 (midnight Wed & Thu; 1am Fri & Sat); 12-11 Sun
☎ (01792) 465300 ⊕ nosignwinebar.com
4 changing beers Ⓗ
Historic narrow bar established in 1690, reputedly a regular haunt of Dylan Thomas. Architectural signs from various periods of the pub's past remain, some dividing the interior into separate bar areas. Quality food and wine are available and there are usually four cask ales on sale. Live music features in the bar on Fridays, Saturdays and often Sundays. Bands also play in the Vault basement later in the evening. Local CAMRA Pub of the Year 2015. ⚲Ⓓ🍴🚆🛜

Potters Wheel ✪
85-86 The Kingsway, SA1 5JE
✪ 8am-midnight (1am Thu-Sat) ☎ (01792) 465113
Adnams Broadside; Fuller's London Pride; Ruddles Best Bitter; Sharp's Doom Bar; changing beers Ⓗ
A city-centre Wetherspoon outlet with a long sprawling bar area offering various seating arrangements, attracting customers of all ages and

backgrounds. An interesting selection of guest beers is kept, with a commitment to local breweries. Cask cider is always available. Photographs feature local dignitaries associated with the area's industrial past, particularly the ceramics and pottery industries. There is a CAMRA board and a beer suggestion box. Ⓓ🚳🍴🚆🛜

Queen's Hotel
Gloucester Place, SA1 1TY (near Waterfront Museum)
✪ 11-11 (11.30 Sat); 12-10.30 Sun ☎ (01792) 521531
Theakston Best Bitter, Old Peculier; 2 changing beers Ⓗ
This vibrant free house is near the Dylan Thomas Theatre, City Museum, National Waterfront Museum and marina. The walls display photographs depicting Swansea's rich maritime heritage. The pub enjoys strong local support and home-cooked lunches are popular. Evening entertainment includes live music on Saturday and a Sunday quiz. This is a rare local outlet for Theakston Old Peculier in addition to a seasonal guest beer often from a local microbrewery. Ⓓ🚳🚆🛜

Uplands Tavern ✪
42 Uplands Crescent, Uplands, SA2 0PG
✪ 11-11 (midnight Fri & Sat) ☎ (01792) 458242
Greene King IPA, Abbot; 2 changing beers Ⓗ
In the heart of Swansea's student quarter, the Tav is a large single-room pub attracting regulars from all walks of life. It is another former haunt of Dylan Thomas, commemorated in a separate snug area. The pub has a deserved reputation for the quality and variety of its live music at weekends. There is a large heated outdoor drinking area at the front. Quiz night is Tuesday. ⚲🚳♣🚆(20,21)🛜

Vivian Arms ✪
104 Gower Road, Sketty, SA2 9BZ (Sketty Cross, jct of A4118 and A4216)
✪ 10.30-11 (midnight Fri & Sat); 12-11 Sun
☎ (01792) 516194
Brains Rev James Gold, Rev James Original, SA; 1 changing beer Ⓗ
Situated on the main crossroads in Sketty, the Vivs is a spacious pub which attracts a wide range of customers young and old. It has a mixture of seating areas, and plenty of TV screens throughout show live sport. There is a small meeting room, and the pub is popular for family dining, with a carvery on Sundays. Live music plays on Fridays, a general knowledge quiz is held on Sundays and a music quiz every other Wednesday. ⓢ⚲Ⓓ🚳🚆(20,21)🛜

Westbourne
1 Brynymor Road, SA1 4JQ
✪ 11-11 (11.30 Tue & Wed; midnight Thu; 12.30am Fri & Sat); 12-11 Sun ☎ (01792) 476637 ⊕ westbourneswansea.com
Greene King Abbot; Sharp's Doom Bar; 4 changing beers Ⓗ
Located on the western fringe of the city centre, this street-corner pub has a single split-level bar with various drinking areas including a heated terrace outside. Home to the first self-service beer wall in Wales and iPad tabletop ordering, it is now the place to go for young and old alike. Four to six ales are always available – customers are able to request a particular beer on the pub's website. A popular quiz is held on Tuesday evening. ⚲Ⓓ🚳🚆(2,3)🛜

Trefforest

Otley Arms 🅛

Forest Road, CF37 1SY (on gyratory system)
✪ 12-midnight (1am Sat) ☎ (01443) 402033
⊕ theotley.co.uk
Otley 01; 5 changing beers (sourced regionally; often Otley) ⊞
Recently refurbished with a log-burning fire, the Otley offers something for all tastes. Popular with university students and locals, there are many comfortable corners of this intimate pub to explore. Five guest beers include two from the Otley range, and the food menu has recently expanded. There is a spring cider festival, and an aptly named Oct-O-bar beer festival. Live music plays on the last Friday of the month. Handy for buses and trains.
ﾐ❶&⇌♣🍴➡ (100,244) ❀

Rickards Arms 🅛

61 Park Street, CF37 1SN
✪ 11-midnight; 12-11 Sun ☎ (01443) 402305
Otley 01; 2 changing beers ⊞
A firm favourite, where students and staff from the nearby university mix with locals and visitors. The cosy atmosphere is enhanced by separate drinking spaces, including a vaulted cellar and upstairs dining area. Famed for its good-value bar food, the breakfasts are a notable feast. Entertainment includes regular quiz nights and music events. Two guest beers are often from the Otley range.
❀❶⇌♣🍴➡ (100,244) ❀ 🛜

Treorchy

Pencelli Hotel 🍷 ✅

Pencae Terrace, CF42 6HL
✪ 2-11 (midnight Thu & Fri); 12-midnight Sat; 12-10.30 Sun; closed Wed ☎ (01443) 775181
6 changing beers (sourced nationally; often Glamorgan) ⊞
It was in the Pencelli Hotel in 1946 that some of the regulars decided to reform the now world-famous Treorchy Male Choir. Seventy years later, it continues to be an excellent community venue. The pub has a central bar serving two large rooms. It hosts a weekly quiz on Monday, pool night on Tuesday and live music Thursday to Saturday. It is easily reached by train, and has ample parking opposite. Local CAMRA branch Pub of the Year 2016. ﾐ❀❶⇌♣🍴➡

Tyla Garw

Boar's Head

Coedcae Lane, CF72 9EZ (600yds from A473 over level crossing)
✪ 4-10 Mon; 12-11; 12-10 Sun ☎ (01443) 225400
9 changing beers (often Dark Star, Oakham, Salopian) ⊞
Recently extended, cosy and welcoming pub with five separate rooms, two set aside for dining, served by a single bar. A tremendous range of beers is available, showcasing all styles from IPA to porter. Staff and locals are always happy to advise on choices. Occasional beer festivals are held, with some beers on gravity. Sunday lunch is popular and booking is advised. The direct walking route from Pontyclun station cuts through a small industrial area. Q ﾐ❀❶&⇌♣P

Upper Church Village

Farmers Arms

St Illtyd Road, CF38 1EB
✪ 3-11; 12-midnight Thu-Sat; 12-10.30 Sun
☎ (01443) 205766
Brains Rev James Original; 1 changing beer (sourced nationally) ⊞
Comfortable village local with one large bar, and a pleasant beer garden and patio outside. The guest beers are often unusual for the locality and frequently from smaller brewers. A popular quiz night is hosted on Tuesdays and live music on alternate Thursdays, but beer and conversation are the main attractions, unless there is rugby on TV.
❀P➡ (90)

Upper Killay

Railway Inn 🅛

553 Gower Road, SA2 7DS
✪ 12-11; 12-10.30 Sun ☎ (01792) 203946
Swansea Deep Slade Dark, Bishopswood Bitter, Three Cliffs Gold, Original Wood; 1 changing beer ⊞
A classic locals' pub set in woodlands at the top end of Clyne Valley. The adjacent former railway line now forms part of Route 4 of the National Cycle Network. In winter the real fire in the lounge provides welcome warmth and cheer. Traditional cider and at least one guest beer are kept alongside the Swansea Brewing Company beers. A large area outside hosts occasional barbecues, music events and boules tournaments in summer.
Q❀♣🍴P➡ (20,21,118)

Wick

Star Inn

Ewenny Road, CF71 7QA
✪ 12 (5 Mon)-11.30; 12-10.30 Sun ☎ (01656) 890080
⊕ thestarinnwick.co.uk
Wye Valley Bitter; 1 changing beer (often Brecon, Evan Evans, St Austell) ⊞
The Star was totally refurbished in 2012, and has returned to its former glory as a Guide regular. It has gained a reputation for excellent food and offers a regularly changing menu. Originally three farm cottages, the interior has a traditional bar and a lounge/diner, with flagstones throughout. The friendly locals will fill you in on the pub's history. Happy hour is Friday 6-8pm. Well-behaved dogs on leads are welcome in the bar.
Qﾐ❀❶♣🍴P➡ (303) ❀

Ynyshir

Ynyshir Hotel 🅛

Ynyshir Road, CF39 0EL
✪ 5 (12 Sat)-midnight; 12-10 Sun ☎ (01443) 686791
2 changing beers (sourced locally; often Bragdy Twt Lol, Grey Trees) ⊞
The Ynyshir, known locally as the Old Pub, is a friendly traditional valleys hostelry on the main road through Ynyshir and on the Pontypridd to Maerdy bus route. Two ales are served, sourced mainly from local brewers. Beer festivals are held in spring and autumn. The snug, with its wooden bar, is of some historic interest. Other rooms include a plainly furnished public bar with a smaller, comfortable lounge area. At the rear is a modest beer garden. Qﾐ❀♣➡ 🛜

Ynystawe

Millers Arms

634 Clydach Road, SA6 5AY (on B4603, ½ mile N of M4 jct 45)

🌍 11.30-11; 12-3, 7-10.30 Sun ☎ (01792) 842614
⊕ millers-arms.co.uk
3 changing beers (often Rhymney) Ⓗ

Friendly community pub with a highly decorative interior including an extensive teapot collection, a photograph of the landlord with Tom Jones, and artwork by Katherine Jenkins. Busy periods require booking for meals, which are good value and home cooked, served in the bar and separate restaurant. In the spring a garden nesting box is on CCTV for twitchers. The pub is on the main bus routes to Swansea Valley and on cycle path Route 43.
🛏❀◑⑃♿P🚌(145,212)

Ystalyfera

Corner House

70 Commercial Street, SA9 2HS

🌍 4-midnight; 3-1am Fri; 12-1am Sat; 12-10.30 Sun
☎ (01639) 849420

2 changing beers (sourced regionally) Ⓗ

Traditional village local, run by the same family for two generations. As the name suggests, it is situated on a corner site on the main (top) road in Ystalyfera. The main bar is to the left as you enter with a separate lounge across the corridor. Live music and karaoke often feature on weekend evenings. A welcome addition in an area where real ale is hard to find. 🛏♣🚌(X50)🐾🛜

Wern Fawr Ⓛ

47 Wern Road, SA9 2LX

🌍 2-5, 7 (6.30 Fri)-11; 7-11 Sat; 12-11 Sun
☎ (01639) 843625
Bryncelyn Holly Hop, Buddy Marvellous, Oh Boy Ⓗ

The brewery tap for Bryncelyn Brewery, this is a rare, unspoilt locals' venue with a central bar serving both the bar and lounge. The bar is a step back in time with an interesting display of old mining, industrial and domestic artefacts. It also has an old stove that the locals have nicknamed 'the nuclear reactor'. The pub is busy on rugby international days and hosts occasional live music. Opening time on Saturdays may be earlier if there is rugby on. ♣🚌(X50)🐾

City Arms, Cardiff

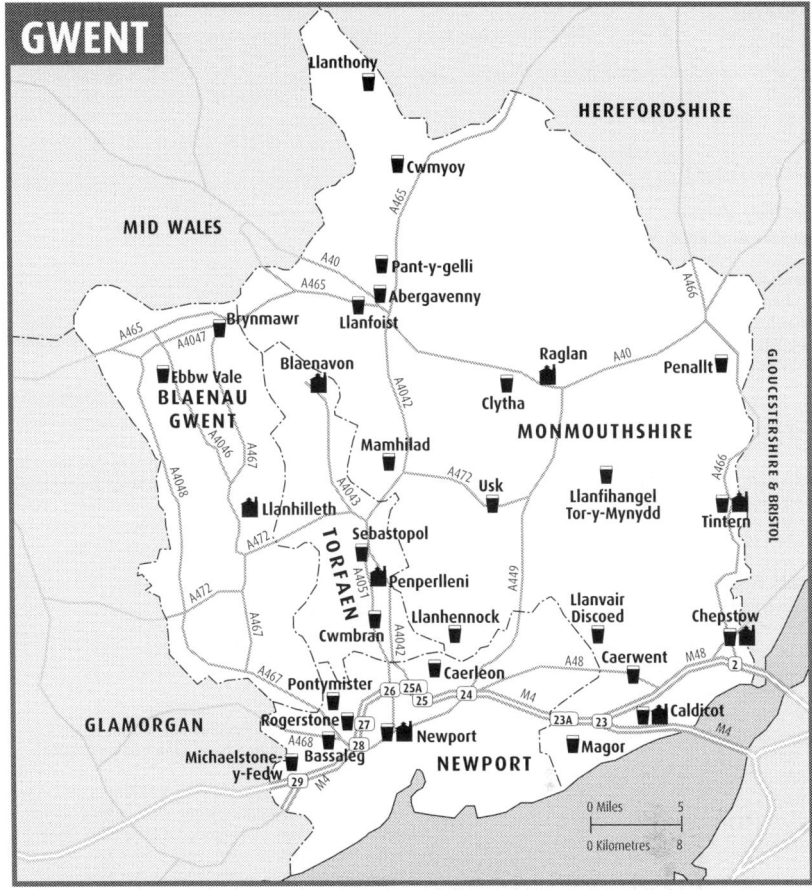

Authority areas covered: Blaenau Gwent UA, Caerphilly UA (part), Monmouthshire UA, Newport UA, Torfaen UA

Abergavenny

Grofield 🅛
Baker Street, NP7 5BT
☼ 5-11 Mon; 11-11.30 ☎ (01873) 858939 ⊕ grofield.com
Rhymney Bitter; Sharp's Doom Bar; 1 changing beer (sourced nationally; often St Austell, Wadworth, Wye Valley) Ⓗ
A busy family-run town-centre pub, opposite the cinema and library. It is becoming well known for the quality of its food, serving lunches Tuesday to Sunday and evening meals Thursday to Saturday until 7.30pm. Frequently changing guest beers come from popular breweries around the country. The garden is a lovely feature and a suntrap on warm days. It is the venue for a summer beer and music festival. Q🏠🕙🐕🕪♣🚪🐾

Station Hotel
37 Brecon Road, NP7 5UH
☼ 5 (2 Wed & Thu)-11; 1-11.30 Fri; 12-11.30 Sat; 11.30-11 Sun ☎ (01879) 854759
Draught Bass; Rhymney Best; Wye Valley HPA; 1 changing beer (sourced nationally) Ⓗ
One of CAMRA's Real Heritage Pubs of Wales, this is a rare example of a place that retains separate bar and lounge areas. The railway disappeared years ago, but the inn itself is largely unchanged. The long bar area is the focus of activity – the clientele a lively mix of local trade and visitors who know the pub by reputation. Conversation is still valued and the pub is at the heart of the community. 🕙♣🅿🚪(3,X4,X43)🐾

Bassaleg

Ruperra Arms ✪
73 Caerphilly Road, NP10 8LJ
☼ 12-midnight ☎ (01633) 894255 ⊕ theruperraarms.co.uk
Brains Bitter; Fuller's London Pride; 3 changing beers (sourced locally) Ⓗ
Small but busy local with an emphasis on quality locally sourced food. Five ales are usually available, at least one from the nearby Tiny Rebel Brewery.

REAL ALE BREWERIES

Baa Chepstow (NEW)
Castles Caldicot
Kingstone Tintern
Mad Dog Penperlleni
Rhymney Blaenavon
Tiny Rebel Newport
Tudor Llanhilleth
Untapped Raglan

While much of the pub is set up for dining, drinkers are welcome in the cosy bar area. The regular food menu is complemented by ever-changing chef's specials. Outside is a small drinking/smoking area next to the modest car park.
Q ☆ ⌂ ⊕ P ☐ (37,50) ⬡

Brynmawr

Hobby Horse
30 Greenland Road, NP23 4DT
⚙ 11.45-3, 7-11; 11.30-midnight Sat; 11.45-10.30 Sun
☎ (01495) 310996
2 changing beers Ⓗ
Situated in a quiet residential street, this family-owned pub is nevertheless only a couple of minutes' walk from the town centre. To the left as you enter is the lounge, partitioned from a small bar. To the right is the restaurant, which links to the bar. The patio at the front is popular with families. Two ales are sourced from micros far and wide and forever changing – expect something different every time you visit. ⌂ ☆ ⌂ ⊕ ⌂ ⅄ ♣ P ☐ ❄ ⬡

Caerleon

Bell Inn ✓
Bulmore Road, NP18 1QQ
⚙ 12-11; 12-10.30 Sun ☎ (01633) 420613
⊕ thebellatcaerleon.co.uk
Sharp's Atlantic; 2 changing beers (sourced nationally; often Caledonian, Cottage) Ⓗ
Beneath the imposing stone façade, the charming low-beamed interior comprises an intimate restaurant, fireside bar and a cosy snug. A popular dining destination with excellent food to savour, there is also plenty here to interest those who enjoy a tipple. The cider choice is exceptional and some guest ales are seldom seen in the area. The pub plays a full part in the Caerleon Arts Festival in July and holds popular beer and cider festivals.
⌂ ☆ ⊕ ♣ ⊕ P ☐ ❄ ⬡

Caerwent

Coach & Horses ✓
Green Lane, NP26 5AX
⚙ 11-11 ☎ (01291) 420352
⊕ caerwent-coachandhorses.co.uk
Brains Rev James; Wye Valley HPA, Dorothy Goodbody's Golden Ale, Butty Bach; 1 changing beer (sourced regionally; often Kingstone, Tiny Rebel, Tomos Watkin) Ⓗ
Central village inn near extensive Roman walls – the Roman site has a CADW (Welsh Government historic environment service) visitor centre. The pub has a traditional public bar with tiled floor, comfortable seating, darts and pool. There is also a cosy lounge, restaurant and tea rooms. Food is sourced primarily from local suppliers, with breakfast served from 10am. The large garden has a patio and play area alongside the Roman walls.
⌂ ☆ ⌂ ⊕ ♣ P ☐ (73) ❄ ⬡

Caldicot

Castle Inn
64 Church Road, NP26 4HW
⚙ 12-11 (midnight Fri & Sat); closed Mon ☎ (01291) 420509
⊕ thecastleinncaldicot.com
2 changing beers (sourced nationally; often Greene King) Ⓗ

In keeping with its location near Caldicot Castle & Country Park, there are miniature cannons near the entrance to this pub while the garden has a large play fort for children. The pleasant low-beamed interior has a lounge/dining room on one side of the bar counter and a cosy bar with a large fireplace as its focal point on the other. Two or three guest ales are sourced from national, regional and family brewers. Food is popular with a good choice from an extensive menu.
⌂ ☆ ⊕ ⅄ P ☐ (74)

Cross Inn
1 Newport Road, NP26 4BG
⚙ 11-11 (12.30am Thu-Sat); 12-11 Sun ☎ (01291) 420692
Greene King IPA; Sharp's Doom Bar; 1 changing beer (sourced regionally) Ⓗ
Thriving pub where the main bar is often a lively place and hosts live bands. A central partition with a wall mounted TV above a fireplace separates the open-plan area from a secluded seating section with an adjacent games area on a higher level at the rear. A small snug is quieter, with comfortable seating. Two resident beers are joined by a guest often sourced from a regional brewery – note the array of pumpclips displayed above the bar.
⌂ ☆ ⅄ ♣ ⊕ P ☐ (62,74) ❄ ⬡

Chepstow

Bell Hanger ✓
St Mary's Street, NP16 5EW
⚙ 8am-midnight ☎ (01291) 637360
Greene King Abbot; Ruddles Best Bitter; Sharp's Doom Bar; 2 changing beers (sourced nationally; often Rhymney) Ⓗ
A converted ironmonger's establishment with the familiar Wetherspoon styling, close to the major tourist attraction of Chepstow Castle. The front entrance leads to a room with a long bar, subdued lighting and semicircular seating areas. A small space with plenty of natural light separates the bar from another spacious room down a flight of stairs. This gives access to the pleasant outdoor area for finer weather, with an entrance from Nelson Street and exit for the railway station.
Q ⌂ ☆ ⊕ ⅄ ⇌ ♣ ☐ ⬡

Chepstow Athletic Club Ⓛ
Mathern Road, Bulwark, NP16 5JJ (off Bulwark Rd)
⚙ 7-11 (11.30 Fri); 12.30-11.30 (midnight summer) Sat; 7-11 Sun ☎ (01291) 622126
Brains SA; Greene King IPA; 2 changing beers (sourced regionally) Ⓗ
CAMRA members are welcome at this well-established sports club, which has been a popular meeting place for local community groups and clubs since the early 1960s. Four good-value ales include two frequently changing guests, often from smaller Welsh breweries. Two low-volume TVs keep sports viewers happy but conversation takes priority. The patio is a good place to enjoy a beer while watching local cricket. The upstairs function room serves one real ale. ⌂ ☆ ⅄ ♣ P ☐

Queen's Head ♈ Ⓛ
Moor Street, NP16 5DD
⚙ 12-2.30 (not Mon-Fri), 5-11; 12-4 Sun; closed Mon ☎ 07793 889613
8 changing beers (sourced regionally; often Castles, Gower, Untapped) Ⓖ
Pioneering micropub, the first in the Gwent area, and already an award winner having clinched

Gwent CAMRA's Town Pub of the Year award for 2016. It has attracted a loyal following among locals and visitors from further afield who enjoy the intimate surroundings and friendly company where conversation dominates. The old adage, enter a stranger and leave a friend, is quite apt here. Enjoy an ever-changing range of mainly Welsh ales and ciders – a blackboard lists what is on. Q❄●🍽

Clytha

Clytha Arms 🍺 🅛

Groesonen Road, NP7 9BW (on B4598 old road between Abergavenny and Raglan)
✿ 12-3 (not Mon), 6-midnight; 12-midnight Fri-Sun
☎ (01873) 840206 ● clytha-arms.com

Brecon Three Beacons; Untapped Sundown; Wye Valley Bitter; 3 changing beers (sourced regionally) 🅷
Formerly a dower house, this award-winning country pub promises a warm welcome and a range of interesting beers. In winter relax at a comfortable table by the roaring log fire and admire the Felinfoel picture on the wall. In summer enjoy the attractive garden and fine views over the rolling Monmouthshire hills. High-quality food is always available – try the bacon, laverbread and cockles on the extensive lunchtime tapas menu.
Q🛏❄🍽🅘❤♣♠♥P🚌(83)❄

Cwmbran

Bush Inn 🅛

Graig Road, NP44 5AN
✿ 4-11 Mon-Wed; 12-11.30 ☎ (01633) 483764
● thebushuppercwmbran.co.uk

2 changing beers (sourced regionally) 🅷
Standing in the shadow of Mynydd Maen with commanding views over Cwmbran and beyond, this cosy pub has a split-level interior reminiscent of two parlours. Old pictures of the locality are a reminder that this was once an industrial community. There is something happening most nights of the week including live music and the popular curry night on Wednesday (booking advisable). The beers are sourced from mainly local or regional brewers while the ciders are primarily from Welsh producers. ❄🍽♣●P🚌❄

John Fielding 🅛 ✓

1 Caradoc Road, NP44 1PP
✿ 7am-midnight (1am Fri & Sat); 8am-midnight Sun
☎ (01633) 833760

Greene King Abbot; Ruddles Best Bitter; Sharp's Doom Bar; 2 changing beers 🅷
John Fielding was a local hero otherwise known as John Williams VC, who survived the Battle of Rorke's Drift (1879) in the Zulu Wars – the pub maintains close links with today's local war veterans. The interior is spacious with areas on several levels where people enjoy the popular Wetherspoon package of food and drink. The pub is a strong supporter of local breweries and there are often interesting Welsh ales on the bar alongside the standard favourites. Q❄🍽🅘❤●P🚌🛜

Mount Pleasant

Wesley Street, NP44 3LX
✿ 12 (4 Mon)-11; 12-midnight Fri & Sat ☎ (01633) 712176
2 changing beers (sourced regionally; often Evan Evans, Kingstone) 🅷

Since taking over two years ago, the owners have transformed this pub. It is open plan with three distinct areas – the bar on the left, a separate raised dining room leading off it and an area to the right popular with groups and families. There is a partly covered patio at the front. The ales are manly from local breweries, with Evan Evans and Kingstone being the most regular. ❄🍽🅘♣P🚌(6)❄

Cwmyoy

Queen's Head

NP7 7NE (near Skirrid Inn, take lane signposted Llanthony; pub is about 1 mile on right) SO311221
✿ 10.30-2 (not Tue or Fri), 6-11; 11-3, 6-11 Sat; 12-4 Sun; closed Wed ☎ (01873) 890241

Celt Experience Celt Native Storm; 1 changing beer (sourced locally) 🅷
A classic example of a remote country pub. Set in the idyllic Llanthony Valley in the Brecon Beacons, this hostelry has served its rural population for generations. Today the locals are joined by walkers and trekkers enjoying green tourism. Flagstone floors and beamed ceilings reflect the pub's venerable age, with a woodburner blasting out heat in winter. Beers from Celt Experience are sometimes joined by other local brews. Q❄🍽P

Ebbw Vale

Picture House ✓

Market Street, NP23 6HP
✿ 8am-11 (midnight Fri & Sat) ☎ (01495) 352810

Greene King Abbot; Ruddles Best Bitter; Sharp's Doom Bar; 2 changing beers (sourced nationally) 🅷
Previously a supermarket built on the site of a former cinema (hence the name), this is now a thriving town-centre pub adjacent to local shops and near the bus station. A wide entrance gives access to an interesting interior on different levels including an upstairs section above a space that looks like a small library. An illustrated history of the locality, including a striking 3D-effect picture of the town, shares wall space with attractive rural artwork. Q❄🍽🅘❤(Town)🚌(X4,22)🛜

Llanfihangel Tor-y-Mynydd

Star Inn ✓

NP15 1DT (near Llansoy)
✿ 4-8 Mon; 5-9 Tue; 12-3, 5-11 Wed-Fri; 12-11 Sat; 12-5 Sun
☎ (01291) 650256 ● thestarllansoy.co.uk

Butcombe Adam Henson's Rare Breed; 1 changing beer (sourced regionally; often Butcombe) 🅷
This pub reopened with new owners in 2014. The public bar has a separate entrance from the restaurant and is comfortably furnished with sofas and a large wood-burning stove. The restaurant serves home-cooked food made to order, and extends into a large conservatory, with three more fireplaces. Disabled access is at the back through the conservatory. The pub produces its own cider and occasionally perry, which are sold seasonally. ❄🍽🅘❤♣●P❄

Llanfoist

Bridge Inn

Merthyr Road, NP7 9LH
✿ 11-11 (midnight Fri & Sat); 12-10.30 Sun
☎ (01873) 854831 ● bridgellanfoist.com
3 changing beers (sourced regionally) 🅷

Set on the roadside at the end of the old bridge across the River Usk, the large grassed garden gives views over the river to Abergavenny and the hills behind. The owners have invested in upgrading the pub's facilities, including the accommodation and kitchens. Guest beers from national breweries are sometimes unusual for the area. Large TV screens show sports fixtures on match days. Beer festivals featuring local breweries are held during the year. ⏰🏠🛏️🍴◀️🏅⬥🅿️🚌(X4)🐾♿🛜

Llanhennock

Wheatsheaf
NP18 1LT (turn right 1 mile along Usk Road heading N from Caerleon; bear left at fork) ST353927
⏰ 11-11; 12-11 (12-4, 8-11 winter) Sun ☎ (01633) 420468
Fuller's London Pride; 2 changing beers (sourced regionally) Ⓗ
With over 30 consecutive years in the Guide under its belt, the Wheatsheaf is a classic example of an unspoilt, traditional country pub. The bar to the right of the entrance is the main area while the bar to the left is more of a snug. Both are adorned with old photographs, bric-a-brac and memorabilia. Outside, you can admire the views, relax in the garden during fine weather or play boules. One of the two guest ales is usually locally produced.
⏰🏠◀️🅰️♣️🅿️🐾

Llanthony

Llanthony Priory Hotel
Mill Farm, NP7 7NN (turn left by Skirrid Mountain Inn, continue for about 6 miles) SO288279
⏰ 11-3, 6-11; 11-11 Sat; 11-10.30 Sun; closed Mon
☎ (01873) 890487 ⊕ llanthonyprioryhotel.co.uk
Felinfoel Double Dragon; 1 changing beer (sourced regionally) Ⓗ
The ruins of an 11th century abbey make a wonderful beer garden for this remote hotel, eight miles into the Black Mountains. Mind your head as you descend into the cellar bar, formerly the abbot's home, to enjoy the ales and the ambience. You will find peace and tranquillity in plentiful supply as you wander the old abbey, a truly original place for exploration. Opening times vary – check before setting out. Q⏰🏠🛏️◀️🅰️🅿️

Llanvair Discoed

Woodlands Tavern
NP16 6LX
⏰ 12-2 (2.30 Sat), 6-11; 12-2 Sun; closed Mon
☎ (01633) 400313 ⊕ thewoodlandstavern.co.uk
3 changing beers (sourced regionally; often Castles, Kingstone) Ⓗ
This comfortable, welcoming and well-modernised village pub, a short detour north from the A48, has long been run by a family team. The chef, who is also the publican, provides admirable good-value food that has gained in reputation and draws customers from all around. Three ales, often including a Bath Ales brew, complement an oft-changing cider. In the bar a fascinating variety of rugby memorabilia, including historic jerseys, emphasises the pub's Welsh heritage. 🏠◀️♿♣️⬥🅿️

Magor

Wheatsheaf Ⓛ ✅
The Square, NP26 3HN

⏰ 10-11 (midnight Fri & Sat); 12-11 Sun ☎ (01633) 880608
4 changing beers (sourced regionally; often Castles Brewery Ltd, Rhymney, Sharp's) Ⓗ
Traditional village pub and a genuine community hub. It has a wide appeal, with diners enjoying the spacious restaurant while drinkers settle with their favourite tipple in the cosy lounge or Tap Room public bar. The interior has character with exposed stonework and low beams. The ale range is drawn from breweries far and near so expect to see a locally brewed ale alongside other guest beers – all are listed on a blackboard near the bar.
⏰🏠◀️♿♣️🅿️🚌(62,74)🐾🛜

Mamhilad

Horseshoe Inn ✅
Old Abergavenny Road, NP4 8QZ
⏰ 12-3, 5-11; 11.30-midnight Fri-Sun ☎ (01873) 880542
⊕ horseshoeinn.org
Tiny Rebel Cwtch; house beer (by Mad Dog); 2 changing beers (sourced nationally) Ⓗ
A welcoming country inn with a good choice of local ales and ciders on offer in the heart of rural Gwent. With a flagstone floor in the main bar area and a smaller dining section at the end of the bar, the pub is well placed to meet the needs of walkers, and is not too far from the Monmouthshire & Brecon canal. A good selection of freshly produced meals is always available. A pub worth seeking out. Q⏰🏠◀️🅰️⬥🅿️🐾🛜

Michaelstone-y-Fedw

Cefn Mably Arms ✅
CF3 6XS
⏰ 12-2.30, 5.30-11 Mon; 12-3.30, 5.30-11.30 Tue-Thu; 12-3.30, 5.30 midnight Fri & Sat; 12-8.30 Sun
☎ (01633) 680347 ⊕ thecefnmablyarms.co.uk
Brains Bitter; Butcombe Gold; Wye Valley HPA; 1 changing beer Ⓗ
Pleasant local pub slightly off the beaten track a couple of miles from the A48 at Castlelton. The interior is divided into three distinct areas, mainly laid out for diners, with a good selection of well-kept ales available. A collection of copper on display is noteworthy. The pub provides a 'get you here' service for locals, but you have to arrange your own journey home. Q⏰🏠◀️🅿️🐾🛜

Newport

Lamb Ⓛ
6 Bridge Street, NP20 4AL
⏰ 10-9 (midnight Wed; 1am Fri & Sat); 1-10 Sun
☎ (01633) 255200 ⊕ thelambnewport.com
Butcombe Bitter; Sharp's Doom Bar; Wye Valley HPA; 2 changing beers (sourced regionally) Ⓗ
Vibrant city-centre pub firmly re-embraced by local drinkers since reopening after a tasteful refurbishment. Be sure to admire the dark tiled exterior before entering the often lively bar. Background music from the jukebox or TV music channels may occasionally intrude on conversation, although the rear section is quieter. Window seats allow you to watch the world go by. The handpumps are kept busy dispensing mainly Welsh guest ales alongside the regular beers. ◀️🚏⬥🚌🛜

Olde Murenger House
52-53 High Street, NP20 1GA
⏰ 12-11; 12-3, 7.30-10.30 Sun ☎ (01633) 263977

Samuel Smith Old Brewery Bitter Ⓗ
No visit to Newport's ale houses is complete without calling into this venerable Tudor-age establishment. The decor is relaxing with much dark wood and matching furnishings – other than old brewery scenes, all manner of things linked with Newport, including sporting greats and the famous Transporter Bridge, are displayed. With no music or TV to distract, settle back and enjoy the ambience and keenly priced ale. Tasty and good-value food is also available. ⬤⬤⇌🖵🐾

Pen & Wig Ⓛ
22-24 Stow Hill, NP20 1JD
✪ 10-11 (midnight Fri); 11-midnight Sat; 12-10.30 Sun
☎ (01633) 666818
Draught Bass; 5 changing beers (sourced regionally; often Brains, Celt Experience, Otley) Ⓗ
Formerly business premises, the interior is a mix of linked sections on different levels, most within sight of a TV for sport. The pub prides itself on showcasing Welsh beers and ciders, and the food offering is appetising and substantial. The large upstairs function room is available for hire and a deck patio at the rear is popular in fine weather. ⊛⬤⇌♣🖐🖵

St Julian Inn ⊘
Caerleon Road, NP18 1QA
✪ 11.30-11.30 (midnight Fri & Sat); 12-11 Sun
☎ (01633) 243548 ⊕ stjulian.co.uk
Wells Bombardier; Young's Bitter; 2 changing beers (sourced regionally; often Bath Ales, Castle Rock, Purity) Ⓗ
Riverside pub in a scenic position, with views towards the countryside and Caerleon. It is nicely set out inside with a bar, comfortable sports section, riverside terrace and a lounge arranged around a central counter. The lounge has wood panelling rescued from a former ocean liner, which gives it a slightly stately feel. The guest ales are often sourced from regional Welsh and West Country breweries. A model of consistency, it has deservedly featured in this Guide for 25 years. 🛏⊛⬤♣P🖵🐾🛜

Urban Tap House
High Street, NP20 1FX
✪ 12-10 (1am Wed & Thu); 11-1am Fri & Sat
☎ (01633) 252538 ⊕ urbantaphouse.co.uk/newport
Tiny Rebel Cereal Killer, Fubar; 4 changing beers (sourced nationally) Ⓗ
This long-awaited Tiny Rebel Brewery venture finally flung open its doors in November 2015 to immediate acclaim after a dry run as a pop-up pub, following major restoration work. Much use of glass and a light decor with contemporary artwork in typical Tiny Rebel style add to the appeal. Downstairs is the Cwtch lounge and a view into the cellar. Tasty burgers and pizzas can be washed down with ales from the host brewery and rare guest ales. ⬤♿⇌🖐🖵🐾🛜

Pantygelli

Crown Inn Ⓛ
Old Hereford Road, NP7 7HR
✪ 12-2.30 (not Mon), 6-11; 12-3, 6-11 Sat; 12-3, 6-10.30 Sun
☎ (01873) 853314 ⊕ thecrownatpantygelli.com
Draught Bass; Rhymney Best; Wye Valley HPA; 1 changing beer (sourced regionally; often Grey Trees, Kingstone, Monty's) Ⓗ

A firm favourite for many years, this family-run gastro-pub has established a strong reputation for excellent beer and food. Its regular beers come in a well-considered range of styles, while the frequently changing guest ales reflect the diversity found in the current Welsh brewery scene. Set between the Sugarloaf and Skirrid mountains, this is excellent walking country. On warm days the large patio provides glorious opportunities for a pint, or an alfresco meal, in a lovely setting. 🛏⊛⬤♣P

Penallt

Boat Inn
Lone Lane, NP25 4AJ
✪ 12-11; closed Tue winter ☎ (01600) 712615
⊕ theboatpenallt.co.uk
Wye Valley Butty Bach; 2 changing beers (sourced regionally; often Butcombe, Goff's, Wickwar) Ⓖ
In an impressive location by the River Wye and accessed from England by footway alongside a former rail bridge, the Boat features a cosy main bar and side room. The cool stillage behind the bar hosts two or three cask ales, and 12 ciders are usually available. Walkers exploring this beautiful valley are fuelled by the pub's generous meals and snacks. Riverside tables and a hillside garden are popular in fine weather. Closing time may be earlier on Sunday or Monday evenings in winter if quiet. 🛏⊛⬤♣🖐P🖵(69)🐾

Pontymister

Commercial Inn Ⓛ ⊘
Commercial Street, NP11 6BA
✪ 11 (10 Sat)-11.30; 12-11.30 Sun ☎ (01633) 612608
⊕ thecommercialpontymister.com
3 changing beers (sourced nationally; often Sharp's, Tiny Rebel) Ⓗ
On the main street in Pontymister, this open-plan pub is heaven for sports lovers, with TVs everywhere all showing different sporting events at the same time – but always except for major events. One of the three ales is usually from Tiny Rebel brewery – sometimes two. Other guest ales are mostly from micros, often breweries with a reciprocal trading arrangement with Tiny Rebel. A draught cider is sometimes added in warmer weather. 🛏⊛⬤♿⇌🖐🖵🛜

Rogerstone

Tredegar Arms ⊘
157 Cefn Road, NP10 9AS
✪ 12 (4 Mon)-11; 12-10.30 Sun ☎ (01633) 547553
Morland Old Speckled Hen Ⓖ**; 2 changing beers (often Brains)** Ⓗ
The Top TA, as it is often called locally, has rightly regained its place in the Guide in the capable hands of an enthusiastic manager. The main lounge at the rear has a dining area and a cosy snug running off it. At the front is a small bar where the regulars congregate. Greene King's Morland Old Speckled Hen is usually on for the regulars. The other two ales change, but with a few favourites on rotation. 🛏⊛⬤⇌♣P🖵(56,R1)🛜

Sebastopol

Open Hearth
Wern Road, NP4 5DR

✪ 11.30-midnight; 12-11.30 Sun ☎ (01495) 763752
Glamorgan Welsh Pale Ale; 3 changing beers (sourced regionally; often Dartmoor, Greene King) Ⓗ
This Monmouthshire & Brecon canalside pub is a perennial favourite and welcoming refreshment stop for walkers, cyclists and boaters – there is a mooring spot nearby. The canal level entrance gives access to the bar, a rear snug and a lounge/dining room. There is a downstairs function room, ample parking and a garden play space for children. Catch it on a busy day and its appeal to all ages, drinkers and diners is obvious. Last entry is 11pm. ➷✺Ⓞ⓭♣Pᵺ❀

Sebastopol Social Club Ⓛ

Wern Road, NP4 5DU (on corner of Wern Rd with Austin Rd)
✪ 12-11 (midnight Fri & Sat); 12-10.30 Sun
☎ (01495) 763808 ⊕ sebastopolsocial.org.uk
Wye Valley HPA; 5 changing beers (sourced regionally; often Cottage, Otley, RCH) Ⓗ
The array of CAMRA awards above the front bar leaves no doubt about this club's commitment to real ale. The range varies but the favourites often return; however, do not be surprised to see a beer you may not have tried before, often from a local or new Welsh brewery. The club is comfortable, with excellent facilities for indoor sport, functions and live entertainment. CAMRA members are welcome subject to entry rules. ✺♣♣♣Pᵺ❀⌗

Tintern

Anchor Inn

NP16 6TE (off A466 at Tintern Abbey)
✪ 9am-11; 12-10.30 Sun ☎ (01291) 689582
⊕ theanchortintern.com
3 changing beers (sourced regionally; often Wye Valley, Kingstone) Ⓗ
River Wye-side pub next to magnificent Tintern Abbey that features the former Cistercian monks' own cider press in its bar. An ale from nearby Kingstone Brewery usually appears alongside two guests, often including a Wye Valley offering, and

cask Old Rosie cider. Good food is served in the bar and in the adjoining restaurant while a well-glazed garden room provides fine views of the beautiful surrounding scenery. The council parking fee can be reclaimed as a discount at the bar.
➷✺Ⓓ♣Pᵺ(69)⌗

Wye Valley Hotel

Monmouth Road, NP16 6SQ
✪ 11-3, 6-11; 12-3, 6.30-10.30 Sun ☎ (01291) 689441
⊕ thewyevalleyhotel.co.uk
Wye Valley HPA, Butty Bach; 1 changing beer (sourced locally; often Kingstone) Ⓗ
A distinctive 1920s independent hotel on the main A466 at the north end of Tintern. The pub has served Wye Valley beers since the brewery's earliest days and the guest is often a locally brewed Kingstone ale. A selection of bottled commemorative beers lines shelves around the bar (not for sale). Home-cooked food is available in the bar and in the separate restaurant. A great stop-off for refreshment while exploring this superbly scenic valley and surrounding hills.
➷✺⇦Ⓞⅅ♿ＡPᵺ(69)❀⌗

Usk

King's Head Hotel

18 Old Market Street, NP15 1AL
✪ 11-11; 11-10.30 Sun ☎ (01291) 672963
⊕ kingsheadusk.com
Fuller's London Pride; Timothy Taylor Landlord; 1 changing beer (sourced nationally; often Draught Bass) Ⓗ
Tucked away in a back street, this pleasant hotel has a history dating back to 1588 and exudes character with its dark decor and fine fireplace in the bar. An appetising range of food, both regular and special dishes, is on the menu, making this a popular place for diners. A long-standing Guide entry, the real ale selection reflects the favourites of local drinkers and a local ale may occasionally appear. Q⇦Ⓓ♿Pᵺ❀⌗

Clytha Arms, Clytha

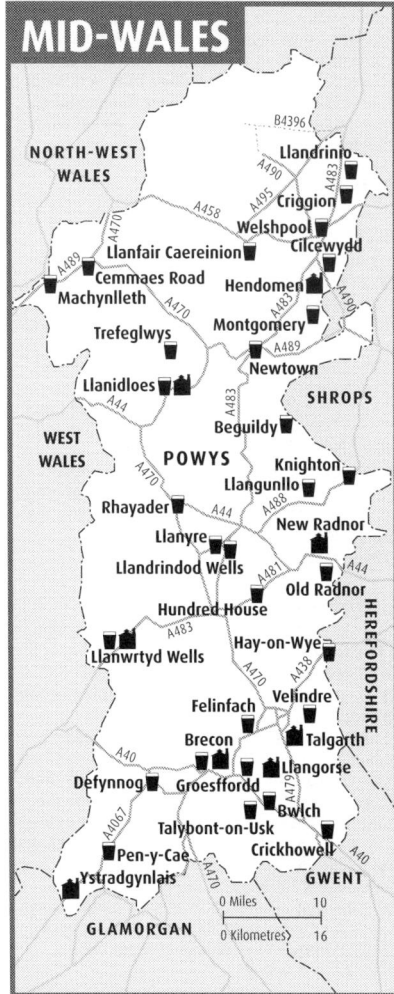

MID-WALES

NORTH-WEST WALES

WEST WALES

POWYS

SHROPS

HEREFORDSHIRE

GWENT

GLAMORGAN

B4396
Llandrinio
Criggion
Welshpool
Cilcewydd
Llanfair Caereinion
Cemmaes Road
Machynlleth
Hendomen
Montgomery
Trefeglwys
Newtown
Llanidloes
Beguildy
Knighton
Llangunllo
Rhayader
New Radnor
Llanyre
Llandrindod Wells
Old Radnor
Hundred House
Hay-on-Wye
Llanwrtyd Wells
Velindre
Felinfach
Brecon
Talgarth
Defynnog
Groesffordd
Llangorse
Bwlch
Talybont-on-Usk
Pen-y-Cae
Crickhowell
Ystradgynlais

0 Miles 10
0 Kilometres 16

Authority area covered: Powys UA

Beguildy

Radnorshire Arms
LD7 1YE

⊘ 12-2, 6-11 (midnight Fri & Sat); 12-3.30, 7-11 Sun; closed Mon ☎ (01547) 510634
2 changing beers (sourced regionally) Ⓗ
The Radnorshire Arms dates back to the 16th century and was probably a drovers' pub at one time. There is a cosy bar with an inglenook, an intimate dining area and a pleasant garden to the side. The beers are from Ludlow and Stonehouse breweries. The pub is popular with diners and offers separate menus for lunchtimes, evenings and Sunday lunches as well as daily specials.
⊛◑PⒹ

Brecon

Brecon Rugby Club
63 The Watton, LD3 7EL

⊘ 5-11; 11-11 Sat & Sun ☎ (01874) 624848
⊕ breconrfc.co.uk
3 changing beers Ⓗ

A founder member of the Welsh RFU, this friendly and welcoming club is open to all. A large main bar with separate lounge is towards the front, and there is a function room with a big screen beyond the bar. Outside is a spacious patio garden and the Brecon Pétanque Club. Beers from local brewers are frequently available plus bottled ciders from Gwynt y Ddraig. The pub is often busy during the rugby season, particularly when Wales are playing. Brecknockshire CAMRA Club of the Year.
⤴⊛◑♣PⒹ⊛❄🔊

Clarence
25 The Watton, LD3 7ED

⊘ 12-midnight (2am Fri & Sat) ☎ (01874) 622810
⊕ clarenceinn.co.uk
Wye Valley Bitter, Butty Bach; 1 changing beer Ⓗ
Two-roomed town-centre community pub with a contemporary, welcoming and relaxed atmosphere. The newly extended front bar tends to be frequented by locals, while the larger back bar is popular with diners. A large TV screen draws a crowd for big sporting events. Outside, the spacious garden is an attraction, especially during the jazz festival. Guest beers are generally sourced from local breweries. ⤴⊛🍴◑♣♠PⒹ❄

Bwlch

New Inn
Brecon Road, LD3 7RQ (on A40 between Brecon and Crickhowell)

⊘ 5-11; 12-11 Sat & Sun ☎ (01874) 730215
⊕ beaconsbackpackers.co.uk
Felinfoel Double Dragon; Wye Valley Butty Bach; 2 changing beers (sourced regionally; often Dark Star, Salopian, Tiny Rebel) Ⓗ
Lively and cosy village pub with a growing local reputation. A comfortable dining area sits to the side of the stone-flagged public bar, with armchairs and settles arranged around a huge fireplace. An always-interesting guest ale supplements the two regulars, and good-value food is served evenings and lunchtimes at weekends. The pub is an excellent base for exploring the surrounding Brecon Beacons and Black Mountains, with bunkhouse accommodation available.
Q⤴⊛🍴◑♣♠PⒹ(X43/43)❄🔊

Cemmaes Road

Dovey Valley Hotel ★
SY20 8JZ

⊘ 6-11; 6-10.30 Sun ☎ (01650) 511335
1 changing beer (sourced locally; often Cwrw Cader, Cwrw Llŷn, Monty's) Ⓗ
Currently undergoing sympathetic restoration to its former glory, this gem of a pub was built to serve the nearby railway. Boasting a nationally important historic interior, it has a cosy main bar and snug with traditional features from the 1870s, including

REAL ALE BREWERIES

Brecon Brecon
Bryncelyn Ystradgynlais
Heart of Wales ⊟ Llanwrtyd Wells
Monty's Hendomen
Radnorshire New Radnor
Rotters ⊟ Talgarth (brewing suspended)
Tydwals Llangorse (NEW)
Waen Llanidloes

the original slate floors and Edwardian-tiled fireplace. It is furnished with a mix of mirrors, brewery memorabilia and other eclectic items. Live music sessions feature now and again. Gwynt y Ddraig cider is available. Food and accommodation are to follow. Q ☺ ♿ ⊛ ▲ ♣ ● P ➡ (X85) ☺ 📶

Cilcewydd

Square & Compass

SY21 8RU

⊛ 4.30 (1 Sat)-11; 12-11 Sun ☎ (01938) 580360

Sharp's Doom Bar; 1 changing beer (sourced regionally) Ⓗ

A rare example of a rural pub that survives on beer sales only, this is a popular community venue situated just off the road and easily missed. It has two rooms – a long main room divided in two by comfortable bench seating with old agricultural photos on the walls, and a second room with wall seating. There are drinking areas outside and gents have the choice of inside or outside toilets. Q ⊛ ♣ P ➡ (71,81) ☺

Crickhowell

Bear Hotel

High Street, NP8 1BW

⊛ 10-11; 11-10.30 Sun ☎ (01873) 810408

⊕ bearhotel.co.uk

Brains Rev James Original; Sharp's Doom Bar; 2 changing beers (sourced regionally; often Bullmastiff) Ⓗ

Originally a 15th-century coaching inn, this is now an award-winning hotel. The multi-roomed bar enjoys grand surroundings with exposed beams, wood panelling, fine settles and an eclectic selection of furnishings and decorations. The two bar rooms have exposed fireplaces, as does one of the side rooms. Food is excellent, with a varied menu featuring much local produce. The hotel is an excellent base for exploring the surrounding Black Mountains and Brecon Beacons National Park. Q ☺ ⊛ ♿ ◑ ♿ ▲ P ➡ (X43/43) ☺ ☺

Criggion

Admiral Rodney Inn

SY5 9AU

⊛ 12-10 (11 Fri & Sat) ☎ (01938) 570313

Wye Valley Butty Bach; 1 changing beer (sourced locally; often Salopian) Ⓗ

This unspoilt rural inn dates back to the mid-1700s and is named after an admiral who harvested local oak to build his ships – he is honoured with a pillar on the adjacent hill. The pub is a base for walkers exploring the area. The single-room interior has a fireplace at both ends and a restaurant area to the right as you enter. Posters of Terry Pratchett's Discworld novels decorate the dining space. Q ☺ ⊛ ◑ ♿ ♣ P ☺

Defynnog

Tanners Arms 🏆

LD3 8SF (on A4067)

⊛ 5-midnight; 12-midnight Fri-Sun ☎ (01874) 638032

⊕ tannersarmspub.com

5 changing beers Ⓗ/Ⓖ

Family-run country pub famous for its warm welcome to customers, set in a delightful village in the Brecon Beacons National Park. It has traded

continuously since 1870 but the original buildings, cottages for workers at the nearby tannery, date from circa 1806. A selection of real ciders is usually on offer alongside home-cooked food. A number of beer and cider festivals are held throughout the year. Multiple local CAMRA branch award winner. ☺ ⊛ ♿ ◑ ▲ ♣ ● P ➡ ☺ 📶

Felinfach

Griffin Ⓛ ✅

LD3 0UB (just off A470 3 miles NE of Brecon)

⊛ 12-11.30 ☎ (01874) 620111

4 changing beers (sourced locally) Ⓗ

The pub's ethos – the simple things in life done well – says it all. A welcoming country pub, restaurant and rooms, the emphasis here is on good beer and excellent food. The multi-roomed layout allows for discrete areas for drinking and dining. The huge fireplace between the bar and the main dining area dominates in winter, while an Aga lurks in a side room, providing warmth throughout the building. The large garden affords superb views of the surrounding mountains. Beers are sourced from local breweries. Q ☺ ⊛ ♿ ◑ ♿ P ➡

Groesffordd

Three Horseshoes ✅

LD3 7SN (just off B4558 in centre of village)

⊛ 12-3 (not Mon), 5-11; 12-11 Fri-Sun ☎ (01874) 665672

⊕ threehorseshoesgroesffordd.co.uk

St Austell Tribute; 2 changing beers (sourced regionally) Ⓗ

Busy village-centre pub in the heart of the Brecon Beacons, boasting superb views from both the front and rear outdoor seating areas. The pub is only a 10-minute walk from the Brynich Lock on the Monmouthshire & Brecon Canal and is a popular stop for boaters and other visitors. Excellent locally sourced food is on offer. Quizzes and other events take place regularly. Brynich Caravan Site and the Brecon YHA are nearby. ☺ ⊛ ◑ ♿ ▲ ♣ ● ☺ 📶

Hay on Wye

Blue Boar

Oxford Road, HR3 5DF

⊛ 9am-11 ☎ (01497) 820884

Hook Norton Hooky; Timothy Taylor Landlord; 2 changing beers (sourced regionally) Ⓗ

Comfortable and friendly pub in the centre of the town famed for books, owned and run by the same family for many years. A large central bar dominates, with two separate seating areas around it, each with a log fire. Two regular beers are usually supplemented by one or two guests. Food is available all day in the bar and the separate dining area. Q ☺ ◑ ♿ ➡ (39) ☺ 📶

Hundred House

Hundred House

LD1 5RY (on A481, near Builth Wells)

⊛ 12-2, 5.30-11; 11-11 Sat & Sun ☎ (01982) 570231

Greene King Abbot; Wye Valley Butty Bach; 1 changing beer (sourced nationally) Ⓗ

Located among rolling Welsh hills, the Hundred House Inn takes its name from the Saxon hundred, which was an administrative area. At one time a

drovers' inn, this is now a traditional pub, well patronised by the local farming community. There is a lounge, locals' bar, pool room with TV (for rugby), restaurant area and beer garden. The pub is welcoming and friendly – afternoon closing times are flexible depending on custom.
Q👶❀🛏◖◗♿⛺♣P

Knighton

Horse & Jockey

Wylcwm Place, LD7 1AE
🕓 11-11 ☎ (01547) 520062 🌐 thehorseandjockeyinn.co.uk
2 changing beers (sourced regionally; often Three Tuns, Wood, Wye Valley) Ⓗ
The pub is of late-medieval origins, set around a courtyard, and was once a coaching inn. It has a large restaurant converted from stables. Owned by the same family since 1989, the building is a pleasing mixture of old and new, with a variety of rooms and seating outside in the courtyard. It offers an extensive food menu featuring fresh local produce plus a pizza menu. There are two or three cask beers, usually from Welsh and border breweries. Q👶❀🛏◖◗⇌🚌

Llandrindod Wells

Arvon Ale House 🏆 Ⓛ

Temple Street, LD1 5DP
🕓 4-10 (11 Fri & Sat); closed Mon & Tue
5 changing beers Ⓗ
The first micropub in this part of Wales and a welcome addition to Llandrindod's pub scene, this former shop premises is small and perfectly formed. This is a proper alehouse for the quiet enjoyment of beer with no distractions. Sensibly priced ales are sourced from Wales, the borders and the Midlands. Two real ciders are also offered plus bottle-conditioned beers from Waen Brewery. Snacks are available. A monthly all-comers folk music session is held on the second and fourth Sunday. Q⇌🍎🚌🐾

Conservative Club

South Crescent, LD1 5DH (opp bandstand)
🕓 11-2, 5.30-11; 11-11.30 Fri & Sat; 11.30-10.30 Sun
☎ (01597) 822126
Brains Bitter; Marston's Pedigree; 1 changing beer (sourced nationally) Ⓗ
Located in the centre of this historic spa town, the Con Club is a regular Guide entry. It has a large lounge, TV room, games bar, snooker and pool tables and a small front patio/smoking area. Until the early 1970s the building was the Lansdown Hotel. Good-value lunches are served Wednesday to Friday and Sunday. CAMRA members are welcome but visitors must be signed in.
Q❀◖◗♿⇌♣🚌📶

Llandrinio

Punch Bowl

SY22 6SG
🕓 12-3 (not Mon-Wed), 5-midnight; 12-3, 5-1am Fri & Sat
☎ (01691) 830247
2 changing beers (often Offa's Dyke, Sharp's, Stonehouse) Ⓗ
Friendly and popular village local, saved by the community from conversion to residential use. Situated in the middle of the village, it has a traditional public bar on the left and a well-appointed restaurant on the right. The pub is home to a number of sports teams including football, cricket, pool, darts and dominoes. It has a large covered area outside at the back. A beer festival is planned in the future. A true community hub.
👶❀◖◗♿♣P🚌(X71,74)🐾📶

Llanfair Caereinion

Goat Hotel

High Street, SY21 0QS (off A485)
🕓 11-11 (midnight Fri & Sat) ☎ (01938) 810428
🌐 thegoathotel.co.uk
3 changing beers (sourced regionally; often Stonehouse, Wood) Ⓗ
Excellent 300-year-old beamed coaching inn with a welcoming atmosphere which attracts both locals and tourists. The plush lounge, dominated by a large inglenook and open fire, has comfortable leather armchairs and sofas. There is a dining room serving home-cooked food and a games room to the rear. The choice of real ale always includes one from Wood Brewery. Q👶❀🛏◖◗⇌♣P🚌(87)🐾

Llangunllo

Greyhound Ⓛ

LD7 1SP (on B4356, off A488)
🕓 4.30-11 (2am Fri); 2-2am Sat; 2-11 Sun; closed Mon & Tue
☎ (01547) 550400
3 changing beers (often Broughs, Six Bells, Wrekin) Ⓗ
This unique 16th-century inn, set in picturesque countryside, is the first stop on the Glyndwr's Way long-distance trail. The beers are usually from Broughs, Six Bells and Wrekin breweries, and the cider is Westons Family Reserve. Beer festivals are held on the May and August bank holidays and regular music sessions are hosted. You are welcome to bring your own food. Opening times are approximate – ring the doorbell any time after midday and with luck you will be served.
❀♣🍎P▯🐾

Llanidloes

Old Mill Ⓛ

40-44 High Street, SY18 6BZ
🕓 11-11; closed Mon & Tue ☎ (01686) 412008
🌐 oldmillbar.co.uk
Waen Pamplemousse; 2 changing beers (sourced regionally; often Waen) Ⓗ
A pub opened in the old premises of the United Services Club, with an eclectic mix of furniture, shelves and bric-a-brac, set around a wood-panelled bar. There are usually at least two Waen beers on offer. It has two rooms – the main carpeted bar with wall seating, sofas and subdued lighting, and a second room with a pool table and piano. Various events are held including food days, children's activities and live music. Encyclopedia pages serve as wallpaper in the gents.
👶❀◖◗♿♣🚌(X75,525)🐾📶

Stag Inn

15 Great Oak Street, SY18 6BU (off A470)
🕓 12-11 (1.30am Fri); 11-1.30am Sat ☎ (01686) 414824
🌐 staginnllanidloes.co.uk
Purple Moose Cwrw Eryri/Snowdonia Ale; 1 changing beer (sourced regionally; often Fuller's, Shepherd Neame) Ⓗ
Friendly town-centre pub offering two real ales and a real cider. The long premises is divided in two –

WALES

the wooden-floored front area has wall seating and a wood-burning stove, the rear area through an archway has comfortable sofas, a pool table and a piano. There is an outside drinking area to the rear. The pub hosts live music at the weekends. Reasonably priced bar snacks are served and takeaway tea and coffee are available.
🚲🏠🍴◑🕭✿♣⬥🚻 (X75,525)🐾🐾 🛜

Llanwrtyd Wells

Neuadd Arms Hotel 🅛
The Square, LD5 4RB
✪ 11-midnight (2am Fri & Sat) ☎ (01591) 610236
🌐 neuaddarmshotel.co.uk
Felinfoel Double Dragon; Heart of Wales Irfon Valley Bitter, Aur Cymru, Welsh Black, Noble Eden Ale; 4 changing beers (sourced locally) 🅗
This large Victorian hotel serves as the tap for the Heart of Wales Brewery. The Bells Bar features a large fireplace and an eclectic mix of furniture. The bells formerly used to summon servants remain on one wall, along with the winners' boards from some of the town's unusual competitions. The lounge bar is a little more formal. The hotel takes part in the town's annual events including a major beer festival in November. A good range of real ciders is kept. Q✿🏠🍴◑🖢≠♣⬥P🐾

Llanyre

Bell Inn
LD1 6DY
✪ 12-2 (not Mon), 6-11; 11.30-2, 6-11 Fri; 12-3 Sun
☎ (01597) 823959 🌐 bellcountryinn.co.uk
2 changing beers 🅗
Built in 1888 by the local Gibson-Watt family on the site of a much older premises, this was originally a Welsh drovers' inn. It was extended in the 1970s and today is more of a restaurant, conference venue and holiday hotel than a pub, the bar recently modernised in open-plan fashion. Two cask-conditioned beers are usually kept – often Brains Rev James Original or Woods Shropshire Lad – plus a guest beer, sourced nationally. The small public bar seems little used. Q🏠◑🕭P🚻

Machynlleth

White Horse
42 Heol Maengwyn, SY20 8DT
✪ 7 (6 Fri)-11; 3-11 Sat; 12-11 Sun; closed Mon
☎ (01654) 702247
Ludlow Gold; 2 changing beers (sourced regionally; often Purple Moose, Three Tuns) 🅗
Traditional town pub opposite Owain Glyndwr's Parliament House with two separate bars. One has darts and a jukebox, the other a pool table and log fire in the winter. The building was destroyed by fire and rebuilt in 1911 with the present magnificent frontage – look above the fireplace in the right-hand bar for before and after pictures. Real cider is sometimes available in the summer. Bar meals are served including Sunday lunches, but times vary so it is best to phone ahead.
🚲✿🏠◑🕭≠♣P🚻 (T2,X28,X85)🐾

Montgomery

Crown Inn
Castle Street, SY15 6PW
✪ 11-11 ☎ (01686) 668533

Brains Rev James Original; Wye Valley Butty Bach; 1 changing beer (sourced regionally; often Three Tuns) 🅗
A traditional local in a town that once supported a multitude of hostelries. The pub is home to a large number of local sports teams. The public bar is long and quite narrow with a pool and games area at the rear. A small snug sits opposite with a large array of trophies in it. There are benches for outdoor drinking. Beware of the low beams in the bar area. Handy for Monty's Brewery visitor centre.
✿⬥♣🚻 (71,81)

Newtown

Railway Tavern
Old Kerry Road, SY16 1BH (off A483)
✪ 11-2, 5-midnight Mon; 11-midnight Tue; 11-2, 7-midnight Wed & Thu, 11-1am Fri & Sat; 11-1am Sun
☎ (01686) 626156
Hancocks HB; 2 changing beers (sourced regionally; often Salopian, Slater's, Three Tuns) 🅗
Another year in the Guide for Dave and Eileen's one-bar local near the station. Two guest beers from regional or small breweries are always on offer. The Railway hosts a number of darts teams and a dominoes team and can get crowded on match nights. The interior is essentially divided in two – a lower bar area and a rear area with wall benches and tables. Note the poster listing over 50 pubs that once operated in Newtown.
Q✿≠♣🚻 (X75)

Sportsman 🅛
17 Severn Street, SY16 2AQ (off A483)
✪ 12-10 Tue; 12-11 Wed & Thu; 12-11.30 Fri & Sat; 12-10 Sun, closed Mon ☎ (01686) 623978 🌐 sportsmannewtown.co.uk
Monty's Old Jailhouse, MPA, Sunshine, Masquerade, Mischief; 3 changing beers (sourced nationally; often Brains, Robinsons, Wychwood) 🅗
This is a Hophouse Inns-managed house and five Monty's beers are available alongside up to three guest ales and a varying number of ciders. The pub is divided into three areas – a snug with comfortable wall seating, a main bar area and a rear tiled games area with pool table, TV and darts. There is a patio at the rear for summer drinking. Welsh Cider Pub of the Year 2014.
Q✿♿≠♣⬥🚻 (X75)🛜

Old Radnor

Harp Inn
LD8 2RH (at Walton on A44 follow signs for Old Radnor and Harp Inn)
✪ 12-3 (not Wed & Thu), 6-11; 12-3, 6-10.30 Sun; closed Mon & Tue ☎ (01544) 350655 🌐 harpinnradnor.co.uk
2 changing beers (sourced regionally; often Hobsons, Three Tuns, Wye Valley) 🅗
Early-15th-century Welsh longhouse commanding a fine view over the Radnor Valley. The building was rescued and restored by the Landmark Trust in 1972 and then sold on in 1983. The interior is a tasteful mix of old and new, including a modern restaurant serving good food made with locally sourced seasonal ingredients. There are occasional steak nights and seasonal tastings. Ales mainly come from regional and local microbreweries and beer festivals are hosted from time to time.
Q🚲✿🏠◑🕭▲♣⬥P🐾🛜

Pen-y-Cae

Ancient Briton

Brecon Road, SA9 1YY (on A4067 N of Abercraf)

🌐 12-midnight ☎ (01639) 730273 ⊕ ancientbriton.co.uk

Wye Valley Butty Bach; 5 changing beers 🅷

Traditional country pub situated on the A4067 in the Brecon Beacons National Park and Forest Fawr Geopark. There are 14 handpumps offering a selection of up to 11 ales and three real ciders. The bar is open plan, with a real log fire in winter. Cyclists and walkers are welcome, with camping and caravan facilities at the rear. The Ancient Briton has won local CAMRA Pub of the Year awards on numerous occasions and is a former CAMRA regional winner. 🌀🏵🛏🍽🕭⚓🅿🚲(X63)🐾🛜

Rhayader

Cornhill Inn

West Street, LD6 5AB (400yds W of clock tower on main A470)

🌐 4-midnight; 12-midnight Sat & Sun ☎ (01597) 810029

Sharp's Doom Bar; Waen TWA; 2 changing beers (sourced nationally) 🅷

Sixteenth-century inn providing a pub experience sometimes lost in this modern world. There are two separate rooms and a cosy log fire in winter, and a lively, friendly atmosphere is assured. The beer range usually includes local and regional beers. Outside are a beer garden and covered smoking area. For many years there was a blacksmith's forge at the rear, now converted into a holiday cottage. Q🌀🏵🛏🕭🚲🐾🛜

Talybont-on-Usk

Star Inn 🍸 🅻

LD3 7YX (on B4558 between Brecon and Crickhowell)

🌐 11.30-3, 5-11.30; 11-11 Fri-Sun ☎ (01874) 676635 ⊕ starinntalybont.co.uk

6 changing beers (often Brecon, Dark Star, Grey Trees) 🅷

Large and lively pub next to the Monmouthshire & Brecon Canal, with a spacious garden that is extremely popular in summer. The beer range varies constantly, with local ales well represented, served alongside locally produced ciders. Live music evenings are held regularly, and quiz nights are popular. Excellent food makes good use of local produce. Twice-yearly beer festivals are well attended. Local CAMRA Pub of the Year many times (2009-15). 🌀🏵🛏🍽🕭⚓🛜🚲(43)🐾🛜

Trefeglwys

Red Lion

SY17 5PH

🌐 5 (2 Fri)-11; 12-midnight Sat; 12-11 Sun

☎ (01686) 430934

Morland Old Speckled Hen; Sharp's Doom Bar; Three Tuns XXX 🅷

Friendly village pub with a pleasant view across the valley. The public bar is wood panelled and has an impressive inglenook with a wood-burning stove. A pool room is accessed off the bar down a couple of steps, and the restaurant is to the right as you enter. There are outside drinking areas to the front and rear. The pub attracts a mixed clientele and has a relaxed atmosphere. 🌀🏵🛏🕭🚲⚓🅿🛜

Velindre

Three Horseshoes

LD3 0SU

🌐 12-3, 6-11; 12-11 Sat & Sun; closed Mon

☎ (01497) 847304

2 changing beers (sourced locally) 🅷

A warm and friendly free house, off the beaten track next to the green in this quiet village location between Talgarth and Hay-on-Wye. The bar area has two smaller rooms off and a separate dining area behind. Two or three guest ales are usually on offer, plus local cider, all at reasonable prices. Good-value snacks and traditional pub food are usually available and Sunday roasts are popular. 🌀🏵🕭⚓🅿🐾

Welshpool

Pheasant Inn

43 High Street, SY21 7JQ

🌐 4-11; 12-11 Fri-Sun ☎ (01938) 553104

2 changing beers (often Salopian, Three Tuns) 🅷

The Pheasant is a Grade II-listed building in a terrace of what were 18th-century town houses. Much-modified internally, it has one long room with a wooden floor and pool and darts at one end. To the rear is a door leading to an outside drinking and smoking area. A third guest beer is usually available at weekends and they are all often from small or regional breweries. 🏵�⚓🚲(X75)🛜

Talbot Inn ⊘

16 High Street, SY21 7JP

🌐 11.30-11 ☎ (01938) 552181

Banks's Bitter; 1 changing beer (sourced nationally) 🅷

Grade II-listed town-centre pub with part of the frontage dating from the 16th century. This black-and-white timbered hostelry survives on wet sales and is sport focused. The right-hand bar has a jukebox and a TV showing live sport. The left is a games room. There is an extensive undercover beer garden and smoking area to the rear, with a number of benches. 🌀🏵⚓🚲⚓🚲(X75)🐾🛜

One hundred years old

I met the other day an old man, who asked me to drink. 'I am not thirsty,' said I, 'and I will not drink with you.' 'Yes, you will,' said the old man, 'for I am this day one hundred years old; and you will never again have the opportunity of drinking the health of a man on his hundredth birthday.' So I broke my word and drank. 'How have you passed your time?' said I. 'As well as I could,' said the old man, 'always enjoying a good thing when it came honestly within my reach; not forgetting to praise God for putting it there'. 'I suppose you were fond of a glass of good ale when you were young'. 'Yes,' said the old man, 'I was, and so, thank God, I am still'. And he drank off a glass of ale. **George Barrow, 1857**

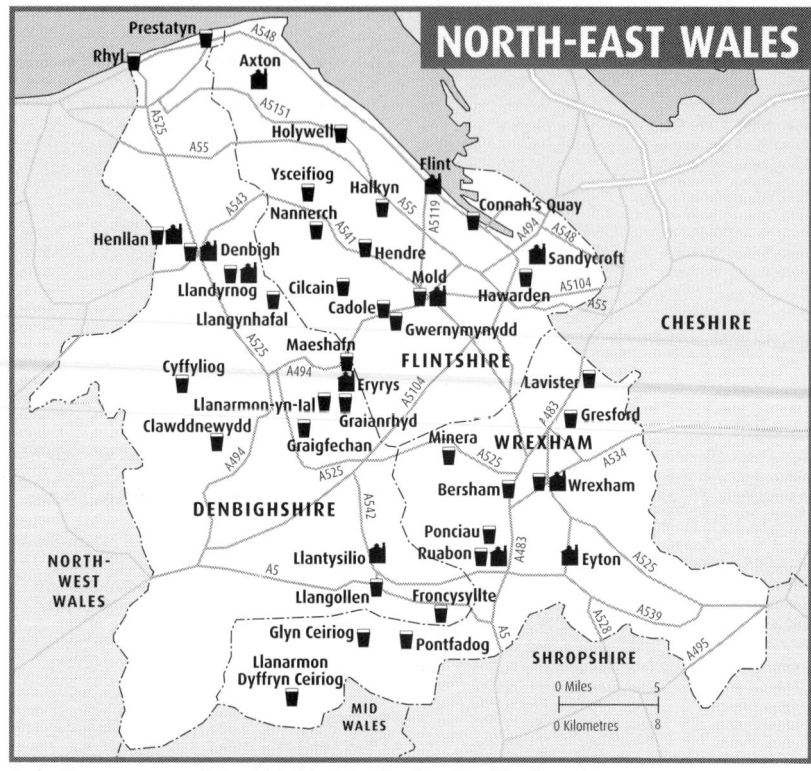

NORTH-EAST WALES

Authority areas covered: Denbighshire UA, Flintshire UA, Wrexham UA

Bersham

Black Lion ✪

Y Ddol, LL14 4HN (off B5099)
🕙 11.30-12.30am ☎ (01978) 290193
🌐 blacklioninnbersham.com
Hydes 1863, Original; 1 changing beer (sourced regionally; often Hydes) Ⓗ
This friendly and welcoming pub, known locally as the Hole in the Wall, celebrates its 20th consecutive year in the Guide. Close to the Clywedog industrial trail, Bersham Heritage Centre and Clywedog River, it is a popular refreshment stop for walkers and tourists. Three rooms are served by the wood-panelled bar, with beers from the Hydes portfolio. A beer and music festival is hosted over the August bank holiday weekend. Hot bar food is available all day. The pub may close early if quiet. ❧🏠🍴&♣🅿🚍(6)🐾🔌

Cadole

Colomendy Arms 🏆

Village Road, CH7 5LL (off A494 Mold-Ruthin road)
🕙 7-11 Mon-Wed; 6-11 Thu; 4-11 Fri; 2-11 Sat & Sun
☎ (01352) 810217
5 changing beers Ⓗ
A wonderful pub in the middle of the village, run by the same family for some 28 years and featuring in the Guide for most of that time. It has two cosy rooms warmed by real fires and festooned with local history and photographs. Five different beers come from far and wide. Be aware that the Black Sheep clock keeps dubious time. The Loggerheads Country Park is close by. Q❀♣🅿🚍🐾

Cilcain

White Horse

Ffordd Y Llan, CH7 5NN (signed from A451 Mold-Denbigh road)
🕙 12-3, 6-11; 12-11 Sat; 12-10.30 Sun ☎ (01352) 740142
Banks's Bitter; 1 changing beer (sourced nationally; often Marston's) Ⓗ
Picturesque country village pub that has been a regular in the Guide for over 20 years. It has a traditional layout with a quarry-tiled public bar featuring a set of antique beer engines and a warm, cosy lounge. Situated beside the Clwydian Range, the pub caters for visitors to the nearby Moel Famau and Offa's Dyke. Q❧🏠🍴&♣🅿🚍(14C)🐾

REAL ALE BREWERIES

Axiom Wrexham
Axton Axton
Big Hand Wrexham
Buzzard Llandyrnog
Denbigh (Bragdy Dinbych) Denbigh
Deva Craft Sandycroft
Erddig 🍺 Wrexham
Facer's Flint
Hafod Mold
Heavy Industry Henllan
Iâl Eryrys
Llangollen 🍺 Llantysilio
McGivern 🍺 Ruabon
New Plassey Eyton
Sandstone Wrexham

Clawddnewydd

Glan Llŷn Inn Ⓛ

Ruthin Road, LL15 2NA (on B5105)
✪ 5-11; 12-midnight Fri & Sat; 12-9 Sun ☎ (01824) 750754
🌐 clawddnewydd.org.uk
2 changing beers (sourced locally) Ⓗ
This pub is now owned and run by the community.
Dating in parts back to the 16th century, it has
been refurbished to include a lounge area with real
fire and stove, a dining room and a separate public
bar. Another extension will provide an additional
dining area and space to set up the community
shop. The Sunday carvery is popular.
Q ☎ ❀ ◖ ⅄ ♣ P ☀ ☂

Connah's Quay

Ship Inn

275 High Street, CH5 4DJ (on B5129)
✪ 3-midnight; 12.30-12.30am Sat & Sun ☎ (01244) 818916
**1 changing beer (sourced locally; often Big Hand,
Deva Craft, Heavy Industry)** Ⓗ
A cheerful, no-frills mock-Tudor-fronted free house
on the main road through the Quay. Open plan, it
has a comfortable front room with a large-screen
TV and hosts weekend karaoke/open mic nights. A
side area has more banquette seating, an upright
piano and reading material. Separate rooms cater
for darts and pool and there is a rudimentary
courtyard out back. Generally only one ale is
available, usually supplied by a local brewer.
☎ ❀ ♣ ♣ ☐ (10,10A,11) ☀

Cyffylliog

Red Lion Hotel Ⓛ

LL15 2DN (4 miles W of Ruthin, off B5105 at Llanfwrog)
✪ 5-10.30 (midnight Fri); 12-midnight Sat; 12-3 Sun; closed
Mon ☎ (01824) 710351 🌐 redlionhotel.biz
**Marston's Burton Bitter, Pedigree; 1 changing beer
(sourced locally)** Ⓗ
Family-run village inn with parts dating back to the
17th century. The focal point is the welcoming
lounge with a bar and open fire. There is a cosy
adjacent dining area and a further dining/function
room. The public bar includes a pool table and TV.
Wednesday quiz nights and Thursday curry nights
are popular. The pub also serves as the village
shop. Q ☎ ◖ ⅄ ♣ P ☀ ☂

Denbigh

Brookhouse Mill Ⓛ

Ruthin Road, LL16 4RD
✪ 12-3, 6-11.30; 12-11 Sun ☎ (01745) 813377
🌐 brookhousemill.co.uk
Conwy Welsh Pride; 2 changing beers Ⓗ
The mill was powered by the River Ystrad, and the
wheel and workings can still be seen in this plush
multi-roomed restaurant. Local breweries are
always represented in the bar. There are function
facilities, regularly used by several societies, and a
well-appointed garden alongside the river. Buses
from Denbigh take you to the door.
☎ ❀ ◖ & ⅄ P ☐ (X5,X50) ☂

Froncysyllte

Aqueduct Inn Ⓛ ✅

Holyhead Road, LL20 7PY (on A5)
✪ 12 (5 Mon-Thu winter)-11 ☎ (01691) 777118
🌐 theaqueductinn.co.uk
**3 changing beers (sourced locally; often Hafod,
Peerless, Stonehouse)** Ⓗ
Friendly and welcoming free house unmissable in
its canary yellow livery. It has a simple three-
roomed layout with a small central bar, games
room and comfortable lounge with woodburner.
The rear verandah offers panoramic views, not
least of the Llangollen Canal as it approaches the
spectacular and world-famous Pontcysyllte
Aqueduct. One Stonehouse ale is always available
plus two local guest beers. There is limited parking
to the side and additional parking down the lane.
☎ ❀ ◖ ♣ P ☐ (64) ☀ ☂

Glyn Ceiriog

Oak

High Street, LL20 7EH
✪ 6-11; 5-midnight Fri; 4-midnight Sat; 12-4 Sun; closed Mon
☎ (01691) 718810 🌐 y-dderwen.co.uk
**Stonehouse Station Bitter; 1 changing beer (often
Brains)** Ⓗ
Friendly community-run free house, committed to
providing a local focus and employment. The Oak
(Y Dderwen in Welsh) is a popular and welcoming
watering hole offering good food and two real
ales, often from local microbreweries. The small
bar serves a simple lounge area with additional
side and dining rooms alongside. Outside is a
pleasant verandah and small car park. In the
Ceiriog Valley there was once a tramway and the
original tramshed and terminus are close by.
☎ ❀ ◖ P ☐ ☀ ☂

Graianrhyd

Rose & Crown

Llanarmon Road, CH7 4QW (on B5430 off A5104)
✪ 4-11; 12-midnight Sat; 12-10.30 Sun ☎ (01824) 780727
🌐 theroseandcrownpub.co.uk
Black Sheep Best Bitter; 2 changing beers Ⓗ
Cosy, traditional and welcoming village pub,
recognised by CAMRA as having a regionally
important historic pub interior. The long bar serves
two rooms – one was the original inn and the other
was converted in the 1960s from the former living
quarters. Guest beers are usually from local
breweries – the many badges behind and above
the bar testify to the variety. Popular with locals
and walkers. Q ☎ ❀ ◖ ⅄ ♣ P ☐ (2) ☀

Graigfechan

Three Pigeons Inn

LL15 2EU (on B5429 about 3 miles from Ruthin)
✪ 5-10.30 Tue; 12-3, 5-11 Wed-Fri; 12-11 Sat; 12-10 Sun;
closed Mon ☎ (01824) 703178 🌐 threepigeonsinn.co.uk
Sharp's Doom Bar; 3 changing beers Ⓗ
Fine old drovers' inn with parts originating from
the 12th century. Original features and open log
fires have been retained, the interior tastefully
decorated throughout. There is an extensive
lounge area with a sports room to one side and a
large dining area to the other. Cellars are ideal for
keeping the cask ale that is still, on occasion,
served direct in jugs. An outdoor area to the rear
has great views over the Vale of Clwyd. Regular
live music and other special events are hosted. A
campsite is adjacent.
☎ ❀ ⌂ ◖ ⅄ ♣ P ☐ (76) ☀ ☂

Gresford

Pant-yr-Ochain ⓛ
Old Wrexham Road, LL12 8TY (off A5156, E from A483 follow signs to The Flash)
✪ 11.30-11; 11.30-10.30 Sun ☎ (01978) 853525
⊕ pantyrochain-gresford.co.uk
Purple Moose Cwrw Eryri/Snowdonia Ale; Stonehouse Off the Rails; Timothy Taylor Landlord; Weetwood Eastgate Ale; house beer (by Phoenix); 3 changing beers (sourced locally) Ⓗ
Lovingly restored 16th-century dower house which retains many historic features and sits beside a small lake within extensive gardens. The central room, dominated by a large double-fronted bar, leads to a variety of seating areas including a garden room, a small snug behind the period inglenook fireplace, and the patio and lawn outside. Hugely popular with diners, food is served all day. Five regular beers are supplemented by three guests, often local, and draught cider is usually available. Q❀❁➊➋❸❹❺❻P❼❽ 🤎

Gwernymynydd

Owain Glyndwr
Glyndwr Road, CH7 5LP (signed 1 mile S of Gwernymynydd off A494)
✪ 5-11; 12-10 Sun ☎ (01352) 752913
Thwaites Wainwright; 1 changing beer Ⓗ
A traditional single-room country pub. A real fire adds to the warm welcome during colder months. The pub is named after the last native Welshman to hold the title Prince of Wales after he led a revolt against English rule in the late-14th/early-15th centuries. The pub's position gives a lovely panoramic view of the surrounding area. The changing guest beer is often from a local brewery such as Hafod. Parking space is limited at busy times. ❀❁➊❸❹❺P 🤎

Halkyn

Blue Bell Inn ⓛ ✔
Rhosesmor Road, CH8 8DL (on B5123)
✪ 3 (5 Wed)-11; 5-midnight Fri; 12-midnight Sat; 12-11 Sun; closed Tue ☎ (01352) 780309 ⊕ bluebell.uk.eu.org
House beer (by Facer's); 2 changing beers (sourced locally) Ⓗ
Situated on Halkyn mountain, the Blue Bell is an excellent community pub with weekly events including free guided walks, conversational Welsh classes and trad jazz on Sunday afternoons. In the bar there is a much-needed post office for the village. There are usually four beers – two house ales from local brewery Facer's (Blue Bell Bitter and Dark Blue Porter) plus two from other local producers. Ciders feature strongly, with three or four regularly available. Local CAMRA Pub of the Year 2015. Q❀❁❸❹❺P❼❽ 🤎

Hawarden

Glynne Arms ⓛ
3 Glynne Way, CH5 3NS
✪ 11-11 (midnight Fri & Sat) ☎ (01244) 569988
⊕ theglynnearms.co.uk
Facer's This Splendid Ale; 3 changing beers (sourced locally; often Big Hand, Facer's, Heavy Industry) Ⓗ
Tastefully restored 200 year-old village-centre pub and eatery. The interior comprises a simply furnished bar area with semicircular counter and wooden furniture, with separate dining areas and an upstairs function room. The pub has strong links to the famous 19th-century politician and Hawarden resident William Gladstone, whose library is in the village. Four mainly locally sourced real ales are available, and the food menu includes local produce from the nearby Hawarden Estate Farm Shop which also sells bottled beers. ❀❁➊➋❸❹❺❻P (4,11) 🤎

Hendre

Y Dderwen (Oak) ⓛ
Denbigh Road, CH7 5QE (on A541)
✪ 7-midnight (1am Fri; 2am Sat) ☎ (01352) 741466
2 changing beers Ⓗ
A roadside pub with a central bar serving two rooms, both with ceilings adorned with impressive collections of pottery. Up to four cask ales are available from north Wales microbreweries including Hafod, Great Orme and Cwrw Llŷn. This 300 year-old pub has a strong community focus, hosting a range of social activities including Welsh singing. It is popular with walkers and visitors to the nearby Clwydian hills. Q❀❁❸❹P (14) 🤎

Henllan

Llindir Inn ⓛ
Llindir Street, LL16 5BH
✪ 12-3 (not Mon-Wed), 5-11; 12-midnight Fri & Sat; 12-11 Sun ☎ (01745) 812188
Heavy Industry Electric Mountain; 1 changing beer (often Heavy Industry Brewing) Ⓗ
Thirteenth-century Grade II-listed rambling thatched inn. On entry you are welcomed by a long bar room with an inglenook fireplace and a comfortable TV lounge offset. Three steps take you up to another bar and a further three steps to a pleasant restaurant. The interior retains its character with old beams, tiled floors, copper and brassware. This is the home of Heavy Industry Brewing situated close by and it serves two of the brewery's cask and one keg beer. Q❀❁➊➋❺P (6) 🤎

Holywell

Market Cross ✔
9-11 High Street, CH8 7LA (on main walkway)
✪ 8am-midnight (1am Fri & Sat) ☎ (01352) 717800
Greene King Abbot; Ruddles Best Bitter; 3 changing beers Ⓗ
Converted in 2011 from a large retail outlet, this small Wetherspoon pub is named after the obelisk of the same name that stood outside. There are many pictures on the walls remembering Holywell and the Greenfield Valley in times gone by. The bar, warmed by a log-burning fire, offers a choice of seating from stools to sofas. Q❀➊❹❻ (X11,11) 🤎

Old Wine Vaults ⓛ
Cross Street, CH8 7LP (at jct of High St & Cross St)
✪ 10-midnight (2am Fri & Sat) ☎ (01352) 714801
Sharp's Doom Bar; 3 changing beers (sourced locally; often Buzzard, Facer's, Heavy Industry) Ⓗ
A town pub with a large open-plan area and two small rooms served by a single bar. There are several TV screens showing sport, with another screen in the smoking area. Three changing local

beers are available. The pub is close to St Winefride's Well, a shrine of unbroken pilgrimage since the 12th century and one of the Seven Wonders of Wales. When local lead mines were still in operation the pub was also the pay office – the safes remain in the bar. ❀♿🖾(X11,11A)❀🦮 🛜

Lavister

Nag's Head
Chester Road, LL12 0DN
❀ 12-11 ☎ (01244) 571034 ⊕ nagsheadlavister.com
Salopian Shropshire Gold; Timothy Taylor Landlord; Wye Valley HPA; 1 changing beer (sourced nationally) Ⓗ
Pleasantly furnished roadside pub with a central bar serving three lounge areas (one set for dining). There are some additional interesting little seating areas and a larger rear dining space. Three regular cask beers plus a changing guest from the Enterprise list are available. A fenced-off patio area to the side offers plenty of outside seating. Parking is fairly limited. The pub claims to be one of the first places where CAMRA members were signed up. 🌄❀🕦♿🅿🖾🦮 🛜

Llanarmon Dyffryn Ceiriog

Hand at Llanarmon
LL20 7LD (end of B4500 from Chirk)
❀ 11-11.30 (1am Fri & Sat); 12-11.30 Sun ☎ (01691) 600666
⊕ thehandhotel.co.uk
2 changing beers (sourced regionally; often Big Hand, Weetwood) Ⓗ
Easily identified by the large wooden statue of a hand outside, this family-run free house sits at the head of the delightful Ceiriog Valley. The cosy bar has seating by a large fire, with a games room and restaurant to the rear. Two real ales are offered, usually one from Weetwood and one from a local brewery. Both food and accommodation are of a high standard – diners are advised to book at busy times. Tourists, walkers, cyclists and dogs are all welcome. Q🌄❀🛏🕦♿🛫🅿🖾(60,64,65)🦮 🛜

Llanarmon-yn-Ial

Raven Inn Ⓛ
Ffordd-Rhew-Ial, CH7 4QE (signed 500yds W of B5430)
❀ 5-10.30 (11 Fri); 12-11 Sat; 12-9 Sun; closed Mon
☎ (01824) 780833 ⊕ raveninn.co.uk
3 changing beers (sourced locally) Ⓗ
Community-run by volunteers since 2009, this delightful old pub goes from strength to strength, with profits used to benefit the community. The bar serves two discrete carpeted areas and a tiled area to one side. The three guest beers are from local breweries, usually including one from sister enterprise, Cwrw Ial Brewery. Excellent locally sourced home-cooked food is served Thursday to Sunday. Three self-catering bedrooms are available. Q🌄❀🛏🕦♿🍴🛫🅿🖾(2)🦮 🛜

Llandyrnog

Kinmel Arms Ⓛ
LL16 4HN
❀ 12-3, 5-11 (9.30 Mon & Tue); 12-midnight Sat; 12-6 Sun
☎ (01824) 790291 ⊕ kinmelarms.com
Thwaites Original, Lancaster Bomber; 2 changing beers Ⓗ

Friendly traditional pub handy for Offa's Dyke path and Moel Arthur iron-age fort. The front bar area features a large woodburner while there are barrel ends from the long-defunct Chester Northgate Brewery displayed to the rear. A large separate dining room is to the right. The guest beers are usually from the local Buzzard and Heavy Industry microbreweries. Q🌄❀🕦♿🛫🅿🖾(76)🦮 🛜

Llangollen

Chainbridge Hotel Ⓛ
Berwyn, LL20 8BS (off B5103)
❀ 11-11; 11-10.30 Sun ☎ (01978) 860215
⊕ chainbridgehotel.com
2 changing beers (sourced locally; often Purple Moose, Stonehouse) Ⓗ
Situated in a picturesque spot directly between the Llangollen Canal and the River Dee, this relaxed hotel has excellent views of the river, the surrounding wooded hills and the preserved Llangollen Heritage Railway. It can be reached by bus or steam train to Berwyn and then across the restored pedestrian chainbridge. It is also a pleasant, half-hour stroll along the canal towpath from the centre of Llangollen. Ales are typically from Stonehouse and Purple Moose breweries. Q🌄❀🛏🕦🛖🚆🅿🖾(T3)🦮 🛜

Ponsonby Arms Ⓛ
Mill Street, LL20 8RY (near steam railway)
❀ 12-midnight ☎ (01978) 447985 ⊕ ponsonbyarms.com
10 changing beers (sourced nationally; often Bank Top, Salopian, Ulverston) Ⓗ
Just east of the north end of the bridge, this welcoming independent free house is run by the team from the nearby Sun Inn. Outside is an extensive beer garden overlooking the river. Up to 10 beers and two ciders are available, with Ulverston and Salopian regularly represented. There is a cask ale promotion every Friday 6-7pm. Quiz night is Tuesday. Opening time can be later in winter. A free ticket for the adjacent council car park can be obtained at the bar. Q🌄❀🛖🚆🍂🛫🅿🖾(5,T3)🦮 🛜

Sun Inn Ⓛ
49 Regent Street, LL20 8HN (400yds E of town centre on A5)
❀ 5-2am (3am Fri); 12-3am Sat; 12-2am Sun summer; 7-2am (3am Fri & Sat) winter ☎ (01978) 860079
5 changing beers (often Bollington, Ulverston) Ⓗ
A lively free house across the River Dee from its sister pub, the Ponsonby Arms. The stone-flagged bar room has two open fires and a games area with pool and table football. A quieter back room can be reached via the seating area outside. Wednesday to Saturday evenings feature live music. Five changing ales, often including Bollington and Ulverston, plus a changing cider, are available. Cask ale promotions are offered at various times Friday to Sunday. ❀🛖🚆🍂🛫🖾(5,T3)🦮 🛜

Llangynhafal

Golden Lion Inn
LL16 4LN (at village crossroads)
❀ 6 (4 Fri & Sat)-11; 12-10.30 Sun; closed Mon
☎ (01824) 790451 ⊕ thegoldenlioninn.com
Thwaites Original; 1 changing beer (sourced locally; often Buzzard) Ⓗ

Traditional and welcoming 18th-century village inn at the foothills of the Clwydian Hills. The bar serves two distinct areas – the bar room with a pool table, and the lounge, which leads down to a dining area. The landlord has been at the helm for over 13 years and takes particular pride in his beers and whiskies. There is a campsite to the rear. A regular in the Bus Route 76 Real Ale Festival.
Q ☺ ⌂ ♪ ⅄ ♣ ♠ P ❑ (76) ❀ 📶

Maeshafn

Miners Arms
Village Road, CH7 5LR (off A494 in village centre)
☼ 12-3 (not Mon & Tue), 6-11.30; 12-11.30 Sat & Sun
☎ (01352) 810464 ⊕ miners-arms-maeshafn.co.uk
Theakston Best Bitter; 2 changing beers (sourced locally) ⊞
Built in the 1820s as part of the development of lead mining in the area, the pub is now popular with hikers visiting local nature reserves. The central bar area has a large wood-burning stove and there is a side room which can accommodate groups. A pleasant area outside at the front of the pub is used for occasional beer and music festivals. The food menu includes daily specials and 'miners mess tin' meals for simpler tastes.
☺ ❀ ⅅ ♣ P ❑ (2) ❀ 📶

Minera

Tyn-Y-Capel Ⓛ
Church Road, LL11 3DA
☼ 5-11; 3-midnight Fri; 12-midnight Sat; 12-10.30 Sun
☎ (01978) 269347 ⊕ tyn-y-capel.com
House beer (by Facer's); 3 changing beers (sourced locally; often Cwrw Llŷn, Heavy Industry) ⊞
Former coaching house run by the local community and staffed mainly by volunteers. Outside, the impressive terrace affords panoramic views of Esclusham Mountain and the surrounding area. The house beer, The Cat in the Capel, is brewed by Facer's and guest ales are usually from Welsh microbreweries such as Big Hand or Heavy Industry. Food is popular and available every day. Opening times may be earlier in summer.
Q ☺ ❀ ⅅ ⅄ ♣ P ❑ ❀ 📶

Mold

Glasfryn Ⓛ
Raikes Lane, CH7 6LR (off A5119 ½ mile N of Mold)
☼ 11-11; 11-10.30 Sun ☎ (01352) 750500
⊕ glasfryn-mold.co.uk
Facer's Flintshire Bitter; Purple Moose Cwrw Eryri/ Snowdonia Ale; house beer (by Brunning & Price); 3 changing beers ⊞
Near Theatre Clwyd and set in its own grounds, this large upmarket pub and restaurant was once the residence for circuit judges attending the nearby court. A total of 12 handpumps supply national and local beers including the Brunning & Price house beer from Phoenix. Food is served all day in three dining areas. The walls are covered with many interesting and unusual pictures. Extensive views over the surrounding countryside from the garden make this a popular venue in summer.
Q ☺ ❀ ⅅ ⅃ P ❑ (28,X44) ❀ 📶

Gold Cape ✔
8-8A Wrexham Street, CH7 1ES (next to Market Square crossroads)

☼ 8am-midnight (1am Fri & Sat) ☎ (01352) 705920
Greene King Abbot; Ruddles Best Bitter; Sharp's Doom Bar; 8 changing beers ⊞
Situated in this historic market town, the Gold Cape is named after a 4,000-year-old peytrel found nearby in 1831 – an impression of the ceremonial cape stands in the entrance to the pub. The walls display pictures of Mold's past, including local poet Daniel Owen. The pub takes part in a twice-yearly bus-based beer festival involving up to 10 pubs in the area. Q ☺ ⅅ ⅄ ♠ ❑ 📶

Nannerch

Cross Foxes Ⓛ
Village Road, CH7 5RD
☼ 6-11; 12-10.30 Sun ☎ (01352) 741464 ⊕ nannerch.com/ cf.html
Buzzard Pale of Clwyd; 2 changing beers ⊞
Set in a charming village close to the church, the Cross Foxes was built by the 18th-century Williams family of Penbedw Estate. It was at one time also a butcher's – the hooks still remain over the bar. The interior has altered very little and divides into four areas – the bar with a large fireplace, where dogs are allowed, a reception bar, lounge and function room. The regular beer is from local brewery Buzzard. Tuesday is curry-and-a-pint night.
Q ☺ ⅅ ⅄ ♣ P ❑ (14) ❀ 📶

Ponciau

Colliers Arms
Chapel Street, LL14 1SE (off B5426)
☼ 7 (4 Fri)-11; 1-11 Sat; 1-10.30 Sun
Facer's Flintshire Bitter; Salopian Oracle; 2 changing beers (sourced regionally; often Deva Craft, Tweed) ⊞
Cherish this spotless, welcoming, family-run free house on a narrow street of terraced housing. The slate-floored front room and snug have banquette and stool seating around cast-iron tables, while a corridor leads to a sofa-laden pool room and lawn with decking. Guest beers, generally from northern micros, are of sensible strength.
☺ ❀ & ♣ ❑ (3,3E) ❀ 📶

Pontfadog

Swan Inn
Llanarmon Road, LL20 7AR (on B4500 next to post office)
☼ 4.30-11; 12-3, 6-11 Sat; 12-3, 7.30-10.30 Sun
☎ (01691) 718273 ⊕ theswaninnpontfadog.co.uk
1 changing beer (sourced nationally; often Conwy, Felinfoel) ⊞
Traditional free house in the scenic Ceiriog valley. The cosy red-tiled bar features a central fireplace, which separates the TV and darts area from the servery. One or two real ales are on the bar, depending upon trade. Food is served in the adjacent Cygnet Restaurant dining room. Five miles from Chirk station, the owners can arrange a taxi. Opening times can vary so please ring to check before visiting. The waiting room for the long-closed tramway is a few doors away.
☺ ⌂ ❀ ⅅ & ♣ P ❑ (64,65) ❀ 📶

Prestatyn

Archies Ⓛ
151 High Street, LL19 9AS

🕔 12-midnight; 12-11 Sun; closed Mon ☎ (01745) 855657
⊕ archiesbar.co.uk
Facer's Flintshire Bitter; 3 changing beers Ⓗ
This modern, family-run pub, situated at the southern end of the High Street, has one room with wall-to-wall TV and a pull-down screen for sports fans. The regular beer is from Facer's Brewery and other beers are often local – one may be from Axton Brewery in which the landlord has an interest. A wide range of traditional British food is available. At the entrance is a decking area suitable for outside drinking. The northern end of Offa's Dyke is nearby. ⬤◑⬤⬤⬤⬤(11,35,36)✧

Halcyon Quest Hotel Ⓛ

17 Gronant Road, LL19 9DT (on A547 just E of town centre)
🕔 3-11 (midnight Fri); 12-midnight Sat; 12-11 Sun
☎ (01745) 852442 ⊕ halcyonquest-hotel.com
Facer's Flintshire Bitter; 3 changing beers (sourced locally) Ⓗ
Known locally as HQ, the Halcyon Quest is located on the southern edge of the town, just off the High Street. It has just one room, packed with sporting memorabilia, including a rowing boat suspended from the ceiling. The garden at the rear, for sunny days, has a covered area. The beer is from local brewery Facer's, backed up by three changing ales. Accommodation is available in nine rooms.
⬤⬤⬤⬤⬤⬤⬤⬤P⬤(35,36)

Rhyl

Cob & Pen

143 High Street, LL18 1UF (close to bus and rail station)
🕔 11-11 (midnight Fri & Sat); 12-11 Sun ☎ (01745) 350446
Banks's Mild; Marston's Burton Bitter, Pedigree; 2 changing beers Ⓗ
Respected and welcoming pub with a central bar and a number of themed seating areas, all decorated imaginatively in recognition of the local heritage. Televised sports events are shown on several large screens. A weekly acoustic night is a popular attraction, as are darts, pool and dominoes. This is one of the few local pubs serving cask-conditioned mild. ⬤⬤◑⬤⬤⬤⬤✧

Ruabon

Bridge End Inn Ⓛ

5 Bridge Street, LL14 6DA
🕔 5 (4 Fri)-11; 12-11 Sat & Sun ☎ (01978) 810881
⊕ mcgivernales.co.uk
8 changing beers (sourced nationally; often Ossett, Rat, Salopian) Ⓗ
Friendly former coaching inn close to the station. A winner of numerous awards since being taken over and completely revitalised by the McGivern family in 2009, including the ultimate accolade of CAMRA National Pub of the Year in 2011. Eight changing cask ales are served, at least one from the on-site McGivern Brewery. Real cider is also available. Families and well-behaved dogs are welcome in the lounge. A hugely popular beer festival is held over the August bank holiday weekend.
Q⬤⬤⬤⬤⬤⬤P⬤⬤⬤✧

Wrexham

Acton Park ✪

Chester Road, LL11 2SN (on A5152, ¾ mile N of town centre)

🕔 11.30-midnight (11 Mon & Tue); 11.30-11 Sun
☎ (01978) 314336
Brains Bitter; Thwaites Wainwright; changing beers (often Purity, Sharp's, Timothy Taylor) Ⓗ
Large open-plan estate pub, well furnished with tables and chairs, with a cosy family dining area with soft seating located towards the rear. A U-shaped bar serves all areas and there are a couple of real fires to keep you warm on winter evenings. Two permanent beers are served alongside up to 10 guests. Real cider is available in summer. On Mondays all beers are reduced in price. There is an accessible WC on the ground floor.
⬤⬤◑⬤P⬤(1)✧

Elihu Yale ✪

44-46 Regent Street, LL11 1RR
🕔 8am-midnight (1am Fri & Sat) ☎ (01978) 366646
Greene King Abbot; Ruddles Best Bitter; Sharp's Doom Bar; 6 changing beers (sourced nationally) Ⓗ
Conveniently located for bus and rail stations, this was formerly the Majestic Cinema. The large room has been divided into discrete areas, including a quieter space near the front. As well as the three regular ales there are usually six guests, typically including one from north Wales, and real cider also features. The standard Wetherspoon food menu is offered with the addition of Welsh dishes. Quiz night is Wednesday, poker night Sunday.
Q⬤◑⬤⬤(Central/General)⬤⬤✧

Royal Oak

35 High Street, LL13 8HY
🕔 12-midnight ☎ (01978) 358547 ⊕ joulesbrewery.co.uk
Joule's Blonde, Pale Ale, Slumbering Monk; 2 changing beers (sourced locally; often Brimstage, Offbeat, Salopian) Ⓗ
Grade II-listed building with a long, narrow interior in traditional Joule's style, with plenty of wood panelling and etched brewery mirrors. The chimney breast above the fireplace displays the head of an eland antelope. Three regular Joule's ales are complemented by seasonal and guest beers, typically from breweries within a 10-mile radius such as Axiom. Real cider is also on handpump. No food is served but you are welcome to bring your own. Darts and traditional board games are available. The rooftop garden is open April to September.
Q⬤⬤⬤(Central/General)⬤⬤⬤⬤✧

Ysceifiog

Fox ★ Ⓛ

Ysceifiog Village Road, CH8 8NJ (signed from B5121)
🕔 4 (1 Sat)-11; 1-10.30 Sun ☎ (01352) 720241
⊕ foxinnysceifiog.co.uk
Brimstage Trappers Hat Bitter; 2 changing beers (often Great Orme, Hafod) Ⓗ
Built around 1730, the Fox is well-worth seeking out and a warm welcome awaits. The interior comprises four small rooms, two for dining. The bar has a sliding door to the public bar that takes you back to the 1930s. A choice of four beers is offered. Identified by CAMRA as having a nationally important historic pub interior, this is a rare classic.
Q⬤⬤◑⬤⬤⬤P✧

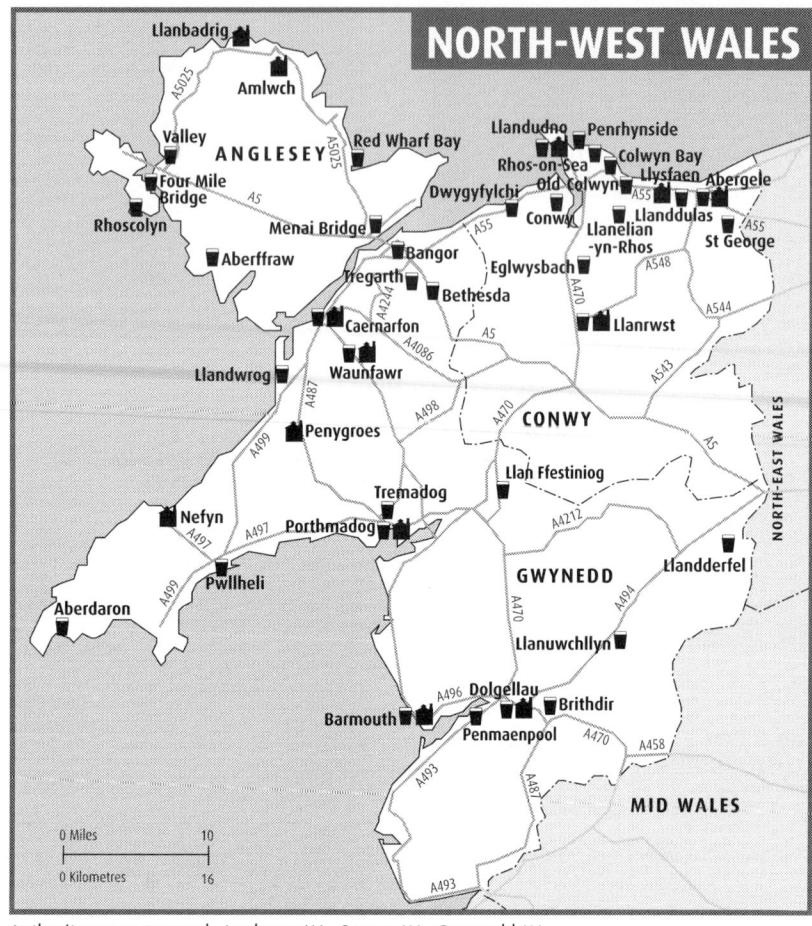

NORTH-WEST WALES

Authority areas covered: Anglesey UA, Conwy UA, Gwynedd UA

Aberdaron

Ty Newydd
LL53 8BE
☼ 11-midnight; 11-10.30 Sun ☎ (01758) 760207
⊕ gwesty-tynewydd.co.uk
Cwrw Llŷn Brenin Enlli; Purple Moose Calon Lan Ⓗ
This hotel is situated at the centre of a picturesque and historic village at the end of the Llŷn Peninsula. Beers are from two local breweries. Freshly caught Bardsey lobster and crab are on the menu, as well as afternoon teas. The Wales coastal footpath passes through the village. Eleven en-suite bedrooms offer stunning sea views. Bus services run from Pwllheli. Q ☼ ⇔ ◑ ▲ ⊟ ⟨

Aberffraw

Crown
Bodorgan Square, LL63 5BX
☼ 12-11; 12-8 Sun; closed Mon & Tue ☎ (01407) 840222
2 changing beers (sourced locally) Ⓗ
Traditional coastal village pub which has benefited from a complete refurbishment. Located in the village square, near the bus stop and post office/shop, it is popular with locals and visitors walking the Anglesey coastal path. The interior comprises a welcoming, cosy lounge bar, separate games room

and a good-sized dining room, with access to the secluded garden area. There are plenty of tables, and secure bicycle parking. Q ☼ ◑ ◐ ⊟ (25,42) ⟨

Abergele

Castle ⦸
67 Water Street, LL22 7SN
☼ 12-midnight ☎ (01745) 823322
Lees Bitter, John Willie's; 1 changing beer (often Lees) Ⓗ

REAL ALE BREWERIES

Bwthyn Llanbadrig
Cader Dolgellau
Conwy Llysfaen
Coppertown Amlwch (NEW)
Great Orme Llandudno
Llŷn Nefyn
Lleu Penygroes
Myrddins 🍺 Barmouth (NEW)
Nant Llanrwst
North Wales Abergele
Old Market Caernarfon
Purple Moose Porthmadog
Snowdonia 🍺 Waunfawr

Large multi-room former Bass pub just off the town centre, built in the 1850s, serving the north-east of the town and acquired by Lees in 2007. It reopened in 2015 following a short closure for an extensive internal refurbishment. The licensees pride themselves on promoting and serving quality real ale. Photographs of old Abergele adorn the walls in the snug/bar area, with two dartboards and a pool table in the games room. Q❄♣🖵(12)🌸🛜

Bangor

Patricks
59 Holyhead Road, LL57 2HE
🕓 11-2am (2.30am Wed & Thu; 3am Fri & Sat)
☎ (01248) 353062 ⊕ patricksbar.com
3 changing beers (sourced regionally) Ⓗ
Situated in upper Bangor, this lively Irish-themed bar is popular with both the locals and students of Bangor University. Numerous TVs display sporting events. There are usually two locally sourced ales and one regional beer on the bar. Note the late opening hours for sport and late-night drinking. On the bus route towards the Menai Straits and near the railway station. ➤🖵

Barmouth

Royal Hotel
LL42 1AB
🕓 12-11 (midnight Sat) ☎ (01341) 280455
4 changing beers Ⓗ
The pub is located beneath the main hotel with access from the main road. The hotel has recently had a major refurbishment including the kitchens. The pub is on two levels, with the main bar next to the entrance, and the lower level primarily for playing pool. There is a beer garden to the rear. Beers are usually from Welsh breweries but occasionally come from just over the border. ❄🅰➤♣🖵🌸

Bethesda

Douglas Arms Hotel ★
High Street, LL57 3AY
🕓 6-11; 3.30-midnight Sat; 1-3, 7-11 Sun ☎ (01248) 600219
Marston's Burton Bitter, Pedigree; 2 changing beers Ⓗ
Built in 1820, this was an important coaching inn on the historic Telford post route from London to Holyhead. The Grade II-listed building is recognised by CAMRA as having a nationally important historic pub interior. The four rooms have not changed since the 1930s and include a snug, lounges and a taproom with a full-size snooker table. Bethesda is convenient for buses to the Ogwen Valley and the surrounding mountains. Q❄🚌♣🍴🖵

Sior
35-37 Carneddi Road, LL57 3SE
🕓 7-midnight; 5-1am Fri; 1-1am Sat; 1-midnight Sun
☎ (01248) 600072
4 changing beers (sourced locally) Ⓗ
A friendly locals' pub in the village of Carneddi just outside Bethesda. A few minutes' drive from the A5, there is plenty of parking nearby. Free of tie, the pub offers a variety of ales from the Marston's range as well as locally brewed beers. There are views across the valley to the local slate quarry, which has the longest zip wire in Britain. Q🖵🌸

Brithdir

Cross Foxes
LL40 2SG (jct of A470 and A487)
🕓 11-midnight ☎ (01341) 421001
Cwrw Cader Gold; 2 changing beers Ⓖ
A refurbished Grade II-listed building situated near the foot of Cader Idris mountain and four miles from the historic town of Dolgellau. Beers are usually from Cader Ales and other local microbreweries. Breakfast is served from 8am and meals are available all day until 9pm. Dogs are welcome in the bar area. The hotel has Welsh Tourist Board 5-star grading. Bus services T2 pass by, but please check times.
Q❄🌸🍴🅰P🖵(T2)🌸🛜

Caernarfon

Black Boy Inn ❷
Northgate Street, LL55 1RW (near marina)
🕓 11-11; 11-11.30 Fri & Sat; 12-10.30 Sun
☎ (01286) 673604
Cwrw Llŷn Brenin Enlli; Draught Bass; 4 changing beers (sourced locally) Ⓗ
The pub is set within the town walls between the marina and castle. This historic town, a World Heritage Site, is well-worth a visit, ending with a welcome pint at the Black Boy. The public bar and small lounge are warmed by roaring fires. Good-value food is served and the guest beer usually comes from Purple Moose. There is a drinking area outside on the traffic-free street. A previous local CAMRA award winner. Q🍴🛏♿➤(WHR)♣🍴🖵

Tafarn Y Porth ❷
5-9 Eastgate Street, LL55 1AG (just off Bangor Rd near Barclays Bank)
🕓 9am-midnight ☎ (01268) 662920
Big Bog Standard Bitter; Greene King Abbot; Ruddles Best Bitter; 2 changing beers Ⓗ
Friendly, welcoming Wetherspoon pub opposite the town walls and close to the castle. It has a large open-plan interior and a spacious partly covered courtyard outside with plenty of seating. The real ale range often includes a beer from the Big Bog Brewing Company in Waunfawr, just a few miles away. The pub's location is handy for the Welsh Highland Railway, which takes you to the heart of Snowdonia. Q❄🍴🅰➤(WHR)♣🍴🖵

Colwyn Bay

Pen-y-Bryn Ⓛ
Pen-y-Bryn Road, LL29 6DD
🕓 11-11; 12-10.30 Sun ☎ (01492) 533360
⊕ penybryn-colwynbay.co.uk
Purple Moose Cwrw Eryri/Snowdonia Ale; house beer (by Phoenix); 4 changing beers (sourced regionally) Ⓗ
Open-plan pub with large bookcases, old furniture and real fires during the winter. The walls are decorated with photographs and memorabilia from the local area. Panoramic views of the Bay of Colwyn and the Great Orme can be admired from the terrace and garden. Food is served throughout the day - the menu is updated daily on the website. A boardroom-style function room, for get-togethers and meetings, has been created in the cellar, opening onto the garden.
Q🌸🍴♿P🖵(24)🛜

Picture House 🅛 ✅

24-26 Prince's Drive, LL29 8LA

⚙ 8am-midnight (1am Fri & Sat) ☎ (01492) 535286

Greene King Abbot; Ruddles Best Bitter; 4 changing beers (sourced regionally) Ⓗ

A Wetherspoon pub in the former Princess Cinema, now a Grade II-listed building, next to Colwyn Bay railway station. Theatre memorabilia adorn the walls of the three-level building, which also has an upper balcony. There are eight handpumps featuring at least one beer from a local brewery, such as Big Bog, Conwy, Great Orme or Purple Moose, plus guest ciders. Local beer festivals and Meet the Brewer promotions, in addition to Wetherspoon's national events, are held throughout the year. Q◐&≠●🚌(12,13,14)🛜

Station 🅛

Abergele Road, LL29 8BP

⚙ 11-11 ☎ (01492) 532818 ⊕ thestationcolwynbay.co.uk

6 changing beers (sourced regionally) Ⓗ

Large town-centre pub originally built around 1870 and reopened in 2015 by the management team from the successful Albert in Llandudno, following an extensive, modern refurbishment and change of name. Food is served throughout the day. Beers are displayed on blackboards near the bar, with third-pint glasses available as well as CAMRA discounts. And with many tables overlooking the street, it is handy for a quick drink while waiting to travel home from the adjacent bus stop. ঌ◐&≠●🚌(12,13,14)🛜

Conwy

Albion Ale House ★ 🅛

Uppergate Street, LL32 8RF

⚙ 12-11 (midnight Fri & Sat) ☎ (01492) 582484

⊕ albionalehouse.weebly.com

8 changing beers (sourced regionally; often Conwy, Great Orme, Nant) Ⓗ

Multi-room pub with a nationally important historic interior superbly refurbished by the current owners. Each room retains original 1920s features and several have wonderful fireplaces. There is no music or TV, just pleasant conversation. The pub is managed by four local brewers – Conwy, Great Orme, Nant and Purple Moose – and showcases their beers as well as guests. There are two guest Welsh ciders and a good selection of wines and malt whiskies. CAMRA awards include branch and Welsh Pub of the Year. Q❀≠♣●🚌(5,19)🐾🛜

Bridge Inn/Y Bont 🅛

Rosehill Street, LL32 8LD

⚙ 12-11 (midnight Fri & Sat) ☎ (01492) 572974

⊕ bridgeinnconwy.co.uk

5 changing beers (sourced regionally; often Conwy, Great Orme, Nant) Ⓗ

The sister pub to the Albion Ale House, this busy, traditional corner inn is within sight of historic Conwy Castle and inside the town walls. It has an open-plan lounge with a central bar area. Local beers come from Bragdy'r Nant, Great Orme, Purple Moose and Conwy breweries, usually including a dark ale. Real Welsh cider is also on handpump. Good-quality food is available lunchtimes and evenings. Thursday is quiz night. Excellent accommodation includes Welsh breakfast. Q🛏◐≠♣●🚌(5,19)🐾🛜

Castle Hotel 🅛

High Street, LL32 8DB

⚙ 11-11; 11.30-10.30 Sun ☎ (01492) 582800

⊕ castlewales.co.uk

Conwy Clogwyn Gold, Welsh Pride; house beer (by Conwy); 2 changing beers (often Conwy) Ⓗ

An old coaching inn dating back to the 15th century, this privately owned hotel is now an upmarket meeting place. One of the partners is Graham Tinsley, head of the Welsh Culinary Team, and excellent food, made from the finest local produce, is served in the bar and restaurant. A local beer from Conwy Brewery, Dawson's Dark, is only available here. The cider is from Gwynt y Ddraig. Q❀🛏◐&≠●P🚌(5,19)🐾🛜

Dolgellau

Torrent Walk Hotel 🅛

Smithfield Street, LL40 1AA

⚙ 11-midnight ☎ (01341) 422858

Purple Moose Cwrw Eryri/Snowdonia Ale; Wychwood Hobgoblin; 3 changing beers Ⓗ

An 18th-century hotel in the narrow streets of the town centre, retaining most of its multi-roomed interior and old fireplaces, although the bar fittings date from circa 1970. Note the Coffee Room etched panel in the door from the lobby to the room on the right. A real cider is always served and up to five ales, mostly from local breweries. Dolgellau is an ideal base for walking in the Cader Idris area. 🛏◐♣●🚌

Dwygyfylchi

Gladstone 🅛 ✅

Ysgubor Wen Road, LL34 6PS

⚙ 12-11 (midnight Fri & Sat) ☎ (01492) 623231

Black Sheep Best Bitter; 3 changing beers Ⓗ

Renowned for its magnificent sea views, this pub has been nicely refurbished but retains many original features including the alcoves and traditional decor, with wood panelling and old photographs. A central bar serves both dining and drinking areas. Comfortable sofas surround a wood-burning stove, and a galleried balcony with tables and booths overlooks the bar. The restaurant offers imaginative food sourced locally. There is a function room, accommodation in six luxury rooms, and the pub has a wedding licence. ❀🛏◐&🅰≠♣P🚌(5,X5)🐾🛜

Eglwysbach

Bee Inn ✅

LL28 5UD

⚙ 12-11; 12-6 Sun; closed Mon & Tue ☎ (01492) 650291

House beer (by Marston's); 2 changing beers (sourced regionally) Ⓗ

This newly refurbished country pub is located in the heart of the Conwy Valley and offers a menu of superb locally sourced home-cooked food. Themed food nights featuring pies or pizzas are also held occasionally and good-value Sunday lunches. The one-roomed bar has a mixture of stone and wood flooring and the walls are adorned with Welsh artwork, Welsh rugby pictures and a selection of musical instruments. Friday is singalong night and open mic nights are sometimes hosted. ঌ❀◐P🚌(25)🛜

Four Mile Bridge

Anchorage Hotel

LL65 2EZ (on B4545, just past bridge to Holy Island)
🌐 11-11; 12-11 Sun ☎ (01407) 740168
⊕ the-anchorage-hotel.com
Draught Bass; Theakston XB; Timothy Taylor Landlord; 2 changing beers 🅗
Family-run hotel situated on Holy Island close to Treaddur Bay. It has a comfortable lounge bar and a large dining area serving a wide selection of meals. The hotel is near some fine sandy beaches and coastal walks. Its proximity to the A55 makes it a useful stopping off point for Holyhead Port. Hourly bus services from Bangor pass by the hotel entrance. Q ➤ 🚃 🕪 ♣ P 🖃

Llan Ffestiniog

Pengwern ✓

Church Square, LL41 4PB
🌐 7-11.30; 5-midnight Fri; 12-midnight Sat & Sun
☎ (01766) 762200 ⊕ pengwern.org.uk
Purple Moose Cwrw Eryri/Snowdonia Ale; 1 changing beer 🅗
This community-run hostelry was formerly an old drovers' inn. It has one regular beer from Purple Moose and guests from other local breweries such as Big Bog, Cwrw Llŷn and Heavy Industry. The pub holds a beer festival over the August bank holiday with around 20 beers. An ideal stop-off for walkers in the local area, and there is a bus stop right outside. Q ❀ 🚃 🕪 ⅋ P 🖃 ♣ 🛜

Llandderfel

Bryntirion Inn 🅛

LL23 7RA (on B4401 4 miles E of Bala)
🌐 11-11; 12-11 Sun ☎ (01678) 530205
⊕ bryntirioninn.co.uk
Purple Moose Cwrw Eryri/Snowdonia Ale; 1 changing beer (sourced locally; often Big Hand, Conwy) 🅗
Former hunting lodge and coaching inn overlooking the River Dee. The single bar services a number of rooms to accommodate diners and families, in addition to the cosy and comfortable bar area with a log fire. There is a small covered courtyard at the rear. The regular beer is from the Purple Moose Brewery range. A second guest beer varies from other local or national brewers. Good-value accommodation is available.
Q ➤ ❀ 🚃 🕪 ⅋ ♣ ♣ P 🖃 (T3) ♣ 🛜

Llanddulas

Valentine ✓

9 Mill Street, LL22 8ES
🌐 3-11; 12-midnight Fri & Sat; 12-11 Sun ☎ (01492) 515898
⊕ valentine-inn.co.uk
Marston's Pedigree; 2 changing beers (sourced regionally) 🅗
At the centre of a semi-rural seaside village this traditional village inn, dating from the 18th century, is built on the site of an old clay cottage. To the left is a well-furnished, comfortable lounge and straight ahead is a separate public bar with TV, both with an open fire in winter. Brewery memorabilia and many old framed photographs relating to the Valentine decorate the walls. An attractive drinking area and walled garden for warmer weather are at the rear.
Q ➤ ❀ ▲ ♣ 🖃 (12,13) ♣ 🛜

Llandudno

Albert 🅛 ✓

56 Madoc Street, LL30 2TW
🌐 11-11; 12-10.30 Sun ☎ (01492) 877188
5 changing beers (sourced regionally) 🅗
Just off the town centre and close to the railway station, this popular pub/restaurant offers five handpulled beers from local and independent breweries and a range of tasty meals throughout the day. The beers on offer are clearly displayed on blackboards above and beside the L-shaped bar, with third-pint glasses available. The decor is modern, with a range of interesting photographs and pictures on display. There is a heated and covered verandah outside at the front.
Q ➤ ❀ 🕪 ⅙ ⇄ ♠ 🛜

Cottage Loaf 🅛 ✓

Market Street, LL30 2SR
🌐 11-11 ☎ (01492) 870762 ⊕ the-cottageloaf.co.uk
Brains Rev James Original; Conwy Welsh Pride; Courage Directors; 2 changing beers (sourced regionally) 🅗
The building was previously a bakery, hence the name. The interior features stone-flagged floors, an impressive fireplace and a raised timber-floored area – much of the wood came from the Flying Foam, a schooner shipwrecked at Llandudno's West Shore. The Loaf is a popular meeting place for people of all ages, with excellent home-cooked food served all day every day. A major refurbishment and extension took place early in 2014, adding a conservatory restaurant area with an enclosed outdoor terrace.
➤ ❀ 🕪 ⇄ ♠ 🖃 (5,12) 🛜

Snowdon

11 Tudno Street, LL30 2HB
🌐 12-11 (11.30 Fri & Sat); 12-10.30 Sun ☎ (01492) 872166
⊕ the-snowdonhotel.co.uk
Draught Bass; 3 changing beers (sourced regionally) 🅗
Attractively refurbished pub just off the town centre near the tram station, with excellent multilingual bar staff. One of the oldest pubs in Llandudno, it is frequently referred to as the locals' local. Four real ales are usually available, with three thirds on offer for the price of a pint if you cannot make up your mind. The interior comprises a large main drinking area and a small side snug – look for the Snowdon mirror above the fireplace. The garden, with fine views of the Great Orme, won Llandudno in Bloom for its floral display.
❀ ♣ ♠ 🖃 (5,12) ♣

Llandwrog

Harp Inn (Ty'n Llan)

LL54 5SY
🌐 12-11; 12-10.30 Sun ☎ (01286) 831071
3 changing beers (sourced locally) 🅗
Hidden on a back road to Dinas Dinlle and Caernarfon airport, this beautiful old stone inn boasts many cosy rooms and a resident parrot called Dylan. The ever-changing beers come from smaller breweries, with one pump in use in winter and two in summer. Legend says there was a tunnel from the cellar to the church – look out for the pirate's grave in the churchyard. 🕪

Llanelian-yn-Rhos

White Lion Inn ✔
LL29 8YA
☼ 11.30-3, 6-11; 11.30-4, 5-11.30 Sat; 12-10.30 Sun; closed Mon ☎ (01492) 515807 ⊕ whitelioninn.co.uk
Marston's Burton Bitter; 2 changing beers (sourced regionally) 🅷
A regular in the Guide for more than 20 years, this 16th-century inn situated in the hills above Old Colwyn, next to St Elian's Church, offers a warm welcome. Gracing the entrance are two white stone lions, leading into the bar area with slate-flagged flooring and large comfortable chairs around the log fires. Decorative stained glass is mounted above the bar in the tiny snug. The restaurant serves delicious home-cooked food. Jazz night is Tuesday, quiz night Thursday.
Q❄🚲🕮🛇🅰♣P🚫📶

Llanrwst

Eagles Hotel 🅛
Ancaster Square, LL26 0LG
☼ 11-11; 12-11 Sun ☎ (01492) 640454
⊕ theeagleshotel.com
2 changing beers (often Nant)
This large town-centre hotel was built in the 18th century and underwent a major refurbishment in 2013. The front entrance is via the car park but there is a small doorway from Ancaster Square which leads into reception. The main bar is off to the left with a second bar beyond, and there is a large restaurant and function room. The two beers on offer are from the nearby Bragdy Nant Brewery.
Q❄🚲🕮🛇🍴⇌♣P🚫(X1,19)🐾📶

Llanuwchllyn

Eagles Inn (Tafarn Yr Eryrod) 🅛
LL23 7UB
☼ 11-11 (midnight Thu-Sat) ☎ (01678) 540278
⊕ yr-eagles.co.uk
3 changing beers (sourced locally; often Cwrw Cader, Purple Moose) 🅷
A friendly welcome awaits visitors to this little gem – an old stone-built village local opposite the church. It retains plenty of historic features including a wonderful stone floor. The bar also serves as a shop and is open most of the day, although hours may be shorter in winter. The adjacent restaurant serves highly rated locally produced food. The patio garden has good mountain views. It is a 10-minute walk to Llanuwchllyn station on the Bala Lake Railway.
🚲🕮🛇🅰⇌(Bala Lake)♣P🚫(T3)🐾📶

Menai Bridge

Anglesey Arms ✔
Mona Road, LL59 5EA (by Menai Suspension Bridge)
☼ 11-11 (midnight Thu-Sat); 12-11 Sun ☎ (01248) 712305
⊕ anglesey-arms.co.uk
Lees Manchester Pale Ale, The Governor, Bitter, John Willie's; 4 changing beers 🅷
Dating back more than 200 years, this old coaching house has been completely refurbished. Just over Telford's famous suspension bridge, it is on the main route to Holyhead and ideally situated for Snowdonia, the Llŷn Peninsula, the resorts of Anglesey and the Irish Ferries. Guest beers and seasonal ales are from the JW Lees list and local

produce is used in most meals. The large rear rooms are available for functions.
Q❄🚲🕮🛇🅰♣P🚫🐾

Liverpool Arms ✔
St George's Pier, LL59 5EY
☼ 12-2, 5-11.30; 12-11.30 Fri-Sun ☎ (01248) 712453
Facer's Flintshire Bitter; Purple Moose Cwrw Eryri/Snowdonia Ale 🅷/🅶, Ochr Tywyll y Mws/Dark Side of the Moose; 1 changing beer 🅷
Refurbished to a high standard, the Livvy has four cask ales on offer and serves good-quality home-cooked food. This nautically themed pub is frequented by locals, students in term time and the local sailing fraternity. A short walk takes you beneath the famous suspension bridge and it is close to the quay for local tourist boats. The Anglesey and Welsh Coast footpaths are nearby.
🚲🕮🛇🚫

Old Colwyn

Red Lion
385 Abergele Road, LL29 9PL
☼ 5-11; 4-midnight Fri; 12-midnight Sat; 12-11 Sun
☎ (01492) 515042
Holden's Black Country Mild; Marston's Burton Bitter; changing beers (sourced nationally) 🅷
This free house serves up to five guest ales from independent and local brewers. It has a cosy L-shaped lounge featuring a real coal fire, antique brewery mirrors and other memorabilia, and a traditional public bar with a pool table, darts and TVs. To the rear is a Victorian-style covered and heated smoking conservatory. The real ale club every Thursday offers nine beers at reduced prices. The traditional pub sign is worth a look.
Q♣🚫(12,13,14)🐾📶

Penmaenpool

George the Third Hotel
LL40 1YD
☼ 11-11 ☎ (01341) 422525 ⊕ georgethethird.co.uk
3 changing beers (sourced regionally) 🅷
The original hotel was constructed in 1650 to serve the local boat-building industry. There are two bars – the main dresser bar and the cellar bar, which is situated on the edge of the estuary and popular with hikers, dog walkers and families. The hotel has 11 en-suite rooms and a large restaurant. An ideal base for walking and touring in this beautiful area of North Wales. 🚲🕮🛇P

Penrhynside

Penrhyn Arms 🅛
Pendre Road, LL30 3BY
☼ 5 (4.30 Thu; 4 Fri; 12 Sat)-11.45; 12-11 Sun ☎ 07780 678927 ⊕ penrhynarms.com
Banks's Bitter; 4 changing beers (sourced regionally) 🅷
This welcoming local free house has up to four guest beers, concentrating on new breweries and new beers, plus a winter ale on gravity at Christmas. The spacious L-shaped bar has pool, darts and a wide-screen TV. The walls are decorated with signed photographs of famous people and numerous awards the pub has won, including local CAMRA Pub of the Year and National Cider Pub of the Year finalist four times. Thursday is cheese night. 🕮🅰♣🚫(12,14,15)🐾

Porthmadog

Australia 🏆
31-35 High Street, LL49 9LR
🕒 12-11 (midnight Fri & Sat) ☎ (01766) 51595
Conwy Welsh Pride; Great Orme Celtica; Nant Munci Nel; Purple Moose Cwrw Eryri/Snowdonia Ale; 8 changing beers (sourced regionally) 🅗
A pub since 1864, the Australia has recently been tastefully refurbished by the co-owners – Purple Moose, Great Orme, Nant and Conwy breweries. It is situated in the centre of town next to the bus stops. Two rooms are served by a long wooden bar with eight handpumps. There is a small outdoor seating area at the back. Near to the Ffestiniog and Welsh Highland Railway station. Local CAMRA Pub of the Year 2016. ⌂🔗🚆🍴🚉🐾

Spooner's Bar
Harbour Station, LL49 9NF
🕒 9am-11; 12-10.30 Sun ☎ (01766) 516032 🌐 festrail.co.uk
4 changing beers 🅗
Spooner's beer range varies, but there are always at least two ales from the local Purple Moose Brewery. Situated in the terminus of the world-famous Ffestiniog and Wesh Highland Railway, steam trains are outside the door most of the year. Food is served every lunchtime, evening meals Tuesday to Saturday, but check first out of season. A former local CAMRA Pub of the Year award winner. Q🛏🕒🍴🅰🚆(WHR)🚉

Pwllheli

Pen Cob ✅
Station Square, LL53 5HG
🕒 7am-11 ☎ (01758) 704970
Greene King Abbot; Ruddles Best Bitter; 4 changing beers 🅗
Wetherspoon pub opened in 2013 opposite the train station at the start (or end) of the scenic Cambrian Line. Formerly a Bon Marche shop, it has been tastefully refurbished and is now a light and airy venue popular with people of all ages. It gets especially busy with locals and tourists at weekends and during the holiday season. The area is popular for sailing. 🛏🕒♿🚆🚉🛜

Red Wharf Bay

Ship Inn ✅
LL75 8RJ (off A5025 between Pentraeth and Benllech)
🕒 11-11; 11-10.30 Sun ☎ (01248) 852568
🌐 shipinnredwharfbay.co.uk
Adnams Broadside; Brains SA; 2 changing beers 🅗
Red Wharf Bay was once a busy port exporting coal and fertilisers in the 18th and 19th centuries. Previously known as the Quay, the Ship enjoys an excellent reputation for its bar and restaurant, with meals served lunchtimes and evenings. It gets busy with locals and visitors in the summer. The garden has panoramic views across the bay to south-east Anglesey. The resort town of Benllech is two miles away and the coastal path passes the front door. Q🛏🕒🍴♿P

Rhos-on-Sea

Hickory's Smokehouse 🅛
9 Llandudno Road, LL28 4TR
🕒 10-midnight ☎ (01492) 550444 🌐 hickorys.co.uk/rhos-on-sea

House beer (by Weetwood); 1 changing beer (sourced locally) 🅗
Formerly known as the Ship, this authentic American smokehouse reopened in 2014 following an extensive and major refurbishment. From the bar you can enjoy the Weetwood house beer or a local real ale (often from Heavy Industry) as well as a range of US and European beers and an extensive range of unusual bourbons. There is a large car park to the rear and an attractive drinking area to one side. An indoor children's playroom is available. 🛏🕒🍴P🚉(12)🐾🛜

Rhoscolyn

White Eagle
LL65 2NJ (off B4545 signed Traeth Beach)
🕒 12-3, 6-11; 12-11 Sat; 12-10.30 Sun ☎ (01407) 860267
🌐 white-eagle.co.uk
Marston's Burton Bitter, Pedigree; Weetwood Eastgate Ale; 2 changing beers 🅗
Saved from closure by new owners, this pub has been renovated and rebuilt with an airy, brasserie-style ambience. It has a fine patio enjoying superb views over Caernarfon Bay and the Llŷn Peninsula to Bardsey Island. The nearby beach offers safe swimming with a warden on duty in the summer months. The pub is also close to the coastal footpath. Excellent food is available lunchtimes and evenings – all day during the school holidays. Q🛏🕒♿🅰♣P

St George

Kinmel Arms
LL22 9BP
🕒 12-3, 6-11 (11.30 Fri & Sat); closed Sun & Mon
☎ (01745) 832207 🌐 thekinmelarms.co.uk
Thwaites Original; 1 changing beer (sourced regionally) 🅗
A 17th-century former coaching inn on the hillside overlooking the sea. A central bar serves a large combined drinking and dining area with a real log fire in one corner and a spacious conservatory at the rear. Guest beers often come from local breweries, plus a cider from Gwynt y Ddraig. The pub has a reputation for good food, and luxury accommodation is available in four comfortable suites. The owner's art gallery and shop is on site. Q🏨🛏🕒♿🍴🐾🛜

Tregarth

Pant Yr Ardd
LL57 4PL
🕒 4 (2 Mon)-midnight; 4-1am Fri; 12-1am Sat; 12-midnight Sun ☎ (01248) 605546
2 changing beers (sourced regionally) 🅗
This pub divides on entry into two rooms either side of the bar. The walls are adorned with pictures of the village from the past. A free house, the ale is sourced mostly from local breweries, but sometimes there will be a national beer. Outside, the beer garden is adjacent to the car park over the road. The inn has been an integral part of the village community for generations and you will always receive a warm welcome here. 🛏P🚉🐾

Tremadog

Union Inn ✅
7 Market Square, LL49 9RB

✪ 12-2, 5.30-12.30am; 12-2, 5.30-11 Sun ☎ (01766) 512748
⊕ union-inn.com
Big Bog Standard Bitter; Great Orme Atlantis; Purple Moose Cwrw Eryri/Snowdonia Ale Ⓗ
Friendly village local situated in the village square, with two separate cosy bars and a restaurant at the rear. The pub has a policy of using locally sourced produce, and the ale range mainly features local beers. Children are welcome and there are board games available. Excellent food is served in the bar and restaurant. Tremadog was the birthplace of Lawrence of Arabia. Frequent bus services pass the building. Q ⧖ ❀ ◑ ♿ ▲ ⇌ ● 🍴 🚍 (1A,T2)

Valley

Valley Hotel ✅
London Road, LL65 3DU
✪ 11.30-11 ☎ (01407) 740203 ⊕ valleyanglesey.co.uk
Tetley Bitter; house beer (by Conwy); 2 changing beers Ⓗ
Owned by Anglesey Inns, the Valley Hotel is in the centre of the town. Food is available all day, with produce sourced from the surrounding area where possible, alongside local Conwy real ales. Two

ground-floor function rooms have wheelchair access, and accommodation is offered in 19 en-suite bedrooms. An ideal base for touring or walking on the island and central for stopovers to or from Holyhead Port to Ireland. ⧖ ❀ ⛺ ◑ P ❀

Waunfawr

Snowdonia Park ✅
Beddgelert Road, LL55 4AQ
✪ 11-11; 11-10.30 Sun ☎ (01286) 650409
⊕ snowdonia-park.co.uk
Snowdonia Trithro, Snowdonia Gold, Carmen Sutra, Cais, Dark and Delicious, Welsh Highland Bitter Ⓗ
Home of the Snowdonia brewery, this is a popular pub for walkers, climbers and families, with children's play areas inside and out. Meals are served all day. The pub adjoins Waunfawr station on the Welsh Highland Railway – stop off here before continuing on one of the most scenic sections of narrow-gauge railway in Britain. There is a large campsite adjacent on the riverside. Local CAMRA Pub of the Year 2014-2015.
Q ⧖ ❀ ◑ ♿ ▲ ♣ ● P 🚍 ❀ 🛜

Kinmel Arms, St George

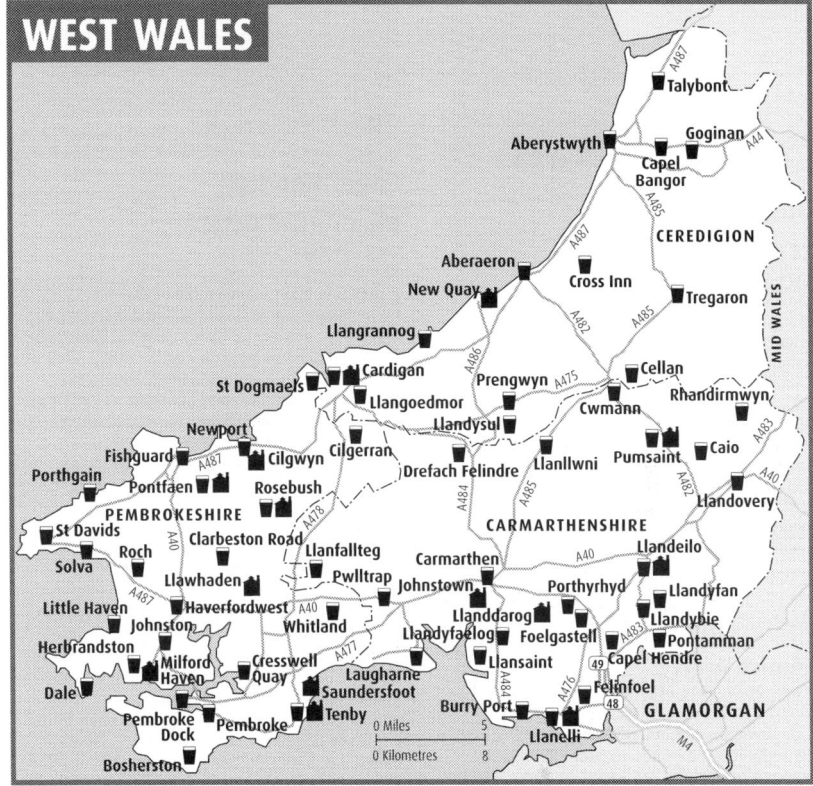

WEST WALES

Authority areas covered: Carmarthenshire UA, Ceredigion UA, Pembrokeshire UA

Aberaeron

Cadwgan Inn

10 Market Street, SA46 0AU (off A487, overlooking harbour)
⏰ 12 (5 Mon)-11; 12-midnight Fri & Sat; 12-5 Sun
☎ (01545) 570149
Hancocks HB; 2 changing beers (sourced nationally; often Bluestone (Pembrokeshire), Celt Experience, Cottage) Ⓗ
Named after the last ship to be built in this attractive Regency planned town, this old-fashioned single-bar pub offers a friendly welcome and lively conversation. It is popular for its sports coverage, mainly rugby and racing. The guest beers are chosen from a wide range of micro and regional breweries. A small pavement drinking area at the front of the building is a suntrap. The free public car park opposite fills up quickly, especially in summer. ❀▲🚌(T1,T5)♣🎵

Aberystwyth

Glengower Hotel 🍺 ✔

3 Victoria Terrace, SY23 2DH (N end of promenade)
⏰ 12-11 ☎ (01970) 626191 ⊕ glengower.co.uk
Mantle Rock Steady; Wye Valley Butty Bach; 3 changing beers (sourced regionally; often Cwrw Cader, Monty's, Purple Moose) Ⓗ
Excellent coastal views can be enjoyed from the suntrap terrace at this newly refurbished seafront hotel. Inside is a light, airy front bar, quieter dining area, and large back room with pool and electronic games. A real cider bar has five handpumps

offering ciders from Gwynt y Ddraig and regional guests. An annual beer festival and raft race is organised over the May bank holiday weekend. Tasty food is locally sourced wherever possible. The hotel closes for a fortnight over Christmas/New Year. Q🍴🐕♿🅿️🚭♣(03)♣🎵🌐

Hen Orsaf

26 Alexandra Road, SY23 1LN
⏰ 8am-midnight (1am Fri & Sat) ☎ (01970) 636080
Greene King Abbot; Ruddles Best Bitter; Sharp's Doom Bar; 6 changing beers (sourced nationally; often Bluestone (Pembrokeshire), Celt Experience, Mantle) Ⓗ
An award-winning conversion of Aberystwyth's 1924-built ex-GWR railway station, this excellent Wetherspoon pub offers up to six guest beers with either a Bluestone or a Mantle beer normally available. Ciders are from Westons and Gwynt y Ddraig. The usual Wetherspoon policies and promotions apply. Trains, buses, and taxis are all adjacent, with a train departure screen in the bar. Outdoor drinking is on the old station concourse within view of the trains. 🐕🌟🍴♿▲🚉🚌🅿️🎵🌐

Ship & Castle

1 High Street, SY23 1JG
⏰ 2-midnight (1am Fri); 12-1am Sat ☎ 07773 778785
Wye Valley HPA, Butty Bach; 3 changing beers (sourced nationally; often Oakham, Tiny Rebel, Wye Valley) Ⓗ
A real ale flagship offering microbrewery guests from the UK and Ireland. Real cider and perry are available from Gwynt y Ddraig, alongside small

amounts of excellent beer in other formats including craft keg, bottles (eg Kernel, Tiny Rebel), and canned beers. A five-pump platter of third-pint measures is available. Well-considered décor reflects the pub's name and history. Mid-week beer festivals in spring and autumn offer extended choice. The venue can be busy on rugby days, but welcoming at all times. ▲⇌♣🕭P🖵😺🛜

Bosherston

St Govans Country Inn
SA71 5DN
🕛 12-3, 6-11; 12-11 Sat & Sun ☎ (01646) 661311
🌐 stgovanscountryinn.webeden.co.uk
Evan Evans Cwrw; 3 changing beers (sourced nationally; often Adnams, Elgood's, Navigation) Ⓗ
With a population of about three hundred, the village lies a short walk from the stunning south Pembrokeshire coast and the Bosherston lily ponds which are renowned for their beauty and varied wildlife. Up to four ales are available in the summer from regional and national brewers. The pub has a comfortable interior, with exposed beams, horse brasses and a large stone fireplace with a logburner giving a cosy feel. It can get busy in the summer months. Q🛏🕭◑🕭🏪A♣P🖵😺🛜

Burry Port

Cornish Arms ♀
1 Gors Road, SA16 0EL
🕛 12-11; 12-10.30 Sun ☎ (01554) 833224
5 changing beers (sourced regionally) Ⓗ
Centrally located in this coastal town and conveniently within 100yds of the train and bus stations. The friendly pub and restaurant is popular with locals and visitors to the area. The bar offers a choice of four real ales, while the restaurant is well-known for its good quality food, specialising in fish dishes. Outside, there is a beer garden and smoking area. Q🛏😺◑▲⇌🖵🛜

Caio

Brunant Arms
Church Street, SA19 8RD (off A482 near Pumsaint)
🕛 12.30 (6 Tue)-10; 12-10 Fri; 12-4 Sun; closed Mon
☎ (01558) 650483
2 changing beers (sourced locally; often Evan Evans) Ⓗ
Family-run pub in the centre of the village near the Dolaucothi Gold Mines. Good food is served until 9pm every day. There are plenty of outdoor pursuits nearby including pony trekking and walks through a large forest. A legendary Welsh wizard is buried in the church opposite. One real ale is offered in winter, two in summer, usually supplied by Evan Evans. Q🛏🛏◑♣🕭

Capel Bangor

Tynllidiart Arms
SY23 3LR
🕛 11.30-3, 5-11; 11.30-11 Fri & Sat; 12-4 Sun; closed Mon
☎ (01970) 880248 🌐 tynllidiartarms.co.uk
Wye Valley Butty Bach; 2 changing beers (sourced regionally; often Purple Moose) Ⓗ
Situated in the charming village of Capel Bangor on the main A44 leading to Aberystwyth, the Tynllidiart Arms offers a warm welcome to tourists and locals alike. The bar area downstairs is perfect for a cosy pint. The restaurant upstairs serves fine British cuisine, locally sourced wherever possible, including a tasty and flexible children's menu. Dogs are welcome downstairs and on the front terrace outside. The bus service finishes early evening. Q🛏😺◑P🖵(525,X47)😺🛜

Capel Hendre

King's Head Hotel Ⓛ
Waterloo Road, SA18 3SF
🕛 4-midnight; 12-midnight Sun ☎ (01269) 842377
2 changing beers (sourced regionally) Ⓗ
Local village pub tucked away just a couple of miles from the former mining town of Ammanford. The main bar has pool and darts, with a sliding door leading to a separate snug. Usually two, sometimes three real ales are sourced from Wales, with Glamorgan and Neath breweries often represented. There is a large car park. 🛏🛏🏪♣🕭P🖵(128,129)😺🛜

Cardigan

Black Lion Hotel
High Street, SA43 1HJ
🕛 10-11 (12.30am Sat); 10-10.30 Sun ☎ (01239) 612532
🌐 theblacklion-hotel.co.uk
2 changing beers (sourced locally; often Mantle) Ⓗ
Dating from 1105, the Black Lion is said to be the oldest coaching inn in Wales. Originally known as a 'grogg shope', it is an ideal stopping point for both visitors and locals. The pub has three separate rooms – a dedicated restaurant, a relaxing coffee room and a traditional bar with a real fire for the colder months. Real ales come from the local Mantle brewery. 🛏◑🖵🛜

Eagle
Castle Street, SA43 3AA
🕛 12-10.30 ☎ (01239) 612046
Felinfoel Cambrian Best Bitter; Mantle Cwrw Teifi Ⓗ
This family-run traditional Welsh pub on the outskirts of Cardigan town welcomes both families and dogs. Real ale and good food are served by friendly and attentive staff. Live bands play regularly and open mic nights are hosted. Live Sky Sports is shown on TV. There is a quiz night each Friday and music sessions every Tuesday. Well-worth venturing over the bridge for. 🛏😺◑♣🕭😺

REAL ALE BREWERIES

Bluestone Cilgwyn
Caffle Llawhaden
Castle Gate Johnstown (NEW)
Coles Family 🍺 Llanddarog
Evan Evans Llandeilo
Felinfoel Llanelli
Friends Arms 🍺 Johnstown
Gwaun Valley Pontfaen
Harbwr Tenby Tenby (NEW)
Jacobi Pumsaint
Little Dragon Milford Haven (NEW)
Mantle Cardigan
Pembrokeshire Saundersfoot
Penlon Cottage New Quay
Seren Rosebush
Tenby Tenby

WALES

Grosvenor

Bridge Street, SA43 1HY SN177459
🌞 11-11 ☎ (01239) 613792
**Greene King Abbot; Sharp's Doom Bar; 1 changing
beer (sourced nationally)** ℍ
Situated on the edge of the town centre next to
Cardigan Castle and the River Teifi, this large pub
offers a good choice of ales, including a selection of
bottled beers. The large open-plan bar/lounge
provides various areas to relax, eat and drink, and
there is an extra room upstairs for dining and
functions. Good-value food is served lunchtimes
and evenings every day. An outdoor patio area
overlooks the river and the revamped quay area.
🌟🏠🕙&♣🚌🛜

Carmarthen

Friends Arms

Old St Clears Road, Johnstown, SA31 3HH
🌞 12-11 (midnight Fri); 11-midnight Sat; 11-11 Sun
☎ (01267) 234073
3 changing beers (sourced locally) ℍ
Excellent local hostelry half a mile from
Carmarthen town centre, with a cosy and friendly
atmosphere and a warm welcome, enhanced by
two open fires. Popular with sports fans, it has Sky
Sports and ESPN, plus pool and darts. Three real
ales are usually offered, with a 10 per cent
discount for CAMRA members. A former local
CAMRA Pub of the Year, it has its own
microbrewery and an out-building fitted out on
two floors with function rooms for meetings and
parties. 🌟🚌 (222,322)🛜

Queen's Hotel

10 Queen Street, SA31 1JR
🌞 10-midnight; 11-8 Sun ☎ (01267) 231800
**5 changing beers (sourced regionally; often Evan
Evans)** ℍ
Town-centre pub near Carmarthenshire county hall
with a bar, lounge and small function room. The
public bar is where you will find the locals and it
has a TV for sporting events. The patio nestles
beneath the castle walls and is a suntrap during the
summer months. Upstairs function rooms are
available, and the local CAMRA branch meets here.
Locally sourced ales include those from the Evan
Evans range. 🌟🏠🕙≈🚌🦊🛜

Stag & Pheasant

34 Spilman Street, SA31 1LQ
🌞 12-11 (midnight Sat) ☎ (01267) 232040
**Ringwood Boondoggle, Fortyniner; Wychwood
Hobgoblin Gold; 1 changing beer (sourced regionally;
often Marston's)** ℍ
A busy locals' pub with a warm and friendly
atmosphere on the main thoroughfare in
Carmarthen, making it a popular venue for tourists
and locals. The pub boasts an excellent beer
garden with outdoor heaters at the rear. The real
ales vary between Fortyniner, Boondoggle and
Hobgoblin Gold alongside another guest Marston's
beer. This is a popular venue for watching sporting
events, with two large TV screens. 🏠&≈♣🚌🛜

Cellan

Fishers Arms

SA48 8HU (on B4343) SN596482
🌞 4.30-11.30 (8 Mon-Wed) ☎ (01570) 422895
Evan Evans Best Bitter ℍ

This friendly pub, dating back to 1580, has a single
room divided into a flagstoned and beamed bar
area and a lounge area with a woodburner. A large
TV screens BT and Sky Sports and there is a games
room with pool and darts. The rear dining room
offers mostly home-made good-value food. Real
cider is available during the summer months. The
garden has a children's play area and hosts charity
barbecues. Opening hours may vary.
🌟🏠&🅰♣🚌P🚌 (585)🦊

Cilgerran

Pendre Inn

High Street, SA43 2SL
🌞 12-11; 12-10.30 Sun ☎ (01239) 614223
Evan Evans Best Bitter, Warrior ℍ
Welcoming, traditional 14th-century pub standing
at the heart of a large village whose attractions
include a castle, wildlife centre and the Teifi Gorge.
The public bar leads to a lounge area and separate
restaurant. Up to two guest beers change regularly
and real cider often makes an appearance. Bar
snacks are generally available, evening meals are
served Wednesday to Saturday only. Sunday lunch
is popular (booking is advisable). 🏠🕙♣🚌P🚌

Clarbeston Road

Cross Inn ✪

SA63 4UL (N of railway station)
🌞 12-midnight (1am Fri & Sat) ☎ (01437) 731506
**Courage Directors; Greene King Abbot; 1 changing
beer (sourced nationally; often Caledonian)** ℍ
Multi-roomed village inn, well-worth seeking out,
with stone and wood floors and original oak beams
in abundance. The beer range is regional and
national. The large bar area housing pool, TV for
sport and jukebox is complemented by two small
snugs and a dining room where reasonably priced
home-cooked food from a largely grill-based menu
is served Thursday to Saturday evenings and
Sunday lunchtime. Outside there are more spacious
drinking areas. A beer festival is held in summer.
Q🌟🏠🕙&♣P🚌 (313,344,432)🦊🛜

Cresswell Quay

Cresselly Arms 🄻

SA68 0TE
🌞 12-3, 5-11; 12-11 Sat; 12-3, 5-10.30 Sun
☎ (01646) 651210
Sharp's Doom Bar ℍ; **Worthington's Bitter** 🄶; **house
beer (by Caffle); 2 changing beers (sourced locally;
often Bluestone (Pembrokeshire), Mantle)** ℍ
Situated on the Cresswell River, this 250-year-old
ivy-covered hostelry is a throwback to the Victorian
age. The homely farm kitchen interior, where a
roaring fire burns in the hearth, is a haven for locals
and visitors alike. Accessible by boat from the
Milford Haven estuary at high tide, the pub also lies
on a series of interesting walking routes. The house
beer from Caffle Brewery is complemented by
Worthington's Bitter dispensed from the cask by
jug. Local CAMRA Pub of the Year 2015.
Q🌟🏠&🅰♣P🚌 (361)

Cross Inn (Llanon)

Rhos yr Hafod Inn

SY23 5NB (at B4337/B4577 crossroads)
🌞 5-11; closed Sun ☎ (01974) 272644

2 changing beers (sourced regionally; often Celt Experience, Evan Evans, Purple Moose) Ⓗ

Now under new management, this friendly and traditional pub has made its return to the Guide. Cosy drinking areas cluster around the small central bar and a larger back room decorated with old photographs of local scenes provides additional seating. Sunny days can be enjoyed either at the front of the pub in the roadside drinking area or in the large rear garden. A traditional turntable and vinyl collection is available for customers to peruse. Quiz nights are regular events. There is ample parking. ♿⌂Å♣P☂

Cwmann

Cwmann Tavern

SA48 8DR SN582473

🕏 4-11; 12-11 Sun; closed Mon ☎ (01570) 423861

⊕ cwmannetavern.co.uk

2 changing beers (sourced nationally; often Cottage) Ⓗ

A former coaching inn dating from the 1600s, within easy walking distance of the town. The stone floors and low beams help create a cosy, comfortable atmosphere. The varied menu (available evenings only in the week) includes pub favourites, interesting specials and vegetarian options. There is a folk night every Thursday with an ever-changing line-up of instruments and styles. ♿⌂◑♿♣●P🚲

Dale

Griffin Inn

SA62 3RB

🕏 12-11 (12-2, 5.30-11 winter); 12.30-2.30, 5.30-10.30 Sun ☎ (01646) 636227

Brains Rev James Original; Evan Evans Cwrw; 1 changing beer (often Evan Evans) Ⓗ

In an enviable location at the water's edge close to the slipway on the Milford Haven waterway, the Griffin is popular with locals and visitors, including those exploring the Pembrokeshire Coast Path. Some of the outside seats are right alongside the water. Inside you can have some fun with table skittles. The village is the centre for a thriving sailing club. The pub has recently won Silver Best Place to Eat in the National Tourism Awards for Wales. Q♿⌂◑♿♣🚲

Drefach Felindre

John Y Gwas

SA44 5XG SN354383

🕏 5-11; 4-midnight Fri; 12-midnight Sat; 12-11 Sun ☎ (01559) 370469 ⊕ johnygwas.co.uk

2 changing beers (sourced regionally; often Bluestone (Pembrokeshire), Draught Bass, Purple Moose) Ⓗ

Early-19th-century village tavern with its striking yellow and black livery that attracts locals and tourists alike with its snugs, a wood-burning stove, quality beer and cider, and a warm welcome, especially for dogs. Two ales are generally offered, sourced mainly from Welsh and/or micro breweries. A wide variety of bottled beers and ciders is also available. A beer festival, showcasing more than 10 different ales, is held over the August bank holiday weekend. Basket meals are available every evening, bar meals on Friday and Saturday evenings. ♿⌂♣●P🚲(460)♨☂

Felinfoel

Harry Watkins

2 Millfield Road, SA14 8HY (on A476)

🕏 12-11; closed Mon ☎ (01554) 776644

⊕ theharrywatkins.co.uk

Ringwood Fortyniner; house beer (by Banks's); 1 changing beer Ⓗ

Renamed after a local rugby hero who features on the pub walls, the pub was originally called the Bear. The open-plan, split-level, family-friendly hostelry has defined dining spaces and a function room, with covered and open drinking areas outside. National cycle and walking paths to the Swiss Valley and beyond are nearby. Quiz nights are Sunday and Wednesday. Good-value food includes a carvery. No car park, but there is usually ample room on the road. ♿⌂◑🚲☂

Fishguard

Globe

28 Main Street, SA65 9HJ

🕏 12-midnight; 12-10.30 Sun ☎ (01348) 873999

⊕ gofishguard.co.uk

Wadworth Horizon, 6X; 1 changing beer (often Bath Ales) Ⓗ

Friendly locals' pub with a varying guest beer served straight from the cask. Home-cooked meals are available most days – with Friday pizza night a regular event (phone to check). A wood-beamed ceiling adds to the cosy atmosphere. In the winter a woodburner in the inglenook fireplace chases away the chills. The well-stocked jukebox features '60s, '70s and '80s music. There is a bijou beer garden for fine days. Q♿⌂♿🚲(T5)♨☂

Pendre Inn

High Street, SA65 9AT (S of town towards Haverfordwest, 300yds from square)

🕏 11 (4 Mon)-midnight; 11-1am Fri & Sat; 12-11.30 Sun ☎ (01348) 874128 ⊕ thependreinn.co.uk

3 changing beers (sourced nationally; often Greene King, Ruddles, St Austell) Ⓗ

Built around 1790, close to the tollgate on the turnpike road to Haverfordwest on the main road south out of town, this friendly traditional pub has a good local following and an established reputation for its beer. Two guest beers change regularly and may come from anywhere in the UK. Pool and darts are played in the large back bar, while the front bar boasts an inglenook fireplace. Meals, available all day in summer, lunchtimes and evenings in winter (not Mon), include home-made specials. Q♿⌂◑Å♣P🚲(T5)♨☂

Foelgastell

Smiths Arms

Heol y Foel, SA14 7EL

🕏 12-11 (11.30 Fri & Sat) ☎ (01269) 842213

⊕ thesmithsarms.co.uk

2 changing beers Ⓖ

This friendly local pub is a handy stopping-off point for travellers, signposted from the A48/M4 to Carmarthen dual carriageway. It is open all day from noon, offering a choice of bar or restaurant menus (no food Sun eve). The beer selection varies, with one or two real ales usually on offer from either local or national breweries. Real cider is often also available. B&B accommodation is ideal for visitors to the nearby National Botanical Gardens of Wales. ♿⌂🛏◑♿●P🚲(166)♨☂

Goginan

Druid Inn

SY23 3NT (on A44 6 miles E of Aberystwyth)
🌍 12-midnight (1am Fri & Sat) ☎ (01970) 880650
Celt Experience Celt Golden; Wye Valley Bitter; 1 changing beer (sourced nationally; often Mantle, Purple Moose, Wood) Ⓗ
A family-run community pub celebrating its 42nd year in this Guide. The dining room and pool room flank the L-shaped main bar where dogs are welcome. Two guest beers are available summer and weekends plus a range of bottled real ales and ciders. Occasional music nights (sometimes with acts of more than local renown) and beer festivals are hosted. Food is popular and high quality (no food Tue). Buses run until early evening Monday to Saturday. Pub-owned B&B can be found next door.
🏃😺🍴🔌♿♣●🅿🚉(525,X47)🐾

Haverfordwest

William Owen Ⓛ ✅

6 Quay Street, SA61 1BG
🌍 8am-midnight (1am Fri & Sat) ☎ (01437) 771900
Caffle Drop Squint; Fuller's London Pride; Greene King Abbot; Ruddles Best Bitter; Sharp's Doom Bar; 2 changing beers (sourced locally; often Bluestone (Pembrokeshire), Mantle) Ⓗ
Pembrokeshire's first and so far only Wetherspoon pub occupies a handsome 19th-century building, formerly a shop, hotel and restaurant, now with a spacious extension to the rear. It was reputedly built in 1856 for Joseph Thomas, a corn and manure merchant, by local architect William Owen. It has also been a saddler's and more recently the Wilton House Hotel. Beer from one of the county's eight breweries is regularly available. The pub offers the chain's standard menu and promotional deals, and is open from 8am for breakfast.
Q🏃😺🔌♿≢🅿🚉🛜

Herbrandston

Taberna Inn Ⓛ

SA73 3TD (3 miles W of Milford Haven)
🌍 12-11 ☎ (01646) 693498 ⊕ taberna.org.uk
Caffle Drop Squint; Moles Best Bitter; 1 changing beer (sourced nationally) Ⓗ
Designed and built in 1963 by a local carpenter and builder with an eye to the area's then rapidly developing oil and petrochemical industry. A bus (service 300) is available from Milford Haven and the marina for visitors and crews looking for a choice of real ales. Local, regional and national beers are available alongside Westons and Moles Black Rat ciders. The pub maintains a list of all the guest beers sold throughout the year. Local CAMRA Cider Pub of the Year 2016.
Q🏃😺🔌♿▲●🅿🚉(300,315)

Johnston

Vine Inn 🏆 Ⓛ

Vine Road, SA62 3NY
🌍 11-2, 6-11; 12-11 Sat & Sun; closed Mon
☎ (01437) 890611
Sharp's Doom Bar; Wye Valley Dorothy Goodbody's Golden Ale; 2 changing beers (sourced regionally; often Mantle, Purple Moose) Ⓗ
First licensed in 1810 to Thomas Evans, this pub has been trading successfully ever since, apart from a

brief closure a few years ago. A smart black-and-white roadside establishment, it has a good local and countywide following. Local and regional guest ales are available. Inside is a long bar area with exposed beams where many pumpclips tell of past and present beer delights. Local CAMRA Pub of the Year for 2014 and 2016. 🏃😺🔌≢●🅿🚉(302,349)

Laugharne

New Three Mariners Inn Ⓛ

Victoria Street, SA33 4SE
🌍 3-11; 12-11 Fri-Sun ☎ (01994) 427426
Changing beers (often Evan Evans) Ⓗ
The building is located in the centre of the historic township of Laugharne and only yards from its early-11th-century castle. Dylan Thomas lived in the town for a number of years and he and his wife Caitlin are laid to rest in the graveyard of St Martin's Church. The pub moved to its current site when the original ale house opposite was converted to a carpentry shop. The pub is popular with locals. Opening hours vary throughout the year. 🏃😺🍴🔌♿♣●🅿🚉🐾🛜

Little Haven

Saint Bride's Inn Ⓛ

St Brides Road, SA62 3UN
🌍 11-midnight ☎ (01437) 781266 ⊕ saintbridesinn.co.uk
Brains Rev James Original; Caffle Darker Side of Pale; Hancocks HB; 2 changing beers (sourced regionally; often Bluestone (Pembrokeshire), Brecon) Ⓗ
Little Haven is a quaint old fishing village in a conservation area of the Pembrokeshire Coast National Park. This family-run pub in the centre of the village is open all year round, selling a range of Welsh and Pembrokeshire ales. It is noted for the ancient well in the cellar. The attractive interior includes a separate dining area, and there are heaters on the patio in the pretty suntrap garden for outdoor drinking. Q🏃😺🔌▲🅿🚉(311,400)🛜

Llandeilo

Angel Hotel

62 Rhosmaen Street, SA19 6EN
🌍 11.30-3, 6-11; closed Sun ☎ (01558) 822765
⊕ angelbistro.co.uk
3 changing beers Ⓗ
Ideally located in the centre of this picturesque Towy Valley town, the Angel ministers to all needs. The main bar is a U-shaped room providing three real ales, mainly from local breweries, and bar meals. At the back is a bistro dating from the 1700s, while the first floor offers a beer garden to the rear and a function room boasting a Michelangelo-inspired hand-painted mural. Themed meal nights and music nights are held regularly. 🏃😺🍴🔌≢●🚉🐾

Cottage Inn

Pentrefelin, SA19 6SD (on A40, 3 miles W of Llandeilo)
🌍 12-11 ☎ (01558) 613374 ⊕ cottageinnbandb.co.uk
Gower Gold; 2 changing beers (sourced locally) Ⓗ
A popular family-run local community pub on the A40. Dating back to the 1850s, it was formerly a coaching inn and a drovers' hostelry. Sky TV is available and the pub gets busy when major sporting events are screened. It has a separate restaurant/function room. At the rear is a spacious covered smoking area and outside is a large car

park with caravanning and camping space. Two or three guest real ales are offered.
Q❄🍴🛏🍺♿P🐾🎵

White Horse

Rhosmaen Street, SA19 6EN
⏣ 11-11; 12-10.30 Sun ☎ (01558) 822424
Evan Evans Best Bitter, Cwrw, Warrior; 2 changing beers Ⓗ
Grade II-listed coaching inn dating from the 16th century. The tap for the local Evan Evans Brewery, this multi-roomed hostelry is popular with all ages. There is a small outdoor drinking area to the front and a large council car park to the rear with access down a short flight of steps. A covered area is available for smokers with its own TV showing sport. Local CAMRA Pub of the Year 2014.
◖≉🚲🚆🚌(103,X13)🐾

Llandovery

King's Head 🄻

1 Market Square, SA20 0AB
⏣ 10-11 ☎ (01550) 720393 ⏥ kingsheadcoachinginn.co.uk
Evan Evans Cwrw; 2 changing beers Ⓗ
Set in the main square of this historic town on the edge of the Brecon Beacons National Park, this former coaching inn dates from the 1700s. It is a popular base for many organisations including the Rotary Club and cattle breeders. Good food ranges from bar meals to à la carte. Guest beers are usually sourced from local Welsh breweries.
Q❄🛏🍴Å≉♣🚌🐾

Llandybie

Ivy Bush

18 Church Street, SA18 3HZ (100yds from church)
⏣ 12-midnight (11 Mon); 11-midnight Sat & Sun
☎ (01269) 850272
Timothy Taylor Landlord; 1 changing beer (sourced regionally) Ⓗ
The oldest pub in the village, this friendly local dates back nearly 300 years. The single-bar room has two comfortable seating areas. Pub games and quizzes are run weekly and a large-screen TV shows sport. Timothy Taylor Landlord is the adopted house ale, usually joined by at least one regularly changing guest. The local bird-watching group holds its meetings here. The railway station nearby is on the scenic Heart of Wales line.
≉🐾P🚆🚌(103,X13)

Llandyfaelog

Red Lion

SA17 5PP (300yds off A484)
⏣ 11-midnight ☎ (01267) 267530
⏥ redlionllandyfaelog.co.uk
2 changing beers Ⓗ
Family-run hostelry that can truly be described as the hub of the community. Alongside the village pub is a separate annexe which hosts concerts and functions for a wide area, including the local choir's practice evenings. The large public bar, with darts and a pool table, is enhanced by a restaurant and a separate family room. Food is served throughout the bar and restaurant. Q❄🛏🍴Å♣🚌(198,X11)

Llandyfan

Square & Compass

SA18 2UD (between Ammanford and Trapp)
⏣ 4 (12 Sat)-11; 12-10.30 Sun ☎ (01269) 850402
Tomos Watkin Old Style Bitter; 2 changing beers Ⓗ
Originally the village blacksmith's, this 18th-century building was converted to a pub in the 1960s. Nestling on the western edge of the Brecon Beacons National Park, it enjoys magnificent local views and plenty of walking opportunities. A traditional family hostelry, it has a wonderful rustic charm and offers a warm, friendly welcome. Usually two, occasionally three, guest beers are available, at least one from a local brewery. Opening hours vary in winter – ring ahead to check.
Q❄🍴♿Å♣🐾P🚆

Llandysul

Porth Hotel

Church Street, SA44 4QS
⏣ 12-3, 6-11; 12-5 Sun ☎ (01559) 362202
⏥ porthhotel.co.uk
Draught Bass Ⓗ; 1 changing beer (sourced locally; often Brecon, Coles Family, Glamorgan) Ⓖ
Originally a 17th-century coaching inn, set on the banks of the River Teifi, this is now a family-run village hotel with a bar, restaurant and function room. The public rooms still retain the original oak beams and panels. Beers from the local Castlegate Brewery are regularly featured alongside ales from other Welsh breweries such as Brecon, Glamorgan, Coles and Gower. ❄🍴🛏🍴P🚌🎵

Llanelli

York Palace ⓥ

51 Stepney Street, SA15 3YA (opp Town Hall Square Gardens)
⏣ 8am-midnight (1am Fri & Sat) ☎ (01554) 758609
Greene King Abbot; Ruddles Best Bitter; Sharp's Doom Bar; 5 changing beers Ⓗ
This former cinema in the town centre is a typical Wetherspoon conversion spread over two levels. The walls are adorned with photographs of local industrial history including Llanelli's famous tin plate industry. Guest beers are often sourced locally and discounted on Mondays. There is easy access to the bus station, and the railway station is a 10-minute walk. Q🍴♿≉🚆🚌🎵

Llanfallteg

Plash

SA34 0UN (off A40 at Llanddewi Velfrey)
⏣ 12 (5 Mon & Tue)-11 ☎ (01437) 563472
Wye Valley Butty Bach; 2 changing beers Ⓗ
At the centre of village life, this terrace-style cottage pub has been an inn for more than 180 years. It holds a quiz night on Tuesday and a number of other special nights throughout the month. The guest beers are usually from small, independent breweries. Home-made food, using locally sourced ingredients, is served, with specials on Wednesdays, Fridays and Saturdays. The disabled entrance is to the rear. A small cottage is available to let. A former local CAMRA Pub of the Year. Q❄🛏🍴Å🐾

Llangoedmor

Penllwyndu

SA43 2LY (on B4570 4½ miles from Cardigan) SN240458
✪ 12-11 ☎ (01239) 682533
Courage Directors; Hancocks HB; 1 changing beer (often Evan Evans) Ⓗ
Old-fashioned ale house standing at an isolated crossroads where Cardigan's evil-doers were once hanged – the pub sign is worthy of close inspection. The cheerful and welcoming public bar retains its quaintness, with a slate floor and inglenook with wood-burning stove. Good home-cooked food including traditional favourites is available all day in the bar and the separate restaurant. Live music plays on the third Thursday evening of the month.
🌣⊛◖♣P🐾

Llangrannog

Pentre Arms Hotel

SA44 6SP (at seaward end of B4321/B4334)
✪ 12-midnight ☎ (01239) 654345 ⊕ pentrearms.co.uk
Gale's Seafarers Ale; St Austell Tribute; 1 changing beer (sourced regionally; often Mantle) Ⓗ
Set on the Wales Coastal Path in a former seafaring village, this pub commands tremendous sea views (also viewable via beach-facing webcam). The main bar is flanked by the games room – with pool, darts and poker on winter Wednesdays – and dining room. A guest beer is available in summer. Live music plays at weekends. Well-behaved dogs are welcome in the bar. The bus service is infrequent and variable.
🌣⊛🚪◖🄰♣🚌(552)🐾🛜

Llanllwni

Talardd Arms

SA39 9DX
✪ 12-2.30, 6-11 ☎ (01559) 395633 ⊕ talardd.com
1 changing beer (sourced regionally; often Evan Evans) Ⓗ
There are records of this old inn dating back to 1626, when drovers would stop for refreshments for man and beast before driving their livestock over Llanllwni Mountain on their way to markets over the border. Sympathetically modernised, Tafarn y Talardd continues to offer a traditional warm and friendly welcome. Live music, quizzes and film nights are organised most Mondays. Evan Evans Cwrw is usually available, switching to Evan Evans Warrior occasionally. 🌣◖♣P🚌🐾🛜

Llansaint

King's Arms

13 Maes yr Eglwys, SA17 5JE
✪ 6-11 Sat; 12-11 Sun; closed Mon-Fri ☎ (01267) 267487
Young's Special; 2 changing beers Ⓗ
A former local CAMRA Pub of the Year, this friendly village hostelry has been a pub for more than 200 years. Situated near an 11th-century church, it is reputedly built from stone recovered from the lost village of St Ishmaels. Music and poetry nights are usually held on the third Friday of the month. The guest beers come from smaller breweries. Good-value home-cooked food is served. Carmarthen Bay Holiday Park is a few miles away.
🌣🚪◖🄳♣P🚌(198)🛜

Newport

Golden Lion Ⓛ

East Street, SA42 0SY (on A487)
✪ 12-midnight; 12-11 Sun ☎ (01239) 820321
⊕ goldenlionpembrokeshire.co.uk
Bluestone Bedrock Blonde; Sharp's Doom Bar; Worthington's Bitter; 1 changing beer (sourced nationally; often Thwaites) Ⓗ
Situated in an area of outstanding natural beauty close to the Pembrokeshire Coast Path, the Golden Lion is another of Newport's sociable locals and is reputed to have its own resident ghost. A number of internal walls have been removed to create a spacious open-plan bar area, with distinct sections helping to retain a cosy atmosphere. Locally caught fish and Welsh Black beef are specialities, served in the bar and restaurant. Car parking space is available on the opposite side of the road.
Q🌣⊛🚪◖🄰♣P🍴🚌(T5)🐾🛜

Llwyngwair Arms

East Street, SA42 0SY (town centre, Newport Square)
✪ 2-11 (12.30am Fri); 12-12.30am Sat; 12-11 Sun
☎ (01239) 820267
Bluestone Bedrock Blonde; Brains Rev James Original; 2 changing beers (often Gower) Ⓗ
A centrally situated stone-built traditional pub within easy reach of the coastal path. It is a Grade II-listed coaching inn built around the early-to mid-19th century, with stabling opposite. The Court Leet, an ancient institution, meets here and the Lady Marcher attends most of its meetings. The annual mayoral ceremony is also held here each November. Q🌣⊛🄳AP🍴🐾🛜

Pembroke

Old King's Arms Ⓛ

Main Street, SA71 4JS
✪ 11-11 ☎ (01646) 683611 ⊕ oldkingsarmshotel.co.uk
Felinfoel Double Dragon; Marston's Old Empire; 2 changing beers (sourced locally; often Bluestone (Pembrokeshire), Evan Evans) Ⓗ
This former coaching inn is allegedly the oldest in Pembroke, dating back to around 1520. The King's Bar, with four handpumps serving local, regional and national beers, is a small room with exposed stone walls, wood beams and a real fire. There is also a lounge with a dining area and a restaurant with space for larger groups. The hotel prides itself on using locally sourced meat and fish in its dishes.
Q🌣⊛🚪◖🄳P🍴🛜

Pembroke Dock

First & Last

London Road, SA72 6TX (on A477)
✪ 10-1am (1.30am Thu-Sat) ☎ (01646) 682687
Brains Rev James Original; Worthington's White Shield; 1 changing beer (sourced nationally; often Skinner's) Ⓗ
Friendly single-bar local run by the same family for 50 years. The walls display an eclectic mix of photos and prints. The guest beer can be from anywhere, local or national, and the food is good pub fare. There is a popular quirky Sunday evening quiz. Formerly the Commercial, the pub acquired its more distinctive name in 1991 to reflect its edge-of-town location. It is handy for the Cleddau Bridge, giving easy access to Haverfordwest, and close to the historic naval dockyard and Irish ferry.
Q🌣⊛◖⇥P🚌(349,356)🛜

Station Inn

Hawkestone Road, SA72 6HN (in station building)
✪ 10.30-3, 6.30-11; 12-2.30, 7-11 Sun ☎ (01646) 621255
Brains Rev James Original; Courage Directors; 2 changing beers (sourced nationally; often Cottage, Otter) Ⓗ
Housed in the town's railway station where trains depart for Carmarthen, Swansea and, on summer Saturdays, far-off Paddington, this town-centre pub is close to both the Irish Ferries terminal and Pembrokeshire Coastal Path. Meals are excellent value (no lunches Mon, evening meals Wed-Sat only). Three real ales are generally on sale, with Young's Bitter a frequent visitor and a new beer every Tuesday. The June beer festival offers around 20 beers. Live music is hosted on Saturday evenings. ☞🏠🕽🕭♿🚲♣🍴P🚃🚘(349)🐾

Pontamman

Red Kite Inn

89 Pontamman Road, SA18 2JD (a little over 1 mile N of Ammanford on main A474 towards Neath)
✪ 12-3, 5-11; 12-11 Sat & Sun; closed Mon & Tue
☎ (01269) 597177 ● theredkiteinn.co.uk
2 changing beers Ⓗ
Previously known as the Perrivale, the pub reopened as the Red Kite Inn (or Y Barcud Coch in Welsh). Two or three real ales are usually available, mostly sourced from Welsh breweries. Live music and quiz nights feature on most weekends. There are a number of quiet corners and a separate restaurant. Meals are served lunchtimes and evenings Wednesday to Saturday, and Sunday lunchtimes. ☞🏠🖴🕽♣P🚘🛜

Pontfaen

Dyffryn Arms ★

SA65 9SE (off B4313)
✪ 11-11 ☎ (01348) 881305
Draught Bass Ⓖ
This much-loved hostelry is the hub of life in a secluded valley whose distinctive cultural traditions include a long history of farmhouse brewing. Recognised as a pub with a nationally important historic interior, it is a reminder of how country inns must once have looked. There is no bar counter – beers are still served by the jug through a sliding serving hatch. Conversation is the main form of entertainment. This is a timeless gem to be treated with respect. Q☞🏠🛡♣🍴P🐾

Porthgain

Sloop Inn

SA62 5BN
✪ 9.30am-11 (midnight Sat) ☎ (01348) 831449
● sloop.co.uk
Brains Rev James Original; Hancocks HB; 1 changing beer (sourced nationally; often Gower, Sharp's) Ⓗ
Situated in the beautiful fishing harbour of Porthgain, this sympathetically renovated old inn has served both the locally based fishing industry and the nearby now-defunct quarry and brickworks. Interesting quarrying, brick-making and shipping artefacts are on display. The Sloop is a popular refreshment stop for walkers on the scenic Pembrokeshire Coast National Park footpath, with stunning beaches and dramatic cliff views nearby. Seasonal fresh fish and local lobster are often on the menu. Q☞🏠🕽🛡♣🍴P🚘🛜

Porthyrhyd

Mansel Arms

Banc y Mansel, SA32 8BS (on B4310 between Porthyrhyd and Drefach)
✪ 5-11; 3-midnight Sat; 12-6 Sun ☎ (01267) 275305
2 changing beers Ⓗ
Friendly 18th-century former coaching inn with wood fires in each room. The original limestone flags have been broken up and used in the fireplace, and low beams have been added to create atmosphere, with numerous jugs hanging from them in the bar. Pool and darts are played in a room to the rear, which was originally used for slaughtering pigs. Beers are varied, with the Young's range always popular as well as local ales. Q☞🕽♣🍴P🚘(129)

Prengwyn

Gwarcefel Arms

SA44 4LU (on crossroads of A475 and B4476) SN424442
✪ 4 (1 Sat)-11; 12-11 Sun ☎ (01559) 363126
● gwarcefel.co.uk
Sharp's Doom Bar; 1 changing beer (sourced nationally; often Evan Evans) Ⓗ
A traditional country inn with a friendly atmosphere where everyone is welcome, including families and dogs. Situated at the junction of five roads in Prengwyn, three miles north of Llandysul, the pub has a main bar with a wood-burning stove, cosy seating, pool table and dartboard. A separate restaurant area, which caters for functions and parties, offers evening meals Thursdays to Saturdays. The beer garden and ample car park are to the rear. ☞🏠🕽♣P🐾🛜

Pumsaint

Dolaucothi Arms

SA19 8UW (on A482 midway between Llanwrda and Lampeter)
✪ 12 (5 Tue)-11; 12-8 Sun; closed Mon ☎ (01558) 650237
1 changing beer Ⓗ
A friendly welcome is assured at this substantial stone-built inn owned by the National Trust and tastefully restored in traditional style. There is an excellent food menu to savour and two ales usually sourced from Welsh breweries alongside real cider. The pub is located close to the National Trust's Dolaucothi Gold Mines. Opening hours may vary so it is advisable to check before travelling. ☞🏠🖴🕽♿🛡♣🍴P🚘🐾🛜

Pwlltrap

White Lion

SA33 4AT
✪ 12-11; 11-10.30 Sun ☎ (01994) 230370
Courage Directors; Greene King Abbot; Shepherd Neame Bishops Finger; Young's Bitter; 1 changing beer (sourced nationally) Ⓗ
This roadside pub, just outside St Clears, is warm and welcoming with a real fire in winter. It has an old-world charm with oak beams and panelled walls, and boasts a large restaurant with good food. Pool and darts are played and a large TV screen shows regular sporting fixtures. The pub organises a range of events throughout the year. Two cask beers are available in winter, four in summer. Q🕽♿🚘(224,322)🐾🛜

Rhandirmwyn

Royal Oak 𝕃

SA20 0NY
⏲ 12-2, 6-11; 12-2, 7-10.30 Sun ☎ (01550) 760201
🌐 theroyaloakinn.co.uk
3 changing beers Ⓗ
Remote, stone-flagged inn with excellent views of the Towy Valley and close to an RSPB bird sanctuary. Originally built as a hunting lodge for the local landowner, it is now a focal point for community activities and popular with fans of outdoor pursuits. The village shop is alongside. Two or three guest beers are offered and good wholesome food comes recommended. There are panoramic views from the beer garden at the side of the pub. Four times local CAMRA Pub of the Year. Q♉🛏◐◑♣🍎P🐾📶

Roch

Victoria Inn

SA62 6AW (on A487)
⏲ 12-2.30, 5-11 Mon & Tue; 12-11 ☎ (01437) 710426
🌐 thevictoriainnroch.com
Black Sheep Ale; 3 changing beers (sourced nationally; often Evan Evans, Marston's) Ⓗ
Only one mile from the vast expanse of Newgale beach, which can be seen from the pub, this little gem is worth seeking out. Dating back to at least 1851, it was reputedly at one time a stop-off for drovers on their way home from market in Haverfordwest. With low doorways and beamed ceilings, and a log fire in winter, it has a warm atmosphere. A popular quiz night is held on Wednesdays, curry-and-a-pint on Fridays. Q♉◐◑▲P🚌(411)📶

Rosebush

Tafarn Sinc

SA66 7QU
⏲ 12-11; closed Mon ☎ (01437) 532214 🌐 tafarnsinc.co.uk
Worthington's Bitter; 1 changing beer (often Evan Evans) Ⓗ
Originally the Precelly Hotel, this Victorian hostelry was built to attract tourists to the Preseli mountains when the Clunderwen to Rosebush railway line was opened. The pub closed in 1992 but was later bought by locals, refurbished and renamed Tafarn Sinc. It is set in the heart of the mountains, with many scenic views to discover whether driving or walking. This pub features in the historic and social life of the area and is full of old-world character and charm. ♉❀◐◑♿▲P🐾

St Davids

Farmers Arms

14-16 Goat Street, SA62 6RF
⏲ 11-midnight ☎ (01437) 721666 🌐 farmersstdavids.co.uk
Brains Rev James Original; Felinfoel Double Dragon; house beer (by Hancocks); 2 changing beers (sourced nationally; often Evan Evans, Sharp's, Wychwood) Ⓗ
A traditional city pub comprising three rooms – the top bar, mainly for dining, the smaller Coxswains room, which is the social meeting place for the St Davids lifeboat crew, and the Glue Pot bar, where the locals tend to gather around the fire. Outside, the patio offers views of the cathedral and has a seasonal bar. Winter opening times vary so please check before you visit. Q♉❀◐◑♿▲♣🍎🚌🐾📶

St Dogmaels

White Hart

Finch Street, SA43 3EA
⏲ 12 (5 Mon & Tue)-11 ☎ (01239) 612099
Felinfoel Double Dragon; Wye Valley Butty Bach; 1 changing beer (often Mantle) Ⓗ
Set in Pembrokeshire's northernmost village, this small, cheery community pub enjoys a good local following. Guest beers change regularly and are often from breweries rarely seen locally. The beach at nearby Poppit Sands marks the northern terminus of the Pembrokeshire Coast Path. The pub is a short walk to St Dogmaels Benedictine Tironensian Abbey and visitor centre, one of Pembrokeshire's most beautiful historic attractions. The restaurant specialises in locally sourced fresh fish and produce. Q♉◐◑♿▲♣P🚌🐾

Solva

Ship

15 Main Street, SA62 6UU (on A487)
⏲ 11-11 ☎ (01437) 721247
Banks's Bitter; Marston's Pedigree; 1 changing beer (sourced nationally; often Marston's) Ⓗ
A traditional black-and-white timbered building both inside and out. Families are made particularly welcome. The Sunday roast is popular and authentic Indian curries are served in the evening. There is a covered and heated outdoor smoking area, and ample parking is available nearby overlooking the picturesque harbour. A former local CAMRA Pub of the Year winner. Winter opening times may vary – check before your visit. ❀🛏◐◑♿▲P🚌(411)📶

Talybont

White Lion (Llew Gwyn) ✔

SY24 5ER
⏲ 12-1am; 12-midnight Sun ☎ (01970) 832245
Banks's Mild, Bitter; 3 changing beers (sourced nationally; often Ringwood, Thwaites, Wychwood) Ⓗ
Set on the village green, this friendly community pub is the hub of village life. The main bar with its old slate floor, heated by a small solid-fuel stove, features an interesting local history display and is flanked by a rear bar and games room. Guest beers are from the Marston's group. Curry-and-a-pint deals are available on Thursdays. Free-for-all music afternoons feature on occasion. Evening and Sunday bus services are limited. ♉❀🛏◐◑♿♣P🚌(T2,X28)🐾📶

Tenby

Buccaneer Inn

St Julian Street, SA70 7AS
⏲ 11-12.30am; 11-11 Sun ☎ (01834) 842273
Harbwr Tenby MV Enterprise, North Star, RFA Sir Galahad; 1 changing beer (sourced regionally; often Glamorgan) Ⓗ
The Buccaneer is in a quaint street which links the town square to the harbour and beaches. The bar area is large but has a cosy feel with beams, stove and Tenby memorabilia adorning the walls. A sunny walled beer garden is to the rear. The pub is the brewery tap for the adjacent Tenby Harbour Brewery, selling its full range of beers. Food is served all day with locally sourced fresh fish on the menu. ♉❀◐◑⥃🚌🐾

Hope & Anchor ⬡

St Julian Street, SA70 7AS

☼ 11-midnight; 11-10.30 Sun ☎ (01834) 842131

Sharp's Doom Bar, Atlantic; 2 changing beers (sourced locally; often Bluestone (Pembrokeshire), Mantle) Ⓗ

Welcoming pub set in the old town on the way down to the harbour. Food is important here and a range of specials supplements the standard menu. The convivial atmosphere and interesting local décor make it an excellent place to relax over a beer. Four guest beers are sourced mainly from Welsh breweries including Evan Evans, Mantle and Purple Moose, while Wye Valley sometimes sneaks over the border. The ciders are Old Rosie and Somerset Tree Shaker. ⏱☸◑▲⇌♿P➾🚆(349)🛜

Tregaron

Talbot

The Square, SY25 6JL

☼ 11-11; 11-10.30 Sun ☎ (01974) 298208 ⊕ ytalbot.com

4 changing beers (sourced regionally; often Evan Evans, Mantle, Purple Moose) Ⓗ

Former drovers' inn of immense character offering a public bar with TV, a small front lounge with an open fire, and a delightful beamed and flagstoned snug with inglenook fireplace. Four real ales are available, always including one from the Mantle Brewery, and a varying selection of cider and perry comes from Gwynt y Ddraig. Excellent locally sourced food includes good vegetarian options. The terrace drinking area has fine views and a memorial to a circus elephant reputedly buried here. Local CAMRA Pub of the Year 2015. Q⏱☸🛏◑♿♣♿P🚆(585,588)🐾🛜

Whitland

Station House Hotel

St Johns Street, SA34 0AP

☼ 9am-1am (2am Fri & Sat) ☎ (01994) 240556

⊕ stationhousewhitland.co.uk

Courage Best Bitter; Worthington's White Shield; 3 changing beers Ⓗ

A smile and a warm welcome are always on tap at this friendly hostelry. Very much a local pub for all ages, there is something for everyone here, with pool and darts teams and bingo on Sunday evenings. A separate small room is available for people looking for a quiet corner. The outside drinking area is partly under cover. Car parking is to the rear and the railway station is close by. ☸◑⇌♣♿P🚆🐾🛜

Royal Oak, Rhandirmwyn

Scotland

ABERDEEN & GRAMPIAN

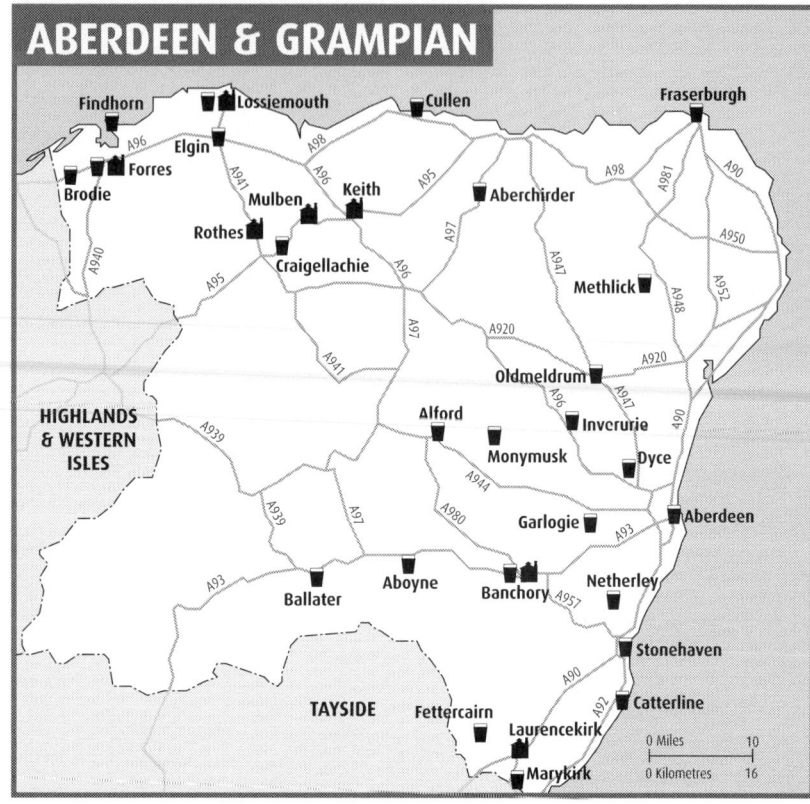

Authority areas covered: Aberdeenshire UA, City of Aberdeen UA, Moray UA

Aberchirder

New Inn

79 Main Street, AB54 7TB
🕔 12 (5 Mon)-12.30am; 12-11 Sun ☎ (01466) 780633
🌐 newinnaberchirder.co.uk
Windswept Wolf 🅖; **5 changing beers (sourced nationally; often Hambleton, Orkney, Windswept)** 🅗
Traditional, welcoming inn with wood-burning stoves, candlelit areas and a vintage atmosphere, offering a changing selection of five quality ales from local and national breweries. A separate dining area provides home-made food using locally sourced produce cooked by the owner – the pork pies come highly recommended. Families with their children are welcome in the dining room until 9pm (booking advised; no food Mon and none Tue lunchtime). Dogs are welcome in the bar. A beer festival is held in September in the large function room. Q🐕🛏🍴◑🚆♿️🅿️🚃(301)☕️🎵🛜

Aberdeen

Aitchies Ale House

10 Trinity Street, AB11 5LY
🕔 8am-10 (11 Fri & Sat); closed Sun ☎ (01224) 575972
McEwan's IPA; Orkney Dark Island 🅗
This small corner bar is the closest real ale outlet to the city rail/bus stations and the Union Square shopping complex. Family-owned, it retains the flavour of an old-fashioned Scottish pub with bar staff wearing traditional white aprons and friendly service second to none. Bar food is basic Scottish pub grub, including roast beef stovies. A good selection of whiskies and Bell's special edition decanters adorn the gantry. Q♿️🚆🍴🛜

Archibald Simpson's ✅

5 Castle Street, AB11 5BQ (E end of Union St)
🕔 8am-midnight (1am Fri & Sat); 9am-midnight Sun
☎ (01224) 621365
Greene King Abbot; Sharp's Doom Bar; 10 changing beers (sourced nationally) 🅗
Wetherspoon pub that is in one of many monumental granite buildings in central Aberdeen designed by local architect Archibald Simpson. It retains many original architectural features. The main room is the high-ceilinged central hall, and there are additional seating areas to the side. The long bar features 12 handpumps offering a variety of beers, frequently from Scottish breweries. There is a narrow outside drinking area on the pavement on Union Street corner. Alcohol is served from 11am. 🛏◑♿️🚆🍴🛜

REAL ALE BREWERIES

Burnside Laurencekirk
Deeside Banchory
Keith Keith
Quiet 🍺 Banchory
Rothes Rothes
six°north Laurencekirk
Spey Valley Mulben
Speyside Craft Forres
Windswept Lossiemouth

Carriages

101 Crown Street, AB11 6HH (nr railway and bus stations)

⊕ 11-2.30, 4.30-midnight; 11-midnight Fri & Sat; 5.30-11 Sun ☎ (01224) 595440 ⊕ brentwood-hotel.co.uk

8 changing beers (sourced nationally; often Orkney, Swannay, Windswept) ⊞

A mirrored downstairs bar in the basement of the modernised Brentwood Hotel, with lots of seating areas and comfortable couches. A winner of several local CAMRA awards, it offers eight changing beers, usually a mix of national brands and Scottish micro beers – tasters are offered if undecided. Lunches are available in the bar and the adjoining restaurant serves good food in the evening. ⍟🏠◑≥P🚫🛜

Grill ♀ ★

213 Union Street, AB11 6BA

⊕ 10-midnight (1am Fri & Sat); 12.30-midnight Sun ☎ (01224) 573530 ⊕ thegrillaberdeen.co.uk

Harviestoun Bitter & Twisted; 3 changing beers (sourced regionally; often Deeside, Fyne Ales, Windswept) ⊞

With an exquisite interior redesigned in 1926 and remaining largely unchanged since, this is the only pub listed in CAMRA's National Inventory of Historic Pub Interiors in the area. For men only until 1975, ladies' toilets were eventually provided in 1998. Situated across from the Music Hall, musicians often visit during concert breaks. Guest ales are frequently from a variety of Scottish micros and the large selection of malts has won the pub several awards. Bar snacks are available. CAMRA Branch Pub of the Year 2016 and Whisky Bar of the Year. ≥🚫🛜

Krakatoa

2 Trinity Quay, AB11 5AA (facing quayside at bottom of Market St)

⊕ 1-midnight; 2-3am Fri & Sat; 2-midnight Sun ☎ (01224) 587602 ⊕ krakatoa.bar

Windswept Weizen; changing beers (sourced regionally; often Cromarty, Fyne Ales, Swannay) ℗

This historic harbourside bar, formerly known as the Moorings and much refurbished recently, has a unique interior and a friendly, varied crowd of regulars. A wide selection of beers mainly from Scottish micros is served on up to 12 American-style fonts to the far left of the bar. There are also two similar banks dispensing various real ciders, keg and Belgian beers. Try some of the exotic specialist cocktails. Live music plays every Friday and Saturday night, when there may be a cover charge, and Wednesday is rock karaoke night. Multiple local CAMRA city Pub of the Year winner and branch Pub of the Year in 2015. ♿≥♣🍴🚫🐾🛜

Prince of Wales ✅

7 St Nicholas Lane, AB10 1HF (in lane opp Marks & Spencer and parallel to Union St)

⊕ 10-midnight (1am Fri & Sat); 11-midnight Sun ☎ (01224) 640597 ⊕ princeofwales-aberdeen.co.uk

House beer (by Inveralmond); 7 changing beers (sourced nationally; often Cromarty, Swannay, Windswept) ⊞

Refurbished in 2016, this is one of the oldest pubs in Aberdeen with possibly the longest bar counter in the city. It has a friendly atmosphere and a large following of regulars. A varied selection of mainly Scottish and some English ales includes the usuals from Greene King/Belhaven and the house beer,

Prince of Wales, and tasters are offered. Folk music is hosted on Sunday evenings and a prize quiz is held on Monday night. Listed in Scotland's True Heritage Pubs, this is a good venue with conversation the only background noise. Food is served until 9pm daily. Q⍟◑≥🚫🛜

Six Degrees North

6 Littlejohn Street, AB10 1FF

⊕ 11-midnight (1am Fri & Sat); 12.30-midnight Sun ☎ (01224) 379192 ⊕ sixdnorth.co.uk

3 changing beers (sourced regionally; often Cromarty, Six Degrees North, Wild Beer) ⊞

A conversion of part of the former college premises, this Belgian beer bar has a two-tiered interior, minimal but comfortable, with exposed granite and modern wooden benches. Upstairs, there is more seating on the balcony. A large blackboard displays the changing range of around 24 Belgian and several locally brewed ales plus up to three cask beers. Beers are mostly served in two-thirds-of-a-pint glasses, with stronger ones in half pints. Over 300 bottled beers are stocked. Live music features on the last Sunday afternoon of the month. Hearty bar snacks are available. Q♿≥🚫🛜(20)🐾🛜

St Machar Bar

97 High Street, Old Aberdeen, AB24 3EN

⊕ 11-11 (midnight Fri); 12.30-11 Sun ☎ (01224) 483079 ⊕ themachar.com

Caledonian Deuchars IPA; 4 changing beers (sourced regionally; often Caledonian) ⊞

The St Machar Bar is a friendly, historic pub located within photogenic Old Aberdeen. It is frequented by students, academics and locals alike from the surrounding university and nearby historic Kings College. A splendid mirror from the long-gone Thomson Marshall Aulton Brewery, which used to be just down the street, adorns the wall. Up to four guest beers, frequently from Scottish micros, are available alongside a comprehensive selection of whiskies. The bar is home to two darts teams. 🐾◑♣🚫🛜

Under the Hammer

11 North Silver Street, AB10 1RJ (off Golden Square)

⊕ 5-midnight (1am Thu); 4-1am Fri; 2-1am Sat; 6-midnight Sun ☎ (01224) 640253

Fyne Ales Jarl; Inveralmond Ossian; 1 changing beer (often Cromarty) ⊞

A welcoming, long-established basement pub located near Golden Square just minutes off Union Street. The pub takes its name from the auction rooms upstairs. Unobtrusive background music plays, allowing for conversation, with no TV to disturb. Convenient for the Music Hall and His Majesty's Theatre, many use it for a pre or post-theatre drink. Frequently changing works by local artists decorate the walls and are for sale. Q≥🛜

Aboyne

Boat Inn

Charleston Road, AB34 5EL (N bank of River Dee next to Aboyne Bridge)

⊕ 11-11 (midnight Fri & Sat) ☎ (01339) 886137 ⊕ theboatinnaboyne.co.uk

3 changing beers (sourced nationally) ⊞

Popular riverside inn with a food-oriented lounge, newly redecorated. Junior diners (and adults) may request to see the model train, complete with sound effects, traverse the entire pub at picture-rail

SCOTLAND

height upon completion of their meal. The local Rotary Club regularly meets here. The public bar has been extended, with a recess at the back which is used for musicians on live music nights, staged twice-monthly on Thursday or Friday evenings. A monthly quiz night is held. Self-catering accommodation is available and one of the rooms has full disabled facilities. Q☆✿⊈◑&A♣P❀✿

Alford

Forbes Arms Hotel
Bridge of Alford, AB33 8QJ (1½ miles from Alford on the A944)
✪ 11 (3.30 Mon & Tue)-11; 11-midnight Fri & Sat
☎ (01975) 562108 ⊕ theforbesarmshotel.co.uk
2 changing beers (often Inveralmond Ossian, or Thrappledouser) Ⓗ
Small fishing-oriented hotel on the banks of the River Don. The public bar has the feel of a dark, wood-lined cave with one end dominated by a projection TV screen used for sporting events. The lounge bar has a warming wood-burning stove and there is a separate restaurant and conservatory dining area with river views. The riverside garden is popular in summer. The Grampian Transport Museum with its own miniature railway is nearby and the Castle Trail and a dry ski slope are also close. ☆✿⊈◑&A♣P❀✿

Ballater

Alexandra Hotel
12 Bridge Square, AB35 5QJ
✪ 11-2.30, 5-midnight; 11-midnight Fri & Sun
☎ (01339) 755376 ⊕ alexandrahotelballater.co.uk
Cairngorm Trade Winds; 2 changing beers (sourced regionally; often Cairngorm, Inveralmond, Orkney) Ⓗ
Originally built as a private home in 1800 and becoming the Alexandra Hotel in 1915, this smart refurbished lounge bar is popular with locals for lunches and suppers and regular bar drinkers too. It is easily spotted on entering the village from Aboyne, with prominent external displays of prior Guide entries. Handy for a stop-off on your way to Braemar for the Highland Games or for a visit with the royals at Balmoral. ☆⊈◑&AP❀✿

Balmoral Bar
1 Netherley Place, AB35 5QE
✪ 11-midnight (1am Thu-Sat); 12.30-midnight Sun
☎ (01339) 755462
Caledonian Deuchars IPA; 1 changing beer (sourced regionally; often Inveralmond) Ⓗ
Smart public bar on a corner opposite the village square. Two large plasma screens show sport and news while the adjacent pool room also has two large screens. An old poster on the wall shows the coach timetable of days gone by from Aberdeen. Evening meals are served only in summer. The pub is under the same ownership as the St Machar Bar in Aberdeen. The guest beer is often from Inveralmond Brewery. ☆◑&A♣⊟✿

Glenaden Hotel
6 Church Square, AB35 5NE
✪ 11-1 (midnight Mon-Wed) ☎ (01339) 755488
3 changing beers (sourced regionally; often Burnside) Ⓗ
On the far side of the town square, this small hotel serves up to three beers, always Scottish, with

Burnside a regular favourite and darker ales preferred by the locals. There may be fewer pumps in use in the winter months. An annual beer festival is held in the function suite to the rear in the autumn. Q☆✿⊈◑&♣P⊟❀✿

Banchory

Douglas Arms Hotel
22 High Street, AB31 5SR
✪ 11-midnight (1am Fri & Sat); 12-midnight Sun
☎ (01330) 822547 ⊕ douglasarms.co.uk
Cairngorm Trade Winds; 2 changing beers Ⓗ
Small hotel, recently upgraded with a new lounge/diner primarily used for bar suppers. The public bar and adjacent snug have plasma TVs for sport and the pool/TV room also has a large screen and is often frequented by the local rugby club and opposition. The bar is a classic Scottish long bar with etched windows and vintage mirrors, and features in CAMRA's Scotland's True Heritage Pubs. To the rear is a large south-facing decking space, ideal for fair-weather drinking. The public bar usually opens from 3pm. Q☆✿⊈◑&A⊟❀✿

Ravenswood Club (Royal British Legion)
25 Ramsay Road, AB31 5TS (up Mount St from A93, then second right)
✪ 11-11 (midnight Fri & Sat) ☎ (01330) 822347
⊕ banchorylegion.com
2 changing beers Ⓗ
Large British Legion club with a comfortable lounge adjoining the pool and TV room and a spacious function room well-used by local clubs and societies as well as members. Darts and snooker are popular and played most evenings. The two handpumps offer excellent value and the beer choice is constantly changing, with ales consistently the best quality in the village. An elevated terrace has fine views of the Deeside hills. Show a copy of this Guide or your CAMRA membership card for entry. ☆✿⊈◑&A♣P

Brodie

Old Mill Inn
IV36 2TD (on main A96 between Forres and Nairn)
✪ 11.30-11; 11.45-11 Sun ☎ (01309) 641605
⊕ oldmillinnbrodie.com
5 changing beers (sourced regionally; often Speyside Craft, Swannay, Windswept) Ⓗ
This gem is a spacious, family-friendly pub-restaurant with a cosy fireside area, smart restaurant, function room and a charming conservatory with views of the old watermill and garden. Up to five ales are available, mainly from Scottish micros. An excellent range of meals is offered with specials changing daily. Live Scottish/Irish instrumental music plays on Sunday evening. Brodie Castle is nearby and the popular Brodie Countryfare is opposite. A beer festival is held in June. Q☆✿⊈◑&AP⊟(10,11)✿

Catterline

Creel Inn
AB39 2UL (on coast off A92, 5 miles S of Stonehaven)
✪ 12-2, 5.30-midnight (1am Fri); 12-1am Sat; 12-midnight Sun; closed Mon Nov-Feb ☎ (01569) 750254
⊕ thecreelinn.co.uk

4 changing beers (sourced regionally; often Cromarty, Inveralmond, Swannay) 🅷
Set in a scenic cliff-top location, the view from the rear garden of this small village inn is not to be missed. Catterline is known as an artists' village, the most famous being Joan Eardley – one of her paintings is on display in the pub along with other artwork. The Creel is primarily a food venue but the bar area serves as the village local with up to four beers on offer, usually from Scottish micros. Todhead Lighthouse, Crawton Bird Sanctuary and Kinneff Old Church are nearby. ⌖❀◐&♣P🏠❀

Craigellachie

Highlander Inn
10 Victoria Street, AB38 9SR (on A95, opp post office)
❀ 12-11 (12.30am Fri & Sat) ☎ (01340) 881446
⊕ whiskyinn.com
3 changing beers (often Rothes, Spey Valley, Windswept) 🅷
One of the top whisky bars in the world and popular with visitors to the area and lovers of the malt alike, the Highlander can be busy during whisky festivals and the tourist season. All food is sourced locally and prepared in the hotel kitchen. An outside decked area with tables and chairs is a delight on a sunny afternoon for dining and drinking. CRAC (Craigellachie Real Ale Club) meets here on the first Wednesday of the month.
Q⌖❀◪◐🛏Å♣P🖥(36)🛜

Cullen

Three Kings
17-21 North Castle Street, AB56 4SA
❀ 5-11 Wed; 12-2, 5-12.30am Thu-Sat; 12-2, 5-11 Sun; closed Mon & Tue ☎ (01542) 840031
3 changing beers (sourced regionally; often Orkney, Windswept) 🅷
Situated close to an impressive but now defunct railway viaduct, this small, family-run pub was converted over 40 years ago from 150-year-old railway workers' cottages. A low-beamed roof and real fire help to create a cosy atmosphere on colder days. There is a separate 25-cover restaurant to the rear and a large outdoor drinking area complete with pétanque courts. Families are welcome, with plenty of toys to keep the children amused. Up to three beers are served, mainly from Scottish micros. Q⌖❀◪◐🛏🖥(35)🛜

Dyce

Granite City ✅
Main Terminal, Aberdeen Airport, AB21 7DU
❀ 6am (8am Sat)-10; 8am-9 Sun ☎ (01224) 725711
Sharp's Doom Bar; 4 changing beers (sourced nationally) 🅷
In the main terminal of Aberdeen Airport, close to the entrance, this Wetherspoon bar is popular with airport staff, travellers and offshore workers. Alcohol is served during all opening times. The walls display informative framed photographs of local personalities including 'The Scottish Samurai' Thomas Blake Glover – one of the prime movers of Japan's industrialisation in the late-19th century. An extensive outdoor area features the Baby Boar, a sculpture carved from a one-ton boulder of local Kemnay granite. ⌖❀◐&🖥(727,27)🛜

Elgin

Drouthy Cobbler ✅
Shepherd's Close, 48A High Street, IV30 1BU
❀ 8am-12.30am (1.30am Fri & Sat) ☎ (01343) 553933
⊕ thedrouthycobbler.co.uk
3 changing beers (sourced regionally; often Windswept, Wooha) 🅷
Smart and elegant, long and narrow bar named after John Shanks, who was a shoemaker and an important figure in the conservation of Elgin Cathedral. Excellent food is on offer including brunch on Sundays. Three ales are on handpump alongside many local bottled beers. A constantly increasing variety of whiskies (now more than 80) and gins is also stocked. There are benches outside in the lane and a small garden area. Alcohol is served from 11am. Q⌖❀◐&🛏

Muckle Cross ✅
34 High Street, IV30 1BU
❀ 8am-midnight (1am Fri & Sat); 9am-11.45 Sun
☎ (01343) 559030
Caledonian Deuchars IPA; Greene King Abbot; Sharp's Doom Bar; 4 changing beers (sourced nationally; often Isle of Skye) 🅷
A small, particularly good and deservedly popular Wetherspoon pub in a former bicycle repair shop with friendly, efficient staff. The long, pleasant room has ample seating, including a family area. Eight handpumps offer a wide range of beers from national and Scottish micros. The pub also stocks a good choice of malt whiskies from more than 20 local distilleries. An extensive menu features healthy options as well as pub grub. Open from 8am (9am Sun) for coffee and breakfast. Q⌖◐&⇌●🖥🛜

Fettercairn

Ramsay Arms
Burnside Road, AB30 1XX
❀ 12-3, 5.30-11; 12-11.30 Fri & Sat; 12.30-11 Sun
☎ (01561) 340334 ⊕ ramsayarmshotel.co.uk
Inveralmond Ossian, Thrappledouser 🅷
In the shadow of the Victoria Commemorative Arch, erected in recognition of the Queen's first trip to the north-east of Scotland, when she spent the night in the hotel, its Victorian heritage lends itself to the cuisine in the open, modern lounge. It is close to Fasque Estate, residence of Sir William Gladstone, and near the visitor centre at the Fettercairn distillery. May close at 10pm in winter depending on custom. ⌖❀🛏◐&P🛜

Findhorn

Crown & Anchor Inn ✅
44 Findhorn, IV36 3YF
❀ 12-10 (11 Fri); 12-midnight Sat; 12-11 Sun
☎ (01309) 690243 ⊕ crownandanchorinn.co.uk
Timothy Taylor Landlord; 1 changing beer 🅷
Spacious, well-kept seaside inn with solid, rustic decor and separate restaurant and dining areas, serving a wide menu of locally sourced food. Outside are many picnic tables and a fine smokooterie for smoking in comfort. The conservatory has splendid views over Findhorn Bay to the Culbin Forest. The pub is popular with locals and summer visitors who come for sailing, camping or strolling along the sands.
Q⌖❀◪◐&Å♣P🖥(31,31B)

Kimberley Inn

94 Findhorn, IV36 3YG

✪ 12-midnight ☎ (01309) 690492 ⊕ kimberleyinn.com

2 changing beers (sourced regionally; often Cairngorm, Houston, Orkney) Ⓗ

Styling itself as Moray's seafood pub, the Kimberley is situated right on the shore of Findhorn Bay, with superb views from the patio outside. The bar is wood-panelled with snugs at either end. Two handpumps dispense a wide variety of beers, mainly from Scottish micros. The menu of home-cooked food features local fish and even local ice cream. Findhorn is a breezy village with views over the sands to the Moray Firth, framed by distant hills. Q☽✿❍Ⓓ & ▲♣Ｐ🚌 (31,31B)

Forres

Mosset Tavern

Gordon Street, IV36 1DL (just off A96 in town centre)

✪ 11-12.30am (1.30am Fri & Sat); 12-midnight Sun

☎ (01309) 672981 ⊕ mossettavern.com

Cairngorm Trade Winds; 4 changing beers (sourced regionally; often Cromarty, Speyside Craft, Swannay) Ⓗ

Described as 'the country pub in the heart of Forres', this smart, extremely popular Scottish lounge bar/restaurant is situated next to the Mosset burn and pond, with swans and ducks. The friendly, efficient staff serve ale from a single handpump in the lounge and four in the spacious, comfortable public bar, where there are pool tables and large screens showing sport. A large function room is also available. Live music plays on Friday evenings, and there is a pub quiz every Tuesday at 8.30pm. ☽✿🚐Ⓓ & ≠♣Ｐ🚌 (10,11)📶

Fraserburgh

Elizabethan Bar & Lounge

36 Union Grove, AB43 9PH

✪ 9.30am-1am; 9am-1am Sun ☎ (01346) 510464

3 changing beers (sourced regionally; often Cairngorm, Kelburn, Loch Ness) Ⓗ

Set in the middle of a housing estate and near the local Academy, with a mock-Tudor exterior, the large bar and lounge have three distinct sections, with sport on TV in two of them. The bar has featured more than 600 different ales over the past few years, as well as over 200 malts – the largest collection in the area. The beach, harbour and lighthouse museum are just a mile away. A former CAMRA Pub of the Year. ☽▲♣Ｐ🚌😺📶

Garlogie

Garlogie Inn

AB32 6RX (on B9125)

✪ 11-2.30, 5-10.30 (11 Fri); 12-11 Sat; 12.30-9 Sun

☎ (01224) 743212 ⊕ garlogieinn.com

1 changing beer (sourced regionally; often Deeside) Ⓗ

This family-run roadside inn dates from the early-19th century. Numerous extensions have been added over time to the original building, including a large restaurant area, and the pub has a reputation for excellent food (booking advised). Drinkers are welcome in the small bar area, with beer served on a single handpump. Drum Castle and Cullerlie Stone Circle are close at hand. Beer is available in the summer months only. Q✿Ⓓ & Ｐ🚌 (X18)📶

Inverurie

Black Bull ✓

50 North Street, AB51 4RS (on B9001 heading N)

✪ 2-11; 12-1am Fri; 11-1am Sat; 11-11 Sun

☎ (01467) 621242

3 changing beers (sourced regionally; often Deeside, Fyne Ales, Inveralmond) Ⓗ

Old staging inn now a family-run small hotel and friendly local pub with a separate pool room. The pub is home to four darts teams and has live music each Saturday and a quiz night on Thursday. One Inveralmond beer is usually served with up to two guests usually from Scottish micros but sometimes from further afield. Bar snacks are served. ✿🚐Ⓓ & ≠♣Ｐ🚌 (41,41A,493)😺📶

Gordon Highlander ✓

West High Street, AB51 3QQ

✪ 9am-11.30 (1am Fri & Sat) ☎ (01462) 626780

Sharp's Doom Bar; 4 changing beers (sourced nationally; often Inveralmond, Strathaven, Windswept) Ⓗ

A fine Wetherspoon pub in a splendid Art Deco building which used to be the Victoria Cinema. The name refers to the famous local regiment, and also to a preserved steam engine named after the regiment, which was based at the now defunct Inverurie Locomotive Works nearby. Both historic references are documented in various displays. The books on the shelves are free to read and take home, with donations welcome. The usual Wetherspoon beer festivals feature. Alcohol is served from 11am. ☽Ⓓ & ≠🚌 (10,37)📶

Lossiemouth

Skerry Brae Hotel

Stotfield Road, IV31 6QS

✪ 12-11 (midnight Fri & Sat) ☎ (01343) 812040

⊕ skerrybrae.co.uk

Windswept Blonde, APA Ⓗ

Modern hotel lounge bar, refurbished and reopened in 2012 after an uncertain future due to RAF cutbacks, with commanding views across the championship golf course, West Beach and the Moray Firth – ideal for sunny days at the coast which can be viewed from the deck and large conservatory. There is a decent selection of malt whiskies in addition to the two regular ales. Hearty food is served all day, every day. Bus stops are close by but beware, all buses go to Elgin but alternate ones run in opposite directions. Q☽✿❍Ⓓ & ▲Ｐ🚌 (33A,33C)😺📶

Marykirk

Marykirk Hotel

Main Street, AB30 1UT

✪ 12-2.30, 5-11; 12-midnight Fri & Sat ☎ (01674) 840239

⊕ marykirkhotel.co.uk

Inveralmond Thrappledouser Ⓗ

Built in the 18th century, this Category C listed building is a former coaching inn in Marykirk, which lies between Montrose and Laurencekirk. It is popular for hunting and fishing, with the river North Esk, one of the top salmon rivers in Scotland, nearby. The hotel holds a children's certificate. Aficionados of old brewery mirrors can find examples from Lochside Brewery in Montrose and Boroughlodge Brewery in Edinburgh. Bus services between Montrose and Laurencekirk stop in the village. ☽✿🚐Ⓓ & ♣Ｐ🚌📶

Methlick

Ythanview Hotel

Main Street, AB41 7DT

🌑 11-2.30, 5-11 (1am Fri); 11-12.30am Sat; 12-11 Sun
☎ (01651) 806235 ⊕ ythanviewhotel.co.uk
**2 changing beers (sourced regionally; often Fyne
Ales, Swannay, Windswept)** Ⓗ

Traditional inn in the village centre, home to the
MCC (Methlick Cricket Club) at Lairds nearby. Log
fires warm both the lounge and the friendly sports-
themed public bar at the rear. The pub is renowned
for the owner Jay's special chicken curry, and steak
night on Thursday is also busy. Meals are available
all day at weekends. Live music and quiz nights
take place on most Saturdays. Beers are exclusively
from Scottish micros. Haddo House, Tolquhon
Castle and Pitmedden Garden are nearby.
🏠🏵🚪◑♣☂🚬(290,291)😺📶

Monymusk

Grant Arms Hotel

AB51 7HJ (Stagecoach 220 bus from Aberdeen or Alford)

🌑 11-11 (11.30 Fri & Sat) ☎ (01467) 651226
⊕ grantarmsmonymusk.com
**Timothy Taylor Landlord; 1 changing beer (sourced
regionally; often Belhaven, Deeside)** Ⓗ

Former coaching inn dating from the 18th century,
with later additions, now a small hotel with lounge
and public bars. A fine display of model trucks can
be seen above the lounge gantries as well as a
small collection of trolls - the Norwegian type!
Situated at the centre of a conservation area, this is
a popular haunt for walkers as well as salmon and
trout fishermen on the River Don. The Pitfichie and
Cairn William mountain bike trails are close by.
Breakfasts are served from 10 to 11.30.
Q🏵🚪◑&♣🚬😺

Netherley

Lairhillock Inn

AB39 3QS (signed off B979, 3 miles S of B9077)

🌑 11-11 (midnight Fri & Sat) ☎ (01569) 730001
⊕ lairhillock.co.uk
Timothy Taylor Landlord; 2 changing beers Ⓗ

The INN sign on the roof of this rambling building
in attractive open countryside makes it easy to spot
from the road. It has a traditional wood-panelled
bar warmed by a large log fire in winter, a lounge
with an open fireplace and a large conservatory
area, popular for dining. A separate function room,
the Crynoch, is also available. Two guest beers (one
in winter) are frequently sourced from Scottish
breweries. Convenient for the attractions of
Stonehaven and Royal Deeside. Q🏠🏵◑&♣P😺

Oldmeldrum

Redgarth

Kirk Brae, AB51 0DJ (outskirts of village, signed off
A947)

🌑 11-3, 5-11 (midnight Fri & Sat); 12-11 Sun
☎ (01651) 872353 ⊕ redgarth.com

**3 changing beers (sourced regionally; often
Cromarty, Fyne Ales, Swannay)** Ⓗ /Ⓖ

This renowned local hotel and pub has imposing
views over the eastern Grampian mountains. A
winner of many local CAMRA awards, it retains a
strong reputation for the imaginative choice of
excellent-quality beers, sourced from many
Scottish micros. A successful blend of popular
family restaurant and marvellous real ale pub, it is
appreciated by a dedicated core of regulars. During
occasional Brewers in Residence evenings, three
handpumped ales may be supplemented by many
more on gravity. Q🏠🏵🚪◑▲♣P🚬(35,X35)📶

Stonehaven

Belvedere Hotel

41 Evan Street, AB39 2ET

🌑 11-11 (1am Fri & Sat) ☎ (01569) 762672
⊕ belvederestonehaven.co.uk
1 changing beer (sourced regionally; often Orkney) Ⓗ

Large Victorian house in the town centre near the
market square, converted to a 10-bedroom hotel
and pub. The bar area is in a modern extension to
the rear of the property, overlooking the large,
secluded walled garden, which is ideal for outdoor
drinking, weather permitting. Dunnottar Castle, the
picturesque harbour and seasonal open-air bathing
pool are close by, as is the original home of the
deep-fried Mars Bar! 🏠🏵🚪◑&▲P🚬😺📶

Marine Hotel 🍽

9-10 Shorehead, AB39 2JY (overlooking harbour)

🌑 11-midnight (1am Fri & Sat) ☎ (01569) 762155
⊕ marinehotelstonehaven.co.uk
**Timothy Taylor Landlord; 5 changing beers (sourced
regionally; often Burnside, Loch Ness, Windswept)** Ⓗ

Small harbourside hotel featuring simple wood
panelling in the bar and a rustic lounge with an
open fireplace. The upstairs restaurant has its own
handpumps. Seating outside offers a splendid view
of the harbour. Two to three beers from the hotel-
owned Six Degrees North brewery at Laurencekirk
are available alongside several Belgian beers on
draught and a massive choice of bottled Belgian
beers. Historic Dunnottar Castle is one mile south
and the open-air bathing pool one mile north.
CAMRA Country Pub of the Year 2016 and winner of
many previous awards. 🏠🏵🚪◑▲🚬😺📶

Ship Inn

5 Shorehead, AB39 2JY (on harbour front)

🌑 11-midnight (1am Fri & Sat) ☎ (01569) 762617
⊕ shipinnstonehaven.com
**2 changing beers (sourced regionally; often
Inveralmond)** Ⓗ

Built in 1771, this harbour-front hotel has a
maritime-themed, wood-panelled bar and a
seating area outside overlooking the water. Two
beers from Scottish breweries are normally offered
and an extensive range of malt whiskies is stocked.
A modern restaurant with panoramic harbour
views is adjacent to the bar, with food served all
day at the weekend. Accommodation is available
in 11 guest rooms. 🏠🏵🚪◑&▲🚬😺📶

SCOTLAND

ARGYLL & THE ISLES

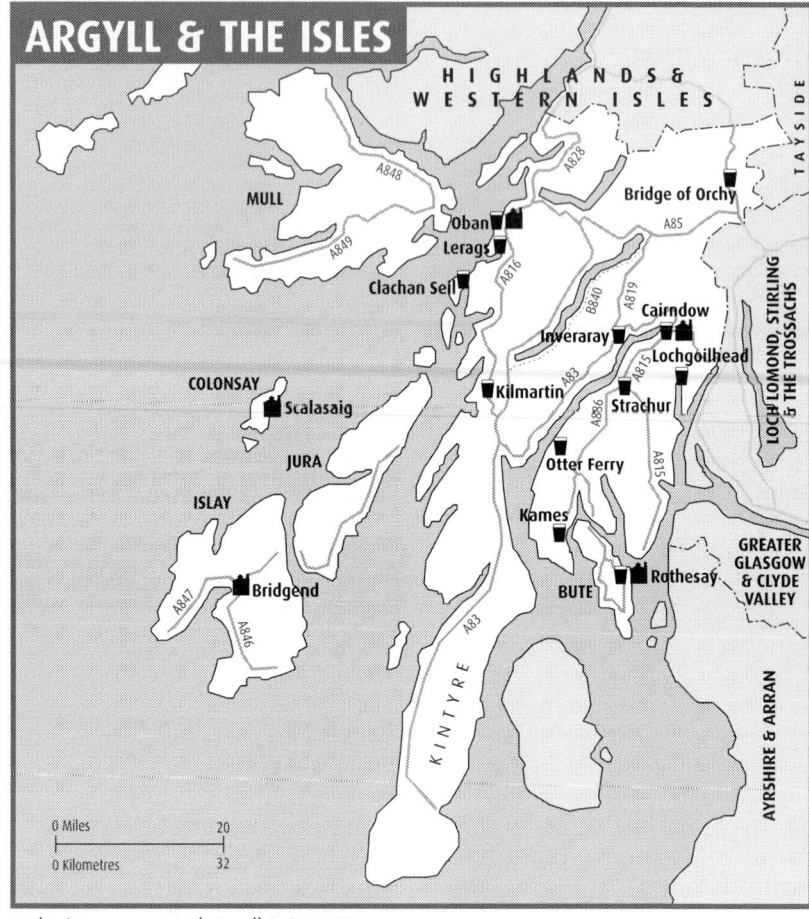

Authority area covered: Argyll & Bute UA

Bridge of Orchy

Bridge of Orchy Hotel ✓
PA36 4AD
☼ 11-10.45 (11.45 Fri & Sat) ☎ (01838) 400208
⊕ bridgeoforchy.co.uk
**Harviestoun Bitter & Twisted; 1 changing beer
(sourced regionally; often Harviestoun)** Ⓗ
Prominent hotel on the A82 heading north before
it climbs up to Rannoch Moor, a popular stopping-
off place on the West Highland Way and at times
busy with walkers. Some take advantage of the
accommodation in the hotel itself, the annexe
behind or in the bunkhouse. The front bar looks
across the road to the mountains beyond while the
restaurant to the rear enjoys panoramic views
across and down Glen Orchy.
ਠ⊛⇦◖▶⇌P♈(915)♣ 🛜

Cairndow

Fyne Ales Brewery Tap Ⓛ
PA26 8BJ (up side road at head of Loch Fyne)
☼ 10-6 ☎ (01499) 600120 ⊕ fyneales.com/brewery-tap
**Fyne Ales Jarl; 4 changing beers (sourced locally;
often Fyne Ales)** Ⓗ
Tastefully converted farm building, part of the
original farm complex which was used to set up

the brewery. The polished granite bar front displays
the people who created the brewery and
ingredients for making the beer. In good weather,
seating in the courtyard allows visitors to view the
work in progress and savour the spectacular
scenery. This is still a working farm and beef from
the Highland cattle is on sale and used to make the
excellent pies. Q ਠ⊛&P♣ 🛜

Stagecoach Inn Ⓛ
PA26 8BN (on slip road off A83)
☼ 11-11 (1am Fri & Sat); 11-midnight Sun
☎ (01499) 600286 ⊕ cairndowinn.com
**2 changing beers (sourced regionally; often Fyne
Ales, Loch Lomond)** Ⓗ
This long-established coaching inn has played host
to many famous people enjoying a rest before the
long climb up Glen Kinglas. Nowadays, visitors can
appreciate the many mountain and woodland
walks or relax viewing the scenery across Loch

REAL ALE BREWERIES
Argyll Oban
Bute Rothesay: Isle of Bute
Colonsay Scalasaig: Isle of Colonsay
Fyne Cairndow
Islay Bridgend: Isle of Islay

Fyne. The friendly bar to one side offers two real ales, though only one is available at quieter times. An archway leads through to an old-world restaurant converted from stables and to a comfortable lounge/function room beyond.
🌣❀🛏🕀🕭👌▲♣🅿🖭 (926,976) 🐾 📶

Clachan Seil

Tigh an Truish Inn 🛈
PA34 4QZ
🌣 11 (12 Sun)-11 summer; 11-2.30, 5-11; 11-11 Fri & Sat; 12-11 Sun winter ☎ (01852) 300242 ⊕ tigh-an-truish.co.uk
2 changing beers (sourced nationally; often Fyne Ales, Orkney) 🅷
The House of the Trousers was allegedly where islanders changed from kilts during the Jacobite risings when visiting the mainland. Now this attractive pub provides an ideal viewing place for the famous Bridge over the Atlantic. The L-shaped bar features a gantry designed like a ship's galley and an unusual high-level bench seat. An iron stove warms the bar in winter while fine weather can be enjoyed in the garden and patio. No meals are available in winter. Q🌣❀🛏🕀🅿🖭 (418) 🐾 📶

Inveraray

George Hotel
Main Street East, PA32 8TT
🌣 11-midnight; 12-midnight Sun ☎ (01499) 302111
⊕ thegeorgehotel.co.uk
2 changing beers (sourced locally; often Fyne Ales) 🅷
Busy, attractive old hotel in a model town setting, owned by the same family for six generations. There are several rooms off the main bar, each with flagstone floors and solid dark-stained wooden furniture, warmed by log fires, giving an old-fashioned ambience. The meals have an emphasis on good-quality local produce and are served throughout, including the popular and lively public bar to one side. The conservatory to the rear hosts weddings in winter.
Q🌣❀🛏🕀🕭👌▲🅿🖭 (926,976) 🐾 📶

Kames

Kames Hotel 🛈
PA21 2AF
🌣 12-midnight ☎ (01700) 811489 ⊕ kames-hotel.com
Fyne Ales Highlander; 1 changing beer (sourced locally; often Fyne Ales) 🅷
Recently refurbished historic hotel full of character, looking down on a small harbour and with stunning views over the Kyles of Bute and beyond. The friendly and lively bar is popular with both locals and visitors, some of whom are seagoing and make use of the hotel's 15 moorings. Meals are freshly prepared and sourced locally where possible, as are the real ales which usually come from nearby Fyne Ales. 🌣❀🛏🕀🖭 (477,478) 🐾 📶

Kilmartin

Kilmartin Hotel 🛈
PA31 8RQ (on A816 10 miles N of Lochgilphead)
🌣 12 (5 winter)-11; 11-1am Fri; 11-midnight Sat; 12-11 Sun
☎ (01546) 510250 ⊕ kilmartin-hotel.com
3 changing beers (sourced regionally; often Caledonian, Loch Lomond, Orkney) 🅷
Sited on the top of a small promontory, overlooking prehistoric Kilmartin Glen on the A816,

this whitewashed hotel is easy to find. The small L-shaped bar has a cosy nook round the fire and pool room to the rear, leading to a beer garden. The dining room to the side serves good wholesome food. This is a convenient refreshment stop following a visit to the local museum or a walk to the nearby ancient stone circles.
🌣❀🛏🕀👌▲🅿🖭 (423) 🐾 📶

Lerags

Barn 🛈
PA34 4SE
🌣 12-11 (1am Fri & Sat); closed Mon-Thu winter
☎ (01631) 564618 ⊕ cologin.co.uk/country-inn
2 changing beers (sourced locally; often Fyne Ales) 🅷
The Barn forms part of a holiday chalet and cottage complex in rugged hills to the south of Oban. The cosy bar, warmed by an iron stove, was formerly a cowshed, though all that remains are the stall dividers used as back rests for the bench seating. To the front, the verandah overlooking the duck pond and play area has been enclosed to provide extra space whatever the weather. CAMRA Argyll Pub of the Year 2015. Q🌣❀🛏🕀▲🅿 🐾 📶

Lochgoilhead

Shore House Inn 🛈
PA24 8AA
🌣 12-11; closed Mon & Tue ☎ (01301) 703340
⊕ theshorehouse.net
Fyne Ales Highlander; 1 changing beer (sourced locally; often Fyne Ales) 🅷
Located at the head of Loch Goil with stupendous views down the loch, there are numerous activity and outdoor centres nearby and the inn makes an ideal stop for visiting the Argyll Forest Park or walking the Cowal Way. The bright and cheerful bar has comfortable wood seating. The restaurant has a varied menu and wood-fired pizza oven. A guest ale is available during the summer. The inn closes from early January until early February.
Q🌣❀🛏🕀👌▲🅿🖭 (302,484) 📶

Oban

Corryvreckan ✔
The Waterfront Centre, Railway Pier, PA34 4LW
🌣 7am-midnight (1am Fri & Sat) ☎ (01631) 568910
Caledonian Deuchars IPA; Greene King Abbot; Sharp's Doom Bar; 6 changing beers (sourced nationally) 🅷
A recently opened Wetherspoon pub named after the famous whirlpool between Jura and Scarba. A modern building between the station and ferry terminals, the large single room has a maritime theme throughout, watched over by a carved sea eagle. The windows to one side provide views across Oban Bay to the islands beyond, ideal for watching the many ferries come and go. Alcohol is served from 11am. 🌣🕀👌🍴🖭 📶

Cuan Mor 🛈
60 George Street, PA34 5SD
🌣 11-11; 12.30-11 Sun ☎ (01631) 565078 ⊕ cuanmor.co.uk
3 changing beers (sourced locally; often Oban Bay) 🅷
This smart, modernised bar and restaurant is set on the harbour, with views across the bay to the ferry terminus and the island of Kerrera. Not surprisingly, there is a strong emphasis on seafood and local produce. For those who prefer a drink only, there is seating around the bar and at the back. Beer is

SCOTLAND

brewed in a back room by the Oban Bay Brewery and there is always one ale available, increasing to three in the summer. ⏩◑➔⇌🖵🛜

Otter Ferry

Oystercatcher Ⓛ

PA21 2DH (on B8000)
🕓 11-11 summer; closed Mon-Fri; 5-11 Sat; 12.30-5 Sun winter ☎ (01700) 821229 ⊕ theoystercatcher.co.uk
2 changing beers (sourced nationally; often Fyne Ales) Ⓗ

Attractive beach-front pub by a former ferry dock set in part of Argyll's Secret Coast on the eastern side of Loch Fyne. The bar and lounge feature real fires, comfortable chairs and two handpumps serving mainly Scottish beers, particularly from Fyne Ales. The quality meals concentrate on local produce and seafood. There are 15 moorings available to motor vessels, RIBS and yacht owners, who are advised to take note of the mile long, sandy beach, Otter Spit. ⏩⛵◑🕭AP🛜

Rothesay

Black Bull Inn

West Princes Street, PA20 9AF (opp harbour)
🕓 11-11 (midnight Fri & Sat); 12.30-11 Sun
☎ (01700) 502366

3 changing beers (sourced regionally) Ⓗ
This ever-popular pub in the centre of town, close to the harbour, is approached from the mainland via the splendid Wemyss Bay rail station and ferry terminal. A fine example of Victorian toilets can be seen close by. This two-bar pub, always popular with yachtsmen, is ideally situated as a meeting point for food and drink before trips to all corners of the island. One of the three ales is brewed locally by Bute Beer Company. ◑🖵🐾🛜

Strachur

Creggans Inn Ⓛ

PA27 8BX (on A815 at N end of village)
🕓 11-11; 12-11 Sun ☎ (01369) 860279
⊕ creggans-inn.co.uk
2 changing beers (sourced locally; often Fyne Ales) Ⓗ
Large whitewashed inn built in the mid-1800s and where the ferry left for Inveraray. The cosy public McPhunn's bar, warmed by a log fire, plays occasional host to the local shinty team. Extra seating has been added and a pool room extends further back. Adjacent dining rooms serve bistro meals concentrating on local and seasonal produce, including seafood. A more extensive menu is available in a separate restaurant.
Q⏩⛵🚃◑P🖵(484,486)🐾🛜

Tigh an Truish, Clachan Seil (Photo: Alan Williamson)

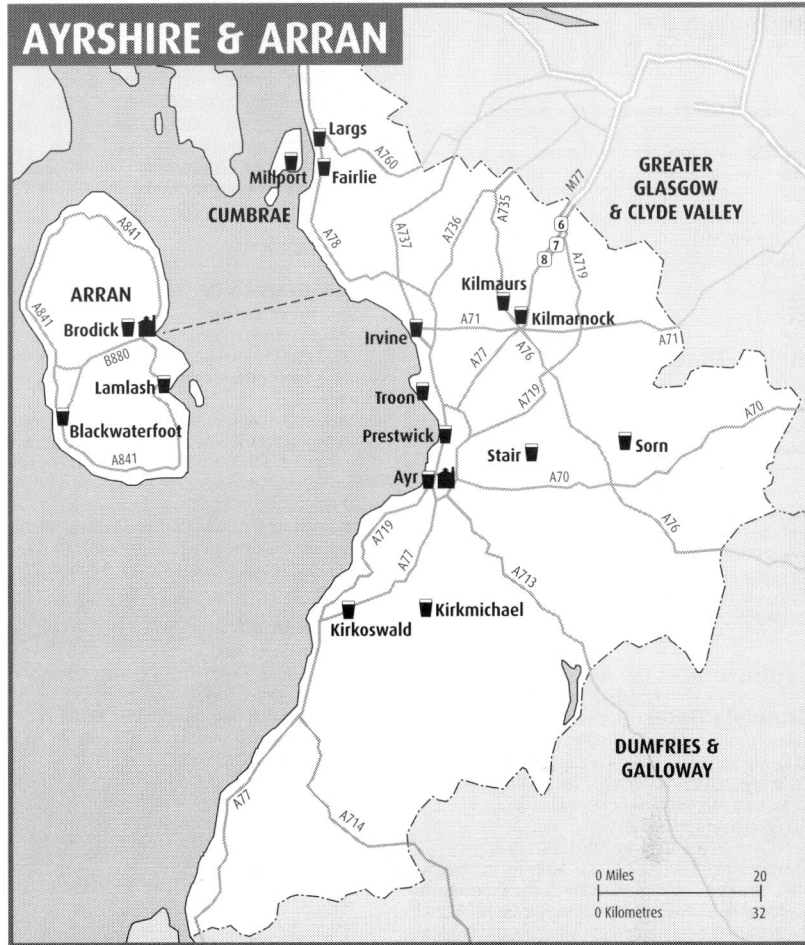

AYRSHIRE & ARRAN

Largs
Millport
Fairlie
CUMBRAE

GREATER GLASGOW & CLYDE VALLEY

ARRAN
Brodick
Lamlash
Blackwaterfoot

Kilmaurs
Kilmarnock
Irvine
Troon
Prestwick
Stair
Sorn
Ayr

Kirkoswald
Kirkmichael

DUMFRIES & GALLOWAY

0 Miles 20
0 Kilometres 32

SCOTLAND

Authority areas covered: East Ayrshire UA, North Ayrshire UA, South Ayrshire UA

Ayr

Chestnuts Hotel

52 Racecourse Road, KA7 2UZ (on A719, 1 mile S of centre)

☼ 10-11 (12.30am Fri & Sat) ☎ (01292) 264393
⊕ chestnutshotel.com

3 changing beers (often Harviestoun, Inveralmond, Kelburn) Ⓗ

Three changing real ales from a range of breweries are offered in the 19th Hole, a delightful oak-beamed hall with an interesting history and a huge collection of whisky water jugs. Excellent food is available in the bar and separate restaurant. Open log fires add to the comfortable atmosphere in winter and a pleasant beer garden is very popular when weather allows. ⏰✿🛏️🍴👶🅿️🚌(9)🛜

Geordie's Byre

103 Main Street, KA8 8BU (N of centre, in Newton area, over river towards Prestwick)

☼ 11-11 (midnight Thu-Sat); 12.30-11 Sun
☎ (01292) 264925

4 changing beers (often Fyne Ales, Kelburn) Ⓐ
CAMRA award-winning 18th-century pub, serving up to four guest ales, sourced from far and wide. It

is one of the few Scottish pubs using traditional Scottish tall founts. Both the public bar and the lounge feature a wealth of memorabilia. A wide selection of malt whiskies and rums is also available. Handy for several local bus routes. Q🚌(2,4,14)🐾🛜

Glen Park Hotel Ⓛ

5 Racecourse Road, KA7 2DG

☼ 10-midnight; 12-midnight Sun ☎ (01292) 263891
Ayr Leezie Lundie, Jolly Beggars; 2 changing beers (often Ayr) Ⓗ

This comfortable lounge bar, in an attractive 1860s B-Listed Victorian building, is the brewery tap for Ayr Brewing Company, situated in the rear of the building. The guest ales are from Ayr Brewing and usually include a seasonal. Bar and restaurant meals are served daily except Monday. Beers are usually available to take away. ⏰✿🛏️👶♿️🚆🅿️🚌(9)🐾🛜

REAL ALE BREWERIES

Arran Brodick: Isle of Arran
Ayr 🍺 Ayr

Wellingtons Bar

17 Wellington Square, KA7 1EZ
🕐 11-12.30am; 12-midnight Sun ☎ (01292) 262794
🌐 welliesbar.weebly.com
3 changing beers (often Fyne Ales, Kelburn) Ⓗ
A large Wellington boot advertises the location of
this basement bar. Close to the seafront, bus
station and local government offices, it attracts
tourists and office workers alike. The Wednesday
evening quiz is popular, and weekend events
include live music or a DJ on Saturday and an
acoustic session on Sunday evening. ◐≠🖰🐾🛜

Blackwaterfoot: Isle of Arran

Kinloch Hotel

KA27 8ET
🕐 12-midnight ☎ (01770) 860444 🌐 bw-kinlochhotel.co.uk
**House beer (by Ayr); 1 changing beer (often Brains,
Caledonian, Theakston)** Ⓗ
Sitting in a quiet and peaceful rural village, this
family hotel offers coastal comfort and spectacular
scenery. The Kinloch has 37 bedrooms, a restaurant
and three refurbished bars. Fabulous local produce
is served including fish and seafood. Facilities
include a heated indoor swimming pool. A beer
festival is held in July.
🛏️🏨◐🕹️🐾♣●P🖰(322,323,324)🐾🛜

Brodick: Isle of Arran

Ormidale Hotel

Knowe Road, KA27 8BY (off A841 at W end of village)
🕐 12.30-2.30 (summer only), 4-midnight; 12-12.30am Sat;
12-midnight Sun ☎ (01770) 302293 🌐 ormidale-hotel.co.uk
**Arran Guid Ale; house beer (by Caledonian); 1
changing beer (often Ayr)** Ⓐ
Beers are served from traditional Scottish tall
founts on the boat-shaped bar, with Arran Blonde
often stocked in summer. Home-cooked meals are
recommended. Discos and folk nights are held, and
the attractive beer garden has views across Brodick
Bay. Accommodation is available all year round.
🛏️🏨◐🕹️♣P🖰(324)🐾🛜

Fairlie

Village Inn Ⓛ

46 Bay Street, KA29 0AL
🕐 11-midnight; 11 (1 winter)-1am Fri & Sat; 12.30-midnight
Sun; closed Mon & Tue winter ☎ (01475) 568432
🌐 villageinnfairlie.co.uk
2 changing beers (often Alechemy, Kelburn) Ⓗ
A popular local serving one or two ales, often from
local breweries. Good-quality reasonably priced
meals are available in the public bar and adjacent
restaurant, which displays sailing pictures
commemorating the famous Fife boatyard which
stood nearby. The pub runs a regular quiz and
occasional live music nights. Children are welcome
until 10pm in the restaurant but the public bar is a
child-free zone. Q🛏️🏨◐🕹️&P🖰(585)🐾🛜

Irvine

Ship Inn

122 Harbour Street, KA12 8PZ
🕐 10-11 (midnight Fri & Sat) ☎ (01294) 279722
🌐 theshipinnirvine.co.uk
2 changing beers (often Ayr) Ⓗ

The Ship is the oldest pub in Irvine, dating back to
1595 and licensed since 1754. It is close to the
Harbour Arts Centre and Magnum Leisure Centre.
There are several dining and drinking areas, all
adorned with maritime murals and bric-a-brac. A
mast forms part of the main bar structure. The pub
has an excellent reputation for food. There is
always one ale from Ayr Brewing Company, two
during the warmer months. Q🛏️🏨◐🕹️&≠🖰🐾🛜

Kilmarnock

Brass & Granite ✅

53 Grange Street, KA1 2DD
🕐 11-midnight (1am Thu-Sat); 12.30-midnight Sun
☎ (01563) 523431
**3 changing beers (often Houston, Inveralmond,
Strathaven)** Ⓗ
Open-plan pub near Kilmarnock town centre and
close to Rugby Park football ground. Guest ales are
usually sourced from local or Cumbrian brewers
and there is also a wide range of draught and
bottled Belgian beers available. Families are
welcome and food is available all day. Several TVs
show live sport and regular quizzes are held on
Sunday, Monday and Wednesday. 🛏️◐🕹️&≠♣🖰🐾🛜

First Edition ✅

50 Bank Street, KA1 1HA
🕐 9am-11 (1am Fri & Sat); 11-11 Sun ☎ (01563) 528833
🌐 firsteditionkilmarnock.co.uk
**Caledonian Deuchars IPA; Courage Best Bitter; 2
changing beers (often Stewart, Strathaven)** Ⓗ
A recently refurbished pub in former local
newspaper offices set in the historic core of the
town. A large, modern pub, it serves food all day in
bright surroundings. Four guest ales are available,
usually including one from a Scottish regional
brewer. 🛏️🏨◐🕹️≠🖰🛜

Kilmaurs

Weston Tavern

27 Main Street, KA3 2RQ
🕐 11-midnight (1am Fri & Sat); 12.30-midnight Sun
☎ (01563) 538805 🌐 westontavern.co.uk
1 changing beer Ⓗ
Classic country pub and restaurant with a tiled
floor, stone walls and a wood-burning fire. It sits
beside the Jougs, a former jailhouse and tollbooth
(jougs were iron collars used to restrain miscreants
and a set still hangs from the walls today). A single
pump dispenses ale from a rotating list of local
breweries. Regular live music and quiz nights are
held. 🏨◐🕹️&≠P🖰(1,13,337)

Kirkmichael

Kirkmichael Arms

3-5 Straiton Road, KA19 7PH
🕐 12-midnight (12.30am Fri & Sat) ☎ (01655) 750200
🌐 kirkmichaelarms.co.uk
2 changing beers (often Ayr) Ⓗ
A friendly country pub at the heart of the
community with a lounge bar and separate dining
room. Two handpumps serve a local Ayr Brewing
Co beer plus a guest. Excellent meals are available,
with food sourced locally where possible. Walkers
and dogs are made welcome, and small functions
are catered for. Q🛏️🏨◐🕹️&♣🖰(358,361)🐾🛜

Kirkoswald

Souter's Inn
47 Main Road, KA19 8HY
🌐 9am-11 (midnight Fri & Sat) ☎ (01655) 760653
🌐 soutersinn.com
Strathaven Trumpeter, Witches Brew Ⓗ
A thatched building that was originally the school that Robert Burns attended, and it was here that he met his first love, Peggy Thompson. Across the road in the graveyard lie the bodies of Tam o' Shanter, Souter Johnnie, Hugh Roger (his teacher) and Burns' grandparents. The pub is almost adjacent to the National Trust for Scotland's Souter Johnnie's Cottage and close to Culzean Castle. Both ales on the bar are from Strathaven Brewery. Their own ice creams are to die for.
🏃😺◗☙♿ΛΡ🚪(60)🛜

Lamlash: Isle of Arran

Drift Inn
KA27 8JN (nr ferry terminal)
🌐 12-11 (midnight Thu; 1am Fri & Sat) ☎ (01770) 600608
🌐 driftinnarran.com
3 changing beers (often Arran, Ayr, Fyne Ales) Ⓗ
Seafront pub with views of the Holy Isle. There are three guest beers in summer, mainly from Arran Brewery, Fyne Ales or Ayr Brewing Co, dropping to one in winter. An extensive range of food is served throughout the day. Closed for three weeks in January. 🏃😺◗♣Ρ🚪(323)🛜

Largs

JG Sharps Bar ✅
34-36 Nelson Street, KA30 8LW (turn off seafront at Nardini's; corner of Nelson St and Boyd St)
🌐 11-midnight (1am Fri & Sat); 12.30-midnight Sun
☎ (01475) 675515 🌐 jgsharps.co.uk
Sharp's Doom Bar; 1 changing beer Ⓗ
A large traditional pub with several drinking areas, an open fire warms the bar area. Good-quality pub meals are served at lunchtime and Friday to Sunday evenings. Games and sport on TV are in evidence and there is occasional live music. There is space for smokers in the beer garden outside.
Q🏃😺◗♿≈♣🚪😺🛜

Millport: Isle of Cumbrae

Fraser's Bar Ⓛ
7 Cardiff Street, KA28 0AS
🌐 11-midnight (1am Thu-Sat) ☎ (01475) 530518
2 changing beers (often Houston, Kelburn) Ⓗ
Welcoming pub close to the pier and an oasis in an otherwise real ale desert. Two handpumps serve a varied range, usually including one from a local brewery, and good-value pub food is available lunchtimes and early evenings. Children are welcome in the lounge until 8pm. Buses meet every ferry from Largs and terminate at the nearby pier. Q🏃😺◗♿Λ♣🚪(320)🛜

Prestwick

Prestwick Pioneer ✅
87 Main Street, KA9 1JS
🌐 8am-midnight (12.30am Fri & Sat) ☎ (01292) 473210
Caledonian Deuchars IPA; Greene King Abbot; Sharp's Doom Bar; changing beers Ⓗ
Modern Wetherspoon named after the first Scottish Aviation Pioneer built in 1947 at the nearby international airport. It has an airy feel with light-wood decor, and features photos of early Open Golf Championships at Prestwick and of Elvis at the nearby airport – the only place in the UK where he stepped foot. Ten handpumps serve local and national ales and food is available all day. Licensed from 10am. 🏃◗♿≈(Town)👜🚪🛜

Sorn

Sorn Inn
35 Main Street, KA5 6HU
🌐 12-2.30, 6-10 (midnight Fri); 12-midnight Sat; 12-10 Sun; closed Mon ☎ (01290) 551305 🌐 sorninn.com
1 changing beer (often Orkney) Ⓗ
Major community hub for residents of this conservation village in East Ayrshire. It has an award-winning restaurant featuring a menu that offers a mix of fine dining and brasserie-style food, much of the ingredients locally sourced. The cosy bar has one handpump usually serving ale from Orkney Brewery. 😺🛏◗♿Ρ🚪(X50,X76)😺🛜

Stair

Stair Inn
KA5 5HW (on B730 7 miles E of Ayr)
🌐 12-11 (1am Fri & Sat) ☎ (01292) 591650 🌐 stairinn.co.uk
1 changing beer (often Fyne Ales, Orkney, Strathaven) Ⓗ
This family-run hotel on the banks of the River Ayr is not accessible by public transport but is well-worth seeking out. The food menu relies heavily on local produce and fish from the inn's own smokehouse is a speciality (booking recommended at weekends). Freshly cooked pizzas are now available, to eat in or take away. Q😺🛏◗♿Ρ🛜

Troon

Bruce's Well ✅
91 Portland Street, KA10 6QN
🌐 12-midnight; 11-1am Fri & Sat ☎ (01292) 311429
Caledonian Deuchars IPA; 2 changing beers (often Greene King, Inveralmond) Ⓗ
A friendly, spacious and comfortable lounge bar, close to Troon town centre and a short walk from the station. The guest ales come from the Belhaven list and change regularly. Unusually, the cellar is situated in a temperature-controlled room off the main bar area. A number of TVs show sport with the volume kept down. ≈🚪(10,14,110)🛜

McKay's ✅
69 Portland Street, KA10 6QU
🌐 10-12.30am; 10-midnight Sun ☎ (01292) 737372
3 changing beers (often Cairngorm, Harviestoun, Inveralmond) Ⓗ
Attractive town-centre bar with a large beer garden which is popular in summer. The ale range varies but beers are usually sourced from Scottish breweries including Harviestoun and Inveralmond. Food is served lunchtimes Monday to Thursday and until 8pm Friday to Sunday. The bar hosts various food themed evenings including a steak night every Wednesday (booking usually required). It also holds local dominoes competitions.
🏃😺◗≈🚪(10,14,110)🛜

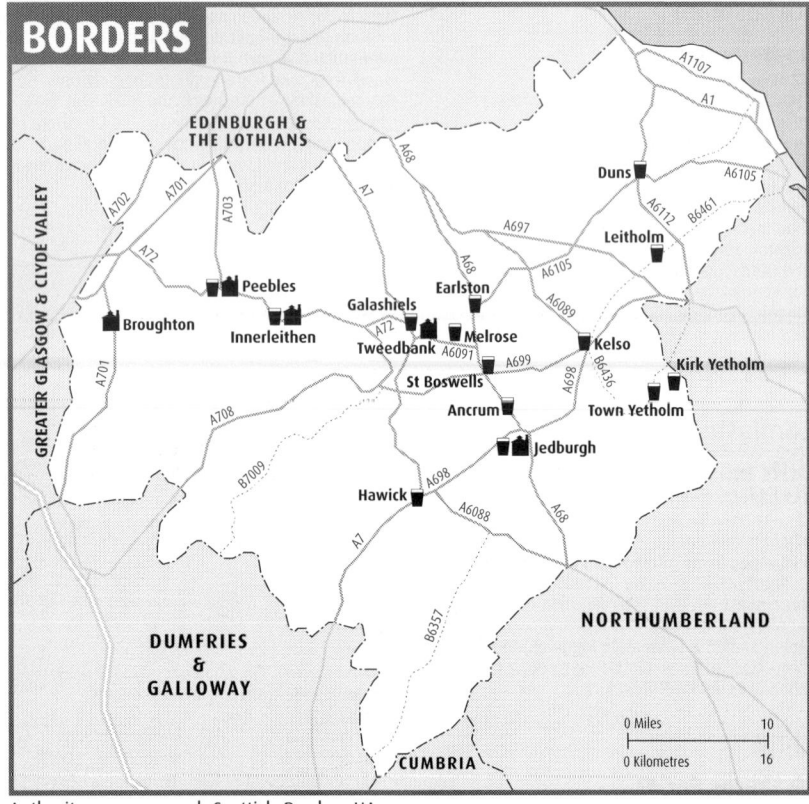

BORDERS

Authority area covered: Scottish Borders UA

Ancrum

Ancrum Cross Keys

The Green, TD8 6XH (on B6400, off A68)
🌣 5-11 (1am Fri & Sat); 12-11 Sun ☎ (01835) 830242
⊕ ancrumcrosskeys.com
4 changing beers (sourced locally; often Born in the Borders) ⊞

Perched on the Ale Water (yes really!), this village local's front bar has remained largely untouched since 1906, retaining pine panelling throughout and a real fire. There is also a comfortable drinking and dining area and a snug at the front. Owned by Born in the Borders Brewery, the food features local produce that is sometimes foraged with a 'plough to platter' ethos matching the brewery's 'plough to pint' philosophy. The garden has a play area. 🌣❀◑🕭🗚♣🅿🚃(25,68)🐾🛜

Duns

Black Bull Hotel

15 Black Bull Street, TD11 3AR (off Market Square)
🌣 11-midnight (1am Fri & Sat); 12-midnight Sun; closed Mon
☎ (01361) 883379 ⊕ blackbullhotelduns.co.uk
3 changing beers (sourced regionally; often Born in the Borders, Knops, Tempest) ⊞

This family-run 200 year-old hotel has a cosy wood-panelled bar that is popular with locals and a lounge that is more suited to families. There is also a restaurant specialising in fresh local produce, with an intimate candlelit atmosphere. The real ales are mainly from smaller Scottish breweries and a beer festival is usually held during the summer. The secluded beer garden has a gazebo and play area. The bedrooms are named after local historic figures. 🌣❀🛏◑🕭♣🅿🚃(60,260)🐾🛜

Earlston

Red Lion ✅

The Square, TD4 6DB
🌣 10-11 (1am Fri & Sat); 11-11 Sun ☎ (01896) 848994
⊕ redlionearlston.co.uk
2 changing beers (sourced regionally; often Born in the Borders, Harviestoun, Stewart) ⊞

Dating from the 1800s, this former coaching inn stands back from the main street in the village centre. The bar has a huge open fire and pool table in the corner. Its styling has a contemporary touch, with tiled floor and mixed seating including high tables and stools. Only one real ale may be on the bar during quiet periods. Food, which is available all day at weekends, is served in the bar and dining room. There is a children's menu. Alcohol is sold from 11am. 🌣❀🛏◑♣🅿🚃🐾🛜

Galashiels

Ladhope Inn ✪
33 High Buckholmside, TD1 2HR (N of centre)
✪ 4-11 (midnight Thu); 3-1am Fri; 11-1am Sat; 12-11 Sun
☎ (01896) 752446
1 changing beer (sourced regionally; often Born in the Borders, Caledonian, Northumberland) Ⓗ
Very much a community hub, this is a comfortable, friendly local with a vibrant Borders atmosphere. Originating circa 1792, it has been altered considerably inside. Now a single room, it is decorated with a large inked map of the Galashiels area and has a wee alcove with a golfing theme. Three TVs ensure the pub is busy during sporting events. Excellent home-made soup is served on Sundays. Children are not allowed.
✿♠️➤♣️🖵🐾🛜

Hawick

Bourtree ✪
22 Bourtree Place, TD9 9HL (NE edge of town centre)
✪ 8am-midnight (1am Fri & Sat) ☎ (01450) 360450
Greene King Abbot; 5 changing beers (sourced nationally) Ⓗ
Built as Hawick Conservative Club in 1897, this listed building has been stunningly transformed into a Wetherspoon pub. The former snooker hall forms the main area, while there are three further areas for quieter or private use. Pictures show a history of Hawick life, including mills, railways, common riding and motorbiking. Regular cask ale and cider promotions and festivals are held. Food is available all day, alcohol is served from 11am.
Q🕭✿🕩🕭♣️🖵🅿🖵(20,95,120)🛜

Exchange Bar (Dalton's)
1 Silver Street, TD9 0AD (off SW end of High St)
✪ 11-11 (1am Fri & Sat); 12.30-11 Sun ☎ (01450) 376067
2 changing beers (sourced regionally; often Born in the Borders) Ⓗ
Hidden away between St Mary's Kirk and the Heart of Hawick Heritage Centre, the pub used to overlook the Corn Exchange, hence the name; however, a previous owner was called Dalton and the name has stuck. It is a Victorian gem with original dark-wood panelling and ornate cornice work. The bar is popular with knowledgable locals and there is a comfy lounge used for parties, Friday karaoke and Sunday folk sessions. Children are not admitted. ♣️🖵(20,95,120)🐾🛜

Innerleithen

St Ronan's Hotel
High Street, EH44 6HF
✪ 12-midnight (12.45am Fri & Sat) ☎ (01896) 831487
1 changing beer (sourced regionally; often Born in the Borders, Hadrian Border, Traquair House) Ⓗ
This village hotel with a smart blue and white exterior takes its name from a local saint. The public bar is long and thin, with a wood-burning stove. Two alcoves in differing styles offer extra seating and a darts area. A pick-up service is available for Southern Upland Way Walkers and packed lunches can be provided. Simple bar snacks are served. A garden play area and indoor games are provided for children. 🕭✿🛏️♠️🅿🖵🐾🛜

Jedburgh

Canon (Exchange Inn)
8 Exchange Street, TD8 6BH
✪ 3-midnight (1am Fri); 12-1am Sat; 12.30-midnight Sun
☎ (01835) 863243
2 changing beers (sourced regionally) Ⓗ
Compact town-centre locals' pub with a traditional atmosphere, featuring a welcoming real fire, original stone wall and dark-wood beams. The long bar has a small alcove-like area at the end. Real ales are usually from Scotland or northern England. The walls are adorned with rugby memorabilia and local history material. Recent renovations are in sympathy with the pub's original layout. Closed on Tuesdays in January and February. 🕭🕭♠️♣️🖵🐾🛜

Kelso

Cobbles Freehouse & Dining
7 Bowmont Street, TD5 7JH (off NE side of town square)
✪ 11.30-11; 11-midnight Fri & Sat; 12-11 Sun
☎ (01573) 223548 ∰ thecobbleskelso.co.uk
2 changing beers (sourced locally; often Tempest) Ⓗ
A friendly gastro-pub offering an interesting and varied choice of dishes, with a warm welcome both for diners and drinkers. Meals are served all day at weekends and there is a children's menu. The lounge bar to the right of the dining area is where the real ales from Tempest can be found – these are listed on a blackboard as pumpclips are not used. Please ask if bringing in a dog.
🕭✿🕩🕭♣️🐾🛜

Rutherfords
38 The Square, TD5 7HL
✪ 12 (4 Mon)-9; 12-10 Fri & Sat ☎ 07803 208460
∰ rutherfordsmicropub.co.uk
4 changing beers (sourced nationally; often Allendale, Born in the Borders, Loch Ness) Ⓖ
In 2015 this tiny shop conversion became the first micropub in Scotland. Sometimes the real ales are from breweries not usually seen locally. There is also a selection of foreign bottled beers and a range of up to eight real ciders. A short but interesting snack menu offers a selection of charcuterie, pies and cheeses from local artisan producers. It may open later on weekdays in winter. Q🕭✿♣️🐾🖵🐾

Kirk Yetholm

Border
The Green, TD5 8PQ
✪ 11.30-11 (1am Fri & Sat summer) ☎ (01573) 420237
∰ borderhotelyetholm.co.uk
House beer (by Hadrian Border); 2 changing beers (sourced nationally; often Born in the Borders, Greene King, Timothy Taylor) Ⓗ
An attractive 260-year-old coaching inn with bar areas and a conservatory restaurant. Popular with walkers, it is at the confluence of several long-distance footpaths. In a tradition from Wainwright's time, those completing the Pennine Way are awarded a free half of Pennine Pint. The inn is noted for its hearty food including a children's menu (served all day on Sunday). Games are provided. Only two real ales may be available in winter. 🕭✿🕩🕭♠️♣️🅿🖵(81)🐾🛜

Leitholm

Plough Inn

Main Street, TD12 4JN

☼ 12-10 (11 Fri & Sat); closed Mon ☎ (01890) 840408

⊕ theploughinnleitholm.co.uk

2 changing beers (sourced nationally; often Born in the Borders) Ⓗ

A delightful inn on the main street of a quiet village, extensively renovated in recent years. The exterior has been returned to the original stonework and the bar and dining room have a bright, modern and welcoming appearance. A large clock is next to the fireplace in the bar. Full meals are served in the evenings and Sunday lunchtime, with a café-style snack menu at other times. ☜✿☎◑♣❄♥

Melrose

George & Abbotsford Hotel

High Street, TD6 9PD

☼ 11-11 (1am Fri & Sat); 12-11 Sun ☎ (01896) 822308

⊕ georgeandabbotsford.co.uk

4 changing beers (sourced locally; often Tempest, Traquair House) Ⓗ

A spacious family-run hotel in the town centre with a comfortable bar and lounges. The owners have carried out much redecoration and refurbishment since their arrival. They are now concentrating on building the real ale portfolio which features interesting beers from both sides of the border, often including Tempest. Cider is available in summer. Regular music sessions are hosted on Wednesdays and weekends. The bar may open later Monday to Thursday in January.
Q☜✿☎◑A♣♥P🚗❄🎵

Peebles

Bridge Inn (Trust) 🏆

Portbrae, EH45 8AW

☼ 11-midnight (1am Thu-Sat); 12-midnight Sun

☎ (01721) 720589

Caledonian Deuchars IPA; 3 changing beers (sourced nationally; often Stewart, Tempest, Timothy Taylor) Ⓗ

Welcoming single-roomed town-centre local, also known as the Trust. The mosaic entrance floor shows it was once the Tweeddale Inn. The bright, comfortable bar is decorated with jugs, bottles, memorabilia of outdoor pursuits and photos of old Peebles. An outdoor heated patio area overlooks the river. The Gents is superb, with well-maintained original Twyford Adamant urinals. There is TV sport and live music on Sunday evening. Children are not admitted. CAMRA Borders Pub of the Year 2016. ✿A♣🚗(X62,62A)❄🎵

Cross Keys ⊘

Northgate, EH45 8RS

☼ 7am-midnight (1am Fri & Sat) ☎ (01721) 723467

6 changing beers (sourced nationally; often Acorn, Sharp's, Wychwood) Ⓗ

Old coaching inn, just off the High Street, now a Wetherspoon pub and hotel. The large, pleasant, low-ceilinged main bar is on the ground floor. A smaller, attractive bar is situated one floor up with easy access to an excellent beer garden. Food is served all day from the extensive Wetherspoon menu. Alcohol is served from 11am (noon Sun). ☜✿☎◑ᗡᗡ♣♥P🚗(X62,62A)🎵

Crown Hotel

High Street, EH45 8SW

☼ 11-midnight (1am Thu-Sat) ☎ (01721) 720239

Stewart Edinburgh Gold; 1 changing beer (sourced locally; often Stewart) Ⓗ

A basic narrow bar that opens out to a seating area with a leather settee and banquettes. There are wooden floors and half-panelled walls throughout. At the back of the bar, down a flight of steps, is a lovely restaurant area with a conservatory. The bar is popular with the locals, who make visitors welcome. Full meals and simple bar snacks are served all day. Live music is hosted occasionally. ☜✿☎◑ᗡᗡ♣🚗(X62,62A)❄🎵

St Boswells

Buccleuch Arms

TD6 0EW (on A68)

☼ 11-11 (1am Fri & Sat); 12-10.30 Sun ☎ (01835) 822243

⊕ buccleucharms.com

2 changing beers (sourced locally; often Born in the Borders, Tempest) Ⓗ

The only hostelry in the village, this well-appointed roadside hotel sits adjacent to the cricket ground and village green. The lounge bar, with its half-panelled walls and large real fire, attracts a mixed clientele including hunters, fishers and shooters, and can be busy at peak times. Meals are served all day in the lounge bar and the bistro offers a more extensive menu – a children's menu is available. Outside is the garden and a play area. ☜✿☎◑ᗡP🚗❄🎵

Town Yetholm

Plough Hotel

High Street, TD5 8RF

☼ 11-midnight (1am Fri & Sat) ☎ (01573) 420215

⊕ theploughhotelyetholm.co.uk

2 changing beers (sourced regionally; often Belhaven, Born in the Borders, Broughton) Ⓗ

A friendly village inn dating from 1710 at the heart of a rural village, which is a haven for walkers with the Pennine Way, St Cuthbert's Way and the Scottish National Trail all nearby. A large wood-burning stove dominates the bar, where the locals are happy to chat with visitors. There is also a separate lounge. Food is served in the bar and the attractive little dining room. Look for the beer garden in summer. ☜✿☎◑A♣P🚗(81)❄🎵

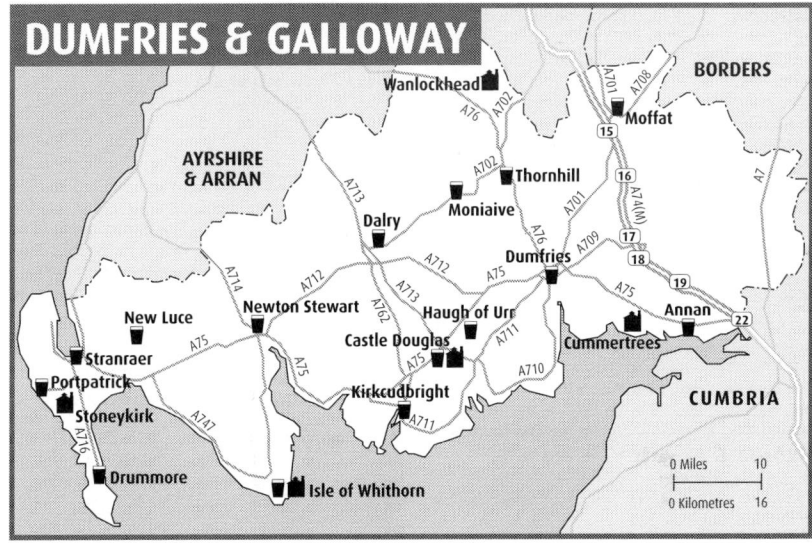

Authority area covered: Dumfries & Galloway UA

Annan

Blue Bell Inn

10 High Street, DG12 6AG

☼ 11-11 (midnight Thu-Sat); 12.30-11 Sun

☎ (01461) 202385

Caledonian Deuchars IPA; 3 changing beers (sourced nationally; often Andrews Ales, Kelburn, Strathaven) Ⓗ

Former coaching inn dating from 1770 at the western entrance to the town. A focus for ale enthusiasts in the area for many years, the pub is also home to many community activities. The interior has traditional features, notably the wood panels with quotations retained from its time as a State Management Scheme pub during World War One. There is a seating area in the courtyard to the rear. Annual beer and cider events are hosted.
ᗺ❀ᵭ🅰️⇌♣🅿️🚉(79,383)❀🛜

Castle Douglas

Sulwath Brewery Tap Room Ⓛ

209 King Street, DG7 1DT

☼ 11-6; closed Sun ☎ (01556) 504525

🌐 sulwathbrewers.co.uk

4 changing beers (sourced locally; often Sulwath) Ⓗ

The visitor centre for Sulwath Brewery, the Tap Room is also popular with local ale lovers. It acts as a showcase for Sulwath beers although not all may be in cask-conditioned form. Occasionally guest ales are served, and one draught cider, usually from Westons, is also available. Brewery tours are offered and there is an annual beer festival.
Q🅰️♣🅿️🚉(500,501)❀

Dalry

Clachan Inn

8-10 Main Street, DG7 3UW

☼ 12-midnight ☎ (01644) 430241 🌐 theclachaninn.co.uk

2 changing beers (sourced nationally; often Ayr, Fyne Ales, Morland) Ⓗ

The Clachan has a reputation for excellent food, cosy, well-equipped bedrooms and a welcoming atmosphere. The menu is varied with excellent daily specials, and the kitchen makes use of local produce including organic lamb and venison. The pub has an attractive traditional main bar, a relaxing lounge bar and a separate restaurant – both bars have wonderfully warming open log fires in winter. A handy stop for walkers on the Southern Upland Way. Q🗢❀🛏️◁🅰️🅿️(520)❀🛜

Drummore

Clashwhannon

DG9 9QE (on A716 S of Stranraer)

☼ 12-midnight summer; 4 (12 Fri-Sun)-11 winter

☎ (01776) 840632 🌐 clashwhannon.co.uk

2 changing beers (often Hadrian Border, Portpatrick, Timothy Taylor) Ⓗ

A friendly and relaxing place, this bar serves the adjacent caravan park and is open all year round. Demand from visitors and locals alike has seen the emergence of real ale in this remote location, close to the Mull of Galloway. There is a bar area plus large family room and restaurant where local produce is served at reasonable prices. Three handpumps are operational in summer, one in winter. Music and variety events feature during the high season. 🗢❀🛏️◁🅰️♣🅿️🚉(407)❀🛜

Dumfries

Cavens Arms

20 Buccleuch Street, DG1 2AH

☼ 11-midnight (11 Mon & Tue); 12-11 Sun

☎ (01387) 252896

Fyne Ales Jarl; Morland Old Speckled Hen; Thwaites Wainwright; 4 changing beers (sourced nationally) Ⓗ

REAL ALE BREWERIES

Andrews Cummertrees

Five Kingdoms 🍺 Isle of Whithorn (NEW)

Lola Rose 🍺 Wanlockhead

Portpatrick Stoneykirk

Sulwath 🍺 Castle Douglas

This busy food-oriented pub is popular with diners for its range of good-value meals, and renovation has created a separate restaurant area providing more space. Drinkers are welcome in the bar area where the atmosphere is like that of a friendly local. Guest ales are from a wide range of breweries including some rarely seen in this locality. There are regular charity quizzes and other theme nights. A frequent winner of local CAMRA awards. Q❶க≢P♠❖

Coach & Horses
66 Whitesands, DG1 2RS
✪ 11-11; 12.30-11 Sun summer; 4 (11 Thu-Sat)-11; 12.30-11 Sun winter ☎ 07746 675349
Draught Bass ⊞
A former coaching inn overlooking the River Nith. It has a pleasant large bar area with a flagstone floor and warming open fire. Live music events are hosted including a folk day on the last Thursday of the month. The Coach is situated next to the Tourist Information Centre and is close to bus routes. It is handy for the many local tourist attractions and car parking. ❀≢P♠❖

New Bazaar
38-39 Whitesands, DG1 2RS
✪ 11-midnight; 12.30-11 Sun summer; 11-7 (midnight Thu-Sat); 12.30-11 Sun winter ☎ (01387) 268776
Theakston XB; 1 changing beer (sourced nationally; often Greene King) ⊞
Former coaching inn beside the River Nith with an attractive airy bar featuring a splendid Victorian gantry displaying an impressive malt whisky collection. The cosy lounge provides a quiet retreat and has a warming coal fire in winter. A small room is available for meetings. The pub is a favourite with football supporters attending nearby Palmerston Park and is ideally situated for car parking, local buses and tourist attractions. There is a pleasant seating area outside. Q❀≢♣P♠❖

Robert the Bruce ✔
81 Buccleuch Street, DG1 2AB
✪ 10-midnight (1am Fri & Sat); 11-midnight Sun ☎ (01387) 270320
Caledonian Deuchars IPA; Greene King Abbot; Ruddles Best Bitter; Sharp's Doom Bar; 3 changing beers (sourced nationally) ⊞
This former Methodist church, sensitively converted by Wetherspoon in 2001, has a relaxed atmosphere and is a popular meeting place in the town centre. Guest ales are from regional and national breweries. The food menu offers a range of good-value meals served all day, every day. There is a pleasant outside seating area to the rear. Alcohol is served from 11am. Q❤❀❶க≢♣P♠❖

Tam o'Shanter
113-117 Queensberry Street, DG1 1BH
✪ 11-11 (midnight Fri & Sat); 12-10 Sun ☎ (01387) 267880
Broughton Clipper IPA; 5 changing beers (sourced regionally; often Broughton) ⊞
A 17th-century coaching inn established in 1630 and which has featured on the Dumfries beer scene for many years. It is a small traditional pub with a main bar and a couple of quiet cosy rooms behind. An upstairs room hosts live music and other functions. It is well positioned just off the High Street serving mainly Broughton beers but has guest ales from other breweries. Q❤≢P♠❖

Haugh of Urr

Laurie Arms Hotel ♥
11-13 Main Street, DG7 3YA
✪ 12-2.30, 5-10 (8 winter); 12-2.30, 5-midnight Wed-Fri; 12-midnight Sat & Sun ☎ (01556) 660246
⊕ haugh-of-urr.com
4 changing beers (sourced regionally; often Fyne Ales, Inveralmond, Strathaven) ⊞
Welcoming family-run pub and restaurant in a charming, quiet village, popular for its range of beers and freshly cooked food featuring local produce. It has a good village-pub atmosphere, enhanced on winter nights by the warming log fire in the bar. Up to four beers are available depending on the season, mainly from independent breweries. National Cycle Route 7 passes nearby. Dumfries and Stewartry CAMRA Pub of the Year winner for 2016. Q❤❀❶♣P♠(501)❖

Isle of Whithorn

Steam Packet Inn ♥ ✔
Harbour Row, DG8 8LL (on B7004 from Whithorn)
✪ 11-11 (12.30am Fri & Sat); 11-11 Sun summer; 11-11 Mon; 11-3, 6-11 Tue-Thu; 11-midnight Fri & Sat; 12-11 Sun winter ☎ (01988) 500334 ⊕ thesteampacketinn.biz
8 changing beers (often Five Kingdoms, Kelburn) ⊞
Traditional family-run hotel overlooking the harbour, welcoming to all including families and pets. The public bar has stone walls and a multi-fuel stove, and there are pictures of the village and maritime events throughout. Four guest ales from a wide variety of breweries and up to four ales from the in-house brewery, Five Kingdoms, are available in both bars. The extensive food menu features local produce – the Sunday hot buffet is a speciality and there are various themed food nights. Q❤❀⊞❶♣●P♠(415)❖

Kirkcudbright

Masonic Arms
19 Castle Street, DG6 4JA
✪ 11-midnight; 12.30-midnight Sun ☎ (01557) 330517
3 changing beers (sourced nationally; often Black Sheep, Sharp's, Wychwood) ⊞
Friendly pub in the town that has been a firm favourite with real ale enthusiasts for many years. The tables and bar fronts are made from old malt whisky casks originating from Islay's Bowmore Distillery. There is a smaller back bar and a garden with a smoking area. Draught Budvar is available along with a choice of over 30 bottled beers from around the world, as well as a selection of more than 100 malt whiskies. Q❀க⛄P♠(431,502)❖

Selkirk Arms Hotel ✔
High Street, DG6 4JQ
✪ 11-11 ☎ (01557) 330402 ⊕ selkirkarmshotel.co.uk
Sulwath The Grace; 2 changing beers (sourced nationally; often Appleby, Parker, Timothy Taylor) ⊞
Refurbished 18th-century hotel with restaurant, bistro and lounge bar that is renowned for locally sourced food, highlighted by the menus and photos of suppliers on the walls. The large garden area with tables is popular in summer. Robert Burns wrote his famous Selkirk Grace at the hotel in 1794. Kirkcudbright is notable for its artistic heritage and houses a number of interesting galleries and museums. Bitburger Drive alcohol-free Pilsner is available on draught. Q❤❀❶க⛄P♠(431,502)❖

Moffat

Star Hotel

44 High Street, DG10 9EF
✪ 11-11 (midnight Thu-Sat); 12-11 Sun ☎ (01683) 220156
⊕ famousstarhotel.co.uk
Sulwath Criffel; 1 changing beer (sourced nationally; often Greene King) Ⓗ
The Famous Star Hotel is recognised by the Guinness Book of Records as the narrowest detached hotel in the world. The building is 20 feet wide and 162 feet long but feels much bigger due to the clever use of internal space. It has been run by the same family for over 30 years and offers excellent service. Moffat is a good base for exploring the Southern Uplands.
🌇🏮🍴🌙👤♿🅿🚪🐾🐱🛜

Moniaive

Craigdarroch Arms Hotel

High Street, DG3 4HN
✪ 12-midnight ☎ (01848) 200205
⊕ craigdarrocharmshotel.co.uk
2 changing beers (sourced nationally; often Caledonian, Sulwath, Timothy Taylor) Ⓗ
The Craigdarroch Arms Hotel has been at the heart of Moniaive's community for over a century. It attracts outdoor enthusiasts including cyclists, anglers and shooters. The village hosts regular music festivals with a varied range of major artists performing in the Marquee Club in the hotel garden. The hotel holds an annual beer festival. The restaurant serves excellent, freshly prepared meals using local produce. Children are welcome.
Q🌇🏮🍴🌙♣🅿🚪(202,212)🐾

New Luce

Kenmuir Arms Hotel

31 Main Street, DG8 0AJ (8 miles N of Glenluce along old military road)
✪ 5-11; closed Mon ☎ (01581) 600218 ⊕ kenmuirarms.com
1 changing beer (often Goose Eye, Houston, Orkney) Ⓗ
Situated in a beautiful village on the banks of the River Luce, this picturesque hotel has well-kept gardens by the river. The public bar offers one real ale all year round, two in summer, sourced from all over the UK. Home-cooked, freshly prepared food is served in the evenings. This is a popular stopping-off point for walkers on the Southern Upland Way and the hotel offers a luggage transfer service. Opening hours vary so check first.
Q🌇🏮🍴🌙👤♣🅿🛜

Newton Stewart

Creebridge House Hotel

Minnigaff, DG8 6NP (on B7079, E of river)
✪ 12-2.30, 6-midnight ☎ (01671) 402121
⊕ creebridge.co.uk
3 changing beers (often Belhaven, Greene King, Sulwath) Ⓗ
This traditional country house hotel close to the town centre is set in three acres of gardens and woodland next to the River Cree. It offers two Greene King ales and occasionally a local Sulwath

brew. A choice of excellent food is available featuring locally sourced meat, game and fish, served in the top-class restaurant and adjacent informal brasserie. The bar and lounge areas have real fires. Occasional dominoes league games, quiz nights and charity events are held.
🌇🏮🍴🌙👤♿🅿🚪(X75,430)🐾🛜

Portpatrick

Crown Hotel

9 North Crescent, DG9 8SX (facing harbour)
✪ 11-midnight (1am Fri & Sat); 12-midnight Sun
☎ (01776) 810261 ⊕ crownportpatrick.com
2 changing beers (often Hadrian Border, Portpatrick, Wells) Ⓗ
Hotel overlooking the picturesque and historic Portpatrick harbour with views on a clear day across to Ireland. The large comfortable bar area at the front is adorned with fine pictures and ornaments and warmed by an open fire. Two regularly changing ales are available from breweries across the UK, including the local Portpatrick Brewery. Live music plays on Friday and Saturday nights, featuring both local and visiting musicians and groups.
🌇🏮🍴🌙👤♿🅲♣🚪(367)🐾🛜

Stranraer

Grapes

4-6 Bridge Street, DG9 7HY
✪ 11-11.30 (midnight Thu-Sat); 12.30-11.30 Sun
☎ (01776) 703386 ⊕ thegrapes1862.co.uk
2 changing beers (often Portpatrick) Ⓗ
Popular historic public bar, with impressive mirror and gantry, that has altered little in over 50 years. It has a separate refurbished snug bar, an upstairs function room with 1930s Art Deco gantry and counter, and a small courtyard with tables and chairs. Regular live music features in the bar on Friday evenings, and occasional music nights in the function room. Two ales are usually on offer, sourced from all over Britain, although there may be just one in winter. 🌇🏮🍺♣🚪🐾🛜

Thornhill

Buccleuch & Queensberry Hotel

112 Drumlanrig Street, DG3 5LU
✪ 11-midnight; 12-midnight Sun ☎ (01848) 323101
⊕ bqahotel.com
2 changing beers (sourced nationally; often Born in the Borders, Broughton, Morland) Ⓗ
Originally built by the Duke of Buccleuch in 1855, the hotel is now family-run. The building has been renovated to create a stylish country hotel in this scenic part of the Nith Valley. The former public bar has reopened to provide a more traditional pub environment. Opening times are for the lounge bar – the public bar opens at 5pm on weekdays and noon at weekends.
Q🌇🏮🍴🌙👤♿🅿🚪(202,246)🐾🛜

SCOTLAND

EDINBURGH & THE LOTHIANS

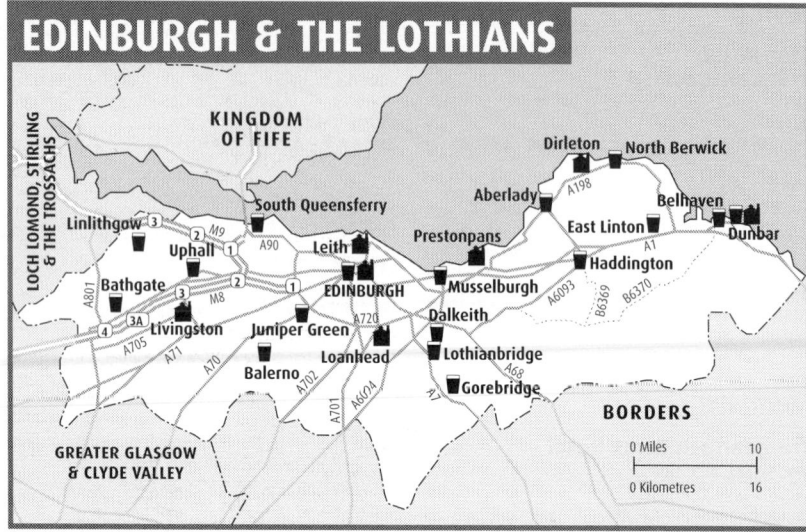

Authority areas covered: City of Edinburgh UA, East Lothian UA, Midlothian UA, West Lothian UA

Aberlady

Ducks Inn
Main Street, EH32 0RE
🕐 12-1am (11 Mon); 12-midnight Sun ☎ (01875) 870682
🌐 ducks.co.uk
Sharp's Doom Bar; 1 changing beer (sourced regionally; often Knops) Ⓗ
A well-appointed village hotel with a bar and restaurants. The comfortable bar is compact and intimate but there are numerous overspill areas, one showing sport on a large TV. The interior is decorated with sporting and brewing memorabilia. Bar games include the exclusive Ducks Challenge putting game. Food is served all day and families are welcome until 8pm, with a children's menu provided. Three real ales are available in summer. Q🕮🏵🍴🍺◐ὃ🅰♣🅿🚃🐾🛜

Balerno

Grey Horse
20 Main Street, EH14 7EH (off A70, in pedestrian area)
🕐 11-11 (midnight Fri & Sat); 12.30-11 Sun
☎ (0131) 449 2888 🌐 greyhorsebalerno.com
5 changing beers (sourced regionally; often Alechemy, Orkney, Stewart) Ⓗ
Traditional stone-built village pub, dating from the 18th century. The cosy public bar retains some original features with wood panelling and a fine Bernard's mirror, and the pleasant lounge has green and red banquette seating. The Chinese restaurant next door is part of the pub and you can enjoy a beer with your meal. One folk and one jazz evening are held each month, often on a Sunday. CAMRA Lothian Pub of the Year runner-up 2016.
Q🕮🏵◐♣🚃🐾

Bathgate

James Young ✅
36-44 Hopetoun Street, EH48 4EU
🕐 8am-midnight (1am Thu-Sat) ☎ (01506) 651600
Caledonian Deuchars IPA; Greene King Abbot; 2 changing beers Ⓗ

Thanks to James Young, Bathgate has a good claim to be known as the home of the oil industry, and this Wetherspoon pub is named in his honour. In 1850, Young set up the world's first commercial oil refinery to process the oil-rich coal from nearby Torbanehill. Major sport is shown on TV, with subtitled news at other times. Music plays on Friday and Saturday evenings. Alcohol is served from 11am (12.30pm Sun), children are welcome until 8pm. 🕮🏵◐ὃ♿🚃🍴🚃(5,31)🛜

Belhaven

Masons Arms
8 High Street, EH42 1NP (1 mile W of Dunbar)
🕐 12-2.30, 6-11; 12-midnight Fri & Sat; 12.30-11 Sun
☎ (01368) 864566
1 changing beer (sourced locally; often Belhaven, Knops, Stewart) Ⓗ
Just a few minutes' walk from Belhaven Brewery, the bright, comfortable bar has a plain wooden floor, bench seating around the walls and is warmed by a real fire in winter. A further small room is used for functions. Outside, the superb beer garden has views to the distant Lammermuir Hills. 🕮🏵🅰♣🚃(X6,253)🐾🛜

Dalkeith

Blacksmith's Forge ✅
Newmills Road, EH22 1DU
🕐 8am-midnight (1am Fri & Sat) ☎ (0131) 561 5100
Greene King Abbot; Sharp's Doom Bar; 6 changing beers (sourced regionally; often Cairngorm, Harviestoun, Stewart) Ⓗ
Large open-plan Wetherspoon pub divided into several areas with a mix of tables and chairs, high tables and booths with bench seating. Changing real ales are often from Scottish breweries. Families are welcome until 10pm for meals, which are served all day. Alcohol is served from 11am (12.30pm Sun). Q🕮🏵◐ὃ♿🚃🛜

Dunbar

Volunteer Arms

17 Victoria Street, EH42 1HP (near swimming pool)
☼ 12-11 (midnight Thu; 1am Fri & Sat); 12.30-midnight Sun
☎ (01368) 862278 ⊕ volunteerarmsdunbar.co.uk
2 changing beers (sourced nationally) Ⓗ
Close to Dunbar harbour, this is a friendly
traditional locals' pub. The two real ales are often
from smaller breweries. Upstairs is a restaurant
serving an excellent, good-value range of food
including a children's menu, with an emphasis on
seafood. Meals are available all day. Dogs must be
on a lead. ⯊❀❍◑Åⲙ♣🖳😸🛱

East Linton

Linton Hotel & Steakhouse

3 Bridge End, EH40 3AF
☼ 12-11 (1am Fri & Sat) ☎ (01620) 860202
⊕ thelintonhotel.co.uk
3 changing beers (sourced regionally) Ⓗ
Small, welcoming, traditional hotel by the historic
brig over the Tyne in a pretty conservation village.
There is a comfortably furnished public bar with at
least one real ale from a Scottish microbrewery. To
the rear is a pleasant coffee/dining lounge while
upstairs is a large restaurant with modern styling.
Food is served all day and the emphasis is on local
produce, especially quality steaks – the owner was
previously a butcher. Six en suite rooms are
available. ⯊❀🚪◑♣🖳(120,X6)😸🛱

Edinburgh: Central

Abbotsford Bar & Restaurant ★

3-5 Rose Street, EH2 2PR
☼ 11-11 (midnight Fri & Sat) ☎ (0131) 225 5276
6 changing beers (sourced regionally) Ⓗ/Ⓐ
A traditional Scottish bar listed on CAMRA's
National Inventory of Historic Pub Interiors. The
magnificent island bar and gantry in dark
mahogany have been a fixture since 1902. The
ornate plasterwork and corniced ceiling are
outstanding and highlighted by concealed lighting.
Six real ales are served, usually from Scottish
microbreweries. There is an extensive food menu,
available all day in the bar. Diners in the restaurant
upstairs can order real ale from downstairs.
Q⯊❀❍◑�¬(Waverley)🖳🛱

Blue Blazer

2 Spittal Street, EH3 9DX (SW of centre)
☼ 11-1am; 12.30-1am Sun ☎ (0131) 229 5030
**7 changing beers (sourced regionally; often
Edinbrew, Fallen, Kelburn)** Ⓗ/Ⓐ
Two-roomed pub with wooden floors, high ceilings
and old brewery window panels – candles in the
evening add to the traditional feel. The pub
specialises in beers from smaller Scottish
breweries. Toasties are available all day. Close to
theatres and cinemas, closing time is later during
August and December. Children are not admitted.
🖳😸🛱

Bow Bar

80 West Bow, EH1 2HH (Old Town, off Grassmarket)
☼ 12-midnight; 12.30-11.30 Sun ☎ (0131) 226 7667
⊕ thebowbar.co.uk
**Alechemy Bowhemia; Cromarty Happy Chappy;
Stewart 80/-; 5 changing beers (sourced nationally;
often Arbor, Swannay, Tempest)** Ⓐ

A re-creation of a classic Scottish one-roomed ale
house, dedicated to traditional Scottish air pressure
dispense and upright drinking. The beers can be
from anywhere in the UK and regular beer festivals
are held in January and June. The walls are
festooned with original brewery mirrors and the
superb gantry does justice to an award-winning
selection of over 300 single malt whiskies and
international bottled beers. Pies, soup and bridies
are available at lunchtime. Children are not
admitted. Q�¬(Waverley)🖳🛱😸🛱

Guildford Arms

1 West Register Street, EH2 2AA (off E end of Princes St)
☼ 11-11 (midnight Thu & Fri); 10-midnight Sat; 10-11 Sun
☎ (0131) 556 4312 ⊕ guildfordarms.com
10 changing beers (sourced nationally) Ⓗ
A large establishment built in the golden age of
Victorian pub design. The high ceiling, cornices and
friezes are spectacular, as are the window arches
and screens. The restaurant is upstairs in a
noteworthy gallery. There is a large standing space
around the canopied bar plus extensive seating
areas. The diverse range of 10 real ales includes
many from Scottish micros, and real cider is
occasionally on handpump. Bar snacks are
available 3-9pm. Alcohol is served from 11am.
⯊◑➬(Waverley)🖳♣🖳😸🛱

Halfway House

24 Fleshmarket Close, EH1 1BX (up steps opp Waverley
station's Market St entrance)
☼ 11-11.30 (midnight Thu; 1am Fri & Sat)
☎ (0131) 225 7101
**4 changing beers (sourced nationally; often
Stewart)** Ⓗ
Cosy, characterful bar hidden halfway down an Old
Town close. Railway memorabilia and current
timetables adorn the interior of this small, often
busy, bar. At the front are tables with window
seats and stools. The rear area has more
comfortable semicircular booth seating. There are
usually four interesting real ales, mainly from
smaller Scottish breweries. Meals and bar snacks
are served all day. The bar may stay open until 1am
during busy times of year.
⯊❀❍◑➬(Waverley)🖳🖳😸🛱

Haymarket ✪

11-14 West Maitland Street, EH12 5DS (W of centre)
☼ 10-midnight (1am Fri & Sat) ☎ (0131) 228 2537
**Caledonian Deuchars IPA; St Austell Nicholson's Pale
Ale; Stewart 80/-; 7 changing beers (sourced
nationally; often Acorn, Harviestoun, Kelburn)** Ⓗ
On the busy corner of the Haymarket, the pub has a
comfortable interior decorated with historic prints

SCOTLAND

REAL ALE BREWERIES

Alechemy Livingston
Andrew Usher 🍺 Edinburgh
Barney's Edinburgh
Belhaven Dunbar
Caledonian Edinburgh
Campervan Edinburgh (NEW)
Edinbrew Livingston
Hanging Bat 🍺 Edinburgh
Kentwood 🍺 Prestonpans
Knops Dirleton
Krafty Brew Edinburgh
Pilot Leith
Stewart Loanhead
Top Out Loanhead

of the pub and locality. An island bar with 12 handpumps overlooks a large central area with a raised mezzanine floor to one side and arches leading through to a restaurant. The real ale range is varied, coming from UK-wide regional and micro breweries. Food is served all day from the Nicholson's menu. Children are welcome if dining. ⏰🛏🌳❶🕽🍴⇌(Haymarket)🅿♿🚲🐱🛜

Holyrood 9A

9A Holyrood Road, EH8 8AE (E edge of Old Town)
🕐 9am-midnight (1am Fri & Sat) ☎ (0131) 556 5044
🌐 theholyrood.co.uk
3 changing beers (sourced nationally; often Fyne Ales) ℗
Popular Old Town bar. The main area features a dark-wood bar, wood flooring and a large Ushers mirror. The beer taps are on the bar's back wall, with real ales to the left and craft keg to the right. There is a constant rotation of interesting real ales, many rare for the city. A further room is to the rear and a smaller snug at the front. Food is available all day with burgers a speciality. Alcohol is served from 11am. ⏰🛏❶⇌(Waverley)🕽🐱🛜

Jolly Judge

7a Lawnmarket, EH1 2PB (Old Town, in James Court)
🕐 12-11 (midnight Mon); 12-midnight Fri & Sat
☎ (0131) 225 2669 🌐 jollyjudge.co.uk
3 changing beers (sourced nationally) ℍ
Comfortable bar with an attractive painted ceiling hidden down an Old Town close just off the Royal Mile. There are steps down to the entrance, as was common in the past. The real ales are often from Scottish or Northumbrian micros and a single but varying real cider is available. A welcome spot for refreshment after visiting the castle. Dogs are permitted after 3pm, but no children inside. Q🌳❶⇌(Waverley)🕽♣🍴🕽🐱🛜

Lock 25

85-87 Fountainbridge, EH3 9PU (½ mile W of centre)
🕐 12-11 (midnight Thu-Sat); closed Sun ☎ (0131) 228 8831
🌐 lock25.co.uk
Caledonian Deuchars IPA; 3 changing beers (sourced nationally) ℍ
The inside is deceptively spacious with an L-shaped bar and seating ranging from high stools to comfortable armchairs. The real ales may be from breweries UK-wide, but are generally Scottish. The cider is from Famer Jims. Home-made meals, including steak and guest ale pie, are served every lunchtime and all day Thursday to Saturday. ⏰🛏❶🌳♿🍴🕽🐱🛜

Oxford Bar ★

8 Young Street, EH2 4JB (New Town, off Charlotte Sq)
🕐 11-midnight (1am Fri & Sat); 12.30-11 Sun
☎ (0131) 539 7119 🌐 oxfordbar.co.uk
Caledonian Deuchars IPA; 3 changing beers (sourced regionally; often Cairngorm, Fyne Ales, Inveralmond) ℍ
A real taste of New Town past, this small, basic, vibrant drinking shop has remained largely unaltered since the late-19th century. The bar counter nearly fills the small front room but there is more space in the side room. It is renowned as one of the favourite pubs of Rebus and his creator Ian Rankin, and a haunt of many other famous and infamous characters over the years. The beers are usually from Scottish breweries. Children are not admitted. Q🕽🍴🐱🛜

Sandy Bell's

25 Forrest Road, EH1 2QH (½ mile S of centre)
🕐 12-1am; 12.30-midnight Sun ☎ (0131) 225 2751
🌐 sandybellsedinburgh.co.uk
Caledonian Deuchars IPA; Harviestoun Bitter & Twisted; Inveralmond Ossian; Orkney Dark Island; 1 changing beer (sourced regionally; often Sonnet 43) ℍ
A part of Edinburgh folklore, the pub has featured on the traditional music scene for many years. An arch, the gantry bar counter and wall panelling are all in dark wood, in contrast to the atmosphere which is far from gloomy. Live folk music plays every night and on Saturday and Sunday afternoons. Bring along an instrument and join in! Children are not admitted. ⇌(Waverley)♣🍴🐱

Thomson's Bar ✅

182-184 Morrison Street, EH3 8EB (W of centre)
🕐 12-11.30 (midnight Thu & Sat; 1am Fri); 4-11.30 Sun
☎ (0131) 228 5700 🌐 thomsonsbaredinburgh.co.uk
6 changing beers (sourced nationally; often Alechemy, Oakham, Swannay) ℍ/Ⓐ
Superb single-roomed bar modelled on the style of Glasgow architect Alexander 'Greek' Thomson. The hand-made gantry and room panelling are inlaid with scenes from Greek mythology. The walls are decorated with rare mirrors, adverts and point of sale material from long-forgotten breweries. The bar is a member of Oakham Ales' Oakademy, and up to six, often hoppy, real ales are served from a variety of breweries. No food is served on Sunday and pies only on Saturday. Children are not admitted. Q🌳❶⇌(Haymarket)🅿♣🍴🐱🛜

Edinburgh: East

Regent ✅

2 Montrose Terrace, EH7 5DL
🕐 12-1am; 12.30-1am Sun ☎ (0131) 661 8198
🌐 theregentbar.co.uk
Caledonian Deuchars IPA; 2 changing beers (sourced nationally) ℍ
Large tenement bar with two rooms, popular with LGBT real ale drinkers. The comfortable seating includes banquettes, leather sofas and armchairs. Beers are served without sparklers on request. The cider is Westons Old Rosie. Bar snacks and simple meals, including good vegetarian and vegan options, are available all day. A novel slant on pub games is the gymnastic pommel horse by the toilets. Children are permitted until 8pm. ⏰❶♣🍴🐱🛜

Edinburgh: North

Kay's Bar ✅

39 Jamaica Street West, EH3 6HF (New Town, off India St)
🕐 11-midnight (1am Fri & Sat); 12.30-11 Sun
☎ (0131) 225 1858 🌐 kaysbar.co.uk
Caledonian Deuchars IPA; Theakston Best Bitter; 5 changing beers (sourced nationally; often Fyne Ales, Loch Ness, Timothy Taylor) ℍ
A cosy and convivial pub that retains many features from its days as a Victorian wine merchant. The pub is decorated with whisky barrels and specialises in malt whisky, with a large selection behind the bar. If the front bar is busy, try the small room at the back. Lunches consist mainly of traditional Scottish fare. Children are not admitted. Dogs are permitted after 2.30pm. Q❶♣🍴🐱🛜

Malt & Hops

45 The Shore, Leith, EH6 6QU
☼ 12-11 (midnight Wed & Thu; 1am Fri & Sat); 12.30-11 Sun
☎ (0131) 555 0083 ⊕ barcalisa.com
8 changing beers (sourced nationally; often Fallen, Hadrian Border, Swannay) Ⓗ
Single-roomed, old-fashioned bar by the Water of Leith dating from 1747. A large collection of pumpclips, many from long-lost breweries and distilleries, hangs from the ceiling along with hop bines that are renewed every harvest. The wide real ales selection has an emphasis on smaller breweries. Meals are served on Friday lunchtime and toasties are always available. Children are welcome until 6pm. ➘⊛◐♣🖵😺🛜

Stockbridge Tap ▾

2-4 Raeburn Place, Stockbridge, EH4 1HN
☼ 12-midnight (1am Fri & Sat); 12.30-midnight Sun
☎ (0131) 343 3000
Alechemy Ritual; Swannay Island Hopping; 5 changing beers (sourced nationally; often Alechemy, Fallen, Oakham) Ⓗ
A specialist real ale house, the pub offers interesting ales from all over the UK and holds occasional beer festivals. The L-shaped room, with bright bar area, boasts mirrors from lost breweries including Murray's and Campbell's. There is plenty of seating and ample space for vertical drinking. No food is served on Monday or Tuesday. Children are not admitted. Closing time may be a little earlier if quiet. CAMRA Edinburgh Pub of the Year 2016 and Scottish Pub of the Year 2015. ◐🖐♣🖵😺🛜

Teuchters Landing

1c Dock Place, Leith, EH6 6LU (2 miles N of centre)
☼ 10.30-1am ☎ (0131) 554 7427 ⊕ aroomin.co.uk/teuchters-landing-bar-edinburgh
Caledonian Deuchars IPA; Fyne Ales Jarl; Inveralmond Ossian; Timothy Taylor Landlord; 2 changing beers (sourced regionally; often Fallen, Knops, Stewart) Ⓗ
Converted from the former waiting room for the Leith to Aberdeen ferry, the attractive bar has a wood-panelled ceiling edged with tiles featuring random Scottish place names from Teuchterland. There are also some smaller rooms and a large conservatory extension that opens out onto a pontoon floating on the Water of Leith. The food menu, available all day, includes meals served in small or large mugs. An excellent selection of malt whiskies is available. Alcohol is served from 11am. ➘⊛◐🖐♣🖵😺🛜

Edinburgh: South

Cask & Barrel (Southside)

24-26 West Preston Street, EH8 9PZ
☼ 12-midnight (1am Fri); 11-1am Sat; 12.30-midnight Sun
☎ (0131) 667 0856
Caledonian Deuchars IPA; Swannay Orkney Best; Tryst Drovers 80/-; 5 changing beers (sourced nationally; often Ayr, Hardknott, Loch Lomond) Ⓗ
Modern re-creation of a Scottish city or tenement bar. The single room, with windows front and back, is divided by a horseshoe bar with a dark-wood gantry adorned with decorative wooden casks. A good place to try real ales from interesting breweries UK-wide. Children are not admitted. CAMRA Edinburgh Pub of the Year runner-up in 2016. 🖵🛜

Cloisters Bar

26 Brougham Street, EH3 9JH (SW of centre)
☼ 12-midnight (1am Fri & Sat); 12.30-midnight Sun
☎ (0131) 221 9997 ⊕ cloistersbar.com
Stewart Pentland IPA, Holy Grale; 7 changing beers (sourced nationally; often Alechemy, Swannay, Thornbridge) Ⓗ
Established in 1995 in the former All Saints Parsonage, many traditional features have been maintained in this warm and friendly bar. The wide range of single malt whiskies, gins and rums does justice to the outstanding gantry. The real ales are generally from interesting breweries UK-wide. Frequent beer festivals and Meet the Brewer events are held. Meals are freshly prepared (no food Mon or Sun eve). Children over five are welcome until 7pm if dining. Q➘◐♣🖵😺🛜

Dagda Bar

93-95 Buccleuch Street, EH8 9NG
☼ 12.30-1am; 1-1am Sun ☎ (0131) 667 9773
House beer (by Broughton); 3 changing beers (sourced regionally; often Oakham, Orkney, Tryst) Ⓗ
A really cosy howff situated in the heart of the university area attracting a wide-ranging clientele. The small single room has banquette seating on three sides and a welcoming U-shaped bar. The beers are often but not exclusively from local breweries, including their own Dagda Ale brewed by Broughton. There is also a good range of whiskies and bottled beers. Children are not admitted. An essential stop on any Southside pub walk. ♣🖵😺🛜

Spylaw Tavern ✪

27 Spylaw Street, Colinton, EH13 0JT (SW edge of city)
☼ 11.30-11.30 (midnight Thu-Sat); 12-11.30 Sun
☎ (0131) 441 2783 ⊕ spylawtavern.co.uk
2 changing beers (sourced nationally) Ⓗ
Attractive, comfortable inn set in an historic village now absorbed by the city. Light-coloured wood gives the bar a bright, airy feel. The lounge and restaurant have a darker decor and windows overlooking the garden and Colinton Dell. Meals are freshly prepared and served all day, including a good range of pies. One of the changing real ales is always an IPA. Beer is served in third and or two-thirds of a pint measures, in addition to full pints and halves. The pub makes an ideal stop when walking the Water of Leith path. ➘⊛◐🖐♣🖵🛜

Edinburgh: West

Athletic Arms (Diggers) ✪

1-3 Angle Park Terrace, EH11 2JX (SW of centre)
☼ 11-1am ☎ (0131) 337 3822
Caledonian Deuchars IPA; Stewart Diggers 80/- Ⓐ**; 4 changing beers (sourced nationally; often Alechemy, Caledonian, Houston)** Ⓗ
Situated between two graveyards, the name Diggers became synonymous with this Edinburgh pub legend which opened in 1897. Banquette seating lines the walls, and a compass drawing in the floor aids the geographically challenged. A smaller back room has a dartboard and further seating – children are welcome here if dining. Quieter now than in its heyday, though packed when Hearts are at home, it continues to extend a warm welcome to locals and visitors alike. The pies are outstanding. ➘♣🖵😺🛜

Golden Rule ✓

30 Yeaman Place, EH11 1BT
✪ 12-midnight (1am Fri); 11-1am Sat; 12.30-midnight Sun
☎ (0131) 229 3413 ⊕ goldenruleedinburgh.co.uk
5 changing beers (sourced nationally; often Drygate, Magic Rock, Stewart) Ⓗ
A split-level Victorian tenement bar close to the Union Canal and the Fountain Park entertainment complex. The pub is a real ale showcase, with a great selection from smaller breweries UK wide. The upstairs bar is pleasantly furnished. The downstairs bar comes into its own at weekends, but real ale has to be brought down from upstairs. There is live music on Saturday evenings and a quiz on Tuesday evenings. Children are not admitted.
✹♣🖩😺🎅

Roseburn Bar ✓

1 Roseburn Terrace, EH12 5NG
✪ 9am-11 (midnight Thu-Sat); 11-11 Sun
☎ (0131) 337 1067 ⊕ roseburnbar.co.uk
Caledonian Deuchars IPA; Fyne Ales Jarl; 2 changing beers (sourced nationally) Ⓗ
A traditional pub that is popular with locals. It boasts high ceilings and a largely wooden interior, with interesting mirrors and period photos on the walls. There are numerous comfortable booths along the walls and two separate lounge areas. Three flatscreen TVs show sporting events, though the volume is typically kept low. Close to Murrayfield Stadium and also handy for Tynecastle Stadium. Children are not admitted. ✹🖘🖩😺

Winstons ✓

20 Kirk Loan, Corstorphine, EH12 7HD (off St Johns Road)
✪ 11-midnight (1am Fri & Sat); 12.30-midnight Sun
☎ (0131) 539 7077 ⊕ winstonslounge.co.uk
Caledonian Deuchars IPA; 3 changing beers (sourced regionally; often Harviestoun, Loch Ness, Swannay) Ⓗ
A comfortable lounge bar in Corstorphine, just over a mile from Murrayfield Stadium and a half mile from the zoo. Set in a small, modern building, this is a warm and welcoming community venue used by old and young alike. The decor features golfing and rugby themes along with historic photos of the area. The beers are usually from a variety of Scottish breweries. Lunchtime meals include wonderful home-made pies (no food Sun). Children are not admitted. ✹🍽😺📶

Gorebridge

Stobsmill Inn (Bruntons)

25 Powdermill Brae, EH23 4HX (S edge of town)
✪ 11-11.30 Mon & Thu; 12-11 Tue; 11-11 Wed; 11-midnight Fri & Sat; 12.30-11.30 Sun ☎ (01875) 820202
1 changing beer (sourced nationally; often Kelburn, Stewart, Tryst) Ⓗ
Built in 1866 as a public house, the single-room wood-floored bar has one area containing a long L-shaped counter lined with stools and another with bench seating, tables and chairs. Wooden panels engraved with sporting scenes hide an intriguingly tiny jug bar. The single real ale is often from a smaller Scottish brewery. Simple bar snacks are available at all times. Over-21s only.
✹≈♣P🖩(29,33)😺📶

Haddington

Golf Tavern

5 Bridge Street, EH41 4AU
✪ 11-11 (midnight Thu); 11-1am Fri & Sat; 11-midnight Sun
☎ (01620) 822327 ⊕ golftavernhaddington.co.uk
1 changing beer (sourced regionally; often Broughton, Knops, Tryst) Ⓗ
A traditional locals' bar nestling behind the Waterside Bistro on the south-east side of the River Tyne. The public bar has a pool table and dartboard. Only one of the two handpumps is in use, featuring a Scottish real ale. The spacious lounge bar acts mainly as a popular restaurant and function room. Food, served in generous portions, is available all day Saturday and until 7pm on Sunday.
🖙🍽🌙🕹♣🖩📶

Tyneside Tavern

10 Poldrate, EH41 4DA (on B6368, 500yds S of centre)
✪ 11-11 (midnight Thu; 1am Fri & Sat); 12.30-11 Sun
☎ (01620) 822221 ⊕ tynesidetavern.com
Caledonian Deuchars IPA; 4 changing beers (sourced nationally; often Alechemy, Born in the Borders, Knops) Ⓗ
An unusual twin-gable-ended building dating from the 18th century. This is a community pub and popular with locals. It has a long, narrow bar with an open fire in winter, and shows sport on TVs. The lounge has tables set for dining, with food served all day Friday to Sunday. The excellent range of real ales is mainly from Scottish micros but some little-known ones from south of the border occasionally appear. 🖙🌙🕹🖩😺📶

Juniper Green

Juniper Green Inn

542 Lanark Road, EH14 5EL
✪ 11-midnight (11 Mon & Tue); 12.30-11 Sun
☎ (0131) 458 5395
Caledonian Deuchars IPA; Timothy Taylor Landlord; 2 changing beers (sourced nationally; often Black Isle, Fuller's, Hadrian Border) Ⓗ
Well-appointed, single-room lounge bar in a late-1800s building, with a strong community spirit. The decor is clean and attractive throughout. Pictures of the old Balerno branch line provide interest. A secluded patio and garden are popular in summer. The menu includes steak pie, chicken, a fish dish and meal deals. Children are not admitted.
Q✹🌙🖩📶

Linlithgow

Platform 3 Ⓛ ✓

1A High Street, EH49 7AB
✪ 10.30-midnight (1am Fri & Sat); 12.30-midnight Sun
☎ (01506) 847405 ⊕ platform3.co.uk
Caledonian Deuchars IPA; 2 changing beers (sourced regionally; often An Teallach, Cairngorm, Harviestoun) Ⓗ
Small, friendly hostelry on the railway station approach, originally the public bar of the hotel next door and renovated in 1998 as a pub in its own right. Two Scottish beers are served in addition to the regular ale. Dogs are welcome, with biscuits 'on tap'. Alcohol is served from 11am (12.30pm Sun). ≈🖩😺📶

Lothianbridge

Sun Inn

EH22 4TR (A7, near Newtongrange)
🕐 11-11 (midnight Fri & Sat) ☎ (0131) 663 2456
🌐 thesuninnedinburgh.co.uk
2 changing beers (sourced regionally; often Alechemy, Kelburn, Stewart) Ⓗ
A well-appointed award-winning gastro-pub built circa 1870 next to the impressive 23-span Waverley Line viaduct. The tasteful interior has a mixture of exposed stone, papered walls, wooden floors and carpets. Meals are served all day on Sundays until 7pm and afternoon teas are available during the week. Space is limited for drinkers at busy times. A major extension is in progress. The bar may close earlier if quiet.
🗝🏠🍴🕽🛒🅿🚆(29,39)🛜

Musselburgh

David MacBeth Moir ✓

Bridge Street, EH21 6AG (opp The Brunton)
🕐 8am-11 (midnight Thu; 1am Fri & Sat) ☎ (0131) 653 1060
Caledonian Deuchars IPA; Sharp's Doom Bar; 8 changing beers (sourced nationally) Ⓗ
Wetherspoon pub named after a local physician and writer, set in a former cinema dating back to 1935. The main door and original features have been beautifully restored, and the vast single-room bar is filled with Art Deco cinema-related artefacts. The long bar counter has 10 handpumps offering a good mix of guest ales and a cider, often Westons Old Rosie. Food is available all day. Alcohol is served from 11am (12.30pm Sun).
Q🗝🏠🍴🕽🛒🚆🛜

Levenhall Arms

10 Ravensheugh Road, EH21 7PP (on B1348, 1 mile E of centre)
🕐 12-11 (midnight Thu; 1am Fri & Sat); 12.30-midnight Sun ☎ (0131) 665 3220
Inveralmond Ossian Ⓐ; 3 changing beers (sourced regionally; often Knops, Stewart) Ⓗ/Ⓐ
A three-roomed hostelry dating from 1830 and close to the racecourse. The lively, cheerfully decorated public bar is half timber-panelled and carpeted. Dominoes is popular here and there is a TV for sporting events. A smaller area leads off, with a dartboard and pictures of old local industries. The pleasant lounge has a hardwood floor and comfortable seating, and is used as an Indian restaurant in the evenings. Expect to find some interesting beers from smaller, mainly Scottish breweries. Q🗝🏠🕽🛒♣🅿🚆🛜

Volunteer Arms (Staggs) 🏆

81 North High Street, EH21 6JE (behind The Brunton)
🕐 12-11 (11.30 Thu; midnight Fri); 11-midnight Sat; 12.30-11 Sun ☎ (0131) 665 9654 🌐 staggsbar.com
Oakham JHB, Bishops Farewell; 9 changing beers (sourced nationally) Ⓗ
Superb pub run by the same family since 1858. The bar and snug are traditional, with wooden floors, wood panelling and mirrors from defunct local breweries. The more modern lounge opens at the weekend. Up to nine guest beers, mostly pale and hoppy but often one darker, change regularly. Local CAMRA branch Pub of the Year 2016 and winner of many previous awards – see the bar wall.
🗝🏠♣🛒🚆🛜

North Berwick

Nether Abbey Hotel

20 Dirleton Avenue, EH39 4BQ (on A198, ¾ mile W of centre)
🕐 11-11 (midnight Thu; 1am Fri & Sat) ☎ (01620) 892802
🌐 netherabbey.co.uk
Knops East Coast Pale; 3 changing beers (sourced nationally; often Stewart, Timothy Taylor, Williams Bros) Ⓗ
Busy, family-run hotel in a stone-built villa, offering a bright, contemporary interior with open-plan rooms. The Fly Half Bar is in a split-level glass extension, with large folding doors opening out onto a suntrap patio for summer drinking. The upper central area, also accessed via the main door, is an award-winning restaurant. Real ales are often from Scottish breweries – sparklers can be removed on request. The Nethers is famous for its good, freshly cooked and locally sourced cuisine, served all day Friday to Sunday.
🗝🏠🍴🕽🛒🅿🚆♿🛜

Ship Inn ✓

7-9 Quality Street, EH39 4HJ
🕐 11-11 (1am Thu-Sat) ☎ (01620) 890699 🌐 50mls.co.uk/ship-inn
Harviestoun Schiehallion; 3 changing beers (sourced nationally; often Greene King, Stewart, Theakston) Ⓗ
Spacious, open-plan bar located beneath a tenement block at the leafy east end of town. The bar area has pine floorboards, a mahogany counter and a dark-stained wood gantry. To the side and rear is a quieter carpeted area. The guest beers often include one with a higher ABV. Sparklers are happily removed on request. The pub is popular for food, with good vegetarian options, served all day until 8pm (6pm winter). 🗝🏠🕽🛒🚆♿🛜

South Queensferry

Anchor Inn

10 Edinburgh Road, EH30 9HR
🕐 11-1am ☎ (0131) 331 3684 🌐 anchor-queensferry.co.uk
Caledonian Deuchars IPA Ⓗ
Busy, single-room, comfortable locals' bar in a building dating from 1886 located in the historic village centre. Banquette seating surrounds the room and a high shelf is adorned with sporting trophies. The pub has a friendly atmosphere and visitors are made welcome. Traditional board games, including dominoes, are often played and occasionally there is live music. Children are not admitted. ♣🚆(63,40,40a)♿🛜

Uphall

Oatridge Hotel 🏆

2-4 East Main Street, EH52 5DA
🕐 11-midnight (1am Sat); 12.30-midnight Sun ☎ (01506) 856465 🌐 theoatridgehotel.co.uk
2 changing beers (sourced nationally; often Alechemy) Ⓗ
The Oatridge was built in 1810 as a coach house and is conveniently situated for travel, with access routes to the east, west and north only minutes away. It is also close to Livingston, where you will find one of Europe's largest discount designer shopping centres. The bar is popular both with local residents and visitors. Local CAMRA branch Pub of the Year 2016. 🏠🕽♣🚆♿

GREATER GLASGOW & CLYDE VALLEY

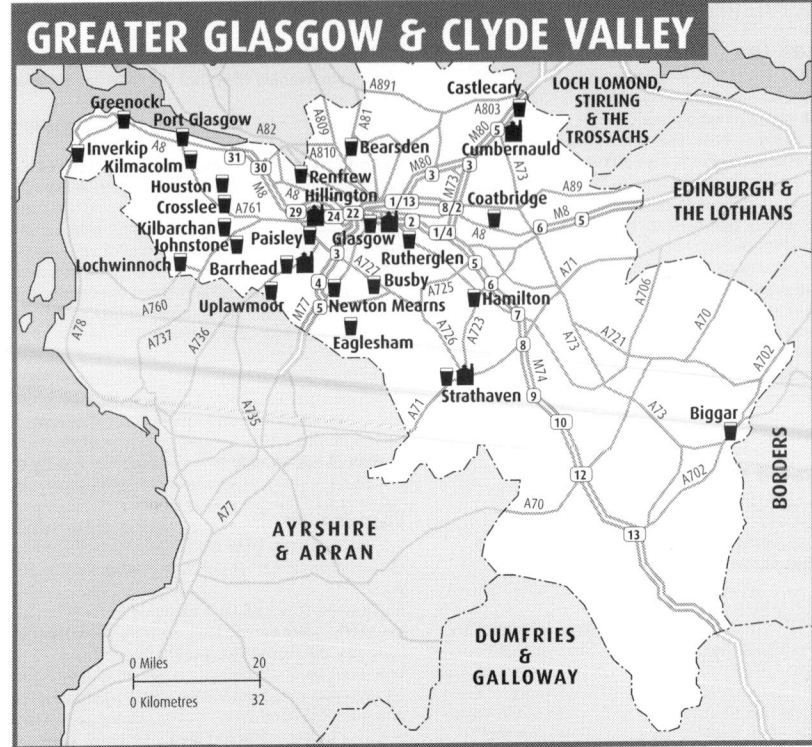

Authority areas covered: City of Glasgow UA, Dunbartonshire UAs, Inverclyde UA, Lanarkshire UAs, Renfrewshire UAs

Barrhead

Cross Stobs Inn L

2-6 Grahamston Road, G78 1NS (jct of B771/B774)
🕑 11-11 (midnight Thu & Sat; 1am Fri); 12.30-11 Sun
☎ (0141) 881 1581
Kelburn Misty Law; 1 changing beer H
Eighteenth-century coaching inn on the road to Paisley. The public bar has a real coal fire and retains much of its original charm with antique furniture and service bells. The spacious lounge is mostly used for dining and leads to an enclosed garden to the rear. There is also an outside drinking area at the front of the pub. A pool room and function suite are situated off the public bar.
🏠🏵️🕪🛒🚲🅿️�(54,101)🛜

Bearsden

Burnbrae ✅

281 Milngavie Road, G61 3EA
🕑 7am-11 (midnight Fri); 8am-11 Sat & Sun
☎ (0141) 942 5951
Morland Old Speckled Hen; 5 changing beers (sourced nationally; often Greene King, Jaw) H
This relatively recently built but old world-style pub restaurant has real fires and oak beams. In front of a Premier Inn, the interior is open plan with several distinct areas mostly used for dining but there is space around the bar for those who only wish to drink. The licensee is enthusiastic about real ale and has begun running a mini festival every Easter with stillage set up in the bar. Alcohol is served from 11am (12.30pm Sun). 🏠🏵️🕪🛒🅿️late(60A)🛜

Biggar

Crown Inn ✅

ML12 6DL
🕑 11-midnight (1am Fri); 12.30-midnight Sun
☎ (01899) 220116 🌐 thecrownbiggar.co.uk
3 changing beers (sourced nationally) H
Small long-established market-town pub situated in rolling hills just north of the Southern Uplands. The friendly, traditional public bar at the front is comfortably furnished and warmed by an open fire. To the rear is a large lounge bar with dining and separate family areas, plus a smaller cosy dining room. The beers mostly come from smaller Scottish breweries. 🏠🏵️🕪🚲(191)

Elphinstone Hotel ✅

145 High Street, ML12 6DL (in centre)
🕑 11-midnight ☎ (01899) 220044 🌐 elphinstonehotel.co.uk
4 changing beers (sourced regionally; often Broughton, Caledonian, Fyne Ales) H
A coaching inn with a history going back over 400 years. The L-shaped public bar, the Elph, has been tastefully renovated while retaining its original character. Customers enjoying a beer or watching live music at weekends are warmed by an impressive logburner and there is a games area at the back. 🕪🚲(191)🐾🛜

Busby

White Cart ✅

61 East Kilbride Road, G76 8HX
🕑 11-11; 12-10 Sun ☎ (0141) 644 2711

3 changing beers Ⓗ
A friendly welcome awaits you at this Chef & Brewer pub. The listed building is bright and spacious, with roaring fires in winter. The emphasis here is on food service but there are four handpumps offering three guest ales and a cider. The patio at the front is popular in the summer and there is an area for families inside.
Q P

Castlecary

Castlecary House Hotel

Castlecary Road, G68 0HD (just off M80 jct 6 and 6A)
11-11 (11.30 Thu-Sat); 12.30-11 Sun ☎ (01324) 840233
castlecaryhotel.com
4 changing beers (sourced nationally; often An Teallach) Ⓗ
This family-run hotel in quiet suburban countryside is not too far from Glasgow city centre, and near the Glasgow-Edinburgh railway viaduct. It is also a handy stopping-off place when walking the Forth & Clyde Canal or Antonine Wall. The Poachers and Wee Bar provide a traditional pub atmosphere with comfortable lounge seating and a good-value bar meal menu. The adjacent restaurant also serves quality food with an emphasis on local produce.
Q P (X37,X39)

Coatbridge

Vulcan ✔

181 Main Street, ML5 3HH (jct with Dunbeth Rd)
8am-midnight (1am Thu-Sat) ☎ (01236) 437972
Sharp's Doom Bar; 5 changing beers (sourced nationally) Ⓗ
Wetherspoon pub named after the first iron-built ship, to reflect the area's industrial past. A full-scale replica is on show at the nearby Summerlee Heritage Park. Unusually for the chain, this building has always been a pub and it is small by Wetherspoon's standards, which helps to give it a more intimate atmosphere. The single room is level apart from a raised area overlooking Main Street, which is useful for small gatherings. Alcohol is served from 11am.
(Sunnyside) P

Crosslee

River Inn

Houston Street, PA6 7AW
11-midnight (1am Fri & Sat); 12.30-midnight Sun
☎ (01505) 613288 riverinn.co.uk
4 changing beers (sourced regionally; often Houston, Kelburn, Orkney) Ⓗ
Open since 2005, the River Inn is a family-friendly restaurant specialising in locally sourced produce. There are three restaurants, a bar area with two handpumps and a garden terrace downstairs and the Brierie Village Bar upstairs, with an additional four handpumps. The owner sponsors local sports clubs and the bar can be busy on Saturday afternoons. P

Eaglesham

Swan Inn

23 Polnoon Street, G76 0BH
11-11 (midnight Thu-Sat) ☎ (01355) 302673
Timothy Taylor Landlord; 1 changing beer (sourced nationally) Ⓗ
A homely country pub in a village setting, dating back to 1832, the Swan retains much of its original character, highlighted by a wooden and stained-glass interior. The excellent home-cooked food is generously portioned, reasonably priced and available throughout the day – the steak pie is a speciality. Q P

Glasgow

Babbity Bowster

16-18 Blackfriars Street, Merchant City, G1 1PE
11-midnight; 12.30-midnight Sun ☎ (0141) 552 5055
babbitybowster.com
1 changing beer (sourced regionally; often Fyne Ales) Ⓗ
Named after a Scottish dance, Babbity Bowster is unique in the Merchant City, situated away from the main hubbub down a quiet street. The café-style room has three real ales from Scottish breweries and the food here reflects the quality of the upstairs restaurant, often offering Scottish game and seafood, with the French chef adding his own touch. A fireplace burns peat in winter while in summer the beer garden has barbecues and a boules alley. Q (High St)

Blackfriars Ⓛ

36 Bell Street, Merchant City, G1 1LG
11-midnight; 12.30-midnight Sun ☎ (0141) 552 5924
blackfriarsglasgow.com
5 changing beers (sourced nationally; often Kelburn) Ⓗ
Popular traditional corner pub in the heart of the Merchant City with a broad clientele. A raised corner overlooks Albion Street while a quiet dining area lies to the rear. The central bar has five handpumps offering ales from across the UK, including many Scottish and local beers. There is a good selection of foreign beers and often real cider. Live bands perform on Tuesday and Sunday nights and a cellar bar hosts a comedy club and other events. (Argyle St)

Bon Accord ✔

153 North Street, Charing Cross, G3 7DA
11-midnight; 12.30-midnight Sun ☎ (0141) 248 4427
bonaccordweb.co.uk
Caledonian Deuchars IPA; Marston's Pedigree; 8 changing beers (sourced nationally; often Lawman, Theakston) Ⓗ
The Bon was an early pioneer on the Glasgow real ale scene and it has maintained its commitment to cask beer, with 10 handpumps on the bar, and winning many awards over the years. It has an interest in the new Lawman Brewery and acts as the brewery tap. The pub also earned the SLTN Whisky Pub of 2015 award, offering a select range of over 400 malts including a special house blend.
(Charing Cross)

REAL ALE BREWERIES

Clockwork Glasgow
Drygate Glasgow
Houston Hillington
Jaw Hillington
Kelburn Barrhead
Lawman Cumbernauld (NEW)
Strathaven Strathaven

Clockwork Beer Co 🅛 ✅
Cathcart Road, Mount Florida, G42 9HB
❂ 11-midnight ☎ (0141) 649 0184
Clockwork Original Amber, Cartside Red, Craft Lager, Oregon IPA, Hampden Roar; house beer (by Clockwork); 4 changing beers (sourced regionally; often Clockwork) 🅐
This spacious southside brewpub with 10 founts dispenses six regular and two seasonal Clockwork ales along with two guests, usually from Scottish breweries. Drinks can be taken to the upstairs bar which opens when events are on at nearby Hampden Park. The pub has a relaxed atmosphere during weekday afternoons but can get busy when sport is shown on the big screen, and evenings and weekends. Events include open mic Monday, quiz night Thursday and live music on the last Friday of the month. ⏳🏵️🍴♿≠(Mount Florida)🅿️�🛈

Curlers Rest ✅
256-260 Byres Road, Hillhead, G12 8SH
❂ 12-midnight ☎ (0141) 341 0737
⊕ thecurlersrestglasgow.co.uk
Caledonian Deuchars IPA; Sharp's Doom Bar; 3 changing beers (sourced nationally) 🅗
Originally a conversion from two 18th-century cottages, this is a large open-plan pub spreading over two floors. There has always been a pub on this site, taking its name from a local curling pond. The real ales are complemented by a selection of world beers. There is a more limited range of ales served in the upstairs bar with its open fire. ⏳🍴♿🚌🍺🛈

Drygate 🅛
85 Drygate, Dennistoun, G4 0UT (off John Knox St)
❂ 11-midnight ☎ (0141) 212 8815 ⊕ drygate.com
Drygate Seven Peaks; 3 changing beers (sourced nationally; often Drygate) 🅗
Large brewpub a short walk east of the city centre, almost in the shadow of Glasgow Cathedral. Four real ales, usually at least two brewed on the premises, are complemented by a large choice of specialist and bottled beers, with beers also available to take away from the in-house bottle shop. Live music and comedy feature regularly in the upstairs beer hall and there is a roof terrace for outdoor drinking. Excellent food is served all day. ⏳🏵️🍴♿≠(High St)🅿️🚌🍺🛈

Edward Wylie ✅
107-109 Bothwell Street, G2 6TS
❂ 7am-11.30 (midnight Fri); 8am-midnight Sat; 8am-11.30 Sun ☎ (0141) 229 5480
Sharp's Doom Bar; 10 changing beers (sourced nationally; often Isle of Skye, Oakham, Williams Bros) 🅗
A large establishment set in the business district close to Glasgow Central station, offering the standard Wetherspoon fare. The modern bar offers a variety of seating. Given the number of pubs in the chain in Glasgow, the staff work hard to source interesting beers and make this venue distinct in an area not short of competition. The hard work has paid off and customers are offered a superb range of nationally sourced beers in excellent condition. Alcohol is served from 11am. Q⏳🏵️🍴♿≠(Central)🚌🍺🛈

Hengler's Circus ✅
351-363 Sauchiehall Street, Charing Cross, G2 3HU
❂ 8am-midnight ☎ (0141) 331 9810

Sharp's Doom Bar; 13 changing beers (sourced nationally) 🅗
Wetherspoon pub on Sauchiehall Street where there is lots of competition from other bars and food outlets. It is creditable that the Hengler stands out from the crowd, particularly in terms of beer. Fourteen handpumps dispense an excellent range of ales from Scotland and beyond. The well-kept beers, knowledgeable staff and eclectic customers are not to be missed, whether you are stopping for a short lunch break or want a longer stay. Alcohol is served from 11am.
Q⏳🍴♿≠(Charing Cross)🚌🍺🛈

Inn Deep
445 Great Western Road, Hillhead, G12 8HH
❂ 12-midnight; 12-11 Sun ☎ (0141) 357 1075
⊕ inndeep.com
3 changing beers (sourced nationally; often Williams Bros) 🅟
Situated in the shadow of Kelvin Bridge, Inn Deep is built into archways beside the old railway station and is accessed by stairs down from the main road which formerly served the ticket office. The pub also opens onto the low-level river walkway where benches provide a pleasant place to sit in good weather. Three beers usually include one from Williams of Alloa with two guests from newer breweries throughout the country. Good food is served. There is a DJ on Friday and Saturday evenings. ⏳🏵️🍴🚌🍴🚌(6,20)🍺🛈

Laurieston Bar ★ 🅛
58 Bridge Street, Tradeston, G5 9HU
❂ 11-11; 12.30-11 Sun ☎ (0141) 429 4528
Fyne Ales Jarl; 2 changing beers (sourced locally; often Fyne Ales, Jaw) 🅗
A friendly family-run local, little has changed at this bar since it was fitted out in the 1960s. The formica-topped tables screwed to the floor and matching horseshoe bar earn the pub an entry in CAMRA's National Inventory of Historic Pub Interiors. The plusher lounge dates from the same period, as does the music, played quietly, from a free jukebox. A traditional pie and peas warmer is served until early evening, with tea and biscuits also available to customers. ≠(Central)🚌🍺🛈

MacGregors Pie & Ale Howff 🅛
5 Blackfriars Street, G1 1PG (off High St down from station)
❂ 11-midnight ☎ (0141) 552 5012
5 changing beers (sourced regionally) 🅗
Cosy pub on the outskirts of Merchant City offering real ales from local and national microbreweries, a well-stocked fridge of beers, and a good range of hand-made savoury pies. Vegetarian pies are also served and all come with baked beans or mushy peas. The pub has two rooms, one a busy bar with darts to the side of the bar and comfortable seating, and the other a slightly larger lounge. Traditional music often creates a friendly and welcoming atmosphere. Q🍴≠(High Street)🍺🛈

Mulberry St
778 Pollokshaws Road, Strathbungo, G41 2AE
❂ 11-11 (midnight Fri & Sat); 12.30-11 Sun
☎ (0141) 424 0858 ⊕ mulberrystbarbistro.com
Harviestoun Bitter & Twisted; 2 changing beers (sourced locally; often Fyne Ales) 🅗
Friendly community pub in a conservation area close to Queens Park. The bar is laid out in a modern style with comfortable seating. In summer

the seating area outside on the pavement quickly fills in fine weather. A varied menu of food is available in the bar and the attached bistro. To augment the real ales there is a variety of foreign bottled beers on offer.
🛏🅃♿⇌(Queens Park)🚉🐾🛜

Pot Still 🄻

154 Hope Street, G2 2TH
✪ 11-midnight ☎ (0141) 333 0980 ⊕ thepotstill.co.uk
4 changing beers (sourced regionally) Ⓗ
This cosy, friendly, family-run pub has a heritage going back almost 150 years. Conveniently near both rail stations and on a main bus route, connoisseurs come from all over the world to sample rare malt whiskies from the hundreds covering numerous shelves. Four handpumps dispense mainly Scottish ales, with lesser-known and new breweries supported. A mezzanine corner provides a retreat when busy. Basic bar food, such as hot pies and beans, is available until 6pm.
🅃⇌(Queen St)🚉🚉🐾🛜

Sir John Moore ✪

Argyle Street, G2 8QW
✪ 8am-midnight; 11-midnight Sun ☎ (0141) 222 1780
Caledonian Deuchars IPA; Greene King Abbot; 6 changing beers (sourced nationally) Ⓗ
Long and narrow with a low ceiling, a family area at one end and a quiet corner at the other, this Wetherspoon pub has a traditional feel. Though modern in style, extensive use of wood prevents it from appearing glitzy. Eight handpumps serve a range of ales from Scotland and south of the border. 🅃♿⇌Ⓡ🍴🚉🛜

Sir John Stirling Maxwell ✪

136-140 Kilmarnock Road, Shawlands, G41 3NN
✪ 8am-midnight ☎ (0141) 636 9024
Caledonian Deuchars IPA; Greene King Abbot; 8 changing beers (sourced nationally; often Kelburn) Ⓗ
Wetherspoon supermarket conversion in an elevated position at the south end of Shawlands shopping centre. Ten handpumps dispense a wide-ranging choice of beers with at least a couple of strong ales on offer. The raised space to the rear is primarily used for dining and is favoured by families. Busy but never raucous, the pub is popular with a mixed clientele and is a good weekend venue. Alcohol is served from 11am.
🛏🅃♿⇌(Shawlands)🍴🚉🛜

State Bar 🏆

148 Holland Street, Charing Cross, G2 4NG (just off Sauchiehall St, opp the Hengler's Circus)
✪ 12-midnight ☎ (0141) 332 2159
House beer (by Stewart Brewing); 6 changing beers (sourced nationally; often Oakham) Ⓗ
A popular city-centre pub which gets busy at lunchtimes and weekends. The changing beers are often ones you might not see elsewhere in Glasgow. This old-fashioned island bar is close to the King's Theatre. There is a weekly blues session on Tuesdays in the main bar and a comedy club in the small bar downstairs on Fridays. Local CAMRA Pub of the Year for 2015.
🅃♿⇌(Charing Cross)🚉🚉🛜

Sweeney's on the Park 🄻

962 Pollokshaws Road, Shawlands, G41 2ET
✪ 12-midnight ☎ (0141) 632 6741
⊕ sweeneysonthepark.com
2 changing beers (sourced locally; often Fyne Ales) Ⓗ

A friendly, modernised pub close to Shawlands Cross and over the road from Queens Park. The popular, traditional bar is complemented by a comfortable lounge which hosts karaoke on Wednesday, a quiz on Sunday and bands most other evenings. No meals are available but a roll and soup is on offer Monday to Friday afternoons and sausage rolls on Friday and Saturday evenings. Dogs are welcome except when the pub is busy at weekends. ♿⇌(Crossmyloof)🚉🐾🛜

Tennent's ✪

191 Byres Road, Hillhead, G12 8TN
✪ 9am-11 (midnight Thu-Sat) ☎ (0141) 339 7203
⊕ thetennentsbarglasgow.co.uk
Brains Rev James; Caledonian Deuchars IPA; Draught Bass; Harviestoun Bitter & Twisted; Stewart Brewing 80/-; Timothy Taylor Landlord; 3 changing beers (sourced nationally) Ⓗ
Long-established pub at the heart of the West End that has undergone many refurbishments over the years but that has retained many original features and kept its character. The rectangular horseshoe bar features 12 handpumps serving nine regular and three guest ales from national breweries. There is a small lounge to one side reached by a short corridor where pictures of the locals are displayed. Good-value meals are served all day.
🅃♿Ⓡ🚉🐾🛜

Three Judges 🄻 ✪

141 Dumbarton Road, Partick, G11 6PR
✪ 11-midnight ☎ (0141) 337 3055 ⊕ threejudges.co.uk
Caledonian Deuchars IPA; 8 changing beers (sourced nationally) Ⓗ
Long-standing corner pub that has won numerous CAMRA awards over the last 25 years. Eight handpumps offer ever-changing ales, especially from new and lesser-known breweries. Another pump serves a real cider or perry. Pork pies are available and food may be brought in from nearby takeaways. This friendly local has a raised front area overlooking Partick Cross where traditional jazz plays on Sunday afternoons and there is a quiet corner at the back. Q⇌(Partick)🚉🐾🚉🐾🛜

Greenock

James Watt ✪

80-92 Cathcart Street, PA15 1DD
✪ 8am-midnight (1am Fri & Sat); 9am-midnight Sun
☎ (01475) 722640
Greene King Abbot; Sharp's Doom Bar; 3 changing beers Ⓗ
Close to the rail and bus stations, this large open-plan Wetherspoon, in a former post office, is named after one of Greenock's famous sons who improved steam engine technology and has the SI unit of power named after him. The chain's standard value-for-money food is available all day and beer festivals are hosted at various times throughout the year. This pub is an oasis in a beer desert. Alcohol is served from 11am.
🅃♿⇌(Central)🛜

Hamilton

George Bar

18 Campbell Street, ML3 6AS
✪ 12-midnight (1am Fri); 12.30-midnight Sun
☎ (01698) 424225

3 changing beers (sourced nationally; often Strathaven) H

This traditional, family-run pub is situated in a pedestrianised area just off the inner ring road in the town. The single-bar room is small but full of character and there is plenty of standing room alongside dining space to enjoy the tasty home-cooked meals (served until 6pm). In warmer weather café-style tables and chairs provide extra seating outside. The kitchen is closed on Sunday but you can help yourself to free soup.
◐&≈(Central)🚗🌼

Houston

Houston Inn

North Street, PA6 7EN
◑ 11-midnight (1am Fri & Sat) ☎ (01505) 614315
🌐 houston-inn.com

Kelburn Goldihops; 2 changing beers (often Belhaven, Kelburn, Stewart) H

Friendly village country inn having an L-shaped bar area with a log fire and a separate restaurant. Three handpumps offer a variety of Scottish and occasionally English beers. There is a quiz night each Wednesday and live music on a Saturday. Only a short drive from Glasgow, the restaurant offers flavoursome traditional food made with locally sourced ingredients. ➰🏠🍴◐&P🚗🌼 ᗡ

Inverkip

Inverkip Hotel

Main Street, PA16 0AS
◑ 11-11 (11.30 Thu-Sat); 12.30-11 Sun ☎ (01475) 521478
🌐 inverkip.co.uk

Fyne Jarl; 1 changing beer H

Small, family-run hotel just a short walk from the large Inverkip Marina, making it an ideal staging post for those just messing about on the river or passing through on the way to Largs and the Ayrshire coast. 🏠🍴◐≈P🚗(578,580)ᗡ

Johnstone

Callum's L

26 High Street, PA5 8AH
◑ 11-11.30 (1am Fri & Sat); 12.30-midnight Sun
☎ (01505) 322925 🌐 callums-bar.com

Kelburn Pivo Estivo; 6 changing beers (often Jaw, Orkney) H

Popular town-centre pub offering a friendly welcome and a comfortable atmosphere. The lounge has an area for dining with themed nights including Thursday curry. There is a small function room available for private parties with occasional live music at weekends. Six changing guest ales are usually available and one permanent from the local Kelburn brewery. ➰◐&≈🚗(36,38)ᗡ

Kilbarchan

Trust Inn

8 Low Barholm, PA10 2ET
◑ 11-midnight; 12-1am Fri & Sat ☎ (01505) 702401
🌐 thetrustinn.com

3 changing beers (often Fuller's, Greene King, Shepherd Neame) H

This small, popular, single-roomed pub in the centre of a conservation village has old local photographs adorning the pub walls. Offering a superior bar food menu and special promotions, it

can be busy at mealtimes. There is live music fortnightly on a Friday night featuring local acts. Children are welcome in the evening until 9pm if dining. ➰◐&🚗(38)ᗡ

Kilmacolm

Pullman Tavern

Elphinstone Court, Lochwinnoch Road, PA13 4LG
◑ 11-11 (midnight Wed); 11-1am Fri & Sat; 12.30-11 Sun
☎ (01505) 874501

1 changing beer H

This Mitchells & Butlers establishment is the only pub in a small conservation village and was converted from a railway station. There is a large seating area outside which is particularly popular in the summer months with families, walkers and cyclists. The national cycle path, which follows the old railway line from Paisley to Gourock, passes by the pub. 🏠◐&P🚗(X7)🌼ᗡ

Lochwinnoch

Brown Bull ᗒ

32 Main Street, PA12 4AH
◑ 12-11 (midnight Fri & Sat); 12.30-11 Sun
☎ (01505) 843250

4 changing beers (sourced regionally) H

This village pub is a family-run free house more than 200 years old and popular with locals and visitors alike. It is located close to Lochwinnoch RSPB nature reserve and Castle Semple visitor centre. Quiz night is Tuesday and live music features every second Sunday. The ales showcase mainly Scottish breweries. At the rear is a quirky outdoor seating area. The popular upstairs restaurant uses local produce and bar meals are also available. Q➰🏠◐&🍴🚗ᗡ

Newton Mearns

Osprey ✔

Stewarton Road, G77 6NP (just off jct 4 M77)
◑ 12-11; 12-10.30 Sun ☎ (0141) 639 7453

3 changing beers (often Caledonian, Sharp's) H/Ⓐ

A country pub oozing rural charm and rustic character. The picturesque surroundings provide the perfect backdrop for savouring beer and hearty food, available all day. Part of the Vintage Inns group, it is near Pollok House and the Burrell Collection of artworks, making it an ideal refreshment stop for art lovers and ale fans alike. Q➰🏠◐&P🚗(44A)🌼ᗡ

Paisley

Bull Inn ★ L ✔

7 New Street, PA1 1XU
◑ 11-midnight (1am Fri & Sat) ☎ (0141) 849 0472
🌐 bullinnpaisley.co.uk

4 changing beers (sourced regionally; often Arran, Kelburn, Loch Lomond) H

Established in 1901 and identified by CAMRA as having a nationally important historic interior, this is the oldest inn in Paisley. The pub retains many original features including stained-glass windows, three small snugs and a spirit cask gantry, and boasts the only original set of spirit cocks left in Scotland. Guest ales are usually Scottish, with an emphasis on the local Arran and Kelburn breweries. ◐&≈(Gilmour St)🚗🌼ᗡ

Harvies Bar Ⓛ

86 Glasgow Road, PA1 3NU
🕑 11-11 (1am Fri); 11-midnight Sat; 12.30-midnight Sun
☎ (0141) 889 0911 ⊕ harviesbar.co.uk
Caledonian Flying Scotsman; Kelburn Goldihops; 1 changing beer Ⓗ

Popular tenement-style local situated on the main Paisley to Glasgow road. The spacious open-plan bar, with raised seating, has three large TV screens showing sport and music videos with the volume turned down low. The pub can get busy during major football matches. Sunday features a quiz night and Wednesday is poker night. Live music or a DJ play occasionally. ◑ᶜ⇌🖥 (9,17,38)🛜

Sandpiper ⊘

Glasgow Airport, PA3 2SW
🕑 4-9.30 ☎ (0141) 842 7858
Caledonian Deuchars IPA; Greene King Abbot; Marston's Pedigree; Sharp's Doom Bar; 4 changing beers (often Broughton, Kelburn, Williams Bros) Ⓗ

Positioned on the ground floor, in the public area of the airport, this Wetherspoon outlet is ideal if you are looking for an ale before heading through security, waiting for family or friends arriving on an incoming flight or, if you are a plane spotter, in need of refreshment. With eight handpumps you are spoiled for choice and can relax watching one of the many TV screens showing 24-hour news or sporting events. Q🚲◑ᶜ♿🍴🖥🛜

Wee Howff

53 High Street, PA1 2AN
🕑 11-11 (11.30 Wed & Thu; 1am Fri; 12.30am Sat); 12.30-11 Sun ☎ (0141) 889 2095
3 changing beers Ⓗ

The Wee Howff has appeared in 25 editions of the Guide and is a haven in an otherwise crowded area of cheap drinking establishments. A small, traditional pub with a loyal regular clientele, the Howff offers up to three guest ales from all corners of the country from a quarterly rotating list. It holds an open mic night on the first Monday of the month and a pub quiz every Thursday. The jukebox caters for the most eclectic of tastes. ⇌(Gilmour St)🖥 (9,36)🛜

Port Glasgow

Waterwheel

Russel Way, Greenock Road, PA14 5DX
🕑 11-11 ☎ (01475) 742167
Marston's Pedigree; 1 changing beer Ⓗ

This is a modern family-friendly food-led Marston's pub/restaurant, situated adjacent to the A8 on the site of the old Lithgow's Kingston shipyard, with great views of the River Clyde. While the focus is on carvery meals which are served all day, up to three handpumps offer a choice of cask ales from the Marston's family of brewers. 🚲◑⇌(Port Glasgow)P

Renfrew

Lord of the Isles ⊘

Unit 21 Xscape, Kings Inch Road, PA4 8XQ
🕑 8am-midnight (1am Fri & Sat) ☎ (0141) 886 8930
Greene King Abbot; 3 changing beers Ⓗ

Purpose-built Wetherspoon establishment attached to the Soar leisure complex at the Braehead shopping centre. The walls display photographs depicting the history of industry on the River Clyde. The outside seating area is south-facing and a suntrap on summer days. Food is available all day and three changing guest ales are on handpump. A short stroll allows you to view the ships docked at Yarrow Shipyard. Alcohol is served from 11am. 🐕◑♿P🖥🛜

Rutherglen

An Ruadh Ghleann ⊘

40-44 Main Street, G73 2HY
🕑 8am-midnight (1am Fri & Sat); closed Sun
☎ (0141) 613 2370
Caledonian Deuchars IPA; Greene King Abbot; Sharp's Doom Bar; 6 changing beers (sourced nationally) Ⓗ

Situated at the west end of the long Main Street, this Wetherspoon pub has friendly staff and locals. Sizeable windows make for a bright, airy atmosphere in this spacious venue. To the rear is a beer garden on two levels, the upper with an awning, which catches the sun all day. Up to six ales are available from 10 handpumps, including changing Scottish beers and guest ales from elsewhere. Alcohol is served from 11am. Q🛜🐕◑♿⇌🖥🛜

Strathaven

Weavers Ⓛ ⊘

1-3 Green Street, ML10 6LT
🕑 4.30 (11 Mon)-midnight; 4.30-1am Thu; 11-1am Fri & Sat; 2-1am Sun ☎ 07749 332914
4 changing beers (sourced nationally; often Strathaven) Ⓗ

Named after the traditional trade of the town, this family-run pub was once part of a much larger hotel and function rooms. It has strong local links and participates in community activities including supporting the nearby Strathaven Ales. The modernised single-room bar, with a cosy space around the fire, is decorated with black and white photographs of film and pop stars. The choice of guest ales is dictated by customers' requests. ♿🖥(254,256)🛜

Uplawmoor

Uplawmoor Hotel Ⓛ

66 Neilston Road, G78 4AF (off A736)
🕑 11-11 (10 Mon & Tue; midnight Fri); 11-10 Sun
☎ (01505) 850565 ⊕ uplawmoor.co.uk
2 changing beers (sourced locally; often Kelburn) Ⓗ

In a tranquil village setting just over 10 miles from Glasgow, the building dates back to the 18th century. It was originally a coaching inn used by travellers and customs officers chasing smugglers en-route between Glasgow and the south-west coast of Scotland. Today the hotel continues to offer travellers the opportunity to relax and explore. The interior is rustic and cosy, with a public bar, pool room and lounge bar. The beer is usually from the local Kelburn Brewing Co. 🚲🐕🛏◑♿P🖥(395,X44B)🐾🛜

Where village statesmen talked with looks profound, And news much older than the ale went round. **Alfred, Lord Tennyson**

HIGHLANDS & WESTERN ISLES

John o' Groats

Thurso

Stornoway

LEWIS

HARRIS

THE
WESTERN
ISLANDS

Ullapool
Dundonell

Dornoch

Gairloch

Kinlochewe

Cromarty

NORTH
UIST

Uig

Fortrose

Munlochy

Nairn

Waternish

Inverness
Cawdor

SKYE

Drumnadrochit
Dores

SOUTH
UIST

Plockton

Carrbridge

Sligachan

Foyers

ABERDEEN & GRAMPIAN

Whitebridge

Aviemore

Cluanie

Kincraig
Newtonmore

Glenfinnan

TAYSITE

Roy Bridge
Fort William

Kinlochleven

Glencoe

0 Miles   20

0 Kilometres   32

ARGYLL & THE ISLES

Authority areas covered: Highland UA, Western Isles UA

Aviemore

Cairngorm Hotel (Cairn Bar) L

77 Grampian Road, PH22 1PE (opp railway station, S of village)

☼ 11-midnight (1am Fri & Sat); 11.30-midnight Sun

☎ (01479) 810233 ⊕ cairngorm.com

Cairngorm Stag, Gold ⊞

Just across the road from the station, the lounge bar of this privately owned hotel, though large, has a cosy feel. The trade is mainly holidaymakers, but the bar is popular with locals and has a large-screen TV showing sport. Decorated with tartan wall coverings, there is a Scottish theme throughout the hotel, and Scottish entertainment features on many afternoons and evenings.

Old Bridge Inn L

Dalfaber Road, PH22 1PU (off B970 S of village)

☼ 12-1am; 12-midnight Sun ☎ (01479) 811137

⊕ oldbridgeinn.co.uk

Cairngorm Stag, Trade Winds; Caledonian Flying Scotsman, Deuchars IPA; 2 changing beers (sourced regionally; often Cairngorm) ⊞

Busy pub, popular with outdoor enthusiasts, serving good-quality food made with locally sourced ingredients. Originally a cottage and now greatly enlarged, it lies on the road to the Strathspey Steam Railway overlooking the River Spey. The two guest handpumps dispense the seasonal offering from the local Cairngorm Brewery

plus another Scottish ale. Live entertainment is hosted twice weekly, including traditional and modern Scottish music and bands. Children are welcome and there is a bunkhouse attached.

Winking Owl L ✔

123 Grampian Road, PH22 1RH (at N end of village)

☼ 11-midnight (1am Thu-Sat); 12.30-midnight Sun

☎ (01479) 812368 ⊕ thewinkingowl.co

Cairngorm Stag, Trade Winds, Wildcat; Caledonian Flying Scotsman, Deuchars IPA; 1 changing beer (sourced locally; often Cairngorm) ⊞

Legendary Aviemore hostelry, known locally as Winky, now under the stewardship of the nearby Cairngorm Brewery. Reputed to be Aviemore's oldest pub, part of the original inn is where Robert Burns had breakfast during his 1787 Highland tour. The interior has been tastefully redecorated and updated without losing the familiar cosy layout. Beers are from Cairngorm and Caledonian via an innovative brewery tie. The creative all-day menu is designed to please all tastes and appetites, including children.

Carrbridge

Cairn Hotel L

Main Road, PH23 3AS (B9153 to N of village)

☼ 12-midnight; 12-1am Fri & Sat; 12.30-midnight Sun

☎ (01479) 841212 ⊕ cairnhotel.co.uk

3 changing beers (sourced regionally; often Cairngorm, Cromarty, Orkney) H
Along the road from the Landmark Adventure Park, the Cairn is a traditional Highland inn with seven guest rooms. It is in the Cairngorm National Park and is popular with both locals and visitors. Freshly cooked, seasonal bar meals are available. Real ales include a beer from the local Cairngorm Brewery, one from either Cromarty or Orkney, and the third will be a different Scottish guest ale with every cask. ➤✿🏠🍺🅿🚪🐾🛜

Cawdor

Cawdor Tavern ✅
The Lane, IV12 5XP (B9090) NH845500
🕐 11-3, 5-11 (11-11 summer); 11-midnight Sat; 12.30-11 Sun
☎ (01667) 404777 🌐 cawdortavern.co.uk
Orkney Northern Light, Red MacGregor, Dark Island; 1 changing beer (sourced regionally; often Orkney) H
Owned by the same family for nearly 20 years, the Cawdor is at the heart of this conservation village, within easy reach of local historic attractions. It has a spacious lounge and cosy public bar, both wood-panelled with log fires, and a large restaurant. Up to five handpumps offer Orkney and Atlas ales – the family also owns the Orkney Brewery at Quoyloo. The pub has a reputation for good food. Q➤✿🍺🔌🐾🅿🚪(252)🛜

Cluanie

Cluanie Inn 🄻
Glenmorriston, IV63 7YW (on A87) NH076117
🕐 8am-11; 12-11 Sun ☎ (01320) 340238 🌐 cluanieinn.com
Loch Ness WilderNESS, HoppyNESS H
Cluanie Inn lies next to the A87, the Road to the Isles, in the centre of the Highlands surrounded by breathtaking mountain scenery, 20 miles from Loch Ness. The hotel is an excellent base for hill walkers and Munro baggers alike, offering a mixture of accommodation from luxury rooms to a clubhouse that sleeps 10. There are no formal camping facilities but wild camping is available locally. Q➤✿🏠🍺🅿⛺🅿🚪(915,916,917)🐾🛜

Dores

Dores Inn 🄻
IV2 6TR (on B862 at jct with B852) NH598348
🕐 11-11 (midnight Fri & Sat); closed Mon winter
☎ (01463) 751203 🌐 thedoresinn.co.uk
4 changing beers (sourced regionally; often Cromarty, Inveralmond, Loch Ness) H
On the north-east side of Loch Ness, just eight miles from Inverness, this inn enjoys spectacular views and is ideal for Nessie spotting. The cosy wood-finished bar serves up to four ales, nearly always from Scottish independent breweries such as Cairngorm, Fyne Ales and Swannay, with an occasional English ale featured. The welcoming, extended dining room offers good food made with locally sourced ingredients and can get busy at times. Open from 10am for tea, coffee and bakes. Q➤✿🍺🅿🚪(16,18D,114)🛜

Dornoch

Dornoch Castle Hotel 🄻
Castle Street, IV25 3SD
🕐 11-11 (1am Fri; 11.45 Sat); 12.30-11 Sun
☎ (01862) 810216 🌐 dornochcastlehotel.com

Cromarty Happy Chappy; 2 changing beers (sourced regionally; often Cairngorm, Cromarty, Orkney) H
It is worth diverting off the A9 to Dornoch just to marvel at the interior of this hotel, parts of which date back to 1577, and since June 2000 under the ownership of the Thompson family. Up to three ales from various Scottish breweries are usually available as well as a massive collection of 300 single malt whiskies. The restaurant has an excellent reputation among locals and visitors. Local attractions include the 13th-century cathedral opposite, golf course and beaches. Q➤✿🏠🍺🅿🅿🚪(X98,X99,25X)🛜

Drumnadrochit

Benleva Hotel 🍺 🄻
Kilmore Road, IV63 6UH (signed from A82) NH513295
🕐 12-midnight (1am Fri); 12.30-11 Sun ☎ (01456) 450080
🌐 benleva.co.uk
7 changing beers (sourced regionally; often Isle of Skye, Loch Ness, Windswept) H
Popular, friendly village inn near Loch Ness, catering for locals and visitors. A 400 year-old former manse, the sweet chestnut outside was once a hanging tree. Eight handpumps dispense three Loch Ness Brewery ales accompanied by guests from the rest of the UK plus a real cider. Lunches, evening meals and Sunday roasts are served. Entertainment includes poker nights, occasional quiz nights and traditional music. Home of the famous Loch Ness Beer Festival in September. ➤✿🏠🍺⛺🐾🅿🚪🐾🛜

Fort William

Ben Nevis Inn 🄻
Achintee Road, Claggan, PH33 6TE (just outside Fort William, signed from A82) NN125729
🕐 12-11 summer; hours vary winter ☎ (01397) 701227
🌐 ben-nevis-inn.co.uk
3 changing beers (sourced locally; often Cairngorm, Isle of Skye) H
Popular with outdoor enthusiasts, the inn is housed in a traditional, stone-built barn at the start of the Ben Nevis mountain path. The bar, with long beer hall-style tables and a warming stove, is a friendly, informal setting, an ideal venue for the regular live music that plays here. Food is served all day, featuring local produce in a mix of traditional favourites and international dishes, complemented by a choice of three real ales from local breweries. Bunkhouse accommodation sleeps up to 20 people. Check ahead for opening hours in winter. Q✿🏠🍺🐾🅿

REAL ALE BREWERIES

An Teallach Dundonell
Black Isle Munlochy
Cairngorm Aviemore
Cromarty Cromarty
Cuillin ■ Sligachan: Isle of Skye
Glenfinnan Glenfinnan
Hebridean Stornoway: Isle of Lewis
Isle of Skye Uig: Isle of Skye
John o'Groats John o'Groats (NEW)
Loch Ness ■ Drumnadrochit
Old Inn ■ Gairloch
Plockton Plockton
River Leven Kinlochleven
Wooha Nairn

SCOTLAND

Cobbs at Nevisport

Airds Crossing, PH33 6EU (beneath Nevisport shop)
🌐 11–midnight (1am Fri & Sat); 12.30–midnight Sun
☎ (01397) 704790 ⊕ cobbs-at-nevisport.co.uk
4 changing beers (sourced regionally; often Isle of Skye, Orkney) Ⓗ
At the start/finish of the West Highland and Great Glen Ways and close to the Nevis range, this large but cosy bar is a popular meeting place for outdoor enthusiasts. Warmed by a large fire, the interior is adorned with classic mountaineering photographs and outdoor gear. Food is served all day in the bar and upstairs restaurant where children are welcome. Four handpumps dispense a changing range of beers from Highlands and Islands breweries. Live music features regularly.
🏮🕸🍴◑&Å≠P🚌🐾🛜

Great Glen ✔

104 High Street, PH33 6AD (S end of pedestrianised area)
🌐 7–midnight (1am Fri & Sat) ☎ (01397) 709910
Adnams Broadside; Caledonian Deuchars IPA; house beer (by Strathaven); 8 changing beers (sourced nationally) Ⓗ
Named after The Great Glen (An Gleann Mor), a stunning 78-mile natural route running from Inverness to Fort William. This is a new-build pub, unusual for Wetherspoon, conveniently situated under a Travelodge. It has a spacious, modern interior with plenty of comfortable sofa seating and an open kitchen. Ten handpumps serve a good many Scottish ales. There is a small decking area up the steps outside with seating. Alcohol is available from 11am (12pm Sun).
🏮🕸🍴◑&≠P🚌🛜

Grog & Gruel Ⓛ ✔

66 High Street, PH33 6AE
🌐 12–11.30 (12.30am Thu-Sat); 12.30 (5 winter)–11.30 Sun
☎ (01397) 705078 ⊕ grogandgruel.co.uk
6 changing beers (sourced locally; often An Teallach, Glenfinnan, Isle of Skye) Ⓗ
Located at the end of the West Highland Way, halfway along the pedestrianised high street, this award-winning traditional ale house is the perfect place to slake your thirst after the 96-mile hike. Up to six beers are served, fewer in winter, predominantly from Scottish independents such as Cairngorm and Swannay. Bar meals and snacks are available all day, with evening meals in the upstairs restaurant. Popular with locals, tourists and outdoor enthusiasts. Regular events include live music, open mic nights and beer festivals.
🏮◑Å≠🍴🚌🛜

Fortrose

Anderson

Union Street, IV10 8TD (on A832)
🌐 4–11.30; closed Sun-Tue winter ☎ (01381) 620236
⊕ theanderson.co.uk
3 changing beers (sourced nationally; often Cromarty, Inveralmond) Ⓗ
Over the past 10 years the bar's three handpumps have offered ales from nearly 400 breweries from all over the UK, with the emphasis on Scottish brews. The shelves groan under the weight of more than 260 malts, 100 Belgian and 30 Mikkeller bottled beers. The restaurant has a well-deserved reputation for excellent meals made with local ingredients. Quiz, music, film and knitting nights all

feature regularly. Wood-burning stoves keep the rooms cosy. The pub closes for four weeks in November/December, opening again just before Christmas. Q🏮🕸🍴◑&Å♣🍴P🚌🐾🛜

Foyers

Craigdarroch Inn (Am Fuaran Bar) Ⓛ

IV2 6XU (B852, turn down towards Lower Foyers, follow signs) NH497207
🌐 11–11 ☎ (01456) 486400 ⊕ hotel-loch-ness.co.uk
2 changing beers (sourced locally; often Loch Ness) Ⓗ
This AA four-star inn on the south side of Loch Ness is perched on a hillside with splendid views over the loch – an ideal base for a spot of monster hunting. Close by are the Falls of Foyers and loch-side/woodland walks. The Am Fuaran Bar (The Well) serves the ales which are mainly from Loch Ness Brewery just over the water. Good seasonal food is available. The hot water and heating are supplied by a biomass wood chip system.
Q🏮🕸🍴◑&Å♣P🚌(16)🐾🛜

Glencoe

Clachaig Inn Ⓛ ✔

PH49 4HX (3 miles SE of village, off A82) NN127567
🌐 11–11 (11.30 Fri; midnight Sat); 12.30–11 Sun
☎ (01855) 811252 ⊕ clachaig.com
10 changing beers (sourced locally; often An Teallach, Cairngorm, Orkney) Ⓗ
A real ale stronghold for decades, you will be spoilt for choice by the wide range of Scottish brews that feature on up to 15 handpumps. There are three bars to enjoy but the popular Boots bar with its wooden benches and upholstered seating around the walls is the one favoured by the climbers, walkers and tourists who come for the stunning surrounding scenery. Plenty of wood-burning stoves keep the place cosy and there is a hearty food menu to enjoy throughout the day.
🏮🕸🍴◑&♣P🛜

Inverness

Castle Tavern Ⓛ

1 View Place, IV2 4SA (top of Castle St)
🌐 11–11am (12.30am Sat); 12–midnight Sun
☎ (01463) 718178 ⊕ castletavern.net
6 changing beers (sourced regionally; often An Teallach, Cromarty, Isle of Skye) Ⓗ
A 73-mile hike along the Great Glen Way or a five-minute stroll from the city centre brings you to this friendly hostelry in a listed building facing the castle and boasting fine views across the River Ness towards the cathedral. Six handpumps dispense a changing range of beers and beer styles, often featuring Scottish independents and local breweries, including Cairngorm and Cromarty. Bar meals are served all day, and there is a separate restaurant on the first floor. A Victorian-style canopy covers the large beer patio.
🏮🕸◑Å≠🚌🛜

Clachnaharry Inn

17-19 High Street, Clachnaharry, IV3 8RB (on A862 Beauly road)
🌐 11–11 (midnight Thu; 1am Fri & Sat); 12–11 Sun
☎ (01463) 239806 ⊕ clachnaharryinn.co.uk
Fyne Ales Jarl; 3 changing beers (sourced nationally; often Cairngorm, Greene King, Timothy Taylor) Ⓗ

Popular with locals and visitors, this friendly 17th-century coaching inn offers high-quality food made with locally sourced ingredients lunchtimes and evenings, and families are welcome. Four handpumps dispense Scottish beers from Inveralmond, Fyne and Cairngorm breweries as well as some from Greene King. The large patio area affords fine views over the Caledonian Canal sea lock and Beauly Firth toward the Munro, Ben Wyvis. Wednesday is quiz night and Thursday has been a Scottish music jam session night for many years. Q ⛽ ✿ ⏺ ◖ ▲ ♣ P � (28,28A) ✿ ⚲

Corriegarth L
5-7 Heathmount Road, IV2 3JU
✿ 11-midnight (1am Fri & Sat); 12-midnight Sun
☎ (01463) 242730 ⊕ corriegarth.com
Caledonian Deuchars IPA; Cromarty Happy Chappy; 2 changing beers (sourced nationally) Ⓗ
One of the Highland capital's oldest private hotels, constructed around 1840, it is situated in the Crown area of Inverness, a few minutes' walk from the city centre, and has six en-suite bedrooms. It has been refurbished to a high standard and is a comfortable, friendly place. In addition to the regular beers there are often two beers from the Punch list. Q ⛽ ✿ ⏺ ◖ & ➡ P ➡ ⚲

Hootananny
67 Church Street, IV1 1ES
✿ 12-1am; 6.30-midnight Sun ☎ (01463) 233651
⊕ hootanannyinverness.co.uk
Black Isle Yellowhammer, Red Kite Ⓗ
Hootananny (meaning celebration or party in Scots) has a fantastic atmosphere and is a popular award-winning pub that celebrates Scottish folk music. Live sessions are hosted round the table or on the raised stage downstairs 9.30pm-midnight every night, and upstairs in the Mad Hatters Lounge 9.30pm-3am Friday and Saturday nights (entry is usually free). Children are welcome provided they are dining. An excellent selection of freshly prepared Scottish food is available. Beer is from the Black Isle Brewery which is certified organic. ⛽ ✿ ◖ & ➡ 🚃

King's Highway ✓
72-74 Church Street, IV1 1EN
✿ 11-1am; 12.30-1am Sun ☎ (01463) 251830
Adnams Broadside; Caledonian Deuchars IPA; Fuller's London Pride; Greene King Abbot; Sharp's Doom Bar; changing beers (often An Teallach, Houston) Ⓗ
This former hotel is now a Wetherspoon pub with a 27-room lodge attached. The vast single-roomed bar is broken up by several pillars and plenty of comfortable seating in alcoves. Up to 10 handpumps serve the regular ales alongside a good mix of guests. Food is standard keenly priced Wetherspoon fare, with breakfast available from 7am. Customers are the typical eclectic mix and the pub gets busy at weekends. ⛽ ➡ ◖ & ➡ P ➡ ⚲

Number 27 L
27 Castle Street, IV2 3DU
✿ 11-11 (12.30am Fri & Sat); 12.30-11 Sun
☎ (01463) 241999
4 changing beers (sourced regionally; often Speyside Craft, Windswept) Ⓗ
Alongside four ales on handpump, this popular city centre bar and restaurant offers a large bottle range including continental brews. A good selection of malt whiskies is also stocked. The venue has a reputation for good food – lunches

range from sandwiches to light bites while the comprehensive evening menu features traditional main courses made with locally-sourced ingredients including venison and steak. ◖ ➡ 🚃 ➡ ⚲

Phoenix Ale House L
106-110 Academy Street, IV1 1LX
✿ 11-midnight (1am Fri & Sat); 12-midnight Sun
☎ (01463) 240300
10 changing beers (sourced nationally; often Cairngorm, Loch Ness, Windswept) Ⓗ
After years of decline, the Phoenix is now a free house and completely refurbished throughout. The iconic island bar has 10 handpumps offering a wide range of Scottish and English ales, always including a couple of LocAles. The comfortable adjoining lounge is a relaxing place to enjoy a meal from the extensive menu. True to the legend, the Phoenix has risen from the ashes. Q ◖ ◖ & ➡ P ➡

Kincraig

Suie Bar L
PH21 1NA (at the head of Loch Insh on B9152) NH829057
✿ 5-11 (1am Fri & Sat) ☎ (01540) 651344
Cairngorm Trade Winds; 2 changing beers (sourced regionally; often Cairngorm, Orkney) Ⓗ
Victorian character lodge located at the south end of the village, run by only the second owner in 108 years. The separate wooden-floored bar features a large wood-burning stove plus a pool table and jukebox. Three pumps dispense a selection of Scottish guests. Close to the River Spey and Loch Insh, the bar is popular with welcoming locals, hill walkers, skiers and cyclists. Traditional Scottish music is hosted regularly and the lodge is available for weekly rental. ✿ ➡ ♣ P ➡ ✿ ⚲

Kinlochewe

Kinlochewe Hotel (Beinn Eighe Bar) L
IV22 2PA (on A832) NH028619
✿ 11-midnight; 12.30-midnight Sun ☎ (01445) 760253
⊕ kinlochewehotel.co.uk
5 changing beers (sourced regionally; often An Teallach, Cromarty, Orkney) Ⓗ
Friendly, family-run 1800s coaching inn. Set in the heart of the magnificent Torridon mountains, at the foot of Beinn Eighe, this is an ideal base for exploring the wild scenery of the north-west Highlands. Freshly cooked seasonal dishes are made with high-quality local produce including seafood, game and beef, with an emphasis on simplicity and flavour. Up to five handpumps dispense ales including Windswept, with a guest in summer, plus Westons Family Reserve cider. A 12-bed bunkhouse is attached.
Q ➡ ◖ & ▲ ♣ P ➡ (700,705,711) ✿ ⚲

Munlochy

Allangrange Arms L ✓
58 Millbank Road, IV8 8NL (on B9161)
✿ 11-11 (1am Fri & Sat); hours vary winter
☎ (01463) 819862 ⊕ allangrangearms.com
Cromarty Happy Chappy; Orkney Red MacGregor Ⓗ
Modern, lodge-themed, family-friendly pub in this Black Isle village. Quality food made with primarily local produce is served daily, except winter Mondays, and a children's menu is available. There

SCOTLAND

is a separate restaurant area. Seating includes cosy booths, and there is a small open-plan lounge with a sofa and large-screen TV for sport. Live music features regularly. Wooden benches outside are pleasant on warmer days.
Q☆⊛🛏🍴◑⅁♿P🚬🐾🌐

Nairn

Braeval Hotel 🅛 ✅
Crescent Road, IV12 4NB (E of village)
⊛ 12-midnight (12.30am Thu-Sat) ☎ (01667) 452341
⊕ braevalhotel.co.uk
9 changing beers (sourced nationally; often Cairngorm, Cromarty, Orkney) 🅗
The family-run Bandstand Bar in the hotel has up to nine handpumps offering a good selection of English and Scottish ales. It hosts the largest independent beer festival in the Highlands every spring with around 140 ales and great live music throughout the 10-day event. Quality food is served in the popular sea-view restaurant. Winner of CAMRA Highland Pub of the Year three times.
Q☆⊛🛏🍴◑⅁♿A⇌♣♠P🚬🌐

Newtonmore

Glen Hotel 🅛
Main Street, PH20 1DD
⊛ 11-midnight; 12.30-midnight Sun ☎ (01540) 673203
⊕ theglenhotel.co.uk
3 changing beers (often Cairngorm, Caledonian) 🅗
Small, welcoming, family-run Edwardian hotel with the Monadhliath and Cairngorm mountain ranges on its doorstep. It has a good local trade and is also popular with outdoor enthusiasts and tourists. There is a large bar room and separate games and dining rooms, with regular quiz and games nights. Up to three handpumps dispense mainly Scottish beers, plus a Westons cider or perry in the summer. An extensive menu includes a good selection of vegetarian dishes. ☆🛏◑⅁♿A⇌P🚬🌐

Plockton

Plockton Hotel ✅
41 Harbour Street, IV52 8TN NG803334
⊛ 11-midnight; 12.30-11 Sun ☎ (01599) 544274
⊕ plocktonhotel.co.uk
House beer (by Inveralmond); 4 changing beers (often Cromarty, Swannay) 🅗
Sheltered by mountains and fanned by the warm air of the Gulf Stream, the hotel is at the edge of Loch Carron and boasts breathtaking views across the bay. Seafood is the speciality on an excellent menu alongside locally reared beef and Highland venison. The village has much to offer and is a regular haunt for outdoor enthusiasts. Brews from a variety of Highland and other Scottish micros are regularly on handpump. Closed throughout January.
Q☆⊛🛏◑⅁♿P🚬🌐

Roy Bridge

Stronlossit Inn 🅛 ✅
Main Street, PH31 4AG (on A86) NN272812
⊛ 11-11.45 (1am Thu-Sat); 12.30-11.45 Sun
☎ (01397) 712253 ⊕ stronlossit.co.uk
3 changing beers (sourced regionally; often Cairngorm, Orkney) 🅗
A roaring log fire warms the cosy bar of this country inn-style hotel, ideally located for enjoying

the seemingly endless range of outdoor pursuits on offer in Lochaber. Three regularly changing Scottish beers are available, often from Highlands and Islands breweries, plus an occasional cider, as well as over 80 Scotch malt whiskies. Freshly prepared food is served all day, locally sourced and taking full advantage of Scotland's natural larder. Ten en suite, high-quality, budget rooms, adjacent to the main hotel, are designed to meet the needs of outdoor enthusiasts. Q☆⊛🛏🍴◑⅁♿A⇌♣P🚬🌐

Thurso

Weigh Inn (Ashes Bar)
Burnside, KW14 7UG (N of town on A9 at A836 jct)
⊛ 12-2.30, 4.30-midnight; 12-midnight Fri-Sun
☎ (01847) 893722 ⊕ weighinn.co.uk
1 changing beer (sourced locally; often Orkney) 🅗
Sitting in two acres of its own grounds and overlooking the Pentland Firth with panoramic views of the Orkney Isles, the hotel is close to the Scrabster to Orkney ferry. The Ashes is the main bar, and there are two other bars used for functions. A single handpump alternates between Orkney Corncrake and another Orkney beer. Occasional live entertainment is hosted in the bar and there are screens for sport. Bar meals are served lunchtimes and evenings. Outside is an enclosed children's play area and a patio with tables and seating. Q☆⊛🛏🍴◑⅁♿A♣P🚬🌐

Ullapool

Argyll Hotel 🅛 ✅
18 Argyll Street, IV26 2UB
⊛ 11-1am; 12-midnight Sun ☎ (01854) 612422
⊕ theargyllullapool.com
4 changing beers (sourced regionally; often An Teallach) 🅗
Busy, small hotel offering breakfast, lunch and dinner all made with locally sourced produce, with good vegetarian and coeliac choices. There are three changing guest ales plus another from the local An Teallach Ale Co. Live music features on Monday and live bands play on Tuesday and weekends March-October. There are three mini beer festivals including a cider and blues music festival in September. A weekly curry night, quiz and poker keep the bar busy. Ideally located for the ferry to the Hebrides. ⊛🛏◑⅁♿A♣♠P🚬🐾🌐

Morefield Motel 🅛
North Road, IV26 2TQ (off A835)
⊛ 12-11 ☎ (01854) 612161 ⊕ morefieldmotel.co.uk
3 changing beers (sourced locally; often Cairngorm) 🅗
Locally caught seafood is the speciality on the menu at this family-run, friendly motel, surrounded by some of the most dramatic and beautiful scenery to be found in the country. Three ales, fewer in winter, are predominantly from local Highlands breweries. The annual Ullapool Beer Festival is held here in October. The Western Isles ferry terminal in the centre of Ullapool is a short distance away. Winter opening hours can vary.
Q⊛🛏◑⅁♿AP🚬🐾🌐

Waternish: Isle of Skye

Stein Inn 🅛 ✅
MacLeod's Terrace, IV55 8GA (N of Dunvegan, on B886)
NG263564

✪ 11-midnight; 11.30-11 Sun summer; 12-11 (midnight Sat); 12.30-11 Sun winter ☎ (01470) 592362 ⊕ steininn.co.uk
3 changing beers (sourced regionally; often Caledonian, Isle of Skye, Loch Ness) Ⓗ

Dating back to the 18th century, this is the oldest inn on Skye, nestling in a row of whitewashed cottages on the shores of Loch Bay, owned and run by the same family for more than 20 years. A large stove warms the cosy low-beamed bar which has fine views over the sea loch to Rubha Maol. In addition to the real ales on offer, the hotel has a selection of over 130 single malt whiskies. Locally caught seafood, landed at the nearby jetty, is served April to October in the bar and restaurant. The guest ale may be from Swannay. For seafarers there are four council moorings.
Q☎⊛🛏🍽◐👤♣P🐾

Whitebridge

Whitebridge Hotel Ⓛ

IV2 6UN (SW of Loch Ness on B862) NH487152
✪ opening hours vary ☎ (01456) 486226
⊕ whitebridgehotel.co.uk
3 changing beers (sourced regionally; often Cairngorm, Cromarty, Loch Ness) Ⓗ

Built in 1899 and located on the 'quiet' side of Loch Ness, this hotel has fishing rights on two local lochs. Inside, the attractive pitch pine-panelled bar, with a welcoming wood-burning stove, has an alcove with a pool table and a separate area used for dining. The traditional pub food is all home cooked. Two ales are usually available, sometimes only one in winter. The hotel has a green tourism policy. Q⊛🛏◐👤♣P🚍(18D,228,301)🐾 ᳇

SCOTLAND

Stein Inn, Waternish: Isle of Skye

KINGDOM OF FIFE

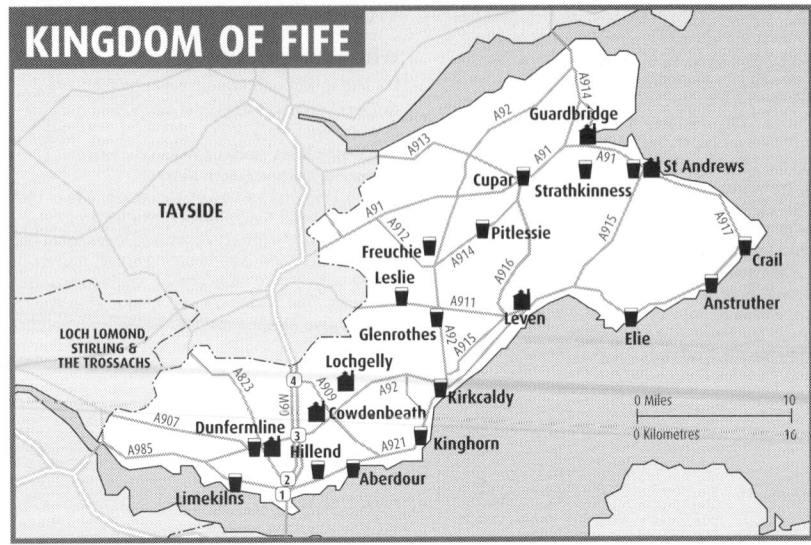

Authority area covered: Fife UA

Aberdour

Foresters Arms 🏆 ✅
35 High Street, KY3 0SJ
✪ 11-midnight (1am Fri); 10-1am Sat ☎ (01383) 860544
🌐 forries.co.uk
Caledonian Deuchars IPA; 3 changing beers (sourced nationally) Ⓗ
A pub at the centre of the community, right in the middle of the village, only minutes away from the railway station. This recently refurbished family-run inn offers a friendly welcome to all and is a welcoming retreat for walkers on the Fife coastal path. It has six handpumps with two dedicated to cider. Warm yourself by the real coal fire and enjoy a good pub lunch. Live music, quizzes and theme nights are held regularly. Kingdom of Fife CAMRA Pub of the Year 2015 and 2016.
❀◑&≠●🖂(7)🐾🕈

Anstruther

Ship Tavern
49 Shore Street, KY10 3AQ
✪ 11-midnight (1am Fri & Sat); 12.30-midnight Sun
☎ (01333) 310347
2 changing beers (sourced nationally; often Eden Mill) Ⓗ
Next door to the famous Anstruther Fish Bar, this traditional pub on the harbour front is a popular meeting place for fishermen, locals and visitors to the museum. The bar has all the character you would expect from a historic fishing village inn. Two varying ales are from the local Eden Mill as well as breweries from all over the UK. Take in the views of the harbour or relax in the comfort of the back room. ◑🛦♣🖂(X60,95)

Crail

Golf Hotel ✅
4 High Street, KY10 3TD
✪ 11-midnight (1am Thu-Sat); 12.30-midnight Sun
☎ (01333) 450206 🌐 thegolfhotelcrail.com
3 changing beers (sourced nationally) Ⓗ

The Golf Hotel is a listed 16th-century coaching inn in a picturesque village in the East Neuk of Fife. The historic bar dates back to 1721, making it one of the oldest in Scotland. The room retains the original low-beamed ceiling, wooden floor and a 16th-century fireplace with a marriage lintel over it bearing the initials of the original owners. Relax with a beer in the garden or enjoy a meal in the restaurant after walking the coastal path.
❀🛏◑🖂(95)🐾🕈

Cupar

Boudingait
43 Bonnygate, KY15 4BU
✪ 11-11 (midnight Thu; 1am Fri & Sat); 11-midnight Sun
☎ (01334) 654681 🌐 theboudingaitcupar.co.uk
2 changing beers (sourced regionally; often Edenmill, Orkney) Ⓗ
This wee gem hidden off Main Street in Cupar is a bustling family-friendly outlet, traditionally decorated with a rustic feel. Two handpulls feature a variety of regional and local ales. A loyalty card is available – ask staff for details. Good home-made pub food made with locally sourced produce is available throughout the day. A quiz night features weekly and live music fortnightly. ◑&≠🖂🕈

Dunfermline

Commercial Inn
13 Douglas Street, KY12 7EB (off High St adjacent to post office)
✪ 10-11 (midnight Fri & Sat) ☎ (01383) 733876

REAL ALE BREWERIES
Beath Cowdenbeath (NEW)
Beeches Lochgelly (brewing suspended)
de bRus 🍺 Dunfermline
Eden St Andrews Guardbridge
Luckie Leven
St Andrews St Andrews

Caledonian Deuchars IPA, Edinburgh Castle 80/-; Courage Best Bitter; Theakston Old Peculier; 3 changing beers (sourced nationally) H
This renowned ale house is situated just off the high street in a historic building dating back to the 1820s. Seven real ales and a cider are always on offer. Good food and friendly service attract an eclectic clientele. Local CAMRA Pub of the Year 2016 finalist, 2014 winner and Scottish finalist 2014. ⬤ ➡ ≢ (Town)⬤🚇

Guildhall & Linen Exchange ✅
79-83 High Street, KY12 7DR
⏰ 8am-midnight (1am Fri & Sat) ☎ (01383) 625960
Caledonian Deuchars IPA; Greene King Abbot; changing beers (sourced nationally) H
A split-level Wetherspoon pub in a category A listed building, decorated throughout with a mix of modern and Art Deco features. Numerous pictures from years gone by depict Dunfermline's and the Guildhall's historic past. Located in the middle of the town's busy retail area, this is a great place to escape for a quick half or two. 🏛️❀🍽️⬤♿≢🚇🛜

Elie

Ship Inn
The Toft, KY9 1DT
⏰ 10.30-11 (midnight Fri & Sat) ☎ (01333) 330246
⊕ shipinn.scot
4 changing beers (sourced regionally; often Eden Mill) H
The ship reopened in 2015 following a major refurbishment including the spectacular first-floor restaurant overlooking Elie Bay. During the summer when the tide is out, beach cricket can be viewed from the beach bar. In inclement weather visitors can relax in the comfort of the bar with open fires and wood-burning stoves. Four handpulls offer a wide range of local, regional and national ales. A Kingdom of Fife Pub of the Year 2016 finalist. ❀🍽️⬤ ♣

Freuchie

Albert Tavern
2 High Street, KY15 7EX
⏰ 5 (12 Fri & Sat)-midnight; 12.30-midnight Sun ☎ 07876 178863
5 changing beers (sourced nationally) H
A multi-award winner, including former Scottish CAMRA Pub of the Year and Kingdom of Fife Pub of the Year. A friendly village local, the Albert was reputedly a coaching inn when nearby Falkland Palace was a royal residence. Wainscot panelling and two old brewery mirrors decorate the walls of the bar. A TV in the lounge screens sport. Five handpumps offer weekly changing beers. Q❀⬤🚇(36,66)♣

Lomond Hills Hotel
High Street, KY15 7EY
⏰ 11-2, 5-midnight; 11-midnight Fri & Sat; 12.30-midnight Sun ☎ (01337) 857329 ⊕ lomondhillshotel.com
2 changing beers (sourced nationally) H
Comfortable country hotel, originally a coaching inn established in 1733, with a marvellous view of the Lomond Hills and handy for visiting Falkland Palace. The small, welcoming public bar sports a carved bar top and wood panelling on the walls. A plasma screen shows football, rugby and golf. Two beers are always available. Meals are served in the

family lounge and a separate dining room. Outside there is a smoking area and beer garden. 🛏️❀🍽️⬤♿P🚇(36,66)

Glenrothes

Golden Acorn ✅
1 North Street, KY7 5NA
⏰ 7am-midnight (1am Fri) ☎ (01592) 751175
Caledonian Deuchars IPA; Greene King Abbot; 7 changing beers (sourced nationally) H
A Wetherlodge decorated with scenes of the local area in days gone by. Real ale is offered on seven handpumps alongside a regular cider, and the standard Wetherspoon beer festivals and special deals are available. Plasma screens show a number of sporting events. Located near the town centre with the bus station only two minutes' walk away. 🛏️❀🍽️⬤♿⬤P🚇🛜

Hillend

Hillend Tavern
37 Main Street, KY11 9ND
⏰ 4 (3 Fri)-midnight; 1-midnight Sat & Sun
☎ (01383) 415391 ⊕ hillendtavern.co.uk
2 changing beers (sourced nationally) H
A small, traditional pub with a warm welcome. A hidden gem not far from Dalegty Bay, it has a spacious room at the back and a large covered area outside. The Hillend offers a wide variety of traditional events, live music, TV sport such as football and rugby, quizzes and karaoke. Two handpulls dispense a wide range of regional and national ales. ❀≢🚇(7,87)♣

Kinghorn

Crown Tavern ✅
55-57 High Street, KY3 9UW
⏰ 11-11.45; 12.30-11.45 Sun ☎ (01592) 890340
2 changing beers (sourced nationally; often Tryst) H
A bustling two-roomed local, also called the Middle Bar, situated to the west of the High Street. Attractive stained-glass panels adorn the windows, and the high ceilings feature ornate plaster work. Mainly a sports bar, two TVs screen a wide range of sporting events. A pool table can be found to the side. Two guest ales from microbreweries throughout the UK are available here. ≢♣⬤🚇(7)

Kirkcaldy

Harbour Bar
471-475 High Street, KY1 2SN
⏰ 11-3, 5-midnight; 11-midnight Thu-Sat; 12.30-midnight Sun ☎ (01592) 264270
6 changing beers (sourced nationally) H
The building dates from around 1870 and was a ship chandlers' before it became a pub in 1924. It is one of just a few pubs to still have the historic jug bar. The lounge is light and airy with ornate cornices. Six handpumps sell up to 20 different beers a week from micros all over Britain. Kingdom of Fife CAMRA Pub of the Year on numerous occasions, a finalist in 2016 and a previous Scottish Pub of the Year winner. Q⬤🚇(X58,X60,X62)♣

Robert Nairn ✅
2-6 Kirk Wynd, KY1 1EH
⏰ 8am-midnight (1am Fri & Sat); 8am-11 Sun
☎ (01592) 205249

Caledonian Deuchars IPA; Greene King Abbot; 4 changing beers (sourced nationally) Ⓗ
A Wetherspoon pub just off the main pedestrianised area of the town with a split-level lounge and pictures of old Kirkcaldy on the walls. Six handpulls dispense a variety of beers and regular Meet the Brewer evenings are hosted. With its central location, this lively pub attracts a mixed clientele, young and old, who all enjoy the real ales. ⓈⓄ♿≠🚃🛜

Leslie

Burns Tavern
184 High Street, KY6 3DB
✪ 12 (11 Fri & Sat)-midnight; 12.30-midnight Sun
☎ (01592) 741345
Timothy Taylor Landlord; 1 changing beer (sourced nationally) Ⓗ
Typical Scottish two-room, main-street local in a town once famous for papermaking. The public bar is on two levels, the lower lively and friendly, the upper with a large-screen TV, pool table and football memorabilia on the walls. The lounge bar is quieter and more spacious. Competitions and quizzes are held weekly, and karaoke on Saturday. Leslie Folk Club plays here on a Sunday. Two beers are usually available in this good honest local.
Q♣♣P🚃(38)♣

Limekilns

Ship Inn
Halketts Hall, KY11 3HJ
✪ 11-11 (midnight Fri & Sat); 12.30-11 Sun
☎ (01383) 872247
3 changing beers (sourced nationally) Ⓗ
Set on the waterfront in a small rural village, this establishment has excellent views across the River Forth. Three guest ales are available, mostly from microbreweries throughout the UK. The bar has a cosy alcove to the left, and a maritime theme features throughout the building. Meals are served lunchtimes with fish and seafood the speciality (booking is essential). A former CAMRA Kingdom of Fife Pub of the Year runner-up. Q❀ⓄP🚃(6)

Pitlessie

Village Inn
Cupar Road, KY15 7SU
✪ 12-2.30, 5-11 (midnight Thu); 12-midnight Fri; 12-11.30 Sat; 12-11 Sun ☎ (01337) 830595 ⊕ pitlessievillageinn.co.uk
3 changing beers (sourced nationally) Ⓗ
Old coaching inn decorated with pictures of the maltings that were once opposite. A lovely real fire helps create a cosy atmosphere in the wood-panelled, stone and plaster-walled interior. The room has a corner bar with bar stools and a separate seating area for bar meals or drinks. There is a large restaurant and separate pool room. Three handpulls offer two ales and a real cider. High teas are served on Sunday afternoon. Ⓞ♣P🚃(X24)

St Andrews

Central Bar ✪
77 Market Street, KY16 9NU
✪ 11-11.45 (midnight Fri & Sat); 12.30-11.45 Sun
☎ (01334) 478296
Courage Best Bitter; Fuller's London Pride; Inveralmond Lia Fail; Theakston Old Peculier; 4 changing beers (sourced nationally) Ⓗ
Busy city-centre pub on one of St Andrews' main streets, full of character and attracting a good mix of students, tourists and locals. It has a Victorian-style island bar, large windows and ornate mirrors, creating a late-19th century feel. A former CAMRA Kingdom of Fife Pub of the Year winner.
Q❀ⓄⓀ🚃🛜

Criterion
99 South Street, KY16 9QW
✪ 11-midnight (1am Fri & Sat); 12.30-midnight Sun
☎ (01334) 474543
Caledonian Deuchars IPA; 6 changing beers (sourced nationally; often Eden Mill) Ⓗ
Lovely local with seating outdoors on the pavement, a big picture window and oak-panelled walls adorned with photographs of St Andrews in days gone by. The pub is renowned for its home-made meals (served until 5pm). Background music plays and a plasma screen shows sport. Open music night on Monday is popular with local artists, and a regular quiz night is hosted during the week. CAMRA Kingdom of Fife Pub of the Year runner-up 2016. ❀Ⓞ♣🚃♣

St Andrews Brewing Co
177 South Street, KY16 9EE
✪ 12-11; 12.30-11 Sun ☎ (01334) 471111
⊕ standrewsbrewingcompany.com
4 changing beers (sourced nationally) Ⓗ
This brewpub showcases a wide range of St Andrews Brewing Co beers in cask, keg and bottles. It has 16 taps, with four dedicated to cask ales which vary between national and St Andrews' ales. The rest of the taps offer cider and beer from all over the UK. Available in third pints so you can try one or two, enjoy your beer downstairs by the fire or upstairs in the beer hall. Ⓞ♿🚃♣🛜

Strathkinness

Tavern
4 High Road, KY16 9RS
✪ 5-11; 5-midnight Fri-Sun ☎ (01334) 850085
⊕ strathkinnesstavern.co.uk
2 changing beers (sourced nationally) Ⓗ
The Tavern has a public bar with a comfortable lounge at one end and a separate quiet library lounge. Two handpulls offer a choice of changing guest ales. Lunches and evening meals are served in the bar and restaurant. Quiz nights are the first and third Tuesday of each month and folk night on a Monday. Tables at the front enjoy lovely views over the river estuary. Q❀Ⓞ♣♣P🚃(64,64A)🛜

Lets have filleted steak and a bottle of Bass for dinner tonight. It will be simply exquisite. I shall love it.' 'But my dear Nella,' he exclaimed, 'steak and beer at Felix's! It's impossible! Moreover, young women still under twenty-three cannot be permitted to drink Bass.'
Arnold Bennett, The Grand Babylon Hotel, 1902

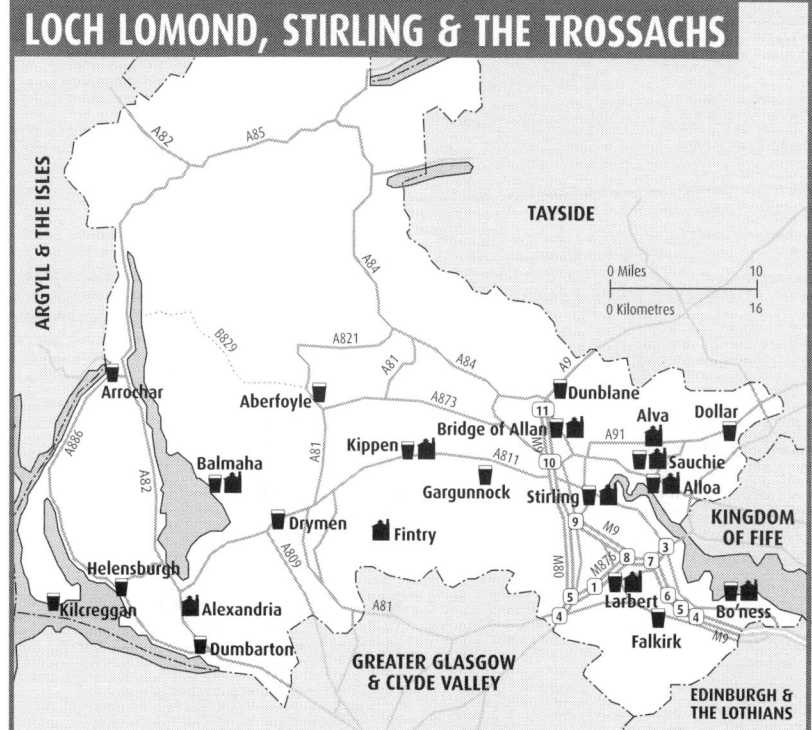

LOCH LOMOND, STIRLING & THE TROSSACHS

Authority areas covered: Argyll & Bute UA (part), Clackmannanshire UA, Falkirk UA, Stirling UA, West Dumbartonshire UA

Aberfoyle

Forth Inn
Main Street, FK8 3UQ
☼ 11-midnight (1am Fri & Sat) ☎ (01877) 382372
⊕ forthinn.com
Harviestoun Schiehallion; 4 changing beers (sourced regionally; often Belhaven, Cairngorm, Fallen) ℍ
This 100-year-old inn is situated by the River Forth within the Trossachs National Park. The cosy wood-panelled bar is decorated with old photographs of the area and is a magnet for tourists and locals alike. The innovative landlord is proud to serve only Scottish ales from up to eight handpumps, with third-pint taster glasses available, and wholesome food featuring locally sourced produce. There is a separate dining room and a 'baronial' dining hall.
Q ♿ ⊛ ♨ ◑ ♿ ♣ P ☐ (C11)

Alloa

Bobbing John ✓
46 Drysdale Street, FK10 1JL
☼ 11-midnight (1am Fri & Sat); 11-11 Sun ☎ (01259) 222590
Caledonian Deuchars IPA; Greene King Abbot; Sharp's Doom Bar; 2 changing beers (often An Teallach, Black Wolf) ℍ
Situated in a traditional three-storey sandstone building, purpose-built in 1895 for the Alloa Co-operative Society, the pub is named after Alloa-born John Erskine who created industrial Alloa, developing the town as a coal mining centre. He was twice Secretary of State for Scotland under Queen Anne; however, his frequent changes of

political allegiance earned him the nickname Bobbing John. Much of the building's existing stone has been retained and a new Victorian shop front reintroduced. Alcohol is served from 11am.
♿ ⊛ ⊛ ◑ ♿ ♣ ☐ ☎

Arrochar

Village Inn ✓
Shore Road, G83 7AX (down A814 from A83 jct)
☼ 11-11 (midnight Fri & Sat); 12-11 Sun ☎ (01301) 702279
⊕ villageinnarrochar.co.uk
Caledonian Deuchars IPA; 3 changing beers (sourced nationally; often Loch Lomond Brewery) ℍ
Attractive pub set back from the road, originally built in 1827 as the local manse. Set on the shore of Loch Long, seating outside at the front provides excellent views across to the Cobbler and Arrochar Alps. A large open log fire and hardwood floor and fittings add to the cosy ambience in the public bar.

REAL ALE BREWERIES

Balmaha 🍺 Balmaha
Black Wolf Stirling
Devon 🍺 Sauchie
Fallen Kippen
Fintry Fintry
Harviestoun Alva
Kinneil Bo'ness
Loch Lomond Alexandria
Tinpot 🍺 Bridge of Allan
Tryst Larbert
Williams Alloa

Food is available all day, served in the bar and adjacent restaurant.
🧒🌞🛏️🍴🕐♿Å♣P🚪(926,976)🛜

Balmaha

Oak Tree Inn 🍺
Main Street, G63 0JQ
🌑 9.30am-midnight (1am Fri & Sat) ☎ (01360) 870357
🌐 theoaktreeinn.co.uk
4 changing beers (often Fallen, Jaw, Loch Lomond) Ⓗ
Balmaha is a picturesque village situated on the quieter eastern shore of Loch Lomond, on the route of the West Highland Way and close to the statue of climber and broadcaster Tom Weir. Meals are served all day in this award-winning pub-restaurant with four handpumps on the bar dispensing local microbrewery ales. There is a large outdoor drinking area under the eponymous oak tree. Alcohol is served from 11am (12.30pm Sun). Local CAMRA Rural Pub of the Year 2016.
🧒🌞🛏️🕐♿P🚪(309)🛜

Bo'ness

Corbie Inn
84 Corbiehall, EH51 0AS
🌑 12-11; 12.30-11 Sun ☎ (01506) 825307 🌐 corbieinn.co.uk
Changing beers (sourced nationally; often Kinneil) Ⓗ
This pub opened in 2011 and has been hand-crafted by the owners. Six ales are usually to be found on handpump, including one from the Kinneil Brew Hoose at the back of the premises. An ideal refreshment stop after a visit to the Bo'ness & Kinneil Railway or the Bo'ness Motor Museum, the pub is also handy for the Hippodrome, Scotland's oldest purpose-built picture house. Very much a community venue and involved in local charity projects, the Corbie was local CAMRA Pub of the Year 2015. Q🧒🌞🕐P🚪

Bridge of Allan

Old Bridge Inn
2 Inverallan Road, FK9 4JA
🌑 closed Mon; 11-midnight; 11-6 Sun ☎ (01786) 833335
🌐 oldbridgeinn.co.uk
Caledonian Deuchars IPA; 2 changing beers (often Fuller's, Theakston) Ⓗ
The Old Bridge Inn was built in 1710 and is an integral part of the early Clachan of Bridge End which, with the river close by, was the site for several mills. The old meal mill across the road has been beautifully restored, as has this pub. It is situated not far from the railway station on the old A9 route beside the River Allan, just off the main street in the town. Q🕐♿🚆P🚪(58)🌺

Dollar

King's Seat 🅥
23 Bridge Street, FK14 7DE
🌑 4-midnight; 12-1am Fri & Sat; 12-midnight Sun
☎ (01259) 742515 🌐 kingsseat.com
Fyne Ales Jarl; Harviestoun Bitter & Twisted; 4 changing beers (sourced nationally; often Fuller's, Harviestoun) Ⓗ
Cosy, welcoming bar and restaurant situated in a quaint old village. Up to six ales and real cider are on offer during the summer, along with bar snacks and restaurant food. Dogs and children are welcome and there are tables and chairs outside

for warmer weather. Occasional barbecues and live folk music are hosted. There are many great walks and attractions nearby. Q🌞🛏️🕐♿Å👜🚪🌺

Drymen

Clachan Inn
2 Main Street, G63 0BG
🌑 11-midnight (1am Fri & Sat); 12.30-midnight Sun
☎ (01360) 660824 🌐 clachaninndrymen.co.uk
2 changing beers (sourced regionally; often Belhaven) Ⓗ
A free house in the same family for over 30 years, this is reputedly the oldest licensed premises in Scotland, dating from 1734, and has been recently renovated while preserving many original features. There are two handpumps dispensing a changing selection of excellent local beers. Visitors can be sure of a warm welcome, and the inn is a popular stop-off for walkers on the West Highland Way and tourists exploring Loch Lomond National Park. Quality food is served all day in the bar and restaurant at this popular pub.
🧒🛏️🕐 ÅP🚪(309)🌺

Dumbarton

Captain James Lang 🅥
97-99 High Street, G82 1PH
🌑 8am-midnight (1am Fri & Sat) ☎ (01389) 742112
Caledonian Deuchars IPA; Greene King Abbot; 8 changing beers (sourced nationally) Ⓗ
An attractive conversion of the old Woolworths, this Wetherspoon pub has various seating areas and a beer garden to the rear overlooking the River Leven. As ever, the pub is full of local ephemera. Captain Lang was a riverboat captain and there is much to see in Dumbarton connected to the town's maritime history. Deuchars and Abbot ales are supported by an ever-changing guest range. Alcohol is served from 11am. 🧒🌞🕐♿🚆🚪🛜

Dunblane

Riverside 🍺
Stirling Road, FK15 9EP
🌑 8am-midnight (1am Fri & Sat); 9am-midnight Sun
☎ (01786) 823318 🌐 theriversidedunblane.co.uk
Caledonian Deuchars IPA; 2 changing beers (sourced regionally; often Loch Ness, Orkney, Strathaven) Ⓗ
Homely, family-friendly venue that is a pub, restaurant and coffee house where you can enjoy a hearty breakfast, a coffee and home-bake or a quality meal, as well as excellent local ale. It has a terrace overlooking Allan Water and is close to the railway station and a short walk from the cathedral. Alcohol is served from 11am. Local CAMRA Pub of the Year 2016. 🧒🕐♿🚆🚪

Tappit Hen 🅥
Kirk Street, FK15 0AL
🌑 11-midnight (1am Fri & Sat) ☎ (01786) 825226
🌐 thetappithen-dunblane.co.uk
Belhaven IPA; 4 changing beers Ⓗ
A traditional single-room pub with the interior separated into different areas by wooden dividers. It is a cosy meeting point for local people as well as a delightful discovery for visitors. It hosts a weekly folk music night on a Tuesday and a real ale festival once or twice a year. Fundraising events in support of local charities are held regularly at this generous community venue. 🚆🚪🌺🛜

Falkirk

Behind the Wall ✅
14 Melville Street, FK1 1HZ
☼ 11-midnight (3am Fri & Sat); 12-midnight Sun
☎ (01324) 633338 ⊕ behindthewall.co.uk
Changing beers (often Fyne Ales, Tryst) Ⓗ
This spacious venue for drinking, dining and entertainment was once a bra factory. Upstairs was previously the Eglesbrech Brewery but is now a two-room real ale and whisky bar, with timber furnishings and a wood-burning stove. When the brewery closed, Eglesbrech became popular for watching sport events, music and comedy, hosting bands and comedians, both local and national. This bar is occasionally closed but ale can be ordered downstairs and staff will get it for you.
&꙱❀◑⇌局 ❧

Wheatsheaf Inn ✅
16 Baxters Wynd, FK1 1PF
☼ 11-midnight (1am Fri & Sat); 12.30-midnight Sun
☎ (01324) 638282 ⊕ thewheatsheaffalkirk.co.uk
Caledonian Deuchars IPA; 3 changing beers (sourced nationally; often Hadrian Border, Ilkley, Knops) Ⓗ
A public house, dating from the late-18th century and retaining much of its original character, found off the High Street via one of the vennels. The wood-panelled bar is furnished in traditional style with plenty of interesting features from the past. Guest ales come from microbreweries in both Scotland and England, with two on offer mid-week and three at the weekend. Tea, coffee and snacks are served daily. A must-visit venue when in the area. ❀⇌局

Gargunnock

Gargunnock Inn
Main Street, FK8 3BW
☼ 12-11; 11-12.30am Fri & Sat; 12.30-11 Sun
☎ (01786) 860333 ⊕ gargunnockinn.co.uk
2 changing beers Ⓗ
Dating from the 1700s, this is now a roomy yet cosy pub and restaurant. The bar has two handpumps offering at least one Scottish ale. There are numerous restaurant rooms and seating areas, two wood-burning stoves and exposed original features. An extensive quality food menu is served throughout – chicken with haggis and Aberdeen Angus steaks are notable. Popular local walks abound close by. The annual beer festival is the second Sunday in August. Q&❀◑♿♣局(12)❧

Helensburgh

Ashton Ⓛ
West Princes Street, G84 8UG
☼ 11-midnight (1am Fri & Sat) ☎ (01436) 675900
Belhaven IPA; 2 changing beers (sourced nationally) Ⓗ
A warm welcome awaits at this genuine local where the bar has been tastefully modernised while retaining its original charm – a carved gantry catches the eye. During recent improvement work the front of the building was opened up to reveal a set of ceramic tiles depicting scenes from Sir Walter Scott's Waverley novels. An ever-changing selection of ales from Scottish microbreweries supported by quality English beers can be enjoyed. Live music is a regular Saturday night feature.
⇌(Central)♣局(1B,316)❀ ❧

Commodore ✅
112-117 West Clyde Street, G84 8ES
☼ 11-11; 12.30-10.30 Sun ☎ (01436) 676924
Caledonian Deuchars IPA; 3 changing beers (sourced nationally) Ⓗ
Situated on the shores of the Gareloch, this recently refurbished pub has views over the Clyde estuary and passing submarines can be seen on a stroll along the front. A bar area with a variety of seating adjoins the restaurant. The pub is less than 10 minutes from Helensburgh Central station and the Glasgow bus service terminates outside. The large garden area can be packed in summer with live music on selected nights. ❀⇌◑♿P局(1B)

Kilcreggan

Kilcreggan Hotel Ⓛ
Argyll Road, G84 0JP (turn off Shore Rd at Donaldson's Brae)
☼ 4-midnight; 11.30-1am Fri & Sat; 12.30-midnight Sun
☎ (01436) 842243 ⊕ kilcregganhotel.com
2 changing beers (sourced nationally) Ⓗ
Set in well-established gardens and perched on an elevated position above the Clyde, the views from the lounge and patio of this venue are stunning. The interior is decorated with a nautical theme. An ever-changing choice of two ales is sourced mostly from Scottish breweries, particularly Orkney, Strathaven and Fyne Ales. The pub can be approached via the ferry from Gourock or the bus from Helensburgh. Opening hours vary in winter.
&❀⇌◑P局(316)❦ ❧

Kippen

Cross Keys
Main Street, FK8 3DN
☼ 12-3, 5-11 (midnight Fri); 12-midnight Sat; 12-11 Sun
☎ (01786) 870293 ⊕ kippencrosskeys.com
House beer (by Fallen); 1 changing beer (sourced locally; often Fallen) Ⓗ
The Cross Keys is a comfortable coaching inn with a rustic feel – the oldest of its kind in Stirlingshire. Situated between Loch Lomond & The Trossachs National Park and Stirling, it is handy as a stopover whether travelling north or south, and an ideal base for walking, cycling, golfing and fishing. A community pub with a traditional feel, it has low ceilings, panelled walls and wood floors, and log fires in winter. The beer garden enjoys fine views in summer. Q&❀⇌◑P局(B12,C12)❧

Larbert

Station Hotel ♟ ✅
2 Foundry Loan, FK5 4AW
☼ 12-11 (midnight Thu; 1am Fri & Sat); 12.30-11 Sun
☎ (01324) 557186 ⊕ thestationhotellarbert.co.uk
5 changing beers (sourced nationally; often Cairngorm, Greene King, Strathaven) Ⓗ
A popular local, situated next to the railway station and on a regular bus route, this hotel prides itself on the support it gives to a number of community groups. Three to five cask ales are usually on offer and efforts are made to provide a variety of local, regional and national ales. There is a games room and large-screen TVs show sporting events.
❀⇌⇌P局(6,7)

SCOTLAND

Sauchie

Mansfield Arms ✔

7 Main Street, FK10 3JR
⚙ 11-midnight ☎ (01259) 722020 ⊕ devonales.com
Devon Original 70/-, Black, IPA, Pride H

Home to the oldest operating microbrewery in the county, this traditional two-bar pub brews four Devon ales which are dispensed via T-bar founts. Family-owned and run, the bar is popular with locals, who enjoy lively banter, and families who come to enjoy a meal in the comfortable lounge. The pub is situated within an ex-mining community and the local colliery inspired the brewery name and beer pump clip artwork. Beer and food are both excellent value for money. The pub is on the Stirling via Alloa circular bus route.
🛏️⊙&P🚲🚌(62,63,H2)🌸

Stirling

Portcullis Hotel

Castle Wynd, FK8 1EG (adjacent to castle esplanade)
⚙ 11-11 (midnight Wed-Sat); 11.30-11 Sun
☎ (01786) 472290 ⊕ theportcullishotel.com
2 changing beers (sourced regionally; often Isle of Skye, Orkney) H

This popular pub at the top of the town was originally the old grammar school building. Exposed stone walls and an open fireplace with ornate surround create a warm ambience in the heart of old Stirling. Close to the castle, it is frequented by tourists while also supported by locals. The pub is renowned for its food and regularly changing selection of Scottish ales from the far north and west. Always busy, diners are advised to reserve a table. Q🛏️🏨⊙&⋈P🛜

Clachan Inn, Drymen (Photo: Andrew Bowden/flickr)

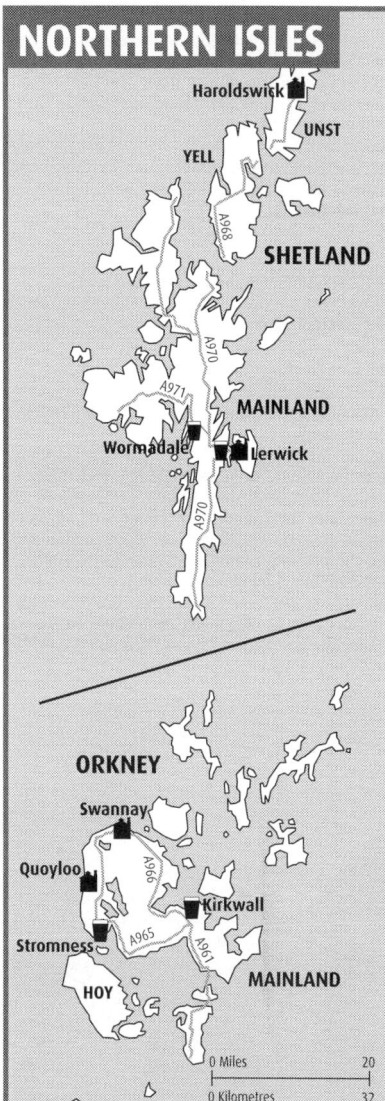

NORTHERN ISLES

Haroldswick

UNST

YELL

SHETLAND

MAINLAND

Wormadale   Lerwick

ORKNEY

Swannay

Quoyloo

Kirkwall

Stromness

MAINLAND

HOY

0 Miles   20
0 Kilometres   32

Authority area covered: Highland UA

Kirkwall: Orkney

Auld Motor Hoose 🏆
26 Junction Road, KW15 1AB
✪ 11-midnight (1am Fri & Sat) ☎ (01856) 871422
🌐 auldmotorhoose.co.uk
Swannay Scapa Special Ⓗ
A friendly pub with a single-room bar featuring lots of motoring memorabilia, car parts and illuminated petrol pump tops. The jukebox tends to blast out rock classics. There is regular live music, mainly at weekends, and the pub is one of the venues for the Orkney Rock Festival. Outside, the patio has a smoking area. Convenient for the bus station close by. CAMRA Northern Isles Pub of the Year 2016.
🏵🚷🍴♣🚪🐾🛜

Bothy Bar (Albert Hotel)
Mounthoolie Lane, KW15 1HW
✪ 11-midnight (1am Sat); 12-midnight Sun
☎ (01856) 876000 🌐 alberthotel.co.uk
Swannay Scapa Special; 2 changing beers (sourced locally; often Orkney, Swannay) Ⓗ
After reconstruction using much of the original materials following a fire a few years ago, this popular bar in the town centre has more space than previously, with intimate alcoves offering some privacy. Handy for buses, North Isles ferries and the shops, it is frequented by locals and after-work drinkers, and features on the weekend circuit. A roaring fire adds warmth in winter. Historic St Magnus Cathedral is close by. Now serving third-pint samplers in a tray of three. There is a premium for half pints. 🛏🍺🚆🐾🛜

Helgi's Bar
14 Harbour Street, KW15 1LE (by harbour)
✪ 12.30-midnight ☎ (01856) 879293 🌐 helgis.co.uk
Swannay Scapa Special; 2 changing beers (sourced locally; often Swannay) Ⓗ
Converted from a former shipping office, this small, smart bar has the look of a modern café with a local stone floor and wood panelling. Set on the harbour front where seafood is landed daily, it is a handy place to fill in time before island hopping on the many ferries to outlying parts. One dark beer is usually available. Special food nights where food is matched with ales are hosted, as well as regular music sessions and Thursday quiz nights. CAMRA Northern Isles Pub of the Year 2015. 🍺🚷🚆🐾🛜

Shore
Shore Street, KW15 1LG (on harbour road)
✪ 3-11 (midnight Fri); 10-midnight Sat; 10-11 Sun
☎ (01856) 872200 🌐 theshore.co.uk
Swannay Scapa Special Ⓗ
A smart, modern bar at the pier head which may be an ideal place to recuperate after a rough ferry crossing from a north isle or possibly the first experience of a Scottish bar for cruise ship passengers. The main street is just round the corner where a wide range of shops can be found and also St Magnus Cathedral, which was founded in 1137 by the Viking Earl Rognvald. Cross over the road to catch a ferry to many other Northern Isles.
🛏🍺🚷♣🚪🐾🛜

Lerwick: Shetland

Captain Flints
Ellesmere Stores, Esplanade, ZE1 0LL
✪ 11-1am ☎ (01595) 692249
1 changing beer (sourced regionally; often Swannay) Ⓗ
Two-floored bar situated above Ellesmere Store with a nautical theme and dark-wood wall panelling. A small stage area to the rear is used for bands at weekends and the upper floor is a games area. There are excellent views of the small boat harbour and the island of Bressay from seating areas closest to the bar. Entry is via a staircase from a door opposite the Market Cross. 🚆

REAL ALE BREWERIES

Lerwick Lerwick: Shetland
Orkney Quoyloo: Orkney
Swannay Swannay: Orkney
Valhalla Haroldswick: Unst

SCOTLAND

Stromness: Orkney

Ferry Inn

10 John Street, KW16 3AD (opp ferry terminal)
☼ 9am-midnight summer; 4-11 (11.30 Fri); 9am-11.30 Sat;
9.30am-11 Sun winter ☎ (01856) 850280 ⊕ ferryinn.com
**Orkney Corncrake; Swannay Sneaky Wee Orkney
Stout, Orkney IPA; 2 changing beers (sourced locally;
often Orkney, Swannay)** Ⓗ
An easy walk from the harbour front, the Ferry Inn
is handy for buses to Kirkwall and the ferry from
Scrabster. Friendly and lively, it is popular with
locals and visitors, including divers who come to
Orkney to explore the sunken German fleet at
Scapa Flow. Various attractions nearby include the
Ring of Brodgar and Scara Brae village. Annual folk
and blues festivals are held, with a marquee
erected outside complete with one ale pump. Out
of season, usually only Scapa Special is on tap.
❀🍴◑ Å♣P🚃(X1)😺🛜

Stromness Hotel

15 Victoria Street, KW16 3AA (opp pier head)
☼ 12-midnight (1am Fri & Sat); 12.30-11 Sun; closed Jan &
Feb ☎ (01856) 850298 ⊕ stromnesshotel.com
**Orkney Corncrake; Swannay Scapa Special; 2
changing beers (sourced locally; often Orkney,
Swannay)** Ⓗ
On the first floor of this imposing hotel you will find
the Hamnavoe Lounge, with windows and a small
balcony giving commanding views of the harbour.
In winter a roaring fire and comfy seating welcome
the visitor and there is a separate whisky bar with
over 100 bottles to choose from. The Flattie Bar
downstairs, open all year round, is complete with a
'flattie' hanging from the ceiling and serves a
Swannay ale. Out of season, there is usually only
Scapa Special on in the lounge. Jazz, blues and beer
festivals are held throughout the year.
🛏❀🍴◑ ÅP🚃(X1)

Wormadale: Shetland

Westings Inn

ZE2 9LJ (8 miles N of Lerwick on A971)
☼ 7.30-10.30; closed Sun-Wed ☎ (01595) 840242
⊕ westings.shetland.co.uk
**3 changing beers (sourced nationally; often Fuller's,
Timothy Taylor)** Ⓗ
Isolated white-painted inn in a stunning location
near the summit of Wormadale Hill, two miles
west of Tingwall airstrip. There are marvellous sea
views from the comfortable lounge, and adjacent
games area, of Whiteness Voe, western Shetland
and the outlying islands. Caravans are welcome
and camping is possible in the pub grounds. Two
ales are usually served in summer, one in winter –
it is advisable to phone ahead to check beer
availability and opening hours. 🛏❀🍴◑ ᴦÅ♣P🛜

Ferry Inn, Stromness: Orkney (Photo: Tom Bastin/flickr)

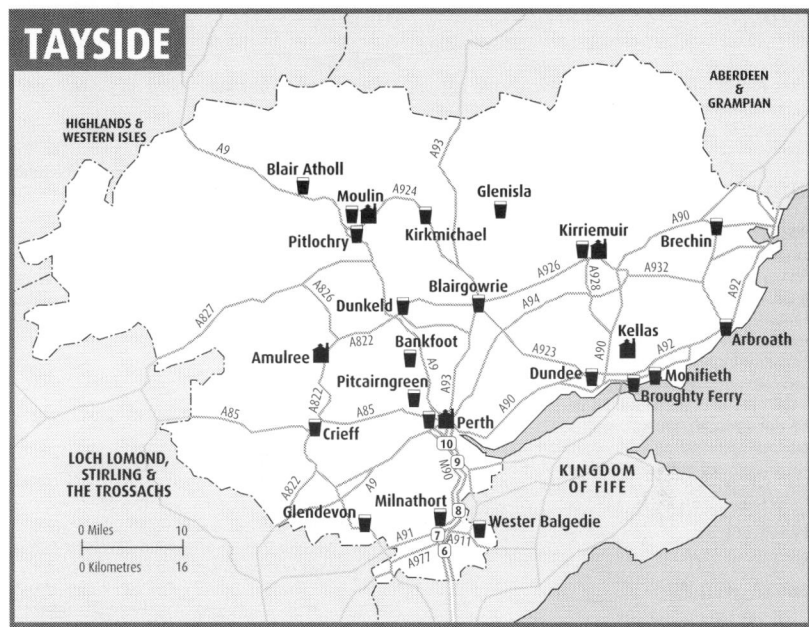

Authority areas covered: Angus UA, City of Dundee UA, Perth & Kinross UA

Arbroath

Corn Exchange ✅
14 Olympic Centre, Market Place, DD11 1HR
☼ 8am-midnight (1am Fri & Sat) ☎ (01241) 432430
Caledonian Deuchars IPA; Greene King Abbot; Sharp's Doom Bar; 3 changing beers Ⓗ
Located just off the High Street, this Wetherspoon pub occupies a 19th-century former corn exchange. Although it is largely open plan there are a number of booths providing some privacy. Boat trips offering fishing or a visit to the 200-year-old Bell Rock lighthouse are available from the nearby harbour. ◖▮➔🖵🛜

Bankfoot

Bankfoot Inn
Main Street, PH1 4AB
☼ 12-2 (not Mon & Tue), 6-11; 12-2, 5-12.30am Fri; 12-12.30am Sat; 12-midnight Sun ☎ (01738) 787243
⊕ bankfootinn.co.uk
3 changing beers (sourced locally) Ⓗ
The hotel has a public bar and a small lounge bar with an adjoining restaurant, warmed by two real fires in winter. The owners are real ale enthusiasts and strongly committed to local breweries. Two ale fests are held each year. Good food is available lunchtimes and evenings Wednesday to Sunday. Quality live folk music features every Wednesday evening. There is outdoor seating at the front and rear of the building. Tayside CAMRA Pub of the Year 2014. ✿🛏◖♣●🖵😺🛜

Blair Atholl

Atholl Arms Hotel
PH18 5SG
☼ 11-11 ☎ (01796) 481205
Moulin Light, Braveheart, Ale of Atholl, Old Remedial Ⓗ

The Atholl Arms has a grand and imposing façade in the Victorian Highland style. The characterful Highland Bothy Bar offers four ales and serves freshly cooked food all day. Blair Atholl and the surrounding area is a popular destination for walking, climbing, biking and sightseeing. 🛏◖≈

Blairgowrie

Ericht Alehouse
13 Wellmeadow, PH10 6ND
☼ 1-11 ☎ (01250) 872469
6 changing beers (sourced regionally) Ⓗ
Classic town-centre pub with a friendly atmosphere. There are two seating areas separated by a well-stocked bar. A wide range of changing ales and ciders caters for all tastes, alongside a dozen gins. No food is served but customers are welcome to bring their own. A winner of Tayside CAMRA Pub of the Year several times over the past decade. ✿♣●🖵😺🛜

Brechin

Caledonian
43 Southesk Street, DD9 6DZ
☼ 5-10 Wed & Thu; 4.30-11.30 Fri; 3-11.30 Sat; 3-11 Sun; closed Mon & Tue ☎ (01356) 624345
3 changing beers (often Houston, Inveralmond) Ⓗ
Named after the privately run railway whose terminus is opposite, the Caledonian features a large bar and dining area. The extensive use of wood creates a warm and inviting interior. In

REAL ALE BREWERIES

Inveralmond Perth
Kirrie Kirriemuir
MòR Kellas
Moulin 🛢 Moulin
Strathbraan Amulree

addition to the regular ales, guest beers sourced by the landlord on trips to Hampshire are frequently available. A wide range of continental bottled beers is also offered. Live folk music on the last Friday of the month is popular. Opening hours are extended in summer. ▶🚌

Broughty Ferry

Fisherman's Tavern ✓

10-16 Fort Street, DD5 2AD
✪ 11-midnight (1am Thu-Sat) ☎ (01382) 775941
⊕ fishermanstavern-broughtyferry.co.uk
7 changing beers (sourced nationally) Ⓗ

Licensed since 1857, this famous hostelry was originally three fishermen's cottages, later converted into a small hotel. The bar is to the right of the entrance, and a snug is to the left, leading to the dining room/lounge, warmed by a real fire. The lounge to the rear has disabled access from Bell's Lane. An annual beer festival is held in late May. A Belhaven/Greene King managed house, the ales come from Scottish and English breweries. ❀🛏◐≢☻⧗

Royal Arch ✓

285 Brook Street, DD5 2DS
✪ 11-midnight (1am Fri & Sat); 12.30-midnight Sun
☎ (01382) 779741
Caledonian Deuchars IPA; 2 changing beers Ⓗ

A popular locally owned pub in the centre of the Ferry. There are three TVs in the public bar for the many sports fans, and good-quality meals are served in the Art Deco lounge. Three handpulls dispense ales from local brewers as well as from all over Britain. The gantry in the public bar was rescued long ago from the demolished Craigour Bar in Dens Road, and the exterior was refurbished in 2014. ❀◐≢🖥☻⧗

Ship Inn

121 Fisher Street, DD5 2BR
✪ 11-11; 12.30-11 Sun ☎ (01382) 214235
⊕ theshipinn-broughtyferry.co.uk
Timothy Taylor Landlord; 2 changing beers Ⓗ

The Ship Inn is a traditional free house on the waterfront at Broughty Ferry, with views over the Tay towards Fife. Dating back to 1847, this cosy retreat has some nautical features and is interesting and atmospheric. Three well-kept real ales are usually available. A range of tasty bar meals is on offer and there is a restaurant upstairs. Pavement seating just outside is pleasant in good weather. ◐≢☻⧗

Crieff

Tower Gastro-pub Ⓛ

81 East High Street, PH7 3JA
✪ 12.30-11; 11-12.30am Fri & Sat; 11-11 Sun
☎ (01738) 650050
Inveralmond Ossian; Strathbraan Head East Ⓗ

This small family-run gastro-pub has been tastefully refurbished by licensees Annie and Bob. The beams and friezes display some interesting and amusing proverbs and quotations. There is a comfortable seating area overlooking the beer garden which has great views south to the Ochil Hills. Attached to the pub are three self-catering apartments. Q❧🛏❀◐🖥(15,47)

Dundee

Bank Bar

7-9 Union Street, DD1 4BN
✪ 11-midnight (10 Mon & Tue); 12.30-7 Sun
☎ (01382) 205037
3 changing beers Ⓗ

A former bank with a collection of themed pictures decorating the walls, it has a bare-boards floor, wooden furnishings and a series of alcoves with tables in the tradition of older Scottish city pubs. Two or three ales are usually available and food is served until 7pm every day. Live music features on most Friday and Saturday nights. ◐≢🖥☻

Phoenix

103 Nethergate, DD1 4DH
✪ 11-midnight ☎ (01382) 200014
Caledonian Deuchars IPA; Timothy Taylor Landlord; 3 changing beers Ⓗ

A traditional pub with great atmosphere and subdued lighting. Sturdy wooden seats and tables and green leather benches give the place character, and there is a rare Ballingall Brewery mirror. Five ales are on offer, and excellent pub food at conservative prices. The location is handy for the Rep Theatre, Dundee Contemporary Arts and Bonar Hall. Warm and cosy, like pubs used to be. ◐≢🖥(73)

Speedwell Bar (Mennie's) ★ ✓

165-167 Perth Road, DD2 1AS
✪ 11-11; 12.30-11 Sun ☎ (01382) 667783
⊕ speedwell-bar.co.uk
3 changing beers Ⓗ

Built in 1903 for James Speed, the bar is known as Mennie's after the family who ran it for more than 50 years. The L-shaped interior is divided by a part-glazed screen and has a magnificent mahogany gantry and counter, dado-panelled walls and an anaglypta Jacobean ceiling. It has two sitting rooms, separated by a glass screen. There are usually three ales to choose from, alongside a selection of Belgian bottled beers and around 150 malt whiskies. You can take in your own food. 🖥(73)☻⧗

Dunkeld

Atholl Arms Hotel

Tay Terrace, Bridgehead, PH8 0AQ
✪ 11-11 ☎ (01350) 727219 ⊕ athollarmshotel.com
3 changing beers (often Inveralmond) Ⓗ

An impressive building standing on the corner of the main street. Three handpulls can be found in the small but friendly public bar. Food is served in the bar and the more formal restaurant. There is a fine view over the River Tay which is just across the road. 🛏◐☻

Taybank Hotel

Tay Terrace, PH8 0AQ
✪ 11-11 ☎ (01350) 727340 ⊕ thetaybank.squarespace.com
Strathbraan Due South, Head East Ⓗ

A fine bar space serving good food and drink, and frequented by folk musicians, which adds to a great atmosphere. There is an open fire and a fine large painting of fiddler Niel Gow on the wall. The excellent outdoor drinking area has good views over the River Tay. Accommodation is available. ❧❀🛏◐P🖥☻

Glendevon

Tormaukin Hotel
FK14 7JY
✪ 11-11 ☎ (01259) 781252 ⊕ tormaukinhotel.co.uk
2 changing beers (often Harviestoun) Ⓗ
This 18th-century former drovers' inn is on the A823 Yetts o' Muckhart to Gleneagles road in a peaceful setting surrounded by the Ochil Hills. It has a comfortable, relaxed atmosphere, with an open fire in winter. Two ales are usually available and wine is also taken seriously. Local venison is a speciality and soups, sandwiches, scones and other snacks are available throughout the day. Q ★ ☕ ◑ ▶

Glenisla

Kirkton of Glenisla Hotel
PH11 8PH
✪ 12-midnight; 12-1am Fri-Sun ☎ (01575) 582223
⊕ glenisla-hotel.com
2 changing beers (sourced locally) Ⓗ
A welcoming hostelry in a magnificent Angus glen. This 17th-century former coaching inn has been refurbished to a high standard but retains a traditional feel. Beer from local breweries is served from two handpumps in the cosy, oak-beamed bar, which features an open log fire. Good-value traditional food is available. ☕ ☕ ◑ ▶ ❀ ♐ ♑

Kirkmichael

Strathardle Inn
PH10 7NS (on A924)
✪ 11-11 ☎ (01250) 881224 ⊕ strathardleinn.co.uk
3 changing beers Ⓗ
Small, friendly hotel with a bar room with a coal fire and horse brasses around the mantelpiece. Up to three ales are available from Scottish micros, and good lunches and evening meals are served. The historic coaching inn, dating back to the late-1700s, has a 700-yard fishing beat on the River Ardle which flows in front of the building. The Cateran Trail is also nearby and the Southern Highlands, Glenshee ski slopes, Deeside and Angus Glens are all within reach. ☕ ❀ ☕ ◑ ▶ P ❀ ♑

Kirriemuir

Airlie Arms
St Malcolm's Wynd, DD8 4HB
✪ 11-midnight (1am Fri & Sat); 12.30-1am Sun
☎ (01575) 218080 ⊕ airliearms.net
2 changing beers Ⓗ
After many years left closed and run-down, this large, B-listed, 18th-century establishment was substantially renovated and reopened in 2015 by the local Ewart family. Real ale has made a welcome appearance, with two handpulls on the bar. Food is served daily in the bar and also in the restaurant Friday to Sunday. ☕ ◑ ▶

Glen Clova Hotel
Glen Clova, DD8 4QS
✪ 11-11 (1am Fri & Sat); 12-1 Sun ☎ (01575) 550350
⊕ clova.com
2 changing beers Ⓗ
Situated near the head of one of Scotland's most beautiful glens and popular with walkers after a day on the hills, the hotel's bar has a large log-fired stove and plenty of character. Two handpumps supply the ale, usually from Scottish breweries.

Local food including lamb and venison is served in the bar and adjoining restaurant. The hotel has a range of accommodation from bunkhouse to en-suite rooms to self-catering luxury lodges. A summer beer festival is held in the field opposite. ☕ ◑ ▶ P

Milnathort

Village Inn
36 Wester Loan, KY13 9YH
✪ 2-11 (midnight Fri); 12-midnight Sat; 12.30-11 Sun
☎ (01577) 863293
Inveralmond Thrappledouser; 2 changing beers (sourced regionally) Ⓗ
Friendly local with a semi open-plan interior featuring classic brewery mirrors and local historic photographs. The comfortable lounge area has low ceilings, exposed joists and stone walls, and the bar area is warmed by a log fire. At the rear is a games room with a pool table. This pub has been family-owned since 1985 and usually serves three beers. Milnathort links some great cycling routes through the Ochils, via Burleigh Castle, to the more leisurely Loch Leven Heritage Trail. ❀ ♿ ♣ ♐

Monifieth

Milton Inn ♗ ✔
Grange Road, DD5 4LU
✪ 12-2.30, 5-11; 12-midnight Fri & Sat; 12-11 Sun; closed
Mon ☎ (01382) 532620 ⊕ themiltoninn.co.uk
3 changing beers (sourced regionally) Ⓗ
The only premises in Monifieth serving real ale, which this traditional inn does with a passion. There are usually three beers to choose from, alongside good home-made food at fair prices. Set back from the road, the large gardens and sunny decked area to the rear provide a nice sheltered spot for a pint in the fresh air, or to enjoy a barbecue. Entertainment features regularly. ❀ ☕ ◑ ⇌ P ♐ ♑

Moulin

Moulin Inn
11-13 Kirkmichael Road, PH16 5EH
✪ 11-11 ☎ (01796) 472196 ⊕ moulininn.co.uk
Moulin Light, Braveheart, Ale of Atholl, Old Remedial Ⓗ
First opened in 1695, the inn is the oldest part of the Moulin Hotel, situated within the village square of an ancient crossroads, just east of Pitlochry. Full of character and charm, it is traditionally furnished and has two log fires. A good choice of home-prepared local fare is available, along with Moulin's own beers, brewed in the old coach house behind the hotel. Outside is an area for dining and drinking in good weather. An ideal base for outdoor pursuits, with several marked walks nearby. Q ☕ ❀ ☕ ◑ ♣ P

Perth

Cherrybank Inn
210 Glasgow Road, PH2 0NA
✪ 11-11 (12.30am Thu-Sat); 12-midnight Sun
☎ (01738) 624349 ⊕ cherrybankinn.co.uk
Inveralmond Ossian; 4 changing beers Ⓗ
A 250-year-old former drovers' inn that is a popular watering hole and stopover for travellers. Six handpulls dispense ales from Inveralmond and

other Scottish independents, which can be enjoyed in the multi-roomed public bar or the larger L-shaped lounge with views up to a woodland walk. Good bar lunches and evening meals are served. The inn has seven well-appointed en-suite rooms, and golf can be arranged for residents.
🏠🍴🛏️🕙🍺🌳♿🅿️🚃(7)🐾🍴🛰

Green Room

97 Canal Street, PH2 6DR
✪ 12-11 (12.30am Thu; 1.30am Fri & Sat); 12-midnight Sun
☎ (01738) 248121 ⊕ thegreenroomperth.com
6 changing beers (sourced nationally) ℍ
Following a major makeover, this establishment now has three bars, one with six handpulls, plus a large selection of bottled beers from around the world. Live entertainment plays seven nights a week, which pulls in plenty of customers. A must-visit venue in Perth for ale enthusiasts, with ales coming from a variety of local, Scottish and national breweries.

Greyfriars

15 South Street, PH2 8PG
✪ 11-11 (11.45 Fri & Sat); 3-11 Sun ☎ (01738) 633036
⊕ perth-bars.co.uk
Inveralmond Lia Fail; 3 changing beers (often Inveralmond) ℍ
Small city-centre lounge bar serving up to four ales, often including an Inveralmond beer. Good-value lunches are available in the bar and an upstairs area. The pub takes its name from the former Greyfriars monastery. Nearby attractions include a Victorian theatre, art gallery, museum and concert hall. This may well be the smallest lounge bar in the Fair City but it has an enviable reputation among locals and visitors as one of the friendliest.
🕙🚃

Kirkside Inn

St John's Place, PH1 5SZ
✪ 11-11 ☎ (01738) 626344
1 changing beer (sourced locally; often Inveralmond) ℍ
An old establishment in the heart of the city, close to the big kirk and known by locals as the Kirky. It was bought in late 2014 by a local man, with real ale – often from Inveralmond – making a welcome appearance on the bar thereafter. The bar area is split between front and back areas and serves filled rolls and soup.

Pitcairngreen

Pitcairngreen Inn

PH1 3LP
✪ 10.30-11 (midnight Fri & Sat) ☎ (01738) 583022
⊕ pitcairngreeninn.co.uk
2 changing beers (sourced locally) ℍ
A fairly large establishment divided into several different areas including a snug warmed by a large

open log fire. The inn has a real enthusiasm for good beer, served on three handpulls. This is the finest place in Tayside to enjoy real ciders and perries, presented professionally and with passion. Good-value, home-cooked food is also available, making use of fresh local produce. The car park is just across the road. Q🕙🍴🕙🍺🅿️🚃(14,15)🐾

Pitlochry

Craigvrack Hotel

38 West Moulin Road, PH16 5EQ
✪ 11-11 ☎ (01796) 472399 ⊕ craigvrack.com
2 changing beers ℍ
Family-run hotel with a warm welcome and a relaxed atmosphere. Two real ales are usually available, with regular customers being influential in the selection. The bar has a pool table at one end and there is a fine view from the window. Seating outside is pleasant in good weather.
🏠🛏️🕙🍽️🅿️🛰

Old Mill Inn

Mill Lane, PH16 5BH
✪ 11-11; 11-midnight Sat & Sun ☎ (01796) 474020
⊕ theoldmillpitlochry.co.uk
Strathbraan Due South, Head East; 2 changing beers (sourced locally; often Strathbraan) ℍ
This is a family-owned and family-run establishment in the town centre. It was built in the 19th century as a mill, with the mill wheel still driven by the stream. Customers can sit beside it in fine weather. The large bar serves a varied selection of three or four guest ales, as well as the regulars from local Scottish microbrewery Strathbraan. 🏠🍴🛏️🕙♿🍽️🍺🅿️🚃🛰

Wester Balgedie

Balgedie Toll Tavern

KY13 9HE (2 miles E of M90 at jct of A911 and B919)
✪ 11-11 (11.30 Thu; 12.30am Fri & Sat); 12.30-11.30 Sun
☎ (01592) 840212
Harviestoun Bitter & Twisted; 1 changing beer (sourced regionally) ℍ
Welcoming and comfortable rural tavern dating from 1534 where travellers had to break their journey to pay tolls. Now much extended, the oldest part of the building, the toll house, is at the southern end. It has three seating areas plus a small bar with low ceilings, oak beams, horse brasses, wooden settles and works of art by a local painter. A good selection of meals and bar snacks is available. The rotating guest beer usually comes from a Scottish independent brewery. 🍴🕙🍺🅿️🚃

Drunken primates

Brehm asserts that the natives of north-eastern Africa catch the wild baboons by exposing vessels with strong beer, by which they are made drunk. On the following morning they (the baboons) were very cross and dismal; they held their aching heads with both hands, and wore a most pitiable expression: when beer was offered them, they turned away in disgust.

Charles Darwin, The Origin of Species, 1859

NORTHERN ISLES

SHETLAND

HIGHLANDS
&
WESTERN ISLES

ABERDEEN
& GRAMPIAN

TAYSIDE

ARGYLL &
THE ISLES

LOCH LOMOND
STIRLING
& THE
TROSSACHS

FIFE

GREATER
GLASGOW &
CLYDE

EDINBURGH & LOTHIANS

AYRSHIRE
& ARRAN

BORDERS

NORTHERN
IRELAND

DUMFRIES &
GALLOWAY

NORTHUMBERLAND

TYNE &
WEAR

ISLE OF
MAN

CUMBRIA

DURHAM

NORTH
YORKSHIRE

LANCASHIRE

WEST
YORKS

EAST
YORKS

MERSEYSIDE

GREATER
MANCHESTER

SOUTH
YORKS

CHESHIRE

DERBYSHIRE

NOTTINGHAM-
SHIRE

LINCOLNSHIRE

NW
WALES

NE
WALES

STAFFORD
SHIRE

LEICESTERSHIRE

NORFOLK

SHROPSHIRE

WEST
MIDLANDS

WARWICK-
SHIRE

NORTHAMPTON-
SHIRE

RUTLAND

CAMBRIDGE-
SHIRE

SUFFOLK

MID
WALES

HEREFORD-
SHIRE

WORCESTER-
SHIRE

BEDFORD-
SHIRE

HERTFORD-
SHIRE

ESSEX

WEST
WALES

GLAMORGAN

GWENT

GLOUCS &
BRISTOL

OXFORD-
SHIRE

BUCKINGHAM-
SHIRE

GREATER
LONDON

BERKSHIRE

SURREY

KENT

WILTSHIRE

HAMPSHIRE

WEST
SUSSEX

EAST
SUSSEX

SOMERSET

CHANNEL
ISLANDS

DEVON

DORSET

ISLE OF
WIGHT

CORNWALL

Northern Ireland
Channel Islands
Isle of Man

NORTHERN IRELAND

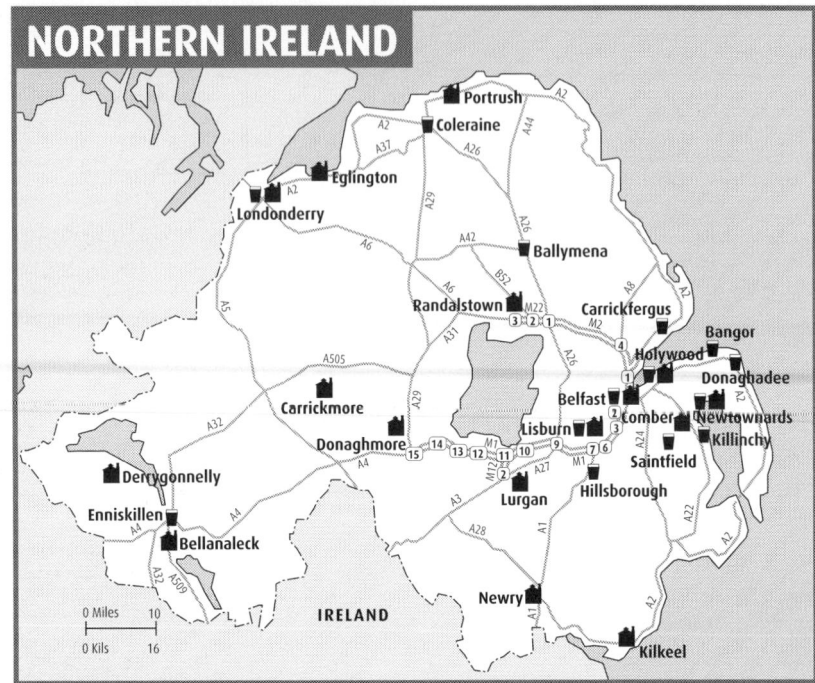

Ballymena

Spinning Mill ✔
17-21 Broughshane Street, BT43 6EB
⚙ 8am-midnight (1am Fri & Sat) ☎ (028) 2563 8985
Adnams Broadside; Greene King Abbot; 2 changing beers (sourced nationally) Ⓗ
This was Wetherspoon's first pub in Northern Ireland and remains the only real ale outlet in town. It is a busy venue with bars upstairs and downstairs. There are plenty of comfortable nooks to sit in and some interesting woodwork to admire. Eight handpumps offer a changing variety of ales. A former local CAMRA Pub of the Year. Alcohol is served from 11.30am (12.30pm Sun).
Q ☕ 🍴 🕸 Å P 🚃 🚆

Bangor

Jenny Watts
41 High Street, BT20 5BE
⚙ 11.30-11 (midnight Fri & Sat); 12.30-10 Sun
☎ (028) 9127 0401 🌐 jennywattsbar.com
1 changing beer (often Hilden)
The oldest public house in town, Jenny Watts retains a traditional feel inside, with a central bar, stone walls and stone flooring, and a beer garden. It has been selling real ale for some years, with one handpump now dispensing a variety of Hilden ales. Good food and live music feature, with jazz in the afternoon on Sundays. Upstairs is Ruby's Lounge. Q ☕ 🐾 🍴 🕸 🚆

Belfast

Botanic Inn
23-27 Malone Road, BT9 6RU
⚙ 11.30-1am; 12-midnight Sun ☎ (028) 9050 9740
🌐 thebotanicinn.com

Whitewater Belfast Ale Ⓗ
Now under new ownership, this large inn is one of Belfast's most popular pubs. As well as the main bar there is also a public bar where ale is cheaper. Good food is served and both bars are usually busy. Sport is shown on the many screens. A student club night is held on Wednesdays with music, sport or other attractions for the younger generation.
Q 🍴 🕸 🚆 (Balmoral) 🚌 (8B)

Bridge House ✔
37-43 Bedford Street, BT2 7EJ
⚙ 8am-midnight (1am Fri & Sat); 12-midnight Sun
☎ (028) 9072 7890
Fuller's London Pride; Greene King Abbot; Sharp's Doom Bar; changing beers Ⓗ
Near the city centre, this is a large Wetherspoon pub. Upstairs is a dining room, while downstairs there are comfy booths and a mixture of regular and craft bar-style tables. Usually busy, the main bar features eight handpumps dispensing a changing variety of real ale. Real cider is also available on gravity. It has been twice CAMRA Northern Ireland Pub of the Year. Alcohol is served from 11.30am (12.30pm Sun). Q ☕ 🍴 🕸 🚆 🚌 🚆

Crown ★ ✔
46 Great Victoria Street, BT2 7BA (opp Europa Hotel and Great Victoria St station)
⚙ 11.30-midnight; 12.30-11 Sun ☎ (028) 9024 3187
Hilden Scullion Irish Ale; St Austell Nicholson's Pale Ale; Whitewater Belfast Ale; 2 changing beers (sourced nationally) Ⓗ
The Crown is renowned for its outstanding interior that dates from 1885. It is also known as a top spot for real ale, with five handpumps serving Nicholson's Pale Ale and local beers from Hilden and Whitewater breweries. Two guest ales vary, especially during the regular beer festivals. Good food is served. Both the bar and upstairs dining

rooms have recently been further restored. A former CAMRA Northern Ireland Pub of the Year.
Q◑🕭&⚲≒🖳

Errigle Inn

312-320 Ormeau Road, BT7 2GE
🕛 11.30-1am; 10-midnight Sun ☎ (028) 9064 1410
🌐 errigle.com
Hilden Scullion's Irish; Shepherd Neame Whitstable Bay Pale Ale; Whitewater Belfast Ale; 1 changing beer (often Farmageddon) Ⓗ
A long-established pub on the south side of the city. The Errigle has increased output of real ale in the past year and now has five handpumps with an emphasis on local ale from Hilden, Whitewater and Farmageddon breweries. Shepherd Neame ales are also available. The handpumps are in the Oak Lounge, a quiet back bar away from the TV sport and music found in other areas of the pub. Q◑&

Kitchen Bar

1 Victoria Square, BT1 4QB (adjacent to shopping centre, Victoria St side)
🕛 11.30-11.30 (midnight Mon; 1am Fri & Sat); 12-6 Sun
☎ (028) 9024 5268 🌐 thekitchenbar.com
Whitewater Maggies Leap IPA Ⓗ
This pub has recently started selling real ale again after a few years without. A large, modern venue, there is some exposed internal brickwork and interesting riveted metal pillars. The centrally positioned bar has one handpump exclusively selling Whitewater beers. Food, music and sport are big draws, attracting daytime shoppers and night-time drinkers alike. A popular location and often extremely busy, especially on Friday and Saturday nights. ◑&≒🖳

Sunflower

65 Union Street, BT1 2JG
🕛 11.30-midnight (1am Thu-Sat); 5-11 Sun
☎ (028) 9023 2474
Hilden Twisted Hop Ⓗ
This is a traditional corner pub, situated north of the city centre, behind Belfast Central Library. Recently renovated and now serving real ale, the bar downstairs is cosy, with one handpump offering a changing array of beers from Hilden brewery. It is a popular live music venue with acts performing in the bar and in the lounge upstairs. A spacious beer garden has been added where pizza is available on Friday and Saturday evenings. Q❀◑🖳

Carrickfergus

Central Bar ⊘

13-15 High Street, BT38 7AN (opp Castle)
🕛 8am-midnight (1am Fri & Sat) ☎ (028) 9335 7840
Fuller's London Pride; Greene King Abbot; Sharp's Doom Bar; 3 changing beers (sourced nationally) Ⓗ
Busy town-centre Wetherspoon pub with a choice between the downstairs bar populated with lively locals and a quieter family dining area upstairs. There are five handpumps on both floors, dispensing the house beers plus up to three guests. The dining area and beer garden enjoy fantastic views which include Belfast Lough and Carrickfergus Castle. It is close to bus and rail stops. Alcohol is served from 11.30am (12.30pm Sun).
Q➺❀◑&≒🖳 (563)

Coleraine

Old Courthouse ⊘

Castlerock Road, BT51 3HP
🕛 8am-midnight (1am Fri & Sat) ☎ (028) 7032 5820
Fuller's London Pride; Greene King Abbot; 2 changing beers (sourced nationally) Ⓗ
One of those Wetherspoon establishments that does not look like a pub at first – it was a courthouse until 1985. Some of the former interior has been retained, including the pillars and distinctive black and white floor tiles. The bar has five handpumps with up to three guest ales and a cider on gravity. Food is available downstairs or on the imposing balcony accessed by a grand staircase. Alcohol is served from 11.30am (12.30am Sunday). Q➺◑&💮

Donaghadee

Moat Inn

102 Moat Street, BT21 0ED
🕛 11.30-11.30; 12.30-10 Sun ☎ (028) 9188 3297
🌐 moatinn.co.uk
Whitewater Belfast Ale; 1 changing beer (sourced locally; often Whitewater) Ⓗ
The Moat Inn has two restaurants, a lounge and public bar, and a beer garden. It is situated on the main road into Donaghadee, a popular coastal tourist destination about 20 miles east of Belfast. There are two handpumps, both in the public bar. Whitewater ales are the mainstay, usually Belfast Ale and Copperhead, though occasionally there is a guest ale on the second pump. The bar is compact and traditional, a pleasant place in which to drink and dine. Q➺❀◑&🖳 (7)

Enniskillen

Linen Hall ⊘

11-13 Townhall Street, BT74 7BD
🕛 8am-midnight (11 Mon & Tue; 1am Sat); 8am-11 Sun
☎ (028) 6634 0910
Greene King Abbot; Sharp's Doom Bar; 3 changing beers (sourced nationally) Ⓗ
This has been a busy Wetherspoon outlet in the centre of town for many years. The long, narrow building has one bar with several drinking areas on different levels. There are five handpumps serving the regular beers and guest ales, with real cider available on gravity. The good-value Wetherspoon food menu is available all day. The area attracts a

REAL ALE BREWERIES

Ards Newtonards
Boundary Belfast (NEW)
Clanconnel Lurgan
Farmageddon Comber (NEW)
Hercules Holywood
Hilden Lisburn
Hillstown Randalstown (NEW)
Inishmacsaint Derrygonnelly
Knockout Belfast
Lacada Portrush (NEW)
Northbound Eglinton (NEW)
Pokertree Carrickmore
Red Hand 🍴 Donaghmore (NEW)
Sheelin Bellanaleck
Station Works Newry (NEW)
Walled City 🍴 Londonderry (NEW)
Whitewater Kilkeel

lot of visitors despite being some 80 miles west of Belfast. Alcohol is served from 11.30am (12.30pm Sun). Q❄️🚲🕊️&P🚭(261)

Hillsborough

Hillside
21 Main Street, BT26 6AE
🌀 12-11.30 (12.30am Fri & Sat); 12-11 Sun
☎ (028) 9268 9233 ⊕ hillsidehillsborough.co.uk
Hilden Nut Brown, Scullion's Irish, Twisted Hop ⊞
This is the oldest pub in Hillsborough and the only one selling real ale, with three handpumps dispensing Hilden ales. The bar sports three different drinking areas and excellent food is served in the bar and restaurant. Live music plays at the weekend and there is a summer beer festival in the pleasant beer garden. The pub also provides a real ale bar when the Oyster festival is on. Q❄️🕊️🌀&🚲(38,238)✪

Holywood

Dirty Duck Ale House ♟
3 Kinnegar Road, BT18 9JN
🌀 12-11 (1am Thu-Sat); 12.30-11 Sun ☎ (028) 9059 6666
⊕ thedirtyduckalehouse.co.uk
3 changing beers (sourced nationally; often Barney's Beer Ltd, Inveralmond, Shepherd Neame) ⊞
Situated on the shores of Belfast Lough, the Dirty Duck is the current CAMRA Northern Ireland Pub of the Year. Three ales are usually available with occasional guests. The house beer, Dirty Duck Ale, is brewed by Hilden. Good food is available both downstairs and in the restaurant upstairs. The pub has a large ship shaped beer garden and a corner celebrating local golfing hero Rory McIlroy. Q❄️🕊️🌀&≉

Killinchy

Daft Eddy's
Sketrick Island, BT23 6QH (2 miles N of Killinchy at Whiterock Bay)
🌀 11.30-11.30 (1am Fri); 12-10.30 Sun ☎ (028) 9754 1615
⊕ dafteddys.co.uk
1 changing beer (sourced locally; often Whitewater) ⊞
This could be Northern Ireland's most remote yet pleasantly situated real ale pub. It is on an island in Strangford Lough about two miles from the nearest town. The main bar has one handpump, exclusively dispensing Whitewater beer. The venue is well-known for the quality of the restaurant – food is locally sourced and seafood is a speciality. Smaller meals are served in the attached coffee bar. With impressive views over the lough, this must be one of the country's treasures. Q❄️🕊️🌀&

Lisburn

Tuesday Bell ✅
4 Lisburn Square, BT28 1TS
🌀 8am-11 (midnight Fri & Sat) ☎ (028) 9262 7390
Fuller's London Pride; Greene King Abbot; Sharp's Doom Bar ⊞
The Tuesday Bell is the main attraction in the city's Lisburn Square shopping development. It tends to get very busy, with locals mainly gathering downstairs and younger people upstairs, where there is background music at the weekend. A total of eight handpumps dispense a range of regular

beers and guests from Wetherspoon's list, sometimes including local ale from Hilden. Real cider is available on gravity. Alcohol is served from 11.30am (12.30pm Sun). Q❄️🕊️🌀&≉🕊️♦P🚭📶

Londonderry

Diamond ✅
23-24 The Diamond, BT48 6HP (centre of walled city)
🌀 8am-midnight (11 Mon & Tue; 1am Fri & Sat)
☎ (028) 7127 2880
Fuller's London Pride; Greene King Abbot; Sharp's Doom Bar; 3 changing beers (sourced nationally) ⊞
The Diamond sits in the main shopping district, one of the city's two Wetherspoon establishments. In an elevated location inside the city walls, this two-storey pub with large bars on both floors has good views from the upper floor. Although spacious inside it can get busy. A total of 10 handpumps dispense a varied range of guest ales alongside the regulars. Real cider is available on gravity. Alcohol is served from 11.30am (12.30pm Sun). Q🌀&≉

Ice Wharf ✅
Strand Road, BT48 7AB
🌀 8am-midnight (1am Thu-Sat) ☎ (028) 7127 6610
Greene King Abbot; Sharp's Doom Bar; 3 changing beers (sourced nationally) ⊞
This is a spacious Wetherspoon hostelry not far from the city's Guildhall Square, looking out on Strand Road. A former hotel, it is now a large single-floor pub with screens dividing the semi-circular bar from the seating area and a series of pillars holding up the ceiling. As well as the regular and guest ales, real cider is available on gravity. Alcohol is served from 11.30am (12.30pm Sun). Q❄️🌀🚭

Newtownards

Spirit Merchant ✅
54-56 Regent Street, BT23 4LP (next to bus station)
🌀 8am-midnight ☎ (028) 9182 4270
Fuller's London Pride; Greene King Abbot; Sharp's Doom Bar; 2 changing beers (sourced nationally) ⊞
This large single-bar Wetherspoon pub on the main street, near to the bus station, retains the feel of a local with knowledgeable and welcoming staff. In addition to the regular beers, up to two changing guest ales are offered from five handpumps. A major feature is the large heated courtyard to the side. Alcohol is served from 11.30am (12.30pm Sun). Q❄️🕊️🌀▲🚭(7)

Saintfield

White Horse
49-53 Main Street, BT24 7AB
🌀 11.30-11.30; 12-10.30 Sun ☎ (028) 9751 1143
⊕ whitehorsesaintfield.com
Whitewater Copperhead, Belfast Ale, Maggies Leap IPA; 1 changing beer ⊞
Although a modern pub, some of the original walls can be seen inside. It is the brewery tap for Whitewater and mainly serves the brewery's beers, with occasional guest ales. Food is a major feature, with a bistro upstairs and the Flaming Crust pizza place downstairs. A popular community pub, live music plays at the weekends. A former CAMRA Northern Ireland Pub of the Year. Q🕊️🌀&🚭(15,215)

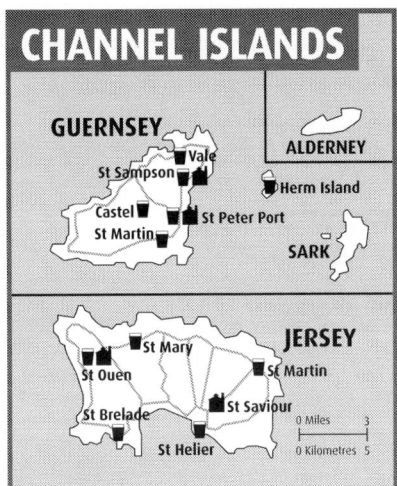

CHANNEL ISLANDS

GUERNSEY
Vale
St Sampson
ALDERNEY
Herm Island
Castel
St Martin
St Peter Port
SARK

JERSEY
St Mary
St Ouen
St Martin
St Saviour
St Brelade
St Helier
0 Miles 3
0 Kilometres 5

GUERNSEY
Castel

Fleur du Jardin ✔
Kings Mills, GY5 7JT
✪ 10.30-11.45 ☎ (01481) 257996 ⊕ fleurdujardin.com
2 changing beers ⊞
A building of unique charm with two bars – one traditional, small and cosy, attached to the restaurant, the other recently renovated in a more contemporary style to create a comfortable, relaxing area to enjoy a beer. A door from this area leads to a large covered patio and out to the garden. Menus in both the bar and restaurant feature fresh local produce. Q ⛲ ⊛ ✇ ◑ ☕ P ⎙ ❀

La Grand Mare Hotel & Golf Club
Vazon Bay, GY5 7LL (on Vazon coast road)
✪ 10-11.45; 12-11.45 Sun ☎ (01481) 256576
⊕ lagrandemare.com
Shepherd Neame Spitfire; 2 changing beers ⊞
The hotel is open all year for guests and locals alike. It is situated opposite the beach at Vazon, one of the popular west coast bays. The Club bar is open every day and there is a large-screen TV showing sport and a fire in the winter months. There is also a separate bar with some comfy seats, attached to the large restaurant. Children are welcome. ⛲ ✇ ◑ ☕ P ⎙ ❀

Rockmount Hotel
Cobo, GY5 7HB
✪ 10.30-midnight; 10.30-12.45am Fri & Sat
☎ (01481) 252778 ⊕ therocky.gg
5 changing beers
The pub has been refurbished but, due to public demand, the public bar, while having a tidy, remains unchanged. There is a taproom for TV sport and a large lounge bar. The lounge is mainly for diners, but there are comfy chairs near the fire for those who just wish to drink. Five handpumps offer a changing range of beers. The lounge opens on to the terrace area, which is lovely in the summer. Q ◑ ☕ ⎙ ❀

Herm Island

Mermaid Tavern ✔
GY1 3HR (travel Trident ferry from St Peter Port to Herm then follow signposts)
✪ 11-10.30; 12-10.30 Sun ☎ (01481) 750050 ⊕ herm.com/mermaid
House beer (by Liberation); 2 changing beers ⊞
A short trip by ferry from Guernsey takes you to Herm. A large courtyard acts as a suntrap in the summer while in winter an open fire creates a cosy atmosphere. Real ale and cider festivals are held twice a year. The house beer is Herm Island Gold and the cider varies. A trip to Herm to discover the island's tranquillity and natural beauty is a must for any visitor to Guernsey. ⛲ ⊛ ◑ ☕ A ♣ ❀ ❀ ❀ 穼

St Martin

Captain's Hotel ✔
La Fosse, GY4 6EF
✪ 11-11 (midnight Fri & Sat); 12-4 Sun ☎ (01481) 238990
⊕ thecaptainshotel.co.uk
Fuller's London Pride; Sharp's Doom Bar ⊞
In a secluded location down a country lane, this is a popular locals' pub with a lively, friendly atmosphere. It has a small raised area in front of the bar furnished with a sofa to make a comfy zone. Good-quality meals can be eaten in the bar or bistro area, or you can take away a pizza. A meat draw is held on Friday. The car park to the rear fills up quickly. ✇ ◑ P ⎙

Les Douvres Hotel ✔
La Fosse, GY4 6ER
✪ 10.30-12.30am ☎ (01481) 238731
⊕ lesdouvreshotel.co.uk
3 changing beers (often Randalls) ⊞
Former 18th-century manor house, set in private gardens in St Martin near the south coast, two-and-a-half miles from St Peter Port, with cliff walks and a tiny fishing harbour. A well-maintained, changing range of beers is offered on two handpumps, and occasionally real cider is also on the bar. Excellent meals are served in the bar and separate restaurant. Live music features on Friday nights and occasional Wednesdays. The venue is popular with locals and visitors. ⊛ ✇ ◑ P ⎙

St Peter Port

Cock & Bull
Lower Hauteville, GY1 1LL
✪ 11-12.45am; closed Sun ☎ (01481) 722660
⊕ cockandbullguernsey.com/home
Changing beers ⊞
Popular pub, just up the hill from the town church, with five handpumps providing a changing range of beer and cider. Seating is on three levels. Live music features throughout the week, with open mic on Tuesday, jazz on Wednesday, Irish on Thursday, baroque once a month on Monday, and on Saturday a silent set – gentle music that won't hinder conversation. A meat draw is held on Friday. Open on Sundays only when rugby is on. ● ⎙ 穼

REAL ALE BREWERIES

Liberation St Saviour: Jersey
Pocket St Ouen: Jersey (brewing suspended)
Randalls St Peter Port: Guernsey
White Rock St Sampsons: Guernsey

ISLANDS

Cornerstone 🄻

2 La Tour Beauregard, GY1 1LQ
🕐 11-12.30am; 12-11 Sun ☎ (01481) 713832
🌐 thecornerstone.gg
5 changing beers (often Liberation, Randalls, White Rock) Ⓗ
Now owned by White Rock Brewery, this café has a small bar area to the front and further seating to the rear. Regular quiz evenings are held and there is a large screen for sporting events. The menu offers a wide range of meals plus daily specials (no food Sun, unless advertised). One handpump is for cider, often local from Rocquette. Visit the website for the current ale and cider selection. Local CAMRA Pub of the Year 2014 and 2015. ◖🍴♿🚲🛜

Pickled Pig (Duke of Normandie Hotel)

Lefebvre Street, GY1 2JP (through arch close to jct of High St with Smith St)
🕐 11-12.45am; 11-11 Sun ☎ (01481) 721431
🌐 dukeofnormandie.com
3 changing beers (often Liberation) Ⓗ
Town-centre hotel just off the High Street. The comfortable hotel bar, newly refurbished, has three rooms with different seating – the bar areas have stools and armchairs. There is an emphasis on dining, with a varied menu of home-made pub classics, but you can come just for the beer. Gluten-free beer is available in bottles and there are gluten-free choices on the food menu. Outside is a courtyard beer garden for warm summer days. 🛏◖♿🚲🛜

Prince of Wales

Manor Place, GY1 2JH
🕐 10.30-12.45am ☎ (01481) 724493 🌐 pow.gg
Randalls St Peter Porter; 1 changing beer Ⓗ
Town-centre pub with bars on two floors, both of which can be accessed from the street or via an internal staircase. There is an outside area on the opposite side of the road open during the summer months (no real ale is served from the garden bar). The ground floor Coal Hole bar has TV sport. Food is tasty, from light bites to pizzas and burgers. ♿◖🍴🚲

St Sampson

Pony Inn ✔

Les Capelles, GY2 4GX (on main road between Guernsey Candles and Oatlands Centre)
🕐 11-11; 10-11 Sat; 12-6.30 Sun; closed Mon
☎ (01481) 244374
Butcombe Gold; 1 changing beer Ⓗ
A good pub with well-maintained beer and generous portions of excellent food served in the main bar, conservatory area and separate family dining room (booking advisable, particularly at weekends). The public bar at the side shows televised sports and has a pool table. Ale can be purchased and passed through from the main bar. The staff are friendly and families are welcome. There is disabled access for wheelchair users. 🚲♿◖🍴♿🚲🚪

Vale

Houmet Tavern ✔

Rousse, GY6 8JR (between Vale Church and Rousse Tower)
🕐 10-12.45am; 10-6 Sun ☎ (01481) 242214
Marston's Pedigree; 2 changing beers Ⓗ

A popular pub, the Houmet has two bars – the Anchor Bar, which is the public bar at the rear with pool and darts, and the Front Bar, which has more of an emphasis on food, and enjoys picturesque views of the north of the island. Only the public bar is open in the afternoon during the week. The same choice of beer is available in both bars. ◖🍴🚲🛜

JERSEY
St Brelade

Old Smugglers Inn ✔

Le Mont du Ouaisne, JE3 8AW
🕐 11-11 ☎ (01534) 741510 🌐 oldsmugglersinn.com
Draught Bass Ⓗ**; Greene King Abbot** Ⓖ**; 2 changing beers (often Skinners)** Ⓗ
Perched on the edge of Ouaisne Bay, the Smugglers has been the jewel of the Jersey real ale scene for many years. Steeped in history, dating back to when pirates were known to enjoy an ale or two here, it is set within granite-built fishermen's cottages with foundations reputedly from the 13th century. Up to four ales are available including one from Skinner's, and mini beer festivals are regularly held. The pub is renowned for its good food and fresh daily specials. Q🛏◖🍴🚲(12,15)♣

St Helier

Forum 🄻 ✔

13 Grenville Street, JE2 4UF
🕐 11-11 ☎ (01534) 768105
Liberation Ale; 3 changing beers (often Box Steam) Ⓗ
On the outskirts of town, the pub is named after the cinema that once stood opposite. It has a modern interior but with a classic feel and includes a number of brass plaques that were taken from the old Royal Court building. Live sport and background music often feature. Three real ales are always available, and a large range of real ciders. A former local CAMRA Pub of the Year. ◖♿🍴🚲(3)♣🛜

Lamplighter 🍸 🄻 ✔

9 Mulcaster Street, JE2 3NJ
🕐 11-11 ☎ (01534) 723119
House beer (by Ringwood); 7 changing beers (often Ringwood, Wells) Ⓗ
A traditional pub with a modern feel. The gas lamps that gave the pub its name remain, as does the original antique pewter bar top. An excellent range of up to eight real ales is available including one from Skinner's, all served on handpump from the cellar. A choice of real ciders is sometimes also on offer. Local and regional CAMRA Pub of the Year 2014, local Pub of the Year 2015, and Jersey branch Pub of the Year 2016. ◖🍴🚲♣🛜

Peirson 🄻 ✔

17 Royal Square, JE2 4WA
🕐 10 (11 Sun)-11 ☎ (01534) 722726
Draught Bass; Liberation Ale Ⓗ**; 1 changing beer** Ⓖ
Nestled in the corner of the Royal Square in the centre of St Helier, the pub is named after Major Francis Peirson and contains historical reminders of the Battle of Jersey in 1781. Two ales are always on handpump plus an occasional additional ale on gravity. Excellent food is served lunchtimes throughout the year, with evening meals also on offer in summer. The pub has a good reputation

with locals and visitors alike. Outside seating is extremely popular in the summer months.
Q✥⚅◖⬥⌂❀

Post Horn ⃝ ✓

Hue Street, JE2 3RE
✪ 10 (11 Sun)-11 ☎ (01534) 872853
Liberation Ale; 3 changing beers (often Butcombe, Liberation) Ⓗ
Busy, friendly pub adjacent to the precinct and five minutes' walk from the Royal Square. Popular at lunchtimes with its own nucleus of regulars, it offers up to four draught ales. The large L-shaped public bar extends into the lounge area with an open fire and TV showing sport. A good selection of freshly cooked food is served. There is a large function room on the first floor, a drinking area outside and a public car park nearby. ✿◖⬥⌂❀⌕

St Martin

Royal

La Grande Route de Faldouet, JE3 6UG
✪ 10 (11 Sun)-11 ☎ (01534) 856289
Draught Bass; Ringwood Best Bitter Ⓗ**; 1 changing beer** Ⓖ
Large, traditional, country-style inn at the centre of St Martin with sizeable public and lounge bars and restaurant area. Owned by Randalls, it has been under the same management for more than 25 years. The interior features traditional furnishings, cosy corners and a real fire in the colder months. Guest ales are from the Marston's range or Skinner's. Quality food is popular with locals and visitors alike, and a good menu is served lunchtimes and evenings until 8.30pm (no food Sun eve). ✥✿◖⬥▲P⌂(3)❀

Rozel Bar & Restaurant ⃝ ✓

La Valle de Rozel, JE3 6AJ
✪ 10 (11 Sun)-11 ☎ (01534) 863478
Draught Bass; Liberation Ale; 1 changing beer (often Ringwood, Skinners) Ⓖ
A charming hostelry tucked away in the north-east corner of the island, under new management as a Liberation Group partner pub. It has a delightful beer garden and an excellent restaurant upstairs. Bar meals are served in the public bar and snug, where there is a real fire in the winter. Locals are friendly if sometimes a little rumbustious.
✥✿◖⬥⌂(3)❀

St Mary

St Mary's Country Inn ⃝ ✓

La Rue des Buttes, JE3 3DS
✪ 10 (11 Sun)-11 ☎ (01534) 482897
Liberation Ale; 3 changing beers (often Butcombe) Ⓗ
An archetypal country inn from the outside, this 17th-century farmhouse is opposite the Norman parish church. Following refurbishment in 2009, the interior is contemporary, with a main bar and an extensive dining area. Four handpumps serve Liberation and three guest beers, and reasonably priced good food is offered daily from an extensive menu. The inn has a comfortable and relaxed atmosphere with seating outside front and rear for when the sun shines. A reasonable walk from the north coast. ✥✿◖⬥P⌂(25,27)❀⌕

St Ouen

Farmers Inn ✓

La Grande Route de St Ouen, JE3 2HY
✪ 10 (11 Sun)-11 ☎ (01534) 485311
Draught Bass; Liberation Ale; 1 changing beer Ⓗ
Situated in the hub of St Ouen, the rustic Farmers Inn is a typical country pub offering up to three ales as well as a locally made cider when available (usually April-July). Traditional pub food is served in generous portions. Best described as a friendly community local, there is a good chance of hearing Jersey French (Jerriais) spoken at the bar.
◖♣P⌂(8,9)

Moulin de Lecq ✓

Le Mont de la Greve de Lecq, JE3 2DT
✪ 11-11 ☎ (01534) 482818 🌐 moulindelecq.com
4 changing beers (often Liberation, Ringwood, Skinners) Ⓖ
Another free house on the island offering a range of real ales, the Moulin is a converted 12th-century watermill situated in the valley above the beach at Greve de Lecq. The waterwheel is still in place and the turning mechanism can be seen behind the bar. A restaurant adjoins the mill. There is a children's play space and a barbecue area used extensively in the summer. Q✥✿◖⬥♥P⌂(9)❀

Spores for thought

Yeast is a fungus, a single cell plant that can convert a sugary liquid into equal proportions of alcohol and carbon dioxide. There are two basic types of yeast used in brewing, one for ale and one for lager. (The yeasts used to make the Belgian beers known as gueuze and lambic are wild spores in the atmosphere). It is often said that ale is produced by 'top fermentation' and lager by 'bottom fermentation'. While it is true that during ale fermentation a thick blanket of yeast head and protein is created on top of the liquid while only a thin slick appears on top of fermenting lager, the descriptions are seriously misleading. Yeast works at all levels of the sugar-rich liquid in order to turn malt sugars into alcohol. If yeast worked only at the top or bottom of the liquid, a substantial proportion of sugar would not be fermented. Ale is fermented at a high temperature, lager at a much lower one. The furious speed of ale fermentation creates the yeast head and with it the rich, fruity aromas and flavours that are typical of the style. It is more accurate to describe the ale method as 'warm fermentation' and the lager one as 'cold fermentation'.

The Year in Beer
2017 Diary

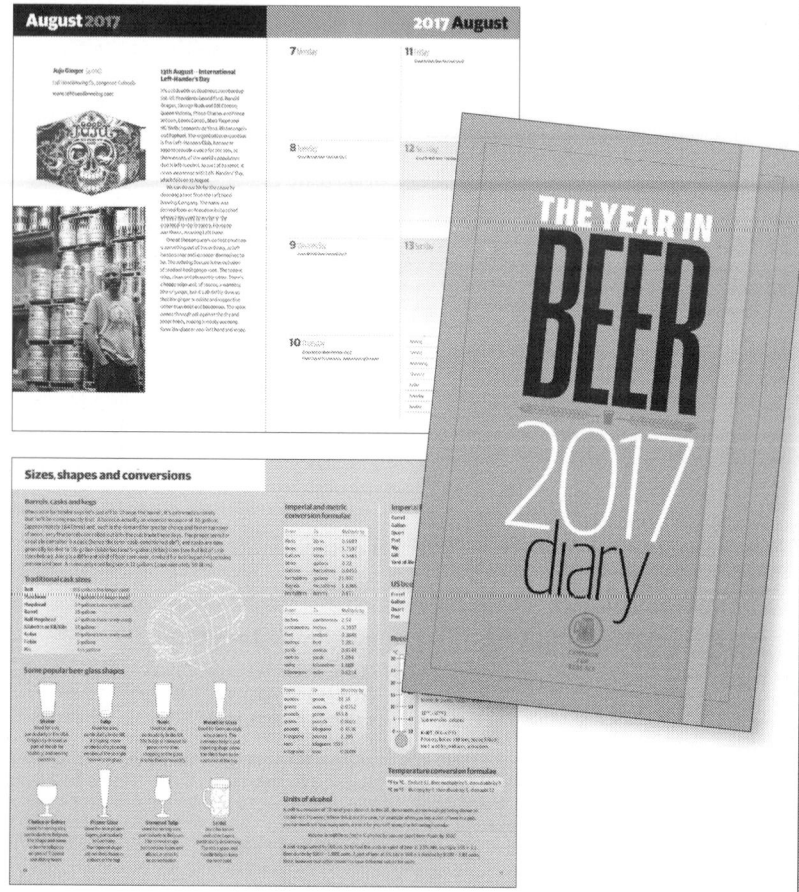

This content-packed diary is based around 52 full-page features linking each week of the year to a beer, brewing or pub theme. This beautiful, practical diary is supplemented by a wealth of further information, including CAMRA's beer festivals, beer storage tips, beer's patron saints and much more.
An essential and attractive publication for the traditional real ale drinker as well as the most style-conscious of beer hipsters.

£9.99 ISBN 978-1-85249-337-0 CAMRA members' price £7.99 144 pages

For this and other books on beer and pubs visit CAMRA's online bookshop at **www.camra.org.uk/books** or call **01727 867201**

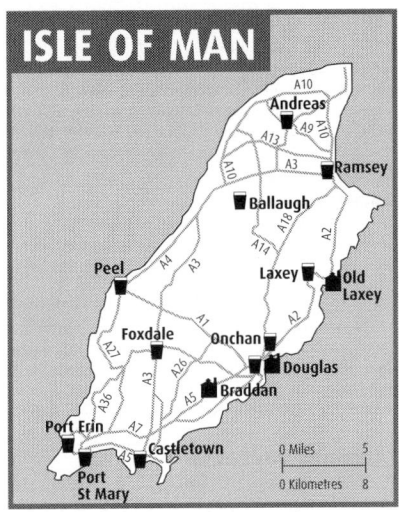

ISLE OF MAN

racing themes. The patio is ideal for watching quayside vessels and waterfront wildlife. This is the only pub in the British Isles to feature on a banknote (to the left of Castle Rushen on the Manx £5 note). Q❀♿Å⇌♣🖵(1,2)❀≋

Sidings

Victoria Road, IM9 1EF (next to railway station)
✿ 11.30-11 (midnight Fri & Sat) ☎ (01624) 823282
Bushy's Castletown Bitter, Ruby (1874) Mild, Bitter; Okell's Bitter; 8 changing beers (sourced nationally) Ⓗ
The Sidings (a former railway ticket office) comprises two large lounges with a newly refurbished games and TV area, and an extensive beer garden at the rear. The 10 handpumps sitting in a straight line along the bar are an impressive sight. Four local ales are available alongside six changing guests sourced from throughout the UK. This CAMRA award-winning pub is a popular stop-off for bus and train travellers alike.
Q❀◑⇌♣P🖵❀≋

Tap Room

Castle Street, IM9 1LF
✿ 12-11 (midnight Fri & Sat) ☎ (01624) 824885
4 changing beers (sourced nationally) Ⓗ
The Tap Room, just off the town square and close to Castle Rushen, was successfully converted from a tapas and wine bar, and can cater for up to 80 diners, with a varied menu. It has four handpumps, with the beers stored and cooled behind the bar area on the same floor – rare for the Isle of Man. Guest ales here are often not found elsewhere on the island. There is a rear courtyard and roof terrace. It may close early on quiet winter evenings. Q❀◑♿⇌♣🖵(1,2)≋

Douglas

Albert Hotel ❷

3 Chapel Row, IM1 2BJ
✿ 10-11 (11.45 Fri & Sat); 12-11 Sun ☎ (01624) 673632
Bushy's Bitter; Okell's Bitter; 2 beers (sourced locally) Ⓗ
The nearest real ale pub to the sea terminal, the Albert is an unspoilt local with many regulars. It has a traditionally laid-out central bar and dark-wood panelling, with a pool table in one room and interesting historic pictures of Steampacket boats in the other. Sport is often on TV but never loud enough to spoil conversation. The drinks are reasonably priced, and the resident beers include those from local breweries Okell's and Bushy's.
Q⇌♣🖵❀≋

Cat with No Tail ❷

Hailwood Court, Governors Hill, IM2 7EA
✿ 12-11 (midnight Fri & Sat) ☎ (01624) 616364
Okell's Bitter; 3 changing beers Ⓗ
A modern pub serving Governors Hill housing estate, situated two miles from central Douglas. The Cat has a public bar with large-screen TV for sport, as well as pool and darts. The large lounge has a conservatory area, popular with families,

Andreas

Grosvenor

Kirk Andreas, IM7 4HE
✿ 12-2.30, 5.30-midnight; 12-8 Sun; closed Mon
☎ (01624) 888007
Okell's Bitter; 1 changing beer (sourced nationally) Ⓗ
The island's most northerly pub has a loyal clientele, and is equally popular for drinking and dining. The Tap Room is a long-established favourite with locals and patrons from further afield, from families to farmers. It is a traditional country bar, with a real sense of relaxed charm and timeless character. Beers are supplied via Okell's brewery and frequently include a guest ale. There is a separate dining section and function room. It may close earlier on quieter winter evenings.
Q❦❀◑♣P🖵❀≋

Ballaugh

Raven ❷

The Main Road, IM7 5EG
✿ 12-11 (midnight Fri & Sat) ☎ (01624) 896128
Okell's Bitter; house beer (by Okells); 2 changing beers (sourced nationally) Ⓗ
Village-centre pub situated on the world famous TT motorcycle circuit at Ballaugh Bridge. There is a comfortable main bar with three separate areas, one mainly for dining, as well as one with a separate games room for pool and darts. Rarely for the island, there is a house brew, Ravens Claw, always on sale. Families are welcome and food is served daily. There are outdoor seating areas, popular in the summer months and when the races are on. Q❦❀◑♿♣P🖵(5,6)❀≋

Castletown

Castle Arms ❷

The Quay, IM9 1LD
✿ 12-11.30 (12.30am Fri & Sat) ☎ (01624) 824673
Okell's Bitter, Dr Okell's IPA; 2 changing beers Ⓗ
An attractive and historic pub, the Castle Arms is also known as the Glue Pot. It is next to Castletown harbour beneath the walls of Castle Rushen and handy for other heritage attractions. Two small ground floor rooms have nautical and Manx motor

REAL ALE BREWERIES

Bushy's Braddan
Hooded Ram Douglas
Okell's Douglas
Old Laxey 🏠 Old Laxey

which leads to an extensive outside seating area overlooking open countryside, with a patio and play area. You will often find up to four ales here including two guests – check what both bars have to offer. ☺☯◐Ⅎよ♣Pᆸ(12,22)☂

Horse & Plough ✓
Isle of Man Business Park, Bradden, IM2 2QZ
✿ 12-11 (midnight Fri & Sat) ☎ (01624) 626060
Okell's Manx Pale Ale, Bitter; 2 changing beers Ⓗ
Modern Heron & Brearley pub serving the IoM Business Park and nearby housing estate. There is ample space for diners, families and drinkers to relax in an informal atmosphere, with a good arrangement of offshoot rooms. The large conservatory is popular for functions and leads to an outside seating area at the rear. There is a pool table and TV sport. An interesting menu accompanies up to four real ales. The pub is increasingly busy following an excellent refurbishment. ☺☯◐Ⅎよ♣Pᆸ☺☂

Old Market Inn
Chapel Row, IM1 2BJ
✿ 9am-11
2 changing beers (often Bushy's)
Under the same ownership for many years, the Market has the smallest bar on the island, serving two separate rooms. What it lacks in size is more than made up for in character, and few pubs like this remain in the British Isles. Two ales, often from Bushy's, are stocked in this friendly hostelry, where the visitor is almost bound to end up in conversation with other drinkers. In close proximity to the bus station and ferry terminal, the pub has an intensely loyal following. Q⇌ᆸ

Prospect Hotel ✓
Prospect Hill, IM1 1ET
✿ 12-11 (midnight Fri & Sat); closed Sun ☎ (01624) 616773
Okell's Bitter; 13 changing beers Ⓗ
Opened in 1857, the pub is in the finance sector of the island's capital. The law courts are in close proximity, and the walls feature many pictures of luminaries of the law profession from the UK and the Isle of Man. Fourteen handpumps, the largest number in one venue on the island, are now well established. Mini beer festivals feature throughout the year. ◐⇌♣●ᆸ☺☂

Queen's Hotel ✓
Queens Promenade, IM2 4NL
✿ 12-midnight (1am Fri & Sat) ☎ (01624) 674438
Okell's Bitter; 3 changing beers Ⓗ
One of just a few remaining pubs situated on Douglas promenade, the refurbished Queen's is popular with visitors and locals alike. There is a great view of Douglas Bay, ferries and trams from the terrace, which has plenty of seating under heated awnings. Inside there are three distinct areas, one with a pool table, two with low-volume TVs featuring sport. Pub grub is served seven days a week and there is live music at the weekends. Q☺☯◐よ⇌♣ᆸ☺☂

Rovers Return
11 Church Street, IM1 2AG
✿ 12-11 (midnight Fri & Sat) ☎ (01624) 676459
Bushy's Ruby (1874) Mild, Bitter; 5 changing beers Ⓗ
The Rovers is a fascinating pub, with handpumps fashioned from fire hoses, a real fire beneath the dartboard, and a shrine to Blackburn Rovers in a back room. The interior comprises an almost

warren-like series of many rooms, with a truly eclectic and loyal clientele. Famously large food portions are available at lunchtimes, and rare and unusual guest ales complement the Bushy's regulars. The pub is tucked away in a narrow street directly behind Douglas Town Hall. ☺◐⇌♣●ᆸ☂

Samuel Webbs ✓
Marina Road, IM1 2HG
✿ 12-midnight (1am Fri & Sat) ☎ (01624) 675595
Okell's Manx Pale Ale, Bitter; 1 changing beer Ⓗ
Sam Webbs is a vibrant town-centre bar, ideally situated for both pre- and post-theatre drinks, as it sits just a few yards away from the Gaiety Theatre. At weekends there is regular live entertainment. Sam's, which returned to real ale some years ago, now usually carries up to three Okell's beers. A popular sports bar and a favourite venue for starting or finishing a tour of Douglas bars. ♣●☂

Terminus Tavern ✓
Strathallan Crescent, IM2 4NR
✿ 12-11 (midnight Fri & Sat) ☎ (01624) 624312
Okell's Bitter; 3 changing beers Ⓗ
Located next to the starting point for the seasonal Manx Electric Railway and horse trams, the Terminus has a comfortable, spacious front bar with alcoves around its large front windows. There is also a side bar for pool and darts, and a large outside seating area with views across Douglas Bay. This award-winning pub is popular for dining throughout the year, but nevertheless retains a local focus. Q☺☯◐よ⇌(MER)♣Pᆸ(25,26,27)☂

Woodbourne Hotel ✓
Alexander Drive, IM2 3QF
✿ 3 (12 Sat & Sun)-midnight ☎ (01624) 676754
Okell's Bitter; 8 changing beers Ⓗ
Large three-bar Victorian local in a residential area within walking distance of Douglas centre. What was once the gents-only bar is now used to promote cask ale, offering a range of Okell's beers alongside four or five guests. The Woody is a popular, friendly pub with a varied clientele and boasts a genuine community spirit, with a proud record of charity fundraising. A regular pub quiz is held on Sunday evening, and there is a separate pool room. Local CAMRA Pub of the Year 2015. Q☺♣●ᆸ☂

Foxdale

Baltic Inn
1 Glentramman Terrace, IM4 3EE
✿ 4 (2 Fri & Sat)-midnight ☎ (01624) 801305
Okell's Manx Pale Ale, Bitter; 1 changing beer (sourced locally) Ⓗ
Quiet, cosy local, with one main room divided into separate seating areas. A roaring real fire in winter adds to the atmosphere. Real ales on handpump supplement bottled Okell's IPA, Maclir and Hooded Ram beers. There are some fascinating historic photos on the walls of Foxdale during the mining boom. This friendly village pub is thriving under new ownership. Q♣☺☂

Laxey

Bridge Inn
6 New Road, IM4 7BE
✿ 12-11 (midnight Fri & Sat) ☎ (01624) 862414
⊕ bridgeinn.im

Bushy's Bitter; Ruddles Best Bitter; 1 changing beer (sourced locally) 🅷
Popular and lively local pub in the centre of the village. The Bridge has been refurbished but retains its friendly atmosphere and continues to serve an excellent pint. It offers occasional live music, wide-screen TV and a pool table. In 1897, after the Snaefell mining disaster in which 20 men perished, the cellar area was used as a temporary morgue. There are rumours of a resident ghost.
🏮🍴◁❶🚲🅿🐾🛏♿🐕☕🛜

Onchan

Manx Arms ✅
Main Road, IM3 1BE
🕙 12-11 (midnight Fri-Sun) ☎ (01624) 675484
Okell's Manx Pale Ale, Bitter; 1 changing beer (sourced nationally) 🅷
Traditional village pub on the main road with a lounge and bar with pub games including pool, darts and dominoes, and a large-screen TV for sport. Rare local historic car racing photographs adorn the walls. A lively and friendly pub, live music features most Saturday evenings as well as an occasional karaoke night. There is an attractive heated patio at the front for smokers and another at the rear next to the large car park.
Q🏮♿♣❶P🚌(3,23)🐾🛜

Peel

Creek Inn ✅
Station Place, IM5 1AT (by harbour)
🕙 10-midnight (12.30am Fri & Sat) ☎ (01624) 842216
🌐 thecreekinn.co.uk
Okell's Bitter; Sharp's Doom Bar; changing beers (often Hooded Ram) 🅷
Traditional harbourside pub popular with locals and tourists, with ample outdoor seating on the edge of the picturesque harbour. The lounge bar has a nautical theme with etched-glass screens featuring sailing ships separating the cosy seating areas. A large selection of ales is on offer to complement the comprehensive food menu. Locally caught Manx queenies (queen scallops) are a speciality, together with locally cured kippers. The pub has live music at the weekends in a second back bar area. 🏮🍴◁❶Ⓐ♣❶🚌(5,6)🐾🛜

Marine Hotel
Shore Road, IM5 1AH
🕙 10-midnight ☎ (01624) 842337 🌐 marinehotelpeel.co.uk
Okell's Bitter; 3 changing beers (sourced locally) 🅷
Popular with all ages, the Marine Hotel overlooks the beach and historic Peel Castle. It has two bar areas, one a traditional drinking corridor, and a large restaurant accessed via a separate entrance, serving excellent, value-for-money meals seven days a week. The venue has developed an increasing reputation for quality ales and ciders in recent years, and the landlord is a staunch supporter of local breweries and cider makers, though guest ales from all over the UK are often available. ◁❶♣❶🚌(5,6)🐾🛜

White House Hotel ✅
2 Tynwald Road, IM5 1LA
🕙 11-midnight ☎ (01624) 842252
🌐 thewhitehousepeel.com

Bushy's Ruby (1874) Mild, Bitter; Moorhouse's Pride of Pendle; Okell's Manx Pale Ale, Bitter; 4 changing beers (sourced nationally) 🅷
The White House, run by the same family for many years, features a public bar area, a separate pool room and a larger room for TV sport and live music at the weekends. In addition there is a separate cosy snug, with a second bar accessed internally via a sliding door. A prolific winner of the Isle of Man CAMRA Pub of the Year award over the last 20 years, the pub has long supported the now-growing cider market on the island.
Q🏮Ⓐ♣❶P🚌(5,6)🐾🛜

Port Erin

Bay Hotel
Shore Road, IM9 6HL
🕙 12-11 (midnight Fri & Sat); 12-11.30 Sun
☎ (01624) 832084
Bushy's Castletown Bitter, Ruby (1874) Mild, Bitter, Old Bushy Tail; 2 changing beers (sourced nationally) 🅷
Bushy's flagship pub is on one of the best beaches on the island. Beach concerts and a promenade patio make the Bay a great summertime venue, with local bands playing in the winter. The full range of Bushy's brews is available, and can be sampled by ordering a tasting tray. The interior comprises four traditional rooms – public bar, quiet room, dining room and band area. Winner of the inaugural Isle of Man CAMRA Cider Pub of the Year competition in 2015. Q🏮🍴🏮◁♿♣❶🐾🛜

Falcon's Nest Hotel
Station Road, IM9 6AF
🕙 11-midnight (12.30am Fri & Sat) ☎ (01624) 834077
🌐 falconsnesthotel.co.uk
Bushy's Bitter; 3 changing beers (sourced nationally) 🅷
The Falcon's Nest Hotel is on the south-west coast in a spectacular location overlooking the beautiful crescent-shaped bay of Port Erin. A free house with two bars, the residents' lounge, also open to the public, is in the true tradition of the public house, where visitors can enjoy a wide choice of guests and local beers relaxing in front of an open fire. The Victorian-style Gladstone restaurant offers an extensive à la carte menu and an ever-popular Sunday lunch carvery. Locally-sourced produce is used wherever possible. Q🍴◁❶♣❶P🚌🐾🛜

Port St Mary

Albert Hotel ♟
Athol Street, IM9 5DS
🕙 11-midnight (1am Fri & Sat); 12-midnight Sun
☎ (01624) 832118
Bushy's Bitter; Okells Bitter; 2 changing beers (sourced nationally) 🅷
A hidden gem in the heart of this coastal village, the Albert boasts impressive views over the harbour. It has a public bar with games area, a cosy lounge bar complete with newly installed wood-burning stove, and an overflow area of tables and seating. Immaculately decorated and furnished, the walls are adorned with many paintings by local artists who use the pub, often depicting local scenes and landscapes. The ideal retreat following a sea fishing trip. Q🏮🍴♣❶P🚌(1,2)🛜

ISLANDS

Shore Hotel

Shore Road, IM9 5LZ

✪ 12-11 (midnight Fri & Sat) ☎ (01624) 832269
⊕ theshore.im

Bushy's Old Bushy Tail; Okell's Bitter; 1 changing beer (sourced nationally) Ⓗ

Large, sturdy building with stunning views over Carrick Bay, also known as Gansey. There is a separate bar with a mixture of seating and tables, and a lounge style area. The wooden bar area is fashioned partly from former door panelling and ships' handrails. Food is served throughout the day in a separate dining section. The outdoor seating area is sheltered from what can be biting winds. This is one of only a few outlets to regularly sell Bushy's Old Bushy Tail. ✤⇔◑●P🚌❄️🐾

Ramsey

Mitre

16 Parliament Street, IM8 1AP

✪ 10-11 (1am Fri & Sat); 10-midnight Sun ☎ (01624) 813257

Bushy's Bitter; Okell's Bitter; house beer (by Okells); 1 changing beer (sourced locally) Ⓗ

Large building, much refurbished in recent years, with views of the quayside, accessible from both the harbour and the main street. There are distinct and separate bars on three levels – the basement Schooner bar is popular with young revellers at the weekend, while live music is hosted in the upstairs bar where the cask ales are to be found. Food is now served here at lunchtimes. The Mitre is a staunch supporter of island breweries, with the house beer, Jough, supplied by Okell's. ◑⇄🐾❄️🌐

Plough

46 Parliament Street, IM8 1AN

✪ 4.30-11.30; 12-12.30am Fri & Sat; 12-11.30 Sun
☎ (01624) 813323

Okell's Bitter; 1 changing beer (sourced nationally) Ⓗ

In the heart of Ramsey's main street and recently substantially refurbished, the Plough stocks a changing guest ale in addition to Okell's Bitter. This small two-roomed pub caters for a mixed clientele, from shoppers taking a break to football fans. The pub is a proud sponsor of Shennaghys Jiu, a Manx music festival held in Ramsey in March/April, and produces bespoke beermats to advertise and celebrate the event. ⇄♣❄️🌐

Trafalgar Hotel ✅

West Quay, IM8 1DW

✪ 11-11 (12.15am Fri & Sat); 11.30-11 Sun
☎ (01624) 814601

Moorhouse's Black Cat; Okell's Bitter; 2 changing beers (sourced nationally) Ⓗ

Traditional, genuine, single-room pub situated on the harbour behind the main shopping street, now under new ownership – the previous landlord having retired after 23 years. A CAMRA Isle of Man branch Pub of the Year finalist on several occasions, the real ales, including guests, are sourced from all over the UK. Friendly, welcoming and always busy, it is particularly popular during TT week and just around the corner from spectacular views of the races. Q⇄♣●🚌(3,5,6)❄️🌐

Raven, Ballaugh (Photo: Tom Stainer)

The Breweries

Breweries overview

Global giants on takeover trail to build a presence in the craft sector

It's an exhilarating time for beer, with new breweries opening and an ever-growing choice for drinkers. But there are worrying storm clouds gathering as global giants jostle for domination and move into the craft beer sector.

The 2016 edition of the *Good Beer Guide* voiced concern at the acquisition of the Meantime Brewery in Greenwich, London, by the world's second-biggest brewer, SABMiller. No figures were released but it was thought SAB paid £80 million for a brewery that enjoys a deserved reputation for its pale ales, properly brewed lagers and American and Belgian-style beers. It later transpired that the global brewer had in fact paid £120 million in order to stake a claim in the craft beer sector.

The ink was still damp on the agreement when SAB itself was the subject of what turned out to be the world's third biggest ever takeover. AB InBev, an American-Belgian-Brazilian conglomerate best known for Budweiser and Stella Artois, bid £71 billion for its arch rival. When the deal is finalised, the merged group will control one third of world beer production.

Problems arose in the summer of 2016 as a result of the UK's decision to leave the European Union. As the pound fell against the dollar, some of the corporate shareholders in SABMiller expressed concern at getting a relatively poor return on their investments. In August 2016, AB InBev said it would prepare a revised offer but, whatever the final outcome, the merger indicates that giant brewers, worried by declining sales in their traditional markets, will be looking to build a stake in the craft movement.

Camden bought

At the same time as AB InBev was attempting to merge with SABMiller, it bought another London craft brewer, Camden Town, for £80 million. A new brewery will be built to expand Camden's production and AB InBev says it plans to build sales of the beers in the London region. It will achieve greater market penetration by undercutting other, smaller producers.

Professor John Colley of Warwick University's Business School has made a study of the way in which global corporations operate and snuff out competition. He says the globals' ability to dominate markets is a result of producing cheaper products. Big brewers enjoy 40 per cent lower costs than the smaller ones and there's even a huge difference between the big- and medium-sized brewers, as the globals are able to buy raw materials, such as malt and hops, in vast bulk. The result is lower costs and lower prices.

Professor Colley says that when AB InBev bought Modelo in Mexico it stripped 20 per cent of costs out of the company. With Beck's in Germany it took out 15 per cent of costs. He estimates that a merger with SABMiller will generate cost savings of $1.4 billion, which amounts to 70 per cent of revenue. Low production costs enable the giant brewers to promote their beers on TV, poster sites and social media at prices smaller brewers cannot match.

The success of the global brewers in the independent sector can be seen at close hand with the sale of Sharp's of Cornwall to Molson Coors in 2011. The Canadian-American group, which bought the former Bass breweries in Burton-on-Trent, has invested £7.5 million in Sharp's and boosted production from 60,000 to 200,000 barrels a year. It has turned Sharp's Doom Bar – much to the chagrin of Greene King and its IPA – into the biggest draught and bottled beer in the country. In spite of many references to Cornwall on the label, the bottled version of Doom Bar is now produced in Burton-on-Trent.

Merger merry-go-round

Back in Greenwich, Meantime went on a dizzying ride on the merger merry-go-round. It was bought by SABMiller, passed to AB InBev and then found itself sold on to Asahi of Japan. Regulators in the United States and the European Union told

Prof John Colley: globals succeed by stripping costs

Molson Coors has turned Sharp's Doom Bar into a huge commercial success but, in doing so, it has diluted the beer's Cornish origins. Bottled versions of Doom Bar are brewed in Burton-on-Trent

AB InBev it had to jettison some of its brands in order to satisfy competition rules. As a result, the group has sold off Grolsch, Peroni, Meantime and the iconic original golden lager, Pilsner Urquell from the Czech Republic.

The frightening power of the giant global brewers can be seen in the way AB InBev has handled the acclaimed Goose Island beers in the United States. Goose Island, renowned for its IPA, Honkers Ale and 312 Urban Wheat, started life as a Chicago brew pub in 1988 and later moved to a bigger plant at Wrigley Field in the city. In 2011, it was bought by Anheuser Busch, the American arm of AB InBev. The main Goose Island beers are now produced at a vast AB plant in Fort Collins, Colorado, at its Canadian subsidiary Labatt, and at a new brewing 'facility' on the East Coast of the United States.

A different yeast culture is used as the original yeast wasn't suitable for big batch brewing: yeast makes a vital contribution to beer flavour. AB has ditched imported Saaz hops from the Czech Republic as a result of its long running trademark dispute with Budweiser Budvar. Goose Island IPA is widely available in bottle in the UK but the name has been reduced to just Goose IPA.

All of this activity will not have been lost on other global players. Heineken has invested in its Caledonian Brewery in Edinburgh, which now has a portfolio of ales along with the award-winning Deuchars IPA. Carlsberg, based in Northampton, distributes a range of ales and imported beers as well as its ubiquitous lager but the Danish owners may regret closing the Tetley plant in Leeds and axing the only national brand ever to be named Champion Beer of Britain – Draught Burton Ale.

Pressures at home

The curious case of Thwaites of Blackburn could be a worrying trend for the future. The Blackburn brewery was founded in 1807 and remains in the hands of descendants of the founder, Daniel Thwaites. For several years it planned to move production to a greenfield site outside the town but, in 2015, it announced it was selling its brewing division, which amounted to 100,000 barrels a year, to Marston's for £25.1 million.

Thwaites produces a few short-run beers on a micro-plant but all its main brands are now supplied to its 350 pubs from Marston's plants in Burton and Wolverhampton. In effect, Thwaites is now a pub company and the fear is that other regional and family breweries, unable to compete with the economies of scale of such national groups as Greene King and Marston's, will follow suit.

A further pressure comes from Progressive Beer Duty which incentivizes production within much smaller breweries (3,000 to 18,000 barrels per year) and disadvantages middle-ranking producers.

Beer choice in Britain has never been better but it would be a dereliction of duty if the *Good Beer Guide* did not warn of possible threats to drinkers' choice. As always, we need to campaign to defend good beer and our brewing heritage.

Thwaites sold its brewing business and it is feared other mid-sized brewers might do the same

How to use the Breweries section

This section lists breweries operating in the United Kingdom, the Isle of Man and the Channel Islands. Breweries are listed in alphabetical order. They include independent companies (regional, family, micro-brewers and brewpubs), national brewers and global groups. If a brewery owns more than one site, these are cross-referenced. Within each brewery entry, regular beers are listed in increasing order of strength. Websites should be consulted when breweries produce occasional or seasonal beers that are available for less than six months of the year. We mention when breweries produce bottle-conditioned beers but do not list or evaluate them: for further information, see CAMRA's *Good Bottled Beer Guide*.

KEY TO BREWERY ENTRIES

BREWERY SYMBOLS

Brewpub: a pub that brews beer on the premises.

Cyclops: the brewery is affiliated with the Cyclops system for describing beers to consumers.

CAMRA tasting notes, supplied by a trained CAMRA tasting panel. Beer descriptions that do not carry this symbol are based on more limited tastings or have been obtained from other sources.

A CAMRA Beer of the Year in 2015.

One of CAMRA's Beers of the Year 2016: a finalist in the Champion Beer of Britain competition held during the Great British Beer Festival in London in August 2016, or in the Champion Winter Beer of Britain competition held earlier in the year.

Serve with tight sparkler: the brewery's beers can be acceptably served through a 'tight sparkler' attached to the nozzle of the beer pump, designed to give a thick collar of foam on the beer.

Do not serve with tight sparkler: the brewery's beers should NOT be served through a tight sparkler. CAMRA is opposed to the growing tendency to serve southern-brewed beers with the aid of sparklers, which aerate the beer and tend to drive hop aroma and flavour into the head, altering the balance of the beer achieved in the brewery. When neither symbol is used it means the brewery in question has not stated a preference.

Brewery tours available: check with individual breweries for details.

Brewery shop: beer available to take away. Check opening hours in advance.

RAIB **Real Ale in a Bottle:** the brewery produces bottle-conditioned beer (known by CAMRA as Real Ale in a Bottle).

Seasonal beers: the brewery produces seasonal beers in addition to its regular range.

V **Vegan:** the brewery produces vegan beers (check with brewery for further details. Not all beers produced may be vegan).

GF **Gluten free:** the brewery produces gluten-free beers (check with brewery for further details. Not all beers produced may be gluten free).

ABBREVIATIONS

OG Stands for Original Gravity, the measure taken before fermentation of the level of 'fermentable material' (malt sugars and added sugars) in the brew. It is only a rough indication of strength and is no longer used for duty purposes.

ABV Stands for Alcohol by Volume, which is a more reliable measure of the percentage of alcohol in finished beer. Many breweries now only disclose ABVs but the Guide lists OGs where available. Often the OG and the ABV of a beer are identical, i.e. 1035 and 3.5 per cent. If the ABV is higher than the OG, i.e. OG

1035, ABV 3.8, this indicates that the beer has been 'well attenuated' with most of the malt sugars turned into alcohol. If the ABV is lower than the OG, this means residual sugars have been left in the beer for fullness of body and flavour: this is rare but can apply to some milds or strong old ales, barley wines and winter beers.

SIBA Indicates a member of the Society of Independent Brewers.

IFBB Indicates a member of the Independent Family Brewers of Britain.

NOTE: The Breweries section was correct at the time of going to press and every effort has been made to ensure that all regularly-available cask-conditioned beers are included.

The Breweries

The breweries listed in this section include micro, small, family, regional, national and global companies. Please use the Beer index (p985) to help locate beers.

1648 SIBA

▤ **Old Stables Brewery, Mill Lane, East Hoathly, East Sussex, BN8 6QB**
☎ (01825) 840830 ⊕ 1648brewing.co.uk

⊠ The 1648 brewery, set up in the old stable block at the King's Head pub in 2003, derives its name from the year of the deposition of King Charles I. One pub is owned and more than 40 outlets are supplied. ‼ ✑ ◆ RAIB

Hop Pocket (OG 1039, ABV 3.7%)

Triple Champion (OG 1041, ABV 4%)
A chestnut-coloured traditional English ale, deeply flavoured and full-bodied.

Signature (OG 1044, ABV 4.4%)
Pale, light, crisply refreshing ale with a bitter aftertaste.

Laughing Frog (OG 1052, ABV 5.2%)
A dark gold-coloured, full-bodied, French/Belgian-style ale. Lightly hopped with a full malty flavour.

3 Brewers SIBA ◉

The Potato Shed, Symonds Hyde Farm, Symonds Hyde Lane, Hatfield, Hertfordshire, AL10 9BB
☎ (01707) 271636 ☎ 07941 854615
⊕ 3brewers.co.uk

⊠ Launched in 2013 by three enthusiastic brewers from St Albans who transformed a former potato shed into an eight-barrel plant brewery. It is located on a working farm and livery and sources fresh water from the farm borehole. The brewery supplies two permanent beers to pubs in and around the St Albans district and also to local beer festivals. Spent malt is turned into compost for the farm. Bottled beer is available through several beer and wine merchants locally. ‼ ✑

Golden (OG 1038, ABV 3.8%)
A refreshing, light gold-coloured beer with a subtle citrus flavour and a hint of sweetness.

Classic English Ale (OG 1040, ABV 4%)
Deep amber in colour with a light hoppy aroma and a rich and rounded malty taste balanced by subtle hoppiness to give a clean, smooth and refreshing ale.

Ruby English Ale (OG 1043, ABV 4.3%)

Special English Ale (OG 1048, ABV 4.8%)
A robust and full-bodied premium ale made with chocolate malt, giving a deep copper colour. English hops give a hint of berries. Well balanced and smooth.

3 Potts (NEW)

8 Russell Avenue, Southport, Merseyside, PR9 7RD
☎ 07926 178707 ⊕ 3potts.co.uk

3 Potts is a 1.8-barrel brewery established in 2015 by Simon and Shona Potts on a part-time basis, creating small batch beers. RAIB

Sprocket IPA (ABV 5.5%)

An amber-coloured IPA with citrus aromas. Well-balanced with a lightly honeyed bitterness.

Furnace (ABV 6.5%)
A single hop stout.

Turbine IIPA (ABV 7.4%)
The big brother to Sprocket IPA, dry-hopped for an upfront citrus aroma.

360° SIBA ◉

Unit 22, Bluebell Business Estate, Sheffield Park, East Sussex, TN22 3HQ
☎ (01825) 722375 ⊕ 360degreebrewing.com

⊠ Brewing began in 2013 using a six-barrel plant. Its beers are available across Sussex, the South East, and London. There are plans to move to larger premises in summer 2016 and to increase the range. ‼ ◆

Pale #39 (ABV 3.9%)
A light-bodied, yet full-flavoured, zesty golden ale.

Sussex #42 (ABV 4.2%)
A traditional, copper-coloured best bitter, aromatic with a clean bitterness.

West Coast Pale Ale (ABV 5%)
A contemporary-style pale ale, heavily hopped with intense tropical fruit flavours and a long bitter finish.

40FT (NEW)

Bootyard, Abbott Street, Dalston, London, E8 3DP

Office: The Printhouse, 18-20 Ashwin Street, Dalston, E8 3DL ⊕ 40ftbrewery.com

Founded by Steve Ryan, Andreas Pettersson, Fredrik Pettersson and Ben Ott, 40FT began brewing in 2015. It is a six-barrel microbrewery, located in a 40-ft shipping container in a disused car park close to Ridley Road Market. No real ale.

4Ts

Unit 20, Manor Industrial Estate, Lower Wash Lane, Latchford, Warrington, Cheshire, WA7 4UA
☎ (01925) 747463 ☎ 07917 730184

Office: 72 Rydal Avenue, Warrington, WA4 6AT
⊕ 4tsbrewery.co.uk

Brewing returned to Warrington in 2015, to bigger premises with scope to increase production of cask, bottles and polypins. The '2 & Nine' mini kit is now located here and beers will be produced on it using this name. 4Ts offers a core range of four beers plus many special brews. Beers are usually available in the Tavern, Warrington. ◆

Pale Ale (OG 1037, ABV 3.7%)
A pale, refreshing session ale. Spicy notes from European hops help make this ale well balanced throughout.

APA (OG 1040, ABV 4%)
An American-style pale ale with spicy and citrus hints throughout with a hint of bitterness at the end, leaving a citrus burst of flavour.

IPA (OG 1046, ABV 4.6%)
Lots of bitterness and bursts of aroma with hints of citrus and passion fruit.

Stout (OG 1050, ABV 5%)
Well-balanced and smooth with biscuit, chocolate and burnt notes at the start, then English hops break through giving a burst of flowery tones.

8 Sail SIBA

Heckington Windmill, Hale Road, Heckington, Lincolnshire, NG34 9JW
☎ (01529) 469308 ☎ 07866 183479
⊕ 8sailbrewery.co.uk

8 Sail Brewery was established in 2010 and operates on a six-barrel brew plant. The brewery nestles in the shadow of Heckington Windmill, Britain's only eight-sailed windmill, from where the brewery takes its name. The mill is now working and helping to mill malted grain for the brewery. The brewery shop stocks bottle-conditioned beers alongside local ciders. 🍺♦ RAIB

Millwright Mild (OG 1038, ABV 3.5%)
Rich, dark malt flavours are lightly balanced with hops. The aroma is chocolaty with a dry roast and liquorice flavour.

Ale (OG 1040, ABV 3.8%)
A refreshing traditional English pale ale.

Windmill Bitter (OG 1040, ABV 3.8%)
An amber-coloured session bitter with a blend of malt and hops.

Blonde (OG 1042, ABV 4%)
A blonde beer, gently hopped to create a refreshing taste.

Merry Miller (OG 1043, ABV 4.1%)
A traditional bitter. Mid brown in colour with a nutty, malty flavour.

Rolling Stone (OG 1044, ABV 4.3%)
A 'stoneground' pale ale using locally grown barley malted at Bairds, Grantham, and milled at the Heckington Windmill.

Golden Ale (OG 1044, ABV 4.4%)
A well-balanced pale beer with a citrus and peach aroma and a dry, slightly tart, citrus-dominated flavour.

King John's Jewels (OG 1045, ABV 4.5%)
A golden ale brewed to commemorate the 800th anniversary of the signing of Magna Carta and the death of King John.

Millstone (OG 1046, ABV 4.5%)
A modern premium bitter with a good balance of malt and hops.

After the Gold Rush (Deacon John Ales)
(OG 1047, ABV 4.6%)
A medium-bodied ale/lager hybrid with a malt character. Mild and fruity with an assertive hop bitterness.

Kibbled (OG 1047, ABV 4.6%)
A well-rounded and balanced red ale with a lightly hopped flavour and malt character.

Windy Miller (OG 1047, ABV 4.6%)
A rich, dark, smooth-flavoured stout brewed with plenty of oat malt.

Damson Porter (OG 1053, ABV 5%)
Damsons are added to give a full-bodied fruitiness to the rich, complex flavours provided by the malts.

Aroma is bitter with caramel malt tones. Flavour is malty and slightly fruity with a bitter finish.

Sail Away (OG 1050, ABV 5%)
Brewed in the style of a German Klsch beer with a good balance of malt and hops.

Victorian Porter (OG 1053, ABV 5%) 🍺
A true porter brewed to a classic Victorian recipe with an aroma of berries, sour fruits and roasted malts and deep, intense, chocolaty flavours giving this dark beer a rich and full-bodied flavour.

Old Colony (Deacon John Ales)
(OG 1052, ABV 5.3%)
An American-style pale ale hopped with a combination of English and American hops.

Black Widow (OG 1054, ABV 5.5%)
A strong, dark ruby mild. Dark malt and liquorice flavours dominate.

John Barleycorn IPA (OG 1053, ABV 5.5%)
Brewed to recreate the taste of an original English IPA using English hops.

AB InBev UK

Porter Tun House, 500 Capability Green, Luton, Bedfordshire, LU1 3LS
☎ (01582) 391166 ⊕ inbev.com

No real ale. As we go to press the takeover for about £70B of SABMiller by A-B InBev, giving it about 30% of the world's beer market with over 400 beer brands, was due to be finalised.

Abbey SIBA 👁

Abbey Brewery, Camden Row, Bath, BA1 5LB
☎ (01225) 444437 ⊕ abbeyales.co.uk

Founded in 1997, Abbey Ales was the first brewery in Bath for over 50 years. It supplies more than 80 regular outlets within a 20-mile radius. It operates four tied houses. ‼♦

Somerset Ale (OG 1038, ABV 3.8%)

Bath Best (OG 1040, ABV 4%)

Bellringer (OG 1042, ABV 4.2%) ◆
A notably hoppy ale, light- to medium-bodied, clean-tasting, refreshingly dry, with a balancing sweetness. Citrus, pale malt aroma and dry, bitter finish.

Abbey Grange

See Llangollen

Abbeydale SIBA 👁

Unit 8, Aizlewood Road, Sheffield, South Yorkshire, S8 0YX
☎ (0114) 281 2712 ⊕ abbeydalebrewery.co.uk

Since starting in 1996, Abbeydale Brewery has grown steadily; it now produces upwards of 130 barrels a week, and recent investment has enabled further growth. 🍺♦

Brimstone (OG 1039, ABV 3.9%)
A russet-coloured bitter beer with a distinctive hop aroma.

Deception (ABV 4.1%)

Moonshine (OG 1041.2, ABV 4.3%)

A well-balanced pale ale with a full hop aroma. Pleasant grapefruit traces may be detected.

Absolution (OG 1050, ABV 5.3%)
A fruity pale ale, deceptively drinkable for its strength. Sweetish but not cloying.

Black Mass (OG 1065, ABV 6.7%)
A strong black stout with complex roast flavours and a lasting bitter finish.

Abstract Jungle (NEW)

Unit 14, Bailey Brook Industrial Estate, Amber Drive, Langley Mill, NG16 4BE ☎ 07481 849332

Office: 2 Manor Farm Mews, Brinsley, Nottinghamshire, NG16 5AG
✉ simon@abstractjunglebrewery.co.uk

Abstract Jungle was established in 2016 by experienced head brewer Simon King, using a custom-built six-barrel plant. ‼ ▆

Pride (OG 1040, ABV 3.9%)
Crisp, clean pale ale brewed with German and American hops. Low mellow bitterness with a tropical aroma.

Jackal (OG 1043, ABV 4.2%)
Traditional-style porter with four different malts and a subtle spicy aroma.

Restless (OG 1045, ABV 4.5%)
A hoppy session beer, resinous and fruity.

Casual (OG 1048, ABV 4.6%)
A bold, complex stout using unrefined chocolate and a hint of blueberries.

Sturdy (OG 1054, ABV 5.6%)
A classic IPA using pale malt and American hops. Pine resinous and citrus fruit.

Acorn SIBA ⊙

Unit 3, Aldham Industrial Estate, Mitchell Road, Wombwell, Barnsley, South Yorkshire, S73 8HA
☎ (01226) 270734 ⊕ acorn-brewery.co.uk

⊚Acorn was set up in 2003 with a 10-barrel expanding to a 20-barrel plant when the brewery moved to larger premises and currently has a 160-barrel a week capacity. All beers are produced using the Barnsley Bitter yeast strain, dating back to the 1850s. ‼ ▆ ◆ RAIB

Yorkshire Pride (OG 1037, ABV 3.7%) ◆
This session beer is golden in colour with pleasing fruit notes. A mouthwatering blend of malt and hops creates a fruity taste which leads to a clean bitter finish.

Barnsley Bitter (OG 1038, ABV 3.8%) ⬚ ▆ ◆
This brown bitter has a smooth malty bitterness throughout with notes of chocolate and caramel. Fruity bitter finish.

Blonde (OG 1040.5, ABV 4%) ◆
A clean-tasting golden-coloured hoppy beer with a refreshing bitter and fruity aftertaste.

Darkness (OG 1042, ABV 4.2%) ▆ ◆
Roast malt and hop aroma in this deep red coloured mild. A slight bitterness in the taste with a smooth finish.

Barnsley Gold (OG 1041.5, ABV 4.3%) ⬚ ◆
This golden ale has fruit in the aroma with a hoppy and fruitiness flavour throughout. A well-hopped, clean, dry finish.

1887 Red (OG 1044, ABV 4.4%)

Old Moor Porter (OG 1045, ABV 4.4%) ▆ ◆
A rich-tasting porter, smooth throughout with a hint of chocolate and liquorice.

Gorlovka Imperial Stout (OG 1058, ABV 6%) ◆
This black stout is rich and smooth and full of chocolate and liquorice flavours with a fruity, creamy finish.

Acton SIBA ⊙

Unit 2, 13b Castle Island Way, North Seaton, Northumberland, NE63 0XL
☎ (01670) 817635 ☎ 07707 703182
✉ actonales1@outlook.com

Formerly known as Gundog, brewing began in 2011. Originally using a 10-barrel plant, the brewery has expanded to a 75-barrel plant brewing four times a week. The Office micropub in Morpeth is connected to Acton Ales and opened in 2014.

Triple Pale Ale (ABV 3.6%)

Northumbrian (ABV 3.8%)

American Dark Knight (ABV 4.1%)

American White Knight (ABV 4.1%)

Golden Cocker (OG 1042, ABV 4.1%)
Dark golden colour with a good nose and citrus and melon finish.

Seahouses Pale (OG 1043, ABV 4.2%)
A pale ale with a clean bitter finish.

Adkin

Correspondence only: c/o 52 Adkin Way, Wantage, Oxfordshire, OX12 9HW ☎ 07709 86149
⊕ adkinbrewery.co.uk

Adkin was established on a 0.5-barrel plant in 2007. A new similar-sized plant was installed in 2013. Twelve brews are produced by prior order. The beers are most easily found at regional beer festivals, but are starting to appear in the local free trade. ‼ ▆ RAIB

Adnams SIBA ⊙

Sole Bay Brewery, East Green, Southwold, Suffolk, IP18 6JW
☎ (01502) 727200 ⊕ adnams.co.uk

⊠ The company was founded by George and Ernest Adnams in 1872. About 50 pubs are owned around East Anglia plus an outpost in London and there is national distribution. Beers are from a new 300-barrel plant within the confines of the present site. ‼ ▆ ◆

Lighthouse (OG 1037, ABV 3.4%) ◆
A quaffable beer with bitterness predominating.

Southwold Bitter (OG 1037, ABV 3.7%) ◆
Aromas of toffee apple, caramel and sulphur. Taste is a complex mix of malt toffee and roast bitterness with hops. Malty bitter and apple flavours linger into the aftertaste.

Old Ale (OG 1044, ABV 4.1%) ⬚ ▆
Aromas of malt and soft cheese, leading into malty and sweet flavours with fruit berries and vanilla. Caramel and roast finish.

Ghost Ship (OG 1046, ABV 4.5%) ▆

A pale ale with an assertive, pithy bitterness and a malty backbone.

Broadside (OG 1049, ABV 4.7%) ◆
Rich, malty aroma with blackberries and dried fruit. Rich and full flavours of malt and fruit, with roast and caramel notes and subtle hops. Well-balanced, long-lasting aftertaste.

Tally Ho (OG 1075, ABV 7%) 🍺 🍾

Adur

Brick Barn, Charlton Court, Mouse Lane, Steyning, West Sussex, BN44 3DG
☎ (01903) 867614

Office: 2 Sullington Way, Shoreham-by-Sea, West Sussex, BN43 6PJ ⊕ adurvalleycoop.com

⊠ Adur Brewery, nestled in the heart of the South Downs, was launched in 2008 on a 5.5-barrel plant, marking the return of brewing to the Adur Valley after an interval of nearly 100 years. The brewery was sold to the Adur Valley Co-Operative Ltd in 2012, including the Adur Brewery name and recipes. A large part of the output is sold as bottle-conditioned beer. ‼ ◆ RAIB

Ropetackle Golden Ale (OG 1036, ABV 3.4%)
A light, golden ale with an initial sweetness and delicate aroma balanced by a dry finish.

Hop Token: Amarillo (OG 1040, ABV 4%)
An amber-coloured bitter with notes of peach and grapefruit in both aroma and taste, a good bitterness and a long, dry finish.

Hop Token: Summit (OG 1040, ABV 4%)

Velocity (OG 1044, ABV 4.4%)
Traditional best bitter with a hoppy aroma and a hint of marmalade in the taste.

Black William (OG 1055, ABV 5%)
A rich, black stout with dark chocolate aroma and roasted flavours.

Robbie's Red (OG 1050, ABV 5.2%)
A strong red-brown ale with an aroma of malt and hops. Slight initial sweetness leads to complex flavours including smoky orange peel and a satisfying bitterness which persists into the long finish.

AJ's 👁

Unit 12, Ashmore Industrial Estate, Longacre Street, Walsall, WS2 8QG ☎ 07860 585911 ⊠ ajs-ales@hotmail.com

⊠ Established in 2015 using a five-barrel plant, AJ's has recently added a further fermenting vessel and a cool room. Brewing takes place regularly three times a week and mainly local Black Country pubs, local wholesalers and Wetherspoon pubs are supplied. ◆

Stuck on Blondes (ABV 3.9%)
Straw-coloured session ale

Best Bitter (ABV 4%)
Fruity, golden-coloured bitter.

SPA (ABV 4.2%)
A smooth pale ale.

Stuck in the Mud (ABV 4.3%)
Smooth, dark stout.

Ruby Red (ABV 4.4%)
A full-bodied ruby ale.

Stuck in the Doghouse (ABV 4.7%)
A bittersweet, golden-coloured ale.

Alcazar

See Basin City

Alchemist

See Golden Duck

Ale House Rock (NEW)

Dean Park, Peebles, EH45 8DD ☎ 07722 388155
⊕ alehouserockbrewery.co.uk

Brewing began in 2016, run by a husband-and-wife team. There are plans to open a micropub on site in 2017.

Smooth Criminal (OG 1039, ABV 3.9%)

Suicide Blonde (OG 1040, ABV 4%)

Bitter Sweet Symphony (OG 1041, ABV 4.1%)

Rock the Cas'Bar (OG 1042, ABV 4.2%)

White Riot (OG 1045, ABV 4.5%)

Storm Bringer IPA (OG 1050, ABV 5%)

Alechemy SIBA

Unit 2c, Young Square, Brucefield Industry Park, Livingston, EH54 9BX
☎ (01506) 413634 ☎ 07748 156973
⊕ alechemybrewing.com

Dr James Davies, a keen craft brewer and chemist, started brewing in 2012. A 12-barrel plant is used. New beers are being produced regularly: see website for details. Beers can be found in pubs across the UK. ◆ RAIB

Starlaw (OG 1040, ABV 3.5%)
Session beer with citrus and tropical fruit character.

Rhapsody (OG 1038, ABV 3.8%)
Extra pale ale.

Ritual (OG 1042, ABV 4.1%) ◆
Well-balanced golden ale. A strong hop character, balanced by malt and fruit with a long and dry finish.

Five Sisters (OG 1045, ABV 4.3%) ◆
Flavoursome tawny beer with excellent balance of malt, hops and fruit plus hints of roast and caramel. Lingering distinctive finish.

Photon (OG 1043, ABV 4.3%)

10 Storey Malt Bomb (OG 1049, ABV 4.5%)
Modern take on a traditional 80/- using 10 different malts.

Bad Day at the Office (OG 1047, ABV 4.5%)
Golden ale dry hopped with Australian varieties.

Miss America (ABV 4.5%)

Black Aye PA (OG 1047, ABV 4.6%) ◆
A dark robust beer with substantial malt and a significant hop character. Roast, caramel and fruit add to the complexity.

Milk Stout (ABV 5.3%)

Citra Burst (OG 1056, ABV 5.4%)

Heavily hopped pale ale bursting with grapefruit and tangerine aromas with a pleasant bitter aftertaste.

AleCraft

c/o Farmers Boy, 134 London Rd, St Albans, Hertfordshire, AL1 1PQ ☎ 07939 634677

Office: 17 Springhill, Nuneaton, Warwickshire, CV10 0NP ⊕ alecraftmanagement.co.uk

AleCraft began brewing in 2012 as a cuckoo brewery utilising the equipment at the Verulam brewery in St Albans. Beers are delivered direct to Yorkshire, the Midlands and the south east. RAIB

Simplicity (OG 1038, ABV 3.6%)
A straw-coloured session bitter with a hoppy nose and flavour.

Sauvin So Good (OG 1039, ABV 4%)
Straw-coloured ale with a massive citrus and gooseberry nose and flavour that lingers through to the long bitter finish.

Night on the Tiles (OG 1044, ABV 4.7%)
Golden-coloured American pale ale with a big hop character.

Bartholomew Porter (OG 1048, ABV 4.8%)
A deep ruby-coloured, almost black ale, with massive chocolate, burnt and roast malt flavours complemented by hops.

Fudgey Porter (OG 1048, ABV 4.8%)
A version of Bartholomew Porter with vanilla fudge added.

High Five (OG 1056, ABV 5.9%)
A combination of five hop varieties gives this IPA a big, generous hop character.

Sonoma (OG 1070, ABV 8%)
An American-style double IPA. Deep golden in colour with a big hop character.

Aleyard (NEW)

Home Farm, Riddlesworth, Norfolk, IP22 2TD ☎ (01953) 681005 ✉ aleyardbrewery@aol.com

Established in 2015, Aleyard is based on a farm, and has a brewing capacity of 2.5 barrels (410 litres). Brewing takes place two or three times a week. All beers are bottle conditioned and are given a minimum six-week, in-bottle conditioning period prior to sale via small, local shops. The beers contain only malted barley (some contain wheat), water, hops and yeast. No finings or chemicals are added during the brewing or fermentation processes. RAIB

Ales of Scilly SIBA

2b Porthmellon Industrial Estate, St Mary's, Isles of Scilly, Cornwall, TR21 0JY
☎ (01720) 423233 ☎ 07810 816681
⊕ alesofscilly.co.uk

⊠ Opened in 2001, Ales of Scilly is the most south-westerly brewery in Britain. Several island pubs are supplied, with occasional exports to mainland beer festivals. ‼☞♦

Schiller (OG 1038, ABV 3.8%)

Challenger (OG 1039, ABV 4.2%)

Alfred's SIBA

Unit 5B, Scylla Industrial Estate, Winnall Valley Road, Winchester, Hampshire, SO23 0LD
☎ (01962) 859999 ⊕ alfredsbrewery.co.uk

Alfred's is a 3.5-barrel brewhouse opened by Steve and Isabelle Haigh in 2012. Steve previously brewed for three other renowned Hampshire breweries. Deliveries are made to pubs within 15 miles of Winchester. ‼☞♦

Saxon Bronze (OG 1038, ABV 3.8%)
Easy-drinking amber-coloured session beer with a crisp finish.

All Day

Salle Brewery Barns 14, 15, 16, Salle Moor Farm, Wood Dalling Road, Salle, Norfolk, NR10 4SB
☎ (01603) 951173 ☎ 07825 604887
⊕ alldaybrewing.co.uk

⊠ Located in former farm buildings, the brewery has established its own hop yard, to be self sufficient in traditional (tall) varieties of hop. Hops are frozen and used to produce a range of green hop beers throughout the year. A tap room and shop are open at weekends and other ad hoc hours. Organic cider is also produced. A changing range of beers is available. ♦V

Drink Me (OG 1053, ABV 5%)
Distinctly hoppy with strong bitterness, but balanced malt and body.

All Hallows

▤ Main Street, Goodmanham, East Yorkshire, YO43 3JA
☎ (01430) 873849 ⊕ goodmanhamarms.co.uk

⊚ Abbie Logozzi, landlady of the Goodmanham Arms, started brewing in 2012 in outbuildings behind the pub. The ex-Goodmanham Brewery Buildings were purchased and a five-barrel plant installed. The brewery name comes from the adjacent 12th-century All Hallows Church. Local legendary characters are used in the naming of some of the beers. Brews are supplied to the pub, beer festivals when requested, and mainly to local free trade. ♦

Peg Fyfe Dark Mild (OG 1040, ABV 3.6%)

Ragged Robyn (OG 1058, ABV 4.8%)
A traditional ruby-coloured heritage ale.

No Notion Porter (OG 1060, ABV 5.6%)

Allendale SIBA ◉

Allen Mills, Allendale, Northumberland, NE47 9EQ
☎ (01434) 618686 ⊕ allendalebrewery.com

⊚ Brewing returned to Allendale in 2006 and the business now supplies more than 300 pubs, shops and restaurants across the North of England from its 10-barrel plant. ‼☞♦

Wagtail Best Bitter (OG 1037, ABV 3.8%) ◗
Amber bitter with spicy aromas and a long, bitter finish.

Golden Plover (OG 1039, ABV 4%) ◗
Light, refreshing, easy-drinking blonde beer with a clean finish.

Pennine Pale (OG 1040, ABV 4%)

A light golden ale, brewed with a trio of American hops for a full citrus fruit flavour and a refreshing finish.

APA (OG 1056, ABV 5.5%)
A full-bodied IPA with citrus and tropical aromas, full of flavour and refreshing bitterness.

Wolf (OG 1053, ABV 5.5%) ◄
Full-bodied red ale with bitterness in the taste giving way to a fruity finish.

Red Rye (OG 1060, ABV 6%)

AllGates ◉

The Old Brewery, Brewery Yard, off Wallgate, Wigan, WN1 1JU
☎ (01942) 234976 ⊕ allgatesbrewery.com

☺ AllGates commenced brewing in 2006 in a fully restored Grade II-listed tower brewery at the rear of Wigan's General Post Office. A modern five-barrel plant is used. Beers are principally delivered to its own nine-pub estate. ‼♦

Florida (OG 1036, ABV 3.6%)
Blonde ale, pale and easy-drinking.

Tag (OG 1036, ABV 3.6%) ◄
Dark brown beer with a malty, fruity aroma. Creamy and malty in taste, with blackberry fruits and a satisfying aftertaste.

California (OG 1037, ABV 3.8%) ◄
A pale yellow beer with a restrained hoppy and fruity aroma. It is clean and fresh-tasting, with hops and fruit in the mouth and a bitter hoppy finish.

Wigan Junction (OG 1038, ABV 3.9%)
A deep golden/copper-coloured traditional session bitter.

Dry Bones (OG 1040, ABV 4%)
Light golden and hoppy with tropical fruits and hints of melon.

Patchcroft (OG 1042, ABV 4.2%)
Pale and fruity.

Allsaints

c/o Coastal Brewery, Unit 10B, Cardrew Industrial Estate, Redruth, Cornwall, TR15 1SS ☎ 07790 274112

Formerly known as Doghouse Brewery, which closed in 2007, Allsaints recommenced production in 2008 using spare capacity at Keltek Brewery. In 2009 the brewery began using spare capacity at Coastal Brewery in Redruth. Brewing is currently suspended.

Almasty

Unit 11, Algernon Industrial Estate, New York Road, Shiremoor, NE27 0NB

⊗ Opened in 2014, this one-man-operated 10-barrel plant produces unfined, unfiltered beers. The brewery tap is the Free Trade Inn, Byker. Pumpclips are made from screen-printed, hand-sawn logs. The beer range continuously changes, with monthly output always including heavily hopped pale ales/IPAs plus saisons, sours, porters and stouts. Outlets are supplied across the UK. A barrel-ageing programme is also in place. ‼♦

Alnwick

Beers are contract brewed by Cumberland and Daleside (qv).

Alphabet SIBA

99 Northern Western Street, Ardwick, Manchester, M12 6JL ☎ 07540 534350 ⊕ alphabetbrewing.co.uk

Alphabet began brewing in 2014 and is situated in Manchester city centre under railway arches. It has a 60-barrel capacity with a 10-barrel kit and focuses mainly on keg-style beers, which are unfiltered and unpasteurised and often in a KeyKeg container. The brewery also bottles its own beers. Cask beers can be supplied for beer festivals.

Alphabeta (NEW)

⊟ Pittcue, 1 The Avenue, Devonshire Square, London, EC2M 4YP
☎ (020) 7324 7770

⊗ Alphabeta is a small in-house brewery contiguous with the Pittcue restaurant. ♦

C (ABV 3.8%)

D (ABV 4.3%)

B (ABV 4.6%)

A (ABV 5.6%)

Amazing (NEW)

⊟ Ship Inn, 65 High Street, Sandgate, Kent, CT20 3AH
☎ (01303) 248525

⊗ Amazing was set up in 2016 using a four-barrel plant and is situated at the Ship Inn, Sandgate. ‼

Cotter VC (ABV 4%)

Amber SIBA

Unit 7, Outram Business Centre, Whiteley Road, Ripley, Derbyshire, DE5 3QL
☎ (01773) 512864 ⊕ amberales.co.uk

⊗ Amber Ales began production in 2006 on a five-barrel plant obtained from the former Firkin brewpub chain. Five core beers and a range of experimental and seasonal ales are produced, all available at the brewery tap, the Talbot Taphouse in Ripley. Around 50 outlets are supplied direct, further afield via distributors. Bottle-conditioned beers are suitable for vegans. ‼ ☛♦ RAIB V

Chocolate Orange Stout (OG 1040, ABV 4%)
Brewed with chocolate malt and curacao orange peel. Bitter chocolate orange in a glass.

Derbyshire Gold (OG 1039, ABV 4%)
Well-hopped, full-flavoured golden ale.

Original Black Stout (OG 1040, ABV 4%)
Traditional stout made with a complex blend of five malts to give a full-flavoured, yet smooth and easy-drinking base with a subtle hop aroma.

Barnes Wallis (OG 1040, ABV 4.1%)
An easy-drinking IPA-style bitter, copper-coloured with a full malt flavour.

Revolution (OG 1047, ABV 4.5%)
Highly-hopped, spicy golden ale with a touch of rye, giving a strong citrus flavour.

Dambuster (OG 1051, ABV 5.5%)
Well-hopped golden ale.

Imperial IPA (OG 1058, ABV 6.5%)
Traditional IPA with a substantial malty base and a big hop profile.

Ambridge

Unit 2a, Priory Piece Business Park, Priory Farm Lane, Inkberrow, Worcestershire, WR7 4HT
☎ (01386) 792191 ☎ 07500 046391
⊕ ambridgebrewery.co.uk

☺ Ambridge commenced brewing in 2013, initially for the family pub, the Bulls Head in Inkberrow. Later that year they acquired the Wyre Piddle Brewery. The beers from both breweries continue to be brewed but during 2013 relocated to a single brew house on the outskirts of the village. On-demand brews supplement the core and seasonal range, and some small-run bottling is carried out.
‼ ◆ RAIB

Sticky Dog (OG 1040, ABV 4%)
A smooth, easy-drinking golden ale with citrus hop aroma and a refreshing, slightly bitter finish.

Honey Bunny (OG 1043, ABV 4.2%)
A light, honey-infused ale, smooth and full-flavoured.

Worcestershire Pale Ale (WPA) (OG 1043, ABV 4.2%)
A premium pale ale with a good balance of hops and malt. Hops carry on from the taste to a bittersweet finish

Citra (OG 1044, ABV 4.4%)
Light and refreshing with a zesty lemon and lime bitter finish.

Jester (OG 1048, ABV 4.8%)
British Jester single-hopped beer with a punchy aroma of grapefruit and tropical fruits. Pale gold with a delicate bitter finish.

Ampthill (NEW) SIBA

Unit D, The Sidings, Station Road, Ampthill, Bedfordshire, MK45 2QY
☎ (01525) 620015 ⊕ ampthillbrewhouse.co.uk

A six-barrel microbrewery established in 2015.
⊨ RAIB

Session Ale (ABV 3.3%)
A lighter ale with a subtle spice and honey aroma ending with a gentle citrus kick.

Golden Ale (ABV 4.1%)
A smooth and refreshing golden ale.

Indian Pale Ale (ABV 4.5%)
A refreshing, distinctly hoppy dark-coloured ale.

An Teallach SIBA ☜

Camusnagaul, Dundonnell, Garve, IV23 2QT
☎ (01854) 633306 ✉ ataleco1@yahoo.co.uk

An Teallach was formed in 2001 by husband-and-wife team David and Wilma Orr, on the family croft on the shores of Little Loch Broom, Wester Ross. More than 60 pubs are supplied. ‼ ◆

Beallach Na Ba (ABV 3.8%) ◣
Golden-amber hoppy brew with some background malts.

Beinn Dearg Ale (OG 1044, ABV 3.8%) ◣
A well-balanced malty, hoppy, sweetish beer with a long, malty bitter aftertaste.

Ale (OG 1042, ABV 4.2%) ◣
A classic pint in the Scottish 80/- tradition. Plenty of malt in the nicely balanced bittersweet taste.

Crofters Pale Ale (OG 1042, ABV 4.2%) ⬚ ◣
A good quaffing, lightly flavoured golden ale. Citrus hops in the taste and with a slight astringency in the finish.

Suilven (OG 1043, ABV 4.3%) ◣
A refreshing yellow brew with plenty of citris fruits and hops throughout.

Kildonan (OG 1044, ABV 4.4%) ◣
Plenty of fruit and a good smack of bitterness in this golden ale.

Anarchy SIBA

Unit 5, Whitehouse Farm Centre, Stannington, Northumberland, NE61 6AW
☎ (01670) 789755 ☎ 07702 810111
⊕ anarchybrewco.com

☺A 10-barrel brewery ran by an enthusiastic team producing a range of hand-crafted beers and lagers with big, bold flavours. ‼ ⊨ RAIB

Smoke Bomb (OG 1043, ABV 3.9%)
A bitter with a light, smoky nose and Bavarian smoked ham and citrus flavours matched with dark, smooth toffee malts.

Blonde Star (OG 1041, ABV 4.1%)
Lemon, grapefruit and passion fruit flavours from the hops combine with pale malts to give a crisp and fresh, light-bodied session blonde.

Citra Star (OG 1041, ABV 4.1%)
Citrus, grapefruit, lemon, lime and passion fruit flavours come from the hops to give a clean, crisp, light-bodied blonde.

Rough Justice (OG 1046, ABV 4.5%)
Resinous pine and orange flavours create a dry and bitter dark red rye beer.

Grin & Bare It (OG 1050, ABV 5%)
A pale wheat beer.

Urban Assault (OG 1050, ABV 5%)
Medium-bodied light red pale ale with heavy notes of lemon, orange and passion fruit in the flavour, followed by a bitter finish.

Crime Scene (OG 1056, ABV 5.5%)
Fruit-flavoured, medium-bodied amber beer made using caramel malts that melt into a long-lasting bitter aftertaste.

Quiet Riot (OG 1063, ABV 6.6%)
Kiwi fruit, lime and orange zest flavours combine to give a big bitterness that is balanced with sweet malts.

Sublime Chaos (OG 1075, ABV 7%)
Liquorice, chocolate and caramel flavoured breakfast stout infused with Ethiopian Guji natural coffee beans backed with dark malts.

Anchor Springs

See Littlehampton

Andrews

1 Railway Cottages, Cummertrees, Annan, DG12 5QG
☎ (01461) 700387 ☎ 07785 613321
✉ aemmerson999@googlemail.com

Andrews Ales began brewing in 2011 and is situated at the family home in Cummertrees. Brewing capacity is three barrels. Cask and bottle-conditioned beers are supplied direct by the brewery to pubs and independent shops. ◆ RAIB

Supus Lupus (OG 1036, ABV 3.6%)
A straw-coloured session ale with a light zesty finish.

Cummertrees Pale Ale (OG 1040, ABV 4%)
Full-bodied IPA-style beer, refreshingly clean and crisp.

Wee Willy Wonky (OG 1042, ABV 4.2%)
A classic British bitter.

Into the Darkness (OG 1046, ABV 4.3%)
A deliciously dark stout made with chocolate and black malts and hopped with classic British varieties. Full-bodied and quaffable.

Andwell SIBA 👁

Andwell Lane, Andwell, Hampshire, RG27 9PA
☎ (01256) 761044 ⊕ andwells.com

⊠ Brewing commenced in 2008 on a 10-barrel plant. It relocated and expanded in 2011 to an idyllic riverside location with a new bespoke 20-barrel plant and offers tours and direct sales from its brewery shop. Beer is distributed within a 40-mile radius to Hampshire, Surrey, Wiltshire, Berkshire, Greater London and the Isle of Wight. More than 200 outlets are supplied. ‼️🚆◆

Resolute Bitter (OG 1038, ABV 3.8%) 🍺
An easy-drinking session bitter. A malty aroma leads into an initially malty flavour with some bitterness and a sweetish finish.

Gold Muddler (OG 1039, ABV 3.9%) 🍺
Light golden standard bitter. Aroma of hops and malt; characteristics carried into the palate with solid bitterness and dry, biscuity finish.

Red Mist (ABV 4.1%) 🍺
Pale brown best bitter brewed for Red Mist Leisure. Predominantly bitter, with a malty backbone and a dry, bitter finish.

King John (OG 1042, ABV 4.2%) 🍺
Malty best bitter, low in hops with short initial bitterness and underlying sweetness, leading to some dryness in the finish.

Rudy Darter (OG 1047, ABV 4.6%) 🍺
A ruby chestnut ale with a hoppy, spicy aroma. The beer has a full-bodied and fruity taste with a dry finish.

Angel SIBA

62a Furlong Lane, Halesowen, West Midlands, B63 2TA ☎ 07986 382919 ⊕ angelales.co.uk

Angel Ales began commercial brewing in 2011 and is expanding outlets. The brewery building has been a Chapel of Rest, a coffin makers' workshop and a pattern makers before becoming a brewhouse. Beers are produced using organic materials where possible, and all stouts are vegan-friendly. ◆ RAIB V

Ale (OG 1042, ABV 4.1%)
Ultra pale and intensely hopped bitter with a citrus nose and lingering bitter finish.

Ginger Stout (OG 1048, ABV 4.8%)
A summer stout produced using fresh ginger root.

Animal

See XT

Anspach & Hobday

118 Druid Street, Bermondsey, London, SE1 2HH
☎ (020) 8617 9510 ⊕ anspachandhobday.com

⊠ Anspach & Hobday began commercial brewing in 2014 using a one-barrel plant, upgrading to 2.5 barrels later that year. In 2016 the brewery was upgraded again to a seven-barrel plant. It is based in an railway arch in Bermondsey. Beer is mostly bottled or kegged with some available cask-conditioned. A brewery taproom is open at weekends. 🚆 RAIB V

Anstey (NEW)

40 Derby Road, Anstey, Leicestershire, LE7 7DJ
☎ 07960 776843 ✉ stuartslessor@me.com

Anstey is a small one-barrel brewery operated on a part-time basis, which commenced brewing in 2015. There are plans for expansion, relocation and to create a brewpub.

Paleface (ABV 4.8%)

Father's Favourite (ABV 5%)

Antoine's (NEW)

The Garden Shed at 25 Ashley Road, Westcott, Dorking, Surrey, RH4 3QJ ☎ 07545 828589
✉ antoine@1beer.co.uk

A tiny brewery producing occasional KeyKegs in a variety of styles.

Appleby

Unit D3, Cross Croft Industrial Estate, Wellhouse Road, Appleby-in-Westmorland, Cumbria, CA16 6HX
☎ (01768) 353846 ⊕ applebybrewery.co.uk

Established by Fred Mills in March 2015 using a former Rolls-Royce storage unit on the outskirts of the town. The beers are available at selected pubs across Cumbria, but mainly in the Eden Valley area. ◆

Senior Moment (OG 1039, ABV 3.9%)
An old-fashioned bitter.

Midlife Crisis (OG 1042, ABV 4.2%)

Appleford

Unit 14, Highlands Farm, High Road, Brightwell-cum-Sotwell, Oxfordshire, OX10 0QX
☎ (01235) 848055 ⊕ applefordbrewery.co.uk

Appleford Brewery opened in 2006 when two farm units were converted to house an eight-barrel plant. Deliveries are made to a number of local outlets, as well as nationally, via the brewery or through wholesalers. ◆ RAIB

Brightwell Gold (OG 1041, ABV 4%)

Power Station (OG 1043, ABV 4.2%)
A copper-coloured, slightly malty bitter.

Arbor SIBA 👁

181 Easton Road, Easton, Bristol, BS5 0HQ
☎ (0117) 329 2711 ⊕ arborales.co.uk

⊗ Arbor Ales began brewing in 2007 and has relocated and expanded several times, most recently in 2015. A wide range of beers is brewed, with particular pride taken in darker ales. 🍽◆RAIB

Motueka (OG 1037, ABV 3.8%)

Triple Hop (OG 1038, ABV 4%)

Oz Bomb (OG 1045, ABV 4.7%)

Devil Made Me Brew It (OG 1056, ABV 5.5%)

Why Kick a Moo Cow (OG 1052, ABV 5.5%)

Yakima Valley (OG 1067, ABV 7%) 🔸
A strong, full-bodied IPA. Hoppy and very fruity. Sweetness which is well balanced with bitterness, lasting into a soft bitter aftertaste.

Arcane Bridge

Arch 5, King Edward Bridge, Newcastle upon Tyne, NE1 3TQ ☎ 07932 774745 ✉ arcanebridge@aol.com

Formerly known as Temptation Brewery. Arcane Bridge began brewing in 2016 using a 5.5-barrel plant, supplying local outlets within a 20-mile radius of the brewery. A tasting bar is located on the premises.

Eden (ABV 4%)

Turncoat (ABV 4.5%)

Bosch (ABV 5.2%)

Archerfield

See Knops

Archers

See Evan Evans

Ards

34b Carrowdore Road, Newtonards, Co Down, BT22 2LX ☎ 07515 558406
✉ ardsbrewing@blackwood34.plus.com

Ards began brewing in 2011 using a 100-litre plant. A five-barrel plant is now in operation, allowing cask production in addition to the increasing range of bottle-conditioned beers. RAIB

Rockin' Goose (OG 1044, ABV 4.4%)

Bally Black (OG 1046, ABV 4.6%)

Hip Hop (OG 1050, ABV 5%)

Carey Man (OG 1051, ABV 5.1%)

Pig Island (OG 1052, ABV 5.2%)

Argyll SIBA

Cuan Mor, 60 George Street, Oban, PA34 5SD
☎ (01631) 564492 ⊕ obanbaybrewery.co.uk

Argyll Breweries was formed in 2010 following the merger of Oban Bay and Isle of Mull breweries,

continuing to trade under those names. Cask production is only at the Oban site. ‼

Kilt Lifter (OG 1039, ABV 3.9%)

Skinny Blonde (OG 1041, ABV 4.1%)

Ginger Jakey (OG 1042, ABV 4.2%)

Skelpt Lug (OG 1042, ABV 4.2%)

Fair Puggled (OG 1045, ABV 4.5%)

Arkell's SIBA IFBB 👁

Kingsdown, Swindon, Wiltshire, SN2 7RU
☎ (01793) 823026 ⊕ arkells.com

Arkells Brewery was established in 1843 by John Arkell and the Arkell family still brew beer in the original Victorian brewhouse every day. The brewery owns 96 pubs in Berkshire, Gloucestershire, Oxfordshire and Wiltshire. Seasonal beers are brewed frequently, often linked to sporting and other national events. ‼🍽◆

Wiltshire Gold (OG 1038, ABV 3.7%)
A light golden-coloured ale with a sweet, malty flavour and a mellow floral hop aroma followed by a distinctive hoppy taste.

3B (OG 1040, ABV 4%) 🔸
A medium brown beer with a strong, sweetish malt/caramel flavour. The hops come through strongly in the aftertaste, which is lingering and dry.

HOPeration IPA (OG 1041, ABV 4.2%)
Pale in colour with a slight golden hue, it has a strong hop aroma with floral and lemon overtones.

Bee's Organic (OG 1045, ABV 4.5%)
Organically grown malted barley, hops and organically produced honey give this golden ale a light, fresh taste.

Moonlight (OG 1046, ABV 4.5%)
Golden auburn in colour with a warm toasty aroma and distinctive citrus hoppy flavour.

Arkwright's

52-54 Aqueduct Street, Preston, Lancashire, PR1 7RE
☎ 07944 912326 ⊕ arkwrightsbrewery.com

Arkwright's began brewing at the rear of the Real Ale Shop on Lovat Road in 2010 using a 2.5-barrel plant. In 2014 the plant was upgraded to a 10-barrel plant previously used by Wolf brewery and moved to a nearby industrial unit. ◆

Arran SIBA

Cladach, Brodick, Isle of Arran, KA27 8DE
☎ (01770) 302353

Office: 100 Wellington Street, Glasgow, G2 6DH
⊕ arranbrewery.com

The brewery opened in 2000 using a 20-barrel plant. Around 300 outlets around the UK are supplied direct. Beers are also produced under the Devil's Dyke Brewery name. ‼🍽◆RAIB

Guid Ale (OG 1038, ABV 3.8%)
A golden, refreshing session ale with a delicate balance of malt and fruit.

Red Squirrel (OG 1038, ABV 3.9%)
Session beer with a balanced malt and hop blend with a hint of liquorice and burnt toffee, and a characteristic nutty aroma.

Dark (OG 1042, ABV 4.3%) ◆
A well-balanced malty beer with plenty of roast and hop in the taste and a dry, bitter finish.

Sunset (OG 1042, ABV 4.4%)
A mid-amber summer ale, light perfumed aroma, good balance of malt, fruit and hops with a pleasant dry finish.

Clyde Puffer (OG 1045, ABV 4.5%)
A stout with a deep dark colour. Sweet and mellow with a low hop taste.

Fireside (OG 1044, ABV 4.7%)
A smooth, malty brew with a pleasant hop character. Bittersweet finish with a hint of ginger.

Blonde (OG 1048, ABV 5%) ◆
A hoppy beer with substantial fruit balance. The taste is balanced and the finish increasingly bitter. An aromatic strong bitter that drinks below its weight.

Brewery Dug (OG 1055, ABV 5.5%)
An American-style IPA with a refreshing citrus body and a dry, lemon-zest bitter finish.

ID (OG 1065, ABV 6%)
A dark, hoppy beer in the style of a dark IPA.

Arrow

c/o Wine Vaults, 37 High Street, Kington, Herefordshire, HR5 3BJ
☎ (01544) 230685 ✉ deanewright@yahoo.co.uk

Brewer Deane Wright built this five-barrel brewery at the rear of the Wine Vaults and started brewing in 2005. The Wine Vaults is the only pub outlet for Arrow Bitter.

Bitter (OG 1042, ABV 4%)

Art Brew

Brightwater Farm, Sutcombe, Devon, EX22 7QE
☎ 07881 783626

⊠ Brewing started in 2008 on a five-barrel plant near the Jurassic Coast. In 2016 the brewery relocated to a new site with a brewery tap in Devon. ◆ RAIB

Milk Stout (OG 1045, ABV 4.5%)

Monkey IPA (OG 1058, ABV 6.4%)
A massively-hopped proper IPA.

Artisan

See Evan Evans

Artisan Brewing

See Pipes

Arundel SIBA 👁

Unit C7, Ford Airfield Industrial Estate, Ford, Arundel, West Sussex, BN18 0HY
☎ (01903) 733111 ⊕ arundelbrewery.co.uk

⊠ Founded in 1992, Arundel Brewery is the historic town's first brewery in 70 years. A seasonal beer is alway available, plus occasional brands in selected months. The brewery opened a shop in 2014, at River Road, Arundel, but beer and other merchandise can also be purchased from the brewery office. ‼ ☰ ◆

Black Stallion (OG 1037, ABV 3.7%) ◆
A dark mild with well-defined chocolate and roast character. The aftertaste is not powerful but the initial flavours remain in the clean finish.

Castle (OG 1038, ABV 3.8%) ◆
A pale tawny beer with fruit and malt noticeable in the aroma. The flavour has a good balance of malt, fruit and hops, with a dry, hoppy finish.

Sussex Gold (OG 1042, ABV 4.2%) ◆
A golden-coloured best bitter with a strong floral hop aroma. The ale is clean-tasting and bitter for its strength, with a tangy citrus flavour. The initial hop and fruit die to a dry and bitter finish.

Sussex IPA (OG 1045, ABV 4.5%)
Formerly known as Heritage IPA. A special bitter with a complex roast malt flavour leading to a fruity, hoppy, bitter-sweet finish.

Stronghold (OG 1047, ABV 4.7%) ◆
A smooth, full-flavoured premium bitter. A good balance of malt, fruit and hops comes through in this rich, chestnut-coloured beer.

Trident (OG 1050, ABV 5%)
An amber-coloured strong beer with a citrus, fruity aroma. The taste is clean and refreshing with a hoppy, fruity flavour and a pleasant dry bitter finish.

Wild Heaven (OG 1052, ABV 5.2%)
A full-flavoured American-style pale ale with strong grapefruit, orange and lime notes and a lingering, dry, bitter finish.

Ascot SIBA 👁

Unit 5, Compton Place Business Centre, Surrey Avenue, Camberley, Surrey, GU15 3DX
☎ (01276) 686696 ⊕ ascot-ales.co.uk

⊠ Ascot Ales started production in 2007 on a four-barrel plant in a small industrial unit. The brewery has successfully expanded over the years.. ‼ ☰ ◆ RAIB V

Alley Cat Ale (OG 1038, ABV 3.8%) ◆
A pale brown session bitter with malt flavours present throughout. Dry with a lasting sharp and bitter finish.

On the Rails (OG 1039, ABV 3.8%) ◆
Chocolaty mild with a notable hop character throughout, bittersweet in the taste and aftertaste, with a dry finish.

Aureole Ale (OG 1039, ABV 4%) ◆
A lemon aroma leads to a dry, bitter taste, with more citrus flavours. Hoppy finish with a hint of sweetness.

Posh Pooch (OG 1042, ABV 4.2%) ◆
A best bitter with balancing biscuity malt sweetness. Some citrus fruitiness and a clean hoppy aftertaste.

Penguin Porter (OG 1045, ABV 4.5%)

Alligator Ale (OG 1047, ABV 4.6%) ◆
Some grapefruit in the aroma, with hop and bitterness in the taste and plenty of balancing biscuit in the aroma and aftertaste.

Single Hop (OG 1045, ABV 4.6%)
Copper-coloured IPA brewed each month showcasing a single hop variety.

Anastasia's Exile Stout (OG 1049, ABV 5%) 🍺 ◆
Burnt coffee aromas lead to a roast malt flavour in this black beer. Notably fruity throughout, with a bittersweet aftertaste.

Rhino Rye (OG 1049, ABV 5%)

Red IPA (OG 1054, ABV 5.5%)
An intensely hopped red IPA, giving a citrus, grapefruit taste.

Anastasia's Imperial Stout (OG 1078, ABV 8%) 🍺

Ash Valley

🍴 Prince of Wales, Green Tye, nr Much Hadham, Hertfordshire, SG10 6JP
☎ (01279) 842139 ☎ 07966 474730
⊕ thepow.co.uk/the-brewery

⊠ The brewery is part of the Prince of Wales pub in Green Tye, run by the landlord. Three regular beers and occasional specials are produced. Most of the beer is sold at the pub and occasional CAMRA beer festivals, and a small amount is swapped with other brewers.

Prince of Wales IPA (OG 1039, ABV 3.9%)
An easy-drinking, well-balanced traditional bitter.

Ash (OG 1041, ABV 4%)
A pale ale brewed with lager malt and a small amount of wheat. All American hops are balanced with local honey.

Best Bitter (OG 1040, ABV 4%)
An easy-drinking best bitter, mid-brown in colour.

Ashdown (NEW) SIBA 👁

Buckhurst Park, Withyham, East Sussex, TN7 4BN
☎ (01892) 770532 ☎ 07530 604064
⊕ ashdownales.co.uk

Brewing began in 2016.

Dawning Light (ABV 3.5%)
A golden-coloured English session bitter with a fruity palate and floral nose.

Blonde (ABV 3.8%)
An amber-coloured ale with grapefruit, citrus aroma, a lemon, grapefruit taste and dry finish.

Blue Sky (ABV 4%)
A best bitter, deep caramel in colour with a fruity aroma.

Morning Dew (ABV 4.3%)
A refreshing pale ale bursting with orange and citrus, backed up with fragrant hops.

Sussex Sunset (ABV 4.5%)
A traditional ruby ale. Its fruity background is complemented by crisp, clean hoppy aromas.

Eagle (ABV 4.7%)
An American-style pale ale, zingy with aromatic hops.

Forest Fire (ABV 4.9%)
An oak-smoked, rich porter.

Royal Gold (ABV 5.1%)
An IPA with citrus and grapefruit flavours complemented by a subtle aroma of spices and cedar.

Ashley Down

15 Wathen Road, St Andrews, Bristol, BS6 5BY

☎ (0117) 983 6567 ☎ 07563 751200
✉ ashleydownbrewery@gmail.com

⊠ Ashley Down began brewing in 2011 using a 5.5-barrel plant in the owner's garage. There are plans for expansion and to relocate to new premises. ◆ RAIB

Remedy (OG 1037.5, ABV 4%) ◆
Characteristics of a dark mild and a red. A pronounced aroma of crystal malt precedes a malty astringent taste with hints of toffee and dark fruit. The aftertaste is thin.

Landlords Best (OG 1040, ABV 4.2%) ◆
Malty best bitter with balancing hops and astringency in the aftertaste.

Pale Ale (OG 1040.5, ABV 4.3%) ◆
Sweet best bitter balanced with hoppy bitterness, which continues to the aftertaste.

Ashleyhay SIBA

New Buildings Farm, Taylors Lane, Ashleyhay, Derbyshire, DE4 4AH ☎ 07708 050019
✉ jim@ashleyhaybrewery.co.uk

⊠ The brewery is situated near the market town of Wirksworth, Derbyshire. Its ales are produced using natural spring water, solar energy and, where feasible, with hops grown on site. Traditional methods are combined with modern hopping techniques. It is planned to move production to a barn at the Royal Oak in Wirksworth while also retaining existing premises.

Citra Pale (OG 1043, ABV 4.3%)

CJ Porter (OG 1048, ABV 4.8%)

Red Tape IPA (OG 1050, ABV 5%)

Knobstick IPA (OG 1053, ABV 5.3%)

Ned's Big Shed (OG 1054, ABV 5.4%)

Ashover SIBA

🍴 Unit 1, Derby Road, Clay Cross, Derbyshire, S45 9AG
☎ 07803 708526 ⊕ ashoverbrewery.com

Ashover Brewery first brewed in 2007 on a 3.5-barrel plant in the garage of the cottage next to the Old Poets' Corner in Ashover. In 2015 it took over the former Brown Ales brewery in nearby Clay Cross, and all regular beers are now brewed there, with the original plant in Ashover being used for special and one-off brews. The brewery caters mainly for the Old Poets' Corner and its sister pub, the Poet & Castle in Codnor. Other local free houses and festivals are also supplied. House beers are also produced for pubs within the Brown Ales group. ‼ RAIB

Light Rale (OG 1038, ABV 3.7%) 🍺 ◆
Light in colour and taste, with initial sweet and malt flavours, leading to a bitter finish and aftertaste.

Poets Tipple (OG 1041, ABV 4%) ◆
Complex, tawny-coloured beer that drinks above its strength. Predominantly malty in flavour, with increasing bitterness towards the end.

Littlemoor Citra (OG 1041, ABV 4.1%)
Clean, pale, crisp and refreshing.

Hydro (OG 1043, ABV 4.2%) ◆

Easy to drink golden beer with a predominantly hoppy aroma. Hop and fruit flavours and an initial sweetness lead to a dry, clean finish and aftertaste.

Rainbows End (OG 1045, ABV 4.5%) ◆
Slightly smooth, bitter golden beer with an initial sweetness. Grapefruit and lemon hop flavours come through strongly as the beer gets increasingly dry towards the finish, ending with a bitter, dry aftertaste.

Coffin Lane Stout (OG 1050, ABV 5%) ◆
Excellent example of the style, with a chocolate and coffee flavour, balanced by a little sweetness. Finish is long and quite dry.

Butts Pale Ale (OG 1055, ABV 5.5%) ◆
Pale and strong yet easy to drink golden bitter. Combination of bitter and sweet flavours mingle with an alcoholic kick, leading to a warming yet bitter finish and aftertaste.

Atlantic

Treisaac Farm, Treisaac, Newquay, Cornwall, TR8 4DX
☎ **(01637) 880326** ⊕ **atlanticbrewery.com**

⊗ Specialist microbrewery producing organic and vegan ales. All ales are unfiltered and finings-free. There are nine core brews including four food-matched Dining Ales developed with Michelin chef Nathan Outlaw. Casks are supplied locally and into London, with bottle-conditioned beers available nationally. ◆ RAIB V

Ale (OG 1038, ABV 3.9%) ◆
A pale amber ale, with good body, sweet malt and hints of vanilla. Well hopped yet balanced, including Cornish Fuggles.

Azores (OG 1042, ABV 4.2%) ◆
Pale brown golden ale. Citrus and resinous hops dominate the aroma and taste with tropical fruits. Refreshing bitterness and dryness throughout.

Earl Grey PA (OG 1045, ABV 4.5%)
Straw-coloured session ale with aromatic bergamot and citrus.

Masala Chai PA (OG 1045, ABV 4.5%)
A pale session ale with classic Indian roadhouse spices and black tea tannins.

Smoked Green Tea PA (OG 1045, ABV 4.5%)
A fresh pale ale with green tea, lightly smoked.

Gold (OG 1043, ABV 4.6%) ◆
Refreshing, crisp golden ale lightly spiced with zingy ginger. Dry finish with the lingering light marmalade of First Gold hops.

Pilgrim (OG 1046, ABV 4.6%) ◆
A ruby-brown beer with a malty nose. Malt dominates the creamy taste and finish balanced by bitter and fruity hops.

Bee Keeper (OG 1046, ABV 4.8%)
A smooth, balanced, golden-coloured honey beer.

Blue (OG 1045, ABV 4.8%) ◆
This dark ruby porter floods the palate with sweet malt, roast coffee, dark chocolate, a soft smokiness and orangey nose.

Red (OG 1047, ABV 5%) ◆
Malty, smooth red ale with nutty flavours and natural cloudiness. Dryness of the hop finish is balanced by sweet malt.

Fistral (OG 1048, ABV 5.2%) ◆

Full-flavoured copper wheat beer. Sweet, stone-fruit flavours blend with biscuit malt and citrus hops. Malt finish with hops and dryness.

Discovery – Easterly (OG 1050, ABV 5.5%) ◆
A golden-coloured pale ale with crisp distinct flavours of lime, chilli and ginger. Sweet malt balances the citrus aroma tones.

Discovery – Northerly (OG 1050, ABV 5.5%) ◆
Rich Cornish porter with blackcurrant and molasses. Full-bodied dark roasted malts, hints of chocolate, ripe blackcurrants and black cherries.

Discovery – Southerly (OG 1050, ABV 5.5%) ◆
Smooth blonde ale with elderflower and lemon. Gentle hops, sweet malt with a floral and citrus zest finish.

Discovery – Westerly (OG 1050, ABV 5.5%) ◆
Red Celtic ale with cinnamon and orange. Full-bodied bitter with gentle citrus marmalade and mild nutty spice flavours.

Atlas

See Orkney

Atom SIBA

Unit 4 Food & Tech Park, Malmo Road, Sutton Fields Industrial Estate, Hull, East Yorkshire, HU7 0FY
☎ **07908 737769** ⊕ **atombeers.com**

Atom is a collaboration between Allan Rice and Sarah Thackray, set up in 2013 in a modern industrial unit north-west of Hull city centre. The 10-barrel brewing equipment, which came from Oban Ales, is supplemented by a fermentation capacity of 120 barrels and a conditioning capacity of 120 barrels.

Schrodingers Cat (OG 1035, ABV 3.5%)
A pale ale brewed using different mashing mechanisms creating a full-bodied, low-ABV hop bomb.

Blonde Ale (OG 1040, ABV 4%)
A fresh, smooth, easy-drinking pale beer with citrus notes.

Camomile (OG 1042, ABV 4.2%)
An easy-drinking ale with a fragrant floral aroma created using the finest camomile from the Blending Rooms in Hull.

Pale Ale (OG 1045, ABV 4.5%)
A malty and hoppy pale ale with bags of flavour.

Dark Alchemy (OG 1049, ABV 4.9%)
A rich, complex malt bill with bitterness and aroma from cardamon and coriander but no hops, creating a porter rich in body, smooth and characterful.

India Pale Ale (OG 1056, ABV 5.6%)
Lots of malt and big juicy hops.

Atomic

▤ **c/o Alexandra Arms, 72-73 St James Street, Rugby, Warwickshire, CV21 2SL**
☎ **(01788) 576194** ☎ **07986 983984**

Office: 1 Lower Hillmorton Road, Rugby, Warwickshire, CV21 3ST ⊕ **atomicbrewery.com**

Atomic started production in 2006 and is run by CAMRA members Keith Abbis and Nick Pugh. Two pubs are owned, the Victoria Inn and the Alexandra

Arms, the brewery being located in the garden of the latter, being the owners' latest acquisition. ‼◆

Strike (OG 1039, ABV 3.7%)
A pale golden ale with a sharp, fruity, aromatic aroma and a good sharp bitter finish.

Fission (OG 1040, ABV 3.9%)
An amber-coloured session ale with a good helping of Cascade hops.

Spectrum (OG 1040, ABV 4%)
Pale golden in colour, with a huge grapefruit nose and aroma.

Dark Matter (OG 1041, ABV 4.1%)
A dark, well-hopped ale with hints of chocolate and a good bitter finish.

Fusion (OG 1042, ABV 4.1%)
A golden-coloured ale with a citrus, hoppy aroma, leading to a good bitter finish.

Half Life (OG 1051, ABV 5%)
A premium IPA, golden in colour with a citrus nose to finish.

Attwell's (NEW)

Unit 6, Crossways Business Park, Canterbury Road, St Nicholas at Wade, Kent, CT7 0PQ ☎ 07966 586642 ⊕ attwellsbrewery.co.uk

⊠ A small, family-run microbrewery based on the Isle of Thanet, Attwell's was established in 2014 and produces beers for the micropubs of East Kent. Brewing is currently suspended.

Attwood

See Worcestershire

Austendyke

The Beeches, Austendyke Road, Weston Hills, Spalding, Lincolnshire, PE12 6BZ ☎ 07866 045778

Austendyke Ales began brewing in 2012 using a seven-barrel plant. The brewery is operated on a part-time basis by brewer Charlie Rawlings and business partner Nathan Marshall, who handles sales. The brewery owns and runs its micropub, the Prior's Oven, Spalding, and serves several locally brewed beers by gravity.

Long Lane (OG 1039, ABV 4%)
A traditional copper-coloured bitter.

Sheep Market (OG 1040, ABV 4%)
A copper-coloured, crisp, easy-drinking ale with a bitter finish.

Bakestraw Bitter (OG 1041, ABV 4.1%)
Pale, hoppy best bitter.

Holbeach High Street (OG 1045, ABV 4.5%)
An old-fashioned, dark-coloured best bitter.

Hogsgate (OG 1050, ABV 5%)
A traditional copper-coloured ale.

Axiom

Unit 4a, Wrexham Enterprise Park, Ash Road, North Wrexham Industrial Estate, Wrexham, LL13 9JT ☎ 07544 280353 ⊕ axiombrewing.co.uk

Brewing commenced in 2014 on a self-built four-barrel plant. A core range of beers is available, as

well as occasional experimental beers and collaboration brews.

Taid's Garden (OG 1043, ABV 4.3%)
Delicate and refreshing.

Conclusion (formerly Dusk) (OG 1049, ABV 4.9%)
Rich and dark with notes of figs, raisins and dark chocolate. Bittersweet.

Axton

Pentre Lane, Axton, CH8 9DH
☎ (01745) 855657 ☎ 07756 636415

Office: Archies Bar, 151 High Street, Prestatyn, LL19 9AS ✉ jamesmcgeown@live.co.uk

☺Axton commenced brewing in 2015 on a 1.5-barrel plant mainly supplying Archies Bar in Prestatyn with regular brews, specials, experimental brews and re-creations of old brewery recipes.

Nicky Nacky Noo (OG 1043, ABV 4.3%)
Made with Crystal and Citra hops, giving a caramel butterscotch aftertaste.

Aylesbury

🍺 83 Bicester Road, Aylesbury, Buckinghamshire, HP19 9AZ
☎ (01844) 239237 ⊕ aylesburybrewhouse.co.uk

⊠ Established in 2011 at the Hop Pole as a sister brewery to Vale (qv). Limited edition, one-off beers are brewed on a weekly basis using the old Vale Brewery 12-barrel kit. ‼🍴◆

Ayr

🍺 5 Racecourse Road, Ayr, KA7 2DG
☎ (01292) 263891
✉ anthony.valenti@btinternet.com

☺Ayr began brewing in 2009 on a five-barrel plant and is located at the Glenpark Hotel. As well as the hotel around 50 other outlets are supplied throughout Scotland and England. ‼◆

Leezie Lundie (OG 1037.5, ABV 3.8%) 🍂
A pale golden session ale with hints of grapefruit and a dry lingering finish.

Jolly Beggars (OG 1041, ABV 4.2%) 🍂
A complex best bitter with plenty of character and lingering malty aftertaste.

Rabbie's Porter (OG 1042.5, ABV 4.3%) 🍺 🍂
A robust, full-bodied porter with well-balanced toffee, fruity malt and a slightly smoky finish.

Towzie Tyke (OG 1044.5, ABV 4.6%)
An amber-coloured ale with a refreshingly dry, long and bitter finish.

B&T SIBA 👁

The Brewery, Shefford, Bedfordshire, SG17 5DZ
☎ (01462) 815080 ⊕ banksandtaylor.com

⊠ Banks & Taylor – now just B&T – was founded in 1982. It produces 12 regular beers, plus monthly specials and occasional beers, in an industrial unit close to the town centre. There are six tied houses, all selling B&T beers plus guest beers and real cider. ‼◆

Two Brewers Bitter (OG 1036, ABV 3.6%) 🍂

Bronze-coloured bitter with citrus hop aroma and taste and a dry finish.

Shefford Bitter (OG 1038, ABV 3.8%) ◆
A pale brown beer with a light hop aroma and a hoppy taste leading to a bitter finish.

Shefford Dark Mild (OG 1038, ABV 3.8%) ◆
A dark beer with a well-balanced taste. Sweetish, roast malt aftertaste.

Golden Fox (OG 1041, ABV 4.1%)
A golden, hoppy ale, dry tasting with a fruity aroma and citrus finish.

Black Dragon Mild (OG 1043, ABV 4.3%) ◆
Black in colour with a toffee and roast malt flavour and a smoky finish.

Dunstable Giant (OG 1044, ABV 4.4%)
Dark tawny bitter with a subtle blend of malt and hops.

Dragon Slayer (OG 1045, ABV 4.5%) 🗎 ◆
A golden beer with a malt and hop flavour and a bitter finish. More malty and less hoppy than is usual for a beer of this style.

**Edwin Taylor's Extra Stout
(OG 1045, ABV 4.5%)** ◆
A complex black beer with a bitter coffee and roast malt flavour and a dry bitter finish.

Fruit Bat (OG 1045, ABV 4.5%) ◆
A warming straw-coloured beer with a generous taste of raspberries and a bitter finish.

Shefford Pale Ale (SPA) (OG 1045, ABV 4.5%) ◆
A well-balanced beer with hop, fruit and malt flavours. Dry, bitter aftertaste.

SOD (OG 1050, ABV 5%)
SOS with caramel added for colour.

SOS (OG 1050, ABV 5%) ◆
A rich mixture of fruit, hops and malt is present in the taste and aftertaste of this beer. Predominantly hoppy aroma.

Baa (NEW) SIBA

Unit 4, Station Road Industrial Estate, Chepstow, NP16 5PF ⊕ baabrewing.com

☺Established in 2015 using an eight-barrel plant with five fermenters and a bright beer tank. ‼️ 🍺

Best Bitter (ABV 4%)
A well-balanced beer with fruity, floral and aromatic hop notes and smooth, mellow maltiness followed by a crisp bitterness.

IPA (ABV 5%)

Bacchus

⊟ Bacchus Hotel, 17 High Street, Sutton-on-Sea, Lincolnshire, LN12 2EY
☎ (01507) 441204 ⊕ bacchushotel.co.uk

Bacchus began brewing in 2010 and now has a two-barrel plant supplying the Bacchus Hotel. New equipment was installed in 2013. ‼️ 🍺 RAIB

1692 (OG 1042, ABV 4.2%)

Sutton Pride (OG 1042, ABV 4.2%)

Best Bitter (OG 1043, ABV 4.3%)

Backyard SIBA ⊙

Unit 8a, Gatehouse Trading Estate, Lichfield Road, Brownhills, Walsall, West Midlands, WS8 6JZ
☎ (01543) 360145 ⊕ tbb.uk.com

☺Backyard began brewing in 2008 and expanded in 2012 to a 12-barrel plant brewing up to 50 barrels a week. Two pubs are owned: the Fountain, Walsall and the Saddlers Arms, Solihull. A 0.5-barrel experimental plant is in operation. ‼️🍺◆

Bitter (OG 1040, ABV 3.8%)
Blonde-style ale, slightly sweet with hints of tangerine and fruit salad.

Hoard (OG 1040, ABV 3.9%)

Blonde (OG 1041, ARV 4.1%)

Gold (OG 1044, ABV 4.4%)
A dark, rich beer full of bitter chocolate and fruit malt character with a full, rounded bitter hop finish.

IPA (OG 1049, ABV 5%)

BAD SIBA ⊙

Unit 3, North Hill Road, Dishforth, North Yorkshire, YO7 3DH
☎ (01423) 324005 ⊕ wearebad.co

Brewing commenced in 2014, originally using a 13-barrel plant, since upgraded to cope with demand. Monthly specials often incorporate seasonal ingredients and the brewery also produces more experimental and radical brews pushing the boundaries of conventional brewing. ‼️◆

Comfortably Numb (ABV 3.8%)
Fruity and slightly bitter, hop-packed with notes of tangerine, mango, grapefruit and pineapple.

Love Over Gold (ABV 4.1%)
A New World-style blonde ale, light and hoppy. Well-balanced with grapefruit and grassy notes.

Wild Gravity (ABV 5.2%)
An IPA with a malty backbone and tropical hop flavours.

Dazed and Confused (ABV 5.5%)
Dark-coloured, rich milk stout with hints of cherry, chocolate, coffee and almond.

Bad Seed SIBA

Unit 6, 6 Rye Close, York Way Industrial Estate, Malton, North Yorkshire, YO17 6YD
⊕ badseedbrewery.co.uk

Started in 2013 by James Broad and Chris Waplington, the four-barrel brewery produces a core range of bottled beers, available across the UK, supplemented by a few specials.

Badger

See Hall & Woodhouse

Baildon SIBA

Unit D, Tong Park Business Centre, Otley Road, Baildon, West Yorkshire, BD17 7QD
⊕ baildonbrewing.co.uk

Brewing began in 2014 using a six-barrel plant. The brewery is run by Leigh Terry, head brewster. ◆

Blonde (ABV 3.6%)
Refreshing, zesty summer ale.

Brunette (ABV 3.9%)
A rounded ruby ale.

Auburn Flame (ABV 4.2%)
A crisp ale with spicy hop and soft fruit flavours.

Bakers Dozen (NEW)

Unit 5, Ketton Business Estate, Pit Lane, Ketton, Leicestershire, PE9 3SZ
☎ (01780) 238180 ⊕ bakersdozenbrewing.co.uk

Brewing takes place on a five-barrel plant installed in 2015 by the owners of the Jolly Brewer, Stamford, where the beers are regularly available. ♦V

Jentacular (OG 1035, ABV 3.5%)

Bearded Archway (OG 1043, ABV 4.6%)
A refreshing, unfined, lemon and lime saison-style beer.

Summertime (OG 1046, ABV 4.6%)
Magnum, Ella and Summer hops complement a malt grist of extra pale and wheat malts.

Electric Landlady (OG 1048, ABV 5%)
Golden ale brewed with Mosaic hops.

Ballard's SIBA 👁

The Old Sawmill, Nyewood, Petersfield, West Sussex, GU31 5HA
☎ (01730) 821362 ⊕ ballards-brewery.co.uk

Launched in 1980 by Mike and Carola Brown at Cumbers Farm, Trotton, Ballard's has been trading at Nyewood since 1988 and now supplies 70-80 outlets. ‼🍺♦RAIB

Midhurst Mild (OG 1034, ABV 3.4%)
Traditional dark mild, well-balanced and refreshing, with a biscuity flavour.

Golden Bine (OG 1038, ABV 3.8%) 🍺
Amber-coloured, clean-tasting bitter. A roast malt aroma leads to a fruity, slightly sweet taste and a dry finish.

Best Bitter (OG 1042, ABV 4.2%) 🍺
A copper-coloured beer with a malty aroma. A good balance of fruit and malt in the flavour gives way to a dry, hoppy aftertaste.

Wild (OG 1047, ABV 4.7%)

Nyewood Gold (OG 1050, ABV 5%)

Wassail (OG 1060, ABV 6%) 🍺
A strong, full-bodied, tawny-red, fruity beer with a predominance of malt throughout, but also an underlying hoppiness.

Balmaha

🍴 Oak Tree Inn, Balmaha, Loch Lomond, G63 0JQ
☎ (01360) 870357 ⊕ oak-tree-inn.co.uk

Balmaha began brewing in 2012 using a one-barrel plant. ‼♦

Baltic Fleet

🍴 Baltic Fleet, 33a Wapping, Liverpool, L1 8DQ
☎ (0151) 709 3116 ⊕ balticfleetpubliverpool.com

👁Wapping brewery was established in 2002 in the cellars of the pub on the waterfront in Liverpool using the old Passageway Brewery plant. A new brewer took over in 2015 and the brewery was renamed to Baltic Fleet. The brewery is concentrating on brewing Summer Ale, but other beers may be produced in the future. RAIB

Summer Ale (OG 1042, ABV 4.2%) 🍺
Refreshing golden beer with floral hops dominating the nose and taste. Some fruit also on the aroma and in the taste. Good bitterness throughout, leading to a dry, bitter aftertaste.

Bank Top SIBA 👁

The Pavilion, Ashworth Lane, Bolton, BL1 8RA
☎ (01204) 595800 ⊕ banktopbrewery.com

👁Bank Top was established in 1995. Since 2002 the brewery has occupied a Grade II-listed tennis pavilion. In 2007 the brewing capacity was doubled with the installation of a new 10-barrel plant and in 2008 David Sweeney became the sole proprietor. Bank Top Brewery Estates was formed in 2010 and now owns two pubs; Bank Top Brewery Tap and Bank Top Ale House. ‼♦

Barley to Beer (OG 1036, ABV 3.6%)
A pale bitter with a citrus lemon and herbal finish.

Sweeneys (OG 1038, ABV 3.8%)
An amber-coloured bitter with a bold, crisp flavour and a delicate, slightly spicy aroma.

Bad to the Bone (OG 1040, ABV 4%)
A tan-coloured beer with floral qualities and delicate citrus notes.

Dark Mild (OG 1040, ABV 4%) 🍺
Dark brown beer with a malt and roast aroma. Smooth mouthfeel, with malt, roast malt and hops prominent throughout.

Flat Cap (OG 1040, ABV 4%) 🍴🍺
Amber ale with a modest fruit aroma leading to a beer with citrus fruit, malt and hops. Good finish of fruit, malt and bitterness.

Gold Digger (OG 1040, ABV 4%) 🍺
Golden coloured, with a citrus aroma, grapefruit and a touch of spiciness on the palate; a fresh, hoppy citrus finish.

Old Slapper (OG 1042, ABV 4.2%)
A quaffable golden-amber beer with citrus, floral and peach notes on the nose. Lightly hopped with a soft fruity taste.

Pavilion Pale Ale (OG 1045, ABV 4.5%) 🍺
A yellow beer with a citrus and hop aroma. Big fruity flavour with a peppery hoppiness; dry, bitter yet fruity finish.

Blonde (OG 1050, ABV 5%)
A pale ale made with a pleasant woody flavour and distinct berry aroma.

Port o' Call (OG 1050, ABV 5%) 🍺
Dark brown beer with a malty, fruity aroma. Malt, roast and dark fruits in the bittersweet taste and finish.

Banks's

Park Brewery, Wolverhampton, West Midlands, WV1 4NY
☎ (01902) 711811 ⊕ bankssbeer.co.uk

Banks's was founded as a firm of maltsters in 1840 and commencing brewing in 1874; it moved to the current Park Brewery the following year. It became the principal brewery of Wolverhampton & Dudley Breweries, founded in 1890 by an amalgamation with two other local companies. Several other breweries were later acquired, notably Hanson's of Dudley in 1943, which continued brewing until 1991. Following the takeover of Marston's of Burton on Trent in 1999, W&DB subsequently adopted this name for the PLC in 2007. While continuing to produce the original Banks's Mild and Bitter beers for which they gained fame throughout the Midlands, many new beers have been developed plus the Single Hop and Revisionist ranges. In recent years, Marston's PLC has taken on contract brewing of several well-known national ales, many being produced at the Banks's site. These include Tetley Bitter, for Carlsberg and the principal Thwaites' brands, which were brewed under licence from 2014; and purchased outright by Marston's the following year. Part of Marston's PLC. !! ➤

Mild (OG 1036, ABV 3.5%) ◆
An amber-coloured, well-balanced, refreshing session beer.

Bitter (OG 1038, ABV 3.8%) ◆
A pale brown bitter with a pleasant balance of hops and malt. Hops continue from the taste through to a bittersweet aftertaste.

Sunbeam (OG 1042, ABV 4.2%)
Zesty golden blonde beer, with refreshing gooseberry and grapefruit citrus hops prominent. A vibrant hop aroma leads to a long clean finish

Brewed for Marston's:

EPA (OG 1036, ABV 3.6%)

Brewed under the Mansfield brand name:

Cask Ale (OG 1038, ABV 3.9%)
A copper-coloured bitter with fruity notes, subtle hop aromas, and a restrained bitterness.

Brewed under the Thwaites brand name:

Original (OG 1036, ABV 3.6%)
A classic copper-coloured, traditional session bitter, with balance between malt flavour and hop bitterness.

Wainwright (OG 1042, ABV 4.1%)
Refreshing golden ale with gentle bitterness and a sweet lemon hop finish.

Lancaster Bomber (OG 1044, ABV 4.4%)
Full-bodied deep amber beer, with a raisin-like sweetness and a noticeable dry hop character.

Contract brewed for Carlsberg:

Mild (OG 1034, ABV 3.3%)

Bitter (OG 1035, ABV 3.7%)
A classic, dry session bitter. A distinct hop character prevails, with a subtle clove-like note.

Gold (OG 1041, ABV 4.1%)
A straw-coloured golden ale. A dry, refreshing citrus/herbal hop character predominates.

Barkston

Orchard House, Saw Wells Court, Barkston Ash, North Yorkshire, LS24 9UJ
☎ **(0845) 224 6324** ☎ **07764 750959**
⊕ **barkstonbrewery.com**

Barkston Brewery is situated in the picturesque village of Barkston Ash, four miles south of Tadcaster. Production started in 2011 experimenting with different malt and hop combinations before settling on the current range of beers. New equipment with increased capacity was installed during 2013. Brewing is currently suspended.

Barlick

🛱 **Greyhound, 61 Manchester Road, Barnoldswick, Lancashire, BB18 5PW**
☎ **(01282) 850670** ⊕ **barlick-brewery.co.uk**

⊛Barlick began brewing in 2012 at the Greyhound in Barnoldswick, where a beer is always available. A four-barrel plant is used. Barlick is the colloquial name for the town. ♦

Barlow

Units 5 & 6, Shippen Rural Business Centre, Church Farm, Barlow, Derbyshire, S18 7TR
☎ **(0114) 289 1767** ⊕ **barlowbrewery.co.uk**

Brewing started in 2009 on a self-built 2.5-barrel plant. Expansion to five-barrel capacity was completed in 2014. Beers are supplied to the Hare & Hounds in Barlow and other local outlets. The brewery acquired its first pub, the Tap House, in 2014. ➤ ♦ RAIB

Heath Robinson (OG 1039, ABV 3.8%)
A traditional dark bitter with a malty background and a balanced, bitter finish.

Betty's Blonde (OG 1042, ABV 4%)
Brewed with a blend of pale malts to give a light golden colour, hopped for subtle citrus and passion fruit flavours with a clean crisp finish.

Beyond the Pale (OG 1042, ABV 4%)
A well-balanced, straw-coloured pale ale. Floral aroma with a light grapefruit taste, a hint of lemon and a light, bitter finish.

Carnival Ale (OG 1042, ABV 4%)
A light, golden pale ale with a citrus finish.

Dark Horse (OG 1043, ABV 4.2%)
Dark-coloured bitter with a coffee aroma and a well-balanced finish.

Three Valleys IPA (OG 1052, ABV 5%)
An American-style IPA bursting with tropical fruit and citrus flavours, with a clean, bitter finish.

Full Monty (OG 1067, ABV 6.5%)
A strong, full-flavoured IPA. Golden in colour with complex passion fruit, citrus and mandarin orange flavours with a warming alcoholic finish.

Anastasia (OG 1076, ABV 7.5%)
Strong, dark and smooth with complex malt flavours, chocolate, coffee and a hint of fruit.

Barn Owl (NEW)

Buildings Farm, Faringdon Road, Gozzard's Ford, Oxfordshire, OX13 6QH ☎ **07724 551086**

⊗ Located in a spacious barn on a farm just outside Abingdon, brewing began in 2016 using a four-barrel plant. Beers are often to be found in the Black Horse in Gozzard's Ford and other local free trade outlets.

Golden Gozzard (OG 1040, ABV 4%)

A light, refreshing golden ale with soft bitterness and a long finish.

Gozzard's Guzzler (OG 1044, ABV 4.4%)
A dark best bitter with a sweetish nose and fruity tones.

Barnet

🕿 Black Horse, Wood Street, High Barnet, Hertfordshire, EN5 4BW
☎ (020) 8449 2230 ⊕ blackhorsebarnet.co.uk

The brewery opened in 2013 using a 2.5-barrel plant located behind the Black Horse pub. Brewing takes place twice a week using traditional recipes taken from the Dead Brewers Society dating back to Victorian times. The beers are supplied mainly to the Black Horse, and in small quantities to other local pubs.

Glory (ABV 3.9%)

Best Bitter (ABV 4.1%)

IPA (ABV 4.5%)

High Speed (ABV 5.1%)

Barney's SIBA

Summerhall Brewery, 1 Summerhall, Edinburgh, EH9 1PL ☎ 07512 253660 ⊕ barneysbeer.com

The only microbrewery in Edinburgh's city centre, Barney's Beer was founded in 2010 and now brews on the site of the original 1800s Summerhall brewery. Summerhall is Edinburgh's centre for the arts and science. ‼RAIB

Good Ordinary Pale Ale (OG 1038, ABV 3.8%)
A gold-coloured, English-style full-bodied bitter.

Extra Pale (OG 1040, ABV 4%)
Light and refreshing blonde beer.

Red Rye (OG 1044, ABV 4.5%)
Copper/dark amber in colour, with a clean, crisp, dry and fruity taste.

Volcano IPA (OG 1049, ABV 5%)
An American-style pale ale, packed with hops.

Barngates SIBA ◉

Barngates, Cumbria, LA22 0NG
☎ (01539) 436575 ⊕ barngatesbrewery.co.uk

◉ Barngates was established in 1997 to supply only the Drunken Duck Inn. It became a limited company in 1999. Expansion over the years plus a new purpose-built 10-barrel plant in 2008 means it now supplies more than 150 outlets throughout Cumbria, Lancashire, Yorkshire and Northumberland. ‼

Pale (OG 1036, ABV 3.3%) ◄
A well-balanced, fruity, hoppy bitter with plenty of flavour for its strength.

Cat Nap (OG 1037, ABV 3.6%) ◄
Pale beer, unapologetically bitter, with a dry astringent finish.

Cracker (OG 1038, ABV 3.9%) ◄
A full-bodied hoppy beer with some balancing sweetness and fruit. There is plenty of taste in this brown beer. Cleverly constructed.

Brathay Gold (OG 1042, ABV 4%) ◄
Attractive, sweet and rich aroma is followed by plenty of fruit and hops then a long bitter finish.

Goodhew's Dry Stout (OG 1045, ABV 4.3%) ◄
The inviting roast aroma leads to an easy-drinking, full-bodied and well-balanced roasty stout.

Tag Lag (OG 1044, ABV 4.4%) ⌕ ◄
This traditional bitter is full on: fruit, noble hops, malt balance, good body with a crisp clean finish.

Red Bull Terrier (OG 1048, ABV 4.8%) ◄
An assertive roasty red beer with full mouthfeel. Initial sweetness and luscious fruit, give way to a lingering bitter finish.

Barrell & Sellers SIBA

Spring Farm, St Cross South Elmham, Harleston, Suffolk, IP20 0NZ
☎ (01986) 783902 ☎ 07788 561455
⊕ barrellandsellers.co.uk

⊠ Brewing began in 2014, producing easy-drinking classic beers using only English-grown hops and malt. The cask beers are supplied to a small number of local pubs and its bottled-conditioned beers are available direct from the brewery, via the website shop or through selected retail outlets. ‼🍴◆RAIB

Barrowden

See Co Pilot

Bartleby's

Coachwerks, 19 Hollingdean Terrace, Brighton, BN1 7HB
☎ (01273) 275012 ☎ 07518 485 342
⊕ bartlebysbrewery.com

Bartleby's began trading in 2014 in Brighton. Since opening it has expanded its distribution to local pubs and has established an on-site shop with home deliveries by veloelectric tricycle. An on-site venue is used for music, community events and art shows. ‼🍴◆V

Bartrams

Rougham Estate, Ipswich Road (A14), Rougham, Suffolk, IP30 9ND ☎ 07768 062581
⊕ bartramsbrewery.co.uk

⊠ Established in 1999, the brewery was moved to Rougham Airfield in 2005 to a building formerly used to pack parachutes during WW2. Its small capacity enables the brewery to produce a great diversity and number of specialist beers including its legendary dark brews. Beers are supplied to a select number of local pubs with the majority of sales being via music festivals and local events. ‼🍴◆RAIB V

Marld (OG 1033, ABV 3.4%)
A traditional mild. Spicy hops and malt with a hint of chocolate, slightly smoky with a light, roasted finish.

Washing Machine Bitter (OG 1036, ABV 3.6%)
A golden bitter.

Adams Ale (OG 1036, ABV 3.7%)

Premier Bitter (OG 1038, ABV 3.7%)
A traditional quaffing ale, full-flavoured but light, dry and hoppy.

Rougham Ready (OG 1038, ABV 3.8%)

A light, crisp bitter, surprisingly full bodied for its strength.

Milkmaid Bitter (OG 1040, ABV 4%)
A copper-coloured traditional bitter.

Thy Last Drop (OG 1040, ABV 4%)

Bee's Knees (OG 1042, ABV 4.2%)
An amber-coloured beer with a floral aroma; honey softness on the palate leads to a crisp, bitter finish.

Captain Bill Bartram's Best Bitter (OG 1048, ABV 4.8%)
Modified from a 100-year old recipe, using full malt and traditional Kentish hops.

Captain's Stout (OG 1049, ABV 4.8%)
Biscuity dark malt leads to a lightly smoked aroma, plenty of roasted malt character, coffee notes and a whiff of smoke.

Cherry Stout (OG 1048, ABV 4.8%)
Sensuous hints of chocolate lead to a subtle suggestion of cherries.

Darkside (OG 1050, ABV 5%)

Suffolk 'n' Strong (OG 1050, ABV 5%)
A light, smooth and dangerously potable strong bitter, well-balanced malt and hops with an easy finish.

Flirtatious Ungulate (OG 1052, ABV 5.2%)

Red Rye Ding Hood (OG 1066, ABV 6.6%)

Comrade Bill Bartram's Egalitarian Anti Imperialist Soviet Stout (OG 1070, ABV 6.9%)
A Russian stout by any other name, a luscious easy-drinking example of the style.

Brewed for Cambridge Rock events:

Cambridge Rock (ABV 3.8%)
A golden-coloured bitter with New World hops.

Brewed for the John Peel Centre, Stowmarket:

John Peel Centre (ABV 3.7%)
A copper-coloured bitter using New World hops.

Barum SIBA

☰ c/o Reform Inn, Pilton, Barnstaple, Devon, EX31 1PD
☎ (01271) 329994 ⊕ barumbrewery.co.uk

⊠ Barum was formed in 1996 by Tim Webster and is housed in a conversion attached to the Reform Inn, which acts as the brewery tap and main outlet. Distribution is exclusively within Devon. ‼☰♦

Original (OG 1044, ABV 4.4%) ◣
A complex beer. The fruity aroma lingers into a sweet, hoppy bitter with a short-lived aftertaste.

EPA (OG 1046, ABV 4.6%)
Very pale golden ale with citrus/grapefruit notes throughout. Clean, dry finish.

Breakfast (OG 1048, ABV 5%)
Copper-coloured, malty premium bitter with a floral nose and a bittersweet finish.

Basin City

☰ Fox & Crown, Church Street, Old Basford, Nottingham, NG6 0GA
☎ (0115) 942 2002

Office: 33 Church Street, Old Basford, Nottingham, NG6 0GA ⊠ basincitybrewers@gmail.com

Set up in 1996, originally as Fiddlers Ales. In 1999 it became Alcazar Brewery on change of ownership. A full mash brewery with a 10-barrel brew length, it is located behind its brewery tap, the Fox & Crown. The brewery and pub changed hands in 2016 when the name of the brewery was changed again and a new portfolio of beers established. ♦

Mustache Petes (ABV 3.8%)

Helter Skelter Highway (ABV 5.2%)

Batemans SIBA IFBB 👁

Salem Bridge Brewery, Mill Lane, Wainfleet, Lincolnshire, PE24 4JE
☎ (01754) 880317 ⊕ bateman.co.uk

😊Bateman's Brewery is one of Britain's few remaining independent family-owned and managed brewers. Established in 1874 it has been brewing award-winning beers for four generations. All tied and managed houses serve cask-conditioned beer. ‼☰♦

XB (OG 1037, ABV 3.7%) ◣
A well-rounded, smooth, malty beer with a blackcurrant fruity background. Hops flourish initially before giving way to a bittersweet dryness that enhances the mellow malty ending.

Gold (OG 1039, ABV 3.9%)
A golden-coloured, refreshing beer with a citrus flavour and aroma, quite dry.

XXXB (OG 1045, ABV 4.5%) ◣
A brilliant blend of malt, hops and fruit on the nose with a bitter bite over the top of a faintly banana maltiness that stays the course. A russet-tan brown classic.

Salem Porter (OG 1048, ABV 4.7%) ◣
A black and complex mix of chocolate, liquorice and cough elixir.

Bath SIBA 👁

Hare House, Southway Drive, Warmley, Bristol, BS30 5LW
☎ (0117) 947 4797 ⊕ bathales.com

⊠ Established in 1995, Bath Ales uses traditional brewing techniques with cutting-edge technology. An experimental brewery produces unusual and fashionable brews under the Beerd brand name. More than 400 regional outlets are supplied. Eleven pubs and sites are operated across the south-west, all but two serving cask ale, and one of which brews its own specials (the Graze Bar & Chophouse, Bath). In July 2016, Bath Ales was bought by St Austell Brewery (qv) which said it would maintain all the Bath Ales beers. ‼☰♦RAIB

Special Pale Ale (OG 1039, ABV 3.7%) ◣
Hoppy, pale golden session bitter. Light citrus aroma with bittersweet flavours and a bitter aftertaste. Some samples may have a hint of caramel.

Prophecy (OG 1040, ABV 3.9%)
Fruity, pine-like aroma, light in colour with a crisp bitter finish.

Gem (OG 1042, ABV 4.1%) 🍾 ◣
Pale brown best bitter with sweet fruit and malt flavours and a hint of caramel. Little aroma but a balanced taste with a short, bitter finish.

Barnsey (OG 1045, ABV 4.5%) ◣

A dark brown old ale with a grainy mouthfeel. Malt, dark fruits and toffee flavours combine to provide sweetness before a lingering bitter finish.

Platform 3 (OG 1044, ABV 4.5%)
A refreshing IPA with tropical fruit aromas, hints of citrus honey flavours and a long bitter finish.

Brewed under the Beerd brand name:

Monterey (OG 1040, ABV 3.9%)
A West Coast-style pale ale brewed with American-sourced hops.

Silver Tip (OG 1046, ABV 4.7%)
A refreshing pale ale with a fruity aroma. The flavour has hints of white wine with a fresh, quick bitter finish.

Bathams IFBB

Delph Brewery, Delph Road, Brierley Hill, West Midlands, DY5 2TN
☎ (01384) 77229 ⊕ bathams.com

☺A classic Black Country small brewery established in 1877. Tim and Matthew Batham represent the fifth generation to run the company. The Vine, one of the Black Country's most famous pubs, is also the site of the brewery. The company has 10 tied houses and supplies around 30 other outlets. Batham's Bitter is delivered in 54-gallon hogsheads to meet demand. ♦

Mild Ale (OG 1036.5, ABV 3.5%) ◆
A fruity, dark brown mild with malty sweetness and a roast malt finish.

Best Bitter (OG 1043.5, ABV 4.3%) ▤ ◆
A pale yellow, fruity, sweetish bitter, with a dry, hoppy finish. A good, light, refreshing beer.

Battledown SIBA ◉

Keynsham Works, Keynsham Street, Cheltenham, Gloucestershire, GL52 6EJ
☎ (01242) 693409 ☎ 07734 834104
⊕ battledownbrewery.com

⊗ Established in 2005 by Roland and Stephanie Elliott-Berry, and joined in 2006 by Ben Jennison-Phillips (ex-Whittingtons), Battledown operates an eight-barrel plant from an old engineering works and supplies more than 250 outlets. Visitors are always welcome. Beer can be purchased directly at the brewery and also via an online shop. ‼▤♦RAIB

Sunbeam (OG 1037, ABV 3.8%)
A golden pale ale with a refreshing aroma and sharp but smooth taste, leaving a dry, hoppy aftertaste which lingers on the palate.

Natural Selection (OG 1041, ABV 4.2%)
A deep golden beer, the malt is evident but gives way to a triple hop addition giving a spicy and slightly citrus finish.

Premium (OG 1046, ABV 4.6%)
A rich amber ale. A malty aroma and taste with a deep, satisfying, full-bodied fruit and malt texture leaving a well-rounded, mellow aftertaste.

Special (OG 1050, ABV 5.2%)
A well-balanced and crisp pale ale.

Black (OG 1070, ABV 7.2%)
A dark, complex, full-bodied stout.

Four Kings (OG 1066, ABV 7.2%)
A strong ale with a heady aroma.

Battlefield (Shrewsbury) (NEW) SIBA

Harlescott Lane, Shrewsbury, SY1 3AH
☎ (01743) 465000 ⊕ battlefieldbrewery.co.uk

Battlefield Brewery began brewing in 2015 using a 25-hectolitre European system. It is located in the famous Battlefield area of Shrewsbury. ‼▤♦

Saxon Gold (OG 1038, ABV 3.8%)
A golden ale with subtle orange marmalade on the nose, crisp maltiness with touches of soft hops and a well-rounded finish.

Citrus Blast (OG 1042, ABV 4.2%)
A citrus ale with lemon and lime on the nose, crisp and easy-drinking with tropical grapefruit flavours from the hops, a hint of orange and zesty lime finish.

1403 (OG 1043, ABV 4.3%)
A light, dry and crisp ale. Slight malt backbone with a subtle citrus/apricot note. The finish from the dry hops leaves you with a grapefruit and slight floral flavour.

1066 (OG 1045, ABV 4.5%)
An easy-drinking dark ale with rich malt and striking hop aromas.

Archers (OG 1049, ABV 4.9%)
A smooth, strong pale ale full of clean malt flavours, with a hoppy finish.

Battlefield

See Tunnel

Bays SIBA ◉

Aspen Way, Paignton, Devon, TQ4 7QR
☎ (01803) 555004 ⊕ baysbrewery.co.uk

⊗ Bays Brewery opened in 2007 in an old steel fabrication unit in Paignton using a 20-barrel plant. The brewery delivers to many pubs, hotels and restaurants in the south-west and further afield. ‼▤♦

Topsail (OG 1040, ABV 4%)

Gold (OG 1042, ABV 4.3%)

Devon Dumpling (OG 1048, ABV 5.1%)

Beachy Head SIBA

Seven Sisters Sheep Centre, Birling Manor Farm, Gilberts Drive, East Dean, East Sussex, BN20 0AA
☎ (01323) 423313

Estates Office: The Green, East Dean, BN20 0BS
⊕ beachyhead.org.uk

⊗ The 2.5-barrel brew plant was installed in 2006. Around 25 outlets are supplied regularly, including three local pubs. The full range of ales (including seasonals) can be sampled at the Tiger Inn in East Dean village, which is the brewery tap. ‼♦RAIB

Lighthouse Ale (OG 1045, ABV 3.5%)

South Downs Ale (OG 1044, ABV 4.4%)

Beachy Original (OG 1045, ABV 4.5%)

Legless Rambler (OG 1050, ABV 5%)

Parsons Porter (OG 1050, ABV 5%)

Bear Claw

Unit 3, Meantime Workshops, Spittal,
Northumberland, TD15 1RG ☎ 07919 276715
⊕ bearclawbrewery.weebly.com

Bear Claw began brewing in 2012 using a two-barrel plant, producing an ever-changing range of mainly highly-hopped cask-conditioned ales and many bottle-conditioned beers, including continental styles. Expansion is planned as demand is high. RAIB

Bear North (NEW)

Old Well House, 322 Wakefield Road, Denby Dale,
West Yorkshire, HD8 8SD
☎ (01484) 767954 ⊕ bearnorthbrewing.co.uk

Glyn Barker, the brewer, was a home brewer for 2.5 years before deciding to brew commercially. Seven bottle-conditioned beers are produced and sold locally at farmers' markets, craft stalls and bottle shops. The output is limited due to the 50-litre brew plant capacity but there are plans for expansion. RAIB

Beardy Monkey (NEW)

22 Thorpe Road, Melton Mowbray, Leicestershire,
LE13 1SG ☎ 07866 477504
✉ tobychaplin71@gmail.com

Beardy Monkey commenced brewing in 2016 using a half-barrel plant which ex-science teacher turned brewer Toby Chaplin operates from the rear of his own house. There are usually eight brews a month. A small number of local outlets and beer festivals are supplied direct. Beers can be designed and brewed to order.

Pale Ale (OG 1040, ABV 3.9%)
A well-balanced, malty brew with a floral hop and soft citrus aftertaste.

Beartown SIBA ◉

Bromley House, Spindle Street, Congleton, Cheshire,
CW12 1QN
☎ (01260) 299964 ⊕ beartownbrewery.co.uk

☺ Beartown began brewing in 1994 and uses a 25-barrel plant. It supplies more than 250 outlets and owns five pubs. The brewery's Navigation in Stockport and the Beartown Tap in Congleton have both been named CAMRA regional pubs of the year. ‼ ⌷ ◆

Best Bitter (OG 1037, ABV 3.7%)
A copper-coloured session beer with a full palate of malt and crisp hops.

Bear Ass (OG 1040, ABV 4%)
Dark ruby-red, malty bitter with good hop nose and fruity flavour with a dry, bitter, astringent aftertaste.

Ginger Bear (OG 1040, ABV 4%)
The flavours from the malt and hops blend with the added bite from the root ginger to produce a quenching blonde ale.

Kodiak Gold (OG 1040, ABV 4%) ◣
Hops and fruit dominate the taste of this crisp yellow bitter and these follow through to the dryish aftertaste. Biscuity malt also comes through on the aroma and taste.

Bearskinful (OG 1042, ABV 4.2%) ◣
Biscuity malt dominates the flavour of this amber best bitter. There are hops and a hint of sulphur on the aroma. A balance of malt and bitterness follow through to the aftertaste.

Bearly Literate (OG 1045, ABV 4.5%)
Golden pale ale. Floral sented and packed with the flavours of summer fruits and lemon, ending with a smooth dryness.

Polar Eclipse (OG 1048, ABV 4.8%) ▣ ◣
Classic black, dry and bitter stout, with roast flavours to the fore. Good hop on the nose follow through the taste into a long, dry finish.

Blackbear (OG 1050, ABV 5%)
Dark ruby-coloured strong mild ale. Subtle roast and malt flavours fill the taste complemented by a mellow sweetness.

Bruins Ruin (OG 1050, ABV 5%)
Deep copper-coloured premium ale. Full of malty character and a palate of sweet, smooth, fruity flavours.

Beat (NEW) SIBA

Old Coach House, Church Road, North Curry, Somerset,
TA3 6LH ☎ 07821 132297

Office: 11 Sydenham Hill, Bristol, BS6 5SL
⊕ beatales.com

⊗ Beat Ales was established by the North Curry Brewery owner's son, Jack Pike. The brewery is currently in the same location but with offices in Bristol. RAIB

Raver (OG 1034, ABV 3.8%)

Mod (OG 1038, ABV 4.3%)

Metal Head (OG 1042, ABV 4.8%)

Rockabilly (OG 1050, ABV 5.3%)

Beath (NEW) SIBA

54 Foulford Road, Cowdenbeath, KY4 9AS ☎ 07792 369678 ⊕ beathbrewing.com

Beath began brewing in 2016, originally with a 20-litre capacity upgraded to 100-litre within a few months. RAIB

AreYouWithMe (ABV 4%)
A red-coloured, citrus tasting ale.

Born Slippy (ABV 4%)

Edelweiss (ABV 4%)
A wheat beer.

Slowly Slipping Under (ABV 4%)

Funkytown (ABV 4.5%)
A fruity IPA.

Beavertown SIBA

Units 17 & 18, Lockwood Industrial Park, Mill Mead
Road, Tottenham Hale, London, N17 9QP
☎ (020) 8525 9884 ☎ 07976 984173
⊕ beavertownbrewery.co.uk

⊗ Beavertown moved into a large industrial unit in 2014 and expanded again in 2015. It is a sizeable craft brewery with six regular beers and many seasonal, one-off and collaboration beers. Most are sold in key-keg, can and keg without filtration or pasteurisation. Real ale is produced on a small plant. 🚉 ◆ RAIB

Beckstones

Upper Beckstones Mill, The Green, Millom, Cumbria, LA18 5HL ☎ 07761 605782
🌐 beckstonesbrewery.co.uk

⊗ On the site of an 18th-century mill, with its own water supply, this five-barrel operation continues to win awards. Beer names have connections to the long-closed Millom Iron Works or local characters; the brewer designs the distinctive pump clips. ◆

Leat (OG 1036, ABV 3.6%) 🍺
A refreshing golden bitter with tangy fruit and a rising hop finish.

Barley Blonde (ABV 3.7%) 🍺
Full-flavoured, beautifully balanced, emphatically fruity, hoppy beer.

Black Dog Freddy Mild (OG 1038, ABV 3.8%) 🍺
A full-bodied, beautifully balanced ruby dark mild, replete with fruit and roast malt.

Border Steeans (OG 1040, ABV 4.1%) 🍺
An old-fashioned style tawny bitter with a sweet start, some bitter notes and plenty of aftertaste.

Iron Town (ABV 4.1%) 🍺
Creamy sweet brown ale full of well-balanced fruit and hop.

Rev Rob (OG 1044, ABV 4.6%) 🍺
A golden beer with a pronounced grapefruit aroma and taste. The hoppy bitterness lasts through to the aftertaste.

Bedlam SIBA

Albourne Estate Farm, Shaves Wood Lane, Albourne, West Sussex, BN6 9DX
☎ (01273) 978015 🌐 bedlambrewery.co.uk

Bedlam brewery operates full time from its own farm estate at the foot of the South Downs National Park, led by German head brewer Fabio Israel. More than 300 pubs and bars are supplied across London and the South East.

Benchmark (ABV 4%)
An amber-coloured best bitter with refreshing bitterness and sweet, fruity notes. The hops are balanced by a rich, malty character, with a hint of chocolate.

Golden (ABV 4.2%)
A session bitter with a bright bitterness on the palate.

IPA (OG 1048, ABV 4.8%)
A rich, full-flavoured IPA.

Porter (OG 1050, ABV 5%)
Plenty of roasted malt aromas and flavours. Rich and dark with a full palate and lasting bittersweet finish.

Beeches

39 The Beeches, Lochgelly, KY5 9QB
☎ (01592) 782474 ☎ 07761 752876
✉ thebeechesbrewery@gmail.com

☺Beeches came into existence from the love of small batch home brewing. Run by a husband and wife team, production started in 2012 using a 10-

gallon plant in a small outbuilding at the rear of the family home. Brewing is currently suspended.

Beer Bores (NEW)

Pixtons Green, Ashwicke, Marshfield, Gloucestershire, SN14 8AL ☎ 07790 715464 🌐 thebeerbores.co.uk

Mark Hempleman-Adams, Paul Clarke-Dabson and Marshall Ewart established Box Steam Brewery in 2004, before selling the business in 2007. However, Mark and Paul missed brewing so much that they set up a three-barrel microbrewery in 2015. Plans are in place to increase capacity with a new six-barrel plant and to distil their own West Country gin. ◆

American Beauty (OG 1035, ABV 3.5%)
A blonde, American-style, malty pale ale with hints of hazelnut and honey.

Toad Stabber (OG 1043, ABV 4.3%)
A traditional, full-flavoured beer, with a crisp, dry aftertaste.

Beer Brothers (NEW)

Unit 1, Gill Lane, Longton, Lancashire, PR4 4SR
☎ 07805 208098 🌐 beerbrothers.co.uk

Brewing started in 2015 using a 120-litre brew plant.

Blonde (ABV 3.8%)
Refreshing session beer with a crisp taste.

IPA (ABV 4%)
A full-bodied and full-flavoured IPA.

Milk Stout (ABV 4%)
Brewed with the addition of lactose. An initial creamy sweet hit on the palate is followed by gentle dark roasted barley bitterness.

Best Bitter (ABV 4.2%)
A golden, smooth, full-bodied malty session ale made with British hops.

Chocolate Porter (ABV 4.3%)
Full-bodied and well-balanced with heavy bitter notes of full roast coffee and dark chocolate. Made with real cocoa.

Altbier (ABV 5%)
A dark copper-coloured ale with a crisp, fruity finish.

Cloudy Wheat Beer (ABV 5.5%)
A German-style, crisp, golden, top-fermented wheat beer.

Dark Wheat Beer (ABV 6.5%)
A dark, lightly carbonated, full-bodied wheat beer with hints of liquorice and tart berries to round off a long-lasting fruity finish.

Beer Engine

Newton St Cyres, Devon, EX5 5AX
☎ (01392) 851282 🌐 thebeerengine.co.uk

⊗ Beer Engine was developed in 1983 and is the oldest continuously working microbrewery in Devon. The brewery is visible behind glass downstairs in the pub. Several outlets are supplied, as well as local beer festivals. ‼◆

Rail Ale (OG 1037, ABV 3.8%) 🍺
A straw-coloured beer with a fruity aroma and a sweet, fruity finish.

Silver Bullet (OG 1040, ABV 4%)
A light, medium-strength summer beer with a bitter aftertaste.

Piston Bitter (OG 1043, ABV 4.3%) ◈
A mid-brown, sweet-tasting beer with a pleasant, bittersweet aftertaste.

Sleeper Heavy (OG 1052, ABV 5.4%) ◈
A red-coloured beer with a fruity, sweet taste and a bitter finish.

Beer Ink (NEW)

Plover Road Garage, Plover Road, Lindley, Huddersfield, West Yorkshire, HD3 3PJ
☎ (01484) 655262

The Beer Ink Brewery Company is based in Lindlay and occupies the premises previously used by the Hand Drawn Monkey Brewery. Ryan Stoppard, owner and brewer, took possession of the brewery and eight-barrel plant in late 2015. The Brewery Tap opened in 2016. ♦

Avant Garde (ABV 4%)
A non-traditional bitter with the floral and fruity flavours of New World hops.

Pin Up (ABV 4%)
A pale ale with aromas and flavours of melon, apricot and lemon zest.

Flagship (ABV 5%)
A floral, fruity and zesty IPA with a mouth drying bitterness.

Noire (ABV 5%)
A stout with coffee, chocolate and toffee flavours.

Two Faced (ABV 7%)
A double IPA, hoppy and fruity.

Beer Me

🍴 Belgian Café, 11-23 Grand Parade, Eastbourne, East Sussex, BN21 3YN
☎ (01323) 729967 ⊕ thebelgiancafe.co.uk

⊗ Beer Me was launched in 2014 by the owners of the Belgian Café in Eastbourne, building on 10 years in the catering industry. It uses a 2.5-barrel plant and produces continental-style beers which are served direct from the brewery. ‼🍴♦

Beer Nouveau

75 Temperance Street, Manchester, M12 6HU
⊕ beernouveau.co.uk

Beer Nouveau started brewing in 2014 in Prestwich, Manchester, on a 42-litre kit that owner Steve built in his garage. In 2015 the brewery relocated, taking over the 6.5-barrel brewing plant in the railway arch previously occupied by Privateer Beers. The original kit has been retained for experimental brews. In 2016 the adjacent arch was acquired, doubling the size of the brewery and tap. RAIB

Prestwich Pale (OG 1038, ABV 3.9%)
A light, hoppy beer with an underlying hint of malty sweetness.

Body Snatcher (OG 1040, ABV 4.4%)
A rich, copper-coloured session beer brewed from classic English bitter ingredients. A slightly sweet malt base sits underneath a fresh, spicy hop aroma.

Dry, crisp and clean hop flavours linger to produce a balanced, bitter aftertaste.

Manchester Sun (OG 1052, ABV 5.3%)
A golden-coloured bitter, light on hops on the nose, but heavy on the palate with a little maltiness.

Satanic Mills (OG 1056, ABV 6.1%)
A full-flavoured stout, smooth and slightly sweet.

Uncle Sam (OG 1057, ABV 6.3%)
Golden amber in colour with a light floral, almost fruity aroma and a massive hop hit on the tongue. Slightly bitter with a dry, slightly biscuity aftertaste.

Beer Refinery

Chapel Court Enterprise Centre, Wervin Road, Wervin, Chester, CH2 4BP ☎ 07939 875308
✉ enquiries@thebeerrefinery.co.uk

⊗ The Beer Refinery is a partnership of 10 engineers, some home brewers, and some just beer lovers. Brewing began in 2014 using a locally built four-barrel plant. 14 outlets are supplied. ‼♦

Beer Studio

See Hydes

Beercraft (NEW)

🍴 Watchmaker's Arms, 84 Goldstone Villas, Hove, East Sussex, BN3 3RU ⊕ beercraftbrighton.co.uk

Beercraft Brighton is a 100-litre pilot kit based out of the Watchmaker's Arms micropub in Hove. Brewing started in 2016 with different beers being produced each time. There are plans for expansion to a full-size plant. ‼

Beerd

See Bath

BEEspoke (NEW)

🍴 Fox, 41 Briggate, Shipley, West Yorkshire, BD17 7BP

Brewing began in 2015 in the cellar of the Fox pub using a one-barrel plant. A gluten-free beer is planned. ‼♦

Plan Bee (ABV 3.8%)
A pale, hoppy session ale.

Beeboppalula (ABV 4.2%)
A traditional, copper-coloured ale.

Shipley Stout (ABV 4.6%)
A rich, smooth stout with chocolate and coffee notes.

Briggate Blonde (ABV 5%)
A blonde, full-bodied strong ale with a resinous hop character.

Clocktower Porter (ABV 5.4%)
A robust porter with vinous aroma and nutty sweetness.

Beeston SIBA

Fransham Road Farm, Beeston, Norfolk, PE32 2LZ

☎ (01328) 700844 ☎ 07768 742763
⊕ beestonbrewery.co.uk

⊠ The brewery was established in 2006 in an old farm building using a five-barrel plant. Brewing water comes from a dedicated borehole and raw ingredients are sourced locally whenever possible. All beers are also available in five-litre mini casks. ‼ RAIB

Squirrel's Nuts (OG 1035, ABV 3.5%) ◗
Cherry, chocolate and vanilla aroma. A malt and cherry sweetness comes to the fore but quickly fades. Short finish.

Bloomers (OG 1039, ABV 4%)

Worth the Wait (OG 1041, ABV 4.2%) ◗
Hoppy throughout with a growing dryness. Complex and grainy with fruit notes, malt and understated bitterness.

Stirling (OG 1045, ABV 4.5%)
Rich, malty, red bitter with toffee notes.

Dry Road (OG 1048, ABV 4.8%)

Village Life (OG 1047, ABV 4.8%) ◗
Copper-coloured with a nutty character. Malty throughout, a bittersweet background gives depth. Strong toffee apple finish.

On the Huh (OG 1048, ABV 5%) ◗
A fruity raisin aroma. A bittersweet maltiness jousts with caramel and roast. A dry hoppiness adds to a strong finale.

Old Stoatwobbler (OG 1065, ABV 6%)

Brewed for Brancaster Brewery:

Brancaster Best (ABV 4.2%)
A refreshing session ale with a touch of citrus on the finish.

Malthouse Bitter (ABV 4.2%)
A mid amber ale with malty character and distinct bitterness on the finish.

Beeston Hop

Gwenbrook Avenue, Beeston, Nottingham, NG9 4BA
⊕ beestonhop.co.uk

A nano-brewery launched in 2015 producing mainly bottle-conditioned beers. Cask beers are occasionally produced for festivals using capacity at other breweries. The beers are unfined, unfiltered and unpasteurised. RAIB V

Belhaven

Brewery Lane, Dunbar, EH42 1PE
☎ (01368) 862734

Office: Spott Road, Dunbar, EH42 1RS
⊕ belhaven.co.uk

☺Belhaven brewery is one of the oldest brewing sites in Scotland. Established in Dunbar in 1719, it brews beers made with water from its own well and local Scottish barley. Part of Greene King PLC. ‼ ⤳

60/- Ale (OG 1030, ABV 2.9%) ◗
A fine example of a Scottish light. This bittersweet, reddish-brown beer is dominated by fruit and malt with a hint of roast and caramel, and increasing bitterness in the aftertaste.

IPA (OG 1038, ABV 3.8%)

A golden ale with refreshing floral and citrus tones produced by a well balanced fusion of malt and hops giving a clean, crisp flavour.

80/- Ale (OG 1040, ABV 4.2%) ◗
One of the last remaining original Scottish 80 Shillings. Malt is the predominant flavour characteristic, though it is balanced by fruit and a little hop. A complex ale, true to the 80/- style.

Black (OG 1041, ABV 4.2%)
A smooth, balanced stout with malty body and roast notes of dark chocolate and coffee.

St Andrew's Ale (OG 1046, ABV 4.9%)
A bittersweet beer with lots of body. The malt, fruit and roast mingle throughout with hints of hop and caramel.

Bell Street

▤ 57-59 Bell Street, Henley-on-Thames, Oxfordshire, RG9 2BA
☎ (01491) 570217 ⊕ bellstreetbrewery.co.uk

Bell Street Brewery opened in 2013 at the rear of Brakspear pub company's refurbished Bull on Bell Street. A four-barrel plant is used. The beers are sold at the pub and through the Brakspear estate. ◆

Brakspear Special (OG 1043, ABV 4.3%)
Tawny-coloured beer with a well-balanced aroma and a hint of sweetness. Full bodied, the initial sweetness gives way to a dry hop bitterness.

Belleville SIBA

36 Jaggard Way, Wandsworth Common, London, SW12 8SG ☎ 07712 298273
⊕ bellevillebrewing.co.uk

Belleville began brewing in 2012. It was formed by a group of parents who met in the playground of a local primary school and specialises in American-style beers. ‼ ◆

Calif-Oregon Amber (ABV 4.2%)

Northcote Blonde (OG 1042, ABV 4.2%) ◗
Smooth, dark golden ale with biscuity character and a trace of hoppy bitterness. Fruit is pineapple, orange and mixed citrus.

Balham Black (ABV 4.6%)

Battersea Brownstone (OG 1048, ABV 4.8%) ◗
Complex beer with chocolate and blackcurrant notes on the nose and palate coupled with a little malty sweetness. Hoppy bitter finish.

Chestnut Porter (OG 1049, ABV 4.9%) ◗
Brown creamy beer with roast and nutty notes throughout and a little hoppiness and fruit. Faintly bitter. Short dry finish.

Commonside Pale Ale (OG 1050, ABV 5%) ◗
A full-flavoured golden beer with hops and fruit throughout. The initial palate is sweet but then the bitterness develops.

Thames Surfer (OG 1057, ABV 5.7%) ◗
Strong pale brown IPA with citrus, hops, honey and spicy notes. There is a long-lasting, faintly hoppy, bitter finish.

Tie-Dye Rye (OG 1054, ABV 5.8%)

THE BREWERIES

Bellinger's SIBA

Station Road, Grove, Oxfordshire, OX12 0DH
☎ (01235) 772255 ⊕ bellingersbrewery.co.uk

⊠ The late Mike Bellinger established the brewery as a family partnership in 2011. Now run by his nephew and son-in-law, it is currently a five-barrel plant and supplies cask ale to around a dozen outlets and many beer festivals. All beers are also bottled and these, plus polypins, are sold in the garage forecourt shop. ‼ ⊑ ♦

Original Bitter (OG 1040, ABV 4.1%)
A light and refreshing, easy-drinking beer with a delicate malt flavour.

Cavalry (OG 1045, ABV 4.6%)
A malty, robust bitter.

IPA (OG 1050, ABV 5%)
Gently hoppy with a lingering bitter taste.

Gallipoli Stout (OG 1053, ABV 5.3%)
A stout with a big chocolate taste.

Belvoir SIBA ◉

Crown Park, Station Road, Old Dalby, Leicestershire, LE14 3NQ
☎ (01664) 823455 ⊕ belvoirbrewery.co.uk

Belvoir (pronounced 'beaver') Brewery was set up in 1995 by former Shipstone's and Theakston's brewer Colin Brown. Long-term expansion has seen the introduction of a 20-barrel plant that can produce 50 barrels a week. There is also a visitor centre incorporating brewery memorabilia, a bar, restaurant and shop (open seven days a week). Around 150 outlets are supplied direct. ‼ ⊑ ♦ RAIB

Dark Horse (OG 1034, ABV 3.4%)
A classic, smooth, dark mild ale.

Whippling (OG 1037, ABV 3.6%)
A light-bodied golden ale. Refreshing with a crisp, dry finish.

Star Bitter (OG 1039, ABV 3.9%) ◄
Reminiscent of the long-extinct Shipstone's Bitter, this mid-brown bitter lives up to its name as it is bitter in taste but not unpleasantly so.

Gordon Bennett (OG 1041, ABV 4.1%)
Light chestnut-coloured beer with a biscuity character and a pleasant hop finish.

Beaver Bitter (OG 1043, ABV 4.3%) ◄
A light brown bitter that starts malty in both aroma and taste, but soon develops a hoppy bitterness. Appreciably fruity.

Old Dalby (OG 1050, ABV 5.1%)
A rich, smooth ruby red strong ale with pleasant hop character.

Contract brewed for Hoskins Brothers:

Hob Bitter (OG 1040, ABV 4%)

IPA (OG 1040, ABV 4%)

Contract brewed for Shipstone's Beer Co Ltd:

Bitter (OG 1036, ABV 3.8%)
Amber-coloured, dry, classic Nottingham-style bitter.

Nut Brown (OG 1041, ABV 4%)

Gold Star (OG 1041, ABV 4.2%)
Smooth, well-balanced blonde ale, clean and crisp with a light, subtle hop finish.

Contract brewed for Steamin' Billy:

Tipsy Fisherman (OG 1036, ABV 3.6%)
Traditional light amber-coloured bitter with a mellow, crisp flavour and a hoppy aftertaste.

Bitter (OG 1043, ABV 4.3%)
A light golden three-hop English bitter with a pronounced floral flavour and aroma followed by a lingering aftertaste.

1485 (OG 1050, ABV 5%)

Skydiver (OG 1050, ABV 5%)
Full-strength mahogany-coloured beer with a fine balance of malty sweetness and hop bitterness. Deceivingly drinkable.

Bendigo (NEW)

c/o Unit 3, Northgate Place, High Church Street, New Basford, Nottingham, NG7 7JT ⊕ bendigobitter.com

Brewing began in 2015. Beers are currently brewed using spare capacity at Robin Hood Brewery (qv) while own premises are sought.

Bitter (ABV 4%)

Beowulf SIBA ◉

Forest of Mercia, Chasewater Country Park, Pool Lane, Brownhills, Staffordshire, WS8 7NL
☎ (01543) 454067 ☎ 07714 291226
⊕ beowulfbrewery.com

Beowulf Brewing Company is based at the Chasewater County Park. Its beers appear as guest ales predominantly in the central region, but also across the country. The brewery's dark beers have a particular reputation for excellence. ‼ ♦ RAIB

Beorma (OG 1038, ABV 3.9%) ◄
A perfectly balanced session ale with a malty hint of fruit giving way to a lingering bitterness. Background spice excites the palate.

Chasewater Bitter (OG 1043, ABV 4.4%) ◄
Golden bitter, hoppy throughout with citrus and hints of malt. Long, mouth-watering, bitter finish.

Chase Buster (OG 1045, ABV 4.5%)
A pale golden bitter.

Dark Raven (OG 1048, ABV 4.5%) ▮ ◄
Dark with apple and bonfire in the aroma. Sweet and smooth like liquid toffee apples with a sudden bitter finish.

Swordsman (OG 1045, ABV 4.5%) ◄
Pale gold, light fruity aroma, tangy hoppy flavour. Faintly hoppy finish.

Folded Cross (OG 1045, ABV 4.6%) ◄
Malt and caramel aromas and tastes with hints of fruity biscuits are nudged aside by the robust hops which give lingering bitter edges.

Hurricane (OG 1041, ABV 4.6%)
A copper-coloured bitter.

Dragon Smoke Stout (OG 1048, ABV 4.7%) ◄
Black with a light brown creamy head. Tobacco, chocolate, liquorice and mixed fruity hints on the aroma. Bitterness fights through the sweet and roast flavours and eventually dominates. Hints of a good port emerge.

Finn's Hall Porter (OG 1049, ABV 4.7%) ◄
Dark chocolate aroma, after-dinner mints, coffee and fresh tobacco. Good bitterness with woodland hints of autumn. Long, late bitterness with lip-drying moreishness.

Heroes Bitter (OG 1046, ABV 4.7%) ◆
Gold in colour, malt aroma, hoppy taste but sweetish finish.

Mercian Shine (OG 1048, ABV 5%) ◆
Amber to pale gold with a good bitter and hoppy start. Plenty of caramel and hops with background malt leading to a good bitter finish with caramel and hops lingering in the aftertaste.

IPA (OG 1074, ABV 7.2%) ◆
Malty aroma with plenty of hops. Sweet malty start, malty middle and hoppy finish. Complex tastes abound with fruit, sweetness and hops all combining to produce a terrific taste, strong and warming.

Berrow

See Towles'

Bespoke SIBA

Unit 5, The Mews, Mitcheldean, Gloucestershire, GL17 0SL
☎ (01594) 546557 ⊕ bespokebrewery.co.uk

⊗ Brewing commenced in 2012 on a 5.5-barrel plant on the site of the former Wintles Brewery. In 2014 capacity was increased to 12 barrels. Speciality-labelled bottles are offered for celebratory occasions. An on-site brewery tap opens on Fridays 2-11; Saturdays 4-11; and Sundays 4-9 pm. ‼🍺◆

Raging Ale (OG 1035, ABV 3.4%)
Light golden session bitter with zesty finish brewed exclusively with British malt and hops.

Leading Light (OG 1035, ABV 3.5%)
A light blonde ale with a refreshing citrus hop finish.

Saved by the Bell (OG 1038, ABV 3.8%)
A light, refreshing session bitter with a spicy hop bite and a light floral aroma from the late hop addition.

King's Shilling (OG 1044, ABV 4.2%)
A mild ale with full malt flavour and a clean, dry finish.

Running the Gauntlet (OG 1046, ABV 4.4%)
Full, malty flavoured bitter with rich roasted undertones balanced with good hop bitterness with spicy blackcurrant aromas from late hopping.

Going Off Half-Cocked (OG 1045, ABV 4.6%)
A spicy hopped golden pale ale.

Money for Old Rope (OG 1049, ABV 4.8%)
Classic stout with rich dry flavours of malt and grain with deep hop bitterness.

Over a Barrel (OG 1052, ABV 5%)
A richly coloured, fruity strong ale with a generous peppery finish.

Betteridge's

Coopers Barn, The Dene, Hurstbourne Tarrant, Hampshire, SP11 0AG ☎ 07771 966058
⊕ betteridgesbrewery.co.uk

Trading since 2014, Betteridge uses a 2.5-barrel plant. Founder and brewer Mark Betteridge brews four core beers using principally English hops and traditional floor-malted barley. Beers are supplied to beer festivals, private events and to a growing

number of pubs in the Test Valley area and occasionally further afield. RAIB

Old Chap (ABV 3.8%)
An easy-drinking, lightly hopped session bitter, amber in colour, with good malt flavour.

Jenny Wren (ABV 4.2%)
A golden-coloured, single hopped beer with a distinctive hop flavour and malty notes.

Private Sector (ABV 4.2%)
A full-flavoured amber-coloured ale.

Serious Black (ABV 4.2%)
A complex enriched stout with coffee, chocolate notes and roast flavours but with some underlying sweetness from added lactose.

Bewdley SIBA

Unit 7, Bewdley Craft Centre, Lax Lane, Bewdley, Worcestershire, DY12 2DZ
☎ (01299) 405148 ⊕ bewdleybrewery.co.uk

⊗ Bewdley began brewing in 2008 on a six-barrel plant in an old school. This was upgraded to a 10-barrel plant in 2014. Brewing experience days are offered – please ring for details. Beers are brewed with a railway theme for the nearby Severn Valley Railway. ‼🍺◆RAIB

Worcestershire Way (OG 1036, ABV 3.6%)
A light beer with citrus notes.

Black 5 Special (OG 1038, ABV 3.8%)

Old School Bitter (OG 1038, ABV 3.8%)
Session bitter with a hoppy finish.

Jubilee (OG 1043, ABV 4.3%)
Pale-coloured beer with a fruit and citrus aroma and a sweet malt taste with underlying citrus.

Sir Keith Park (OG 1045, ABV 4.5%)
Pale amber in colour, full-bodied and fruity with a balanced flavour followed by a long, hoppy finish.

2857 (OG 1050, ABV 5%)

Worcestershire Sway (OG 1050, ABV 5%)
A stronger version of Worcestershire Way, slightly sweeter with more body.

William Mucklow's Dark Mild (OG 1060, ABV 6%)
Dark in colour with a malty, sweetish fruity flavour and a slight liquorice finish.

Bexar County

8 Belgic Square, Padholme Road, Peterborough, Cambridgeshire, PE1 5XF
☎ (07934) 722584 ☎ 07934 722584
⊕ bexarcountybrewery.com

Bexar was established in 2013, brewing American-style beers. V

Poquito Pequeno (OG 1040, ABV 3.5%)

Prospect (OG 1048, ABV 4.5%)

Phantasmagorical (OG 1075, ABV 7.4%)

Bexley SIBA 👁

18 Manford Industrial Estate, Erith, Kent, DA8 2AJ
☎ (01322) 337368 ⊕ bexleybrewery.co.uk

Opened in 2014, the brewery produces regular and seasonal brews from a six-barrel plant with two conical fermenters. The beers are conditioned for at least seven days prior to release. Brewer Cliff

Murphy and wife Jane also undertake weekend off-sales of the distinctive 'parakeet'-labelled bottled beers on site. ‼️🍴◆

Golden Acre (OG 1042, ABV 4%) ◆
Golden ale with citrus aroma. Flavour is of grapefruit, spicy hops and a strong bitterness, continuing in the dry, fruity finish.

Bexley's Own Beer (OG 1044, ABV 4.2%) ◆
Pale brown best bitter with apple notes and a little sweetness. Trace of hops and bitterness in flavour and finish.

Redhouse Premium (OG 1042, ABV 4.2%)
A rich-flavoured pale ale, with a clean finish and late hop bitterness.

US Cascade Pale Ale (ABV 4.7%)
An amber-coloured ale with a taste and aroma of lemon citrus and pine, with a malty, biscuity finish.

Big Bog SIBA

74 Venture Point West, Evans Road, Speke, Merseyside, L24 9PB
☎ (0151) 558 0290 ⊕ bigbog.co.uk

Big Bog was established in 2011 by Paul Jefferies of Hydes Brewery. The brewery, which used to share its site with the Snowdonia Parc brewpub, underwent rapid expansion in 2013. In 2016 the brewery moved to its present location in Speke. ◆

Bog Standard Bitter (OG 1036, ABV 3.6%)
A light-coloured session beer with medium bitterness and a distinctive hoppy finish.

Blonde Bach (ABV 3.9%)
A pale-coloured ale with citrus/grapefruit notes.

Hinkypunk (OG 1041, ABV 4.1%)
Hoppy beer with intense citrus notes. Extremely pale in colour.

Welsh Pale Ale (OG 1042, ABV 4.2%)
Tawny-coloured classic British ale with medium bitterness and a dry finish.

Swampy (OG 1044, ABV 4.7%)
Ruby red in colour with a robust bitterness that is offset by a slightly sweet finish owing to the inclusion of muscovado sugar in the recipe.

Bog Trotter (OG 1051, ABV 5.3%)
Rich chestnut in colour with a hint of roasted flavours from black malt which are offset by classic spicy hop notes.

Quagmire (OG 1058, ABV 6%)
A strong but deceptively easy-drinking beer, mid-brown in colour with a medium to high bitterness.

Bog Super IPA (OG 1068, ABV 7%)
An IPA with a tawny colour, great strength and robust bitterness.

Big Clock SIBA

🍴 Grants, 1 Manchester Road, Accrington, Lancashire, BB5 2BQ
☎ (01254) 393938 ⊕ thebigclockbrewery.co.uk

Brewing commenced in 2014. A 6.5-barrel plant is used.

Sunny Boy (OG 1038, ABV 3.8%)
A deep golden hoppy ale with a floral, herbal taste and nose.

100 (OG 1040, ABV 4%)

Pals (OG 1040, ABV 4%)
Easy-drinking light blonde bitter with a floral nose.

Dirty Blonde (OG 1042, ABV 4.2%)
Blonde beer with blackcurrant, lemon and spicy flavours.

Dark Knight (OG 1045, ABV 4.5%)
A velvety stout with a spicy, liquorish taste.

Big Hand SIBA

Unit A1, Abbey Close, Redwither Business Park, Wrexham, LL13 9XG
☎ (01978) 660709 ☎ 07946 514238
⊕ facebook.com/BigHandBrewing

☺Big Hand is a family owned and run brewery that began brewing in 2013 using a 10-barrel plant. It opens on the first Friday of each month for its Weekend Wind Down event where you can enjoy beer served from a bar in the brewery itself. In 2014 its award-winning beer, King's Bane, featured in the Stranger's Bar in the House of Commons. The brewery sponsors the Focus Wales music festival in Wrexham. ‼️🍴◆

Solaris (OG 1035.9, ABV 3.7%)

King's Bane (OG 1038, ABV 3.9%) ◆
A clean-tasting malty bitter with a fruity aroma and peppery hops evident in the full, smooth mouthfeel.

Seren (OG 1038, ABV 3.9%)
American-style pale ale, light and malty.

Melyn (OG 1039, ABV 4%) ◆
A malty, hoppy beer with a faint fruit aroma and bittersweet taste. The initial sweet malt flavours combine with hoppy bitterness in the aftertaste.

Bastion (OG 1041, ABV 4.2%) ◆
A dry, malty best bitter, mahogany in colour with a full mouthfeel. Biscuity flavours and faint roast notes feature throughout.

Tyn-y-Capel Ale (OG 1041, ABV 4.2%)

Domino (OG 1046, ABV 4.4%) ◆
A smooth and fruity stout, quite hoppy and roasty with hints of berries in the initial sweetness leading to a satisfying hoppy finish.

Havok (OG 1049, ABV 5%)
Intense American-style pale ale with strong grapefruit flavours.

Bad Gorilla (OG 1060, ABV 6%)
A strong, dark mild, sweet yet dry.

Big Lamp

Grange Road, Newburn, Newcastle upon Tyne, NE15 8NL
☎ (0191) 267 1689 ⊕ biglampbrewers.co.uk

☺Big Lamp started in 1982 and relocated in 1997 to a 55-barrel plant in a former water pumping station. It is the oldest microbrewery in the north-east of England. Around 160 outlets are supplied and two pubs are owned, one of which (the Keelman) is attached to the brewery. ‼️◆RAIB

Sunny Daze (OG 1036, ABV 3.6%) ◆
Golden, hoppy session bitter with a clean taste and finish.

Bitter (OG 1039, ABV 3.9%) ◆
A clean-tasting bitter, full of hops and malt. A hint of fruit with a good, hoppy finish.

Lamplight Bitter (OG 1042, ABV 4.2%)
Crisp, light, refreshing ale with a dry aftertaste.

Summerhill Stout (OG 1044, ABV 4.4%) ◆
A rich, tasty stout, dark in colour with a lasting rich roast character. Malty mouthfeel with a lingering finish.

Prince Bishop Ale (OG 1048, ABV 4.8%) ◆
A refreshing, easy-drinking bitter. Golden in colour, full of fruit and hops. Strong bitterness with a spicy, dry finish.

Premium (OG 1052, ABV 5.2%) ◆
Hoppy ale with a good bitter finish.

Keelman Brown (OG 1057, ABV 5.7%)
A full-bodied ale with a hint of toffee.

Big Rabbit SIBA ◉

Unit 1, Butterleigh Sawmill, Butterleigh, Cullompton, Devon, EX15 1PP
☎ (01884) 308633 ☎ 07926 191089

Office: Olde Mill Limited, 12 East Street, Suite 101, Epsom, Surrey, KT17 1HX ⊕ oldemill.co.uk

⊠ Part of Olde Mill Ltd, of London Cider Company fame, Big Rabbit commenced brewing in 2014 in a former rural sawmill. There are plans for bottle-conditioned beers during the coming year. The brewery often uses locally sourced ingredients and Herefordshire hops. The company also produces cider. ◆

Unit 1 Red Ale (ABV 4%)

Wild West Country (ABV 4%)

Black Annie (ABV 4.5%)

Orange Elephant IPA (ABV 4.5%)

Hedgerow Hooligan (ABV 5%)

Hop Fodder (ABV 5.1%)

Big Shed

2 Muckleton Lane, Shawbury, Shrewsbury, SY4 4HF
☎ (01939) 250678 ⊕ bigshedbrewery.co.uk

Big Shed Brewery opened in 2014 on a smallholding in rural North Shropshire using a new 20-barrel plant and brewing in a traditional manner. Three mainstream beers are produced. ◆

Battlefield Gold (OG 1038, ABV 3.8%)

Engineers Best (OG 1042, ABV 4.2%)
Golden-coloured pale ale with a restrained malt flavour and a hint of sweetness and a light citrus element.

Tyger Tyger IPA (OG 1045, ABV 4.5%)

Big Smoke SIBA ◉

⊟ Antelope, 87 Maple Road, Surbiton, Surrey, KT6 4AW
☎ (020) 8339 9721 ☎ 07859 884190
⊕ bigsmokebrew.co.uk

⊠ Big Smoke is a purpose-built brewery established in 2014 in courtyard buildings behind the Antelope pub, Surbiton. The five-barrel brew kit is used twice weekly; a range of core beers and bi-monthly ales are available in the Antelope, the Sussex Arms in Twickenham, the Lyric in Soho, the Express in Brentford and occasionally in other local pubs and at beer festivals. ◆V

Solaris Session Pale Ale (ABV 3.8%) ◆
Unfined golden ale with bitter grapefruit flavour, some malt and a long, dry, bitter finish. Hoppy fruity nose.

Dark Wave Porter (ABV 5%)

Electric Eye Pale Ale (ABV 5%)

Underworld Milk Stout (ABV 5%) ◆
A sweet, smooth stout with hints of chocolate and coffee in the taste.

Biggar (NEW)

Queens Arms Courtyard, Biggar Village, Barrow-in-Furness, Cumbria, LA14 3YG
☎ (01229) 474335 ⊕ biggarbrewing.co.uk

This 2.5-barrel brewery, an independent co-operative of several shareholders, opened in late 2015 in the courtyard of the Queens Arms in Biggar Village on Walney Island. The beer names are themed on Barrow's shipbuilding heritage, and the brewery logo features a representation of Barrow's dockside cranes, a strong visual motif of the town's history.

Mikasa (ABV 3.6%)
A dark mild with a slight hint of chocolate.

Vanguard (OG 1041, ABV 3.8%)

Oriana (ABV 4.2%)

Billericay SIBA

⊟ Essex Beer Shop, 54c Chapel Street, Billericay, Essex, CM12 9LS
☎ (01277) 500121 ☎ 07788 373129
⊕ billericaybrewing.co.uk

Billericay Brewing opened at its present site in 2014, having brewed at Pitfield the previous year. A micropub and beershop are next door. ‼ ⊟ ◆ RAIB

Zeppelin (OG 1037, ABV 3.8%)
Easy-drinking session ale with slight smoky notes.

Blonde (OG 1040, ABV 4%)

Dickie (OG 1041, ABV 4.2%)
A balanced amber-coloured ale with biscuit notes.

Rhythm Stick (OG 1047, ABV 4.8%)
Hoppy, rich ale with caramel flavours.

A Mild with no Name (OG 1055, ABV 5.5%)
An easy-drinking strong mild.

Chapel Street Porter (OG 1059, ABV 5.9%)
Rich, dark porter with chocolate and coffee flavours.

Mayflower Gold (OG 1064, ABV 6.5%)
A hoppy IPA.

Binghams SIBA

Unit 10, Tavistock Industrial Estate, Ruscombe, Berkshire, RG10 9NJ
☎ (0118) 934 4376 ⊕ binghams.co.uk

⊠ Binghams began brewing in 2010, producing 40 firkins in each batch. The brewery is situated in an industrial unit on the site of a former brickworks – hence the name of one of the beers. Head brewer Chris Bingham is a member of the local branch of CAMRA and had extensive experience in homebrewing and a local brewery prior to starting up. ‼ ⊟ RAIB

Twyford Tipple (OG 1040, ABV 3.7%)
Tawny-coloured bitter with a good balance of malt
and hops in the flavour and a citrus hop finish.

Brickworks Bitter (OG 1047, ABV 4.2%)
Chestnut-coloured best bitter with a sweetish,
malty nose. Hops balance the maltiness to give a
well-rounded flavour with a slightly nutty hint and
a sweet, earthy aftertaste.

Coffee Stout (OG 1056, ABV 5%)
A mellow beer with dark malts that complement
the coffee flavour.

Doodle Stout (OG 1056, ABV 5%)
A blend of dark malts provide a complex character.
Named after the brewery dog, a Labradoodle
called Stout.

Ginger Doodle Stout (OG 1056, ABV 5%)
A dark stout with a subtle hint of ginger which
rounds off the bitterness.

Hot Dog Chilli Stout (OG 1056, ABV 5%)
Doodle Stout with a hint of chilli to provide a warm
glow on the aftertaste.

Space Hoppy IPA (OG 1052, ABV 5%)
Pale golden and packed with hops to create a
complex flavour and a long citrus finish.

Vanilla Stout (OG 1052, ABV 5%) 🍂
Infused with vanilla pods that complement the
dark malts to create a smooth-drinking, dark stout.

Bingley SIBA

**Unit 2, Old Mill Yard, Shay Lane, Wilsden, West
Yorkshire, BD15 0DR**
☎ (01535) 274285 ⊕ bingleybrewery.co.uk

Bingley is a small, family-run brewery that opened
in 2014 using a six-barrel plant. It is located in a
rural setting in the village of Wilsden, part of
Bingley Rural Ward. More than 20 outlets are
supplied. ‼

Goldy Locks Blonde (ABV 4%)
Refreshing citrus aroma and a delicate toffee
aftertaste.

Centennial (ABV 4.4%)

1848 Stout (ABV 4.8%)
A creamy stout made using roasted malts with
hints of chocolate and liquorice and a bitter finish.

Blantyre Red (ABV 5%)
A robust, full-bodied red ale.

Jamestown APA (ABV 5.4%)
Slightly spicy American-style pale ale with distinct
piny notes on the palate and an aroma of
grapefruit with a hint of apricot.

Warrior (ABV 5.8%)

Birchover (NEW)

📗 Red Lion, Main Street, Birchover, Derbyshire,
DE4 2BN
☎ (01629) 650363 ⊕ red-lion-birchover.co.uk

Brewing commenced in 2016 at the Red Lion Inn.
The pub's own well water is used.

Bircher Best (ABV 3.9%)
An amber-coloured best bitter.

Cork-Stone (ABV 4.5%)
Refreshingly bitter, golden blonde ale with a
pleasant dry finish.

Bird Brain

30 Hailgate, Howden, East Yorkshire, DN14 7SL
☎ (01430) 432166 ☎ 07790 615915
✉ birdbrainbrewery@tiscali.co.uk

☺Bird Brain began brewing in 2009 on a two-
barrel plant expanded to four barrel capacity in
2012. Brewing twice a month, the brewery
supplies local pubs and beer festivals. ♦

Shiny (OG 1038, ABV 3.9%)

Howden Bittern (OG 1039, ABV 4%)

Bishop Nick SIBA 👁

33 East Street, Braintree, Essex, CM7 3JJ
☎ (01376) 349605 ⊕ bishopnick.com

⊗ Bishop Nick was launched in 2011 by Nelion
Ridley, a member of the family that started
Ridley's brewery near Chelmsford in 1842. In 2013
a new brewery was established in Braintree using
a 20-barrel plant. 🍴♦RAIB

Ridley's Rite (OG 1036, ABV 3.6%)

Heresy (OG 1041, ABV 4%)

1555 (OG 1043, ABV 4.3%)

Bishop's Crook SIBA

**51 Woodcroft Close, Penwortham, Lancashire,
PR1 9BX ☎ 07516 478003**
⊕ bishopscrookbrewery.com

A small brewery based at the home of one of the
owners, it started brewing commercially in late
2013 and currently has just a handful of regular
outlets.

Galaxy (OG 1037, ABV 3.7%)
A light pale ale with citrus and passion fruit
flavours.

Withy Way (OG 1038, ABV 3.8%)
A light pale ale with floral, citrus and tropical
flavours.

Ah Fuggit (OG 1040, ABV 4%)
A copper-coloured ale brewed with traditional
English hops with a citrus twist.

Initiate (OG 1040, ABV 4%)
A golden ale with strong citrus and tropical fruit
flavours.

Lancashire's Invaders (OG 1042, ABV 4.2%)
A refreshing amber-coloured ale, well hopped and
providing a burst of grapefruit, lemon and pine.

Bishop's Stortford

**c/o Prince of Wales, Green Tye, Much Hadham,
Hertfordshire, SG10 6JP**
☎ (01279) 503224

Correspondence: **24 Trinity Street, Bishop's Stortford,
Hertfordshire, CM23 3TJ**
✉ bishopsstortfordbrewery@hotmail.co.uk

⊗ Established in 2012, the brewery has produced
beer on various other brewer's equipment. Since
the start of 2014 the brewery has used spare
capacity at Ash Valley Brewery (qv) in Green Tye,
Hertfordshire. ♦

Stortford Pale Ale (OG 1039, ABV 3.8%)

Stortford Sunrise (OG 1041, ABV 3.8%)

A refreshing golden ale, with a subtle hint of Belgian witbier.

Stortford Sunset (OG 1042, ABV 3.8%)
A complex beer with a golden hue. Triple hopping is completed with American Simcoe for a long, firm finish.

Stortford Citra (OG 1039, ABV 3.9%)
A light golden ale with a good balance of malt and citrus hops.

Bishop's Stortford Bitter (OG 1040, ABV 4.1%)
Classic copper-coloured bitter with a complex balance of malts and hopped with English Fuggles.

Bitter End

See Tirril

Black Bear

≣ c/o Bear Inn, 8-10 North Street, Wiveliscombe, Somerset, TA4 2JY
☎ (01984) 623537 ✉ liquidbrighton@hotmail.com

Originally named East Stratton, brewing began in 2014 and was based at the Northbrook Arms in East Stratton, Hampshire. The brewery relocated and was renamed in 2015. Seasonal beers are planned.

Wivey Best (ABV 3.8%)
Copper-coloured bitter, brewed with Cascade and Northdown hops.

Wivey Pure (ABV 3.8%)
A golden version of Wivey Best

Black Cat SIBA

Unit 12, Knights Business Centre, Squires Farm Industrial Estate, Palehouse Common, Framfield, East Sussex, TN22 5RB
☎ (01825) 840879 ☎ 07909 916813
⊕ blackcat-brewery.com

⊠ Black Cat began brewing in 2011 in Groombridge using a 2.5-barrel plant, supplying three to four local pubs. It has now relocated to Framfield, expanded and is owned and run by husband-and-wife team, Paul and Kate Wratten. ♦RAIB

Tip Top (OG 1039, ABV 3.2%)
Smooth-tasting beer that belies its low alcohol content.

Hopsmack (OG 1045, ABV 4%)
A golden beer, refreshing and hoppy with citrus overtones.

Original (OG 1046, ABV 4.2%)
A hoppy, bitter, amber-coloured beer balanced with malt.

Nine Tails (OG 1053, ABV 4.9%)
A dark-coloured winter warmer.

Crossale (OG 1050, ABV 5.1%)
An ale/lager cross, full-flavoured and refreshing.

Tsar Imperial Stout (OG 1072, ABV 6.8%)
A robust stout made with real chocolate.

Black Country SIBA 👁

≣ Rear of Old Bulls Head, 1 Redhall Road, Lower Gornal, West Midlands, DY3 2NU

☎ (01384) 401820

Office: 69 Third Avenue, Pensnett Trading Estate, Kingswinford, West Midlands, DY6 7FD
⊕ blackcountryales.co.uk

Originally brewing at the rear of the Old Bulls Head since 2004, the brewery relocated in 2015. Beers are also brewed under the Thomas Guest Brewing Company name. ‼♦

Bradley's Finest Golden (OG 1040, ABV 4.2%)
A straw-coloured quaffing beer with a bold citrus hop aroma, fruity balanced sweetness and a lingering, refreshing aftertaste.

Pig on the Wall (OG 1042, ABV 4.3%)
A refreshing chestnut brown beer with a complex flavour of light hops giving way to a bittersweet blend of roasted malt. Suggestions of chocolate and coffee undertones.

Fireside (OG 1047, ABV 5%)
A well-rounded premium bitter, amber in colour, clean in taste leading to a pleasant, dry finish.

Black Dog

See Hambleton

Black Falls

See Neath

Black Flag

Unit 4D Bridge Road Industrial Estate, Goonhavern, Cornwall, TR4 9QL
☎ (01872) 858004 ⊕ blackflagbrewery.com

⊠ Black Flag began brewing in 2013 using an eight-barrel plant. Much use is made of New Zealand and US hops. ♦RAIB

Chameleon (OG 1038, ABV 3.8%) 🍺
Golden ale. Grassy and floral hops throughout. Punchy lemon citrus flavour with apricot and peaches. Bitter, dry and crisp finish.

Fang (OG 1040, ABV 4%) 🍺
Light amber-coloured best bitter with hop aroma. Orange and tart grapefruit throughout, balanced by light malt. Light hop bitter finish.

Naughty Pilchard (OG 1040, ABV 4%) 🍺
Pale brown best bitter with malt aroma. Malt flavour with a sharp bite of hops. Dry, malty and citrus finish.

Mosiac IPA (OG 1055, ABV 5.7%)
Single hopped IPA. Masses of fruity citrus hops, tones of mango.

White Cross IPA (OG 1057, ABV 5.7%) 🍺
Amber beer with fruity and malty aroma. Powerful hop bitterness with fruit sweetness, grapefruit and apple. Dry and bitter finish.

Saison (OG 1052, ABV 6.1%)
Traditional Belgian-style farmhouse pale ale, smooth and malty. Crisp, gentle aftertaste with the medium-intensity spiciness of Dupont yeast.

Black Hole SIBA

Unit 63GF, IMEX Business Park, Shobnall Road, Burton upon Trent, Staffordshire, DE14 2AU

☎ (01283) 619943 ☎ 07812 812953
⊕ blackholebrewery.co.uk

⊠ Black Hole was established in 2007 with a purpose-built 10-barrel plant in the former Ind Coope bottling stores. Fermenting capacity was increased in 2012 to enable the production of up to four brews per week. Around 600 outlets, mainly in the Midlands, are supplied direct, and many more via wholesalers. The brewery was bought by the owners of Mr Grundy's Brewery (qv) in 2014. ‼◆

Bitter (OG 1040, ABV 3.8%) ⬗
Amber glow and malt and spicy hop aroma. Fresh lively session beer hopped to give a clean, crisp finish of hoppy dryness and a touch of astringency.

Cosmic (OG 1044, ABV 4.2%) ⬗
Almost golden with an initial malt aroma. The complex balance of malt and English hops gives lingering tastes of nuts, fruit and dry, hoppy bitterness.

Red Dwarf (OG 1045, ABV 4.5%) ⬗
Red as named with a sweet shop start of sugary sweet fruits with citrus centres. Malt is elbowed aside by the hops which dominate the tongue-tickling bitter end.

Supernova (OG 1048, ABV 4.8%) ⬗
Pure gold. Like marmalade made from Seville oranges and grapefruit, the aroma mimics the sweet start but gives into the hops which deliver a dry, lingering bitter finish.

Cyborg (OG 1055, ABV 5.5%) ⬗
Malty aroma, sweet start building to a sweet but hoppy finish. Mouthwateringly bitter.

Milky Way (OG 1059, ABV 6%) ⬗
Honey and banana nose advises the sweet taste but not the sweet, dry spicy finish from this wheat beer.

Black Horse SIBA ⬿

26 Nottingham Court, Nottingham Road, Louth, Lincolnshire, LN11 0WB
☎ (01507) 354331 ☎ 07557 789060

Office: Freshwater Cottage, 2 Chapel Brow, Charlesworth, Glossop, Derbyshire, SK13 5HH
⊕ blackhorsebrewing.co.uk

☺Black Horse is a five-barrel microbrewery situated in the Lincolnshire Wolds. There is a retail outlet and fully licensed bar at the brewery. A range of events, including tasting sessions and beer festivals, are held throughout the year. Beers can be found across the county and beyond. ☞◆

Mild Midlander (OG 1034, ABV 3.4%)
A dark, rich and creamy mild with notes of roasted coffee.

Lincolnshire Traditional Bitter (OG 1038, ABV 3.8%)
A traditional English session bitter with a smooth finish.

Where's My Fiorucci (OG 1038, ABV 3.8%)
Amber-coloured session beer with delicate malt flavours and a slightly spicy aroma.

Saturday's Blonde (OG 1042, ABV 4%)
A delicate pale ale bittered with carefully selected citrus hops, leaving a subtle yet refreshing aftertaste.

Pleasant Blonde (OG 1042, ABV 4.2%)

Refreshing blonde ale with a clean citrus hop flavour and flowery grapefruit aroma.

Black Frog (OG 1044, ABV 4.4%)
Dark English ale with complex malt flavours, nicely bittered with a slight smoky aroma.

Queens (OG 1040, ABV 4.4%)
Full-bodied golden ale.

Nicholas De Luda (OG 1050, ABV 5.4%)
A rich, dark, old-style English stout, full-bodied and packed with flavour.

Thanks Pa (OG 1057, ABV 6%)
Traditional strength IPA with a floral bouquet and citrus finish.

Black Iris SIBA

Unit 1, Shipstone Street, New Basford, Nottingham, NG7 6GJ
☎ (0115) 979 1936 ✉ blackirisbrewery@gmail.com

Black Iris began brewing in 2011 using a six-barrel plant behind the Flowerpot pub in Derby. It expanded to a brand new 10-barrel plant in 2014 and relocated to premises in Nottingham. ‼◆

Snake Eyes (OG 1038, ABV 3.8%) ⬗
Golden-coloured ale with an intense hoppy aroma and taste with a lingering bitter finish.

Bleeding Heart (OG 1044, ABV 4.5%) ⬗
Red rye malty ale balanced with roast and hops and a bitter finish.

Better the Devil You Know (OG 1053, ABV 5.5%)
Pale, citrus Australian-style IPA with big fruity aromas and a lingering bitterness.

Black Isle

Old Allengrange, Munlochy, Ross-shire, IV8 8NZ
☎ (01463) 811871 ⊕ blackislebrewery.com

☺Black Isle Brewery was set up in 1998 in the heart of the Scottish Highlands. It expanded substantially in 2011 with a new brewhouse and bottling line. All beers are organic with Soil Association certification. ‼☞◆

Yellowhammer (OG 1038, ABV 3.9%) ⬗
A refreshing, hoppy golden ale with light hop and passion fruit throughout. A short, bitter finish.

Red Kite (OG 1042, ABV 4.2%) ⬗
Tawny ale with light malt on the nose and some fruit on the palate. Slight sweetness in the taste and a short, bitter finish.

Heather Honey (OG 1045, ABV 4.6%) ⬗
Sweet, honey-flavoured brew.

Porter (OG 1046, ABV 4.6%) ⬗
A hint of liquorice and burnt chocolate on the nose and a creamy mix of malt and fruit in the taste.

Blonde (OG 1046, ABV 5%)

Black Market (NEW)

▤ The Workman's, 43 High Street, Warsop, Nottinghamshire, NG20 0AE ☎ 07824 363373/ 360773

Beers first appeared from Black Market in 2016. The 2.5-barrel plant is situated in the basement of the brewery tap, the Workman's. Further beers are planned.

Imposter (OG 1033.5, ABV 3.7%)

Pale session ale with citrus notes.

Illicit (OG 1041.5, ABV 4.7%)
Hoppy pale ale with grapefruit notes.

Insane (ABV 5.8%)
A strong golden ale.

Black Metal

Unit 3, 6b Dryden Road, Loanhead, EH20 9LZ
☎ (0131) 623 3411 ☎ 07711 295385
⊕ blackmetalbrewery.com

Black Metal Brewery was established in 2012 by two old friends, originally brewing from home. A 1000-litre plant is now used, sharing equipment at Top Out (qv) brewery. ♦RAIB V

Black Paw SIBA

Unit 4, Westgate Road, Bishop Auckland, County Durham, DL14 7AX
☎ (01388) 602144 ☎ 07557 020664
⊕ blackpawbrewery.co.uk

Black Paw began brewing in 2011 using a 12-barrel plant and now supplies pubs across the North-east of England. Occasional open days are held. ♦

Bishop's Best (OG 1038, ABV 3.8%)
Tasty session bitter with a slight hint of chocolate.

Paw's Gold (OG 1040, ABV 4%)
A rich golden bitter with the malt and hop taste coming through.

Archbishop's Ale (OG 1041, ABV 4.1%)
Full-flavoured and smooth.

Polar Paw (OG 1044, ABV 4.4%)
Bittersweet dark ale with a pleasant hoppy aroma and aftertaste.

Dark Seam (OG 1050, ABV 5%)
A dark and full-flavoured beer with definite chocolate taste and a hint of coffee.

IPA (OG 1050, ABV 5%)
Amber-coloured ale, brewed to an American recipe. There is a strong, complex aroma and a refreshing bitter finish.

Black Rock SIBA

Unit 6c, Empire Way, Tregoniggie Industrial Estate, Falmouth, Cornwall, TR11 4SN
☎ (01326) 379477 ⊕ blackrockbrewing.com

⊗ Black Rock began brewing in 2013, producing just one beer. It now has a range of four beers, which are available in Five Degrees West in Falmouth and a number of other local outlets. Relocation to larger premises within Falmouth is planned. ♦RAIB

Endless IPA (ABV 3.8%)
A pale straw-coloured ale.

Pale Ale (OG 1042, ABV 4.2%) ◥
Light-tasting golden best bitter with faint hop aroma. Hops, tropical fruits, honey and earthy malt flavours. Persistent fruity aftertaste.

Deep (OG 1048, ABV 5%) ◥
Earthy, light hop and malt aroma. Strong hop bitterness in the mouth balanced by sweet fruit. Pear flavour aftertaste.

Black IPA (OG 1058, ABV 6%) ◥

Strong black porter with roast malt throughout. Smooth, rich flavours of raisins and cloves. Moderate hop bitterness, fading slowly.

Black Sheep SIBA ◉

Wellgarth, Masham, Ripon, North Yorkshire, HG4 4EN
☎ (01765) 689227 ⊕ blacksheepbrewery.co.uk

☺Established in 1992 by Paul Theakston, a member of Masham's famous brewing family, in the former Wellgarth Maltings, using the traditional Yorkshire Square fermenting system, the company now supplies around 600 free trade outlets, with national exposure through pubcos and wholesale channels, but owns no pubs. Production is 75% cask with the remainder bottled. Paul has now handed over operations to his sons. ‼◨♦

Best Bitter (OG 1038, ABV 3.8%) ◥
A hoppy and fruity beer with strong bitter overtones, leading to a long, dry, bitter finish.

Golden Sheep (OG 1039, ABV 3.9%)
A balanced blonde beer with a dry and refreshing bitterness. Light golden in colour with fresh citrus fruit flavours and a clean, crisp finish.

Ale (OG 1044, ABV 4.4%)
A premium bitter with robust fruit, malt and hops.

Riggwelter (OG 1059, ABV 5.9%) ▮◥
A fruity bitter, with complex underlying tastes and hints of liquorice and pear drops leading to a long, dry, bitter finish.

Black Tap (NEW)

▤ **Beech House, 6 Church Green East, Redditch, Worcestershire, B98 8BP**
☎ (01527) 549997 ⊕ blacktap.co.uk

Originally based in Staffordshire, Black Tap relocated to Redditch in 2015, now operating as a brewpub with a focus on serving high-quality cask ales, designed and brewed on site.

Not Lager (OG 1040, ABV 4%)
Smooth, easy-drinking beer with a citrus hop aroma and a refreshing, not too bitter finish.

Morning Glory (OG 1043, ABV 4.3%)
A hoppy beer with orange, citrus and herbal notes.

Golden Arrow (OG 1044, ABV 4.4%)
A single hop beer with bold characteristics including peach, mango, lemon and pine flavours and aromas.

Black Tor SIBA

Unit 5, Gidley's Industrial Estate, Christow, Exeter, Devon, EX6 7QB
☎ (01647) 252120 ⊕ blacktorbrewery.co.uk

Brewing began on this site in 1998 under the Scattor Rock name using a five-barrel plant. The brewery changed hands in 2009, trading under the Gidley's name, before another change of hands in 2013 when it became Black Tor. It changed hands again in 2015. The brewery is situated in the Teign Valley in the beautiful East Dartmoor National Park. Outlets are supplied in Devon and on the Cornwall border. Five beers are regularly produced, with plans for seasonal beers in the future.

Pride of Dartmoor (OG 1040, ABV 4%)
A mid-brown session bitter with a gentle floral aroma and pleasant taste.

Raven (OG 10420, ABV 4.2%)

Devonshire Pale Ale (OG 1044, ABV 4.5%)

Tor Ale (OG 1047, ABV 4.8%)
A deep golden brown ale with a hoppy aroma and sweet malty finish.

Templer's IPA (OG 1054, ABV 5.6%)
Classic IPA flavours with a gentle dark fruit twist.

Black Wolf SIBA ⊚

Unit 7c, Bandeath Industrial Estate, Throsk, Stirling, FK7 7NP
☎ (01786) 817000 ⊕ blackwolfbrewery.com

☺ Established in 2005, and now owned by VC2 Brands, the brewery is located in a former torpedo factory on the shores of the River Forth. In 2014 the brewery changed its name from Traditional Scottish Ales to Black Wolf Brewery and rebranded its range of beers. ♦

Nevis (OG 1040, ABV 4%)

RoK (OG 1040, ABV 4%)

Florida Black (OG 1045, ABV 4.5%)

Glencoe (OG 1045, ABV 4.5%)

William Wallace (OG 1045, ABV 4.5%)

Lomond Gold (OG 1050, ABV 5%)

Valente's Double Espresso (OG 1060, ABV 6%)

BlackBar

Unit B3, Button End Industrial Estate, Harston, Cambridgeshire, CB22 7GX
☎ (01223) 872131 ☎ 07811 499914
⊕ blackbar.co.uk

⊗ BlackBar was established in 2011. Around 10 outlets, mostly in the Cambridge area, are supplied direct. Mini-casks are also available. ‼ ╤ ♦ RAIB

Bitter (ABV 3.6%)
A malty, tawny brown-coloured bitter with a noble hop finish.

Blacklight (ABV 4%)
A blonde beer with hops on the nose.

Porteur (ABV 4%)
A malty, brown-coloured porter.

Black Economy (ABV 4.6%)

Blackbeck

☷ Blackbeck Inn, Blackbeck, Cumbria, CA22 2NY
☎ (01946) 841661 ⊕ blackbeckbrewery.co.uk

A five-barrel brewery, established in 2009 and owned by a father-and-daughter team, producing handcrafted ales using English malts and hops. Beers have fairground themed names and are also available in bottles and mini casks. ♦

Belle (OG 1038, ABV 3.8%) ◣
Sweet, tasty, dark mild.

Trial Run (OG 1037, ABV 3.8%) ◣
A fresh and fruity yellow beer with a lasting hoppy finish.

Blackedge SIBA ⊚

Moreton Mill, Hampson Street, Horwich, BL6 7JH

☎ (01204) 692976 ☎ 07795 654895
⊕ blackedgebrewery.co.uk

⊗ Blackedge Brewery, established in 2011, is a traditional five-barrel brewery producing handcrafted ales using only natural ingredients. No extracts or pellets are used in the brewing process. A core range of 10 beers is permanently available with special seasonal ales brewed monthly. The brewery also houses its own bar. ‼ ╤ ♦ RAIB

Session (OG 1038, ABV 3.5%)
A golden session bitter, surprisingly full bodied with a grapefruit flavour and aroma.

HoP (OG 1039, ABV 3.8%)
Generously hopped to give a clean, dry, refreshing and hoppy citrus, floral-flavoured session beer.

Black (OG 1047, ABV 4%)
A velvety stout with intense roasted barley flavours and rich undertones of chocolate and coffee with a liquorice finish.

Pike (OG 1042, ABV 4%)
A pale ale with plenty of sweet citrus hop flavour.

American Pale Ale (OG 1043, ABV 4.2%)
Light hoppy beer made using American hops giving intense citrus aromas.

Platinum (OG 1046, ABV 4.4%)
Blonde ale, light in colour, lightly hopped to give a clean, citrus flavour and a sweet citrus aroma.

BLONDe (OG 1046, ABV 4.5%)
Full-flavoured, full-bodied blonde ale, well hopped to give a clean, crisp fruity flavour and aroma.

Dark Rum (OG 1045, ABV 4.6%)
Dark rich porter with roasted coffee and chocolate flavours, hints of liquorice and finished with sweetness from dark rum.

IPA (OG 1047, ABV 4.7%)
Full-bodied, full-flavoured and well-balanced hoppy and intensely citrus IPA with a grapefruit aroma.

Black Port (OG 1045, ABV 4.9%) ◣
Black beer with a malty, fruity aroma. Rich, with chocolate and dark fruits to taste with a slightly drier finish.

Blackhill SIBA

Unit 1a, Pontop Business Park, Harelaw Industrial Estate, Stanley, County Durham, DH9 8HN
☎ (01207) 230632 ☎ 07905 788286
⊕ blackhillbrewery.com

Blackhill began brewing in 2012 using spare capacity at Geltsdale Brewery. In 2013 it moved to its own premises using a 10-barrel plant. Beers are named after Durham coal mining seams and are available on rotation. ♦

Blackjack SIBA

36 Gould Street, Manchester, M4 4RN
☎ (0161) 819 2767 ⊕ blackjack-beers.com

☺ Blackjack started brewing in 2012 using a 4.5-barrel plant, producing a large range of regular beers, many using Belgian and farmhouse yeasts. Beers are named with a playing card theme, and are widely available in the local free trade as well as further afield. A number of house beers are brewed for selected pubs. ♦ RAIB V

Pokies (OG 1036, ABV 3.6%)
Extra pale New Zealand-hopped session bitter.

Shuffled Deck (OG 1039, ABV 3.9%)
Aromas are marmalade with pine and grapefruit. Flavours are woody with sweet citrus and bitter grapefruit with a dry finish.

Bramling Cross (OG 1040, ABV 4%)
Single hopped best bitter.

New Deck (OG 1042, ABV 4.2%)
A crisp hoppy ale with a satisfying finish.

Solitaire (OG 1042, ABV 4.3%)
A pale session ale with a blend of lager malt and Maris Otter, simply hopped with delicate US and German varieties.

First Deal (OG 1044, ABV 4.4%)
A ruby ale with a dried fruit aroma and flavours of berries, earthy malts, and a spicy, bitter finish.

Small Saison (OG 1042, ABV 4.5%)
Spicy and dry.

Double Bluff (OG 1048, ABV 4.8%)
An amber ale with full aroma and bitter notes.

River (OG 1049, ABV 4.8%)
Brown ale with farmhouse yeast.

Beginners Luck (OG 1050, ABV 5%)
All-American Cascade-hopped pale ale. Punchy fruit aroma with a golden IPA bitterness and colour.

Schafkopf (OG 1050, ABV 5%)
A German wheat beer.

Stout (OG 1050, ABV 5%)
Aroma is roasted malts and chocolate syrup. Flavour is similar with a hint of maple syrup and light bitter hops. Finish is slightly fruity.

Aces High (OG 1055, ABV 5.5%)
Aroma has some ripe citrus notes of melon and orange. Flavour is sweet, with mild grass and pine, along with more ripe tangerine and melon.

Black Maria (OG 1057, ABV 5.8%)
A dark ale with a hoppy aroma, light body and a stout-like colour.

Dragon's Tears (OG 1054, ABV 5.8%)
A jasmine tea infused golden Saison.

Four of a Kind (OG 1060, ABV 6.2%)
American-style IPA, hopped with a blend of four US varieties.

Brewed for the Crescent, Salford:

Crescent Ale (ABV 4%)

Brewed for the Jack in the Box, Altrincham:

House Pale (ABV 4%)
English-hopped pale ale.

Brewed for the Moorbrook, Preston:

Moorbrook Pale Ale (ABV 3.9%)
A citrus pale ale.

Blackmore

▤ Trooper Inn, Golden Hill, Stourton Caundle, Dorset, DT10 2JW
☎ (01963) 362405 ✉ kevinstaunton@aol.com

⊗ This small 0.5-barrel brewpub began brewing in 2011, in the adjacent garage. Beers are brewed only for the pub.

Ale (OG 1038, ABV 3.8%)

Pale (OG 1042, ABV 4.2%)

Blackwater

See Salopian

Blindmans SIBA

Talbot Farm, Leighton, Frome, Somerset, BA11 4PN
☎ (01749) 880038 ⊕ blindmansbrewery.co.uk

Established in 2002 in a converted milking parlour and purchased by its current owners in 2004, this five-barrel brewery has its own water spring. The range of ales is regularly on tap at the Cornerhouse, Frome. ‼️ ☛◆

Buff (OG 1036, ABV 3.6%)
Amber-coloured, smooth session beer.

Golden Spring (OG 1040, ABV 4%)
Fresh and aromatic straw-coloured beer, brewed using selected lager malt.

Mine Beer (OG 1042, ABV 4.2%)
Full-bodied, copper-coloured, blended malt ale.

Icarus (OG 1045, ABV 4.5%)
Fruity, rich, mid-dark ruby ale.

Bloomsbury

▤ Perseverance, 63 Lamb's Conduit Street, Bloomsbury, London, WC1N 3NB
☎ (020) 7405 8278

Based in the cellar of the Perseverance pub, brewing began in 2015. ◆

Best Bitter (ABV 4.1%)

Pale Ale (ABV 4.1%)

Blue Anchor SIBA

▤ 50 Coinagehall Street, Helston, Cornwall, TR13 8EL
☎ (01326) 562821 ⊕ spingoales.com

⊗ 15th-century thatched brewpub, the oldest continuously brewing plant in the country. Home of the famous Spingo ales, which are produced from the well water beneath the pub. ‼️ ☛◆RAIB

Flora Daze (OG 1040, ABV 4%) ◟
Brown best bitter with light hoppy aroma and balanced malt, fruit and hops in the mouth. Lingering, bitter hop finish.

Jubilee IPA (OG 1045, ABV 4.5%) ◟
Copper-coloured best bitter with fruity hop aroma. Biscuit malt and fresh hop bitter taste. Long, bitter finish with rising dryness.

Ben's Stout (OG 1048, ABV 4.8%) ◟
Creamy black stout with coffee roast aroma. Roast malt with liquorice and cherry flavours. Sweet finish with apples and cloves.

Spingo Middle (OG 1050, ABV 5%) ◟
Sweet and creamy, brown, strong bitter. Dried fruit and roast in aroma. Malt flavour throughout with plums, apples and melon.

Spingo Special (OG 1066, ABV 6.6%) 🍶 ◟
Smooth, red, strong old ale. Red wine aroma. Powerful flavours of sweet stone fruits, malt and hops. Vinous but delicate.

Blue Bear SIBA 👁

Unit 5, Empire House, 11 New Street, Smethwick, West Midlands, B66 2AJ

☎ (0121) 565 5622 ✉ info@bluebearbrewery.com

⊕ Blue Bear brewery, formerly in Worcestershire, relocated to an industrial unit in Smethwick on the outskirts of Birmingham. The nine-barrel plant produces a selection of beers, most of it under contract for the now defunct Highgate & Davenports brewery of Walsall. Much of the beer is keg but cask-conditioned beers are now being promoted. ♦

Contract brewed under the Highgate & Davenports brand name:

Highgate Dark Mild (OG 1036.8, ABV 3.4%)

Davenports Original Bitter (OG 1041.8, ABV 4%)

Blue Bee SIBA

Unit 29-30, Hoyland Road Industrial Estate, Sheffield, South Yorkshire, S3 8AB ⊕ bluebeebrewery.co.uk

Blue Bee was established in 2010. The 10-barrel brewery was acquired by Reet Ales Pubs Ltd in 2014 and supplies beer to the free trade throughout Yorkshire and the East Midlands. The core range of beers is complemented by an ever-changing range of specials. ‼♦

Hillfoot Best Bitter (OG 1040, ABV 4%)
Traditional, dark chestnut-coloured, fruity best bitter.

Reet Pale (OG 1040, ABV 4%)
Pale with floral and citrus flavours leading to a dry, bitter finish.

American 5 Hop (OG 1043, ABV 4.3%)
Pale ale brewed with five different American hop varieties.

Ginger Beer (OG 1048, ABV 4.8%)
A pale ale with the addition of fiery ginger.

Tempest Stout (OG 1048, ABV 4.8%)
Rich, well-balanced stout with hints of coffee and chocolate leading to a bitter finish.

Blue Bell

⊟ Cranesgate South, Whaplode St Catherine, Lincolnshire, PE12 6SN
☎ (01406) 504300 ☎ 07788 136663
⊕ thebluebell.net

⊕Founded in 1998 behind the Blue Bell pub, the brewery is now back under the ownership of the pub after several years as a separate business. Beers are only available at the pub and to private customers. ‼♦RAIB

New Honesty (OG 1040, ABV 4.1%)
A traditional beer, smooth with a full-bodied bitterness.

Old Honesty (OG 1040, ABV 4.1%)
Traditional brew with a full-bodied, rounded bitterness.

Ingle Dingle Ale (OG 1054, ABV 5.1%)
Mid-brown in colour, malty and slightly sweet.

Blue Bell Brewhouse

⊟ Blue Bell Cider House, Warings Green Road, Warings Green, Warwickshire, B94 6BP ☎ 07922 554181 ✉ rnrbrewhouse@outlook.com

⊠ A two-barrel plant set up in 2013 by Mark Shepherd to resurrect on-site brewing at the Blue

Bell Cider House (brewing ceased in 1968). Brewster Lynn Crossland, who joined in 2014, continues the tradition of female brewers in the original brewhouse, producing a core range of pale ales plus seasonal specials, solely for the Blue Bell and local festivals. The brewery likes to experiment with unusual flavours, and using ingredients foraged from local hedgerows. Beer names are motorcycle or music themed. ♦V

Dragonfly Pale Ale (OG 1038, ABV 3.8%)

Starfire Pale Ale (OG 1040, ABV 4%)

Harley Barley American Pale Ale (OG 1042, ABV 4.2%)

Blue Cow

⊟ High Street, South Witham, Lincolnshire, NG33 5QB
☎ (01572) 768432 ⊕ bluecowinn.co.uk

⊕Blue Cow is a traditional 13th-century pub with a brewery. The beer is only available in the pub or at CAMRA beer festivals. ‼

Best Bitter (OG 1038, ABV 3.8%)
Hoppy, golden ale, with a fresh initial taste.

Blue Monkey SIBA

10 Pentrich Road, Giltbrook Industrial Park, Giltbrook, Nottinghamshire, NG16 2UZ
☎ (0115) 938 5899 ⊕ bluemonkeybrewery.com

⊕ Blue Monkey was established in 2008 as a 10-barrel plant but moved in 2010 to a bigger site to meet increasing demand. It now brews around 15,000 pints a week to supply more than 200 local outlets and selected national distributors. The name stems from a nickname for the blue flames that used to rise from the chimneys of Stanton Ironworks, a prominent local foundry. ‼▰

Marmoset (OG 1038, ABV 3.6%) ◆
Highly hopped citrus-flavoured golden beer with a dry, bitter finish.

Chimp Chim-in-Nee (ABV 3.8%)
Pale and intensely hoppy beer, with tropical fruit aromas and a thirst-quenching bitterness

BG Sips (OG 1041, ABV 4%) ◆
Pale golden hoppy beer, brewed mainly with Brewers Gold hops. Very fruity and bitter.

Sanctuary (OG 1041.8, ABV 4.1%) ⬡ ◆
Copper-coloured malty beer with German and American hops.

99 Red Baboons (OG 1042, ABV 4.2%) ◆
Red in colour with a malty fruitiness. Not overly hoppy.

Right Turn Clyde (OG 1043.3, ABV 4.3%) ◆
Golden hoppy ale, citrus fruit aroma and taste, lingering dry bitter finish.

Infinity (OG 1045.7, ABV 4.6%) ⬡ ▰ ◆
Golden ale packed with Citra hops.

Guerrilla (OG 1052, ABV 4.9%) ◆
A creamy stout, full of roast malt flavour and a slightly sweet finish.

Ape Ale (OG 1052, ABV 5.4%) ◆
Intensely hopped, strong golden ale with a dry, bitter finish

Blueball

Kash 22, 22 Church Street, Frodsham, Cheshire, WA6 6QW
☎ (01928) 733116

⊕Blueball originally started brewing as Bridgewater Brewery in 2010 behind a homebrew shop in Frodsham. The business relocated to Runcorn and expanded later the same year using a five-barrel plant. A bar and restaurant, Kash, opened in Chester in 2011. In 2013 the brewery relocated to a newly opened second bar in Frodsham called Kash 22. In 2015 the bar was subleased to a former employee, but Blueball brewing continues on the premises. ⬛♦RAIB

Indie Girl (OG 1036, ABV 3.8%)
A pale golden ale with a citrus and tropical fruit aroma. The finish is clean and dry with a long, hoppy aftertaste.

1492 American Pale Ale (OG 1040, ABV 4.5%)

Zeppelin (OG 1053, ABV 5.5%)

Spank (Industrial IPA) (OG 1059, ABV 6%)
Sweetish strong ale.

Bluestone (Lancashire) SIBA

Unit 6, Daniel Street Industrial Estate, Whitworth, Lancashire, OL12 8BX
☎ (01706) 853009 ☎ 07802 792536
⊕ bluestonebrewery.co.uk

Bluestone is a small 3.5-barrel brewery using traditional methods including 'double dropping' fermentation. Brewing currently only takes place at the weekend.

Quarryman's Stout (OG 1041, ABV 4%)
A black stout, full of traditional flavour.

EPA (English Pale Ale) (OG 1042, ABV 4.2%)
A traditional dry pale ale with strong malt and hop flavours.

Night Hops Stout (OG 1043, ABV 4.2%)
Dark dry stout with a good hop flavour through the roasted malt, liquorice and spice.

AKA (Amber Kitchen Ale) (OG 1043, ABV 4.4%)
Based on an old recipe, a mild/brown ale, lightly hopped with a caramel and liquorice malty flavour.

Spodden Pilsner (OG 1048, ABV 4.4%)
A full-bodied Bohemian-style Pilsner. Hoppy and full-flavoured.

Bluestone (Pembrokeshire) SIBA

Tiriet, Cilgwyn, Pembrokeshire, SA42 0QW
☎ (01239) 820833 ⊕ bluestonebrewing.co.uk

A family-run business established in 2013 on a working organic hill farm in the Preseli Hills within the Pembrokeshire Coast National Park. The 10-barrel brewery has been installed in a renovated 200-year-old stone barn, which doubles as a cold store and office. The brewery uses water from a private supply which filters down through the Preseli Hills. Numerous local outlets are supplied as well as wholesalers around the UK. ‼⬛♦RAIB

Rockhopper (OG 1039, ABV 3.9%)
A classic pale, amber-coloured bitter, with a light malt base and a spicy fruitiness from the hops.

Crystal Ruby (OG 1042, ABV 4.2%)

A balanced blend of rich malty flavours with a touch of caramelised grain.

Bedrock Blonde (OG 1040, ABV 4.5%)
A straw-coloured blonde ale with creamy soft and malt flavours.

Elderflower Blonde (OG 1040, ABV 4.5%)
Straw-coloured, delicately hopped, and finished with a delicate hint of elderflower.

Hammerstone IPA (OG 1044, ABV 4.5%)
A modern IPA providing a fruity, effervescent and refreshing golden ale.

Moonstone (OG 1046, ABV 4.6%)
A full-bodied dark porter. Spicy bitterness complements chocolate and nut flavours.

Rocketeer (OG 1046, ABV 4.6%)
A traditional full-bodied bitter with a rich, malty base.

Blythe SIBA

Blythe House Farm, Lichfield Road, Hamstall Ridware, Staffordshire, WS15 3QQ ☎ 07931 290879/07483 248723 ⊕ blythebrewery.co.uk

⊗ Blythe began brewing in 2003 using a 2.5-barrel plant in a converted barn. 15 outlets are supplied direct. ‼♦RAIB

Ridware Pale (OG 1042, ABV 4.3%) ◀
Bright and golden with a bitter floral hop aroma and citrus taste. Good and hop-sharp, bitter and refreshing. Long, lingering bite with ripples of citrus across the tongue.

Chase Bitter (OG 1044, ABV 4.4%) ◀
Fresh fruity aroma touched by malt from this amber beer. Sweet biscuity start with caramel support and fruit hints. Hops emerge and intensify to give a satisfyingly bitter finish.

Staffie (OG 1044, ABV 4.4%) ◀
Hoppy and grassy aroma with hints of sweetness from this amber beer. A touch of malt at the start is soon overwhelmed by hops. A full hoppy, mouthwatering finish.

Palmers Poison (OG 1045, ABV 4.5%) ◀
Refreshing darkish beer. Tawny but light headed. Coffee truffle aroma, pleasingly sweet to start but with a good hop mouthfeel.

Johnsons (OG 1056, ABV 5.2%) ▱◀
Black with a thick head. Refreshingly hoppy and full bodied with lingering bitterness of chocolate, dates, coal smoke and liquorice.

Bohem (NEW)

227 Whittington Road, Bowes Park, London, N22 8YW
☎ (020) 8888 5226 ☎ 07999 014294
⊕ bohembrewery.co.uk

No real ale.

Bollington SIBA

▤ **Adlington Road, Bollington, Cheshire, SK10 5JT**
☎ (01625) 575380 ⊕ bollingtonbrewing.co.uk

⊗ Bollington began brewing in 2008 with the Vale Inn, Bollington, as the brewery tap. The Park Tavern, Macclesfield, and the Cask Tavern, Poynton, are also owned. All three pubs serve mainly Bollington beers. Around 40 outlets are supplied direct. ‼♦RAIB

Long Hop (OG 1039, ABV 3.9%)
Pale lager-style bitter with fruity, refreshing hops.

Ginger Brew (OG 1041, ABV 4.1%)
A classic ginger bitter with a hoppy bitter flavour and a smooth taste with fresh root ginger added at the end.

White Nancy (OG 1038, ABV 4.1%)
Pale-coloured light bitter with a good hoppiness and light body.

Best (OG 1041, ABV 4.2%)
A hoppy bitter. Clean and crisp with a light golden colour and a refreshing, bitter aftertaste.

Dinner Ale (OG 1042, ABV 4.3%)
Deep copper-coloured, traditional-style bitter with a fresh, slightly fruity nose and a dry, hoppy finish.

Oat Mill Stout (OG 1049, ABV 5%)
An oatmeal stout with a twist. A hoppy bitter taste keeps the sweetness in check and allows for a fine dark beer.

Eastern Nights (OG 1056, ABV 5.6%)
A pale gold-coloured balanced IPA with a modest hop content. Easy-drinking for the strength.

Bolthole (NEW)

2a Shipley Road, Westbury on Trym, Bristol, BS9 3HS
☎ 07771 902393 ⊕ bolthole.beer

The brewery was set up in 2015, running from the owner's premises in North Bristol. A range of five beers is regularly produced, with occasional specials. Most of the production is bottle-conditioned and sold at local farmers' markets.
🍺♦ RAIB

Bond (NEW)

Units 3 & 4, Gardeners Green Farm, Heathlands Road, Wokingham Without, Berkshire, RG40 3AS
☎ (01344) 775450 ☎ 07986 460504
⊕ bondbrews.co.uk

⊠ Bond Brews was established in 2015 using a six-barrel plant. Beers are delivered to pubs within a 30-mile radius and there are plans to open a brewery shop. ♦ RAIB

Goldi-hops (OG 1039, ABV 3.9%)
A refreshing amber-coloured pale ale with a malty and delicately citrusy nose, followed by a bitter flavour and a long, dry, bitter finish.

Best of British (OG 1040, ABV 4%)
A tawny best bitter with malt and fruit on the nose, dry fruity flavours balancing the bitterness, followed by a touch of blackcurrant in the aftertaste.

Railway Porter (OG 1045, ABV 4.5%)
An easy-drinking dark brown porter with a reddish tint and a subtle toasty maltiness with a gently lingering fruity finish.

Boot (NEW)

⬢ 12 Boot Hill, Repton, Derbyshire, DE65 6FT
☎ (01283) 346047 ⊕ thebootbeer.co.uk

A six-barrel microbrewery installed at the rear of the Boot Inn in Repton, home of the eponymous public school, during 2015. The brewery supplies the three pubs within the group and a small number of free trade outlets. ‼🍺♦

Repton Cross (ABV 3.7%)
Session bitter with a smooth mouthfeel and hints of nutty roasted malt character. Good dry finish with a hint of bitterness.

Clod Hopper (ABV 3.9%)
A hoppy, golden-coloured pale ale. Citrus dominated, soft and smooth with a climax of hoppiness, hints of caramel and an enduring, bitter finish.

Bitter (ABV 4.3%)
A well-balanced, traditional English ale with a fresh citrus/spicy aroma, malty palate and clean, crisp bitterness.

Wellington (ABV 4.5%)
An amber-coloured ale from a blend of dark and light malts deliver a smooth, velvety flavour with a pronounced hop.

Tuffer's Old (ABV 4.6%)
A satisfying porter with cappuccino, chocolate, dark fruits and vibrant fresh peel aromas. The mouthfeel is velvety and rich, with notes of coffee, chocolate and hazelnuts, and warming alcohol and cocoa in the finish.

Beast of Bloodstock (ABV 6.6%)
Full-bodied and rounded, moderately hopped with a rich dark chocolate and caramel character.

Bootleg IFBB

⬢ Horse & Jockey, 9 The Green, Chorlton-cum-Hardy, M21 9HS
☎ (0161) 860 7794 ⊕ horseandjockeychorlton.com

⊠ Situated in the Horse & Jockey Inn on the Green, the brewery is in a tiny space above the dining room, where evidence remains of a historic brewery. The beers are available in the pub and selected Joseph Holt outlets. ‼♦

Fool's Gold (OG 1039, ABV 3.9%)

Chorlton Pale Ale (OG 1040, ABV 4%)
A refreshing blonde beer with a hint of citrus and a long, dry finish.

Urban Fox (OG 1042, ABV 4.2%)

Bootlegger (NEW)

⬢ The Bootlegger, 3 Amersham Hill, High Wycombe, Buckinghamshire, HP13 6NQ
☎ (01494) 525457 ⊕ thebootleggerpub.co.uk/brewco

A small-scale brewery operating out of the Bootlegger pub in High Wycombe. It currently produces five bottle-conditioned beers. Cask-conditioned beer may be available in the future. RAIB

Born in the Borders SIBA ◉

Lanton Mill, Jedburgh, TD8 6ST
☎ (01835) 830495 ☎ 07802 416494
⊕ bornintheborders.com

Born in the Borders Brewery is Scotland's original plough-to-pint brewery, and started brewing as Scottish Borders Brewery in 2011 using barley from its own farm. Beyond its core range of ales, recent projects include the brewery's 'Wild Harvest' initiative, which sources locally foraged ingredients for its ales. The brewery has recently launched a visitor centre, offering brewery tours, a café/

restaurant and retail units featuring Borders beer, produce and food. !! ☛ ♦

Foxy Blonde (OG 1037.5, ABV 3.8%)
Brewery-grown barley and a complex mixture of hops combine to create a golden ale bursting with citrus and floral flavours.

Game Bird (OG 1039.5, ABV 4%) 🍺 🍴
An amber ale with a balance of malty sweetness and late summer fruit with a long and easy finish.

Holy Cow (OG 1041, ABV 4.2%)
Hints of dark malt combine with a long floral finish.

Gold Dust (OG 1041.5, ABV 4.3%)
A light IPA with a big burst of hop aroma.

Dark Horse (OG 1044, ABV 4.5%)
A classic dark ale that has overtones of coffee and chocolate with a surprisingly spicy finish that lingers on the tongue.

Borough (Lancaster) SIBA

Brook Street, Lancaster, LA1 1SL ☎ 07912 679761 ⊕ theboroughbrewery.co.uk

☺ Borough Brewery moved from the cellar of the Borough, a free house in the centre of Lancaster, in 2016. A 2.5-barrel plant is used to create four regular beers. ♦V

Pale (OG 1038, ABV 3.7%) ◗
Dry, refreshing, up-front hoppy bitter beer.

Bitter (OG 1040, ABV 4%) ◗
Sweet, malty bitter with caramel flavours and light hop balance.

Summertime Dark (OG 1040, ABV 4%) ◗
A rich, dark, sweet mild with gentle roast.

Wintertime Dark (OG 1050, ABV 5%) ◗
Well-balanced, roasty dry stout with full body and lingering finish.

Borough (Neath) SIBA ◉

🏠 2 New Henry Street, Neath, SA11 1PH
☎ (01639) 644902 ☎ 07577 461915
⊕ boroughbreweryneath.com

☺Opened in 2014, the brewery was built by the landlord Kevin Davies in a converted outbuilding at the rear of the pub. Beers are named primarily after the local coal and steel industry. !! ☛ RAIB

Welsh Gold (OG 1038, ABV 3.8%)
A stout with hints of chocolate and nut in the taste and a slightly bitter finish.

Bit 'o' Sweet (OG 1042, ABV 4.2%)
A light brown-coloured malty beer, with a biscuit taste and a subtle aroma backed with the taste of British hops.

Iron Runner (OG 1042, ABV 4.3%)
Best bitter with a roasted nutty aftertaste.

Triple Bleeder (OG 1046, ABV 4.3%)
Amber-coloured bitter ale with a dry, hoppy taste.

IPA (OG 1044, ABV 4.4%)
Strong tasting with a crisp, clean mouth feel.

Full Blast (OG 1050, ABV 4.7%)
Golden-coloured, fruity, zesty ale.

Puddlers Peril (OG 1048, ABV 4.8%)
A copper-coloured strong ale with a malt aroma and a distinct hoppy aftertaste.

Nut Red Coke (OG 1051, ABV 4.9%)
Chestnut-coloured ale with malt overtones.

Pit Head Porter (OG 1058, ABV 5.4%)
A full-bodied porter with nutty overtones and a hint of chocolate in the aftertaste.

Borough Arms

🏠 33 Earle Street, Crewe, Cheshire, CW1 2BG
☎ (01270) 254999 ⊕ borougharmscrewe.co.uk

☺A two-barrel brewery opened in 2005 to supply the pub but with beers occasionally available at festivals. Occasional brewing restarted in 2016 after a break. !! ♦

Boss SIBA ◉

14 Worcester Court, Mannesmann Close, Llansamlet, Swansea, SA7 9FD
☎ (01792) 790726 ☎ 07825 525735
⊕ bossbrewing.co.uk

⊗ The brewery opened in 2015 by Roy Alkin and Sarah John, using a 10-barrel plant. There are plans to expand and to provide bottling and casking facilities. 100 outlets are supplied. A brewpub and shop are also planned. ♦RAIB

Blonde (OG 1040, ABV 4%)
Aromas of pine, exotic spice and grapefruit peel, and grapefruit and pine flavours, with a clean, bitter finish.

Best (OG 1042, ABV 4.2%)
A deep copper-coloured session beer with a soft, earthy, floral nose and hints of orange zest ending with a gentle dryness.

Brawn (OG 1043, ABV 4.4%)
A hoppy golden ale with lychee and sherbet flavours and a dry, hoppy, balanced finish.

Blaze (OG 1045, ABV 4.5%)
Floral, herbal aroma gives way to a zingy citrus, spicy flavour.

Bare (OG 1050, ABV 5%)
A lager-style beer with a clean, spicy finish.

Black (OG 1050, ABV 5%)
Roasted coffee and chocolate aromas, with flavours of fire-roasted nuts, toffee and chocolate.

Brave (OG 1055, ABV 5.5%)
Tropical fruit, elderflower and rose aromas, with flavours of grapefruit, citrus and pine.

Bosun's SIBA ◉

Unit 20, Wakefield Commercial Park, 97 Bridge Road, Horbury Bridge, West Yorkshire, WF4 5NW ☎ 07703 535735 / 07513 112188 ⊕ bosunsbrewery.co.uk

The first brew was produced in 2013 by a father-and-son team who have both served in the armed forces. The regular beers are produced on a 10-barrel plant with some given military themed names. !! ♦

Horbury Blond (OG 1039, ABV 3.9%)
A straw-coloured bitter.

Maiden Voyage (OG 1039, ABV 3.9%)
Chestnut brown-coloured traditional English ale.

Bermuda Triangle (OG 1041, ABV 4.1%)
Fruity golden ale with a soft citrus aroma and flavour.

Botley SIBA

Botley Mills, Mill Hill, Botley, Hampshire, SO30 2GB
☎ (01489) 784867 ☎ 7909337212
⊕ botleybrewery.com

⊗ Botley Brewery was established in 2010 and uses a five-barrel plant. ♦RAIB

Hampshire Bitter (OG 1038, ABV 3.8%)
Yorkshire-style amber session bitter.

Mill (OG 1038, ABV 3.8%)
A light session bitter, copper in colour, with a fresh aftertaste.

Cobbett's (OG 1045, ABV 4.5%)
A light, fruity golden ale with a clean, bitter finish.

Bottle Brook

Church Street, Kilburn, Belper, Derbyshire, DE56 0LU
☎ (01332) 880051 ☎ 07971 189915

⊗ A sister brewery to Leadmill (qv), Bottle Brook was established in 2005 using a 2.5-barrel plant on a tower gravity system. New World hops are predominantly used. The core range of beers is supplemented by one-off brews.

Columbus (OG 1040, ABV 4%)

Heanor Pale Ale (OG 1041, ABV 4.2%)

Roadrunner (OG 1047, ABV 4.8%)

Mellow Yellow (OG 1054, ABV 5.7%)

Rapture (OG 1058, ABV 5.9%)

Sand in the Wind (OG 1060, ABV 6.1%)

Boudicca (NEW)

Tunstead Road, Hoveton, NR12 8QN ☎ 07864 321732
⊕ boudiccabrewing.co.uk

⊗ Boudicca was set up in 2015 and exclusively produces vegan beers from organic ingredients. Further beers are planned. ♦V

Three Tails (OG 1036.5, ABV 3.9%)
A classic, amber-coloured English bitter with a touch of peppery spicyness in the hop character. Gentle on the nose, with sweet fruit, malt and hops, and a lasting finish.

Golden Torc (OG 1039.5, ABV 4.3%)
A hoppy golden ale with a good malt base, bitterness and a hint of grapefruit/citrus. Subtle hop aroma and strong hop flavours lead into a lasting finish.

Spiral Stout (OG 1045, ABV 4.6%)
A traditional full-bodied stout with an aroma of dark autumnal berries, and undertones of coffee and dark chocolate. Gentle lingering dry roast finish with a hint of smoke.

Prasto's Porter (OG 1053.5, ABV 5.2%)
Dark fruit and hops on the nose, with hints of roast malt and smoke. Full-bodied in the mouth. A dry and subtle smoky finish with fruit and hop notes.

Boundary (NEW)

Unit A5, 310 Portview Trade Centre, Newtownards Road, Belfast, BT4 1HE ⊕ boundarybrewing.coop

Boundary is a cooperative brewery based in Belfast. Three regular cask ales are supplemented by a number of special edition beers released a few times a year, which are sold directly to cooperative members and some retail outlets. ♦

APA (OG 1035, ABV 3.5%)

Export Stout (OG 1070, ABV 7%)

IPA (OG 1070, ABV 7%)

Bournemouth

Unit 6, 4-6 Abingdon Road, Nuffield Industrial Estate, Poole, Dorset, BH17 0UG
☎ (01202) 280405 ⊕ bournemouthbrewery.co.uk

Brewing began in 2013 using a one-barrel plant but has since increased capacity to seven barrels. Most of the beer is sold directly from the brewery and the brewery's own pub, the Smuggler's Run, in Poole. A small proportion goes to other local pubs and beer festivals. ‼🍴♦

Sandbanks (OG 1038, ABV 3.9%)
A session bitter with a slighty malty taste.

Wessex Wobble (OG 1041, ABV 4.3%)
Best bitter with a mildly hoppy taste.

Golden Grains (OG 1044, ABV 4.6%)
A pale golden beer with a mild sweetness and a strong hop flavour.

Sandbanks Export (OG 1052, ABV 5.7%)
Sweeter, maltier and hoppier version of Sandbanks Bitter.

Battleaxe (OG 1058, ABV 6.3%)
Lots of dark malts rounded off with powerful hops.

Sandbanks Extra Reserve (OG 1059, ABV 6.6%)
Strong, well-aged beer emphasising the hops.

Bowland SIBA ⊙

Holmes Mill, Greenacre Street, Clitheroe, Lancashire, BB7 1EB
☎ (01200) 443592 ⊕ bowlandbrewery.com

⊙ Founded in 2003, this family-run brewery moved to Clitheroe in 2015. There are plans to redevelop the site, including the addition of a visitor centre. The beers are supplied to pubs and clubs across the north-west of England. 🍴♦RAIB

Pheasant Plucker (OG 1038, ABV 3.7%)
A copper-coloured bitter with rounded blackcurrant flavours and a malty aftertaste.

Gold (OG 1039, ABV 3.8%)
A hoppy, golden bitter with intense grapefruit flavours and aromas.

AONB (Ale of Outstanding Natural Beauty) (OG 1040, ABV 4%)
A straw-coloured refreshing ale with a delicate gooseberry flavour and aroma.

Hen Harrier (OG 1040, ABV 4%) 🍺
The malty start belies what comes next: fruity, sweet, hoppy bitter with a long-lasting finish comprising all the previous elements.

Buster IPA (OG 1046, ABV 4.5%)
Well balanced, medium bodied and rounded. Generous American hops provide long tropical undertones.

Bowman SIBA ⊙

Wallops Wood, Sheardley Lane, Droxford, Hampshire, SO32 3QY
☎ (01489) 878110 ⊕ bowman-ales.com

⊗ Brewing started in 2006 in converted farm buildings. The brewery supplies more than 100 outlets. A new 40-barrel plant came on line in 2013, which is now working alongside the original 20-barrel plant. In addition to the standard beers, a range of seasonal brews and monthly specials is produced. !! ⬛ ♦ RAIB

Swift One (OG 1038, ABV 3.8%) 🍺
Easy-drinking bitter, well balanced with sweet maltiness leading to a bittersweet finish and slightly dry, hoppy aftertaste.

Meon Valley Bitter (OG 1040, ABV 3.9%)

Yumi (OG 1039, ABV 3.9%)
A fairly bitter beer, rich amber in colour.

Wallops Wood (OG 1040, ABV 4%) 🍺
No particular flavour dominates this well-crafted beer. Malt flavours throughout balanced by toffee notes, sweetness and a slightly dry finish.

Bowness Bay

Grosvenor House, Stramongate, Kendal, Cumbria, LA9 4BD ☎ 07768 116794
⊕ bownessbaybrewing.co.uk

Bowness Bay Brewery moved to Kendal in 2015, increasing capacity from 5 to 13 barrels. The original five-barrel plant has been retained for smaller experimental brews while the new eight-barrel plant is used for the brewery's main output. The brewery now has its own tap house, the Factory Tap.

Amazon Amber (OG 1038, ABV 3.8%)
A distinctive partnering of oranges and spiced berries; light, tasty ale.

Swallow Gold (OG 1039, ABV 3.9%)
A golden ale with smooth floral hints of apricot, lime and peach.

Swan Blonde (OG 1039, ABV 4%) 🍺
A sweet malty start with a finish dominated by hop bitterness.

Term IPA (OG 1043, ABV 4.3%)
A crisp, full-flavoured golden ale with a well-balanced hoppiness and caramel sweetness giving a deep smooth finish.

Swift Best (OG 1044, ABV 4.5%) 🍺
A tawny bitter where caramel sweetness dominates, leading to a gentle bitter finish.

Swan Black (OG 1046, ABV 4.6%) 🍺
Stout-like beer with a fruity raisiny middle, grainy mouthfeel and roast bitter finish.

Esperance (OG 1062, ABV 6.2%)
A classic caramel-tinged abbey ale. Maple syrup flavours combine with surprisingly light fruitiness.

Box Social (NEW) SIBA

Units 1-3, Winnings Courtyard, Newburn, Newcastle upon Tyne, NE15 9RU ☎ 07803 791761
⊕ boxsocial.pub

Launched in 2015, this family-run brewery has a license and is open to the public most days (12-9pm). !! ⬛ ♦

Convive Blond (ABV 3.9%)
A light blonde session ale.

Kaffir (ABV 4.2%)
A lime leaf session IPA.

India Brown Ale (ABV 5.6%)
A brown ale with West Coast American hops.

Box Steam SIBA 👁

The Midlands, Holt, Wiltshire, BA14 6RU
☎ (01225) 782700 ⊕ boxsteambrewery.com

⊗ The brewery was founded in 2004 and boasts a Fulton steam-fired copper, hence the name. New ownership since 2006 meant expansion and increased capacity with the brewery moving to larger premises in Holt in 2011. Two Wiltshire pubs are owned and more than 100 outlets supplied. !! ⬛ ♦

Tunnel Vision (OG 1040.5, ABV 4.2%)
A well-rounded, light amber-coloured bitter. Clean tasting, with a slight bitterness in the finish.

Piston Broke (OG 1045, ABV 4.5%)
A full-bodied, deep golden ale with a refreshing, hoppy, citrus palate and a subtle fruit-hop aroma.

Brack'N'Brew (NEW)

▤ Brackenrigg Inn, Watermillock, Cumbria, CA11 0LP
☎ (01768) 486206 ⊕ brackenriginn.co.uk

Brewing started in 2015 in a converted 16th-century stable overlooking Ullswater. Brewing takes place three times a week on a four-barrel plant.

Ullswater Gold (ABV 3.2%)
A mildly bitter, light and crisp golden ale packed with citrus aroma and a hint of spice.

Blonde (ABV 3.8%)
A blonde beer with a hoppy nose with hints of grapefruit and a dry, refreshing aftertaste.

Bitter (ABV 4.1%)
A traditional session ale, rich caramel in colour with a mellow honey aroma. Moderate hop bitterness is compensated for with sweetness and a hint of roast malt.

Bradfield SIBA 👁

Watt House Farm, High Bradfield, Sheffield, South Yorkshire, S6 6LG
☎ (0114) 285 1118 ⊕ bradfieldbrewery.co.uk

⊛ Established in 2005, Bradfield is a family-run business, based on a working farm in the Peak District using pure Millstone Grit springwater. In 2009 the brewery bought its first brewery tap, the Nags Head, Loxley. ⬛ ♦ RAIB

Farmers Bitter (OG 1039, ABV 3.9%)
A traditional copper-coloured malt ale with a floral aroma.

Farmers Blonde (OG 1041, ABV 4%)
Pale, blonde beer with citrus and summer fruit aromas.

Farmers Stout (OG 1045, ABV 4.5%)
A dark stout with roasted malts and flaked oats and a subtle, bitter hop character.

Bradford

▤ 22 Rawson Road, Westgate, Bradford, BD1 3SQ
☎ (01274) 379054 ⊕ bradfordbrewery.com

⊛ The brewery was established in 2015, seeing the return of brewing to Bradford city centre for the first time in 60 years. It is based in newly converted, former factory buildings and uses a 10-barrel plant. The beers are available at the on-site Brewfactory pub, where a feature glass wall allows visitors to view the brewery in operation. ‼ ⌦

Original (ABV 4.2%)

Brains IFBB ◉

Crawshay Street, Cardiff, CF10 1SP
☎ (029) 2040 2060 ⊕ sabrain.com

◉ Brains was established in 1882 at the Old Brewery, moving to the former Hancock's brewery site in 1999. The company has remained in family ownership and runs over 270 pubs throughout Wales, the Midlands and the West Country and is heavily involved in sponsoring Welsh sport. A new microbrewery within the existing site has produced an ever-increasing range of new beers, which have proved popular within the Brain's estate. ♦

Dark (OG 1035.5, ABV 3.5%) ◀
A tasty, classic dark brown mild, a mix of malt, roast, caramel with a background of hops. Bittersweet, mellow and with a lasting finish of malt and roast.

Bitter (OG 1036, ABV 3.7%) ◀
Amber coloured with a gentle aroma of malt and hops. Malt, hops and bitterness combine in an easy-drinking beer with a bitter finish.

Rev James Gold (OG 1041, ABV 4.1%)

SA (OG 1042, ABV 4.2%) ◀
A mellow, full-bodied beer. Gentle malt and hop aroma leads to a malty, hop and fruit mix with a balancing bitterness.

SA Gold (OG 1042, ABV 4.2%) ◀
A golden ale with a hoppy aroma. Well balanced with a zesty hop, malt, fruit and balancing bitterness; a similar satisfying finish.

Rev James Rye (OG 1043, ABV 4.3%)

Rev James (OG 1045.5, ABV 4.5%) ⬚ ◀
A faint malt and fruit aroma with malt and fruit flavours in the taste, initially bittersweet. Bitterness balances the flavour and makes this an easy-drinking beer.

Contract brewed for Molson Coors:

M&B Brew XI (OG 1036, ABV 3.6%)

Hancock's HB (OG 1037, ABV 3.7%)

Worthington's Bitter (OG 1037, ABV 3.7%)

Brakspear ◉

Eagle Maltings, The Crofts, Witney, Oxfordshire, OX28 4DP
☎ (01993) 890800 ⊕ brakspear-beers.co.uk

Brakspear beers have been brewed in Oxfordshire since 1779. They continue to be traditionally crafted at the Wychwood Brewery (qv) in the historic market town of Witney using the original Victorian square fermenters and the renowned 'double drop' fermenting system. Part of Marston's PLC. ‼ ⌦ ♦

Bitter (OG 1035, ABV 3.4%)
A classic copper-coloured pale ale with a big hop resins, juicy malt and orange fruit aroma, intense hop bitterness in the mouth and finish, and a firm maltiness and tangy fruitiness throughout.

Oxford Gold (OG 1040, ABV 4%)
A golden ale with a hoppy and zesty aroma and a full, fruity flavour.

Brampton SIBA ◉

Units 4 & 5, Chatsworth Business Park, Chatsworth Road, Chesterfield, Derbyshire, S40 2AR
☎ (01246) 221680 ⊕ bramptonbrewery.co.uk

◉ The original Brampton Brewery closed in 1955. In 2007 a new brewery was established, and brewing commenced on an eight-barrel plant. Two tied houses are situated close to the brewery. ‼ ⌦ ♦ RAIB

Golden Bud (OG 1037, ABV 3.8%) ◀
Crisp and refreshing golden bitter with a pleasant balance of citrus, sweetness and bitter flavours. Light and easy to drink.

1302 (OG 1040, ABV 4%)
A sweeter pale ale.

Griffin (OG 1040, ABV 4.1%)
A pale, slightly sweet summer ale.

Best (OG 1041, ABV 4.2%) ◀
Classic, drinkable bitter with a predominantly malty taste, balanced by caramel sweetness and a developing bitterness in the aftertaste.

Impy Dark (OG 1047, ABV 4.3%) ◀
Strong roasted coffee aroma and a rich flavour of vine fruit and chocolate combine to make this a tasty mild ale.

Jerusalem (OG 1046, ABV 4.6%)
The rich and roasted malt notes defy the pale colour in this special bitter.

Tudor Rose (OG 1045, ABV 4.6%)
A well-balanced and creamy pale ale with good hop nose and mouthfeel.

Mild (OG 1054, ABV 4.9%) ▣
Premium dark mild. Warming, rich and roasted, and packed full of character and flavour.

Wasp Nest (OG 1049, ABV 5%) ◀
Strong and complex with malt and hop flavours and a caramel sweetness.

Speciale (OG 1056, ABV 5.8%)
An IPA-style ale, the fruity hoppiness is balanced beautifully by the residual sweetness of such a strong ale.

Brancaster

See Beeston

Brandon SIBA

76 High Street, Brandon, Suffolk, IP27 0AU
☎ (01842) 878496 ☎ 07876 234689
⊕ brandonbrewery.co.uk

Brandon started brewing in 2005 on the site of an old dairy situated on the Suffolk-Norfolk border. Beers are based on traditional styles which include unique recipes and incorporate locally sourced ingredients. ‼ ⌦ RAIB

Breckland Gold (OG 1038, ABV 3.8%)
A delicate, smooth, slightly spicy taste and a dry, lingering, malty finish.

Old Rodney (OG 1040, ABV 4%) ◀

Damson jam aroma precedes a flavoursome balance of malt, fruit and hops in this tawny best bitter. Gently fading finish.

Paddys Pride (OG 1040, ABV 4%)
A dark ruby mild, smooth malt flavours ending with a little roast bitterness.

Saxon Gold (OG 1040, ABV 4%)
A pale, golden beer with a subtle aroma of hops. The taste is a clean, crisp mix of spice and bitter fruits with a dry, hoppy finish.

Strawberry Wheat (OG 1040, ABV 4%)
A pale ale brewed with torrified wheat and pulped strawberries.

Waxies Dargle (OG 1040, ABV 4%)
A copper-coloured ale with rich malt flavours and a good hoppiness.

Molly's Secret (OG 1041, ABV 4.1%)
A pale ale based on an old recipe.

Norfolk Poacher (OG 1041, ABV 4.1%) ◣
A rich malty roast aroma that follows through to flavours of malt, hops, fruit and sweetness. Upstanding sweetness in a long, complex finish.

Royal Ginger (OG 1041, ABV 4.1%)
A refreshing summer ale with a distinctive mix of malt and hoppy spice, balanced with a gentle ginger flavour and finish.

Gun Flint (OG 1042, ABV 4.2%)
Roasted malts are used to produce a malty, chocolate flavour. This combines well with spicy, citrus hops to give a dry, bittersweet, roasted malt finish.

Wee Drop of Mischief (OG 1042, ABV 4.2%)
An amber-coloured premium bitter. Gentle malt flavours give way to a delightful hop character and a dry, increasingly bitter aftertaste.

Rusty Bucket (OG 1044, ABV 4.4%) ◣
Aromas of figs and malt with dried fruit, and flavours of malt and hops, leading to a bitter, biscuity aftertaste. A well-balanced traditional best bitter.

Grumpy Bastard (OG 1045, ABV 4.5%)

Slippery Jack (OG 1045, ABV 4.5%)
A dark brown stout. Complex but well-balanced flavours of roasted grain and hop bitterness. Dry with a lingering, pleasantly bitter finish.

'Old on to Your 'at (OG 1047, ABV 4.7%)
Dark amber in colour, big malt flavours overlaid with a tangy fruit bitterness.

Nappertandy (OG 1050, ABV 5%)
A reddish amber beer, full-bodied with a malty aroma. Crisp and spicy with an underlying citrus flavour and a dry, malty, bitter fruit finish.

Brandy Cask

▤ Brandy Cask, 25 Bridge Street, Pershore, Worcestershire, WR10 1AJ
☎ (01386) 552602

☺Brewing started in 1995 in a refurbished bottle store in the garden of the pub. Brewery and pub now operate under one umbrella, with brewing carried out by the owner/landlord. Beers are only supplied to the pub. ‼◆

Whistling Joe (OG 1036, ABV 3.6%) ◣

A sweet, fruity, copper-coloured beer that has plenty of contrast in the aroma. A malty balance lingers but the aftertaste is not dry.

Brandysnapper (OG 1040, ABV 4%) ◣
Golden brew with low alpha hops. Plenty of fruit and hop aroma leads to a rich taste in the mouth and a lingering aftertaste.

John Baker's Original (OG 1048, ABV 4.8%) ◣
A superb blend of flavours with roasted malt to the fore. The rich hoppy aroma is complemented by a complex aftertaste.

Branscombe Vale SIBA ◉

Branscombe, Devon, EX12 3DP
☎ (01297) 680511 ⊕ branscombevalebrewery.co.uk

⊗ The brewery was set up in 1992 in cowsheds at the back of a farm owned by the National Trust, overlooking the sea at Branscombe. The then two partners converted the sheds, digging their own well. In 2008 a new 25-barrel plant was shoehorned in through the roof to increase capacity, including bottling some of the range. ◆RAIB

Mild (OG 1036, ABV 3.7%) ⌷
A black session mild ale.

Branoc (OG 1038, ABV 3.8%) ◣
Pale brown with a malt and fruit aroma and a hint of caramel. Malt and bitter taste with a dry, hoppy finish.

Drayman's Best Bitter (OG 1042, ABV 4.2%)
A mid-brown beer with hop and caramel notes and a lingering finish.

Summa This (OG 1040, ABV 4.2%)
Amber-coloured, with digestive biscuit notes and a floral hop.

BVB Best Bitter (OG 1045, ABV 4.6%) ◣
Red/brown coloured beer with a fruity aroma and taste, and a bitter/dry finish.

Summa That (OG 1049, ABV 5%)
Light golden beer with a clean, refreshing taste and a long hoppy finish.

Brass Castle SIBA

10a Yorkersgate, Malton, North Yorkshire, YO17 7AB
☎ (01653) 698683 ☎ 07563 579723
⊕ brasscastlebrewery.co.uk

The brewery is based in the centre of Malton with a 12-barrel plant, having begun life on a one-barrel kit in the owner's garage. The brewery welcomes visitors and hosts a bottle/homebrew shop alongside its tap room. ‼ ⌷◆RAIB GF V

Cliffhanger (OG 1040, ABV 3.8%)
A refreshing hop-laden golden ale with citrus notes.

Northern Blonde (OG 1043, ABV 4%)
Malt-forward blonde ale.

Tail Gunner (OG 1042, ABV 4%)
A dry-hopped rye session ale with a reddish hue.

Hazelnut Mild (OG 1044, ABV 4.2%)
A five-malt nut-brown mild with a delicate hazelnut aroma.

Mosaic (OG 1044, ABV 4.3%)

Oatmeal Pale (OG 1046, ABV 4.6%)

Snoweater (OG 1050, ABV 4.8%)

Brass Lager (OG 1053, ABV 5.3%)
A malt-forward Vienna-style lager.

Bad Kitty (OG 1061.5, ABV 5.5%)
A chewy, chocolate, vanilla-flavoured porter.

Eclipse (OG 1061, ABV 5.7%)
A citrus hop punch is followed by a light roasty aftertaste.

Sunshine (OG 1061, ABV 5.7%) 🍺
A full-bodied IPA.

Burnout (OG 1062, ABV 5.8%)
A robust peat-smoked porter.

Black Forest (OG 1064, ABV 6%)
A velvety stout with added cocoa and cherries.

Heretic (OG 1061, ABV 6.4%)

Braunton SIBA

Unit 9, Chivenor Business Park, Braunton, Barnstaple, Devon, EX31 4AY ☎ 07551 870925 ⊕ brauntonbrewery.co.uk

⊠ After some small-scale brewing, Braunton was established in 2014. Commercial brewing began in early 2015. The brewery has moved to new premises and uses a six-barrel plant. Three beers are currently produced, with plans to expand the range. ‼ RAIB

#1 Pale (OG 1039, ABV 3.8%)
Clean, crisp, refreshing pale ale with long hop overtones.

#2 Bitter (OG 1041, ABV 4%)
Well-rounded, easy-drinking bitter, with malted caramel giving way to a delicate hop aroma.

#3 IPA (OG 1042, ABV 4.2%)
Well-balanced light malts and dry English hops.

Braydon

See Castle Combe

Brecon SIBA

8A, Brecon Enterprise Park, Brecon, Powys, LD3 8BT ☎ (01874) 620800 ⊕ breconbrewing.co.uk

Brecon was established in 2011 by Buster Grant. Seasonal and special beers are also available including beers from the Genesis Project: see website. A brewery tap, in the town centre, opened in 2016. ‼ 🍺 ♦ RAIB

Three Beacons (OG 1030, ABV 3%) 🍺
A low-ABV American-style pale ale, golden hued, full bodied and extensively hopped with six different varieties.

Welsh Beacons (OG 1037, ABV 3.7%)
A golden bitter with a gentle floral bitterness and a full flavour.

Dark Beacons (OG 1038, ABV 3.8%)

Copper Beacons (OG 1041, ABV 4.1%)
A copper-coloured best bitter, smooth with well-balanced fruit and hop flavours.

Gold Beacons (OG 1042, ABV 4.2%)
Deep golden ale, with soft, well-defined bitterness balancing a blend of malts.

Orange Beacons (OG 1043, ABV 4.3%)

Red Beacons (OG 1050, ABV 5%)
Premium red IPA, smooth, well hopped and complex.

Brentwood SIBA 👁

Calcott Hall Farm, Ongar Road, Brentwood, Essex, CM14 5RE
☎ (01277) 200483 ⊕ brentwoodbrewing.co.uk

⊠ Since its launch in 2006 Brentwood has steadily increased its capacity and distribution, relocating to a new purpose-built brewery unit in 2013 with a visitor centre. Seasonal and special beers are also available including more unusual beer styles under the Elephant School brand name. ‼ 🍺 ♦ RAIB

BBC2 (OG 1030, ABV 2.5%)
Full-bodied mid-brown bitter with dry tropical citrus flavour.

IPA (OG 1039, ABV 3.7%)
A lightly hopped, pale session beer.

Marvellous Maple Mild (OG 1038, ABV 3.7%) 🍺
Dark brown mild with a hint of maple syrup.

Best (OG 1042, ABV 4.2%)
A traditional, light-coloured best bitter, with a well-rounded flavour and aroma.

Gold (OG 1043, ABV 4.3%)
A heavily hopped golden beer with a fruity taste and bitter finish.

Hope & Glory (ABV 4.5%)
A well-balanced bitter with full malt flavours and light hops, leaving a pleasing end note and lingering bitterness.

Lumberjack (ABV 5.2%)
A strong, slightly sweet, full-bodied bitter with a rounded, hoppy finish.

Chockwork Orange (OG 1067, ABV 6.5%)
A deep chocolate malty beer brewed with oranges and matured to provide a classic old ale-style beer.

Brewed for The Shackleton:

Centenary (ABV 3.7%)
A lightly-hopped pale ale.

Snuggery (ABV 4.3%)
A rich golden ale with fruity hops and a slightly sweet malt character.

South! (ABV 4.5%)
A light golden ale with a citrus tang.

The Boss (ABV 4.5%)
A full-bodied red bitter with rich malt flavours.

Nimrod (ABV 5.2%)
A slightly sweet, strong ale.

Endurance (ABV 6.5%)
A chocolaty old ale with added oranges for extra tang.

Brew Buddies (NEW)

Unit 14, Highlands Farm Business Park, Highlands Hill, Swanley Village, Kent, BR8 7NA ☎ 07962 369717 ⊕ brew-buddies.co.uk

⊠ Established by two friends in 2015, Brew Buddies operates on a six-barrel plant set up in a post-war farm building. Free trade outlets in Kent and further afield are supplied, as well as local beer festivals. ‼

Brew By Numbers

79 Enid Street, London, SE16 3RA
☎ (020) 7237 9794 ☎ 07528 684105
⊕ brewbynumbers.com

Brew By Numbers is a small brewery established in 2012. In 2015 a bespoke 12-barrel brewhouse was created, and a pilot kit is used to test new ideas and recipes and to create limited-release batches. The vegan-friendly beers are bottled on site, with primary fermentation yeast carried over. Each beer is also sold by number, the first part relating to the style of beer and the second to the recipe within that style. ⊫ RAIB V

Brew Company

See Exit 33

Brew Foundation (NEW) SIBA ◉

c/o Wincle Brewery, Toll Barn, Wincle, Cheshire, SK11 0QE
☎ (0114) 282 3098 ☎ 07545 618894

Office: 18 Jarrow Road, Sheffield, South Yorkshire, S11 8YB ⊕ thebrewfoundation.co.uk

A father-and-son brewery, currently using spare capacity at Wincle Brewery (qv).

Little Bitter That (ABV 3.8%)
A satisfying fruity hop taste and aroma, balanced against a strong malt backbone.

Hops & Dreams (ABV 4%)
A session IPA, easy-drinking with a citrus, floral and tropical hoppy flavour and aroma.

Hop & Glory (ABV 4.9%)
A clean, fresh IPA with tropical fruit flavours and floral, citrus aromas.

Brew Shack (NEW)

Unit 3, Old Manor Farm Buildings, 187 Leigh Road, Wimborne Minster, Dorset, BH21 2BC ☎ 07580 120258 ✉ info@thebrewshack.co.uk

⊠ Brewing began in 2015 on a 1.5-barrel plant in purpose-built premises. Experimental and seasonal beers are planned to complement the regular range.

Amber Gambler (OG 1040, ABV 4%)
A medium-bodied, well-balanced, hoppy amber session bitter.

Pale Ale (OG 1045, ABV 4.5%)
Golden, crisp and hoppy pale ale with smooth bitterness.

Eight Grain Porter (OG 1050, ABV 5%)
A sweet brown porter with complex roasted malt flavour.

5 a Day IPA (OG 1055, ABV 5.5%)
A traditional English-style IPA with big resinous hoppy flavours and aroma.

Sump Oil Stout (OG 1060, ABV 6%)
Rich, full-bodied stout with big roasted flavours and a smooth, hoppy, bitter finish.

Brewdog

Balmacassie Industrial Estate, Ellon, AB41 8BX
☎ (01358) 724924 ⊕ brewdog.com

Established in 2007 by James Watt and Martin Dickie. Thirteen UK bars and three overseas bars are owned, with more bars and a new warehouse planned for 2015. Most of the output is bottled, with some keg production. In July 2016 the brewery launched a KeyKeg version of its Dead Pony ale. ‼ ⊨

Brewhouse & Kitchen

🏠 **Bedford (NEW): 115 High Street, Bedford, MK40 1NU**
☎ (01234) 342931

Bristol: 31-35 Cotham Hill, Clifton, Bristol, BS6 6JY
☎ (0117) 973 3793

Cheltenham (NEW): Unit 7, The Brewery, St Margaret's Road, Cheltenham, GL50 4EQ ☎ (01242) 509946

Dorchester: 27 Weymouth Avenue, Dorchester, DT1 1QY ☎ (01305) 265551

Gloucester (NEW): Unit R1, St Anne Walk, Gloucester Quay, GL1 5SH ☎ (01452) 222965

Highbury: 2a Corsica Street, London, N5 1JJ ☎ (020) 7226 1026

Islington: 5 Torrens Street, London, EC1V 1NQ
☎ (020) 7064 9943

Poole: 3 Dear Hay Lane, Poole, BH15 1NZ ☎ (01202) 771246

Portsmouth: 26 Guildhall Walk, Portsmouth, PO1 2DD
☎ (023) 9289 1340

Southbourne (NEW): 147 Parkwood Road, Southbourne, BH5 2BN ☎ (01202) 055209

Southampton (NEW): 47 Highfield Lane, Southampton, SO17 1QD ☎ (023) 8055 5566

Sutton Coldfield (NEW): 8 Birmingham Road, Sutton Coldfield, B72 1QD ☎ (0121) 796 6838

Wilmslow (NEW): 6-12 Swan Street, Wilmslow, SK9 1HE ☎ (01625) 441850
⊕ brewhouseandkitchen.com

⊠ Brewing started in 2013 in Portsmouth, the first in the growing Brewhouse & Kitchen chain. There are now 12 brewpubs, with more planned, each producing its own particular range of beers and with its brewery on open display in the bar area, following the B&K style. Local freehouses and beer festivals can be supplied. Carry outs and 'Brewery Experience' days are available at all venues. ‼◆V

Brewmeister

See Keith

Brewshed SIBA

1 Tayfen Road, Bury St Edmunds, Suffolk, IP32 6BH
☎ (01284) 848066 ⊕ brewshedbrewery.co.uk

⊠ Brewshed began brewing in 2011 using a five-barrel plant in the buildings located behind the Beerhouse, one of its pub outlets. There are plans to move to a new 12-barrel plant. A number of other beers are brewed occasionally, as capacity permits.

Pale (OG 1040, ABV 3.9%)

Best (OG 1044, ABV 4.3%)

American Blonde (OG 1055, ABV 5.5%)

Brewshine

4 Littledale, Kendal, Cumbria, LA9 7SG ☎ 07817 873997 ⊕ brewshine.co.uk

Brewing began in 2014 using a nine-gallon plant situated in a garage in Kendal. There are plans for expansion.

Silly Billy (OG 1038, ABV 3.8%)
A smooth copper-coloured bitter with balanced flavours and a caramel finish.

Billonde (OG 1040, ABV 4%)
A light citrus fruity flavour. Very refreshing.

Billy Goat Ale (OG 1040, ABV 4%)
Dark amber in colour with a rich malty taste. Well balanced with hops to leave a dry, caramel-chocolate finish.

Billyonaires Gold (OG 1040, ABV 4%)
A light refreshing beer with a citrus fruity flavour.

Brewsmith SIBA

Unit 11, Cuba Industrial Estate, Ramsbottom, BL0 0NE ☎ (01706) 829390 ⊕ brewsmithbeer.co.uk

Brewsmith is a 10-barrel microbrewery established in 2014 by the Smith family – James, Jennifer and Ted. ‼◆RAIB

Bitter (OG 1039, ABV 3.9%)
A pale session bitter. Moderate bitterness, pronounced floral/citrus hop aromas.

Gold (ABV 4.2%)
A golden ale. Moderate bitterness with a hint of marmalade.

Pale Ale (OG 1042, ABV 4.2%)
A refreshingly bitter and hoppy pale ale.

Anvil Ale (OG 1045, ABV 4.5%)
A full-bodied dark bitter with pine and fruit aromas.

APA (ABV 5%)
Pale ale with resinous pine, grapefruit and floral aromas.

Oatmeal Stout (OG 1052, ABV 5.2%)
A full-bodied, richly textured stout.

IPA (OG 1060, ABV 6%)
Rich mouthfeel, big hop aromas, long, dry bitter finish.

Brewster's SIBA 👁

Unit 5, Burnside, Turnpike Close, Grantham, Lincolnshire, NG31 7XU ☎ (01476) 566010 ⊕ brewsters.co.uk

⊠ Brewster is the old English term for a female brewer and Sara Barton is a modern example. Originally established in the Vale of Belvoir in 1998 and moving to Grantham in 2006, Brewster's produces a range of traditional and innovative beers with two regularly changing ranges: Wicked Women (4.8%) and WhimsicAles (4.0%). ‼🍺◆

Hophead (OG 1036, ABV 3.6%) ❧
This amber beer has a floral/hoppy character; hops predominate throughout before finally yielding to grapefruit in the lasting dry finish.

Marquis (OG 1038, ABV 3.8%) ❧
A well-balanced and refreshing session bitter with maltiness and a dry, hoppy finish.

Hopticale Illusion (OG 1040, ABV 4%)

A deep red beer with a big hop flavour, balanced with roast malts to give a flavoursome session brew.

Aromantica (OG 1042, ABV 4.2%)
A touch of roast malt for a light amber brew with a slightly sweet nutty flavour, tropical hop notes and aromas of lime and passion fruit. Refreshingly long aromatic finish.

Hop a Doodle Doo (OG 1043, ABV 4.3%) ⬡
A copper-coloured ale with a rich, full-bodied feel and fruity hop character.

Decadence (OG 1044, ABV 4.4%)
A golden ale with a hint of malt sweetness with passion fruit and grapefruit aromas on the nose. First taste gives a complex zesty hop palate leading to a fresh herby finish.

Aromatic Porter (OG 1045, ABV 4.5%)
A rich roasty dark porter with citrus and tropical fruit hop flavours.

Stilton Porter (OG 1049, ABV 4.9%)
A rich roast-flavoured porter with spicy hop flavours.

Briarbank SIBA

▤ 70 Fore Street, Ipswich, Suffolk, IP4 1LB ☎ (01473) 284000 ⊕ briarbank.org

The Briarbank Brewing Company was established in 2013, and is situated on the site of the old Lloyds Bank on Fore Street. The brewery is a small two-barrel plant. The bar above offers the range of beers. ‼◆

Briar Bitter (ABV 3.7%)
A traditional copper-coloured English bitter.

Brick SIBA

Arch 209, Blenheim Grove, Peckham, London, SE15 4QL ⊕ brickbrewery.co.uk

Brick began brewing in 2013. A brewery tap room is open on Saturdays from 12-6pm. The beers brewed vary from week to week. Local pubs, bars and restaurants are also supplied.

Sir Thomas Gardyner (OG 1038, ABV 3.8%) ❧
Unfined golden ale. Grapefruit and orange peel dominate, overlaid with hops lingering in the dry finish; increasing bitterness on drinking.

Blenheim Black (OG 1053, ABV 5.3%) ❧
Roasted notes throughout with black cherry and blackcurrant and a trace of hops. Finish is bitter and dry with some malt.

Brick House

Patcham, Brighton, BN1 8HQ ☎ 07708 384604 ✉ brickhousebrewingco@gmail.com

⊛Brick House has grown organically from humble homebrewing beginnings and plans to continue in this vein. Current output is a single firkin and 24 bottles a week. There are plans to upscale to a 100-litre kit with output of two firkins a week. RAIB

Session IPA (ABV 4%)

Bricknell (NEW)

67 Bricknell Avenue, Hull, East Yorkshire, HU5 4ET

☎ (01482) 446563 ☎ 07729 722953
⊕ bricknellbrewery.co.uk

Commercial brewing began in 2015, the brewery is currently at 150 litres and brews once or twice a week following 19th-century recipes. Most of the beer is bottle conditioned, with occasional casks produced. RAIB V

Bridestones SIBA

Smithy Farm, Long Causeway, Blackshaw Head, Hebden Bridge, West Yorkshire, HX7 7JB
☎ (01422) 847104 ⊕ bridestonesbrewing.co.uk

☺Bridestones, situated close to a rock outcrop from which it takes its name, started brewing in 2006 and currently supplies more than 60 outlets. Its brewery tap is the New Delight Inn in Blackshaw. ◆RAIB

Sandstone (OG 1039, ABV 3.9%) ◈
Amber-coloured session bitter with equal amounts of malt, fruit and bitterness. Initial balance gives way to a more bitter aftertaste.

Pennine Gold (OG 1043, ABV 4.3%) ◈
Good hop aroma and flavour; fruity, refreshing and easy-to-drink best bitter.

Bridge

▤ The Bridge, Woodhead Road, Holmbridge, West Yorkshire, HD9 2NQ
☎ (01484) 687652 ☎ 07970 779762

Brewing began in 2014 using a 2.5-barrel plant, in premises at the Bridge pub in Holmbridge. It produces beers for the pub and also for its companion pub, Brambles, in Holmfirth.

Bridgehouse SIBA

Airedale Heifer, Bradford Road, Sandbeds, Keighley, West Yorkshire, BD20 5LY

Office: Unit 1, Aireworth Mills, Aireworth Road, Keighley, West Yorkshire, BD21 4DH ☎ (01535) 601222 ⊕ bridgehousebrewery.co.uk

Bridgehouse began brewing in 2010 using a 10-barrel plant. The brewery purchased the recipes and branding of Old Bear Brewery in 2014 and moved into its premises in Keighley. In 2015 the brewery relocated again, to its present address. ‼◆

Blonde (OG 1040, ABV 4%) ◈
A strong fruity aroma with a sharp burst of grapefruit on the tongue and a touch of sweetness in the background. Bitter finish.

Aired Ale (OG 1042, ABV 4.2%) ◈
Brown beer with malty aroma. Malt, hops and fruit in equal balance with lingering fruitiness in a long bitter finish.

Porter (OG 1045, ABV 4.5%) ◈
Dark brown beer with red hints. Aromas of malt and liquorice lead to coffee and wine fruit flavours which carry through to a dry finish.

Holy Cow (OG 1057, ABV 5.6%) ◈
Light brown strong ale with juicy malt and full hop flavour, citrus overtones. Light hop aroma and a bitter, slightly astringent finish.

Brewed under the Old Bear brand name:

Yorkshire Ale (OG 1042, ABV 4.2%) ◈

A malty robust best bitter with slight fruit aroma. Sweet fruitiness follows through into the bitter aftertaste

Bridgetown

▤ Albert Inn, Bridgetown Close, Totnes, Devon, TQ9 5AD
☎ (01803) 863214 ⊕ albertinntotnes.com/bridgetown-brewery

⊗ Bridgetown started brewing in 2008 on a 2.5-barrel plant. ‼◆RAIB

Albert Ale (OG 1039, ABV 3.8%)

Totnes Hemp (OG 1040, ABV 4%)

Bitter (OG 1042, ABV 4.2%)

Cheeky Blonde (OG 1044, ABV 4.5%)

Shark Island Stout (OG 1044, ABV 4.5%)

Bridlington

▤ Telegraph Inn, 110 Quay Road, Bridlington, East Yorkshire, YO16 4JB
☎ (01262) 674592

Bridlington was founded in 2014 and is based in an outhouse in the beer garden of the Telegraph Inn. Following a pause in production, the brewery recommenced brewing in 2016. Both the Telegraph Inn and the Pack Horse in Bridlington are owned.

Briggs

c/o Unit 1, Waterhouse Mill, 65-71 Lockwood Road, Huddersfield, West Yorkshire, HD1 3QU ☎ 07427 668004 ⊕ briggssignatureales.weebly.com

Nick Briggs, a former member of the brewing team at Mallinson's and former head brewer at Elland, has branched out on his own producing his first brew on the Mallinson's plant. Now producing various regular, rotating, modern, hop-forward beers. ▰

Northern Soul (OG 1038, ABV 3.8%)
Pale bitter with a citrus and zesty aroma from an abundance of American hops.

Brighton Bier SIBA

Unit 20, Bell Tower Industrial Estate, Roedean Road, Brighton, East Sussex, BN2 5RU ☎ 07515 956976 ⊕ brightonbier.com

Brighton Bier was established in 2012. Originally based at the Hand in Hand pub in Brighton, it moved into new premises in 2014 with the opening of a new 15-barrel brewery. Beers are available throughout the South-east, and increasingly across the country. The brewery also part-owns the Brighton Beer Dispensary pub in Brighton with Late Knights Brewery.

Thirty Three (OG 1035, ABV 3.3%)

Brighton Bier (ABV 4%)

West Pier (OG 1042, ABV 4%)

Underdog (ABV 4.2%)

IPA (OG 1062, ABV 5%)

No Name Stout (ABV 5%)

Grand Porter (ABV 5.2%)

Brightside SIBA

Unit 10, Dale Industrial Estate, Radcliffe, M26 1AD
☎ (0161) 725 9644 ☎ 07870 207442
⊕ brightsidebrewing.co.uk

Brightside is an 18-barrel plant established in 2010 which began commercial production in 2011. It moved from the back room of the family bakery into dedicated industrial premises in 2013 and has expanded twice since then. ♦ RAIB V

The Beast (OG 1038, ABV 3.6%)
Copper-coloured beer, fairly malty with stone fruit flavours and a slight herbal character.

Odin (OG 1038, ABV 3.8%)
A fresh, light-bodied blonde ale brewed with a blend of American hops to give a fruity, citrus flavour and moderately bitter finish.

Our Town (OG 1040, ABV 4%)
A copper-coloured beer brewed with tropical fruit-flavoured hops to create maltiness and depth of flavour.

B-Side (OG 1042, ABV 4.2%)
Light and refreshing with fruity notes and gentle malty, lightly bitter finish.

Best Bitter (OG 1044, ABV 4.3%)
A dark amber-coloured traditional best bitter made from a blend of three hops showing a great depth of flavour.

Underworld (OG 1049, ABV 4.4%)
A drier, medium-bodied porter brewed with predominantly English hops. Bitter with aromas of coffee and dried fruit.

Darkside Stout (OG 1052, ABV 4.6%)
A jet black stout with espresso coffee and dark chocolate flavours, with more than a touch of smoke on the finish. More hops than are usual for a stout enhance the roast malt bitterness.

Manchester Skyline (OG 1044, ABV 4.6%)
Lager malt, wheat and four speciality malts give a deep golden colour and complex flavour.

Maverick IPA (OG 1047, ABV 4.8%)
Light amber in colour but with a weighty rich malty base and punchy citrus hop character. Refreshingly bitter but not overpowering.

Amarillo (OG 1048, ABV 5%)
The broad blend of malts create a complex grain profile to complement a single hop variety. A dry, light amber-coloured beer, liberally hopped without being overwhelmingly bitter.

Brightwater

9 Beaconsfield Road, Claygate, Surrey, KT10 0PN
☎ (01372) 462334 ☎ 07802 316389
⊕ brightbrew.co.uk

⊠ Brightwater is a stainless steel five-barrel brewery with two six-barrel fermenters, situated at the rear of a domestic property. Established in 2013, it supplies its own brewery tap (Platform 3) outside Claygate station, plus other local Surrey and South London pubs.

Little Nipper (OG 1033, ABV 3.3%) ◆
A rather thin hoppy bitter with a hint of a citrus taste and a bitter, slightly dry finish.

Top Notch (OG 1035, ABV 3.5%) ◆

Citrus notes dominate the aroma of this mid brown bitter. It has a reasonably well-balanced taste with some bitterness in the finish.

Daisy Gold (OG 1040, ABV 4%) ◆
Gold-coloured ale with a moderate tropical fruit hoppy character and some balancing malt leading to a bittersweet finish.

Wild Orchid (OG 1040, ABV 4%)
Dark oatmeal porter enhanced with a Madagascan vanilla pod in each cask giving the beer fragrant vanilla undertones.

All Citra (OG 1043, ABV 4.3%)
Bitter with a distinctly citrus flavour.

Brigstock

7 Park Walk, Brigstock, Northamptonshire, NN14 3HH
☎ (01536) 373428 ⊕ brigstockbrewhouse.co.uk

Philip Wilks began brewing in 2012 on a small 52-litre plant using natural spring water from a local limestone aquifer. Six regular beers are brewed, mostly available bottle-conditioned but occasionally in cask. RAIB

Brimstage SIBA

Home Farm, Brimstage, CH63 6HY
☎ (0151) 342 1181 ☎ 07870 968323
⊕ brimstagebrewery.com

Brewing started in 2006 on a 10-barrel plant in a redundant farm dairy in the heart of the Wirral countryside. This is Wirral's first brewery since the closure of the Birkenhead Brewery in the late 1960s. Around 60 outlets supplied across the Wirral, Merseyside, Cheshire and North Wales. ‼♦

Sandpiper Light Ale (OG 1036.5, ABV 3.6%)
Brewed with Citra hops, this session beer is well-balanced, light and refreshing with tropical fruit flavours.

Trappers Hat Bitter (OG 1037.5, ABV 3.8%)
Gold-coloured with a complex bouquet. It provides a mouthful of fruit zest, with hints of orange and grapefruit. A refreshingly hoppy session brew.

Rhode Island Red Bitter (OG 1039, ABV 4%) ◆
Red, smooth and well-balanced malty beer with a good dry aftertaste. Some fruitiness in the taste.

Scarecrow Bitter (OG 1041, ABV 4.2%)
Orange marmalade in colour, this well-balanced session brew has a distinct citrus fruit bouquet and a bitter finish.

Brinkburn Street (NEW) SIBA

Unit 1, Maling Court, Hoults Yard, Walker Road, Byker, Newcastle upon Tyne, NE6 2HL
☎ (0191) 260 0688 ⊕ brinkburnstreebrewery.co.uk

Brewing began in 2015, much influenced by West Coast USA beer styles. Citrus flavours and highly-hopped bitterness is a feature of many of its beers.

Fools Gold Session (ABV 3.8%)

The Pursuit of Hoppiness Session (ABV 3.9%)

Byker Brown Ale (ABV 4.8%)

TINO (ABV 4.8%)

Briscoe's

16 Ash Grove, Otley, West Yorkshire, LS21 3EL
☎ (01943) 466515 ✉ briscoe.brewery@talktalk.net

☺The brewery was launched in 1998 by microbiologist/chemist Dr Paul Briscoe in the cellar of his house with a one-barrel brew length. Dr Briscoe is currently producing one brew per week on his original plant, while several beers are produced on an irregular basis.

Chevin Bitter (OG 1039, ABV 3.8%)
Golden, hoppy bitter.

Otley Gold (OG 1040, ABV 3.9%)

Lighter Shade of Pale (OG 1040, ABV 4%)

Bristol Beer Factory SIBA

Unit A, The Old Brewery, Durnford Street, Ashton, Bristol, BS3 2AW
☎ (0117) 902 6317

Office: Bristol Beer Factory, c/o Tobacco Factory, Raleigh Road, Southville, Bristol, BS3 1TF
⊕ bristolbeerfactory.co.uk

🔲 A 30-barrel micro-brewery in a part of the former Ashton Gate Brewing Co, which closed in 1933. 50 outlets are supplied and output and brewing capacity are steadily increasing. !! 🍴 ◆ RAIB

Nova (OG 1040, ABV 3.8%) 🍺
Citrus hop aroma to this straw-coloured, light-bodied and bitter session ale. Hop-led taste with lemon fruit and pale malt following into a bitter hop aftertaste.

Seven (OG 1043, ABV 4.2%) 🍺
Mid-brown best bitter with a fruity aroma. Balanced malt and hops with hints of fruit and caramel flavours. Malt and bitterness remain on the aftertaste.

Enigma (OG 1044, ABV 4.4%)
A low bitterness red ale with speciality malt and crystal rye flavours, and aromatic, fruity hops.

Milk Stout (OG 1049, ABV 4.5%) 🍺
Sweet, full-bodied black stout with lactose creaminess. Finishes with smoky roast bitterness.

Independence (OG 1046, ABV 4.6%) 🍺
Strong, hoppy aroma and initial flavour. Sweet fruitiness follows, leading to a bitter hoppy finish. Well-balanced with impressive flavour for its strength.

Britman

The Stables, Atelier Suite, Burton Manor, Burton, Cheshire, CH64 5SJ ☎ 07925 875836
✉ britmanbreweryburtonmanor@gmail.com

Britman is a small, quirky independent brewery established in 2013. It brews to the Reinheitsgebot, German purity law, and produces vegetarian-friendly beers. The brewery has been recognised by the Sustainable Restaurants Association as a sustainable product, all spent grain is sent to happy pigs locally. ◆

Best Bitter (OG 1044, ABV 4.5%)
Smooth, light and pleasantly bitter.

London Porter (OG 1043, ABV 4.5%)
Dark, hoppy and slightly bitter with a treacle and coffee aftertaste.

Golden Ale (OG 1044, ABV 4.6%)
A true golden ale, hoppy and slightly bitter with a mild, sweet aftertaste.

Kolsch Style (OG 1045, ABV 4.8%)
A refreshing and tasty Kolsch-style beer.

IPA (OG 1049, ABV 5.2%)
A fresh and hoppy balanced ale with a slightly bitter finish.

Brixton SIBA

Arch 547, Brixton Station Road, Brixton, London, SW9 8PF
☎ (020) 3609 8880 ☎ 07761 436757
⊕ brixtonbrewery.com

Located in a railway arch in central Brixton, the brewery opened in 2013. The bulk of the production is currently bottled, but cask-conditioned ales feature as occasional guests in several pubs in the Brixton area. Beers are generally named after places in Brixton. 🍴◆RAIB

Reliance Pale Ale (OG 1042, ABV 4.2%) 🍺
Grapefruit and hops are present throughout this refreshing golden ale. Dry aftertaste with a hint of bitterness.

Effra Ale (OG 1045, ABV 4.5%) 🍺
Dry copper-coloured best bitter with hops and a trace of citrus in the flavour and finish, which is bitter.

Atlantic APA (OG 1054, ABV 5.4%) 🍺
Hops and fruit throughout this smooth yellow-coloured beer. There is a dry bitterness in the flavour and finish.

Electric IPA (OG 1065, ABV 6.5%)
Full-bodied IPA; balances malty sweetness and hoppy bitterness, with a floral, citrus and tropical fruit hit.

Brockley SIBA

31 Harcourt Road, Brockley, London, SE4 2AJ
☎ 07814 584338 ⊕ brockleybrewery.co.uk

Established in 2013 by a group of local beer enthusiasts who installed a five-barrel plant in a converted builder's workshop. The brewery concentrates on supplying outlets within a five-mile radius. Fermenting vessels were added in 2016, enabling the brewery to experiment with short runs of more specialist beer styles alongside its regular beers. A refurbished bar is open from 12-6pm on Saturdays. 🍴◆

Golden Ale (OG 1038, ABV 3.8%) 🍺
A hoppy golden ale with some citrus throughout and a bitter finish. Trace of caramelised malt.

Pale Ale (OG 1041, ABV 4.1%) 🍺
Well-balanced and dry, hoppy best bitter with some apricot fruit overlaid with biscuit malt.

Porter (OG 1043, ABV 4.3%) 🍺
Roast malt with a hint of blackcurrant becoming more hoppy and bitter late in the taste and aftertaste.

Red Ale (OG 1048, ABV 4.8%)
A deep red ale; the malty backbone is complemented by a distinctive hoppy aroma.

Brodie's SIBA

816a High Road, Leyton, London, E10 6AE ☎ 07828 498733 ⊕ brodiesbeers.com

⊠ Siblings James and Lizzie began commercial brewing in 2008 on a five-barrel plant at the back of the William IV pub in East London. Beers are available at the William IV and their small chain of family-owned pubs as well as other local outlets. ‼ ◆ RAIB

Citra (OG 1031, ABV 3.1%) ◥
Citrus and tropical fruit in aroma and flavour, which is dry, bitter and faintly sweet. Bitterness grows on drinking.

Kiwi (ABV 3.8%) ◥
A smooth-drinking yellow-coloured beer. Flavour is malty sweet overlaid by green fruit, a little hops and a bitter character.

Bethnal Green Bitter (OG 1040, ABV 4%) ◥
A brown-coloured, refreshing but full-bodied bitter with a malty sweetness. Finish is dry with an increasing bitterness.

Old Street Pale Ale (OG 1050, ABV 5%) ◥
Hops and citrus fruit are balanced in this golden beer by the bitterness, a biscuity sweetness and a creamy mouthfeel.

California (OG 1053, ABV 5.3%) ◥
Smooth yellow-coloured beer with a citrus fruit aroma. Sweet citrus fruit is balanced with bitterness on the palate and aftertaste.

Broughs

Unit 26, Steel Drive, Fordhouse Road Industrial Estate, Bushbury, Wolverhampton, West Midlands, WV10 9XD ☎ 07814 158292

Office: 192 Staveley Rd, Wolverhampton, West Midlands, WV1 4RL ✉ broughsltd@yahoo.co.uk

☺Broughs is a family-run brewery which began trading in 2008 using spare capacity at several breweries around the West Midlands region. In 2011 it moved into rented premises at the former Butlers Springfield brewery (1873-1991). Redevelopment of the site in 2015 forced Broughs to relocate to more modern premises. It continues to brew three times a week on its five-barrel plant. More than thirty outlets in the West Midlands, Staffordshire and Shropshire are supplied direct. ‼ ◆ RAIB

Original (OG 1036, ABV 3.6%)
A pale, easy-drinking session bitter, well-balanced with refreshing English hops.

Springfield (OG 1040, ABV 4%)
A light golden-coloured session ale with a subtle clean taste created by an unusual blend of English and European hops.

Light Pale Ale (OG 1043, ABV 4.3%)
Light, smooth and creamy ale with a subtle bitter finish.

Blonde (OG 1046, ABV 4.6%)
A contemporary hoppy and fruity pale yellow-coloured ale.

India Pale Ale (OG 1048, ABV 4.8%)
Traditional strong IPA bursting with a sweet, fruity, hoppy flavour. Followed by pleasant spices and bitterness to finish.

Superior (OG 1050, ABV 5%) 🗖

A strong, dark mild with a sweet malty finish. Mainly brewed throughout Autumn/Winter.

Sledgehammer (OG 1056, ABV 5.6%)
Traditional strong English IPA, dark gold in colour and full of flavour with a subtle hop finish.

Broughton SIBA

Broughton, ML12 6HQ
☎ (01899) 830345 ⊕ broughtonales.co.uk

☺Founded in 1979, Broughton Ales was then one of the first microbreweries. Broughton has developed since then and though more than 60% of production goes into bottle for sale in Britain and abroad, it retains a sizeable range of cask ales. All beers are suitable for vegetarians. ‼ ☰ ◆

Hopopotamus (OG 1038, ABV 3.8%)

Greenmantle (OG 1038, ABV 3.9%)
A dark bittersweet ale with a pleasant hop aftertaste.

Brewer's Gold (OG 1060, ABV 4%)

Clipper IPA (OG 1042, ABV 4.2%)
A light-coloured, crisp, hoppy beer with a clean aftertaste.

Merlin's Ale (OG 1042, ABV 4.2%) ◥
A well-hopped, fruity flavour is balanced by malt in the taste. The finish is bittersweet, light but dry.

Dark N'Cloudy (OG 1046, ABV 4.4%)

Exciseman's 80/- (OG 1046, ABV 4.6%)
A traditional 80/- cask ale. A dark, malty brew. Full drinking with a good hop aftertaste.

Jeddart Justice (OG 1046, ABV 4.7%)

Dark Dunter (OG 1050, ABV 4.8%)
Bursting with oatmeal and chocolate aromas complemented by dark roasted malts and a rich aftertaste.

Proper IPA (OG 1050, ABV 5%)

6.2 IPA (OG 1060, ABV 6%)
With quadruple the hops of a typical IPA, this dark chestnut brown example has a bold citrus aroma and a biscuit and bitter aftertaste.

Old Jock (OG 1070, ABV 6.7%) 🗖
Strong, sweetish and fruity in the finish.

Brown

See Ashover

Brown Cow

Brown Cow Road, Barlow, North Yorkshire, YO8 8EH
☎ (01757) 618947 ⊕ browncowbrewery.co.uk

☺Brewing since 1997, Brown Cow has won awards at many festivals. Keith and Sue Simpson operate a six-barrel plant at its maximum capacity of 17 barrels per week. Handcrafted cask beers brewed using traditional methods are delivered direct from the brewery. Beers are also brewed for Suddaby's. ◆ RAIB

Sessions (OG 1033, ABV 3.6%)
A pale, hoppy session beer with a refreshing finish and citrus notes in the aftertaste.

Bitter (OG 1038, ABV 3.8%)

Copper-coloured classic bitter brewed with English hops. Round and full in flavour with a smooth finish.

White Dragon (OG 1039, ABV 4%)
A pale, aromatic beer with a good level of bitterness, citrus undertones and a clean finish.

Scruff's Gold (OG 1041, ABV 4.2%)
Well-balanced golden traditional English ale, round and full-flavoured with a smooth finish.

Captain Oates Mild (OG 1044, ABV 4.5%)
A dark mild with complex mix of malts and oats. Well-balanced with undertones of coffee and chocolate.

Mrs Simpsons Thriller in Vanilla (OG 1049, ABV 5.1%)
A rich porter brewed with fresh vanilla pods complementing the dark malts.

Broxbourne SIBA

Unit 12c, Reeds Farm Estate Office, Roxwell Road, Writtle, Essex, CM1 3ST ⊕ broxbournebrewery.co.uk

Broxbourne began brewing in 2013 using a two-barrel plant. Bottle-conditioned beers are also produced under the Fallen Angel brewery name. Production moved from Hertfordshire to Essex in 2015. RAIB

Ginger Beer (OG 1035, ABV 4%)
Traditionally made ginger beer with an old fashion style to give it a strong, sweet taste with a smooth finish.

Cowgirl Gold (OG 1045, ABV 4.2%)

Angry Ox Bitter (OG 1047, ABV 4.8%)

Brewed under the Fallen Angel Brewery name:

Fire in the Hole (OG 1046, ABV 4.9%)
A chilli beer.

Black Death (OG 1052, ABV 5.2%)
A jet black stout infused with Naga chilli.

Brunning & Price

See Phoenix

Brunswick SIBA ◉

⊟ 1 Railway Terrace, Derby, DE1 2RU
☎ (01332) 410055 ☎ 07534 401352
⊕ brunswickbrewingcompany.co.uk

⊗ Derby's oldest brewery, it is a 10-barrel tower plant built as an extension to the Brunswick Inn in 1991. Bought by Everards in 2002, the brewery is now run separately yet in conjunction with the pub. It supplies the inn, Everards, wholesalers and the free trade within 100 miles. Brunswick also swaps with other breweries. !! ♦ RAIB

White Feather (OG 1038, ABV 3.6%)
Pale yet full-bodied session beer, easy-drinking with a citrus twist.

Triple Hop (OG 1040, ABV 4%)
Straw-coloured ale with a bitter astringency.

The Usual (OG 1042, ABV 4.2%)
A traditional English malty best bitter, smooth with hints of toffee.

Railway Porter (OG 1045, ABV 4.3%)

A classic dark porter, lightly hopped with chocolate and coffee notes.

Rocket (OG 1047, ABV 4.7%)
A 'New World' IPA, the use of US and Pacific hops imparts citrus, apricot and mango flavours.

Black Sabbath (OG 1058, ABV 6%)
A strong dark ale with finely balanced flavours of liquorice, coffee and chocolate.

Bryncelyn

Unit 303, Ystradgynlais Workshops, Trawsffordd Road, Ystradgynlais, SA9 1BS
☎ (01639) 841900
✉ bryncelynbrewery@hotmail.co.uk

☺Opened in 1999, the brewery relocated to its present premises in 2008 with a six-barrel plant acquired from Webbs Brewery of Ebbw Vale. The owner is fond of Buddy Holly and this is reflected in beer names. !! ♦ RAIB

Holly Hop (OG 1039, ABV 3.9%) ◤
Pale amber with a hoppy aroma. A refreshing hoppy, fruity flavour with balancing bitterness; a similar lasting finish. A beer full of flavour for its gravity.

Buddy Marvellous (OG 1040, ABV 4%) ◤
Dark brown with an inviting aroma of malt, roast and fruit. A gentle bitterness mixes roast with malt, hops and fruit, giving a complex, satisfying and lasting finish.

Oh Boy (OG 1045, ABV 4.5%) ◤
An inviting aroma of hops, fruit and malt, and a golden colour. The tasty mix of hops, fruit, bitterness and background malt ends with a long, hoppy, bitter aftertaste. Full-bodied and drinkable.

Brythonic (NEW)

Tyersall Annexe, The Hudnalls, St Briavels, Gloucestershire, GL15 6RT ☎ 07766 652837
✉ doug.morgan@hotmail.co.uk

One of the new breed of nanobreweries, having begun brewing in a Bristol suburb on a small scale in 2015, the brewery relocated in 2016 to the Gloucestershire/Welsh border village of St Briavels. Brewing is temporarily suspended. RAIB

Bucks Star

23 Twizel Close, Stonebridge, Milton Keynes, Buckinghamshire, MK13 0DX
☎ (01908) 590054 ⊕ bucksstar.beer

⊗ Possibly the first microbrewery to be solar-powered from panels on the brewery roof, Bucks Star opened in 2015 using a 10-barrel, purpose-built plant. Only organic malt is used and no sugars or syrups are added. The beers are distributed to local pubs, restaurants and garden centres. !! ⊨ RAIB V

No. 1 (OG 1040, ABV 4%)
A deep golden-coloured beer with a good balance between malt and hops. It has a light, dry and refreshing character with a lingering bitter finish.

Bude SIBA

Unit 1, Kings Hill Industrial Estate, Bude, Cornwall, EX23 8QN

☎ (01288) 359937 ☎ 07414 660787
⊕ budebrewery.co.uk

⊠ Originally established in 2011 near Launceston as Fry's Brewery, and now relocated to Bude, it started beer production under the Bude Brewery name in 2014.

Neet (OG 1037, ABV 3.7%)

Porthbud (OG 1040, ABV 4%)

Haven (OG 1042, ABV 4.2%) ◆
Tawny-coloured best bitter with hop aroma. Balanced hop and malt character with notes of apple, cranberry, cherry, marmalade and honey.

Summerleaze (OG 1047, ABV 4.7%) ◆
Refreshing pale brown strong bitter. Sweet malt with stone fruit flavours balanced by hops, becoming bitter.

Black Rock (OG 1051, ABV 5.1%) ◆
Red porter with malt aroma. Sweet roast malt and stone fruit flavours with bitterness. Malt, hops and dry bitter finish.

Buffy's SIBA

Rectory Road, Tivetshall St Mary, Norfolk, NR15 2DD
☎ (01379) 676523 ⊕ buffys.co.uk

⊠ Established in 1993, Buffy's brewing capacity is 20 barrels. The brewery owns two pubs, the Wicklewood Cherry Tree and the Foulden White Hart. Barley for all brewing is grown in Norfolk. Around 100 outlets are supplied. ◆ RAIB

Norfolk Terrier (OG 1038, ABV 3.8%) ◆
A strong plummy aroma leads into a sweet malty beginning. Caramel notes add depth to a long fruity finish.

Beagle (OG 1040, ABV 4%)

Mild (OG 1042, ABV 4.2%) ◆
Complex with a smooth but grainy feel. Caramel and blackcurrant initially bolster the heavy malt influence. Short malty finish.

Polly's Folly (OG 1043, ABV 4.3%) ◆
Well-balanced with a definitive malty spine. Elderberry notes and a long, dry, bittersweet finale.

Hopleaf (OG 1044.5, ABV 4.5%) ◆
A gentle hop nose. Strawberries mingle with the hops as the malt gently subsides to leave a bittersweet, dry finish.

Mucky Duck (OG 1044, ABV 4.5%) ◆
Roasted malt throughout with a sweet fruitiness giving depth without becoming dominant. Chewy mouthfeel and lingering finish.

India (OG 1046, ABV 4.6%)

Norwegian Blue (OG 1049, ABV 4.9%) ◆
Nutty caramel aroma. A well-balanced mix of malt and bitterness with caramel, hops, and sweetness. Strong, increasingly bitter finish.

Ale (OG 1055, ABV 5.5%)

9X (OG 1089, ABV 9%)

Bull Lane

See Stables

Bullards 👁

7 The Arches, Bracondale, Trowse Millgate, Norwich, NR1 2EF
☎ (01603) 624072 ⊕ bullardsbeers.co.uk

Beers were originally produced by Redwell brewery. Bullards is now a separate company sharing premises and brewer but not brewing kit. ◆

No. 4: Session IPA (OG 1041, ABV 3.8%)
A golden, juicy session beer packed full of American hops.

No. 5: Best Red Bitter (OG 1040, ABV 4%)
A deep red-coloured, malty bitter.

No. 1: East Coast Pale Ale (OG 1042, ABV 4.2%) ◆
Grapefruit and lemon join the hoppy signature to create a distinctive, easy-drinking brew. Well-balanced, complex strong finish.

No. 6: Rye Pale Ale (OG 1045, ABV 4.4%)
A brown rye ale brewed with spicy English and American hops.

No. 3: Amber Ale (OG 1047, ABV 4.7%)
A malty, amber-coloured ale with hints of caramel as well as peppery and fruity hops.

No. 2: India Pale Ale (OG 1058, ABV 6%)
A deep-copper coloured ale with a frothy white head, full of rich caramel and burnt brown sugar flavours with a bitter orange aroma.

Bullfinch

Units 886-887, Rosendale Road, Herne Hill, London, SE24 9EH ☎ 07899 795823
⊕ thebullfinchbrewery.co.uk

Bullfinch began brewing in 2014 using a 2.5 barrel plant, upgraded in 2015 to a five-barrel one. Production is mainly keg but cask and bottle-conditioned beers are available. ‼ ⚑ RAIB

RosendAle (OG 1039, ABV 3.8%)

South Eastern Bloc Stout (OG 1060, ABV 5.2%)

Bullmastiff SIBA

14 Bessemer Close, Leckwith, Cardiff, CF11 8DL
☎ (029) 2066 5292 ✉ bob.bullmastiff@live.co.uk

The brewery has recently been purchased following the retirement of the founders Bob and Paul Jenkins. The new brewster, Ramphai, is believed to be the only Thai brewster currently brewing in the UK. The beers are still brewed using the founders' recipes and are available in south-east Wales, with the JD Wetherspoon Bears Head in Penarth serving as the informal brewery tap. ◆

Welsh Red (OG 1048, ABV 4.8%)

Son of a Bitch (OG 1062, ABV 6%) ◆
A complex, warming amber ale with a tasty blend of hops, malt and fruit flavours, with increasing bitterness.

Bumpmill

The Cottage, Hallfieldgate, Shirland, Derbyshire, DE55 6AG
☎ (01773) 830431 ⊕ bumpmillbrewery.co.uk

A four-barrel family brewery located in a converted building overlooking the beautiful Amber Valley. The name comes from the site of an old Bump Mill close by – bump was coarse cotton used to make wicks for candles. Bumpmill has one tied house, Stanley's micro pub in Matlock. ♦

Moonraker (OG 1038, ABV 3.8%)

Drops of Jupiter (OG 1040, ABV 4%)
A blonde ale with grapefruit notes, leading to a slightly bitter finish.

Lola (OG 1040, ABV 4%)
Easy-drinking session pale ale.

Heart of Gold (OG 1042, ABV 4.2%)

Thunder Road (OG 1044, ABV 4.4%)
Copper-coloured premium bitter. Full-bodied chocolate and roast malt with a smooth finish.

Glory Daze (OG 1045, ABV 4.5%)

Dakota (OG 1048, ABV 5%)

Buntingford SIBA

Greys Brewhouse, Therfield Road, Royston, Hertfordshire, SG8 9NW
☎ **(01763) 250749** ☎ **07879 698541**
⊕ **buntingford-brewery.co.uk**

⊗ Brewing commenced on the current site in 2005 and has expanded to a capacity of around 60 barrels per week. Two regular beers are brewed year round alongside occasional brews and various themed specials. The beers are brewed using water from an on-site well and all liquid waste is treated in a reed bed. The brewery is located on a conservation farm and there is a wide variety of bird life visible from the doors of the brewhouse, often including rare and endangered species. !! ♦

Highwayman (OG 1036, ABV 3.6%)

Twitchell (OG 1038, ABV 3.8%) ⏚ ▮

Burley Street

▤ **Fox & Newt, 7-9 Burley Street, Leeds, LS3 1LD**
☎ **(0113) 245 4527** ⊕ **burleystreetbrewhouse.co.uk**

☺Burley Street Brewhouse is in the cellar of the Fox & Newt pub where the first brewery was installed by Whitbread in the 1980s. The freehold was purchased by the current owners and brewing recommenced in 2010 and then again, after a two-year break, in 2015 by the team from the Whippet Brewing Company. The Pack Horse at Woodhouse is the only other outlet supplied.

The Brickyard (OG 1038, ABV 3.7%)
A traditional Yorkshire bitter.

Laguna Seca (OG 1041, ABV 4%)
A blonde beer with a grapefruit flavour. Its initial sweetness and full body are balanced by a dry, fruity citrus finish.

Burning Sky SIBA

Place Barn, The Street, Firle, East Sussex, BN8 6LP
☎ **(01273) 858080** ⊕ **burningskybeer.com**

⊗ Burning Sky started brewing in 2013 using a 15-barrel plant, based on the Firle Estate in the South Downs. It is owned and run by Mark Tranter (ex-Dark Star head brewer). Brewing takes place four days a week. The brewery has its own yeast strains suited to the beer styles. It specialises in pale ales and Belgian-inspired farmhouse beers and has an extensive barrel-aging programme. RAIB

Plateau (OG 1035, ABV 3.5%)
Pale gold in colour, with a crisp malt edge and sharp bitterness. Full in flavour, zesty and refreshing.

Aurora (OG 1056, ABV 5.6%)
A premium strength pale ale, with a blend of malts to provide a juicy backbone and a pale amber colour it has a resinous mouthfeel plus big citrus and tropical fruit flavours, which are prominent, yet well balanced.

Devil's Rest IPA (OG 1070, ABV 7%)
A full strength IPA named after a nook on the South Downs near the brewery. It has a burnt orange colour and full flavour.

Burnside SIBA

Laurencekirk Business Park, Laurencekirk, Aberdeenshire, AB30 1EY
☎ **(01561) 377316** ⊕ **burnsidebrewery.co.uk**

Burnside began brewing in 2010 using a 2.5-barrel plant and by 2012 had expanded to a 10-barrel plant. Since then the focus has been to establish the brand and range of cask-conditioned ales locally and to develop a range of bottle-conditioned beers. Further development to expand is scheduled. !! ☛ RAIB

Black Katz (OG 1036, ABV 3.6%)

No. 1 Pale Ale (OG 1036, ABV 3.6%)
A well-balanced pale ale.

3-BULLZ (OG 1038, ABV 3.8%)

Mad Dogz (OG 1038, ABV 3.8%) ◣
Slight mix of roasted malt and citrus hop session brew.

Golden X (OG 1042, ABV 4.1%)
An easy-drinking best bitter.

Wild Rhino (OG 1045, ABV 4.5%)

Chieftains Export (OG 1048, ABV 4.6%)
A classic export 80/- ale.

India Pale Ale (OG 1049, ABV 4.8%)
A fruity, hoppy IPA.

After Dark (OG 1050.5, ABV 5%)
A double chocolate oatmeal stout.

M-PIRE (OG 1052, ABV 5.2%) ◣
Sweetish peachy hoppy brew. Very warming.

Stealth (OG 1058, ABV 6%)
A full-bodied rich dark ale.

Burscough SIBA

c/o Hop Vine, Liverpool Road North, Burscough, Lancashire, L40 4BY
☎ **(01704) 893799** ☎ **07831 225656**
⊕ **burscoughbrewery.co.uk**

Burscough commenced brewing in 2010 in old stable buildings in the courtyard to the rear of the Hop Vine. It is currently brewing on a four-barrel plant but plans are underway to relocate and to expand. ♦

Flat Rib Mild (OG 1036, ABV 3.6%)
A classic mild, dark and satisfying.

Priory Gold (OG 1038, ABV 3.8%) ◣
A sweet and fruity, lightly bittered, easy-drinking session beer.

Duke of Lancaster (OG 1040, ABV 4%) ◣

Brown beer with a roast bitter finish.

Mere Blonde (OG 1040, ABV 4%)
A pale, full-flavoured, thirst quenching golden ale with a light bitterness and a prominent citrus hop aroma. The malt undertones in the body are complemented by a full hop flavour which gives way to a massive grapefruit finish.

Ringtail (OG 1042, ABV 4.2%)
A ruby red ale. Full bodied with a prominent bitterness and a delightful malt character. A noticeable grassy aroma with hints of marmalade and molasses.

Black Canon Stout (OG 1045, ABV 4.5%)
A dark and luscious stout, full flavoured with hints of coffee and liquorice in the finish, named after the Augustine Friars who inhabited Burscough Priory in the 12th Century.

Mug Billy (OG 1045, ABV 4.5%)
A traditional best bitter. Light amber in colour, easy drinking with a noticeable bitterness.

Wailing Willy (OG 1050, ABV 5%)
A premium pale beer with a slightly fruity taste.

Thorougood (OG 1051, ABV 5.1%)
A dangerously drinkable ale. Golden in colour with a citrus finish.

Sutler's IPA (OG 1055, ABV 5.5%)
A powerful amber-coloured heavily-hopped ale. A sharp lip smacking prominent bitterness gives way to a massive aroma with hints of grapefruit and other citrus fruits.

Burton Bridge SIBA ◉

24 Bridge Street, Burton upon Trent, Staffordshire, DE14 1SY
☎ (01283) 510573 ⊕ burtonbridgebrewery.co.uk

⊛The brewery was established in 1982 by Bruce Wilkinson and Geoff Mumford and owns five pubs in the local area, including its CAMRA award-winning brewery tap. More than 300 outlets are supplied direct. ‼ ☞ ♦ RAIB

Golden Delicious (OG 1037, ABV 3.8%) ◄
A Burton classic with sulphurous aroma and well-balanced hops and fruit. An apple fruitiness, sharp and refreshing start leads to a lingering mouth-watering bitter finish with a hint of astringency. Light, crisp and refreshing.

Sovereign Gold (OG 1040, ABV 4%) ◄
Sweet caramel aroma with a grassy hop start with malt overtones. Fresh and fruity with a bitterness that emerges and continues to develop.

XL Bitter (OG 1039, ABV 4%) ◄
Another Burton classic with sulphurous aroma. Golden with fruit and hops and a characteristic lingering aftertaste hinting of toffee apple sweetness.

XL Mild (OG 1040, ABV 4%)

Bridge Bitter (OG 1041, ABV 4.2%) ◄
Gentle aroma of malt and fruit. Good balanced start finishing with a robust hop mouthfeel.

Burton Porter (OG 1044, ABV 4.5%) ◄
Chocolate aromas and sweet, smooth taste of smoky roasted grain and coffee.

Damson Porter (OG 1044, ABV 4.5%)

Draught Burton Ale (OG 1048, ABV 4.8%) ◄

Fruity orange aroma leads to hoppy start, hop and fruit body then fruity aftertaste. Dry finish with fruity hints

Bramble Stout (OG 1049, ABV 5%)

Stairway to Heaven (OG 1049, ABV 5%) ◄
Golden bitter. A perfectly balanced beer. The fruity and hoppy start leads to a hoppy body with a mouthwatering finish.

Top Dog Stout (OG 1049, ABV 5%) ◄
Black and rich with a roast and malty start. Fruity and abundant hops give a fruity, bitter finish with a mouth-watering edge. Also available as Bramble Stout.

Festival Ale (OG 1054, ABV 5.5%) ◄
Caramel aroma with plenty of hop taste balanced by a full-bodied malty sweetness.

Thomas Sykes (OG 1095, ABV 10%) ◄
Kid in a sweetshop aroma. Rich, fruity spirited tastes – warming and dangerously drinkable.

Burton Old Cottage IFBB

Unit 10, Eccleshall Business Park, Hawkins Lane, Burton upon Trent, Staffordshire, DE14 1PT ☎ 07909 931250 ⊕ oldcottagebeer.co.uk

⊛The brewery was originally installed in the old Heritage Brewery. When the site was taken over, it moved to a modern industrial unit. The brewery was sold in 2005, the following year saw heavy investment in new production and storage facilities by the new owners. ‼ ♦

Oak Ale (OG 1044, ABV 4%) ◄
Tawny-coloured, full-bodied bitter. A sweet start with balanced fruit gives way to a slight roast taste with some caramel for interest. A dry, hoppy finish satisfies the palate.

Chestnut (OG 1042, ABV 4.2%)
A dark session ale with a touch of bitterness and a pleasant, full aftertaste.

Stout (OG 1047, ABV 4.7%) ◄
Roast aroma with background fruit, roast tastes with gentle sweetness. Bitterness develops surprisingly from the sweet start to leave a sharp edged mouthfeel. Roast throughout with a malt background.

Pastiche (OG 1050, ABV 5.2%)
A smooth, balanced ale with a complex taste and aroma.

Halcyon Daze (OG 1050, ABV 5.3%) ◄
Tawny-coloured and creamy with touches of hop, fruit and malt aroma. Fruity taste and finish.

Burton Town (NEW) SIBA

10 Broadlands, Burton on Trent, Staffordshire, DE13 0EU
☎ (01283) 350350 ☎ 07701 067046 ⊕ burton.town

⊗ Burton Town began brewing in 2015 with a capacity of 40 litres in head brewer Rich Catlin's garage. Initial focus has been on strong, dark beers, which are supplied to local pubs. ‼

Burtonwood

Bold Lane, Burtonwood, Warrington, Cheshire, WA5 4TH
☎ (01925) 220022 ⊕ thomashardybrewery.co.uk

Thomas Hardy's only brewery was acquired by Molson Coors in 2015. Currently producing no real ale.

Bushy's SIBA

Mount Murray Brewery, Mount Murray, Braddan, Isle of Man, IM4 1JE
☎ (01624) 661244 ⊕ bushys.com

☺Launched in 1986 as a brewpub, Bushys relocated in 1990 when demand outgrew capacity. Bushys goes one step further than the Manx Pure Beer Law preferring the German Reinheitsgebot (Pure Beer Law) that excludes sugar. ‼◆

Castletown Bitter (OG 1035, ABV 3.5%)
A light, golden beer full of floral and citrus hints. A refreshing session beer.

Ruby (1874) Mild (OG 1035, ABV 3.5%) ◆
Classic full-bodied malty ruby mild with sweet caramel flavours throughout, and well-balanced hops.

Bitter (OG 1038, ABV 3.8%) ◆
A traditional malty and hoppy beer with good balance. The fruit lasts through to the bitter finish.

Old Bushy Tail (OG 1045, ABV 4.5%)
A reddish-brown beer with a pronounced hop and malt aroma, the malt tending towards treacle. Slightly sweet and malty on the palate with distinct orange tones. The full finish is malty and hoppy with a hint of toffee.

Butcher's Dog (NEW)

Unit 10D, Twydale Business Park, Skerne Road, Driffield, East Yorkshire, YO25 6JX
☎ (01377) 254032 ☎ 07525 050644
⊕ thebutchersdog.co.uk/brewery

Butcher's Dog is an independantly-owned microbrewery using a one-barrel plant. Beers are available within a 30-mile radius of Driffield.

Yorkshire Tyke Bitter (ABV 3.8%)

Black Spot Stout (ABV 4.6%)
A complex dry stout made with a unique blend of seven malts.

One-0-One Pale Ale (ABV 4.6%)
A pale ale with citrus notes.

Peppa's Pawter (ABV 4.7%)
A dark red-coloured ale combining fine malts with black treacle and First Gold hops.

Kukar IPA (ABV 5.8%)

Butcombe SIBA ⟨◉⟩

Cox's Green, Wrington, Somerset, BS40 5PA
☎ (01934) 863963 ⊕ butcombe.com

⊗ Originally established in 1978, Butcombe was bought by the Jersey-based Liberation Group for a reported £15m in 2015. It moved to a new purpose-built brewery with a 150-barrel plant in 2005. Around 500 outlets are supplied direct and similar numbers via wholesalers and pub companies. The brewery has an estate of 17 freehouses. ‼▰◆

Adam Henson's Rare Breed
(OG 1038, ABV 3.8%) ◆

Sulphurous aroma with undertones of unripe fruit combine in this thin-bodied ale. Bitterness and astringency dominate and continue into the finish.

Bitter (OG 1039, ABV 4%) ◆
Bitter tawny ale. Malt with hops and ripe fruit contribute to a well-balanced flavour. Long, refreshing bitter aftertaste.

Gold (OG 1045, ABV 4.4%) ◆
Amber golden ale with light aroma of fruit and hops, leading to well-balanced flavours of malt, pale fruit and hops. Bitter aftertaste.

Bute

15-17 Columshill Street, Rothesay, Isle of Bute, PA20 0DN
☎ (01700) 504260 ☎ 07980 259511
⊕ butebrewco.co.uk

Situated in the centre of Rothesay on the Isle of Bute, brewing began in 2015. Beers are supplied to several local outlets, and further afield. Beer festivals are also supplied. ‼

Scalpsie Blonde (OG 1038, ABV 3.8%)
A refreshing session beer with tropical tastes of lime and lychee.

Red (OG 1042, ABV 4.2%)
A fruity ale with a pleasant caramel body.

The Maids (OG 1043, ABV 4.3%)
A malty beer with a smooth bitterness and hint of passionfruit.

Butts SIBA

Northfield Farm, Wantage Road, Great Shefford, Berkshire, RG17 7BY
☎ (01488) 648133 ⊕ buttsbrewery.com

⊗ The brewery was set up in a converted barn in 1994. In 2002 the brewery took the decision to become dedicated to organic production; all the beers brewed use organic malted barley and organic hops and are certified by the Soil Association. ▰◆RAIB

Jester (OG 1036, ABV 3.5%) ◆
A pale brown-coloured session bitter with a hoppy aroma and a hint of fruit. The taste balances malt, hops, fruit and bitterness with a hoppy aftertaste.

Traditional (OG 1040, ABV 4%)
A pale brown-coloured bitter that is quite soft on the tongue with hoppy citrus flavours accompanying a gentle bittersweetness. A long, dry aftertaste is dominated by fruity hops.

Barbus Barbus (OG 1046, ABV 4.6%) ◆
Golden ale with a fruity hoppy aroma and a hint of malt. Hops dominate taste and aftertaste, accompanied by fruitiness and bitterness, with a hint of balancing sweetness.

Buxton SIBA

Units 4, Staden Business Park, Staden Lane, Buxton, Derbyshire, SK17 9RZ
☎ (01298) 244200 ☎ 07754 015743
⊕ buxtonbrewery.co.uk

Buxton Brewery was set up in 2009 as a five-barrel brewery and now currently operates on a 24-barrel plant. Water is drawn from its own borehole. Its brewery tap is in Buxton and it exports to 25 countries. ◆RAIB

Moor Top (OG 1038, ABV 3.6%)
Pale ale heavily hopped with US Chinook hops imparting refreshing grapefruit bitterness.

Rednik Stout (OG 1045, ABV 4.1%)
Classic stout with big roast malt character.

SPA (Special Pale Ale) (OG 1041, ABV 4.1%)
A single-hopped beer showcasing US Citra hops.

Axe Edge (OG 1065, ABV 6.8%)
An IPA with a big tropical and zesty fruit nose and palate.

Buzzard

Speddyd Farm, Llandyrnog, LL16 4LE ☎ 07972 202880 ⊕ buzzardbrewery.co.uk

Brewing commenced in 2013 on a 2.5-barrel plant in a former farm building. 30-50 pubs are supplied within a 30-mile radius. There are plans to start bottling beer. ♦

Hoppin' Buzzard (OG 1038, ABV 3.9%)

HPA (OG 1038, ABV 3.9%)

Village Bitter (OG 1039, ABV 3.9%) ◕
A malty session bitter with a dry taste and subtle hop characteristics leading to a bitter finish.

Best Bitter (OG 1042, ABV 4.2%)

Pale of Clwyd (OG 1042, ABV 4.2%) ◕
A light and fruity best bitter with a sweetish initial taste and a hoppy, dry finish.

Vale Ale (OG 1045, ABV 4.5%) ◕
A dark brown-coloured best bitter, smooth and malty with a dry, hoppy finish.

Old Buzzard (OG 1050, ABV 5.3%)
Mid to dark brown-coloured traditional strong ale with a good balance of malt and hops.

Bwthyn

Llanbadrig, LL67 0LN

Bwthyn began brewing in 2014 producing bottle-conditioned beers only. RAIB

By the Horns SIBA

Unit 25, Summerstown, London, SW17 0BQ
☎ (020) 3417 7338 ⊕ bythehorns.co.uk

⊠ By the Horns began brewing in 2012 using a 5.5-barrel plant, since upgraded to a 12-barrel. It is located in an industrial unit near Wimbledon Stadium. The brewery tap is open six days a week (Tue-Sun) and hosts regular events. ⇟

Stiff Upper Lip (OG 1038, ABV 3.8%) ◕
A classic amber-coloured bitter, well balanced with hops to the fore and a hint of citrus. Dry bitter finish.

Mayor of Garratt (OG 1042, ABV 4.3%) ◕
Amber-coloured best bitter with sweet biscuit and orange fruit flavour. Long, dry finish with some bitterness and peppery hop.

Diamond Geezer (OG 1049, ABV 4.9%) ◕
Malty, hoppy red ale with blackcurrant, citrus and faint roast notes. Bitterness develops and builds in the aftertaste.

Lambeth Walk (OG 1051, ABV 5.1%) ▯ ◕

Well-balanced black porter with hops and a little fruit throughout. The roasted bitterness is complemented by the malt notes.

Byatt's SIBA

Unit 10, Lythalls Lane Industrial Estate, Lythalls Lane, Coventry, CV6 6FL
☎ (024) 7663 7996 ⊕ byattsbrewery.co.uk

☺ Byatts, established in 2011 and located on the north side of Coventry, was the first commercial brewery in the city for over 80 years. It supplies the West Midlands area, expanding into other regions. ♦ RAIB

XK Dark (OG 1038, ABV 3.5%) ▯ ◕
Smoky aromas then a mass of varied tastes ending in diminishing hop and roast.

Coventry Bitter (OG 1039, ABV 3.8%)

Big Cat (OG 1042, ABV 4%)

Phoenix Gold (OG 1043, ABV 4.2%)

Madagascar Stout (OG 1043, ABV 4.4%)

Urban Red (OG 1047, ABV 4.5%)

Regal Blond (OG 1053, ABV 5.2%)

C&C Wellpark

Wellpark Brewery, 161 Duke Street, Glasgow, G31 1JD

No real ale. ‼

Cader SIBA

Unit 4, Marian Mawr Enterprise Park, Dolgellau, LL40 1UU ☎ 07931 734655 ⊕ caderales.com

Cader Ales was founded in 2012 by a husband-and-wife team. It was expanded in 2013 to its present five-barrel capacity. It is situated close to the centre of the picturesque market town of Dolgellau. ‼

Gold (OG 1038, ABV 3.8%)
A light, hoppy golden ale with a subtle aroma of honey, lemon and tarragon.

Idris Bitter (OG 1041, ABV 4.1%)
Traditional bitter with caramel and spicy notes.

Tallyllyn Pale Ale (OG 1044, ABV 4.4%)
A classic IPA, refreshingly bitter with citrus and floral notes.

Glasdir Copper (OG 1045, ABV 4.5%)
A deep, copper-coloured ale with spicy tones and malty finish with a touch of caramel.

Red Bandit (OG 1050, ABV 5%)
A warm ruby-coloured ale based on a traditional recipe with spicy berry aromas.

Caffle

The Old School, Llawhaden, SA67 8DS
☎ (01437) 541502 ⊕ cafflebrewery.co.uk

⊠ Caffle began brewing in 2013 using a four-barrel plant producing ale in small batches, mainly for the local market. Further beers are planned. ‼ ⇟ RAIB

Skirp Gold (OG 1039, ABV 3.8%)
Golden ale with fruity, spicy aromas. Bitter grapefruit flavour.

Quay Ale (OG 1044, ABV 4%)

An amber-coloured ale, caramel with a light, hoppy citrus flavour. Balanced slightly to the malty side.

Sholly Amber (OG 1043, ABV 4%)
Light chestnut in colour with a good malt/hop balance.

Kift Blonde (OG 1044, ABV 4.3%)
Straw-coloured, with citrus and floral notes, flavoured with nettle tips.

In The Grip (OG 1052, ABV 4.7%)
A warming ale, ruby red in colour. Malty and slightly sweet with caramel tones.

Skaddly Puck (OG 1048, ABV 4.8%)
An IPA using a blend of hops to give a distinctive hoppy citrus flavour.

Drop Squint (OG 1052, ABV 5.2%)
Light golden in colour, smooth and clean-tasting with honey, malt and biscuit flavours.

Cairngorm SIBA ⊚

Unit 12, Dalfaber Industrial Estate, Aviemore, PH22 1ST
☎ (01479) 812222 ⊕ cairngormbrewery.com

☺Cairngorm produces six regular cask beers using a 20-barrel plant. Now with its own bottling line and a capacity of 140 barrels, the free trade is supplied as far as the central belt and nationally via wholesalers. !!🍺♦

Nessies Monster Mash (OG 1040, ABV 4.1%) 🍺
A traditional English-type bitter with plenty of bitterness and strong malt flavour and a fruity background. Lingering bitterness in the aftertaste with diminishing sweetness.

Stag (OG 1040, ABV 4.1%) 🍺
A best bitter with plenty of roast and hop throughout. This tawny-coloured brew also has plenty of malt in the lingering bittersweet aftertaste.

Trade Winds (OG 1043, ABV 4.3%) 🍺
Citrus fruit, hop and elderflower nose leads to hints of grapefruit in the mouth. The bitter sweetness in the taste lasts through the long, lingering aftertaste.

Black Gold (OG 1044, ABV 4.4%) 🍾 🍺
Roast malt dominates throughout, slight smokiness in aroma leading to a liquorice and blackcurrant background taste giving it a background sweetness. A long, dry bitter finish.

Cairngorm Gold (OG 1044, ABV 4.5%) 🍺
Fruit and hops to the fore with a hint of caramel in this sweetish brew. Also known as Sheepshaggers Gold.

Highland IPA (OG 1049, ABV 5%) 🍺
Refreshing light-coloured, citrus-hopped IPA.

Wildcat (OG 1049.5, ABV 5.1%) 🍾 🍺
A full-bodied warming strong bitter. Malt predominates but there is an underlying hop character through to the well-balanced aftertaste. Drinks dangerously less than its strength.

Caledonian ⊚

42 Slateford Road, Edinburgh, EH11 1PH
☎ (0131) 337 1286 ⊕ caledonianbeer.com

☺The brewery was founded by Lorimer and Clark in 1869 and was sold to Vaux of Sunderland in 1919. In 1987 the brewery was saved from closure

by a management buy-out and became independent. The brewery was purchased by S&N in 2004 and became part of Heineken in 2008. Monthly guest beers are produced which are sometimes of an unusual style, as well as a rolling programme of special beers covering each of the seasons. A pilot plant, Wee George, within the main brewery was opened in 2015 to allow small scale brews of new recipes. !!♦

Flying Scotsman (OG 1039.5, ABV 3.5%) 🍺
Well-balanced, malty beer with bittersweet character. Similar to a Scottish 80/-, but drier and with more hop bitterness.

Deuchars IPA (OG 1039.5, ABV 3.8%) 🍺
Golden session ale with hop aroma and dry bitter finish. Balanced, with malt adding body and fruit a balancing sweetness.

Edinburgh Castle 80/- (OG 1042.4, ABV 4.1%) 🍺
A predominantly malty, brown beer with soft roast and caramel throughout. Fruit gives sweetness, typical of a Scottish 80/-.

Golden XPA (OG 1044, ABV 4.3%) 🍺
Nicely balanced golden ale with malt and fruit throughout. Hops come to the fore in the increasingly dry, bitter aftertaste.

Calverley's SIBA

23a Hooper Street, Cambridge, CB1 2NZ
☎ (01223) 312370 ☎ 07769 537342
⊕ calverleys.com

⊠ This small central Cambridge brewery was started in 2013 by Sam Calverley and his brother Tom. The one-barrel plant is located in an old industrial unit close to the city centre and mainly supplies local pubs and beer festivals. !!🍺

The Ninth (ABV 3.8%)
A wheat beer, lightly hopped with US hops.

Citra & Simcoe Pale Ale (ABV 4.5%)

The Eighth (ABV 4.7%)
An unfined wheat beer hopped with Cascade and Centennial.

Best Bitter (ABV 4.8%)
A smooth amber-coloured ale with a good balance of malt and subtle bittering hops.

Calvors SIBA ⊚

Home Farm, Coddenham Green, Suffolk, IP6 9UN
☎ (01449) 711055 ⊕ calvorsbrewery.com

Calvors Brewery was established in 2008 and brews four craft lagers, as well as cask-conditioned beers. V

Lodestar Festival Ale (OG 1038, ABV 3.8%)
A rich golden straw-coloured ale with a gentle sweetness and a honey aroma. Lightly hopped and well-balanced.

Smooth Hoperator (OG 1040, ABV 4%)
A pale ale combining four different malts to give a copper colour and a background sweetness. Well-rounded and easy-drinking.

Cambridge

🏠 Cambridge Brew House, 1 King Street, Cambridge, CB1 1LH
☎ (01223) 858155 ⊕ thecambridgebrewhouse.com

⊗ Brewing began in 2013. ♦

King's Parade (OG 1040, ABV 3.8%) ⬥
A good traditional English bitter with moderate biscuity malt and resiny hop throughout and a hint of caramel. Dry finish.

Misty River (OG 1043, ABV 4.2%) ⬥
Golden beer dominated by grapefruit on nose, palate and lingering dry aftertaste.

Night Porter (OG 1046, ABV 4.4%) ⬥
A creamy black/red-coloured beer luxuriating in a blend of dark chocolate and coffee, softened by raisins.

Cambrinus

See Liverpool Organic

Camden Town

55-59 Wilkin Street Mews, Kentish Town, London, NW5 3NN
☎ (020) 7485 1671 ⊕ camdentownbrewery.com

⊗ No real ale. Bought by A-B InBev in 2016 for reportedly £85M. A modern, automated brewhouse situated in five railway arches underneath Kentish Town West railway station, NW5, with two other arches as storage areas, and six conditioning tanks outside. There is a brewery tap on site, in one arch. The majority of its output is in keg form. The brewery was bought by AB InBev in 2016. ‼

Camerons ⊚

Lion Brewery, Stranton, Hartlepool, County Durham, TS24 7QS
☎ (01429) 852000 ⊕ cameronsbrewery.com

⊚Founded in 1865, Camerons was bought in 2002 by Castle Eden. The brewery has a pub estate of 70+, including the Head of Steam pubs. Contract brewing and bottling also take place. ‼ ⎚ ♦

Best Bitter (OG 1036, ABV 3.6%) ⬥
A light bitter, but well-balanced, with hops and malt.

Camerons IPA (OG 1038, ABV 3.8%)
A straw-coloured, light IPA.

Strongarm (OG 1041, ABV 4%) ⬥
A well-rounded, ruby-red ale with a distinctive, tight creamy head; initially fruity, but with a good balance of malt, hops and moderate bitterness.

Trophy Special (OG 1040, ABV 4%)
An amber ale, slightly sweet and malty, fruity and hoppy.

Gold Bullion (OG 1043, ABV 4.3%)
Gold-coloured, full-bodied ale with a good hop flavour.

Contract brewed for Heineken:

Bitter (OG 1035, ABV 3.8%)

Campervan (NEW) SIBA

Edinburgh ☎ 07786 566000

Office: PO Box 28626, Comely Bank, Edinburgh, EH4 9DQ ⊕ campervanbrewery.com

Campervan began brewing in 2016 in a private garage but also in a 1973 VW campervan, hence

the name. The van is used as a mobile sales outlet at beer festivals and other outdoor events.

Blonde Voyage (OG 1038, ABV 3.8%)

All Shook Up (OG 1040, ABV 4%)

Mutiny on the Bounty (OG 1042, ABV 4.2%)

Cannon Royall IFBB

🏠 **Fruiterer's Arms, Uphampton Lane, Uphampton, Worcestershire, WR9 0JW**
☎ (01905) 621161 ⊕ cannonroyall.co.uk

Cannon Royall's first brew was in 1993 in a converted cider house behind the Fruiterer's Arms. The brewery supplies a number of mainly local outlets. ‼♦RAIB

Fruiterers Mild (OG 1037, ABV 3.7%) ⬥
Dark-coloured beer with malty aromas leading to a fruity mix of bitter hops and sweetness, and a short, balanced aftertaste.

Hunny Bear (OG 1038, ABV 3.8%)

King's Shilling (OG 1038, ABV 3.8%) ⬥
A golden bitter that packs a citrus hoppy punch throughout.

Arrowhead Bitter (OG 1039, ABV 3.9%) ⬥
A powerful punch of hops attacks the nose before the feast of bitterness. The memory of this golden brew fades too soon.

Comfortably Stout (OG 1041, ABV 4%)
Full flavoured, slightly dry, light stout.

Arrowhead Extra (OG 1043, ABV 4.3%)
A Fuggles hop punch leads to a smooth palate and pleasant finish with a good malt balance.

Blond Bombshell (OG 1043, ABV 4.3%)

Grapeshot (OG 1043, ABV 4.3%)
Gold-coloured with a citrus bite.

Hood (OG 1043, ABV 4.3%)

Slap Ale (OG 1043, ABV 4.3%)
Pale ale with a hoppy palate that is not overpowering.

Teddy Bear (OG 1043, ABV 4.3%)
Pale, easy-drinking bitter.

Canopy SIBA

Arch 1127, Bath Factory Estate, 41 Norwood Road, Herne Hill, London, SE24 9AJ ☎ 07792 463386
⊕ canopybeer.com

⊗ Canopy started brewing in 2014 and opened a tap room in 2015. ‼♦RAIB V

Sunray Pale Ale (ABV 4.2%)
A light-coloured ale; refreshing and hoppy.

Full Moon Porter (ABV 5%)
Rich flavours of chocolate, caramel and coffee with light hop notes on the finish.

Ruskin Wheat Beer (ABV 5.4%)
A German-style wheat beer with zesty flavours and fruity overtones.

Brockwell IPA (ABV 5.6%)
A hoppy, easy-drinking pale ale.

Milkwood Amber Ale (ABV 7.2%)
A Belgian-style amber-coloured beer with a full, robust and fruity flavour.

Canterbury Ales SIBA

Unit 7, Stour Valley Business Park, Ashford Road, Chartham, Kent, CT4 7HF
☎ (01227) 732541 ☎ 07944 657978
⊕ canterbury-ales.co.uk

⊠ Brewing commenced in 2010. The eight-barrel plant was supplied by PBC Brewery Installations.
‼◆

The Wife of Bath's Ale (OG 1038, ABV 3.9%) ◄
A golden beer with strong bitterness and grapefruit hop character, leading to a long, dry finish.

The Reeve's Ale (OG 1040, ABV 4.1%)

The Miller's Ale (OG 1044, ABV 4.5%)

Canterbury Brewers ◉

▤ **Foundry Brew Pub, White Horse Lane, Canterbury, Kent, CT1 2RU**
☎ (01227) 455899 ⊕ thefoundrycanterbury.co.uk

⊠ Canterbury Brewers started brewing in 2011, situated in the Foundry brewpub (formerly a Victorian foundry) in the heart of Canterbury. 2013 saw an increase in capacity to a four-barrel plant. 16 beers are usually available all year round, with a small core range and many seasonal beers and specials. Several events and festivals are run throughout the year, including the Kent Green Hop Festival. The company also runs the nearby City Arms. Experimental brews are planned using brewing yeasts isolated from the walls of the monk's brewhouse at nearby St Augustine's Abbey.
‼◆RAIB

Foundryman's Gold (OG 1040, ABV 4%)
A golden ale with strong aromas of citrus and elderflower with a subtle lingering bitterness.

GB (OG 1040, ABV 4.1%)

Foundry Torpedo (OG 1044, ABV 4.5%)
A straw-coloured ale with an explosive, crisp finish.

Little Red Rye (OG 1043, ABV 4.5%)
Citra, Chinook and Centennial hops deliver flavour and aroma, with spice from the rye malt.

Streetlight Porter (OG 1059, ABV 5.8%)
Dark, malty porter with strong coffee-chocolate notes and a liquorice finish. It has a strong, sweet grist which gives balance to the coffee and spicy hop.

Cap House

444-446 Bradford Road, Batley, West Yorkshire, WF17 5LW
☎ (01924) 479909 ☎ 07981 858270
⊕ caphousebrewery.co.uk

☺Cap House began in 2011 using a 2.5-barrel plant as a joint venture between Peter Lister, who has a plastics business at the location, and Gary Wardman of the Reindeer Inn in Overton, which is the brewery tap. ◆

Miners A Pint (OG 1038, ABV 3.8%)
A tangy session bitter with a smooth mouthfeel balanced by a toffee undertone and a deep, dry finish with lingering fruit notes.

Hey Blondie (ABV 4.2%)

Hoppylicious (OG 1040, ABV 4.2%)

A light, hoppy beer, well-balanced with a fruity taste. Refreshing citrus and grapefruit flavours for a bittersweet finish.

Temptress (OG 1054, ABV 5.6%)
A rich ruby-coloured beer with a smooth finish, fruity nut/toffee aroma and tangy palate.

Captain Cook SIBA ◉

▤ **White Swan, 1 West End, Stokesley, North Yorkshire, TS9 5BL**
☎ (01642) 710263 ⊕ captaincookbrewery.com

☺The Captain Cook Brewery is located within the 18th-century White Swan pub. The brewery, which started in 1999, has a four-barrel plant. ‼◆

Botany Bay (OG 1040, ABV 4%)
A light ale with a hint of grapefruit and spruce.

Sunset (OG 1040, ABV 4%)
A smooth, light ale with hint of citrus flavours.

Slipway (OG 1042, ABV 4.2%)
A light-coloured, full-flavoured, hoppy ale with a smooth malt aftertaste.

Endeavour (OG 1043, ABV 4.3%)
Brown-coloured ale with a bitter finish.

Black Porter (OG 1044, ABV 4.4%)
Chocolate notes and dominant roast flavours lead to a dry, bitter finish.

IPA (OG 1051, ABV 5.1%)

Carbon Smith

80 North Western Street, Manchester, M12 6DY
☎ 07518 106487 ⊕ carbonsmith.co.uk

⊠ Carbon Smith started brewing in a fourth-floor tenement flat bedroom in Edinburgh before moving to a small unit in Newington with a self-built and designed two-barrel plant. It moved to a archway near Piccadilly station in Manchester in 2016. There are plans for expansion to a 10-barrel plant. ◆

Carlisle SIBA ◉

Unit 2, 12a Kingstown Broadway, Kingstown Industrial Estate, Carlisle, Cumbria, CA3 0HA
☎ (01228) 532928 ☎ 07423 595921

Office: Spinners Arms, Cummersdale, Carlisle, Cumbria, CA2 6BD ⊕ thespinnersarms.org.uk

☺Carlisle is a family-run brewery established in 2013. Initially using a 2.5-barrel plant in a shed behind the owner's freehouse, by 2015 it had expanded to a 10-barrel plant in an industrial unit. The brewery strongly favours English hops and malts. Beer is available in the Spinners Arms and other local outlets. ‼◆

Pale Ale (OG 1039, ABV 3.8%)
A traditional session pale ale; light and crisp. Biscuit tastes come through from the malts with bitterness from the hops making it refreshingly well-balanced.

Spun Gold (OG 1043, ABV 4.2%)
A sweet-tasting, red-coloured beer. Hops follow on to build the flavour and complement the balanced finish.

Flaxen (OG 1042, ABV 4.5%)

Complex flavours mingle in the mouth with a background of bitterness.

Magic Number (OG 1045, ABV 4.5%)
A premium bitter, soft and smooth with caramel and toffee flavours. Lightly bittered to give a refreshing malty beer.

Nut Brown (OG 1048, ABV 4.7%)
A full-flavoured, rounded, nutty tasting beer with hops adding to the overall fruitiness. Chestnut-coloured, it builds up a warm, sweet nutty flavour with hops lingering in the mouth.

Oatmeal Stout (OG 1048, ABV 4.7%)
A soft, rounded stout with coffee, chocolate and dark smoke aromas.

The Carlisle Experiment (ABV 5.6%)

Carlsberg ◉

Jacobsen House, 140 Bridge Street, Northampton, NN1 1PZ
☎ (01604) 668866 ⊕ carlsberg.co.uk

International lager brewery, which, while brewing no real ale, is a major distributor of cask beer. The Tetley real ales are brewed under contract by Marston's.

Castle SIBA

Unit 9a-7, Restormel Industrial Estate, Liddicoat Road, Lostwithiel, Cornwall, PL22 0HD ☎ 07880 349032
⊕ castlebrewery.co.uk

The brewery was established in 2007 using a one-barrel plant by Andy White, formally with Keltek Brewery. It was sold to Theo Corfield on Andy's retirement in 2012. ♦ RAIB

Golden Gauntlet (OG 1040, ABV 4%)

Cornish Best Bitter (OG 1042, ABV 4.2%)

Once a Knight (OG 1050, ABV 5%)

Castle Combe SIBA ◉

The Brewhouse, Preston West Farm, Preston, Wiltshire, SN15 4DX
☎ (01249) 892900 ⊕ castlecombebrewery.co.uk

⊗ Brewing began on a farm in Wiltshire in 2009 using a five-barrel plant under the Braydon Ales name. A change of ownership in 2014 saw a name change and a new beer range. More than 50 outlets are supplied direct, mostly as guest ales, with further outlets via the SIBA Beerflex scheme. ‼♦

Bybrook Bitter (OG 1034, ABV 3.5%)
Pale single malt/single hop easy-drinking beer with a citrus taste.

Pendulum Pale Ale (OG 1037, ABV 3.8%)
Well-hopped, full-bodied golden bitter.

Doing Little Bitter (OG 1040, ABV 4.1%)
Light copper-coloured ale with a gentle bitter taste from the English hops.

Circuit Bitter (OG 1043, ABV 4.4%)
Chestnut-coloured, well-balanced premium bitter.

Dark Lane Porter (OG 1055, ABV 5.5%)
Called a porter but is in fact a creamy milk stout. Full-flavoured but easy drinking for its strength.

Castle Gate (NEW)

Unit 13, Cillefwr Industrial Estate, Johnstown, SA31 3RB
☎ (01267) 468150
✉ castlegatebrewery@outlook.com

Castle Gate began brewing in 2015 using a five-barrel plant. Pubs and shops are supplied in Southwest Wales. RAIB

Best Bitter (ABV 4.4%)
Traditional, easy-drinking bitter. A smooth, malty ale with hints of caramel, chocolate and fruitiness.

Towy Gold (ABV 4.4%)
A clean, crisp and refreshing light straw-coloured ale with a hit of hop bitterness.

Merlin's Own (ABV 5.2%)
A well-balanced, refreshing golden pale ale.

Castle Rock SIBA ◉

Queensbridge Road, Nottingham, NG2 1NB
☎ (0115) 985 1615 ⊕ castlerockbrewery.co.uk

☺ Castle Rock was established in 1998. Since then capacity has steadily increased with the largest expansion taking place in 2010, which gave a total capacity of 360 barrels per week. Beers are distributed through its estate of 21 pubs and further afield through wholesalers. Four different beers are brewed each year to support the Nottinghamshire Wildlife Trust and a unique Nottinghamian Celebration Ale is brewed quarterly. The Traffic Street Specials, an offshoot range of experimental beers, are also brewed at Castle Rock, all of which are unfined and vegan friendly. A visitor centre opened in 2011 adjacent to the brewery tap, the Vat & Fiddle. ‼♦ RAIB V

Sheriff's Tipple (OG 1034, ABV 3.4%) ◣
Tawny-coloured malty beer with Goldings hops.

Black Gold (OG 1037, ABV 3.8%) ◣
A dark ruby mild. Full-bodied and fairly bitter.

Harvest Pale (OG 1037, ABV 3.8%) ◣
Pale yellow-coloured beer, full of hop aroma and flavour. Refreshing with a mellowing aftertaste.

Red Riding Hood (OG 1042.5, ABV 4.3%) ◣
Reddish brown-coloured fruity bitter with initial malt, caramel and hops leading to a lasting malty, bitter finish.

Preservation Fine Ale (OG 1044, ABV 4.4%) ◣
A traditional copper-coloured English best bitter with malt predominant. Fairly bitter with a residual sweetness.

Sherwood Reserve (OG 1045, ABV 4.5%) ◣
An earthy yet smooth-tasting dark stout with a smoked roastiness through to a roast bitter finish.

Elsie Mo (OG 1045, ABV 4.7%) ▣ ◣
A strong golden ale with floral hops evident in the aroma. Citrus hops are mellowed by a slight sweetness.

Midnight Owl (OG 1055, ABV 5.5%) ⬡ ▣ ◣
Black IPA with roast malts, fruity hops and a slightly sweet finish.

Screech Owl (OG 1055, ABV 5.5%) ▣ ◣
A classic golden IPA with an intensely hoppy aroma and bitter taste with a little balancing sweetness.

Brewed for Cooper & Griffin Beer Co:

Vulcan Bomber (ABV 3.8%)

Castles SIBA 👁

Symondscliffe Way, Caldicot, NP26 5PW
☎ (01291) 422032 ☎ 07825 992604
⊕ castlesbrewery.co.uk

Brewing began in 2014. Capacity increased in 2015 to seven barrels and a brewery shop, selling bottle-conditioned ales, was opened. 🍺RAIB

Court Jester (OG 1038, ABV 3.8%)
A refreshing session pale ale.

White Knight (OG 1041, ABV 4.1%)
American-style pale ale, peach in smell and vibrant in taste.

Portcullis (OG 1042, ABV 4.2%)
A russet brown-coloured ale producing a vibrant tropical fruit smell. Full-bodied with a malty yet rounded taste.

Kings Reserve (OG 1043, ABV 4.3%)
Amber-coloured ale brewed with a blend of malts. An orange, dry taste.

Bishop's Secret (OG 1045, ABV 4.5%)
A dark mild, fruity on the nose, giving a malty finish.

Black Smith (OG 1046, ABV 4.6%)
A stout, rich in malt and roasted barley with a hint of liquorice.

Ironclad (OG 1052, ABV 5%)
A traditional IPA, full-flavoured with a peach aroma.

Castor SIBA

30 Peterborough Road, Castor, Cambridgeshire, PE5 7AX
☎ (01733) 380337 ⊕ castorales.co.uk

This three-barrel brewery, established in 2009, is located in a specially converted outhouse in the garden of the founder brewer. The Prince of Wales Feathers in Castor village features the beers on a permanent basis, along with other local outlets and national beer festivals. ‼♦

Durobrivae (OG 1037, ABV 3.7%)

Hopping Toad (OG 1040, ABV 4.1%)
A light golden bitter, the pale malt is balanced by bittering and aroma hops giving a refreshing citrus flowery finish with a fruity aftertaste.

Old Scarlet (OG 1045, ABV 4.6%)
A complex grain bill produces a ruby-coloured malty beer balanced by subtle hops with a fine aroma and citrus finish.

Cathedral Heights SIBA 👁

Unit 12, Churchill Business Park, Bracebridge Heath, Lincoln, LN4 2HD
☎ (01522) 530661 ☎ 07432 266783
⊕ chbrewery.co.uk

Cathedral Heights was established by Steve Marston in 2011, brewing on a nine-gallon plant in his kitchen. In 2013, after a year out of production, the brewery relocated to a business unit in Bracebridge Heath where a 2.5-barrel plant was installed. On and off sales are available and a local delivery service is offered.

Lincoln Pale (OG 1037, ABV 3.8%)
A light and refreshing pale ale with a hoppy finish.

Churchills Pride (OG 1038, ABV 3.9%)

A copper-coloured ale bittered using Target hops with a dash of Fuggles to finish.

Strait IPA (OG 1039, ABV 3.9%)
A gold-coloured, slightly citrus single-hop beer.

BBH Bitter (OG 1042, ABV 4.3%)
A hoppy, refreshing golden bitter.

Devils Nightmare (OG 1042, ABV 4.3%)
A smooth, dark mild, sweet and malty.

Steep Hill (OG 1041, ABV 4.3%)
A dark copper-coloured ale with malty tones and a fruity finish.

Castle Dungeon (OG 1050, ABV 5.4%)
A full-bodied stout with added chocolate.

Caveman

The Cave (below The George & Dragon), 1 London Road, Swanscombe, Kent, DA10 0LQ ☎ 07900 234644 ⊕ cavemanbrewery.co.uk

Caveman began brewing in 2012 and moved to its current site beneath the George & Dragon pub in 2013 using a four-barrel plant. It is named for the local discovery in the 1930s of skull fragments from a Palaeolithic human, then the oldest remains found in the UK. Beers can be found nationwide through various wholesalers with direct supply to London, Kent and parts of Sussex. ♦RAIB

Palaeolithic (OG 1038, ABV 3.8%)
A pale ale with Cascade hops and some slight malt sweetness.

Citra (OG 1042, ABV 4.1%)
A hoppy pale ale with a malt character that lets the citrus flavours from American Citra hops shine through. A refreshing session beer.

Neanderthal (OG 1044, ABV 4.4%)
An ale full of roast and caramel malt flavours and traditional Kent hops.

Caythorpe SIBA

⧉ c/o Black Horse, 29 Main Street, Caythorpe, Nottinghamshire, NG14 7ED
☎ (0115) 966 4933 ☎ 07807 583724
⊕ caythorpebrewery.co.uk

Established in 1996 using a 2.5-barrel plant in a building at the rear of the Black Horse pub, the brewery upgraded to a six-barrel plant in 2010. ‼

Dark Gem (OG 1033.3, ABV 3.5%) 🍺
Subtly hopped dark mild, initial malt and roast taste, chocolaty mouthfeel and slight bitter finish.

One Swallow (OG 1034, ABV 3.6%)
Golden session bitter, crisp and well hopped.

Cocker Beck (OG 1034.7, ABV 3.7%)
Copper-coloured, light-flavoured bitter.

Dover Beck (OG 1037, ABV 4%) 🍺
Pale brown-coloured, well-balanced session bitter. Initial malt is offset by a slight hoppy bitterness.

Outlaw (OG 1039, ABV 4%)
Smooth bitterness with a light orange citrus hop finish.

Stout Fellow (OG 1040, ABV 4.2%)
A dark stout, brewed with roasted barley to give a roast character.

Classic (OG 1042, ABV 4.6%)

Traditional copper-coloured premium bitter, malty and well hopped.

Cerddin SIBA

▤ c/o Cross Inn, Maesteg Road, Cwmfelin, CF34 9LB
☎ (01656) 732476 ☎ 07949 652237
⊕ cerddinbrewery.co.uk

Established in 2010 using a 2.5-barrel plant with conditioning and malting rooms in a converted garage adjacent to the owner's pub, now enlarged to a four-barrel plant. Beer is usually only available in the pub. ‼◆RAIB

Solar (OG 1040, ABV 4%)
A red-coloured beer with a good level of bitterness and a blackcurrant aftertaste.

Oops (OG 1043, ABV 4.3%)
Straw-coloured beer, initial hoppy dryness leads to a fairly sweet aftertaste.

Cascade (OG 1047, ABV 4.8%)
A single-hopped, straw-coloured beer with a citrus finish.

Lighter Shade of Pale (OG 1050, ABV 5.2%)

Cerne Abbas SIBA ◉

North End Farm, Venn Lane, Chideock, Dorset, DT6 6JY
☎ 07506 303407

Office: The Mill House, Mill Lane, Cerne Abbas, Dorset, DT2 7LB ⊕ cerneabbasbrewery.com

⊗ Established in 2014 by Vic Irvine and Jodie Moore using a five-barrel plant. The beers are made as naturally as possible using local, chalk-filtered water. The brewery supplies locally to pubs. ◆

Responsibly (OG 1035, ABV 3.2%)

Ale (OG 1040, ABV 3.8%)
Triple-hopped and well-balanced tawny-coloured ale. Has a supple middle with a fuller mouthfeel and refreshing finish.

Blonde (OG 1042, ABV 4.2%)
Single-hopped blonde ale.

Gurt Stout (OG 1058, ABV 6.2%)
Silky smooth, full-bodied and rich stout.

Chadlington (NEW)

Chapel Road, Chadlington, Oxfordshire, OX7 3LZ
⊕ chadlingtonbrewery.com

Chadlington began brewing in 2015. At present only one beer is brewed, supplied to the local area.

Golden Ale (ABV 4%)

Chadwick's

Unit 16, Castle Mills, Aynam Road, Kendal, Cumbria, LA9 7DE ☎ 07983 543724 ⊕ chadwicksbrewery.co.uk

☺Chadwick's Brewery is based in the historic town of Kendal. Established in 2014 it is situated on the old Goodacre Carpets site.

Castle Mills Mild (OG 1036, ABV 3.6%) ◆
A well-balanced and traditional fruity, dark mild.

Kirkland Blonde (OG 1036, ABV 3.6%) ◆
A brown ale with a slightly bitter finish.

Miller Bridge Bitter (OG 1040, ABV 4%)

A dark mahogany-coloured ale, packed full of malty and caramel flavours.

Castle Pale (OG 1042, ABV 4.2%)
A pale, straw-coloured beer with a citrus taste and aroma from American hops and a pleasant dry finish.

Chalk Hill

▤ Rosary Road, Norwich, NR1 4DA
☎ (01603) 477078 ⊕ thecoachthorperoad.co.uk

⊠ Chalk Hill began production in 1993 on a 15-barrel plant. It supplies local pubs and festivals. ‼◆

Tap Bitter (OG 1036, ABV 3.6%) ◆
Well-balanced with a light, hoppy character in both aroma and taste. Malt provides contrast. Short dry and bitter finish.

CHB (OG 1042, ABV 4.2%) ◆
Malty with fruity cooking apple notes, hoppy bittersweet background. A gentle malt aroma and sticky mouthfeel. Long finish.

Gold (OG 1043, ABV 4.3%) ◆
A light, hoppy nose. Grapefruit, banana and hops mingle in a well-balanced beginning. The finish develops a growing bitterness.

Dreadnought (OG 1049, ABV 4.9%) ◆
A rich, resinous aroma introduces a heavy malty brew. Raisin and plum with a sweet malty backbone. Singularly abrupt ending.

Chantry SIBA

Unit 1, Callum Court, Gateway Industrial Estate, Parkgate, Rotherham, South Yorkshire, S62 6NR
☎ 07815 727285 ⊕ chantrybrewery.co.uk

☺Brewing returned to Rotherham with the opening of Chantry in 2012 using the latest brewing technology in a 20-barrel state of the art plant built by Sheffield-based Moeschle UK. ‼

New York Pale (OG 1039, ABV 3.9%)
A pale session bitter with a refreshing citrus taste and a crisp bitter finish.

Iron & Steel Bitter (OG 1040, ABV 4%)
Chestnut-coloured with complex spicy flavours of dark fruits and a clean finish. An easy-drinking Yorkshire session bitter.

Diamond Black Stout (OG 1045, ABV 4.5%)
Full-bodied dry stout with a bitter finish, spicy with hints of liquorice and dark berries.

Chapel

Dinesfield, Chapel Lane, Criftins, Shropshire, SY12 9LZ
☎ (01691) 690412 ☎ 07928 682174
⊕ chapelbrewery.co.uk

Chapel began brewing in 2013 using a one-barrel plant behind the owner's bungalow. In 2016 the brewery moved to larger premises across the road. Occasional specials are brewed for festivals.

Angels Share (OG 1040, ABV 4%)

Miracle (OG 1044, ABV 4.4%)

Babylon (OG 1048, ABV 5%)

Chapel Street

⊟ Thatched House, Ball Street, Poulton-le-Fylde, Lancashire, FY6 7BG
☎ (01253) 891063 ⊕ thatchedhousepoulton.co.uk

This four-barrel plant is situated in the coach house of the award-winning Thatched House pub in Poulton-le-Fylde and has been brewing almost to capacity since opening in 2014. High local demand means that the whole of production is sold in the pub plus at a few selected beer festivals. ◆

Brewhouse Blonde (OG 1038, ABV 3.8%)
Blonde session ale with aromas of citrus, lemon and pine.

Cream Stout (OG 1041, ABV 4.1%)

Elderflower (OG 1041, ABV 4.1%)

Brewhouse Gold (OG 1042, ABV 4.2%)

Double Hopped (OG 1042, ABV 4.2%) ◀
Gently-hopped golden ale with a smooth body and slight sweetness to the taste.

American Pale (OG 1048, ABV 4.8%) ◀
Thin-bodied but pleasant pale ale, with a moderate hopped taste and a slightly astringent aftertaste.

Charnwood SIBA ⊚

22 Jubilee Drive, Loughborough, Leicestershire, LE11 5XS
☎ (01509) 218666 ☎ 07872 651561
⊕ charnwoodbrewery.co.uk

☺Charnwood is a family-run 10-barrel brewery established in 2014 in a former mozzarella factory. Beers are available in many local pubs. The front of the building has been fitted out as a shop, bar and reception area, with large glass windows giving a good view into the brewery. ‼�◆

Salvation (OG 1038, ABV 3.8%)
A light, refreshing golden beer with tropical fruit, citrus and floral flavours. American hops create a citrus aroma and crisp, clean bitterness on the finish.

Vixen (OG 1040, ABV 4%)
A well-balanced, copper-coloured best bitter with subtle hints of honey, spice and hedgerow fruits. Late added hops deliver a fruity nose and finish.

Checkstone (NEW)

⊟ First & Last Inn, 10 Church Street, Exmouth, Devon, EX8 1PE
☎ (01395) 263275

Checkstone Brewery, named after the Checkstone reef outside the Exe Estuary, is a one-barrel plant inside the First & Last pub, Exmouth, established in 2016. Further beers are planned, named after various sea features around Exmouth. ◆

Conger Rocks (OG 1043, ABV 3.7%)
A traditional mild with a good balance of malt and hops.

Cheddar SIBA ⊚

Winchester Farm, Draycott Road, Cheddar, Somerset, BS27 3RP
☎ (01934) 744193 ⊕ cheddarales.co.uk

⊗ Established in 2006 in the heart of the Mendips, Cheddar Ales has expanded capacity to enable it to

brew up to 100 barrels a week. Production is split approximately 75% cask-conditioned ale with the remainder bottle conditioned. Its bottling plant produces around 120,000 bottles annually. Around 450 outlets are supplied. ‼▐◆RAIB

Bitter Bully (OG 1038.5, ABV 3.8%) ◀
Light session bitter with flowery hops on the nose and a dry, bitter finish.

Gorge Best (OG 1040, ABV 4%) ◀
Malty bitter with caramel and fruit notes followed by a short bittersweet aftertaste.

Potholer (OG 1043.5, ABV 4.3%) ◀
A well-balanced golden ale with fruit and sweetness throughout and some bitterness to finish.

Totty Pot (OG 1044.5, ABV 4.5%) ◀
Roasted malts dominate this smooth, well-flavoured porter. Hints of coffee and rich fruits follow with a well-balanced bitterness.

Crown & Glory (OG 1045, ABV 4.6%)

Goat's Leap (OG 1054.5, ABV 5.5%)

Cheeky Imp

Unit 1, 127a Station Road, Waddington, Lincolnshire, LN5 9QT ☎ 07884 022236
✉ yellowbellyale@me.com

☺Cheeky Imp started brewing on a part-time basis in 2015 with a 0.5-barrel brewery. A move to a 2.5-barrel plant in Skellingthorpe is planned. RAIB

Cheshire Brew Brothers SIBA ⊚

Unit 6, Stanney Mill Industrial Estate, Dutton Green, Ellesmere Port, Cheshire, CH2 4SA ☎ 07890 567582
⊕ cheshirebrewbrothers.co.uk

Brewing began in 2014. The brewery is run by two friends who call themselves the Brew Bros after being inspired by a beer trip to Belgium.

Chester Gold (ABV 3.6%)
Deep gold in colour with a soft, citrus, honey taste and floral, honey aroma.

Earl's Eye Amber (ABV 3.8%)
Dry, hoppy and fruity amber ale with a spicy, malty aroma.

Roodee Dark (ABV 4%)
Deep red porter with a hoppy, dry, coffee taste and roasted, malty aroma.

Cheshire Best Bitter (ABV 4.5%)
A traditional bitter, malty, lightly spicy and dry with a sweetening aftertaste.

Cheshire Brewhouse SIBA

Units 5 & 6, Daneside Business Park, Riverdane Road, Congleton, Cheshire, CW12 1UN
☎ (01260) 274788 ⊕ cheshirebrewhouse.co.uk

☺Cheshire Brewhouse was established in 2012 using a five-barrel plant, expanding in 2014 to a 10-barrel one. The business has taken over adjacent premises and the brewery is now capable of producing 160 firkins a week. Bottling is carried out on site. ‼◆

Cheshire Gap (ABV 3.8%)
A light English pale ale.

Cheshire Set (ABV 4%)

A pale and refreshing ale.

Engine Vein (ABV 4.2%)
A traditional copper-coloured best bitter.

Lindow (ABV 4.5%)
A lighter take on stout; malty and easy drinking with a hint of espresso and dark chocolate balanced with vine fruits.

DBA (ABV 4.6%)
A Burton-style bitter. Strong and malty with a peppery finish.

Chew Valley

Sunningdale, Hillcrest, Pensford, Somerset, BS39 4AS
⊕ chewvalleybrewery.co.uk

⊠ The brewery opened in 2014 using a one-barrel plant supplying the Chew Valley and surrounding areas. Production has been suspended at the brewery premises; bottled beer and occasional casks are contract-brewed elsewhere while new premises are sought.

Chiltern SIBA ◉

Nash Lee Road, Terrick, Aylesbury, Buckinghamshire, HP17 0TQ
☎ (01296) 613647 ⊕ chilternbrewery.co.uk

⊠ Founded in 1980, Chiltern was one of the first microbreweries in the country and is the oldest independent brewery in Buckinghamshire and the Chiltern Hills, growing from a capacity of five to its present 15-barrel plant. Now run by the second generation of the Jenkinson family, George and Tom, it supplies around 100 outlets including its own brewery tap, the Farmers' Bar, at the historic King's Head in Aylesbury. ‼ ⇒ ♦ RAIB

Pale Ale (OG 1037, ABV 3.7%) ◣
A pale amber-coloured, refreshing beer with a slight fruit aroma, leading to a good malt/bitter balance in the mouth. The aftertaste is bitter and dry.

Black (OG 1040, ABV 3.9%)
Dark treacle tones, hints of roast barley and well hopped. Rich smooth flavours abound leading to a light, rewarding finish.

Beechwood Bitter (OG 1043, ABV 4.3%) ◣
This pale brown beer has a balanced butterscotch/toffee aroma, with a slight hop note. The taste balances bitterness and sweetness, leading to a long bitter finish.

Chippenham (NEW)

Unit 109, The Citadel, Bath Road, Chippenham, Wiltshire, SN15 2AB ⊕ chippenhambrewery.co.uk

Established in Chippenham in 2016, initially with a core range of three ales.

Founders Gold (ABV 4.2%)
Straw-coloured best bitter with refreshing citrus notes.

Bustards Bitter (ABV 4.4%)
A classic best bitter, copper in colour, with a complex taste of juicy malts.

Chipper Ale (ABV 4.5%)
A pale bronze-coloured beer generously hopped to give a peppery citrus flavour.

Chorlton

69 North Western Street, Ardwick, Manchester, M12 6DX ⊕ chorltonbrewingcompany.com

Founded in 2014 by Londoner Mike Marcus, lack of available space means that despite the name the brewery is in fact based in Ardwick. Mike is passionate about sour beers and yeast experiments inspired by classic European beer styles. The vegan-friendly beers are neither filtered or pasteurised and are generally available in can, keg-keg and occasionally bottles. RAIB V

Church End SIBA ◉

Ridge Lane, Warwickshire, CV10 0RD
☎ (01827) 713080 ⊕ churchendbrewery.co.uk

⊠ The brewery started in 1994 in an old coffin shop in Shustoke. It moved to the present site and upgraded to a 10-barrel plant in 2001 with further expansion to a 20-barrel plant in 2008. Many one-off specials and old recipe beers are produced. Beers are available at the Brewery Tap, Ridge Lane, and its sister pub, the George & Dragon, Stoke Golding. ‼ ⇒ ♦ RAIB

Poachers Pocket (OG 1036, ABV 3.5%)

Cuthberts (OG 1038, ABV 3.8%) ◣
A refreshing, hoppy beer, with hints of malt, fruit and caramel taste. Lingering bitter aftertaste.

Goats Milk (OG 1038, ABV 3.8%)

Gravediggers Ale (OG 1038, ABV 3.8%) ▤

What the Fox's Hat (OG 1044, ABV 4.2%) ⬡ ◣
A beer with a malty aroma, and a hoppy and malty taste with some caramel flavour.

Vicar's Ruin (OG 1044, ABV 4.4%) ◣
A straw-coloured best bitter with an initially hoppy, bitter flavour, softening to a delicate malt finish.

Stout Coffin (OG 1046, ABV 4.6%)

Fallen Angel (OG 1050, ABV 5%)

Church Farm SIBA ◉

Church Farm, Budbrooke, Warwickshire, CV35 8QL
☎ 07939 607027 ⊕ churchfarmbrewery.co.uk

Brewing began in 2012 using a plant converted from the farm's old milk processing equipment. A new 20-barrel gas fired plant was commissioned in 2016 to meet growing demand. Beers are brewed from local ingredients and the water comes from the farm's own well. Main trading area is a 30-mile radius from Warwick. ♦ RAIB

Old Pal (OG 1038, ABV 3.6%)
A pale, golden ale. Slight flowery hop aroma and mouthfeel, with a smooth, mellow taste and long-lasting finish.

Pale Ale (OG 1036, ABV 3.6%)
Hoppy, easy-drinking bitter with a tangy finish.

Ren's Pride (OG 1044, ABV 4%)
An amber-coloured best bitter with a slightly sweet taste. The distinctive initial flavour comes from a complex array of malts.

Brown's Porter (OG 1042, ABV 4.2%)
A porter with a smooth coffee taste and a long lasting, creamy aftertaste.

Harry's Heifer (OG 1044, ABV 4.2%)

A light amber-coloured best bitter with slight floral notes.

IPA (OG 1050, ABV 5%)
Light amber-coloured, hoppy IPA. Easy-drinking but full of flavour with slight fruit and toffee notes.

Church Hanbrewery (NEW)

Tithe Barn South, Church Hanborough, Oxfordshire, OX29 8AB
☎ (01993) 886603 ☎ 07907 272617
⊕ churchhanbrewery.com

Church Hanbrewery was established in 2015, producing a range of bottled beers. **RAIB**

J Church

⊟ Black Prince, 15 Abington Square, Northampton, NN1 4AE

Julian Church started brewing in 2009 at the Alexandra Arms in Kettering. In 2014 the brewery moved to bigger premises in an old dairy at Cransley near Kettering. It was relocated to the Black Prince, Northampton, in 2016. **‼**

More Tea Vicar (OG 1037, ABV 3.7%)

Gold Testament (OG 1036, ABV 3.9%)

Lion's Den (OG 1040, ABV 4%)

Martyr (OG 1040, ABV 4.1%)
An amber-coloured beer with a caramel flavour and a light, bitter finish.

Freaky Sheep (OG 1045, ABV 4.5%)

Hymn Moosic (OG 1045, ABV 4.5%)

Wonky Spire (OG 1047, ABV 4.7%)

Ciren

⊟ Twelve Bells, 12 Lewis Lane, Cirencester, Gloucestershire, GL7 1EA
☎ (01285) 652230 ☎ 07702 489589
⊕ twelvebellscirencester.com/comcirencester-ales-brewery.html

Ciren Ales is a small microbrewery at the rear of the Twelve Bells pub in Cirencester, established in 2012. The brewer is the owner, Steve. **‼ ♦**

Bells Bitter (OG 1040, ABV 3.8%)
Light brown bitter with a hoppy taste.

Bellend Blonde (OG 1044, ABV 4.2%)
A light, citrus, fruity beer.

Bells Best Mate (OG 1044, ABV 4.2%)
A dark, full-flavoured beer.

City of Cambridge

See Wolf

Clanconnel

Unit 5 , 2 New Line, Gibson's Hill, Lurgan, Co Armagh, BT66 8TA ☎ 07711 626770

Office: PO Box 316, BT65 9AZ
⊕ clanconnelbrewing.com

Clanconnel started producing bottled beer in 2008. Cask-conditioned beer is occasionally available.

Clark's SIBA 👁

Westgate Brewery, Wakefield, West Yorkshire, WF2 9SW
☎ (01924) 373328 ☎ 07801 922473 ⊕ hbclark.co.uk

☺Founded in 1906, Clark's ceased brewing during the 1960s/70s but resumed cask ale production in 1982 and now delivers to around 220 outlets throughout the Midlands and the north of England using its own wholesale network of depots. Its two pubs serve cask ale. A new range of ales was introduced in 2014 called Merrie City Craft Beers. **‼ ♦**

Classic Blonde (OG 1039, ABV 3.9%)
Pale straw-coloured beer with a fruity aroma and light spicy taste.

Brewed under the Merrie City Craft Beers name:

Atlantic Hop (OG 1040, ABV 4%)

Cascadian (OG 1040, ABV 4%)

Crystal Gold (OG 1042, ABV 4.2%)

Clarkshaws SIBA

Arch 283, Belinda Road, off Coldharbour Lane, Loughborough Junction, London, SW9 7DT ☎ 07989 402687 ⊕ clarkshaws.co.uk

Clarkshaws is a small brewery established in 2013 focusing on using ingredients sourced in the UK and on reducing beer miles. The beers are suitable for vegetarians and are accredited by the Vegetarian Society. All beers are unfined and may be hazy.

Gorgon's Alive (OG 1040, ABV 4%) ♦
Unfined golden-coloured beer with spicy hops throughout. The flavour has hints of orange and peach with a dry bitterness.

Phoenix Rising (OG 1040, ABV 4%) ♦
Tawny beer with a creamy toffee nose. Bananas, pineapple, hops and caramel flavours. Dryish, short, fruity, biscuit finish.

Strange Brew No. 1 (OG 1040, ABV 4%) ♦
Easy-drinking, yellow-coloured pale ale. Flavour is of peppery hops, tropical fruits and biscuit sweetness with a trace of bitterness.

Hellhound IPA (OG 1056, ABV 5.5%) ♦
Spiced and citrus notes in this unfined amber beer with a bitterness in the flavour and finish, which is dry.

Clearsky (NEW)

48 Lisnagowan Road, Dungannon, BT70 3LH

Established in 2013. Beers are contract brewed by an undisclosed brewer.

Rowlock (OG 1045, ABV 4.5%)

Fulcrum (OG 1050, ABV 5%)

Clearwater SIBA

Unit 1, Little Court, Manteo Way, Gammaton Road, Bideford, Devon, EX39 4FG
☎ (01237) 420492 ⊕ clearwaterbrewery.co.uk

⊗ Clearwater began brewing in 1999 using a 10-barrel brewery, relocating from Great Torrington to Bideford in 2014. It regularly supplies more than 250 outlets across the South west and increasingly supplies national wholesalers with its Devon's Own labelled beers. **!! ♦ RAIB**

Best Bitter (OG 1037.3, ABV 3.5%)
A traditional brown ale with hints of blackcurrant. Well-balanced and hoppy with a bitter finish.

Real Smiler (OG 1037, ABV 3.7%)
Gold-coloured, crisp and hoppy session beer.

Devon Dympsy (OG 1039, ABV 4%)
A smoky, smooth chestnut-coloured ale with a lemon aroma and a citrus edge.

Proper Ansome (OG 1041, ABV 4.2%)
Full-flavoured dark beer, full of malty goodness.

Submariner (OG 1042.9, ABV 4.2%)
Pale gold in colour. Clean, crisp and hoppy with a fresh grapefruit zestiness and lingering hint of bitterness.

Devon Darter (OG 1043, ABV 4.5%)
A fruity beer, copper in colour with an aroma of grapes, a nutty taste and a lingering light bitterness on the tongue.

Cliff Quay

Unit 1, Meadow Works, Kenton Road, Debenham, Suffolk, IP14 6RT
☎ (01728) 861213 ⊕ cliffquay.co.uk

⊠ Cliff Quay was established in 2008 by former Wychwood brewer Jeremy Moss and John Bjornson (owner of the Earl Soham Brewery) in part of the historic Tolly Cobbold brewery in Ipswich. In 2012 the brewery relocated to Debenham, a small, picturesque market town, due to redevelopment of the former brewery site. Now re-established alongside Earl Soham brewery, with shared shop and offices. **!! ☛ ♦**

Bitter (OG 1034, ABV 3.4%) ◆
Pleasantly drinkable, well-balanced malty sweet bitter with a hint of caramel, followed by a sweet/malty aftertaste. A good flavour for such a low gravity beer.

Anchor Bitter (OG 1040, ABV 4%)

Black Jack Porter (OG 1042, ABV 4.2%) ◆
Unusual dark porter with a strong aniseed aroma and rich liquorice and aniseed flavours, reminiscent of old-fashioned sweets. The aftertaste is long and increasingly sweet.

Tolly Roger (OG 1042, ABV 4.2%) ◆
Well-balanced, highly drinkable, mid-gold summer beer with a bittersweet hoppiness, some biscuity flavours and hints of summer fruit.

Tumblehome (OG 1047, ABV 4.7%)

Sea Dog (OG 1053, ABV 5.5%)
A strong, hoppy beer bursting with the flavours of lemon and grapefruit with a full maltiness in contrast.

Dreadnought (OG 1065, ABV 6.5%)

Clockwork

▤ 1153-1155 Cathcart Road, Glasgow, G42 9HB
☎ (0141) 649 0184 ⊕ clockworkbeercompany.co.uk

☺ Established in 1997, Clockwork is owned by Thistle Pub Company III. The beers are stored in cellar tanks where fermentation gases from the conditioning vessel blanket the beers (but not under pressure). A wide range of ales, lagers and specials is produced. Most beers are naturally gassed while the Craft Lager is pressurised. The establishment has parted ways with its previous managing company, Maclays, and in mid 2014 the pub underwent a full refurbishment. **!! ♦**

Original Amber (OG 1038, ABV 3.8%)
Malts create an underlying sweetness balanced by a combination of hops.

Cascade Parade (OG 1042, ABV 4.2%)
Single and dry hopped with the classic Cascade, this beer is floral and dry with a slight spice.

Cartside Red (OG 1044, ABV 4.4%)
Classic red ale with a twist. German malts and American hops combine for a deep berry-like finish.

Craft Lager (OG 1048, ABV 4.8%)
Classic lager conditioned longer than usual with a generous amount of hops to produce a surprisingly crisp, almost sweet taste.

RunAbout Stout (OG 1050, ABV 4.9%)
Freshly ground coffee and oats add a real depth to this stout. Intense roasted flavours are balanced with a silky smooth finish.

Seriously Ginger (OG 1050, ABV 5%)

Oregon IPA (OG 1054, ABV 5.5%)
American-style IPA with a big citrus bite.

Hampden Roar (OG 1058, ABV 6%)
Complex dark ale with an elaborate bittersweet undertone.

Clouded Minds SIBA ⊚

Unit 5B, Brailes Industrial Estate, Winderton Road, Lower Brailes, Warwickshire, OX15 5JW ☎ 07530 998149 ⊕ cloudedminds.co.uk

Brewing began in 2013, using spare capacity at various breweries around London and Derbyshire. In 2015 the brewery moved to its own site near Banbury using a 10-barrel plant. The London area is mainly supplied but also some outlets in Birmingham, Nottinghamshire, Derbyshire and some national pub chains. Wholesalers distribute the beers more widely. **RAIB**

Catholic's Choice (OG 1028, ABV 2.8%)
Hints of grapefruit through a citrus flavour and aroma. Herbal and moderately dry.

N29 (OG 1036, ABV 3.7%)
A citrus pale ale brewed with a small percentage of rye malt.

N253 (OG 1037, ABV 3.9%)
An oatmeal American pale ale. Fruity and resiny.

N18 (OG 1038, ABV 4%)
A pale ale with mild citrus, pine and resin elements.

Luppol (OG 1040, ABV 4.2%)
A refreshing ale with a good bitter finish.

Clout Stout (OG 1048, ABV 4.5%)
Velvet mouthfeel with an aroma of roasted malts, cocoa, dried fruits and figs. Mildly sweet and sour with a smoky and bitter finish.

Hazelnutter (OG 1048, ABV 5%)
Well-balanced, smooth American brown ale brewed with organic Italian hazelnuts.

Elisir (OG 1052, ABV 5.3%)
Caramel and biscuit taste from the malts balanced by a generous amount of hops. Fruity.

Black Pike (OG 1057, ABV 6.1%)
A highly-hopped black IPA.

Dolce Vita (OG 1058, ABV 6.2%)
West Coast American-style IPA. Fruity and mildly spicy with a dry finish.

Double Clout Stout (OG 1064, ABV 6.6%)
Rich and smooth coffee stout.

Cloudwater

Units 7-8 Piccadilly Trading Estate, Manchester, M1 2NP
☎ (0161) 661 5943 ⊕ cloudwaterbrew.co

Set up in 2015 in the former Ancoats goods depot, Cloudwater specialises in modern, seasonal beers with four distinct line-ups each year using local or seasonally available ingredients. ♦

Clun SIBA ◉

⚑ **White Horse Inn, The Square, Clun, Shropshire, SY7 8JA**
☎ (01588) 640305 ⊕ whi-clun.co.uk

Formerly a tiny brewery, capacity was increased to 2.5 barrels in 2010. Established behind the White Horse in Clun, beers are produced for the pub and increasingly the local trade. ♦

Loophole (OG 1035, ABV 3.5%)
A dry, hoppy, light-coloured beer with a crisp flavour.

Clun Pale (OG 1040, ABV 4.1%)
Pale, clean-tasting bitter beer.

Citadel (OG 1065, ABV 5.9%)
A hoppy strong ale with a hefty bitterness. Golden in colour the rich and fruity malt flavours are met head on by intense hop bitterness and aroma which give rise to a long-lasting dry finish.

Co Pilot

Unit 4, Sam Brown Industrial Units, Dog and Gun Lane, Whetstone, Leicestershire, LE8 6LJ ☎ 07342 040567 ✉ martinjallsopp@gmail.com

⊗ Blencow Brewery was established in 1998 at the Exeter Arms in Barrowden, Rutland. In 2005 Martin Allsopp bought the pub and brewery and renamed the latter as Barrowden. In 2016 Martin sold the pub and relocated the brewery to an industrial unit on the outskirts of Leicester, adopting the name Co Pilot. 🍺♦

Pilot (OG 1028, ABV 2.6%)

Beech (OG 1040, ABV 3.8%)

Own Gear (OG 1040, ABV 4%)

Hop Gear (OG 1046, ABV 4.4%)

Coach House SIBA ◉

Wharf Street, Howley, Warrington, Cheshire, WA1 2DQ
☎ (01925) 232800 ⊕ coach-house-brewing.co.uk

☺Established in 1991 by three former employees of Greenall Whitley Brewery, the brewery was bought by Martin Bailey in 2015. The 40-barrel plant produces up to 240 barrels per week. A wide range of seasonal and special occasion beers is produced. ♦

Coachman's Best Bitter (OG 1037, ABV 3.7%) ◀
A well-hopped, malty bitter, moderately fruity with a hint of sweetness and a peppery nose.

Gunpowder Mild (OG 1037, ABV 3.8%) ◀
Biscuity dark mild with a blackcurrant sweetness. Bitterness and fruit dominate with some hints of caramel and a slightly stronger roast flavour.

Honeypot Bitter (OG 1037, ABV 3.8%)
A medium-bodied golden bitter, lightly hopped. Brewed with Cheshire honey.

Farrier's Best Bitter (OG 1038, ABV 3.9%)
A smooth, tawny-coloured beer, slightly sweet but with rich hop flavours developed in the mouth.

Cromwells Best Bitter (OG 1040, ABV 4%)
Amber-coloured, well-balanced beer with a smooth, clean-hopped finish.

Cheshire Gold (OG 1042, ABV 4.1%)
A pale golden beer with a pine lemon crispness.

Dick Turpin (OG 1042, ABV 4.2%) ◀
Malty, hoppy pale brown beer with some initial sweetish flavours leading to a short, bitter aftertaste. Sold under other names as a pub house beer.

Flintlock Pale Ale (OG 1044, ABV 4.4%)
A pale golden beer, light on the palate with a touch of sweetness in the finish.

Innkeeper's Special Reserve (OG 1045, ABV 4.5%) ◀
A dark, full-flavoured bitter. Quite fruity, with a strong, bitter aftertaste.

Postlethwaite (OG 1045, ABV 4.6%)
A distinctive dry and fruity pale ale. Traditionally dry hopped to give a fine hop aroma.

Posthorn Premium (OG 1050, ABV 5%)
A rich straw-coloured smooth premium ale. The beer has a robust malty palate and well-balanced bitterness with a complexity of flavours.

Coastal SIBA

Unit 10B, Cardrew Industrial Estate, Redruth, Cornwall, TR15 1SS
☎ (01209) 212613 ☎ 07875 405407
⊕ coastalbrewery.co.uk

⊗ Established in 2006, Coastal operates from a five-barrel plant. An adjacent bottle shop and micropub sells a selection of its beers. 🍺♦RAIB

Cornish Bronze (OG 1037, ABV 3.7%)
A traditional session bitter.

Hop Monster (OG 1038, ABV 3.7%) ◀
Powerfully hoppy golden ale with grassy grapefruit and marmalade flavours. Quite sweet, somewhat dry. Rising dryness and bitterness in the finish.

Handliner (OG 1040, ABV 4%) ◀
Red-coloured best bitter with faintly roasted malt aroma. Smoky malt taste balanced by hop bitterness and gentle dryness, finishing bitter.

Merry Maidens Mild (OG 1040, ABV 4%) ◀
A black mild. Smooth and creamy with roasted malt, charcoal and liquorice sweetness fading slowly to a refreshing dry finish.

Angelina (OG 1042, ABV 4.1%) ◀
Golden ale with delicate floral aroma. Grassy, citrus hops with sweet grapefruit, marmalade and apricot throughout. Crisp, dry, fruity finish.

Golden Hinde (OG 1044, ABV 4.3%) ◀

Golden ale with orange marmalade aroma. Apricot and citrus fruit flavours with dominant bitter and grassy hop. Refreshing long finish.

Pier Porter (OG 1043, ABV 4.3%)
A full-bodied porter. Heavy malt flavour gives way to a malt character.

Poseidon Extra (OG 1046, ABV 4.5%) ◆
Yellow-coloured golden ale. Oranges and lemons aroma. Strong bitterness and grassy hops with grapefruit notes. Long bitter and dry finish.

Cornish Cascade (OG 1050, ABV 5%) ◆
Golden ale with hoppy aroma. Strong citrus hop taste, bitter and fruity with sweet malt. Long bitter and dry finish.

Cornish Porter (OG 1050, ABV 5%) ◆
Black porter with strong roast malt and hop nose. Intense bitter roast malt flavour with a hop balance. Finish becoming dry.

St Pirans Porter (OG 1060, ABV 6%)
A traditional, full-bodied porter using seven different malts. Roasty, toasty malt notes mix with abundant hops.

Erosion (OG 1077, ABV 7.5%) ◆
After an aroma promising roast caramel this powerful, warming dark old ale bursts with molasses and roast malt. Liquorice adds to the finish.

Kernow Imperial Stout (OG 1090, ABV 9%)
This full-flavoured, warming dark stout bursts with molasses and roast malts. Roast caramel adds to the dry stout finish.

Colchester SIBA

Viaduct Brewhouse, Unit 16, Wakes Hall Business Centre, Wakes Colne, Essex, CO6 2DY
☎ (01787) 829422 ⊕ colchesterbrewery.com

⊠ Set up in 2012 by three friends, Tom Knox, Roger Clark and Andy Bone, using the double drop fermentation process. Popular during the early 20th century this process requires additional brewing vessels in a two-tier system resulting in clean beer with pronounced flavours. ‼ ⎈ ◆ RAIB

Table Ale (OG 1038, ABV 3.6%)
A session bitter, rich amber in colour.

AK Pale (OG 1039, ABV 3.7%)
A mildly-hopped pale ale. Fresh and fruity.

Metropolis (OG 1040.5, ABV 3.9%)
A golden hoppy beer, full-flavoured with a long, spicy finish.

Braggot (OG 1042, ABV 4%)
An easy-drinking honey beer.

Jack Spitty's Smuggler's Ale (OG 1041.5, ABV 4%)

No. 88 (OG 1042, ABV 4%)
A dark amber-coloured malty bitter.

No. 1 (OG 1042.5, ABV 4.1%) 🗄 🎁
A classic English best bitter, copper in colour.

Pontisbright (OG 1042.5, ABV 4.1%)
A mahogany-coloured ale, with hops providing fruit on the palate and a long, lingering bitter finish.

Drizzle (OG 1043.5, ABV 4.2%)

Red Diesel (OG 1043.5, ABV 4.2%)
Red-coloured best bitter, well-balanced with a long, rich finish.

Romani ite Domum (OG 1045, ABV 4.3%)
A hoppy golden ale.

Trinovantes Gold (OG 1044.5, ABV 4.3%)

Anne Downes (OG 1045.5, ABV 4.4%)
Dark brown-coloured bitter, full and fruity with a lingering hoppy finish.

Brazilian Coffee & Vanilla Porter (OG 1048, ABV 4.6%)

Double Brown Ale (OG 1048, ABV 4.6%)
Dark brown in colour, malty, sweetish and balanced.

Old King Coel London Porter (OG 1052, ABV 5%)

Coles Family

🍴 **White Hart Thatched Inn & Brewery, Llanddarog, Carmarthen, SA32 8NT**
☎ (01267) 275395 ⊕ thebestpubinwales.co.uk

The brewery is based at the ancient White Hart Inn, built in 1371, which historically had a brewery on site. Brewing started again in 1999 on a nine-gallon plant. A one-barrel plant was fitted in 2000 and in 2012 the brewery was opened to the public. Many unique ales are brewed throughout the year with cider also produced. ◆

Merlins (OG 1040, ABV 4%)
A rich, creamy stout.

Swn Y Dail (OG 1040, ABV 4%)

Golden Ale (OG 1042, ABV 4.2%)

Llanddarog (OG 1042, ABV 4.2%)

Cwrw Blasus (OG 1044, ABV 4.4%)

Collingham SIBA

Brooklands, Leeds Road, Collingham, Leeds, West Yorkshire, LS22 5AA
☎ (01937) 573096 ☎ 07538 431921
⊕ collinghamales.co.uk

☺ Microbrewery based in the village of Collingham, brewing handcrafted ales for the local community. The owner was formerly head brewer at one of Yorkshire's most prestigious, regional family breweries. ◆

Blonde (OG 1038, ABV 3.8%)
Crisp and refreshing blonde ale with a fruity, citrus kick.

Journeyman (OG 1039, ABV 3.9%) ◆
A modern bitter with good balance of hops and malt from start to finish, amber in colour.

Artisan's Choice (OG 1043, ABV 4.4%) ◆
Golden ale with a light hoppy bitterness which is balanced by sweetness; some fruit, especially citrus, is evident throughout

Colonsay SIBA

The Brewery, Scalasaig, Isle of Colonsay, PA61 7YT
☎ (01951) 200190 ⊕ colonsaybrewery.co.uk

Colonsay began brewing in 2007 on a five-barrel plant. Beer is mainly bottled or brewery conditioned for the local trade. RAIB

Combined Brewers SIBA 👁

The Brewery, Totworth Business Park, Falfield, Gloucestershire, GL12 8HQ
☎ (01454) 269421 ⊕ combinedbrewers.co.uk

⊠ In 2014, Cotswold Spring Brewing Co merged with Severn Vale Brewing Co, both originally established in 2005, to form Combined Brewers Ltd. The breweries relocated to new, purpose-built premises in 2015 – a new 30-barrel and the five-barrel plant from Severn Vale were installed and are both operational, using water supplied by its own borehole. The Cotswold Spring and Severn Vale brands are still brewed separately. ‼ ☛ ♦ RAIB

Brewed under the Cotswold Spring Brewery name:

OSM (OG 1039, ABV 3.9%)
A complex mild, initially dry with a bitter sweetness. Chocolate notes and a long finish.

Stunner (OG 1041, ABV 4%) 🍺
Spicy biscuit aromas blend into hoppy and pale fruit flavours. Refreshing, hoppy and slightly astringent finish.

Codger (OG 1042, ABV 4.2%) 🍺
Quite bitter with a slightly malty background. Hops throughout give lasting bitterness which complements the hints of dark fruit flavour.

Aviator (OG 1050, ABV 5%)

Brewed under the Severn Vale Brewery name:

Nibley Ale (OG 1039, ABV 3.8%)
A light and refreshing ale.

Dursley Steam Bitter (OG 1043, ABV 4.2%)
A refreshing golden ale full of flowery hops.

Luverley Jub'lee (OG 1043, ABV 4.2%)
A well-balanced golden best bitter with bold fruity hops in the finish.

Severn Swans (a-Swimming) (OG 1048, ABV 4.7%)
Dark ruby ale with slightly spicy malt notes and robust hoppy bitter aftertaste.

Severn Sins (OG 1053, ABV 5.2%)
A jet-black stout with a dry roast malt flavour with hints of chocolate and liquorice.

TSB (Thornbury Special Bitter) (OG 1060, ABV 6.3%)
Rich and powerful IPA with a robust bitterness followed by a fruity marmalade finish.

Compass SIBA 👁

7 Clare Terrace, Carterton, Oxfordshire, OX18 3ES
☎ (01993) 846846 ⊕ compassbrewery.com

⊠ Compass began brewing in 2009 using spare capacity at other breweries. Brewing still takes place at North Cotswold Brewery (qv), although Compass owns its own site at Carterton, which is used for bottling, casking and kegging. Beers are hard to find as there are only two local outlets.
♦ RAIB

Isis Pale Ale (OG 1041, ABV 4.1%)
Malty aromas on a backdrop of hops. Sweet malt with some fruity esters and a gentle bitterness that lingers.

Baltic Night Stout (OG 1048, ABV 4.8%)
Well-balanced roasted bitterness with a hoppy, floral aroma. Roasted barley gives it a hint of coffee and a long, dry cocoa finish.

King's Shipment IPA (OG 1060, ABV 6%)
A strong IPA with hoppy bitterness balanced with malty sweetness. Dry hopped with oak chips. Based on East London Bow Brewery's IPA brewed in the 1790s for shipment to India.

Concertina SIBA

☰ 9a Dolcliffe Road, Mexborough, South Yorkshire, S64 9AZ
☎ (01709) 580841 ✉ concertina@btconnect.com

☺ Concertina started in 1992 in the cellar of a club once famous as the home of a long-gone concertina band. The plant produces up to eight barrels a week for the club and other occasional direct outlets and the wider trade, via beer wholesalers. ‼ ♦

Club Bitter (OG 1038, ABV 3.9%) 🍺
A fruity session bitter with a good bitter flavour.

Bengal Tiger (OG 1043, ABV 4.6%) 🍺
Light amber ale with an aromatic hoppy nose followed by a combination of fruit and bitterness.

Concrete Cow

59 Alston Drive, Bradwell Abbey, Milton Keynes, Buckinghamshire, MK13 9HB
☎ (01908) 316794 ☎ 07889 665745
⊕ concretecowbrewery.co.uk

⊠ Concrete Cow opened in 2007 on a 5.5-barrel plant. The beers are named after aspects of local history. The brewery supplies pubs, farmers' markets, local shops and restaurants. English single malt also available. ‼ ☛ ♦ RAIB

Pail Ale (OG 1036, ABV 3.7%)
A light-coloured ale brewed using lager malt.

Fenny Popper (OG 1039, ABV 4%)
A light-coloured, zesty ale.

Cock 'n' Bull Story (OG 1041, ABV 4.1%)
A dark amber-coloured malty beer.

Coniston SIBA 👁

Coppermines Road, Coniston, Cumbria, LA21 8HL
☎ (01539) 441133 ⊕ conistonbrewery.com

☺ A 10-barrel plant started in 1995 behind the Black Bull Inn in Coniston, it now brews 40 barrels a week and supplies numerous outlets locally and nationally. Some bottle-conditioned Coniston beers are brewed using Hepworth's Horsham plant, others are bottled on site. ‼ ☛ RAIB

Oliver's Light Ale (OG 1035, ABV 3.4%) 🍺
A fruity, hoppy, straw-coloured bitter with plenty of flavour for its strength.

Bluebird Bitter (OG 1036, ABV 3.6%) 🍺
A yellow-gold, predominantly hoppy and fruity beer, well-balanced with some sweetness and a rising bitter finish.

Asrai (OG 1039, ABV 4%) 🍺
Crisp on the palate, a gently hopped beer with a full-bodied finish.

Bluebird Premium XB (OG 1040.5, ABV 4.2%) 🍺
Well-balanced, hoppy and fruity golden bitter. Bittersweet in the mouth with dryness building.

Old Man Ale (OG 1040.5, ABV 4.2%) ◆
Delicious fruity, winey beer with a complex, well-balanced richness.

Special Oatmeal Stout (OG 1045, ABV 4.5%) ◆
A well-balanced, easy-drinking stout, fruity with a balanced ratio of malt to hop bitterness. A good starting point for novice stout drinkers.

K7 (OG 1045, ABV 4.7%) ⬚ ◆
Balanced, fruity hoppy bitter, plenty of body and a long, hoppy, bitter finish.

Thurstein Pilsner (OG 1044.5, ABV 4.8%) ◆
True to style; mild but unusually sweet, with a hoppy fruitiness.

Blacksmiths Ale (OG 1047.5, ABV 5%) ◆
A tawny ale which holds both roastiness and fruitiness in a pleasing balance.

Infinity IPA (OG 1055, ABV 6%) ◆
High impact strong bitter. Fruity aromas persist in the powerful but well-balanced hoppiness and sweetness with nothing being lost in the finish.

No. 9 Barley Wine (OG 1087.5, ABV 8.5%) ◆
Hops and alcohol dominate with appropriate sweetness and fruit on the tongue. A full-bodied and beautifully balanced beer.

Connoisseur

(Rear of) Wolverhampton House, 121-125 Church Street, St Helens, Merseyside, WA10 1AJ ☎ 07921 838831 ⊕ rainfordshow.co.uk/connoisseur/index

Connoisseur Ales launched in 2014, but is built on many years' brewing experience. The team behind the brewery, Mark, Gillian and Kevin Yates, formerly ran Liverpool's Baltic Fleet and the Albion in Warrington.

Bloody Mild (ABV 3.7%)
A well-balanced dark mild with aromatic hops.

The Usual (ABV 3.8%)
A traditional ale with characteristic hop bitterness.

Ninkasia (ABV 4%)
All American hops provide big bitterness atop a crisp and smooth blend of pale malts.

Ruby Ruby Ruby Ruby (ABV 4.1%)
A well-balanced ale with a malty character.

Lucem Light Ale (ABV 4.3%)
A hoppy ale with a distinctive nose and floral citrus taste.

Sparkling WIT (ABV 4.6%)
Complex malt flavours and a hint of chocolate.

Bete Noir Dry Stout (ABV 5%)
Full-flavoured dry stout with coffee, chocolate and a hint of smoke. A creamy oatmeal-like body with a delicate molasses and spice nose.

Ex Terra Lupus IPA (ABV 5.6%)
A clean, crisp pale ale with a well-balanced hop profile.

Conquest

See Whitby

Consall Forge (NEW)

3 Railway Cottages, Consall Forge, Staffordshire, ST9 0AJ

A one-barrel brewery set in the heart of the Staffordshire Moorlands adjacent to the Churnet Valley Railway. The Black Lion at Consall Forge is a regular outlet.

Dark Ruby Mild (OG 1050, ABV 5.2%)

Equilibrium (OG 1054, ABV 6%)
Traditional stout with flavours of coffee and molasses.

Consett Ale Works SIBA ◉

⊟ Grey Horse Inn, 115 Sherburn Terrace, Consett, County Durham, DH8 6NE
☎ (01207) 591540 ⊕ thegreyhorse.co.uk

The brewery opened in 2006 in the stables of a former coaching inn at the rear of the Grey Horse, Consett's oldest pub. The name commemorates the historic Consett Steel Works that closed in 1980. The brewery expanded in 2007 to cope with demand. Over 100 outlets are supplied direct. Recent investment includes new barrel stock. ‼◆

Steel Town Bitter (OG 1039, ABV 3.8%)

White Hot (OG 1040, ABV 4%)

Cast Iron (OG 1040, ABV 4.1%)

Consett Stout (OG 1045, ABV 4.3%)

Men of Steel (OG 1045, ABV 4.3%)

Red Dust (OG 1045, ABV 4.5%)

Conwy SIBA

Unit 2, Ty Mawr Enterprise Park, Tan y Graig Road, Llysfaen, LL29 8UE
☎ (01492) 514305 ⊕ conwybrewery.co.uk

☺Conwy started brewing in 2003, and was the first brewery in Conway for at least 100 years. In 2013 it increased capacity and moved to bigger premises in Llysfaen. Around 100 outlets are supplied. Beers are also produced under the West Coast Brewery brand showcasing modern beer styles. ‼ ⏚ ◆ RAIB

Clogwyn Gold (OG 1037, ABV 3.6%) ◆
A full-flavoured golden ale featuring strong citrus fruit flavours throughout. Hoppy bitterness dominates the full mouthfeel and lasting finish.

Minera Mountain Ale (OG 1040, ABV 4%)
Copper-coloured, light and crisp ale with a hint of heather.

Welsh Pride (OG 1040, ABV 4%)
A clean-tasting malty bitter. Fruit in aroma and taste with a crisp, grainy mouthfeel and a lingering hoppy, bitter aftertaste.

Beachcomber Blonde (OG 1042, ABV 4.2%)
Crisp, dry refreshing ale with a delicate grapefruit flavour.

Oatmeal Stout (OG 1043, ABV 4.3%)

Honey Fayre (OG 1044, ABV 4.5%)
Golden best bitter with a hint of honey sweetness balanced by an increasingly hoppy, bitter finish. A slightly watery mouthfeel for a beer of this strength.

Rampart (OG 1046, ABV 4.5%) ◆
A dark, fruity beer with a sweetish initial taste. Fruit flavours accompanied by the underlying hoppiness continue into the bittersweet aftertaste.

Cooper & Griffin

See Castle Rock and Pheasantry

Copper Dragon IFBB 👁

Unit 3 & 4, Enterprise Way, Airedale Business Park, Skipton, North Yorkshire, BD23 2TZ
☎ (01756) 701289 ⊕ copperdragon.uk.com

☺ Copper Dragon was established in 2003 and relocated to its present address in 2015. The 30-barrel plant is of a twin-vessel, Bavarian design and the brewery has its own bore-hole water supply. Three core beers are supplemented by a range of limited edition ales. A brewery tap bar is open one Friday a month (check website for details). In addition two regular beers are produced under the Greyhawk Brewery name and a small plant is to be installed to allow the brewer to specialise in more niche artisan products. Beers are available nationally. ‼️💻◆

Best Bitter (OG 1036, ABV 3.8%) ◈
A traditional Yorkshire bitter with a malty aroma, a hoppy bitter taste with hints of fruit and a bitter finish.

Golden Pippin (OG 1037, ABV 3.9%) ◈
This golden ale has a citrus aroma and flavour. The dry, bitter astringency increases in the aftertaste.

Scotts 1816 (OG 1041, ABV 4.1%) ◈
This best bitter is fruity and malty with a bitter finish. Look for hints of nuts, tropical fruits and vanilla in the aroma and taste.

Under the Greyhawk Brewery name:

Blonde Obsession (OG 1040, ABV 4%)
A full-flavoured blonde ale.

Broadwing Stout (OG 1047, ABV 4.8%)
A smooth, dark English stout.

Coppertown (NEW)

Unit D, Site 7, Business Park, Amlwch, LL68 9BX
☎ (01407) 832564

Brewing began in 2015. Beers are produced for the island county of Anglesey.

Anglesey Bitter (OG 1038, ABV 3.8%)

Anglesey Gold (OG 1040, ABV 4%)

Anglesey Best (OG 1045, ABV 4.5%)

Corinium

Cirencester, Gloucestershire, GL7 2HB ☎ 07716 826467 ⊕ coriniumales.co.uk

⊗ Corinium Ales was launched in 2012. The one-barrel plant has recently been relocated to newly refurbished ex-dog kennels in Cirencester. The award-winning beers are mainly available bottle-conditioned and make up the brewer's 'Roman Collection' but cask-conditioned production of the beers is increasing. ◆RAIB

Corinium Gold (OG 1043, ABV 4.2%)
An easy-drinking fruity ale with a mellow blend of malt and hops and a soft bitter finish.

Bodicacia (OG 1045, ABV 4.7%)
A full-bodied pale ale with a long-lasting citrus finish.

Centurion (OG 1051, ABV 4.7%)
A rich, malty stout with toasty chocolate undertones. Lightly hopped, leaving a well-rounded aftertaste.

Ale Caesar (OG 1050, ABV 5%)
A well-hopped IPA with a tropical fruit aroma balanced with a pleasing bitterness.

Cornish Chough SIBA

Trethvas Farm, Lizard, Cornwall, TR12 7AR
☎ (01326) 290908

⊗ Cornish Chough, the most southerly brewery on the UK mainland, commenced brewing in 2011 at its present location on Trethvas Farm, Lizard village. The brewery has its own borehole and draws water from between two seams of serpentine rock. ‼️RAIB

Serpentine (OG 1042, ABV 4%) ◈
Light-bodied tawny best bitter with gentle malt and ripe fruit aroma. Strongly malty in taste with sweetness and a delicious bitterness plus a hint of grapefruit that lingers into a dry finish.

Kynance Blonde (OG 1039, ABV 4.2%) ◈
Refreshing golden ale with crisp, hop taste and light bitterness. Lemon, peach and honey flavours and a hoppy finish.

Cadgwith Crabber (OG 1043, ABV 4.3%) ◈
Smooth copper-coloured best bitter. Biscuit malt balanced with citrus hop character, apples, toffee and vanilla. Gentle fruity and astringent finish.

Fire Raven (OG 1047, ABV 4.7%) ◈
Black porter with hop aroma. Velvety roasted barley with bitter chocolate and liquorice. Faint sweet malt and hops. Short finish.

Lizard Storm (OG 1048, ABV 4.8%) ◈
Smooth, red strong bitter with malty fruitiness in the taste. Apples and hops balance the malt. Lingering sweet, fruity finish.

Kilcobben IPA (ABV 5%)

Cornish Crown SIBA

End Unit, Badger's Cross Farm, Badger's Cross, Penzance, Cornwall, TR20 8XE
☎ (01736) 449029 ☎ 07870 998986
⊕ cornishcrown.co.uk

⊗ Cornish Crown began brewing in 2012 on a six-barrel plant and is based on a farm high above Mounts Bay. It was established by the brewer and landlord of the Crown Inn in Penzance, which acts as the brewery tap. Beer is available in local outlets and can be found as far away as the Southampton Arms in London. RAIB

Mousehole (OG 1039, ABV 3.9%) ◈
Refreshing copper-coloured bitter with a hop aroma. Biscuit malt and bitter hops in the mouth, becoming drier in the finish.

St Michaels (OG 1040, ABV 4%) ◈
Copper-coloured best bitter with a dry bitter aftertaste. Flavours of apple and tropical fruits with moderate hop bitterness and malt.

Causeway (OG 1041, ABV 4.1%) ◈
Copper-coloured best bitter with light fragrant nose. Biscuit malt and hops with damson and rum butter flavours. Bitter, dry finish.

One Hop One Grain (OG 1041, ABV 4.1%) ◈

Amber-coloured best bitter with hops dominant from aroma to finish. Taste balanced by malt, marmalade, caramel. Refreshing dry, bitter finish.

Honeyfuggle (OG 1043, ABV 4.5%) ◆
Yellow-coloured hoppy beer with sweet honey and malt in the mouth. Hop aroma and a bitter finish with some dryness.

SPA (OG 1048, ABV 4.8%) ◆
Heavily-hopped, refreshing golden strong bitter with biscuit malt and stone fruits in the mouth. Finish is bitter, hoppy and dry.

Porter (OG 1053, ABV 5.2%) ◆
Black vanilla porter with roast malt aroma. Smooth chocolate, liquorice, deep plum and black cherry, laced with cream. Burnt coffee aftertaste.

IPA (OG 1055, ABV 5.5%) ◆
Amber-coloured strong bitter with hop nose. Powerful hop bitter taste, persistent malt. Orange marmalade, lemon and peach. Bitter, dry finish.

Red IPA (OG 1057, ABV 5.9%) ◆
Strong, brown beer with hops, vine fruit and honey aroma. Rich, sweet malt and fruit cake. Long bitter, dry finish.

Corvedale SIBA 👁

🏠 Sun Inn, Corfton, Shropshire, SY7 9DF
☎ (01584) 861239 ⊕ corvedalebrewery.co.uk

☺Brewing started in 1999 behind the pub. Landlord Norman Pearce is also the brewer and uses only British malt and hops, with water from a local borehole. Bottle-conditioned beers are suitable for vegetarians and vegans. ‼️◆RAIB V

Dale Ale (OG 1040, ABV 4%)
Aromas of smoky molasses and dates with fruity, nutty toffee tastes.

Fuggles Gold (OG 1042, ABV 4.2%)

Golden Dale (OG 1043, ABV 4.2%)

Katie's Pride (OG 1040, ABV 4.3%)

Norman's Pride (OG 1043, ABV 4.3%)
An amber-coloured beer with a refreshing, slightly hoppy taste and a bitter finish.

Farmer Rays Ale (OG 1045, ABV 4.5%)
A clear, ruby bitter with a smooth malty taste.

Oatmeal Stout (OG 1045, ABV 4.5%)

Pax Ale (OG 1045, ABV 4.5%)

St George's Stout (OG 1045, ABV 4.5%)

Dark & Delicious (OG 1045, ABV 4.6%)
A dark ruby beer with hops on the aroma and palate, and a sweet aftertaste.

Cotleigh SIBA

Ford Road, Wiveliscombe, Somerset, TA4 2RE
☎ (01984) 624086 ⊕ cotleighbrewery.com

Established in 1979, Cotleigh is based in the historic brewing town of Wiveliscombe. It supplies direct to 750 pubs, 200 retailers and selected wholesalers. A visitor centre is planned. ‼️🍺◆RAIB

Harrier (OG 1035, ABV 3.5%)
A light and golden beer with a delicate floral and fruity aroma for a refreshing sweet and slightly hoppy finish.

Tawny Owl (OG 1038, ABV 3.8%) ◆

Well-balanced, tawny bitter with malt and fruity aroma, major malt taste followed by hop fruit, developing to satisfying bitter finish.

25 (OG 1040, ABV 4%)
A pale golden beer with a fresh aroma and fruit-filled finish.

Commando Hoofing (OG 1040, ABV 4%)
A pale golden beer, refreshing and slightly sparkling.

Golden Seahawk (OG 1042, ABV 4.2%) ◆
Well-hopped golden ale with flowery hop aroma and fruity hop flavour, clean mouthfeel, leading to a dry, hoppy finish.

Barn Owl (OG 1045, ABV 4.5%) ◆
Mid-brown beer with well balanced malt and hop aroma; a smooth, full-bodied taste where hops dominate, balanced by malt.

Honey Buzzard (OG 1045, ABV 4.5%)
Uses honey from David Pearce Honey Farm situated just a mile from the brewery. A smooth creamy and chocolate palate offers a subtle bittersweet finish.

Old Buzzard (OG 1048, ABV 4.8%)
A traditional dark ale, deep copper red in colour with the roasted chocolate malt giving a dry nutty flavour with hints of biscuit. The finish in the mouth is dry, smoky and smooth.

Cotswold SIBA

College Farm, Stow Road, Bourton-on-the-Water, Gloucestershire, GL54 2HN
☎ (01451) 824488 ☎ 07760 889100
⊕ cotswoldbrewing.com

An independent producer of lager and speciality beers. The brewery was established in 2005 and moved to its current location in 2010. More than 60 outlets are supplied. ‼️◆RAIB

Cask (OG 1040, ABV 4%)
Copper-coloured, well-hopped, easy-drinking ale.

Cotswold Lion SIBA

Grain Store 5, Dowmans Farm, Coberley, Gloucestershire, GL53 9QY
☎ (01242) 870164

Grain Store 5Dowmans FarmCoberley, Near Cheltenham, GL53 9QY ⊕ cotswoldlionbrewery.co.uk

⊠ Brewing began in 2012 using a 10-barrel plant located in a grain store on a farm in the Cotswolds. Established by John Kemp, former head brewer at Nailsworth Brewery, and Andy Forbes, formerly of Festival Brewery. RAIB

Shepherd's Delight (OG 1036, ABV 3.6%)
A light session ale, crisp and full of citrus flavours.

Hogget (OG 1039, ABV 3.8%)
A copper-coloured best bitter. Fruity and light on the citrus with a hint of spice.

Best in Show (OG 1042, ABV 4.2%)
Plenty of blackberry fruit with a hint of honey.

Golden Fleece (OG 1044, ABV 4.4%)
A twist on an IPA, filled with Jamaican fruit.

Drover's Return (OG 1050, ABV 5%)
A strong ruby-coloured bitter.

Cotswold Spring

See Combined Brewers

Cottage 👁

The Old Cheese Dairy, Hornblotton Road, Lovington, Somerset, BA7 7PS
☎ (01963) 240551 ⊕ cottagebrewing.co.uk

⊠ The brewery was established in 1993 in West Lydford and moved to larger premises in 1996, doubling brewing capacity at the same time. In 2001 a 30-barrel plant was installed. Around 1,500 outlets are supplied. A visitor centre and shop are planned. ‼◆

Southern Bitter (OG 1039, ABV 3.7%)
Gold-coloured beer with malt and fruity hops on the nose. Malt and hops in the mouth with a long, fruity bitter finish.

Pacific (OG 1040, ABV 4%)
A gold-coloured ale with a vibrant hop aroma and finish.

Duchess (OG 1042, ABV 4.2%)
A tawny-coloured ale with a balanced bitter finish and distinctive spicy aroma.

Golden Arrow (OG 1045, ABV 4.5%)
A hoppy golden bitter with a powerful floral bouquet, a fruity, full-bodied taste and a lingering dry, bitter finish.

Goldrush (OG 1051, ABV 5%)
A deep golden premium ale. Well-balanced with a distinctive and vibrant aroma.

Norman's Conquest MM (OG 1050, ABV 5%)
A dark, mature, smooth ale. Full-bodied with hints of chocolate, bitter orange and vine fruits.

Cotton End

⧉ Pomfret Arms, 10 Cotton End, Northampton, NN4 8BS
☎ (01604) 765544

⊠ Brewing began in 2014 on a small brewplant located in an outhouse behind the Pomfret Arms, focusing on experimental and specialist beer styles for sale in the pub and at local beer festivals. Customers are invited to suggest beers for brewing.

Country Life SIBA

The Big Sheep, Abbotsham, Bideford, Devon, EX39 5AP
☎ (01237) 420808 ☎ 07971 267790
⊕ countrylifebrewery.co.uk

Country Life is based at the Big Sheep tourist attraction. The brewery offers a beer show and free samples in the shop during the peak season (Apr-Oct). A 15.5-barrel plant was installed in 2005, making Country Life the biggest brewery in north Devon. Around 100 outlets are supplied. ‼◆RAIB

Old Appledore (OG 1037, ABV 3.7%)
A Classic Session beer, a real depth of taste. Maris Otter and Roasted malts combine with Fuggles and Golding hops. ?Multi award winning ale?

Reef Break (OG 1039, ABV 4%)
Maris Otter and Roasted malt with Challenger Hops giving this popular beer a gentle sweet malty taste.

Shore Break (OG 1042, ABV 4.4%)
A favourite with the younger drinker and in the warm summer months as it is a very light easy drinking refreshing ale. ?Multi award winning ale?

Black Boar/Board Break (OG 1044, ABV 4.5%)
Maris otter and black malt, combined with Fuggles and Golding hop's makes this an easy drinking porter. Smokey and rich on the nose, coffee and toffee notes.

Golden Pig (OG 1046, ABV 4.7%)
Maris Otter, crystal and wheat malts, with Challenger as the main hop. ?CHAMPION BEER BRITAIN 2011 SILVER? ?Multi award winning ale?

Country Bumpkin (OG 1058, ABV 6%)
Maris Otter and Chocolate malt along with Challenger hops, giving a malty full-flavoured, smooth taste.

CrackleRock SIBA

The Old Cooperage, High Street, Botley, Hampshire, SO30 2EA ☎ 07733 232806 ⊕ cracklerock.co.uk

⊠ CrackleRock began brewing in 2014 at the Old Cooperage in the centre of Botley with experienced head brewer Andy Ingram. In 2015 the Taproom bar opened (Thu-Sun). ‼🍴◆

Crackerjack (OG 1039, ABV 3.8%)
Clean-tasting, light and hoppy ale.

Barleycorn (OG 1043, ABV 4.2%)
Well-balanced traditional English bitter.

Gold Rush (OG 1046, ABV 4.5%)
A premium golden ale with a full, deep, malty flavour and good hop balance.

Crafty Shag (OG 1050, ABV 5%)
A strong, full-bodied, well-balanced ale.

Craddock's

⧉ Duke William, 25 Coventry Street, Stourbridge, West Midlands, DY8 1EP
☎ (01384) 440202 ⊕ craddocksbrewery.com

⊠ Craddock's is located to the rear of the award-winning pub, the Duke William. It is a four-barrel plant selling exclusively to its three pubs; the Duke William, the Plough & Harrow, Stourbridge and the King Charles, Worcester. ‼◆RAIB

Saxon Gold (OG 1041, ABV 4%)

Crazy Sheep (OG 1045, ABV 4.5%)

Hop & Glory (OG 1045, ABV 4.5%)

Troll (OG 1052, ABV 5.4%)
A deceptively strong, sophisticated golden ale, with a bittersweet taste, and dry hop finish.

Craft (NEW)

Part Street, Southport, Merseyside, PR8 1BD ☎ 07870 160934 ⊕ thecraftbrewery.org

A small-batch microbrewery producing beers and ales using traditional techniques. ◆

Templar's Tipple (ABV 4.2%)
A porter with an aroma of caramel, toffee and chocolate with a slight hint of aniseed.

Brethren's Brew (ABV 4.5%)
A speciality ale with an aroma of caramel, toffee and oak with a slight hint of rum. It delivers a malty

vanilla and oak taste, with subtle hints of sweet rum.

Labour to Refreshment (ABV 4.5%)
A full-flavoured, hoppy IPA, light and strong with a balanced sweetness followed by a refreshingly dry hoppy finish.

Master's Maul (ABV 4.5%)
A full, smooth malt flavour with a rich, amber colour and fruity aromas accompanying a balance of malty tastes. A balanced sweetness followed by a refreshingly dry finish.

Crafty Beers

The Stables, Hall Farm, Newmarket, Cambridgeshire, CB8 0TY
☎ (01223) 813938 ⊕ craftybeers.co.uk

⊠ Crafty Beers are brewed by Robert Beardsmore in an old stable building situated between Cambridge and Newmarket. Brewing started in 2012 at the Carpenter's Arms, Great Wilbraham. The move to larger premises in 2016 was made to increase brewing capacity. Beer is available at a number of pubs in and around Cambrige. RAIB V

Mild Mannered (OG 1041, ABV 3.5%)
Dark mild with a pleasant balance of sweet malt and tempered bitterness.

Sixteen Strides (OG 1037, ABV 3.8%)
Generously hopped pale ale with plenty of citrus aroma.

Carpenter's Cask (OG 1042, ABV 4.2%) ◆
A well-balanced, amber-coloured brew with biscuit malt character giving way to hops on the palate and a long finish.

Wilbraham (OG 1044, ABV 4.3%)
Amber-coloured ale with rich malt flavours and good balancing bitterness. Subtle hop aroma with the characteristic earthy notes of Fuggles.

Sauvignon Blonde (OG 1044, ABV 4.4%)
An aromatic golden ale.

Crafty Brewing SIBA ◉

Thatched House Farm, Loxhill, Dunsfold, Surrey, GU8 4BW
☎ (01483) 271814 ☎ 07702 305595
⊕ craftybrewing.co.uk

⊠ Situated on Luke Herman's family farm behind Dunsfold aerodrome, Crafty's base has an historic connection with the Canadian troop presence during WW2. Crafty now supplies nearly 100 pubs across the region plus local events and markets. RAIB

Loxhill Biscuit (OG 1038, ABV 3.8%)
Well-balanced session golden ale with floral notes.

Dunsfold Best (OG 1040, ABV 4%)
An English ale made with classic English hops, grain and yeast.

Crafty One (OG 1042, ABV 4.2%)
A pale straw-coloured beer; smooth, complex and refreshing.

Heady Steady Go (OG 1045, ABV 4.5%)
An American pale ale.

Crafty Devil

Unit K, Papermill Business Park, Papermill Road, Cardiff, CF11 8DH
☎ (029) 2021 8099 ⊕ craftydevilbrewing.co.uk

Crafty Devil began brewing in 2014 in the district of Canton. It moved to new premises in 2015, which increased its capacity to 3.5 barrels per week. It currently only produces bottled and KeyKeg beers but cask-conditioned beer can be arranged by special request, particularly for local beer events.

Crafty Pint

⬛ c/o Half Moon, 130 Northgate, Darlington, County Durham, DL1 1QS
☎ (01325) 469965 ☎ 07804 305175
⊕ thecraftypint.co.uk

The Crafty Pint Brewery was established in 2013 in the cellar of the Half Moon in Darlington. Originally a 10 gallon brew length, it was upgraded to a one barrel plant in 2015. Occasional one-off beers are brewed solely for the pub with a few other outlets being occasionally supplied. ◆

Tawny Mild (OG 1040, ABV 4%)

Porter (OG 1045, ABV 4.5%)

Crane (NEW)

Unit 4, Lawrence Hill Industrial Park, Croydon Street, Bristol, BS5 0EB ☎ 07811 441588 ⊕ cranebeer.com

Brewing began in 2014, inspired by Bristol's industrial and maritime heritage, which is reflected in the brewery's name and beer range. All beers are unfined, unfiltered and unpasteurised. ◆

Atom (OG 1042, ABV 4.3%)
Refreshing amber-coloured ale with a berry, citrus and pine hop character.

Glow (OG 1046, ABV 4.5%)
Session strength IPA with a clean malt backbone and crisp citrus hops.

Boom (OG 1062, ABV 6.2%)
American-style IPA, crisp and citrus with peach and passion fruit aromas.

Cake (OG 1067, ABV 6.6%)
Complex stout using vanilla beans, cocoa nibs and locally roasted espresso.

Crate SIBA

Unit 7, White Building, Queens Yard, Hackney Wick, London, E9 5EN ☎ 07834 275687
⊕ cratebrewery.com

Crate is a brewery and pizzeria opened in 2012 and situated in a canalside former print factory. RAIB

Best Bitter (OG 1045, ABV 4.3%)

Stout (OG 1057, ABV 5.7%)

Credence (NEW) SIBA

Unit 16b, Coquet Enterprise Park, Amble, Northumberland, NE65 0PE
☎ (01665) 714855 ⊕ credencebrewing.co.uk

Credence began brewing in 2015.

Pale (ABV 3.8%)

A modern take on a best bitter with sweet biscuit flavours balanced with floral, blackcurrant and spicy hop notes.

Blonde (ABV 4%)
A complex blonde ale with refreshing citrus notes on a floral backdrop. Smooth and refreshing.

Porter (ABV 4.4%)
A smooth, robust porter with 11 varieties of barley, rye and wheat.

American Pale (ABV 4.5%)
A well-balanced ale with complex citrus and tropical hop notes.

Red (ABV 5%)
Well-balanced light red-coloured beer, single-hopped for a delicate yet complex flavour and aroma profile.

IPA (ABV 5.5%)
A crisp, clean and hoppy IPA with a good malt balance.

Cromarty

Davidston, Cromarty, IV11 8XD
☎ (01381) 600440 ⊕ cromartybrewing.co.uk

Cromarty began brewing in 2011 in a purpose-built brewhouse. Additional fermenters were installed in 2014 and again in 2015 to meet demand. ‼ ☛◆

Atlantic Drift (OG 1035, ABV 3.5%) ◆
Good citrus hop flavour throughout.

Hit the Lip (OG 1037, ABV 3.8%) ◆
A mouth puckering grapefruit hoppy brew with a dry finish.

Happy Chappy (OG 1040, ABV 4.1%) ◆
A golden ale with plenty of hop character. Floral citrus hop aroma with a good bitter taste, which increases in aftertaste.

Kowabunga (OG 1046, ABV 4.6%) ◆
Refreshing golden peachy hoppy brew.

Red Rocker (OG 1048.5, ABV 5%) ▯ ◆
Red-coloured rye speciality hop monster with a malty background leading to a bitter finish.

Rogue Wave (OG 1052, ABV 5.7%) ◆
Easy-drinking, strong, grapefruit hoppy bitter.

Ghost Town (OG 1058, ABV 5.8%) ◆
Dark roasted malty brew with blackcurrant and liquorice background.

AKA IPA (OG 1067, ABV 6.7%) ◆
Strong IPA with a smooth citrus hoppy taste.

Cronx SIBA

Unit 6, Vulcan Business Centre, Vulcan Way, New Addington, CR0 9UG
☎ (01689) 809093 ☎ 07793 974395
⊕ thecronx.com

Cronx began brewing in 2012 and is the first commercial brewery in the area since 1954. ‼ ☛◆

Standard (ABV 3.8%) ◆
Easy-drinking brown-coloured bitter with sweetish fudge and spicy hoppiness notes throughout. A malty bitter finish with a dryness that remains.

Kotchin (ABV 3.9%) ◆
Grapefruit beer with pleasant hoppy notes. A little sweetness is balanced by a crisp bitter finish that grows on drinking.

Nektar (ABV 4.5%)
A pale ale brewed using Marynka hops from Poland.

Entire (ABV 5.2%) ◆
Dark brown-coloured porter with chocolate roast notes in the aroma, flavour and finish. The fruit character is of caramelised raisins.

Crooked Brook

Office: The Briars, Copthorne Bank, Copthorne, West Sussex, RH10 3QZ ☎ 07595 262247
⊕ crookedbrook.co.uk

⊗ Crooked Brook was established in 2014 and under new ownership since 2015. A one-barrel pilot plant is used. Many one-off beers are brewed, with two regular ales available.

Prizefighter Best Bitter (OG 1046, ABV 4.3%)

Cascade Carousel APA (OG 1049, ABV 4.6%)

Cropton

See Great Yorkshire

Cross Bay ◉

White Lund Industrial Estate, Morecambe, Lancashire, LA3 3PT
☎ (01524) 39481 ⊕ crossbaybrewery.co.uk

☺Cross Bay commenced brewing in 2011 on a 28-barrel brew plant and has a brewing capacity of 168 barrels a week. ‼ ☛◆

Halo (OG 1037, ABV 3.6%) ◆
A crisp and hoppy, pale bitter.

Nightfall Bitter (OG 1038, ABV 3.8%) ◆
A sweet, malty, gently-hopped bitter with some fruit.

Sunshine (OG 1040, ABV 4%)
Smooth blonde beer with forest fruits on the nose.

Sunset Blonde (OG 1043, ABV 4.2%) ◆
Sweet and fruity best bitter with a rising bitter finish.

Dusk Ruby Ale (OG 1045, ABV 4.5%)
A ruby ale, roasted bitter body with hints of cocoa, following through with a red berry aroma.

Zenith (OG 1049.5, ABV 5%) ◆
Gentle bitterness and fruity sweetness with some astringency in the finish.

Crossed Anchors (NEW)

▤ c/o Grapevine, 2 Victoria Road, Exmouth, Devon, EX8 1DL
☎ (01395) 222208 ☎ 07980 806582
⊕ crossedanchors.co.uk

⊗ Crossed Anchors was established in 2015, with the beer initially produced using spare capacity at another brewery. In 2016 a six-barrel plant became operational in the old stables of the Grapevine in Exmouth town centre. ◆

Smash (ABV 3.8%)
A single-hopped pale ale.

American Pale Ale (ABV 4%)
A citrus, golden-coloured pale ale.

Black IPA (ABV 4.1%)

A dark Anglo-American style beer.

Dark Mild (ABV 4.1%)
An easy-drinking mild ale.

Three Cs Gold (ABV 4.3%)
Triple-hopped golden ale.

Red Right Hand (ABV 4.6%)
A fruity pale ale.

Weisse Guy (ABV 5%)
A German-style wheat beer.

Crouch Vale SIBA

23 Haltwhistle Road, South Woodham Ferrers, Essex, CM3 5ZA
☎ (01245) 322744 ⊕ crouchvale.co.uk

⊠ Founded in 1981 by two CAMRA enthusiasts, Crouch Vale is now well established as a major player in Essex brewing, having moved to larger premises in 2006. The company is also a major wholesaler of cask ale from other independent breweries, which it supplies to more than 100 outlets, as well as beer festivals throughout the region. A tap room opened on the brewery site in 2016. One tied house, the Queen's Head in Chelmsford, is owned. ‼ �¬ ♦ RAIB

Blackwater Mild (OG 1037, ABV 3.7%) ◣
A dark bitter rather than a true mild. Roasty and increasingly bitter towards the end.

Essex Boys Best Bitter (OG 1038, ABV 3.8%)
Full bodied, traditional-style mid-brown session beer.

Brewers Gold (OG 1040, ABV 4%) ◣
Pale golden ale with a striking citrus nose. Sweet fruit and bitter hops are well matched throughout.

Yakima Gold (OG 1042, ABV 4.2%)
Golden ale, earthily aromatic and highly drinkable.

Amarillo (OG 1050, ABV 5%)
A premium golden ale with hop aromas and a lasting spicy and orange flavour.

Crown

See Wood Street

Cryptic SIBA ◉

3 Carrington Field Street, Heaviley, Stockport, SK1 3JN
☎ (0161) 222 8840 ☎ 07932 545939
⊕ crypticales.co.uk

⊠ Cryptic Ales was founded in 2014 using a 10-barrel plant after discussion between four quiz team members. Further ales are planned. A one-barrel plant is used for experimental and speciality beers under the Cryptic Labs brand name.

Anagram (OG 1037, ABV 3.5%)
A golden session ale with a hoppy and fruity aroma. It has a refreshing and light, dry finish.

1049 Dead (OG 1047, ABV 4.9%)
A dark, fruity mild with a chocolate taste.

Enigma (OG 1046, ABV 5%)
A deep golden pale ale. A spicy and citrus aroma is followed by a full-bodied, well-hopped honeyed taste.

Tip of the Tongue (OG 1041, ABV 5%)

A copper-coloured premium bitter with a toffee and chocolate aroma. It delivers a malty gentle bitterness.

Acrostic (OG 1047, ABV 5.1%)
A dark porter with a fruity aroma. Made with just one hop variety, it has a liquorice and creamy coffee taste.

Crystalbrew SIBA ◉

Building 40, British Aerospace Business Park, Saltgrounds Road, Brough, East Yorkshire, HU15 1EQ
☎ 07773 938380

Office: 88 Highfields, South Cave, Brough, East Yorkshire, HU15 2AJ ⊕ crystalbrew.co.uk/beerfinder

◉ Brewing began in 2014 using an eight-barrel plant. The brewery is named in honour of Hull University's world famous Crystal Group, whose pioneering research led to the production of the liquid crystals that are an essential part of modern life. The brewer, a chemical scientist and microbiologist, has strong links to the group. ‼

Anzac Pale (OG 1034, ABV 3.8%)
A dry, fresh session ale using New Zealand and American hops.

Crystal Belle (OG 1034, ABV 3.8%)
A light-bodied blonde session ale with a floral aroma and hints of fruit and spices to taste.

Hawk Pale Ale (OG 1035, ABV 3.8%)
A golden session ale with a hint of caramel for a light, fruity taste with honey notes.

Summer Breeze (OG 1034, ABV 3.8%)
A pale and bitter session beer, light in body.

Jade (ABV 4%)
A refreshing American-style pale beer with a hoppy and citrus character.

Crystal Blond (OG 1039, ABV 4.5%)
A thirst-quenching, well-hopped blonde ale with complex grapefruit and orange citrus flavours.

Indian Summer IPA (OG 1048, ABV 5.2%)
A well-hopped golden ale with good maltiness.

Cuillin

☰ Sligachan Hotel, Sligachan, Carbost, Isle of Skye, IV47 8SW
☎ (01478) 650204 ☎ 07795 250808
⊕ sligachan.co.uk

◉ The five-barrel brewery opened in 2004 and is situated in central Skye at the foot of the Cuillin mountains. The water from the Cuillins provides a distinctive colour and taste to the ales. The brewery is closed in winter. ‼ ♦

Cullercoats SIBA ◉

Westfield Court, 19 Maurice Road Industrial Estate, Wallsend, Tyne & Wear, NE28 6BY
☎ (0191) 252 8765 ☎ 07895 692881

Office: 17 St Oswins Avenue, Cullercoats, NE30 4PH
⊕ cullercoatsbrewery.co.uk

◉ Ex-solicitor Bill Scantlebury established Cullercoats in 2011 and brews twice a week. ♦

Shuggy Boat Blonde (OG 1039, ABV 3.8%)
A refreshing blonde beer. Smooth and fresh.

Lovely Nelly (OG 1039, ABV 3.9%)

A full-bodied amber-coloured session beer, with a biscuit malt flavour balanced with a smooth hop bitterness.

Jack the Devil (OG 1045, ABV 4.5%)
A rich, dark chestnut-coloured ale, with a good balance of malty nuttiness and a fresh, hoppy aroma.

Shuggy Boat Blonde Special (OG 1050, ABV 5%)

Rocket Brigade (OG 1054, ABV 5.5%)
An authentic English pale ale, strong and bitter yet easy drinking.

Cumberland SIBA 👁

The Forge, Great Corby, Cumbria, CA4 8LR
☎ (01228) 560899 ☎ 07747 841671
⊕ cumberlandbreweries.co.uk

👁Cumberland was established in 2009 with a bespoke 10-barrel plant and is situated in a building at the heart of the village, previously the farriers shop from 1833. The brewery was purchased by American brewer Alltech in 2015 and expansion is planned. ‼

Corby Ale (OG 1038, ABV 3.8%) 🍺
A fruity session beer with sweetness leading to gentle bitterness in the aftertaste.

Corby Amber (OG 1040, ABV 4%) 🍺
A gentle brown ale; mild, fruity and sweet.

Corby Blonde (OG 1042, ABV 4.2%) 🍺
Melon fruit hoppiness gives a light, refreshing drink.

Corby Noir (OG 1044, ABV 4.5%) 🍺
Fruity aroma, sweet roast middle and dry finish.

Corby Fox (OG 1048, ABV 4.7%) 🍺
A pleasing brown ale with a slight bitter finish.

Cumbrian Legendary SIBA 👁

Old Hall Brewery, Hawkshead, Cumbria, LA22 0QF
☎ (01539) 436436 ⊕ cumbrianlegendaryales.com

👁First established in 2003, the brewery is located in an idyllic position in a renovated barn on the shores of Esthwaite Water. The success of Loweswater Gold has meant the brewery is thriving. ‼♦

Esthwaite Bitter (OG 1038.5, ABV 3.8%) 🍺
Robust refreshing bitter with plenty of hops, lasting well into the finish.

Langdale (OG 1040, ABV 4%) 🍺
Fresh grapefruit aromas with hoppy fruity flavours and crisp long hop finish, make for a well-balanced beer.

Grasmoor Dark Ale (OG 1043, ABV 4.3%) 🍺
Dark fruity beer with complex character and roast nutty tones leading to a short, refreshing finish.

Loweswater Gold (OG 1041, ABV 4.3%) 🍺
A dominant fruity body develops into a light bitter finish. A beer that belies its strength.

American Invasion (OG 1047, ABV 5%) 🍺
Well-balanced, gold-coloured beer with big hop impact and long fruity finish.

Cwm Rhondda

Fforch Farm, Cemetry Road, Treorchy, Glamorgan, CF42 6TF

☎ (01443) 777491 ⊕ cwmrhonddaales.co.uk

Situated on a farm on a hillside in the Rhondda valley, brewing commenced in 2015 on a 2.5-barrel plant using water from its own well. The beer names are related to the Rhondda's rich mining heritage. Following the installation of a bio-mass boiler there are plans for expansion.

Shmae But (OG 1039, ABV 3.8%)

Boyo (OG 1046, ABV 4.5%)

Tommy Box (OG 1044, ABV 4.5%)

Daleside SIBA 👁

Camwal Road, Starbeck, Harrogate, North Yorkshire, HG1 4PT
☎ (01423) 880022 ⊕ dalesidebrewery.com

👁Opened in 1991 in Harrogate with a 20-barrel plant, the brewery delivers direct to a range of outlets including pubs, restaurants and farm shops from Newcastle to Chesterfield as well as nationally via wholesalers. 🍺♦

Bitter (OG 1039, ABV 3.7%) 🍺
Pale brown in colour, this well-balanced, hoppy beer is complemented by fruity bitterness and a hint of sweetness, leading to a long, bitter finish.

Blonde (OG 1040, ABV 3.9%) 🍺
A pale golden beer with a predominantly hoppy aroma and taste, leading to a refreshing hoppy, bitter but short finish.

Old Leg Over (OG 1043, ABV 4.1%)
Well-balanced mid brown refreshing beer that leads to an equally well-balanced fruity bitter aftertaste.

Square Rigger IPA (ABV 4.5%)
Light amber-coloured IPA using three different hops to give a floral aroma.

Monkey Wrench (OG 1055, ABV 5.3%)
Premium ale, deep chestnut red in colour with a spicy fruit aroma and warming spicy flavour.

Dancing Cows (NEW) SIBA 👁

Sadlers Farm Workshops, Lower Pennington Lane, Lymington, Hampshire, SO41 8AL
☎ (01590) 676071 ☎ 07952 639465
⊕ dancingcows.co.uk

Dancing Cow is a small-batch brewery and distillery close to the Lymington-Keyhaven Nature Reserve, sourcing local grains, hops, herbs and spices. Operated by former owner of Bowland Brewery in Lancashire and inspired by a trip to Lake Michigan to bring a fresh outlook on brewing. New recipes are being developed constantly. RAIB

Lighthouse (ABV 3.8%)
A golden ale with grapefruit flavours and aromas.

Pony (ABV 4%)
A traditional amber-coloured ale with rounded fruit flavours and good malt character.

Admiral (ABV 4.5%)
A traditional best bitter with subtle orange notes from the Mandarina hops.

Dancing Duck SIBA 👁

1 John Cooper Buildings, Payne Street, Derby, DE22 3AZ

☎ (01332) 205582 ☎ 07581 122122
⊕ dancingduckbrewery.com

Dancing Duck was established in 2010 by Rachel Mathews using a 10-barrel brew plant. Its name comes from the local greeting 'ay up me duck'. The brewery operates two local pubs, the Exeter Arms and the New Zealand Arms. ♦

Quack Addict (OG 1040.7, ABV 3.8%)
Deep chestnut-coloured fruity ale with a good malt character.

Ay Up (OG 1039.5, ABV 3.9%)
A pale ale session bitter. Subtle malt and floral notes are matched with citrus hop, rounded off with a slightly dry finish.

Waitangi (OG 1041.3, ABV 4%)
An easy-drinking, crisp and clean pale ale, subtle malt character is balanced with zesty lemon and lime hops.

Ginger Ninja (OG 1042, ABV 4.1%)
Quaffable, refreshing ale. Well-balanced with a pleasant aroma, citrus notes from the hops and a subtle ginger flavour.

Nice Weather 4 Ducks (OG 1042, ABV 4.1%)
Copper-coloured fruity ale. Blackberry, strawberry and floral rose notes with just the right amount of malt character.

Sapphire (OG 1042.8, ABV 4.2%)
A pale summer ale with a fruit aroma, citrus flavour and spicy finish.

22 (OG 1044.1, ABV 4.3%)
A well-balanced best bitter with good malty flavour and dark fruit notes, offset by a strong hop with a clean finish.

DCUK (OG 1043.6, ABV 4.3%)
A pale session ale with a fruity aroma. A juicy citrus flavour with hints of orange, mango, lemon and pine.

Dark Drake (OG 1051.2, ABV 4.5%) 🗍
Malty caramel and liquorice flavours combine well in a smooth-drinking, velvety oatmeal stout with a freshly roasted coffee and tea finish.

Waddle It Be? (OG 1045.2, ABV 4.5%)
Pale ale with a complex mouthfeel and intense fruity flavours of oranges, peaches and blackcurrants with a spicy black pepper kick. A good aroma and a balanced level of bitterness.

Gold (OG 1047.5, ABV 4.7%)
A modern IPA with powerful hoppy bitterness and aroma balanced with strong malt notes. English hops give peppery, plum-like and orange zest flavours.

Amberillo (OG 1047.2, ABV 4.8%)
An easy-drinking amber ale. Earthy aromatic hops are balanced with biscuit malt flavours leading to a spicy, peppery finish.

Indian Porter (OG 1051.8, ABV 5%)
Smoky bonfire flavours with a spicy hop and pleasant warming afterglow.

Wot the Duck? (OG 1051.8, ABV 5%)
A vanilla infused porter.

Seduction (OG 1051.3, ABV 5.2%)
A malt-led beer, dark fruity flavours are followed by a lingering powerful American hop.

Abduction (OG 1053, ABV 5.5%)

A myriad of tropical flavours in harmonious balance with a good level of hoppy bitterness, a malt character and clean finish.

Imperial Drake (OG 1068, ABV 6.5%)
A velvety oatmeal stout with a freshly roasted coffee and toffee finish.

Dancing Man

⬢ Wool House, Town Quay, Southampton, Hampshire, SO14 2AR
☎ (023) 8083 6666 ⊕ dancingmanbrewery.co.uk

⊗ Dancing Man began brewing in 2011 in the Platform Tavern. In 2015 the brewery moved to the historic Wool House in order to expand and include an onsite bar and restaurant. One-off and rare brews are available throughout the year. ♦ RAIB

Pilgrim's Pale Ale (OG 1039, ABV 3.9%)
A pale golden ale with tropical fruit aromas, a smooth bitter flavour and a clean and crisp finish.

Congo Driftwood (OG 1042, ABV 4.2%)
A modern pale ale with the addition of fresh mango and papaya in the fermenter, which delivers unique tropical flavours.

Jack O'Diamonds (OG 1045, ABV 4.5%)
Complex malt bodied red ale. Lots of American hops play off the malt body to give a fruity, rich beer.

Fiddler's Jig (OG 1047, ABV 4.8%)
A rich malt body, with fruity hop flavours.

Last Waltz (OG 1052, ABV 5.3%)
A black IPA with an intense hoppy nose with tropical fruit notes, a smoky roasted malt flavour and a dry bitter finish.

Big Casino (OG 1056, ABV 5.7%)
Pine and citrus fruit aroma with a warming malt body and a smooth bitterness with juicy hop flavours.

Dancing Men

⬢ Hill House Inn, The Hill, Happisburgh, Norfolk, NR12 0PW
☎ (01692) 650004 ☎ 07818 038768
⊕ hillhouseinn.co.uk

⊗ Brewing began in 2014 at the 16th-century Hill House Inn on Happisburgh's fast-eroding clifftop. The microbrewery is named in honour of a famous Sherlock Holmes story written by Sir Arthur Conan Doyle after he visited the pub in 1903. The five-barrel plant was acquired from Bees Brewery after its partial destruction during the tidal surge events in Walcott in 2013. ‼♦

After The Storm (ABV 3.8%)
An easy-drinking session beer with a slightly peaty finish.

Famous Norfolk Broads (ABV 3.8%)
Amber-coloured session beer with well-balanced sweetness and bitter flavours leaving the palate refreshed and cleansed.

Soggy Seagull (ABV 4.2%)
A well-balanced fruity and refreshing clean-tasting ale.

Knight's Noggin (ABV 4.8%)
A dark porter-style beer packed with toasted toffee malt flavours.

Cliffhanger (ABV 5.1%)

A pale, single hop premium ale, deceptively easy-drinking with a smooth honey finish.

Dark Horse SIBA

Coonlands Laithe, Hetton, North Yorkshire, BD23 6LY
☎ (01756) 730555 ⊕ darkhorsebrewery.co.uk

☺Dark Horse began brewing in 2008. The brewery is based in an old hay barn within the Yorkshire Dales National Park. More than 30 outlets are supplied direct. ‼

Craven Bitter (OG 1038, ABV 3.8%) ◀
Well-balanced bitter with biscuity malt and fruit on the nose continuing into the taste. Bitterness increases in the finish.

Hetton Pale Ale (OG 1041, ABV 4.2%) ◀
Golden, well-balanced, full-bodied, with hoppy bitterness on the palate overlaying a malty base and a spicy citrus character.

Night Jar (OG 1042, ABV 4.2%)

Dark Star SIBA 👁

22 Star Road, Partridge Green, West Sussex, RH13 8RA
☎ (01403) 713085 ⊕ darkstarbrewing.co.uk

⊠ Dark Star started in the cellar of the Evening Star in Brighton and in 2010 moved to its current premises using a 45-barrel plant. Copies of classic European, American or old English beer styles are regularly produced. ‼ ⚏ ♦ RAIB

The Art of Darkness (OG 1040, ABV 3.5%)
A low gravity beer with classic roast flavours and a hint of sweetness.

Hophead (OG 1040, ABV 3.8%) 🗂 ◀
A golden-coloured bitter with a fruity/hoppy aroma and a citrus/bitter taste and aftertaste. Flavours remain strong to the end.

Partridge Best Bitter (OG 1042, ABV 4%)
Traditional Sussex-style best bitter.

Espresso (OG 1048, ABV 4.2%)
Freshly ground Arabica coffee beans are added to the copper for a few minutes after the boil of this rich black beer.

American Pale Ale (OG 1048, ABV 4.7%)
American-style pale ale, full of the aroma of hops.

Festival (OG 1052, ABV 5%)
A bronze-coloured bitter with a smooth mouthfeel and freshness.

Original (OG 1052, ABV 5%) 🗂
A dark, strong and bitter beer.

Revelation (OG 1057, ABV 5.7%) 🗂 🥫

Imperial (OG 1070, ABV 10.5%) 🥫
A densely rich beer with a dark brown head. It has toffee and berry-like aromas and a velvet-like mouth-feel with complex burnt flavours. Warming with a long lasting wine-like finish.

DarkTribe

⧓ Dog & Gun, High Street, East Butterwick, Lincolnshire, DN17 3AJ
☎ (01724) 782324 ⊕ darktribe.co.uk

☺A small brewery was built during the summer of 1996 in a workshop at the bottom of his garden by Dave 'Dixie' Dean. In 2005 Dixie bought the Dog &

Gun pub and moved the 2.5-barrel brewing equipment there. The beers generally follow a marine theme, recalling Dixie's days as an engineer in the Merchant Navy and his enthusiasm for sailing. Local outlets are supplied. ‼ ♦

Dixie's Mild (OG 1034, ABV 3.6%)
Reddish-brown mild ale with a sweet malty aroma and some roasted notes. A hint of chocolate and berries in the flavour.

Honey Mild (OG 1032, ABV 3.6%)
Dark brown mild ale, brewed with additional honey. Some roasted notes.

Pieces of 8 (OG 1033, ABV 3.6%)
Light amber-coloured brew with Bramling Cross hops.

Three Point Six (OG 1033, ABV 3.6%)

Full Ahead (OG 1034, ABV 3.8%) ◀
A malty smoothness is backed by a slightly fruity hop that gives a good bitterness to this amber-brown bitter.

Captain Floyd (OG 1035, ABV 3.9%)
Pale golden session beer.

Ruddy L (OG 1035, ABV 3.9%)

Albacore (OG 1036, ABV 4%)
Refreshing pale golden bitter.

Sternwheeler (OG 1037, ABV 4.2%)
Pale and golden, with plenty of hops.

Old Gaffer (OG 1038, ABV 4.5%)
Full-flavoured traditional best bitter.

Dartmoor SIBA 👁

The Brewery, Station Road, Princetown, Devon, PL20 6QX
☎ (01822) 890789 ⊕ dartmoorbrewery.co.uk

⊠ Formerly named Princetown, Dartmoor Brewery was established in 1994 and is the highest brewery in England at 1,465 feet above sea level. In 2006 the brewery moved to a new purpose-built building and in 2012 capacity was increased to 360 barrels a week by the addition of another 60-barrel fermenter with a further increase in 2013. All beer is brewed using Dartmoor and Devon-grown barley. ‼ RAIB

Best (OG 1037, ABV 3.7%)
An amber-coloured ale with a citrus fruit character.

IPA (OG 1039.5, ABV 4%) ◀
There is a flowery hop aroma and taste with a bitter aftertaste to this full-bodied, amber-coloured beer.

Dragon's Breath (OG 1044, ABV 4.4%)
Deep ruby brown in colour, rich and full bodied with an aftertaste of morello cherries.

Legend (OG 1043.5, ABV 4.4%)
A classic, smooth, full-flavoured and well-balanced beer with a crisp malt fruit finish. Golden brown in colour with an aroma of fresh baked bread with a hint of spice.

Jail Ale (OG 1047.5, ABV 4.8%) ◀
Well-balanced beer with hints of malt, caramel and fruit leading to a full-flavoured bitter beer. Pleasant bittersweet finish.

Darwin SIBA

1 West Quay Court, Sunderland Enterprise Park,
Sunderland, Tyne & Wear, SR5 2TE
☎ (0191) 549 9450 ⊕ darwinbrewery.com

☺Established in 1994, Darwin Brewery is based in
purpose-built premises in Sunderland with a 3.5-
barrel brew plant. The brewery supports students
on Brewlab brewing courses at the university, who
produce many unique specialist and international
beers, often available locally. A range of
established Darwin beers are also produced, some
based on analysis of historic recipes or student
initiatives. !! ◆ RAIB

Evolution (OG 1039, ABV 4%)
A copper-coloured bitter.

Beagle Blonde (OG 1040, ABV 4.1%)
A golden ale with refreshing citrus hops leading to
a dry, bitter finish.

Rolling Hitch (OG 1051, ABV 5.2%)
An IPA with a flowery and citrus aroma.

Galapagos Stout (OG 1058, ABV 6%)
A smooth chocolate stout brewed with oats to
provide a solid body and bittersweet finish.

Extinction Ale (OG 1084, ABV 8.3%) 🍶 🍺

Dawkins SIBA

Unit 2, Lawnwood Industrial Units, Lawnwood Road,
Easton, Bristol, BS5 0EF
☎ (0117) 955 9503 ⊕ dawkins-ales.co.uk

⊠ The established Dawkins Taverns group of
independent Bristol pubs bought the Matthews
Brewery in 2009. After brewing outside Bristol for a
number or years, Dawkins has now moved to
premises in Easton, Bristol. The new premises
incorporate licensed facilities. !! ◆ RAIB

Bristol Blonde (OG 1036, ABV 3.8%)
Pale gold beer with citrus aroma and flavour with
tones of vanilla.

Bristol Best (OG 1040, ABV 4%)
Copper-coloured with malty aroma. Malt flavour
with biscuity tones and bitter finish.

Tremendous Delicious (OG 1042, ABV 4.2%)
Amber-coloured beer with biscuity malt aroma and
flavour, and a bitter finish.

Bristol Gold (OG 1043, ABV 4.4%)
Golden ale with slightly spicy fruit aroma and
flavour.

Resolution IPA (OG 1046, ABV 5%)
A gold-coloured IPA with mango and grapefruit
flavours.

de bRus

🇪 The Bruery, 25 Canmore Street, Dunfermline,
KY12 7NU
☎ (01383) 747757 ⊕ debrusbrewery.com

☺Located near Dunfermline's city centre and just
along the road from the renowned Alhambra
Theatre, the brewery opened in 2013. 🍺

IPA (OG 1042, ABV 4.2%)

Scottish Lager (OG 1043, ABV 4.3%)

Oatmeal Stout (OG 1044, ABV 4.4%)

Nut Brown Ale (OG 1045, ABV 4.5%)

Blond Ale (OG 1050, ABV 5%)

Decent (NEW) SIBA

Unit 1, LHS Gate House, Hamm Moor Lane,
Addlestone, Surrey, KT15 2SD ☎ 07711 917975
⊕ decentbrewery.co.uk

Brewing began in 2015.

Propeller Pale Ale (ABV 3.5%)
A session pale ale with a light, crisp taste.

Walrus Strong Ale (ABV 5.3%)

Deeply Vale

Unit 24, Peel Industrial Estate, Chamberhall Street,
Bury, BL9 0LU
☎ (0161) 761 7334 ☎ 07736 936973
⊕ deeplyvalebrewery.com

☺Deeply Vale is a family-run business established
in 2012 using a 2.5-barrel plant. The brewery's
name immortalises the Deeply Vale area near Bury,
famed for legendary 1970s music festivals.

Helles Deep (ABV 3.9%)
A well-balanced beer with spicy, herbal hop
aromas and enough bitterness in the finish to dry
the palate.

Citra Storm (ABV 4%)
A session ale bursting with the flavours and aromas
of lemon and grapefruit.

Deeply Red (ABV 4.2%)
Gentle red fruit and light spice aroma. Fruity and
smooth, with slight spice and astringency from the
rye.

Golden Vale (OG 1041, ABV 4.2%)
A complex but well-balanced bitterness with a
slight caramel finish. Fairly fruity aroma. The
flavour is refreshing, robust and satisfyingly malty.

Deeply Blonde (ABV 4.5%)
An easy-drinking citrus and tropical fruit explosion.

DV8 (OG 1050, ABV 4.8%)
Smooth, easy-drinking breakfast stout.

Deeside ☉

Lochton of Leys, Banchory, AB31 5QB
☎ (01339) 883777 ☎ 07765 124162

Office: Escape Business Technologies, 5 Carden Place,
Aberdeen, AB10 1UT ⊕ deesidebrewery.co.uk

Originally established as Hillside Brewery in 2005,
it quickly expanded and was renamed Deeside
Brewery in 2006. The company was sold in 2012
and moved to new premises in 2013. RAIB

Swift (OG 1038, ABV 3.8%) 🍺
Light, citrus, hoppy session ale.

Macbeth (OG 1042, ABV 4.1%)

Rye (ABV 4.8%) 🍺
Rye flavour throughout with some roast caramel
and hops.

IPA (ABV 5.2%)

Degrees Plato

Netil Market, 23 Westgate Street, London, E8 3RL
☎ 07460 693206 ⊕ dplato.com

No real ale.

Denbigh

Crown Workshop, Crown Lane, Denbigh, LL16 3SY
☎ (01745) 817021 ⊕ bragdybinbych.co.uk

Brewing commenced in 2012 at the rear of the Hope & Anchor pub. The brewery relocated in 2015 to a dedicated brewhouse in the town. Beers are mainly bottle-conditioned for markets and fairs but also supplied cask-conditioned to the pub. ♦ RAIB

Earls Folly (OG 1042, ABV 3.6%)

John the Thumb (OG 1038, ABV 3.6%)

Goblin Tower (OG 1038, ABV 3.8%)

Cwrw Dewi Sant (St David's Ale) (OG 1050, ABV 4.3%)

Cadlas Ceiliogod (Cock Pit) (OG 1045, ABV 4.5%)
A medium, tawny-coloured bitter. Well-hopped, with caramel and malt highlights.

Cwrw Du'nbych (Denbigh Black) (OG 1050, ABV 5%)
A traditional Celtic black porter. Brewed with patent black malt for a rich, roasted flavour and hints of muscovado.

No X (OG 1044, ABV 5.3%)
A cask-conditioned lager.

I Presume Ale (IPA) (OG 1050, ABV 5.5%)

Dent SIBA

Hollins, Cowgill, Dent, Cumbria, LA10 5TQ
☎ (01539) 625326 ⊕ dentbrewery.co.uk

☺Dent was set up in 1990 in a converted barn next to a former farmhouse in the Yorkshire Dales National Park. In 2005 the brewery was completely refurbished and capacity expanded. One pub is owned. More than 150 outlets are supplied direct. ‼☛

Golden Fleece (OG 1035, ABV 3.7%) ◆
Light, hoppy and fruity, with a bitter aftertaste.

Station Porter (OG 1042, ABV 3.8%) ◆
A veritable malt feast for the beer's strength. A complex porter ending with roast highlights.

Aviator (OG 1039, ABV 4%) ◆
This amber ale is characterised by citrus, caramel and hop flavours that evolve into a bitter finish.

Rambrau (OG 1042, ABV 4.5%)
A cask-conditioned lager brewed using lager malt and Hallertauer hops. It is a clean, crisp and refreshing lager-style beer.

Ramsbottom Strong Ale (OG 1042, ABV 4.5%) ◆
A well-balanced malty best bitter.

Kamikaze (OG 1047, ABV 5%) ◆
Hops and fruit dominate this full-bodied, golden, strong bitter, with a dry bitterness growing in the aftertaste.

T'owd Tup (OG 1056, ABV 6%) 🍺 ◆
A rich, full-flavoured, strong stout with a coffee aroma. The dominant roast character is balanced by a warming sweetness and a raisin fruitcake taste that lingers on into the finish.

Derby SIBA 👁

Masons Place Business Park, Nottingham Road, Derby, DE21 6AQ
☎ (01332) 365366 ☎ 07887 556788
⊕ derbybrewing.co.uk

A family-run microbrewery, established in 2004 in the old Masons Paintworks Varnish Shed by head brewer Trevor Harris, founder and former brewer at the Brunswick Inn, Derby (qv). The business has grown over the years and four pubs are now owned around Derby. More than 400 outlets are supplied including major retailers. In addition to the core range there are at least four new beers each month which includes the new monthly Craft Collection range. ‼☛♦

Hop Till You Drop (OG 1039, ABV 3.9%)
A polished blonde brew with fruity overtones and a dry finish.

Triple Hop (OG 1041, ABV 4.1%)
A classic pale ale, well-balanced with a combination of triple hop varieties.

Business As Usual (OG 1044, ABV 4.4%)
An easy-drinking, copper-coloured beer. Well-balanced, smooth and malty with a satisfying finish.

Double Mash (OG 1046, ABV 4.6%)
A balanced ruby brew, crafted using the double mash brewing process.

Penny's Porter (OG 1046, ABV 4.6%)
A rich, dark, robust brew, with a good hop balance.

Old Friend (OG 1047, ABV 4.7%)
A classic well-rounded brew, balanced and full bodied.

Dashingly Dark (OG 1048, ABV 4.8%)
A smooth, dark brew with complex flavours and a chocolate roasted finish.

Mercia IPA (OG 1050, ABV 5%)

Old Intentional (OG 1050, ABV 5%)
A full-bodied, malty premium beer rich chestnut in colour. Well-balanced with a delicate sweet aroma and smooth finish.

Quintessential (OG 1058, ABV 5.8%)
Complex and well-rounded with fruit and citrus flavours.

Derventio SIBA

The Brew Shed, Darley Abbey Mills, Darley Abbey, Derbyshire, DE22 1DZ
☎ (01332) 380199 ☎ 07975 944242
⊕ derventiobrewery.co.uk

⊗ Derventio Brewery was established in 2005 and first brewed in 2006 at Trusley Brook Farm. In 2011 the six-barrel brewery relocated to the Grade I-listed Mill Complex, which is part of the Derwent Valley Mills World Heritage Site. The brewery tap can be hired for private parties. A popular 'Day with the Brewer' is available, by prior arrangement. The brewery is one of the founding members of the Derbyshire Brewers Collective. ‼☛♦

Minerva (OG 1036.8, ABV 3.8%)

Emperors Whim (OG 1040.7, ABV 4.2%)
Golden ale, hoppy with a long, bitter finish.

Gold (OG 1040.7, ABV 4.2%)
A pale bitter with subtle character and an outstanding hoppy finish with lemon and pine notes.

Centurion (OG 1041.7, ABV 4.3%)
An amber-coloured bitter with a hoppy aftertaste.

King Arthur (OG 1041.7, ABV 4.3%)

Brown-coloured bitter with sweet biscuit malt flavours and a smooth, balanced hop bitterness.

Et tu Brutus (OG 1043.6, ABV 4.5%)
Dark ale, smooth but with a long, bitter finish.

Feast (OG 1046.5, ABV 4.8%)
IPA giving dry and fruity aftertastes.

Cleopatra (OG 1048.4, ABV 5%)
A complex beer rounded off with First Gold hops and a hint of apricot.

Venus (OG 1048.4, ABV 5%)
A light-coloured, well-balanced and smooth premium ale with a light, fragrant hop finish.

Barbarian (OG 1053.3, ABV 5.5%)
Dark and smooth with a lingering subtle hop finish.

Derwent SIBA

Units 2a-2c, Station Road Industrial Estate, Silloth, Cumbria, CA7 4AG
☎ (01697) 331522 ⊕ derwentbrewery.co.uk

☺ Derwent was set up in 1996 in Cockermouth and moved to Silloth in 1998. Owners Mark and Allie bought the brewery in 2013. A large range of ales is produced, available throughout the north of England. ◆ RAIB

Cote Light (OG 1034, ABV 3.6%)

Carlisle State Bitter (OG 1036, ABV 3.7%) ◥
Malty, biscuity, hoppy beer with a gold colour.

W&M Mild (OG 1036, ABV 3.7%)

Parsons Pledge (OG 1039, ABV 4%) ◥
Amber ale with a biscuity tang and a slightly fruity finish.

Blonde (OG 1039, ABV 4.2%)

Reaper (OG 1042, ABV 4.3%)

Mutineer (OG 1043, ABV 4.4%)

W&M Pale Ale (OG 1042, ABV 4.4%) ◥
A sweet, fruity, hoppy beer with a bitter finish.

Marshall Port Stout (OG 1054, ABV 5.2%)

Deva Craft

Unit 14, Engineer Park, Babbage Road, Sandycroft, CH5 2QD
☎ (01244) 630670 ☎ 07841 384143
⊕ devacraftbeer.co.uk

☺Deva Craft was set up in 2014 by father-and-son team Ade and Nick Gilbody. Brewing started in 2015 on a five-barrel plant. Beers are available in many outlets throughout North Wales and Cheshire. ‼

Nemesis (OG 1040, ABV 4%)

Gladius (ABV 4.1%)

Equinox (OG 1044, ABV 4.7%)

Pandemonium (ABV 5.5%)

Duel IPA (ABV 5.6%)

Deverell's

Unit 16, Globe Industrial Estate, Grays, Essex, RM17 6ST ☎ 07843 627791 ⊕ deverellsbrewery.com

Established in 2012 using a 2.5-barrel plant, Deverell's was the first commercial brewer in Thurrock since Charringtons acquired and closed

Seabrooks Brewery more than 80 years ago. The brewery operates its own pub, the Traitors Gate, Grays. Special monthly brews are available exclusively for the pub. It also contract brews for a Chelmsford-based company selling beers under its own brand names. A move is planned to new premises, which have been obtained and are being renovated, which will increase capacity to six-barrels. ◆ RAIB

Rock 'n' Rolla (OG 1040, ABV 4%)

Redemption (ABV 4.5%)
Full-flavoured amber-coloured ale. Sweet with caramel notes and a well-balanced hop profile.

Devil's Dyke

See Arran

Devon

◾ **Mansfield Arms, 7 Main Street, Sauchie, Clackmannanshire, FK10 3JR**
☎ (01259) 722020 ⊕ devonales.com

☺Established in 1992 to produce cask ales for the Mansfield Arms, Sauchie, Devon is the oldest operating brewery in the county. A second pub, the Inn at Muckhart, was purchased in 1994 and the only beers sold there are from the Devon Ales brewery. The brewery is now selling beer to the open market. ‼

Original (70/-) (OG 1038, ABV 3.8%)
A full-bodied session ale with a prominent malty flavour and a distinct hoppiness.

Black (OG 1042, ABV 4.2%)

IPA (OG 1042, ABV 4.2%)

Pride (OG 1046, ABV 4.8%)

Devon Earth SIBA

Buckfastleigh, Devon ☎ 07927 397871

Office: 7 Fernham Terrace, Torquay Road, Paignton, Devon, TQ3 2AQ ✉ info@devonearthbrewery.co.uk

⊗ Devon Earth was launched in 2008 on a 2.5-barrel plant located on the banks of the River Dart on the edge of Dartmoor and is run on a part-time basis. It supplies beer festivals and pubs mainly in the Torbay area. ◆

Devon Earth (OG 1042, ABV 4.2%)
A light, refreshing summer ale with a satisfying bitter finish.

Grounded (OG 1047, ABV 4.7%)
A well-rounded traditional session ale.

Lost in the Woods (OG 1052, ABV 5.2%)
A dark, full-flavoured porter with roasted malt flavours and a touch of liquorice.

Devon's Own

See Clearwater

Dhillon's SIBA ◉

14a Hales Industrial Estate, Rowleys Green Lane, Longford, West Midlands, CV6 6AL
☎ (024) 7666 7413 ⊕ dhillonsbrewery.com

Originally named Lion Heart, the brewery was established in 2014 on an industrial unit near the Ricoh Arena, using a five-barrel plant. Personalised bottled beers are produced for weddings and other special occasions. Production is currently suspended. ◆ RAIB

Dickens

🍺 Great Expectations, 33 London Street, Reading, RG1 4PS
☎ (0118) 950 3925
✉ greatexpectations@relaxinnz.co.uk

⊠ A 2.5-barrel microbrewery situated in the Great Expectations pub, Reading, it went into full production in 2015. Its beers are named after Dickens' characters and are only available at the pub.

Mr Bumble (OG 1039, ABV 3.8%)
A golden ale with a citrus and fruity flavour balanced with honey and malt undertones.

Artful Dodger (OG 1042, ABV 4%)
A bitter with biscuit and malt undertones and a long bitter finish.

Chuzzlewit (OG 1045, ABV 4.3%)
A Belgian-style witbier. Pale amber in colour, with a hint of banana in the aroma.

Old Curiosity (OG 1049, ABV 4.8%)
A cross-over between a porter and a dry Irish stout. It has a malty, dark chocolate flavour with a toffee aftertaste.

Sikes (OG 1052, ABV 5%)
An American-style IPA. Golden amber with a sweet and fruity aroma. Smooth and creamy with a lightly sharp and fruity taste.

Dickensian

See Target

Dicks (NEW)

c/o All Hallows Brewery, Goodmanham, East Yorkshire, YO43 3JA ☎ 07792 417564

Office: 7 Pickering Grange, Brough, East Yorkshire, HU15 1GY ☎ (01482) 667329
✉ dick@dicksbrewery.co.uk

☺Brewing began in 2016 using spare capacity at All Hallows Brewery (qv). Further beers are planned.

Big Head Bitter (ABV 3.8%)
A traditional Yorkshire session bitter.

Digfield SIBA

Lilford Ldge Farm, Barnwell, Northamptonshire, PE8 5SA
☎ (01832) 273954 ⊕ digfield-ales.co.uk

⊠ Digfield Ales started brewing in 2005 on a five-barrel plant, which was later expanded to seven barrels. Increased demand led to a move to larger premises in 2012, still in the Barnwell area. A reed bed effluent system has been installed and brewing capacity increased to 15 barrels with new equipment. More than 40 free houses are supplied.
◆

Fools Nook (OG 1037, ABV 3.8%) ◄

The floral aroma, dominated by lavender and honey, belies the hoppy bitterness that comes through in the taste of this golden ale. A fruity balance lasts.

Chiffchaff (OG 1038, ABV 3.9%)
An amber-gold pale ale with a distinct hoppy aroma.

Barnwell Bitter (OG 1039, ABV 4%) ◄
A fruity aroma introduces a beer in which sharp bitterness is balanced by dry, biscuity malt.

Old Crow Porter (OG 1042, ABV 4.3%)
A traditional, rich, full-bodied porter with a balanced roasted malt finish.

Shacklebush (OG 1044, ABV 4.5%) ◄
This amber brew begins with a balance of malt and hop on the nose which develops on the palate, complemented by a mounting bitterness. Good dry finish with lingering malt notes.

Mad Monk (OG 1047, ABV 4.8%) ◄
Fruity beer with bitter, earthy hops in evidence.

Dog & Rabbit (NEW)

41 Norham Close, Brunswick Green, Wideopen, Tyne & Wear, NE13 7HS ☎ 07528 676310
⊕ dogandrabbitbrewery.co.uk

Dog & Rabbit began brewing in 2015. Beers are available at the Dog & Rabbit micropub in Whitley Bay. RAIB

Dominion SIBA

Unit Z, New House Farm, Little Laver Road, Moreton, Essex, CM5 0JE
☎ (01277) 890580 ☎ 07931 120806
⊕ dominionbrewerycompany.com

⊠ Dominion was established in 2012 by Andy Skene, renting the premises and Pitfield brand names from the founder of Pitfield, Martin Kemp. All Pitfield beers are certified organic by the Soil Association and vegan by the Vegan Society. ⬩⬩ RAIB V

The Few (ABV 3.5%)
A pale beer brewed to a 1949 Cobbold Brewery of Ipswich recipe using hops from the original hop fields.

Theodore Pinchbeck's Spurious Stout (ABV 4.2%)
A medium-bodied, chocolaty, dark stout.

Woodbine Racer (OG 1042, ABV 4.2%)
A golden beer brewed using English and American hops.

Canada (ABV 4.9%)
A dark red beer, robust and hoppy with a long-lasting bitter finish.

Amber Porter (ABV 5.5%)
A dark beer with biscuity, coffee flavours.

Mad Trappiste (OG 1095, ABV 10%)
A Belgian Trappist-style red-coloured beer, aged in cognac casks and deliberately soured to result in a beer with a complex flavour.

Brewed under the Pitfield Brewery brand name:

Light Ale (OG 1036, ABV 3.6%)

Bitter (OG 1036, ABV 3.7%)

Lager (OG 1037, ABV 3.7%)

Chococino Dark Beer (OG 1038, ABV 4%)

Shoreditch Stout (OG 1040, ABV 4%)

Eco Warrior (OG 1043, ABV 4.5%) ◈
Golden ale with a vivid, citrus hop aroma. The hop character is balanced with a delicate sweetness in the taste, followed by an increasingly bitter finish.

Red Ale (OG 1046, ABV 4.8%) ◈
Complex beer with a full, malty body and strong hop character.

1850 London Porter (OG 1048, ABV 5%) ◈
Big-tasting dark ale dominated by coffee and forest fruits. The finish is dry but not acrid.

Ginger Beer (ABV 5%)
Sweet, malty beer with a good hit of ginger.

N1 Wheat Beer (OG 1048, ABV 5%)

1837 India Pale Ale (OG 1065, ABV 7%)
A true IPA, strong in alcohol, with lots of hops, a light copper-coloured beer with floral aroma.

Imperial Chocolate Stout (OG 1070, ABV 7.3%)
A traditional stout with overtones of chocolate.

1890 Stock Ale (ABV 10%)
Sweet malt flavours with hints of sherry and whisky.

Doncaster

☷ 7 Young Street, Doncaster, South Yorkshire, DN1 3EL
☎ (01302) 376436 ☎ 07770 958394
⊕ doncasterbrewery.co.uk

Established in 2012 and initially based at an industrial unit in Kirk Sandall, Doncaster, the brewery moved to new premises in the centre of Doncaster in 2014 and opened a micropub tap room. ◆

Sand House (OG 1038, ABV 3.8%)

Cheswold (OG 1042, ABV 4.2%)

Gold Cup (OG 1045, ABV 4.5%)

First Aviation (OG 1050, ABV 5%)

Donnington ◉

Upper Swell, Stow-on-the-Wold, Gloucestershire, GL54 1EP
☎ (01451) 830603 ⊕ donnington-brewery.com

Thomas Arkell bought a 13th-century watermill in 1827 and began brewing on the site in 1865; the waterwheel is still in use. Thomas's descendant Claude owned and ran the brewery until his death in 2007, supplying 20 outlets direct. It has now passed to Claude's cousin, James Arkell, also of Arkells Brewery, Swindon (qv). ☷ RAIB

BB (OG 1035, ABV 3.6%) ◈
A pleasant amber bitter with a slight hop aroma, a good balance of malt and hops in the mouth and a bitter aftertaste.

Gold (OG 1041, ABV 4%)
A golden ale with a citrus flavour followed by a rounded malt finish.

SBA (OG 1045, ABV 4.4%) ◈
Malt dominates over bitterness in the subtle flavour of this premium bitter, which has a hint of fruit and a dry, malty finish.

Dorking SIBA

Engine Shed, Dorking West Station Yard, Station Road, Dorking, Surrey, RH4 1HF
☎ (01306) 877988 ⊕ dorkingbrewery.com

⊗ Dorking started brewing in 2008 and supplies an increasing number of local pubs and clubs. New fermenters were purchased in 2013 and brewing takes place at least twice a week. ‼☷◆

Gold (OG 1042, ABV 3.8%)

Pilcrow Pale (ABV 4%)

DB Number One (OG 1045, ABV 4.2%) ◈
Hoppy best bitter with underlying orange fruit notes. Some balancing malt sweetness in the taste leads to a dry bitter finish.

Red India Ale (OG 1051, ABV 5%)

Buffalo Buffalo (OG 1052, ABV 5.1%)

Dorset SIBA ◉

Unit 7, Hybris Business Park, Warmwell Road, Crossways, Dorset, DT2 8BF
☎ (01305) 777515 ⊕ dbcales.com

⊗ Founded in 1996, Dorset Brewing Company relocated from Hope Square, Weymouth, once the old Devenish and Groves breweries site, to new purpose-built premises in 2010. In 2008 it took over the running of Dorchester's brewpub, Tom Brown's (Goldfinch Brewery). Beers are available in local pubs and selected outlets throughout the south west. ‼◆

Dorset Knob (OG 1039, ABV 3.9%) ◈
Complex bitter ale with strong malt and fruit flavours despite its light gravity.

Tom Brown's (OG 1039, ABV 4%)
A pale bitter with a fruity nose. The taste is bittersweet with malt, fruit and some hop. Complex aftertaste.

Jurassic (OG 1040, ABV 4.2%) ◈
Clean-tasting, easy-drinking bitter. Well balanced with lingering bitterness after moderate sweetness.

Yachtsman (OG 1048, ABV 4.7%)
A pale golden bitter-tasting beer with hints of vanilla and honey in the aroma and aftertaste.

Durdle Door (OG 1046, ABV 5%) ◈
A tawny hue and fruity aroma with a hint of pear drops and good malty undertone, joined by hops and a little roast malt in the taste. Lingering bittersweet finish.

Brewed under the Goldfinch Brewery name:

Flashman's Clout (OG 1045, ABV 4.5%)

Dorset Piddle

See Piddle

Double Top SIBA

Unit 4, Kilton Terrace, Worksop, Nottinghamshire, S80 2DQ ☎ 07973 521824

Office: the Mallard, Station Approach, Carlton Road, Worksop, S81 7AG ⊕ doubletopbrewery.co.uk

◉Double Top procured a 2.5-barrel plant in 2012, with fermenting capacity for 7.5 barrels a week.

This was expanded to a five-barrel plant in 2015 with a fermenting capacity of 20 barrels. It caters for its brewery tap, the Mallard on Platform 1 of Worksop railway station, and for regional beer festivals and free houses. ‼◆

Nelson Mild (OG 1037, ABV 3.5%) 🗂
A traditional dark mild with a delicate balance of malts.

Golden Arrow (OG 1038, ABV 3.9%)
A golden ale with citrus notes.

Shanghai (OG 1041, ABV 4.2%)
A light, hoppy session ale.

Adonis (OG 1042, ABV 4.3%)
A pale bitter with a dry, biscuity finish.

Treble 20 (OG 1043, ABV 4.5%)
Straw-coloured, hoppy and bitter.

Bad Boy (OG 1047, ABV 4.6%)
Chestnut-coloured bitter, sweet in taste.

Citra Tip (OG 1050, ABV 5.2%)
An American-hopped pale ale.

Madhouse (OG 1055, ABV 5.2%)
A modern-style porter.

IPA (OG 1055, ABV 5.5%)
A deep golden-coloured strong IPA.

Old Stoneface (OG 1058, ABV 6%)
A black treacle stout.

Dove Street SIBA

82 St Helens Street, Ipswich, Suffolk, IP4 2LB
☎ (01473) 211270 ☎ 07880 707077
⊕ dovestreetbrewery.co.uk

⊗ Dove Street began brewing in 2011 using a 2.5-barrel plant in a garage opposite the Dove Street Inn. The Dove Street Inn, its sister pub and beer festivals are supplied. ‼🍺

Underwood Mild (OG 1033, ABV 3.2%)
Dark, traditional, thirst-quenching mild, packed with flavour and aroma.

Gladstone Guzzler (OG 1037, ABV 3.6%)
Easy-drinking, light-coloured bitter with a hoppy flavour.

Bitter (OG 1038, ABV 3.7%)
A traditional bitter with a dry finish.

Citra (OG 1039, ABV 3.9%)
Light beer with a dry citrus flavour.

Incredible Taste Fantastic Clarity (OG 1041, ABV 4%)
Golden-coloured hoppy session beer; clean, clear and crisp.

Dove Elder (OG 1042, ABV 4.1%)
Traditionally brewed speciality beer.

Thirsty Walker (OG 1047, ABV 4.6%)
A well-balanced bitter.

Old Ipswich Liquor (OG 1055, ABV 5.5%)
Aged for deep complex flavours, chocolate and liquorice notes with a long, well-rounded finish.

Dow Bridge SIBA 👁

2-3 Rugby Road, Catthorpe, Leicestershire, LE17 6DA
☎ (01788) 869121 ⊕ dowbridgebrewery.co.uk

Dow Bridge commenced brewing in 2001 and takes its name from a local bridge where Watling

Street spans the River Avon. The brewery uses English whole hops and malt with no adjuncts or additives. More than 50 outlets are supplied direct. ‼◆RAIB

Bonum Mild (OG 1035, ABV 3.5%) 🌢
Complex dark brown, full-flavoured mild, with strong malt and roast flavours to the fore and continuing into the aftertaste, leading to a long, satisfying finish.

Acris (OG 1037, ABV 3.8%)
A classic session bitter.

Centurion (OG 1039, ABV 4%)
Copper-coloured, well-rounded best bitter. Good balance of malt and hops in the flavour.

Legion (OG 1041, ABV 4.1%)
Golden hoppy ale. A good balance of malt and fruity hop on the nose and palate.

Ratae'd (OG 1041, ABV 4.3%) 🌢
Tawny-coloured, full-bodied beer with bitter hop flavours against a grainy background, leading to a long, bitter and dry aftertaste.

Dark (OG 1042, ABV 4.4%)
A strong, dark, full-bodied ale with roast malt giving hints of chocolate.

Gladiator (OG 1046, ABV 4.5%)
Ruby chestnut-coloured, well-balanced beer. Smooth and malty, but with a bitter, dry finish. Some fruit aroma and slight toffee sweetness.

Fosse Ale (OG 1046, ABV 4.8%)
Well-balanced premium beer with caramel and burnt toffee flavours leading to a hoppy, dry finish.

Praetorian Porter (OG 1048, ABV 5%)
Dark, rich, full-bodied porter. Slightly sweet with hoppy undertones.

Onslaught (OG 1049, ABV 5.2%)
A deep ruby-coloured strong ale. A good balance of fruit and hops with rich flavours and aroma.

Downlands SIBA 👁

Unit Z (2a), Mackley Industrial Estate, Small Dole, West Sussex, BN5 9XE
☎ (01273) 495596 ⊕ downlandsbrewery.com

⊗ A 10-barrel brewery set up in 2012 distributing beers across the south-east of England. ‼◆

Root Thirteen (OG 1033, ABV 3.6%)
Crisp, light golden ale that layers floral zesty aromas over a grapefruit and citrus flavour.

Best (OG 1042, ABV 4.1%)
A traditional and interesting malty, fruity, best bitter.

Dark (OG 1042, ABV 4.1%)
A mahogany-coloured session stout; smoky, vanilla and velvet.

Pale (OG 1041, ABV 4.1%)

Bramber (OG 1047, ABV 4.5%)
Powerfully-hopped American-style amber ale.

Devils Dyke Porter (OG 1052, ABV 5%)
Toffee, chocolate and smoky flavours are complemented by a subtle hint of marmalade.

Devils Dyke Salted Caramel (OG 1052, ABV 5%)
The sweetness of caramel enriches the already present chocolate and coffee flavours with a surprising hint of salt in the finish.

Downton SIBA

Unit 11, Batten Road, Downton Industrial Estate, Downton, Wiltshire, SP5 3HU
☎ (01725) 513313 ⏚ downtonbrewery.com

⊠ Downton was set up in 2003. The brewery has a 20-barrel brew length and produces around 1,500 barrels a year. Around 100 outlets are supplied direct. Eight regular beers are produced together with speciality and experimental beers. 🚃 RAIB

New Forest Ale (OG 1037, ABV 3.8%) ◄
An amber-coloured bitter with subtle aromas leading to good hopping on the palate. Some fruit and predominate hoppiness in the aftertaste.

Quadhop (OG 1038, ABV 3.9%) ◄
Pale golden session beer, initially hoppy on the palate with some fruit and a strong hoppiness in the aftertaste.

Elderquad (OG 1039, ABV 4%) ◄
Golden yellow bitter with a floral fruity aroma leading to a good well-hopped taste with hints of elderflower. Dryish finish with good fruit and hop balance.

Honey Blonde (OG 1041, ABV 4.3%) ◄
Straw-coloured golden ale, easy drinking with initial bitterness giving way to slight sweetness and a lingering balanced aftertaste.

Nelson's Delight (OG 1044, ABV 4.5%)
An amber bitter full of hoppy character and a rich resinous aroma. Underlying sweetness and strength provided by the addition of navy rum.

Dark Delight (OG 1053, ABV 5.5%) ◄
A strong dark brown best bitter, malt and roast in the aroma and on the palate initially, giving way to a balanced lingering aftertaste with noticeable hoppiness.

Chocolate Orange Delight (OG 1052, ABV 5.8%)
A speciality old ale with pronounced chocolate flavours. A pleasant orange addition combines perfectly in this delightfully different offering.

IPA (OG 1063, ABV 6.8%) ◄
Golden yellow strong bitter with good balance of hops and fruit, slight sweetness and some malt notes, all through to the aftertaste.

Dragonfly SIBA

☰ George & Dragon, 183 High Street, Acton, London, W3 9DJ
☎ (020) 8992 3712 ☎ 07788 859450
⏚ dragonflybrewery.co.uk

⊠ Brewing began in 2014 with a Chinese-built brewing kit installed in the back bar of the George & Dragon. The pub is supplied along with other outlets in the same pub group. ♦

2 O'Clock Ordinary (OG 1043, ABV 4%) ◄
Pale brown best bitter with hops and fruit aroma and flavour, with a bitterness that is present in the finish.

Early Doors (OG 1042, ABV 4.3%) ◄
Dark golden best bitter with grapefruit and hops building and lingering in the dry-bitter finish, balanced by some malty sweetness.

Draycott (Cambridgeshire)

Low Farm, 30 Mill Road, Buckden, Cambridgeshire, PE19 5SS

☎ (01480) 812404 ☎ 07740 374710
⏚ draycottbrewery.co.uk

The brewery is located in an old farm complex and was set up by Jon and Jane Draycott in 2009. Only one-pint bottle-conditioned beers are produced. RAIB

Draycott (Derbyshire) SIBA

Ladywood Lodge Farm, Spondon Road, Dale Abbey, Derbyshire, DE7 4PS ☎ 07834 728540
✉ draycottbrewingcompany@yahoo.co.uk

⊠ Small microbrewery established in 2014, supplying local pubs and beer festivals. Relocation to new premises in 2015 saw beer range and capacity increased.

Gold Nugget (OG 1038, ABV 3.8%)
Light-coloured lager-style beer with a refreshing citrus taste.

Butcher's Bitter (OG 1042, ABV 4.2%)
Traditional bitter brewed with caramel notes and a hint of nut.

California Steam Beer (OG 1042, ABV 4.2%)
American-style red beer. Dry and refreshing with a hint of citrus.

Kentucky Common Ale (OG 1042, ABV 4.2%)
American-style amber bitter with big flavours.

Miller's Beer (OG 1042, ABV 4.2%)
Dark-coloured bitter with complex flavours.

Driftwood SIBA

☰ Driftwood Spars Hotel, Trevaunance Cove, St Agnes, Cornwall, TR5 0RT
☎ (01872) 552591 ⏚ driftwoodsparsbrewery.co.uk

⊠ Brewing since 2000 on a custom-built five-barrel plant, the brewery has since expanded to incorporate additional fermentation and conditioning capacity plus a brewery shop and visitor centre with annual production now standing at 1,300 barrels. Monthly specials are produced for selected circulation only. Besides the pub, other outlets and beer festivals are supplied. ‼ 🚃 ♦ RAIB

Bawden Rocks (OG 1037, ABV 3.8%) ◄
Smooth copper-coloured bitter, aromatic hops and refreshing biscuit malt and bitterness with Seville orange and plum fruit. Dry, crisp finish.

Blackheads Mild (OG 1037, ABV 3.8%) ◄
Refreshing dark mild with roast malt aroma. Malt and sweet caramel follow burst of damson and liquorice. Dry, bitter end.

Lewsey Lou's (OG 1038, ABV 3.8%)

Red Mission (OG 1038, ABV 3.8%)

Blue Hills Bitter (OG 1039, ABV 4%) ◄
Medium-bodied refreshing bitter with a hoppy aroma. Flowery, grassy hops dominate the flavour to the end with gentle biscuity malt.

Booskor (OG 1042, ABV 4.2%) ◄
Smooth red mild with light roast malt throughout. Sweetness, toffee apples, roast nuts and stone fruits. Malty finish, slightly dry.

Forest Blond (OG 1044, ABV 4.3%) ◄
Yellow ale with apple and woody aroma. Bitter lemon, apricot, melon and elderflower with grassy hop bitterness, sweetness and perfumed esters.

Badlands Bitter (OG 1047, ABV 4.8%) ◄

Red winter warmer, rich in sweet malt, figs and raisins balanced by hoppiness, finishing with fruit esters, bitterness and dryness.

Bolster's Blood Porter (OG 1049, ABV 5%)
A rich, dark, chocolaty, malty porter with a slight bitter finish.

Lou's Brew (OG 1049, ABV 5%) ◆
Golden beer with strong lemon and grapefruit flavours, bitterness and dryness throughout. Long, tangy finish with hop bitterness fading lastly.

Alfie's Revenge (OG 1060, ABV 6.5%) 🍷 ◆
Brown old ale with malt, sweet fruit aroma and flavours, balanced by spicy hop bitterness. Fruity finish with rising astringency.

Drink Up (NEW) SIBA

Central Workshops, Off Longworth Road, Horwich, BL6 7DB ☎ 07539 112018 ✉ dubrew@outlook.com

Brewing began in 2015. The brewery produces modern, progressive beer styles. ◆

dubALT (OG 1050, ABV 5%)

dubFIRE (OG 1050, ABV 5%)

dubFIRE ACE (OG 1050, ABV 5%)

dubWEST (OG 1050, ABV 5%)

Drone Valley (NEW)

Unstone Industrial Complex, Main Road, Unstone, Derbyshire, S18 4AB ☎ 07794 277091

Office: 63 Alexander Road, Dronfield, S18 2LD ⊕ dronevalleybrewery.com

☺Community-owned five-barrel brewery that began brewing commercially in 2016. The brewery is entirely volunteer operated and welcomes new members and investors. ◆ RAIB

Dronny Bottom Bitter (ABV 3.7%)
A traditional English bitter.

Gosforth Gold (ABV 4%)
A pale straw-coloured beer with a full body for its strength. Well-balanced with a citrus hop finish.

Coal Aston Porter (ABV 4.5%)
A smooth, fruity porter.

Fanshaw Blonde (ABV 4.8%)
An American-hopped IPA.

Stubley Stout (ABV 5%)
A rich, smooth stout.

IPA (ABV 5.2%)
A classic English IPA, deep amber in colour with a rich malt base and generously hopped, giving a full mouthfeel and a dry bitter finish.

Drygate SIBA

🍴 85 Drygate, Glasgow, G4 0UT
☎ (0141) 212 8810 ⊕ drygate.com

Restaurant, bar and microbrewery, Drygate is a joint venture of Tennent's and Williams Bros, though operationally independent. The on-site brewery began production in 2014. A core range of keg and bottled beers has been launched. The brewery is also committed to cask-conditioned ale, at least one permanent cask is on at all times. ‼ ◆ RAIB

Pale Duke (OG 1041, ABV 4%)

Reflex (ABV 4.2%)

Seven Peaks (ABV 5%)

Dukeries SIBA

Carlton Forest Distribution Centre, Unit 6, Blyth Road, Worksop, Nottinghamshire, S81 0TP
☎ (01909) 731171 ☎ 07584 305027
✉ phil.owen@dukeriesbrewery.co.uk

☺Founded in 2012 and located in the heart of the Dukeries in Nottinghamshire using a five-barrel plant. ◆

Elsi Pale (OG 1036, ABV 3.6%)
Traditional chestnut-coloured bitter with slight nutty flavour mixed with hints of fruit leading to a dry bitter finish.

Havana Crest (OG 1037, ABV 3.7%)
A session bitter using two different English hop varieties.

Blonde (OG 1038, ABV 3.8%)
Blonde ale with citrus notes and low level bitterness ensuring a clean, crisp feel throughout.

A Ray of Sunshine (OG 1041, ABV 4.2%)
A fruity beer; tropical fruits throughout with a clean, fresh feel on the palate.

Castle Hill (OG 1041, ABV 4.2%)
Well-hopped bitter, balanced throughout, offering soft malt flavours with a smooth, mellow bitter finish.

De Lovetot (OG 1041, ABV 4.2%)
Golden pale ale. Well-balanced with citrus fruit aroma leading to a bitter finish.

Lady Matilda (OG 1044, ABV 4.5%)
American pale ale brewed with citrus notes and medium bitterness.

Mining Stout (OG 1044, ABV 4.5%)
A dark-coloured beer full of deep, strong character. Bursting with robust rich flavours leading to a well-balanced, dry finish.

IPA (OG 1046, ABV 4.9%)
A traditional English IPA, full of complex hop character.

Farmers Branch (OG 1047, ABV 5%)
This pale strong ale is zesty with fresh, clean citrus notes.

Lord Furnival (OG 1049, ABV 5.3%)
Strong ale with lemon citrus notes and a dry finish.

Gunsmoke (OG 1050, ABV 5.5%)
Russet-coloured beer with hints of chocolate and liquorice with a soft, dry finish.

Bess of Hardwick (OG 1052, ABV 5.7%)
An American pale ale with floral, citrus flavours in abundance and herbal characteristics.

Dunham Massey

100 Oldfield Lane, Dunham Massey, WA14 4PE
☎ (0161) 929 0663 ⊕ dunhammasseybrewing.co.uk

☺Opened in 2007, Dunham Massey brews traditional North-western ales using only English ingredients. Around 30 outlets are supplied direct, along with the brewery tap, Costello's Bar, Altrincham. A sister brewery, Lymm (qv), opened in 2013 with Costello's Bar in Stockton Heath tied to both breweries. 🍴 ◆ RAIB

Little Bollington Bitter (OG 1037, ABV 3.7%) ◆
Straw-coloured light ale with malt and citrus fruit taste and a dry, bitter finish.

Chocolate Cherry Mild (OG 1040, ABV 3.8%)
A speciality beer, it has the all dark chocolate, coffee and liquorice flavours of a dark mild blended with a dry, bittersweet cherry flavour.

Dunham Dark (OG 1040, ABV 3.8%) ◆
Dark brown beer with malty aroma. Fairly sweet, with malt, some roast, hop and fruit in the taste and finish.

Dunham Light (OG 1040, ABV 3.8%)
A creamy, malty, easy-drinking, light mild.

Big Tree Bitter (OG 1041, ABV 3.9%)
A session bitter, golden in colour and full-bodied, with a good balance of hops and malt.

Obelisk (OG 1040, ABV 3.9%)
Light and hoppy, but not too bitter, with hints of citrus and grapefruit.

Dunham Milk Stout (OG 1051, ABV 4%)
A classic, full-bodied, sweet stout with a creamy, roast malt character.

Landlady (OG 1040, ABV 4%)
A light, refreshing, biscuity, dry ale, with a spicy hop finish.

Dunham Stout (OG 1046, ABV 4.2%)
A creamy, full-bodied, all English dry stout, with a classic bitter, burnt, dark roast flavour.

Stamford Bitter (OG 1045, ABV 4.2%)
A golden, full-bodied bitter with a complex blend of hops, giving a slightly dry finish.

Deer Beer (OG 1047, ABV 4.5%)
A clean, full-bodied, malty English ale, with a hint of toffee, and a distinct hop finish.

Cheshire IPA (OG 1047, ABV 4.7%)
A fairly strong, pale, hoppy and bitter beer.

Dunham Porter (OG 1056, ABV 5.2%) 🍺
A classic old-style English porter; creamy, full-bodied and packed with flavour.

East India Pale Ale (OG 1062, ABV 6%)
A stronger IPA brewed in the traditional East India style, using all English ingredients. Light and hoppy.

Dunham Gold (OG 1070, ABV 7.2%)
A Belgian-style ale. Strong, light and fruity, with a hoppy finish.

Dunscar Bridge SIBA

Unit 13a, Dunscar Bridge Business Park, Blackburn Road, Bolton, BL7 9PQ
☎ (01204) 563516 ⊕ dunscarbridge.co.uk

☺Brewing began in 2009. In 2012 a 25-barrel plant was installed in a new brewery within the business park at Dunscar Bridge, Bolton. The brewery supplies several of the groups own pubs plus Wetherspoon outlets in the North-west. ‼

Dunscar Blonde (ABV 3.8%)

Dunscar Gold (ABV 4%)

Lancashire Stout (ABV 4%)
A full-bodied flavour with biscuity aromas and a dry bitter, roasted taste.

Dunscar Best Bitter (ABV 4.1%)
A smooth beer, lightly caramelised and distinctly hoppy with a slightly dry finish. A generous

collection of aromas from wood and pine to soft fruits and roasted coffee, combining to create a distinct yet gentle ale.

Dunscar Amber Ale (ABV 4.5%)

Durham SIBA

Unit 6a, Bowburn North Industrial Estate, Bowburn, County Durham, DH6 5PF
☎ (0191) 377 1991 ⊕ durhambrewery.co.uk

☺Established in 1994, the Durham Brewery has a portfolio of around 40 beers, some permanent, some on rotation with new beers appearing regularly. The oldest brewery in County Durham, beers are available in the North East and West Yorkshire. ‼ 🍺 RAIB V

Magus (OG 1036, ABV 3.8%) ◆
Pale malt gives this brew its straw colour but the hops define its character, with a fruity aroma, a clean bitter mouthfeel, and a lingering, dry, citrus-like finish.

Citra Nova (OG 1039, ABV 3.9%)
Massive hop bouquet with a lively, fresh grape bitterness.

Pale Ice (OG 1039, ABV 3.9%)
A refreshing and bitter pale beer with a floral aroma.

Apollo (OG 1040, ABV 4%)
Pale, aromatic and hoppy American IPA. Full-flavoured and refreshing with grapefruit notes.

Black Velvet (OG 1040, ABV 4%)
A dark beer with rich coffee and roast flavours.

White Gold (OG 1040, ABV 4%)
A floral hop aroma and grapefruit body.

White Amarillo (OG 1041, ABV 4.1%)
Easy-drinking, clean and satisfying beer.

Columbus IPA (OG 1042, ABV 4.2%)
Full-bodied and hoppy American IPA. Peachy aroma with a grapefruit body.

White Velvet (OG 1042, ABV 4.2%)

Evensong (OG 1050, ABV 5%)

White Stout (OG 1072, ABV 7.2%)
A pale stout. Full-bodied and strong with a floral and resinous character.

Dynamite Valley (NEW)

Viaduct Works, Frog Hill, Ponsanooth, Cornwall, TR3 7JW ☎ 07775 570235

Dynamite Valley was set up in 2015 following a successful Crowdfunder campaign. The brewery is located near a historic gunpowder site near Falmouth. Local outlets are supplied along with the brewery's own Beer Café. Collaboration brews are welcomed. 🍺

Gold Rush (OG 1040, ABV 4%)

TNT IPA (OG 1048, ABV 4.8%)

Black Charge (OG 1051, ABV 5.1%)
A sweet oatmeal stout.

Prospector (OG 1052, ABV 5.2%)
A Bavarian wheat beer.

Earl Soham SIBA

Meadow Works, Cross Green, Debenham, Suffolk, IP14 6RP
☎ (01728) 861213 ∰ earlsohambrewery.co.uk

⊠ Earl Soham was set up behind the Victoria pub in 1984 and continued there until 2001 when the brewery relocated, moving again in 2013 to Debenham. The Victoria and the Station in Framlingham both sell the beers on a regular basis, as does the Brewery Tap in Ipswich. When there is spare stock, beer is supplied to local free houses and as many beer festivals as possible. 30 outlets are supplied and two pubs are owned. ‼ ⛟ ♦ RAIB

Gannet Mild (OG 1034, ABV 3.3%) ◄
A beautifully balanced mild, sweet and fruity flavour with a lingering, coffee aftertaste.

Victoria Bitter (OG 1037, ABV 3.6%) ◄
A light, fruity, amber session beer with a clean taste and a long, lingering hoppy aftertaste.

Elizabeth Ale (OG 1040, ABV 4.2%)
A clean, bitter premium beer.

Sir Roger's Porter (OG 1042, ABV 4.2%) ◄
Roast/coffee aroma and berry fruit introduce a full-bodied porter with roast/coffee flavours. Dry roast finish.

Albert Ale (OG 1045, ABV 4.4%)
Hops dominate every aspect of this beer, but especially the finish. A fruity, astringent beer.

Brandeston Gold (OG 1045, ABV 4.5%) ◄
Sharp, clean flavour, malty/hoppy and heavily laden with citrus fruit. Malty finish.

East London SIBA

Unit 45, Fairways Business Centre, Lammas Road, London, E10 7QB
☎ (020) 8539 0805 ∰ eastlondonbrewing.com

⊠ The East London Brewing Company is a 10-barrel microbrewery run by a husband-and-wife team. It has been producing ales for pubs, bars, restaurants and off-licences since 2011. ♦ RAIB

Orchid (OG 1040, ABV 3.6%) ◄
Delicate vanilla on nose and flavour. Fruity overtones coupled with cocoa dark roast character that is present in the finish.

Pale Ale (OG 1042, ABV 4%) ◄
Amber best bitter with spicy hops, bitter lemon, tropical fruits and biscuit that are there in the dry aftertaste.

Foundation Bitter (OG 1044, ABV 4.2%) ◄
Well-balanced brown best bitter with fresh green fruity hop in aroma and flavour with caramelised pineapple. Short bitter marmalade finish.

Nightwatchman (OG 1046, ABV 4.5%) ◄
Dark ruby-brown complex best bitter. Peach, caramelised fruit, toffee balanced by bitter, nutty and roasted malt flavours. Dry aftertaste.

Cowcatcher American Pale Ale (OG 1045, ABV 4.8%) ◄
Fruity, hoppy, rich golden ale with honey sweetness, mango and hints of passion fruit lingering in the dry bitter finish.

Jamboree (OG 1048, ABV 4.8%) ◄
Golden strong bitter with grassy and woody hop aroma. Flavour has spice with kiwi and sweet biscuit. Dry bitter finish.

Quadrant Oatmeal Stout (OG 1063, ABV 5.8%) ◄
Smooth, rich oatmeal stout with liquorice, mocha and caramelised fruit. Roasted coffee aroma. A dry, slightly roast bitter finish lingers.

East Stratton

See Black Bear

Eccleshall

See Slater's

Eden SIBA

Brougham Hall, Brougham, Cumbria, CA10 2DE
☎ (01768) 210565 ☎ 07729 677692
∰ edenbrewery.com

Set up in 2011, Eden Brewery is now run by Jason Hill, assisted by Linda and Chris. The five barrel brewery is located in the Old Brewery at historic Brougham Hall and has the capacity to brew 45 barrels per week. ♦

Best (OG 1039, ABV 3.8%) ◄
A tawny beer with a hoppy beginning, a malty, bittersweet middle and a gentle finish.

Fuggle (OG 1039, ABV 3.8%) ◄
Initially sweet, a gently-hopped pale beer with a more bitter finish.

Dynamite (OG 1040, ABV 4%)
A hoppy blonde ale with good flavour and aroma.

Atomic Blonde (OG 1041, ABV 4.1%)
A hoppy, thirst quenching session ale.

Gold (OG 1042, ABV 4.2%) ◄
Gentle fruity and honey aromas to start leading to a well-balanced sweet beer with a lasting hoppy finish.

First Emperor (OG 1046, ABV 4.6%) ◄
Fruity beer with balanced malt and hops and a hint of butterscotch combining to a rich bitter finish.

Eden St Andrews SIBA

Main Street, Guardbridge, KY16 0UU ☎ 07786 060013 ∰ edenbrewerystandrews.com

☺The brewery was established in 2012 using a five-barrel plant in part of the former Guardbridge paper mills. In 2014 a new 20-barrel plant and distillery was installed. ‼ ⛟ RAIB

St Andrews Blonde (OG 1040, ABV 3.8%)

19th (OG 1041, ABV 3.9%)

Clock Brew (OG 1045, ABV 4.3%)

1882 Lager (OG 1048, ABV 4.5%)

Seggie Porter (OG 1053, ABV 5.5%) 🍷

Edenfield

▤ Rostron Arms, 1 Market Place, Edenfield, Lancashire, BL0 0JZ
☎ (01706) 821756

Edenfield commenced brewing in 2014.

Old Red Dog (OG 1039, ABV 3.9%)
An amber-coloured bitter with a slight dry aftertaste.

Edinbrew SIBA 👁

Unit 5, Knightsridge East Industrial Estate, Livingston, West Lothian, EH54 8RA ☎ 07736 680755
⊕ edinbrew.beer/index

☺Edinbrew opened in 2016 within a small industrial estate in the Knightsridge area of Livingston. The brewery, operated by Ross Hamilton, who trained at the Milestone Brewery, uses a 5.5-barrel plant. At present the ales are supplied to outlets in the Edinburgh area. ‼

Divided City (OG 1043, ABV 3.8%)

Red Alert (ABV 3.8%)

Friendly Fire (ABV 4.3%)

85 Shilling (ABV 4.6%)

Industrial (OG 1054, ABV 5%)

Edmunds (NEW)

▤ Edmunds Brewhouse, 106-110 Edmund Street, Birmingham, B3 2ES
☎ (0121) 200 2423 ⊕ edmundsbrewhouse.co.uk

Brewing began in 2015 at Edmunds Brewhouse in the heart of Birmingham's financial district.

Gold Hop (ABV 4.2%)

American IPA (ABV 4.5%)

Pale Ale (ABV 5%)

Eight Arch SIBA

Unit 3A, Stone Lane Industrial Estate, Wimborne, Dorset, BH21 1HB
☎ (01202) 889254 ☎ 07554 445647
⊕ 8archbrewing.co.uk

Brewing commenced in 2015 on a five-barrel plant situated in a unit on a small industrial estate on the outskirts of Wimborne. Local pubs and clubs are supplied. ▆RAIB

Bowstring Bitter (ABV 3.8%)

Parabolic Pale Ale (ABV 4.5%)

Corbel (ABV 5.5%)

Electric Bear (NEW) SIBA 👁

Unit 12, Maltings Trading Estate, Locksbrook Road, Bath, BA1 3JL
☎ (01225) 424088 ⊕ electricbearbrewing.com

Electric Bear began brewing in 2015 using a purpose-built 15-barrel plant. It brews classic beer styles with a modern twist. Pubs in the South West can obtain its beers direct from the brewery, or nationally via an increasing range of wholesalers. ♦

Persuasion (OG 1038, ABV 3.8%)

Elemental (OG 1042, ABV 4.4%)

Livewire (OG 1052, ABV 5.4%)

Elephant School

See Brentwood

Elgood's SIBA IFBB 👁

North Brink Brewery, Wisbech, Cambridgeshire, PE13 1LW
☎ (01945) 583160 ⊕ elgoods-brewery.co.uk

⊠ The North Brink brewery was established in 1795. Owned by the Elgood family since 1878, the fifth generation are now involved in running the business. Elgood's has approximately 30 tied pubs within a 50-mile radius of the brewery and a substantial free trade. Lambic style beers have been produced recently using the brewery's old open cooling trays as fermenting vessels. Off sales are available all year round from the brewery office when the visitor centre is closed. ‼ ▆♦

Black Dog (OG 1036.8, ABV 3.6%) ◣
Black-red mild with liquorice and chocolate. Dry roast finish.

Cambridge Bitter (OG 1037.8, ARV 3.8%) ◣
Fruit and malt on the nose with increasing hops and balancing malt on the palate. Dry finish.

Golden Newt (OG 1041.5, ABV 4.1%) ◣
Golden ale with floral hops and sulphur aroma. Floral hops and a fruity presence on a bittersweet background lead to a short, muted hoppy and fruity finish.

EP (OG 1043.8, ABV 4.3%)
A premium robust ale with a wonderful aroma of hops and malt.

Elixir

Unit 2c, Brucefield Industry Park, Livingston, EH54 9BX ☎ 07760 330122 ⊕ elixirbrew.com

Elixir Brew Company is an award-winning experimental brewery that produces beers using New World hops, unusual ingredients and novel techniques. Established in 2012, Elixir beers are produced at a variety of breweries throughout the UK, including frequent collaborations with the host brewers.

Elland SIBA 👁

Units 3-5, Heathfield Industrial Estate, Heathfield Street, Elland, West Yorkshire, HX5 9AE
☎ (01422) 377677 ⊕ ellandbrewery.co.uk

☺Orginally formed in 2002 as Eastwood & Sanders by the amalgamation of the Barge & Barrel and West Yorkshire Breweries, the company was renamed Elland in 2006 to reinforce its links with the town. The brewery has a capacity of 50 barrels (200 firkins) a week. Ownership hanged hands in 2016 and further expansion is planned. ‼♦RAIB

Chinook (OG 1039, ABV 3.9%)

White Prussian (OG 1039, ABV 3.9%) ◣
A straw-coloured, lightly flavoured, easy-drinking and refreshing lager-style speciality beer.

Blonde (OG 1041, ABV 4%) ◣
Creamy yellow-coloured, hoppy ale with hints of citrus fruits. Pleasantly strong bitter aftertaste.

Beyond the Pale (OG 1042, ABV 4.2%) ◣
Gold-coloured, robust, creamy beer with ripe aromas of hops and fruit. Bitterness predominates in the mouth and leads to a dry, fruity and hoppy aftertaste.

Nettlethrasher (OG 1044, ABV 4.4%) ◣

Grainy amber-coloured beer. A rounded nose with some fragrant hops notes followed by a mellow nutty and fruity taste and a dry finish.

1872 Porter (OG 1065, ABV 6.5%) ⬚ ▣ ◆
Creamy, full-flavoured porter. Rich liquorice flavours with a hint of chocolate from roast malt. A soft but satisfying aftertaste of bittersweet roast and malt.

Elliswood ◉

Unit 3, Southways Industrial Estate, Coventry Road, Hinckley, Leicestershire, LE10 0NJ
☎ (01455) 635239 ☎ 07795 954392

Office: 24 Leicester Road, Hinckley, Leicestershire, LE10 1LS ⊕ elliswoodbrewery.co.uk

Founded in 2013 by Tracy Ellis and Phil Woodward and taken over in 2016 by Darren and Louise Lavender, who continue to brew using the David Porter 5.5-barrel system with a capacity to brew twice weekly.

Englands Finest (OG 1038, ABV 3.8%)
A golden, heavily-hopped session bitter with tropical hints of peach and melba.

Hansom Ale (OG 1036, ABV 3.9%)
Traditional easy-drinking session ale.

Best of Both (OG 1040, ABV 4%)
A clean, refreshing pale ale with mild floral aroma.

Conny Quaffer (OG 1041, ABV 4.1%)
Deep golden in colour with a crisp, clean biscuit taste.

Barrel of Laughs (OG 1042, ABV 4.2%)
Copper-coloured beer, well-balanced with spicy vanilla undertones. A slight bitterness all the way through with a sweet, pleasant aftertaste.

Just One More (OG 1042, ABV 4.2%)
A citrus beer with blackberry and grapefruit undertones.

Jolly Jack Tar (OG 1047, ABV 4.3%)
A rich, creamy milk stout with a smooth chocolate aftertaste.

Nelson's Right Arm (OG 1044, ABV 4.5%)
A deep dark red-coloured beer with heavy hints of autumn fruits.

Royal Standard 1485 (OG 1047, ABV 4.8%)
A deep red-coloured bitter with a sweet toffee taste and caramel undertones.

Legless (OG 1048, ABV 4.9%)
Gold in colour and easy on the palate, made with wheat to give a full-bodied beer. Undertones of blackberry and spice.

Last Porter Call (OG 1051, ABV 5.1%)
A modern robust porter with a malty palate, depth and complexity. A spicy, earthy aroma giving a subtle almond taste.

Shipwrecked (OG 1054, ABV 5.4%)
Bronze-coloured, crisp, dry ale with a smooth, clean, hoppy taste and a slight smell of lemons. Fruity and malty.

Elmtree SIBA

Snetterton Brewery, Unit 10, Oakwood Industrial Estate, Harling Road, Snetterton, Norfolk, NR16 2JU
☎ (01953) 887065 ☎ 07939 549241
⊕ elmtreebeers.co.uk

⊠ Established in 2007 Elmtree brews on a six-barrel plant. More than 120 free trade outlets are supplied direct. Bespoke beers for individual pubs are also brewed. ‼ ⇥ ◆ RAIB V

Burston's Cuckoo (OG 1038, ABV 3.8%) ◆
Gentle malt airs. Biscuity sweet beginning with delicate lime hints. Full-bodied, short, sweet finish.

Bitter (OG 1041, ABV 4.2%)
A well-balanced, copper-coloured crisp beer, the early malt notes give way to a distinctively complex hop finish.

Mad Maudie (OG 1044, ABV 4.5%)
A clear, fresh ale. The unusual hop combination imparts a light hint of white wine.

Norfolk's 80 Shilling Ale (OG 1044, ABV 4.5%) ◆
Roast malt and caramel provide balance to an inherent hoppy bitterness. A mix of well-balanced flavours. Finish becomes chewy.

Snetterton Scary Tree (OG 1044, ABV 4.5%)
A tan-coloured beer, complex bitterness combined with a hoppy aroma.

Dark Horse (OG 1050, ABV 5%) ◆
Jet black with roast dominating both aroma and taste. A fruity, prune-like background gives depth. Increasingly malty finish.

Golden Pale Ale (OG 1048, ABV 5%) ◆
Full-bodied with a swirling malty aroma. Lime fruit adds depth to the sweet malty character. Short sweetening finish.

Nightlight Mild (OG 1057, ABV 5.7%) ◆
A heavy mix of liquorice, roast and malt infuses aroma and first taste. A sweet spiciness slowly develops.

Elusive (NEW)

Unit 5, Marino Way, Hogwood Lane Industrial Estate, Finchampstead, Berkshire, RG40 4RF
☎ (0118) 973 2153 ☎ 07917 541718
⊕ elusivebrewing.com

Established in 2016, Elusive is a five-barrel brewery located on the Hampshire/Berkshire border.

Cherrywood Road (ABV 3.8%)
A lightly smoked ruby mild.

Starship Fleet (ABV 4.2%)
An English pale ale.

EMAL (NEW)

10 Hogsbrook Units, Woodbury Salterton, Devon, EX5 1PY ☎ 07988 849644 ⊕ emalbrewery.co.uk

EMAL began brewing in 2016 and is a family-run business sharing premises with Powderkeg Brewery (qv). Beer names are influenced by the historic Roman city of Exeter.

Castra (ABV 3.5%)
A session pale ale with light malt base, gentle bitterness and a well-rounded, hoppy finish.

Isca Gold (ABV 4%)
An easy-drinking golden ale balancing a hint of caramel sweetness with a gentle bitter finish, and a fruity hop aroma.

Legio (ABV 4.5%)
A full-bodied, mahogany-coloured ale with sweet caramel notes, balanced bitterness and a crisp hop finish.

Empire SIBA

The Old Boiler House, Unit 33, Upper Mills,
Slaithwaite, Huddersfield, West Yorkshire, HD7 5HA
☎ (01484) 847343 ☎ 07966 592276
⊕ empirebrewing.com

☺Empire Brewing was set up 2006 in a mill on the
bank of the scenic Huddersfield Narrow Canal, close
to the centre of Slaithwaite. In 2011 the brewery
upgraded from a five-barrel to a 10-barrel plant.
Beers are supplied to local free houses and through
independent specialist beer agencies and
wholesalers. !! ◆RAIB

Golden Warrior (OG 1039.5, ABV 3.8%)
Pale bitter, quite fruity with a sherbet aftertaste,
moderate bitterness.

Strikes Back (OG 1041, ABV 4%)
Pale golden session bitter with a hoppy aroma and
good hop and malt balance with a citrus flavour,
light on the palate.

Valour (OG 1042.5, ABV 4.2%)

Longbow (OG 1043, ABV 4.3%)

Imperium (OG 1050, ABV 5.1%)

Emsworth Brewery

Rear of 16 West Street, Emsworth, Hampshire,
PO10 7DY ☎ 07717 510294
⊕ theemsworthbrewery.co.uk

⊠ Michael and Hilary Bolt began their family-run
brewery in 2012 on a 2.5-barrel plant, obtained
from Oban Ales, in a shed behind an antiques shop
in Emsworth. ◆

Slipper (OG 1040, ABV 3.9%)

Wayfarer (OG 1042, ABV 4.1%)

Fairfield (OG 1042, ABV 4.2%)

Emsworth Brewhouse (NEW)

44 Hollybank Lane, Emsworth, Hampshire, PO10 7UE
☎ 07852 000865 ⊕ theemsworthbrewhouse.co.uk

Launched in 2015, the Emsworth Brewhouse
originally used a half-barrel plant but upgraded in
2016. A small number of pubs are supplied direct.

Ennerdale SIBA

Church Row, Rowrah, Cumbria, CA26 3XS
☎ (01946) 862977 ☎ 07918 626652
⊕ ennerdalebrewery.co.uk

☺Ennerdale started brewing in 2010 as a 10-barrel
brewery in a converted barn. In 2016 the brewery
moved to larger premises with plans for expansion.
Beers are distributed throughout the north of
England and south Scotland. !!◆

Blonde (OG 1039, ABV 3.8%) ◄
A sweet, fruity, light-coloured beer with gentle
bitterness.

Darkest (OG 1044, ABV 4.2%) ◄
Sweet, roasty black mild with a fruity, hoppy
flavour.

Wild Ennerdale (OG 1043, ABV 4.2%)
Amber in colour with a fruity base and spicy finish
yielding a good hop aroma and well rounded
bitterness.

Enville SIBA

Coxgreen, Hollies Lane, Enville, DY7 5LG
☎ (01384) 873728 ⊕ envilleales.com

⊠ Enville Brewery is sited on a picturesque
Victorian, Grade II-listed farm complex, using
natural well water, traditional steam brewing and
a reed and willow effluent plant. Enville Ale is
infused with honey and is from a 19th-century
recipe for beekeeper's ale passed down from the
former proprietor's great-great aunt. !!☰♦

LPA (Light Pale Ale) (OG 1039, ABV 4%)
Traditional session bitter; dry and golden with a
mellow, hoppy flavour.

Nailmaker Mild (OG 1041, ABV 4%)
A well-defined hop aroma and underlying
sweetness give way to a dry finish.

Simpkiss (OG 1039, ABV 4%)

Cherry Blonde (OG 1042, ABV 4.2%)
A light blonde bitter, delicately infused with
essence of cherry to produce a Belgian-style fruit
beer. Dry, hoppy and refreshing with a bitter finish.

Saaz (OG 1042, ABV 4.2%) ◄
Golden lager-style beer. Lager bite but with more
taste and lasting bitterness. The malty aroma is late
arriving but the bitter finish, balanced by fruit and
hops, compensates.

White (OG 1041, ABV 4.2%) ◄
Yellow in colour with a malt, hops and fruit aroma.
Hoppy but sweet finish.

Ale (OG 1044, ABV 4.5%) ◄
Sweet malty aroma and taste, honey becomes
apparent before bitterness finally dominates.

Old Porter (OG 1044, ABV 4.5%) ◄
Black with a creamy head and sulphurous aroma.
Sweet and fruity start with touches of spice. Good
balance between sweet and bitter, but hops
dominate the finish.

Ginger Beer (OG 1045, ABV 4.6%) ◄
Golden bright with gently gingered tangs. A
drinkable beer with no acute flavours but a
satisfying aftertaste of sweet hoppiness.

Epping

See Dominion

Erddig SIBA ⊚

⊟ Unit 56 Clywedog Road, North Wrexham Industrial
Estate, Wrexham, LL13 9XN
☎ (01978) 664478 ☎ 07967 585514
⊕ erddibrewery.co.uk

☺Erddig began brewing in 2014 using equipment
from the Llangollen Brewery.

Penny Farthing (OG 1039, ABV 3.9%) ◄
Light and refreshing with a sweetish initial taste
and a citrus bitter finish.

Squires Best (OG 1042, ABV 4.2%) ◄
A bittersweet golden ale, yellow in colour with
citrus fruit notes in aroma and taste.

Errant (NEW) SIBA ⊚

Arch 8, King Edward Bridge, off Pottery Lane,
Newcastle upon Tyne, NE1 3TQ ☎ 07736 333303
⊕ errantbrewery.com

⊗ Brewing began in 2015. ♦

Knight (OG 1039, ABV 3.5%)

Clever Girl (OG 1045, ABV 4.1%)

Future Sailor (ABV 4.2%)

Dillon (ABV 4.8%)

Ahab (ABV 5%)

Tusk (OG 1051, ABV 5.2%)

Essex Street

🍴 46 Essex Street, London, WC2R 3JF
☎ (020) 7936 2536 ⊕ templebrewhouse.com

☺Opened in 2014 within the Temple Brew House pub. The pub company also operates sister brewpubs in London, Bath, Bristol, Cambridge and Norwich. ‼♦

Tempale (ABV 3.8%)

The Gavel (ABV 4.3%)

Evan Evans SIBA

The New Brewery, 1 Rhosmaen Street, Llandeilo, Carmarthenshire, SA19 6LU
☎ (01558) 824455 ⊕ evan-evans.com

☺Evan Evans opened in 2004. Brewing capacity is now 8,000 barrels per annum. Eight pubs are owned. It is Wales' first Soil Association organic-approved brewery. In 2009 the brewery bought Archers Brewery of Swindon's brands and now brew all of Archer's regular and seasonal ales. However, the Archer's range may soon be contracted out to be brewed at Wessex Brewery. Other seasonal beers under the Artisan, WH Buckley and Porter Street brands are also brewed, the latter brand in anticipation of setting up a new brewery on the eastern outskirts of London. ‼🍽♦

BB (Best Bitter) (OG 1036, ABV 3.6%)
An easy-drinking best bitter. Malty with a clean hop palate.

J Buckley Original Best (OG 1040, ABV 4%)

Welsh Pale Ale (WPA) (OG 1040, ABV 4%)
Golden ale, with hints of tropical fruits and a malty finish.

Cwrw (OG 1043, ABV 4.2%)
Rich, malty flavour with a distinct fruity palate.

Warrior (OG 1046, ABV 4.6%)
A classic premium ale, distinctive and full bodied. Malty and fruity with a dry hop finish.

Everards SIBA ◉

Castle Acres, Narborough, Leicestershire, LE19 1BY
☎ (0116) 201 4100 ⊕ everards.co.uk

Established by William Everard in 1849, Everards brewery remains an independent family-owned company. Four core ales are brewed as well as a range of monthly beers. Everards owns a pub estate of more than 170 tenanted houses throughout the Midlands. ‼🍽♦

Beacon Bitter (OG 1036, ABV 3.8%) ◥
Light, refreshing, well-balanced pale amber-coloured bitter in the Burton style.

Sunchaser Blonde (OG 1038, ABV 4%) ◥

A golden brew with a sweet, lightly-hopped character. Some citrus notes to the fore in a quick finish that becomes increasingly bitter.

Tiger Best Bitter (OG 1041, ABV 4.2%) ◥
A mid-brown, well-balanced best bitter crafted for broad appeal, benefiting from a long, bittersweet finish.

Original (OG 1050, ABV 5.2%) ◥
Full-bodied, mid-brown strong bitter with a pleasant rich, grainy mouthfeel. Well-balanced flavours, with malt slightly to the fore, merging into a long, satisfying finish.

Evesham

17 Oat Street, Evesham, Worcestershire, WR11 4PJ
☎ (01386) 443628 ✉ mrsyschembri@gmail.co.uk

☺ Evesham Brewery is located in the former Green Dragon pub. Beer is produced as required by demand from the brewery's own pub. Other local outlets are supplied.

Exe Valley SIBA ◉

Land Farm, Silverton, Exeter, Devon, EX5 4HF
☎ (01392) 860406 ⊕ exevalleybrewery.co.uk

Exe Valley was established as Barron's Brewery in 1984. The brewery is located in a converted barn overlooking the Exe Valley and Dartmoor hills. Locally sourced malt and English hops are used, along with the brewery's own spring water. Around 100 outlets are supplied within a 45-mile radius of the brewery. Beers are also available nationally via wholesalers. ♦RAIB

Bitter (OG 1036, ABV 3.7%) ◥
Mid-brown bitter, pleasantly fruity with underlying malt through the aroma, taste and finish.

Barron's Hopsit (OG 1040, ABV 4.1%) ◥
Straw-coloured beer with strong hop aroma, hop and fruit flavour and a bitter hop finish.

Dob's Best Bitter (OG 1040, ABV 4.1%) ◥
Pale brown best bitter with delicate malty aroma. Well-balanced, sweet, hoppy taste. Malt and sweet finish along with fruit.

Devon Glory (OG 1046, ABV 4.7%) ◥
Mid-brown, fruity-tasting beer with a sweet, fruity finish.

Mr Sheppard's Crook (OG 1046, ABV 4.7%) ◥
Smooth, full-bodied, mid-brown beer with a malty-fruit nose and a sweetish palate leading to a bitter, dry finish.

Exeter Old Bitter (OG 1046, ABV 4.8%) ◥
Mid-brown old ale with a rich fruity taste and slightly earthy aroma and bitter finish.

It's Phil's Ale (OG 1046, ABV 4.8%)
Deep golden-coloured beer with a hoppy flavour.

Winter Glow (OG 1056, ABV 6%) 🍂 ◥
A rich, full bodied, strong ale. Predominantly malty with a hint of chocolate/coffee on the nose, sweet taste and lingering aftertaste.

Exeter SIBA

Unit 1, Cowley Bridge Road, Exeter, Devon, EX4 4NX
☎ (01392) 823013 ⊕ exeterbrewery.co.uk

Exeter Brewery, formerly Topsham & Exminster, began brewing in 2003. In 2012 the brewery moved to a larger site in Exeter. Around 650 outlets are supplied throughout Devon, Somerset, Dorset and the east of Cornwall. ♦

Lighterman (OG 1036, ABV 3.5%)
A light copper-coloured ale. Fruity malt flavour with a traditional bitter finish.

Avocet (OG 1038.5, ABV 3.9%) ◄
An amber-coloured ale with caramel nose, bitter taste and fruity aftertaste.

'fraid Not (OG 1040, ABV 4%)
A golden hoppy beer. A distinct clean citrus bitterness and lasting dry finish.

Ferryman (OG 1041, ABV 4.2%)
Classic copper-coloured session ale. Well-balanced, sweet, warm malt flavour. Crisp bitter finish.

County Best (OG 1045, ABV 4.6%)
Premium strength best bitter. Rich malt fruity flavour. Smooth bittersweet finish.

Darkness (OG 1050, ABV 5.1%) ◄
Smooth, creamy stout with hints of chocolate and coffee. Roast and caramel pervade the aroma, taste and lingering finish.

Exit 33

Unit 7, 106 Fitzwalter Road, Sheffield, South Yorkshire, S2 2SP
☎ (0114) 270 9991 ⊕ exit33.beer

☺This eight-barrel brewery was founded in Sheffield in 2008 as Brew Company but rebranded in 2014. The brewer is also a joint partner at the Harlequin pub. Regular house beers are brewed for local pubs. ♦

Simcoe (OG 1037, ABV 3.8%)
A pale session bitter with a passion fruit, apricot and pine aroma from the hops and sharp, juicy flavour.

Blonde (OG 1039, ABV 4%)
A light-coloured, easy-drinking session beer brewed with German lager hops.

Thirst Aid (OG 1038.8, ABV 4%)
A light, clean-drinking session ale with a juicy, hop forward flavour.

Mosaic (OG 1039.7, ABV 4.1%)
A pale ale showcasing a single hop variety.

New England Best (OG 1041, ABV 4.2%)
Rich, smooth beer with a distinctive malty base, a rich flavour and dark colouring.

Hop Monster (OG 1043.6, ABV 4.5%)
Hoppy golden ale with resinous pink grapefruit, biting citrus and soft floral characters and a long bitter finish.

Yellow Rose (OG 1044, ABV 4.5%)
A golden ale with a floral and fruity character.

Frontier IPA (OG 1045.5, ABV 4.7%)
Straw-coloured, crisp and dry with a bitter aftertaste.

Stout (OG 1048.4, ABV 5%)
A dark, roasted traditional stout. The initial flavour hints of cocoa followed by delicate coffee and molasses with a silky, thick mouthfeel.

Exmoor SIBA ◉

Golden Hill Brewery, Old Brewery Road, Wiveliscombe, Somerset, TA4 2PW

☎ (01984) 623798 ⊕ exmoorales.co.uk

Somerset's largest brewery was founded in 1980 in the old Hancock's brewery, which closed in 1959. In 2015 Exmoor moved to new and larger premises within 100 yards of the original site, thus doubling brewing capacity. Around 250 outlets in the South-west are supplied and others nationwide via wholesalers and pub chains. ‼♦

Ale (OG 1039, ABV 3.8%) ◄
Mid-brown, medium-bodied session bitter. Mixture of malt and hops in the aroma and taste lead to a hoppy, bitter aftertaste.

Fox (OG 1043, ABV 4.2%)
A mid-brown beer with a slight maltiness on the tongue, followed by a burst of hops with a lingering bittersweet aftertaste.

Gold (OG 1045, ABV 4.5%) ◄
Yellow/golden best bitter with good balance of malt and fruity hop on the nose and palate. Sweetness follows through. Bitter finish.

Stag (OG 1050, ABV 5.2%) ◄
A pale brown beer with a malty taste and aroma, and a bitter finish.

Beast (OG 1066, ABV 6.6%)
A dark brew with a complex, long aftertaste.

Facer's

A8-9, Ashmount Enterprise Park, Aber Road, Flint, CH6 5QT ☎ 07713 566370 ⊕ facers.co.uk

Facer's is the oldest existing brewery in Flintshire. Ex-Boddington head brewer Dave Facer ran the brewery single handed from its launch in 2003 until he took on his first employee in 2008 and expanded to twice the floor space. Around 100 outlets are supplied. ‼♦

Mountain Mild (OG 1035, ABV 3.3%) ▤ ◄
A fruity dark mild, not too sweet, with underlying roast malt flavours and a full mouthfeel for its low ABV.

Clwyd Gold (OG 1034, ABV 3.5%) ◄
Clean-tasting session bitter, mid-brown in colour with a full mouthfeel. The malty flavours are accompanied by increasing hoppiness in the bitter finish.

Flintshire Bitter (OG 1035, ABV 3.7%) ◄
Well-balanced session bitter with a full mouthfeel. Some fruitiness in aroma and taste with increasing hoppy bitterness in the dry finish.

Abbey Original (OG 1038, ABV 4%) ◄
A sweetish golden beer with a good hop and fruit aroma, juicy taste and a dry hoppy finish.

Abbey Red (OG 1038, ABV 4%) ◄
A darker version of Abbey Original, copper-coloured with a sweet, malty taste and a bittersweet aftertaste.

North Star Porter (OG 1042, ABV 4%) 🖰 ▤ ◄
Dark, smooth porter-style beer with good roast notes and hints of coffee and chocolate. Some initial sweetness and caramel flavours followed by a hoppy, bitter aftertaste.

Sunny Bitter (OG 1040, ABV 4.2%) ◄
An amber-coloured beer with a dry taste. The hop aroma continues into the taste where some faint fruit notes are also present. Lasting dry finish.

DHB (Dave's Hoppy Beer) (OG 1041, ABV 4.3%) ◄

A dry-hopped version of Splendid Ale with some sweet flavours also coming through in the mainly hoppy, bitter taste.

This Splendid Ale (OG 1041, ABV 4.3%) ◆
Refreshing tangy best bitter, yellow in colour with a sharp hoppy, bitter taste. Good citrus fruit undertones with hints of grapefruit throughout.

Landslide (OG 1047, ABV 4.9%) ◆
Full-flavoured, complex premium bitter with tangy orange marmalade fruitiness in aroma and taste. Long-lasting hoppy flavours throughout.

Fallen Angel

See Broxbourne

Fallen Brewery

Station House, Kippen, Stirlingshire, FK8 3JA ☎ 07507 862167 ⊕ fallenbrewing.co.uk

Fallen began brewing in 2014 using a 10-barrel plant. ◆ RAIB

Odyssey (OG 1040, ABV 4.1%)

Dragonfly (OG 1046, ABV 4.6%)

Blackhouse (OG 1052, ABV 5%)

Grapevine (OG 1054, ABV 5.4%)

Falstaff SIBA ⊙

⧇ 24 Society Place, Normanton, Derby, DE23 6UH
☎ (01332) 342902 ☎ 07947 242710
⊕ falstaffbrewery.co.uk

⊠ Attached to the Falstaff freehouse, the brewery dates from 1999 but was refurbished and re-opened in 2003 under new management. Themed special beers are produced all year round, including exclusive specials for the Babington Arms, Derby. ◆

3 Faze (OG 1040, ABV 3.8%)
Light gold in colour with a malt and honey nose. Smooth malt flavours lead to a clean, balanced malt and hop finish.

Fist Full of Hops (OG 1044, ABV 4.5%)
Golden amber in colour, powerful hop aromas with citrus undertones. Complex mouth-filling hop flavours and a long hop-filled aftertaste.

Phoenix (OG 1045, ABV 4.7%) ◆
A smooth, tawny ale with fruit and hop, joined by plenty of malt in the mouth. A subtle sweetness produces a drinkable ale.

Smiling Assassin (OG 1050, ABV 5.2%)
Dark amber in colour with a fruity malt nose. Fruity malt flavours and a fruity finish with hops coming through at the end.

Darkside (OG 1056, ABV 6%)
A strong black mild with ruby tones. Dark chocolate and plum aromas with fruity bitter chocolate flavours and hints of coffee in the finish.

Good, Bad & Drunk (OG 1057, ABV 6.2%)
Tawny-coloured, full-bodied ale with a fruity, bittersweet aftertaste and hints of caramel.

Faringdon

⧇ 1 Park Road, Faringdon, Oxfordshire, SN7 7BP
☎ (01367) 241480 ⊠ swanfaringdon@yahoo.co.uk

⊠ Faringdon opened in 2010 using a one-barrel plant; brewing on a larger-scale began in 2011. The beers are brewed by Stuart Bruton and supplied to the brewery tap, the Swan. ‼ ◆ RAIB

Folly Ale (OG 1039.5, ABV 4%)
A traditional English bitter, copper-coloured, fruity and sweet with late bitterness from the hops.

PGA (OG 1039, ABV 4%)
Mid amber in colour with sweet undertones and a hoppy aftertaste.

Farmageddon (NEW)

25 Ballykeigle Road, Comber, BT23 5SD
⊕ farmageddonbrewery.com

Brewing began in 2014. All beers are unfiltered with no preservatives and are suitable for vegans. RAIB V

Farmer's

See Maldon

Farr (NEW) SIBA ⊙

The Courtyard, Samuels Farm, Coleman Green Lane, Wheathampstead, Hertfordshire, AL4 8ER ☎ 07734 857881 ⊕ farrbrew.com

Farr Brew was started in 2015 on a 0.5-barrel plant by two friends, Nick Farr and Matt Elvidge. Demand led to a move in 2016 and an upgrade to a 10-barrel plant. ◆ RAIB

Our Greatest Golden (OG 1041, ABV 4.1%)
A dark golden ale with a well-rounded but not overpowering bitterness.

The Best Bitter (ABV 4.2%)
A dark traditional bitter with a hint of caramel.

Our Most Potent Porter (OG 1044, ABV 4.4%)
A complex porter with honey and treacle notes, a deep chocolate nose and a rich, fruity flavour.

Farriers Arms

⧇ The Forstal, Mersham, Kent, TN25 6NU
☎ (01233) 720444 ⊕ thefarriersarms.com

Brewing commenced in 2010 in this brewpub owned by a consortium of villagers. ‼ ◆

Farriers 1606 (OG 1038, ABV 3.7%)

Fat (NEW)

11 East Bridge Street, Crook, County Durham, DL15 9BJ
☎ (01388) 311551 ⊕ fatbrewer.com

Brewing began in 2015.

Pale Ale (OG 1035.5, ABV 3.6%)

Rouge (OG 1037, ABV 3.8%)

Blonde (OG 1039, ABV 4%)

Crimson (OG 1047, ABV 4.8%)

Fat Cat

⧇ Fat Cat Brewery Tap, 98-100 Lawson Road, Norwich, NR3 4LF

☎ (01603) 788508 ☎ 07795 633368
⊕ fatcatbrewery.co.uk

⊠ Fat Cat Brewery was founded by the owner of the Fat Cat free house in Norwich. Brewing started in 2005 at the Fat Cat's sister pub, the Fat Cat Brewery Tap, under the supervision of former Woodforde's owner Ray Ashworth. ‼ ♦ RAIB

Bitter (OG 1038, ABV 3.8%) ◄
Gold-coloured with a grapefruit and sulphur aroma. A mix of malt, citrus and hop with a dry bitter ending.

Hell Cat (OG 1040, ABV 4.1%) ◄
Clementines and hops anchor this lively but full bodied brew. A strong bittersweet but satisfying finale.

Top Cat (OG 1047, ABV 4.7%) ◄
A complex malt, caramel, and blackberry aroma leads into a similarly creamy beginning which continues to a richly satisfying finish.

Marmalade Cat (OG 1055, ABV 5.5%) ◄
Rich and complex with malt and marmalade dominating every corner. Copper-coloured and grainy with a solid bitter finale.

Fat Pig SIBA

▤ 2 John Street, Exeter, Devon, EX1 1BL
☎ (01392) 437217 ⊕ fatpig-exeter.co.uk

⊠ Brewing commenced in 2013 using a 2.5-barrel plant to supply the Fat Pig and its sister pub the Rusty Bike in Exeter. ♦

Pigasus Brown Ale (OG 1039, ABV 3.9%)

Pigmalion Bitter (OG 1042, ABV 4.2%)

John Street Ale (OG 1043, ABV 4.3%)

Ham 69 ESB (OG 1048, ABV 4.8%)

Phat Nancys IPA (OG 1051, ABV 4.8%)

Faversham Steam

See Shepherd Neame

Felinfoel SIBA

Farmers Row, Felinfoel, Llanelli, SA14 8LB
☎ (01554) 773357 ⊕ felinfoel-brewery.com

Founded in the 1830s, the company is still family-owned and is now the oldest brewery in Wales. The present buildings are Grade II*-listed and were built in the 1870s. It supplies cask ale to half its 84 houses, though some use top pressure dispense, and to approximately 350 free trade outlets. ‼ ▤ ♦

IPA (OG 1036, ABV 3.6%)
A golden pale ale.

Celtic Pride (OG 1045, ABV 3.9%)
A light, golden premium ale with a bright, clean flavour and citrus overtones.

Double Dragon (OG 1042, ABV 4.2%) ◄
This pale brown beer has a malty, fruity aroma. The taste is also malt and fruit with a background hop presence throughout. A malty and fruity finish.

Stout (OG 1048, ABV 5%)
A Welsh stout created with a subtle blend of chocolate malt giving a predominantly roast barley flavour and a rich, creamy head.

Fell

Unit 27, Moor Lane Business Park, Flookburgh, Cumbria, LA11 7NG
☎ (01539) 558980 ☎ 07967 503689
⊕ fellbrewery.co.uk

⊠ Fell Brewery was founded in 2012 by homebrewer Tim Bloomer and friend Andrew Carter, brewing beers inspired by their travels in the US and Belgium.

YOLO (OG 1035, ABV 3.7%) ◄
A yellow-coloured, highly drinkable, hoppy session bitter with a long, drying bitter finish.

Cascadian (OG 1039, ABV 4%)
Traditional US-style pale ale made with Cascade hops.

Nectar (OG 1038, ABV 4.2%)
Intensely hoppy American pale ale.

Robust Porter (OG 1051, ABV 4.8%) ◄
Roast dominates throughout; fruit comes through on drinking, with a dry and bitter finish.

Tinderbox IPA (OG 1059, ABV 6.3%)
A strongly-hopped IPA with an initial sweetness leading to a lingering bitter aftertaste.

Fellows

2 Leopold Walk, Cottenham, Cambridgeshire, CB24 8XS
☎ (01954) 250262 ⊕ fellowsbrewery.co.uk

⊠ Fellows began production in 2010 though brewer Mark Burton had been developing recipes for a year or so before. Five regular beers are available with plans for a series of special ales. Beers are increasingly visible in the local free trade.

Cambridge Fellow (OG 1038, ABV 3.8%)
A golden session ale which uses just Challenger hops and is light and clean-tasting.

Gulping Fellow (OG 1042, ABV 4.2%)
A dry bitter finish complements the spicy hop character of this well-balanced best bitter.

Burton Snatch (OG 1048, ABV 4.8%)
Blonde ale with a citrus aroma and refreshing mouthfeel. A hint of wet leather completes the finish.

Jolly Fellows (OG 1050, ABV 5%)
Full-bodied, clean-tasting premium bitter.

Clever Fellow (OG 1052, ABV 5.2%)
Malt loaf and toffee flavours combine with back of the tongue bitterness to achieve a balanced richness.

Felstar

Felsted Vineyards, Crix Green, Felsted, Essex, CM6 3JT
☎ (01245) 361504 ☎ 07546 096374
⊕ felstarbrewery.co.uk

⊠ Felstar Brewery opened in 2001 with a five-barrel plant based in the old bonded warehouse of the Felsted Vineyard. A small number of outlets are supplied. ‼ ▤ ♦ RAIB

Felstar (OG 1036, ABV 3.6%)
Amber-coloured session bitter with an aroma of traditional English hops and a long bitter finish.

Summer Light (OG 1038, ABV 3.8%)

Old Essex (OG 1039, ABV 3.9%)

Crix Forest (OG 1040, ABV 4%)
A toasty dark mild with hints of berries, a hoppy nose and a bitter finish.

Lightburst (OG 1040, ABV 4%)

Witchcraft (OG 1044, ABV 4.4%)

Good Knight (OG 1050, ABV 5%)
A dark porter with gentle smoky and spicy flavours balancing the bitter hoppiness.

Hoppy Hen (OG 1050, ABV 5%)
An old ale with rich malty and spicy flavours and strong hoppy nose and bitter finish from American hops.

Pecking Order (OG 1050, ABV 5%)

Fernandes

⚑ 5 Avison Yard, Kirkgate, Wakefield, West Yorkshire, WF1 1UA
☎ (01924) 291709 ∰ ossett-brewery.co.uk

☺Opened in 1997 and housed in a 19th-century malthouse, Ossett Brewing Company purchased the brewery and tap in 2007 but independent brewing continues. Around 90 different beers are brewed each year. The tap sells Fernandes and Ossett beers as well as guest ales; the former are more widely available through Ossett's supply chain. ‼◆

Malt Shovel Mild (OG 1038, ABV 3.8%)
A dark, full-bodied, malty mild with roast malt and chocolate flavours, leading to a lingering, dry, malty finish.

Ale to the Tsar (OG 1042, ABV 4.1%)
A pale, smooth, well-balanced beer with some sweetness leading to a nutty, malty and satisfying aftertaste.

Centaur (OG 1045, ABV 4.5%)
A dry, pale ale with balanced notes of orange zest, coriander and pine.

Black Voodoo (OG 1050, ABV 5.1%)
Smooth, full-bodied black stout with chocolate, orange and vanilla flavours coming through.

Double Six (OG 1062, ABV 6%)
A powerful, dark and rich strong beer with an array of malt, roast malt and chocolate flavours and a strong, lasting malty finish, with some hoppiness.

Fierce (NEW)

Unit 46, Howe Moss Avenue, Dyce, AB21 0GP
∰ fiercebeer.com

Initially started by an enthusiastic home brewer, the brewery re-located to a factory unit in 2016. Production is currently KegKeg and bottles.

Fighting Cocks (NEW)

⚑ Fighting Cocks, 308 Red Lees Road, Burnley, BB10 4RQ
☎ (01282) 428255 ∰ ninosfightingcocks.co.uk

This brewery set up behind Nino's Italian restaurant started brewing in 2015.

FILO

⚑ The Old Town Brewery, Torfield Cottage, 8 Old London Road, Hastings, East Sussex, TN34 3HA
☎ (01424) 420212 ∰ filobrewing.co.uk

⊠ The brewery at the First In Last Out public house was established in 1985, with the current owners taking over in 1988. In 2011 the brewery relocated two minutes' walk away, remaining in the Old Town. The First In Last Out (FILO) is still supplied direct together with pubs throughout Sussex and Kent. ‼◆

Mike's Mild (OG 1035, ABV 3.4%)

Crofters (OG 1037, ABV 3.8%)

Churches Pale Ale (OG 1042, ABV 4.2%)

Old Town Tom (OG 1044, ABV 4.5%)

Gold (OG 1050, ABV 4.8%)

Fintry

23 Main Street, Fintry, Stirlingshire, G63 0XA
☎ (01360) 860224 ☎ 07833 662820
✉ bill@fintrymusos.co.uk

⊠ Fintry Brewing was established in 2013 in premises at the Fintry Inn. After expansion in 2015, it now uses an eight-barrel plant with a capacity of 2,600 litres a week. The beers are named after local hills and streams. ‼◆

Cringate Gold (OG 1037, ABV 3.7%)

Clachertyfarlie (OG 1039, ABV 3.9%)

Stronend (OG 1039, ABV 3.9%)

Knockbuckle (OG 1041, ABV 4.1%)

Meikle Bin (OG 1041, ABV 4.1%)

Firebird SIBA ◉

Old Rudgwick Brickworks, Lynwick Street, Rudgwick, West Sussex, RH12 3UW
☎ (01403) 823180 ∰ firebirdbrewing.co.uk

⊠ Firebird began brewing in 2013 and has grown rapidly with new beers, new vessels, and extended warehouse and an expanded team of seven people. ‼ ⬛◆RAIB

Heritage XX (OG 1041, ABV 4%)
A fresh, hoppy, full-bodied beer.

No. 79 (OG 1043, ABV 4.3%)
A pale, full-bodied and fruity golden ale.

Old Ale XXXX (OG 1045, ABV 4.5%)
A smooth, bittersweet dark ale with hints of roasted chocolate.

Paleface APA (OG 1053, ABV 5.2%)
A zesty, aromatic American pale ale.

Firebrick SIBA ◉

Units 10 & 11, Blaydon Business Centre, Cowen Road, Blaydon, Tyne & Wear, NE21 5TW
☎ (0191) 447 6543 ∰ firebrickbrewery.com

Firebrick began brewing in 2013 on a 2.5-barrel plant. Expansion in 2014 saw a new 14.5-barrel plant installed. Beers are available at selected pubs between North Yorkshire and the Scottish Borders. ◆

Blaydon Brick (OG 1038, ABV 3.8%)

Coalface (OG 1039, ABV 3.9%)

Tyne Nine (OG 1039, ABV 3.9%)

Pagan Queen (OG 1038, ABV 4%)

Trade Star (OG 1040, ABV 4.2%)

Stella Spark (OG 1041, ABV 4.4%)

Elder Statesman (OG 1044, ABV 4.5%)

Toon Broon (OG 1045, ABV 4.6%)

Firefly

Firefly, 54 Lowesmoor, Worcester, WR1 2SE
☎ (01905) 616996 ☎ 07525 445988
✉ thefirefly@hotmail.co.uk

⊗ A pub microbrewery, Firefly started brewing in 2012 using a 0.5-barrel plant. Brewing takes place from October to March. Each beer is unique as different recipes are used each time. ♦

Firehouse

Unit 8a, Harrison Way, Dowland Business Park, Manby, Lincolnshire, LN11 8UX ☎ 07956 405089
⊕ firehouse-brewery.co.uk

☺ Firehouse was founded by Jason Allen in 2014 and uses a 2.5-barrel plant.

Mainwarings Mild (ABV 3.6%)
A dark, malty mild based on a wartime recipe.

FGB (ABV 3.9%)

Woodman Pale Ale (ABV 4.4%)
Pale yellow-coloured, fruity, sweetish session bitter with a dry, hoppy finish.

Wobbly Weasel (ABV 4.9%)
Complex ale, rich and fruity in the mouth with an intense bittersweet finish.

Firestorm

See Wharfe Bank

First Chop SIBA ◉

Unit 3, Trinity Row, Trinity Way, Salford, M3 5EN
☎ 07970 241398 ⊕ firstchopbrewingarm.com

First Chop Brewing Arm was established in 2012 at the Outstanding Brewery in Bury. Production was transferred to Salford in 2013 and the brewery now uses an eight-barrel plant situated in a railway arch, which also contains a secret garden and reggae sound system.

AVA (OG 1034, ABV 3.5%)
A hoppy blonde session ale.

MIA (OG 1035, ABV 3.5%)
A session ale with bags of malt and hop character.

DOC (OG 1038, ABV 4.1%)
A pale ale with big hoppy flavours and a pleasant lingering bitterness.

HOP (OG 1038, ABV 4.1%)
A pale ale with massive hop flavours.

TEA (OG 1048, ABV 5%)
A full-bodied pale ale.

SIP (OG 1052, ABV 5.4%)
A full-bodied strong pale ale with tropical fruit flavours.

SYL (OG 1064, ABV 6.4%)
A black IPA.

Fish Key (NEW)

1 Granite Quay, Looe, Cornwall, PL13 1DX

☎ (01726) 870007 ☎ 07814 019250

Fish Key started production in 2016. Three local outlets are supplied at present.

Hop2It (OG 1039, ABV 4%)

Hip Hop (OG 1044, ABV 4.5%)

Fisher's (NEW)

45 Wyatt Close, High Wycombe, Buckinghamshire, HP13 5YX ⊕ fishersbrew.co.uk

Established in 2013 and operating out of his garage at home, owner and brewer Mike Fisher hopes to move to larger premises and expand to a six-barrel plant. Beers are supplied to two pubs in High Wycombe, the Bootlegger and Sausage Tree. RAIB

Five Kingdoms

Steam Packet Inn, Harbour Row, Isle of Whithorn, DG8 8LL
☎ (01988) 500334 ⊕ thesteampacketinn.biz

☺Five Kingdoms was established in 2015 by Alistair Scoular, owner of the Steam Packet Inn, using a 2.5-barrel plant. The pub, selected beer festivals and a few local outlets are supplied. Bottle-conditioned beers are planned. ♦

Dr Rudi's Blonde (OG 1040, ABV 4%)
Refreshing, hoppy and light ale with a long bitter finish.

Pale (OG 1045, ABV 4.5%)
Refreshing session ale with floral and citrus notes and a clean, crisp finish.

Captain Morrison IPA (OG 1052, ABV 5.2%)
Hoppy, American-style IPA.

Bisby Blonde (OG 1054, ABV 5.4%)
A refreshing, hoppy golden ale with a long finish.

Dark Storm Stout (OG 1066, ABV 6.8%)
Smooth, strong stout with dark chocolate notes and a hoppy background.

Five Oh

83 Agecroft Road West, Prestwich, M25 9RF ☎ 07772 243089 ✉ fiveohbrewco@sky.com

Five Oh began brewing in 2014 on a small scale focusing on bottled beers, which are based on international styles or have some unusual ingredients. Some of its range is suitable for vegans. Beers are available from selected specialists in Manchester's Northern Quarter and Prestwich. RAIB

Five Points SIBA ◉

3 Institute Place, Hackney Downs, London, E8 1JE
☎ (020) 8533 7746 ⊕ fivepointsbrewing.co.uk

Five Points commenced brewing in 2013 on a 10-barrel plant in the heart of Hackney. Based in a railway arch under Hackney Downs Railway Station, the brewery takes its name from the five-way junction where Dalston Lane, Amhurst Road and Pembury Road meet, the Five Points. Beers are available unfiltered in bottles. RAIB

Pale Ale (OG 1044, ABV 4.4%) ✎
Strong, fruity, bitter golden-coloured ale with citrus and tropical fruit fading in the aftertaste, where the bitterness lingers.

Railway Porter (ABV 4.8%) ◆
Roasted black malt throughout creating a dry roasted finish, softened by a treacle sweetness. Some caramelised fruit and peppery hops.

Red Rye (ABV 6%) ◆
Treacle notes on nose and flavour linger in the dry bitterness, which builds on drinking. The mouthfeel is creamy.

Five Towns

651 Leeds Road, Outwood, Wakefield, West Yorkshire, WF1 2LU
☎ (01924) 781887
✉ malcolmbastow@googlemail.com

⊕Five Towns began production on a 2.5-barrel plant in 2008 and mostly supplies outlets in Yorkshire. ◆ RAIB

Outwood Bound (OG 1040, ABV 4.2%)
A chestnut-coloured beer with a toffee nose and strong, dry, bitter finish.

Callum's Best (OG 1041, ABV 4.6%)
A dark-coloured bitter with a full flavour and bitter finish.

Ponte Carlo Stout (OG 1048.7, ABV 4.6%)
Bitter chocolate and malt aromas, smooth malt and chocolate with a hint of liquorice in the mouth and a dry, bittersweet finish.

Niamh's Nemesis (OG 1053, ABV 5.7%)
A full-bodied IPA with hints of grapefruit before a dry finish.

Fixed Wheel SIBA ⊙

Unit 9, Long Lane Trading Estate, Long Lane, Blackheath, West Midlands, B62 9LD ☎ 07766 162794 ⊕ fixedwheelbrewery.co.uk

⊠ Set up in 2014 by cycling and brewing enthusiasts Scott Povey and Sharon Bryant, this full mash brewery is situated on a trading estate on the Blackheath/Halesowen border. It brews three times a week using an eight-barrel plant. ‼ ◆ RAIB

Chain Reaction Pale Ale (OG 1042, ABV 4.2%)
A session ale with orange and citrus flavours.

Blackheath Stout (OG 1050, ABV 5%)
A full-bodied, fruity stout with an oaky bitterness and a smooth, creamy, dark fruits finish.

No Brakes IPA (OG 1059, ABV 5.9%)
An American-style IPA packed full of classic American hops delivering upfront fruity citrus flavours. English Maris Otter adds some balance to the hops with a touch of sweetness.

Carbon Black IPA (OG 1060, ABV 6%)
A black IPA, intensely hoppy on the palate with huge tropical aroma and flavours.

Flack Manor SIBA ⊙

8 Romsey Industrial Estate, Greatbridge Road, Romsey, Hampshire, SO51 0HR
☎ (01794) 518520 ⊕ flackmanor.co.uk

⊠ Flack Manor commenced brewing in 2010 using a 20-barrel plant purchased from Canada. The brewery employs the 'double drop' method of fermentation. Beers are supplied to local outlets within approximately 30 miles of Romsey. ‼ ➤ ◆ RAIB

Flack's Double Drop (OG 1037, ABV 3.7%) ◆
Brown session bitter. Hops and some bitterness in the taste with more hoppiness and some malt in a long finish.

Flack Catcher (OG 1045, ABV 4.4%) ◆
Well-balanced best bitter with malty nose and citrus hints. Hoppy taste balanced with fruity sweetness and a lingering finish.

Hedge Hop (OG 1050, ABV 4.9%)
Deep, biscuity maltiness balanced with exotic fruit and spicy flavours.

Flash

Moss Top Farm, Moss Top Lane, Flash, Staffordshire, SK17 0TA ✉ flashbrewery@hotmail.com

The brewery is located high in the Peak District and was founded by two friends who brew on a part-time basis. All natural ingredients are used including spring water and seaweed finings, which make the beer suitable for vegans. Due to the altitude a brick boiler was found and is used in the brewing process rather than electrical equipment. Three bottle-conditioned beers are produced and are sold at Leek market, which is the only sales outlet. RAIB V

Flipside SIBA ⊙

The Brewhouse, Private Road No. 2, Colwick, Nottinghamshire, NG4 2JR
☎ (0115) 987 7500 ☎ 07958 752334
⊕ flipsidebrewery.co.uk

⊠ Andrew and Maggie Dunkin established their six-barrel brewery in an industrial unit in Colwick in 2010. With production at full capacity the brewery expanded to 12 barrels in 2013 and relocated to a larger adjacent unit. In 2012 the Flipping Good Beer Shop opened, which also operates online. In 2014 Flipside's brewery tap opened, the Volunteer in nearby Carlton. Other pubs are also operated in the local area. ‼ ➤ ◆ RAIB

Sterling Pale (OG 1039, ABV 3.9%) ◆
Golden ale with a citrus aroma and hoppy taste, leading to a bitter and peppery finish.

Dark Denomination (OG 1041, ABV 4%)
Well-rounded, mildly-hopped beer. Chocolate and caramel malt flavours combine delicately with blackcurrant hop flavours to produce a strikingly tasty ale.

Copper Penny (OG 1043, ABV 4.2%)
An easy-drinking session bitter. Light brown, moderately bitter but with good hop flavours, ending with a hint of tangerine.

Golden Sovereign (OG 1043, ABV 4.2%)
A golden session ale. Refreshingly bitter with dry biscuit flavours. American hops are added to produce a pleasant citrus and grapefruit flavour in the finish.

Franc in Stein (OG 1043, ABV 4.3%) ◆
Golden ale with a floral hop aroma, leading to a hoppy and bitter finish.

Random Toss (OG 1044, ABV 4.4%)
A refreshing pale ale with lemon and lime tropical fruit flavours.

Kopek Stout (OG 1046, ABV 4.5%) ◆

Full-bodied dark stout with a coffee aroma and assertive roast flavours throughout and a balanced bitterness.

Flipping Best (OG 1046, ABV 4.6%) ◆
Brown-coloured malty strong bitter with lasting malt, bitterness and subtle hop flavours.

Dusty Penny (OG 1052, ABV 5%)
A full-bodied porter bursting with chocolate and caramel malt flavours, rounded off with bitterness provided by traditional English hops.

Clippings IPA (OG 1062, ABV 6.5%)
A traditional IPA, golden in colour with crushed gooseberry and bitter white wine hop flavours.

Russian Rouble (OG 1072, ABV 7.3%) ◆
Strong dark stout with balanced malt, roast and fruit flavours.

Flowerpots SIBA

◼ **Brandy Mount, Cheriton, Hampshire, SO24 0QQ**
☎ **(01962) 771534** ⊕ **flowerpotscheriton.co.uk**

⊗ Flowerpots began production in 2006. Brewster Catherine Bate heads the brewing team. Many local outlets are supplied direct. ◆

Perridge Pale (OG 1035.5, ABV 3.6%) ◆
Pale, easy-drinking golden ale. Honey-scented with high hops, grapefruit and bitterness throughout. Crisp with some citrus notes.

Bitter (OG 1038, ABV 3.8%) ◆
Dry, earthy hop flavours balanced by malt. Good bitterness with some hop in aroma and sharp, bitter finish. Refreshing bitter.

Goodens Gold (OG 1046, ABV 4.8%) ◆
Complex full-bodied golden ale, bursting with hops and citrus fruit and a snatch of sweetness, leading to a long, dry finish.

Flying Monk SIBA ⊚

Unit 1, Bradfield Manor Farm, Hullavington, Wiltshire, SN14 6EU
☎ **(01666) 838415** ☎ **07896 600901**
⊕ **theflyingmonkbrewery.co.uk**

⊗ Established in 2014, the Flying Monk uses a 20-barrel plant and supplies to some 200 outlets regionally and utilises national wholesalers. 🚚◆

Elmers (OG 1040, ABV 3.8%)
A pale bitter.

Habit (OG 1045, ABV 4.2%)
An amber-coloured traditional best bitter with a contrast of sweet and bitter hop flavours.

Birdman (OG 1049, ABV 4.7%)
A refreshing golden-coloured premium bitter, well-hopped and full bodied.

Fool Hardy SIBA

◼ **Hope Inn, 118 Wellington Road North, Heaton Norris, SK4 2LL**
☎ **(0161) 637 6191** ⊕ **foolhardyales.co.uk**

☺ Martin and Samantha Wood bought the Hope Inn in 2012 and installed the brewery in the cellar. The beers first went on sale in 2013. In 2014 the brew kit was upgraded, almost doubling capacity to 4.5 barrels. A sister pub, Spring Gardens in Marple Bridge, opened in 2016. Local festivals are also supplied. ‼◆ RAIB

Jack's Ripper (OG 1034, ABV 3.4%)
A smooth, complex and dark oatmeal stout.

Rhidonkulous (OG 1037, ABV 3.7%)
A pale session ale with zesty citrus notes.

Rash Dash (OG 1038, ABV 3.8%)
A rich copper-coloured beer with a light floral aroma. Initial toffee flavour immediately gives way to a bombardment of hops that linger for a long aftertaste.

Ravenous Romp (OG 1038, ABV 3.8%)
A contemporary twist on the traditional bitter, brewed with New World hops.

Rival Blond (OG 1039, ABV 4%)
A pale blonde session ale, hoppy and zesty with distinct fruity flavours from the New Zealand hops.

Rou Shou (OG 1042.4, ABV 4.3%)
A clean-drinking, sweet, refreshing pale ale with a strong floral aroma and elderflower notes.

Risky Blond (OG 1042, ABV 4.4%)
An easy-drinking golden ale with a good balance of hops, subtle hints of citrus and a well-rounded finish.

Reckless Danger (OG 1054, ABV 5%)
A sweet-tasting beer with bitterness poking through. A clean, hoppy finish and moderate aftertaste.

Russian Roulette (OG 1049, ABV 5%)
A crisp, hoppy, distinctive and bitter IPA.

Force

Unit 2, Global Business Park, Wilkinson Road, Cirencester, Gloucestershire, GL7 1YZ ☎ **07532 097050** ⊕ **forcebrewery.com**

Force Brewery was established in 2014 using a four-barrel gravity-fed brew plant. Carry-out ales are available direct from the brewery, which hosts regular tours and is a licensed venue for events. ‼ RAIB

Chasing Leather (OG 1041, ABV 4%)
An aromatic pale ale packed with the grapefruit smack of Chinook hops.

Yankee Zulu (OG 1039, ABV 4%)
A golden bitter. Subtle, spicy bitterness and mellow, floral aromas are given by the blend of hops.

Ephemeral Tan (OG 1046, ABV 4.5%)
A bronze-coloured ale, with a touch of caramel and a spiciness on the palate.

Thunderball (OG 1051, ABV 5%)
A robust stout. Deep, roasty flavours are met with a gentle smoothness from the aroma of the Phoenix hop.

Forge SIBA

Ford Hill Forge, Hartland, Devon, EX39 6EE
☎ **(01237) 440015** ☎ **07837 487800**
⊕ **forgebrewery.co.uk**

⊗ This multi award-winning brewery was set up near Bideford in Devon by Dave Lang, who commenced brewing in 2008 using a five-barrel plant. There are plans for relocation. ◆ RAIB

Discovery (OG 1039, ABV 3.8%) ◆

Light and hoppy beer with a dominant bitter aftertaste. Hops on the nose and throughout the flavour, becoming faintly dry.

Devon Maid (OG 1040, ABV 4%)

Hartland Blonde (OG 1040, ABV 4%)
A light, hoppy beer with citrus notes.

Litehouse (OG 1042, ABV 4.3%)
Golden in colour, hints of elderflower with a citrus bite.

IPA (OG 1044, ABV 4.5%)
A light, hoppy beer with grapefruit and citrus notes.

Ascension (OG 1046, ABV 4.6%)
Amber-coloured beer with complex hop notes.

Rev Hawker (OG 1046, ABV 4.6%)

Dreckly (OG 1046, ABV 4.8%)
A warm, ruby-coloured strong premium ale fortified with gorse and heather, rich in malt with a spicy aroma and a malty aftertaste.

Handsome (OG 1048, ABV 5.1%)
A light brown-coloured, well-balanced, hoppy beer.

Foundry

See Canterbury Brewers

Four Candles SIBA

⬛ 1 Sowell Street, St Peters, Kent, CT10 2AT ☎ 07947 062063 ⊕ thefourcandles.co.uk

⊠ Based in the cellar of the micro pub of the same name, Four Candles uses a 2.5-barrel plant and produces up to 10 nine-gallon casks with each brew. Never brewing the same ale twice, the brewery supplies the micro pub, which is named after the celebrated Two Ronnies sketch.

Fourpure SIBA 👁

22 Bermondsey Trading Estate, Rotherhithe New Road, London, SE16 3LL
☎ (020) 3744 2141 ⊕ fourpure.com

Fourpure began brewing in 2013. Beers are available in cans and kegs, unfiltered, unpasteurised and unfined. Occasional bottle-conditioned beers are also available. ⌷RAIB

Fownes

25 Clarence Street, Upper Gornal, West Midlands, DY3 1UL ☎ 07790 766844

Office: 42 The Ridgeway, Sedgley, West Midlands, DY3 3UR ⊕ fownesbrewing.co.uk

☺The brewery was established in 2012 by James and Tom Fownes in premises to the rear of the Jolly Crispin in Upper Gornal. It expanded to a three-barrel plant in 2014. Beers are available in the Jolly Crispin and a number of free houses in the Midlands. ‼◆RAIB

Elephant Riders (OG 1039, ABV 3.9%)

Gunhild (OG 1041, ABV 4%)
A honey ale.

Origin (OG 1040, ABV 4%)

Crispin's Ommer (OG 1038, ABV 4.1%)

Frost Hammer (OG 1047, ABV 4.6%)
A pale ale with a bitter dryness punctuated by a strong grapefruit aroma.

Ulfsberg Cross (OG 1045, ABV 4.8%)
A traditional bitter made using only Bramling Cross hops.

Firebeard's Old Favourite No. 5 Ruby Ale (OG 1051, ABV 5%)
A rich ruby-coloured mild ale full of malty flavour with fruity notes.

Prophets of Doom (OG 1049, ABV 5%)

Troll Hunter (OG 1051, ABV 5.3%)

King Korvak's Saga (OG 1058, ABV 5.4%) ▮
A traditional porter with roast chocolate flavours.

Fox

⬛ 22 Station Road, Heacham, Norfolk, PE31 7EX
☎ (01485) 570345 ⊕ foxbrewery.co.uk

⊠ Based in an old cottage adjacent to the Fox & Hounds pub, Fox Brewery was established in 2002 and now supplies around 30 outlets as well as the pub. All the Branthill beers are brewed from barley grown on Branthill Farm and malted at Crisps in Great Ryburgh. A hop garden next to the brewery, trialled during 2009, has been enlarged. ‼ ⌷◆RAIB

Branthill Best (OG 1037, ABV 3.9%)

Red Knocker (OG 1037, ABV 3.9%)
Copper-coloured and malty beer.

LJB (OG 1040, ABV 4%) ◀
A well-balanced malty brew with a hoppy, bitter background. Long finish with a growing sultana-like fruitiness.

Bullet (OG 1042, ABV 4.2%)
Pale golden yellow-coloured beer with resinous hop aroma and tropical fruit flavours.

Branthill Norfolk Nectar (OG 1043, ABV 4.3%)

Warrior (OG 1043, ABV 4.4%)

Cascade (OG 1051, ABV 5%)

Nelson's Blood (OG 1049, ABV 5.1%)
A liquor of beers. Red-coloured and full-bodied. Made with Nelson's Blood rum.

IPA (OG 1051, ABV 5.2%)

Foxfield SIBA

⬛ Prince of Wales, Foxfield, Cumbria, LA20 6BX
☎ (01229) 716238 ⊕ princeofwalesfoxfield.co.uk

☺Foxfield is a 4.5-barrel plant in old stables attached to the Prince of Wales. Several other outlets are supplied. Tiger Tops in Wakefield is also owned. The beer range constantly changes. Dark Mild is suitable for vegans. ‼◆V

Dark Mild (OG 1040, ABV 3.7%) ◀
Traditional dark mild, low hop bitterness is compensated for with sweetness and roast malts.

Franklins SIBA

1066 Country Brewery, Pebsham Farm Industrial Estate, Pebsham Lane, Bexhill-on-Sea, East Sussex, TN40 2RZ
☎ (01424) 731066 ⊕ franklinsbrewery.co.uk

⊠ Franklins brews on a 10-barrel kit in a converted milking barn in the Sussex countryside. Steve

Medniuk is sole owner. Beers are supplied throughout the South east, London and beyond. There are plans for expansion to a 15-barrel kit, and bottle-conditioned beers will soon be available. ‼

English Garden (OG 1042, ABV 3.8%)
A hoppy, golden ale perfect for session drinking.

Mumma Knows Best (OG 1043, ABV 4.1%)
A refreshing traditional English best bitter, rich in mango, lemon and earthy pine.

Citra IPA (OG 1056, ABV 5.5%)
Single-hopped IPA, bursting with citrus and lychee flavours and aroma.

Smoked Porter (OG 1052, ABV 5.5%)
A rich, intense, satisfying porter made with oatmeal. Added chipotle chillies accentuate the smokiness and provide a touch of heat.

Free Radical (NEW)

SK4 4AG ☎ 07575 538385
✉ freeradicalbrewco@gmail.com

Production began in 2016 using spare capacity at breweries around Manchester.

Freedom SIBA

1 Park Lodge House, Bagots Park, Abbots Bromley, Staffordshire, WS15 3ES
☎ (01283) 840721 ⊕ freedomlager.com

No real ale. Freedom specialises in producing hand-crafted English lagers, all brewed in accordance with the German Reinheitsgebot purity law. Six beers are currently produced and pale ale was introduced in 2016. ‼ ⇶

Freeminer

Whimsey Road, Steam Mills, Cinderford, Gloucestershire, GL14 3JA
☎ (01594) 827989 ⊕ freeminerbrewery.co.uk

Founded by Don Burgess in 1992, Freeminer – previously Freeminer Brewery – changed hands in 2006 but Don Burgess remained in post. Bottle-conditioned beers are available (brewed for the Co-op). Co-op beers are now brewed with barley grown on Co-op farms and malted at Warminster. Fairtrade and organic beers are also produced, with limited edition cask versions available for Fairtrade fortnight. Brewing is temporarily suspended. ♦ RAIB

Freewheelin'

Shed 3, South Park, Peebles, EH45 9ED ☎ 07802 175826 ⊕ freewheelinbrewery.co.uk

Freewheelin' began brewing in 2013. ♦

Blonde (OG 1040, ABV 3.8%)

XX Bitter (OG 1044, ABV 4.2%)

Dizzy Blonde (OG 1045, ABV 4.3%)

Ruby (OG 1046, ABV 4.4%)

Frensham SIBA

The Old Dairy, Pierrepont Home Farm, The Reeds, Frensham, Surrey, GU10 3BS
☎ (01252) 793956 ☎ 07505 798380
⊕ frenshambrewery.co.uk

⊠ Set in the Surrey countryside, Frensham is a microbrewery situated in a 17th-century restored barn on a working dairy farm. The brewery is due to move to a new premises (on the other side of the courtyard) in 2016 featuring a new brewery tap room with events taking place on occasional Saturday evenings. ⇶♦

Soul (OG 1038, ABV 3.8%)
A light, floral session beer with biscuit orange notes.

Rambler (OG 1039, ABV 3.9%)
A golden, refreshing session ale, fruity hops with an oak edge give rise to a satisfying bitterness. A well-rounded and interesting combination of both floral and hop aromas make for an easy, light beer.

Forager (OG 1045, ABV 4.5%)
Rich copper-coloured ale. A complex floral aroma with subtle oak/vanilla notes, offset with a caramel/spicy hop balance. Lingering bitter finish.

Friday Beer

Unit 4, Link Business Centre, Malvern, Worcestershire, WR14 1UQ
☎ (01684) 572648 ⊕ thefridaybeer.com

Founded in 2011, the Friday Beer Co primarily produces bottle-conditioned ales, selling across the Three Counties. Available cask-conditioned in a small number of local pubs. ‼ ⇶RAIB

Jubilee (OG 1034, ABV 3.1%)
Full of flavour and easy-drinking modern session mild.

Summer Hill Blonde (OG 1043, ABV 4.3%)

Pinnacle (OG 1046, ABV 4.5%)

Black Hill Stout (OG 1052, ABV 4.7%)
A smooth, sweet stout full of complex malty flavours.

Friday Gold (OG 1054, ABV 5.6%)
A refreshing golden ale with a smooth texture and flavour and a slight taste of citrus.

Friends Arms

▤ Old St Clears Road, Johnstown, SA31 3HH
☎ (01267) 234073 ⊕ thefriendsarms.co.uk

⊠ Friends Arms Brewery opened in 2011 on the premises of the Friends Arms, a traditional local community pub, which acts as the brewery tap. Brewing is sporadic so before embarking on a journey to sample the beers an enquiry to check availability is recommended.

Frog Island SIBA

The Maltings, Westbridge, St James Road, Northampton, NN5 5HS
☎ (01604) 587772 ⊕ frogislandbrewery.co.uk

Established in 1994, Frog Island specialises in beers with personalised bottle labels, available by mail order. The brewery changed hands in 2013 and is now run by husband-and-wife team Paul Burchell and Zoe Cushnie. Around 40 free trade outlets are supplied as well as some Everards pubs. ‼ ♦ RAIB

Best Bitter (OG 1038, ABV 3.8%) ◗
Blackcurrant and gooseberry enhance the full malty aroma with pineapple and papaya joining on the tongue. Bitterness develops in the fairly long finish.

Lock, Stock & Barrel (OG 1040, ABV 4%)
A rounded bittersweet malt taste is complemented by the hops, which lead to a refreshing bitter finish.

Shoemaker (OG 1043, ABV 4.2%) ◈
An orange aroma of fruity hops is balanced by malt. Citrus and hoppy bitterness last into a long, dry finish. Amber in colour.

Amber Daze (OG 1043, ABV 4.3%)
An amber-coloured beer with an orange citrus aftertaste.

TOC (That Old Chestnut Porter) (OG 1044, ABV 4.4%)
A smooth, easy-drinking porter-style beer with subtle roasted notes. Cascade hops bring a sweet spiciness to the beer while Target hops contribute bitterness to the dry, malty finish.

Natterjack (OG 1048, ABV 4.8%) ◈
Deceptively robust, golden and smooth. Fruit and hop aromas fight for dominance before the grainy astringency and floral palate give way to a long, dry aftertaste.

Fire Bellied Toad (OG 1048, ABV 5%) ◈
Amber-gold brew with a long bitter/fruity finish. Huge malt and hop flavours have a hint of apples.

Croak & Stagger (OG 1054, ABV 5.6%) ◈
The initial honey/fruit aroma is quickly overpowered by roast malt then bitter chocolate and pale malt sweetness on the tongue. Gentle, bittersweet finish.

Front Row SIBA

Unit 1 Hopkins Close, Greenfield Farm Industrial Estate, Congleton, Cheshire, CW12 4TR
☎ (01260) 289055 ☎ 07861 718673
⊕ frontrowbrewing.co.uk

After starting operations on a 2.5-barrel plant in 2012, Front Row expanded to an eight-barrel plant in 2014 to meet demand. Beers are available nationally through brewery swaps and wholesalers. ‼◆

Crouch (OG 1039, ABV 3.8%)

Touch (OG 1037, ABV 4%)

Pause (OG 1049, ABV 4.5%)

Engage (OG 1047, ABV 4.8%)

Collapsed (OG 1051, ABV 5.6%)

Frontier

See Lenton Lane

Froth Blowers SIBA

Unit W34, Hastingwood Industrial Park, Wood Lane, Erdington, West Midlands, B24 9QR ☎ 07908 056009
⊕ frothblower.co.uk

⊗ Froth Blowers began brewing in 2013. The brewery now has the capacity to brew 20 barrels at a new site only metres away from its current site. The new capacity will be used when needed; otherwise the existing six-barrel plant is still operational. ◆

Piffle Snonker (OG 1038, ABV 3.8%)
A light blonde beer with a floral nose and sweet start but a bitter finish.

Bar-King Mad (OG 1042, ABV 4.2%)

Wellingtonian (OG 1043, ABV 4.3%)
A pale ale made with two New Zealand hops.

John Bull's Best (OG 1044, ABV 4.4%)
A golden, balanced bitter, using traditional British malts and hops.

Gollop With Zest (OG 1045, ABV 4.5%)
A blonde beer with a floral start and a citrus finish.

Hornswoggle (OG 1050, ABV 5%)
A full-bodied blonde beer with a floral nose and sweetish start, soon replaced by a dry and satisfying bitterness.

Fugelestou

See Fulstow

Fuggle Bunny SIBA 👁

Unit 1, Meadowbrook Park Industrial Estate, Station Road, Holbrook, South Yorkshire, S20 3PJ
☎ (0114) 248 4541 ☎ 07813 763347
⊕ fugglebunnybrewhouse.co.uk

This husband-and-wife team commenced brewing in 2014. The brewery name arose from a combination of an English hop (Fuggle) and the image of a rabbit (synonymous with rebirth and resurrection) symbolising the rebirth of brewing in Sheffield following the wholesale closure of major breweries in the city during the 1990s. ‼🍴

Chapter 5 Oh Crumbs (OG 1038, ABV 3.8%)
Amber-coloured with hints of spice, cedar and pine. Sweet caramel and biscuity flavours give a distinctive finish.

Chapter 2 Cotton Tail (OG 1040, ABV 4%)
Uplifting, fruity aromas of lychees and citrus with a dry, hoppy finish.

Chapter 6 Hazy Summer Daze (OG 1042, ABV 4.2%)
Totally tropical with mango, lime, apricot, melon, lychees and grapefruit with fresh floral aromas.

Chapter 8 Jammy Dodger (OG 1045, ABV 4.5%)
A ruby red ale with hints of blackberries, liquorice and caramel and a malty undertone.

Chapter 1 New Beginnings (OG 1049, ABV 4.9%)
Amber-coloured classic bitter with a sweet edge of honey and spice leading to a dry hoppy aftertaste.

Chapter 3 Orchard Gold (OG 1050, ABV 5%)
Golden ale with hints of spice and honey and an earthy undertone.

Chapter 7 Russian Rare-Bit (OG 1050, ABV 5%)
Dark, malty and complex with an intriguing twist of chocolate, coffee and liquorice aromas. British hops lend bittering qualities.

Chapter 4 24 Carrot (OG 1060, ABV 6%)
Smooth aromas of citrus and blackberry with a spicy blanket of malt flavoured hoppiness.

Fulflood Arms

▤ **28 Cheriton Road, Winchester, Hampshire, SO22 5EF**
☎ (01962) 842996
✉ thefulfloodarms@hotmail.co.uk

Established in 2012 in a Greene King pub using a one-barrel plant, the brewery now uses a 1.5-barrel kit. The beer is supplied to the Fulflood Arms pub or its sister pub, the Queen Inn. Brewing is currently suspended.

Full Mash SIBA

17 Lower Park Street, Stapleford, Nottinghamshire, NG9 8EW
☎ (0115) 949 9262 ⊕ fullmash.net

⊛Brewing commenced in 2003, and since then the brewery has grown steadily, with a gradual expansion in outlets and capacity. ♦

Horse & Jockey (OG 1039, ABV 3.8%) ◄
Easy-drinking golden ale with moderate hoppy aroma and finish.

Seance (OG 1041, ABV 4%) ◄
Predominantly hoppy golden beer, with a refreshing bitter finish.

Illuminati (OG 1043, ABV 4.2%) ◄
Gently hopped golden ale with initial hops and bitterness giving way to a short bitter finish.

Wheat Ear (OG 1043, ABV 4.2%)
Pale, clear wheat beer, fruity and aromatic.

Warlord (OG 1045, ABV 4.4%) ◄
Amber-coloured beer with an initial malt taste leading to a dry bitter finish.

Apparition (OG 1046, ABV 4.5%) ◄
A pale, hoppy bitter brewed with Brewers Gold hops.

Nevermore (OG 1047, ABV 4.6%)
Well-rounded stout with soft roast chocolate flavours.

Manhaton Pale?? (OG 1053, ABV 5.2%)
Refreshing, pale American-style IPA with a complex citrus aroma and big hop finish.

Bhisti (OG 1063, ABV 6.2%)
Strong IPA with a warning kick of bitterness.

Fuller's 👁

Griffin Brewery, Chiswick Lane South, London, W4 2QB
☎ (020) 8996 2000 ⊕ fullers.co.uk

⊗ Fuller, Smith and Turner's Griffin Brewery has stood on the same site in Chiswick for more than 350 years. The partnership from which the company now takes its name was formed in 1845 and members of the founding families are still involved in running the company today. At the end of 2005 Fuller's announced an agreed acquisition of Hampshire brewer George Gale. The company now operates 362 pubs and hotels. Fuller's stopped brewing at the Gale's Horndean site in 2006 and all the brands, including some seasonals, are now brewed at Chiswick. ‼ ⌦ ♦ RAIB

Chiswick Bitter (OG 1034.5, ABV 3.5%) ◄
Refreshing pale brown bitter with some citrus notes on the palate fading in the aftertaste, which is hoppy and slightly dry. Aroma is of hops with a trace of biscuit.

London Pride (OG 1040.5, ABV 4.1%) ◄
Well-balanced, smooth best bitter with orange citrus fruit, malt and hops in aroma and flavour, which linger into a slightly bitter aftertaste. Honey and toffee develop as the beer matures.

Bengal Lancer (OG 1049.5, ABV 5%) ◄
Rich, creamy and well-balanced pale brown IPA with a gold hue. Hops with a dryish bitterness

harmonise with the fruit and malty sweetness that linger into the aftertaste.

ESB (OG 1054, ABV 5.5%) ◄
Bitter orange marmalade with hops, creamy toffee and some raisins are all present in this multifaceted strong brown bitter. A satisfying long, bitter, dry finish balanced by a malty sweetness.

Brewed under the Gale's brand name:

Seafarers Ale (OG 1036.8, ABV 3.6%) ◄
A pale brown bitter, predominantly malty, with a refreshing balance of fruit and hops that lingers into the aftertaste, where a dry bitterness unfolds.

HSB (OG 1050, ABV 4.8%) ◄
Dates and dried fruit with some spicy hops in the nose adding to the caramelised orange and treacle in the flavour of this smooth brown beer. Malty throughout with a bittersweet finish.

Fulstow

🍺 **13 Thames Street, Louth, Lincolnshire, LN11 7AD**
☎ (01507) 608202 ⊕ fulstowbrewery.com

Fulstow operates on a 2.5-barrel plant and started brewing in Fulstow in 2004, before moving to Louth in 2006. 'Fugelestou Ales' are one-off beers produced along with the regular range, all only available at the brewery tap, the Gas Lamp Lounge in Louth. ‼ ⌦ RAIB

Common (OG 1038, ABV 3.8%)
A copper-coloured, medium-bodied beer with a strong hop character and malt discernable in the taste.

Marsh Mild (OG 1039, ABV 3.8%)
Traditional mild with a malty aroma. Chocolate malt on the palate with toffee and caramel overtones.

Northway IPA (OG 1042, ABV 4.2%)
A clean, crisp ale with a citrus aroma; hoppy with a dry finish.

Pride of Fulstow (OG 1045, ABV 4.5%)
Copper-coloured bitter with a ripe malt taste in the mouth and a good hop balance. A dry finish with blackcurrant fruit notes.

Sledgehammer Stout (OG 1077, ABV 8%)
A strong, dark stout with raisin and liquorice and roast barley notes balanced by a strong hop flavour.

Funfair

🍺 **Chequers Inn, Toad Lane, Elston, Nottinghamshire, NG23 5NS**
☎ (01636) 525257 ☎ 07971 540186
⊕ funfairbrewingcompany.co.uk

Funfair was launched in 2004 in Holbrook, relocated to Ilkeston, Derbyshire then relocated again in 2012 to the Chequers Inn in Elston, where a new 10-barrel plant is used. The Chequers also serves as the brewery tap. More than 40 outlets are supplied. ‼ ♦ RAIB

Gallopers (OG 1037, ABV 3.8%)
A well-hopped, pale session bitter.

Teacups (OG 1040, ABV 4%)
A traditional ginger beer.

Waltzer (OG 1044, ABV 4.5%)
Copper-coloured, easy-drinking bitter.

Brandy Snap (OG 1046, ABV 4.7%)
A golden ale containing root ginger.

Dive Bomber (OG 1047, ABV 4.7%)
Refreshing, straw-coloured premium ale.

Dodgem (OG 1047, ABV 4.7%)
Golden premium pale ale with a unique blend of hops.

Fuzzy Duck SIBA

18 Wood Street, Poulton Industrial Estate, Poulton-le-Fylde, Lancashire, FY6 8JY ☎ 07904 343729 ⊕ fuzzyduckbrewery.co.uk

Fuzzy Duck was established in 2006 as a commercial home-based brewery. It relocated to Poulton-le-Fylde later that year, expanding capacity to an eight-barrel plant. The brewery delivers over a wide area of North west England and Yorkshire. ‼◆

Golden Cascade (OG 1038, ABV 3.8%)
Golden-coloured ale brewed with Cascade hops for a citrus flavour and floral aroma.

Mucky Duck (OG 1042, ABV 4%)
Dark stout, slightly sweet with chocolate and coffee notes from the roasted malt.

Pheasant Plucker (OG 1042, ABV 4.2%)
Amber-coloured beer with a slightly spicy taste and a citrus finish.

Cunning Stunt (OG 1044, ABV 4.3%)
Amber-coloured beer with a blackcurrant and herbal aroma.

Ruby Duck (OG 1053, ABV 5.3%)
Dark ruby-coloured beer with a rich full body and complex fruit flavours.

Fyne SIBA

Achadunan, Cairndow, PA26 8BJ
☎ (01499) 600120 ⊕ fyneales.com

☺Fyne Ales has been brewing since 2001 and is situated at the head of Loch Fyne. In 2012 an on-site brewery tap was added. Expansion has allowed for the production of experimental brews. FyneFest runs annually, celebrating local fare and showcasing other breweries. ‼🍴◆RAIB

Jarl (OG 1038, ABV 3.8%) 🍺
A light, golden ale with strong citrus notes.

Maverick (OG 1040.5, ABV 4.2%) �
Full-bodied, roasty, tawny best bitter. It is balanced, fruity and well hopped.

Hurricane Jack (OG 1042.5, ABV 4.4%)
Smooth golden ale, deep citrus flavours which mellow to a lingering citrus bitter finish.

Vital Spark (OG 1042.5, ABV 4.4%)
A rich, dark beer that shows glints of red. The taste is clean and slightly sharp with a hint of blackcurrant.

Avalanche (OG 1043.5, ABV 4.5%) �
This true golden ale starts with stunning citrus hops on the nose. Well-balanced with good body and fruit balancing a refreshing hoppy taste, it finishes with a long bittersweet aftertaste.

Highlander (OG 1046, ABV 4.8%) �
Full-bodied, bittersweet ale with a good dry hop finish. In the style of a heavy although the malt is

less pronounced and the sweetness ebbs away to leave a bitter, hoppy finish.

Sublime Stout (OG 1067, ABV 6.8%)
A stout with a hint of liquorice on the aftertaste.

Zombier (OG 1067, ABV 6.9%)
An aroma of molasses, toffee and dark fruits, plum and cherry. The taste is heavily roasted, coffee and chocolate as well as liquorice, molasses and dark fruits, toffee and chocolate. A slightly sticky, sweet finish with a lingering chocolate taste.

Superior IPA (OG 1070, ABV 7.1%)
A full-bodied IPA with an oily mouthfeel. The aroma of apricot and pine resin is present, giving a dusty, hoppy bitterness. A dry, fruity and hoppy aftertaste.

G2 SIBA ◉

Unit 5, Ashford Works, Brunswick Road, Cobbs Wood, Ashford, Kent, TN23 1EH
☎ (01233) 630277 ⊕ g2brewing.com

Formerly known as Spencer's, the brewery was set up in 2012 by Brian Spencer, a retired space rocket fuel engineer. The brewery came under new ownership in 2014 when its name was changed to G2 Brewing. The brewery was upgraded and commercial production recommenced in 2015. Outlets are supplied across the South east and in London. Further expansion is planned.

Vela Blonde (OG 1038, ABV 4.2%)

Otava IPA (OG 1040, ABV 4.4%)

Crux Premium (OG 1044, ABV 4.8%)

Gadds

See Ramsgate

Gale's

See Fuller's

Gaol (NEW) SIBA

The Old Lock Up, 46 North End, Wirksworth, Derbyshire, DE4 4FG ☎ 07981 220734
✉ sam.salt@gmail.com

A small brewery established in 2015. Beer recipes are still in development.

Garden City (NEW)

🏠 22 The Wynd, Letchworth, Hertfordshire, SG6 2EN
☎ 07932 739558 ⊕ gardencitybrewery.co.uk

Brewing began in 2016. The brewery is located in a café bar, with the beers being served on gravity along with guest ales from breweries around the UK.

Gargoyles

See Isca

Gas Dog

🏠 Noel's Arms, 31 Burton Street, Melton Mowbray, Leicestershire, LE13 1AE ☎ 07921 260063

Office: 9 Westview, Somerby, Leicestershire, LE14 2QH ⊕ gasdogbrewery.co.uk

Gas Dog began brewing in 2013 at the same premises as Parish Brewery, but using a separate 0.5-barrel plant. In 2014 it relocated to an outbuilding at the rear of the Noel's Arms in Melton Mowbray and in 2016 upgraded to a 2.5-barrel plant. ♦

Peaky Blinder (OG 1037, ABV 3.7%)
A light, bitter session ale.

Hello Dolly (OG 1038, ABV 3.8%)
An old-fashioned, amber-coloured session bitter.

Bitter (OG 1040, ABV 4%)
A copper-coloured traditional bitter.

Gates Burton

Reservoir Road, Burton upon Trent, Staffordshire, DE14 2BP
☎ (01283) 532567
✉ gatesburtonbrewery@talktalk.net

⊛The Gates Burton Brewery was established in 2011 using a one-barrel plant. This has now expanded to a three-barrel kit. ‼♦

Reservoir (OG 1048, ABV 4.6%) ◈
Pale brown in colour with a malty aroma and roast hint. Caramel and malt lead to a sweet hop balanced taste. Hops arrive late on the palate to urge another mouthful.

Damn (OG 1050, ABV 5%)
Smooth-drinking ruby ale with chocolate malt tones. Delicately hopped with a subtle, sweet finish.

Reservoir Gold (OG 1075, ABV 7.5%)
Full-bodied, amber-coloured ale. Finely balanced with roast barley and subtly hopped. A sweet, smooth finish.

Geeves SIBA

Unit 12 Grange Lane Industrial Estate, Carrwood Road, Stairfoot, Barnsley, South Yorkshire, S71 5AS
☎ 07859 039259 ⊕ geevesbrewery.co.uk

Geeves began brewing in 2011 using a 5.5-barrel plant with recipes developed when the owners lived on a narrow boat. ‼♦RAIB

Rococo (OG 1037, ABV 3.6%)
A smooth, dark mild with a hint of chocolate. Aromas are cocoa, dark fruits and berries with a subtle but lingering bitter finish.

Topaz Session Pale (OG 1040, ABV 3.8%)
A light summery pale with a soft citrus palate.

Renaissance (OG 1040, ABV 4.1%)
A deep red ale packed with sweet malts giving flavours of dark fruits and molasses while American Willamette hops bring a diverse array of spicy earthiness, lemon citrus and hints of floral apricot and peach.

Aurelian (OG 1043, ABV 4.2%)
An English golden ale. Fresh, leafy English hops dominate with flavours of sweet, tangy orange citrus and a refreshingly crisp and bitter finish.

Captain Gingerbread (OG 1043, ABV 4.3%)
A naturally hazy wheat beer infused with ginger. Spicy and refreshing with a hint of citrus.

Clear Cut (OG 1044, ABV 4.4%)
An extra pale ale with bags of American hops for a real citrus kick.

Smokey Joe Stout (OG 1050, ABV 5%)
A blend of several dark malts create this rich, bold stout. Expect flavours of black coffee, dark chocolate and a lingering smokiness. A combination of hops gives a spicy, oaky finish.

Fully Laden (OG 1060, ABV 6%)
An IPA with strength and a juicy, citrus, sweet floral taste and aroma with a satisfying bitterness.

Geipel

Pant Glas Llangwm, Corwen, LL21 0RN
☎ (01490) 420838 ☎ 07549 526287 ⊕ geipel.co.uk

Geipel commenced brewing in 2013 producing classic German-style, unpasteurised and unfiltered beers in keg and bottle form only, mainly supplying bars and off-licences in North Wales and Greater Manchester. RAIB

George N Porter

See under Porter

George Samuel

Spennymoor, County Durham
☎ (01609) 882464 ☎ 07840 892751
⊕ georgesamuelbrewingcompany.co.uk

A small, two-barrel brewery originally set up at the Duke of Wellington pub in the small village of Welbury near Northallerton, and named after the brewer's two sons. It has now moved to a private address in Spennymoor.

By George She's Got It (OG 1036, ABV 3.6%)
A blonde session ale with a good hoppy punch.

Brew It Again Sam (OG 1042, ABV 4.2%)

Golden Wellingtons (OG 1050, ABV 5%)
Golden premium ale with a bittersweet character.

George Wright

See under Wright

George's SIBA

Common Road, Great Wakering, Essex, SS3 0AG
☎ (01702) 826755 ☎ 07771 871255
⊕ georgesbrewery.com

⊠ George's Brewery and Hop Monster Brewing Company (qv) are owned by the same brewer, using the same plant. George's concentrates on traditional styles and Hop Monster on the more unusual. A taproom/micropub called Mawson's has now opened in Southend. ‼🍺♦RAIB

Wallasea Wench (OG 1037.5, ABV 3.6%)
Pale copper-coloured, easy-drinking, low bitterness with a smooth flavour.

Wakering Gold (OG 1039.5, ABV 3.8%)
Bursting with fresh hop aroma; a refreshing blend of English and American hops.

Best (OG 1041, ABV 4%)
Copper-coloured session bitter.

Cockleboats (OG 1039, ABV 4%)

Broadsword (OG 1046, ABV 4.7%)

Ruby/copper-coloured with a malty smooth start and a well-balanced dry finish.

Gertie Sweet

See New Plassey

Ghost (NEW)

Unit D, Tong Business Centre, Otley Road, Baildon, West Yorkshire, BD17 7QD
☎ (0113) 418 2002 ☎ 01896 097882
⊕ ghostbrewing.co.uk

Ghost Brewing Co is the creation of Steve Crump and James Thompson.

Wraith (ABV 3.8%)
A light pale ale with citrus peel and passion fruit aromas. Oats produce a velvet smooth texture.

Spectre (ABV 4.4%)
A session IPA, fruity and moreish with spiced lemon and strawberry notes.

Phantom (ABV 5.3%)

Gipsy Hill SIBA

Unit 11, Hamilton Road Industrial Estate, 160 Hamilton Road, West Norwood, London, SE27 9SF
☎ (020) 8761 9061 ⊕ gipsyhillbrewing.com

Founded in 2014, Gipsy Hill is a small, independent microbrewery producing mainly for the local market in London. A tap room is open to the public at weekends. ♦ RAIB

Beatnik (ABV 3.8%) 🍺
Golden ale with tropical fruit, citrus and hops aroma, which continue into the crisp, hoppy and moderately bitter taste.

Southpaw (ABV 4.2%) 🍺
Pale brown best bitter with hops, oranges and hints of caramel in aroma and flavour. Bitterness builds in the finish.

Wayfarer (ABV 4.6%) 🍺
Well-balanced porter with dark roast and spicy hop aroma. Roast continues in the taste, with sweetness balanced by bitterness.

Glamorgan SIBA 👁

Unit J, Llantrisant Business Park, Llantrisant, CF72 8LF
☎ (01443) 406080

☺Formerly known as the Kite Brewery, this 30-barrel plant is now well established since its move to Llantrisant in 2013. The brewing team produces a well-developed range of year-round and seasonal ales with additional special brews to mark notable events. Distribution across South, West and Mid Wales is undertaken by sister company Glamorgan Beer Company and further afield by selected wholesalers. 🍺♦

Cwrw Gorslas/Bluestone Bitter (OG 1040, ABV 4%)
A well-rounded bitter delivering softly roasted undertones to a malty body, complemented by a smooth and robust hoppiness from nose to finish.

Welsh Pale Ale (OG 1042, ABV 4.1%)
A crisp pale ale, light gold in colour, and full of bright citrus aromas and flavours. Finishes dry, fruity and hoppy.

Jemimas Pitchfork (OG 1044, ABV 4.4%)

Thunderbird (OG 1045, ABV 4.5%)

Glastonbury

Unit 11, Wessex Park, Somerton Business Park, Somerton, Somerset, TA11 6SB
☎ (01458) 272244 ⊕ glastonburyales.com

Glastonbury Ales was established in 2002 on a five-barrel plant. In 2006 the brewery changed ownership and has now expanded to a 20-barrel plant. ‼🍺♦

Mystery Tor (OG 1040, ABV 3.8%) 🍺
Golden bitter with floral hop and fruit on the nose and palate, sweetness giving way to bitter hop finish. Full-bodied.

Lady of the Lake (OG 1042, ABV 4.2%) 🍺
Full-bodied amber best bitter with hops balanced by fruity malt flavour and a hint of vanilla. Clean, bitter hop aftertaste.

Love Monkey (OG 1042, ABV 4.2%)
Golden ale loaded with zesty fruity hops and a variety of malts. Refreshing fruity notes finally succumb to a robust body.

Black As Yer 'At (OG 1043, ABV 4.3%)

Hedge Monkey (OG 1048, ABV 4.6%)
A well-rounded, deep amber-coloured bitter. Malty, rich and hoppy.

Golden Chalice (OG 1048, ABV 4.8%)
Light and golden best bitter with a robust malt character.

Thriller Cappuccino Porter (OG 1050, ABV 5%)

Glenfinnan

Sruth A Mhuilinn, Glenfinnan, PH37 4LT
☎ (01397) 704309 ☎ 07999 261010
⊕ glenfinnanbrewery.co.uk

☺Glenfinnan opened in 2007 and operates on a four-barrel plant. It produces around 600 litres per week during the tourist season. Further expansion is planned. ♦

Gold Ale (OG 1040, ABV 3.8%)

Standard Ale (OG 1044, ABV 4.2%)

Glens of Antrim (NEW)

10 Murlough Road, Ballycastle, BT64 6RG
☎ (028) 2076 9696

Founded in 2014 and based at Murlough near Ballycastle, it currently has three bottled beers on offer. No real ale. ♦

Glentworth

Glentworth House, Crossfield Lane, Skellow, Doncaster, South Yorkshire, DN6 8PL
☎ (01302) 725555

☺The brewery was founded in 1996 and is housed in former dairy buildings. The five-barrel plant supplies more than 80 pubs. Production is concentrated on mainly light-coloured, hoppy ales. ♦

Globe

144 High Street West, Glossop, Derbyshire, SK13 8HJ
☎ (01457) 852417 ⊕ globepub.co.uk

Globe was established in 2006 by Ron Brookes on a 2.5-barrel plant in an old stable behind the Globe pub. Grandson Toby now has a major role in the brewery under the watchful eye of Ron. The beers are mainly for the pub but special one-off brews are produced for beer festivals. ◆

Amber (OG 1040, ABV 3.9%)

Blondie (OG 1039, ABV 3.9%)

Stout (OG 1040, ABV 3.9%)

Comet (OG 1043, ABV 4.3%)

Gloucester SIBA

Fox's Kiln, West Quay, The Docks, Gloucester, GL1 2LG
☎ (01452) 668043 ☎ 07503 152749
⊕ gloucesterbrewery.co.uk

⊗ Situated in the historic Gloucester Docks, brewing began in 2011. The brewery has recently expanded into larger premises in the Dock area to cope with increased demand while retaining and sympathetically restoring their original converted stables site for experimental brews and a bar named Tank. The full range of beers is regularly available in pubs throughout Gloucestershire and further afield, notably Bristol. A new beer is brewed on a bi-monthly basis as part of a craft ale range. ‼ ⛽ RAIB

Priory Pale (OG 1037, ABV 3.7%)
A refreshing hoppy ale with citrus and tropical notes.

Gold (OG 1040, ABV 3.9%)
A crisp, hoppy golden ale.

Cascade (OG 1042, ABV 4.2%)
Big malty backbone with bold Cascade hops.

Mariner (OG 1042, ABV 4.2%)
A smooth, malty and hoppy copper-coloured session ale.

Galaxy (OG 1052, ABV 5.2%)
A golden ale bursting with hop character.

Goacher's

Unit 8, Tovil Green Business Park, Burial Ground Lane, Tovil, Maidstone, Kent, ME15 6TA
☎ (01622) 682112 ⊕ goachers.com

A traditional brewery that uses only malt and Kentish hops for all its beers. Phil and Debbie Goacher have concentrated on brewing good wholesome beers without gimmicks. Two tied houses and around 30 free trade outlets in the mid-Kent area are supplied. Special is brewed for sale under house names. ‼ ◆

Real Mild Ale (OG 1033, ABV 3.4%) ◄
A rich, flavourful mild with moderate roast barley and a generous helping of chocolate malt.

Fine Light Ale (OG 1036, ABV 3.7%) ◄
A pale, golden brown bitter with a strong, floral, hoppy aroma and aftertaste. A hoppy and moderately malty session beer.

Special/House Ale (OG 1037, ABV 3.8%)

Best Dark Ale (OG 1040, ABV 4.1%) ◄
Dark in colour but light and quaffable in body, this ale features hints of caramel and chocolate malt throughout.

Crown Imperial Stout (OG 1044, ABV 4.5%) ◄
A good, well-balanced roasty stout, dark and bitter with just a hint of caramel and a lingering creamy head.

Gold Star Strong Ale (OG 1050, ABV 5.1%) ◄
A strong pale ale.

Goddards SIBA 👁

Barnsley Farm, Bullen Road, Ryde, Isle of Wight, PO33 1QF
☎ (01983) 611011 ⊕ goddardsbrewery.com

⊗ Anthony Goddard established what is now the oldest active brewery on the Isle of Wight in 1993. Originally occupying an 18th-century barn, a new brewery was built in 2008, quadrupling its capacity, which has since been further increased. Goddard's remain a locally-focused business distributing ales on the Isle of Wight and the easily accessible counties of southern England. ◆

Ale of Wight (OG 1037, ABV 3.7%)
An aromatic, fresh and zesty pale beer.

Scrumdiggity (OG 1039, ABV 4%) ◄
Well-balanced session beer that maintains its flavour and bite with compelling drinkability.

Wight Squirrel (OG 1042.5, ABV 4.3%)
A russet-coloured best bitter with an initial dry taste on the palate.

Fuggle-Dee-Dum (OG 1047, ABV 4.8%) ◄
Brown-coloured strong ale with plenty of malt and hops.

Godstone (NEW)

Osney Lodge Farm, Byers Lane, Blindley Heath, Surrey, RH9 8JH ☎ 07791 570731

Office: 3 Willow Way, Godstone, Surrey, RH9 8NQ
⊕ thegodstonebrewers.com

⊗ Godstone Brewers was established in 2015 with a one-barrel plant and has already moved to larger premises on the same farm. Beers are named on local themes. It supplies the nearby Fox & Hounds, Tilburstow Hill, and micropubs in Surrey and Kent.
◆ RAIB V

Trenchman's Hop (OG 1041, ABV 3.8%)
A pale bitter with a good balance of malt and hops.

Pondtail Pale (OG 1044, ABV 4.1%)
Citrus and exotic fruit flavours predominate from the American hops used.

Polly Paine's Porter (OG 1070, ABV 6.5%)
Full-bodied and complex with caramel, coffee and chocolate notes.

Goff's SIBA

9 Isbourne Way, Winchcombe, Gloucestershire, GL54 5NS
☎ (01242) 603383 ⊕ goffsbrewery.com

⊗ Goff's is a family concern that has been brewing cask-conditioned ales since 1994. The ales are available regionally in more than 200 outlets and nationally through wholesalers. ◆

Jouster (OG 1040, ABV 4%) ◄

A tawny-coloured ale, with a light hoppiness in the aroma. It has a good balance of malt and bitterness in the mouth, underscored by fruitiness, with a clean, hoppy aftertaste.

Tournament (OG 1038, ABV 4%) ◆
Dark golden in colour, with a pleasant hop aroma. A clean, light and refreshing session bitter with a pleasant hop aftertaste.

White Knight (OG 1046, ABV 4.7%) ◆
A well-hopped bitter with a light colour and full-bodied taste. Bitterness predominates in the mouth and leads to a dry, hoppy aftertaste.

Golcar

60a Swallow Lane, Golcar, West Yorkshire, HD7 4NB
☎ (01484) 644241 ☎ 07970 267555
⊕ golcarbrewery.co.uk

☺Golcar started brewing in 2001 and production has increased from 2.5 barrels to five barrels a week. The brewery owns one pub, the Rose & Crown at Golcar, and occasionally supplies other outlets in the local area. ‼

Dark Mild (OG 1034, ABV 3.4%) ◆
Dark mild with a light roasted malt and liquorice taste. Smooth and satisfying.

Town End Bitter (OG 1039, ABV 3.9%) ◆
Amber bitter with a hoppy, citrus taste with fruity overtones and a bitter finish.

Pennine Gold (OG 1038, ABV 4%)
A hoppy and fruity session beer.

Guthlac's Porter (OG 1047, ABV 5%)
A robust all grain and malty working man's porter.

Golden Duck SIBA

Unit 2, Redhill Farm, Top Street, Appleby Magna, Leicestershire, DE12 7AH ☎ 07846 295179
⊕ goldenduckbrewery.com

Golden Duck began brewing in 2012 using a five-barrel plant. It is run by the father-and-son team of Andrew and Harry Lunn. Beers have a cricket-related theme and are always available in Mushroom Hall, Albert Village. Beers are also contract brewed for Alchemist Brewery. ◆RAIB

LFB (Lunns First Brew) (OG 1043, ABV 4.3%)
Traditional golden hoppy session ale with citrus overtones.

Wristy Fitzy (OG 1046, ABV 4.6%)
Deceptively smooth and rich chestnut ale. Hoppy but with slight malty overtones.

Lunnys No. 8 (OG 1048, ABV 4.8%)
Hoppy bitter with a fruity and lasting aroma.

Golden Triangle SIBA

Unit 9, Watton Road, Norwich, NR9 4BG
☎ (01603) 757763 ☎ 07976 281132
⊕ goldentriangle.co.uk

⊗ Golden Triangle, named after an area of Norwich, has been brewing modern, hop-forward ales on a 10-barrel plant since 2011. The brewery moved to the current premises in 2012, and continue to add new beers to its range. Beers are mainly found in pubs across Norwich. ◆

City Gold (OG 1038, ABV 3.8%) ◆

A lemony hop aroma introduces a mix of citrus, hop, and bitterness. Finish develops a dry astringency.

Mosaic City (OG 1038, ABV 3.8%) 🍺
Light golden ale with a distinctive flavour and plenty of body.

Citropolis (OG 1039, ABV 3.9%)
A golden ale, light, refreshing and zesty with citrus hop notes and fruity aroma.

Bonny's Gold (OG 1040, ABV 4%)
Golden ale with a definite American citrus hop profile. The hops work well with a good malt backbone.

Black Hops IBA (OG 1047, ABV 4.6%) ◆
Intense hop and cherry aroma. Complex mix of malt, cherry and bitterness dominated by hops. Challenging, increasingly bitter ending.

Red Square (OG 1046, ABV 4.6%)
A red ale with a balanced complex flavour, which develops into a strong, hoppy finish.

Hop Lobster (OG 1053, ABV 5.5%)
A strong golden ale with plenty of citrus hop character.

Golden Valley

Moorhampton Farm, Abbeydore, Herefordshire
☎ 07828 935675

Office: Unit 7, Three Elms Trading Estate, Hereford, HR4 9PU

Occasional brewing began in 2015 in Abbeydore, Herefordshire.

DPA (Dore Pale Ale) (OG 1040, ABV 4%)

Bitter (ABV 4.2%)

Knock 'em Back (OG 1044, ABV 4.4%)

Goldmark SIBA ◉

Unit 23, The Vinery, Arundel Road, Poling, West Sussex, BN18 9PY
☎ (01903) 297838 ☎ 07900 555415
⊕ goldmarks.co.uk

⊠ Ex-biochemist and home brewer Mark Lehmann began commercial brewing in 2013 using an 11-barrel plant. Beers are available in many outlets nationwide. ‼RAIB

Ebony Mild (OG 1035, ABV 3.5%)
Black, spicy mild with hints of chocolate, coffee and toffee.

Liquid Gold (OG 1040, ABV 4%)
A refreshing, full-bodied golden beer with bursts of fruit and citrus.

Pheonix (OG 1041, ABV 4.1%)
A brown ale with hints of toffee, caramel and a smooth hop finish.

Red IPA (OG 1043, ABV 4.3%)
A triple-hopped red ale using caramelised red German malt.

American Hop Idol (OG 1040, ABV 4.4%)
A pale ale using six American hop varieties balanced with roasted malt.

Warrior (OG 1046, ABV 4.6%)
A brown ale with hints of honey, caramel and ending with a smooth hop note.

Black Lion Porter (OG 1048, ABV 4.8%)

A rich, smooth, satisfying black porter with chocolate hints and a coffee end note.

Vertigo Craft Lager (OG 1048, ABV 4.8%)

Goldstone SIBA 👁

The Forge, Ditchling Common Industrial Estate, Streat Lane, Ditchling, East Sussex, BN6 8SG
☎ (01444) 257053

Office: 257 Dyke Road, Hove, East Sussex, BN3 6PA
⊕ goldstonebrewery.co.uk

⊠ Located in an old forge in the South Downs, Goldstone is the brainchild of Mark Francis, who, while running a bar in Brussels, fell in love with the vast selection of Belgian beers. The brewery is named after a 20-ton rock found in Sussex, believed to have been used by druids for worship.

Old Charmer (OG 1041, ABV 4.1%)
An assertive bitterness and tropical fruit and spicy aroma, which makes for a light, thirst quenching ale.

Ruddy Duck (OG 1041, ABV 4.1%)
Medium-bodied dark ale with notes of caramel, chocolate and coffee.

Beacon Best Bitter (OG 1042, ABV 4.2%)
A well-balanced amber ale in the style of a traditional best bitter; there is maltiness on the palate with a pleasant dry, bitter finish.

Cascade (OG 1044, ABV 4.4%)
An American-style ale with strong citrus aromas.

East Slope Ale (OG 1044, ABV 4.4%)
Golden ale with a smooth, light hoppy flavour.

Amarillo (OG 1045, ABV 4.5%)
Golden American-style ale with strong aromas of grapefruit and gooseberry and a dry bitter finish.

Good Chemistry (NEW)

6 Beaconsfield Road, Clifton, Bristol, BS8 2TS
☎ (0117) 903 9930 ⊕ goodchemistrybrewing.co.uk

Good Chemistry was established by Bob Carey and Kelly Sidgwick in an old warehouse in 2015, using a 10-barrel plant. RAIB

Jimmy Porter (ABV 3.2%)
Full-bodied porter despite its strength. Brewed with eight different malts to give chocolate, coffee, caramel and dried fruit flavours.

Big Bang (ABV 4.4%)
An American pale-style beer with a bitter taste and a darker colour than most pale ales.

Quercus Alba (ABV 5.3%)
A beer brewed with rye and fermented over oak chips producing a woody flavour.

Goodall's

▤ The Lodge, 88 Crewe Road, Alsager, Staffordshire, ST7 2JA
☎ (01270) 873669
⊠ goodalls.brewery@hotmail.co.uk

Goodall's began brewing in 2010 at the Lodge in Alsager using a 2.5-barrel plant. Mainly seasonal ales are brewed. ‼◆

Goody SIBA

Bleangate Brewery, Braggs Lane, Herne, Kent, CT6 7NP
☎ (01227) 361555 ⊕ goodyales.co.uk

Goody began brewing in 2012 using a 10-barrel plant. Only locally grown Kent hops are used and a wood-burning boiler is used to heat the water for the brews using wood from its copse, thereby minimising the use of non-renewable fuel. ◆RAIB

Good Evening (OG 1034, ABV 3.4%)
A smooth, dark mild with a tinge of chocolate.

Genesis (OG 1035, ABV 3.5%)
A dark ruby-coloured ale with a full flavour and lasting bitter finish.

Good Health (OG 1038, ABV 3.6%)
A honey-coloured golden ale with a fresh hoppy finish and undertone of zesty orange.

Good Life (OG 1040, ABV 3.9%)
Fresh tasting pale ale, bursting with citrus flavours and a host of golden hops.

Good Heavens (OG 1042, ABV 4.1%)
Amber-coloured, hoppy ale made with Pilgrim hops.

Good Sheppard (OG 1045, ABV 4.5%)
Deep amber-coloured ale with a warm vanilla twist on the palate and a soft feel on the tongue.

Goodness Gracious Me (OG 1047, ABV 4.8%)
Robust and citrus flavoured, highly-hopped IPA.

Goose Eye SIBA

Ingrow Bridge, South Street, Keighley, West Yorkshire, BD21 5AX
☎ (01535) 605807 ⊕ goose-eye-brewery.co.uk

☺Goose Eye is a family-run brewery supplying 60-70 regular outlets, mainly in North and West Yorkshire and Lancashire. The beers are available through national wholesalers and pub chains. At the time of going to press the brewery is looking for new premises. ◆

Springwell (OG 1036, ABV 3.6%)

Barm Pot Bitter (OG 1038, ABV 3.8%) ◥
Bitter, hop and fruit flavours dominate this golden session bitter, over a malty base. Increasingly dry and bitter finish.

Bitter (OG 1038, ABV 3.9%) ◥
Traditional Yorkshire brown session bitter, well-balanced malt and hops with a pleasingly bitter finish.

Blackmoor (OG 1040, ABV 4%)
A dark session beer.

Chinook Blonde (OG 1042, ABV 4.2%) ◥
An increasingly tart bitter finish follows assertive grapefruit hoppiness in the aroma and tropical flavours in this satisfying brew.

Golden Goose (OG 1045, ABV 4.5%) ◥
A straw-coloured beer, light on the palate with a smooth and refreshing hoppy finish.

Over & Stout (OG 1052, ABV 5.2%) ◥
A full-bodied stout with roast and malt flavours mingling with hops, dark fruit and liquorice on the palate. Look also for tart fruit on the nose and a growing bitter finish.

Pommies Revenge (OG 1052, ABV 5.2%) ◥

Golden strong bitter combining grassy hops, a cocktail of fruit flavours, a peppery hint and a hoppy, bitter finish.

Goosnargh SIBA

Horns Inn, Horns Lane, Goosnargh, Lancashire, PR3 2FJ
☎ (01772) 864382 ⊕ yehornsinn.co.uk

Brewing began in 2013 using a five-barrel plant in a tiny outbuilding at Horns Inn. Most of the equipment came from the Grindleton Brewery, which closed in 2010. The beer is served at the pub and in local free houses. ‼◆

Pale (OG 1034.5, ABV 3.6%)
A pale ale with American and Polish hops. A session beer.

Truckle (OG 1035, ABV 3.7%)

Red (OG 1036, ABV 3.9%)
Ruby-red ale with a slightly earthy flavour.

Bit o'Blonde (OG 1038, ABV 4%)
A light ale, crisp and clean. English hops provide a taste of summer.

Gold (OG 1037, ABV 4%)
A golden beer, light but hoppy, with a zesty finish.

Gower SIBA ◉

Crofty Industrial Estate, Crofty ☎ 07967 484356
⊕ gowerbrewery.com

⊗ Established in 2011 on a five-barrel brew plant at the Greyhound Inn in Llanrhidian, Gower moved to a new 20-barrel brewery in Crofty in 2015. ◆

Brew 1 (OG 1039, ABV 3.8%)
Honey-coloured ale with a pronounced floral aroma.

Black Diamond (OG 1042, ABV 4.2%)
A full-bodied Welsh porter, smoky, chocolate and liquorice flavours, with subtle spicy bittering hops.

Best Bitter (OG 1045, ABV 4.5%)
A traditional honey-coloured ale with a full-bodied, balanced malty flavour and crisp, lingering bite of hop.

Gold (OG 1045, ABV 4.5%)
Thirst quenching golden ale, refreshing citrus flavours and hop aromas.

Rumour (OG 1050, ABV 5%)
Strong ruby red ale, with complex tastes and aromas, produced from a delicate mix of malts and hops.

Power (OG 1052, ABV 5.5%)

Grafters SIBA

Half Moon, 23 High Street, Willingham by Stow, Lincolnshire, DN21 5JZ
☎ (01427) 788340 ⊕ graftersbrewery.com

☺ Brewing started on a 2.5-barrel plant in 2007 in a converted garage adjacent to the owner's freehouse, the Half Moon. 2013 saw an upgrade to a 10-barrel plant. ‼◆

Moonlight (OG 1038, ABV 3.6%)
A light, citrus beer.

Traditional (OG 1040, ABV 3.7%)
A traditional beer, fairly light in colour but with a light, hoppy finish.

Over The Moon (OG 1041.5, ABV 4%)
Brewed in the manner of a traditional-style bitter.

Pale (OG 1043.5, ABV 4%)

Best (ABV 4.2%)

Darker Side of the Moon (OG 1043, ABV 4.2%)
A dark, red-hued beer. Classed as a strong mild with a deceptively smooth, chocolaty taste.

Cascade (OG 1044.5, ABV 4.4%)

Wobble Gob (OG 1048, ABV 4.9%)
A deep ruby-coloured beer. A blend of hops gives this beer a slightly floral and roasted taste.

Grafton SIBA ◉

Walters Yard, Unit 4, Claylands Industrial Estate, Worksop, Nottinghamshire, S81 7DW
☎ (01909) 476121 ☎ 07436 282779

Office: 8 Oak Close, Crabtree Park Estate, Worksop, S80 1BH ✉ susanhale1865@gmail.com

☺ Grafton is a 12-barrel brewery established in 2007. The brewery tap is the Grafton Hotel, Worksop. A new brewery, visitor centre and shop opened in 2014. ‼◆

Framboise (OG 1038, ABV 4%) ◆
Golden ale with a raspberry aroma and taste, leading to a sweet and slightly bitter finish.

Silhouette (OG 1038, ABV 4%)
A pale beer, the addition of vanilla pods gives a unique vanilla flavour.

Lady Julia (OG 1041, ABV 4.3%)
A golden ale. Wheat and barley produce a crisp beer with a floral hop aroma.

Bananalicious (OG 1043, ABV 4.5%)
Mid brown ale with a banana and toffee aftertaste.

Lady Catherine (OG 1043, ABV 4.5%)
A pale ale with delicate citrus flavours and a pleasant bitterness from the hops on the tongue.

Lady Ruby (OG 1043, ABV 4.5%)
A dark ruby-coloured ale made with cherries. Hint of cherries on the nose and on the palate. A bitter start which then finishes with a cherry bomb on the back of the tongue. An easy-drinking ale.

Apricot Jungle (OG 1046, ABV 4.8%)
A fruity, golden beer with honey, apricot and almond notes. The sweetness is balanced by hop bitterness.

Blondie (OG 1046, ABV 4.8%)
A strong, golden-coloured beer with an aroma dominated by citrus notes. Hops and fruit on the palate are balanced by malt, leading to a hoppy finish with soft fruit flavours.

Caramel Stout (OG 1048, ABV 5%)

Coco Loco (OG 1048, ABV 5%) ◆
Dark-coloured, smooth-drinking ale, infused with coconut; gentle bitterness.

Charioteer (OG 1063, ABV 6.5%)
An easy-drinking strong beer. Subtle, with citrus flavours, giving a berry aroma and fruity flavour, with a hint of malty sweetness, leading to a smooth, long finish.

Grain SIBA

South Farm, Tunbeck Road, Alburgh, Norfolk, IP20 0BS

☎ (01986) 788884 ⊕ grainbrewery.co.uk

⊠ Grain Brewery was launched in 2006 by Geoff Wright and Phil Halls in a converted dairy in the Waveney Valley. It upgraded to a 15-barrel plant in 2012. Four pubs are owned, the Plough and the Cottage, both in Norwich, the Spread Eagle, Ipswich, and the Corn Hall Bar, Diss. ‼ ⌷ ◆ RAIB

Oak (OG 1038, ABV 3.8%) ◆
A balanced mix of malt and hops with marmalade overtones. A hint of molasses in the short sharp ending.

ThreeOneSix (OG 1039, ABV 3.9%) ◆
Hops mingle with a citrus marmalade bite in both aroma and taste. Long, strong finish with growing malty bitterness.

Blonde Ash (OG 1040, ABV 4%) ◆
Banana notes flow through this sweet smoky brew. Yellow-hued with a grainy mouthfeel and a quick fruity finale.

Best Bitter (OG 1042, ABV 4.2%) ◆
A well-balanced, complex bitter. A complex mix of flavours with malt and hops ably supported by caramel and bitterness.

Redwood (OG 1043, ABV 4.3%) ◆
Heavy blackcurrant airs give way to a rich, fruity bitterness with malt overtones. Copper-coloured, crisp and satisfying.

Lignum Vitae (OG 1065, ABV 6.5%) ◆
Powerful, complex and rich throughout. Malt and hops vie with tropical fruit and bitterness for dominance. Challenging and rewarding throughout.

Grainstore SIBA ◉

⬛ Station Approach, Oakham, Rutland, LE15 6RE
☎ (01572) 770065 ⊕ grainstorebrewery.com

☺ Grainstore, the smallest county's largest brewery, has been in production since 1995, founded by Tony Davis and Mike Davies. After 30 years in the industry Tony decided to set up his own business after finding a derelict Victorian railway grainstore building. Now retired, he has handed the reins to his son, William. More than 200 outlets are supplied. ‼ ◆

Rutland Bitter (OG 1032, ABV 3.4%)
A well-balanced session beer, light in colour and taste.

Rutland Panther (OG 1034, ABV 3.4%) ◆
A reddish-black mild with malt and roast flavours.

Cooking (OG 1036, ABV 3.6%) ◆
Tawny-coloured beer with malt and hops on the nose and a pleasant grainy mouthfeel. Hops and fruit flavours combine to give a bitterness that continues into a long finish.

Red Kite (OG 1038, ABV 3.8%)
A deep red-coloured beer.

Steelback IPA (OG 1042, ABV 4.2%)
A full-bodied golden IPA.

Triple B (OG 1042, ABV 4.2%) ◆
Initially hops dominate over malt in both the aroma and taste, but fruit is there, too. All three linger in varying degrees in the sweetish aftertaste of this brown brew.

GB Best (OG 1043, ABV 4.3%)

A light beer with pronounced floral flavour and aroma.

Gold (OG 1045, ABV 4.5%)
A refreshing light golden brew with mellow malt sweetness finely balanced by the smooth bitterness, subtle flavours and floral hop aromas.

Ten Fifty (OG 1050, ABV 5%) ◆
Pungent banana and malt notes on the nose. On the palate, rich malt and fruit is joined by subtle hop on a bittersweet base. Dry malt aftertaste with some fruit.

Rutland Beast (OG 1053, ABV 5.3%)
A strong mild ale, with a complex flavour of chocolate/coffee notes and raisins and autumn fruits.

Nip (OG 1073, ABV 7.3%)
A well-balanced barley wine with a blend of sweetness and hop bitterness. Smooth and warming with raisins and winter fruit as the dominant flavour notes.

Grampus

⬛ Grampus Inn, Lee Bay, Ilfracombe, Devon, EX34 8LR
☎ (01271) 862906 ⊕ thegrampus-inn.co.uk

⊠ Grampus was opened in 2014 at the back of the Grampus Inn by Bill Harvey, the owner. It is a small plant using traditional brewing methods, but combining some unique and unusual ingredients. At present, most production is sold though the pub, with just a few casks going to local pubs. ◆ RAIB

Bitter (OG 1039, ABV 4%)
A standard session bitter with a good hop finish.

Ale (OG 1042, ABV 4.4%)
A best bitter with a slightly fuller hop feel and increased hop finish.

Granite Rock

Unit 19, Kernick Road Industrial Estate, Penryn, Cornwall, TR10 9EP
☎ (01326) 379251 ☎ 07436 817974
⊕ graniterockbrewery.co.uk

⊠ Granite Rock was established in 2013 as a brewery and home brew shop. Located on an industrial estate in Penryn, the two-barrel plant currently supplies the free trade in west Cornwall. ‼ ⌷ ◆ RAIB

Penryn Company Pale Ale (OG 1040, ABV 4%)
A light, hoppy session beer.

Summer Solstice (OG 1040, ABV 4%)
A golden ale, refreshing and light.

Bronescombe's Vision (OG 1048, ABV 5.2%) ◆
Well-balanced, red-coloured strong bitter with malt and hop aroma. Strong malt flavour, hop bitterness, some sweetness. Refreshing bitter, dry finish.

Glasney College Porter (OG 1050, ABV 5.4%) ◆
Black porter with roast malt aroma. Full-bodied taste of creamy coffee and dark chocolate, liquorice and pear drops. Light finish.

Great Central (NEW)

Unit B, Marlow Road Industrial Estate, Leicester, LE3 2BQ ☎ 07522 673066 ⊕ gcbrewery.co.uk

A five-barrel brewery that began production in 2015 in the disused Dem Bones plant. Brewer Neil Rowley installed new equipment and supplies 12 outlets across the Midlands.

Goyle (ABV 3.1%)

Crompton (ABV 3.3%)

Warship (ABV 4.2%)

Hoover (ABV 5%)

Kettle (ABV 5%)

Great Heck SIBA

Harwinn House, Main Street, Great Heck, North Yorkshire, DN14 0BQ
☎ (01977) 661430 ☎ 07723 381002
⊕ greatheckbrewery.co.uk

☺Great Heck began production in 2008 in a converted slaughterhouse. The brewery moved across the road to a converted cottage in 2012 and now produces its regular beers on a 15-barrel plant with capacity for 45 barrels per week. ‼◆

Chopper (OG 1037, ABV 3.8%)
A pale session beer.

Angel (OG 1037, ABV 3.9%)
A clean, dry and moderately bittered pale ale with loads of American aroma hops.

Dave (OG 1038, ABV 3.9%)
A dark session bitter with a satisfying roasty taste.

Navigator (OG 1039, ABV 3.9%)
Traditional mahogany-coloured session bitter with subtle yet exotic hop aromas.

Blonde (OG 1043, ABV 4.3%)
A well-balanced blonde beer with a zesty finish.

Voodoo Mild (OG 1043, ABV 4.3%)
Rich, black mild bursting with flavour from the roasted malts.

Citra (OG 1043, ABV 4.5%)
Refreshing golden ale brewed with Citra hops giving characteristic tropical fruit flavours and aroma.

Simcoe (OG 1043, ABV 4.5%)
Refreshing golden ale with tropical fruit flavours and aroma.

Amish Mash (ABV 4.7%)
A cloudy wheat beer with notes of banana, clove and fruity hop.

Treasure IPA (OG 1045, ABV 4.8%)
Smooth golden IPA with moderate bitterness and distinctive tropical fruit notes.

Treason Stout (OG 1054, ABV 5.4%)
An unfined wheat stout.

Vanilla Wheat Stout (OG 1054, ABV 5.4%)
An unfined far from traditional stout with vanilla pods in the brew giving a subtle balance of flavours. Smooth and satisfying.

Shankar IPA (OG 1055, ABV 5.9%)
A pale, hoppy fruity beer with a clean, zesty finish.

Black Jesus (OG 1060, ABV 6.5%)
A black IPA.

Yakima IPA (OG 1070, ABV 7.4%)
Deep golden in colour, low in bitterness, the alcohol balances the fruity hop flavours and aromas.

Great Newsome SIBA ◉

Great Newsome Farm, South Frodingham, Winestead, East Yorkshire, HU12 0NR
☎ (01964) 612201 ⊕ greatnewsomebrewery.co.uk

☺Nestled in the Holderness countryside, Great Newsome began brewing in 2007 in renovated farm buildings. A range of beers is now brewed using barley from the farm and brewing can be seen from a newly-built viewing area. Beer is distributed throughout the UK and overseas. ‼☰◆

Sleck Dust (OG 1037, ABV 3.8%)
Straw-coloured, refreshingly bitter session beer with floral aroma and subtle dry finish.

Ploughman's Pride (OG 1042, ABV 4.2%)
Dark, rich malty ale with liquorice tones.

Pricky Back Otchan (OG 1042, ABV 4.2%)
Hoppy golden bitter with fresh citrus aroma.

Frothingham Best (OG 1042, ABV 4.3%)
Dark amber best bitter with a subtle dry finish.

Holderness Dark (OG 1042, ABV 4.3%)
Dark, strong mild. Malty notes with a hint of sweetness.

Jem's Stout (OG 1044, ABV 4.3%)
Dark, smooth beer with smoky, roasted malt flavours and aroma.

Great Oakley SIBA ◉

Ark Farm, High Street South, Tiffield, Northamptonshire, NN12 8AB
☎ (01327) 351759 ☎ 07850 327658
⊕ greatoakleybrewery.co.uk

The brewery commenced production in 2005 in Great Oakley and relocated to Tiffield in 2012. It is run by husband-and-wife team Phil and Hazel Greenway. More than 60 outlets are supplied, including the George, Tiffield, which is the brewery tap. ‼◆RAIB

Welland Valley Mild (OG 1037, ABV 3.6%)
A dark, traditional mild. Full of flavour.

Wagtail (OG 1040, ABV 3.9%)
Light-coloured with a unique bitterness derived from New Zealand hops.

Wot's Occurring (OG 1040, ABV 3.9%)
A mid-golden session bitter with a subtle hop finish.

Walter Tull (OG 1040, ABV 4%)
A golden beer brewed with three different hops.

Tiffield Thunderbolt (OG 1043, ABV 4.2%)
A pale beer brewed with New Zealand hops.

Harpers (OG 1044, ABV 4.3%)
Traditional mid-brown bitter with a malty taste and slight hints of chocolate and citrus in the finish.

Gobble (OG 1045, ABV 4.5%)
Straw-coloured beer with a pleasant hop aftertaste.

Delapre Dark (OG 1047, ABV 4.6%)
A dark, full-bodied ale made from five different malts.

Abbey Stout (OG 1051, ABV 5%)
A dark, rich stout brewed with generous amounts of roast barley and German hops

Tailshaker (OG 1051, ABV 5%)
A complex golden ale with a great depth of flavour.

Great Orme SIBA

Builder Street, Llandudno, LL30 1DR
☎ (01492) 330680 ⊕ greatormebrewery.co.uk

Great Orme began in 2005 on a five-barrel plant, situated in the Conwy Valley. It has recently moved to larger premises in the Victorian seaside town of Llandudno, within sight of the Great Orme from which the brewery takes its name. It now brews on an 18-barrel plant. Around 100 outlets are supplied. ♦

Welsh Gold (OG 1036, ABV 3.6%) ◄
A pale brown malty session bitter with a dry taste. Some hoppy flavours develop in the bitter aftertaste.

Welsh Black (OG 1042, ABV 4%) ☐ ◄
Smooth-tasting dark beer with roast coffee notes in aroma and taste. Sweetish in flavour and having some characteristics of a mild ale with hoppiness also present in the aftertaste.

Orme (OG 1042, ABV 4.2%) ◄
Malty best bitter with a dry finish. Faint hop and fruit notes in aroma and taste, but malt dominates throughout.

Celtica (OG 1045, ABV 4.5%) ◄
Yellow in colour with a zesty taste full of citrus fruit flavours. Some initial sweetness followed by peppery hops and a bitter finish.

Red Dragon (OG 1045, ABV 4.5%) ◄
A light-brown best bitter with a sweet malty taste accompanied by faint fruit notes and peppery hops in the finish.

Ynys Mon (OG 1045, ABV 4.5%) ◄
A copper-coloured, malty best bitter with a smooth sweetish taste and a satisfying finish.

Great Western SIBA ◉

▤ **Stream Bakery, Bristol Road, Hambrook, Bristol, BS16 1RF**
☎ (0117) 957 2842 ⊕ gwbrewery.co.uk

⊠ Great Western is a 12-barrel brewery set up in 2008 by Kevin Stone in a former bakery. The property has been renovated resulting in a bespoke showpiece brewery retaining many of the building's original features. The brewery owns a single pub – the Rising Sun, Frampton Cotterell – and 500 outlets are supplied. ‼ ▤ ♦

HPA (OG 1040, ABV 4%) ◄
Hoppy yellow bitter with clean citrus flavours leading to a lingering astringent finish.

Maiden Voyage (OG 1040, ABV 4%) ◄
An amber bitter with a light aroma of malt and fruit which continues to the palate before leading to a strong bitter finish.

Bees Knees (OG 1041, ABV 4.2%) ◄
Golden-coloured beer, bitter with malt nose and flavour and some honey. Lasting astringent bitter aftertaste.

Exhibitionist (OG 1044, ABV 4.5%)

Classic Gold (OG 1044, ABV 4.6%) ◄
Golden ale with subtle aromas of pale malt and fruits. Citrus fruits with balanced hop and malt character with a lingering bitter finish.

Old Higby (OG 1045, ABV 4.8%) ◄

Full-bodied malty bitter with roast notes on the nose. Hints of fruit flavour give way to a bitter hop finish with some astringency throughout.

Moose River (OG 1047, ABV 5%)
A full-bodied IPA.

Great Yorkshire

Cropton, North Yorkshire, YO18 8HH
☎ (01751) 417330
⊕ thegreatyorkshirebrewery.co.uk

Great Yorkshire took over the Cropton Brewery in 2012 concentrating on the production of keg Yorkshire Lager and Yorkshire Blackout. Check the website for limited edition and other cask ales. ‼ ♦ RAIB

Yorkshire Pale (OG 1038, ABV 3.8%)
A New World-style pale ale, light and smooth with the flavours of mango and pineapple.

Yorkshire Classic (OG 1043.5, ABV 4%)
Light chestnut-coloured beer with a smooth, malty taste balanced with complex biscuit flavours.

Yorkshire Golden (OG 1045, ABV 4.2%)
A refreshing golden beer with hints of caramel and mouthwatering honey-like sweetness.

Yorkshire Blackout (OG 1051, ABV 5%)

Green Dragon

▤ **Green Dragon, 29 Broad Street, Bungay, Suffolk, NR35 1EF**
☎ (01986) 892681

The Green Dragon pub was purchased in 1991 and the rear converted to a brewery. In 1994 the plant was expanded and moved to a converted barn. The doubling of capacity allowed the production of a larger range of ales. ‼ ♦

Chaucer Ale (OG 1037, ABV 3.8%)

Gold (OG 1045, ABV 4.4%)

Bridge Street Bitter (OG 1045, ABV 4.5%)

Strong Mild (OG 1054, ABV 5.5%)
A dark, ruby-coloured ale. Plum and dark chocolate on the nose with a rich and smooth taste full of dark malt notes. It is mildly hopped to allow the malt character to prevail.

Green Duck

▤ **Unit 13, Gainsborough Trading Estate, Rufford Road, Stourbridge, West Midlands, DY9 7ND**
☎ (01384) 377666 ⊕ greenduckbrewery.co.uk

Green Duck began brewing in 2012 and relocated to its present site in Stourbridge in 2013. Experimental beers are brewed alongside a core range. The brewery has an onsite brewery tap, the Badelynge Bar, where the brewing equipment can be viewed through a glass partition. Private parties and quarterly beer festivals are hosted. ‼ ♦

Drunken Duck (OG 1039, ABV 3.9%)
Straw-coloured ale with a lemon and lime edge.

Duck & Cover (OG 1041, ABV 4%)
Pine and subtle grapefruit hop tones with a tropical fruit finish.

Sitting Duck (OG 1040, ABV 4%)
A pale ale, hoppy and straw-like.

Duck Blonde (OG 1042, ABV 4.2%)

Brewed with passion fruit and New World hops for a refreshing burst of fruit flavours, with a long, sweet finish.

Duck Under (OG 1042, ABV 4.5%)
A strong malt backbone with an intense hop flavour delivers a well-balanced ale with a bitter citrus finish.

Duck & Dive (OG 1059, ABV 5.9%)
An American-style IPA with a floral flavour and pronounced grapefruit taste.

Duck Dastardly (OG 1056, ABV 5.9%)
A classic stout with a good body. Chocolate and roasted coffee on the nose and palate.

Green Jack SIBA 👁

Argyle Place, Love Road, Lowestoft, Suffolk, NR32 2NZ
☎ (01502) 562863 ⊕ green-jack.com

⊗ After 10 years at Oulton Broad, Green Jack moved to the Triangle Tavern, Lowestoft in 2003 and then to a nearby 35-barrel plant in 2009. One pub is owned and more than 150 outlets supplied.
‼ ◆ RAIB

Waxwing (OG 1038, ABV 3.9%)

Orange Wheat Beer (OG 1041, ABV 4.2%) 🍷 ◆
Marmalade aroma with a hint of hops, leading to a well-balanced blend of sweetness, hops and citrus with a malt background. Mixed fruit flavours in the aftertaste.

Trawlerboys Best Bitter (OG 1045, ABV 4.6%) 🍷 ◆
Tawny beer with aroma of apple, sultana and malt plus hints of caramel and hops. Rich fig and plum base with malt and roast overtones. Strong finish with a sticky mouthfeel.

Lurcher Stout (OG 1046, ABV 4.8%) 🍷 ◆
Pleasant malt, roast and fruit aromas. Blackberry, raisin and port flavours. Long, dry bitter roast finish.

Rising Sun (OG 1047, ABV 4.8%)

Red Herring (OG 1048, ABV 5%)

Gone Fishing ESB (OG 1052, ABV 5.5%)

Mahseer IPA (OG 1056, ABV 5.8%)

Ripper Tripel (OG 1074, ABV 8.5%)

Baltic Trader Export Stout (OG 1092, ABV 10.5%)

Green Mill SIBA

🍺 **Harewood Arms, 2 Market Street, Broadbottom, SK14 6AX** ☎ 07967 656887 ⊕ greenmillbrewery.com

☺Green Mill started brewing in 2007 on a 2.5-barrel plant and moved in 2010 to the Cask & Feather in Rochdale. The brewery relocated again in 2013 to the Harewood Arms in Broadbottom. A number of occasional beers are brewed. Around 40 outlets are supplied. ◆

Gold (OG 1035, ABV 3.6%)
A quaffable golden session bitter.

Chief (OG 1041, ABV 4.2%)
A smooth, pale bitter with American hop varieties.

Citrus Snap (OG 1040, ABV 4.2%)
A copper-coloured bitter with lots of citrus notes.

Old Git (OG 1040, ABV 4.2%)
A complex, well-hopped golden ale.

Talisman (OG 1040, ABV 4.2%)
A straw-coloured golden ale with tropical fruit notes.

Pot Black Porter (ABV 4.4%)

Smokey Joe (ABV 4.4%)
A porter with a strong smoky taste.

Flavia (OG 1042, ABV 4.5%)
A blonde beer with a fresh hop aroma brewed with lager malt, leading to a clean dry finish.

Northern Lights (OG 1045, ABV 4.5%)
A pale, well-hopped premium bitter.

Big Chief (OG 1052, ABV 5.5%)

Greene King 👁

Westgate Brewery, Westgate Street, Bury St Edmunds, Suffolk, IP33 1QT
☎ (01284) 763222

Office: Abbot House, Westgate Street, Bury St Edmunds, Suffolk, IP33 1QT ⊕ greeneking.co.uk

⊗ Greene King has been brewing in the market town of Bury St Edmunds since 1799. It brews its beers using water drawn from artesian chalk wells below its brewhouse as well as local East Anglia malt. ‼ 🍺 ◆ RAIB

XX Mild (OG 1035, ABV 3%)
A dark mild with a sweet and roast flavour.

IPA (OG 1036, ABV 3.6%) ◆
Hop-infused fruit cake aromas. Complex flavours of malt, caramel and hop with both sweetness and bitterness. A lingering mellow aftertaste with blackberries.

London Glory (OG 1041.1, ABV 4%)
Rich, fruity and full of flavour.

IPA Gold (OG 1041, ABV 4.1%)
A deep golden ale with a blend of tropical fruits, mango and spicy notes.

Abbot (OG 1049, ABV 5%) ◆
Strong malt, toffee and caramel aromas. Rich malty caramel flavours with vine fruit and a little hop bite. Heavy, sweet finish with a subtle hint of bitterness in the aftertaste.

IPA Reserve (OG 1055.5, ABV 5.4%)
A full-bodied amber ale. Grapefruit and orange citrus tones combine with the floral and herbal hop notes and lead to a dry bitter finish.

Brewed under the Hardys & Hansons brand name:

Bitter (OG 1038, ABV 3.9%)
A balance of sweetness and bitterness that combines with a subtle hop character. A distinctive beer with a full finish.

Olde Trip (OG 1043, ABV 4.3%)
A rich, toffee flavoured beer with a fruity character and a clean, bitter finish.

Brewed under the Morland brand name:

Original Bitter (OG 1039, ABV 4%)
A subtle malt and fruit character and a pronounced bitter finish.

Old Golden Hen (OG 1038.6, ABV 4.1%)
Light golden beer brewed using the Galaxy hop to give tropical fruit notes.

Old Speckled Hen (OG 1045, ABV 4.5%) ◆
Smooth, malty and fruity, with a short finish.

Brewed under the Ruddles brand name:

Best Bitter (OG 1037, ABV 3.7%) ◆
An amber/brown beer, strong on bitterness but with some initial sweetness, fruit and subtle, distinctive hop. Dryness lingers in the aftertaste.

County (OG 1043, ABV 4.3%) ◆
Sweet, malty and bitter, with a dry and bitter aftertaste.

Brewed under the Tolly Cobbold brand name:

English Ale (OG 1033.6, ABV 2.8%)
Amber-coloured ale brewed using a complex mix of hops to offer balanced bitterness with strong tropical notes.

Greenfield SIBA 👁

Unit 8, Waterside Mills, Greenfield, Saddleworth, OL3 7NH
☎ (01457) 879789 ⊕ greenfieldbrewery.co.uk

😊Greenfield was launched in 2002 and is situated in an old spinning mill next to the River Chew on the edge of the Peak District National Park. Spring water from the National Park is used for brewing. It is open to the public and supplies beer to them and to more than 100 outlets. ‼🍴◆

Greenfield (OG 1039, ABV 3.8%)

Silver Owl (OG 1042, ABV 4%)
A golden-amber beer with a smell of citrus fruits and hints of vanilla – oranges, dryness and lightly hopped taste.

Thirst Born (OG 1041, ABV 4.1%)
Floral citrus smell with malt and hops. Taste of citrus, peach and floral malt.

Dobcross Bitter (OG 1041, ABV 4.2%)
An amber-coloured beer with lemon flavours and a dry finish.

Copper Caskade (OG 1042, ABV 4.3%)
Full-bodied, copper-coloured beer with a hoppy finish. The final flavours reveal both citrus and fruit tones.

Vanilla Stout (OG 1048, ABV 5.2%)
A black stout brewed with initial flavours of both chocolate and coffee, giving way to a natural vanilla finish, created by the use of real vanilla pods during the cask maturation stage.

Greenodd

🍺 Ship Inn, Main Street, Greenodd, Cumbria, LA12 7QZ ☎ 07782 655294
✉ greenoddbrewery@yahoo.co.uk

😊Established in 2010 at the Ship Inn on a two-barrel plant. The majority of production goes to the Ship with the remainder going to local free trade. ‼◆

Kiln (OG 1038, ABV 3.8%)

Blonde (OG 1040, ABV 4%)

Citra (OG 1040, ABV 4%) ◆
An enticing hoppy and fruity aroma precedes this hoppy bitter beer, with its fruity sweetness.

Best Bitter (OG 1041, ABV 4.1%)

Roundabout (OG 1043, ABV 4.3%)

Cascade (OG 1045, ABV 4.5%)

Coal Wharf (OG 1046, ABV 4.6%)
Full-bodied stout with chocolate malt to the fore.

Greg's

🍺 Dambusters Inn, 23 High Street, Scampton, Lincolnshire, LN1 2SD
☎ (01522) 730123

Greg's is a microbrewery launched in 2013 on the premises of the Dambusters Inn. Initially brewing just for the pub, the beers are now available in a few nearby pubs. ◆

Dambusters Ale (OG 1036, ABV 3.6%)
A fresh, hoppy pale ale with citrus tones and a light bitterness.

Scampton Ale (OG 1042, ABV 3.8%)

Mayson (OG 1045, ABV 4.2%)
A rich smooth best bitter.

Traf. Algar (OG 1045, ABV 5%)
A golden India pale ale.

Grey Friars SIBA

Featherstone Hall Farm, New Road, Featherstone, Staffordshire, WV10 7NW
☎ (01785) 840093 ☎ 07966 361443

Office: 17 Cranbrooks, Wheaton Aston, Staffordshire, ST19 9PZ ⊕ greyfriarsbrewery.co.uk

Established in 2014 and using equipment originally from Upham Brewery in Hampshire, the three-barrel plant is installed in a barn, formerly used as a snooker room and which still contains the original wood panelling.

Bobby (OG 1049, ABV 4%)

Auld Jock (OG 1047, ABV 4.7%)
Golden ale with a sweet initial taste, a hint of citrus and clean finish on the palate.

Grey Trees 👁

Unit 5-6, Gasworks Road, Aberaman, CF44 6RS
☎ (01685) 267077 ⊕ greytreesbrewing.com

Grey Trees began brewing at the Red Cow Inn in 2011 on the outskirts of Aberdare and relocated to its present location in 2013, upgrading to a 10-barrel plant originally used by Breconshire, with five fermentation vessels. It supplies an increasing number of local outlets, as well as those in other parts of South Wales. There are a number of open nights throughout the year (see website for details). ‼RAIB

Caradogs (OG 1038, ABV 3.9%)
Copper in colour, with a crisp flavour and dry finish.

Black Road Stout (OG 1040, ABV 4%)
A dark, smooth stout with delicate roasted flavours and a bittersweet aftertaste.

Diggers Gold (OG 1040, ABV 4%) 🍶
A modern golden ale? with fresh citrus aromas and a subtle bitterness.

Drummer Boy (OG 1042, ABV 4.2%)

Valley Porter (OG 1046, ABV 4.6%)
Warming and rich, with notes of dark fruits, coffee, chocolate and hazelnuts.

JPR Pale (OG 1046, ABV 4.7%)
Traditional British pale ale.

Afghan Pale (OG 1054, ABV 5.4%)
Brewed in the style of an American pale ale, full-flavoured, crisp and thirst quenching.

Greyhawk

See Copper Dragon

Greyhound SIBA 👁

Watershed, Smock Alley, West Chiltington, RH20 2QX
☎ 07973 625510 ⊕ greyhoundbrewery.co.uk

⊗ Greyhound was established in 2015. During its first year the reclaimed equipment was expanded to create a 7.5 barrel capacity, brewing up to three times a week. Husband-and-wife team Sarah and Nick Allen have a design and craft background, which comes across in the striking graphics on pumpclips and bottle labels. ‼◆RAIB

Good Ordinary Bitter (OG 1038, ABV 3.8%)
A classic English-style session bitter with a nutty flavour and subtle bitterness.

Blonde Bird (OG 1041, ABV 3.9%)
A refreshing pale ale with a well-rounded dry finish and a subtle lemon aroma.

Amber Eyes (OG 1040, ABV 4.2%)
A rich and well-balanced golden amber ale with complex floral aromas, rounded light biscuit malt flavours and a bitter finish.

Special B46 (OG 1044, ABV 4.6%)
A rich, dark amber ale with a good balance of warm biscuit malt flavours moving towards toast and blackberry, which linger on the palate assisting a clean, hoppy finish.

Gribble

🍴 Gribble Inn, Oving, West Sussex, PO20 2BP
☎ (01243) 786893 ⊕ gribbleinn.co.uk

⊗ Established in 1980 using a five-barrel plant, the Gribble Brewery is the longest-serving brewpub in the Sussex area, independently owned and run by the licensees. A number of local outlets are supplied. 🍺◆

CHI PA (OG 1040, ABV 3.8%)

Ale (OG 1041, ABV 4.1%)

Fuzzy Duck (OG 1045, ABV 4.3%)

Reg's Tipple (OG 1050, ABV 4.8%)
A smooth nutty flavour with a pleasant afterbite.

Plucking Pheasant (OG 1052, ABV 5%)

Pig's Ear (OG 1058, ABV 6%)

Wobbler (OG 1058, ABV 7.2%)

Griffin

🍴 Church Road, Shustoke, Warwickshire, B46 2LB
☎ (01675) 481205 ⊕ griffininnshustoke.co.uk

Brewing started in 2008 in the old coffin shop premises adjacent to the Griffin Inn. The five-barrel brewery is a venture between Griffin licensee Mick Pugh and his son Oliver. Most output goes to the pub, but free trade presence is increasing. Occasional experimental brews are produced. ‼◆

Dark Mild (OG 1030, ABV 3%)
Dry, assertive mild with a good roast character.

Yeti (OG 1047, ABV 4.7%)
A light-coloured pale ale, with a grapefruit aftertaste.

Black Magic Woman (OG 1050, ABV 5%)

Shoot to Thrill (OG 1050, ABV 5%)

GT

Unit 5, The Old Aerodrome, Chivenor Business Park, Braunton, Devon, EX31 4AY
☎ (01271) 267420 ☎ 07909 515170 ⊕ gtales.co.uk

⊗ GT Ales started in Barnstaple in 2013, producing only bottle-conditioned beers, before relocating to larger premises in Braunton in 2015. It now also brews cask ale. A brand new five-barrel plant purchased from Oban Ales in Scotland has been installed. More than 30 local outlets are supplied. ‼◆RAIB

Thirst of Many (OG 1043, ABV 4.2%)
Amber-coloured best bitter with a fruity and slightly caramel taste.

North Coast IPA (OG 1045, ABV 4.3%)
American-style IPA with strong tropical fruit aroma and taste. Triple-hopped to give a long and complex, sweet, fruity hop finish.

Blonde Ambition (OG 1044, ABV 4.5%)
Golden ale with good hop and citrus/gooseberry notes and a floral aroma.

Dark Horse Milk Stout (OG 1048, ABV 4.5%)

Crimson Rye'd (OG 1048, ABV 4.8%)
A speciality beer with a distinct red colour. Strong, fruity malted taste and good fruity residual hop finish.

Gun SIBA 👁

Hawthbush Farm, Gun Hill, East Sussex, TN21 0JY
☎ (01323) 700200 ☎ 07900 683355
⊕ gunbrewery.co.uk

⊗ Gun Brewery is located on a beautiful 140-acre organic mixed farm in the Sussex Weald. It generates much of its own power from a 15-kW solar array and heating comes from a wood-powered boiler. Spent grains keep the local livestock happy and all the water used for brewing comes from the brewery's own spring. More than 20 outlets are supplied. RAIB V

Scaramanga Extra Pale (OG 1038, ABV 3.9%)

Parabellum Milk Stout (OG 1057, ABV 4.1%)

Project Babylon Pale Ale (OG 1044, ABV 4.6%)

Zamzama IPA (OG 1060, ABV 6.5%)

Gun Dog SIBA

Unit 5b, Great Central Way, Woodford Halse, Northamptonshire, NN11 3PZ
☎ (01327) 264095 ☎ 07834 374751
⊕ gundogales.co.uk

Gun Dog is a family-run brewery established in 2012. A six-barrel plant is used to brew modern crafted ales with a nod to brewing traditions of the past. Beers are available in a number of pubs and shops locally. ‼🍺◆RAIB

Jack's Spaniels (OG 1038, ABV 3.8%)
A floral, refreshing blonde ale.

Booze Hound (OG 1042, ABV 4.2%)
A copper-coloured IPA with a slightly sweet taste and a bitter twist.

Lord Barker (OG 1042, ABV 4.2%)

Rich, dark, smooth and well-balanced stout with a chocolate nose, round taste in the mouth and a clean finish.

Bad to the Bone (OG 1045, ABV 4.5%)
A light brown-coloured English bitter. Biscuit undertones are balanced with a fruity hop finish.

Gundog

See Acton

Gwaun Valley

Kilkiffeth Farm, Pontfaen, SA65 9TP
☎ (01348) 881304 ⊕ gwaunvalleybrewery.co.uk

Gwaun Valley began brewing in 2009 on a four-barrel plant in a converted granary. The brewery offers views of the Preseli Hills and has a camp site, a holiday cottage and pitches for five caravans. Folk music sessions are held every Saturday evening. Each year a Bluegrass Festival is held at the brewery over a July weekend. ‼ ⟵

Farmhouse Ale (OG 1040, ABV 4%)
A malty ale with a smooth, balanced character.

Golden Bitter Ale (OG 1040, ABV 4%)
A smooth, bitter ale with a strong hoppy flavour and a crisp finish.

Light Ale (OG 1040, ABV 4%)
Refreshing and easy drinking, with citrus undertones and a clean finish.

St Davids Special (OG 1040, ABV 4%)
A light fruity beer with a refreshing citrus flavour.

Valley Brew (OG 1040, ABV 4.1%)
Double-hopped bitter ale with a mellow taste and balanced sweetness.

Blodwen (OG 1043, ABV 4.3%)
Creamy full-bodied bitter, ruby red in colour with a hint of caramel.

Cascade (OG 1043., ABV 4.3%)
A refreshing, clear, hoppy pale ale.

Calon Lan (OG 1044, ABV 4.5%)
Rich and malty with medium body and a bittersweet aftertaste.

King of the Road (OG 1045, ABV 4.5%)
A full-bodied, smooth classic light chestnut-coloured ale with a well-balanced finish.

Pembrokeshire Best Bitter (OG 1045, ABV 4.5%)
A full-flavoured, malty bitter ale with a hoppy finish.

Gyle 59 SIBA

The Brewery, Sadborow Estate Yard, Thorncombe, Dorset, TA20 4PW
☎ (01297) 678990 ☎ 07833 204543 ⊕ gyle59.co.uk

⊠ Gyle 59 is a 10-barrel brewery that began commercial production in 2014. All beers are unfined and available cask and bottle-conditioned. Bottling takes place on site with bottles being available by mail order. A brewery bar is open on Saturdays 10am-4pm. ‼ ⟵ ♦ RAIB V

Take it Easy (OG 1029, ABV 2.5%)
A light and refreshing session beer.

Freedom Hiker (OG 1038, ABV 3.7%)
Tropical Thunder (OG 1033.7, ABV 3.7%)

Toujours (OG 1042, ABV 4%)
Happy Daze (OG 1040, ABV 4.1%)
A wheat beer with a hint of banana and coriander.

Halcyon Daze (OG 1046.5, ABV 5%)
Pale & Bitter (OG 1046, ABV 5%)
A strong pale ale.

IPA (OG 1050, ABV 5.3%)
Dorset Gipa (OG 1050, ABV 5.4%)
A ginger infused IPA.

Dark & Bitter (OG 1054, ABV 5.8%)
Starstruck (OG 1060, ABV 6.6%)
A fruity porter enhanced by the addition of star anise.

The Favourite (OG 1060, ABV 6.6%)
A smooth, rich porter.

Double IPA (OG 1063, ABV 7.3%)

Hackney SIBA

Arch 358, Laburnum Street, Hackney, London, E2 8BB
☎ (020) 3489 9595 ⊕ hackneybrewery.co.uk

⊠ Founded in 2011, Hackney Brewery is the oldest brewery in the area. Weekly cask-conditioned specials are available locally. RAIB

Golden Ale (OG 1041, ABV 4%) ◗
Perfumed hops, honey and fruit balanced by a dry, pleasant bitterness that builds as the fruit and hops diminish.

Best Bitter (OG 1044, ABV 4.4%) ◗
Pale brown beer with a sweet citrus aroma and full, smooth mouthfeel. Citrus and floral hops on the palate.

American Pale Ale (OG 1045, ABV 4.5%)
A light copper-coloured pale ale with a sweet citrus aroma and full, smooth mouthfeel. Classic American hops on the finish.

Hadham (NEW) SIBA

Unit 6C, Hadham Industrial Estate, Church End, Little Hadham, SG11 2DY
☎ (01279) 771916 ☎ 07715 001222
⊕ hadhambrewery.co.uk

Hadham began brewing in 2015 using a 15-barrel plant. It uses only English hops and malt and brews with natural spring water found on site. Outlets are supplied within a 25-mile radius of the brewery.

18ct Golden Ale (ABV 3.7%)
A well-balanced ale with a crisp finish.

First Brew Ale (ABV 4%)
Dark ale with roasted coffee, toffee and chocolate flavours and a bittersweet balance.

Hadrian Border SIBA

Unit 5, The Preserving Works, Newburn Industrial Estate, Shelley Road, Newburn, Newcastle upon Tyne, NE15 9RT
☎ (0191) 264 9000 ⊕ hadrian-border-brewery.co.uk

Originally based at the Four Rivers site in Newcastle, the brewery relocated to Newburn in 2011 with a new 30-barrel brew plant to meet increased demand. Core brands, available nationally via wholesalers, are popular throughout

Tyneside, Northumberland, Edinburgh, Glasgow and Yorkshire. ‼ ♦ RAIB

Tyneside Blonde (OG 1037, ABV 3.9%) ◄
Refreshing blonde ale with zesty notes and a clean, fruity finish.

Farne Island Pale Ale (OG 1038, ABV 4%) ◄
A copper-coloured bitter with a refreshing malt/hop balance.

Flotsam (OG 1038, ABV 4%)
Bronze-coloured with a citrus bitterness and a distinctive floral aroma.

Secret Kingdom (OG 1042, ABV 4.3%)
Dark, rich and full-bodied, slightly roasted with a malty palate ending with a pleasant bitterness.

Coast to Coast (OG 1041.5, ABV 4.4%)
Light amber and hoppy beer with a nice malt balance.

Reiver's IPA (OG 1042, ABV 4.4%)
Golden bitter with a clean citrus palate and aroma with subtle malt flavours breaking through at the end.

Jetsam (OG 1043, ABV 4.5%)

Northumbrian Gold (OG 1044, ABV 4.5%)
Light golden-coloured ale with a biscuit malt flavour countered with floral and aromatic hops.

Grainger Ale (OG 1045, ABV 4.6%)
A pale-coloured ale, well-balanced with a refreshing bitter finish.

Hafod

Old Gas Works, Gas Lane, Mold, CH7 1UR
☎ (01352) 752719 ☎ 07901 386638
⊕ welshbeer.com

☺Hafod began brewing in 2011 on a small scale and moved to new premises in 2014, retaining the original kit for low volume brewing. A number of speciality beers using ingredients from the local upland areas and heathlands are also produced on a limited basis. ♦ RAIB

Hopper (OG 1040.5, ABV 3.8%) ◄
A full-flavoured session bitter with a mouthwatering taste of peppery hops and a lasting dry finish.

Sunrise (OG 1037, ABV 3.8%)
Pale and refreshing with citrus fruit flavours.

Moel Famau Ale (OG 1039, ABV 4.1%) ◄
A speciality dark ale brewed using local heather giving a dry, roasty taste with underlying sweet malt flavours.

H:E (OG 1040.5, ABV 4.3%) ◄
A clean-tasting best bitter, pale and hoppy with hints of vanilla in the dry taste.

Moel Fenlli (OG 1045, ABV 4.4%)
A speciality golden ale made with heather honey.

Moel Arthur (OG 1046, ABV 4.5%)
A fruity ale crafted with Clwydian Range bilberries.

Landmark (OG 1046, ABV 4.7%)
Copper-coloured ale with juicy malt flavours.

Hammer (OG 1059, ABV 6.6%) ◄
A sweet, strong bitter full of tropical fruits in aroma and taste, balanced by a powerful hoppy finish.

Dubbel (OG 1069, ABV 7.2%)
Dark Belgian Trappist-style beer.

Hairy Brewers (NEW)

Venture Garage, Belper Road, Holbrook, Derbyshire, DE56 0SX ☎ 07415 209489 ⊕ hairybrewersales.co.uk

The brewery was established in 2015. This eight-barrel plant was born from two bearded friends and their love for fine ale, with six years of experience already in the brewing trade. Beers are available in the Derbyshire area with an increasing demand further afield.

Hair Of The Dog (ABV 3.8%)
Traditional English bitter with a good balance of malt and hops. Full-bodied and rich on the palate, the malt gives a gentle caramel aroma with a spiced aromatic bitter finish.

Blonde Bombshell (ABV 4.3%)
Well-balanced, straw-coloured ale. A floral aroma leads to a citrus taste blast and a thirst quenching bitter finish.

Devils Whiskers (ABV 5.2%)

Dead Beard IPA (ABV 5.5%)
A deceptively easy-drinking, rich golden ale. A grapefruit and mango aroma and soft, smooth sweetness lead to a crisp, dry, hoppy bitter grapefruit finish.

Hale's

Walters Yard, Unit 3, Claylands Industrial Estate, Worksop, Nottinghamshire, S81 7DW ☎ 07436 282779 ✉ susanhale1865@gmail.com

Owners Suzi and Richard Hale founded the brewery in 2013, initially producing small test brews sold at the Grafton Hotel, Worksop. ♦

Sacred Heart (OG 1034, ABV 3.6%)
Golden-coloured session ale, low in strength but with bags of flavour.

Grey Heart (OG 1038, ABV 4%)
A hazy beer infused with Earl Grey. With bergamot and jasmine overtones, followed by a refreshing gentle citrus flavour.

Black Heart (OG 1048, ABV 5%)
A black IPA packed with intense flavours followed by a smooth roast background.

Half Moon SIBA ⊙

Forge House, Main Street, Ellerton, East Yorkshire, YO42 4PB
☎ (01757) 288977 ☎ 07741 400508
⊕ halfmoonbrewery.co.uk

Established in 2013 by Tony and Jackie Rogers, the brewery is based in the original blacksmith's forge next to their house. A five-barrel plant is used. ♦

Winter's Mild (OG 1033, ABV 3.3%)
Classic easy-drinking mild.

F'Hops Sake (OG 1039, ABV 3.9%)
Pale session bitter with a fruity and hoppy aftertaste.

Lunar (OG 1047, ABV 5.5%)
A refreshing golden bitter, intense hop aroma, with a fine malt flavour, and hints of caramel followed by a floral hop aftertaste.

THE BREWERIES

Halfpenny

Crown Inn, High Street, Lechlade, Gloucestershire, GL7 3AE
☎ (01367) 252198 ⊕ halfpennybrewery.co.uk

⊗ Halfpenny was established in 2008 on a four-barrel plant at the Crown at Lechlade, visible in a glazed outbuilding, and has since expanded to a third fermentation vessel. Beers are mainly brewed for the pub but some appears in the local free trade. !! ⊫ RAIB

Revival (OG 1040, ABV 3.6%)

Phoenix (OG 1041, ABV 3.7%)

Prospector (OG 1040, ABV 4%)

Thames Tickler (OG 1040, ABV 4%)
A pleasant session ale, easy to drink, full of subtle character and light on the tongue.

PDA (OG 1043, ABV 4.5%)
A traditional, premium strength ale, well-balanced and full-bodied.

Halifax Steam

The Conclave, Southedge Works, Brighouse Road, Hipperholme, West Yorkshire, HX3 8EF ☎ 07506 022504 ⊕ halifax-steam.co.uk

⊕Brewing since 1999, the five-barrel plant supplies only the brewery tap, the Cock o' the North. A range of permanent beers and around 200 different rotating beers are brewed, including the only rice beers in the country. 10-12 Halifax Steam beers are available in the pub at any one time, plus occasional guests on a fair trade basis. ♦

Aussie Kiss (OG 1038, ABV 3.8%)
Light beer with a hoppy flavour and finish.

Selene (OG 1040, ABV 4%)

Uncle Jon (OG 1043, ABV 4.3%) ◄
Roast predominates in this creamy, dark brown stout. The finish is smooth with no harsh edges.

Childcatcher (OG 1048, ABV 4.8%)
Deceptive pale, smooth-drinking beer with a citrus hop aroma and flavour.

Hall & Woodhouse (Badger) IFBB ◉

Bournemouth Road, Blandford St Mary, Blandford Forum, Dorset, DT11 9LS
☎ (01258) 452141 ⊕ hall-woodhouse.co.uk

⊗ Hall & Woodhouse has been brewing in the heart of the Dorset countryside since 1777. As one of the leading independent brewers in the UK, Hall & Woodhouse is well known for its range of award-winning ales brewed under the Badger brand and its estate of more than 200 pubs across the south of England. The brewery, owned and run by the seventh generation of the Woodhouse family, brews with Dorset spring water filtered through the Cretaceous chalk downs and drawn-up 120 feet from the its own wells. Badger cask ales are available exclusively in Hall & Woodhouse public houses. !! ⊫ ♦

K&B Sussex Bitter (OG 1036, ABV 3.5%) ◄
Traditional, lightly-hopped, easy-drinking session bitter with hints of malt and caramel and the traditional Badger fruit flavour predominating in the lingering bitter aftertaste.

Badger First Call (OG 1041, ABV 4%) ◄

Good example of a best bitter with good, but not over-powering, hop aromas and flavours and a good bittersweet aftertaste.

Tanglefoot (OG 1047, ABV 4.9%) ◄
Relatively sweet-tasting and deceptive, given its strength. Pale malt provides caramel overtones and bittersweet finish.

Hambleton SIBA ◉

Melmerby Green Road, Melmerby, North Yorkshire, HG4 5NB
☎ (01765) 640108 ⊕ hambletonales.co.uk

◉ Established in 1991 on the banks of the River Swale in the Vale of York, after several moves Hambleton now occupies purpose-built premises. Capacity is 100 barrels a week with a monthly special supplementing the core range. Village Brewer and Black Dog beers are contract brewed and a bottling line handles brands for other brewers. !! ♦ GF

Yorkshire Session Bitter (OG 1038.5, ABV 3.8%)
A golden bitter with a good balance of malty and refreshing citrus notes leading to a mellow, tangy finish.

Stallion Premium Bitter (OG 1041, ABV 4.2%) ◄
A premium bitter, moderately hoppy throughout and richly balanced in malt and fruit, developing a sound and robust bitterness, with earthy hops drying the aftertaste.

Stud Golden Ale (OG 1042.5, ABV 4.3%) ◄
A strongly bitter beer, with rich hop and fruit. It ends dry and spicy.

Nightmare Porter (OG 1050, ABV 5%) ◄
This full-flavoured beer satisfies all parts of the palate. Strong roast malts dominate, but hoppiness rears out of this complex blend.

Contract brewed for Black Dog Brewery, Whitby:

Whitby Abbey Ale (OG 1037.5, ABV 3.8%)

Schooner (OG 1041.5, ABV 4.2%)

Rhatas (OG 1045, ABV 4.6%)

Contract brewed for Village Brewer:

White Boar (OG 1037.5, ABV 3.8%)

Bull (OG 1039, ABV 4%)

Hamelsworde

41b Kirkby Road, Hemsworth, West Yorkshire, WF9 4BA ☎ 07530 669332 ⊕ hamelsworde.co.uk

◉ TThe brainchild of enthusiastic home brewer Dan Jones, his beers were originally brewed using a 50-litre boiler in a converted garage. A one-barrel plant was installed in 2013, which has now been moved into a converted shop with a tap house at the front. ♦ RAIB

Spanish Stout (OG 1045, ABV 4.2%)
A traditional stout with strong roasted flavours and a sweet liquorice taste complemented by aniseed.

Haley's Comet (OG 1047, ABV 4.5%)
A fresh, light summery ale with a citrus aroma and taste.

Jumping Pirate (OG 1051, ABV 4.9%)
A light golden ale in a Bavarian style. Floral, pine and citrus notes make this a complex beer which is smooth on the finish.

Colin Brown Ale (OG 1054, ABV 5.2%)
A fruity hop aroma leads on to a malty, nutty bittersweet flavour with a long dry aftertaste while the late addition of hops create a unique citrus burst.

Scalded Shoulder (OG 1054, ABV 5.2%)
A golden wheat beer, single-hopped with Saaz and finished with coriander and orange.

Cherokee America IPA (OG 1063, ABV 6%)
A copper-coloured IPA with a strong, fruity hop aroma.

Hammerpot SIBA

Unit 30, The Vinery, Arundel Road, Poling, West Sussex, BN18 9PY
☎ (01903) 883338 ⊕ hammerpot-brewery.co.uk

⊠ Hammerpot started brewing in 2005 using a five-barrel plant, which was upgraded to 10 barrels in 2011. The brewery supplies as far as London and Southampton. ♦ RAIB

Shooting Star (OG 1038, ABV 3.8%)

HPA (OG 1044, ABV 4.1%)
A light, golden, tangy pale ale with a full, fresh hop flavour.

Red Hunter (OG 1046, ABV 4.3%)
A ruby red-coloured bitter with a full-bodied, rich character. A premium bitter that drinks smoothly, leaving a fine lace in the glass.

Woodcote (OG 1047, ABV 4.5%)
A tangy amber bitter with a pleasant, dry finish.

Brighton Belle (ABV 4.6%)
Pale amber bitter. Fresh floral hops notes, spicy orange, crisp grapefruit and a hint of caramel.

Bottle Wreck Porter (OG 1047, ABV 4.7%)
A traditional pitch black porter with coffee, chocolate and rich roast malt flavours.

Madgwick Gold (OG 1050, ABV 5%)
A golden ale with a fresh citrus spice hop aroma and a refreshing, thirst-quenching finish.

Hammerton SIBA ◉

Unit 8 & 9 Roman Way Industrial Estate, 149 Roman Way, Barnsbury, London, N7 8XH
☎ (020) 3302 5880 ⊕ hammertonbrewery.co.uk

Hammerton Brewery began brewing in London in 1868. It ceased to brew in the late 1950s and the brewery was later demolished. In 2014, a member of the Hammerton family decided to resurrect the family name in brewing. A 15-barrel plant is used. RAIB

N1 (OG 1044, ABV 4.1%) ◣
Refreshing smooth pale ale. Honey, some citrus and pineapple flavours, fading in the finish where a spicy, hoppy bitterness builds.

Life on Mars (OG 1045, ABV 4.6%)
Red ale with the taste of berry and caramel and an aroma of grapefruit, pine and earth hop.

N7 (OG 1052, ABV 5.2%) ◣
Cocoa throughout with a pleasant sweetness, balanced by a lingering dark-roast dryness and a raisin fruitiness. A trace of liquorice.

Oyster Stout (OG 1057, ABV 5.3%) ◣
Liquorice and fruit on the palate. Dry finish with a little dark roast character and a touch of caramelised fruit.

Handley's

⬚ Willow Tree, Front Street, Barnby in the Willows, Newark, Nottinghamshire, NG24 2SA
⊕ willowtreebarnby.co.uk

⊛ Handley's began brewing in 2011 on a 0.5-barrel plant installed behind the Willow Tree pub. Beer is mostly sold in the pub, with at least one being on pump at all times, and can occasionally be found at local beer festivals.

Hanging Bat

⬚ c/o 133 Lothian Road, Edinburgh, EH3 9AB
☎ (0131) 229 0759 ⊕ thehangingbat.com

⊠ Brewing began in 2012 from within the Hanging Bat bar using a 50-litre brew kit from the United States.

Hanlons SIBA ◉

Hill Farm, Half Moon Village, Newton St Cyres, Devon, EX5 5AE
☎ (01392) 851160 ⊕ hanlonsbrewery.com

⊠ Formerly known as O'Hanlons, the brewery moved to Half Moon, near Exeter, in 2013. The building comprises a shop, bar and restaurant. ‼ ⧉ ♦

Firefly (OG 1035, ABV 3.7%) ◣
Malty and fruity light bitter. Hints of orange in the taste.

Copper Glow (OG 1042, ABV 4.2%)
Copper-coloured ale with a hint of toffee and a light bitterness. A malty, fruity taste combines with the perfume of rich roast barley. Full of flavour and easy drinking.

Dry Stout (OG 1043, ABV 4.2%) ◣
A dark, malty, well-balanced stout with a dry, bitter finish and plenty of roast and fruit flavours up front.

Yellowhammer (OG 1041, ABV 4.2%) ◣
A thin, pale yellow beer dominated by hops. The aftertaste is bitter and dry.

Port Stout (OG 1041, ABV 4.8%) ⧉ ◣
Black beer with roast malt aroma that remains in the taste but gives way to hoppy bitterness in the aftertaste.

Stormstay (OG 1048, ABV 5%)
A toffee and floral hop nose and hints of tangerine. Malt, caramel and biscuit nestle with the hoppy aroma.

Happy Valley SIBA

8 Hazelhurst Drive, Bollington, Cheshire, SK10 5QT
☎ 07758 512080 ⊕ happyvalleybrewery.co.uk

⊠ Happy Valley was established in 2010 by David and Nicola Hughes using a 2.5-barrel plant. Pubs are supplied in Cheshire, Derbyshire, Greater Manchester and Staffordshire. ‼ ♦

Little Mill Town (OG 1036, ABV 3.6%)
A traditional dark mild.

Small & Mighty (OG 1036, ABV 3.6%)

A clean, crisp and refreshing ale with a lasting floral, citrus aroma and a hint of lemon.

Sworn Secret (OG 1038, ABV 3.8%)
Pale straw-coloured ale with a strong hop character. It has a pleasant hoppy nose with a citrus aftertaste.

Little Rascal (OG 1039, ABV 3.9%)
A light, well-balanced golden session ale with a lingering citrus and grapefruit aftertaste.

Five Rings (OG 1040, ABV 4%)
Crisp, clean-tasting ale brewed with three aroma hops.

Lazy Daze (OG 1042, ABV 4.2%)
Golden-coloured ale made with a hoppy finish.

Black Out XO Rum Porter (OG 1044, ABV 4.4%)
A dark, full-bodied porter with a deep, intense malty flavour. Dark roasted and chocolate malts with a lingering aroma of oak aged rum.

Black Magic (OG 1046, ABV 4.6%)
A full-bodied stout.

Tie the Knot (OG 1050, ABV 5%)
A straw-coloured strong bitter with malt tastes and a big hop character.

Dangerously Dark (OG 1056, ABV 5.6%)
A black IPA.

Bollywood IPA (OG 1058, ABV 5.9%)
A full-bodied, straw-coloured IPA with rounded malt flavours blended with bitterness and a big hop character. Deep and intensely rich taste.

Harbour SIBA

Trekillick Farm, Kirland, Bodmin, Cornwall, PL30 5BB
☎ (01208) 832131 ☎ 07870 305063
⊕ harbourbrewing.com

⊗ Harbour is an innovative brewery founded on the outskirts of Bodmin in 2011. Brewed using local spring water, the regular beers are established in an increasing number of outlets. A new 30-barrel plant was installed in 2016. ♦

Light (OG 1037, ABV 3.7%) ♠
Light, golden ale with hop aroma. Hops dominate the taste with some pineapple, citrus and pear drops. Hoppy, dry finish.

Amber (OG 1037.5, ABV 4%) ♠
Pale brown bitter with a floral hop aroma. Peach and citrus flavours with biscuit malt. Quite sweet taste and finish.

IPA (OG 1048.5, ABV 5%) ♠
Amber-coloured ale with a heady citrus hop aroma. Hoppy bitter taste and finish with citrus fruits but subdued malt.

Porter (OG 1055, ABV 5.5%) ♠
Smooth, creamy, black porter with roast malt aroma. Malty, smoky and sweet followed by a bitter tang. Sweet finish.

Pale (OG 1059, ABV 6%) ♠
Amber ale with powerful citrus hop aroma. Intense citrus hop flavour with marmalade, orange and bitterness. Hoppy, dry finish.

Harbwr Tenby (NEW)

Sargeants Lane, St Julian Street, Tenby, SA70 7BU
☎ (01834) 845797 ⊕ harbwr.wales

Brewing commenced in 2015 on a five-barrel plant in an outbuilding of the Buccaneer Inn, Tenby. A small plant within the brewery is used for experimental one-off brews. Beers are available in the pub, at the nearby Hope & Anchor and further afield. ‼♦

MV Enterprise (OG 1040, ABV 4%)
A refreshing, citrus pale ale with spicy, herbal bitterness finished with a floral and zesty aroma.

North Star (OG 1042, ABV 4.2%)
Smooth malty amber ale blending herbal bitterness, finishing with spicy blackcurrant and lemon aroma.

RFA Sir Galahad (OG 1046, ABV 4.6%)
A ruby-coloured ale with a deep, complex malt character. Four different hop varieties provide cedar, grapefruit and floral aromas.

Harby (NEW)

⊟ Bottle & Glass, 5 High Street, Harby, Nottinghamshire, NG23 7EB
☎ (01522) 703438
✉ email@bottleandglassharby.com

Harby Brewstore is a four-barrel malt extract brewery established in 2015 and located at the Bottle & Glass in Harby that began brewing in 2015. Most output goes to the three pubs in the small Wig & Mitre pub group, currently Wig & Mitre in Lincoln, Caunton Beck in Caunton and the Bottle & Glass itself.

Lifford Bitter (ABV 3.9%)

Ashworth Ale (ABV 4.2%)

Queen Eleanor IPA (ABV 4.5%)

Hardknott SIBA

Unit 10, Devonshire Road Industrial Estate, Millom, Cumbria, LA18 4JS
☎ (01229) 779309 ⊕ hardknott.com

☺Hardknott began brewing in 2005 at the Woolpack Inn in Boot. The brewery relocated to Millom and expanded in 2010. It supplies beers both nationally and internationally, in a variety of formats. The 16-hectolitre brewhouse is complemented with modern multi-purpose fermentation tanks and a bottling line. ‼♦RAIB

Katalyst (OG 1035, ABV 3.8%) ♠
An assertively hoppy, bitter beer, with a sweet, fruity taste which diminishes in the finish.

Lux Borealis (OG 1035, ABV 3.8%) ♠
Fruity, hoppy aromas lead to a well-balanced middle with hops increasing in the finish.

Continuum (OG 1036, ABV 4%) ♠
An amber-coloured beer with pronounced hops and bitterness right through to the aftertaste. Some maltiness in the aroma and taste.

Brownian Motion (OG 1042, ABV 4.5%)

Nuclear Sunset (OG 1039.5, ABV 4.7%)
A wheat beer made with orange peel, orange juice, coriander and nutmeg.

Dark Energy (OG 1046, ABV 4.9%) ♠
A hoppy aroma leads to a dry hoppy beer with plenty of roast.

Code Black (OG 1052, ABV 5.6%) ♠

High impact hops and roast malt leave a lasting impression.

Azimuth (OG 1052, ABV 5.8%) ◥
Floral and fruity esters and lots of interesting hops and some complex bitterness create a fascinating tasting erxperience.

Infra Red (OG 1058, ABV 6.2%)
Hints of toffee and popcorn. Citrus fruits dominate.

Hardys & Hansons

See Greene King

Haresfoot SIBA ◉

2 River Park Industrial Estate, Billet Lane, Berkhamsted, Hertfordshire, HP4 1HL
☎ (01442) 862878 ⊕ haresfoot.com

⊠ Brewing returned to the heart of Berkhamsted in 2014 after an absence of 100 years. The brewery, established by a consortium of eight local businessmen, is situated in an industrial unit close to the Grand Union Canal using a dual channel 12 and 2.5-barrel plant. During 2015 a range of short run, limited edition beers was introduced under the White Label brand. The owners plan to move to a new site in 2017. **!!** ▅◆

Wild Boy (OG 1037.5, ABV 3.7%)
A quaffable modern pale ale hopped to give floral and citrus aromas. Smooth malt and vanilla in the mouth give way to long bittersweet notes.

Sundial Golden Ale (OG 1038, ABV 3.8%)
A refreshing light golden ale with generous late hopping leading to an undercurrent of exotic fruits.

Lock Keeper's Launch Ale (OG 1039, ABV 3.9%)
A complex blend of malts with a hoppy edge and delicate fruit notes, leading to a long bittersweet aftertaste.

Stardusst (OG 1042.5, ABV 4.2%)
A red-coloured beer with fruit and floral aromas and a nutty sweetness rounded off with a crisp finish.

Conqueror's Premium Bitter (OG 1043, ABV 4.4%)
A full-bodied bitter with roasted barley creating a chestnut-coloured ale with a lingering malty taste and rounded bitter finish.

Totem American IPA (OG 1042, ABV 4.5%)
American-style IPA with citrus flavours and hop aromas well balanced by subtle malt character.

Harrogate SIBA

41 Claro Court Business Centre, Harrogate, North Yorkshire, HG1 4BA ☎ 07774 891664
⊕ harrogatebrewery.co.uk

Started in 2013, the brewery also uses the name Spa Town Ales on the pumpclips for its range of ales.

Tewit Well Ale (OG 1041, ABV 4.1%)
Copper-coloured traditional Yorkshire bitter tasting of malt, spices and orange peel.

Stray Ale (OG 1042, ABV 4.2%)
Golden ale with a spicy flavour and lingering hop finish.

Pinewoods Pale Ale (OG 1044, ABV 4.4%)
Pale beer with citrus flavours.

No. 5 Porter (OG 1053, ABV 5.3%)
A rich, fruity dark beer with roasted malt, fruit and spice.

Kursaal Porter (OG 1054, ABV 5.4%)
A rich, bittersweet example of the style, tasting of espresso, liquorice and chocolate.

The Pump Room (OG 1054, ABV 5.4%)
Ruby brown-coloured, rich, dark and fruity beer.

Hart Family

The 1833 Brewery, 21 Nene Court, The Embankment, Wellingborough, Northamptonshire, NN8 1LD
☎ (01933) 228324 ☎ 07891 212476
⊕ hartfamilybrewers.com

⊠ Hart Family Brewers was established in 2012 using an eight-barrel plant. It is owned and operated by Rob and Sarah Hart, who are indulging their passion after a combined 25 years in the drinks industry. Recent expansion, including a third fermenter, gives weekly production of up to 38 barrels. **!!** ▅RAIB

House Beer (OG 1036, ABV 3.6%)
A classic country bitter.

Harts No. 1 (OG 1043, ABV 4.1%)
A tawny-coloured premium bitter with fruity, malty aromas and grassy citrus notes. Fresh and fruity on the palate with spicy bitterness and citrus, hay-like aromas on the refreshing finish.

Harts No. 9 (OG 1044, ABV 4.3%)
A golden beer, light and refreshing with spicy grapefruit aromas. Fresh and light on the palate with pithy grapefruit flavours supported by biscuity malt.

Harts No. 3 (OG 1047, ABV 4.7%)
A fruity, ruby-coloured beer with full malty, spicy aromas. Full and forward on the palate with rounded, rich malty flavours supported by gentle spicy hoppiness.

Harts No. 8 (OG 1052, ABV 5%)
A dark beer with bold toasted fruit aromas and hints of espresso. Full and warming roasted fruit and molasses flavours balanced by bitter coffee, chocolate and spice aromas over a long finish.

Pale (OG 1052, ABV 5%)
Strong bitter beer. Biscuity malt complemented by a marked orange-scented bitterness.

Hart of Preston SIBA

Unit 5, Oxhey Trading Estate, Greenbank Street, Preston, Lancashire, PR1 7PH
☎ (01772) 437651 ⊕ hartbreweryltd.co.uk

◉Hart opened in 1995 behind the Cartford Hotel in Little Eccleston. In 2010 the brewery relocated to Preston. It supplies a number of local outlets and arranges exchanges with other microbreweries. **!!** ◆RAIB

Bat Out of Hell (OG 1036, ABV 3.6%)

Temptress (OG 1036, ABV 3.6%)

Lancashire Best Bitter (OG 1039, ABV 3.9%)

Pale Ale (OG 1039, ABV 3.9%)

Dishy Debbie (OG 1040, ABV 4%)

Ice Maiden (OG 1040, ABV 4%) ◥
Hoppy, crisp, straw-coloured bitter with floral notes and a dry finish.

Lord of the Glen (OG 1042, ABV 4.2%)

Hart of Stebbing

White Hart, High Street, Stebbing, Essex, CM6 3SQ
☎ (01371) 856383 ⊕ hartofstebbingbrewery.co.uk

The brewery was established in 2007 by Nick Eldred, who is also the owner of the White Hart pub where the brewery is based. At present only the White Hart and local beer festivals are supplied. ◆

Hart IPA (OG 1035, ABV 3.5%)

Harthill Village

Union Street, Harthill, South Yorkshire, S26 7YH
☎ 07736 246474 ⊕ harthillbrewery.co.uk

Brewing began in 2013 using a five-barrel plant supplying local pubs, clubs and shops. ◆

Ace of Harts (OG 1039, ABV 3.9%)
A traditional, well-balanced amber bitter with a subtle malty sweetness and spicy, fruity aroma.

Hart Stopper (OG 1040, ABV 4%)
Hoppy blonde ale with a fresh aroma of citrus and berry fruits with hints of zest and spice.

Hart's Desire (OG 1044, ABV 4.4%)
An amber-coloured premium ale with a fresh aroma of citrus with floral and spicy notes balanced with biscuity, malty, sweet flavours.

Dark Hart (OG 1048, ABV 4.8%)
A rich, smooth, full-bodied dark ale with a toffee, malty sweetness and a dry, biscuity fullness complemented by the spicy, blackcurrant aroma.

Dark Hart Festival Reserve (OG 1065, ABV 6.5%)
Premium version of Dark Hart with an increased intensity of flavour and hoppy finish.

Hartshorns

Unit 4, Tomlinsons Industrial Estate, Alfreton Road, Derby, DE21 4ED ☎ 07830 367125
⊕ hartshornsbrewery.com

Hartshorns began brewing in 2012 using a six-barrel plant installed by brothers Darren and Lindsey Hartshorn. In 2015 the brewery acquired its first pub, the Little Chester Ale House, Derby. ▬

Ignite (OG 1039, ABV 3.9%)

Highgate (OG 1044, ABV 4.3%)
Smooth, easy-drinking, copper-coloured ale. Well-balanced malt sweetness with fruity hop flavour and a well-rounded bitterness.

Porter (OG 1045, ABV 4.5%)

Brooklyn Nights (OG 1052, ABV 5.4%)
A punchy American brown ale with a complex malt base.

Shakademus (OG 1052, ABV 5.4%)
Full-bodied with a citrus hop bite, a satisfying premium golden ale.

Apocalypse (OG 1055, ABV 6.2%)
Surprisingly easy-drinking golden ale with a clean bitter finish. Refreshingly crisp and packed with hop character.

Harveys IFBB 👁

Bridge Wharf Brewery, 6 Cliffe High Street, Lewes, East Sussex, BN7 2AH

☎ (01273) 480209 ⊕ harveys.org.uk

Established in 1790, this independent family brewery operates from the banks of the River Ouse in Lewes. A major development in 1985 doubled the brewhouse capacity and subsequent additional fermenting capacity has seen production rise to more than 38,000 barrels a year. There is also a microbrewery on site used to brew special beers including replicating old Lewes Brewery recipes using the County Town Beers name. Harveys supplies real ale to all its 48 pubs and 550 free trade outlets in the south-east. !! ▬ ◆ RAIB

R (ABV 2.8%)

Sussex XX Mild Ale (OG 1030, ABV 3%) ◄
A dark copper-brown colour. Roast malt dominates the aroma and palate leading to a sweet, caramel finish.

IPA (OG 1033, ABV 3.5%)

Sussex Wild Hop (OG 1037, ABV 3.7%)

Sussex Best Bitter (OG 1040, ABV 4%) ◄
Full-bodied brown bitter. A hoppy aroma leads to a good malt and hop balance, and a dry aftertaste.

Old Ale (OG 1043, ABV 4.3%)

Olympia (OG 1042, ABV 4.3%)

Armada Ale (OG 1045, ABV 4.5%) ◄
Hoppy amber best bitter. Well-balanced fruit and hops dominate throughout with a fruity palate.

Harviestoun SIBA 👁

Harviestoun Brewery, Alva Industrial Estate, Alva, FK12 5DQ
☎ (01259) 769100 ⊕ harviestoun.com

Harviestoun has grown from one-man brewing in a bucket in the back of a shed in 1983 to a 60-barrel, multi-award-winning brewery today. With a reputation for experimentation, the brewery adds around eight to ten short-run seasonals to its core range of two ales. !! ▬ ◆ RAIB

Bitter & Twisted (OG 1039, ABV 3.8%) ◄
Refreshingly hoppy beer with fruit throughout. A bittersweet taste with a long bitter finish. A golden session beer.

Schiehallion (OG 1048, ABV 4.8%) ▮ ◄
A Scottish cask lager, brewed using a lager yeast and Hersbrucker hops. A hoppy aroma, with fruit and malt, leads to a malty, bitter taste with floral hoppiness and a bitter finish.

Harwich Town

Station Approach, Harwich, Essex, CO12 3NA
☎ (01255) 551155 ⊕ harwichtown.co.uk

Brewing started in 2007 on a five-barrel plant next to Harwich Town railway station. The brewer is a CAMRA member and former customs officer. Beers are named after local landmarks, characters or events. 50 outlets are supplied. The brewery holds a beer festival in July and a festival special is brewed for the Harwich & Dovercourt Bay Winter Ale Festival in December. !! ▬ ◆ RAIB

Bay Bitter (OG 1036, ABV 3.6%)

Ha'penny Mild (OG 1036, ABV 3.6%)

EPA 100 (OG 1038, ABV 3.8%)

Leading Lights (OG 1038, ABV 3.8%)

Ganges (OG 1040, ABV 4%)

Misleading Lights (OG 1040, ABV 4%)

Bathside Battery Bitter (OG 1042, ABV 4.2%)

Redoubt Stout (OG 1042, ABV 4.2%)

Parkeston Porter (OG 1045, ABV 4.5%)

Lighthouse Bitter (OG 1048, ABV 4.8%)

Phoenix APA (OG 1052, ABV 5%)

Hastings SIBA

Unit 12, Conqueror Industrial Estate, Moorhurst Road, St Leonards-on-Sea, East Sussex, TN38 9NB
☎ (01424) 572050 ⊕ hastingsbrewery.co.uk

⊠ Hastings is a small five-barrel brewery established in 2010, exclusively producing unfined beers suitable for vegetarians and vegans. Brewing is currently suspended. RAIB V

Hattie Brown's (NEW)

Unit 1, The Sidings, Victoria Avenue Industrial Estate, Swanage, Dorset, BH19 1AU
☎ (01929) 439229

⊠ Hattie Brown's began brewing in 2014 at Wessex brewery. In 2015 it moved to its present location. Beers are produced for the Square & Compass in Worth Matravers, and occasionally for local beer festivals.

Mustang Sally (OG 1042, ABV 4.2%)
A full-flavoured, well-balanced best bitter with good floral hop aroma.

Hawkshead SIBA ⊙

Mill Yard, Staveley, Cumbria, LA8 9LR
☎ (01539) 822644 ⊕ hawksheadbrewery.co.uk

☺ The brewery takes its name from the village in which it was founded in 2002. It outgrew its original barn and so moved to Staveley in 2006 to a purpose-built 20-barrel brewery. Capacity has been increased several times since, a new micro packaging plant added and the Beer Hall, the brewery tap, developed as a showcase for real ale. A kitchen serves 'beer tapas' to complement the beer. Pubs are supplied directly throughout the north and further afield to selected outlets.
!! ▄ ◆ RAIB

Iti (OG 1036, ABV 3.5%) ◣
A beer packed with grapefruit aroma and taste. Well-balanced with a long lasting, hoppy bitter finish.

Windermere Pale (OG 1036, ABV 3.5%) ◣
Crisp and fruity yellow beer with hints of melon and grapefruit and a strong bitter aftertaste.

Bitter (OG 1037, ABV 3.7%) 🗂 ▣ ◣
Well-balanced, thirst-quenching beer with fruit and hops aroma, leading to a lasting bitter finish.

Red (OG 1042, ABV 4.2%) ◣
An impressive colour for this richly flavoured beer; lots of fruitiness and good hop flavour with a lingering aftertaste.

Lakeland Gold (OG 1043, ABV 4.4%) 🗂 ◣
Fresh, well-balanced fruity, hoppy beer with a clean bitter aftertaste.

Dry Stone Stout (OG 1044, ABV 4.5%) ◣

Black, dry, bitter stout with an astringent, roast finish.

Great White (OG 1048, ABV 4.8%)
A spiced wheat beer brewed with coriander seeds and orange peel.

Brodie's Prime (OG 1048, ABV 4.9%) ◣
Complex, dark brown beer with plenty of malt, fruit and roast taste. Satisfying full body with clean finish.

Cumbrian Five Hop (OG 1050, ABV 5%) 🗂 ◣
A robust hoppy bitter with citrus hops and fruity middle.

Lakeland Lager (OG 1045, ABV 5%)
A cask-conditioned lager.

NZPA (OG 1056, ABV 6%) ▣ ◣
A hoppy bitter with a sweet, fruity taste and a resounding dry bitter finish.

IPA (OG 1065, ABV 7%)
A modern IPA, amber in colour, with huge hop flavours.

Haworth Steam

🍺 Rose & Crown, 2 Westgate, Cleckheaton, West Yorkshire, BD19 5ET
☎ (01535) 646059 ☎ 07974 483310
⊕ haworthsteambrewery.co.uk

☺ Established in 2011 using a five-barrel plant, the brewery now has online sales and a café, bar and bistro in Haworth acting as the brewery tap. There are plans to increase both beer range and production. ▄

True Tyke (OG 1038, ABV 3.8%)
Amber-coloured Yorkshire bitter with creamy biscuit notes and a distinctive breadiness.

WD Austerity (OG 1038, ABV 3.8%)
Blonde ale with plenty of cereal and digestive biscuit on the nose. Creamy malt body giving a floral finish.

Ironclad 957 (OG 1043, ABV 4.3%)
Stout with caramel and raisin to the nose and a little drying smoke on the finish.

Fallwood XXXX (OG 1052, ABV 5.2%)
Full-bodied ale full of roasted barley and hops. Toffee-apple red in colour.

Hay Rake

Blackstone Edge Old Road, Littleborough, OL15 0JX
☎ (01706) 379689 ☎ 07775 792684
⊕ hayrakebrewery.info

Mark Wickham, the landlord of the Rake Tapas Restaurant, resurrected the Hay Rake microbrewery in 2013. The Rake brewed its own beer during the reign of Queen Victoria but stopped in 1901. Mark is keen to revive the tradition of locally-brewed ale.

Dawn's Hopping Mad (OG 1038, ABV 3.8%)
A blend of five hops with a hint of chilli and ginger.

Dawn's Called Thyme (OG 1040, ABV 4%)
Citrus with a blend of thyme and fresh peaches.

Early Dawn (OG 1041, ABV 4.1%)
An IPA using a blend of four hops with a hint of honey and lemongrass.

Dawn's Dark Side (OG 1044, ABV 4.4%)
A blend of four hops with molasses and coriander.

THE BREWERIES

Dawn's Autumn Gold (OG 1045, ABV 4.5%)
A blend of four hops with a hint of liquorice and golden syrup.

Haywood Bad Ram SIBA

Callow Top Holiday Park, Buxton Road, Sandydrook, Ashbourne, Derbyshire, DE6 2AQ
☎ (01335) 344020 ☎ 07974 948427
⊕ callowtop.co.uk/callow-top-brewery

⊗ Established in 2003, the brewery was based in a converted barn but a new brewery and bottling plant became operational in 2012. One pub is owned (on site) and several other outlets are supplied. ‼ ☛ RAIB

Thoroughbred Bad Ram (OG 1038, ABV 3.8%)
A refreshing straw-coloured ale with a crisp bite and spice and flowery notes.

Dr Samuel Johnson (OG 1044, ABV 4.5%)
A slightly fruity and refined spicy flavour.

Callow Top Imperial IPA (OG 1050, ABV 5.2%)
A full-bodied, rich ale with a fruity and slightly citrus aftertaste.

Healey's

🏠 Wellington Inn, Main Street, Loppergarth, Cumbria, LA12 0JL
☎ (01229) 582388

Healey's began brewing in the Wellington in 2012 using a custom-made 2.5-barrel stainless steel plant, which can be viewed through full-length windows in the pub.

Golden (OG 1037, ABV 3.6%) ◆
A fruity, moderately bitter light ale.

True Brit (OG 1037, ABV 3.6%)
A golden bitter made with all English hops and a hint of roasted malt.

Dark Mild (OG 1038, ABV 3.7%) ◆
Dark mild with a reddish hue. Roast flavours at outset mingle with fruit and sweetness in the middle. A drier finish completes the beer.

Blonde (OG 1040, ABV 4%) ◆
Aromatic bitter, sweet and tasty from the start with increasing hops and a dry bitter finish.

Best (OG 1042, ABV 4.2%)
Traditional-style best bitter with developing good hop bitterness. Fruity middle and a touch of roast bitterness balance the underlying sweetness.

Loppergarth Pale Ale (OG 1048, ABV 5%)
A well-hopped strong bitter in the style of the original IPA. Late hopped for added aroma.

Heart of Wales

🏠 Stables Yard, Zion Street, Llanwrtyd Wells, LD5 4RD
☎ (01591) 610236 ⊕ heartofwalesbrewery.co.uk

☺The brewery was set up with a six-barrel plant in 2006 in old stables at the rear of the Neuadd Arms Hotel. Beers are brewed using water from the brewery's own borehole. Seasonal brews celebrate local events such as the World Bogsnorkelling Championships. Cambrian Heart Ale was commissioned by and is brewed for the Cambrian Mountains Initiative, inspired by the Prince of Wales, which aims to promote and support rural producers and communities in the region.
‼ ☛ ◆ RAIB V

Irfon Valley Bitter (OG 1038, ABV 3.6%)

Aur Cymru (OG 1040, ABV 3.8%)

Bitter (OG 1042, ABV 4.1%)
A light chestnut-coloured bitter in the Northern style, it has a fine, smooth balance between malt and hop.

Big Red Chopper (OG 1043, ABV 4.3%)
A rich, red ruby ale. Brewed in collaboration with the Wales Air Ambulance, a donation of 10p for every pint sold supports the service's Big Red Chopper.

Welsh Black (OG 1045, ABV 4.4%) ⌂
A full-flavoured, complex and smooth stout.

Cambrian Heart Ale (OG 1045, ABV 4.5%)
Light golden brown ale with a refreshing fruity body and lots of hops in the finish.

Noble Eden Ale (OG 1046, ABV 4.6%)
A dark brown-coloured premium ale bursting with fruit and malt, with just a hint of chocolate.

Inn-stable (OG 1065, ABV 6.8%)
A powerful ale with a warming malty body and a smooth finish.

Heathen

Grape & Grain, 51 The Broadway, Haywards Heath, West Sussex, RH16 3AS
☎ (01444) 456217 ☎ 07825 429428
⊕ heathenbrewers.co.uk

Located in the basement of the Grape & Grain off-licence and delicatessen, brewing began in 2014 using a full mash, two-barrel plant. Local outlets and beer festivals are supplied. ‼ ◆ RAIB

ipaD (OG 1055, ABV 4.5%)
A dark IPA.

Rhubarb (OG 1044, ABV 4.5%)
A best bitter brewed with honey and rhubarb.

Porter (OG 1055, ABV 5%)
A rich, well-hopped porter.

Chemistry (OG 1050, ABV 5.5%)
A Belgian-style wheat beer.

Iceni Genie (OG 1057, ABV 5.5%)
An English pale ale.

West Coast (OG 1049, ABV 5.5%)
A honeyed West Coast-style IPA.

Honey (OG 1060, ABV 6%)
An IPA with copious amounts of Greek honey.

Heathton

c/o Old Gate, Heathton, Shropshire, WV5 7EB

Old Gate, Heathton, WV5 7EB

This brewery is planned to be resurrected at the Old Gate pub, but its three beers are produced at present in three different breweries, and served only in the Old Gate. Brewing is currently suspended.

Heavy Industry SIBA

The Old Slaughterhouse, Denbigh Street, Henllan, LL16 5AR
☎ (01745) 816316 ☎ 07812 346466

The Old Slaughterhouse Denbigh St, Henllan, LL16 5AR
⊕ heavyindustrybrewing.com

Established in 2012, Heavy Industry is an award-winning brewery using a 10-barrel plant situated in an old slaughterhouse in the village of Henllan. ♦

Diawl Bach (OG 1036.5, ABV 3.8%) ◥
Citrus fruit flavours feature strongly in this uncompromising, hoppy bitter. The acerbic, tart taste continues long into the aftertaste

Electric Mountain (OG 1036.5, ABV 3.8%) ◥
A full-bodied session bitter, dry and well-balanced with a satisfying hoppy finish.

Freak Chick (OG 1042, ABV 4.5%)
This red malty beer gives an earthy, spicy and zesty character by a complex blend of five hops that is balanced by the sweetness of the malts.

High Voltage (OG 1042, ABV 4.5%) ◥
A dry, bitter beer full of citrus fruit, hoppy flavours which dominate the taste and lasting bitter finish.

Nelsons Eye (OG 1042, ABV 4.5%) ◥
Heavily hopped with a strong, sharp bitter taste. Citrus fruit notes, mainly grapefruit, in the aroma and palate continue into the hoppy, bitter aftertaste.

Nos Smoked Porter (OG 1045, ABV 4.5%)
This well-hopped dark porter gives wreaths of smoke mingled with coffee and roast notes.

77 (OG 1046, ABV 4.9%) ▨ ◥
A strong bitter with a powerful smack of fruit and hops. Tangy fruit flavours and hoppy bitterness feature strongly in the aroma, taste and finish.

Collaborator (OG 1046, ABV 5%) ◥
A smooth and satisfying dark, hoppy beer. The juicy malty taste is quite roasty and leads to a dry, hoppy aftertaste.

Pigeon Toed Orange Peel (OG 1048.5, ABV 5.2%)
A half wheat beer, citrus notes complemented by a tangy hoppy aftertaste.

Dr Jekyll's Last Waltz (OG 1055, ABV 5.5%)
Black IPA, brewed in collaboration with Black Cloak Brewing, boasting toasted coconut and dark roasted chocolate liquorice notes.

Hebridean

10 Shell St, Stornoway, Isle of Lewis, HS1 2BS
☎ (01851) 700123 ⊕ hebridean-brewery.co.uk

⊛After a hiatus, the brewery has reopened in new premises with the same 14-barrel brew kit as before. At present the output is almost entirely bottled.

Celtic Black Ale (OG 1036, ABV 3.9%)
A dark ale full of flavour, balancing an aromatic hop combined with a subtle bite and a pleasantly smooth caramel aftertaste.

Clansman Ale (OG 1036, ABV 3.9%)
A light Hebridean beer, brewed with Scottish malts and lightly hopped to give a subtle bittering.

Seaforth Ale (OG 1042, ABV 4.2%) ◥
A light, quaffable beer with a delicate nose. A complex mixture of biscuity malt and fruit in the taste leads to a lasting, bittersweet finish.

**Islander Strong Premium Ale
(OG 1044, ABV 4.8%)** ◥
A malty, fruity strong bitter drinking dangerously below its ABV.

Berserker Export Pale Ale (OG 1068, ABV 7.5%) ◥
This malty, fruity winter warmer is packed full of flavour, with toffee apple and caramel notes right through to the long, satisfying aftertaste.

Hedge Row (NEW)

115 Lynfield Drive, Haworth Road, Bradford, West Yorkshire, BD9 6EP ☎ 07714 435599
✉ hedgerowbrewingco@gmail.com

Hedge Row was established in 2015 by young, enthusiastic brewer Michael Coffey after gaining experience in local breweries. It is located in a back garden shed with a brew length of a half barrel.

Bradford's Wrath (OG 1041, ABV 3.9%)
Traditional Yorkshire session bitter.

Daisy Hill Blonde (OG 1043, ABV 4%)
Zesty, quaffable blonde ale with a biscuity dry finish.

Pale Ale (OG 1048, ABV 4.8%)
Well-balanced pale ale with a pronounced floral character.

Sweet Michael (OG 1060, ABV 5.6%)
Distinctive, malty stout.

Hedgedog (NEW) SIBA ⟨⊙⟩

Stroude Farm, Stroude Road, Virginia Water, Surrey, GU25 4BY ☎ 07500 808090 ⊕ hedgedog.co.uk

Marc and Andrew Sage took their passion for beer and brewing and quit their day jobs to start a small brewery in 2013.

Amber (ABV 3.9%)
Amber-coloured ale with malty, caramel and fruity notes. Refreshing and light with well-balanced moderate bitterness.

Brown (ABV 5%)
Rich brown in colour with hazy red highlights. On the nose there are notes of brown sugar, mild roasted malt and a touch of cocoa. A mild hop bitterness and tart hint provides balance.

Heidrun (NEW)

Inn House Brewery, 449 Great Western Road, Glasgow, G12 8HH ✉ hello@valhallasgoat.com

A small batch brewery with beers contract brewed by Drygate Brewery (qv). RAIB V

Heineken Royal Trafford

Royal Brewery, 201 Denmark Road, Manchester, M15 6LD

Brews Kronenbourg (for owner Carlsberg) and Fosters brands among others. No real ale.

Hellhound

Sycamore Farm, Somersham Road, Bramford, Suffolk, IP8 4NN
☎ (01473) 831200 ☎ 07850 076202
⊕ hellhoundbrewery.co.uk

Hellhound was established in 2009, initially producing bottled beers. In 2014 the brewery relocated to its current site, a farm in Bramford with its own private water supply. Around 100 outlets are supplied across East Anglia. ♦

Thunderstruck (ABV 3.5%)
A wheat beer with notes of banana, bubble gum and cloves.

Twisted Sister (ABV 3.5%)
A pale ale with a tropical fruit finish.

Black Shuck (OG 1040, ABV 3.9%)
A breakfast stout, brewed with rolled oats and pressed coffee.

Dirty Blond (OG 1039, ABV 3.9%)
A blonde beer with a citrus finish.

Soul Survivor (OG 1055, ABV 5.7%)
An IPA with tropical notes.

Helm Bar (NEW)

Ellerholme, Appleby-in-Westmorland, Cumbria, CA16 6JG ☎ 07736 364478 ⊕ helmbarbrews.com

Inspired by a passion for strong, distinctive beers from the US Pacific North West and Belgium, Helm Bar currently brews small batch beers using the highest quality grain and hops. RAIB

Jabberwock (ABV 5.2%)

Ghost Tractor (ABV 5.3%)
Robust porter with German beech-smoked malt finished with a hint of vanilla.

Jub Jub (ABV 5.5%)

Bandersnatch (ABV 6%)
An American IPA – mid brown, bitter and dry-hopped.

Vorpel Blade (ABV 6.4%)

Helmsley SIBA 👁

18 Bridge Street, Helmsley, North Yorkshire, YO62 5DX
☎ (01439) 771014 ☎ 07525 434268

☺Located within the North York Moors National Park, brewing began in 2014. The brewery has a viewing gallery, tasting room and brewery tap. Local pubs are supplied. RAIB

Yorkshire Legend (ABV 3.8%)

Striding the Riding (ABV 4%)

Howardian Gold (ABV 4.2%)

Honey (ABV 4.5%)

H!PA (ABV 5.5%)

Hen House

The Old Dairy, Walliscote Farm, High Street, Whitchurch-on-Thames, Oxfordshire, RG8 7EP
⊕ henhousebrewery.co.uk

Hen House began brewing in 2012 on a 30-litre plant. Only bottle-conditioned beers are produced, available from the brewery shop and the Wallingford Local Producers' Market every Saturday. ☛ ♦ RAIB

Hepworth SIBA 👁

The New Brewery, Stane Street, North Heath, West Sussex, RH20 1DJ
☎ (01403) 269696 ⊕ hepworthbrewery.co.uk

⊠ Hepworth's was established in 2001 with draught beer brewing beginning in 2003 using Sussex malt and hops. 274 outlets are supplied. Originally situated in Horsham, a new brewery site in North Heath opened in 2016. ‼ ☛ ♦ RAIB

Traditional Sussex Bitter (OG 1035, ABV 3.5%) ◄
A fine, clean-tasting amber session beer. A bitter beer with a pleasant fruity and hoppy aroma that leads to a crisp, tangy taste. A long, dry finish.

Pullman First Class Ale (OG 1041, ABV 4.2%) ◄
A sweet, nutty maltiness and fruitiness are balanced by hops and bitterness in this easy-drinking, pale brown best bitter. A subtle bitter aftertaste.

Prospect Organic (OG 1045, ABV 4.5%)
A well-balanced and traditional brew.

Classic Old Ale (OG 1046, ABV 4.8%)
A traditional winter brew, rich with a variety of roasted malts balanced with sweetness and the bitterness of Admiral hops.

Iron Horse (OG 1048, ABV 4.8%) ◄
There's a fruity, toffee aroma to this light brown, full-bodied bitter. A citrus flavour balanced by caramel and malt leads to a clean, dry finish.

Hercules

Unit 5b, Harbour Court, Heron Road, Sydenham, Holywood, Belfast, BT3 9HB
☎ (028) 9036 4516 ⊠ niall@herculesbrewery.com

The original Hercules Brewing Company, founded in the 19th century, was one of 13 breweries in Belfast at the time. The company has been re-established to produce small batch brews using old brewing traditions. Its output is all under the Yardsman brand name.

Yardsman IPA (OG 1043, ABV 4.3%)

Yardsman Lager (OG 1048, ABV 4.8%)

Yardsman Belfast Pale Ale (OG 1056, ABV 5.6%)

Here Be Monsters

22 Paris Road, Scholes, West Yorkshire, HD9 1UA
☎ (07792) 174863 ☎ 07792 174863
⊕ herebemonstersbrewery.co.uk

A small brewery producing only bottle-conditioned beers from a one-barrel plant. RAIB

Hereford SIBA

⬚ 88 St Owen Street, Hereford, HR1 2QD
☎ (01432) 342125 ⊠ jfkenyon@aol.com

☺Hereford began life as the Spinning Dog Brewery in 2000, changing its name in 2010. It is now primarily a brew pub but supplies outlets on request, usually by social media. ‼ ♦ RAIB

Herefordshire Owd Bull (OG 1039, ABV 3.9%)
A good session beer with an abundance of hops and bitterness. Dry, with a citrus aftertaste.

Dark (OG 1040, ABV 4%)
A dark, malty mild with a hint of bitterness and a touch of roast caramel. A smooth, drinkable ale.

Herefordshire Light Ale (HLA) (OG 1040, ABV 4%)
A crisp, light, refreshing ale made with Herefordshire hops.

Celtic Gold (OG 1045, ABV 4.5%)

A bright gold-coloured best bitter, full of fruit and blackcurrant flavours.

Mutley's Revenge (OG 1048, ABV 4.8%)
A strong, smooth, hoppy beer, amber in colour. Full-bodied with a dry, citrus aftertaste.

Mutts Nuts (OG 1050, ABV 5%)
A dark, strong ale, full bodied with a hint of a chocolate aftertaste.

Heritage (NEW) SIBA

National Brewery Centre, Horninglow Street, Burton upon Trent, Staffordshire, DE14 1NG
☎ (01283) 777006
⊕ heritagebrewingcompany.co.uk

☺The new name for William Worthington's Brewery. The plant was installed by Molson Coors but it has been sold to Leisure Solutions, owners of the brewery centre. Molson Coors has retained the Worthington brand name, which cannot be used by Heritage. The 25-barrel plant, run by master brewer Steve Wellington, specialises in recreating classic beers from the former Bass range. ‼ ⌷

Victoria Pale Ale (OG 1035, ABV 3.5%)
Light but full flavoured, rich amber in colour.

Charrington Oatmeal Stout (OG 1040, ABV 4%)
Mellow and drinkable, yet full bodied stout.

Offilers' Best Bitter (OG 1042, ABV 4%)
Amber-coloured with a light hop finish.

St Modwens Golden Ale (OG 1041, ABV 4.1%)
Refreshing but not too bitter with subtle malted wheat biscuit taste.

Charrington IPA (OG 1045, ABV 4.5%)
Deep amber in colour with a creamy foam and a pleasant hoppy bite leading to a smooth, malty flavour and a lingering bitterness.

Masterpiece IPA (OG 1054, ABV 5.4%)
Aromatic hops, toasted cereal notes and hints of smoke and spice enhanced by fragrant fruity character and a top note of fresh bread. A full, luxurious mouthfeel combines with a subtle peppery character.

Hermitage

Heathwaite, Slanting Hill, Hermitage, Berkshire, RG18 9QG
☎ (01635) 200907 ☎ 07980 019484
⊕ hermitagebrewery.co.uk

⊠ Brewing began in 2013 in the village of Hermitage, West Berkshire, using a 0.5-barrel plant. The owner, Richard Marshall, taught food science at degree level and has been brewing his own beers for more than 40 years. Bottle-conditioned beers are sold in local shops and post offices. Casks are supplied to some independent pubs as well as local beer festivals. New beers are frequently introduced. RAIB

Tom Herrick's

The Stable House, Main Street, Carlton on Trent, Nottinghamshire, NG23 6NW ☎ 07877 542331
⊠ tomherricksbrewery@hotmail.com

Tom Herrick installed his bespoke 2.5-barrel stainless steel brewery at the front of his premises during 2014 and began small scale commercial brewing in 2015. The brewery is only operated on a part-time basis with output going to festivals and local pubs.

Bomber Command (OG 1045, ABV 4.2%)
A pale copper ale, full-bodied and malty with a delicate, well-balanced hop profile

Hesket Newmarket SIBA

Old Crown Barn, Back Green, Hesket Newmarket, Cumbria, CA7 8JG
☎ (01697) 478066 ⊕ hesketbrewery.co.uk

☺Founded in 1988, and bought by a co-operative in 1999 to preserve a community amenity. All the beers are named after local fells, except for Doris' 90th Birthday Ale. ‼ ♦

Haystacks (OG 1037, ABV 3.7%) ⬧
Light, easy-drinking, thirst-quenching blonde beer; very pleasant for its strength.

Skiddaw Special Bitter (OG 1037, ABV 3.7%)
An amber-coloured session beer, malty throughout, well-balanced with a dry finish.

Red Pike (OG 1038, ABV 3.8%)
A dark red ale with complex malty backbone but with plenty of hop flavour, balanced with a big hit of hops. The hop blend gives notes of resin and pine as well as some citrus and fruit.

Black Sail (OG 1042.1, ABV 4%) ⬧
A sweet stout with roast flavours

Helvellyn Gold (OG 1039, ABV 4%) ⬧
Complex hoppy and fruity beer with malt presence and refreshing finish.

High Pike (OG 1042, ABV 4.2%) ⬧
A traditional style bitter; fruity with a dry finish.

Doris' 90th Birthday Ale (OG 1045, ABV 4.3%)
Fruity premium beer.

Scafell Blonde (OG 1043, ABV 4.4%) ⬧
A hoppy, sweet, fruity, pale-coloured bitter.

Brim Fell (OG 1047, ABV 4.5%)
A light copper-coloured IPA. Enough body to back up the hop bitterness, and a little residual sweetness from the malt balances the beer well. A light malt giving way to floral and citrus hops.

Catbells Pale Ale (OG 1050, ABV 5%) ⬧
Golden ale with a nice balance of fruity sweetness and bitterness, almost syrupy but with an unexpectedly dry finish.

Old Carrock Strong Ale (OG 1060, ABV 6%) ⬧
Red-brown strong ale, vine-fruity in flavour with a slightly astringent finish.

Hetton Law (NEW)

Hetton Law Farm, Lowick, Northumberland, TD15 2UL
☎ (01289) 388558 ☎ 07889 457140
⊕ hettonlawbrewery.co.uk

Brewing began in 2015 using a 2.5-barrel plant. Run by retired dentists Judith and Nicholas Grasse, it uses local spring water and locally grown Golden Promise malt, which gives the beers a distinctive character. ♦

Hetton Harvest (ABV 3.9%)

Hetton Howler (ABV 4.2%)
A traditional bitter with a rich, malty taste and hoppy overtones.

Hetton Hare-raiser (ABV 5.2%)

THE BREWERIES

A light, golden and hoppy beer.

Hewitt's

c/o Brentwood Brewery, Calcott Hall Farm, Ongar Road, Brentwood, Essex, CM15 9HS ☎ 07949 565424

Office: 40 Marconi Road, Chelmsford, Essex, CM1 1QD ⊕ hewittsbrewery.co.uk

Hewitt's was founded in 2010, using spare capacity at Brentwood Brewery (qv). Brewing is currently suspended.

Hexagon (NEW)

PO Box 174, Marple, SK6 9BR ☎ 07903 264243 ⊕ hexagonbrew.co.uk

Hexagon is a small brewery which started production of bottle-conditioned beers in 2015 using a 100-litre brew kit. RAIB

Hexhamshire SIBA ⊙

Leafields, Ordley, Northumberland, NE46 1SX ☎ (01434) 606577 ⊕ hexhamshire.co.uk

Hexhamshire was founded in 1993 and is run by one of the founding partners family, who also run the brewery tap, the Dipton Mill. Outlets are supplied direct and via the SIBA Beerflex scheme.

Devil's Elbow (OG 1036, ABV 3.6%) ◀
Amber brew full of hops and fruit, leading to a bitter finish.

Shire Bitter (OG 1037, ABV 3.8%) ◀
A good balance of hops with fruity overtones, this amber beer makes an easy-drinking session bitter.

Blackhall English Stout (OG 1040, ABV 4%)
A pleasant bitter beer with a strong roast malt flavour.

Devil's Water (OG 1041, ABV 4.1%) ◀
Copper-coloured best bitter, well-balanced with a slightly fruity, hoppy finish.

Whapweasel (OG 1048, ABV 4.8%) ◀
A smooth, hoppy beer with a fruity flavour. Amber in colour, the bitter finish brings out the fruit and hops.

Old Humbug (OG 1055, ABV 5.5%)

High House Farm SIBA

Matfen, NE20 0RG
☎ (01661) 886192 ⊕ highhousefarmbrewery.co.uk

The brewery was founded in 2003 by a Brewlab graduate on a working farm with a visitor centre, brewery shop and function room. This has now expanded to include a restaurant and a wedding venue. More than 350 regional outlets are supplied with beers made using many ingredients from the farm. ‼ ⬛ ♦

Sundancer (OG 1036, ABV 3.6%)

Pullet Please (OG 1037, ABV 3.7%)
A pale golden refreshing ale with a delicate grapefruit nose and a crisp, dry finish. An easy-drinking bitter.

Auld Hemp (OG 1038, ABV 3.8%) ◀
Tawny-coloured ale with hop, malt and fruit flavours and a good bitter finish.

Nel's Best (OG 1041, ABV 4.2%) ◀

Golden, hoppy ale full of flavour with a clean, bitter finish.

Matfen Magic (OG 1046.5, ABV 4.8%) ◀
Well-hopped brown ale with a fruity aroma. Malt and chocolate overtones with a rich, bitter finish.

High Peak (NEW) SIBA

41a Market Street, Chapel-en-le-Frith, Derbyshire, SK23 0HP ☎ 07936 174364 ⊕ highpeakbrewco.com

High Peak is a microbrewery based in Chapel-en-le-Frith on the edge of the Peak District that specialises in hand crafted, small batch, unfined, unfiltered and unpasteurised beers in batches of 600 litres. There is no core range of beers as set recipes are not followed.

High Weald SIBA ⊙

Bulrushes Business Park, Coombe Hill Road, East Grinstead, West Sussex, RH19 4LZ ☎ 07836 291430

Office: 23 Hermitage Road, East Grinstead, RH19 2BP ⊕ highwealdbrewery.co.uk

⊠ Established in 2013, High Weald Brewery has grown to a four-barrel plant size. The brewery supplies local (and not so local) free houses, shops and festivals and is increasing direct sales at farmers' and community markets. Further expansion of both the beer range and capacity is planned.

Chronicle (OG 1038, ABV 3.8%)

Greenstede (OG 1040, ABV 4%)
A refreshing golden ale.

Charcoal Burner (OG 1043, ABV 4.3%)
A traditional English stout. Roasted malts bring a rich, satisfying flavour, combined with the velvety smoothness from generous quantities of oats.

First Gold IPA (OG 1056, ABV 5.6%)
A punchy and zesty IPA with a bitter orange flavour, resinous aroma and a long, smooth finish.

Highland

See Swannay

Highwood

See Tom Wood (under W)

Hilden SIBA

Hilden House, Hilden, Lisburn, Co Antrim, BT27 4TY ☎ (028) 9266 0800 ⊕ hildenbrewery.co.uk

☺Established 1981, Hilden is Ireland's oldest independent brewery. Now in the second generation of family ownership, the beers are widely distributed across the UK. The beers are regularly available in Wetherspoon outlets in Northern Ireland. ‼ ⬛ ♦

Nut Brown (OG 1038, ABV 3.8%)

Ale (OG 1038, ABV 4%) ◀
An amber-coloured beer with an aroma of malt, hops and fruit. The balanced taste is slightly slanted towards hops, and hops are also prominent in the full, malty finish.

Barney's Brew (OG 1043, ABV 4.2%)

Belfast bap wheat beer, spiced with cardamom, coriander and black pepper.

Irish Stout (OG 1043, ABV 4.3%)

Scullion Irish Ale (OG 1046, ABV 4.6%)

Scullion's Irish (OG 1045, ABV 4.6%)
A bright amber ale, initially smooth with a slight taste of honey that is balanced by a long, dry aftertaste that lingers on the palate.

Twisted Hop (OG 1047, ABV 4.7%)

Halt (OG 1058, ABV 6.1%)
A premium traditional Irish red ale with a malty, mild hop flavour.

Hill Island

Unit 7, Fowlers Yard, Back Silver Street, Durham, DH1 3RA ☎ 07740 932584
✉ mike@hillisland.freeserve.co.uk

⊕Established in 2002, the brewery name is a literal translation of Dunholme from which Durham is derived. It is situated in the Fowlers Yard complex by the banks of the Wear in the heart of Durham City. Beers can be crafted exclusively for individual pubs. Beer festivals take place at the brewery each month. ‼️🍽️♦

Peninsula Pint (OG 1036.5, ABV 3.7%)
Blonde and hoppy with a zesty aroma.

Bitter (OG 1039, ABV 3.9%)
A red/gold-coloured bitter with pronounced caramel flavour and zesty bitterness.

Stout for the Count (OG 1040, ABV 4%)
A traditional full-bodied stout. Almost black in colour with roast coffee flavours and a clean hop bitterness.

Neptune's Gold (OG 1042, ABV 4.2%)
Subtle bitterness balanced with hop flavours and a hint of tropical fruit.

Cathedral Ale (OG 1042, ABV 4.3%)
Ruby red in colour with hints of roast malts and crisp bitterness.

ThaIPA (OG 1043, ABV 4.3%)

Griffin's Irish Stout (OG 1045, ABV 4.5%)
Black and bitter, a traditional Irish-style stout.

Hillfire (NEW) SIBA

23 Edison Road, Aylesbury, Buckinghamshire, HP19 8TE
☎ (01296) 338521 ⊕ hillfirebrewing.com

⊗ Hillfire commenced brewing in 2016 using a 2.5-barrel plant. Sole owner and CAMRA member Neil Coxhead brews once a week. Further beers and direct sales are planned.

California Gold (ABV 4.3%)

Hillside SIBA 👁

Holly Bush Farm, Ross Road, Longhope, Gloucestershire, GL17 0NG
☎ (01452) 830222 ☎ 07905 246189
⊕ hillsidebrewery.com

⊗ A six-barrel plant in a reconstructed farm dairy that started in 2011. A 200-foot bore hole produces pure water rich in minerals ideally suited to brewing. The regular beers are supplemented by

limited run specials that explore different styles and flavours. ‼️🍽️♦RAIB

Over the Hill (OG 1042, ABV 3.5%)
Full-bodied, single-hopped dark mild, with Bramling Cross hops complementing the cocoa and roast malt character.

Pinnacle (OG 1038, ABV 3.8%)
A good session beer with a fresh and fruity finish.

Legless Cow (OG 1044, ABV 4.2%)
A well-balanced and full-flavoured best bitter.

Legend of Hillside (OG 1047, ABV 4.7%)
A rich pale ale with strong hop finish.

Hillstown (NEW)

128 Glebe Road, Randalstown, BT41 3DT
⊕ hillstownbrewery.com

Brewing began in 2014 in a converted barn on a farm in Randalstown producing bottle-conditioned beers. ♦RAIB

Hilltop (NEW)

🍽 Sheffield Road, Conisbrough, South Yorkshire, DN12 2AY
☎ (01709) 868811 ☎ 07947 146746
⊕ thehilltophotel.co.uk

Established in 2016, Hilltop Brewery is a 3.5-barrel plant in the recently refurbished outbuildings of the Hilltop Hotel in Conisbrough. ‼️♦

Classic Bitter (OG 1039, ABV 3.9%)

Blonde (OG 1040, ABV 4%)

Golden Ale (OG 1042, ABV 4.2%)

Stout (OG 1045, ABV 4.5%)

Porter (OG 1047, ABV 4.7%)

IPA (OG 1050, ABV 5%)

Hobsons SIBA 👁

Newhouse Farm, Tenbury Road, Cleobury Mortimer, Shropshire, DY14 8RD
☎ (01299) 270837 ⊕ hobsons-brewery.co.uk

Established in 1993 in a former sawmill, Hobsons relocated to a farm site with more space in 1995. A second brewery, bottling plant and a warehouse have been added along with significant expansion to the first brewery. Beers are supplied within a 50-mile radius. The brewery has an onsite wind turbine and utilises environmental sustainable technologies where possible. ‼️🍽️RAIB

Mild (OG 1034, ABV 3.2%) 🌾
A classic mild. Complex layers of taste come from roasted malts that predominate and give lots of flavour.

Twisted Spire (OG 1036, ABV 3.6%)
Vibrant blonde beer with a light fizz and sweet floral aroma bringing bursts of refreshing flavour and crisp, dry finish.

Best (OG 1038.5, ABV 3.8%) 🌾
A pale brown to amber, medium-bodied beer with strong hop character throughout. It is consequently bitter, but with malt discernible in the taste.

Old Prickly (OG 1042, ABV 4.2%)
Pale ale full of hop flavour with floral and citrus notes and a lingering but subtle bitterness.

Town Crier (OG 1044, ABV 4.5%)
A full-flavoured, crisp golden ale with a hint of sweetness, complemented by subtle hop flavours, leading to a dry finish.

Hogarths SIBA

Hogarths, 37-41 Churchgate, Bolton, BL1 1HU
☎ (01204) 386964

Microbrewery located in the old kitchen of a Bolton pub of the same name.

Beer Street (ABV 3.8%)
A session ale with good hop balance.

Liberty (ABV 3.8%)
A light, fruity bitter.

Hoggleys

See Phipps

Hogs Back SIBA ◉

Manor Farm, The Street, Tongham, Surrey, GU10 1DE
☎ (01252) 783000 ⊕ hogsback.co.uk

⊗ This traditionally-styled brewery, established in 1992, boasts an extensive range of award-winning ales. The shop sells all the brewery's beers and related merchandise plus over 400 beers and ciders from around the world. In 2014 the brewery planted hops on neighbouring farmland, restoring the ancient Farnham White Bine variety. ‼🍺♦RAIB

HBB (OG 1039, ABV 3.7%) 🍺
Biscuity aroma with some hops and lemon notes. Well-balanced, plenty of hop in the mouth with a long-lasting, dry bitter aftertaste.

TEA (OG 1044, ABV 4.2%) 🗂 🍺
A tawny-coloured best bitter with toffee and malt present in the nose. A well-rounded flavour with malt and a fruity sweetness.

Hop Garden Gold (OG 1048, ABV 4.4%) 🍺
Full-bodied with an aroma of malt, hops and fruit. Hoppy bitterness grows in an increasingly dry aftertaste with a hint of sweetness.

A Over T (OG 1094, ABV 9%) 🍺
A full-bodied, tawny-coloured barley wine. The malty aroma with hints of vanilla lead to a well-balanced taste where the hops cut through the underlying sweetness and dominate in the finish.

Holden's SIBA IFBB ◉

George Street, Woodsetton, Dudley, West Midlands, DY1 4LW
☎ (01902) 880051 ⊕ holdensbrewery.co.uk

☺A family brewery spanning four generations, Holden's began life as a brewpub in 1915. Continued recent expansion sees 20 tied pubs, a new brewhouse and a shop. ‼🍺♦

Black Country Mild (OG 1037, ABV 3.7%) 🍺
A good, red/brown mild; a refreshing, light blend of roast malt, hops and fruit, dominated by malt throughout.

Black Country Bitter (OG 1039, ABV 3.9%) 🗂 🍺
A medium-bodied, golden ale; a light, well-balanced bitter with a subtle, dry, hoppy finish.

Golden Glow (OG 1045, ABV 4.4%)

A pale golden beer with a subtle hop aroma plus gentle sweetness and a light hoppiness.

Special (OG 1052, ABV 5.1%) 🍺
A sweet, malty, full-bodied amber ale with hops to balance in the taste and in the good, bittersweet finish.

Holsworthy

Unit 5, Circuit Business Park, Clawton, Devon, EX22 6RR
☎ (01566) 783678 ☎ 07879 401073
⊕ holsworthyales.co.uk

⊗ Holsworthy Ales began brewing in 2011 using a six-barrel plant, serving the local rural community. ‼🍺♦RAIB

Mine's a Mild (OG 1035, ABV 3.5%)
A traditional English mild with a rich, malty taste.

Original (OG 1038, ABV 3.8%)
A session bitter, full-flavoured from initial aroma through to lingering aftertaste.

Sunshine (OG 1040, ABV 4%)
Golden ale, easy-drinking with fruity flavours.

Muck 'n' Straw (OG 1044, ABV 4.4%) 🍺
Smooth copper-coloured beer with strong hoppiness. Robust yet easy drinking. Hop aroma leads to a strongly hopped bitter with dry aftertaste.

Make Me Hoppy (OG 1046, ABV 4.7%)
Classic modern IPA, triple hopped for a big flavour.

Tamar Black (OG 1048, ABV 4.8%) 🍺
Complex black stout, smooth and creamy. Roast pervades from nose through to aftertaste with definite coffee and hints of liquorice.

Hop on the Run (OG 1048, ABV 5%)
An American IPA with a strong citrus hit.

Old Market Monk (OG 1059, ABV 6.1%)
Belgian-style ale, lots of coriander, orange peel and German hops.

Holt SIBA IFBB ◉

The Brewery, Empire Street, Cheetham, Manchester, M3 1JD
☎ (0161) 834 3285 ⊕ joseph-holt.com

☺The brewery, established in 1849 by Joseph and Catherine Holt, is still a family-run business and is now in the hands of the great, great-grandson of the founder. It supplies approximately 150 free trade outlets as well as its own estate of 120 tied pubs. 🍺

Mild (OG 1033, ABV 3.2%) 🍺
A dark brown/red beer with a fruity, malty nose. Roast, malt, fruit and hops in the taste, with strong bitterness for a mild, and a dry malt and hops finish.

IPA (OG 1038, ABV 3.8%) 🍺
Golden bitter with biscuity malt, hops and restrained lemony notes. Dry bitter finish.

Mellors (OG 1039, ABV 3.8%)
A citrus blonde ale with hop flavours of lemon and blackcurrant.

Bitter (OG 1040, ABV 4%) 🍺
Copper-coloured beer with malt and hops in the aroma. Malt, hops and fruit in the taste with a bitter and hoppy finish.

Two Hoots (OG 1043.8, ABV 4.2%)
A well-balanced, light, crisp and refreshing ale with a hint of citrus.

50 Gyle (OG 1044, ABV 4.4%)
An American-hopped IPA with hop flavours of berries, tropical fruit and citrus.

Holy Well

4 Barnfield Close, Egerton, Bolton, BL7 9UP ☎ 07949 179338 ⊕ holywellbrewing.com

Holy Well is a nanobrewery and the brewing sister to the Crafty Ales company, which sells beer from Lancashire microbreweries at local farmers' markets and online. RAIB

Hooded Ram SIBA

Hills Meadow, Douglas, Isle of Man, IM3 1LE
☎ (01624) 612464 ⊕ hoodedram.com

⊕Brewing began in 2013 on a 2.5-barrel plant. Expansion in 2014 saw an increase to a 10-barrel plant. Beers are available cask-conditioned throughout the island and bottle-conditioned beers are sold directly through the brewery shop and in some local off-licences and restaurants/bars. ‼☰RAIB

Rams Head Bitter (OG 1037, ABV 3.7%)

Sovereign Ram Single Hop (OG 1037, ABV 4.1%)

Amber Ram (OG 1038, ABV 4.3%)

Cascade (OG 1045, ABV 4.5%)

Jack The Ram Stout (OG 1044, ABV 4.7%) ◆
Roast dominates the aroma and taste, with bitterness coming through in the finish. Plenty of body from the sweetness and fruit, make this an easy drinking stout.

Mosaic Single Hop Pale Ale (OG 1044, ABV 5%)

Pacifica – Cascadian Dark Ale (OG 1050, ABV 5%)

Little King Louis IPA (OG 1054, ABV 6%)

Hook Norton SIBA IFBB ◉

Brewery Lane, Hook Norton, Oxfordshire, OX15 5NY
☎ (01608) 737210 ⊕ hooky.co.uk

⊠ One of the finest examples of a Victorian tower brewery and the oldest independent brewery in Oxfordshire, Hook Norton has been brewing since 1849. The current premises were built in 1900 and still house much of the original machinery, including a 25hp steam engine, which operates occasionally. Shire horses are used to make deliveries to the local pubs in Hook Norton and the surrounding area. Remaining family-owned, it combines its brewing heritage with a modern approach. ‼☰◆RAIB

Hooky Mild (OG 1033, ABV 2.8%) ◆
A chestnut brown, easy-drinking mild. A complex malt and hop aroma give way to a well-balanced taste, leading to a long, hoppy finish that is unusual for a mild.

Hooky (OG 1036, ABV 3.5%) ◆
A classic golden session bitter. Hoppy and fruity aroma followed by a malt and hops taste and a continuing hoppy finish.

Lion (OG 1043, ABV 4%)
A complex fruity nose and bittersweet finish.

Old Hooky (OG 1048, ABV 4.6%) ◆
A strong bitter, tawny in colour. A well-rounded fruity taste with a balanced bitter finish.

Hop & Cleaver

⊟ 44 Sandhill, Newcastle upon Tyne, NE1 3JF
☎ (0191) 261 1037 ⊕ hopandcleaver.com

Established in 2014 the brewery is situated in the Hop & Cleaver pub, where the brewing equipment is on view. Its constantly changing beer range is supplied solely to the pub. ◆

Hop & Stagger SIBA

⊟ 3 West Castle Street, Bridgnorth, Shropshire, WV16 4AB
☎ (01746) 763962 ⊕ hopandstaggerbrewery.co.uk

Hop & Stagger began brewing in 2012 having set up a 2.5-barrel plant at the White Lion Inn, Bridgnorth, initially brewing a range of bitters and occasional seasonal ales exclusively for the pub. ◆

Simpson's Original (OG 1038, ABV 3.6%)

Golden Wander (OG 1042, ABV 4.1%)
A crisp, pale golden ale with fruity notes and a light hopped finish.

Pure Amber (OG 1045, ABV 4.5%)
A zesty light-coloured ale.

Hop Art SIBA ◉

The Brewery, Blacknest Industrial Park, Blacknest Road, Blacknest, Hampshire, GU34 4PX
☎ (01252) 364436

Office: Newtown House, 38 Newtown Road, Liphook, GU30 7DX ⊕ hopartbrewery.com

⊠ Hop Art was established in 2014 with a brand new, custom-built 10-barrel plant. There is capacity to brew three times a week at present, with plans to increase to daily production. 80 outlets are supplied. ‼☰◆RAIB

Hoppy Blonde (OG 1044, ABV 4.3%) ◆
Golden, well-hopped bitter with lemon aroma and touch of sweetness to balance the predominantly dry finish. A refreshing beer.

Red Cap (ABV 4.4%)
Amber red-coloured ale with a balanced malty character.

Golden IPA (OG 1057, ABV 5.2%)
Heady, hop-charged and full of flavour.

Hop Back SIBA

Units 22-24, Batten Road Industrial Estate, Downton, Salisbury, Wiltshire, SP5 3HU
☎ (01725) 510986 ⊕ hopback.co.uk

⊠ Founded in 1987, Hop Back owns 10 pubs and distributes nationally. The flagship beer, Summer Lightning, has won numerous CAMRA awards. ‼☰◆RAIB GF V

GFB (OG 1035, ABV 3.5%) ◆
A light gold refreshing session bitter. The hoppy aroma leads to bitterness initially, lasting through to the finish with some fruit.

Citra (OG 1040, ABV 4%)

A single hop blonde ale with a light, crisp bitterness leading to a refreshing lemon and grapefruit aftertaste and a smooth, dry finish.

Crop Circle (OG 1041, ABV 4.2%) ◈
A pale yellow best bitter with a fragrant hop aroma, complex hop, fruit and citrus flavours with a balanced hoppy, bittersweet aftertaste.

Spring Zing (OG 1041, ABV 4.2%)
A pale, aromatic and hoppy beer.

Taiphoon (OG 1041, ABV 4.2%) ◈
A clean-tasting, light, fruity beer with hops and fruit on the aroma, complex hop character and lemongrass notes in the taste, slight sweetness balanced with some astringency in the aftertaste.

Entire Stout (OG 1044, ABV 4.5%) ◈
A smooth, rich, ruby-black stout with strong roast and malt aromas and flavours, with a long bittersweet and malty aftertaste.

Summer Lightning (OG 1048, ABV 5%) ◈
Golden-coloured strong bitter with a hoppy aroma and slightly astringent bitterness in the taste, balanced with some fruit sweetness, in the dry aftertaste.

Hop Fuzz SIBA

Unit 8, Riverside Industrial Estate, West Hythe, Kent, CT21 4NB ☎ 07730 768881 ⏚ hopfuzz.co.uk

Hop Fuzz was started by two friends in 2011, it is situated on an industrial estate next to the Royal Military Canal (and a main cycle route) at West Hythe. Major expansion took place in 2014. The brewery is environmentally friendly, using solar power and supplying feed to the local animal park. In 2016 the brewery tap, Unit One, opened at the entrance to the estate. ◆

Yellow Zinger (OG 1038, ABV 3.7%)

Martello (OG 1038, ABV 3.8%)

English (OG 1044, ABV 4%)

Goldsmith's (OG 1042, ABV 4%)

Old American Pale (OG 1042, ABV 4.2%)

Northern Star (OG 1044, ABV 4.4%)

Hoppybomb (OG 1049, ABV 5%)

Hop Kettle SIBA

⬗ Red Lion, 74 High Street, Cricklade, Wiltshire, SN6 6DD
☎ (01793) 750776 ⏚ hopkettlebrewery.co.uk

Brewing began in 2012 using a four-barrel plant. The brewery is situated in a stone barn behind the Red Lion Inn, Cricklade. Many beer styles are brewed with some being barrel-aged in whisky and rum casks on site. There are plans to introduce an area that will allow people to dine among the brewing equipment. ◆

North Wall (OG 1043, ABV 4.2%)

Hop King

Eastern Avenue, Reading, Berkshire, RG1 5SF
✉ hopkingbrewingcompany@gmail.com

A 1.25-barrel nanobrewery which started up in 2014. It produces unfiltered, unpasteurised and naturally-carbonated beers available in both

KeyKeg and bottle-conditioned. Brewing is currently suspended. **RAIB**

Hop Monster

See George's

Hop Studio SIBA ◉

3 Handley Park, Elvington Industrial Estate, York Road, Elvington, North Yorkshire, YO41 4AR
☎ (01904) 608029 ⏚ thehopstudio.co.uk

Brewing began in 2012 using a 10-barrel plant situated in an industrial unit just outside York. Seasonal and experimental beers are produced, including some conditioned in wooden casks and some brewed with partners. Outlets in Yorkshire are supplied direct and the rest of the UK via wholesalers. ◆**RAIB**

Hop Stuff SIBA

Unit 7, Gunnery Terrace, Cornwallis Road, Woolwich, London, SE18 6SW
☎ (020) 8854 9509 ☎ 07850 086461
⏚ hopstuffbrewery.com

Hop Stuff began brewing in 2013. ◆

Fusilier (OG 1041, ABV 4.3%) ◈
Biscuity malty best bitter with spicy hop notes. Finish is sweetish, slightly dry with a faint bitterness. Rich, smooth mouthfeel.

Pale (OG 1045, ABV 4.5%) ◈
Slightly dry amber bitter with a complex hop character throughout. Citrus notes in the flavour and finish, which is bitter.

Renegade IPA (OG 1056, ABV 5.6%) ◈
Smooth, dark-gold IPA with grapefruit and spiced hops aroma and flavour. Warm, lingering finish that is bitter and dry.

Hop Yard

The Yard, Lewes Road, Forest Row, East Sussex, RH18 5AA
☎ (01342) 824272 ☎ 07769 313410
⏚ hopyardbrewing.co.uk

⊠ Hop Yard began brewing in 2014 using a 100-litre brew plant. Cask-conditioned Golden Ale is now brewed using spare capacity at Westerham Brewery (qv). The original plant is used for bottle-conditioned and test brews. Further beers are planned. It has a brewery bar and supplies local outlets. **RAIB**

Golden Ale (OG 1050, ABV 5%)
A medium-bodied ale with hop flavours.

Hopcraft

See Pixie Spring

Hopdaemon SIBA

Unit 1, Parsonage Farm, Seed Road, Newnham, Kent, ME9 0NA
☎ (01795) 892078 ⏚ hopdaemon.com

Tonie Prins originally started brewing in Tyler Hill near Canterbury in 2000 and moved to a new site in Newnham in 2005. The brewery currently supplies more than 100 outlets and is working at full capacity. ‼ ◆ RAIB

Golden Braid (OG 1039, ABV 3.7%) ◣
A refreshing golden session bitter with a good blend of bittering and aroma hops underpinned by pale malt.

Incubus (OG 1041, ABV 4%) ◣
A well-balanced, copper-hued best bitter. Pale malt and a hint of crystal malt are blended with bitter and slightly floral hops to give a lingering hoppy finish.

Skrimshander IPA (OG 1045, ABV 4.5%)
An aromatic copper-coloured pale ale with a refreshing taste and fruity finish.

Green Daemon (OG 1048, ABV 5%)
A golden beer with tropical fruit aromas and a crisp, clean finish. Brewed in the style of a Bavarian Helles (light lager).

Leviathan (OG 1057, ABV 6%)
A strong ruby ale with spicy hop aromas and a rich, malty finish.

Hope

76 Corringham Road, Stanford-le-Hope, Essex, SS17 0AE ☎ 07903 793223 ⊕ hopebrewery.co.uk

☒ Hope was founded in 2013 using a 0.25-barrel plant, expanding to 2.5-barrels in 2014 using the old kit as a pilot plant. There are plans for relocation and further expansion. ◆ RAIB

SX Pale (OG 1040, ABV 3.9%)

Strangely SX (OG 1041, ABV 4%)

SX Dark (OG 1042, ABV 4.2%)

SX Gold (OG 1042, ABV 4.2%)

SX Demon (OG 1044, ABV 4.4%)

SX Devil (OG 1044, ABV 4.4%)

SX Porter (OG 1049, ABV 4.6%)

SX Dragon (OG 1049, ABV 5%)

Hope Valley

Losehill Hall Youth Hostel, Castleton, Derbyshire, S33 8WB

Brewing started in 2009 in the former Castleton Youth Hostel but moved to its present location in 2012 when this closed. The two-barrel plant was formerly used by Edale. Only limited supplies are brewed and these are sold exclusively on the bar in the youth hostel when available.

Hophurst SIBA

**Unit 8, Hindley Business Centre, Platt Lane, Hindley, WN2 3PA
☎ (01942) 522333 ⊕ hophurstbrewery.co.uk**

☺ Hophurst Brewery was started in 2014 by Stuart Hurst, whose passion for producing craft ales combined with 20 years of supporting businesses and re-skilling unemployed people created a unique social enterprise brewery that employs people over the age of 50 and guides them through their training programme in the Wigan area. Six core beers are produced. ◆

Flaxen (OG 1038, ABV 3.7%)

A pale golden ale with a fresh, earthy hoppy aroma with hints of honey and a long, refreshing finish. An easy-drinking session ale.

Campfire (OG 1042, ABV 3.9%)
A dark mild with a smoky, malty taste and aromas of roasted coffee and chocolate.

Joust (OG 1040, ABV 4%)
A refreshing citrus pale ale. Well-rounded with flavours of spice, citrus and zesty orange.

Twisted Vine (OG 1041, ABV 4.1%)
A golden bitter with citrus hoppy aromas of grapefruit and passion fruit.

Cosmati (OG 1042, ABV 4.2%)
A hoppy, citrus golden ale with unique flavours of blueberry, citrus and tropical fruit.

Debonair (OG 1052, ABV 4.9%)
A robust stout with flavours of roasted coffee, liquorice and an aftertaste of pleasant bitterness.

Hopjacker (NEW)

**⊟ Dronfield Arms, 91 Chesterfield Road, Dronfield, Derbyshire, S18 2XE ☎ 07841 487247
⊕ hopjacker.co.uk**

☺ Established in 2015 in the old restaurant space beneath the Dronfield Arms. Hopjacker specialises in unfined, vegan-friendly, hop-forward beers. ‼ V

The Mark (OG 1034, ABV 3.5%)

The Long Con (OG 1037, ABV 3.8%)

The Grifter (OG 1043, ABV 4.6%)

The Kansas City Shuffle (OG 1050, ABV 5.5%)

The Score (OG 1063, ABV 6.8%)

Hops & Glory

**⊟ Hops & Glory, 382 Essex Road, London, N1 3PF
☎ (020) 7226 2277**

Brewing occasionally takes place for the pub on the brew kit previously used by the Solvay Society (qv).

Hopshackle SIBA

**Unit F, Bentley Business Park, Blenheim Way, Northfields Industrial Estate, Market Deeping, Lincolnshire, PE6 8LD
☎ (01778) 348542 ⊕ hopshacklebrewery.co.uk**

☺ Hopshackle was established in 2006 using a five-barrel plant. A 10-barrel plant was installed in 2015. More than 40 outlets are supplied direct. ‼ ◆ RAIB

Simarillo (OG 1037, ABV 3.8%)
Burnished gold in colour with an aroma of citrus and soft fruits. The taste is tangy fruit with blackberry, plum and pineapple.

Zen (OG 1037, ABV 3.8%)
Brown-coloured, traditional, full-flavoured/bodied bitter. Malty and fruity with a bittersweet finish.

American Pale Ale (OG 1042, ABV 4.3%)
An amber-coloured ale with a fruity, zesty aroma. The taste is citrus hop with background gooseberry and lychees and a dry bitter finish.

Hopnosis (OG 1050, ABV 5.2%)
Golden beer with a strong aroma of sweet malt and fruit. The taste is of strong citrus and tropical fruits with a dry finish.

Double Momentum (OG 1068, ABV 7%) 🍷
Golden-amber beer with an aroma of vinous fruit with a hoppy edge. It has a coarse white head and a taste of malt, pineapple, melon, and warming alcohol, with a bitter finish.

Hopstar SIBA

Unit 9, Rinus Business Park, Grimshaw Street, Darwen, Lancashire, BB3 2QX ☎ 07933 590159
⊕ hopstarbrewery.co.uk

☺Hopstar first brewed in 2004 on a 2.5-barrel plant and expanded in 2010 to a new unit with a six-barrel plant. More than 100 outlets are supplied around Lancashire and the Greater Manchester area. The brewery tap is Number 39 in Darwen.
‼♦RAIB

Chilli (OG 1039, ABV 3.8%)

Dizzy Danny Ale (OG 1039, ABV 3.8%)

Dark Knight (OG 1041, ABV 4%)

JC (OG 1041, ABV 4%)

Lancashire Gold (OG 1041, ABV 4%)

Lush (OG 1041, ABV 4%)

Saaz Blonde (OG 1038, ABV 4%)

Smokey Joe's Black Beer (OG 1041, ABV 4%)

Hornbeam SIBA

1-1c Grey Street, Denton, Manchester, M34 3RU
☎ (0161) 320 5627 ☎ 07984 443383
⊕ hornbeambrewery.com

☺Hornbeam began brewing in 2007 on an eight-barrel plant. ‼🍽♦RAIB

Mary Rose (OG 1037, ABV 3.8%)
Chestnut-coloured bitter, with an initial citrus taste, and floral, grassy notes in the finish.

Orange Blossom (OG 1038, ABV 3.8%)
Zesty and hoppy, golden pale ale.

Top Hop Best Bitter (OG 1041, ABV 4.2%)
Full-bodied with malt appeal and ample bitterness.

Black Coral Stout (OG 1043, ABV 4.5%)
A smooth, dry roast malt. Dark and full-bodied with a rich, creamy head. Satisfying with a subtle bitterness.

Horncastle

▤ Old Nicks Tavern, 8 North Street, Horncastle, Lincolnshire, LN9 5DX
☎ (01507) 526862 ⊕ horncastleales.co.uk

Brewing began in 2014 using a 3.75-barrel plant. The brewery is situated in Old Nicks Tavern with beer being available in the pub plus other Lincolnshire outlets. A bottling plant is planned.
‼🍽

Midnight Tempter (OG 1036.5, ABV 3.6%)
Smooth roasted flavours with a hoppy edge.

Damned Deceiver (OG 1038, ABV 3.8%)
Smooth, rich, chestnut-coloured beer with a full body.

Wicked Blonde (OG 1039, ABV 3.9%)

Angel of Light (OG 1039.5, ABV 4%)
Light and malty beer with a nutty follow through.

Lilith's Lust (OG 1040.5, ABV 4.1%)

Traditional reddish bitter, malty and full bodied.

Satan's Fury (OG 1040.5, ABV 4.1%)
Full-bodied, fruity IPA with a dark golden colour.

Sacrificed Soul (OG 1042, ABV 4.3%)
Chestnut-coloured, full-bodied bitter with caramel flavours and a slight sweet edge.

Lucifer's Desire (OG 1046, ABV 4.8%)
Deep golden beer with citrus flavours and hoppy follow through.

Hornes (NEW) SIBA

19b Station Road, Bow Brickhill, Buckinghamshire, MK17 9JU
☎ (01908) 647724 ⊕ hornesbrewery.co.uk

A purpose-built six-barrel brewery established in 2015 and producing a range of beers called Triple Goat after the three goats kept in a paddock at the brewery. There is no shop, but beers can be purchased at the brewery. RAIB

Dark Fox (OG 1039, ABV 3.8%)
A rich, malty brown-coloured brew with burnt notes and a lasting dry bitter finish.

Triple Goat Pale Ale (OG 1039, ABV 3.9%)
Easy-drinking golden beer, bitter with hints of grapefruit.

Triple Goat Porter (OG 1047, ABV 4.6%)
Dark brown, sweet and fruity giving way to a lasting bitterness with hints of liquorice.

Triple Goat IPA (OG 1049, ABV 5%)
Deep golden beer, well-balanced with notes of orange and a touch of spice.

Hoskins Brothers

See Belvoir

Houston SIBA 👁

Unit 6, Kelvingate, Hillington, G52 4GA
☎ (0141) 810 4549 ⊕ houstonbrewery.co.uk

Established in 1997, the brewery was attached to the Fox & Hounds pub and restaurant but relocated in 2016 to its current address. Beers are delivered throughout Britain either direct or via a network of distributors. ‼🍽♦

APA (OG 1039, ABV 3.7%) 🍷
A pale, refreshing citrus ale. Zingy and fresh with a hoppy aroma and intense fruit taste.

Killellan Bitter (OG 1037, ABV 3.7%) 🍃
A light session ale, with a floral hop and fruity taste. The finish of this amber beer is dry and quenching.

Blonde Bombshell (OG 1040, ABV 4%)
A gold-coloured ale with a fresh hop aroma and rounded maltiness.

Peter's Well (OG 1042, ABV 4.2%) 🍃
Well-balanced fruity taste with sweet hop, leading to an increasingly bittersweet finish.

Slainte (OG 1043, ABV 4.3%)
Challenger hops explode on the nose leaving an aroma of malt and hops. The taste is long and deep with mature fruit notes that linger.

Tartan Terror (OG 1045, ABV 4.5%)

Howard Town SIBA

Hawkshead Mill, Hope Street, Glossop, Derbyshire, SK13 7SS
☎ (01457) 869800 ⊕ howardtownbrewery.co.uk

Established in 2005, this eight-barrel, award-winning brewery moved to its current location in 2007. An on-site bar caters for members' evenings and open days. Bottle-conditioned beers are suitable for vegetarians. ‼ ☟ ◆ RAIB

Mill Town Mild (OG 1038, ABV 3.5%)
Dark and lightly hopped with hints of toffee and coffee.

Longdendale Lights (OG 1039, ABV 3.9%)
A light-bodied, blonde refreshing ale.

Monk's Gold (OG 1040, ABV 4%)
A golden session ale with subtle orange notes.

Wren's Nest (OG 1041, ABV 4.2%)
Citrus, floral hops dominate this uncompromising bitter.

Super Fortress (OG 1044, ABV 4.4%)
Tasty, well-balanced, premium chestnut bitter with malty caramel notes and fruity hops.

Glott's Hop (OG 1050, ABV 5%)
A strong and assertively bitter, straw-coloured ale with citrus notes.

Dark Peak (OG 1064, ABV 6%)
Strong and dark with a hint of liquorice and a warming rum kick.

Howling Hops

⊟ Unit 9a, Queen's Yard, White Post Lane, Hackney Wick, London, E9 5EN
☎ (020) 3583 8262 ⊕ howlinghops.co.uk

⊗ Brewing began in 2012. A wide range of cask and bottle-conditioned beers is produced, with four cask beers usually available at any one time. Originally brewing at the Cock Tavern in Hackney, a new plant opened in 2015 in Hackney Wick, serving a couple of real ales along side 10 large tank beers. RAIB

Mild (ABV 3.3%)

Pale Ale (ABV 3.8%)

Light Ale (ABV 4.2%)

Pale XX (ABV 5%)

Ruby Red (ABV 5%)

Smoked Porter (ABV 5.2%)

IPA (ABV 6%)

Old London Stout (ABV 6%)

Hoxne SIBA

Unit 12, Forge Business Centre, Palgrave, IP22 1AP
☎ 07563 558889 ⊕ hoxnebrewery.co.uk

Hoxne Brewery is a small village produer handcrafting real ales in small batches. The beers can be found in numerous pubs around East Anglia and at the brewery's own micropub, the Jolly Porters at Diss railway station. ◆ RAIB

Flat Cap Mild (ABV 3.1%)

Goldbrook Pale Ale (ABV 3.8%)

Old Forge Amber (ABV 4%)

Suffolk Punch Bitter (ABV 4.5%)

Sarah Hughes

⊟ Beacon Hotel, 129 Bilston Street, Sedgley, West Midlands, DY3 1JE
☎ (01902) 883381 ⊕ sarahhughesbrewery.co.uk

Traditional Black Country Victorian tower brewery, taken over by Sarah Hughes in 1921. Brewing ceased in the 1950s and recommenced in 1987. The original grist case and rare open-topped copper give a unique character to the brews. The Beacon Hotel is the brewery tap. ‼ ◆

Pale Amber (OG 1038, ABV 4%)
A well-balanced beer, initially slightly sweet but with hops close behind.

Sedgley Surprise (OG 1048, ABV 5%) ◥
A bittersweet, medium-bodied, hoppy ale with some malt.

Dark Ruby Mild (OG 1058, ABV 6%) ◥
A dark ruby strong ale with a good balance of fruit and hops, leading to a pleasant, lingering hops and malt finish.

Humpty Dumpty SIBA

Church Road, Reedham, Norfolk, NR13 3TZ
☎ (01493) 701818 ☎ 07843 248865
⊕ humptydumptybrewery.co.uk

⊠ Established in 1998, this 11-barrel, award-winning brewery continues to grow and expand its range of beers. The on-site shop sells bottled beer from the brewery and local cider. ‼ ☟ ◆ RAIB

Little Sharpie (OG 1039, ABV 3.8%) ◥
Aroma redolent with fresh peach and apricot. Hoppy character with a bitter backlash and biscuity undertones. Long, dry, hoppy finish.

Lemon & Ginger (OG 1041, ABV 4%)
An amber-coloured, crisp ale with a ginger and lemon tang.

Swallowtail (OG 1041, ABV 4%) ◥
Fruity airs introduce this amber-gold ale. Hops reinforce the citrus backbone and grainy mouthfeel. A pleasant, slowly drying finish.

Ale (OG 1043, ABV 4.1%) ◥
A hoppy vanilla fudge edge in both nose and taste. Malt provides balance as a gentle bitterness quickly recedes. Lengthy finish.

Broadland Sunrise (OG 1044, ABV 4.2%) ◥
Hoppy throughout with a strong malt and bitter background. A grainy mouthfeel, hoppy aroma and long, strong finale.

Red Mill (OG 1045, ABV 4.3%) ◥
A peppery redcurrant nose and grainy mouthfeel. Bittersweet base with vine fruit adding depth and gravity. Long sherry-like finish.

Reedcutter (OG 1045, ABV 4.4%) ◥
A sweet, malty beer, golden hued with a gentle malt background. Smooth and full-bodied with a quick, gentle finish.

Cheltenham Flyer (OG 1046, ABV 4.6%) ◥
A full-flavoured golden, earthy bitter with a long, grainy finish. A strong hop bitterness dominates throughout. Little evidence of malt.

**EAPA (East Anglian Pale Ale)
(OG 1046, ABV 4.6%)** ◥

Amber gold with an orange marmalade nose. A bittersweet caramel beginning slowly dries out as malty nuances fade away.

Norfolk Nectar (OG 1046, ABV 4.6%) ◆
Honey notes wrap around all other flavours and aromas. Hops and caramel give a counterpoint to the rich, sweet base.

Hungry Bear

10-14 Stonegate Road, Leeds, West Yorkshire, LS6 4HY
☎ (0113) 274 0241 ⊕ thehungrybear.co.uk

Hungry Bear began brewing in 2013 in the upstairs rooms of the Hungry Bear restaurant. A wide range of ales is produced in batches of about 70 litres, which are bottled and conditioned on site and supplied to the restaurant. ‼ RAIB V

Hunsbury Craft

23 Limefields Way, East Hunsbury, Northamptonshire, NN4 0SA
☎ (01604) 766228 ☎ 07798 907242
✉ johngeorgemargetts@tiscali.co.uk

Hunsbury Craft was established in 2010 using a 0.5-barrel plant, increasing to 2.25-barrel plant to meet demand.

Best Bitter (OG 1040, ABV 3.9%)

Copper (OG 1041, ABV 4.2%)

JD's Robust Porter (OG 1051, ABV 5.4%)

Mel's Mild (OG 1054, ARV 5.4%)

Magic (OG 1058, ABV 5.6%)

Young Chick (OG 1060, ABV 6%)

Old Rooster (ABV 7.1%)

Hunters SIBA ⊚

Bulleigh Barton Farm, Ipplepen, Devon, TQ12 5UA
☎ (01803) 873509 ☎ 07540 657115
⊕ thehuntersbrewery.co.uk

⊠ Hunters began brewing in 2008. The award-winning brewery has a 60-barrel brew length and 4,000 gallon fermenting capacity. A bottling, labelling and packing plant means it can turn out 3,000 bottle-conditioned beers per hour; this coupled with a dedicated conditioning room is enabling Hunters to bottle for others as well as itself. ‼ ⇛ ◆

Crack Shot (OG 1038, ABV 3.8%)
Good malt feel in the mouth, dry, tangy bitter finish.

Best (OG 1040, ABV 4%)

Crispy Pig (OG 1042, ABV 4%)
Speciality beer with a hint of apples.

Half Bore (OG 1040, ABV 4%)
Brewed with Devon honey for a full, malty flavour.

Devon Dreamer (OG 1042, ABV 4.1%)
Smooth and refreshing session ale.

Pheasant Plucker (OG 1044, ABV 4.3%)
Full-flavoured with a bittersweet finish.

Royal Hunt (OG 1055, ABV 5.5%)

Black Jack (OG 1062, ABV 6%)
Triple-hopped stout made with Devon honey.

Full Bore (OG 1070, ABV 6.8%)

Hurns

See Tomos Watkin (under W)

Hurst SIBA ⊚

Western Road, Hurstpierpoint, West Sussex, BN6 9SP
☎ 07866 438953 ✉ hurstbrewery@hotmail.co.uk

Hurst is a four-barrel microbrewery, founded in 2012 but reviving a name dating back to 1862. More than 100 outlets are supplied between south London and Brighton. The brewery has now opened a bottling unit at Blacklands Farm and a new 12-barrel fermenter is in the process of being commissioned. ‼◆

Founders Best Bitter (ABV 4.2%)
A nutty brown in colour with a rounded malty taste and suffused with subtle caramel.

1862 Premium Bitter (ABV 4.8%)

Watchtower (ABV 5.5%)
A strong, dark porter with a distinctive bitterness created by highly roasted malts, and a rich, creamy head.

Husk (NEW)

Unit 58a, Railway Arches, North Woolwich Road, West Silvertown, London, E16 2AA
☎ (020) 7474 3827 ☎ 07803 271160
⊕ huskbrewing.com

Commercial brewing began in 2016 after the husband-and-wife team outgrew their kitchen. RAIB

Pale Ale (OG 1050, ABV 5.1%)
A New World-style pale ale with stone fruit flavours and aromas and a decent malty body.

Hydes ⊚

The Beer Studio, 30 Kansas Avenue, Salford, M50 2GL
☎ (0161) 226 1317 ⊕ hydesbrewery.com

☺ Hydes has been a regional brewer since 1863 with its focus on cask ales to be supplied to their own tied estate of around 60 pubs, as well as to the wholesale and free trade. Four main ranges of beer are produced: Hydes; the Beer Studio – a monthly changing beer using rare and unusual hops and malts; the Lowry Collection – a bi-monthly changing beer celebrating the Salford artist L.S. Lowry; and Provenance, a changing bi-monthly world beer. ◆

1863 (OG 1033.5, ABV 3.5%) ◆
Lightly-hopped, pale brown session beer with some hops, malt and fruit in the taste and a short, dry finish.

Old Indie (OG 1033.5, ABV 3.5%) ◆
Dark brown/red in colour, with a fruit and malt nose. Taste includes biscuity malt and green fruits, with a satisfying aftertaste.

Original (OG 1036.5, ABV 3.8%) ◆
Pale brown beer with a malty nose, malt and an earthy hoppiness in the taste, and a good bitterness through to the finish.

Iâl SIBA 👁

Pant Du Road, Eryrys, CH7 4DD ☎ 07956 440402
🌐 cwrwial.com

Cwrw Iâl Community Brewery is run as a social enterprise assisted by EU funding with all profits used for local community projects. The 10-barrel plant is situated in a former truck maintenance workshop and first brewed in 2014. It supplies outlets along the North Wales coast, Borders, Cheshire and Manchester.

The Volunteer (OG 1037, ABV 3.8%)
Light copper-coloured session ale.

Haul Gwyn Extra Pale Ale (OG 1040, ABV 4%)
Lager malts and wheat combine to make this single hop pale beer.

Tailwhip (OG 1040, ABV 4%)
An easy-drinking, British-hopped golden ale.

Kia Kaha! (OG 1043, ABV 4.3%)

Limestone Cowboy (OG 1045, ABV 4.5%)
Hop-forward, robust, deep copper-coloured ale.

Pothole Porter (OG 1054, ABV 5.1%)
Black and roasted with the addition of British grown hops.

Iceni SIBA

Foulden Road, Ickburgh, Norfolk, IP26 5HB
☎ (01842) 878922 ☎ 07949 488113
🌐 icenibrewery.co.uk

Iceni was launched in 1995 by Brendan Moore. The brewery is also the headquarters of the East Anglian Brewers Co-op (EAB). ‼♦RAIB

Fine Soft Day (OG 1038, ABV 4%) 🍂
Golden-hued with toffee notes throughout. A creamy, lightly-hopped backdrop softly sinks into a pleasant sweetness.

Idle SIBA

🍺 **White Hart Inn, Main Street, West Stockwith, Nottinghamshire, DN10 4EY**
☎ (01427) 892672 ☎ 07949 137174
🌐 theidlebrewery.co.uk

👁The brewery began production in 2007 and is situated in a converted stable at the back of the White Hart Inn, which Brian Cooper, the brewer, now owns, alongside the River Idle. ‼♦

Golden Crown (OG 1038, ABV 3.8%)

Dog (OG 1041, ABV 4.2%)
A copper-coloured ale, moderately hoppy with a good balance of malt and hops leading to a bitter finish.

Sod (OG 1041, ABV 4.2%)
Light golden ale which has a deep fruity aroma and a well-balanced bittering.

Tongue (OG 1041, ABV 4.2%)

Black & Tan (OG 1042, ABV 4.3%)

Black Abbot (OG 1044, ABV 4.6%)
A black ale with deep roasted notes.

Idle Landlord (OG 1044, ABV 4.6%)
A dark brown ale with plenty of body, a malty flavour and a caramel/coffee finish.

Idle Valley SIBA 👁

Barham House, Aurillac Way, Hallcroft Industrial Estate, Retford, Nottinghamshire, DN22 7PX
☎ (01777) 860327 ☎ 07850 228383
🌐 idlevalleybrewing.com

Idle Valley began brewing in 2014 using a 1.46-barrel plant. A core range of five beers has been developed. High demand plus the opening of the Idle Valley Tap in Retford means the brewery upgraded to a 12-barrel plant in 2016. RAIB

Summer Breeze (ABV 3.8%)
A refreshing and hoppy golden ale.

Vacant Gesture (ABV 3.8%)
A light, fresh and hoppy blonde beer.

Jaded Pioneer (ABV 4.1%)
Medium-bodied pale ale with a citrus nose and a crisp, dry, citrus taste.

Torpid Expression (ABV 4.1%)
A deep copper-coloured beer that has a fruity and toffee aroma and a malty and toffee taste.

Coconut Shy PA (ABV 4.2%)
A coconut pale ale.

Indolent Philosopher (ABV 5.3%)
A dark stout with a relatively light body. Roast notes include chocolate and coffee. Not overpowering but smooth and moreish.

Unpretentious Declarant (ABV 5.6%)
Copper-coloured with a tropical and hoppy aroma. The beer is crisp, hoppy and bitter tasting with a citrus flavour.

Ilkley SIBA 👁

The New Brewery, Ashlands Road, Ilkley, West Yorkshire, LS29 8JT
☎ (01943) 604604 🌐 ilkleybrewery.co.uk

👁Ilkley brewery was founded in 2009 and now produces up to 160 barrels per week. The brewery consistently wins awards and last year produced over 40 different beers. It continues to expand, having acquired a new unit on the same site in 2016. ‼♦RAIB

Mary Jane (OG 1036, ABV 3.5%)
A crisp, pale ale with citrus aromas.

Rombald (ABV 4.6%)
An American amber ale with crisp and fruity hop flavours.

Hanging Stone (ABV 5%)
Rich and creamy, with a bitter finish of forest fruits and coffee.

Crossroads IPA (ABV 5.4%)
Aromas of orange rind and citrus peel with a dry, spicy finish.

Imperial

🍺 **Arcadia Hall, Cliff Street, Mexborough, South Yorkshire, S64 9HU**
☎ (01709) 584000 ☎ 07428 422703
✉ imperialclub@hotmail.co.uk

👁Brewing began in 2010 using a six-barrel tower brewery system located in the basement of the Imperial Club, Mexborough. Beer is available in the club as well as local outlets. ‼♦RAIB

Bitter (OG 1039, ABV 3.9%)

Blonde (OG 1040, ABV 4%)

Darkness (OG 1040, ABV 4%)

Bees Knees (OG 1043, ABV 4.2%)

Hop Bomb (OG 1042, ABV 4.2%)

IPA (OG 1052, ABV 5.5%)

Stout (OG 1054, ABV 5.8%)

Incredible SIBA

214-224 Broomhill Road, Brislington, Bristol, BS4 5RG
☎ 07780 977073 ⊕ incrediblebrewingcompany.com

⊠ Incredible Brewing specialises in producing small batches of beer using a 2.5-barrel plant. Established in 2014 by Stephen Hall, it promotes experimental beers and traditional recipes. ‼ ♦ RAIB V

Pale Ale (OG 1040, ABV 4.2%)

Milk Stout (OG 1044, ABV 4.4%)

Amber Ale (OG 1052, ABV 5.2%)

Black IPA (OG 1056, ABV 5.6%)

Indian Pale Ale (OG 1056, ABV 5.6%)

Imperial IPA (OG 1085, ABV 8.2%)

Independent Lakeland

See Strands and Yates

Indian

119b Baltimore Trading Estate, Baltimore Road, Great Barr, B42 1DD ⊕ indianbrewery.com

This six-barrel brewery, established in 2005 as the Tunnel Brewery at the Lord Nelson Inn, relocated to the picturesque stable block at Red House Farm in 2011. In 2015 the owners of Tunnel Brewery went their separate ways, with Mike Walsh retaining the brewery and renaming it the Indian Brewery. Later that year the Indian Brewery was sold to new owners and relocated to the outskirts of Birmingham. ‼

Summer (ABV 4%)

IPA (ABV 4.9%)

Bombay Honey (ABV 5%)

Indigenous SIBA

Peacock Cottage, Main Street, Chaddleworth, Berkshire, RG20 7EH
☎ (01488) 505060 ⊕ indigenousbrewery.co.uk

⊠ An occasional and informal microbrewer for many years, Kevin Brady established Indigenous in 2014, increasing production using a 2.5-barrel plant. Availability is restricted to local pubs, shops and an increasing number of regional beer festivals. ‼ ⊒

Forager's Gold (OG 1040, ABV 4%)
A crisp, golden ale with a slight amber touch. Smooth and refreshing with caramel notes.

Summer Solstice (OG 1042, ABV 4.1%)
A straw-coloured pale ale with a fresh, hoppy aroma coupled with a subtle bitterness and a long, dry finish.

Old Cadger (OG 1046, ABV 4.5%)

Rich malts and fruity hops combine to produce a balanced, full-flavoured beer.

Monocle (OG 1049, ABV 4.6%)
A smooth stout with a malty aroma and a slightly dry finish.

Moonstruck (OG 1051, ABV 4.8%)
Brewed in the classic 1850 London Porter-style, this beer has plenty of chocolate and coffee notes, complemented by a subtle bitterness and smooth finish.

Nosey Parker (OG 1058, ABV 5.5%)
A strong ruby-red mild with a sweet malty base and a hint of hops.

AMMO Belle (OG 1055, ABV 5.6%)
A well-hopped American pale ale that delivers lots of fruity notes, a floral aroma, and a moderately dry finish.

Inishmacsaint

7 Drumadown Road, Drumskimly, Derrygonnelly, Co Fermanagh, BT93 6DN
☎ (028) 6864 1031 ✉ gordyfallis@hotmail.com

⊠ Inishmacsaint is a small-scale brewery that has been in production since 2009. A larger brew plant is now in use producing a range of bottle-conditioned beers. RAIB

INNformal SIBA

⊒ Five Bells, Baydon Road, Wickham, RG20 8HH
☎ (01488) 657300 ⊕ fivebellswickham.co.uk

⊠ INNformal was established in 2015 in a purpose-built building behind the Five Bells pub in Wickham. A bore hole in the pub garden supplies water for the 2.5-barrel plant. A secondary 0.5-barrel kit is used for experimental brews. Beers are supplied mainly to the Five Bells and the John O'Gaunt, Hungerford. ‼ ♦

INNHouse Bitter (OG 1041, ABV 4.1%)
A nutty bitter using traditional English hops, with a biscuit flavour.

INNDeep (OG 1049, ABV 5%)
A robust stout with bitter overtones of chocolate and coffee.

San FrINNcisco (OG 1059, ABV 6%)
West Coast American-style IPA, hoppy with hints of citrus and a bitter finish.

Innis & Gunn

Canning Street, Edinburgh, EH3 8EG
☎ (0131) 272 2782 ⊕ innisandgunn.com

See Inveralmond.

Instant Karma

⊒ 4 John St, Clay Cross, Derbyshire, S45 9NQ
☎ (01246) 250366 ⊕ instantkarmabrewery.co.uk

Instant Karma began brewing in 2012 using a five-barrel plant with a brew length of 15 barrels per week. The brewery is part of the Rykneld Turnpyke brewpub..

Test Brew Number One! (OG 1039, ABV 3.9%)

Test Brew Number Two! (OG 1045, ABV 4.5%)

Sutra IPA (OG 1053, ABV 5.5%)

Interbrew UK

Porter Tun House, Capability Green, Luton, Bedfordshire, LU1 3LS
☎ (01582) 391166

Interbrew (Magor): Magor Brewery, Magor, NP26 3DA

Interbrew (Samlesbury): Cuerdale Lane, Samlesbury, Lancashire, PR5 0XD

UK subsidiary of A-B InBev. No real ale.

Intrepid SIBA ⟨◉⟩

Unit 12, Vincent Works, Brough, Derbyshire, S33 9HG
☎ (01433) 621851 ☎ 07870 777594 ⊕ intrepid.beer

⊕Based in the Hope Valley in the Peak District of Derbyshire, Intrepid commenced brewing in 2014 using an eight-barrel plant. ‼ ⊑

Explorer (OG 1038, ABV 4%)
A refreshing blonde beer with fruity aromas and a crisp, dry finish.

St Bernard (OG 1044, ABV 4.4%)
A malty ale with oak and vanilla aromas and caramel and biscuit flavours.

Porter (OG 1049, ABV 4.8%)
A traditional East India porter but using modern hops for a less bitter finish.

Traveller (OG 1049, ABV 5.4%)
American-style IPA brewed with a fruity flavour and bitter finish.

Inveralmond SIBA ⟨◉⟩

22 Inveralmond Place, Inveralmond Industrial Estate, Perth, PH1 3TS
☎ (01738) 449448 ✉ info@inveralmond-brewery.co.uk

⊕Established in 1997, Inveralmond was the first brewery in Perth for more than 30 years. Around 250 outlets are supplied. In 2016, Innis & Gunn, the Edinburgh company that specialises in oak-aged beers, bought Inveralmond following a successful crowdfunding scheme that raised £3 million. I&G had planned to build a new brewing operation but decided instead to buy the Perth brewery, where the current 30-barrel plant will be expanded, with a new maturation plant for the I&G beers. I&G makes no real ale but the Inveralmond range will continue. ‼ ⊑ ♦

Fair Maid (OG 1036, ABV 3.6%) ◀
A well-balanced Scottish ale with fruit and malt tones. Hops provide an increasing bitterness in the finish.

Ossian (OG 1042, ABV 4.1%) ◀
Well-balanced best bitter with a dry finish. This full-bodied amber ale is dominated by fruit and hop with a bittersweet character although excessive caramel can distract from this.

Thrappledouser (OG 1043, ABV 4.3%) ◀
A refreshing amber beer with reddish hues. The crisp, hoppy aroma is finely balanced with a tangy but quenching taste.

Lia Fail (OG 1048, ABV 4.7%) ◀
A dark, robust, full-bodied beer with a deep malty taste. Smooth texture and balanced finish.

Rascal London Porter (OG 1056, ABV 5.6%)

Ironbridge

See Wrekin

Irving SIBA ⟨◉⟩

Unit G1, Railway Triangle, Walton Road, Portsmouth, Hampshire, PO6 1TQ
☎ (023) 9238 9988 ⊕ irvingbrewers.co.uk

⊗ Established in 2007 by former Gale's brewer Malcolm Irving using a 15-barrel plant. Around 120 outlets are supplied in Hampshire, Sussex and Surrey with beers available further afield through beer swaps with other breweries. ‼ ⊑ ♦

Frigate (OG 1039, ABV 3.8%) ◀
Satisfying session bitter. Hoppy, with a floral aroma and initial sweetness, leading to bitterness and a smooth, slightly dry finish.

Type 42 (OG 1042, ABV 4.2%)
A robust best bitter with a deep ruby red hue balancing sweet hedgerow berry notes with a long, roasted malt finish and a deep bitterness.

Admiral Stout (OG 1042.5, ABV 4.3%)
A classic dark oatmeal stout, deep black in colour with a smooth, rounded malt flavour balanced with a strong bitterness.

Invincible (OG 1048, ABV 4.6%) ◀
Tawny-coloured strong bitter. Sweet and fruity with underlying maltiness throughout and gradually increasing dryness, contrasting with the sweet finish.

Iron Duke (OG 1053, ABV 5.3%)
A refreshing, well-balanced strong IPA. Hoppy – but not overly so.

Irwell Works SIBA

Irwell Street, Ramsbottom, BL0 9YQ
☎ (01706) 825019 ⊕ irwellworksbrewery.co.uk

⊕Irwell Works started brewing in 2010 in a building dating from 1888 that once housed the Irwell Works Steam, Tin, Copper & Iron Works. It now houses a six-barrel plant. A bar opened on the first floor in 2011. ‼

Lightweights & Gentlemen (OG 1031, ABV 3.2%) ◀
Light, refreshing pale ale with some fruitiness and a hoppy, bitter finish.

Tin Plate (OG 1033, ABV 3.6%)
Brewed as a traditional dark mild, low in strength and a rich creamy flavour but with a slight bitterness to contrast.

Copper Plate (OG 1036, ABV 3.8%) ◀
Traditional northern bitter. Copper-coloured with a satisfying blend of malt and hops and good bitterness.

Richard Mason 1888 (OG 1039, ABV 4%)
A mid-strength single-hopped beer with a mild bitterness and pleasant mildly-hopped aftertaste.

Costa del Salford (OG 1039, ABV 4.1%)
A hoppy summer ale, light in colour with bags of flavour.

Steam Plate (OG 1042, ABV 4.3%)
A golden best bitter with medium bitterness balanced with a slight sweetness.

Iron Plate (OG 1043, ABV 4.4%) ◀

Roast malt in the aroma is joined by hop and a toasty bitterness in the taste and finish.

Mad Dogs & Englishmen (OG 1052, ABV 5.5%)
Export-style pale ale hopped in the style of an IPA. Little sweetness for its strength and a strong hop character make this a smooth, easy-drinking beer.

Isca SIBA

Court Farm, Holcombe, Devon, EX7 0JT ☎ 07773 444501 ⊕ iscaales.co.uk

Isca Ales has developed a niche market by bottling a lot of production and supplying beer festivals outside its region. **RAIB V**

Citra (OG 1038, ABV 3.8%)
Light, refreshing beer with grapefruit aroma leading to a dry bitter finish.

Dawlish Summer (OG 1038, ABV 3.8%)
Light beer with a hoppy aroma.

Golden Ale (OG 1038, ABV 3.8%)
A golden bitter with a hoppy aroma.

Dawlish Bittter (OG 1042, ABV 4.2%)
Classic English bitter full of English hops.

Glorious Devon (OG 1044, ABV 4.4%)
The combination of three hops gives a grassy hop aroma with hoppy aftertaste.

Holcombe Gold (OG 1045, ABV 4.5%)
Golden beer full of English and American hops leading to a dry bitter finish.

Dawlish Pale (OG 1050, ABV 5%)
Grassy hop aroma with intense hoppy aftertaste.

Achilles Ale (OG 1054, ABV 5.4%)
A dark, strong, malty ale.

Isfield SIBA 👁

Unit 16, New Place Farm, Framfield, East Sussex, TN22 5RH
☎ (01825) 750633 ☎ 07803 716758
Office: Imperial Cottage, Station Road, Isfield, TN22 5UJ ✉ enquiries@isfieldbrewing.co.uk

⊠ Isfield began brewing in 2012 using a five-barrel plant. ♦

Bitter (OG 1039, ABV 3.7%)
A chestnut-coloured session bitter, fruity and malty aroma with a biscuit sweet taste.

Amberescent (OG 1040, ABV 4%)
A pale amber-coloured best bitter with caramel notes and an orange citrus hop finish.

Straw Blond (OG 1042, ABV 4.1%)

Ethel Red (OG 1043, ABV 4.4%)
Red/amber-coloured bitter with a smooth finish.

Toad in the Ale (OG 1050, ABV 4.8%)

Stiltwalker (OG 1050, ABV 5.2%)

Flapjack (OG 1055, ABV 5.3%)

Isla Vale

17 Westbrook Gardens, Margate, Kent, CT9 5DJ
☎ (01843) 292451 ☎ 07980 174616
⊕ islavalealesmiths.co.uk

⊠ Established in 2014 from a residential address in Westbrook (Margate) supplying local micro-pubs.

There are plans to expand the brewery and increase the range of ales. ♦

Golding Delicious (OG 1038, ABV 3.8%)
A light copper-coloured session ale with a slight malty sweetness.

Hopping Mad (ABV 4%)
A traditional session bitter with a variety of hops, complex aromas and malty flavours.

Cock-A-Snook (ABV 4.6%)
A dark golden-coloured session ale with good hop aroma and hints of fruit.

Natural Blonde (ABV 4.7%)
A refreshing blonde ale, initial floral notes with a lasting hoppy bitterness throughout.

Befuggled (OG 1052, ABV 5.2%)
A rich, malty ale, with plenty of hops.

IPA (ABV 5.5%)
A modern take on a traditional IPA using a variety of New World hops. A hint of fruit with an intense hoppy aroma and flavour.

Brewed for the Wheel Alehouse, Birchington-on-Sea:

Bosun's Best (ABV 4.2%)

Island SIBA

Dinglers Farm, Yarmouth Road, Newport, Isle of Wight, PO30 4LZ
☎ (01983) 821731 ⊕ isleofwightbrewery.com

⊠ Island Brewery is the realisation of Tom Minshull's ambition to brew real ales to complement the existing family-owned drinks distribution business. Brewing commenced in 2010 using a 12-barrel brewery. More than 100 outlets are supplied direct. ‼♦

Nipper Bitter (OG 1038, ABV 3.8%)
Straw-coloured, light and refreshing with a distinguishable balance of malt and hops and a satisfying after bite.

Wight Gold (OG 1040, ABV 4%)
Golden brown in colour with rounded malt and hops throughout.

Yachtsmans Ale (OG 1042, ABV 4.2%)
Chestnut-coloured ale with a rich, malty mouthfeel and hop aroma.

Wight Diamond (OG 1046, ABV 4.4%)

Wight Knight (OG 1045, ABV 4.5%)
Strong, full-bodied beer.

Vectis Venom (OG 1048, ABV 4.8%)
Easy-drinking with an underlying smoothness.

Earls RDA (OG 1052, ABV 5%)
Rich yet understated stout, with strong espresso aftertaste.

Islay SIBA

The Brewery, Islay House Square, Bridgend, Isle of Islay, PA44 7NZ
☎ (01496) 810014 ⊕ islayales.com

☺Brewing started on a four-barrel plant in a converted tractor shed in 2004. The brewery shop is next door. The island is more famous for its whisky, but the brewery has established itself as a must-see place for those visiting the eight working distilleries. ‼ 🍺♦ RAIB

Isle of Mull

See Argyll

Isle of Purbeck SIBA

⧈ Manor Road, Studland, Dorset, BH19 3AU
☎ (01929) 450227 ⊕ isleofpurbeckbrewery.com

⊠ Founded in 2003, the brewery is situated in the grounds of the Bankes Arms Hotel, overlooking Studland Bay on the Jurassic Coast. A 10-barrel plant is used. The core beers are available nationwide via exchange swaps with other microbrewers. ◆ RAIB

Purbeck Best Bitter (OG 1036, ABV 3.6%) ◈
A classic malty best bitter with rich malt aroma and taste and smooth malty bitter finish.

Force Four (OG 1040, ABV 4%)
A balanced, smooth-drinking beer packed with sweet and delicious roasted malt flavours with a subtle whisper of spicy hops.

Fossil Fuel (OG 1040, ABV 4.1%) ◈
Amber-coloured bitter with a complex aroma with a hint of pepper; rich malt dominates the taste, leading to a smooth, dry finish.

Solar Power (OG 1043, ABV 4.3%) ◈
Tawny mid-range ale brewed using Continental hops. Well-balanced flavours combine to provide a strong bitter taste but short, dry finish.

Studland Bay Wrecked (OG 1044, ABV 4.5%) ◈
Deep red ale with slightly sweet aroma reflecting a mixture of caramel, malt and hops that lead to a dry, malty finish.

Purbeck IPA (OG 1047, ABV 4.8%) ◈
Mid-brown beer with hop/malt balance in the flavour and a long, dry aftertaste

Isle of Skye SIBA

The Pier, Uig, Isle of Skye, IV51 9XP
☎ (01470) 542477 ⊕ skyebrewery.co.uk

☺The Isle of Skye Brewery was established in 1995. Originally a 10-barrel plant, it was upgraded to 20 barrels in 2004. Further expansion is planned. ☕◆

Skye Light (OG 1038, ABV 3.8%) ◈
A slightly hoppy nose leads to a powerful hop and fruit taste and a sharp finish.

Skye Otter Ale (OG 1041, ABV 4%)

Tarasgeir (OG 1040, ABV 4%) ◈
The peat roasted barley dominates giving a mellow, peaty whisky taste.

The Thistle and the Fern (OG 1041, ABV 4%) ◈
Good mix of hops and malt with a bitter, earthy background

Tiny Angels (OG 1040, ABV 4%)

Young Pretender (OG 1039, ABV 4%) ◈
A fruity, full-bodied golden ale, predominantly hoppy and fruity. The bitterness in the mouth is also balanced by summer fruits and hops, continuing into the lingering bitter finish.

Skye Red (OG 1041, ABV 4.2%) ◈
A light, fruity nose with a hint of caramel leads to a hoppy, malty, fruity flavour and a dry, bittersweet finish.

Skye Gold (OG 1041.5, ABV 4.3%) ◈

Porridge oats are used to produce this speciality beer. Well-balanced, it has a refreshingly soft fruity, bitter flavour with an oat background.

Skye Black (OG 1044, ABV 4.5%) 🍺 ◈
A complex, tasty brew. Full-bodied with a malty richness. Malt holds sway but there are plenty of hops and fruit to be discovered in its varied character.

Skye IPA (OG 1046, ABV 4.5%) ◈
Well-balanced with a good malty background and complemented with Sorachi hops.

Skye Blaven (OG 1047, ABV 5%) ◈
A well-balanced strong amber bitter with kiwi fruit and caramel in the nose and a lingering, sharp bitterness.

Cuillin Beast (OG 1066, ABV 7%) ◈
A winter warmer; sweet and fruity, and much more drinkable than the strength would suggest. Plenty of caramel throughout with a variety of fruit on the nose.

Itchen Valley SIBA

Unit D, Prospect Commercial Park, Prospect Road, Alresford, Hampshire, SO24 9QF
☎ (01962) 735111 ⊕ itchenvalley.com

⊠ Established in 1997, Itchen Valley moved to new premises in 2006 with a 20-barrel plant. More than 350 pubs are supplied, with wholesalers used for further distribution. ‼ 🍺 ◆ RAIB

QED (OG 1041, ABV 4.1%) ◈
Copper-coloured best bitter with a hint of crystal malt and a pleasant bitter aftertaste.

Hampshire Rose (OG 1042, ABV 4.2%)
A golden amber ale. Fruit and hops dominate the taste throughout, with a good mouthfeel.

Pure Gold (OG 1046, ABV 4.8%) ◈
Aromatic, hoppy, strong bitter. Golden-coloured, with initial maltiness and grapefruit counter-balanced with some sweetness, leading to dry finish.

Jacobi SIBA

Penlanwen Farm, Pumsaint, Carmarthenshire, SA19 8RR
☎ (01558) 650605 ⊕ jacobibrewery.co.uk

Brewing started in 2006 in a converted barn. There is no brewery tap, but regular outlets for the beers are Dolaucothi in Pumpsaint and Blue Bell in Llandovery. ◆

Gold Miner (OG 1038, ABV 3.9%)
Golden light ale with floral flavours reminiscent of elderflower, and a clean bitter finish.

Red Squirrel (OG 1044, ABV 4.3%)
Chestnut-coloured bitter with fruit undertones and a dry bitter finish.

Dr Harries Dark Magic (OG 1050, ABV 4.7%) 🍺
Dark, rich, old-style ale, smooth with a dark chocolate bitter finish.

James & Kirkman

⧈ 4 Wakefield Road, Pontefract, West Yorkshire, WF8 4HN
☎ (01977) 702231
✉ jamesandkirkmanbrewery@gmail.com

Brewing began in 2013 behind the Robin Hood pub using a 2.5-barrel plant.

Stallion (OG 1038, ABV 3.8%)
Deep copper in colour, this best bitter has light toffee and chocolate tastes from the malts and a well-balanced bitterness, with a floral and pine finish.

Magnificent Blonde (OG 1041, ABV 4.1%)
A pale blonde refreshing ale with a crisp, clean bitterness, floral notes and fruity finish.

Bunny Hop (OG 1042, ABV 4.2%)
A hoppy beer, crisp and refreshing, with a distinctive grapefruit flavour.

Mine's a Blonde (OG 1045, ABV 4.5%)
A crisp and refreshing hoppy pale ale, well-balanced with a fruity and citrus flavour and pungent grapefruit, lychee and gooseberry aroma.

Victorian Stout (OG 1056, ABV 5.6%)
Full-bodied, malty stout with chocolate and hints of toffee and roast malt. A good clean bitterness with lasting dried fruit and cherry aroma, and a slightly dry finish.

James Street

City Pub Company, 14 James Street West, Bath, BA1 2BX
☎ (01225) 805609 ⊕ thebathbrewhouse.com

The James Street Brewery opened in 2013 and is owned by the City Pub Company (West), which owns several other pubs, including brewpubs in Cambridge and London. The compact plant is on the ground floor of the Bath Brewhouse, with the conditioning tanks on the first floor. The company's other pub, the Cork in Bath, is also supplied.

Gladiator (OG 1040, ABV 3.8%)
Hazy pale brown beer with little aroma. Thin, sweetish flavour with some malt. Dry aftertaste.

Emperor (OG 1044, ABV 4.4%)
Golden beer with little aroma. A little caramel and fruit in the flavour, but dryness and bitterness is dominant. Dry astringent aftertaste.

Ostiarius (OG 1055, ABV 5.7%)

Jaw SIBA

Unit 9, The Centre Point, 67b Montrose Avenue, Hillington Industrial Estate, Hillington, G52 4LA
☎ (0141) 237 5840 ⊕ jawbrew.co.uk

Brewing began in 2014. RAIB

Drop (OG 1042, ABV 4.2%)

Surf (OG 1043, ABV 4.3%)

Drift (OG 1047, ABV 4.6%)

Wave (OG 1048, ABV 4.7%)

Jennings

Castle Brewery, Cockermouth, Cumbria, CA13 9NE
☎ (01900) 820362 ⊕ jenningsbrewery.co.uk

Jennings Brewery was established as a family concern in 1828 in the village of Lorton. The company moved to its present location in 1874. Pure Lakeland water is still used for brewing, drawn from the brewery's own well. Part of Marston's PLC.

Dark Mild (OG 1031, ABV 3.1%)
A well-balanced, dark brown mild with a malty aroma, strong roast taste, not over-sweet, with some hops and a slightly bitter finish.

Bitter (OG 1035, ABV 3.5%)
A malty beer with a good mouthfeel that combines with roast flavour and a hoppy finish.

Cumberland Ale (OG 1038, ABV 4%)
A tawny, hoppy beer with a dry aftertaste.

Cocker Hoop (OG 1044, ABV 4.6%)
Full-bodied complex bitter beer with plenty of hops and a rising bitter finish.

Sneck Lifter (OG 1051, ABV 5.1%)
A strong, dark brown ale with a complex balance of fruit, malt, sweet and roast flavours through to the finish

Jo C's SIBA

The Old Store, Walsingham Road, West Barsham, Norfolk, NR21 9NP
☎ (01328) 863854 ⊕ jocsnorfolkale.co.uk

Starting in 2010, Jo Coubrough (the county's only brewster) established a 10-barrel brewery in a former farm building in Norfolk. The beers are available in Flying Kiwi Inns, other free trade outlets, and at the brewery.

Norfolk Kiwi (OG 1038.5, ABV 3.8%)
Yellow, hop dominated bitter. Citrus notes vie with bitterness to add depth. Quick, slightly astringent finish.

Bitter Old Bustard (OG 1045, ABV 4.3%)
A mixture of malt and caramel on the nose is joined by a dark fruitiness in the flavour. Quick finish.

Knot Just Another IPA (OG 1052, ABV 5%)
A light amber-coloured and well-balanced strong bitter.

John o'Groats (NEW)

The Old Fire Station, John o'Groats, KW1 4YR ☎ 07825 729680 ⊕ johnogroatsbrewery.co.uk

Brewing began in 2015 using a four-barrel plant.

Swelkie (OG 1040, ABV 4%)
Refreshing golden session ale. Light biscuit overtones and a malty finish.

Duncansby (OG 1044, ABV 4.5%)

Jolly Sailor SIBA

Olympia Hotel, 77 Barlby Road, Selby, North Yorkshire, YO8 5AB
☎ (01757) 268918 ☎ 07923 635755
⊕ jolly-sailor-brewery.webplus.net

Jolly Sailor began brewing in 2012 at Ricall Business Park, a former mine site near York. Production was moved to the Olympia Hotel, Selby, in 2013, where the regular beers are always available and increasingly in other local pubs.

Bullseye Bitter (OG 1039, ABV 3.8%)

Jolly Blonde (OG 1036.5, ABV 3.8%)

Jolly Scotsman's Bitter (OG 1038, ABV 3.8%)
A fruity amber ale with citrus notes.

Yellow Jersey (OG 1036, ABV 3.8%)
A pale ale brewed with English hops.

Cue Brew (OG 1040, ABV 4%)
A dark mild.

Jollyboat SIBA

Coach House, Buttgarden Street, Bideford, Devon, EX39 2AU
☎ (01237) 424343

⊠ Established in 1995, the brewery is named after a sailor's leave vessel and all the beers have a nautical theme. Most outlets supplied are in Devon. !!♦

Mainbrace (OG 1042, ABV 4.2%) ◥
Pale brown brew with a rich, fruity aroma and a bitter taste and aftertaste.

Plunder (OG 1049, ABV 4.8%)
Red/brown beer with an aromatic nose, a good balance of malt, hops and fruit present throughout, leading to a bitter finish.

Joule's SIBA ◉

The Brewery, Great Hales Street, Market Drayton, Shropshire, TF9 1JP
☎ (01630) 654400 ⊕ joulesbrewery.co.uk

Re-established in 2010, following a break of 40 years, Joule's is situated in Market Drayton and uses its own mineral water. It runs a collection of 40 pubs across the region. !!♦

Blonde (OG 1038, ABV 3.8%)
Light, refreshing and aromatic, this well-balanced blonde delivers a crisp, clean palate coupled with a pleasing aroma of citrus fruit.

Pale Ale (OG 1042, ABV 4.1%)
Full-bodied and balanced with a pleasant bitter finish. Brewed using the original Joule's recipe dating back to 1779.

Slumbering Monk (OG 1045, ABV 4.5%)
Full-bodied with complex malt and nut character, this bright copper ale has hints of caramel which give a round, soft smoothness to the palate.

Junction

🏠 1 Baildon Road, Baildon, West Yorkshire, BD17 6AB

Junction is a microbrewery established in 2012 in the cellar of the Junction pub in Baildon, brewing around 300 gallons a week. Beer is sold in the pub and other local outlets. RAIB

Tommy's Tipple (OG 1037, ABV 3.7%)
A chestnut-coloured session bitter; smooth-tasting with a hoppy finish.

Blonde (OG 1040, ABV 4%)
A blonde session bitter, offering a big flavour and dry finish.

Dark Thoughts (OG 1046, ABV 4.6%)
Porter with roasted, nutty flavours and hops, giving a bitter edge.

Keith SIBA

Unit R, Isla Bank Mills, Keith, AB55 5DD
☎ (01542) 488006 ⊕ keithbrewery.co.uk

Formerly known as Brewmeister and established in 2012, the brewery was renamed Keith Brewery in 2015. Beer is mainly available in bottles in selected specialist off-licenses but cask-conditioned beer is available to a few outlets and beer festivals. The Brewmeister brand name is kept for export-only orders. ♦RAIB

Herr Keith (OG 1044, ABV 4.5%)
A wheat beer with honey notes.

Larger Keith (OG 1048, ABV 4.5%)
Cask-conditioned lager.

Pale Keith (OG 1048, ABV 5%)
Hoppy beer with hints of pineapple and exotic fruits.

Stout Keith (OG 1048, ABV 5%)
Coffee stout made with chocolate and coffee beans.

Sir Keith (OG 1096, ABV 10.1%)
Slightly sweet but hoppy with a fruity aroma and complex malty character.

Kelburn SIBA ◉

10 Muriel Lane, Barrhead, G78 1QB
☎ (0141) 881 2138 ⊕ kelburnbrewery.com

⊠ Kelburn is an award-winning family business established in 2002. !!♦

Goldihops (OG 1038, ABV 3.8%) ◥
Well-hopped session ale with a fruity taste and a bitter finish.

Pivo Estivo (OG 1038, ABV 3.9%)

Misty Law (OG 1040, ABV 4%)
A dry, hoppy amber ale with a long-lasting bitter finish.

Red Smiddy (OG 1040, ABV 4.1%) ◥
This bittersweet ale predominantly features an intense citrus hop character that assaults the nose and continues into the flavour, balanced perfectly with fruity malt.

Regnitz (OG 1042, ABV 4.4%)

Dark Moor (OG 1044, ABV 4.5%) 🗒
A dark, fruity ale with undertones of liquorice and blackcurrant.

Jaguar (OG 1043, ABV 4.5%) 🗒

Cart Noir (OG 1046, ABV 4.8%)

Cart Blanche (OG 1048, ABV 5%) ◥
A golden, full-bodied ale. The assault of fruit and hop camouflages the strength of this easy-drinking ale.

Kelham Island SIBA

23 Alma Street, Sheffield, South Yorkshire, S3 8SA
☎ (0114) 249 4804

Office: Prospect House, 17 Alma Street, Sheffield, South Yorkshire, S3 8RY ⊕ kelhambrewery.co.uk

☺Opened in 1990 behind the Fat Cat pub, the brewery moved to new purpose-built premises in 1999. The old building is used as a visitor centre. A brewery shop is housed with new offices in nearby Prospect House. !!🛒♦RAIB

Best Bitter (OG 1038, ABV 3.8%)
Classic amber Yorkshire bitter with spicy, earthy aromas and a sweet, refreshing, malty finish.

Pride of Sheffield (OG 1040.5, ABV 4%)
A full-flavoured amber-coloured bitter.

Easy Rider (OG 1041.8, ABV 4.3%) ◥

A pale, straw-coloured beer with a sweetish flavour and delicate hints of citrus fruits. A beer with hints of flavour rather than full-bodied.

Riders on the Storm (OG 1045, ABV 4.5%)
A robust golden pale ale with berry notes and slight roasted notes.

Pale Rider (OG 1050, ABV 5.2%) ◆
A full-bodied, straw-coloured pale ale, with a good fruity aroma and a strong fruit and hop taste. Its well-balanced sweetness and bitterness continue in the finish.

Kelpaul (NEW)

c/o 88 St Owen Street, Hereford, HR1 2QD ☎ 07941 027134

Office: 1 Churchway Cottage, Holmer, Hereford, HR1 1LL ✉ kelpaulbrewco@gmail.com

⊗ Kelpaul is a cuckoo brewery using Hereford Brewery's 10-barrel plant since 2015. Around 10 outlets across Herefordshire are supplied. ◆ RAIB

Autumn Amber (OG 1036, ABV 3.8%)

Madagascar Mild (OG 1036, ABV 3.8%)
A dark, lightly-hopped, full-flavoured mild. A complex, rich roast malt flavour with a hint of berries and chocolate overlaid with smooth Madagascar vanilla throughout.

Sunshine Session (OG 1036, ABV 3.8%)
A light, refreshing pale ale with a hint of spicy lemon marmalade on the aroma, an instant hit of grapefruit bitterness on the first taste, leading to pleasant grassy, nutty notes and a floral aftertaste.

Autumn Gold (OG 1036, ABV 4%)
A refreshing golden ale. Fresh aroma with a creamy citrus hit on first taste, leading to rich, refreshing fruity flavours and a pleasant astringent aftertaste.

Bonneville (OG 1041, ABV 4.4%)
A well-rounded, moderately-hopped, easy-drinking bitter ale. A malty aroma with green tea notes, giving way to a flavour comprising classic hop earthiness and hints of blackcurrant and grapefruit.

Lambretta (OG 1044, ABV 4.9%)
A smooth, well-hopped pale ale. Initial sweet bitterness gives way to a smooth finish, which belies its strength.

Keltek SIBA ◉

Cardrew Way, Redruth, Cornwall, TR15 1SS
☎ (01209) 313620

Office: Unit 5, Kernick Business Park, Annear Road, Penryn, Cornwall, TR10 9EW ⊕ keltekbrewery.co.uk

⊗ Keltek, meaning 'Celtic' in Cornish, was founded in 1997 by Stuart Heath. It started life as a 2.5-barrel plant in Stuart's disused stable block on the Roseland Peninsula but several moves and expansions means it is now based in Redruth and has the capacity to brew more than 250 barrels a week. In 2013 Keltek acquired four pubs in south-west Cornwall, becoming only the second brewery in Cornwall to own its own estate of public houses. ⛟ ◆ RAIB

Even Keel (OG 1034, ABV 3.4%) ◆

Pale brown session bitter. Light malt and hop taste with apple, plum and pear drops. Gentle dry and bitter finish.

Golden Lance (OG 1038, ABV 4%) ◆
Gold bitter with slight fruity aroma. Grassy citrus hops, apples, gentle malt, hints of elderflower and butterscotch. Long bitter finish.

Magik (OG 1040, ABV 4%) ◆
Copper-coloured best bitter. Sweet honey-like flavour with toffee butterscotch. Quite malty with balancing English hop bitterness. Bitter citrus hop finish.

King (OG 1049, ABV 5.1%) ◆
Pale brown strong bitter. Vine fruits and malt aroma. Sweet summer fruits, esters and biscuit malt balanced by hop bitterness.

Beheaded (OG 1068, ABV 7.5%) ◆
Smooth, brown strong old ale. Christmas pudding with port wine. Smoked peat, figs and plums. Sweet, fruity finish, lightly dry.

Brewed for Roseland Brewery:

Cornish Shag (OG 1037, ABV 3.8%)
A copper-coloured session beer.

Kemptown

⬛ 33 Upper St James's Street, Kemptown, Brighton, East Sussex, BN2 1JN ☎ 07967 681203

☺ Founded in 1989, the brewery is the smallest commercially operating tower brewery in the world. The beers are exclusively available on site at the Hand in Hand brewpub and are brewed by the team behind Brighton Bier. ‼

Kemptown (OG 1040, ABV 4%)
A light session ale. Crisp and hoppy.

Ye Olde Trout (OG 1045, ABV 4.5%)
A golden brown beer with fruity aromas and a dry finish.

Kendal

⬛ Tanners Yard, Kendal, Cumbria, LA9 4DH
☎ (01539) 733803 ⊕ burgundyswinebar.co.uk

☺ Kendal Brewing Company was established in 2011. Brewing take place twice a week. ‼

Mountain Medicine (OG 1037, ABV 3.7%)
Amber-coloured, gently-hopped traditional session bitter.

Eleven Bells (OG 1039, ABV 3.9%)
A light, well-hopped beer with a citrus finish.

Pale Ale (OG 1042, ABV 4.2%)
A traditional pale ale, fruity with a long, dry finish.

Gold (OG 1043, ABV 4.3%)
A fresh, dry ale with a hoppy finish.

Grisleymires Stout (OG 1048, ABV 4.8%)
A dark chocolate taste with a bitter finish.

Dr Mannings Red Winter Ale (OG 1057, ABV 5.7%)
Dark red in colour with a smooth chocolate taste and slightly hoppy finish.

Kendrick's SIBA

Coalpit Lane, Willey, Warwickshire, CV23 0SL
☎ (01788) 833469 ☎ 07912 481250
⊕ kendricksbrewing.co.uk/

☺The brewery, formerly Wood Farm Brewery, opened in 2011 and was taken over and renamed by Linden and Jane Kendricks in 2015. The brewery can be viewed from the bar of the visitor centre, which has an outside patio area with tables, and is set in 36 acres of Warwickshire countryside. **‼◆RAIB**

1823 Mild (OG 1035, ABV 3.5%)

Twickers (OG 1037, ABV 3.7%)

Webb Ellis (OG 1038, ABV 3.8%)

Playon (OG 1040, ABV 4%)

Scrum (OG 1040, ABV 4%)

Best Bitter (OG 1042, ABV 4.2%)

Victorious (OG 1042, ABV 4.2%)

Union (OG 1046, ABV 4.6%)

No. 8 (OG 1050, ABV 5%)

Kennet & Avon SIBA

34 Old Broughton Road, Melksham, Wiltshire, SN12 8BX
☎ **(01225) 707111 ⊕ kennetandavonbrewery.co.uk**

Kennet & Avon began brewing in 2014, with the beers originally being brewed by Wessex Brewery (qv) while the plant was under construction. The brewery relocated to its present site in 2015. The beers are available at the owner's micropub, the Vaults in Devizes, the Bowbridge Lock, Stroud, and in outlets throughout the West Country. A specialist craft beer shop has been built selling beers from all over the world, with a tap room and beer garden planned. **RAIB GF**

Pillbox (OG 1039, ABV 4%)
A light, refreshing ale with a hoppy bite.

Dundas (OG 1041, ABV 4.2%)
A copper-coloured best bitter with a pleasant bitterness and citrus hoppy aroma.

Rusty Lane (OG 1044, ABV 4.4%)
A rust-coloured Irish-style red ale with rounded toffee malt flavour and floral hop finish.

Bruce (OG 1048, ABV 4.8%)
A rich, dark porter with an underlying roasted chocolate maltiness and slight coffee aroma.

Caen Hill Hop (OG 1050, ABV 5%)
A strong golden ale with a powerful floral hop flavour.

Savernake (OG 1053, ABV 5.3%)
Full-bodied black beer with aromas of liquorice, roast coffee and chocolate, and a delicate, pleasant aftertaste.

Crofton IPA (OG 1054, ABV 5.4%)
A traditional, strong beer with exotic fruit flavours and a light bitter finish.

Kent SIBA ◉

The Long Barn, Birling Place Farm, Stangate Road, Birling, Kent, ME19 5JN
☎ **(01634) 780037 ⊕ kentbrewery.com**

Kent Brewery was founded in 2010 by Toby Simmonds (ex-brewer from Dark Star) and Paul Herbert. Originally brewed at Larkins, a 10-barrel plant has been in operation at the Birling site since 2011. More than 200 outlets are supplied direct, mainly throughout Kent, Sussex and London. **◆RAIB**

Session Pale (OG 1037, ABV 3.7%)

A light and hoppy session beer with hints of citrus and elderflower.

Black Gold (OG 1040, ABV 4%)
Dark beer with the easy-drinking qualities of a golden ale.

Pale (OG 1040, ABV 4%)
A full-flavoured and aromatic pale ale.

Cobnut (OG 1041, ABV 4.1%)
Generously-hopped, dark and nutty.

KGB (Kent Golding Bitter) (OG 1041, ABV 4.1%)

Zingiber (OG 1041, ABV 4.1%)
American hops with ginger for a fruity and warming light beer.

Brewers Reserve (OG 1050, ABV 5%)
A strong hop flavour of citrus and resin with a delicate malt background.

Beyond the Pale (OG 1054, ABV 5.4%)
A full-flavoured golden pale ale with a powerful punch of hops.

Enigma (OG 1055, ABV 5.5%)
A highly-hopped black IPA with a soft malt body.

Twelfth Night (ABV 7.4%) 🍺

Kentwood

▤ 227-229 High Street, Prestonpans, EH32 9BE
⊕ kentwoodbrewing.com

A microbrewery was installed at the award-winning pub, the Prestoungrange Gothenburg, in 2004. In 2015 the Kentwood Brewery took ownership of the five-barrel plant. Visitors to the pub are able to see the brewing process through windows separating the brewery and the main bar. Ales from the traditional Fowler's Ales range are also produced under the 'Kentwood at the Goth' label.

Kernel SIBA

Arch 11, Dockley Road Industrial Estate, Dockley Road, London, SE16 3SF
☎ **(020) 7231 4516 ⊕ thekernelbrewery.com**

Kernel was established in 2010 by Evin O'Riordain and moved to larger premises in 2012 to keep up with demand. The brewery produces bottle-conditioned beers, as well as the occasional cask, and has won many awards for its wide, ever-changing range of beers. Beers are available from the brewery on a Saturday as well as an exclusive selection of pubs around the country. **☛RAIB**

Keswick SIBA ◉

The Old Brewery, Brewery Lane, Keswick, Cumbria, CA12 5BY
☎ **(01768) 780700 ⊕ keswickbrewery.co.uk**

Keswick, owned by Sue Jefferson, began brewing in 2006 using a 10-barrel plant on the site of a brewery that closed in 1897. Outlets include Middle Ruddings Hotel in Braithwaite, the Dog & Gun, Keswick, and many other Lakeland pubs. **‼☛◆**

Gold (OG 1035, ABV 3.6%)

Bitter (OG 1036, ABV 3.7%)

Park Your Thirst (OG 1038, ABV 3.9%)

Thirst Run (OG 1041, ABV 4.2%) 🍺

A well-balanced golden beer that maintains its fruitiness from start to finish.

Thirst Quencher (OG 1042, ABV 4.3%)
A refreshing pale ale with an exotic fruit and citrus aroma.

KSB (Keswick Special Bitter) (OG 1047, ABV 4.8%)
Full malt flavour with notes of chocolate and roast barley.

Dark Horse (OG 1057, ABV 6%)
A dark, rich and malty ale.

Thirst Celebration (OG 1065, ABV 7%)

Kew

477 Upper Richmond Road West, East Sheen, London, SW14 7PU
☎ (020) 8878 9415 ⊕ kewbrewery.co.uk

⊠ Established in 2015, Kew is a family-run, independent brewery situated less than a mile from, and inspired by, the world-famous Royal Botanic Gardens at Kew. ‼ ☛ ♦ RAIB

Botanic (ABV 3.8%) ⬟
Tawny bitter with malt and a little hop aroma. Sweet malt flavour and finish with a trace of bitter hop.

Chocolate Milk Stout (ABV 3.9%) ⬟
Strong chocolate note to aroma which continues into a dry, bitter taste and dry finish. A hint of sweetness.

Petersham Porter (ABV 4.3%) ⬟
Dark chocolate character in the aroma and flavour, which is malty with toffee, treacle and blackberry notes. Dry bitter finish.

Sandycombe Gold (ABV 4.4%)
Pale golden ale. Crisp, hoppy and refreshing, with a lingering bitterness and big fruit and spice hop aroma.

Pagoda Pale (ABV 4.5%)

Richmond Rye (ABV 4.5%) ⬟
Dry amber beer with hints of tangerine and spice. Bitter hops throughout with a touch of caramel in the aroma.

Keystone SIBA

Old Carpenters Workshop, Berwick St Leonard, Wiltshire, SP3 5SN
☎ (01747) 820426 ⊕ keystonebrewery.co.uk

⊠ Set up in 2006 with a 10-barrel plant, the brewer aims to be as sustainable and efficient as possible, brewing traditional southern English-style beers using local ingredients. The beers are available in the brewery-run Benett Arms, Tisbury. Around 150 other outlets are also supplied. ‼ ☛ ♦

Bedrock (OG 1035, ABV 3.6%) ⬟
Copper-coloured bitter, hops and malt in the aroma, followed by fruit and bitterness in the taste. Long, lingering aftertaste.

Gold Hill (OG 1039, ABV 4%) ⬟
Amber-coloured bitter with floral/citrus aroma, clean tasting with balanced bittersweet taste right through to the aftertaste, which has a slightly hoppy astringency.

Large One (OG 1041, ABV 4.2%) ⬟

Copper-coloured malty best bitter, fruit and bitterness to the fore initially, long fruit and bitter hop flavours to the finish.

Kiln

4 Alexandra Road, Burgess Hill, West Sussex, RH15 0EW ☎ 07800 556729 ⊕ thekilnbrewery.co.uk

Kiln brewery was set up by two friends in 2014. It produces two beers at present, with more planned. The beers are available locally.

Boardwalk (OG 1050, ABV 4.5%)
Golden-orange in colour; the aroma has citrus, pine and hop notes. Citrus fruit features in the taste with a crisp bitter finish.

Brewlin Rouge (OG 1050, ABV 5.1%)
Red-gold in colour, with a gentle hop aroma and complex malt flavour.

King Alfred

11 Mill Rise, Bourton, Dorset, SP8 5DH
☎ (01747) 840967 ✉ kingalfredales@aol.com

⊠ King Alfred is a 0.5-barrel garage brewery that started production in 2012. It currently brews about once a month. A few local pubs and beer festivals are supplied.

871 (OG 1043, ABV 4.3%)
Mid-brown malty bitter with balanced hop flavours.

Saxon Gold (OG 1048, ABV 4.8%)
Mid-gold bitter with prominent hop flavours and aroma.

King Street (NEW)

▤ Riverside House, Welsh Back, Bristol, BS1 4RR
☎ (0117) 405 8948

Office: The City Pub Company (West) Plc, Essel House, 2nd Floor, 29 Foley Street, London, W1W 7TH
⊕ kingstreetbrewhouse.co.uk

⊠ The King Street Brew House is owned by the The City Pub Company (West) which has several pubs and brewpubs around the country. The compact brewery is on the ground floor, with the fermenting vessels and conditioning tanks in the basement. It also supplies the company's other pub in Bristol, the Prince Street Social. ‼ ♦ RAIB

Socks & Sandals (OG 1039, ABV 3.8%)

Pasty Git (OG 1043, ABV 4.2%)

Red Rye (OG 1046, ABV 4.6%)

Shaft (OG 1055, ABV 5.5%)

King's Cliffe

Unit 10, Kingsmead, Station Road, King's Cliffe, Northamptonshire, PE8 6YH ☎ 07843 288088
⊕ kcbales.co.uk

⊠ In 2014, exactly 100 years after the last brewery in King's Cliffe ceased brewing, village resident Jeremy O'Neill set up this new venture. It currently produces five barrels a week. ‼ ♦

5C (OG 1038, ABV 3.8%)

No. 10 (OG 1040, ABV 4%)

66 Degrees (OG 1046, ABV 4.6%)

K2 (OG 1055, ABV 5.5%)

Kings Clipstone

Keepers Bothy, Kings Clipstone, Nottinghamshire,
NG21 9BT
☎ (01623) 823589 ☎ 07790 190020
⊕ kingsclipstonebrewery.co.uk

Located in the heart of Sherwood Forest, Kings
Clipstone began brewing in 2012 using a five-
barrel plant. The owners, David and Daryl Maguire,
brew a range of core beers plus one-off brews and
seasonals. Beers are available nationwide to
freehouses, festivals and wholesale markets. ‼◆

Palace Pale (OG 1036, ABV 3.6%)
Golden ale which is light and crisp with a
refreshing taste.

Hop On (OG 1039, ABV 3.8%)
A pale and refreshing session beer with fruity hops.

Moonbeam (OG 1042, ABV 4.2%)
A mid-strength chestnut-coloured bitter with a full
flavour and well-rounded finish.

Sire (OG 1043, ABV 4.2%)
A well-rounded beer with a clean bitter finish.

Queen Bee (OG 1051, ABV 5.1%)
A ruby-red strong ale, classically rich and smooth.

Kings Head

⊟ Kings Head, 132 High Street, Bildeston, Suffolk,
IP7 7ED
☎ (01449) 741434 ⊕ bildestonkingshead.co.uk

⊗ Kings Head has been brewing since 1996 in an
old cart lodge at the back of the pub. Under new
ownership since 2008, the three-barrel plant brews
fortnightly. ‼◆

Bildeston Best (OG 1036, ABV 3.6%)
Traditional best. Well-hopped with a malty
sweetness and dry finish.

Brettvale Gold (ABV 3.6%)

Kingstone SIBA

Tintern, NP16 7NX
☎ (01291) 680111 ⊕ kingstonebrewery.co.uk

Kingstone Brewery is located in the Wye Valley
close to the famous Tintern Abbey. Brewing began
on a four-barrel plant in 2005. Special brews are
marketed under the Hapax Brewing Co label.
‼◆RAIB

Tewdric's Tipple (OG 1038, ABV 3.8%)
An ale with a dry, bitter character and a tangy core.

Challenger (OG 1040, ABV 4%)
A smooth, richly-hopped ale with a malty nose and
toffee undertones.

Gold (OG 1040, ABV 4%)
A straw-coloured smooth ale with citrus notes and
a balanced, hoppy finish.

Llandogo Trow (OG 1042, ABV 4.2%)
A ruby-red ale, triple hopped, with a smooth, fruity
finish.

Premium Stout (OG 1044, ABV 4.4%)
A smooth, rich stout with a bitter finish.

Classic (OG 1045, ABV 4.5%)
A balanced, distinctly hoppy, dry ale with a floral
nose and a smooth, well-balanced finish.

1503 (OG 1048, ABV 4.8%)
A deep chestnut red-coloured, lightly-hopped ale
bursting with complex rich flavours.

Abbey Ale (OG 1051, ABV 5.1%)
An amber-coloured, full-flavoured ale. The hoppy
edge is balanced by a smooth, malty richness.

Humpty (OG 1058, ABV 5.8%)
An IPA with a slightly sweet, floral nose, a
balanced level of malt supporting the hops and
finally a subtle but slightly citrus finish.

Kinneil

84 Corbiehall, Bo'ness, EH51 0AS ☎ 07789 204008
⊕ kinneilbrew.co.uk

⊚Kinneil began brewing in 2011 using a 2.5-barrel
plant. The brewery is adjacent to the Corbie Inn but
separately owned.

Wonderful Jake (OG 1037, ABV 3.6%)

Katie Wearie's (OG 1039, ABV 3.8%)

Wayfinder (OG 1038, ABV 3.8%)

Pennvael Amber (OG 1042, ABV 4%)

Kincardine Sunset (OG 1042, ABV 4.1%)

Caer Edin Dark (OG 1044, ABV 4.2%)

Kinver SIBA ◉

Unit 1, Britch Farm, Rocky Wall, Kinver, Staffordshire,
DY7 5NW ☎ 07715 842676 ⊕ kinverbrewery.co.uk

⊚Established in 2004, Kinver produces a wide
range of different beer styles including one-off
specials. The brewery relocated in 2012 to a new
10-barrel plant on the edge of Kinver due to
increased demand. Around 30 outlets are supplied
direct including several in Kinver. ‼◆RAIB

Light Railway (OG 1038, ABV 3.8%) ⬩
Straw-coloured session beer. A fruity and malty
start quickly gives way to well-hopped bitterness
and lingering hoppy aftertaste.

Cavegirl Bitter (OG 1040, ABV 4%)
Pale straw-coloured, balanced bitter.

Edge (OG 1041, ABV 4.2%) ⬩
Amber with a malty aroma. Sweet fruity start with
a hint of citrus marmalade in the spicy edged malt;
lasting hoppy finish that is satisfyingly bitter.

Noble (OG 1043, ABV 4.5%) ⬩
Fruity hop aroma. Fruity start then the grassy hops
give a sharp bitter finish with malt support.

Maybug (OG 1045, ABV 4.8%)
German-style cask-conditioned lager beer brewed
with Tettnang hops.

Half Centurion (OG 1047, ABV 5%) ▤ ⬩
A golden best bitter; malty before the American
Chinook hop takes command to give a balanced
hoppy finish and provide the great aftertaste.

Black Ram Stout (OG 1048, ABV 5.2%)
Full-bodied, roasty dark stout.

Khyber (OG 1054, ABV 5.8%) ⬩
Golden strong bitter with a hop bite that
overwhelms the fleeting malty sweetness and
drives through to the long dry finish.

Over the Edge (OG 1068, ABV 7.5%) ▤
Complex, strong, golden winter ale.

Kirkby Lonsdale SIBA

Unit 2F, Old Station Yard, Kirkby Lonsdale, LA6 2HP
☎ (01524) 272221 ☎ 07793 149999
⏣ kirkbylonsdalebrewery.com

⊛Kirkby Lonsdale is a family-run business established in 2009 on a six-barrel plant. ♦

Tiffin Gold (OG 1036, ABV 3.6%) ◆
A full-flavoured, grapefruity, hoppy and bitter beer with a dry finish.

Stanley's Pale Ale (OG 1038, ABV 3.8%) ◆
Hops dominate this sweet and fruity, well-balanced beer.

Ruskins Bitter (OG 1039, ABV 3.9%) ◆
A tawny bitter with a distinctive aroma of fruit and malt. The clean, hoppy flavour is well-balanced with fruity sweetness leading to a sustained bittersweet finish.

Singletrack (OG 1040, ABV 4%) ◆
Crisp citrus hops predominate in a well-balanced beer with a pleasant bitter finish.

Radical Red (OG 1042, ABV 4.2%) ◆
Malty beer with a caramel sweetness that is balanced by a bitter finish.

Monumental Blonde (OG 1045, ABV 4.5%) ◆
Distinctly hoppy, a fruity, sweet, pale-coloured, full-bodied bitter.

Jubilee Stout (OG 1055, ABV 5.5%) ◆
Rich, well-balanced stout with malt. A long aftertaste retains the complexity and is surprisingly refreshing.

Westmorland Pale Ale (OG 1060, ABV 6.2%)
A pale ale with fruity, spicy hop flavours and aroma together with a delicate hint of chocolate malt.

Imperial Dragon (OG 1080, ABV 8.2%)
Dry-hopped, dangerously drinkable IPA.

Kirkstall SIBA

Unit 6, Canal Wharf, Wyther Lane, Kirkstall, Leeds, West Yorkshire, LS5 3BT
☎ (0113) 345 8835 ⏣ kirkstallbrewerycompany.com

⊛Brewing began in 2011 at a site within yards of the original Kirkstall Brewery beside the Leeds-Liverpool canal with nearby Kirkstall Abbey and lost local industries providing inspiration for the beer names. There are plans to move to a new site. The beer range can always be found at the Kirkstall Bridge Inn nearby. ‼♦

BYB (Best Yorkshire Bitter) (OG 1036, ABV 3.5%)

Pale Ale (OG 1040, ABV 4%) ◆
A refreshing golden-coloured bitter beer with citrus hop flavours, zesty bitterness especially in the finish, which is lingering.

Three Swords (OG 1045, ABV 4.5%) ◆
Pithy grapefruit flavours characterise this light-coloured golden ale; plenty of hops from the start to the lingering finish.

Dissolution IPA (OG 1050, ABV 5%) ◆
Full-flavoured – hops lead the charge with bitter fruit just behind.

Black Band Porter (OG 1055, ABV 5.5%) ◆
Dark, smooth and rich with a full aroma and big flavour. Generous fruity taste, hints of chocolate and liquorice.

Generous George (OG 1060, ABV 6%)

Kirrie

Bon Scott Brewery, 8 Bon Scott Place, Kirriemuir, Angus, DD8 4LD ☎ 07855 808975 ⏣ kirrie-ales.co.nf

Established in 2014, Kirrie Ales microbrewery is situated in the picturesque town of Kirriemuir, birthplace of J. M. Barrie, creator of Peter Pan, and gateway to the Angus Glens. The brewery space measures only 8 by 9 feet. 70-80 litres a day are produced RAIB

Fruity Wee Blonde (OG 1037, ABV 3.8%)
American-style IPA with plenty of grapefruit and other citrus flavours but not overly dry and bitter.

Hoppy Daze (OG 1039, ABV 4%)
A well-balanced classic session IPA.

Red from the Shed (OG 1044, ABV 4.5%)
Scottish 80/- style with subtle fruit notes on the finish.

Thrums Best (OG 1044, ABV 4.5%)
A well-balanced bitter with hints of orange on the finish.

Kissingate

Pole Barn, Church Lane Farm Estate, Church Lane, Lower Beeding, West Sussex, RH13 6LU
☎ (01403) 891335 ☎ 07909 975664

Office: 2 Drury Close, Maidenbower, Crawley
⏣ kissingate.co.uk

⊗ Kissingate was founded in 2010 by husband-and-wife team Gary and Bunny Lucas using an eight-barrel plant. In 2012 the brewery moved into a new purpose-built barn conversion. Brewing capacity is 24 barrels. ‼🍺♦

Storyteller (OG 1036, ABV 3.5%)

Sussex (OG 1040, ABV 4%)

Moon (OG 1045, ABV 4.5%)
A gold-coloured beer with a taste of lightly roasted malts, late autumn apples and a lingering hop bitterness.

Old Tale Porter (OG 1045, ABV 4.5%)
A classic, full-flavoured London porter.

Mandarina Red (OG 1048, ABV 4.8%)
A complex red-coloured IPA with multiple flavour layers of malt and prominent citrus fruits. Pine and citrus bitter finish.

Chennai (OG 1050, ABV 5%)

Smelter's Stout (OG 1052, ABV 5.1%)

Power Blue (OG 1058, ABV 5.5%)

Mary's Ruby Mild (OG 1064, ABV 6.5%)
Deep ruby in colour with gentle aromas of well-aged Port. Intense and rounded malt flavours and a light and floral hop aftertaste.

Kitchen Garden

Old Walled Garden, Sheffield Park, East Sussex, TN22 3QX
☎ (01825) 790775 ⏣ kitchengardenbrewery.co.uk

Kitchen Garden is a small one-barrel plant producing only bottle-conditioned ales, all suitable for vegetarians. It is situated in a Victorian walled kitchen garden at Sheffield Park. The beers are available from the brewery shop and at several outlets in Sussex including Middle Farm, Firle. Brewing is currently suspended. 🍺♦RAIB

Kite

See Glamorgan

Knockout (NEW)

Unit 10, Alanbrooke Park, Alexander Road, Belfast, BT6 9HB

Commercial brewing began in 2015. RAIB

Knops SIBA

The Walled Garden, Archerfield Estate, Dirleton, EH39 5HQ ☎ 07949 879147 ⊕ knopsbeer.co.uk

⊛Knops began brewing in 2010 under contract. In 2013 it moved to new premises on the Archerfield Estate at Dirleton on the East Lothian coastline with an 11-barrel plant. Beers are based on modern interpretations of traditional styles and are bottled in-house. Cask-conditioned beers are available widely in Eastern Scotland and the Glasgow area. ‼RAIB

East Coast Pale (OG 1039, ABV 3.8%)
A light aromatic session beer brewed with a mixture of British and European hops.

Musselburgh Broke (OG 1045, ABV 4.5%)
Modern interpretation of a 19th century style. Full malt flavour with a clean, brisk finish.

California Common (OG 1048, ABV 4.6%)
A deep golden ale with a clean hop finish and light toffee notes followed by a lingering bitterness.

India Pale Ale (OG 1047, ABV 5%)
Light golden ale with a citrus and apricot aroma. Well-balanced by a smooth, honeyed malt backbone.

Black Cork (OG 1066, ABV 6.5%)
An intensely dark beer with a prominent chocolate/coffee bitterness and hop aroma.

Contract brewed for Archerfield Fine Ales:

Golden Ale (OG 1039, ABV 3.8%)

Dark Ale (OG 1046, ABV 4.7%)

India Pale Ale (OG 1047, ABV 5%)

Krafty Brew

11 Stewartfield, Edinburgh, EH6 5RQ
☎ (0131) 555 7189 ⊕ kraftybrew.com

A small brewery specialising in 'brew it yourself' and 'own-label' products. A range of bottle-conditioned beers is sold under the Krafty brand name. Some cask-conditioned beer is available at the brewery's pub, Woodland Creatures in Leith, which was acquired in 2015. RAIB

Lacada (NEW)

7a Victoria Street, Portrush, BT56 8DL
☎ (028) 7082 5684 ⊕ lacadabrewery.com

Lacada is a co-operative brewery established in 2015.

Giant's Organ (OG 1045, ABV 4.5%)

Sorley Boy's Stash (OG 1045, ABV 4.5%)

Stranded Bunny (OG 1045, ABV 4.5%)

Lacons SIBA ◉

Falcon Brewery, Main Cross Road, Great Yarmouth, Norfolk, NR30 3NZ

☎ (01493) 850578 ⊕ lacons.co.uk

⊠ Lacons has a rich history dating back to 1760. The brewery was closed by Whitbread in the 1960s. In 2010 a beer distributor, J.V. Trading, looked into the possibility of reopening the brewery, and acquired its trading name and yeast strains. The new brewery opened in 2013. Beers are available through free trade outlets across East Anglia and beyond. The brewery has strong ties to the original company, and also produces a range of 'Heritage' ales reflecting the brewery's original beers. ‼▤◆RAIB

Encore (OG 1038, ABV 3.8%) ◣
Grapefruit and hops dominate throughout. Well-balanced, with soft sweetness contributing to a gently tapering finish.

Pale Ale (OG 1039, ABV 3.9%) ◣
Strong fruity aroma. Well-rounded orange marmalade character enhanced by hops and malt. Piquant bitter ending.

Falcon Ale (OG 1042, ABV 4.2%)
A classic dark bitter, well-balanced with complex, lightly spiced flavours. The finish is balanced between fruitiness and bitterness.

Legacy (OG 1043, ABV 4.4%) ◣
Malty nose with some biscuit and orange maltiness. Malt, hop and citrus beginning. Increasingly bitter finish.

Affinity (OG 1046, ABV 4.8%)
A full-bodied, chestnut-coloured ale, complex passion fruit and lychee tartness leaps forward, followed by a balance of fruit and malt.

Audit (OG 1072, ABV 8%)
A strong, dark copper-coloured barley wine with a prominent flavour of berry fruit, laced with pronounced spice. The finish is warming, smooth and sweet.

Laine

▤ Brighton: North Laine Bar & Brewhouse, 27 Gloucester Place, Brighton, East Sussex, BN1 4AA

☎ (01273) 683666

Acton: Aeronaut, 264 Acton High Street, Acton, London, W3 9BH ☎ (020) 8993 4242

Battersea: Four Thieves, 51 Lavender Gardens, Battersea, London, SW11 1DJ ☎ (020) 7223 6927

Hackney: People's Park Tavern, 360 Victoria Park Road, Hackney, London, E9 7BT ☎ (020) 8533 0040

Laine launched its first brewery in 2012, in Brighton, using a five-barrel plant based within the North Laine pub, which is owned by the drinkinbrighton pub group. The brewing equipment and process can be viewed from the bar. In 2013 a sister brewery was opened in Acton, London, with the brewing equipment - three fermenters producing 60 firkins of beer a week - visible behind the left-hand bar. Since then two more Laine breweries have been established in London, in Hackney (2014) and Battersea (2015). Beers vary in each establishment. ‼▤

LAM

9 River View, Sandford-on-Thames, Oxfordshire,
OX4 4YF ☎ 07913 061025 ⊕ lambrewing.com

LAM began brewing in 2014 on a 50-litre plant.
Bottle-conditioned beers are produced, and are
available at farmers' markets and the brewery.
♦ RAIB

Lancaster SIBA ◉

Lancaster Leisure Park, Wyresdale Road, Lancaster,
LA1 3LA
☎ (01524) 848537 ⊕ lancasterbrewery.co.uk

⊚Lancaster began brewing in 2005. The brewery
moved to new premises in 2010 and installed a
larger 60-barrel brewing plant. As well as the
regular beers, seasonal beers are brewed under
the T'ales from the Brewhouse name. !! ⌷ ♦ V

Amber (OG 1037, ABV 3.6%) ◄
Amber malt flavours lead to an increasingly
astringent bitter finish.

Blonde (OG 1041, ABV 4%) ◄
A pale, gently-hopped, easy-drinking, mild bitter
with an astringent finish.

Black (OG 1045, ABV 4.5%) ◄
A satisfying and robust, roast bitter beer with hints
of sweet fruitiness.

Red (OG 1047, ABV 4.8%) ◄
Sweet start with lasting roast malts leads to a
satisfying bitter finish.

Landlocked

⊟ Beehive, 151 Peasehill, Ripley, Derbyshire, DE5 3JN
☎ 07845 609585 ✉ brewhousemike@gmail.com

Landlocked began brewing in 2014 using a five-
barrel plant in outbuildings behind the Beehive Inn
in Ripley. The beers can be found in the Beehive,
the Honeypot bar, the Five Lamps and other local
freehouses. ♦ RAIB

Honeypot Pale (OG 1036, ABV 4%)
Pale golden ale brewed with a touch of honey.

Island IPA (OG 1044, ABV 4.7%)
A golden IPA, powerfully hopped.

A & E (OG 1064, ABV 7.4%)
An amber-coloured IPA, strong and powerful.

Landlord's Friend

⊟ Kershaw House Inn, Luddenden Lane,
Luddendenfoot, West Yorkshire, HX2 6NW
☎ (01422) 882222 ✉ landfriendbeers@aol.co.uk

Landlord's Friend began brewing in 2010 using a
2.5-barrel plant. Local pubs can be supplied directly
and wholesalers may also stock the beers. ♦

Last Leaf (ABV 4%)
Golden-coloured and fruity with a hint of dryness in
a grainy malt finish.

Mr Cuddle (ABV 4%)
Combines coriander with a malt base and light
spicy notes.

Chestnuts Roasting (ABV 4.1%)
Chestnut-coloured beer, malty with nutty hints.
Dryish and malty finish.

Mr Webster's Brown Ale (ABV 4.2%)

Moderate malty aroma with molasses, caramel and
toffee. Flavour is sweetish, with some nutty malts
and a touch of toffee.

Mr JK's Itish (ABV 4.4%)
Rich, black body with roast coffee and nut flavours
and a bitter, dry finish.

Not Just For Mother (ABV 4.5%)
Light bodied with a blend of malt and hops.

Langham SIBA

Old Granary, Langham Lane, Lodsworth, West Sussex,
GU28 9BU
☎ (01798) 860861 ⊕ langhambrewery.co.uk

⊠ Langham was established in 2006 in an 18th-
century granary barn and is set in the heart of West
Sussex with fine views of the rolling South Downs.
It is owned by Lesley Foulkes and James Berrow
who brew and run the business. The brewery is a
10-barrel steam-heated plant and more than 200
outlets are supplied. !! ⌷

Halfway to Heaven (OG 1035, ABV 3.5%)
A chestnut-coloured beer with a balanced biscuit
maltiness and citrus and fruit hop character with a
hint of spice.

Saison (OG 1039, ABV 3.9%)
A zesty, unfined Saison-style beer, light and well
hopped.

Hip Hop (OG 1038, ABV 4%)
A blonde beer – clean and crisp. The nose is loaded
with floral hop aroma while the pale malt flavour is
overtaken by a dry and bitter finish.

Sundowner (OG 1042, ABV 4.2%)
A deep golden beer. The nose has tropical fruit,
pineapple and citrus notes with a smooth maltiness
in the background. There is a balanced dry and
bitter finish with floral hop aroma.

Best (OG 1043, ABV 4.5%)
A tawny-coloured classic best bitter with well-
balanced malt flavours and bitterness.

Arapaho (OG 1046, ABV 4.9%)
An American pale ale.

**LSD (Langham Special Draught)
(OG 1049, ABV 5.2%)**
An auburn beer with rich, complex flavours and a
deep red glow. The sweet maltiness is balanced
with spicy hop aromas and a dry finish.

Black Swallow (OG 1055, ABV 6%)
A black IPA.

Langton SIBA ◉

Grange Farm, Welham Road, Thorpe Langton,
Leicestershire, LE16 7TU
☎ (01858) 540116 ☎ 07840 532826
⊕ langtonbrewery.co.uk

Established in 1999 in outbuildings behind the Bell
Inn, East Langton, the brewery relocated in 2005 to
a converted barn at Thorpe Langton, where a four-
barrel plant was installed. Further expansion in
2010 significantly increased capacity. !! ♦ RAIB

Caudle Bitter (OG 1039, ABV 3.9%) ◄
Copper-coloured session bitter that is close to pale
ale in style. Flavours are relatively well-balanced
throughout with hops slightly to the fore.

Inclined Plane Bitter (OG 1042, ABV 4.2%)

A straw-coloured bitter with a citrus nose and long, hoppy finish.

Hop On (OG 1044, ABV 4.4%)
A premium bitter, deep chestnut in colour with a good balance of flavours and aroma.

Scarecrow (OG 1044, ABV 4.4%)
Smooth, well-balanced, slightly fruity and sweet.

Bowler Strong Ale (OG 1048, ABV 4.8%)
A strong traditional ale with a deep red colour and a hoppy nose.

Bullseye (OG 1050, ABV 4.8%)
Intensely dark stout with flavours of liquorice and chocolate.

Langwith (NEW) SIBA

Unit 16, Hermitage Way, Hermitage Way Industrial Estate, Mansfield, Nottinghamshire, NG18 5ES
☎ (01623) 740607 ⊕ langwithbrewing.co.uk

New, purpose-built six-barrel brewhouse that opened in 2016. A 100-litre pilot plant is also utilised for small run and experimental brews. Bottle-conditioned beers are planned.

Larkins SIBA

Larkins Farm, Hampkins Hill Road, Chiddingstone, Kent, TN8 7BB
☎ (01892) 870328

⊠ Larkins brewery was founded by the Dockerty family in Rusthall in Kent in 1986, on the site of the original Royal Tunbridge Wells Brewery. In 1988 the brewery relocated to Larkins Farm in Chiddingstone, where the brewery still resides. Production of its three main brews and two seasonal ales has steadily increased. All beers now include hops grown on Larkins Farm itself. All ales are delivered direct to around 40-50 pubs and restaurants within a 20-mile radius of the brewery. ‼◆

Traditional Ale (OG 1035, ABV 3.4%)
Tawny in colour, a full-tasting hoppy ale with plenty of character for its strength.

Pale (ABV 4.2%)
Pleasantly hoppy pale ale with a soft, fruity rather than astringent aftertaste.

Best (OG 1045, ABV 4.4%) ◆
Full-bodied, slightly fruity and unusually bitter for its gravity.

Late Knights

21 Southey Street, Penge, London, SE20 7JD ☎ 07786 830368 ⊕ lateknightsbrewery.co.uk

⊠ Originally using spare capacity at Truefitt Brewery in Middlesbrough in 2012, Late Knights began brewing using a six-barrel plant in an old converted slaughterhouse in London in 2013. ▆◆

Crack of Dawn (ABV 3.7%) ◆
Amber-coloured hoppy beer with strong citrus notes. Flavour has a faint maltiness and bitterness. Aftertaste is bitter and fractionally dry.

Hop of the Morning (ABV 4.2%) ◆
Strong black roast bitter character in the aroma and flavour with some coffee notes and fruit. Long, bitter, dry finish.

Old Red Eyes (ABV 4.5%) ◆

Reddish brown beer with a clean hop flavour and hints of citrus and butterscotch. Finish is hoppy and dryish.

Worm Catcher (ABV 5%) ◆
Amber-coloured beer with a honey marmalade sweetness and a bitterness that builds and lingers in the slightly dry finish.

Lawman (NEW) SIBA

Cumbernauld
☎ (0141) 212 9570 ☎ 07872 525762
⊕ lawmanbrew.co.uk

Lawman began brewing in 2015 using a five-barrel brew plant located in an industrial unit near Cumbernauld town centre. ◆

Pixel Bandit (OG 1040, ABV 4%)
A thirst-quenching session ale with predominate flavours of lemongrass and tangerine and a citrus aroma.

Steadfast Koln-ish Bier (OG 1044, ABV 4.4%)
A session cask lager with an elderflower twist.

Onyx (OG 1048, ABV 4.8%)
A full-bodied stout, marked with a clean coffee bitterness and a dark chocolate finish.

Horizon APA (OG 1052, ABV 5.2%)
A deep golden-coloured American-style pale ale, packed with tropical fruits and pine.

Weatherall IPA (OG 1064, ABV 6.4%)
A modern take on the traditional IPA; heavily-hopped providing a complex orange marmalade bitterness and full flavour.

Leadmill

Unit 3, Heanor Small Business Centre, Adams Close, Heanor, Derbyshire, DE75 7SW ☎ 07971 189915
✉ leadmill@fsmail.net

⊠ Set up in Selston in 1999, Leadmill moved to Denby in 2001 and again in 2010 to Heanor. A sister brewery to Bottle Brook (qv), the brewery tap is at the Old Oak, Horsley Woodhouse. ◆

Langley Best (OG 1036, ABV 3.6%)

Mash Tun Bitter (OG 1036, ABV 3.6%)

Old Oak Bitter (OG 1037, ABV 3.7%)

B52 (OG 1050, ABV 5.2%)

Slumdog (OG 1058, ABV 5.9%)

Leafy Hollow (NEW)

Ferkins Barn, Lower Burlone, Washaway, Cornwall, PL30 3AJ ☎ 07592 310182
✉ leafyhollowbrewery@yahoo.com

This nanobrewery was established in 2015 and brews bottle-conditioned beers by hand crafting without machinery, using traditional methods and containing no modern chemicals. RAIB

Leamside SIBA

▆ **Three Horseshoes, Pit House Lane, Leamside, County Durham, DH4 6QQ**
☎ (0191) 584 2394
⊕ threehorseshoesleamside.co.uk

Brewing began in 2012 using a 2.5-barrel plant. Beers are available at the Three Horseshoes as well as its three sister pubs.

Adventure (OG 1038, ABV 3.8%)
A deep golden-coloured session bitter. Soft fruit flavours and well-balanced medium bitterness.

Alexandrina (OG 1041, ABV 4.2%)
Light gold in colour. Initial bitterness gives way to citrus fruit flavours.

Brockwell (OG 1042, ABV 4.2%)
A straw-coloured pale ale with tropical fruit flavours.

Five Quarter (OG 1052, ABV 4.5%)
Silky smooth mouthfeel with berry fruit flavours and hints of coffee and chocolate.

Nicholson's American Pale Ale (ABV 5.1%)

Leatherbritches

⊟ Brewery Yard, Tap House, Annwell, Smisby, Derbyshire, LE65 2TA ☎ 07976 279253
⊕ leatherbritches.co.uk

☺The brewery, founded in 1993 in Fenny Bentley, has relocated and expanded over the years, moving to its current address in 2011. Both the Tap House Brewery (qv) and Leatherbritches brew on the same plant but the two businesses are separate. ‼ ♦ RAIB

Goldings (OG 1036, ABV 3.6%)
A light golden beer with a flowery hoppy aroma and a bitter finish.

Lemongrass & Ginger (OG 1036, ABV 3.8%) 🖰
Pale and hoppy ale infused with lemon grass and ginger. Crisp and refreshing.

Ashbourne Ale (OG 1040, ABV 4%)
A pale bitter brewed with a crisp, lasting taste.

Doctor Johnsons (OG 1040, ABV 4%)
A mid-brown ale, not heavily hopped but full-bodied with some caramel flavour.

Scoundrel (OG 1040, ABV 4.1%)
Full-bodied porter, with a well-rounded sweet finish.

Dovedale (OG 1044, ABV 4.4%)
A copper-coloured bitter with a crisp finish.

Ginger Helmet (OG 1047, ABV 4.7%)

Hairy Helmet (OG 1047, ABV 4.7%)
A pale bitter, well hopped but with a sweet finish.

Ashbourne IPA (OG 1047, ABV 4.9%)

Bespoke (OG 1048, ABV 5%)
Full-bodied, well-rounded premium bitter.

Stouter (OG 1049, ABV 5.2%)
Stout with a coffee and vanilla taste.

Porter (OG 1052, ABV 5.5%)

Scary Hairy (OG 1057, ABV 5.9%)

Scary Hairy Export (OG 1064, ABV 7.2%)
Strong pale bitter with a bitter, dry finish.

Leazes Lane

⊟ Trent House, 1-2 Leazes Lane, Newcastle upon Tyne, NE1 4QT
☎ (191) 261 2154

Leazes Lane began brewing in 2013 using a one-barrel plant. Beer is only available in the pub.

Ledbury SIBA

Gazerdine House, Hereford Road, Ledbury, Herefordshire, HR8 2PZ
☎ (01531) 671184 ☎ 07957 428070
⊕ ledburyrealales.co.uk

☺Brewing began in 2012. Beers are produced using locally-sourced ingredients whenever possible. Distribution is generally within a 15-mile radius of the brewery. ‼ ♦

Bitter (OG 1038, ABV 3.8%)
A traditional copper colour with a noticeably bitter start and an enjoyable finish with hints of spice and citrus.

Dark (OG 1039, ABV 3.9%)
Has a chocolate and coffee start with a smooth, mellow finish with notes of spice, marmalade and honey.

Gold (OG 1040, ABV 4%)
A golden bitter, well-balanced with a honey and fruit finish.

Leeds SIBA 👁

⊟ 3 Sydenham Road, Holbeck, Leeds, West Yorkshire, LS11 9RU
☎ (0113) 244 5866 ⊕ leedsbrewery.co.uk

☺Production began in 2007 using a 20-barrel plant. The largest independent brewer in the city, it uses a unique strain of yeast originally used by a defunct West Yorkshire brewery. Seven pubs are owned and around 300 outlets are supplied direct. A separate brew plant is situated in the Leeds Brewery Tap. In July 2016 Camerons of Hartlepool (qv) bought the Leeds' pub estate. ♦

Pale (OG 1037.5, ABV 3.8%) 🍂
Hops and fruit, sometimes citrus or lemon, mix with a sweetness through to the bitter hoppy finish, light gold in colour.

Yorkshire Gold (OG 1040, ABV 4%) 🍂
Plenty of zesty citrus flavours, a burst of hops and a long-lasting bitter finish make this a refreshing beer.

Best (OG 1041, ABV 4.3%) 🍺🍂
A pleasing mix of malt and hops makes this smooth, copper-coloured, bittersweet beer very drinkable.

Midnight Bell (OG 1047.5, ABV 4.8%) 🍂🍺🍂
A full-bodied strong mild, deep red to dark brown in colour. Malty caramel character with chocolate being present throughout.

Leek

See Staffordshire

Lees IFBB 👁

Greengate Brewery, Middleton Junction, Manchester, M24 2AX
☎ (0161) 643 2487 ⊕ jwlees.co.uk

☺Family-owned since its foundation by John Lees in 1828, the brewery has a tied estate of around 150 pubs, mostly in north Manchester, Cheshire, Lancashire and North Wales. The vast majority serve cask beer. The current head brewer is a family member. ‼

Brewer's Dark (OG 1032, ABV 3.5%) ◄
Formerly GB Mild, this is a dark brown beer with a malt and caramel aroma. Creamy mouthfeel, with malt, caramel and fruit flavours and a malty finish. Becoming rare.

Manchester Pale Ale (OG 1038, ABV 3.7%) ◄
Yellow in colour, with malt, hops and a good bitterness throughout.

The Governor (OG 1038, ABV 3.8%)
Malty auburn/amber beer with floral and citrus notes and a clean, dry finish.

Bitter (OG 1037, ABV 4%) ◄
Copper-coloured beer with malt and fruit in aroma, taste and finish.

John Willie's (OG 1041, ABV 4.5%)
A well-balanced, full-bodied premium bitter.

Moonraker (OG 1073, ABV 6.5%) ⛁ ◄
A reddish-brown beer with a strong, malty, fruity aroma. The flavour is rich and sweet, with roast malt, and the finish is fruity yet dry.

Left Bank

Blackhorse Workshop, 1-2 Sutherland Road Path, Walthamstow, London, E17 6BX ☎ 07815 849523
⊕ leftbankbrewery.co.uk

⊗ Brewing began in 2013 under the name of Wilcumestowe Brewery at the Hornbeam Café. It moved to the Blackhorse Workshop in 2014 on a 0.5-barrel plant, and now supplies the workshop and local events. Expansion is planned. ‼♦RAIB

Pale Ale (ABV 4.5%)

Milk Stout (ABV 5.1%)

Sorachi Saison (ABV 5.4%)

Left Handed Giant

Unit 9, Wadehurst Industrial Park, St Philips Road, St Philip's, Bristol, BS2 0JE
☎ (0117) 318 2102 ⊕ lefthandedgiant.com

Launched in 2015, Left Handed Giant is a cuckoo brewery using spare capacity at other local breweries. It has its own 200-litre plant on which it brews experimental beers and collaborations with other breweries. The brewery shares premises with Big Deer Distribution, where there is a tap room. Beers are available both locally and nationally. The head brewer, Richard Poole, is a former home brewer and also has his own nanobrewery, Rocket Science (qv).

Pale (OG 1039, ABV 4.1%)

Duet (OG 1044, ABV 4.8%)

Red 5 (OG 1048, ABV 5%)

Lactose Tolerant (OG 1059, ABV 5.1%)

USPA (OG 1053, ABV 5.5%)

Leighton Buzzard SIBA ◉

Unit 23, Harmill Industrial Estate, Grovebury Road, Leighton Buzzard, Bedfordshire, LU7 4FF ☎ 07538 903753 ⊕ leightonbuzzardbrewingcompany.co.uk

The first brewery to operate in Leighton Buzzard for over 100 years. Established in 2014 by local CAMRA member and home brew enthusiast Jon d'Este-Hoare, the first beers were upscaled versions of his home brews. ‼➤♦

Borrowers Bitter (OG 1038, ABV 3.6%)
A light brown, easy-drinking session ale.

Narrow Gauge (OG 1040, ABV 3.9%)
A golden ale, light and refreshing with a dry bitter taste and crisp citrus finish.

Restoration Ale (OG 1049, ABV 4.6%)
A mid-brown beer, fruity and refreshing.

Rebel Yell (OG 1053, ABV 5%)
A black IPA offering initial smooth richness of the malt quickly followed by sharp, dry hops.

Black Buzzard (OG 1061, ABV 5.8%)
A complex, robust porter.

Leila Cottage SIBA

🍺 Countryman, Chapel Road, Ingoldmells, Skegness, Lincolnshire, PE25 1ND
☎ (01754) 872268
✉ countryman_inn@btconnect.com

Leila Cottage started brewing in 2007 and is now using a 2.5-barrel plant. The brewery is situated at the Countryman pub – Leila Cottage was the original name of the building before it became a licensed club and more recently a pub. The history of the Countryman and the brewery is on display in the pub. ‼➤RAIB

Leila's Lazy Days (OG 1040, ABV 3.6%)
A light IPA, easy-drinking with a slight citrus taste and light caramel edge.

Ace Ale (OG 1040, ABV 3.8%)
A typical session bitter with a reasonable roast malt body and a gentle hop bitterness.

Lincolnshire Life (OG 1040, ABV 4.2%)
A dark, full-bodied, malty bitter with a toffee aroma and taste.

Leila's One Off (OG 1045, ABV 5.1%)
Dark, full-bodied bitter which verges on being a stout.

Leith Hill

🍺 c/o Plough Inn, Coldharbour Lane, Coldharbour, Surrey, RH5 6HD
☎ (01306) 711793 ⊕ ploughinn.com

⊗ Leith Hill was established in 1996 at the Plough Inn using home-made equipment and was moved to converted storerooms at the rear in 2001, increasing capacity to 2.5 barrels in 2005. All beers brewed are sold only on the premises. ‼RAIB

Crooked Furrow (OG 1038, ABV 3.8%) ◄
Malty beer, with some balancing hop bitterness. Pale brown with an earthy malty aroma and a long, dry and bittersweet aftertaste.

Lenton Lane

Unit 5G, The Midway, Lenton Industrial Estate, Nottingham, NG7 2TS
☎ (0333) 003 5008

3 Saddlers Gate, Radcliffe-on-Trent, NG12 2NU
⊕ lentonlane.co.uk

⊗ Lenton Lane began brewing in 2014 under the name Frontier, after taking over the brewing plant at the Flower Pot pub in Derby, which had originally been home to the Headless Brewery. Lenton Lane changed its name in 2016 and relocated to a purpose-built brewery in Nottingham, with new plant. ♦

Gold Rush (OG 1037, ABV 4%)

Pioneer (OG 1040, ABV 4.3%)
A golden, crisp, hoppy pale ale with a dry finish.

Ramification (OG 1042, ABV 4.5%)
Traditional bitter. The official beer of the Derby County FC supporters club.

Atlas Stout (OG 1046, ABV 5%)
A full-bodied rich, dry stout. Coffee and chocolate notes give way to a dry finish.

Lerwick SIBA

Staneyhill, North Road, Lerwick, Shetland, ZE1 0QA
☎ (01595) 694552 ☎ 07738 948336
⊕ lerwickbrewery.co.uk

Lerwick Brewery was established in 2011 using a 12-barrel plant and sits at the very edge of the North Atlantic. Originally only brewing keg beer, a cask-conditioned range was launched in 2015.

Shetland Pale Ale (ABV 3.8%)

Azure (ABV 4.3%) ◈
Refreshing, grapefruity, hoppy, golden bitter.

IPA (ABV 5%)
A hoppy, fruity IPA with a biscuity malt background.

Tushkar Oatmeal Stout (ABV 5.5%)
A smooth and slightly sweet mouthfeel, chocolate and coffee top notes, a light bitterness and a balancing roundness.

Leyden

🍺 **Lord Raglan, Walmersley Old Road, Nangreaves, BL9 6SP**
☎ (0161) 764 6680 ⊕ lordraglannangreaves.co.uk

☺Leyden was established in 1999 at the Lord Raglan pub. Both the pub and the free trade are supplied. ‼♦

Black Pudding (OG 1040, ABV 3.8%)
A dark brown, creamy mild with a malty flavour, followed by a balanced finish.

Nanny Flyer (OG 1040, ABV 3.8%)
A drinkable session bitter with an initial dryness, and a hint of citrus, followed by a strong, malty finish.

Florence Nightingale (OG 1043, ABV 4%)
A smooth and refreshing light copper-coloured beer. Citrus flavours dominate

Balaclava (OG 1040, ABV 4.2%)
A brown-coloured session bitter with malty and hoppy flavours.

Brewers Gold (OG 1042, ABV 4.2%)
A golden bitter with a citrus tinge and slight hoppiness.

Light Brigade (OG 1042, ABV 4.2%) ◈
Copper in colour with a citrus aroma. The flavour is a balance of malt, hops and fruit, with a bitter finish.

Rammy Rocket (OG 1042, ABV 4.2%)
A smooth, straw-coloured ale.

Oyster Stout (OG 1043, ABV 4.5%)
A dark red-coloured beer with a hint of chocolate. Smooth and quaffable.

Raglan Sleeve (OG 1047, ABV 4.6%) ◈
Dark red/brown beer with a hoppy aroma and a dry, roasty, hoppy taste and finish.

Crowning Glory (OG 1068, ABV 6.8%)
A smooth-tasting beer, belying its strength.

Liberation ⊚

Tregear House, Longueville Road, St Saviour, Jersey, JE2 7WF
☎ (01534) 764089 ⊕ liberationgroup.com/brewery

⊗ The Liberation Brewery is located at Longueville, just outside St Helier using a 40-barrel and an 8-barrel plant. Its multi-award-winning flagship beer, Liberation Ale, is now regularly seen on the mainland, as well as on the other Channel islands. 68 pubs are owned with around two-thirds of these serving cask ale. In July 2016 Liberation, including Butcombe (qv), was bought by Caledonia Investments, which said it would expand sales of Butcombe beers and add to its pub estate. ‼♦

Ale (OG 1039, ABV 4%)
Golden beer with a hint of citrus on the nose.

IPA (OG 1047, ABV 4.8%)
Traditional IPA with a coriander-style citrus hop flavour and a crisp, balanced finish.

Lincoln Green SIBA ⊚

Unit 5, Enterprise Park, Wigwam Lane, Hucknall, Nottingham, NG15 7SZ
☎ (0115) 963 4233 ☎ 07748 111457
⊕ lincolngreenbrewing.co.uk

☺Anthony Hughes established the Lincoln Green Brewing Company in 2012 using a 10-barrel plant. Locally-sourced ingredients are used to create five regular beers and, in addition, seasonal and special brews are available that link to local and national events. The brewery takes its name from the colour of dyed woollen cloth associated with the legend of Robin Hood. 🍴♦RAIB

Marion (OG 1038, ABV 3.8%) 🍴 ◈
Subtly-hopped golden ale with a citrus aroma and a dry bitter finish.

Tantalum (OG 1038, ABV 3.8%)

Archer (OG 1040, ABV 4%)

Flerovium (OG 1040, ABV 4%)

Hood (OG 1042, ABV 4.2%) ◈
Tawny-coloured ale with balanced hops and bitterness.

Little John (OG 1043, ABV 4.3%) ◈
Malty best bitter, well-balanced with hops and bitterness throughout

Sherwood (OG 1044, ABV 4.4%)
A pale ale with orange citrus aroma and biscuit malt.

Tuck (OG 1047, ABV 4.7%) ◈
Full-bodied and rich dark ale with roast and malt flavours throughout.

Quarterstaff (OG 1053, ABV 5%)
A rich, full-bodied stout with flaked barley and generous blackcurrant hop bitterness.

Buttermuch (OG 1057, ABV 5.5%)
Butterscotch sweetness is balanced by hop bitterness in this dark, creamy ale.

Sheriff (OG 1055, ABV 5.5%) ◈

Golden, full-bodied IPA, citrus hop taste and bitterness balanced throughout.

Indium (OG 1059, ABV 5.9%)

Lincolnshire SIBA 👁

Unit 3, 39 Monks Way, Lincoln, LN2 5LN
☎ (0845) 094 5784 ☎ 07508 554890
🌐 lincolnshirebrewingco.co.uk

An events company that operates mobile bars, in 2014 it started brewing for its own bars and has since expanded into the free trade. A three-barrel plant brews both cask and bottle-conditioned beers, with bottling carried out in-house. Beers can be found at local fairs, shows and markets. RAIB

Great Tom (OG 1037, ABV 3.7%)
A dark ale with elements of chocolate and coffee on the nose. It has a fruity and dark malt mouthfeel, with a long, but soft bitter finish.

Spicy Sausage (OG 1041, ABV 4.1%)
An amber ale, with a sharp bitterness and dry finish.

Friendly Rottweiler (OG 1045, ABV 4.5%)
A light, crisp ale with a subtle hoppy taste.

Cheeky Imp (OG 1046, ABV 4.6%)
Caramel notes and hoppy aromas gives this ale a good mouthfeel and slightly sweet taste.

Linfit

🍺 Sair Inn, 139 Lane Top, Linthwaite, Huddersfield, West Yorkshire, HD7 5SG
☎ (01484) 842370

😊A 19th-century brewpub that started brewing again in 1982. The beer is only available at the Sair Inn.

Bitter (ABV 3.7%)

Gold Medal (ABV 4.2%)

Special (ABV 4.3%)

Swift (ABV 4.5%)

Autumn Gold (ABV 4.7%)

Old Eli (ABV 5.4%)

Leadboiler (ABV 6.6%)

Lion Heart

See Dhillon's

Lion's Tale SIBA

🍺 Red Lion, High Street, Cheswardine, Shropshire, TF9 2RS
☎ (01630) 661234 ✉ cheslion96@yahoo.co.uk

The brewery building was purpose-built in 2005 and houses a 2.5-barrel plant. Jon Morris and his wife Shiela have owned the Red Lion since 1996. ♦RAIB

Blooming Blonde (OG 1041, ABV 4.1%)

Chesbrewnette (OG 1045, ABV 4.5%)

Lionbru (OG 1045, ABV 4.5%)

Lister's SIBA 👁

The Old Dairy, Ford Lane, Ford, West Sussex, BN18 0DF

☎ (01903) 739117 ☎ 07775 853412
🌐 listersbrewery.com

Brewing began in 2012 using a 0.25-barrel kit. The brewery relocated in 2014 and expanded to a five-barrel plant.

Best Bitter (ABV 3.9%)

Golden Ale (ABV 4.1%)

Limehouse Porter (ABV 4.1%)

IPA (ABV 4.3%)

Special (ABV 4.6%)

Little Beer SIBA 👁

Building 3, 14-15 Midleton Road, Guildford, Surrey, GU2 8XW
☎ (01483) 497201 ☎ 07941 061241
🌐 littlebeer.co.uk

⊠ Little Beer Corporation is a Guildford-based 10-barrel brewery that produces premium bottled, cask-conditioned and keg beers. It is run by Jim Taylor, who is also majority owner, alongside around 300 local shareholders. A monthly beer club (including beer, food and music) is for paid membership only. ‼ ☛RAIB

Little & Often (OG 1030, ABV 3%)
A crystal rye IPA with a malty flavour.

Little Haka (OG 1035, ABV 3.5%) 🍺
An easy-drinking session ale. Predominantly bitter but with with a good malt character and light hoppy tones.

Little Tenderness (OG 1040, ABV 4%) 🍺
A pale brown beer, with a solid malt backbone, a light hoppiness and subtle fruit flavours.

Little Smooth (OG 1045, ABV 4.5%)
A full-flavoured milk stout.

Little Slow (OG 1050, ABV 5%) 🍺
A Vienna-style lager. An initially malty aroma leads to fruitiness in the tasty with good hoppiness and a dry, spicy finish.

Little Vienna (OG 1050, ABV 5%)
A biscuity session lager with a floral aroma.

Little Snug (OG 1054, ABV 5.4%) 🍺
Copper-coloured bitter, brewed with chestnuts, which make for a rich, smooth flavour. A slightly dry bitter finish.

Little Wild (OG 1058, ABV 5.9%) 🍺
A red IPA, rich and full-flavoured with strong hop character, balanced with solid maltiness and a dry bitter finish.

Little Brew 👁

15-16 Auster Road, Clifton Moor, North Yorkshire, YO30 4XA 🌐 littlebrew.co.uk

Brewing began in 2012 using a one-barrel plant in the Camden area of London. In 2014 they relocated to the Clifton Moor, York.

Gold (OG 1047, ABV 4.2%)

Ruby (OG 1050, ABV 4.6%)

Porter (OG 1054, ABV 5%)

IPA (OG 1058, ABV 5.5%)

Extra Porter (OG 1060, ABV 5.7%)

Little Bush

▤ 51 Brook Lane, Marehay, Derbyshire, DE5 8JA
☎ (01773) 570830 ⊕ hollybushmarehay.co.uk

⊗ A four-barrel plant, located in the cellar of the Hollybush pub in the village of Marehay, Little Bush commenced brewing in 2015.

Black Bush Stout (ABV 4%)

Fuggler (ABV 5.2%)

Little Dragon (NEW) SIBA

Unit 3, Havens Head Business Park, Milford Haven, SA73 3LD ☎ 07879 400313

Morgan Coe established the Little Dragon Brewery in 2015 using a five-barrel plant. It is located in an industrial unit close to the historic port of Milford Haven. The beers are unfiltered and no finings are used unless requested. ⬛◆RAIB

Cleddau Gold (OG 1044, ABV 4.4%)
A golden ale full of hop flavour without the strong citrus notes of some pale ales.

Jack Sound (OG 1044, ABV 4.4%)
Good malt/chocolate notes with a balanced hop character.

Pembrokeshire Pale (OG 1045, ABV 4.5%)
A pale ale with strong hop notes providing a bright, fresh flavour.

Little London (NEW)

Unit 6B, Ash Park Business Centre, Ash Lane, Little London, Hampshire, RG26 5FL
☎ (01256) 533044 ☎ 07785 225468
⊕ littlelondonbrewery.com

⊗ Brewing began in 2015 using a six-barrel plant. Three fermentation vessels ensure a production capability of 60 firkins per week, with capacity for expansion.

Doreen's Dark (OG 1035, ABV 3.2%)
Treacle-coloured with a creamy contrasting head and hints of liquorice and coffee, but a dry finish.

Red Boy (OG 1036, ABV 3.7%)
A light, balanced session bitter with a delicate hop aroma and subtle hop flavours on the palate.

Hoppy Hilda (OG 1039, ABV 3.8%)
A light golden ale.

Pryde (OG 1040.5, ABV 4.2%)
A fruity, dark amber best bitter with caramel and toffee aromas and spicy hop notes.

Ash Park Special (OG 1048, ABV 4.9%)
A russet-coloured ale with malt and raisin on the nose. Slightly sweet with a long finish.

Little Valley SIBA 👁

Unit 3, Turkey Lodge Farm, New Road, Cragg Vale, Hebden Bridge, West Yorkshire, HX7 5TT
☎ (01422) 883888 ⊕ littlevalleybrewery.co.uk

☺Little Valley began brewing in 2005 on a 10-barrel plant. All beers are organic and vegan, and Ginger Pale Ale uses Fairtrade ingredients. Around 300 outlets are supplied. Several beers are contract brewed for Suma Wholefoods and in 2012 the brewery was contracted by the Benedictine Order of Ampleforth Abbey to brew and bottle their Ampleforth Abbey Beer (ABV 7%). ⬛◆RAIB

Withens Pale Ale (OG 1037, ABV 3.9%) ◈
Creamy, gold-coloured, refreshingly light ale. Floral, spicy hop aroma, lightly-flavoured with hints of lemon and grapefruit. Clean, bitter aftertaste.

Ginger Pale Ale (OG 1037, ABV 4%) ◈
Full-bodied speciality ale. Ginger predominates in the aroma and taste. It has a pleasantly powerful, fiery and spicy finish.

Cragg Vale Bitter (OG 1039, ABV 4.2%) ◈
Grainy, pale brown session bitter, light on the palate with a delicate flavour of malt and fruit and a bitter finish.

Hebden's Wheat (OG 1043, ABV 4.5%) ◈
A pale yellow, creamy wheat beer with a good balance of bitterness and fruit, a hint of sweetness but with a lasting, dry finish.

Vanilla Porter (ABV 4.5%) ◈
Dark, complex speciality beer. Fresh taste of vanilla dominates both the aroma and taste. Smooth mellow finish.

Stoodley Stout (OG 1044, ABV 4.8%) ◈
Dark brown creamy stout with a rich roast aroma and fruity, chocolate, roast flavours. Well-balanced with a clean bitter finish.

Tod's Blonde (OG 1045, ABV 5%) ◈
Bright yellow, grainy, speciality beer with a citrus hop start and a dry finish. Fruity, with a hint of spice. Similar in style to a Belgian blonde beer.

Moor Ale (OG 1055, ABV 5.5%) ◈
Tawny in colour with a full-bodied taste. It has a strong malty nose and palate with hints of heather and peat-smoked malt. Well-balanced with a bitter finish.

Python IPA (OG 1055, ABV 6%) ◈
Amber-coloured grainy beer with a complex bitter fruit palate subtly balance by a malty sweetness, leading to a strongly lingering bitter aftertaste.

Littlehampton SIBA

▤ Tap & Barrel, 2-13 Duke Street, Littlehampton, West Sussex, BN17 6EU
☎ (01903) 715111 ⊕ littlehamptonbrewery.co.uk

Previously known as Anchor Springs, The Littlehampton Brewery is situated in the Tap & Barrel Bar & Restaurant, with the brew plant visible behind the bar. ⬛◆RAIB

LA Gold (OG 1039.5, ABV 3.7%)

Mild (OG 1045.5, ABV 3.8%)

Worthing's Best Bitter (OG 1045, ABV 4%)

Riptide (OG 1045, ABV 4.1%)

Undercurrent (ABV 4.2%)

Hornblower (OG 1045, ABV 4.5%)

Black Pearl (ABV 5.2%)

Old Mothers Ruin (OG 1063, ABV 6%)

Littleover (NEW) SIBA

Unit 9, Robinson Industrial Estate, Shaftesbury Street, Derby, DE23 8NL
☎ (01332) 987100 ☎ 07449 586811
⊕ littleoverbrewery.co.uk

Littleover was established in 2015, using a new six-barrel plant from PBC installations. Three beers are brewed, with more planned.

Gold (ABV 3.8%)
Pale, golden session ale with a subtle hoppy aroma.

King George's Bitter (ABV 4%)
Traditional bitter, the subtle malty bitterness leads to a refreshing crisp finish.

Crest (ABV 4.4%)
Malty chestnut-coloured best bitter, with a clean fresh taste and a light fruity aroma.

Liverpool Craft SIBA

62-64 Bridgewater Street, Liverpool, L1 0AY
☎ (0151) 236 9400 ⊕ liverpoolcraftbeer.com

☺Liverpool Craft began brewing in 2011 using a 10-barrel plant, relocating to the other side of the city centre in 2015. A visitor centre is planned. The brewery regularly supplies arts and music venues as well as local pubs. Swaps with other breweries make the beers available further afield. ◆RAIB

Liverpool Organic SIBA

39 Brasenose Road, Liverpool, L20 8HL
☎ (0151) 933 9660 ⊕ liverpoolorganicbrewery.com

⊠ Liverpool Organic started brewing in 2009. Outlets are supplied around the extended Merseyside area. The brewery also supports many local beer festivals and also runs festivals of its own including the largest beer event in Liverpool. Beers are also brewed under the name of the now defunct Cambrinus brewery. ‼◆RAIB

Cascade (OG 1038, ABV 3.8%)
An intensely-hopped light session bitter.

Joseph Williamson (OG 1039, ABV 4%)
Traditional malty bitter. Floral elements build to a smooth, satisfying finish.

Liverpool Pale Ale (OG 1039, ABV 4%)
Dry, hoppy notes with floral complexity giving way to spicy tones and a slightly creamy malt finish.

Bier Head (OG 1040, ABV 4.1%)
Sharp, hoppy foretaste with complex spice and crisp malt tones, building to a rich, mellow aftertaste.

24 Carat Gold (OG 1041, ABV 4.2%)
Generously hopped with a bitterness that builds steadily towards a lingering finish with spicy orange notes.

Liverpool Stout (OG 1048, ABV 4.3%)
Strong, dark and dry stout with a smooth, spicy finish.

William Roscoe (OG 1042, ABV 4.3%)
Hoppy and fruity with a hint of dryness and bitterness building to a crisp and slightly earthy malt finish.

Honey Blond (OG 1043, ABV 4.5%)
A subtle and not cloyingly sweet honey aftertaste married to a solid malt backbone and a good hoppy character.

Josephine Butler (OG 1043, ABV 4.5%)
Initial citrus hops followed by elderflower fruit and pale, biscuity malt with a refreshing, sharp finish.

Kitty Wilkinson (OG 1047, ABV 4.5%)
Vanilla, butterscotch and chocolate combine in the roasted malty taste with a fairly dry finish and a generous cocoa bitterness.

Empire Ale (OG 1056, ABV 5.3%)
A strong ruby ale with a slightly sweet finish.

Shipwreck IPA (OG 1066, ABV 6.5%)
Grapefruit, aniseed and peach notes feature in the hoppy bite that builds to tropical fruit and generous pine bitterness in the finish.

Imperial Russian Stout (OG 1078, ABV 7.4%)
Featuring a rich, strong, hoppy bitterness with a full-bodied sweetness and bitter coffee finish with a little fruity malt on the aftertaste.

Brewed under the Cambrinus Brewery name:

Deliverance (OG 1042, ABV 4.2%)
Pale gold beer with a sharp, hoppy taste.

Endurance (OG 1044, ABV 4.3%)
A beer with vanilla notes.

Lizard

The Old Nuclear Bunker, Pednavounder, Cornwall, TR12 6SE
☎ (01326) 281135 ⊕ lizardales.co.uk

⊠ Launched in 2004, Lizard Ales is now based at former RAF Treleaver, a massive disused nuclear bunker in the countryside near Coverack on the Lizard Peninsula. Specialising in bottle-conditioned ales, it mainly supplies west Cornwall. ‼RAIB

Kernow Gold (OG 1037, ABV 3.7%)

Bitter (OG 1041, ABV 4.2%) ◆
Pale brown beer with aroma of ripe apples. Roast malt with fruit esters balanced by bitterness. Bitter finish with dryness.

Frenchman's Creek (OG 1042, ABV 4.8%)

An Gof (OG 1049, ABV 5.2%) ◆
Robust and smooth tawny ale dominated by malt in the mouth with a hint of smoke. Fruity hops follow on into the bitter finish.

Llangollen SIBA

▤ **Abbey Grange Brewing Ltd, Abbey Grange Hotel, Horseshoe Pass Road, Llantysilio, LL20 8DD**
☎ (01978) 861916 ⊕ llangollenbrewery.com

Brewing began in 2010 on a 2.5-barrel plant. The brewery was updated and upgraded in 2014. ‼RAIB

Grange No.1 (OG 1032, ABV 3.2%)

Wrexham Borders Bitter (OG 1039, ABV 3.9%)
A pale ale, fruity notes, hay-like and distinctively hoppy.

Bitter (OG 1042, ABV 4.2%)

Holy Grail (OG 1043, ABV 4.3%)

Welsh Black (OG 1055, ABV 5.5%)
Chocolate and toffee notes with a hoppy finish.

Lleu

Unit A9, Penygroes Industrial Estate, Penygroes, LL54 6DB
☎ (01286) 882561 ☎ 07756 547650
⊕ bragdylleu.co.uk

Brewing began in 2014 using a 1.25-barrel plant. The beer reflects the Welsh folklore tales of the Mabinogi in both name and character.

Blodeuwedd (OG 1036, ABV 3.6%)

Lleu (OG 1040, ABV 4%)
Full-bodied ale with a good mouthfeel and a lasting and satisfying hoppy aftertaste. Good, easy drinking session bitter.

Llŷn

Unit 6, Ffordd Dewi Sant, Nefyn, Gwynedd, LL53 6EG
☎ 07792 050134 ⊕ cwrwllyn.com

⊛The brewery is a co-operative of 12 friends that began brewing in 2011 producing 44 barrels per week. There are firm plans for a new brewery, incorporating a gas combustion system. ‼

Y Brawd Houdini (OG 1036, ABV 3.8%)
A summer-style ale, citrus and flowery.

Brenin Enlli (OG 1038, ABV 4%) ◗
A fruity bitter, the initial malty taste leads to a hoppy, bitter aftertaste.

Cwrw Glyndwr (OG 1040, ABV 4%) ◗
A full-bodied and well-balanced amber beer, quite fruity with a good hoppy finish.

Seithenyn (OG 1040, ABV 4.2%) ◗
A fruity golden ale with a tangy citrus taste and a dry hoppy finish.

Cochyn (OG 1043, ABV 4.5%)
Ruby Welsh ale.

Loch Lomond SIBA

Block 1, Unit 5, Lomond Industrial Estate, Alexandria, G83 0TL
☎ (01389) 755698 ☎ 07891 920213
⊕ lochlomondbrewery.com

Established in 2011 by Fiona and Euan MacEachern, it is the only brewery around Loch Lomond. ‼ ▰ ◆

Bonnie'n' Bitter (OG 1036, ABV 3.6%)
A blonde, easy-drinking bitter with a citrus flavour and full-rounded bitterness.

The West Highland Way (OG 1038, ABV 3.8%)
A light ale with fruity flavours.

Bonnie & Blonde (OG 1040, ABV 4%)
A light, refreshing ale with a well-rounded citrus flavour.

The Ale of Leven (OG 1045, ABV 4.5%)
An amber-coloured beer with a slight sweetness and spicy bitterness.

Silkie Stout (OG 1050, ABV 5%)
A black stout with chocolate-orange spicy notes.

Kessog Dark Ale (OG 1052, ABV 5.2%)
Dark with warm spicy flavours.

Loch Ness

≣ Blarmor, Drumnadrochit, IV63 6UG
☎ (01456) 450726 ⊕ lochnessbrewery.com

⊛Brewing began in 2011 using a two-barrel plant in the grounds of the Benleva Hotel. The brewery moved in 2012 to nearby premises using an eight-barrel plant. Beers are available in the local area, central Scotland and northern England plus exports to Italy, South Africa, US and Russia. There are plans for expansion. ‼ ▰ ◆

GoldenNESS (OG 1036, ABV 3%) ◗
Grapefruity, hoppy bitter.

LightNESS (OG 1039, ABV 3.9%) ◗
Golden, refreshing, hoppy bitter with a hint of lemons and grapefruit.

WilderNESS (OG 1039, ABV 3.9%) ◗
Fruity, hoppy brew with a slight malt background. Bittersweet turning to a more bitter finish.

CaithNESS (OG 1044, ABV 4%) ◗
Golden amber-coloured, citrus, hoppy and bittersweet taste with a sweeter finish. Made with honey and porridge oats

SaaziNESS (OG 1042, ABV 4%) ◗
Refreshing, golden, light citrus and hop flavoured lager using Saaz hops.

RedNESS (OG 1042, ABV 4.2%) ◗
Red-brown in colour with a good mix of malt and hops and a raspberry background in this bittersweet brew.

LochNESS (OG 1044, ABV 4.4%) ◗
A malty, fruity, sweetish brew in the 80/- style. Hints of chocolate and blackcurrant.

DarkNESS (OG 1052, ABV 4.5%) ◗
Roasted chocolate malt with a blackcurrant and liquorice background. Thick brown head all the way to the bottom.

InverNESS (OG 1042, ABV 4.5%) ◗
Golden, hoppy brew with a slight sweetness in the background.

HoppyNESS (OG 1050, ABV 5%) ◗
Golden, smooth, citrus and hoppy brew. The initial sweetness turns to a bitter finish. Does not drink its strength.

**MadNESS – One Hop Beyond
(OG 1050, ABV 5%)** ◗
A brown-coloured hoppy bitter.

SmokieNESS (OG 1050, ABV 5%) ◗
Red, malty brew with sweetness from the honey and a slight smoky/spicy background from the ginger.

NESStonia (OG 1060, ABV 6.4%)

NESStrovia (OG 1090, ABV 8.5%)

Prince of DarkNESS (OG 1095, ABV 10%) ◗
Creamy, heavy on malt with roast, chocolate and liquorice flavours coming through.

Loddon SIBA ◉

Dunsden Green Farm, Church Lane, Dunsden, Oxfordshire, RG4 9QD
☎ (0118) 948 1111 ⊕ loddonbrewery.com

⊠ This family-run brewery was established in 2002, in a brick-and-flint barn that was originally a grain store. The custom-built 17-barrel plant typically produces 120 barrels per week, and supplies more than 500 outlets far and wide. Popular open evenings are held quarterly. ‼ ▰ ◆

Hoppit (OG 1036.2, ABV 3.5%) ◗
Hops dominate the aroma of this drinkable, light-coloured session beer. Malt and hops create a balanced taste and a pleasant bitterness carries through to the aftertaste.

Reading Best (OG 1041.5, ABV 4%)

**Gravesend Shrimpers Bitter
(OG 1042.8, ABV 4.1%)**

Hullabaloo (OG 1043.8, ABV 4.2%) ◗

A hint of fruit in the initial taste develops into a balance of hops and malt in this well-rounded, medium-bodied bitter with a bitter aftertaste.

Ferryman's Gold (OG 1045.8, ABV 4.4%) ◄
Golden-coloured with a strong hoppy character throughout, accompanied by fruit in the taste and aftertaste.

Bamboozle (OG 1049.5, ABV 4.8%) ◄
Full-bodied and well balanced. Distinctive bittersweet flavour with hop and caramel to accompany.

Forbury Lion (OG 1056.5, ABV 5.5%)
A malty IPA with a strong complex hop finish.

Lola Rose

▤ Wanlockhead Inn, Wanlockhead, ML12 6UZ
☎ (01659) 74535 ☎ 07500 663405
⊕ lola-rose-brewery.co.uk

Lola Rose is based in the family-run Wanlockhead Inn, situated in the scenic Lowther Hills of the Scottish Lowlands. Local outlets only are supplied at present. RAIB

Blonde (OG 1041, ABV 4.1%)

Stout (OG 1042, ABV 4.2%)

Red Ale (OG 1043, ABV 4.3%)

London Beer Factory SIBA

Unit 4, 160 Hamilton Road, West Norwood, London, SE27 9SF ☎ 07760 290489
⊕ thelondonbeerfactory.com

The London Beer Factory started brewing in 2014 using a 20-barrel plant. Local outlets are supplied. A tap room is open to the public at weekends.

Chelsea Blonde (ABV 4.3%) ◄
Grapefruit dominates the flavour and aroma with trace of spiciness and a dry bitterness balanced by a little honey sweetness.

Sayers Stout (ABV 4.5%)

Paxton Pale Ale (ABV 5%)

London Beer Lab (NEW)

c/o Arch 283, Belinda Road, Coldharbour Lane, Loughborough Junction, London, SW9 7DT
☎ (020) 8001 6552 ☎ 07948 160953
Office: Arch 41, Nursery Road, London, SW9 8BP
⊕ londonbeerlab.com

London Beer Lab began brewing in 2015. Initially offering only KegKeg and bottled beers, it has recently started cask-conditioned beer production. Spare capacity is used at Clarkshaws (qv).

London Brewing

▤ Bohemia, 762-764 High Road, North Finchley, London, N12 9QH
☎ (020) 8446 0294 ⊕ londonbrewing.com

⊠ London Brewing Co began brewing in 2011 at the Bull in Highgate using a 2.5-barrel plant. In 2014 it acquired its second pub, the Bohemia in North Finchley, at which brewing began in 2015 in a new 6.5-barrel brewhouse. The Bull was sold in the summer of 2016 to concentrate all production at the North Finchley site. ♦

High Rise (OG 1040, ABV 3.9%) ◄
A fruity, yellow-coloured ale with a bitter character balanced by a fudge sweetness and a touch of lemon/lime peel.

Beer Street (OG 1042, ABV 4%) ◄
Well-balanced, copper-brown best bitter with the hoppy bitterness underpinned by the caramelised malt character. Fruit is present throughout.

Vista (OG 1047, ABV 4.7%) ◄
Smooth brown best bitter. Some nutty notes with hints of chocolate balanced by fruit. Lingering, dry bitter finish.

Skyline (OG 1053, ABV 5.3%) ◄
Pale brown beer with a honey sweetness and a some soft fruit notes. Sweetness is balanced by a bitter dryness.

Never Mind the Kent Hops (OG 1056, ABV 5.5%)
A complex malt profile of dark fruits and clean amber malts. Hop aroma is of pine and resin.

Long Arm (NEW)

▤ Ealing Park Tavern, 222 South Ealing Road, Ealing, London, W5 4RL
☎ (020) 8758 1879 ☎ 07857 257970
⊕ ealingparktavern.com

A brewpub on the Brentford/Ealing border. Beers are also available across London and at the ETM chain of bars and restaurants. ‼

Lucky Penny (OG 1041, ABV 4%) ◄
Smooth, dark golden ale with a sweet and lightly fruity flavour followed by a sharply dry, strong bitter finish.

Birdie Flipper (OG 1045, ABV 4.5%)

IPA OK (OG 1051, ABV 5.5%) ◄
Fruity brown beer with a malty toffee sweetness and bitter hop character that is also in the dry finish.

Shadow Wolf (OG 1054, ABV 5.5%)
A smoked stout.

Long Lane

Correspondence: Unit 2, Redhill Farm, Top Street, Appleby Magna, Leicestershire, DE12 7AH
☎ (01530) 813800

Opened in 2010 at the Matchless Homebrew shop in Colville, with beers brewed by passionate brewster Ann Saunders. In 2014 the brewery was closed and beers are now brewed by Ann's son utilising spare capacity at Golden Duck Brewery (qv). All beers are available bottle-conditioned; however cask-conditioned beers can be produced to order. Beers are available at various farmers' markets in the area. RAIB

Long Man SIBA ◉

Church Farm, Litlington, East Sussex, BN26 5RA
☎ (01323) 871850 ☎ 07976 777992
⊕ longmanbrewery.com

⊠ Long Man began brewing in 2012 using a 20-barrel stainless steel plant. Hops and grain are sourced locally with a view to using home-grown barley, as well as a traditional strain of Sussex yeast. ‼

Long Blonde (OG 1039, ABV 3.8%)

A light-coloured golden ale with a distinctive hoppy aroma and crisp, clean bitterness on the finish. Smooth, light and refreshing.

Best Bitter (OG 1040, ABV 4%)
Well-balanced with a complex bittersweet malty taste, fragrant hops and a characteristic long, deep finish. A traditional Sussex-style best bitter.

Copper Hop (ABV 4.2%)

Old Man (OG 1048, ABV 4.3%)
Dark beer with soft malt notes of coffee and chocolate combined with a pleasant light hoppiness creating a rich, full tasting old ale.

Sussex Pride (OG 1045, ABV 4.5%)
A classic strong pale ale. Bronze-coloured with a fruity nose and full round flavours.

American Pale Ale (OG 1046, ABV 4.8%)
A triple-hopped American pale ale with a pleasant citrus fruit aroma and characteristic robust bitterness.

Longden

See Shropshire Brewer

Longdog SIBA

Unit A1, Moniton Trading Estate, West Ham Lane, Worting, Hampshire, RG22 6NQ
☎ (01256) 324286 ☎ 07827 618733
⏚ longdogbrewery.co.uk

⊗ Longdog was established in 2011 using a six-barrel plant. The name is inspired by the owner's greyhound. ‼⏚♦

Bunny Chaser (OG 1036, ABV 3.6%)
A dark copper-coloured session bitter with plenty of malt in the mouth and a good whack of bitterness.

Golden Poacher (OG 1038, ABV 3.9%) ♦
A fruity nose with plenty of hops, balanced by a malty sweetness in the flavour. The hops build to a faint astringent finish.

Red Runner (OG 1042, ABV 4.2%)
A fruity and hoppy mahogany-coloured best bitter.

Kismet (OG 1045, ABV 4.5%)

Lamplight Porter (OG 1048, ABV 5%) 🍾 ♦
Smoky and drier than many, with strong roast flavours giving way to a blackberry taste and slightly vinous finish.

Longhill

Longhill Cottage, Whitstone, Cornwall, EX22 6UG
☎ (01288) 341466

⊗ Longhill began brewing in 2011 using a 0.5-barrel plant, upgraded in 2012 to a four-barrel plant to meet demand. The beers are named with a wind theme. Eight outlets are supplied direct.

Whistler (OG 1038, ABV 3.8%) ♦
Smooth pale brown bitter with little aroma. Gentle balance of caramel malt, bitter hops and sweet fruit. Slowly fading bittersweet finish.

Westerly (OG 1040, ABV 4%) ♦
Copper-coloured best bitter with malt and toffee aroma. Mainly malt and caramel flavour. Light finish with malt, fruit and bitterness.

Gale Force (OG 1048, ABV 4.8%) ♦

Copper-coloured strong bitter. Malt and almonds aroma. Malty flavours with toffee and nuts. Short, malty, dry finish with stone fruit.

Hurricane (OG 1048, ABV 4.8%)

Loose Cannon SIBA

Unit 6, Suffolk Way, Abingdon, Oxfordshire, OX14 5JX
☎ (01235) 531141 ⏚ lcbeers.co.uk

Loose Cannon began brewing in 2010 using a 15-barrel plant, reviving Abingdon's brewing history after the Morland Brewery closed in 2000. Beers can be found in an increasing number of local pubs, with the Chester in Oxford acting as the brewery tap. Popular brewery evenings take place on the first Tuesday of the month. ‼⏚♦

Gunners Gold (OG 1034.5, ABV 3.5%)
Golden, easy-drinking session ale with a subtle peach flavour.

Abingdon Bridge (OG 1041, ABV 4.1%)
Full-flavoured and smooth, with well-rounded hop bitterness and a floral aroma.

Abingdon Bridge XB (OG 1043, ABV 4.5%)
Copper-coloured with medium bitterness and hints of lychee.

Porter (OG 1054, ABV 5%)
Moderately sweet with hints of dark chocolate and a smooth espresso finish.

India Pale Ale (OG 1053, ABV 5.4%)
Balanced floral aroma and fruity taste with a smooth bitter kick and a warming quality.

Lord Conrad's

Unit 21, Dry Drayton Industrial Estate, Scotland Road, Dry Drayton, Cambridgeshire, CB23 8AT ☎ 07736 739700 ⏚ lordconradsbrewery.co.uk

⊗ Lord Conrad's was established in 2007 and moved to Dry Drayton in 2011 using a 2.5-barrel plant. One permanent outlet is supplied, the Abbot's Elm in Abbots Ripton, along with other local free houses and beer festivals. The brewery adheres strongly to 'green' principles, using low energy systems, recycled materials and local ingredients. ‼⏚

Stoat Warbler (OG 1035, ABV 3.4%)

Zulu Dawn (OG 1037, ABV 3.5%)

Hedgerow Hop (OG 1039, ABV 3.7%)
An amber-coloured ale made with locally picked hops.

Lickety Split (OG 1038, ABV 3.8%)
Sweet, malty brown ale, light but not overly hoppy.

Conkerwood (OG 1044, ABV 4%)
Dark porter with hints of liquorice.

Gubbins (OG 1040, ABV 4%)

Slap N'Tickle (OG 1042, ABV 4.3%)

Zulu (OG 1047, ABV 4.5%)
A strong black bitter.

Pheasant's Rise (OG 1050, ABV 5%)
Smoky, woody traditional strong ale.

Stubble Burner (OG 1050, ABV 5%)
A straw-like beer with a good earthy nose and a well-balanced, fruity bitterness.

Lord's (NEW)

c/o Golcar Brewery, 60a Swallow Lane, Golcar, West Yorkshire, HD7 4NB ☎ 07976 974162 ⊕ lordsbrewing.com

Established in 2015, Lords is the brain child of three brothers-in-law, Ben, John and Tim. Brewing takes place using spare capacity at the Golcar Brewery (qv). ♦

Tithe House Bitter (ABV 3.9%)
A light copper-coloured session bitter with subtle malt flavours balanced by English hops. It has a soft malt and caramel base with a mellow pine and grapefruit flavour.

Expedition Pale Ale (ABV 4%)
Pale and delicately hopped. Refreshing with citrus notes.

Mount Helix West Coast Pale (ABV 5%)
A crisp malt base with citrus, pine and floral overtones.

Havelock IPA (ABV 6.5%)
Golden-coloured beer, both sharp and rich on the palate with a juicy, herbal finish.

Lost Industry (NEW)

Nutwood Trading Estate, Sheffield, S6 1NJ
☎ (0114) 231 6393 ⊕ lostindustrybrewing.com

Lost Industry began brewing in 2015. A wide range of beer styles is brewed.

LoveBeer SIBA

95 High Street, Milton, Oxfordshire, OX14 4EJ
☎ 07889 455845 ⊕ lovebeerbrewery.com

Jim Southey has been brewing ale since 2013 and became fully licensed as a brewery in 2014. The 0.5-barrel plant supplies local pubs such as the Nags Head in Abingdon, the regular beer festival at the Plum Pudding in Milton, and local farm shops.

Doctor Roo (OG 1038, ABV 3.7%)
A balanced, light pale ale. Late flavour hops contribute a zesty, tropical flavour.

Molly's Malt (OG 1041, ABV 4%)
A well-hopped amber ale with a caramel biscuit aroma and hints of citrus.

Purdy Peculiar (OG 1054, ABV 5.4%)
A smooth, dark and smoky stout with hints of molasses and black treacle.

Monty's Jem (OG 1058, ABV 5.6%)
A traditional ale with full body and good hop flavour with a hint of lime or mandarin.

Lovibonds

Rear of 19-21 Market Place, Henley-on-Thames, Oxfordshire, RG9 2AA
☎ (01491) 576596 ⊕ lovibonds.com

Lovibonds was founded by Jeff Rosenmeier in 2005 and is named after Joseph William Lovibond, who invented the Tintometer to measure beer colour. The beers are unfiltered and unpasteurised, but served with top pressure. Currently brewing on the kit at Old Luxters (qv), its ownn brewery is being built near Henley. ‼ ⌱

Luckie

Unit 4, Block 5, Banbeath Industrial Estate, Leven, KY8 5HD ☎ 07979 364906 ⊕ luckie-ales.com

Luckie Ales was established in 2009 and is an artisan microbrewery specialising in handcrafted Scottish beers and historic British Ales. Brewing moved to Markinch in 2012, operating on a one-barrel plant. The brewery was sold in 2016, and relocated to new premises in Leven. RAIB

Ludlow SIBA 👁

The Railway Shed, Station Drive, Ludlow, Shropshire, SY8 2PQ
☎ (01584) 873291
⊕ theludlowbrewingcompany.co.uk

Established in 2006, the brewery occupies a converted railway sidings shed. Brews are produced using a 20-barrel brewing plant. The premises also function as a brewery tap, visitor centre and events area. ‼ ⌱

Best (OG 1037, ABV 3.7%)
An amber-coloured, well-balanced session beer with a banana, pineapple and toffee aroma and a resinous, dry finish.

Blonde (OG 1040, ABV 4%)
A pale blonde ale, aromatic and well hopped.

Gold (OG 1041, ABV 4.2%)
A yellow-coloured ale with a papaya, pineapple and lemon aroma and a soft, full-bodied, creamy taste.

Black Knight (OG 1045, ABV 4.5%)
A ruby-black stout with a smoky, liquorice aroma and sweet, roasted nutty flavour.

Boiling Well (OG 1045.5, ABV 4.7%)
A chestnut-coloured beer with a grassy aroma of autumn fruit and a full-bodied, sweet then dry taste.

Stairway (OG 1047, ABV 5%)
A gold-coloured beer with a grassy, citrus floral aroma and a sharp, sweet, full-bodied taste.

LWC

Beers brewed under the Gray's brand name by Marston's PLC

Lyme Regis SIBA

Mill Lane, Lyme Regis, Dorset, DT7 3PU
☎ (01297) 444354

Office: 15a Broad Street, Lyme Regis, Dorset, DT7 3QE
⊕ lymeregisbrewery.com

⊗ Lyme Regis Brewery, formerly known as Town Mill, began brewing in 2010 using a four-barrel plant in a part of the mill that at one time housed the Lyme Regis electricity generator, although historic use of the building was as a brewer's malthouse. The outside area is now licensed and is proving popular. Contract brewing is carried out for other breweries. ‼ ⌱ RAIB

Cobb (OG 1041, ABV 3.9%)
An amber/brown bitter with a full flavour and traditional-tasting fruity hop finish.

Lyme Gold (OG 1042, ABV 4.2%)

A pale summer ale, easy-drinking with a refreshing citrus aroma.

Town Mill Best (OG 1045, ABV 4.5%)
A reddish brown bitter with a fruit and nut flavour.

Black Ven (OG 1050, ABV 5%)
A dark brown porter with a pronounced depth of flavour, enhanced with the blackcurrant fruitiness of the hops.

Revenge (OG 1052, ABV 5.3%)
A traditional IPA with a well-balanced hop and spiced fruit flavour.

Lymestone SIBA 👁

The Brewery, Mount Road, Stone, Staffordshire, ST15 8LL
☎ (01785) 817796 ☎ 07891 782652
🌐 lymestonebrewery.co.uk

☺Lymestone commenced brewing in 2008. Rapid growth has seen the beers supplied direct to 300 outlets, with beer also being available via wholesalers. The brewery opened its first pub in 2012, the Lymestone Vaults, Newcastle-under-Lyme. ‼🍺♦

Stone Cutter (OG 1037, ABV 3.7%) 🍺
Hoppy and grassy aroma, clean, sharp and refreshing. A hint of caramel start then intense bitterness emerges with a good bitter aftertaste and touch of mouthwatering astringency.

Stone Faced (OG 1040, ABV 4%)
Subtle citrus and toffee flavours balanced by a hoppy aroma and bitter finish.

Foundation Stone (OG 1047, ABV 4.5%) 🍺
An IPA-style beer. Faint biscuit and chewy, juicy fruits burst on to the palate then the spicy hops pepper the taste buds to leave a dry bitter finish.

Ein Stein (OG 1052, ABV 5%)
A pale, citrus, hoppy ale.

Stone the Crows (OG 1056, ABV 5.4%) 🍺
A rich, dark beer. Fruit, roast and hops abound to leave a deep, lingering bitterness from the hop mix.

Abdominal Stoneman (OG 1072, ABV 7%)
An American pale ale with a crisp hop base and massive hoppy finish.

Lymm

18 Bridgewater Street, Lymm, Cheshire, WA13 0AB
☎ (0161) 929 0663 ✉ info@lymmbrewing.co.uk

☺Lymm is a small, family-run brewery, launched in 2013. Located in an old post office, the brewing equipment is downstairs in what used to be the mess rooms with a brewery tap upstairs in what was the sorting office/post office counter. A sister brewery to Dunham Massey (qv), a joint bar opened in 2013, Costello's Bar, Stockton Heath. ♦

Bitter (OG 1040, ABV 3.8%)
A light, refreshing, medium-bodied session bitter, with a good balance of malt and hops.

Bridgewater Blonde (OG 1041, ABV 4%)
Light, delicate, hoppy, subtle and refreshing.

Heritage Trail Ale (OG 1046, ABV 4.5%)
An easy-drinking, well-balanced best bitter, fruity with a light, crisp hop.

Dam Strong Ale (OG 1071, ABV 7.2%)

Belgian-style ale – strong, malty and fruity with a dry finish.

Lytham SIBA

8 Cambell's Court, Lord Street, St Annes, Lancashire, FY8 2DF
☎ (01253) 725440 🌐 lythambrewery.co.uk

☺Lytham is a well-established, family-run brewery that began brewing in 2007. ‼♦

Amber (OG 1037, ABV 3.6%)
A traditional malty beer using English hops.

Blonde (OG 1038, ABV 3.8%)
Smooth golden ale with a dry finish.

Gold (OG 1042, ABV 4.2%)
A golden beer with a fruity aroma and lasting bitter finish.

Royal (OG 1044, ABV 4.4%)
A full-bodied English ale with a crisp fruity aroma and a smooth, dry finish.

Stout (OG 1046, ABV 4.6%)
Dark, rich, roasty, full-bodied stout.

IPA (OG 1054, ABV 5.6%)
A pale bitter with a fresh, sweet, hoppy flavour leading to a long, dry finish.

McGivern

🏠 c/o The Bridge End Inn, 5 Bridge Street, Ruabon, LL14 6DA
☎ (01978) 810881 ☎ 07891 676614
🌐 mcgivernales.co.uk

☺The brewery was established in 2008 and was originally based at the brewer's home in Wrexham but moved in 2011 to the award winning Bridge End Inn in Ruabon using a 2.5-barrel plant. ♦

Bridge Bitter (OG 1039, ABV 3.9%)

Bridge Pale (OG 1039, ABV 3.9%)

Pyramid Porter (OG 1045, ABV 4.5%)
Hoppy Porter with chocolate undertones.

Gambit (OG 1047, ABV 4.7%)

Enigma (OG 1050, ABV 5%)

McMullen SIBA IFBB 👁

26 Old Cross, Hertford, SG14 1RD
☎ (01992) 584911 🌐 mcmullens.co.uk

⊗ McMullen, Hertfordshire's oldest independent brewery, was founded in 1827. Under the banner of the Whole Hop Brewery (the name emphasising the company's continuing policy of using only traditional brewing materials) eight or more seasonal beers are produced a year. All 135 pubs, now spread across south-east England, serve cask beer. ‼♦

AK (OG 1035, ABV 3.7%) 🍺
A pleasant mix of malt and hops leads to a distinctive, dry aftertaste that isn't always as pronounced as it used to be.

Cask Ale (OG 1039, ABV 3.8%)
A well-balanced, light and refreshing ale with subtle biscuity flavours mixed with citrus hop notes.

Country Bitter (OG 1042, ABV 4.3%) 🍺

A full-bodied beer with a well-balanced mix of malt, hops and fruit throughout.

IPA (OG 1047, ABV 4.8%)
A strong bitter with deep rich flavours created with specially kilned amber malts.

Macclesfield (NEW) MACC

76 Brown Street, Macclesfield, Cheshire, SK11 6RY

A small-batch 100-litre brewery producing bottled beers using seasonal ingredients.

Maclay

See Clockwork

Mad Cat SIBA

Brogdale Farm, Brogdale Road, Faversham, Kent, ME13 8XU
☎ **(01795) 597743** ☎ **07960 263615**
⊕ **madcatbrewery.co.uk**

Mad Cat was established in 2012 by Peter Meaney in a refurbished cold store using an eight-barrel plant. The site is shared with the National Fruit Collection. !! ☲ ◆

Redhead (ABV 3.9%)

Crispin Ale (ABV 4%)

Mild Disobedience (ABV 4%)

Golden IPA (ABV 4.2%)

Platinum Blonde (ABV 4.2%)

Special Relationship (ABV 4.8%)

Mad Dog SIBA

Shed 4, Unit 9, Park Farm, Plough Road, Penperlleni, NP4 0AL ☎ **07703 731197**

Office: 75 Brynhyfryd, Croesyceiliog, NP44 2LN
⊕ **maddogbrew.co.uk**

Brewing began in 2014 based at the brewer's home in Cwmbran. The brewery relocated in 2015 expanding to a brew length of five barrels. An upgrade to larger premises on the same site later the same year has enabled a significant increase in production capacity.

John Peel (OG 1040, ABV 4%)
A full-bodied stout with flavours of chocolate and infused with fresh orange peel, finishing on a spicy note.

Afternoon Sunshine (OG 1042, ABV 4.2%)
Golden in colour with the aroma of citrus and tangerine then followed by tastes of tropical fruits and finishing with a subtle spicy note.

Now In a Minute (OG 1042, ABV 4.2%)
A traditional Welsh red ale with flavours of sweet chocolate and citrus.

Dirty Dog (OG 1045, ABV 4.5%)
Brown-coloured, with flavours of chocolate, orange and grapes.

Bohemian Hipster (OG 1049, ABV 4.9%)
Pale ale giving flavours of lemongrass and pine needles.

Bark Like a Bird (OG 1052, ABV 5.2%)

Deep red in colour with bitterness to mellow out the sweet chocolate followed by tropical fruits and citrus.

Submissable Anarchy (OG 1064, ABV 6.4%)
A golden ale brewed with local honey, with added flavours of citrus and crushed juniper berries.

Mad Hatter

Unit 1, Palmer Hill Building, 15-37 Caryl Street, Liverpool, L8 5SQ ☎ **07474 797450**
⊕ **madhatterbrewing.co.uk**

Mad Hatter began brewing in 2013 combining traditional techniques with new flavours and approaches to brewing. Most of the output is bottled or keg with cask-conditioned beers making an occasional appearance around Merseyside or at beer festivals. In 2014 the brewery relocated to Liverpool's Baltic Triangle.

Madrigal

The Manor House, Manor Green, Lynmouth, Devon, EX35 6EN ☎ **07857 560677** ⊕ **madrigalbrewery.co.uk**

⊠ The brewery was established in 2014 in the village of Combe Martin. It has now relocated to larger premises in Lynmouth in 2016 to help meet increased demand. ◆RAIB V

Garland (OG 1036, ABV 3.5%)
A wheat beer with hints of fruits from the tropics.

Surfer Rosa (OG 1036, ABV 3.6%)
Unique ale, made with English hops and a spicy red rye malt.

Burning House (OG 1042, ABV 4%)
Speciality beer with a smoky flavour. Dark brown in colour with a smooth mouthfeel and gradual smoke and hop finish.

Fossil (OG 1043, ABV 4%)
A well-rounded amber ale.

Severed Hand (OG 1041, ABV 4.1%)
Velvety porter beer.

Hanged Man (OG 1042, ABV 4.2%)
Well-rounded stout made with raw cacao nibs. Smooth, soft taste with slight spicy notes.

Monkey's Fist (OG 1048, ABV 5%)
Smooth with a hint of chocolate and slight orange taste.

North Coast Voodoo (OG 1050, ABV 5%)
An aromatic IPA with a fruity aroma and gradual hop finish.

Wheatear (OG 1048, ABV 5.1%)
Wheat beer made with fresh ginger and coriander.

Magic Rock SIBA

Units 1-4, Willow Lane, Huddersfield, West Yorkshire, HD1 5EB
☎ **(01484) 649823** ⊕ **magicrockbrewing.com**

Magic Rock began brewing in 2011 in the Old Bed Factory attached to the Rockshop Wholesale Company in Huddersfield. In 2015 the brewery relocated to its present address. ◆RAIB

Ringmaster (OG 1038, ABV 3.9%)
Pale ale with a floral/grassy aroma and citrus hops.

Rapture (OG 1044.5, ABV 4.6%)

Full-bodied red ale, with grapefruit and pine aromas, pithy orange, and a rich, malty body.

High Wire (OG 1051, ABV 5.5%)
West coast-style pale ale, with mango, lychee and grapefruit flavours.

Dark Arts (OG 1057, ABV 6%) 🗍
Chocolate, liquorice, blackberry and fig flavours with a long, roasted, bitter finish.

Magpie SIBA ⌾

Unit 4, Ashling Court, Ashling Street, Nottingham, NG2 3JA ☎ 07738 762897 ⊕ magpiebrewery.com

⌾ Launched in 2006, this six-barrel plant was upgraded to 10 barrels in 2016. The brewery maintains a large core range, plus seasonal and one-off beers. ♦RAIB

Hoppily Ever After (OG 1035, ABV 3.8%) ◥
Golden bitter, gently hopped with biscuit malt flavours and a bitter finish.

Angry Bird (OG 1039, ABV 4%) ◥
Ruby-coloured ale with a malty aroma, fruit taste and balanced with a bitter finish.

Flyer (OG 1038.8, ABV 4.1%)
A light golden ale with a fruity and slightly spicy flavour.

Best (OG 1040.7, ABV 4.2%) ◥
A malty, traditional pale brown best bitter, with balancing hops giving a bitter finish.

Raven Stout (OG 1044, ABV 4.4%) ◥
Dark stout with roast coffee aroma and taste leading to a dry bitter finish.

Thieving Rogue (OG 1042, ABV 4.5%) ◥
A hoppy golden ale with a long-lasting, bitter finish.

Pica Porter (OG 1049.4, ABV 5%)
Rich and creamy dark porter with coffee, raisin and chocolate flavours.

Jay IPA (OG 1048.6, ABV 5.2%)
Mature hops, citrus fruit nose with a balance of hops and malt in the mouth with a smooth, hoppy aftertaste.

Maidstone

Unit 11, The Old Brewery, Rocky Hill, London Road, Maidstone, Kent, ME16 0DZ ☎ 07736 149014 ⊕ maidstonebrewing.co.uk

⊠ A four-barrel brewery situated in the former stable block of the old Style & Winch brewery in Maidstone. Test brewing commenced in 2013 and the first beer went on sale in 2015. Further beers are planned across a range of styles to be made available locally, particularly at the Flower Pot pub in Maidstone.

First Light (OG 1040, ABV 3.9%)
A pale ale with a slightly sweet initial taste and a dry, bitter finish.

Eight (OG 1052, ABV 4.5%)
A smooth, dark ale with gentle bitterness, a hint of chocolate and medium hop aroma.

Maldon SIBA

Stable Brewery, Silver Street, Maldon, Essex, CM9 4QE ☎ (01621) 851000 ⊕ maldonbrewing.co.uk

⊠ Established in 2002, this family-run brewery is tucked away behind the 14th-century Blue Boar Hotel. The six-barrel plant is at full production serving more than 50 outlets including many Gray & Sons houses and the brewery's micropub on the High Street. ▰♦RAIB

Farmer's IPA (OG 1036, ABV 3.6%)
A crisp IPA based on an old Ridley's recipe.

Drop of Nelson's Blood (OG 1038, ABV 3.8%)
An easy-drinking bitter. A tot of brandy is added to each cask.

Hotel Porter (OG 1041, ABV 4.1%)
A classic stout with a smoky tang.

Pucks Folly (OG 1038, ABV 4.2%)
A pale golden ale with a spicy character and pineapple in the aroma and taste.

Farmer's Golden Boar (OG 1050, ABV 5%)
An amber-coloured beer with a hoppy aroma.

Essex Strong Ale (OG 1053, ABV 5.3%)
An American-style pale ale, slightly sweet.

Dark Horse (OG 1064, ABV 6.6%)
A chestnut-coloured bitter, smooth but with spice in the finish.

Mallard SIBA

Unit A, Maythorne, Nottinghamshire, NG25 0RS ☎ 07811 193930 ✉ stevenhussey@tiscali.co.uk

⌾ 2.25-barrel brewery run by Steve Hussey and Alison Ryan, brewing for their own pub, the Cross Keys in Upton, and local outlets in and around the county. ‼♦RAIB

Duck 'n' Dive (OG 1039, ABV 3.7%) ◥
A bitter, pale golden beer, with a dry finish.

Golden Duck (OG 1039, ABV 3.9%)
A golden beer, complex and hoppy.

Quackpot (ABV 4%)
A copper-coloured traditional bitter.

Feather Light (OG 1040, ABV 4.1%) ◥
A straw-coloured lager-style beer with a hoppy taste and aroma.

Specduckular (OG 1042, ABV 4.2%)
A golden ale with malty undertones.

Spittin' Feathers (OG 1040, ABV 4.4%)
A traditional English ale.

Drake (ABV 4.5%)
A copper-coloured, full-bodied beer.

Mallinson's

Unit 1, Waterhouse Mill, 65-71 Lockwood Road, Huddersfield, West Yorkshire, HD1 3QU ☎ (01484) 654301 ☎ 07850 446571 ⊕ drinkmallinsons.co.uk

⌾ The brewery was originally set up in 2008 on a six-barrel plant by CAMRA members Tara Mallinson and Elaine Yendall. The company moved to new premises in 2012 after trial brewing its core beers on a new 15-barrel plant for several weeks. ‼♦RAIB

Malt SIBA

Collings Hanger Farm, 100 Wycombe Road, Prestwood, Buckinghamshire, HP16 0HP ☎ (01494) 865063 ☎ 07815 187113 ⊕ maltthebrewery.co.uk

⊗ Opened in 2012 in a converted dairy, the 10-barrel brewery has conservation at its heart; from the use of local ingredients, to spent grain sent to the local farm. The ales are also used in pies and sausages. ‼ ☛ ♦ RAIB

Missenden Pale (OG 1035, ABV 3.6%)
Easy to drink session ale, light amber in colour.

Dark Ale (OG 1038, ABV 3.9%)
Smooth, mild and drinkable. Full of deep malt tones.

Golden Ale (OG 1038, ABV 3.9%)
Light and refreshing with a citrus finish.

Starry Nights (ABV 4%)
A light, fruity ale.

Prestwood's Best (OG 1043, ABV 4.4%)
Classic-style bitter with a dry finish.

IPA (OG 1048, ABV 5%)
Aromatic with a bitter finish.

Malvern Hills SIBA

15 West Malvern Road, Malvern, Worcestershire, WR14 4ND
☎ (01684) 560165 ⊕ malvernhillsbrewery.co.uk

⊗ Founded in 1998 in an old quarrying dynamite store and now an established presence in the Three Counties, Birmingham and the Black Country. The core brews are supplemented by seasonals and specials, the latter typically brewed for local community events. ‼ ♦

Beacon Gold (OG 1035, ABV 3.7%)

Feelgood (OG 1036, ABV 3.8%)

Radar Love (OG 1038, ABV 4%)
Straw-coloured beer with notable but not overpowering hops.

Priessnitz Plzen (OG 1040, ABV 4.3%) ◗
A mix of soft fruit and citrus give this straw-coloured brew its quaffability, making it ideal for quenching summer thirsts.

Black Pear (OG 1042, ABV 4.4%) ◗
A sharp citrus hoppiness is the main constituent of this golden brew that has a long, dry aftertaste.

Manchester (NEW)

66 North Western Street, Manchester, M12 6DX
☎ (0161) 273 6167 ⊕ manchesterbrewing.co.uk

Brewing commenced in 2016 in a railway arch on Manchester's 'beer mile' with an eight-barrel plant producing cask-conditioned and KegKeg beers. Local pubs and beer festivals are supplied.

Factory Pale Ale (ABV 4%)
Straw-coloured pale ale with a dry bitterness.

Cuts Like a Buffalo (ABV 4.5%)
An American pale ale.

Mad Carew (ABV 5.9%)
A modern IPA brewed with Antipodean and American Hops.

Manning (NEW) SIBA

Lower Overton Farm, Overton Road, Congleton, Cheshire, CW12 3QW ☎ 07946 278018
⊕ manningbrewers.co.uk

A family-owned and run brewery using only British hops, opened in 2015.

Woah Man (ABV 3.8%)
A clean-drinking golden pale ale with a floral aroma.

Man Up! (ABV 4%)
A chestnut-coloured malty session beer, lightly hopped allowing the sweetness of the malt to come through.

Cave-Man (ABV 4.2%)
A well-balanced bitter with a refreshing hop character. A light caramel colour and bitter crisp finish with some blackberry hop aromas, and a lasting gentle bitterness.

Mantle SIBA ⊚

Unit 16, Pentood Industrial Estate, Cardigan, SA43 3AG
☎ (01239) 623898 ☎ 07552 609909
⊕ mantlebrewery.com

Mantle began brewing in 2013 using a 10-barrel plant. Honing their skills brewing traditional beers for the local market, Ian and Dominique Kimber have now branched out into New World hops to extend their portfolio. Pubs throughout South and West Wales are supplied direct, select wholesalers delivering further afield. ‼ ☛ ♦

Rock Steady (OG 1038, ABV 3.8%)
Golden session ale with great depth of flavour. Satisfying and refreshing.

MOHO (OG 1041.5, ABV 4.3%)
Robust and aromatic Welsh pale ale, finely balanced and full flavoured.

Cwrw Teifi (OG 1045, ABV 4.5%)
Full-bodied, malt-driven best bitter with a well balanced and pleasant hop finish.

Dark Heart (OG 1052, ABV 5.2%)
Rich, dark and smooth porter with a hint of spice.

Marble SIBA

41 Williamson Street, Manchester, M4 4JS
☎ (0161) 819 2694 ⊕ marblebeers.com

⊚ Marble began brewing in 1997 at the Marble Arch Inn in Manchester but now brews at a larger 12-barrel plant in a nearby unit, producing vegan beers. It supplies its own three pubs and more than 70 other outlets. ‼ ♦ RAIB V

Pint (OG 1038.5, ABV 3.9%)
Dry session bitter with notes of citrus and grapefruit. Plenty of character.

Manchester Bitter (OG 1040.5, ABV 4.2%) ◗
Yellow beer with a fruity and hoppy aroma. Hops, fruit and bitterness on the palate and in the finish.

Lagonda IPA (OG 1047, ABV 5%) 🍴 ◗
Golden yellow beer with a spicy, fruity nose. Fruit, hops and malt in the mouth, with a dry fruitiness continuing into the bitter aftertaste.

Ginger 5.1 (OG 1047.5, ABV 5.1%)
This full-bodied, copper-coloured beer displays a delicate blend of cloves, coriander and heaps of fiery ginger.

Chocolate Marble (OG 1054.5, ABV 5.5%) 🍴
Brewed with an emphasis on chocolate malts; tasting of coffee, cocoa and liquorice with a quenching, bitter finish.

THE BREWERIES

Dobber (OG 1056.5, ABV 5.9%)
A dark golden IPA with pronounced hop character and smooth biscuit base, offset by fruit aroma.

Earl Grey IPA (OG 1065, ABV 6.8%) 🍺
With timed additions of Earl Grey during fermentation, the result is a citrus fruit aroma, smooth texture, with hop notes complemented by bergamot and a light tannic finish.

Maregade (NEW)

🍺 Cock Tavern, Mare Street, Hackney, London, E8 1EJ
⊕ maregade.com

Microbrewery in the basement of the Cock Tavern in Hackney. ♦

Amber (ABV 4.3%)

Vanilla Milk Stout (ABV 4.5%)

Blonde Pale (ABV 4.8%)

Pale (ABV 5.2%)

Market Harborough (NEW)

71 St Mary's Road, Market Harborough,
Leicestershire, LE16 7DS
☎ (01858) 461682 ⊕ mhbrew.co.uk

Brewing commenced in 2015 on a six-barrel plant. Beers are supplied to a limited number of pubs and shops in the area. 🚂 ♦ RAIB

Best Bitter (ABV 3.8%)
A complex malty backbone with traditional English hops.

Hoppy Pale (ABV 4.1%)
Crisp, refreshing, pale and bursting with citrus hop notes.

XX Bitter (ABV 4.2%)
A copper-coloured bitter with a soft bitterness and pronounced hop aroma.

Harboro Red (ABV 4.5%)
A deep red-coloured ale balancing malt against a lingering bitterness.

Premium Brown (ABV 5.1%)
A modern brown ale with chocolate and caramel malt flavours.

IPA (ABV 6.3%)
An English IPA, smooth and deceptively strong with a long hoppy finish.

Marlpool

5 Breach Road, Marlpool, Derbyshire, DE75 7NJ
☎ (01773) 711285 ☎ 07963 511855
⊕ marlpoolbrewing.co.uk

Marlpool was set up by brothers Andy and Chris McAuley in 2010 using a 2.5-barrel plant situated in an old slaughterhouse. The majority of the beer is sold through its own micro pub built into the old butcher's shop attached to the brewery. The remainder is sold to local outlets. ‼ ♦ RAIB

Blind Boris (OG 1038, ABV 3.5%)
A traditional dark mild.

Otters Pocket (OG 1040, ABV 4%)
Easy-drinking, smooth amber ale.

Scratty Ratty (OG 1044, ABV 4.4%)
Pale ale, lightly hopped with a bitter, dry finish.

Frank (OG 1045, ABV 4.5%)

A dark red ale, fairly bitter.

Derbyshire Classic (OG 1048, ABV 4.8%)
Premium amber bitter.

Black Oss (OG 1058, ABV 5.4%)
A black porter.

Marston's 👁

Shobnall Road, Burton upon Trent, Staffordshire, DE14 2BW
☎ (01283) 531131 ⊕ marstons.co.uk

☺Marston's has been brewing cask beer in Burton since 1834 and the current site is the home of the only working Burton Union fermenters, housed in rooms known as the Cathedral of Brewing. Burton Unions were developed in the 19th century to cleanse the new style of pale ale yeast. Only Pedigree is fermented in the Unions but yeast from the system is used to ferment the other Marston's branded beers. Marston's continues to take contract brewing, and brews the iconic cask beer Draught Bass on behalf of AB Inbev. ‼ 🚂 RAIB

Burton Bitter (OG 1037, ABV 3.8%) 🍺
Overwhelming sulphurous aroma supports a scattering of hops and fruit with an easy-drinking sweetness. The taste develops from the sweet middle to a satisfyingly hoppy finish.

**Pedigree New World Pale Ale
(OG 1038, ABV 3.8%)**
A mellow, understated bitterness is complemented by peach, apricot, melon and passion fruit flavours. A light citrus tingle follows, leading to a fragrant and refreshing finish.

Pedigree (OG 1043, ABV 4.5%) 🍺
Pale brown with a sweet hoppy aroma. Malt with a dash of hop flavours give a satisfying tasty finish.

Old Empire (OG 1057, ABV 5.7%) 🍺
Sulphur dominates the gentle malt aroma. Malty and sweet to start but developing bitterness with fruit and a touch of sweetness. A balanced aftertaste of hops and fruit leads to a lingering bitterness.

For AB InBev:

Draught Bass (OG 1043, ABV 4.4%) 🍺
Hints of caramel aroma and taste, lightly hopped for a short bitter finish.

Martland Mill SIBA

Unit 5 Otterwood Square, Martland Mill, Wigan, WN5 0LF
☎ (01942) 665656 ⊕ martlandmillbrewery.co.uk

☺Founded in 2014 by a husband-and-wife team using a six-barrel brew plant, the brewery is located close to the town centre of Martland Mill Park. Numerous local outlets are supplied including the brewery tap, the Tap 'n' Barrel in Wigan, opened in 2015. ♦

Chonkin Feckle (OG 1038, ABV 3.8%)
A golden yellow-coloured ale with a citrus hop aroma, floral notes and pine finish.

Spinners Gold (OG 1038, ABV 3.8%)
A golden ale with well-balanced hoppiness, a pleasant citrus taste and a hint of spiciness.

Clogmaker (OG 1043, ABV 4%)
A rich, golden, full-bodied ale with a refreshing fruity flavour and an inkling of cedar and honey.

Lancashire Loom (OG 1046, ABV 4%)
A light golden ale bursting with a real fruit punch of grapefruit, lychees and lemon with a slight floral note.

D Day Dodger (OG 1046, ABV 4.1%)
A red-hued beer with subtle malt aromas, a refreshing rounded bitterness and a crisp, clean, fruity finish.

George 'n' Dragon (OG 1052, ABV 4.8%)
A smooth, full-bodied ale with honey flavours and a well-balanced pine hop aroma.

MASH SIBA ◉

Middle Barn, Burcot Farm, East Stratton, Hampshire, SO21 3DZ
☎ (01962) 795023 ⊕ mashbrewery.com

⊗ MASH began brewing in 2013 using a one-barrel plant. A new 10-barrel plant was installed in 2014. RAIB

Pale (OG 1035, ABV 3.8%)
A pale ale with a subtle aroma and a long bitter finish.

Copper (OG 1037, ABV 3.9%)
A copper-coloured beer with fruity, peachy aromas and a dry bitter flavour.

Gilt (OG 1038, ABV 4.1%)
A golden ale with citrus orange aroma and spice. Dry bitter finish.

Amber (OG 1042, ABV 4.3%)
A well-balanced beer with floral aromas.

Ruby (OG 1045, ABV 4.8%)
A red-coloured ale with a malty, full-bodied finish.

Chocolate Stout (OG 1047, ABV 5%)
A rich, black stout with roasted malt and burnt coffee flavours. Dark chocolate is added during the brew.

Matlock Wolds Farm SIBA

South Barn, Cavendish Road, Farm Lane, Matlock, Derbyshire, DE4 3GZ ☎ 07852 263263 ⊕ woldsfarm.co.uk

Brewing began in 2014 using a 50-litre kit. Production is mostly bottle-conditioned and available locally. Cask-conditioned beers are available by arrangement. The brewery expanded to a 250-litre kit in 2015. RAIB

The Bitter End (OG 1034, ABV 3.4%)
Ruby-coloured ale with a rich, malty background. Earthy, grassy hop flavours and notes of chocolate, nuts and pine with a long, bitter finish.

Apogee (OG 1038, ABV 3.8%)
Medium-bodied amber ale with fruit and citrus aromas. Flavours include orange and grapefruit combined with a light bitterness.

Simcoe (OG 1038, ABV 3.8%)
Aromas of pine and apricot with earthy citrus flavours and hints of tropical fruit leading to a strong bitter finish. Complex for a single hop ale.

Riber Gold (OG 1043, ABV 4.3%)
Traditional medium-bodied golden ale with floral and apricot aromas, hints of tropical fruit and a complex finish.

100cc (OG 1049, ABV 4.9%)

Rounded, light chestnut ale with a malty aroma complemented by orange and pine. Huge citrus flavours with orange and lemon coming through a good bitterness from the hops.

Classic Porter (OG 1049, ABV 4.9%)
Full-bodied and almost black in colour, with a chocolate aroma and hint of vanilla. Full of roasted malt, coffee and a lingering bitterness.

Mauldons SIBA ◉

Black Adder Brewery, 13 Church Field Road, Sudbury, Suffolk, CO10 2YA
☎ (01787) 311055 ⊕ mauldons.co.uk

The Mauldon family started brewing in Sudbury in 1795. The brewery with 26 pubs was bought by Greene King in the 1960s. The current business, established in 1982, was bought by Steve and Alison Sims in 2000. They relocated to a new brewery in 2005, with a 30-barrel plant that has doubled production. One pub is owned and around 150 outlets are supplied. ‼ ⬛ ♦

Micawber's Mild (OG 1035, ABV 3.5%) ◥
Light, easy-drinking mild. Malty smoothness with a rich roast flavour turns into a caramel liquorice aftertaste.

Moletrap Bitter (OG 1038, ABV 3.8%) ◥
Pleasant fulfilling ale, with a dark fruity aroma, sticky toffee mouthfeel and a sweetness that gives depth to the flavour.

Silver Adder (OG 1042, ABV 4.2%) ◥
Light, fruity aroma, dry hoppiness and citrus fruit with rich honey in the taste, and a long, fruity, sweet aftertaste. Refreshing and well balanced.

Suffolk Pride (OG 1048, ABV 4.8%) ◥
A full-bodied, copper-coloured beer with a good balance of malt, hops and fruit in the taste.

Suffolk Punch (OG 1048, ABV 4.8%)

Black Adder (OG 1053, ABV 5.3%) ⬛ ◥
Malty, roasty aroma leads to a well-balanced, full-bodied beer, malty with roast and dark, soft fruit overtones.

Maule SIBA

42 Rothersthorpe Avenue, Northampton, NN4 8JH
⊕ maulebrewing.com

Brewing began in 2014 on a self-built plant. Production is mainly unfiltered keg and bottle-conditioned beers, but cask-conditioned ales are occasionally produced for festivals. Most output is supplied to London outlets. RAIB

Maxim SIBA ◉

1 Gadwall Road, Rainton Bridge South, Houghton-le-Spring, Tyne & Wear, DH4 5NL
☎ (0191) 584 8844 ⊕ maximbrewery.co.uk

◉Rising from the ashes of Sunderland brewer Vaux, Maxim was set up with a 20-barrel plant in Houghton-le-Spring in 2007. More than 100 outlets are supplied direct and two pubs are owned. ‼ ⬛ ♦

Lambtons (OG 1039, ABV 3.8%)
Smooth golden ale with citrus and hoppy flavours.

Samson (OG 1040, ABV 4%)
Traditional chestnut brown best bitter, with a caramel taste and a balance of bitterness.

THE BREWERIES

Ward's Best Bitter (OG 1040, ABV 4%)
A tawny copper-coloured best bitter, with a sweet toasted biscuit flavour, slightly hoppy, slightly fruity.

Swedish Blonde (OG 1042, ABV 4.2%)
This smooth beer is very light in colour, with a refreshing and complex grapefruit flavours on the palate.

Double Maxim (OG 1048, ABV 4.7%)
A smooth and well-balanced brown ale with a fruity, caramel, malty, nutty taste and a hint of sweetness.

American Pride IPA (OG 1055, ABV 5.2%)

Maximus (OG 1062, ABV 6%)
Dark ruby-coloured full-bodied premium ale. Sweet with a liquorice flavour, caramel and dark fruits.

Mayflower

🍴 Dochertys, 14 Upper Dicconson Street, Wigan, WN1 2AD ☎ 07984 404567
✉ info@mayflowerbeer.co.uk

Originally established in Standish in 2001 as a 2.5-barrel plant, which was acquired by the current owner in 2007. Between 2012 and 2016 brewing was undertaken at various guest breweries but a new five-barrel plant has now been established at the rear of the owner's pub.

Maypole

North Laithes Farm, Wellow Road, Eakring, Nottinghamshire, NG22 0AN ☎ 07971 277598
⊕ maypolebrewery.co.uk

☺The brewery opened in 1995 in a converted 18th-century farm building. After changing hands in 2001 it was bought by the former head brewer, Rob Neil, in 2005. ♦

Midge (OG 1035, ABV 3.5%)
Pale, brewed with bags of American hops, lasting bitter finish.

Little Weed (OG 1037, ABV 3.8%)
Deep golden in colour, subtle bitterness from a blend of hops.

Celebration (OG 1038, ABV 4%)
Amber-coloured traditional English ale, slightly nutty overtones.

Gate Hopper (OG 1040, ABV 4%)
Cascade hops give this golden ale a floral aroma and lingering hoppy bitterness.

Hop Fusion (OG 1040, ABV 4.2%)

Major Oak (OG 1042, ABV 4.4%)
A well-balanced, red/brown, full-bodied bitter, hints of fruit and burnt malt.

Wellow Gold (OG 1044, ABV 4.6%)
Refreshing blonde ale, citrus flavours on the nose and aftertaste.

Meantime 👁

Lawrence Trading Estate, Blackwall Lane, London, SE10 0AR
☎ (020) 8293 1111

Office: Norman House, 110-114 Norman Road, London, SE10 9EH ⊕ meantimebrewing.com

⊗ Founded in 2000, Meantime brews a wide range of continental style beer and traditional English bottle-conditioned ales. Two pubs are owned. In 2010 the brewery relocated to larger premises in Greenwich. Its other plant, the Old Brewery at the Old Royal Naval College, Greenwich has been closed since the take over by SABMiller in 2015. Meantime has since been sold to Asahi of Japan.
‼ ☛ RAIB V

Melbourn

All Saints Brewery, All Saints Street, Stamford, Lincolnshire, PE9 2PA
☎ (01780) 752186

No real ale. A famous Stamford brewery that opened in 1825 and closed in 1974. It re-opened in 1994 and is owned by Samuel Smith of Tadcaster (qv). Melbourn brews four handcrafted, organic fruit beers (Cherry, Strawberry, Apricot and Raspberry) using the antique steam-driven brewing equipment. The beers are all organic, sold in bottles only. They are not bottle-conditioned. ‼ V

Melwood SIBA

7 Stanley Grange, Knowsley Park, Merseyside, L34 4AR
☎ (0151) 214 3340 ☎ 07545 265283
⊕ melwoodbeer.co.uk

Melwood began brewing in 2013 using a five-barrel plant in an old dairy that used to house the Cambrinus Brewery. In 2016 the brewery moved to bigger premises in nearby old kennels on the Knowsley Estate. Husand-and-wife team John and Julie Marsen have now been joined by brewer Stan Shaw. Monthly specials are available in the Icons of Rock series. ♦

Lovelight (OG 1038, ABV 3.8%)
Light, hoppy blonde beer. Bold and refreshing with bags of hop aroma and a crisp, biting flavour.

Equinox (OG 1040, ABV 4%)
English pale session bitter.

Deadhead (OG 1041, ABV 4.1%)
A hazy, hoppy beer with a robust yet fruity flavour and aroma.

Citradelic (OG 1051, ABV 5.1%)
A light pale ale with grapefruit, lychee and gooseberry aromas.

Merlin SIBA

3 Spring Bank Farm, Congleton Road, Arclid, Cheshire, CW11 2UD
☎ (01477) 500893 ☎ 07812 352590
⊕ merlinbrewing.co.uk

☺ Established in 2010 using an eight-barrel plant in a farm unit just outside Sandbach. The beers are principally supplied to outlets within a 30-mile radius. The brewery helps its environment by disposing of spent grain and water on the farm.
‼ ♦ RAIB

Merlin's Gold (OG 1038, ABV 3.8%)
Light golden ale with rounded floral citrus flavours.

Excalibur (OG 1039, ABV 3.9%)
A light-coloured session ale. Bitter, hoppy flavours are accompanied by a faint sweetness.

Spellbound (OG 1040, ABV 4%)

A full-flavoured bitter, light chestnut in colour with a dry finish.

The Wizard (OG 1042, ABV 4.2%)
A hoppy, bitter, golden-coloured ale with generous hints of grapefruit flavour.

Dark Magic (OG 1048, ABV 4.8%)
A strong, full-bodied dark mild with a caramel aftertaste.

Dragonslayer (OG 1056, ABV 5.6%)
A dark brew with complex flavours.

Merrie City

See Clark's

Merrimen SIBA ◉

Unit 12, Litchborough Industrial Estate, Northampton Road, Litchborough, Northamptonshire, NN12 8JB ☎ (01327) 831308 ☎ 07414 007999 ⊕ merrimen.co.uk

Merrimen commenced brewing on an eight-barrel plant in 2013. All beers are named on a 'Merri' theme. Outlets include JD Wetherspoon, SIBA, pubs and off-licences in Northampton, Coventry, Warwick and surrounding areas. ♦RAIB

Merri Gold (OG 1034, ABV 3.5%)
A pale golden ale with grapefruit and gentle malt aroma, with a light spice and citrus taste.

Merri One (OG 1035, ABV 3.6%)
A light amber ale with medium bitterness, combining three spicy hops.

Hail Merri (OG 1036, ABV 3.8%)
Deep amber in colour, with a fruity, floral and malty aroma, with a biscuit, bitter taste and a dry finish.

Merri Weather (OG 1038, ABV 4%)
Rich golden beer with five hops, creating a refreshing flavour.

Be Merri (OG 1042, ABV 4.5%)
Premium amber bitter, roasted chocolate malt, and a smooth, rounded taste.

Merry Miner ◉

Unit 20-21, Grendon House Farm, Grendon, Warwickshire, CV9 3DT ☎ 07811 932721 ⊕ merryminerbrewery.com

Merry Miner commenced brewing in 2010. The brewery is based in farm buildings on the outskirts of the village of Grendon, near Atherstone. The brewery and beers are named after the brewer's former occupation. Also brews under the name of Morgans. !!♦

Miners Best Bitter (OG 1035, ABV 3.7%)
A pale, smooth, traditional best bitter with a crisp bitter aftertaste.

Warwickshire's Finest (OG 1036, ABV 3.8%)
Light amber session bitter.

Self Rescuer (OG 1039, ABV 3.9%)
Deep golden in colour with a pleasing bitterness and a smooth, malty aftertaste.

Davy's Lamp (OG 1038, ABV 4%)
Pale, full-flavoured bitter.

Bevin Boys (OG 1039, ABV 4.1%)

An American-style IPA, full of character and aromas, with a pleasant finish.

Cap Lamp (OG 1039, ABV 4.2%)
Mid gold in colour. Refreshing with a crisp bitterness.

Deputy Drop (OG 1040, ABV 4.3%)

Going Underground (OG 1041, ABV 4.4%)

Pit Pony (OG 1041, ABV 4.5%)

Methane (OG 1045, ABV 5%)
Light golden bitter with a citrus bitter finish.

Brewed under the Morgans brand name:

Chedhams Ale (OG 1036, ABV 3.8%)
Dark golden. Tangy with a bitter fruit taste and a tart, hoppy aftertaste. Finishes dry.

Mersea Island

Rewsalls Lane, East Mersea, Essex, CO5 8SX ☎ 07970 070399 ⊕ merseabrewery.co.uk

⊠ The brewery was established at Mersea Island Vineyard in 2005. The brewery supplies several local pubs on a guest beer basis as well as most local beer festivals. It holds its own festival of Essex-produced ales over the four-day Easter weekend. ➤RAIB

Mersea Mud (OG 1036, ABV 3.8%)
An easy-drinking mild with a refreshingly malty flavour.

Yo Boy! (OG 1038, ABV 3.8%)
A session bitter with a long-lasting bitterness on the finish.

Gold (OG 1043, ABV 4.4%)
A refreshing, golden Pilsner-style beer.

Monkeys (OG 1044, ABV 4.4%)
Sweet, lightly smoky and roasted in aroma with smoky, fruity and light herbal flavours.

Skippers (OG 1047, ABV 4.8%)
Dark amber in colour with a good malty flavour and a smooth hop bitterness.

Oyster Stout (OG 1048, ABV 5%)
A traditional oyster stout with the addition of local Mersea Island oysters.

Middle Earth

Rowditch Inn, 246 Uttoxeter New Road, Derby, DE22 3LL ☎ 07504 304564

53 Springfield Road, Etwall, DE65 6JZ ⊕ mebrewco.com

Set up in 2011, Middle Earth uses the 3.75-barrel plant based at the Rowditch Inn in Derby (also used by the Rowditch Brewery, qv). Steve Twells (the Rowditch brewer) established Middle Earth as a separate venture to utilise spare plant capacity to produce different brews for free trade sale. Following the successful start of its first micropub, the brewery will concentrate on house ales and one stout, with all other products to be brewed periodically.

Prancing Pony (OG 1039, ABV 3.9%)
Golden session bitter. Very bitter with a sharp grapefruit flavour and a pepper aroma.

Rivendale (OG 1044, ABV 4.3%)

Honey Dragon (OG 1044, ABV 4.5%)
Balanced golden bitter, with subtle honey notes.

Black Rose (OG 1048, ABV 4.6%)
Chocolate predominates in this stout, with complex malt flavours combined with subtle ginger.

Mighty Oak

14b West Station Yard, Spital Road, Maldon, Essex, CM9 6TW
☎ (01621) 843713 ⊕ mightyoakbrewing.co.uk

⊠ Mighty Oak was formed in 1996 and has expanded considerably following a move to Maldon in 2001. Current capacity is 8,000 barrels a year following the acquisition of two adjacent buildings and enlarged plant. 420 outlets are supplied. Twelve monthly ales are brewed to a theme, which for 2017 is trees. ‼️⊨◆

IPA (OG 1031.5, ABV 3.5%) ◆
Light-bodied, pale session bitter. Hop notes are initially suppressed by a delicate sweetness but the aftertaste is more assertive.

Oscar Wilde (OG 1039.5, ABV 3.7%) 🍺 ◆
Roasty dark mild with suggestions of forest fruits and dark chocolate. A sweet taste yields to a more bitter finish.

Captain Bob (OG 1039.5, ABV 3.8%)
A traditional deep amber-coloured bitter with a fruity and hoppy aroma. A slight sweet maltiness balances an easy-going bitterness, followed by hints of gooseberry, elderflower and grape in the finish.

Maldon Gold (OG 1039.5, ABV 3.8%) ◆
Pale golden ale with a sharp citrus note moderated by honey and biscuity malt.

Kings (OG 1042.6, ABV 4.2%)
A deep golden beer with hoppy fruitiness and orange, nectarine and passion fruit flavours lasting into the finish.

Saxon Strong (OG 1062, ABV 6.5%)
An amber-coloured ale with malt flavours balanced by a strong hop finish. The flavour is caramel and dark berry with hints of wood and toffee.

Mile Tree SIBA

Mile Tree Lane, Wisbech, Cambridgeshire, PE13 4TR
☎ 07858 930363 ⊕ miletreebrewery.co.uk

Mile Tree began brewing in 2012 using a five-barrel plant. Local outlets and beer festivals are supplied. ◆ RAIB

Adventurer (OG 1040, ABV 4%)
Golden, full-flavoured beer with a ripe, generous fruitiness and a fresh, light hop character.

Wellstream (OG 1049, ABV 4.9%)
Ruby brown in colour, full-bodied malty beer with a deep, bittersweet finish.

Milestone SIBA 👁

Great North Road, Cromwell, Newark, Nottinghamshire, NG23 6JE
☎ (01636) 822255 ⊕ milestonebrewery.co.uk

☺Established in 2005, Milestone currently brew on a 12-barrel plant. More than 150 outlets are supplied. ‼️⊨◆ RAIB

Liberty Ale (OG 1037, ABV 3.7%)
Straw-coloured session ale infused with American hops.

Lion's Pride (OG 1038, ABV 3.8%)
Copper-coloured session ale.

Sherwood Pale Ale (OG 1039, ABV 3.9%)

Classic Dark Mild (OG 1040, ABV 4%)

Shine On (OG 1039, ABV 4%)
Straw-coloured session ale with floral and citrus notes.

Loxley Ale (OG 1042, ABV 4.2%)
Golden brew with a subtle hint of honey.

Black Pearl (OG 1043, ABV 4.3%)
A traditional Irish-style stout.

Crusader (OG 1044, ABV 4.4%)

Rich Ruby (OG 1044, ABV 4.5%)
Rich, smooth, creamy Celtic red ale.

American Pale Ale (OG 1046, ABV 4.6%)
A blonde, hoppy, citrus ale.

Colonial Pale Ale (OG 1048, ABV 4.8%)
Light in colour, brewed in the style of a US West Coast pale ale.

Olde English (OG 1049, ABV 4.9%)
Full-bodied winter warmer with a pleasing nutty finish.

Magna Carta Ale (OG 1050, ABV 5%)

Raspberry Wheat Beer (OG 1055, ABV 5.6%)
Continental-style ale infused with fresh fruit.

Milk Street SIBA 👁

⚑ Griffin, 25 Milk Street, Frome, Somerset, BA11 3DB
☎ (01373) 467766 ⊕ milkstreetbrewery.co.uk

⊠ Milk Street was established in 1999 in a former 'private' cinema situated behind the Griffin pub. The cinema is long gone and now houses the brewery, which expanded in 2005 and is capable of producing 30 barrels a week. It mainly produces for its own estate of three outlets and direct delivery to pubs in a 30-mile radius. Wholesalers are used to distribute the beers further afield. ‼️◆

Same Again (ABV 3.9%)
A session ale.

Funky Monkey (OG 1040, ABV 4%)
Copper-coloured summer ale with fruity flavours and aromas. A dry finish with developing bitterness and an undertone of citrus fruit.

The Usual (OG 1045, ABV 4.4%)
Aromas of pear drops and orange marmalade give way to a well-rounded fruitiness and hints of caramel in the taste. The slight sweetness is balanced by a dry, bitter, grainy finish, with hints of raspberry.

Zig-Zag Stout (OG 1046, ABV 4.5%)
A dark ruby stout with characteristic roastiness and dryness with bitter chocolate and citrus fruit in the background.

Beer (OG 1049, ABV 5%)
A blonde beer with musky hoppiness and citrus fruit on the nose, while more fruit surges through on the palate before the bittersweet finish.

Mill Valley (NEW)

Woodroyd Mills, Cleckheaton, BD19 3AF
☎ (0113) 815 1624 ☎ 07565 229560
⊕ millvalleybrewery.co.uk

Ⓐ Brewing began in 2016. Initially using a three-barrel plant, since upgraded to six barrels. ‼

Luddite Ale (ABV 4.2%)

Mill Blonde (ABV 4.2%)

Mill Bitter (ABV 4.3%)

Luddite Dark (ABV 4.6%)

Millis (Dartford Wobbler) SIBA ◉

Dartford Wobbler Brewery, St Margaret's Farm, St Margaret's Road, South Darenth, Kent, DA4 9LB
☎ (01322) 866233 ⊕ dartfordwobbler.com

Ⓐ John and Miriam Millis started with a 0.5-barrel plant at their home in Gravesend. Demand outstripped the facility and Millis moved in 2003 to its current location – a former farm cold store – using a 10-barrel plant. It now supplies to around 40 outlets within a 50-mile radius. ◆ RAIB

Curiously Dark (ABV 3.6%)
A dark mild with a roasted malt flavour and some background fruit notes, leading to a dry aftertaste.

Guinea Guzzler (OG 1037, ABV 3.7%)
Pale, easy-drinking, fruity session beer.

Penny Red (ABV 3.9%)
A red-coloured beer with pungent hop notes, a dry finish and a malty base.

Peddler's Best (ABV 4%)
A copper-coloured bitter with floral fruit notes and a dry, oaky finish.

Golden Wobbler (OG 1041, ABV 4.1%)
A pale gold beer with a hoppy citrus aroma. Grapefruit and light spice flavours in the taste.

Dartford Wobbler (OG 1043, ABV 4.3%)
A tawny-coloured, full-bodied best bitter with complex malt and hop flavours and a long, clean, slightly roasted finish.

Millstone SIBA ◉

Unit 4, Vale Mill, Micklehurst Road, Mossley, OL5 9JL
☎ (01457) 835835 ⊕ millstonebrewery.co.uk

Established in 2003 by Nick Boughton and Jon Hunt, the brewery is located in an 18th-century textile mill. The eight-barrel plant produces a range of pale, hoppy beers and a traditional stout. More than 40 regular outlets are supplied. ◆

Vale Mill (OG 1039, ABV 3.9%)
A pale gold session bitter with a floral and spicy aroma building on a crisp and refreshing taste.

Three Shires Bitter (OG 1040, ABV 4%) ◣
Yellow-coloured beer with hop and fruit aroma. Fresh citrus fruit, hops and bitterness in the taste and aftertaste.

Tiger Rut (OG 1040, ABV 4%)
A pale, hoppy ale with a distinctive citrus/grapefruit aroma.

Stout (OG 1045, ABV 4.5%)
A traditional dry stout; pale chocolate malt, roasted barley, and hint of sweetness to the aroma.

True Grit (OG 1050, ABV 5%)
A well-hopped strong ale with a mellow bitterness and a citrus/grapefruit aroma.

Brewed for the Rising Sun, Mossley:

Rising Sunsation (OG 1047, ABV 4.7%)

A pale, dry bitter with hints of pine.

Milltown SIBA

The Brewery, The Old Railway Goods Yard, Scar Lane, Milnsbridge, West Yorkshire, HD3 4PE ☎ 07946 589645 ⊕ milltownbrewing.co.uk

Ⓐ Milltown began brewing in 2011 using a four-barrel plant. ‼◆

Golden Hop (OG 1037, ABV 3.8%)

Slubbers Gold (OG 1040, ABV 4.2%)

Milton SIBA

Pegasus House, Pembroke Avenue, Waterbeach, Cambridgeshire, CB25 9PY
☎ (01223) 862067 ⊕ miltonbrewery.co.uk

⊠ The brewery has grown steadily since it was founded in 1999. In 2012 the brewery moved to larger premises in the village of Waterbeach. It now operates pubs in Cambridge, London, Peterborough and Norwich through a sister company. ‼

Minotaur (OG 1035, ABV 3.3%) ◣
A dark ruby mild with liquorice and raisin fruit throughout. Light, dry finish.

Dionysus (OG 1037, ABV 3.6%) ◣
Yellow-coloured bitter with a good balance of biscuity malt and citrus hop. Some malt and hops linger on the long, dry aftertaste.

Justinian (OG 1039, ABV 3.9%) ◣
Straw-coloured bitter with pink grapefruit hop character and light malt softness. Dry finish.

Pegasus (OG 1043, ABV 4.1%) ◣
Malty, amber-coloured, medium-bodied bitter with faint hops. Bittersweet aftertaste.

Sparta (OG 1043, ABV 4.3%) ◣
A yellow/gold best bitter with floral hops, kiwi fruit and balancing malt softness which fades to leave a long, dry finish.

Nero (OG 1050, ABV 5%) ◣
A complex black beer comprising a blend of milk chocolate, raisins and liquorice. Roast malt and fruit completes the experience.

Cyclops (OG 1055, ABV 5.3%)
Deep copper-coloured ale, with a rich, hoppy aroma and full body; fruit and malt notes develop in the finish.

Marcus Aurelius (OG 1075, ABV 7.4%) ◣
A powerful black brew brimming with raisins and liquorice. Big balanced finish.

Mitchell Krause

See Tractor Shed

Mithril

Mithril, Aldbrough St John, North Yorkshire, DL11 7TL
☎ (01325) 374817 ☎ 07889 167128
⊕ mithrilales.co.uk

Ⓐ Mithril started brewing in 2010 in old stables opposite the brewer's house on a 2.5-barrel plant. Owner/brewer Pete Fenwick, a well-known craft brewer, brews twice a week to supply the local area of Darlington and Richmond. A new beer is brewed every week. ♦

Dere Street (OG 1039, ABV 3.8%)
Amber-coloured bitter with a fruity, malty sweetness and a smooth, hoppy finish.

A66 (OG 1041, ABV 4%)
A crisp, refreshing, satisfying golden beer. A dry bitterness, with a lingering citrus and spicy hop taste and aroma.

Flower Power (OG 1043, ABV 4.3%)
A pale ale with massive citrus, fruity hop flavour. Hints of grapefruit and floral on the tongue from the late addition of elderflower.

Mix

3 Cemmaes Court Road, Hemel Hempstead, Hertfordshire, HP1 1ST ⊕ mlxbrewery.co.uk

⊗ A small brewery established in 2013 and based in a domestic garage. Beer is produced in small batches allowing for an ever-changing range.

Mobberley SIBA

Unit 2, Barncroft Farm, Woodend Lane, Mobberley, Cheshire, WA16 7LZ
☎ (01565) 872609 ☎ 07879 771209
⊕ mobberleyfineales.co.uk

⊗ Mobberley began brewing in 2011 in an old milking parlour on a working farm in the heart of the Cheshire countryside. ♦

HedgeHopper (OG 1039, ABV 3.8%)
A golden refreshing fine ale, light and aromatic.

RoadRunner (OG 1039, ABV 3.8%)
A light-coloured pale ale with a delicate, lightly spicy finish.

WhirlyBird (OG 1040, ABV 4%)
Pale ale, sweet yet full bodied, with a smooth, subtle, zesty finish.

Moles SIBA ◉

5 Merlin Way, Bowerhill, Melksham, Wiltshire, SN12 6TJ
☎ (01225) 708842 ⊕ molesbrewery.com

Moles was established in 1982 by Roger Catte, a former Ushers brewer, using his nickname for the brewery. 10 pubs are owned, all serving cask beer. More than 200 outlets are supplied direct. ‼ ➑ ♦

Tap Bitter (OG 1035, ABV 3.5%)
A session bitter with a smooth, malty flavour and clean bitter finish.

Gold (OG 1038, ABV 3.8%)
Golden, refreshing hoppy beer with a citrus zest flavour and tropical fruit aroma.

Best Bitter (OG 1040, ABV 4%)
A well-balanced, amber-coloured bitter, clean, dry and malty with some bitterness, and delicate floral hop flavour.

Elmo's Fire (OG 1044, ABV 4.4%)
Medium-bodied pale ale. Refreshingly bitter with a fruity, spicy aroma from the hops, balanced by the malt, leaving a long bitter finish.

Landlords Choice (OG 1045, ABV 4.5%)
A dark, strong, smooth porter, with a rich fruity palate and malty finish.

Rucking Mole (OG 1045, ABV 4.5%)
A chestnut-coloured premium ale, fruity and malty with a smooth bitter finish.

Mole Catcher (OG 1050, ABV 5%)
A copper-coloured ale with a spicy hop aroma and taste, and a long bitter finish.

Molson Coors ◉

Molson Coors (Burton): 137 High Street, Burton upon Trent, Staffordshire, DE14 1JZ
☎ (01283) 511000

Molson Coors (Tadcaster): Tower Brewery, Wetherby Road, Tadcaster, North Yorkshire, LS24 9SD
⊕ molsoncoorsbrewers.com

Molson Coors is the result of a merger between Molson of Canada and Coors of Colorado, US. Coors established itself in Europe in 2002 by buying part of the former Bass brewing empire, when Interbrew (now A-B InBev) was instructed by the British government to divest itself of some of its interests in Bass. Coors owns several cask ale brands. It brews 110,000 barrels of cask beer a year (under licensing arrangements with other brewers) and also provides a further 50,000 barrels of cask beer from other breweries. In 2011 Molson Coors bought Sharp's brewery in Cornwall (qv) in a bid to increase its stake in the cask beer sector. No cask ale is produced in Burton.

Moncada SIBA ◉

Unit 1, Buspace Studios, Conlan Street, London, W10 5AT
☎ (020) 8964 0829 ⊕ moncadabrewery.co.uk

⊗ Moncada began brewing in 2011 using a six-barrel plant. ♦ RAIB

Notting Hill Bitter (ABV 3.7%) �‣
Brown bitter with a good balance of hops and sweetness and a pleasant finish.

Notting Hill Blonde (ABV 4.2%) ➣
Continental-style golden beer with a smooth mouthfeel, sweetish with a touch of honey and fruity hops. Short, crisp finish.

Notting Hill Amber (ABV 4.7%) ➣
Full-bodied, creamy, amber-coloured beer with the citrus aroma and flavour well balanced by the sweet biscuit character.

Notting Hill Porter (ABV 5%) ➣
Rich black porter with dark roast bitterness and black treacle, which linger in the finish. Some faint hoppy notes.

Notting Hill Stout (ABV 5%) ➣
A dry, malty beer with roast, caramel and a little malty sweetness. The pleasant aftertaste is long and lingering.

Notting Hill Ruby Rye (ABV 5.2%) ➣
Sweetish ruby red beer with a full, fruity aroma, a creamy mouthfeel and a little roast throughout.

Mondo

86-92 Stewarts Road, London, SW8 4UG
☎ (020) 7720 0782 ☎ 07453 312170
⊕ mondobrewingcompany.com

⊗ The brewery opened in 2015 using a 10-hectolitre brew kit. A taphouse has been added. ‼ ♦

Monty's SIBA 👁

Unit 1, Castle Works, Hendomen, Montgomery, SY15 6HA
☎ (01686) 668933 🌐 montysbrewery.co.uk

Monty's began brewing in 2009 and was the first brewery in Montgomeryshire since the Eagle brewery in Newtown closed in 1990. Three pubs are leased by the brewery's sister company, Hophouse Inns: Sportsman in Newtown, Powis Arms in Lydbury North and the Cottage Inn in Montgomery. The Cottage also acts as Monty's visitor centre and a microbrewery on the premises is planned. ♦ RAIB GF

Old Jailhouse (OG 1039.5, ABV 3.9%)
Copper-coloured bitter with a good blend of malt and hops.

Midnight (OG 1040, ABV 4%)
A dark, smooth, creamy stout.

Moonrise (OG 1040, ABV 4%)
A copper-coloured, gently malty, well-balanced traditional brew.

MPA (OG 1040.5, ABV 4%)
Pale ale with a good bitter character.

Sunshine (OG 1041, ABV 4.2%)
A golden, hoppy, floral/citrus ale with a pleasantly dry finish.

Masquerade (OG 1046, ABV 4.6%)
A gluten-free premium golden bitter with tropical fruit flavour and hoppy aroma.

Mischief (OG 1050, ABV 5%)
Strong golden ale with a good balance of malt and hop bitterness.

Magnitude (OG 1075.5, ABV 7.5%)
A premium strong golden ale. Smooth with a hint of sweetness in the finish.

Moody Goose (NEW)

King William IV, 114 London Road, Braintree, Essex, CM77 7PU
☎ (01376) 567755
🌐 ign1407423026.site-fusion.co.uk

The brewery is run by Angus and Marian and is located in the grounds of the King William IV Public House in Braintree. Brewing began in 2015 using a four-barrel plant supplying the pub.

Arbor Gold (ABV 3.7%)
A golden ale with floral and fruity aromas. Smooth with slight malt and a green hop finish.

Pigs Head in a Pottage Pot (ABV 3.8%)
A traditional-style ruby ale with plenty of malt and hops giving a pleasant bitter finish.

Stark Mild (ABV 4.2%)
A ruby mild with a gentle blend of malt and fruit and a dry, hoppy finish.

Fibonacci (ABV 5.1%)
A pale ale with a sweet malt taste with malt and fruit aromas and a gentle hoppy finish.

moogBREW (NEW)

1 Copeland Cottages, Marsh Lane, Taplow, Berkshire, SL6 0DF ☎ 07941 241954 ✉ moogbrew@gmail.com

⊠ Situated in a converted garden shed, this 100-litre brewery was set up in 2016 and replaced

contract brewing of its beers by XT Brewing (qv). Two imported stainless steel conical fermenters are used to brew two regular and four seasonal beers. Distribution is targeted to within a five-mile radius of the brewery. ♦

Royal Standard Pale (ABV 3.8%)

Porter (ABV 4.7%)

Moonchild (NEW)

2 Church Gate, Petrockstow, Devon, EX20 3HL
☎ 07585 914120

Moonchild was established in 2016 by Fred and Sophie Caure. All beers are unfined, unfiltered and unpasteurised. Small batch brews are also planned. ♦ RAIB

Bird Of Paradise (OG 1035, ABV 3.5%)
A pale wheat beer.

Gypsy Queen Baltic Porter (OG 1055, ABV 5.5%)
Raisins, dark fruit and chocolate, with a slight hint of roasted coffee.

Harvest Home Red Rye (OG 1055, ABV 5.5%)
Light spices and coffee, with a generous amount of New World hops, adding a fruity note.

IPA (OG 1060, ABV 6%)

Moonshine

Hill Farm, Shelford Road, Fulbourn, Cambridgeshire, CB21 5EQ ☎ 07906 066794

Office: 28 Radegund Road, Cambridge, CB1 3RS
🌐 moonshinebrewery.co.uk

⊠ Established in 2004, the brewery produces up to 20 barrels a week. Locally produced ingredients are used including water from the brewery's own well and barley grown on the farm where the brewery is based. CAMRA beer festivals are supplied throughout the country, with 30 local outlets supplied direct. ♦ RAIB

Trumpington Tipple (OG 1036, ABV 3.6%)
Deep amber ale, medium malt flavours, fragrant hop aroma.

Cambridge Pale Ale (OG 1038, ABV 3.8%)
Golden beer, light to the palate with a dry, citrus finish.

Shelford Crier (OG 1038, ABV 3.8%)

Harvest Moon Mild (OG 1040, ABV 3.9%)

Barton Bitter (OG 1040, ABV 4%) 🍂
Pale brown in colour with red and amber highlights, balanced malt and hops and a fruity backdrop on both nose and palate. A bittersweet flavour dries as fruit and sweetness diminish.

Blueberry Ale (OG 1040, ABV 4.2%)

Cambridge Best Bitter (OG 1041, ABV 4.2%)

Nightwatch Porter (OG 1043, ABV 4.5%)

Black Hole Stout (OG 1048, ABV 5%)

Hot Numbers Coffee Stout (OG 1057, ABV 5.5%)
Dark roasted malt with balanced coffee and hops. The addition of lactose adds sweetness to the flavour.

Chocolate Orange Stout (OG 1068, ABV 6.7%) 🍺

Wheat Wine Ale (OG 1091, ABV 10.5%)
A barley wine produced using wheat instead of barley.

Moonstone

⧮ Ministry of Ale, 9 Trafalgar Street, Burnley, Lancashire, BB11 1TQ
☎ (01282) 830909 ⊕ moonstonebrewery.co.uk

⊛ A small, three-barrel brewery, based in the front room of the Ministry of Ale pub. Brewing started in 2001 and beer is only available in the pub. ‼

Black Star Dark (OG 1037, ABV 3.4%)

Moor SIBA

Days Road, Bristol, BS2 0QS ☎ 0117 ☎ (941 4460)
⊕ moorbeer.co.uk

⊗ Moor Beer was founded in 1996, originally brewing in Ashcott. Since being relaunched in 2007 in Long Sutton the brewery has gone through a steady expansion programme, resulting in the relocation to larger premises in central Bristol featuring a shop and brewery tap. All beers are produced without isinglass finings and are naturally hazy. ‼ ⧮ ♦ RAIB

Revival (OG 1038, ABV 3.8%)
An immensely hoppy and refreshing pale ale.

Nor'Hop (OG 1041, ABV 4.1%)

So'Hop (OG 1041, ABV 4.1%)

Raw (OG 1043, ABV 4.3%) ◥
Pale brown best bitter with a powerful aroma. Bitter orange fruit with a hint of tropical lychee on the tongue. Sweetish background and a bitter finish.

Amoor (OG 1045, ABV 4.5%)
Rich porter with chocolate and nut flavours to the fore and a balancing bitterness.

Dark Alliance (OG 1045, ABV 4.5%)
Hoppy coffee stout.

Illusion (OG 1045, ABV 4.5%)
Session strength version of a black IPA, powerfully hopped.

Confidence (OG 1046, ABV 4.6%)
Hoppy American-style red ale.

Ported Amoor (OG 1047, ABV 4.7%)
Amoor with added Reserve Port.

Radiance (OG 1048, ABV 5%)

Smokey Horyzon (OG 1050, ABV 5%) ◥
A speciality beer made using smoked rye. Hoppy, pale brown, strong ale with plenty of body, balanced by sweetness of unfermented rich dry rye malt and incredibly smoky.

Stout (OG 1050, ABV 5%)

Return of the Empire (OG 1057, ABV 5.7%)

B-Moor (OG 1060, ABV 6%)
A rich porter, with flavours of blueberry chocolate cheesecake.

Hoppiness (OG 1065, ABV 6.5%)

Old Freddy Walker (OG 1073, ABV 7.3%) ▨
Rich, dark, strong ale with a fruity, complex taste, leaving a fruitcake finish.

Moorhouse's SIBA ⊙

The Brewery, Moorhouse Street, Burnley, Lancashire, BB11 5EN
☎ (01282) 422864 ⊕ moorhouses.co.uk

Established in 1865 as a soft drinks manufacturer, the brewery started producing cask-conditioned ale in 1978. A new brewhouse and visitor centre opened in 2012. The company owns three pubs. ‼♦

Black Cat (OG 1036, ABV 3.4%) ◥
A dark mild-style beer with delicate chocolate and coffee roast flavours and a crisp, bitter finish.

Premier Bitter (OG 1036, ABV 3.7%) ◥
A clean and satisfying bitter aftertaste rounds off this well-balanced, hoppy, amber-coloured session bitter.

Pride of Pendle (OG 1040, ABV 4.1%) ▨ ◥
Well-balanced amber best bitter with a fresh initial hoppiness and a mellow, malt-driven body.

Blond Witch (OG 1045, ABV 4.5%) ◥
A light ale, fruity with lasting finish.

Pendle Witches Brew (OG 1050, ABV 5.1%) ◥
Well-balanced, full-bodied, malty beer with a long, complex finish.

Moorstone (NEW) SIBA

Axna Farm, Horndon, Devon, PL19 9NF
☎ (01822) 810418 ☎ 07738 098572
✉ moorstonebrewery@btinternet.com

Paul and Joanna Barton began brewing in 2016 using a 2.5-barrel plant.

Wheal Betsy (OG 1041, ABV 4.1%)
A light, refreshing golden best bitter with a strong malty finish and well-balanced, subtle lemon citrus hop aroma.

Ruby Red (OG 1050, ABV 4.7%)
Brewed with oats, this deep red, full-bodied porter has a silky smooth mouthfeel and a long-lasting finish with hints of chocolate and coffee.

MòR SIBA

Old Mill, Kellas, DD5 3PD ☎ 07884 346351
⊕ morbrewing.co.uk

Retired lifeboat coxswain Jim Hughan teamed up with family friend Ross Niven to establish the 2.5-barrel brewery in 2012. Just over a year later it expanded to a 4.3-barrel plant with five fermenters. In 2016 Matt Forrest joined the business as a co-director following Ross' retirement. ‼♦ RAIB

MòR Calm & Wise (ABV 3.4%)
A pale straw-coloured session ale with citrus notes and a dry finish.

MòR Tea Vicar? (OG 1038, ABV 3.8%)
A pale amber session bitter with a pleasant balance of malt and hops.

MòR Scode (ABV 4%)
A light citrus session ale with overtones of grapefruit and a smooth finish.

MòR Ish! (OG 1042, ABV 4.2%)
A light ale with a malty, fruity aroma and well-balanced, controlled bitter finish.

MòR Please! (OG 1045, ABV 4.5%)
A clean-tasting, full-bodied golden bitter bursting with malt and hops with just a hint of honey.

MòR Ticia (ABV 4.5%)
A full-bodied stout with a hint of coffee and a dark chocolate aftertaste.

Mordue SIBA 👁

Units D1 & D2, Narvic Way, Tyne Tunnel Estate, North Shields, Tyne & Wear, NE29 7XJ
☎ (0191) 296 1879 ⊕ morduebrewery.com

👁In 1995 the Fawson brothers revived the Mordue Brewery name (the original closed in 1879). High demand required moves to larger premises and replacing the original five-barrel plant with a 20-barrel one. The beers are distributed nationally and 300 outlets are supplied direct. ‼ ▦ ◆ RAIB

Five Bridges (OG 1038, ABV 3.6%) ◆
Crisp, golden beer with a good hint of hops, the bitterness carries on in the finish. A good session bitter.

Northumbrian Blonde (OG 1040, ABV 4%) ◆
A blonde beer with a citrus aroma and hoppy finish.

Workie Ticket (OG 1045, ABV 4.5%) ◆
Complex tasty bitter with plenty of malt and hops, long satisfying bitter finish.

Radgie Gadgie (OG 1048, ABV 4.8%) ◆
Strong, easy-drinking bitter with plenty of fruit and hops.

IPA (OG 1051, ABV 5.1%) ◆
Easy-drinking golden ale with plenty of hops, the bitterness carries on in the finish.

Morgans

See Merry Miner

Morland

See Greene King

Morton

Unit 10, Essington Light Industrial Estate, Essington, Staffordshire, WV11 2BH ☎ 07988 69647

Office: 96 Brewood Road, Coven, Staffordshire, WV9 5EF ⊕ mortonbrewery.co.uk

👁The family-run brewery was established in 2006 on a three-barrel, purpose-built plant. 20 outlets are supplied direct plus various beer festivals and a selection is always available at the brewery's own micropub, Hail to the Ale. ‼ ◆ RAIB

Essington Dark Mild (OG 1036, ABV 3.6%)

Essington Bitter (OG 1037, ABV 3.8%)
Fruity, hoppy session ale.

Merry Mount (OG 1037, ABV 3.8%)

Essington Blonde (OG 1039, ABV 4%)
Thirst-quenching pale ale using American hops.

Essington Ale (OG 1041, ABV 4.2%)
Refreshing golden session ale.

Jelly Roll (OG 1041, ABV 4.2%)
Dry-hopped best bitter.

Essington Gold (OG 1044, ABV 4.4%)
A refreshing golden ale.

Essington Supreme (OG 1046, ABV 4.6%)
A premium brown ale, dark and sweet.

Scottish Maiden (OG 1045, ABV 4.6%)
A malty premium bitter.

Essington IPA (OG 1046, ABV 4.8%)

A pale, hoppy IPA.

Moulin

⌂ 2 Baledmund Road, Moulin, Pitlochry, PH16 5EL
☎ (01796) 472196

Correspondence: Moulin Hotel, 11-13 Kirkmichael Road, Moulin, Pitlochry, PH16 5EH
⊕ moulinhotel.co.uk

👁The brewery opened in 1995 to celebrate the Moulin Hotel's 300th anniversary. Two pubs are owned and four outlets are supplied. ‼ RAIB

Light (OG 1036, ABV 3.7%) ◆
Thirst-quenching, straw-coloured session beer, with a light, hoppy, fruity balance, ending with a gentle, hoppy sweetness.

Braveheart (OG 1039, ABV 4%) ◆
An amber bitter, with a delicate balance of malt and fruit and a Scottish-style sweetness.

Ale of Atholl (OG 1043.5, ABV 4.5%) ◆
A reddish, quaffable, malty ale, with a solid body and a mellow finish.

Old Remedial (OG 1050.5, ABV 5.2%) ◆
A distinctive and satisfying dark brown old ale, with roast malt to the fore and tannin in a robust taste.

Mountain Hare

⌂ Mountain Hare Inn, Brynna Road, Brynnau Gwynion, CF35 6PG
☎ (01656) 860453 ⊕ mountainhare.co.uk

👁Paul Jones, licensee of the Mountain Hare, finally realised his ambition of installing a brewery in his family-owned pub. A 1.5-barrel custom-built brewing plant was installed in the pub and the beer first went on sale in 2013, supplying only the pub itself. There are plans for expansion to meet demand.

Gold (OG 1041, ABV 4.1%)
A golden, well-hopped bitter. The blend of three hops provides initial citrus in the mouth giving way to a satisfying bitter finish.

Far Shores IPA (OG 1043, ABV 4.3%)
A well-balanced, pale brown hoppy ale.

Mouselow Farm

3 Mouselow Farm, Dinting, Derbyshire, SK13 7QQ
☎ 07920 048252 ✉ glossopowl@btinternet.com

Mouselow Farm began brewing in 2013 using a 2.5-barrel plant housed in a converted barn. Brewing is on a part-time basis. Local free houses, clubs and beer festivals are supplied. ◆

Golden Gosling (OG 1037, ABV 3.6%)
Light, delicately-hopped bitter.

Cluckstar (ABV 3.7%)
Light, copper-coloured session beer, medium hopped.

Udder the Influence (OG 1041, ABV 4%)
Medium-hopped session bitter using a five-hop combination.

Flying Goose (ABV 4.2%)
A premium bitter with a hoppy character.

Mr Grundy's SIBA

⊟ Georgian House Hotel, 34 Ashbourne Road, Derby, DE22 3AD
☎ (01332) 349806 ⊕ mrgrundysbrewery.co.uk

The brewery opened in 2010 using a four-barrel plant which was made-to-measure to fit into a converted hotel bedroom. Beers are produced for the company's own tavern (Mr Grundy's) and hotels.

Trench Foot (OG 1038, ABV 3.8%)
Darkish-coloured ale with strong malt flavours and some bitterness.

Passchendaele (OG 1039, ABV 3.9%)
A straw-coloured pale, sharp bitter with citrus overtones.

Big Willie (OG 1043, ABV 4.3%)
Thirst-quenching golden ale packed with a lasting dry bitter finish.

Bullet (OG 1043, ABV 4.3%)
Dark ale with a treacle aroma and a smooth rounded taste.

The Red Baron (OG 1043, ABV 4.3%)
A rich, malty, dark red bitter with strong caramel overtones, lightly hopped to allow the malt flavours to permeate.

No Man's Land (OG 1045, ABV 4.5%)
Dark-coloured yet hoppy beer, retaining the soft malty flavours of a traditional bitter.

Mr Majolica

Units 7a & 15, Thurrock Enterprise Centre, Maidstone Road, Grays, Essex, RM17 6NF ☎ 07834 539761 ⊕ mrmajolica.co.uk

⊗ A family-run microbrewery situated in Grays town centre, Mr Majolica began brewing in 2014 on a 2.5-barrel plant. Pubs and clubs are supplied around Essex, north Kent and east London.

Buccaneer (ABV 3.8%)
An amber-coloured session ale.

Phantom (ABV 4%)
A black porter made from a complex mix of malts.

Vanguard (ABV 4.1%)
An easy-drinking ale, light brown in colour.

Enterprise (ABV 4.5%)
A pale ale.

Evolution (ABV 4.8%)
A hearty red/brown-coloured ale.

Muirhouse

Unit 1, Enterprise Court, Manners Avenue, Manners Industrial Estate, Ilkeston, Derbyshire, DE7 8EW
☎ 07916 590525 ⊕ muirhousebrewery.co.uk

Muirhouse was established in 2009 in a domestic garage in Long Eaton. It expanded in 2011 to an industrial unit in Ilkeston using a 7.5-barrel plant. ‼ ◆ RAIB

Summit Hoppy (OG 1041, ABV 4%)
A pale session beer.

Magnum Mild (OG 1045, ABV 4.5%)
A dark, smooth strong mild.

Pirate's Gold (OG 1045, ABV 4.5%)
Golden beer with hint of caramel.

Hat Trick IPA (OG 1052, ABV 5.2%)

Mulberry Duck

Elan Portway, Burghill, Herefordshire, HR4 8NF
☎ 07740 468675 ⊕ mulberryduck.co.uk

Mulberry Duck opened in 2012 in a former dairy using a 3.75-barrel plant. Beers are supplied to the local free trade.

Golden Sparkle (OG 1038, ABV 3.8%)

Copper Bottom (OG 1041, ABV 4.1%)

Mumbles SIBA 👁

Unit 8, Clarion Court, Clarion Close, Swansea Enterprise Park, Swansea, SA6 8RF
☎ (01792) 792612 ☎ 07757 109938

Office: 23 Oakland Road, Mumbles, SA3 4AQ
⊕ mumblesbrewery.co.uk

⊗ Mumbles was established in 2011 and began brewing in 2013. The beers are supplied to numerous pubs in South Wales and the Bristol area. In 2014 brewing took place using spare capacity at other local breweries but a permanent home was found in 2015 using a 10-barrel plant installed on Swansea's Enterprise Park. Director/brewer Rob Turner has initiated collaborative projects with other breweries, including Hopcraft and Grey Trees. ◆

Mile (OG 1039, ABV 4%)
A light-coloured, hoppy session bitter.

Gold (OG 1042, ABV 4.3%)
A light, refreshing, thirst-quenching pale ale with lingering lemon and lime flavours.

Oystermouth Stout (OG 1043, ABV 4.4%)
A rich, creamy head and dark roasted malt flavours distinguish this classic stout, with real oysters added.

Lifesaver Strong Bitter (OG 1048, ABV 4.9%)
A smooth, malty, bronze-coloured ale, easy-drinking with a clean hop finish.

India Pale Ale (OG 1052, ABV 5.3%)
A traditional IPA, light gold in colour with a distinct marmalade taste and aroma. Easy-drinking, well-rounded and full bodied.

Musket SIBA

Unit 7, Loddington Farm, Loddington Lane, Linton, Kent, ME17 4AG ☎ 07967 127278
⊕ musketbrewery.co.uk

Musket began production in 2013 in refurbished mushroom sheds at Loddington Farm, in the heart of the Kent countryside. In the 1700s the local area was used for military training camps for what seemed like the inevitable invasion from France, hence the brewery and beer names. ◆

Trigger (OG 1032, ABV 3.6%)
A hoppy, easy-drinking session ale.

Fife & Drum (OG 1034, ABV 3.8%)
A golden ale with tastes and aromas of spice, honey, marmalade, floral and the merest hint of wild blackcurrant.

Flintlock (OG 1037, ABV 4.2%)
A best bitter with spicy orange undertones and just a hint of marmalade.

Muzzleloader (OG 1044, ABV 4.5%)
Smoky and dark in colour, with the faint spicy aroma of orange.

Myrddins (NEW)

≣ Church Street, Barmouth, LL42 1EH
☎ (01341) 388060 ✉ myrddins@talktalk.net

Established in 2016, Myrddins is a small brewery within a café bar in the centre of Barmouth.

Nailsworth

≣ Village Inn, The Cross, Nailsworth, Gloucestershire, GL6 0HH ☎ 07963 200768
⊕ nailsworth-brewery.co.uk

After 96 years commercial brewing returned to Nailsworth in 2004. Beers are sold mainly at the Village Inn above the brewery and at its new outlet, the Star Inn, Fishponds, Bristol. ‼ ♦ RAIB

Alestock (OG 1036, ABV 3.6%)
A light-coloured ale full of elderflower notes.

Mayor's Bitter (OG 1042, ABV 4.3%)
A best bitter with malt textures complemented by a long-lasting taste of blackcurrant.

Old Rocky (OG 1044, ABV 4.4%)
Light IPA-style beer with loads of grapefruit flavour.

Town Crier (OG 1046, ABV 4.5%)
A premium ale with delicate grassy and floral overtones.

Red October (OG 1049, ABV 4.9%)
A ruby-coloured, rich and malty, well-balanced strong bitter.

Naked Brewer

≣ Corner Pin, Palmerston Street, Westwood, Nottinghamshire, NG16 5HY ☎ 07908 531901
✉ cornerpinwestwood@hotmail.co.uk

The brewery was set up in 2010 in a skittle alley behind the Corner Pin pub and can be viewed from the function room. Beer is mainly brewed for the pub but is occasionally supplied to beer festivals or for swaps with other brewpubs. ‼ ♦

Hopsession (OG 1038, ABV 3.8%)
A light amber bitter retaining a smooth creamy head, with a strawlike aroma and crisp bitter finish.

Blush (OG 1045, ABV 4.5%)
A dark ruby bitter with caramel undertones and a mid bitter finish.

Palindrome (OG 1048, ABV 4.7%)
Smooth creamy porter with a mellow bitter finish.

Nant SIBA

Penrhwylfa, Maenan, Llanrwst, LL26 0UF ☎ 07723 036862 ⊕ bragdynant.co.uk

⊗ Nant commenced brewing in 2007 with a plant purchased from the Yorkshire Dales Brewery. Capacity is currently 10-15 nine gallon firkins a week. ♦ RAIB

Brenin (OG 1038, ABV 3.8%)
A light golden session ale with balanced hops and malt.

Cwrw Chwarel (OG 1036, ABV 3.8%)

Pale gold session ale.

Cwrw Coryn (OG 1042, ABV 4.2%)
Traditional amber-coloured beer. Slightly malty with good bitter overtones.

Chwaden Aur (OG 1043, ABV 4.3%)
Golden orange-coloured ale with a citrus aroma and full mouthfeel. Grapefruit and lemon citrus taste balance with biscuity malt for a long, fruity finish.

Rwster (OG 1046, ABV 4.6%)
Deep copper-coloured, sweet and malty ale.

Mwnci Nel (OG 1055, ABV 5.5%)
A special dark ale, not excessively sweet but dominated by burnt chocolate flavours, balanced with hops.

Navigation SIBA

≣ Trent Navigation Inn, 17 Meadow Lane, Nottingham, NG2 3HS
☎ (0115) 986 9877 ⊕ navigationbrewery.com

Brewing began in 2012 in the old stable block of the Trent Navigation Inn. The brewery is owned by sister company Great Northern Inns and supplies cask beers to the pubs in its estate. ‼

Britannia (OG 1038, ABV 3.8%) ♠
Tawny-coloured, malty bitter.

New Dawn Pale (OG 1039, ABV 3.9%) ♠
Golden-coloured ale with initial fruit and hops and a bitter finish.

Golden Anchor (OG 1041.8, ABV 4.3%) ♠
A golden best bitter.

Eclipse (OG 1043.5, ABV 4.4%) ♠
Dark roast stout aroma and aftertaste with bitterness and some sweetness.

Classic IPA (OG 1050, ABV 5.2%) ♠
Golden IPA, hoppy and bitter throughout.

Apus (OG 1054, ABV 5.5%)
American-style IPA, deceptively drinkable with a lasting aftertaste.

Naylor's SIBA 👁

Midland Mills, Station Road, Cross Hills, North Yorkshire, BD20 7DT
☎ (01535) 637451 ⊕ naylorsbrewery.com

☺The Naylor brothers started brewing in 2005 at the Old White Bear pub in Cross Hills. The brewery moved to Midland Mills in 2006 and transferred to a larger unit on the same site in 2012. Occasional restaurant evenings and comedy nights are held in the upstairs private function room. 70 outlets are regularly supplied and around 1,000 on an occasional basis. ‼ ➟ ♦

Aire Valley Bitter (OG 1037, ABV 3.8%) ♠
Predominantly malty traditional mid-brown bitter with subtle fruit and hops in the nose and taste and a growing bitter finish.

Velvet (OG 1039, ABV 3.9%) ♠
Chocolate and roast aromas and flavours predominate in this dark brown mild which has an increasingly roast bitter finish.

Brew 1919 (OG 1039, ABV 4%)

Pinnacle Blonde (OG 1041.5, ABV 4.3%) ♠

Hoppy, fruity aroma followed by grassy hop and tropical fruit flavours. The finish remains hoppy with a bitter, fruity edge.

Black & Tan (OG 1042, ABV 4.4%) ◆
Dark brown best bitter with a roast edge and a hop hit. Liquorice and a malty sweetness lead to a bitter finish.

Old Ale (OG 1054, ABV 5.9%)
A smooth beer with sweet maltiness, balanced by subtle bitterness. Strong but easy drinking.

Neath

Endeavour Close, Port Talbot, SA12 7PT ☎ 07772 468436 ⊕ neathales.co.uk

Neath Ales was established in 2009 and produces a range of single hop variety beers. Some beers are released under the Black Falls brand name. ◆ RAIB V

Firebrick (OG 1042, ABV 4.2%)
Amber-coloured best bitter with British hop flavour and aroma.

Witch Hunter (OG 1042, ABV 4.2%)
Well-balanced ruby ale with roasted malt and hop fruit flavours.

Deliverance (OG 1045, ABV 4.5%)
Smooth bronze-coloured beer.

Dewi Sant (OG 1048, ABV 4.8%)
A pale ale with a nicely balanced hop fruit flavour.

Gold (OG 1050, ABV 5%)
Citrus/grapefruit hop aroma and flavour dominate this golden ale.

Black (OG 1055, ABV 5.5%)
A strong black ale with dark malt flavours balanced by aggressive hopping rates.

Green Bullet (OG 1060, ABV 6%)
IPA with massive hop aroma and flavour.

Neatishead (NEW)

⬛ White Horse Inn, The Street, Neatishead, Norfolk, NR12 8AD
☎ (01692) 630828
⊕ thewhitehorseinnneatishead.com

⊗ Brewing began in 2015 at the White Horse Inn. The brew kit can be viewed through glass from the restaurant. Beer is only available in the pub at present. A range of semi-regular beers are brewed with at least one ever-changing ale.

Neepsend (NEW)

Units 1-3, Lion Works, Mowbray Street, Sheffield, South Yorkshire, S3 8EN
☎ (0114) 276 3406 ☎ 07545 323427
✉ gavin@neepsendbrewco.com

☺Established in 2015 by James Birkett, Richard Appleton and Gavin Martin after taking over Little Ale Cart Brewery and moving to new premises in Sheffield's 'Valley of Beer'. A 10-barrel plant is used, supplying beers locally, including to the company's own pubs, Sheaf View, the Blake Hotel and the Wellington. Members of the Sheffield Brewers Cooperative. ◆

Blonde (OG 1039, ABV 4%)
Easy-drinking session blonde with a short finish.

IPA (OG 1047, ABV 5%)

Assertive bitterness balanced by fruity hop flavours with a dry finish.

Stout (OG 1049, ABV 5.2%)
Rich, full-bodied and robust dry stout with roasty notes of coffee and dark chocolate.

Nelson SIBA

Unit 2, Building 64, The Historic Dockyard, Chatham, Kent, ME4 4TE
☎ (01634) 832828 ⊕ nelsonbrewery.co.uk

☺Based in Chatham's Historic Dockyard and brewing on a nautical theme, the brewery supplies award-winning ales direct to more than 330 outlets. ‼ 🍽 ◆ RAIB

Pieces of Eight (OG 1040, ABV 3.8%)
A light, refreshing ale with full-flavoured hops and a hint of chocolate aftertaste.

Admiral IPA (OG 1040, ABV 4%)
A traditional IPA with a combination of citrus flavours on the palate.

Midshipman Dark Mild (OG 1040, ABV 4%)
A dark mild leaving a roasted aftertaste on the palate.

Trafalgar Bitter (OG 1040, ABV 4.1%)

Powder Monkey (OG 1043, ABV 4.3%)
A golden ale with a smooth aftertaste which leaves a sweetness on the palate.

Friggin' in the Riggin' (OG 1046, ABV 4.5%)
Premium bitter with smooth malt flavour and bittersweet aftertaste.

Pursers Pussy Porter (OG 1051, ABV 4.8%)

Nelsons Blood (OG 1062, ABV 6%)
A strong, malty ale with mellow roast tones, slightly nutty and fruity with a warm aftertaste.

Nene Valley SIBA

Oundle Wharf, Station Road, Oundle, Station Road, PE8 4DE
☎ (01832) 272776 ⊕ nenevalleybrewery.com

⊗ Established in 2011, a bespoke 15-barrel plant was installed in former Water Board premises on expansion in 2012. Further expansion in 2016 has doubled the floorspace allowing an increase in fermentation vessels. A brewery tap, Tap & Kitchen, opened on the same site in 2014. ‼ 🍽 ◆ RAIB GF

Simple Pleasures Ale (OG 1036, ABV 3.6%)
A light, clean and refreshing beer with a pleasing citrus hop aroma and flavour.

Lone Star (OG 1037, ABV 3.7%)

Blonde Session Ale (OG 1037, ABV 3.8%)

Dark Horse (OG 1040, ABV 3.8%)
A dark ruby mild with roasted grains giving hints of chocolate, coffee and liquorice.

Jim's Little Brother (OG 1038, ABV 3.8%)
A session strength IPA, warmly golden with pleasant passionfruit and grapefruit hop flavours.

Bitter (OG 1040, ABV 4.1%) 🍺 ◆
Floral hop and malt aroma introduces a full, clean biscuit malt taste balanced by bitterness and some fruit, ending with a long malt and bitter finish.

Starless Stout (OG 1042, ABV 4.2%)

Smooth oat stout, refreshing dark grain flavours with a slight hop bite to finish.

Australian Pale (OG 1044, ABV 4.4%)
A rich golden ale with a floral aroma preceding citrus and tropical fruit flavour from the Australian hops.

Release the Chimps (OG 1045, ABV 4.4%)

DXB Special Bitter (OG 1045, ABV 4.6%)
Chestnut in colour with plenty of maltiness. Balanced with late-hopped spicy character.

Grapefruit Saison (OG 1051, ABV 5.1%)

Big Bang Theory (OG 1051, ABV 5.3%)
Well-balanced pale ale with a huge hop aroma giving way to malty sweetness and a gentle bitter finish.

Jim Irving Pale (OG 1056, ABV 5.6%)
Full-bodied, with a malty taste backed with heaps of zesty hop flavour.

Bible Black (OG 1065, ABV 6.5%)
Initial rich and fruity flavours give way to a chocolate and roasted finish.

Fenland Farmhouse Saison (OG 1057, ABV 7.2%)
Refreshing Belgian-style ale with a hint of spice.

Mid-week Bender (OG 1070, ABV 7.4%)

Neon Raptor (NEW)

Stumble Inn, 37 Tamworth Rd, Long Eaton, Derbyshire, NG10 1JF ☎ 07415 273048

Office: 133 Green Lane, Derby, DE1 1RZ ✉ neontigerbrewingco@gmail.com

Neon Raptor was established in 2016 and uses spare capacity at the Songbird Brewery (qv).

Neptune (NEW)

1 Sefton Lane, Maghull, Merseyside, L31 8BX ☎ (0151) 222 3908 ⊕ neptunebrewery.com

Neptune began brewing in 2016, upgrading from a one-barrel plant to six barrels. **V**

Riptide (ABV 3.6%)

Brown Ale (ABV 3.7%)

Triton (ABV 4.4%)

Amberjack (ABV 4.5%)

King of the Sea (ABV 4.7%)

Abyss (ABV 5%)

Jack May (ABV 6.3%)

Ness (NEW)

🏠 c/o Old Three Pigeons, Nesscliffe, Shropshire, SY4 1DB ☎ (01743) 741279 ✉ info@3pigeons.co.uk

⊠ Brewing commenced in 2015 at the Three Pigeons pub using a two-barrel plant.

Humphrey's Tipple (OG 1039, ABV 3.9%)

Nethergate SIBA

Growler Brewery, The Street, Pentlow, Essex, CO10 7JJ ☎ (01787) 283220 ⊕ nethergatebrewery.co.uk

⊠ Starting at Clare in 1986 the brewery moved to Pentlow, Essex in 2005, where after large growth

there is still room to expand. The brewery name, under new owners, was changed to Growler but in 2014 original owner Dick Burge returned and restored Nethergate. ‼️🍴♦

IPA (OG 1036, ABV 3.5%) ◈
Bitter-tasting session beer with some fruit and malt balancing the predominate hop character. Dry aftertaste.

Priory Mild (OG 1036, ABV 3.5%) ◈
A 'black bitter' rather than a true mild. Strong roast and bitter tastes dominate throughout.

Umbel Ale (OG 1039, ABV 3.8%) ◈
Pleasant, easy-drinking bitter, infused with coriander, which dominates.

Growler Bitter (OG 1040, ABV 3.9%) ◈
Light tasting, sweetish and fruity session beer.

Suffolk County Best Bitter (OG 1041, ABV 4%) ◈
Dark bitter with roast grain tones off-setting biscuity malt and powerful hoppy, bitter notes.

Stour Valley Gold (OG 1043, ABV 4.2%)
A light golden ale, smooth and refreshing with a well-rounded bitterness. Hoppy with a slightly fruity taste in the finish.

Old Growler (OG 1051, ABV 5%) ◈
Well-balanced porter in which roast grain is complemented by fruit and bubblegum.

Umbel Magna (OG 1051, ABV 5%) ◈
Old Growler flavoured with coriander. The spice is less dominant than in Umbel Ale, with some of the weight and body of the beer coming through.

New Bristol

20a Wilson Street, Bristol, BS2 9HH ☎ 07837 976871 ⊕ newbristolbrewery.co.uk

⊠ Brothers Tom and Noel commenced brewing in 2013 on a five-barrel plant. Capacity has since been increased to fifteen barrels. All beers are unfined, unfiltered and unpasteurised. ♦ RAIB

365 (OG 1041, ABV 4%)
A session bitter with plenty of up front malt and toffee, married with Challenger, Fuggles and Cascade hops.

Oolala (OG 1040, ABV 4.2%)
An amber-coloured beer balanced by sweet spicy notes with hints of citrus and herbs and the zest of 60 lemons.

Beer Du Jour (OG 1046, ABV 4.6%) ◈
A bittersweet, strong bitter with citrus fruit aromas and flavours which continue in the aftertaste.

New Inn

🏠 New Inn, 112 Roberttown Lane, Roberttown, Liversedge, West Yorkshire, WF15 7NP ☎ (01924) 402069 ⊕ thenewinnroberttown.com

Brewing commenced in 2012 using a half-barrel brew plant located in the cellar of the New Inn, Liversedge. The beer is produced in wood-clad vessels by Andrew Kenyon, the son of ex-brewer at the Riverhead Brewery, Joe Kenyon. ♦

Pale Bob (OG 1038, ABV 3.8%)

Golden Bob (OG 1040, ABV 4%)
A golden beer with a refreshing aftertaste.

Rusty Bob (OG 1045, ABV 4.5%)

A smooth, malty, traditional Yorkshire bitter packed with flavour and a slightly bitter aftertaste.

Bobcastle Brown (OG 1046, ABV 4.6%)
A dark brown ale, smooth and easy-drinking with a pleasant bitter aftertaste.

Bobmeister (OG 1049, ABV 4.9%)
Lager-based golden ale with German hops for a full flavour.

Bombay Bob (OG 1060, ABV 6%)
A strong, pale beer full of flavours with ginger, cardamom and mint to the fore.

New Lion SIBA

Station Road, Totnes, Devon, TQ9 5JR
☎ (01803) 226277 ⊕ lioncraftbrewery.com

⊗ The original Lion Brewery closed in 1926 and was restarted in 2013 by four local business people. The only memorabilia found for the old brewery is a mirror for the 'Celebrated Totnes Stout', which the brewery revived. Experimental brews are tested through customers in the Bay Horse, Totnes. There is a commitment to providing apprenticeship opportunities and work experience for people with learning difficulties. ♦ RAIB

Mane Event (OG 1039, ABV 3.8%)
A golden brown, well-balanced modern session bitter.

TQ9 (OG 1042, ABV 4.2%)
A golden and refreshing summer ale with a hint of Earl Grey.

Totnes Stout (OG 1045, ABV 4.4%)
Silky and smooth due to the addition of oats, this stout offers a good mouthfeel coupled with deep roasted and coffee notes. Unfined.

Pandit IPA (OG 1046, ABV 4.9%)
A citrus and floral nose. These flavours are complemented on the palate by a well-defined, biscuity malt character.

New Plassey

Eyton, LL13 0SP ☎ 07769 155874
✉ plassey.brewery@gmail.com

Plassey brewery was founded in 1985 on the 250-acre Plassey Estate. Following the merger of Plassey and the Gertie Sweet Brewery in 2012, the New Plassey Brewery was formed.

New World Pale (OG 1039, ABV 3.9%)
A pale beer, well-balanced with a hoppy bite.

Plassey Bitter (OG 1040, ABV 4%) ◆
Smooth and malty best bitter, reddish brown in colour, with a good hop and fruit balance and a dry finish.

Midnight Mild (OG 1042, ABV 4.2%)
A medium strength mild with a fullness of character and flavour. Dark and subtle.

Offa's Dyke (OG 1043, ABV 4.3%)
Pale, crisp and refreshing bitter.

Dusky Maiden Stout (OG 1044, ABV 4.4%)
A dark, complex-flavoured stout.

Deep Porter (OG 1045, ABV 4.5%)
A smooth, deep brown porter.

Cherry Diva (OG 1047, ABV 4.7%)
A pale beer with a subtle flavour of Maraschino cherry.

Cwrw Tudno (OG 1050, ABV 5%)
A pale, strong bitter.

Dragons Breath (OG 1060, ABV 6%) ◆
Well-balanced strong bitter. Plum fruit in aroma with the initial sweetness followed by a powerful smack of hops and fruit.

New River (NEW) SIBA

Unit 47, Hoddesdon Industrial Centre, Pindar Road, Hoddesdon, Hertfordshire, EN11 0FF
☎ (01992) 446200 ⊕ newriverbrewery.co.uk

⊗ New River commenced brewing in 2015, operating with all new equipment and using fresh yeast. Around six local pubs are supplied regularly plus beer festivals. ‼♦

London Tap (OG 1038, ABV 3.8%)

Riverbed Red (OG 1041, ABV 4.2%)

Five Inch Drop (OG 1044, ABV 4.6%)

Newark SIBA ⊙

77 William Street, Newark, Nottinghamshire, NG24 1QU ☎ 07804 609917 ⊕ newarkbrewery.co.uk

Newark Brewery was established in 2012 on the site of a former maltings using an eight-barrel plant. The bulk of production is supplied to local pubs. Its brewery tap is the Ram in Castle Gate, Newark.

Best (OG 1038, ABV 3.8%)
Deep copper in colour with a biscuity malt nose. Sweet toffee dominates the palate with a long, fruity finish.

NPA (Newark Pale Ale) (OG 1039, ABV 3.8%)
Pale gold in colour, citrus lemon on the nose, leading to a fruity finish.

BLH4 (OG 1040, ABV 4%)

Norwegian Blue (OG 1040, ABV 4%)
Deep gold in colour. Grapefruit and citrus orange on the nose. Malty lemon on the palate with a long finish.

Winter Gold (OG 1040, ABV 4%)
Dry golden ale with bittersweet lemon citrus flavours.

Pure Gold (OG 1045, ABV 4.5%)
A rich gold in colour with biscuit and burnt orange on the nose leading to a soft biscuit finish.

Summer Gold (OG 1045, ABV 4.5%)
Deep gold in colour with a strong, sweet citrus nose. The lime character and light malt balance produce a lasting finish.

Phoenix (OG 1048, ABV 4.8%)
Russet brown in colour, slight spice and roasted malt on the nose, with a fruity treacle, full-bodied finish.

5.5 (OG 1055, ABV 5.5%)
Deep gold strong ale, strong honey on the nose with sweet soft fruits on the finish.

Newbridge

Unit 3, Tudor House, Moseley Road, Bilston, West Midlands, WV14 6JD ☎ 07970 456052
⊕ newbridgebrewery.co.uk

First established in 2014, the five-barrel plant incorporates six original Grundy cellar tanks. Since first installed, the brewery has undergone a number of modifications and improvements and is now in regular production.

Little Fox (OG 1042, ABV 4.2%)

Solaris (OG 1045, ABV 4.5%)

Indian Empire (OG 1051, ABV 5.1%)

Newby Wyke SIBA

Unit 24, Limesquare Business Park, Alma Park Road, Grantham, Lincolnshire, NG31 9SN
☎ (01476) 565682 ⊕ newbywyke.co.uk

⊠ The brewery is named after a Hull trawler skippered by brewer Rob March's grandfather. It started life in 1998 as a 2.5-barrel plant in a converted garage then moved to premises behind the Willoughby Arms, Little Bytham. In 2009 it moved back to Grantham with a brew length of 10 barrels. ‼◆

Banquo (OG 1036, ABV 3.8%)
Pale blonde in colour with a full hoppy taste and a long, fruity finish.

Orsino (OG 1037, ABV 4%)
A blonde ale with a bright, fruity citrus and mango taste moving to a soft citrus hop finish.

Comet (OG 1039, ABV 4.1%)
Single-hopped amber ale, slight malt undertones with a gooseberry citrus fruit finish.

Kingston Topaz (OG 1039, ABV 4.2%)
A single-hopped ale with floral undertones.

Black Beerd (OG 1040, ABV 4.3%)
Oat malt stout with a balanced malt palate and fruit undertones.

Bear Island (OG 1043, ABV 4.6%)
A blonde beer with a hoppy aroma and a crisp, dry finish.

White Squall (OG 1044, ABV 4.8%) ◆
Blonde-hued with a hoppy aroma. Generous amounts of hop are well-supported by a solid malty undercurrent. An increasingly bittersweet tang makes itself known towards the finish.

Nine Standards

See Settle

Ninety-Ninety (NEW)

Side End Cottage, Macclesfield Road, Kettleshulme, Cheshire, SK23 7QU ✉ ninety90brewco@gmail.com

Brewing began in 2016 using spare capacity at RedWillow Brewery (qv) in Macclesfield.

No. 18 Yard

See Shepherd Neame

Nobby's SIBA

▤ **Unit 2, Cottingham Way, Thrapston, Northamptonshire, NN14 4PL**
☎ (01832) 730800 ⊕ nobbysbrewery.co.uk

Paul 'Nobby' Mulliner started commercial brewing in 2004 on a 2.5-barrel plant at the rear of the Alexandra Arms, Kettering. The brewery relocated to the Ward Arms, Guilsborough, in 2007 where a

14-barrel plant was installed at the rear and subsequently expanded. The full range of beers is bottled in-house. 2014 saw another move to larger premises in Thrapston. ‼➾◆RAIB

Claridges Crystal (OG 1036, ABV 3.6%)
Pale summer ale, crisp and fresh with a slightly citrus hop finish.

Guilsborough Guzzler (OG 1036, ABV 3.6%)
An easy-drinking, malty auburn ale with a gentle hop finish.

Best (OG 1037, ABV 3.8%)
A session ale with a good hop finish.

Guilsborough Gold (OG 1041, ABV 4%)
Golden ale with full-bodied, well-balanced traditional hop finish.

Wild West (OG 1046, ABV 4.6%)
Mahogany-coloured beer, full and flavoursome.

Tow'd Navigation (OG 1067, ABV 6.1%)
Dark, strong ale. Rich malt and hops and wonderfully warming.

Nook SIBA

▤ **Riverside, 7b Victoria Square, Holmfirth, West Yorkshire, HD9 2DN**
☎ (01484) 682373 ⊕ thenookbrewhouse.co.uk

☺The Nook Brewhouse is built on the foundations of a previous brewhouse dating back to 1754, next to the River Ribble. Two brewery taps are supplied, one with a restaurant whose dishes are matched with the beer brewed on site. A history room with renovated archives dating back to the 1700s and a brewery shop are planned. ‼

Yorks (OG 1037, ABV 3.7%) ◆
A well-balanced bitter with light malt and hop aroma and hop and fruit in the taste, developing in strength. A good session beer.

Baby Blond (OG 1038, ABV 3.8%)
A pale ale packed with hop flavours and citrus notes for a refreshing finish.

Rescue Red (OG 1038, ABV 3.8%)
A deep red ale, subtly hopped to give a floral aroma and finish that are balanced with the rich malt base.

Best (OG 1040.5, ABV 4.2%) ◆
An easy-drinking best bitter with hints of malt and floral hops in the aroma. The taste has an abundance of hops and fruit and a pleasant, crisp, malty aftertaste.

Blond (OG 1042.5, ABV 4.5%) ◆
A golden ale with intense hop and fruit tastes, which lessen in the aftertaste.

Oat Stout (OG 1052, ABV 5.2%)
A distinctive stout that gains it rich flavour and full body from the whole oats added to every brew which help impart dark chocolate and liquorice notes.

Norfolk SIBA ◉

Moon Gazer Barn, Harvest Lane, Hindringham, Norfolk, NR21 0PW
☎ (01328) 878495 ⊕ norfolkbrewhouse.co.uk

⊠ Brewing began in 2012 using a 10-barrel plant. The brewery is owned and run by Rachel and David Holliday. Chalk-filtered water is used from the brewery's own well. ‼◆

Moon Gazer Amber Ale (OG 1040, ABV 4%)
An amber-coloured ale with a full-bodied bitterness, fruity overtones and a smooth, lasting finish.

Moon Gazer Golden Ale (OG 1040, ABV 4%)
A golden ale with a fresh, citrus aroma. Well-hopped with fruit and hop flavour carrying through to the refreshing, crisp, dry finish.

Moon Gazer Ruby Ale (OG 1040, ABV 4%)
A ruby-coloured bitter with a rich, spicy, roasted aroma and a full malty body, resulting in a full-bodied mouthfeel.

Moon Gazer Dark Mild (OG 1051, ABV 4.9%)
A strong dark mild with a subtle blackcurrant aroma. Full-bodied with a rich, fruity, sweet finish.

Moon Gazer Gold IPA (OG 1051, ABV 5%)
A well-hopped IPA, fruity with a building bitterness leading to a crisp, dry finish.

Norland

c/o Bridestones Brewery, Smithy Farm, Long Causeway, Blackshaw Head, West Yorkshire, HX7 7JB
☎ 07475 085385 ✉ norlandbeersltd@outlook.com

Founded in 2014, Norland uses spare capacity at Bridestones Brewery (qv).

Barnstormers (OG 1040, ABV 3.8%) ◆
Amber-coloured, refreshing session bitter. Mellow fruity flavour with hints of caramel that linger into the aftertaste, where a dry bitterness unfolds.

Moorish Mild (OG 1042, ABV 4%) ◆
Malty, caramel and fruit flavours combine in a smooth-drinking, refreshing , tawny-coloured mild with a lingering toffee finish.

Showcase (ABV 4.2%) ◆
A full-bodied and well-rounded red ale. The hoppy taste is balanced by smooth malt and mellow fruit, leading to a long, dry finish.

North (NEW)

Unit 6, Taverner's Walk Industrial Estate, Sheepscar Grove, Leeds, West Yorkshire, LS7 2PT
☎ (0113) 345 3290 ⊕ northbrewing.com

☺Brewing began in 2015, originally supplying the North Bar group of bars in Leeds. It has since grown and supplies other outlets. ‼ ☒ ◆

Prototype (ABV 3.8%)
A session beer; light citrus with a floral and herbal aroma.

Sputnik (ABV 5%)

Transmission (ABV 6.9%)

North Cotswold SIBA ◉

Unit 3, Ditchford Farm, Stretton-on-Fosse, Warwickshire, GL56 9RD
☎ (01608) 663947 ⊕ northcotswoldbrewery.co.uk

☺North Cotswold started in 1999 as a 2.5-barrel plant, which was upgraded in 2000 to 10 barrels. ☒ ◆ RAIB

Windrush Ale (OG 1036, ABV 3.6%)
A thirst-quenching, amber-coloured session bitter, brewed with English hops for a traditional taste. A malty, slightly sweeter palate.

Moreton Mild (OG 1038, ABV 3.8%)

A classic dark mild with a nutty palate.

Cotswold Best (OG 1040, ABV 4%)
An easy-drinking, copper-coloured best bitter.

Shagweaver (OG 1045, ABV 4.5%)
A pale hoppy bitter made with a trio of New Zealand hops.

Hung, Drawn 'n' Portered (OG 1050, ABV 5%) ▣
Strong, dark-coloured porter with a malty finish.

North Curry

The Old Coach House, Gwyon House, Church Road, North Curry, Somerset, TA3 6LH ☎ 07928 815053
⊕ thenorthcurrybrewerycouk.com

☒ The brewery opened in 2006 and is attached to one of the oldest properties in North Curry, where brewing last took place in the village in the 1920s. Beers are available at farmers markets in Taunton and Minehead and in local shops. ◆ RAIB

Howzat (OG 1036, ABV 3.7%)
A golden ale with fruity hop flavours and a smooth aftertaste.

Curry Gold (OG 1038, ABV 3.9%)
A golden ale with a fruity aroma. Maize flakes are added to give a smooth sweetness in contrast to the bitter hops.

Red Heron (OG 1041, ABV 4.3%)
A full-bodied, malty-flavoured ale, balanced by hop bitterness.

The Withyman (OG 1042, ABV 4.6%)
The malty flavour has a bitterness and punch from the fruity hops.

Level Headed (OG 1043, ABV 4.7%)
A traditional old English ale made with chocolate malt. Dark ruby in colour, rich and full of flavour.

Alfred's Stout (OG 1047, ABV 5.1%)
A black, dry stout with a robust flavour.

North Riding (Brewery)

Unit 9, Betton Business Park, Racecourse Road, East Ayton, Scarborough, North Yorkshire, YO13 9HD
☎ (01723) 864845 ☎ 07930 843868
⊕ northridingbrewery.com

Brewing commenced in 2015 on a 10-barrel plant with four core beers. ◆ RAIB

USA Session IPA (OG 1039, ABV 3.8%)
A pale and hoppy session IPA using three different American hops.

Cascade Pale Ale (OG 1042, ABV 4%)
A US-hopped pale ale with unique citrus qualities.

Mosaic Pale Ale (OG 1044, ABV 4.3%)
Packed with blueberry and citrus flavours.

Citra Pale Ale (OG 1045, ABV 4.5%)
Easy-drinking premium pale ale with a grapefruit and lemon taste and aroma.

North Riding (Brewpub)

⌷ North Marine Road, Scarborough, North Yorkshire, YO12 7HU
☎ (01723) 370004 ⊕ northridingbrewpub.com

Brewing commenced in 2011 using a two-barrel plant situated in the cellar of the pub, which is now brewing to capacity with three fermenting vessels. ◆ RAIB

Peasholm Pale Ale (OG 1042, ABV 4.3%)
Pale and hoppy ale with a citrus bitterness and a long, smooth finish.

North Union (NEW)

Matrix Business Centre, Nobel Way, Dinnington, Sheffield, South Yorkshire, S25 3QB
☎ (01909) 547033 ⊕ northunionbrewing.co.uk

Brewing began in 2016 using spare capacity at Harthill Village Brewery (qv). No real ale.

North Wales

Tan-y-Mynydd, Moelfre, Abergele, LL22 9RF ☎ 0800 083 4100 ⊕ northwalesbrewery.net

John Wood established his brewery in 2007. In 2012 a bore hole was drilled to supply water for brewing. Mead and soft drinks are also produced. RAIB

Bodelwyddan Bitter (OG 1038, ABV 3.8%)

Chilli Beer (OG 1040, ABV 4%)

Dandelion & Burdock (OG 1040, ABV 4%)

Abergele Ale (OG 1050, ABV 5%)

Welsh Stout (OG 1052, ABV 5.2%)

North Yorkshire SIBA

Pinchinthorpe Hall, Pinchinthorpe, North Yorkshire, TS14 8HG
☎ (01287) 630200 ⊕ nybrewery.co.uk

☺Founded in Middlesbrough in 1989 the brewery moved to Pinchinthorpe Hall, a moated, listed medieval estate near Guisborough in 1998. Its own spring water produces a distinctive flavour. More than 100 trade outlets are supplied. Most cask beers are organic with some occasional beers not so. More than 20 different beers are produced: please see website for full list. ‼ ☞ ♦ RAIB

Northbound (NEW) SIBA

Campsie Industrial Estate, McLean Road, Eglinton, BT47 3XX ⊕ northboundbrewery.com

The brewery was established in 2015, producing bottle-conditioned beers. RAIB

Northern Alchemy

The Lab, The Cumberland Arms, St James Street, Newcastle upon Tyne, NE6 1LD ☎ 07834 386333 ⊕ wearenorthernalchemy.com

Brewing began in 2014. Production is mostly keg but some cask-conditioned beer is available.

Northern FC

🏳 McCracken Park, Great North Road, Gosforth, Newcastle upon Tyne, NE3 2DT
⊕ northernfootballclub.co.uk

Established in 2012 to supply the clubhouse for the Northern RUFC. The range is developing.

Northern Monk SIBA ◉

The Old Flax Store, Marshalls Mill, Holbeck, Leeds, West Yorkshire, LS11 9YJ

☎ (0113) 243 6430 ⊕ northernmonkbrewco.com

Based in a Grade II-listed mill building in the centre of Leeds, Northern Monk started brewing as cuckoo brewers in 2013 and set up at the new site in 2014 using a 10-barrel plant.

True North (OG 1037, ABV 3.7%) ◂
Hops dominate this dark gold beer, but there is a bitterness which builds in strength then lingers in the finish.

Monacus NZ Pale Ale (OG 1045, ABV 4.5%) ◂
Floral hops and citrus fruits are present throughout; the finish of this yellow-coloured beer is lingering and dry.

Northumberland SIBA ◉

Accessory House, Barrington Road, Bedlington, Northumberland, NE22 7AP
☎ (01670) 822112 ⊕ northumberlandbrewery.co.uk

☺Brewing began in 1996 in Ashington using a five-barrel plant. Relocation and expansion mean that the brewery now uses a 10-barrel plant and has an on-site brewery tap, Fuggles. 30-40 barrels are brewed each week of a wide range of ales. ‼ ♦

Pit Pony (OG 1039, ABV 3.8%)

Fog on the Tyne (OG 1040.5, ABV 4.1%)

Norton

Norton Priory, Tudor Road, Manor Park, Runcorn, Cheshire, WA7 1SX
☎ (01928) 716971 ☎ 07767 354674
⊕ nortonbrewing.com

Situated within the grounds of Norton Priory, the brewery was created as a social enterprise by Halton Borough Council to provide employment opportunities for people with learning disabilities, autism and other disabilities. It opened in 2011 with a 2.5-barrel plant and began bottling in 2012.

Noss Beer Works SIBA

Unit 6, Ash Court, Pennant Way, Lee Mill, Devon, PL21 9GE ☎ 07977 479634 ⊕ nossbeerworks.co.uk

⊠ Noss Beer Works, based in Lee Mill, was formed in 2012 using a six-barrel plant. The beers are made from only the finest locally sourced hops and malts. ‼ RAIB

Black Rock (ABV 4%)
A black IPA with liquorice, citrus and caramel notes. Slightly bitter aftertaste.

Church Ledge (OG 1040, ABV 4%)
A late hopped blonde IPA, light, hoppy and zesty.

Mew Stone (OG 1043, ABV 4.3%)
A copper-coloured ale, well-balanced and refreshing.

Ebb Rock (OG 1049, ABV 4.9%)
A full-bodied, dark copper-coloured beer.

Nottingham SIBA ◉

Plough Inn, 17 St Peter's Street, Radford, Nottingham, NG7 3EN
☎ (0115) 942 2649 ☎ 07815 073447
⊕ nottinghambrewery.co.uk

The former owners of the Bramcote and Castle Rock Breweries re-established the Nottingham

Brewery in 2000 in a purpose-built brewhouse behind the Plough Inn. Philip Darby and Niven Balfour set out to revive the brands of the original Nottingham Brewery, closed by Whitbread in the 1950s, with a view to supplying local outlets within the LocAle ethos. ‼

Rock Ale Bitter Beer (OG 1038, ABV 3.8%) 🗌 ◆
A pale and bitter, thirst-quenching, hoppy beer with a dry finish.

Rock Ale Mild Beer (OG 1038, ABV 3.8%) 🗌 ◆
A reddish-black malty mild with some refreshing bitterness in the finish.

Legend (OG 1040, ABV 4%) ◆
A fruity and malty pale brown bitter with a touch of sweetness and bitterness.

Extra Pale Ale (OG 1042, ABV 4.2%) ◆
A hoppy and fruity golden ale with a hint of sweetness and a long-lasting bitter finish.

Dreadnought (OG 1045, ABV 4.5%) ◆
Well-balanced best bitter. Blend of malt and hops give a rounded, fruity finish.

Bullion (OG 1047, ABV 4.7%) ◆
A refreshing premium golden ale. Brewed with a single malt variety, it is triple-hopped and exceptionally bitter.

Supreme (OG 1052, ABV 5.2%) ◆
A strong, amber, fruity ale. A touch of malt in the taste is followed by a sweet and slightly hoppy finish.

Brewed for the Broadway Cinema Cafébar, Nottingham:

Broadway Reel Ale (OG 1044, ABV 4.4%)
Hoppy, amber best bitter. Occasionally found at beer festivals.

Brewed for the Trent Bridge Inn, West Bridgford:

Trent Bridge Inn Ale (OG 1038, ABV 3.8%)
Tawny, traditionally-hopped bitter.

Nutbrook

6 Hallam Way, West Hallam, Derbyshire, DE7 6LA
☎ 0800 458 2460 ⊕ nutbrookbrewery.com

Nutbrook was established in 2007. In addition to a regular range, special beers are brewed to order for domestic and corporate clients. The brewery's unique 'Design-a-Beer' system allows customers to design and brew their own beer. On Saturdays cask-conditioned beer is sold at Oakfield Farm, Stanley Common. ‼ ⟲ RAIB

The Mild Side (OG 1036, ABV 3.6%)
Golden mild with a traditional malt taste and fruit tones.

Responsibly (OG 1041, ABV 4%)
A light bronze-coloured, crisp beer with a fruity flavour.

Banter (OG 1040.8, ABV 4.5%)
A light golden yellow beer, with a traditional hoppy taste and floral notes.

Daft Apeth (ABV 4.5%)
A pale yellow-coloured beer brewed with English hops.

More (OG 1047, ABV 4.8%)
Dark beer with a subtle red tint, burnt roasted barley taste and sweet bitterness.

Black Beauty (OG 1054, ABV 5%)

A traditional milk stout with a secret ingredient giving undertones of chocolate, honey and nuts.

The Perfect Fifth (OG 1047.8, ABV 5%)
A strong pale ale with honey tones.

Moderation (ABV 5.5%)
A golden ale with subtle flavours and medium bitterness.

D. O'Brien

Unit 13, Enderby Road Industrial Estate, Whetstone, Leicestershire, LE8 6HZ
☎ (0116) 286 3166 ⊕ dobrienbrewery.co.uk

D. O'Brien commenced brewing in 2016 using a four-barrel plant. One regular beer is produced along with a rotating selection of seasonal and one-off brews. The brewery also supplies fresh brewing ingredients to home brewers via its online shop. ◆

Fearless City Ale (OG 1043, ABV 4.5%)
A golden beer with a firm and smooth bitterness with subtle lemon and citrus from the hops.

O'Hanlon's

See Hanlons

Oakham SIBA ⊚

🏠 2 Maxwell Road, Woodston, Peterborough, Cambridgeshire, PE2 7JB
☎ (01733) 370500 ⊕ oakhamales.com

⊗ The brewery started in 1993 in Oakham, Rutland, and moved to Peterborough in 1998. The brewery's main production site is a 75-barrel plant. An additional six-barrel plant is located at its city-centre brewpub, which makes special and one-off brews. Around 350 outlets are supplied and four pubs are owned. ‼ ⟲ ◆ RAIB

JHB (OG 1038, ABV 3.8%) ◆
Straw-coloured golden ale dominated by citrus hop character throughout. Long dry, slightly astringent finish.

Inferno (OG 1039, ABV 4%) ◆
The citrus hop character of this straw-coloured brew begins on the nose and builds in intensity on the palate. Clean, dry, citrus finish.

Citra (OG 1042, ABV 4.2%) ◆
Refreshing grapefruit and peach aroma and flavour characterise this golden ale. Bittersweet palate gives way to a long, dry aftertaste.

Scarlet Macaw (OG 1043, ABV 4.4%)
Tart gooseberry and soft peach on the nose and intense bitter finish.

Bishops Farewell (OG 1046, ABV 4.6%) ◆
Powerfully citrus, the hops and fruit on the aroma of this golden/yellow beer become bittersweet on the palate. Zesty citrus aftertaste.

Oakleaf SIBA ⊚

Unit 7, Clarence Wharf Industrial Estate, Mumby Road, Gosport, Hampshire, PO12 1AJ
☎ (023) 9251 3222 ⊕ oakleafbrewing.co.uk

⊗ Ed Anderson set up Oakleaf with his father-in-law, Dave Pickersgill, in 2000. The brewery stands on the side of Portsmouth harbour. Some 350 outlets are supplied direct with national deliveries via wholesalers. ‼ ☞ ♦ RAIB

Heart of Gold (OG 1038, ABV 3.8%)
An easy-drinking golden ale with a hint of spices and balanced sweetness.

Quercus Folium (OG 1040, ABV 4%)
A traditional mid-brown bitter with an inital malty flavour leading to a long, hoppy finish.

Nuptu'ale (OG 1042, ABV 4.2%) ◗
An intense spicy, floral aroma leads to a complex hoppy taste. Well-balanced with malts and citrus flavours and a hint of sweetness.

Hole Hearted (OG 1048, ABV 4.7%) ◗
Amber-coloured with a strong floral hop aroma. Continuing into the flavour, with some malt, leading to a long, bittersweet finish.

**I Can't Believe It's Not Bitter
(OG 1048, ABV 4.9%)**
Clean and crisp with a fruity aftertaste.

India Pale Ale (OG 1053, ABV 5.5%)
This beer is initially dry and bitter. Full-flavoured and complex marmalade/aniseed notes to follow, which leaves a lingering bitterness on the palate.

Brewed for Suthwyk Ales:

Old Dick (OG 1038, ABV 3.8%) ◗
Pleasant, clean-tasting pale brown bitter. Easy-drinking and well-balanced.

Liberation (OG 1042, ABV 4.2%)
Light-coloured with a soft, berry fruit flavour.

Skew Sunshine Ale (OG 1046, ABV 4.6%) ◗
An amber-coloured beer. Initial hoppiness leads to a fruity taste and finish.

Palmerston's Folly (OG 1050, ABV 5%)
A clear wheat and barley beer. Slightly dry with a hint of honey in the aftertaste.

Oakwood (NEW)

Northfield Crescent, Wells-next-the-Sea, Norfolk, NR23 1LP ☎ 07512 111211 ⊕ oakwoodbrewery.com

Oakwood brewery was established in 2015. After producing beers on a small scale from home the brewer decided to turn his hobby into a full time job. Barley is locally-grown by Teddy Maufe at Branthill Farm on the Holkham Estate in Norfolk. RAIB

Oban Bay

See Argyll

Occasional

Roosters of Babylon, Babylon Lane, Babylon Lane, Devon, EX5 4DT ☎ 07506 355318
⊕ occasionalbrewing.co.uk

The Occasional Brewing Company was established in 2014. It currently concentrates on producing bottle-conditioned beers, although the occasional cask does get into the trade. Beers can be found at a number of local retailers, at farmers' markets and other events. RAIB

Odcombe

🍺 Masons Arms, 41 Lower Odcombe, Odcombe, Somerset, BA22 8TX
☎ (01935) 862591 ⊕ masonsarmsodcombe.co.uk

Odcombe opened in 2000, but closed a few years later. It re-opened in 2005 with assistance from Shepherd Neame (qv). Brewing takes place once a week and beers are available only in the Masons Arms. ‼ ♦

No. 1 (OG 1040, ABV 4%)
A traditional best bitter.

Spring (OG 1042, ABV 4.1%)
Amber ale, light and hoppy with floral notes.

Roly Poly (OG 1042, ABV 4.3%)
A ruby-coloured beer with juniper berries and star anise.

Odyssey

🍺 Brockhampton Brewery, Oast House Barn, Whitbourne, Herefordshire, WR6 5SH
☎ (01885) 483496 ☎ 07918 553152
⊕ odysseybrewco.com

⊠ This six-barrel brewery was bought in 2014 by Alison and Mitchell Evans, who also own the Beer in Hand in Hereford. The original building, a restored barn on a National Trust estate, has been retained. ☞

Syren (OG 1039, ABV 3.9%)

Mo' Citra (OG 1040, ABV 4%)

Little India Pale Ale (OG 1045, ABV 4.5%)

Latte Stout (OG 1062, ABV 5.4%)

Nirvana (OG 1052, ABV 5.4%)

31st State (OG 1049, ABV 5.8%)

Crowd Control (OG 1060, ABV 6%)
Massively-hopped West Coast IPA.

Cookie Monster (OG 1045, ABV 6.5%)
Chocolate raisin, cinnamon and oatmeal cookie stout.

Offa's Dyke

🍺 Chapel Lane, Trefonen, Shropshire, SY10 9DX
☎ (01691) 656889

☺Established in 2007, the brewery and adjoining pub straddle the old England/Wales border, Offa's Dyke. The Olde Vaults and adjacent Ironworks in Oswestry serve as alternative brewery taps.
‼ ☞ ♦ RAIB

Barley Gold (OG 1038, ABV 3.6%)
A full-bodied session bitter. Bitterness with hops and fruit. Lingering bitterness.

Offa's Pride (OG 1040, ABV 3.8%)
A well-rounded bitter with a fruity finish.

Thirst Brew (OG 1042, ABV 4%)
A malty premium bitter with a bitter finish.

Grim Reaper (OG 1050, ABV 5%)
Dark and smooth with a rich flavour. Roast and chocolate dominate the aroma. Not too sweet for its gravity.

Offbeat SIBA

Units 4-5, Thomas Street, Crewe, CW1 2BD ☎ 07502 096438 ⏺ offbeatbrewery.com

☺Offbeat began brewing in 2010 and in 2016 scaled down to a two-barrel plant focusing on local sales and its own bar in the brewery. The brewery tap is open Thursday and Friday evenings. A monthly open night is held the first Friday of the month with live music. ‼ ⛟ ◆ RAIB

Outlandish Pale (OG 1037.8, ABV 3.9%)
A pale session beer with a burst of lemon hoppiness on the palate.

Kooky Gold (OG 1041, ABV 4.1%)
Light, golden session ale, easy-drinking with a low bitterness.

Odd Ball Red (OG 1040.4, ABV 4.2%)
A ruby-coloured ale with a bold fruitiness and masses of Columbus hops giving a spicy flavour and finish.

Disfunctional Functional IPA (ABV 4.8%)
A heavily-hopped IPA.

Out of Step IPA (OG 1055.3, ABV 5.8%)
An American-style IPA. Generously hopped with abundant citrus flavours leading to a dry, bitter finish.

Okell's SIBA 👁

Kewaigue, Douglas, Isle of Man, IM2 1QG ☎ (01624) 699400 ⏺ okells.co.uk

☺Founded in 1874 by Dr Okell, this is the main brewery on the island and moved in 1994 to a new, purpose-built plant at Kewaigue. All the beers are produced under the Manx Brewers' Act. ‼ ◆

MPA (Manx Pale Ale) (OG 1036, ABV 3.6%) ◄
A golden-coloured, fruity session bitter with background sweetness and a rising hoppy finish.

Bitter (OG 1035, ABV 3.7%) ◄
A gently bittered, sweet beer with some fruit and malt flavours.

Olaf (OG 1040, ABV 3.9%)
Deep black in colour with aromas of coffee and liquorice.

Dr Okell's IPA (OG 1044, ABV 4.5%) ◄
A clean, fruity, sweetish bitter with an alcoholic bite.

Alt (OG 1050, ABV 4.9%)
A copper-coloured beer with a fresh flavour, with hints of gooseberry and citrus.

Steam (OG 1052, ABV 5%)
Dark gold in colour, with a citrus, herb, sherbet and resin aroma and a spicy, bitter palate.

Old Bear

See Bridgehouse

Old Bog

🍺 Masons Arms, 2 Quarry School Place, Headington, OX3 8LH
☎ (01865) 764579 ✉ theoldbog@hotmail.co.uk

Originally established in 2005 behind the Masons Arms, Headington, the brewer is again producing Old Bog beers at the pub after a short spell of brewing them at the Old Forge brewery. The beers, when available, are sold at the Masons Arms (generally at weekends) and occasionally at local beer festivals. A number of one-off brews appear throughout the year. ◆

Half Wit (OG 1045, ABV 4.5%)
A malty, amber-coloured wheat beer.

Quarry Goldish (OG 1046, ABV 4.6%)
Golden ale with mild fruit notes and a sweet finish.

Wheat Beer (OG 1050, ABV 5%)
Pale gold in colour with a light citrus hoppiness.

Monstrous Mild (OG 1056, ABV 5.6%)
Strong, smooth, dark mild with fruity and malty tastes.

Old Cannon

🍺 86 Cannon Street, Bury St Edmunds, Suffolk, IP33 1JR
☎ (01284) 768769 ⏺ oldcannonbrewery.co.uk

⊗ The former St Edmunds Head pub re-opened in 1999 as the Old Cannon Brewery complete with a unique state-of-the-art brewery housed in the bar area. A growing number of outlets are supplied across East Anglia. ‼ ◆

Best Bitter (OG 1037, ABV 3.8%) ◄
Traditional East Anglian bitter. Rich, hoppy aroma and bitterness dominate throughout with just a hint of sweetness in the aftertaste.

Gunner's Daughter (OG 1052, ABV 5.5%) ◄
A well-balanced strong ale with a complexity of hop, fruit, sweetness and bitterness in the flavour, and a lingering hoppy, bitter aftertaste.

Old Chimneys

Hopton End Farm, Church Road, Market Weston, Suffolk, IP22 2NX
☎ (01359) 221411/221013
⏺ oldchimneysbrewery.com

Old Chimneys opened in 1995, moving to a converted farm building in 2001. Most of the beers are named after rare species found nearby. ‼ ⛟ ◆ RAIB

Military Mild (OG 1035, ABV 3.3%) ◄
A rich, dark mild with good body for its gravity. Sweetish toffee and light roast bitterness dominate, leading to a dry aftertaste.

Great Raft Bitter (OG 1040, ABV 4%)
Pale copper bitter bursting with fruit. Malt and hops add to the sweetish fruity flavour, which is rounded off with hoppy bitterness in the aftertaste.

Black Rat Stout (OG 1048, ABV 4.4%)
Roast malt and coffee flavours with body and sweetness from added lactose.

Golden Pheasant (OG 1044, ABV 4.5%)
Pale, dry bitter with citrus, apple and malt balanced with robust hop bitterness.

Arrowhead (OG 1047, ABV 4.8%)
A premium dark, ruby ale with smooth, malty tones.

Old Cross

🍺 Old Cross Tavern, 8 St Andrew Street, Hertford, SG14 1JA
☎ (01992) 583133

⊗ The microbrewery was set up in 2008 and is located within the pub. Owner Nigel Beviss brews solely for the Old Cross Tavern. A range of beers is produced during the year including beers brewed with single variety hops. One of these is usually available at the bar. ♦

Gertcha! (OG 1039, ABV 3.9%)

Old Dairy SIBA ◉

Units 2 & 3, Tenterden Station Estate, Station Road, Tenterden, Kent, TN30 6HE
☎ (01580) 763867 ⊕ olddairybrewery.com

⊗ Old Dairy was founded in 2009. It relocated from Rolvenden in 2014 to larger premises near the Kent & East Sussex Railway in Tenterden in order to increase brewing capacity. There is a brewery shop offering discounts to CAMRA members. ‼ ╤ ♦ RAIB

Red Top (OG 1038, ABV 3.8%) ◗
A sweetish copper-coloured bitter with hints of caramel and a subtle hop character.

Ak1911 (OG 1041, ABV 4.1%)
Brewed to a historic recipe of a long lost Kent brewery. East Kent Goldings hops give a pleasant fruity character, balanced with a sweet, biscuity malt and hints of honey.

Copper Top (OG 1041, ABV 4.1%)
Dark, full-flavoured best bitter.

Gold Top (OG 1043, ABV 4.3%) ◗
A well-balanced golden ale with a good blend of malt and hops followed by a long, bittersweet finish.

Blue Top (OG 1048, ABV 4.8%) ◗
Rich and full-bodied, this pale brown ale has a long bittersweet finish and a hint of aroma hop.

Snow Top (OG 1060, ABV 6%) 🍺
Malty and fruity winter ale brewed for Christmas.

Old Forge

🍺 Radnor Arms, 32 Coleshill, Coleshill, Oxfordshire, SN6 7PR
☎ (01793) 861575 ⊕ oldforgebrewery.co.uk

⊗ Old Forge began brewing in a converted outbuilding at the Radnor Arms in 2010 using a four-barrel plant. ‼ ♦ RAIB

Anvil Ale (OG 1037, ABV 3.8%)
Light session ale, amber-coloured with traditional bitterness.

Blacksmith's Gold (OG 1042, ABV 4%)
Refreshing straw-coloured ale with citrus notes and a hoppy floral finish.

Hammer & Tongs (OG 1043, ABV 4.2%)
Ruby chestnut in colour, bitter yet mellow in taste.

Sledgehammer (OG 1048, ABV 5%)
Deep red, full-bodied premium ale with hints of chocolate and caramel.

Old Inn

🍺 Old Inn, Flowerdale Glen, Gairloch, IV21 2BD
☎ (01445) 712006 ⊕ theoldinn.net

Brewing began in 2010 using a 150-litre plant. ♦

Erradale IPA (OG 1041, ABV 4.2%)

The Blind Piper (OG 1046, ABV 4.6%)

Old Laxey

🍺 Shore Hotel Brew Pub, Old Laxey, Isle of Man, IM4 7DA
☎ (01624) 863214 ⊕ shorehotel.im

Beer brewed on the Isle of Man is brewed to a strict Beer Purity Act. Additives are not permitted to extend shelf life, nor are chemicals allowed to assist with head retention. Old Laxey's beer is sold mostly through the adjacent Shore Hotel. ‼

Bosun Bitter (OG 1038, ABV 3.8%)
Crisp and fresh with a hoppy aftertaste.

Old Luxters

Chiltern Valley Vineyard, Hambledon, Henley-on-Thames, RG9 6JW
☎ (01491) 638330 ⊕ chilternvalley.co.uk

Situated in a 17th-century barn beside the Chiltern Valley Vineyard. Old Luxters is a traditional brewery established in 1990 and was awarded a Royal Warrant of Appointment in 2007. The core range is bottle-conditioned beers. ‼ ╤ ♦ RAIB

Old Market

Old Market Hall, Palace Street, Caernarfon, LL55 1RR

Situated in a 19th-century former market hall building, close to Caernarvon Castle. The six-barrel plant can be viewed within the premises. The beer is usually only available in the Old Market Hall bar, but may sometimes be found in other local outlets.

A55 (OG 1042, ABV 4.2%)

Genius (OG 1052, ABV 5.2%)

Old Mill SIBA

Mill Street, Snaith, East Yorkshire, DN14 9HU
☎ (01405) 861813 ⊕ oldmillbrewery.co.uk

Opened in 1983 in a 200-year-old former malt kiln and corn mill, the brew-length is 60 barrels. The brewery is building a tied estate, now standing at 18 houses. Beers can be found nationwide through wholesalers and around 80 free trade outlets are supplied direct. ‼ ♦

Traditional Mild (OG 1034, ABV 3.4%) ◗
A satisfying roast malt flavour dominates this easy-drinking dark mild.

Traditional Bitter (OG 1038.5, ABV 3.8%) ◗
A malty nose is carried through to the initial flavour. Bitterness runs throughout.

Blonde Bombshell (OG 1042, ABV 4%)
A straw-coloured beer, easy drinking due to delicate and refreshing fruity flavours.

Red Goose (OG 1042, ABV 4.2%)
A rich, ruby-coloured, malty beer.

Old Curiosity (OG 1044.5, ABV 4.5%) ◗
Slightly sweet amber brew, malty to start with. Malt flavours all the way through.

Bullion (OG 1047.5, ABV 4.7%) ◗
The malty and hoppy aroma is followed by a neat mix of hop and fruit tastes within an enveloping maltiness. Dark brown/amber in colour.

Old Pie Factory SIBA ◉

Montague Road, Warwick, CV34 5LW

THE BREWERIES

☎ (01926) 402100 ⊕ oldpiefactorybrewery.co.uk

☺Old Pie Factory began brewing in 2011 using a 5.5-barrel plant. The brewery is located at Underwood Wines and is a joint venture between Underwood Wines, the Old Fourpenny Shop Hotel in Warwick and the Case is Altered in Five Ways.

Bitter (OG 1038.5, ABV 3.9%)
Classic English session bitter with only English ingredients.

Pale (OG 1040, ABV 4.1%)
Light and refreshing straw-coloured ale with pleasing hoppy notes.

Old Sawley SIBA

🏠 White Lion, 352 Tamworth Road, Sawley, Derbyshire, NG10 3AT ☎ 07722 311209 ⊕ oldsawley.com

Old Sawley Brewing Company was established in 2013, initially on a half-barrel plant but expansion to a 10-barrel plant is planned. The brewery supplies Midland beer festivals local pubs and further afield. ‼☰◆

Tollbridge Porter (OG 1049, ABV 4.5%)

Old School SIBA

Holly Bank Barn, Crag Road, Warton, Lancashire, LA5 9PL
☎ (01524) 740888 ☎ 07515 376700
⊕ oldschoolbrewery.co.uk

☺A 12-barrel brewery, founded in 2012, located in a renovated 400-year-old former school outbuilding overlooking the picturesque village of Warton. Beer is mainly sold to free houses within a 40-mile radius. ‼◆

Hopscotch (OG 1037, ABV 3.7%) 🍺
Initially hoppy, astringency builds in this satisfying beer, ending with a bitter finish.

Textbook (OG 1039, ABV 3.9%)

Detention (OG 1041, ABV 4.1%) 🍺
Light, malty bitter, sweetish middle with a gentle finish.

Headmaster (OG 1045, ABV 4.5%)
A dark, strong best bitter. It mixes a complex malty flavour with a blackcurrant aroma, leaving a subtle, sweet, nutty aftertaste.

Old Spot

Manor Farm, Station Road, Cullingworth, Bradford, West Yorkshire, BD13 5HN
☎ (01535) 691144 ⊕ oldspotbrewery.co.uk

☺Old Spot, named after the owner's sheepdog, started brewing in 2005. The beers are available locally with the acting brewery tap, the George Hotel in Cullingworth, being the main outlet. ‼◆

Light But Dark (OG 1043, ABV 4%)
Chestnut-coloured bitter with a slight malty taste and pleasant bitter finish. An ideal session beer.

Spot Light (OG 1040, ABV 4.2%) 🍺
This smooth-drinking golden ale has a slightly fruity, hoppy aroma leading to a well-balanced fruity hop flavour with hints of pineapple and a long, bittersweet finish.

Inn-Spired (OG 1043, ABV 4.3%)

Light-coloured bitter with a light, hoppy taste and a slight, fruity finish.

OSB (OG 1042, ABV 4.5%)
A golden-coloured, full-bodied bitter.

Spot O'Bother (OG 1060, ABV 5.5%)
Porter with a chocolate ice cream taste and slight liquorice bitterness to finish. A complex brew.

Old Tree

SILO Restaurant, 39 Upper Gardener Street, Brighton, BN1 4AN ☎ 07413 064346
⊕ old-tree-oz74.squarespace.com

Old Tree Brewery, part of the Old Tree Co-operative, is based in the zero-waste Silo restaurant in Brighton. As brewers, makers and gardeners the group has envisioned a production process for drinks production that contributes to land regeneration. RAIB

Old Worthy

Broughton, ML12 6HQ ☎ 07955 113083
⊕ oldworthybeer.co.uk

☺Brewing takes place on a 10-barrel plant. The beers are designed to be drunk as a 'half 'n' half', a beer served with a dram of whisky on the side. The malt used is sourced from Scottish whisky distilleries. 200 outlets are supplied.

Wee XP (OG 1045, ABV 4.4%)

Wee Blonde (OG 1048, ABV 4.7%)

The Old Worthy (OG 1050, ABV 5%)

Wild Bill's Aces & Eights (OG 1050, ABV 5%)

A Midnight Caper (OG 1050, ABV 5.5%)

Mighty XP (OG 1060, ABV 6%)

Olde Potting Shed

Collingdon Buildings, Collingdon Road, High Spen, Rolands Gill, Tyne & Wear, NE39 2EQ
☎ (01207) 545577

Olde Potting Shed began brewing in 2013 using a five-barrel plant.

Cygnet (ABV 4%)

Dark Wing (ABV 4.3%)

Swan Song (ABV 4.8%)

Olde Swan

🏠 89 Halesowen Road, Netherton, Dudley, West Midlands, DY2 9PY
☎ (01384) 253075

☺A famous brewpub best known as Ma Pardoe's after the matriarch who ruled it for years. The pub has been licensed since 1835 and the present brewery and pub were built in 1863. Brewing continued until 1988 and restarted in 2001. ‼◆

Original (OG 1034, ABV 3.5%) 🍺
Straw-coloured light mild, smooth but tangy, and sweetly refreshing with a faint hoppiness.

Dark Swan (OG 1041, ABV 4.2%) 🍺
Smooth, sweet dark mild with late roast malt in the finish.

Entire (OG 1044, ABV 4.4%) 🍺

Faintly hoppy, amber premium bitter with sweetness persistent throughout.

NPA (Netherton Pale Ale) (OG 1048, ABV 4.8%)
A pale and hoppy ale.

Bumble Hole Bitter (OG 1052, ABV 5.2%) ◀
Sweet, smooth amber ale with hints of astringency in the finish.

Oldershaw SIBA 👁

Heath Lane, Barkston Heath, Grantham, Lincolnshire, NG32 2DE
☎ (01476) 572135 ⊕ oldershawbrewery.com

☺Oldershaw Brewery has been brewing since 1997. Owned and run by brewster Kathy Britton, it is a nine-barrel plant and brews in the region of 500,000 pints a year. The brewery produces around 20 different beers of varying styles. ‼☰♦

Heavenly Blonde (OG 1038, ABV 3.8%)
Pale blonde session beer, packed with zesty tropical fruits with a crisp, dry finish.

Newton's Drop (OG 1041, ABV 4.1%) ◀
Balanced malt and hops but with a strong bitter, lingering taste in this mid-brown beer.

Great Expectations (OG 1040, ABV 4.2%)
A pale gold beer with citrus rich hops.

Grantham Stout (OG 1043, ABV 4.3%)
Dark brown and smooth with rich roast malt notes and warming, fruity, complex flavours.

Mosaic Blonde (OG 1041, ABV 4.3%)
Satisfying lager-style beer. Powerfully citrus and tropical.

Posh Blonde (OG 1041, ABV 4.3%)
Crisp lager-style beer, enhanced by fruity floral and citrus infused notes.

Old Boy (OG 1047, ABV 4.8%) ◀
A full-bodied amber ale, fruity and bitter with a hop/fruit aroma. The malt that backs the taste dies in the long finish.

Blonde Volupta (OG 1050, ABV 5%)
Gold-coloured, zesty premium beer packed with complexity and intense tropical fruit flavours, leading to a crisp, dry finish.

Alchemy (OG 1052, ABV 5.3%)
A premium golden bitter, easy-drinking and well-balanced with tropical citrus notes and subtle French toast malts.

American Hopquad (OG 1053, ABV 5.5%)
A fresh IPA, with a rich blend of American hops. Sharp citrus and herbal notes, light amber ale on a warm toasted malt base. A distinct orange aroma leads to a crisp finish.

Ollie's (NEW)

616 Newport Road, Cardiff, CF3 4FG ☎ 07896 296259

Ollie's was established in 2016 using a 100-litre brew kit producing bottled beers. Cask-conditioned beers are planned.

On the Edge

Woodseats, Sheffield, South Yorkshire ☎ 07854 983197 ⊕ ontheedgebrew.com

On the Edge started brewing commercially in 2012 using a 0.5-barrel plant in the brewer's home.

Brewing takes place once a week. Three local pubs are supplied as well as beer festivals. There is no regular beer list as new brews are constantly being tried.

One Mile End SIBA

Unit 2, Compass West Estate, West Road, London, N17 0XL ☎ 07912 411147

Correspondence: White Hart Brewpub, 1-3 Mile End Road, London, E1 4TP ⊕ the-white-hart.co.uk/index.php

Three-barrel plant brewing for the White Hart Pub in Mile End and the trade. A brew plant still exists at the White Hart.

Opa Hay's

Glencot, Wood Lane, Aldeby, Norfolk, NR34 0DA
☎ (01502) 679144 ☎ 07916 282729
⊕ engelfineales.com

Opa Hay's began brewing in 2008. It is a small, family-run microbrewery, taking its name from the brewer's great grandfather. Only traditional brewing methods are used, with ingredients that are, where possible, sourced locally. ♦RAIB

Engels Fruity Little Number (ABV 3.6%) ◀
Powerful citrus/grapefruit aroma with malt and hops. Smoky sweetish flavours with fruit notes, and a fruity, hoppy aftertaste.

Engel's Best Bitter (ABV 4%)
A triple-hopped aromatic beer, an old fashioned traditional English ale.

Matilda's Revenge (ABV 4.3%)

SEMP (Samuel Engels Meister Pils) (ABV 4.8%)
A Pilsner-style beer, light in colour with a hoppy aroma.

Liquid Bread (ABV 5.2%)
Bavarian-style wheat beer, naturally cloudy, with a distinct aroma of cloves and banana.

Orbit

Arches 225 & 228, 39a Fielding Street, Walworth, London, SE17 3HD ☎ 07885 663842
⊕ orbitbeers.com

Established in 2014, Orbit is a microbrewery producing keg and bottle-conditioned beers. RAIB

Orkney SIBA 👁

Quoyloo, Stromness, Orkney, KW16 3LT
☎ (01667) 404555 ☎ 07721 013227

Office: Sinclair Breweries Ltd, Cawdor, IV12 5XP
⊕ sinclairbreweries.co.uk

☺Orkney was established in 1988 in an old village school building. Having incorporated sister brewery Atlas (qv), it moved next door in 2010 to enable an increase in capacity and the completion of an award-winning visitor centre in 2012. ‼☰♦

Raven (OG 1038, ABV 3.8%) ▣ ◀
A well-balanced quaffable bitter. Malty fruitiness and bitter hops last through to the long, dry aftertaste.

Dragonhead (OG 1040, ABV 4%) ◀
A strong, dark malt aroma flows into the taste. The roast malt continues to dominate the aftertaste,

and blends with chocolate to develop a strong, dry finish.

Northern Light (OG 1040, ABV 4%) ◄
A well-balanced golden ale with a real smack of fruit and hops in the taste and an increasing bitter aftertaste.

Red MacGregor (OG 1040, ABV 4%) ◄
This tawny red ale has a powerful smack of fruit and a clean, fresh mouthfeel. Generally a well balanced bitter.

Corncrake (OG 1042, ABV 4.1%) ◄
A straw-coloured beer with soft citrus fruits and a floral aroma.

Puffin Ale (OG 1045, ABV 4.5%) ◄
Bittersweet mix of some malts and plenty of hops.

Dark Island (OG 1045, ABV 4.6%) ◄
The roast malt and chocolate character varies, making the beer hard to categorise as a stout or an old ale. A sweetish roast malt taste leads to a long-lasting roasted, slightly bitter, dry finish.

Skull Splitter (OG 1080, ABV 8.5%) 🗐 🖿 ◄
An intense velvet malt nose with hints of apple, prune and plum. The hoppy taste is balanced by satin smooth malt with sweet, fruity, spicy edges, leading to a long, dry finish with a hint of nut.

Brewed for Atlas Brewery:

Wayfarer (OG 1044, ABV 4.4%) ◄
Full of citrus fruits and hops.

Golden Amber (OG 1045, ABV 4.5%) ◄
Refreshing hops, honey, marmalade and grapefruit to the fore with a dry, hoppy finish.

Blizzard (OG 1047, ABV 4.7%) ◄
Light on malts and hops with ginger and spices coming through.

Ossett SIBA 👁

Kings Yard, Low Mill Road, Ossett, West Yorkshire, WF5 8ND
☎ (01924) 261333 ⊕ ossett-brewery.co.uk

☺Ossett began brewing in 1998, moving to a new site in 2005. An extra 40-barrel fermenter was added in 2014, increasing total brewing capacity to 280 barrels a week. The brewery owns 23 pubs, five of which are 'Hop'-branded bars – larger city centre venues with real ale and live music – in Wakefield, Leeds, Sheffield, York and Saltaire. ‼🍽♦

Pale Gold (OG 1038, ABV 3.8%)
A refreshing pale ale with a light, hoppy aroma.

Big Red Bitter (OG 1042, ABV 4%) 🖿
Deep red, malty Yorkshire bitter.

Inception (OG 1043, ABV 4%)
A deep golden, full-bodied ale made from a blend of five malts. Moderately bitter but with a powerful hop aroma.

Silver King (OG 1041, ABV 4.3%)
A lager-style beer with a crisp, dry flavour and citrus fruity aroma.

Treacle Stout (OG 1050, ABV 5%) 🖿
A rich and robust stout. The addition of black treacle gives intense depth and roasted malts impart a coffee flavour. Generous amounts of hops add a dry citrus finish to this complex black ale.

Excelsior (OG 1051, ABV 5.2%)

A strong pale ale with a full, mellow flavour and a fresh, hoppy aroma with citrus/floral characteristics.

Otherton

Audley, Staffordshire ☎ 07921 717154
⊕ othertonales.co.uk

Brewing commenced in 2014 on a cuckoo basis at Offbeat Brewery (qv), Crewe but in 2016 operations moved to a site in Audley, Staffordshire. The range of beers, produced roughly once a month, varies throughout the year. ♦

Otley SIBA 👁

Unit 39, Albion Industrial Estate, Pontypridd, Mid Glamorgan, CF37 4NX
☎ (01443) 480555 ⊕ otleybrewing.co.uk

☺Otley Brewing was established in 2005 and since then the brewery has almost tripled in size, taking over adjacent industrial units. There is now an on-site shop. The beers are supplied to many outlets across South Wales and in the London area.
‼🍽♦RAIB

O1 (OG 1038, ABV 4%) 🖿 ◄
A pale golden beer with a hoppy aroma. The taste has hops, malt, fruit and a thirst-quenching bitterness. A satisfying finish completes this beer.

O2 Croeso (OG 1040, ABV 4%)
Light golden ale full of citrus hop aromas. Dry hopped with American hops.

O4 Colombo (OG 1038, ABV 4%)
A golden, hoppy ale.

O3 Boss (OG 1042, ABV 4.4%)
Chestnut red-coloured bitter using American hops for bitterness and aroma.

O12 Thai Bo (OG 1045, ABV 4.6%)
Clear wheat beer with lemongrass, lime leaf and galangal.

O5 Hop Angeles (OG 1047, ABV 4.8%)
An American red ale.

O9 Blonde (OG 1047, ABV 4.8%)
Clear wheat beer flavoured with roasted orange peel, coriander and cloves.

O7 Weissen (OG 1048, ABV 5%)
Cloudy German-style wheat beer.

O10 Oxymoron (OG 1047, ABV 5.5%)
A black IPA.

O6 Porter (OG 1063, ABV 6.6%)

O11 Motley Brew (OG 1072, ABV 7.5%)
Double IPA with big hop aromas and high bitterness giving a classic IPA mouthfeel.

Otter SIBA 👁

Mathayes, Luppitt, Honiton, Devon, EX14 4SA
☎ (01404) 891285 ⊕ otterbrewery.co.uk

⊠ Otter Brewery is a family-run brewery set high up in the Blackdown Hills. Environmental responsibility lies at the heart of the brewery's ethos. Otter's eco cellar has been built underground and is naturally chilled. The beers are made from the brewery's own springs and locally sourced ingredients. ‼♦

Bitter (OG 1036, ABV 3.6%) 🗐 ◄

Well-balanced amber session bitter with a fruity nose and bitter taste and aftertaste.

Amber (OG 1038.5, ABV 4%) 🍺
A well-balanced bitter with hints of tropical fruit and spice – sometimes with a note of ginger.

Bright (OG 1039, ABV 4.3%) 🍺
Pale yellow/golden ale with a strong fruit aroma, sweet, fruity taste and bittersweet finish.

Ale (OG 1043, ABV 4.5%) 🍺
A brown ale with malty aroma, a malty bitter taste leading to a malty/bitter aftertaste.

Head (OG 1054, ABV 5.8%) 🍺
Fruity aroma and taste with a pleasant bitter finish. Dark brown and full-bodied.

Oud Craft (NEW)

c/o Dulcimer, 567 Wilbraham Road, Manchester, M21 0AE
☎ (0161) 860 6444 ✉ brewedbyoud@gmail.com

Established in 2015, Oud Craft Brewery was set up by the team behind Dulcimer Bar, Chorlton-cum-Hardy, and Saison, West Didsbury, using spare capacity at Outstanding Brewing Company (qv).

Wandering Eye (ABV 4.3%)

Under the Red Sky (ABV 5.2%)

Ouseburn Valley

11 Dilston Terrace, Gosforth, Tyne & Wear, NE3 1XX
☎ 07932 677899 ⊕ ouseburnvallleybrewery.co.uk

Ouseburn Valley started in the owner's garage in 2010, and in 2011 the plant was moved to the cellar of the Brandling Villa Pub where both capacity and beer range were increased. After a flood in 2012, brewing is back in the owner's garage. ♦

Armstrong Bitter (OG 1042, ABV 4.1%)
Rich yellow-coloured ale with a light, spicy aroma with soft caramel overtones, and a long bitter finish.

Golden Ale (OG 1044, ABV 4.4%)
Dark gold in colour with light hop aroma, sweet malty taste with a smooth finish.

India Pale Ale (OG 1047, ABV 4.7%)
Pale gold in colour with a strong hop aroma and a long dry finish.

Milk Stout (OG 1047, ABV 4.7%)
Dark beer with a liquorice aroma, and a sweet liquorice and slightly coffee taste.

American Honey (OG 1049, ABV 5%)
Rich dark gold-coloured ale with a sweet honey taste and very strong dry hop aroma.

Out There SIBA

Unit 4, Foundry Lane Industrial Estate, Newcastle upon Tyne, NE6 1LH ☎ 07946 579534
⊕ outtherebrewing.com

Out There was established in 2012 by Steve Pickthall. Branding and beer names are themed around the 1950s space race. In 2016 capacity tripled with the installation of a new plant.

Space is the Place (OG 1034, ABV 3.5%)

An amber coloured table beer with a cream head. The aroma is digestive biscuits and brown bread with a sweet malt flavour and floral notes.

Laika (OG 1049, ABV 4.8%)
A straw-coloured cloudy body with a frothy white head. The aroma is citrus with a hint of custard cream biscuits and the flavour of the orange peel and spices liven the pale malt base.

Celestial Love (OG 1051, ABV 5.1%)
A rich red body with an off white creamy head. The aroma is caramel with a hint of malt loaf and the taste is sweet malt with floral and grapefruit hop flavours.

Outlaw

See Rooster's

Outstanding SIBA 👁

Britannia Mill, Cobden Street, Bury, Lancashire, BL9 6AW
☎ (0161) 764 7723 ⊕ outstandingbeers.com

Born of an aspiration to create outstanding beers and established in 2008, the brewery operates a dual system, brewing on a 15-barrel plant and using a 2.5-barrel plant for special and experimental brews. Selective free trade accounts are supplied nationally. ♦

3.9 (OG 1036, ABV 3.9%)
Pale, light and hoppy beer with a smooth, mellow bitterness and a fresh passion fruit aroma.

UltraPale (OG 1041, ABV 4.1%)
An aromatic golden ale. Not too bitter.

Red (OG 1045, ABV 4.4%)
A traditional red/copper-coloured bitter with a light malt body balanced with a hop bitterness.

Blond (OG 1044, ABV 4.5%)
A pale ale, citrus and refreshing.

IPA (OG 1058, ABV 5.5%)
A complex pale golden IPA, dry and bitter..

Stout (OG 1061, ABV 5.5%)
A smooth, jet black stout, dry and bitter. Balanced roasted barley flavours with a hint of liquorice.

Imperial IPA (OG 1065, ABV 7.4%) 🍺
A golden, dry, strong and hoppy beer.

Oxted (NEW)

Flower Farm, Oxted Road, Godstone, Surrey, RH9 8BP
☎ 07867 541700 ⊕ theoxtedbrewery.co.uk

⊠ Oxted Brewery was established in 2016 at a farm in Godstone using a new two-barrel plant. Open events at the brewery are usually held once a month and produce is available from the farm shop. 🍴♦ RAIB

Hopfather (OG 1038, ABV 3.8%)

Single Hop (OG 1037, ABV 3.8%)

Amber (OG 1039, ABV 3.9%)

Pacific Red (OG 1043, ABV 4.3%)

Black Perle (OG 1044, ABV 4.4%)
A black lager.

IPA (OG 1048, ABV 4.9%)

Padstow SIBA

The Brewery, Unit 4a, Trecerus Industrial Estate,
Padstow, Cornwall, PL28 8RW
☎ (01841) 532169 ☎ 07834 924312
⊕ padstowbrewing.co.uk

⊗ The brewery started commercially in 2013 using
a 0.5-barrel plant. Owners Des and Caron Archer,
Caron being the brewster, have since installed a
custom-built 10-barrel plant. Beer festivals and an
increasing number of local outlets are supplied.
‼ ☛ ◆ RAIB

Pale Ale (OG 1037, ABV 3.6%) ◆
Golden beer with assertive hop aroma. Citrus hops
dominate the taste with bitterness and dryness.
Hoppy, refreshing and crisp finish.

Kor Dorgel (OG 1040, ABV 4%)

Pilot (OG 1040, ABV 4%) ◆
Tawny old ale with malt aroma. Biscuit malt
dominates the taste with apple fruit and liquorice
notes. Malty, bitter finish.

Windjammer (OG 1042, ABV 4.3%) ◆
Copper-coloured best bitter. Biscuit malt with pear
drops and delicate stone fruits. Bitterness grows
and lasts well into the finish.

Lobster Tale (OG 1044, ABV 4.5%)

Pride (OG 1044, ABV 4.5%) ◆
Tawny with added honey. Malt dominates
throughout with some toffee sweetness and light
roast notes balanced by bitterness, plums and
hops.

IPA (OG 1046, ABV 4.8%) ◆
Amber strong bitter. Fully hopped on nose and
taste with orange bitterness. Sweet finish with
citrus hops and faintly dry.

May Day (OG 1048, ABV 5%) ◆
Golden ale with powerful citrus hop aroma and
flavour. Grapefruit and moderate bitterness.
Strong, grassy hop finish with dryness.

Sundowner (OG 1060, ABV 6.5%) ◆
Strong gold ale with fruity hop aroma. Dominant
apricot with citrus hops and malt flavours. Quite
bitter, slightly sweet and dry.

Palmers SIBA IFBB 👁

The Old Brewery, West Bay Road, Bridport, Dorset,
DT6 4JA
☎ (01308) 422396 ⊕ palmersbrewery.com

⊗ Palmers is Britain's only thatched brewery and
dates from 1794. It is situated in Bridport, the heart
of the Jurassic Coast in south-west Dorset. The
company continues to make substantial
investment in its 54 tenanted pubs, all serving cask
ale. An additional 400 outlets are supplied. ‼ ☛

Copper Ale (OG 1036, ABV 3.7%) ◆
Beautifully balanced, copper-coloured light bitter
with a hoppy aroma.

Best Bitter (OG 1040, ABV 4.2%) ◆
Hop aroma and bitterness stay in the background in
this predominately malty best bitter, with some
fruit on the aroma.

Dorset Gold (OG 1046, ABV 4.5%) ◆
More complex than many golden ales thanks to a
pleasant banana and mango fruitiness on the
aroma that carries on into the taste and aftertaste.

200 (OG 1052, ABV 5%) ◆

This is a big beer with a touch of caramel
sweetness adding to a complex hoppy, fruit taste
that lasts from the aroma well into the aftertaste.

Tally Ho! (OG 1057, ABV 5.5%) 🍴 ◆
A complex dark old ale. Roast malts and treacle
toffee on the palate lead in to a long, lingering
finish with more than a hint of coffee.

Panther

Unit 1, Collers Way, Reepham, Norfolk, NR10 4SW
☎ 07766 558215 ⊕ pantherbrewery.co.uk

⊗ Panther began brewing in 2010 on an industrial
estate near the old railway station, formerly the
home of Reepham Brewery. ‼ ☛ ◆ RAIB

Mild Panther (OG 1035, ABV 3.3%) ◆
A smooth, malty character with notes of chocolate.

Ginger Panther (OG 1037, ABV 3.7%) ◆
Refreshingly clean ginger wheat beer with a
distinct fiery kick.

Golden Panther (OG 1039, ABV 3.7%) ◆
Flowing malt notes throughout supported by
orange hop airs. Gently tapering finish lapses into a
growing dry bitterness.

Honey Panther (OG 1044, ABV 4%) ◆
A gentle flowing brew with honey and malt
throughout. Malt, caramel and hop. Amber-
coloured with a tapering bittersweet finale.

Red Panther (OG 1041, ABV 4.1%) ◆
Full-flavoured brew. Solidly malty in both aroma
and taste. Hops, and a residual sweetness, provide
balance.

Black Panther (OG 1050, ABV 4.5%) ◆
This dark ale is full-flavoured, smooth and complex.
It has a bittersweet balance that leads to a dry
finish.

Beast of the East (OG 1052, ABV 5.5%)
An amber IPA, refreshing, with floral and grapefruit
hop notes.

Paradigm SIBA

4d Green End Farm, 93a Church Lane, Sarratt,
Hertfordshire, WD3 6HH
☎ (01923) 291215 ⊕ paradigmbrewery.com

⊗ Founded by two friends, Neil Hodges and Rob
Atkinson, Paradigm went into production in 2015.
Its five-barrel plant is located in an industrial unit
on a farm. One-off beers are also brewed. The
brewery and beer names are based on corporate
jargon and buzzwords. ‼ ◆

Low Hanging Fruit (OG 1036, ABV 3.7%)
Refreshing beer with citrus flavours, particularly
tangerine and grapefruit.

Touch Point (OG 1039, ABV 3.9%)
A light-coloured, hoppy, pale ale.

Win-Win (OG 1044, ABV 4.2%)

Synergy (OG 1052, ABV 5.1%)
A full-bodied, fruity IPA.

Paradise

🏠 Bird in Hand, Trelissick Road, Hayle, Cornwall,
TR27 4HY
☎ (01736) 753974
✉ birdinhand@paradisepark.org.uk

⊗ Brewing first started in 1981 under the name Paradise Brewery, named after its location, the Paradise Bird Park. The name was changed to Wheal Ale in 1995. Brewing ceased in 2004 but restarted in 2009 under the original Paradise name. ‼◆

Bitter (OG 1043, ABV 4.3%) ◣
Copper-coloured best bitter with malty and fruity aroma. Malty and sweet body, heavy fruity flavour with toffee. Apple finish.

Artist (OG 1055, ABV 5.2%) ◣
Full-bodied tawny ale with faint aroma of malt. Heavy sweet malt and bubblegum esters in the mouth with a balance of hops. Dryness and bitterness in the finish.

Parish

■ 6 Main Street, Burrough on the Hill, Leicestershire, LE14 2JQ
☎ (01664) 454801 ☎ 07715 369410
✉ bazbrewery@gmail.com

Parish began in 1983 and now operates on a 20-barrel plant, with capacity to brew a further 12 barrels. The brewery is located in a 400-year-old building next to Grants Freehouse, which stocks the full range of beers. Other local outlets are also supplied and one-off brews are produced for beer festivals. ‼RAIB

PSB (OG 1038, ABV 3.9%)
Hoppy session beer with malty aftertaste.

Burrough Bitter (OG 1047, ABV 4.8%)
Darker version of PSB with a good balance of malt and hops. Reddish brown in colour.

Poachers Ale (OG 1060, ABV 6%)
Deep rub-coloured, full-bodied, malty blended beer.

Baz's Bonce Blower (OG 1098, ABV 12%) ⬡
Strong, dark beer with a rich, malty character.

Park SIBA ◉

95 Elm Road, Kingston-upon-Thames, Surrey, KT2 6HX ☎ 07932 624395

Office: 38 St Georges Road, Kingston-upon-Thames, Surrey, KT2 6DN ⊕ theparkbrewery.com

⊗ The Park Brewery was founded in 2014 in a former greengrocer's premises, using a one-barrel plant. Four cask ales are regularly produced, and a much wider bottled range is available through the local off trade but also appears occasionally in cask form at beer festivals and local pubs. After expanding from one to four barrels during 2015 there are plans for expansion and relocation. ◆RAIB

Killcat Pale (OG 1037, ABV 3.7%) ◣
Unfined golden bitter with grapefruit throughout and a strong, hoppy, bitter flavour and finish, which is dry and slightly tart.

Gallows Gold (OG 1044, ABV 4.4%) ◣
Unfined hoppy golden ale with citrus notes. Bitterness develops in the taste and finish, which has some pineapple fruitiness.

Spankers IPA (OG 1055, ABV 5.5%) ◣
An amber-coloured, hoppy, citrus, dry golden ale with a similar finish and a touch of dry bitterness.

Dark Hill (OG 1058, ABV 5.8%)

Parker

Unit 3 Gravel Lane, Banks, Lancashire, PR9 8BY
☎ (01704) 620718 ☎ 07949 797889
⊕ theparkerbrewery.co.uk

☺Parker was established in 2014 using a 25-litre plant, and has since expanded to a five-barrel plant producing both cask-conditioned ales and bottled beers. ‼RAIB

Centurion Pale Ale (OG 1040, ABV 3.9%)
A light, refreshing pale ale with zesty fruit flavours with a crisp, dry and hoppy finish.

Barbarian Bitter (OG 1040, ABV 4.1%)
Golden traditional ale with notes of caramel. Smooth and well balanced, an easy drinking ale.

Saxon Red Ale (OG 1046, ABV 4.5%)
Ruby red in colour. A smooth beer packed full of warm fruit flavours and a subtle hint of spice on the finish.

Viking Blonde (OG 1042, ABV 4.5%)
A blonde ale with subtle hints of blackcurrant leaf and summer berry fruit flavours with a refreshing, full, crisp finish.

Dark Spartan Stout (OG 1052, ABV 5%)
Silky smooth stout with hints of chocolate and coffee.

Partizan SIBA

8 Almond Road, South Bermondsey, London, SE16 3LR
☎ (020) 8127 5053 ☎ 07708 263931
⊕ partizanbrewing.co.uk

Partizan began brewing in 2012. Each brew is different, but they are based on a variety of international styles and all are vegan-friendly and bottled by hand on site. ☛RAIB V

Partners SIBA ◉

The Brew House, 589 Halifax Road, Hightown, Liversedge, West Yorkshire, WF15 8HQ
☎ (01924) 457772 ⊕ partnersbrewery.co.uk

☺Partners was formed in 2011 following the purchase of the long-established Anglo Dutch Brewery by Richard Sharp. The brewery moved into newly renovated premises in 2015 and invested in a new, 15-barrel, state-of-the-art brewery to meet increased demand for its beers. Partners owns three pubs, the Brew House in Hightown, Halfway House in Morley and the Shant in Halifax. ‼◆

Working Class Hero (OG 1038, ABV 3.8%)
A bitter tasting session beer with a strong, hoppy aftertaste.

Blonde (OG 1039, ABV 3.9%)
A blonde, crisp, aromatic session beer.

Cascade (OG 1040, ABV 4%)
A light and refreshing beer with a citrus and blackcurrant nose.

Triple Hop (OG 1042, ABV 4.2%)
A triple-hopped APA, refreshing with good bitterness and a hoppy aftertaste.

Ghost (OG 1043, ABV 4.5%)
A pale, full-bodied bitter with a fresh, gentle nose, taken over by a smooth hop and citrus finish.

Tabatha (OG 1054, ABV 6%) ◣

Golden-coloured, Belgian-style Tripel with a strong, fruity, hoppy and bitter character. Powerful and warming, slightly thinnish, with a bitter, dry finish.

Patriot

Upcott Farm, Bicknoller, Somerset, TA4 4EY

Office: c/o Farmer's Arms, Combe Florey, Somerset, TA4 3HZ ⊕ thepatriotbrewery.co.uk

⊗ Patriot began brewing in 2010 using a four-barrel brew plant. The brewery relocated to Combe Florey, Somerset, in 2015, with the beers regularly on sale at the adjacent Farmer's Arms pub. ‼ ⌷

Morris (OG 1038, ABV 3.8%)

Kiwi (OG 1041, ABV 4.1%)

Pug IPA (OG 1057, ABV 5.6%)

Peak SIBA

Barn Brewery, Chatsworth, Bakewell, Derbyshire, DE45 1EX
☎ (01246) 583737 ⊕ peakales.co.uk

☺Peak Ales opened in 2005 in former derelict farm buildings on the Chatsworth estate aided by a DEFRA Rural Enterprise Scheme grant and support from trustees of Chatsworth Settlement. Main beer production moved to a new facility at Ashford in the Water in 2014 to increase capacity. Beers are available throughout the Peak District and beyond. ‼ ◆

Swift Nick (OG 1038, ABV 3.8%) ◖
Easy-drinking, copper coloured bitter with balanced malt and hops and a gentle, hoppy, bitter finish.

Bakewell Best Bitter (OG 1041, ABV 4.2%) ◖
Full-bodied tawny bitter with a hoppy bitterness against a malty background, leading to a hoppy, dry aftertaste.

Chatsworth Gold (OG 1045, ABV 4.6%) ▣ ◖
Speciality beer made with honey, which gives a pleasant sweetness leading to a hop and malt finish.

Peakstones Rock SIBA ◉

Peakstones Farm, Cheadle Road, Alton, Staffordshire, ST10 4DH ☎ 07891 350908 ⊕ peakstonesrock.co.uk

⊗ Peakstones Rock was established in 2005 with a five-barrel brewery located on a farm in the Peak District Park. The plant was expanded to 10-barrel capacity in 2009. The brewery supplies an expanding free trade market in the North Midlands and surrounding areas. ‼ ◆ RAIB

Nemesis (OG 1042, ABV 3.8%) ◖
Biscuity aroma with some hop background. Sweet start, sweetish then hops emerge to give a fruity middle. Bitterness develops slowly to a tongue tingling finish.

Pugin's Gold (OG 1043, ABV 4%)

Chained Oak (OG 1045, ABV 4.2%)
A copper-coloured beer with a bitter finish and hop aroma.

Alton Abbey (OG 1051, ABV 4.5%)

Black Hole (OG 1048, ABV 4.8%) ▣ ◖

Grassy aroma with malt background. Hops hit the mouth and intensify. Bitterness lingers with some mouth-watering astringency.

Oblivion (OG 1055, ABV 5.5%)

Peerless SIBA ◉

The Brewery, 8 Pool Street, Birkenhead, Merseyside, CH41 3NL
☎ (0151) 647 7688 ⊕ peerlessbrewing.co.uk

Peerless began brewing in 2009 and is under the directorship of Steve Briscoe. Beers are sold through festivals, local pubs and the free trade. ‼ ◆

Fusion (ABV 3.5%)
Easy-drinking session strength pale ale.

Pale (OG 1036, ABV 3.8%)
Pale session ale. Good initial bitterness and a hint of grapefruit on the finish.

Triple Blonde (OG 1040, ABV 4%)
Blonde beer with a fruity, citrus finish.

Paxtons Peculiar (ABV 4.1%)
This copper-coloured ale is a complex array of malt, hints of chocolate and fruity citrus overtones.

Chestnut Ale (ABV 4.3%)
Classic brown ale, full-bodied with good bitterness and a distinctive malt flavour.

Crystal Maze (ABV 4.4%)
A ruby ale. Good bitterness and a hint of fruit on the finish.

Gold (ABV 4.4%)
A well-balanced golden ale with initial hop bitterness. The distinct citrus fruit and hop aroma leads to a crisp, dry finish.

Storr Lager (OG 1042, ABV 4.8%)
A fresh citrus hop finish and pleasant malt backbone.

Oatmeal Stout (OG 1050, ABV 5%)
Full-bodied black stout. The use of oats gives a good mouthfeel and dark malts provide lots of backbone with toffee and caramel tones. There is an element of sweetness to balance the bitterness from the roast malts.

Red Rocks (OG 1047, ABV 5%)
Full-bodied ruby ale. Rich malt flavours combine with the hops for a beer with fruity overtones.

Knee-Buckler IPA (ABV 5.2%)
Initial hop bitterness is matched with a hint of sweetness.

Full Whack (OG 1054, ABV 6%)
Bitterness and a fruity hop finish is derived from a combination of hops.

Tectonic (ABV 6.2%)
A deep honey-coloured ale with lots of hop aroma and flavour.

Pells (NEW)

⊟ c/o Elephant & Castle, White Hill, Lewes, East Sussex, BN7 2DJ ⊕ pellsbrewingcoop.org

⊗ A brewing co-operative established in 2015. All beers are sold through the Elephant & Castle pub in Lewes.

House IPA (ABV 6.4%)

Pembrokeshire

The Ridgeway, Saundersfoot, SA69 9JU
☎ (01834) 813574
⊕ pembrokeshirebrewingco.co.uk

Opened in 2014 with a 2.5-barrel, full-mash plant, the brewery plans to install a Burton Union system, making it the second of only two in the country and one of three in the world. The range of beers can be sampled in the brewery tap while watching the brewing process through a glass partition. Beer festivals and musical events are held every month. ⬛

Cariad (OG 1039, ABV 3.9%)
Copper-coloured beer, full-bodied with a citrus aroma.

Daft Bass (OG 1041, ABV 4.1%)
A flagship beer with a balanced mixture of malt and hops.

Pale Ale (OG 1041, ABV 4.1%)
A refreshingly hoppy, full-bodied pale ale with a subtle character of its own.

Black Bart (OG 1045, ABV 4.5%)
A rich stout with a balanced blend of roasted barley and robust hops.

**SSA (Saundersfoot Supreme Ale)
(OG 1045, ABV 4.5%)**
A full-bodied premium bitter.

Knocker (OG 1050, ABV 5%)

IPA (OG 1060, ABV 6%)

Penlon Cottage

Panteg Farm, New Quay, SA45 9TL
☎ (01545) 561492 ⊕ penlon.biz

After 10 years' operation, Penlon Cottage, strongly focussed on an ethos of sustainability, changed hands in 2014 and in early 2015 moved to new premises nearby, where re-equipment and facilities for visitors are planned. It produces mainly bottle-conditioned beers. RAIB

Pennine SIBA

Well Hall Farm, Well, North Yorkshire, DL8 2PX
☎ (01677) 470111 ⊕ pennine-brewing.co.uk

☺Pennine began brewing in Batley in 2012 using an 18-barrel lager plant complete with lauter [filtration] tun. In 2013 the brewery relocated to Well, near Masham. ‼◆

Amber Necker (OG 1039, ABV 3.9%)
A session beer with a smooth and creamy texture and hoppy aftertaste.

Best Bitter (OG 1040, ABV 3.9%)

Hair of the Dog (OG 1036, ABV 3.9%)
Bright blonde with a good aroma and smooth, refreshing aftertaste.

Real Blonde (OG 1041, ABV 4%)
Well-balanced blonde ale with a mouthwatering fruity aftertaste.

Natural Gold (OG 1043, ABV 4.2%)

Penpont

Inner Trenarrett, Altarnun, Launceston, Cornwall, PL15 7SY

☎ (01566) 86069 ⊕ penpontbrewery.co.uk

⊗ Penpont opened in 2008 and has steadily increased the range and production since then. The brewery has also won a number of awards. Its beers are available in pubs across Cornwall.
‼ ⬛◆RAIB

St Nonna's (OG 1037, ABV 3.7%) ◕
Tawny session bitter with floral nose and balanced malt and hop bitterness throughout with roast and sweet notes. Bitter finish.

Cornish Arvor (OG 1040, ABV 4%) ◕
Well-balanced tawny best bitter. Principally bitter with fruity sweetness and some malt. Bitter hop-fruit finish.

Creation Pale Ale (OG 1039.2, ABV 4.2%) ⬛ ◕
Gold-coloured bitter with hop aroma. Quite hoppy taste with sweet peach, citrus zing and roast malt. Bitter, slightly dry finish.

Shipwreck Coast (OG 1044, ABV 4.4%) ◕
Golden ale with a citrus aroma. Powerful lemon citrus hop dominates the taste and finish with bitterness and fruits. Faint dryness.

Roughtor (OG 1047, ABV 4.7%) ◕
Copper strong bitter with malt and citrus hop aroma. Hop bitterness balanced by malt, plum and marmalade. Bitter, dry finish.

Beast of Bodmin (OG 1046.5, ABV 5%) ◕
Brown strong bitter with malt aroma. Smooth roast malt, chestnuts and complex fruits in the mouth. Refreshing malty, bitter finish.

Stormer IPA (OG 1046.7, ABV 5.2%)

Pentrich SIBA

Unit B, Asher Lane Business Park, Asher Lane, Pentrich, Derbyshire, DE5 3RB
☎ (01773) 741700
✉ pentrichbrewingco@gmail.com

Two former home brewers began producing beer for sale in their garage in Pentrich, before moving to share the plant of the Landlocked Brewing Co at the Beehive Inn, Ripley in 2014. In 2016, after purchasing the brewing kit from Nutbrook Brewery, the brewery moved into its own premises. ◆RAIB

1817 (OG 1045, ABV 4.5%)
A full-bodied amber ale with a dry fruit aroma, and a pleasing bitter finish.

Cut Your Teeth (OG 1050, ABV 5%)
A hoppy session IPA, bright gold in colour.

Three Graves (OG 1060, ABV 6%)
A strong, dark porter, made using only British ingredients.

Penzance

▤ Star Inn, Crowlas, Penzance, Cornwall, TR20 8DX
☎ (01736) 740375
⊕ penzancebrewing.wordpress.com

⊗ Owner Peter Elvin began brewing in 2008 on a self-built five-barrel plant in the old stable block of the Star Inn. The fermentation capacity has since been expanded, increasing the volume and range of beers produced. Production is now at full capacity of 1,400 barrels a year. Besides the pub, selected outlets and beer festivals are supplied.
‼◆

Mild (OG 1042, ABV 3.6%) ◀
Creamy dark brown mild with smoky malt aroma.
Roast coffee and sweet malt dominate the palate,
balanced by light bitterness.

Crowlas Bitter (OG 1037, ABV 3.8%) ◀
Refreshing copper session bitter with light malt
aroma. Light biscuit maltiness and hops. Lingering
finish of malty bitterness with dryness.

Potion No. 9 (OG 1039, ABV 4%) ◀
Golden ale with floral, grapefruit hops dominating
nose and taste. Big bitter taste grows into a
complex grapefruit, apricot finish.

Brisons Bitter (OG 1043, ABV 4.5%) ◀
Tawny best bitter with malt aroma. Malt dominates
the taste with sweetness, fruits and bitterness.
Malt finish with sweet toffee.

Liberty (OG 1049, ABV 5%)

Trink (OG 1048, ABV 5.2%) ◀
Golden ale with a grapefruit nose. Powerful,
punchy and astringent hop flavours with grapefruit
marmalade and peaches. Bittersweet and hoppy
finish.

American Pale Ale (OG 1052, ABV 5.7%)

IPA (OG 1058, ABV 6%) ◀
Smooth golden strong bitter with hoppy aroma.
Strong hop bitterness which continues into the
finish is balanced by sweet malt.

Scilly Stout (OG 1067, ABV 7%) ◀ ◀
Dark brown, full-bodied and creamy stout. Burnt
malt, liquorice, chicory and prunes taste. Long,
bittersweet finish with strong roast malt.

People's

**Mill House, Mill Lane, Thorpe-next-Haddiscoe,
Norfolk, NR14 6PA**
☎ (01508) 548706 ✉ peoplesbrewery@mail.com

⊠ A one-barrel brewery associated with the
community-owned Queen's Head pub in Thurlton,
which takes most of its draught output.

Norton Pale Ale (OG 1038, ABV 3.8%)
Brewed to emphasis the bitterness and flavour of
English hops.

Raveningham Bitter (OG 1039, ABV 3.9%)
Traditional English biter with a good malt flavour
and bitter finish.

Thurlton Gold (OG 1042, ABV 4.2%)
Pale ale with distinctive hop flavours.

Cascade (OG 1044, ABV 4.5%)
Cascade hops give this golden beer its
characteristic flavour.

Thorpe Old (OG 1049, ABV 5%)
A dark, strong ale made with roasted malts that
complement the bitter hops.

Pheasantry SIBA 👁

▋ High Brecks Farm, Lincoln Road, East Markham,
Nottinghamshire, NG22 0SN
☎ (01777) 872728 ☎ 07948 976749
⊕ pheasantrybrewery.co.uk

☺Pheasantry began brewing in 2012 using a new
10-barrel plant from Canada. Situated in a listed
barn on a farm, the brewery and visitor centre
incorporate a wedding and events venue, with the
brewery visible through glass partitions. It supplies

some 200 pubs and retail outlets in
Nottinghamshire, Lincolnshire and South Yorkshire.
‼ ⍤

Best Bitter (OG 1038, ABV 3.8%) ⍟
Smooth-tasting, copper-coloured beer, with
medium bitterness and sweetness. It has a light,
spicy aroma.

Pale Ale (OG 1040, ABV 4%)
A pale-coloured, smooth-tasting beer with floral
and citrus notes and a dry finish.

Ringneck Amber Ale (OG 1041, ABV 4.1%) ◀
Amber-coloured best bitter, initial malt and
caramel leading to a brief bitter, dry finish.

Dark Ale (OG 1042, ABV 4.2%)
A smooth, soft, satisfying dark ale with malty
flavours, balanced bitterness and a velvety texture.

Lincoln Tank Ale (OG 1042, ABV 4.2%)
Amber-coloured, well-hopped beer.

Dancing Dragonfly (OG 1050, ABV 5%)
Refreshing blonde beer with exotic fruit flavours.

Brewed for Cooper & Griffin Beer Co:

Blue Steel Nuclear Ale (ABV 5%)

Philsters (NEW)

**Beehive Brewery, Beehive Cottage, Little Haseley,
Oxfordshire, OX44 7LH** ☎ 07747 827489
⊕ philsters.co.uk

⊠ Named after the owner/brewer's nickname,
this small 60-litre brewery was established in
2015. It supplies local pubs, including the Plough,
Great Haseley and the White Rabbit, Oxford. There
are plans to increase production when funding and
premises become available. ♦

Haseley Gold (OG 1039, ABV 4.1%)
A golden light ale with a good balance of malt and
hops, giving an initial bright, fresh bitterness, with
soft woody, honey notes following.

Boosh (OG 1041, ABV 4.5%)
A light copper-coloured best bitter with an easy-
drinking, crisp, dry bitter finish to balance the rich
malts.

Haseley Rising (OG 1041, ABV 4.5%)
A pale ale using traditional English hops to give an
intensely bitter, grassy, spicy clean hop hit.

GlassBlower (ABV 4.6%)
A traditional best bitter re-crafted with a secret
ingredient.

Phipps SIBA 👁

**The Albion Brewery, 54 Kingswell Street,
Northampton, NN1 1PR**
☎ (01604) 946606 ☎ 07803 295154
⊕ phipps-nbc.co.uk

Originally founded in Towcester in 1801, Phipps
had been brewing in Northampton since 1817 until
taken over by Watney Mann, who closed the
brewery in 1974. The company name and recipes
were acquired and in 2008 the first Phipps draught
beer reappeared after 40 years, brewed to the
original recipe at Grainstore Brewery (qv) in
Oakham. The Albion Brewery site, once owned by
Phipps, was acquired and a new 15-barrel brewing
plant installed in 2014 to enable Phipps beers to be
once again brewed in the town. Hoggleys brewery,
which was established in 2002, merged with

Phipps NBC at the end of 2013 and all Hoggleys beers are now brewed on the Phipps plant, with the former Hoggleys plant sold to Merrimen Brewing (qv). ‼♦RAIB V

Diamond Ale (OG 1037, ABV 3.7%)
A light amber harvest ale.

Red Star (OG 1038, ABV 3.8%)
A malty, sweet, dark beer. Based on a pre-WW2 session beer.

Midsummer Meadow (OG 1039, ABV 3.9%)
A golden ale with modern aromatic hops.

IPA (OG 1043, ABV 4.3%)
A pale amber best bitter recreated from an old Phipps recipe. A residual malt sweetness and the grapefruit note from the hops gives a fine, fresh, crisp finish.

Ratliffe's Celebrated Stout (OG 1043, ABV 4.3%)
A creamy, well-balanced stout with just a hint of bitterness.

Steam Roller (OG 1045, ABV 4.4%)
A chestnut-coloured malty ale with smoky notes on the finish.

Becket's Honey Ale (OG 1045, ABV 4.5%)
A dark, sweet and malty beer brewed with local honey.

Bison Brown (OG 1046, ABV 4.6%)
Strong, smooth and sweet brown ale.

Gold Star (OG 1050, ABV 5.2%)
An export pale ale.

Brewed for Hoggleys Brewery:

Mill Lane Mild (OG 1040, ABV 4%)

Northamptonshire Bitter (OG 1040, ABV 4%)
A straw-coloured bitter brewed with pale malt only.

Reservoir Hogs (OG 1042, ABV 4.3%)
Mid golden in colour, hoppy and refreshing.

Pump Fiction (OG 1045, ABV 4.5%)
Light copper-coloured, complex but easy drinking.

Indian Summer IPA (OG 1050, ABV 5%)
A hoppy, full-bodied IPA.

Solstice Stout (OG 1050, ABV 5%)
A rich, full-flavoured stout made with a wide range of malts.

Yuletide Ale (OG 1068, ABV 7.2%) 🍾

Phoenix SIBA 👁

Green Lane, Heywood, OL10 2EP
☎ (01706) 627009 ✉ tony@phoenixbrewery.co.uk

☺Established in Ellesmere Port in 1982, Oak Brewery moved to the old Phoenix Brewery in Heywood and adopted the name in 1991. It now supplies 400-500 outlets plus wholesalers. Restoration of the old brewery, built in 1897, is ongoing. ♦

Hopsack (OG 1038, ABV 3.8%)
A light-drinking, hoppy session beer.

Navvy (OG 1039, ABV 3.8%) 🍺
Amber beer with a citrus fruit and malt nose. Good balance of citrus fruit, malt and hops with bitterness coming through in the aftertaste.

Monkeytown Mild (OG 1039, ABV 3.9%)
Dark-coloured mild with fruitiness, bitterness and a smooth, full malt finish.

Arizona (OG 1040, ABV 4.1%) 🍺
Yellow in colour with a fruity and hoppy aroma. A refreshing beer with citrus, hops and good bitterness, and a shortish, dry aftertaste.

Spotland Gold (OG 1041, ABV 4.1%)
A pale, hoppy beer with a lingering bitter finish.

Pale Moonlight (OG 1042, ABV 4.2%)
Quite bitter with lingering grassy hop finish.

Black Bee (OG 1045, ABV 4.5%)
Brewed with honey, this porter has a malty aroma, which tastes of dark fruit, honey and a hint of coffee.

White Monk (OG 1045, ABV 4.5%) 🍺
Yellow beer with a citrus fruit aroma, plenty of fruit, hops and bitterness in the taste, and a hoppy, bitter finish.

Thirsty Moon (OG 1046, ABV 4.6%) 🍺
Tawny beer with a fresh citrus aroma. Hoppy, fruity and malty with a dry, hoppy finish.

West Coast IPA (OG 1046, ABV 4.6%) 🍺
Golden in colour with a hoppy, fruity nose. Strong hoppy and fruity taste and aftertaste with good bitterness throughout.

Double Gold (OG 1050, ABV 5%)
Full-bodied, premium bitter.

Wobbly Bob (OG 1060, ABV 6%) 🍺
A red/brown beer with malty, fruity aroma and creamy mouthfeel. Strongly malty and fruity in flavour, with hops and a hint of herbs. Both sweetness and bitterness are evident throughout.

Brewed for Brunning & Price Pub Co:

Original (ABV 3.8%)

Pickled Pig (NEW) SIBA

Unit 5, Staunton Industrial Estate, Staunton in the Vale, Nottinghamshire, NG13 9PE ☎ 07484 734768 ⊕ pickledpigbrewers.co.uk

Pickled Pig was established in 2015 utilising the 2.5-barrel plant previously used at Copthorne Brewery.

Barnstormer (ABV 3.7%)
A well-rounded, chestnut-coloured beer with a burnt toffee flavour.

Commando (ABV 3.8%)
Chestnut-coloured session beer with a tight creamy head.

Pigs Can Fly (ABV 3.9%)
Straw-coloured session ale with a slight citrus taste.

Apache (ABV 4%)
Copper-coloured with caramel undertones.

The Chase (ABV 4.2%)
A smooth, slightly spicy beer with hints of burnt sugar.

Piggy Bling (ABV 4.4%)
A golden hoppy ale with herbal and floral tones.

Grenade (ABV 4.6%)
Dark-coloured beer with chocolate aromas and undertones of liquorice.

Pictish

Unit 9, Canalside Industrial Estate, Rochdale, OL16 5LB

THE BREWERIES

☎ (01706) 522227 ⊕ pictish-brewing.co.uk

☺The brewery was established in 2000 and supplies around 60 free trade outlets in the North-west and West Yorkshire. Famed for the consistency and clarity of its brews and the ever-changing single hop series of beers. ◆

Brewers Gold (OG 1038, ABV 3.8%) ◈
Yellow in colour, with a hoppy, fruity nose. Soft maltiness and a strong hop/citrus flavour lead to a dry, bitter finish.

Talisman IPA (OG 1042, ABV 4.2%)
A golden IPA. Well hopped with a blend of US and European hops, without being overpowering. A solid session ale.

Alchemists Ale (OG 1043, ABV 4.3%) ◈
Yellow beer with generous hop and fruit on the nose and palate. Good bitter hop finish.

Piddle SIBA

Unit 24, Enterprise Park, Piddlehinton, Dorset, DT2 7UA
☎ (01305) 849336 ☎ 07730 436343
⊕ piddlebrewery.co.uk

▨ Established in 2007 with its name coming from the Piddlehinton location. In 2011 the brewery moved to larger premises. New owners took over in 2014. Beers are available in pubs and other outlets across Dorset and beyond. ◆

Martyr's Relief (OG 1038, ABV 3.5%)

Piddle (OG 1043, ABV 4.1%)
An amber-coloured, full-bodied beer that is slightly sweet but malty with a fruity nose leading to a resinous hoppy flavour with a twist of citrus fruit, giving way to a dry bitter finish.

Cocky (OG 1047, ABV 4.7%)
Bright, light and golden in colour with a refreshing hoppy zing and a lasting bitterness.

Slasher (OG 1053, ABV 5.1%)
Blonde, lager-style beer. Light, with hops chosen for their floral aroma and flavour. Slightly sweet with a refreshing, dry bitter finish.

Pied Bull

⊟ Pied Bull Hotel, 57 Northgate Street, Chester, CH1 2HQ
☎ (01244) 325829 ⊕ piedbull.co.uk

☺Pied Bull began brewing in 2011 using a one-barrel plant. Beer is mainly for in-house consumption but local beer festivals are supplied and occasional brewery swaps occur. ◆

Sensibull (OG 1039, ABV 3.8%)
Session ale brewed with a rounded malt base balanced against a light hop profile.

Gullabull (OG 1040, ABV 3.9%)
A pale ale with a big pink grapefruit aroma.

Pied Eyed (OG 1040, ABV 4%)
A well-balanced session bitter with a malty foretaste and a pleasant hoppy aftertaste.

Quaffabull (OG 1039, ABV 4%)
A refreshing light pale ale with hints of citrus.

Bulls Hit (OG 1055, ABV 4.3%)
A refreshing, light golden ale with plenty of American and New Zealand hops.

Matador (OG 1049, ABV 5%)

A rich, malt-driven ale featuring an aromatic hop profile.

Sitting Bull (OG 1050, ABV 5%)
An American-style IPA.

Black Bull Porter (OG 1060, ABV 5.2%) ⬚
A classic porter brewed to a local recipe dating from 1865, using a blend of six malts and English hops to give a dry coffee flavour.

Redbull (OG 1057, ABV 5.5%)
A rich, deep red ale with a chocolate undertone. Dry hopped for a fruity finish.

Pig & Porter

18h Chapman Way, Tunbridge Wells, Kent, TN2 3EF
☎ (01424) 893519 ⊕ pigandporter.co.uk

Originally brewing at several microbreweries in Sussex and Kent, brewing has taken place on its own plant in Tunbridge Wells since 2013 using a 10-barrel plant. ◆

Ashburnham Pale Ale (ABV 3.8%)

Red Spider Rye (ABV 5.5%)

Pig Iron SIBA

Unit 3, Venture Way, Brierley Hill, West Midlands, DY5 1RG ☎ 07816 018777 ⊕ pigironbrewingco.co.uk

☺Set up in 2015, this three-barrel plant is situated on the edge of the Merry Hill shopping centre. The brewer, from a former baking family, acquired the kit from Brewmeister in Northern Scotland. The brewery supplies free trade outlets within 15 miles of the brewery and the brewer's home. ◆

Blonde (OG 1038, ABV 3.8%)
A smooth, light blonde ale with the addition of honey.

EPA (OG 1042, ABV 4.2%)
Floral, grapefruit, pine and cedar flavours with a spicy honey aroma give this golden-coloured beer a smooth, light texture and a subtle hop flavour.

IPA (OG 1042, ABV 4.2%)
A traditional hoppy IPA.

APA (OG 1045, ABV 4.5%)
Citrus, blackcurrant and grapefruit flavours are pronounced in this American-style IPA.

Pig Pub

⊟ Pig In Muck, Manor Road, Claybrooke Magna, Leicestershire, LE17 5AY
☎ (01455) 202859 ⊕ piginmuck.com/brewery

Brewing began in 2013 using a two-barrel plant. Beers are available in the Pig in Muck and the Criterion in Leicester. Special beers are brewed for the pub by customers.

Weiner Bitter (OG 1038, ABV 3.8%)
A straw-coloured session bitter. Hoppy and fruity throughout with a compounding bitterness culminating on a a distinct dryness at the finish.

Pig Out (OG 1039, ABV 3.9%)
Dark amber beer with a pleasant bitterness and fruity citrus finish.

Claybrooke Bitter (OG 1042, ABV 4.2%)
A full bodied dark amber ale with a malty aroma. It starts bitter, with a hint of fruit and a soft hop flavour to finish.

Pigs Best Bitter (OG 1042, ABV 4.2%)
A golden brown beer with a hint of citrus. The fresh hoppiness comes through at the end with a malt finish.

Pigeon Fishers

Unit B1, Devonshire Buildings, Works Road, Hollingwood, Chesterfield, Derbyshire, S43 2PE
☎ 07506 000989 ⊕ pigeonfishers.com

Pigeon Fishers was founded by Ade Cole in 2014 with the help of co-directors Neil Turner and Kathy Chadwick. Originally using a one-barrel plant donated by Thornbridge Brewery, it upgraded to a 2.5-barrel plant from Barlow Brewery later in the year. ♦

Poacher's Thirst (OG 1039, ABV 4%)
An easy-drinking amber ale, full of malt and hops.

Cynosure (OG 1045, ABV 4.6%)
A smooth-drinking floral and citrus beer with a strawberry and cherry finish.

Pikefields (OG 1052, ABV 5.2%)
An American-style pale ale, hoppy with malty middle notes and a citrus finish.

Pilgrim SIBA

11 West Street, Reigate, Surrey, RH2 9BL
☎ (01737) 222651 ⊕ pilgrim.co.uk

⊠ Pilgrim was the first microbrewery in Surrey, set up in 1982 in Woldingham before moving to its current premises in Reigate in 1984. The original owner, Dave Roberts, is still in charge. Beers are sold to around 40 local outlets. ‼🍴♦

Quench (OG 1037, ABV 3.6%)
A light ale with a floral, lime note.

Surrey Bitter (OG 1038, ABV 3.7%) 🍴
Pineapple, grapefruit and spicy aromas. Biscuity maltiness with a hint of vanilla balanced by a hoppy bitterness and refreshing bittersweet finish.

Progress (OG 1041.5, ABV 4%) 🍴
Well-rounded, tawny-coloured bitter. Predominantly sweet and malty with an underlying fruitiness and hint of toffee, balanced with a subdued bitterness.

Quest (OG 1045, ABV 4.3%)

Pilot (Leith)

22 Jane Street, Leith, EH6 5HD
☎ (0131) 561 4267 ⊕ pilotbeer.co.uk

Pilot started brewing in 2013 in an industrial unit in Leith using a salvaged five-barrel plant. Graduates of the Heriot-Watt University Brewing degree course, the owners infuse a number of flavours in their hop-forward beers. Distribution is to the Edinburgh area. Beers are mostly unfiltered and unfined.

Blond (OG 1047, ABV 4%)
A modern fresh and zesty pale ale with a smooth, full body, and a huge tropical fruit hit.

Vienna Pale (OG 1043, ABV 4.6%)
A take on the classic Vienna lager style. Light and dry with a delicate yet earthy, herbal flavour, followed up with an easy, rounded bitterness.

Iced Tea Ale (OG 1048, ABV 5%)

A refreshing amber beer brewed with a uniquely produced tea blend.

Mochaccino Stout (OG 1069, ABV 5.5%)
A rich, dark milk stout infused with an exclusive coffee roast, organic cocoa nibs and Madagascan vanilla. Lactose gives a sweet silkiness and body to this opulent beer.

India Pale (OG 1060, ABV 6.4%)
Complex spice, maple and caramel flavours join with huge floral, pine and grassy hop notes, all finished off with a powerful yet smooth bitterness.

Pilot (Swansea)

▤ 726 Mumbles Rd, Mumbles, Swansea, SA3 4EL
☎ 07897 895511 ⊕ thepilotbrewery.co.uk

The Pilot Brewery began production on its 2.5-barrel plant in 2013. It is located at the rear of the Pilot Inn on the Mumbles sea front. The output is mainly for the Pilot Inn but can be found at festivals and other select outlets.

Revolver (OG 1040, ABV 4%)
Pale ale, with varying hops in each brew. ·

Gold (OG 1044, ABV 4.4%)

Black Storm (OG 1045, ABV 4.5%)

Wrecker (OG 1050, ABV 5%)
With an initial chocolate taste, this dark beer develops a clean, refreshing maltiness.

Pin-Up SIBA

Unit 3, Block 3, Chalex Industrial Estate, Manor Hall Road, Southwick, Brighton, West Sussex, BN42 4NH
☎ (01273) 411127 ☎ 07888 836892
⊕ pinupbrewingco.com

⊠ Pin-Up began brewing in 2011. The brewery moved from Crowborough to Southwick, near Brighton, in 2014 and uses a five-barrel plant. ♦RAIB

Honey Brown (OG 1039, ABV 4%)

Session IPA (OG 1040, ABV 4.1%)

Summer Pale (OG 1040, ABV 4.1%)

Red Head (OG 1041, ABV 4.2%)

Milk Stout (OG 1044, ABV 4.5%)

Pipes

183a Kings Road, Cardiff, CF11 9DF ☎ 07776 382244
⊕ pipesbeer.co.uk

Formerly known as Artisan, the brewery was established in 2008. All beers are unfiltered, without additives or preservatives and suitable for vegans. The main output is bottled and keg beers, although cask-conditioned beers are occasionally produced. 🍴♦V

Bavarian Style Wheat Beer (OG 1053, ABV 5.3%)

American IPA (OG 1056, ABV 5.6%)

Pitfield

See Dominion

Pixie Spring/Hopcraft

Unit C1, Coed Cae Lane Industrial Estate, Pontyclun, CF72 9HG ☎ 07814 255943 ⊕ pixiespring.com

Pixie Spring began brewing in 2011 in the Wheatsheaf, Llantrisant. In 2012 there was a joining of forces with Gazza Prescott of Steel City Brewing and a move to the present 12-barrel plant. Output under the Pixie Spring banner is restricted to a few regular beers, whereas the Hopcraft brand is used for mostly one-off, well-hopped recipes, although many beers are now semi-permanent. The brewery opened the Hopbunker, a cellar bar in the centre of Cardiff, in 2015.

Plain SIBA

17c Deverill Trading Estate, Sutton Veny, Wiltshire, BA12 7BZ
☎ (01985) 841481 ⊕ plainales.co.uk

⊠ Plain Ales started production in 2008 on a 2.5-barrel plant in a garage, and expanded to a 10-barrel plant in 2011 to keep up with demand for its award-winning ales. !! ♦

Sheep Dip (OG 1040, ABV 3.8%)
A session ale with a zesty start leading to a dry and hoppy finish.

Innocence (OG 1042, ABV 4%)
A straw-coloured, fragrant bitter.

Innspiration (OG 1042, ABV 4%) 🗇
A traditional copper-coloured, easy-drinking bitter.

Inntrigue (OG 1044, ABV 4.2%)
Ruby-coloured best bitter with flavours of woodland berries and a whisper of dark chocolate.

Inncognito (OG 1053, ABV 4.8%) 🗇 🏶
A flavoursome stout; sweet, roasted malt, aged port and mature fruits of the vine.

Inndulgence (OG 1055, ABV 5.2%)
A dark ruby porter with coffee, chocolate and a hint of smoke.

Plassey

See New Plassey

Platform 5 SIBA

🖥 Railway Brewhouse, 197 Queen Street, Newton Abbot, Devon, TQ12 2BS
☎ (01626) 437140 ⊕ platform5brewing.co.uk

⊠ Platform 5 was established in 2013 using a six-barrel plant. The Railway Inn is supplied along with Molloys in Teignmouth and Torquay. This family-run brewery is situated in part of an enclosed alley under the disused Platform 5 of Newton Abbot station.

The Coaster (OG 1040, ABV 4%)
A light and refreshing session ale.

The Antelope (OG 1043, ABV 4.3%)
A hoppy pale ale.

The Whistleblower (OG 1046, ABV 4.6%)

Western Gold (OG 1048, ABV 4.8%)
A strong golden ale.

IPA (OG 1050, ABV 5%)
A strong IPA brewed with English and American hops.

Plockton

5 Bank Street, Plockton, IV52 8TP
☎ (01599) 544276 ☎ 07823 322043
⊕ theplocktonbrewery.com

The brewery started trading in 2007 and expanded to a 2.5-barrel plant in 2009. Bottle-conditioned beers are available and are suitable for vegetarians. !! ♦ RAIB

Ciste Dhubh (OG 1040, ABV 3.9%) 🌢
Excellent mix of malts and hops in this dark brew. Initial bitter turning bittersweet.

Bay (OG 1047, ABV 4.6%) 🌢
A well-balanced, tawny-coloured best bitter with plenty of hops and malt which give a bittersweet fruity flavour.

Fiddlers Fancy (OG 1046, ABV 4.6%) 🌢
Refreshing grapefruit aroma and taste turning to a more malty finish.

Poachers

439 Newark Road, North Hykeham, Lincolnshire, LN6 9SP
☎ (01522) 807404 ☎ 07954 131972
⊕ poachersbrewery.co.uk

☺Brewing started in 2001 on a five-barrel plant. In 2006 it was downsized to 2.5-barrel and relocated to outbuildings at the rear of the brewer's home. 2011 saw capacity returned to five barrels. Regular outlets in Lincolnshire and surrounding counties are supplied direct; outlets further afield via wholesalers. !! !!

Trembling Rabbit Mild (OG 1034, ABV 3.4%)
Rich, dark mild with a smooth, malty flavour and a slightly bitter finish. Local honey used.

Shy Talk Bitter (OG 1037, ABV 3.7%)
A crisp tasting session beer, pale golden in colour. Refreshing with citrus overtones.

Rock Ape (OG 1038, ABV 3.8%)
Traditional brown-coloured session bitter produced from English ingredients.

Pride (OG 1040, ABV 4%)
Amber-coloured bitter brewed using East Kent Goldings hops.

Bog Trotter (OG 1042, ABV 4.2%)
An amber, full-flavoured, malty beer with a bitter aftertaste.

Lincoln Best (OG 1042, ABV 4.2%)
A flowery, hop-nosed, brown beer with a well-balanced but bitter taste that stays with the malt, becoming more apparent in the drying finish.

Billy Boy (OG 1044, ABV 4.4%)
A rich, full-flavoured brown beer.

Imp Ale (OG 1044, ABV 4.4%)
Copper-coloured, fruity and floral with a bitter finish.

Black Crow Stout (OG 1045, ABV 4.5%)
A full-bodied stout that has an aftertaste that lingers. Burnt toffee and caramel flavours come to the fore.

Hykeham Gold (OG 1045, ABV 4.5%)
A cask-conditioned lager.

Monkey Hanger (OG 1045, ABV 4.5%)
A ruby-red bitter, smooth, fruity flavour balanced by the bitter hops.

Jock's Trap (OG 1050, ABV 5%)
A strong, pale brown bitter. A hoppy, well-balanced beer with a slightly dry fruit finish.

Trout Tickler (OG 1055, ABV 5.5%)
A strong ruby bitter with intense flavour and character, sweet undertones with a hint of chocolate. A rich, malty beer.

Pocket

La Croix Farm, La Rue de la Croix, St Ouen, Jersey, JE3 2HA ☎ 07797 771931
✉ jerseybeer@jerseymail.co.uk

⊗ As the name implies, Pocket Brewery began in 2011 on a small scale. Brewing was undertaken occasionally on demand with the beers available locally in bottle-conditioned form and sometimes in cask at local freehouses and beer festivals. Brewing is currently suspended. RAIB

Pokertree

The Brewhouse, 357b Drumnakilly Road, Carrickmore, Co Tyrone, BT79 9JY
☎ (028) 8076 1923 ⊕ pokertreebrewing.co.uk

Opened in 2014, Pokertree brews small batch beers using all natural and, where possible, local ingredients. RAIB

Ghrain Golden Ale (OG 1045, ABV 4.5%)

Seven Sisters Treacle Oat Stout (OG 1052, ABV 5.2%)

Red Earl Ruby Ale (OG 1055, ABV 5.5%)

Dark Nirvana (OG 1065, ABV 6.5%)

Pope's

73a, Blackpole Trading Estate West, Worcester, WR3 8TJ
☎ (01905) 755016 ✉ popesbrew@btconnect.com

Pope's is a family-run brewery established in 2012. A 4.5-barrel brew plant is used with brewing taking place twice a week, supplying the local free trade and further afield. Beer names are influenced by the local area. Brewery and pizzeria open from 4-11pm Fridays. ‼ ⬤ ◆ RAIB

Nut Brown Ale (OG 1036, ABV 3.6%)

Hop Market (OG 1038, ABV 3.8%)

Worcester Gold (OG 1040, ABV 4%)

Hope & Glory (OG 1046, ABV 4.6%)

Pope's Yard

477-479 Whippendell Road, Watford, Hertfordshire, WD18 7PU
☎ (01923) 224182 ⊕ popesyard.co.uk

Pope's Yard began commercial brewing in 2012 using a one-barrel plant. Relocation in 2015 also meant expansion to a five-barrel plant with a one-barrel pilot plant. RAIB

Luminaire (OG 1041, ABV 3.9%)
Hints of citrus, passion fruit and pineapple with a classic bitter finish.

Quartermaster (OG 1044, ABV 4.4%)

Club Hammer Stout (OG 1060, ABV 5.5%)

A stout with chocolate sweetness and roasted flavours balanced by hop bitterness and aroma.

Strong Dark Mild (OG 1063, ABV 6.8%)

Galaxian IPA (OG 1066, ABV 7.4%)

Poppyland

46 West Street, Cromer, Norfolk, NR27 9DS
☎ (01263) 513992 ☎ 07887 389804
⊕ poppylandbeer.com

Established in 2012 by museum curator and geologist Martin Warren as a working retirement project, the two-barrel Poppyland Brewery produces adventurous, unfiltered and vegan-friendly beers. Many of the beers are gluten-free, most are experimental and brewed with local wild ingredients such as damson, sea purslane, wild hops and dandelions. ⬤ RAIB GF V

Porter Street

See Evan Evans

George N Porter

Whitley Bay, Tyne & Wear, NE26 1AP
☎ (0191) 290 2134 ☎ 07980 842087
✉ gnporterbrewing@gmail.com

George N Porter is a 2.5-barrel microbrewery established in 2012. Brewing is currently suspended.

Portobello SIBA

Unit 6, Mitre Bridge Industrial Estate, Mitre Way, Kensington, London, W10 6AU
☎ (020) 8969 2269 ⊕ portobellobrewing.com

⊗ Portobello began brewing in 2012 using a 10-barrel plant. ◆

Pale (OG 1040, ABV 4%) 🍺
Golden, well-balanced best bitter with citrus and spiced hops. Biscuit sweetness fades in the clean, dry finish, becoming bitter.

Star (OG 1044, ABV 4.3%) 🍺
Pale brown malty best bitter with a sweetish nose, a fruity flavour and a bitter finish. Hints of nut on the palate and some hops throughout.

APA (OG 1050, ABV 5%) 🍺
Full-bodied, straw-coloured strong ale. The honey sweetness and soft citrus fruit balanced by bitter hops. Dry aftertaste.

Portpatrick

The Neuk, Stoneykirk, DG9 9EF ☎ 07826 542149
⊕ portpatrick-brewery.co.uk

☺The brewery opened in 2015 using a 1.5-barrel brew plant in converted space in outbuildings. ◆ RAIB

16-21 (OG 1040, ABV 3.8%)

Dorn Rock (OG 1043, ABV 4.3%)

Fog Horn (OG 1048, ABV 4.8%)

Potbelly SIBA 👁

Sydney Street Entrance, Kettering, Northamptonshire, NN16 0JA
☎ (01536) 410818 ☎ 07834 867825
⊕ potbelly-brewery.co.uk

Potbelly started brewing in 2005 on a 10-barrel plant and supplies some 200 outlets. The brewery has won numerous awards for its beers. ‼ 🍺♦RAIB

Best (OG 1036.9, ABV 3.8%)
A traditional chestnut-coloured bitter.

Lager Brau (OG 1037.4, ABV 3.9%)

Hop-Trotter (OG 1039, ABV 4.1%)
Golden in colour, spicy aromas and citrus notes.

Beijing Black (OG 1045, ABV 4.4%)
A strong dark mild.

Pigs Do Fly (OG 1041, ABV 4.4%)
A single-hopped, light golden ale.

Bellowhead Hedonism (OG 1045, ABV 4.5%)
A light-coloured bitter with a citrus, hoppy finish, brewed with the help of Bellowhead, a local band.

Captain Pigwash (OG 1050, ABV 5%)
An easy-drinking dark porter.

SOAB (OG 1048, ABV 5%)
A fruity and malty bitter.

Crazy Daze (OG 1050, ABV 5.5%)
A light golden bitter with hidden strength.

Powderkeg (NEW) SIBA

10 Hogsbrook Units, Woodbury Salterton, Devon, EX5 1PY
☎ (01395) 488181 ⊕ powderkegbeer.co.uk

⊗ Powderkeg was established in 2015 brewing small batches of beer. It combines International beer styles with new ingredients sourced from around the world.

**Speak Easy Transatlantic Pale Ale
(OG 1041.5, ABV 4.3%)**
Uniting robust malt and huge fruitiness with balanced bitterness and a clean finish.

Poynton (NEW)

🍺 Royal British Legion Club, St George's Road West, Poynton, Cheshire, SK12 1JY ☎ 07771 722403

The Poynton Brewery was established in 2015 by Colin Bavens and Andy King, located at the Poynton Legion Club. Around 20 pubs, clubs and bars are supplied in the Stockport, Altrincham, East Cheshire and Macclesfield areas.

Fireside (ABV 3.2%)
A full-bodied, nutty brown ale.

Maid in Cheshire (ABV 3.7%)
A light, zesty bitter.

Aurora (ABV 3.9%)
A session bitter. Light and refreshing.

Vulcan (ABV 4.2%)

Dark Side (ABV 4.5%)
Dark, not overly bitter porter with hints of chocolate and coffee.

Prescott SIBA

Unit 1, The Bramery Business Park, Alstone Lane, Cheltenham, Gloucestershire, GL51 8HE ☎ 07526 934866 ⊕ prescottales.co.uk

Prescott Ales was established in 2008, and brews on a traditional 25-barrel plant, clad in wood, brass and copper. It takes its name from the famous Prescott Hill Climb, which is also the home of the UK Bugatti Owners Club. In 2015, a number of craft ales brewed under the Super-6 banner was introduced. ‼♦

Hill Climb (OG 1039.5, ABV 3.8%)
A late-hopped, straw-coloured IPA-style session beer with a refreshing fruity finish.

Chequered Flag (OG 1042, ABV 4.1%)
A generously-hopped amber ale with a malty finish.

Track Record (OG 1044, ABV 4.4%)
A fruity, light, copper-coloured best bitter, with a slightly sweet finish.

Grand Prix (OG 1050, ABV 5.2%)
A dark amber-coloured strong ale with a rich, smooth finish.

Preseli

See Tenby

Pressure Drop

Unit 19, Bohemia Place, Hackney, London, E8 1DU
☎ (020) 8533 0614 ⊕ pressuredropbrewing.co.uk

Pressure Drop is run by three partners who were home brewers but began commercial brewing in 2013 using a five-barrel plant and a small pilot kit. RAIB

Street Porter (ABV 5.2%) 🍺
Roast notes and a bitter character dominate this black porter. Long, enjoyable aftertaste.

Prestonpans

See Kentwood

Prior's Well (NEW)

Unit 8, Block 21, Old Mill Lane Industrial Estate, Mansfield, Nottinghamshire, NG19 9BG

Originally established in a National Trust building on the Clumber Park Estate, but brewing ceased there in 2014. The brewery was subsequently sold and the five-barrel plant relocated to a new site in Mansfield, where brewing recommenced in 2016.

Priory Gold (ABV 4.7%)

Resurrected (ABV 4.8%)

Problem Child

🍺 Wayfarer Inn, Alder Lane, Parbold, Lancashire, WN8 7NL
☎ (01257) 464600 ☎ 07588 736926
⊕ problemchildbrewing.co.uk

Problem Child began brewing in 2013, at the Wayfarer Inn, Parbold, owned by Johnny and Rachel Birkett. The brewery name originates from the family history of the Wayfarer. ‼

Scallywag (OG 1039, ABV 3.7%)

One Night Stand (OG 1038, ABV 3.8%)

Rascal (OG 1039, ABV 3.8%)

Tantrum (OG 1040, ABV 4%)

Little Punk (OG 1048, ABV 4.2%)

Rapscallion (OG 1046, ABV 4.2%)

Scoundrel (OG 1046, ABV 4.6%)

Good Spankin' (OG 1055, ABV 5.1%)

Prospect SIBA ⟨◉⟩

Unit 11, Bradley Hall Trading Estate, Bradley Lane, Standish, WN6 0XQ
☎ (01257) 421329 ⊕ prospectbrewery.com

⊛Prospect Brewery was founded in 2007 and relocated to its present premises in 2010, expanding to a 12-barrel plant. The brewery owns a local bar, Wigan Central, where its beers are available. ♦

Silver Tally (OG 1037, ABV 3.7%)
A clean, pale golden bitter with citrus aromas and a full hop flavour with a dry bitter finish.

Whatever! (OG 1040, ABV 3.8%)
Pale bitter packed with hop flavour and aroma.

Nutty Slack (OG 1039, ABV 3.9%) 📭 ◄
Dark brown mild ale with malt and fruit in the aroma. Creamy and chocolaty on the palate, with both malt and fruit in evidence. Malty and moderately bitter finish.

Pioneer (OG 1040, ABV 4%)
A light-bodied amber beer with aromas of dry pale malt and earthy hops.

Cascade Blonde (OG 1039, ABV 4.1%)
A yellow/gold beer with zesty citrus notes; clean-tasting and refreshing lemon notes.

Blinding Light (OG 1042, ABV 4.2%)
A pale, refreshing beer with citrus and spicy notes.

Gold Rush (OG 1045, ABV 4.5%)
A deep golden ale with hoppy and bitter flavours, light fruity notes and a grassy, floral finish.

Big John (OG 1047, ABV 4.8%)
A dark stout bursting with smoky liquorice flavour with a satisfying bitter aftertaste.

Pumphouse (NEW)

Green Man Pub, The Barn, Toppesfield, Essex, CO9 4DR ☎ 07421 994518
⊕ pumphousecommunitybrewery.com

⊠ Community-owned brewery established in 2015 with a two-barrel brewing capacity. Brewing is on a regular basis by a professional head brewer supported by members of the local community working on a voluntary basis. ♦

Bitter (OG 1037, ABV 3.6%)

Toppesfield Tap (OG 1037, ABV 3.6%)
Well-hopped, well-balanced session bitter.

Black (OG 1041, ABV 4%)

Gold (OG 1041, ABV 4.2%)

Purity SIBA ⟨◉⟩

The Brewery, Upper Spernal Farm, Spernal Lane, Great Alne, Warwickshire, B49 6JF
☎ (01789) 488007 ⊕ puritybrewing.com

⊛Brewing began in 2005 in a purpose-designed plant housed in converted barns. The brewery incorporates an environmentally-friendly effluent treatment system. It supplies the free trade within a 70-mile radius, plus London postcodes, and delivers to more than 500 outlets. ‼️🍴♦

Pure Gold (OG 1039.5, ABV 3.8%) 📭
An easy-drinking beer with a dry and bitter finish.

Mad Goose (OG 1042.5, ABV 4.2%)
Light copper in colour with a zesty hop character with citrus overtones.

Pure UBU (OG 1044.8, ABV 4.5%)
A distinctive premium amber-coloured beer. Well-balanced and full-flavoured.

Purple Moose SIBA ⟨◉⟩

Madoc Street, Porthmadog, LL49 9DB
☎ (01766) 515571 ⊕ purplemoose.co.uk

Purple Moose opened in 2005 using a 10-barrel plant in a former iron works in the coastal town of Porthmadog. In 2013 a new 40-barrel plant was installed, significantly increasing production. The names of the beers reflect local history and geography. ‼️🍴♦

Cwrw Eryri/Snowdonia Ale
(OG 1035.3, ABV 3.6%) ◄
Golden, refreshing bitter with citrus fruit hoppiness in aroma and taste. The full mouthfeel leads to a long-lasting, dry, bitter finish.

Cwrw Madog/Madog's Ale
(OG 1037, ABV 3.7%) 🗃 ◄
Full-bodied session bitter. Malty nose and an initial nutty flavour but bitterness dominates. Well-balanced and refreshing with a dry roastiness on the taste and a good dry finish.

Cwrw Ysgawen/Elderflower
(OG 1039, ABV 4%) ◄
A pale and refreshing elderflower beer with a good citrus fruit aroma, bittersweet taste, and a zesty, hoppy, mouthwatering finish.

Cwrw Glaslyn/Glaslyn Ale
(OG 1040.5, ABV 4.2%) ◄
Refreshing light and malty amber-coloured ale. Plenty of hop in the aroma and taste. Good smooth mouthfeel leading to a slightly chewy finish.

Ochr Tywyll y Mws/Dark Side of the Moose
(OG 1045, ABV 4.6%) 🗃 📭 ◄
A dark, complex beer, quite hoppy and bitter with roast undertones. Malt and fruit flavours also feature in the smooth taste and dry finish.

Q

16 The Ringway, Queniborough, Leicestershire, LE7 3DL ☎ 07762 300240 ⊕ qbrewery.co.uk

Q is a microbrewery based in Queniborough in a converted building behind the house of head brewer Tim Lowe. It was established in 2014 and uses a 0.5-barrel brew kit, producing a firkin and a pin from each batch brewed. Beers are brewed on demand.

Quantock SIBA 👁

Westridge Way, Broadgauge Business Park, Bishops Lydeard, Somerset, TA4 3RU
☎ (01823) 433812 ⊕ quantockbrewery.co.uk

Quantock is a family-run brewery that started trading in 2008 on an eight-barrel plant. The brewery supplies beers to outlets throughout the South-west and further afield via wholesalers. Beers are available to the public direct from the brewery and via online sales from the website.
♦ RAIB

Ale (OG 1036, ABV 3.8%)
An amber-coloured beer with a fruity, full-bodied flavour with a dry finish to the palate. The blend of English hops creates a balanced, fruity character with a delicate spicy aroma.

Ginger Cockney (OG 1037, ABV 4%)
A copper-coloured ale, generously hopped and with a hint of fresh ginger.

Rorke's Drift (OG 1039, ABV 4.2%)
A light, refreshing lager-style beer, a fruit-filled experience with a delicate citrus aroma. Brewed in support of The Royal Engineers Association (REA) with five pence from every pint being donated to the Association.

Sunraker (OG 1039, ABV 4.2%)
A pale straw-coloured beer, light and refreshing with a delicate, clean grassy hop finish.

Wills Neck (OG 1040, ABV 4.3%)
This bright golden ale has a rich, malty flavour and is late hopped to produce a prominent aroma with hints of grapefruit and cherries and a lasting bitterness on the palate.

White Hind (OG 1042, ABV 4.5%)
A chestnut-coloured best bitter brewed from a blend of three malts to give a full-bodied, malty flavour with the roast malt coming through and a dry finish. The beer is generously hopped, producing a biscuity, spicy aroma.

Royal Stag IPA (OG 1056, ABV 6%)
A copper-coloured beer with a malty and fruity flavour, generously hopped giving a smoky aroma with hints of banana and toffee.

UXB (OG 1088, ABV 9%)
A strong beer, slightly sweet with a full, malty flavour.

Quantum

Unit 4, Victoria Works, Hempshaw Lane, Stockport, SK1 4LG ☎ 07976 032465
⊕ quantumbrewingcompany.co.uk

☺The brewery was established in 2011 using a five-barrel plant on the site of the former Shaws Brewery. It brews short-run beers and one-off specials mainly for the local free trade and Wetherspoon outlets. ‼

Quartz SIBA 👁

Archers, Alrewas Road, Kings Bromley, Staffordshire, DE13 7HW
☎ (01543) 473965 ⊕ quartzbrewing.co.uk

☺Quartz was established in 2005 by Scott and Julia Barnett. Around 50 outlets are supplied direct.
‼ 🍺 ♦

Blonde (OG 1038, ABV 3.8%) 🍺

Little aroma, gentle hop and background malt. Sweet with unsophisticated sweetshop tastes.

Crystal (OG 1040, ABV 4.2%) 🍺
Sweet aroma with some fruit and yeasty Marmite hints. Hoppiness begins but dwindles to a bittersweet finish.

Extra Blonde (OG 1042, ABV 4.4%) 🍺
Sweet malty aroma with a touch of fruit. Sweet start, smooth with a hint of hops in the sugary finish.

Heart (OG 1045, ABV 4.6%) 🍺
Pale brown with some aroma of fruit and malt. Gentle tastes of fruit and hops eventually appear to leave a bitter finish.

Cracker (OG 1050, ABV 5%)
Chestnut in colour with a slight roasted aroma, smooth fruit notes leaving a dry hop finish.

Queen Inn SIBA

🏠 **28 Kingsgate Road, Winchester, Hampshire, SO23 9PG**
☎ (01962) 853898 ⊕ thequeeninnwinchester.co.uk

Brewing began in 2014 using a 1.5-barrel brew plant. At present beers are only brewed for the pub.

St Cross Ale (ABV 4.1%)

Queen's Head

🏠 **Queen's Head, 66 Acton Street, London, WC1X 9NB**
☎ (020) 7713 5772

Situated in the basement of the Queen's Head pub, brewing began in 2014. Beer is mainly keg and supplied direct to the pub. Bottle-conditioned ales are planned. Brewing is currently suspended.

Quercus

See Salcombe

Quiet

🏠 **Buchanan's Bistro, Woodend Barn, Burn O'Bennie, Banchory, Aberdeenshire, AB31 5QA**
☎ (01330) 826530 ✉ bistro@buchananfood.com

Quiet Brewery is situated at Buchanan's Bistro. Beers are available bottle-conditioned only and are supplied to the bistro and local outlets. ♦ RAIB

Quirky (NEW)

Unit 1a, Fusion Point, Ash Lane, Garforth, Leeds, West Yorkshire, LS25 2HG ☎ 07425 133199
⊕ quirkyales.com

☺Established in 2015, Quirky Ales brews only five or so nine-gallon firkins at a time. However, expansion is planned as investment in new equipment and premises is underway and a small tap room is due to open.

Bitter (ABV 4%)
A chestnut-coloured session bitter, well-balanced and easy-drinking.

Long Hop (ABV 4%)
A dry, clean base with a citrus and refreshing taste.

Porter (ABV 4%)

A dark, rich beer with a malty start and a fruity finish. Smooth and easy-drinking.

Ruby (ABV 4%)
A ruby-coloured ale with a smooth finish.

Saazy Blonde (ABV 4%)
A refreshing ale made using Saaz hops.

Gold (ABV 4.1%)
An easy-drinking golden IPA with a citrus flavour and caramel finish.

Blonde (ABV 4.2%)
A crisp, refreshing beer with hints of tropical fruit and a citrus aftertaste.

Classic (ABV 5.7%)
A dark, smooth beer made with roasted malt.

Radlett (NEW) SIBA

Watling Street Beer, Hilfield Farm, Hilfield Lane, Aldenham, Hertfordshire, WD25 8DD ☎ 07713 841936 ⊕ watlingstreetbeer.com

Brewing began in 2015 in Aldenham village and relocated to an old farm building on Hilfield Farm in 2016 to allow for expansion to a 10-barrel plant. There is an on-site bar and functions occur on a regular basis including comedy nights.

Golden Ale (ABV 3.8%)
A light-coloured ale with citrus notes.

Premium (ABV 4.2%)
A best bitter using roasted malt.

Radnorshire SIBA

Timberworks, Brookside Farm, Mutton Dingle, New Radnor, LD8 2SU
☎ (01544) 350456 ☎ 07789 909748
✉ info@radnorhillsholidaycottages.com

Radnorshire is a microbrewery set up in 2012 in a barn on the grounds of a farm offering holiday cottage accommodation. It uses its own spring water. Drinkers staying at the cottages are supplied as well as a few local pubs. ‼ ☞

Whimble Gold (OG 1038, ABV 3.8%)
Light and hoppy golden ale.

Four Stones (OG 1040, ABV 4%)
A light amber ale with a subtle maltiness.

Smatcher Tawny (OG 1042, ABV 4.2%)
Mellow, tawny-coloured best bitter.

Water-Break-Its-Neck (ABV 5.7%)
A well-hopped IPA.

Rail Ale

Schooner, South Shore Road, Gateshead, Tyne & Wear, NE8 3AF ☎ 07758 653510

Established in 2013, and based at the Schooner pub, Rail Ale is the first microbrewery in Gateshead. Beers are available at the Schooner and other local outlets, and are named with a railway theme. Brewing is currently suspended.

Amber Aspect (OG 1039, ABV 3.8%)
A traditional, refreshing amber bitter.

Night Train (OG 1040, ABV 4%)
Black in colour, dry hopped giving a smooth velvet taste.

Railway Tavern

58 Station Road, Brightlingsea, Essex, CO7 0DT

The brewery started life as a kitchen-sink affair in 1998. In 2012 the brewery was completely refurbished; a two-barrel plant is used to create a selection of dark beers suitable for vegetarians. ‼

Crab & Winkle Mild (OG 1036, ABV 3.6%) ◆
Thin-bodied mild with a pear drop aroma and a rather roasty taste. The aftertaste is slightly ash-like with suggestions of bitter chocolate.

Bladderwrack Stout (OG 1047, ABV 4.7%) ◆
Full-bodied stout with an intense roast grain character that is initially underpinned by subtle sweetness, which subsides to leave a drier finish.

Ramsbottom Craft SIBA 👁

1 Heapworth Avenue, Ramsbottom, BL0 9EH
☎ 07976 263344 ⊕ ramsbottombrewery.com

Brewing began in 2011 from a microbrewery in owner Matt Holmes's converted garage. 2014 saw production go full-time and the bottling side of the business moved to a bespoke unit, creating more room to expand the brewery. Larger premises are now being sought due to increased demand.
◆ RAIB V

NS IPA (OG 1037, ABV 3.4%)

Rammy Red (OG 1039, ABV 3.6%)
Classic red ale with dominant roasted malt and a hint of smoke.

Stellar IPA (OG 1040, ABV 3.7%)
Refreshing, medium-bodied ale with intensely fruity finish.

Waterfall Pale (OG 1041, ABV 3.9%)

Ye Old Gold (OG 1041, ABV 3.9%)

Bumble's Honeyed Ale (OG 1039, ABV 4%)
Elderflower and honey based EPA.

Rammy Ale (OG 1041, ABV 4%)
A session bitter using Styrian and Goldings hops.

Flaori Maori (OG 1042, ABV 4.1%)
Balanced session ale, initial light malt gives way to increasingly red fruit finish.

Chocolate Porter (OG 1043, ABV 4.2%)
A brown porter. Cocoa steep giving mocha notes.

Yankie Lip Smacka (OG 1042, ABV 4.2%)

Fat Lady Stout (OG 1043, ABV 4.3%)
Dark brown, almost black stout with a hint of roast in the aroma and a smooth taste.

Crafty Ram (OG 1045, ABV 4.4%)

Gift o'Gold (OG 1046, ABV 4.5%)
Copper/golden ale with a floral aroma and flavour notes of honey, spice and vanilla.

Oh, Sunny Day (OG 1046, ABV 4.5%)
A pale yellow-coloured mellow ale with balanced malt sweetness and fruitiness.

Liquorice Root Stout (OG 1052, ABV 4.6%)
Dark, sweet flavours and a deep, earthy liquorice, lasting finish.

Mango Beach (OG 1054, ABV 5.5%)
American pale ale using Amarillo hops.

THE BREWERIES

Ramsbury SIBA 👁

Stockclose Farm, Aldbourne, Wiltshire, SN8 2NN
☎ (01672) 541407 ☎ 07843 289527
⊕ ramsbury.com/brewery

Ramsbury started brewing in 2004 using a 10-barrel plant and is situated high on the Marlborough Downs in Wiltshire. The brewery uses home-grown barley from the Ramsbury Estate. Expansion in 2014 saw an upgrade to a 30-barrel plant with a visitor centre and a well to provide the water. A distillery that uses grains grown on the estate became operational in 2015. ‼🍴♦

Bitter (OG 1036, ABV 3.6%)
Amber-coloured beer with a smooth, delicate aroma and flavour.

Deerstalker (OG 1040, ABV 4%)
Amber coloured best bitter with smooth bitter finish.

Kennet Valley (OG 1041, ABV 4.1%)
A light amber, hoppy bitter with a long, dry finish.

Flint Knapper (OG 1042, ABV 4.2%)
Rich amber in colour with a malty taste.

Gold (OG 1045, ABV 4.5%)
A rich, golden-coloured beer with a light, hoppy aroma and taste.

Red Velvet (OG 1046, ABV 4.6%)
A red-coloured American IPA, full of flavour and character.

Chalk Stream (OG 1050, ABV 5%)
A pale, lightly-hopped premium ale.

Belapur IPA (OG 1055, ABV 5.5%)

Ramsgate SIBA 👁

1 Hornet Close, Pyson's Road Industrial Estate, Broadstairs, Kent, CT10 2YD
☎ (01843) 868453 ⊕ ramsgatebrewery.co.uk

Ramsgate was established in 2002 at the back of a Ramsgate pub. In 2006 the brewery moved to its current location, allowing for increased capacity and bottling. ‼🍴♦RAIB

Gadds' No. 7 Bitter Ale (OG 1037, ABV 3.8%)

Gadds' Seasider (OG 1042, ABV 4.3%)

Gadds' No. 5 Best Bitter Ale (OG 1043, ABV 4.4%)

Gadds' No. 3 Kent Pale Ale (OG 1047, ABV 5%)

Gadds' Faithful Dogbolter Porter (OG 1054, ABV 5.6%)

RAN SIBA

Unit 8, Ormonde Street, Fenton, Stoke-on-Trent, Staffordshire, ST4 3NP ☎ 07843 092620
⊕ ranales.co.uk

RAN Ales began brewing in 2014 using a one-barrel kit in the garage to the rear of the owner's house. It relocated in 2015 to larger, purpose-built premises nearby, increasing capacity to 2.5 barrels. ♦

Coppa Flya (OG 1040, ABV 4%)
A copper-coloured bitter with a dry finish and a complementary caramel aftertaste.

American Pale Ale (OG 1045, ABV 4.5%)

Flya (OG 1045, ABV 4.5%)

Easy-drinking session ale. Amber in colour with a malty bitterness.

Hedge Hopper (OG 1045, ABV 4.5%)
A light golden-coloured bitter with refreshing fruity notes.

Owd Flya (OG 1050, ABV 5%) 🍂
Malt and roast aromas. Liquorice flavours, sweet finish with gentle hops.

Cherry Chilli Stout (OG 1053, ABV 5.3%)

Rum 'n' Raisin Stout (OG 1053, ABV 5.3%) 🍂
Chocolate aroma with cocoa. Sweet fruity start with hoppy background which develops to a mouthwatering finish.

Stout (OG 1053, ABV 5.3%)
Rich and flavoursome dark ale with hints of coffee and chocolate.

Randalls SIBA

La Piette Brewery, St Georges Esplanade, St Peter Port, Guernsey, GY1 3JG
☎ (01481) 720134 ⊕ randallsbrewery.com

Randalls has been brewing in Guernsey since 1868. The company was bought out in 2006 and moved into a modern, purpose-built brewery in 2008. 19 pubs are owned and a further 70 outlets are supplied. ‼♦

Range (NEW)

Unit N4, Lympne Industrial Estate, Otterpool Lane, Lympne, Kent, CT21 4LR
☎ (01303) 238420 ⊕ rangealesbrewery.co.uk

⊗ Range Ales was planned and set up in 2016 by two friends over a few pints in their local. The brewery name comes from associations with the Hythe small arms ranges nearby, which provides the names of the beers. It is a four-barrel plant with two fermenters and produces beers designed to suit local tastes. Currently supplying pubs and clubs in the Hythe and Folkestone areas. ‼

Golden Shot (ABV 3.7%)
A hoppy, citrus flavoured beer.

Double Tap (ABV 4.1%)
Based on an original Burton recipe – a sweetish beer with a gentle hop aftertaste.

Rat

🏠 Rat & Ratchet, 40 Chapel Hill, Huddersfield, West Yorkshire, HD1 3EB
☎ (01484) 542400 ☎ 07906 279038
✉ ratandratchet@ossett-brewery.co.uk

☺The Rat & Ratchet was originally established as a brewpub in 1994. Brewing ceased and it was purchased by Ossett Brewery (qv) in 2004. Brewing re-started in 2011 with a capacity of 30 barrels per week. A wide range of occasional beers with Rat themed names supplements the regular ales. ♦

Rat Attack (OG 1038, ABV 3.8%)
A pale golden session beer with a powerful citrus aroma.

White Rat (OG 1040, ABV 4%)
A pale, hoppy ale with an intensely aromatic and resinous finish.

Black Rat (OG 1047, ABV 4.5%)

A porter with burnt, coffee and chocolate malt character. Slightly sweet on the palate, but moderate bitterness and a fruity/spicy aroma.

King Rat (OG 1050, ABV 5%)
A unique white wine hop aroma. Bitterness is high, but balanced by a residual malty sweetness.

Rat Against the Machine (OG 1071, ABV 7%)
A massively hopped IPA.

Raw SIBA

Units 3 & 4, Silver House, Adelphi Way, Staveley, Derbyshire, S43 3LJ
☎ (01246) 475445 ⊕ rawbrew.com

Raw began brewing in 2010 using a five-barrel plant from Prospect Brewery of Wigan. Specials are available including the Xtreme range, which are one-off brews that push the ingredients a little further. ‼◆

Baby Ghost IPA (OG 1039, ABV 3.9%)
Powerful citrus-hopped session IPA.

Blonde Pale (OG 1039, ABV 3.9%)
Refreshing pale ale with German hops for a dry lager style.

JR Best Bitter (OG 1042, ABV 4.2%)
Traditional brown bitter with sweet biscuit malt flavours. Smooth, balanced bitterness.

Dark Peak Stout (OG 1045, ABV 4.5%)
Easy-drinking stout with plenty of malt flavours. English hopped for a smooth, bitter finish.

Edge Pale Ale (OG 1045, ABV 4.5%)
Pale ale with balanced bitterness and a citrus aroma.

Anubis Porter (OG 1051, ABV 5.2%) ▣
Smooth roast malt and mild coffee flavours with a lingering bitterness and gentle hop aroma.

Grey Ghost IPA (OG 1056, ABV 5.9%) ⬚
Powerful IPA with citrus and grapefruit flavours. Smooth and deceptively easy to drink.

RCH SIBA ◉

West Hewish, Somerset, BS24 6RR
☎ (01934) 834447 ⊕ rchbrewery.com

⊠ The brewery was originally installed in the early 1980s behind the Royal Clarence Hotel, Burnham-on-Sea. Since 1993 brewing has taken place in a former cider mill at West Hewish. A 30-barrel plant was installed in 2000. RCH supplies 150 outlets and the award-winning beers are available nationwide through its own wholesaling company, which also distributes beers from other small independent breweries. ➽◆RAIB

Hewish IPA (OG 1036, ABV 3.6%) ◈
Thinnish session bitter with plenty of malt, hops and pale fruit on the nose and palate. An astringent finish.

Hewish Mild (OG 1036, ABV 3.6%) ▣ ◈
Black mild with light roast nose. Hints of roast malt and slight apple taste with an astringent finish.

PG Steam (OG 1039, ABV 3.9%) ◈
A tawny beer with a hint of unripe fruit and some malt in the flavour. Bitterness and astringency throughout.

Pitchfork (OG 1043, ABV 4.3%) ▣ ◈

Some citrus aroma is followed by a bitter, hoppy taste with grapefruit notes. Finishes with an astringent and bitter aftertaste.

Chocolate Slug (OG 1045, ABV 4.5%)
A velvety smooth porter with added chocolate that features strongly in the smooth finish.

Old Slug Porter (OG 1046, ABV 4.5%) ▣ ◈
Powerful aroma of roast and dark fruit which continues into the roast malt flavours. Bitter, slightly astringent finish.

East Street Cream (OG 1050, ABV 5%) ◈
Brown beer which is low in flavour for the strength, with an astringent finish.

Double Header (OG 1053, ABV 5.3%) ◈
A strong, full-bodied golden bitter with a citrus taste and fruity hop nose. Has a bitter, astringent finish.

Firebox (OG 1060, ABV 6%) ◈
Strong golden bitter with complex hoppy and fruity aroma. Sweet apple flavours give way to a lingering bitter aftertaste.

Reality

127 High Road, Chilwell, Nottingham, NG9 4AT
☎ 07801 539523
✉ alandenismonaghan@hotmail.com

Reality began brewing in 2010 in the unused space of an IT business, hence the pun on Real-ITy. Beers are mainly themed around the brewery name and can be found locally and occasionally at beer festivals across the country.

Virtuale Reality (OG 1039, ABV 3.8%)
A pale session brew.

No Escape (OG 1043, ABV 4.2%)

Bitter Reality (OG 1044, ABV 4.3%)
A copper-coloured bitter.

Stark Reality (OG 1046, ABV 4.5%)
An amber-coloured bitter with a hint of rum.

Reality Czech (OG 1047, ABV 4.6%)

Rebel SIBA

Century House, Kernick Industrial Estate, Penryn, Cornwall, TR10 9EP
☎ (01326) 617780 ⊕ rebelbrewing.co.uk

⊠ Rebel began brewing in 2011. It expanded to a nine-barrel plant with a shop and bar in 2012, supplying local pubs. In 2015 an 18-barrel plant was installed to meet demand. ‼◆RAIB

Surfbum IPA (OG 1034, ABV 3.5%)
Golden-coloured, fragrant session ale with masses of citrus hoppiness.

Gold (OG 1038, ABV 3.8%) ◈
Refreshing golden ale with a light hop and fruit nose. Sweet grapefruit and citrus marmalade throughout. Bitter and slight dry finish.

Bal Maiden (OG 1041, ABV 4%) ◈
Pale brown best bitter with malt aroma. Full malt and bitter ale with apple and lemon flavours. Lingering bittersweet finish.

Sail Ale Golden Ale (OG 1041, ABV 4%) ◈
Gold-coloured best bitter. Balanced malt and bitter, grapefruit citrus hop flavour. Malt fades, with grassy hops and rising dryness at the end.

Penryn Pale Ale (OG 1043, ABV 4.3%) ◆
Amber-coloured best bitter with hop and mango nose. Bitter taste, fruit, biscuit malt and toffee. Short, fresh hop bitter finish.

Bullhorn Black Lager (OG 1049, ABV 4.9%)

80/- Scotch Ale (OG 1051, ABV 5%) ◆
A dark brown porter with roast malt aroma. Roast and biscuit malt balanced by sweet plum and bitterness. Long finish.

**Mexi-Cocoa Choc-Vanilla Stout
(OG 1085, ABV 8.5%)** ◆
Black speciality beer heavily infused with chocolate and vanilla. Roast caramel nose. Smooth velvety taste of intense roast malt, sweet chocolate and fruit.

Rebellion SIBA

Marlow Brewery, Bencombe Farm, Marlow Bottom, Buckinghamshire, SL7 3LT
☎ (01628) 476594 ⊕ rebellionbeer.co.uk

⊠ Established in 1993, Rebellion has grown steadily with one site move and several expansion projects, including an on-site shop. It currently brews approximately 70,000 pints per week, supplying more than 400 local pubs and clubs within a 30-mile radius of Marlow. ‼️🍺◆

IPA (OG 1039, ABV 3.7%) ◆
Copper-coloured bitter, sweet and malty, with resinous and red apple flavours. Caramel and fruit decline to leave a dry, bitter and malty finish.

Smuggler (OG 1042, ABV 4.2%) ◆
A red-brown beer, well-bodied and bitter with an uncompromisingly dry, bitter finish.

Mutiny (OG 1046, ABV 4.5%) ◆
Tawny in colour, this full-bodied best bitter is predominantly fruity and moderately bitter, continuing to a dry finish.

Rectory SIBA

Streat Hill Farm, Streat Hill, Streat, East Sussex, BN6 8RP
☎ (01273) 890570 ✉ rectoryales@hotmail.com

⊠ Rectory was founded in 1995 by the Rev Godfrey Broster to generate funds for the maintenance of his three parish churches. 107 parishioners are shareholders. ‼️◆

Rector's Pleasure (ABV 3.8%)
A bitter session beer.

Rector's Light Relief (OG 1045, ABV 4.5%)
Golden ale with a fresh, floral aroma and distinctly hoppy, bitter characteristics.

Rector's Porter (ABV 5%)

Rector's Revenge (OG 1050, ABV 5%)
Traditional brown-coloured strong bitter with good balance of malt and hops and a long, bitter finish.

Red 👁

Unit 1, The Orchard, Garden Farm, The Town, Great Staughton, Cambridgeshire, PE19 5BE ☎ 07557 207013 ⊕ redbrewery.com

Red Brewery was established using a four-barrel plant in 2012 in a converted farm building in the village of Great Staughton. ◆RAIB

One Brown Mouse (OG 1041, ABV 4%)
A brown-coloured session ale with caramel and toffee flavours.

Pathfinder (OG 1045, ABV 4.8%)
A blonde ale with orange and grapefruit citrus notes.

Sundial Gold (OG 1046, ABV 4.8%)
Golden ale with balanced, deep hop character. Citrus with a light hop finish.

White Duck (OG 1045, ABV 4.8%)
Pale, highly-hopped ale wit grapefruit and melon flavours.

Staughton Bitter (OG 1050, ABV 5.2%)
Copper-coloured hoppy bitter with light fruit tastes.

Kangaroo (OG 1053, ABV 5.4%)
Garnet-coloured winter ale. Light hop, floral and slightly sweet.

Valhalla (OG 1053, ABV 5.5%)
Bronze-coloured strong beer with rounded fruit flavours.

Red Cat SIBA 👁

Unit 10, Sun Valley Business Park, Winnall Close, Winchester, Hampshire, SO23 0LB
☎ (01962) 863423 ☎ 07824 876489
⊕ redcatbrewing.co.uk

Red Cat was established in 2014 by Andy Mansell and Iain McIntosh using an 11-barrel plant. It supplies Hampshire and bordering counties. A small bar in the brewery sells a range of products. 🍺

Prowler Pale (OG 1034.5, ABV 3.6%)
A light, straw-coloured session bitter. Slightly fruity with hints of hops.

Bitter (OG 1037, ABV 3.7%) ◆
A fresh, hoppy bitter, light brown in colour with an enticing hoppy aroma and a lasting dryness throughout.

Scratch (ABV 4%)

Best (OG 1042.3, ABV 4.2%)
A traditional best bitter, this beer has a deep red/bronze colour and a rounded, malty flavour with not too much bitterness or hop notes.

Mr M's Porter (OG 1050, ABV 4.5%)
A complex beer, which gives aromas of chocolate, vanilla and soft Greek coffee. Full in the mouth yet surprisingly easy to drink.

TomCat (OG 1044.4, ABV 4.7%)
A golden premium ale with a full hop flavour that is not overly bitter.

MaCavity (OG 1055.5, ABV 5.3%)

Red Fox SIBA

The Chicken Sheds, Upp Hall Farm, Salmons Lane, Coggeshall, Essex, CO6 1RY
☎ (01376) 563123 ⊕ redfoxbrewery.co.uk

Red Fox began brewing in 2008 and has continued to expand in line with increasing demand. Brewery experience days are available. ‼️◆RAIB

Mild (OG 1037, ABV 3.6%)
A classic dark, full-flavoured mild with hints of chocolate and a deep roast barley flavour.

IPA (OG 1038, ABV 3.7%)

An East Anglian-style, copper-coloured beer with a delicate flavour.

Bitter (OG 1039, ABV 3.8%)
A traditional-style bitter, which perfectly balances malt and fruit flavours.

Hunter's Gold (OG 1040, ABV 3.9%)
A golden beer with a delicate citrus aroma.

Best Bitter (OG 1040, ABV 4%)
A light brown bitter with a full flavour and malty backbone. A classic best bitter.

Coggeshall Gold (OG 1041, ABV 4%)
An aromatic golden beer, packed full of citrus and exotic fruit flavours. Unusually for a beer of this style it does not have a bitter finish.

Surrex Gold (OG 1041, ABV 4.1%)
A highly-hopped, aromatic beer. Pink grapefruit and peach aromas abound leading to a slightly bitter finish.

Black Fox Porter (OG 1046, ABV 4.8%) 🍷 🍴
A rich black beer packed with malty flavour and undertones of chocolate.

Wily Ol' Fox (OG 1050, ABV 5.2%)
An aromatic amber traditional IPA made from English hops and malt, with a soft fruity palate.

Red Hand (NEW)

🍺 38 Main Street, Donaghmore, County Tyrone, BT70 3EZ ☎ 07748 637056

Established in 2013, Red Hand Brewing Company forms part of the award-winning Brewers House pub in Donaghmore, County Tyrone.

Pale Ale (ABV 5%)

Red Rock SIBA

Higher Humber Farm, Bishopsteignton, Devon, TQ14 9TD
☎ (01626) 879738 ⊕ redrockbrewery.co.uk

⊠ Red Rock first started brewing in 2006 with a four-barrel plant and upgraded in 2011 to a 7.5-barrel one. It is based in a converted barn on a working farm using locally-sourced malt, fresh hops and the farm's own spring water. It has a bar and can accommodate private functions. ‼ 🍴 ♦ RAIB

Back Beach (OG 1038, ABV 3.8%)
A golden beer with a crisp, clean finish.

Red Rock (OG 1041, ABV 4.2%)
A well-balanced best bitter.

Red Shoot

🍺 Toms Lane, Linwood, Ringwood, Hampshire, BH24 3QT
☎ (01425) 475792 ⊕ redshoot.co.uk

⊠ The 2.5-barrel brewery was commissioned in 1998 and can be viewed from inside the pub. All the output is currently sold in the pub.

New Forest Gold (OG 1038, ABV 3.8%)
A refreshing golden ale with a light, floral, citrus taste, moving towards a burnt toffee finish.

Muddy Boot (OG 1042, ABV 4.2%)
A dark mild. Molasses and some chocolate malt.

Tom's Tipple (OG 1048, ABV 4.8%)
A copper-coloured strong malty bitter, with some citrus balance to the toffee and malt flavours.

Red Squirrel SIBA 👁

Unit 24, Boxted Farm, Berkhamsted Road, Potten End, Hertfordshire, HP1 2SQ
☎ (01442) 256970 ⊕ redsquirrelbrewery.co.uk

⊠ Red Squirrel started brewing in Hertford in 2004 using a 10-barrel plant. In 2011 it moved to Potten End near Hemel Hempstead to brand new premises and has subsequently expanded production. It launched a crowd-funding programme in 2016 to raise funds for further growth. ‼ ♦ RAIB

Red Dawn Mild (OG 1037.7, ABV 3.7%)
Dark red in colour with mellow and nutty overtones and a smooth and rounded palate.

Hopfest (OG 1037, ABV 3.8%)
Pale, golden ale with a floral/citrus aroma and elderflower notes.

Legally Blonde (OG 1040, ABV 4%)
Hops give a fresh, citrus flavour with herbal, floral and buttery notes.

Conservation Bitter (OG 1040, ABV 4.1%)
A chestnut brown traditional bitter with a hoppy, fruity bitterness and biscuit flavours with a hint of spice and chocolate.

Mr Squirrel (OG 1042.9, ABV 4.3%)
A chestnut red bitter, lightly hopped with a creamy texture. Hints of caramel and vanilla complement the slightly hoppy and malty overtones.

Jack Black (OG 1047.7, ABV 4.8%)
A black IPA featuring the hop profile of an IPA and the dark colour of a porter.

London Porter (OG 1048, ABV 5%)
Dark brown/black porter with a good balance of chocolate and roasted barley. Full-bodied on the palate with bittersweet liquorice and rich chocolate flavours and a creamy finish.

Redwood American IPA (OG 1051, ABV 5.4%)
Based on a secret Michigan recipe, golden orange in colour, with complex hoppy aromas, floral/citrus tones and a long, lingering finish.

Red Star (NEW) SIBA 👁

54b Stephenson Way, Formby Business Park, Formby, Merseyside, L37 8EG
☎ (01704) 461120 ☎ 07899 904270
⊕ redstarbrewery.co.uk

Production started in 2015 using a 10-barrel plant. Pubs and bars are supplied in Merseyside and the wider North west region.

Formby Blonde (ABV 3.9%)
A light ale with an orange peel finish.

Formby IPA (ABV 4%)
A session IPA with a hint of elderflower.

Lakota (ABV 4.1%)
An amber-coloured ale with a smooth, sweet edge.

Havana Moon (ABV 4.2%)
An oatmeal stout with notes of chocolate, coffee and raisins.

Samba (ABV 4.7%)
A premium golden ale.

Hurricane (ABV 4.8%)
A premium copper-coloured ale with a bittersweet finish.

Weissbier (ABV 5.3%)

A naturally cloudy wheat beer with big orange and coriander flavours and European hops.

Partisan (ABV 5.4%)
Dark chestnut in colour. A smooth and malty finish follows mocha and caramel flavours.

Redchurch

275-276 Poyser Street, Bethnal Green, London, E2 9RF
☎ (020) 3487 0255 ☎ 07968 173097
⊕ theredchurchbrewery.com

Redchurch was established in 2011 using an eight-barrel plant and is situated in a pair of units under the railway arches in Bethnal Green. The brewery produces seven beers at present, in KegKeg and bottles, for both the domestic and export markets. There are ongoing plans for expansion. 🖷 ◆ RAIB

Redemption SIBA

Unit 16, Compass West Industrial Estate, 33 West Road, Tottenham, London, N17 0XL
☎ (020) 8885 5227 ⊕ redemptionbrewing.co.uk

⊗ Redemption began brewing in 2010 on a 12-barrel plant. In 2016 it moved into a larger unit with a 30-barrel plant and a tasting room (open to the public on Saturdays). Most of the beer is supplied in cask to pubs in north and central London and to beer festivals. ‼ 🖷 ◆ RAIB

Trinity (OG 1036.6, ABV 3%) 🍺
Refreshing golden beer with strong citrus notes throughout. The strong bitterness is softened by a little sweet malt character.

Pale Ale (OG 1037.5, ABV 3.8%) 🍺
Well-balanced amber bitter with peppery hops and citrus throughout. Sweet toffee and fruit fades in the slightly dry, bitter finish.

Hopspur (OG 1044.5, ABV 4.5%) 🍺
Smooth, brown best bitter. Sweet coffee roast notes, a little nuttiness with resinous hops on the flavour. Dry bitter finish.

Urban Dusk (OG 1044.5, ABV 4.6%) 🍺
Full-bodied brown best bitter; chocolate and fudge in the aroma and flavour overlaid with citrus. Lingering dry bitter finish.

Friendship Porter (OG 1051.5, ABV 5.1%) 🍺
Sweetish, smooth porter. Liquorice, treacle and caramelised fruit balances the dry, dark roast coffee and chocolate notes in the flavour.

Big Chief (OG 1052.5, ABV 5.5%) 🍺
Golden ale with a smooth mouthfeel and a strong fruity aroma, flavour and finish, which is also dry and bitter.

Redscar SIBA

⊟ c/o Cleveland Hotel, 9-11 High Street West, Redcar, North Yorkshire, TS10 1SQ
☎ (01642) 513727 ☎ 07828 855146
⊕ redscar-brewery.co.uk

☺ Redscar first brewed in 2008. In 2014 it increased its capacity to a five-barrel plant. The brewery supplies the hotel, local pubs and beer festivals. ‼ ◆

Jazz (OG 1040, ABV 4%)
Light-coloured session beer, delicately hopped with three varieties.

Poison (OG 1040, ABV 4%)
A dark, full-bodied ale.

Beach (OG 1050, ABV 5%)

Redwell SIBA

7 The Arches, Bracondale, Trowse Millgate, Norwich, NR1 2EF
☎ (01603) 624072 ⊕ redwellbrewing.com

⊗ Redwell began brewing in 2013 using a 10-barrel plant. Production is mostly keg or bottled but occasional cask-conditioned ales are produced for beer festivals or by special request for local outlets. ‼

RedWillow SIBA

The Lodge, Sutton Garrison, Byrons Lane, Macclesfield, Cheshire, SK11 7JW
☎ (01625) 502315 ⊕ redwillowbrewery.com

☺ Established in 2010 by home brewer Toby McKenzie and his wife Caroline. In 2015 brewing moved to a larger, purpose-built unit on the same site, close to the centre of Macclesfield. The award-winning beers are distributed nationwide and are available from the brewery's own RedWillow bar in Macclesfield. Experimental brews are branded under the Faithless and Clueless labels. ◆ RAIB

Seamless (OG 1034, ABV 3.6%)
A light and hoppy pale ale.

Headless (OG 1037, ABV 3.9%)
Refreshingly floral pale ale with a restrained orange-led bitterness and a light, straw colour.

Mirthless (OG 1037, ABV 3.9%)
A refreshing, easy-drinking pale ale with a smooth finish.

Feckless (OG 1040, ABV 4.1%)
A classic best bitter, rich toffee and malt balanced with subtle hop flavours.

Directionless (OG 1041, ABV 4.2%)
A balanced and easy-drinking session ale, warm amber in colour, with candied orange fruitiness.

Wreckless (OG 1046, ABV 4.8%)
This pale ale is loaded with hops providing massive amounts of tropical fruit, with a clean finish.

Heartless (OG 1048, ABV 4.9%)
A dry, balanced bitterness and a long espresso finish.

Sleepless (OG 1052, ABV 5.4%)
Rich toffee malt flavours followed by juicy hops, with a long, clean bitter finish.

Smokeless (OG 1055, ABV 5.7%) 🍺
A smooth, smoky porter infused with chipotles.

Shameless (OG 1055, ABV 5.9%)
An American-style IPA.

Ageless (OG 1065, ABV 7.2%)
American-style IPA with a huge hit of mango, lychee and pineapple, and a long, clean bitter finish.

Reedley Hallows SIBA

Unit B3, Farrington Close, Farrington Road Industrial Estate, Burnley, Lancashire, BB11 5SH ☎ 07963 038220 ⊕ reedley-hallows-brewery.co.uk

☺Brewing started on this four-barrel plant in 2012. Having moved to larger premises the brewery now has nine fermenters to cope with demand. ‼

Old Laund Bitter (OG 1038, ABV 3.6%)
A good session beer, smooth and creamy with a distinctive hoppy aftertaste.

Filly Close Blonde (OG 1040, ABV 3.9%)
A well-balanced ale, bitter and spicy with a good fruity finish.

Pendleside (OG 1042, ABV 4%)
A light-coloured beer with hints of tropical fruits and a spicy aftertaste.

Monkholme Premium (OG 1042, ABV 4.2%)
A premium golden ale, smooth with a hoppy taste throughout.

New Laund Dark (OG 1044, ABV 4.4%)
A dark stout, sweet with a smoky, bitter finish.

Griffin IPA (OG 1045, ABV 4.5%)
Well-hopped classic IPA balanced with traditional malty sweetness.

Nook of Pendle (OG 1050, ABV 5%)
An amber, warming ale with a dried fruit and malty aroma. Tropical fruits in the taste with a bittersweet finish.

Regather (NEW)

57-59 Club Garden Road, Sheffield, South Yorkshire, S11 8BU
☎ (0114) 273 1258 ⊕ regather.net/food-drink/regather-brewery

When Ed (proprietor of craftalekits.com) met Gareth (director of co-op Regather) they discovered a shared interest... the result was Regather Brewery. Current brewer Jim Danson uses Sheffield's smallest microbrewery to produce a series of strong, idiosyncratic one-off brews. Beers are bottle conditioned and available at all Regather events. RAIB V

Remedy (NEW)

▤ 10-11 Market Place, Stockport, SK1 1EW
☎ (0161) 477 1842
⊕ remedybarandbrewhouse.co.uk

Opened in 2016, the 1.5-barrel plant is located in a glazed-off area in the main bar of the Remedy pub in Stockport. The brewery supplies the pub and local festivals. There are plans for further beers.

Broomstick Bitter (OG 1040, ABV 4.4%)
Traditional amber-coloured session ale.

Bone Orchard Stout (OG 1052, ABV 5%)
A full-bodied, easy-drinking Irish stout with a tight, creamy head and moderate bitterness.

Tai-pan IPA (OG 1056, ABV 5.5%)
An American-style IPA with a noticeable bitterness.

Reunion (NEW) SIBA ◉

Unit 17, Vector Park, Forest Road, Feltham, TW13 7EJ
☎ 07818 014430 ⊕ reunionales.com

⊠ Reunion Ales was founded in 2015 by Francis Smedley using a Moeschle 10-barrel plant. Beers are available across the south-west of London. There are plans for a tap room. ‼◆

Opening Gambit (OG 1038, ABV 3.8%)

A well-balanced session ale. A hoppy nose is followed by a smooth, malty mouthfeel and aromatic hops on the nose. Hoppy bitterness leads to a dry finish.

Frost Fair (OG 1044, ABV 4.5%)
A dark ale with berry, pine and spicy notes.

Talwar (OG 1042, ABV 4.5%)
A pale, straw-coloured ale with a resinous aroma. Clean-tasting with a well-balanced bittersweet flavour and a hint of coriander.

Incredible Pale Ale (OG 1047, ABV 5%)
A pale ale with a resinous, fruity nose and light body.

Revolutions SIBA

Unit B7, Whitwood Enterprise Park, Speedwell Road, Whitwood, West Yorkshire, WF10 5PX
☎ (01977) 552649 ☎ 07801 701089
⊕ revolutionsbrewing.co.uk

Revolutions began brewing in 2010. All beers are musically inspired, reflecting formats from the analogue era mainly brewed to 3.3% (33 rpm), 3.9% (EP), 4.5% (45 rpm) and 6.0% (C60). The Rewind 33 series of monthly specials references music from 33 years ago. ‼◆

Cocker Yorkshire Ale (OG 1040, ABV 3.9%)
Pale brown/golden ale; fruity with moderate levels of bitterness.

EP Session Pale (OG 1040, ABV 3.9%)
A pale ale with balanced levels of sweetness and bitterness with a crisp, lemony hop finish.

Clash London Porter (OG 1047, ABV 4.5%)
A complex, dark, malty beer rounded off with a smooth hop finish.

Go-Go American Pale (OG 1044, ABV 4.5%)
A golden pale ale hopped with three American citrus-floral hops.

Pretender NZ Blonde (OG 1045, ABV 4.5%)
A blonde ale with medium levels of bitterness and with pine, lemon and lime hop notes.

Amnesiac English IPA (OG 1058, ABV 6%)
Full-flavoured IPA hopped with an orange finish.

Manifesto Strong Stout (OG 1059, ABV 6%)
A rich, dark stout.

Rhymney SIBA

Gilchrist Thomas Industrial Estate, Blaenavon, NP4 9RL
☎ (01685) 722253 ⊕ rhymneybreweryltd.com

☺Rhymney first brewed in 2005. The 75-hectolitre plant was sourced from Canada. Around 220 outlets are supplied. In 2012 the brewery relocated to Blaenavon with a new brewing centre and visitor facility. An expanding tied estate now consists of eight pubs, all in South Wales. ‼ ▰ RAIB

Hobby Horse (OG 1038, ABV 3.8%)

Dark (OG 1040, ABV 4%)

Best (OG 1037, ABV 4.1%)

Bevans Bitter (OG 1042, ABV 4.2%)

Bitter (OG 1043, ABV 4.5%)

Export Ale (OG 1050, ABV 5%)

Richmond SIBA

Station Brewery, Station Yard, Richmond, North Yorkshire, DL10 4LD
☎ (01748) 828266 ⊕ richmondbrewing.co.uk

😊 Richmond opened in 2008 in the Victorian station complex beside the River Swale. The brewery's output is split between cask-conditioned (60%) and bottled ales (40%). Beers are available in the local area in the Hildyard Arms in Colburn, Bolton Arms in Leyburn and the Castle Tavern in Richmond. Ownership changed in 2013. ‼ ⊫ ◆ RAIB

SwAle (OG 1035, ABV 3.7%)
A dark mild with slightly more bitterness than a traditional mild.

Station Ale (OG 1039, ABV 4%)
Light golden bitter brewed using hedgerow hops.

Greyfriars Stout (OG 1042, ABV 4.2%)

Dale Strider (OG 1043, ABV 4.5%)

Stump Cross Ale (OG 1046, ABV 4.7%)
Dark, malty and full-flavoured beer.

Ridgeside SIBA

Unit 24, Penraevon 2 Industrial Estate, Meanwood, Leeds, West Yorkshire, LS7 2AW ☎ 07595 380568
⊕ ridgesidebrewery.co.uk

😊 Ridgeside began brewing in 2010 using a four-barrel plant. Regular outlets are supplied around Leeds and beers can be found across West and North Yorkshire. ◆

Jailbreak (OG 1038, ABV 3.8%)
A pale session beer.

Cascadia (OG 1041, ABV 4.1%)
A single hop pale ale.

Stonegate (OG 1043, ABV 4.4%)
A cask Pilsner, pale and well-hopped. Grassy, floral and refreshing.

Black Night (OG 1050, ABV 5%) ◥
Dark brown, full-bodied stout with roasted malts starting strong but gradually overtaken by a chocolate sweetness.

Stargazer (OG 1049, ABV 5%)
A light amber-coloured IPA. Bitter, pithy and aromatic.

Ridgeway ◉

Beer Counter Ltd, South Stoke, Oxfordshire, RG8 0JW
☎ (01491) 873474 ⊕ ridgewaybrewery.co.uk

Set up by ex-Brakspear head brewer Peter Scholey, Ridgeway specialises in bottle-conditioned beers, although cask beers are occasionally offered for festivals and locally. At present the beers are brewed by Peter using his own ingredients on plant at Hepworth's brewery (qv). Construction of Ridgeway's own brewery is planned.

Ringwood ◉

Christchurch Road, Ringwood, Hampshire, BH24 3AP
☎ (01425) 471177 ⊕ ringwoodbrewery.co.uk

⊗ Ringwood was bought in 2007 by Marstons for £19 million. Production has been increased to 50,000 barrels a year. Some 750 outlets are supplied. Ringwood beers are now available in

Marston's pubs all over the country. Part of Marston's PLC. ‼ ⊫ ◆

Razor Back (OG 1038, ABV 3.8%) ◥
A malty session bitter with strong toffee notes in the aroma, leading to a short, bittersweet finish. Malt tends to dominate throughout.

Boondoggle (OG 1042, ABV 4.2%)
A golden beer, full of zesty hop flavours and aromas.

Fortyniner (OG 1049, ABV 4.9%) ◥
A caramel, biscuity aroma, with hints of damson, lead to a sweet but well-balanced taste with malt, fruit and hop flavours.

Old Thumper (OG 1055, ABV 5.1%) ◥
A powerful, sweet, copper-coloured beer. A fruity aroma preludes a sweet, malty taste with fruit and caramel and a bittersweet aftertaste.

Ripple Steam SIBA

Parsonage Farm, Vale Road, Sutton, Kent, CT15 5DH
☎ 07917 037611 ⊕ ripplesteambrewery.co.uk

Ripple Steam began brewing commercially on a farm in Kent in 2012. ◆

Milk Stout (ABV 3.5%)

Best Bitter (ABV 4.1%)

Green Hopped IPA (ABV 4.5%)

IPA (ABV 4.5%)

Rising Sun (NEW)

⊟ **Rising Sun, 235 Stockport Road, Mossley, OL5 0RQ**
☎ (01457) 238236 ⊕ risingsunmossley.co.uk

😊 Brewing began in 2016 using a two-barrel plant at the side of the Rising Sun. The beers are primarily produced for sale in the pub. In addition to the regular beer, various other brews are produced on demand.

Builder's Craic (ABV 3.8%)
A golden, creamy, smooth traditional session bitter.

River Leven

Lab Road, Kinlochleven, PH50 4SG
☎ (01855) 831519 ☎ 07901 873273
⊕ riverlevenales.co.uk

River Leven was established in 2011 in the former carbon bunker of the aluminium smelter factory in Kinlochleven. Only pure malt cask-conditioned ale is produced.

Blonde (OG 1040, ABV 4%)
A clean-tasting, pale golden beer with hints of citrus.

Traditional IPA (OG 1040, ABV 4%)
The distinctive, traditional British bittering hops combine with the nutty flavour of the malt to produce this copper-coloured, classic British ale.

Riverhead

⊟ **2 Peel Street, Marsden, Huddersfield, West Yorkshire, HD7 6BR**
☎ (01484) 841270 (Pub) ⊕ ossett-brewery.co.uk

😊 Riverhead is a brewpub that opened in 1995. Ossett Brewing (qv) purchased the site in 2006 but runs it as a separate brewery. It has since opened the Dining Room on the first floor, which uses Riverhead beers in its dishes. Many different beers are produced on a rotating basis. !! ♦

Butterley Bitter (OG 1038, ABV 3.8%)
A light and refreshing traditional Yorkshire bitter.

March Haigh (OG 1046, ABV 4.6%)
Malty and full-bodied traditional premium ale with moderate bitterness and spicy hop aroma.

Redbrook Premium (OG 1055, ABV 5.5%)
A reddish-brown, full-bodied and malty strong ale with a mellow palate and gently spice aroma.

Riverside (NEW)

Unit 6, Beeding Court Business Park, Shoreham Road, Upper Beeding, West Sussex, BN44 3TN
☎ (01903) 898030 ⊕ riversidebreweryltd.co.uk

Riverside began brewing in 2015 using a five-barrel plant.

Steyning Stinker (OG 1042, ABV 4%)
A slight fruity, spicy edge to this beer is complemented by earthy and smoky notes.

Beeding Best Bitter (OG 1037, ABV 4.2%)
A best bitter with pine and floral characteristics and just a hint of liquorice.

Sneaky Steamer (OG 1050, ABV 5.1%)
Four different hops are used giving this beer pine/floral notes with a hint of grapefruit.

Tubbers' Tipple (OG 1051, ABV 5.6%)
A premium bitter with earthy, spicy characteristics and just a hint of honey.

Riviera (NEW)

4 Yonder Meadow, Stoke Gabriel, Devon, TQ9 6QE
✉ waldronalan@yahoo.com

Riviera started brewing commercially in 2015 using a one-barrel plant.

RBC Best (ABV 3.8%)
A lightly-hopped session ale.

Gold (ABV 4.2%)
Citrus and refreshing.

Porterhead (ABV 4.3%)
A dark ruby ale.

Rivington (NEW)

Cunliffe Farm, New Road, Anderton, Lancashire, PR6 9EY ☎ 07989 165370 ⊕ rivingtonbrewing.co.uk

☺ Established in 2015, operating from a dairy farm and initially using a 1.5-barrel plant. This has been replaced with a 4.5-barrel plant and 80% of production is now cask conditioned. A number of local outlets are supplied direct from the brewery. RAIB

Most Excellent (ABV 3.9%)

Bodacious (ABV 4.6%)

Robin Hood SIBA

Unit 3, Northgate Place, High Church Street, New Basford, Nottingham, NG7 7JT ☎ 07804 499462 ⊕ robinhoodbrewery.com

Robin Hood began brewing in 2012, originally using spare capacity at another brewery. It moved to its own premises in 2013 using a 5.5-barrel plant. ♦

Major Oak (OG 1038, ABV 3.8%)
Dark chestnut-coloured mild with a smooth caramel malt taste and just a hint of hop finish.

Maid Marian Extra Pale (OG 1039, ABV 3.9%)
Pale straw-coloured ale with overtones of honey, balanced with a hint of hop aroma and bitterness.

Robin Hood (OG 1040, ABV 4%)
A traditional English ale, light brown in colour with the distinctive aroma and taste of English hops and malt, with a smooth, dry finish.

Wolfshead (OG 1040, ABV 4%)
Dark golden amber ale, honey and nut flavours to the forefront in the malt and a lingering hop finish.

Golden Archer (OG 1042, ABV 4.2%)
Deep golden ale, hints of orange in the aroma with a fruity hop taste and bitter edge for balance.

Will Scarlet (OG 1042, ABV 4.2%)
Red-coloured ale with spicy hop overtones and port like flavours.

Friar Tuck Stout (OG 1044, ABV 4.4%)
Dark and malty with coffee and chocolate flavours balanced out with a hint of hop background.

Outlaw (OG 1044, ABV 4.4%)
Golden ale with floral citrus hop aroma and crisp hop finish.

Fool King Ale (OG 1045, ABV 4.5%)
Deep golden ale combining flavoursome malts with fruity and bitter hops.

The Sheriff Of Nottingham (OG 1046, ABV 4.6%)
A tawny-coloured special ale, initial fruity hop flavour developing into a satisfying bitterness to finish.

Little John Strong (OG 1050, ABV 5%)
Deep gold-coloured strong ale. Full-bodied with an aroma and taste of barley wine to start, then developing a bitter, hoppy but balanced finish.

Templar (OG 1060, ABV 6%)
Golden, highly-hopped IPA. Deceptively smooth and malty with highly aromatic and fruity hop character.

The Black Death Plague Ale (OG 1085, ABV 8.5%)
Black ale with dark, smoky malts and flavours of liquorice, black coffee and bonfire toffee and a hint of bitterness.

Robinsons SIBA IFBB ◉

Unicorn Brewery, Lower Hillgate, Stockport, Cheshire, SK1 1JJ
☎ (0161) 612 4061 ⊕ robinsonsbrewery.com

☺Robinsons has been brewing since 1838 and the business is still owned and run by the family. It has an estate of around 300 pubs stretching from Cheshire to Cumbria and out to North Wales; this is subject to ongoing disposal and refurbishment programmes. In addition to the published seasonal range a series of one-off 'White Label' beers are produced every 2-3 months. !! ➤ ♦

Wizard (OG 1037, ABV 3.7%)
A well-balanced, crisp and refreshing session beer.

Dizzy Blonde (OG 1037, ABV 3.8%)

THE BREWERIES

A straw-coloured summer ale with a distinctive hop aroma. A light, refreshing beer with a clean, zesty, hop-dominated palate complemented by a crisp, dry finish.

Hartleys XB (OG 1040, ABV 4%) ◀
An overly sweet and malty bitter with a bitter citrus peel fruitiness and a hint of liquorice in the finish.

Cumbria Way (OG 1040, ABV 4.1%)
A pronounced malt aroma with rich fruit notes. Rounded malt and hops in the mouth, long dry finish with citrus fruit notes. Brewed for the Hartley's estate in Cumbria.

Cwrw'r Ddraig Aur (OG 1041, ABV 4.1%)

Unicorn (OG 1041, ABV 4.2%) ◀
Amber beer with a fruity aroma. Malt, hops and fruit in the taste with a bitter, malty finish.

Trooper (OG 1048, ABV 4.8%) ◀
Well-balanced amber beer with malt and hops in aroma and taste.

Double Hop (OG 1050, ABV 5%) ◀
Pale brown beer with malt and fruit on the nose. Full hoppy taste with malt and fruit, leading to a hoppy, bitter finish.

Old Tom (OG 1079, ABV 8.5%) 🍾 ◀
A full-bodied, dark beer with malt, fruit and chocolate on the aroma. A complex range of flavours includes dark chocolate, full maltiness, port and fruits and lead to a long, bittersweet aftertaste.

Rock & Roll

Unit 2, 60 Regent Place, Hockley, Birmingham, B1 3NJ ☎ 07922 554181
✉ rnrbrewhouse@outlook.com

⊠ The Rock & Roll brewery started life as Birmingham's only rooftop pub brewery, set up by experienced brewer Mark Shepherd using a two-barrel plant. In 2014 brewster Lynn Crossland joined and now does most of the brewing. In 2016 the brewery moved and expanded to a six-barrel plant in Birmingham's historic Jewellery Quarter in order to increase capacity. ‼ ♦ V

Brew Springsteen (OG 1042, ABV 4.2%)
A pale ale with honey.

Thirst Aid Kit (OG 1042, ABV 4.2%)

Mash City Rocker (OG 1045, ABV 4.5%)

Rock Mill (NEW)

2a Rock Mill Lane, New Mills, Derbyshire, SK22 3BN
☎ 07971 747050

Office: 81-83 Bridge Street, New Mills, Derbyshire, SK22 4DN ✉ rbpine@hotmail.co.uk

⊠ Rock Mills is a microbrewery established by Ray Barton in 2016, next door to his cabinet-making business. V

Mermaids Pool (OG 1035, ABV 3.5%)
A golden ale.

Stars & Stripes (OG 1035, ABV 3.8%)
An American-style pale ale.

Strange Ways (OG 1038, ABV 4%)
A straw-coloured bitter.

Inbetweener (OG 1050, ABV 5.3%)
A pale rye beer, amber in colour.

Rock the Boat (NEW) SIBA 👁

6 Little Crosby Village, Little Crosby, Merseyside, L23 4TS
☎ (0151) 924 7936 ☎ 07727 959356
⊕ rocktheboatbrewery.co.uk

Rock the Boat began brewing in 2015 in a converted 16th-century wheelwright's workshop in Little Crosby village. The beers can be found in a variety of pubs and clubs in the Crosby and Waterloo area, Liverpool city centre and as far as Chorley in Lancashire.

Liverpool Light (OG 1037, ABV 3.4%)
A blonde session ale with subtle, fruity hop flavours.

(Sittin' on) The Dock (OG 1042, ABV 3.5%)
A dark, smooth ale with treacle.

Dazzle (OG 1039, ABV 3.6%)
Pale golden beer bursting with hop flavour, smooth in the mouth with a long bitter finish.

Bootle Bull (OG 1042, ABV 3.8%)
A traditional-style bitter, light brown in colour. A smooth, malty ale balanced with a good hop character, which is evident in the finish.

Mussel Wreck (OG 1041, ABV 3.9%)
A subtle blend of malt and hops creates an easy-drinking, smooth ale. Fruity hop flavours with a short bitter finish.

Waterloo Sunset (ABV 4.2%)
Full-bodied beer with rye malt. Hop combinations give a subtle orange marmalade flavour.

Rocket Town (NEW)

Hole in the Wall, 14-15 Horsemarket, Darlington, County Durham, DL1 5PT
☎ (01325) 466720
✉ rockettownbrewery@hotmail.com

Rocket Town began brewing in 2015.

Black IPA (ABV 3.8%)

Rocket Kolsch (ABV 4%)

Dirty Bumble (ABV 4.2%)

Second Burn (ABV 4.2%)

Maple Dog (ABV 4.4%)

Lift Off (ABV 4.5%)

DPA (ABV 5.2%)

Rockin' Robin SIBA

Campfield Farm, Haste Hill Road, Boughton Monchelsea, Kent, ME17 4LR
☎ (01622) 747106 ☎ 07787 416110
⊕ rockinrobinbrewery.co.uk

Brewing began in 2011 using a one-barrel plant in a garden shed. It moved to its current location in 2014. Outlets throughout Kent, Sussex and the south-east London borders are supplied, including several micropubs. ‼ 🍺 ♦

Hoppin' Robin (OG 1036, ABV 3.7%)
A traditional English session bitter with full malt, fruit in the mouth and Kentish hops on the tongue.

Reliant Robin (OG 1036, ABV 3.7%)
An auburn-coloured classic session bitter. Its richness is delivered from four malts, with

traditional hop notes on the palate and a fresh, spicy finish.

RPA (OG 1038, ABV 3.9%)
A light but refreshing pale ale.

Robin Redbest (OG 1041, ABV 4%)
Light amber in colour with initial good hop flavour moving to a pleasant malty finish.

Rocka Hula (OG 1039, ABV 4%)
A pale ale with a fruity and slightly spicy taste.

Reckless Robin (OG 1044, ABV 4.5%)
A strong bitter that delivers a fresh, hoppy punch, well-balanced with soft fruit malt.

Rockingham SIBA

Blatherwycke, Northamptonshire, PE8 6YN
☎ (01832) 280722

Office: 25 Wansford Road, Elton, Cambridgeshire, PE8 6RZ ⊕ rockinghamales.co.uk

⊠ Rockingham is a small brewery established in 1997 that operates from a converted farm building near Blatherwycke, Northamptonshire, with a two-barrel plant producing a prolific range of beers. It supplies half a dozen local outlets. ◆

Forest Gold (OG 1039, ABV 3.9%)
A hoppy blonde ale with citrus flavours. Well-balanced and clean finishing.

Hop Devil (OG 1040, ABV 3.9%)
Six hop varieties give this golden ale a bitter start and fruity finish.

White Rabbit (OG 1040, ABV 4%)
Light golden ale with a bitter start and a tropical fruit finish.

Saxon Cross (OG 1041, ABV 4.1%)
A golden/red-coloured ale with a nutty coffee aroma and fruit and blackcurrant undertones.

Fruits of the Forest (OG 1043, ABV 4.3%)
A multi-layered beer in which summer fruits and several spices compete with a big hop presence.

Dark Forest (OG 1050, ABV 5%)
A dark and complex beer, similar to a Belgian Dubbel, with malty/smoky flavours that give way to a fruity, bitter finish.

Rocky Head

Unit 16, Glenville Mews, Kimber Road, Southfields, London, SW18 4NJ
☎ (020) 8875 9917
⊕ sites.google.comsiterockyheadbrewery

Rocky Head is a microbrewery set up in 2012 by a group of friends inspired by the American craft brewing scene. A range of vegan-friendly bottle-conditioned beers is brewed on a five-barrel plant. RAIB

Romney Marsh

Unit 7, Jacks Park, Cinque Ports Road, New Romney, Kent, TN28 8AN
☎ (01797) 362333 ☎ 07796 176011
⊕ romneymarshbrewery.com

⊠ A 12-barrel, family-run brewery founded in 2015 by former Come Dine with Me executive producer Matt Calais. Beer is supplied to outlets throughout Kent and East Sussex. ‼ ☛ RAIB

Marsh Gold (OG 1038, ABV 3.8%)
Orange and lemon citrus flavours.

Romney Golden Ale (OG 1037, ABV 3.9%)
A golden ale with honey, citrus and marmalade hop flavours.

Romney Best (OG 1038, ABV 4%)
Biscuit and chocolate malts with blackcurrant hop notes.

Cinque Porter (OG 1040, ABV 4.2%)
Gentle orange hop notes with roasted barley, crystal and chocolate malts.

Romney Amber Ale (OG 1041, ABV 4.4%)
Citrus and tropical hop flavours with a hint of caramel.

Rooster's SIBA ⊙

Unit 3, Grimbald Park, Wetherby Road, Knaresborough, North Yorkshire, HG5 8LJ
☎ (01423) 865959 ⊕ roosters.co.uk

⊙ Rooster's was founded in 1993 by Sean and Alison Franklin. The brewery was acquired by the Fozard family in 2011 when Sean and Alison retired. One off and occasional experimental beers are also brewed under the Outlaw Brewing Co name. ‼◆

Buckeye (OG 1035.5, ABV 3.5%)
An easy-drinking, well-hopped pale ale, with an orange citrus fruit aroma and a refreshing level of bitterness.

Highway 51 (OG 1036.5, ABV 3.7%)
Juicy tropical fruit flavours come to the fore in this pale session ale, backed with a hint of citrus and a grapefruit finish.

YPA (Yorkshire Pale Ale) (OG 1039.5, ABV 4.1%)
A pale, aromatic summer ale that offers delicate peachy and berry fruit flavours.

Yankee (OG 1041, ABV 4.3%) ◣
A straw-coloured beer with a delicate, fruity aroma leading to a well-balanced taste of malt and hops with a slight evidence of sweetness, followed by a refreshing, fruity/bitter finish.

Fort Smith (OG 1048, ABV 5%)
A bold IPA with tropical and passion fruit aromas and a lasting, bitter finish.

Baby-Faced Assassin (OG 1058, ABV 6.1%)
An IPA with aromas of mango, apricot, grapefruit and mandarin orange, along with a lasting, juicy, tropical fruit bitterness.

Roseland

c/o Roseland Inn, Philleigh, St Mawes, Cornwall, TR2 5NB
☎ (01872) 580254 ☎ 07977 472484
⊕ roselandinn.co.uk

⊠ Established in 2009 by its owner/brewer at the Roseland Inn, St Mawes, with the beers mostly named after local birds and available in the pub. Beers are contract brewed at Keltek Brewery (qv). Please see Keltek for beer list. ☛

Rossendale

🏠 Griffin Inn, 84 Hud Rake, Haslingden, Lancashire, BB4 5AF
☎ (01706) 214021 ⊕ rossendalebrewery.co.uk

⊕Formerly known as Pennine Ales, the brewery acquired the brew plant previously used by Porter Brewing Co in 2007 and is based in the cellar of the Griffin Inn in Haslingden.

Floral Dance (OG 1040, ABV 3.8%)
A pale and fruity session beer.

Hameldon Bitter (OG 1040, ABV 3.8%)
A dark traditional bitter with a dry and assertive character that develops in the finish.

Ale (OG 1045, ABV 4%)
A malty aroma leads to a complex, malt dominated flavour, supported by a dry, increasingly bitter finish.

Glen Top Bitter (OG 1040.5, ABV 4%)
A citrus, full-bodied, pale beer. Intentionally not over hopped with quite a dry aftertaste.

Halo Pale (OG 1045, ABV 4.5%)
A citrus, pale ale brewed with Cascade aroma hops, finishing with a slightly bitter aftertaste.

Pitch Porter (OG 1050, ABV 5%)
A full-bodied, rich beer with a slightly sweet, malty start, counter balanced with sharp bitterness and a roast barley dominance.

Sunshine (OG 1055, ABV 5.3%)
A hoppy and bitter golden beer with a citrus character. The lingering finish is dry and spicy.

Rother Valley SIBA

Gate Court Farm, Station Road, Northiam, East Sussex, TN31 6QT
☎ (01797) 252922 ☎ 07798 877551
⊕ rothervalleybrewery.co.uk

⊠ Rother Valley Brewing Co was established in Northiam in 1993, overlooking the Rother Levels and the Kent & East Sussex Railway. Established and new hop varieties are grown on the farm and also sourced locally. Brewing is split between cask and an ever-increasing range of filtered bottled beers. Around 100 outlets are supplied direct and through wholesalers. ‼◆

Honeyfuzz (OG 1038, ABV 3.8%)
A pale bitter flavoured with Sussex honey, subtle but not sweet with a citrus twang on the finish.

Smild (OG 1038, ABV 3.8%)
A full-bodied, dark, creamy mild with hints of chocolate.

Level Best (OG 1040, ABV 4%) ◗
Full-bodied, tawny session bitter with a malt and fruit aroma, malty taste and a dry, hoppy finish.

Copper Ale (OG 1041, ABV 4.1%)
A copper-coloured ale with a good balance of malt and hops.

Hoppers Ale (OG 1044, ABV 4.4%)
A copper-coloured ale. The initial burst of hop is followed by a pleasant caramel taste.

Boadicea (OG 1045, ABV 4.5%)
A straw-coloured beer with a delicate, fruity flavour.

Blues (OG 1050, ABV 5%)

Rothes

77 New Street, Rothes, AB38 7BJ ☎ 07336 233634
⊕ therothesbrewery@sky.com

⊠ Situated in the heart of the Spey Valley, Rothes began producing commercially in 2014. Initially producing only bottle-conditioned beers, cask ales are now also brewed, with an output of up to 800 litres a week. RAIB

Rotters

🏠 Tower Hotel, Talgarth, LD3 0BW
☎ (01874) 711253 ⊕ rottersbrewery.co.uk

⊕Rotters brewery was established in 2010. Brewing is currently suspended. ‼◆

Round Tower SIBA

Unit 11a, Robjohns House, Navigation Road, Chelmsford, Essex, CM2 6ND
☎ (01245) 807343 ☎ 07905 255909
⊕ roundtowerbrewery.co.uk

Round Tower began brewing in 2013, the first brewery in Chelmsford since Grays & Sons ceased brewing in 1974. Former home brewer Simon Tippler started on a small scale but has now expanded to a brew length of five barrels. Several local pubs are supplied and the beers can also be found in the Grays & Sons estate and other selected free houses. RAIB

Stout (OG 1043, ABV 4.3%)
A rich and complex stout.

Slipstream (OG 1053, ABV 5.4%)
A black IPA.

Rowditch

🏠 Rowditch Inn, 246 Uttoxeter New Road, Derby, DE22 3LL
☎ (01332) 343123

⊠ The Rowditch Brewery was established in 2010 and is a 3.75-barrel plant situated on the premises of the Rowditch pub. One-off ales are periodically available. ◆

St Stephens (OG 1038, ABV 3.6%)
Citrus-flavoured, golden, very bitter ale.

More Beer (OG 1045, ABV 4.5%)

R.P.A (OG 1047, ABV 4.7%)
Balanced golden bitter.

Rowett

Storrs Cottage, The Square, North Thoresby, Lincolnshire, DN36 5QL
☎ (01472) 841080 ⊕ rowettbrewing.com

Founded in 2014 as a commercial 1.5-barrel nanobrewery, Rowett Brewing supplies its beers to pubs in Grimsby and the Lincolnshire Wolds. ◆RAIB

Six Hour Lunch (ABV 4.2%)
A classic amber-coloured bitter.

Oak Barrel Stout (OG 1056, ABV 5.2%)
A rich oatmeal stout. Oak whiskey barrel aged.

Rowton SIBA ◉

Stone House, Rowton, Telford, Shropshire, TF6 6QX
☎ 07746 290995 ⊕ rowtonbrewery.com

Rowton is a father and son team that was established in 2008 on a four-barrel plant in an old cow shed on the owner's farm. The water is drawn from a borehole on site. ♦

Moonstruck Mild (OG 1033, ABV 3.3%)

Pure Gold (OG 1038, ABV 3.8%)

Bitter (OG 1040, ABV 3.9%)

Portly Stout (OG 1045, ABV 4.5%)
A smooth, flavoursome stout fortified with port.

RPM (NEW)

▤ 118 High Street, Weston-super-Mare, BS23 1HP
☎ (01934) 632629

Office: 19 Orchard Street, Weston Super-Mare, BS23 1RG

⊗ Established in 2015 and operating on a 10-gallon system out of the Brit Bar in Weston-super-Mare.

Black Dog (ABV 4.2%)
A rich porter with hints of coffee, vanilla, spice and molasses.

Rtwo Dtoo

▤ Steamhouse, Station Road, Urmston, M41 9SB
☎ (0161) 748 6487 ⊕ thesteamhouse.co.uk

The unusual name of this brewery comes from the triumvirate who run it – Rob, Ron and Danny (two 'R's and a 'D' too). Established in 2013 and located at the Steamhouse pub in Urmston.

Ruddles

See Greene King

Rudgate SIBA ◉

2 Centre Park, Marston Moor Business Park, Tockwith, York, North Yorkshire, YO26 7QF
☎ (01423) 358382 ⊕ rudgatebrewery.co.uk

☺Rudgate began brewing in 1992 on a disused WWII airfield that was chosen because of its water suitability. The original brewery was in a former ammunition building, expanding into a modern facility in 2011. Traditional methods are followed using a full mash infusion system and fermentation is achieved using its own strain of Yorkshire brewing yeast. ♦

Jorvik Blonde (OG 1036, ABV 3.8%)
Blonde ale with a balanced hoppy bitterness and a crisp, fruity finish.

Viking (OG 1036, ABV 3.8%) ◣
An initially warming and malty, full-bodied beer, with hops and fruit lingering into the aftertaste.

Battleaxe (OG 1040, ABV 4.2%) ◣
A well-hopped bitter with slightly sweet initial taste and light bitterness. Complex fruit character gives a memorable aftertaste.

Ruby Mild (OG 1041, ABV 4.4%) ⌂ ◣
Nutty, rich ruby ale, stronger than usual for a mild.

Volsung (OG 1046, ABV 5%)
A premium bitter, golden-coloured with distinctive lemon on the nose.

York Chocolate Stout (OG 1049, ABV 5%)
Deep, rich stout with complex balanced flavours and a subtle chocolate finish.

IPA (OG 1053, ABV 5.2%)
Initially bittersweet, well-balanced complex fruit, hints of citrus and a bitter, hoppy finish.

Runaway

Unit 4, Millgate, Dantzic Street, Manchester, M4 4JW
☎ (0161) 832 2628 ☎ 07505 237078
⊕ therunawaybrewery.com

Runaway began brewing in 2014 using a 5.5-barrel plant producing KeyKeg and bottle-conditioned beers. All beers are unfiltered and unpasteurised. ♦ RAIB

Ryedale SIBA

Hardings House, Hardings Lane, Cross Hills, North Yorkshire, BD20 7AD
☎ (01535) 637026 ☎ 07850 510859
⊕ ryedalebrewing.co.uk

Rydale began brewing in 2013 using a four-barrel plant, supplying pubs in the local area.

Angler (ABV 3.8%)
Blonde ale with light bitterness and a pleasant, light, hoppy aftertaste.

Gold (ABV 3.8%)
Golden ale with a hoppy taste.

Pale (ABV 3.8%)
Light-coloured, clean, refreshing ale with a slightly hoppy taste.

Rambler (ABV 3.8%)
Dark chestnut-coloured bitter, creamy with a well-balanced, smooth, hoppy aftertaste.

Bitter (ABV 4%)

Stout (ABV 4.3%)

S&P

Homestead, Drayton Lane, Horsford, Norfolk, NR10 3AN ☎ 07552 300768 ⊕ spbrewery.co.uk

⊗ Production commenced in 2013 using a 10-barrel plant constructed upon land once owned by prominent Norfolk brewers Steward & Patteson (1800-1965), hence the name. Locally produced malts are used as is water from the brewery's own borehole. ‼

Topaz Blonde (OG 1038, ABV 3.7%)
A golden-coloured beer with a citrus aroma and grapefruit taste. A crisp bitter finish.

Afterglow (OG 1041.6, ABV 3.9%)
A full-bodied, well-balanced amber ale.

Between the Posts (OG 1040.2, ABV 3.9%)

Barrack Street Bitter (OG 1041, ABV 4%) ◣
A refreshing amber ale. A gentle hop aroma sits comfortably with the malty biscuit flavour. An increasingly bitter finish.

First Light (OG 1042, ABV 4.1%) ◣
A light golden beer. A strong citrus aroma and deep hoppy flavour is complemented by a lingering bitter finish.

Dennis (OG 1042, ABV 4.2%)
A rich amber bitter with a well-balanced malty sweetness.

Eve's Drop (OG 1046, ABV 4.3%) ◣

A well-balanced golden brown ale. Hops and malts dominate with a peppery mouthfeel giving way to lingering sweetness.

Darkest Hour (OG 1047, ABV 4.4%)
Roasted barley gives a faint coffee aroma and taste to this full-bodied Irish stout.

Nasha IPA (OG 1050, ABV 5%)
A persistent head sits atop a rich amber ale with well-balanced malty sweetness.

Sacre Brew

≣ Unit 13, Monmore Road, Wolverhampton, WV1 2TZ
☎ 07413 432120 ⊕ sacrebrew.com

Sacre Brew is a small, artisanal 1.2-barrel microbrewery based at the Hungry Bistro in Wolverhampton. Beers are supplied to pubs across the West Midlands as well as to the bistro. **RAIB V**

Saddleworth

≣ Church Inn, Church Lane, Uppermill, Oldham,
OL3 6LW
☎ (01457) 820902 ⊕ churchinnsaddleworth.co.uk

☺Saddleworth started brewing in 1997 in a 120-year old brewhouse at the Church Inn. Brewery and inn are set above a valley overlooking Saddleworth Moor. Brewing capacity was significantly expanded in 2011 with a new 13-barrel plant. ♦

Mild (OG 1038, ABV 3.6%)

St George's Bitter (OG 1038, ABV 3.8%)
Quite dry and bitter, with some citrus and nutty notes.

Sadler's SIBA 👁

≣ Unit 2, Conyers Trading Estate, Station Drive, Lye,
West Midlands, DY9 8ER
☎ (01384) 895230 ⊕ sadlersales.co.uk

☺Third and fourth generation brewers John and Chris Sadler re-opened this historic brewery in 2004. The brewery tap house was built and opened in 2006 next to the brewery. Around 250 outlets are supplied. A new 30-barrel plant, visitor centre, shop and tasting room opened in 2015. ‼️🍺

JPA (OG 1038, ABV 3.8%)
A pale, hoppy bitter with a crisp and zesty lemon undertone.

Mellow Yellow (OG 1041, ABV 4.1%)
A pale ale brewed with plenty of hop and honey.

Worcester Sorcerer (OG 1043, ABV 4.3%)
Brewed with English hops and barley with hints of mint and lemon, creating a floral aroma and crisp bitterness.

Thin Ice (OG 1045, ABV 4.5%)
A pale ale. Bitter but with an orange and lemon finish.

Peaky Blinder (OG 1046, ABV 4.6%)
A black IPA; dark, refreshing and hoppy.

Boris Citrov (OG 1047, ABV 4.7%)
A punchy orange marmalade ale, leading to a sweet, crisp and fruity finish.

Hop Bomb (OG 1050, ABV 5%)
A powerful IPA. A balanced malt sweetness supports the epic hop aroma and flavour explosion.

Red IPA (OG 1057, ABV 5.7%)

Mud City Stout (OG 1066, ABV 6.6%)
Rich, full-bodied strong stout brewed with raw cocoa, fresh vanilla pods, oats, wheat and dark malts.

Saffron SIBA

The Cartshed, Parsonage Farm, Henham, Essex,
CM22 6AN
☎ (01279) 850923 ☎ 07980 972067
⊕ saffronbrewery.co.uk

⊠ Founded in 2005, the brewery was upgraded to a 15-barrel plant in early 2008 and re-located to a converted barn at Parsonage Farm, with a purpose-built reed bed for environmentally-friendly disposal of waste products. 40 outlets are supplied direct. ‼️♦RAIB

IPA (OG 1036, ABV 3.6%)

Citra (ABV 3.8%)
A light golden ale with grapeberry aromas and a crisp gooseberry finish.

Dawn Til Dusk (ABV 3.8%)
A traditional copper-coloured bitter with hints of citrus and biscuit maltiness.

Ramblers Tipple (OG 1040, ABV 3.9%)
A rich, copper-coloured bitter with toffee and caramel flavours.

Brewhouse Bell (OG 1041, ABV 4%)
Golden amber in colour with citrus and hop flavours balancing well for a clean, fresh finish.

Littlebury Lighthouse (OG 1043, ABV 4.2%)

Blonde (OG 1044, ABV 4.3%)
A light golden ale with a delicate balance of citrus and smooth, malty flavours and a crisp finish.

Squires Gamble (OG 1044, ABV 4.3%)
Traditional-style copper ale; soft, mellow, full-flavoured and hoppy with citrus and biscuit hints.

Porter (ABV 5.2%)
A ruby porter with rich chocolate and coffee aromas. Ruby port and red grape juice create a soft fruit and spice finish.

St Andrew's (Norwich) (NEW)

≣ City Pub Co, 41 St Andrews Street, Norwich,
NR2 4TP
☎ (01603) 305995 ☎ 07976 652410
⊕ standrewsbrewhouse.com

⊠ A city centre brewpub opened in 2015 in the premises formerly occupied by Delaney's Irish Bar. ‼️♦

Cork-Cutters Best Bitter (OG 1038, ABV 3.8%)
Best bitter with an earthy, spicy, biscuity aroma but a sweet, malty but fruity finish.

Wensum Ale (OG 1038, ABV 3.8%)

Grocers Ghost IPA (OG 1040, ABV 4.2%)
A hoppy ale with a floral, citrus aroma with long-lasting hints of grapefruit and spice.

St Andrews (St Andrews) SIBA

Unit 7 Bassaguard Business Park, St Andrews,
KY16 8AL ☎ 07879 399441
⊕ standrewsbrewingcompany.com

Established in 2012, St Andrews Brewing Company produces bottle-conditioned beers that are available across Fife and Scotland. Beers are brewed in small batches of just 750 bottles. Cask beers are supplied to a number of local outlets including the brewery tap in St Andrews, opened in 2013. RAIB

The Wee Blonde (OG 1035, ABV 3.7%)
Gentle blonde ale with light citrus hops, hints of fruit, and a floral aroma.

Seventy Bob (OG 1037, ABV 3.8%)
A traditional 70/- brown ale with toffee and malt aromas leading to nutty chocolate, toast and caramel flavours, rounded off with a subtle and balanced bitter finish.

Fife Gold (OG 1040, ABV 4.2%)
Straw yellow in colour with a fresh, floral aroma backed up with a citrus punch of lemon, lime and grapefruit coming through from a blend of hops.

Crail Ale (OG 1043, ABV 4.5%)
A bright golden ale with long-lasting citrus and floral flavours.

Oatmeal Stout (OG 1043, ABV 4.5%)
A smooth, full-bodied Scottish oatmeal stout. Strong coffee, chocolate and dark fruit flavours balanced against a blend of hops to create a rich, silky aftertaste.

Neuk Ale (OG 1046, ABV 4.6%)
A Scotch ale-style beer. Dark mahogany in colour with rich, dark fruit, chocolate and roast coffee flavours. A long-lasting bitter aftertaste ties together with a fresh finish.

Eighty Bob (OG 1046, ABV 4.8%)
A traditional Scottish 80/- ale. Complex malt flavours dominate.

India Pale Ale (OG 1048, ABV 5%)
Bold IPA with a big hop kick and a depth of orange and tropical fruit flavours that are both refreshing and complex.

St Austell SIBA 👁

63 Trevarthian Road, St Austell, Cornwall, PL25 4BY
☎ (01726) 74444 ⊕ staustellbrewery.co.uk

⊠ Founded in 1851, St Austell Brewery remains family owned. Its cask beers are available in all its pubs, and throughout the UK. The brewery hosts its own Celtic beer festival in November each year. A visitor centre with a 10-barrel small batch plant has recently opened. !! ☰ ♦ RAIB

Cornish Best Bitter (OG 1035, ABV 3.5%) ◈
Light, refreshing copper-coloured bitter with a malt aroma. Gentle biscuit malt and hops flavour with low bitterness. Bitter, dry finish.

Trelawny (OG 1039, ABV 3.8%) ◈
Tawny bitter with aroma of hops and stone fruits. Hop bitterness and some citrus develop into caramel-malt sweetness. Refreshing, crisp finish.

Nicholson's Pale Ale (OG 1040, ABV 4.1%) ◈
Amber best bitter. Lightly roast malt and hops dominate the taste with sweet fruit tones. Dry bitterness rises in the finish.

Tribute (OG 1043, ABV 4.2%) ◈
Pale brown best bitter with malt and hop aroma. Dominant hop bitterness with biscuit malt, ending refreshingly bitter and dry.

Proper Job (OG 1046, ABV 4.5%) ◈

Golden IPA with resinous hop aroma. Copious citrus fruits with bitterness and a crisp hop, bitter and grapefruit finish, becoming dry.

HSD (OG 1052, ABV 5%) 🗂 ◈
Malt and stone fruit aroma leads into rich, balanced fruit, caramel, bitterness and malt, which last into the long finish.

1913 Cornish Stout (OG 1052, ABV 5.2%) ◈
Velvet black stout with roast coffee aroma. Powerful roast malt with vine fruit and esters. Roast, dry and bitter finish.

St George's SIBA

The Old Bakery, Bush Lane, Callow End, Worcestershire, WR2 4TF
☎ (01905) 831316 ⊕ stgeorgesbrewery.co.uk

The brewery was established in 1998 in old village bakery premises and acquired in 2006 by Duncan Ironmonger, who owns three nearby pubs. The brewery supplies local free houses and wholesalers for a wider distribution. !! ♦

By George (OG 1036, ABV 3.6%)
A clean-drinking pale golden session ale with a strong floral aroma and citrus hop notes.

Friar Tuck (OG 1040, ABV 4%)
A golden bitter with a smooth, refreshing bitter taste and citrus character.

Lazy Days (OG 1042, ABV 4.1%)
A light golden-coloured ale with a mellow floral hop aroma followed by a distinctive hoppy taste.

Worcester Sauce (OG 1043, ABV 4.3%)
A chestnut-coloured ale with a hoppy aroma and a strong bitter finish.

Dream Weaver (OG 1045, ABV 4.5%)

Charger (OG 1046, ABV 4.6%)
A light golden beer with a citrus blast and a hint of grapefruit.

Dragons Blood (OG 1048, ABV 4.8%)
A ruby-coloured beer with a hint of chocolate. An earthy and slightly spicy aroma.

St Ives (NEW)

Trenwith Burrows, St Ives, Cornwall, TR26 1GD
☎ (01736) 793488 ☎ 07702 311595
⊕ stives-brewery.co.uk

Owner Marco Amura started the brewery in 2010, though all beers at the time were produced under licence by various local breweries. In 2015 a two-storey brewery was constructed with a 10-barrel plant, incorporating a visitor centre and gift shop plus a 60-seat café, with production at the site beginning in 2016. RAIB

Pale Ale (OG 1036, ABV 3.6%)

Harbourside Light Ale (OG 1038, ABV 3.8%)

Boilers (OG 1040, ABV 4%)

Knill by Mouth (OG 1048, ABV 5%)

St Judes (NEW)

🏠 2 Cardigan Street, Ipswich, Suffolk, IP1 3PF
☎ (01473) 413334 ☎ 07879 360879
⊕ stjudestavern.com

⊠ The brewery resumed brewing in 2015 on a newly installed 10-barrel plant. Run by Frank Walsh and Colleen Seymour, the beers are sold mainly through their Ipswich tavern, but can occasionally be found further afield through a distribution agreement with Nethergate. The core range is supplemented by frequent one off and special beers.

Devereaux Porter (OG 1043, ABV 4.2%)
An easy-drinking porter with a well-rounded flavour.

Gainsborough Bitter (OG 1044, ABV 4.4%)
An amber-coloured bitter, full-bodied with a hoppy aftertaste.

John Orford Brown Ale (OG 1050, ABV 4.8%)
An old-fashioned brown ale with a rich, sweet flavour.

Coachmans Whip (OG 1052, ABV 5.2%)
A strong, complex bitter with a powerful fruity flavour and a long bitter finish.

St Peter's SIBA ◉

St Peter's Hall, St Peter South Elmham, Suffolk, NR35 1NQ
☎ (01986) 782322 ⊕ stpetersbrewery.co.uk

⊠ St Peter's Brewery is based adjacent to a moated medieval hall near Bungay, Suffolk. Established in 1996 it concentrates in the main on bottled beer/keg (85% of capacity) but has a rapidly increasing cask market. Two pubs are owned. 50% of production is exported to 50 countries worldwide. ‼♣♦GF

Best Bitter (OG 1037, ABV 3.7%) ♣
A complex but well-balanced hoppy brew. A gentle hop nose introduces a singular hoppiness with supporting malt notes and underlying bitterness. Other flavours fade to leave a long, dry, hoppy finish.

Mild (OG 1037, ABV 3.7%) ♣
Heady aroma of caramelised blackberries and black toffee. Complex flavours with caramel, blackberries, hops and an astringent bitterness. Long, sustained finish with a roast coffee bitterness; increasingly dry.

Golden Ale (OG 1040, ABV 4%) ♣
Amber-coloured, full-bodied, robust ale. A strong hop bouquet leads to a mix of malt and hops combined with a dry, fruity hoppiness. The malt quickly subsides, leaving creamy bitterness.

Organic Best (OG 1041, ABV 4.1%) ♣
A dry and bitter beer with a growing astringency. Pale brown in colour, it has a gentle hop aroma which makes the definitive bitterness surprising.

G-Free (OG 1048, ABV 4.2%)
A pale gold gluten-free ale with aromas of citrus and mandarin.

Ruby Red (OG 1043, ABV 4.3%)
A tawny red ale with subtle malt undertones and a distinctive spicy hop aroma.

Organic Ale (OG 1045, ABV 4.5%) ♣
A rich toffee apple aroma and a smooth grainy feel. Malt and caramel initially match the dry, hoppy bitterness. As the flavours mature, liquorice dryness develops. Full-bodied.

Grapefruit Beer (OG 1047, ABV 4.7%) ♣
With a strong aroma and taste of grapefruit, this refreshing beer is a superb example of a fruit beer.

IPA (OG 1055, ABV 5.5%)

A full-bodied, highly hopped pale ale with a zesty character.

Salamander SIBA

22 Harry Street, Dudley Hill, Bradford, West Yorkshire, BD4 9PH
☎ (01274) 652323 ⊕ salamanderbrewing.co.uk

⊠ Salamander first brewed in 2000 in a former pork pie factory. An expansion in 2004 increased capacity to 40 barrels per week. Direct deliveries are made to around 100 outlets in Yorkshire, Cumbria, Lancashire, Manchester, Derbyshire, Leicestershire and Lincoln. ‼♦

Axolotl (OG 1038, ABV 3.9%)

Mudpuppy (OG 1042, ABV 4.2%) ♣
A well-balanced, copper-coloured best bitter with a fruity, hoppy nose and a bitter finish.

Golden Salamander (OG 1045, ABV 4.5%) ♣
Citrus hops characterise the aroma and taste of this golden premium bitter, which has malt undertones throughout. The aftertaste is dry, hoppy and bitter.

Salcombe SIBA ◉

Unit 2M, South Hams Business Park, Churchstow, Devon, TQ7 3QH
☎ (01548) 854888

⊠ Quercus began trading in 2007, using an eight-barrel brew plant, before being sold to local residents John Tiner and Mike George in 2012. A complete rebranding occurred in 2016, with a name change to Salcombe Brewing Company, and all beers were relaunched. A new, purpose-built 20-barrel brewery and visitor centre at nearby Ledstone Cross is planned. ‼♣♦

Devon Amber (OG 1038, ABV 3.8%)
A classic bitter. Amber in colour with a dry, hoppy aroma and flavour and a sweet malt backbone.

Gold (OG 1042, ABV 4.2%)
A light, refreshing straw-coloured ale with a hop aroma and taste and a long hoppy finish.

Shingle Bay (OG 1042, ABV 4.2%)
A light, easy-drinking ale with a fruity aroma and flavour. Smooth to the taste with a crisp finish.

Seahorse (OG 1044, ABV 4.4%)
A smooth-drinking ale, deep gold in colour, with a spicy hop character.

Lifesaver (OG 1048, ABV 4.8%)
A refreshing ale, deep copper in colour, with a smack of citrus and orange peel and a malty flavour. A dry citrus finish with a taste of liquorice.

Salopian SIBA ◉

The Old Station Yard, Station Road, Hadnall, Shropshire, SY4 3DD
☎ (01743) 248414 ⊕ salopianbrewery.co.uk

⊛The brewery was established in 1995 in an old dairy on the outskirts of Shrewsbury but moved in 2014 to its new location in an industrial unit in the village of Hadnall, where it now produces more than 150 barrels a week. Salopian also brews under the Blackwater Brewery name. ‼♣♦RAIB

Shropshire Gold (OG 1037, ABV 3.8%) ⌖ ▯
A light, copper-coloured ale with an unusual blend of body and dryness.

Oracle (OG 1040, ABV 4%) 🍺 📋 🥄
Citrus aromas lead to an impressive dry and increasing citrus taste.

Darwins Origin (OG 1042, ABV 4.3%) 🍺 📋
A light copper-coloured ale with a striking hop profile, which is balanced by a refined malt finish.

Hop Twister (OG 1044, ABV 4.5%)
A premium bitter with a citrus flavour and complex hop finish. Refreshing and crisp.

Lemon Dream (OG 1043.5, ABV 4.5%)
A light gold ale brewed with wheat malt and subtly flavoured with fresh lemons.

Golden Thread (OG 1048, ABV 5%) 🍺
A bright gold ale. Strong and quite bitter but well balanced.

Kashmir (OG 1053.5, ABV 5.5%)

Automaton (OG 1068, ABV 7%)

Saltaire SIBA 👁

Unit 6, County Works, Dockfield Road, Shipley, West Yorkshire, BD17 7AR
☎ (01274) 594959 ⊕ saltairebrewery.co.uk

☺Launched in 2006, Saltaire is an award-winning brewery based in a former Victorian power station. A mezzanine bar gives visitors views of the brewing plant and the chance to taste the beers. A brewery tap and shop opened in 2014. More than 600 pubs are supplied across West Yorkshire and the north of England. 🍴♦

South Island Pale (OG 1035, ABV 3.5%) 🥄
This golden-coloured bitter has an intensely hoppy aroma which follows through to a well-balanced fruity, citrus, hop flavour and a long, hoppy finish.

Pride (OG 1039, ABV 3.9%)
A deep gold-coloured beer with a toasty malt flavour and rich, spicy hop flavours.

Blonde (OG 1040, ABV 4%) 🍺 🥄
This straw-coloured beer is slightly sweet and well-rounded with fruit, malt and hops in the taste and a fruity, hoppy finish.

Elderflower Blonde (OG 1040, ABV 4%) 🥄
An easy-drinking, smooth, golden-coloured ale with subtle elderflower aroma leading to a pleasant elderflower fruit taste and a long, refreshing finish.

Raspberry Blonde (OG 1040, ABV 4%)
Refreshing blonde ale infused with a hint of raspberries.

Blackberry Cascade (OG 1046, ABV 4.8%)
Cascade hops infused with a hint of blackberries.

Cascade Pale Ale (OG 1046, ABV 4.8%) 🥄
A well-balanced golden bitter with smooth mouthfeel, floral hop aromas and pronounced bitterness, culminating in a long, dry finish and dry aftertaste.

Cascadian Black (OG 1046, ABV 4.8%) 🥄
A well-rounded, smooth, dark strong bitter with a hoppy aroma. The flavour is strong on hops and malt with a slight liquorice hint. The aftertaste is long, liquorice and strongly hoppy.

Triple Chocoholic (OG 1048.5, ABV 4.8%) 🍺 📋 🥄
A creamy, dark brown, roast, chocolate stout with a dry bitter finish and a rich chocolate aroma.

Sambrook's SIBA 👁

Units 1-3, Yelverton Road, Battersea, London, SW11 3QG
☎ (020) 7228 0598 ⊕ sambrooksbrewery.co.uk

⊠ Sambrook's was founded by Duncan Sambrook and David Welsh in 2008, supplying its award-winning ales throughout London. The brewery bar hosts regular events. ‼🍴♦RAIB

Wandle (OG 1038.5, ABV 3.8%) 📋 🥄
Dryness balances the rounded sweetish malt flavour of this fruity, quaffable pale brown bitter. Some peach and citrus notes.

Pumphouse Pale (OG 1041.5, ABV 4.2%) 🥄
Refreshing golden beer with a hint of citrus aroma becoming more pronounced on the palate, lingering into the bitter finish.

Junction (OG 1045.5, ABV 4.5%) 📋 🥄
Smooth, full-bodied brown best bitter. Fruit and spicy hoppy aroma and flavour, lingering in the dry, slightly bitter finish.

Powerhouse Porter (OG 1050, ABV 4.9%) 🥄
Dark brown porter with a pleasant roasted malt nose with some sultana, blackcurrant and treacle character. Dry roasted finish.

Sandiway (NEW)

Blakemere Village, Chester Road, Sandiway, Cheshire, CW8 2EB
☎ (01606) 301000 ⊕ sandiwayales.co.uk

☺Sandiway began brewing in 2015 using a five-barrel plant in the premises of the former Blakemere Brewery at Blakemere Village Craft Centre. Aimed at local trade, outlets include the on-site shop called 'Wee Howff'. Beers are also available at the No. 4 Bar in Winsford and limited outlets throughout Cheshire and surrounding areas. ‼🍴

Hop Salvo (OG 1037, ABV 3.8%)
Light session bitter with citrus flavours.

Hop Schism (OG 1040, ABV 4.1%)
Golden ale with a hint of orange peel.

Hop Sepia (OG 1041, ABV 4.3%)
Copper-coloured ale with liquorice/caramel hints.

Hop Secret (OG 1043, ABV 4.5%)
A dark porter with coffee notes.

Sandstone SIBA 👁

Unit 5, Wrexham Enterprise Park, Preston Road, off Ash Road, North Wrexham Industrial Estate, Wrexham, LL13 9JT
☎ (01978) 664805 ☎ 07851 001118
⊕ sandstonebrewery.co.uk

☺Sandstone Brewery was established as a four-barrel plant in 2008. More than 60 outlets in north Wales and north-west England are supplied. The brewery was taken over by new owners in 2013 with the existing portfolio retained and a number of new beers added. ‼♦

Edge (OG 1039, ABV 3.8%) 🥄
A satisfying session ale, this pale, dry, bitter beer has a full mouthfeel and a lingering hoppy finish that belies its modest strength.

Onyx Dragon (OG 1040, ABV 4%)

Coal black in colour with hints of chocolate, toffee and caramel.

Post Mistress (OG 1046, ABV 4.4%) ◆
A full-bodied, smooth, premium bitter, ruby-red in colour, with a rich, mellow taste. Good combination of malt, hops and fruit in aroma and initial taste leading to a lasting, satisfying finish.

Racing Dragon (OG 1044, ABV 4.4%)

Twisted Dragon (OG 1058, ABV 5.8%)

Savour (NEW)

Office: 10 Stephenson Drive, Windsor, Berkshire, SL4 5LG ⊕ savourbeer.com

Inspired by the farmhouse beers of Belgium and Northern France, Savour was founded in 2013 and focusses mainly on bottle-conditioned beers. Beers are brewed in small batches at either Compass Brewing (qv) in Oxfordshire or at Firebrand Brewing in Cornwall. **RAIB**

Sawbridgeworth SIBA

≣ 81 London Road, Sawbridgeworth, Hertfordshire, CM21 9JJ
☎ (01279) 722313 ☎ 07446 960409
⊕ thegatepub.net

⊠ Set up in 2000 by owners Tom and Gary Barnett, the brewery is situated behind the Gate Inn. Tom is a former professional footballer whose clubs included Crystal Palace. Brewing is carried out by ex-Nethergate brewer Bob Renvoise. **!!◆**

Manor Mild (OG 1034, ABV 3.4%)

IPA (OG 1038, ABV 3.8%)

Selhurst Park Flyer (OG 1038, ABV 3.8%)

Gold (OG 1040, ABV 4%)

Is It Yourself (OG 1042, ABV 4.2%)

Dragon's Blood (OG 1043, ABV 4.3%)

Saxon City

Glebe Farm Industrial Estate, Stoke Edith, Herefordshire, HR1 4HG
☎ (01432) 890688 ⊕ herefordcasks.co.uk

☺Brewing began in 2010 in a vacant unit adjoining a cask factory using a six-barrel plant by PBC Brewery Installations. Brewing is currently suspended.

Scarborough SIBA

Unit 1b, Stadium Works, Barry's Lane, Scarborough, North Yorkshire, YO12 4HA
☎ (01723) 367506 ⊕ scarboroughbrewery.co.uk

Scarborough Brewery was established in 2010 using a one-barrel plant. In 2011 commercial brewing began using a 10-barrel plant from Wold Top Brewery. Beers can be found at its brewery tap, the Valley Bar in Scarborough, and nationwide via wholesalers. ◆

Blonde (OG 1038, ABV 3.8%)
Easy-drinking pale session beer with a subtle citrus flavour and hoppy aroma.

Cascades (OG 1041, ABV 4.1%)
Pale straw-coloured beer with a zesty, citrus flavour and floral, hoppy aroma.

Chinook (OG 1041, ABV 4.1%)
Straw-coloured pale beer with spicy bitter flavours and a fruity, hoppy aroma.

Citra (OG 1042, ABV 4.2%)
Refreshing and light, pale golden beer with citrus aromas.

Sealord (OG 1043, ABV 4.3%)
Golden ale brewed with a combination of hops that give subtle hints of lime, grapefruit and melon.

Stout (OG 1046, ABV 4.6%)
Full-bodied dark stout with a bitter chocolate aroma.

American Pale (OG 1050, ABV 5%)
American-style golden beer with a crisp, hoppy taste and floral aroma.

Schoolhouse SIBA

Unit 1, Cleveland Industrial Estate, Darlington, County Durham, DL1 2PB
☎ (01325) 461812
✉ gannaway@schoolhousebrewery.co.uk

☺Schoolhouse began brewing in 2013 on a six-barrel plant. The brewery does not artificially enhance the mineral content of its brewing water, ensuring its beer reflects the geology of the North East. **!!**

The Equation (ABV 4.2%)
A black bitter, deceptively light and smoky.

The Bike Shed (ABV 4.4%)
A blonde bitter with zesty hoppiness.

Triple Science (ABV 4.4%)
An amber-coloured bitter.

Equation+ (ABV 4.5%)
Equation but with the addition of North Yorkshire heather honey.

Scottish Borders

See Born in the Borders

Scribbler's SIBA ◉

7 Lime Grove, Stapleford, Nottinghamshire, NG9 7GF
☎ (0115) 875 1759 ☎ 07780 662244
⊕ scribblers-ales.com

Scribbler's was established in 2014 by Richard Nettleton, an author (hence the name) and Roger Frost. The 4.5-barrel plant was constructed by the owners, the fermentation and mash tun converted from old ice cream vessels. The copper came from Grafton Brewing Co (qv). Beer names are based on classic book titles.

Beerfest at Tiffanys (OG 1046, ABV 3.8%)
Traditional English session bitter with a slightly spicy aftertaste.

Hoppy Potter and the Goblet of Ale (OG 1048, ABV 4.2%)
Light-coloured ale with with citrus hop aromas.

Masher In The Rye (OG 1053, ABV 4.8%)
Golden-coloured American-style ale made with a dash of rye malt.

Rubecca (OG 1053, ABV 4.8%)
Smooth ruby-coloured beer with hints of chocolate.

One Brew Over The Cuckoo's Nest (OG 1058, ABV 5.3%)

Beyond Reasonable Stout (OG 1068, ABV 6%)

Seren SIBA

Syfnau House, Rosebush, SA66 7QY
☎ (01437) 532098 ⊕ serenbrewing.com

⬣ Seren is an award-winning nanobrewery on the edge of the Preseli Mountains in North Pembrokeshire. Beers are crafted on a small scale, however a large scale expansion is planned, with a new brewery to be built. RAIB

Bluestone IPA (OG 1042, ABV 4.2%)
A gold-coloured beer with citrus and tropical hop aromas and flavours.

Ink Spot (OG 1042, ABV 4.2%)
Citrus and pine plays over roast flavours.

Blackstone Stout (OG 1045, ABV 4.5%)

Factory Steam (OG 1045, ABV 4.5%)
A steam brewed, full-bodied, copper-coloured best bitter. Fruity, with a firm bitterness and biscuity malt notes.

Browncoat (OG 1047, ABV 4.7%)
American-style brown ale. Grapefruit aroma and flavour, with a malty backbone with hints of chocolate.

Indian Ink (OG 1062, ABV 6.5%)
A black IPA. Citrus and pine plays over a touch of roast.

West Wales IPA (OG 1062, ABV 6.5%)
Full strength American-style IPA. Gold in colour with citrus and tropical hop aroma and flavour.

Serious (NEW)

Unit C5, Fieldhouse Industrial Estate, Fieldhouse Road, Rochdale, OL12 0AA
✉ jenny@seriousbrewing.co.uk

Established in 2015 and run by a husband-and-wife team. The focus is on producing high quality beers drawing influences from traditional British ales, US craft beers and artisinal Belgian beers. ♦ RAIB

Moonlight (ABV 4.5%)
A silky smooth stout with chocolate notes and a bitter hop finish.

Redsmith (ABV 4.5%)
A copper-coloured IPA.

Settle SIBA

Unit 8, The Sidings, Settle, North Yorkshire, BD24 9RP
☎ (01729) 824936 ⊕ settlebrewery.co.uk

Settle Brewery is located in a small industrial unit adjacent to Settle railway station. Brewing started in 2013 using a new 12-barrel Johnsons kit. Brewer Ian Simkins originally brewed at Nine Standards Brewery in Kirkby Stephen. More than 40 outlets across Cumbria, the Yorkshire Dales, West Yorkshire and North Lancashire are supplied. The beers are also available through wholesalers. ‼♦

Blonde (OG 1036, ABV 3.6%)
A delicate straw-coloured beer with a subtle blend of fruit and spice flavours and citrus overtones.

Mainline (OG 1037.5, ABV 3.8%)
A refreshing, delicately fruity golden IPA-style beer with a little bit of sweetness.

Attermire IPA (OG 1041, ABV 4.2%)

A session IPA.

Contract brewed for Nine Standards Brewery:

No. 4 Amber Ale (OG 1037, ABV 3.7%)
A dark amber bitter with a fruity, spicy nose.

No. 1 Golden Ale (OG 1040, ABV 4.1%)
A golden ale with a hint of blackcurrant.

No. 2 Pale Ale (OG 1042, ABV 4.3%)
A classic pale ale with a strong hoppy aroma.

No. 3 Porter (OG 1048, ABV 4.7%)
A robust porter with caramel and coffee notes and smoky undertones.

Seven Bro7hers SIBA ◉

33 Waybridge Enterprise Centre, Daniel Adamson Road, Salford, M50 1DS
☎ (0161) 637 9929 ☎ 07968 538572
⊕ sevenbro7hers.com

Brewing began in 2014 using a 10-barrel plant.

Session (ABV 3.8%)
A session ale delivering massive citrus aromas and tropical fruit flavours. A light malt base gives strawberry and elderflower undertones on the palate.

EPA (ABV 4.8%)
An English pale ale. Golden in colour with a floral, tropical fruit aroma. The flavour is sweet with tropical fruit notes and a sweet caramel finish.

IPA (ABV 5%)
A classic American-style IPA that is bitter rather than sweet. Massively hopped, giving a rich, flavoursome base with grapefruit and floral undertones and a full aroma bursting with citrus.

Stout (ABV 5.2%)
A dark, silky beer made with a huge hit of roasted coffee and chocolate, combined with fruity hop undertones. Star anise is added to give a distinctive but subtle liquorice character.

Severn Vale

See Combined Brewers

Shackleton

See Brentwood

Shalford SIBA ◉

Hyde Farm, Shalford ☎ 07749 658512

Correspondence: PO Box 10411, Braintree, Essex, CM7 5WP ☎ (01371) 850925
⊕ shalfordbrewery.co.uk

Shalford began brewing in 2007 on a five-barrel plant at Hyde Farm in the Pant Valley in Essex. More than 50 outlets are supplied direct. ♦ RAIB

1319 Mild (OG 1037, ABV 3.7%)
Roast malt and chocolate sweetness with a slight bitter finish.

Barnfield Pale Ale (OG 1038, ABV 3.8%) ◣
Pale-coloured but full-flavoured, this is a traditional, hoppy bitter rather than a golden ale. Malt persists throughout, with bitterness becoming more dominant towards the end.

Braintree Market Ale (OG 1040, ABV 4%)

Traditional, easy-drinking session ale with a hoppy, lingering, dry finish.

Levelly Gold (OG 1040, ABV 4%)
Golden bitter with a pleasant finish.

Stoneley Bitter (OG 1042, ABV 4.2%) ◥
Dark amber session beer whose vivid hop character is supported by a juicy, malty body. A dry finish.

Hyde Bitter (OG 1047, ABV 4.7%) ◥
Stronger version of Barnfield, with a similar but more assertive character.

Levelly Black (OG 1048, ABV 4.8%)
A dark, heavy, well-hopped ale with a grainy toffee taste topped with a thick creamy head.

Rotten End (OG 1065, ABV 6.5%)
Strong beer with slightly sweet, nutty undertones and a bitter edge to finish.

Shardlow 👁

The Old Brewery Stables, British Waterways Yard, Cavendish Bridge, Leicestershire, DE72 2HL
☎ (01332) 799188 ✉ nev@shardlowbrewery.co.uk

👁On a site associated with brewing since 1819, Shardlow delivers to more than 100 outlets throughout the East Midlands and is also one of the largest UK cider distributors. Reverend Eaton is named after a scion of the Eaton brewing family, Rector of Shardlow for 40 years. The brewery tap is the Blue Bell Inn at Melbourne, Derbyshire. Prolific supplier of beers to local beer festivals. ‼ ♦ RAIB

Chancellors Revenge (OG 1036, ABV 3.6%)
A light-coloured, refreshing, full-flavoured and well-hopped session bitter.

Cavendish Dark (OG 1037, ABV 3.7%)
A mild, well-balanced beer with a hoppy aftertaste.

Golden Hop (OG 1041, ABV 4.1%)
Golden, sweet tasting beer, dry hopped for added aroma.

Kiln House (OG 1041, ABV 4.1%)
A refreshing golden ale with a lingering bitter finish.

Narrow Boat (OG 1043, ABV 4.3%)
A pale amber bitter, with a short, crisp, hoppy aftertaste.

Cavendish Bridge (OG 1045, ABV 4.5%)
Pale amber premium bitter. Refreshing, clean and fruity with a pleasing bitter finish.

Cavendish Gold (OG 1045, ABV 4.5%)
Pale gold, bright and clean tasting. A full-bodied ale with pronounced bitterness and complexity.

Reverend Eaton (OG 1045, ABV 4.5%)
A smooth, medium-strong bitter, full of malt and hop flavours with a sweet aftertaste.

Mayfly (OG 1048, ABV 4.8%)
Fruit notes predominate together with a pronounced malty aroma. Easy-drinking but strong.

Five Bells (OG 1050, ABV 5%)
Dark, rich, ruby-coloured ale, powerful and bittersweet to the palate. Coffee notes complete the profile.

Whistlestop (OG 1050, ABV 5%)
A smooth and surprisingly strong pale beer.

Sharp's 👁

Pityme Business Centre, Rock, Cornwall, PL27 6NU
☎ (01208) 862121 ⊕ sharpsbrewery.co.uk

⊗ Sharp's was bought for £20 million by Molson Coors in 2011. The brewery was founded in 1994 and within 15 years had grown from producing 1,500 barrels a year to 60,000. £7.5 million of investment from Molson Coors has brought the capacity up to 200,000 barrels a year. The company owns one pub, the Mariners at Rock, and delivers beer to more than 1,200 outlets across the south of England via temperature-controlled depots in Bristol and London. Molson Coors has stressed that it will maintain production in Cornwall. Part of Molson Coors PLC. ➤ ♦ RAIB

Cornish Coaster (OG 1035.2, ABV 3.6%) ◥
Refreshing copper bitter. Gentle balance of biscuit malt, fruit and sweetness. Fruit in the finish with bitterness and faint dryness.

Doom Bar (OG 1038.5, ABV 4%) ◥
Tawny brown bitter with gentle fruit aroma. Balanced taste of biscuit malt, resinous hops with apple, strawberry and plum fruits.

Atlantic (OG 1043, ABV 4.2%) ◥
Gold best bitter with fragrant hop aroma. Orange citrus with caramel sweetness balanced by malt and bitterness. Tropical fruit hints.

Own (OG 1042.5, ABV 4.4%) ◥
Brown best bitter with English hop and malt aroma. Fruity, hoppy taste with malt and bitter roasted biscuit, finishing dry.

Special (OG 1048.5, ABV 5%) ◥
A tawny strong bitter with hops and caramel aroma. Sweet malty taste, with fruit and light roast throughout, becoming dry.

Shed

Broadfields, Pewsey, Wiltshire, SN9 5DT
☎ (01672) 564533 ☎ 07769 812643
⊕ shedales.com

Shed Ales was launched in 2012 operating from a one-barrel plant in a converted garden shed. The brewery currently produces four core ales and several bespoke ales, available at selected local outlets (including the brewery owned Shed Alehouse a micropub in Pewsey). A house beer is produced for The Royal Oak at Great Wishford. ♦

Dig It (OG 1037.5, ABV 3.7%)

Patrick's Best (OG 1039, ABV 3.8%)

Some Light (OG 1041, ABV 3.8%)
A refreshing blonde beer with a light, earthy hop aroma and flavour.

Dibber (OG 1042.5, ABV 4.2%)
Light amber with a biscuit malt and citrus hop aroma. Easy-drinking with a good balance of malt and fruity hop notes and dry finish.

Sheelin

178 Derrylin Road, Bellanaleck, County Fermanagh, BT92 2BA ☎ 07730 432232 ⊕ sheelin.com

Sheelin was established by brewer and chemist Dr George Cathcart in 2013. Beer is mainly available in bottles.

Blonde (OG 1045, ABV 4.5%)

IPA (OG 1045, ABV 4.5%)

Red (OG 1045, ABV 4.5%)

Stout (OG 1045, ABV 4.5%)

Sheffield SIBA

Unit 111, JC Albyn Complex, Burton Road, Sheffield, South Yorkshire, S3 8BT
☎ (0114) 272 7256 ⊕ sheffieldbrewery.com

☺Sheffield began brewing in 2006 in the former Blanco polish works using a 10-barrel plant. The brewery operates on the tower principal in premises which also are also used as a venue for corporate or social gatherings. ‼

Crucible Best (OG 1038, ABV 3.8%)
A well-balanced session best bitter.

Five Rivers (OG 1038, ABV 3.8%)
Easy-drinking, straw-coloured session ale. The hoppy aroma carries through to the finish.

Blanco Blonde (OG 1042, ABV 4.2%)
A continental lager-style beer.

Porter (OG 1045, ABV 4.4%)
A dark porter with rich chocolate, malty and caramel flavours.

Forgemasters (OG 1038, ABV 4.8%)

IPA (OG 1048, ABV 5%)

Shepherd Neame IFBB ⊙

17 Court Street, Faversham, Kent, ME13 7AX
☎ (01795) 532206 ⊕ shepherdneame.co.uk

⊗ Shepherd Neame traces its history back to 1698, making it the oldest continuous brewer in the country, though brewing probably began even earlier. The 1914 oak mash tuns are still operational. The company has 350 tied houses in the south east, nearly all selling cask ale. More than 2,000 other outlets are also supplied. The cask beers are made with Kentish hops, and water from the brewery's own artesian well. There is a microplant to brew ales for special occasions and product development. These beers are available in selected pubs. The company also brews cask ales under the Faversham Steam Brewery and No. 18 Yard Brewhouse names. ‼ ▬ ◆RAIB

Master Brew (OG 1032, ABV 3.7%) ◥
A distinctive bitter, mid-brown in colour, with a hoppy aroma. Well-balanced, with a nicely aggressive bitter taste from its hops, it leaves a hoppy/bitter finish, tinged with sweetness.

Whitstable Bay Pale Ale (OG 1038, ABV 3.9%)
A full-bodied, fruity ale with a subtle bitterness and glorious grapefruit and pine aromas.

Kent's Best (OG 1036, ABV 4.1%)
A robust bitter which merges the biscuity sweetness of English malt with the fruity, floral bitterness of locally-grown hops.

Spitfire Gold (OG 1039, ABV 4.1%)
A well-balanced golden ale with tropical fruit and pine aromas, and a subtle bitterness.

Spitfire (OG 1036, ABV 4.2%)
A well-balanced British bitter. Hints of marmalade, red grapes and pepper, with warm, mellow malts. A fruity finish with hints of spice and raspberry.

Bishops Finger (OG 1046, ABV 5%)

A strong ale with a complex hop aroma reminiscent of lemons, oranges and bananas combined with malt, molasses and toffee. Refreshing with a good malt character tinged with a lingering bitterness.

Sherfield Village SIBA

Goddards Farm, Goddards Lane, Sherfield on Loddon, Hampshire, RG27 0EL ☎ 07906 060429
⊕ sherfieldvillagebrewery.co.uk

Sherfield Village started brewing in 2011, based in a converted barn on a working dairy farm. The brewery uses a five-barrel plant, supplying local pubs and regional festivals. As well as its regular beers, numerous seasonal and one-off specials are available. Extensive use is made of New World hops (prefixed SOLO), particularly those from New Zealand. Dry-hopped versions of single-hop beers are usually available. ◆RAIB

Threesome (OG 1030, ABV 3%)
Copper-coloured session beer with a long hoppy finish.

SOLO Southern Gold (OG 1040, ABV 4%)
A golden beer with a citrus flavour and a floral nose.

SOLO Green Bullet (OG 1042, ABV 4.3%) ◥
A strong lemony nose, with hops dominating the taste building to a strong aftertaste with a big astringent hit at the end.

SOLO Single Hop (OG 1042, ABV 4.3%)
A golden ale which uses a single hop variety that changes every month, thereby subtly changing the beer characteristics.

Hoppy Harrington (OG 1046, ABV 4.7%)
A mid-brown strong bitter. It has a complex, sweetish flavour and a satisfying hoppy finish.

Pioneer Stout (OG 1048, ABV 5%)
A black stout, with a hint of vanilla.

ShinDigger

Office: 170 Vie Building, 185 Water Street, Manchester, M3 4JU ⊕ shindiggerbrewing.co

Established in 2012, ShinDigger is the project of two former Manchester University students. Output is predominantly keg. Contract brewed in Cumbria, the beer is mostly available in the Manchester area.

Shiny SIBA

Unit 10, Old Hall Mill Business Centre, Little Eaton, Derbyshire, DE21 5EJ
☎ (01332) 902809

Brewing commenced in 2012 using a six-barrel plant sited in the beer garden of the Furnace Inn. After initially brewing solely for the pub, 2014 saw an increase in scale and output, with beers distributed across most of the country. A second 12-barrel brew plant was built in 2015 to increase capacity and host a visitor centre and shop. ◆RAIB V

New World (OG 1039, ABV 3.7%)
Golden in colour with powerful citrus hop flavours.

Pail (OG 1041, ABV 4%)

Wrench (OG 1045, ABV 4.4%)
A full-bodied stout.

THE BREWERIES

4 Wood (OG 1045, ABV 4.5%)
Traditional, well-balanced light chestnut ale with a delicate hop finish.

Affinity (OG 1046, ABV 4.6%)
Strong golden bitter with lots of fruity hops.

Tomahawk (OG 1058, ABV 6%)
Refreshing American-style brown IPA with citrus flavour and aromas.

Ship Inn

▤ Ship Inn, Newton Square, Low Newton-by-the-Sea, Northumberland, NE66 3EL
☎ (01665) 576262 ⊕ shipinnewton.co.uk

Brewing commenced in 2008 on a 2.5-barrel plant. The brewery now produces 7.5 barrels per week. All regular beers are brewed in constant rotation but are only available on the premises. A special beer (4.2% ABV) is brewed for every 100 brews. ◆ RAIB

Sandcastles at Dawn (OG 1038, ABV 3.8%)
A pale session beer, light and crisp with a delicate floral finish.

Sea Coal (OG 1040, ABV 4%)
A dark wheat beer with mild coffee and bittersweet chocolate, and a berry fruit finish.

Sea Wheat (OG 1040, ABV 4%)
A pale crisp, sharp English-style wheat beer, with a citrus burst and strong grapefruit flavours.

Ship Hop Ale (OG 1042, ABV 4.2%)
A light copper-coloured ale, dry with hints of orange and marmalade.

Dolly Daydream (OG 1043, ABV 4.3%)
A classic premium bitter with a slight toffee edge and subtle vine fruit finish.

Shipstones

See Belvoir

Shoes SIBA

▤ Three Horseshoes Inn, Norton Canon, Hereford, HR4 7BH
☎ (01544) 318375

Established in 1994. The beers are brewed from malt extract and are normally only available at the Three Horseshoes. Each September Canon Bitter is brewed with green hops fresh from the harvest. !! RAIB

Norton Ale (OG 1038, ABV 3.6%)

Canon Bitter (OG 1040, ABV 4.1%)

Peploe's Tipple (OG 1060, ABV 6%)

Farrier's Ale (OG 1114, ABV 15%)

Shortts Farm SIBA

Shortts Farm, Thorndon, Suffolk, IP23 7LS ☎ 07900 268100 ⊕ shorttsfarmbrewery.com

Shortts Farm Brewery was established in 2012 by Matt Hammond on what has been the family farm for over a century. A five-barrel brewing plant is used. All of the beers are based around a musical theme inspired by a love of real ale and music. RAIB

Strummer (OG 1038, ABV 3.8%)

An amber ale. Easy drinking, light and hoppy with a good malty character.

Blondie (OG 1040, ABV 4%)

Skiffle (OG 1047, ABV 4.5%)
Chestnut in colour. A complex and malty, rich bitter with a good balance of hops over malt.

Indie (OG 1048, ABV 4.8%)

Shotover SIBA

Coopers Yard, Manor Farm Road, Horspath, Oxfordshire, OX33 1SD
☎ (01865) 604620 ☎ 07710 883273
⊕ shotoverbrewing.com

⊠ A family-owned and -run brewery four miles from Oxford city centre. It began brewing in 2009 and supplies outlets in the Oxford area. Bottle-conditioned beers are available and suitable for vegetarians. Cask ale suitable for vegetarians can also be supplied. !! ⋤ ◆ RAIB

Prospect (OG 1040, ABV 3.7%)
A flavoursome local bitter, packed with hops.

Trinity (OG 1040, ABV 4.2%)
Pale gold in colour with an intense grapefruit hop character.

Scholar (OG 1047, ABV 4.5%)
Deep copper-coloured premium bitter combining a silky malt base with a mixture of oranges, grapefruit and spiciness. It delivers a satisfying bitter finish.

Shottle Farm

School House Farm, Lodge Lane, Shottle, Derbyshire, DE56 2DS
☎ (01773) 550056 ☎ 07877 723075
⊕ shottlefarmbrewery.co.uk

Located in the hills above Belper, the Grade II-listed farm is part of the Chatsworth Estate. Family-run, Shottle Farm Brewery has been in production since 2011 with a 10-barrel plant. It has an onsite bar, the Bull Shed. The brewery regularly supplies the George & Dragon, Belper, plus other outlets in the county. ◆ RAIB

Shottlecock (OG 1034.9, ABV 3.6%)
Single malt light ale with local honey. In the summer the honey is replaced with home-made elderflower syrup.

Black Peggy (OG 1037.8, ABV 3.9%)
Smooth, easy-drinking stout with chocolate malt and oatmeal. Light bodied with pleasing hints of liquorice.

Shottle Pale Ale (OG 1037.8, ABV 4%)
Pale ale with a hint of citrus, brewed with local honey.

BOB (Best of Both) (OG 1038.8, ABV 4.1%)
A full-flavoured cask-conditioned lager.

Eight Shilling (OG 1038.8, ABV 4.1%)
A rich, dark beer. Smooth and malty. Full-bodied, pleasant aftertaste with undertones of treacle and caramel.

Shottle Gold (OG 1041.7, ABV 4.3%)
Golden ale with a floral aroma and a fruity hint of citrus lemon. Crisp and easy-drinking with a clean white head.

Dilks (OG 1048.4, ABV 5%)

Smooth and well-balanced amber ale with a slight sweetness and hint of citrus.

Shoulder of Mutton

See Weldon

Shropshire Brewer SIBA 👁

Red Lion, Longden Common, Shropshire, SY5 8AE
☎ (01743) 718889 ☎ 07958 007551
⊕ theshropshirebrewer.com

👁Formerly known as Longden Brewing Company, Shropshire Brewer has been in production since 2013. In 2014 a new five-barrel plant was installed. Four regular beers are produced, with beer names inspired by local legends. The beers are usually available at the Red Lion (the brewery tap) and in a number of free houses in Shropshire. ♦

The Golden Arrow (OG 1038, ABV 3.8%)
A pale ale of moderate strength, but with an abundance of hop character.

Sawn Off (OG 1042, ABV 4%)
A copper-coloured best bitter.

Spire Dancer (OG 1044, ABV 4.2%)

Rope Slider (OG 1044, ABV 4.4%)

Shugborough SIBA

Shugborough Estate, Milford, Staffordshire, ST17 0XB
☎ (01782) 823447 ⊕ shugborough.org.uk

Brewing in the original brewhouse at Shugborough, home of the Earls of Lichfield, restarted in 1990, but a lack of expertise led to the brewery being a static museum piece until Titanic Brewery of Stoke-on-Trent (qv) began helping in 1996. ‼

Signature Brew SIBA 👁

Unit 25, Leyton Business Centre, Etloe Road, Leyton, London, E10 7BT
☎ (020) 7684 4664

Office: Workshop 45, Hackney Downs Studio, Hackney, London, E8 2BT ⊕ signaturebrew.co.uk

Signature Brew have been brewing beer inspired by music since 2011. Originally using spare capacity at a number of breweries, a successful crowd funding initiative has resulted in it owning its own brewery in Leyton. Special seasonal beers are brewed in collaboration with music artists. 🍴♦RAIB

Session (OG 1042, ABV 4%) 🍺
Refreshing bitter with spicy hop on the nose and palate balanced by a malty sweetness and a lingering bitterness.

Signature Pale (OG 1033, ABV 4.1%) 🍺
Golden beer using pale malts with a little wheat. The American hops give the beer its fruity character.

Black Vinyl Stout (OG 1046, ABV 4.2%) 🍺
Rich cocoa roasted notes predominate on the palate balanced by some sweetness and American hops giving lightness to the flavour.

Red Wedge (OG 1047, ABV 4.7%)

Backstage IPA (OG 1054, ABV 5.6%) 🍺

Amber-coloured, unfined IPA with fruity hops and a bitterness, overlaid with some banana and biscuity malty notes. Lingering dry finish.

Silhill SIBA

Oak Farm, Silhill Brewery Ltd, Solihull, West Midlands, B92 0JB
☎ (0845) 519 5101 ☎ 07977 444564

Correspondence: PO Box 15739, Solihull, West Midlands, B93 3FW ⊕ silhillbrewery.co.uk

⊠ Established in 2010, Silhill is a small independent brewery based in premises just outside Solihull town centre using a 10-barrel plant. Bottling operations commenced in 2015. Beers are available in Solihull, Birmingham and Stratford-upon-Avon as well as in Malmaison restaurants. ‼RAIB

Gold Star (OG 1039, ABV 3.9%)
An amber-coloured ale. Malty and smooth, finishing with a delicate honey note.

Blonde Star (OG 1041, ABV 4.1%)
A refreshing, sweet citrus pale ale.

Pure Star (OG 1043, ABV 4.3%)
A chestnut-coloured ale, warm and well-balanced, with a hint of chocolate.

North Star (OG 1047, ABV 4.5%)
An American raspberry oatmeal stout.

Silks (NEW)

Wash Farm, Queen Street, Sible Hedingham, Essex, CO9 3RH
☎ (01787) 275513 ☎ 07921 654910
⊕ silksbrewery@co.uk

Silks is a five-barrel microbrewery producing hand-crafted ales in small batches. Established in 2015, it is based on a North Essex farm in a converted grain store. ♦RAIB

Veteran Campaigner (ABV 3.8%)
An amber-coloured session beer.

Whacker Payne (ABV 3.8%)
A golden beer, crisp and refreshing with subtle citrus hints.

Old Man Shirv (ABV 4.5%)
Copper-coloured premium ale, smooth and fruity.

Silver Street

▤ Clarence Hotel, 2 Silver Street, Bury, BL9 0EX
☎ (0161) 763 9399 ⊕ theclarence.co.uk

Silver Street began brewing in 2014 at the Clarence Hotel in Bury. ♦

Session (OG 1039, ABV 3.9%)
Well-balanced session ale with an interesting blend of hops; tangerine and blackcurrant notes.

One (OG 1040, ABV 4%)
A pale ale with plenty of hop.

Ruby, Ruby, Ruby, Ruby (OG 1047, ABV 4.7%)
Deep ruby ale. Plenty of malty, biscuity tastes plus jammy, plummy notes with a fruity nose.

EQ (OG 1048, ABV 4.9%)

Silverstone

Shacks Barn Farm, Silverstone, Northamptonshire, NN12 8TB
☎ (01908) 565652 ☎ 07918 031464
⊕ silverstonerealale.com

This traditional tower brewery, which is located near the celebrated motor racing circuit, opened in 2008. With a change of hands in 2015 the brewery has re-engineered its range of real ales, which are available in casks and bottles. ‼◆

Ignition (ABV 3.4%)
Floral, hoppy blonde ale which delivers a zesty powerful taste for its strength.

Pitstop (ABV 3.9%)
Session bitter with a mellow bitter flavour, with undertones of lime.

Chequered Flag (OG 1043, ABV 4.3%)
Full-bodied amber IPA with a complex taste and citrus finish.

Octane (ABV 4.8%)
A stronger ale, rich with hints of honey and toffee and a mellow, slightly coffee-like aroma.

Simpsons

White Swan, Eardisland, Herefordshire, HR6 9BD
☎ (01544) 388635 ⊕ simpsonsfineales.co.uk

Tim Simpson acquired the White Swan in 2011 and set up the brewery at the rear of the pub in 2013. Beers are currently served in the White Swan, and locally to the free trade. A bottling facility is now in operation to supply local county shows. ◆

Golden Cock (OG 1037, ABV 3.7%)

Red Leg (OG 1043, ABV 4.3%)

Black Grouse (OG 1045, ABV 4.5%)

Old English (OG 1047, ABV 4.7%)

Sinclair

See Orkney

Siren Craft SIBA

Unit 1, Hogwood Industrial Estate, Weller Drive, Finchampstead, Berkshire, RG40 4QZ
☎ (0118) 973 0929 ⊕ sirencraftbrew.com

⊠ Siren Craft is a 40-barrel brewery, established in 2013 and extended in 2014 and 2015. An extensive barrel-aging programme commenced in 2013 with many interesting beers produced. A balance of cask, keg and bottles is distributed throughout Europe. ‼◆RAIB

Undercurrent Oatmeal Pale Ale (OG 1042, ABV 4.5%)
A pale ale with spicy, grassy aromas and a taste of grapefruit and apricot.

Soundwave IPA (OG 1056, ABV 5.6%)
An American-style West Coast IPA: golden, immensely hoppy and with grapefruit, peach and mango flavours.

Liquid Mistress Red IPA (OG 1061, ABV 5.8%)
An American-style red ale: burnt raisins and crackers balanced by a citrus grapefruit and peach spark.

Broken Dream Breakfast Stout (OG 1072, ABV 6.5%)
A breakfast stout with a gentle touch of smoke, coffee and chocolate. Deep and complex.

Six Bells SIBA

▤ Church Street, Bishop's Castle, Shropshire, SY9 5AA
☎ (01588) 638930 ⊕ sixbellsbrewery.co.uk

The Six Bells Brewery started in 1997 using a five-barrel plant. It supplies customers both within Shropshire and over the border in Wales. A new 12-barrel plant opened in 2010. ‼◆

Noggin' (OG 1037, ABV 3.8%)
A pale, fairly hoppy bitter.

Ow Do! (OG 1040, ABV 4%)
Rich amber-coloured beer, full of spicy, fruity character.

Spikey Blonde (OG 1040, ABV 4%)

Cloud Nine (OG 1043, ABV 4.2%)
Golden ale, well-hopped with citrus notes throughout.

six°north

Reekie House, Aberdeen Road, Laurencekirk, AB30 1AG
☎ (01561) 377047 ☎ 07840 678243
⊕ sixdnorth.co.uk

⊠ Established in 2013, the brewery brews beers in the Belgian tradition, using a purpose-built 470-hectolitre plant. Depending on beer style, the beers are supplied as cask or keg as appropriate. ‼

Six O'Clock

Gould Street, Manchester, M4 4RN
⊕ sixoclockbeer.co.uk

Six O'Clock began brewing in 2013 and has its own plant on the premises of BlackJack Brewery (qv). The plant is just over one barrel and is in full production. There is direct distribution to pubs in Manchester city centre and further afield through Glassworks Distribution. ‼

Overtime (OG 1042, ABV 4.2%)
A light, hoppy pale ale.

Annuit Coeptis (OG 1048, ABV 4.8%)
An American pale ale.

Union (OG 1048, ABV 5%)
A robust IPA.

Sixpenny SIBA

The Dairy Building, Manor Farm, Sixpenny Handley, Dorset, SP5 5NU
☎ (01725) 762006 ⊕ sixpennybrewery.co.uk

⊠ Established in 2007, the brewery has been located in Sixpenny Handley since 2009 but is planning to move to a new site at Holwell Farm in Cranborne. The new premises will house the 20-barrel plant along with a larger area for the brewery shop and bar (the Sixpenny Tap). More than 50 outlets are supplied including house beers to local Wetherspoon pubs. ‼▰◆

6d Best Bitter (OG 1042, ABV 3.8%)
A well-balanced ale with a rounded malt flavour that leads to a pleasantly bitter and hoppy finish.

6d Gold (OG 1044, ABV 4.2%)
A golden ale, slightly citrus flavoured with a distinct hoppy, floral aroma.

Addlestone Ale (OG 1044.5, ABV 4.2%)
Copper-coloured premium best bitter with good balance of malt and hops.

SAM fm Ale (OG 1044, ABV 4.2%)
A well-balanced, amber-coloured best bitter.

6d IPA (OG 1053, ABV 5.2%)
Traditional IPA with a powerful hop character and a long, rounded malt finish.

Skinner's SIBA ◉

Riverside, Newham Road, Truro, Cornwall, TR1 2DP
☎ (01872) 271885 ⊕ skinnersbrewery.com

⊗ Award-winning brewery established in 1997. The brewery moved to bigger premises in 2003, opening a shop and visitor centre. The 25-barrel plant produces 25,000 hectolitres a year, using local Cornish barley only. ‼️➤◆

Copper Ale (OG 1038, ABV 3.6%) ◈
Smooth copper bitter with malt and fruity hop aroma. Balanced flavour of malt and bitter citrus marmalade hops, becoming dry.

Cornish Trawler (OG 1038, ABV 3.8%) ◈
Amber ale with malt, toffee and hop aroma. Complex bitter grassy hop, strawberries and sweet malt. Long bittersweet finish becoming dry.

Betty Stogs (OG 1040, ABV 4%) ◈
Copper-coloured best bitter with gentle hop aroma. Balance of light citrus hops and apple, sweet malt and bitterness. Long finish.

Heligan Honey (OG 1040, ABV 4%) ◈
A pale brown beer containing Cornish honey. Citrus hop zing balanced by sweet honey and bitterness. Lingering bittersweet, dry aftertaste.

Hops n Honey (OG 1040, ABV 4%) 🍺
A pale brown beer containing Cornish honey. Citrus hop zing balanced by sweet honey and bitterness. Lingering bittersweet, dry aftertaste.

River Cottage EPA (OG 1040, ABV 4%) ◈
Gold best bitter with floral hop aroma. Robust hops, sweet fruit, bitterness and malt flavours. Hoppy, rising bitter, dry finish.

Lushingtons (OG 1041, ABV 4.2%) ◈
Yellow golden ale with citrus hop aroma. Strong citrus hops dominate. Bitter with sweetness, tropical fruits. Long, dry, citrus finish.

Cornish Knocker (OG 1044, ABV 4.5%) ◈
Refreshing golden ale with fragrant apple and hop aroma. Citrus hops, malt and summer fruit flavours. Bitter and astringent finish.

Pennycomequick (OG 1046, ABV 4.5%) ◈
Creamy smooth, dark brown stout with roast grain aroma. Heavy roast coffee, malt, fig and cherry flavours. Roast, dry finish.

Porthleven (OG 1048, ABV 4.8%) 🗄️◈
Golden ale with elderflower nose. Smooth citrus hop taste with bitter grapefruit and honey tones. Bitter, dry, citrus hop finish.

7 Hop (OG 1050, ABV 5%) ◈
Smooth golden ale. Strong hop aroma and heavy punch of grapefruit citrus hops throughout. Marmalade and stone fruits. Bitter, dry finish.

Slater's SIBA IFBB ◉

St Albans Road, Common Road Industrial Estate, Stafford, ST16 3DR
☎ (01785) 257976 ⊕ slatersales.co.uk

☺The brewery was opened in 1995 and in 2006 moved to new, larger premises. It has won numerous awards from CAMRA and SIBA and supplies a large number of outlets. 2015 saw Slater's celebrate its 20th anniversary. ‼️➤

Bitter (OG 1035.5, ABV 3.6%)
Amber in colour with a hop and malt aroma. Hoppiness develops into a long, dry finish.

Rye IPA (OG 1038.5, ABV 3.8%)

Top Totty (OG 1039, ABV 4%) ◈
Yellow hued with a fruit and hop nose. Big malty start leads to citrus hints with mouthwatering edges. Dry finish with tangs of lingering lemon bitterness.

Premium (OG 1042.5, ABV 4.4%) ◈
Pale brown bitter with malt and caramel aroma. Malt and caramel taste supported by hops and some fruit provide a warming descent and satisfyingly bitter mouthfeel.

Smoked Porter (OG 1046, ABV 4.8%) ◈
Nose full of smoke, bonfire tastes with bacon. Hops break out to a bitter finish.

Western (OG 1048, ABV 4.9%)
A pale ale with a heady hop aroma and chewy, aromatic finish.

Haka (OG 1049, ABV 5.2%) ◈
Exotic aromas of tropical fruits lead to a sweet, fruity start with background bitterness. This erupts into a mouthy bitterness with a long finish.

Slaughterhouse SIBA

🏭 Bridge Street, Warwick, CV34 5PD
☎ (01926) 490986 ☎ 07951 842690
⊕ slaughterhousebrewery.com

☺Production began in 2003 on a four-barrel plant in a former slaughterhouse. Around 30 outlets are supplied. The brewery premises are licensed for off-sales direct to the public. In 2010 Slaughterhouse opened its first pub, the Wild Boar in Warwick. ‼️

Saddleback Best Bitter (OG 1038, ABV 3.8%)
Amber-coloured session bitter with a distinctive hop flavour.

Extra Stout Snout (OG 1044, ABV 4.4%)

Boar D'eau (OG 1045, ABV 4.5%)

Wild Boar (OG 1052, ABV 5.2%)

Sleaford

21 Pride Court, Enterprise Park, Sleaford, Lincolnshire, NG34 8GL ☎ 07867 366929
✉ sleafordbrewery@gmail.com

Sleaford was established in 2010 and came under new ownership in 2013. It is a family-run brewery creating small batch craft beers on a one-barrel plant. Production ceased in late 2015, with consideration being given to moving the equipment to Nottingham, closer to the owner's home. ◆RAIB

Slightly Foxed SIBA

Unit 25, Asquith Bottom Mill, Sowerby Bridge, West
Yorkshire, HX6 3BS ☎ 07412 008221
⊕ slightlyfoxedbrewery.co.uk

☺Slightly Foxed launched in 2011 as a venture
between an award-winning landlord and a local
businessman. Originally using spare capacity at
Brass Monkey Brewery, Slightly Foxed bought the
brewery in 2012. ♦

Howlin Fox (OG 1035, ABV 3.5%) ◄
Easy-drinking, crisp and refreshing session beer.
Hoppy with a light, fruity citrus palate followed by
a mellow finish.

Slightly Foxed (OG 1038, ABV 3.8%)
Pale golden, light and refreshing beer with a spicy,
grapefruit flavour, a light, fruity floral aroma and a
clean, dry finish.

Flying Fox (OG 1043, ABV 4.3%)
Pale and hoppy bitter with a touch of apricot
flavour.

Fox Glove (OG 1043, ABV 4.3%)
A golden-coloured premium best bitter with a full-
bodied fruity flavour and fruit aromas.

Urban Fox (OG 1048, ABV 4.8%) ◄
Well-balanced, dark-coloured London porter.
Chocolate nose with a rich, fruity roast flavour and
a mild aftertaste.

Bengal Fox (OG 1052, ABV 5.2%)
A bright golden-coloured beer with a complex
combination of pine, citrus and vanilla flavours.

Prairie Fox (OG 1052, ABV 5.2%) ◄
An American-style pale ale. Plenty of hops on the
nose. It has a mildly spicy and predominately citrus
palate followed by a mellow and dry aftertaste.

Small Paul's

27 Briar Close, Gillingham, Dorset, SP8 4SS
☎ (01747) 823574 ✉ smallbrewer@btinternet.com

⊗ Launched in 2006, this half-barrel brewery is
located in the owner's garage. There are usually
two brews a month. A small number of local pubs
and clubs are supplied direct and beers can be
designed and brewed to order. ♦

Gylla's Gold (OG 1039, ABV 3.8%) ◄
Drinkable session ale. Mild fruit hop aromas lead to
bitter hop flavours and a lingering dry hop
aftertaste.

Amber Nectar (OG 1042, ABV 4.2%)
Amber-coloured, full-bodied best bitter. Slightly
citrus aroma with balanced malt and spicy hop
flavours and a bitter finish.

Invicta (OG 1042, ABV 4.2%)
Pale, aromatic and hoppy with a long bitter finish.
Named after a fishing fly.

Challenger II (OG 1044, ABV 4.3%)
A copper-coloured, slightly sweet, malty bitter.

Wyvern (OG 1044, ABV 4.4%) ◄
Red-brown, well-balanced best bitter with malt
and caramel flavours and short, bittersweet finish.

Gillingham Pale (OG 1045, ABV 4.5%) ◄
Fruity, caramel aromas lead to complex bitter
flavours and short, dry finish.

Small World SIBA

Unit 10, Barncliffe Business Park, Near Bank, Shelley,
West Yorkshire, HD8 8LU
☎ (01484) 602805 ☎ 07540 319326
⊕ smallworldbeers.com

The brewery is situated in the picturesque
Barncliffe valley in rural Shelley. The beers are
brewed on a 20-barrel plant using spring water
from an on-site bore hole. There is a small bar on
site. ‼

Barncliffe Bitter (OG 1037, ABV 3.7%)
Pleasant, light-drinking bitter with fruit and citrus
notes and a lasting bitterness through the finish.

Long Moor Pale (OG 1039, ABV 3.9%)
Pale ale with grapefruit and citrus notes, and a
light bitter finish.

Spike's Gold (OG 1043, ABV 4.4%)
Smooth, well-balanced golden ale with fruit and
hop flavours through to the finish.

Thunderbridge Stout (OG 1051, ABV 5.2%)
Traditional dry stout with roast flavours giving way
to smooth coffee undertones and a sharp, dry
finish.

Twin Falls (OG 1051, ABV 5.2%)
Full-bodied pale ale with fruity aroma, strong
tropical fruit and hop taste.

Joseph Herbert Smith

▤ Fox Inn, Hanley Broadheath, Worcestershire,
WR15 8QS
☎ (01886) 853189 ☎ 07527 066474
⊕ jhstraditionalbrewery.com

☺The brewery was established in Staffordshire in
2007 by Jonathan Smith. In 2008 it relocated to
barns adjacent to the Fox Inn. All equipment is gas
fired and ingredients are sourced locally where
possible. ‼♦

Amy's Rose (OG 1040, ABV 4%)

Foxy Lady (OG 1043, ABV 4.3%)

Samuel Smith

High Street, Tadcaster, North Yorkshire, LS24 9SB
☎ (01937) 832225 ⊕ samuelsmithsbrewery.co.uk

☺Fiercely independent, family-owned company.
Tradition, quality and value are important, resulting
in brewing without any artificial additives. All real
ale is supplied in wooden casks. A bottle-
conditioned beer (Yorkshire Stingo, ABV 8%) is only
available in specialist off-licences. RAIB

Old Brewery Bitter (OG 1040, ABV 4%)
Malt dominates the aroma, with an initial burst of
malt, hops and fruit in the taste, which is sustained
in the aftertaste.

Tom Smith

101 Barnwell Street, Kettering, Northamptonshire,
NN16 0JF
☎ (01536) 399859 ☎ 07956 051922
⊕ tomsmithales.co.uk

Tom Smith Brewery was established in 2012 by
Mark Smith in an industrial unit in Kettering. It
relocated to Corby in 2013 and then back to
Kettering in 2016. Brewing is currently suspended.
♦ RAIB

John Smith's

The Brewery, Tadcaster, North Yorkshire, LS24 9SA
☎ (01937) 832091 ⊕ heineken.com

No real ale. The brewery was built in 1879 by a relative of Samuel Smith (qv). John Smith's became part of the Courage group in 1970 before being taken over by S&N and now Heineken UK. Major expansion has taken place, with 11 new fermenting vessels installed. Traditional Yorkshire Square fermenters have been replaced by conical vessels. John Smith's cask Magnet has been discontinued. John Smith's Bitter in cask form is brewed under contract by Cameron's Brewery (qv) in Hartlepool.

Snaggletooth

Rear of 11 Pole Lane, Darwen, Lancashire, BB3 3LD
☎ 07810 365701 ⊕ snaggletoothbrewing.com

Snaggletooth was established in 2012 by three beer geeks with a passion for crafting ales. A 2.5-barrel plant is used at the Hopstar Brewery (qv) in Darwen, Lancashire.

Allotropic Pale Ale (ABV 3.8%)
A pale ale with floral and citrus notes.

Three Amigos (ABV 3.9%)

Deja Brewed (OG 1040, ABV 4%)
Refreshing ale with floral, spicy and citrus flavours.

Rolling Maul (ABV 4.1%)
Pale ale with bursts of floral and citrus finish.

'Cos I'm a Lobster (OG 1044, ABV 4.2%)
Summery red ale with subtly roasted malts.

Snowdonia

🛏 **Snowdonia Parc Brewpub and Campsite, Waunfawr, Caernarfon, LL55 4AQ**
☎ (01286) 650409 ⊕ snowdonia-park.co.uk

Snowdonia started brewing in 1998 in a two-barrel brewhouse. The brewing is now carried out by the owner, Carmen Pierce. The beer is brewed solely for the Snowdonia Park pub and campsite.

Gwyrfai (OG 1037, ABV 3.8%)
Tawny in colour with bitterness from traditional hop varieties.

Trithro (OG 1038, ABV 3.8%)

Gold (OG 1040, ABV 4%)
A refreshing ale with citrus notes.

Theodore Stout (OG 1040, ABV 4.1%)
A robust stout with roast flavours complemented by a full-bodied and smooth mouthfeel. The hops lend a tart bitterness to the dry espresso-like finish. The complex coffee aromas mingle with light liquorice notes.

Carmen Sutra (OG 1043, ABV 4.4%)

Cais (OG 1045, ABV 4.8%)
A dark beer with rich flavours and balanced bitterness.

Dark & Delicious (OG 1046, ABV 5%)
Rich, dark and complex with an outstanding depth of flavour.

Welsh Highland Bitter (OG 1048, ABV 5.2%)
A traditional premium strong ale that is malty and full. A slight sweetness extends into the finish of this mid-brown, balanced beer.

Ixion Addiction (OG 1060, ABV 6%)
A strong ruby-coloured ale.

Snowhill (NEW)

Snowhill Cottage, Snow Hill Lane, Scorton, Lancashire, PR3 1BA
☎ (01524) 791352

☺Snowhill was established in 2015 by Nigel Stokes following several years of small scale brewing. It uses a 1.5-barrel plant. A one-man operation, Nigel brews 3-4 times per month to supply pubs in North-west Lancashire. An environmentally-friendly set-up sees the spent grain feeding local cattle and waste water treated through a small reed bed. ♦

Pale (OG 1037, ABV 3.7%)
A fruity pale yellow-coloured beer with intense Citra hop flavours and a fairly bitter aftertaste.

Gold (OG 1039, ABV 3.9%)
Fruit and malt dominate, with a bitter-dry finish.

Best Bitter (OG 1042, ABV 4.2%)
Rich, malty and fruity, with a pronounced bitter finish.

Black Magic IPA (OG 1042, ABV 4.2%)
A complex black IPA, with a hoppy aroma and taste, with hints of roast.

Solvay Society

Cuckoo Hall Brewery, Unit 8, Aldborough Hall Farm, Aldborough Hatch, Essex, IG2 7TD

Solvay Society began brewing in 2014 in the cellar of a Walthamstow pub using a small 0.5-hectolitre kit. In 2015 it transferred the equipment to the Hops & Glory pub in north London. In 2016 the brewery moved again, taking over the old equipment from the Ha'penny Brewery in Aldborough Hatch. Production is mostly keg but bottle-conditioned beer is also available. RAIB

Son of Sid

🛏 **Chequers, 71 Main Road, Little Gransden, Cambridgeshire, SG19 3DW**
☎ (01767) 677348 ⊕ sonofsid.co.uk

⊠ Son of Sid was established in 2007. The three-barrel plant is situated in a separate room at the back of the pub and can be viewed from a window in the lounge bar. It is named after the father of the current landlord, who ran the pub for 42 years. His son has carried the business on for the past 24 years as a family-run enterprise. Beer is sold in the pub and at local beer festivals. ‼ ▇ RAIB

English Ale (OG 1035, ABV 3.5%)
Traditional English ale with a clean, malty taste and a good hop character.

Muck Cart Mild (OG 1035, ABV 3.5%) ◥
Black mild with a resounding roast malt presence and a caramel background in aroma and taste. There is some sweetness but the balance is predominantly dry and bitter, with increasing bitterness in the aftertaste.

Golden Shower (OG 1039, ABV 3.9%)
Full-bodied golden beer with a light hop character and a defined maltiness.

Fine Ale Furlong (OG 1043, ABV 4.3%)
Malty, easy-drinking premium bitter.

Songbird

▤ Stumble Inn, 37 Tamworth Rd, Long Eaton, Derbyshire, NG10 1JF
☎ (0115) 972 4529 ☎ 07912 601475
⊕ songbirdbrewery.co.uk

Songbird was founded in 2013, with production beginning in 2014. A two-barrel plant is used, situated at the rear of the Stumble Inn.

Double Bass (OG 1042, ABV 4.2%)
Malty, brown-coloured traditional bitter.

Melody Pale (OG 1044, ABV 4.5%)
Light in colour, a sweet, hoppy ale.

Ale House Rock (OG 1047, ABV 4.8%)
Traditional porter. Rich and dark with outstanding depth of flavour.

Sonnet 43 SIBA ◉

Durham Road, Coxhoe, County Durham, DH6 4HX
☎ (0191) 377 3039 ⊕ sonnet43.com

☺Sonnet 43 began brewing in 2012. The name and brewing ethos is inspired by the most famous work of poet Elizabeth Barratt Browning who was born nearby. A limited edition beer range is brewed. The brewery has five outlets and supplies extensively to the free trade. ☛

Abolition (OG 1038, ABV 3.8%)
Medium bodied amber ale with sourdough and nut aromas, and a slightly bitter aftertaste.

Seraphim (OG 1041, ABV 4.1%)
A golden, straw-coloured wheat-style beer with a sweet, delicate, floral aroma.

The Raven (OG 1046, ABV 4.3%)
Dark beer brewed with Bourbon, cocoa and oats to give a rich, full-bodied, chocolaty bitterness.

The Aurora (OG 1044, ABV 4.4%)
Strong pale ale with a complex hoppy aroma, and a delicate fruity malt taste.

Impressment (OG 1055, ABV 5.4%)
Full-bodied bronze-coloured ale with a spicy and peppery aroma, and a fruity, malty and spicy flavour.

South Hams SIBA

Stokeley Barton Farm, Stokenham, Devon, TQ7 2SE
☎ (01548) 581151 ⊕ southhamsbrewery.co.uk

☒ The brewery moved to its present site, a milking parlour, in 2003, with a 10-barrel plant and plenty of room to expand. It supplies more than 60 outlets in south Devon. Wholesalers are used to distribute to other areas. Three pubs (one being the brewery tap) are owned. ‼ ♦ RAIB

Devon Pride (OG 1039, ABV 3.8%)
A dark amber-coloured beer, smooth to drink with a malty palate.

Wild Blonde (OG 1044, ABV 4.4%)

Hopnosis (OG 1046, ABV 4.5%)

Eddystone (OG 1050, ABV 4.8%)
A golden IPA with a distinct fruity aroma and a fruity palate.

Pandemonium (OG 1054, ABV 5%)

South Lakes (NEW)

Unit 30, Ulverston Auction Mart, North Lonsdale Road, Ulverston, Cumbria, LA12 0AU ☎ 07795 363523
✉ aaronpos1@hotmail.com

South Lakes began brewing on a 1.5-barrel plant in 2016, in a part of the Auction Mart in Ulverston. The brewer is experimenting with a range of beers.

Rakau (OG 1048, ABV 4.7%)
A strong blonde ale bursting with hops and fruit.

American Pale Ale (OG 1050, ABV 4.8%)
A rich golden ale with lots of citrus.

Southbourne

45 Poole Hill, Bournemouth, BH2 5PW
☎ (01202) 471190 ☎ 07845 795464
⊕ southbourneales.co.uk

☒Jennifer Tingay, former technologist and brewer for Ringwood, began brewing in 2013 using spare capacity at Town Mill brewery in Lyme Regis. Using crowdfunding she secured the lease of a former nightclub on Bournemouth's West Cliff and in 2016 transferred the brewery there. A bar, the Angel's Den, is planned. Crowdfunding is continuing to support the project. ♦

Paddlers (OG 1037, ABV 3.6%)
A light but balanced session bitter with moderate hop characteristics.

Sunbather (OG 1040, ABV 4%)
A red-coloured ale with moderate hop bitterness and flavour but with toffee notes in the distinctive malt flavour.

Headlander (OG 1043, ABV 4.2%)
Floral aroma and full hop bitterness is balanced with malt.

Beachcomber (OG 1058, ABV 5.7%)
A full-flavoured brown ale with a good malt and hop balance.

SouthDowns

See Downlands

Southport SIBA

Unit 3, Enterprise Business Park, Russell Road, Southport, Merseyside, PR9 7RF ☎ 07748 387652
⊕ southportbrewery.co.uk

☺Southport Brewery was established in 2004 on a five-barrel plant. Outlets are supplied in Southport, North-west England and nationally. ♦

Cyclone (OG 1039.5, ABV 3.8%)
A bronze-coloured bitter with a fruity blackcurrant aftertaste.

Sandgrounder Bitter (OG 1039.5, ABV 3.8%)
Pale, hoppy session bitter with a floral character.

Dark Night (OG 1040.5, ABV 3.9%)
A dark traditional mild.

Carousel (OG 1041.5, ABV 4%)
A refreshing, floral, hoppy best bitter.

Golden Sands (OG 1041.5, ABV 4%)
A golden-coloured, triple-hopped bitter with citrus flavour.

Natterjack (OG 1043.5, ABV 4.3%)

A premium bitter with fruit notes and a hint of coffee.

Southsea (NEW)

Southsea Castle, Clarence Esplanade, Southsea, Hampshire, PO5 3PA ☎ 07939 063970 ⊕ southseabrewing.co.uk

⊠ Launched in 2016, Southsea Brewing is located in an old ammunition storage room within the walls of a coastal defence fort built by Henry VIII in 1544. All beers are unfined, unfiltered and unpasteurised and bottled on site. ‼ RAIB

Southwark SIBA ◉

46 Druid Street, London, SE1 2EZ ☎ (020) 3302 4190 ⊕ southwarkbrewing.co.uk

⊠ A further addition to the burgeoning Bermondsey brewing scene, Southwark Brewing Company opened in 2014 focussing on cask ales. A tap room is open Thursday-Sunday. ☕♦

London Pale Ale (OG 1038.5, ABV 4%) ◕
Pale golden-coloured, smooth beer. Sweet biscuity malt is balanced by pineapple and pithy citrus. Dry aftertaste with a building bitterness.

Potters' Fields Porter (OG 1040, ABV 4%) ◕
Dark brown porter. Raisins, prunes and cocoa in the flavour and aroma fading in the dry roast bitter aftertaste.

Bermondsey Best (OG 1042, ABV 4.4%) ◕
A well-balanced best bitter with the fruity notes developing in the finish, which is bitter. Some malty notes on the palate.

Gold (OG 1047, ABV 5.2%) ◕
Pleasant earthy hop on the nose and palate becoming peppery in the finish. Sweet pink grapefruit and orange pith flavour.

Harvard (OG 1049, ABV 5.5%) ◕
Honey with sweet orange and grapefruit marmalade character are present in this rich, smooth pale brown beer. Dry bitter finish.

Spa Town

See Harrogate

Spencer's

See G2

Sperrin SIBA

▤ Birmingham Road, Ansley, Warwickshire, CV10 9PQ ☎ (024) 7639 2305 ☎ 07917 772208 ⊕ sperrinbrewery.co.uk

Sperrin began brewing in 2012 and is situated by the side of the Lord Nelson Inn. A brewery was first established there in 1868. Beers are also available at its sister pub, the Blue Boar in Mancetter. ‼♦RAIB

Ansley Mild (OG 1035, ABV 3.5%)
Old traditional recipe giving a rich, roast, malty-flavoured mild.

Head Hunter (OG 1038, ABV 3.8%)
Triple-hopped amber-coloured ale with slight fruity hints and a pleasant dry finish.

Band of Brothers (OG 1042, ABV 4.2%)
Hoppy and full-flavoured golden ale with long-lasting, smooth, citrus and refreshing overtones.

Third Party (OG 1048, ABV 4.8%)
Malty ruby-coloured ale with a floral aroma and hints of fruit and spice.

Thick as Thieves (OG 1068, ABV 6.8%)
Smooth stout, rich in hops with an array of roasted chocolate malts giving a smooth liquorice well-balanced finish.

Spey Valley

Mains of Mulben, Mulben, Keith, AB55 6YH ☎ 07780 655199 ⊕ speyvalleybrewery.co.uk

⊠ Pilot brewery was founded in 2007 at Mulben Mains Farm. Originally using a two-barrel plant from Loch Ness Brewery, it now brews on a 20-barrel plant at a new site in Mulben. ♦

Sunshine on Keith (OG 1036, ABV 3.5%) ◕
Wheaty with a light bitter hop.

David's Not So Bitter (OG 1046, ABV 4.4%) ◕
Light brown with a good mix of malts, hops and red fruits.

Stillman's IPA (OG 1047.6, ABV 4.6%) ◕
Amber-coloured, hoppy bitter with a whisky background.

1814 (OG 1050, ABV 5%)

Spey Stout (OG 1055, ABV 5.4%) ◕
A thick, dark and malty stout with a smoky background.

Speyside Craft

2 Greshop Road, Forres, IV36 2GU ☎ (01309) 358082 ☎ 07854 053277 ⊕ speysidecraftbrewery.com

Based in a traditional whisky-producing area, Speyside Brewery uses the same water that goes into the production of Scottish whiskies. A number of local outlets are supplied. A donation from sales of Bottlenose Bitter goes to help support the work of the Whale & Dolphin Conservation Society. ♦

Bow Fiddle Blonde (OG 1038, ABV 3.8%)

Bottlenose Bitter (OG 1041, ABV 4.1%) ◕
Slightly citrus, hoppy bitter.

Randolph's Leap (OG 1049, ABV 4.9%)

Moray IPA (OG 1055, ABV 5.5%)

Findhorn Killer Red IPA (OG 1056, ABV 5.6%)

Spire SIBA

Bull Paddock Farm, Sutton Lane, Sutton Scarsdale, Derbyshire, S44 5UW ☎ (01246) 807940 ⊕ spirebrewing.co.uk

☺Originally set up in 2006, the Spire brand came under the ownership of a long-standing CAMRA member in 2014 and the new-look brewery relocated to Sutton Scarsdale. The old 15-barrel plant has been replaced with a new 15-barrel brewery and bottling plant added. More than 100 outlets are supplied direct. ☕♦RAIB

Whiter Shade (OG 1039, ABV 4%)
Pale straw-coloured session bitter with a subtle lemon hop finish. It is refreshingly smooth with a well-balanced malt flavour.

Dark Side (OG 1043, ABV 4.3%) ◆
Complex and satisfying ruby mild with coffee aroma and toffee flavours. Dark and sweet.

Chesterfield Best Bitter (OG 1044, ABV 4.5%) ◆
Classic brown strong bitter with malt and fruit flavours and a hint of caramel and chocolate in the finish. There is a little bitterness in the aftertaste.

Jailbreak IPA (OG 1054, ABV 5.4%)
A slight floral and assertive nose. The distinct peach flavour accompanies a hint of malty sweetness before a pleasant bitterness. This light copper ale finishes dry with notes of tea and cedar spice.

Yaroslavna Stout (OG 1063, ABV 6%)
Robust roast flavour complemented by a full-bodied and smooth mouthfeel. It is filled with rich complex coffee aromas mingled with light liquorice notes. The bitterness of the hops and roasted barley balance the slight sweetness in the finish.

Spitting Feathers SIBA 👁

Common Farm, Waverton, Cheshire, CH3 7QT
☎ (01244) 332052 ☎ 07974 348325
⊕ spittingfeathers.org

☺Spitting Feathers was established in 2005. The brewery is located in a sandstone building set around a cobbled yard. Around 200 local outlets are supplied. A range of occasional beers are brewed to old recipes under the Heritage Ales brand. ‼◆

Session Beer (OG 1035, ABV 3.6%)
A golden session bitter. Traditional English malts and hops combine to make this a well-balanced and satisfying beer.

Thirstquencher (OG 1038, ABV 3.9%) ◆
Powerful hop aroma leads into the taste. Bitterness and a fruity citrus hop flavour fight for attention. A sharp, clean golden beer with a long, dry, bitter aftertaste.

Special Ale (OG 1041, ABV 4.2%) ◆
Complex tawny-coloured beer with a sharp, grainy mouthfeel. Malty with good hop coming through in the aroma and taste. Hints of nuttiness and a touch of acidity. Dry, astringent finish.

Old Wavertonian (OG 1043, ABV 4.4%) ◆
Creamy and smooth stout. Full-flavoured with coffee notes in aroma and taste. Roast and nut flavours throughout, leading to a hoppy, bitter finish.

Springhead SIBA 👁

Robin Hood Site, Main Street, Laneham, Retford, Nottinghamshire, DN22 0NA
☎ (01777) 228080 ☎ 07720 461655
⊕ springhead.co.uk

☺Springhead Brewery opened in 1990, moving to bigger premises three years later and, to meet increased demand, expanded to a brew length of 50 barrels in 2003. In 2011 the brewery relocated to its current address. Around 500 outlets are supplied direct and the brewery owns five pubs. Brewery tours start and finish at Meg's Bar, which is part of the brewery building and you can watch the brewery in operation from the bar. ‼ 🍺◆V

Outlawed (OG 1040, ABV 3.8%)
A triple-hopped easy drinking American-style pale ale, with a citrus aroma.

Drop O' The Black Stuff (OG 1041, ABV 4%)

A smooth, dark easy-drinking porter.

Robin Hood (OG 1041, ABV 4%)
A chestnut-brown traditional bitter with a good head and plenty of hops.

Maid Marian (OG 1045, ABV 4.5%)
A pale golden beer with a fruity orange aroma and a dry finish.

Leveller (OG 1047, ABV 4.8%)
Brewed in the style of Belgian abbey ale, with a dark, smoky intense flavour with a toffee finish.

Roaring Meg (OG 1052, ABV 5.5%)
A smooth classic IPA. Golden, with a citrus honey aroma and a dry finish.

Squawk

Unit 4, Tonge Street, Ardwick, Manchester, M12 6LY
☎ 07590 387559 ⊕ squawkbrewingco.com

Squawk initially cuckoo-brewed on the Hand Drawn Monkey plant in Huddersfield in 2013, with the first brew from the Manchester site being in 2014. The eight-barrel plant is located in a railway arch in Ardwick. **RAIB**

Espresso Stout (OG 1060, ABV 6.5%)
A smooth, rich beer with an espresso flavour.

Stables

⊟ Beamish Hall Country House Hotel, Beamish, County Durham, DH9 0YB
☎ (01207) 288750 ⊕ beamish-hall.co.uk/stables

Stables was established as part of a £1 million development of an old stable block of Beamish Hall, converting a disused building to a restaurant and eight-barrel microbrewery. The hotel is supplied plus the Sun Inn at Beamish Museum. Beers are also brewed under the Bull Lane Brewery name. ‼◆

Beamish Hall Best Bitter (OG 1038, ABV 3.8%)

Old Miner Tommy (OG 1037, ABV 3.8%)

Bobby Dazzler (OG 1042, ABV 4.2%)

Coppy Lane (OG 1043, ABV 4.2%)

Silver Buckles (OG 1044, ABV 4.4%)

Beamish Burn (OG 1045, ABV 4.5%)

Bell Tower (OG 1052, ABV 5%)

Staffordshire

12 Churnet Court, Cheddleton, Staffordshire, ST13 7EF
☎ (01538) 361919 ☎ 07971 808370
⊕ staffordshirebrewery.co.uk

No real ale. Brewing started in 2002 and the brewery has steadily increased in capacity since. A 20-barrel brew plant was completed in 2011. The brewery was renamed from Leek Brewery in 2013 at which time cask production ceased, being replaced by filtered, pasteurised bottled beers only. Cask-conditioned ales are brewed for Wicked Hathern Brewery Ltd using a six-barrel plant. ‼

Brewed for Wicked Hathern Brewery:

Albion Special (OG 1042, ABV 4%)
Light copper in colour with a nutty aroma and a smoky, malty taste.

Hawthorn Gold (OG 1045, ABV 4.6%)

A light golden, easy-drinking beer with a good balance of hops and malt.

Staggeringly Good SIBA

Unit 3, St Georges Industrial Estate, Rodney Road, Southsea, Hampshire, PO4 8SS
☎ (023) 9229 7033 ☎ 07881 943452
⊕ staggeringlygood.com

⊗ Brewing began in 2014, originally using spare capacity at other breweries. In 2015 a 10-barrel plant at its own premises came on stream. ‼ ➦ ◆ RAIB

Staggersaurus (OG 1039, ABV 4%)
A deep golden ale with summer fruit aromas and grapefruit on the palate. It has a light bitterness which quickly softens, giving a refreshing finish.

ThaiRannoCitrus (OG 1048, ABV 5%)
A pale ale with distinct lime and peach flavours and aromas, balanced by a hoppy bitterness.

Post Impact Porter (OG 1057, ABV 5.4%)
A rich porter with roasted malts and hints of espresso and dark chocolate.

VelociRapture (OG 1060, ABV 6.5%)
An American-style IPA with a strong fruit character and bitterness. A well-rounded, crisp and refreshing ale.

Stamps SIBA

The Basement, 17 Boundary Street, Everton, Liverpool, L5 9UB ☎ 07779 000094
⊕ stampsbrewery.co.uk

⊛ Brewing began in 2012 on an environmentally-friendly brew plant: power for brewing comes from 52 solar panels and a biomass boiler, used grain is sent to a local city farm for animal feed and rainwater is recycled and used for floor cleaning. The beers are named after famous world postage stamps. ‼ ➦

Blonde Moment (OG 1037, ABV 3.6%)
A pale-coloured beer with a smooth floral and citrus aroma and flavour. A good session beer.

Bondi Blonde (OG 1037, ABV 3.7%)
A pale, full-flavoured blonde beer. Flowers and citrus evident.

Ahtanum (OG 1039, ABV 3.9%)
Pale ale with a strong hint of citrus.

Mail Train (OG 1042, ABV 4.2%)
A traditional bitter, hoppy with a noticeable bitterness and a malt character.

The Russian (OG 1040, ABV 4.2%)
A copper-coloured ale with a hoppy finish.

Swedish Blonde (OG 1041, ABV 4.3%)
A session ale with a strong hint of citrus.

Inverted Jenny (OG 1046, ABV 4.6%)
Golden in colour with a grassy and floral bouquet and a noticeable tinge of caramel.

Flying Cloud (OG 1052, ABV 5.2%)
A strong American-style lager beer.

Penny Black (OG 1055, ABV 5.5%)
Robust porter with hints of chocolate.

Stancill SIBA ◉

Unit 2, Oakham Drive, off Rutland Road, Sheffield, South Yorkshire, S3 9QX
☎ (0114) 275 2788 ☎ 07809 427716

⊛ Stancill began brewing in 2014 and is named after the first head brewer and co-owner. It is situated on the doorstep of the late Cannon Brewery, taking advantage of the soft Yorkshire water. ‼

Barnsley Bitter (OG 1037.5, ABV 3.8%)

Blonde (OG 1038.5, ABV 3.9%)

India (ABV 4%)

No. 7 (OG 1042, ABV 4.3%)

Stainless (ABV 4.3%)

Porter (OG 1042.5, ABV 4.4%)

Black Gold (ABV 5%)

Stanway

Stanway House, Stanway, Gloucestershire, GL54 5PQ
☎ (01386) 584320 ⊕ stanwaybrewery.co.uk

⊛ Stanway is a small brewery founded in 1993 with a five-barrel plant that confines its sales to the Cotswolds area (15 to 20 outlets). The brewery is the only known plant in the country to use wood-fired coppers for all its production. ◆

Stanney Bitter (OG 1042, ABV 4.5%) ◈
A light, refreshing, amber-coloured beer, dominated by hops in the aroma, with a bitter taste and a hoppy, bitter finish.

Star SIBA

Unit D, Bentley Business Park, Northfields Industrial Estate, Market Deeping, Lincolnshire, PE6 8LD
☎ (01778) 380480 ☎ 07885 666836
✉ starbrewco@gmail.com

⊗ Star commenced production in 2014 using a 10-barrel brew plant. It has since expanded capacity to 20 barrels. Star Beers are now available in the JD Wetherspoons chain as well as being distributed all over the UK by wholesalers. ‼◆

Comet (OG 1038.5, ABV 3.8%)
Well-hopped blond ale.

Meteor (OG 1040, ABV 4%)
Traditional amber ale.

Galaxy (OG 1044, ABV 4.4%)
Crisp, golden best bitter.

Station 119

Rokeby Old Hall, Wilby, Eye, Suffolk, IP21 5LF
☎ 07766 701440 ⊕ station119.co.uk

Brewing started in 2014 using a two-barrel plant. The focus is firmly towards American craft style and all the beers have hop dominant flavours. Beers are available locally from Snape Maltings, Marlesford Farm Shop/cafe and the White Horse, Sweffling. RAIB

Station Works (NEW)

Camlough Road, Newry, Northern Ireland, BT35 6JP

A sister brewery to Cumberland Breweries, brewing began in 2013.

The Foxes Rock (OG 1042, ABV 4.2%)

Finn (OG 1045, ABV 4.5%)

Steamin' Billy

See Belvoir

Steel City

c/o Toolmakers Brewery, 6-8 Botsford Street, Sheffield, South Yorkshire, S3 9PF
⊕ steelcitybrewing.co.uk

⊗ Steel City was established in 2009 and brews once or twice a month. Brewing activity was originally based at the Brew Company before moving on to Little Ale Cart's premises for three years. It currently uses spare capacity at Toolmakers Brewery (qv).

Stewart SIBA

26a Dryden Road, Bilston Glen Industrial Estate, Loanhead, EH20 9LZ
☎ (0131) 440 2442 ⊕ stewartbrewing.co.uk

☺Established in 2004 by Steve and Jo Stewart. The brewery moved to a larger, custom-built brewery in 2013 with a brand new 50-hectolitre plant. Increased capacity enables the brewing team to experiment with seasonal and one-off beers. It also runs Natural Selection Brewing, a collaboration with Heriot Watt students. Beers are distributed throughout the UK, although they are mainly sold in south-east Scotland. !! ♙ ♦ RAIB

Jack Back (OG 1039, ABV 3.7%)
A pale, hoppy beer with strong citrus and tropical fruit aromas. The taste is light, crisp and refreshing.

Pentland IPA (OG 1040, ABV 3.9%) ♠
A pleasing, hoppy, golden session ale. The dry bitter taste is well balanced by sweetness from the malt, and fruit flavours. The aftertaste is dry with a lingering bitterness.

Crossfire (OG 1045, ABV 4.3%)
A golden IPA. Pine and citrus aromas on the nose with a distinct malt profile and a crisp bitterness in its complex flavour profile.

80/- (OG 1044, ABV 4.4%) ♠
A traditional Scottish heavy. The complex profile is dominated by malt with fruit flavours giving the sweetish character typical of this beer style. Hops provide a gentle balancing bitterness that intensifies in the dry finish.

Edinburgh Gold (OG 1048, ABV 4.8%) ♠
A full-bodied but easy-drinking Continental-style golden ale. Bitterness from the hop character is strong in the finish and complemented in the taste by a little sweetness from malt, and fruit flavours.

Sticklegs

Primrose Farm, Hall Road, Great Bromley, Essex, CO7 7TR ☎ 07971 138038 ⊕ sticklegs.co.uk

⊗ Sticklegs was established in 2008 at the Cross Inn, Great Bromley. The brewery expanded and relocated to Elmstead Market, where it continued to grow. In 2016 it moved to Primrose Farm and

plans to hold events there. Both a two and a six-barrel plant are used. The brewery is owned and run by Phil Reeve and his wife Linda, the brewster. !!

Malt Shovel Mild (OG 1032, ABV 3.4%)

Old Forge Bitter (OG 1038, ABV 3.8%)

Stour Gold (OG 1040, ABV 3.8%)

Bar'King (ABV 4%)

Tendring 100 (OG 1041, ABV 4%)

Elmstead Stout (OG 1046, ABV 4.8%)

Nemesis (OG 1048, ABV 5%)

Stocklinch

Unit 3, Manor Farm, Stocklinch, Somerset, TA19 9JG
☎ 07711 479917 ⊕ stocklinchales.co.uk

⊗ Established in 2012 in a converted farm building, Stocklinch uses a five-barrel plant supplying a number of local outlets. The brewery is licensed to open for a few days each month, mainly at weekends, which compensates for the lack of a village pub. !! ♙ ♦

Ramblers Gold (OG 1038, ABV 3.8%)
Refreshing light golden beer with a slight aftertaste of grapefruit.

Jakes (OG 1040, ABV 4%)

Gunner Boyce (OG 1042, ABV 4.2%)

Jakes Special (OG 1045, ABV 4.5%)

Ramblers Gold Extra (OG 1045, ABV 4.5%)

Rusty Boiler (OG 1045, ABV 4.5%)
Mid brown best bitter, strong fruity flavours with a lick of caramel.

Black Smock (OG 1050, ABV 5%)
Dark beer with a strong, rich taste of chocolate liquorice and coffee, with a hint of blackcurrant.

Stockport SIBA ⊙

Arch 14, Heaton Lane, Stockport, SK4 1AQ
☎ (0161) 477 1084 ☎ 07442 530728
⊕ stockportbrewingcompany.com

☺Previously sharing equipment at another local brewery, Stockport Brewing Co installed its own eight-barrel plant in 2014. HMRC accreditation was gained and brewing commenced in the same year. The brewery now has a regular brewing capacity of 100 firkins a week, producing more than 15 different ales. The beers are available at over 100 pubs across the North-west. !! ♙ ♦

Cascade (ABV 4%)
Light in colour, gently hopped giving a slight citrus flavour.

Bitter Lemon (ABV 4.2%)
A straw-coloured hoppy beer with a bitter lemon finish.

Crown Best Bitter (ABV 4.2%)
Amber-coloured ale with a smooth, hoppy taste and a dry finish.

Stock Porter (ABV 4.8%)
Liquorice and malty nose with coffee and chocolate notes.

Heaton Rifles (ABV 6.6%)
A volley of hops burst through the malt base.

Stockton

28 Light Pipe Hall Road, Stockton on Tees, County Durham, TS18 4AH
☎ (01642) 678334
⊕ stocktonbrewingcompany.co.uk

Stockton Brewing Co started production in 2015 based in an industrial unit. It uses a 2.5-barrel plant. RAIB

Rocket (ABV 4.3%)
Ruby ale with a lightly hopped and refreshing taste, and a subtle smokiness on the finish.

Black Swann (ABV 5%)
An oatmeal stout with a creamy mouthfeel and chocolate notes, with a dry finish.

New World Order (ABV 6.2%)
An IPA-style beer with a light caramel body, and a powerful hoppy aroma and character.

Stod Fold SIBA ⊙

Stod Fold Farm, Hays Lane, Halifax, West Yorkshire, HX2 8UL
☎ (01224) 245951 ☎ 07870 498324
⊕ stodfoldbrewing.com

Stod Fold was founded by childhood friends Paul Harris and Angus Wood. They designed and built the brewery themselves and the result is a fully integrated, bespoke, computer-controlled, state of the art 10-barrel plant. The brewery is not open to the public but once a month is open to trade partners only.

Gold (OG 1038, ABV 3.8%) ◆
A refreshing, hoppy and fruity session ale. It has a crisp bitter aftertaste.

Amber (OG 1042, ABV 4.2%) ◆
Well-balanced best bitter. Overtones of fruit and hops. Easy-drinking with a mild bitter finish.

Blonde (OG 1045, ABV 4.5%) ◆
Smooth-tasting fruity beer with a lingering dry finish. Easy-drinking.

Stokesley

See Wainstones

Stonehenge SIBA ⊙

The Old Mill, Mill Road, Netheravon, Salisbury, Wiltshire, SP4 9QB
☎ (01980) 670631 ⊕ stonehengeales.co.uk

The brewery was founded in 1984 in what was originally a water-driven mill built in 1914. In 1993 the company was bought by Danish master brewer Stig Andersen and now supplies more than 300 outlets. From 2013 a new borehole, accessing the Salisbury Plain aquifer, has been supplying the brewery's water. It is of such pristine quality that the brewery now bottles and sells it under the Stonehenge name. !! ◆

Spire Ale (OG 1037, ABV 3.8%) ◆
A pale golden-coloured session bitter with an initial bitterness giving way to a well-rounded bitter aftertaste with discernible fruit balance.

Pigswill (OG 1039, ABV 4%) ◆
A tawny-coloured session bitter with an initial pleasant hop aroma and slight bitterness to the taste moving to a well-rounded bitter finish with slight malt and fruit in the finish.

Heel Stone (OG 1042, ABV 4.3%) ◆
A copper-coloured best bitter with some malt and fruit in the aroma continuing into the initial taste along with pleasant hoppiness. Medium bodied with plenty of flavour in the aftertaste with noticeable malt, fruit and hops.

Great Bustard (OG 1046, ABV 4.8%) ◆
A copper-brown coloured strong bitter. Complex malt and fruit flavours at first with a long fruit and bitter aftertaste.

Danish Dynamite (OG 1048, ABV 5%) ◆
Golden-coloured strong bitter with good hop and fruit aromas. Complex flavours in the initial taste with a beautifully balanced, full-bodied aftertaste with hops and fruit to the fore.

Stonehouse SIBA

Stonehouse, Weston, Oswestry, Shropshire, SY10 9ES
☎ (01691) 676457 ⊕ stonehousebrewery.co.uk

Stonehouse was established in 2007 and operates a 22-barrel plant. The brewery was based in former chicken sheds and is next to the preserved Cambrian railway line. A new building includes a bar and visitor centre. Direct delivery is within 30 miles of the brewery. !! ⊨ RAIB

Sunlander (OG 1037, ABV 3.7%)
Pale with a balance of citrus and floral hops.

Station Bitter (OG 1041, ABV 3.9%)
A traditional, amber-coloured bitter. A full-bodied session beer with a perfect balance of fruity hops and roasted malt.

Cambrian Gold (OG 1042, ABV 4.2%)
A deep golden-coloured fruity beer with a subtle, dry finish.

Wheeltapper's Wheatbeer (OG 1043, ABV 4.5%)
A refreshing golden wheat beer with hints of coriander and lemon zest.

KPA (OG 1047, ABV 4.6%)
A crisp pale ale with a herby, floral note.

Off the Rails (OG 1048, ABV 4.8%)
A rich and malty premium bitter, with a classic British hop flavour.

Stoney Ford (NEW)

Crown Lodge, Crown Street, Ryhall, Rutland, PE9 4HQ
⊕ stoneyfordbrewco.co.uk

Stoney Ford Brewers was established in 2016 by Tim Nicol and Simon Watson, using a 2.5-barrel plant. Only English hops and malt are used. Local pubs are supplied.

PE9 Paradise Pale (ABV 4%)
Soft and rounded English pale ale with pronounced bitterness, a definitive hoppy flavour and the aromas of a traditional English ale.

All Saints Almighty Amber (ABV 4.2%)
Dark amber ale with a gentle bitterness and a resinous, marmalade and orange, aromatic and citrus bite.

Storm SIBA

2 Waterside, Macclesfield, Cheshire, SK11 7HJ
☎ (01625) 431234 ⊕ stormbrewing.co.uk

⊙Storm Brewing was founded in 1998, operating from an old ICI boiler room. In 2001 it moved to its current location, which until 1937 was a pub called the Mechanics Arms. More than 60 outlets are supplied. ◆ RAIB

Beauforts Ale (OG 1038, ABV 3.8%)
Golden brown, full-flavoured session bitter with a lingering hoppy taste.

Desert Storm (OG 1040, ABV 3.9%)
Amber-coloured beer with a smoky flavour of fruit and malt.

Bosley Cloud (OG 1041, ABV 4.1%) ◣
Dry, golden bitter with peppery hop notes throughout. Some initial sweetness and a mainly bitter aftertaste. Soft, well-balanced and quaffable.

Ale Force (OG 1042, ABV 4.2%) ◣
Amber, smooth-tasting, complex beer that balances malt, hop and fruit on the taste, leading to a roasty, slightly sweet aftertaste.

Downpour (OG 1043, ABV 4.3%)
A pale ale with a full, fruity flavour, a hint of apple and a sightly hoppy aftertaste.

PGA (OG 1044, ABV 4.4%) ◣
Light, crisp, lager-style beer with a balance of malt, hops and fruit. Moderately bitter and slight dry aftertaste.

Hurricane Hubert (OG 1045, ABV 4.5%)
A dark beer with a refreshing full, fruity hop aroma and a subtle bitter aftertaste.

Silk of Amnesia (OG 1047, ABV 4.7%) ◣
Smooth, premium, easy-drinking bitter. Fruit and hops dominate throughout. Not too sweet, with a good lasting finish.

Red Mist (OG 1049, ABV 4.8%)
A dark red/black porter with fruity notes and a hoppy finish.

Stowey

Old Cider House, 25 Castle Street, Nether Stowey, Somerset, TA5 1LN
☎ (01278) 732228 ⊕ stoweybrewery.co.uk

Somerset's smallest brewery was established in 2006, primarily to supply the owners' guesthouse and to provide beer to participants on 'real ale walks' run from the accommodation. The brewery also runs brewery workshop courses and supplies seasonal brews to the village pubs on a guest beer basis. !! ◆

Nether Ending (OG 1044, ABV 4.2%)

Strands

☰ Strands Inn, Nether Wasdale, Cumbria, CA20 1ET
☎ (01946) 726237 ⊕ strandshotel.com

⊙ Strands Brewery is a six-barrel plant with a 30-barrel fermentation capacity. The majority of beers are available bottle conditioned. Six of the beers are available on the bar of the Strands Inn at all times. !! ◆ RAIB

Pied Piper (OG 1030, ABV 2.7%) ⌂ ◣
Lots of traditional mild characteristics: malty, caramel, roast, sweet and fruity.

Green Bullet (OG 1037, ABV 3.5%)
A light and creamy wheat beer.

Responsibly (OG 1038, ABV 3.7%)

Clean-tasting, heavily-hopped and lightly smoked beer.

Brown Bitter (OG 1039, ABV 3.8%) ◣
A complex tasting brown beer with a lingering bitter aftertaste.

Errmmm... (OG 1039, ABV 3.8%) ◣
A complex, traditional bitter.

Red Screes (OG 1047, ABV 4.5%) ◣
An interesting, rich-tasting, smooth, strong bitter; full-flavoured with plenty of roast and malt tastes.

T'errmmm-inator (OG 1050, ABV 5%) ◣
A smooth, dark brown, roast-led beer. Full-bodied and well-balanced.

Brewed for Independent Lakeland Breweries:

Gold Wing (OG 1040, ABV 4%)
A clean, crisp and dry golden ale with delicate citrus aromas and a flavoursome finish.

Dark Knight (OG 1050, ABV 5%)
A dark-coloured, well-balanced ale.

Stratford Upon Avon SIBA ⊙

Warwick Road, Stratford-upon-Avon, Warwickshire, CV37 0NT ☎ 07866 495232 ⊕ sua-brewery.co.uk

Stratford Upon Avon is the first brewery in Stratford since Flowers in the 1960s. It was established by Richard Williams in 2014 on his family farm, which lies on the River Avon. The brewery has been developed around an environmentally-friendly approach, using the farm's own small solar farm, wind turbine and bore hole. ◆

Stratford Gold (OG 1038, ABV 3.8%)

Louis's Pale Ale (OG 1040, ABV 4%)

Malty Pig Bitter (OG 1044, ABV 4.4%)
A malty but well-hopped ale with biscuity flavours.

Stratford IPA (OG 1045, ABV 4.5%)
A full-bodied ale with hints of honey and citrus fruits.

Dark Star Porter (OG 1046, ABV 4.6%)
A full-bodied ale with hints of coffee and chocolate.

Strathaven SIBA ⊙

Craigmill Brewery, Sandford Road, Strathaven, ML10 6PB
☎ (01357) 520419 ⊕ strathavenales.com

Strathaven Ales is a 10-barrel brewery on the River Avon close to Strathaven and was converted from the remains of a 16th-century mill. The range is distributed throughout Scotland and the north of England. !! ☰ ◆

Craigmill Mild (OG 1035, ABV 3.5%)

Clydesdale (OG 1038, ABV 3.8%)

Duchess Anne (ABV 3.9%)

Avondale (OG 1048, ABV 4%)

Old Mortality (OG 1046, ABV 4.2%)

Claverhouse (OG 1046, ABV 4.5%)

Strathbraan SIBA

Deanshaugh, Amulree, PH8 0EB
☎ (01350) 725264 ☎ 07747 857908
✉ strathbraan.bry@btinternet.com

Straathbraan began brewing in 2012 using a 10-barrel plant.

Due South (OG 1038, ABV 3.8%)

Head East (OG 1042, ABV 4.2%)

Stringers SIBA

Unit 3, Low Mill Business Park, Ulverston, Cumbria, LA12 9EE
☎ (01229) 581387 ⊕ stringersbeer.co.uk

Stringers is a small, family-run brewery. Brewing started in 2008 on a five-barrel plant run on 100% renewable energy. ◆ RAIB GF V

Plan B (OG 1036, ABV 3.7%) ◄
An easy-drinking, zingy, pale thirst quencher.

No. 2 Stout (OG 1042, ABV 4%) ◄
A robust, drying stout full of roast and hop bitterness.

Yellow Lorry (OG 1039, ABV 4%)

The North Will Rise Again (OG 1046, ABV 4.9%)

Turbine Porter (OG 1058, ABV 5.1%)

Victoria IPA (OG 1053, ABV 5.5%)
Spicy, tropical fruit from the hops, then some bitter marmalade, with a definite bitter finish.

Brewed for Independent Lakeland Breweries:

Wolf Warrior (OG 1035, ABV 3.5%) ◄
A hoppy aroma and a fruity, full-bodied taste of hops, finishes with a drying bitterness.

Stroud SIBA ⟨⊙⟩

Unit 11, Phoenix Works, London Road, Thrupp, Gloucestershire, GL5 2BU
☎ (01453) 887122 ⊕ stroudbrewery.co.uk

⊠ Established in 2006, Stroud Brewery supports the local economy and does not sell its organic bottled beers through supermarkets. The ales are sold in 40-50 pubs, independent retailers and the brewery shop. ‼ ☛ ◆ RAIB

Tom Long (OG 1039, ABV 3.8%)
Amber-coloured session beer with a spicy citrus aroma.

OPA (Organic Pale Ale) (OG 1041, ABV 4%)
A refreshing, golden-coloured organic ale with a delicate apple aroma.

Budding (OG 1045, ABV 4.5%)
Pale ale with a grassy bitterness, sweet malt and floral aroma.

Stubborn Mule (NEW)

Old Heyes Road, Timperley, WA15 6EN ☎ 07730 515251 ⊕ stubbornmulebrewery.com

Brewing began in 2015, producing mainly bottled beers to micro pubs, specialist beer shops and restaurants in the Manchester area. Cask-conditioned beer is supplied to festivals.

Stumptail

North Street, Great Dunham, Norfolk, PE32 2LR
☎ (01328) 701042 ✉ stumptail@btinternet.com

⊠ Stumptail began commercial home-brewing in 2011 using a 100-litre plant. Bottle-conditioned beers are produced with cask-conditioned versions

brewed to order. Only the west Norfolk area is supplied. RAIB

Stumpy's

See Yates'

Suddaby's

See Brown Cow

Sulwath SIBA

⊟ The Brewery, 209 King Street, Castle Douglas, DG7 1DT
☎ (01556) 504525 ⊕ sulwathbrewers.co.uk

☺ Sulwath started brewing in 1995. The beers are supplied to markets as far away as Devon in the south and Aberdeen in the north. The brewery has a fully licensed brewery tap. Cask ales are sold to around 100 outlets and four wholesalers. ‼ ☛ ◆ RAIB

Cuil Hill (OG 1039, ABV 3.6%) ◄
Distinctively fruity session ale with malt and hop undertones. The taste is bittersweet with a long-lasting, dry finish.

Tri-ball (OG 1039, ABV 3.9%)
A fresh, crisp blonde ale.

The Grace (OG 1044, ABV 4.3%)
A refreshing, rich ale with a full-bodied flavour that balances the caramel undertones.

Black Galloway (OG 1046, ABV 4.4%)

Criffel (OG 1044, ABV 4.6%) ◄
Full-bodied beer with a distinctive bitterness. Fruit is to the fore of the taste with hops becoming increasingly dominant in the taste and finish.

Galloway Gold (OG 1049, ABV 5%) ◄
A cask-conditioned lager that will be too sweet for many despite being heavily hopped.

Knockendoch (OG 1047, ABV 5%) ◄
Dark, copper-coloured, reflecting a roast malt content, with bitterness from Challenger hops.

Solway Mist (OG 1052, ABV 5.5%)
A naturally cloudy wheat beer. Sweetish and fruity.

Summer Wine

The Old Furnace, Unit 15 Crossley Mills, New Mill Road, Honley, West Yorkshire, HD9 6QB
☎ (01484) 665466 ⊕ summerwinebrewery.co.uk

☺ Brewing commenced in 2006 on a 10-gallon kit with an emphasis on bottle-conditioned beer. A 2007 upgrade saw a 0.5-barrel plant installed and in 2008 the brewery expanded to a six-barrel plant. Over 500 outlets are supplied direct.

Resistance (OG 1037, ABV 3.7%)
Dark ruby mild with a malty body and hints of caramel, cocoa and bitter roasted barley combined with a light, fruity hop character.

Zenith (OG 1040, ABV 4%)
Pale golden beer with floral aroma and a crisp bitter finish.

Barista (OG 1048, ABV 4.8%)
A rich, coffee flavoured stout.

Teleporter (OG 1050, ABV 5%)

A porter with a creamy body and cocoa, caramel and vanilla flavours.

Oregon (OG 1055, ABV 5.5%)
American-style pale ale with grapefruit, sherbet, spicy and floral aroma, malty body and hoppy finish.

Rogue Red Hop Ale (OG 1058, ABV 5.8%)
Deep ruby red ale with good body and tasty flavour and finish.

Diablo (OG 1060, ABV 6%)
A strong IPA with tropical fruit aroma and flavours.

Summerskills SIBA ◉

15 Pomphlett Farm Industrial Estate, Broxton Drive, Billacombe, Plymouth, Devon, PL9 7BG
☎ (01752) 481283 ⊕ summerskills.co.uk

⊠ Established in a vineyard in 1983 at Bigbury-on-Sea, Summerskills moved to its present site in 1985 and is the oldest brewery in Plymouth. Wholesalers and pub companies perform national distribution and the beers regularly appear in a selection of local outlets. ♦ RAIB

Start Point (OG 1036, ABV 3.7%)
Golden ale with a clean and fresh nose. Sweet up front with a delicate bitter finish.

Westward Ho! (OG 1040, ABV 4.1%)
Golden amber-coloured beer. Initial light fruity taste, followed by a zesty and fruity finish.

Best Bitter (OG 1042, ABV 4.3%) ◆
A mid-brown beer, with plenty of malt and hops through the aroma, taste and finish. A good session beer.

Tamar (OG 1042, ABV 4.3%)
A tawny-coloured bitter with a fruity aroma and a hop taste and finish.

Devon Dew (OG 1044, ABV 4.5%)
Honey yellow in colour with a floral, clean malty aroma. Sweet lemon up front, with a long grapefruit finish. Mildly hopped.

Menacing Dennis (OG 1045, ABV 4.5%)
Golden amber in colour, with aromas of dark malt and hops, and a slight hint of liquorice.

Bolt Head (OG 1046, ABV 4.7%)
Ruby red premium beer. Sweet rum-like aroma, full fruit taste, followed by a citrus orange finish.

Whistle Belly Vengeance (OG 1047, ABV 4.7%)
Russet brown-coloured with a smoky, caramel aroma and a rich, sharp chocolate taste.

Ninja (OG 1049, ABV 5%)

First Light (OG 1054, ABV 5.5%)
Bright amber-coloured strong summer ale. Initial toffee taste, followed by an orange and sherbet finish.

Indiana's Bones (OG 1055, ABV 5.6%)
Russet brown in colour, with a smoky, fresh hop aroma. Full-bodied, with a roast burnt and slightly sweet taste.

Sunbeam

52 Fernbank Road, Leeds, West Yorkshire, LS13 1BU
☎ 07772 002437 ⊕ sunbeamales.co.uk

☺Sunbeam ales was established in a back-to-back house in Leeds in 2009 with commercial brewing beginning in 2011. Since moving capacity has increased to a two-barrel plant based in a garage. The core range of ales, available in West and North Yorkshire at present, are brewed on rotation once a week with occasional brews every six weeks or so. ♦

Surfing Monkey

31 Fairwater Grove West, Cardiff, CF5 2JN ☎ 07412 365789 ⊕ surfingmonkeybrewery.com

Brewing began in 2014 utilising a large garage at the rear of a private house. Further beers are planned.

Blown-out Baboon (OG 1038, ABV 3.8%)
A pale session ale, finished with late bitterness on the tongue.

Offshore Howler (OG 1040, ARV 4%)
Cloudy wheat beer with orange and coriander.

Messed up Macaque (ABV 5%)
Light in colour with a sweet and sour taste.

Surrey Hills SIBA

Denbies Wine Estate, London Road, Dorking, Surrey, RH5 6AA
☎ (01306) 883603 ⊕ surreyhills.co.uk

⊠ Surrey Hills began brewing in 2005 near Shere, moving to Dorking in 2011. Nearly 95% of production is sold within 15 miles of the brewery. The beers have won several local and national awards. ‼ ☲ ♦

Ranmore (OG 1039, ABV 3.8%) 🍺 🍂
A light session beer. An earthy hoppy nose leads into a grapefruit and hoppy taste and a clean, bitter finish.

Shere Drop (OG 1043, ABV 4.2%) 🍺 🍴 🍂
A hoppy ale with some balancing malt. A pleasant citrus aroma and a noticeable fruitiness in the taste, with some sweetness.

Gilt Complex (OG 1047, ABV 4.6%)

Greensand IPA (OG 1047, ABV 4.6%) 🍴 🍂
A strong flavoured and easily drinkable IPA, with intense grapefruit and hops in the aroma and taste and soft citrus finish.

Collusion (OG 1053, ABV 5.2%)

Suthwyk

See Oakleaf

Swan (NEW)

Unit 17, Rural Enterprise Centre, Brunel Road, Leominster, Herefordshire, HR6 0LX
☎ (01568) 617709 ☎ 07508 207928
⊕ swanbrewery.co.uk

Swan Brewery was established in 2016 by Jimmy Swan and partner Gill Bullock on a 10-barrel plant in Leominster. Jimmy was previously head brewer at Wye Valley Brewery.

Cygneture Ale (OG 1037, ABV 3.6%)
Chestnut-coloured session beer.

Gold (OG 1040, ABV 4%)

Amber (OG 1044, ABV 4.4%)
A malt forward beer with wheat and flaked maize in the mix.

Swan on the Green

⊟ Swan on the Green, West Peckham, Kent, ME18 5JW
☎ (01622) 812271 ⊕ swan-on-the-green.co.uk

The brewery was established in 2000 in an old coal shed behind the Swan on the Green pub using a two-barrel plant. ‼♦

Fuggles Pale (OG 1037, ABV 3.6%)

Trumpeter Best (OG 1041, ABV 4%)

Cygnet (OG 1048, ABV 4.2%)

Bewick Swan (OG 1052, ABV 5.3%)

Swannay SIBA

Swannay Brewery, Swannay by Evie, Orkney, KW17 2NP
☎ (01856) 721700 ⊕ swannaybrewery.com

☺Originally named Highland Brewing Co, brewing began in 2006 at the redundant Swannay dairy on Orkney mainland's exposed north-western tip. Two brewing plants are utilised, a five and a twenty barrel. Founder Rob is assisted by son Lewis plus a further small team of passionate beer lovers. ‼☞♦

Orkney Best (OG 1038, ABV 3.6%) ◣
A refreshing, light-bodied, low gravity golden beer bursting with hop, peach and sweet malt flavours. The long, hoppy finish leaves a dry bitterness.

Island Hopping (OG 1039, ABV 3.9%) ◣
Fruity hoppiness with some caramel with a lasting bitter aftertaste.

Dark Munro (OG 1040, ABV 4%) ◣
The nose presents an intense roast hit which is followed by summer fruits in the mouth. The strong roast malt continues into the aftertaste.

Scapa Special (OG 1042, ABV 4.2%) ⌑ ▣ ◣
A good copy of a typical Lancashire bitter, full of bitterness and background hops, leaving your mouth tingling in the lingering aftertaste.

**Sneaky Wee Orkney Stout
(OG 1044, ABV 4.2%)** ⌑ ◣
Bags of malt and roast with a mixed fruit berry background. Dry bitter finish.

Pale Ale (OG 1047, ABV 4.7%)

Orkney IPA (OG 1048, ABV 4.8%) ◣
A traditional bitter, with light hop and fruit flavour throughout.

Duke IPA (OG 1053, ABV 5.2%)
Assertively hopped, American-style IPA.

Orkney Blast (OG 1058, ABV 6%) ◣
Plenty of alcohol in this warming strong bitter/ barley wine. A mushroom and woody aroma blossoms into a well-balanced smack of malt and hop in the taste.

Swansea SIBA

⊟ Joiners Arms, 50 Bishopston Road, Bishopston, Swansea, SA3 3EJ
☎ (01792) 232658

☺Opened in 1996, Swansea was the first commercial brewery in the area for almost 30 years. Two regular outlets are supplied along with other pubs in the South Wales area. ‼♦

Deep Slade Dark (OG 1034, ABV 4%)

A dark brown-coloured beer with a reddish hue with a nutty, malty taste. The aroma is malty with a little roast.

Bishopswood Bitter (OG 1043, ABV 4.3%) ◣
A delicate aroma of hops and malt in this pale brown ale. The taste is a balanced mix of hops and malt with a growing hoppy bitterness ending in a lasting bitter finish.

Three Cliffs Gold (OG 1042, ABV 4.7%) ◣
A golden beer with a hoppy and fruity aroma, a hoppy taste with fruit and malt, and a quenching bitterness. The pleasant finish has a good hop flavour and bitterness.

Original Wood (OG 1046, ABV 5.2%) ◣
A full-bodied, pale brown beer with an aroma of hops, fruit and malt. A complex blend of these flavours with a firm bitterness ends with increasing bitterness.

Taddington

Blackwell Hall, Blackwell, Buxton, Derbyshire, SK17 9TQ
☎ (01298) 85734

No real ale. Taddington started brewing in 2007, and brews one Czech-style unpasteurised lager in two different strengths: Moravka (ABV 4.4% and 5%), which is available on draught. Taddington also supplies an unfiltered version of Moravka called Moravka Kvasnicove.

Talke O' Th' Hill

Merelake Road, Talke, Staffordshire, ST7 1UE
☎ 07875 951399 ⊕ talkeothhill.co.uk

Talke O' Th' Hill began brewing in 2011 using a two-barrel brew plant based on a family farm on the Staffordshire/Cheshire border. The brewery is based on two floors in the old farm buildings. ♦

Citrade (OG 1043, ABV 4.4%)

Potter's Porter (OG 1044, ABV 4.4%)

First Porter Call (OG 1045, ABV 4.5%)

Tally Ho! SIBA

14 Market Street, Hatherleigh, Devon, EX20 3JN
☎ (01837) 810306 ☎ 07532 105871
⊕ tallyhobrewery.co.uk

⊠ The Tally Ho! brewery was recommissioned in 2015 by four brewing enthusiasts, after a number of years lying dormant. A recent investment has allowed expansion. As well as the pub, other local free houses and other establishments are supplied.

Ruby EPA (OG 1038, ABV 3.8%)
A dark ale with a long chocolate bite.

Ukulale (OG 1042, ABV 4.2%) ◣
Subtle aromas leading to a pleasantly balanced beer with clean hop flavours and bitter taste.

Tanners (NEW)

⊟ The Old Stables, White Hart Inn, The Square, Wiveliscombe, Somerset, TA4 2JP
☎ (01984) 623344 ⊕ tannersales.co.uk

Tanners was established in 2015 on a five-barrel plant in the old stables at the rear of the White Hart Inn, Wiveliscombe. Two pubs are owned.

Big Horse (ABV 3.8%)
A copper-coloured traditional bitter.

TA Gold (ABV 4.2%)
An easy-drinking golden beer.

Box O' Frogs (ABV 4.5%)
Rich, golden-coloured hoppy beer, with intense citrus notes and rich bitterness.

TAP (NEW)

Marsden Estate, Rendcomb, Gloucestershire, GL7 7EX
☎ 07931 920988 ⊕ tapbrewerygloucestershire.com

⊠ TAP is a microbrewery established near Cirencester in 2015. It prides itself on sourcing materials and services locally, with malt from Warminster, hops from Worcester and the beer labels produced in Cirencester. !! ♦ RAIB

Glow (OG 1040, ABV 4%)
A golden ale, with a smooth and malty character, a peachy aroma and a hoppy finish.

Ruby (OG 1042, ABV 4.2%)
A ruby-coloured best bitter with a unique fruitiness, a warming bitterness and a hoppy finish.

Tap East SIBA

⬛ 7 International Square, Montfichet Road, The Great Eastern Market, Westfield Stratford City, Stratford, London, E20 1EE
☎ (020) 8555 4467 ⊕ tapeast.co.uk

⊠ Tap East is located in Westfield Stratford City shopping centre opposite the main entrance to Stratford International Station. Brewing began in 2011. One-off and collaborative beers with other breweries are also produced. ➤ ♦ V

Tonic Ale (OG 1032, ABV 3%) ◥
A refreshing golden ale with strong citrus throughout. Faint biscuit notes and a bitter dry aftertaste.

East End Mild (OG 1037, ABV 3.5%) ◥
Dark mild that has roast and a little fruit and treacle on the palate fading in the shortish dry finish.

JWB (OG 1040, ABV 3.8%)
Bitter with a malty back bone and a good dose of hops.

APA (OG 1043, ABV 4.3%) ◥
Yellow-coloured beer with citrus throughout and a dash of pineapple. Bitterness grows on drinking, balanced by a little sweetness.

Coffee in the Morning (OG 1059, ABV 5.3%) ◥
Black porter with coffee dominating the aroma and flavour and lingering in the dry bitter finish. Trace of liquorice.

IPA (OG 1054, ABV 5.3%)

Smokestack Porter (ABV 6.5%)

Tap House

⬛ Tap House, Annwell Lane, Smisby, Derbyshire, LE65 2TA
☎ (01530) 413604 ☎ 07528 145217
⊕ taphouse-smisby.co.uk

⊠ Established in 2010, this purpose-built brewery supplies beers to its two pubs, the Tap House, Smisby, and the Kings Arms, Coleorton, as well as to pubs across Derbyshire and Leicestershire.

Leatherbritches Brewery (qv) shares the same brewery plant and brewer but the two businesses are run independently.

Ashby Pride (OG 1038, ABV 3.8%)
A light, quaffable, session beer.

Tap House Gold (OG 1042, ABV 4%)
A light, hoppy, golden ale.

Kingdom (OG 1046, ABV 4.5%)
A chestnut-coloured beer with a hint of caramel.

Malt Teaser (OG 1046, ABV 4.6%)
A rich crimson beer full of malt flavours with a light toffee aftertaste.

Dark & Dangerous (OG 1048, ABV 5%)
A delicious dark and complex porter with subtle chocolate flavours.

Tapped SIBA 👁

⬛ Sheffield: Sheffield Tap, Platform 1b, Sheffield Station, Sheaf Street, Sheffield, S1 2BP
☎ (0114) 273 7558

Leeds: Leeds Tap, 51 Boar Lane, Leeds, LS1 5EL
☎ 0113 2441953 ⊕ tappedbrewco.co.uk

Brewing began in 2013 after the old Edwardian dining rooms were converted into an onsite brewery with a viewing gallery at the Sheffield Tap pub. The beer is supplied via the company's specialist beer wholesale business, Pivovar. A further on-site brewery opened at the Leeds Tap in 2014.

Ale (OG 1035, ABV 3.5%)

Mojo (OG 1036, ABV 3.6%)
A clear crisp light pale ale.

Rodeo (OG 1039, ABV 4%)

Stout (OG 1041, ABV 4%)
English dry stout with a bitter, slightly sour finish.

Bramling (OG 1042, ABV 4.2%)
Golden best bitter taking its character from the classic hop variety.

Liberty (OG 1052, ABV 5.2%)
Rich dark treacle stout with subtle bitterness and hop aroma.

Bullet (OG 1059, ABV 5.9%)
Strong IPA with fruit candy aroma.

Tapstone

11 Bartlett Park, Millfield, Chard, Somerset, TA20 2BB
☎ (01460) 929156 ☎ 07969 651998
⊕ tapstone.co.uk

⊠ Founded in 2015, Tapstone is a modern brewery, using renewable energy and focusing on hop-forward beers. The brewery was custom built around a unique brewing process that preserves delicate hop oils – making beers with a saturated hop flavour. It has commenced growing Centennial hops about two miles from the brewery.

Sea Monster (OG 1042, ABV 4.2%)
A fresh and fruity pale ale with a crisp citrus base and tropical flavours of gooseberry and lime.

Kush Kingdom (OG 1050, ABV 5%)
Orange-coloured beer with fruit and citrus flavours and a complex resiny mouthfeel.

Opium Wars (OG 1056, ABV 5.6%)

Target 👁

Roden Nurseries, Roden Lane, Roden, Shropshire, TF6 6BP
☎ (01952) 770882 ☎ 07766 387488
✉ geoff@targetbrewery.com

Formally known as Dickensian, Target Brewery was renamed in 2015. Brewing takes place on a 15-barrel plant based in an old vehicle storage shed. The beers are named around Shropshire legends. ♦

Golden (OG 1039, ABV 3.9%)
A light ale, golden in colour, medium-bodied with sweet malty finish.

Marmid Gold (OG 1039, ABV 3.9%)
A well-balanced traditional bitter.

Hop Rankin (OG 1042, ABV 4.2%)
A classic blonde beer with plenty of body but maintaining a light crisp finish.

Wrekin Giant (OG 1042, ABV 4.2%)
A pale ale packed with hoppy flavours, giving a clean dry finish and a distinctive fruity kick.

Equinox (OG 1045, ABV 4.5%)
An American-style pale ale delivers a clean hoppy flavour with a dry and subtle spicy finish.

Rock Steady (OG 1045, ABV 4.5%)
A golden ale delivering a fruity and tropical slightly spicy flavour.

Tarn Hows SIBA

Low Bield, Knipe Fold, Outgate, Cumbria, LA22 0PU
☎ (01539) 436409 ☎ 07935 789581
⊕ tarnhowsbrewery.com

A small micro-brewery near Hawkshead specialising in traditional British ales using oak casks that provide a further dimension to the beer flavour.

Pigling Blonde (OG 1039, ABV 3.8%)
Blonde ale with peach and caramel notes.

Beertrix Porter (ABV 4%)
A traditional porter-style beer, with liquorice and vanilla flavours from the oak casks.

Grized Ale (OG 1041, ABV 4.2%)
Old ale-style, moderately dark beer with a hint of smoked malts, and warming hints of wood, wine and pine.

Puddled Duck (OG 1051, ABV 5.2%)
A dark golden-coloured IPA.

Tatton SIBA

Unit 7, Longridge Trading Estate, Knutsford, Cheshire, WA16 8PR
☎ (01565) 750747 ☎ 07738 150898
⊕ tattonbrewery.co.uk

😊Tatton is a family-run business based in the heart of Cheshire. Brewing commenced in 2010 using a steam-fired, custom-built 15-barrel brewhouse. Occasional beers are also brewed. It supplies pubs throughout Cheshire and the North-west. ‼🍺♦

Ale (OG 1036, ABV 3.7%)
An easy-drinking session ale with a rich copper colour. It has a full malty/toffee flavour balanced by a soft bitterness and hoppy, fruity taste and aroma.

Blonde (OG 1039, ABV 4%)

A clean tasting, smooth pale ale with a fine hop aroma.

Best (OG 1040.5, ABV 4.2%)
A classic light amber-coloured best bitter with a clean malt flavour and fine hop character.

Gold (OG 1046, ABV 4.8%)
A golden special ale with a maltiness backed by a robust hop character.

Tavernale

🍺 Bridge Tavern, 7 Akenside Hill, Newcastle upon Tyne, NE1 3UF
☎ (0191) 232 1122 ⊕ thebridgetavern.com

A two-barrel plant supplies beers to the Bridge Tavern only. All beers brewed are one-offs. ♦

Tavy SIBA

Unit 9, Porsham Close, Beliver Industrial Estate, Roborough, Plymouth, Devon, PL6 7DB ☎ 07971 411727

Office: 15 Hawkmoor Parke, Bovey Tracey, Devon, TQ13 9NL ⊕ tavyales.co.uk

⊠Committed to producing premium handcrafted small batch beers using a combination of traditional and modern brewing techniques and local ingredients, Tavy Ales is a six-barrel microbrewery situated in Plymouth. With a focus on sustainability, spent grain is taken to a local farm for animal feed. ‼♦RAIB

Best Bitter (OG 1043, ABV 4.3%)
A full-bodied chestnut brown beer with a well-rounded complex malt flavour and early bitterness.

Ideal Pale Ale (OG 1048, ABV 4.8%)
A pale golden beer loaded with citrus flavour, balanced bitterness and body. It has a strong floral and hoppy aroma.

Porter (OG 1052, ABV 5.2%) 🍺
Creamy black porter with malted roast aromas, leading to roasted caramel taste and refreshing, complex malt, roast and caramel aftertaste.

Timothy Taylor SIBA IFBB 👁

Knowle Spring Brewery, Keighley, West Yorkshire, BD21 1AW
☎ (01535) 603139 ⊕ timothy-taylor.co.uk

😊An independent, family-owned company established in 1858, Timothy Taylor has occupied the Knowle Spring site since 1863. Pennine spring water is used to brew its award-winning ales that are served in 18 tied pubs as well as more than 300 directly delivered outlets. Expanded brewing facilities opened on the main site in 2011.

Dark Mild (OG 1034, ABV 3.5%) 🍺
Malt and caramel dominate throughout in this sweetish beer with background hop and fruit notes.

Golden Best (OG 1033, ABV 3.5%) 🍺
Refreshing amber coloured traditional Pennine mild. A delicate fruit hoppy aroma leads to a fruity taste with underlying hops and malt. Fruity finish.

Boltmaker (OG 1038, ABV 4%) 🍷🍺🍺
Tawny bitter combining, hops fruit and biscuity malt. Lingering, increasingly bitter aftertaste. Formerly and sometimes still sold as Best Bitter.

Landlord (OG 1042, ABV 4.3%) 🏆 ◥
A tasty bitter combining citrus peel aromas, malt and grassy hops, marmalade sweetness and a long bitter finish.

Ram Tam (OG 1043, ABV 4.3%) ◗ ◥
A black beer with red highlights topped by a coffee coloured head. Burnt caramel on the nose, sweetish caramel taste leading to a light sweet finish.

Taylors

◻ London Tavern, Church Street, Attleborough, Norfolk, NR17 2AH ☎ 07871 773206
✉ taylorsbrewery@gmail.com

⊗ Brewing began in 2014, primarily to supply the London Tavern but the beers are now supplied to beer festivals and the free trade. A range of special beers are brewed for the annual Old Buckenham Air Show.

Number One (ABV 3.9%)

Second Coming (ABV 3.9%)
A well-balanced traditional English session bitter.

Dogtooth (ABV 4%)

English Pale Ale (OG 1040, ABV 4%)

Remember Me (OG 1044, ABV 4.4%)
Malty beer with a caramel note and a dry finish.

Stitched Up (ABV 4.7%)

Teignworthy SIBA

The Maltings, Teign Road, Newton Abbot, Devon, TQ12 4AA
☎ (01626) 332066 ⊕ teignworthybrewery.com

Teignworthy Brewery opened in 1994 within Tuckers historic maltings building. The 20-barrel plant produces 50 barrels a week using malt from Tuckers and supplies around 300 outlets in Devon and Somerset. ‼ ◄ ◆ RAIB

Neap Tide (OG 1038, ABV 3.8%)

Reel Ale (OG 1039.5, ABV 4%) ◥
Clean, sharp-tasting bitter with lasting hoppiness; predominantly malty aroma.

Gun Dog (OG 1043.5, ABV 4.3%)
A light bronze coloured ale with a flowery, fruity aromatic finish.

Spring Tide (OG 1043.5, ABV 4.3%) ◥
An excellent, full and well-rounded, mid-brown beer with a dry, bitter taste and aftertaste.

Old Moggie (OG 1044.5, ABV 4.4%)
A golden, hoppy and fruity ale.

Beachcomber (OG 1045.5, ABV 4.5%) ◥
A pale brown beer with a light, refreshing fruit and hop nose, grapefruit taste and a dry, hoppy finish.

Teme Valley SIBA 👁

◻ Talbot, Bromyard Road, Knightwick, Worcestershire, WR6 5PH
☎ (01886) 821235 ☎ 07792 394151
⊕ temevalleybrewery.co.uk

⊙Teme Valley was established in 1997 to brew beer for the Talbot, Knightwick. Only hops grown in Herefordshire and Worcestershire are used in brewing. Cask and bottle-conditioned beers are

supplied throughout the West Midlands and Marches. ‼ ◆ RAIB

T'Other (OG 1035, ABV 3.5%) ◥
Refreshing amber beer offering an abundance of flavour in the fruity aroma, followed by a short, dry bitterness.

This (OG 1037, ABV 3.7%) ◥
Dark gold brew with a mellow array of flavours in a malty balance.

That (OG 1041, ABV 4.1%) ◥
A rich fruity nose and a wide range of hoppy and malty flavours in this copper-coloured best bitter.

Talbot Blond (OG 1042, ABV 4.4%)

Tempest SIBA

Block 11, Units 1 & 2, Tweedbank Industrial Estate, Tweedbank, TD1 3RS
☎ (01896) 759500 ⊕ tempestbrewingco.com

Based in a former dairy, Tempest was set up in 2010 by Gavin Meiklejohn, brewer and co-proprietor of the Cobbles Inn in Kelso, which is the brewery tap. In 2015 the brewery moved from Kelso to new premises at Tweedbank. Gavin's focus is on bold flavours and ingredients to produce interesting styles based on classic and New World beers. ‼ ◆ RAIB

Armadillo (OG 1039, ABV 3.8%)
Waves of zesty citrus are amplified with hops for added flavour.

Cascadian (OG 1039, ABV 3.9%)
Light citrus hoppy session-style ale.

White Light (OG 1047, ABV 4.7%)
American hop hitter with a smooth citrus finish.

Elemental (OG 1053, ABV 5.1%)
Smooth robust porter.

Long White Cloud (OG 1053, ABV 5.6%)
Extra pale ale, light and refreshing.

Tenby SIBA

Unit 15, The Salterns, Tenby, Pembrokeshire, SA70 8EQ
☎ (01834) 218090 ☎ 07410 169447
⊕ tenbybrewingco.com

Tenby Brewing Co uses a six-barrel plant, formerly known as the Preseli Brewery. Two young brewers purchased, relocated and renamed the plant, and have introduced an impressive and interesting range of beers. Cask and bottled beers are supplied to outlets in Pembrokeshire, neighbouring counties and further afield. Spent grain is fed to animals at a local eco farm and through energy savings the brewery plans to become carbon neutral in the near future. RAIB

West Coast Rocks (OG 1040, ABV 3.8%)
A malty body with a hint of spiced blackberry.

Pembrokeshire Promise (OG 1046, ABV 4.5%)
An extra special bitter with hints of caramel, complex grain and mellow bitter hops.

Barefoot Blonde (OG 1041, ABV 4.6%)
A refreshing, clean, crisp blonde, infused with kaffir lime leaves.

Black Flag Porter (OG 1055, ABV 5.6%)
Full of character, with coffee and chocolate and a hint of vanilla spiced rum.

Thame

📧 East Street, Thame, Oxfordshire, OX9 3JS
☎ (01844) 218202
✉ thamebrewery@btinternet.com

⊗ This one-barrel brewery was set up in 2009 by Peter Lambert and Oak Taverns in the old stables at the Cross Keys. Beer is produced for the Cross Keys and beer festivals, and includes many one-off brews.

Mr Splodge's Mild (OG 1037, ABV 3.8%)

Hoppiness (OG 1042, ABV 4.2%)

Thames Side (NEW) SIBA

Unit 7, Tims Boatyard, Timsway, Staines-upon-Thames, Surrey, TW18 3JY ☎ 07749 204242
⊕ thamessidebrewery.co.uk

Thames Side was founded in 2015 by Andy Hayward using a four-barrel plant. Beer is supplied to the local area as well as into central London. Beers are named after birds found on or near the River Thames. ◆

Harrier Bitter (ABV 3.4%)

Heron Bitter (ABV 3.7%)

White Swan Pale Ale (ABV 4.5%)

Egyptian Goose IPA (ABV 4.8%)

That Little Brewery

134 London Road, St Albans, AL1 1PQ
☎ (01727) 869230

3 Tudor Road, St Albans, AL3 6AY
⊕ thatlittleplace.co.uk

That Little Brewery produces two bottle-conditioned beers available at That Little Place restaurant in Harpenden. Cask-conditioned beer is available at the Farmer's Boy in St Albans, and at beer festivals. RAIB

Theakston 👁

The Brewery, Masham, North Yorkshire, HG4 4YD
☎ (01765) 680000 ⊕ theakstons.co.uk

☺After several years under the control of other companies Theakston is now owned by four brothers, grandsons of Thomas Theakston, the son of the company's founder who built the brewery in 1875. A new fermentation room was built in 2004 to provide additional flexibility and capacity, and further capacity was added in 2006. All Theakston beers are now brewed in Masham. ‼◆

Best Bitter (OG 1038, ABV 3.8%)
A golden-coloured beer with a full flavour that lingers pleasantly on the palate. With a good bitter/sweet balance, this beer has a robust hop character, citrus and spicy.

Black Bull Bitter (OG 1037, ABV 3.9%) ◆
A distinctively hoppy aroma leads to a bitter, hoppy taste with some fruitiness and a short bitter finish.

Lightfoot (OG 1041, ABV 4.1%)

XB (OG 1044, ABV 4.5%)
A sweet-tasting bitter with background fruit and spicy hop. Some caramel character gives this ale a malty dominance.

Old Peculier (OG 1057, ABV 5.6%) ◆
A full-bodied, dark brown, strong ale. Slightly malty but with hints of roast coffee and liquorice. A smooth caramel overlay and a complex fruitiness leads to a bitter chocolate finish.

Third Eye (NEW)

The Mill, Hurst House Farm Barn, Halfpenny Lane, Heskin, Lancashire, PR7 5PR ☎ 07871 870015
⊕ thirdeyebrewery.co.uk

☺Third Eye began brewing in 2015 using a 1.5-barrel plant. Local specialist real ale outlets and beer festivals are supplied direct. Seasonal and bottled beers are planned.

Session Ale (OG 1041, ABV 3.9%)
A hop forward pale ale with some residual sweetness and body to balance out the hops.

Thirst Class

Unit 16, Station Road Industrial Estate, Reddish, Stockport, SK5 6ND
☎ (0161) 431 3998 ⊕ thirstclassale.co.uk

☺Thirst Class opened in 2014 in the centre of Stockport using a purpose-built two-barrel plant, constructed by award-winning brewer Richard Conway. In 2015 the brewery relocated to larger premises and installed a 10-barrel plant. Four core beers are brewed, along with a number of speciality one-off brews. All the beers are available bottle-conditioned. ◆RAIB

Pale and Interesting (OG 1043, ABV 3.4%)
English bitter with a rich, malty body and a clean, bitter finish.

Stockport Common Beer (OG 1053, ABV 4.9%)
California steam beer with grapefruit and pine flavours and a crisp, clean finish.

Stocky Oatmeal Stout (OG 1057, ABV 5.5%)
Smooth, full-bodied oatmeal stout with notes of coffee and chocolate.

Hoppy Couple IPA (OG 1060, ABV 6.3%)
American-style IPA. Rich copper in colour with a big citrus hop aroma and flavour.

Thomas Guest

See Black Country

John Thompson

📧 Ingleby, Melbourne, Derbyshire, DE73 7HW
☎ (01332) 862469 ⊕ johnthompsoninn.com

⊗ Established by John Thompson in 1977 as an addition to the John Thompson Inn, which he converted from a 15th-century farmhouse in 1968, and is now run by his son Nick. JTS XXX is Derbyshire's longest continuously brewed ale. ‼◆

JTS XXX (OG 1041, ABV 4.1%)

Gold (OG 1045, ABV 4.5%)

Thorley & Sons (NEW)

30 East Street, Ilkeston, Derbyshire, DE7 5JB ☎ 07899 067723 ✉ dylan.thorley1@yahoo.co.uk

Thorley & Sons began brewing commercially in 2015 on a 1.5-barrel plant located in an old coach house at the rear of brewer Dylan Thorley's house.

Pale & Interesting (ABV 4.5%)
Easy-drinking pale ale with a subtle hint of citrus in the taste.

Thornbridge SIBA ◉

Riverside Business Park, Buxton Road, Bakewell, Derbyshire, DE45 1GS
☎ (01629) 815999 ⊕ thornbridgebrewery.co.uk

⊛The first Thornbridge craft beers were produced in 2005 using a 10-barrel brewery, housed in the grounds of Thornbridge Hall. The beers have gained considerable success with over 300 consumer and industry awards being won. A 30-barrel brewery opened in Bakewell 2009. The original site continues to develop new, seasonal and speciality beers. 200 outlets are supplied direct. 12 pubs are managed and owned. ‼ ⌷ ♦ RAIB

Wild Swan (OG 1035, ABV 3.5%) ◈
Extremely pale yet flavoursome and refreshing beer. Plenty of lemony citrus hop flavour, becoming increasingly dry and bitter in the finish and aftertaste.

Brother Rabbit (OG 1035, ABV 4%)
Lemon zest in colour with a clean, hoppy aroma, a resinous finish and some bitterness

Lord Marples (OG 1041, ABV 4%) ◈
Smooth, traditional, easy-drinking bitter. Caramel, malt and coffee flavours fall away to leave a long, bitter finish.

Ashford (OG 1043, ABV 4.2%)
A brown ale with a floral hoppiness, a smooth, malty kick and a delicate coffee finish.

Kipling (OG 1050, ABV 5.2%) ◈
Golden pale bitter with aromas of grapefruit and passion fruit. Intense fruit flavours continue throughout, leading to a long bitter aftertaste.

Jaipur IPA (OG 1055, ABV 5.9%) ◈
Flavoursome IPA packed with citrus hoppiness that's nicely counterbalanced by malt and underlying sweetness and robust fruit flavours.

Saint Petersburg Imperial Russian Stout (OG 1073, ABV 7.4%) ◧ ◈
Good example of an imperial stout. Smooth and easy to drink with raisins, bitter chocolate and hops throughout, leading to a lingering coffee and chocolate aftertaste.

Three B's SIBA ◉

▤ Black Bull, Brokenstone Road, Blackburn, Lancashire, BB3 0LL
☎ (01254) 581381 ⊕ threebsbrewery.co.uk

Robert Bell acquired the Black Bull in 2011 and the brew pub now supplies 50 outlets. A bottling plant has been installed and bottle-conditioned beers will be available in supermarkets. ‼ ♦ RAIB

Bee Thrifty (OG 1036, ABV 3.4%)
A light and refreshing amber-coloured beer.

Stoker's Slake (OG 1038, ABV 3.6%) ◈
Lightly roasted coffee flavours are in the aroma and the initial taste. A well-rounded, dark brown mild with dried fruit flavours in the long finish.

Honey Bee (OG 1039, ABV 3.7%)
A golden honey beer with honey apparent in both aroma and taste.

Bobbin's Bitter (OG 1038, ABV 3.8%)

A golden bitter with warm aromas of nutty grain and a full, fruity flavour with a light, dry finish.

Bee Blonde (OG 1041, ABV 4%)
A distinctive, pale bitter with a light, dry, balance of grain and hops and a delicate finish with citrus fruits.

Black Bull (OG 1042, ABV 4%)
Dark ruby with a red bitter, rich character with a hint of chocolate. A unique beer brewed for consumption at the source.

Weavers Brew (ABV 4%)
A pale blonde beer with a hop flavour.

Fettlers Choice (ABV 4.2%)
An amber-coloured beer with a smooth, light taste.

Tackler's Tipple (OG 1044, ABV 4.3%)
A dark best bitter with full hop flavour, biscuit tones on the tongue and a deep, dry finish.

Black Bull Lager (ABV 4.5%)
A cask lager brewed all year round.

Doff Cocker (OG 1045, ABV 4.5%) ◈
Yellow with a hoppy aroma and initial taste giving way to subtle malt notes and orchard fruit flavours. Crisp, dry finish.

Pinch Noggin (OG 1046, ABV 4.6%)
A dark, strong best bitter with full hop flavour and a long aftertaste.

Knocker Up (OG 1047, ABV 4.8%) ◈
A smooth, rich, creamy porter. The roast flavour is foremost without dominating and is balanced by fruit and hop notes.

Shuttle Ale (OG 1050, ABV 5.2%)
A rustic-coloured traditional strong pale ale.

Three Blind Mice

Unit W10, Black Bank Business Park, Black Bank Road, Little Downham, Cambridgeshire, CB6 2UA
☎ 07912 875825 ✉ blindmice3@btinternet.com

Three Blind Mice began brewing in 2014 using a five-barrel plant, supplying outlets in Cambridgeshire. An ever-changing range of beers is brewed throughout the year. ♦

Table Liquor (ABV 2.8%)
Very dry, light bitter pale ale with a big hop punch.

Faintest Idea (ABV 3.5%)

Lonely Snake (ABV 3.5%)

Corumbo (ABV 4.2%)

Yankee Kangaroo (ABV 4.3%)

Generation Red (ABV 4.5%)
Ruby coloured with subtle roasted malt character, nicely balanced with both fruity and resinous hop flavours.

Pale Ale No 1 (ABV 4.5%)
Well balanced and hoppy with citrus notes.

Black Bank Porter (ABV 4.7%)
A porter with roasted malt, coffee and chocolate, and a bitter finish.

Odds & Sods (ABV 5.2%)

Dirty Goulash (ABV 8.2%)
Rum-infused strong ale, rum flavours balance nicely with the sweet, roasted malt backbone.

Three Castles

Unit 12, Salisbury Road Business Park, Pewsey, Wiltshire, SN9 5PZ
☎ (01672) 564433 ☎ 07725 148671
⊕ threecastlesbrewery.co.uk

Three castles is an independent, family-run brewery which was established in 2006. ‼ 📼 ♦ RAIB

Barbury Castle (OG 1039, ABV 3.9%)
A balanced, easy-drinking pale ale with a hoppy, spicy palate.

Saxon Archer (OG 1040, ABV 4%)

Vale Ale (OG 1043, ABV 4.3%)
Golden-coloured ale with a fruity palate and strong floral aroma.

Corn Dolly (OG 1047, ABV 4.7%)

Three Daggers SIBA 👁

Westbury Road, Edington, Westbury, Wiltshire, BA13 4PG
☎ (01380) 830940 ⊕ threedaggersbrewery.com

⊗ Three Daggers Brewery was established in 2013 using a 2.5-barrel brew plant in a farm shop next to a popular roadside pub. Malt is sourced locally from Warminster Maltings and hops from Charles Faram in Herefordshire. Cask ales are produced for the pub. Bottled beers and take outs are available in the farm shop. ‼ ♦ RAIB

Daggers Blonde (OG 1037, ABV 3.6%)

Daggers Ale (OG 1041, ABV 4.1%)
A refreshingly malty ale with a dry, hoppy finish.

Daggers Edge (OG 1047, ABV 4.7%)
A full-bodied, well-balanced strong bitter.

Three Fiends (NEW) SIBA

Brookfield Farm, 148 Mill Moor Road, Meltham, West Yorkshire, HD9 5LN ☎ 07810 370430
⊕ threefiends.co.uk

The brewery was set up by three friends in 2015 and is based in one of the outbuildings at Brookfield Farm. The current two-barrel plant is in the process of being upgraded. Beers are available around Huddersfield and at CAMRA beer festivals.

Two Face (ABV 4%)
An easy-drinking session ale with floral, citrus and honey-like tones.

Boomer (ABV 4.3%)
Heavily-hopped and malty dark ale.

Dark Side (ABV 5.3%)
A black IPA with a smooth chocolaty start, leading to an increasingly bitter finish.

Little Devil (ABV 5.3%)
An easy-drinking American-style pale ale.

Three Kings SIBA

🮲 14 Prospect Terrace, North Shields, Tyne & Wear, NE30 1DX ☎ 07580 004565
⊕ threekingsbrewery.co.uk

Three Kings started in 2012 using a 2.5-barrel plant, upgrading to a five-barrel one in 2013. A core range of beers is brewed, with previous occasional beers being brewed again on request. House specials are brewed for for Oddfellows in

North Shields, Rockcliffe in Whitley Bay and the Bridge Hotel, Newcastle. ♦

Billy Mill (OG 1040, ABV 4%)

Gallowgate Raw (OG 1045, ABV 4.4%)

Ring of Fire (OG 1048, ABV 4.5%)

Three Legs

7 Burnt House Farm, Udimore Road, Brede, East Sussex, TN31 6BX ☎ 07783 973161
⊕ thethreelegs.co.uk

⊗ Three Legs was started in 2015 by three friends who met studying wine-making and viticulture at university. Initially a nanobrewery, it has expanded to a four-barrel plant, in a converted farm barn. 10 local pubs and two Brighton bottle shops are supplied. Beers are available in cask and bottle-conditioned form from the on-site shop. ‼ 📼 RAIB

Pale (OG 1033, ABV 3.7%)
American hopped, light in body and crisp.

Gold (OG 1034, ABV 3.8%)
English hopped, biscuity session golden ale

Dark (OG 1045, ABV 4%)
Stout style, full bodied with flavours of coffee and chocolate.

Red (OG 1048, ABV 4.2%)
A well-balanced, fruity beer with a lifting bitterness.

Amber (OG 1048, ABV 4.9%)
Malt driven, medium bodied with caramel and toffee flavours.

English IPA (OG 1053, ABV 5.5%)

Three Peaks

Scar Top, Buck Haw Brow, Settle, North Yorkshire, BD24 0DJ
☎ (01729) 822939 ☎ 07795 358932

7 Craven Terrace, Settle, BD24 9DB
⊕ threepeaksbrewery.co.uk

⊗ Formed in 2006, Three Peaks is run by husband and wife team Colin and Susan Ashwell assisted by Andrew Murphy. Four regular beers are brewed on their five-barrel plant with an occasional beer. ♦

Pen-y-Ghent Bitter (OG 1040, ABV 3.8%) 🍂
The malty character of this mid-brown session bitter is balanced by fruit in the aroma and taste. The finish is malty and hoppy.

Ingleborough Gold (OG 1041, ABV 4%) 🍂
This golden coloured best bitter is hoppy throughout with fruit in the aroma and taste and a hoppy bitter finish.

Whernside Pale Ale (OG 1042, ABV 4.2%)

Blea Moor Porter (OG 1045, ABV 4.5%)

Three Shires (NEW) SIBA 👁

Unit 10, Park Boulevard, Worcester, WR2 4GD
☎ 07964 196194 ⊕ threeshiresbrewery.co.uk

Three Shires began brewing in 2014 on a hand-built plant in Worcester. Local outlets are supplied.

Kenelm (OG 1041, ABV 3.8%)
Golden in colour with a smoky aroma and initial sweetness giving way to a malt whiskey flavour

with peat and fruit undertones. Dry hop and peaty finish.

Hafren (OG 1043, ABV 4%) ◆
Copper-coloured bitter with a dry, fruity, caramel aroma, slightly roasted malt flavour with a hint of cucumber, and a dry hop, malt and caramel finish.

Three Sods SIBA 👁

Bethnal Green Working Men's Club, 42 Pollard Row, Bethnal Green, London, E2 6NB ☎ 07544 422236
⏺ threesodsbrewery.com

⊠ Based in a working men's club in East London, Three Sods specialises in small batch beers produced using a range of malts and hops from around the world. Head brewer David Jonsson Buttery is currently part-time but hopes to brew full time.

Session (OG 1044, ABV 4.4%)
Light and hoppy IPA, packed full of fruity notes including grapefruit, with a massive bitter finish.

Red Rocket Rye (OG 1046, ABV 4.6%)
Classic English ale with deep dry flavours and a hint of smoke and light spiciness from the rye.

Mud Puddler Black IPA (OG 1050, ABV 4.9%)
Black IPA with light, hoppy flavours of coffee and mint with a light spiciness.

Belgian Bugger (OG 1051, ABV 5%)
Belgian-inspired beer with a hint of wheat and a massive floral and grassy hop hit.

Three Tuns SIBA 👁

🛏 **Salop Street, Bishop's Castle, Shropshire, SY9 5BN**

16 Market Square, Bishops Castle, SY9 5BW
⏺ threetunsbrewery.co.uk

Brewing on this site started in the 16th century and was licensed in 1642. A small-scale tower brewery from late 19th century survives. Three Tuns was one of only four pub breweries still running in 1970s. ‼ 🍴 ◆ RAIB

Mild (OG 1040, ABV 3.4%)
Tawny-coloured winter beer with burnt and roasted flavours and a rich maltiness.

Rantipole (OG 1036, ABV 3.7%)

1642 Bitter (OG 1042, ABV 3.8%)
A golden ale with a light, nutty maltiness and spicy bitterness.

Solstice (OG 1037, ABV 3.9%)
Pale straw-coloured summer beer. Light malty quality; medium strength, crisp fruity bitterness, with citrus and straw flavours. Smooth mellow presentation.

XXX (OG 1046, ABV 4.3%) ◆
A pale, sweetish bitter with a light hop aftertaste that has a honey finish.

Stout (OG 1048, ABV 4.4%)
Old fashioned-style stout.

Cleric's Cure (OG 1059, ABV 5%)
A light tan coloured ale with a malty sweetness. Strong and spicy with a floral bitterness.

Steampunk (OG 1065, ABV 6.5%)
A rich dark and fiery barley wine with flavours of liquorice, ginger, caramel and roasted malts lasting through into strong bitter finish.

XXXXXXX Strong Ale (OG 1095, ABV 9.5%)

Thurstons (Horsell) SIBA 👁

The Courtyard, 102c High Street, Horsell, Surrey, GU21 4ST
☎ (01483) 729555 ☎ 07789 936784
⏺ thurstonsbrewery.co.uk

⊠ Originally based in the Crown, Horsell, Thurstons moved next door in 2014 when the brewery upgraded to a 4.5-barrel plant. The core beer range is supplemented by seasonal and occasional brews. The brewery supplies cask beers to pubs across Surrey and bottles to local stores and restaurants. ◆ RAIB

Horsell Best (OG 1040, ABV 3.8%) ◆
Traditional, well balanced bitter, initially malty with strong caramel flavours throughout and balancing bitterness, becoming drier in the finish.

Horsell Gold (OG 1040, ABV 3.8%) ◆
Light fruit and slightly nutty aroma, lead to some bitterness and malt, which soon fades into a light bitter finish.

Stedmans Ale (OG 1042, ABV 4.1%) ◆
Thurston's original beer, golden in colour with citrus and caramel aroma, and malt and hops more pronounced in the taste.

Milk Stout (OG 1055, ABV 4.5%) ◆
Smooth, sweet stout, with a chocolaty flavour. A sweet malty flavour with a pleasant sharpness and a slightly dry finish.

Thwaites IFBB 👁

Star Brewery, PO Box 50, Blackburn, Lancashire, BB1 5BU
☎ (01254) 686868 ⏺ danielthwaites.com

☺In 2015, Thwaites sold its brewing division to Marston's for £25.1 million. Wainwright and Lancaster Bomber, while still bearing the Thwaites logo, are now owned and brewed by Marston's in Wolverhampton. Marston's also bought Thwaites's free trade business, its distribution depot and dray fleet. The company's Original Bitter and the Occasional Range of beers are also brewed by Marston's. The Blackburn brewery, founded in 1807, closed in 2014 with production of 100,000 barrels a year transferred to Marston's Wolverhampton plant. Thwaites' micro-brewery is still operational in Blackburn brewing Thwaites Best Cask (TBC), Nutty Black and the Signature Range plus other seasonal and trial cask brews. There are plans to build a new brewery at Mellor Brook. Around 300 pubs are owned with most selling real ale. See Banks's. ‼ ◆ RAIB

Nutty Black (OG 1036, ABV 3.3%)
Traditional, malty, dark mild with caramel notes and a slightly bitter finish.

Thwaites Best Cask (OG 1038, ABV 3.8%)
Well-balanced, traditional, amber bitter.

Ticketybrew SIBA 👁

16 Waterloo Court, Stalybridge, SK15 2AU ☎ 07970 093665 ⏺ ticketybrew.co.uk

☺Ticketybrew opened in 2013 using a five-barrel plant, producing cask and bottle-conditioned beers brewed using a Belgian yeast strain. RAIB V

Jasmin Green Tea (OG 1038, ABV 3.8%)
A light and refreshing ale brewed with jasmine phoenix pearls green tea and lemon peel. Hop bitterness is complemented by fresh lemon rind.

Munchner (ABV 4.3%)
Mixing malty caramel sweetness with hops; a traditional beer is given a new lease of life with the spicy flavours of Belgian yeast.

**Rose and Ginger Wheat Beer
(OG 1044, ABV 4.5%)**
A beer with the unique aroma of roses, balanced by a subtle kick of fresh ginger.

Pale Ale (OG 1050, ABV 5.3%)
Hops are balanced with a sweetness provided by Belgian yeast.

Blonde (OG 1047, ABV 5.6%)
A blonde ale with soft floral and fruit on the nose, and a spicy, fruity and yeasty flavour.

Tigertops

**22 Oakes Street, Flanshaw, Wakefield, West Yorkshire, WF2 9LN
☎ (01229) 716238 ☎ 07951 812986
✉ tigertopsbrewery@hotmail.com**

☺Tigertops was established in 1995 by Stuart Johnson and his wife Lynda who, as well as owning the brewery, run the Foxfield brewpub in Cumbria (qv). The brewery is run on their behalf by Barry Smith supplying five regular outlets. Seasonal and experimental beers are also brewed. ♦

Tiley's

**⬛ Salutation Inn, Ham, Gloucestershire, GL13 9QH
☎ (01453) 810284 ⊕ the-sally-at-ham.com**

⊗ This 2.5-barrel microbrewery was established in an outbuilding of the award-winning Salutation Inn in 2015. Brewery open days or 'Brew Sessions' regularly take place, where invited local brewers tweak their own brews slightly for sale in the pub. Further beers are planned.

Pale Ale (OG 1042, ABV 4.2%)
Pale and hoppy.

Porter (OG 1046, ABV 4.6%)
A rich and chocolaty coffee porter.

Best Bitter (OG 1048, ABV 4.8%)
A strong premium bitter.

Tillingbourne SIBA

**Old Scotland Farm, Staple Lane, Shere, Surrey, GU5 9TE
☎ (01483) 222228 ⊕ tillybeer.co.uk**

⊗ Tillingbourne began in 2011 on a farm site previously used by Surrey Hills Brewery using its old 17-barrel plant. Around 25 local outlets are supplied. ‼⬛♦

The Source (OG 1033, ABV 3.3%) ◈
Light and crisp golden ale with strong grapefruit flavours. Packed full of citra hops and drinking well above its strength.

Black Troll (OG 1035, ABV 3.7%) ◈
A black bitter in which initial roast notes are eventually overpowered by citrus hop through to the finish.

Bouncing Bomb (ABV 3.8%)

AONB (OG 1036, ABV 4%) ◈
Golden ale in which citrus hop dominates throughout. Some balancing malt in the aroma and taste, however.

Falls Gold (OG 1037, ABV 4.2%) ◈
While hops dominate, balancing malt is evident throughout. Hints of grapefruit in the aroma and taste lead to a dry finish.

Hop Troll (OG 1045, ABV 4.8%) ◈
Golden ale with big hop flavours together with peach and apricot. Sweet, fruity taste leads to a floral bitter finish.

Summit (ABV 6%)

Time and Tide

Statenborough Farm, Felderland Lane, Eastry, Kent, CT14 0BX ☎ 07739 868256

Office: 10 Herschell Road, East Walmer, Deal, Kent, CT14 7SQ ⊕ timeandtidebrewing.co.uk

Time and Tide began brewing in 2013 using spare capacity at Ripple Steam Brewery (qv). In 2015 it obtained its own 20-barrel brewhouse in Eastry. Production is in KeyKeg or cans. ♦

Tindall

Toad Lane, Seething, Norfolk, NR35 2EQ

Tindall Ales began brewing in 1998. It was originally based in Ditchingham but moved to its current location towards the end of 2001. ♦

Best Bitter (OG 1037, ABV 3.7%)

Fuggled Up (OG 1037, ABV 3.7%)

Mild (OG 1037, ABV 3.7%)

Liberator (OG 1038, ABV 3.8%)

Alltime (OG 1040, ABV 4%)

Mundham Mild (OG 1040, ABV 4%)

Ditchingham Dam (OG 1042, ABV 4.2%)

Seething Pint (OG 1043, ABV 4.3%)

Norwich Dragon (OG 1046, ABV 4.6%)

Honeydo (OG 1050, ABV 5%)

Tinpot

**⬛ Allanwater Brewhouse, Queens Lane, Bridge of Allan, Stirlingshire, FK9 4NY
☎ (01786) 834555 ☎ 07831 224242
⊕ bridgeofallan.co.uk**

☺Tinpot opened in 2009 using a one-barrel plant designed to brew speciality beers, and started supplying CAMRA beer festivals in 2010. In 2014 the brewery capacity was increased to a 1.5-barrel plant. The beer range varies depending on season and demand and is expanding every year.
‼⬛♦RAIB

Gold Pot 70/- (OG 1042, ABV 3.9%)

Choc Pot 80/- (OG 1046, ABV 4.5%)

Pot Black (OG 1052, ABV 5%)

Procrastination (OG 1060, ABV 6%)
A hoppy IPA brewed by Stirling University Craft Beer Society.

Tinshed

Justice Close Farm, Tilbrook Road, Kimbolton, Cambridgeshire, PE28 0JW ☎ 07585 551499
⊕ tinshedbrewery.com

Tinshed Brewery was established in 2014 using a home-made four-barrel set-up. The brewery is run by three close friends from the village of Kimbolton and produces four core beers and seasonal specials, available in cask and bottles. Local pubs, clubs, beer festivals and shops are supplied. Beer in bottles and cask is also availabe direct from the brewery. ‼ ♦ RAIB

Skinny Pig (OG 1039, ABV 3.8%)
Burnished gold in colour with a light hoppy aroma, malt balances with hop, producing a complex spiced flavour, complemented by a sweet, long, dry finish.

Golden Weasel (OG 1040, ABV 4%)
A full-flavoured refreshing light bitter with a clean, fresh finish.

Old Smokey (OG 1041, ABV 4.1%)
A copper-coloured beer with an initial kiss of malt, followed by a classic hop aroma and a long dry nutty finish.

Black Stoat (OG 1045, ABV 4.8%)
Deep black stout full of roast malts. It is slightly bitter, allowing the malts to dominate the pallet with a short dry finish.

Tintagel SIBA

Condolden Farm, Tintagel, Cornwall, PL34 0HJ
☎ (01840) 213371 ⊕ tintagelbrewery.co.uk

⊠ This 7.5-barrel brewery was established in 2009 in a redundant milking parlour on the highest farm in Cornwall, and some 80 outlets are now supplied direct. ☛ ♦ RAIB

Castle Gold (OG 1038, ABV 3.8%) ◆
Heavily hopped golden ale. Citrus hops and noticeable malt taste. Bitterness throughout with citrus and stone fruits. Lingering dry finish.

Cornwall's Pride (OG 1040, ABV 4%) ◆
Tawny best bitter with peaty malt aroma. Nutty malt then hop bitterness with complex flavours. Bitterness and rising dry finish.

Arthur's Ale (OG 1044, ABV 4.4%) ⌐ ◆
Copper best bitter with malt aroma. Best bitter and golden ale combined. Malt, stone fruit sweetness and citrus hop bitterness.

Poldark Ale (OG 1045.8, ABV 4.5%) ◆
Tawny strong mild. Assertive malty flavour with light caramel, roast notes and sweetness balanced by fruity hop bitterness. Caramel malt finish.

Harbour Special (OG 1048.9, ABV 4.8%) ◆
Brown strong bitter with ripe fruity, malty aroma. Rich nutty malt, stone fruits and esters taste, finishing bitter and dry.

Merlins Muddle (OG 1052, ABV 5.2%) ◆
Tawny old ale with assertive sweetness but faint bitterness. Malt dominates aroma and taste with treacle, citrus and summer fruits.

Tiny Rebel SIBA

Unit 12 & 12A, Maes Glas Industrial Estate, Greenwich Road, Newport, NP20 2NN

☎ (01633) 547378 ☎ 07980 798268
⊕ tinyrebel.co.uk

☺ Tiny Rebel opened in 2012. It operates on a 12-barrel brew plant consisting of 10 fermentation and two conditioning tanks. Beers are available in cask, bottle and keg. Bottling is done by a contractor. 'Cwtch' which is Welsh for 'cuddle' was awarded CAMRA's Champion Beer of Britain 2015. There are two tied houses in Cardiff and in Newport. ☛♦

Cereal Killer (OG 1033, ABV 3%)
Golden, light, hoppy beer, with rolled oats and a trio of hops.

One Inch Punch (OG 1039, ABV 3.9%)
Golden American-style session beer with big tropical hits of flavours.

Flux (OG 1039, ABV 4%)

Hank (OG 1038, ABV 4%) ▮

Morning Glory (OG 1044, ABV 4%)
A low ABV stout described as breakfast in a glass: milk, dark chocolate, coffee and rolled oats, making a dark yet light-bodied beer.

Fubar (OG 1041, ABV 4.4%) ⌐
Floral hoppy flavours up front, leading into a dry spicy bitterness on the back.

Loki (OG 1044, ABV 4.5%) ▮
A black IPA. Tropical and resinous aromas dominate with crisp-like citrus flavours and moderate bitterness.

Loki Lite (OG 1044, ABV 4.5%)
An IPA with citrus aromas and tropical fruit punch flavours. It's moderate in bitterness and refreshing on the palate.

XLPA (OG 1042, ABV 4.5%)

Billabong (OG 1045, ABV 4.6%)

Cwtch (OG 1045, ABV 4.6%) ⌐ ▮
Welsh red ale with a fresh hit of hops that complements the caramel flavours of the malts.

The Full Nelson (OG 1046, ABV 4.8%)

Dirty Stopout (OG 1052, ABV 5%)
Complex smoked oak stout packed with hops to provide an equalising bitterness that adds another layer of depth.

Bonsai (OG 1062, ABV 6.5%)

Hadouken (OG 1069, ABV 7.4%) ⌐ ▮

Tipples

Unit 3 The Mill, Wood Green, Salhouse, Norfolk, NR13 6NY
☎ (01603) 721310 ⊕ tipplesbrewery.com

⊠ Tipples was established in 2004 on a six-barrel brew plant. In addition to a full range of cask ales, an extensive range of bottled beers is produced, which can be found in some farmers markets and supermarkets in Norfolk. ♦ RAIB

Hanged Monk (OG 1038, ABV 3.8%) ◆
Strong roast and malt notes dominate the aroma and taste. A grainy mouthfeel with caramel and a growing vinous finish.

Sundown (OG 1040, ABV 3.9%) ◆
Berries and malt introduce this smooth creamy bitter. Bitterness gives depth to the fruity malt core as it slowly sweetens.

Redhead (OG 1042, ABV 4.2%) ◗
Malt and hops in both nose and palate. Toffee in the initial taste gives way to an increasing bitterness.

Brewers Progress (OG 1046, ABV 4.6%) ◗
Solid and malty with strong caramel and vanilla support. Smooth and creamy with added depth by a bitter blackcurrant fruitiness.

Moonrocket (OG 1050, ABV 5%) ◗
A complex golden brew. Malt, hop, bitterness and a fruity sweetness swirl round in an ever-changing kaleidoscope of flavours.

Tír Dhá Ghlas

▤ Cullins Yard, 11 Cambridge Road, Dover, Kent, CT17 9BY
☎ (01304) 211666 ⊕ cullinsyard.co.uk

⊠ Brewing began in 2012 using a two-barrel plant. Beers only available in Cullins Yard bar/restaurant and occasionally at the nearby Royal Cinque Ports Yacht Club, particularly when they are holding beer festivals.

Tirril SIBA

Red House, Long Marton, Cumbria, CA16 6BN
☎ (01768) 361846 ⊕ tirrilbrewery.co.uk

☺Established in 1999, Tirril Brewery has twice outgrown its premises. Capacity has grown to 60 barrels. It has over 170 outlets, 100 of which regularly stock the beer. One pub is owned. Contract brewing is also carried out for Bitter End Brewery. ‼◆

Original Bitter (OG 1038.5, ABV 3.8%)
Lightly-hopped, golden brown session beer.

Ullswater Blonde (OG 1038.5, ABV 3.8%)
A golden, easy-drinking session beer.

Langdale Light Ale (ABV 3.9%)
A traditional, mildly-hopped ale.

Old Faithful (OG 1040, ABV 4%) ◗
Initially bitter, gold-coloured ale with an astringent finish.

1823 (OG 1041, ABV 4.1%)
A full-bodied session bitter with a gentle bitterness.

Academy Ale (OG 1041.5, ABV 4.2%)
A dark, full-bodied, traditional rich and malty ale.

Borrowdale Bitter (OG 1041.5, ABV 4.2%)
An amber ale with a nice bite.

Windermere IPA (ABV 4.3%)
A pale and hoppy IPA using New World hops.

Red Barn Ale (OG 1043, ABV 4.4%)
A ruby red ale with a strong hop finish.

Titan

c/o Golden Eagle, 6 St Katherine's Court (off Agard Street), Derby, DE22 3AY
☎ (01332) 298465 ☎ 07749 556837
⊕ titanbrewery.co.uk

⊠ Set-up by former Mr Grundy's brewers in 2014. A pub has been acquired, the Golden Eagle, Derby. The brewery is in the process of obtaining a commercial unit but at present the beers are brewed using spare capacity at Mr Grundy's Brewery (qv).

Bitter (OG 1036.8, ABV 3.8%)
Dark, malty and smooth.

Pale (OG 1038.7, ABV 4%)
Light, fruity and moreish.

Gold (OG 1043.5, ABV 4.5%)

Ruby (OG 1044.6, ABV 4.6%)

Stout (OG 1066, ABV 4.8%)
Dark, oaty and caramel.

IPA (OG 1048.5, ABV 5%)
Golden, full-flavoured and hoppy.

Titanic SIBA ◉

Callender Place, Burslem, Stoke-on-Trent, Staffordshire, ST6 1JL
☎ (01782) 823447 ⊕ titanicbrewery.co.uk

☺Founded in 1985 and named after Captain Smith, a Potteries man and the captain of the Titanic. One of the earliest microbreweries, Titanic has grown into a local brewer with a small, constantly expanding tied pub estate and supplies free trade customers across the Midlands and the North-west. 2014 saw a major investment in the brewery and brewhouse creating a brewery shop and sample room. ‼◆RAIB

Mild (OG 1036, ABV 3.5%) ◗
Fresh fruity hop aroma leads to a caramel start then a rush of bitter hoppiness ending with a lingering dry finish.

Steerage (OG 1039.5, ABV 3.8%) ◗
Pale yellow bitter. Flavours start with hops and fruit but become zesty and refreshing in this light session beer with a long, dry finish.

Lifeboat (OG 1040, ABV 4%) ◗
Dark brown with fruit, malt and caramel aromas. Sweet start, malty and caramel middle with hoppiness developing into a fruity and dry lingering finish.

Anchor Bitter (OG 1042, ABV 4.1%) ◗
Amber beer with a spicy hint to the fruity start that says go to the rush of hops for the dry bitter finish.

Iceberg (OG 1042, ABV 4.1%) ◗
Yellow gold sparkling wheat beer with a flowery start leading to a great hop crescendo.

Cherry Dark (OG 1045, ABV 4.4%)

Cappuccino Stout (OG 1046, ABV 4.5%)

Chocolate and Vanilla Stout (OG 1047, ABV 4.5%) ◗
Chocoholic paradise with real coffee and vanilla support. Cocoa, sherry and almonds lend depth to this creamy, drinkable 'Heaven in a glass' stout.

Stout (OG 1046, ABV 4.5%) ▥ ◗
Roasty, toasty with tobacco, autumn bonfires, chocolate and hints of liquorice; perfectly balanced with a bitter, dry finish reminiscent of real coffee.

White Star (OG 1048, ABV 4.5%) ◗
Hints of cinnamon apple pie are found before the hops take over to give a bitter edge to this well balanced refreshing fruity beer.

Plum Porter (OG 1051, ABV 4.9%) ▭ ▥ ◗
Dark brown with a powerful fruity aroma. A sweet plum fruitiness gives way to a gentle bitter finish.

Captain Smith's Strong Ale
(OG 1054, ABV 5.2%) ◆
Red brown and full bodied, lots of malt and roast
with a hint of honey but a strong bittersweet finish.

Toll End

⊟ c/o Waggon and Horses, 131 Toll End Road, Tipton,
West Midlands, DY4 0ET ☎ 07903 725574

The four-barrel brewery opened in 2004. With the
exception of Phoebe's Ale, named after the
brewer's daughter, all brews commemorate local
landmarks, events and people. ‼ RAIB

William Perry (OG 1043, ABV 4.3%)

Black Bridge (OG 1044, ABV 4.4%)

Phoebe's Ale/PA (OG 1047, ABV 4.7%)

Power Station (OG 1049, ABV 4.9%)
Cask-conditioned lager.

Retribution (OG 1052, ABV 5.2%)
Traditional pale ale with a bitter hoppy taste.

Charlie Blackout Stout (OG 1058, ABV 5.4%)

Tollgate SIBA

Unit 1, Southwood House Farm, Staunton Lane, Calke,
Leicestershire, LE65 1RG
☎ (01283) 229194 ⊕ tollgatebrewery.com

⊠ This six-barrel brewery was founded in 2005 on
the site of the old Brunt & Bucknall Brewery in
Woodville, but relocated to new premises on the
National Trust's Calke Park estate in 2012. Around
150 outlets are supplied direct. Bottle-conditioned
beer is suitable for vegans and constitutes nearly
30% of production. ‼ ◆ RAIB V

California Steam (OG 1041, ABV 4.2%)
Pale golden beer brewed in the style of a West
Coast beer.

Tollgate Bitter (OG 1041, ABV 4.3%)
A smooth, easy-drinking bitter.

Darkwood Bitter (OG 1042, ABV 4.4%)
A traditional dark amber bitter.

Ashby Pale (OG 1043, ABV 4.5%)
A light, refreshing beer with a citrus finish.

Red Star IPA (OG 1043, ABV 4.5%)
A classic, hoppy IPA.

Billy's Best Bitter (OG 1044, ABV 4.6%)
Dark amber-coloured best bitter.

Red McAdy (OG 1043, ABV 5%)
Whisky-conditioned northern ale.

Tolly Cobbold

See Greene King

Tom Herrick's

See under H

Tombstone SIBA

6 George Street, Great Yarmouth, Norfolk, NR30 1HR
☎ 07584 504444 ⊕ tombstonebrewery.co.uk

⊠ Tombstone was established in 2013 and is run
by former home brewer Paul Hodgson. The original

brewery backed onto the town cemetery, inspiring
the name. The brewery has now relocated to the
rear of its brewery tap, the Tombstone Saloon.
Around 30 outlets are supplied in and around
Yarmouth and several in Norwich. All the beers
have a Wild West theme.

Ale (OG 1038, ABV 3.7%)
A light golden ale with subtle citrus tones of
oranges and lemons.

Arizona (OG 1040, ABV 3.9%) ◆
Gentle butterscotch airs. Strong bitter backbone
with hints of lemon and malt. Increasingly dry
finish.

Texas Jack (OG 1040, ABV 4%) ◆
Toffee apple and vanilla aroma. Caramel leads the
smooth complex mix of flavours. A bittersweet
fruitiness continues to the end.

Regulators (OG 1040, ABV 4.1%)
A golden hoppy ale with a bitter, dry finish.

Gunslinger (OG 1044, ABV 4.3%)
Golden ale with a caramel, nutty finish.

Lone Rider (OG 1044, ABV 4.3%)
A hoppy deep ruby ale.

Stagecoach (OG 1044, ABV 4.4%)
Smooth dark and malty ale, with a hit of liquorice

Cherokee (OG 1045, ABV 4.5%)
Amber-coloured with fruity overtones and aroma.

Big Nose Kate (OG 1054, ABV 5.3%)
A ruby-coloured ale. Malty and fruity with a subtle
passion fruit taste.

6 Shooter (ABV 6.6%)
Floral beer with fresh orchard fruits and citrus
undertones.

Tomos & Lilford

Unit 14, Heritage Business Park, Wick Road, Llantwit
Major, CF61 1YU
☎ (01446) 796905 ☎ 07779 132647

Office: 117 Boverton Road, Llantwit Major, CF61 1YA
✉ tomos.lilford@gmail.com

⊠ Tomos & Lilford was launched in 2013 by keen,
experimental home brewers Rolant Tomos and
brothers Rob and James Lilford. The brewery
supplies pubs and clubs across the Vale of
Glamorgan and further afield. All point of sale
material is bilingual. ◆

Cob (OG 1040, ABV 4%)
A malty session beer with creamy, nutty notes.

Triple Hop (OG 1040, ABV 4%)
American-style session bitter.

Personal Best (ABV 4.5%)
Malty session beer with creamy, nutty notes.

Gaucho (OG 1050, ABV 5%)
An IPA with a long smooth finish, based on an old
recipe, brewed using wheat and a South American
herb tea.

Rosemary Ale (ABV 5%)
Very pale, refreshing ale, bursting with the flavours
of honey and rosemary.

Hay (OG 1052, ABV 5.2%)
An English-style IPA with added hay for sweetness
and aroma.

Tonbridge SIBA

Unit 19, Branbridges Industrial Estate, East Peckham, Kent, TN12 5HF
☎ (01622) 871239 ⊕ tonbridgebrewery.co.uk

⊗ Tonbridge Brewery was launched in 2010 using a four-barrel plant, expanding in 2013 to a 12-barrel plant. It is owned and run jointly by Paul Bournazian and Mark Gardner and produces cask conditioned ales using predominantly Kent-grown hops. The full range of ales is also available in five-litre mini casks. Pubs and shops are supplied throughout Kent and also parts of Surrey, Sussex, Essex and South-east London. ‼

Golden Rule (OG 1037, ABV 3.5%)
Hoppy golden ale with a light, crisp body and delicate floral aroma.

Traditional Ale (OG 1038, ABV 3.6%)
Easy drinking and refreshing ale with a light fruity hop taste and aroma.

Coppernob (OG 1039.5, ABV 3.8%)
A fairly dry, rich, copper-coloured ale with a robust fruity flavour.

Alsace Gold (OG 1041.5, ABV 4%)
Single hopped golden ale. A light caramel maltiness is balanced with a delicate floral hoppiness.

Rustic (OG 1041.5, ABV 4%)
Deep bronze-coloured, rich-tasting country ale. The hops give a delicate spicy taste and aroma.

Weald Amber (OG 1041, ABV 4%)
Medium dry amber-coloured ale with a stone fruit/marmalade finish.

Blonde Ambition (OG 1043.5, ABV 4.2%)
Crisp, refreshing, fully flavoured blonde ale with spicy and citrus notes.

Ebony Moon (OG 1044, ABV 4.2%)
A rich porter with a pronounced maltiness balanced with a light bitterness.

Old Chestnut (OG 1045, ABV 4.4%)
Full-bodied, chestnut-coloured ale with a malty base and a berry/honey finish.

Union Pale (OG 1047, ABV 4.7%)
An American-style premium pale ale with rich malt flavours balanced by citrus and tropical fruit aromas.

Toolmakers SIBA

6-8 Botsford Street, Sheffield, South Yorkshire, S3 9PF
☎ 07956 235332 ⊕ toolmakersbrewery.com

Toolmakers is a family-run brewery established in 2013 in an old tool-making factory. Beers are brewed on a five-barrel plant and are available in local pubs as well as at the adjacent Forest pub which is owned by the brewery. ‼

Lynch Pin (OG 1040, ABV 4%)
A slightly darker best bitter with caramel undertones.

G Philips Driver (OG 1042, ABV 4.2%)

Sonic Screwdriver (OG 1042, ABV 4.2%)
A light beer with floral aromas and a citrus taste.

Bottom Filter (OG 1043, ABV 4.3%)

Fine Finish (OG 1043, ABV 4.3%)
A nicely-balanced blonde ale with lots of body and a good hoppy flavour.

Pin Hammer (OG 1043, ABV 4.3%)
A nicely-balanced traditional beer with a good soft finish.

Toffee Hammer (OG 1043, ABV 4.3%)
Well-balanced beer with caramel hints of chocolate and liquorice.

Black Edge (OG 1052, ABV 5.2%)
A dark chocolate, flavoursome beer.

Top Out SIBA

Unit 3, 6b Dryden Road, Loanhead, EH20 9LZ
☎ (0131) 440 0270 ☎ 07742 234970
⊕ topoutbrewery.com

Brewing began in 2013 using a six-barrel plant. Initially focusing on mostly bottle-conditioned output, the brewery has expanded into brewing cask beer for the on-trade. The beer range is currently being developed and additional fermentation capacity is being installed. Top Out is a host to cuckoo brewery Black Metal and also contract brews for Secret Herb Garden. ♦ RAIB

Staple (OG 1037, ABV 4%)

Smoked Porter (OG 1060, ABV 5.6%)

The Cone (OG 1058, ABV 6.8%)

Top-Notch

Haywards Heath, West Sussex, RH16 1UQ ☎ 07963 829368 ⊕ topnotchbrewing.co.uk

The one-barrel brewery is situated in a converted residential outbuilding in Haywards Heath. RAIB

Hop Festival (OG 1038, ABV 3.9%)
A light and refreshing ale with a hoppy citrus flavour and floral aroma.

Royal Fanfare (OG 1046, ABV 4.6%)
Medium-bodied with a subtly sweet malt taste and floral, gently spiced hop flavours and aromas.

Flare-Path (OG 1053, ABV 5.5%)
Toasted caramel and malty sweetness balanced with a smooth grapefruit bitterness, tropical fruitiness and citrus aroma.

#BONZER (OG 1055, ABV 5.9%)
A dark IPA. Strong, roasty bittering with a bold tropical fruit flavour and citrus hit.

Topsham SIBA

Globe Hotel, Fore Street, Topsham, Devon, EX3 0DP
☎ (01392) 874818 ⊕ topsham-ales.co.uk

⊗ Topsham Ales has operated since 2010 in premises within the Globe Hotel. It is run solely by volunteers, being one of only a handful of co-operatively owned breweries in the UK. Brewing takes place once a fortnight and also some bottling. The beer is sold locally. ‼

Bitter (OG 1036, ABV 3.7%)
A deep amber bitter with toffee and floral aroma and a light malt and caramel taste, with lingering hoppy notes.

Torrside (NEW)

New Mills Marina, Hibbert Street, New Mills, Derbyshire, SK22 3JJ ☎ 07539 149175
⊕ torrside.co.uk

Torrside was established by three home-brewing friends in 2015, using a ten-barrel commercial plant in a warehouse at the refurbished New Mills marina. 30-40 outlets are supplied from Sheffield to Manchester via High Peak. All beers are unfined. ■◆V

Euro-Hop (ABV 4.5%)

West Of The Sun (ABV 4.5%)

I'm Spartacus (ABV 6%)

Totally Brewed SIBA ◉

Units 8 & 9, Meadow Lane Fruit and Veg Market, Clarke Road, Nottingham, NG2 3JJ ☎ **07702 800639**
⊕ **totallybrewed.com**

☺Totally Brewed began brewing in 2014 using a seven-barrel plant previously used at White Dog Brewery. A diverse range of hop-forward beers are produced including seasonal and one-off brews. ◆

Slap in the Face (OG 1040, ABV 4%) ◈
Golden-coloured ale with citrus fruit hop aroma and taste with a dry bitter finish.

Crazy Like A Fox (OG 1045, ABV 4.5%) ◈
Copper-coloured malty best bitter with a caramel aroma and a gentle bitter finish.

Papa Jangle's Voodoo Stout (OG 1046, ABV 4.5%) ◈
Full bodied dark stout oozing complex malt tastes throughout.

Punch in the Face (OG 1047, ABV 4.8%) ◈
Golden coloured ale, assertive hop aroma leading to grapefruit and malt taste with a hoppy bitter finish.

Four Hopmen of the Apocalypse (OG 1047, ABV 5.2%) ◈
Immense big hopped fruity golden ale, moderate bitterness with a lasting hoppy finish.

Captain Hopbeard (OG 1050, ABV 5.5%) ◈
Amber-coloured ale with citrus hops aplenty with a strong bitter finish.

Totem

11 Cleaveland Rise, Ogwell, Newton Abbot, Devon, TQ12 6FF
☎ **(01626) 330358** ✉ **totembrewing@gmail.com**
No real ale.

Totnes

☰ **59a High Street, Totnes, Devon, TQ9 5PB**
☎ **(01803) 849290** ☎ **07974 828971**
✉ **richard.kidd@idnet.net.uk**

The brewery is situated at the rear of a bistro/bar in Totnes. It has a portfolio of three main ales plus additional specials.

Ink (OG 1050, ABV 5.2%)
A chocolate malted porter with burnt toffee notes.

Spanner Hand (OG 1052, ABV 5.2%)
A sweet and strong English pale ale.

Ziggy's Chin (OG 1052, ABV 5.3%)
A bitter rye pale ale, well-hopped with New Zealand hops.

Towcester Mill SIBA

The Mill, Chantry Lane, Towcester, Northamptonshire, NN12 6AD
☎ **(01327) 437060** ☎ **07812 366369**
⊕ **towcestermillbrewery.co.uk**

⊠ A five-barrel brew plant situated at the Old Mill in Towcester, brewing a range of beers. There is a brewery tap and shop on site. ‼■◆

Crooked Hooker (OG 1038, ABV 3.8%)
Amber session ale with a satisfying bitter finish.

Mill Race (OG 1040, ABV 3.9%)
Blonde beer with a herbal and grapefruit finish.

Bell Ringer (OG 1044, ABV 4.4%)
Golden ale with subtle malt tones, and orange and citrus notes from the hops.

Black Fire (OG 1050, ABV 5.2%)
Dark ale with dark fruit aromas.

Tower SIBA

Old Water Tower, Walsitch Maltings, Glensyl Way, Burton upon Trent, Staffordshire, DE14 1PZ
☎ **(01283) 562888** ⊕ **towerbrewery.co.uk**

☺Tower was established in 2001 by John Mills, formerly a brewer at Burton Bridge, in a converted derelict water tower of Thomas Salt's Brewery. The conversion was given a Civic Society award for the restoration of a historic building in 2001. Tower has 20 regular outlets. ‼■◆

Thomas Salt's Burton Ale (OG 1035, ABV 3.5%)

Bitter (OG 1042, ABV 4.2%) ◈
Gold coloured with a malty, caramel and hoppy aroma. A full hop and fruit taste with the fruit lingering. A bitter and astringent finish.

Gone for a Burton (OG 1046, ABV 4.6%)

Imperial Pale Ale (OG 1050, ABV 5%)

Towles' SIBA

Unit 11, Circuit 32, Easton Road, Easton, Bristol, BS5 0DB
☎ **(0117) 321 3188** ⊕ **towlesfineales.co.uk**

⊠ Towles' is a 10-barrel brewery built in the tower style and run by Andrew and Anna Towle. They purchased Berrow Brewery in 2011 and brewing commenced on the site in Easton in 2012. The Berrow beers will continue to be brewed, along with their own beers. The brewery includes a shop and tasting room. ‼■◆RAIB

Old Smiler (OG 1041, ABV 4.1%) ◈
Slight aroma of malt. Taste is malty with a little pale fruit. Malty aftertaste.

Berrow Copper Leaf (OG 1042, ABV 4.2%) ◈
A beer with a malty aroma and taste. Some dark fruit. Malty aftertaste.

Ma Beese's Chocolate Stout (OG 1065, ABV 6.9%)

Town Mill

See Lyme Regis

Townes

☰ **Speedwell Inn, Lowgates, Staveley, Chesterfield, Derbyshire, S43 3TT**

☎ (01246) 472252

Townes Brewery, which started in 1994, has been situated in the rear of the Speedwell Inn at Staveley since 1997. After the retirement of brewer Alan Wood in 2013, Lawrie and Nicoleta Evans have continued brewing to the same recipes on the five-barrel plant. ◆

Speedwell Bitter (OG 1039, ABV 3.9%) 🍺
Straw-coloured session bitter with little aroma. Initially quite sweet leading to a bitterness developing in the long, slightly astringent aftertaste.

Staveley Cross (OG 1043, ABV 4.3%) 🍺
Amber gold best bitter with a faint banana aroma. Hoppy with bitterness present throughout, culminating in a short, dry, slightly astringent aftertaste.

Pynot Porter (OG 1045, ABV 4.5%) 🍺
Red-brown porter with a faint malt and roast coffee aroma. Roast malt flavours combine with vine fruit, becoming increasingly bitter towards the finish.

Double Bagger (OG 1049, ABV 5%)

Townhouse

Units 1-4, Townhouse Studios, Townhouse Farm, Alsager Road, Audley, Staffordshire, ST7 8JQ ☎ **07976 209437** ✉ **j.nixon2@btinternet.com**

Townhouse was set up in 2002 with a 2.5-barrel plant. In 2004 the brewery scaled up to five barrels. Demand is growing rapidly and in 2006 two additional fermenting vessels were added. Bottling is planned. ◆

Enigma (OG 1035, ABV 3.5%)

Styrian Pale (OG 1035, ABV 3.5%)

Rye Pale Ale (OG 1035, ABV 3.6%)

Flowerdew (OG 1039, ABV 4%) 🍺
Golden with a wonderful floral aroma. Fabulous flavour of flowery hops delivering a crisp hoppy bite and presenting a lingering taste of flowery citrus waves.

Meridian Mild (OG 1039, ABV 4%)

Barney's Stout (OG 1043, ABV 4.5%) 🍺
Roast chocolate and toffee nose atop this black stout. Sweet start becoming bitter at the end, with velvety roast throughout.

Armstrong Ale (OG 1045, ABV 4.8%)
A rich, fruity ruby red beer with a hoppy, dry finish.

Gladstone Strong Ale (OG 1048, ABV 5%)

Track

5 Sheffield Street, Manchester, M1 2ND
☎ **(0161) 273 4832** ☎ **07725 692096**
⊕ **trackbrewing.co**

Track Brewing Co is a microbrewery based in the heart of Manchester. Brewing began in 2014 using a nine-barrel plant plant. A varied range of beers is produced. ‼🍻◆

Sonoma (OG 1040, ABV 3.8%)
A light pale ale with late citrus and juicy fruit aromas.

Ozark (OG 1044, ABV 4.4%)

A balanced, refreshing, dry-hopped American-style pale ale. A pale malt backbone is accentuated with juicy hops for a light, easy drinking finish.

Mazama (OG 1052, ABV 5.5%)
A classic take on an IPA. Primarily dry hopped, to give a spicy, citrus aroma.

Toba (OG 1054, ABV 5.6%)
Oatmeal stout with a chocolate and coffee flavour.

Tractor Shed SIBA

The Tractor Shed, Calva Brow, Workington, Cumbria, CA14 1DB
☎ **(01900) 68860** ⊕ **tractor-shed.co.uk**

☺Set up in 2009, as Mitchell Krause, beers were originally contract brewed. A new brewery opened in 2013 in an old tractor shed on the family farm, and the brewery was renamed in 2014. Initially focusing on bottled and kegged continental-style beers, the first cask-conditioned beer was produced in 2014. Hefeweiss is also available bottle-conditioned. Brewery shop on site with tours and events by appointment. Tractor Shed now contract brews various beers for Shindigger, mostly for bottle and keg. ‼RAIB

Traditional Scottish

See Black Wolf

Traffic Street Specials

See Castle Rock

Traquair House SIBA

Traquair House, Innerleithen, EH44 6PW
☎ **(01896) 830323** ⊕ **traquair.co.uk/ traquair-house-brewery**

The 18th century brewhouse is based in one of the wings of the 1,000-year-old Traquair House, Scotland's oldest inhabited house. All the beers are oak-fermented and 60% of production is exported. ‼🍻◆

Bear Ale (OG 1050, ABV 5%)

Treboom SIBA

Millstone Yard, Main Street, Shipton-by-Beningbrough, North Yorkshire, YO30 1AA
☎ **(01904) 471569** ☎ **07761 608662**

c/o Nova Scotia Cottage, Acaster Malbis, YO23 2PY
⊕ **treboom.co.uk**

Treboom began in 2011 using a 10-barrel plant with the output going mainly to pubs within a 50-mile radius. ◆

Tambourine Man (OG 1038.5, ABV 3.9%)
A deep golden ale with a hint of maltiness complemented by fruit flavours from the hops.

Yorkshire Sparkle (OG 1039, ABV 4%)
A really pale ale with a fresh citrus taste.

Kettle Drum (OG 1042, ABV 4.3%)
Copper-coloured ale with a distinct fruitiness, and robust hop flavours leading to a clean finish.

Hop Britannia (OG 1050, ABV 5%)

A hoppy, strong pale ale. Honey in colour, with intense citrus fruit and spice notes.

Tremethick (NEW)

Grampound, TR2 4QY ☎ 07726 427775
⊕ tremethick.co.uk

Tremethick began brewing in 2015. Having brewed in small batches in a garage or using spare capacity at other breweries, a new building was completed and 5.5-barrel plant commissioned in 2016. Further beers are planned. RAIB

Pale Ale (OG 1043, ABV 4.3%)
Medium-bodied pale brown best bitter with light malt on the nose and a grainy mouthfeel. A crisp, drinkable beer with sweet malt and fruit flavours and a gentle finish.

Très Bien

36B The Manor, Main Street, Tur Langton, Leicestershire, LE8 0PJ ☎ 07976 310860
⊕ tresbienbrewery.com

⊠ Très Bien began brewing in 2014 on a two-barrel plant, supplying a small selection of pubs throughout Leicestershire. What began life as a fictional brewery for the labels of home-brew Christmas presents now exists as an actual small one-man brewery brewing a regularly-changing variety of beers.

Ponytail Pale Ale (OG 1034, ABV 3.4%)
Very light and hoppy golden ale with a strong citrus aroma.

Killer Whale (OG 1040, ABV 3.8%)
An easy-drinking light and hoppy session pale ale with citrus and floral aromas and a delicate bitterness.

Cascade (OG 1048, ABV 4.5%)
A single hoped pale ale, light and golden in colour with pronounced floral aromas.

Chinook (OG 1048, ABV 4.5%)
Notable citrus and pine aromas feature in this golden, single hoped pale ale.

Citra Special Pale Ale (OG 1046, ABV 4.5%)
A citrus-flavoured single hopped golden ale with tropical and mango flavours.

Simcoe Special Pale Ale (OG 1046, ABV 4.5%)
A straw-coloured single hopped golden ale with a pronounced tropical aroma.

Porter (OG 1052, ABV 5%)
A smoky and chocolaty porter.

Tring SIBA

Dunsley Farm, London Road, Tring, Hertfordshire, HP23 6HA
☎ (01442) 890721 ⊕ tringbrewery.co.uk

Founded in 1992, Tring Brewery moved to its present site in 2010. It brews more than 130 barrels a week, producing a core range of nine beers augmented by monthly and seasonal specials, most taking their names from local myths and legends. The brewery uses international hop varieties in its monthly specials. ‼ ⬛ ◆ RAIB

Side Pocket for a Toad (OG 1035, ABV 3.6%)
A straw-coloured ale with citrus notes and floral aroma, and a crisp dry finish.

Brock Bitter (OG 1036, ABV 3.7%)
A mid-brown quaffing ale with a hint of sweetness and caramel.

Mansion Mild (OG 1036, ABV 3.7%)
Smooth and creamy dark ruby mild with a fruity palate and gentle late hop.

Drop Bar Pale Ale (OG 1039, ABV 4%)
A dry hopped pale ale with a biscuit malt base and citrus aroma.

Ridgeway (OG 1039, ABV 4%)
Balanced malt and hop flavours give way to a dry, flowery hop aftertaste.

Moongazing (OG 1042, ABV 4.2%)
Red-hued ale with a rounded bitterness and a hoppy aftertaste.

Pale Four (OG 1048, ABV 4.6%)
A light and satisfying golden ale brewed with a blend of four hop varieties and an American yeast.

Tea Kettle Stout (OG 1047, ABV 4.7%)
Rich and complex traditional stout with a hint of liquorice and moderate bitterness.

Colley's Dog (OG 1051, ABV 5.2%)
Dark but not over-rich, strong yet drinkable, this premium ale has a long dry finish with overtones of malt and walnuts.

Death or Glory (OG 1074, ABV 7.2%) ⬛
A strong, dark, aromatic barley wine.

Trinity (NEW)

Wakefield Wildcats Rugby League Ground, Doncaster Road, Wakefield, West Yorkshire, WF1 5EY ☎ 07885 219811

Office: 3 George Street, Outwood, Wakefield, West Yorkshire, WF1 2LR ⊕ trinitybrewing.co.uk

Trinity is housed at the rear of the Wakefield Wildcats Rugby League ground. Brewing began in 2015 and the beers are rugby themed. Partner Neil Land was previously proprietor of Whitley Bridge brewery and partner Steve Locking is a stainless steel fabricator.

Trinity Ales

Church Road, Gisleham, Suffolk, NR33 8DS
☎ (01502) 743121 ⊕ trinity-ales.co.uk

⊠ Trinity Ales was launched in 2009 using a four-barrel plant. It uses pure spring water from its own ancient well along with locally sourced ingredients. Pubs, restaurants, retail outlets and festivals are supplied throughout Suffolk, and beyond. RAIB

Wishing Well (OG 1039, ABV 3.8%)
A light golden ale. Richly hopped to give a smooth honey aftertaste.

Highlight (OG 1040, ABV 4%)
A smooth amber ale, rich in flavour.

Black Street Smithy (OG 1045, ABV 4.5%)
A strong, dark porter with smoky notes.

Gisleham Gold (OG 1045, ABV 4.5%)
A straw-coloured ale with a distinctive citrus flavour.

Trinity Gold (OG 1045, ABV 4.5%)
A rich copper-coloured beer with a well-rounded flavour.

Triple fff SIBA

Magpie Works, Station Approach, Four Marks, Alton, Hampshire, GU34 5HN
☎ (01420) 561422 ⊕ triplefff.com

⊠ Established in 1997 close to a stop on the Watercress Line, the brewery and all the beers except Alton's Pride are named following a musical theme. The fff refers to fortissimo, meaning louder or stronger. Brewing on a 50-barrel plant since 2006, multiple CAMRA awards have been won. Two pubs are owned: the Railway Arms, Alton, and the White Lion, Aldershot. ‼ ⛟ ◆ RAIB

Alton's Pride (OG 1039, ABV 3.8%) ⬦ ◥
Full-bodied session biter. An initially malty flavour fades as citrus notes and hoppiness take over, leading to a lasting hoppy/bitter finish.

Pressed Rat & Warthog (OG 1039, ABV 3.8%) ⬦ ▣ ◥
Toffee aroma with hints of blackcurrant and chocolate lead to a well-balanced flavour with roast, fruit and malt vying with the hoppy bitterness.

Moondance (OG 1042, ABV 4.2%) ◥
An aromatic citrus hop nose, balanced by bitterness and sweetness in the mouth. Bitterness increases in the finish as fruit declines.

Truefitt

3 Carcut Road, Lawson Industrial Estate, Middlesbrough, TS3 6QL ☎ 07883 072389
✉ matt@truefittbrewing.co.uk

☺Truefitt began brewing in 2012 using a four-barrel plant producing up to 16 barrels a week. ◆ RAIB V

Erimus Pale Ale (OG 1041, ABV 3.9%)
A pale session beer with a crisp aroma, floral and citrus notes and a bitter finish.

North Riding Bitter (OG 1042, ABV 4%)
A traditional bitter, loaded with hops, giving the beer an earthy nuttiness.

Ironopolis Stout (OG 1051, ABV 4.7%)
A bold stout packed full of chocolate and roast malt.

Mydilsburgh IPA (OG 1052, ABV 5%)
A well-hopped IPA with a spicy, dry finish.

Truman's SIBA

The Eyrie, 2&3 Stour Road, London, E3 2NT
☎ (020) 8533 3575 ⊕ trumansbeer.co.uk

The legendary East London brewery Truman's was reborn in 2013, 24 years after the original Brick Lane brewery's closure in 1989. The new brewery is a 40-barrel plant in Hackney Wick, just a stroll down the Roman Road from the original site. The original Truman's yeast, recovered from the National Collection of Yeast Cultures, is used. ◆ RAIB

Swift (OG 1040.5, ABV 3.9%) ◥
Well balanced golden bitter with hops and a trace of grapefruit on the nose and palate and a bitter finish.

Runner (OG 1040, ABV 4%) ◥
Traditional brown best bitter with spicy hoppy aroma and flavour fading in the dry aftertaste. Some marmalade fruity notes.

Lazarus (OG 1043, ABV 4.2%) ◥
Well-balanced very pale golden ale with peaches and straw aroma, refreshing grassy and citrus flavour, continuing into the short finish.

Zephyr (ABV 4.4%) ◥
Pale brown smooth beer with a slightly dry roasted character on the palate and a bitter finish. Touch of orange and hops.

Tryst SIBA

Lorne Road, Larbert, FK5 4AT
☎ (01324) 554 000 ⊕ trystbrewery.co.uk

Tryst started production in 2003. A large range of beers is produced, all available in cask and bottles. Supermarkets across the UK are supplied. ‼ ⛟ ◆ RAIB

Brockville Dark (OG 1039, ABV 3.8%)
A full-tasting session ale with hints of liquorice and roasted grains.

Brockville Pale (OG 1039, ABV 3.9%)
A pale golden session ale, smooth on the palate.

Hop Trial (OG 1040, ABV 3.9%)
Beer brewed with lager malt and a changing hop profile.

Bla'than (OG 1041, ABV 4%)
A strong floral nose and refreshing taste, enhanced with elderflower and pale malts.

Drovers 80/- (OG 1041, ABV 4%)
A traditional, well-malted 80/- with an element of sweetness. A gentle nose complements a smooth finish.

Carronade Pale Ale (OG 1043, ABV 4.2%) ▣
A pale ale bursting with citrus flavours.

Sherpa Porter (OG 1044, ABV 4.4%)

German Hops Pils (OG 1045, ABV 4.5%)

V.I.P (OG 1046, ABV 4.5%)
Light brown best bitter with a deep hop taste and floral nose.

Zetland Wheatbier (OG 1046, ABV 4.5%)
Refreshing cloudy wheat beer with a distinctive banana nose.

RAJ IPA (OG 1055, ABV 5.5%) ▣
IPA with balanced flavours, and a hoppy aroma and palate.

Tudor SIBA ◉

Unit A, Llanhilleth Industrial Estate, Llanhilleth, Gwent, NP13 2RX
☎ (01495) 214808 ☎ 07971 015844
⊕ tudorbrewery.co.uk

☺ Tudor is a family-run, four-barrel plant that began brewing in 2012. Beers are available in cask and bottle, with several local pubs supplied, in addition to others further afield. RAIB

Blorenge (OG 1038, ABV 3.8%)
A light, pale ale with a fresh citrus undertone.

Black Mountain Stout (OG 1039, ABV 4%) ▣

IPA (OG 1039, ABV 4%)
A classic IPA with a sharp, hoppy, grapefruit finish.

Skirrid (OG 1040, ABV 4.2%)
A full-flavoured dark beer.

Sugarloaf (OG 1044, ABV 4.7%)

A rounded full-bodied ale with smooth caramelised undertones.

Winter Cheer (OG 1046, ABV 5%)
A dark ale infused with ground ginger, lemon rind, honey, cinnamon and nutmeg.

Black Rock (OG 1050, ABV 5.6%)
A dark ale with a rich aroma and dark appearance, and a smooth chocolate-coffee aftertone.

Tunnel SIBA ⊙

Correspondence: The Old Stable Block, Red House Farm, Nuneaton Road, Ansley, Nuneaton, Warwickshire, CV10 0QU ☎ 07765 223110
⊕ tunnelbrewery.co.uk

The six-barrel brew kit has been sold to Indian Rrwery (qv) and relocated to the Great Barr area of Birmingham. Beers continue to be brewed under the Tunnel & Battlefield Brewery brand names at various local breweries. Plans are underway to open a new brewery. ‼️ ☒ ♦ RAIB

Percheron (OG 1037, ABV 3.7%)
Refreshing, citrus, pale golden ale.

Late Ott (OG 1040, ABV 4%)
Dark golden session bitter with a fruity nose and perfumed hop edge. The finish is dry and bitter.

Trade Winds (OG 1045, ABV 4.6%)
An aromatic, copper-coloured beer with an aroma of hops and a clean, crisp hint of citrus, followed by fruity malts and a dry finish full of scented hops.

Parish Ale (OG 1047, ABV 4.7%)
A reddish-amber, malty ale with a slight chocolate aroma, becoming increasingly fruity as the hops kick in. Smooth, gentle hop bitterness in the finish.

Shadow Weaver (OG 1046, ABV 4.7%)
A dark stout with chocolate and roasted coffee on the tongue, developing through slight fruit into a dry, mellow, bitter finish.

Fields of Gold (OG 1048, ABV 5%)
Pale-coloured beer with a hoppy taste and a floral nose.

Nelson's Column (OG 1051, ABV 5.2%)
A ruby red, strong old English ale.

East India Pale Ale (OG 1058, ABV 5.9%)
Traditional-style old English IPA. Robust in flavour with a good hit of hops.

Turners

Highfield Farm, The Broyle, Ringmer, East Sussex, BN8 5AR
☎ (08456) 892689 ☎ 07896 598172
⊕ turnersbrewery.com

☒ Turners began brewing in 2012, initially at a brewery in Hampshire. The brewery is now based on a farm outside Ringmer. Spent grain is fed to the farm's cattle. Beers are available at local pubs and in bottles for sale direct from the brewery. Brewing is currently suspended.

Turnstone

20 West Cliff, Whitstable, Kent, CT5 1DN ☎ 07807 262662 ✉ turnstoneales@outlook.com

☒ Turnstone Ales is a small, 0.5-barrel home-based brewery set up in 2014 by a part-time teacher. The beers are supplied in cask to two local

pubs while the bottle-conditioned versions are available at local outlets and on the brewers bottle stall at Faversham market. RAIB

Turpin

Turpins Lodge, Lodge Farm, Tadmarton Heath Road, Hook Norton, Oxfordshire, OX15 5DQ
☎ (01608) 737033
✉ turpinbrewery@btconnect.com

☒ Brewing started in 2013. A number of local pubs are supplied regularly, as well as a few pubs further afield in Rugby and Birmingham. Seasonal beers are available. ♦

Golden Citrus (OG 1042, ABV 4.2%)
A bright golden beer with a pronounced citrus character. Full-tasting yet easy drinking, it has a good body and a strong, lasting bitter hop finish

Turpin's (NEW) SIBA ⊙

▤ The Med, 59 Perne Road, Cambridge, CB1 3RX
☎ (01223) 240808 ⊕ turpinsbrewery.co.uk

Turpin's is a microbrewery based inside the Med pub in Cambridge. The brewery can be viewed from the bar.

Meditation (ABV 4.3%)
Smooth pale ale with citrus aromas.

Cambridge Black (ABV 4.6%)
A stout with a unique full-bodied taste.

Tweed SIBA ⊙

Unit D1C, Newton Business Park, Talbot Road, Newton, Hyde, Greater Manchester, SK14 4UQ
☎ (0161) 368 8608 ⊕ tweedbrewing.com

Tweed began brewing in 2014 and expanded to bottle production in 2015. Beers are available in Manchester, particularly the Northern Quarter. ♦

Six Points (ABV 3.7%)
Amber ale packed with a delicate spice and pleasant bitterness.

Pale Ale (ABV 3.8%)
Straw in colour with early pine and cedar notes which make way for a subtle honey finish.

Twickenham SIBA ⊙

Unit 6, 18 Mereway Road, Twickenham, TW2 6RG
☎ (020) 8241 1825 ⊕ twickenham-fine-ales.co.uk

☒ Established in 2004, Twickenham Fine Ales is London's oldest microbrewery. Operating a 25-barrel plant, it is the first brewery in Twickenham since the 1920s. ‼️ ☒ ♦

Sundancer (OG 1037, ABV 3.7%) 🍺
Light zesty golden ale with citrus notes dominating from beginning to end. Finish is bitter but balanced by biscuity sweetness.

Grandstand Bitter (OG 1038, ABV 3.8%) 🍺
Pale brown beer with peach, citrus and malt on the palate, fading in the bitter, slightly dry finish.

Redhead (OG 1040, ABV 4.1%) 🍺
A creamy, chestnut brown best bitter with interesting sweet caramel hints and a mild, short, roasted bitter finish.

Naked Ladies (OG 1043, ABV 4.4%) 🍺

Refreshing dark golden ale with a touch of spicy hop in the flavour but fruit dominates with a lasting bitterness.

Twisted SIBA 👁

Unit 8, Commerce Business Centre, Commerce Close, Westbury, Wiltshire, BA13 4LS
☎ (01373) 864441 ☎ 07512 261914
⊕ twisted-brewing.com

⊠ Twisted began brewing in 2014 using a new six-barrel plant. Outlets in west Wiltshire and north Somerset are supplied. ♦

Rider (OG 1041, ABV 4%)
A triple-hopped amber-coloured ale. Light, flavoursome and well-balanced.

Conscript (OG 1043, ABV 4.2%)
A golden-coloured ale with a soft fruit aroma and floral notes.

Pirate (OG 1043, ABV 4.2%)
A classic English best bitter, pale copper-coloured with an aroma of roasted malt and coffee, with undertones of nutty fruit cake.

Gaucho (OG 1048, ABV 4.6%)
Ruby-coloured ale with aromas of soft fruits, coffee and a hint of chocolate, with a long-lasting finish.

Twisted Barrel

⬛ **Unit 5, Fargo Village, Far Gosford Street, Coventry, CV1 5ED**
☎ (024) 7610 1701 ⊕ twistedbarrelale.co.uk

⊠ Commencing commercial production as a pico-brewery in 2013 using a brew length of 60 litres, Twisted Barrel expanded to a six-barrel brewery and moved to its new location in Fargo Village in 2015. A brewery tap house opened to the public in 2015. beer is mostly sold through the brewery tap, but other local outlets also supplied. ‼ 🍴 ♦ RAIB V

Beast Of A Midlands Mild (OG 1044, ABV 3.8%)

God's Twisted Sister (OG 1050, ABV 4.1%)

Inspired (OG 1046, ABV 4.5%)

Sine Qua Non (OG 1046, ABV 4.5%)

The Saison From Another Place (OG 1051, ABV 5.6%)

Call of Korriban (OG 1056, ABV 6%)

In Amber Clad (OG 1059, ABV 6%)

Twisted Oak SIBA 👁

Yeowood Farm, Iwood Lane, Wrington, Bristol, BS40 5NU ☎ 07917 457797
⊕ twistedoakbrewery.co.uk

⊠ Twisted Oak began brewing in 2012 using a five-barrel plant situated in a former agricultural building, on a working farm in the north Somerset countryside. The business is run by Keith and Deb Hayles who brew small batches of special and unique real ale. ♦ RAIB

Fallen Tree (OG 1039, ABV 3.8%) 🌶
Superb bittersweet session bitter. Aroma and flavour of hops and ripe fruit. Complex and satisfying bitter astringent finish.

Wild Wood (OG 1040, ABV 4%) 🌶

Little aroma. Very smooth, with flavours of hops and fruit and a little malt. Minimal aftertaste.

Old Barn (OG 1045, ABV 4.5%) 🌶
Fruity red ale. Well balanced flavour with a very long bitter finish.

Spun Gold (OG 1045, ABV 4.5%) 🍽 🌶
Classic golden ale with a soft mouthfeel. Spicy notes to the fruity malt aroma and flavour. Hops in the aroma develop into a bitter finish.

Two Beach SIBA

Ness Cove, Shaldon, Devon, TQ14 0HP
☎ (01626) 873427 ⊕ odetruefood.com/brewery

Two Beach began brewing in 2013 using the plant previously used at Ringmore Craft Brewery. They now produce three regular ales, with the occasional seasonal beer being available. ♦

ODE Ale (OG 1042, ABV 4.2%)
A light amber ale with a citrus twist. The hop flavour is finely balanced with strong hints of elderflower.

Shaldon Shag Ale (OG 1042, ABV 4.2%)
The aroma is light malt and summer fruits, with a hint of caramel. The taste is fruity, zesty hops with a well-balanced finish.

Oarsome Ale (OG 1047, ABV 4.6%)
A dark amber ale with flavoursome hoppy tones. The aroma is full of hops and barley, with a hint of sweet fruit. Smooth and easy on the palate with deep caramel flavours.

Two by Two SIBA

Unit 19, Point Pleasant Industrial Estate, Wallsend, Tyne & Wear, NE28 6HA ☎ 07723 959168

14 Albany Gardens, Whitley Bay, NE26 2DY
✉ twobytwobrewing@gmail.com

Brewing began in 2014 using a five-barrel plant in Wallsend on Tyneside. ♦ RAIB

Two Cocks

Church Lane, Enborne, Berkshire, RG20 0HB
☎ (01635) 38295 ☎ 07876 594501
⊕ twococksbrewery.com

⊠ The brewery was established in 2011 after wild hops were found growing in the farm's hedgerows. A 180-feet deep borehole supplies water for the brewery. Many local and regional outlets are regularly supplied. Most beer names refer to the 1st Battle of Newbury in the English Civil War.

Diamond Lil (OG 1035, ABV 3.2%)
A light and fruity golden ale developed for the 2012 Jubilee.

1643 Cavalier (OG 1039, ABV 3.8%)
A light, refreshing, thirst-quenching golden ale.

1643 Leveller (OG 1040, ABV 3.8%)
A malty session bitter brewed with a single variety of old English hop.

1643 Musket Bitter (OG 1039.9, ABV 3.8%)
A smooth, flavour-packed session ale.

1643 Roundhead (OG 1042, ABV 4.2%)
A full bodied, smooth best bitter.

1643 Puritan (OG 1049, ABV 4.5%)
A dark stout with notes of caramel and chocolate.

1643 Viscount (OG 1054, ABV 5.6%)
An unusually fruity strong beer.

Two Rivers SIBA

2 Sluice Bank, Denver, Downham Market, Norfolk,
PE38 0EQ
☎ (01366) 380131 ☎ 07518 099868
⊕ denverbrewery.co.uk

Two Rivers was established in 2012 by John Nash.
Bottled-conditioned ale has been available since
establishment of the brewery and cask ales have
been produced since 2013. All beers are suitable
for vegans and vegetarians. ‼◆RAIB V

Miners Mild (OG 1032, ABV 3.1%)
Easy drinking tawny mild, with good malt
character, light finish and chocolate notes.

Hares Hopping (OG 1041, ABV 4.1%)
Refreshing clean-flavoured bitter with a distinctive
late bitterness and a dry finish.

Kiwi Kick (ABV 4.1%)
A golden bitter with a pleasant hop aroma and an
exciting zesty hop finish.

Denver Diamond (OG 1047, ABV 4.4%)
Full-bodied beer with a bitter and malt taste and a
grassy, slightly floral aromatic character.

Porters Pride (OG 1050, ABV 5%)
Full-bodied and well-balanced porter, with a slight
sweetness cutting through the smooth malt. Coffee
and chocolate aromas and taste are rounded off
with a liquorice and vanilla finish.

Norfolk Stoat (OG 1050, ABV 5.8%)
Distinctive, full flavoured, silky, dark oatmeal stout
with a well-balanced, subtle burnt edge.

Two Roses SIBA

Unit 9, Darton Business Park, Barnsley Road, Darton,
South Yorkshire, S75 5QX ☎ 07780 701254
⊕ tworosesbrewery.co.uk

⊛Two Roses started in brewing 2011 using an 8-
barrel plant installed in a former carpet factory. The
core beers are supplemented during the year with
special brews. ‼🍴◆

Full Nelson (OG 1038, ABV 3.8%)

Chinook (OG 1040, ABV 4%)

Marynka (OG 1040, ABV 4%)

Heron Porter (OG 1041, ABV 4.2%)

Legacy (OG 1041, ABV 4.2%)

Two Towers SIBA

29 Shadwell Street, Birmingham, B4 6HB
☎ (0121) 439 3738 ☎ 07795 247059
⊕ twotowersbrewery.co.uk

⊠ Established in 2010, the 10-barrel brewery is
named after the famous Birmingham landmarks.
Most of the production is bottle conditioned with
cask making up about 40%. The regular ales are
supplemented by six rotating specials. The brewery
also creates bespoke brews for special events,
mainly local in nature. ‼🍴◆RAIB

Baskerville Bitter (OG 1038, ABV 3.8%)
Full bodied bitter with a blend of four hops,
providing a complex but beautifully balanced ale.

Complete Muppetry (OG 1043, ABV 4.3%)

Chamberlain Pale Ale (OG 1042, ABV 4.5%)
A crisp light ale loaded with grapefruit flavours
with a long hoppy finish.

Jewellery Porter (OG 1049, ABV 5%)
A full-bodied wholesome stout with a thick and
slightly chocolate texture underlined with long,
fulfilling English hops.

Birmingham Special Ale (OG 1043, ABV 5.4%)
Maltly strong bitter with a full body, reflecting the
flavours and characteristics of traditional English
ales.

Two Tribes (NEW) ◉

3-5 Jubilee Estate, Foundry Lane, Horsham, West
Sussex, RH13 5UE
☎ (01403) 272102 ⊕ twotribesbrewing.com

Two Tribes began brewing in 2015. Beers are
available in KeyKeg and cans under its own label,
and in collaboration with others, notably Island
Records and Bison Beer. A range of cask-
conditioned beer is also available under the Two
Tribes Unbarred name.

Twt Lol (NEW) SIBA

Unit B27, Trefforest Industrial Estate, Pontypridd,
Glamorgan, CF37 5YB
☎ (07966) 467295 ⊕ twtlol.com

Bragdy Twt Lol opened in 2015 using a 10-barrel
plant. It brews three core ales and a developing
range of seasonal beers. Total capacity is currently
80 firkins a week, with the potential to expand to
160. All of its branding is produced in both Welsh
and English. ‼🍴◆

Glog (OG 1043, ABV 4%)
A bitter, malty beer with caramel/toffee flavours.

**Cwrw'r Afr Serchog (Horny Goat Ale)
(OG 1040, ABV 4.2%)**
A golden ale with pine and citrus flavours, brewed
with horny goat weed, a herb used in traditional
Chinese medicine.

**Pewin Ynfytyn (Crazy Peacock)
(OG 1045, ABV 4.8%)**
A hoppy golden ale made with a hint of caramel
malt, dry hopped.

Tydd Steam SIBA

Manor Barn, Kirkgate, Tydd Saint Giles,
Cambridgeshire, PE13 5NE
☎ (01945) 871020 ☎ 07932 726552
⊕ tyddsteam.co.uk

⊠ Tydd Steam Brewery opened in 2007 in a
converted agricultural barn. The brewery is named
after two farm steam engines. A 15-barrel plant
was installed in 2011. Around 70 outlets are
supplied direct. ‼◆

Barn Ale (OG 1038, ABV 3.9%) 🍺
A golden bitter that has good biscuity malt aroma
and flavour, balanced by spicy hops. Long, dry,
fairly astringent finish.

Piston Bob (OG 1044, ABV 4.6%) 🍺
Malt and faint hops on the aroma progress through
to a malty flavour complemented by a balance of
hops and fruit. A long, dry finish rounds off this
amber strong bitter.

Tydwals (NEW)

Ty Newyth Farm, Llangorse, LD3 9LD ☎ 07851 958254

Tydwals began brewing in 2015, on the premises occupied by Redstone brewery, which closed in 2014. The brewery is named after a family ancestor.

Drysllwyn Bitter (OG 1043, ABV 4.5%)

Cennan Gold (OG 1049, ABV 5%)

Dinefer Porter (OG 1053, ABV 5.5%)

Tyne Bank SIBA

**Unit 11, Hawick Crescent, St Lawrence Road, Newcastle upon Tyne, NE6 1AS
☎ (0191) 265 2828 ☎ 07989 426604
⊕ tynebankbrewery.co.uk**

⊗ Tyne Bank began brewing in 2011. Five core beers are produced, as well as specials and seasonals. Beer is available to buy from the brewery shop. ‼️🛒♦

Single Blonde (OG 1037, ABV 3.5%)
A light ale with a slightly dry bitterness and hints of vanilla.

Pacifica (OG 1040, ABV 4%)
A well-hopped pale ale.

Monument (OG 1041, ABV 4.1%)
Smooth, balanced bitter with a berry fruit character.

Dark Brown Ale (OG 1042, ABV 4.2%)
Newcastle-brewed dark brown ale.

Silver Dollar (OG 1050, ABV 4.9%)
Hoppy American-style ale with lasting bitterness and a citrus kick.

Uffa

**🍴 White Lion Inn, Lower Street, Lower Ufford, Suffolk, IP13 6DW
☎ (01394) 460770 ⊕ uffordwhitelion.co.uk/brewery**

Uffa began brewing in 2011 using a 2.5-barrel plant. It is situated next to the White Lion pub in a converted coach house. ♦

Fox (OG 1037, ABV 3.7%)

Golden Hoard (OG 1038, ABV 3.7%)
A golden ale with a spicy taste and earthy aromas.

Raedwald (OG 1037, ABV 3.7%)
A bitter, golden pale ale with a crisp, refreshing citrus flavour.

Longboat (OG 1051, ABV 4.7%)
A light brown, hoppy ale, bursting with citrus and caramel flavours.

Uley

**The Old Brewery, 31 The Street, Uley, Gloucestershire, GL11 5TB
☎ (01453) 860120 ⊕ uleybrewery.com**

⊗ Uley started brewing in 1833 as Price's Brewery. After a long gap, the premises were restored and Uley Brewery opened in 1985. It has its own spring water, which is used to mash Tucker's Maris Otter malt, and boiled with Herefordshire hops. Uley

delivers to 40-50 outlets in the Cotswold area while brewing to capacity. ♦

Hogshead Cotswold Pale Ale (OG 1035, ABV 3.5%) 🍺
A pale-coloured, hoppy session bitter with a good hop aroma and a full flavour for its strength, ending in a bittersweet aftertaste.

Bitter (OG 1040, ABV 4%) 🍺
A copper-coloured beer with hops and fruit in the aroma and a malty, fruity taste, underscored by a hoppy bitterness. The finish is dry, with a balance of hops and malt.

Laurie Lee's Bitter (OG 1045, ABV 4.5%) 🍺
A copper-coloured, full-flavoured, hoppy bitter with some fruitiness and a smooth, long, balanced finish.

Old Ric (OG 1045, ABV 4.5%) 🍺
A full-flavoured, hoppy bitter with some fruitiness and a smooth, balanced finish. Distinctively copper-coloured, this is the house beer for the Old Spot Inn, Dursley.

Old Spot Prize Strong Ale (OG 1050, ABV 5%) 🍺
A ruby ale with an initial strong malty sweetness that develops into a smooth dry malty finish. A beer that is deceptively easy to drink.

Pig's Ear Strong Beer (OG 1050, ABV 5%) 🍺
A golden pale ale with an initial refreshing taste with a hint of fruitiness that develops into a light malty finish. A smooth quaffable strong ale.

Ulverston

**Lightburn Road, Ulverston, Cumbria, LA12 0AU
☎ (01229) 586870 ☎ 07840 192022
⊕ ulverstonbrewingcompany.com**

☺ The brewery occupies the octagonal bullring of the old livestock market. There is a bar that overlooks the brew-plant which opens by prior arrangement and during some local festivals. Some beers have a Laurel and Hardy theme: Stan Laurel was born in Ulverston. ‼️🛒♦

Flying Elephants (OG 1037, ABV 3.7%) 🍺
Clean, refreshing yellow bitter, sweet and fruity with a dry citrus finish.

Celebration Ale (OG 1039, ABV 3.9%) 🍺
Yellow fruity bitter with hints of tangerine and a notably sustained dry finish.

Harvest Moon (OG 1039, ABV 3.9%) 🍺
A well-balanced, pale, hoppy bitter.

Another Fine Mess (OG 1040, ABV 4%) 🍺
A refreshing gold-coloured bitter. Initially fruity but with a rising bitterness.

Laughing Gravy (OG 1040, ABV 4%) 🍺
Smooth and grainy brown bitter with a good mix of flavours.

Lonesome Pine (OG 1042, ABV 4.2%) 🍺
A fresh and fruity pale gold beer; honeyed, lemony and resiny with an increasingly bitter finish.

Fra Diavolo (OG 1043, ABV 4.3%) 🍶

UnBarred

**33 Bolsover Road, Hove, East Sussex, BN3 5HQ
☎ 07850 070471 ⊕ unbarredbrewery.com**

⊗ UnBarred uses a purpose-built brewery in the owner's garden. It produces beers in limited small batches, with some collaborations with other brewers and the local community including beekeepers and coffee shops. Six outlets are supplied. ‼ RAIB

Benchmark (OG 1046, ABV 4.7%)

Unsworth's Yard SIBA

4 Unsworth's Yard, Ford Road, Cartmel, Cumbria, LA11 6PG ☎ 07810 461313 ⊕ unsworthsyard.co.uk

☺Unsworth's Yard opened in 2011, brewing on a five-barrel plant. The brewery produces beers named after historic figures and legends associated with the Cartmel area. Beers are available in Cartmel pubs and other local outlets as well as the brewery's visitor centre. ‼ 🍺

Freedom Under Law (OG 1037, ABV 3.5%)
A light but full-flavoured amber ale with a bitter finish.

J C Dickinson's The Land of Cartmel (OG 1038, ABV 3.7%) ◆
Bitter pale ale, fruity and hoppy with some grapefruit.

Cartmel Peninsula (OG 1039, ABV 3.8%)
A mellow and sweet English bitter.

Crusader Gold (OG 1041, ABV 4.1%)
A crisp and refreshing golden ale with a subtle citrus finish.

Cartmel Wharf Sandpiper (OG 1038, ABV 4.3%)
A crisp, light blonde beer.

Sir Edgar Harrington's Last Wolf (OG 1045, ABV 4.5%) ◆
Well balanced rich fruity, tawny ale with gentle bitterness.

The Flookburgh Cockler (OG 1057, ABV 5.7%)
Smooth, rich and dark with roasted and mocha flavours.

Untapped SIBA ◉

Unit 6, Little Castle Farm Business Park, Raglan, Monmouthshire, NP15 2BX ☎ (01291) 690074 ☎ 07988 197794 ⊕ untappedbrew.com

Untapped was established in 2009. Beers were intitally brewed at Whittingtons Brewery in Newent, Gloucestershire, but in 2013 they moved to their own plant in Raglan. The Whittingtons range of bottled beers are also brewed here. Untapped has developed its own core range of ales and also experimental brews created primarily for the bottled market. ‼ 🍺 ◆ RAIB

Border Bitter (OG 1036.8, ABV 3.8%)

Sundown (OG 1038.8, ABV 4%)

Monnow (OG 1038.3, ABV 4.2%)

U.P.A. (OG 1043.6, ABV 4.5%)

Triple S (OG 1048.4, ABV 4.9%)

Crystal (OG 1052.3, ABV 6%)

Upham SIBA ◉

Stakes Farm, Cross Lane, Upham, Hampshire, SO32 1FL ☎ (01489) 861383 ⊕ uphambrewery.co.uk

⊠ Upham began brewing in 2009 and expanded to a 30-barrel plant in 2013. It owns 15 pubs and supplies more than 250 outlets. Beer is available in boxes and casks from the shop. 🍺 ◆ RAIB

Tipster (OG 1036, ABV 3.6%) ◆
An easy drinking and light golden ale. Initial hoppiness and fruit is balanced by maltiness that lasts into the finish.

Punter (OG 1039, ABV 4%)
Light amber ale with a sweet and floral hop aroma. The flavour balances refreshing bitterness and maltiness with a dry fruity finish.

Stakes (OG 1045, ABV 4.8%)
A full-bodied ale with striking bitterness, grapefruit and toffee flavours and a hoppy finish.

Urban Island (NEW) SIBA

Unit 28, Limberline Industrial Estate, Limberline Spur, Portsmouth, Hampshire, PO3 5DZ ☎ (023) 9266 8726 ⊕ urbanislandbrewing.uk

⊠ Urban Island is a family-run brewery which began production in 2015 on a bespoke five-barrel purpose-built plant. The range is distributed throughout Hampshire and the South east. The brewery offers on-site sales, including a bar. ‼

DSB/Dolly's Special Beer (OG 1045, ABV 4.6%)
A light, refreshing ale, slightly fruity with a bitter hop finish.

Porter 28 (OG 1056, ABV 5%)
A combination of seven malts give gentle hints of smokiness and chocolate, with a roasted finish.

High & Dry (OG 1056, ABV 5.5%)
An American-hopped IPA with an earthy base and citrus finish.

Andrew Usher

⊟ 32b West Nicolson Street, Edinburgh, EH8 9DD ☎ (0131) 667 1757 ⊕ ushersofedinburgh.co.uk

Formerly Usher's of Edinburgh, the renamed Andrew Usher & Co started brewing in 2015 and is based in a bar of the same name.

Vagrant

Correspondence: Gould Street, Manchester, M4 4RN ☎ 07939 032080 ⊕ vagrantbrewing.com

A cuckoo brewery, established in 2014, using spare capacity at other breweries based around Manchester.

Vale SIBA ◉

Tramway Business Park, Ludgershall Road, Brill, Buckinghamshire, HP18 9TY ☎ (01844) 239237 ⊕ valebrewery.co.uk

⊠Established in 1995 and initially based in Haddenham, Vale moved to Brill in 2007. In 2010 it expanded to 20-barrel brew plant. Five pubs are owned, including the Hop Pole where sister brewery the Aylesbury Brewhouse (qv) opened in 2011. ‼ 🍺 ◆ RAIB

Brill Gold (OG 1035, ABV 3.5%)
Golden session ale with a full malt flavour, well balanced with fruity, slightly citrus hop aromas and a soft bitterness.

Best IPA (OG 1036, ABV 3.7%) ◆
This pale amber beer starts with a slight fruit aroma. This leads to a clean, bitter taste where hops and fruit dominate. The finish is long and bitter with a slight hop note.

Black Swan Mild (OG 1038, ABV 3.9%)
Dark and smooth with hints of chocolate and coffee on the nose and a malty, dry finish.

Wychert Ale (OG 1038, ABV 3.9%)
A traditional Thames Valley beer. Woody flavours are notable in this malty beer with a finish of port and berries on the nose.

VPA/Vale Pale Ale (OG 1042, ABV 4.2%)
An assertive, dry, hoppy ale with a citrus nose, combined with a pronounced malt background.

Red Kite (OG 1043, ABV 4.3%)
Refreshing, chestnut beer with a bitter finish.

Black Beauty Porter (OG 1044, ABV 4.4%) ◆
A very dark ale, the initial aroma is malty. Roast malt dominates initially and is followed by a rich fruitiness, with some sweetness. The finish is increasingly hoppy and dry.

Gravitas (OG 1047, ABV 4.8%)
A strong pale ale packed with hop and citrus flavours, rounded off by a dry, malty, biscuit finish. There is a pronounced hop aroma throughout.

Valhalla

Haroldswick, Unst, Shetland, ZE2 9TJ
☎ (01957) 711658 ⊕ valhallabrewery.co.uk

Valhalla was set up by husband and wife team Sonny and Sylvia Priest in 1997. A bottling plant was installed in 1999. A new brewery building was officially opened in 2012, converted from part of the former RAF SaxaVoord camp at Haroldswick. ‼◆

White Wife (OG 1038, ABV 3.8%) ◆
Predominantly malty aroma with hop and fruit, which remain on the palate. The aftertaste is increasingly bitter.

Old Scatness (OG 1038, ABV 4%)
A light bitter brewed with Bere, an ancient strain of barley which was common in Shetland until the middle of the last century.

Simmer Dim (OG 1039, ABV 4%) ◆
A light golden ale, named after the long Shetland twilight. The sulphur features do not mask the fruits and hops of this well-balanced beer.

Island Bere (OG 1044, ABV 4.2%)

Auld Rock (OG 1043, ABV 4.5%) ◆
A full-bodied, dark Scottish-style best bitter, it has a rich malty nose but does not lack bitterness in the long dry finish.

Sjolmet Stout (OG 1048, ABV 5%) ◆
Full of malt and roast barley, especially in the taste. Smooth, creamy, fruity finish, not as dry as some stouts.

Verulam

🍺 Farmers Boy, 134 London Road, St Albans, Hertfordshire, AL1 1PQ
☎ (01727) 860535 ⊕ farmersboy.co.uk

⊠ Established in 1997 and situated behind the Farmers Boy, the brewery produces beers for the pub, where a selection of beers is always available.

Beer is also supplied locally and to CAMRA festivals. Beers are also produced under the Ale Craft name (founded in 2012) for the free trade. ‼RAIB

Half Nelson (OG 1029, ABV 2.8%)
A straw-coloured, low gravity beer with a big hop flavour and character.

Black Mild (OG 1033, ABV 3.3%)
Easy-drinking dark mild with rich dark malt tones.

Farmer's Delight (OG 1036, ABV 3.9%)
Straw-coloured beer with a distinct hop aroma and flavour.

Run o't' Mill (OG 1041, ABV 3.9%)
Copper-coloured session beer with a balanced flavour.

Farmers Joy (OG 1043, ABV 4.5%)
Ruby, almost black beer, with a combination of dark malt roast and citrus hop flavours.

Citra Hit (OG 1046, ABV 4.6%)
Pale ale with big hop character throughout.

Vibrant Forest SIBA

Unit 3, Gordleton Business Park, Hannah Way, Bowling Green, Lymington, Hampshire, SO41 8JD
☎ (01590) 681094 ☎ 07921 753109
⊕ vibrantforest.co.uk

⊠ Located in the New Forest, Vibrant Forest began brewing commercially in 2011 using a one-barrel plant. This award-winning brewery has progressed to a 10-barrel capacity. ‼🍺◆RAIB

Summerlands (OG 1036, ABV 3.5%)
An IPA-style bitter, well-hopped with balanced malt flavours.

Nova Foresta (OG 1038, ABV 3.8%)
A refreshing well-hopped light amber English bitter with a spicy fruitiness balanced by a pleasant maltiness.

Flying Saucer (OG 1041, ABV 4.3%)
A full-flavoured golden ale with fruity, floral and citrus-like flavours. Fresh and very hoppy with a long bitter finish.

Cydonia (OG 1046, ABV 4.7%)
Grapefruit, citrus and pine flavours are balanced by a sweet maltiness.

Farmhouse Ale (OG 1043, ABV 5%)
A light golden ale with slightly peppery and spicy aromas, subtle bitter and fruity flavours, and a dry finish.

Pale Ale (OG 1047, ABV 5%)
A golden ale that is brewed with a single rotating hop variety.

Oat & Coffee Stout (OG 1060, ABV 5.7%)
A rich, jet black, roasty stout with a smooth texture, made with freshly roasted Columbian coffee beans.

Metropolis (OG 1100, ABV 6%)
A hoppy black IPA, with flavours of citrus and tropical fruits underneath a complex mix of chocolate and balanced bitterness.

Kaleidoscope (OG 1060, ABV 6.5%)
American-style IPA. Intense citrus hops are abundant in this flavour-packed premium beer.

Village Brewer

See Hambleton

Village Brewer: Brew 22

🏠 22 Coniscliffe Road, Darlington, County Durham, DL3 7RG
☎ (01325) 354590 ⊕ villagebrewer.co.uk

☺One-barrel microbrewery, established in 2013, which has been brewing on a regular basis since 2015. The plant is also used to produce the malt wash for the distilling of gin and vodka on site. The beer strength and style varies from brew to brew.

Violet Cottage

🏠 Gwaelod-y-Garth Inn, Main Road, Gwaelod y Garth, CF15 9HH
☎ (029) 2081 0408

⊠ The brewery was established in 2012 in a converted outbuilding at the rear of the Gwaelod-y-Garth Inn, within the grounds of the licensee's private house. Occasional collaborations with Swansea brewery take place. All brews are subject to availability as the brewer decides. Most of the production is sold within the pub. ◆

VIP SIBA

Unit E, Hawkshill Business Park, Lesbury, Alnwick, Northumberland, NE66 3PG ☎ 07545 885352
⊕ thevillageinnpub.co.uk

Brewing began in 2012 using a five-barrel plant to serve the owner's pub, the Village Inn in Longframlington, and the local free trade. Around 150 outlets are supplied.

Village Bike (OG 1040, ABV 4%)

Village Copper (OG 1042, ABV 4.2%)

Village Ghost (OG 1045, ABV 4.5%)

Vocation (NEW) SIBA ⊙

Unit 8, Craggs Country Business Park, New Road, Cragg Vale, Hebden Bridge, West Yorkshire, HX7 5TT
☎ (01422) 410810 ⊕ vocationbrewery.com

☺Vocation began brewing in 2015 on a bespoke 20-barrel plant. The brewery is located high above Hebden Bridge, with a brewery shop selling both draught and bottled beer. 🍺

Bread & Butter (ABV 3.9%)
Pale gold bitter with a floral aroma; smooth and rounded with fresh flavours and aromas of pine, peach, lychee and citrus fruits.

Heart & Soul (ABV 4.5%) ◄
A golden ale with a strong citrus aroma. Hops dominate taste and aftertaste.

Pride & Joy (ABV 5.3%) ◄
Flavoursome IPA packed with citrus hoppiness. A hint of sweetness gives way to a mellow aftertaste.

Divine & Conquer (ABV 6.5%) ◄
Roast malt aroma and taste giving way to a hoppy and vinous mouthfeel. This Black IPA has a smooth, slightly sweet finish.

Life & Death (ABV 6.5%)
An American-style IPA with flavours of tropical and citrus fruits and a lingering bitterness, set against a smooth, malty backbone.

VOG SIBA

Unit 8a, Atlantic Trading Estate, Barry, CF63 3RF
☎ (01446) 730757 ⊕ vogbrewery.co.uk

☺Created in 2005, the founders handed over the reins to a new team in 2015 who have rebranded the brewery and added new beers. An experimental 'New Tricks' range of beers has also been introduced. ◆RAIB

Light Headed (OG 1040, ABV 4%)
A well balanced tawny bitter with a complex malt recipe delivering a fruity caramel character.

Sesiwn (OG 1041, ABV 4.1%)
A classic best bitter, malty sweetness leads to a dry bitter finish.

South Island (OG 1042, ABV 4.2%)
Dry, bitter and refreshing pale ale with a big punch from heavy late hopping.

Dark Matter (OG 1044, ABV 4.4%) 🍺
Easy going, rich and smooth blackcurrant porter with liquorice and chocolate notes from the complex dark roasted malts, balanced by late hop addition.

Nugget (OG 1044, ABV 4.4%)
A floral, golden summer ale, with subtle aromas from hop and dried elderflower.

Decadence (OG 1046, ABV 4.6%)
An IPA underpinned by a big malt character, but with a tropical citrus punch.

Dakota Red (OG 1054, ABV 5.4%)
A full-bodied, American-style red ale, backed up by heavy late hopping.

Volden

35a Neville Road, Croydon, CR0 2DS ⊕ volden.co.uk

⊠ Volden produce beer for the Antic pub group in South London. In addition to the regular range, a number of seasonal and special brews are produced. ◆

Session Ale (OG 1037, ABV 3.8%) ◄
Amber bitter with caramel and orange aroma. Lemon marmalade and sweetish malty biscuit that fades to a bitter dryish finish.

Pale Ale (ABV 4.6%)
A straw-coloured pale ale.

Wadworth SIBA IFBB ⊙

Northgate Brewery, Devizes, Wiltshire, SN10 1JW
☎ (01380) 723361 ⊕ wadworth.co.uk

⊠ Established in 1885 by Henry Wadworth, this impressive market town brewery is one of few remaining producers to sell beer locally in oak casks. Traditional horse-drawn drays deliver beer daily around Devizes. Wadworth has 250 pubs throughout southern England. ‼🍺◆RAIB

Wadworth IPA (OG 1035, ABV 3.6%)
A classic session beer with malt-led flavours.

Horizon (OG 1039, ABV 4%)
A pale gold beer with zesty citrus and hop aromas and a crisp, tangy finish on the palate.

6X (OG 1040.5, ABV 4.1%) ◄
Copper-coloured ale with a malty and fruity nose, and some balancing hop character. The flavour is

similar, with some bitterness and a lingering malty, but bitter finish.

Bishops Tipple (OG 1048, ABV 5%)
A golden brew giving well-balanced hop bitterness and a clean finish.

Swordfish (OG 1047.5, ABV 5%)
A full-bodied, deep copper-coloured ale flavoured with Pusser's Rum.

Waen SIBA

Unit 7, Maesyllan Industrial Estate, Llanidloes, Powys, SY18 6YU
☎ (01686) 627042 ⊕ thewaenbrewery.co.uk

Waen began brewing in 2009. Increased demand saw the brewery increase from a five-barrel to a 20-barrel plant and relocate to Llanidloes. Outlets across the UK and Europe are supplied, both direct and via wholesalers. In 2014 its first bottle shop and bar, the Gravity Station, opened in Cardiff and in 2015 another Gravity Station was opened in Swansea. !! ♦ RAIB

Lemon Drizzle (OG 1037, ABV 3.7%)
A floral and aromatic pale ale with a long-lasting finish.

Festival Gold (OG 1042, ABV 4.2%)
A well-hopped beer.

Pamplemousse (OG 1040, ABV 4.2%) 🍶
Pale ale with a fresh and zingy, lingering finish.

Landmark (OG 1048, ABV 5.5%)
IPA with a full on-hop bitterness and a crisp citrus bite.

Chili Plum Porter (OG 1067, ABV 6.1%)
Sumptuous fruity porter with rich dark fruit flavours and warm chilli tingle.

Snowball (OG 1073, ABV 7%)
Dark chocolate, vanilla and coconut stout.

Wagtail

New Barn Farm, Wilby Warrens, Old Buckenham, Norfolk, NR17 1PF
☎ (01953) 887133 ⊕ wagtailbrewery.com

Wagtail Brewery went into full-time production in 2006. All beers are now only available bottle-conditioned and all are suitable for vegetarians and vegans. RAIB

Wainstones SIBA ◉

Unit 9, Terry Dicken Industrial Estate, Station Road, Stokesley, North Yorkshire, TS9 7AE ☎ 07885 240226 ⊕ stokesleybrewing.co.uk

Wainstones began brewing in 2010 using a 2.5-barrel plant set up in an industrial unit in Stokesley, trading as the Stokesley Brewing Company.

Amber (OG 1038, ABV 3.8%)
Distinctive light golden ale with moderate bitterness and a pleasant floral nose.

Sandstone (OG 1040, ABV 4%)
Traditional brown-coloured ale with moderate bitterness and a pleasant aftertaste.

Ironstone (OG 1042, ABV 4.2%)
A classic rich and full of flavour ale with a smooth aftertaste.

Copper (OG 1043, ABV 4.3%)

Steel River (OG 1043, ABV 4.3%)
Traditional full-flavoured chestnut-coloured ale with medium bitterness.

Jet (OG 1045, ABV 4.5%)
An unusual black ale, full of flavour with an excellent hoppy aftertaste.

Transporter (OG 1045, ABV 4.5%)
A dark porter with a creamy head and a deep malty taste.

Walled City (NEW)

🏠 70 Ebrington Square, Londonderry, BT47 6FA
☎ (028) 7134 3336 ⊕ walledcitybrewery.com

Restaurant-based brewery established in 2015. Beers are brewed on site.

Wit (ABV 4%)

Boom (OG 1042, ABV 4.2%)

Kick (OG 1045, ABV 4.5%)

Stitch (ABV 5%)

Wantsum SIBA

Units 22, 23 & 25, Sparrow Way, Lakesview International Business Park, Hersden, Kent, CT3 4AL
☎ (01227) 714702 ⊕ wantsumbrewery.co.uk

⊗ Wantsum was established in 2009 by James Sandy and takes its name from the nearby Wantsum Channel. In 2012 a new plant was installed and in 2015 two new fermenters added to increase brewing capacity. Outlets are supplied throughout Kent and the Home Counties. !! ♦ RAIB

More's Head (OG 1034, ABV 3.5%)
A chestnut-coloured bitter, with malt and roasted grains balanced against fruit and floral hops with a hint of citrus.

1381 (OG 1036, ABV 3.8%)
A light amber-coloured IPA with delicate citrus and herbal aromas.

Black Prince (OG 1036.5, ABV 3.9%)
A rich, full bodied Kentish mild, smooth on the palate with subtle hop notes.

Imperium (OG 1037, ABV 4%)
A deep amber best bitter. Smooth biscuit malts and rich hoppy nose balance this beer perfectly.

Fortitude (OG 1039, ABV 4.2%)
A bitter with a deep, malty body and a pronounced hop finish.

One Hop (OG 1040, ABV 4.2%)
A single hop beer – the hop is changed every couple of months.

Dynamo (OG 1043, ABV 4.3%)
A crisp, light, golden ale, fruity and floral with an orange citrus twist.

Yellow Tail (OG 1040, ABV 4.5%)
A pale-coloured fruity ale with a hint of vanilla and mild malt flavours.

Black Pig (OG 1044, ABV 4.8%)
Adapted from a Russian Imperial porter recipe, this beer is smooth with burnt chocolate and smoky malt notes mixed with delicate hop bitterness and floral notes.

Red Raddle (OG 1049, ABV 5%)

Ruby red premium bitter. A biscuit and toasted malt base supports a broad, hoppy and smooth finish.

Golgotha (OG 1047, ABV 5.5%)
A rich, deep and broad malt base gives this stout a long, smooth finish. Hops are prominent on the nose with blackcurrant, liquorice and cedar.

Ravening Wolf (OG 1052, ABV 5.9%)
A light amber strong pale ale. Toasted biscuit and rye malt flavours support a pine lemon hop crispness with a hint of vanilla.

Wapping

See Baltic Fleet

Warwickshire SIBA 👁

Bakehouse Brewery, Queen Street, Cubbington, Warwickshire, CV32 7NA
☎ (01926) 450747 ⊕ warwickshirebeer.co.uk

A six-barrel brewery in a former village bakery which has been in operation since 1998. Bottled beers are available from local farm shops, garden centres, wine specialists, supermarkets, as well as from the brewery direct and its four pubs.
🚩 ♦ RAIB

Shakespeare County (OG 1034, ABV 3.4%)
A refreshing deep copper-coloured ale with a fruity, spicy and floral aroma. Full-bodied, soft and hoppy to taste.

Fusilier (OG 1039, ABV 3.9%)
A traditional classic bitter with a fruity, hoppy, malty aroma and sharp, light and malty taste.

Darling Buds (OG 1041, ABV 4%)
A refreshing real ale alternative to lager, brewed with lager malt.

Duck Soup (OG 1043, ABV 4.2%)
A copper-coloured beer with rich malty overtones.

Lady Godiva (OG 1042, ABV 4.2%)
An aromatic golden ale, with honey and malt on the nose. A slightly sweet, biscuity maltiness is balanced by hop bitterness, with a lingering bitterness in the finish.

Golden Bear (OG 1049, ABV 4.9%)
An assertive golden brown beer characterised by a long lasting slightly resiny bitterness. The finish is fruity and warming with hints of spice and orange.

Rugby Ball Stitcher IPA (OG 1051, ABV 5%)
A smooth yet hoppy IPA with a pale golden colour.

Kingmaker (OG 1055, ABV 5.5%)
A rich, fruity, amber-coloured beer. A fruity, malty, toffee aroma leads onto a palate with overtones of spice and caramel. A warming alcoholic dry finish.

Watermill SIBA 👁

🏠 **Watermill Inn, Ings, Cumbria, LA8 9PY**
☎ (01539) 821309 ☎ 07831 873300
⊕ lakelandpub.co.uk

☺Watermill was established in 2006 in a purpose-built extension to the inn. The beers have a canine theme, dogs being welcome in the main bar of the pub. The brewery was extended in 2008 with a new brewery planned within the grounds ‼♦

Collie Wobbles (OG 1037.5, ABV 3.7%)

A pale gold bitter with a slight citrus taste. A good hop and malt balance gives way to a dry finish.

Black Beard (OG 1038, ABV 3.8%) 🐾
Full bodied fruity dark mild with hints of chocolate.

A Bit'er Ruff (OG 1041.5, ABV 4.1%) 🐾
Hops dominate this beer. There is some fruit and sweetness but the bitter flavours take charge.

Ruff Justice (OG 1041, ABV 4.2%)
A malty golden ale, well-balanced with caramel, light floral hops and a fresh, dry finish.

Windermere Blonde (OG 1041.5, ABV 4.2%) 🐾
Light and creamy, fruity and sweet with good hop balance, forms a very satisfying beer.

Isle of Dogs (OG 1044, ABV 4.5%) 🐾
A complex fruity bitter with lasting flavours in the finish

Wruff Night (OG 1047.5, ABV 5%) 🐾
Straw-coloured, sweet and fruity, uncomplicated beer with bitterness in a short-lived aftertaste.

Dogth Vader (OG 1050, ABV 5.1%) 🐾
Intensely flavoursome porter: malt, caramel, roast, fruit and hops all vie for attention.

Shih Tzu Faced (OG 1063.5, ABV 7%) 🍾 🐾
Incredibly well balanced, a warming rich experience. Starting with a fruity aroma, leading to plenty of middle and finish, enhanced with a hint of sprit.

Tomos Watkin SIBA

Unit 3, Alberto Road, Century Park, Valley Way, Swansea Enterprise Park, Swansea, SA6 8RP
☎ (01792) 797300 ⊕ tomoswatkin.com or hurns.co.uk

☺Brewing started in 1995 in converted garages in Llandeilo using a 10-barrel plant. The brewery moved to bigger premises in Swansea in 2000 and the plant increased to a 50-barrel capacity. Over 60% of production is bottled beers (not bottle conditioned). More than 600 outlets are currently supplied. ‼🚩♦

Cwrw Braf (OG 1038, ABV 3.7%)
A clean-drinking, amber-coloured ale with a light bitterness and gentle hop aroma.

Blodwens Beer (OG 1045, ABV 4.5%)
Light blonde beer, with delicate creamy finish with a hint of citrus.

Old Style Bitter/OSB (OG 1045, ABV 4.5%) 🐾
Amber-coloured with an inviting aroma of hops and malt. Full bodied; hops, fruit, malt and bitterness combine to give a balanced flavour continuing into the finish.

Watling Street

See Radlett

Watts Brewing?

🏠 **Magnet Freehouse, 51 Wellington Road North, Stockport, SK4 1HJ**
☎ (0161) 429 6287 ⊕ themagnetfreehouse.co.uk

☺Brewing began in 2014 on the premises of the Magnet freehouse. No regular beers. Speciality beers are brewed to suit the season, and are mostly sold in the pub. ♦

Waveney

▪ Queen's Head, Station Road, Earsham, Norfolk, NR35 2TS
☎ (01986) 892623 ✉ lyndahamps@aol.com

⊗ Established at the Queen's Head in 2004, the five-barrel brewery produces three beers, regularly available at the pub along with other free trade outlets. ♦

East Coast Mild (OG 1037, ABV 3.8%) ◣
A traditional mild with distinctive roast malt aroma and red-brown colouring. A sweet, plummy malt beginning quickly fades as a dry roasted bitterness begins to make its presence felt.

Lightweight (OG 1039, ABV 3.9%) ◣
A gentle beer with a light but well-balanced hop and malt character. A light body is reflected in the quick, bitter finish. Golden hued with a distinctive strawberry and cream nose.

Welterweight (OG 1042, ABV 4.2%)

Weal SIBA

Unit 6, Newpark Business Park, London Road, Chesterton, Newcastle under Lyme, Staffordshire, ST5 7HT
☎ (01782) 565635 ☎ 07980 606966
⊕ wealales.co.uk

Weal Ales is a microbrewery established in 2014 on a one-barrel plant. It expanded to a six-barrel plant in 2015 and is now also bottling its beers. RAIB

Sqweal (OG 1040, ABV 3.9%)
A refreshing golden ale, smooth and well bodied with a slight hoppy flavour and a hint of caramel in the aftertaste.

Weally Hopper (OG 1042, ABV 4.2%)
A light and refreshing pale ale. It has a defining floral and citrus aroma with a dry and bitter finish.

Weller Weal (OG 1044, ABV 4.6%)
A pale ale with a citrus finish.

Weal Noir (OG 1050, ABV 4.8%)
A rich and warming porter, with a roast malt flavour throughout and a subtle hint of spice.

Unweal Stout (OG 1052, ABV 5%)
A robust traditional stout with rich chocolaty and roast malt flavours.

Potters Weal (OG 1056, ABV 5.5%)
A strong traditional bitter with a solid malty backbone with caramel hints throughout.

Weard'ALE

▪ Hare & Hounds, 24 Front Street, Westgate, County Durham, DL13 1RX
☎ (01388) 517212

Brewing commenced in the Hare & Hounds in 2010. The beers are mainly sold on the premises but some have found their way to nearby beer festivals and other local pubs.

Beer Wulf (OG 1038, ABV 3.8%)

Challenger (OG 1038, ABV 3.8%)
A sharp and tasty bitter.

Gold (OG 1038, ABV 3.8%)
Refreshing beer, with light appearance but surprising body.

Fell Over (ABV 4%)

Lighter-bodied, mellow and refreshing session bitter.

Chilled Nights (OG 1044, ABV 4.4%)

Dark Nights (ABV 4.4%)
Dark and full flavoured beer.

Weatheroak SIBA

Unit 7, Victoria Works, Birmingham Road, Studley, Warwickshire, B80 7AP
☎ (0121) 445 4411 (eve) ☎ 07798 773894

Victoria Works, 33 Redditch Road, Studley, Redditch, B80 7AU ⊕ weatheroakbrewery.co.uk

⊗ The brewery was set up in 1997 at Weatheroak Hill. It is now in a spacious factory unit in Studley. Weatheroak supplies 40 outlets. Its brewery tap is the Victoria Works nearby. ‼♦

St Udley Mild (OG 1034, ABV 3.4%)

Light Oak (OG 1036, ABV 3.6%) ◣
This straw-coloured quaffing ale has lots of hoppy notes on the tongue and nose, and a fleetingly sweet aftertaste.

Ale (OG 1041, ABV 4.1%) ◣
The aroma is dominated by hops in this golden-coloured brew. Hops also feature in the mouth and there is a rapidly fading dry aftertaste.

Victoria Works (OG 1043, ABV 4.3%)
A pale hoppy bitter with a citrus finish.

Redwood (OG 1047, ABV 4.7%)
A rich, tawny, strong but mellow beer with a short-lived sweet fruit and malt balance.

Keystone Hops (OG 1050, ABV 5%) ◣
A golden yellow beer that is surprisingly easy to quaff given the strength. Fruity hops are the dominant flavour without the commonly associated astringency.

Weatheroak Hill SIBA

▪ Coach & Horses, Weatheroak Hill, Alvechurch, Worcestershire, B48 7EA
☎ (01564) 823386

Weatheroak Hill brews at the busy Coach & Horses pub and restaurant near Alvechurch. It brews four regular beers and a number of seasonals including single hop IPAs with variable hops. ‼♦

Hill Top Bitter (OG 1034, ABV 3.4%)

Gold (OG 1035, ABV 3.5%)

Icknield Pale Ale (OG 1038, ABV 3.8%)

Single Hop IPA (OG 1041, ABV 4.1%)

Bitter (WHB) (OG 1042, ABV 4.2%)

Cofton Common (OG 1049, ABV 4.9%)

King O' the Hill (OG 1054, ABV 5.4%)

Websters

▪ 73 Bridgnorth Road, Wollaston, West Midlands, DY8 3PZ
☎ (01384) 440315 ✉ info@grahams-place.co.uk

☺Microbrewery set up to the side of Graham's Place in 2014. Currently brewing with malt extract, full mash beers are planned. All beers are sold though the pub including some one-off specials.

GPA (OG 1045, ABV 4.5%)

Tarty Sara (OG 1051, ABV 5.1%)
Well-hopped, stronger version of GPA.

Weetwood SIBA

The Brewery, Common Lane, Kelsall, Cheshire, CW6 0PY
☎ (01829) 752377 ⊕ weetwoodales.co.uk

☺Weetwood Ales began brewing in 1992 in a barn in the tiny hamlet of Weetwood. In 2011 it moved to a new 30-barrel plant. Under new ownership since 2014, there are plans to further increase capacity and broaden the beer range. Around 300 pubs are supplied throughout the North west and north Wales.

Southern Cross (ABV 3.6%)
A hoppy beer, pale golden in colour with fresh pine and lemon hop characteristics.

Bitter (OG 1038.5, ABV 3.8%) ◄
Pale brown beer with an assertive bitterness and a lingering dry finish. Despite initial sweetness, peppery hops dominate throughout.

Mad Hatter (OG 1038.5, ABV 3.9%)
A red-brown beer with spicy and floral notes, and fruity and malty flavours throughout.

Cheshire Cat (OG 1040, ABV 4%) ◄
Pale, dry bitter with a spritzy lemon zest and a grapy aroma. Hoppy aroma leads through to the initial taste before fruitiness takes over. Smooth creamy mouthfeel and a short, dry finish.

Eastgate (OG 1043.5, ABV 4.2%) ◄
Well-balanced and refreshing clean amber beer. Citrus fruit flavours predominate in the taste and there is a short, dry aftertaste.

Old Dog (OG 1045, ABV 4.5%) ◄
Robust, well-balanced amber beer with a slightly fruity aroma. Rich malt and fruit flavours are balanced by bitterness. Some sweetness and a hint of sulphur on nose and taste.

Oregon Pale (ABV 4.5%)
Pale in colour, medium-bodied with big flavours of citrus and grapefruit. A well-balanced and refreshing session beer.

Ambush (OG 1047.5, ABV 4.8%) ◄
Full-bodied malty, premium bitter with initial sweetness balanced by bitterness and leading to a long-lasting dry finish. Blackberries and bitterness predominate alongside the hops.

Oast House (OG 1050, ABV 5%) ◄
Straw-coloured, crisp, full-bodied and fruity golden ale with a good dry finish.

Weighbridge SIBA

⬛ Penzance Drive, Swindon, Wiltshire, SN5 7JL
☎ (01793) 881500 ⊕ weighbridgebrewhouse.co.uk

⊠ The Weighbridge micro-brewery is based within the Weighbridge Brewhouse Restaurant and Bar, in the building which was formerly the home of Archer's brewery and once part of Swindon Railway Works. Established in 2011 under the ownership of Anthony and Allyson Windle, with the brewing skills of Mark Wallington, former Archer's brewer, and his deputy Tim Sherad. Take outs are available. ‼◆

Brinkworth Village (OG 1038, ABV 3.6%)

A light hoppy refreshing ale with a floral, spicy aroma. Easy-drinking session beer.

Weighbridge Best (OG 1044, ABV 4.3%)
A light copper coloured ale with a full palate and a spicy fruit aroma. A good bitter ale but with a malty aftertaste.

Pooley's Golden (OG 1048, ABV 4.7%)
A robust golden ale, full bodied with plenty of bitterness and with an unusual gooseberry aroma. The aftertaste is an excellent balance of the malt and hop.

Weird Beard SIBA

Unit 5, Boston Business Park, Trumpers Way, Hanwell, W7 2QA
☎ (0203) 645 2711 ⊕ weirdbeardbrewco.com

⊠ Brewing began in 2013 on an industrial estate in Hanwell. The plant has expanded again with two new 20-barrel fermenters in addition to six 10-barrel ones. Beer is mostly sold bottle-conditioned or in KeyKeg, but some is available cask conditioned. RAIB

Dark Hopfler (OG 1043, ABV 2.5%)
A hoppy dark beer with pine and chocolate on the nose. Roasted malt and sweet cocoa flavours carry into the taste which is balanced with resinous hop bitterness.

Little Things That Kill (OG 1044, ABV 3.8%) ◄
Hoppy, fruity golden ale which varies in flavour as the hops that are used can alter.

Black Perle (OG 1058.5, ABV 4.5%) ◄
Coffee milk stout with roast notes throughout this full favoured sweetish black beer. Finish has some black roast bitter dryness.

Mariana Trench (OG 1048, ABV 5.3%) ◄
Passionfruit and citrus are noticeable throughout this malty sweet golden beer. Bitterness builds and lingers overlaid by dryness.

Decadence Stout (OG 1062, ABV 5.5%) ◄
Orange with some black treacle sweetness balances the dry chocolate and coffee character that lingers pleasantly with the bitterness developing.

Hive Mind (OG 1052, ABV 5.5%)
Hoppy red ale with a subtle honey aroma and sweetness. A dry, biscuit finish complements the caramel flavours of the malts.

K*ntish Town Beard (OG 1054, ABV 5.5%)

Hit The Lights (OG 1056, ABV 5.8%)
A clean, bitter IPA with lots of fruity hop character.

Fade to Black (OG 1063, ABV 6.5%) ◄
Balanced black IPA with some fruitiness. The beer contains crystal rye and chocolate malt, which gives roast coffee notes throughout.

Welbeck Abbey SIBA ◉

Brewery Yard, Welbeck, Nottinghamshire, S80 3LT
☎ (01909) 512539 ☎ 07921 066274
⊕ welbeckabbeybrewery.co.uk

Welbeck Abbey opened in 2011. The microbrewery is housed in a listed barn at the centre of the Welbeck country estate, and the brew plant was previously used at Kelham Island. Head brewer Claire Monk trained at the Kelham Island Brewery after studying microbiology at Sheffield

University. A range of different beer styles is produced, according to local demand. ‼

Henrietta (OG 1035, ABV 3.6%)
Low-strength beer with a bitter note and citrus and grassy nose.

Red Feather (OG 1040, ABV 3.9%)
A traditional dark amber ale with subtle notes of caramel and toffee.

Harley (OG 1038, ABV 4.3%)
Lightly citrus pale ale.

Portland Black (OG 1043, ABV 4.5%) ⬚ ◆
Black ale with a roast malt aroma and taste throughout, and a well balanced bitterness

Cavendish (OG 1046, ABV 5%) ◆
Golden in colour with a smooth hoppy and malt mouthfeel and a lingering hoppy bitter finish.

Weldon

Bencroft Grange, Bedford Road, Rushden, Northamptonshire, NN10 0SE

Office: 12 Chapel Road, Weldon, Northamptonshire, NN17 3HP ☎ (01536) 601016
⊕ weldonbrewery.co.uk

Originally started brewing in 2014 on a two-barrel plant at the Shoulder of Mutton in Weldon, after which the brewery was originally named. In 2016 the premises and 3.5-barrel kit of the former Copper Kettle brewery in Rushden was purchased and became the main production facility, with the brewery being renamed Weldon. The original plant at the Shoulder of mutton has been retained and is used for small runs and test batches. ◆

Dragline (OG 1040, ABV 3.9%)
Golden ale, light and crisp with delicate fruit and floral notes.

Rosie's Sweatbox (OG 1042, ABV 4.2%)
A rich and tasty dark ale.

Windmill (OG 1042, ABV 4.2%)

Galvy Stout (ABV 4.7%)
A classic stout with hints of coffee, chocolate and liquorice.

Charles Wells IFBB 👁

The Brewery, Havelock Street, Bedford, MK40 4LU
☎ (01234) 272766 ⊕ charleswells.co.uk

☺Charles Wells has a long heritage of brewing in the heart of Bedfordshire since 1876. It remains a family-run brewery. In 2006 Wells merged its brewing and brands division with Young's of Wandsworth when the London brewery closed and the company became known as Wells & Young's. Both run their own pub estates under their family names. In 2014, however, the brands became wholly owned by Charles Wells, which has restored its original company name. It runs an estate of more than 200 pubs and brews beers for the Young's pub company. In 2007, Wells bought the Courage brands from Scottish & Newcastle (now Heineken UK) and added the former McEwan's and Younger's brands in 2011. ‼ ◆ RAIB

Wells Eagle IPA (OG 1035, ABV 3.6%) ◆
A refreshing, amber session bitter with pronounced citrus hop aroma and palate, faint malt in the mouth, and a lasting dry, bitter finish.

Wells Bombardier (OG 1041, ABV 4.1%) ◆

A heavy aroma of malt and raspberry jam. Traces of hops and bitterness are quickly submerged under a smooth, malty sweetness. A solid, rich finish.

Wells Bombardier Burning Gold (OG 1037, ABV 4.1%)

Brewed under the Courage brand name:

Best Bitter (OG 1038, ABV 4%)
Good fullness mixed with a bitter/fruity palate, finished off with a good mouthfeel.

Director's (OG 1043, ABV 4.8%)
A rich, fruity and fully bodied chestnut-coloured classic ale.

Brewed under the McEwan's brand name:

IPA (OG 1037, ABV 4%)
A classic full-bodied, hoppy ale that delivers a citrus fruit aroma and a dry, refreshing finish.

Signature (OG 1043, ABV 4.8%)
Chestnut brown beer with an appealing aroma of citrus, biscuits and spice.

Brewed under the Young's brand name:

Bitter (OG 1034, ABV 3.7%) ◆
This light drinking amber bitter has citrus initially on the palate with sweet malt and a hint of hops that linger into a slightly dry and bitter finish.

London Gold (OG 1037, ABV 4%) ◆
A dark gold beer with a smooth mouthfeel. Citrus and malt in the low aroma, coming through more strongly on the palate and aftertaste with a little peach. Dry finish.

Special (OG 1043, ABV 4.5%) ◆
Pale brown in colour, this rounded best bitter has citrus throughout plus some slight creamy toffee, which balances the bitterness that grows in the aftertaste.

Weltons SIBA

1 Mulberry Trading Estate, Foundry Lane, Horsham, West Sussex, RH13 5PX
☎ (01403) 242901/251873 ⊕ weltonsbeer.co.uk

⊗ Ray Welton moved the brewery into a factory unit in 2003. Over 70 different beers are brewed every year. Pubs throughout the South-east and London are supplied. ‼ ◆ RAIB V

Pride 'n' Joy (OG 1028, ABV 2.8%) ◆
A light brown bitter with a slight malty and hoppy aroma. Fruity with a pleasant hoppiness and some sweetness in the flavour, leading to a short malty finish.

Horsham Pale (OG 1037, ABV 3.7%)
Amber-coloured beer, bitter but with a huge aroma.

Sussex Pride (OG 1040, ABV 4%)

Old Cocky (OG 1043, ABV 4.3%)

Old Harry (OG 1051, ABV 5.2%)

Churchillian Stout (OG 1066, ABV 6.6%)
Hints of burnt toast, balanced by good levels of hops with a long finish.

Wensleydale SIBA

Unit F, Manor Road, Bellerby, North Yorkshire, DL8 5QH
☎ (01969) 622463 ☎ 07765 596666
⊕ wensleydalebrewery.co.uk

THE BREWERIES

⊚Wensleydale was set up in 2003 and currently operates on a 5-barrel plant. It was taken over by Geoff Southgate and Carl Gehrman in 2013. Around 100 outlets are supplied direct. ‼ 🍺 ◆RAIB

Rowley Mild (OG 1032, ABV 3.2%) 🍺
Chocolate and toffee aromas lead into what, for its strength, is an impressively rich and flavoursome taste. The finish is pleasantly bittersweet.

Bitter (OG 1036, ABV 3.7%) 🍺
Intensely aromatic, straw-coloured ale offering a superb balance of malt and hops on the tongue.

Falconer (OG 1038, ABV 3.9%)
A copper-coloured fruity, malt-based session ale, with a long, bitter, dry finish.

Semer Water (OG 1040, ABV 4.1%)
Pale best bitter with tempting citrus aromas. The clean, hoppy nose is balanced by a light, malty sweetness.

Gamekeeper (OG 1042, ABV 4.3%)
A copper-coloured best bitter, with huge spicy hop flavours and a nourishing juicy malt flavour. Balanced to perfection.

Black Dub (OG 1043, ABV 4.4%)
Black and silky oat stout enriched with roast barley, chocolate malt and malted oats.

Gold (OG 1044, ABV 4.5%)
Light golden, best bitter with aromatic and spicy hop flavours.

Poacher (OG 1048, ABV 5%) 🍺
Citrus flavours dominate both aroma and taste in this pale, smooth, refreshing beer; the aftertaste is quite dry.

Wentwell

Unit 16, Perkins Industrial Estate, Mansfield Road, Derby, DE21 4PW ☎ 07900 475755 ⊕ wentwellbrewery.com

Wentwell Brewery was established in 2011 and began commercial brewing on a one-barrel set-up in the owner's garage, before moving to a three-barrel plant in a new commercial premises. Occasional seasonals and one-off beers are brewed. ◆RAIB

Jeremiah Mild (OG 1035, ABV 3.3%)
Smooth, dark and malty, with a lot of body.

Derby Pale Ale (OG 1039, ABV 3.8%)
A very pale straw-coloured hoppy bitter.

Derbyshire Gold (OG 1039, ABV 3.9%)
A light, refreshingly hoppy and zesty session beer.

Justice for Gingers (OG 1040, ABV 4%)
A pale bitter infused with ginger.

Little Tick (OG 1040, ABV 4%)
Straw-coloured bitter, triple hopped for a fuller flavour.

Farm Hands' Bitter (OG 1042, ABV 4.1%)
A rich copper-coloured best bitter with a smooth rounded flavour and nicely balanced bitterness.

Barrel Organ Blues (OG 1046, ABV 4.5%)
Golden-brown full-bodied premium bitter with a rich, malty flavour and aroma.

Nellie's Best (OG 1050, ABV 5.3%)
A full-flavoured strong bitter brewed with molasses.

Wessex

Rye Hill Farm, Longbridge Deverill, Wiltshire, BA12 7DE
☎ (01985) 844532
✉ wessexbrewery@tinyworld.co.uk

⊠ Wessex was established in 2001 and moved to its current location in 2004. 15 local outlets are supplied. Beers are also available through selected wholesalers. Beers are occasionally contract brewed when capacity permits. ◆

Stourton Pale Ale (OG 1038, ABV 3.5%)
A very pale, hoppy session beer with plenty of character.

Potter's Ale (OG 1038, ABV 3.8%)
A classic session bitter.

Longleat Pride (OG 1040, ABV 4%)
A pale, hoppy bitter.

Kilmington Best (OG 1041, ABV 4.2%)
Slightly sweet amber best bitter, with balanced malt and hop characteristics.

Warminster Warrior (OG 1045, ABV 4.5%)
Full-flavoured premium bitter.

Golden Apostle (OG 1048, ABV 4.8%)

Russian Stoat (OG 1080, ABV 9%)
Dark, strong and obvious.

West

🮲 Binnie Place, Glasgow Green, Glasgow, G40 1AW
☎ (0141) 550 0135 ⊕ westbeer.com

No real ale. Brewery-bar and restaurant, producing German-style beer to the Bavarian Purity Law. Beers are usually served under pressure, but not pasteurised. Four regular beers are produced. ‼◆

West Berkshire SIBA ⊚

The Flour Barn, Frilsham Home Farm Units, Yattendon, Berkshire, RG18 0XT
☎ (01635) 202968 ⊕ wbbrew.com

⊠ West Berkshire was established in 1995. Based in Yattendon, it has a 50-barrel brewhouse, office and shop. Following the appointment in 2014 of David Bruce as chairman, the brewery plans to move a larger site nearby, which will enable it to do bottling, labelling and canning on-site. A core range of cask ales is supplied in the south of England. ‼ 🍺 ◆RAIB

**Mr Chubb's Lunchtime Bitter
(OG 1041, ABV 3.7%)** 🍺
A drinkable, balanced, session bitter. A malty caramel note dominates aroma and taste and is accompanied by a nutty bittersweetness and a hoppy aftertaste.

Maggs' Magnificent Mild (OG 1041, ABV 3.8%) 🍺
Silky, full-bodied, dark mild with a creamy head. Roast malt aroma is joined in the taste by caramel, sweetness and mild, fruity hoppiness. Aftertaste of roast malt with balancing bitterness.

Good Old Boy (OG 1043, ABV 4%) 🍺
Well-rounded, tawny bitter with malt and hops dominating throughout. A balancing bitterness accompanies the taste and aftertaste.

Mr Swift's Pale Ale (OG 1043, ABV 4%)
A golden, fruity bitter.

Dr Hexter's Healer (OG 1051, ABV 5%) ⬦
An amber strong bitter with malt, caramel and hops in the aroma. Taste is a balance of malt, caramel, fruit, hops and bittersweetness. Caramel, fruit and bittersweetness dominate the aftertaste.

West Coast

See Conwy

West End

🏠 68-70 Braunstone Gate, Leicester, LE3 5LG
☎ 07875 745302
✉ thewestendbrewery@gmail.com

👁A brewpub in Leicester's West End which opened in 2016 with a 2.5-barrel plant. The regular beer is supplemented by changing specials inspired by the seasons and available ingredients. ⬦

Copper (OG 1043, ABV 4.3%)
Copper-coloured best bitter with caramel flavours and an earthy finish.

IPA (OG 1050, ABV 5.2%)
An initial bitter kick gives way to a rounded finish.

Westerham SIBA 👁

Grange Farm, Pootings Road, Crockham Hill, Kent, TN8 6SA
☎ (01732) 864427 ⊕ westerhambrewery.co.uk

The brewery was established in 2004 at the National Trust's Grange Farm, and is housed in a former dairy. More than 500 outlets are supplied in Kent, Surrey, Sussex and London. Gluten free bottled beers are available. ⬦ RAIB

Finchcocks Original (OG 1036.2, ABV 3.5%)
Mid-gold session beer. Citrus notes on the palate with a hint of biscuit and resiny hoppiness.

Grasshopper Kentish Bitter (OG 1039, ABV 3.8%)
A dark, malty bitter with nutty, roasted notes from the chocolate malt.

Summer Perle (OG 1038.5, ABV 3.8%)
Golden ale with a spicy, refreshing finish.

Spirit of Kent (OG 1039.5, ABV 3.8%)
Crisp golden ale with floral and fruity notes. Complex tropical fruit and citrus flavours blend with the sweet malt. Assertive dry hop notes on the finish.

British Bulldog (OG 1040, ABV 4.1%)
A rich, full-bodied best bitter with a massive aroma and a palate of jammy fruit, biscuity malt and bitter hop resins.

1965 (OG 1047.5, ABV 4.8%)
A clean, refreshing bitter with a full-bodied flavour.

Hop Rocket IPA (OG 1052, ABV 5.5%)
Traditional IPA with plum jam and blackcurrant aroma and palate, balanced by sappy malt and a long, lingering bitter, fruity finish.

Audit Ale (OG 1061, ABV 6.2%)
Wonderful, hoppy, strong and bitter.

Brewed for the Spirit Pub Company:

Taylor Walker 1730 Special Pale Ale (OG 1040, ABV 4%)
Lemon balm, honey and blackcurrant flavours merge with grassy, earthy and botanical tones to create a perfectly balanced ale.

Westmorland (NEW)

Kendal, Cumbria ☎ 07554 562662

Office: Mint Street, Kendal, Cumbria, LA9 6DS
✉ westmorlandbrewery@yahoo.com

Westmorland began brewing in 2016 using a one-barrel plant.

WH Buckley (NEW)

See Evan Evans

Whaley Bridge

Unit 8, Furness Vale Business Centre, Furness Vale, Derbyshire, SK23 7SW ☎ 07890 455279
⊕ whaleybridgebrewery.co.uk

Whaley Bridge was set up by a former home brewer and launched commercially in 2012. The brewery moved to new premises in 2015, and a new six-barrel purpose built plant was installed. Local free houses and eateries are supplied. RAIB

Hockerley Ruby Ale (OG 1040, ABV 4%)
A fruity ruby ale with a hoppy aroma and a hint of treacle.

Anakena (OG 1042, ABV 4.2%)
A pale and tropical summer ale.

Buxworth Ale (OG 1042, ABV 4.2%)
Fruity and flowery ale, with a hint of spice and a hoppy finish.

Goyt Valley (OG 1044, ABV 4.4%)
An earthy golden ale with slightly spicy notes.

Stoneheads (OG 1047, ABV 4.8%)
Complex ale with a taste of citrus, a honey finish and a hoppy aroma.

Rapa Nui (OG 1047, ABV 4.9%)
A pale amber ale with subtle spice and a hint of orange.

Wharfe Bank SIBA 👁

Unit 4, Pool Business Park, Pool Road, Pool-in-Wharfedale, LS21 1EG
☎ (0113) 284 2392 ⊕ wharfebankbrewery.co.uk

👁Wharfe Bank commenced brewing in 2010 using a 20-barrel plant in a converted paper mill on the banks of the River Wharfe. The regular range of beers is complemented by two distinct series of monthly specials often featuring unusual ingredients or rare beer styles. A separate range of beers is also brewed under the Firestorm Brewing Company brand name. ‼⬦

Dragon Slayer (OG 1039, ABV 3.8%)
An English-hopped, copper-coloured traditional ale, well-balanced and easy-drinking.

Magellan (OG 1042, ABV 4%)
Tropical fruit and blueberry flavours with a crisp, dry finish.

Red Angel (OG 1045, ABV 4.2%)
Amber-coloured rye ale. Subtle spice and biscuit notes from the rye malt are complemented by big American hop flavours.

Wharfedale SIBA

Back Barn, 16 Church Street, Ilkley, West Yorkshire, LS29 9DS
☎ (01943) 609587 ⊕ wharfedalebrewery.com

Wharfedale began brewing in 2012 using spare capacity at Five Towns brewery in Wakefield. Brewing moved to Ilkley in 2013 using a 2.5-barrel plant located at the rear of the Flying Duck pub. Special 'one-off' beers are brewed in addition to the core range.

Wharfedale Black (OG 1037, ABV 3.7%)
A smooth, well-balanced, rich, dark mild ale with lasting flavour and subtle hints of chocolate, coffee and liquorice.

Wharfedale Blonde (OG 1039, ABV 3.9%)
A straw-coloured session blonde ale with lingering citrus and grapefruit flavours and a fresh satisfying bitter finish.

Wharfedale Best (OG 1040, ABV 4%)
A traditional chestnut coloured Yorkshire bitter. Subtle malt flavours give way to a floral spicy hoppiness and a mild bitter finish.

Whim SIBA

Whim Farm, Hartington, Derbyshire, SK17 0AX
☎ (01298) 84991 ⊕ whimales.co.uk

Whim opened in 1993 in outbuildings at Whim Farm. The beers are available in 50-70 outlets and the brewery's tied house, the Wilkes Head in Leek. ♦

Arbor Light (OG 1035, ABV 3.6%)
Light-coloured bitter, sharp and clean with lots of hop character and a delicate light aroma.

Hartington Bitter (OG 1039, ABV 4%)
A light, golden-coloured, well-hopped session beer. A dry finish with a spicy, floral aroma.

Earl Grey Bitter (OG 1042, ABV 4.2%)
Traditional full-bodied deep golden brown-coloured ale, with complex malt and dry hop flavours.

Hartington IPA (OG 1045, ABV 4.5%)
Pale and light-coloured beer, smooth on the palate allowing malt to predominate. Slightly sweet finish combined with distinctive light hop bitterness.

Flower Power (OG 1053, ABV 5.3%)
Light, golden-coloured beer with a flowery hop aroma, citrus with mild spice on the palate and a dry, bitter finish.

Whistling Kite SIBA

35a Buccleuch Street, Kettering, Northamptonshire, NN16 9EE ☎ 07891 956055

23 New Road, Geddington, Northamptonshire, NN14 1AT ✉ phillipsjez@aol.com

Located in a former shoe factory, this six-barrel plant was established in 2013 by Jez Phillips. It supplies a number of local outlets. ♦

Starry Kite (OG 1038, ABV 3.6%)
Dark ruby beer with roast and biscuit notes.

Jai Ho (OG 1038, ABV 3.8%)
A light IPA with a tangy finish.

Wet Your Whistle (OG 1040, ABV 3.8%)
A well-rounded mahogany-coloured session bitter.

Little Squirt (OG 1039, ABV 3.9%)
A copper-coloured bitter with a tangy hop bitterness.

Honeymoon (OG 1041, ABV 4%)
A golden ale with mellow honey tones.

Eleanor's Ise (OG 1041, ABV 4.2%)
Pale golden ale brewed with lager hops.

Comfort and Joy (OG 1046, ABV 4.6%)
A festival ale, figgy pudding in a glass.

Whitby SIBA

Unit 2b, Larpool Lane Industrial Estate, Whitby, North Yorkshire, YO22 4LX ☎ 07516 116377
⊕ whitby-brewery.com

Whitby brewery was established in 2012 under the Conquest name by a local team who built the brewery from scratch. The brewery supplies to local pubs. ⚑

Abbey Blonde (OG 1036, ABV 3.6%)
A golden blonde ale with a zesty finish and strong notes of toffee.

Whaler (OG 1040, ABV 4%)
A fruity pale ale with a malty, citrus flavour and a not too intense bitter finish.

Saltwick Nab (OG 1044, ABV 4.2%)
A full bodied ruby red ale with a pleasantly fruity finish.

Black Death (OG 1045, ABV 4.5%)

Jet Black (OG 1047, ABV 4.5%)
A finely balanced porter packed with liquorice, coffee and sweet toffee.

Brewed for the Station Inn, Whitby:

Platform 3 (OG 1038, ABV 3.6%)
Nutty pale ale with a smooth citrus finish.

White Horse SIBA

3 Ware Road, White Horse Business Park, Stanford-in-the-Vale, Oxfordshire, SN7 8NY
☎ (01367) 718700 ⊕ breweryoxfordshire.co.uk

White Horse was founded in 2004. The brewery now has its own pub in Oxford, the Royal Blenheim, as well as supplying outlets nationally. ⚑♦

Bitter (OG 1038.7, ABV 3.7%)
Golden bitter, well-hopped with a clean, fruity finish.

Black Beauty (OG 1043.2, ABV 3.9%)
Rich deep ruby mild.

Village Idiot (OG 1041.8, ABV 4.1%)
A blonde ale with a complex hop aroma and taste.

Dark Blue Oxford University Ale (OG 1045, ABV 4.3%)
Dark chestnut-coloured beer.

Wayland Smithy (OG 1047.1, ABV 4.4%)
A red-brown ale with a biscuit flavour that is balanced with a spicy hop finish.

White Park SIBA

Perry Hill Farm, Bourne End Road, Cranfield, Bedfordshire, MK43 0BA
☎ (01223) 911357 ⊕ whiteparkbrewery.co.uk

⊠ White Park is a family business established in 2007 on a five-barrel plant. Spent malt is recycled as feed for rare breed cattle. 60 outlets are supplied direct. In 2009 the brewery began bottling, and supplies direct to pubs and local stores. ◆

Park Light (ABV 3.6%)
A nutty English IPA with a sweet hop aroma balanced with a crisp, dry taste.

White Gold (OG 1037, ABV 3.8%)
A golden session ale. Gentle malt flavour giving rise to floral hoppiness.

Cranfield Best (ABV 4.2%)
Traditional best bitter with a complex biscuity malt flavour.

Oast House (ABV 4.8%)
A light yellow-coloured zesty pale ale with four varieties of hop.

Malt Store (OG 1047, ABV 5%)
A malty, strong English ale.

Moonshine (OG 1050, ABV 5.2%)
A citrus strong pale ale brewed in the Trappist style.

White Rock SIBA

Units 6 & 7, Dysons Complex, Southside, St Sampsons, Guernsey, GY2 4QJ
☎ (01481) 249920 ☎ 07911 760302
⊕ whiterockbrewery.gg

White Rock began brewing in 2013 in a modern industrial unit in the north of the island and supplies the limited free trade on the island as well as a small number of tied houses. There are plans for a bottling line. ‼

Pushang (OG 1038, ABV 3.8%)
Golden ale with a light floral aroma and subtle sweetness which provides for a generous length of flavour.

Wonky Donkey (OG 1047, ABV 4.7%)
A distinctive hoppy bitter with hints of citrus. Quite bitter on the tongue initially, it settles nicely at the finish.

Lost Tourist (OG 1050, ABV 5.3%)
A full strength IPA with a very hoppy, citrus and slightly caramel flavour.

White Rose SIBA

119 Chapel Road, Burncross, Chapeltown, Sheffield, South Yorkshire, S35 1QL
☎ (0114) 297 6150
✉ whiterose.brewery@btinternet.com

☺Gary Sheriff, former head brewer at Wentworth Brewery, set up White Rose in 2007. It shares the Little Ale Cart Brewery's premises behind the Wellington in Sheffield. Some equipment is used jointly but White Rose uses its own fermenters. ‼◆

Original Blonde (OG 1040, ABV 4%)

Stairway to Heaven (OG 1044, ABV 4.3%)

Raven (ABV 4.6%)

Whitewater

40 Tullyframe Road, Kilkeel, Co Down, Northern Ireland, BT34 4RZ

☎ (028) 4176 9449 ⊕ whitewaterbrewery.com

Established in 1996, Whitewater is now the biggest brewery in Northern Ireland. One pub is owned, the White Horse in Saintfield, Co. Down. ‼◆

Copperhead (OG 1037, ABV 3.7%)

Crown and Glory (OG 1038, ABV 3.8%)

Belfast Black (OG 1042, ABV 4.2%)

Belfast Ale (OG 1046, ABV 4.5%)

Maggie's Leap IPA (OG 1047, ABV 4.7%)
Triple hopped IPA with powerful hop and fruit aromas. Full-bodied, rich and complex.

Clotworthy Dobbin (OG 1050, ABV 5%)

Whitstable SIBA

Little Telpits Farm, Woodcock Lane, Grafty Green, Kent, ME17 2AY
☎ (01622) 851007 ⊕ whitstablebrewery.co.uk

Whitstable Brewery was founded in 2003. It currently provides all the beer for the Whitstable Oyster Company's three restaurants, their hotel and a brewery tap as well as supplying cask ale to pubs all over Kent, London and Surrey. ◆

Native Bitter (OG 1036, ABV 3.7%) ◥
A classic copper-coloured Kentish session bitter with hoppy aroma and a long, dry bitter hop finish.

Renaissance Ruby Mild (OG 1038, ABV 3.7%)
Deep ruby in colour, this classic mild has a nutty taste with a gentle roast malt aroma.

East India Pale Ale (OG 1040, ABV 4.1%) ◥
A well-hopped golden IPA with good grapefruit aroma, hop character and lingering bitter finish.

Oyster Stout (OG 1045, ABV 4.5%)
Rich, dry deep chocolate and mocha flavours.

Pearl of Kent (OG 1043, ABV 4.5%)
A light-coloured, well-rounded premium golden ale with tropical fruit flavours.

Winkle Picker (OG 1042, ABV 4.5%)
A beautifully balanced amber best bitter. A pleasant maltiness is offset by a firm but not overpowering bitterness, and delightful orange flavours.

Kentish Reserve (OG 1047, ABV 5%)
Reddish amber-coloured premium bitter. Malty notes with flavours of peaches and plums, ending on a note of rich ruby port.

Whittington's SIBA 👁

Three Choirs Vineyards Ltd, Newent, Gloucestershire, GL18 1LS
☎ (01531) 890555 ⊕ whittingtonbrewery.co.uk

⊠ Whittington's started in 2003, using a purpose-built, five-barrel plant producing 20 barrels a week. The legendary Dick Whittington came from nearby Pauntley, hence the name and feline theme. The beers are available from local outlets. 🍺◆RAIB

Why Not

27 Redfern Road, Norwich, NR7 9RB
☎ (01603) 300786 ⊕ thewhynotbrewery.co.uk

Why Not began brewing 2005 on a 1.5-barrel plant located to the rear of the house of proprietor Colin Emms. In 2006 the brewery was extensively upgraded, doubling in capacity. In 2011 the brewery was moved to a new location in Thorpe St Andrew. The beers are available bottle-conditioned but can be supplied in polypins or firkins to order. **RAIB**

Wally's Revenge (OG 1040, ABV 4%) ◆
An overtly bitter beer with a hoppy background. The bitterness holds on to the end as an increasing astringent dryness develops.

Roundhead Porter (OG 1045, ABV 4.5%)
A traditional old-style London porter.

Cavalier Red (OG 1047, ABV 4.7%) ◆
Explosive fruity nose belies the gentleness of the taste. The summer fruit aroma dominates this red-gold brew. A sweet, fruity start disappears under a quick, bitter ending.

Norfolk Honey Ale (OG 1050, ABV 5%)
A golden beer with a honey nose. A definite hop edge leaves a honey aftertaste.

Chocolate Nutter (OG 1056, ABV 5.5%)

Wibblers SIBA

Goldsands Road, Southminster, Essex, CM0 7JW
☎ (01621) 772044 ⊕ wibblers.com

⊠ Wibblers was established in 2007 and expanded to a 20-barrel plant in 2009. In 2016 the brewery moved to new premises in Southminster, where there are plans to install a tap room and four new fermenters. Production is currently 45-barrels per week. More than 100 outlets are supplied including many Gray & Sons pubs. Real cider is also produced. ‼ ▇ ◆ RAIB

Dengie IPA (OG 1037, ABV 3.6%)
Malty, full-flavoured beer with gentle bitterness and balanced sweetness.

Apprentice (OG 1039, ABV 3.9%)
Amber session beer with a hoppy aroma and light, malty taste.

Dengie Dark (OG 1039, ABV 4%)
Smooth, light malty beer with subtle bitterness and balancing sweetness.

Dengie Gold (OG 1040, ABV 4%)
A golden beer with a refreshing hop punch, citrus aroma and balanced bitterness.

Hop Black (OG 1041, ABV 4%)
A dark bitter that tastes light and hoppy.

Dengie Best (OG 1041, ABV 4.1%)
A pale ale with a balance of malty mouthfeel and peppery hop bitterness.

Crafty Stoat (OG 1056, ABV 5.3%) 🍺

Wicked Hathern

See Staffordshire

Wickwar Wessex SIBA ◉

Old Brewery, Station Road, Wickwar, Gloucestershire, GL12 8NB
☎ (01454) 292000 ⊕ wickwarbrewing.com

The brewery was established as a 10-barrel brewery in 1990, expanding to 40 barrels in 2004. 350 outlets are supplied on a regular basis and the beers are available nationally through most distributors and SIBA. ‼ ▇ ◆

BOB (OG 1040, ABV 4%) ◆
Amber-coloured, this has a distinctive blend of hop, malt and apple/pear citrus fruits. The slightly sweet taste turns into a fine, dry bitterness, with a similar malty-lasting finish.

Cotswold Way (OG 1042, ABV 4.2%) ◆
Amber-coloured, it has a pleasant aroma of pale malt, hop and fruit. Good dry bitterness in the taste with some sweetness. Similar though less sweet in the finish, with good hop content.

Falling Star (OG 1045, ABV 4.2%)
A golden premium beer with a floral aroma and a light malty finish.

Wild Beer SIBA

Lower Westcombe Farm, Evercreech, Somerset, BA4 6ER
☎ (01749) 838742 ☎ 07968 721841
⊕ wildbeerco.com

Brewing began in 2012 using a 24-hectolitre plant. Cask, keg and bottle-conditioned beers are available. ◆ RAIB

Bibble (OG 1042, ABV 4.2%)

Scarlet Fever (OG 1048, ABV 4.8%)

Fresh (OG 1055, ABV 5.5%)

Madness IPA (OG 1068, ABV 6.8%)

Wild Boar SIBA

🍴 **Wild Boar, Crook Road, Bowness-on-Windermere, Cumbria, LA23 3NF**
☎ (08458) 504604 ⊕ englishlakes.co.uk

⊠ Brewing began in 2013 on a microbrewery at the Wild Boar, a large, traditional Lakeland luxury hotel. ◆

Blonde Boar (OG 1037, ABV 3.7%)
A light, refreshing ale. Low in bitterness, this beer delivers a zesty, fruity aroma with a light, clean body.

Mad Pig Ale (OG 1039, ABV 4%)
A classic session ale with a dry body.

Hogsheads 54 (OG 1054, ABV 5.5%)
A hoppy IPA. Flavours of citrus and pine give way to a bitter but clean finish.

Wild Card SIBA

Unit 7, Ravenswood Industrial Estate, Shernhall Street, Walthamstow, E17 9HQ ☎ 07982 402650
⊕ wildcardbrewery.co.uk

⊠ Wild Card began brewing in 2013, initially using spare capacity at several breweries in and around London. It now has its own six-barrel plant in Walthamstow. ▇

Wild Card Pale (ABV 3.6%)

Jack of Clubs (ABV 4.5%) ◆
Initially malty but the hops and bitter flavours develop in the red-coloured beer. Traces of blackberries.

King of Hearts (ABV 4.5%)
Blond beer, well-bittered and dry-hopped.

Ace of Spades (ABV 4.7%)
A porter with flavours of caramel and coffee.

Queen of Diamonds (ABV 5%)

A continuously-hopped IPA with citrus flavours.

Wild Horse SIBA

Unit 4, Cae Bach Builder Street, Llandudno, LL30 1DR
☎ (01492) 868292 ⊕ wildhorsebrewing.co.uk

No real ale. Small brewery concentrating on supplying KeyKeg and bottled beers to local bars and off-licences.

Wild Weather SIBA ◉

Unit 19, Easter Park, Benyon Road, Silchester,
Hampshire, RG7 2PQ
☎ (0118) 970 1837 ⊕ wildweatherales.com

Wild Weather was established in 2013 on the Hampshire/Berkshire border. American and other New World hops are used to create distinctive ales.
⏚ ◆ RAIB

Sundowner (OG 1035, ABV 3.4%)
A light golden beer with subtle floral and fruity notes.

Big Muddy (OG 1038, ABV 3.8%)
Tawny session beer where smooth malty bitterness combines with floral spicy and mild citrus hoppy overtones.

Black Night (OG 1039, ABV 3.9%)
A dark mild, with a light taste that rapidly develops into a complex blend of rich malt and hop flavours and a hint of caramel. The aftertaste is long, dry, hoppy and toasty.

Little Wind (OG 1042, ABV 4.2%)
A deep amber ale with a touch of copper.

Stormbringer (OG 1044, ABV 4.5%)
Malty and hoppy.

Shepherd's Warning (OG 1056, ABV 5.6%)
A smooth, rich IPA with a wonderful hit of hoppy grapefruit, peach and mango flavours.

Williams SIBA ◉

New Alloa Brewery, Kelliebank, Alloa, FK10 1NT
☎ (01259) 725511 ⊕ williamsbrosbrew.com

☺Brothers Bruce and Scott Williams started brewing Heather Ale in 1988. A range of indigenous, historic ales have been added since. Hundreds of cask ale outlets are supplied worldwide. ‼◆

Gold (OG 1040, ABV 3.9%)
Golden session beer with a crisp mouth-feel and lemony hop aromas with suggestions of grapefruit and orange.

Harvest Sun (OG 1041, ABV 3.9%)
A straw gold-coloured ale with a pleasant citrus aroma that gives way to a balanced and satisfyingly bitter finish.

Fraoch Heather Ale (OG 1041, ABV 4.1%) ◣
The unique taste of heather flowers is noticeable in this beer. A fine floral aroma and spicy taste give character to this drinkable speciality beer.

Black (OG 1042, ABV 4.2%) ⏚ ⬛
A light-bodied, rich dark ale in the style of Czech dark lagers. Aromatic and full-flavoured with coffee and chocolate undertones and a lovely blackcurrant aroma.

Birds & Bees (OG 1044, ABV 4.3%)

A bright, golden ale with a late infusion of fresh elderflowers and lemon zest. Fruity, aromatic and deliciously refreshing.

Cock O' the Walk (OG 1042, ABV 4.3%)
A classic red ale.

Kelpie (OG 1045, ABV 4.4%)
A rich dark chocolate ale, which has the aroma of a fresh Scottish sea breeze and a distinctive malty texture.

Red (OG 1045, ABV 4.5%)
Rich ruby red beer with toffee flavours and citrus hop aromas and a medium dry finish.

Joker IPA (OG 1050, ABV 5%)
A well-balanced IPA, golden in the glass, fruity on the nose with hints of cedar.

Seven Giraffes (OG 1051, ABV 5.1%)
Classic IPA with late infusion of elderflower. The aroma is elderflower, citrus hops and sweet caramel. Biscuity malt flavours are balanced with hop bitterness, lemon, and a lingering floral elderflower aftertaste.

Midnight Sun (OG 1058, ABV 5.6%)
A rich, black, smooth porter with an after bite of fresh root ginger.

Willy Good Ale!

The Old Forge, Hartley Farm, Winsley, Bradford on
Avon, Wiltshire, BA15 2JB ☎ 07711 364202
⊕ willygoodale.com

⊠ This award-winning brewery was set up by well-travelled Will Southward in 2010. While in North America, Will discovered a taste for well-hopped beers, and a flair for flavours. The brewery at Hartley Farm quickly out-grew demand and expanded to a six-barrel plant in 2011. Local pubs, shops and restaurants are supplied directly, with beer festivals, parties and weddings also catered for. ⏚ ◆ RAIB

Willy Hop (OG 1040, ABV 4%)
A dry hopped amber ale with a medium body and rich toasted/caramel overtones.

Beerier Beer (OG 1042, ABV 4.2%)
A light single hop English amber ale with a medium body and vanilla overtones.

High Fives (OG 1048, ABV 5%)
A light but hoppy pale ale with hints of grapefruit.

Hopadelic (OG 1048, ABV 5%)
An American-style IPA with a citrus taste and floral aroma.

Willy Brown (OG 1048, ABV 5%)
A rich, malty nut brown ale.

Wheat a Second (OG 1050, ABV 5.2%)
Wheat ale with a hint of orange and coriander.

Willy's

⊟ 17 High Cliff Road, Cleethorpes, Lincolnshire,
DN35 8RQ
☎ (01472) 602145

The brewery opened in 1989 to provide beer mainly for its in-house pub in Cleethorpes, although some beer is sold in the free trade. It has a five-barrel plant with maximum capacity of 15 barrels a week. The brewery can be viewed at any time from pub or street. ‼◆

Original (OG 1039, ABV 3.9%) ◆
A light brown 'sea air' beer with a fruity, tangy hop on the nose and taste, giving a strong bitterness tempered by the underlying malt.

Wilson Potter SIBA

Unit E2 Hanson Close, Middleton, Manchester, M24 2QZ
☎ (0161) 654 6446 ⊕ wilsonpotterbrewery.co.uk

⊚Wilson Potter is a six-barrel microbrewery established in 2011 by two former home brewers, Kathryn Harrison and Amanda Seddon. Cask beers are delivered across the North west, and further afield via wholesale distributors. RAIB

Cascale (OG 1038, ABV 3.7%)
Pale and hoppy beer.

Don't Fall (OG 1039, ABV 3.9%)
A light, hoppy pale ale made using lager malt.

Tandle Hill (OG 1040, ABV 3.9%)
A blonde beer with strong citrus flavours and aroma.

Bon Don Doon (OG 1042, ABV 4.2%)
A refreshing pale ale with hints of lemon.

In the Black (OG 1048, ABV 4.2%) 🍺
A fruity beer with roast malt and liquorice notes, and a sweet liquorice and roast finish.

Ruby Red (OG 1047, ABV 4.4%)
An easy-drinking rich ruby ale with a full-bodied malty berry taste and a floral hop finish.

Wimbledon SIBA ⊚

8 College Fields, Prince George's Road, London, SW19 2PT
☎ (020) 3674 9786 ⊕ wimbledonbrewery.com

⊠ Set up by Mark Gordon after a 23 year career in the City, Wimbledon began production in 2015 with former Young's brewer, Derek Prentice at the helm of a brand new 30-barrel plant. The initial range is focused on the finest English ingredients with further seasonal brews and a range of more experimental 'New World' beers to come. ‼◆RAIB

Common PA (ABV 3.7%) ◆
Well-balanced gold coloured bitter mandarin and hoppy flavours and aroma. Floral note in the lingering finish with some dry bitterness.

Tower SPA (ABV 4.6%) ◆
Fruit and honey aroma. Flavour has a balanced malt and hoppy character with bittersweet finish with some fading orange notes.

Quartermaine IPA (ABV 5.8%) ◆
Amber beer with slight sweetness complementing citrus and summer fruits plus spicy hops. Fruit, spice and bittersweet finish. Hoppy nose.

Wincle SIBA

Tolls Farm Barn, Dane Bridge, Wincle, Cheshire, SK11 0QE
☎ (01260) 227777 ☎ 07701 075368
⊕ winclebeer.co.uk

⊚Wincle Beer Company was set up in 2008 in a redundant milking parlour on a working farm located within the Peak District National Park. The brewery now operates from a new 15-barrel plant in Wincle. ‼🍺◆RAIB

Wincle Waller (OG 1038, ABV 3.8%)
A pale and refreshing beer with a distinctive hop character.

Rambler (ABV 4%)
A well-balanced beer with malt and autumn fruit hoppiness.

Sir Philip (OG 1041, ABV 4.2%)
Amber-coloured premium bitter with a light malty overtone, balanced by hops.

Wibbly Wallaby (OG 1043, ABV 4.4%)
A full-bodied golden beer with fruity hop overtones and a dry, slightly biscuity finish.

Burke's Special (ABV 5%)
A chestnut coloured English special bitter with a full malty and fruity taste.

Windermere

See Watermill

Windsor & Eton SIBA ⊚

Unit 1, Vansittart Estate, Duke Street, Windsor, Berkshire, SL4 1SE
☎ (01753) 854075 ⊕ webrew.co.uk

⊠ Four friends, including two fully-qualified brewers, set up the brewery in 2010 though their brewing experience goes back to the original Courage Brewery. The purpose-built plant is 18 barrels, which produces cask, keg and bottled beers for around 250 outlets in London and the Thames Valley area. ‼🍺◆

ParkLife (OG 1037, ABV 3.2%)
A full-flavoured light ale with a citrus aroma and taste.

Knight of the Garter (OG 1036.5, ABV 3.8%) ◆
Hoppy golden ale with grapefruit notes. Dry refreshing finish.

Windsor Knot (OG 1039, ABV 4%) 🍺
Amber ale with a grapefruit aroma. An initially sweet malt and fruit taste is followed by a mild, bittering finish.

Guardsman (OG 1041, ABV 4.2%)
A tangy best bitter, tawny in colour, with a fresh hoppy finish mellowed with the use of oak during conditioning.

Conqueror (OG 1049, ABV 5%) ◆
A black IPA. Malty and hoppy with berry notes. A full, rounded, slightly dry finish.

Windswept SIBA ⊚

Unit B, 13 Coulardbank Industrial Estate, Lossiemouth Moray, Lossiemouth, IV31 6NG
☎ (01343) 814310 ☎ 07896 897944
⊕ windsweptbrewing.co.uk

Windswept began brewing in 2012 usinga 10-barrel plant installed by John Trow of Oban Ales. It is situated near the gates of RAF Lossiemouth and run by two former Tornado pilots who are CAMRA members. ‼RAIB

Blonde (OG 1039, ABV 4%) ◆
Smooth, golden, citrus hoppy brew with hints of grapefruit.

APA (OG 1046, ABV 5%) ◆
Amber peachy fully hopped brew.

Weizen (OG 1052, ABV 5.2%) ◆
Cloudy wheat beer full of bananas and pear drops with a hint of spices.

Wolf (OG 1064, ABV 6%) 🍴 ◆
Dark, strong tasting, roasted malty brew with coffee background.

Typhoon (OG 1062, ABV 6.2%)

Windy SIBA

🍴 Volunteer Inn, New Road, Seavington St Michael, Somerset, TA19 0QE
☎ (01460) 240126 ⊕ thevolly.co.uk

The brewery was established in 2011. The name stems from the time when alterations were carried out to the back of the pub and the workmen suffered extremes of varying weather conditions. ◆

Tornado (OG 1039, ABV 3.9%)
Traditional brown-coloured bitter.

Southerly (OG 1042, ABV 4%)
A pale golden ale with a fruity aftertaste.

Flurry (OG 1042, ABV 4.1%)

Hurricane (OG 1043, ABV 4.2%)
American-style IPA.

Northerly (OG 1050, ABV 4.8%)

Winning Post

🍴 Winning Post Pub, 6 Pope Iron Road, Worcester, WR1 3HB
☎ (01905) 21178

A small pub brewery established in 2014.

Ken Porter (OG 1037, ABV 3.7%)

Kevin Tully (OG 1039, ABV 3.9%)

Tick Tack Tommy Moore (OG 1040, ABV 4%)

John Mason (OG 1042, ABV 4.2%)

Winster Valley

🍴 Brown Horse Inn, Winster, Cumbria, LA23 3NR
☎ (01539) 443443 ⊕ winstervalleybrewery.co.uk

☺Winster Valley was established in 2009 using a 2.5-barrel plant at the Brown Horse Inn in Winster. ‼

Dark Horse (OG 1035, ABV 3.5%)
A dark warming mild with soft mouthfeel and roasted malt aromas.

Hurdler (OG 1035, ABV 3.5%)
A golden ale with a hint of sweetness on the nose tilted towards the hops and soft malty flavour.

Best Bitter (OG 1036, ABV 3.7%)
Smooth full bodied beer, with a roasted malt flavour and a hint of caramel.

Lakes Blonde (OG 1037, ABV 3.7%) ◆
An uncomplicated fruity, hoppy bitter.

Old School (OG 1037, ABV 3.9%)
Full-tasting pale ale, with floral aroma on the finish.

Chaser (OG 1041, ABV 4.1%)
Smooth chestnut red ale, with caramel and toffee notes and a sweet bitter finish.

Winter's

8 Keelan Close, Norwich, NR6 6QZ
☎ (01603) 787820 ⊕ wintersbrewery.co.uk

Winter's was established in 2001 by David Winter, who had previous award-winning success as brewer for both Woodforde's and Chalk Hill breweries. Winter's ales have won many awards, with David now passing his brewing knowledge to his son, Mark, an award-winning brewer in his own right. ◆

Mild (OG 1036.5, ABV 3.6%) ◆
Classic red-brown mild with a nutty roast character. A well balanced mix of malt caramel, and roast. Lingering bitter finish.

Cloudburst (OG 1037.5, ABV 3.7%) ◆
Copper coloured with a malty nose. A bitter beginning with malt and hop notes ends in a long, dry, finale.

Bitter (OG 1038.5, ABV 3.8%) ◆
A well-balanced amber bitter. Hops and malt are balanced by a crisp citrus fruitiness. A pleasant hoppy nose with a hint of grapefruit. Long, sustained, dry, grapefruit finish.

Geniuss (OG 1041.5, ABV 4.1%) ◆
A dark brown stout that has a smooth mouthfeel with a grainy edge. Roast dominates throughout but is balanced by a mix of malt, a bittersweet fruitiness and an increasingly nutty finish.

Golden (OG 1041.9, ABV 4.1%) ◆
Just a hint of hops in the aroma. The initial taste combines a dry bitterness with a fruity apple buttress. The finish slowly subsides into a long, dry bitterness.

Revenge (OG 1047.9, ABV 4.7%) ◆
Blackcurrant notes give depth to the inherent maltiness of this pale brown beer. A bittersweet background becomes more pronounced as the fruitiness gently wanes.

Storm Force (OG 1053, ABV 5.3%) ◆
A well-defined, sweetish brew. Hops and vine fruit give depth to the malty backbone of this pale brown strong beer. All flavours hold up well as the finish develops a warming softness.

Wiper & True

2 – 8 York Street, St Werburghs, Bristol, BS2 9XT
☎ (0117) 941 2501 ⊕ wiperandtrue.com

Originally launched in 2012 by Michael Wiper as a cuckoo brewery, Wiper & True has operated since 2015 using its own 20-barrel plant. It produces an ever-changing range of bottle-conditioned beers, with a small amount going into casks. The beers are available locally in Bristol/Bath, nationally and internationally. RAIB

Wishbone (NEW) SIBA ◉

2a Worth Bridge Industrial Estate, Chesham Street, Keighley, West Yorkshire, BD21 4LG ☎ 07867 419445
⊕ wishbonebrewery.co.uk

Founded by a husband and wife team in 2015, Wishbone brews on a modern 10-barrel plant based in a mill shed which used to be part of Sir James Hill Textiles. A core range of six beers is supplied to a variety of local outlets.

Blonde (OG 1037, ABV 3.6%)

A very pale straw coloured blonde ale.

Bandit (OG 1038, ABV 3.8%)
A session strength easy-drinking all American-hopped pale ale.

Rascal (OG 1040, ABV 4%)

Abyss (OG 1048, ABV 4.3%)
A rich dark stout, with subtle hopping.

Gumption (OG 1046, ABV 4.5%)
A classic British hopped malty best bitter with caramel toffee notes.

Divination (OG 1057, ABV 5.6%)
American-hopped IPA, heavily dry hopped.

Witham

c/o The Chicken Sheds, Upp Hall Farm, Salmons Lane, Coggeshall, Essex, CO6 1RY
☎ (01376) 563123 ☎ 07824 698235
✉ glenn.ackerman@orange.net

Brewing started in 2012, using a 0.5-barrel plant at the Woolpack Inn, Witham. In 2015 the began using spare capacity at the Red Fox Brewery (qv). The beer continues to be available at the Woolpack. One-off beers are occasionally made.

Scruffy (OG 1049, ABV 3.9%)
A dark mild ale.

No Name (OG 1043, ABV 4.3%)
A traditionally brewed best bitter.

Wizard ◉

Unit 4, Lundy View, Mullacott Cross Industrial Estate, Ilfracombe, EX34 8PY
☎ (01271) 867260 ✉ bruce@wizardbrewery.co.uk

Established in 2003 in Warwickshire and moving to Devon in 2007, the brewery was taken over by Bruce Hutton and his team, who have also taken over the Pier Brewery Tap & Grill in Ilfracombe. Brewing is currently suspended. !!◆

Wobbly SIBA

Unit 22c, Beech Business Park, Tillington Road, Hereford, HR4 9QJ
☎ (01432) 355496 ☎ 07702 739357
⊕ wobblybrewing.co.uk

Wobbly began brewing in 2013 using a 2.5-barrel plant and is an off-shoot of AJP Process Pipework. There is a small on-site bottling plant in production. The beers are available in several pubs in Worcestershire. ◆RAIB

Gold (OG 1036.5, ABV 4.2%)
A lightly hopped traditional golden brown bitter.

Welder (OG 1046.5, ABV 4.8%)
A golden-coloured strong bitter.

Wold Top SIBA ◉

Hunmanby Grange, Wold Newton, Driffield, East Yorkshire, YO25 3HS
☎ (01723) 892222 ⊕ woldtopbrewery.co.uk

☺An integral part of Hunmanby Grange Farm, Wold Top brewed its first ale in 2003 and uses home and Wolds-grown malting barley and chalk filtered water from the farm's own borehole. The range includes special edition cask and bottled beers plus a gluten-free beer, Against the Grain.

The brewery installed a bottling line in 2008 and contract bottles for other breweries. ◆RAIB GF

Bitter (OG 1036, ABV 3.7%)
A crisp, clean, aromatic session bitter. Full-flavoured with a long, hoppy finish.

Anglers Reward (OG 1039, ABV 4%)
A refreshing golden pale ale with a fruity bitterness and lingering aftertaste.

Headland Red (OG 1042, ABV 4.3%)
A red ale with a mellow malty flavour.

Against The Grain (OG 1045, ABV 4.5%)
A full flavoured bitter beer with refreshing bitterness and citrus aftertaste.

Wold Gold (OG 1046, ABV 4.8%)
A light-coloured summer beer with a soft, fruity flavour and a hint of spice.

Scarborough Fair IPA (OG 1060, ABV 6%)
Strong, well hopped ale.

Wolf SIBA ◉

Decoy Farm, Old Norwich Road, Besthorpe, Attleborough, Norfolk, NR17 2LA
☎ (01953) 457775 ⊕ wolfbrewery.com

⊗ The brewery was founded in 1996 on a 20-barrel plant, which was upgraded to a 25-barrel plant in 2006. In 2009 the brewery installed a Moravek bottling plant with an output capability of 2,000 bottles per hour. It moved to its current site in 2013. More than 300 outlets are supplied. ☛◆

Edith Cavell (OG 1037, ABV 3.7%)
A hoppy thirst-quenching beer with a fruity finish.

Golden Jackal (OG 1039, ABV 3.7%) ◄
A hoppy, citrus nose and first taste. Increasingly dry bitter ending as citrus notes fade.

Lavender Honey (OG 1037, ABV 3.7%) ◄
Malty caramel aroma leads into a bittersweet beginning with background honey notes. A long drying finish.

Wolf In Sheep's Clothing (OG 1039, ABV 3.7%) ◄
A malty, dark berry bouquet. Malt, with a bitter background, is the dominant flavour of this clean-tasting beer.

RAF Collection Battle of Britain
(OG 1039, ABV 3.9%) ⬠◄
Signally malty throughout, a complex brew with caramel, vine fruit, and an initial sweetness. Dramatic quick bitter finale.

Wolf Ale (OG 1039, ABV 3.9%)
A copper-coloured, full-bodied ale.

Lupus Lupus (OG 1042, ABV 4.2%) ◄
Hops, with a citrus edge, dominate both aroma and taste. A biscuity background disappears quickly in a short sharp finish.

Sirius Dog Star (OG 1044, ABV 4.4%) ◄
Roast, coffee and caramel aroma flows into a similar first taste. Big mouthfeel with a slightly sour caramel enhanced finale.

Sly Wolf (OG 1041, ABV 4.4%)
Pale, refreshing ale brewed with American hops, infused with lime.

Straw Dog (OG 1045, ABV 4.5%) ◄
Delicately flavoured with a fruity character. A redcurrant aroma gives way to marmalade and hops. A strong increasingly bitter finale.

Norfolk Pride (OG 1045, ABV 4.6%)
A mellow and exotic amber-coloured ale.

Mad Wolf (OG 1048, ABV 4.7%)
Smooth, dark and malty ale.

Granny Wouldn't Like It (OG 1049, ABV 4.8%) ◆
Complex, with a malty bouquet. Increasing bitterness is softened by malt as a gentle, fruity sweetness adds depth.

Woild Moild (OG 1048, ABV 4.8%) ◆
Heavy and complex with malt, vine fruit, bitterness and roast notes vying for dominance. Increasingly dry finish.

Contract brewed for City of Cambridge Brewery:

Boathouse (OG 1037, ABV 3.7%)
A light copper-coloured session bitter with a pleasant aroma from the unique blend of hops and malt.

Hobson's Choice (OG 1041, ABV 4.2%)
A pale-coloured ale with a refreshing hoppy aftertaste.

Atom Splitter (OG 1045, ABV 4.5%)
A golden ale bursting with hoppy flavours.

Parkers Piece (OG 1050, ABV 5%)
A chestnut coloured fruity beer with a long lasting hop bitterness.

Wollaton

Unit 4, Balloon Woods Industrial Estate, Coventry Lane, Wollaton, Nottingham, NG9 3GJ ☎ 07879 664702

Lenton Business Centre, Lenton Boulevard, Nottingham, NG7 2BY ⊕ thewollatonbreweryco.co.uk

Wollaton is a 1,000 litre brewery that started production in 2013 producing just bottled beers. Production of cask or keg beers is being considered.

Wood SIBA ⟨⊙⟩

Wistanstow, Craven Arms, Shropshire, SY7 8DG
☎ (01588) 672523 ⊕ woodbrewery.co.uk

The brewery opened in 1980 in buildings next to the Plough Inn, still the brewery's only tied house. Steady growth over the years included the acquisition of the Sam Powell Brewery and its beers in 1991. Around 200 outlets are supplied. ‼◆

Parish Bitter (OG 1038, ABV 3.8%) ◆
A blend of malt and hops with a bitter aftertaste. Pale brown in colour.

Shropshire Lass (OG 1040, ABV 4%)
A golden ale with zesty bitterness.

Beauty (OG 1042, ABV 4.2%)
Mid amber-coloured beer. Fruity hops give a lingering bitter aftertaste together with a well rounded maltiness.

Shropshire Lad (OG 1045, ABV 4.5%)
A strong, well-rounded bitter.

Wood Farm

See Kendrick's

Woodcote Manor (NEW)

Kidderminster Road, Dodford, Worcestershire, B61 9DY
☎ (01527) 558141 ☎ 07779 166174
⊕ woodcotemanor.com

▨ Woodcote Manor opened in 2015 in former dairy outbuildings attached to the brewer's house. The 20-barrel plant came from Pembrokeshire brewery, and is run by a keen home brewer who turned his hobby into a business. The regular beers use locally-sourced ingredients, including own grown hops, and are distributed to a number of local pubs. ◆RAIB

Supreme Pale Ale (ABV 4.1%)
A well-balanced golden orange-coloured ale, with a malty, soft citrus and mango aroma. The flavour is malt biscuit with a touch of passionfruit, and a light bitter finish.

Squire's Gold (ABV 4.5%)
Golden beer with aromas of sweet grain, honey and dried fruit. It has a bitter but smooth taste, with a lingering flavour of toasted malt, fresh hops and a hint of fruit.

Tom Wood's SIBA ⟨⊙⟩

Melton High Wood Farm, Melton High Wood, Melton Ross, Lincolnshire, DN38 6AA
☎ (01652) 680001 ⊕ tom-wood.com

The Tom Wood range of beers is brewed in the 60-barrel Highwood plant. The range consists of three permanent beers and quarterly seasonal beers. ◆

Best Bitter (OG 1035.5, ABV 3.5%) ◆
A good citrus, passion fruit hop dominates the nose and taste, with background malt. A lingering hoppy and bitter finish.

Lincoln Gold (OG 1041, ABV 4%)
Pale bitter with a fruity aroma and slightly zesty flavour but retaining malt characteristics.

Bomber County (OG 1046, ABV 4.8%) ◆
An earthy malt aroma but with a complex underlying mix of coffee, hops, caramel and apple fruit. The beer starts bitter and intensifies to the end.

Wooden Hand ⟨⊙⟩

Unit 3, Grampound Road Industrial Estate, Grampound Road, Cornwall, TR2 4TB
☎ (01726) 884596 ⊕ woodenhand.co.uk

▨ Wooden Hand was founded in 2004, and changed hands in 2015. The brewery now supplies around 50 outlets with a high percentage of production being sold further afield via wholesalers. A bottling line was installed in 2005, which also contract-bottles for other breweries.

Pirates Gold (OG 1040.6, ABV 4%) ◆
Yellow best bitter with hop aroma. Burst of hops with malt and bitterness, with caramel and fruit. Dry, bitter finish.

Cornish Gribben (OG 1041.6, ABV 4.1%)
A distinctive well hopped beer, with citrus and fruit notes. Well-balanced bittersweet finish.

Cornish Buccaneer (OG 1043.6, ABV 4.3%) ◆
Tawny best bitter with malt aroma. Strong grainy malt balanced by bitter hops and dryness which rise to the finish.

Black Pearl (OG 1050.6, ABV 4.5%)
A rich, nutty stout with good hop balance and dry chocolate finish.

Cornish Mutiny (OG 1048.6, ABV 4.8%) ◄
Tawny strong bitter with malt aroma. Sweet, biscuit malt and bitterness dominate the taste with fruit and dryness. Short finish.

Woodforde's SIBA 👁

Broadland Brewery, Woodbastwick, Norfolk, NR13 6SW
☎ (01603) 720353 ⊕ woodfordes.co.uk

⊗ Founded in 1981 by two members of the Homebrewers' Society, Woodforde's is named after Parson Woodforde, the 18th century Norfolk diarist with a penchant for real ale. In 1989 the brewery moved to its current home at Woodbastwick, where it has its own boreholes and brews using locally-grown Maris Otter. Investment in 2001 and 2008 more than doubled the production capacity. The brewery tap is located next-door, and over 600 outlets are supplied on a regular basis. New owners took over in 2016. ‼🍴♦RAIB

Mardler's (OG 1036, ABV 3.5%) ◄
Chocolate and roast aromas introduce this well-balanced dark mild. Vanilla, caramel and malt boost the dominant roast and chocolate flavours.

Wherry (OG 1037.5, ABV 3.8%) 🍺 ◄
Amber-coloured with an orange citrus nose. A swirling mix of malt, hops, citrus and bitterness combine into a tangy marmalade dryness.

Once Bittern (OG 1040, ABV 4%) ◄
A light malty nose. A dark marmalade tang gives an edge to the dominant malt character. Long bittersweet ending

Sundew (OG 1039, ABV 4.1%) ◄
Hops emerge from a mix of malt, fruit and bitterness to provide a cutting edge to both taste and aroma.

Reedlighter (OG 1040, ABV 4.2%)
A dry-hopped American-style pale ale.

Bure Gold (OG 1043, ABV 4.3%) ◄
A well balanced blend of malt and hop with significant banana, caramel and bitter contributions. Crisp and easy drinking.

Nelson's Revenge (OG 1045, ABV 4.5%) ◄
An infusion of vine fruit, malt and hops provide a rich, rewarding experience. A sweet, Madeira-like finale.

Norfolk Nog (OG 1047, ABV 4.6%) ◄
Echoes of Pontefract cake dominate. A plummy sweetness is aided by a dry bitterness and a hint of caramel

Wooha SIBA

Unit 8A1, Balmakeith Business Park, Nairn, IV12 5QR
☎ (01667) 459929 ☎ 07811 260732
⊕ woohabrewing.com

Wooha opened in 2015 using a 10-barrel plant. It specialises in producing bottle-conditioned ales. Cask-conditioned beers are brewed on demand for beer festivals. Pubs and retail outlets are supplied locally, in Nairn, and across Scotland. RAIB

IPA (ABV 6.2%) ◄
Malty background but with a strong hop character in this red IPA.

Worcester

Arch 49, Cherry Tree Walk, Worcester, WR1 3AU
☎ 07906 432049 ⊕ worcesterbrewingco.co.uk

A six-barrel brewery in the heart of Worcester. The brewer is very keen to only use traditional British hops.

Gyle 2 (OG 1040, ABV 4%)
Pale gold bitter packing a hop punch.

Gyle 1 (OG 1045, ABV 4.5%)
Light amber-coloured, fruity ale.

Worcestershire SIBA 👁

Hartlebury Brewery, Station Road, Hartlebury, Worcestershire, DY11 7YJ
☎ (01299) 253617
⊕ worcestershirebrewingcompany.co.uk

☺Worcestershire Brewing Co was established in 2011 as Attwood Ales on a new 10- barrel plant to the rear of the Tap House, a conversion of the original Hartlebury station ticket office. It has five tied pubs. Beers are sold direct to free houses, clubs and pub companies in Worcestershire and the West Midlands. ♦

Golden (OG 1038, ABV 3.8%)
A refreshing golden beer, packed with fruity, hoppy flavours. It has malty herbal aroma with a hint of orange.

Attwood's Pale Ale (OG 1039, ABV 4%)
A traditionally-brewed crisp, light and refreshing IPA, with clean bitterness and a delicious hoppy aroma.

Nectar Bitter (OG 1043, ABV 4.2%)
Light golden-coloured bitter which is well balanced with a gentle sweetness throughout.

Copper Hopper (OG 1045, ABV 4.5%)
A triple hopped copper ale, with a tropical fruit character.

World's End

🍺 **Crown Inn, 60 Wilcot Road, Pewsey, Wiltshire, SN9 5EL**
☎ (01672) 562653 ⊕ thecrowninnpewsey.com

⊗ World's End Ales was established in 2009 on a one-barrel plant at the rear of the Crown Inn in Pewsey. World's End is the 18th-century name for the area in which the brewery is located. ‼♦

Marilyn (OG 1037, ABV 3.7%)

Diana (OG 1039, ABV 3.9%)

Mercian Incursion (OG 1039, ABV 4%)

Bitterus Magnus (OG 1041, ABV 4.1%)
A well-balanced, chestnut-coloured ale with a good malt, low bitter flavour and a sweet finish.

Best Bitter (ABV 4.5%)

Pewsey Mild (OG 1048, ABV 4.8%)
This dark-coloured mild is full of roasted malt flavours, with a sweet finish.

Worsthorne SIBA

Unit 11 Siberia Mill, Holgate Street, Brierncliffe, Lancashire, BB10 2HQ
☎ (01282) 422588 ☎ 07815 708289
⊕ worsthornebrewingcompany.co.uk

Worsthorne began brewing in 2011 using a 5.5-barrel plant. Over 150 outlets are now supplied. The brewery moved to larger premises behind the original building in 2014. The brewery has opened a visitor centre and there are plans to expand to a 10-barrel plant. !!♦

Worsthorne Gold (OG 1036, ABV 3.6%)
Lightly bittered golden ale with a spicy aroma.

Packhorse (OG 1037, ABV 3.7%)
Pale amber ale with subtle earthy bitterness and floral spicy finish.

Foxstones (OG 1039, ABV 3.9%)
Traditional style amber bitter with well balanced hoppy aroma and lingering floral aftertaste.

Some Like It Blond (OG 1039, ABV 3.9%)
A blond beer, brewed using German hops, with a lingering dry aftertaste.

Hop the Mayflower (OG 1040, ABV 4%)
A light fruity bitter.

Redman (OG 1042, ABV 4.2%)
Smooth well-flavoured light bitter. Overtones of honey and citrus with satisfying aftertaste and subtle lingering bitterness

Trust the Clarets (OG 1043, ABV 4.3%)
Light golden bitter brewed for Burnley football club's Clarets Trust.

Old Trout (OG 1045, ABV 4.5%)
Well flavoured red/brown ale.

Blackthorn Stout (OG 1049, ABV 4.9%)
Rich dark stout with distinct chocolate and liquorice flavours, a hint of ripe berries and a smooth bitter aftertaste.

Colliers Clog (OG 1055, ABV 5.5%)
A strong pale ale lightly bittered with spicy overtones and citrus finish.

Worthington's

See Heritage

Wrekin

🏠 54 Market Street, Wellington, TF1 1DT
☎ (01952) 260683 ☎ 07795 517903
⊕ ironbridgebrewery.co.uk

☺Wrekin Brewing Company (formerly Ironbridge Brewery) was established in 2014 at the Pheasant in Wellington, having relocated from Ironbridge, where it was first established in 2008. A 12-barrel plant is used with the majority of production supplying the brewery's two pubs. Wenlock Stout is on limited supply and is stored for four weeks and supplied in oak casks. Experience days are available.

Blond (OG 1037, ABV 3.6%)

Wrekin Best Bitter (OG 1039, ABV 3.9%)

Wrekin Pale Ale (OG 1040, ABV 4%)

Kiwi Pale Ale (OG 1043, ABV 4.2%)

Ironbridge Gold (OG 1045, ABV 4.4%)

Wenlock Stout (OG 1052, ABV 5.1%)

Wrexham Lager

42 St Georges Crescent, Wrexham, LL13 8DB

☎ (01978) 266222
✉ enquiries@wrexhamlager.co.uk

No real ale.

Wriggle Valley SIBA

Frankham Lane, Ryme Intrinseca, Dorset, DT9 6JT
☎ 07952 198777 ⊕ wrigglevalleybrewery.co.uk

⊗ Wriggle Valley began brewing in 2014. It is based in a converted garage at the owner's house. A three-barrel plant is used to brew twice a week. Beers are mainly supplied in pins and can be found within 15 miles of the brewery. ♦RAIB

Ryme Rambler (OG 1040, ABV 4%)
A tawny-coloured ale.

Dorset Pilgrim (ABV 4.2%)
Session bitter with a good level of bitterness and some fruit.

Copper Hoppa (OG 1047, ABV 4.5%)
A full-bodied dark copper-coloured ale with big fruit aromas and flavour.

Valley Gold (ABV 4.5%)
A refreshing golden ale.

George Wright SIBA

Unit 11, Diamond Business Park, Sandwash Close, Rainford, Merseyside, WA11 8LY
☎ (01744) 886686 ⊕ georgewrightbrewing.co.uk

George Wright started production in 2003. The original 2.5-barrel plant was replaced by a five-barrel one, which has since been upgraded again to 25 barrels with production of 200 casks a week. !!🍺♦

Drunken Duck (OG 1040, ABV 3.9%) 🍺
Fruity gold-coloured bitter beer with good hop and a dry aftertaste. Some acidity.

Long Boat (OG 1040, ABV 3.9%) 🍺
Good hoppy bitter with grapefruit and an almost tart bitterness throughout. Some astringency in the aftertaste. Well-balanced, light and refreshing with a good mouthfeel and long, dry finish.

Blonde Moment (OG 1040, ABV 4%)
A premium blonde beer. Very light in colour, herbal nose with a sweet aftertaste.

Mild (OG 1042, ABV 4%)

Pipe Dream (OG 1044, ABV 4.3%) 🍺
Refreshing hoppy best bitter with a fruity nose and grapefruit to the fore in the taste. Lasting dry, bitter finish.

Pure Blonde (OG 1045, ABV 4.6%)
A premium blonde ale, light and hoppy, giving an earthy hop flavour.

Cheeky Pheasant (OG 1047, ABV 4.7%)
Light amber in colour, distinctive fruit, malty taste with a sweet aftertaste.

Roman Black (OG 1047, ABV 4.8%)
A dark premium ale, smooth and creamy leaving a long, malty, sweet taste.

Blue Moon (OG 1048, ABV 5%) 🍺
Easy-drinking, strong, gold-coloured beer. Good malt/bitter balance and well hopped.

Mocne Piwo (OG 1051, ABV 5.1%)
Strong ale, light amber in colour with a hoppy aftertaste.

Northern Lights (OG 1049, ABV 5.1%)
Strong ale, amber in colour. A strong citrus taste is balanced by the bitter hop.

Wychwood ⊚

Eagle Maltings, The Crofts, Witney, Oxfordshire, OX28 4DP
☎ (01993) 890800 ⊕ wychwood.co.uk

Wychwood brewery is located in the Cotswold market town of Witney. The brewers take inspiration from the myths and legends associated with the ancient medieval Wychwood forest to create a range of award-winning, characterful ales. Part of Marston's PLC. !!♥◆

Hobgoblin Gold (OG 1042, ABV 4.2%)
A golden beer full of malty flavours, with a refreshing bitterness and zesty aroma.

Hobgoblin (OG 1045, ABV 4.5%)
A ruby beer with well-balanced malt flavours combined with a crisp, refreshing hop bitterness.

Wye Valley SIBA ⊚

Stoke Lacy, Herefordshire, HR7 4HG
☎ (01885) 490505 ☎ 07970 597937
⊕ wyevalleybrewery.co.uk

⊕Founded in 1985 at Canon Pyon, the award-winning brewery is now situated in Stoke Lacy. Regarded as a successful regional brewery, a new brewhouse was commissioned in 2013 and it is now operational. !!≒RAIB

Bitter (OG 1037, ABV 3.7%) ◆
A beer whose aroma gives little hint of the bitter hoppiness that follows right through to the aftertaste.

The Hopfather (ABV 3.9%)
A smooth ale with a spicy, honey, pine and grapefruit flavours.

HPA (OG 1040, ABV 4%) ◆
A pale, hoppy, malty brew with a hint of sweetness before a dry finish.

Golden Ale (OG 1042, ABV 4.2%)
A light, gold-coloured ale with a good hop character throughout.

Butty Bach (OG 1046, ABV 4.5%)
A burnished gold, full-bodied premium ale.

Wholesome Stout (OG 1046, ABV 4.6%) ◆
A smooth and satisfying stout with a bitter edge to its roast flavours. The finish combines roast grain and malt.

Dorothy Goodbody's Glorious IPA (OG 1058, ABV 6%)
A strong golden ale with pronounced hop character.

Wylam SIBA

Palace of Arts, Exhibition Park, Newcastle upon Tyne, NE2 4PZ
☎ (01661) 853377 ⊕ wylambrewery.co.uk

⊕Wylam commenced brewing in 2000 on a 4.5-barrel plant. Originally brewing in Heddon-on-the-Wall in Northumberland, the brewery moved to Newcastle upon Tyne in 2016 with a new 30-barrel brew kit. The brewery tap is open Thursday and Friday evenings and all day Saturday. !!≒◆

Bitter (OG 1039, ABV 3.8%) ◆
A refreshing, copper-coloured, hoppy bitter with a clean, bitter finish.

Galaxia (OG 1039, ABV 3.9%)

Gold Tankard (OG 1040, ABV 4%) ◆
Fresh clean flavour, full of hops. This golden ale has a hint of citrus in the finish.

Collingwood (OG 1041, ABV 4.1%)
Soft bodied, honey-coloured beer with a sweet tangerine aroma, citrus and pine flavours and a dry and bitter finish.

Writer's Block (OG 1041, ABV 4.1%)
Pale gold beer with a citrus nose. Full of hops with a bitter finish.

Angel (OG 1044, ABV 4.3%)
A well balanced bitter with a citrus character in the aroma and finish. Commissioned to mark the 10th anniversary of the Angel of the North sculpture.

Red Kite (OG 1046.5, ABV 4.5%)
A ruby ale in the style of a traditional 'scotch'. The hops are balanced by residual maltiness to give subtle hop character and a rich palate.

Haugh Porter (OG 1046, ABV 4.6%) ◆
A dark, satisfying porter, smooth, full of character and complex flavours with hints of chocolate, liquorice and malt.

Wyre Piddle

See Ambridge

XT SIBA

Notley Farm, Chearsley Road, Long Crendon, Buckinghamshire, HP18 9ER
☎ (01844) 208310 ⊕ xtbrewing.com

⊠ XT started brewing in 2011 with a British-built 18-barrel plant. It supplies direct to pubs in Buckinghamshire, Oxfordshire and the Midlands. The brewery shop sells its bottle-conditioned beers and locally-made cider. A range of limited edition, one-off brews is produced under the Animal Brewing Co name. !!≒◆RAIB

Four (OG 1037, ABV 3.8%)
A balanced, mellow session amber ale with pine and citrus hop notes.

One (OG 1041, ABV 4.2%)
Pale blonde beer with dry citrus, lemon and spice notes.

Three (OG 1041, ABV 4.2%)
An American-style pale ale with citrus and pine flavours, light biscuit malt character.

Two (OG 1041, ABV 4.2%)
Golden ale with chewy juicy malts and mellow balanced hop character.

Eight (OG 1045, ABV 4.5%)
A full-bodied, dark porter with roast malt, coffee and bitter chocolate notes.

Fifteen (OG 1044, ABV 4.5%)
English hopped IPA, pale amber with caramel malt notes and a lasting floral, grassy hop character.

Six (OG 1045, ABV 4.5%)
A rich, ruby red beer with a strong malt character and soft citrus hop finish.

Thirteen (OG 1044, ABV 4.5%)

A red ale, brewed with a range of citrus aromatic hops selected from around the Pacific rim.

Five (OG 1052, ABV 5.5%)
An American-style amber ale with intense hop character on a full bodied malt base.

XPA (OG 1055, ABV 5.9%)
A pale, golden American-style IPA with a clean malt character and an intense mix of aromatic fruity hops.

Xtreme

Unit 21, Alfric Square, Maxwell Road, Woodston, Peterborough, Cambridgeshire, PE2 7JP ☎ 07427 661839 ⊕ xtremeales.com

⊠ Founded in 2013, this independent, family-run brewery initially started brewing on a one-barrel plant in Turves. Demand has meant a move to bigger premises in Peterborough using a 2.5-barrel plant. A number of local pubs and beer festivals are supplied around the area. In addition to its regular range, the brewery specialises in developing one-off brews for festivals and occasions such as the annual Whittlesey Straw Bear festival in January. ‼◆

Route 701 (ABV 4%)

Space Pigeon (ABV 4%)

Dancing Pigeon (ABV 4.2%)

Pigeon Ale (OG 1043, ABV 4.3%)

Milk Stout (ABV 4.5%)

Chocolate Stout (OG 1050, ABV 5%)

Evil Pigeon (OG 1055, ABV 5.5%)

Yard of Ale

≣ Surtees Arms, Chilton Lane, Ferryhill, County Durham, DL17 0DH
☎ (01740) 655724 ☎ 07540 733513
⊕ thesurteesarms.co.uk

Established in 2008, the 2.5-barrel microbrewery supplies ales to its brewery tap, the Surtees Arms, beer festivals and to a growing number of pubs from North Tyne to South Tees. ‼◆RAIB

One Foot In The Yard (OG 1044, ABV 4.5%)
Premium golden ale. Fruity on the nose and palate with a sweet finish.

Yates SIBA

Ghyll Farm, Westnewton, Cumbria, CA7 3NX
☎ (01697) 321081 ⊕ yatesbrewery.co.uk

⊛The first of Cumbria's new generation of breweries, established in 1986 and owned by Graeme and Caroline Baxter. It brews using a 20-barrel brewhouse and uses a limited number of site-grown hops. There is a reed bed effluent system. It began brewing speciality lager in 2015. ‼◆

Bitter (OG 1036, ABV 3.7%) ⬠ ◗
A well-balanced, full-bodied bitter, golden in colour with complex hop bitterness. Good aroma and distinctive flavour.

Golden Ale (OG 1038, ABV 3.9%) ◗
Skilful use of lager malt and hops results in a pale beer with a light bitterness; melon fruit and a clean, refreshing finish.

Sun Goddess (OG 1041, ABV 4.2%) ◗
A complex, full-bodied beer, packed with tropical fruit.

Contract brewed for Independent Lakeland Breweries:

Entente Cordiale (OG 1040, ABV 3.9%)
A flavoursome, hoppy beer, using a combination of French and English hops.

Black Wasp (OG 1043, ABV 4.5%)
Lightly hopped, dark, smooth and rich beer with malt flavours of liquorice and chocolate.

Yates' SIBA

Unit 4C, Langbridge Business Centre, Newchurch, Isle of Wight, PO36 0NP
☎ (01983) 867878 ⊕ yates-brewery.co.uk

Brewing started in 2000 on a five-barrel plant and was upgraded to a 10-barrel plant in 2009. Stumpys Brewery was bought out by Yates in 2009 and Old Stumpy (ABV 4.5%) and Tumbledown (ABV 5%) are now produced on request. ‼◆RAIB

Best Bitter (OG 1039, ABV 3.8%)

Golden Bitter (OG 1040, ABV 4%)

Undercliff Experience (OG 1040, ABV 4.1%)
An amber ale with a bittersweet malt and hop taste and a dry, lemon edge that dominates the bitter finish.

Sunfire (OG 1042, ABV 4.3%)
Full-bodied bitter with a strong citrus aroma and bitter taste.

Blonde Ale (OG 1045, ABV 4.5%)

Holy Joe (OG 1050, ABV 4.9%)

Dark Side of the Wight (OG 1049, ABV 5%)
Bitter, malty beer with milk chocolate and plenty of orange fruit. Bitter roasted perfumed finish.

TropicAle (OG 1050, ABV 5%)
Brewed using hops grown at the Ventnor Botanic Gardens on the Isle of Wight.

Special Draught (OG 1056, ABV 5.5%)

Y.S.D. (OG 1056, ABV 5.5%)
Strong golden-coloured beer with fruit notes and a dry bitter hoppy aftertaste.

Wight Old Ale (OG 1060, ABV 6%)
A deep ruby ale with a smooth taste.

Yelland Manor

Lower Yelland Farm, Yelland, Barnstaple, Devon, EX31 3EN
☎ (01271) 860355 ☎ 07770 267592
✉ yellandmanor@gmail.com

Located on the Taw Estuary and close to the Tarka Trail, this is a five-barrel plant in a converted milking parlour. The brewery began production in 2013 and now supplies a small number of local pubs and hotels. The brewery is usually open to the public on Saturday afternoons in summer.

Standard (OG 1043, ABV 4.2%)

Classic (OG 1045, ABV 4.4%)
Traditional English best bitter.

Yeovil SIBA 👁

Unit 5, Bofors Park, Artillery Road, Lufton Trading Estate, Yeovil, Somerset, BA22 8YH
☎ (01935) 414888 ⊕ yeovilales.com

⊗ Yeovil Ales was established in 2006 using an 18-barrel plant. ‼ ☞ ♦ RAIB

Glory (OG 1039, ABV 3.8%)
A well-balanced bitter with citrus hop notes.

Star Gazer (OG 1042, ABV 4%)
Dark copper bitter with a late-hopped floral aroma.

Summerset (OG 1041, ABV 4.1%)
Blonde ale with fruity hop finish.

Lynx Wildcat (OG 1044, ABV 4.3%)

Stout Hearted (OG 1045, ABV 4.3%)

Ruby (OG 1047, ABV 4.5%)
Red bitter with rich malt depth.

POSH IPA (OG 1052, ABV 5.4%)
A strong IPA with a fruity body and hoppy finish.

Yetman's

Bayfield Farm Barns, Bayfield Brecks Farm, Bayfield, Norfolk, NR25 7DZ ☎ 07774 809016 ⊕ yetmans.net

A 2.5-barrel plant built by Moss Brew was installed in restored medieval barns near Holt in 2005. The brewery supplies local free trade outlets. RAIB

Red (OG 1036, ABV 3.8%)

York SIBA 👁

12 Toft Green, York, North Yorkshire, YO1 6JT
☎ (01904) 621162 ⊕ york-brewery.co.uk

York started production in 1996. It was the first brewery in the city for 40 years. It was acquired by Mitchell's of Lancaster in 2008. Five pubs are owned in York and Leeds. The 20-barrel plant has a viewing platform overlooking the conditioning and fermenting rooms. ‼ ☞ ♦

Guzzler (OG 1036, ABV 3.6%) ◀
Refreshing golden ale with dominant hop and fruit flavours developing throughout.

Yorkshire Terrier (OG 1041, ABV 4.2%) ◀
Refreshing and distinctive amber/gold brew where fruit and hops dominate the aroma and taste. Hoppy bitterness remains assertive in the aftertaste.

Centurion's Ghost Ale (OG 1051, ABV 5.4%) ◀
Dark ruby in colour, full-tasting with mellow roast malt character balanced by light bitterness and autumn fruit flavours that linger into the aftertaste.

Burton beer makes me blithe,
French wine makes me sick.
I'm devoted to ale,
And to ale I will stick.
Henceforth let the grape
To the barleycorn bow;
Here's to success to the farmer,
And God speed the plough.
Traditional

Yorkshire SIBA

Brewery Wharf, The Old Fruit Market, 70 Humber Street, Hull, East Yorkshire, HU1 1TU
☎ (01482) 618000 ☎ 07850 494990
✉ guy@yorkshirebrewing.co.uk

⊕ Brewing started in 2012 in the Old Fruit Market Quarter of Hull using a six-barrel plant. Two of the beers are named in honour of the Holy Trinity Church in Hull. A bottling plant, tours and a retail outlet are established. Festivals and local outlets are supplied. ‼ ☞ ♦ RAIB

Mutiny (OG 1036, ABV 3.6%)

Supernatural Blonde (OG 1041, ABV 4.1%)

Mosaic (OG 1042, ABV 4.2%)
Easy-drinking session bitter with a mango, peach and tangerine finish.

Blackjack (OG 1046, ABV 4.5%)
A complex stout fortified with fresh blackberries, providing lasting fruit and chocolate characteristics.

Moondance (OG 1045, ABV 4.5%)
Refreshing golden ale infused with passion fruit.

Oregon Gold (OG 1045, ABV 4.5%)
Traditionally cloudy Belgian-style wheat beer, brewed with coriander and curacao oranges.

Yorkshire Passion (OG 1045, ABV 4.5%)

Raspberry Tipple (OG 1048, ABV 4.8%)

Strawberry Blonde (OG 1048, ABV 4.8%)
Traditionally cloudy Belgian-style wheat beer, infused with strawberries.

Waverider (OG 1052, ABV 5.2%)
A complex West Coast-style IPA.

Shangri-la (OG 1067, ABV 6.7%)
A double IPA with a lingering grapefruit finish.

Yorkshire Dales

Abbey Works, Askrigg, North Yorkshire, DL8 3JT
☎ (01969) 622027 ☎ 07818 35592
⊕ yorkshiredalesbrewery.com

⊕ Situated in the heart of the Yorkshire Dales, brewing started in a converted milking parlour in 2005. In 2016 the brewery moved to larger premises on the edge of the village. Installation of a five-barrel plant increased capacity to 20 barrels a week. Over 150 pubs are supplied throughout the north of England. ♦ RAIB

Butter Tubs (OG 1037, ABV 3.7%)
A pale golden beer with a dry bitterness complemented by strong citrus flavours and aroma.

Askrigg Bitter (OG 1038, ABV 3.8%)

Leyburn Shawl (OG 1038, ABV 3.8%)
A crisp, dry, pale ale with an underlying sharpness.

Buckden Pike (OG 1040, ABV 3.9%)
A refreshing blonde beer with a crisp, fruity finish.

Nappa Scarr (OG 1041, ABV 4%)
A golden ale with citrus and peach flavours throughout.

Muker Silver (OG 1041, ABV 4.1%)
A blonde lager-style ale, very crisp with a sharp, hoppy finish.

Askrigg Ale (OG 1043, ABV 4.3%)

A pale golden ale with intense aroma that generates a crisp, dry flavour with a long, bitter finish.

Garsdale Smokebox (OG 1057, ABV 5.6%)
A complex ale created using smoked and dark malts. Rich chocolate and coffee flavours compliment the smokiness.

Yorkshire Heart SIBA

The Vineyard, Pool Lane, Nun Monkton, North Yorkshire, YO26 8EL
☎ (01423) 330716 ☎ 07838 030067
⊕ yorkshireheart.com

☺Yorkshire Heart has been brewing since 2011 and is situated adjacent to the Yorkshire Heart vineyard and winery, not far from York. Seven regular ales are produced. ‼♦

Lightheart (OG 1033, ABV 3.3%)
A pale ale full of fresh citrus flavours.

Hearty Bitter (OG 1037, ABV 3.7%)
A sparkling amber brown bitter with roasted malt aromas.

Hearty Mild (OG 1039, ABV 4%)
A richly flavoured mild with hints of nuts and chocolate and a natural residual sweetness.

SilverHeart IPA (OG 1039, ABV 4%)
An IPA with a slight citrus taste.

J.R.T. Best Bitter (OG 1041, ABV 4.2%)
Golden ale with a refreshing taste and flavour.

Blackheart Stout (OG 1047, ABV 4.8%)
Stout with chocolate and liquorice flavours.

Heartger Lager (OG 1047, ABV 5%)
Brewed using lager malts and citrus hops.

Young's

See Charles Wells (under W)

Zeitgeist (NEW)

c/o Crown & Kettle, 2 Oldham Road, Manchester, M4 5FE ⊕ zeitgeistbrew.co.uk

Established in 2015 by Jason, Paul and Sean, a pub landlord, an architectural assistant and an undergraduate, using spare capacity at Runaway Brewery (qv). No real ale.

Zerodegrees

⊟ Blackheath: 29-31 Montpelier Vale, Blackheath, London, SE3 0TJ

Bristol: 53 Colston Street, Bristol, BS1 5BA ☎ (0117) 925 2706

Cardiff: 27 Westgate Street, Cardiff, CF10 1DD ☎ (029) 2022 9494

Reading: 9 Bridge Street, Reading, RG1 2LR ☎ (0118) 959 7959

Brewing started in 2000 in Greenwich, London and now four brewpubs are owned, each incorporating a state-of-the-art, computer-controlled, German plant producing unfiltered and unfined ales and lagers. All beers use natural ingredients and are suitable for vegetarians, and are served from tanks using air pressure (not CO2). Wheat Ale at Bristol is now brewed as a Hefeweizen and not in the Belgian style as before. ♦

Mango (OG 1040, ABV 4%)
Mango-flavoured wheat beer with plenty of sweetness throughout, bitterness and some lingering astringency. Pale in colour, served cold and cloudy, fruit and yeast lead the aroma.

Wheat Ale (OG 1045, ABV 4.2%)
Powerful wheat aromas and flavour. Hints of coriander, clove and lemon on the nose. Fruity sweetness follows with a short citrus aftertaste.

Pale Ale (OG 1046, ABV 4.6%)
American style ale with hops, malt and a hint of caramel on the nose. Sweet malty taste with a peppery finish.

Black Lager (OG 1048, ABV 4.8%)
Czech-style beer with roast malt aromas and flavours and a long bittersweet aftertaste.

Pilsner (OG 1048, ABV 4.8%) ⑤
Clean refreshing lager in the European style with hints of sweetness. Short bitter finish.

Zymurgorium

Unit 19, Irlam Business Centre, Soapstone Way, Irlam, M44 6RA ⊕ zymurgorium.com

The UKs first craft meadery and Manchester's first distillery. In combination with the brewery it was established in Irlam in 2013. Most of its output is in bottled form.

SIBA's Beerflex scheme

In 2002 the Society of Independent Brewers (SIBA) launched a direct delivery scheme, now renamed Beerflex, which enables its members to deliver beer to individual pubs rather than to the warehouses of pub companies.

Before the scheme came into operation, small craft brewers could only sell beer to the national pubcos if they delivered beer to their depots. In one case, a brewer in Sheffield was told by Punch Taverns that the pubco would only take his beer if he delivered it to a warehouse in Liverpool and then returned to pick up the empty casks. In the time between delivery and pick-up, some of the beer would have been delivered by Punch to...Sheffield.

The scheme has been such a success that Beerflex is now a separate but wholly owned subsidiary of SIBA. See **www.siba.co.uk/dds_site**

Closed breweries

The following breweries have closed, gone out of business or suspended operations since the 2016 Guide was published:

Abbey Ford, Chertsey, Surrey
Abbot, Dunfermline, Kingdom of Fife
Anglesey, Llanerchmedd, North West Wales
Axholme, Crowle, Lincolnshire
Barearts, Todmorden, West Yorkshire
Baseline, Small Dole, West Sussex
Ben Rhydding, Ilkley, West Yorkshire
Birds, Bromsgrove, Worcestershire
Blackawton, Totnes, Devon
Blakemere, Sandiway, Cheshire
Bob's, Healey, West Yorkshire
Boggart Hole Clough, Manchester, Greater Manchester
Bondgate, Hexham, Northumberland
Bottle Cap, Aberdeen, Aberdeen & Grampian
Brightlingsea, Brightlingsea, Essex
Britannia, Forty Green, Buckinghamshire
Cats, Shennington, Oxfordshire
Celt Experience, Caerphilly, Glamorgan
Clipper, Bridgnorth, Shropshire
Combe Martin, Combe Martin, Devon
Copper Kettle, Rushden, Northamptonshire
Coppice Side, Heanor, Derbyshire
Copthorne, Darlton, Nottinghamshire
Coquetdale, Rothbury, Northumberland
Corfe Castle, Wareham, Dorset
Cranky Cobbler, Kingsthorpe, Northamptonshire
Delavals, Whitley Bay, Tyne & Wear
Dronfield, Sheffield, South Yorkshire
DT, Upwey, Dorset
Eastbury, Baydon, Wiltshire
Fakir, Norwich, Norfolk
Fisher, Noke, Oxfordshire
Florence, SE24: Herne Hill, Greater London

Frodsham, Frodsham, Cheshire
Frontier, Derby, Derbyshire
Gambling Man, Willington, County Durham
Garage, Plympton St Maurice, Devon
Hand Drawn Monkey, Huddersfield, West Yorkshire
Handmade, Capel Dewi, West Wales
Hardhead, Pensilva, Cornwall
Havant, Havant, Hampshire
Heath Village, Heath, Derbyshire
Honest Brew, SE20: Penge, Greater London
Hoptimists, Wormley, Surrey
Jarrow, Jarrow, Tyne & Wear
Jones the Brewer, Whitney-on-Wye, Herefordshire
Just a Minute, Spennymoor, County Durham
King Beer, Horsham, West Sussex
Knaresborough, Knaresborough, North Yorkshire
Kubla, Lydeard St Lawrence, Somerset
Latimer, Kettering, Northamptonshire
Little Ale Cart, Sheffield, South Yorkshire
London Fields, Hackney, Greater London
Madcap, Annan, Dumfries & Galloway
Malmesbury, Royal Wootton Bassett, Wiltshire
Masters, Greenham, Somerset
Medieval, Colston Bassett, Nottinghamshire
Mill Green, Sudbury, Suffolk
Monkey Chews, SE15: Peckham, Greater London
Moorside, Kirkbymoorside, North Yorkshire
Naked Beer, Lancing, West Sussex
North Star, Ilkeston, Derbyshire

Oates, Halifax, West Yorkshire
Ordnance City, Ashcott, Somerset
Oxfordshire, Marsh Gibbon, Oxfordshire
Potton, Potton, Bedfordshire
Private Brewery of Bob, St Albans, Hertfordshire
Privateer, Manchester, Greater Manchester
Red Even, Coleshill, Warwickshire
Red Ink, Greenham, Somerset
Redball, Chester, Cheshire
Redstone, Llangorse, Mid Wales
Riverside, Wainfleet All Saints, Lincolnshire
Rocket Science, Yate, Gloucestershire
Rusty Prop, Romsey, Hampshire
Severn Vale, Dursley, Gloucestershire
Shed, Hockley Heath, West Midlands
Sportsman, Huddersfield, West Yorkshire
Star Inn Community, Higher Broughton, Greater Manchester
Strawman, SE15: Peckham, Greater London
Sultan, SW19: Wimbledon, Greater London
Sunny Republic, Winterborne Kingston, Dorset
Terrace, Aylburton, Gloucestershire
Thirstin, Honley, West Yorkshire
Abraham Thompson, Barrow-in-Furness, Cumbria
Tipsy Angel, Warrington, Cheshire
Vens, Rawreth, Essex
Wall's, Northallerton, North Yorkshire
Wellcross, Upholland, Lancashire
Wentworth, Wentworth, South Yorkshire
Wood Street, Sheffield, South Yorkshire
Woodlands, Stapeley, Cheshire

Future breweries

The following new breweries have been notified to the Guide and will start to produce beer during 2016/2017. In a few cases, they were in production during the summer of 2016 but were too late for a full listing:

4Four, Llanfallteg, West Wales
71, Dundee, Tayside
Ainsty, Malton, North Yorkshire
Alehouse & Kitchen, Worthing, West Sussex
Barrow Green, Oxted, Surrey
Beardface & Bines, Cardiff, Glamorgan
Black Brook, Mold, North East Wales
Black Swan, Leeds, West Yorkshire
Bloomfield, Blackpool, Lancashire
Brew York, York, North Yorkshire
Brewhouse & Kitchen, Bournemouth, Dorset
Broadway, Shifnal, Shropshire
Bullhouse, Newtownards, Northern Ireland
Burton Road, Manchester, Greater Manchester
Camel, St Austell, Cornwall
Cask, Lincoln, Lincolnshire
Castle Eden, Seaham, County Durham
Chicken Foot, Bonsall, Derbyshire
Criterion, Leicester, Leicestershire
Dronfield, Chesterfield, Derbyshire
Emmanuales, Sheffield, South Yorkshire
Enfield, N18: Upper Edmonton, Greater London
Ethical, Mauchline, Ayrshire & Arran
Ewhurst, Ewhurst Green, East Sussex
Flash House, North Shields, Tyne & Wear
Forth Bridge, Edinburgh, Edinburgh & the Lothians
Gemstone, Maidstone, Kent
Golden Owl, Leeds, West Yorkshire

Grasshopper, Nottingham, Nottinghamshire
Great North Eastern, Gateshead, Tyne & Wear
Harvest, Camberley, Surrey
Hells Kettle, Darlington, County Durham
Hop Forge, Lledrod, West Wales
Horbury, Horbury, West Yorkshire
Ignition, SE13: Lewisham, Gtr London
Inkspot, SW16: Streatham, Gtr London
Inner Bay, Inverkeithing, Kingdom of Fife
JAM, Chester-le-Street, County Durham
Jolly Boys, Penistone, South Yorkshire
Karrock, Brampton, Cumbria
Laid Back, Crewe, Cheshire
Lemming, Offchurch, Warwickshire
Little Critters, Sheffield, South Yorkshire
Little Ox, Freeland, Oxfordshire
Load of Hay, NW3: Haverstock Hill, Greater London
Lucky 7, Hay-on-Wye, Herefordshire
Marko Paulo, W13: Northfields, Greater London
Melin, Pontypool, Gwent
Mercian, Buxton, Derbyshire
Mitchell's Hop House, Sheffield, South Yorkshire
Morton Collins, Ryhill, West Yorkshire
Moseley, Moseley, West Midlands
NauticAles, Ramsgate, Kent
New Religion, Cwmbran, Gwent
Northallerton, Northallerton, North Yorkshire

Oast House, Penparcau, Mid Wales
Old Pump, Dronfield, Derbyshire
Papworth, Papworth Everard, Cambridgeshire
Pershore, Pershore, Worcestershire
Pit Top, Hexham, Northumberland
Isaac Poad, Cattal, North Yorkshire
Purple Cow, Kettering, Northamptonshire
Ribble, Leyland, Lancashire
Salisbury, Bournemouth, Dorset
Seal Bay, Cardigan, West Wales
Secret Herb Garden, Loanhead, Edinburgh & the Lothians
Sentinel, Sheffield, South Yorkshire
Spotty Dog, Daventry, Northamptonshire
Stannary, Tavistock, Devon
Stardust, High Wycombe, Buckinghamshire
Steam Punk, Castleford, West Yorkshire
Stratford St Mary Swan, Stratford St Mary, Suffolk
Tarn 51, Normanton, West Yorkshire
Tin Miner's, St Ives, Cornwall
Treen's, Ponsanooth, Cornwall
True North, Sheffield, South Yorkshire
Urban Chicken, Ilkeston, Derbyshire
Westwood, Denton, Greater Manchester
Whippet, Leeds, West Yorkshire
Wily Fox, Wigan, Greater Manchester
Woodbine, Waltham Abbey, Essex
Woodbury, Woodbury Salterton, Devon
Y Maerun, Cardiff, Glamorgan

Indexes & Further Information

Places index

PLACES INDEX

Beers index

These beers refer to those in bold type in the breweries section (beers in regular production) and so therefore do not include seasonal, special or occasional beers that may be mentioned elsewhere in the text.

B52 Leadmill 837
Baby Blond Nook 867
Baby Ghost IPA Raw 893
Baby-Faced Assassin Rooster's 901
Babylon Chapel 746
Back Beach Red Rock 895
Backstage IPA Signature Brew 913
Bad to the Bone Bank Top 701
   Gun Dog 802
Bad Boy Double Top 769
Bad Day at the Office
   Alechemy 690
Bad Gorilla Big Hand 712
Bad Kitty Brass Castle 728
Badger First Call Hall &
   Woodhouse (Badger) 804
Badlands Bitter Driftwood 770
Bakestraw Bitter Austendyke 699
Bakewell Best Bitter Peak 880
Bal Maiden Rebel 893
Balaclava Leyden 840
Balham Black Belleville 709
Bally Black Ards 695
Baltic Night Stout Compass 753
Baltic Trader Export Stout Green
   Jack 799
Bamboozle Loddon 845
Bananalicious Grafton 795
Band of Brothers Sperrin 919
Bandersnatch Helm Bar 812
Bandit Wishbone 964
Banquo Newby Wyke 867
Banter Nutbrook 870
Bar'King Sticklegs 922
Bar-King Mad Froth Blowers 787
Barbarian Bitter Parker 879
Barbarian Derventio 766
Barbury Castle Three Castles 933
Barbus Barbus Butts 739
Bare Boss 723
Barefoot Blonde Tenby 930
Barista Summer Wine 925
Bark Like a Bird Mad Dog 849
Barley to Beer Bank Top 701
Barley Blonde Beckstones 707
Barley Gold Offa's Dyke 871
Barleycorn CrackleRock 757
Barm Pot Bitter Goose Eye 794
Barn Ale Tydd Steam 946
Barn Owl Cotleigh 756
Barncliffe Bitter Small World 916
Barnes Wallis Amber 692
Barney's Brew Hilden 814
Barney's Stout Townhouse 941
Barnfield Pale Ale Shalford 909
Barnsey Bath 704
Barnsley Bitter Acorn 689
   Stancill 921
Barnsley Gold Acorn 689
Barnstormer Pickled Pig 883
Barnstormers Norland 869
Barnwell Bitter Digfield 767
Barrack Street Bitter S&P 903
Barrel of Laughs Elliswood 775
Barrel Organ Blues Wentwell 956
Barron's Hopsit Exe Valley 777
Bartholomew Porter AleCraft 691
Barton Bitter Moonshine 859
Baskerville Bitter Two Towers 946
Bastion Big Hand 712
Bat Out of Hell Hart of Preston 807
Bath Best Abbey 688
Bathside Battery Bitter Harwich
   Town 809

Battersea Brownstone
   Belleville 709
Battleaxe Bournemouth 724
   Rudgate 903
Battlefield Gold Big Shed 713
Bavarian Style Wheat Beer
   Pipes 885
Bawden Rocks Driftwood 770
Bay Bitter Harwich Town 808
Bay Plockton 886
Baz's Bonce Blower Parish 879
BB (Best Bitter) Evan Evans 777
BB Donnington 768
BBC2 Brentwood 728
BBH Bitter Cathedral Heights 745
Be Merri Merrimen 855
Beach Redscar 896
Beachcomber Blonde Conwy 754
Beachcomber Southbourne 918
   Teignworthy 930
Beachy Original Beachy Head 705
Beacon Best Bitter Goldstone 794
Beacon Bitter Everards 777
Beacon Gold Malvern Hills 851
Beagle Blonde Darwin 764
Beagle Buffy's 736
Beallach Na Ba An Teallach 693
Beamish Burn Stables 920
Beamish Hall Best Bitter
   Stables 920
Bear Ale Traquair House 941
Bear Ass Beartown 706
Bear Island Newby Wyke 867
Bearded Archway Bakers
   Dozen 701
Bearly Literate Beartown 706
Bearskinful Beartown 706
Beast Of A Midlands Mild Twisted
   Barrel 945
Beast of Bloodstock Boot 722
Beast of Bodmin Penpont 881
Beast of the East Panther 878
The Beast Brightside 732
Beast Exmoor 778
Beatnik Gipsy Hill 791
Beauforts Ale Storm 924
Beauty Wood 965
Beaver Bitter Belvoir 710
Becket's Honey Ale Phipps 883
Bedrock Blonde Bluestone
   (Pembrokeshire) 721
Bedrock Keystone 832
Bee Blonde Three B's 932
Bee Keeper Atlantic 698
Bee Thrifty Three B's 932
Beeboppalula BEEspoke 708
Beech Co Pilot 751
Beechwood Bitter Chiltern 748
Beeding Best Bitter Riverside 899
Bee's Knees Bartrams 704
Bee's Organic Arkell's 695
Beer Du Jour New Bristol 865
Beer Street Hogarths 816
   London Brewing 845
Beer Wulf Weard'ALE 953
Beer Milk Street 856
Beerfest at Tiffanys Scribbler's 908
Beerier Beer Willy Good Ale! 961
Beertrix Porter Tarn Hows 929
Bees Knees Great Western 798
   Imperial 824
Befuggled Isla Vale 826
Beginners Luck Blackjack 719
Beheaded Keltek 830
Beijing Black Potbelly 888

Beinn Dearg Ale An Teallach 693
Belapur IPA Ramsbury 892
Belfast Ale Whitewater 959
Belfast Black Whitewater 959
Belgian Bugger Three Sods 934
Bell Ringer Towcester Mill 940
Bell Tower Stables 920
Belle Blackbeck 718
Bellend Blonde Ciren 749
Bellowhead Hedonism
   Potbelly 888
Bellringer Abbey 688
Bells Best Mate Ciren 749
Bells Bitter Ciren 749
Benchmark Bedlam 707
   UnBarred 948
Bengal Fox Slightly Foxed 916
Bengal Lancer Fuller's 788
Bengal Tiger Concertina 753
Ben's Stout Blue Anchor 719
Beorma Beowulf 710
Bermondsey Best Southwark 919
Bermuda Triangle Bosun's 723
Berrow Copper Leaf Towles' 940
Berserker Export Pale Ale
   Hebridean 811
Bespoke Leatherbritches 838
Bess of Hardwick Dukeries 771
Best Bitter AJ's 690
   Ash Valley 697
   Baa 700
   Bacchus 700
   Ballard's 701
   Barnet 703
   Bathams 705
   Beartown 706
   Beer Brothers 707
   Black Sheep 717
   Bloomsbury 719
   Blue Cow 720
   Brightside 732
   Britman 733
   Buzzard 740
   Calverley's 741
   Camerons 742
   Castle Gate 744
   Clearwater 750
   Copper Dragon 755
   Courage (Charles Wells) 955
   Crate 758
The Best Bitter Farr 779
Best Bitter Frog Island 786
   Gower 795
   Grain 796
   Greenodd 800
   Hackney 802
   Hunsbury Craft 822
   Kelham Island 829
   Kendrick's 831
   Lister's 841
   Long Man 846
   Market Harborough 852
   Moles 858
   Old Cannon 872
   Palmers 878
   Pennine 881
   Pheasantry 882
   Red Fox 895
   Ripple Steam 898
   Ruddles (Greene King) 800
   Snowhill 917
   St Peter's 906
   Summerskills 926
   Tavy 929
   Theakston 931

Tiley's 935
Tindall 935
Tom Wood's 965
Winster Valley 963
World's End 966
Yates' 969
Best Dark Ale Goacher's 792
Best in Show Cotswold Lion 756
Best IPA Vale 949
Best of Both Elliswood 775
Best of British Bond 722
Best Bollington 722
  Boss 723
  Brampton 726
  Brentwood 728
  Brewshed 729
  Dartmoor 763
  Downlands 769
  Eden 773
  George's 790
  Grafters 795
  Healey's 810
  Hobsons 815
  Hunters 822
  Langham 836
  Larkins 837
  Leeds 838
  Ludlow 847
  Magpie 850
  Newark 866
  Nobby's 867
  Nook 867
  Potbelly 888
  Red Cat 894
  Rhymney 897
  Tatton 929
Bete Noir Dry Stout
  Connoisseur 754
Bethnal Green Bitter Brodie's 734
Better the Devil You Know Black
  Iris 716
Betty Stogs Skinner's 915
Betty's Blonde Barlow 702
Between the Posts S&P 903
Bevans Bitter Rhymney 897
Bevin Boys Merry Miner 855
Bewick Swan Swan on the
  Green 927
Bexley's Own Beer Bexley 712
Beyond the Pale Barlow 702
  Elland 774
  Kent 831
Beyond Reasonable Stout
  Scribbler's 909
BG Sips Blue Monkey 720
Bhisti Full Mash 788
Bibble Wild Beer 960
Bible Black Nene Valley 865
Bier Head Liverpool Organic 843
Big Bang Theory Nene Valley 865
Big Bang Good Chemistry 794
Big Casino Dancing Man 762
Big Cat Byatt's 740
Big Chief Green Mill 799
  Redemption 896
Big Head Bitter Dicks 767
Big Horse Tanners 928
Big John Prospect 889
Big Muddy Wild Weather 961
Big Nose Kate Tombstone 938
Big Red Bitter Ossett 876
Big Red Chopper Heart of
  Wales 810
Big Tree Bitter Dunham
  Massey 772

Big Willie Mr Grundy's 862
The Bike Shed Schoolhouse 908
Bildeston Best Kings Head 833
Billabong Tiny Rebel 936
Billonde Brewshine 730
Billy Boy Poachers 886
Billy Goat Ale Brewshine 730
Billy Mill Three Kings 933
Billy's Best Bitter Tollgate 938
Billyonaires Gold Brewshine 730
Bircher Best Birchover 714
Bird Of Paradise Moonchild 859
Birdie Flipper Long Arm 845
Birdman Flying Monk 784
Birds & Bees Williams 961
Birmingham Special Ale Two
  Towers 946
Bisby Blonde Five Kingdoms 782
Bishop's Best Black Paw 717
Bishops Farewell Oakham 870
Bishops Finger Shepherd
  Neame 911
Bishops Tipple Wadworth 951
Bishop's Secret Castles 745
Bishop's Stortford Bitter Bishop's
  Stortford 715
Bishopswood Bitter Swansea 927
Bison Brown Phipps 883
Bit 'o' Sweet Borough (Neath) 723
Bit o'Blonde Goosnargh 795
Bitter (WHB) Weatheroak Hill 953
Bitter Bully Cheddar 747
The Bitter End Matlock Wolds
  Farm 853
Bitter Lemon Stockport 922
Bitter Old Bustard Jo C's 828
Bitter Reality Reality 893
Bitter Sweet Symphony Ale House
  Rock 690
Bitter & Twisted Harviestoun 808
Bitter Arrow 696
  Backyard 700
  Banks's 702
  Bendigo 710
  Big Lamp 712
  Black Hole 716
  BlackBar 718
  Boot 722
  Borough (Lancaster) 723
  Brack'N'Brew 725
  Brains 726
  Brakspear 726
  Brewsmith 730
  Bridgetown 731
  Brown Cow 734
  Bushy's 739
  Butcombe 739
  Cliff Quay 750
  Daleside 761
  Dove Street 769
  Elmtree 775
  Exe Valley 777
  Fat Cat 780
  Flowerpots 784
  Gas Dog 790
  Golden Valley 793
  Goose Eye 794
  Grampus 796
  Hardys & Hansons (Greene
  King) 799
  Hawkshead 809
  Heart of Wales 810
  Hill Island 815
  Holt 816
  Imperial 823

  Isfield 826
  Jennings 828
  John Smith's (Camerons) 742
  Keswick 831
  Ledbury 838
  Lees 839
  Linfit 841
  Lizard 843
  Llangollen 843
  Lymm 848
  Nene Valley 864
  Okell's 872
  Old Pie Factory 874
  Otter 876
  Paradise 879
  Pitfield (Dominion) 767
  Pumphouse 889
  Quirky 890
  Ramsbury 892
  Red Cat 894
  Red Fox 895
  Rhymney 897
  Rowton 903
  Ryedale 903
  Shipstone's (Belvoir) 710
  Slater's 915
  Steamin' Billy (Belvoir) 710
  Tetley (Banks's) 702
  Titan 937
  Topsham 939
  Tower 940
  Uley 947
  Weetwood 954
  Wensleydale 956
  White Horse 958
  Winter's 963
  Wold Top 964
  Wye Valley 968
  Wylam 968
  Yates 969
  Young's (Charles Wells) 955
Bitterus Magnus World's End 966
Bla'than Tryst 943
Black 5 Special Bewdley 711
Black Abbot Idle 823
Black Adder Mauldons 853
Black Annie Big Rabbit 713
Black As Yer 'At Glastonbury 791
Black Aye PA Alechemy 690
Black Band Porter Kirkstall 834
Black Bank Porter Three Blind
  Mice 932
Black Bart Pembrokeshire 881
Black Beard Watermill 952
Black Beauty Porter Vale 949
Black Beauty Nutbrook 870
  White Horse 958
Black Bee Phoenix 883
Black Beerd Newby Wyke 867
Black Boar/Board Break Country
  Life 757
Black Bridge Toll End 938
Black Bull Bitter Theakston 931
Black Bull Lager Three B's 932
Black Bull Porter Pied Bull 884
Black Bull Three B's 932
Black Bush Stout Little Bush 842
Black Buzzard Leighton
  Buzzard 839
Black Canon Stout Burscough 738
Black Cat Moorhouse's 860
Black Charge Dynamite Valley 772
Black Coral Stout Hornbeam 820
Black Cork Knops 835
Black Country Bitter Holden's 816

Chapter 3 Orchard Gold Fuggle Bunny 787
Chapter 4 24 Carrot Fuggle Bunny 787
Chapter 5 Oh Crumbs Fuggle Bunny 787
Chapter 6 Hazy Summer Daze Fuggle Bunny 787
Chapter 7 Russian Rare-Bit Fuggle Bunny 787
Chapter 8 Jammy Dodger Fuggle Bunny 787
Charcoal Burner High Weald 814
Charger St George's 905
Charioteer Grafton 795
Charlie Blackout Stout Toll End 938
Charrington IPA Heritage 813
Charrington Oatmeal Stout Heritage 813
Chase Bitter Blythe 721
Chase Buster Beowulf 710
The Chase Pickled Pig 883
Chaser Winster Valley 963
Chasewater Bitter Beowulf 710
Chasing Leather Force 784
Chatsworth Gold Peak 880
Chaucer Ale Green Dragon 798
CHB Chalk Hill 746
Chedhams Ale Morgans (Merry Miner) 855
Cheeky Blonde Bridgetown 731
Cheeky Imp Lincolnshire 841
Cheeky Pheasant George Wright 967
Chelsea Blonde London Beer Factory 845
Cheltenham Flyer Humpty Dumpty 821
Chemistry Heathen 810
Chennai Kissingate 834
Chequered Flag Prescott 888 Silverstone 914
Cherokee America IPA Hamelsworde 805
Cherokee Tombstone 938
Cherry Blonde Enville 776
Cherry Chilli Stout RAN 892
Cherry Dark Titanic 937
Cherry Diva New Plassey 866
Cherry Stout Bartrams 704
Cherrywood Road Elusive 775
Chesbrewnette Lion's Tale 841
Cheshire Best Bitter Cheshire Brew Brothers 747
Cheshire Cat Weetwood 954
Cheshire Gap Cheshire Brewhouse 747
Cheshire Gold Coach House 751
Cheshire IPA Dunham Massey 772
Cheshire Set Cheshire Brewhouse 747
Chester Gold Cheshire Brew Brothers 747
Chesterfield Best Bitter Spire 920
Chestnut Ale Peerless 880
Chestnut Porter Belleville 709
Chestnut Burton Old Cottage 738
Chestnuts Roasting Landlord's Friend 836
Cheswold Doncaster 768
Chevin Bitter Briscoe's 733
CHI PA Gribble 801
Chief Green Mill 799
Chieftains Export Burnside 737

Chiffchaff Digfield 767
Childcatcher Halifax Steam 804
Chili Plum Porter Waen 951
Chilled Nights Weard'ALE 953
Chilli Beer North Wales 869
Chilli Hopstar 820
Chimp Chim-in-Nee Blue Monkey 720
Chinook Blonde Goose Eye 794
Chinook Elland 774 Scarborough 908 Très Bien 942 Two Roses 946
Chipper Ale Chippenham 748
Chiswick Bitter Fuller's 788
Choc Pot 80/- Tinpot 935
Chockwork Orange Brentwood 728
Chococino Dark Beer Pitfield (Dominion) 767
Chocolate Cherry Mild Dunham Massey 772
Chocolate Marble Marble 851
Chocolate Milk Stout Kew 832
Chocolate Nutter Why Not 960
Chocolate Orange Delight Downton 770
Chocolate Orange Stout Amber 692 Moonshine 859
Chocolate Porter Beer Brothers 707 Ramsbottom Craft 891
Chocolate Slug RCH 893
Chocolate Stout MASH 853 Xtreme 969
Chocolate and Vanilla Stout Titanic 937
Chonkin Feckle Martland Mill 852
Chopper Great Heck 797
Chorlton Pale Ale Bootleg 722
Chronicle High Weald 814
Church Ledge Noss Beer Works 869
Churches Pale Ale FILO 781
Churchillian Stout Weltons 955
Churchills Pride Cathedral Heights 745
Chuzzlewit Dickens 767
Chwaden Aur Nant 863
Cinque Porter Romney Marsh 901
Circuit Bitter Castle Combe 744
Ciste Dhubh Plockton 886
Citadel Clun 751
Citra Burst Alechemy 690
Citra Hit Verulam 949
Citra IPA Franklins 786
Citra Nova Durham 772
Citra Pale Ale North Riding (Brewery) 868
Citra Pale Ashleyhay 697
Citra & Simcoe Pale Ale Calverley's 741
Citra Special Pale Ale Très Bien 942
Citra Star Anarchy 693
Citra Storm Deeply Vale 764
Citra Tip Double Top 769
Citra Ambridge 693 Brodie's 734 Caveman 745 Dove Street 769 Great Heck 797 Greenodd 800 Hop Back 817

Isca 826
Oakham 870
Saffron 904
Scarborough 908
Citrade Talke O' Th' Hill 927
Citradelic Melwood 854
Citropolis Golden Triangle 793
Citrus Blast Battlefield (Shrewsbury) 705
Citrus Snap Green Mill 799
City Gold Golden Triangle 793
CJ Porter Ashleyhay 697
Clachertyfarlie Fintry 781
Clansman Ale Hebridean 811
Claridges Crystal Nobby's 867
Clash London Porter Revolutions 897
Classic Bitter Hilltop 815
Classic Blonde Clark's 749
Classic Dark Mild Milestone 856
Classic English Ale 3 Brewers 687
Classic Gold Great Western 798
Classic IPA Navigation 863
Classic Old Ale Hepworth 812
Classic Porter Matlock Wolds Farm 853
Classic Caythorpe 745 Kingstone 833 Quirky 891 Yelland Manor 969
Claverhouse Strathaven 924
Claybrooke Bitter Pig Pub 884
Clear Cut Geeves 790
Cleddau Gold Little Dragon 842
Cleopatra Derventio 766
Cleric's Cure Three Tuns 934
Clever Fellow Fellows 780
Clever Girl Errant 777
Cliffhanger Brass Castle 727 Dancing Men 762
Clipper IPA Broughton 734
Clippings IPA Flipside 784
Clock Brew Eden St Andrews 773
Clocktower Porter BEEspoke 708
Clod Hopper Boot 722
Clogmaker Martland Mill 852
Clogwyn Gold Conwy 754
Clotworthy Dobbin Whitewater 959
Cloud Nine Six Bells 914
Cloudburst Winter's 963
Cloudy Wheat Beer Beer Brothers 707
Clout Stout Clouded Minds 750
Club Bitter Concertina 753
Club Hammer Stout Pope's Yard 887
Cluckstar Mouselow Farm 861
Clun Pale Clun 751
Clwyd Gold Facer's 778
Clyde Puffer Arran 696
Clydesdale Strathaven 924
Coachman's Best Bitter Coach House 751
Coachmans Whip St Judes 906
Coal Aston Porter Drone Valley 771
Coal Wharf Greenodd 800
Coalface Firebrick 781
Coast to Coast Hadrian Border 803
The Coaster Platform 5 886
Cob Tomos & Lilford 938
Cobb Lyme Regis 847
Cobbett's Botley 724
Cobnut Kent 831
Cochyn Llŷn 844

Dunham Gold Dunham Massey *772*
Dunham Light Dunham Massey *772*
Dunham Milk Stout Dunham Massey *772*
Dunham Porter Dunham Massey *772*
Dunham Stout Dunham Massey *772*
Dunscar Amber Ale Dunscar Bridge *772*
Dunscar Best Bitter Dunscar Bridge *772*
Dunscar Blonde Dunscar Bridge *772*
Dunscar Gold Dunscar Bridge *772*
Dunsfold Best Crafty Brewing *758*
Dunstable Giant B&T *700*
Durdle Door Dorset *768*
Durobrivae Castor *745*
Dursley Steam Bitter Severn Vale (Combined Brewers) *753*
Dusk Ruby Ale Cross Bay *759*
Dusky Maiden Stout New Plassey *866*
Dusty Penny Flipside *784*
DV8 Deeply Vale *764*
DXB Special Bitter Nene Valley *865*
Dynamite Eden *773*
Dynamo Wantsum *951*

E

Eagle Ashdown *697*
EAPA (East Anglian Pale Ale) Humpty Dumpty *821*
Earl Grey Bitter Whim *958*
Earl Grey IPA Marble *852*
Earl Grey PA Atlantic *698*
Earl's Eye Amber Cheshire Brew Brothers *747*
Earls Folly Denbigh *765*
Earls RDA Island *826*
Early Dawn Hay Rake *809*
Early Doors Dragonfly *770*
East Coast Mild Waveney *953*
East Coast Pale Knops *835*
East End Mild Tap East *928*
East India Pale Ale Dunham Massey *772*
Tunnel *944*
Whitstable *959*
East Slope Ale Goldstone *794*
East Street Cream RCH *893*
Eastern Nights Bollington *722*
Eastgate Weetwood *954*
Easy Rider Kelham Island *829*
Ebb Rock Noss Beer Works *869*
Ebony Mild Goldmark *793*
Ebony Moon Tonbridge *939*
Eclipse Brass Castle *728*
Navigation *863*
Eco Warrior Pitfield (Dominion) *768*
Eddystone South Hams *918*
Edelweiss Beath *706*
Eden Arcane Bridge *695*
Edge Pale Ale Raw *893*
Edge Kinver *833*
Sandstone *907*
Edinburgh Castle 80/- Caledonian *741*
Edinburgh Gold Stewart *922*
Edith Cavell Wolf *964*

Edwin Taylor's Extra Stout B&T *700*
Effra Ale Brixton *733*
Egyptian Goose IPA Thames Side *931*
Eight Grain Porter Brew Shack *729*
Eight Shilling Shottle Farm *912*
Eight Maidstone *850*
XT *968*
The Eighth Calverley's *741*
Eighty Bob St Andrews (St Andrews) *905*
Ein Stein Lymestone *848*
Elder Statesman Firebrick *782*
Elderflower Blonde Bluestone (Pembrokeshire) *721*
Saltaire *907*
Elderflower Chapel Street *747*
Elderquad Downton *770*
Eleanor's Ise Whistling Kite *958*
Electric Eye Pale Ale Big Smoke *713*
Electric IPA Brixton *733*
Electric Landlady Bakers Dozen *701*
Electric Mountain Heavy Industry *811*
Elemental Electric Bear *774*
Tempest *930*
Elephant Riders Fownes *785*
Eleven Bells Kendal *830*
Elisir Clouded Minds *750*
Elizabeth Ale Earl Soham *773*
Elmers Flying Monk *784*
Elmo's Fire Moles *858*
Elmstead Stout Sticklegs *922*
Elsi Pale Dukeries *771*
Elsie Mo Castle Rock *744*
Emperor James Street *828*
Emperors Whim Derventio *765*
Empire Ale Liverpool Organic *843*
Encore Lacons *835*
Endeavour Captain Cook *743*
Endless IPA Black Rock *717*
Endurance Cambrinus (Liverpool Organic) *843*
Shackleton (Brentwood) *728*
Engage Front Row *787*
Engel's Best Bitter Opa Hay's *875*
Engels Fruity Little Number Opa Hay's *875*
Engine Vein Cheshire Brewhouse *748*
Engineers Best Big Shed *713*
Englands Finest Elliswood *775*
English Ale Son of Sid *917*
Tolly Cobbold (Greene King) *800*
English Garden Franklins *786*
English IPA Three Legs *933*
English Pale Ale Taylors *930*
English Hop Fuzz *818*
Enigma Bristol Beer Factory *733*
Cryptic *760*
Kent *831*
McGivern *848*
Townhouse *941*
Entente Cordiale Independent Lakeland (Yates) *969*
Enterprise Mr Majolica *862*
Entire Stout Hop Back *818*
Entire Cronx *759*
Olde Swan *874*
EP Session Pale Revolutions *897*
EP Elgood's *774*

EPA (English Pale Ale) Bluestone (Lancashire) *721*
EPA 100 Harwich Town *808*
EPA Barum *704*
Marston's (Banks's) *702*
Pig Iron *884*
Seven Bro7hers *909*
Ephemeral Tan Force *784*
EQ Silver Street *913*
The Equation Schoolhouse *908*
Equation+ Schoolhouse *908*
Equilibrium Consall Forge *754*
Equinox Deva Craft *766*
Melwood *854*
Target *929*
Erimus Pale Ale Truefitt *943*
Erosion Coastal *752*
Erradale IPA Old Inn *873*
Erммmm... Strands *924*
ESB Fuller's *788*
Esperance Bowness Bay *725*
Espresso Stout Squawk *920*
Espresso Dark Star *763*
Essex Boys Best Bitter Crouch Vale *760*
Essex Strong Ale Maldon *850*
Essington Ale Morton *861*
Essington Bitter Morton *861*
Essington Blonde Morton *861*
Essington Dark Mild Morton *861*
Essington Gold Morton *861*
Essington IPA Morton *861*
Essington Supreme Morton *861*
Esthwaite Bitter Cumbrian Legendary *761*
Et tu Brutus Derventio *766*
Ethel Red Isfield *826*
Euro-Hop Torrside *940*
Eve's Drop S&P *903*
Even Keel Keltek *830*
Evensong Durham *772*
Evil Pigeon Xtreme *969*
Evolution Darwin *764*
Mr Majolica *862*
Ex Terra Lupus IPA Connoisseur *754*
Excalibur Merlin *854*
Excelsior Ossett *876*
Exciseman's 80/- Broughton *734*
Exeter Old Bitter Exe Valley *777*
Exhibitionist Great Western *798*
Expedition Pale Ale Lord's *847*
Explorer Intrepid *825*
Export Ale Rhymney *897*
Export Stout Boundary *724*
Extinction Ale Darwin *764*
Extra Blonde Quartz *890*
Extra Pale Ale Nottingham *870*
Extra Pale Barney's *703*
Extra Porter Little Brew *841*
Extra Stout Snout Slaughterhouse *915*

F

F'Hops Sake Half Moon *803*
Factory Pale Ale Manchester *851*
Factory Steam Seren *909*
Fade to Black Weird Beard *954*
Faintest Idea Three Blind Mice *932*
Fair Maid Inveralmond *825*
Fair Puggled Argyll *695*
Fairfield Emsworth Brewery *776*
Falcon Ale Lacons *835*
Falconer Wensleydale *956*

Fruits of the Forest Rockingham *901*
Fruity Wee Blonde Kirrie *834*
Fubar Tiny Rebel *936*
Fudgey Porter AleCraft *691*
Fuggle Eden *773*
Fuggle-Dee-Dum Goddards *792*
Fuggled Up Tindall *935*
Fuggler Little Bush *842*
Fuggles Gold Corvedale *756*
Fuggles Pale Swan on the Green *927*
Fulcrum Clearsky *749*
Full Ahead DarkTribe *763*
Full Blast Borough (Neath) *723*
Full Bore Hunters *822*
Full Monty Barlow *702*
Full Moon Porter Canopy *742*
The Full Nelson Tiny Rebel *936*
Full Nelson Two Roses *946*
Full Whack Peerless *880*
Fully Laden Geeves *790*
Funky Monkey Milk Street *856*
Funkytown Beath *706*
Furnace 3 Potts *687*
Fusilier Hop Stuff *818* Warwickshire *952*
Fusion Atomic *699* Peerless *880*
Future Sailor Errant *777*
Fuzzy Duck Gribble *801*

G

G Philips Driver Toolmakers *939*
G-Free St Peter's *906*
Gadds' Faithful Dogbolter Porter Ramsgate *892*
Gadds' No. 3 Kent Pale Ale Ramsgate *892*
Gadds' No. 5 Best Bitter Ale Ramsgate *892*
Gadds' No. 7 Bitter Ale Ramsgate *892*
Gadds' Seasider Ramsgate *892*
Gainsborough Bitter St Judes *906*
Galapagos Stout Darwin *764*
Galaxia Wylam *968*
Galaxian IPA Pope's Yard *887*
Galaxy Bishop's Crook *714* Gloucester *792* Star *921*
Gale Force Longhill *846*
Gallipoli Stout Bellinger's *710*
Gallopers Funfair *788*
Galloway Gold Sulwath *925*
Gallowgate Raw Three Kings *933*
Gallows Gold Park *879*
Galvy Stout Weldon *955*
Gambit McGivern *848*
Game Bird Born in the Borders *723*
Gamekeeper Wensleydale *956*
Ganges Harwich Town *809*
Gannet Mild Earl Soham *773*
Garland Madrigal *849*
Garsdale Smokebox Yorkshire Dales *971*
Gate Hopper Maypole *854*
Gaucho Tomos & Lilford *938* Twisted *945*
The Gavel Essex Street *777*
GB Best Grainstore *796*
GB Canterbury Brewers *743*
Gem Bath *704*

Generation Red Three Blind Mice *932*
Generous George Kirkstall *834*
Genesis Goody *794*
Genius Old Market *873*
Geniuss Winter's *963*
George 'n' Dragon Martland Mill *853*
German Hops Pils Tryst *943*
Gertcha! Old Cross *873*
GFB Hop Back *817*
Ghost Ship Adnams *689*
Ghost Town Cromarty *759*
Ghost Tractor Helm Bar *812*
Ghost Partners *879*
Ghrain Golden Ale Pokertree *887*
Giant's Organ Lacada *835*
Gift o'Gold Ramsbottom Craft *891*
Gillingham Pale Small Paul's *916*
Gilt Complex Surrey Hills *926*
Gilt MASH *853*
Ginger 5.1 Marble *851*
Ginger Bear Beartown *706*
Ginger Beer Blue Bee *720* Broxbourne *735* Enville *776* Pitfield (Dominion) *768*
Ginger Brew Bollington *722*
Ginger Cockney Quantock *890*
Ginger Doodle Stout Binghams *714*
Ginger Helmet Leatherbritches *838*
Ginger Jakey Argyll *695*
Ginger Ninja Dancing Duck *762*
Ginger Pale Ale Little Valley *842*
Ginger Panther Panther *878*
Ginger Stout Angel *694*
Gisleham Gold Trinity Ales *942*
Gladiator Dow Bridge *769* James Street *828*
Gladius Deva Craft *766*
Gladstone Guzzler Dove Street *769*
Gladstone Strong Ale Townhouse *941*
Glasdir Copper Cader *740*
Glasney College Porter Granite Rock *796*
GlassBlower Philsters *882*
Glen Top Bitter Rossendale *902*
Glencoe Black Wolf *718*
Glog Twt Lol *946*
Glorious Devon Isca *826*
Glory Daze Bumpmill *737*
Glory Barnet *703* Yeovil *970*
Glott's Hop Howard Town *821*
Glow Crane *758* TAP *928*
Go-Go American Pale Revolutions *897*
Goat's Leap Cheddar *747*
Goats Milk Church End *748*
Gobble Great Oakley *797*
Goblin Tower Denbigh *765*
God's Twisted Sister Twisted Barrel *945*
An Gof Lizard *843*
Going Off Half-Cocked Bespoke *711*
Going Underground Merry Miner *855*
Gold Ale Glenfinnan *791*
Gold Beacons Brecon *728*
Gold Bullion Camerons *742*
Gold Cup Doncaster *768*

Gold Digger Bank Top *701*
Gold Dust Born in the Borders *723*
Gold Hill Keystone *832*
Gold Hop Edmunds *774*
Gold Medal Linfit *841*
Gold Miner Jacobi *827*
Gold Muddler Andwell *694*
Gold Nugget Draycott (Derbyshire) *770*
Gold Pot 70/- Tinpot *935*
Gold Rush CrackleRock *757* Dynamite Valley *772* Lenton Lane *840* Prospect *889*
Gold Star Strong Ale Goacher's *792*
Gold Star Phipps *883* Shipstone's (Belvoir) *710* Silhill *913*
Gold Tankard Wylam *968*
Gold Testament J Church *749*
Gold Top Old Dairy *873*
Gold Wing Independent Lakeland (Strands) *924*
Gold Atlantic *698* Backyard *700* Batemans *704* Bays *705* Bowland *724* Brentwood *728* Brewsmith *730* Butcombe *739* Cader *740* Chalk Hill *746* Dancing Duck *762* Derventio *765* Donnington *768* Dorking *768* Eden *773* Exmoor *778* FILO *781* Gloucester *792* Goosnargh *795* Gower *795* Grainstore *796* Green Dragon *798* Green Mill *799* John Thompson *931* Kendal *830* Keswick *831* Kingstone *833* Ledbury *838* Little Brew *841* Littleover *843* Ludlow *847* Lytham *848* Mersea Island *855* Moles *858* Mountain Hare *861* Mumbles *862* Neath *864* Peerless *880* Pilot (Swansea) *885* Pumphouse *889* Quirky *891* Ramsbury *892* Rebel *893* Riviera *899* Ryedale *903* Salcombe *906* Sawbridgeworth *908* Snowdonia *917* Snowhill *917* Southwark *919* Stod Fold *923* Swan *926*

Gunpowder Mild Coach House *751*
Gunslinger Tombstone *938*
Gunsmoke Dukeries *771*
Gurt Stout Cerne Abbas *746*
Guthlac's Porter Golcar *793*
Guzzler York *970*
Gwyrfai Snowdonia *917*
Gyle 1 Worcester *966*
Gyle 2 Worcester *966*
Gylla's Gold Small Paul's *916*
Gypsy Queen Baltic Porter
 Moonchild *859*

H

H:E Hafod *803*
H!PA Helmsley *812*
Ha'penny Mild Harwich Town *808*
Habit Flying Monk *784*
Hadouken Tiny Rebel *936*
Hafren Three Shires *934*
Hail Merri Merrimen *855*
Hair Of The Dog Hairy Brewers *803*
Hair of the Dog Pennine *881*
Hairy Helmet Leatherbritches *838*
Haka Slater's *915*
Halcyon Daze Burton Old
 Cottage *738*
 Gyle 59 *802*
Haley's Comet Hamelsworde *804*
Half Bore Hunters *822*
Half Centurion Kinver *833*
Half Life Atomic *699*
Half Nelson Verulam *949*
Half Wit Old Bog *872*
Halfway to Heaven Langham *836*
Halo Pale Rossendale *902*
Halo Cross Bay *759*
Halt Hilden *815*
Ham 69 ESB Fat Pig *780*
Hameldon Bitter Rossendale *902*
Hammer & Tongs Old Forge *873*
Hammer Hafod *803*
Hammerstone IPA Bluestone
 (Pembrokeshire) *721*
Hampden Roar Clockwork *750*
Hampshire Bitter Botley *724*
Hampshire Rose Itchen Valley *827*
Hancock's HB Brains *726*
Handliner Coastal *751*
Handsome Forge *785*
Hanged Man Madrigal *849*
Hanged Monk Tipples *936*
Hanging Stone Ilkley *823*
Hank Tiny Rebel *936*
Hansom Ale Elliswood *775*
Happy Chappy Cromarty *759*
Happy Daze Gyle 59 *802*
Harboro Red Market
 Harborough *852*
Harbour Special Tintagel *936*
Harbourside Light Ale St Ives *905*
Hares Hopping Two Rivers *946*
Harley Barley American Pale Ale
 Blue Bell Brewhouse *720*
Harley Welbeck Abbey *955*
Harpers Great Oakley *797*
Harrier Bitter Thames Side *931*
Harrier Cotleigh *756*
Harry's Heifer Church Farm *748*
Hart IPA Hart of Stebbing *808*
Hart Stopper Harthill Village *808*
Hart's Desire Harthill Village *808*
Hartington Bitter Whim *958*
Hartington IPA Whim *958*

Hartland Blonde Forge *785*
Hartleys XB Robinsons *900*
Harts No. 1 Hart Family *807*
Harts No. 3 Hart Family *807*
Harts No. 8 Hart Family *807*
Harts No. 9 Hart Family *807*
Harvard Southwark *919*
Harvest Home Red Rye
 Moonchild *859*
Harvest Moon Mild
 Moonshine *859*
Harvest Moon Ulverston *947*
Harvest Pale Castle Rock *744*
Harvest Sun Williams *961*
Haseley Gold Philsters *882*
Haseley Rising Philsters *882*
Hat Trick IPA Muirhouse *862*
Haugh Porter Wylam *968*
Haul Gwyn Extra Pale Ale Iâl *823*
Havana Crest Dukeries *771*
Havana Moon Red Star *895*
Havelock IPA Lord's *847*
Haven Bude *736*
Havok Big Hand *712*
Hawk Pale Ale Crystalbrew *760*
Hawthorn Gold Wicked Hathern
 (Staffordshire) *920*
Hay Tomos & Lilford *938*
Haystacks Hesket Newmarket *813*
Hazelnut Mild Brass Castle *727*
Hazelnutter Clouded Minds *750*
HBB Hogs Back *816*
Head East Strathbraan *925*
Head Hunter Sperrin *919*
Head Otter *877*
Headland Red Wold Top *964*
Headlander Southbourne *918*
Headless RedWillow *896*
Headmaster Old School *874*
Heady Steady Go Crafty
 Brewing *758*
Heanor Pale Ale Bottle Brook *724*
Heart of Gold Bumpmill *737*
 Oakleaf *871*
Heart & Soul Vocation *950*
Heart Quartz *890*
Heartger Lager Yorkshire Heart *971*
Heartless RedWillow *896*
Hearty Bitter Yorkshire Heart *971*
Hearty Mild Yorkshire Heart *971*
Heath Robinson Barlow *702*
Heather Honey Black Isle *716*
Heaton Rifles Stockport *922*
Heavenly Blonde Oldershaw *875*
Hebden's Wheat Little Valley *842*
Hedge Hop Flack Manor *783*
Hedge Hopper RAN *892*
Hedge Monkey Glastonbury *791*
HedgeHopper Mobberley *858*
Hedgerow Hooligan Big
 Rabbit *713*
Hedgerow Hop Lord Conrad's *846*
Heel Stone Stonehenge *923*
Heligan Honey Skinner's *915*
Hell Cat Fat Cat *780*
Helles Deep Deeply Vale *764*
Hellhound IPA Clarkshaws *749*
Hello Dolly Gas Dog *790*
Helter Skelter Highway Basin
 City *704*
Helvellyn Gold Hesket
 Newmarket *813*
Hen Harrier Bowland *724*
Henrietta Welbeck Abbey *955*

Herefordshire Light Ale (HLA)
 Hereford *812*
Herefordshire Owd Bull
 Hereford *812*
Heresy Bishop Nick *714*
Heretic Brass Castle *728*
Heritage Trail Ale Lymm *848*
Heritage XX Firebird *781*
Heroes Bitter Beowulf *711*
Heron Bitter Thames Side *931*
Heron Porter Two Roses *946*
Herr Keith Keith *829*
Hetton Hare-raiser Hetton
 Law *813*
Hetton Harvest Hetton Law *813*
Hetton Howler Hetton Law *813*
Hetton Pale Ale Dark Horse *763*
Hewish IPA RCH *893*
Hewish Mild RCH *893*
Hey Blondie Cap House *743*
High & Dry Urban Island *948*
High Five AleCraft *691*
High Fives Willy Good Ale! *961*
High Pike Hesket Newmarket *813*
High Rise London Brewing *845*
High Speed Barnet *703*
High Voltage Heavy Industry *811*
High Wire Magic Rock *850*
Highgate Dark Mild Highgate &
 Davenports (Blue Bear) *720*
Highgate Hartshorns *808*
Highland IPA Cairngorm *741*
Highlander Fyne *789*
Highlight Trinity Ales *942*
Highway 51 Rooster's *901*
Highwayman Buntingford *737*
Hill Climb Prescott *888*
Hill Top Bitter Weatheroak Hill *953*
Hillfoot Best Bitter Blue Bee *720*
Hinkypunk Big Bog *712*
Hip Hop Ards *695*
 Fish Key *782*
 Langham *836*
Hit The Lights Weird Beard *954*
Hit the Lip Cromarty *759*
Hive Mind Weird Beard *954*
Hoard Backyard *700*
Hob Bitter Hoskins Brothers
 (Belvoir) *710*
Hobby Horse Rhymney *897*
Hobgoblin Gold Wychwood *968*
Hobgoblin Wychwood *968*
Hobson's Choice City of Cambridge
 (Wolf) *965*
Hockerley Ruby Ale Whaley
 Bridge *957*
Hogget Cotswold Lion *756*
Hogsgate Austendyke *699*
Hogshead Cotswold Pale Ale
 Uley *947*
Hogsheads 54 Wild Boar *960*
Holbeach High Street
 Austendyke *699*
Holcombe Gold Isca *826*
Holderness Dark Great
 Newsome *797*
Hole Hearted Oakleaf *871*
Holly Hop Bryncelyn *735*
Holy Cow Born in the Borders *723*
 Bridgehouse *731*
Holy Grail Llangollen *843*
Holy Joe Yates' *969*
Honey Bee Three B's *932*
Honey Blond Liverpool Organic *843*
Honey Blonde Downton *770*

I

Mill Town Mild Howard Town *821*
Mill Botley *724*
Miller Bridge Bitter
  Chadwick's *746*
The Miller's Ale Canterbury
  Ales *743*
Miller's Beer Draycott
  (Derbyshire) *770*
Millstone 8 Sail *688*
Millwright Mild 8 Sail *688*
Mine Beer Blindmans *719*
Mine's a Blonde James &
  Kirkman *828*
Mine's a Mild Holsworthy *816*
Minera Mountain Ale Conwy *754*
Miners A Pint Cap House *743*
Miners Best Bitter Merry
  Miner *855*
Miners Mild Two Rivers *946*
Minerva Derventio *765*
Mining Stout Dukeries *771*
Minotaur Milton *857*
Miracle Chapel *746*
Mirthless RedWillow *896*
Mischief Monty's *859*
Misleading Lights Harwich
  Town *809*
Miss America Alechemy *690*
Missenden Pale Malt *851*
Misty Law Kelburn *829*
Misty River Cambridge *742*
Mo' Citra Odyssey *871*
Mochaccino Stout Pilot (Leith) *885*
Mocne Piwo George Wright *967*
Mod Beat *706*
Moderation Nutbrook *870*
Moel Arthur Hafod *803*
Moel Famau Ale Hafod *803*
Moel Fenlli Hafod *803*
MOHO Mantle *851*
Mojo Tapped *928*
Mole Catcher Moles *858*
Moletrap Bitter Mauldons *853*
Molly's Malt LoveBeer *847*
Molly's Secret Brandon *727*
Monacus NZ Pale Ale Northern
  Monk *869*
Money for Old Rope Bespoke *711*
Monkey Hanger Poachers *886*
Monkey IPA Art Brew *696*
Monkey Wrench Daleside *761*
Monkey's Fist Madrigal *849*
Monkeys Mersea Island *855*
Monkeytown Mild Phoenix *883*
Monk's Gold Howard Town *821*
Monkholme Premium Reedley
  Hallows *897*
Monnow Untapped *948*
Monocle Indigenous *824*
Monstrous Mild Old Bog *872*
Monterey Beerd (Bath) *705*
Monty's Jem LoveBeer *847*
Monument Tyne Bank *947*
Monumental Blonde Kirkby
  Lonsdale *834*
Moon Gazer Amber Ale
  Norfolk *868*
Moon Gazer Dark Mild Norfolk *868*
Moon Gazer Gold IPA Norfolk *868*
Moon Gazer Golden Ale
  Norfolk *868*
Moon Gazer Ruby Ale Norfolk *868*
Moon Kissingate *834*
Moonbeam Kings Clipstone *833*

Moondance Triple fff *943*
  Yorkshire *970*
Moongazing Tring *942*
Moonlight Arkell's *695*
  Grafters *795*
  Serious *909*
Moonraker Bumpmill *737*
  Lees *839*
Moonrise Monty's *859*
Moonrocket Tipples *937*
Moonshine Abbeydale *688*
  White Park *959*
Moonstone Bluestone
  (Pembrokeshire) *721*
Moonstruck Mild Rowton *903*
Moonstruck Indigenous *824*
Moor Ale Little Valley *842*
Moor Top Buxton *740*
Moorbrook Pale Ale Blackjack *719*
Moorish Mild Norland *868*
Moose River Great Western *798*
Moray IPA Speyside Craft *919*
More Beer Rowditch *902*
More Tea Vicar J Church *749*
More Nutbrook *870*
More's Head Wantsum *951*
Moreton Mild North Cotswold *868*
Morning Dew Ashdown *697*
Morning Glory Black Tap *717*
  Tiny Rebel *936*
Morris Patriot *880*
Mosaic Blonde Oldershaw *875*
Mosaic City Golden Triangle *793*
Mosaic Pale Ale North Riding
  (Brewery) *868*
Mosaic Single Hop Pale Ale
  Hooded Ram *817*
Mosaic Brass Castle *727*
  Exit 33 *778*
  Yorkshire *970*
Mosiac IPA Black Flag *715*
Most Excellent Rivington *899*
Motueka Arbor *695*
Mount Helix West Coast Pale
  Lord's *847*
Mountain Medicine Kendal *830*
Mountain Mild Facer's *778*
Mousehole Cornish Crown *755*
MPA (Manx Pale Ale) Okell's *872*
MPA Monty's *859*
Mr Bumble Dickens *767*
Mr Chubb's Lunchtime Bitter West
  Berkshire *956*
Mr Cuddle Landlord's Friend *836*
Mr JK's Itish Landlord's Friend *836*
Mr M's Porter Red Cat *894*
Mr Sheppard's Crook Exe
  Valley *777*
Mr Splodge's Mild Thame *931*
Mr Squirrel Red Squirrel *895*
Mr Swift's Pale Ale West
  Berkshire *956*
Mr Webster's Brown Ale Landlord's
  Friend *836*
Mrs Simpsons Thriller in Vanilla
  Brown Cow *735*
Muck 'n' Straw Holsworthy *816*
Muck Cart Mild Son of Sid *917*
Mucky Duck Buffy's *736*
  Fuzzy Duck *789*
Mud City Stout Sadler's *904*
Mud Puddler Black IPA Three
  Sods *934*
Muddy Boot Red Shoot *895*
Mudpuppy Salamander *906*

Mug Billy Burscough *738*
Muker Silver Yorkshire Dales *970*
Mumma Knows Best Franklins *786*
Munchner Ticketybrew *935*
Mundham Mild Tindall *935*
Mussel Wreck Rock the Boat *900*
Musselburgh Broke Knops *835*
Mustache Petes Basin City *704*
Mustang Sally Hattie Brown's *809*
Mutineer Derwent *766*
Mutiny on the Bounty
  Campervan *742*
Mutiny Rebellion *894*
  Yorkshire *970*
Mutley's Revenge Hereford *813*
Mutts Nuts Hereford *813*
Muzzleloader Musket *863*
MV Enterprise Harbwr Tenby *806*
Mwnci Nel Nant *863*
Mydilsburgh IPA Truefitt *943*
Mystery Tor Glastonbury *791*

N

N1 Wheat Beer Pitfield
  (Dominion) *768*
N1 Hammerton *805*
N18 Clouded Minds *750*
N253 Clouded Minds *750*
N29 Clouded Minds *750*
N7 Hammerton *805*
Nailmaker Mild Enville *776*
Naked Ladies Twickenham *944*
Nanny Flyer Leyden *840*
Nappa Scarr Yorkshire Dales *970*
Nappertandy Brandon *727*
Narrow Boat Shardlow *910*
Narrow Gauge Leighton
  Buzzard *839*
Nasha IPA S&P *904*
Native Bitter Whitstable *959*
Natterjack Frog Island *787*
  Southport *918*
Natural Blonde Isla Vale *826*
Natural Gold Pennine *881*
Natural Selection Battledown *705*
Naughty Pilchard Black Flag *715*
Navigator Great Heck *797*
Navvy Phoenix *883*
Neanderthal Caveman *745*
Neap Tide Teignworthy *930*
Nectar Bitter Worcestershire *966*
Nectar Fell *780*
Ned's Big Shed Ashleyhay *697*
Neet Bude *736*
Nektar Cronx *759*
Nel's Best High House Farm *814*
Nellie's Best Wentwell *956*
Nelson Mild Double Top *769*
Nelson's Blood Fox *785*
Nelson's Column Tunnel *944*
Nelson's Delight Downton *770*
Nelson's Revenge
  Woodforde's *966*
Nelson's Right Arm Elliswood *775*
Nelsons Blood Nelson *864*
Nelsons Eye Heavy Industry *811*
Nemesis Deva Craft *766*
  Peakstones Rock *880*
  Sticklegs *922*
Neptune's Gold Hill Island *815*
Nero Milton *857*
Nessies Monster Mash
  Cairngorm *741*
NESStonia Loch Ness *844*

NESStrovia Loch Ness *844*
Nether Ending Stowey *924*
Nettlethrasher Elland *774*
Neuk Ale St Andrews (St Andrews) *905*
Never Mind the Kent Hops London Brewing *845*
Nevermore Full Mash *788*
Nevis Black Wolf *718*
New Dawn Pale Navigation *863*
New Deck Blackjack *719*
New England Best Exit 33 *778*
New Forest Ale Downton *770*
New Forest Gold Red Shoot *895*
New Honesty Blue Bell *720*
New Laund Dark Reedley Hallows *897*
New World Order Stockton *923*
New World Pale New Plassey *866*
New World Shiny *911*
New York Pale Chantry *746*
Newton's Drop Oldershaw *875*
Niamh's Nemesis Five Towns *783*
Nibley Ale Severn Vale (Combined Brewers) *753*
Nice Weather 4 Ducks Dancing Duck *762*
Nicholas De Luda Black Horse *716*
Nicholson's American Pale Ale Leamside *838*
Nicholson's Pale Ale St Austell *905*
Nicky Nacky Noo Axton *699*
Night Hops Stout Bluestone (Lancashire) *721*
Night Jar Dark Horse *763*
Night Porter Cambridge *742*
Night on the Tiles AleCraft *691*
Night Train Rail Ale *891*
Nightfall Bitter Cross Bay *759*
Nightlight Mild Elmtree *775*
Nightmare Porter Hambleton *804*
Nightwatch Porter Moonshine *859*
Nightwatchman East London *773*
Nimrod Shackleton (Brentwood) *728*
Nine Tails Black Cat *715*
Ninja Summerskills *926*
Ninkasia Connoisseur *754*
The Ninth Calverley's *741*
Nip Grainstore *796*
Nipper Bitter Island *826*
Nirvana Odyssey *871*
No. 1: East Coast Pale Ale Bullards *736*
No. 1 Golden Ale Nine Standards (Settle) *909*
No. 1 Pale Ale Burnside *737*
No. 1 Bucks Star *735* Colchester *752* Odcombe *871*
No. 10 King's Cliffe *832*
No. 2: India Pale Ale Bullards *736*
No. 2 Pale Ale Nine Standards (Settle) *909*
No. 2 Stout Stringers *925*
No. 3: Amber Ale Bullards *736*
No. 3 Porter Nine Standards (Settle) *909*
No. 4 Amber Ale Nine Standards (Settle) *909*
No. 4: Session IPA Bullards *736*
No. 5: Best Red Bitter Bullards *736*
No. 5 Porter Harrogate *807*
No. 6: Rye Pale Ale Bullards *736*
No. 7 Stancill *921*

No. 79 Firebird *781*
No. 8 Kendrick's *831*
No. 88 Colchester *752*
No. 9 Barley Wine Coniston *754*
No Brakes IPA Fixed Wheel *783*
No Escape Reality *893*
No Man's Land Mr Grundy's *862*
No Name Stout Brighton Bier *731*
No Name Witham *964*
No Notion Porter All Hallows *691*
No X Denbigh *765*
Noble Eden Ale Heart of Wales *810*
Noble Kinver *833*
Noggin' Six Bells *914*
Noire Bent Ink *708*
Nook of Pendle Reedley Hallows *897*
Nor'Hop Moor *860*
Norfolk Honey Ale Why Not *960*
Norfolk Kiwi Jo C's *828*
Norfolk Nectar Humpty Dumpty *822*
Norfolk Nog Woodforde's *966*
Norfolk Poacher Brandon *727*
Norfolk Pride Wolf *965*
Norfolk Stoat Two Rivers *946*
Norfolk Terrier Buffy's *736*
Norfolk's 80 Shilling Ale Elmtree *775*
Norman's Conquest MM Cottage *757*
Norman's Pride Corvedale *756*
North Coast IPA GT *801*
North Coast Voodoo Madrigal *849*
North Riding Bitter Truefitt *943*
North Star Porter Facer's *778*
North Star Harbwr Tenby *806*
Silhill *913*
North Wall Hop Kettle *818*
The North Will Rise Again Stringers *925*
Northamptonshire Bitter Hoggleys (Phipps) *883*
Northcote Blonde Belleville *709*
Northerly Windy *963*
Northern Blonde Brass Castle *727*
Northern Light Orkney *876*
Northern Lights George Wright *968*
Green Mill *799*
Northern Soul Briggs *731*
Northern Star Hop Fuzz *818*
Northumbrian Blonde Mordue *861*
Northumbrian Gold Hadrian Border *803*
Northumbrian Acton *689*
Northway IPA Fulstow *788*
Norton Ale Shoes *912*
Norton Pale Ale People's *882*
Norwegian Blue Buffy's *736* Newark *866*
Norwich Dragon Tindall *935*
Nos Smoked Porter Heavy Industry *811*
Nosey Parker Indigenous *824*
Not Just For Mother Landlord's Friend *836*
Not Lager Black Tap *717*
Notting Hill Amber Moncada *858*
Notting Hill Bitter Moncada *858*
Notting Hill Blonde Moncada *858*
Notting Hill Porter Moncada *858*
Notting Hill Ruby Rye Moncada *858*

Notting Hill Stout Moncada *858*
Nova Foresta Vibrant Forest *949*
Nova Bristol Beer Factory *733*
Now In a Minute Mad Dog *849*
NPA (Netherton Pale Ale) Olde Swan *875*
NPA (Newark Pale Ale) Newark *866*
NS IPA Ramsbottom Craft *891*
Nuclear Sunset Hardknott *806*
Nugget VOG *950*
Number One Taylors *930*
Nuptu'ale Oakleaf *871*
Nut Brown Ale de bRus *764* Pope's *887*
Nut Brown Carlisle *744* Hilden *814* Shipstone's (Belvoir) *710*
Nut Red Coke Borough (Neath) *723*
Nutty Black Thwaites *934*
Nutty Slack Prospect *889*
Nyewood Gold Ballard's *701*
NZPA Hawkshead *809*

O

01 Otley *876*
010 Oxymoron Otley *876*
011 Motley Brew Otley *876*
012 Thai Bo Otley *876*
02 Croeso Otley *876*
03 Boss Otley *876*
04 Colombo Otley *876*
05 Hop Angeles Otley *876*
06 Porter Otley *876*
07 Weissen Otley *876*
09 Blonde Otley *876*
Oak Ale Burton Old Cottage *738*
Oak Barrel Stout Rowett *902*
Oak Grain *796*
Oarsome Ale Two Beach *945*
Oast House Weetwood *954* White Park *959*
Oat & Coffee Stout Vibrant Forest *949*
Oat Mill Stout Bollington *722*
Oat Stout Nook *867*
Oatmeal Pale Brass Castle *727*
Oatmeal Stout Brewsmith *730* Carlisle *744* Conwy *754* Corvedale *756* de bRus *764* Peerless *880* St Andrews (St Andrews) *905*
Obelisk Dunham Massey *772*
Oblivion Peakstones Rock *880*
Ochr Tywyll y Mws/Dark Side of the Moose Purple Moose *889*
Octane Silverstone *914*
Odd Ball Red Offbeat *872*
Odds & Sods Three Blind Mice *932*
ODE Ale Two Beach *945*
Odin Brightside *732*
Odyssey Fallen Brewery *779*
Off the Rails Stonehouse *923*
Offa's Dyke New Plassey *866*
Offa's Pride Offa's Dyke *871*
Offilers' Best Bitter Heritage *813*
Offshore Howler Surfing Monkey *926*
Oh Boy Bryncelyn *735*
Oh, Sunny Day Ramsbottom Craft *891*

Piggy Bling Pickled Pig 883
Pigling Blonde Tarn Hows 929
Pigmalion Bitter Fat Pig 780
Pigs Best Bitter Pig Pub 885
Pigs Can Fly Pickled Pig 883
Pigs Do Fly Potbelly 888
Pigs Head in a Pottage Pot Moody Goose 859
Pigswill Stonehenge 923
Pike Blackedge 718
Pikefields Pigeon Fishers 885
Pilcrow Pale Dorking 768
Pilgrim Atlantic 698
Pilgrim's Pale Ale Dancing Man 762
Pillbox Kennet & Avon 831
Pilot Co Pilot 751
    Padstow 878
Pilsner Zerodegrees 971
Pin Hammer Toolmakers 939
Pin Up Beer Ink 708
Pinch Noggin Three B's 932
Pinewoods Pale Ale Harrogate 807
Pinnacle Blonde Naylor's 863
Pinnacle Friday Beer 786
    Hillside 815
Pint Marble 851
Pioneer Stout Sherfield Village 911
Pioneer Lenton Lane 840
    Prospect 889
Pipe Dream George Wright 967
Pirate Twisted 945
Pirate's Gold Muirhouse 862
Pirates Gold Wooden Hand 965
Piston Bitter Beer Engine 708
Piston Bob Tydd Steam 946
Piston Broke Box Steam 725
Pit Head Porter Borough (Neath) 723
Pit Pony Merry Miner 855
    Northumberland 869
Pitch Porter Rossendale 902
Pitchfork RCH 893
Pitstop Silverstone 914
Pivo Estivo Kelburn 829
Pixel Bandit Lawman 837
Plan B Stringers 925
Plan Bee BEEspoke 708
Plassey Bitter New Plassey 866
Plateau Burning Sky 737
Platform 3 Bath 705
    Whitby 958
Platinum Blonde Mad Cat 849
Platinum Blackedge 718
Playon Kendrick's 831
Pleasant Blonde Black Horse 716
Ploughman's Pride Great Newsome 797
Plucking Pheasant Gribble 801
Plum Porter Titanic 937
Plunder Jollyboat 829
Poacher Wensleydale 956
Poachers Ale Parish 879
Poachers Pocket Church End 748
Poacher's Thirst Pigeon Fishers 885
Poets Tipple Ashover 697
Poison Redscar 896
Pokies Blackjack 719
Polar Eclipse Beartown 706
Polar Paw Black Paw 717
Poldark Ale Tintagel 936
Polly Paine's Porter Godstone 792
Polly's Folly Buffy's 736
Pommies Revenge Goose Eye 794
Pondtail Pale Godstone 792

Ponte Carlo Stout Five Towns 783
Pontisbright Colchester 752
Pony Dancing Cows 761
Ponytail Pale Ale Très Bien 942
Pooley's Golden Weighbridge 954
Poquito Pequeno Bexar County 711
Port o' Call Bank Top 701
Port Stout Hanlons 805
Portcullis Castles 745
Ported Amoor Moor 860
Porter 28 Urban Island 948
Porter Bedlam 707
    Black Isle 716
    Bridgehouse 731
    Brockley 733
    Cornish Crown 756
    Crafty Pint 758
    Credence 759
    Harbour 806
    Hartshorns 808
    Heathen 810
    Hilltop 815
    Intrepid 825
    Leatherbritches 838
    Little Brew 841
    Loose Cannon 846
    moogBREW 859
    Quirky 890
    Saffron 904
    Sheffield 911
    Stancill 921
    Tavy 929
    Tiley's 935
    Très Bien 942
Porterhead Riviera 899
Porters Pride Two Rivers 946
Porteur BlackBar 718
Porthbud Bude 736
Porthleven Skinner's 915
Portland Black Welbeck Abbey 955
Portly Stout Rowton 903
Poseidon Extra Coastal 752
Posh Blonde Oldershaw 875
POSH IPA Yeovil 970
Posh Pooch Ascot 696
Post Impact Porter Staggeringly Good 921
Post Mistress Sandstone 908
Posthorn Premium Coach House 751
Postlethwaite Coach House 751
Pot Black Porter Green Mill 799
Pot Black Tinpot 935
Pothole Porter Ial 823
Potholer Cheddar 747
Potion No. 9 Penzance 882
Potter's Ale Wessex 956
Potter's Porter Talke O' Th' Hill 927
Potters Weal Weal 953
Potters' Fields Porter Southwark 919
Powder Monkey Nelson 864
Power Blue Kissingate 834
Power Station Appleford 695
    Toll End 938
Power Gower 795
Powerhouse Porter Sambrook's 907
Praetorian Porter Dow Bridge 769
Prairie Fox Slightly Foxed 916
Prancing Pony Middle Earth 855
Prasto's Porter Boudicca 724
Premier Bitter Bartrams 703
    Moorhouse's 860

Premium Brown Market Harborough 852
Premium Stout Kingstone 833
Premium Battledown 705
    Big Lamp 713
    Radlett 891
    Slater's 915
Preservation Fine Ale Castle Rock 744
Pressed Rat & Warthog Triple fff 943
Prestwich Pale Beer Nouveau 708
Prestwood's Best Malt 851
Pretender NZ Blonde Revolutions 897
Pricky Back Otchan Great Newsome 797
Pride 'n' Joy Weltons 955
Pride & Joy Vocation 950
Pride of Dartmoor Black Tor 717
Pride of Fulstow Fulstow 788
Pride of Pendle Moorhouse's 860
Pride of Sheffield Kelham Island 829
Pride Abstract Jungle 689
    Devon 766
    Padstow 878
    Poachers 886
    Saltaire 907
Priessnitz Plzen Malvern Hills 851
Prince Bishop Ale Big Lamp 713
Prince of DarkNESS Loch Ness 844
Prince of Wales IPA Ash Valley 697
Priory Gold Burscough 737
    Prior's Well 888
Priory Mild Nethergate 865
Priory Pale Gloucester 792
Private Sector Betteridge's 711
Prizefighter Best Bitter Crooked Brook 759
Procrastination Tinpot 935
Progress Pilgrim 885
Project Babylon Pale Ale Gun 801
Propeller Pale Ale Decent 764
Proper Ansome Clearwater 750
Proper IPA Broughton 734
Proper Job St Austell 905
Prophecy Bath 704
Prophets of Doom Fownes 785
Prospect Organic Hepworth 812
Prospect Bexar County 711
    Shotover 912
Prospector Dynamite Valley 772
    Halfpenny 804
Prototype North 868
Prowler Pale Red Cat 894
Pryde Little London 842
PSB Parish 879
Pucks Folly Maldon 850
Puddled Duck Tarn Hows 929
Puddlers Peril Borough (Neath) 723
Puffin Ale Orkney 876
Pug IPA Patriot 880
Pugin's Gold Peakstones Rock 880
Pullet Please High House Farm 814
Pullman First Class Ale Hepworth 812
Pump Fiction Hoggleys (Phipps) 883
The Pump Room Harrogate 807
Pumphouse Pale Sambrook's 907
Punch in the Face Totally Brewed 940
Punter Upham 948

Redhead Mad Cat *849*
Tipples *937*
Twickenham *944*
Redhouse Premium Bexley *712*
Redman Worsthorne *967*
RedNESS Loch Ness *844*
Rednik Stout Buxton *740*
Redoubt Stout Harwich Town *809*
Redsmith Serious *909*
Redwood American IPA Red
Squirrel *895*
Redwood Grain *796*
Weatheroak *953*
Reedcutter Humpty Dumpty *821*
Reedlighter Woodforde's *966*
Reef Break Country Life *757*
Reel Ale Teignworthy *930*
Reet Pale Blue Bee *720*
The Reeve's Ale Canterbury
Ales *743*
Reflex Drygate *771*
Regal Blond Byatt's *740*
Regnitz Kelburn *829*
Reg's Tipple Gribble *801*
Regulators Tombstone *938*
Reiver's IPA Hadrian Border *803*
Release the Chimps Nene
Valley *865*
Reliance Pale Ale Brixton *733*
Reliant Robin Rockin' Robin *900*
Remedy Ashley Down *697*
Remember Me Taylors *930*
Renaissance Ruby Mild
Whitstable *959*
Renaissance Geeves *790*
Renegade IPA Hop Stuff *818*
Ren's Pride Church Farm *748*
Repton Cross Boot *722*
Rescue Red Nook *867*
Reservoir Gold Gates Burton *790*
Reservoir Hogs Hoggleys
(Phipps) *883*
Reservoir Gates Burton *790*
Resistance Summer Wine *925*
Resolute Bitter Andwell *694*
Resolution IPA Dawkins *764*
Responsibly Cerne Abbas *746*
Nutbrook *870*
Strands *924*
Restless Abstract Jungle *689*
Restoration Ale Leighton
Buzzard *839*
Resurrected Prior's Well *888*
Retribution Toll End *938*
Return of the Empire Moor *860*
Rev Hawker Forge *785*
Rev James Gold Brains *726*
Rev James Rye Brains *726*
Rev James Brains *726*
Rev Rob Beckstones *707*
Revelation Dark Star *763*
Revenge Lyme Regis *848*
Winter's *963*
Reverend Eaton Shardlow *910*
Revival Halfpenny *804*
Moor *860*
Revolution Amber *692*
Revolver Pilot (Swansea) *885*
RFA Sir Galahad Harbwr Tenby *806*
Rhapsody Alechemy *690*
Rhatas Black Dog (Hambleton) *804*
Rhidonkulous Fool Hardy *784*
Rhino Rye Ascot *697*
Rhode Island Red Bitter
Brimstage *732*

Rhubarb Heathen *810*
Rhythm Stick Billericay *713*
Riber Gold Matlock Wolds
Farm *853*
Rich Ruby Milestone *856*
Richard Mason 1888 Irwell
Works *825*
Richmond Rye Kew *832*
Rider Twisted *945*
Riders on the Storm Kelham
Island *830*
Ridgeway Tring *942*
Ridley's Rite Bishop Nick *714*
Ridware Pale Blythe *721*
Riggwelter Black Sheep *717*
Right Turn Clyde Blue Monkey *720*
Ring of Fire Three Kings *933*
Ringmaster Magic Rock *849*
Ringneck Amber Ale
Pheasantry *882*
Ringtail Burscough *738*
Ripper Tripel Green Jack *799*
Riptide Littlehampton *842*
Neptune *865*
Rising Sun Green Jack *799*
Rising Sunsation Millstone *857*
Risky Blond Fool Hardy *784*
Ritual Alechemy *690*
Rival Blond Fool Hardy *784*
Rivendale Middle Earth *855*
River Cottage EPA Skinner's *915*
River Blackjack *719*
Riverbed Red New River *866*
Roadrunner Bottle Brook *724*
RoadRunner Mowberley *858*
Roaring Meg Springhead *920*
Robbie's Red Adur *690*
Robin Hood Robin Hood *899*
Springhead *920*
Robin Redbest Rockin' Robin *901*
Robust Porter Fell *780*
Rock 'n' Rolla Deverell's *766*
Rock Ale Bitter Beer
Nottingham *870*
Rock Ale Mild Beer
Nottingham *870*
Rock Ape Poachers *886*
Rock the Cas'Bar Ale House
Rock *690*
Rock Steady Mantle *851*
Target *929*
Rocka Hula Rockin' Robin *901*
Rockabilly Beat *706*
Rocket Brigade Cullercoats *761*
Rocket Kolsch Rocket Town *900*
Rocket Brunswick *735*
Stockton *923*
Rocketeer Bluestone
(Pembrokeshire) *721*
Rockhopper Bluestone
(Pembrokeshire) *721*
Rockin' Goose Ards *695*
Rococo Geeves *790*
Rodeo Tapped *928*
Rogue Red Hop Ale Summer
Wine *926*
Rogue Wave Cromarty *759*
RoK Black Wolf *718*
Rolling Hitch Darwin *764*
Rolling Maul Snaggletooth *917*
Rolling Stone 8 Sail *688*
Roly Poly Odcombe *871*
Roman Black George Wright *967*
Romani ite Domum
Colchester *752*

Rombald Ilkley *823*
Romney Amber Ale Romney
Marsh *901*
Romney Best Romney Marsh *901*
Romney Golden Ale Romney
Marsh *901*
Roodee Dark Cheshire Brew
Brothers *747*
Root Thirteen Downlands *769*
Rope Slider Shropshire Brewer *913*
Ropetackle Golden Ale Adur *690*
Rorke's Drift Quantock *890*
Rose and Ginger Wheat Beer
Ticketybrew *935*
Rosemary Ale Tomos & Lilford *938*
RosendAle Bullfinch *736*
Rosie's Sweatbox Weldon *955*
Rotten End Shalford *910*
Rou Shou Fool Hardy *784*
Rouge Fat *779*
Rough Justice Anarchy *693*
Rougham Ready Bartrams *703*
Roughtor Penpont *881*
Roundabout Greenodd *800*
Roundhead Porter Why Not *960*
Route 701 Xtreme *969*
Rowley Mild Wensleydale *956*
Rowlock Clearsky *749*
Royal Fanfare Top-Notch *939*
Royal Ginger Brandon *727*
Royal Gold Ashdown *697*
Royal Hunt Hunters *822*
Royal Stag IPA Quantock *890*
Royal Standard 1485
Elliswood *775*
Royal Standard Pale
moogBREW *859*
Royal Lytham *848*
RPA Rockin' Robin *901*
Rubecca Scribbler's *908*
Ruby (1874) Mild Bushy's *739*
Ruby Duck Fuzzy Duck *789*
Ruby English Ale 3 Brewers *687*
Ruby EPA Tally Ho! *927*
Ruby Mild Rudgate *903*
Ruby Red AJ's *690*
Howling Hops *821*
Moorstone *860*
St Peter's *906*
Wilson Potter *962*
Ruby Ruby Ruby Ruby
Connoisseur *754*
Ruby, Ruby, Ruby, Ruby Silver
Street *913*
Ruby Freewheelin' *786*
Little Brew *841*
MASH *853*
Quirky *891*
TAP *928*
Titan *937*
Yeovil *970*
Rucking Mole Moles *858*
Ruddy Duck Goldstone *794*
Ruddy L DarkTribe *763*
Rudy Darter Andwell *694*
Ruff Justice Watermill *952*
Rugby Ball Stitcher IPA
Warwickshire *952*
Rum 'n' Raisin Stout RAN *892*
Rumour Gower *795*
Run o't' Mill Verulam *949*
RunAbout Stout Clockwork *750*
Runner Truman's *943*
Running the Gauntlet
Bespoke *711*

Shepherd's Delight Cotswold Lion 756
Shepherd's Warning Wild Weather 961
Shere Drop Surrey Hills 926
The Sheriff Of Nottingham Robin Hood 899
Sheriff Lincoln Green 840
Sheriff's Tipple Castle Rock 744
Sherpa Porter Tryst 943
Sherwood Pale Ale Milestone 856
Sherwood Reserve Castle Rock 744
Sherwood Lincoln Green 840
Shetland Pale Ale Lerwick 840
Shih Tzu Faced Watermill 952
Shine On Milestone 856
Shingle Bay Salcombe 906
Shiny Bird Brain 714
Ship Hop Ale Ship Inn 912
Shipley Stout BEEspoke 708
Shipwreck Coast Penpont 881
Shipwreck IPA Liverpool Organic 843
Shipwrecked Elliswood 775
Shire Bitter Hexhamshire 814
Shmae But Cwm Rhondda 761
Shoemaker Frog Island 787
Sholly Amber Caffle 741
Shoot to Thrill Griffin 801
Shooting Star Hammerpot 805
Shore Break Country Life 757
Shoreditch Stout Pitfield (Dominion) 768
Shottle Gold Shottle Farm 912
Shottle Pale Ale Shottle Farm 912
Shottlecock Shottle Farm 912
Showcase Norland 868
Shropshire Gold Salopian 906
Shropshire Lad Wood 965
Shropshire Lass Wood 965
Shuffled Deck Blackjack 719
Shuggy Boat Blonde Special Cullercoats 761
Shuggy Boat Blonde Cullercoats 760
Shuttle Ale Three B's 932
Shy Talk Bitter Poachers 886
Side Pocket for a Toad Tring 942
Signature Pale Signature Brew 913
Signature 1648 687
McEwan's (Charles Wells) 955
Sikes Dickens 767
Silhouette Grafton 795
Silk of Amnesia Storm 924
Silkie Stout Loch Lomond 844
Silly Billy Brewshine 730
Silver Adder Mauldons 853
Silver Buckles Stables 920
Silver Bullet Beer Engine 708
Silver Dollar Tyne Bank 947
Silver King Ossett 876
Silver Owl Greenfield 800
Silver Tally Prospect 889
Silver Tip Beerd (Bath) 705
SilverHeart IPA Yorkshire Heart 971
Simarillo Hopshackle 819
Simcoe Special Pale Ale Très Bien 942
Simcoe Exit 33 778
Great Heck 797
Matlock Wolds Farm 853
Simmer Dim Valhalla 949
Simpkiss Enville 776

Simple Pleasures Ale Nene Valley 864
Simplicity AleCraft 691
Simpson's Original Hop & Stagger 817
Sine Qua Non Twisted Barrel 945
Single Blonde Tyne Bank 947
Single Hop IPA Weatheroak Hill 953
Single Hop Ascot 696
Oxted 877
Singletrack Kirkby Lonsdale 834
SIP First Chop 782
Sir Edgar Harrington's Last Wolf Unsworth's Yard 948
Sir Keith Park Bewdley 711
Sir Keith Keith 829
Sir Philip Wincle 962
Sir Roger's Porter Earl Soham 773
Sir Thomas Gardyner Brick 730
Sire Kings Clipstone 833
Sirius Dog Star Wolf 964
Sitting Bull Pied Bull 884
Sitting Duck Green Duck 798
Six Hour Lunch Rowett 902
Six Points Tweed 944
Six XT 968
Sixteen Strides Crafty Beers 758
Sjolmet Stout Valhalla 949
Skaddly Puck Caffle 741
Skelpt Lug Argyll 695
Skew Sunshine Ale Suthwyk (Oakleaf) 871
Skiddaw Special Bitter Hesket Newmarket 813
Skiffle Shortts Farm 912
Skinny Blonde Argyll 695
Skinny Pig Tinshed 936
Skippers Mersea Island 855
Skirp Gold Caffle 740
Skirrid Tudor 943
Skrimshander IPA Hopdaemon 819
Skull Splitter Orkney 876
Skydiver Steamin' Billy (Belvoir) 710
Skye Black Isle of Skye 827
Skye Blaven Isle of Skye 827
Skye Gold Isle of Skye 827
Skye IPA Isle of Skye 827
Skye Light Isle of Skye 827
Skye Otter Ale Isle of Skye 827
Skye Red Isle of Skye 827
Skyline London Brewing 845
Slainte Houston 820
Slap Ale Cannon Royall 742
Slap in the Face Totally Brewed 940
Slap N'Tickle Lord Conrad's 846
Slasher Piddle 884
Sleck Dust Great Newsome 797
Sledgehammer Stout Fulstow 788
Sledgehammer Broughs 734
Old Forge 873
Sleeper Heavy Beer Engine 708
Sleepless RedWillow 896
Slightly Foxed Slightly Foxed 916
Slipper Emsworth Brewery 776
Slippery Jack Brandon 727
Slipstream Round Tower 902
Slipway Captain Cook 743
Slowly Slipping Under Beath 706
Slubbers Gold Milltown 857
Slumbering Monk Joule's 829
Slumdog Leadmill 837

Sly Wolf Wolf 964
Small & Mighty Happy Valley 805
Small Saison Blackjack 719
Smash Crossed Anchors 759
Smatcher Tawny Radnorshire 891
Smelter's Stout Kissingate 834
Smild Rother Valley 902
Smiling Assassin Falstaff 779
Smoke Bomb Anarchy 693
Smoked Green Tea PA Atlantic 698
Smoked Porter Franklins 786
Howling Hops 821
Slater's 915
Top Out 939
Smokeless RedWillow 896
Smokestack Porter Tap East 928
Smokey Horyzon Muor 860
Smokey Joe Stout Geeves 790
Smokey Joe Green Mill 799
Smokey Joe's Black Beer Hopstar 820
SmokieNESS Loch Ness 844
Smooth Criminal Ale House Rock 690
Smooth Hoperator Calvors 741
Smuggler Rebellion 894
Snake Eyes Black Iris 716
Sneaky Steamer Riverside 899
Sneaky Wee Orkney Stout Swannay 927
Sneck Lifter Jennings 828
Snetterton Scary Tree Elmtree 775
Snow Top Old Dairy 873
Snowball Waen 951
Snoweater Brass Castle 728
Snuggery Shackleton (Brentwood) 728
So'Hop Moor 860
SOAB Potbelly 888
Socks & Sandals King Street 832
SOD B&T 700
Sod Idle 823
Soggy Seagull Dancing Men 762
Solar Power Isle of Purbeck 827
Solar Cerddin 746
Solaris Session Pale Ale Big Smoke 713
Solaris Big Hand 712
Newbridge 867
Solitaire Blackjack 719
SOLO Green Bullet Sherfield Village 911
SOLO Single Hop Sherfield Village 911
SOLO Southern Gold Sherfield Village 911
Solstice Stout Hoggleys (Phipps) 883
Solstice Three Tuns 934
Solway Mist Sulwath 925
Some Light Shed 910
Some Like It Blond Worsthorne 967
Somerset Ale Abbey 688
Son of a Bitch Bullmastiff 736
Sonic Screwdriver Toolmakers 939
Sonoma AleCraft 691
Track 941
Sorachi Saison Left Bank 839
Sorley Boy's Stash Lacada 835
SOS B&T 700
Soul Survivor Hellhound 812
Soul Frensham 786
Soundwave IPA Siren Craft 914
The Source Tillingbourne 935

South Downs Ale Beachy Head *705*
South Eastern Bloc Stout Bullfinch *736*
South Island Pale Saltaire *907*
South Island VOG *950*
South! Shackleton (Brentwood) *728*
Southerly Windy *963*
Southern Bitter Cottage *757*
Southern Cross Weetwood *954*
Southpaw Gipsy Hill *791*
Southwold Bitter Adnams *689*
Sovereign Gold Burton Bridge *738*
Sovereign Ram Single Hop Hooded Ram *817*
SPA (Special Pale Ale) Buxton *740*
SPA AJ's *690*
    Cornish Crown *756*
Space Hoppy IPA Binghams *714*
Space is the Place Out There *877*
Space Pigeon Xtreme *969*
Spanish Stout Hamelsworde *804*
Spank (Industrial IPA) Blueball *721*
Spankers IPA Park *879*
Spanner Hand Totnes *940*
Sparkling WIT Connoisseur *754*
Sparta Milton *857*
Speak Easy Transatlantic Pale Ale Powderkeg *888*
Specduckular Mallard *850*
Special Ale Spitting Feathers *920*
Special B46 Greyhound *801*
Special Draught Yates' *969*
Special English Ale 3 Brewers *687*
Special Oatmeal Stout Coniston *754*
Special Pale Ale Bath *704*
Special Relationship Mad Cat *849*
Special Battledown *705*
    Holden's *816*
    Linfit *841*
    Lister's *841*
    Sharp's *910*
    Young's (Charles Wells) *955*
Special/House Ale Goacher's *792*
Speciale Brampton *726*
Spectre Ghost *791*
Spectrum Atomic *699*
Speedwell Bitter Townes *941*
Spellbound Merlin *854*
Spey Stout Spey Valley *919*
Spicy Sausage Lincolnshire *841*
Spike's Gold Small World *916*
Spikey Blonde Six Bells *914*
Spingo Middle Blue Anchor *719*
Spingo Special Blue Anchor *719*
Spinners Gold Martland Mill *852*
Spiral Stout Boudicca *724*
Spire Ale Stonehenge *923*
Spire Dancer Shropshire Brewer *913*
Spirit of Kent Westerham *957*
Spitfire Gold Shepherd Neame *911*
Spitfire Shepherd Neame *911*
Spittin' Feathers Mallard *850*
Spodden Pilsner Bluestone (Lancashire) *721*
Spot Light Old Spot *874*
Spot O'Bother Old Spot *874*
Spotland Gold Phoenix *883*
Spring Tide Teignworthy *930*
Spring Zing Hop Back *818*
Spring Odcombe *871*

Springfield Broughs *734*
Springwell Goose Eye *794*
Sprocket IPA 3 Potts *687*
Spun Gold Carlisle *743*
    Twisted Oak *945*
Sputnik North *868*
Square Rigger IPA Daleside *761*
Squire's Gold Woodcote Manor *965*
Squires Best Erddig *776*
Squires Gamble Saffron *904*
Squirrel's Nuts Beeston *709*
Sqweal Weal *953*
SSA (Saundersfoot Supreme Ale) Pembrokeshire *881*
Staffie Blythe *721*
Stag Cairngorm *741*
    Fxmoor *778*
Stagecoach Tombstone *938*
Staggersaurus Staggeringly Good *921*
Stainless Stancill *921*
Stairway to Heaven Burton Bridge *738*
    White Rose *959*
Stairway Ludlow *847*
Stakes Upham *948*
Stallion Premium Bitter Hambleton *804*
Stallion James & Kirkman *828*
Stamford Bitter Dunham Massey *772*
Standard Ale Glenfinnan *791*
Standard Cronx *759*
    Yelland Manor *969*
Stanley's Pale Ale Kirkby Lonsdale *834*
Stanney Bitter Stanway *921*
Staple Top Out *939*
Star Bitter Belvoir *710*
Star Gazer Yeovil *970*
Star Portobello *887*
Stardusst Haresfoot *807*
Starfire Pale Ale Blue Bell Brewhouse *720*
Stargazer Ridgeside *898*
Stark Mild Moody Goose *859*
Stark Reality Reality *893*
Starlaw Alechemy *690*
Starless Stout Nene Valley *864*
Starry Kite Whistling Kite *958*
Starry Nights Malt *851*
Stars & Stripes Rock Mill *900*
Starship Fleet Elusive *775*
Starstruck Gyle 59 *802*
Start Point Summerskills *926*
Station Ale Richmond *898*
Station Bitter Stonehouse *923*
Station Porter Dent *765*
Staughton Bitter Red *894*
Staveley Cross Townes *941*
Steadfast Koln-ish Bier Lawman *837*
Stealth Burnside *737*
Steam Plate Irwell Works *825*
Steam Roller Phipps *883*
Steam Okell's *872*
Steampunk Three Tuns *934*
Stedmans Ale Thurstons (Horsell) *934*
Steel River Wainstones *951*
Steel Town Bitter Consett Ale Works *754*
Steelback IPA Grainstore *796*
Steep Hill Cathedral Heights *745*
Steerage Titanic *937*

Stella Spark Firebrick *782*
Stellar IPA Ramsbottom Craft *891*
Sterling Pale Flipside *783*
Sternwheeler DarkTribe *763*
Steyning Stinker Riverside *899*
Sticky Dog Ambridge *693*
Stiff Upper Lip By the Horns *740*
Stillman's IPA Spey Valley *919*
Stilton Porter Brewster's *730*
Stiltwalker Isfield *826*
Stirling Beeston *709*
Stitch Walled City *951*
Stitched Up Taylors *930*
Stoat Warbler Lord Conrad's *846*
Stock Porter Stockport *922*
Stockport Common Beer Thirst Class *931*
Stocky Oatmeal Stout Thirst Class *931*
Stoker's Slake Three B's *932*
Stone the Crows Lymestone *848*
Stone Cutter Lymestone *848*
Stone Faced Lymestone *848*
Stonegate Ridgeside *898*
Stoneheads Whaley Bridge *957*
Stoneley Bitter Shalford *910*
Stoodley Stout Little Valley *842*
Storm Bringer IPA Ale House Rock *690*
Storm Force Winter's *963*
Stormbringer Wild Weather *961*
Stormer IPA Penpont *881*
Stormstay Hanlons *805*
Storr Lager Peerless *880*
Stortford Citra Bishop's Stortford *715*
Stortford Pale Ale Bishop's Stortford *714*
Stortford Sunrise Bishop's Stortford *714*
Stortford Sunset Bishop's Stortford *715*
Storyteller Kissingate *834*
Stour Gold Sticklegs *922*
Stour Valley Gold Nethergate *865*
Stourton Pale Ale Wessex *956*
Stout Coffin Church End *748*
Stout Fellow Caythorpe *745*
Stout for the Count Hill Island *815*
Stout Hearted Yeovil *970*
Stout Keith Keith *829*
Stout 4Ts *688*
    Blackjack *719*
    Burton Old Cottage *738*
    Crate *758*
    Exit 33 *778*
    Felinfoel *780*
    Globe *792*
    Hilltop *815*
    Imperial *824*
    Lola Rose *845*
    Lytham *848*
    Millstone *857*
    Moor *860*
    Neepsend *864*
    Outstanding *877*
    RAN *892*
    Round Tower *902*
    Ryedale *903*
    Scarborough *908*
    Seven Bro7hers *909*
    Sheelin *911*
    Tapped *928*
    Three Tuns *934*

Titanic 937
Titan 937
Stouter Leatherbritches 838
Strait IPA Cathedral Heights 745
Stranded Bunny Lacada 835
Strange Brew No. 1
Clarkshaws 749
Strange Ways Rock Mill 900
Strangely SX Hope 819
Stratford Gold Stratford Upon
Avon 924
Stratford IPA Stratford Upon
Avon 924
Straw Blond Isfield 826
Straw Dog Wolf 964
Strawberry Blonde Yorkshire 970
Strawberry Wheat Brandon 727
Stray Ale Harrogate 807
Street Porter Pressure Drop 888
Streetlight Porter Canterbury
Brewers 743
Striding the Riding Helmsley 812
Strike Atomic 699
Strikes Back Empire 776
Stronend Fintry 781
Strong Dark Mild Pope's Yard 887
Strong Mild Green Dragon 798
Strongarm Camerons 742
Stronghold Arundel 696
Strummer Shortts Farm 912
Stubble Burner Lord Conrad's 846
Stubley Stout Drone Valley 771
Stuck on Blondes AJ's 690
Stuck in the Doghouse AJ's 690
Stuck in the Mud AJ's 690
Stud Golden Ale Hambleton 804
Studland Bay Wrecked Isle of
Purbeck 827
Stump Cross Ale Richmond 898
Stunner Cotswold Spring
(Combined Brewers) 753
Sturdy Abstract Jungle 689
Styrian Pale Townhouse 941
Sublime Chaos Anarchy 693
Sublime Stout Fyne 789
Submariner Clearwater 750
Submissable Anarchy Mad
Dog 849
Suffolk 'n' Strong Bartrams 704
Suffolk County Best Bitter
Nethergate 865
Suffolk Pride Mauldons 853
Suffolk Punch Bitter Hoxne 821
Suffolk Punch Mauldons 853
Sugarloaf Tudor 943
Suicide Blonde Ale House
Rock 690
Suilven An Teallach 693
Summa That Branscombe Vale 727
Summa This Branscombe Vale 727
Summer Ale Baltic Fleet 701
Summer Breeze Crystalbrew 760
Idle Valley 823
Summer Gold Newark 866
Summer Hill Blonde Friday
Beer 786
Summer Light Felstar 780
Summer Lightning Hop Back 818
Summer Pale Pin-Up 885
Summer Perle Westerham 957
Summer Solstice Granite Rock 796
Indigenous 824
Summer Indian 824
Summerhill Stout Big Lamp 713
Summerlands Vibrant Forest 949

Summerleaze Bude 736
Summerset Yeovil 970
Summertime Dark Borough
(Lancaster) 723
Summertime Bakers Dozen 701
Summit Hoppy Muirhouse 862
Summit Tillingbourne 935
Sump Oil Stout Brew Shack 729
Sun Goddess Yates 969
Sunbather Southbourne 918
Sunbeam Banks's 702
Battledown 705
Sunchaser Blonde Everards 777
Sundancer High House Farm 814
Twickenham 944
Sundew Woodforde's 966
Sundial Gold Red 894
Sundial Golden Ale Haresfoot 807
Sundown Tipples 936
Untapped 948
Sundowner Langham 836
Padstow 878
Wild Weather 961
Sunfire Yates' 969
Sunlander Stonehouse 923
Sunny Bitter Facer's 778
Sunny Boy Big Clock 712
Sunny Daze Big Lamp 712
Sunraker Quantock 890
Sunray Pale Ale Canopy 742
Sunrise Hafod 803
Sunset Blonde Cross Bay 759
Sunset Arran 696
Captain Cook 743
Sunshine on Keith Spey Valley 919
Sunshine Session Kelpaul 830
Sunshine Brass Castle 728
Cross Bay 759
Holsworthy 816
Monty's 859
Rossendale 902
Super Fortress Howard Town 821
Superior IPA Fyne 789
Superior Broughs 734
Supernatural Blonde
Yorkshire 970
Supernova Black Hole 716
Supreme Pale Ale Woodcote
Manor 965
Supreme Nottingham 870
Supus Lupus Andrews 694
Surf Jaw 828
Surfbum IPA Rebel 893
Surfer Rosa Madrigal 849
Surrex Gold Red Fox 895
Surrey Bitter Pilgrim 885
Sussex #42 360° 687
Sussex Best Bitter Harveys 808
Sussex Gold Arundel 696
Sussex IPA Arundel 696
Sussex Pride Long Man 846
Weltons 955
Sussex Sunset Ashdown 697
Sussex Wild Hop Harveys 808
Sussex XX Mild Ale Harveys 808
Sussex Kissingate 834
Sutler's IPA Burscough 738
Sutra IPA Instant Karma 824
Sutton Pride Bacchus 700
SwAle Richmond 898
Swallow Gold Bowness Bay 725
Swallowtail Humpty Dumpty 821
Swampy Big Bog 712
Swan Black Bowness Bay 725
Swan Blonde Bowness Bay 725

Swan Song Olde Potting Shed 874
Swedish Blonde Maxim 854
Stamps 921
Sweeneys Bank Top 701
Sweet Michael Hedge Row 811
Swelkie John o'Groats 828
Swift Best Bowness Bay 725
Swift Nick Peak 880
Swift One Bowman 725
Swift Deeside 764
Linfit 841
Truman's 943
Swn Y Dail Coles Family 752
Swordfish Wadworth 951
Swordsman Beowulf 710
Sworn Secret Happy Valley 806
SX Dark Hope 819
SX Demon Hope 819
SX Devil Hope 819
SX Dragon Hope 819
SX Gold Hope 819
SX Pale Hope 819
SX Porter Hope 819
SYL First Chop 782
Synergy Paradigm 878
Syren Odyssey 871

T

T'errmmm-inator Strands 924
T'Other Teme Valley 930
T'owd Tup Dent 765
TA Gold Tanners 928
Tabatha Partners 879
Table Ale Colchester 752
Table Liquor Three Blind Mice 932
Tackler's Tipple Three B's 932
Tag Lag Barngates 703
Tag AllGates 692
Tai-pan IPA Remedy 897
Taid's Garden Axiom 699
Tail Gunner Brass Castle 727
Tailshaker Great Oakley 797
Tailwhip Iâl 823
Taiphoon Hop Back 818
Take it Easy Gyle 59 802
Talbot Blond Teme Valley 930
Talisman IPA Pictish 884
Talisman Green Mill 799
Tally Ho Adnams 690
Tally Ho! Palmers 878
Tallyllyn Pale Ale Cader 740
Talwar Reunion 897
Tamar Black Holsworthy 816
Tamar Summerskills 926
Tambourine Man Treboom 941
Tandle Hill Wilson Potter 962
Tanglefoot Hall & Woodhouse
(Badger) 804
Tantalum Lincoln Green 840
Tantrum Problem Child 889
Tap Bitter Chalk Hill 746
Moles 858
Tap House Gold Tap House 928
Tarasgeir Isle of Skye 827
Tartan Terror Houston 820
Tarty Sara Websters 954
Tawny Mild Crafty Pint 758
Tawny Owl Cotleigh 756
**Taylor Walker 1730 Special Pale
Ale** Spirit (Westerham)
(Westerham) 957
Tea Kettle Stout Tring 942
TEA First Chop 782
Hogs Back 816

BEERS INDEX

1019

Worsthorne Gold Worsthorne 967
Worth the Wait Beeston 709
Worthing's Best Bitter
Littlehampton 842
Worthington's Bitter Brains 726
Wot the Duck? Dancing Duck 762
Wot's Occurring Great Oakley 797
Wraith Ghost 791
Wrecker Pilot (Swansea) 885
Wreckless RedWillow 896
Wrekin Best Bitter Wrekin 967
Wrekin Giant Target 929
Wrekin Pale Ale Wrekin 967
Wrench Shiny 911
Wren's Nest Howard Town 821
Wrexham Borders Bitter
Llangollen 843
Wristy Fitzy Golden Duck 793
Writer's Block Wylam 968
Wruff Night Watermill 952
Wychert Ale Vale 949
Wyvern Small Paul's 916

X

XB Batemans 704
Theakston 931
XK Dark Byatt's 740
XL Bitter Burton Bridge 738
XL Mild Burton Bridge 738
XLPA Tiny Rebel 936
XPA XT 969
XX Bitter Freewheelin' 786
Market Harborough 852
XX Mild Greene King 799
XXX Three Tuns 934
XXXB Batemans 704
XXXXXXX Strong Ale Three
Tuns 934

Y

Y Brawd Houdini Llŷn 844
Y.S.D. Yates' 969
Yachtsman Dorset 768
Yachtsmans Ale Island 826
Yakima Gold Crouch Vale 760
Yakima IPA Great Heck 797
Yakima Valley Arbor 695
Yankee Kangaroo Three Blind
Mice 932
Yankee Zulu Force 784
Yankee Rooster's 901
Yankie Lip Smacka Ramsbottom
Craft 891
Yardsman Belfast Pale Ale
Hercules 812
Yardsman IPA Hercules 812
Yardsman Lager Hercules 812
Yaroslavna Stout Spire 920
Ye Old Gold Ramsbottom Craft 891
Ye Olde Trout Kemptown 830
Yellow Jersey Jolly Sailor 828
Yellow Lorry Stringers 925
Yellow Rose Exit 33 778
Yellow Tail Wantsum 951
Yellow Zinger Hop Fuzz 818
Yellowhammer Black Isle 716
Hanlons 805
Yeti Griffin 801
Ynys Mon Great Orme 798
Yo Boy! Mersea Island 855
YOLO Fell 780
York Chocolate Stout Rudgate 903
Yorks Nook 867

Yorkshire Ale Old Bear
(Bridgehouse) 731
Yorkshire Blackout Great
Yorkshire 798
Yorkshire Classic Great
Yorkshire 798
Yorkshire Gold Leeds 838
Yorkshire Golden Great
Yorkshire 798
Yorkshire Legend Helmsley 812
Yorkshire Pale Great Yorkshire 798
Yorkshire Passion Yorkshire 970
Yorkshire Pride Acorn 689
Yorkshire Session Bitter
Hambleton 804
Yorkshire Sparkle Treboom 941
Yorkshire Terrier York 970
Yorkshire Tyke Bitter Butcher's
Dog 739
Young Chick Hunsbury Craft 822
Young Pretender Isle of Skye 827
YPA (Yorkshire Pale Ale)
Rooster's 901
Yuletide Ale Hoggleys
(Phipps) 883
Yumi Bowman 725

Z

Zamzama IPA Gun 801
Zen Hopshackle 819
Zenith Cross Bay 759
Summer Wine 925
Zephyr Truman's 943
Zeppelin Billericay 713
Blueball 721
Zetland Wheatbier Tryst 943
Zig-Zag Stout Milk Street 856
Ziggy's Chin Totnes 940
Zingiber Kent 831
Zombier Fyne 789
Zulu Dawn Lord Conrad's 846
Zulu Lord Conrad's 846

Award winning pubs
Local CAMRA Pubs of the Year

The Pub of the Year competition is judged by CAMRA members. Each of the CAMRA branches votes for its favourite pub: criteria include the quality and choice of real ale, atmosphere, customer service and value. The pubs listed below are current winners of the title; look out for the ♀ next to the entries in the Guide.

England

♀ Bedfordshire
Castle, Bedford
Fox, Carlton
New Inn Ale House & Kitchen, Biggleswade
Black Lion, Leighton Buzzard

♀ Berkshire
Fox & Hounds, Caversham
King Charles Tavern, Newbury
Queen's Head, Wokingham

♀ Buckinghamshire
White Horse, Hedgerley
Crown Inn, Little Missenden
Wheatsheaf, Maids Moreton

♀ Cambridgeshire
Crown Inn, Ashley
Drayman's Son, Ely
Falcon, Huntingdon
Woolpack, Peterborough

♀ Cheshire
Lodge, Alsager
Olde Cottage Inn, Chester
Helter Skelter, Frodsham
Cask Tavern, Poynton
Eight Towers, Widnes
Old Dancer, Wilmslow

♀ Cornwall
Hole in the Wall, Bodmin

♀ Cumbria
Prince of Wales, Foxfield
Drovers Rest, Monkhill
Beer Hall, Staveley
Strands Inn, Nether Wasdale

♀ Derbyshire
Rykneld Turnpyke, Clay Cross
Brunswick Inn, Derby
Old Oak Inn, Horsley Woodhouse
Miners Arms, Hundall
Dewdrop, Ilkeston
Stanley's Alehouse, Matlock
Devonshire Arms, South Normanton
Old Dog, Thorpe

♀ Devon
Queen's Arms, Brixham
Foxhound Inn, Brixton
Grove Inn, Kings Nympton
Fortescue Hotel, Plymouth

♀ Dorset
Firkin Shed, Bournemouth
Bottle Inn, Marshwood

♀ Durham
Quakerhouse, Darlington
Old Elm Tree, Durham
Dun Cow, Seaton
Golden Smog, Stockton-on-Tees

♀ Essex
Hop Beer Shop, Chelmsford
Three Elms, Chignal St James
Victoria Inn, Colchester
Compasses, Great Totham
Theobald Arms, Grays
Alma Inn, Harwich
Mayflower, Leigh-on-Sea
Fox & Hounds, Steeple Bumpstead

♀ Gloucestershire & Bristol
Volunteer Tavern, Bristol
Craven Arms, Brockhampton
Salutation Inn, Ham

♀ Hampshire
Prince of Wales, Farnborough
Royal Oak, Fritham
Hole in the Wall, Portsmouth
Wonston Arms, Wonston

♀ Herefordshire
Chase Inn, Upper Colwall

♀ Hertfordshire
Queen's Head, Allens Green
Land of Liberty, Peace & Plenty, Heronsgate
Half Moon, Hitchin
Woodman, Wild Hill

♀ Isle of Wight
King Harry's Bar, Shanklin

♀ Kent
Wrong Turn, Barfrestone
Bell Inn, Ivychurch
Cock Inn, Luddesdown
Rifle Volunteers, Maidstone
Yard of Ale, St Peter's
Windmill, Sevenoaks Weald
Paper Mill, Sittingbourne
Tankerton Arms, Tankerton
King's Arms, Upper Upnor

♀ Lancashire
Shepherds Hall Ale House, Chorley
Limeburners Arms, Nether Kellet
Swan with Two Necks, Pendleton
Thatched House, Poulton le Fylde
Heatons Bridge Inn, Scarisbrick

♀ Leicestershire
Wheel Inn, Branston
Lime Kilns, Burbage
King's Head, Leicester
White Hart, Loughborough
Stilton Cheese, Somerby

♀ Lincolnshire
Castle Inn, Castle Bytham
Elm Cottage, Gainsborough
White Hart, Ludford
Dambusters Inn, Scampton
Royal Oak, Snitterby
Clickem Inn, Swinhope

♀ Greater London
Harp, WC2: Charing Cross
Colley Rowe Inn, Collier Row
Bohemia, N12: North Finchley
Bree Louise, NW1: Euston
Hope, Carshalton
Penny Farthing, Crayford
Dog & Bull, Croydon
One Inn the Wood, Petts Wood
Pelton Arms, SE10: East Greenwich
Trafalgar, SW19: Merton
Masons Arms, Teddington
Fox, W7: Hanwell

♀ Greater Manchester
Pi, Altrincham
Great Ale at the Market, Bolton
Grocers, Cadishead
Cheshire Ring Hotel, Hyde
White Lion, Leigh
Baum, Rochdale
Boar's Head, Stockport
Wigan Central, Wigan

♀ Merseyside
Gallaghers Pub & Barber's Shop, Birkenhead
Cask, Liverpool: Stoneycroft
Cricketers Arms, St Helens

♀ Norfolk
Fat Cat Tap, Norwich
King's Arms, Shouldham

♀ Northamptonshire
George at Tiffield, Tiffield
Coach & Horses, Wellingborough

♀ Northumberland
Curfew, Berwick upon Tweed
Office, Morpeth

Nottinghamshire
White Lion, Kimberley
Railway Inn, Mansfield
Just Beer Micropub, Newark
BeerHeadZ, Retford
Staunton Arms, Staunton in the Vale

Oxfordshire
Horse & Groom, Caulcott
Bird in Hand, Henley-on-Thames
Cross Keys, Thame
Lamb & Flag, Oxford
Royal Oak, Wantage

Rutland
Fox, North Luffenham

Shropshire
Black Boy, Bridgnorth
Royal Oak, Ellerdine Heath
Prince of Wales, Shrewsbury
Pheasant Inn, Telford: Wellington

Somerset
Brewers Arms, South Petherton

Staffordshire
Burton Bridge Inn, Burton upon Trent
Harrows Inn, Coven
Cat Inn, Enville
Tavern, Denstone
Cross Keys Hotel, Hednesford
Earl Grey Inn, Leek
Green Man, Milwich
Hopinn, Newcastle-under-Lyme
Market Vaults, Tamworth

Suffolk
Oakes Barn, Bury St Edmunds
Vine, Hopton
Stanford Arms, Lowestoft
White Horse, Sweffling

Surrey
Surrey Oaks, Newdigate
Barley Mow, Shepperton
Regent, Walton on Thames
White Hart, Tongham

East Sussex
Gardener's Arms, Lewes
Tower, St Leonards on Sea

West Sussex
Malt Shovel, Horsham
Inglenook, Pagham
Brooksteed Alehouse, Worthing

Tyne & Wear
Fitzgeralds, Newcastle upon Tyne:
   City Centre
Steamboat, South Shields

Warwickshire
Lord Nelson Inn, Ansley
Angel Ale House, Atherstone
Old Bakery, Kenilworth
Rugby Tap, Rugby
Stratford Alehouse,
   Stratford-upon-Avon
Wild Boar, Warwick

West Midlands
Bull's Head, Barston
Inn on the Green, Birmingham:
   Acocks Green
Bishop Vesey, Boldmere
Vine, Brierley Hill
Broomfield Tavern, Coventry
Swan, Halesowen
Black Country Arms, Walsall
Hail to the Ale, Wolverhampton

Wiltshire
Three Crowns, Chippenham
Red Lion, Cricklade
Earl of Normanton, Idmiston
Winchester Gate, Salisbury
Benett Arms, Semley

Worcestershire
Robin Hood, Drayton
Coach & Horses, Harvington
Weavers Real Ale House,
   Kidderminster
Imperial Tavern, Worcester

East Yorkshire
Butchers Dog, Driffield
Goodmanham Arms, Goodmanham
Whalebone, Hull
Jemmy Hirst at the Rose & Crown,
   Rawcliffe

North Yorkshire
Downe Arms, Castleton
10 Devonshire Place, Harrogate
George & Dragon, Hudswell
Dr Phil's Real Ale House,
   Middlesbrough
Sun Inn, Pickering
Stumble Inn, Scarborough
Talbot Arms, Settle
Rook & Gaskill, York

South Yorkshire
Doncaster Brewery Tap, Doncaster
Crown Inn, Elsecar
Beehive, Harthill
New York Tavern, Rotherham
Kelham Island Tavern, Sheffield:
   Kelham Island

West Yorkshire
Robin Hood, Altofts
Sportsman, Huddersfield
Kirkstall Bridge Inn, Leeds: Kirkstall
Fleece, Pudsey
New Inn, Roberttown
Hop, Saltaire
Firehouse, Sowerby Bridge
George Inn, Upper Denby

Wales

Glamorgan
Hopbunker, Cardiff
Mumbles Ale House, Mumbles
Golden Lion, Penarth
Pontardawe Inn, Pontardawe
Pencelli Hotel, Treorchy

Gwent
Queen's Head, Chepstow
Clytha Arms, Clytha

Mid-Wales
Tanners Arms, Defynnog
Arvon Ale House, Llandrindod Wells
Star Inn, Talybont-on-Usk

North-East Wales
Colomendy Arms, Cadole

North-West Wales
Australia, Porthmadog

West Wales
Glengower Hotel, Aberystwyth
Cornish Arms, Burry Port
Vine Inn, Johnston

Scotland

Aberdeen & Grampian
Grill, Aberdeen
Marine Hotel, Stonehaven

Borders
Bridge Inn (Trust), Peebles, Borders

Dumfries & Galloway
Laurie Arms Hotel, Haugh of Urr
Steam Packet Inn, Isle of Whithorn

Edinburgh & The Lothians
Stockbridge Tap, Edinburgh: North
Volunteer Arms (Staggs),
   Musselburgh
Oatridge Hotel, Uphall

Greater Glasgow & Clyde Valley
State Bar, Glasgow
Brown Bull, Lochwinnoch

Highlands & Western Isles
Benleva Hotel, Drumnadrochit

Kingdom of Fife
Foresters Arms, Aberdour

**Loch Lomond, Stirling
& The Trossachs**
Riverside, Dunblane
Station Hotel, Larbert
Oak Tree Inn, Balmaha, Loch Lomond

Northern Isles
Auld Motor Hoose, Kirkwall: Orkney

Tayside
Milton Inn, Monifieth

Northern Ireland

Dirty Duck Ale House, Holywood

Channel Islands

Jersey
Lamplighter, St Helier

Isle of Man

Albert Hotel, Port St Mary

Readers' recommendations

Suggestions for pubs to be included or excluded

All pubs are regularly surveyed by local branches of the Campaign for Real Ale to ensure they meet the standards required by the *Good Beer Guide*. If you would like to comment on a pub already featured, or on any you think should be featured, please fill in the form below (or a copy of it), and send it to the address indicated. Alternatively, email **gbgeditor@camra.org.uk**. Your views will be passed on to the branch concerned. Please mark your envelope/email with the county where the pub is, which will help us to direct your comments efficiently.

Pub name:

Address:

Reason for recommendation/criticism:

Pub name:

Address:

Reason for recommendation/criticism:

Pub name:

Address:

Reason for recommendation/criticism:

Your name and address:

Please send to: [Name of county] Section, Good Beer Guide,
230 Hatfield Road, St Albans, Hertfordshire AL1 4LW

Have your say

Feedback on the Good Beer Guide

We are always trying to improve the *Good Beer Guide* for our readers and we welcome your feedback. If you have any suggestions for how the *Good Beer Guide*, Good Beer Guide e-book, mobile app or sat-nav POI could be improved, please let us know. Simply fill out the form below (or a copy of it) and send it to the address indicated, or make your comments on our website at: **www.camra.org.uk/gbg-feedback**. Thank you.

Colour sections:

Pubs section:

Brewery section:

Good Beer Guide e-book:

Good Beer Guide mobile app:

Good Beer Guide sat-nav POI:

What other suggestions do you have?

Please send to: Good Beer Guide – Have your say,
230 Hatfield Road, St Albans, Hertfordshire AL1 4LW

Outside influences

Even wine countries are switching to beer

The world of beer changes at bewildering speed. Old styles are revived and transformed while new beers push wide the boundaries of brewing. While a great deal of attention has been devoted to the United States in recent years, with more than 4,000 craft breweries and a vast array of styles, the beer revolution is now making an impact in mainland Europe and in the most surprising countries.

Italy, famous as a major wine-producing nation, now has some 900 breweries and the number is expected to rise to four figures at any time. Many of the breweries are tiny and are often no more than brewpubs, but others are growing at a fast rate. The pacesetter is Baladin in Piozzo in the Piedmont region, founded by Teo Musso who has opened bars throughout the country, including Rome and Milan. Annual festivals in those two cities offer a wide range of beers and, as Italians cheerfully admit they have no beer heritage to fall back on, they embrace such styles as Belgian Dubbels and Tripels, with IPAs and pale ales based on British and American versions. At a Rome festival called Fermentazione in autumn 2015, *Good Beer Guide* editor Roger Protz spoke to a large audience on the subject of IPA and also met monks at a local monastery who have been inspired to brew a beer based on the Belgian Trappist model.

Beer law challenged

For centuries, German brewers have concentrated on fine lagers and wheat beers, with specialities such as Alt and Kölsch from Düsseldorf and Cologne – all brewed according to the 16th-century Purity Law, the *Reinheitsgebot*. But the law, which lays down that malted grain, hops, yeast and water can only be used to make beer, is being challenged by a new wave of young brewers. They are keen to widen the appreciation of beer with brews that are spiced or have the likes of vanilla, coffee, fruit and other unmalted ingredients added.

The much-travelled India Pale Ale is also making an appearance in Germany. In Berlin, Stone Brewing of California, one of the Top 10 American craft breweries, has opened a brewery, beer garden and 800-seater restaurant on the site of a former gas works at Marienpark. The complex, which cost 20 million euros, will sell fresh, unpasteurised beer throughout Europe and the UK. With a bow to local convention, it will produce a Vanilla Weisse – wheat beer with vanilla added – and will further challenge the Purity Law with a Vanilla Porter.

But it will also offer hoppy versions of IPA to Berliners with Ruination IPA, Go To IPA and Cali-Belgique IPA. The brewery can be found at Marienpark: U-Bahn Alt-Mariendorf.

On a much smaller scale, three young Americans – David Spengler, Tom Crozier and Matthew Walthall (pictured below) – have also brought IPA to the attention of not only Berliners but also fellow Americans, Brits and Australians living and working in the cosmopolitan city. Their Vagabund Brauerei has a small bar attached where All-Star IPA (5.8%) and Double Imperial IPA (7.5%) boom with the citrus fruit notes of American hops: 3 Antwerpener Strasse: U-Bahn Seestrasse.

IPA has also reached into the deeply conservative south in Bavaria. And Union, a co-operative brewery run by beer-loving families, is producing unfiltered and unpasteurised beers including Sunday Easy IPA, Handwerk Everyday IPA and Friday Über IPA – described as 'not for Woosies'. Also in Bavaria, a long-running brewery, Shönram, brews a 7.8% India Pale Ale that has a sharply different character to the American versions in Berlin as it uses a German hop, Mandarin, which delivers a delicate spicy and herbal note.

IPA has also made an appearance in Belgium. The best-known version comes from Achouffe, a rural brewery in the Ardennes, famous for its Smurf-like gnome logo. Its IPA is a mouthful in every way: Chouffe Houblon Dobbelen IPA Triple, which weighs in at a redoubtable 9%: the name translates as Double Hops, with Triple indicating an extra strong beer. Other Belgian brewers producing IPAs include Belle-Fleur, Den Triest and Excalibur.

Traditional influences

As we show in the British beer styles section (pages 28–31), two Belgian styles making an impact in the UK and the U.S. are Saison and Sour. Saison, also known as Farmhouse Beer, is almost exclusively brewed in the French-speaking region of Wallonia

Sardinian brewers at Rome festival

American Vagabund Brauerei trio, brewing IPA in Berlin

and was originally a seasonal ale – hence the name – produced by farmers to refresh their labourers during harvest time. The beers are now made commercially, with the best-known versions coming from Dupont, a family-owned brewery based on a former farm.

In sharp contrast to 'hop forward' modern IPAs, a true Saison has a rich biscuit malt character but with a good balance of peppery and spicy hops. The beers were, after all, designed to not only refresh people during hard farm work but also to provide much-needed protein and sustenance.

Sours are based on the famous and enigmatic Belgian style of Lambic, which is beer made as a result of 'wild' or spontaneous fermentation, with air-borne yeasts attacking the sugars in the mash of barley malt and wheat. Once fermentation is under way, the beer is transferred to wooden casks, usually obtained from wine makers in France and Portugal, where more yeasts trapped in the wood add to the conversion of malt sugars to alcohol.

Belgian Lambic brewers don't appreciate the label 'sour' and say their beers, in common with dry Brut champagne, are acidic rather than sour. But American brewers have developed the term sour and have been followed by a growing number of British producers. In other countries, brewers are following another Belgian tradition of adding fruit – often cherries and raspberries – to make fruit Lambic or Fruit Sours.

> ❛ Sours are based on the famous and enigmatic Belgian style of Lambic, which is beer made as a result of 'wild' or spontaneous fermentation ❜

Lager beer, for long a derided style in the UK among beer lovers, is enjoying an improved reputation as a number of craft brewers make proper cold-conditioned and aged beers in the European tradition. The pacesetter is Freedom in Staffordshire, which is installing additional equipment to keep pace with demand. In Glasgow, Petra Wetzel from Franconia in Germany, has proved to Scots that there is an alternative to the ubiquitous Tennent's with lagers and wheat beers at WEST, Glasgow Green. Her beers are made in strict observance of the *Reinheitsgebot*.

Petra came to Glasgow to study law. Her father, from the famous brewing town of Bamberg, came to visit her and was so appalled at the taste of Tennent's that he raised the funds to set his daughter up in a brew pub.

Collaborative brewing

Collaboration brewing is becoming a major trend, where two breweries combine their skills to produce challenging new beers. The undoubted pacesetter in this movement is Mikkel Borg Bjersø, the founder of Mikkeler in Copenhagen. He is described as a 'gypsy brewer', roaming the world to brew amazing beers with fellow brewers in Europe and the United States. He widens the boundaries and perceptions of beer with brews made with avocado leaves, black torte beans, maize, grated chocolate, syrup and chillis. An IPA brewed with the Anchorage Brewery in Alaska was aged in French oak wine barrels and fermented with Brettanomyces, the 'wild yeast' used by Belgian Lambic brewers.

If you ask Mikkel if he brews other IPAs, he answers: 'We make them all the time' – and they are produced all round the world. But IPA was a beer designed to travel!

A fascinating collaboration beer available to sample in the UK is the result of a partnership between Thornbridge in Derbyshire and the renowned American brewmaster Garrett Oliver at Brooklyn Brewery in New York City. Working with Thornbridge head brewer Rob Lovatt, Oliver developed a beer that was aged for 18 months in American Bourbon barrels with the addition of lees – sediment – from cider maker Tom Oliver in Herefordshire. Wild yeasts and friendly bacteria add to the fermentation and ageing process.

The result is a 10% beer called Serpent that has notes of beer, cider and whisky. For further information go to **www.thornbridgebrewery.co.uk** – but be warned, a 750ml bottle will set you back £15.

Serpent: Collaboration brew between Brooklyn and Thornbridge breweries

Books for beer lovers

CAMRA'S Beer Anthology

Edited by Roger Protz

An anthology of excerpts from literature, television, film and music about beer, pubs and drinking. Roger Protz, in themed chapters and using easily digested quotations, demonstrates how deeply beer and pubs are woven into the DNA of British culture. The book runs the gamut of culture, from Eastenders to Dickens, and is ideal for the casual reader looking for beer-based entertainment or for the more studious one who wants to gather a sense of how Britain's national drink – and the consumption of it – have been represented in many media.

£9.99 ISBN: 978-1-85249-333-2 CAMRA members' price: £7.99

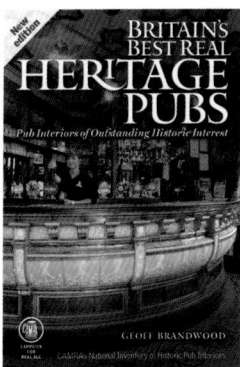

Britain's Best Real Heritage Pubs

2nd Edition

Geoff Brandwood

This definitive listing is the result of 25 years' research by CAMRA to discover pubs that are either unaltered in 70 years or have features of truly national historic importance. Fully revised from the 2013 edition, the book boasts updated information and a new set of evocative illustrations. Among the 260 pubs, there are unspoilt country locals, Victorian drinking palaces and mighty roadhouses. The book has features describing how the pub developed, what's distinctive about pubs in different parts of the country, how people a century ago could expect to be served drinks at their table, and how they used the pub for take-out sales in the pre-supermarket era. There is a bonus listing of 70 pubs that, while not meeting CAMRA's national criteria for a heritage pub, will still thrill visitors with their historic ambience.

£9.99 ISBN: 978-1-85249-334-9 CAMRA members' price: £7.99

The Year in Beer 2017 Diary

This content-packed diary is based around 52 full-page features linking each week of the year to a beer, brewing or pub theme. This beautiful, practical diary is supplemented by a wealth of further information, including CAMRA's beer festivals, beer storage tips, beer's patron saints and much more. An essential and attractive publication for the traditional real ale drinker as well as the most style-conscious of beer hipsters.

£9.99 ISBN: 978-1-85249-337-0
CAMRA members' price: £7.99

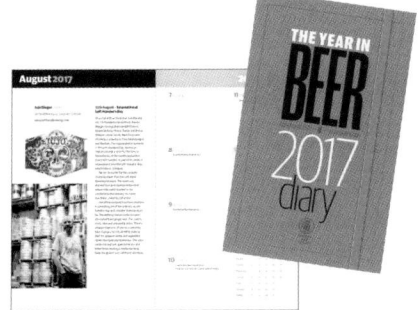

CAMRA'S Beer Knowledge

Jeff Evans

With this absorbing, pocket-sized book, packed with beer facts, feats, records, stats and anecdotes, you'll never be lost for words at the pub again. More than 200 entries cover the serious, the silly and the downright bizarre from the world of beer. Inside this pint-sized compendium you'll find everything from the biggest brewer in the world to the beers with the daftest names. A quick skim before a night out and you'll always have enough beery wisdom to impress your friends.

£9.99 ISBN: 978-1-85249-338-7 CAMRA members' price: £7.99
Publishes October 2016

London's Best Beer, Pubs & Bars – 2nd Edition
Des de Moor

The essential guide to London beer, completely revised for 2015. *London's Best Beer, Pubs & Bars* is packed with detailed maps and easy-to-use listings to help you find the best places to enjoy perfect pints in the capital. Laid out by area, the book will be your companion in exploring the best pubs serving the best British and world beers. Additional features include descriptions of London's rich history of brewing and the city's vibrant modern brewing scene, where brewery numbers have more than doubled in the last three years. The venue listings are fully illustrated with colour photographs and include a variety of real ale pubs, bars and other outlets, with detailed information to make planning any excursion quick and easy.

'...meticulously researched and open-minded' Will Hawkes, *The Independent*

£12.99 ISBN 978-1-85249-323-36 CAMRA members' price £10.99

CAMRA's 101 Beer Days Out
Tim Hampson

Revised and updated for 2015, *101 Beer Days Out* is the perfect handbook for the beer tourist wanting to explore beer, pubs and brewing in the UK. From brewery tours to rail-ale trails, beer festivals to hop farms, brewing courses to historic pubs, Britain has a huge variety of beer experiences to explore and enjoy. *101 Beer Days Out* is ordered geographically, so you can easily find a beer day out wherever you are in Britain, and includes full visitor information, maps and colour photography, with detailed information on opening hours, local landmarks and public transport links to make planning any excursion quick and easy.

£12.99 ISBN 978-1-85249-328-8 CAMRA members' price £10.99

CAMRA's So, You Want to Be a Beer Expert?
Jeff Evans

More people than ever are searching for an understanding of what makes a great beer, and this book meets that demand by presenting a hands-on course in beer appreciation, with sections on understanding the beer styles of the world, beer flavours, how beer is made, the ingredients, and more. Uniquely, *So, You Want to Be a Beer Expert?* doesn't just relate the facts, but helps readers reach conclusions for themselves. Key to this are the interactive tastings that show readers, through their own taste buds, what beer is all about. CAMRA's *So, You Want to Be a Beer Expert?* is the ideal book for anyone who wants to further their knowledge and enjoyment of beer.

£12.99 ISBN 978-1-85249-322-6 CAMRA members' price £10.99

Yorkshire Pub Walks
Bob Steel

This is a pocket-sized, traveller's guide to some of the best walking and finest pubs in Yorkshire. The walks are grouped geographically and explore some of the region's fascinating historical and literary heritage as well as its thriving brewing scene. The book contains essential information about local transport and accommodation. The walks include: Settle and Upper Ribblesdale; Whitby to Robin Hood's Bay; Brontë country: Haworth and Ponden; Sheffield: Kelham Island and the 'valley of beer' and Hull's old town: a fishy trail. The book covers towns and cities as well as rural areas, i.e. Beverley; Hull; Leeds; Sheffield and York.

£9.99 ISBN: 978-1-85249-329-5 CAMRA members' price: £7.99

An offer for CAMRA members
Join the Good Beer Guide Privilege Club

Being a CAMRA member brings many benefits, not least a big discount on the *Good Beer Guide*. You can take advantage of an even bigger discount and get further benefits by taking out an annual subscription to the Good Beer Guide Privilege Club.

Privilege Club benefits:

- Get your copy of the new Guide before publication and before any other sales are dispatched
- Pay just £10 for your copy, including all postage and packaging costs* (RRP £15.99)
- Receive the *Good Beer Guide* sat-nav POI files free
- Never have to worry about missing a new Guide as everything is taken care of with one simple Direct Debit
- Help to fund CAMRA directly, allowing us to continue to campaign for real ale and community pubs

Privilege Club subscriptions are paid annually by Direct Debit. Club members **receive the Good Beer Guide automatically every year** around two weeks before before the official publication date and before any other postal sales are processed. Privilege Club members receive the book at a lower price than other CAMRA members (for instance, the 2016 Guide was sold to Privilege Club subscribers for just £10 including postage & packing. *The standard CAMRA members' price is £11.00 plus £2.50 postage & packing).

So sign up now and be sure of receiving your copy early every year. Simply visit **www.camra.org.uk/gbg-privilege-club** and follow the online instructions.

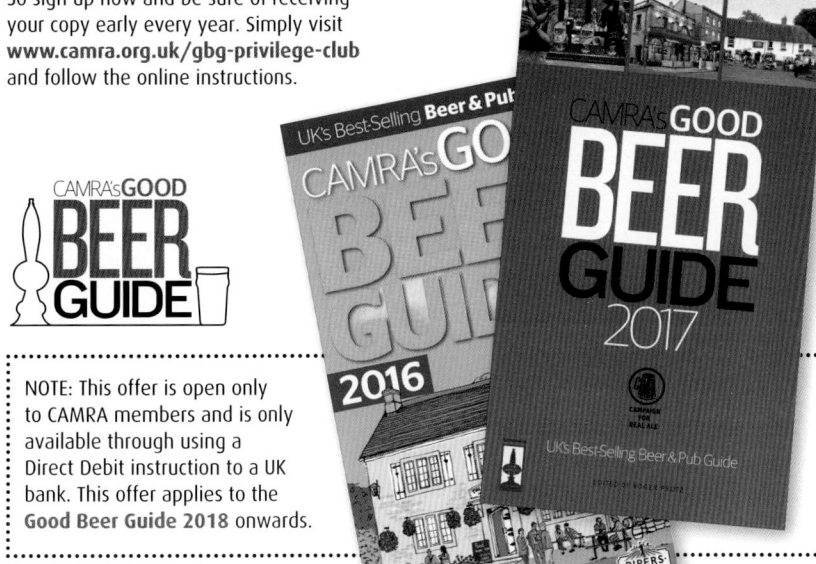

NOTE: This offer is open only to CAMRA members and is only available through using a Direct Debit instruction to a UK bank. This offer applies to the **Good Beer Guide 2018** onwards.

Get the ALL NEW Good Beer Guide app to...

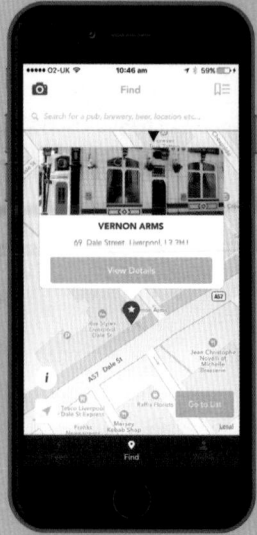
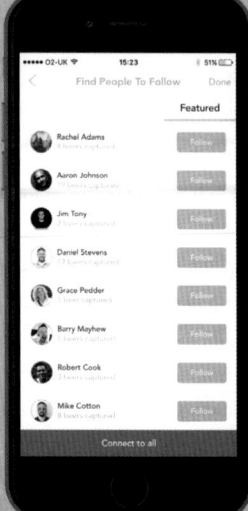
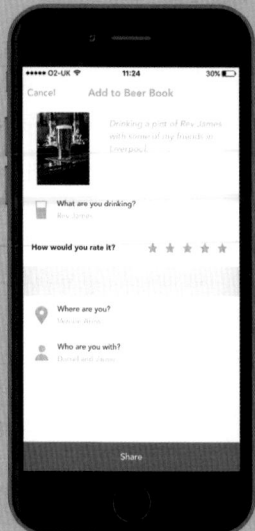

FIND

pubs · breweries · beers

CONNECT

to other beer fans

SHARE

beer experiences

Available now on the App Store and on Google Play™

CAMRA's **GOOD**
BEER
GUIDE

For further information and to keep updated visit **www.camra.org.uk/gbg-mobile**

Good Beer Guide digital editions

 The *Good Beer Guide* is also available in digital formats, including an all-new mobile app, an e-book and a sat-nav download. Together, these offer the perfect solution to pub-finding on the move. To discover more, scan the QR code or visit **www.camra.org.uk/gbg**.

NEW! Good Beer Guide mobile app

The new Good Beer Guide mobile app for Apple and Android™ devices provides detailed information on local *Good Beer Guide* pubs, breweries and beers wherever you are or wherever you are going. Social media integration lets you share your beer experiences with other users. Features include:[†]

- Search results with full pub descriptions and detailed visitor information for 4,500 pubs listed in the *Good Beer Guide* plus basic information for 31,000 other real ale pubs all over the UK, collated by CAMRA

- Detailed information on all UK real-ale breweries and their regular beers along with hundreds of CAMRA tasting notes

- Custom functions allow you to mark your favourite pubs, breweries and beers and write and share your own personal reviews

- Pump-clip recognition feature along with photo capture

- Can be used on multiple devices and platforms under one account

- Social media functions and improved search functionality for non-subscribers

For more information visit **www.camra.org.uk/gbg-mobile**

[†]App is free to download with an in-app subscription required for full features.
NOTE: Standard network charges apply when using the app.

Good Beer Guide e-book

The *Good Beer Guide 2017* is available as an e-book in the widely compatible ePUB and Kindle formats. It offers the following key features:

- Portable, electronic version of the printed Guide

- Fully interactive, searchable content in ePUB and Kindle formats, compatible with iPad, Kindle and many other e-readers

- Includes full-colour* features and images from the printed book, as well as complete pubs and breweries listings

- Active e-mail and web links within entries*

- Postcode links to Google maps to help you navigate*

*Where e-reader allows

 ePUB  amazonkindle

Good Beer Guide sat-nav POI files

Priced at just £2.99, the Good Beer Guide POI (Points of Interest) file allows users of TomTom, Garmin and Navman sat-nav systems to see the locations of all the 4,500 current *Good Beer Guide* pubs and all the UK's real-ale breweries and plan routes to them.

For more information and to download visit **http://www.camra.org.uk/gbg-sat-nav**

Join the Campaign!

CAMRA, the Campaign for Real Ale, is an independent not-for-profit, volunteer-led consumer group. We promote good-quality real ale and pubs, as well as lobbying government to champion drinkers' rights and protect local pubs as centres of community life.

CAMRA has over 180,000 members from all ages and backgrounds, brought together by a common belief in the issues that CAMRA deals with and their love of good-quality British beer. From just £24 a year – that's less than a pint a month – you can join CAMRA and enjoy the following benefits:

- A monthly colour newspaper (*What's Brewing*) and award-winning quarterly magazine (*BEER*) containing news and features about beer, pubs and brewing.

- Free or reduced entry to over 160 national, regional and local beer festivals.

- Money off many of our publications including the *Good Beer Guide* and the *Good Bottled Beer Guide*.

- A 10% discount on all holidays booked with Cottages.com and Hoseasons, a 10% discount with Beer Hawk, plus much more.

- £20 worth of J D Wetherspoon real ale vouchers* (40 x 50 pence off a pint).

- Discounts in thousands of pubs across the UK through the CAMRA Real Ale Discount Scheme.

- 15 months membership for the price of 12 for new members paying by Direct Debit**

For more details about member benefits please visit **www.camra.org.uk/benefits**

If you feel passionately about your pint and about pubs, join us by visiting www.camra.org.uk/join or calling 01727 798 440

For the latest campaigning news and to get involved in CAMRA's campaigns visit www.camra.org.uk/campaigns

---

**CAMPAIGN
FOR
REAL ALE**

*Joint members receive £20 worth of J D Wetherspoon vouchers to share. **15 months membership for the price of 12 is only available the first time a member pays by Direct Debit. NOTE: Membership prices and benefits are subject to change.